Hoover's Handbook of

Private Companies

2010

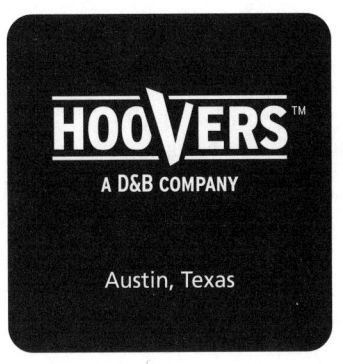

HOOVERS™
A D&B COMPANY

Austin, Texas

Hoover's Handbook of Private Companies 2010 is intended to provide readers with accurate and authoritative information about the enterprises covered in it. Hoover's researched all companies and organizations profiled, and in many cases contacted them directly so that companies represented could provide information. The information contained herein is as accurate as we could reasonably make it. In many cases we have relied on third-party material that we believe to be trustworthy, but were unable to independently verify. We do not warrant that the book is absolutely accurate or without error. Readers should not rely on any information contained herein in instances where such reliance might cause financial loss. The publisher, the editors, and their data suppliers specifically disclaim all warranties, including the implied warranties of merchantability and fitness for a specific purpose. This book is sold with the understanding that neither the publisher, the editors, nor any content contributors are engaged in providing investment, financial, accounting, legal, or other professional advice.

The financial data (Historical Financials sections) in this book are from the companies profiled or from trade sources deemed to be reliable. Hoover's, Inc., is solely responsible for the presentation of all data.

Many of the names of products and services mentioned in this book are the trademarks or service marks of the companies manufacturing or selling them and are subject to protection under US law. Space has not permitted us to indicate which names are subject to such protection, and readers are advised to consult with the owners of such marks regarding their use. Hoover's is a trademark of Hoover's, Inc.

Copyright © 2010 by Hoover's, Inc. All rights reserved. No part of this book may be reproduced or transmitted in any form or by any means, electronic or mechanical, including by photocopying, facsimile transmission, recording, rekeying, or using any information storage and retrieval system, without permission in writing from Hoover's, except that brief passages may be quoted by a reviewer in a magazine, in a newspaper, online, or in a broadcast review.

10 9 8 7 6 5 4 3 2 1

Publishers Cataloging-in-Publication Data

Hoover's Handbook of Private Companies 2010

    Includes indexes.

    ISBN 978-1-57311-137-9

    ISSN 1073-6433

    1. Business enterprises — Directories. 2. Corporations — Directories.

HF3010 338.7

Hoover's Company Information is also available on the Internet at Hoover's Online (www.hoovers.com). A catalog of Hoover's products is available on the Internet at www.hooversbooks.com.

The Hoover's Handbook series is produced for Hoover's Business Press by:

Sycamore Productions, Inc.
5808 Balcones Drive, Suite 205
Austin, Texas 78731
info@sycamoreproductions.com

Cover design is by John Baker. Electronic prepress and printing are by Sheridan Books, Inc., Ann Arbor, Michigan.

U.S. AND WORLD BOOK SALES

Hoover's, Inc.
5800 Airport Blvd.
Austin, TX 78752
Phone: 512-374-4500
Fax: 512-374-4538
e-mail: orders@hoovers.com
Web: www.hooversbooks.com

EUROPEAN BOOK SALES

William Snyder Publishing Associates
5 Five Mile Drive
Oxford OX2 8HT
England
Phone & fax: +44-186-551-3186
e-mail: snyderpub@aol.com

Hoover's, Inc.

Founder: Gary Hoover
President: Hyune Hand
EVP Marketing and Business Development: Peter Poulin
VP Business Excellence: Jeffrey A. (Jeff) Cross
VP Technology: Mamie Jones
VP Business Development: Heidi Tucker
VP Advertising Sales and Operations: Mark Walters
VP Sales: Tom Wickersham
Leader e-Commerce and Books: Dan Tharp
Leader New Business Acquisitions: Amy Bible
Leader Human Resources: Robin Pfahler

(For the latest updates on Hoover's, please visit: http://hoovers.com/global/corp)

EDITORIAL

Managing Editor: Margaret L. Harrison
Senior Editors: Adrianne Argumaniz, Larry Bills, Jason Cother, Barbara-Anne Mansfield, Greg Perliski, Barbara Redding, Dennis Sutton
Team Leads: Danny Cummings and Matt Saucedo
Editors: Chelsea Adams, Adam Anderson, Jenn Barnier, Victoria Bernard, Alex Biesada, Joe Bramhall, James Bryant, Anthony Buchanan, Ryan Caione, Jason Cella, Catherine Colbert, Tami Conner, Nancy Daniels, Jeff Dorsch, Bobby Duncan, Lesley Epperson, Rachel Gallo, Jenni Gilmer, Chris Hampton, Stuart Hampton, Jim Harris, Laura Huchzermeyer, Chris Huston, Donna Iroabuchi, Ellen Jacobs, Jessica Jimenez, Linnea Anderson Kirgan, Sylvia Lambert, Anne Law, Josh Lower, John MacAyeal, Kathryn Mackenzie, Rebecca Mallett, Erin McInnis, Michael McLellan, Barbara Murray, Nell Newton, Lynett Oliver, Tracey Panek, Peter Partheymuller, Rachel Pierce, David Ramirez, Diane Ramirez, Mark Richardson, Melanie Robertson, Patrice Sarath, Amy Schein, Nikki Sein, Seth Shafer, Lee Simmons, Paula Smith, Anthony Staats, Tracy Uba, Vanessa Valencia, Ryan Wade, Randy Williams, David Woodruff
QA Editors: Carrie Geis, Rosie Hatch, Diane Lee, John Willis
Editorial Customer Advocates: Adi Anand and Kenny Jones

HOOVER'S BUSINESS PRESS

Distribution Manager: Rhonda Mitchell
Customer Support and Fulfillment Manager: Michael Febonio

ABOUT HOOVER'S, INC. – THE BUSINESS INFORMATION AUTHORITY™

Hoover's, a D&B company, provides its customers the fastest path to business with insight and actionable information about companies, industries, and key decision makers, along with the powerful tools to find and connect to the right people to get business done. Hoover's provides this information for sales, marketing, business development, and other professionals who need intelligence on U.S. and global companies, industries, and the people who lead them. Hoover's unique combination of editorial expertise and one-of-a-kind data collection with user-generated and company-supplied content gives customers a 360-degree view and competitive edge. This information, along with powerful tools to search, sort, download, and integrate the content, is available through Hoover's (http://www.hoovers.com), the company's premier online service. Hoover's is headquartered in Austin, Texas.

Abbreviations

AFL-CIO – American Federation of Labor and Congress of Industrial Organizations

AMA – American Medical Association

AMEX – American Stock Exchange

ARM – adjustable-rate mortgage

ASP – application services provider

ATM – asynchronous transfer mode

ATM – automated teller machine

CAD/CAM – computer-aided design/computer-aided manufacturing

CD-ROM – compact disc – read-only memory

CD-R – CD-recordable

CEO – chief executive officer

CFO – chief financial officer

CMOS – complimentary metal oxide silicon

COO – chief operating officer

DAT – digital audiotape

DOD – Department of Defense

DOE – Department of Energy

DOT – Department of Transportation

DRAM – dynamic random-access memory

DSL – digital subscriber line

DVD – digital versatile disc/digital video disc

DVD-R – DVD-recordable

EPA – Environmental Protection Agency

EPS – earnings per share

ESOP – employee stock ownership plan

EU – European Union

EVP – executive vice president

FCC – Federal Communications Commission

FDA – Food and Drug Administration

FDIC – Federal Deposit Insurance Corporation

FTC – Federal Trade Commission

GATT – General Agreement on Tariffs and Trade

GDP – gross domestic product

HMO – health maintenance organization

HR – human resources

HTML – hypertext markup language

ICC – Interstate Commerce Commission

IPO – initial public offering

IRS – Internal Revenue Service

ISP – Internet service provider

kWh – kilowatt-hour

LAN – local-area network

LBO – leveraged buyout

LCD – liquid crystal display

LNG – liquefied natural gas

LP – limited partnership

Ltd. – limited

mips – millions of instructions per second

MW – megawatt

NAFTA – North American Free Trade Agreement

NASA – National Aeronautics and Space Administration

Nasdaq – National Association of Securities Dealers Automated Quotations

NATO – North Atlantic Treaty Organization

NYSE – New York Stock Exchange

OCR – optical character recognition

OECD – Organization for Economic Cooperation and Development

OEM – original equipment manufacturer

OPEC – Organization of Petroleum Exporting Countries

OS – operating system

OSHA – Occupational Safety and Health Administration

OTC – over-the-counter

PBX – private branch exchange

PCMCIA – Personal Computer Memory Card International Association

P/E – price to earnings ratio

RAID – redundant array of independent disks

RAM – random-access memory

R&D – research and development

RBOC – regional Bell operating company

RISC – reduced instruction set computer

REIT – real estate investment trust

ROA – return on assets

ROE – return on equity

ROI – return on investment

ROM – read-only memory

S&L – savings and loan

SEC – Securities and Exchange Commission

SEVP – senior executive vice president

SIC – Standard Industrial Classification

SOC – system on a chip

SVP – senior vice president

USB – universal serial bus

VAR – value-added reseller

VAT – value-added tax

VC – venture capitalist

VoIP – Voice over Internet Protocol

VP – vice president

WAN – wide-area network

Contents

Companies Profiled

Companies Profiled (continued)

Companies Profiled (continued)

Companies Profiled (continued)

Companies Profiled (continued)

About Hoover's Handbook of Private Companies 2010

With this 2010 edition, *Hoover's Handbook of Private Companies* celebrates its 15th year as one of the premier sources of business information on privately held enterprises in the US.

Publishing current, relevant information about nonpublic companies can be a challenge, as many of them see secrecy as a competitive strategy, but we continue to do the hard work of compiling the information you need.

In this edition we bring you the facts on 900 of the largest and most influential enterprises in the US. Entries feature overviews of company operations, up to five years of financial information, product information, and lists of company executives as found in Hoover's huge database of company information. Some larger and more visible companies will feature an additional History section.

HOOVER'S ONLINE FOR BUSINESS NEEDS

In addition to Hoover's widely used MasterList and Handbooks series, comprehensive coverage of more than 40,000 business enterprises is available in electronic format on our Web site at www.hoovers.com. Our goal is to provide our customers the fastest path to business with insight and actionable information about companies, industries, and key decision makers, along with the powerful tools to find and connect to the right people to get business done. Hoover's has partnered with other prestigious business information and service providers to bring you all the right business information, services, and links in one place.

We welcome the recognition we have received as the premier provider of high-quality company information — online, electronically, and in print — and continue to look for ways to make our products more available and more useful to you.

Hoover's Handbook of Private Companies is one of our four-title series of handbooks that covers, literally, the world of business. The series is available as an indexed set, and also includes *Hoover's Handbook of American Business, Hoover's Handbook of World Business*, and *Hoover's Handbook of Emerging Companies*. This series brings you information on the biggest, fastest-growing, and most influential enterprises in the world.

We believe that anyone who buys from, sells to, invests in, lends to, competes with, interviews with, or works for a company should know all there is to know about that enterprise. Taken together, this book and the other Hoover's products and resources represent the most complete source of basic corporate information readily available to the general public.

HOW TO USE THIS BOOK

This book has four sections:

1. "Using Hoover's Handbooks" describes the contents of our profiles and explains the ways in which we gather and compile our data.

2. "A List-Lover's Compendium" contains lists of the largest and fastest-growing private companies. The lists are based on the information in our profiles, or compiled from well-known sources.

3. The company profiles section makes up the largest and most important part of the book — 900 profiles of major private enterprises, arranged alphabetically.

4. Three indexes complete the book. The first sorts companies by industry groups, the second by headquarters location. The third index is a list of all the executives found in the Executives section of each company profile.

As always, we hope you find our books useful. We invite your comments via phone (512-374-4500), fax (512-374-4538), mail (5800 Airport Boulevard, Austin, Texas 78752), or e-mail (custsupport@hoovers.com).

The Editors,
Austin, Texas,
January 2010

Using Hoover's Handbooks

SELECTION OF THE COMPANIES PROFILED

The 900 enterprises profiled in this book include the largest and most influential private enterprises in America. Among them are:

- private companies, from the giants (Cargill and Koch) to the colorful and prominent (Bad Boy Worldwide Entertainment and L.L. Bean)
- mutuals and cooperative organizations owned by their customers (State Farm Insurance, Ace Hardware, Ocean Spray Cranberries)
- not-for-profits (Red Cross, Kaiser Permanente, Smithsonian Institution)
- joint ventures (Motiva Enterprises, Dow Corning)
- partnerships (PricewaterhouseCoopers, Baker & McKenzie)
- universities (Columbia, Harvard, University of California)
- government-owned corporations (US Postal Service and New York City's Metropolitan Transportation Authority)
- and a selection of other enterprises (National Basketball Association, AFL-CIO, Texas Lottery Commission).

ORGANIZATION

The profiles are presented in alphabetical order. You will find the commonly used name of the enterprise at the beginning of the profile; the full, legal name is found in the Locations section. If a company name is also a person's name, such as Henry Ford Health System or Mary Kay, it will be alphabetized under the first name; if the company name starts with initials, for example, L.L. Bean or S.C. Johnson, look for it under the combined initials (in the above examples, LL and SC, respectively).

Basic financial data are listed under the heading Historical Financials. The annual financial information contained in the profiles is current through fiscal year-ends occurring as late as October 2009. We have included certain nonfinancial developments, such as officer changes, through December 2009.

OVERVIEW

In the first section of the profile, we have tried to give a thumbnail description of the company and what it does. The description will usually include information on the company's strategy, reputation, and ownership. We recommend that you read this section first.

HISTORY

This extended section, which is available for some of the larger and more well-known companies, reflects our belief that every enterprise is the sum of its history and that you have to know where you came from in order to know where you are going. While some companies have limited historical awareness, we think the vast majority of the enterprises in this book have colorful backgrounds. We have tried to focus on the people who made the enterprises what they are today. We have found these histories to be full of twists and ironies; they make fascinating reading.

EXECUTIVES

Here we list the names of the people who run the company, insofar as space allows. In the few cases where available, we have shown the ages and pay of key officers. In some instances the published data is for the previous year, although the company has announced promotions or retirements since year-end. The pay represents cash compensation, including bonuses, but excludes stock option programs.

Although companies are free to structure their management titles any way they please, most modern corporations follow standard practices. The ultimate power in any corporation lies with the shareholders, who elect a board of directors, usually including officers or "insiders," as well as individuals from outside the company. The chief officer, the person on whose desk the buck stops, is usually called the chief executive officer (CEO). Often, he or she is also the chairman of the board.

As corporate management has become more complex, it is common for the CEO to have a "right-hand person" who oversees the day-to-day operations of the company, allowing the CEO plenty of time to focus on strategy and long-term issues. This right-hand person is usually designated the chief operating officer (COO) and is often the president of the company. In other cases one person is both chairman and president.

A multitude of other titles exists, including chief financial officer (CFO), chief administrative officer, and vice chairman. We have always tried to include the CFO, the chief legal officer, and the chief human resources or personnel officer.

The people named in the Executives section are indexed at the back of the book.

The Executives section also includes the name of the company's auditing (accounting) firm, where available.

LOCATIONS

Here we include the company's full legal name and its headquarters, street address, telephone and fax numbers, and Web site, as available. The back of the book includes an index of companies by headquarters locations.

In some cases we have also included information on the geographic distribution of the company's business, including sales and profit data. Note that these profit numbers, like those in the Products/Operations section below, are usually operating or pretax profits rather than net profits. Operating profits are generally those before financing costs (interest income and payments) and before taxes, which are considered costs attributable to the whole company, rather than to one division or part of the world. For this reason the net income figures (in the Historical Financials section) are usually much lower, since they are after interest and taxes. Pretax profits are after interest but before taxes.

Headquarters for companies that are incorporated in Bermuda, but whose operational headquarters are in the US, are listed under their US address.

PRODUCTS/OPERATIONS

This section contains selected lists of products, services, brand names, divisions, subsidiaries, and joint ventures. We have tried to include all of a company's major lines and all familiar brand names.

The nature of this section varies by company and the amount of information contained in Hoover's storehouse of business information. If the company publishes sales and profit information by type of business, we have included it.

COMPETITORS

In this section we have listed companies that compete with the profiled company. This feature is included as a quick way to locate similar companies and compare them. The universe of competitors includes all public companies and all private companies with sales in excess of $500 million. In a few instances we have identified smaller private companies as key competitors.

HISTORICAL FINANCIALS

Here we have tried to present as much data about each enterprise's financial performance as we could compile in the allocated space. The information varies somewhat from industry to industry and is less complete in the case of private companies that do not release data. (We have always tried to provide annual sales and employment, although in some instances those numbers are simply not available.) There are a few industries, venture capital and investment banking, for example, for which revenue numbers are not reported as a rule. In the case of private companies that do not publicly disclose financial information, we have sometimes used estimates of sales and other statistics when reliable sources are available.

The following information is generally present.

A five-year table, with relevant annualized compound growth rates, covers:
- Sales — fiscal year sales (year-end assets for most financial companies)
- Net income — fiscal year net income (before accounting changes)
- Net profit margin — fiscal year net income as a percent of sales (as a percent of assets for most financial firms)
- Employees — fiscal year-end or average number of employees

The information on the number of employees is intended to aid the reader interested in knowing whether a company has a long-term trend of increasing or decreasing employment. As far as we know, we are the only company that publishes this information in print format.

The numbers on the left in each row of the Historical Financials section give the month and the year in which the company's fiscal year actually ends. Thus, a company with a March 31, 2009, year-end is shown as 3/09. The last item in the Financials section is a graph, which for private companies shows net income, or, if that is unavailable, sales.

Key year-end statistics are included in this section for insurance companies and companies required to file reports with the SEC. They generally show the financial strength of the enterprise, including:
- Debt ratio (long-term debt as a percent of shareholders' equity)
- Return on equity (net income divided by the average of beginning and ending common shareholders' equity)
- Cash and cash equivalents
- Current ratio (ratio of current assets to current liabilities)
- Total long-term debt (including capital lease obligations)
- Fiscal year sales for financial institutions.

Hoover's Handbook of

Private Companies

A List-Lover's Compendium

The 300 Largest Companies by Sales in
Hoover's Handbook of Private Companies 2010

Rank	Company	Sales ($ mil.)
1	General Motors	148,979
2	Cargill, Incorporated	116,579
3	Koch Industries	100,000
4	US Postal Service	74,932
5	State Farm Mutual	61,300
6	California State Board of Equalization	49,950
7	Cellco Partnership	49,332
8	Kaiser Permanente	40,300
9	Carlson Companies	38,075
10	Bechtel Group	31,400
11	Mars, Incorporated	30,000
12	Liberty Mutual	28,855
13	National Institutes of Health	28,461
14	HCA Inc.	28,374
15	PricewaterhouseCoopers	28,185
16	Platinum Equity	27,500
17	Deloitte Touche Tohmatsu	27,400
18	Ernst & Young Global	24,500
19	Publix Super Markets	24,110
20	Nationwide Mutual Insurance	22,962
21	KPMG International	22,690
22	Northwestern Mutual Life Insurance	21,923
23	IGA, Inc.	21,000
24	U.S. Foodservice	19,810
25	Massachusetts Mutual Life Insurance	19,301
26	C & S Wholesale Grocers	19,000
27	Delphi Automotive	18,060
28	Teacher Retirement System of Texas	18,002
29	NBC Universal	16,969
30	New York Life Insurance	16,830
31	Love's Travel Stops	16,500
32	Health Care Service Corporation	16,025
33	Tenaska, Inc.	16,000
34	University of California	15,465
35	Cox Enterprises	15,400
36	H-E-B	15,000
37	Meijer, Inc.	13,700
38	Ascension Health	13,489
39	ARAMARK Corporation	13,470
40	Environmental Protection Agency	13,152
41	Highmark Inc.	13,002
42	FMR LLC	12,937
43	USAA	12,912
44	Chevron Phillips Chemical	12,828
45	TIAA-CREF	12,740
46	Kinder Morgan	12,095
47	Land O'Lakes	12,039
48	Dairy Farmers of America	11,700
49	Energy Future Holdings	11,364
50	Transammonia, Inc.	11,200
51	Reyes Holdings	11,000
52	Blue Cross Blue Shield of Michigan	10,680
53	Wakefern Food	10,600
54	Tennessee Valley Authority	10,382
55	CCA Global Partners	10,200
56	Harrah's Entertainment	10,127
57	JM Family Enterprises	10,100
58	Enterprise Rent-A-Car	10,100
59	Capital Group Companies	9,900
60	The Regence Group	8,930
61	California Physicians' Service	8,898
62	First Data Corporation	8,811
63	Army and Air Force Exchange	8,705
64	EmblemHealth, Inc.	8,612
65	Blue Cross and Blue Shield of Florida	8,532
66	Catholic Healthcare West	8,402
67	Southern Wine & Spirits	8,400
68	Sutter Health	8,281
69	Catholic Health Initiatives	8,245
70	State University of New York	8,151
71	Cumberland Farms	8,100
72	CDW Corporation	8,070
73	Giant Eagle	8,020
74	Peter Kiewit Sons'	8,000
75	S.C. Johnson	8,000
76	Horizon Healthcare	7,963
77	Menard, Inc.	7,800
78	Hilton Worldwide	7,770
79	Sinclair Oil	7,750
80	QuikTrip Corporation	7,700
81	Advance Publications	7,630
82	Guardian Life Insurance	7,472
83	Mayo Foundation	7,222
84	New York State Lottery	7,175
85	Alticor Inc.	7,100
86	Providence Health & Services	7,026
87	National Football League	6,900
88	Associated Wholesale Grocers	6,900
89	American Family Insurance	6,743
90	Gordon Food Service	6,700
91	RaceTrac Petroleum	6,680
92	Yale University	6,651
93	Keystone Foods	6,540
94	Major League Baseball	6,500
95	Partners HealthCare System	6,478
96	Federal Home Loan Bank of Atlanta	6,419
97	Thrivent Financial	6,413
98	Trinity Health	6,300
99	New York City Health and Hospitals	6,213
100	Colonial Group	6,200
101	Hy-Vee, Inc.	6,200
102	Bloomberg L.P.	6,100
103	Hexion Specialty Chemicals	6,093
104	Metropolitan Transportation Authority	5,932
105	Delta Dental Plan	5,900
106	U.S. Premium Beef	5,847
107	University of Michigan	5,821
108	Allegis Group	5,740
109	Wawa, Inc.	5,700
110	MacAndrews & Forbes	5,700
111	Guardian Industries	5,600
112	SunGard Data Systems	5,596
113	CH2M HILL Companies	5,590
114	Meadowbrook Meat Company	5,500
115	Kohler Co.	5,500
116	Adventist Health System	5,496
117	Dow Corning	5,450
118	Ergon, Inc.	5,430
119	Graybar Electric	5,400
120	McKinsey & Company	5,330
121	Pension Benefit Guaranty Corporation	5,325
122	Ryerson Inc.	5,310
123	Avaya Inc.	5,279
124	McJunkin Red Man Holding	5,260
125	Freescale Semiconductor	5,226
126	Blue Cross (NC)	5,200
127	Apex Oil	5,200
128	Mansfield Oil	5,100
129	Save Mart Supermarkets	5,100
130	Kinray Inc.	5,100
131	Gulf States Toyota	5,100
132	Unisource Worldwide	5,000
133	Auto-Owners Insurance Group	4,951
134	H Group Holding	4,921
135	Stanford University	4,905
136	Center Oil	4,900
137	Hearst Corporation	4,810
138	Wegmans Food Markets	4,800
139	National Cancer Institute	4,793
140	Realogy Corporation	4,725
141	Clark Enterprises	4,700
142	Tishman Realty & Construction	4,690
143	Neiman Marcus	4,601
144	Charmer Sunbelt	4,600
145	Southwire Company	4,600
146	Oxbow Corporation	4,500
147	Massachusetts State Lottery	4,480
148	Sheetz, Inc.	4,410
149	Pro-Build Holdings	4,400
150	RNDC Texas	4,400

Rank	Company	Sales ($ mil.)	Rank	Company	Sales ($ mil.)	Rank	Company	Sales ($ mil.)
151	National Basketball Association	4,400	201	Burlington Coat Factory Warehouse	3,424	251	McCarthy Building Companies	2,900
152	Levi Strauss	4,303	202	Raley's	3,400	252	CUNA Mutual	2,890
153	Perdue Incorporated	4,300	203	Bass Pro Shops	3,400	253	Novant Health	2,887
154	The Scoular Company	4,300	204	Swift Transportation	3,400	254	Hunt Consolidated	2,870
155	Hallmark Cards	4,300	205	Parsons Corporation	3,400	255	Drummond Company	2,870
156	Battelle Memorial Institute	4,181	206	Factory Mutual Insurance	3,365	256	University of Washington	2,853
157	Salvation Army	4,157	207	Hensel Phelps Construction	3,337	257	Memorial Hermann Healthcare System	2,841
158	Whiting-Turner Contracting	4,150	208	JohnsonDiversey, Inc.	3,316	258	DeBruce Grain	2,830
159	Manor Care	4,130	209	ServiceMaster	3,311	259	Cornell University	2,826
160	Unified Grocers	4,105	210	US Oncology	3,304	260	Columbia University	2,820
161	Eby-Brown Company	4,100	211	Bonneville Power Administration	3,269	261	Zachry Holdings	2,800
162	Booz Allen Hamilton	4,100	212	Goodwill Industries	3,250	262	DeMoulas Super Markets	2,800
163	Ohio State University	4,090	213	Castle Harlan	3,245	263	Quintiles Transnational	2,800
164	Mutual of Omaha	4,073	214	Gilbane, Inc.	3,210	264	Rich Products	2,800
165	Catholic Healthcare Partners	4,045	215	Red Cross	3,204	265	Amsted Industries	2,800
166	Pacific Mutual	4,010	216	Black & Veatch	3,200	266	Sammons Enterprises	2,800
167	The Renco Group	4,000	217	Vanguard Health Systems	3,200	267	Sentara Healthcare	2,776
168	Kingston Technology	4,000	218	Medline Industries	3,190	268	Navy Federal Credit Union	2,772
169	Golden State Foods	4,000	219	New York Power Authority	3,185	269	J.E. Dunn Construction Group	2,760
170	Banner Health	3,971	220	CHRISTUS Health	3,168	270	National Hockey League	2,747
171	OSI Restaurant Partners	3,963	221	Golub Corporation	3,140	271	Securian Financial	2,746
172	Grant Thornton International	3,956	222	LPL Investment Holdings	3,117	272	Salt River Project	2,739
173	Red Apple Group	3,950	223	Dot Foods	3,100	273	Vanderbilt University	2,733
174	St. Joseph Health System	3,944	224	Structure Tone	3,100	274	Flex-N-Gate	2,720
175	Catholic Health East	3,926	225	Pennsylvania Lottery	3,089	275	Services Group of America	2,700
176	University of Illinois	3,900	226	Intermountain Health Care	3,049	276	Ag Processing	2,685
177	Roundy's Supermarkets	3,900	227	Howard Hughes Medical Institute	3,029	277	M. A. Mortenson	2,684
178	Ace Hardware	3,864	228	International Data Group	3,020	278	SSM Health Care	2,682
179	Jones Financial Companies	3,859	229	Jefferson Health System	3,010	279	Group Health Cooperative	2,665
180	InterTech Group	3,800	230	OSI Industries	3,000	280	Momentive Performance Materials	2,639
181	Texas Lottery	3,775	231	Ashley Furniture	3,000	281	University of Chicago	2,624
182	Sisters of Mercy Health System	3,748	232	MAINES Paper & Food Service	3,000	282	Leprino Foods	2,620
183	Tauber Oil	3,736	233	WinCo Foods	3,000	283	Mary Kay	2,600
184	Schneider National	3,700	234	JR Simplot	3,000	284	Spectrum Health System	2,596
185	Henry Ford Health System	3,690	235	Advocate Health Care	3,000	285	Harvard Pilgrim Health Care	2,591
186	Stater Bros.	3,674	236	ABC Supply	3,000	286	Sentry Insurance	2,588
187	Brightstar Corp.	3,570	237	Software House	3,000	287	Asplundh Tree Expert	2,580
188	H.T. Hackney	3,550	238	Glazer's Wholesale Drug Company	3,000	288	Golden Horizons	2,580
189	Walsh Group	3,530	239	Sports Authority	2,980	289	Wilbur-Ellis Company	2,577
190	Schwan Food	3,530	240	Boise Cascade	2,978	290	University of California, Davis	2,571
191	Port Authority of New York and New Jersey	3,528	241	Chick-fil-A	2,960	291	Fairview Health Services	2,567
192	Georgia Lottery	3,519	242	Grocers Supply	2,950	292	World Wide Technology	2,560
193	AllianceBernstein L.P.	3,514	243	O'Neal Steel	2,930	293	Graham Packaging	2,559
194	CalPERS	3,514	244	Alex Lee	2,920	294	Do it Best	2,546
195	Berry Plastics	3,513	245	General Parts	2,910	295	Allina Hospitals	2,534
196	MedStar Health	3,502	246	University of Alabama System	2,900	296	Travelport Limited	2,527
197	Central National-Gottesman	3,500	247	Sabre Holdings	2,900	297	University of Southern California	2,524
198	California Dairies Inc.	3,500	248	Schreiber Foods	2,900	298	Quality King Distributors	2,500
199	Harvard University	3,482	249	Tube City IMS	2,900	299	Schnuck Markets	2,500
200	Consolidated Electrical Distributors	3,430	250	JELD-WEN, inc.	2,900	300	Truman Arnold	2,500

The 300 Largest Employers in
Hoover's Handbook of Private Companies 2010

Rank	Company	Employees	Rank	Company	Employees	Rank	Company	Employees
1	US Postal Service	663,238	51	Golden Horizons	41,000	101	Henry Ford Health System	21,500
2	ARAMARK Corporation	260,000	52	FMR LLC	40,000	102	St. Joseph Health System	21,500
3	General Motors	243,000	53	Jones Financial Companies	40,000	103	24 Hour Fitness	21,410
4	HCA Inc.	191,000	54	Menard, Inc.	40,000	104	Schneider National	21,400
5	Kaiser Permanente	167,300	55	Ohio State University	39,120	105	Perdue Incorporated	21,000
6	Deloitte Touche Tohmatsu	165,000	56	University of Michigan	37,925	106	Jefferson Health System	20,700
7	Carlson Companies	160,000	57	Genesis HealthCare	37,700	107	University of New Mexico	20,210
8	Cargill, Incorporated	159,000	58	Wegmans Food Markets	37,000	108	PETCO Animal Supplies	20,100
9	PricewaterhouseCoopers	155,693	59	Giant Eagle	37,000	109	Hearst Corporation	20,000
10	Delphi Automotive	146,600	60	Catholic Healthcare Partners	36,925	110	Battelle Memorial Institute	20,000
11	Publix Super Markets	144,000	61	Nationwide Mutual Insurance	36,023	111	JELD-WEN, inc.	20,000
12	KPMG International	136,896	62	Red Cross	35,000	112	C & S Wholesale Grocers	20,000
13	Ernst & Young Global	135,000	63	City University of New York	33,642	113	SunGard Data Systems	20,000
14	Hilton Worldwide	130,000	64	Freeman Decorating Services	32,200	114	Lifetouch Inc.	20,000
15	University of California	127,368	65	Life Care Centers	31,000	115	MacAndrews & Forbes	19,800
16	Ascension Health	107,000	66	Grant Thornton International	30,662	116	University of Minnesota	19,274
17	OSI Restaurant Partners	105,000	67	University of California, Davis	30,086	117	Vanguard Health Systems	19,200
18	IGA, Inc.	92,000	68	Kohler Co.	30,000	118	Highmark Inc.	19,000
19	Goodwill Industries	86,000	69	Duke University Health System	29,826	119	Bon Secours Health System	19,000
20	Cellco Partnership	85,800	70	Sisters of Mercy Health System	29,500	120	Guardian Industries	19,000
21	State University of New York	83,547	71	Laureate Education	28,500	121	Booz Allen Hamilton	19,000
22	Harrah's Entertainment	80,000	72	IAC North America	28,245	122	Roundy's Supermarkets	19,000
23	Cox Enterprises	77,000	73	University of Washington	28,198	123	Iowa Health System	18,923
24	Catholic Health Initiatives	70,760	74	Asplundh Tree Expert	27,589	124	University of Alabama System	18,785
25	Koch Industries	70,000	75	Advance Publications	27,200	125	Claire's Stores	18,700
26	Mars, Incorporated	70,000	76	ServiceMaster	27,000	126	National Institutes of Health	18,627
27	State Farm Mutual	68,600	77	Texas A&M University System	26,876	127	University of Rochester	18,531
28	H-E-B	68,000	78	First Data Corporation	26,600	128	Indiana University	18,427
29	Enterprise Rent-A-Car	65,000	79	Burlington Coat Factory Warehouse	26,580	129	University of Wisconsin-Madison	18,374
30	Platinum Equity	60,000	80	U.S. Foodservice	26,000	130	Columbia Sussex	18,250
31	Meijer, Inc.	60,000	81	CHRISTUS Health	25,000	131	William Beaumont Hospital	18,050
32	Manor Care	60,000	82	Banner Health	25,000	132	Amtrak	18,000
33	Sitel Corporation	60,000	83	University of Illinois	24,513	133	Hobby Lobby	18,000
34	Salvation Army	59,651	84	Advocate Health Care	24,500	134	Environmental Protection Agency	18,000
35	Mayo Foundation	57,000	85	University of Missouri	24,013	135	Schwan Food	18,000
36	Hy-Vee, Inc.	55,000	86	Day & Zimmermann	24,000	136	Nypro Inc.	18,000
37	Catholic Health East	54,000	87	SSM Health Care	24,000	137	Central Parking	18,000
38	Delaware North Companies	50,000	88	CH2M HILL Companies	24,000	138	Fairview Health Services	18,000
39	Chick-fil-A	50,000	89	Golub Corporation	23,892	139	Stater Bros.	18,000
40	Wakefern Food	50,000	90	Federal Prison Industries	23,152	140	University of Southern California	18,000
41	Catholic Healthcare West	50,000	91	MedStar Health	23,000	141	Neiman Marcus	18,000
42	Sutter Health	47,892	92	Wheaton Franciscan Services	23,000	142	Avaya Inc.	18,000
43	Liberty Mutual	45,000	93	Quintiles Transnational	23,000	143	Health Care Service Corporation	17,500
44	Providence Health & Services	45,000	94	University of Nebraska	23,000	144	BayCare Health System	17,400
45	Trinity Health	44,500	95	Intermountain Health Care	23,000	145	Forstmann Little & Co.	17,034
46	Bechtel Group	44,000	96	Freescale Semiconductor	22,900	146	Sentara Healthcare	17,000
47	Army and Air Force Exchange	43,658	97	Allina Hospitals	22,347	147	Partners HealthCare System	16,981
48	Adventist Health System	43,000	98	SavaSeniorCare	22,000	148	AMC Entertainment	16,800
49	H Group Holding	42,000	99	USAA	21,900	149	General Parts	16,800
50	Knowledge Learning	42,000	100	Vanderbilt University	21,502	150	Memorial Hermann Healthcare	16,500

SOURCE: HOOVER'S, INC., DATABASE, DECEMBER 2009

Rank	Company	Employees	Rank	Company	Employees	Rank	Company	Employees
151	Vanderbilt University Medical Center	16,230	201	Massachusetts Mutual Life Insurance	12,000	251	US Oncology	9,600
152	Bass Pro Shops	16,000	202	K-VA-T Food Stores	12,000	252	Grocers Supply	9,550
153	ShopKo Stores	16,000	203	S.C. Johnson	12,000	253	Guitar Center	9,540
154	Wawa, Inc.	16,000	204	Yale University	11,750	254	Big Y Foods	9,500
155	InterTech Group	16,000	205	Discount Tire	11,652	255	Blue Cross and Blue Shield of Florida	9,500
156	ClubCorp USA	16,000	206	Tennessee Valley Authority	11,584	256	Baptist Health South Florida	9,374
157	Sports Authority	15,825	207	Mohegan Tribal Gaming Authority	11,575	257	OSI Industries	9,200
158	McKinsey & Company	15,600	208	Flex-N-Gate	11,500	258	Amsted Industries	9,200
159	Cornell University	15,558	209	Parsons Corporation	11,500	259	Land O'Lakes	9,100
160	Zachry Holdings	15,500	210	Sheetz, Inc.	11,500	260	Arctic Slope Regional Corporation	9,000
161	Clayton, Dubilier & Rice	15,500	211	The Renco Group	11,400	261	Marsh Supermarkets	9,000
162	Hallmark Cards	15,500	212	Realogy Corporation	11,400	262	APi Group	9,000
163	Harvard University	15,302	213	Levi Strauss	11,400	263	Sabre Holdings	9,000
164	Raley's	15,000	214	SAS Institute	11,019	264	Capital Group Companies	9,000
165	Volunteers of America	15,000	215	ADESA, Inc.	11,000	265	Infor Global Solutions	9,000
166	New York Life Insurance	15,000	216	Quad/Graphics, Inc.	11,000	266	Crown Equipment	9,000
167	Peter Kiewit Sons'	15,000	217	CompuCom Systems	11,000	267	Cook Group	9,000
168	Schnuck Markets	15,000	218	Scripps Health	11,000	268	U.S. Premium Beef	8,900
169	Turner Industries	15,000	219	Blue Cross (SC)	11,000	269	NTK Holdings	8,800
170	Inova Health System Foundation	15,000	220	Montefiore Medical Center	11,000	270	Ceridian Corporation	8,776
171	University of Chicago	14,772	221	Southern Wine & Spirits	11,000	271	Dart Container	8,500
172	Resurrection Health Care	14,409	222	TA Delaware	11,000	272	Key Safety Systems	8,500
173	Spectrum Health System	14,400	223	Alex Lee	10,900	273	Allegis Group	8,500
174	Amscan Holdings	14,130	224	Michigan State University	10,900	274	Source Interlink Companies	8,500
175	Columbia University	14,113	225	JohnsonDiversey, Inc.	10,800	275	New England Alliance for Health	8,392
176	Ashley Furniture	14,000	226	Iasis Healthcare	10,775	276	Energy Future Holdings	8,150
177	Koch Foods	14,000	227	Sisters of Charity of Leavenworth Health System	10,770	277	Graybar Electric	8,100
178	Fry's Electronics	14,000	228	QuikTrip Corporation	10,745	278	American Family Insurance	8,071
179	Berry Plastics	13,800	229	Beall's Inc.	10,700	279	Schottenstein Stores	8,050
180	Keystone Foods	13,700	230	Affinia Group	10,576	280	The Methodist Hospital System	8,000
181	International Data Group	13,640	231	ValleyCrest Companies	10,500	281	Heico Companies	8,000
182	ContiGroup Companies	13,500	232	Bloomberg L.P.	10,500	282	U.S. Xpress	8,000
183	University of Kentucky	13,500	233	Sequa Corporation	10,340	283	Yates Companies	8,000
184	Castle Harlan	13,450	234	Walsh Group	10,300	284	Bose Corporation	8,000
185	Pro-Build Holdings	13,204	235	Reyes Holdings	10,300	285	Temple University	7,996
186	Johns Hopkins Health System	13,000	236	Foster Poultry Farms	10,000	286	Les Schwab Tire Centers	7,900
187	Alticor Inc.	13,000	237	WinCo Foods	10,000	287	Red Apple Group	7,800
188	Estes Express Lines	13,000	238	Milliken & Company	10,000	288	Kinder Morgan	7,800
189	GNC Corporation	12,862	239	JR Simplot	10,000	289	Ardent Health	7,745
190	MediaNews Group	12,700	240	Dow Corning	10,000	290	University of Iowa Hospitals and Clinics	7,625
191	Colliers International	12,700	241	Andersen Corporation	10,000	291	Atlantic Express Transportation	7,600
192	Brookshire Grocery	12,700	242	Follett Corporation	10,000	292	Haworth, Inc.	7,500
193	Taylor Corporation	12,500	243	University of Maryland Medical System	10,000	293	TIAA-CREF	7,500
194	Novant Health	12,500	244	REI	10,000	294	McWane, Inc.	7,500
195	Yale New Haven Health System	12,176	245	Stanford University	9,821	295	Eddie Bauer	7,427
196	Real Mex Restaurants	12,085	246	Pella Corporation	9,800	296	Graham Packaging	7,400
197	CareGroup, Inc.	12,000	247	Catalent Pharma Solutions	9,800	297	Rich Products	7,300
198	Gordon Food Service	12,000	248	Baker & McKenzie	9,700	298	Biomet, Inc.	7,220
199	Keane Inc.	12,000	249	Black & Veatch	9,600	299	Port Authority of New York and New Jersey	7,127
200	Alsco, Inc.	12,000	250	HVM L.L.C.	9,600	300	Solo Cup	7,100

The *Inc.* 500 Fastest-Growing Private Companies in America

Rank	Company	Headquarters	Sales Growth Increase (%)*
1	Northern Capital Insurance	Miami, FL	19,812.2
2	National Retirement Partners	San Juan Capistrano, CA	13,416.4
3	Harley Stanfield	Washington, DC	13,350.4
4	Perfect Fitness	Mill Valley, CA	12,749.3
5	IntegraClick	Sarasota, FL	12,654.4
6	Kiva Systems	Woburn, MA	10,399.0
7	Freedom Health	Tampa, FL	10,035.3
8	One Technologies	Dallas, TX	9,946.4
9	MediaTrust	New York, NY	9,481.1
10	Criterion Systems	Vienna, VA	8,433.6
11	ProKarma	Beaverton, OR	8,311.4
12	Canopy Financial	San Francisco, CA	7,929.1
13	MedVantx	San Diego, CA	7,898.5
14	Skullcandy	Park City, UT	6,251.6
15	Centuria	Dulles, VA	5,968.8
16	Snap Fitness	Chanhassen, MN	5,906.8
17	P3S	San Antonio, TX	5,898.4
18	MonaVie	South Jordan, UT	5,883.0
19	ITA International	Yorktown, VA	5,778.9
20	Working Media Group	New York, NY	4,782.4
21	Blue Entertainment Sports Television	Louisville, KY	4,685.3
22	vAuto	Oak Brook, IL	4,659.9
23	BancVue	Austin, TX	4,645.5
24	InsuranceAgents.com	Columbus, OH	4,582.2
25	Ahura Scientific	Wilmington, MA	4,564.8
26	Ruckus Wireless	Sunnyvale, CA	4,540.1
27	SDV Solutions	Toano, VA	4,345.6
28	SFP	Leawood, KS	4,321.3
29	iCore Networks	McLean, VA	3,924.0
30	StarTex Power	Houston, TX	3,794.3
31	FedStore	Rockville, MD	3,748.8
32	ID Experts	Beaverton, OR	3,632.9
33	ARK Solutions	Chantilly, VA	3,537.4
34	Revel Consulting	Kirkland, WA	3,531.2
35	Diapers.com	Montclair, NJ	3,473.8
36	ICS	Vienna, VA	3,431.0
37	GourmetGiftBaskets.com	Manchester, NH	3,260.5
38	Oil Chem Technologies	Sugar Land, TX	3,251.7
39	ReachLocal	Woodland Hills, CA	3,217.2
40	mSpot	Palo Alto, CA	3,189.4
41	Xtreme Consulting Group	Redmond, WA	3,092.5
42	Nutricap Labs	Farmingdale, NY	2,899.7
43	FTEN	New York, NY	2,863.7
44	Enalasys	Calexico, CA	2,813.7
45	HMS Technologies	Martinsburg, WV	2,750.8
46	Royal Buying Group	Lisle, IL	2,748.4
47	Service Financial	Whitefish Bay, WI	2,706.2
48	Aqua Superstore	Port Charlotte, FL	2,694.6
49	Echo Global Logistics	Chicago, IL	2,667.0
50	Bridgepoint Education	San Diego, CA	2,645.4
51	Direct Exteriors	Maple Grove, MN	2,559.4
52	Mission Essential Personnel	Columbus, OH	2,537.9
53	Clear Harbor	Alpharetta, GA	2,469.6
54	Broadnet Teleservices	Highlands Ranch, CO	2,358.4
55	EffectiveUI	Denver, CO	2,333.9
56	Namaste Solar	Boulder, CO	2,243.1
57	ReSource Pro	New York, NY	2,239.5
58	Allegiance	South Jordan, UT	2,235.7
59	Hardwire	Pocomoke City, MD	2,235.1
60	Clarisonic	Bellevue, WA	2,197.1
61	International Checkout	Santa Monica, CA	2,191.2
62	DeviceAnywhere	San Mateo, CA	2,103.8
63	Sirsai	Redmond, WA	2,076.9
64	Workway	Burbank, CA	2,058.1
65	Lifematters	Bethesda, MD	2,051.1
66	StoreBoard Media	New York, NY	2,025.7
67	iSeatz	New Orleans, LA	1,983.6
68	1 Source Consulting	Washington, DC	1,971.4
69	Radiation Technical Services	New Orleans, LA	1,957.2
70	Electronic Payments	Calverton, NY	1,953.5
71	SmartPrice Sales & Marketing	Schaumburg, IL	1,951.8
72	SolutionSet	Palo Alto, CA	1,931.8
73	Adlucent	Austin, TX	1,908.4
74	US Media Consulting	Miami, FL	1,898.7
75	Simply Canvas	Kent, OH	1,896.4
76	2Pi Solutions	Washington, DC	1,895.1
77	Technical and Project Engineering	Kingstowne, VA	1,890.5
78	High Street Partners	Annapolis, MD	1,872.9
79	Remedy Roofing	Katy, TX	1,871.7
80	Suntiva Executive Consulting	Falls Church, VA	1,868.4
81	Flipswap	Torrance, CA	1,839.7
82	NWN	Waltham, MA	1,800.2
83	Connexion Technologies	Cary, NC	1,784.7
84	ClinAssure	Irvine, CA	1,743.0
85	Summit Tech Consulting	Atlanta, GA	1,740.8
86	Prep Sportswear	Seattle, WA	1,728.3
87	Pangea3	New York, NY	1,718.1
88	AtLast Fulfillment	Denver, CO	1,708.6
89	Charles F. Day & Associates	Davenport, IA	1,678.4
90	CSI	Oklahoma City, OK	1,673.5
91	American Correctional Solutions	Orange, CA	1,659.0
92	Instant Tax Service	Dayton, OH	1,658.0
93	TSS-Radio	Chicago, IL	1,651.3
94	TeraThink	Reston, VA	1,611.5
95	Robinson Radio	Glen Allen, VA	1,609.8
96	Celergo	Deerfield, IL	1,581.2
97	Bug Music	Los Angeles, CA	1,564.5
98	KBW Financial Staffing & Recruiting	Bedford, NH	1,546.1
99	Nexcelom Bioscience	Lawrence, MA	1,521.9
100	C&I Engineering	Richland, WA	1,513.2

*Average annual sales growth measured over a three-year period.

SOURCE: *INC.*, SEPTEMBER 1, 2009

The *Inc.* 500 Fastest-Growing Private Companies in America (continued)

Rank	Company	Headquarters	Sales Growth Increase (%)	Rank	Company	Headquarters	Sales Growth Increase (%)
101	Zeon Solutions	Milwaukee, WI	1,506.4	151	Reuseit	Chicago, IL	1,190.5
102	Market Tech	Scotts Valley, CA	1,496.5	152	CPX Interactive	Westbury, NY	1,187.6
103	Technatomy	Fairfax, VA	1,491.3	153	World Pac Paper	Cincinnati, OH	1,182.4
104	FireFold	Concord, NC	1,490.7	154	College Hunks Hauling Junk	Tampa, FL	1,179.1
105	Conferencing Advisors	Capistrano Beach, CA	1,480.7	155	Global Wedge	Riverside, CA	1,175.1
106	WBS Connect	Denver, CO	1,476.5	156	SendOutCards	Salt Lake City, UT	1,173.4
107	Dicom Solutions	Irvine, CA	1,473.9	157	OraMetrix	Richardson, TX	1,170.9
108	oDesk	Menlo Park, CA	1,470.2	158	BlueStar Energy Services	Chicago, IL	1,170.0
109	Innovative Foods	Wilmington, MA	1,463.7	159	Payscape Advisors	Atlanta, GA	1,161.8
110	National Positions	Agoura Hills, CA	1,455.6	160	TowerCo	Cary, NC	1,155.8
111	BlackLine Systems	Calabasas, CA	1,452.5	161	Campus Habitat	New York, NY	1,152.4
112	MacUpdate	Traverse City, MI	1,443.3	162	Packet360	Glen Allen, VA	1,147.6
113	BabyEarth	Round Rock, TX	1,440.1	163	Angel Staffing	San Antonio, TX	1,138.5
114	Rockett Interactive	Cary, NC	1,429.9	164	Mediaspectrum	Burlington, MA	1,133.2
115	eCardio Diagnostics	The Woodlands, TX	1,424.6	165	EVO^2	San Mateo, CA	1,129.0
116	Latshaw Drilling & Exploration	Tulsa, OK	1,419.0	166	Smiley Media	Austin, TX	1,126.3
117	Centro	Chicago, IL	1,418.7	167	The Neat Company	Philadelphia, PA	1,121.2
118	Improving Enterprises	Dallas, TX	1,417.1	168	Visible Technologies	Seattle, WA	1,120.6
119	Solvern Innovations	Baltimore, MD	1,415.5	169	Future Ads	Irvine, CA	1,114.7
120	Bosh Global Services	Newport News, VA	1,415.0	170	Kaydon Group	Taunton, MA	1,113.1
121	Atlas Properties	Fort Worth, TX	1,412.5	171	GeBBS Healthcare Solutions	Englewood Cliffs, NJ	1,110.0
122	TAG Employer Services	Phoenix, AZ	1,396.0	172	PriceSpective	Blue Bell, PA	1,109.8
123	CJ Environmental	Sharon, MA	1,394.5	173	GlobalTranz	Phoenix, AZ	1,104.8
124	Triplefin	Cincinnati, OH	1,383.0	174	MicroTech	Vienna, VA	1,102.9
125	Headspring Systems	Austin, TX	1,366.3	175	Senior Whole Health	Cambridge, MA	1,099.9
126	ERT	Annapolis Junction, MD	1,354.6	176	AtTask	Orem, UT	1,097.1
127	Affiliate Media	Irvine, CA	1,353.5	177	Troon Construction	Mesa, AZ	1,096.0
128	GlowTouch Technologies	Louisville, KY	1,350.2	178	GuardianEdge	San Francisco, CA	1,073.3
129	Sensor Technologies	Red Bank, NJ	1,348.1	179	Logik	Washington, DC	1,067.1
130	Heritage Makers	Provo, UT	1,342.8	180	Catapult Consultants	Arlington, VA	1,062.7
131	Genesis Today	Austin, TX	1,314.3	181	Spectraforce Technologies	Raleigh, NC	1,005.5
132	Vizio	Irvine, CA	1,313.0	182	The Chip	Newhall, CA	1,060.0
133	Clear Align	Eagleville, PA	1,305.3	183	Hyper Interactive Media	Draper, UT	1,057.7
134	Property Solutions International	Provo, UT	1,295.6	184	Walz Group	Temecula, CA	1,057.0
135	Glispa	St. Paul, MN	1,295.2	185	Code Shred	Island Park, NY	1,055.9
136	VitalWear	South San Francisco, CA	1,285.2	186	cPrime	Foster City, CA	1,053.4
137	XCEND Group	Brighton, MI	1,266.2	187	Torrey Hills Technologies	San Diego, CA	1,051.7
138	U.S. Energy Development	Getzville, NY	1,260.3	188	iContact	Durham, NC	1,049.4
139	SingleSource Property Solutions	Canonsburg, PA	1,253.4	189	Nova USA Wood Products	Portland, OR	1,041.2
140	Go Internet Media	Santa Clara, CA	1,241.9	190	DMS International	Silver Spring, MD	1,025.7
141	Zumasys	Irvine, CA	1,234.1	191	Realty ONE Group	Las Vegas, NV	1,024.3
142	Syndero	San Francisco, CA	1,222.2	192	Milestone Metals	Fairfax, VA	1,024.1
143	Loeffler Randall	New York, NY	1,220.7	193	Ignify	Cerritos, CA	1,023.0
144	G5 Search Marketing	Bend, OR	1,208.5	194	Generational Equity	Dallas, TX	1,022.7
145	Remote Medical International	Seattle, WA	1,206.6	195	See Kai Run	Woodinville, WA	1,021.1
146	Pallet Central Enterprises	Atlanta, GA	1,203.0	196	Monoprice	Rancho Cucamonga, CA	1,016.1
147	The Glenture Group	Northbrook, IL	1,201.4	197	Stream Energy	Dallas, TX	1,014.3
148	AB Star Group	Newark, CA	1,198.8	198	eMason	Clearwater, FL	1,009.8
149	Golden Key Group	Centreville, VA	1,194.9	199	JSymmetric	Atlanta, GA	1,008.7
150	Capital City Technologies	Suwanee, GA	1,190.9	200	TechCFO	Atlanta, GA	1,006.6

The *Inc.* 500 Fastest-Growing Private Companies in America (continued)

Rank	Company	Headquarters	Sales Growth Increase (%)	Rank	Company	Headquarters	Sales Growth Increase (%)
201	Kimball Concepts	Chandler, AZ	1,004.6	251	Big Fish Games	Seattle, WA	880.0
202	U.S. Gas & Electric	North Miami Beach, FL	1,003.7	252	US Aluminum Services	Orlando, FL	877.8
203	The Groop	Los Angeles, CA	999.9	253	Cali Bamboo	San Diego, CA	877.1
204	Alteris Renewables	Wilton, CT	999.0	254	APN Consulting	Princeton, NJ	873.4
205	The Snack Factory	Princeton, NJ	997.4	255	Britstan Technology	Brea, CA	873.0
206	Ingenious	Houston, TX	995.3	256	MindSmack.com	New York, NY	869.3
207	Interbank FX	Salt Lake City, UT	987.9	257	Metal Mafia	New York, NY	866.7
208	Environmental Design & Construction	Washington, DC	967.3	258	GATR Technologies	Huntsville, AL	866.1
209	FriendFinder Networks	Boca Raton, FL	966.4	259	The Winvale Group	Washington, DC	866.0
210	ACI Estate	Doylestown, PA	964.0	260	Media Two Interactive	Clayton, NC	865.7
211	Quantum Retail	Minneapolis, MN	963.4	261	ChemSol	Minnetonka, MN	863.0
212	EGB Systems & Solutions	Stamford, CT	961.5	262	Ali International	Los Angeles, CA	862.3
213	Texas Physical Therapy Specialists	San Antonio, TX	957.9	263	Charlesson	Oklahoma City, OK	858.0
214	MBS Dev	Englewood, CO	955.0	264	SkyMira	Milford, CT	855.3
215	Lurn	Gaithersburg, MD	950.8	265	Carahsoft Technology	Reston, VA	854.2
216	BrightStar	Gurnee, IL	944.5	266	Children's Progress	New York, NY	854.1
217	Sand Creek Post & Beam	Wayne, NE	943.0	267	Outskirts Press	Parker, CO	850.5
218	Total Attorneys	Chicago, IL	938.3	268	MediGain	Dallas, TX	844.4
219	Demandforce	San Francisco, CA	936.2	269	Eco-Products	Boulder, CO	843.9
220	Cities2Night.com	Philadelphia, PA	935.4	270	Extrakare	Norcross, GA	834.6
221	The Knowland Group	Salisbury, MD	933.6	271	SkyBox-USA	Juno Beach, FL	833.5
222	Audigy Group	Vancouver, WA	933.0	272	Bills.com	San Mateo, CA	833.1
223	Carchex	Hunt Valley, MD	932.5	273	5LINX Enterprises	Rochester, NY	831.8
224	Celestar	Tampa, FL	932.5	274	Smarsh	Portland, OR	831.4
225	Plus1 Marketing	Columbia, MO	928.6	275	OnTimeSupplies.com	Atlanta, GA	830.4
226	United States Construction	Pompano Beach, FL	927.2	276	Search Wizards	Atlanta, GA	827.5
227	Jobs2Web	Minnetonka, MN	925.3	277	U.S. Tax Advantage	Evanston, IL	822.1
228	Strategic Systems	Dublin, OH	923.6	278	Kingfisher Systems	Alexandria, VA	821.9
229	MensRedTag.com	Joliet, IL	922.4	279	Accelera Solutions	Falls Church, VA	821.4
230	Cyrus Innovation	New York, NY	919.7	280	Strike Construction	Spring, TX	821.3
231	Dirt Pros EVS	Plantation, FL	918.3	281	SoDel Concepts	Bethany Beach, DE	820.5
232	Covario	San Diego, CA	917.7	282	C.L. Carson	Austin, TX	820.4
233	Pandigital	Dublin, CA	917.2	283	Reveal Imaging Technologies	Bedford, MA	818.1
234	Diplomat Specialty Pharmacy	Swartz Creek, MI	917.2	284	Anytime Fitness	Hastings, MN	815.5
235	The Analysis Group	Falls Church, VA	915.2	285	Custom Tree Care	Topeka, KS	809.1
236	Johnny Cupcakes	Weymouth, MA	914.3	286	Corporate Brokers	Annapolis, MD	806.3
237	eIQnetworks	Acton, MA	904.5	287	TerraCycle	Trenton, NJ	803.4
238	HostGator.com	Houston, TX	896.4	288	Rally Software	Boulder, CO	801.8
239	Logical Innovations	Richmond, VA	894.4	289	Winshuttle	Bothell, WA	801.1
240	Ocenture	Jacksonville, FL	894.2	290	The Paquin Healthcare Companies	Celebration, FL	799.7
241	Hillard Heintze	Chicago, IL	892.3	291	Canyon Construction	Frederick, MD	798.8
242	BargainLocks	North Canton, OH	891.7	292	Best Practice Systems	Centennial, CO	798.2
243	ePsolutions	Austin, TX	889.9	293	Data Processing Services	Suwanee, GA	797.3
244	NetSteps	American Fork, UT	889.7	294	Dynalabs	St. Louis, MO	795.3
245	American Bancard	Boca Raton, FL	887.8	295	Simplion Technologies	San Jose, CA	794.3
246	Source Technologies	Albuquerque, NM	884.9	296	Rapid7	Boston, MA	794.1
247	Volusion	Simi Valley, CA	884.5	297	Genband	Plano, TX	791.6
248	2Is	Walpole, MA	883.9	298	MIR3	San Diego, CA	791.6
249	USfalcon	Morrisville, NC	881.0	299	Alatec	Huntsville, AL	790.2
250	Thrustmaster of Texas	Houston, TX	880.0	300	BoxTone	Columbia, MD	789.6

The *Inc.* 500 Fastest-Growing Private Companies in America (continued)

Rank	Company	Headquarters	Sales Growth Increase (%)	Rank	Company	Headquarters	Sales Growth Increase (%)
301	EMS	Houston, TX	785.2	351	Secure-24	Southfield, MI	704.1
302	Array Information Technology	Greenbelt, MD	781.4	352	Mystikal Solutions	San Antonio, TX	698.5
303	Cowan & Associates	Arlington, VA	781.1	353	Red Bricks Media	San Francisco, CA	698.4
304	Power Home Technologies	Raleigh, NC	781.0	354	LesserEvil Brand Snack	Village of Tuckahoe, NY	696.6
305	PowerON Services	Roseville, CA	779.2	355	FURminator	Fenton, MO	695.2
306	Access Technology Solutions	Provo, UT	777.6	356	Spine & Sport	Rincon, GA	693.6
307	Health Diagnostics	Melville, NY	775.8	357	Sittercity	Chicago, IL	692.8
308	WaterFilters.net	Zumbrota, MN	774.4	358	Enrich IT	Alpharetta, GA	692.3
309	Systems Made Simple	Syracuse, NY	771.8	359	Ignited Discovery	Arlington, VA	691.8
310	Berlin Building Supply	Berlin, WI	767.8	360	Sage Management	Hanover, MD	691.8
311	Forward Edge	Cincinnati, OH	765.7	361	Aurora Contractors	Ronkonkoma, NY	691.6
312	Premier Integrity Solutions	Russell Springs, KY	765.5	362	Fusion Systems	Burr Ridge, IL	691.0
313	Lead Flash	Delray Beach, FL	762.9	363	TableTopics	Berkeley, CA	688.0
314	EscapeWire Solutions	Buffalo, NY	762.5	364	AnswerLab	San Francisco, CA	686.9
315	Rapid Air Systems	Milwaukee, WI	761.7	365	AJ Riggins	Dallas, TX	686.5
316	Pop Labs	Houston, TX	761.5	366	Securit	Flushing, NY	685.7
317	Timeshare Relief	Torrance, CA	758.4	367	Sensis	Los Angeles, CA	684.5
318	Findaway World	Solon, OH	755.3	368	Raven Rock Workwear	Dayton, OH	683.7
319	Intermark Media	Woodbury, NY	754.5	369	Mindbody	San Luis Obispo, CA	682.4
320	Borrego Solar Systems	El Cajon, CA	754.4	370	Ovation Health & Life Services	Dallas, TX	679.2
321	Geo-Solutions	New Kensington, PA	752.9	371	Adayana	Indianapolis, IN	677.5
322	Impact Group	Saint Louis, MO	751.5	372	Triad Digital Media	Tampa, FL	677.2
323	Utility Integration Solutions	Lafayette, CA	744.0	373	Commcare Pharmacy	Fort Lauderdale, FL	675.4
324	Morgan Borszcz Consulting	Ashburn, VA	741.4	374	Zipcar	Cambridge, MA	674.8
325	Portfolio Creative	Columbus, OH	741.3	375	Polaris Direct	Hooksett, NH	674.6
326	MindFire	Irvine, CA	738.9	376	McLane Advanced Technologies	Temple, TX	670.9
327	Millennium Pharmacy Systems	Wexford, PA	737.5	377	Castle Rock Innovations	Chicago, IL	669.1
328	Devcon Group	Monument, CO	735.7	378	ESET	San Diego, CA	667.4
329	Angarai	Largo, MD	735.0	379	Torres Advanced Enterprise Solutions	Arlington, VA	667.0
330	Softek International	Edison, NJ	734.5	380	Quest Products	Libertyville, IL	666.6
331	Dogswell	Los Angeles, CA	733.2	381	Kirtas Technologies	Victor, NY	666.5
332	ESC Select	Amherst, NY	730.3	382	GS5	Dumfries, VA	663.3
333	Bluefish Wireless Management	Indianapolis, IN	727.4	383	Knowledge Marketing	Plymouth, MN	661.9
334	Simplex Healthcare	Brentwood, TN	727.4	384	Infusionsoft	Gilbert, AZ	661.5
335	Aasent Mortgage	Atlanta, GA	726.7	385	Landscape Masterpiece	Carlsbad, CA	658.6
336	Network Innovations	Chicago, IL	726.5	386	Libsys	Naperville, IL	658.2
337	Investor Relations International	Sherman Oaks, CA	723.7	387	Tactile Systems Technology	Minneapolis, MN	657.4
338	Squarespace	New York, NY	723.3	388	RAC Enterprise	West Hazleton, PA	655.7
339	Show Media	New York, NY	722.5	389	Lead Research Group	Huntington Beach, CA	652.9
340	U.S. Energy Services	Plymouth, MN	722.0	390	JBCStyle	New York, NY	650.2
341	SkinCareRx	Salt Lake City, UT	720.9	391	Reliable Environmental Transport	Bridgeport, WV	650.0
342	Pfister Energy	Paterson, NJ	720.9	392	Five Nines Technology	Lincoln, NE	649.1
343	BriMar Wood Innovations	Goshen, IN	719.3	393	Embassy International	Rockwall, TX	643.8
344	FTrans	Atlanta, GA	718.4	394	CyberData Technologies	Herndon, VA	643.0
345	iCrossing	Scottsdale, AZ	714.7	395	SoftNice	Allentown, PA	640.9
346	VST Consulting	Iselin, NJ	713.4	396	Engineering & Computer Simulations	Orlando, FL	640.0
347	Zebra Imaging	Austin, TX	712.8	397	SEF Stainless Steel	Baltimore, MD	638.9
348	Gold Star Mortgage Financial Group	Ann Arbor, MI	712.8	398	Tableau Software	Seattle, WA	638.9
349	Innovative Analytics	Kalamazoo, MI	709.9	399	MegaMeeting.com	Sherman Oaks, CA	638.8
350	Calnet	Reston, VA	705.3	400	Animax Entertainment	Van Nuys, CA	638.8

The *Inc.* 500 Fastest-Growing Private Companies in America (continued)

Rank	Company	Headquarters	Sales Growth Increase (%)
401	Most Brand Development and Advertising	Aliso Viejo, CA	638.1
402	Mountain Khakis	Charlotte, NC	638.0
403	Iverify	Charlotte, NC	637.0
404	Iplex	Alpharetta, GA	637.0
405	Digitaria	San Diego, CA	634.8
406	Saturna Capital	Bellingham, WA	634.0
407	Economic Modeling Specialists	Moscow, ID	631.3
408	Disability Group	Los Angeles, CA	626.9
409	Bomgar	Ridgeland, MS	626.8
410	The Watchery	Cedarhurst, NY	623.5
411	EAD	Omaha, NE	621.8
412	MaxTorque	Limerick, ME	620.3
413	Select Engineering	Tulsa, OK	620.0
414	Alpha Card Services	Huntingdon Valley, PA	620.0
415	Travel Ad Network	New York, NY	619.6
416	Ignite Media Solutions	Oldsmar, FL	618.0
417	Granicus	San Francisco, CA	617.9
418	Spring2 Technologies	Sandy, UT	617.9
419	Futura Builders Group	Jamaica, NY	617.6
420	BIAS Corporation	Atlanta, GA	616.7
421	Tellico Electric	Lenoir City, TN	612.8
422	Oak Grove Technologies	Raleigh, NC	612.6
423	PeopleShare	Philadelphia, PA	611.2
424	Bulk TV & Internet	Raleigh, NC	610.7
425	HealthDataInsights	Las Vegas, NV	610.3
426	IndSoft	St. Charles, IL	608.8
427	Sensible Micro	Odessa, FL	608.2
428	DyKnow	Indianapolis, IN	606.9
429	NeoPhotonics	San Jose, CA	606.8
430	Defender Direct	Indianapolis, IN	605.4
431	Gravity Payments	Seattle, WA	599.4
432	Integrated Mortgage Solutions	Houston, TX	597.9
433	Rennen International	South Ozone Park, NY	596.3
434	A & D Home Health Solutions	Newington, CT	594.2
435	101 Financial	Kahuku, HI	593.0
436	The Select Group	Raleigh, NC	591.3
437	Decypher Technologies	San Antonio, TX	585.1
438	American Unit	Frisco, TX	584.9
439	UniTek USA	Blue Bell, PA	583.3
440	Deemsys	Gahanna, OH	582.9
441	Ratchet	Minneapolis, MN	581.9
442	Culmen International	Alexandria, VA	581.5
443	Wise Men Consultants	Houston, TX	580.9
444	CommonPlaces e-Solutions	Hampstead, NH	580.8
445	Camp Bow Wow	Boulder, CO	580.2
446	Meridian Partners	Miami Beach, FL	580.2
447	Electronic Check Services	Springfield, MO	579.6
448	Hydra	Beverly Hills, CA	579.1
449	Xenosoft Technologies	Dallas, TX	576.2
450	RigNet	Houston, TX	573.2
451	Fortis Construction	Portland, OR	572.8
452	RightStar Systems	Vienna, VA	571.5
453	Battle Resource Management	Clarksville, MD	566.9
454	Orbis Clinical	Woburn, MA	566.9
455	Complete Office	Seattle, WA	566.0
456	CrankyApe.com	Cannon Falls, MN	565.5
457	Cardinal Technologies	Bethesda, MD	565.0
458	Luxor	Stafford, TX	563.5
459	Cactus Custom Analog Design	Chandler, AZ	561.2
460	Blue Streak Partners	New York, NY	559.5
461	SwaddleDesigns	Seattle, WA	558.6
462	LaserGifts	Prescott, AZ	556.4
463	NewsGator	Denver, CO	554.5
464	H&H Steel Fabricators	Dallas, TX	554.4
465	M2 Media Group	Stamford, CT	554.1
466	MotionPoint	Coconut Creek, FL	553.2
467	Oompa Toys	Madison, WI	552.3
468	The Coding Source	Los Angeles, CA	551.5
469	Planet Fitness	Dover, NH	551.4
470	DOMA Technologies	Virginia Beach, VA	550.9
471	iVision	Atlanta, GA	550.8
472	Ironbridge Consulting	Arlington, VA	550.4
473	Virpie	Southbury, CT	550.0
474	Aribex	Orem, UT	549.7
475	InfoSync Services	Wichita, KS	549.1
476	Monsoon	Portland, OR	547.7
477	James Ray International	Carlsbad, CA	547.4
478	Valudor Products	Rancho Santa Fe, CA	545.8
479	Inphi	Westlake Village, CA	547.3
480	Electronic Cash Systems	Rancho Santa Margarita, CA	544.1
481	Select Marketing Solutions	Gurnee, IL	543.2
482	Mad*Pow	Portsmouth, NH	541.2
483	Concorde Construction	Charlotte, NC	541.0
484	New Era Portfolio	Austin, TX	540.3
485	AdaQuest	Bellevue, WA	539.4
486	CareNet	San Antonio, TX	537.4
487	The Media Crew	Orlando, FL	536.7
488	DiscountOfficeItems.com	Columbus, WI	536.2
489	ScienceLogic	Reston, VA	535.8
490	KBK Technologies	Deerfield Beach, FL	535.3
491	Foundation Systems	San Francisco, CA	533.6
492	Netcordia	Annapolis, MD	533.9
493	MidSouth Geothermal	Memphis, TN	532.6
494	Incipio Technologies	Irvine, CA	532.1
495	WhiteHat Security	Santa Clara, CA	530.9
496	Single Digits	Manchester, NH	530.4
497	GyanSys	Indianapolis, IN	530.2
498	Mpell Solutions	Carlsbad, CA	530.2
499	HealthCareSeeker.com	Boonton, NJ	529.0
500	Spinnaker	Denver, CO	528.5

The *Forbes* Largest Private Companies in the US

Rank	Company	Sales ($ mil.)	Rank	Company	Sales ($ mil.)	Rank	Company	Sales ($ mil.)
1	Cargill	106,300	51	Keystone Foods	6,540	101	Roundy's Supermarkets	3,900
2	Koch Industries	100,000	52	Bloomberg	6,100	102	Edward Jones	3,860
3	Chrysler	47,600	53	Hexion Specialty Chemicals	6,090	103	Michaels Stores	3,820
4	GMAC Financial Services	35,450	54	McKinsey & Co.	6,000	104	Hyatt Hotels Corporation	3,800
5	Bechtel	31,400	55	Wawa	5,830	105	InterTech Group	3,800
6	Mars	30,000	56	DeBruce Grain	5,760	106	VWR Funding	3,760
7	HCA	28,370	57	Allegis Group	5,740	107	Stater Bros.	3,750
8	PricewaterhouseCoopers	26,200	58	MBM	5,700	108	Schneider National	3,700
9	Publix Super Markets	24,110	59	Guardian Industries	5,600	109	Neiman Marcus Group	3,640
10	Ernst & Young	21,400	60	SunGard Data Systems	5,600	110	Burlington Coat Factory	3,570
11	US Foodservice	19,810	61	CH2M Hill Cos.	5,590	111	Brightstar	3,570
12	C&S Wholesale Grocers	19,330	62	Kohler	5,500	112	H.T. Hackney	3,550
13	Flying J	18,000	63	Ergon	5,430	113	Walsh Group	3,530
14	Pilot Travel Centers	17,280	64	Graybar Electric	5,400	114	Schwan Food	3,530
15	Love's Travel Stops & Country Stores	16,500	65	Aleris International	5,300	115	Raley's	3,530
16	Tenaska Energy	16,000	66	McJunkin Red Man	5,260	116	Central National-Gottesman	3,500
17	TransMontaigne	15,950	67	Freescale Semiconductor	5,230	117	Eby-Brown	3,500
18	Cox Enterprises	15,400	68	Gulf States Toyota	5,100	118	Belk	3,500
19	H.E. Butt Grocery	15,100	69	Kinray	5,100	119	McCarthy Building Cos.	3,480
20	Meijer	13,880	70	Save Mart Supermarkets	5,000	120	Hensel Phelps Construction	3,440
21	Toys "R" Us	13,720	71	Unisource Worldwide	5,000	121	Parsons	3,440
22	Fidelity Investments	12,900	72	Hearst	4,810	122	Consolidated Elec Distributors	3,430
23	Aramark	12,470	73	Charmer Sunbelt Group	4,800	123	Bass Pro Shops	3,400
24	Enterprise Rent-A-Car	12,100	74	Wegmans Food Markets	4,800	124	Colonial Group	3,400
25	Reyes Holdings	11,800	75	Clark Enterprises	4,700	125	Swift Transportation	3,400
26	Energy Future Holdings	11,360	76	Tishman Construction	4,690	126	JohnsonDiversey	3,320
27	Platinum Equity	11,350	77	Perdue	4,600	127	ServiceMaster	3,310
28	Transammonia	11,210	78	Southwire	4,600	128	US Oncology	3,300
29	Dollar General	10,460	79	International Automotive Components	4,500	129	Golub	3,300
30	JM Family Enterprises	10,100	80	Oxbow	4,500	130	Sheetz	3,240
31	Kiewit Corporation	10,040	81	Levi Strauss & Co.	4,400	131	Gilbane	3,210
32	Harrah's Entertainment	9,370	82	Booz Allen Hamilton	4,400	132	Black & Veatch	3,200
33	Performance Food Group	9,300	83	Mansfield Oil	4,400	133	Vanguard Health Systems	3,200
34	Cumberland Farms	8,900	84	Pro-Build Holdings	4,400	134	Berry Plastics	3,190
35	S.C. Johnson & Son	8,880	85	Republic National Distributing	4,400	135	Medline Industries	3,190
36	First Data	8,810	86	J.R. Simplot	4,400	136	LPL Investment Holdings	3,120
37	Murdock Holding Company	8,490	87	NewPage	4,360	137	Dot Foods	3,100
38	Southern Wine & Spirits	8,400	88	Carlson Cos	4,330	138	E&J Gallo Winery	3,100
39	Alticor	8,200	89	Scoular	4,300	139	J. D. Heiskell & Co.	3,100
40	Giant Eagle	8,150	90	Avaya	4,200	140	International Data Group	3,050
41	CDW	8,070	91	Tribune Company	4,200	141	Structure Tone	3,030
42	Menard	7,900	92	WinCo Foods	4,200	142	Sports Authority	3,030
43	Hilton Worldwide	7,770	93	Whiting-Turner Contracting	4,150	143	Alex Lee	3,000
44	Sinclair Oil	7,750	94	Manor Care	4,130	144	Ashley Furniture Industries	3,000
45	QuikTrip	7,730	95	Hallmark Cards	4,020	145	Glazer's Wholesale Drug	3,000
46	Advance Publications	7,630	96	Golden State Foods	4,000	146	OSI Group	3,000
47	Capital Group Cos.	7,630	97	Kingston Technology Company	4,000	147	Sabre Holdings	3,000
48	Hy-Vee	7,050	98	Renco Group	4,000	148	Boise Cascade	2,980
49	Gordon Food Service	6,800	99	OSI Restaurant Partners	3,960	149	Grocers Supply	2,950
50	RaceTrac Petroleum	6,680	100	Red Apple Group	3,950	150	O'Neal Steel	2,930

SOURCE: *FORBES*, OCTOBER 28, 2009

The *Forbes* Largest Private Companies in the US (continued)

Rank	Company	Sales ($ mil.)	Rank	Company	Sales ($ mil.)	Rank	Company	Sales ($ mil.)
151	Amsted Industries	2,910	186	Travelport	2,530	221	Foster Farms	2,200
152	General Parts	2,910	187	Biomet	2,500	222	HP Hood	2,200
153	JELD-WEN	2,900	188	Andersen	2,500	223	Merit Energy	2,200
154	Schreiber Foods	2,900	189	Bausch & Lomb	2,500	224	Skadden, Arps	2,200
155	ABC Supply	2,880	190	Hunt Construction Group	2,500	225	Affinia Group	2,180
156	Hunt Consolidated/Hunt Oil	2,870	191	Schnuck Markets	2,500	226	Ingram Industries	2,160
157	Drummond	2,870	192	SHI International	2,440	227	Metals USA	2,160
158	M. A. Mortenson	2,830	193	Camac International	2,430	228	Brasfield & Gorrie	2,140
159	Demoulas Super Markets	2,800	194	Discount Tire	2,410	229	Flex-N-Gate	2,140
160	Quintiles Transnational	2,800	195	Boston Consulting Group	2,400	230	W. L. Gore & Associates	2,130
161	Rich Products	2,800	196	Ebsco Industries	2,400	231	WinWholesale	2,110
162	Sammons Enterprises	2,800	197	Fry's Electronics	2,400	232	84 Lumber	2,100
163	Zachry Construction	2,800	198	Smart & Final	2,400	233	Infor	2,100
164	J.E. Dunn Construction Group	2,760	199	J M Smith	2,360	234	Newegg.com	2,100
165	G-I Holdings	2,750	200	Parsons Brinckerhoff	2,340	235	Plastipak Holdings	2,100
166	Interstate Bakeries	2,700	201	Day & Zimmermann	2,320	236	Young's Market	2,050
167	Services Group of America	2,700	202	Iasis Healthcare	2,320	237	Bartlett & Co.	2,040
168	Houchens Industries	2,700	203	Guitar Center	2,300	238	Kum & Go	2,030
169	Ben E. Keith	2,700	204	Arctic Slope Regional	2,300	239	Univision Communications	2,020
170	Quality King Distributors	2,680	205	Life Care Centers of America	2,290	240	Vizio	2,010
171	Follett	2,660	206	Brookshire Grocery	2,270	241	Roll International	2,010
172	Apex Oil	2,640	207	NTK Holdings	2,270	242	D&H Distributing	2,000
173	Leprino Foods	2,600	208	Quad/Graphics	2,270	243	Bashas'	2,000
174	Maines Paper & Food Service	2,600	209	AMC Entertainment	2,270	244	Heico Cos.	2,000
175	Mary Kay	2,600	210	Academy Sports & Outdoors	2,260	245	Holiday Companies	2,000
176	Cooper-Standard Automotive	2,600	211	SAS Institute	2,260	246	J.M. Huber	2,000
177	Graham Packaging Holdings	2,580	212	Sequa	2,250	247	Sun Products	2,000
178	Golden Living	2,580	213	West Corp.	2,250	248	UniGroup	2,000
179	Asplundh Tree Expert	2,580	214	Dresser	2,240			
180	Wilbur-Ellis	2,580	215	ShopKo Stores	2,220			
181	Reader's Digest Association	2,560	216	Soave Enterprises	2,220			
182	Rosen's Diversified	2,560	217	Genesis HealthCare	2,210			
183	World Wide Technology	2,560	218	Bi-Lo Holdings	2,200			
184	Petco Animal Supplies	2,550	219	Delaware North Cos.	2,200			
185	Milliken & Co.	2,540	220	Electro-Motive Diesel	2,200			

Top 20 Universities

Rank	School
1	Harvard University
1	Princeton University
3	Yale University
4	California Institute of Technology
4	Massachusetts Institute of Technology
4	Stanford University
4	University of Pennsylvania
8	Columbia University
8	University of Chicago
10	Duke University
11	Dartmouth College
12	Northwestern University
12	Washington University in St. Louis
14	Johns Hopkins University
15	Cornell University
16	Brown University
17	Emory University
17	Rice University
17	Vanderbilt University
20	University of Notre Dame

Ranked by composite score, including such factors as graduation and retention rates, faculty resources, and student-to-faculty ratio.

SOURCE: *U.S. NEWS AND WORLD REPORT*, AUGUST 19, 2009

Top 20 US Foundations

Rank	Name	State	Assets ($ mil.)
1	Bill & Melinda Gates Foundation	WA	38,921.0
2	The Ford Foundation	NY	11,184.7
3	J. Paul Getty Trust	CA	10,837.3
4	The Robert Wood Johnson Foundation	NJ	10,730.5
5	W. K. Kellogg Foundation	MI	8,058.1
6	The William and Flora Hewlett Foundation	CA	6,289.0
7	Lilly Endowment Inc.	IN	5,718.8
8	John D. and Catherine T. MacArthur Foundation	IL	5,014.1
9	The California Endowment	CA	4,657.2
10	The David and Lucile Packard Foundation	CA	4,650.9
11	The Rockefeller Foundation	NY	4,615.4
12	Gordon and Betty Moore Foundation	CA	4,509.7
13	The Andrew W. Mellon Foundation	NY	4,363.6
14	Tulsa Community Foundation	OK	3,740.2
15	The Kresge Foundation	MI	3,100.0
16	The Starr Foundation	NY	2,801.7
17	Carnegie Corporation of New York	NY	2,662.7
18	The Susan Thompson Buffett Foundation	NE	2,517.6
19	The Annenberg Foundation	CA	2,487.7
20	The Harry and Jeanette Weinberg Foundation, Inc.	MD	2,480.3

SOURCE: THE FOUNDATION CENTER (WWW.FOUNDATIONCENTER.ORG), NOVEMBER 19, 2009

Top 20 US Law Firms

Rank	Law Firm	2008 Gross Revenue ($ mil.)	Number of lawyers
1	Skadden, Arps, Slate, Meagher & Flom	2,200.0	1,994
2	Baker & McKenzie	2,188.0	3,626
3	Latham & Watkins	1,923.0	2,102
4	Jones Day	1,540.0	2,348
5	Sidley Austin	1,489.5	1,702
6	White & Case	1,467.0	2,074
7	Kirkland & Ellis	1,400.0	1,333
8	Mayer Brown	1,294.0	1,801
9	Weil, Gotshal	1,231.0	1,190
10	Greenberg Traurig	1,204.0	1,734
11	DLA Piper US	1,178.0	1,380
12	Morgan, Lewis	1,120.5	1,363
13	Dewey & LeBoeuf	1,030.5	1,268
14	Paul, Hastings	986.0	1,062
15	Sullivan & Cromwell	985.0	665
16	Reed Smith	979.5	1,484
17	McDermott Will	966.0	1,055
18	Cleary Gottlieb	965.0	993
19	K&L Gates	959.5	1,552
20	Gibson, Dunn	957.0	923

SOURCE: *AMERICAN LAWYER*, MAY 1, 2009

Top 20 Tax & Accounting Firms by US Revenue

Rank	Firm	Headquarters	2008 US Revenue ($ mil.)
1	Deloitte & Touche	New York	10,980.0
2	Ernst & Young	New York	8,232.1
3	PricewaterhouseCoopers	New York	7,578.3
4	KPMG	New York	5,679.0
5	RSM/McGladrey & Pullen	Bloomington, MN	1,467.6
6	Grant Thornton	Chicago	1,210.3
7	BDO Seidman	Chicago	659.0
8	CBIZ/Mayer Hoffman McCann	Cleveland	553.1
9	Crowe Horwath	Oak Brook Terrace, IL	493.0
10	BKD	Springfield, MO	358.0
11	Moss Adams	Seattle	336.0
12	Plante & Moran	Southfield, MI	291.9
13	Clifton Gunderson	Peoria, IL	247.0
14	J.H. Cohn	Roseland, NJ	245.0
15	UHY Advisors	Chicago	239.1
16	Reznick Group	Bethesda, MD	219.6
17	Virchow Krause & Co.	Madison, WI	216.0
18	Dixon Hughes	High Point, NC	207.0
19	LarsonAllen	Minneapolis	201.0
20	Marcum & Kliegman	Melville, NY	182.6

SOURCE: *ACCOUNTING TODAY*, MARCH 16, 2009

Hoover's Handbook of

Private Companies

The Companies

24 Hour Fitness

If you're holding too much weight, 24 Hour Fitness Worldwide has the solution. It owns and operates more than 450 fitness centers that offer aerobic, cardiovascular, and weight lifting activities to the company's more than 3 million members. Some facilities also feature squash, racquetball, and basketball courts; swimming pools; steam and sauna rooms; tanning rooms; and whirlpools. It is one of the only fitness chains open 24 hours a day. The centers are located in more than 15 states in the US, as well as throughout Asia. Forstmann Little & Co owns 24 Hour Fitness, which was founded in 1983.

The chain has a history of linking with sports stars to open co-branded clubs such as 24 Hour Fitness — Lance Armstrong and 24 Hour Fitness — Magic Johnson. In 2008 the club expanded into New York City with the launch of three 24 Hour Fitness — Derek Jeter clubs in Manhattan. The New York Yankees star is an equity partner and has a role in the design of the clubs.

In addition to these celebrity partnerships, the company has teamed with NBC to create the reality TV show *The Biggest Loser*. In 2009 the network renewed the show for a seventh season.

Internationally, 24 Hour Fitness has about 25 clubs in Asia, including Hong Kong, Malaysia, Singapore, and Taiwan, as well as mainland China. Its Asian clubs operate under the brand name California Fitness.

The company was founded by chairman Mark Mastrov, who opened his first athletic club in San Leandro, California. Financier Theodore J. Forstmann bought the company for $1.6 billion in 2005.

EXECUTIVES

CEO: Carl C. Liebert III
EVP and CFO: Jeffrey N. (Jeff) Boyer, age 51
Chief Marketing Officer: Tony Wells
VP Personal Training: Christopher W. Gurtcheff
Auditors: Deloitte & Touche

LOCATIONS

HQ: 24 Hour Fitness Worldwide, Inc.
12647 Alcosta Blvd., 5th Fl., San Ramon, CA 94583
Phone: 925-543-3100   **Fax:** 925-543-3200
Web: www.24hourfitness.com

Selected Club Locations

Asia
  Hong Kong
  Malaysia
  Singapore
  Taiwan
US
  Arizona
  California
  Colorado
  Florida
  Hawaii
  Kansas
  Missouri
  Nebraska
  New Jersey
  Nevada
  New York
  Oregon
  Tennessee
  Texas
  Utah
  Washington

PRODUCTS/OPERATIONS

Selected Amenities

Baby sitting
Basketball courts
Cardio equipment
Group exercise classes
Personal trainers
Swimming pools
Weight training equipment

Selected Co-branded Clubs

Andre Agassi Signature Clubs
Lance Armstrong Signature Clubs
Derek Jeter Signature Clubs
Magic Johnson Signature Clubs
Shaquille O'Neal Signature Clubs

COMPETITORS

Bally Total Fitness	Lady of America
Crunch Fitness	Physical Property Holdings
Curves International	The Sports Club
Equinox Holdings	World Gym
Gold's Gym	YMCA
Jazzercise	YWCA

HISTORICAL FINANCIALS

Company Type: Private

Income Statement				FYE: December 31
	REVENUE ($ mil.)	**NET INCOME** ($ mil.)	**NET PROFIT MARGIN**	**EMPLOYEES**
12/07	1,280	—	—	21,410
12/06	1,840	—	—	11,000
12/05	1,077	—	—	19,660
12/04	1,004	—	—	—
12/03	1,000	—	—	16,000
Annual Growth	6.4%	—	—	7.6%

Revenue History

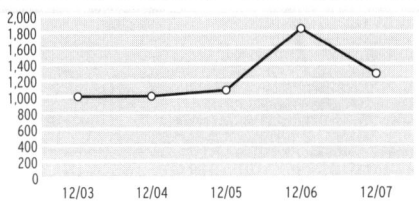

84 Lumber

With its utilitarian stores (most don't have heat or air conditioning), 84 Lumber has built itself up to be a leading low-cost provider of lumber and building materials and services. Through about 320 stores in more than 35 states, the company, which is the nation's largest privately held building-materials retailer, sells lumber, siding, drywall, windows, and other supplies, as well as plans to construct decks, garages, and houses. Its 84 Components subsidiary operates about a dozen manufacturing plants that make floor and roof trusses and wall panels. Its stores are mainly in the Northeast, Midwest, and South; the firm also sells products internationally. CEO Joseph Hardy Sr. founded 84 Lumber in 1956.

The slump in the new home construction market has hit 84 Lumber like a two-by-four to the head. Its sales plunged to about $2 billion in 2008, a drop of some 30% over the previous year. (The company had reached nearly $4 billion in sales two years earlier.) In response to decreased demand, the building supplies retailer closed and consolidated more than 100 stores across the US, including some in core markets. It also cut about 4,600 jobs, including more than 100 positions at its headquarters. The downturn has pre-empted plans of opening about 120 new stores by the end of 2009, which aimed to extend 84 Lumber's reach to more than 40 states. The company also mothballed several of its component plants until market conditions improve.

Although 84 Lumber was founded to serve professionals, the retailer had attempted to attract more do-it-yourself (DIY) consumers before refocusing its efforts on professional builders and remodelers (about 95% of sales). As a result, it is particularly vulnerable to the downturn in housing starts.

While the professional market is less profitable and more cyclic than the DIY segment, it has the advantage of being less crowded with big-box competitors, such as The Home Depot and Lowe's.

The company has also expanded to provide professional services, including financing, risk insurance, and travel through 84 Travel. Its 84 Lumber Installed Sales business provides installation services for windows, doors, and framing and roofing jobs.

HISTORY

In 1956 Joseph Hardy Sr. opened the first 84 Lumber store in Eighty Four, Pennsylvania, a town near Pittsburgh. Hardy epitomized the bare-bones approach, keeping a tight rein on his company and paying cash for new building sites.

The strategy was successful, and for the next two decades 84 Lumber prospered, growing steadily to more than 350 stores in the early 1980s. But the 1980s brought trouble, not only for 84 Lumber but also within the Hardy family. Paul Hardy, the second-eldest son, left the company after continued sparring with Hardy Sr. Another son, Joe Hardy Jr., seemed to be his father's handpicked successor: He had worked for 84 Lumber since 1967, rising to the level of COO. However, Joe Jr. and Joe Sr. clashed and under pressure from his father, Joe Jr. resigned in 1988.

Joe Sr. also underwent a transformation during this time, opening his once-tight purse strings to buy himself an honorary English title — lord of the manor of Henley-in-Arden — for about $170,000. In 1987 he paid $3.1 million to purchase a retreat in southwestern Pennsylvania, the Nemacolin Woodlands. He placed the renovation of the resort (at the cost of some $100 million) in the hands of his daughter Maggie, who was in her early twenties at the time.

While Hardy was transforming, so was 84 Lumber. The company started moving away from its traditional approach in an attempt to gain a piece of the budding yuppie market. This approach, along with an ill-timed expansion, led to a loss of customers and falling profits. Earnings fell from $52 million in 1987 to $22 million in 1989.

84 Lumber started to right itself in 1991. Hardy transferred stock to Maggie, his heir apparent. While running luxury resort Nemacolin Woodlands, Maggie strove to emulate her father's business style, including obscenity-laced

staff meetings. 84 Lumber shut stores and returned to its basic operating scheme as a low-cost provider of lumber in small towns. The company also added do-it-yourself (DIY) building kits for kitchens and baths that year, and it expanded that DIY concept a year later in 1992, with home building kits.

Under new president Maggie, 84 Lumber's sales topped the $1 billion mark in 1993 and the company refocused on its professional contractor customers. The company first shipped its building materials internationally in 1996 (to New Zealand) and added customers in China, South Korea, Switzerland, and Australia in the late 1990s.

In 1997 84 Lumber opened Maggie's Building Solutions Showroom, a 7,500-sq.-ft. remodeling center featuring upscale home products. By that year 84 Lumber was the US's largest dealer of building supplies to professional contractors.

In a further effort to attract contractors' business, 84 Lumber introduced a builder financing program in 1999 and began converting some of its stores to an 84-Plus store format, in which its traditional lumberyard setup is matched with a 10,000-sq.-ft. hardware store.

In an effort to reach more professionals, the company increased outside sales staff by 25% in 2000. The next year the company bought 15 stores from Payless Cashways, which went out of business, a move that extended 84 Lumber's operations to Oklahoma, Nevada, and Nebraska.

The company added two red-letter dates to its company history in 2002. On April 3 of that year, 84 Lumber opened 20 new stores throughout the US, increasing its store count by 5%. Thanks in part to added revenue from those stores, on December 7, 2002, company cash registers went past the $2 billion mark in sales for the year.

In June 2004, 84 Lumber opened a distribution center in Auburn, New York. The facility supplies vinyl siding and roofing materials to stores in Rochester and Syracuse.

To help fund its future growth in May 2007 the company completed a $200 million sale/lease-back deal with Spirit Finance Corporation covering 53 stores and a manufacturing facility. Also in May 84 Lumber acquired two Denver-area companies (JAC & Co. and Front Range Panel).

Between January and April 2008, the building supplies retailer closed or consolidated more than 100 stores across the US.

EXECUTIVES

CEO: Joseph A. Hardy Sr.
President: Maggie Hardy Magerko
CFO: Dan Wallach
EVP Store Operations: Frank Cicero
SVP National Sales: Brian Sento
Divisional VP, Western Division: David Cochran
Divisional VP, Southeast Division: Billy Ball
Divisional VP, Central Division: Harry Streyle
Divisional VP, Northeast Division: Ed McKenzie
VP Human Resources: Jim Guest
VP Marketing and Public Relations: Jeff Nobers
VP Installed Sales and Component Manufacturing: Mike McCrobie
Director Purchasing: Mitch Wagner

LOCATIONS

HQ: 84 Lumber Company
1019 Rte. 519, Eighty Four, PA 15330
Phone: 724-228-8820 **Fax:** 724-228-8058
Web: www.84lumber.com

PRODUCTS/OPERATIONS

Selected Products

Doors
Drywall
Flooring
Insulation
Lumber
Plywood
Project kits
  Decks
  Garages
  Gazebos
  Houses
  Pole buildings
Roofing
Room additions
Siding
Skylights
Trim
Trusses
Ventilation
Windows

COMPETITORS

Ace Hardware
Builders FirstSource
Building Materials Holding
Carter Lumber
Do it Best
Foxworth-Galbraith Lumber
Grossman's
HD Supply
Home Depot
Lowe's
McCoy Corp.
Menard
Stock Building Supply
Sutherland Lumber
True Value

HISTORICAL FINANCIALS

Company Type: Private

Income Statement

FYE: First Sunday following December 31

	REVENUE ($ mil.)	NET INCOME ($ mil.)	NET PROFIT MARGIN	EMPLOYEES
12/08	2,100	—	—	4,500
12/07	3,100	—	—	7,000
12/06	3,920	—	—	9,500
12/05	4,000	—	—	10,500
12/04	3,460	—	—	8,000
Annual Growth	(11.7%)	—	—	(13.4%)

Revenue History

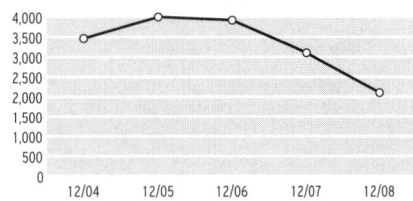

AARP

Turn 50 and the doors of the AARP will open for you, as they have for 40 million current members. On behalf of its members, the not-for-profit AARP acts as an advocate on public policy issues, publishes information (including the monthly *AARP Bulletin* and the bimonthly *AARP The Magazine,* and through Spanish language media), promotes community service, and works with business partners to offer products and services (including discounts on insurance and travel). The group is organized into some 2,400 local chapters throughout the US. Royalties from businesses eager to reach AARP members account for about 40% of the group's revenue; membership dues ($16 per year) account for about 25%.

AARP may not be the most exclusive club around, but it is one of the most powerful. As the largest advocacy group in the US, the organization has a loud (and sometimes feared) voice on Capitol Hill, in part because older people tend to vote in greater relative numbers than many other segments of the population. AARP policy recommendations address such issues as the national budget, Medicare, elder abuse, and Social Security.

Employers who engage in age discrimination are likely to hear from the AARP, which joins about three age discrimination cases each year. In 2009 the advocacy group joined as co-counsel in a class-action age discrimination lawsuit brought against Seagate Technology. Other corporations that AARP has met in court include 3M, Goodyear Tire & Rubber Co., Sprint, and Ford Motor Co.

The group has worked to attract baby boomers with its 50+ campaign, which began in 2000. In 2003 AARP developed a 10-year agenda designed to address the effects of the first wave of boomers reaching age 65 in 2011. Concerns for the 50+ set include Medicare reforms, improved consumer protections and financial security, and employment opportunities for older workers. As concerns about funding for Social Security become more urgent, AARP intends to continue to make its voice heard.

In 2007 AARP expanded its insurance offerings, through partnerships with Aetna and UnitedHealth Group. The AARP-branded products includes policies designed to supplement Medicare coverage and policies intended to cover people ages 50 to 64.

In 2009 the organization launched Government Watch, an interactive website designed to allow older Americans to hold Congress and the Obama Administration accountable on key issues that affect them. In a move the may help AARP diversify its membership, the group named A. Barry Rand, a former head of Avis Group and executive at Xerox, as its new CEO in April. Rand is the first African-American to lead the organization.

HISTORY

Ethel Andrus, a retired Los Angeles high school principal who founded the National Retired Teachers Association (NRTA) in 1947, founded the American Association of Retired Persons (AARP) in 1958 with the assistance of Leonard Davis, a New York insurance salesman who had helped her find an underwriter for the NRTA. The new organization's goal: to "enhance the quality of life" for older Americans and "improve the image of aging."

Andrus offered members the same low rates for health and accident insurance provided to NRTA members. She also started publishing AARP's bimonthly magazine, *Modern Maturity*, in 1958. The organization's first local chapter opened in Youngstown, Arizona, in 1960. Still an insurance man, Davis formed Colonial Penn Insurance in 1963 to take over the AARP account. Andrus led the AARP and its increasingly powerful lobby for the elderly until her death in 1967.

With criticism of Colonial Penn mounting in the 1970s (critics charged the organization was little more than a front for the insurance company), Prudential won AARP's insurance business in 1979. The NRTA merged with AARP in 1982, and the following year it lowered the membership eligibility age from 55 to 50. The organization continued to expand its offerings, adding an auto club and financial products such as mutual funds and expanded insurance policies. The organization also started a federal credit union for members in 1988, but despite rosy projections, it ceased operations two years later.

AARP forked over $135 million to the IRS in 1993 as part of a settlement regarding the tax status of profits from some of its activities, but the dispute remained unresolved. AARP switched insurance providers again in 1996 (New York Life) and started offering discounted legal services. Also that year, AARP said it would let HMOs offer managed-care services to members. The plan drew objections over its potential violation of Medicare anti-kickback laws and AARP developed a revised payment plan in 1997.

AARP's image was bruised in 1998 when Dale Van Atta wrote a scathing account of the organization, *Trust Betrayed: Inside the AARP*. The book accused the organization of operating out of lavish accommodations, acting as a shill for businesses to hawk their wares, and concealing a drop in membership. The next year, recognizing that nearly a third of its members were working, the organization dropped the American Association of Retired Persons moniker and began to refer to itself by the AARP abbreviation.

To end the long-running dispute with the IRS, AARP reached a settlement over its alleged profit-making enterprises by creating a new taxable subsidiary called AARP Services in 1999. The following year AARP initiated a five-year plan to attract aging baby boomers. AARP launched its *My Generation* magazine in 2001; two years later the organization combined *My Generation* with its *Modern Maturity* magazine to form a single publication: *AARP The Magazine*.

In 2005 the group's lobbying efforts focused on Social Security reform proposals and a new prescription drug benefit for Medicare recipients.

In 2009 A. Barry Rand, former head of Avis Group Holdings, succeeded Bill Novelli as CEO of AARP. Novelli had held the position for eight years.

EXECUTIVES

Chairman: Bonnie M. Cramer
CEO: A. Barry Rand, age 64
President and Director: Jennie Chin Hansen
COO: Thomas C. Nelson
EVP and Chief Communications Officer:
  Kevin Donnellan
EVP State Operations: Harroll (Hop) Backus
EVP and Chief Brand Officer: Emilio Pardo
EVP and CFO: Robert R. Hagans Jr., age 50
EVP and Chief People Officer: Ellie Hollander
EVP Social Impact Group: Nancy A. LeaMond
EVP Policy and Strategy: John Rother
President, AARP Foundation: Robin Talbert

President and CEO, AARP Services, Inc.: John Wider
Group Executive Officer (GEO), Member Value:
  Shereen Remez
General Counsel: Joan S. Wise
President-Elect and Director: W. Lee Hammond
Auditors: KPMG LLP

LOCATIONS

HQ: AARP
  601 E St. NW, Washington, DC 20049
Phone: 202-434-7700   **Fax:** 202-434-7710
Web: www.aarp.org

PRODUCTS/OPERATIONS

2008 Sales

	% of total
Royalties	52
Membership dues	20
Advertising	9
Program income	7
Federal & other grants	7
Contributions	3
Other	2
Total	**100**

Selected Operations and Programs

AARP Andrus Foundation (gerontology research)
AARP Bulletin (monthly news update)
AARP Driver Safety (classroom refresher)
AARP Legal Services Network
AARP Services (taxable product management,
  marketing, and e-commerce subsidiary)
AARP The Magazine (bimonthly magazine)
Financial Planning
Public Policy Institute
Research Information Center
Senior Community Service Employment Program
Tax-Aide

HISTORICAL FINANCIALS

Company Type: Not-for-profit

Income Statement

	REVENUE ($ mil.)	NET INCOME ($ mil.)	NET PROFIT MARGIN	EMPLOYEES
				FYE: December 31
12/08	1,257	99	7.8%	2,330
12/07	1,255	108	8.6%	1,867
12/06	1,010	(31)	—	1,849
12/05	936	—	—	—
12/04	878	—	—	—
Annual Growth	9.4%	—	—	12.3%

2008 Year-End Financials

Debt ratio: 214.0%   Current ratio: —
Return on equity: —   Long-term debt ($ mil.): 230
Cash ($ mil.): —

Net Income History

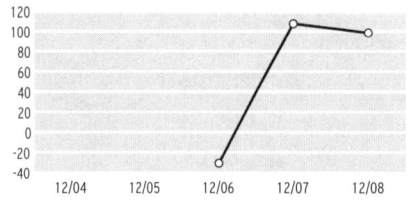

ABC Supply

American Builders & Contractors Supply Co. (better known as ABC Supply) has put roofs over millions of heads. A leading supplier of roofing, siding, windows, gutters, doors, and other exterior building products, ABC Supply operates about 380 outlets in 45 states and the District of Columbia. The company carries its own brand of products under the Amcraft name, as well as offering products from outside vendors. ABC Supply markets its products to builders and professional contractors. The family-owned business was founded in 1982 by the late Ken Hendricks, the son of a roofer.

When Hendricks died in 2007 he was succeeded as chief executive by David Luck, who had joined the firm as president and COO in 1998. Hendricks' wife, Diane, took over as chairman.

ABC Supply plans to build a nationwide network of wholesale distribution centers through acquisitions. The company hopes to expand its network to 500 branches and reach $5 billion in sales (up from about $3 billion in 2006) by 2012. To this end, the company in 2009 acquired building products wholesaler Chesapeake Siding and Roofing, which has two locations in Virginia and North Carolina. In 2007 it purchased Ashley Aluminum, an aluminum and building materials wholesale distributor with nearly 50 outlets in Florida, Texas, Alabama, and Georgia.

ABC Supply is one of about 20 diverse companies owned by Hendricks Holding.

EXECUTIVES

Chairman: Diane M. Hendricks, age 62
President and CEO: David A. Luck
EVP and COO: Keith Rozolis, age 46
CFO, Treasurer, VP, Secretary, and Director:
  Kendra A. Story
VP Organizational Development: Kim Hendricks
VP Branch Operations: Kevin Hendricks
VP and CIO: Kathy Murray
VP Divisional Operations: Brent Fox
VP Manufacturing Operations: Brad Money
Director Business Development: Mary Groessl
Director Marketing and Business Intelligence:
  Mike Schwarz
Auditors: Ernst & Young LLP

LOCATIONS

HQ: American Builders & Contractors Supply Co., Inc.
  1 ABC Pkwy., Beloit, WI 53511
Phone: 608-362-7777   **Fax:** 608-362-2717
Web: www.abc-supply.com

PRODUCTS/OPERATIONS

Selected Products

Roofing materials
Siding materials
Tools and equipment
Windows and doors

COMPETITORS

Beacon Roofing	Huttig Building Products
Bradco Supply	Lowe's
Building Materials Holding	North Pacific Group
Emco Corporation	Pacific Coast Building
Guardian Building	Products
Products	PrimeSource Building
HD Supply	

HISTORICAL FINANCIALS

Company Type: Private

Income Statement

FYE: December 31

	REVENUE ($ mil.)	NET INCOME ($ mil.)	NET PROFIT MARGIN	EMPLOYEES
12/08	3,000	—	—	5,800
12/07	2,630	—	—	5,243
12/06	2,990	—	—	5,431
12/05	2,597	—	—	5,144
12/04	2,042	—	—	4,128
Annual Growth	10.1%	—	—	8.9%

Revenue History

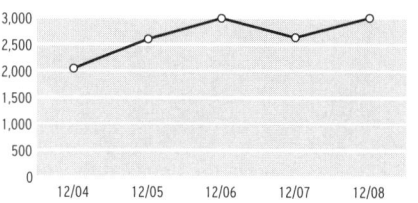

LOCATIONS

HQ: Academy of Motion Picture Arts and Sciences
8949 Wilshire Blvd., Beverly Hills, CA 90211
Phone: 310-247-3000 **Fax:** 310-859-9351
Web: www.oscars.org

PRODUCTS/OPERATIONS

Selected Members

Actors
Art directors
Cinematographers
Composers and lyricists
Directors
Documentary filmmakers
Executives
Film editors
Makeup artists and hairstylists
Music
Producers
Public relations
Short films and feature animators
Sound editors
Visual effects artists
Writers

LOCATIONS

HQ: Academy of Television Arts & Sciences, Inc.
5220 Lankershim Blvd.
North Hollywood, CA 91601
Phone: 818-754-2800 **Fax:** 818-761-2827
Web: www.emmys.org

Ace Hardware

Luckily, Ace has John Madden up its sleeve. Despite the growth of warehouse-style competitors, Ace Hardware has remained a household name, thanks to ads featuring Madden, a former Oakland Raiders football coach and retired TV commentator. By sales the company is the #1 hardware cooperative in the US, ahead of Do It Best. Ace dealer-owners operate about 4,600 Ace Hardware stores, home centers, and lumber and building materials locations in all 50 US states and about 60 other countries. From about 15 warehouses Ace distributes such products as electrical and plumbing supplies, garden equipment, hand tools, housewares, and power tools. Its paint division is also a major paint manufacturer in the US.

Amid the global economic downturn, Ace said its business has been fortunate because of its "relative recession resistance." Although the company's network of retail stores has been shrinking, its profits have remained relatively steady. In 2008 about 120 Ace Hardware stores opened while about 240 closed, but as it turned out, sales at new stores have outpaced those at closed locations.

The company is making strides to boost its bottom line, starting with helping shoppers locate hard-to-find items. In 2009 Ace launched Aisle411, a free product-location service that can be accessed via phone, similar to dialing for information. The company launched the service after learning that shoppers who were unable to find a product either left (about 20% of the time) or asked store associates for assistance (about 60%), which created a high demand for staff attention.

Challenged by big-box chains such as The Home Depot and Lowe's, Ace rolled out its "next generation" store concept, which involves signage with detailed product descriptions and different flooring to set off departments, among other features. The company is also focusing on opening smaller neighborhood stores to entice customers who would rather not drive to edge-of-town big-box chains.

In 2007 CEO Ray Griffith sent a letter to Ace's retailers, saying the company was considering changing from a cooperative to a traditional corporation to become more competitive and to better fuel growth. Shortly after, the company announced an accounting shortfall of about $150 million, or nearly half of its equity, which was uncovered while Ace prepared to convert formats. The error turned out to be an accident by a mid-level employee, but the company ended up calling off the conversion until the lost equity is restored. Ace hopes to make up the shortfall by assessing store owners with a variance allocation charge.

Academy of Motion Pictures

And the Oscar goes to . . . the Academy of Motion Picture Arts and Sciences (AMPAS). The not-for-profit organization promotes the movie industry by recognizing excellence, fostering cultural progress, providing a forum for various crafts, and cooperating in technical research. It is best known for the annual Academy Awards in which a Britannia metal trophy (known as the Oscar) is awarded for outstanding achievement in the motion picture industry. The more than 6,000 AMPAS members (who pick the Oscar winners) represent 15 branches of the industry, including actors, directors, producers, and executives. The organization was founded in 1927 and is governed by seven officers and a board of governors.

EXECUTIVES

Chairman: Fay Kanin, age 92
Vice Chairman: Arthur Hamilton
President and Trustee: Sid Ganis
Executive Administrator: Ric Robertson
First VP and Trustee: Robert Rehme
VP and Trustee: Hawk Koch
VP and Trustee: Kathleen Kennedy
VP and Trustee: Donn Cambern
Film Department Coordinator: D. J. Ziegler
Program Coordinator, Nicholl Fellowships: Greg Beal
Director Marketing: Janet Weiss
Director Communications: Leslie Unger
Treasurer and Trustee: Tom Sherak
Secretary and Trustee: Cheryl Boone Isaacs
Executive Director and Executive Secretary of the Board of Trustees: Bruce Davis
Awards Coordinator: Torene Svitil
Academy Film Archive Director: Michael Pogorzelski
Director Membership: Kimberly Roush
Auditors: PricewaterhouseCoopers LLP

Academy of Television Arts & Sciences

And the award for best organization that honors the television industry goes to: the Academy of Television Arts & Sciences (ATAS). ATAS, which has more than 13,000 members, presents the annual Emmy Awards and sponsors various television-related conferences and activities. The organization also oversees the Daytime and L.A. Area Emmy Awards, publishes *emmy* magazine, manages archival and educational programs through its ATAS Foundation, and operates Web sites such as emmys.tv and emmys.com. The Emmy statuette features a winged woman holding an atom aloft to symbolize the melding of art and science. The award's name is a deviation of "Immy," an early television camera. ATAS was founded in 1946.

The organization's members are divided into about 30 peer groups, including animation, cinematographers, daytime programming, makeup, performers, and writers. Benefits of membership include Emmy voting, travel and other discounts, and seminars and educational activities. ATAS also hosts private film screenings, family events, and behind-the-scenes functions for TV shows.

EXECUTIVES

Chairman and CEO: John Shaffner
First Vice Chair: Nancy Bradley Wiard
Second Vice Chair: Brian Seth Hurst
COO: Alan Perris
CFO and Chief Administrative Officer: Frank Kohler
SVP Awards: John Leverance
VP Marketing: Laurel Whitcomb
Secretary: Sheila Manning
Director of Membership: Barbara Chase
Director of Human Resources: Gregory Sims
Chairman, Academy Foundation: Jerry Petry
Vice Chair, Los Angeles Area: Hal Eisner
Executive Director, Foundation: Terri Clark
Treasurer: Donna Kanter

HISTORY

A group of Chicago-area hardware dealers — William Stauber, Richard Hesse, Gern Lindquist, and Oscar Fisher — decided in 1924 to pool their hardware buying and promotional costs. In 1928 the group incorporated as Ace Stores, named in honor of the superior WWI fliers dubbed aces. Hesse became president the following year, retaining that position for the next 44 years. The company also opened its first warehouse in 1929, and by 1933 it had 38 dealers.

The organization had 133 dealers in seven states by 1949. In 1953 Ace began to allow dealers to buy stock in the company through the Ace Perpetuation Plan. During the 1960s Ace expanded into the South and West, and by 1969 it had opened distribution centers in Georgia and California — its first such facilities outside Chicago. In 1968 it opened its first international store in Guam.

By the early 1970s the do-it-yourself market began to surge as inflation pushed up plumber and electrician fees. As the market grew, large home center chains gobbled up market share from independent dealers such as those franchised through Ace. In response, Ace and its dealers became a part of a growing trend in the hardware industry — cooperatives.

Hesse sold the company to its dealers in 1973 for $6 million (less than half its book value), and the following year Ace began operating as a cooperative. Hesse stepped down in 1973. In 1976 the dealers took full control when the company's first Board of Dealer-Directors was elected.

After signing up a number of dealers in the eastern US, Ace had dealers in all 50 states by 1979. The co-op opened a plant to make paint in Matteson, Illinois, in 1984. By 1985 Ace had reached $1 billion in sales and had initiated its Store of the Future Program, allowing dealers to borrow up to $200,000 to upgrade their stores and conduct market analyses. Former head coach John Madden of the National Football League's Oakland Raiders signed on as Ace's mouthpiece in 1988.

A year later the co-op began to test ACENET, a computer network that allowed Ace dealers to check inventory, send and receive e-mail, make special purchase requests, and keep up with prices on commodity items such as lumber. In 1990 Ace established an International Division to handle its overseas stores. (It had been exporting products since 1975.) EVP and COO David Hodnik became president in 1995. That year the co-op added a net of 67 stores, including a three-store chain in Russia. Expanding further internationally, Ace signed a five-year joint-supply agreement in 1996 with Canadian lumber and hardware retailer Beaver Lumber. Hodnik added CEO to his title in 1996.

Ace fell further behind its old rival, True Value, in 1997 when ServiStar Coast to Coast and True Value merged to form TruServ (renamed True Value in 2005), a hardware giant that operated more than 10,000 outlets at the completion of the merger.

Late in 1997 Ace launched an expansion program in Canada. (The co-op already operated distribution centers in Ontario and Calgary.) In 1999 Ace merged its lumber and building materials division with Builder Marts of America to form a dealer-owned buying group to supply about 2,700 retailers. Ace gained 208 member outlet stores in 2000, but saw 279 member outlets terminated. The next year it gained 220, but lost 255.

Sodisco-Howden bought all the shares of Ace Hardware Canada in February 2003. To better serve international members, Ace opened its first international buying office, in Hong Kong, in April 2004.

In all, the company added 131 new stores in 2005. That year, after 33 years with the company, David F. Hodnik retired as president and CEO of Ace Hardware. He was succeeded by COO Ray A. Griffith.

EXECUTIVES

Chairman: David S. Ziegler
President and CEO: Ray A. Griffith, age 54
CFO: Dorvin D. Lively, age 49
EVP: Rita D. Kahle
SVP Retail Operations: Kenneth L. (Ken) Nichols
SVP, General Counsel, and Secretary:
Arthur J. (Art) McGivern
VP Merchandising, Marketing, and Advertising:
Lori L. Bossmann
VP Supply Chain: Daniel C. (Dan) Prochaska
VP Information Technology: Michael G. (Mike) Elmore
VP Business Development: John Venhuizen, age 37
VP Retail Support: William J. (Bill) Bauman
VP Human Resources: Jimmy Alexander
VP Retail Operations: Kane Calamari
Senior Creative Specialist: Andrew Vitellaro
Media Contact and Public Relations:
Christopher Boniface
Auditors: KPMG LLP

LOCATIONS

HQ: Ace Hardware Corporation
2200 Kensington Ct., Oak Brook, IL 60523
Phone: 630-990-6600   **Fax:** 630-990-6838
Web: www.acehardware.com

2008 Sales

	$ mil.	% of total
US	3,651.3	94
Other countries	212.9	6
Total	**3,864.2**	**100**

PRODUCTS/OPERATIONS

2008 Sales

	$ mil.	% of total
Merchandise	3,540.7	92
Retail	323.5	8
Total	**3,864.2**	**100**

COMPETITORS

84 Lumber
Akzo Nobel
Benjamin Moore
Building Materials Holding
Costco Wholesale
Do it Best
Fastenal
Grossman's
Handy Hardware Wholesale
Home Depot
Kmart
Lowe's
McCoy Corp.
Menard
Northern Tool
Orgill
Reno-Depot
Sears
Sherwin-Williams
Stock Building Supply
Sutherland Lumber
True Value
United Hardware Distributing
Wal-Mart

HISTORICAL FINANCIALS

Company Type: Cooperative

Income Statement		FYE: Saturday nearest December 31		
	REVENUE ($ mil.)	NET INCOME ($ mil.)	NET PROFIT MARGIN	EMPLOYEES
12/08	3,864	86	2.2%	4,800
12/07	3,971	87	2.2%	4,800
12/06	3,770	107	2.8%	5,000
12/05	3,466	100	2.9%	4,976
12/04	3,289	102	3.1%	5,000
Annual Growth	4.1%	(4.2%)	—	(1.0%)

Net Income History

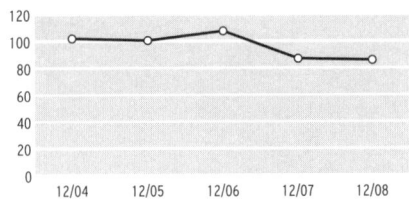

ADESA, Inc.

ADESA (Auto Dealers Exchange Services of America) doesn't sell cars, it sells fleets of cars to dealers. The firm offers used- and salvage-vehicle redistribution services to automakers, lessors, and dealers in the US, Canada, and Mexico. ADESA operates about 60 whole car auction sites; it also offers such ancillary services as logistics, inspections, evaluation, titling, and settlement administration. The company collects fees from buyers and sellers on each auction and from its extra services. Its AFC (Automotive Finance Corporation) unit offers dealer floor-plan financing services from more than 85 locations. ADESA was acquired by KAR Auction Services in 2007. KAR, a holding company, went public in late 2009.

In its bid to become the top vehicle-auction firm, KAR raised $300 million in a December 2009 IPO, hoping that the move would allow it to eclipse its rivals (Manheim and Copart), expand internationally, and pay off debt.

In January 2008 ADESA acquired Dent Demon, a paintless dent repair service in Indiana. Other reconditioning services provided by ADESA include body work, detailing, glass repair, light mechanical work, tire and key replacement, and upholstery repair. In June 2008 it acquired Live Global Bid (LGB), a provider of Internet-based auction software and services. (ADESA, which uses LGB's technology, previously owned about 18% of the firm.)

The company agreed in September 2008 to sell its real estate portfolio to First Industrial Realty Trust for $82 million. ADESA will lease back the land at eight of the sites, as ADESA wanted more financial flexibility to reinvest funds back into its core business.

Founded in 1989, ADESA was acquired in 2007 by a group of private equity firms, including Kelso & Company, GS Capital Partners, ValueAct Capital, and Parthenon Capital. The company's

$3.7 billion purchase price included about $700 million in debt. Following the acquisition, the group integrated ADESA's operations with those of Insurance Auto Auctions (IAA), a fellow automotive salvage auction provider (and former rival of ADESA), under the KAR umbrella. IAA operates about 150 salvage auction sites in the US.

EXECUTIVES

President and CEO: Thomas J. (Tom) Caruso, age 50
EVP Operations and Finance: Paul Lips
**EVP Customer Strategies and Analytics; Chief
  Economist:** Tom Kontos
EVP Corporate Development: Warren Byrd
EVP Sales and Marketing: Robert (Bob) Rauschenberg
SVP Operations and Strategic Improvement:
  David Vignes
VP Legal: Michelle Mallon
VP Marketing: Carol Sewell
VP Operations, AutoVIN: John Hoctor
VP Dealer Consignment: Tim Zierden
Gregg Maidment
VP Commercial Sales and Operations: Jeff Bescher
VP e-Business Sales and Operations: Jason Ferreri
President, Specialty Sales: Jane Morgan
President, AutoVIN: Dennis Jones
Financial Controller: Kara Paciorek
Executive Director Sales: David Carlucci
Auditors: KPMG LLP

LOCATIONS

HQ: ADESA, Inc.
  13085 Hamilton Crossing Blvd., Carmel, IN 46032
Phone: 317-815-1100   **Fax:** 317-249-4651
Web: www.adesa.com

2008 Auction Sites

	No.
US	138
Canada	12
Total	**150**

PRODUCTS/OPERATIONS

2008 Locations

	No.
ADESA	61
AFC	88
Total	**149**

COMPETITORS

ADESA PA
Autobytel
Columbus Fair Auto Auction
Copart
Cox Enterprises
eBay
Pittsburgh Independent Auto Auction
Ritchie Bros. Auctioneers

HISTORICAL FINANCIALS

Company Type: Subsidiary

Income Statement   FYE: December 31

	REVENUE ($ mil.)	NET INCOME ($ mil.)	NET PROFIT MARGIN	EMPLOYEES
12/08	1,123	131	11.7%	11,000
12/07	678	82	12.0%	11,000
Annual Growth	65.8%	60.7%	—	0.0%

Net Income History

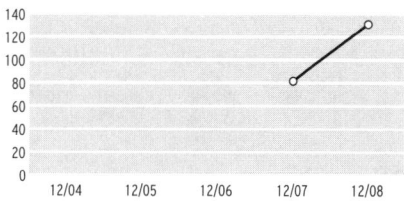

	12/04	12/05	12/06	12/07	12/08

Advance Publications

The drumbeat urging this company forward is the drone of printing presses. Advance Publications is a leading newspaper and magazine publisher with several dozen titles. Its portfolio of about 20 newspapers includes *The Star-Ledger* (New Jersey), *The Cleveland Plain Dealer*, and namesake *Staten Island Advance*, as well as more than 40 weekly titles published by American City Business Journals. Through Condé Nast, Advance Publications owns a bevy of magazines including *The New Yorker*, *Vanity Fair*, and *Wired*. Other operations and interests include online content (Condé Nast Digital) and cable television. Patriarch Sam Newhouse started the family-owned business with the purchase of the *Staten Island Advance* in 1922.

Through acquisitions, creative development, aggressive promotion, and dogged determination, Advance Publications has built a formidable estate of media properties. Its newspapers serve generally smaller markets in about 10 states, while its magazine empire has focused on special interest topics such as fashion, food, interior decorating, and technology. Along the way, the Newhouse family, led by brothers Si and Donald, have become true media moguls and rank among such publishing elite as the Grahams (The Washington Post Company), the Hearsts (Hearst Corporation), and the Sulzbergers (New York Times).

Advance Publications' focus on editorial content means most of its revenue comes from advertising and subscriptions. However, the publishing business has been in decline for several years as readers turn to the Internet and other sources for their news and information. The downturn in the economy has only added to those problems. In response, the company has looked for ways to reduce operating costs at its papers and magazines, including staff cuts and mandatory furloughs. Its flagship *Star-Ledger* laid off about 40% of its workforce late in 2008.

Condé Nast, meanwhile, has had to shutter some of its under-performing titles. In 2009 the unit closed its venerable *Gourmet* magazine (launched in 1940) along with *Cookie* and *Modern Bride*. Other casualties have included *Domino* and *Condé Nast Portfolio*. (The company kept Portfolio.com alive under the auspices of American City Business Journals.) Advance Publications has been investing in online media through Condé Nast Digital. The subsidiary operates Web sites including Epicurious.com, STYLE.com, and the WiredDigital family of sites.

One bright spot has been the company's interests in cable television. Affiliate Advance/Newhouse controls more than 25% of Discovery Communications (DCI), a leading programmer

with popular networks such as Animal Planet, the Science Channel, and its flagship Discovery Channel. DCI went public in 2008 after Advance/Newhouse combined its interests with those of Liberty Media chief John Malone. Advance/Newhouse also owns cable system operator Bright House Networks through a partnership with Time Warner Cable.

HISTORY

Solomon Neuhaus (later Samuel I. Newhouse) got started in the newspaper business after dropping out of school at age 13. He went to work at the *Bayonne Times* in New Jersey and was put in charge of the failing newspaper in 1911; he managed to turn the paper around within a year. In 1922 he bought the *Staten Island Advance* (founded in 1886) and formed the Staten Island Advance Company in 1924. After buying up more papers, he changed the name of the company to Advance Publications in 1949. By the 1950s the company had local papers in New York, New Jersey (including *The Star-Ledger*), and Alabama.

In 1959 Newhouse bought magazine publisher Condé Nast as an anniversary gift for his wife. (He joked that she had asked for a fashion magazine, so he bought her *Vogue*.) His publishing empire continued to grow with the addition of the *Times-Picayune* (New Orleans) in 1962 and *The Cleveland Plain Dealer* in 1967. In 1976 the company paid more than $300 million for Booth Newspapers, publisher of eight Michigan papers and *Parade Magazine*.

Newhouse died in 1979, leaving his sons Si and Donald to run the company, which encompassed more than 30 newspapers, a half-dozen magazines, and 15 cable systems. The next year Advance bought book publishing giant Random House from RCA. Si resurrected the Roaring Twenties standard *Vanity Fair* in 1983 and added *The New Yorker* under the Condé Nast banner in 1985. The Newhouses scored a victory over the IRS in 1990 after a long-running court battle involving inheritance taxes. Condé Nast bought Knapp Publications (*Architectural Digest*) in 1993 and Advance later acquired American City Business Journals in 1995.

In 1998 the company sold the increasingly unprofitable Random House to Bertelsmann for about $1.2 billion. It later bought hallmark Internet magazine *Wired* (though it passed on Wired Ventures' Internet operations). That year revered *New Yorker* editor Tina Brown, credited with jazzing up the publication's content and increasing its circulation, left the magazine; staff writer and Pulitzer Prize winner David Remnick was named as Brown's replacement.

In 1999 Advance joined Donrey Media Group (now called Stephens Media Group), E.W. Scripps, Hearst Corporation, and MediaNews Group to purchase the online classified advertising network AdOne (later named PowerOne Media). It also bought Walt Disney's trade publishing unit, Fairchild Publications (now Fairchild Fashion Group), for $650 million.

In 2001 Condé Nast bought a majority stake in Miami-based Ideas Publishing Group (Spanish language versions of US magazines; its name was later changed to Condé Nast Americas). Also that year Advance bought four golf magazines, including *Golf Digest*, from the New York Times Company for $430 million. It also picked up *Modern Bride* magazine from PRIMEDIA in 2002. Richard Diamond, a Newhouse relative who'd been publisher of the *Staten Island Advance* since 1979, died in 2004. The following year, Condé Nast launched home magazine *Domino* and lifestyle title *Cookie* targeting the mommy set.

Affiliate Advance/Newhouse combined its stake in cable programmer Discovery Communications with the interests of John Malone (head of Liberty Media) in 2008 to spin off Discovery as a public company. A downturn in the economy that year led to a sharp decline in ad revenue for many of Advance Publications' newspaper and magazine titles. *The Star-Ledger* was forced to cut about 40% of its workforce to reduce costs. Condé Nast, meanwhile, shuttered several titles in 2009, including *Cookie*, *Domino*, *Gourmet*, and *Modern Bride*.

EXECUTIVES

Chairman and CEO; Chairman Condé Nast Publications: Samuel I. (Si) Newhouse Jr., age 82
President: Donald E. Newhouse, age 80
Publisher Staten Island Advance: Caroline Harrison
President and CEO American City Business Journals: Whitney Shaw
Chairman Advance.net: Steven Newhouse, age 52
CEO Parade Publications: John E. (Jack) Haire, age 56
President CondéNet Nast Digital: Sarah Chubb
President Advance Internet: Peter Weinberger
CEO Condé Nast: Charles H. (Chuck) Townsend
CFO Advance Publications and President Advance Finance Group LLC: Thomas S. (Tom) Summer, age 55
Group President Consumer Marketing, Condé Nast: Robert (Bob) Sauerberg

LOCATIONS

HQ: Advance Publications, Inc.
950 Fingerboard Rd., Staten Island, NY 10305
Phone: 718-981-1234 **Fax:** 718-981-1456
Web: www.advance.net

PRODUCTS/OPERATIONS

Selected Operations

Newspapers
 The Cleveland Plain-Dealer
 The Oregonian (Portland)
 The Star-Ledger (Newark, New Jersey)
 Staten Island Advance (New York)
 The Times-Picayune (New Orleans)
Magazines
 Allure
 Architectural Digest
 Bon Appétit
 Condé Nast Traveler
 Details
 Glamour
 Golf Digest
 GQ
 Lucky
 Men's Vogue
 The New Yorker
 Self
 Teen Vogue
 Vanity Fair
 Vogue
 W
 Wired
Other interests
 Bright House Networks (cable system operator)
 Discovery Communications (cable television channels, 25%)

COMPETITORS

American Express	New York Times
Crain Communications	News Corp.
Gannett	North Jersey Media
Hearst Corporation	Philadelphia Media
Lagardère Active	Time Inc.
McClatchy Company	Tribune Company
MediaNews	Washington Post
Meredith Corporation	

HISTORICAL FINANCIALS

Company Type: Private

Income Statement FYE: December 31

	ESTIMATED REVENUE ($ mil.)	NET INCOME ($ mil.)	NET PROFIT MARGIN	EMPLOYEES
12/08	7,630	—	—	27,200
12/07	7,970	—	—	29,100
12/06	7,700	—	—	28,000
12/05	7,315	—	—	30,000
Annual Growth	**1.4%**	**—**	**—**	**(3.2%)**

Revenue History

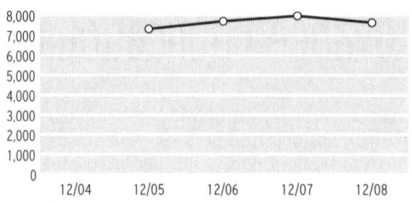

Advanced Drainage Systems

Work at Advanced Drainage Systems (ADS) isn't going down the drain, it *is* the drain. ADS manufactures high-density polyethylene (HDPE) pipes for storm and sanitary sewers, agricultural drainage, road and highway construction, and residential and commercial development. The corrugated HDPE lineup runs from culverts to drains, fittings, grates, grease interceptors, and leaching chambers. ADS even offers a green building mix of products. Customers are mining and timber operators as well as engineers in highway construction and waste management systems. ADS products lie under fabled US athletic turf and recreation sites such as Augusta National, Dodger Stadium, and Lambeau Field. ADS is an employee-owned company.

Customers' pipe preferences continue to drive ADS. Targeting public works, ADS pushes for new service approval of its pipes' structural strength and flow efficiency. Federal regulations have helped; state governments receiving federal monies must consider drainage materials beyond steel and concrete. Although competitors in the concrete industry disagree with the rule's application to HDPE, ADS' N-12 and N-12 HP pipe offerings received a nod from The Florida Department of Transportation (FDOT) in 2008. Money-saving features of ADS corrugated HDPE pipe, and its role in completing the job on time, have also contributed to winning civil construction contracts. Because a large amount of pipe can be loaded with each delivery, lowering truck transportation emissions, the products' reduced environmental impact is being highlighted, too. Pressing these benefits, ADS landed the storm water drainage system project for Utah's Interstate Highway-15 reconstruction in 2001, and the state's New Ogden Weber (NOW) County widening and repair in 2008.

The company acquired the remaining 50% interest in StormTech in 2009. StormTech, which makes chemically-resistant underground stormwater chambers, was created as a 50/50 partnership between ADS and Infiltrator Systems.

ADS takes aim at broadening its market dominance by expanding its product lineup. Also in 2009 the company inked an exclusive marketing agreement with Inlet & Pipe Protection's storm water inlet filter units, a promising growth market in plastic building products. This move fell on the heels of a deal to act as the sole sales and marketing arm of BaySaver Technologies' product line. In 2005 ADS picked up regional rival Hancor, creating the world's largest HDPE corrugated plastic pipe company.

The company, which was founded in 1966, operates over 40 domestic and international manufacturing facilities. It also has 30 distribution centers in the US and reportedly sells $1 billion of corrugated pipe per year.

EXECUTIVES

Chairman, President, and CEO; Chairman and CEO, Hancor: Joseph A. (Joe) Chlapaty, age 63
CFO; EVP Finance, Hancor: Mark B. Sturgeon
EVP Engineering; VP Engineering, Hancor: Tom Fussner
EVP Sales; EVP Sales, Hancor: Bob Klein
EVP Manufacturing; EVP Manufacturing, Hancor: Jim Baich
VP International Operations; VP International Operations, Hancor: Ewout Leeuwenburg
Director Marketing; Director Marketing, Hancor: Tori L. Durliat
Director Human Resources; Director Human Resources, Hancor: Erick Piscopo

LOCATIONS

HQ: Advanced Drainage Systems, Inc.
4640 Trueman Blvd., Hilliard, OH 43026
Phone: 614-658-0050 **Fax:** 614-658-0204
Web: www.ads-pipe.com

PRODUCTS/OPERATIONS

Select Markets Served

Agriculture
Green Building
Landfill/Waste Disposal Management
Mining
On-Site Septic System
Residential/Commercial Drainage
Retention/Detention Systems
Road & Highway Drainage
Sanitary Sewers
Storm Sewer
Timber
Turf & Recreation

COMPETITORS

Charlotte Pipe & Foundry
CONTECH
Diamond Plastics
Enerfab
J-M Manufacturing
NIBCO

HISTORICAL FINANCIALS

Company Type: Private

Income Statement

FYE: December 31

	REVENUE ($ mil.)	NET INCOME ($ mil.)	NET PROFIT MARGIN	EMPLOYEES
12/08	1,200	—	—	4,000
12/07	1,200	—	—	4,000
12/06	1,200	—	—	3,900
12/05	1,200	—	—	3,800
Annual Growth	0.0%	—	—	1.7%

Revenue History

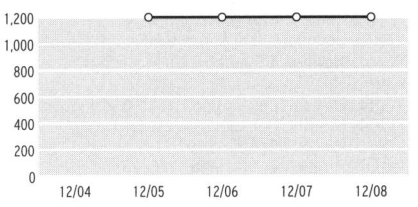

Advanced Lighting Technologies

And then there was metal halide light. More closely than other technologies, Advanced Lighting Technologies' (ADLT) metal halide simulates sunlight. Through subsidiary Venture Lighting, ADLT makes metal halide lamps and ballast systems. ADLT touts an energy-efficient lineup including lamp components, power supplies, and lamp-making equipment for commercial and industrial needs. Vertically integrated, ADLT's APL Engineered Materials arm makes the metal halide salts used in its products and also sells the salts to other manufacturers. ADLT's Deposition Sciences makes passive optical telecommunications devices and thin film deposition equipment. The company is owned by private equity firm Saratoga Partners.

Operating through five subsidiaries, ADLT looks to develop a spectrum of complementary competencies that tap growth markets demanding "green" lighting materials, components, and systems. Its technological expertise focuses on a breadth of applications — fiber-optic lighting, telecommunications, automotive, and commercial and residential operations. To this end ADLT bought Auer Lighting GmbH, a division of Schott AG, in 2007. The investment added a strong arm in building general and specialized lighting components for digital projection, stage, medical, and automotive lighting.

ADLT's direction to diversify vertically is influenced by its past financial troubles and current ownership. The company emerged from Chapter 11 in late 2003 after refinancing was provided by Saratoga Lighting Holdings, an affiliate of the New York-based Saratoga Partners.

EXECUTIVES

Non-Executive Chairman: Robert Cizik, age 77
CEO and Director: Wayne R. Hellman, age 62
COO and Director: Sabu Krishnan, age 50
EVP and CFO: Wayne J. Vespoli, age 47
VP: Lee A. Bartolomei, age 69
VP: James L. Schoolenberg, age 65
Plant Manager: John Larker
Public Relations: David Wypasek
Finances: Lisa Barry
Human Resources: Michelle Guarino
Auditors: Grant Thornton LLP

LOCATIONS

HQ: Advanced Lighting Technologies, Inc.
32000 Aurora Rd., Solon, OH 44139
Phone: 440-519-0500   **Fax:** 440-519-0501
Web: www.adlt.com

COMPETITORS

Corning
EI Products
GE
Havells Sylvania
JDS Uniphase
LSI Industries
Magnetek
Nortel Networks
OSRAM
Philips Electronics

Advanstar Communications

Advanstar Communications offers a constellation of business-to-business publishing and marketing services related to fashion, life sciences, and powersports. The company has a portfolio of nearly 70 print publications and directories and some 270 electronic publications and Web sites. It also stages nearly 140 expositions, conferences, and other events annually. Titles include *Motor Age*, *Medical Economics*, and *Dermatology Times*; trade shows include apparel show MAGIC Marketplace; and marketing offerings include direct-mail services and custom publishing. A consortium of investors led by private-equity firm Veronis Suhler Stevenson owns Advanstar.

In 2008 Advanstar Communications launched digital editions for three health care titles. *RN*, *Healthcare Traveler*, and *LocumLife* joined *Drug Topics* and *Geriatrics* in offering readers instant access to an online version of each print issue. The company did so in order to expand audience engagement and reach beyond print circulation to other relevant disciplines, international providers, and students.

The company was previously owned by DLJ Merchant Banking Partners III, the merchant banking affiliate of Donaldson, Lufkin & Jenrette (now part of Credit Suisse Group). In 2007 Veronis Suhler Stevenson acquired the firm for more than $1 billion; Citigroup Private Equity and New York Life Capital Partners were co-sponsors in the deal.

EXECUTIVES

Chairman: James M. (Jim) Alic
CEO: Joseph (Joe) Loggia
EVP Finance and CFO: Theodore S. (Ted) Alpert
EVP Powersports, Dental and Veterinary:
Daniel M (Danny) Phillips
EVP Exhibitions: Anthony (Tony) Calanca
EVP Corporate Development: Eric I. Lisman, age 51
EVP Fashion; President, Magic International:
Chris DeMoulin
EVP Licensing, Market Development, and Europe:
Georgiann DeCenzo
EVP Healthcare, Pharmaceutical, and Science:
R. Steven (Steve) Morris
VP and General Counsel: Ward D. Hewins
VP; Chief Merchandising Officer, Fashion:
André Warren
VP Human Resources: Nancy Nugent
VP Information Technology: J. Vaughn
VP, Treasurer, and Controller: Shelbie O'Brien
VP Media Operations: Francis Heid
Director Corporate Marketing: Lorelyn Eaves
Manager Corporate Marketing and Communications:
Susannah George
Auditors: PricewaterhouseCoopers LLP

LOCATIONS

HQ: Advanstar Communications Inc.
6200 Canoga Ave., 2nd Fl.
Woodland Hills, CA 91367
Phone: 818-593-5000   **Fax:** 818-593-5020
Web: www.advanstar.com

PRODUCTS/OPERATIONS

Selected Products and Services

Marketing services
Classified advertising
Database marketing
Direct mail services
Directories
Guides and reference books
Reprints
Trade, business, and professional publications
Trade shows and conferences

Selected Trade Shows and Conferences

International Powersports Dealer Expo (powersports accessories trade show)
MAGIC Marketplace (men's apparel trade show)

Selected Publications

Auto Body Repair News
Dental Product Reports
Dermatology Times
DIRTsports
Medical Economics
Motor Age
Pharmaceutical Technology

COMPETITORS

Access Intelligence
BravoSolution US
Crain Communications
Fairchild Fashion Group
Freeman Decorating Services
George P. Johnson
Hanley Wood
Harte-Hanks
IHS
Informa
International Data Group
Lebhar-Friedman
McGraw-Hill
The Nielsen Company
Penton Media
Reed Elsevier Group
Thomas Publishing
United Business Media
Wolters Kluwer

Advantis Real Estate Services

Advantis Real Estate Services (aka GVA Advantis or Advantis/GVA) knows its advantage is in commercial real estate. A member of global partnership GVA Worldwide, the company offers brokerage, project management, and strategic consulting services to commercial property owners and developers, primarily in the southeastern US. It also leases and manages more than 30 million sq. ft. of commercial space including office, industrial, and retail properties. The company has about 15 offices in the Southeast and Mid-Atlantic. A private equity firm led by real estate developer Jeffrey T. Neal acquired a controlling interest in GVA Advantis in 2008.

The sale came three years after management bought out the firm from Florida real estate development company St. Joe. Former CBRE Canada chairman Richard Pogue took over as president of GVA Advantis, whose headquarters moved from Atlanta to Washington, DC.

EXECUTIVES

Chairman and CEO: Jeffrey T. Neal
President: Thomas W. (Tim) Hague
COO: Robert L. Brumm
SVP, Human Resources: Karen McWeeny
President, Advantis Construction Company:
 Paul Thomann
Principal and Executive Director, Corporate Services:
 Scott W. Nelson

LOCATIONS

HQ: Advantis Real Estate Services Company
 888 16th St. NW, Ste. 800, Washington, DC 20006
Phone: 202-204-7039
Web: www.advantisgva.com

Selected Offices

Atlanta
Destin, FL
Durham, NC
Fredricksburg, VA
Jacksonville, FL
Newport News, VA
Norfolk, VA
Orlando, FL
Panama City, FL
Richmond, VA
Tallahassee, FL
Tampa
Tysons Corner, VA
Washington, DC

COMPETITORS

Carter
CB Richard Ellis
Cushman & Wakefield
Divaris Real Estate
Donohoe Companies
Flagler Development
Great Atlantic Management
Grubb & Ellis
Inland Group
Jones Lang LaSalle
Lincoln Property
Opus Corp.
Stiles
Weichert Realtors

Adventist Health System

Adventist Health's mission is to serve the community, and boy does it! One of the country's largest faith-based hospital systems, not-for-profit Adventist Health System runs about 40 hospitals and some 20 nursing homes, as well as nearly 30 home health care agencies. Its acute care hospitals have more than 6,500 beds combined, and its long-term care facilities offer just about 2,000 beds. It operates in 12 states mostly in the Southeast, with Florida being its key market. The organization's Florida Hospital division includes 17 hospitals serving the state via more than 1,400 beds. The health system is sponsored by the Seventh-Day Adventist Church as part of that denomination's legacy of providing health care.

Despite its already considerable size, the system continues to grow its services and facilities through both affiliation agreements and new construction. Between 2008 and 2009 Adventist Health built or began building new hospitals in Daytona Beach and Orlando, Florida, and Bolingbrook, Illinois.

The health system also embarked on a number of construction projects designed to expand the services offered at existing facilities, including a second cardiac catheterization lab at its Florida Hospital Flagler and a Heart & Vascular Institute at Adventist GlenOaks Hospital in Glendale Heights, Illinois.

Adventist Health's hospitals in Texas (Central Texas Medical Center and Metroplex Health System) have entered into affiliation agreements in recent years that give them greater access to physician specialists and services. Central Texas Medical Center entered into an agreement with St. David's Healthcare in late 2008. Metroplex Health System and Scott & White Healthcare entered into a similar agreement that same year to grow medical services in the communities each of them serve.

EXECUTIVES

Chairman: Max A. Trevino
President, CEO, and Director: Donald L. Jernigan, age 62
CFO and Director: Terry D. Shaw
President and CEO, Florida Hospital and Florida Division: Lars D. Houmann, age 49
President and CEO, Multi-State Division and Director:
 Richard K. (Rich) Reiner
SVP Finance; Senior Finance Officer, Florida Hospital:
 Lewis A. Seifert
SVP Finance and Senior Financial Officer:
 Paul C. Rathbun
SVP and Treasurer: Gary C. Skilton
SVP Business Development, Risk Management, and Chief Compliance Officer: Sandra K. Johnson
SVP Clinical Effectiveness and Chief Medical Officer:
 Loran D. Hauck
SVP and Chief Clinical Officer: Carlene Jamerson
SVP Information Services and CIO: John W. McLendon
SVP Managed Care: John R. Brownlow
SVP Administration and Director:
 Robert R. Henderschedt
VP Human Resources: Donald G. (Don) Jones
VP Finance and Corporate Controller:
 Amy L. Zbaraschuk

LOCATIONS

HQ: Adventist Health System
 111 N. Orlando Ave., Winter Park, FL 32789
Phone: 407-647-4400   **Fax:** 407-975-1469
Web: www.adventisthealthsystem.com

Selected Facilities

Colorado
 Avista Adventist Hospital (Louisville)
 Littleton Adventist Hospital
 Parker Adventist Hospital
 Porter Adventist Hospital (Denver)
Florida
 Adventist Care Center – Courtland (Orlando)
 Adventist Care Centers (Orlando)
 Adventist Health System (Winter Park)
 Chapel Home Health (Zephyrhills)
 East Orlando Health & Rehab Center
 Florida Hospital Altamonte (Altamonte Springs)
 Florida Hospital Apopka
 Florida Hospital Celebration Health (Celebration)
 Florida Hospital DeLand
 Florida Hospital East Orlando
 Florida Hospital Fish Memorial (Orange City)
 Florida Hospital Flagler (Palm Coast)
 Florida Hospital Heartland Medical Center (Sebring)
 Florida Hospital Kissimmee
 Florida Hospital Lake Placid
 Florida Hospital Oceanside (Ormond Beach)
 Florida Hospital Orlando
 Florida Hospital Winter Park Memorial Hospital
 Sunbelt Health & Rehab Center – Apopka
 Zephyr Haven Health & Rehab Center (Zephyrhills)
Georgia
 Gordon Hospital (Calhoun)
 Emory-Adventist Hospital (Smyrna)
Illinois
 Adventist Bolingbrook Hospital
 Adventist GlenOaks Hospital (Glendale Heights)
 Adventist Hinsdale Hospital
 Adventist La Grange Memorial Hospital
Kansas
 Shawnee Mission Medical Center
Kentucky
 Manchester Memorial Hospital
North Carolina
 Park Ridge Hospital (Fletcher)
Tennessee
 Jellico Community Hospital
 Takoma Regional Hospital (Greeneville)
Texas
 Central Texas Medical Center (San Marcos)
 Huguley Memorial Medical Center (Fort Worth)
 Metroplex Adventist Hospital (Killeen)
 Rollins Brook Community Hospital (Lampasas)
Wisconsin
 Chippewa Valley Hospital (Durand)

PRODUCTS/OPERATIONS

2008 Patient Visits

	No. (thou.)	% of total
Outpatient Visits	2,170	55
ER Visits	940	24
Home Health Visits	530	13
Admissions	300	8
Nursing Home Patients	5	—
Total	**3,945**	**100**

COMPETITORS

Ascension Health
Catholic Health East
Catholic Health Initiatives
Catholic Healthcare Partners
Community Health Systems
HCA
Health Management Associates
Kindred Healthcare
Mount Sinai Medical Center of Florida
Orlando Health
Tenet Healthcare
Universal Health Services

HISTORICAL FINANCIALS

Company Type: Not-for-profit

Income Statement

FYE: December 31

	REVENUE ($ mil.)	NET INCOME ($ mil.)	NET PROFIT MARGIN	EMPLOYEES
12/08	5,496	234	4.2%	43,000
12/07	4,835	360	7.5%	43,000
12/06	4,969	325	6.5%	43,000
12/05	4,637	251	5.4%	43,000
12/04	4,379	236	5.4%	—
Annual Growth	5.8%	(0.3%)	—	0.0%

Net Income History

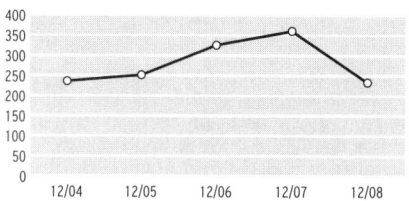

Advocate Health Care

Advocating wellness in Chicagoland from Palos Heights to Palatine, Advocate Health Care is an integrated health care network with more than 200 sites serving the Chicago area. Advocate's operations include about a dozen acute and specialty care hospitals (including Christ Medical Center, Hope Children's Hospital, and Lutheran General Hospital) with more than 3,300 beds, as well as community health clinics and home health care and hospice services. The health system includes the largest physician network of primary care physicians, specialists, and subspecialists in the state. Advocate Health and BroMenn Healthcare System have announced they intend to merge.

BroMenn Healthcare System, which has some 2,000 employees and has been in business for more than 110 years, would become a part of the Advocate system while retaining its name and identity. The merger — which could happen by mid-2010 — would expand Advocate's reach beyond the Chicago area, making the health system a statewide presence. Bromenn Healthcare comprises two full-service hospitals, a medical group of providers and clinics, and a provider network consisting of nearly 400 health care providers.

Around the same time BroMenn Healthcare and Advocate announced they plan to merge, Advocate added to its already hefty size by acquiring the 280-bed Condell Medical Center for $180 million. Condell Medical had been seeking a buyer due to financial difficulties. Advocate plans to eventually expand Condell's emergency services and patient capacity.

The following year the health network grew again and bolstered its staff base and outpatient network by acquiring the Midwest Physician Group for $12.5 million.

Along with providing the full spectrum of health care services, Advocate Health has a clinical laboratory joint venture, ACL Laboratories, with Aurora Health Care. ACL provides analytical and diagnostic testing services for both companies' facilities.

Advocate Health has ties to both the Evangelical Lutheran Church in America and the United Church of Christ. The system also has teaching affiliations with area medical schools such as the University of Illinois at Chicago and the University of Chicago Pritzker School of Medicine. Advocate Health was formed in 1995.

EXECUTIVES

Chairperson: John F. Timmer, age 61
Vice Chairperson: Lynn Crump-Caine, age 53
President, CEO, and Director:
James H. (Jim) Skogsbergh
EVP and COO; Interim President, Advocate Lutheran General Hospital and Advocate Lutheran General Children's Hospital: William P. (Bill) Santulli
SVP, CFO, and Treasurer: Dominic J. Nakis
SVP Strategic Planning and Growth: Scott Powder
SVP, General Counsel, and Corporate Secretary: Gail D. Hasbrouck
SVP Communications and Government Relations: Anthony (Tony) Mitchell
SVP Information Systems and CIO: Bruce Smith
SVP Human Resources: Ben Grigaliunas
SVP Mission and Spiritual Care:
Rev Jerry A. Wagenknecht
Chief Development Officer; President, Advocate Charitable Foundation: Susan J. Ell
VP Communication and Government Relations: Kelly Jo Golson
CEO, Advocate Physician Partners:
Martin F. (Marty) Manning, age 54
Auditors: Ernst & Young

LOCATIONS

HQ: Advocate Health Care
2025 Windsor Dr., Oak Brook, IL 60523
Phone: 630-572-9393 **Fax:** 630-990-4752
Web: www.advocatehealth.com

PRODUCTS/OPERATIONS

Selected Locations

Advocate Bethany Hospital
Advocate Christ Medical Center
Advocate Condell Medical Center
Advocate Good Samaritan Hospital
Advocate Good Shepherd Hospital
Advocate Health Centers
Advocate Home Health Services
Advocate Hope Children's Hospital
Advocate Illinois Masonic Medical Center
Advocate Illinois Masonic Physician Group
Advocate Lutheran General Hospital
Advocate Lutheran General Children's Hospital
Advocate Medical Group
Advocate Physician Partners
Advocate South Suburban Hospital
Advocate Trinity Hospital

COMPETITORS

Alexian Brothers Health System
Central DuPage Hospital
Children's Memorial Hospital
Covenant Ministries
Elmhurst Memorial Healthcare
Gottleib Memorial Hospital
HCA
Hospital Sisters Health System
KishHealth
Lake Forest Hospital Foundation
Loyola University Health System
Mercy Hospital and Medical Center
NorthShore University HealthSystem
Northwest Community Healthcare
Northwestern Memorial HealthCare
Pronger Smith
Provena Health
Rush System for Health
Silver Cross Hospital
Sinai Health System
SSM Health Care
University of Chicago Medical Center

HISTORICAL FINANCIALS

Company Type: Not-for-profit

Income Statement

FYE: December 31

	REVENUE ($ mil.)	NET INCOME ($ mil.)	NET PROFIT MARGIN	EMPLOYEES
12/08	3,000	—	—	24,500
12/07	3,457	—	—	30,000
12/06	3,268	—	—	29,100
12/05	2,974	—	—	29,600
12/04	2,780	—	—	24,500
Annual Growth	1.9%	—	—	0.0%

Revenue History

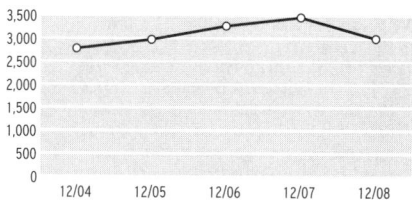

Aerospace Corporation

A not-for-profit company, The Aerospace Corporation provides space-related research, development, and advisory services, primarily for US government programs. Its chief sponsor is the US Air Force, and its main customers have included the Space and Missile Systems Center of Air Force Space Command and the National Reconnaissance Office. Other clients have included NASA and the National Oceanic and Atmospheric Administration, as well as commercial enterprises, universities, and international organizations. Areas of expertise include launch certification, process implementation, systems engineering, and technology application. The Aerospace Corporation was established in 1960 and operates through about 20 offices.

The US relies on space systems for intelligence, communications, navigation, and weather, making Aerospace's mission assurance and systems engineering services vital to national security. Among the company's projects are work on the next generation of satellites, including the Global Positioning System IIF, Space Based Space Surveillance, Advanced Extremely High Frequency, Wideband Global Satcom, and Space Based Infrared System programs. These new satellites will provide new capabilities and replace systems from the 1970s and 1980s.

Scientists at The Aerospace Corporation also have been developing a nanosatellite to test high-efficiency solar cells under space conditions. Solar cells, made by Spectrolab (a subsidiary of Boeing Space and Intelligence Systems) and EMCORE, convert sunlight into electricity. The nanosatellite, only 14 pounds, is one of many such small satellites pioneered by Aerospace. Compared to larger satellites, nanosatellites are less expensive to launch and operate.

Officially, The Aerospace Corporation operates a federally funded research and development center, or FFRDC, for the Air Force. The Aerospace FFRDC is one of more than 40 established to help government agencies with tasks related to aviation, defense, energy, health and human services, space, and tax administration.

EXECUTIVES

Chairman: Peter B. Teets
Vice Chairman: Thomas S. Moorman Jr.
President, CEO, and Trustee: Wanda M. Austin
SVP, General Counsel, and Secretary:
  Malissia R. Clinton
SVP National Systems Group: Manuel De Ponte
SVP Engineering and Technology Group:
  Rami R. Razouk
SVP Space Systems Group: David J. Gorney
VP, CFO, and Treasurer: Dale E. Wallis
VP and CIO: William C. (Willie) Krenz
VP Civil and Commercial Operations: Gary P. Pulliam
VP Program Assessment: John R. (Jack) Wormington
VP Space Launch Operations: Ray F. Johnson
VP National Systems Group: Bernard W. Chau
Principal Director NOAA Programs: W. J. Hussey
Principal Director Treasury Directorate: D. M. Wong
Principal Director Finance: J. W. Ford
Principal Director Corporate Communications
  Directorate: S. K. Steele
Principal Director Commercial, International, and
  Homeland Security Programs: M. N. Rochlin
Director Risk Management: D. G. Rhyne
General Manager, Human Resources Division:
  C. M. Lazar-Morrison
Auditors: Deloitte & Touche LLP

LOCATIONS

HQ: The Aerospace Corporation
  2350 E. El Segundo Blvd., El Segundo, CA 90245
Phone: 310-336-5000   **Fax:** 310-336-7055
Web: www.aero.org

Affiliated Foods

This company helps keep pantries stocked in the Panhandle and elsewhere. Affiliated Foods is a leading wholesale distribution cooperative that supplies about 700 member grocery stores and restaurants in Texas, New Mexico, and four other states. It distributes fresh produce, meat, and non-food products, as well as dairy products and beverages through its Plains Dairy unit. Its Tri State Baking Company supplies bread and other baked goods. In addition, Affiliated Foods owns a stake in private-label products supplier Western Family Foods. The company was founded in 1946 as Panhandle Associated Grocers, which merged with South Plains Associated Grocers to form Affiliated Foods in 1968.

EXECUTIVES

President: George Lankford
CFO: Tammie Coffee
Director, Non-Foods: Steve Paul
Director, Operations, Tri State Baking Company:
  Doug Perrett
Director, Produce: Harold Callaway
Director, Meat: Bob Cota
Director, Information Technology: Michael Lindley
Director, Corporate Purchasing: Joe Self
Director, Human Resources: Gene Blackburn
Director, Advertising: David Campsey
Controller: Kim Clark
President, Plains Dairy: Dub Garlington
President, Tri State Baking Company: Jim Ravenscraft
Auditors: Johnson Moore & Associates, PC

LOCATIONS

HQ: Affiliated Foods Inc.
  1401 W. Farmers Ln., Amarillo, TX 79118
Phone: 806-372-3851   **Fax:** 806-372-3647
Web: www.afiama.com

COMPETITORS

Affiliated Foods Midwest
Associated Wholesale Grocers
C & S Wholesale
Grocers Supply
GSC Enterprises
IGA
McLane
Nash-Finch
SUPERVALU

HISTORICAL FINANCIALS

Company Type: Cooperative

Income Statement

	REVENUE ($ mil.)	NET INCOME ($ mil.)	NET PROFIT MARGIN	EMPLOYEES
9/08	1,137	—	—	1,200

FYE: September 30

Affinia Group

Affinia Group caters to those with an affinity for car parts. The company is a leading designer, manufacturer, and distributor of aftermarket vehicular components. "Aftermarket" refers to the network of vendors existing to sell vehicle components intended to replace the stock manufacturer's parts. Affinia's products, which are sold in 19 countries worldwide, consist of brake, filtration, and chassis parts and are made for passenger cars; sport utility vehicles (SUVs); light, medium, and heavy trucks; and off-highway vehicles. Its brand names are well known in the industry and include AIMCO, McQuay-Norris, Nakata, Quinton Hazell, Raybestos, and WIX.

Affinia's customers, who are primarily large aftermarket distributors and retailers (who then sell to professional technicians and installers), include CARQUEST, NAPA, and Federated Auto Parts. In addition, the company provides private-label and co-branded components for Federated and Automotive Distribution Network (ADN).

In 2008 the company added more than 1 million sq. ft. of manufacturing space when it purchased 85% of HBM Investment, the parent of Chinese drum and rotor maker Longkou Haimeng Machining. Haimeng gives Affinia access to aftermarket and OEM customers in Asia and Europe.

EXECUTIVES

Chairman: Larry W. McCurdy, age 73
President, CEO, and Director: Terry R. McCormack,
  age 58, $733,333 total compensation
SVP and CFO: Thomas H. Madden, age 59,
  $351,225 total compensation
SVP, General Counsel, and Secretary: Steven E. Keller,
  age 50
VP and CIO: James E. Burdiss, age 57
VP Commercial Distribution, South America:
  Jorge C. Schertel, age 57, $423,172 total compensation
VP Human Resources: Timothy J. Zorn, age 56
VP Commercial Distribution, Europe:
  Roderick Ashby-Johnson, age 64
VP Business Development: Patrick M. Manning, age 36
President, Global Brake and Chassis Group:
  H. David Overbeeke, age 47,
  $1,105,353 total compensation
President, Global Filtration: Keith A. Wilson, age 47,
  $434,446 total compensation
Auditors: Deloitte & Touche LLP

LOCATIONS

HQ: Affinia Group Intermediate Holdings Inc.
  1101 Technology Dr., Ann Arbor, MI 48108
Phone: 734-827-5400   **Fax:** 734-827-5402
Web: www.affiniagroup.com

2008 Sales

	% of total
US	63
South America	19
Europe	18
Total	**100**

PRODUCTS/OPERATIONS

2008 Sales by Product Group

	% of total
Filtration	33
Brake	31
Commercial distribution	29
Chassis	7
Total	**100**

COMPETITORS

Cardone Industries
CLARCOR
Cummins
Donaldson Company
Federal-Mogul
Genuine Parts
Honeywell International
United Components

HISTORICAL FINANCIALS

Company Type: Private

Income Statement				FYE: December 31
	REVENUE ($ mil.)	NET INCOME ($ mil.)	NET PROFIT MARGIN	EMPLOYEES
12/08	2,178	(3)	—	10,576
12/07	2,138	6	0.3%	9,507
12/06	2,160	(5)	—	10,497
12/05	2,132	(30)	—	11,678
12/04	2,089	24	1.1%	12,400
Annual Growth	1.0%	—	—	(3.9%)

2008 Year-End Financials

Debt ratio: 170.8%
Return on equity: —
Cash ($ mil.): —

Current ratio: —
Long-term debt ($ mil.): 608

Net Income History

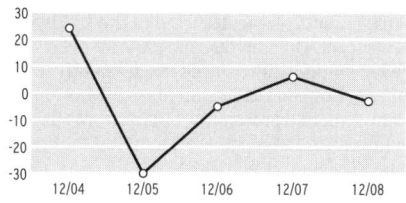

Affinion Group

Through its partners and affiliations, Affinion Group aims to make fans of its customers' customers. The company operates membership and loyalty programs on behalf of corporate clients seeking to strengthen their ties to consumers. It specializes in launching a variety of media services — through direct mail and the Internet — and packaging these benefits to its clients' customers. Programs overseen include AutoVantage, Buyers Advantage, and Travelers Advantage. Overall, the group offers its programs to about 61 million members worldwide through more than 5,500 partners; it has offices in Europe, South Africa, and the US. The group is owned by investment firm Apollo Management.

Of all of Affinion's thousands of partners, the company depends the most on Bank of America and JPMorgan Chase; the two have been marketing with Affinion for over a decade, with JPMorgan accounting for 10% of its overall revenue in 2008. The company is engaged in 12 individual contracts with JPMorgan.

Affinion's growth strategy largely involves expanding its international operations, most notably in the European retail, travel services, cable, and Internet markets.

Proceeds of the company's 2007 IPO were used to alleviate debt and pay fees owed to Apollo Management for advisory and consulting services.

EXECUTIVES

Chairman, President, and CEO: Nathaniel J. Lipman, age 44
EVP and CFO: Todd H. Siegel, age 39
EVP Global Operations: John Kitzie
EVP Product Development: Tom Smith
EVP and General Counsel: Leonard P. Ciniello, age 46
EVP and COO: Robert G. (Bob) Rooney, age 51
EVP Marketing Services: Michael P. (Mike) Rauscher
EVP Client Solutions: Bill Graham
EVP Business Development and Strategic Marketing: Wayne Conte
EVP Support Services: Mary Rusterholz
SVP and Chief Accounting Officer: Brian J. Dick
SVP Communications and Brand: James T. Hart
President, Affinion Loyalty Solutions: Marti Beller
President and CEO, North America: Thomas J. (Tom) Rusin, age 40
President and CEO, Affinion International Limited: Steven E. (Steve) Upshaw, age 38
Director Corporate Communications: Todd Smith
Auditors: Deloitte & Touche LLP

LOCATIONS

HQ: Affinion Group, Inc.
100 Connecticut Ave., Norwalk, CT 06850
Phone: 203-956-1000   **Fax:** 203-956-8502
Web: www.affiniongroup.com

2008 Sales

	$ mil.	% of total
US	1,155.7	82
UK	143.2	10
Other countries	111.0	8
Total	**1,409.9**	**100**

PRODUCTS/OPERATIONS

2008 Sales

	$ mil.	% of total
Membership products	712.6	50
Insurance & package products	375.1	27
International products	254.2	18
Loyalty products	72.2	5
Adjustment	(4.2)	—
Total	**1,409.9**	**100**

Selected Membership Products and Services

AutoVantage
Buyers Advantage
Clever Clubhouse
CompleteHome
Great Fun
Great Options
HealthSaver
Hot-Line
ID Secure
Just For Me
National Card Registry
Netmarket.com
PC SafetyPlus
Pet Privileges
Privacy Guard
Shoppers Advantage
Small Business Central (SM)
Travelers Advantage
Wallet Security

Selected Partners

1-800-FLOWERS
Bank of America
CompUSA
Choice Hotels
HSBC
GMAC
JPMorgan Chase
Royal Bank of Scotland
Société Générale
Staples
Priceline

COMPETITORS

Access Plans USA
AEGON Direct Marketing Services
AIG
Assurant
Carlson Marketing
Hospitality Marketing Concepts
Intersections Inc.
Loyalty Management
Maritz Loyalty Marketing
Provell
Q Interactive
Rewards Network
Student Advantage
Vertrue
Webloyalty.com

HISTORICAL FINANCIALS

Company Type: Private

Income Statement				FYE: December 31
	REVENUE ($ mil.)	NET INCOME ($ mil.)	NET PROFIT MARGIN	EMPLOYEES
12/08	1,410	(89)	—	3,550
12/07	1,321	(191)	—	3,300
12/06	1,138	(453)	—	3,000
12/05	1,199	(89)	—	3,000
12/04	1,531	376	24.6%	—
Annual Growth	(2.0%)	—	—	5.8%

2008 Year-End Financials

Debt ratio: —
Return on equity: —
Cash ($ mil.): —

Current ratio: —
Long-term debt ($ mil.): 1,361

Net Income History

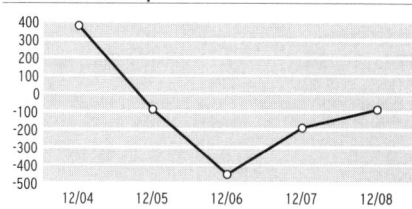

Affinity Group

Recreation is serious business for Affinity Group (AGI). The direct marketing firm sells goods and services through its membership and discount buyers clubs, such as Good Sam, Coast to Coast Resorts, Camp Club USA, and President's Club. It offers RV products (air conditioners, sanitation systems, furnishings) not usually found in general merchandise stores through about 80 Camping World specialty shops across the US, as well as via mail-order catalog and online. AGI also organizes related trade shows and publishes magazines and travel guides, from which it derives subscription fees and ad sales revenue. Chairman Steve Adams is the majority owner of both AGI and, through another entity, RV retailer FreedomRoads.

Membership clubs and membership-based products and services are primary revenue drivers for AGI, contributing about three-quarters of its income. The company's membership clubs have an average renewal rate of about 70% while the renewal rate of its membership-based products and services category (emergency roadside assistance, RV insurance, extended warranty) is about 90%.

With nearly 2 million club members, AGI hopes to continue growing by adding new customers to its database, in an effort to cross-sell its products and services. As it turns out, Camping World and President's Club, its discount buyers club, account for about 60% of the company's new database additions.

Despite tightened credit markets and the US recession, the company expects RV ownership, which is often contingent on factors related to the economy, to increase. Over a five-year period ending in 2010, RV ownership is expected to grow by 20%, according to the National Survey of the RV Consumer by the University of Michigan.

The economic downturn in the US has put the brakes on AGI's retail expansion strategy. In 2009 the company added one Camping World store, and in 2008 it opened five. AGI plans to consolidate underperforming store locations as consumers scale back their spending habits. In previous years AGI added 15 to 20 locations annually to its retail network.

Besides its dues-paying members, AGI also has a subscriber base of about 5 million in aggregate circulation, as well as 1 million in paid circulation, for its nearly 40 publications.

EXECUTIVES

Chairman: Stephen Adams, age 71
President, CEO, and Director: Michael A. Schneider, age 54, $585,740 total compensation
SVP and CFO: Thomas F. Wolfe, age 47, $294,553 total compensation
SVP Products and Services: Prabhuling Patel, age 62, $303,073 total compensation
SVP Human Resources: Laura A. James, age 52
President and SVP, Membership Clubs and Multimedia Division: Joseph (Joe) Daquino, age 49, $280,561 total compensation
President Retail Operations, Camping World: John A. Sirpilla, age 42, $469,778 total compensation
CEO and President, Camping World: Marcus A. Lemonis, age 35
SVP Business Development and General Counsel, Camping World: Brent Moody, age 47
Auditors: Ernst & Young LLP

LOCATIONS

HQ: Affinity Group, Inc.
2575 Vista Del Mar, Ventura, CA 93001
Phone: 805-667-4100   **Fax:** 805-667-4419
Web: www.affinitygroup.com

PRODUCTS/OPERATIONS

2008 Sales

	$ mil.	% of total
Retail	291.1	55
Membership services	152.6	29
Media	82.4	16
Total	**526.1**	**100**

Selected Publications

American Rider
ATV Sport
Bass & Walleye Boats
Boating Industry
Camping Life
MotorHome
Powerboat
PowerSports Business
Rider
RV Business
RV View

SnowGoer
Snow Week
TrailerBoats
Trailer Life
Ultimate Snowmobile Buyers Guide
Watercraft World
Woodall's Tenting Directory
Woodall's Specials

COMPETITORS

International Leisure
Kampgrounds of America
Outdoor Resorts
REI
Thousand Trails

HISTORICAL FINANCIALS

Company Type: Private

Income Statement

FYE: December 31

	REVENUE ($ mil.)	NET INCOME ($ mil.)	NET PROFIT MARGIN	EMPLOYEES
12/08	526	(112)	—	1,814
12/07	562	19	3.4%	2,003
12/06	515	(5,731)	—	2,006
12/05	486	11	2.2%	1,842
12/04	465	10	2.2%	1,800
Annual Growth	**3.2%**	**—**	**—**	**0.2%**

2008 Year-End Financials

Debt ratio: —   Current ratio: —
Return on equity: —   Long-term debt ($ mil.): 280
Cash ($ mil.): —

Net Income History

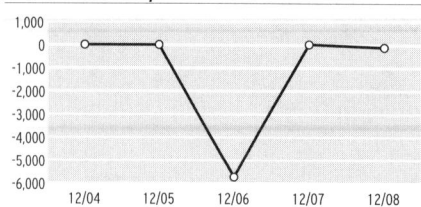

AFL-CIO

Talk about spending a long time in labor: The AFL-CIO (American Federation of Labor and Congress of Industrial Organizations) has been focused on the task for more than a century. The AFL-CIO is an umbrella organization for more than 55 autonomous national and international unions. Altogether, the AFL-CIO represents more than 10 million workers — ranging from actors and airline pilots to marine engineers and machinists — and fights to improve wages and working conditions. The organization charters 51 state federations and about 525 central labor councils. Union members generally receive about 30% higher pay and more benefits than non-members.

The organization's membership has been decreasing, due in part to the decline in manufacturing jobs and the increased use of temporary workers and automation. Despite president John Sweeney's aggressive plans to increase recruiting, the Teamsters and the Service Employees International Union (SEIU) left the AFL-CIO in 2005 over the issues of plummeting membership

and the future course of the labor movement. They took 3.3 million members with them.

Along with Sweeney, the AFL-CIO's executive council comprises more than 45 executives. As part of the organization's emphasis on corporate responsibility, it devotes blogs, reports, videos, and other mediums to discuss the retail environment, such as the dominance of Wal-Mart. It also monitors executive pay through its Executive PayWatch reports and case studies.

HISTORY

The American Federation of Labor (AFL) was formed in 1886 in Columbus, Ohio, by the merger of six craft unions and a renegade craft section of the Marxist-oriented Knights of Labor. Samuel Gompers, a New York cigar factory worker who headed the AFL until his death in 1924, initiated the AFL's pragmatic focus: to work within the economic system to increase wages, improve working conditions, and abolish child labor.

Gompers' successes incensed employers, whose arsenal, supported by the US courts and public opinion, included injunctions, government-backed police forces to crush strikes, and the Sherman Anti-Trust Act (used to assail union monopoly powers).

WWI's production needs boosted AFL membership to 4 million by 1919. Labor clashes with management were widespread in the 1920s amid the fear of Bolsheviks. As part of open-shop drives, employers replaced strikers with southern African-Americans and Mexican workers.

The Great Depression brought more supportive public and pro-labor laws, including the National Industrial Recovery Act (NIRA, 1933), which allowed union organizing and collective bargaining. After NIRA was declared unconstitutional, the Wagner Act (1936) restated many of NIRA's provisions and established the legal basis for unions.

Union power split in 1935 when AFL coal miner John L. Lewis began organizing unskilled workers. Lewis and his allies, expelled from the AFL, formed the Congress of Industrial Organizations (CIO, 1938) and enjoyed success in unionizing the auto, steel, textile, and other industries. By 1946 the AFL and CIO had 9 million and 5 million members, respectively.

Amid postwar concern over rising prices, communist infiltration, and union corruption, Congress passed the Taft-Hartley Act in 1947 (which outlawed closed shops). The new climate of hostility led the AFL (headed by plumber George Meany) and the CIO (headed by autoworker Walter Reuther) to merge in 1955. The AFL-CIO soon expelled the Teamsters and other unions on charges of corruption. (The Teamsters reaffiliated in 1987.)

AFL-CIO membership jumped after President Kennedy gave federal employees the right to unionize (1962); state, county, and municipal workers soon followed.

Union membership, which peaked in the mid-1940s with more than a third of the US labor force, was particularly hurt by a jump in imported goods in the 1970s and automation's triumph over manual labor in the 1980s. Legislation supported by the AFL-CIO included a law requiring 60 days' notice for plant closings (1988) and the Family Medical Leave Act (1993). But labor lost its battle against NAFTA (North American Free Trade Agreement), which it feared would export jobs to Mexico.

In 1995 John Sweeney, former head of the Service Employees International Union (SEIU), became president of the AFL-CIO in its first contested election. Under Sweeney the union spent $35 million in advertising in 1996 to draw attention to issues. After years with little focus on organizing, in 1997 the AFL-CIO launched a massive campaign to organize construction, hospital, and hotel workers in Las Vegas, and committed a third of its budget to recruiting and reorganizing. It supported the Teamsters' successful strike against UPS in 1997 and in 1998 threw its weight behind the Air Line Pilots Association's walkout on Northwest Airlines. It approved a restructuring plan in 1999 and the next year spent significant time and money rallying members all across the US in support of losing presidential candidate Al Gore. In 2002 AFL-CIO announced its pledge of $750 million to create affordable housing in New York City.

At the group's 2005 convention, the Teamsters and the SEIU broke ranks over Sweeney's inability to stem the tide of falling membership. They joined a rival group, Change to Win Coalition, led by SEIU's Andrew Stern.

EXECUTIVES

President: Richard L. Trumka, age 60
EVP: Arlene Holt Baker
President, Building and Construction Trades Department: Mark H. Ayers
President, United Mine Workers of America: Cecil E. Roberts Jr.
President, American Federation of Teachers: Randi Weingarten
National President, American Federation of Government Employees: John Gage, age 62
President, Office and Professional Employees International Union: Michael Goodwin, age 67
President, Communications Workers of America: Larry Cohen, age 57
President, Screen Actors Guild: Alan Rosenberg
National President, National Association of Letter Carriers: William H. (Bill) Young
General President, Sheet Metal Workers International Association: Michael J. (Mike) Sullivan
Secretary and Treasurer: Elizabeth (Liz) Shuler
General Counsel: Jonathan (Jon) Hiatt

LOCATIONS

HQ: AFL-CIO
815 16th St. NW, Washington, DC 20006
Phone: 202-637-5000   **Fax:** 202-637-5323
Web: www.aflcio.org

Ag Processing

Soy far, soy good for Ag Processing (AGP), one of the largest soybean processors in the world. AGP's chief soybean products include vegetable oil and commercial animal feeds. The agricultural cooperative provides grain marketing and transportation services for its 250,000 members. The cooperative also offers corn-based ethanol and soybean oil-based bio-fuels, fuel additives, and solvents. The co-op's owners include member-farmers in the US and Canada. Mostly midwestern farmers, AGP's members are represented through about 200 local and regional co-ops. AGP owns Masterfeeds, a Canadian animal feed company; it is also a major shareholder in the Venezuelan poultry company Proagro.

The co-op, which operates nine soybean processing plants, turns its products into food ingredients, such as lecithin and meat extenders for ground beef. To capitalize on new EPA emission limits and mandates, the co-op lobbies to increase retail demand for ethanol. Additionally, AGP is promoting methyl ester, a by-product of soy oil refining, for use as a clean fuel and fuel additive, agricultural spray, and non-toxic solvent to replace petroleum-based products.

In order to reposition its grain assets to better serve its customers, in 2008 the co-op sold its AGP Grain Ltd. subsidiary (including elevator and terminal operations located in Minnesota and North Dakota) to Columbia Grain.

In 2007 the co-op's board rejected a hostile takeover bid made by Ag Processors Alliance (APA). APA was formed exclusively to take over AGP and consisted of the leadership of Ag and Food Associates of Omaha, an investment banking firm that manages the project on behalf of an investment group that has a specific interest and expertise in agricultural operations.

HISTORY

Seeking strength in numbers, Ag Processing (AGP) was formed in 1983 when agricultural cooperatives Land O' Lakes and Farmland Industries merged their money-losing soybean operations into similarly struggling Boone Valley Cooperative.

Separately, AGP's six soybean mills had been unable to compete successfully against each other and larger corporations. The entire industry had been hampered by the Soviet grain embargoes imposed by the US in 1973 and 1979, and US government policies had contributed to increased competition from heavily subsidized soy producers in Argentina and Brazil. Soy exports from the US had fallen dramatically, leading to a production capacity surplus.

Collectively, AGP was able to attract a stronger management staff than its predecessors had; it hired 21-year Archer Daniels Midland (ADM) veteran James Lindsay as CEO and general manager. With operations scattered over four states, AGP placed its headquarters in Omaha, Nebraska — chosen for its central location and close proximity to the co-op's main bank.

In its first two years, AGP cut employee rolls by 20% and scaled back production, thus trimming costs and squeezing higher prices for finished products. A turnaround came quickly, and in 1985 members received a dividend from the co-op's $8 million pretax profit. That year AGP purchased two Iowa plants from AGRI Industries.

AGP dismantled two plants in 1987. By the next year the co-op witnessed an increase in domestic demand and had resumed selling to the Soviet Union. It generated additional sales by further processing soybean oil into food-grade products like hydrogenated oil and lecithin.

With an eye on diversification and value-added products, by 1991 AGP had expanded to eight soybean plants and two vegetable oil refineries; it also acquired the feed and grain business of International Multifoods that year through an 80%-owned joint venture with ADM. The acquisition included 29 feed plants in the US and Canada, 26 retail centers, 18 grain elevators, and the brands Supersweet and Masterfeeds. In 1994 AGP formed feed manufacturer Consolidated Nutrition, a 50-50 joint venture with ADM.

Consolidated Nutrition introduced a Swine Operations program in 1996. The program quickly grew through the development of PORK PACT, a

partnership to serve pork producers. (The co-op has since exited the swine business.) The next year AGP's grain division sold nine grain elevators in Ohio and Indiana to Cargill. That year the co-op gained control of Venezuelan feed manufacturer Proagro.

By 1998 passage of the Freedom to Farm Act and growing demand had spurred soybean planting. The co-op in 1998 opened an additional processing plant in Emmetsburg, Iowa, followed by another in Eagle Grove, Iowa. AGP sold off its pet food operations in 1998 to Windy Hill, which was later acquired by Doane Pet Care Enterprises. Also that year Consolidated Nutrition combined its Master Mix and Supersweet feed brands into the Consolidated Nutrition label.

In 1999 the company added the Garner-Klemme-Meservey cooperative to its grain operations. It opened a new plant late that year in St. Joseph, Missouri, to make value-added products such as hardfat (used in emulsifiers).

In 2001 AGP sold its 50% share of Consolidated Nutrition to ADM. In 2002 the co-op's Masterfeeds business acquired four feed mills and a merchandising operation from Saskatchewan Wheat Pool (now Viterra). In 2003 AGP opened the Port of Grays Harbor vessel-loading terminal in Aberdeen, Washington.

The company formed a subsidiary, AgGrowth Products, to market crop nutrients manufactured by Bio Tech Nutrients in 2005. Also that year, the company announced facility expansions for its ethanol, biodiesel, and soybean processing operations.

EXECUTIVES

Chairman: Bradley T. (Brad) Davis
Vice Chairman: Lowell D. Wilson
CEO and General Manager: Martin P. (Marty) Reagan
SVP Refined Vegetable Oils: David E. Tegeder
SVP Engineering: Charles A. (Chuck) Janiszewski
SVP Marketing and Soybean and Corn Processing: Gregory (Greg) Twist
SVP Human Resources: Judith V. (Judy) Ford
SVP Information Systems: Michael C. (Mike) Reed
SVP Operations and Research: Richard P. (Dick) Copeland
SVP Corporate and Member Relations: Michael L. Maranell
SVP Industrial Products and Government Relations: John B. Campbell
SVP Transportation: Terry J. Voss
Group VP Animal Nutrition; President, Masterfeeds: Robert J. Flack
Group VP Finance, CFO, Assistant Secretary, and Assistant Treasurer: J. Keith Spackler
VP and Corporate Controller: Dennis Rademacher
VP, Corporate General Counsel, and Assistant Secretary: Larry J. Steier
Treasurer, Secretary, and Director: Dean B. Isaacson
Auditors: Deloitte & Touche LLP

LOCATIONS

HQ: Ag Processing Inc
12700 W. Dodge Rd., Omaha, NE 68154
Phone: 402-496-7809   **Fax:** 402-498-2215
Web: www.agp.com

PRODUCTS/OPERATIONS

Selected Brands

AMINOPLUS (dairy feed additive)
BYN (crop nutrient)
Masterfeeds (feeds, Canada)
Progtinal/Proagro (poultry and feed, Venezuela)
SOYGOLD (bio-diesel, solvents, fuel additives)

Selected Exported Products
Barley
Corn
Distillers dried grains (DDGS)
Feeding peas
High protein soybean meal
Lecithin
Low protein soybean meal
Oats
Soybean hulls
Soybean oil
Soybeans
Sunflowers
Wheat

Selected Operations
Commercial feeds
Food (lecithin, soybean oil, vegetable oil)
Grain
Industrial products (ethanol, methyl ester)
Soybean processing

COMPETITORS
Abengoa Bioenergy	Griffin Industries
ADM	GROWMARK
AGRI Industries	J. D. Heiskell & Company
Agrium	Lake Area Corn Processors
Andersons	Land O'Lakes Purina Feed
Badger State Ethanol	Liberty Vegetable Oil
Bunge Limited	Little Sioux Corn
Bunge Milling	MFA
Cargill	Omega Protein
CHS	Owensboro Grain
Corn Products	Scoular
International	Southern States
DeBruce Grain	SunOpta

A.G. Spanos

Spanning the land from California to Florida, A. G. Spanos Companies bridges many operations — from building, managing, and selling multifamily housing units to constructing master-planned communities, as well as developing land and building commercial space. With divisions and operations in about 10 states, the firm has built about 2 million sq. ft. of office space properties, 120,000-plus apartment homes, and more than 400 developments. Other operations include mixed-use development and property management. Alex Spanos, owner of the NFL's San Diego Chargers, operates the company with his sons Dean (president and CEO) and Michael Spanos (EVP).

In 1951 Alex Spanos quit his job as a baker at his father's bakery to found his first business, A.G. Spanos Agricultural Catering Service. He moved into real estate in 1956 and built his first apartment building in 1960.

But real estate and football are just the beginning. The Spanos family also has a taste for wine: It owns the Spanos Berberian Winery and Bell Wine Cellars in Napa Valley, and it plans to grow and acquire additional vineyards and winery assets.

EXECUTIVES
Founder: Alexander Gus (Alex) Spanos, age 86
President and CEO: Dean A. Spanos, age 59
CFO: Jeremiah T. Murphy, age 65

EVP: Charlie Raffo
EVP: Michael A. Spanos, age 47
SVP Land Development: David R. Nelson
VP Marketing and Sales: Nick Faklis
Financial Officer: Steven L. Cohen
Director Public Relations and Communications:
 Natalia Orfanos

LOCATIONS
HQ: A. G. Spanos Companies
 10100 Trinity Pkwy., 5th Fl., Stockton, CA 95219
Phone: 209-478-7954   **Fax:** 209-473-3703
Web: www.agspanos.com

Divisions
Arizona
Colorado
Florida
Georgia
Kansas and Missouri
Nevada
New York and North Carolina
Northern and Central California
Southern California
Texas

PRODUCTS/OPERATIONS

Other Ownership Interests
Bell Wine Cellars
San Diego Chargers National Football League Team
Spanos Berberian Wine Company

COMPETITORS
Avatar Holdings
Castle & Cooke
Irvine Company
SunCor Development
Trammell Crow Residential

AgFirst Farm Credit Bank

AgFirst puts farmers first. A large and growing agricultural lender, AgFirst Farm Credit Bank operates through 22 farmer-owned cooperatives in 15 eastern states and Puerto Rico. It offers more than $20 billion in loans to some 80,000 farmers, ranchers, rural homeowners, and agribusiness owners. The lender originates real estate, operating, and rural home mortgage loans. Additionally, it offers crop, life, and timber insurance; equipment leasing; tax services; record keeping; and other products and services designed to meet customers' business and personal needs. The bank does not accept deposits; it raises money by selling bonds and notes on the capital markets.

AgFirst is a member of the largest agricultural lending organization in the US, Farm Credit System (FCS), which provides more than $160 billion in loans to farmers and agribusinesses across the nation.

One of its more active units, Capital Markets, arranges and participates in loans for agribusinesses. Its Correspondent Lending unit (formerly Secondary Mortgage Market) buys, sells, and services agricultural and rural home loans.

EXECUTIVES
Chairman: Paul M. House
Vice Chairman: M. Wayne Lambertson
President and CEO: F. A. (Andy) Lowrey,
 $874,398 total compensation
EVP and COO: Leon T. (Timmy) Amerson
EVP and Chief Administrative and Legislative Officer:
 Thomas S. Welshs
SVP and CIO: Benjamin F. Blakewood
SVP and Chief Lending Officer: William L. Melton
SVP and General Counsel: Frederick T. Mickler III
SVP and CFO: Charl L. Butler
Marketing Manager: Rhonda Uzzolino
Auditors: PricewaterhouseCoopers LLP

LOCATIONS
HQ: AgFirst Farm Credit Bank
 1401 Hampton St., Columbia, SC 29201
Phone: 803-799-5000   **Fax:** 803-254-1776
Web: www.agfirst.com

PRODUCTS/OPERATIONS

2008 Sales
	$ mil.	% of total
Interest		
Loans	1,027.6	76
Investment securities & other	305.9	22
Noninterest		
Loan fees	8.6	1
Other	7.2	1
Investment losses	(10.9)	—
Total	**1,338.4**	**100**

COMPETITORS
AgriBank
Agstar
Alabama Farmers Cooperative
Bank of Granite
COUNTRY Financial
Farm Credit Services of Mid-America
Farmer Mac
National Rural Utilities Cooperative
Nationwide Agribusiness
Rabo AgriFinance
United Producers

HISTORICAL FINANCIALS
Company Type: Cooperative

Income Statement FYE: December 31
	ASSETS ($ mil.)	NET INCOME ($ mil.)	INCOME AS % OF ASSETS	EMPLOYEES
12/08	29,911	217	0.7%	—
12/07	26,927	192	0.7%	—
12/06	24,412	190	0.8%	—
12/05	20,483	164	0.8%	—
12/04	16,888	180	1.1%	—
Annual Growth	15.4%	4.8%	—	—

2008 Year-End Financials
Equity as % of assets: —
Return on assets: 0.8%
Return on equity: —
Long-term debt ($ mil.): 28,053
Sales ($ mil.): 1,338

Net Income History

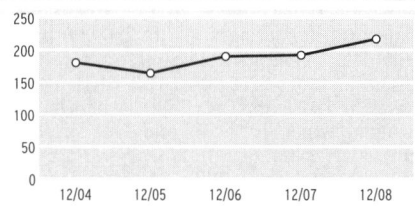

AgriBank, FCB

AgriBank puts the "green" in green acres. A financial intermediary, AgriBank provides wholesale lending and business services to Farm Credit System (FCS) associations in America's heartland. Established by Congress in 1916, the FCS is a nationwide network of cooperatives that provides loans and financial services for farmers, ranchers, agribusiness owners, timber producers, and rural homeowners. Farm Credit System's co-ops write loans for land, equipment, and other farm operating costs; they in turn own AgriBank. Formed in 1992, AgriBank also provides credit to rural electric, water, and telephone systems.

Located in St Paul, Minnesota, AgriBank serves the Seventh Farm Credit District, which operates in 15 states stretching from Ohio to Wyoming and Minnesota to Arkansas.

It is organized along three lines of business: wholesale, business services, and retail. Providing district associations with wholesale products and services is its primary focus; however, it also offers a wide range of business services including information technology, portfolio risk management, retail product and processing support, and human resources.

EXECUTIVES

Chairman: Thomas (Tom) Klahn
Vice Chairman: Keri Votruba
CEO: L. William (Bill) York,
 $729,000 total compensation
SVP and CFO: Brian J. O'Keane, age 41
SVP Credit and Chief Credit Officer: Ross B. Anderson
SVP, CIO, and Chief Risk Officer: Bill Johnson
SVP Business and Market Strategies:
 Gregory J. (Greg) Taylor
VP and Controller: Jeff Moore
VP Human Resources: Sandi Schmiesing
VP and Treasurer: Martin Fischer
VP Wholesale Lending and Relationship Management:
 Greg Elwood
VP and General Counsel: William J. (Bill) Thone
VP Audit: Donald W. (Don) Theuninck
Auditors: PricewaterhouseCoopers LLP

LOCATIONS

HQ: AgriBank, FCB
 375 Jackson St., St. Paul, MN 55101
Phone: 651-282-8800 **Fax:** 651-282-8666
Web: www.agribank.com

2008 Loan Distribution by State

	% of total
Iowa	11
Illinois	9
Minnesota	9
Nebraska	8
Indiana	6
Michigan	6
Ohio	6
Tennessee	6
Wisconsin	6
Missouri	5
South Dakota	5
Arkansas	4
Kentucky	4
North Dakota	4
Wyoming	1
Other states	10
Total	**100**

PRODUCTS/OPERATIONS

2008 Sales

	$ mil.	% of total
Interest income		
Loans	2,085.5	84
Investment securities	284.6	12
Non-interest income		
Loan prepayment fees	30.4	1
Business services income	19.3	1
Miscellaneous income & other gains, net	53.1	2
Total	**2,472.9**	**100**

2008 Loan Distribution by Commodity

	% of total
Crops	41
Residential & investor real estate	9
Cattle	9
Dairy	7
Hogs	6
Other	28
Total	**100**

COMPETITORS

AgFirst
Agstar
Alabama Farmers Cooperative
CHS
Farmer Mac
National Rural Utilities Cooperative
Nationwide Agribusiness
Rabo AgriFinance
United Producers

HISTORICAL FINANCIALS

Company Type: Cooperative

Income Statement

	ASSETS ($ mil.)	NET INCOME ($ mil.)	INCOME AS % OF ASSETS	EMPLOYEES
12/08	63,286	329	0.5%	—
12/07	52,264	183	0.3%	—
12/06	47,007	163	0.3%	—
12/05	39,867	139	0.3%	—
12/04	36,175	157	0.4%	—
Annual Growth	**15.0%**	**20.3%**	**—**	**—**

FYE: December 31

2008 Year-End Financials

Equity as % of assets: —
Return on assets: 0.6%
Return on equity: —
Long-term debt ($ mil.): —
Sales ($ mil.): 2,473

Net Income History

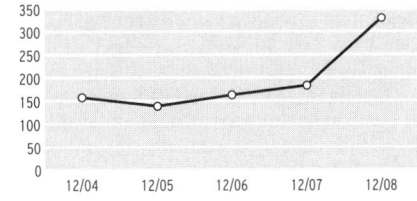

Alabama Farmers Cooperative

Alabama Farmers Cooperative (AFC) provides farmers in the Yellowhammer State a full range of agricultural supplies and services, including feed, fertilizer, seed, grain storage, and marketing, along with home-gardening items such as seeds and hardware. The co-op, which boasts 46 member associations, also serves members in parts of Florida, Georgia, and Mississippi. AFC owns Bonnie Plant Farms, one of the largest suppliers of vegetable plants and annual flowers in the US. Its Anderson's Peanuts division was sold to Birdsong in 2007. Originally called the Tennessee Valley Fertilizer Cooperative, it was established in 1936.

EXECUTIVES

Chairman: Larry Bennich
Vice Chairman: Lawrence Smith
President and CEO: Tommy Paulk
EVP and COO: Roger Pangle
Secretary, Treasurer, and CFO: Dan Groscost
CIO: Wayne Holt
VP Feed, Farm, and Home: Steve Moore
VP Grain: John Gamble
VP and General Manager, Anderson's Peanut:
 Dennis Finch
VP and Manager, Cooperative Financial Services:
 Bill Eubanks
VP and General Manager, Bonnie Plant Division:
 Dennis Thomas
VP Management Services: James Fudge
VP Human Resources: Tina Johnson
Director Public Relations and Advertising: Jim Allen

LOCATIONS

HQ: Alabama Farmers Cooperative, Inc.
 121 Somerville Rd. SE, Decatur, AL 35601
Phone: 256-353-6843 **Fax:** 256-350-1770
Web: www.alafarm.com

PRODUCTS/OPERATIONS

Sales Segments

Grain
Feed, Farm, & Home
 Feed
 Animal Health
 Lawn & Garden
 Hardware & TBA
Peanut
Gin
Plant

COMPETITORS

Ag Processing
Andersons
CHS
Jimmy Sanders
Scoular
Southern States
Tennessee Farmers Co-op

Alberici Corporation

Alberici helped shape the St. Louis skyline; it now sets its sights — or its construction sites — across North America. Alberici Corporation, parent of Alberici Constructors, encompasses a group of enterprises with a presence in North America, Central America, South America, and Europe. Operations include construction services, building materials, and steel fabrication and erection units. Alberici offers general contracting, design/build, construction management, demolition, and specialty contracting services. It also offers facilities management. The Alberici family still holds the largest share of the employee-owned firm, founded in 1918 by John S. Alberici.

Alberici serves markets including automotive, energy, health care, industrial, manufacturing, and wastewater treatment. Its subsidiary Gunther-Nash provides construction services to the mining industry. Another division, Vertegy, specializes in construction consulting for green and sustainable projects.

The company has a joint venture with the Washington Division of URS Corporation to build a $900 million cement plant in Missouri for Holcim (US). The plant will be one of the largest in the world. Alberici also was chosen to help improve the New Orleans levee system. Some of Alberici's completed projects include casinos for Ameristar, modernized and new facilities for Anheuser-Busch, and factories for Boeing.

EXECUTIVES

Chairman: John S. Alberici
CFO, Alberici Group: Gregory T. (Greg) Hesser
SVP Administration and Contract Review Officer, Alberici Group: James E. (Jim) Frey
VP and General Manager, Vertegy: Thomas A. Taylor
VP and General Counsel: Trevor Ladner
CIO and VP, Support Services: Frank C. Kropiunik
VP Employee Services: Denay Davis
VP and General Manager, Hillsdale Fabricators: Michael W. (Mike) Burke
VP and General Manager, Kienlen Constructors: Matt Grieshaber
VP and Market Leader, Healthcare and General Building, Alberici Constructors; President, Alberici Constructors, Ltd. (Canada): Alan D. (Dave) Gough
CEO and President; President, Alberici Constructors, Inc.: Gregory J. (Greg) Kozicz

LOCATIONS

HQ: Alberici Corporation
8800 Page Ave., St. Louis, MO 63114
Phone: 314-733-2000 **Fax:** 314-733-2001
Web: www.alberici.com

PRODUCTS/OPERATIONS

Selected Markets

Automotive
Building
Energy
Green building
Health care
Industrial
Manufacturing/food and beverage
Mining infrastructure
Steel fabrication
Water and wastewater treatment

COMPETITORS

Aker Construction
Barton Malow
Bechtel
Black & Veatch
DPR Construction
Fluor
Fred Weber
Hensel Phelps
Hoffman Corporation
Hunt Construction
Jacobs Engineering

McCarthy Building
Parsons Corporation
Peter Kiewit Sons'
TIC Holdings
Turner Corporation
Tutor Perini
Walbridge Aldinger
Walsh Group
Washington Division
Zachry Inc.

HISTORICAL FINANCIALS

Company Type: Private

Income Statement

FYE: December 31

	REVENUE ($ mil.)	NET INCOME ($ mil.)	NET PROFIT MARGIN	EMPLOYEES
12/08	1,300	—	—	—
12/07	1,150	—	—	415
12/06	1,030	—	—	511
12/05	1,033	—	—	511
Annual Growth	**8.0%**	**—**	**—**	**(9.9%)**

Revenue History

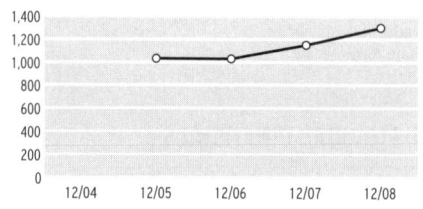

Albertsons LLC

Call it the incredible shrinking grocery chain. Albertsons LLC (formerly Albertson's) runs some 235 Albertsons supermarkets in Arizona, Arkansas, Colorado, Florida, Louisiana, New Mexico, and Texas. That's all that remains of what was once the nation's #2 supermarket operator with about 2,500 stores. Stung by competition, the firm sold itself in 2006 to a consortium that included rival grocer SUPERVALU, drugstore chain CVS, investment firm Cerberus Capital Management, and Kimco Realty for about $9.7 billion. SUPERVALU and CVS cherry-picked the company's best supermarket and drugstore assets. Subsequent divestments, including 132 stores in Northern California and 50 stores in Florida, further shrunk the company.

Albertsons' recent history has been marked by divestitures and total retreat from some markets, including California and Utah. Most recently, the grocery chain closed five stores and a distribution center in the Denver area in fall 2009. The closings left the company with only about 25 stores in Colorado. (Albertsons had struggled there with competition from larger rivals King Soopers and Safeway.) Previous big divestments include about half of its supermarkets in Florida to Publix Super Markets, which left the grocer with only about 35 stores in the Sunshine State. In 2008 Albertsons sold 72 of its Express fuel centers in Arizona, Colorado, Louisiana, and Texas to Valero Energy Corp. and another 30 fuel

centers in Florida to Reb Oil, to better focus its energies on its core grocery and pharmacy business.

To tap the pharmacy niche, Albertsons in October 2008 launched its Rxtra Savings Program. Soon thereafter, in January 2009, the grocery chain expanded its generic-drug discount program to include more than 500 medicines.

Albertsons isn't retreating on every front, however. In early 2009 it announced plans to invest significantly to remodel more than 20% of the stores in its Texas division, which includes about 100 supermarkets in Texas, Arkansas, and Louisiana. The company has little choice but to invest in the long-neglected locations or see its market share shrink even further. In key markets such as Texas, where it competes with regional heavyweight H-E-B and Kroger, and Florida, dominated by Publix and a resurgent Winn-Dixie, Albertsons faces stiff competition from larger, more successful grocery chains. Indeed, CEO Robert Miller contends that Albertsons, which acquired a store in Louisiana in early 2009, is looking for growth opportunities. He has also said that Albertsons' Texas and Southwest divisions are not on the selling block. Following the sale of the Florida stores to Publix, the future of the remaining stores there is less certain.

Other investors in Albertsons LLC include Schottenstein Stores, Lubert-Adler Partners, and Klaff Realty LP.

HISTORY

J. A. "Joe" Albertson, Leonard Skaggs (whose family ran Safeway), and Tom Cuthbert founded Albertson's Food Center in Boise, Idaho, in 1939. Albertson, who left his position as district manager for Safeway to run the store, thought big from the start. The 10,000-sq.-ft. store was not only eight times the size of the average competitor, it also offered an in-store butcher shop and bakery, one of the country's first magazine racks, and homemade "Big Joe" ice-cream cones. The men ended their partnership in 1945, the year Albertson's was incorporated, and by 1947 it operated six stores in Idaho.

The company opened its first combination food store and drugstore, a 60,000-sq.-ft. superstore, in 1951 and began locating stores in growing suburban areas. Albertson's went public to raise expansion capital in 1959 and by 1960 had 62 stores in Idaho, Oregon, Utah, and Washington. The food retailer acquired Greater All American Markets (1964), a grocery chain based in Downey, California, and Semrau & Sons (1965) of Oakland, which aided the company's thrust into the California market.

Albertson's and the Skaggs chain (by this time run by L. S. Skaggs Jr.) reunited temporarily in 1969, financing six Skaggs-Albertson's food-and-drug-combination stores. (The partnership dissolved in 1977, with each side taking half of the units.) By 1986 the company had reached $5 billion in sales, a fivefold increase over 1975.

The company purchased 74 Jewel Osco combination food stores and drugstores (mostly in Arkansas, Florida, Oklahoma, and Texas) from American Stores in 1992. Co-founder Albertson died in 1993 at age 86.

In 1997 the United Food and Commercial Workers union, which represents supermarket employees, sued Albertson's, alleging the company forced employees to work overtime without pay. (It was settled in 1999, resulting in a $22 million charge.) Also in 1997 Albertson's began selling gasoline at a few stores. In 1999 the grocer revisited its roots when it acquired American

Stores (Skaggs' successor), which operated more than 1,550 stores in 26 states. To obtain regulatory approval for the $12 billion deal, Albertson's sold 145 stores in overlapping markets in three states (most were in California).

In 2001 Larry Johnston, former CEO of GE Appliances, took over as chairman and CEO of Albertson's. Facing increasing competition (especially from Wal-Mart), Johnston announced in March 2002 aggressive restructuring plans that included job cuts and closing 95 stores in underperforming markets, specifically Memphis and Nashville, Tennessee, and Houston and San Antonio, Texas.

Already allowing customers to order drugs online (from its online drugstore, Savon.com) and groceries in Seattle, Albertson's expanded its online operations to San Diego in 2001 and in early 2002 to Los Angeles, San Francisco, and parts of Oregon and Washington. Albertson's exited the New England drugstore market in 2002 when it sold 80 New England Osco stores to Brooks Pharmacy.

A four-and-a-half month strike by grocery workers in Southern California ended in March 2004. The dispute pitted workers' demands for continued generous health care coverage vs. management's call for cost cuts to remain profitable in the face of Wal-Mart's entry into the Southern California grocery market. In April Albertson's completed the acquisition of JS USA Holdings, which runs Shaw's and Star Markets stores in New England, from UK grocer J Sainsbury. The deal to buy Shaw's was worth about $2.4 billion (cash and leases).

In June 2006 Albertson's was sold to a consortium that included SUPERVALU, CVS, Cerberus Capital Management, and Kimco for about $9.7 billion. Following the acquisition and the divvying up of Albertson's assets, the surviving company went private and changed its name to Albertsons LLC. Concurrently, Johnston left Albertsons and was succeeded by Robert Miller, chairman of drugstore chain Rite Aid and the former head of Fred Meyer for eight years in the 1990s. Of the company's 27 price-impact Super Saver stores, 25 closed their doors in mid-2006. Also, in June, the company put about 45 stores on the auction block. (It was announced in late 2006 that discount apparel retailer Ross Stores would acquire these stores.) In July the company shut down its online shopping service Albertsons.com.

In 2007 Albertsons sold 132 grocery stores and two distribution centers in Northern California and Nevada to Save Mart Supermarkets for an undisclosed amount. Albertsons also sold eight of its stores in Wyoming to SUPERVALU in 2008. The divestments continued with the sale of 49 supermarkets in Florida to Publix Super Markets for about $500 million. Also in 2008 Albertsons sold about 100 of its Express fuel centers in Arizona, Colorado, Florida, Louisiana, and Texas to Valero Energy and Reb Oil.

EXECUTIVES

CEO: Robert (Bob) Miller
CFO: Richard J. (Rick) Navarro, age 57
CIO: Mark Bates
Chief Strategic Officer: Justin Dye
SVP and General Counsel: Paul Rowan
SVP Marketing and Merchandising: Bob Butler
SVP Distribution Operations: Michael (Mike) McCarthy
SVP Human Resources and Labor Relations: Andrew Scoggin
President Florida: Wayne A. Denningham
President Southwest: Shane Dorcheus
President Dallas Fort Worth: William Emmons

LOCATIONS

HQ: Albertsons LLC
250 Parkcenter Blvd., Boise, ID 83706
Phone: 208-395-6200 **Fax:** 208-395-6349
Web: albertsonsmarket.com

2009 Stores

	No.
Southwest division	113
Dallas-Fort Worth division	99
Florida division	36
Total	**248**

COMPETITORS

Costco Wholesale	Rite Aid
H-E-B	Safeway
IGA	Walgreen
King Soopers	Wal-Mart
Kmart	Whole Foods
Kroger	Winn-Dixie
Publix	

Alex Lee

Wholesale groceries is only part of the story for this company. Alex Lee is a leading wholesale distributor of food and other products to retailers and foodservice operators. Through Merchants Distributors, Inc. (MDI), it supplies food and related merchandise to more than 600 retailers in more than a half-dozen states, mostly in the Southeast. Its Institutional Food House (IFH) unit is a foodservice supplier serving customers in the hospitality industry. Alex Lee also operates a chain of more than 100 grocery stores through Lowe's Food Stores, and it provides warehousing services through Consolidation Services. Alex and Lee George started the company in 1931; the George family continues to control Alex Lee.

The company joined with Canadian meat processor Vantage Foods to open a $21 million meat packaging plant in 2007. The facility serves Alex Lee's grocery stores, as well as its MDI wholesale distribution operation.

Alex Lee began diversifying its operations in the 1960s when it acquired IFH. It bought the Lowe's Food chain in 1984 and formed its Consolidation Services warehousing and logistics outsourcing subsidiary in 1998.

EXECUTIVES

Chairman and CEO: Boyd L. George, age 67
President: Dennis G. Hatchell
EVP and CFO: Ronald W. Knedlik
VP Information Systems: Jay Schwarz
VP Human Resources: Robert Vipperman
President, Merchants Distributors, Inc.: Matt Saunders
President, Institution Food House, Inc.: Gerald Davis
President, Lowe's Food Stores, Inc.: Steve Hall

LOCATIONS

HQ: Alex Lee, Inc.
120 4th St. SW, Hickory, NC 28602
Phone: 828-725-4424 **Fax:** 828-725-4435
Web: www.alexlee.com

Alion Science and Technology

Alion creates alliances between science and big government. Alion Science and Technology is a development and research company that provides consulting and technology services, primarily to federal agencies. The majority of its revenues come from contracts with the US Department of Defense (DOD), especially the Navy. The company specializes in areas including naval architecture and marine engineering, manufacturing engineering services, wargaming, lab support and chemical decontamination, military transformation analysis, and wireless communications engineering. The employee-owned Alion operates from offices and facilities throughout the US, generally near government military bases and other installations.

The DOD accounts for some 85% of Alion's sales. The company plans to expand its client base to include more federal civilian agencies as well as commercial customers.

It is also growing through acquisitions. In 2006 it bought program management and engineering services firm Anteon from General Dynamics, systems engineering firm BMH Associates, management consultancy Washington Consulting, and the high-speed vessel design technology assets of Australia-based International Catamaran Designs (INCAT). The following year it acquired the assets of logistics and inventory tracking firm LogConGroup, which expanded Alion's high-value tracking operations.

EXECUTIVES

Chairman and CEO: Bahman Atefi, age 55
EVP and COO: Stacy Mendler, age 45
SVP, Acting CFO, Assistant Treasurer, and Executive Director Financial Operations: Michael J. Alber, age 51
Chief Administrative Officer: Patricia A. Weaver
SVP; Deputy Manager Engineering and Information Technology: Robert D. (Rob) Hirt
SVP; Manager Engineering and Information Technology: Walter E. (Buck) Buchanan III, age 58

COMPETITORS

ALDI
Associated Wholesale Grocers
Ben E. Keith
BI-LO
C & S Wholesale
Food Lion
Harris Teeter
H.T. Hackney
Ingles Markets
Kroger
K-VA-T Food Stores
MAINES
McLane
Meadowbrook Meat Company
Nash-Finch
Performance Food
SUPERVALU
SYSCO
U.S. Foodservice
Wal-Mart
Winn-Dixie

SVP; Deputy Manager Defense Operations Integration:
Richard E. (Tex) Brown III
SVP, General Counsel, and Secretary:
James C. (Jim) Fontana, age 50
SVP Engineering and Integration Solutions Sector
Manager: Scott Fry, age 59
SVP and Defense Operations and Integrations Sector
Manager: David Ohle
Manager Corporate Development: Steve Kimmel
Government Relations Director: Tim Cook
Auditors: Deloitte & Touche LLP

LOCATIONS

HQ: Alion Science and Technology Corporation
1750 Tysons Blvd., Ste. 1300, McLean, VA 22102
Phone: 703-918-4480   **Fax:** 703-714-6508
Web: www.alionscience.com

PRODUCTS/OPERATIONS

2008 Sales

	$ mil.	% of total
Naval architecture & marine engineering	313.5	42
Defense operations	140.1	19
Industrial technology solutions	115.6	16
Modeling & simulation	70.6	10
Chemical, biological, nuclear & environmental sciences	53.7	7
Information technology	31.8	4
Wireless communications	14.2	2
Total	**739.5**	**100**

COMPETITORS

Accenture
Battelle Memorial
BearingPoint
Booz Allen
CACI International
CAE Inc.
Capgemini
Computer Sciences Corp.
Evans & Sutherland
GE
General Dynamics
HP Enterprise Services
IBM
Lockheed Martin
ManTech
Northrop Grumman
Perot Systems
SAIC
SRA International
Unisys

HISTORICAL FINANCIALS

Company Type: Private

Income Statement
FYE: September 30

	REVENUE ($ mil.)	NET INCOME ($ mil.)	NET PROFIT MARGIN	EMPLOYEES
9/08	740	(25)	—	3,266
9/07	738	(43)	—	3,400
9/06	509	(31)	—	3,575
9/05	369	(40)	—	2,508
9/04	270	(15)	—	1,880
Annual Growth	28.7%	—	—	14.8%

Net Income History

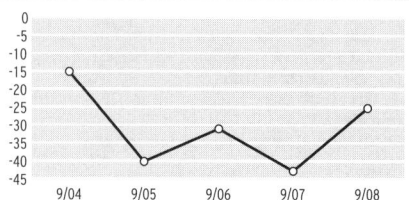

0				
-5				
-10				
-15				
-20				
-25				
-30				
-35				
-40				
-45				
9/04	9/05	9/06	9/07	9/08

Allbritton Communications

This company has a real affinity for the Alphabet Network. Allbritton Communications is a leading television broadcaster with about 10 TV stations, all affiliated with Walt Disney's ABC television network. The stations serve markets in Alabama, Arkansas, Oklahoma, Pennsylvania, South Carolina, and Virginia, as well as Washington, DC. The company also owns and operates a 24-hour cable news channel (News-Channel 8) that serves the nation's capitol, and it operates Politico.com, a Web site and companion newspaper offering political news and opinion. Joe Allbritton started the family-owned business in 1975.

While Allbritton's primary business is still anchored by its TV stations, the company launched Politico (operated through Capitol News Company) in 2007 as part of an effort to expand its media profile in Washington, DC. The site became a popular destination for news and political junkies during the Presidential election the following year. Politico is also augmenting its advertising revenue by contracting with newspapers such as the *Atlanta Journal-Constitution* (owned by Cox Newspapers) to supply local and regional news.

EXECUTIVES

Chairman and CEO: Robert L. Allbritton, age 39
Vice Chairman, President, and COO:
Frederick J. (Fred) Ryan Jr., age 53
EVP and Director: Barbara B. Allbritton, age 71
SVP and CFO: Stephen P. Gibson, age 43
SVP Legal and Strategic Affairs and General Counsel:
Jerald N. Fritz, age 57
VP and Controller: Elizabeth A. Haley
VP Sales: James C. Killen Jr., age 46
Auditors: PricewaterhouseCoopers LLP

LOCATIONS

HQ: Allbritton Communications Company
1000 Wilson Blvd., Ste. 2700, Arlington, VA 22209
Phone: 703-647-8700   **Fax:** 703-236-9268

PRODUCTS/OPERATIONS

2008 Sales

	% of total
Local & national advertising	83
Subscriber fees	5
Political advertising	3
Trade & barter	3
Network compensation	1
Other	5
Total	**100**

Selected Operations

Television stations
KATV (ABC; Little Rock, AR)
KTUL (ABC; Tulsa, OK)
WBMA (ABC; Birmingham, AL)
WCFT (ABC; Tuscaloosa, AL)
WCIV (ABC; Charleston, SC)
WHTM (ABC; Harrisburg, PA)
WJLA (ABC; Washington, DC)
WJSU (ABC; Anniston, AL)
WSET (ABC; Roanoke-Lynchburg, VA)
Other
NewsChannel 8 (cable news channel; Washington, DC)
The Politico (newspaper)

COMPETITORS

E. W. Scripps
Fox Entertainment
Gannett
Hearst Television
Media General
National Journal
National Review
NBC
Newport Television
News World Communications
Nexstar Broadcasting
Schurz Communications
Sinclair Broadcast Group
Tribune Company
Washington Post

Allegis Group

Clients in need of highly skilled technical and other personnel might want to take the pledge of Allegis. One of the world's largest staffing and recruitment firms, Allegis Group has about 300 offices in North America and Europe. Among its companies are Aerotek (engineering, automotive, and scientific professionals), Stephen James Associates (recruitment for accounting, financial, and cash management positions), and TEKsystems (information technology staffing and consulting). Other Allegis units include sales support outsourcer MarketSource. Chairman Jim Davis helped found the company (originally known as Aerotek) in 1983 to provide contract engineering personnel to two clients in the aerospace industry.

In 2008 Allegis expanded its international operations when it acquired legal search firm Major, Lindsey & Africa and India-based IT recruitment firm TVA Infotech Pvt., Ltd. Closer to home, Allegis added executive recruiting and human resources outsourcing to its offerings with the purchase of InSearch Worldwide in October 2008. InSearch Worldwide is part of Allegis Group Services. In January 2009 Allegis' Stephen James Associates beefed up its presence on the East Coast with the acquisition of professional recruiting firm Stafford Paige.

Growth for Allegis, however, has been put on hold due to the recession. Directly affected by the decline in demand for workers for some of its key industries — banking and finance, accounting, human resources, and sales and marketing — Allegis was forced to cut 10% of its workforce in February 2009.

EXECUTIVES

Chairman: James C. (Jim) Davis
EVP Human Resources: Neil Mann
SVP and COO: Jeff Moore
CFO: Paul Bowie
CIO: Kevin Apperson
President, Aerotek: Tom Thornton
General Counsel: Randy Sones

LOCATIONS

HQ: Allegis Group, Inc.
7301 Parkway Dr., Hanover, MD 21076
Phone: 410-579-4800   **Fax:** 410-540-7556
Web: www.allegisgroup.com

PRODUCTS/OPERATIONS

Selected Subsidiaries

Aerotek
  Aerotek Automotive
  Aerotek Aviation, LLC
  Aerotek Canada
  Aerotek CE
  Aerotek Commercial Staffing
  Aerotek E&E
  Aerotek Energy Services
  Aerotek Germany
  Aerotek Netherlands
  Aerotek Professional Services
  Aerotek Scientific, LLC
  Aerotek United Kingdom
Allegis Group Canada
Allegis Group Europe
Allegis Group India
Allegis Group Services
InSearch Worldwide
Major, Lindsey & Africa
MarketSource, Inc
Stephen James Associates
TEKsystems
  TEKsystems Canada
  TEKsystems Germany
  TEKsystems Netherlands
  TEKsystems United Kingdom

COMPETITORS

Adecco
ASG Renaissance
CDI
Curran Partners
ExecuNet
Heidrick & Struggles
Horton International
Innovative Management Solutions Group
Kelly Services
Korn/Ferry
Manpower
MPS
Randstad Holding
RDL Corporation
Robert Half
Snelling Staffing
Spherion
Volt Information

HISTORICAL FINANCIALS

Company Type: Private

Income Statement				FYE: December 31
	REVENUE ($ mil.)	NET INCOME ($ mil.)	NET PROFIT MARGIN	EMPLOYEES
12/08	5,740	—	—	8,500
12/07	5,570	—	—	10,000
12/06	5,000	—	—	8,000
12/05	4,400	—	—	7,000
12/04	3,600	—	—	6,000
Annual Growth	12.4%	—	—	9.1%

Revenue History

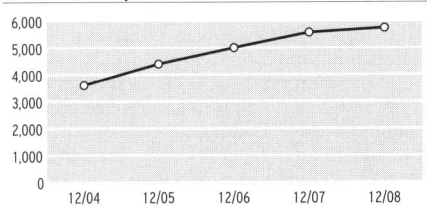

Alliance Laundry

Laundry day can't come often enough for Alliance Laundry Holdings (ALH). Through its wholly owned subsidiary, Alliance Laundry Systems, the company makes commercial laundry equipment used in laundromats, multi-housing laundry facilities (apartments, dormitories, military bases), and on-premise laundries (hotels, hospitals, prisons). Its washers and dryers are made under the brands Speed Queen, UniMac, Huebsch, IPSO, and Cissell. They're sold in North America and in 90 countries. Investment firm Teachers' Private Capital (private equity arm of Ontario Teachers' Pension Plan) acquired more than 91% of ALH for about $450 million in 2005. The company was founded in 1908.

To expand its laundry business overseas, ALS in mid-2006 bought Laundry System Group NV's Commercial Laundry Division headquartered in Belgium. The division, which has operations in the US and Belgium, makes and markets commercial washer/extractors, ironers, and tumble dryers under the Ipso and Cissell names. During 2008 ALS considered strategic acquisitions — domestically and internationally.

EXECUTIVES

Chairman: Shael J. Dolman, age 37
President and COO: Michael D. Schoeb, age 47, $663,723 total compensation
CEO and Director: Thomas F. (Tom) L'Esperance, age 60, $1,207,397 total compensation
SVP Sales, North America: Jeffrey J. (Jeff) Brothers, age 62, $618,499 total compensation
VP and CFO: Bruce P. Rounds, age 52, $635,942 total compensation
VP, Chief Legal Officer, and Secretary: Scott L. Spiller, age 58
VP Engineering: Robert J. Baudhuin, age 47
VP and Corporate Controller: Robert T. Wallace, age 52
VP Strategic Projects: William J. Przybysz, age 63
VP Customer Support: Richard L. Pyle, age 44
Treasurer and Assistant Secretary: Jeffrey Thoms
Auditors: PricewaterhouseCoopers LLP

LOCATIONS

HQ: Alliance Laundry Holdings LLC
119 Shepard St., Ripon, WI 54971
Phone: 920-748-3121   **Fax:** 920-748-4334
Web: www.comlaundry.com

2008 Sales

	% of total
US	71
Other countries	29
Total	**100**

PRODUCTS/OPERATIONS

2008 Sales

	$ mil.	% of total
Equipment & service parts	451.0	98
Equipment financing	9.3	2
Total	**460.3**	**100**

2008 Sales

	$ mil.	% of total
Commercial laundry	337.9	68
European operations	79.7	16
Service parts	52.6	11
Consumer laundry	22.8	5
Total	**460.3**	**100**

COMPETITORS

American Dryer
Electrolux
GE Consumer & Industrial
Miele
Whirlpool

HISTORICAL FINANCIALS

Company Type: Private

Income Statement				FYE: December 31
	REVENUE ($ mil.)	NET INCOME ($ mil.)	NET PROFIT MARGIN	EMPLOYEES
12/08	460	16	3.4%	1,572
12/07	443	10	2.2%	1,653
12/06	366	(3)	—	1,517
12/05	297	(1)	—	1,312
12/04	281	12	4.2%	1,312
Annual Growth	13.1%	7.1%	—	4.6%

2008 Year-End Financials

Debt ratio: 212.6%   Current ratio: —
Return on equity: —   Long-term debt ($ mil.): 310
Cash ($ mil.): —

Net Income History

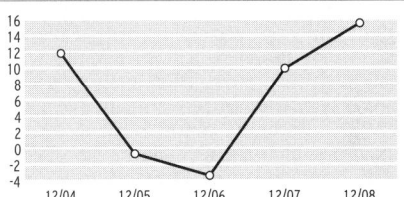

AllianceBernstein L.P.

AllianceBernstein has tons of funds. As one of the world's largest investment managers, the company (formerly Alliance Capital Management) administers about 170 domestic and international mutual funds. Institutional customers, including public retirement funds, employee benefit plans, foundations, endowments, government entities, and insurance firms, account for a majority of the firm's approximately $400 billion in assets under management. For retail investors, the company provides private client services, managed accounts, annuities, retirement plans, and college savings plans. AllianceBernstein also owns money manager and research firm Sanford C. Bernstein.

Dealing with a decline of more than 40% of its assets under management due to market depreciation and client outflows, AllianceBernstein cut more than 10% of its workforce in 2008. As a result of the depreciation, a greater proportion of the company's assets under management (around 40%) are invested in fixed-income products. Near the end of the year, Peter Kraus was named chairman and CEO of the company, succeeding the retiring Lewis Sanders who had held the post for five years.

Active in North America, Europe, Asia, Australia, and South Africa, AllianceBernstein has offices in more than 25 cities. French insurer AXA holds nearly 60% of AllianceBernstein; publicly traded AllianceBernstein Holding owns more than 30%.

HISTORY

Alliance Capital Management began in 1962 as the management department of Donaldson, Lufkin & Jenrette (now part of Credit Suisse (USA)). The company opened its first international office in the UK in 1978. Also that year the company introduced its first money market fund. In 1983 the company debuted its first mutual fund. The Equitable acquired Alliance as part of its DLJ acquisition in 1985.

In an attempt to raise money, cash-strapped Equitable sold 40% of the company in a 1988 public offering of Alliance stock. The company acquired Shields Asset Management in 1994 and bought Cursitor-Eaton two years later. Poor performance of the Cursitor unit forced the company to take a $121 million charge in 1997.

In 1998 the Taxpayer Relief Act of 1997 removed Alliance's Master Limited Partnership tax status and increased the company's tax rate to that of a regular partnership, a 3.5% increase. The next year the company organized a holding company and transferred its operations and old name to a new limited partnership, Alliance Capital Management Holding, to help provide tax relief for parent company The Equitable (renamed AXA Financial in 1999).

The firm continued to bolster its reputation as a global investor, expanding its operations in Asia, Europe, the UK, and South America, where it targeted privatized pension funds. As deregulation opened the Japanese mutual fund market in 1998, the company worked to rapidly establish a major presence there. Alliance's global vision played into the strategy of its ultimate parent, AXA. As one of the world's largest insurers, AXA began building its brand, using Alliance to help establish itself in global financial services.

In 2000 the company bought money manager Sanford C. Bernstein, a firm noted for its research.

In 2003 Alliance came under investigation as instances of improper market-timing trades came to light. The firm's president, the head of its mutual fund distribution unit, and some additional employees were ousted amidst the scandal. In late 2003 the company reached a $600 million settlement with regulators, also agreeing to cut its fund fees and freeze the rates at that level for a five-year period.

AllianceBernstein sold its cash management business to Federated Investors in 2005; the sale included the assets under management of 22 third-party-distributed money-market funds.

EXECUTIVES

Chairman and CEO: Peter S. Kraus, age 56
COO and Global Head Distribution: David A. Steyn, age 49
EVP and Head of Institutional Investments: Gregory J. Teneza, age 42
EVP and Head of Global Operations: Richard G. Taggart, age 48
EVP and Chief Investment Officer: Sharon E. Fay, age 48, $3,531,356 total compensation
EVP, Head of Global Value Equities, and Chairperson, US Large Cap Value Equity Investment Policy Group: Marilyn G. Fedak, age 62, $3,531,356 total compensation
EVP and General Counsel: Laurence E. Cranch, age 62
EVP; Chairman and CEO, SCB LLC: James A. Gingrich, age 50
EVP and CEO, AllianceBernstein Limited; Head, Global/International Growth Equities: Christopher M. Toub, age 49
EVP and Head of US Large-Cap Growth: James G. Reilly, age 47
EVP and CTO: Lawrence H. (Larry) Cohen, age 47
EVP: Robert M. Keith, age 48

EVP and Chief Investment Officer, Fixed Income: Jeffrey S. (Jeff) Phlegar, age 42
EVP; Head of Bernstein Global Wealth Management: Thomas S. Hexner, age 52
EVP and Chief Talent Officer, Talent Development and Human Resources: Lori Massad, age 44
SVP and CFO: Robert H. Joseph Jr., age 61, $1,350,897 total compensation
SVP and Controller: Edward J. Farrell, age 48
Auditors: PricewaterhouseCoopers LLP

LOCATIONS

HQ: AllianceBernstein L.P.
1345 Avenue of the Americas, New York, NY 10105
Phone: 212-969-1000 **Fax:** 212-969-2229
Web: www.alliancebernstein.com

2008 Sales

	% of total
US	64
International	36
Total	**100**

PRODUCTS/OPERATIONS

2008 Sales

	$ mil.	% of total
Investment advisory & services fees	2,839.5	74
Institutional research services	471.7	12
Distribution revenues	378.4	10
Net interest & dividend income	55.2	1
Other	118.6	3
Investment losses	(349.2)	—
Total	**3,514.2**	**100**

2008 Sales by Segment

	$ mil.	% of total
Institutional investment services	1,240.7	33
Retail services	1,227.6	32
Private client services	849.8	23
Institutional research services	471.7	12
Adjustments	(275.6)	—
Total	**3,514.2**	**100**

2008 Assets under Management

	% of total
Institutional investment services	63
Retail services	22
Private client services	15
Total	**100**

COMPETITORS

Affiliated Managers Group
AIG
AIG Retirement Services
American Century
BlackRock
Capital Group
Eaton Vance
Federated Investors
FMR
Franklin Resources
GAMCO Investors
ING
Invesco
Janus Capital
Legg Mason
MFS
Neuberger Berman
Nuveen
Principal Financial
Raymond James Financial
T. Rowe Price
UBS Financial Services
The Vanguard Group
Waddell & Reed

HISTORICAL FINANCIALS

Company Type: Private

Income Statement

FYE: December 31

	ASSETS ($ mil.)	NET INCOME ($ mil.)	INCOME AS % OF ASSETS	EMPLOYEES
12/08	8,503	839	9.9%	4,997
12/07	9,369	1,260	13.5%	5,580
12/06	10,601	1,109	10.5%	4,914
12/05	9,491	868	9.1%	4,312
12/04	8,779	705	8.0%	4,100
Annual Growth	(0.8%)	4.4%	—	5.1%

2008 Year-End Financials

Equity as % of assets: —
Return on assets: 9.4%
Return on equity: —
Long-term debt ($ mil.): —
Sales ($ mil.): 3,514

Net Income History

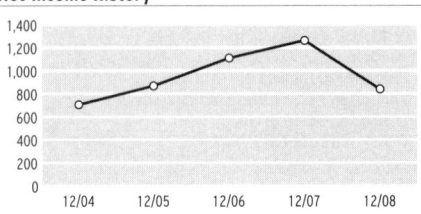

Allied Systems

Carrying millions of cars, trucks, and SUVs every year, Allied Systems Holdings leads the North American automobile-hauling market. Subsidiary Allied Automotive Group moves vehicles with a fleet of about 3,400 tractor-trailer rigs, which it operates from about 90 terminals in the US and Canada. Vehicles are transported from manufacturing plants, railway distribution points, ports, and auctions to auto dealers and car rental companies. Automakers, including industry leaders such as Chrysler, Ford, General Motors, Honda, and Toyota, are the company's main customers. Investment firm Yucaipa Companies owns a controlling stake in Allied Systems Holdings.

Yucaipa participated in a financial restructuring of Allied Systems Holdings and wound up with a controlling interest when the holding company emerged from Chapter 11 bankruptcy protection in 2007.

Success in the car-hauling business is tied directly to new vehicle production and sales, and slumping sales for the top US-based automakers have put the brakes on Allied's revenues. The company cited a drop in new vehicle production, an increase in fuel costs, and wage and benefit obligations to unionized employees as reasons for its bankruptcy filing in 2005. Many of those same issues returned to plague Allied Systems Holdings in 2008. Historic financial problems in the auto industry — including trips through Chapter 11 for giant General Motors and Chrysler in 2009 — made trouble for anciliary businesses including Allied Systems Holdings. In July 2009, Allied Systems Holdings laid off about 120 workers in Michigan as GM closed a medium-duty truck plant in Flint. The company hopes to maintain its market share by holding onto its longstanding customers.

Through its Axis Group unit, Allied Systems Holdings provides vehicle-related logistics services, but the actual hauling of cars, trucks, and SUVs accounts for the vast majority of the company's overall sales.

Allied Systems Holdings has worked over the years to incorporate Christian values into its business. Toward that end, the company has assigned a chaplain to each of its terminals to counsel employees as requested.

EXECUTIVES

Chairman: Robert J. Rutland, age 67
President, CEO, and Director: Mark Gendregske, age 48
EVP and CFO: Thomas H. (Tom) King, age 54
EVP, General Counsel, and Secretary: Thomas M. Duffy, age 48
SVP and Director: Guy W. Rutland IV, age 45
SVP Service Operations: Keith M. Rentzel
SVP Information Systems: Larry G. Parks
SVP Human Resources: Brenda Ragsdale
SVP Maintenance and Procurement: Robert Ferrell
SVP Field Operations: Joseph V. (Joe) Marinelli, age 48
Group VP, Labor Relations: Robert L. Hutchison
President, Axis Group: John Harrington
Auditors: KPMG LLP

LOCATIONS

HQ: Allied Systems Holdings, Inc.
2302 Parklake Dr., Bldg. 15, Ste. 600
Atlanta, GA 30345
Phone: 404-373-4285   **Fax:** 404-370-4206
Web: www.alliedholdings.com

COMPETITORS

Burlington Northern Santa Fe
Cassens
CSX
Jack Cooper Transport
JHT Holdings
Norfolk Southern
United Road Services
UPS Supply Chain Solutions
Waggoners Trucking

Allina Hospitals

Allina Hospitals and Clinics is a not-for-profit health care system — focused on protecting people's #1 asset — their good health. The health system owns and operates about a dozen hospitals, a network of nearly one hundred clinics and specialty centers, and 15 pharmacies. Its vast system of provider locations serve residents throughout Minnesota and western Wisconsin, providing disease prevention programs along with specialized inpatient and outpatient services. Allina's Aspen Medical Group division also operates a range of outpatient clinics providing primary and specialty care, as well as more than two dozen nursing homes. Allina is led by CEO Ken Paulus, who previously served as the system's COO.

Combined, Allina's hospitals have nearly 2,000 licensed beds. The largest hospital in the group is Abbott Northwestern Hospital, with more than 600 beds, followed by United Hospital, which has about 450 beds. Five of Allina's hospitals are in the Minneapolis/St. Paul metropolitan area (where the system has about a 33%

share of the health care market), five are scattered throughout the rest of Minnesota, and one is in western Wisconsin.

The system's wide-ranging locations combined with its huge number of facilities prompted Allina to embark on a multi-year initiative (which it wrapped up in late in 2009) to install electronic medical records (EMR) at all of its hospitals and clinics. The installation gives medical providers the ability to track a patient's progress through any of the myriad health care settings operated by Allina.

EMR also gives patients access to coordinated care between the different providers, as well as the ability to see portions of their medical records and lab results online. Patients can also schedule appointments and make use of a number of health and wellness tools, all via the Internet.

Despite Allina's already hefty size, in 2009 the health system forged a partnership with retail clinic provider, MinuteClinic, which offers basic health care at CVS Caremark stores. Through the agreement the two organizations will refer patients to each other, with an eye toward providing the appropriate level of care to each company's patients. For example, if a patient shows up at the emergency room with non-emergent symptoms, such as a cold or allergies, he could be referred to a nearby MinuteClinic for care, and likewise, conditions not covered in the basic care clinics can be sent to an Allina hospital for more comprehensive care.

The two medical providers will also create an interface between their EMR systems to share data when a patient is referred to either company's facilities.

EXECUTIVES

Chairperson: Dean Phillips
Vice Chairperson: Christine A. Morrison
President, CEO and Director: Kenneth (Ken) Paulus, age 50
EVP and CFO: Duncan P. Gallagher
EVP, Philanthropy: Sid Mallory
EVP Strategy and Organizational Performance: Sandy Schmitt
EVP Ambulatory Services: Robert A. Wieland
General Counsel: Elizabeth T. Smith
Chief Clinical Officer: Penny Ann Wheeler
Chief Administrative Officer: Gary J. Strong
CIO and VP, Information Services: Robert Plaszcz
Auditors: Deloitte & Touche LLP

LOCATIONS

HQ: Allina Hospitals and Clinics
2925 Chicago Ave., Minneapolis, MN 55407
Phone: 612-775-5000   **Fax:** 612-863-5667
Web: www.allina.com

PRODUCTS/OPERATIONS

Selected Hospitals

Abbott Northwestern Hospital (Minneapolis, MN)
Buffalo Hospital (Buffalo, MN)
Cambridge Medical Center (Cambridge, MN)
Mercy Hospital (Coon Rapids, MN)
New Ulm Medical Center (New Ulm, MN)
Owatonna Hospital (Owatonna, MN)
Phillips Eye Institute (Minneapolis, MN)
River Falls Area Hospital (River Falls, WI)
St. Francis Regional Medical Center (Shakopee, MN)
United Hospital (St. Paul, MN)
Unity Hospital (Fridley, MN)

COMPETITORS

Bethesda Hospital
Catholic Health Initiatives
CentraCare Health
Children's Hospitals and Clinics of Minnesota
Fairview Health
Hazelden
HealthEast Care System
Mayo Foundation
Methodist Hospital (MN)
North Memorial Health Care
Park Nicollet Health Services
Regions Hospital
St. John's Hospital (Minnesota)
University of Minnesota Medical Center

HISTORICAL FINANCIALS

Company Type: Not-for-profit

Income Statement				FYE: December 31
	REVENUE ($ mil.)	NET INCOME ($ mil.)	NET PROFIT MARGIN	EMPLOYEES
12/08	2,534	—	—	22,347

Allison Transmission

You can't have a tractor pull without Allison Transmission. Allison builds automatic transmissions for commercial vehicles. Its customers include makers of everything from garbage trucks and city transit buses to military vehicles and dump trucks. Allison also makes a line of electric drives for use primarily on buses and shuttles, and remanufactures automatic transmissions for the commercial replacement aftermarket. Allison also builds transmissions for GM's Silverado HD and GMC Sierra HD pickups. In 2007 General Motors sold Allison to The Carlyle Group and Onex Corp. for $5.6 billion. GM kept one Allison plant that builds transmissions for its light trucks.

Teaming up with Remy International, Allison developed a hybrid transmission used to power buses that can be found on the streets of Seattle.

In addition to its US headquarters, Allison maintains regional headquarters in Brazil, China, India, Japan, and the Netherlands. The company has 1,500 dealer and distributor locations in 80 countries around the world.

The company was established in 1915 as the Indianapolis Speedway Team Company. Later known as the Allison Engineering Company, after founder Jim Allison (who also was a founder of the Indianapolis Motor Speedway), the company was sold to GM in 1929, the year after Allison's death.

EXECUTIVES

Chairman and CEO: Lawrence E. (Larry) Dewey
CFO: David S. Graziosi, age 40
VP Engineering: Laurie Tuttle
Executive Director, Military Programs: Bryan Stephens
Director Transmission Programming: Randy Kirk
Director Public Relations and Communication: Eric Dickerson

LOCATIONS

HQ: Allison Transmission, Inc.
4700 W. 10th St., Indianapolis, IN 46222
Phone: 317-242-5000
Web: www.allisontransmission.com

COMPETITORS

Eaton
Enova Systems
Magna International
Twin Disc
Valeo
ZF Friedrichshafen

HISTORICAL FINANCIALS

Company Type: Private

Income Statement				FYE: December 31
	REVENUE ($ mil.)	NET INCOME ($ mil.)	NET PROFIT MARGIN	EMPLOYEES
12/07	2,400	—	—	2,800

Allstates WorldCargo

No relation to insurance giant Allstate, Allstates WorldCargo uses its "good hands" to provide freight forwarding and logistics services. The company arranges the transportation of its customers' cargo by plane, ship, and truck. Rather than maintaining its own transportation assets, Allstates WorldCargo uses a network of air, ocean, and over-the-road carriers. The company operates from a network of about 20 offices in the US, and it maintains agents and relationships with freight forwarders in Europe, South America, and the Asia/Pacific region. Freight forwarding within the US accounts for most of the company's sales. Company founder Joseph Guido owns 58% of Allstates WorldCargo.

To grow, Allstates World Cargo intends to continue to invest in information technology. The company has implemented systems that improve its ability to track freight and manage inventory.

Besides its freight forwarding business, Allstates WorldCargo generates revenue from a subsidiary, Audiogenesis Systems, that distributes protective clothing and other safety equipment to employees of a pharmaceutical company.

Audiogenesis Systems bought Allstates Air Cargo in a reverse acquisition in 1999, and the combined company took the name Allstates WorldCargo. Guido, a former freight supervisor for AMR's American Airlines, founded Allstates Air Cargo in 1961. CEO Sam DiGiralomo, a veteran employee of Audiogenesis Systems and its predecessor, Genesis Safety Systems, owns 12% of Allstates WorldCargo.

EXECUTIVES

President and CEO: Sam DiGiralomo, age 65
EVP, COO, and Director: Barton C. Theile, age 62
CFO, Secretary, Treasurer, and Director:
Craig D. Stratton, age 57
Auditors: Cowan, Gunteski & Co., P.A.

LOCATIONS

HQ: Allstates WorldCargo, Inc.
4 Lakeside Dr. South, Forked River, NJ 08731
Phone: 609-693-5950   **Fax:** 609-693-5550
Web: allstates-worldcargo.com

COMPETITORS

CEVA Logistics
C.H. Robinson Worldwide
DHL
Expeditors
FedEx Trade Networks Transport & Brokerage
Lakeland Industries
Menlo Worldwide
Mine Safety Appliances
UPS Supply Chain Solutions
UTi Worldwide

Alsco, Inc.

Alsco tells its clients, "It pays to keep clean," and then provides the uniforms, linens, and related products to achieve that goal. Operating from some 120 sites in 10 countries worldwide, the company (whose name stands for American linen supply company) supplies clean towels, linens, and uniforms to the medical and hospitality industries, among others. It also manufactures, rents, and sells uniforms, provides workplace restroom services, launders specialized garments, and manages gown rooms at high-tech sites. The company expanded in 2006 by buying the assets of National Linen and Uniform Service. Founded in 1889 by George Steiner, Alsco is owned and operated by the Steiner family.

EXECUTIVES

Co-President: Robert Steiner
Co-President: Kevin Steiner
CFO: Jim Kearns
VP Operations, Alsco North America: Steve Larson
Director Information Systems: Larry Tomsic
Director Sales and Marketing: Jim Divers
Director Human Resources: Tim Weiler
Manager National Sales: Russ Meredith

LOCATIONS

HQ: Alsco, Inc.
505 E. South Temple, Salt Lake City, UT 84102
Phone: 801-328-8831   **Fax:** 801-363-5680
Web: www.alsco.com

PRODUCTS/OPERATIONS

Selected Products and Services

Cold weather gear	Laundry
Drum covers	Medical apparel
Dust bags	Restroom service
Filter belts	Restroom supplies
Garments	Towel service
Gown room management	Towels
Gowns	Uniform rental
Hospitality/restaurant apparel	Uniform sales
Kitchen matting	Vacuum filters

COMPETITORS

Angelica Corporation	JohnsonDiversey
ARAMARK	Rentokil Initial
Cintas	ServiceMaster
Crothall Services	Sodexo USA
Davis Service	Superior Uniform Group
Ecolab	Swisher Hygiene
G&K Services	Tranzonic
Healthcare Services	UniFirst
ISS A/S	

Alticor Inc.

At the core of Alticor, there is Amway. Alticor was formed in 2000 as a holding company and operates five businesses: direct-selling giant Amway, Web-based sales firm Amway Global (formerly Quixtar), Amway Hotel Corp. (corporate development for Alticor and affiliates), upscale cosmetics company Gurwitch Products, and Access Business Group (manufacturing, logistics services). Access Business' biggest customers are Amway and Amway Global, but Access also serves outsiders.

Amway, which accounts for most of Alticor's revenues, sells more than 450 different products through some 3 million independent distributors. Alticor is owned by Amway founders, the DeVos and Van Andel families.

Alticor expanded its cosmetics portfolio by inking a deal in July 2006 to acquire Gurwitch Products from The Neiman Marcus Group. Gurwitch, the licensee of Laura Mercier cosmetics, makes and markets luxury cosmetics and skin care items. As part of the deal, Gurwitch Products became a wholly owned subsidiary of Alticor. The acquisition gives Alticor a foothold in upscale cosmetics and offers its hefty direct sales ranks growth opportunities. For Gurwitch the deal breathes new life into its Laura Mercier business.

The company also owns the Amway Grand Plaza Hotel, located in Grand Rapids, Michigan. The hotel houses the state's first AAA Five-Diamond-designated restaurant, the 1913 Room.

EXECUTIVES

Chairman: Steve Van Andel
President: Doug DeVos
COO, Access Business Group LLC: Al Koop
EVP and CFO: Russell A. (Russ) Evans
EVP, Greater China and Southeast Asia, Amway:
Eva Cheng
EVP; EVP, Quixtar and EVP, Amway Corporation:
Jim Payne
VP and Managing Director, Quixtar: Steve Lieberman
VP Public Policy: Richard Holwill
VP Human Resources: Kelly Savage
Chief Marketing Officer: Candace S. Matthews, age 50
Corporate General Counsel: Michael Mohr
Manager Brand Communications: Glen Myers
Corporate Communications: Mike Smith
President and Representative Director, Japan and Korea, Amway: David D. Ussery, age 73
CEO, Gurwitch Products: Janet Gurwitch

LOCATIONS

HQ: Alticor Inc.
7575 Fulton St. East, Ada, MI 49355
Phone: 616-787-1000   **Fax:** 616-682-4000
Web: www.alticor.com

PRODUCTS/OPERATIONS

Selected Amway Products
Catalog Products
    Appliances
    Electronics
    Fashions
    Home furnishings
    Office supplies
    Toys
Home Care Products
    Dishwashing liquid
    Laundry detergent
    Multi-purpose cleaner
Home Living/Home Tech Products
    Cookware
    Water-treatment systems
Nutrition and Wellness Products
    Beverages
    Dietary supplements
    Meals
    Snacks
    Weight-control products
Personal Care Products
    Body washes
    Deodorants
    Hair care products
    Lotions
    Toothpaste
Skin Care and Cosmetics Products
    Cleansers
    Color cosmetics
    Moisturizers
    Toners

COMPETITORS

Avon	Kao
Bath & Body Works	L'Oréal
Brown-Forman	MacAndrews & Forbes
CCL Industries	Mary Kay
Clorox	Newell Rubbermaid
Colgate-Palmolive	Nikken
Daiei	Nu Skin
Estée Lauder	PFSweb
Fingerhut	Procter & Gamble
Forever Living	S.C. Johnson
GNC	Shaklee
Henkel	Tupperware Brands
Johnson & Johnson	Unilever

AMC Entertainment

AMC Entertainment shines when the lights go down. The #2 movie theater chain in the US (behind Regal Entertainment), the company owns more than 300 theaters housing some 4,600 screens, most of which are in megaplexes (units with more than 14 screens and stadium seating). The majority of its theaters can be found throughout the US and Canada; about a dozen theaters are in China (Hong Kong), France, and the UK. The firm is part owner (more than 25%) of MovieTickets.com, along with Hollywood Media and rivals Cineplex and National Amusements, among others. The company bought rival Loews Cineplex in 2006, significantly boosting its holdings. AMC is controlled by J.P. Morgan Partners and Apollo Management.

AMC generates about 70% of its revenue from ticket sales, while more than 25% is from the concession stand. More than 75% of its screens are located in megaplex theatres. The company also sells digitally projected on-screen advertising and pre-show entertainment videos through its National CineMedia joint venture with Regal and Cinemark.

AMC is also in the process of converting all of its theaters to digital cinema. In order to do so it has entered a joint venture with Cinemark and Regal called Digital Cinema Implementation Partners, which operates under the goal of establishing a business plan for digital cinema. The company is also installing 100 MPX digital IMAX projection systems at locations in more than 30 major US markets, including Chicago, Houston, Los Angeles, and New York. AMC expects the installation to be completed by the end of 2011.

In 2009 Gerardo Lopez became CEO of the company. A former executive at Starbucks, Lopez replaced the retiring Peter Brown, who had been with the theater chain for nearly 20 years. In 2008 AMC Entertainment dropped plans for an IPO as a result of the weak market for new equities. Also that year the company exited Mexico when it sold its interests in Grupo Cinemex, which then operated 44 theatres with 493 screens, primarily in the Mexico City metropolitan area. In 2007 AMC Entertainment sold its 9% share in online ticket Fandango to Comcast for some $20 million.

An investment vehicle controlled by affiliates of CCMP Capital and Apollo Advisors purchased AMC Entertainment for about $2 billion in 2004.

EXECUTIVES

Chairman: Aaron J. Stone, age 36
CEO and Director: Gerardo I. (Gerry) Lopez, age 50
EVP, CFO, and Director, American Multi-Cinema:
  Craig R. Ramsey, age 56
EVP International Operations, AMC Entertainment International: Mark A. McDonald, age 50
EVP US and Canada Operations, American Multi-Cinema: John D. McDonald, age 51
SVP, General Counsel, and Secretary: Kevin M. Connor, age 45
SVP Strategic Development and Marketing:
  Frank W. Rash III
SVP Human Resources: Keith Wiedenkeller
VP Technology and Systems: Dan Huerta
VP National Sales: Scott Wall
VP Finance: Michael W. Zwonitzer, age 44
VP and Chief Accounting Officer: Chris A. Cox, age 42
VP Corporate Communications: Sun Dee Larson
VP Marketing: Zach Baze
President, AMC Film Programming:
  Samuel D. (Sonny) Gourley
President Programming: Robert J. Lenihan
Auditors: PricewaterhouseCoopers LLP

LOCATIONS

HQ: AMC Entertainment Inc.
  920 Main St., Kansas City, MO 64105
Phone: 816-221-4000   **Fax:** 816-480-4617
Web: www.amctheatres.com

2009 Sales

	$ mil.	% of total
US	2,184.7	96
International	80.8	4
Total	**2,265.5**	**100**

2009 US Holdings

	Theaters	Screens
California	42	651
Texas	22	437
Florida	23	392
New Jersey	24	310
New York	27	279
Illinois	18	271
Michigan	13	214
Georgia	12	189
Arizona	9	183
Washington	14	149
Pennsylvania	12	142
Maryland	13	136
Massachusetts	10	129
Missouri	8	117
Virginia	7	113
Ohio	5	86
Colorado	4	74
Louisiana	5	68
Minnesota	4	64
North Carolina	3	60
Oklahoma	3	60
Kansas	2	48
Indiana	3	42
Connecticut	2	36
Nebraska	1	24
Washington, DC	3	22
Kentucky	1	20
Wisconsin	1	18
Arkansas	1	16
South Carolina	1	14
Utah	1	9
Total	**294**	**4,373**

2009 International Holdings

	Theaters	Screens
Canada	8	184
China	2	13
France	1	14
The UK	2	28
Total	**13**	**239**

PRODUCTS/OPERATIONS

2009 Sales

	$ mil.	% of total
Admissions	1,580.3	70
Concessions	626.3	28
Other	58.9	2
Total	**2,265.5**	**100**

COMPETITORS

Brenden Theatre
Carmike Cinemas
Cinemark
Cineplex Galaxy
Clearview Cinemas
Hoyts Cinemas
IMAX
Kerasotes ShowPlace
Laemmle Theatres
Landmark Theatres
Marcus Corporation
National Amusements
Pacific Theatres
Regal Entertainment

HISTORICAL FINANCIALS

Company Type: Private

Income Statement
FYE: Thursday nearest March 31

	REVENUE ($ mil.)	NET INCOME ($ mil.)	NET PROFIT MARGIN	EMPLOYEES
3/09	2,266	(81)	—	16,800
3/08	2,333	43	1.9%	20,200
3/07	2,462	117	4.7%	22,900
3/06	1,687	(216)	—	21,400
3/05	1,699	(80)	—	22,200
Annual Growth	7.5%	—	—	(6.7%)

Net Income History

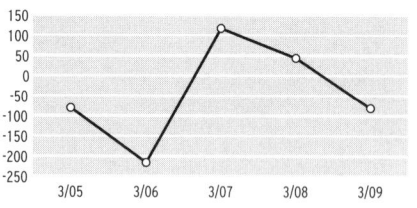

LOCATIONS

HQ: America Chung Nam, Inc.
1163 Fairway Dr., City of Industry, CA 91789
Phone: 909-839-8383 **Fax:** 909-869-6310
Web: www.acni.net

COMPETITORS

Caraustar Recovered Fiber Group
International Paper
Smurfit-Stone Container
Weyerhaeuser

HISTORICAL FINANCIALS

Company Type: Private

Income Statement
FYE: December 31

	REVENUE ($ mil.)	NET INCOME ($ mil.)	NET PROFIT MARGIN	EMPLOYEES
12/08	1,363	—	—	200

America Chung Nam

Ever wondered where all that paper to be recycled goes? If this company is any indication, it goes to China. America Chung Nam is the largest exporter of recovered paper in the US and a leading exporter in Europe and Asia. The company exports recovered fiber sources to Chinese paper mills where they can be converted into fiberboard, cardboard, and packaging. The company sources its fiber through exclusive relationships with recycling facilities, waste management companies, and distribution centers throughout North America, Asia, and Europe. America Chung Nam was founded in 1990 by Yan Cheung and Ming Chung Liu. The pair also own and manage China's largest packaging manufacturer, Nine Dragons Paper.

Recognizing the demand for packaging materials driven by China's product exports and having a ready source for fiber materials through America Chung Nam, Ms. Cheung established Nine Dragons Paper in 1996 to great success. America Chung Nam supplies the fiber materials, which Nine Dragons converts into the packaging material that is used to ship various Chinese products to consumers across the world. Once delivered, the packaging is again ripe for recycling and export back to China.

EXECUTIVES

President and CEO: Yan Cheung
CFO: Kevin Zao
Chief Executive Officer, Worldwide Marketing: Peter Wang
Managing Director, Europe and UK: Wade Schuetzeberg
Deputy CEO Asia Pacific Region: Teresa Cheung

American Bar Association

The American Bar Association (ABA) doesn't have anything to do with alcohol, except maybe defending drunken drivers. The group seeks to promote improvements in the American justice system and develop guidelines for the advancement of the legal profession and education. It provides law school accreditation, continuing education, legal information, and other services to assist legal professionals. Its roster of more than 400,000 members includes judges, court administrators, law professors, and nonpracticing lawyers. All lawyers in good standing with any US state or territory bar are eligible for membership. The ABA cannot discipline lawyers, nor can it enforce its rules; it can only develop guidelines.

The ABA releases about 100 books and 60 magazines, journals, and newsletters in various formats through its ABA Publishing division. Popular materials run the gamut of topics, from administrative practices for lobbyists to immigration law guides for criminal lawyers to leadership and empowerment for women lawyers. Publications are for sale on the ABA's online store.

HISTORY

One hundred lawyers from 21 states met in Saratoga, New York, in 1878 and drafted the constitution for the American Bar Association. As the ABA grew over the next hundred years, it came to influence the direction of legal education and the nomination and confirmation of judicial candidates. This brought the ABA into the political arena where its stance on controversial issues politicized the group and opened it to charges of partisan bias.

Its activities also have led to lawsuits (imagine that), including a 1993 suit by the Massachusetts School of Law claiming that the ABA's law school accreditation practices impinged on the university's right to set school policy. The Justice Department agreed, saying the ABA's requirements raised costs without improving educational quality, so in 1995 the association changed its accreditation process.

Its influence over judicial nominations took a beating in 1997 when the Senate Judiciary Committee announced that it would no longer await ABA pronouncements before acting on a nomination. The ABA's accreditation process came under fire again in 1998 when the government agency that oversees educational accreditation agencies threatened to penalize or terminate the ABA unless its accreditation policies complied with federal law. Supreme Court Justice Clarence Thomas levied his own attack in 1999 by charging that the ABA's political platforms compromised its objectivity in reviewing judicial nominations.

The ABA joined with the Federal Bar Association in 2001 to support a pay increase for federal judges. In 2002 the ABA voted to recommend that alleged terrorists tried before military tribunals should be guaranteed the same legal protections as criminal defendants in US courts.

EXECUTIVES

Chair, House of Delegates: William (Bill) Hubbard
President: H. Thomas Wells Jr.
President-Elect: Carolyn Lamm
Executive Director and COO: Henry F. White Jr.
Secretary: Bernice Donald
Treasurer: Alice E. Richmond
Auditors: Ernst & Young LLP

LOCATIONS

HQ: American Bar Association
321 N. Clark St., Chicago, IL 60610
Phone: 312-988-5000 **Fax:** 312-988-5177
Web: www.abanet.org

PRODUCTS/OPERATIONS

Selected Committees, Forums, and Other Groups

Coalition for Justice
Commission on Domestic Violence
Commission on Mental and Physical Disability Law
Commission on Racial and Ethnic Diversity in the Profession
Death Penalty Moratorium Implementation Project
Forum Committee on Affordable Housing and Community Development Law
Forum Committee on Entertainment and Sports Industries
Law Student Division
Office of the President
Section of Administrative Law and Regulatory Practice
Section of Business Law
Senior Lawyers Division
Special Committee on Gun Violence
Standing Committee on Election Law
Standing Committee on Judicial Independence
Standing Committee on Lawyers' Professional Liability
Standing Committee on Legal Assistants
Standing Committee on Pro Bono and Public Service
Young Lawyers Division

American Cancer Society

The American Cancer Society (ACS) seeks to end cancer suffering. Dedicated to the elimination of cancer, the not-for-profit organization is staffed by professionals and more than 2 million volunteers at some 3,400 local units across the country. ACS is the largest source of private cancer research funds in the US. Recipients of the society's funding include more than 40 Nobel Prize laureates. In addition to research, the ACS supports detection, treatment, and education programs. The organization encourages prevention efforts with programs such as the Great American Smokeout. Patient services include moral support, transportation to and from treatment, and camps for children who have cancer.

The ACS took its fight against cancer overseas in partnership with the Lance Armstrong Foundation during the summer of 2009. The two anticancer groups are joining forces at the LIVESTRONG Global Cancer Summit to be held in Dublin, Ireland, in August. The goal of the meeting is to empower and support cancer survivors worldwide and create a survivor advocacy movement.

The ACS has generated considerable income by marketing its name for antismoking nicotine patches and orange juice, and is contemplating even more lucrative deals. Program services, including research, prevention, detection/treatment, and patient support, account for about three-quarters of expenses; the rest goes to administration and fund raising.

The organization has seen double-digit growth in online monetary gifts, although online giving still is a small percentage of overall giving.

HISTORY

Concerned over the lack of progress in detecting and treating cancer, a group of 10 physicians and five laymen met in New York City in 1913 to form the American Society for the Control of Cancer (ASCC). Because public discussion of cancer was taboo, the group struggled with how to educate people without raising unnecessary fears. Some physicians even preferred keeping knowledge of the disease from the public. In the 1920s the ASCC began sponsoring cancer clinics and collecting statistics on the disease. By 1923 some states reported improvements in early diagnosis and treatment. In 1937 the ASCC started its first nationwide public education program, with the help of volunteers known as the Women's Field Army. President Franklin Roosevelt named April National Cancer Control Month, a practice since followed by every president.

By 1944 some cancer rates were rising but the word "cancer" still couldn't be mentioned on radio. Mary Lasker, wife of prominent ad executive Albert Lasker, was instrumental in getting information about cancer broadcast. At her insistence, in 1945 the newly renamed American Cancer Society began donating at least 25% of its budget to research. The society raised $4 million in its first major national fund-raising campaign.

The link between smoking and lung cancer became known after a study in the early 1950s by ACS medical director Charles Cameron. That information became part of the Surgeon General's Report of 1964. In 1973 an ACS branch in Minnesota held the first Great American Smokeout to encourage people to quit smoking.

The ACS backed the 1971 congressional bill that inaugurated the War on Cancer. The society was attacked in the 1970s for emphasizing cures rather than prevention because, critics claimed, research would reveal environmental causes from industrial products made by companies with connections to ACS directors. In the 1970s and 1980s, the ACS backed tougher restrictions on tobacco and, in response to earlier criticism, directed research toward prevention as well as treatment. The society played a major role in the 1989 airline smoking ban.

John Seffrin, a former Indiana University professor, was named CEO of ACS in 1992. The first of several genetic breakthroughs came in the 1990s when ACS grantees isolated genes believed to be responsible for triggering various types of cancer. In 1995 the ACS accused the tobacco industry of infiltrating its offices in the 1970s and using its papers to aid in the early marketing of low-tar cigarettes.

In 1996 the ACS announced that new data showed a drop in the US cancer death rate for the first time ever. The ACS entered agreements with SmithKline Beecham (NicoDerm antismoking patches) and the Florida Department of Citrus in 1996 to allow the use of the American Cancer Society name in marketing.

The proposed $369 billion settlement between the attorneys general of 40 states and the tobacco industry was big news in 1997. The ACS had wanted more concessions, such as a $2-per-pack tax increase, more power for industry regulation by the FDA, and underage use rate-reduction targets for smokeless tobacco products as stringent as those for cigarettes.

In 1998 the ACS launched a $5 million national advertising campaign to combat what it saw as "misleading" information spread by the tobacco industry. It argued before the Supreme Court in 1999 to help the FDA gain control over cigarette production and distribution. In 2000 ACS restructured its $50-million-a-year research program to increase the size of individual grants; it also awarded its largest-ever award, $1.7 million, to study the side effects of cancer treatment. ACS filed petitions to the FDA the next year urging it to regulate new tobacco products marketed as being safer than traditional cigarettes. In 2002 ACS and The Robert Wood Johnson Foundation launched the Center for Tobacco Cessation to help people quit smoking. ACS published strategic guides the following year to help countries in the early stages of tobacco control.

EXECUTIVES

Chairman: G. Van Velsor Wolf Jr.
Vice Chairman: Stephen L. Swanson
Chair-Elect: George W. P. Atkins
CEO: John R. Seffrin
Deputy CEO: Donald Thomas
President and Director: Elizabeth T. H. (Terry) Fontham
COO: Patricia M. (Pat) Felts, age 57
CFO: Catherine E. Mickle
Interim Chief Mission Officer: Terry Music
Chief Medical Officer: Otis W. Brawley, age 49
First VP and Director: Edward E. Partridge
Second VP and Director: W. Phil Evans
Secretary and Director: Cynthia M. LeBlanc
Senior Director Communications and Media Advocacy: Steven C. Weiss
Treasurer and Director: Nancy S. Brakensiek
President, American Cancer Society Foundation: Robert D. (Rob) Mitchell III
President-Elect and Director: Alan G. Thorson
Auditors: Ernst & Young LLP

LOCATIONS

HQ: American Cancer Society, Inc.
250 Williams St., Ste. 600, Atlanta, GA 30303
Phone: 404-320-3333 **Fax:** 404-982-3677
Web: www.cancer.org

PRODUCTS/OPERATIONS

Selected Patient Services Programs

Children's Camps (for children and teens with cancer; some for siblings)
Hope Lodge (housing assistance)
I Can Cope (education and support classes on living with cancer)
Look Good . . . Feel Better (cosmetics and beauty techniques for women experiencing side effects of cancer treatment)
Man To Man Prostate Cancer Support
Pamphlets and brochures for cancer patients and their families
Reach to Recovery (support for women with breast cancer and their families)
Road to Recovery (transportation services)

Selected Public Education Programs and Publications

Great American Smokeout (national stop-smoking-for-a-day event)
Making Strides Against Breast Cancer (fund-raiser)
Relay for Life (fund-raiser)

Selected Research Grants and Awards

Clinical research professorships
Clinical research training grants
Institutional research grants
Postdoctoral fellowships
Research opportunity grants
Research professorships

American Crystal Sugar

Call it saccharine, but for American Crystal Sugar, business is all about sharing. This sugar-beet cooperative is owned by some 2,900 growers in the Red River Valley of North Dakota and Minnesota who farm more than one-half million owned and contracted acres of cropland. American Crystal, formed in 1899 and converted into a co-op in 1973, divides the 35-mile-wide valley into five districts, each served by a processing plant. The plants produce sugar, molasses, and beet pulp. American Crystal's products are sold internationally to industrial users and to retail and wholesale customers under the Crystal name, as well as under private labels through marketing co-ops United Sugars and Midwest Agri-Commodities.

Company subsidiary Sidney Sugars operates a processing facility in Montana. Sidney owns a plant in Wyoming that is leased to another sugar cooperative.

American Crystal holds the controlling interest in the corn-sweetener joint venture ProGold, which leases its facility to Cargill for the production of high-fructose corn syrup.

The company also sells agri-products and sugar-beet seeds, and leases a corn milling plant for the production of high-fructose corn syrup, the sweetener of choice for almost all US food and beverage manufacturers.

EXECUTIVES

Chairman: Francis L. Kritzberger, age 64
Vice Chairman: Neil C. Widner, age 58
President and CEO: David Berg, age 55,
$1,600,012 total compensation
COO: Joseph J. (Joe) Talley, age 49,
$780,039 total compensation
VP Finance and CFO: Thomas S. Astrup, age 41,
$716,160 total compensation
VP Administration: Brian F. Ingulsrud, age 46,
$578,794 total compensation
**Controller, Chief Accounting Officer, Assistant
Treasurer, and Assistant Secretary:** Teresa A. Warne,
age 39
Manager Treasury Operations and Assistant Secretary:
Lisa M. Maloy, age 45
Manager Accounting and Systems: Ronald K. Peterson,
age 54
Secretary: Daniel C. Mott, age 50
Treasurer and Assistant Secretary: Samuel S. M. Wai,
age 55
**Director Economic Analysis, Assistant Secretary, and
Assistant Treasurer:** David L. Malmskog, age 52
**Manager Finance Administration, Assistant Secretary,
and Assistant Treasurer:** Mark L. Lembke, age 53
Auditors: Eide Bailly LLP

LOCATIONS

HQ: American Crystal Sugar Company
101 N. 3rd St., Moorhead, MN 56560
Phone: 218-236-4400   **Fax:** 218-236-4422
Web: www.crystalsugar.com

PRODUCTS/OPERATIONS

2009 Sales

	$ mil.	% of total
Sugar	1,176.3	98
Leasing	23.9	2
Total	**1,200.2**	**100**

Selected Joint Ventures and Subsidiaries

Joint ventures
  Midwest Agri-Commodities Company
  Progold L.L.C.
  United Sugars Corporation
Subsidiaries
  Crab Creek Sugar Company
  Crystech, LLC
  Sidney Sugars Incorporated

COMPETITORS

ADM
Alberto-Culver
Alexander & Baldwin
Amalgamated Sugar
C&H Sugar
Cargill
Cumberland Packing
Florida Crystals
Holly Sugar
Imperial Sugar
M A Patout
Merisant Worldwide
Michigan Sugar Company
Nippon Beet Sugar
NutraSweet
Südzucker
SMBSC
Sterling Sugars
Sugar Cane Growers Cooperative of Florida
Sugar Foods
Tate & Lyle
U.S. Sugar
Western Sugar Cooperative

HISTORICAL FINANCIALS

Company Type: Cooperative

Income Statement

FYE: August 31

	REVENUE ($ mil.)	NET INCOME ($ mil.)	NET PROFIT MARGIN	EMPLOYEES
8/09	1,200	536	44.7%	1,369
8/08	1,233	543	44.0%	1,361
8/07	1,222	601	49.2%	1,380
8/06	1,006	445	44.3%	1,306
8/05	966	373	38.7%	1,337
Annual Growth	**5.6%**	**9.5%**	**—**	**0.6%**

Net Income History

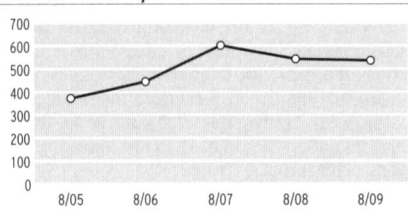

American Family Insurance

Even confirmed bachelors can get insured through American Family Insurance. The company specializes in property/casualty insurance, but also offers life and health coverage, as well as investment and retirement-planning products. The company operates in about 20 states, primarily in the midwestern and western US. It is among the largest US mutual companies that concentrates on auto insurance (State Farm is the biggest). American Family Insurance also provides coverage for homeowners and farmers, as well as restaurants, contractors, and other businesses. Through the company's consumer finance division, agents can also offer their customers home equity and personal lines of credit.

The company's health insurance products include HSA (health savings account), Medicare supplement, and short-term medical care plans. In 2009 the company began phasing out its own line of individual health products and began marketing the policies of affiliate American Enterprise Mutual.

American Family Insurance sells its insurance products through a network of nearly 4,000 independent agents. Unlike many of its competitors, the company has said it has no plans to demutualize and has steadily grown its equity and assets.

In a turbulent economic environment, and after experiencing high levels of catastrophe and storm-loss coverage in 2008 and previous years, the company is focused on improving operational efficiencies, being prudent in investment choices, and beefing up customer service functions.

The company was founded by insurance salesman Herman Wittwer in 1927 as Farmers Mutual Automobile Insurance Company to provide auto insurance to farmers in Wisconsin. The American Family moniker came into use in the 1960s.

HISTORY

In 1927 Herman Wittwer founded Farmers Mutual Automobile Insurance to sell coverage to Wisconsin farmers. As farms became mechanized in the 1920s, the insurance market grew. Low-density rural traffic reduced the potential for accidents, a fact that attracted Wittwer and others, such as State Farm (founded in 1922) to serve similar markets. Wittwer also noted that rural Wisconsin's severe winters made cars unusable for a good part of the year, further reducing risk.

Farmers Mutual grew despite the Depression and WWII, spreading to Minnesota (1933); Missouri (1939); Nebraska and the Dakotas (1940); and Indiana, Iowa, and Kansas (1943). The war years were generous to insurers: Rising incomes allowed people to insure their cars, but rationing programs limited use of the cars. The postwar suburban boom — when cars became a necessity rather than a luxury — also helped auto insurers.

Growing prosperity for single-earner households in the 1950s helped boost the demand for life insurance. In 1958 Farmers Mutual formed American Family Life Insurance. The company wrote $1.6 million in insurance on its first day in the life insurance business. During that decade, Farmers Mutual moved into Illinois.

The 1960s brought growth and change. To capture more auto business, it founded American Standard Insurance to write nonstandard auto insurance. The firm also launched consumer finance operations for insurance customers and noncustomers alike, departing from standard industry practice by selling through agents rather than offices. In 1963, in recognition of its growing diversification, Farmers Mutual changed its name to American Family Mutual Insurance.

During the 1970s and 1980s, the firm strengthened its infrastructure and added regional offices. It moved into Arizona and later formed American Family Brokerage to fill in gaps in its own coverage by obtaining insurance for clients through other insurers.

During this period American Family suffered cultural pains. It moved beyond its traditional rural clientele and into the urban unknown as it sought to increase its market share. In 1981 community groups questioned whether the company was adequately serving racially mixed neighborhoods. In 1988 the US Justice Department began investigating allegations that the firm engaged in redlining (offering inferior or no service for minority neighborhoods); a class-action suit based on similar claims was filed in 1990. The suit went all the way to the Supreme Court, which ruled that insurance sales must comply with the Fair Housing Act.

The company had begun rectifying its practices before the case was decided. Nevertheless, when American Family settled the case in 1995, it agreed to pay a $14.5 million settlement plus about $2 million in court costs. Part of the settlement was to compensate people who had suffered from the company's discrimination. But most of the money went to fund community programs begun in 1996 to promote home ownership among minorities. In 1997 trouble came from within and without: One lawsuit claimed the company falsely promised to shrink premiums as policies earned dividends, and two dissident agents filed a civil complaint for wrongful termination (the latter case was settled the next year).

The company's profits tumbled in 1998 due to severe storms in Minnesota and Wisconsin. The next year American Family expanded its operations in Colorado and moved into Cleveland.

In 2000 Wisconsin was again pounded by hail, high winds, and floods. American Family Insurance announced $100 million in expected losses from the event. Streamlining claims processing, the company closed nine of its offices in 2001.

American Family Insurance grew its policy count by almost 10% in 2002, but the volatile stock market hurt the company's net result. By 2004 the company had regained financial strength to the tune of $4.2 billion in policyholder equity, primarily due to record gains in operations.

Where property/casualty insurers along US coastlines were hard hit during the 2005 hurricane season, American Family rode that year out comfortably. However, the company paid out $1.1 billion in storm losses in the wake of hail and windstorms that hit the midwestern US during 2006.

EXECUTIVES

Chairman and CEO: David R. Anderson
CFO and Treasurer: Daniel R. Schultz
EVP: Jerry G. Rekowski
EVP: Mary L. Schmoeger
EVP: Mark V. Afable
EVP: Bradley J. Gleason
EVP: Gerry W. Benusa
SVP and Chief Legal Officer: Christopher S. Spencer
VP Human Resources: Daniel J. Kelly
VP and Controller: Kari E. Grasee
VP Public Relations: Richard A. Fetherston
President, COO, and Director: Jack C. Salzwedel
Auditors: PricewaterhouseCoopers LLP

LOCATIONS

HQ: American Family Insurance Group
   6000 American Pkwy., Madison, WI 53783
Phone: 608-249-2111   **Fax:** 608-243-4921
Web: www.amfam.com

PRODUCTS/OPERATIONS

2008 Revenues

	$ mil.	% of total
Property & casualty premiums	5,818.5	86
Investment income	561.2	8
Life (AFLIC) premiums	318.2	5
Finance charges	6.2	—
Other	38.5	1
Total	**6,742.6**	**100**

Selected Subsidiaries

American Family Brokerage, Inc.
American Family Financial Services, Inc. (AFFS)
American Family Insurance Company
American Family Life Insurance Company (AFLIC)
American Family Mutual Insurance Company
American Family Securities, LLC
American Standard Insurance Company of Ohio
American Standard Insurance Company of Wisconsin
Amfam, Inc.

COMPETITORS

AIG	MetLife
Allstate	Mutual of Omaha
American Financial	Nationwide
Cincinnati Financial	Ohio Casualty
COUNTRY Financial	Old Republic
Farmers Alliance	Progressive Corporation
Farmers Group	Prudential
GEICO	Safeco
General Casualty	State Farm
The Hartford	Travelers Companies
Liberty Mutual	USAA
Lincoln Financial	

HISTORICAL FINANCIALS

Company Type: Mutual company

Income Statement				FYE: December 31
	ASSETS ($ mil.)	NET INCOME ($ mil.)	INCOME AS % OF ASSETS	EMPLOYEES
12/08	15,502	(298)	—	8,071
12/07	16,004	82	0.5%	8,482
12/06	15,477	24	0.2%	8,237
12/05	14,637	672	4.6%	8,135
12/04	13,641	564	4.1%	8,238
Annual Growth	3.2%	—	—	(0.5%)

2008 Year-End Financials

Equity as % of assets: 26.9%   Long-term debt ($ mil.): —
Return on assets: —   Sales ($ mil.): 6,743
Return on equity: —

Net Income History

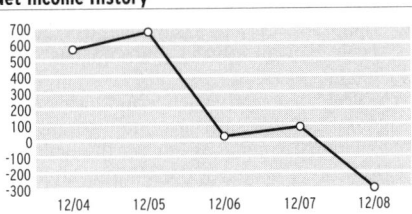

American Library Association

Shhhh! The American Library Association (ALA) is a not-for-profit that works to develop, promote, and improve library and information services. Governed by an elected council, the ALA works with libraries of all types, from public to academic to prison. The more than 67,000-member organization consists of 11 divisions, as well as affiliated organizations and chapters in all 50 states, all working to advance ALA causes, such as Banned Books Week, an annual event promoting awareness about efforts to ban certain books from libraries. The ALA's Washington, DC, branch office tries to influence federal legislative policy to ensure the public's right to free access to information. The group was founded in 1876.

EXECUTIVES

Executive Director: Keith Michael Fiels
President: Camila A. Alire
President-Elect: Roberta A. Stevens
Director Operations and Support: Alex Companio
Director Information Technology and Telecommunication Services: Sherri L. Vanyek
Director Office for Information Technology Policy: Alan Inouye
Director Office of Diversity: Miguel Figueroa
Director Public Information Office: Mark R. Gould
Director Office for Literacy and Outreach Services: Satia M. Orange
Director Development Office: Kim Olsen-Clark
Director Office for Accreditation: Karen L. O'Brien

Director Office of Chapter and International Relations: Michael P. Dowling
Director Office for Library Advocacy: Marci Merola
Director Membership Development: John F. Chrastka
Director Human Resources: Cynthia Vivian
Director Office of Government Relations: Lynne E. Bradley
Secretariat: Eileen R. Hardy
Controller: Russell D. (Russ) Swedowski
Treasurer: Rodney M. (Rod) Hersberger

LOCATIONS

HQ: American Library Association
   50 E. Huron St., Chicago, IL 60611
Phone: 312-944-6780   **Fax:** 312-440-9374
Web: www.ala.org

American Media

These publications cover gossip and good health. American Media is the nation's top publisher of tabloid newspapers and magazines, including *National Enquirer* and *Star*. It also publishes women's health magazine *Shape*, as well as a number of other magazines such as *Flex, Men's Fitness,* and *Natural Health*. In addition to publishing, American Media offers distribution services to other publishers to get their periodicals in the racks at supermarkets throughout the US and Canada. American Media is owned by a group of investment firms including Angelo, Gordon & Co.

American Media has struggled for the past several years with declining readership and advertising, despite attempts to revamp its core publications, *Star* and *National Enquirer*, into celebrity gossip papers. The company also labors under mounting debt as a result of its $350 million acquisition of several fitness magazines from Weider Publications (formerly part of Weider Health & Fitness) in 2003.

In an effort to avoid bankruptcy, the company restructured its debt early in 2009 by selling a 95% stake to Angelo, Gordon and a group of other bondholders. American Media had been owned by EMP Group LLC, a holding company controlled by private equity firms Evercore Partners and Thomas H. Lee.

The company has also put several of its titles on the auction block, including *Country Weekly, Muscle & Fitness, Flex, Muscle & Fitness Hers,* and Spanish language paper *Mira!* It sold the tabloid *Weekly World News* in 2008 to a private investment group led by former National Lampoon executive Neil McGinness. The company hopes the disposals will help it focus on its core publications and it plans to use the funds to pay down debt. In addition, American Media moved the editorial headquarters of the *Enquirer* from New York City back to Florida as part of a cost-cutting move.

Meanwhile, American Media is trying to expand its holdings to include online publishing operations. It formed a joint venture with Integrity Multimedia in 2008 to acquire and operate the Web site Radar Online. It hopes to build the site into a destination for pop culture and celebrity news. The deal came as Integrity had pulled the plug on a print version of *Radar* magazine.

EXECUTIVES

Chairman and CEO: David J. Pecker, age 57
EVP Finance, Chief Accounting Officer, and Treasurer: Chris Polimeni
EVP and Chief Marketing Officer: Kevin Hyson, age 59
EVP and Co-Publishing Director, AMI Enthusiast Group: Laya Clark
EVP and Co-Publishing Directors, AMI Enthusiast Group: Chris Scardino
EVP: John Swider, age 49
EVP Consumer Marketing: David W. (Dave) Leckey, age 56
EVP and Managing Editor, RadarOnline: David Perel
SVP and CIO: Dave Thompson
VP and Publisher, Men's Fitness: Marc Richards
VP and Publisher, Star Magazine: David Jackson
President and CEO, DSI: Michael J. (Mike) Porche, age 52
Human Resources: Ken Slivken
General Counsel: Michael Antonello
Auditors: Deloitte & Touche LLP

LOCATIONS

HQ: American Media, Inc.
1000 American Media Way, Boca Raton, FL 33464
Phone: 561-997-7733
Web: www.americanmediainc.com

PRODUCTS/OPERATIONS

2008 Sales

	$ mil.	% of total
Circulation	271.7	55
Advertising	181.5	37
Other	37.6	8
Total	**490.8**	**100**

2008 Sales

	$ mil.	% of total
Tabloids	140.7	28
Celebrity publications	127.7	26
Women's health & fitness	85.5	17
Distribution services	33.0	7
Other	112.6	22
Adjustments	(8.7)	—
Total	**490.8**	**100**

Selected Publications

Newspapers
  Globe
  National Enquirer
  National Examiner
Celebrity publications
  Country Weekly
  Star
Women's health and fitness
  Fit Pregnancy
  Shape
Other
  Flex
  Men's Fitness
  Mira!
  Muscle & Fitness
  Muscle & Fitness Hers
  Natural Health
  Sun

COMPETITORS

Bauer Publishing USA
Condé Nast
Lagardère Active
Meredith Corporation
Northern and Shell
Rodale
Time Inc.
TMZ
Wenner Media

American Medical Association

The AMA knows whether there's a doctor in the house. The American Medical Association (AMA) prescribes the standards for the medical profession. The membership organization's activities include advocacy for physicians, promoting ethics standards in the medical community, and improving health care education. Policies are set by the AMA's House of Delegates, which is made up mainly of elected representatives. The AMA also publishes books and products for physicians, is a partner in the Medem online physician network, sells medical malpractice insurance, and helps doctors fight legal claims. The organization was founded in 1847 by a physician to establish a code of medical ethics. The AMA has some 236,000 members.

The group has been an active and vocal participant concerning health care and insurance reform. National campaigns, such as the "Voice for the Uninsured," waged by the AMA call attention to deficiencies in our health care system.

As part of the AMA, affiliated groups have sprouted to support the association and fund some of its efforts. The American Medical Association Alliance is a large grassroots group established to support and represent physician spouses. The AMA Foundation, founded in 1950, funds medical education, research, and service through its focus on health care. AMA extends its reach internationally through its AMA Office of International Medicine, established in 1978.

EXECUTIVES

President: J. James Rohack
CEO and EVP: Michael D. Maves
COO: Bernard L. Hengesbaugh
CFO: Denise Hagerty
SVP and Chief Marketing Officer: Marietta Parenti
SVP Membership, Publishing, and Business Services: Robert A. Musacchio
SVP Human Resources and Corporate Services: Robert W. (Bob) Davis
SVP Professional Standards: Modena H. Wilson
SVP Advocacy Group: Richard A. Deem
SVP Scientific Publications and Multimedia Applications, and Chief Editor, JAMA: Catherine D. De Angelis
VP Governance and Program Support: Robin J. Menes
VP Executive Offices and Chief, Staff: Jon Burkhart
VP External Communications: Michael Lynch
General Counsel: Jon Ekdahl
Director Media Relations: Brenda Craine
Auditors: Deloitte & Touche LLP

LOCATIONS

HQ: American Medical Association
515 N. State St., Chicago, IL 60610
Phone: 312-464-5000   **Fax:** 312-464-4184
Web: www.ama-assn.org

PRODUCTS/OPERATIONS

2008 Revenues

	$ mil.	% of total
Royalties & credentialing products	65.0	23
Books, newsletters & online product sales	50.4	18
Membership dues	44.0	16
Insurance commissions	32.9	12
Advertising	31.1	11
Other publishing revenue	18.1	6
Subscriptions	15.0	5
Investments	12.7	5
Grants & other	12.3	4
Sponsored revenue	0.3	—
Equity in profit of unconsolidated subsidiary	0.2	—
Total	**282.0**	**100**

HISTORICAL FINANCIALS

Company Type: Association

Income Statement

FYE: December 31

	REVENUE ($ mil.)	NET INCOME ($ mil.)	NET PROFIT MARGIN	EMPLOYEES
12/08	282	(100)	—	1,155
12/07	290	50	17.4%	1,121
12/06	286	25	8.8%	1,114
12/05	280	—	—	—
12/04	270	—	—	—
Annual Growth	**1.1%**	—	—	**1.8%**

Net Income History

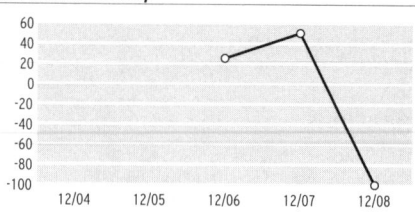

American Seafoods

With operations in the northern Pacific (*i.e.*, in the Bering Sea and Aleutian Islands), American Seafoods Group casts a bountiful net. The company offers frozen and processed fish such as Alaska pollock, Pacific whiting, Pacific cod, sea and bay scallops, haddock, sole, and farm-raised tilapia and catfish. It operates its own fleet of ships that process and freeze the catch while at sea, as well as a fleet of transport trucks. American Seafoods' land-based operations in Massachusetts makes breaded seafood products. It sells its fish under the American Pride and Frionor brand names in North America, Asia, and Europe.

American Seafoods' customers include retail food operations and club stores, wholesalers, restaurants, and foodservice operators. The company also harvests fish eggs (roe) for sale to markets mainly in Japan. It operates sales offices in the US, Japan, and Europe.

Due to poor catfish sales and subsequent falling prices for the product, in 2009 the company sold its Alabama-based Southern Pride Catfish farming operations to Heartland Catfish in Mississippi.

EXECUTIVES

Chairman and CEO: Bernt O. Bodal, age 55
CFO and Treasurer: Brad D. Bodenman, age 45
Chief Legal Officer and General Counsel:
  Matthew D. Latimer, age 40
VP Sales: Robert Hatcher
VP Development, American Pride Seafoods: David Bleth
VP IT: Dar Khalighi
VP Sales: Thomas Wilson
VP Human Resources: Tammy French
VP: Benny Bishop
VP Treasury and Compliance: Glenn Sumida
VP Finance and Administration, American Pride
  Seafoods: Bob Myatt
President, American Pride Seafoods and American
  Seafoods International: John Cummings, age 53
President, American Seafoods Company:
  Inge Andreassen, age 45
Auditors: KPMG LLP

LOCATIONS

HQ: American Seafoods Group LLC
  Marketplace Tower, 2025 1st Ave., Ste. 900
  Seattle, WA 98121
Phone: 206-374-1515   **Fax:** 206-374-1516
Web: www.americanseafoods.com

PRODUCTS/OPERATIONS

Selected Products and Species Used

Fishmeal
  Alaska pollock
  Pacific whiting
  Yellowfin sole
Fillet block
  Alaska pollock
  Pacific cod
  Pacific whiting
Headed + Gutted (H+G)
  Flathead sole
  Rock sole
  Yellowfin sole
Roe
  Alaska pollock
  Pacific cod
Shatterpack fillets
  Alaska pollock
  Pacific cod
Surimi
  Alaska pollock
  Pacific whiting

COMPETITORS

Alyeska Seafoods
Arrowac Fisheries
Icelandic Group
Icicle Seafoods
Maruha Nichiro
Nippon Suisan Kaisha
North Pacific Seafoods
Ocean Beauty Seafoods
Pacific Seafood Group
Red Chamber Co.
Santa's Smokehouse
Seafreeze
Thai Union
Trident Seafoods

HISTORICAL FINANCIALS

Company Type: Private

Income Statement				FYE: December 31
	REVENUE ($ mil.)	NET INCOME ($ mil.)	NET PROFIT MARGIN	EMPLOYEES
12/08	600	—	—	—
12/07	550	—	—	—
Annual Growth	9.1%	—	—	—

Revenue History

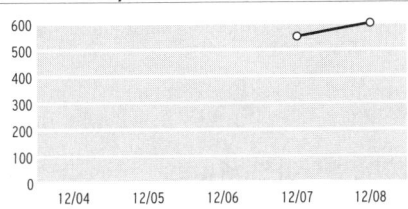

American Tire Distributors

American Tire Distributors Holdings' business starts where the rubber meets the road. The company, through its American Tire Distributors (ATD) unit, is one of the largest independent tire wholesalers in the US. Offerings include the flagship brands of industry leaders Bridgestone, Continental, Goodyear, and Michelin, as well as budget brands and private-label tires. Tires account for about 90% of the company's sales. ATD also markets custom wheels and tire service equipment. It maintains about 100 distribution centers that serve independent tire dealers, retail chains, and auto service facilities in some 40 states. Investment firm Investcorp owns the company.

To focus on wholesale tire operations, ATD is fine-tuning its business lines. The company in June 2009 unloaded its retail chain of more than 25 Autotire Car Care Centers to Monro Muffler Brake for $10 million. The stores, which are located in the St. Louis area, were part of ATD's $75 million acquisition of Am-Pac Tire Dist. from Tokyo-based ITOCHU. (The distribution centers that were also part of the Am-Pac purchase were integrated into ATD's network.)

The company has grown steadily over the years by picking up smaller regional players. Its network of distribution centers has expanded in the South, especially in Texas and Oklahoma, thanks to the 2008 acquisitions of Am-Pac Tire Dist. and Remington Tire Distributors (dba Gray's Wholesale Tire). In 2007 ATD purchased distribution centers in Colorado, Florida, Louisiana, and Texas.

COO William Berry took over as the firm's president and CEO in April 2009, succeeding chairman Dick Johnson. Leaving the company with retirement in mind, Johnson will retain his position as chairman of ATD until 2011.

Investcorp bought ATD in 2005 and formed American Tire Distributors Holdings in conjunction with the acquisition.

EXECUTIVES

Chairman: Richard P. (Dick) Johnson, age 61
President and CEO: William E. (Bill) Berry, age 54
EVP and CFO: David L. Dyckman, age 44
EVP, General Counsel, and Secretary:
  J. Michael (Mike) Gaither, age 56

SVP Marketing: Ron Sinclair
SVP Procurement: Dan Seitler
SVP Administration and Pricing: Jason Shannon
SVP Sales: Roland Boyette
SVP Eastern Division Manager: Keith Calcagno
SVP Sales: Daniel K. (Dan) Brown, age 55
SVP Operations: John Flowers
SVP Western Division Manager: Jim Williams
SVP Marketing and Procurement:
  Phillip E. (Phil) Marrett, age 58
Auditors: PricewaterhouseCoopers LLP

LOCATIONS

HQ: American Tire Distributors Holdings, Inc.
  12200 Herbert Wayne Ct., Ste. 150
  Huntersville, NC 28078
Phone: 704-992-2000   **Fax:** 704-992-1384
Web: www.americantiredistributors.com

PRODUCTS/OPERATIONS

2008 Sales

	% of total
Tires	91
Custom wheels	5
Equipment, tools & supplies	4
Total	**100**

Selected Products

Equipment, tools and supplies (valve stems, auto lifts)
Tires
Wheel covers
Wheel Wizard (computer program allowing customers to virtually see wheel types on their vehicle)

COMPETITORS

Dealer Tire
TBC
TCI Tire Centers
Treadways
Wal-Mart

HISTORICAL FINANCIALS

Company Type: Private

Income Statement			FYE: Saturday nearest December 31	
	REVENUE ($ mil.)	NET INCOME ($ mil.)	NET PROFIT MARGIN	EMPLOYEES
12/08	1,961	10	0.5%	2,900
12/07	1,878	1	0.1%	2,400
12/06	1,578	(5)	—	2,100
12/05	1,151	(2)	—	2,127
12/04	1,282	25	1.9%	2,071
Annual Growth	11.2%	(21.1%)	—	8.8%

Net Income History

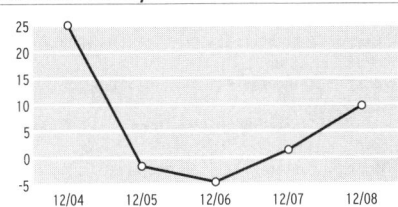

American United Mutual Insurance

There are 50 states, but only OneAmerica. American United Mutual Insurance Holding Company is primarily a life insurer whose operating units do business under the OneAmerica Financial Partners banner. The company offers individual life insurance, disability and long-term-care coverage, and annuities. For businesses the company offers employee benefits, medical stop-loss coverage, retirement plans, and group life insurance. Its subsidiaries include American United Life Insurance, The State Life Insurance Company, OneAmerica Securities, Pioneer Mutual Life Insurance, and R.E. Moulton. The company operates in 49 states and Washington, DC.

The insurer restructured into mutual holding company ownership in 2000, a move that has not only given it a more favorable tax status, but has allowed it to form and acquire stock subsidiaries.

Flagship insurer American United Life was formed in the 1936 merger of United Mutual Life Insurance and American Central Life Insurance.

As OneAmerica, the company has an appetite for acquisitions. Purchases include the life, long-term care, and annuity business of Golden Rule Insurance (2005); medical stop-loss insurer R.E. Moulton and the group life and disability insurance business of The Union Central Life Insurance Company (2003); and Pioneer Mutual Life Insurance (2002).

The company had agreed to acquire mutual life insurer Shenandoah Life in 2008, but OneAmerica terminated the deal the following year shortly before Shenandoah Life was placed in receivership by the state of Virginia due to financial difficulties brought on by the US mortgage and credit crises.

American United Mutual Insurance Company exited the reinsurance business in 2002.

EXECUTIVES

Chairman, President, and CEO: Dayton H. Molendorp, age 62
Chairman Emeritus: Jerry D. Semler
CFO, OneAmerica Financial: J. Scott Davison
SVP and Chief Actuary: David A. Brentlinger
SVP Retirement Services, OneAmerica Financial: William F. Yoerger
SVP Investments, OneAmerica Financial: G. David Sapp
SVP Individual Operations, OneAmerica; President, State Life: Mark A. Wilkerson
SVP Corporate Finance, OneAmerica Financial: Constance E. Lund
SVP Human Resources, OneAmerica Financial: Mark C. Roller
VP and Chief Marketing Officer, OneAmerica Financial: Brian J. Lauber
VP Strategic Planning, OneAmerica Financial: Victoria I. Yamasaki
VP Systems and CIO, OneAmerica Financial: Emet C. Talley
VP Employee Benefits Division: Leonard A. Cavallaro
General Counsel and Corporate Secretary, OneAmerica Financial: Thomas M. Zurek
Auditors: PricewaterhouseCoopers LLP

LOCATIONS

HQ: American United Mutual Insurance Holding Company
1 American Sq., Indianapolis, IN 46206
Phone: 317-285-1111   **Fax:** 317-285-1728
Web: www.aul.com

PRODUCTS/OPERATIONS

2008 Revenues

	$ mil.	% of total
Net investment income	584.2	52
Premiums & other considerations	342.9	30
Policy & contract charges	181.0	16
Realized investment losses	(20.6)	—
Other income	22.4	2
Total	**1,109.9**	**100**

Selected Subsidiaries and Affiliates

American United Life Insurance Company (life insurance and annuities)
OneAmerica Securities, Inc. (broker and investment advisor)
Pioneer Mutual Life Insurance Company (individual life insurance and annuities)
R.E. Moulton, Inc. (stop-loss insurance; group life, health and disability insurance)
The State Life Insurance Company (individual long-term care insurance)

COMPETITORS

Aetna
CNA Financial
John Hancock Financial Services
Lincoln Financial Group
MassMutual
MetLife
Mutual of America
Nationwide Financial
New York Life
Northwestern Mutual
Ohio National
Principal Financial
Prudential
Reliance Standard
Securian Financial
Security Benefit Group
Unity Mutual Life

HISTORICAL FINANCIALS

Company Type: Mutual company

Income Statement

FYE: December 31

	ASSETS ($ mil.)	NET INCOME ($ mil.)	INCOME AS % OF ASSETS	EMPLOYEES
12/08	18,494	40	0.2%	—
12/07	19,921	88	0.4%	—
12/06	18,491	68	0.4%	—
12/05	17,607	62	0.4%	—
12/04	15,028	56	0.4%	1,800
Annual Growth	**5.3%**	**(8.5%)**	**—**	**—**

2008 Year-End Financials

Equity as % of assets: —
Return on assets: 0.2%
Return on equity: —
Long-term debt ($ mil.): —
Sales ($ mil.): 1,110

Net Income History

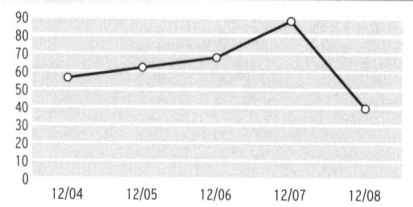

Amscan Holdings

Amscan Holdings caters to the party animal in all of us. The company makes party goods, such as balloons, invitations, piñatas, stationery, and tableware, and supplies party superstores and other retailers worldwide. It operates production and distribution facilities in Asia, Australia, Europe, and North America. Amscan also markets its products through about 900 company-owned or franchised stores in the US, Puerto Rico, and Dubai. Shops operate under the Party City, Party America, Factory Card & Party Outlet, and Halloween USA banners, among others. Amscan is a subsidiary of AAH Holdings, which is controlled by Berkshire Partners and Weston Presidio.

Amscan has grown its retail business primarily through acquisitions. In 2007 the company purchased Factory Card & Party Outlet for $72 million. The chain operates as a separate entity. Other significant deals include Amscan's acquisitions of Party City in 2005 and Party America in 2006.

To strengthen its presence, Amscan in 2009 planned to open at least five company-owned retail stores, and it expected franchisees would add up to 10 locations. The company also streamlined its operations in 2008, selling four retail stores in the Salt Lake City market to Zurcher's Merchandise Company, a regional operator of party supply shops. As part of the deal, Zurcher's entered into a seven-year agreement to purchase merchandise from Amscan.

Halloween helps to scare up revenues for the retailer near the end of the year. The ghoulish holiday's decorations and related merchandise typically account for about 20% of Amscan's annual sales. To capitalize on its top selling season, the company operates about 150 temporary stores under the Halloween USA banner, primarily from September through November. It also offers an array of Halloween-related merchandise throughout the year at its other stores.

Although its generates about 15% of its wholesale revenue from international operations, Amscan is banking on opportunities in Asia, Canada, Europe, Mexico, and the UK to push that figure upward. The company looks to expand its distribution network and broaden its offerings for local holidays and tastes to achieve this end.

Berkshire and Weston Presidio sold a nearly 40% stake in the company to global buyout fund Advent International in August 2008.

EXECUTIVES

Chairman: Robert J. (Rob) Small, age 42
CEO and Director: Gerald C. (Jerry) Rittenberg, age 57, $3,729,400 total compensation
President, COO, and Director: James M. Harrison, age 57, $2,909,000 total compensation
CFO: Michael A. Correale, age 51, $666,700 total compensation
Auditors: Ernst & Young LLP

LOCATIONS

HQ: Amscan Holdings, Inc.
80 Grasslands Rd., Elmsford, NY 10523
Phone: 914-345-2020   **Fax:** 914-345-3884
Web: www.amscan.com

2008 Sales

	$ mil.	% of total
Domestic	1,499.4	95
Foreign	83.5	5
Eliminations	(23.2)	—
Total	**1,559.7**	**100**

PRODUCTS/OPERATIONS

2008 Stores

	No.
Company-owned	643
Franchised	273
Total	**916**

2008 Sales

	$ mil.	% of total
Retail	653.4	37
Wholesale	1,099.1	63
Adjustments	(192.8)	—
Total	**1,559.7**	**100**

2008 Sales

	% of total
Party goods & stationery	77
Metallic balloons	20
Gifts	3
Total	**100**

Selected Products

Party goods
  Candles
  Cascades and centerpieces
  Crepe
  Cutouts
  Flags and banners
  Latex balloons
  Party favors
  Piñatas
Stationery
  Baby and wedding memory books
  Decorative tissues
  Gift wrap, bows, and bags
  Invitations, notes, and stationery
  Photo albums
  Ribbons
  Stickers and confetti
Metallic balloons
  18-inch standard
  Bouquets
  Sing-A-Tune
Gifts
  Ceramic giftware
  Decorative candles
  Decorative frames
  Mugs

COMPETITORS

American Greetings
Celebrate Express
CSS Industries
CTI Industries
Garden Ridge
Hallmark
iParty
Kmart
Michaels Stores
Solo Cup
Target
Walgreen
Wal-Mart

HISTORICAL FINANCIALS

Company Type: Private

Income Statement

FYE: December 31

	REVENUE ($ mil.)	NET INCOME ($ mil.)	NET PROFIT MARGIN	EMPLOYEES
12/08	1,560	41	2.6%	14,130
12/07	1,247	19	1.5%	12,569
12/06	1,015	6	0.6%	8,138
12/05	418	12	2.9%	6,720
12/04	399	8	1.9%	1,750
Annual Growth	**40.6%**	**51.4%**	**—**	**68.6%**

2008 Year-End Financials

Debt ratio: 134.3%
Return on equity: —
Cash ($ mil.): —
Current ratio: —
Long-term debt ($ mil.): 551

Net Income History

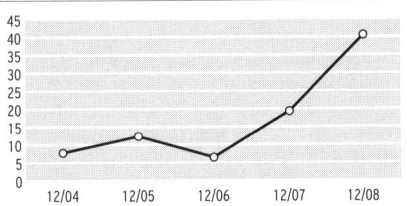

Amsted Industries

Wilbur and Orville Wright's first flight might never have succeeded without an assist from Amsted Industries' Diamond Chain subsidiary. A maker of bicycle and industrial roller chains, Diamond Chain produced the propeller chain for the Wright brothers' aircraft. The company's three diverse segments manufacture highly engineered industrial components for locomotive and railcar manufacturers, automotive OEMs, and construction and building markets. Amsted is a major force in making freight car undercarriages. Its main subsidiaries include ASF-Keystone, Griffin Pipe Products, and Means Industries. Employee-owned, Amsted has nearly 50 plants worldwide. North American customers account for 85% of the company's sales.

Amsted operations are underpinned by a history of making cast-steel components including wheels and tapper roller bearings for railroad companies, a lineup of vehicular parts such as steering and transmission components, and industrial supplies like pressure and sewer pipe, and cooling towers and evaporative condensers.

The company's product mix has grown primarily through acquisition. However Amsted's deal for FM Industries (a subsidiary of Progress Rail Services) in 2005 went particularly sour. The acquisition effectively removed Amsted's only railroad competitor in new end-of-car cushioning units (EOCCs). Customers cried foul claiming that the lack of competition spurred excessive pricing practices. The US Department of Justice agreed and forced Amsted to divest the assets from its purchase. In addition, Amsted was required to grant a perpetual license for its own intellectual property in EOCCs to any company that wanted to compete in making this piece of railroad equipment.

Founded as American Steel Foundries in 1902, the company united the strength of eight steel foundries across the East and Midwest. In 1962 the company decided to emphasize its manufacturing diversity, and changed its name to Amsted Industries.

EXECUTIVES

Chairman, President, and CEO: W. Robert Reum, age 66
VP People: Shirley J. Whitesell
VP Finance and CFO: Thomas E. (Tom) Bergmann, age 42
VP, General Counsel, and Secretary: Stephen R. Smith
VP and Treasurer: Matthew J. Hower
VP and Senior Tax Counsel: Marilyn D. Franson
Controller: Steven E. Obendorf
President, Burgess-Norton: Brett Vasseur
President Business Systems, Amsted Rail: Dave Liming
President, Baltimore Aircoil:
  Steven S. (Steve) Duerwachter
President, Consolidated Metco: Edward (Ed) Oeltjen
President, Amsted Rail: John Wories Jr.
President, Griffin Pipe Products: Paul T. Ciolino
President, Means Industries, Inc.: D. W. (Bill) Shaw
Auditors: PricewaterhouseCoopers

LOCATIONS

HQ: Amsted Industries Incorporated
  2 Prudential Plaza, 180 N. Stetson St., Ste. 1800
  Chicago, IL 60601
Phone: 312-645-1700   **Fax:** 312-819-8494
Web: www.amsted.com

PRODUCTS/OPERATIONS

Selected Products by Division

ASF-Keystone, Inc.
  Cast-steel freight car components
  Discharge gates
  Draft and draw gears
  Dynamic brake components
  Hot coiled steel springs and buffers
  Valves
Baltimore Aircoil Company (B.A.C.)
  Cooling towers
  Evaporative condensers
  Heat exchangers
  Ice thermal storage systems
  Industrial fluid coolers
Brenco Inc.
  Railroad track anchoring systems
  Tapered roller bearings
Burgess-Norton Manufacturing Company (BN)
  Gray and ductile iron castings
  Piston pins
  Powder metal parts
  Rocker arms and assemblies
Consolidated Metco, Inc. (ConMet)
  Aluminum permanent mold and die castings
  Axle hubs
  Door sill assemblies
  Fifth wheels and assemblies
  Instrument panels
  Sleeper cab accessories
  Spring brake flanges and pistons
  Structural molded plastic products
  Suspension components
  Transmission housings
Diamond Chain Company
  Roller chains
Griffin Pipe Products Co.
  Ductile iron pressure pipes and fittings
  Ductile iron sewer pipes
Griffin Wheel Company Inc.
  Cast steel railroad wheels
Means Industries, Inc.
  One-way clutches
  Stamped metal components
  Steering column components
  Transmission components
Unit Anchor Co.
  Railroad anchors

Amtrak

America's ambivalence toward intercity rail travel is reflected in Amtrak. The National Railroad Passenger Corporation, better known as Amtrak, carries about 29 million passengers a year. It provides intercity offerings as well as commuter rail services in several major markets. The carrier's system includes about 21,000 route miles of track, most of which is owned by freight railroads. Amtrak serves more than 500 destinations in 46 states, the District of Columbia and three Canadian provinces. Ridership and sales are on the rise, but Amtrak, a for-profit company, has never been profitable. Controlled by the US Department of Transportation, Amtrak depends on subsidies from the federal government to operate.

Through the years, some government officials have called for Amtrak to be self-sufficient, and the railroad's annual requests for federal money tend to be the subject of considerable debate in Congress. After a Bush administration proposal to end subsidies, break up Amtrak, and turn over passenger rail operations to local authorities failed to gain traction, rising gasoline prices led some lawmakers to push for an increase in Amtrak appropriations. In October 2008 President Bush signed legislation into law that funds Amtrak for five years with about $13 billion — almost double the amount of funding in the past.

Despite traveling a rocky road for many years, Amtrak had its best financial year in company history in 2008, with an almost $2 billion boost in ticket sales and the company transported about 29 million passengers in 2008 — 11% more than the year prior. Travel and ticket revenues along Amtrak's Northeast corridor posted double-digit increases in 2008.

Another boon for the rail carrier was the $1.3 billion of stimulus money earmarked for Amtrak that President Obama authorized in February 2009. With those funds, Amtrak is required to modernize infrastructure and its fleet, including returning about 100 rail cars to service. Besides Amtrak's dedicated portion of the federal money, another $8 billion is up for grabs by state programs for high-speed rail and other rail services. The Obama administration has promised an ongoing investment of about $1 billion annually for high-speed rail projects.

Before the stimulus funding, Amtrak already had been investing in its infrastructure, particularly in the northeastern US, where the company owns most of the track that it uses in the Boston-to-Washington, DC, corridor. Another focus has been a route between Philadelphia and Harrisburg, Pennsylvania, where Amtrak has worked with state authorities to make improvements needed to enable the railroad to offer high-speed service. High-demand routes in California, the Chicago area, and the Pacific Northwest also have been targeted for upgrades.

Transportation industry veteran Joseph Boardman took the helm as CEO and president in November 2008 following the resignation of Alex Kummant. Boardman, who was previously administrator of the Federal Railroad Administration, will serve for one year while the company searches for a permanent replacement.

HISTORY

US passenger train travel peaked in 1929, with 20,000 trains in operation. But the spread of automobiles, bus service, and air travel cut into business, and by the late 1960s only about 500 passenger trains remained running in the country. In 1970 the combined losses of all private train operations exceeded $1.8 billion in today's dollars. That year Congress passed the Rail Passenger Service Act, which created Amtrak to preserve America's passenger rail system. Although railroads were offered stock in the corporation for their passenger equipment, most just wrote off the loss.

Amtrak began operating in 1971 with 1,200 cars, most built in the 1950s. Although the company lost money from the outset ($153 million in 1972), it continued to be bankrolled by Uncle Sam, despite much criticism. Amtrak ordered its first new equipment in 1973, the year it also began taking over stations, yards, and service staff. The company didn't own any track until 1976, when it purchased hundreds of miles of right-of-way track from Boston to Washington, DC.

After a 1979 study showed Amtrak passengers to be by far the most heavily subsidized travelers in the US, Congress ordered the company to better utilize its resources. The 1980s saw Amtrak leasing its rights-of-way along its tracks in the Northeast corridor to telecommunications companies, which installed fiber-optic cables, and beginning mail and freight services for extra revenue.

In the early 1990s Amtrak faced a number of challenges: Midwest flooding, falling airfares, and safety concerns over a number of rail accidents, particularly the 1993 wreck of the Sunset Limited near Mobile, Alabama, in which 47 people were killed (the worst accident in Amtrak's history). In 1994 Amtrak's board of directors (at Congress' behest) adopted a plan to be free of federal support by 2002.

Amtrak's board of directors was replaced by Congress in 1997 with a seven-member Reform Board appointed by President Clinton. Chairman and president Thomas Downs resigned that year, and Tommy Thompson, then governor of Wisconsin, took over as chairman. Former Massachusetts governor Michael Dukakis was named vice chairman, and George Warrington stepped in as Amtrak's president and CEO.

Technical problems in 1999 delayed Amtrak's introduction of the Acela high-speed train in the Northeast until late 2000, when service began in the Boston-Washington corridor. In 2001 Amtrak pitched a 20-year plan, involving an annual outlay of $1.5 billion in federal funds, for expanding and modernizing its passenger service to help alleviate highway and airport congestion nationwide.

Thompson left the Amtrak board in 2001 after he was named US secretary of health and human services.

In 2002 Warrington resigned and was replaced by David Gunn, who formerly headed the metropolitan transit systems in New York and Toronto. Gunn began moving to cut costs, and he worked to secure new federal money to avert a threatened shutdown of rail service in July 2002. In 2004 the company exited the mail-carrying business, which had not been profitable.

Gunn was fired in November 2005, however, and chief engineer David Hughes was named interim president and CEO. He left the company after Alexander Kummant was made president and CEO in September 2006.

EXECUTIVES

Chairman: Thomas C. Carper
Vice Chairman: Donna McLean
President, CEO, and Director: Joseph H. Boardman
COO: William L. (Bill) Crosbie
CFO: D.J. Stadtler
CIO: Ed Trainor
VP Security Strategy and Special Operations:
William Rooney
VP Labor Relations: Joseph M. Bress
VP, General Counsel, and Corporate Secretary:
Eleanor D. Acheson
VP Strategic Partnerships and Business Development:
Anne Witt
VP Human Resources and Diversity Initiatives:
Lorraine A. Green
VP Policy and Development: Stephen J. Gardner, age 52
VP Marketing and Product Management:
Emmett H. Fremaux
VP Government Affairs and Corporate
Communications: Joseph H. (Joe) McHugh
Chief Risk Officer: James McDonnell
Auditors: KPMG LLP

LOCATIONS

HQ: National Railroad Passenger Corporation
60 Massachusetts Ave. NE, Washington, DC 20002
Phone: 202-906-3000   **Fax:** 202-906-3306
Web: www.amtrak.com

PRODUCTS/OPERATIONS

2008 Sales

	$ mil.	% of total
Passenger-related	1,955.4	80
Commuter	129.6	5
Other	340.5	14
State capital payments	27.3	1
Total	**2,452.8**	**100**

COMPETITORS

HISTORICAL FINANCIALS

Company Type: Government-owned

Income Statement				FYE: September 30
	REVENUE ($ mil.)	NET INCOME ($ mil.)	NET PROFIT MARGIN	EMPLOYEES
9/08	2,453	(1,133)	—	18,000
9/07	2,153	(1,121)	—	19,000
9/06	2,043	(1,068)	—	19,000
9/05	1,886	(1,192)	—	19,000
9/04	1,865	(1,309)	—	19,700
Annual Growth	7.1%	—	—	(2.2%)

Net Income History

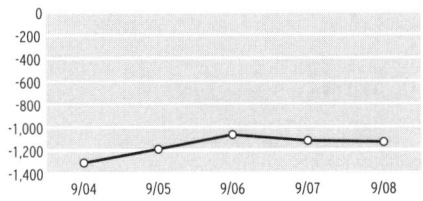

AmWINS Group

AmWINS is rarely at a loss when it comes to insurance. The company is among the largest wholesale insurance brokers in the US (along with Swett & Crawford and Crump). The group sells insurance products —including property/casualty, group benefits, and specialty coverage — to retail brokers across the country. It also provides underwriting of specialty insurance products for niches including armored cars, broadcasters, and Domino's franchise owners. The company offers additional services such as administration and actuarial services for some products. Private equity firm Parthenon Capital acquired a majority stake in AmWINS in 2005.

AmWINS property/casualty brokerage division accounts for nearly three-quarters of sales; however, its fastest-growing units (primarily through acquisitions) are its group benefits and underwriting businesses. The group benefits division administers retiree health plans, provides claims administration, and offers pharmacy benefit management services. AmWINS operates the group benefits division through its BrokerNetUSA, National Employee Benefit Companies, and WEB-TPA businesses.

AmWINS has grown its holdings of niche underwriters through a number of acquisitions over the past few years. In 2007 AmWINS purchased London American General Agency, which provides commercial transportation underwriting for limousines and truckers. AmWINS expanded even further into underwriting with the 2008 acquisition of Beacon Risk Strategies, a Seattle-based underwriter that specializes in protecting companies and their health plans from unexpected catastrophic claims.

Then, in 2009, AmWINS acquired American Stop Loss Insurance Brokerage Services, Health Benefit Solutions Insurance, and National Insurance Wholesalers; merged them, and in one fell swoop created the nation's largest wholesale broker of medical stop loss insurance.

Earlier acquisitions include Stewart Smith Group, the US wholesale insurance unit of

Willis Group Holdings; that deal was part of an industry-wide trend in which retail insurance brokers (such as Willis) divested wholesale holdings to remove any appearance of a conflict of interest.

Former chairman Ernie Telford and CEO Steve DeCarlo founded American Wholesale Insurance Group in 2002 by combining several specialty wholesale insurance firms. AmWINS proposed an initial public offering in 2006, but withdrew its registration in 2007.

EXECUTIVES

CEO: M. Steven (Steve) DeCarlo
President: W.H. (Skip) Cooper
VP, CFO, and Secretary: Scott M. Purviance
General Counsel: Donna L. Hargrove
Director of Human Resources: Kristin L. Downey
President, Transportation Underwriters: Joe Hutelmyer
President, BrokerNetUSA: Paul E. Morse
President, Woodus K. Humphrey & Co.: Dick Chilvers
President, AmWINS Program Underwriters:
 Ben Francavilla
President, Brokerage Division: James Drinkwater
President, Property Risk Services: Tom Spinner Jr.
President, AmWINS Healthcare: Mike Walton
President, Group Benefits Division:
 Samuel H. (Sam) Fleet
Auditors: PricewaterhouseCoopers LLP

LOCATIONS

HQ: AmWINS Group, Inc.
 4725 Piedmont Row Dr., Ste. 600
 Charlotte, NC 28210
Phone: 704-749-2700　　**Fax:** 704-943-9000
Web: www.amwins.com

Selected Operations

American Equity Underwriters
Beacon Risk Strategies
BrokerNetUSA
NEBCO
Web TPA
Woodus K. Humphrey & Company

COMPETITORS

Aon
Arthur Gallagher
Brown & Brown
Burns & Wilcox
CRC Insurance
Crump Group
Marsh & McLennan
Swett & Crawford
Willis Group

Anaheim Ducks

Officially these Ducks are no longer Mighty, but they are still a pretty good hockey team. Formerly known as The Mighty Ducks of Anaheim, the Anaheim Ducks Hockey Club joined the National Hockey League as an expansion team in 1993. Anaheim made its first playoff appearance in 1997 and reached the Stanley Cup finals in 2003 (losing to the New Jersey Devils); the team captured its first NHL championship in 2007. The Ducks franchise was originally granted to entertainment goliath Walt Disney, which

named the team after its 1992 hockey film, *The Mighty Ducks*. Billionaire Henry Samueli — who co-founded computer chip maker Broadcom — and his wife Susan purchased the franchise from Disney in 2005.

With a Stanley Cup championship under its belt and a playoff contender on the ice, the Ducks team has continued to draw capacity crowds at Honda Center in Anaheim. The arena, previously known as the Arrowhead Pond of Anaheim, was renamed in 2006 when American Honda Motor Co. signed a 15-year, $60 million naming-rights deal. That was the same year Samueli changed the name of the team for the start of the 2006-07 season to help market the hockey franchise to new fans.

The team's owner has been suspended by the NHL, however, pending the outcome of a criminal case involving stock options backdating at Broadcom. The former chairman of the company, Samueli, has been charged with lying to investigators looking into the $2.2 billion financial scandal.

Disney's short-lived flirtation with professional sports, which also included the Anaheim Angels baseball team (now carrying the labor-intensive moniker Los Angeles Angels of Anaheim), was a strategy designed to create new revenue streams while providing programming for its television stations. ABC and ESPN, both Disney-owned networks, paid $600 million for the television rights to NHL games, but ratings were so poor that they dropped out of the broadcast scheme following the 2004 season. The media company sold the Angels in 2003.

EXECUTIVES

CEO; Chairman, Anaheim Arena Management:
 Michael Schulman
EVP and COO; President and CEO, Anaheim Arena Management: Tim Ryan
EVP and General Manager: Bob Murray
SVP and Chief Marketing Officer: Bob Wagner
Head Coach: Randy Carlyle
VP Sales and Marketing: Steve Obert
VP Finance: Doug Heller
VP Human Resources: Kim Kutcher
Director Fan Development: Matt Savant
Director Marketing: Tracie Jones
Director Finance: Mike McGee
Director Sales and Marketing: Michael Williams
Director Media and Communications: Alex Gilchrist
Director Human Resources: Jenny Price
Director Broadcasting: Aaron Teats

LOCATIONS

HQ: Anaheim Ducks Hockey Club, LLC
 2695 E. Katella Ave., Anaheim, CA 92806
Phone: 714-704-2700　　**Fax:** 714-704-2754
Web: www.anaheimducks.com

PRODUCTS/OPERATIONS

Championship Trophies
Stanley Cup (2007)
Clarence S. Campbell Bowl (2003, 2007)

COMPETITORS

Dallas Stars
Los Angeles Kings
Phoenix Coyotes
San Jose Sharks

Andersen Corporation

Windows of opportunity open daily for Andersen, a well-known maker of wood-clad windows and patio doors in North America. Andersen offers window designs from hinged, bay, and double-hung to skylight, gliding, and picture windows. Its Renewal by Andersen subsidiary provides start-to-finish window renewal services, including in-home consultations, in more than 100 markets in the US. Subsidiary EMCO Doors makes storm and screen doors. Through independent and company-owned distributorships (including its Andersen Logistics division), Andersen sells to homeowners, architects, builders, designers, and remodelers. The company is owned by the Andersen family, the Andersen Foundation, and company employees.

Andersen competes in the marketplace by building strong brand recognition for its products. The company offers products that are available in more than 600,000 unique shapes and styles; it builds some 12 million doors and windows annually from more than 15 factories.

Acquisitions, too, play an important role in the company's growth strategy. In 2006 it bought Silver Line Building Products, a maker of vinyl window products. The move was a departure for Andersen, which had hitherto concentrated on its wooden windows. (Vinyl is the fastest-growing segment of the window industry.) The previous year, the company bought Eagle Window & Door, a maker of aluminum clad windows and patio doors.

Other units include Canada-based roof window and skylight maker and distributor Dashwood Industries, and specialty window manufacturer KML Windows. Through its Aspen Research subsidiary, Andersen analyzes composite materials development, product life-cycle management, and waste elimination and reclamation.

Andersen's annual profit-sharing program has been in operation since it was established in 1914, with the exception of the Depression-era years from 1929 to 1936.

HISTORY

Danish immigrant Hans Andersen and his two sons, Fred and Herbert, founded Andersen in 1903. Andersen's first words in English, "All together, boys," became the company motto. Andersen arrived in Portland, Maine, in 1870 and worked as a lumber dealer and manufacturer. In the 1880s he bought a sawmill in St. Cloud, Minnesota, and later managed one in Hudson, Wisconsin. When the Hudson mill owners asked him to let workers go during the off season, Andersen refused and then resigned. He subsequently launched his own lumber business — Andersen Lumber Company — in 1903 and hired some of the men who had been laid off. He opened a second lumberyard, in Afton, Minnesota, in 1904.

Andersen and his sons revolutionized the window industry in the early 1900s by introducing a standardized window frame with interchangeable parts. Buoyed by success, the Andersens sold their lumberyards in 1908 to focus on the window-frame business. (Andersen purchased lumberyards again in 1916 before exiting the lumberyard business for good in the 1930s.) Around 1913 the company moved from Hudson to South Stillwater (now Bayport), Minnesota.

Thrifty Hans launched the company's first (and the US's third) profit-sharing plan shortly before his death in 1914. Herbert became VP, secretary, treasurer, and factory manager, and Fred became president. Herbert died in 1921 (at age 36), but Fred proved to be a versatile and capable successor. Among his accomplishments, Fred came up with the tag line "Only the rich can afford poor windows."

In 1929 the company changed its name to Andersen Frame Corporation. In the following decade Andersen introduced a number of innovations, including Master Frame (a frame with a locked sill joint, 1930); a casement window, the industry's first complete factory-made window unit (1932); and a basement window (1934). The company adopted its current name in 1937.

Andersen introduced the gliding window concept in the early 1940s. It also launched the Home Planners Scrap Book consumer ad campaign in 1943. During the 1950s Andersen's new products included the Flexivent awning window, which featured welded insulating glass that served as an alternative to traditional storm windows. In the 1960s the company produced a gliding door and introduced the Perma-Shield system. The system featured easy-to-maintain vinyl cladding to protect wood frames from weathering. By 1978 Perma-Shield products accounted for three-quarters of sales. Fred, who had run the company as president until 1960 and had subsequently held the positions of chairman and chairman emeritus, died in 1979 at age 92.

Between 1984 and 1994 the company increased its sales threefold by introducing additional customized and state-of-the-art products, including patio doors. In 1995 it launched Renewal by Andersen, a retail window-replacement business.

Andersen acquired former long-term strategic partner Aspen Research (materials testing, research, and product development) in 1997. Among its jointly developed products is Fibrex, a composite material used in replacement windows. Also in 1997 the company moved its international division office from Bayport, Minnesota, to the Minnesota World Trade Center in St. Paul to help boost its export drive.

In 1998 company veteran Donald Garofalo succeeded Andersen's president and CEO Jerold Wulf, who retired after 39 years with the company. Andersen reinforced its company-owned distributorships in 1999 when it bought millwork distributors Morgan Products (now Andersen Logistics) and Independent Millwork.

Expanding its product offerings, Andersen purchased privately held EMCO Enterprises (storm doors and accessories, Iowa) in 2001. Other acquisitions from 1993 to 2003 included Dashwood Industries (windows, skylights, roof windows, doors; Canada) and KML Windows (architectural windows and doors, Canada). The company also opened a new production facility in Menomonie, Wisconsin.

At the close of 2002, Andersen's COO James Humphrey was promoted to president, becoming the company's ninth president; he gained the added role of chief executive the next year.

Andersen celebrated its 100th year in 2003, publishing a book on its history, and the company kicked off a community project to build 100 Habitat for Humanity homes throughout North America over a period of five years (it met that goal in 2007).

EXECUTIVES

Chairman and CEO: James E. (Jim) Humphrey
President and COO: Jay Lund
EVP and CFO: Philip (Phil) Donaldson
SVP and Chief Administrative Officer: Mary D. Carter
SVP and Chief Sales and Marketing Officer:
 Craig Evanich
SVP and General Counsel: Alan Bernick
SVP; General Manager, New Traditional Products
 Division: Mary J. Schumacher
SVP and General Manager, Architectural Products
 Division: David (Dave) Beeken
VP Sales: Vic Springer
Manager Marketing: Blaine Verdoorn
Manager Corporate Affairs: Susan Roeder
Director Corporate Communications:
 Maureen McDonough
President, Renewal by Andersen: Paul Delahunt
President, Silver Line: T. Randall (Randy) Iles

LOCATIONS

HQ: Andersen Corporation
 100 4th Ave. North, Bayport, MN 55003
Phone: 651-264-5150   **Fax:** 651-264-5107
Web: www.andersenwindows.com

PRODUCTS/OPERATIONS

Selected Products and Brands

Doors
 Patio doors
  Art glass
  Frenchwood Collection (gliding, hinged, and
   outswing)
  Narroline gliding patio doors
  Perma-Shield gliding patio doors
 Screen doors
 Storm doors

Windows
 Aluminum-clad
 Art glass
 Awning
 Basement
 Bay and bow
 Casement
 Double-hung
 Fixed
 Gliding
 Horizontal sliding
 Picture
 Skylights and roof windows
 Transom
 Utility
 Wood
 Wood-clad

Selected Market Segments and Customers

Commercial (architects and building owners)
Home improvement (professional remodelers and do-it-
 yourselfers)
New residential construction (builders and contractors)
Replacement (homeowners)

Selected Companies

Andersen Logistics
Aspen Research Corporation (R&D of composite
 materials, adhesives, and coatings)
Dashwood Industries Ltd. (roof windows and skylights,
 distribution, Canada)
Eagle Window & Door (aluminum clad wood windows
 and patio doors)
EMCO Doors (all-season/storm doors and accessories)
KML Windows Inc. (architecturally designed windows
 and entranceways, Canada)
Silver Line Building Products (vinyl windows and patio
 doors)

COMPETITORS

Atrium Companies
Champion Window
Crystal Window & Door Systems
GBO
Great Lakes Window
JELD-WEN
Marshfield DoorSystems
MI Windows and Doors
Milgard Manufacturing
Pella
Ply Gem
Royal Group
Sierra Pacific Industries
Simonton Windows, Inc.
Thermal Industries
TRACO
Weather Shield Manufacturing

HISTORICAL FINANCIALS

Company Type: Private

Income Statement

	REVENUE ($ mil.)	NET INCOME ($ mil.)	NET PROFIT MARGIN	EMPLOYEES
12/08	2,500	—	—	10,000
12/07	3,000	—	—	13,000
12/06	3,000	—	—	14,000
12/05	3,000	—	—	16,000
12/04	2,500	—	—	8,500
Annual Growth	0.0%	—	—	4.1%

FYE: December 31

Revenue History

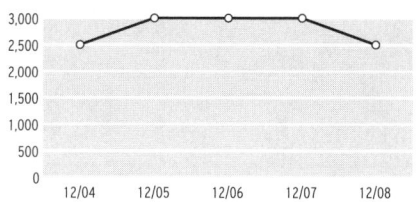

Apex Oil

Always at the top of its game, Apex Oil sells, stores, and distributes petroleum products. Its range of refined products includes asphalt, biodiesel, kerosene, fuel oil, diesel fuel, heavy oil, gasoline, and bunker fuels. The company's terminals are primarily located on the East Coast and Gulf Coast, in California, and in the Midwest. Internationally, Apex Oil has operations in the Bahamas, Monaco, and the Netherlands. The company's subsidiaries include Apex Towing, a tug boat and barge business; Petroleum Fuel and Terminal, a storage and truck rack operation; and Enjet (oil and carbon black marketing). Apex Oil is controlled by CEO Tony Novelly.

To free up cash, in 2009 Petroleum Fuel and Terminal sold its 680,000-barrel petroleum storage assets in Weirton, West Virginia to a subsidiary of World Point Terminals, also controlled by Novelly, for $9.1 million.

Apex Oil was founded in 1932 by Samuel Goldstein. Apex Oil paid $550 million for Clark Oil and Refining in 1981. Financially strapped, it sold that company in 1994.

EXECUTIVES

CEO: P. Anthony (Tony) Novelly, age 65
President and Bulk Activity, Heavy Oil:
  Edwin L. (Ed) Wahl
EVP and General Counsel: Douglas D. Hommert
VP and Treasurer: John L. Hank Jr.
Director IT: Dave Paul
Material Safety Data Sheets: Chris Casnelli
Controller: Jeffrey D. Baltz
Ethanol: Doug Berhorst
Human Resources and Benefits: Julie Cook

LOCATIONS

HQ: Apex Oil Company, Inc.
  8235 Forsyth Blvd., Ste. 400, Clayton, MO 63105
Phone: 314-889-9600   **Fax:** 314-854-8539
Web: www.apexoil.com

PRODUCTS/OPERATIONS

Major Products
Asphalt
Biodiesel
Bunker fuels
Carbon black
Diesel fuel
Fuel oil
Gasoline
Heavy oil
Kerosene

Selected Subsidiaries and Affiliates
Apex Towing Company (tugs and barges)
Clark Oil Trading Company
Enjet, Inc. (oil and carbon black)
Petroleum Fuel and Terminal Co. (storage and truck racks)
Trinidad Resort and Club

COMPETITORS

Chemoil
Crown Central
Getty Petroleum Marketing
Global Partners
Koch Industries, Inc.
Marathon Oil
Tauber Oil
U.S. Oil

APi Group

Holding company APi Group has a piece of the action in five business sectors: construction services, fire protection, special systems, manufacturing, and materials distribution. APi has more than 30 subsidiaries, which operate as independent companies. Services provided by the company's construction subsidiaries include energy conservation; electrical, industrial, and mechanical contracting; industrial insulation; and overhead door installation. Other units install fire protection systems, fabricate structural steel, and distribute building materials. The family-owned company was founded in 1926 by Reuben Anderson, father of chairman Lee Anderson.

EXECUTIVES

Chairman: Lee R. Anderson Sr.
President and CEO: Russell (Russ) Becker
COO: Paul Grunau
CFO and Treasurer: Gregory J. Keup, age 50
VP, Construction: Mark Udager
VP, Distribution: John deGrood
VP, Tessier's: Gopal Vyas
VP, Api Electric: Jeff Tyllia
VP Operations, APi Electric: Floyd Cochran
VP, International Fire Protection: Ronnie Davidson
VP, NYCO: Richard (Rick) Hansen
VP, Construction: Jerald P. (Jerry) Pederson
VP, Vipond Systems Group: Michael (Mike) Godara
VP Industrial, APi Electric: Todd Lyden
VP, Vipond Fire Protection: Grant R. Neal
VP and Controller: Scott Hatfield
VP Operations, Vipond Fire Protection:
  Bernie M. Beliveau

LOCATIONS

HQ: APi Group, Inc.
  2366 Rose Place, St. Paul, MN 55113
Phone: 651-636-4320   **Fax:** 651-636-0312
Web: www.apigroupinc.com

APi Group has more than 100 offices, plants, and warehouses in the US, Canada, and the UK.

PRODUCTS/OPERATIONS

Selected Subsidiaries
Fabrication and Manufacturing
  Anco Products, Inc. (flexible air ducts)
  Industrial Fabricators, Inc. (industrial silencers)
  LeJeune Steel Company (structural steel fabrication)
  Wisconsin Structural Steel Company
Fire Protection Systems
  Alliance Fire Protection, Inc.
  APi National Service Group
  Davis-Ulmer Sprinkler Company
  Delta Fire Systems, Inc.
  International Fire Protection, Inc.
  Rich Fire Protection Co, Inc.
  Security Fire Protection Company
  United States Fire Protection Company
  VFP Fire Systems, Inc.
  Viking Automatic Sprinkler Company
  Vipond Fire Protection, Inc. (Canada)
  Vipond Fire Protection, Ltd. (UK)
  Western States Fire Protection, Inc.
Materials Distribution
  APi Distribution (insulation and construction materials)
  ASDCO (construction materials)
Specialty Construction Services
  APi Construction Company (industrial insulation)
  APi Electric (electrical contracting)
  APi Supply, Inc. (rental, sales, service of aerial work platforms)
  Classic Industrial Services, Inc. (full-service merit shop specialty contractor)
  Doody Mechanical, Inc. (mechanical contracting, including heating, ventilation, and air-conditioning)
  Garage Door Store (residential and commercial garage and specialty doors)
  Grunau Company, Inc. (mechanical and fire protection systems)
  Industrial Contractors, Inc. (energy industry contracting)
  The Jamar Company (mechanical and specialty contracting)
  Larson Electric Systems, Inc. (electrical contracting)
  Tessier's Inc. (heating, ventilating, air conditioning installation)
  Twin City Garage Door Company (installation and servicing of overhead doors)
Systems
  APi Systems Group (fire and gas detection and security systems provider)
  Communications Systems, Inc. (security systems integration)
  Halon Banking Systems
  Northern Fire & Communication (fire alarm and communications equipment)
  Vipond Systems Group, Inc. (fire alarm and communications equipment)

COMPETITORS

ADT Worldwide
Comfort Systems USA
EMCOR
Integrated Electrical Services
Irex
John E. Green
TDIndustries
Team
Turner Industries

HISTORICAL FINANCIALS

Company Type: Private

Income Statement				FYE: December 31
	REVENUE ($ mil.)	NET INCOME ($ mil.)	NET PROFIT MARGIN	EMPLOYEES
12/08	1,600	—	—	9,000
12/07	1,000	—	—	9,000
12/06	900	—	—	5,000
Annual Growth	33.3%	—	—	34.2%

Revenue History

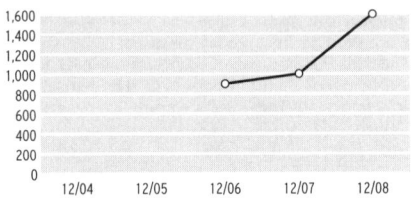

Appleton Papers

Paper is the apple of Appleton Papers' eye. The company manufactures a variety of specialty paper products through two divisions: technical papers and performance packaging. Its top product is carbonless paper (sold under the NCR Paper brand), which is used for business invoices. Appleton also makes paper embedded with security technologies and thermal paper used in point-of-sale receipts and coupons, gaming and transportation tickets, shipping labels, and medical charts. Performance packaging products include plastic films used for packaging in the food processing, household goods, and industrial products industries. Customers in the US account for about three-quarters of sales.

Appleton operates paper mills and converting plants in Ohio, Pennsylvania, and Wisconsin. It maintains distribution centers in the US, Canada, the Netherlands, and the UK. The company's papers are sold to merchant distributors that stock and redistribute those products globally. They are also sold to printers and converters that cut, print, or further process the paper for different end user needs.

Appleton Papers is 100% employee-owned. In 2001 Appleton's employees invested $107 million of their retirement funds to provide the equity portion of an $810 million buyout of the company from its France-based owner ArjoWiggins (then known as Arjo Wiggins Appleton).

The company restructured its operations in 2005 to streamline costs and position the company for growth. It also acquired packaging company New England Extrusion that year.

Its international division was formed in 2005 to focus on sales and marketing of its carbonless and thermal papers in more than 70 countries.

Part of its effort to focus on core North American products included the sale of its Bemrose subsidiary, which it had acquired with the hopes of expanding into the UK market. In 2008 Appleton sold BemroseBooth to American Industrial Acquisition Corporation, a private equity firm.

EXECUTIVES

Chairman, President, and CEO, Appleton Papers and PDC: Mark R. Richards, age 49
VP Finance, CFO, and Treasurer; CFO and Treasurer, PDC: Thomas J. Ferree, age 51
VP Marketing and Strategy: Kent E. Willetts, age 51
VP Business Development: Ted E. Goodwin
VP and General Manager, Performance Packaging: M. Kathleen (Kathy) Bolhous, age 49
VP Operations, Technical Papers Division: David B. Williams
VP Global Sales and General Manager, International Division: Sarah T. Macdonald, age 44
Controller and Assistant Treasurer; Controller, PDC: Jeffrey J. Fletcher, age 56
Auditors: PricewaterhouseCoopers LLP

LOCATIONS

HQ: Appleton Papers Inc.
825 E. Wisconsin Ave., Appleton, WI 54911
Phone: 920-734-9841 **Fax:** 920-991-7365
Web: www.appletonideas.com

2008 Sales

	$ mil.	% of total
US	695.8	72
Other countries	268.8	28
Total	**964.6**	**100**

PRODUCTS/OPERATIONS

2008 Sales

	$ mil.	% of total
Technical papers		
Coated solutions	538.0	56
Thermal papers	280.3	29
Security papers	34.0	3
Performance packaging	112.3	12
Total	**964.6**	**100**

Selected Products

Coated solutions
  Carbonless paper
    Credit card receipts
    Invoices
    NCR Paper
  Coated products
    Design and print applications
    Point-of-sale displays
Thermal and advanced technical products
  Non-thermal products
  Thermal business products
    Point-of-sale receipts and coupons
    Label products
    Lotteries and gaming tickets
    Tags for airline baggage
    Tickets
Security products
  Business documents
  Checks
  Government documents
Secure and specialized print services
  High-integrity mailing and niche publishing
  Mass transit and car parking tickets
  Security printed vouchers and payment cards
Performance packaging
  Flexible packaging materials
  Multilayered films

Selected Subsidiaries

American Plastics
C&H Packaging
New England Extrusion

COMPETITORS

ArjoWiggins	Kanzaki Specialty Papers
Asia Pulp & Paper	Mitsubishi Paper Mills
Bemis	Oji Paper
Boise Cascade	Pliant Corporation
Cascades Inc.	Printpack
De La Rue	Ricoh Company
Glatfelter	Rio Tinto Alcan
Howard Smith Paper	Winpak

HISTORICAL FINANCIALS

Company Type: Private

Income Statement				FYE: Saturday nearest December 31
	REVENUE ($ mil.)	NET INCOME ($ mil.)	NET PROFIT MARGIN	EMPLOYEES
12/08	965	(97)	—	2,210
12/07	963	(6)	—	3,001
12/06	1,087	11	1.0%	3,144
12/05	1,047	(3)	—	3,238
12/04	990	(25)	—	3,406
Annual Growth	(0.6%)	—	—	(10.2%)

Net Income History

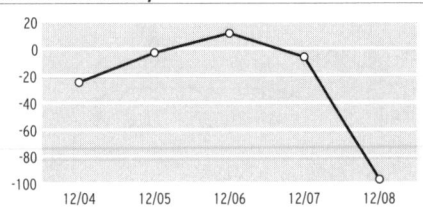

ARAMARK Corporation

Keeping employees fed and clothed is one mark of this company. ARAMARK is the world's #3 contract foodservice provider (behind Compass Group and Sodexo) and the #2 uniform supplier (behind Cintas) in the US. It offers corporate dining services and operates concessions at many sports arenas and other entertainment venues, while its ARAMARK Refreshment Services unit is a leading provider of vending and beverage services. The company also provides facilities management services. Through ARAMARK Uniform and Career Apparel, the company supplies uniforms for health care, public safety, and technology workers. Founded in 1959, ARAMARK is owned by an investment group led by chairman and CEO Joseph Neubauer.

A leader in its industry, the company continues to look for opportunities to expand not only its client base, but also to expand the number of services it supplies for its existing customers. In 2008 its concessions unit inked a deal with SMG Management to provide food and beverage services at more than 30 concert venues. ARAMARK is also targeting such industry segments as correctional facilities and health care operators.

Keen on international expansion, the company has focused on Europe and Asia, including the burgeoning market in China where it provided foodservices for the 2008 Olympic Games in Beijing. That same year ARAMARK acquired The Patman Group, expanding its reach into India. International markets now account for more than 25% of the company's revenue.

With backing from such investment firms as CCMP Capital, Thomas H. Lee Partners, and Warburg Pincus, Neubauer took the company private in 2007 for $8.3 billion, including the assumption of $2 billion in debt. (The executive already owned 40% of ARAMARK.) The deal marked the second such transaction for the company, having been taken private by Neubauer and a management group in the 1980s.

EXECUTIVES

Chairman and CEO: Joseph (Joe) Neubauer, age 67
EVP and CFO; Group Executive, ARAMARK Uniform and Career Apparel: L. Frederick Sutherland, age 57
EVP; President, ARAMARK Uniform and Career Apparel (AUCA): Thomas J. (Tom) Vozzo, age 46
EVP Human Resources: Lynn B. McKee, age 53
EVP; Group President, Global Food, Hospitality, and Facilities Services: Andrew C. Kerin, age 45
EVP and Chief Globalization Officer; President, ARAMARK International: Ravi K. Saligram, age 52
SVP, Controller, and Chief Accounting Officer: Joseph M. (Joe) Munnelly, age 44
SVP and Treasurer: Christopher S. (Chris) Holland, age 42
Corporate Executive Chef, Sports and Entertainment: Brian Stapleton
Auditors: KPMG LLP

LOCATIONS

HQ: ARAMARK Corporation
ARAMARK Tower, 1101 Market St.
Philadelphia, PA 19107
Phone: 215-238-3000   **Fax:** 215-238-3333
Web: www.aramark.com

2008 Sales

	$ mil.	% of total
US	9,998.0	74
International	3,472.2	26
Total	**13,470.2**	**100**

PRODUCTS/OPERATIONS

2008 Sales

	$ mil.	% of total
Food & support services		
North America	8,924.9	66
International	2,783.0	21
Uniform & career apparel	1,762.3	13
Total	**13,470.2**	**100**

Selected Operations

Food and support services
  ARAMARK Convention Centers
  ARAMARK Correctional Services
  ARAMARK Education
  ARAMARK Facility Services
  ARAMARK Food Services
  ARAMARK Harrison Lodging (conference centers)
  ARAMARK Healthcare
  ARAMARK Higher Education
  ARAMARK Innovative Dining Solutions
  ARAMARK Parks and Destinations
  ARAMARK Refreshment Services (vending services)
  ARAMARK Sports and Entertainment
Uniform and career apparel
  ARAMARK Cleanroom Services
  ARAMARK Uniform & Career Apparel
  Galls (tactical equipment and apparel)

COMPETITORS

ABM Industries	Elior
Alsco	G&K Services
Angelica Corporation	Healthcare Services
Autogrill	ISS A/S
Centerplate	Sodexo
Cintas	SSP
Compass Group	UniFirst
Delaware North	

HISTORICAL FINANCIALS

Company Type: Private

Income Statement			FYE: Friday nearest September 30	
	REVENUE ($ mil.)	**NET INCOME** ($ mil.)	**NET PROFIT MARGIN**	**EMPLOYEES**
9/08	13,470	40	0.3%	260,000
9/07	12,384	31	0.2%	250,000
Annual Growth	8.8%	27.8%	—	4.0%

Net Income History

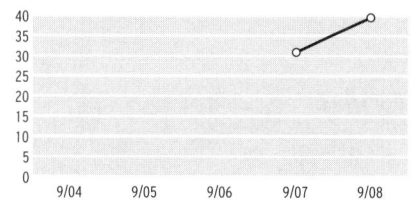

	9/04	9/05	9/06	9/07	9/08

Archstone

Archstone (formerly Archstone-Smith) is the cornerstone of Tishman Speyer and Lehman Brothers' real estate partnership. Acquired by Tishman and Lehman for $22 billion in 2007, the firm is one of the largest apartment investment companies in the US. It owns about 84,000 apartment units in areas such as Washington, DC (about 40% of its portfolio); California; New York; Seattle; and Boston. The company also offers extended-stay properties through Oakwood Worldwide. Development and investment advice is offered through its Archstone Real Estate Advisory Services arm. Lehman filed for bankruptcy in 2008 and could sell some $32 billion in real estate assets.

Before the Chapter 11 bankruptcy, which was brought on by the subprime mortgage crisis, Lehman and Archstone already had begun selling off assets, especially in the San Francisco area, to raise cash and reduce debt. Lehman's deal to buy Archstone and take it private in the first place was an example of risks Lehman took in the property market.

Archstone had been growing through acquisitions. In 2005 Archstone acquired a portfolio of 36 apartment communities from affiliates of furnished and corporate housing provider Oakwood for some $1.5 billion. It also bought three highrise apartment buildings in Manhattan and began construction on a fourth. The company dipped its toe in European real estate, buying an 11-building portfolio in Germany in anticipation of the nation's economic recovery and privatization of multifamily housing.

Archstone continued its expansion in Manhattan in 2006 with the purchase of a 13-story apartment building for $110 million. That year the REIT also expanded its holdings in Germany with the acquisition of Deutsche WohnAnlage GmbH (deWAG) for $649 million.

In 2009 the company launched its Archstone Real Estate Advisory Services division, which is focused on helping lenders and investors develop their multifamily and mixed-use assets.

Archstone got its start in 1963. Then named Archstone Communities, the company acquired DC-based apartment property owner Charles E. Smith Residential in 2001.

EXECUTIVES

Chairman and CEO: R. Scot Sellers, age 52
COO: Charles E. (Chaz) Mueller Jr., age 45
CFO: Gerald R. (Gerry) Morgan, age 45
Chief Development Officer: Alfred G. (Al) Neely, age 60
EVP Operations: David Brackett
EVP Operations, East Region: Matthew T. (Matt) Smith
Group VP Operations: Sally Matheu
President, U.S. Operations: Jack R. Callison, age 38
Managing Director, Archstone B.V.: Dana K. Hamilton, age 39
Chief Information and Marketing Officer: Daniel E. Amedro, age 51
General Counsel and Secretary: Caroline Brower, age 59
Auditors: KPMG LLP

LOCATIONS

HQ: Archstone
9200 E. Panorama Cir., Ste. 400
Englewood, CO 80112
Phone: 303-708-5959   **Fax:** 303-708-5999
Web: www.archstoneapartments.com

COMPETITORS

AMLI Residential
Apartment Investment and Management
Associated Estates Realty
AvalonBay
Boston Capital
BRE Properties
Colonial Properties
Equity Residential
Essex Property Trust
Gables Residential Trust
Intergroup
Lincoln Property
Post Properties
UDR

Arctic Slope Regional Corporation

The Inupiat people have survived the Arctic for centuries, and now they're surviving in the business world. The Inupiat-owned Arctic Slope Regional Corporation (ASRC) was set up to manage 5 million acres on Alaska's North Slope after the Alaska Native Claims Settlement Act in 1971 cleared the way for oil development in the area. ASRC gets more than two-thirds of sales from its energy services subsidiary (ASRC Energy Services) and its petroleum refining and marketing unit (Petro Star). Other operations include construction, engineering, and governmental services.

ASRC represents 10,000 members/shareholders in eight villages on the North Slope of Alaska:

Anaktuvuk Pass, Atqasuk, Barrow, Kaktovik, Nuiqsut, Point Hope, Point Lay, and Wainwright. The company seeks to adhere to Inupiat traditional values of protecting the land, the environment, and the native culture while developing economic programs.

ASRC has its head office in Barrow, with a major administrative office in Anchorage. It has other subsidiary offices in the lower 48 states.

EXECUTIVES

Chairman: Rex A. Rock Sr.
Vice Chairman: Molly Pederson
President, CEO, and Director:
  Roberta (Bobbi) Quintavell
SEVP and COO: Mark W. Kroloff
EVP and CFO: Kristin Mellinger
First VP and Director: George Sielak
Second VP and Director: George T. Kaleak
Third VP and Director: Raymond Paneak
VP, Operations: Forrest (Deano) Olemaun
VP Administration and Shareholder Relations:
  Flossie Chrestman
VP Government Affairs: Oliver Leavitt
VP and General Counsel: Alma McClellan Upicksoun
VP Lands and Natural Resources and Director:
  Richard Glenn
Director Communications: Mary Gasperlin
Treasurer and Director: Crawford Patkotak
Secretary and Director: Mary Ellen Ahmaogak
Auditors: KPMG LLP

LOCATIONS

HQ: Arctic Slope Regional Corporation
  3900 C St., Ste. 801, Anchorage, AK 99503
Phone: 907-339-6000   **Fax:** 907-339-6028
Web: www.asrc.com

Arctic Slope Regional Corporation has US offices in Alaska, Arizona, California, Maryland, New Mexico, and Oregon. It also has operations in Mexico and Venezuela.

PRODUCTS/OPERATIONS

Selected Subsidiaries

Energy services
  Alaska Petroleum Contractors
  ASRC Energy Services
  ASRC Parsons Engineering, LLC.
  Global Power and Communications
  Houston Contracting Company-Alaska, Ltd.
  Natchiq Sakhalin Ltd.
  Omega Service Industries, Inc.
  Tri Ocean Engineering, Ltd.

Engineering and construction
  Arctic Slope Construction, Inc.
  ASCG, Inc.
  ASCG Inspection, Inc.
  ASCG of New Mexico
  McLaughlin Water Engineers, Ltd.
  SKW/Eskimos, Inc.

Manufacturing
  Puget Plastics Corporation
  Puget Plastics S.A. de C.V. (Mexico)
  Triquest Puget Plastics, LLC

Petroleum refining and marketing
  Kodiak Oil Sales Inc. (North Pacific Fuel)
  Petro Star, Inc.
  Petro Star Valdez, Inc. (Valdez refinery)
  Sourdough Fuel, Inc.
  Valdez Petroleum Terminal (North Pacific Fuel)

Technical services
  Arctic Slope World Services, Incorporated
  ASRC Aerospace Corp.
  ASRC Communications, Ltd.

Other operations
  Alaska Growth Capital Bidco Inc.
  Barrow Cable Television
  Eskimos, Inc.
  Tundra Tours, Inc.

COMPETITORS

Alaska Communications Systems
Baker Hughes
Halliburton
Nabors Industries
Noble
Schlumberger
Smith International
Tesoro
Tesoro Alaska
T-Mobile USA

HISTORICAL FINANCIALS
Company Type: Private

Income Statement
FYE: December 31

	REVENUE ($ mil.)	NET INCOME ($ mil.)	NET PROFIT MARGIN	EMPLOYEES
12/08	2,300	—	—	9,000
12/07	1,778	—	—	6,000
12/06	1,701	—	—	6,000
12/05	1,567	—	—	6,000
12/04	1,201	—	—	6,500
Annual Growth	17.6%	—	—	8.5%

Revenue History

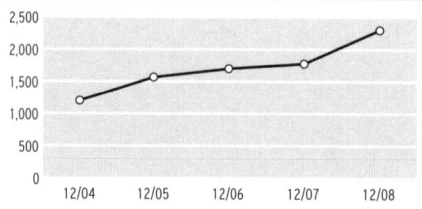

Ardent Health

Ardent Health Services is passionate about healing the body. The company operates seven acute care hospitals and a number of specialty care facilities in the southern US. Its facilities are located in New Mexico, where the company operates as the Lovelace Health System, and in Oklahoma, where it operates the Hillcrest Medical Center and other hospitals and clinics. Ardent Health Services' facilities also include physician group practices and medical pathology laboratories. In addition, it operates the Lovelace Health Plan, which serves some 220,000 members in New Mexico. Welsh, Carson, Anderson & Stowe owns a controlling stake in Ardent Health Services.

The company has been slimming down its portfolio of medical facilities to focus on acute and specialty care in the New Mexico and Oklahoma markets. Ardent sold its interest in Samaritan Hospital in Lexington, Kentucky, to partner Associated Healthcare Systems in 2005, and it sold its stake in Summit Hospital in Baton Rouge, Louisiana, to the Ochsner Clinic Foundation in 2007. Ardent has also consolidated inpatient care at its downtown Albuquerque location, leaving only outpatient services at its Gibson, New Mexico, hospital.

A deal with Oklahoma State University transferred ownership of the Oklahoma State University Medical Center from Ardent to a public trust in 2009. Tulsa hospital operator St. John Health System took over management of the facility.

Ardent has undergone a little bit of growth, however. In 2007 the company completed construction of the Bailey Medical Center, a new 75-bed acute care community hospital in Owasso, Oklahoma. It also added an orthopedic center at the Hillcrest Medical Center that year, and added 20 patient beds in a renovation construction effort at the 100-bed Lovelace Westside Hospital in Albuquerque, New Mexico.

Ardent was founded in 1993 as Behavioral Healthcare Corporation (BHC), which had six behavioral treatment centers at the outset. Investment firm Welsh, Carson, Anderson & Stowe acquired majority ownership of BHC in 2001 and renamed the company as Ardent Health Systems. Ardent sold off its 20 behavioral health care facilities to Psychiatric Solutions in 2005 in order to focus on its acute care hospitals and specialty health care facilities.

EXECUTIVES

President and CEO: David T. Vandewater, age 55
CFO: Kerry Gillespie
Chief Accounting Officer: Clint B. Adams
SVP Financial Operations: Jim Schnuck
SVP Human Resources and Administration:
  Neil Hemphill
SVP, General Counsel, and Secretary:
  Steven C. (Steve) Petrovich
VP and CIO: Mark Gillum
VP Communications: Kevin Gwin
President, Albuquerque Division: Ron Stern
President, Oklahoma Division: Earl Denning
Auditors: KPMG LLP

LOCATIONS

HQ: Ardent Health Services LLC
  1 Burton Hills Blvd., Ste. 250, Nashville, TN 37215
Phone: 615-296-3000   **Fax:** 615-296-6351
Web: www.ardenthealth.com

PRODUCTS/OPERATIONS

Selected Operations

New Mexico (Lovelace Health System)
  Gibson Medical Center (outpatient clinic)
  Lovelace Health Plan (health insurance)
  Lovelace Medical Center (acute care hospital)
    Lovelace Rehabilitation Hospital
  Lovelace Westside Hospital (acute care hospital)
  Lovelace Women's Hospital (acute specialty hospital)

Oklahoma
  Bailey Medical Center (acute care hospital)
  Cushing Regional Hospital (acute care hospital)
  Henryetta Medical Center (acute care hospital)
  Hillcrest Medical Center (dba Hillcrest Healthcare
    System, acute care hospital and clinics)
    Oklahoma Heart Institute
  Utica Park Clinic (outpatient facility)

COMPETITORS

Catholic Health Initiatives
CIGNA
Community Health Systems
Deaconess Health Care
Holy Cross Hospital
INTEGRIS Health
LifePoint Hospitals
MedCath
Presbyterian Healthcare Services
Saint Francis Health System
St. John Health System

HISTORICAL FINANCIALS
Company Type: Private

Income Statement

	REVENUE ($ mil.)	NET INCOME ($ mil.)	NET PROFIT MARGIN	EMPLOYEES
				FYE: December 31
12/08	1,800	—	—	7,745
12/07	1,650	—	—	8,500
12/06	1,670	—	—	9,942
12/05	1,731	—	—	8,800
12/04	1,607	—	—	15,900
Annual Growth	2.9%	—	—	(16.5%)

Revenue History

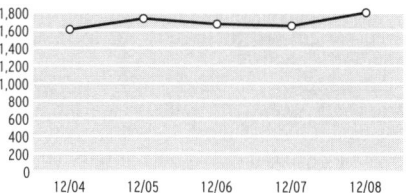

Arizona Chemical

Arizona Chemical is always pining for more business. The company is among the world's largest fractionators (separators) of crude tall oil (from the Swedish word *talloja*, or pine oil). It manufactures such pine tree-based chemicals as fatty acids, rosin esters, and terpenes. These chemicals are used to manufacture a wide variety of products, including adhesives, household cleaners, hydraulic fluids, inks, paints, personal care products, and plastics. Arizona Chemical was formed in 1930 by paper products maker International Paper (IP) and American Cyanamid and now is owned by private equity group Rhone Capital. Tall oil is a byproduct of paper making.

The company operates a number of manufacturing plants in the US and Europe; it also maintains R&D facilities in the US as well as in the Netherlands. Arizona Chemical's sales offices and distribution centers are in Asia, Europe, Latin America, and the US. It added to its European manufacturing base with the 2009 acquisition of the German natural resins maker Abieta Chemie, which supplies raw materials to makers of synthetic rubber.

International Paper underwent a corporate reorganization designed to slim down the paper giant's operations beginning in 2005. The re-org included the 2007 sale of Arizona Chemical to Rhone Capital for $485 million.

EXECUTIVES

President and CEO: Cornelis K. (Kees) Verhaar, age 55
VP and Managing Director, Europe: Juhani Tuovinen
VP and General Counsel: Bo Segers
VP Human Resources and Communications: David (Dave) Cowfer
VP Tax and Treasury: Glenda Haynes
VP and General Manager, North America: Gary Reed
Auditors: Deloitte & Touche LLP

LOCATIONS

HQ: Arizona Chemical Company
4600 Touchton Rd. East, Ste. 500
Jacksonville, FL 32246
Phone: 904-928-8700 **Fax:** 904-928-8779
Web: www.arizonachemical.com

PRODUCTS/OPERATIONS

Selected Products and Brands
Adhesives
  Dispersions
  Hot melt polyamides
  Hydrocarbon-based adhesive resins
  Rosin tackifiers
  Terpene resin tackifiers
Inks and Coatings
  Additives
  Hydrocarbon-based ink resins
  Polyamides
  Resinates
  Rosin resins
Oleochemicals
  Dimer acids
  Ester products
  Hydrogenated castor oil derivatives (CENWAX)
  Oleo fatty acids
  Tall oil products
  Terpenes
Special Products
  Arizona polymer additives
  Digital ink resins (Unirez)
  Specialty gellants (Uniclear)

COMPETITORS

Akzo Nobel
Eastman Chemical
Georgia-Pacific Chemicals
Hexion
MeadWestvaco

HISTORICAL FINANCIALS
Company Type: Private

Income Statement

	REVENUE ($ mil.)	NET INCOME ($ mil.)	NET PROFIT MARGIN	EMPLOYEES
				FYE: December 31
12/07	1,000	—	—	1,400
12/06	769	—	—	1,400
12/05	692	—	—	1,600
12/04	672	—	—	1,600
12/03	625	—	—	1,600
Annual Growth	12.5%	—	—	(3.3%)

Revenue History

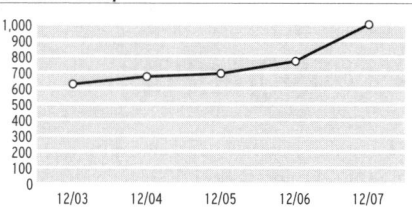

Army and Air Force Exchange

Be all that you can be and buy all that you can buy at the PX (Post Exchange). The Army and Air Force Exchange Service (AAFES) runs more than 3,100 facilities — including PXs and BXs (Base Exchanges) — at US Army and Air Force bases in more than 30 countries (including Iraq), all 50 US states, and five US territories. Its presence ranges from tents to shopping centers, including 175 retail stores, 1,300 fast-food outlets (brands like Burger King and Taco Bell), movie theaters, beauty shops, and gas stations. AAFES serves active-duty military personnel, reservists, retirees, and their family members. Although it's a government agency under the DOD, it receives less than 5% of its funding from the department.

While the AAFES receives little federal money, it pays neither taxes nor rent to occupy US government property. Its retail prices average about 20% less than the competition, and about two-thirds of AAFES's profits go into Morale, Welfare, and Recreation (MWR) programs for amenities such as libraries and youth centers. In 2008 AAFES generated more than $264 million in profits to fund the MWR program. Other profits are used to renovate or build new stores.

Active military personnel head AAFES, but its staff consists mostly of military family members and other civilians. Some 25% of its 43,000 AAFES associates in 2009 are family members.

AAFES shops are facing increased competition from Wal-Mart Stores, which is luring soldiers off base with its low prices. To better compete with discounters, AAFES has begun adding dollar sections to about 150 of its stores worldwide.

With the pledge "We Go Where You Go," AAFES is a multi-channel retailer offering catalog and online shopping as well as retail stores. Its Exchange Online Store and Exchange Online Mall average a savings of 10-20% on more than 18 million items.

HISTORY

During the American Revolution, peddlers known as sutlers followed the Army, selling items such as soap, razors, and tobacco. The practice lasted until after the Civil War, when post traders replaced sutlers. This system was replaced in 1889 when the War Department authorized canteens at military bases.

The first US military exchanges were established in 1895, creating a system to supply military personnel with personal items on US Army bases around the world. The exchanges were run independently, with each division creating a Post Exchange (PX) to serve its unit. The post commander would assign an officer to run the PX (usually along with other duties) and would decide how profits were spent.

In 1941 the Army Exchange Service was created, and the system was reorganized. A five-member advisory committee made up of civilian merchandisers was created to provide recommendations for the reorganization. The restructuring made the system more like a chain store business. The independent PXs were bought by the War Department from the individual military organizations that ran them. Civilian personnel were brought in to staff the PXs, and a brigadier general was named to head an executive staff made up of Army officers and civilians that provided centralized control of the system. The Army also created a special school to train officers to run the PXs.

Sales at the PXs skyrocketed during WWII; a catalog business was added so soldiers could order gifts to send home to their families. The Department of the Air Force was established in 1947, and the exchange system organization was renamed the Army and Air Force Exchange Service (AAFES) the next year.

In 1960 the government allowed the overseas exchanges to provide more luxury items in an effort to keep soldiers from buying foreign-made goods. By the time the military had been cranked up again for the Vietnam War, big-ticket items such as TVs, cameras, and tape recorders were among the exchanges' best-sellers. In 1967 AAFES moved its headquarters from New York City to Dallas.

By 1991 the exchanges were open to the National Guard and the Reserve; AAFES's customer base had grown to 14 million. When the military began downsizing during the 1990s following the end of the Cold War, AAFES's customer base shrank by 35%.

AAFES stores sold more than $12 million in pornographic materials in 1995. The House of Representatives passed the Military Honor and Decency Act the next year prohibiting the sale of pornography on US military property, including AAFES stores; this ban was struck down as unconstitutional in 1997. That year AAFES was approved as a provider of medical equipment covered by federal CHAMPUS/TRICARE insurance. It also created a Web site to offer online shopping in 1997.

The Supreme Court upheld the porn ban in 1998; the Pentagon banned the sale of more than 150 sexually explicit magazines (such as *Penthouse*), while a military board permitted the continued sale of certain publications (including *Playboy*). Maj. Gen. Barry Bates took over as AAFES's Commander and CEO in 1998. To better battle other retailers, that year AAFES announced its stores would offer best-price guarantees, matching prices of local stores and refunding price differences if customers found lower prices within 30 days of buying products.

In 1999 AAFES expanded to Macedonia and Kosovo, providing its services to military personnel in Operation Joint Guardian. In 2000 Bates was replaced as AAFES commander and CEO by Maj. Gen. Charles J. Wax.

Maj. Gen. Kathryn Frost became commander and CEO when Wax stepped down in August 2005.

Brigadier General Keith L. Thurgood assumed duties as AAFES commander in August 2007.

EXECUTIVES

Chairman: Richard Y. Newton III
Deputy Commander and Director EEO:
 Francis L. (Fran) Hendricks
COO: Michael P. (Mike) Howard
Chief of Staff: Col. Virgil Williams
Chief Staff: Thomas M. Baker
Senior Enlisted Advisor to Commanding General:
 Jeffry Helm
Commander and Director: Maj. Gen. Keith L. Thurgood
Executive Secretary and Director: Gregg Cox
Auditors: Ernst & Young LLP

LOCATIONS

HQ: Army and Air Force Exchange Service
 3911 S. Walton Walker Blvd., Dallas, TX 75236
Phone: 214-312-2011   **Fax:** 214-312-3000
Web: www.aafes.com

PRODUCTS/OPERATIONS

Selected Merchandise and Services
Barber and beauty shops
Books, newspapers, and magazines
Catalog services
Class Six stores
Concessions
Food facilities (mobile units, snack bars, name-brand fast-food franchises, and concession operations)
Gas stations and auto repair
Military clothing stores
Movie theaters
Retail stores
Vending centers

COMPETITORS

7-Eleven	Kroger
Amazon.com	METRO AG
Best Buy	Sears
Costco Wholesale	Supercuts
J. C. Penney	Target
Kmart	Wal-Mart

HISTORICAL FINANCIALS
Company Type: Government agency

Income Statement
FYE: Saturday nearest January 31

	REVENUE ($ mil.)	NET INCOME ($ mil.)	NET PROFIT MARGIN	EMPLOYEES
1/08	8,705	442	5.1%	43,658
1/07	8,921	428	4.8%	45,000
1/06	8,667	378	4.4%	45,000
1/05	8,352	474	5.7%	48,000
1/04	7,905	485	6.1%	47,323
Annual Growth	2.4%	(2.3%)	—	(2.0%)

2008 Year-End Financials
Debt ratio: —   Current ratio: —
Return on equity: —   Long-term debt ($ mil.): 0
Cash ($ mil.): —

Net Income History

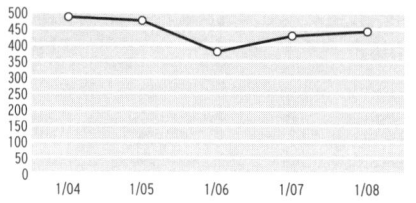

Ascension Health

Ascension Health has ascended to the pinnacle of not-for-profit health care. As the largest Catholic hospital system in the US, and thus one of the top providers of charity care in the nation, the organization's health care network consists of 65 general hospitals, along with a dozen long-term care, acute care, rehabilitation, and psychiatric hospitals. Ascension Health also operates nursing homes, community clinics, and other health care providers. Its network of medical facilities spans 20 states and the District of Columbia. The organization's facilities have more than 16,800 licensed beds.

Consistent with its not-for-profit status, Ascension Health provides millions of dollars in "community benefit," a vaguely defined term that includes charity care to the indigent and uninsured, costs not covered by Medicaid, and other community health programs. Ascension Health recorded more than $925 million in community benefit costs in 2008.

Ascension Health is engaged in system-wide efforts to improve patient safety at its facilities, vowing to reduce preventable deaths from hospital-acquired infections, surgical and drug complications, birth trauma injuries, and other avoidable circumstances. The organization also advocates for expanded access to health care and has set a goal of guaranteed access to care in all its markets by the year 2020. It is working in partnership with local governments and private groups (persuading doctors to add some uninsured patients to their rolls, for instance) to achieve that goal.

But alongside its role as a mission-driven organization, Ascension Health is also a large business, and it has used its business savvy to make it one of the nation's largest and most successful health care organizations. It has consistently pruned money-losing operations, including the divestiture in 2006 of St. Joseph Hospital of Augusta, Georgia, to Triad (now part of Community Health Systems).

Ascension Health is not afraid of growth, and it has snapped up hospitals and health systems to expand its geographic footprint and market share. It bought Eastern Health System, a three-hospital group in Birmingham, in 2007 and merged it with its existing St. Vincent's Health System. The same year it became co-owner of Via Christi Health System in Wichita, Kansas, and it has also agreed to an affiliation of its Columbia St. Mary's system in Milwaukee with Froedtert & Community Health. A plan to re-enter the Boston market by acquiring Caritas Christi fell through in 2007.

To actually make a little money on the side, Ascension joined with Catholic Health Initiatives and Catholic Health East, to create investment firm Ascension Health Ventures (AHV). AHV has built a portfolio of investments in the medical technology and service sector that have the potential to improve health care delivery, but that will also reap financial rewards for Ascension Health and its partners. AHV was the second such venture for Ascension Health, which set up a wholly owned fund in 2001.

HISTORY

The Daughters of Charity order was formed in France in 1633 when St. Vincent de Paul recruited a rich widow (St. Louise de Marillac) to care for the sick on battlefields and in their homes.

Elizabeth Ann Seton, America's first saint (canonized 1974), brought the order to the US. In 1809 Seton earned the title of Mother and started the Sisters of Charity. The Sisters adopted the vows of the Daughters of Charity, adding "service" to them in 1812.

The Sisters officially became part of the Daughters of Charity in 1850. The Daughters cared for soldiers during the Civil War and were responsible for training Florence Nightingale. In the late 1800s the Daughters pioneered exclusive provider arrangements (similar to today's managed care contracts) with railroads, lumber camps, and the like. During the next 100 years, the order furthered its mission of caring for the sick and the poor. To support their efforts, the nuns founded hospitals (44 by 1911), schools, and other charity centers.

In 1969 the charity association formed a health care services cooperative, which became the Daughters of Charity National Health System (DCNHS).

DCNHS operated as two regional institutions (one based in Maryland, the other in Missouri) until 1986, when the systems merged. The first task was to balance their holy mission with the need to make money. With competition from managed care companies increasing, DCNHS responded by cutting staff and diversifying into nursing homes and retirement centers.

The Daughters of Charity's western unit combined its six hospitals in California with Mullikin Centers (a physician-owned medical group) in 1993 to form one of the largest health care associations in the state.

DCNHS expanded its network in 1995 by merging its hospitals with and becoming a co-sponsor of San Francisco-based Catholic Healthcare West. That year it joined with Catholic Relief Services to operate a hospital in war-torn Angola.

In 1996 DCNHS dropped a proposed merger of its struggling 221-bed Carney Hospital in Boston with Quincy Hospital because the municipally owned Quincy facility was required by law to provide abortions. Instead, DCNHS sold Carney Hospital to Caritas Christi Health Care System (owned by the Boston Roman Catholic archdiocese), one of about a dozen hospital sales by DCNHS in the mid-1990s.

DCNHS reorganized its leadership in 1997, creating SVP positions for system direction and policy and for program development to strengthen and update its programs. In 1998 Sister Irene Kraus, who had founded DCNHS and led it through its expansion, died.

In 1999 DCNHS merged with fellow Catholic caregiver Sisters of St. Joseph Health System, then Michigan's largest health care system, to form Ascension Health.

In 2000 Ascension saw the collapse of a five-hospital merger in Florida between subsidiary St. Vincent's Health System and Baptist Health System. The organization also launched the Voice for the Voiceless initiative, which combined private monies and federal grants to fund programs for the uninsured in Detroit, New Orleans, and Austin, Texas.

In response to rising health care costs, Ascension merged with national Catholic health care provider Carondelet Health System in 2003.

EXECUTIVES

Chair: Sister Kathleen Kelly
President and CEO: Anthony R. (Tony) Tersigni, age 58
Chief Medical Officer: David B. Pryor
SVP and Chief Supply Chain Officer: Scott Caldwell
SVP and CFO: Anthony J. (Tony) Speranzo
SVP Legal Services and General Counsel:
 Joseph R. Impicciche
SVP Mission Integration: Sister Maureen McGuire
SVP and CIO; CEO, Ascension Health Information Services: Mark D. Barner
SVP and Program Executive, Project Symphony:
 Ann Esposito
SVP Organizational Development and Human Resources: Challis M. Lowe, age 63
SVP System Support Services and Chief Risk Officer:
 James K. Beckmann Jr.
VP Communications: Stephen D. (Steve) LeResche
President, Healthcare Operations and COO:
 Robert J. (Bob) Henkel, age 55
Senior Executive Assistant to the President:
 Sister Bernice Coreil
Chief Investment Officer: David E. Erickson
Director: John O. (Jack) Mudd
Auditors: Ernst & Young LLP

LOCATIONS

HQ: Ascension Health
 4600 Edmundson Rd., St. Louis, MO 63134
Phone: 314-733-8000 **Fax:** 314-733-8013
Web: www.ascensionhealth.org

Selected Hospitals

Alabama
 Providence Hospital (Mobile)
 St. Vincent's Hospital (Birmingham)
Arizona
 Carondelet Holy Cross Hospital
 Carondelet St. Joseph's Hospital (Tucson)
 Carondelet St. Mary's Hospital (Tucson)
Arkansas
 DePaul Health Center (Dumas)
 St. Elizabeth Health Center (Gould)
Connecticut
 Hall-Brooke Behavioral Health Services (Westport)
 St. Vincent's Medical Center (Bridgeport)
District of Columbia
 Providence Hospital
Florida
 Sacred Heart Children's Hospital (Pensacola)
 Sacred Heart Hospital of the Emerald Coast (West Destin)
 Sacred Heart Hospital of Pensacola (Pensacola)
 Sacred Heart Women's Hospital (Pensacola)
 St. Vincent's Medical Center (Jacksonville)
Georgia
 Walton Rehabilitation Hospital (Augusta)
Idaho
 St. Joseph Regional Medical Center (Lewiston)
Illinois
 Saint Anthony Hospital (Chicago)
Indiana
 Saint John's Health System (Anderson)
 St. Elizabeth Ann Seton Hospital (Boonville)
 St. Joseph Hospital (Kokomo)
 St. Mary's Warrick Hospital (Boonville)
 St. Vincent Carmel Hospital
 St. Vincent Clay Hospital (Brazil)
 St. Vincent Frankfort Hospital
 St. Vincent Jennings Hospital (North Vernon)
 St. Vincent Indianapolis Hospital
 St. Vincent Mercy Hospital (Elwood)
 St. Vincent Randolph Hospital (Winchester)
 St. Vincent Williamsport Hospital
Louisiana
 The Daughters of Charity Health Center (New Orleans)
Maryland
 Sacred Heart Hospital (Cumberland)
 St. Agnes HealthCare (Baltimore)
Michigan
 Borgess-Lee Memorial Hospital (Dowagiac)
 Borgess Medical Center (Kalamazoo)
 Borgess-Pipp Health Center (Plainwell)
 Brighton Hospital
 CareLink of Jackson
 Genesys Regional Medical Center (Grand Blanc)
 Providence Hospital (Southfield)
 St. John Hospital and Medical Center (Detroit)
 St. John Macomb Hospital (Warren)
 St. John North Shores Hospital (Harrison Township)
 St. John Oakland Hospital (Madison Heights)
 St. Mary's of Michigan Medical Center (Saginaw)
 St. Mary's of Michigan — Standish Hospital
 St. Joseph Health System (Augres)
Missouri
 St. Joseph Medical Center (Kansas City)
 St. Mary's Medical Center (Blue Springs)
New York
 Mount St. Mary's Hospital and Health Center (Lewiston)
 Our Lady of Lourdes Memorial Hospital (Binghamton)
 St. Mary's Hospital (Amsterdam)
 St. Mary's Hospital (Troy)

Pennsylvania
 Good Samaritan Regional Medical Center (Pottsville)
Tennessee
 Baptist Hickman Community Hospital (Centerville)
 Baptist Hospital (Nashville)
 Middle Tennessee Medical Center (Murfreesboro)
 Saint Thomas Health Services System (Nashville)
Texas
 Dell Children's Medical Center of Central Texas (Austin)
 Providence Health Center (Waco)
 Seton Edgar B. Davis Hospital (Luling)
 Seton Highland Lakes Hospital (Burnet)
 Seton Medical Center (Austin)
 Seton Medical Center Williamson (Round Rock)
 Seton Northwest Hospital (Austin)
 Seton Southwest Hospital (Austin)
 University Medical Center Brackenridge (formerly Brackenridge Hospital, Austin)
Washington
 Lourdes Medical Center (Pasco)
Wisconsin
 Columbia St. Mary's (Milwaukee)
 Columbia St. Mary's Ozaukee Campus (Mequon)
 Orthopaedic Hospital of Wisconsin (Glendale)
 Sacred Heart Rehabilitation Institute (Milwaukee)

COMPETITORS

Catholic Health East
Catholic Health Initiatives
Catholic Healthcare Partners
Catholic Healthcare West
Community Health Systems
Detroit Medical Center
Golden Horizons
HCA
Health Management Associates
HealthSouth
Henry Ford Health System
Kindred Healthcare
Life Care Centers
MedStar Health
Tenet Healthcare
Trinity Health (Novi)
Universal Health Services
University of Maryland Medical System

HISTORICAL FINANCIALS

Company Type: Not-for-profit

Income Statement

FYE: June 30

	REVENUE ($ mil.)	NET INCOME ($ mil.)	NET PROFIT MARGIN	EMPLOYEES
6/08	13,489	—	—	107,000
6/07	12,322	—	—	106,000
6/06	11,263	—	—	106,000
6/05	10,861	—	—	107,000
6/04	10,046	—	—	106,000
Annual Growth	7.6%	—	—	0.2%

Revenue History

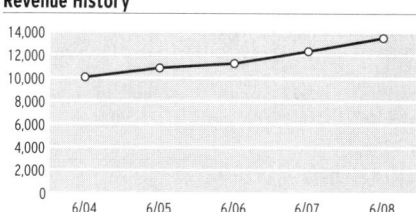

Ashley Furniture

Not to be confused with Laura Ashley, this Ashley is more interested in peddling leather and wood than toile and chenille. Ashley Furniture Industries, one of the nation's largest furniture manufacturers, makes and imports upholstered furniture, as well as leather and hardwood pieces. The company licenses its name to more than 350 Ashley Furniture HomeStores located in the US, as well as Canada, Mexico, and Japan. These stores are independently owned and sell only Ashley Furniture-branded products. Founded by Carlyle Weinberger in 1945, Ashley Furniture is owned by father-and-son duos Ron and Todd Wanek and Chuck and Ben Vogel.

The company has three operating divisions: Ashley Casegoods, Ashley Upholstery, and Millennium. About 45% of the company's furniture is manufactured in Asia. Overall, Ashley maintains 3 million sq. ft. of manufacturing facilities at half a dozen locations.

In an industry hurt by sluggish consumer spending amid the global economic downturn, Ashley is looking ahead to better times. The company announced in July 2009 that it would be expanding its Southern California distribution operations by about 500,000 sq. ft. The move gives the furniture firm a footprint spanning some 1.5 million sq. ft. Tightened credit markets and reduced revenues have stalled commercial growth in many industries, but it has also freed up (and in many cases lowered the rents on) warehouse space for those able to afford it.

Ashley's bid to expand follows about 200 job cuts from its Mississippi production plants in 2008. The firm said the workforce reduction was necessary to stay competitive. The furniture industry has been suffering through falling demand in recent years because of the US recession and housing market slowdown.

To take its retail business forward, Ashley tapped former Wickes Furniture president and CEO John Disa in January 2009 to be president of its Ashley Furniture HomeStore division. Disa succeeds Chuck Spang, who stepped into a new role as president of HomeStore licensing.

EXECUTIVES

Chairman: Ronald G. (Ron) Wanek, age 67
President and CEO: Todd Wanek, age 45
CFO: Gino Mangione
CIO: Dwain Jansson
VP International: Shari Wagner
VP Visual: Dave Mattea
VP and General Merchandise Manager: Kris Woodcock
Director Corporate Marketing: Nicole Jordan
Human Resources Manager: Jim Dotta
President, Ashley Furniture HomeStore Licensing: Chuck Spang
President, Ashley Furniture HomeStore: John Disa
President, Casegoods Division: Rob Hoffman

LOCATIONS

HQ: Ashley Furniture Industries, Inc.
1 Ashley Way, Arcadia, WI 54612
Phone: 608-323-3377   **Fax:** 608-323-6008
Web: www.ashleyfurniture.com

COMPETITORS

Bassett Furniture
Berkline BenchCraft
Brown Jordan International
Ethan Allen
Euromarket Designs
Furniture Brands International
Havertys
Home Meridian
Hooker Furniture
IKEA
Kimball International
Klaussner Furniture
La-Z-Boy
Natuzzi
Rowe Fine Furniture
Williams-Sonoma

HISTORICAL FINANCIALS

Company Type: Private

Income Statement				FYE: December 31
	ESTIMATED REVENUE ($ mil.)	NET INCOME ($ mil.)	NET PROFIT MARGIN	EMPLOYEES
12/08	3,000	—	—	14,000
12/07	3,430	—	—	17,000
12/06	3,120	—	—	14,600
12/05	2,550	—	—	13,400
12/04	2,000	—	—	11,000
Annual Growth	10.7%	—	—	6.2%

Revenue History

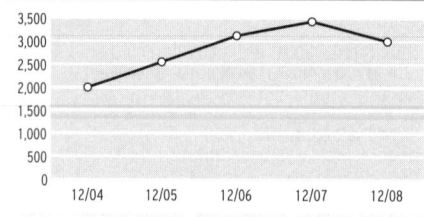

ASI Computer Technologies

ASI Computer Technologies is a wholesale distributor of computer software, hardware, and accessories. It offers more than 8,000 products, including PCs, modems, monitors, networking equipment, and storage devices. ASI sells to more than 20,000 resellers throughout North America. The company's vendor partners include such companies as AMD, Intel, Microsoft, Samsung, and Western Digital. Its services include custom systems integration and contract assembly. The company also markets a line of computers and configures custom computer systems under its own Nspire brand. ASI was established in 1987 by Christine Liang, the company's president, who owns ASI.

ASI customers include resellers, retailers, systems integrators, and OEMs. It has operations in North America and Asia.

In 2009 ASI opened a 20,000-sq.-ft. systems integration center within its large logistics facility in Southaven, Mississippi, located near Memphis. The center makes desktop and notebook computers, servers, network-attached data storage equipment, and specialty products, such as digital signs.

EXECUTIVES

Chairman and CEO: Marcel Liang
President: Christine Liang
EVP North America Sales: Brian Clark
VP Finance: Bill Chen
VP Product Management: Cathy Wang
VP Business Development: Henry Chen
VP Marketing: Kent Tibbils
VP Human Resources and Administration: Crystal Yuan
Director Program Management: Shelly L. Schroeder
Director Technical Services: Vince Tartalia
Director Operations: Mike Jackson

LOCATIONS

HQ: ASI Computer Technologies, Inc.
48289 Fremont Blvd., Fremont, CA 94538
Phone: 510-226-8000   **Fax:** 510-226-8858
Web: www.asipartner.com

PRODUCTS/OPERATIONS

Selected Products

Accessories
Cables
Cameras
Cases
CD-ROM drives
Central processing units
Controller cards
DVD drives
Fans
Floppy drives
Hard drives
Keyboards
Memory
Mice
Modems
Monitors
Motherboards
MP3 players
Multimedia products
Network connectivity products
Notebooks
Optical drives
PCs
Power supplies
Printers
Projectors
Removable drives and media
Scanners
Software
Sound cards
Speakers
Storage devices
Tape back-up products
Video cards
Zip drives

COMPETITORS

Agilysys
Arrow Electronics
ASCII Group
Avnet
Bell Microproducts
CompuCom
Continental Resources
D&H Distributing
En Pointe
Flextronics
Ingram Micro
Merisel
MicroAge
MTM Technologies
New Age Electronics
SED International
Softmart
Software House
Supercom
SYNNEX
Tech Data

HISTORICAL FINANCIALS
Company Type: Private

Income Statement				FYE: December 31
	REVENUE ($ mil.)	NET INCOME ($ mil.)	NET PROFIT MARGIN	EMPLOYEES
12/08	1,300	—	—	800
12/07	1,300	—	—	800
12/06	1,110	—	—	850
12/05	1,110	—	—	600
12/04	1,060	—	—	500
Annual Growth	5.2%	—	—	12.5%

Revenue History

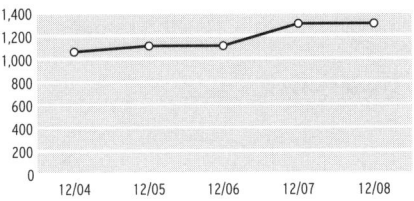

Asplundh Tree Expert

How much wood would a woodchuck chuck, if a woodchuck could chuck wood? A lot, if the woodchuck were named Asplundh. One of the world's leading tree-trimming businesses, Asplundh clears tree limbs from power lines for utilities and municipalities throughout the US and in Canada, Australia, and New Zealand. Asplundh also offers utility-related services such as line construction, meter reading, and pole maintenance; in addition, the company has branched out into fields such as billboard maintenance, traffic signal and highway lighting construction, and vegetation control for railroads and pipelines. The Asplundh family owns and manages the company, which was founded in 1928.

One of the competitive pressures driving Asplundh is the growing use of alternative methods for managing the tree elimination process. As a result, the company competes with companies such as Dow AgroSciences and Bayer CropScience which provide herbicide applications and other chemical methods for eliminating plants and trees.

In 2008 Asplundh sold its Central Locating Service unit, which finds and marks underground utility lines, to a group led by investment firm Kohlberg & Company. Kohlberg at the same time acquired a Central Locating Service rival, SM&P Utility Resources, and the utility locating companies have been combined as components of a new company, United States Infrastructure, in which Asplundh holds a minority stake.

EXECUTIVES

Chairman and CEO: Christopher B. Asplundh
President: Scott M. Asplundh
Manager Field Personnel: Joseph (Joe) Lee
Manager Corporate Communications: Patti Chipman
Treasurer and Secretary: Joseph P. Dwyer

LOCATIONS

HQ: Asplundh Tree Expert Co.
708 Blair Mill Rd., Willow Grove, PA 19090
Phone: 215-784-4200   **Fax:** 215-784-4493
Web: www.asplundh.com

COMPETITORS

Arbor Tree Surgery
Bayer CropScience
Control Group
Davey Tree
Dow AgroSciences
Excel Landscape
Lewis Tree
Quanta Services

HISTORICAL FINANCIALS
Company Type: Private

Income Statement				FYE: December 31
	REVENUE ($ mil.)	NET INCOME ($ mil.)	NET PROFIT MARGIN	EMPLOYEES
12/08	2,580	—	—	27,589
12/07	2,370	—	—	28,606
12/06	2,400	—	—	28,831
12/05	2,366	—	—	24,000
12/04	2,080	—	—	28,638
Annual Growth	5.5%	—	—	(0.9%)

Revenue History

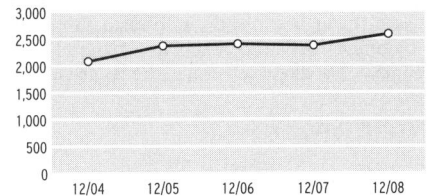

Associated Electric Cooperative

Associated Electric Cooperative makes the connection between power and cooperatives. The utility provides transmission and generation services to its six member/owner companies, which in turn provide power supply services to 51 distribution cooperatives in three Midwest states. (The distribution cooperatives have a combined customer count of more than 850,000.) Associated Electric operates 9,280 miles of power transmission lines and has more than 5,220 MW of generating capacity from interests in primarily coal- and gas-fired power plants and from wholesale energy transactions with other regional utilities.

The cooperative has 158 interconnections and 21 interconnection agreements. It is engaged in the wholesale transmission business with 71 investor-owned and municipal utilities, electric cooperatives, power marketing firms and regional transmission organizations.

Founded in 1961, Associated Electric supplies wholesale power to 39 distribution cooperatives in Missouri, three in southeast Iowa, and nine in northeast Oklahoma.

EXECUTIVES

CEO and General Manager: James J. Jura
President, Board of Directors: O. B. Clark
CFO: David W. McNabb
CIO: Ronald H. Murphy
VP, Board of Directors: Emery O. Geisendorfer Jr.
Director Member Services and Corporate Communications: Joseph E. Wilkinson
Director Engineering and Operations: Roger S. Clark
Director Human Resources: David P. Stump
Director Power Production: Duane D. Highley
General Counsel: Patrick A. Baumhoer
Treasurer: Charles C. Baile
Secretary: R. Layne Morrill
Special Assistant to the CEO and General Manager: Michael M. (Mike) Miller
Special Assistant to the CEO and General Manager: Keith E. Hartner
Auditors: KPMG LLP

LOCATIONS

HQ: Associated Electric Cooperative Inc.
2814 S. Golden, Springfield, MO 65801
Phone: 417-881-1204   **Fax:** 417-885-9252
Web: www.aeci.org

PRODUCTS/OPERATIONS

Member Transmission and Distribution Cooperatives

Central Electric Power Cooperative
KAMO Power
M&A Electric Power Cooperative
Northeast Missouri Electric Power Cooperative
NW Electric Power Cooperative Inc.
Sho-Me Power Electric Cooperative

COMPETITORS

Ameren
Empire District Electric
Great Plains Energy
Westar Energy

HISTORICAL FINANCIALS
Company Type: Cooperative

Income Statement				FYE: December 31
	REVENUE ($ mil.)	NET INCOME ($ mil.)	NET PROFIT MARGIN	EMPLOYEES
12/07	909	21	2.3%	645
12/06	865	16	1.8%	640
12/05	873	11	1.2%	640
12/04	798	18	2.2%	620
12/03	756	11	1.4%	591
Annual Growth	4.7%	17.9%	—	2.2%

2007 Year-End Financials

Debt ratio: 385.6%
Return on equity: —
Cash ($ mil.): —
Current ratio: —
Long-term debt ($ mil.): 1,170

Net Income History

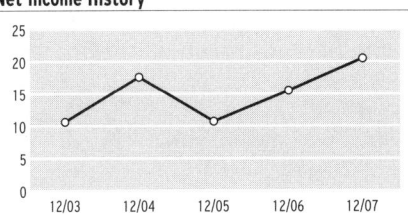

Associated Food Stores

This business makes sure there's plenty of grub for the Wild West. Associated Food Stores is a leading regional cooperative wholesale distributor that supplies groceries and other products to about 600 independent supermarkets in eight Western states. It also offers a variety of support services for its member-owners, including market research, real estate analysis, store design, technology procurement, and training. In addition, Associated Food Stores owns a stake in Western Family Foods, a grocery wholesalers' partnership that produces Western Family private-label goods. The co-op was formed in 1940 by Donald Lloyd, then president of the Utah Retail Grocers Association, and 34 other retailers.

EXECUTIVES

President and CEO: Richard A. (Rich) Parkinson
VP and CFO: Robert (Bob) Obray
VP Trade Relations: Richard L. (Dick) King
President AFS Insurance: Don Noyes
President Associated Retail Stores: Dave Wirthlin
Produce Buyer: Darin Larkin
Corporate Secretary: Lezlie Sanders
Manager Facilities: Tim Conner
Auditors: Deloitte & Touche LLP

LOCATIONS

HQ: Associated Food Stores, Inc.
1850 W. 2100 South, Salt Lake City, UT 84119
Phone: 801-978-8697   **Fax:** 801-974-0484
Web: www.afstores.com

COMPETITORS

AMCON Distributing
C & S Wholesale
GSC Enterprises
McLane
Nash-Finch
Safeway
SUPERVALU
Unified Grocers
URM Stores
Wal-Mart

HISTORICAL FINANCIALS

Company Type: Cooperative

Income Statement			FYE: Saturday nearest March 31
	REVENUE ($ mil.)	**NET INCOME** ($ mil.)	**NET PROFIT MARGIN**	**EMPLOYEES**
3/08	1,632	—	—	2,000

Associated Materials

Vinyl has never gone out of style at Associated Materials (AM). The company makes and distributes vinyl siding and windows, as well as aluminum and steel siding, aluminum trim coil, and accessories. Products are marketed under the brand names of Alside, Gentek, and Revere. They are sold through about 125 supply centers and 250 independent distributors in the US and Canada. (AM generates about 70% of its sales through its supply stores.) Its top customers include contractors, remodelers, and architects. The retailer also makes UltraGuard-branded vinyl fencing and railing. AM is indirectly owned by AMH Holdings, which is controlled by Investcorp and Harvest Partners.

Vinyl siding makers such as AM compete for exterior wall-cladding business with fiber cement, stone veneer, stucco, brick, and other masonry manufacturers. Particularly in the Southwest region, the economic climate of the vinyl siding industry has declined, causing companies such as AM and rivals Ply Gem Industries and CertainTeed to close plants. To this end, AM relocated some of its manufacturing operations in 2008 to facilities in the Northeast and Midwest, where demand for vinyl siding is greater.

Raw materials that are used in AM's products — vinyl resin, aluminum, steel, glass, window hardware, and packaging materials — are purchased through contracts with resin suppliers. To counter the rising costs of raw materials, the company has likewise bumped up its prices.

EXECUTIVES

Chairman: Ira D. Kleinman, age 52
President and CEO: Thomas N. (Tom) Chieffe, age 51, $1,104,101 total compensation
SVP Operations: Warren J. Arthur, age 41, $233,081 total compensation
VP Human Resources: John F. Haumesser, age 44, $274,152 total compensation
VP, CFO, Treasurer, and Secretary: Stephen E. Graham, age 51
VP Sales: David L. King
President, Alside Supply Centers: Robert M. Franco, age 55, $370,610 total compensation
Auditors: Ernst & Young LLP

LOCATIONS

HQ: Associated Materials, LLC
3773 State Rd., Cuyahoga Falls, OH 44223
Phone: 330-929-1811   **Fax:** 330-922-2354
Web: www.associatedmaterials.com

PRODUCTS/OPERATIONS

2008 Sales

	$ mil.	% of total
Vinyl windows	380.3	34
Vinyl siding	254.6	22
Metal products	213.2	19
Third-party manufactured products	210.6	18
Other	75.3	7
Total	**1,134.0**	**100**

COMPETITORS

Alcoa Home Exteriors	Owens Corning Sales
Andersen Corporation	Ply Gem
CertainTeed	Royal Group
James Hardie Industries	Silver Line Building
JELD-WEN	Products
Louisiana-Pacific	Timber Truss Housing

HISTORICAL FINANCIALS

Company Type: Private

Income Statement			FYE: Saturday nearest December 31	
	REVENUE ($ mil.)	**NET INCOME** ($ mil.)	**NET PROFIT MARGIN**	**EMPLOYEES**
12/08	1,134	21	1.9%	2,800
12/07	1,204	40	3.3%	3,625
12/06	1,250	33	2.7%	5,009
12/05	1,174	22	1.9%	3,872
12/04	1,094	(11)	—	3,137
Annual Growth	0.9%	—	—	(2.8%)

2008 Year-End Financials

Debt ratio: 73.9%   Current ratio: —
Return on equity: —   Long-term debt ($ mil.): 221
Cash ($ mil.): —

Net Income History

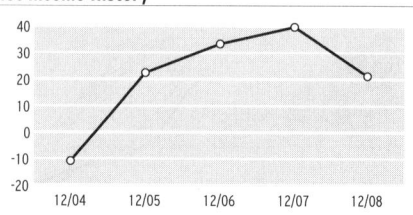

Associated Milk Producers

Associated Milk Producers Inc. (AMPI) might wear a cheesy grin, but it churns up solid sales. The dairy cooperative transforms some 6 billion pounds of milk into butter, cheese, fluid milk, and other dairy products each and every year. A regional co-op with some 3,600 member/farmers from Iowa, Minnesota, Nebraska, North and South Dakota, and Wisconsin, AMPI operates 15 manufacturing plants. In addition to its State Brand and Cass-Clay brand, Associated Milk Producers also makes private-label products for food retailers, fast-food restaurants (including McDonald's), and other foodservice operators. It also makes dairy ingredients for food manufacturers.

In 2007 AMPI acquired cheese and milk producing co-op, Cass-Clay Creamery, located in North Dakota. Consisting of farmers in Wisconsin, Minnesota, Iowa, Nebraska, Missouri, South Dakota, North Dakota and Montana, the acquisition added some 200 members to AMPI. The acquisition also enlarged the co-op's product line, adding ice cream, yogurt, dips, sour cream, and juice to AMPI's mix.

HISTORY

In 1969, faced with declining milk consumption and a subsequent drop in income, about 100 dairy cooperatives in the Midwest and the South merged to form Associated Milk Producers Incorporated (AMPI). AMPI elected John Butterbrodt, from a Wisconsin co-op, as the first president. Co-ops throughout the central US clamored to join, and AMPI became the largest US dairy co-op within two years of its formation.

Almost from the beginning, AMPI became embroiled in the two main controversies involving dairy co-ops: monopolistic practices and political contributions. In 1972 consumer advocate Ralph Nader alleged that the three main dairy co-ops — AMPI, Dairymen, and Mid-America Dairymen — had illegally contributed $422,000 to President Nixon's reelection campaign in an attempt to obtain higher price supports (enacted in 1971) and an agreement that the administration would drop antitrust suits against the co-ops. Watergate investigators subpoenaed Nixon's tapes, and AMPI was accused of bribery, destruction of evidence, and attempting to achieve "complete market dominance." In 1974 it pleaded guilty to making illegal political contributions in 1968, 1970, and 1972. By 1975 three former AMPI employees had been convicted of various charges and Butterbrodt had resigned.

The co-op spent the last half of the 1970s quietly reorganizing. In 1982 a suit for monopolistic practices, originally filed in 1971 by the National Farmers Organization (NFO), finally reached the federal courts. The case was decided in favor of AMPI and two other large co-ops, but before the year was out an appeals court reversed the decision, saying AMPI and its co-defendants had conspired to eliminate competitive sellers of milk. (The US Supreme Court subsequently upheld the appeals court ruling.)

Business soured in the early 1990s, and despite successfully lobbying the Department of Agriculture to strengthen dairy price supports, AMPI posted losses. Despite heavy spending in Congress, AMPI watched decades of government support to dairy farmers fall away as the 1996 Farm Bill established free-market agriculture.

Faced with falling prices, deregulation, and foreign competition, in 1997 AMPI entered into consolidation talks with three of its dairy co-op brethren: Mid-America Dairymen, Milk Marketing, and Western Dairymen Cooperative. AMPI's Southern Region, which primarily produced fluid milk, decided to join the new co-op, Dairy Farmers of America; members of its Northern Region, which focused on hard products, stayed put, renaming itself North Central AMPI to reduce confusion during the transition. However, the co-op officially readopted the original name in 1999.

High butterfat prices in 1998 helped the co-op post record earnings during its first year after the separation. Amid wild consolidations within the dairy industry, in mid-1999 AMPI made a modest merger with the Glencoe Butter & Produce Association. The small regional cooperative based in Glencoe, Minnesota, brought a cheese production plant and 1,000 new members to AMPI. In 2000 a Minnesota cooperative, the Fremont Cooperative Creamery Association, sold its plant and added its 40 members to AMPI rolls.

AMPI's 93,000-sq.-ft. plant in New Ulm, Minnesota, is the biggest butter barn in the US and was originally able to whip up nearly 20,000 pounds of butter per hour. However, a fire at the plant in 2004 melted nearly 3 million pounds of butter and left the facility badly damaged. AMPI has since rebuilt the plant. It reopened in 2005.

EXECUTIVES

Chairman: Paul Toft
Vice Chairman: Roger Lyon
President and CEO: Ed Welch
VP Public Affairs: Sheryl Doering Meshke
Director Marketing: Jim Walsh
Director Quality Assurance: Tom Honse

Director Human Resources: Geoff Davies
Director Fluid Marketing: Neil Gulden
Secretary and Director: Phil Johnson
Treasurer and Director: Dale Hoffman
Manager, Dawson and Paynesville: Matt Quade
Manager, New Ulm: Bill Swan
Manager, Arlington Division: Jerry Johnson
Manager, Fargo: Keith Pagel
Manager, Rochester Division: Jim Kleva
Manager, Freeman and Sanborn: Mike Wolkow
Manager, Jim Falls Division: John Breene
Manager, Blair Division: Mark Frederixon

LOCATIONS

HQ: Associated Milk Producers Inc.
315 N. Broadway, New Ulm, MN 56073
Phone: 507-354-8295   **Fax:** 507-359-8651
Web: www.ampi.com

PRODUCTS/OPERATIONS

Selected Products

Butter
Cheese
Fluid milk
Nacho cheese sauce
Nonfat dry milk
Pudding

Selected Services

AMPI Political Action Committee (PAC)
Bulk tank cultures
Complete field service
Daily component and somatic cell testing
Dairy farm product delivery
Direct deposit
Early equity revolvement for retired members
Equipment financing
Grassroots lobbying
Group life insurance
Milk contracting
Milk Market Loss program
Milker training
Milking system analysis
Milking time evaluation
Online milk test results
Web site resources
Young Cooperator (YC) program

COMPETITORS

Bel Brands USA
BelGioioso Cheese
Dairy Farmers of America
Dairylea
Dean Foods
Ellsworth Cooperative
Foremost Farms
Great Lakes Cheese
Kemps, LLC
Kraft Foods
Land O'Lakes
Leprino Foods
Marathon Cheese
MMPA
Prairie Farms Dairy
Saputo
Sargento
Schreiber Foods

Associated Press

This just in: The Associated Press (AP) is reporting tonight and every night wherever news is breaking. AP is one of the world's largest news gathering organizations, with about 240 news bureaus in nearly 100 countries. It provides news, photos, graphics, and audiovisual services that reach people daily through print, radio, television, and the Web. In addition to traditional news services, it operates international television news service APTN (AP Television News), photo archives, and an interactive news service (AP Digital). It also offers advertising management and distribution services. The not-for-profit cooperative is owned by 1,500 US daily newspaper members.

With print publishing struggling against declining readership, falling advertising revenues, and the rise in popularity of digital media, AP reduced member rates in 2009. Also that year it cut some 90 jobs, instituted a hiring freeze, and bought out about 100 employees. It has additionally announced that it is considering a plan to begin charging fees for some content. New products AP is exploring include premium-priced information on certain topics and charging customers to get news earlier. In previous efforts to help the bottom line, AP cut costs when it consolidated its print, broadcast, and digital sales and marketing units in 2008. The restructuring was part of an effort to streamline the distribution of news in order to gain greater efficiencies.

All total, AP serves 1,700 newspapers and 5,000 radio and television outlets in the US, many of which are members. It also has approximately 8,500 newspaper, radio, and television subscribers in more than 100 countries. In recent years AP has shifted its focus from providing content to newspapers; some of the company's biggest customers now include media outlets such as Google, MSN, and Yahoo!. AP's Online Video Network (OVN) service provides news video to AP member and customer Web sites.

In 2009 AP launched AP Mobile News, a multimedia service for wireless devices such as iPhones and Blackberries that offers access to global, international, and local news. More than 1,000 members are using the service, and monthly traffic has reached some 40 million page views. Also in response to new media formats, AP joined with Nintendo in 2007 to launch a news channel for the game maker's Wii console.

A group of New York newspapers founded the AP in 1846 in order to chronicle the US-Mexican War more efficiently. The founding papers include *The New York Sun*, *The Journal of Commerce*, *The Courier and Enquirer*, *The New York Herald*, and *The Express*.

HISTORY

The Associated Press traces its roots to 1846, when *New York Sun* publisher Moses Yale Beach agreed to share news arriving by telegraph about the Mexican-American War with four other New York newspapers. The cooperative news gathering effort was later established as the AP, which began selling wire reports to other papers and started creating regional associations. Adapting to changing technologies and public interests, AP began covering sports, financial, and public interest stories in the 1920s and was selling news reports to radio stations in the 1940s. Advancements during WWII included using transatlantic cable and radio-teletype circuits to deliver news and photos.

In the late 1960s AP and Dow Jones introduced services to improve business and financial reporting. AP improved photo delivery, reception, and storage in the 1970s with the advent of Laserphoto and the Electronic Darkroom. It began transmitting news by satellite and offering color photographs to newspapers in the 1980s. In 1985 Louis Boccardi took over the job as president and CEO of AP.

AP adjusted to the media-heavy culture of the 1990s by launching the APTV international news video service and the All News Radio network in 1994. It then moved onto the Internet with The WIRE in 1996 and began offering online access to its Photo Archive in 1997. It bought Worldwide Television News in 1998, combining it with APTV to form AP Television News Limited (APTN). The following year it purchased the radio news contracts of UPI after the rival organization announced it was getting out of broadcast news.

In 2000 AP created an Internet division, AP Digital, to focus on marketing news to online providers. The cooperative continued its Internet focus the following year, launching AP Online en Español (news for Spanish-language Web sites) and AP Entertainment Online (multimedia entertainment news for Web sites). Also that year AP bought the Newspaper Industry Communication Center from the Newspaper Association of America.

In 2002 the company launched an expanded editorial partnership with Dow Jones Newswires, increasing the amount of financial news distributed on AP wires. Later that year it acquired Capitolwire, a provider of state government news. Boccardi stepped down as CEO in 2003, handing the reins to former *USA TODAY* publisher Tom Curley.

In 2004 AP relocated from Rockefeller Plaza (its home for the last 65 years) to a new headquarters on the west side of Manhattan that features a 105,000-sq.-ft. newsroom and serves as a central hub of digital news streams.

The company moved to strengthen its sports information coverage in 2005, merging its AP MegaSports operation with News Corporation's STATS, Inc. to form STATS, LLC, a 50-50 joint venture that provides sports-related information, content, and statistical analysis.

EXECUTIVES

Chairman: William D. (Dean) Singleton, age 58
Vice Chairman: Mary E. Junck, age 61
President and CEO: Thomas (Tom) Curley, age 60
SVP and CFO: Kenneth J. (Ken) Dale, age 52
SVP International Business: James M. (Jim) Donna, age 62
SVP Global Technology and VP Product Development: Lorraine Cichowski
SVP and Executive Editor: Kathleen Carroll
SVP Americas Media Markets and Global New Media: Sue A. Cross, age 48
SVP Sales and Marketing and Chief Revenue Officer: Thomas R. (Tom) Brettingen, age 60
SVP Global Product Development: Jane Seagrave, age 54

VP and Director Corporate Communications: Ellen Hale
VP and Director Strategic Planning: James M. Kennedy
VP Human Resources: Jessica Bruce, age 43
VP Global Technology Operations: Kurt Rossi
VP Sales, Europe, the Middle East, and Asia: Daisy Veerasingham
VP Global Security: C. Daniel (Danny) Spriggs
VP and General Counsel: Srinandan (Sri) Kasi, age 43
VP Images: Ian Cameron, age 52
VP Newspaper Markets: Thomas E. Slaughter
VP Marketing Operations: Joy Jones, age 38
Auditors: Ernst & Young LLP

LOCATIONS

HQ: The Associated Press
450 W. 33rd St., New York, NY 10001
Phone: 212-621-1500   **Fax:** 212-621-5447
Web: www.ap.org

PRODUCTS/OPERATIONS

Selected Products and Services

AP Digital News (Internet and wireless news delivery)
AP Images (photo services)
APTN (AP Television News, international television news service)
ENPS (electronic news production system)
Online Video Network (video content distribution)
STATS (sports-related content)

COMPETITORS

Agence France-Presse	Gannett
Bloomberg L.P.	Getty Images
Business Wire	New York Times
Comtex News	PR Newswire
Corbis	Reuters
Dow Jones	Tribune Company
E. W. Scripps	UPI

Associated Wholesale Grocers

Associated Wholesale Grocers (AWG) knows its customers can't live on bread and milk alone. The second largest retailer-owned cooperative in the US (behind Wakefern Food Corporation), AWG supplies more than 2,500 member-stores in about 25 states with a wide array of grocery items from its eight distribution facilities. In addition to its wholesale operation, AWG offers a variety of business services to its members, including marketing and merchandising programs, insurance, and store design. It also operates about 10 grocery store brands, including Country Mart and Homeland, and it owns a small number of supermarkets. AWG was founded by a group of independent grocers in 1924.

As a member-owned cooperative, AWG not only supplies its member stores with goods and services, but those independent retailers also benefit from profits generated by the business. The company focuses on expanding its membership by attracting additional independent retailers to its distribution network, as well as through selected acquisitions. It purchased certain assets from Little Rock, Arkansas-based Affiliated Foods Southwest (AFS) in 2009, adding about a dozen new stores. AFS had filed for bankruptcy and liquidated its assets that year.

AWG is also continuing to build sales for its private-label products such as Best Choice and Always Save. In addition to marketing the products as lower-cost alternatives to brand-name products, the co-op has been investing in efforts to make sure the quality of its private-label items matches competing national brands.

Operating in a fragmented business, AWG competes with a large number of local and regional suppliers, as well as distributors of specialty items. The food wholesale business also has its share of national giants, including C & S Wholesale, Nash-Finch, and the wholesale operations of supermarket operator SUPERVALU.

Company veteran Jerry Garland was promoted to CEO in 2009. He replaced longtime chief Gary Phillips, who retired that year.

HISTORY

About 20 Kansas City, Kansas-area grocers met in a local grocery in 1924 and organized the Associated Grocers Company to get better deals on purchases and advertising. They elected J. C. Harline president, and each chipped in a few hundred dollars to make their first purchases. It took a while to find a manufacturer who would sell directly to them; a local soap maker was finally convinced, and others gradually followed.

In 1926 the group was incorporated as Associated Wholesale Grocers (AWG). It outgrew two warehouses in four years, finally moving to a 16,000-sq.-ft. facility big enough to add new lines and more products. Membership doubled between 1930 and 1932 as grocers moved from ordering products a year ahead to the new wholesale concept, and members took seriously the slogan: "Buy, Sell, Buy Some More." They met every week to plan how to sell their products, and buyer and advertising manager Harry Small gave sales presentations and advertising ideas (his trade-in plan for old brooms sold more than two train-carloads of brooms in two weeks). Heavy newspaper advertising also paid off; AWG topped $1 million in sales in 1933.

The cooperative made its first acquisition in 1936, buying Progressive Grocers, a warehouse in Joplin, Missouri; a second warehouse named Associated Grocers was acquired the next year in Springfield, Missouri. AWG continued building and expanding warehouses, and annual sales were at $11 million by 1951.

Louis Fox became CEO in 1956. Fox maximized year-end rebates for members, led several acquisitions, and formed a new subsidiary for financing stores and small shopping centers where AWG members had a presence (Supermarket Developers). Sales increased nearly fifteen-fold to over $200 million in his first 15 years.

James Basha, who succeeded Fox when he retired in 1984, saw sales reach $2.4 billion by the time of his own retirement in 1992. Basha was followed by former COO Mike DeFabis, once a deputy mayor of Indianapolis.

DeFabis orchestrated several acquisitions, including 41 Kansas City-area stores — most of which were quickly bought by members — from bankrupt Food Barn Stores in 1994 and 29 Oklahoma stores and a warehouse from Safeway spinoff Homeland Stores in 1995 (members bought all the stores).

AWG's nonfood subsidiary, Valu Merchandisers Co., was established in 1995; its new Kansas warehouse began shipping health and beauty aids and housewares the following year to help members battle big discounters. Members narrowly defeated a proposal in late 1996 to convert the cooperative into a public company. Proponents promptly petitioned for a second vote, which was defeated early the next year.

AWG veteran Doug Carolan succeeded DeFabis in 1998, becoming only the fifth CEO in the cooperative's history. The company bought five Falley's and 33 Food 4 Less stores in Kansas and Missouri from Fred Meyer in 1998 for $300 million. In a break with tradition, AWG began operating the stores rather than selling them to members.

In 2000, after a months-long labor dispute with the Teamsters was resolved, Carolan left AWG. The company's CFO, Gary Phillips, was named president and CEO later that year. In 2001 the company debuted a new format, ALPS (Always Low Price Stores) — small stores that carry a limited selection of grocery top-sellers. Also that year AWG's Kansas City division began distributing to more than 10 new stores that had formerly been served by Fleming, at the time the #1 US wholesale food distributor.

In 2002 supermarket operator Homeland Stores, which operates stores in Oklahoma, emerged from bankruptcy as a fully owned subsidiary of AWG.

Introducing a "dollar" section in its stores in 2004 proved successful, leading AWG to expand the category to more than 1,000 food and non-food items. The following year it merged the corporate offices of its Homeland and Food 4 Less chains.

AWG took steps to expand its capacity and its territory in 2007 when it acquired a distribution center in Fort Worth from Albertsons. The cooperative also took on supply operations for Albertsons locations in Arkansas, Louisiana, and Texas. CEO Phillips retired in 2009 and was succeeded by AWG veteran Jerry Garland.

EXECUTIVES

Chairman: Bob Hufford
President and CEO: Jerry Garland, age 58
COO: Michael (Mike) Rand
EVP and CFO: Robert C. (Bob) Walker
SVP and Division Manager, Oklahoma: Steve Arnold
SVP and Division Manager, Kansas City:
  William A. (Bill) Quade
SVP and Division Manager, Kansas City: Gary Jennings
SVP, Grocery Products: Dennis Kinser, age 64
SVP, Perishables: Lucky Hicks
SVP and Division Manager, Nashville: Milton Milam
SVP, General Counsel, and Corporate Secretary:
  Frances Pellegrino Puhl, age 59
SVP, Real Estate and Store Engineering:
  Scott Wilmoski, age 56
VP and CIO: Keith Martin
VP, Corporate Sales: Bill Lancaster, age 69
VP, Corporate Human Resources: Frank Tricamo
President, Valu Merchandisers: Ken Nemeth
President and CEO, Benchmark Insurance Company:
  Bill Morrison
Auditors: KPMG LLP

LOCATIONS

HQ: Associated Wholesale Grocers, Inc.
  5000 Kansas Ave., Kansas City, KS 66106
Phone: 913-288-1000   **Fax:** 913-288-1587
Web: www.awginc.com

COMPETITORS

Affiliated Foods	GSC Enterprises
Affiliated Foods Midwest	Kroger
Alex Lee	McLane
Associated Grocers, Inc.	Nash-Finch
C & S Wholesale	Spartan Stores
Central Grocers	SUPERVALU
Dearborn Wholesale	Wal-Mart
Grocers	

HISTORICAL FINANCIALS
Company Type: Cooperative

Income Statement				FYE: Last Saturday in December
	REVENUE ($ mil.)	NET INCOME ($ mil.)	NET PROFIT MARGIN	EMPLOYEES
12/08	6,900	—	—	—
12/07	5,700	—	—	—
12/06	5,000	—	—	—
12/05	5,000	—	—	—
12/04	4,570	—	—	—
Annual Growth	10.8%	—	—	—

Revenue History

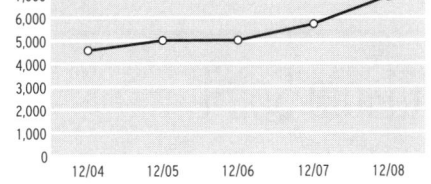

Associated Wholesalers

Grocery stores can profit from an association with this business. Associated Wholesalers, Inc., (AWI) is a retailer-owned cooperative that supplies a wide array of food and non-food products to independent grocers and convenience stores along the eastern seaboard from distribution centers in Pennsylvania and New Jersey. It distributes broadline grocery products, bakery goods, meat and dairy items, fresh produce, and frozen foods, as well as a full line of general merchandise products. Its White Rose Foods unit serves supermarkets and grocers in the New York City area, as well as in New Jersey and New England. AWI also operates more than a dozen supermarkets, mostly under the Shurfine Markets banner.

AWI took a major expansion step in 2006 when it acquired Di Giorgio Corporation, the parent holding company of White Rose Foods. The deal increased the company's geographic reach and added about 500 new grocers to its customer base.

EXECUTIVES

Chairman: Stewart E. Hartman Jr.
President and CEO: J. Christopher (Chris) Michael
EVP, Marketing and Merchandising: Bernie Ellis
EVP, Logistics: Robert Rippley

VP, Finance: Thomas C. Teeter
VP, Risk: W. Douglas Hager
VP, Procurement: Donald (Don) Tiesenga
VP, Store Development and Sales: James Cartin
VP, Information Systems: Glenn D. Kriczky
VP, Retail Operations: Steve Hunsinger
VP, Sales, Retail Development, Customer Service, and
  Pharmacy: Charles Yahn
Human Resources: Audrey Schein
President, White Rose: Joseph Fantozzi
Auditors: Beard Miller Company LLP

LOCATIONS

HQ: Associated Wholesalers, Inc.
  Route 422, Robesonia, PA 19551
Phone: 610-693-3161   **Fax:** 610-693-3171
Web: www.awiweb.com

COMPETITORS

Ahold USA
Associated Grocers of New England
C & S Wholesale
Dot Foods
Key Food
Krasdale Foods
Kroger
Nash-Finch
Pathmark Stores
SUPERVALU
Wakefern Food

HISTORICAL FINANCIALS
Company Type: Cooperative

Income Statement				FYE: July 31
	REVENUE ($ mil.)	NET INCOME ($ mil.)	NET PROFIT MARGIN	EMPLOYEES
12/08	1,100	—	—	2,100

A.T. Kearney

With roots going back to the founding of McKinsey & Company in 1926, A.T. Kearney has established a place for itself in the management consulting pantheon. Today's A.T. Kearney operates from offices in about 35 countries around the world. It offers consulting in a variety of areas, including growth strategies, IT strategies, and supply chain management. Clients have come from a wide range of industries, including automotive, financial services, health care, and utilities. A.T. Kearney is owned by its management team. The consulting firm took its current name in 1946 from that of Andrew T. Kearney, one of McKinsey's first partners.

A.T. Kearney hopes to grow by using its geographic reach to gain more business from clients with operations in multiple countries. As part of an environmental sustainability initiative, the firm aims to expand its use of collaborative technology to reach across geographic regions, in order to reduce consultants' travel and thus minimize the firm's overall carbon footprint. Lessons from the internal sustainability efforts are being applied to the firm's work for its customers, particularly on issues related to supply chains.

At the same time, A.T. Kearney is once again flexing its muscles as an independent consultancy after having operated under the wing of systems integrator and data management company HP Enterprise Services (formerly Electronic Data Systems) from 1995 until it was acquired by managers in January 2006.

EXECUTIVES

Chairman and Managing Officer: Paul A. Laudicina, age 57
COO; Managing Director, Asia Pacific: John Yoshimura
CFO: Dan A. DeCanniere
Chief Human Resources Officer: Peter (Pete) Pesce, age 58
VP Financial Institutions Group: Michael C. (Mike) Kim
VP Financial Institutions Group: Srini Venkateswaran
Partner and Leader, Financial Institutions Group: Rajiv Shah
Partner, Automotive Practice, Detroit: Bill Windle
Managing Director, North America: Michael J. (Mike) Tower, age 45
Head, European Region: Johan Aurik
General Counsel: Mark Berlind
Auditors: KPMG LLP

LOCATIONS

HQ: A.T. Kearney, Inc.
222 W. Adams St., Chicago, IL 60606
Phone: 312-648-0111   **Fax:** 312-223-6200
Web: www.atkearney.com

PRODUCTS/OPERATIONS

Selected Industries Served

Aerospace and defense
Automotive
Communications and high tech
Consumer industries and retail
Energy and process industries
Financial institutions
Pharmaceuticals and health care
Public sector
Transportation
Utilities

Selected Services

Enterprise services transformation
Growth strategies
Innovation and complexity management
IT strategies
Marketing and sales strategies
Manufacturing strategies
Merger and acquisition strategies
Procurement and analytic services
Strategic supply management
Supply chain management
Supply management services
Sustainability

COMPETITORS

Accenture
Bain & Company
BearingPoint
Booz Allen
Boston Consulting
Capgemini
Celerant Consulting
Computer Sciences Corp.
Deloitte Consulting
IBM Global Services
Infosys Consulting
McKinsey & Company
PA Consulting
Roland Berger

HISTORICAL FINANCIALS

Company Type: Private

Income Statement

FYE: December 31

	REVENUE ($ mil.)	NET INCOME ($ mil.)	NET PROFIT MARGIN	EMPLOYEES
12/07	785	—	—	2,500
12/06	798	—	—	2,500
12/05	700	—	—	2,500
12/04	806	—	—	—
12/03	846	—	—	4,000
Annual Growth	(1.9%)	—	—	(11.1%)

Revenue History

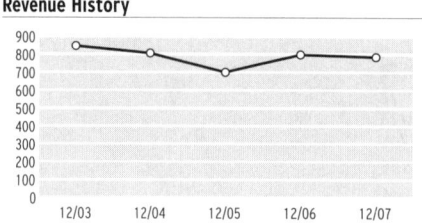

Atlanta Spirit

This company serves spirited Atlanta sports fans. Atlanta Spirit owns and operates two of the city's professional sports franchises, the Atlanta Hawks basketball team and the Atlanta Thrashers hockey team. The Hawks were formed in 1946, joined the National Basketball Association in 1949, and moved to Atlanta from St. Louis in 1968. The Thrashers joined the National Hockey League as an expansion franchise in 1999. Atlanta Spirit also operates Philips Arena, which serves as home for both teams. The sports investment partnership includes entrepreneurs Steve Belkin, Bruce Levenson, and Michael Gearon Jr.

Belkin and his partners have been embroiled in a public feud over the ownership of Atlanta Spirit since late in 2005. After a lawsuit, an injunction, and power plays of all sorts over the signing of guard Joe Johnson, Belkin originally agreed to sell his 30% stake in Atlanta Spirit to the other owners, but he has been battling in the courts over how to effect the sale.

Amid the turmoil, CEO Bernie Mullin left Atlanta Spirit in early 2008, followed by CFO Bill Duffy and several other top executives. A committee handles day-to-day operations at the firm, reporting to the estranged ownership group.

Atlanta Spirit acquired the sports franchises in 2004 for $250 million from Turner Sports, a unit of Time Warner's Turner Broadcasting.

EXECUTIVES

Owner: Michael Gearon Jr.
SVP Booking and Events, Philips Arena: Trey Feazell
SVP Broadcast and Corporate Partnerships: Tracy White
VP Finance: Phil Ebinger
VP and Chief Legal Officer: Scott Wilkinson
VP Operations: Patrick Lane
VP and Assistant General Manager Basketball Operations: Gary Fitzsimmons
VP Basketball: Dominique Wilkins

VP Public Relations: Arthur Triche
VP Business Development: David Lee
VP Marketing, Advertising, and Branding: Jim Pfeifer
President, Philips Arena: Bob Williams
Counsel: Melissa Linsky
Director Basketball Operations: Michael (Mike) McNeive
Manager Broadcast Services: Diana Corbin

LOCATIONS

HQ: Atlanta Spirit, LLC
101 Marietta St. NW, Ste. 1900, Atlanta, GA 30303
Phone: 404-878-3800
Web: www.atlantaspirit.com

COMPETITORS

Atlanta Braves
Atlanta Falcons
Atlanta Motor Speedway
Herschend Entertainment
Six Flags Over Georgia

HISTORICAL FINANCIALS

Company Type: Private

Income Statement

FYE: December 31

	REVENUE ($ mil.)	NET INCOME ($ mil.)	NET PROFIT MARGIN	EMPLOYEES
12/08	170	—	—	—
12/07	139	—	—	—
12/06	134	—	—	—
12/05	87	—	—	—
12/04	83	—	—	—
Annual Growth	19.6%	—	—	—

Revenue History

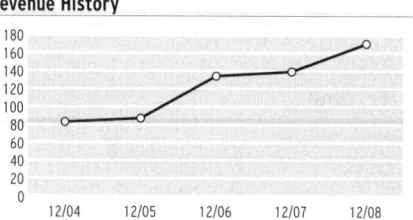

Atlantic Express Transportation

Driving with thousands of schoolchildren in the back seat, or rows of seats, doesn't bother Atlantic Express Transportation. The company serves about 100 school districts throughout the US with a fleet of some 5,600 vehicles. School bus services account for about 90% of the company's sales. In addition, Atlantic Express provides paratransit services (transportation of people with disabilities) in New York City and offers charter, express, and fixed-route bus services, mainly as a contractor for New York's Metropolitan Transportation Authority. Investment firm Greenwich Street Capital owns a controlling stake in Atlantic Express, which was founded in 1964.

Contracts with the New York City Department of Education, which represent a little more than half of the company's overall revenue, have been extended through 2010. Typically Atlantic Express has been able to renew contracts in order to ensure a steady revenue stream: More than 95% of its contracted revenue comes from customers who have worked with the company for five years or longer.

EXECUTIVES

President and CEO: Domenic Gatto, age 60
COO, Secretary, and Treasurer: Jerome (Jerry) Dente, age 63
CFO: Nathan Schlenker, age 70
EVP: Noel Cabrera, age 49
Auditors: BDO Seidman, LLP

LOCATIONS

HQ: Atlantic Express Transportation Corp.
7 North St., Staten Island, NY 10302
Phone: 718-442-7000   **Fax:** 718-442-7672
Web: www.atlanticexpress.com

Selected Operating Locations
California
Illinois
Massachusetts
Missouri
New Jersey
New York
Pennsylvania

PRODUCTS/OPERATIONS

2008 Sales

	$ mil.	% of total
School bus	386.3	89
Paratransit & transit	47.2	11
Total	**433.5**	**100**

COMPETITORS

FirstGroup America
MV Transportation
National Express Group
STA
Veolia Transportation

HISTORICAL FINANCIALS
Company Type: Private

Income Statement

	REVENUE ($ mil.)	NET INCOME ($ mil.)	NET PROFIT MARGIN	EMPLOYEES	FYE: June 30
6/08	434	(34)	—	7,600	
6/07	429	(17)	—	7,600	
6/06	414	(30)	—	8,100	
6/05	364	(42)	—	—	
6/04	364	57	15.6%	—	
Annual Growth	**4.5%**	**—**	**—**	**(3.1%)**	

2008 Year-End Financials

Debt ratio: —
Return on equity: —
Cash ($ mil.): —
Current ratio: —
Long-term debt ($ mil.): 191

Net Income History

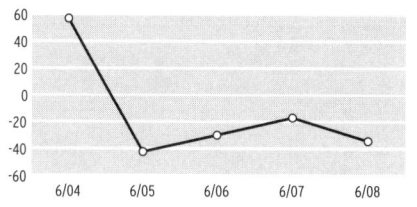

Atrium Companies

The way to Atrium's heart? Right through that sliding door. Atrium Companies makes and distributes vinyl and aluminium windows and patio doors for residential use. The company's brand names include Atrium, HR Windows, Champion Window, Superior Windows, and Darby Doors. It also makes the SafeHarbor brand of hurricane-resistant windows, doors, and shutters. The company's products are sold to the wholesale and retail markets. Atrium also offers installation and repair services. The company operates more than 50 manufacturing facilities and distribution centers throughout North America. Atrium was founded in 1948 and is majority-owned by investment firm Kenner & Company.

Housing and construction setbacks, particularly in Florida, and a worsening economy have prompted the company to rejigger operations. It closed plants in Connecticut, Arizona, and Florida in 2007 and 2008. In addition, it closed most of its sales and distribution offices in Florida in an effort to shift away from its direct-to-dealer sales model, and it sold its Miniature Die Casting window components subsidiary to cut costs. On the other hand, Atrium strengthened its Canadian operations with the 2007 acquisition of North Star Vinyl Windows and Doors.

EXECUTIVES

Chairman: Larry T. Solari, age 67
President and CEO: Gregory T. (Greg) Faherty
EVP and COO: Robert E. Burns
VP and CFO: Wayne Terry
SVP Human Resources: D. D. (Gus) Agostinelli
SVP, General Counsel, and Secretary:
Philip J. (Phil) Ragona
VP and CIO: Larry Freed
VP Marketing: Mark Gallant
President, Central Region: Art Steinhafel
President, R. G. Darby and Total Trim: Cliff Darby
President, Eastern Region: Robert Ractliffe
President, Western Region: Pete Venerdi
Treasurer: Patrick Coffee
Corporate Controller: Amber Vaught
Auditors: Deloitte & Touche LLP

LOCATIONS

HQ: Atrium Companies, Inc.
3890 W. Northwest Hwy., Ste. 500, Dallas, TX 75220
Phone: 214-630-5757   **Fax:** 214-630-5001
Web: home.atrium.com

PRODUCTS/OPERATIONS

Selected Products
Aluminum impact-resistant windows
Aluminum sliding patio doors
Awning windows
Bow windows
Patio enclosures
Picture windows
Single-hung windows
Slider windows
Vinyl deck rails
Vinyl sliding patio doors

Selected Subsidiaries
Danvid Window Company
Dow-Tech Plastics
HR Windows
North Star Windows & Doors
R.G. Darby Co., Inc.
Superior Engineered Products Corporation
Thermal Industries, Inc.
West Coast Custom Finish Inc.

COMPETITORS

Andersen Corporation
Crystal Window & Door Systems
Great Lakes Window
International Aluminum
JELD-WEN
Kolbe & Kolbe
Masco
Masonite
MI Windows and Doors
Milgard Manufacturing
MW Manufacturers
Pella
Silver Line Building Products
Simonton Windows, Inc.
Therma-Tru
TRACO
Weather Shield Manufacturing

HISTORICAL FINANCIALS
Company Type: Private

Income Statement

	REVENUE ($ mil.)	NET INCOME ($ mil.)	NET PROFIT MARGIN	EMPLOYEES	FYE: December 31
12/08	600	—	—	4,000	
12/07	700	—	—	5,100	
12/06	840	—	—	6,000	
12/05	800	—	—	7,000	
12/04	800	—	—	6,300	
Annual Growth	**(6.9%)**	**—**	**—**	**(10.7%)**	

Revenue History

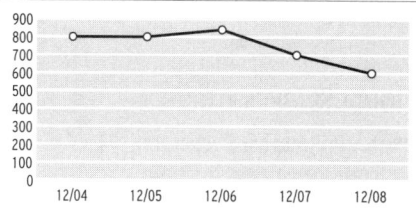

Austin Industries

Belying its name, Austin Industries is actually based in Dallas. The company provides civil, commercial, and industrial construction services in the southern half of the US. Its oldest subsidiary, Austin Bridge & Road, provides road, bridge, and parking lot construction across Texas. (It built the longest bridge in Texas, the Queen Isabella Causeway.) Subsidiary Austin Commercial builds office buildings, technology sites, hospitals, and other commercial projects. The group's Austin Industrial arm provides construction, maintenance, and electrical services for the chemical, refining, power, and manufacturing industries. The employee-owned company was founded in 1918.

The company, which has nearly $2 billion in annual revenue, has been involved in building many notable projects in the South and Southwest. Austin Bridge & Road's largest project to date is the four-level interchange in Texarkana, Texas. The $180 million project included work on 10 miles of frontage roads and reconstruction of several area bridges.

Austin Commercial's prize project, the Omni Fort Worth, includes more than 1 million sq. ft. of hotel, meeting, and event space. Other Austin Commercial projects include the American Airlines Center in Dallas, the Consolidated Rental Agency Complex at Hartsfield Jackson Airport in Atlanta, and the Irving Convention Center. The subsidiary also has been tapped to build a new $425 million terminal at Los Angeles International Airport.

Austin Industries is committed to workplace diversity. It has a unit devoted to diversity affairs, which seeks women-owned, minority-owned, and disadvantaged companies with which to do business or to provide mentorships.

EXECUTIVES

President and CEO: Ronald J. (Ron) Gafford, age 59
CFO: JT Fisher
CIO: Stan Smith
VP Human Resources and Treasurer:
 James (Jim) Schranz
President, Austin Commercial: David B. Walls
President, Austin Industrial: Barry Babyak
President, Austin Bridge & Road:
 James R. (Jim) Andoga
Director Corporate Communications: Lori E. Brakhage
General Counsel: Charles Hardy
Manager Communications: Kay Bishop
Corporate Controller: Dana Bartholomew

LOCATIONS

HQ: Austin Industries, Inc.
 3535 Travis, Ste. 300, Dallas, TX 75204
Phone: 214-443-5500
Web: www.austin-ind.com

PRODUCTS/OPERATIONS

Selected Projects and Customers

Austin Commercial
 ACME Brick Headquarters (Ft. Worth, TX)
 Alamo County Community College District (Universal City, TX)
 AMD Fab 25 (Austin, TX)
 AMD Lone Star Campus (Austin)
 American Airlines Center (Dallas)
 American Airlines Terminal, Miami International Airport
 Bank of America Plaza (Dallas)
 Burlington Northern Santa Fe Command Station and Headquarters (Ft. Worth)
 Chase Tower (Dallas)
 Children's Medical Center Legacy (Plano, TX)
 Citigroup North Texas expansion (Irving, TX)
 Dallas Convention Center (2002 expansion)
 Federal Reserve Automation System Consolidation (data center, Dallas)
 Hartfield Jackson Airport, Consolidated Rental Agency Complex (Atlanta)
 Irving Convention Center (Irving, TX)
 Marriott Hotel & Golf Club (Ft. Worth)
 Museum of Living Art at the Fort Worth Zoo
 Omni Fort Worth
 Presbyterian Hospital of Plano Tower III (Plano, TX)
 Taylor Place (ASU dormitories, Phoenix)
 TCU Recreation Center (Ft. Worth)
 UNT Chemistry Building (Denton, TX)
 UNT School of Public Health (Ft. Worth)
 UT Applied Computational Engineering & Sciences Building (Austin)
 UT Executive Education and Conference Center (Austin)
 UT Southwestern Medical Center T. Boone Pickens Biomedical Building and Conference Center (Dallas)
 W Austin

Austin Industrial
 Augusta Service Company (contract services)
  DSM Chemicals
  DSM Resins
  Nylon Polymer
  W.R. Grace
 BP Exploration, Gas-to-Liquids Test Facility (Nikiski, AK)
 Nordic Biofuels Ethanol Plant (Ravenna, NE)
Bridge & Road
 Barksdale Bridge (Shreveport, LA)
 Dallas North Tollway at Oak Lawn
 Dallas Area Rapid Transit (DART) Blue Line Expansion
 Elm Fork (railroad bridge, Dallas)
 Port Isabella Causeway (Cameron County, TX)
 Texarkana, IH-30 (bridges, turnarounds, flyover ramps; Texarkana, TX)
 Westpark Tollway (flyover ramps, Houston)

COMPETITORS

Balfour Beatty
Bechtel
Beck Group
Brasfield & Gorrie
Choate Construction
Flintco
Fluor
Granite Construction
Halliburton
Hardin Construction
Hensel Phelps Construction
Hunt Construction
JC General Contractors
J.F. Shea
MYR Group
Peter Kiewit Sons'
Rooney Holdings
Shaw Group
Skanska
Sundt
Swinerton
Turner Corporation
Turner Industries
Vecellio & Grogan
Zachry Inc.

HISTORICAL FINANCIALS

Company Type: Private

Income Statement

FYE: December 31

	REVENUE ($ mil.)	NET INCOME ($ mil.)	NET PROFIT MARGIN	EMPLOYEES
12/08	2,000	—	—	6,000
12/07	1,700	—	—	5,600
12/06	1,310	—	—	6,000
12/05	1,359	—	—	6,000
12/04	1,230	—	—	5,300
Annual Growth	12.9%	—	—	3.1%

Revenue History

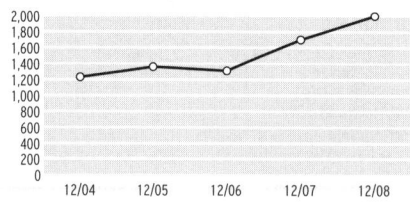

Auto-Owners Insurance Group

There's more to Auto-Owners Insurance Group than the name implies. In addition to auto coverage, the company provides a range of personal property/casualty and life insurance products including disability and annuities. Auto-Owners Insurance operates through its aptly named subsidiaries (including Auto-Owners Life Insurance, Home-Owners Insurance, and Property-Owners Insurance Company). Its Southern-Owners Insurance subsidiary offers property/casualty insurance in Florida. Auto-Owners Insurance also sells commercial auto, liability, and workers' compensation policies. Established in 1916, the company operates in 25 states nationwide and is represented by some 35,000 independent agents in about 6,000 agencies.

Most of the company's revenues come from Florida and Michigan. Auto-Owners is focused on growing its business by establishing strong relationships with independent agents and by diversifying its product offerings.

The company has also been expanding through new construction, opening regional offices in Jackson, Tennessee; Fargo, North Dakota; and Pittsburgh. In 2009 it opened two more offices in Utah and Kentucky. Auto-Owners Insurance also opened a data center to house document processing and premium payment processing near its headquarters in Michigan. In addition, the company is considering a more than $1 million expansion of its corporate complex that would include building a three-story facility on about 140 acres. The expansion would begin in 2012 and be wrapped up two years later.

EXECUTIVES

Chairman and CEO: Ron H. Simon
President: Jeffrey F. Harrold
EVP: Rodney Rupp

LOCATIONS

HQ: Auto-Owners Insurance Group
 6101 Anacapri Blvd., Lansing, MI 48917
Phone: 517-323-1200   **Fax:** 517-323-8796
Web: www.auto-owners.com

PRODUCTS/OPERATIONS

Selected Subsidiaries

Auto-Owners Insurance Company (group's largest property & casualty insurer; 25 states)
Auto-Owners Life Insurance Company (life insurance; 25 states)
Home-Owners Insurance Company (property & casualty; Michigan and Ohio)
Owners Insurance Company (property & casualty; 24 states)
Property-Owners Insurance Company (property & casualty; Indiana and Michigan)
Southern-Owners Insurance Company (property & casualty; Florida)

COMPETITORS

ACE Limited
AIG
Allstate
American Family Insurance
American National Property And Casualty
Century-National Insurance
CNA Financial
Farmers Group
GEICO
Hanover Insurance
The Hartford
Mercury General
MetLife
Nationwide
Progressive Corporation
Prudential
Safeco
State Farm
Travelers Companies

HISTORICAL FINANCIALS

Company Type: Private

Income Statement

	REVENUE ($ mil.)	NET INCOME ($ mil.)	NET PROFIT MARGIN	EMPLOYEES
12/08	4,951	206	4.2%	3,400
12/07	4,802	467	9.7%	3,400
12/06	5,074	634	12.5%	3,400
12/05	5,001	623	12.5%	3,300
12/04	4,714	191	4.0%	3,270
Annual Growth	1.2%	1.9%	—	1.0%

FYE: December 31

Net Income History

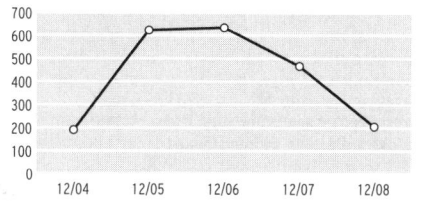

Avaya Inc.

Avaya helps to tie the corporate world together. The company's communication equipment and software integrates voice and data services for customers including large corporations, government agencies, and small businesses. Avaya's office phone systems incorporate IP telephony, messaging, Web access, and interactive voice response. The company offers a wide array of consulting, integration, and managed services through its Avaya Global Services unit. It sells directly and through distributors, resellers, systems integrators, and telecom service providers. Avaya was acquired by Silver Lake Partners and TPG Capital for $8.2 billion in 2007.

Consolidation in the telecommunications equipment sector had fueled speculation that Avaya was a takeover target, either for private equity investors or competitors such as Cisco Systems and Nortel Networks. Silver Lake and TPG paid $17.50 a share to purchase Avaya. In 2008 Avaya announced that Kevin Kennedy, CEO of optical networking specialist JDS Uniphase,

will take over as CEO of Avaya in 2009. The company's current CEO, Cisco veteran Charles Giancarlo, will become chairman.

Avaya continues to utilize both a direct sales force and partners to market its wares, but the company's sales strategy has seen it place increasing emphasis on building its channel sales.

The company has supplemented its internal product development with a string of acquisitions. It bought audio conferencing systems maker Spectel in late 2004 and Nimcat Networks, a developer of peer-to-peer communications software, in 2005. Avaya acquired mobile device communications software developer Traverse Networks in 2006.

In 2009 it announced plans to purchase the enterprise solutions business of bankrupt competitor Nortel for $475 million. The company says that the acquisition will enable it to expand its channel partner network and bolster its product and service offerings.

Avaya continues to sell traditional communications equipment with an eye toward helping customers with legacy voice products migrate to converged, IP-based systems.

EXECUTIVES

Chairman: Charles H. (Charlie) Giancarlo, age 51
President and CEO: Kevin J. Kennedy, age 53
SVP and CFO: Anthony J. (Tony) Massetti, age 49
SVP and President, Global Communications Solutions: Stuart Wells
SVP and CIO: Lorie Buckingham, age 49
SVP; President, Operations: Jim Chirico
SVP Global Business Operations: Micky S. Tsui
SVP Human Resources: Roger C. Gaston, age 50
SVP Marketing: Vance Williams LaVelle
SVP Strategy and Technology: Karyn Mashima, age 55
SVP Manufacturing, Logistics, and Procurement: Francis M. (Fran) Scricco, age 60
SVP; President, Avaya Global Services: Chris Formant
SVP; President, Global Communications: Alan E. Baratz, age 54
VP, Treasurer and Investor Relations: Matthew W. Booher
President, Avaya Labs: Ravi Sethi
President, Avaya Global Services: Christopher M. (Chris) Formant, age 51
Chief Administrative Officer: Pamela F. Craven, age 55
Auditors: PricewaterhouseCoopers LLP

LOCATIONS

HQ: Avaya Inc.
211 Mount Airy Rd., Basking Ridge, NJ 07920
Phone: 908-953-6000   **Fax:** 908-953-7609
Web: www.avaya.com

PRODUCTS/OPERATIONS

Selected Products

Global Communications Solutions
  Communications systems
    Appliances, Mobile, and Small Systems Division (traditional and IP phones, wireless devices, phone accessories)
    Customer Service Applications Division (contact center hardware and software)
    Unified Communications Division (Avaya Communications Portal, modular messaging, multimedia conferencing, video, IP soft phones)
  Converged voice applications
    Media gateways
    Media servers
    Session Initiation Protocol (SIP) enablement services
    Voice and data infrastructure management tools
    Voice application software

Avaya Global Services
  Applications design and integration
  Business communications strategy development and planning
  Communications support and network monitoring
  Globalization planning
  IP migration
  Managed business communications services
  Security consulting and integration

COMPETITORS

3Com
Aastra Technologies
Accenture
Active Voice, LLC
Alcatel-Lucent
Aspect Software
Cisco Systems
Computer Sciences Corp.
Comverse Technology
Ericsson
IBM Global Services
Microsoft
Mitel Networks
NEC
Nokia Siemens Networks
Nortel Networks
Panasonic Corporation of North America
Polycom
Unisys

Bad Boy Worldwide Entertainment Group

From music to fashion to food, Bad Boy Worldwide Entertainment Group sells attitude and image. The company oversees the business interests of its founder, owner, and CEO Sean "Diddy" Combs, a music impresario, fashion designer, and business mogul. Combs' core business is Bad Boy Records, founded in 1994 with Craig Mack and the late Notorious B.I.G., which produces such artists as Yung Joc, Danity Kane, and Cassie, as well as the music of Diddy himself. The label is 50% owned by Warner Music Group (WMG). Combs also markets branded clothing through Sean John Clothing and operates two upscale restaurants called Justin's (named after Combs' oldest son) in New York City and Atlanta.

Diddy, who has also gone by the monikers Puffy, Puff Daddy, and most recently P. Diddy, is active in a variety of projects that complement his expanding media and fashion portfolio. In 2009 he launched "P. Twitty TV," which added a video blog component to his Twitter messages. The previous year the entrepreneur acquired the fashion label ENYCE from Liz Claiborne.

Bad Boy Worldwide Entertainment Group's other recent activities include teaming with MTV Networks to produce TV shows such as the reality series *Making the Band, Taquita & Kaui*, and *Run's House*. In addition, the company partnered with HBO for *P. Diddy Presents: The Bad Boys of Comedy*, a series starring underground comedians performing before a live audience at the Brooklyn Academy of Music.

Combs' sixth album, *Last Train To Paris*, is scheduled for a 2010 release through Bad Boy

Records. The label was originally a joint venture between Combs and Arista Records, an imprint of Sony Music Entertainment (formerly Sony BMG). Arista, however, eventually dropped the label due to lagging sales. Bad Boy Records formed a partnership with WMG in 2005 to distribute albums through its Atlantic Records unit. The $30 million distribution deal gave WMG a 50% stake in the record company.

EXECUTIVES

Chairman and CEO, Bad Boy Worldwide Entertainment Group and Sean John Clothing; CEO, Blue Flame Marketing and Advertising: Sean (Diddy) Combs, age 39
President, Bad Boy Records: Harve Pierre
CFO: Derek Ferguson
EVP Brand Development and Licensing, Sean John Clothing: Jeff Tweedy
SVP Radio Promotion, Bad Boy Records: Mel Smith
General Manager, Blue Flame Marketing and Advertising: Dia Simms, age 34
Senior Director A&R, Bad Boy Records: Conrad Dimanche
National Director Mix Show and Club Promotion, Bad Boy Records: Henry Polanco
Director A&R, Bad Boy Records: Shannon Lawrence

LOCATIONS

HQ: Bad Boy Worldwide Entertainment Group
  1710 Broadway, New York, NY 10019
Phone: 212-381-1540   **Fax:** 212-381-1599
Web: www.badboyonline.com

PRODUCTS/OPERATIONS

Selected Operations

Bad Boy Records
Blue Flame Marketing + Advertising
Justin's (restaurant)
Sean John Clothing

Selected Bad Boy Artists

Aasim
Cassie
Danity Kane
Day26
Diddy
Elephant Man
Notorious B.I.G.
Yung JOC

COMPETITORS

Armani
Capitol Records
Columbia Records
Epic Records
FUBU
Hugo Boss
Interscope Geffen A&M
Island Def Jam
Motown Records
Roc Apparel
Rush Communications
Tommy Boy
Zomba

HISTORICAL FINANCIALS

Company Type: Private

Income Statement				FYE: December 31
	REVENUE ($ mil.)	NET INCOME ($ mil.)	NET PROFIT MARGIN	EMPLOYEES
12/08	300	—	—	600
12/07	500	—	—	—
Annual Growth	(40.0%)	—	—	—

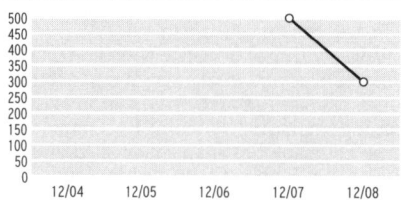
Badger State Ethanol

Badger State Ethanol hopes to badger gasoline consumers into using its ethanol. The company manufactures fuel-grade ethanol (a performance-enhancing gasoline additive derived from processing corn into ethyl alcohol) at the rate of about 50 million gallons per year at its plant in Wisconsin. Its ethanol is marketed through distributor Murex; the firm has also opened a retail fuel station. Badger State Ethanol also sells 125,000 tons a year of distiller's grains (an animal feed supplement) and carbon dioxide, two by-products of ethanol production. The company was formed in 2000 and opened its ethanol plant in 2002.

EXECUTIVES

Chairman: Nathan (Nate) Klassy
CFO: James (Jim) Leitzinger, age 53
President, General Manager, and Director: Gary L. Kramer, age 60
VP and Director: David Kolsrud, age 60
Office Manager: Cindy Sigafus
Manager Maintenance: Bill Jacobson
Plant Manager: Kurt Koller
Director, Distiller's Sales and Marketing: George Drewry
Administrative Assistant and Safety Director: Laurie Cannova
Commodity Manager: Erik Huschitt
Secretary and Director: Kevin Malchine
Auditors: Grant Thornton LLP

LOCATIONS

HQ: Badger State Ethanol, LLC
  820 W. 17th St., Monroe, WI 53566
Phone: 608-329-3900   **Fax:** 608-329-3866
Web: www.badgerstateethanol.com

COMPETITORS

Abengoa Bioenergy
ADM
Ag Processing
Cargill
Iogen Corporation
Lake Area Corn Processors
Little Sioux Corn Processors
Northern Growers
Pacific Ethanol
United Wisconsin

Bain & Company

Bain aims to be ready when corporate titans need a little direction. One of the world's leading management consulting firms, Bain & Company offers a wide array of services aimed at increasing efficiency and streamlining business processes. The firm also consults on strategic business issues, such as potential mergers and acquisitions and private equity investments; services include due-diligence preparation. In addition, Bain consultants address topics such as information technology, marketing, and performance improvement. With more than 3,500 consultants, the firm operates from more than 35 offices in about two dozen countries. It was founded in 1973 by Boston Consulting Group alumnus Bill Bain.

As companies have become more savvy about what consulting firms can and cannot do, as well as more sensitive to costs, they have started to demand smaller engagements that will produce specific business improvements, and less "big picture" consulting. For its part, Bain measures success by its ability to improve clients' financial results.

Although founded by the same individuals, Bain & Company and investment firm Bain Capital are separate entities.

EXECUTIVES

Chairman: Orit Gadiesh, age 58
Worldwide Managing Director: Steve Ellis
Head of Global Energy Practice: Peter Parry
Managing Director, Chicago: Michael Collins
Managing Director, San Francisco and Palo Alto: Tom Holland
Managing Director, Atlanta: Alan Colberg
Managing Partner, São Paulo: Giovanni Fiorentino
Managing Partner, China: Michael Thorneman
Worldwide Senior, Director Public Relations: Cheryl Krauss
Director, Global Human Capital: Elizabeth Corcoran
Treasurer: Andrew J. Frommer

LOCATIONS

HQ: Bain & Company, Inc.
  131 Dartmouth St., Boston, MA 02116
Phone: 617-572-2000   **Fax:** 617-572-2427
Web: www.bain.com

PRODUCTS/OPERATIONS

Selected Practice Areas

Change management
Corporate renewal
Corporate strategy
Cost and supply chain management
Customer strategy and marketing
Growth strategy
IT
Mergers and acquisitions
Organization
Performance improvement
Private equity

COMPETITORS

Accenture	IBM
A.T. Kearney	Keane
BearingPoint	McKinsey & Company
Booz Allen	Oliver Wyman
Boston Consulting	PA Consulting
Capgemini	Perot Systems
Computer Sciences Corp.	Roland Berger
Deloitte Consulting	Towers Perrin

HISTORICAL FINANCIALS

Company Type: Private

Income Statement

	ESTIMATED REVENUE ($ mil.)	NET INCOME ($ mil.)	NET PROFIT MARGIN	EMPLOYEES
12/07	1,640	—	—	4,083
12/06	1,310	—	—	3,550
12/05	1,130	—	—	3,200
Annual Growth	20.5%	—	—	13.0%

FYE: December 31

Revenue History

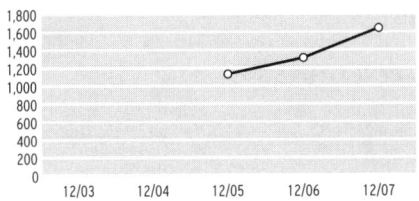

Baker & McKenzie

Baker & McKenzie believes big is good and bigger is better. One of the world's largest law firms, it has about 3,900 attorneys practicing from some 70 offices — from Bangkok to Berlin to Buenos Aires — in almost 40 countries. It offers expertise in a wide range of practice areas, including antitrust, intellectual property, international trade, mergers and acquisitions, project finance, and tax law. Baker & McKenzie's client list includes big companies from numerous industries, including banking and finance, construction, and technology, as well as smaller enterprises.

Baker & McKenzie is known for the geographic scope of its practice — some 80% of the firm's attorneys work outside the US. The firm touts its widespread network of offices as an advantage for clients with multinational interests.

The vast scale of Baker & McKenzie's operations increases the firm's exposure to liability, however, and that concern led Baker & McKenzie to reorganize itself as a Swiss Verein in 2004. Under the new structure, which is used by accounting firms such as Deloitte Touche Tohmatsu, Baker & McKenzie's member firms operate as separate entities, insulating the parent firm from liability. Baker & McKenzie was the first international law firm to organize itself under a Verein structure.

HISTORY

Russell Baker traveled from his native New Mexico to Chicago on a railroad freight car to attend law school. Upon graduation in 1925 he started practicing law with his classmate Dana Simpson under the name Simpson & Baker. Inspired by Chicago's role as a manufacturing and agricultural center for the world and influenced by the international focus of his alma mater, the University of Chicago, Baker dreamed of creating an international law practice. He began developing an expertise in international law, and in 1934 Abbott Laboratories retained him to handle its worldwide legal affairs. Baker was on his way to fulfilling his dream.

Baker joined forces with Chicago litigator John McKenzie in 1949, forming Baker & McKenzie. In 1955 the firm opened its first foreign office in Caracas, Venezuela, to meet the needs of its expanding US client base. Over the next 10 years it branched out into Asia, Australia, and Europe, with offices in London, Manila, Paris, and Tokyo. Baker's death in 1979 neither slowed the firm's growth nor changed its international character. The next year it expanded into the Middle East and opened its 30th office in 1982 (Melbourne). To manage the sprawling law firm, Baker & McKenzie created the position of chairman of the executive committee in 1984.

In late 1991 the firm dropped the Church of Scientology as a client, losing an estimated $2 million in business. It was speculated that pressure from client Eli Lilly (maker of the drug Prozac, which Scientologists actively oppose) influenced the decision. In 1992 Baker & McKenzie was ordered to pay $1 million for wrongfully firing an employee who later died of AIDS. (The case became the basis for the 1993 film *Philadelphia*.) The firm fought the verdict but eventually settled for an undisclosed amount in 1995.

In 1994 Baker & McKenzie closed its Los Angeles office (the former MacDonald, Halsted & Laybourne; acquired 1988) amid considerable rancor. Also that year a former secretary at the firm received a $7.1 million judgment for sexual harassment by a partner. (A San Francisco Superior Court judge later reduced the award to $3.5 million.)

John Klotsche, a senior partner from the firm's Palo Alto, California, office, was appointed chairman in 1995. The following year the firm began a major expansion into California's Silicon Valley as part of an initiative to serve technology companies around the world. It also expanded its Warsaw, Poland, office through a merger with the Warsaw office of Dickinson, Wright, Moon, Van Dusen & Freman.

In 1998 Baker & McKenzie formed a special unit in Singapore to deal with business generated by the financial troubles in Asia. The opening of offices in Taiwan and Azerbaijan in 1998 brought the firm's total number of offices to 59. Klotsche stepped down in 1999 as the firm celebrated its 50th anniversary; Christine Lagarde replaced him. In early 2001 Baker & McKenzie created a joint venture practice with Singapore-based associate firm Wong & Leow. Also that year it merged with Madrid-based Briones Alonso y Martin to create the largest independent law firm in Spain.

Lagarde stepped down as executive chairman in 2004, and John Conroy was chosen to lead the firm.

EXECUTIVES

Chairman: John J. Conroy Jr.
Global COO: Greg Walters
Global CFO: Robert S. Spencer
Global Director Information Systems: Martin Telfer
Global Director Practice Groups: Dave Southern
Global Director Talent Management: Vicki Kelley
Global Director Knowledge Management: Michael Campbell
Global Director Communications: Mark Bain
Member Executive Committee, Hong Kong: Tan Poh Lee
Member Executive Committee, London: Beatriz P. de Araujo
Member Executive Committee, San Francisco: Peter J. Engstrom
Member Executive Committee, Mexico City: Raymundo E. Enriquez
Member Executive Committee, Dallas: Alan G. Harvey

Regional Operating Officer, Latin America: Leon J. Sacks
Regional Operating Officer, North America: Joseph Plack
Regional Operating Officer, Asia Pacific: Paul Malliate
Regional Operating Officer, Europe, Middle East, and Central Asia: Kate Stonestreet
General Counsel: Edward J. Zulkey
Manager Marketing, North America: Heidi Bouldin
Senior Public Relations Coordinator: Jessica Benzon

LOCATIONS

HQ: Baker & McKenzie
1 Prudential Plaza, 130 E. Randolph Dr., Ste. 2500
Chicago, IL 60601
Phone: 312-861-8800 **Fax:** 312-861-8823
Web: www.bakernet.com

PRODUCTS/OPERATIONS

Selected Practice Areas

Antitrust and trade
Banking and finance
Corporate
Dispute resolution
Employment
Insurance
Intellectual property
International/commercial
IT/communications
Major projects and project finance
Pharmaceuticals and health care
Real estate, construction, environment, and tourism
Tax

COMPETITORS

Clifford Chance
DLA Piper
Jones Day
Kirkland & Ellis
Latham & Watkins
Mayer Brown
McDermott Will & Emery
Shearman & Sterling
Sidley Austin
Skadden, Arps
Sullivan & Cromwell
Weil, Gotshal & Manges
White & Case

HISTORICAL FINANCIALS

Company Type: Private

Income Statement

	REVENUE ($ mil.)	NET INCOME ($ mil.)	NET PROFIT MARGIN	EMPLOYEES
6/09	2,110	—	—	9,700
6/08	2,190	—	—	9,700
6/07	1,829	—	—	9,600
6/06	1,522	—	—	9,503
6/05	1,352	—	—	8,500
Annual Growth	11.8%	—	—	3.4%

FYE: June 30

Revenue History

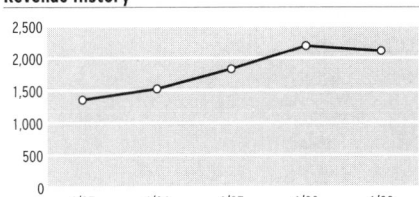

Baker & Taylor

If you've strolled through a library recently, you likely saw a lot of Baker & Taylor (B&T) without knowing it. The #1 book supplier to libraries, B&T primarily serves two types of markets. Its core business distributes books, calendars, music, games, and DVDs to thousands of school, public, and specialty libraries worldwide. The firm's retail unit supplies storefront and Internet book and music retailers, as well as independent booksellers, with a million book titles and about 385,000 DVD and CD titles. On the Internet (where it formerly operated as Informata.com) B&T offers B2B e-commerce fulfillment services. Investment firm Willis Stein & Partners sold the company to Castle Harlan in 2006.

Leadership changes in mid-2008 are taking the company in a new direction. The firm is focusing on its more profitable library and education business, and trimming its exposure to the retail market, especially home entertainment retail.

Castle Harlan bought B&T for about $455 million for its direct-to-home distribution for Internet retailers and its library-based business model. Castle Harlan's belief that B&T's library business and its Internet retailing wholesale segment would continue to grow spurred the deal to buy the company.

B&T's YBP Library Services unit offers acquisition and collection management support services to libraries. It supplies public and school libraries with both paper-based and digital books. B&T's fulfillment customers include companies such as Amazon.com and barnesandnoble.com. The retail unit also handles the company's international operations.

B&T offers automatic shipping of books by popular authors (mailed as soon as they are published), and its J.A. Majors Company subsidiary is a major supplier of medical books to the educational and professional health markets.

The company acquired most of Advanced Marketing Services' assets in 2007, boosting its customer service offerings.

EXECUTIVES

Chairman and CEO: Thomas I. (Tom) Morgan, age 55
President: Marshall A. (Arnie) Wight
EVP and CFO: Jeff Leonard
EVP Marketing: Kimberly (Kim) Kuo
EVP Strategic Business Development:
  Robert C. (Bob) Nelson
SVP Operations: Gary Dayton
SVP and CIO: Matt Carroll
SVP Retail and International Sales:
  William (Bill) Preston
SVP Information Systems Development: Dan Johnson
SVP Human Resources: Rick Mark
VP Book Merchandising: John Lindsay
President, Baker & Taylor Retail: David K. Cully, age 49
President, Baker & Taylor Institutional: George Coe

LOCATIONS

HQ: Baker & Taylor, Inc.
  2550 W. Tyvola Rd., Ste. 300, Charlotte, NC 28217
Phone: 704-998-3100   **Fax:** 704-998-3316
Web: www.btol.com

PRODUCTS/OPERATIONS

Selected Products and Services

Accessories
Calendars
Cataloging database (B&T MARC)
CD-ROM and Internet database and ordering software (Title Source II)
CDs
DVDs
Games
Hardcover and paperback books
Library acquisition and collection management services (YBP Library Services)
Medical books (J.A. Majors Company)
Spoken-word media
Standing-order service (Compass)
Videos

COMPETITORS

Alliance Entertainment
Dawson Holdings
East Texas Distributing
Educational Development
Follett
Ingram Content
Ingram Industries
Levy Home Entertainment
Media Source
Navarre
Rentrak
Scholastic
Source Interlink

Baker Botts

Baker Botts is a Lone Star legal legend. The law firm's history stretches back to 1840, when founding partner Peter Gray was admitted to the bar of the Republic of Texas. The firm became Baker & Botts after Walter Browne Botts and James Addison Baker (great-grandfather of former US Secretary of State and current partner James A. Baker III) joined the partnership. The firm has some 800 lawyers in about a dozen offices worldwide. Over the years Baker Botts has represented numerous clients from the energy industry, including Exxon Mobil and Halliburton. The firm practices in such areas as corporate, intellectual property, and tax law.

In 2009 Baker & Botts expanded its international footprint when it opened an office Abu Dhabi, its third office in the Middle East. Over the years the company has provided merger and acquisition services as well as consultation on oil and gas field development. It has also assisted chemical plants in the region with methods for expansion.

EXECUTIVES

Managing Partner: Walter J. (Walt) Smith
CFO: Lydia Companion
Director Information Technology: Mark Hendrick
Chief Administrative Officer: Mark White
Senior Partner: James A. Baker III
Partner-in-Charge, New York: Lee D. Charles
Partner-in-Charge, CIS: Steven (Steve) Wardlaw
Partner-in-Charge, Austin: James W. (Jim) Cannon Jr.
Partner-in-Charge, Beijing: John T. Kuzmik
Partner-in-Charge, Houston: Maria Wyckoff Boyce
Partner-in-Charge, Dallas: Jack L. Kinzie
Partner-in-Charge, Washington, D.C.:
  James A. (Jamie) Baker IV
Director Attorney Recruiting and Development:
  Rachel Koenig
Director Human Resources: Roger Walter
Director Client Relations: Catherine Austin
Manager Public Relations: Michael A. (Mike) Cinelli
Director Knowledge Services: Tracy Hallenberger

LOCATIONS

HQ: Baker Botts L.L.P.
  1 Shell Plaza, 910 Louisiana St., Houston, TX 77002
Phone: 713-229-1234   **Fax:** 713-229-1522
Web: www.bakerbotts.com

PRODUCTS/OPERATIONS

Major Practice Areas

Corporate
Environmental
Global Projects
Intellectual Property
Litigation
Tax

COMPETITORS

Akin Gump
Andrews Kurth
Bracewell & Patterson
Fulbright & Jaworski
Thompson and Knight
Vinson & Elkins

HISTORICAL FINANCIALS

Company Type: Partnership

Income Statement

FYE: December 31

	REVENUE ($ mil.)	NET INCOME ($ mil.)	NET PROFIT MARGIN	EMPLOYEES
12/08	614	—	—	—
12/07	578	—	—	—
12/06	503	—	—	—
12/05	365	—	—	—
12/04	420	—	—	1,601
Annual Growth	9.9%	—	—	—

Revenue History

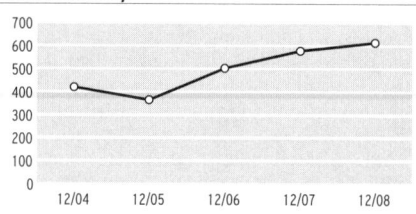

Banner Health

Hoist this Banner high! Banner Health is one of the largest secular not-for-profit health systems in the US. The organization operates more than 20 hospitals (with nearly 4,000 beds). It also operates clinics, nursing homes, clinical laboratories, ambulatory surgery centers, home health agencies, and other health care-related organizations, including physician practices and a captive insurance company. Banner Health also participates in medical research in areas such as Alzheimer's disease and spinal cord injuries through its Banner Research division. The company provides services in seven states in the western US; its largest concentration of facilities is in Arizona.

In 2009 Banner Health became one of the first not-for-profit hospital operators to begin reinsuring its employees after it won approval from the US Labor Department to reinsure employee benefits through its captive insurance company,

Samaritan Insurance Funding. The move allowed Banner Health to diversify its risk, improve cash flow, and lower life insurance costs by about half a million dollars a year.

Banner Health derives the majority of its revenue (about 65%) from third-party payors, such as commercial insurance and managed care agreements. Medicare and Medicaid, plus a small portion of self-pay patients, make up the remainder of Banner Health's income.

In 2008 Banner Health acquired Sun Health, a fellow Arizona care provider with two hospitals in Phoenix, as well as research and health insurance programs.

The health system also grows through construction. Banner Health is nearly always engaged in some sort of construction, renovation, or upgrade at its numerous facilities. The organization has more than $1 billion in construction projects in progress or completed in recent years. The system has expanded its facilities at Banner Baywood Medical Center, Banner Del E. Webb Medical Center, Banner Desert Medical Center, Banner Thunderbird Medical Center, Cardon Children's Medical Center, and McKee Medical Center.

Banner Health has also partnered with M.D. Anderson Cancer Center to build a comprehensive cancer center in Phoenix. Services will include medical oncology, radiation oncology, surgical oncology, pathology, laboratory, diagnostic imaging, as well as other supportive clinical services. M.D. Anderson will have clinical oversight for all aspects of care delivery.

Banner Health is also building one of the country's largest simulation education centers Banner Corporate Center-Mesa. Simulation education is an expanding field in which medical students (as well as already licensed doctors, nurses, and emergency-service providers) use computerized mannequins to improve their surgical or other medical skills.

EXECUTIVES

Chairman: Mark N. Sklar
President, CEO, and Director: Peter S. Fine
EVP and Chief Administrative Officer:
  Ronald R. (Ron) Bunnell
EVP and Chief Medical Officer: John Hensing
SVP and CFO: Dennis Dahlen
SVP, General Counsel, and Secretary: David M. Bixby
SVP Information Technology and CIO:
  Michael S. (Mike) Warden
SVP and Chief Talent Officer: Ed Oxford
System VP Clinical Delivery: Kathy Scott
Regional VP Physician Resources: Don Maloney
Regional VP Human Resources: Tom Koelbl
VP Design and Construction: Kip Edwards
System Director Public Relations: Bill Byron
Chief People Officer: Sandra Herr

LOCATIONS

HQ: Banner Health
  1441 N. 12th St., Phoenix, AZ 85006
Phone: 602-495-4000
Web: www.bannerhealth.com

Selected Facilities

Alaska
  Fairbanks Memorial Hospital (Fairbanks)
Arizona
  Banner Baywood Medical Center (Mesa)
    Banner Heart Hospital
  Banner Desert Medical Center (Mesa)
    Banner Children's Hospital
  Banner Estrella Medical Center (Phoenix)
  Banner Gateway Medical Center (Gilbert)
  Page Hospital (Page)
  Banner Good Samaritan Medical Center (Phoenix)
  Banner Thunderbird Medical Center (Glendale)
California
  Banner Lassen Community Hospital (Susanville)
Colorado
  East Morgan County Hospital (Brush)
  North Colorado Medical Center (Greeley)
  McKee Medical Center (Loveland)
  Sterling Regional MedCenter (Sterling)
Kansas
  St. Luke Hospital and Living Center (Marion)
Nebraska
  Ogallala Community Hospital (Ogallala)
Nevada
  Banner Churchill Community Hospital (Fallon)
Wyoming
  Community Hospital (Torrington)
  Platte County Memorial Hospital (Wheatland)
  Washakie Medical Center (Worland)

PRODUCTS/OPERATIONS

2008 Sales

	$ mil.	% of total
Net patient service	3.7	95
Other	0.2	5
Total	**3.9**	**100**

COMPETITORS

Catholic Healthcare West
Community Health Systems
HCA
Iasis Healthcare
Inova
John C. Lincoln Health Network
MedCath
Memorial Health System of East Texas
Northern Arizona Healthcare
Phoenix Children's Hospital
Poudre Valley Health System
Providence Health & Services
Scottsdale Healthcare
St. Joseph Health System
Tenet Healthcare
Texas Health Resources
University Medical Center
Vanguard Health Systems
Yuma Regional Medical Center

HISTORICAL FINANCIALS

Company Type: Not-for-profit

Income Statement				FYE: December 31
	REVENUE ($ mil.)	NET INCOME ($ mil.)	NET PROFIT MARGIN	EMPLOYEES
12/08	3,971	—	—	25,000

Baptist Health South Florida

Baptist Health South Florida is a not-for-profit health care organization composed of six Miami-area hospitals, as well as numerous outpatient centers. Its flagship facility, Baptist Hospital, has more than 550 beds and provides a comprehensive range of medical and surgical services. The systems also includes South Miami Hospital, with 445 beds, as well as several smaller inpatient facilities in surrounding communities. In all, Baptist Health South Florida hospitals contain around 1,500 beds. In addition to its inpatient services, the organization provides outpatient care, including ambulatory surgery, urgent care, diagnostic imaging, and home health services.

EXECUTIVES

Chairman: Rev David W. Cleeland
President and CEO: Brian E. Keeley
COO: D. Wayne Bracken
CFO: Ralph E. Lawson
EVP and Chief Administrative Officer: George W. Foyo
Corporate VP Marketing and Public Relations:
  Joanne (Jo) Baxter
Director General Thoracic Surgery and Thoracic Surgical Oncology: Mark Dylewski
Corporate VP and Chief Diversity Officer:
  Ricardo Forbes

LOCATIONS

HQ: Baptist Health South Florida
  6855 Red Rd., Coral Gables, FL 33143
Phone: 786-662-7000   **Fax:** 786-662-7334
Web: www.baptisthealth.net

PRODUCTS/OPERATIONS

Selected Facilities

Baptist Children's Hospital
Baptist Hospital of Miami
Doctors Hospital
Homestead Hospital
Mariners Hospital
South Miami Hospital

COMPETITORS

Broward Health
Catholic Health East
HCA
Miami Children's Hospital
Mount Sinai Medical Center of Florida
Public Health Trust
South Broward Hospital District
University of Miami Hospital

HISTORICAL FINANCIALS

Company Type: Not-for-profit

Income Statement				FYE: September 30
	REVENUE ($ mil.)	NET INCOME ($ mil.)	NET PROFIT MARGIN	EMPLOYEES
9/08	1,518	—	—	9,374

Barry-Wehmiller

With Barry-Wehmiller, you get the whole package. The company manufactures and supplies packaging, corrugating, paper converting, filling, and labeling automation equipment primarily for the food and beverage industry. The company conducts business around the world through 10 divisions including Accraply (labeling machinery), Barry-Wehmiller Company (bottle washers and pasteurizers), HayssenSandiacre (packaging systems), PneumaticScaleAngelus (bottle fillers and cappers), FleetwoodGoldco-Wyard (conveyor systems), and Central Bottling International (industrial manufacturing equipment). Other Barry-Wehmiller units offer IT, engineering. and design consulting services.

Originally a provider of conveying equipment to St. Louis malt houses, Barry-Wehmiller Companies was founded by Thomas Barry and Alfred Wehmiller in 1885. Ownership passed from the Wehmiller family to the Chapman family in 1963, and the Chapmans continue as the majority owners.

Acquisitive Barry-Wehmiller has grown its annual revenues to more than $1 billion, with roughly one-quarter of sales from overseas markets. The enterprise serves customers that include Anheuser-Busch, PepsiCo, and Polaris Industries.

Since 1987 the company has acquired more than 45 companies. Acquisitions in 2005 included the engineering division of UK-based Central Bottling International (packaging equipment and products for the food and beverage industries); Green Bay, Wisconsin-based Paper Converting Machine Company; and Owings Mills, Maryland-based AMBEC Inc. (stainless steel conveyance systems).

In late 2006 the company acquired the UK-based Sandiacre Rose Forgrove (SRF), a packaging machinery manufacturer owned by Molins. SRF was combined with Hayssen Packaging Technologies to form HayssenSandiacre. In 2008 the company furthered developed its business in Europe by establishing a HayssenSandiacre sales and service office in the Netherlands.

In early 2007 Barry-Wehmiller acquired (through subsidiary Thiele Technologies) SWF Companies, a packaging machinery manufacturer previously owned by Dover Corporation. The acquisition positioned Thiele as one of the largest system manufacturers of robotic packaging.

Also in 2007 the company bought Stanford Products, a manufacturer of slitting, rewinding, and inspection equipment for the packaging and converting industries. Stanford Products also made machinery for turning out shrink sleeve labels. Barry-Wehmiller integrated the business with its Accraply division.

The company's significant period of growth continued in 2008 when it acquired Apollo Sheeters. The business joined MarquipWard-United, Barry-Wehmiller's division devoted to designing and manufacturing of advanced sheeting, corrugating, and finishing equipment.

EXECUTIVES

Chairman and CEO: Robert H. (Bob) Chapman, age 63
VP, CFO, and Director: James W. (Jim) Lawson
President, Hayssen Packaging: Daniel Jones
President, Thiele Technologies: Laurence (Larry) Smith
President, Pneumatic Scale: William Morgan
President and CEO, Paper Converting Machine Company and MarquipWardUnited:
Timothy J. (Tim) Sullivan
President and CEO, Fleetwood Goldco Wyard and Group President, Design Group: Phil Ostapowicz
President, Accraply: Gregory J. (Greg) Tschida
President and Managing Partner, Barry-Wehmiller International Resources: Vasant Bennett
Practice Head, Knowledge Management and Multimedia Services, Barry-Wehmiller:
Krishnakumar (KK) Krishnan
Practice Head, Global Marketing, Barry-Wehmiller International Resources:
Rajmohan (Raj) Madhusoodanan
Director International Human Resources: Donn Boyer
Treasurer: Micheal (Mike) Zaccarello
Director Corporate Communications: Kim Hutton

LOCATIONS

HQ: Barry-Wehmiller Companies, Inc.
8020 Forsyth Blvd., St. Louis, MO 63105
Phone: 314-862-8000   **Fax:** 314-862-8858
Web: www.barry-wehmiller.com

PRODUCTS/OPERATIONS

Selected Operations
Engineering/consulting
Barry-Wehmiller Design Group, Inc. (high-speed, complex, automated manufacturing and packaging system design)
Barry-Wehmiller International Resources (IT consulting and engineering services)
Stahlman Group (facility and infrastructure design, process engineering, and construction management services)
Converting equipment
Paper Converting Machine Company (PCMC)
Coaters
Narrow web in-line printing systems
Nonwovens converting equipment
Tissue converting equipment
Wide web flexo printing, coating, and laminating
Corrugating equipment
MarquipWardUnited, Inc. (corrugating, sheeting, and finishing equipment)
Packaging equipment
Accraply, Inc. (packaging label machinery)
Barry-Wehmiller Company (bottle washers and pasteurizers)
Central Bottling International Limited (CBI, reconditioned and used bottle-filling and packaging machinery)
FleetwoodGoldcoWyard (conveyer systems)
HayssenSandiacre (form/fill/seal packaging machinery)
PneumaticScaleAngelus (fillers, cappers, seamers, and labelers)
Thiele Technologies, Inc. (packaging systems)

COMPETITORS

Bradman Lake
Graphic Packaging Holding
Impaxx
Industria Macchine Automatiche
Menasha
Rexam
Semco Technologies
Sencorp Inc
Tetra Laval
Traco Manufacturing

HISTORICAL FINANCIALS
Company Type: Private

Income Statement
FYE: December 31

	REVENUE ($ mil.)	NET INCOME ($ mil.)	NET PROFIT MARGIN	EMPLOYEES
12/08	1,100	—	—	5,200
12/07	1,200	—	—	5,000
Annual Growth	(8.3%)	—	—	4.0%

Revenue History

1,200				
1,000				
800				
600				
400				
200				
0				
12/04	12/05	12/06	12/07	12/08

Bartlett and Company

When the cows come home, Bartlett and Company will be ready. The company's primary business is grain merchandising, but it also runs cattle feedlots, mills flour, and sells feed and fertilizer. Bartlett operates grain storage facilities, terminal elevators, and country elevators in the midwestern US, including locations in Kansas, Iowa, Missouri, and Nebraska. Bartlett also operates flour mills and feed stores in the Midwest and along the East Coast; its cattle operations are based in Texas. The Bartlett and Company Grain Charitable Foundation makes financial gifts to local causes. Founded in 1907 as Bartlett Agri Enterprises, the company is still owned by the founding Bartlett family.

EXECUTIVES

Chairman: Paul D. Bartlett Jr.
President and CEO: James B. (Jim) Hebenstreit, age 62
CIO: Jack Moran
VP, Secretary, and Treasurer: Arnold F. (Arnie) Wheeler
VP Human Resources: Bill Webster
President, Bartlett Grain: William J. Fellows
President, Bartlett Milling and Bartlett Cattle:
John Gillcrist

LOCATIONS

HQ: Bartlett and Company
4900 Main St., Ste. 1200, Kansas City, MO 64112
Phone: 816-753-6300   **Fax:** 816-753-0062
Web: www.bartlettandco.com

PRODUCTS/OPERATIONS

Selected Subsidiaries
Bartlett Cattle Company, L.P.
Bartlett Grain Co Southwest, L.P.
Bartlett Grain Company, L.P.
Bartlett Milling Company, L.P.
Bartlett Specialty Grains

COMPETITORS

ADM
Ag Processing
AzTx Cattle
Cactus Feeders
Cargill
CHS
ContiGroup
DeBruce Grain
Friona Industries
GROWMARK
King Ranch
Scoular

HISTORICAL FINANCIALS

Company Type: Private

Income Statement				FYE: December 31
	REVENUE ($ mil.)	NET INCOME ($ mil.)	NET PROFIT MARGIN	EMPLOYEES
12/08	2,040	—	—	700
12/07	1,510	—	—	700
12/06	1,100	—	—	750
Annual Growth	36.2%	—	—	(3.4%)

Revenue History

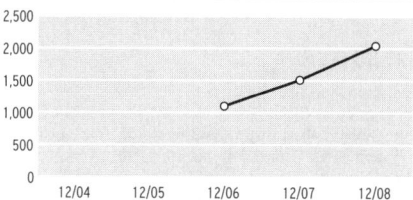

Barton Malow

Barton Malow scores by building end zones and home plates. The construction management and general contracting firm, which has built its share of sporting facilities, also makes points for its schools, hospitals, offices, and plants. The company offers design/build services ranging from the pre-planning stage to completion throughout the US and Mexico. Projects have included the Detroit Institute of Arts and Cultural Center and the Baltimore Orioles stadium. Barton Malow provides architecture and engineering services, and its Barton Malow Rigging unit installs process equipment and machinery. Carl Osborn Barton founded the employee-owned firm as C.O. Barton Company in 1924.

Barton Malow has historically had a relationship with the steel and auto industries, but over the years has expanded into new sectors and geographic markets. In 2008 the company acquired Florida-based L.C. Gaskins Construction Company, which specializes in the federal market sector. Today Barton Marlow operates about a dozen offices, mostly in the East Coast.

The family of CEO Ben Maibach III, a third-generation Barton Malow executive, owns a controlling interest in the company.

EXECUTIVES

Chairman, President, and CEO: Ben C. Maibach III
EVP, Chief Legal Officer, and Secretary:
  Thomas (Tom) Porter
EVP and COO: Lester (Les) Snyder III
SVP and CFO: Lori R. Howlett
CIO: Phil Go
Chief Marketing Officer: Sheryl B. Maibach
SVP Sports Facilities: Harvey Oliva
SVP Southern and Western Regions:
  Aleksei (Alex) Ivanikiw
VP Corporate Affairs: Doug Maibach
VP Energy and Environmental: Geoff Murken
VP Human Resources: Jim Nahrgang
Senior Director Business Development:
  Robert L. Stempien
Communications Director: Janet Cohen
Public Relations Manager: Anne-Marie Poltorak
Auditors: Grant Thornton LLP

LOCATIONS

HQ: Barton Malow Company
  26500 American Dr., Southfield, MI 48034
Phone: 248-436-5000   **Fax:** 248-436-5001
Web: www.bmco.com

PRODUCTS/OPERATIONS

Primary Services

Architecture/Planning
Building Information Management (BIM)
Concrete Trades
Construction Management
Design/Build
Facility Audits
Facility Services
General Contracting
Interior Design
Interiors Trades
Preconstruction
Program Management
Rigging/Millwright
Technology Consulting

COMPETITORS

Alberici
BE&K
Clark Enterprises
Fluor
Gilbane
Hensel Phelps
H.J. Russell
Hunt Construction
M. A. Mortenson
McCarthy Building
Skanska USA Building
Turner Corporation
Walbridge Aldinger
Walsh Group
Whiting-Turner

Bass Pro Shops

Bass Pro Shops (BPS) knows how to reel in shoppers. The company operates about 60 Outdoor World stores in the US and Canada that sell boats, firearms, equipment, and apparel for most outdoor activities. Stores feature archery ranges, fish tanks, bowling lanes, billiards tables, and dining areas. BPS also catches shoppers at home with its catalogs, online store, and TV and radio programs. The first Outdoor World store (in Missouri) has been one of the state's biggest tourist attractions since it opened in 1981. The company owns Tracker Marine (boat manufacturing) and American Rod & Gun (sporting goods wholesale) and runs an 850-acre resort in the Ozark Mountains. Founder John Morris owns BPS.

While other retailers are reporting lower foot traffic amid the US recession, BPS is experiencing the opposite. In 2008 the company lured more than 100 million people to its stores — an increase over the previous year and six times the number of visitors to Disney World. The reason for the increase, the company says, is that camping vacations and related outdoor activities have surged in popularity as people scale back their spending. Sales of firearms, camping equipment, and fishing gear remained healthy at BPS, but the firm has had a hard time moving its own brand of boats.

To keep pace with the uptick in demand, the outdoor products merchant plans to open about five new stores in existing markets, including Alabama, California, and Georgia. It has also taken steps to attract more female consumers, launching its first catalog for women in 2007. (The company mails about 125 million copies of its seasonal and specialty catalogs and flyers each year.)

EXECUTIVES

Founder: John L. (Johnny) Morris, age 60
President and COO: James (Jim) Hagale
CIO: Shawn Morin
VP Human Resources: Mike Roland
VP Marketing: Stan Lippleman
Manager Corporate Public Relations and Outdoor Education: Larry L. Whiteley
Director Conservation: Martin MacDonald
Corporate Maintenance Manager: Mark Kueck

LOCATIONS

HQ: Bass Pro Shops, Inc.
  2500 E. Kearney, Springfield, MO 65898
Phone: 417-873-5000   **Fax:** 417-873-4672
Web: www.basspro.com

PRODUCTS/OPERATIONS

Other Operations

American Rod & Gun (sporting goods wholesale)
Bass Pro Shops (sporting goods catalog)
Bass Pro Shops Collections (catalog aimed at women)
Bass Pro Shops Outdoor World (magazine, radio and TV programs)
Big Cedar Lodge (resort)
Outdoor World (retail stores)
Tracker Marine (sport boat manufacturing)

COMPETITORS

Academy Sports & Outdoors
Cabela's
Cruise America
Dick's Sporting Goods
Gander Mountain
Hibbett Sports
Kmart
L.L. Bean
MarineMax
Orvis Company
REI
Sears
Sports Authority
Sportsman's Guide
Sportsman's Warehouse
Wal-Mart
West Marine
Winmark

HISTORICAL FINANCIALS

Company Type: Private

Income Statement

	ESTIMATED REVENUE ($ mil.)	NET INCOME ($ mil.)	NET PROFIT MARGIN	EMPLOYEES
12/08	3,400	—	—	16,000
12/07	2,650	—	—	14,000
12/06	2,660	—	—	13,000
12/05	1,915	—	—	12,500
12/04	2,050	—	—	11,300
Annual Growth	13.5%	—	—	9.1%

FYE: December 31

Revenue History

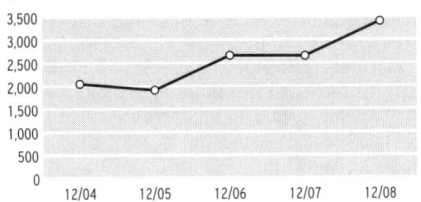

Battelle Memorial Institute

When you use a copier, hit a golf ball, or listen to a CD, you're using technologies developed by Battelle Memorial Institute. The nonprofit trust operates one of the world's largest research enterprises, with more than 20,000 scientists, engineers, and staff serving 1,100 corporate and government customers annually. Battelle owns research facilities in the US and Switzerland and manages or co-manages several Department of Energy-sponsored labs, including Brookhaven National Laboratory, Oak Ridge National Laboratory, Idaho National Laboratory, and Pacific Northwest National Laboratory. Established by the family of Gordon Battelle, an early leader in the steel industry, the institute began operations in 1929.

While contract research and development remains the core activity of the company, Battelle is becoming more and more involved in managing operations for about a half-dozen laboratories for the government. Battelle operates Idaho National Laboratory through Battelle Energy Alliance, a partnership formed with BWX Technologies, Washington Group International, Electric Power Research Institute, and a consortium of universities including MIT, Ohio State, and the University of Idaho.

With offices in Japan and Korea, Battelle expanded its international reach to include India in 2008. The company formed a partnership in 2007 with oil and gas company PETRONAS to operate a renewable energy lab in Kuala Lumpur, Malaysia.

Through its Battelle Ventures subsidiary, the company also serves as a nesting ground for new businesses formed to commercialize discoveries and technologies Battelle owns or to which it has rights.

Originally formed to promote metallurgy and related industries, the institute — which conducts nearly $4 billion in research and development each year — has diversified into researching other areas such as agriculture, energy, software, and medicine. Among other notable milestones, Battelle's research was instrumental in developing the photocopy machine, optical digital recording (used with compact discs), and bar codes.

Battelle is led by CEO and President Jeffrey Wadsworth, a former metallurgist who started at Battelle in 2002 and served as director of Oak Ridge National Laboratory.

HISTORY

Battelle Memorial Institute was founded with a $1.5 million trust willed by Gordon Battelle, who died in 1923. Battelle was a champion of research for the advancement of humankind, and before taking his father's place as president of several Ohio steel mills, he had funded a former university professor's successful work to extract useful chemicals from mine waste. Battelle's mother, upon her death in 1925, left the institute an additional $2.1 million. The institute opened in 1929.

The institute took on perhaps the most important project in its history in 1944 when it helped an electronics company's patent lawyer, Chester Carlson, find practical uses for his invention, called xerography. Eventually Battelle developed the first photocopy machine, and in 1955 it sold the patent rights for the machine to Haloid (now Xerox) in exchange for royalties.

During WWII Battelle worked on uranium refining for the Manhattan Project, and in the early 1950s it established the world's first private nuclear research facility. The company also set up operations in Germany and Switzerland.

The tax man came knocking in 1961, questioning the tax-free status of some of Battelle's activities. The organization eventually had to pay $47 million. In 1965 Battelle developed a coin with a copper core and a copper-and-nickel-alloy cladding for the US Treasury.

As the result of a ruling that reinterpreted a clause in Gordon Battelle's will, in 1975 the institute gave $80 million to philanthropic enterprises. This ruling, coupled with the taxes that the organization was still unaccustomed to paying, forced Battelle to re-examine its strategy.

Battelle co-developed the Universal Product Code (the bar code symbol found today on nearly all consumer goods packaging) in the 1970s. The institute also landed a lucrative contract from the US Department of Energy (DOE) to manage its commercial nuclear waste isolation program.

In 1987 Battelle chose Douglas Olesen — a 20-year veteran of the institute — to replace retiring CEO Ronald Paul. The company signed an extension with the DOE in 1992 to run its Pacific Northwest Laboratory (which it has operated since 1965).

An Ohio court in 1997 approved a seven-page agreement with the institute outlining the key principles that must be followed according to Gordon Battelle's will. This agreement replaced the 1975 decree and ended more than 20 years of scrutiny by the state attorney general's office.

In 1998 the DOE contracted Brookhaven Science Associates — a partnership between the State University of New York and Battelle — to operate Brookhaven National Laboratory. That year a Battelle contract to dispose of Vietnam War-era napalm drew national attention when subcontractor Pollution Control Industries backed out of the project, citing safety concerns. Under Battelle's direction, Houston-based GNI Group took the 3.4 million gallons of napalm off the US Navy's hands.

Battelle and the University of Tennessee in 1999 won a five-year contract to operate the US government's Oak Ridge National Laboratory. That year the institute made several breakthroughs in cancer research, including FDA approval to test an inhalation delivery system for treating lung cancer.

In 2000 the company spun off OmniViz (data mining software) and Battelle Pulmonary Therapeutics (pulmonary and drug delivery technology) as wholly owned subsidiaries. In 2001 Battelle chose former Kodak EVP and chief technology officer Carl Kohrt to replace Olesen. Kohrt retired in January 2009 and was replaced by Jeffrey Wadsworth, who has worked for the company since 2002.

Battelle and several partners, including BWX Technologies, Washington Group International, and Electric Power Research Institute, won a 10-year contract in 2004 to operate Idaho National Laboratory, a research facility focusing on nuclear energy research and related technologies.

EXECUTIVES

Chairman: John B. McCoy Jr.
President and CEO: Jeffrey (Jeff) Wadsworth, age 59
EVP Global Laboratory Operations: Ron Townsend
EVP and CFO: I. Martin Inglis
SVP; Director Global Laboratory Operations, Pacific Northwest National Laboratory: Michael Kluse
SVP; Director Global Laboratory Operations, Oak Ridge National Laboratory: Thomas E. Mason
SVP, General Counsel, and Secretary: Russell P. (Russ) Austin
SVP Corporate Relations: Anthony T. Hebron
SVP International Partnerships: Richard C. Adams
SVP Energy Technology Global Business: Donald P. McConnell
SVP Health and Life Sciences Global Business: Barbara L. Kunz
SVP National Security Global Business: Stephen E. Kelly
SVP Organizational Development: Robert W. Smith Jr.
SVP; Director Global Laboratory Operations, Idaho National Laboratory: John J. Grossenbacher
Treasurer: Gwendolyn C. VonHolten
Manager National Media Relations: Katy Delaney, age 43

LOCATIONS

HQ: Battelle Memorial Institute
505 King Ave., Columbus, OH 43201
Phone: 614-424-6424   **Fax:** 614-424-5263
Web: www.battelle.org

PRODUCTS/OPERATIONS

Selected Laboratories and Research Facilities

Battelle Biomedical Research Center (West Jefferson, OH)
Battelle Eastern Science and Technology Center (Aberdeen, MD)
Battelle Frederick Operations (Frederick, MD)
Battelle Geneva Operations (Geneva, Switzerland)
Brookhaven National Laboratory (Upton, NY)
Human Factors Transportation Center (Seattle)
Idaho National Laboratory (Idaho Falls, ID)
Lawrence Livermore National Laboratory (Livermore, CA)
Marine Science Laboratory (Sequim, WA)
National Renewable Energy Laboratory (Golden, CO)
Oak Ridge National Laboratory (Oak Ridge, TN)
Battelle Duxbury Operations (Duxbury, MA)
Pacific Northwest National Laboratory (Richland, WA)

Exploded-tip paintbrush (nylon brush for Wooster Brush Co., 1950)
Golf ball coatings (1965)
Heat Seat (microwaveable stadium cushion, 1990s)
Holograms (work began in the 1970s)
Insulin injection pen (for Eli Lilly, 1990s)
Oil spill outline monitor (1992)
PCB-cleaning chemical process (1992)
Photocopy machine (with Haloid, 1940s)
Plastic breakdown process (1990s)
"Sandwich" coins (copper/copper-and-nickel-alloy cladding design for US Treasury, 1965)
SenSonic toothbrush (with Teledyne/WaterPik, 1990s)
Smart cards (cards embedded with tiny computer chips that store information, 1980s)
Universal Product Code (co-creator; bar code, 1970s)

COMPETITORS

Argonne National Laboratory
Berkeley Lab
Charles Stark Draper Laboratory
Sarnoff
Southwest Research Institute

Bausch & Lomb

Eyes are the windows to profit for Bausch & Lomb. The eye care company is best known as a leading maker of contact lenses and lens care solutions (including the PureVision and ReNu brands). In addition to its lens products, Bausch & Lomb makes prescription ophthalmic drugs Lotemax, Alrex, and Minims, along with over-the-counter vitamins and drops through its pharmaceuticals division. Its surgical unit makes equipment for cataract, refractive (LASIK laser vision correction), and other ophthalmic surgeries. Bausch & Lomb markets its products in more than 100 countries worldwide. The company is owned by private equity firm Warburg Pincus.

Bausch & Lomb was taken private by Warburg Pincus in 2007 in a deal worth about $4.5 billion. A few months later, in early 2008, Ronald Zarrella retired as CEO and chairman and was replaced by former Johnson & Johnson executive Gerald Ostrov.

Bausch & Lomb is boosting its surgery business in order to cash in on the boom in cataract and corrective eye surgeries. It acquired intraocular lens maker eyeonics, which makes products used to surgically replace cataract-affected lenses, in 2008. The following year the company signed a licensing agreement for the development of intraocular lenses (used in cataract and vision correction surgery) with Santen Pharmaceutical.

Bausch & Lomb's pharmaceuticals division makes prescription and over-the-counter ophthalmic drugs, as well as vitamins for ocular health. Its vitamin product line includes products for age-related macular degeneration and dry eye; the company has expanded the line with a vitamin for diabetics. The division also sells prescription anti-inflammatory/anti-infective Zylet, and plans to develop more proprietary prescription drugs over the long term.

To grow its European pharmaceutical distribution reach, the company acquired the pharmaceuticals portfolio and distribution operations of Italy's Group Tubilux in 2009.

Bausch & Lomb announced development collaborations with CrystalGenomics and Galapagos in 2008, and it entered a co-marketing agreement with Pfizer regarding several ophthalmic drugs made by both firms in 2009. Later that year, bacterial conjunctivitis (pink eye) treatment Besivance received FDA approval; the drug will be marketed by Bausch & Lomb and Pfizer in the US.

The company is still dealing with fallout over the recall of its ReNu with MoistureLoc lens care solution. Bausch & Lomb halted sales on what had been its lead product in 2006, following an outbreak of serious fungal eye infections. The company has already spent more than $250 million to settle some 600 lawsuits and is still litigating others. However, more painful than the settlements was its loss of dominance in the lens cleaning market.

HISTORY

In 1853 German immigrant Jacob Bausch opened a small store in Rochester, New York, to sell European optical imports. Henry Lomb soon became a partner by lending Bausch $60.

Bausch & Lomb's first major breakthrough came with Bausch's invention of Vulcanite (a hard rubber) eyeglass frames. The company fitted the frames with European lenses, and by 1880 had a New York City sales office. Bausch & Lomb later began making microscopes, binoculars, and telescopes.

The company incorporated in 1908 as Bausch & Lomb Optical Co. In 1912 Jacob's son, William Bausch, became one of the few to make optical-quality glass in the US. During WWI Bausch & Lomb supplied the military with lenses for binoculars, searchlights, rifle scopes, and telescopes.

The Army Air Corps commissioned the company in 1929 to create lenses to reduce sun glare for pilots. Bausch & Lomb responded with Ray-Ban sunglasses; they were made available to the public in 1936 and went on to become a company mainstay. Bausch & Lomb went public in 1938.

The company won an Oscar in the 1950s for its Cinemascope lens; it won government contracts for lenses used in satellite and missile systems in the 1960s. Bausch & Lomb also bought such firms as Ferson Optics (1968) and Reese Optical (1969). It began concentrating on contact lenses after the FDA approved its soft lenses in 1971.

In 1981 Daniel Gill, who had helped build the soft contact lens business, became CEO. He sold the company's prescription eyeglass services and industrial instruments units and diversified into medical products and research.

Earnings soared in the 1990s with foreign expansion and acquisitions, including Steri-Oss (dental implants); the Curel and Soft Sense skin care lines from S.C. Johnson & Son; Award, a Scottish manufacturer of disposable contacts (1996); and Arnette Optic Illusions sport sunglasses (1996).

However, Gill's insistence on double-digit growth contributed to a dubious ethical climate in which some executives used questionable tactics to put more sales on the books. This led to an SEC probe (closed in 1997 with no fines or penalties assessed) and a shareholder lawsuit (settled in 1997 for $42 million). That year, the company also paid $1.7 million to settle a class

action lawsuit alleging Bausch & Lomb was marketing one type of contact lens under several different product names with varying prices. Gill resigned under fire in 1995 and was replaced by outside director William Waltrip; he turned the reins over to William Carpenter in 1997.

Noncore divisions were sold (oral care and dental implant businesses in 1996; skin care line to Kao subsidiary Andrew Jergens in 1998) and 1,900 jobs were cut. In 1999 the company sold its sunglasses unit to Luxottica, and Charles River Laboratories to an affiliate of Donaldson, Lufkin & Jenrette.

Ronald Zarrella became chairman and CEO of Bausch & Lomb in 2001, after seven years with General Motors.

More than 700 people fell victim to a rare and dangerous fungal infection while using Bausch & Lomb's ReNu with MoistureLoc contact lens solution between 2005 and 2006. The company recalled the product, which had been its leading brand. Expenses associated with the recall hurt the company's bottom line, as well as its stock price. A desire to keep any settlement expenses out of the public eye contributed to the company's decision to go private in 2007.

Former J&J executive Gerald Ostrov took over as CEO in 2008 following Bauch & Lomb's acquisition by private equity firm Warburg Pincus.

EXECUTIVES

Chairman Emeritus: Ronald L. Zarrella, age 59
Chairman and CEO: Gerald M. Ostrov, age 59
CFO and Corporate VP: Brian J. Harris
SVP Research and Development and Chief Scientific Officer: Praveen Tyle, age 49
Corporate VP and Chief Medical Officer: Brian Levy, age 56
SVP and President, Asia Region: Dwain L. Hahs, age 57
SVP Customer Service and Information Technology and CIO: Alan H. Farnsworth, age 57
Corporate VP and Chief Technology Officer: John W. Sheets Jr.
Corporate VP; President, Asia Pacific: David N. Edwards
Corporate VP; Global President, Vision Care: Peter (Pete) Valenti III
Corporate VP and EVP Global Business Operations and Process Excellence: Michael Gowen
Corporate VP and Chief Compliance Officer: Susan A. Roberts
Corporate VP Global Surgical: Henry C. Tung, age 50
Corporate VP; President, Europe, Middle East, and Africa: John H. Brown
Corporate VP Global Operations and Engineering: Gerhard Bauer, age 53
Corporate VP Public Affairs and Human Resources: Paul H. Sartori
Corporate VP and Global President, Surgical Products: J. Andy Corley
Corporate VP Communications and Investor Relations: Barbara M. Kelley, age 63
VP Human Resources, Global Research and Development: Michelle Graham
VP and General Counsel: A. Robert D. Bailey, age 46
Corporate Secretary: Jean F. Geisel
Director Investor Relations: Daniel L. Ritz
Auditors: PricewaterhouseCoopers LLP

LOCATIONS

HQ: Bausch & Lomb Incorporated
1 Bausch & Lomb Place, Rochester, NY 14604
Phone: 585-338-6000   **Fax:** 585-338-6007
Web: www.bausch.com

PRODUCTS/OPERATIONS

Selected Products and Brands

Contact lenses
  Boston (hard contact lenses)
  Optima 38/SP
  Optima Toric (corrects astigmatism)
  PureVision
  PureVision Multi-Focal (bifocal soft contact lenses)
  PureVision Toric (corrects astigmatism)
  SilSoft (for children and adults who have had cataract surgery)
  SofLens59 (two-week replacement soft contact lenses)
  SofLens Multi-Focal (bifocal soft contact lenses)
  SofLens Daily Disposable (disposable soft contact lenses)
  SofLens Toric (corrects astigmatism)

Lens care
  ReNu

Pharmaceuticals
  Alaway (antihistamine)
  Collyrium (eye wash)
  Liposic (dry eye)
  Lotemax (anti-inflammatory)
  Muro (anti-inflammatory)
  Ocuvite (ocular vitamins)
  Opcon-A (antihistamine and redness relief)
  Zylet (anti-inflammatory and anti-infective)

Cataract and vitreoretinal
  Crystalens (intraocular lens for cataract surgery)
  Millennium Microsurgical System (vitreoretinal surgery)
  SofPort (foldable intraocular lens)
  Stellaris (cataract surgery system)

Refractive surgery
  Zyoptix (LASIK system)

COMPETITORS

Abbott Medical Optics
Advanced Vision Research
Akorn
Alcon
Allergan
CIBA VISION
CooperVision
Escalon Medical
Essilor International
LaserSight
Paradigm Medical
Pfizer
STAAR Surgical
Vistakon

HISTORICAL FINANCIALS

Company Type: Private

Income Statement				FYE: Last Saturday in December
	REVENUE ($ mil.)	NET INCOME ($ mil.)	NET PROFIT MARGIN	EMPLOYEES
12/08	2,500	—	—	2,500
12/07	2,500	—	—	13,000
Annual Growth	0.0%	—	—	(80.8%)

Revenue History

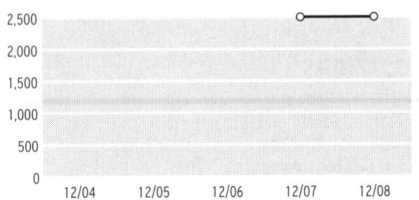

	12/04	12/05	12/06	12/07	12/08

BayCare Health System

BayCare Health System takes care of folks lounging (or limping) on the bay in the Sunshine State. Established in 1997, the health system operates ten hospitals (about 2,700 beds) that serve residents of Tampa Bay and surrounding areas in Florida. Its member hospitals (eight full-service acute-care facilities and two specialty units) are grouped together into the Morton Plant Mease Health Care, St. Anthony's Health Care, and St. Joseph's-Baptist Health Care systems. The system offers a wide variety of specialty services ranging from orthopedics to cancer care to women's services. The health system also operates area ambulatory and outpatient clinics, and it provides visiting nurse home health care services.

BayCare's St. Joseph's-Baptist system is building a new hospital, to be dubbed St. Joseph's Hospital-North, that will feature 75 inpatient beds and surgery, outpatient, and emergency care facilities. The facility is scheduled to open in 2010.

EXECUTIVES

President and CEO: Stephen R. Mason
CFO: Tommy Inzia
CIO: Lindsey Jarrell
Chief Marketing and Strategy Officer: Stewart Schaffer, age 57
VP Clinical Transformation: Cathy Menkiena
VP Human Resources: Craig Brethauer
CEO, Morton Plant Mease Health Care: Philip K. Beauchamp
President, Morton Plant Mease Health Care: Glenn Waters
President and CEO, St. Joseph's Hospital: Isaac Mallah
President, St. Anthony's Health Care: William (Bill) Ulbricht
Director Communications: Amy Lovett

LOCATIONS

HQ: BayCare Health System
  16255 Bay Vista Dr., Clearwater, FL 33760
Phone: 727-820-8200
Web: www.baycare.org

PRODUCTS/OPERATIONS

Selected Facilities

Morton Plant Mease Health Care
  Mease Countryside Hospital
  Mease Dunedin Hospital
    BayCare Alliant Hospital (long-term acute hospital)
  Morton Plant Hospital
  Morton Plant North Bay Hospital
St. Anthony's Health Care
  St. Anthony's Hospital
St. Joseph's Health Care
  St. Joseph's Hospital
  St. Joseph's Children's Hospital of Tampa
  St. Joseph's Women's Hospital
  South Florida Baptist Hospital

COMPETITORS

Adventist Health System
Ascension Health
Bayfront Health
HCA
Iasis Healthcare
Lakeland Regional Medical Center
Tampa General Hospital

HISTORICAL FINANCIALS

Company Type: Private

Income Statement				FYE: September 30
	REVENUE ($ mil.)	NET INCOME ($ mil.)	NET PROFIT MARGIN	EMPLOYEES
9/08	1,734	—	—	17,400

Beall's Inc.

Residents of the Sun Belt have been known to leave their homes with Beall's on. The retail holding company operates through subsidiaries Beall's Department Stores, Beall's Outlet, and Burkes Outlet Stores in a dozen states. It has more than 560 stores (about 200 are in Florida) located throughout states in the southern and western US, including Arizona, California, Georgia, and Louisiana. Products range from off-price clothing and footwear for men and women to cosmetics, gifts, and housewares. Each chain has its own online shopping destination. The family-owned company was founded in 1915 by the grandfather of chairman Bob Beall (pronounced "Bell").

Hard economic times are proving to be pretty good times for Beall's, which plans to open more than 20 new stores in five southeastern states by the end of 2009. The company is focusing on its budget-priced outlet stores, which have proven popular during this recession, as opposed to its more moderately priced department stores. The retailer is also benefiting from the demise of other retailers, including Goody's, Linens 'n Things, and Mervyn's.

Stores operating under the Bealls name in Alabama, New Mexico, and Texas are owned by Stage Stores and are not affiliated with Beall's, Inc.

EXECUTIVES

Chairman: Robert M. (Bob) Beall II
CEO: Stephen M. Knopik
COO: Richard Judd
CFO: Dan Love
CIO: Joe Iannello
VP Human Resources: Dan Doyle
VP Advertising and E-Commerce: Gwen Bennett
VP Product Development: Janet (Jan) Longo
President, Outlet Stores: Conrad Szymanski
President, Department Stores: Lana C. Krauter
Director Public and Goverment Affairs: Bill Webster

LOCATIONS

HQ: Beall's Inc.
  1806 38th Ave. East, Bradenton, FL 34208
Phone: 941-747-2355   **Fax:** 941-746-1171
Web: www.beallsinc.com

COMPETITORS

Bed Bath & Beyond
Costco Wholesale
Dillard's
The Gap
J. C. Penney Company
Kohl's
Macy's
Nordstrom
Ross Stores
Sears
Stage Stores
Target
Wal-Mart

Beaulieu Group

Doing business as Beaulieu of America, the closely held Beaulieu Group rolls out a line of berber, commercial, and indoor/outdoor (nonwoven, turf) carpet. Chances are you have had Beaulieu underfoot; the company is the third-largest carpet manufacturer in the world. Through its dealers, carpets are distributed to home improvement chains, including The Home Depot and Lowe's Companies, and commercial contractors. The company's facilities operate in North America and Australia. Consumer brands include Beaulieu, Coronet, and Hollytex. The company markets commercial products under the Bolyu (high-end), Cambridge (value), and Aqua (hospitality) labels. The Beaulieu Group is controlled by the Bouckaert family.

The company courts the growing demand by consumer and commercial markets for eco-friendly products. Beaulieu's initiatives include purchasing renewable energy to power its plants, and incorporating recycled plastic bottles in its polyester (PET) fiber carpet.

Beaulieu of America founders and owners Carl Bouckaert and Mieke Hanssens (formerly known as Mieke Bouckaert) stepped down from the company's day-to-day operations in 2007 when Beaulieu pleaded guilty to tax fraud. In a global settlement, it agreed to pay over $32 million.

EXECUTIVES

Chairman: Carl M. Bouckaert
CEO: Ralph Boe
CFO: Del Land
EVP Sales and Marketing: Jeff Meadows
VP Marketing: Mike McAllister
Director Human Resources: Bernadette Martin

LOCATIONS

HQ: Beaulieu Group, L.L.C.
    1502 Coronet Dr., Dalton, GA 30720
Phone: 706-876-2900   **Fax:** 706-695-6237
Web: www.beaulieu-usa.com

COMPETITORS

Armstrong	Milliken
Dixie Group	Mohawk Industries
Interface, Inc.	Shaw Industries

HISTORICAL FINANCIALS

Company Type: Private

Income Statement

FYE: December 31

	ESTIMATED REVENUE ($ mil.)	NET INCOME ($ mil.)	NET PROFIT MARGIN	EMPLOYEES
12/07	1,100	—	—	5,850
12/06	1,200	—	—	6,500
12/05	1,100	—	—	8,300
Annual Growth	0.0%	—	—	(16.0%)

Revenue History

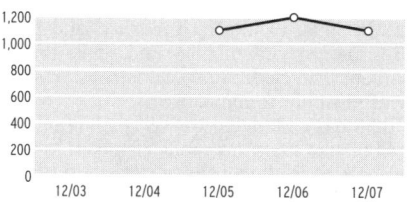

Bechtel Group

Whether the job is raising an entire city or razing a nuclear power plant, you can bet the Bechtel Group will be there to bid on the business. The engineering, construction, and project management firm was named the US's #1 contractor (ahead of Fluor) by *Engineering News-Record* for 11 consecutive years. It operates worldwide and has participated in such historic projects as the construction of Hoover Dam and the cleanup of the Chernobyl nuclear plant. Bechtel's Oil, Gas & Chemical business unit and Bechtel National, its government contracts group, are its leading revenue producers. The group is in its fourth generation of leadership by the Bechtel family, with chairman and CEO Riley Bechtel at the helm.

Bechtel has made a name for itself by participating in mega-projects. In addition to providing its core project management and design services, it offers such services as environmental restoration and remediation, telecommunications infrastructure (installing cable-optic networks and constructing data centers), and project financing through Bechtel Enterprises.

Bechtel National is the prime contractor for design and construction of the Hanford Vitrification Plant in Washington State, one of the DOE's most complex cleanup projects. The project's aim is to treat 53 million gallons of high-level radioactive waste stored at the Hanford site.

Among Bechtel's more traditional (perhaps notorious) infrastructure projects was its involvement in the "Big Dig," Boston's Central Artery/Tunnel project. Bechtel, in a joint venture with Parsons Brinckerhoff, served as lead contractor on the $14.6 billion project, which was the subject of much dispute over cost overruns and safety issues. After a death occurred in which the ceiling collapsed on a motorist, the National Transportation Safety Board said that Bechtel was partially at fault. Bechtel/Parsons Brinckerhoff paid a $450 million settlement which included a provision removing any criminal liability.

In Europe, the group has expanded its rail business by working on High Speed One, the high-speed rail line connecting London with the Channel Tunnel and the UK's first major new railroad project in a century. It is also managing the upgrade of the UK's West Coast main line and has joined a consortium to renovate part of London's 140-year-old subway. The group provides telecommunications services to US government entities through its Bechtel Federal Telecoms unit.

Bechtel has completed projects in some 50 countries on all seven continents. It was one of the companies that received contracts to help rebuild Iraq's infrastructure beginning in 2003, but it exited that country in 2006 as its contracts expired.

Current projects include a 411-MW combined-cycle power plant in Russia, an Alaska-Canada natural gas pipeline, the Queensland Curtis LNG project in Australia, and the Rio Tinto Alcan aluminum smelter project in British Columbia. The company is also a leading bidder on a pending project to expand the Panama Canal.

HISTORY

In 1898, 25-year-old Warren Bechtel left his Kansas farm to grade railroads in the Oklahoma Indian territories, then followed the rails west. Settling in Oakland, California, he founded his own contracting firm. Foreseeing the importance of roads, oil, and power, he won big projects such as the Northern California Highway and the Bowman Dam. By 1925, when he incorporated his company as W.A. Bechtel & Co., it ranked as the West's largest construction company. In 1931 Bechtel helped found the consortium that built Hoover Dam.

Under the leadership of Steve Bechtel (president after his father's death in 1933), the company obtained contracts for large infrastructure projects such as the San Francisco-Oakland Bay Bridge. Noted for his friendships with influential people, including Dwight Eisenhower, Adlai Stevenson, and Saudi Arabia's King Faisal, Steve developed projects that spanned nations and industries, such as pipelines in Saudi Arabia and numerous power projects. By 1960, when Steve Bechtel Jr. took over, the company was operating on six continents.

In the next two decades, Bechtel worked on transportation projects — such as San Francisco's Bay Area Rapid Transit (BART) system and the Washington, DC, subway system — and power projects, including nuclear plants. After the 1979 Three Mile Island accident, Bechtel tried its hand at nuclear cleanup. With nuclear power no longer in vogue, it focused on other markets, such as mining in New Guinea (gold and copper, 1981-84) and China (coal, 1984). Bechtel's Jubail project in Saudi Arabia, begun in 1976, raised an entire industrial port city on the Persian Gulf.

The US recession and rising developing-world debt of the early 1980s sent Bechtel reeling. It cut its workforce by 22,000 and stemmed losses by piling up small projects.

Riley Bechtel, great-grandson of Warren, became CEO in 1990. After the 1991 Gulf War, Bechtel extinguished Kuwait's flaming oil wells and worked on the oil-spill cleanup. During that decade it also worked on such projects as the Channel tunnel (the Chunnel) between England and France, pipelines in the former Soviet Union, and the new airport in Hong Kong.

Bechtel was part of the consortium contracted in 1996 to build a high-speed passenger rail line between London and the Chunnel. International Generating (InterGen), Bechtel's joint venture with Pacific Gas and Electric (PG&E), was chosen to help build Mexico's first private power plant. In 1996 Bechtel bought PG&E's share of InterGen, then sold a 50% stake in InterGen to a unit of Royal Dutch Shell in early 1997.

In 1998 Bechtel joined Battelle and Electricité de France in project management of a long-term plan to stabilize the damaged reactor of the Chernobyl nuclear plant in Ukraine.

The next year Bechtel was hired to decommission the Connecticut Yankee nuclear plant.

Bechtel expanded its telecommunications operations in 2001 to provide turnkey network implementation services in Europe, the Middle East, and Asia. In 2002 Bechtel was called on to work on the UK's rail system, taking over management of the upgrade of the West Coast main line from financially troubled Railtrack. As part of a consortium with UK facilities management giants Jarvis and Amey, Bechtel began work that year on a 30-year project to modernize part of London's aging subway system.

In 2005 Bechtel and joint venture partner Shell Oil sold InterGen, its power production joint venture, to AIG Highstar Capital for about $1.75 billion.

EXECUTIVES

Chairman Emeritus: Stephen D. (Steve) Bechtel Jr., age 84
Chairman and CEO: Riley P. Bechtel, age 57
Vice Chairman: Adrian Zaccaria, age 64
President, COO, and Director: Bill Dudley, age 57
CFO and Director: Peter Dawson
President, Nuclear Power: Carl Rau
President, Bechtel National: David Walker
President, Oil, Gas, and Chemicals Business Unit: Jim Jackson
President, Mining and Metals Global Business Unit: Andy Greig
President, Power Global Business Unit: Jack Futcher
President, Renewables and New Technology: Ian Copeland
President, Bechtel Systems & Infrastructure: Scott Ogilvie
President, Civil Global Business Unit, and Director: Mike Adams
Manager Construction: Walker Kimball
Manager Project Management: Dick McIlhattan
Manager Engineering, Procurement & Construction Functions, and Human Resources: John MacDonald
Manager Engineering: Tom Patterson
Manager Rail Business Unit: Tom McCarthy
Manager Infrastructure Business Unit: Carl Strock
Manager Media Relations: Francis Canavan
CIO and Manager Information Systems and Technology: Geir Ramleth
General Counsel, Secretary and Director: Judith Miller
Auditors: PricewaterhouseCoopers LLP

LOCATIONS

HQ: Bechtel Group, Inc.
50 Beale St., San Francisco, CA 94105
Phone: 415-768-1234   **Fax:** 415-768-9038
Web: www.bechtel.com

PRODUCTS/OPERATIONS

Selected Services

Construction
Engineering
Financing and development
Procurement
Project management
Safety
Technology

Selected Markets

Civil infrastructure (airports, rail, highways, heavy civil)
Communications (wireless and other telecommunications)
Mining and metals
Oil, gas, and chemicals (design and construction for chemical, petrochemical, LNG and natural gas plants, and pipelines)
Power electrical (gas, oil, coal, and nuclear power plants)
U.S. government services (defense, space, demilitarization, security, nuclear, and environmental restoration and remediation services)

COMPETITORS

Aker Solutions
AMEC
Balfour Construction
Black & Veatch
Bouygues
CH2M HILL
Chiyoda Corp.
EIFFAGE
Fluor
Foster Wheeler
Halliburton
HOCHTIEF
Hyundai Engineering
ITOCHU
Jacobs Engineering
Kajima
Lummus Technology

Marelich Mechanical
Parsons Corporation
Peter Kiewit Sons'
RWE
Schneider Electric
Shaw Group
Siemens AG
Skanska
SNEF
Technip
Tutor Perini
Uhde
URS
VINCI
Washington Division
Weston

HISTORICAL FINANCIALS

Company Type: Private

Income Statement

FYE: December 31

	REVENUE ($ mil.)	NET INCOME ($ mil.)	NET PROFIT MARGIN	EMPLOYEES
12/08	31,400	—	—	44,000
12/07	27,000	—	—	42,500
12/06	20,500	—	—	40,000
12/05	18,100	—	—	40,000
12/04	17,378	—	—	40,000
Annual Growth	**15.9%**	**—**	**—**	**2.4%**

Revenue History

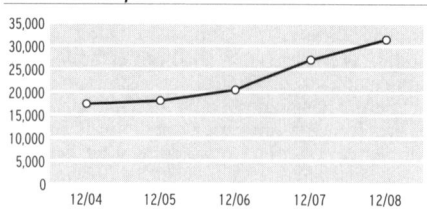

Belden & Blake

It may sound like a law firm, but Belden & Blake is in fact an energy company that obeys the laws of supply and demand in the oil and gas market. It acquires properties, explores for and develops oil and gas reserves, and gathers and markets natural gas in the Appalachian and Michigan basins. In 2008 Belden & Blake reported interests in 4,550 gross wells, and leases on about 562,100 net acres, and it owned and operated 1,660 miles of gas gathering lines. The company had estimated proved reserves of 223 billion cu. ft. of gas equivalent. Belden & Blake is controlled by Capital C Energy Operations, itself controlled by EnerVest Ltd.

EnerVest Operating acts as operator for most of Belden & Blake's oil and gas wells and its related gathering systems and production facilities (4,006 wells, or 88% of gross wells representing 97% of its estimated proved developed reserves).

The company's strategy is to drill in low risk formations and in underexploited formations in the Appalachian and Michigan basins. In 2008 Belden & Blake drilled 98 gross development wells. In 2009 its focus was in three areas: operational reworking and enhancement programs and Marcellus Shale recompletions, Knox exploration in Ohio, and new drilling in Pennsylvania.

EXECUTIVES

President and CEO: John B. Walker, age 63
EVP and CFO: James M. Vanderhider, age 50
SVP, COO, and Director: Kenneth (Ken) Mariani, age 47
VP Exploration: Mark L. Barnhill, age 53
VP Accounting: Frederick J. Stair, age 49
VP Land and Legal and Secretary: Sandra K. Fraley, age 43
VP Operations: Barry K. Lay, age 52
VP Engineering: David M. Elkin, age 43
Auditors: Deloitte & Touche LLP

LOCATIONS

HQ: Belden & Blake Corporation
1001 Fannin St., Ste. 800, Houston, TX 77002
Phone: 713-659-3500

PRODUCTS/OPERATIONS

2008 Sales

	$ mil.	% of total
Oil & gas	145.4	92
Gas gathering & marketing	12.2	8
Other	0.8	—
Total	**158.4**	**100**

COMPETITORS

Cabot Oil & Gas
EQT Corporation
Petroleum Development
Quicksilver Resources
Range Resources
Sharpe Resources

HISTORICAL FINANCIALS

Company Type: Private

Income Statement

FYE: December 31

	REVENUE ($ mil.)	NET INCOME ($ mil.)	NET PROFIT MARGIN	EMPLOYEES
12/08	158	(29)	—	0
12/07	126	(35)	—	0
12/06	159	52	32.8%	0
12/05	155	17	11.1%	134
12/04	102	13	12.5%	180
Annual Growth	**11.7%**	**—**	**—**	**—**

Net Income History

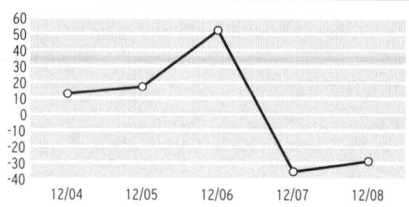

Belk, Inc.

Belk is busy bulking up. Already the nation's largest privately owned department store chain, Belk now operates more than 300 stores in some 15 states, following its 2006 purchase of the Parisian chain from Saks. Previously, Belk acquired Saks' McRae's and Proffitt's divisions. Belk stores are located primarily in the Southeast and Mid-Atlantic (the Carolinas, Florida, and Georgia) states and offer mid-priced brand-name and private-label apparel, shoes, jewelry, cosmetics, gifts, and home furnishings. Its stores usually anchor malls or shopping centers in small to midsized markets and target 35-to-54-year-old middle- and upper-income women. The Belk family runs the show and owns most of the company.

Belk has completed the rebranding of 25 of the Parisian stores acquired from Saks in October 2006 to the Belk banner. (Previously, it sold four of the acquired stores to The Bon-Ton

Stores and disposed of about a dozen others.) In fiscal 2009, during which revenues decreased more than 8%, the company opened eight new stores and expanded several other locations. However, given the current hostile retail climate, Belk has scaled back its growth plans for fiscal 2010, with only three new stores and three expansions planned. Belk is focusing its expansion efforts in midsized markets and suburbs surrounding large cities.

The retailer also launched its own fine jewelry business in 2007 under the "Belk and Co. Fine Jewelers" name and operates jewelry departments under that brand in about half of its stores.

Larger Belk stores may also contain hair salons, spas, restaurants, and optical centers.

HISTORY

William Henry Belk didn't mind being known as a cheapskate. At 26 he opened his first store, New York Racket, in 1888 in Monroe, North Carolina. He nicknamed the tiny shop "The Cheapest Store on Earth" and created the slogan "Cheap Goods Sell Themselves." In 1891 Belk convinced his brother John to give up a career as a doctor and join him in the retail business.

The new company, Belk Brothers, opened stores in North and South Carolina, often with partners who were family members or former employees, resulting in many two-family store names such as Belk-Harry and Hudson-Belk.

The Belks formed a partnership with the Leggett family (John's in-laws) in 1920. But feuding between the two families led to a split in 1927. The Leggetts agreed that the Belk family could keep a 20% share of the Leggett stores. John died the next year.

A strict no-credit policy worked in William's favor during the Depression, when he was able to buy out his more lenient competitors for rock-bottom prices. The shrewd businessman grew the chain from 29 stores in 1929 to about 220 stores by 1945, employing concepts such as a no-haggling policy and easy returns. William died in 1952.

That year one of his six children, William Henry Jr., opened a Belk-Lindsey store in Florida using a new format that featured, among other things, an Oriental design. Most of his siblings balked at the store's new look, but William Jr. opened another store in 1953 following the same format.

Two years later four of William Jr.'s siblings — John, Irwin, Tom, and Sarah — cut ties with the Florida stores and formed Belk Stores Services to organize their other stores. Angry at the rebuke, William Jr. and another brother, Henderson, sued the rest of the family, but they later dropped the lawsuit. In 1956 Belk Stores, with John at the helm, bought out 50-store rival chain Effird.

John had political ambitions and was elected mayor of Charlotte, North Carolina, in 1969, despite attempts by his brother William Jr. to foil the campaign. He remained mayor until 1977. Tom became the company's president in 1980.

Belk Stores continued to hold its own in the 1980s against larger department store chains on the prowl for acquisitions, but the company was stung by family discord and a loose ownership structure. Some relatives sold Belk stores to competitors such as Proffitt's (now Saks Inc.) and Dillard's. Irwin and his family, discouraged about the company's direction, sold their stock to John. In 1996 the Leggetts came back into the fold when Belk Stores bought out their 30-store chain.

Tom died in 1997 after complications from gall bladder surgery. His three sons, Tim, Johnny, and McKay, stepped up as co-presidents but continued to answer to their Uncle John, the CEO. Also in 1997 Belk Stores closed its struggling 13 Tags off-price outlets.

A year later the firm reorganized and brought all 112 separate corporations under one company, streamlining accounting (previously it had to fill out tax forms for all 112 businesses) and other operations.

In 1999 Belk formed Belk National Bank in Georgia to manage its credit card operations. The company closed four of its distribution centers in 2001, consolidating their operations into its new Blythewood, South Carolina, center.

After serving over 50 years as the company's CEO and close to 25 years as chairman, John Belk retired in May 2004. Nephew Tim Belk was named the new chairman and CEO, and his brothers McKay and Johnny were promoted to co-presidents of the company.

In July 2005 Belk acquired the Proffitt's and McRae's department store business from Saks Inc. for about $622 million. At the time, Proffitt's/McRae's operated 47 stores in 11 southeastern states.

In January 2006 Belk sold its private-label credit card business, with about $300 million in receivables, to an affiliate of GE Consumer Finance for about $321 million. (Concurrently, GE Consumer Finance purchased the Proffitt's and McRae's proprietary credit card account from HSBC.) In October Belk paid $285 million for Saks Inc's. 38-store Parisian department store chain, which has a presence in nine states in the Midwest and Southeast.

The company's acquisition of Migerobe, Inc. in June 2006 for about $19 million brought another niche for the retailer. Migerobe had leased and operated fine jewelry departments in 35 of Belk's stores. In early 2007 Belk began expanding its fine jewelry operations when its contract with Finlay Fine Jewelry Corp. expired. Belk hired a couple of Migerobe executives to lead its jewelry team.

In 2007 the company trimmed its store count by about a dozen stores and exited the Indiana and Ohio markets.

EXECUTIVES

Chairman and CEO: Thomas M. (Tim) Belk Jr., age 54, $1,407,533 total compensation
Co-President, COO, and Director: John R. (Johnny) Belk, age 50, $1,165,761 total compensation
Co-President, Chief Merchandising Officer, and Director: H. W. McKay Belk, age 52, $1,169,681 total compensation
EVP, General Counsel, and Secretary: Ralph A. Pitts, age 55, $886,636 total compensation
EVP and CFO: Brian T. Marley, age 52, $786,038 total compensation
EVP Human Resources: Adam M. Orvos, age 44
SVP and Director Stores, Northern Division: Bill Roberts
SVP and Director Stores, Northern Division: Gary Pierce
VP and Controller: Rodney F. Samples, age 45
President Merchandising and Marketing: Kathryn (Kathy) Bufano, age 56
Auditors: KPMG LLP

LOCATIONS

HQ: Belk, Inc.
2801 W. Tyvola Rd., Charlotte, NC 28217
Phone: 704-357-1000   **Fax:** 704-357-1876
Web: www.belk.com

2009 Stores

	No.
North Carolina	72
Georgia	47
South Carolina	37
Florida	30
Alabama	22
Tennessee	23
Virginia	20
Mississippi	17
Texas	13
Arkansas	7
Kentucky	5
West Virginia	4
Louisiana	4
Maryland	2
Oklahoma	3
Missouri	1
Total	**307**

PRODUCTS/OPERATIONS

2009 Sales

	% of total
Women's apparel	37
Cosmetics, shoes & accessories	31
Men's apparel	16
Home	10
Children's apparel	6
Total	**100**

Selected Private Labels

Be Inspired	Mary Jane's Farm
Biltmore Estate for Your Home	Meeting Street
	ND (New Directions)
Choices	Pro Tour
Cook's Tools	Red Camel
Home Accents	Saddlebred
J.Khaki	Sophie Max
Kim Rogers	W.H. Belk
Madison Studio	

COMPETITORS

Bromberg's	Sears
Dillard's	Stein Mart
J. C. Penney	Target
Kohl's	TJX Companies
Macy's	Wal-Mart

Ben E. Keith

Ben E. Keith is your bud if you like eating out and drinking brew. A leading food and beverage distributor, the company supplies its 22,000 customers, including restaurants, hotels, schools, and other institutional foodservice operators in 11 Southern states with a bevy of food and non-food products from its six distribution centers. Ben E. Keith is also one of the largest Anheuser-Busch distributors, delivering beer to customers in some 60 Texas counties. Founded in 1906 as Harkrider-Morrison, the company assumed its current name in 1931 in honor of Benjamin Ellington Keith, who served as the firm's president until 1959. It is controlled by Robert and Howard Hallam.

The company has been expanding its foodservice operation, opening a new distribution facility in Amarillo in 2007. The company has also laid plans to build another facility in Houston.

It has recently added more beer to its beverage products in 2008, acquiring Texas craft and import beer distribution operations of CR Goodman. The acquisition added 60 craft and import breweries to Ben E. Keith's portfolio.

In 2008 the company acquired Dallas-based Winn Meat Company, which added to its foodservice offerings. Its other foodservice companies include Markon Cooperative produce and Admiral of the Fleet seafood.

EXECUTIVES

Chairman and CEO: Robert Hallam
President and COO: Howard Hallam
CFO and Treasurer: Mel Cockrell
EVP Purchasing and National Accounts, Ben E. Keith Foods: Jim Lavender
SVP Sales, Ben E. Keith Foods: Ron Boyd
VP and Controller: Jerry Hall
VP: John Hallam
VP: Robert Hallam Jr.
VP Information Services: Jim Stone
VP and Treasurer: Gordon Crow
Corporate Secretary and General Counsel: Stewart D. (David) Greenlee
Director Human Resources: Sam Reeves
Director Credit: Richard Grasso
Director Produce and Dairy and Sales Training, Ben E. Keith Foods: David Werner
Director Risk Management: Daryl Wigington
President Food Division: Michael (Mike) Roach

LOCATIONS

HQ: Ben E. Keith Company
601 E. 7th St., Fort Worth, TX 76102
Phone: 817-877-5700   **Fax:** 817-338-1701
Web: www.benekeith.com

Selected Distribution Locations
Beverage division
  Abilene, TX
  Commerce, TX
  Dallas
  Denton, TX
  Llano, TX
  Palestine, TX
  Waco, TX

Food division
  Albuquerque, NM
  Amarillo, TX
  Dallas
  Little Rock, AR
  Oklahoma City
  San Antonio

COMPETITORS

Brown Distributing
Clark National
Glazer's Wholesale Drug
Glazier Foods
MAINES
McLane Foodservice
Meadowbrook Meat Company
MillerCoors
Performance Food
Republic National Distributing Company
Silver Eagle
Southern Wine & Spirits
SYSCO
UniPro Foodservice
U.S. Foodservice

Berry Plastics

Berry Plastics makes bunches and bunches of plastic products. The company is a leading maker of injection-molded plastic products. Its lineup includes drink cups, bottles, closures, tubes and prescription containers, stretch films, plastic sheeting, tapes, and housewares. Customers range from health care and personal care industries to restaurants, agricultural, industrial, construction, aerospace, and automotive, to name a few. The company operates 68 strategically located manufacturing facilities and has extensive distribution capabilities. Apollo Management and Graham Partners acquired Berry Plastics in 2006; Apollo owns approximately 75% of the company.

Shoring up against the recession in 2008 and 2009, Berry considers that buying and allying are the way to survive and prosper. In December 2009 Berry acquired specialty film and flexible packaging company Pliant Corporation; the acquisition brings 16 global manufacturing facilities to Berry's operation. The company plans to integrate Pliant into its structure as the Specialty Films Division. Pliant's former COO R. David Corey will head the division.

One of the most important raw materials for Berry is polyethylene resin; approximately 1.2 billion pounds are used annually. Based on the need for this material, the company maintains strong relationships with suppliers Chevron, DAK Americas, Dow, DuPont, Eastman Chemical, Exxon Mobil, Flint Hills Resources, and Sunoco. Other core materials include natural and butyl rubber, chemicals and adhesives, paper and packaging materials, polyester, raw cotton, linerboard and kraft, woven and nonwoven cloth, and foil, which are sourced from a broader number of companies.

As good as Berry's supply relationships were, rising prices for plastic resin in 2008 forced cost reductions. The company shut down underperforming manufacturing facilities in Mexico (tapes/coatings) and Canada (rigid closed top). The workforce in the Alabama production facility (tapes/coatings) was reduced, and a number of employees were shuttled to other Berry facilities.

The company also uses its acquisitions to build and hold market positions, expand product lines, and reduce manufacturing and overhead costs through operating synergies and introduction of advanced processes. In 2007 the company acquired Captive Holdings, the parent company of Captive Plastics (Captive), from First Atlantic Capital, for $500 million in cash. Captive manufactures blow-molded bottles and injection-molded closures for the food, health care, spirits, and personal care markets. Similar strategic acquisitions have included Rollpak Acquisition Corporation (Rollpak), a flexible film manufacturer, and MAC Closures (MAC), a fully integrated manufacturer of injection molded plastic caps and closures serving pharmaceutical, personal care, and household and industrial chemical industries. In November 2008 Berry scored Erie Plastics, a custom injection molder. The deal brought Erie Plastics out of bankruptcy protection (filed in September 2008) and offers Berry additional capacity in plastics packaging and components. Subsequently, Berry agreed to acquire Superfos Packaging. The 2009 deal will give Berry a plant ready to churn out open-top plastic containers for an array of goods, such as food and household and industrial chemicals.

Technology and new products provide a mainstay for growth, as well. The company's four operating divisions — rigid open top, rigid closed top, flexible films, and tapes and coatings — are manufactured using primary molding methods including injection, thermoforming, compression, tube extrusion, and blow molding. These processes begin with raw plastic pellets and resins, which are then converted into finished products. Berry spent $13.9 million on R&D in 2008 and has major technical centers and quality laboratories for product testing and experimenting in Pennsylvania, Massachusetts, and Louisiana. These centers drive prototypes of new ideas as well as conduct research and development for new products and processes.

The company's investment in developing and commercializing flexible products and manufacturing technologies has paid off. Examples include the X-FLEX Blast Protection System, a peel-and-stick film that absorbs energy during significant blast events and reduces injury to military personnel within a battle zone. Other examples are Berry's stretch film technology, which is capable of producing 11-layer stretch film; Thermo-ply Total Structural Sheathing (formaldehyde-free); Barricade Dry Step synthetic roofing underlayment with Breathe Dry Technology; Twistrand Technology (twisted fibers for more traction); and Ruffies PRO duct and masking tape for consumer applications. In 2008 Berry utilized Power Efficiency Corporation, a clean tech company that uses E-Save Technology to improve the efficiency of its electric motors and to conserve energy and reduce CO_2 emissions.

Responding to consumer demand, Berry is expanding its thermoforming business. In 2008 it added a cup and lid line capability to its facility, as well as a line of clear cold cups. The company plans an $80 million expansion of its thermoforming operations, with a targeted startup in the first quarter of 2010.

Apollo Management and Graham Partners acquired Berry Plastics from Goldman Sachs and J.P. Morgan for $2.25 billion in September 2006. The company then moved into the flexible packaging industry by merging with another Apollo-controlled company, Covalence Specialty Materials. Covalence is the former plastics and adhesives business of Tyco that was also acquired by Apollo in 2006. The two Apollo-controlled companies combined in a stock-for-stock merger transaction in April 2007, with the surviving entity retaining the Berry Plastics name.

EXECUTIVES

Chairman and CEO: Ira G. Boots, age 54, $1,493,662 total compensation
President and COO: Ralph B. Beeler, age 55, $1,138,643 total compensation
EVP, CFO, Secretary, and Treasurer: James M. (Jim) Kratochvil, age 52, $793,651 total compensation
EVP and Controller: Mark Miles
EVP Commercial Development: Randall J. (Randy) Hobson, age 44, $509,721 total compensation
VP Human Resources: Bill Harness
VP Operations, Tapes and Coatings: Terri Pitcher
President, Tapes and Coatings: Thomas E. (Tom) Salmon, $648,688 total compensation
President, Rigid Open Top Division: Glenn A. Unfried, age 38, $484,691 total compensation
Executive Assistant and Media Contact: Diane Tungate
Auditors: Ernst & Young LLP

LOCATIONS

HQ: Berry Plastics Corporation
101 Oakley St., Evansville, IN 47710
Phone: 812-424-2904 **Fax:** 812-424-0128
Web: www.berryplastics.com

PRODUCTS/OPERATIONS

2008 Sales

	$ mil.	% of total
Flexible Film	1,092.2	31
Rigid Open Top	1,053.2	30
Rigid Closed Top	853.4	24
Tapes/Coatings	514.3	15
Total	**3,513.1**	**100**

Selected Product Lines

Agricultural Film
Bottles
Building Products
Catering
Closures
Containers
Corrosion Protection
Custom Films
Cutlery & Meal Kits
Drink Cups
Drop Cloths
FIBC
Flexible Packaging
Home & Party
Institutional Can Liners
Lids
Overcaps
Prescription
Sheeting
Stretch Film
Tapes
Trash Bags
Tubes

Available Services

Berry Design Center
Creative Services
Decorating Services
Global Services
Technical Services

COMPETITORS

3M
AEP Industries
Alcoa
AptarGroup
Berlin Packaging
Dart Container
DENSO
Dopaco
Graham Packaging
Huhtamäki
Huhtamaki Foodservice
Inteplast
International Paper
Intertape Polymer
Letica
Omni Industries Holdings
Owens-Illinois
Pactiv
Pliant Corporation
Poly-America
Polytainers
Portola Packaging
Rexam
Shurtape Technologies
Sigma Plastics
Silgan
Silgan White Cap
Solo Cup
WinCup

HISTORICAL FINANCIALS

Company Type: Private

Income Statement

FYE: September 30

	REVENUE ($ mil.)	NET INCOME ($ mil.)	NET PROFIT MARGIN	EMPLOYEES
9/08	3,513	(101)	—	13,800
9/07*	3,055	(116)	—	12,700
12/06	1,432	(75)	—	6,600
12/05	1,170	20	1.7%	6,800
12/04	814	23	2.8%	4,550
Annual Growth	**44.1%**	**—**	**—**	**32.0%**

*Fiscal year change

Net Income History

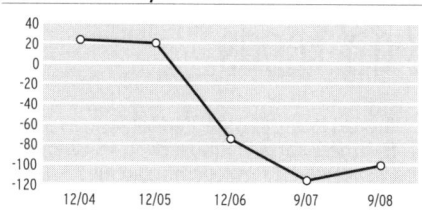

Berwind Corporation

Founded in 1886 to mine Appalachian coal, Berwind began leasing its mining operations in 1962 to fund investments in new ventures. Berwind Corporation gives autonomy to the management teams of its portfolio companies while adding investment fuel to their financial fires. The company's portfolio includes Elmer's Products, maker of Elmer's Glue, Krazy Glue, and other products; specialty chemicals companies CRC and Colorcon; and promotional products firm National Pen. Berwind Property Group (or BPG Properties) owns more than 30 million sq. ft. of residential, multi-family, student, retail, hotel, and industrial properties. The Berwind family owns Berwind Corporation.

In 2008 BPG bought Boston Capital Real Estate Investment Trust, which owns around a dozen apartment buildings totalling 2.7 million sq. ft.

Berwind's venture capital arm, Inflection Point Ventures (IPV), funds early-stage telecommunications and information technology concerns. Another unit, Berwind Natural Resources, still holds coal, natural gas, and timber rights in Kentucky, Pennsylvania, Virginia, and West Virginia.

The company takes full ownership of its investment companies. It looks for target companies that show steady growth, international operations, and companies with high growth margins.

EXECUTIVES

President and CEO: Michael B. McClelland
CFO: Van Billet, age 55
CEO, National Pen: Dave Thompson
President and COO, ECCO: Chris Thompson
CEO, Consumer Group; CEO, Elmer's Products: Timothy M. (Tim) Callahan
CEO, ECCO: Ed Zimmer
CIO, National Pen: Ed Fares

CFO, National Pen: Ted Heininger
VP Global Sales and Marketing, ECCO: Mike Scoll
VP Engineering, ECCO: Mike Lindstrom

LOCATIONS

HQ: Berwind Corporation
3000 Centre Sq. West, 1500 Market St.
Philadelphia, PA 19102
Phone: 215-563-2800 **Fax:** 215-575-2314
Web: www.berwind.com

PRODUCTS/OPERATIONS

Selected Operations

Berwind Natural Resources (land and resource management)
Colorcon (specialty chemical products)
CRC Industries (specialty chemical products)
Elmer's Products (consumer adhesives)
Inflection Point Ventures (venture capital)
National Pen Co. (promotional products)

COMPETITORS

Apollo Advisors
Berkshire Income Realty
Bruckmann, Rosser, Sherrill & Co.
Jordan Company
Vulcan

HISTORICAL FINANCIALS

Company Type: Holding company

Income Statement

FYE: December 31

	ESTIMATED REVENUE ($ mil.)	NET INCOME ($ mil.)	NET PROFIT MARGIN	EMPLOYEES
12/07	1,470	—	—	3,565
12/06	1,710	—	—	3,500
12/05	1,629	—	—	3,500
Annual Growth	**(5.0%)**	**—**	**—**	**0.9%**

Revenue History

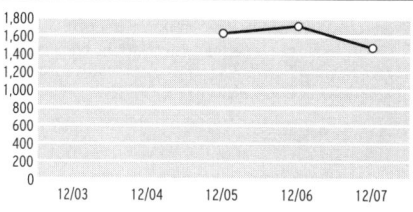

Best Western

Western hospitality has really spread. Begun in 1946 by hotelier M. K. Guertin and named for its California origins, Best Western has more than 4,000 independently owned and operated hotels (including 2,200-plus in the US, Canada, and the Caribbean), making it the world's largest hotel brand (by number of rooms). Hotels sport its flag in about 80 countries and territories; Australia and the UK have the most outside the US. The company has about 100 Best Western Premier branded hotels in Asia and Europe, which offer a higher level of amenities and services. Best Western is organized as a not-for-profit membership association, with most of its sales coming from monthly fees and annual dues.

The company is expanding its global presence, especially in Asia, where the chain plans to have more than 200 hotels by 2010. In addition, through a licensing agreement in India, Best Western also expects to add 100 new hotels per year there through the next decade. In 2008 Best Western broke ground on its first hotel in Dubai, the Best Western Residences. The brand also opened its first hotels in Colombia (Best Western Cyan Suites in Medellin) and Suriname (Best Western Elegance Hotel in Paramaribo), and secured plans for its first hotel in Haiti. In addition, the Best Western Premier Hotel Krakow opened in Poland.

In North America, in 2008 the company opened its first Atrea upper-midscale business hotel in San Antonio, Texas, and its first LEED-certified hotel, the Best Western Inn and Suites at Dinosaur Ridge, in Golden, Colorado. (The Leadership in Energy and Environmental Design certification is from the US Green Building Council.) Also that year Best Western opened its first hotel in New York City's Chinatown, the Best Western Bowery Hanbee Hotel. In Canada, Best Western opened the Best Western Fredericton Hotel and Suites, its first property in Fredericton, New Brunswick.

While the travel industry is facing hard times as a result of the economic recession, the company claims that its hotels are benefiting from companies who are looking to cut costs by moving their hotel business to the mid-market sector. For example, Best Western requires its hoteliers to provide complimentary Internet and local phone calls.

EXECUTIVES

Chairwoman: Beth Campbell
Vice Chairman: P. G. West
President and CEO: David T. Kong
CFO: Mark Straszynski
SVP Marketing and Sales: Dorothy Dowling
SVP Distribution and Strategic Services and CIO: Scott Gibson
VP Design and Supply: Richard (Rich) Bennett
VP North American Development: Mark E. Williams
VP Information Systems Operations: David Velasquez
VP and General Counsel: Lawrence M. (Larry) Cuculic, age 52
VP Human Resources: Barbara Bras
VP International Operations: Suzi Yoder MacDonald
VP International Operations, Asia: Glenn de Souza
VP Brand Management and Member Services: Ron Pohl
VP Marketing: Renee Ryan
Secretary, Treasurer, and Director: Julie Montmaneix
Director External Communications: Troy Rutman
Auditors: Mukai, Greenlee & Company, P.C.

LOCATIONS

HQ: Best Western International, Inc.
6201 N. 24th Pkwy., Phoenix, AZ 85016
Phone: 602-957-4200   **Fax:** 602-957-5641
Web: www.bestwestern.com

Sales Office Locations

Atlanta	Orlando
Bangkok	Rio de Janeiro
Beijing	Sao Paolo
Bogota	San Diego
Buenos Aires	Santiago
Chicago	Seattle
Dallas	Seoul
Dubai	Singapore
Hong Kong	St. Louis
London	Sydney
Los Angeles	Tel-Aviv
Mexico City	Tokyo
Miami	Toronto
Milan	Washington, DC
New York City	

COMPETITORS

Accor
Carlson Hotels
Choice Hotels
HVM
InterContinental Hotels
La Quinta
Marriott
Scandic Hotels
ShoLodge
Sunburst Hospitality
Wyndham Worldwide

Big Y Foods

Why call it Big Y? Big Y Foods began as a 900-sq.-ft. grocery at a Y intersection in Chicopee, Massachusetts. It now operates about 55 supermarkets throughout Massachusetts and Connecticut. Most of its stores are Big Y World Class Markets, offering specialty areas such as bakeries and floral shops, as well as banking. The rest consist of Big Y Supermarkets and a single gourmet food and liquor store called Table & Vine in Springfield, Massachusetts. Some Big Y stores provide child care, dry cleaning, photo processing, and even propane sales, and their delis and food courts offer to-go foods. Big Y is owned and run by the D'Amour family and is one of New England's largest independent supermarket chains.

In July 2009 the company began offering up to a 14-day supply of free select generic antibiotics at its 33 in-store pharmacies to shoppers with a Big Y Express Savings Club card. (National chains, such as Wal-Mart stores, have long offered deals on pharmaceuticals.) Big Y also offers health services, such as flu shot clinics and screenings, at its pharmacies.

Jumping on the organic/natural foods and local foods bandwagons, Big Y offers produce from local growers, and the grocery chain's smaller Fresh Acres format (launched in 2006) offers fresh, natural, and easy-to-prepare foods.

EXECUTIVES

Chairman and CEO: Donald H. D'Amour
President and COO: Charles L. D'Amour
CFO: William (Bill) White
SVP Merchandising: Daniel (Dan) Lescoe
VP Information Systems: John N. Sarno
VP Fresh Foods: Michael P. D'Amour
VP Marketing and Corporate Strategies: Antonio F. Gomes
VP Employee Services: Jack Henry
VP Corporate Communications: Claire H. D'Amour-Daley
VP Store Operations: William P. Hogan
VP Legal Affairs and Government Relations: Michael S. Gold
Director IRT Infrastructure: Bruce W. Bailly
Director Food Safety: Casimir M. Tryba
Director Supply Chain Management: Edward D. Burke
Director Grocery Sales: Peter M. Dudis
Director Loss Prevention: Mark L. Gaudette
Director Risk Management: James Kacmarcik
Director Store Design and Purchasing: John W. Jendza
Director Facilities Management: Anthony P. Coppola
Auditors: Deloitte & Touche LLP

LOCATIONS

HQ: Big Y Foods, Inc.
2145 Roosevelt Ave., Springfield, MA 01102
Phone: 413-784-0600
Web: www.bigy.com

2009 Stores

	No.
Massachusetts	32
Connecticut	25
Total	**57**

PRODUCTS/OPERATIONS

Selected Products and Services

Babysitting
Bakery
Banking
Bottle redemption
Coin sorting and counting
Deli
Dry cleaning
Florist
General merchandise
Gourmet food
Knife sharpening
Liquor
Lottery tickets
Meat
Money orders
Phone cards
Photo processing
Postage stamps
Poultry
Produce
Propane
Seafood
Sushi
Western Union
Wine

COMPETITORS

BJ's Wholesale Club	Rite Aid
Costco Wholesale	Shaw's
Cumberland Farms	Stop & Shop
CVS Caremark	SUPERVALU
DeMoulas Super Markets	Target
Golub	Walgreen
Hannaford Bros.	Wal-Mart

Bill & Melinda Gates Foundation

You don't have to be one of the world's richest men to make a difference with your charitable gifts — but it helps. Established by the chairman of Microsoft and his wife, the Bill & Melinda Gates Foundation works in developing countries to improve health and reduce poverty, and in the US to support education and libraries nationwide and children and families in the Pacific Northwest. With an endowment of about $29.5 billion in 2009 (down from $38 billion in 2007), the foundation is the largest in the US. Investor Warren Buffett has announced plans to give the Bill & Melinda Gates Foundation about $30 billion worth of Berkshire Hathaway stock in installments, the first of which was received in 2006.

The Buffett gift will be spread over a number of years. (The $30 billion figure represents the value of the stock when the gift was announced in June 2006.) As a result of Buffett's gift, the Gates Foundation predicted a steep increase in grant making. Indeed, despite a sizeable hit to its endowment due to the crisis in the financial markets, the philanthropic organization plans to increase spending from $3.3 billion in 2008 to $3.8 billion in 2009.

With the Buffett giving program comes a challenge, however: Starting in 2009, the foundation has to annually give away 100% of Buffett's contribution from the previous year. Not a bad problem to have, but the foundation is working to expand its staff and revamp its processes in order to take advantage of the new opportunity. Global economic development efforts are expected to gain additional support.

As part of its response to the Buffett gift, the foundation restructured itself in November 2006. Its assets were transferred to the Bill & Melinda Gates Foundation Trust, which will receive future contributions of Berkshire Hathaway stock and will be overseen by the Gateses as trustees. Money will pass from the trust to the Bill & Melinda Gates Foundation, which will make grants. Buffett joined the Gateses as a trustee of the Bill & Melinda Gates Foundation — but not of the asset trust, thus separating him from decisions about the disposition of the trust's Berkshire Hathaway shares.

The foundation also announced that it would give away all of its assets within 50 years of the deaths of Buffett, then 76; Bill Gates, then 51; and Melinda Gates, then 42. Bill Gates previously had said he would like to give away most of his fortune while he is still living, and he is scaling back his duties at Microsoft in order to spend more time at the foundation.

The Gates Foundation is co-funding a study called The *Joys and Dilemmas of Wealth* scheduled for release in the fall of 2008. The study will survey American households worth $25 million or more with the goal of encouraging charitable giving by the rich.

The Bill & Melinda Gates Foundation was formed in 2000 in a combination of two related philanthropies: The William H. Gates Foundation (established in 1994) and the Gates Learning Foundation.

HISTORY

Bill Gates created the William H. Gates Foundation in 1994 with $106 million. During the next four years he added about $2 billion to the charity. He appointed his father the head of the foundation, which at first was housed in Bill Gates Sr.'s basement. In 1997 Gates established the Gates Learning Foundation (originally called the Gates Library Foundation), a philanthropic effort to improve library systems. It was Gates's goal to improve technology and Internet access at libraries, which some critics saw as a way for him to plant Microsoft software at libraries nationwide. Patty Stonesifer, a former executive at Microsoft, ran the organization from an office above a pizza parlor.

Bill and his wife, Melinda French Gates, contributed some $16 billion to the foundation in 1999. In 2000 Gates decided to merge his two charity programs into one entity, the Bill & Melinda Gates Foundation, to be run by the elder Gates and Stonesifer.

In early 2000 Gates made another $5 billion gift of stock to the foundation. Also that year the foundation pledged $10 million toward construction of an underground visitors center at Capitol Hill in Washington, DC. The Bill &

Melinda Gates Foundation donated another $10 million in 2001 to be awarded over three years to the Hope for African Children Initiative, to help African children affected by AIDS. In 2002 the Bill & Melinda Gates Foundation pledged more than $100 million over 10 years to reduce the spread of AIDS in India. The foundation awarded a $70 million grant to the departments of genome sciences and bioengineering at the University of Washington in 2003.

The Bill & Melinda Gates Foundation donated $750 million to be given over 10 years to the Global Alliance for Vaccines & Immunization in 2005. This follows a $750 million gift to the organization when it was established in 2000.

In June 2006 investor Warren Buffett announced plans to give the Bill & Melinda Gates Foundation about $30 billion over a number of years. Buffett's 2006 and 2007 gifts to the Bill & Melinda Gates Foundation were worth about $1.6 billion and $1.7 billion, respectively.

In September 2008 Patty Stonesifer, who had served as CEO of the foundation since its inception, was succeeded by Jeff Raikes, a 27-year Microsoft veteran.

EXECUTIVES

Co-Chair: William H. (Bill) Gates III, age 53
Co-Chair: William H. (Bill Sr.) Gates Sr., age 83
Co-Chair: Melinda F. Gates, age 44
CEO: Jeffrey S. (Jeff) Raikes, age 51
CFO: Alexander S. Friedman
Chief of Staff, Global Health Program: Neil McDonnell
Chief of Staff, Executive Office: Andrea Voytko
Chief Administrative Officer: Martha Choe
Chief Communications Officer: Kate James
Chief Human Resources Officer: Franci Phelan
General Counsel and Secretary: Connie Collingsworth
President, U.S. Program: Allan C. Golston
President, Global Development Program:
 Sylvia Matthews Burwell, age 43
Director HIV, Global Health Program: Stefano Bertozzi
Director Education, U.S. Program: Vicki L. Phillips
Director Operations, U.S. Program: Diane de Ryss
Director, Foundation Communications: Robert Rosen
Director of Operations Global Development Program:
 Jim Bormley
Director Education, Postsecondary Success, and Special Initiatives, U.S. Program:
 Hillary C. Pennington
Director Financial Services for the Poor, Global Development Program: Bob Christen
Director Policy and Advocacy, Global Development Program: Mark Suzman
President, Global Health Program:
 Tadataka (Tachi) Yamada, age 63
Director Impact Planning and Improvement:
 Fay Twersky
Auditors: KPMG LLP

LOCATIONS

HQ: Bill & Melinda Gates Foundation
 1551 Eastlake Ave. East, Seattle, WA 98102
Phone: 206-709-3100   **Fax:** 206-709-3180
Web: www.gatesfoundation.org

PRODUCTS/OPERATIONS

Selected Beneficiaries
Alliance for Cervical Cancer Prevention ($3.9 million over two years)
Gay City Health Project ($30,000 over three years)
Global Alliance for Vaccines & Immunization ($1.5 billion over 15 years)
Global Health Council ($4.8 million over three years)
Helen Keller International ($5 million over five years)
International Planned Parenthood Federation ($8.8 million over five years)
International Tuberculosis Foundation ($1.9 million over five years)

International Vaccine Institute ($40 million over five years)
Library and Information Commission ($4.2 million over one year)
National Institute of Child Health and Human Development ($15 million over five years)
Oxfam ($2.9 million over four years)
Pacific Institute for Women's Health ($1 million over three years)
Population Council ($4 million over two years)
Portland Children's Museum ($600,000 over three years)
United Negro College Fund ($1 billion over 20 years)
US Fund for UNICEF ($15 million over five years)

HISTORICAL FINANCIALS
Company Type: Foundation

Income Statement

	REVENUE ($ mil.)	NET INCOME ($ mil.)	NET PROFIT MARGIN	EMPLOYEES
12/08	(5,836)	(9,809)	—	760
12/07	8,082	—	—	626
12/06	5,704	—	—	457
12/05	1,864	—	—	270
12/04	3,344	—	—	234
Annual Growth	—	—	—	34.2%

FYE: December 31

Revenue History

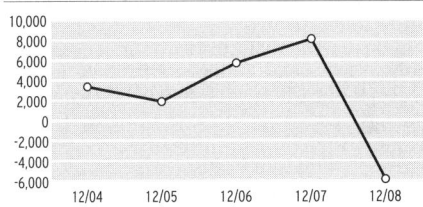

Biomet, Inc.

When the leg bone and the knee bone don't connect so well anymore, Biomet may have a solution. Orthopedic specialists use the medical devices made by Biomet, whose wares include reconstructive products (hips, knees, and shoulders), dental implants, bone cement systems, orthopedic support devices, and operating-room supplies. Through its EBI subsidiary, the firm also sells fixation devices (bone screws and pins), electrical bone-growth stimulators, and bone grafting materials. Subsidiary Biomet Microfixation markets implants and bone substitute material for craniomaxillofacial (head and face) surgeries. Biomet is controlled by LVB Acquisition, which is owned by a group of private equity firms.

Reconstructive devices account for more than 70% of Biomet's sales, and the US is its biggest market (about 60% of sales); Europe accounts for more than 25%. Products are marketed to hospitals, surgeon practices, and other medical facilities through direct and commissioned sales representatives, as well as through wholesale distributors.

The company distributes its products in some 90 countries worldwide, but it is looking to expand its geographical presence, particularly in Asia and Latin America. Biomet also avidly pursues research and development efforts to expand its product offerings.

For example, in 2009 Biomet acquired Cartilix, a company that has developed proprietary cartilage repair technology. The company fits with Biomet's plan to expand its sports medicine segment and gives the company a possible interventional treatment for pre-arthritic patients. The ChonDux cartilage regeneration technology is set to enter clinical trials.

In 2007 Biomet was acquired by LVB for more than $11 billion. The private equity consortium includes Blackstone Group, Goldman Sachs, KKR, TPG Capital, and former CEO Dane Miller. UK medical device company Smith & Nephew had also made a bid but was rejected in favor of the slightly lower private equity offer. Biomet had been on the auction block for more than a year.

HISTORY

In 1977 Niles Noblitt, Dane Miller, and two others established Biomet to design orthopedic products, a field then dominated by divisions of large pharmaceutical companies; the founders hoped that Biomet (the name links "biological" and "metal") could — because of its focus and small size — grow unhindered by bureaucratic red tape. The company's discovery that contractors making Biomet-designed products were selling them to competitors inspired the move into manufacturing.

Biomet went public in 1982. The company acquired Orthopedic Equipment in 1985, gaining access to the UK market. In 1988 it engineered the hostile takeover of Electro-Biology. Biomet acquired Effner GmbH (orthopedic devices, Germany) in 1991 and Walter Lorenz Surgical Instruments in 1992. Two years later the company acquired Kirschner Medical, a producer of joint-replacement products for hips, knees, and shoulders. Biomet founded Biomet Europe in 1995 to strengthen and centralize its international marketing effort. In 1996 the company was hit with a $36 million judgment in a patent dispute. The award was vacated three years later.

In 1998 the company formed a 50-50 joint venture with Merck KGaA to distribute orthopedic products in Europe. The deal gave Biomet its first crack at licensing both Merck's existing biomaterial orthopedic products (outside Europe) and future products developed by the joint venture.

The company continued moving into genetically engineered products with a 1999 agreement to distribute tissue-repair and -regeneration products developed by Selective Genetics. It also bought Implant Innovatives (later renamed 3i), which sells dental reconstructive implants. Also that year Biomet lost a breach of contract suit (relating to a distribution agreement) brought by Orthofix, which won a $49 million judgment.

In 2000 Biomet introduced a host of new products, including the SpineLink Cervical System, the Opti-rom Elbow Fixator, and the RC Needle Kit. The company continued to push out new products the following year.

In 2004 Biomet acquired Interpore, a maker of orthopedic biomaterials and specialty fixation devices, expanding the company's product offerings within the reconstructive surgery market. Biomet had difficulty integrating the acquisition into its EBI subsidiary, however, and separated some of the Interpore/EBI operations in 2006.

After nearly 30 years at Biomet, Dane Miller retired as president and CEO in March 2006. Daniel P. Hann served in the top spot on an interim basis until Jeffrey Binder was appointed president and CEO of Biomet early the following year. Suffering from disappointing earnings results, the company also hired Morgan Stanley in 2006 to help it consider its options. (This later resulted in the company's going-private transaction.)

In the year that followed, Biomet also revealed that it had backdated some stock options given to executives, a scandal that predictably resulted in some top-level resignations, shareholder lawsuits, and a restatement of earnings. Department of Justice officials also were investigating Biomet (along with several rivals) over payments to orthopedic surgeons who use the company's hip and knee replacements; the company settled with the DOJ in 2007, agreeing to pay about $27 million in fines.

EXECUTIVES

President, CEO, and Director: Jeffrey R. Binder, age 46, $6,234,134 total compensation
SVP Quality, Regulatory, and Clinical Affairs: Robert E. Durgin, age 50
SVP; President, Biomet 3i: Maggie Anderson, age 44
SVP; President, Biomet Orthopedics: Jon Serbousek, age 48, $2,014,850 total compensation
SVP and CFO: Daniel P. (Dan) Florin, age 45, $1,449,854 total compensation
SVP, General Counsel, and Secretary: Bradley J. Tandy, age 50
SVP; President, Biomet Trauma and Biomet Spine: Glen A. Kashuba, age 46, $1,806,190 total compensation
SVP; President, Biomet Europe, Middle East, and Africa: Roger P. van Broeck, age 60, $1,821,718 total compensation
SVP; President, Biomet SBU Operations: Gregory W. Sasso, age 47
SVP Human Resources: Peggy Taylor, age 53
SVP Worldwide Operations: Robin T. Barney, age 48
VP and Chief Compliance Officer: Sujata Dayal
VP Public Affairs: Bill Kolter
Auditors: Ernst & Young LLP

LOCATIONS

HQ: Biomet, Inc.
56 E. Bell Dr., Warsaw, IN 46582
Phone: 574-267-6639   **Fax:** 574-267-8137
Web: www.biomet.com

2009 Sales

	$ mil.	% of total
US	1,527.9	61
Europe	711.7	28
Other regions	264.5	11
Total	**2,504.1**	**100**

PRODUCTS/OPERATIONS

2009 Sales

	$ mil.	% of total
Reconstructive products	1,851.0	74
Fixation products	234.1	9
Spinal products	222.1	9
Other	196.9	8
Total	**2,504.1**	**100**

Selected Product Lines

Reconstructive products
  Bone cement and cement delivery systems
  Dental reconstructive implants
  Joint replacement systems (knees, hips, shoulders)
  Patient matched implants (custom)
  Platlet separation systems
Fixation products
  Bone substitute materials
  Craniomaxillofacial fixation systems
  Electrical stimulation devices (non-spinal)
  External fixation devices
  Internal fixation devices (nails, plates, screw, and pins)

Spinal products
  Orthobiologics (allograft)
  Spinal fusion stimulation systems
  Spinal fixation systems
Other
  Arthroscopy products
  Operating room supplies
  Orthopedic soft goods and braces

Selected Subsidiaries

Biomet 3i, LLC (dental reconstructive implants)
Biomet Biologics, LLC (orthobiologics)
Biomet Europe BV (Netherlands, European headquarters)
Biomet Microfixation, LLC (craniomaxillofacial fixation systems)
Biomet Orthopedics, LLC (joint replacements)
Biomet Sports Medicine, LLC (arthroscopy products)
EBI, LLC (dba Biomet Bracing, Biomet Osteobiologics, Biomet Spine, Biomet Trauma, fixation and electrical stimulation devices)
Interpore Spine Ltd. (dba Interpore Cross, biomaterials)

COMPETITORS

Aesculap, Inc. USA	Medtronic
Amedica	Nobel Biocare
Arthrex	Orthofix
ArthroCare	OrthoLogic
Astra Tech (Sweden)	Smith & Nephew
Codman & Shurtleff	Straumann
CONMED Corporation	Stryker
DePuy	Synthes
DJO	Wright Medical Group
Ethicon	Zimmer Holdings
Exactech	

HISTORICAL FINANCIALS

Company Type: Private

Income Statement

	REVENUE ($ mil.)	NET INCOME ($ mil.)	NET PROFIT MARGIN	EMPLOYEES
5/09	2,504	(749)	—	3,548
5/08	2,135	(964)	—	7,220
Annual Growth	17.3%	—	—	(50.9%)

FYE: May 31

Black & Veatch

Black & Veatch provides the ABCs of construction, engineering, and consulting. The international group is one of the largest private companies in the US. It specializes in infrastructure development for the energy, water, environmental, federal, and telecommunications markets, and engages in all phases of building projects, including design and engineering, financing and procurement, and construction. Among the company's services are environmental consulting, operations and maintenance, security design and consulting, management consulting, and IT services. Projects include coal, nuclear, and combustion turbine plants; drinking water and coastal water operations; and wireless and broadband installation.

The group's operations in the global water markets affect water quality and quantity throughout the water cycle: from source to treatment, to delivery, to wastewater collection and treatment. A key player in water treatment and wastewater treatment design, Black & Veatch's water sector division works with utilities, governments, and industries worldwide. The company acquired MJ Gleeson's water engineering division in the UK in 2006. The move more than doubled Black & Veatch's water industry business.

Black & Veatch expanded its technology capabilities in 2009 with an agreement to acquire Arista Consulting & Technologies, a San Diego-based systems application programming integrator. Financial details were not disclosed.

In 2008 Black & Veatch launched Smart Utility, a new set of electric infrastructure services aimed at the development and implementation of smart grid technologies. The new technologies are designed to enhance reliability, reduce power consumption, and integrate power generation sources such as solar arrays and wind turbines.

Founded in 1915 in Kansas City, Missouri, by engineers E. B. Black and Tom Veatch, the firm is now employee-owned and has more than 100 offices worldwide.

EXECUTIVES

Chairman, President, and CEO:
Leonard C. (Len) Rodman, age 60
CFO and Director: Karen L. Daniel, age 51
Chief Human Resources Officer: Shirley Gaufin
Chief Administrative Officer: Howard G. Withey
SVP, CTO, and Chief Knowledge Officer:
John G. Voeller
CIO and SVP: Phillip B. (Brad) Vaughan
VP Global Marketing, Branding and Communications:
Fredrik Winterlind
VP Corporate Development: Bart Schubert
VP Government Affairs: Paul Weida
General Counsel: Timothy W. Triplett
President, Telecommunications: Martin G. Travers
President, Enterprise Management Solutions:
Rodger E. Smith
President and CEO, B&V Energy; Director:
O. H. (Dean) Oskvig
President, Federal Services Division:
William R. (Bill) Van Dyke, age 61
President, Strategic Sales & Marketing: Kim I. Mastalio
President, Construction & Procurement:
Haldon E. (Hal) Smith
President and CEO, Black & Veatch Water; Director:
Daniel W. (Dan) McCarthy
Auditors: KPMG LLP

LOCATIONS

HQ: Black & Veatch Holding Company
11401 Lamar Ave., Overland Park, KS 66211
Phone: 913-458-2000 **Fax:** 913-458-2934
Web: www.bv.com

PRODUCTS/OPERATIONS

Market Sectors
Energy
Air quality control
Coal
Combustion turbine
Gas, oil, and chemicals
Hydropower
IGCC
Nuclear
Power delivery
Renewables
Water
Conveyance systems and tunneling services
Drinking water
Hydropower
River and coastal management
Wastewater
Water resources

Telecommunications
Broadband wireline
Cyber and physical security
Telecom for smart utilities
Utility automation
Utility telecommunications
Site acquisition services
Wireless
Management consulting
Integrated strategy development
Process improvement
Technology application services
Federal
Civil works
Disaster support
Facilities
Federal design-build
Management programs
Security
Environmental
Air quality
Compliance management
Due diligence
Field studies/investigations
Permitting
Prevention plans
Remediation
Siting
Water/wastewater
Watershed analysis and restoration

COMPETITORS

AECOM	Malcolm Pirnie
AMEC	McDermott
Balfour Beatty	Michael Baker
Bechtel	Mott MacDonald
Burns & McDonnell	MWH Global
Burns and Roe	Parsons Brinckerhoff
CH2M HILL	Parsons Corporation
Costain	Shaw Group
EA Engineering	SNC-Lavalin
Fluor	Tetra Tech
Foster Wheeler	TIC Holdings
Halcrow Group	Washington Division
HNTB Companies	Zachry Inc.
Louis Berger	

HISTORICAL FINANCIALS

Company Type: Private

Income Statement

FYE: December 31

	REVENUE ($ mil.)	NET INCOME ($ mil.)	NET PROFIT MARGIN	EMPLOYEES
12/08	3,200	—	—	9,600
12/07	3,200	—	—	9,600
12/06	2,200	—	—	8,600
12/05	1,573	—	—	7,500
12/04	1,400	—	—	6,800
Annual Growth	**23.0%**	**—**	**—**	**9.0%**

Revenue History

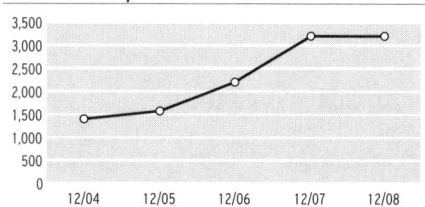

Bloomberg L.P.

What do you do when you've conquered Wall Street? You become mayor of the city the famous financial district calls home. After leading his financial news and information company to success, Michael Bloomberg left to run the Big Apple. His namesake company remains a leader in the market for business media. Its core product, the Bloomberg Professional, is a service terminal that provides real-time financial news, market data, and analysis. The company also has a syndicated news service, publishes magazines (including the newly acquired *BusinessWeek*), and disseminates business information via Bloomberg Television, radio, and the Web. Michael Bloomberg founded the company in 1981; he owns a majority of the firm.

In 2009 Bloomberg turned heads when it acquired *BusinessWeek* from The McGraw-Hill Companies. *BusinessWeek* has been suffering amid an economic recession and the public's waning interest in weekly print magazines, where advertising pages have dropped significantly, and experts have questioned Bloomberg's interest in the title. Bloomberg executives state that the purchase will strengthen the company's consumer-branded content and expand its reach (*BusinessWeek* has about 4.8 million readers each week). The sale price was not disclosed.

The consumer brand supplements Bloomberg's flagship product, Bloomberg Professional, which serves some 250,000 customers in more than 150 countries. Terminals account for some 85% of the company's business. It charges a monthly fee per terminal for multiple system clients; its data can be accessed on PCs and mobile phones via the company's Bloomberg Anywhere offering. Bloomberg also distributes financial news and information through other media channels in an effort to build its brand and keep up with fierce competition.

Such competition only intensified when Thomson bought Reuters for $17 billion in 2008 to form the world's largest financial data company. Months after the Thomson Reuters deal closed, Bloomberg hired Norman Pearlstine, the former top editor of *Time* and *The Wall Street Journal*, to the newly created position of chief content officer of Bloomberg. The move emphasized the company's focus on its editorial staff, which nearly doubled from 1,200 employees in 2001 to 2,300 in 2008.

However, in 2009 Bloomberg laid off some 60 people in the company's unprofitable TV and radio operations. As part of the cuts, the company canceled the *Night Talk* TV show. A sign of the dismal state of the economy, the move marks the first-ever major round of layoffs since the company's founding.

After the departure of former CEO Lex Fenwick, who stepped down to oversee Bloomberg Ventures, the company brought in Daniel Doctoroff (a former deputy mayor under Bloomberg) as its new president in 2008.

Merrill Lynch sold its 20% stake back to Bloomberg for more than $4 billion in 2009.

HISTORY

By the mid-1970s ambitious Michael Bloomberg had worked his way up to head of equity trading and sales at New York investment powerhouse Salomon Brothers. He left Salomon in 1981, just after the firm went private, cashing out with $10 million for his partnership interest.

Bloomberg founded Innovative Marketing Systems and spent the next year developing the Bloomberg terminal, which allowed users to manipulate bond data. In 1982 he pitched it to Merrill Lynch, which bought 20 machines. Regular production of the terminals began in 1984, and in 1985 Merrill Lynch invested $39 million in the company to gain a 30% stake. The company prospered during the 1980s boom, and over time the data, not the machines, became the heart of the business, which was renamed Bloomberg L.P. in 1986.

The company weathered the stock market crash of 1987, opening offices in London and Tokyo. Bloomberg made its entry into news-gathering and delivery in 1990 when Bloomberg News began broadcasting on its terminals. The company built its news organization from scratch, hiring away reporters from such publications as *The Wall Street Journal* and *Forbes*. Bloomberg bought a New York radio station in 1992 and converted it to an all-news format. The next year it built an in-house TV studio and created a business news show for PBS. A satellite TV station followed in 1994, along with the *Bloomberg Personal Finance* magazine.

In 1995 Bloomberg began offering business information via its Web site. The company also introduced the Bloomberg Tradebook, an electronic securities-trading venue designed to compete with Instinet. (In 1997 Tradebook was approved by the SEC for use in connection with some Nasdaq-listed stocks.) Bloomberg also started offering its services to subscribers in a PC-compatible format and selling its data to other news purveyors, such as LexisNexis (an online information service).

In 1996 the company went further into financial publishing, issuing *Swap Literacy: A Comprehensive Guide* and *A Common Sense Guide to Mutual Funds*. That year Michael Bloomberg bought back 10% of the company from Merrill Lynch for $200 million, giving Bloomberg L.P. an estimated market value of $2 billion.

When Bridge Information Systems bought Dow Jones Markets from Dow Jones in 1998, Bridge surpassed Bloomberg in number of financial information terminals installed, bumping Bloomberg from the #2 spot into third place. But Bloomberg continued expanding its offerings through strategic agreements with Internet companies such as America Online and CNET Networks, and through the introduction of new magazines such as *Bloomberg Money* in 1998 as well as *On Investing* and *Bloomberg Wealth Manager* in 1999.

The company expanded its presence in the Spanish-language market in 1999 through its agreement with CBS Telenoticias to produce a TV news program (*Noticiero Financiero*). In 2000 Bloomberg joined with Merrill Lynch to make Merrill Lynch's institutional e-commerce portal available to Bloomberg customers

In 2005 the company left Park Avenue and moved into the new Bloomberg Tower on Lexington Avenue. The 53-story building is also home to retail and residential space. Mayor Bloomberg was re-elected in 2005; he was re-elected again in 2009.

Merrill Lynch sold its 20% ownership stake in Bloomberg back to the company in 2009. Later that year the company acquired *Business-Week* magazine.

EXECUTIVES

Chairman: Peter T. Grauer, age 63
President and Director: Daniel L. (Dan) Doctoroff
CEO, Multimedia Group: Andrew R. (Andy) Lack, age 62
Chief Marketing Officer: Maureen A. McGuire, age 57
Chief Content Officer: Norman Pearlstine
Head Sales, Americas: Max Linnington
Head Sales, Europe, Africa, Middle East:
 Jean-Paul (J.P.) Zammitt
Head Sales, Asia and Pacific: Gerard Francis
Head Product Development: Thomas (Tom) Secunda
Head Bloomberg.com: Kevin Krim
Head Global Corporate Communications:
 Judith A. Czelusniak
Editor-in-Chief and Head News:
 Matthew (Matt) Winkler, age 53
Founder: Michael R. (Mike) Bloomberg, age 67

LOCATIONS

HQ: Bloomberg L.P.
 731 Lexington Ave., New York, NY 10022
Phone: 212-318-2000
Web: www.bloomberg.com

PRODUCTS/OPERATIONS

Selected Products and Services

Bloomberg Anywhere (mobile phone and PC access)
Bloomberg Hardware (terminal includes keyboard, flat-panel monitors, and audio/video conferencing tools)
Bloomberg Markets Magazine (content for and about professional investors)
Bloomberg News (syndicated news service)
Bloomberg Professional (24-hour, real-time financial information system)
 Bloomberg Data License (financial database service)
 Bloomberg Roadshows (presentation service)
 Bloomberg Tradebook (equities trading technology)
 Bloomberg Trading Systems (Bloomberg information combined with trading technology)
Bloomberg Radio (syndicated radio news service)
Bloomberg Television (24-hour news channel and syndicated reports)
Bloomberg.com (Web site)
BusinessWeek (consumer magazine)

COMPETITORS

Agence France-Presse
Associated Press
Dow Jones
Economist Group
FactSet
Financial Times
Forbes
Interactive Data
Intex Solutions
Intuit
MarketWatch
Morningstar
Newsweek
Pearson plc
TheStreet.com
Thomson Reuters
U.S. News & World Report
Wall Street Journal

HISTORICAL FINANCIALS

Company Type: Private

Income Statement

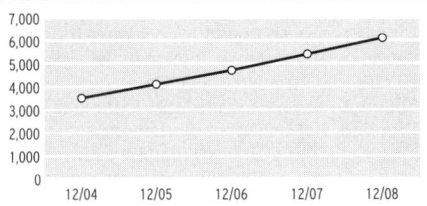

Revenue History

FYE: December 31

	REVENUE ($ mil.)	NET INCOME ($ mil.)	NET PROFIT MARGIN	EMPLOYEES
12/08	6,100	—	—	10,500
12/07	5,400	—	—	10,800
12/06	4,700	—	—	9,500
12/05	4,100	—	—	8,200
12/04	3,500	—	—	8,000
Annual Growth	14.9%	—	—	7.0%

Blue Cross and Blue Shield Association

The rise of managed health care has had some of its members singing the blues, but the Blues — with more than 100 million members nationwide — aren't complaining. The Blue Cross and Blue Shield Association is a federation of independent health insurance companies who license the Blue Cross and Blue Shield brand names. Member companies — of which there are about 40 — own the rights to sell Blue-branded health plans within defined regions. The Association coordinates some national programs such as BlueCard, which allows members of one franchisee to have coverage in other service areas, and the Federal Employee Program, which covers more than half of federal government employees, retirees, and their families.

The Blue licensees cover customers in all 50 states plus the District of Columbia and Washington, DC; the brand is also registered internationally. The Association administers a program, BlueWorldwide Expat, that provides coverage for US citizens working abroad.

The Association strives to improve its resource offerings for member companies, employers, health care providers, and consumers, including enhanced information technology, wellness, and consumer education programs. Affiliate Blue Cross and Blue Shield Foundation on Health Care conducts research on health care issues in cooperation with health plans, universities, and government agencies.

In 2007 the Association was approved under a Federal Savings Bank charter to provide health-related banking services through its Blue Healthcare Bank.

These days, most of the Blues companies are healthy and profitable, after a tough decade in the 1990s that led to a continuing series of rate hikes, as well as consolidation, conversions to for-profit status, and product innovations, among other strategies.

WellPoint, the largest Blues company and the largest for-profit health insurer in the nation, has grown by buying up for-profit Blues plans (or converting them to for-profit status). It has also acquired a number of non-Blue subsidiaries, such as American Imaging Management, though it is required to get two-thirds of its insurance revenue from Blue products to keep its Blue Cross Blue Shield license.

As profits at the Blues companies have grown, the Association and its franchisees have come in for criticism over high executive pay and other perceived excesses. However, as economic trends have caused difficulty in the financial and insurance industries in 2008 and 2009, the lofty profitability of some Blue Cross and Blue Shield providers may begin to crumble.

HISTORY

Blue Cross was born in 1929, when Baylor University official Justin Kimball offered schoolteachers 21 days of hospital care for $6 a year. A major plan feature was a community rating system that based premiums on the community claims experience rather than members' conditions.

The Blue Cross symbol was devised in 1933 by Minnesota plan executive E. A. van Steenwyck. By 1935 many of the 15 plans in 11 states used the symbol. Many states gave the plans nonprofit status, and in 1936 the American Hospital Association formed the Committee on Hospital Service (renamed the Blue Cross Association in 1948) to coordinate them.

As Blue Cross grew, state medical societies sponsored prepaid plans to cover doctors' fees. In 1946 they united under the aegis of the American Medical Association (AMA) as the Associated Medical Care Plans (later the Association of Blue Shield Plans).

In 1948 the AMA thwarted a Blue Cross attempt to merge with Blue Shield. But the Blues increasingly cooperated on public policy matters while competing for members, and each Blue formed a not-for-profit corporation to coordinate its plan's activities.

By 1960 Blue Cross insured about a third of the US. Over the next decade the Blues started administering Medicare and other government health plans, and by 1970 half of Blue Cross' premiums came from government entities.

In the 1970s the Blues adopted such cost-control measures as review of hospital admissions; many plans even abandoned the community rating system. Most began emphasizing preventive care in HMOs or PPOs. The two Blues finally merged in 1982, but this had little effect on the associations' bottom lines as losses grew.

By the 1990s the Blues were big business. Some of the state associations offered officers high salaries and perks but still insisted on special regulatory treatment.

But as lower-cost plans attracted the hale and hearty, the Blues' customers became older, sicker, and more expensive. With their quasi-charitable status and outdated rate structures, many Blues lost market share.

The Blues fought back by updating their technology and rate structures, merging among themselves, creating for-profit subsidiaries, forming alliances with for-profit enterprises, or (in some cases) dropping their not-for-profit status and going public — while still using the Blue Cross Blue Shield name.

Blue Cross of California became the first chapter to give up its tax-free status when it was bought by WellPoint Health Networks, a managed care subsidiary it had founded in 1992.

Half the nation's Blues formed an alliance called BluesCONNECT in 1997, competing with national health plans by offering employers one nationwide benefits organization.

In 1998 Blues in more than 35 states sued the nation's big cigarette companies to recoup costs of treating smoking-related illnesses. In a separate lawsuit, Blue Cross and Blue Shield of Minnesota received nearly $300 million from the tobacco industry.

In 2000, after years of discussions, the New York attorney general permitted Empire Blue Cross and Blue Shield to convert to for-profit status.

In 2004 Anthem (now called WellPoint) and WellPoint Health Networks announced plans to merge, becoming the largest for-profit health insurer in the nation. WellPoint acquired Empire Blue Cross and its parent WellChoice in 2005.

EXECUTIVES

President and CEO: Scott P. Serota
SVP Clinical Affairs and Chief Medical Officer: Allan M. Korn
SVP Human Resources and Administrative Services: William J. (Bill) Colbourne
SVP BHI and CIO: Doug Porter
SVP and CFO: Robert J. (Bob) Kolodgy
SVP National Programs: Steve W. Gammarino
SVP, Corporate Secretary, and General Counsel: Roger G. Wilson
SVP Strategic Services: Maureen Sullivan
SVP Office of Policy and Representation: Alissa Fox
VP Business Informatics and Blue Health Intelligence: Shirley S. Lady
VP Business Development: Jody Voss
VP Federal Relations: Jack Ericksen
VP Federal Employee Program: Jena L. Estes
VP and CTO: William B. O'Loughlin
VP Brand Strategy and Marketing Services: Jennifer Vachon
VP Inter-Plan Programs: Frank Coyne
Auditors: PricewaterhouseCoopers LLP

LOCATIONS

HQ: Blue Cross and Blue Shield Association
225 N. Michigan Ave., Chicago, IL 60601
Phone: 312-297-6000   **Fax:** 312-297-6609
Web: www.bcbs.com

PRODUCTS/OPERATIONS

2008 Health Care Members

	Members (mil.)	% of total
PPO	71.6	70
HMO	14.8	14
Traditional indemnity	11.7	11
POS (point-of-service)	4.8	5
Total	**102.9**	**100**

Selected Blue Cross and Blue Shield Licensees

Arkansas Blue Cross and Blue Shield
Blue Cross and Blue Shield of Alabama
Blue Cross and Blue Shield of Arizona
Blue Cross and Blue Shield of Delaware
Blue Cross and Blue Shield of Florida
Blue Cross and Blue Shield of Kansas
Blue Cross and Blue Shield of Louisiana
Blue Cross and Blue Shield of Massachusetts
Blue Cross and Blue Shield of Michigan
Blue Cross and Blue Shield of Minnesota
Blue Cross and Blue Shield of Mississippi
Blue Cross and Blue Shield of Kansas City
Blue Cross and Blue Shield of Montana
Blue Cross and Blue Shield of Nebraska
Blue Cross and Blue Shield of North Carolina
Blue Cross and Blue Shield of North Dakota
Blue Cross and Blue Shield of Rhode Island
Blue Cross and Blue Shield of South Carolina
Blue Cross and Blue Shield of Tennessee
Blue Cross and Blue Shield of Wyoming
Blue Cross and Blue Shield of Vermont
Blue Cross & Blue Shield de Uruguay
BlueCross BlueShield of Panama
Blue Cross of Northeastern Pennsylvania
Blue Shield of California
Capital BlueCross (Pennsylvania)
CareFirst
   CareFirst Blue Cross and Blue Shield (District of Columbia)
   CareFirst Blue Cross and Blue Shield of Maryland
Excellus BlueCross BlueShield of New York
Hawaii Medical Service Association
Health Care Service Corporation
   Blue Cross and Blue Shield of Illinois
   Blue Cross and Blue Shield of New Mexico
   Blue Cross and Blue Shield of Oklahoma
   Blue Cross and Blue Shield of Texas
HealthNow New York
   BlueCross and BlueShield of Western New York
   BlueShield of Northeastern New York
Highmark Blue Cross Blue Shield (Pennsylvania)
   Mountain State Blue Cross and Blue Shield (West Virginia)
Horizon Blue Cross and Blue Shield of New Jersey
Idaho Blue Cross
Independence Blue Cross (Pennsylvania)
   La Cruz Azul de Puerto Rico
Premera Blue Cross (Alaska and Washington)
The Regence Group
   Regence BlueCross and BlueShield of Oregon
   Regence BlueCross BlueShield of Utah
   Regence BlueShield of Idaho
   Regence BlueShield (Washington)
Triple-S (Puerto Rico)
Wellmark
   Wellmark Blue Cross and Blue Shield of South Dakota
   Wellmark Blue Cross and Blue Shield of Iowa
WellPoint
   Anthem Blue Cross and Blue Shield of Colorado
   Anthem Blue Cross and Blue Shield of Connecticut
   Anthem Blue Cross and Blue Shield of Indiana
   Anthem Blue Cross and Blue Shield of Kentucky
   Anthem Blue Cross and Blue Shield of Maine
   Anthem Blue Cross and Blue Shield of Nevada
   Anthem Blue Cross and Blue Shield of New Hampshire
   Anthem Blue Cross and Blue Shield of Ohio
   Anthem Blue Cross and Blue Shield of Virginia
   Blue Cross and Blue Shield of Georgia
   Blue Cross and Blue Shield of Missouri
   BlueCross BlueShield of Wisconsin
   California Blue Cross (Anthem Blue Cross)
   Empire Blue Cross and Blue Shield of New York

COMPETITORS

Aetna
AMERIGROUP
Centene
CIGNA
Coventry Health Care
Health Net
Humana
Kaiser Foundation Health Plan
Molina Healthcare
UnitedHealth Group
WellCare Health Plans

Blue Cross and Blue Shield of Florida

Blue Cross and Blue Shield of Florida (BCBSF) is the state's largest and oldest health insurance provider. The company provides a wide range of health insurance products and related services to some 8 million members in Florida. Its health plan policies include HMO, PPO, traditional indemnity, and supplemental Medicare. BCBSF also provides accident and dismemberment, long-term care, dental, disability, and workers' compensation insurance. Other services include the administration of pharmacy programs, health savings accounts, and flexible spending accounts. The company is a not-for-profit mutual insurance firm owned by its policyholders. It is an independent Blue Cross and Blue Shield Association licensee.

Founded in 1944, BCBSF operates in one of the most competitive health care markets in the nation primarily due to the state's population growth. The company's HMO products are offered through subsidiaries Capital Health Plan and Health Options. Some of its supplemental insurance products, such as its life and disability insurance offerings, are provided through Life and Specialty Ventures, a joint venture with Arkansas Blue Cross and Blue Shield that includes Florida Combined Life Insurance Company.

The company's strategy for keeping its competitors at bay consists of using the specialty insurance product offerings of its various subsidiaries to complement its core health plans, thus providing a one-stop employee benefits shop. It also regularly introduces new products, especially products targeting low-income customers such as health plan discount cards and specialized plans for at-risk communities. The company also opened two retail stores in 2007 and 2008 to help promote its products and improve customer service.

BCBSF expanded in 2009 through the acquisition of the Florida Health Care Plan, which serves some 53,000 members in Flagler and Volusia counties, from the Halifax Hospital Medical Center. The purchase aimed to expand its operations in the growing Daytona Beach area.

BCBSF also has operations outside of the insurance arena, such as human resources consulting and staffing services provided by its Incepture subsidiary. Another unit, Availity, is an electronic medical records administration joint venture with Humana and HCSC.

EXECUTIVES

Chairman and CEO: Robert I. Lufrano
EVP and COO: Arnold (Duke) Livermore
EVP, Chief Administrative Officer, and CFO: R. Chris Doerr
Chief Human Resource Officer and SVP Human Services Group: Robert (Bob) Wall
Chief Marketing Executive: Craig Thomas
Chief Strategy Officer: John Kaegi
SVP, CIO, and CEO, Incepture: Jeannette Ekh
SVP, General Counsel, and Corporate Secretary: Charles S. Joseph
SVP Public Affairs: Cyrus M. (Russ) Jollivette
SVP Delivery System: Joyce Kramzer
SVP Sales, Distribution, and Local Markets: Michael Guyette
VP Channel Service Organization: Lynn Esposito
VP Corporate Services: Lanny Felder
VP Local Markets: Jonathan Anderson
VP Corporate Communications: Sharon Wamble-King
VP Regulatory Affairs and Public Policy: Randy Kammer
VP Business Process Optimization: Elana Schrader
VP Community Relations; Executive Director, The Blue Foundation for a Healthy Florida: Susan B. Towler
VP and Chief Medical Officer: Jonathan Gavras
Director Business Communications: Lisa Acheson Luther
Director External Communications: John Herbkersman
Auditors: PricewaterhouseCoopers LLP

LOCATIONS

HQ: Blue Cross and Blue Shield of Florida, Inc.
4800 Deerwood Campus Pkwy.
Jacksonville, FL 32246
Phone: 904-791-6111   **Fax:** 904-905-6638
Web: www.bcbsfl.com

PRODUCTS/OPERATIONS

Selected Subsidiaries and Affiliates

Availity, L.L.C. (joint venture with Humana and HCSC for electronic medical records)
Blue Foundation for a Healthy Florida, Inc. (philanthropy)
Capital Health Plan (HMO and Medicare Advantage)
Health Options, Inc. (HMO and Medicare Advantage)
First Coast Service Options, Inc. (third-party Medicare adminstration)
Incepture Inc. (staffing and consulting)
Life and Specialty Ventures, LLC (joint venture with Arkansas Blue Cross and Blue Shield; life, dental, accounts, and disability)
 Florida Combined Life Insurance Agency
 Florida Combined Life Insurance Company, Inc.
 USAble Life
Navigy, Inc. (consulting)
Novitas Health (joint venture with Arkansas BCBS, capability development)

COMPETITORS

Aetna	MetCare
AvMed Health Plans	Total Health Care
CIGNA	UnitedHealth Group
Health First Health Plans	Vista South Florida
Humana	WellCare Health Plans

HISTORICAL FINANCIALS

Company Type: Not-for-profit

Income Statement

FYE: December 31

	REVENUE ($ mil.)	NET INCOME ($ mil.)	NET PROFIT MARGIN	EMPLOYEES
12/08	8,532	137	1.6%	9,500
12/07	8,347	214	2.6%	6,500
12/06	7,470	—	—	8,500
Annual Growth	6.9%	(36.0%)	—	5.7%

Net Income History

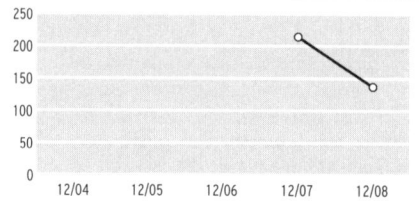

Blue Cross and Blue Shield of Kansas City

Blue Cross and Blue Shield of Kansas City provides health care insurance and related services for about 880,000 members in 32 counties in Kansas and Missouri. Its Good Health HMO subsidiary is a for-profit health maintenance organization that serves more than 58,000 members. Another subsidiary, Blue-Advantage Plus of Kansas City, is a Medicaid HMO serving customers in nine counties in the Kansas City area. Blue Cross and Blue Shield of Kansas City has other operations providing non-Blue life and disability insurance, third-party administration services, and provider network rental services.

Founded in 1932, the company is the largest not-for-profit health insurance provider in the state.

Blue Cross and Blue Shield of Kansas City offers a variety of commercial and individual health plans, including HMO, PPO, and high-deductible health plans, as well as supplemental Medicare coverage. Its ChamberCHOICE plan is aimed at small businesses and has about 60,000 members.

EXECUTIVES

Chairman: William C. Nelson, age 71
Vice Chairman: Janice C. Kreamer
President, CEO, and Director: Tom E. Bowser
SVP and President and CEO, PHP and PWC: Bryan R. Camerlinck
EVP and COO: John W. Kennedy
EVP and Chief Marketing Officer: Roger L. Foreman
EVP and Chief Administrative Officer: Peter K. Yelorda
EVP and Chief Member Services and Subsidiary Officer: David R. Gentile
VP and CFO: Marilyn T. Tromans
VP and General Counsel: Richard J. Kastner
VP Human Resources: Sherri L. Enright
VP and Senior Medical Director: Blake J. Williamson
VP Community Relations: Alice M. Ellison
VP Corporate Services: Tama S. Putthoff
VP and Chief Actuary: Bryan F. Miller
VP Group Marketing: Danette K. Wilson
VP Customer Service: Nancy M. Creasy
VP and Medical Director: Loretta M. Britton
Secretary and Director: Melvin L. Glazer

LOCATIONS

HQ: Blue Cross and Blue Shield of Kansas City
1 Pershing Sq., 2301 Main St.
Kansas City, MO 64108
Phone: 816-395-2222   **Fax:** 816-395-2726
Web: www.bcbskc.com

PRODUCTS/OPERATIONS

Selected Products and Services

Blue Card (national account health plan)
BlueSaver (high-deductible health plan)
ChamberCHOICE (small business group health plan)
Medicare supplemental insurance
Preferred-Care Blue Premium (PPO plan)
USAble Life (life and disability insurance)

Selected Subsidiaries

Blue-Advantage Plus of Kansas City (Medicaid HMO)
EPOCH (third-party administration for self-funded groups)
Good Health HMO (for-profit HMO)
New Directions Behavioral Health (behavioral health benefit management and employee assistance programs)
Preferred Health Professionals (provider network rental)
Premier Work-Comp Management (workers' compensation provider network)

COMPETITORS

Aetna
CIGNA
Heartland Health
Mercy Health Plans
Preferred Health Systems
UnitedHealth Group

HISTORICAL FINANCIALS

Company Type: Not-for-profit

Income Statement

FYE: December 31

	REVENUE ($ mil.)	NET INCOME ($ mil.)	NET PROFIT MARGIN	EMPLOYEES
12/08	1,838	—	—	1,000

Blue Cross (LA)

The Bayou State's largest health insurer, Blue Cross and Blue Shield of Louisiana provides health insurance products and related services to more than 1.1 million members across Louisiana. Established in 1934, the company is an independent licensee of the Blue Cross and Blue Shield Association and has offices throughout the state. Blue Cross and Blue Shield of Louisiana offers HMO, PPO, supplemental Medicare, and traditional indemnity plans, as well as the BlueSaver high-deductible plan with a health savings account. Its HMO Louisiana subsidiary offers a point-of-service (POS) plan that provides some out-of-network benefits. Customers include both individuals and employer groups.

In addition to medical coverage, Blue Cross and Blue Shield of Louisiana sells group life and disability insurance through its Southern National Life Insurance Company subsidiary.

Despite disruptions caused by Hurricane Katrina in 2005, the company has managed to continue growing its medical membership. As a result of the storm, however, it has had to reconstitute its provider network, which was decimated when Katrina shut down hospitals and forced doctors and other health care providers to relocate outside the state.

EXECUTIVES

Chairman: Charles B. (Brent) McCoy
Vice Chair: C. Richard Atkins
Interim President and CEO: Mike Reitz
EVP and COO: Peggy B. Scott
SVP and Chief Medical Officer: James J. Carney
SVP Benefits Administration: Allison Young
SVP and General Counsel: Michele Calandro
SVP and CIO: Worachote (Ob) Soonthornsima
SVP Human Resources: Todd G. Schexnayder
SVP Healthcare System Quality: Sabrina Heltz
VP Corporate Communications: John Maginnis
Secretary and Director: Ann H. Knapp

LOCATIONS

HQ: Blue Cross and Blue Shield of Louisiana
5525 Reitz Ave., Baton Rouge, LA 70809
Phone: 225-295-3307   **Fax:** 225-295-2054
Web: www.bcbsla.com

PRODUCTS/OPERATIONS

Selected Products
Health plans
  BlueChoice 65 (Medicare supplemental insurance)
  Blue Max (major medical plan for individuals)
  BlueSaver (high-deductible health plan)
  GroupCare (group PPO plan)
  HMO plans from HMO Louisiana
  PremierBlue (group PPO plan)
  RxBLUE (Medicare prescription drug coverage)
Other
  Group dental insurance
  Group term life insurance
  Long-term disability insurance
  Short-term disability insurance

COMPETITORS

Aetna
CIGNA
Coventry Health Care
Health Net
Humana
UnitedHealth Group

HISTORICAL FINANCIALS
Company Type: Not-for-profit

Income Statement
FYE: December 31

	REVENUE ($ mil.)	NET INCOME ($ mil.)	NET PROFIT MARGIN	EMPLOYEES
12/08	2,115	49	2.3%	—
12/07	1,946	66	3.4%	1,600
12/06	1,764	78	4.4%	1,555
12/05	1,626	111	6.8%	—
12/04	1,497	81	5.4%	—
Annual Growth	9.0%	(11.8%)	—	2.9%

Net Income History

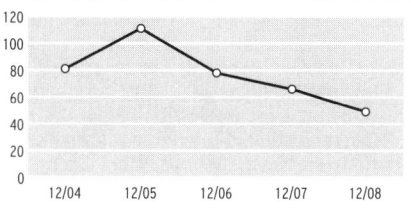

Blue Cross and Blue Shield of Massachusetts

The dominant health insurer in the Bay State, Blue Cross and Blue Shield of Massachusetts (BCBSMA) covers some 3 million members. The company, an independent licensee of the Blue Cross and Blue Shield Association, offers a variety of individual and employer-sponsored health care plans, including HMO (HMO Blue), PPO (Blue Care Elect), and point-of-service (Blue Choice) plans, as well as various hybrid options and personal spending accounts to cover out-of-pocket costs. BCBSMA also provides dental, vision, and prescription drug coverage. The health care firm was founded in 1937.

In response to sweeping health care reforms passed in Massachusetts in 2006, BCBSMA has introduced several new products (called Commonwealth Choice plans) intended for individuals required to purchased insurance coverage under the new law. While the state's reform laws have succeeded in providing coverage to nearly all of the state's residents, government agencies are considering new reform measures to curb the state's rising medical costs.

The company has been pushing information technology as a means to keep medical costs lower and improve care. In 2008, for example, it partnered with Google Health, the online medical records initiative of Google, to allow its members to import their insurance claims into their Google Health profiles. In addition, BCBSMA expanded its e-Prescribing program in 2008 and 2009 to allow more doctors to prescribe medicines online, thus increasing the safety and efficiency of medication administration. Other cost-control measures include the promotion of consumer wellness and healthy lifestyle programs.

EXECUTIVES

Chairman, President, and CEO:
  Cleve L. Killingsworth Jr., age 56
EVP and Chief Legal Officer: Sandra L. (Sandy) Jesse
EVP and CFO: Allen P. Maltz
EVP Sales, Marketing, Service, and Information Technology: Stephen R. (Steve) Booma
EVP Health Care Services: Andrew Dreyfus
SVP and Chief Strategy Officer: Vinod K. (Vin) Sahney
SVP Public, Government, and Regulatory Affairs and Chief Government and Public Affairs Officer:
  Jay Curley
SVP and Chief of Staff, Executive Office:
  John Schoenbaum
SVP and Chief Human Resources Officer:
  Ann S. Anderson
SVP and Chief Physician Executive: John A. Fallon
SVP Corporate Relations and Corporate Secretary:
  Fredi Shonkoff
Auditors: Ernst & Young LLP

LOCATIONS

HQ: Blue Cross and Blue Shield of Massachusetts, Inc.
  LandMark Center, 401 Park Dr., Boston, MA 02215
Phone: 617-246-5000   **Fax:** 617-246-4832
Web: www.bcbsma.com

PRODUCTS/OPERATIONS

Selected Health Plans
Access Blue (open access HMO plan)
Blue Care Elect (PPO plan)
Blue Choice (point-of-service plan)
Blue Medicare PFFS PlusRx (private-fee-for-service Medicare Advantage plan)
Consumer Choice Blue (high-deductible plan with personal spending account)
Essential Blue YA (low-cost, young adult plan)
HMO Blue (statewide managed care)
Medex (Medicare supplemental plan)
Medicare HMO Blue (Medicare Advantage plan)
Medicare PPO Blue (Medicare Advantage plan)

COMPETITORS

Aetna	Health New England
CIGNA	MVP Health Plan
ConnectiCare	Neighborhood Health Plan
Dental Service of Massachusetts	Senior Whole Health
	Tufts Health Plan
Fallon Community Health	UnitedHealth Group
Harvard Pilgrim	

HISTORICAL FINANCIALS
Company Type: Not-for-profit

Income Statement
FYE: December 31

	REVENUE ($ mil.)	NET INCOME ($ mil.)	NET PROFIT MARGIN	EMPLOYEES
12/08	2,229	84	3.8%	3,878
12/07	2,267	146	6.4%	3,878
12/06	2,098	157	7.5%	3,983
12/05	1,977	128	6.5%	4,038
12/04	4,928	243	4.9%	—
Annual Growth	(18.0%)	(23.4%)	—	(1.3%)

Net Income History

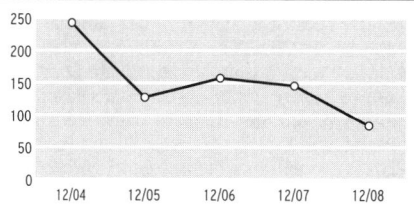

Blue Cross Blue Shield of Michigan

Blue Cross Blue Shield of Michigan is Michigan's leading health benefits organization, serving some 4.7 million members residing in the state or employed by companies headquartered there. The company's insurance offerings include traditional indemnity, PPO, and POS plans, in addition to its Blue Care Network HMO plans. It also offers consumer-directed Flexible Blue plans paired with health savings accounts, as well as options for individual buyers and Medicare beneficiaries. The not-for-profit organization is an independent licensee of the Blue Cross and Blue Shield Association.

Like most health plans, Blue Cross Blue Shield of Michigan (BCBSM) has combated the rise of health care costs with a combination of rate hikes, new product offerings that shift the burden of cost to members, and programs that encourage healthy lifestyles and the use of lower-cost alternatives such as generic drugs.

It entered the Medicare Part D market in 2006, offering prescription drug plans to seniors. It also revamped its product lineup for individual buyers that year and acquired the M-CARE health plan (150,000 members) from the University of Michigan Health System for about $260 million.

The organization has also launched a long-term care insurance subsidiary, called LifeSecure, which is licensed throughout most of the country. It has partnered with the state of Michigan to provide children's insurance through the MIChild program, and it provides funding for charity care at hospitals and for low-income clinics.

Facing heavy losses in its individual policy segment, the company announced a cost-reduction program in early 2009 that will include job cuts, salary freezes, and other spending reductions.

As part of its plan to give customers access to more competitive products, later that year it sold its DenteMax dental benefits unit to Dental Network of America (DNoA), a subsidiary of Health Care Service Corporation. BCBSM members will continue to have access to the combined national network of dentists.

HISTORY

The history of prepaid medical care began in 1929, when Baylor University Hospital administrator Justin Kimball developed a plan to offer schoolteachers 21 days of hospital care for $6 a year. Fundamental to the plan was a community rating system, which based premiums on the community's claims experience rather than subscribers' conditions.

A similar program was started in Michigan in 1938 when a group of hospitals formed the Michigan Society for Group Hospitalization, which became the Michigan Hospital Service and later became a chapter of the national Blue Cross association. The health care plan was funded by local hospitals and private grants. (A group of private donors, including Oldsmobile automotive founder Ransom Olds, loaned the group $5,000.)

The state insurance commission approved tax-exempt status for the Michigan Blue Cross in 1939. Nine days after opening a three-person office in Detroit, Blue Cross landed its first cus-

tomer, insurance company John Hancock Mutual Life. John Hancock's Detroit branch manager became the first subscriber, paying $1.90 per month for 21 days of hospitalization coverage for his family of eight.

Due in part to the addition of Chrysler, Ford, and General Motors to its health plans, Blue Cross grew from less than 1 million members in the 1940s to more than 3 million in the 1950s. In 1945 it began to offer coverage for individuals; 14 years later the association started to offer policies to seniors who were ineligible for group coverage. Blue Cross took over operation of Michigan's Medicare program in 1966.

Michigan's Blue Cross merged with longtime partner Blue Shield in 1975 to create Blue Cross Blue Shield of Michigan, with a total of 5 million subscribers. Blue Shield, a prepayment plan that covered doctors' services, had been started in 1939 by the Michigan State Medical Society (a group of Michigan physicians).

As overseas competition forced automakers to cut their employment rolls, Blue Cross Blue Shield of Michigan's membership contracted. BCBSM chairman John McCabe, realizing the need to generate additional revenue, pushed for an end to the company's not-for-profit status in the 1980s but was rejected by the Michigan legislature. This failure was at least partially behind McCabe's resignation in 1987.

The struggling Michigan Blues moved toward profitability in 1994 when the state legislature specially authorized its $291 million purchase of the for-profit State Accident Fund, the state's workers' compensation program. It also lost its large but hard-to-manage state Medicare contract to Blue Cross Blue Shield of Illinois (now Health Care Service Corporation). In 1996 the company reorganized, with a division for Michigan residents and one for nationwide accounts. In 1997 BCBSM continued its efforts to increase revenue by acquiring private health management company Preferred Provider Organization of Michigan, which operates in Michigan and nearby states. BCBSM president and CEO Richard Whitmer announced that he was willing to compete with other Blues in bordering states.

In 1998 Blue Cross Blue Shield of Michigan consolidated four regional HMOs into a single statewide HMO, the Blue Care Network. Costs of the merger and growing losses in drug coverage constrained earnings, but were counterweighted by returns on assets invested in the stock market. In 1999 and 2000 the company rankled Detroit's small business owners with double-digit premium hikes.

Blue Cross Blue Shield of Michigan sold its for-profit subsidiary Preferred Provider Organization of Michigan to regional health plan provider HMS Healthcare in 2004.

EXECUTIVES

Chairman: Gregory A. (Greg) Sudderth
Vice Chairman: Spencer C. Johnson
President, CEO, and Director: Daniel J. Loepp
EVP Health Care Value Enhancements: Kevin L. Seitz
EVP and CFO; President, Emerging Markets: Mark R. Bartlett
SVP, Chief of Staff, and CIO: Joseph H. Hohner
SVP and Chief Actuarial Officer: J. Paul Austin
SVP and General Counsel: Lisa S. DeMoss
SVP Human Resources: Darrell E. Middleton
SVP Subsidiary Operations; President and CEO, Blue Care Network of Michigan: Jeanne H. Carlson
SVP Subsidiary Operations; President and CEO, Accident Fund Insurance Company of America: Elizabeth R. Haar

SVP Health Care Value and Provider Affiliation and Chief Medical Officer: Thomas L. Simmer
SVP Operations and Hospital Relations: Robert Milewski
SVP Group Sales and Corporate Marketing: Kenneth R. (Ken) Dallafior
VP and Treasurer: Carolynn Walton
VP, General Auditor, and Corporate Compliance: Michele Samuels
VP, Corporate Secretary, and Services: Tricia A. Keith
VP Corporate Communications: R. Andrew Hetzel
CEO and Executive Director, Blue Cross Blue Shield of Michigan Foundation: Ira Strumwasser
President and CEO, LifeSecure Holdings: E. Lisa Wendt
Auditors: Deloitte & Touche LLP

LOCATIONS

HQ: Blue Cross Blue Shield of Michigan
600 E. Lafayette Blvd., Detroit, MI 48226
Phone: 313-225-9000   **Fax:** 313-225-6764
Web: www.bcbsm.com

PRODUCTS/OPERATIONS

Selected Products

BCN Advantage (Medicare Advantage HMO)
Blue Care Network (HMO)
Blue Choice (point-of-service plan)
Blue Preferred PPO
Blue Preferred Plus PPO
First Dollar (traditional indemnity plan)
Flexible Blue (consumer-directed plan)
Individual Care Blue (individual health plan)
LifeSecure (long-term care insurance)
Medicare Plus Blue (Medicare Advantage plan with prescription drug coverage)
Value Blue (basic health coverage for individuals)

COMPETITORS

Aetna
CIGNA
Health Alliance Plan of Michigan
HealthPlus of Michigan
Humana
OmniCare Health Plan
Total Health Care
UnitedHealth Group

HISTORICAL FINANCIALS

Company Type: Not-for-profit

Income Statement

FYE: December 31

	REVENUE ($ mil.)	NET INCOME ($ mil.)	NET PROFIT MARGIN	EMPLOYEES
12/08	10,680	(145)	—	7,000
12/07	9,849	177	1.8%	8,945
12/06	8,687	243	2.8%	7,047
12/05	8,151	295	3.6%	—
12/04	8,044	411	5.1%	—
Annual Growth	7.3%	—	—	(0.3%)

Net Income History

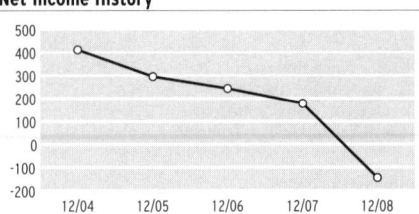

Blue Cross (NC)

Blue Cross and Blue Shield of North Carolina (BCBSNC) provides health care insurance products and related services to about 3.5 million members in North Carolina. The company's health plans include Blue Care (HMO) and Blue Options (PPO), as well as consumer-directed plans that couple a high-deductible policy with a health savings account. BCBSNC also provides dental, life, disability, long-term care, and Medicare supplemental insurance, as well as prescription drug coverage. The company's Partners National Health Plans subsidiary offers Medicare Advantage health plans. BCBSNC is a licensee of the Blue Cross and Blue Shield Association.

North Carolina's largest health insurer, the company maintains a provider network that includes nearly 5,000 primary care doctors, 15,000 specialists, and more than 100 hospitals.

Like many health insurers, BCBSNC is focused on enlisting its members in health improvement programs — including fitness programs and health screenings — that it hopes will lower medical costs over the long run.

EXECUTIVES

Chairman: Jeffrey L. Houpt
CEO and Trustee: Robert J. (Bob) Greczyn Jr.
President and COO: J. Bradley (Brad) Wilson, age 56
CFO: Gerald Petkau
Chief Administrative Officer, General Counsel, and Corporate Secretary: Maureen K. O'Connor
SVP Commercial and Governmental Operations: Ian Gordon
SVP and Chief Medical Officer: Don Bradley
CIO and SVP Information Services: Alain Hughes
SVP Human Resources: Fara Palumbo
VP Health Policy: Barbara Morales Burke
VP Total Benefits: Gayle Sauer
VP Document Operations and Electronic Solutions: Josh Duffy
VP Corporate Communications: Lynne Garrison
President, BCBSNC Foundation: Kathy Higgins
Chief Sales and Marketing Officer: John T. Roos
Media Contact: Mark Stinneford
Auditors: PricewaterhouseCoopers LLP

LOCATIONS

HQ: Blue Cross and Blue Shield of North Carolina
1830 US 15-501 North, Chapel Hill, NC 27514
Phone: 919-489-7431   **Fax:** 919-765-7818
Web: www.bcbsnc.com

PRODUCTS/OPERATIONS

Selected Products

Dental Blue (dental insurance)
Blue Advantage (PPO)
Blue Care (HMO)
Blue Medicare Supplement (Medicare supplemental coverage)
Blue Medicare Rx (Medicare prescription drug coverage)
Blue Medicare HMO (Medicare Advantage plan)
Blue Medicare PPO (Medicare Advantage plan)
Blue Options (high-deductible plan with health savings account)

COMPETITORS

Aetna
Celtic Insurance
CIGNA
Coventry Health Care
North Carolina Mutual
UnitedHealth Group

HISTORICAL FINANCIALS

Company Type: Not-for-profit

Income Statement

FYE: December 31

	REVENUE ($ mil.)	NET INCOME ($ mil.)	NET PROFIT MARGIN	EMPLOYEES
12/08	5,200	—	—	4,900
12/07	4,900	—	—	4,700
12/06	4,407	—	—	4,000
Annual Growth	8.6%	—	—	10.7%

Revenue History

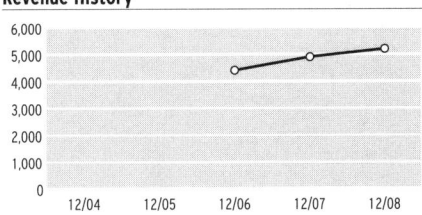

Blue Cross (SC)

Blue Cross and Blue Shield of South Carolina provides health insurance and related services to about 1 million members in South Carolina. Its BlueChoice HealthPlan is an HMO offering managed care plans to some 200,000 members. Other group offerings include PPO plans (Preferred Blue), traditional indemnity coverage (Simply Blue), and a consumer-driven plan (Blue-by-Design). For individual buyers, the firm provides Personal BluePlans, Medicare supplemental coverage, and Medicare Advantage PPO and private-fee-for-service plans. The company also has life and property/casualty insurance subsidiaries, as well as a government health programs division.

The government programs unit administers managed care contracts for Medicare, Medicaid, and TRICARE (for military families). Its operating companies include Palmetto GBA, which specializes in managing Medicare benefit plans, and PGBA, which handles TRICARE contracts.

The company's other subsidiaries include Companion Property & Casualty Group, a provider of commercial property/casualty insurance and claims management services, and Companion Life, which sells group life and disability policies. It sold subsidiary Companion Technologies (now HealthPort Technologies), which offered health care information technology services, to private investment firms ABRY Partners and Thurston Group in 2007.

That same year Blue Cross and Blue Shield of South Carolina established its Companion Global Healthcare subsidiary. The new division provides appointment and travel arrangement services to health plan members seeking care overseas, supporting the "medical tourism" trend of underinsured US residents seeking lower-cost care in other nations.

The company traces its roots back to the formation of the not-for-profit South Carolina Hospital Service Plan in 1946, which later became Blue Cross of South Carolina. The Blue Shield organization entered South Carolina in 1949, and the two entities merged to form Blue Cross Blue Shield of South Carolina in 1971.

EXECUTIVES

Chairman and CEO: M. Edward Sellers, age 64
President: David S. Pankau
CFO: Robert Leichtle
EVP and CIO: Stephen K. Wiggins
EVP and Chief Legal Officer: Judith M. Davis
SVP Large Groups: Matthew M. (Matt) Shaffer
SVP Small Groups and Individual: James A. Deyling
SVP National Alliance: Michael Griggs
VP and Chief Actuary: Will Shrader
VP Federal Affairs: George Johnson
President, BlueChoice HealthPlan of South Carolina: Mary Mazzola Spivey
Assistant VP Corporate Marketing Communications and Public Relations: Kim Wellman

LOCATIONS

HQ: Blue Cross and Blue Shield of South Carolina
2501 Faraway Dr., Columbia, SC 29219
Phone: 803-788-0222   **Fax:** 803-264-8077
Web: www.southcarolinablues.com

PRODUCTS/OPERATIONS

Selected Products and Services

Ancillary products
  Flexible spending acounts (FSAs)
  Wellness programs
Business health plans
  Blue-by-Design
  BlueChoice HealthPlan (HMO)
  Blue Health Fund
  Consumer Health Plans
  Preferred Blue (PPO)
  Simply Blue
Dental coverage
Federal and state employee plans
Individual and family health plans
  Medicare Advantage
  Medicare supplements
  Personal Blue Plans
  TRICARE
Life and disability insurance
Mental health and substance abuse benefits
Property/casualty insurance

COMPETITORS

Aetna
Carolina Care Plan
CIGNA
Coventry Health Care
Health Net
Humana
Unison Health Plan
UnitedHealth Group

HISTORICAL FINANCIALS

Company Type: Not-for-profit

Income Statement

FYE: December 31

	REVENUE ($ mil.)	NET INCOME ($ mil.)	NET PROFIT MARGIN	EMPLOYEES
12/08	1,535	—	—	11,000

Blue Diamond Growers

Blue Diamond Growers is one nutty business. Some 3,000 California almond growers belong to the cooperative, which is a top global player in the tree nut market. The company sells almonds and almond products, hazelnuts, macadamia, pistachio, and other nuts to food and candy makers, the foodservice industry, and food retailers. Blue Diamond Growers has developed products such as Almond Breeze, an almond-based, lactose-free milk substitute; Nut Thins crackers; and special cuts and flavored varieties of the nuts. The co-op, formed in 1910, sells its products throughout the US and in more than 90 other countries. It operates processing plants, receiving stations, and retail nut stores in California and Oregon.

In resonse to demands for healthier products, the company has introduced 100-calorie portion packs and a line of oven-roasted nuts.

In 2000 Blue Diamond Growers purchased the world's largest macadamia nut producer, MacFarms of Hawaii; it sold MacFarms to Sparks Corp. and Greater Pacific Food Holdings in 2003.

EXECUTIVES

Chairman: Clinton Shick
Vice Chairman: Dale Van Groningen
President and CEO: Douglas D. Youngdahl
CFO: Robert S. Donovan, age 47
Human Resources, Salida Office: Sheryl Guzman
Director Public Affairs: Susan Brauner
Director Employee Services: George Johnson
Director Marketing: Al Greenlee
Director Member Relations: Dave Baker
Senior Planning: David Hills
General Manager Export Sales: Bill Morecraft
General Manager Industrial Operations: Bruce Lish
Auditors: KPMG LLP

LOCATIONS

HQ: Blue Diamond Growers
1802 C St., Sacramento, CA 95814
Phone: 916-442-0771   **Fax:** 916-446-8461
Web: bluediamond.com

PRODUCTS/OPERATIONS

Selected Products and Brands

Almond Breeze (nut milk)
  Refrigerated
  Sweetened
  Unsweetened
Bold Flavors
  Jalapeno Smokehouse
  Lime 'n Chili
  Maui Onion & Garlic
  Salt & Black Pepper
  Salt 'n Vinegar
  Wasabi & Soy Sauce
Cooking and Baking
  Sliced Almonds
  Slivered Almonds
  Whole Almonds
Nut Thins (crackers)
  Almond
  Cheddar Cheese
  Country Ranch
  Hazelnut
  Pecan
  Smokehouse
Oven-Roasted
  Cinnamon Brown Sugar
  No Salt
  Sea Salt
  Vanilla Bean
Traditional Flavors
  Honey Roasted
  Jordan
  Roasted Salted
  Smokehouse
  Whole Natural

COMPETITORS

Arcade Industries
Beer Nuts
Calcot
Diamond Foods
Dole Food
Golden West Nuts
Harvest Manor Farms
John Sanfilippo & Son
Meridian Nut Growers
ML Macadamia Orchards
Paramount Farms
Primex International
Stewart & Jasper Orchards
SunWest Foods
Tejon Ranch

Blue Tee

Blue Tee has stayed out of the rough through diversification. The company, which operates through its many subsidiaries, distributes steel and scrap metal and manufactures a variety of industrial equipment. Blue Tee's Brown-Strauss Steel subsidiary is a leading distributor of structural steel products (beams, pipe, tubing) in the western US. Other operations include AZCON (scrap metal sales and rail cars and parts), GEFCO (portable drilling rigs), Standard Alloys (pump parts), and Steco (dump-truck trailers). Union Tractor provides replacement parts for construction and transportation equipment in western Canada. Blue Tee is owned by its employees.

Founder and chairman Richard Secrist resigned as CEO in 2009 and was replaced by president William Kelly. Secrist founded the company in 1986 and built it up through acquisitions.

Later that year, Brown-Strauss bought Kansas distributor B-S Steel, marking the company's eastern-most location. Brown-Strauss saw the move as a way to break into the Midwestern market.

EXECUTIVES

Chairman: Richard A. Secrist
President and CEO: William M. Kelly, age 60
EVP Finance and Secretary: David P. Alldian
EVP, Steco Trailers: Greg Haub
Group VP, Metals Operations and President, PUMPSTAR: Richard A. Secrist Jr.
Executive Director Benefit Plans:
  Annette Marino D'Arienzo
Controller and Assistant Secretary: Thomas Caruso
Treasurer and Assistant Secretary: Jerry D'Auria

LOCATIONS

HQ: Blue Tee Corp.
250 Park Ave. South, New York, NY 10003
Phone: 212-598-0880   **Fax:** 212-598-0896
Web: www.bluetee.com

PRODUCTS/OPERATIONS

Selected Subsidiaries

AZCON Corporation (ferrous and nonferrous scrap; rail cars, locomotives, and parts; relay and reroll rail)
Brown-Strauss Steel (steel distribution, including angles, beams, channels, pipe, and tubing)
GEFCO (The George E. Failing Company, portable drilling rigs)
Pumpstar (truck-mounted concrete boom pumps)
Standard Alloys (pump parts and repairs)
Steco (dump trailers, transfer trailers, and trailer parts)
Union Tractor Ltd. (Canada)
  Delta Warehouses (replacement parts for construction and transportation equipment)
  United Diesel Injection (parts and service for fuel-injection systems and turbochargers)

COMPETITORS

A. M. Castle
APi Group
Dover Corp.
Furukawa
Kreher Steel
OmniSource
Philip Services
Reliance Steel
RTI International Metals
Russel Metals
Supreme Industries
Trinity Industries
TTX
Utility Trailer
Wescast Industries

HISTORICAL FINANCIALS

Company Type: Private

Income Statement				FYE: December 31
	REVENUE ($ mil.)	**NET INCOME** ($ mil.)	**NET PROFIT MARGIN**	**EMPLOYEES**
12/08	1,549	—	—	875
12/07	1,103	—	—	1,050
12/06	852	—	—	—
12/05	699	—	—	—
12/04	741	—	—	—
Annual Growth	20.3%	—	—	(16.7%)

Revenue History

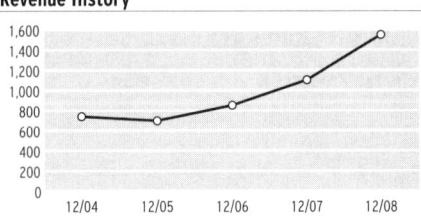

Boise Cascade

Boise Cascade Holdings (BCH) makes and distributes lumber, plywood, particleboard, and engineered products such as wood I-joists and laminated lumber. It also operates about 30 wholesale building material distribution centers throughout the US that sell a broad line of building materials, including those made by the company. To better focus on its core wood products and building materials distribution businesses, the firm sold its paper, packaging, and newsprint businesses in 2008. Formerly part of Boise Cascade Corporation (now OfficeMax), BCH is controlled by private investment firm Madison Dearborn Partners.

BCH sold its paper, packaging, and newsprint businesses, which operate as publicly traded Boise Inc., to Aldabra 2 Acquisition for nearly $2 billion in cash and securities. As part of the deal, BCH owns 49% of Boise Inc's. shares. The slowdown in the US housing market led to lower sales for the remaining wood products and building materials distribution business segments.

Because of reduced demand for its products in the housing market, BCH closed a plywood manufacturing center in Oregon in 2009. It has also scaled back manufacturing at its other facilities to keep inventories in line with decreasing sales figures.

Boise Cascade had a long history as the Boise Cascade Corporation; however, the company's assets were purchased by Madison Dearborn Partners in 2004, forming BCH. The old Boise Cascade Corporation's office products distribution business changed its name to OfficeMax Incorporated. OfficeMax owns about 20% of BCH; management and Madison Dearborn Partners own the rest.

In 2009 CFO Tom Carlile was named Boise Cascade's CEO. He succeeds Duane McDougall, who remains as chairman.

HISTORY

Boise Cascade got its start as the old Boise Cascade Corporation in 1957 with the merger of two small lumber companies — Boise Payette Lumber Company (based in Boise, Idaho) and Cascade Lumber Company (Yakima, Washington). The business diversified in the 1960s under the leadership of Robert Hansberger, moving into office-products distribution in 1964. A number of acquisitions followed, including Ebasco Industries (1969), a consulting, engineering, and construction firm. By 1970 Boise Cascade had made more than 30 buys to diversify into building materials, paper products, real estate, recreational vehicles (RVs), and publishing.

In the early 1970s the company suffered a timber shortage as its access to public timberlands dwindled. Its plans to develop recreational communities in California, Hawaii, and Washington met opposition from residents, causing Boise Cascade to scrap all but six of the 29 projects.

In 1972 high costs related to the remaining projects left the company in debt. John Fery replaced Hansberger as president that year and sold companies not directly related to the company's core forest-product operations.

In the late 1980s and early 1990s, Boise sold more nonstrategic operations, including its Specialty Paperboard Division in 1989. It sold more than half of its corrugated-container plants in 1992 to focus on manufacturing forest products and distributing building materials and office supplies.

Boise Cascade also sold its wholesale office-product business in 1992 to focus on direct sales to big buyers such as IBM and Boeing. The company sold off its Canadian subsidiary, Rainy River Forest Products, during 1994 and 1995. Resurgent paper prices resulted in a profit in 1995, Boise Cascade's first since 1990.

Also in 1995, in a move into the international paper market, Boise Cascade signed a joint venture agreement with Shenzhen Leasing to form Zhuhai Hiwin Boise Cascade, a Chinese manufacturer of carbonless paper. That year it sold a minority stake in Boise Cascade Office Products (BCOP) to the public.

The company sold its coated-papers business to paper and packaging heavyweight Mead in 1996 for $639 million. The following year Boise began harvesting its first quick-growth cottonwood trees (specially grown to cut the cost of harvesting from traditional slow-growth hardwood plantations). Also in 1997 BCOP bought Jean-Paul Guisset, an office-products direct marketer in France. Although this acquisition boosted sales and increased the company's European presence, company profits suffered that year because of weak paper prices.

The low price of paper in 1998 prompted the company to close four sawmills and a research and development center. Restructuring costs associated with the closures and a fire at the company's Medford, Oregon, plywood plant led to a net income loss for the year.

In 1999 Boise bought Wallace Computer Services, a contract stationer business, and broadened its building-supply distribution network nationwide by acquiring Furman Lumber, a building-supplies distributor. In 2000 Boise Cascade completed the purchase of the 19% of Boise Office Solutions that it didn't already own. The company also sold its European office products operations for $335 million and then turned around and purchased the Blue Star Business Supplies Group of US Office Products in Australia and New Zealand for about $115 million.

Because of the decline in federal timber sales, in 2001 the company closed its plywood mill and lumber operations in Emmett, Idaho, and a sawmill in Cascade, Idaho. In 2002 lagging profits prompted Boise to implement cost-cutting procedures. In 2003 the company pinned its hopes for growth on the office product segment with the acquisition of OfficeMax for nearly $1.2 billion in cash and stock. The deal put Boise Cascade's office products business on par with industry leaders Staples and Office Depot.

Investment firm Madison Dearborn Partners purchased Boise Cascade's paper, forest products, and timberland assets for $3.7 billion in October 2004 and changed the name of the company to Boise Cascade Holdings, L.L.C. Thomas Stephens became the new CEO. The firm filed an IPO registration statement and converted from a Delaware limited liability company to a Delaware corporation named Boise Cascade Company, but canceled the IPO in May 2005. It converted back to a limited liability company status and reinstated its Boise Cascade Holdings, L.L.C. name in December 2005.

In 2008 the firm sold its paper, packaging and newsprint, and transportation businesses, which now operate as publicly traded Boise Inc., to Aldabra for about $1.6 billion. Also that year Duane McDougall replaced the retiring Tom Stephens as chairman and CEO. Stephens had held those titles since 2004.

EXECUTIVES

Chairman: Duane C. McDougall, age 57, $97,402 total compensation
CEO and Director: Thomas E. Carlile, age 58, $1,441,158 total compensation
SVP, CFO, and Treasurer: Wayne M. Rancourt, age 46
VP Human Resources and Communications: John Sahlberg, age 55
VP and Controller: Bernadette M. Madarieta, age 33
VP and General Counsel: David Gadda, age 61, $629,432 total compensation
VP, Boise Wood Products: Thomas (Tom) Corrick
VP and Operations Manager, Boise Building Materials Distribution: Nick A. Stokes
Director Strategic Planning and Internal Audit: Kelly Hibbs
President, Boise Building Materials Distribution: Stanley R. (Stan) Bell, age 62, $1,542,990 total compensation
President, Wood Product Manufacturing: Thomas A. (Tom) Lovlien, age 53, $1,060,987 total compensation
Auditors: KPMG LLP

LOCATIONS

HQ: Boise Cascade Holdings, L.L.C.
    1111 W. Jefferson St., Ste. 900, Boise, ID 83702
Phone: 208-384-6161
Web: www.bc.com

PRODUCTS/OPERATIONS

2008 Sales

	$ mil.	% of total
Building materials distribution	2,108.5	71
Wood products	520.5	17
Paper	244.5	8
Packaging & newsprint	102.2	4
Other	1.8	—
Total	**2,977.5**	**100**

Selected Products and Operations

Building material distribution
    Composite decking
    Engineered wood products (EWP)
    Framing accessories
    Insulation
    Lumber
    Oriented strand board (OSB)
    Plywood
    Roofing
    Siding
Wood
    Dimension lumber
    Engineered wood products (EWP)
    Laminated veneer lumber
    Plywood
    Ponderosa pine lumber

COMPETITORS

84 Lumber
BlueLinx
Builders FirstSource
Georgia-Pacific
Guardian Building Products Distribution
HD Supply
Lowe's
Pacific Coast Building Products
Potlatch
PrimeSource Building
Stock Building Supply
Temple-Inland
Weyerhaeuser

HISTORICAL FINANCIALS
Company Type: Private

Income Statement   FYE: December 31

	REVENUE ($ mil.)	NET INCOME ($ mil.)	NET PROFIT MARGIN	EMPLOYEES
12/08	2,978	(288)	—	4,600
12/07	5,414	128	2.4%	10,042
12/06	5,780	72	1.2%	10,191
12/05	5,907	121	2.0%	10,155
12/04	5,735	94	1.6%	10,494
Annual Growth	(15.1%)	—	—	(18.6%)

Net Income History

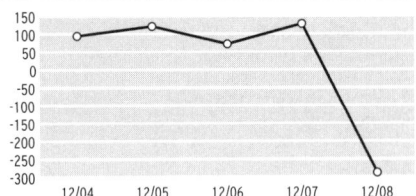

Bon Secours Health System

Bon Secours Health System provides succor to the poor and sick. The Roman Catholic health care organization, sponsored by the Bon Secours Ministries, set up its first hospital in Baltimore in 1919. Today, Bon Secours Health System includes nearly 20 hospitals with some 4,400 licensed acute care beds. The organization's facilities are in seven states in the eastern US, from New York to Florida. In addition to its acute care facilities, the health care system operates numerous nursing homes and assisted-living facilities with about 1,500 beds, as well as outpatient centers, hospices, and home health care agencies.

Bon Secours Health System has been ridding itself of its unprofitable facilities and has exited several geographic markets entirely. In 2007 it sold Detroit's Bon Secours Hospital and its Michigan nursing homes to Beaumont Hospitals. It also ended its Bon Secours Cottage Health Services joint venture, selling its stake to partner Henry Ford Health System.

It left New Jersey, where it had operated St. Mary Hospital, in 2007. It had threatened to close down the money-losing hospital, but St. Mary was saved when Hoboken city officials offered to run it as a public hospital.

Despite its asset sales, Bon Secours plans to continue to grow its operations in existing and new communities, targeting expansion in ambulatory care, elderly services, and home health and hospice. The health system has opened several new ambulatory care centers in existing service territories and it is conducting renovation and expansion efforts at some of its hospital facilities.

The company has also initiated information technology restructuring efforts; it has developed a new clinical information management system

(electronic medical records), ConnectCare, which is being implemented at its facilities in gradual stages.

In 2007 the company transitioned from operating under the sponsorship of the Sisters of Bon Secours to the Bon Secours Ministries.

EXECUTIVES

Chairperson: Sister Patricia A. (Pat) Eck
President, CEO, and Director: Richard J. (Rich) Statuto, age 50
COO: Donald E. (Don) Strange
CFO: Katherine A. (Kathy) Arbuckle
COO, Bon Secours St. Mary's Hospital: Tom Koenig
EVP Sponsorship: Sister Anne M. Lutz
EVP Organization Effectiveness: Timothy J. Davis
SVP Sponsorship: Sister Rose Marie Jasinski
SVP Performance Management:
  Richard A. (Dick) Hanson
SVP Corporate Services: Edward (Ed) Boyer
VP Human Resources: David D. Jones
VP Operations and Finance: Janice Burnett
CIO and VP Information Systems: Skip Hubbard
Director Marketing and Communications: Diana Stager

LOCATIONS

HQ: Bon Secours Health System, Inc.
  1505 Marriottsville Rd., Marriottsville, MD 21104
Phone: 410-442-5511   **Fax:** 410-442-1082
Web: www.bshsi.com

Selected Facilities
Florida
  Bon Secours St. Petersburg Health System
    Bon Secours — Maria Manor Nursing Care and Rehabilitation Center (St. Petersburg)
    Bon Secours Place at St. Petersburg
Kentucky
  Bon Secours Kentucky Health System
    Our Lady of Bellefonte Hospital (Ashland)
Maryland
  Bon Secours Baltimore Health System
    Bon Secours Hospital (Baltimore)
    Bon Secours Washington Village (Baltimore)
    Community Institute of Behavioral Sciences (Baltimore)
    Hollins Terrace/Benet House (Baltimore)
New York
  Bon Secours Charity Health System
    Bon Secours Community Hospital (Port Jervis)
    Good Samaritan Hospital (Suffern)
    St. Anthony Community Hospital (Warwick)
  Bon Secours New York Health System
    Schervier Nursing Care Center (Riverdale)
Pennsylvania
  Altoona Regional Health System (Altoona, joint venture)
South Carolina
  Bon Secours St. Francis Health System, Inc.
    St. Francis Hospital (Downtown and Eastside Campuses, Greenville)
    Roper St. Francis Healthcare (Charleston, joint venture)
Virginia
  Bon Secours Hampton Roads Health System
    Bon Secours Maryview Nursing Care Center (Suffolk)
    DePaul Medical Center (Norfolk)
    Mary Immaculate Hospital (Newport News)
    Maryview Medical Center (Portsmouth)
    Province Place (Norfolk and Portsmouth)
    St. Francis Nursing Care Center (Newport News)
  Bon Secours Richmond Health System (joint venture)
    Memorial Regional Medical Center (Mechanicsville)
    Richmond Community Hospital (Richmond)
    St. Francis Medical Center (Midlothian)
    St. Mary's Hospital (Richmond)

COMPETITORS

Adventist HealthCare
Appalachian Regional Healthcare
Carilion Clinic
Catholic Health East
Centra Health, Inc.
Christiana Care
Conemaugh Health System
Franklin Square Hospital Center
GBMC Healthcare
Greenville Hospital System
Highlands Health
Inova
Johns Hopkins Medicine
MediSys Health Network
MedStar Health
New York City Health and Hospitals
Novant Health
Riverside Health System (Virginia)
Sentara Healthcare
St. Agnes HealthCare
University of Maryland Medical System
Virginia Hospital Center

HISTORICAL FINANCIALS
Company Type: Not-for-profit

Income Statement   FYE: August 31

	REVENUE ($ mil.)	NET INCOME ($ mil.)	NET PROFIT MARGIN	EMPLOYEES
8/08	2,437	—	—	19,000

Bonneville Power Administration

Bonneville Power Administration (BPA) keeps the lights on in the Pacific Northwest. The US Department of Energy power marketing agency operates a 15,190-mile high-voltage transmission grid that delivers about 35% of the electrical power consumed in the region. The electricity that BPA wholesales is generated primarily by 31 federal hydroelectric plants and one private nuclear facility. BPA also purchases power from other hydroelectric, gas-fired, and wind and solar generation facilities in North America. Founded in 1937, the utility sells power to about 150 primary customers, mainly public and investor-owned utilities.

BPA's strategy calls for it to maintain an efficient and reliable power supply by operating a transmission system that can integrate and transmit power from multiple generating sources, while mitigating the system's impacts on fish and wildlife.

EXECUTIVES

Administrator and CEO: Stephen J. (Steve) Wright
COO: Anita Decker
EVP and CFO: David J. Armstrong
CIO: Larry D. Buttress
Chief Technical Officer: Scott Ducar
Chief Supply Chain Officer: Ann Scholl
Chief Risk Officer: Samuel Cannady

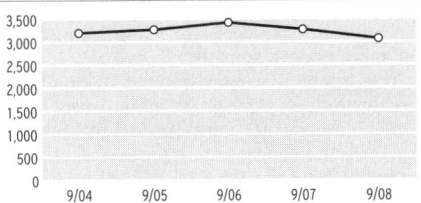
Booz Allen Hamilton

For more than 95 years, consultants at Booz Allen Hamilton have been helping US government agencies operate more efficiently at home and abroad. The firm provides a wide range of management consulting and technology integration services; its specialties include information technology, operations, organization and change, program management, strategy, training programs, and systems engineering. Booz Allen has worked for such agencies as the Department of Defense, the Federal Aviation Administration, and the Internal Revenue Service. Investment firm The Carlyle Group owns a majority interest in the consulting firm, which traces its roots to 1914.

Though focused on US government clients, Booz Allen nevertheless undertakes a variety of engagements. Key markets include civil government agencies responsible for energy, finance, health, and transportation, as well as defense and national security agencies. Clients also include international development entities, such as the World Bank, and nongovernmental organizations, such as foundations and universities.

Booz Allen formerly worked for commercial as well as government clients. But the firm separated its commercial- and government-related businesses in July 2008 as part of a deal in which The Carlyle Group paid about $2.5 billion for control of the government arm, which retained the Booz Allen name. The firm's commercial arm was spun off as a separate entity, Booz & Company, which is owned by its officers.

The goal of the separation was to enable each operating business to better focus on its core market. Just as the commercial and government units did when they operated under common ownership, however, Booz Allen and Booz & Company will work together on engagements when it makes sense to do so.

HISTORY

Edwin Booz graduated from Northwestern University in 1914 with degrees in economics and psychology and started a statistical analysis firm in Chicago. After serving in the army during WWI, he returned to his firm, renamed Edwin Booz Surveys. In 1925 Booz hired his first full-time assistant, George Fry, and in 1929 he hired a second, James Allen. By then the company had a long list of clients, including U.S. Gypsum, the *Chicago Tribune*, and Montgomery Ward, which was losing a retail battle with Sears, Roebuck and Co.

In 1935 Carl Hamilton joined the partnership, and a year later it was renamed Booz, Fry, Allen & Hamilton. The firm prospered well into the next decade by providing advice based on "independence that enables us to say plainly from the outside what cannot always be said safely from within," according to a company brochure.

During WWII the firm worked increasingly on government and military contracts. Fry opposed the pursuit of such work for consultants and left in 1942. The firm was renamed Booz, Allen & Hamilton. Hamilton died in 1946, and the following year Booz retired (he died in 1951), leaving Allen as chairman. He successfully steered the firm into lucrative postwar work for clients such as Johnson Wax, RCA, and the US Air Force.

A separate company, Booz, Allen Applied Research, Inc. (BAARINC), was formed in 1955 for technical and government consulting, including missile and weaponry work, as well as consulting with NASA. By the end of the decade, *Time* had dubbed Booz Allen "the world's largest, most prestigious management consultant firm." The partnership was incorporated as a private company in 1962, and in 1967 commissioner Pete Rozelle requested its services for the merger of the National Football League and American Football League.

When Allen retired in 1970, Charlie Bowen became the new chairman, and the company went public. However, as the economy stalled during the energy crisis, spending for consultants plunged. Jim Farley replaced Bowen in 1975, and the company was taken private again in 1976. A turnaround was engineered, and the firm was soon helping Chrysler through its 1979 bailout and developing strategies for the breakup of AT&T in 1984.

Booz Allen again experienced trouble in the 1980s after Farley instituted a competition to select his successor. Michael McCullough was eventually chosen in 1984, but the 10-month election process turned into a dogfight that pitted partner against partner, taking an enormous toll on morale. McCullough began restructuring the firm along industry lines, creating a department store of services in an industry characterized by boutique houses. The turmoil was too much, and by 1988 nearly a third of the partners had quit.

William Stasior became chairman in 1991 and reorganized Booz Allen yet again, splitting it down public and private sector lines. Allen died in 1992, the same year the firm moved to McLean, Virginia. The company began privatization work in the former Soviet Union and in Eastern Europe in 1992 and continued to emphasize government business, including contracts with the IRS (1995) for technology modernization and with the General Services Administration (1996) to provide technical and management support for all federal telecommunications users.

In 1998 the company won a 10-year, $200 million contract with the US Defense Department to establish a scientific and technical data warehouse. Ralph Shrader was appointed CEO in early 1999; Stasior retired as chairman later that year. Booz Allen acquired Scandinavian consulting firm Carta in 1999 and formed a venture capital firm for startups with Lehman Brothers in 2000. The company announced in late 2000 that it would spin off Aestix, its e-commerce business, but reconsidered amid a general economic slowdown and hostile IPO market. (The unit was integrated back into Booz Allen in 2002.)

Booz Allen saw an increase in work related to defense and national security after the terrorist attacks of September 11, 2001. Engagements included work related to the reconstruction of Iraq (as a subcontractor on telecommunications projects managed by Lucent), and in 2003 Booz Allen was awarded a contract from the US Health Resources and Services Administration to help establish and operate a bioterrorism technical support center.

In 2008 Booz Allen spun off its commercial consulting business as an independent firm, Booz & Company. The spinoff was part of a transaction in which investment firm The Carlyle Group acquired a controlling interest in Booz Allen's government-related consulting business, which retained the Booz Allen name.

EXECUTIVES

Chairman and CEO: Ralph W. Shrader, age 65
SVP, Chief Administrative Officer, CFO, and Director:
Samuel R. (Sam) Strickland
SVP and Chief Legal Officer: C. G. Appleby
VP and Chief Personnel Officer: Horacio Rozanski
**VP and Client Service Officer, National Geospatial
Intelligence Agency:** John Lueders
**VP and Officer in Chief, National Reconnaissance
Office Market:** Carol Staubach
VP and Head, Economic and Business Analysis:
Robert Makar
VP Advanced Enterprise Integration:
Gregory G. (Greg) Wenzel
**VP and Client Service Officer, Navy and Marine Corps
Business:** David J. (Dave) Karp
Lead VP Information Technology, Security Market:
James (Jim) Manchisi
VP and CIO: Frank S. Smith III
VP and Head, Information Analysis Center:
Robert J. (Bob) Lamb
VP and Client Service Officer, Environmental Business:
Molly Finn
**VP and Principal Manager, Diplomacy and International
Development Business:** Donald L. (Don) Pressley

LOCATIONS

HQ: Booz Allen Hamilton Inc.
8283 Greensboro Dr., McLean, VA 22102
Phone: 703-902-5000 **Fax:** 703-902-3333
Web: www.boozallen.com

PRODUCTS/OPERATIONS

Selected Markets

Civil government
Benefits and entitlements
Federal finance
International development and diplomacy
Defense
Air Force
Army
Joint staff and combatant commands
Navy and Marine Corps
Office of the Secretary of Defense and defense agencies
Space
Energy
Environment
Health
Health informatics
Health not-for-profit/nongovernmental organizations
International public health
US public health
Homeland security
Intelligence
Law enforcement
Not-for-profit/nongovernmental organizations
Transportation
Aviation infrastructure
Highways and automotive technology
Passenger rail and mass transit

Selected Practice Areas

Assurance and resilience
Economic and business analysis
Information technology
Modeling and simulation
Organization and strategy
Supply chain and logistics
Systems engineering and integration

COMPETITORS

Accenture	HP Enterprise Services
A.T. Kearney	IBM
BAE SYSTEMS	Lockheed Martin
Bain & Company	MAXIMUS
BearingPoint	McKinsey & Company
Boston Consulting	Northrop Grumman
CACI International	PA Consulting
Capgemini	PRTM Management
Computer Sciences Corp.	Raytheon
Deloitte Consulting	Towers Perrin
General Dynamics	Unisys

Booz & Company

Created from the commercial consulting arm of venerable Booz Allen Hamilton, Booz & Company was spun off in 2008 as part of a transaction in which Booz Allen sold a controlling stake in its US government consulting unit to The Carlyle Group. Booz & Company emerged as an independent firm, owned by its officers. The firm's consultants work with businesses, governments, and other organizations from more than 55 offices around the world. Booz & Company's specialties include corporate finance, IT, mergers and acquisitions, and organization. The commercial consulting business has counted the New York Stock Exchange, Deutsche Post, and publishing giant Wolters Kluwer among its clients.

EXECUTIVES

Chairman: Joe Saddi
CEO: Shumeet Banerji
CFO and Partner: Douglas G. (Doug) Swenson
SVP and Director: Steven B. Wheeler
SVP and Director: Gary L. Neilson
VP and Director: Christian Burger
Partner, Japan: Steven Veldhoen
Managing Partner, Greater China: Edward C. Tse
Partner and Managing Director, Nordic: Torsten Moe
**Managing Partner, Australia, New Zealand, and South
East Asia:** Timothy (Tim) Jackson
Managing Director, Italy: Fernando Flavio Napolitano,
age 44
Managing Director, North America: Cesare R. Mainardi
Senior Partner and Head South Latin America:
Ivan De Souza

LOCATIONS

HQ: Booz & Company
101 Park Ave., 18th Fl., New York, NY 10178
Phone: 212-697-1900 **Fax:** 212-551-6732
Web: www.booz.com

PRODUCTS/OPERATIONS

Selected Industries Served

Aerospace and Defense
Automotive
Chemicals
Consumer Products
Energy and Utilities
Financial Services
Government Departments and Ministries
Health
Industrials
Media and Entertainment
Oil & Gas
Private Equity
Retail
Technology
Telecommunication
Transportation

COMPETITORS

Accenture
A.T. Kearney
Bain & Company
BearingPoint
Boston Consulting
McKinsey & Company
PA Consulting
Towers Perrin

HISTORICAL FINANCIALS

Company Type: Private

Income Statement
FYE: March 31

	ESTIMATED REVENUE ($ mil.)	NET INCOME ($ mil.)	NET PROFIT MARGIN	EMPLOYEES
3/08	1,100	—	—	3,300

Bose Corporation

Bose has been making noise in the audio products business for some time. The firm is one of the world's leading manufacturers of speakers for the home entertainment, automotive, and pro audio markets. It makes a variety of consumer models for stereo systems and home theaters, including its compact Wave radio system. For sound professionals, Bose offers loudspeakers and amplifiers, as well as products designed for musicians. Bose sells its products at 100-plus factory and showcase stores and through affiliated retailers. The company is using its expertise to branch out into other markets. Founder Amar Bose, a former professor of electrical engineering at Massachusetts Institute of Technology, owns the company.

Stung by the recession and the downturn in spending on high-end products, Bose cut 1,000 jobs, or about 10% of its workforce in early 2009. The layoffs were in select areas, including manufacturing and at its Massachusetts headquarters.

The company has eight manufacturing plants and 16 international subsidiaries. One new subsidiary, ElectroForce Systems Group, offers advanced test instruments for materials research and product development.

Bose has built a reputation for making high-quality products through its commitment to research in electronics and acoustical engineering. The expertise of its engineers proved invaluable to the Boston Convention & Exhibition Center, which brought in Bose to revamp its public address system.

Its research focus has taken the company into new fields in recent years: Bose has been developing an electromagnetic suspension system for automobiles since the 1980s and in 2004 it acquired testing equipment maker EnduraTEC. Taking advantage of the popularity of Apple's iPod, Bose introduced the SoundDock digital music system in 2004.

EXECUTIVES

Chairman and CEO: Amar G. Bose, age 76
President: Bob Maresca
CIO: Rob Ramrath
VP Bose Europe: Nic A. Merks
VP Manufacturing: Bryan Fontaine

VP Human Resources: John C. Ferrie
VP Manufacturing: Thomas Beeson
VP; President, Bose Japan: Sumiyoshi Sakura
VP Sales: Debi Aubee
VP Finance: Daniel A. Grady, age 68
VP Research and Director: Thomas A. Froeschle
Director Global Marketing: Jeff Lawson
Director Product Development: Ken Jacob
General Counsel and Secretary: Mark E. Sullivan
Treasurer: Mario J. Cornacchio Jr.
Director of Public Relations: Carolyn Cinotti
Auditors: PricewaterhouseCoopers LLP

LOCATIONS

HQ: Bose Corporation
The Mountain, Framingham, MA 01701
Phone: 508-879-7330   **Fax:** 508-766-7543
Web: www.bose.com

PRODUCTS/OPERATIONS

Selected Products

Automotive sound systems
Aviation and military headsets
Home entertainment
  Headphones and headsets
  Home stereo speakers
  Home theater speakers
  Multimedia speakers
  Outdoor and marine speakers
  SoundDock for iPod
  Wave systems
Professional audio
  Amplifiers
  Loudspeakers

COMPETITORS

Bosch Communications   Pioneer Corporation
Boston Acoustics   Polk Audio
Cambridge SoundWorks   QSC Audio
Eminence Speaker   Rockford
Harman International   Rodin
JVC KENWOOD   Sony USA
Klipsch   SpeakerCraft
Koss   Stanton Group
Mitek Corporation

Boston Consulting Group

Global corporations are willing to give much more than a penny for the thoughts of Boston Consulting Group (BCG). One of the world's top-ranked consulting practices, BCG operates from about 65 offices in more than 35 countries in the Americas, Europe, and the Asia/Pacific region. The firm's 4,300 consultants offer a wide array of services, mainly to large corporate clients. BCG's practice areas include branding and marketing, corporate finance, globalization, and information technology. Founded in 1963 by industry pioneer Bruce Henderson, the firm is owned by its employees.

BCG is noted for developing consulting concepts such as "time-based competition" (rapid response to change) and "deconstruction" (an end to vertical integration). Over the years, CEO Hans-Paul Bürkner has worked to distinguish the firm from competitors such as McKinsey & Company and Bain & Company in an effort to win consulting engagements in a tight economy. One area of focus is China, where BCG is working to expand its staff. The firm also specializes in a wide area of practice areas, which helps it somewhat shield itself from being susceptible to the economic downturns affecting specific industries.

EXECUTIVES

Chairman Emeritus: John S. Clarkeson, age 66
Chairman: Carl W. Stern, age 63
President and CEO: Hans-Paul Bürkner
CFO: Debbie Simpson
Global Leader, Technology and Communications Practice: Ron Nicol
Global Leader, Energy Practice: Ivan Marten
Global Leader, Global Advantage Practice: David Michael
Global Leader, Operations Practice: Joe Manget
Global Leader, Insurance Practice: Heiner Leisten
Global Leader, Financial Institutions Practice: David Rhodes
Global Leader, Public Sector Practice: Larry Kamener
Global Leader, Industrial Goods Practice: Josef Rick
Global Leader, Information Technology Practice: Wolfgang Thiel
Global Leader, Corporate Development Practice: Daniel Stelter
Global Leader, Organization Practice: Andrew Dyer
Global Leader, Health Care Practice: Marty Silverstein
Global Leader, Consumer Practice: Patrick Ducasse
Global Leader, Marketing and Sales Practice: Miki Tsusaka
General Counsel and Risk Management Head: Jeremy Barton
Chairman, Europe and Middle East: Bjørn Matre
Chairman, North and South America: Rich Lesser

LOCATIONS

HQ: The Boston Consulting Group Inc.
1 Exchange Place, 31st Fl., Boston, MA 02109
Phone: 617-973-1200   **Fax:** 617-973-1339
Web: www.bcg.com

PRODUCTS/OPERATIONS

Selected Practice Areas

Branding
Corporate finance
E-commerce
Globalization
Information technology
Innovation
Intellectual property
Marketing and sales
Operations
Organization
Post-merger integration
Strategy

COMPETITORS

Accenture
Arthur D Little
A.T. Kearney
Bain & Company
BearingPoint
Booz Allen
Computer Sciences Corp.
Deloitte Consulting
HP Enterprise Services
IBM
McKinsey & Company
Monitor Group
PA Consulting
Perot Systems
PRTM Management
Roland Berger
Towers Perrin

HISTORICAL FINANCIALS

Company Type: Private

Income Statement				FYE: December 31
	ESTIMATED REVENUE ($ mil.)	NET INCOME ($ mil.)	NET PROFIT MARGIN	EMPLOYEES
12/08	2,400	—	—	6,000
12/07	2,332	—	—	6,000
12/06	1,800	—	—	6,270
12/05	1,500	—	—	5,500
Annual Growth	17.0%	—	—	2.9%

Revenue History

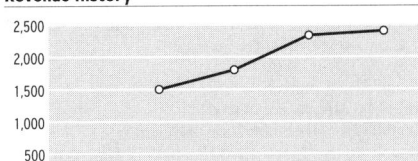

Boston Red Sox

You might say this team is now a curse on the other clubs in Major League Baseball. Boston Red Sox Baseball Club operates one of the oldest and most storied franchises in the major leagues. Founded as a charter member of the American League in 1901, the team owns seven World Series titles but at one time suffered through an 86-year championship drought popularly attributed to "The Curse of the Bambino." Boston broke The Curse in 2004 and then won its seventh championship three years later. Red Sox fans root for their home team at venerable Fenway Park, the oldest pro baseball stadium in the country. Businessman John Henry leads a group that has owned the Red Sox franchise since 2002.

Boston's rise to the top ranks of baseball has come mostly thanks to the deep pockets of its owner, who has spent lavishly to stock the BoSox roster with talent. Before making its run for the 2007 World Series, the team signed Japanese pitcher Daisuke Matsuzaka to a six-year, $52 million contract (plus a $51 million "negotiating fee" paid to Matsuzaka's former team, the Sebu Lions) and later inked former Los Angeles Dodger J. D. Drew to a five-year, $70 million deal.

Henry, who previously controlled the Florida Marlins, and his partners (including The New York Times Company) paid about $660 million for the storied franchise, a record sum at the time for a baseball team. (That amount was surpassed in 2009 when Tom Ricketts purchased the Chicago Cubs for $840 million.) The new ownership group upgraded the team's 90-year-old stadium with new concessions areas and seats atop the Green Monster — the left field wall which measures 37 feet high.

Henry's partnership, known as New England Sports Ventures, also owns an 80% stake in New England Sports Network along with Boston Bruins owner Jeremy Jacobs.

EXECUTIVES

Chairman: Thomas C. (Tom) Werner
Vice Chairman: David I. Ginsberg
Vice Chairman: Phillip H. Morse
Principal Owner: John W. Henry
President and CEO: Larry Lucchino, age 64
CFO: Steve Fitch
EVP and General Manager: Theo Epstein
EVP and Chief Sales and Marketing Officer:
  Samuel (Sam) Kennedy
SVP Planning and Development: Janet Marie Smith
SVP International Scouting: Craig Shipley
SVP Business Affairs: Jonathan Gilula
SVP Fenway Affairs: Lawrence C. (Larry) Cancro
**SVP Corporate Relations; Executive Director, Red Sox
  Foundation:** Meg Vaillancourt
VP Human Resources and Administration: Mary Sprong
Director Information Technology:
  Stephen P. (Steve) Conley
VP and Club Counsel: Jennifer Flynn
VP Public Affairs: Susan Goodenow
VP and Team Historian: Dick Bresciani
VP and Club Counsel: Elaine Weddington Steward
Manager: Terry John Francona
Director Player Development: Mike Hazen

LOCATIONS

HQ: Boston Red Sox Baseball Club Limited Partnership
4 Yawkey Way, Boston, MA 02215
Phone: 617-267-9440   **Fax:** 617-375-0944
Web: boston.redsox.mlb.com

The Boston Red Sox play at 37,373-seat capacity Fenway
Park in Boston.

PRODUCTS/OPERATIONS

Championship Titles
World Series (1903, 1912, 1915-16, 1918, 2004, 2007)
American League Pennant (1903-04, 1912, 1915-16,
  1918, 1946, 1967, 1975, 1986, 2004, 2007)

COMPETITORS

Baltimore Orioles
New York Yankees
Tampa Bay Rays
Toronto Blue Jays

HISTORICAL FINANCIALS

Company Type: Private

Income Statement  FYE: December 31

	REVENUE ($ mil.)	NET INCOME ($ mil.)	NET PROFIT MARGIN	EMPLOYEES
12/08	269	—	—	—
12/07	263	—	—	—
12/06	234	—	—	—
12/05	206	—	—	—
12/04	220	—	—	—
Annual Growth	5.2%	—	—	—

Revenue History

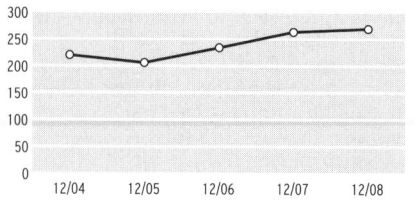

Boston University

With colleges and universities thick on the ground in Boston, Boston University (BU) amounts to more than a hill of beans. Founded as a Methodist seminary in 1839, the private university has more than 32,000 students at its campus on the banks of the Charles River. It offers approximately 250 undergraduate, graduate, doctorate, and special degree programs at more than 15 colleges and schools. BU counts Nobel laureates Elie Wiesel (peace), Derek Walcott (literature), Sheldon Glashow (physics), and Osamu Shimomura (chemistry) among its more than 3,900 faculty members.

EXECUTIVES

Chairman: Robert A. Knox, age 57
Vice Chairman: David F. D'Alessandro, age 58
President and Trustee: Robert A. Brown, age 57
Provost: David K. Campbell
EVP: Joseph P. Mercurio
VP Financial Affairs and Treasurer: Martin J. Howard
VP Operations: Gary W. Nicksa
VP Enrollment and Student Affairs: Laurie Pohl
VP and Associate Provost Research:
  Andrei E. Ruckenstein
VP Government and Community Affairs:
  Edward M. King
VP Administrative Services: Peter Fiedler
VP Marketing and Communications: Stephen P. Burgay
VP Information Systems and Technology:
  Tracy Schroeder
VP Development and Alumni Relations:
  Scott G. Nichols
VP, General Counsel, and Secretary Board of Trustees:
  Todd L. C. Klipp
Dean of Students: Kenneth Elmore
Chief Investment Officer: Pamela L. Peedin
Auditors: PricewaterhouseCoopers LLP

LOCATIONS

HQ: Boston University
  1 Sherborn St., Boston, MA 02215
Phone: 617-353-2000   **Fax:** 617-353-4048
Web: www.bu.edu

PRODUCTS/OPERATIONS

Selected Schools and Colleges
College of Arts and Sciences
College of Communication
College of Engineering
College of General Studies
Goldman School of Dental Medicine
Graduate School of Arts and Sciences
Metropolitan College (continuing education)
Sargent College of Health & Rehabilitation Sciences
School of Education
School of Hospitality Administration
School of Law
School of Management
School of Medicine
School of Public Health
School of Social Work
School of Theology
The University Professors Program

Boy Scouts of America

Scouts enter dens as Tigers and eventually take flight as Eagles. Boy Scouts of America (BSA), one of the nation's largest youth organizations, has about 3 million youth members and more than 1 million adult leaders in its ranks. BSA offers educational and character-building programs emphasizing leadership, citizenship, personal development, and physical fitness. In addition to traditional scouting programs (Tiger, Cub, Webelos, and Boy Scouts, ranging up to Eagle rank), it offers the Venturing program for boys and girls ages 14-20. BSA generates revenue through membership and council fees, supply and magazine sales, and contributions. The organization was founded by Chicago publisher William Boyce in 1910.

In 2009 the organization announced it would be building a high adventure base in West Virginia. High adventure bases offer Scouts a range of outdoor activities, including backpacking, camping, canoeing, and diving. BSA operates bases in Florida, Minnesota, and New Mexico.

BSA programs remain popular, but membership growth in the organization's units has stalled. The organization has a strategic plan that involves reaching out to new groups of parents and students. To this end, BSA has developed and maintained relationships with civic, religious, and fraternal organizations across the US, including those that serve African-American, Asian, and Latino families. It has also analyzed Generation X and Millennial parents, in order to determine how to best bring scouting to their communities.

EXECUTIVES

Chief Scout Executive: Robert J. (Bob) Mazzuca
National President: John Gottschalk, age 66
National Commissioner: Tico A. Perez
COO and Assistant Chief Scout Executive:
  Wayne Brock
CFO and Assistant Chief Scout Executive: Jim Terry
EVP: Rex W. Tillerson, age 57
VP Marketing: Nathan Rosenberg
VP Human Resources: James S. Turley
VP Council Solutions: Terrence P. (Terry) Dunn
VP Administration: Randall Stephenson
VP Outdoor Adventures: Jack Furst
VP Development: Drayton McLane Jr., age 73
VP Supply: O. Temple Sloan Jr., age 70
Group Director Council Solutions: Gary Butler
Group Director Administration: Nate Langston
Group Director Supply: Michael (Mike) Ashline
Group Director Human Resources: Al Morin
Group Director, Innovation and Strategy:
  Fred Meijering
Group Director Marketing: Stephen Medlicott
Chairman, World Scout Committee:
  William F. (Rick) Cronk
Auditors: PricewaterhouseCoopers LLP

LOCATIONS

HQ: Boy Scouts of America
  1325 W. Walnut Hill Ln., Irving, TX 75015
Phone: 972-580-2000   **Fax:** 972-580-7870
Web: www.scouting.org

PRODUCTS/OPERATIONS

2008 Youth Membership

	No.
Cub Scouts	1,665,635
Boy Scouts	844,939
Venturers	261,075
Varsity Scouts	60,940
Total	**2,832,589**

HISTORICAL FINANCIALS

Company Type: Not-for-profit

Income Statement				FYE: December 31
	REVENUE ($ mil.)	NET INCOME ($ mil.)	NET PROFIT MARGIN	EMPLOYEES
12/08	151	(20)	—	—
12/07	175	32	18.4%	500
12/06	195	65	33.2%	500
12/05	181	26	14.3%	500
12/04	270	—	—	500
Annual Growth	(13.6%)	—	—	0.0%

Net Income History

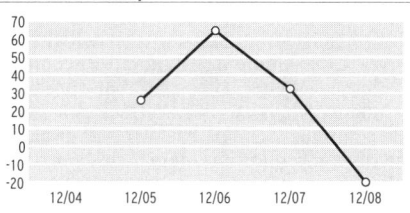

Bozzuto's Inc.

Bozzuto's is a leading wholesale grocery distribution company that supplies food and non-food products to independent supermarkets belonging to the IGA network in New Jersey, New York, Pennsylvania, and in New England. The company distributes a full line of grocery items, including meat products, produce, and frozen food, as well as household goods and other general merchandise. It carries goods sold under both the IGA and Hy-Top labels, in addition to national brands. Bozzuto's also owns about 10 supermarkets in Connecticut and Massachusetts operating under the Adams Super Food Stores banner. The company, founded in 1945, is owned and operated by the Bozzuto family.

During 2008 Bozzuto's struck a supplier deal with Big Y Foods, a regional supermarket operator with more than 50 stores. The supermarkets had previously been supplied by C&S Wholesale Grocers.

EXECUTIVES

Chairman, President, and CEO: Michael A. Bozzuto
EVP Retail Development: George Motel
SVP Merchandising, Advertising, and Procurement:
  Steve Heggelke
VP Deli, Bakery, and Dairy: Robert Cohen
VP Information Technology: John Keeley
VP Finance: Robert H. (Bob) Wood
VP Sales: Dan Brock
VP Retail Systems and e-Commerce: Steve Methvin
Director Human Resources: Lilly Branco
Manager Marketing: Buddy McLean
Distribution Center Supervisor: Chris Griffin
Director Advertising and Communication: Amy Yeager
Corporate Secretary and Assistant Treasurer:
  Patricia S. (Pat) Houle

LOCATIONS

HQ: Bozzuto's Inc.
  275 School House Rd., Cheshire, CT 06410
Phone: 203-272-3511   **Fax:** 203-250-2954
Web: www.bozzutos.com

COMPETITORS

Associated Grocers of New England
Associated Wholesalers
C & S Wholesale
Krasdale Foods
McLane
Nash-Finch
Pine State Trading
Shaw's
Stop & Shop
SUPERVALU
Wakefern Food

Bradco Supply

Bradco Supply offers building contractors everything they need to put a roof over their clients' heads. The company distributes roofing, siding, windows, and other building materials through about 130 locations in 30 states under several names, including Admiral Building Products, Bak-A-Lum, FlexMaster, and H. Verby. It is one of the nation's largest distributors of roofing materials for commercial use. Bradco also exports its construction materials to the Caribbean, Europe, Latin America, and the Middle East. In 2008 private equity firm Advent International acquired a majority interest in Bradco Supply from founder Barry Segal and his family.

Bradco Supply has been growing its network of building products distributors through acquisitions in recent years. In 2009 the company purchased Denver-based Premier Supply and New York-based Quality Roofing Supplies. It acquired Admiral Building Products, a major Firestone roofing materials distributor in New England, in early 2008. As part of their purchase agreements, the companies were allowed to continue operating under their own names.

Following the Advent transaction later in 2008, Admiral Building Products founder Ted Boylan joined Bradco Supply as its CEO. He succeeded the retiring Segal, who started Bradco Supply in 1966. Segal's sons Brad and Martin remain with the company as president and vice president, respectively. The Segal family retains a minority stake in the business.

EXECUTIVES

Chairman and CEO: Tom Karol
President: Bradley (Brad) Segal
CFO: Joe Stacy
VP Operations: John Morrison
VP Sales: Tom Adams
VP Acquisitions: Martin Segal
General Counsel: Michael L. Weinberger
Controller: John Gray
Manager Information Systems: Joe Hradil
Manager Human Resources: Gary Schneid
Manager Marketing: Paul Barsa

LOCATIONS

HQ: Bradco Supply Corp.
  34 Englehard Ave., Avenel, NJ 07001
Phone: 732-382-3400   **Fax:** 732-382-6577
Web: www.bradcosupply.com

PRODUCTS/OPERATIONS

Selected Subsidiaries

Admiral Building Products (roofing materials)
Bak-A-Lum (building materials, cabinets, countertops)
Bradco Metals (metal roofing systems)
Bradco Tapered Express (tapered roof design)
FlexMaster (building products)
Posey Steel & Supply (metals and building materials)
Quality Roofing Supply (roofing materials)

COMPETITORS

ABC Supply
Beacon Roofing
CRH
Guardian Building Products Distribution
Huttig Building Products
North Pacific Group
PrimeSource Building

HISTORICAL FINANCIALS

Company Type: Private

Income Statement				FYE: December 31
	REVENUE ($ mil.)	NET INCOME ($ mil.)	NET PROFIT MARGIN	EMPLOYEES
12/08	1,600	—	—	2,000
12/07	1,700	—	—	2,600
12/06	1,920	—	—	3,100
12/05	1,760	—	—	3,200
12/04	1,340	—	—	3,250
Annual Growth	4.5%	—	—	(11.4%)

Revenue History

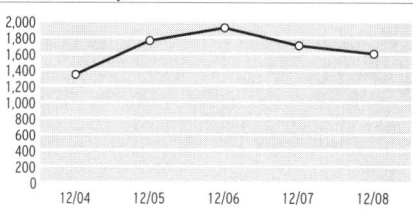

BrandsMart USA

The only thing that isn't big about Interbond Corporation of America (dba BrandsMart USA) is its geographic scope. The company runs five BrandsMart USA stores in South Florida and three in the Atlanta area that each stock more than $8 million in merchandise. BrandsMart USA discount stores sell a wide selection of brand-name consumer electronics, including appliances, camcorders, cameras, car stereos, computers, DVD players, home theater components, phones, printers, and TVs. BrandsMart USA also offers delivery and installation services and store-branded credit cards. Chairman Robert Perlman founded the company in 1977.

In 2008 the consumer electronics retailer launched a recycling service that allows consumers to exchange unwanted cell phones, MP3 players, cameras, gaming devices, global positioning systems, and car audio players for store gift cards through a partnership with Consumer Electronics Exchange.

BrandsMart USA stores are known for their brightly lit interiors and neon-colored price tags, as well as their noisy bustling atmospheres. The stores offer a "no lemon guarantee" that allows customers to have a product replaced if it experiences the same verified problem three times in six months. The price protection policy guarantees prices 30 days from date of purchase.

EXECUTIVES

Chairman: Robert Perlman
President: Michael Perlman
CFO: Eric Beazley
EVP: Lary Sinewitz
SVP Operations: Larry Levine
SVP White Goods: Randy Johnson
SVP Sales: Bobby Johnson
VP Marketing: Ellen Stevens
VP Sales, Atlanta: Harlan Russo
VP Human Resources: Janet Witczak
VP Merchandising: Angus Bryan
Chief Merchandising Marketing Officer:
 Richard Wallace
Auditors: Kaufman, Rossin & Co.

LOCATIONS

HQ: Interbond Corporation of America
 3200 SW 42nd St., Hollywood, FL 33312
Phone: 954-797-4000   **Fax:** 954-797-4061
Web: www.brandsmartusa.com

2008 Stores

	No.
Florida	5
Georgia	3
Total	**8**

COMPETITORS

Best Buy
Costco Wholesale
Fry's Electronics
Home Depot
RadioShack
Sears
Wal-Mart

Brasfield & Gorrie

If the South will rise again, Brasfield & Gorrie should have something to do with it. One of the leading construction companies in the Southeast, Brasfield & Gorrie builds high rises and hotels, bridges and churches, hospitals and malls. Other projects include industrial plants, water and wastewater treatment facilities, and schools. Commercial and industrial construction together account for most of its revenues; the company is a leading health care facilities contractor. Brasfield & Gorrie provides general contracting, design/build, and construction management services. Founded in 1922 by Thomas C. Brasfield, the company was sold to owner Miller Gorrie (chairman and CEO) in 1964.

Projects included the I-59/I-20 replacement bridge in Alabama that was destroyed in 2004 when a tanker truck carrying diesel fuel crashed and burned. Brasfield & Gorrie and the other contractors replaced the bridge almost a month ahead of schedule.

Brasfield & Gorrie has offices in Atlanta; Birmingham, Alabama; Nashville, Tennessee; Jacksonville and Orlando, Florida; and Raleigh, North Carolina.

EXECUTIVES

Chairman and CEO: M. Miller Gorrie, age 73
President: M. James (Jim) Gorrie
CFO: Randall J. Freeman
CIO: Tom Garrett
VP and COO: Jeffrey I. (Jeff) Stone
VP and General Counsel: Charles (Chip) Grizzle
VP and Director Career Development: Charles Mason
Director Operations: Marty Hardin
Corporate Marketing Director: Missy Heard
President, Corporate Planning and Administration:
 Jim Hughey
President, East Region: Rob Taylor
Auditors: PricewaterhouseCoopers

LOCATIONS

HQ: Brasfield & Gorrie, LLC
 3021 7th Ave. South, Birmingham, AL 35233
Phone: 205-328-4000   **Fax:** 205-251-1304
Web: www.brasfieldgorrie.com

PRODUCTS/OPERATIONS

Portfolio

Clubhouses
Education
Healthcare
Industrial
Mixed-Use
Multi-Family
Office
Parking
Religious
Retail
Sports & Leisure
Treatment

COMPETITORS

Alberici	Doster Construction
B. L. Harbert	Hardin Construction
Barton Malow	H.J. Russell
Batson-Cook	Hoar Construction
BE&K	McCarthy Building
Beck Group	Skanska USA Building
Bovis Lend Lease	Turner Corporation
Brice Building	Whiting-Turner
Choate Construction	

HISTORICAL FINANCIALS

Company Type: Private

Income Statement				FYE: December 31
	REVENUE ($ mil.)	NET INCOME ($ mil.)	NET PROFIT MARGIN	EMPLOYEES
12/08	2,140	—	—	3,200
12/07	2,006	—	—	3,000
12/06	1,980	—	—	2,939
12/05	1,645	—	—	2,743
12/04	1,260	—	—	2,267
Annual Growth	14.2%	—	—	9.0%

Revenue History

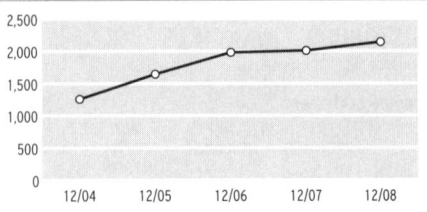

Brightstar Corp.

Brightstar shines in the constellation of telecommunications distributors. The company distributes wireless communications products, including cell phones and accessories, wireless data equipment, and prepaid wireless products. The company offers inventory management, logistics, fulfillment, customized packaging, and assembly services, as well as supply chain and reverse logistics services. It distributes cell phones made by the likes of Motorola, Kyocera, Samsung, LG, and Sony Ericsson. With operations in more than 40 countries, the company serves network operators, retailers, and resellers in the Americas, Europe, Asia, and the Asia/Pacific region. Brightstar was founded in 1997 by CEO Marcelo Claure.

The company has been expanding its presence across Europe through Brightstar Europe, a joint venture that it formed with computer products distributor Tech Data. The joint venture, also a distribution company, has been growing rapidly since its formation in 2008. In its first year, it expanded its operations into the Germany, commenced distribution of Microsoft's Windows Mobile product in Europe, and began offering Blackberry products and services to its European client base.

EXECUTIVES

Chairman, President, and CEO: R. Marcelo Claure
COO: Michael (Mike) Cost
CFO: Dennis Strand
CTO: David A. (Dave) Stritzinger
Chief Strategy Officer and Director:
 Andrew S. Weinberg
SVP and Corporate Controller: Arlene Vargas, age 39
VP, Global Marketing and Press Relations: Sally Lange
CEO, Brightstar US: Denise Gibson
President and COO US: Patrick Stokes
President, Brightstar Europe: Rod Millar
President, Brightstar Latin America:
 Juan Carlos Archila
President, Integrated Supply Chain Solutions:
 Harry Lagad
Auditors: Deloitte & Touche LLP

LOCATIONS

HQ: Brightstar Corp.
9725 NW 117th Ave., Ste. 300, Miami, FL 33178
Phone: 305-421-6000
Web: www.brightstarcorp.com

COMPETITORS

Axesstel
Brightpoint Inc.
CLST Holdings
Hello Direct
InfoSonics
Ingram Micro
Phones International
SED International
Tech Data
Telular
TESSCO
Tricell

HISTORICAL FINANCIALS

Company Type: Private

Income Statement

FYE: December 31

	REVENUE ($ mil.)	NET INCOME ($ mil.)	NET PROFIT MARGIN	EMPLOYEES
12/08	3,570	—	—	2,101
12/07	4,400	—	—	3,500
12/06	3,590	—	—	1,684
12/05	2,252	—	—	1,441
Annual Growth	16.6%			13.4%

Revenue History

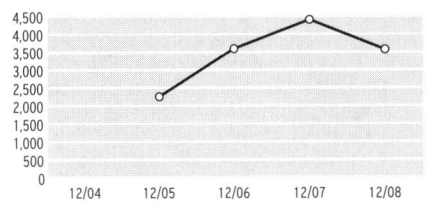

Broadcast Music, Inc.

If you are a composer or musician, Broadcast Music, Inc. (BMI) is here to see that your royalties are paid. The not-for-profit organization collects licensing fees from a host of outlets and venues (such as radio stations, TV programs, Web sites, restaurants, and nightclubs) and distributes them to the more than 375,000 songwriters, composers, and music publishers it represents. Its catalog of compositions includes more than 6.5 million works by a diverse range of artists including Carrie Underwood, the Foo Fighters, Shakira, Herbie Hancock, and Kanye West. BMI was founded in 1939.

BMI is working to eliminate online piracy and ensure that its clients get a cut of the proceeds when their music is downloaded on the Internet. The organization monitors music played over the Web and has created a digital licensing center to license music played online. BMI's New Media unit also makes deals related to the use of music in podcasts and mobile phone ringtones.

EXECUTIVES

Chairman: Cecil L. Walker
President, CEO, and Director: Del R. Bryant
EVP and COO: John Cody
SVP Licensing: Michael O'Neill
SVP Performing Rights: Alison Smith
SVP Government Relations: Fred Cannon
SVP Finance and CFO: Bruce Esworthy
SVP Operations and Information Technology: Milton T. (Milt) Loughlin
SVP Writer/Publisher Relations: Phillip R. Graham
SVP International: Ron Solleveld
SVP and General Counsel: Marvin Berenson
VP Corporate Planning: Jodi H. Saal
VP International Operations and Information Technology: Edward Oshanani
VP Legal Affairs: Joseph J. DiMona
VP Legal and Corporate Secretary: Stuart Rosen
Assistant VP Human Resources: Pat Belfield

LOCATIONS

HQ: Broadcast Music, Inc.
320 W. 57th St., New York, NY 10019
Phone: 212-586-2000   **Fax:** 212-245-8986
Web: www.bmi.com

PRODUCTS/OPERATIONS

Selected Artists Represented

The Beatles	Kid Rock
Black Eyed Peas	Little Richard
Chuck Berry	Jennifer Lopez
David Bowie	Marilyn Manson
Brooks & Dunn	matchbox twenty
James Brown	Tim McGraw
Dave Brubeck	Sarah McLachlan
Mariah Carey	Moby
Eric Clapton	Willie Nelson
Sheryl Crow	Santana
Dixie Chicks	Smash Mouth
Eagles	Sting
Eminem	Shania Twain
Elton John	

HISTORICAL FINANCIALS

Company Type: Not-for-profit

Income Statement

FYE: June 30

	REVENUE ($ mil.)	NET INCOME ($ mil.)	NET PROFIT MARGIN	EMPLOYEES
6/08	901	—	—	—
6/07	839	—	—	—
6/06	779	—	—	—
6/05	728	—	—	—
6/04	673	—	—	700
Annual Growth	7.6%	—	—	—

Revenue History

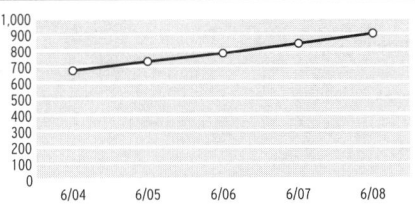

Broder Bros.

Selling clothes had been in the genes of sportswear distributor Broder Bros. for years. Begun as a haberdashery in 1919, it evolved from making hats and gloves into a leading distributor of imprintable sportswear distributing more than products under 35 retail brands, including adidas Golf, Champion, and Dickies, and private labels and operates under the Broder, Alpha, and NES divisions. Its private labels include Devon & Jones, Desert Wash, Harvard Square, and others. Customers, mostly small US retailers, order merchandise through seasonal catalogs or online. Private investment firm Bain Capital has held a majority interest of the company since May 2000, when the Broder family sold the firm.

In response to the weakening retail economy in the US, declining demand for its higher-priced products, and credit issues, Broder Bros. in late 2008 cut about 140 jobs in its distribution and call centers, as well as some management positions. In April 2009 the company began looking into strategic alternatives in an effort to iron out its liquidity troubles ahead of a looming debt deadline in the fall.

Since being acquired by Bain Capital, Broder Bros. has been busy adding to its portfolio. The company acquired the assets of Amtex Imports, a competitor based in Northlake, Illinois, for $6.8 million in September 2006.

The company caters to more than 75,000 customers. Clients include advertising specialty companies, screen printers, embroiderers, and specialty retailers that purchase Broder Bros. products (blank T-shirts, sweatshirts, polo shirts, outerwear, caps, bags, and more) to embellish for their clients.

EXECUTIVES

CEO and Director: Thomas (Tom) Myers, age 60, $355,223 total compensation
CFO: Martin J. (Marty) Matthews, age 37, $224,400 total compensation
EVP and COO: Norman (Norm) Hullinger, age 49, $226,600 total compensation
SVP Marketing: Girisha Chandraraj, age 34, $205,541 total compensation
VP Sales: Christopher Blakeslee, age 31
VP Merchandising: Andrea Engel
Marketing Communications Specialist: Kirwei Lo
Auditors: PricewaterhouseCoopers LLP

LOCATIONS

HQ: Broder Bros., Co.
6 Neshaminy Interplex, 6th Fl., Trevose, PA 19053
Phone: 215-291-6140   **Fax:** 800-521-1251
Web: www.broderbros.com

PRODUCTS/OPERATIONS

2008 Sales

	$ mil.	% of total
Alpha	448.1	48
Broder	362.1	39
NES	115.8	13
Total	**926.0**	**100**

2008 Sales

	% of total
Trade brands	79
Private-label brands	12
Exclusive or near-exclusive brands	9
Total	**100**

COMPETITORS

Anvil Holdings
Concept One Accessories
Delta Apparel
Fruit of the Loom
Gildan Activewear
Hanesbrands
PremiumWear
Russell Corporation
VF

HISTORICAL FINANCIALS

Company Type: Private

Income Statement

FYE: December 31

	REVENUE ($ mil.)	NET INCOME ($ mil.)	NET PROFIT MARGIN	EMPLOYEES
12/08	926	(69)	—	1,326
12/07	929	(124)	—	1,743
12/06	959	(8)	—	1,799
12/05	978	—	—	1,571
12/04	877	—	—	1,498
Annual Growth	1.4%	—	—	(3.0%)

2008 Year-End Financials

Debt ratio: —
Return on equity: —
Cash ($ mil.): —
Current ratio: —
Long-term debt ($ mil.): 380

Net Income History

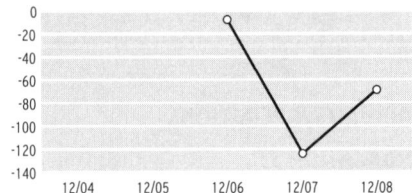

| 12/04 | 12/05 | 12/06 | 12/07 | 12/08 |

Brookshire Brothers

From its roots in East Texas, Brookshire Brothers operates more than 100 supermarkets and convenience stores from Louisiana to Central Texas. The regional grocery company primarily operates under the Brookshire Brothers banner, but some of its supermarkets operate under the B&B Foods name. Nearly all of the stores feature outlets selling Conoco gasoline (the company is one of Conoco's largest distributors). Brookshire Brothers is not affiliated with Brookshire Grocery of Tyler, Texas. The companies share a common ancestry dating back to 1921, but a split between the founding brothers in the late 1930s resulted in separate grocery chains. Formerly family-owned, the grocery chain is now 100% employee owned.

Convenience stores account for about 15% of the company's total sales. They operate under the Pick It Up banner. Brookshire Brothers acquired Polk Oil, the operator of some 30 Polk's Pick It Up convenience stores, in July 2007. Following the purchase, Brookshire Brothers launched a new super convenience-store format that offers fresh produce, meat, a pharmacy, and an in-store medical clinic. The super c-stores, which measure about 8,700 sq. ft., are located in areas too small to support a large supermarket. The company also operates Tobacco Barn outlets, which sell a variety of tobacco products.

In September 2009 Brookshire Brothers acquired Kaine's Grocery, the operator of a single store in Buna, Texas.

EXECUTIVES

Chairman: Milton Hixson
President, CEO, and Director: Jerry Johnson
COO, EVP Retail Operations, and Director: Jack Gabriel
SVP Distribution and Transportation: Edgar Burton
VP Marketing: Kevin Flanagan
VP Retail Operations: John Schumacher
Director Petroleum Marketing: Carl Polk
Director Payroll: Billie Warnasch
Director Public Relations: Gloria McDonald
District Director: John Alston
Director Personnel: Emily Watts

LOCATIONS

HQ: Brookshire Brothers, Ltd.
   1201 Ellen Trout Dr., Lufkin, TX 75904
Phone: 936-634-8155
Web: www.brookshirebrothers.com

PRODUCTS/OPERATIONS

2009 Stores

	No.
Brookshire Brothers	73
Pick It Up	29
Total	**102**

COMPETITORS

7-Eleven
Fiesta Mart
Foodarama Supermarkets
Gerland's Food Fair
H-E-B
Kroger
Randall's
Valero Energy
Wal-Mart

Brookshire Grocery

By selling staples, specialties, and Southern hospitality, Brookshire Grocery Co. has grown into a chain of about 155 Brookshire's, Super 1 Food, and Olé Foods supermarkets in Texas, Arkansas, Louisiana, and Mississippi. The company also owns three distribution centers, a dairy, and BGC Manufacturing, its private-label manufacturing unit. Brookshire's stores average about 40,000 sq. ft., while its warehouse-style Super 1 Foods stores average 80,000 sq. ft. More than 110 of Brookshire Grocery's stores have pharmacy departments. Originally part of the Brookshire Brothers grocery chain (dating back to 1921), the company split from it in 1939. The Brookshire family is still among the company's owners.

The regional grocery chain's fast-growing BGC Manufacturing (formerly South West Foods) business makes private-label goods for Brookshire stores under the Goldenbrook Farms, Food Club, Valu Time, and Full Circle brands. BGC began distributing LeCarb, a reduced-carbohydrate frozen dessert in 2001, eventually selling the brand to HP Hood. In early 2009 BGC launched another frozen confection, Supreme Blend, in organic and natural food stores nationwide. Dairy products contribute about $75 million of BGC Manufacturing's $88 million in annual sales.

To better compete with Wal-Mart Supercenters, among other rivals, the Texas grocer has added its own Health & Harmony line of organic and natural foods and other specialty food items, and is touting low prices. To that end, its newest store format is named ALPS (for Always Low Price Store) a discount-store prototype.

The regional grocer also seeks to please the state's sizable Hispanic population with a pair of Olé Foods stores, which cater to Hispanic shoppers. To court NASCAR fans, Brookshire Grocery operates an on-site track store in a tent at the Texas Motor Speedway.

CEO Marvin Massey retired in 2007. He was succeeded by Rick Rayford, a 35-year veteran and former EVP of Brookshire Grocery.

EXECUTIVES

CEO: Rick Rayford
EVP, CFO, and Controller: Tim King
SVP and Chief Marketing Officer: Rick Ellis
SVP and Category Management Officer: Randy Duke
SVP Corporate Development: Greg Nordyke
SVP and CIO: Gary Butler
SVP Super 1 Foods Division: Pete Leung
VP Category Management Grocery: Ron Oran
VP, Manufacturing: James (Jim) Pitner
VP, Distribution: Hugh Kirksey
VP Materials Management: Jerry Nick
VP, Corporate Asset Protection: Ed Van Fleet
VP and District Manager: Jerry Jarrard
President, Marketing Group: Brad Brookshire

LOCATIONS

HQ: Brookshire Grocery Company
   1600 W. South West Loop 323, Tyler, TX 75701
Phone: 903-534-3000   **Fax:** 903-534-2206
Web: www.brookshires.com

PRODUCTS/OPERATIONS

2009 Stores

	No.
Brookshire's Food Stores	124
Super 1 Foods	29
Olé Foods Stores	2
ALPS (Always Low Price Store)	1
Total	**156**

Selected Private-Label Brands

Brookshire's Meats (deli and other meats)
Dairy Pride (dairy products)
Economize (milk)
Flavor Pride (beverages)
Food Club (milk, dairy products, orange juice)
Full Circle (organic milk and orange juice)
Goldenbrook Farms (premium dairy and frozen foods)
Premier Mountain (water)
Tasty Bakery (baked goods)
Sunnybrook Farms (fresh produce)

COMPETITORS

Blue Bell
Dean Foods
E-Z Mart Stores
Fiesta Mart
H-E-B
Kmart
Kroger
Minyard Group
National Dairy Holdings
Randall's
SUPERVALU
Target
Wal-Mart
Whole Foods

Brookstone, Inc.

Need a putting green for the office? How about an alarm clock set to respond to your spoken commands? Then Brookstone is the place for you. It sells gifts, gadgets, and other doodads targeted primarily to men through more than 300 stores in more than 40 states, Washington, DC, and Puerto Rico. The company's functional yet unique product categories include audio and technology, health and fitness, home and office, and travel. Brookstone also sells its wares online and through its name-brand catalog. Because gifts contribute to most of its sales, the company operates temporary kiosks during the busy Father's Day and December holiday seasons. The company is owned by Osim International.

Brookstone is banking its success on the regular introduction of new and updated gizmos and gifts. To further this objective, the company plans to expand its selection of proprietary products and increase sales to corporate and wholesale customers.

To shore up its balance sheet amid the worldwide financial downturn, the retailer has been working to refocus its approach. Brookstone in 2008 cut back on purchases and advertising as consumer spending and traffic in US shopping malls has slowed. The company looks to further pare expenses in 2009 through payroll, advertising, and leases on commercial space.

With the demise of competitor Sharper Image, Brookstone in 2008 capitalized on the situation with a limited-time offer that gave holders of Sharper Image gift cards a 25% discount on items. (Sharper Image, now called TSIC, has since closed its retail stores, but continues to sell its products in other stores.)

CEO Lou Mancini resigned his position in early 2009, and EVP Philip Roizin stepped in to serve as interim president and chief executive. While conducting its search for a new leader, Brookstone said it will not exclude Roizin, who has served as the company's finance and administration EVP since 1996.

A consortium led by Singapore-based lifestyle products company Osim International acquired the company for nearly $420 million and took it private in 2005.

To stay competitive, Osim founder Ron Sim said his firm is "always on the lookout for more mergers and acquisitions" to complement its retail and lifestyle businesses. He hinted that Osim could be adding a sportswear brand.

EXECUTIVES

Chairman: Jackson P. Tai, age 58
President, CEO, and Director: Ronald D. (Ron) Boire, age 48
EVP Store Operations: George H. Sutherland, age 47
EVP Finance and Administration and CFO: Philip W. Roizin, age 50
SVP Business Development: Jim Rabbitt
VP Business Development: William Ellis, age 66
VP Marketing: Steven C. Strickland, age 45
VP Human Resources: Carol A. Lambert, age 54
VP and General Merchandising Manager: M. Rufus (Rudy) Woodard Jr., age 51
VP and General Manager Direct Marketing: Gregory B. (Greg) Sweeney, age 53
VP Distribution and Logistics and CIO: Steven P. Brigham
Auditors: Ernst & Young LLP

LOCATIONS

HQ: Brookstone, Inc.
1 Innovation Way, Merrimack, NH 03054
Phone: 603-880-9500 **Fax:** 603-577-8005
Web: www.brookstone.com

PRODUCTS/OPERATIONS

Selected Categories and Products

Audio and technology
 Audio
 Lighting
Health and fitness
 Bedding
 Footwear
 Home comfort
 Massagers
 Massage chairs
 Personal accessories
 Personal care
Home and office
 Backyard leisure
 Games
 Kitchen
 Stationery
Travel
 Auto/Tools
 Travel

COMPETITORS

Bed Bath & Beyond	Provide Gifts
Best Buy	RadioShack
Eddie Bauer llc	Relax the Back
Hammacher Schlemmer	Restoration Hardware
Levenger	SkyMall
L.L. Bean	TSIC
Neiman Marcus	Williams-Sonoma

HISTORICAL FINANCIALS

Company Type: Private

Income Statement

FYE: Saturday nearest December 31

	REVENUE ($ mil.)	NET INCOME ($ mil.)	NET PROFIT MARGIN	EMPLOYEES
12/08	497	(148)	—	—
12/07	563	6	1.1%	3,504
12/06	512	2	0.3%	3,278
12/05*	441	(4)	—	—
1/05	499	21	4.3%	3,016
Annual Growth	(0.1%)	—	—	5.1%

*Fiscal year change

2008 Year-End Financials

Debt ratio: —
Return on equity: —
Cash ($ mil.): —
Current ratio: —
Long-term debt ($ mil.): 174

Net Income History

Bureau of National Affairs

The Bureau of National Affairs (BNA) is a leading provider of legal and regulatory information. The company publishes advisory and research reports, books, newsletters, and other publications covering economic, health care, labor, public policy, and tax issues for professionals in business and government. It has a staff of 600 reporters, editors, and legal experts who gather information from around the country. BNA delivers its information online and through print and electronic products, some available through subscription services such as LexisNexis and Thomson Reuter's Westlaw. Founded in 1929, BNA was incorporated as an employee-owned company in 1946. It is the country's oldest fully employee-owned company.

BNA also produces financial planning and tax software (BNA Software), provides commercial printing services (McArdle Printing), and offers information for tax planning and compliance (Tax Management Inc.). Large law firms are BNA's largest market, and electronic products account for more than 70% of the company's legal and regulatory subscription offerings. BNA plans to complete the migration of its products to its next-generation Web platform, BWD, by the end of 2009.

The company's sales were not significantly affected by a weak economy in 2008, and BNA has continued to develop new products. That year it launched the commercial real estate law product, *Real Estate Law & Industry Report*, which provides news and analysis about the real estate market crash. Responding to a decline in the live conference business, BNA is focusing on its audio conference program, which produces more than 75 live events annually.

Also in 2008 the company merged two of its subsidiaries: Institute of Management and Administration (IOMA) and Kennedy Information, both of which provide information to management consultants, executive and corporate recruiters, and investor relations professionals. While products are continued to be marketed under the IOMA and Kennedy Information brands, the combined entity is legally known as BNA Subsidiaries, LLC. The merger was designed to reduce costs and increase operating efficiencies.

EXECUTIVES

Chairman and CEO: Paul N. Wojcik, age 60, $995,031 total compensation
President, COO, Publisher, Editor-in-Chief, and Director; President, Tax Management: Gregory C. McCaffery, age 48, $731,358 total compensation
VP, Corporate Secretary, and Director: Cynthia J. Bolbach, age 61
VP and CFO: Robert P. Ambrosini, age 52, $347,166 total compensation
VP Resource Management: Carol A. Clark, age 52, $449,911 total compensation
VP, General Counsel, and Director: Eunice L. Bumgardner, age 48, $347,166 total compensation
President, McArdle Printing: Lisa Arsenault
President, STF Services: Michael Smith
President, Kennedy Information and Institute of Management Administration (IOMA): Joseph Bremner
President, BNA International: Alan Edmunds
President, BNA Washington: Elizabeth (Betti) Brown
Controller: James R. Schneble, age 54
Treasurer: Gilbert S. Lavine, age 57
Auditors: BDO Seidman, LLP

LOCATIONS

HQ: The Bureau of National Affairs, Inc.
1801 S. Bell St., Arlington, VA 22202
Phone: 703-341-3000   **Fax:** 800-253-0332
Web: www.bna.com

PRODUCTS/OPERATIONS

Selected Subsidiaries and Brands

BNA International (international tax and legal information)
BNA Software (tax, financial planning, and fixed asset management software)
Institute of Management and Administration (information for management consultants, executive and corporate recruiters, and investor relations officers)
Kennedy Information (information for management consultants, executive and corporate recruiters, and investor relations officers)
The McArdle Printing (printing services)
Tax Management Inc. (taxation and financial accounting information)

Selected Products

Alternative Investment Law Report
Benefits Practice Center
BNA Corporate Tax Analyzer
Consulting
Health Law & Business Library
International HR Decision Support Network
North American Tax Handbook
Patent, Trademark, and Copyright Laws
Portfolios
Real Estate Law & Industry Report
World Climate Change Report

Selected Specialty Areas

Corporate law and business
Employee benefits
Employment and labor law
Environment, health and safety
Health care
Human resources
Intellectual property
Litigation
Tax and accounting

COMPETITORS

BLS	Inside Washington
CCH Incorporated	National Journal
EB	Reed Elsevier Group
H&R Block	Thomson Reuters
IHS	US Census Bureau
Informa	Wolters Kluwer

HISTORICAL FINANCIALS

Company Type: Private

Income Statement

FYE: December 31

	REVENUE ($ mil.)	NET INCOME ($ mil.)	NET PROFIT MARGIN	EMPLOYEES
12/08	352	31	8.9%	1,745
12/07	352	88	25.0%	1,719
12/06	345	20	5.7%	1,728
12/05	329	24	7.3%	1,729
12/04	321	23	7.0%	1,802
Annual Growth	2.3%	8.6%	—	(0.8%)

2008 Year-End Financials

Debt ratio: —
Return on equity: —
Cash ($ mil.): —
Current ratio: —
Long-term debt ($ mil.): 24

Net Income History

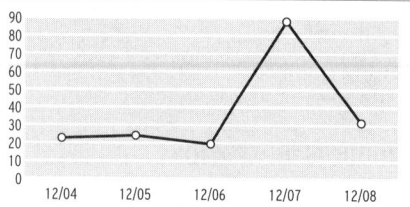

	12/04	12/05	12/06	12/07	12/08

Burlington Coat Factory Warehouse

Burlington Coat Factory Warehouse has two *de facto* mottos: "not affiliated with Burlington Industries" (thanks to a 1981 trademark-infringement lawsuit settlement) and "We sell more than coats." The company operates about 435 no-frills retail stores offering off-price current, brand-name clothing. Although it is one of the nation's largest coat sellers, the stores also sells children's apparel, bath items, furniture, gifts, jewelry, linens, and shoes. The business operates under the names Burlington Coat Factory (98% of sales), Cohoes Fashions, MJM Designer Shoes, and Super Baby Depot in some 45 states and Puerto Rico. Founded in 1972, Burlington is owned by affiliates of buyout firm Bain Capital.

Under the terms of the buyout, Bain Capital in 2006 acquired all of Burlington Coat Factory's outstanding shares for about $2.1 billion. (The family of founder Monroe Milstein owned about 62% of Burlington Coat Factory prior to the acquisition.)

Burlington Coat Factory's off-price niche is popular with consumers looking for bargains in today's tough economy. The company is locked in a competitive battle with TJX Companies (operator of the T.J. Maxx and Marshalls chains) and Ross Stores, both of which are larger than it is. To grow, and ideally steal market share from its larger rivals, Burlington Coat Factory is focusing on offering superior customer service and opening new stores in high-traffic locations.

As part of its growth plan, the firm recently acquired the leases for about two dozen former Value City Department Stores in Ohio, Pennsylvania, New Jersey, and Maryland and has reopened under the Burlington Coat Factory banner.

The retailer is best known for its year-round selection of about 10,000 to 20,000 discounted coats (compared to about 1,500 to 2,000 coats at the typical department store). Burlington Coat Factory takes less of a markup than its department store competition and has lower profit margins than other clothing retailers. It buys the coats early in the season (up to five months before department store rivals) to lock in lower prices.

The company has a new leader. Thomas Kingsbury in late 2008 was named president and CEO of Burlington Coat Factory Warehouse, succeeding Mark Nesci who retired. Prior to joining the company, Kingsbury was a SEVP at Kohl's.

HISTORY

Russian-Jewish immigrant Abe Milstein and a partner started coat wholesaler and manufacturer Milstein and Feigelson in 1924. Abe's son, Monroe, was a quick study. He graduated from New York University with a business degree in 1946 at age 19 and started his own coat and suit wholesaling business called Monroe G. Milstein, Inc. His mother provided free labor at her son's company six days a week to keep the business alive. Abe ended his partnership in 1953 and joined his son's business.

Family relations were strained temporarily in 1972, when Monroe disregarded his father's advice not to buy a faltering coat factory outlet store in Burlington, New Jersey. (Abe believed that his son did not have enough retailing experience.) Monroe, however, thought owning a retail store would provide a guaranteed sales outlet for their merchandise, and he bought Burlington Coat Factory for $675,000 (using $60,000 of his wife Henrietta's savings). His company also adopted the Burlington Coat Factory Warehouse moniker as its own.

To become less dependent on the season-specific coat business, the company soon expanded its merchandise mix by adding a children's division (started by Henrietta, deceased in 2001) and subleased departments. It opened a second store in Long Island, New York, in 1975.

Settling a trademark dispute with fabric maker Burlington Industries in 1981, Burlington Coat Factory agreed to say in advertising — as it does to this day — that the two companies are not affiliated. The 31-store company went public two years later, using the money it raised to open almost 30 stores that year. As part of its expansion in the 1980s, Burlington Coat Factory opened stores in warmer climates such as Texas and Florida.

The firm tried to grow through acquisitions that decade but failed in its attempts to buy a number of department store retailers. It made a successful bid in 1989 for New York discount retailer Cohoes.

Burlington Coat Factory's sales topped the $1 billion mark for the first time in fiscal 1993. Also that year the company bought Boston-based off-price family apparel chain Decelle. It then opened its first store outside the US (in Mexico) and tried new stand-alone store concepts based on successful in-store departments such as Luxury Linens and Baby Depot. A warm winter in 1994 hurt the company: Profits fell by two-thirds, and it sold off inventory for two years afterward.

The company pulled a line of men's parkas in late 1998 after a Humane Society investigation revealed that the coats were trimmed with hair from dogs killed inhumanely in China. Burlington Coat Factory launched a baby gift registry in 2000, and later that year opened a silk floral division in selected stores. In 2001 the company acquired 16 stores formerly occupied by bankrupt Montgomery Ward. Burlington Coat Factory began operating MJM Designer Shoes in fiscal 2002, opening nine of the stand-alone specialty shoe stores. The company closed its Decelle stores in 2003 but converted most of them to the Burlington Coat Factory and Cohoes names while launching 25 new stores in 2004 (most under the Burlington Coat Factory moniker).

In 2005 the company opened two Super Baby Depot stores. Burlington Coat Factory was acquired by the Boston-based private equity firm Bain Capital Partners in April 2006 for about $2.1 billion.

In fiscal year 2006 the company opened three MJM Designer Shoes stores. The company's two stand-alone Luxury Linens stores were shut down and instead operate as departments within Burlington Coat Factory stores.

In December 2008 Thomas Kingsbury was named president and CEO of Burlington Coat Factory Warehouse, succeeding Mark Nesci who retired after 37 years with the retailer. Prior to joining the company, Kingsbury was a SEVP at Kohl's.

EXECUTIVES

President, CEO, and Director:
Thomas A. (Tom) Kingsbury, age 56, $1,606,000 total compensation
EVP and CFO: Todd Weyhrich, age 46, $979,595 total compensation
CTO: Michael (Mike) Prince
EVP Stores: Fred Hand, $915,983 total compensation
EVP and Chief Accounting Officer: Marc D. Katz, age 44, $965,058 total compensation
EVP, General Counsel, and Secretary: Paul C. Tang, age 56
EVP Supply Chain: Charles (Charlie) Guardiola, $729,959 total compensation
SVP Information Systems: Brad H. Friedman
VP Store Planning: Gerry Incollingo
VP Stores: Evanne Cuccorelli
VP Advertising: H. Robert Greenbaum
VP Fashion and Branding: Jason Somerfield
VP e-Learning and Task Management: Gloria Johnson
VP Logistics: Lorenzo Figueroa
VP Operations and Administration:
Albert (Al) Cuccorelli
VP Real Estate: Robert Grapski, age 57
VP Recruiting: Sarah Orleck
VP Baby Depot: David Cestaro
VP Facilities Management: Jerry Lupia
VP, Chief Accounting Officer, and Treasurer:
Robert L. (Bob) LaPenta Jr., age 55

Chief Marketing Officer: Garry Graham
Director Human Resources: Judy Mascio
Auditors: Deloitte & Touche LLP

LOCATIONS

HQ: Burlington Coat Factory Warehouse Corporation
1830 Rte. 130 N., Burlington, NJ 08016
Phone: 609-387-7800 **Fax:** 609-387-7071
Web: www.burlingtoncoatfactory.com

PRODUCTS/OPERATIONS

2009 Stores

	No.
Burlington Coat Factory Warehouse	415
MJM Designer Shoes	15
Cohoes Fashions	2
Super Baby Depot	1
Total	**433**

Selected Store Banners

Burlington Coat Factory Warehouse (off-price clothing, accessories, linens, bath items, gifts)
Cohoes Fashions (upscale apparel and accessories)
MJM Designer Shoes (designer and fashion shoes)
Super Baby Depot (accessories, clothes, furniture for babies and toddlers)

COMPETITORS

Babies "R" Us	Nordstrom
Bed Bath & Beyond	Payless ShoeSource
Belk	Retail Ventures
Bon-Ton Stores	Ross Stores
Dillard's	Saks
Dress Barn	Sears
DSW	Stein Mart
Filene's Basement	Syms
J. C. Penney	Target
Kohl's	TJX Companies
Macy's	Wal-Mart

HISTORICAL FINANCIALS

Company Type: Private

Income Statement

	REVENUE ($ mil.)	NET INCOME ($ mil.)	NET PROFIT MARGIN	EMPLOYEES
5/08	3,424	(49)	—	26,580
5/07	3,442	(47)	—	28,005
5/06	3,439	67	1.9%	26,500
5/05	3,200	106	3.3%	25,000
5/04	2,878	68	2.3%	24,000
Annual Growth	4.4%	—	—	2.6%

FYE: Saturday nearest May 31

2008 Year-End Financials

Debt ratio: 457.5%   Current ratio: —
Return on equity: —   Long-term debt ($ mil.): 1,480
Cash ($ mil.): —

Net Income History

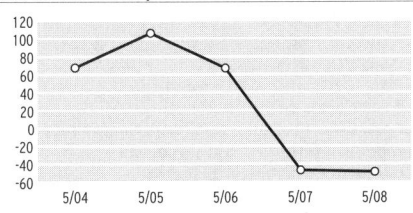

Burns & McDonnell

It may sound like a law firm, but Burns & McDonnell provides construction services, not legal advice. A top design/build firm in the US, the company provides engineering, architectural, construction, environmental remediation, and consulting services. It is one of the leading constructors of electric transmission and distribution infrastructure, airports, and fossil fuel and chemical plants. The company also serves the government, manufacturing, health care, and water and wastewater sectors, among others. Burns & McDonnell has about 20 offices throughout the US.

The company was founded in Kansas City in 1898 by Clinton Burns and Robert McDonnell. The employee-owned firm's first major project (secured in 1900) was a combined water and light plant for Iola, Kansas.

EXECUTIVES

Chairman, President, and CEO: Greg M. Graves, age 51
SVP and General Manager, Infrastructure Group:
James (Jim) Foil
VP and Chief Administrative Officer: Denny Scott
VP, Treasurer, and CFO: Mark Taylor
VP and CTO: Greg Gould
VP, Environmental Group: Stephen (Steve) Linneman
VP, Business and Technology Services Group: Jeff Greig
Associate VP Human Resources: Melissa Wood
President, Energy Group: Ray Kowalik
President, Regional Office Group: Paul Fischer
President, Process and Industrial Group:
John E. Nobles
President, Aviation and Facilities Group:
David Yeamans
President, Electrical Transmission and Distribution Group: Walt Womack
President, Construction Group and Director:
Don Greenwood
Director Corporate Safety and Health: Robert Coker
Director Corporate Marketing: H. Joseph (Joe) Brooks

LOCATIONS

HQ: Burns & McDonnell, Inc.
9400 Ward Pkwy., Kansas City, MO 64114
Phone: 816-333-9400   **Fax:** 816-822-3412
Web: www.burnsmcd.com

COMPETITORS

Bechtel
Black & Veatch
Burns and Roe
Fluor
Foster Wheeler
HNTB Companies
Jacobs Engineering
Michael Baker
Parsons Corporation
Sargent & Lundy
Shaw Group
Terracon
URS
Washington Division

California Dairies Inc.

Herding dairies to give them greater "ag"-gregate strength has made California Dairies one of the largest dairy cooperatives in the US. California Dairies' 620 members provide the co-op with more than 18 billion pounds of milk a year. Its plants process milk, cheese, butter, and powdered milk. California Dairies' subsidiaries include Challenge Dairy Products (retail, foodservice, and ingredient products) and Los Banos Foods (cheddar cheese ingredients for food manufacturing). California Dairies is also a majority owner of DairyAmerica, which markets dairy products, including some 60% of all the milk powder produced in the US. The company exports its products to some 40 countries worldwide.

California Dairies was formed as the result of the 1999 merger of three California dairy cooperatives — California Milk Producers, Danish Creamery Association, and San Joaquin Valley Dairymen. In addition to its headquarters in Visalia, California, the co-op operates five production plants in the state.

EXECUTIVES

Chairman: George Borba
First Vice Chairman: Tony Mendes
Second Vice Chairman: Gerben Leyendekker
President and CEO: Richard L. Cotta
Treasurer and Director: Duane Matheron
Secretary and Director: Steve Maddox

LOCATIONS

HQ: California Dairies Inc.
2000 N. Plaza Dr., Visalia, CA 93291
Phone: 559-625-2200   **Fax:** 559-625-5433
Web: www.californiadairies.com

PRODUCTS/OPERATIONS

Selected Products
Bulk butter
Milk powder
  Dry buttermilk
    Extra grade sweet cream
    Grade A sweet cream
  Dry whole milk
    Extra grade 26%
    Extra grade 28.5%
  Non-fat dry milk
    Extra grade low heat
    Extra grade medium heat
    Extra grade high heat
    Grade A low heat
    Grade A medium heat
    Grade A high heat

COMPETITORS

Agri-Mark	Foremost Farms
Agropur Cooperative	Foster Dairy Farms
Associated Milk Producers	Humboldt Creamery
Berkeley Farms	J.M. Swank
Dairy Farmers of America	Kraft Food Ingredients
Dairy Manufacturers	Land O'Lakes
Danisco A/S	Main Street Ingredients
Darifair Foods	Nestlé
Darigold, Inc.	Northwest Dairy
Dean Foods	Schreiber Foods
Denali Flavors	Sodiaal
Emmi	

HISTORICAL FINANCIALS
Company Type: Cooperative

Income Statement				FYE: April 30
	REVENUE ($ mil.)	NET INCOME ($ mil.)	NET PROFIT MARGIN	EMPLOYEES
4/08	3,500	—	—	755

California Physicians' Service

California Physicians' Service, which operates as Blue Shield of California, provides health insurance products and related services to some 3.4 million members in the state of California. The not-for-profit mutual organization's health insurance products include HMO, PPO, dental, and Medicaid or Medicare supplemental plans for individuals, families, and employer groups. Accidental death and dismemberment, executive medical reimbursement, life insurance, vision, and short-term health plans are provided by the company's Blue Shield of California Life & Health Insurance subsidiary. Blue Shield of California has more than 20 locations across California.

Blue Shield of California is an independent Blue Cross and Blue Shield Association member. The company was established in 1939 by the California Medical Association House of Delegates. The company's provider network has grown to include some 65,000 primary and specialty physicians and 350 hospitals. Blue Shield of California is growing its patient wellness programs to promote preventative care; it is also improving its information technology systems.

In 2009 the company scaled back its coverage under the Federal Employee Health Benefits Program. It exited coverage in northern California, but will continue to cover federal employees residing in Tulare County.

The company has come under fire from California agencies and lawmakers, including the Los Angeles city attorney, for the alleged improper rescinding of customer policies after they become ill. It settled charges with California's Department of Insurance by agreeing to reinstate nearly 700 consumer policies in 2009.

EXECUTIVES

Chairman, President, and CEO: Bruce G. Bodaken
SVP and Chief Medical Officer: Meredith Mathews
EVP and COO: Paul Markovich
EVP and CFO: Heidi Fields, age 54
SVP and CIO: Elinor C. MacKinnon
SVP and Chief Executive, Individual, Small Group, and Government Business Unit: Karen Vigil
SVP Human Resources: Marianne Jackson
SVP Customer Operations: Rob Geyer
SVP, General Counsel, and Secretary: Seth A. Jacobs
SVP Mid/Large and Specialty Benefits Business Unit: David S. Joyner
SVP Network Management: Juan Davila
SVP and Chief Actuary: Edward C. (Ed) Cymerys
SVP Labor and Public and Strategic Accounts; SVP, CalPERS: Janet Widmann
VP Public Affairs: Tom Epstein
President and CEO, Blue Shield of California Foundation: Crystal Hayling

LOCATIONS

HQ: California Physicians' Service
50 Beale St., San Francisco, CA 94105
Phone: 415-229-5000   **Fax:** 415-229-5070
Web: www.blueshieldca.com

PRODUCTS/OPERATIONS

Selected Products
Health Plans
  Access+HMO
  Active Start
  Balance
  Dental HMO
  Dental PPO
  Essential
  Healthy Families
  Medicare Advantage
  Medicare Supplement
  Shield Savings
  Shield Spectrum PPO
  Vital Shield
  Vital Shield Plus
Other Plans
  Accidental death and dismemberment
  Group term life
  Individual term life
  Vision

COMPETITORS

Aetna
Alameda Alliance for Health
CIGNA
Community Health Group
Delta Dental Plan
Health Net of California
Kaiser Foundation Health Plan
L. A. Care Health Plan
Molina Healthcare
SCAN Health Plan
Sharp Health Plan
UnitedHealth Group
WellPoint

HISTORICAL FINANCIALS
Company Type: Not-for-profit

Income Statement				FYE: December 31
	REVENUE ($ mil.)	NET INCOME ($ mil.)	NET PROFIT MARGIN	EMPLOYEES
12/08	8,898	307	3.5%	4,800
12/07	8,364	318	3.8%	4,500
12/06	8,150	382	4.7%	4,500
12/05	7,519	330	4.4%	4,300
12/04	6,846	334	4.9%	—
Annual Growth	6.8%	(2.1%)	—	3.7%

Net Income History

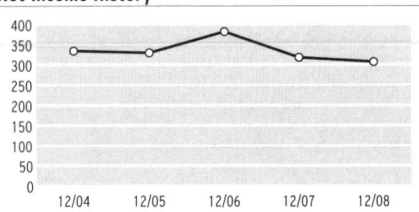

California State Board of Equalization

All things being equal, the California State Board of Equalization has a corner on the gold in the Golden State. The board administers the state's tax and fee programs, including sales and usage, property, and special taxes, which together provide about one-third of the state's annual tax revenue. The board-administered monies support state and local government programs and services in corrections and social welfare, hospital and health care, housing, law enforcement, natural resource management, schools and universities, and transportation. The board operates roughly 25 field offices throughout California and out-of-state offices in Chicago, Houston, and New York City.

Members of the board, who serve concurrent four-year terms, constitute the US's only elected tax commission. One member is elected from each of California's four Equalization Districts. The state controller also gets a seat. The Board of Equalization's executive director is appointed by the five board members and directs more than 3,800 agency employees.

EXECUTIVES

Chair: Judy Chu
Vice Chair: Betty T. Yee
Executive Director: Ramon J. Hirsig
Chief, Financial Management Division: Caroline Cabias
CIO, Technology Services Division: Anna Brannen
Chief, Excise Taxes Division: Lynn Bartolo
Chief, Tax Policy Division: Jeff McGuire
Chief, Human Resources Division: Lisa Fien
Chief, Investigations Division: Gilbert Haas Jr.
Chief, Legislative Research Division: Margaret S. Shedd
Chief, Fuel Taxes Division: Edward King
Chief, Administrative Support Division: Charlene Yount
Chief Counsel: Kristine Cazadd

LOCATIONS

HQ: California State Board of Equalization
450 N St., Sacramento, CA 95814
Phone: 916-445-6362　　**Fax:** 916-324-3984
Web: www.boe.ca.gov

California State University System

California State University (CSU) turns students into teachers. The university traces its roots to the state's teaching colleges and trains the majority of California's teachers and staff. CSU is neck-and-neck with the State University of New York (SUNY) as the nation's largest university system. And it's growing. CSU's enrollment has ballooned to about 450,000. Those students are spread out among CSU's 23 campuses in cities such as Bakersfield, Los Angeles, San Francisco, and San Jose. CSU primarily awards bachelor's and master's degrees in nearly 360 subject areas, leaving most higher levels of study to the University of California (UC) system.

In 2007 CSU got into the business of handing out PhD's when it launched its own independent education doctorate program.

CSU has been developing strategies to cope with an expected enrollment increase of about 40% through 2010 — what it calls Tidal Wave II. The first waves started with more than 20,000 additional students flooding the system in the fall of 2001. To battle the crippling influx of new students, CSU began offering distance education programs, which teach students via teleconferencing and the Internet. Other strategies involve adding a summer semester to create year-long schooling, and expanding the use of off-campus centers.

However, in 2008 skyrocketing enrollment and limited state funding caught up with the system and CSU announced plans to reduce its enrollment by accepting some 10,000 fewer students for the 2009-10 school year. Other university programs also are on the chopping block as CSU faces a $50 million budget reduction.

HISTORY

In 1862 San Francisco's Normal School, a training center for elementary teachers, became California's first state-founded school for higher education. Six students attended its first classes, but there were 384 by 1866. It later moved to San Jose to escape the bustle of San Francisco.

In the late 1880s State Normal Schools opened in Chico, San Diego, and San Francisco, followed in 1901 by California State Polytechnic Institute, which offered studies in agriculture, business, and engineering. Other new colleges included Fresno State (1911) and Humboldt State (1913). Most of the schools offered four-year programs and admitted any student with eight years of grammar school education.

The Normal Schools were renamed Teachers Colleges in 1921 to reflect their role in teacher education. Two years later the colleges began awarding bachelor of arts degrees in education.

In 1935 the schools were renamed State Colleges and expanded into liberal arts. In 1947 they were authorized to confer master's degrees in education.

After WWII, students on the GI Bill helped increase enrollment, and campuses opened in Los Angeles, Sacramento, and Long Beach. The prospect of the first baby boomers reaching college age prompted the founding of more campuses in the late 1950s. Russia's 1957 launch of Sputnik spurred additional focus on science and math at all education levels. The next year the colleges began awarding master's degrees in subjects unrelated to teacher education.

During the Red Scare, the system's first chancellor, Buell Gallagher, was accused by the press of being soft on communism. Other faculty were subpoenaed to appear before the House Committee on Un-American Activities.

In 1961 the system became the California State Colleges (CSC) and the board of trustees was created, giving the schools more independence from state government. In 1969 student and faculty groups seeking ethnic studies departments went on strike in San Francisco; the unrest closed the campus.

In 1972 CSC became known as the California State University and Colleges. Ten years later it adopted California State University as its name.

Barry Munitz became chancellor in 1991, taking over a system that had become oppressive due to a heavy-handed administration. Munitz, who came from corporate America, brought his business sense to the university and increased private fund raising, among other activities. He used words like "consumer" and "product" to describe his job. Munitz also increased tuition, which caused enrollments to drop from 1991-1995.

CSU added two new campuses in 1995, including CSU Monterey Bay, the first military base to be converted into a university since the end of the Cold War.

In 1997 Charles Reed was named to replace Munitz as chancellor, effective the following year. That year CSU proposed the California Educational Technology Initiative (CETI), a plan to build high-speed computer and telephone networks linking its campuses. CETI failed in 1998 after Microsoft and other investors pulled out. In 1999, after lengthy contract negotiations between Reed and faculty members failed to produce accord over teacher salaries and employment conditions, Reed imposed his own merit-based plan. The faculty responded with official rebukes and a vote of no confidence in Reed. The two sides eventually settled on a new three-year contract with provisions that salary and benefits may be negotiated annually.

The rancor over pay continued in 2000 when the California Faculty Association issued a report claiming women were discriminated against and the merit system was inherently unfair. CSU issued its own report denying the charges. In 2001 Reed, stirring up more controversy, began a new quest that would allow CSU to offer doctorate degrees. The move was bitterly opposed by the competing University of California system. In 2002 CSU started a program funded by a federal grant to reduce the harmful effects of alcohol on its students.

EXECUTIVES

Chair: Jeffrey L. Bleich
Vice Chair: Herbert L. Carter
Chancellor: Charles B. Reed, age 68
Chief of Staff: William Dermody
Executive Vice Chancellor and Chief Academic Officer:
Gary W. Reichard
Executive Vice Chancellor and CFO: Richard P. West
Vice Chancellor Business and Finance:
Benjamin F. Quillian Jr.
Vice Chancellor Human Resources: Gail E. Brooks
Vice Chancellor University Relations and Advancement:
Garrett P. Ashley
Associate Vice Chancellor Academic Affairs:
Keith O. Boyum
Assistant Vice Chancellor, Federal Relations: Jim Gelb
Assistant Vice Chancellor Public Affairs: Claudia Keith
Assistant Vice Chancellor, Advocacy and Institutional Relations: Karen Yelverton-Zamarripa
General Counsel: Christine Helwick, age 62
University Auditor: Larry Mandel
Communications Specialist, Office of the Chancellor:
Teresa Ruiz
Auditors: KPMG LLP

LOCATIONS

HQ: California State University System
    401 Golden Shore St., Long Beach, CA 90802
Phone: 562-951-4000   **Fax:** 562-951-4956
Web: www.calstate.edu

California State University Campuses

California Maritime Academy
California Polytechnic State University, San Luis Obispo
California State Polytechnic University, Pomona
California State University
  Bakersfield
  Channel Islands
  Chico
  Dominguez Hills
  East Bay
  Fresno
  Fullerton
  Long Beach
  Los Angeles
  Monterey Bay
  Northridge
  Sacramento
  San Bernardino
  San Marcos
  Stanislaus
Humboldt State University
San Diego State University
San Francisco State University
San Jose State University
Sonoma State University

PRODUCTS/OPERATIONS

Selected Majors

Agriculture
Anthropology
Asian studies
Business administration
Chemistry
Communications
Computer science
Economics
Education
History
Latin American studies
Mathematics
Nursing
Philosophy
Physics
Psychology
Public administration
Theater arts

California Steel Industries

California Steel Industries (CSI) doesn't use forensic evidence, but its work does involve a steel slab. The company uses steel slab produced by third parties to manufacture steel products such as hot-rolled and cold-rolled steel, galvanized coils and sheets, and electric resistance weld (ERW) pipe. Its customers include aftermarket automotive manufacturers, oil and gas producers, roofing makers, tubing manufacturers, and building suppliers. CSI serves the western region of the US. The company operates slitting, shearing, coating, and single-billing services for third parties. Japan's JFE Holdings and Brazilian iron ore miner Companhia Vale do Rio Doce (Vale) each own 50% of CSI.

It buys more than two-thirds of its steel slab from ArcelorMittal subsidiary Lazaro Cardenas, in Mexico; ArcelorMittal Tubarão, in Brazil; and Australia's Bluescope Steel. The purchased slab is transported to the Port of Los Angeles and then sent by train to CSI's facilities. Effectively all of its products are sold within the US.

EXECUTIVES

Chairman: Masakazu Kurushima, age 60, $211,625 total compensation
President and CEO: Vicente Wright, age 56, $254,736 total compensation
EVP Finance and CFO: Ricardo Bernandes, age 45, $366,846 total compensation
EVP Operations: Toshiyuki (Ted) Tamai, age 57, $335,604 total compensation
VP Administration and Corporate Secretary: Brett Guge, age 54, $402,525 total compensation
Manager Communications: Kyle Schulty
Auditors: Ernst & Young LLP

LOCATIONS

HQ: California Steel Industries, Inc.
    14000 San Bernardino Ave., Fontana, CA 92335
Phone: 909-350-6200   **Fax:** 909-350-6398
Web: www.californiasteel.com

PRODUCTS/OPERATIONS

2008 Production

	% of total
Hot Rolled	36
Galvanized	34
Electric Resistance Welded (ERW) pipe	20
Cold Rolled	10
Total	**100**

COMPETITORS

AK Steel Holding Corporation
Evraz Inc
Nucor
O'Neal Steel
Steel Dynamics
Steelscape
Ternium Mexico
USS-POSCO Industries

HISTORICAL FINANCIALS

Company Type: Joint venture

Income Statement			FYE: December 31	
	REVENUE ($ mil.)	NET INCOME ($ mil.)	NET PROFIT MARGIN	EMPLOYEES
12/08	1,511	13	0.9%	911
12/07	1,283	(1)	—	933
12/06	1,359	109	8.0%	931
12/05	1,234	43	3.5%	938
12/04	1,257	109	8.7%	944
Annual Growth	4.7%	(40.9%)	—	(0.9%)

2008 Year-End Financials

Debt ratio: 59.0%
Return on equity: —
Cash ($ mil.): —

Current ratio: —
Long-term debt ($ mil.): 185

Net Income History

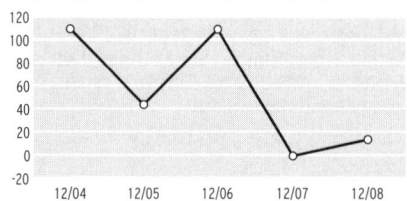

Callison Architecture

Callison Architecture provides services such as architectural design, consulting, graphic and interior design, and master planning for retail, mixed-use, multifamily residential, hospitality, health care, and corporate projects all over the world. The company, founded in 1975, also has a division dedicated to consulting and technical audit services for data centers and mission-critical facilities. A new real estate analysis and planning service was added in 2007. Callison's US clients have included Boeing, The Gap, Hewlett-Packard, Microsoft, NIKE, Nordstrom, Starwood Hotels and Resorts, and Washington Mutual.

International clients include the Bank of China, Harrods (UK), Mass Transit Railway Corporation (Hong Kong), IKEA (Sweden), Falabella Department Store (Chile), The Seibu Department Stores (Japan), LG Department Stores (Korea), and Central Pattana (Thailand).

Callison has offices around the world including Dallas, London, Los Angeles, New York, Seattle, and Shanghai. The company opened an office in Mexico City in 2007 after acquiring AGI Mexico — a small, full-service design firm.

World Architecture magazine ranked Callison as the top retail design firm in the US in 2008, a position which the company has held since 2003.

EXECUTIVES

Chairman: Robert J. (Bob) Tindall
President: John T. Bierly
COO: Tom Bahn
CFO: Craig Parker
EVP: Paula Stafford
EVP: Steven E. Epple
Managing Director: Leigh Dennis
Principal-in-Charge, Retail Mixed-Use Studio: Stephen L. (Steve) Dwoskin
Principal-in-Charge, International and Commercial Markets: William F. (Bill) Gartz
Principal: Michael Hebrant
Principal; Director Design, Callison Shanghai: Zivko Penzar
Marketing and Communications Director: Kipepeo Brown
President, Callison Real Estate Strategies: Yves Mizrahi

LOCATIONS

HQ: Callison Architecture, Inc.
    1420 5th Ave., Ste. 2400, Seattle, WA 98101
Phone: 206-623-4646   **Fax:** 206-623-4625
Web: www.callison.com

Callison Architecture has principal US offices in Seattle, New York, and Santa Monica, California. It has international offices in London and Shanghai.

PRODUCTS/OPERATIONS

Selected Services

Architecture
Feasibility and development analysis
Fixture design
Graphic design
Interior design
Landlord services
Master planning
Medical planning
Operational analysis
Program management
Programming
Purchasing
Real estate consulting
Sustainable design
Tenant strategy and planning
Visual merchandising
Workplace consulting

CalPERS

California's public-sector retirees already have a place in the sun; CalPERS gives them the money to enjoy it. CalPERS is the California Public Employees' Retirement System, the largest public pension system in the US. It manages retirement and health plans for nearly 2 million beneficiaries (employees, retirees, and their dependents) from more than 2,500 government agencies and school districts. Although the system's beneficiaries are current or former employees of the Golden State, CalPERS brings its influence to bear in all 50 states and beyond.

With more than $190 billion in assets in its investment funds, CalPERS uses its clout to sway such corporate governance issues as company performance, executive compensation, and even social policy. In the absence of a strong federal effort to purge corporations of corruption, CalPERS has often acted as a force for reform, urging companies to remove conflicts of interest and make themselves more accountable to shareholders, employees, and the public. CalPERS is also a powerful negotiator for such services as insurance; rates established by the system serve as benchmarks for employers throughout the nation.

Most of CalPERS' revenue comes from its enormous investment program: It has interests in US and foreign securities, oil and energy, real estate, and even hedge funds and venture capital activities. CalPERS has steadily increased its investments in private equity, looking to take ownership stakes in more firms. It owns stake in such prestigious entities as The Carlyle Group, Apollo Management, and Blackstone.

Fred Buenrostro retired as CEO in 2008. Anne Stausboll, who'd been serving as CalPERS' interim chief investment officer and was previously California's Chief Deputy Treasurer, was named his successor. She is the fund's first female CEO.

Shortly after Buenrostro's retirement, CalPERS reported one of its worst performances in years, partly due to its investments in undeveloped land earlier in the decade.

Troubles continued in 2009. CalPERS had nearly a quarter of its assets wiped out due to the collapse of the market. In order to cover the losses, CalPERS proposed a plan to have cities and counties make higher contributions to the system. CalPERS also sued three credit rating agencies in 2009 — blaming them for a big chunk of its losses.

During the coming years CalPERS may be forced to sell assets, as it is expected to be hit with a wave of early retirements by middle-aged workers. The fund plans to sell some of its US stocks, which have been declining, in exchange for emerging markets such as India and China.

CalPERS' board consists of six elected, three appointed, and four designated members (director of the state's Department of Personnel Administration, state controller, state treasurer, and a member of the State Personnel Board).

HISTORY

The state of California founded CalPERS in 1931 to administer a pension fund for state employees. By the 1940s the system was serving other public agencies and educational institutions on a contract basis.

When the Public Employees' Medical and Hospital Care Act was passed in 1962, CalPERS added health coverage. The fund was conservatively managed in-house, with little exposure to stocks. Despite slow growth, the state used the system's funds to meet its own cash shortfalls.

CalPERS became involved in corporate governance issues in the mid-1980s, when California treasurer Jesse Unruh became outraged by corporate greenmail schemes. In 1987 he hired as CEO Wisconsin pension board veteran Dale Hanson, who led the movement for corporate accountability to institutional investors.

In the late 1980s CalPERS moved into real estate and Japanese stocks. When both crashed around 1990, Hanson came under pressure. CalPERS was twice forced to take major writedowns for its real estate holdings and turned to expensive outside fund managers, but its investment performance deteriorated and member services suffered.

Legislation in 1990 enabled CalPERS to offer long-term health insurance. Governor Pete Wilson's 1991 attempt to use $1.6 billion from CalPERS to help meet a state budget shortfall resulted in legislation banning future raids. CalPERS made its first direct investment in 1993, an energy-related infrastructure partnership with Enron.

CalPERS suffered in the 1994 bond crash. That year Hanson resigned amid criticism that his focus on corporate governance had depressed fund performance. The system moved to an indexing strategy.

In 1996 the system teamed with the Asian Development Bank to invest in the Asia/Pacific region; it took a major hit in the Asian financial crisis the next year, but used the downturn as an opportunity to expand its position there in undervalued stocks. In 1998 CalPERS pressured foreign firms to adopt more transparent financial reporting methods.

In 2000 CalPERS said it would sell off more than $500 million in tobacco holdings; it then invested the same amount in five biotech funds, its first foray into the sector.

In 2001 California state controller and CalPERS board member Kathleen Connell successfully sued the system for not following state-sanctioned rules regarding pay increases. CalPERS was forced to cut salaries for investment managers, a move that prompted chief investment officer Daniel Szente to resign.

In 2003 CalPERS agreed to a record $250 million settlement relating to an age-discrimination suit brought by the Equal Employment Opportunity Commission. Also that year CalPERS clamored for (and got) the resignation of New York Stock Exchange (NYSE) chairman Richard Grasso. CalPERS and others claimed Grasso's pay of $140 million a year made it impossible for him to effectively monitor the exchange's member companies for corruption.

CalPERS found itself on the receiving end of a corporate governance issue in 2004 when a media group sued, demanding CalPERS make public the fees it pays to venture capital firms and hedge funds. CalPERS settled the suit by disclosing the fees.

Also in 2004 the president of CalPERS' board, Sean Harrigan, was ousted when the State Personnel Board voted to remove him as its representative. Harrigan had drawn the ire of the business community because of his labor ties and because, under his leadership, the board had withheld votes for directors of most of the companies in which CalPERS invests.

EXECUTIVES

CEO: Anne Stausboll, age 52
President, Board of Administration: Rob Feckner
Chief Office Governmental Affairs: Melanie Moreno
Chief Actuary: Ronald L. (Ron) Seeling
Chief Compliance Officer: Sherry Johnstone
Chief, Customer Service and Education Division:
  Ron Kraft
Chief, Policy and Program Development: Ken Nitschke
Chief, Member Services Division: Darryl Watson
Chief Investment Officer: Joseph Dear
**Assistant Executive Officer, Member and Benefit
  Services Branch:** Kathie Vaughn
**Assistant Executive Officer, Actuarial and Employer
  Services Branch:** Kenneth W. Marzion
Assistant Executive Officer, Health Benefits:
  Gregory A. Franklin
Assistant Chief, Office of Governmental Affairs:
  Danny Brown
**Assistant Executive Officer, Information Technology
  Sercices:** Teri Bennett
Assistant Executive Officer, Administrative Services:
  John Hiber
Assistant Division Chief, Public Affairs:
  Brad W. Pacheco
General Counsel: Peter H. Mixon
Auditors: Macias, Gini & Company LLP

LOCATIONS

HQ: California Public Employees' Retirement System
  Lincoln Plaza, 400 Q St., Sacramento, CA 95811
Phone: 916-795-3829   **Fax:** 916-795-4001
Web: www.calpers.ca.gov

PRODUCTS/OPERATIONS

Investment Portfolio by Type

	% of total
Domestic equity	31
Domestic debt securities	24
International equity	20
Alternative investments	10
Real estate	9
Inflation linked	2
Short-term investments	2
International debt securities	2
Total	**100**

HISTORICAL FINANCIALS

Company Type: Government-owned

Income Statement

FYE: June 30

	ASSETS ($ mil.)	NET INCOME ($ mil.)	INCOME AS % OF ASSETS	EMPLOYEES
6/08	276,658	—	—	2,300
6/07	303,995	—	—	2,154
6/06	254,763	—	—	1,924
6/05	235,759	—	—	1,924
6/04	198,633	—	—	1,687
Annual Growth	8.6%	—	—	8.1%

Asset History

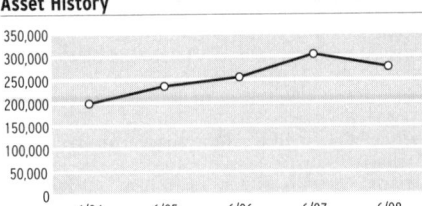

350,000				
300,000				
250,000				
200,000				
150,000				
100,000				
50,000				
0				
	6/04	6/05	6/06	6/07	6/08

C & S Wholesale Grocers

C&S Wholesale Grocers is at the bottom of the food chain — and likes it that way. The company is the second-largest wholesale grocery distributor in the US (behind SUPERVALU), supplying goods to some 5,000 independent supermarkets, major supermarket chains (including Safeway), mass marketers, and wholesale clubs. It distributes more than 53,000 items, including groceries, produce, and non-food items from its more than 70 distribution centers in a dozen states. C&S Wholesale also operates dozens of grocery stores and liquor outlets through its Southern Family Markets division. Israel Cohen started the family-owned company with Abraham Siegel in 1918.

C&S Wholesale has become a giant in the wholesale distribution business through its focus on serving retail chains with a variety of services allied to distribution. The company's affiliated ES3 logistics business provides warehousing and supply-chain management services for such retailers as Pathmark and Safeway and also for food manufacturers such as Unilever. Its diversified portfolio of services not only offers a lucrative stream of revenue but it has also helped protect the company from bankruptcies in the retail grocery industry.

Looking to streamline operations, C&S inked a 10-year partnership with Great Atlantic & Pacific Tea (A&P) in 2008, combining their supply agreements into one. The deal, which includes Pathmark's supply agreement, represents an effort for both companies to streamline their distribution operations. C&S has also been expanding its distribution business through targeted acquisitions, including its purchase of Penn Traffic's wholesale food distribution division late in 2008.

C&S also expanded its retail operations in 2009 when its Southern Family division acquired Bruno's Supermarkets out of bankruptcy. The $50 million deal added more than 30 Bruno's and Food World stores to its portfolio.

HISTORY

Israel Cohen and Abraham Siegel began C&S Wholesale Grocers in 1918 in Worcester, Massachusetts. Cohen ran the company for more than 50 years after buying out Siegel in 1921. It became a family concern in 1972 when Cohen turned the company over to his son Lester, who soon brought in his sons, Jim and Rick.

C&S Wholesale expanded over the years, growing along with its customers. It had $98 million in sales in 1981, the year its skyrocketing growth began. Also in 1981 Rick, now the company's chairman, president, and CEO, engineered a move to Brattleboro, in southern Vermont, where it had better access to interstate highways and a larger workforce.

After attending a seminar hosted by management whiz Tom Peters, in 1987 Cohen set up self-managed teams of three to eight employees who would act as small business units responsible for a customer's order from the time it was received to when it was delivered. Team members were paid for the amount of time they worked and were given bonuses for error-free operations and penalties for errors or damaged goods. His plan saw an immediate response in terms of increased sales, and by 1992 C&S Wholesale had more than $1 billion in sales. Rick bought out his father in 1989 and the next year became the company's single shareholder when he bought out his brother.

C&S Wholesale started its produce business in 1990 (by 1994 it was the major purchaser of locally grown fruits and vegetables) and began making plans to build an 800,000-sq.-ft. refrigerated warehouse near a scenic highway in Brattleboro. However, it ran up against environmentalists and Vermont's Act 250 environmental impact law, and eventually dropped its original plan, opting instead to expand at its headquarters.

In 1992 the wholesaler offered plans for a smaller, revised warehouse, but again met opposition. After a two-year battle, C&S Wholesale gave up and said it would build elsewhere. (Most of its employees and warehouses are now in Massachusetts and New Jersey.)

The following year C&S Wholesale welcomed 127 Grand Union stores and several East Coast Wal-Mart stores as customers. The next year the company picked up another 103 Grand Union stores; Grand Union said it was closing two distribution centers and shifting distribution to C&S Wholesale in a deal worth $500 million a year. A $650 million-per-year contract with Edwards stores was inked in 1996, the year C&S Wholesale's sales topped $3 billion.

The company acquired ice-cream distributor New England Frozen Foods in 1997. Continuing its move toward the mid-Atlantic, C&S Wholesale took over the distribution and supply operations of New Jersey-based grocery chain Pathmark Stores in 1998 for $60 million. In 1999 C&S Wholesale purchased Shaw's Supermarkets' Star Markets' wholesale division and moved into Pennsylvania with a facility in York.

In 2001 the company, through affiliate GU Markets, bought most of the assets of one of its biggest customers, bankrupt The Grand Union Company. C&S acquired about 170 of Grand Union's 197 stores in the purchase. It transferred most of the stores to third-party purchasers.

In 2002 C&S Wholesale formed a new holding company, called C&S Holdings, and reorganized its management to better oversee its various businesses. That summer the company acquired the grocery distribution operations of TOPS Markets, which until 2007 was a division of Dutch supermarket giant Royal Ahold.

C&S acquired the New England operations of SUPERVALU in 2003. In 2005 C&S acquired the warehouse facilities and distribution functions of supermarket chains BI-LO and Bruno's. It used the stores to gain a foothold into the southeastern market, as well as a platform for developing new supply-chain processes. Later that year, C&S subsidiary Southern Family Markets bought more than 100 BI-LO and Bruno's stores.

EXECUTIVES

Chairman and CEO: Richard B. (Rick) Cohen
EVP Operations: Scott Charlton
EVP Process Engineering and CIO: Joe Caracappa
EVP, General Counsel, and Secretary: Michael (Mike) Newbold
EVP Procurement and Merchandising: Robert (Bob) Palmer
EVP Human Resources: Bruce Johnson
SVP Corporate Construction and Engineering: Dennis Mead
SVP Facilities and Automation: Ted Speas
SVP Chain Sales and Customer Service: Marilyn Tillinghast
SVP Perishable: Michael Papaleo
SVP and General Manager, Southern Family Markets: Jeffrey Burkhead
SVP Warehouse Operations: Paul Moshovetis
SVP Merchandising, Marketing, and Trade Relations: Tracy Moore
SVP Mergers and Acquisitions and Business Enhancements: Jim Weidenheimer
SVP Perishable Procurement: Albert Grimaldi
SVP Warehouse Operations: Peter Fiore
Director Corporate Giving: Gina Goff

HQ: C & S Wholesale Grocers, Inc.
7 Corporate Dr., Keene, NH 03431
Phone: 603-354-7000 **Fax:** 603-354-4690
Web: www.cswg.com

PRODUCTS/OPERATIONS

Selected Customers
A&P Food Mart
Big Y Foods
BJ's Warehouse
Demoulas
Giant Food Stores
Great American
Pathmark
Safeway
SavMart/Foodmax
Shaw's
Stop and Shop
Target
TOPS

States Served
Alabama
California
Connecticut
Hawaii
Maryland
Massachusetts
New Hampshire
New Jersey
New York
Pennsylvania
South Carolina
Vermont

COMPETITORS

Alex Lee
Associated Wholesale Grocers
Associated Wholesalers
Bozzuto's
GSC Enterprises
H.T. Hackney
Kroger
McLane
Nash-Finch
SUPERVALU
Wakefern Food
Wal-Mart

HISTORICAL FINANCIALS
Company Type: Private

Income Statement
FYE: September 30

	REVENUE ($ mil.)	NET INCOME ($ mil.)	NET PROFIT MARGIN	EMPLOYEES
9/08	19,000	—	—	20,000
9/07	19,500	—	—	17,000
9/06	18,000	—	—	20,000
9/05	15,200	—	—	18,000
9/04	13,600	—	—	12,000
Annual Growth	8.7%	—	—	13.6%

Revenue History

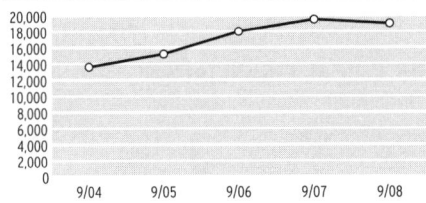

Capital Group Companies

If mutual fund firms were described like potential romantic partners in lonely hearts ads, The Capital Group Companies might be marriage material. The mutual fund firm, founded in 1931, is quiet (they don't advertise or grant many interviews), stable (it prides itself on consistency and believes investment decisions should not be taken lightly), and faithful (most of its investments and its executives are long-term). Subsidiary Capital Research and Management manages The American Funds, a family of about 30 mutual funds that ranks among the largest groups of mutual funds by assets in the US. Other Capital Group units offer mutual funds in Canada and Europe, and investment trusts in Japan.

Capital Group has some $850 billion in assets under management. The company, which mainly sells its products through financial advisers and other third parties, has more than 20 offices worldwide.

Additional activities include portfolio management for institutional investors, personal investment management for high-net-worth individuals and families, recordkeeping for small-company retirement plans, and private equity investing.

Capital Group's philosophy of staying under the radar has kept it relatively unscathed by troubles that have rocked the financial services industry in recent years, while remaining one of the largest US mutual fund firms. However, stock market declines have caused the company's assets to fall, in turn affecting management fees. In 2009 Capital Group announced layoffs totaling some 14% of its total workforce; no portfolio managers or analysts were affected.

EXECUTIVES
President: Philip de Toledo
SVP and Treasurer; SVP, Capital International: Jim Brown
SVP, Capital International; Research Director, Capital Global Private Equity: Lam Nguyen-Phuong
SVP, Capital International: Koenraad C. Foulon
VP, Capital International Research: Ashley Dunster
Chairman, Capital Group International and Capital Guardian Trust Company: David I. Fisher
Chairman, Capital International: Shaw B. Wagener
Chairman and Portfolio Manager, Capital Guardian: Shelby Notkin
Chief Administrative Officer, Personal Investment, Capital Guardian: Karen Skinner-Twomey
Director of Media Relations: Chuck Freadhoff
President, Personal Investment Management, Capital Guardian: John B. Emerson

LOCATIONS
HQ: The Capital Group Companies, Inc.
333 S. Hope St., 53rd Fl., Los Angeles, CA 90071
Phone: 213-486-9200 **Fax:** 213-486-9217
Web: www.capgroup.com

PRODUCTS/OPERATIONS

Selected Subsidiaries
Capital Bank and Trust (recordkeeping for small-company retirement plans in the US)
Capital Guardian (institutional asset management)
Capital International Asset Management
Capital International, Inc. (private equity investments)
Capital International K.K. (Japan)
Capital Research and Management

COMPETITORS
AllianceBernstein
American Century
AXA Financial
FMR
Franklin Resources
Invesco
Janus Capital
Legg Mason
MFS
Principal Financial
Putnam
T. Rowe Price
Van Kampen Investments
The Vanguard Group

CapRock Communications

CapRock Communications provides satellite communications services where others fear to tread. The company's network enables the secure transmission of voice, data, and video primarily for customers operating in remote locations or harsh environments such as offshore drilling platforms or mining sites. Clients come from such industries as construction, maritime, military, mining, and energy exploration. The company's SeaAccess Communications service provides broadband networking to ships at sea. CapRock operates a global communications network in cooperation with other satellite fleet operators. It has teleports and support centers in Angola, Brazil, Indonesia, Mexico, Norway, the UK, and the US.

CapRock changed the name of its Arrowhead Global Solutions division (acquired in 2007) to CapRock Government Solutions in 2009 before integrating its operations into the CapRock corporate structure. The unit serves customers in the defense, intelligence, and civilian government sectors. Also that year CapRock Government Solutions announced a new field communications service for military and civilian customers called CommandAccess. The new offering is intended to bridge the gap between commercial subscription services and portable, rugged military-grade communications systems.

The company's key contracts for 2009 included a multiyear deal to install satellite gear on Norway-based energy company Statoil's new drilling ship and to provide its satellite communications services and manage network operations. It also agreed to provide satellite connectivity to remote drilling sites for the Jakarta-based oil and gas unit of Genting Oil & Gas Limited.

In addition to satellite connections CapRock provides systems integration and project management services, including engineering design, equipment installation, and testing.

EXECUTIVES
Chairman and CEO: Peter Shaper
COO: Douglas A. Tutt
CFO: Hank M. Winfield
CTO: Philip Harlow
VP Global Energy Services Sales: Aldo Rodriguez
VP Engineering: David Bunting

VP Global Project Management: James Rickaby
VP Corporate Development: Bill Weakley
VP and General Manager, North America: Ron Wagnon
VP and General Counsel: Alan B. Aronowitz
VP Global Operations: Ron Long
President, Maritime: Pal Jensen
President, Global Energy Services: Keith Johnson
President, CapRock Government Solutions:
  Thomas E. (Tom) Eaton Jr.

LOCATIONS

HQ: CapRock Communications, Inc.
  4400 S. Sam Houston Pkwy. East
  Houston, TX 77048
Phone: 832-668-2300   **Fax:** 832-668-2388
Web: www.caprock.com

COMPETITORS

Eutelsat	RigNet
Globalstar	SES Group
Inmarsat	SkyTerra
Iridium Satellite	Stratos
ORBCOMM	Telenor

HISTORICAL FINANCIALS

Company Type: Private

Income Statement

FYE: December 31

	REVENUE ($ mil.)	NET INCOME ($ mil.)	NET PROFIT MARGIN	EMPLOYEES
12/07	235	—	—	650
12/06	119	—	—	450
12/05	104	—	—	392
12/04	91	—	—	388
12/03	51	—	—	210
Annual Growth	46.8%	—	—	32.6%

Revenue History

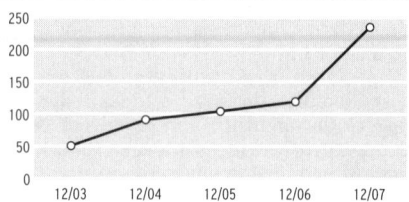

CareerBuilder LLC

CareerBuilder constructs new careers by bringing employers and potential employees together through the Web. The company's CareerBuilder Network consists of its flagship site careerbuilder.com, as well as affiliated career sites including the *Los Angeles Times* and MSN Careers. CareerBuilder.com allows job seekers access to the Mega Job Search to peruse more than 1 million job openings, and more than 300,000 employers tap into its database consisting of over 30 million resumes. The company also conducts surveys and polls through the Web paneling of its vast database. Newspaper publisher Gannett owns a controlling stake in CareerBuilder, which was founded in 1995.

Like other job recruiters, CareerBuilder has struggled as the global economic downturn caused many employers to pull back from posting job notices. CareerBuilder itself laid off about 300 workers — or about 15% — in December 2008. Most of the layoffs were in the company's small business segment.

In early 2008, CareerBuilder expanded its product offerings when it launched Personified, an independent consulting firm focusing on the relationship between a company's hiring practices and its work performance. Personified provides employee acquisition and retention; recruitment outsourcing; corporate culture development; and employment branding services. Also in 2008 CareerBuilder expanded its operations in Europe with the acquisition of French online recruiter Lesjeudis.com.

Besides Gannett, which owns a 51% stake in CareerBuilder, the job site's shareholders include newspaper companies Tribune (31%) and McClatchy (14%), plus Microsoft (4%).

The Microsoft investment, made in 2007, enabled CareerBuilder to extend its partnership with MSN Careers through 2013. Under the agreement, CareerBuilder will pay MSN more than $440 million over seven years in order to be featured as the Web site's primary job search engine.

EXECUTIVES

President, CEO, and Director:
  Matthew W. (Matt) Ferguson, age 42
CFO: Kevin Knapp
CTO: Eric Presley
VP Business Development: Hope Gurion
VP Government Solutions: Chuck Loeher
VP Human Resources: Rosemary Haefner
Chief Marketing Officer: Richard Castellini
General Counsel: Alex Green
Senior Director Online Products: Liz Harvey
President, Personified: Mary Delaney
President, CareerBuilder North America:
  Brent Rasmussen
President, Recruiter Business Unit, Canada:
  Todd McCormick
President, Europe, Middle East and Africa:
  Farhan Yasin

LOCATIONS

HQ: CareerBuilder LLC
  200 N. LaSalle St., Ste. 1100, Chicago, IL 60631
Phone: 773-527-3600   **Fax:** 773-399-6313
Web: www.careerbuilder.com

COMPETITORS

craigslist
Dice
HotJobs
Kelly Services
Monster.com
Vault, Inc.

HISTORICAL FINANCIALS

Company Type: Joint venture

Income Statement

FYE: December 31

	REVENUE ($ mil.)	NET INCOME ($ mil.)	NET PROFIT MARGIN	EMPLOYEES
12/07	768	—	—	2,000
12/06	672	—	—	1,800
12/05	495	—	—	1,500
12/04	280	—	—	900
12/03	160	—	—	550
Annual Growth	48.0%	—	—	38.1%

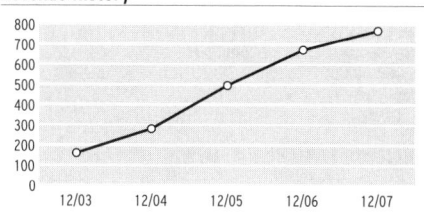

CareGroup, Inc.

Thanks to CareGroup, there's well-being in Beantown. Formed through the 1997 union of several Boston-area health care organizations, CareGroup serves Massachusetts residents through its flagship facility, the 620-bed Beth Israel Deaconess Medical Center, and three other hospital campuses. With about 1,000 beds total, the system provides a comprehensive range of general acute care as well as specialty care in a number of areas, such as orthopedics, diabetes, and cardiovascular disease. It is also involved in biomedical research and medical education; Beth Israel Deaconess and Mount Auburn Hospital are both teaching facilities for Harvard University's medical school.

EXECUTIVES

President and CEO: Paul F. Levy
CFO: John T. Szum
CIO: John D. Halamka, age 46
SVP, Human Resources: Lisa Zankman

LOCATIONS

HQ: CareGroup, Inc.
  109 Brookline Ave., Boston, MA 02215
Phone: 617-975-5000
Web: www.caregroup.org

PRODUCTS/OPERATIONS

Selected Hospitals

Beth Israel Deaconess Medical Center
Beth Israel Deaconess Hospital Needham
Mount Auburn Hospital
New England Baptist Hospital

COMPETITORS

Baystate Health
Boston Medical Center
Cambridge Health Alliance
Caritas Christi
Children's Hospital Boston
Partners HealthCare
Southcoast Health
Winchester Healthcare

HISTORICAL FINANCIALS

Company Type: Private

Income Statement

FYE: September 30

	REVENUE ($ mil.)	NET INCOME ($ mil.)	NET PROFIT MARGIN	EMPLOYEES
9/08	2,076	—	—	12,000

Cargill, Incorporated

Cargill may be private, but it's highly visible. The US's second-largest private corporation (after Koch Industries), Cargill's diversified operations include grain, cotton, sugar, petroleum, and financial trading; food processing; futures brokering; health and pharmaceutical products; agricultural services such as animal feed and crop protection; and industrial products including biofuels, oils and lubricants, starches, and salt. The company is one of the leading grain producers in the US, and its Excel unit is one of the top US meatpackers. Cargill's brands include Diamond Crystal (salt), Gerkens (cocoa), Honeysuckle White (poultry), Sterling Silver (fresh meats), and Nutrena (dog and cat food).

Being private doesn't mean Cargill is cut off from the world. The agribusiness giant has operations in 67 countries throughout the world. Along with its grain and meatpacking businesses, Cargill is a commodity trader. It is also a global supplier of oils, syrups, flour, and other products used in food processing.

Long the largest private company in the US, it lost that the #1 title when conglomerate Koch Industries acquired forest products maker Georgia-Pacific Corp in 2005. But Cargill is still a powerhouse. It is involved in petroleum trading, financial trading, futures brokering, and shipping. To focus on processing, Cargill sold its seed operations and coffee trading business and part of its steel business. It formed a joint venture with Hormel Foods to market fresh beef, along with pork, under the Always Tender brand. Cargill is also a major US supplier for McDonald's, providing the burger behemoth with eggs, oils, sauces, and beef products.

Cargill has a partnership with Coca-Cola to produce and market the sweetener Rebiana, which is said to sweeten without adding calories, while at the same time producing a natural flavor. It is made from the South American herb, stevia. Coke wants to put it in its beverages; Cargill sees uses in yogurt, cereal, ice cream, candy, and, perhaps table-top use. Rebiana received regulatory approval in the US for general use in food and beverages at the end of 2008.

Cargill is looking for additional growth opportunities in the world of bio-plastics. It reclaimed full control of its NatureWorks subsidiary in 2009, acquiring the 50% stake of former joint venture partner Teijin. NatureWorks makes commercial biopolymers, focusing on applications in eco-friendly products.

Long-time CEO Warren Staley retired in 2007. Cargill's board chose 33-year company veteran, president, and COO Gregory Page to replace Staley. Page stated that he hopes to make Cargill, an historically tight-lipped company, more visible. Later that year, Page was appointed chairman of the company.

HISTORY

William W. Cargill founded Cargill in 1865 when he bought his first grain elevator in Conover, Iowa. He and his brother Sam bought grain elevators all along the Southern Minnesota Railroad in 1870, just as Minnesota was becoming an important shipping route. Sam and a third brother, James, expanded the elevator operations while William worked with the railroads to monopolize transport of grain to markets and coal to farmers.

Around the turn of the century, William's son William S. invested in a number of ill-fated projects. William W. found that his name had been used to finance the projects; shortly afterward, he died of pneumonia. Cargill's creditors pressed for repayment, which threatened to bankrupt the company. John MacMillan, William W.'s son-in-law, took control and rebuilt Cargill. It had recovered by 1916 but lost its holdings in Mexico and Canada. MacMillan opened offices in New York (1922) and Argentina (1929), expanding grain trading and transport operations.

In 1945 Cargill bought Nutrena Mills (animal feed) and entered soybean processing; corn processing began soon after and grew with the demand for corn sweeteners. In 1954 Cargill benefited when the US began making loans to help developing countries buy American grain. Subsidiary Tradax, established in 1955, became one of the largest grain traders in Europe. A decade later, Cargill began trading sugar by purchasing sugar and molasses in the Philippines and selling them abroad.

Cargill made its finances public in 1973 (as a requirement for its unsuccessful takeover bid of Missouri Portland Cement), revealing it to be one of the US's largest companies, with $5.2 billion in sales. In the 1970s it expanded into coal, steel, and waste disposal and became a major force in metals processing, beef, and salt production.

To placate family heirs who wanted to take Cargill public, CEO Whitney MacMillan, grandson of John, created an employee stock plan in 1991 that allowed shareholders to cash in their shares. He also boosted dividends and reorganized the board, reducing the family's control. MacMillan retired in 1995 and non-family member Ernest Micek became CEO and chairman.

The firm bought Akzo Nobel's North American salt operations in 1997, becoming the #2 US salt company. Micek resigned as CEO that year and was replaced by Warren Staley. Also in 1999 Cargill fessed up to misappropriating some genetic seed material from rival Pioneer Hi-Bred, killing the $650 million sale of its North American seed assets to Germany's AgrEvo.

In 2004 the company announced the discovery of genetic markers in cattle that predict whether or not a specific steer will produce good-tasting meat. Also that year Cargill combined its crop-nutrition segment with phosphate fertilizer maker IMC Global to form a new, publicly traded company called Mosaic. Cargill owns about 66% of the company. This is the first time privately held Cargill has ventured into the public sector.

In 2005 Cargill acquired The Dow Chemical Company's interest in the two companies' 50-50 plastics business joint venture, Cargill Dow LLC, and renamed it NatureWorks. It also broke ground for its first oil refinery in Russia.

Cargill introduced Meadowlands Farms ground beef at food retailers throughout the US later in 2007. The introduction marked the company's first foray into the nationally branded hamburger market. However, Cargill was forced to recall meat products twice that year because of *E. coli* contamination. The first involved more than 800,000 pounds of frozen beef patties. More than 1 million pounds of fresh ground beef was involved in the second recall.

In 2008 Cargill added to its sugar business, announcing the construction of its first sugar refinery. The operation is a 50-50 joint venture between Cargill and Louisiana agricultural cooperative Sugar Growers and Refiners.

EXECUTIVES

Chairman and CEO: Gregory R. (Greg) Page, age 57
EVP: David M. Larson
SVP: Paul D. Conway
SVP: William A. (Bill) Buckner
SVP and CFO: David W. MacLennan, age 50
SVP: Richard D. Frasch, age 54
Corporate VP, General Counsel, and Corporate Secretary: Steven C. Euller
Corporate VP and Treasurer: Jayme D. Olson
Corporate VP, Operations: Tom Hayes
Corporate VP Corporate Affairs: Bonnie E. Raquet
Corporate VP, Research and Development: Christopher P. (Chris) Mallett
Corporate VP and CIO: Rita J. Heise
Corporate VP and Controller: Galen G. Johnson, age 62
Corporate VP Human Resources: Peter Vrijsen, age 55
President, Cargill Meat Solutions and President, Cargill Case Ready Beef: Jody Horner
President, Cargill Beef: John Keating
President, Cargill Energy, Transportation, and Industrial Group: Thomas (Tom) Intrator
Auditors: KPMG LLP

LOCATIONS

HQ: Cargill, Incorporated
15407 McGinty Rd. West, Wayzata, MN 55391
Phone: 952-742-7575   **Fax:** 952-742-7393
Web: www.cargill.com

PRODUCTS/OPERATIONS

Selected Products and Services

Agriculture and Animal Nutrition
  Agricultural commodity trading
  Animal nutrition
  Crop production
  Sugar refining
Financial and Risk Management
  Investment
  Risk Management
Food
  Baking and cereals
  Beverages
  Chocolates and confections
  Dairy products
  Health, nutrition, and organic
  Meat and poultry
  Prepared foods
  Salt
  Snacks
Health and Pharmaceutical
  Health, nutrition, and organic
  Pharmaceuticals
Industrial
  Biobased polyols
  Biofuels
  Deicing products and surface overlays
  Fermentation solutions
  Oils and lubricants
  Power and gas
  Salt
  Soy-based candle waxes
  Starches and derivatives
  Steel and ferrous raw materials

Selected Joint Ventures and Operations

Freeman's of Newent Ltd (chicken processing, UK)
Frontier Agriculture (UK)
Horizon Milling
Progressive Baker
Renessen Feed & Processing
Sun Valley (chicken processing, UK)

COMPETITORS

Abengoa Bioenergy	King Arthur Flour
ADM	Koch Industries, Inc.
Ag Processing	Kraft Foods
Amalgamated Sugar	Lake Area Corn Processors
American Animal Health	Land O'Lakes
American Crystal Sugar	Land O'Lakes Purina Feed
American Steel	Mars, Incorporated
Asia Food & Properties	Mars Petcare
Aventine	Merck
Badger State Ethanol	Merisant Worldwide
BASF SE	Michigan Sugar Company
Bayer Animal Health	Monsanto Company
Beef Products	Morton Salt
BioFuel Energy	Nestlé Purina PetCare
Blyth	Nippon Steel
Bunge Limited	Northern Growers
Butterball	Nucor
C&H Sugar	NutraSweet
Casco	Omega Protein
Chaparral Energy	Pacific Ethanol
CHS	Palm Restaurants
COFCO	Perdue Incorporated
Coleman Natural Foods	Pfizer
ConAgra	Phibro Animal Health
ContiGroup	Raeford Farms
Corn Products	Rohm and Haas
International	Royal Canin
Cumberland Packing	Royal Schouten Group
Danisco A/S	Südzucker
Dean Foods	Sara Lee North American
Del Monte Foods	Retail
Dow Chemical	Sime Darby
DuPont	SMBSC
DuPont Agriculture &	Smithfield Foods
Nutrition	Sterling Sugars
Eight in One Pet Products	Sugar Cane Growers
Ellison Meat Company	Cooperative of Florida
Evialis	Sugar Foods
Faultless Starch	Tate & Lyle
Florida Crystals	Tate & Lyle Ingredients
General Mills	Teva Pharmaceuticals
Hershey	Tyson Foods
Hill's Pet Nutrition	United Salt
Holly Sugar	United States Steel
Iams	U.S. Sugar
Imperial Sugar	Viterra Inc.
IOI Corporation	Western Beef
JBS	Western Sugar Cooperative
Jennie-O	Yankee Candle

HISTORICAL FINANCIALS

Company Type: Private

Income Statement

FYE: May 31

	REVENUE ($ mil.)	NET INCOME ($ mil.)	NET PROFIT MARGIN	EMPLOYEES
5/09	116,579	3,334	2.9%	159,000
5/08	120,439	3,951	3.3%	160,000
5/07	88,266	2,343	2.7%	158,000
5/06	75,208	1,537	2.0%	149,000
5/05	71,066	2,103	3.0%	124,000
Annual Growth	13.2%	12.2%	—	6.4%

Net Income History

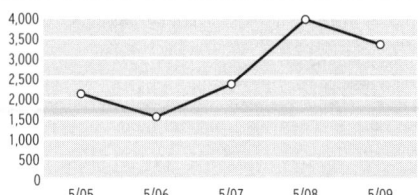

Carlson Companies

Carlson Companies began in 1938 as the Gold Bond Stamp Company, but has evolved into a leisure services juggernaut. The company owns 55% of travel giant Carlson Wagonlit. Its Carlson Hotels Worldwide owns and operates more than 1,000 hotels in some 70 countries under brands such as Radisson, Country Inns & Suites By Carlson, and Park Plaza. In addition, its Carlson Restaurants Worldwide includes the T.G.I. Friday's and Pick Up Stix chains. Chairman Marilyn Carlson Nelson and director Barbara Carlson Gage, daughters of founder Curtis Carlson, each own half of the company.

In 2009 Carlson Companies sold its Carlson Marketing business to Canada-based loyalty management firm Groupe Aeroplan in a deal worth some $175 million. Carlson made the sale in order to focus on the growth of its core hotel, restaurant, and travel businesses. The divestiture followed another key disposal — the company's Carlson Leisure Group included a variety of leisure and franchise travel holdings, including cruise-specialty operations Cruise Holidays, SeaMaster Cruises, and Cruise Specialists, as well as online operations such as Fly4Less.com, CruiseDeals.com, and SinglesCruise.com. In 2008 those assets were sold to Carlson Leisure Group's management team.

Also in 2008 Carlson Wagonlit president and CEO Hubert Joly replaced Marilyn Carlson Nelson as CEO of Carlson Companies. Nelson remains chairman. The Carlsons are one of the first families of business in Minnesota, and Nelson regularly makes the list of the most powerful women in corporate America. She and her son Curtis Nelson are engaged in a legal battle. The younger heir was fired from his position as COO of the company and is suing his mother, asking for a larger share of the company and claiming he deserves the CEO position. Carlson Nelson claims that her son is not suited for the position, citing his past problems with alcohol and substance abuse in a counter suit.

Barbara Carlson Gage runs the family foundation (the Curtis L. Carlson Family Foundation). As a result of the economic recession wrecking havoc on the tourism and travel industry, the Carlson sisters saw their combined fortune drop to $1.7 billion in 2008 (down from $2.2 billion the previous year).

HISTORY

Curtis Carlson, the son of Swedish immigrants, graduated from the University of Minnesota in 1937 and went to work selling soap for Procter & Gamble in the Minneapolis area. In 1938 he borrowed $55 and formed Gold Bond Stamp Company to sell trading stamps. His wife, Arleen, dressed as a drum majorette and twirled a baton to promote the concept. By 1941 the company had 200 accounts. Business was slowed by WWII but took off in the 1950s. During the 1960s the company began diversifying into other enterprises such as travel, marketing, hotels, and real estate.

Gold Bond Stamp bought the Radisson Hotel in Minneapolis in 1962 and began expanding the chain. The company adopted the Carlson Companies name in 1973. Carlson Companies continued expanding its holdings during the 1970s, buying the 11-unit T.G.I. Friday's chain, as well

as a chain of Country Kitchen family restaurants (sold in 1997).

In 1979 Carlson bought First Travel Corp., which owned travel agency Ask Mr. Foster and Colony Hotels. Carlson Companies slowed the pace of its acquisitions in the 1980s. Hired in 1984, Juergen Bartels changed the hospitality division's strategy from building and owning hotels to franchising and managing them. This enabled Carlson to weather the crash that followed the 1980s hotel building boom.

The company took T.G.I. Friday's public to fund expansion in 1983, but it reacquired all outstanding shares in 1989. It launched its cruise ship business in 1992, when the luxury liner SSC *Radisson Diamond* set sail.

Carlson made a major international advance in 1994 when it formed joint venture Carlson Wagonlit Travel, with France's Accor. In 1997 it expanded into the luxury hotel business when it bought Regent International from Four Seasons. In a nod to its roots, the company also unveiled the Gold Points Reward guest loyalty system to reward customers who frequent its hotels and restaurants.

In 1998 Curtis Carlson appointed his daughter, Marilyn Carlson Nelson, as the company's chief executive (he remained chairman). The following year Carlson Companies merged its UK leisure travel business with UK-based travel and financial services firm Thomas Cook. Founder Curtis Carlson died that year and Nelson added chairman to her title. The company later filed to spin off its T.G.I. Friday's unit as Carlson Restaurants Worldwide.

Carlson Companies sold its 22% stake in Thomas Cook Holdings in 2001 to German tour company C&N (which then changed its name to Thomas Cook AG). In mid-2001 the company bought 52-unit Asian restaurant chain Pick Up Stix. The following year Carlson Companies announced a major expansion initiative into the Asia/Pacific region. The company bought customer-based business strategy firm Peppers & Rogers in 2003, and the next year completed the purchase of the business travel subsidiary of Maritz Travel.

In early 2008 the company sold several leisure and franchise travel holdings that operated under the Carlson Leisure Group banner. Later that year Hubert Joly replaced Marilyn Carlson Nelson as CEO. Nelson remains chairman.

In 2009 the company sold Carlson Marketing.

EXECUTIVES

Chairman: Marilyn Carlson Nelson, age 69
President, CEO, and Director; President and CEO, Carlson Hotels Worldwide: Hubert Joly, age 50
EVP and Chief Administrative Officer: Jim T. Porter
EVP and CFO: Trudy Rautio, age 56
EVP and General Counsel: William A. (Bill) Van Brunt
EVP, Business Unit Liaison; President and CEO, Carlson Marketing: Jeffrey A. (Jeff) Balagna, age 48
President, Engagement and Events, Carlson Marketing: Fay Beauchine
President and CEO, Carlson Restaurants Worldwide: Nicholas P. (Nick) Shepherd
President and CEO, Carlson Wagonlit Travel: Douglas (Doug) Anderson, age 54
Franchise and Managed Hotel Development, Carlson Hotels Worldwide: Janelle Russenberger
VP Responsible Business, Carlson Hotels Worldwide: Carmen Baker
Director Public Relations, Carlson Marketing: Barry Wegener
Director Public Relations, Regent Hotels & Resorts: Tom Polski
Director Public Relations, Carlson Restaurants Worldwide: Amy Freshwater

LOCATIONS

HQ: Carlson Companies, Inc.
701 Carlson Pkwy., Minnetonka, MN 55305
Phone: 763-212-4000　　**Fax:** 763-212-2219
Web: www.carlson.com

PRODUCTS/OPERATIONS

Selected Operations

Hotel brands
　Country Inns & Suites By Carlson
　Park Inn Hotels
　Park Plaza Hotels & Resorts
　Radisson Hotels & Resorts
　Regent International Hotels
Restaurants
　Pick Up Stix
　T.G.I. Friday's
Travel
　Carlson Wagonlit Travel (55%)

COMPETITORS

American Express
Applebee's
BCD Travel
Brinker
Darden
Denny's
Diamond Resorts
Fairmont Raffles
Four Seasons Hotels
Hilton Worldwide
Hyatt
Marriott
Mitchells & Butlers
O'Charley's
Omni Hotels
OSI Restaurant Partners
Ritz-Carlton
Starwood Hotels & Resorts

HISTORICAL FINANCIALS

Company Type: Private

Income Statement				FYE: December 31
	REVENUE ($ mil.)	NET INCOME ($ mil.)	NET PROFIT MARGIN	EMPLOYEES
12/08	38,075	—	—	160,000
12/07	39,800	—	—	160,000
12/06	37,100	—	—	176,000
12/05	34,400	—	—	—
12/04	30,700	—	—	190,000
Annual Growth	5.5%	—	—	(4.2%)

Revenue History

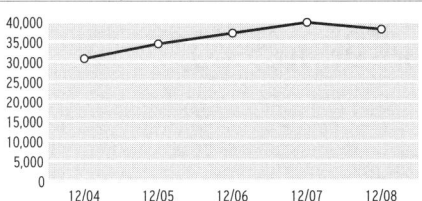

The Carlyle Group

The Carlyle Group, with some $85 billion under management, is one of the world's largest private investment firms. Undertakings include management-led buyouts, minority equity investments, real estate, venture capital, and leveraged finance opportunities in the energy and power, consumer and retail, and technology and business services industries. Other sectors it focuses on include financial services, health care, infrastructure, aerospace and defense, automotive, transportation, telecommunications, and media. Since its founding in 1987, The Carlyle Group has made some 900 investments; it maintains offices in about 20 countries and oversees more than 60 private equity, real estate, and leveraged buyout funds.

Affiliate Carlyle Capital went under in 2008 when creditors, including some of the world's biggest investment banks, began liquidating their assets. The company had invested in triple-A rated mortgages but did not have enough collateral to cover its debt. The Carlyle Group extended a $150 million line of credit to the company, but ultimately, it wasn't enough. Later that year the firm closed another hedge fund, Blue Wave, when its assets fell by one-third.

Also in 2008 The Carlyle Group announced that it would cut about 100 jobs, or some 10% of its workforce. Most of the cut positions will be from the firm's accounting, human resources, legal, and other back-office departments. However, in the spirit of making lemonade from lemons, the company formed a new fund that year to invest in troubled securities, companies, and other distressed investments.

The widespread recession hasn't spared Carlyle's portfolio companies either. Hawaiian Telecom filed for Chapter 11 bankruptcy protection in late 2008. The following year, German auto parts maker Edscha filed for insolvency for its 14 European plants.

Although the majority of its money is in North America, The Carlyle Group also has investments in Asia and Europe, and has been making inroads in Brazil, the Middle East, North Africa, and Russia. The company traditionally has been known for turning small acquisitions into big companies, but during a boom in private equity investing earlier this decade, The Carlyle Group began to make bigger and bigger deals. It has stakes in some 200 firms, including Dunkin' Brands, Hertz, and The Nielsen Company.

In 2008 the company announced plans to pay some $2.5 billion for a majority stake in the government operations of Booz Allen Hamilton, which provides consulting services to the US Department of Defense and other government agencies at home and abroad.

It purchased Allison Transmission for some $5.6 billion and home care operator Manor Care for nearly $5 billion in 2007. Additionally, the company joined with Bain Capital and Clayton, Dubilier & Rice to buy HD Supply, the wholesale construction supply business of The Home Depot, for around $8.5 billion.

California Public Employees' Retirement System (CalPERS) owns more than 5% of Carlyle; the government of Abu Dhabi owns another 7.5%. The rest is owned by a group of individuals, most of whom are managing directors at Carlyle.

HISTORY

In 1987 T. Rowe Price director Edward Mathias brought together David Rubenstein, a former aide to President Carter; Stephen Norris and Daniel D'Aniello, both executives with Marriott; William Conway Jr., the CFO of MCI; and Greg Rosenbaum, a VP with a New York investment firm. They pooled their experience along with a load of money from T. Rowe Price Associates, Alex. Brown & Sons (now Deutsche Banc Alex. Brown), First Interstate (acquired by Wells Fargo), and Pittsburgh's Mellon family to form a buyout firm.

Named after the Carlyle Hotel in New York, the firm opted to make Washington, DC, its headquarters so it wouldn't get lost in the crowd of New York investment firms. The company spent its first years investing in a mish-mash of companies, using Norris' and D'Aniello's Marriott experience primarily on restaurant and food service companies (including Mexican restaurant chain Chi-Chi's).

In 1989 it wooed the well-connected Frank Carlucci, who had served as President Reagan's secretary of defense, to join the group. Soon thereafter, Carlyle began making more high-profile deals. That year it acquired Coldwell Banker's commercial real estate operations (sold 1996) and Caterair International, Marriott's airline food services (sold 1995).

Carlucci helped redirect the firm's focus to the downsizing defense industry. Among its targets were Harsco (1990), BDM International (1991), and LTV's missile and aircraft units (1992). Carlyle helped overhaul their operations and make them attractive to the industry's elite, including Boeing and Lockheed Martin.

As the company's reputation grew, so did its cast of players. Among its new backers were James Baker and Richard Darman (both Reagan and Bush administration alums) and investor George Soros, who chipped some $100 million into the Carlyle Partners L.P. buyout fund. With the help of its "access capitalists" such as Baker and Saudi Prince al-Waleed bin Talal (the firm helped add to his fortune in a 1991 Citicorp stock transaction), Carlyle made deals in the Middle East and Western Europe (including a bailout of Euro Disney) in the mid-1990s.

While the firm continued to acquire defense companies (aircraft castings maker Howmet in 1995), it picked up a grab bag of holdings, such as natural food grocer Fresh Fields Markets (1994; sold 1996); the quick turnaround helped build Carlyle's war chest. The firm also began investing in industrial-cleanup companies, seeing increased government spending as a major opportunity for profit. In 1999, the firm acquired automobile engine parts manufacturer Honsel International Technologies in Germany's first public-to-private transaction. (It later sold this investment to Ripplewood Holdings in 2004.)

Formerly a list of who's-who in aerospace and defense, Carlyle has unloaded many of its assets in the sector, retooled its management board, and made its undertakings more transparent, in part due to suspicions regarding its dealings with Saudi investors (including the bin Laden family) in a post-9/11 world.

Out went the likes of former US President George H.W. Bush, former British Prime Minister John Major, former Secretary of State James Baker, and former US Secretary of Defense Frank Carlucci. They were replaced by business leaders such as Lou Gerstner, the former IBM CEO, former SEC chairman Arthur Levitt, and David Calhoun, a former vice chairman of GE.

EXECUTIVES

Founding Partner and Managing Director:
David M. Rubenstein
**Founding Partner and Managing Director; Chairman,
Carlyle Investment Committees:**
William E. Conway Jr., age 57
Managing Director and CFO: Peter H. Nachtwey
Managing Director and General Counsel:
Jeffrey W. Ferguson
Managing Director and Chief Accounting Officer:
Curt Buser
Mannaging Director and Head Human Resources:
Lori R. Sabet
Chairman, Global Buyouts: Gregory L. Summe, age 52
**Principal, Director, Global Communications and
Corporate Spokesman:** Christopher W. Ullman

LOCATIONS

HQ: The Carlyle Group, L.P.
1001 Pennsylvania Ave. NW, Washington, DC 20004
Phone: 202-729-5626   **Fax:** 202-347-1818
Web: www.carlyle.com

PRODUCTS/OPERATIONS

Selected Portfolio Companies

Aerospace and Defense
DHS Technologies, LLC
Gardner Group, Ltd.
Sequa Corporation
Vought Aircraft Industries, Inc.
Wesco Holding, Inc.

Automotive and Transportation
Allison Transmission, Inc.
Hertz Corporation
United Components, Inc.
United Road Towing, Inc.

Consumer and Retail
Alliance Boots plc
American Achievement Corporation
Babela Restaurant Management Co. Ltd.
Britax Childcare Holdings Limited
China Pacific Insurance (Group) Co. Ltd.
Dunkin' Brands, Inc.
Harrah's Entertainment, Inc.
Mattress Giant Corporation
Oriental Trading Company
Xstep (China) Company Limited
Zhejiang Kaiyuan Hotel Managemetn Co., Ltd.

Energy and Power
Coastal Carolina Clean Power LLC
Collingwood Ethanol, L.P.
Dresser, Inc.
Frontier Drilling ASA
Green Earth Fuels, LLC
HongHua Group Holding
International Logging, Inc.
Kinder Morgan, Inc.
Stallion Oilfield Services
Titan Specialties, Ltd.
Vantage Energy, LLC
Voice Construction Ltd.

Health Care
BioReliance Corporation
Claris Lifesciences Limited
LifeCare Holdings, Inc.
Manor Care
MedPointe, Inc.
Primary Health, Inc.
Proteus Biomedical, Inc.
Qualicaps Group
Transport Pharmaceuticals, Inc.

Industrial
China Forestry Holdings Group
Chongquing Polycomp International Corporation
Comark Building Systems, Inc.
East River Biochemical Group
Gardner Group Ltd.
Goodman Global, Inc.
Goodyear Engineered Products
Hawkeye Group
International Aluminum Corporation
John Maneely Company
PQ Corporation
Specialty Manufacturing Company
StrionAir, Inc.
Taylor-Wharton International
Wastequip, Inc.
Zodiac Marine & Pool

Technology and Business Services
Apollo Global
Authentix, Inc.
BFinance
bigmouthmedia GmbH
Blackboard, Inc.
Booz Allen Hamilton, Inc.
CPU Technology, Inc.
Carefx, Corp.
Catapult Learning LLC
China Real Estate Network
CompuDyne Corporation
Compusearch Software Systems
Flexcom Company Limited
Freescale Semiconductor, Inc.
Housing Development Finance Corp.
Infomax Optical
Liquid Engines, Inc.
Mainstream Data, Inc.
Nitride Semiconductor Co., Ltd
Open Solutions, Inc.
Panasas, Inc.
Rhythm NewMedia Inc.
SchoolNet, Inc.
SmartTrust AB
StrionAir, Inc.
Supercircuits, Inc.
TLI Incorporated
TOPIA Education, Inc.
Verari Systems, Inc.
Viator, Inc.
ZCom Company Limited (China)

Telecom and Media
AMC Entertainment, Inc.
Focus Media Holdings
Hawaiian Telecom
Health Central Network, Inc.
Hyundai Communications & Network
Insight Communications Company
The Nielsen Company
Time Share Advertising & Communications Co. Ltd.
WILLCOM, Inc.

COMPETITORS

Blackstone Group
CD&R
Forstmann Little
Goldman Sachs
HM Capital Partners
Investcorp
KKR
Thomas H. Lee Partners
TPG

Carolina Hurricanes

Carolina Hurricanes Hockey Club is a professional hockey franchise that represents North Carolina in the National Hockey League. The team earned its first and only Stanley Cup championship in 2006. Originally founded in 1971 as the New England Whalers of the World Hockey Association (WHA), the team joined the NHL as the Hartford Whalers in 1979. Peter Karmanos, founder and chairman of Compuware, led a group that acquired the team in 1994, relocating it first to Greensboro, North Carolina, before settling in Raleigh in 1999.

EXECUTIVES

CEO and Governor: Peter (Pete) Karmanos Jr., age 66
President and General Manager: Jim Rutherford
CFO: Michael (Mike) Amendola
Director Information Technology: Glenn Johnson
Head Coach: Paul Maurice, age 42
VP and Assistant General Manager: Jason Karmanos
VP and General Manager, RBC Center: Davin Olsen
Director Corporate Sales: Mike Hurley
Director Marketing and Brand Development:
Ben Aycock
Director Media Relations: Mike Sundheim
Director Ticket Sales: Kyle Prairie
**Associate Head Coach and Director Player
Development:** Ron Francis

LOCATIONS

HQ: Carolina Hurricanes Hockey Club
1400 Edwards Mill Rd., Raleigh, NC 27607
Phone: 919-467-7825   **Fax:** 919-462-7030
Web: www.caneshockey.com

PRODUCTS/OPERATIONS

Championship Trophies
Stanley Cup (2006)
Prince of Wales Trophy (2002, 2006)

COMPETITORS

Atlanta Thrashers
Florida Panthers
Tampa Bay Lightning
Washington Capitals

Carpenter Co.

It's a cushy job for Carpenter Co., making polyurethane foam and chemicals and polyester fiber used as cushioning by the automotive, bedding, floor covering, packaging, and furniture industries. The company started out making foam rubber; it now also manufactures air filters, expanded polystyrene building materials, and a tire fill product used as a replacement for air in off-road construction vehicles. Carpenter also sells consumer products — which include craft fiber products, mattress pads, and pillows — through retailers. The company has facilities throughout North America and Europe. Carpenter, which was founded in 1948 by E. Rhodes Carpenter, is owned by chairman and CEO Stanley Pauley.

EXECUTIVES

CEO: Stanley F. Pauley
COO: Stanley Yukevich
CFO: Michael (Mike) Lowery
Managing Director, Dumo: Hendrick Kesteloot

LOCATIONS

HQ: Carpenter Co.
5016 Monument Ave., Richmond, VA 23230
Phone: 804-359-0800   **Fax:** 804-353-0694
Web: www.carpenter.com

PRODUCTS/OPERATIONS

Selected Products

Air filter media
Bedding
Carpet cushion
Chemicals
Chemical systems
Consumer products
Expanded polystyrene systems
Flexible foam packaging
Furniture
Polyester fiber
Tire products

COMPETITORS

British Vita
Dash Multi-Corp
FXI
Henry Company
MTI Global
Owens Corning Sales
PMC Global
The Woodbridge Group

HISTORICAL FINANCIALS

Company Type: Private

Income Statement			FYE: December 31
	REVENUE ($ mil.)	NET INCOME ($ mil.)	NET PROFIT MARGIN	EMPLOYEES
12/07	1,650	—	—	5,900
12/06	1,710	—	—	5,675
12/05	1,456	—	—	5,900
12/04	1,300	—	—	6,000
12/03	1,200	—	—	6,000
Annual Growth	8.3%	—	—	(0.4%)

Revenue History

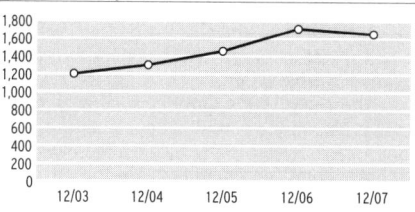

Castle Harlan

Castle Harlan is a private equity firm that has investments in restaurant chains, industrial and manufacturing firms, shipping and transportation support companies, and other concerns in the US and Australia. The hands-on company sniffs out established enterprises with steady earnings; it often partners with the existing management of an acquired business, places directors on its board, and eventually seeks a profitable exit. Castle Harlan owns stakes in about a dozen companies in all. Its restaurant holdings include well-known names Perkins & Marie Callender's and Morton's. The firm was co-founded in 1987 by Leonard Harlan and chairman John Castle, a former CEO of Donaldson, Lufkin & Jenrette.

Castle Harlan has raised more than $3 billion since its inception. Investors in the company's private equity funds include pension funds, college endowments, banks, insurance companies, and wealthy families.

In 2009 the company purchased a 75% stake in Australian financial adviser Centric Wealth. The previous year it bought Anchor Drilling Fluids USA, a provider of drilling fluids and fluid-handling services to the oil and gas drilling industry, for a reported $250 million from American Capital.

Castle Harlan more than doubled its investments in steel castings maker AmeriCast (sold to Australian manufacturer Bradken for nearly $290 million in 2008) and tubular products manufacturer RathGibson (sold to DLJ Merchant Banking for $440 million in 2007). Castle Harlan and its Australian affiliate, CHAMP Private Equity, also did well with the divesture of United Malt Holdings in 2009. The fourth-largest producer of malt was sold to GrainCorp for some $655 million.

Acquisitions in 2006 included BRAVO! Development, which operates Bravo! Cucina Italiana restaurants and Brio Tuscan Grilles; and DVD distributor Baker & Taylor, acquired for some $455 million from fellow private equity firm Willis Stein & Partners.

EXECUTIVES

Chairman and CEO: John K. Castle, age 68
Vice Chairman: Gary B. Appel
President: Justin B. Wender, age 39
SVP and CFO: Lewis A. Raibley III
SVP and Chief Financial and Administrative Officer: Howard Weiss
VP: Anand T. Philip
VP and Controller: Sylvia F. Rosen
Controller, CHAMP Funds: Gary D. Bialik
Office Manager: Beverly Fox
Senior Managing Director: David B. Pittaway, age 57
Senior Managing Director: William M. Pruellage, age 35
Senior Managing Director: Howard D. Morgan, age 47
Senior Managing Director: Marcel Fournier

LOCATIONS

HQ: Castle Harlan, Inc.
150 E. 58th St., New York, NY 10155
Phone: 212-644-8600   **Fax:** 212-207-8042
Web: www.castleharlan.com

PRODUCTS/OPERATIONS

Selected Portfolio Companies

Ames True Temper (lawn and garden tools)
Anchor Drilling Fluids USA, Inc. (onshore drilling, US)
Associated Packaging Technologies (frozen food packaging)
Baker & Taylor (book, music, and DVD distributor)
Bravo Development (restaurant chains)
Caribbean Restaurants, LLC (Burger King franchises, Puerto Rico)
Morton's Restaurant Group, Inc.
Perkins & Marie Callender's, Inc.

COMPETITORS

Berkshire Hathaway
The Carlyle Group
CD&R
Charterhouse Group
Forstmann Little
HM Capital Partners
Jordan Company
KKR
Leonard Green
Madison Dearborn
NexCen Brands
Thomas H. Lee Partners
TPG
Vulcan

HISTORICAL FINANCIALS

Company Type: Private

Income Statement			FYE: December 31
	REVENUE ($ mil.)	NET INCOME ($ mil.)	NET PROFIT MARGIN	EMPLOYEES
12/08	3,245	—	—	13,450

Catalent Pharma Solutions

Catalyst + talent = Catalent. At least, that's the brand Catalent Pharma Solutions is trying to convey to ensure its customers' success. The company provides contract development and manufacturing of oral (soft and hardshell capsules), topical (ointment applicators), sterile (syringes), and inhaled (nasal sprays) drug delivery products to pharmaceutical and biotechnology companies in some 100 countries. Catalent also provides packaging services, using bottles, pouches, and strips used to hold tablet, powder, and liquid medicines. Catalent operates 30 facilities worldwide. The company was formed in 2007 when The Blackstone Group acquired Cardinal Health's pharmaceutical technologies segment for $3.3 billion.

After establishing its independence, Catalent then set its strategic direction by reorganizing its business into three main segments: oral technologies, sterile technologies, and packaging technologies. The company divested its hormone manufacturing facilities in New Mexico and France in 2008 and 2009 because neither was core to its future growth.

On the flip side, Catalent opened a facility near Belgium specifically designed to double the production of prefilled flu vaccine syringes, thereby enhancing its sterile technologies business. Already it operated prefilled syringe plants in North Carolina and France, which are helping the company keep pace with customer demand in Europe, Japan, and the US. The company announced plans in 2008 to divest the North Carolina facility, which didn't measure up to its growth and profitability standards.

In 2009 the company brought in GE executive John Chiminski to take over the roles of president and CEO from George Fotiades, who remains as chairman.

Key customers for the company's outsourced development, manufacturing, packaging, and regulatory consulting services include Pfizer, Johnson & Johnson, and Genentech.

EXECUTIVES

Chairman: George L. Fotiades, age 56, $778,585 total compensation
President, CEO, and Director: John R. Chiminski, age 45, $2,284,723 total compensation
SVP and CFO: Matthew M. (Matt) Walsh, age 43, $1,341,602 total compensation
Group President, Oral Technologies: Thomas J. Stuart, age 48, $799,860 total compensation
Group President, Development and Clinical Services: Scott Houlton, age 42
Group President, Packaging Services: David Heyens, age 53
Group President, Sterile Technologies and SVP Global Sales & Marketing: Will Downie
SVP Human Resources: Harry F. Weininger, age 58
SVP Information Technology: Roy Satchell, age 50
SVP Global Quality and Regulatory Affairs: Edward C. Theile, age 65
SVP Global Quality and Regulatory Affairs: Sharon Johnson
SVP, General Counsel, and Secretary: Samrat S. (Sam) Khichi, age 42, $634,232 total compensation
SVP Global Operations: Steve Leonard
VP Corporate Development and Strategy and Investor Relations Officer: Cornell Stamoran
Auditors: Ernst & Young LLP

LOCATIONS

HQ: Catalent Pharma Solutions, Inc.
14 Schoolhouse Rd., Somerset, NJ 08873
Phone: 732-537-6200   **Fax:** 732-537-6480
Web: www.catalent.com

2008 Sales

	$ mil.	% of total
Europe	885.8	48
US	691.5	37
Other	268.5	15
Adjustments	(17.8)	—
Total	**1,828.0**	**100**

PRODUCTS/OPERATIONS

2008 Sales

	$ mil.	% of total
Oral technologies	1,039.0	56
Packaging services	531.3	28
Sterile technologies	301.0	16
Adjustments	(43.3)	—
Total	**1,828.0**	**100**

COMPETITORS

Charles River Laboratories
Covance
DRAXIS
Hyaluron
K-V Pharmaceutical
MDS
Nektar Therapeutics
Omnicare Clinical Research
PAREXEL
Patheon
Pharmaceutical Product Development
Soft Gel Technologies

HISTORICAL FINANCIALS

Company Type: Private

Income Statement				FYE: June 30
	REVENUE ($ mil.)	NET INCOME ($ mil.)	NET PROFIT MARGIN	EMPLOYEES
6/08	1,828	(540)	—	9,800
6/07	1,704	(125)	—	10,000
6/06	1,612	51	3.2%	—
6/05	1,517	14	0.9%	—
Annual Growth	6.4%	—	—	(2.0%)

Net Income History

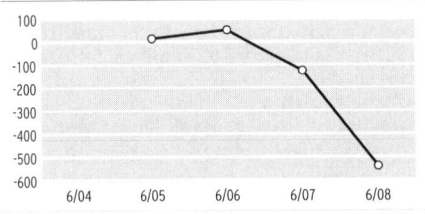

Catholic Health East

Catholic Health East marries the physical and the spiritual in its vast network of not-for-profit health care facilities. As one of the largest religious health systems in the country, Catholic Health East carries out its mission of healing the sick through more than 30 acute-care hospitals, 25 freestanding and hospital-based long-term care facilities, about 15 assisted living homes, and numerous behavioral health and rehabilitation centers. Operating in 11 states along the East Coast from Maine to Florida, Catholic Health East is also one of the country's largest providers of home health care services. The health care organization is sponsored by nine religious congregations and Hope Ministries.

Catholic Health East was founded in 1998 when three regional Catholic health systems joined forces. It has since grown its network by adding affiliated hospitals to its network, including the 2008 addition of Saint Michael's Medical Center in Newark, New Jersey, and the Minnie G. Boswell Memorial Hospital, an acute-care facility in Greene County, Georgia.

Catholic Health East also grows through partnerships like the one it formed in late 2008 with Deborah Heart and Lung Center to develop a satellite emergency department on Deborah's campus in New Jersey. The $4 million emergency department, scheduled to open in 2010, would be operated by Lourdes Medical Center, a Catholic Health East affiliate, and is part of a plan to expand care services in Burlington County.

HISTORY

It was three easy pieces that made up Catholic Health East in 1997. Allegany Health System, Eastern Mercy Health System, and Sisters of Providence Health System operated almost entirely in separate, but adjacent, geographic areas on the East Coast, overlapping only in Florida.

Catholic Health East's history goes as far back as 1831, when the Sisters of Mercy was founded in Dublin, Ireland, by Catherine McAuley, who established a poorhouse using her inheritance. Some of the sisters hopped the Pond in 1843, establishing the first Catholic hospital in the US, the Mercy Hospital of Pittsburgh, four years later. Over the years the Sisters of Mercy expanded throughout the US. By 1991 there were 25 Sisters of Mercy congregations; they united that year under the newly formed Institute of the Sisters of Mercy of the Americas.

The Sisters of Providence came from Kingston, Ontario, to found the first hospital in Holyoke, Massachusetts. Having established their own ministry, the sisters in Holyoke became a separate congregation in 1892. The congregation expanded slowly, moving into North Carolina in 1956, eventually forming the Sisters of Providence Health System.

A Polish nun, Mother Colette Hilbert, formed a new congregation in Pittsburgh in 1897 after the other members of her former parish were recalled to Poland. The new congregation entered health care in 1926, establishing a home for the elderly in New York. In honor of Hilbert's favorite saint, the order became the Franciscan Sisters of St. Joseph in 1934.

The Franciscan Sisters of St. Joseph and the Sisters of Mercy united in the ministry that became Pittsburgh Mercy Health System in 1983. In 1986 the congregations formed Eastern Mercy Health System as a holding company for the health concern. The consolidation served to cut costs, as well as to preserve the organization's religious mission.

The Franciscan Sisters of Allegany congregation got its start in 1859 teaching children in Buffalo, New York. In 1883 the order took over St. Elizabeth Hospital in Boston, expanding its health care services ministry throughout New York, New Jersey, and Florida by the 1930s. In 1986 the sisters organized the operations as Allegany Health System.

In the early 1990s Catholic health care systems underwent a round of consolidation. Allegany Health Systems and Eastern Mercy Health Systems combined services, aiming to lower costs through economies of scale.

The mid-1990s also brought consolidation, but this time operational costs weren't the major problem; Catholic health systems across the nation were facing a shortage of sisters. To have a sufficient number of sisters to keep the "Catholic" in Catholic health care, the three health systems merged in 1997, becoming Catholic Health East.

After the merger, the company continued to build its network through acquisitions, including Mercy Health in Miami (1998) and a suffering, secular Cooper Health System in Camden, New Jersey (1999). In 2000 it gained control of two troubled hospitals in Palm Beach, Florida, only to sell them the following year. Catholic Health East remains focused on reducing costs even as it continues to expand.

EXECUTIVES

Chairperson: Jacquelyn Kinder
President and CEO: Robert V. Stanek
CIO: Donette Herring
EVP and Chief Medical Officer: Thomas L. Garthwaite, age 60
EVP and CFO: Peter L. (Pete) DeAngelis Jr.
EVP Acute Care Division: Judith M. (Judy) Persichilli
EVP Mission Integration: Sister Juliana M. Casey
VP Finance and Growth, Continuing Care Management Services Network: Kelly Hopkins
VP Leadership Development: Anita K. Jensen
VP Clinical Transformation: Kathleen Meredith
VP Business Development: Scott Ash
VP, Mission and Ethics: Philip J. Boyle
VP, Claims Services and Clinical Loss Prevention: Kathleen Young
VP, Risk Management Services and Chief Risk Officer: Theodore Schlert
VP, Systems Communications: Scott Share
VP, Legal Services and General Counsel: Michael C. Hemsley
VP, Capital Strategy and Management: Randal Schultz
Director Human Resources and Administration: Susan Tillman-Taylor
Executive Director, Global Health Ministry: Sister Mary Jo McGinley
President and CEO, Continuing Care Management Services Network: John Capasso
Auditors: PricewaterhouseCoopers LLP

LOCATIONS

HQ: Catholic Health East
3805 W. Chester Pike, Ste. 100
Newtown Square, PA 19073
Phone: 610-355-2000   **Fax:** 610-271-9600
Web: www.che.org

Selected Facilities

Alabama
    Mercy Medical (rehabilitation and nursing care, Daphne)
Connecticut
    Mercy Community Health (nursing care and senior living facilities, West Hartford)
Delaware
    St. Francis Healthcare Services (Wilmington)
Florida
    BayCare Health Systems (Clearwater)
    Holy Cross Hospital (Fort Lauderdale)
    Mercy Hospital (Miami)
Georgia
    Saint Joseph's Health System (Atlanta)
    St. Mary's Health Care System, Inc. (Athens, GA)
Massachusetts
    Sisters of Providence Health System (Springfield)
Maine
    Mercy Health System of Maine (Portland)
New Jersey
    Lourdes Health System (Camden)
    Saint Michael's Medical Center (Newark)
    St. Francis Medical Center (Trenton)
New York
    Catholic Health System (Buffalo)
    St. James Mercy Health System (Hornell)
    St. Peter's Health Care Services (Albany)

North Carolina
    St. Joseph of the Pines (senior living facility, Southern Pines)
Pennsylvania
    Maxis Health System (Carbondale)
    Mercy Health System of Southeastern Pennsylvania (Conshohocken)
    St. Mary Medical Center (Langhorne)

PRODUCTS/OPERATIONS

2008 Key Catholic Health Services

	No. of facilities
Acute-care hospitals	34
Home health/hospice agencies	32
Long-term care (hospital-based & freestanding)	25
Assisted-living facilities	14
Psychiatric & rehabilitation facilities	8
Continuing-care retirement communities	4
Long-term care hospitals	4
Total	**121**

COMPETITORS

Albany Medical Center
Albert Einstein Healthcare Network
Ascension Health
Baptist Health South Florida
Baystate Medical Center
Bon Secours Health
Capital Health System
Catholic Health Initiatives
Christiana Care
Community Health Systems
HCA
Health Management Associates
Kaleida Health
Sun Health
Tenet Healthcare
Universal Health Services
University Health Care System
University of Miami Hospital
University of Pennsylvania Health System

HISTORICAL FINANCIALS

Company Type: Not-for-profit

Income Statement

FYE: December 31

	REVENUE ($ mil.)	NET INCOME ($ mil.)	NET PROFIT MARGIN	EMPLOYEES
12/08	3,926	(540)	—	54,000
12/07	4,365	255	5.8%	54,000
12/06	4,183	199	4.8%	50,000
12/05	4,246	219	5.2%	43,000
12/04	4,035	205	5.1%	43,000
Annual Growth	(0.7%)	—	—	5.9%

2008 Year-End Financials

Debt ratio: 88.2%
Return on equity: —
Cash ($ mil.): —

Current ratio: —
Long-term debt ($ mil.): 1,745

Net Income History

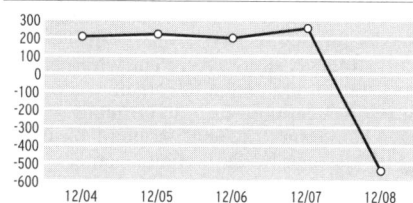

Catholic Health Initiatives

For Catholic Health Initiatives (CHI), returning sick people to good health is more than a business — it's a mission. Formed in 1996 through the merger of three Catholic hospital systems, the giant not-for-profit organization is the second-largest Catholic hospital operator in the US, just behind Ascension Health. It operates more than 70 hospitals and 40 long-term care, assisted-living, and senior residential facilities in 20 states from Washington to Maryland. Its hospitals range from large urban medical centers to small critical-access hospitals in rural areas. All told, the health system has more than 14,000 acute-care beds. It is sponsored by a dozen different congregations of nuns.

The organization grew in 2007 through several new affiliations. It bought 38-bed Enumclaw Regional Hospital, which became part of Washington State's Franciscan Health System; and its Kentucky-based Saint Joseph HealthCare system gained Mary Chiles Hospital, later renamed Saint Joseph Mount Sterling. CHI's largest addition, however, came with the acquisition of Saint Clare's Health System, a four-hospital system operating in northwest New Jersey, from Marian Health System.

Catholic Health Initiatives, along with other not-for-profit hospitals, came under some pressure from Congress in 2006, as federal officials tried to determine whether such hospitals provided enough benefit to their communities (by treating the poor and uninsured, among other things) to earn their tax-exempt status. In anticipation of increased congressional scrutiny, CHI adopted an updated system for reporting their contributions to their communities; the system was developed by the Catholic Health Association, an organization of not-for-profit health systems to which CHI belongs.

HISTORY

In 1860 the Sisters of St. Francis established a hospital in Philadelphia, laying the foundation for a larger health care organization. In 1981 Franciscan Health System was formally established to be a national holding company for Catholic hospitals and related organizations. By the mid-1990s the system consisted of 12 member and two affiliate hospitals and 11 long-term-care facilities located in the mid-Atlantic states and the Pacific Northwest.

Sisters of Charity of Cincinnati and the Sisters of St. Francis Perpetual Adoration of Colorado Springs co-sponsored The Sisters of Charity Health Care Systems, incorporated in 1979 as a multi-institutional health care network. By the mid-1990s the system included 20 hospitals in Colorado, Kentucky, Nebraska, New Mexico, and Ohio.

Three congregations collaborated to form Catholic Health Corporation in 1980, one of the first such health care partnerships between religious communities within the Roman Catholic Church in the US. By 1996 this coalition operated 100 health care facilities in 12 states.

The development of modern managed care health care systems put pressure on the smaller Catholic hospital operations, so the three systems established Catholic Health Initiatives

(CHI) in 1996 as a national entity serving five geographic regions. Patricia Cahill, a lay health care veteran who previously served the Archdiocese of New York, was appointed president and CEO of CHI. The following year CHI absorbed the 10-hospital Sisters of Charity of Nazareth Health Care System, based in Bardstown, Kentucky (founded in a log cabin in 1812).

That year CHI continued to seek new partnerships to improve efficiency. With Alegent Health it formed provider network Midwest Select with nearly 200 hospitals, marketing discounted rates to businesses. CHI allied with the Daughters of Charity to form for-profit joint venture Catholic Healthcare Audit Network to provide operational, financial, compliance, and information systems audits, as well as due diligence reviews. CHI also joined insurance joint venture NewCap Insurance with the Daughters of Charity and Catholic Health East; the firm allowed CHI to operate independently of commercial insurers.

CHI made a secular tie-in with the University of Pennsylvania Health System in 1998, whereby the university's system would offer care through five Catholic hospitals (CHI made plans to transfer these hospitals to Catholic Health East in 2001). The next year CHI announced its first loss, due to lackluster performance in the Midwest. During 2000 the company responded by streamlining operations and changing management, resulting in a positive bottom line. In 2001 it sold three hospitals in Pennsylvania, one in Delaware, and one in New Jersey to Catholic Health East.

EXECUTIVES

Chair, Board of Stewardship: Phyllis Hughes
President, CEO, and Trustee (Board of Stewardship): Kevin E. Lofton
EVP and COO: Michael T. Rowan
SVP Finance and Treasury and CFO: Colleen M. Blye
SVP and CIO: Michael O'Rourke
SVP and Chief Human Resource Officer, Kentucky: Herbert J. Vallier
SVP, Chief Nursing Officer, and Interim Chief Medical Officer: Kathleen D. Sanford
SVP and Division Executive Officer: Jeffrey S. Drop
SVP, National Business Lines: Paul W. Edgett III
SVP and Group Executive Officer: M. Elizabeth O'Brien
SVP, Performance Management: Susan M. Peach
SVP, Legal Services and General Counsel: Mitch H. Melfi
SVP Mission: Rev Thomas R. Kopfensteiner
SVP Sponsorship and Governance: Sister Peggy Ann Martin
SVP Advocacy: M. Colleen Scanlon
SVP Performance Management: Susan E. Peach
SVP Strategy and Business Development: John F. DiCola
SVP and Group Executive Officer: David J. Goode
SVP Communications: Joyce M. Ross
Director, Public Policy: Marcia Desmond
Auditors: Ernst & Young LLP

LOCATIONS

HQ: Catholic Health Initiatives
1999 Broadway, Ste. 4000, Denver, CO 80202
Phone: 303-298-9100   **Fax:** 303-298-9690
Web: www.catholichealthinit.org

COMPETITORS

Adventist Health System
Allina Hospitals
Ascension Health
Baptist Health (Arkansas)
Baptist Healthcare System
BryanLGH Medical Center
Catholic Healthcare Partners
Denver Health and Hospital Authority
Exempla Healthcare
Golden Horizons
HCA
Health Alliance
Kettering Health Network
Life Care Centers
MedCath
Memorial Health System (Colorado)
Methodist Health System
MultiCare Health System
OhioHealth
Tenet Healthcare
Universal Health Services
University of Colorado Hospital

HISTORICAL FINANCIALS

Company Type: Not-for-profit

Income Statement

	REVENUE ($ mil.)	NET INCOME ($ mil.)	NET PROFIT MARGIN	EMPLOYEES
				FYE: June 30
6/08	8,245	32	0.4%	70,760
6/07	7,732	902	11.7%	65,296
6/06	8,077	687	8.5%	65,070
6/05	7,091	461	6.5%	54,044
6/04	6,121	770	12.6%	53,459
Annual Growth	7.7%	(54.8%)	—	7.3%

Net Income History

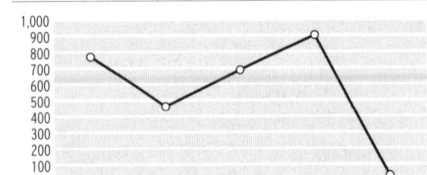

Catholic Healthcare Partners

Catholic Healthcare Partners (CHP) performs acts of healing in the Midwest. One of the nation's largest not-for-profit health systems, CHP offers health care services primarily in Ohio but also in Indiana, Kentucky, Pennsylvania, and Tennessee through some 100 organizations. Facilities include more than 30 hospitals, over a dozen long-term care facilities, affordable housing for the elderly, and wellness centers. CHP also offers physician practices and hospice and home health care. The system is cosponsored by the Sisters of Mercy South Central and Mid-Atlantic communities; the Sisters of the Humility of Mary of Villa Maria, Pennsylvania; the Franciscan Sisters of the Poor; and Covenant Health Systems.

The health care system utilizes its religious philanthropic background combined with modern medical technologies to provide comprehensive patient care. CHP organizes its operations into nine regions to better serve the communities where its facilities are located. Its acute and non-acute inpatient facilities have a total of 7,400 beds. Specialized health care services include cancer, cardiology, radiology, laboratory, surgical, and women's health care.

In 2009 CHP agreed to acquire Jewish Hospital in Cincinnati from The Health Alliance for some $180 million. Jewish Hospital will become part of CHP's Mercy Health Partners Southwest Ohio Region division. Later that year it agreed to purchase the troubled Tyler Memorial Hospital, which will be renamed Mercy Tyler and operate under the Mercy Health Partners Northeast Region network in Pennsylvania.

The health network's St. Mary's Health division was renamed Mercy Health Partners Tennessee in 2008 after St. Mary's merged with the acquired Baptist Health System of East Tennessee. CHP also grows through expansion and renovation efforts at its existing facilities.

EXECUTIVES

Chair: James C. (Jim) Patton
Vice Chair: Cathleen P. Eldridge
President, CEO, and Trustee: Michael D. Connelly
COO: A. David Jimenez
EVP and Chief Administrative Officer: Jane Durney Crowley
EVP and Divisional CEO; President and CEO, Mercy Health Partners, Northern Region: Steven L. (Steve) Mickus
SVP and CFO: James R. (Jim) Gravell Jr.
SVP; President and CEO, Humility of Mary Health Partners: Robert W. (Bob) Shroder
SVP; President and CEO, West Central Ohio Health Partners and St. Rita's Medical Center: James P. Reber
SVP; Divisional CEO, Humility of Mary Health Partners and Mercy Health Partners, Southwest Ohio: James E. (Jim) May
SVP and Divisional CEO; President and CEO, Mercy Health Partners, Tennessee and Kentucky: Debra K. London
SVP and General Counsel: Michael A. Bezney
SVP and CIO: Rebecca (Becky) Sykes
SVP Insurance and Physician Services: R. Jeffrey (Jeff) Copeland
SVP Mission and Values Integration: Sister Doris Gottemoeller
SVP Human Resources; Interim CEO, Mercy Health Partners, Northeast Region: John M. Starcher Jr.
SVP Talent Management and Diversity: Jon C. Abeles
Auditors: Ernst & Young LLP

LOCATIONS

HQ: Catholic Healthcare Partners
615 Elsinore Place, Cincinnati, OH 45202
Phone: 513-639-2800   **Fax:** 513-639-2700
Web: www.health-partners.org

PRODUCTS/OPERATIONS

2008 Sales

	$ mil.	% of total
MHP-Northern	847.4	20
MHP-Southwest Ohio	745.1	17
MHP-Tennessee	618.9	14
Humility of Mary Health Partners	601.9	14
West Central Ohio Health Partners	382.8	9
Community Mercy Health Partners	311.9	7
Community Health Partners	230.5	5
MHP-Kentucky	210.9	5
MHP-Northeast	170.5	4
Home office & other	223.7	5
Adjustments	(298.9)	—
Total	**4,044.7**	**100**

Selected Regions and Facilities

Community Health Partners (Lorain, Ohio)
  Allen Community Hospital
  Community Regional Medical Center

Community Mercy Health Partners (Springfield, Ohio)
  Mercy Memorial Hospital
  Springfield Regional Medical Center Fountain
  Springfield Regional Medical Center High

Humility of Mary Health Partners (Youngstown, Ohio)
  St. Elizabeth Boardman Health Center
  St. Elizabeth Health Center
  St. Joseph Health Center

Mercy Health Partners Kentucky Region (Paducah, Kentucky)
  Lourdes Hospital
  Marcum & Wallace Memorial Hospital

Mercy Health Partners Northeast Region (Scranton, Pennsylvania)
  Mercy Hospital Scranton
  Mercy Special Care Hospital

Mercy Health Partners Northern Region (Toledo, Ohio)
  Mercy Hospital of Defiance
  Mercy St. Anne Hospital
  Mercy St. Charles Hospital
  Mercy St. Vincent Medical Center
    Mercy Children's Hospital
  Mercy Tiffin Hospital
  Mercy Willard Hospital

Mercy Health Partners Southwest Ohio Region (Cincinnati, Ohio)
  Mercy Hospital Anderson
  Mercy Hospital Clermont
  Mercy Hospital Fairfield
  Mercy Hospital Mt. Airy
  Mercy Hospital Western Hills

Mercy Health Partners Tennessee Region (formerly St. Marys Health and Baptist Health; Knoxville, Tennessee)
  Baptist Hospital of Cocke County
  Baptist Hospital West
  St Mary's Jefferson Memorial Hospital
  St. Mary's Medical Center
  St. Mary's Medical Center North
  St. Mary's Medical Center of Campbell County
  St. Mary's Medical Center of Scott County

West Central Ohio Health Partners (Lima, Ohio)
  Institute for Orthopaedic Surgery
  St. Rita's Medical Center

COMPETITORS

AdCare
Adventist Health System
Ascension Health
Catholic Health Initiatives
Cincinnati Children's Hospital
HCA
Kindred Healthcare
LifePoint Hospitals
Methodist Healthcare
Mount Carmel Health
National HealthCare
OhioHealth
Premier Health Partners
SavaSeniorCare
St. Elizabeth Healthcare
Tenet Healthcare
TriHealth
Universal Health Services

HISTORICAL FINANCIALS

Company Type: Not-for-profit

Income Statement

FYE: December 31

	REVENUE ($ mil.)	NET INCOME ($ mil.)	NET PROFIT MARGIN	EMPLOYEES
12/08	4,045	(548)	—	36,925
12/07	3,715	97	2.6%	36,925
12/06	3,511	136	3.9%	34,280
12/05	3,361	154	4.6%	35,000
12/04	3,158	171	5.4%	—
Annual Growth	6.4%	—	—	1.8%

Net Income History

Catholic Healthcare West

Catholic Healthcare West (CHW) has steadily grown to become the largest private, not-for-profit health care provider in the state of California. Sponsored by six congregations of nuns, CHW operates a network of more than 40 acute-care facilities located in the Golden State and, to a lesser extent, in Arizona and Nevada. Those facilities house about 8,800 acute care beds, as well as 900 skilled nursing beds. CHW provides home health and hospice services through agencies in California and Nevada. It also operates emergency and specialty clinics, imaging centers, and medical labs, as well as managed care and wellness programs.

Like most hospital operators, CHW relies on reimbursements from health plans, including Medicare and Medicaid (about 45% of sales), managed care companies, and commercial insurers. The health network also serves private pay customers and provides charity care to qualifying patients. Inpatient services account for about two-thirds of patient revenues, with outpatient services provided at hospitals and clinics making up the remainder.

CHW is expanding some facilities and adding new ones in high-growth areas. Acquisitions have included both religious-group affiliated and community hospitals. In 2007 the organization added the independent 380-bed Saint Mary's Regional Medical Center in Reno, Nevada, to its stable of hospitals. The acquisition included several outpatient clinics and a regional HMO.

In 2009 two of the company's sponsoring congregations merged into a larger regional organization: The Sisters of Mercy communities in Auburn and Burlingame, California, became part of the Sisters of Mercy of the Americas West Midwest Community headquartered in Omaha, Nebraska. The other Catholic sponsoring groups are located in California, Michigan, Texas, and Wisconsin. The six congregations are responsible for appointing CHW's corporate officers.

HISTORY

Catholic Healthcare West traces its roots to 1857, when the Sisters of Mercy founded St. Mary's Hospital in San Francisco. The order expanded in that area, and in 1986 two different communities of the Sisters of Mercy merged their hospitals into an organization with one retirement home and 10 hospitals from the Bay Area to San Diego. Declining membership in Roman Catholic religious orders, combined with consolidation in the field, led the orders to see merger as their only route to survival.

Rising medical costs, slow payers, and merger expenses dropped the organization's combined net income to $20 million in 1988 (from nearly $58 million in 1986). One of the hardest-hit CHW affiliates was Mercy Healthcare Sacramento, which lost $4.2 million between 1986 and 1987. In 1988 Mercy Healthcare restructured along regional lines.

The next year the Sisters of St. Dominic brought two hospitals into the alliance. CHW launched the Community Economic Assistance program, which provided $220,000 in grants to 16 human service and health care agencies in its first year.

CHW continued to add facilities, including AMI Community Hospital in Santa Cruz, California, in 1990. Since CHW already owned the area's only other acute care hospital, Dominican Santa Cruz Hospital, CHW in 1993 was ordered not to acquire any more acute care hospitals in Santa Cruz County without FTC approval.

As the trend to managed care became a stampede in the 1990s, CHW moved more into preventive care and began reining in costs through productivity improvement plans. It continued to add hospitals, including tax-supported institutions trying to compete with national for-profit systems.

The network increased its medical clout in 1994 by allying with San Diego-based Scripps, one of the state's largest HMO systems. In 1995 the Daughters of Charity Province of the West realigned its six-hospital operation with CHW. The next year the Dominican Sisters (California), Dominican Sisters of St. Catherine of Siena (Wisconsin), and Sisters of Charity of the Incarnate Word allied their California hospitals with CHW. New community hospitals included Bakersfield Memorial, Sierra Nevada Memorial (Grass Valley), and Sequoia Hospital (Redwood City).

Charity and cost-consciousness clashed in 1996 when union members staged a walkout to protest nonunion outsourcing of vocational nursing, housekeeping, and kitchen jobs. This dispute was settled, but CHW continued to be a target for union organizers, with a bitter battle against the Service Employees International Union (SEIU) starting in 1998.

CHW agreed in 1996 to merge with Samaritan Health Systems (now Banner Health System) in a move that would have made CHW one of the US's top five providers, but the deal fell apart in 1997. In 1998 CHW merged with UniHealth, a group with eight facilities in Los Angeles and Orange counties. Mounting costs forced CHW to post a loss, and in 1999 it cut some managerial positions and reorganized to recover.

The year 2000 brought CHW more problems with labor relations: SEIU argued that the organization was resistant to unionization. Continued losses led the organization to implement major restructuring the following year, as its 10 regional divisions were consolidated into four.

In 2001 CHW stepped up donations, grants, and other sponsorship efforts designed to benefit areas served by its hospitals and clinics. However, the rapid expansion that made the system a name in the California health care industry also left it bloated. Rising health care costs and trouble with its physician management groups cut deeply into earnings.

Two years later the company parted ways with one of its sponsoring organizations, the Franciscan Sisters of the Sacred Heart of Frankfort, Illinois. The sponsorship ended when CHW closed St. Francis Medical Center of Santa Barbara.

In 2004 CHW joined other Catholic hospitals in announcing plans to charge uninsured patients the same rates charged to patients on Medicare, Medicaid, and other government-funded health care programs. The announcement came, in part, as a response to criticism that hospitals across the country charge uninsured patients much higher rates for services and aggressively seek payment.

And in 2006 CHW settled a class action lawsuit alleging that it had historically overcharged uninsured patients. As part of the settlement, CHW agreed to give hundreds of millions of dollars in refunds and bill adjustments to more than 750,000 patients.

EXECUTIVES

Chair: Jarrett Anderson
Vice Chair: Tessie Guillermo
President, CEO, and Director: Lloyd H. Dean, age 58
EVP, Chief Corporate Officer, and CFO:
  Michael D. Blaszyk
EVP and Co-COO: Marvin O'Quinn
EVP and Co-COO: William J. (Bill) Hunt
SVP and Chief Administrative Officer: Elizabeth Shih
SVP and Chief Strategy Officer: Charles P. Francis
SVP and CIO: Benjamin R. (Ben) Williams
SVP Human Resources: Ernest Urquhart
SVP and Chief Medical Officer: Robert L. Wiebe
SVP and General Counsel: Derek F. Covert
SVP Sponsorship and Mission Integration:
  Bernita McTernan
SVP Managed Care: John Wray
Auditors: Deloitte & Touche LLP

LOCATIONS

HQ: Catholic Healthcare West
  185 Berry St., Ste. 300, San Francisco, CA 94107
Phone: 415-438-5500   **Fax:** 415-438-5724
Web: www.chwhealth.org

Selected Facilities

Arizona
  Barrow Neurological Institute (Phoenix)
  Chandler Regional Medical Center
  Mercy Gilbert Medical Center
  St. Joseph's Hospital and Medical Center (Phoenix)

California
  Arroyo Grande Community Hospital
  Bakersfield Memorial Hospital
  California Hospital Medical Center (Los Angeles)
  Community Hospital of San Bernardino
  Dominican Hospital (Santa Cruz)
  French Hospital Medical Center (San Luis Obispo)
  Glendale Memorial Hospital and Health Center
  Marian Medical Center (Santa Maria)
  Mark Twain St. Joseph's Hospital (San Andreas)
  Mercy General Hospital (Sacramento)
  Mercy Hospital of Bakersfield
  Mercy Hospital of Folsom
  Mercy Medical Center Merced Community Campus
  Mercy Medical Center Merced Dominican Campus
  Mercy Medical Center Mt. Shasta
  Mercy Medical Center Redding
  Mercy San Juan Medical Center (Carmichael)
  Mercy Southwest Hospital (Bakersfield)
  Methodist Hospital of Sacramento
  Northridge Hospital Medical Center
  Oak Valley Hospital (Oakdale)
  Saint Francis Memorial Hospital (San Francisco)
  Sequoia Hospital (Redwood City)
  Sierra Nevada Memorial Hospital (Grass Valley)
  St. Bernardine Medical Center (San Bernardino)
  St. Elizabeth Community Hospital (Red Bluff)
  St. John's Pleasant Valley Hospital (Camarillo)
  St. John's Regional Medical Center (Oxnard)
  St. Joseph's Behavioral Health Center (Stockton)
  St. Joseph's Medical Center (Stockton)
  St. Mary Medical Center (Long Beach)
  St. Mary's Medical Center (San Francisco)
  Woodland Healthcare
Nevada
  Saint Mary's Regional Medical Center (Reno)
  St. Rose Dominican Hospital Rose de Lima Campus
    (Henderson)
  St. Rose Dominican Hospital San Martín Campus (Las
    Vegas)
  St. Rose Dominican Hospital Siena Campus
    (Henderson)

PRODUCTS/OPERATIONS

2009 Sales

	$ mil.	% of total
Patients	8,234.2	92
Premiums	485.3	6
Contributions	22.0	—
Health-related activities	12.2	—
Other	204.2	2
Total	**8,957.9**	**100**

Sponsoring Organizations

Congregation of the Dominican Sisters of St. Catherine of Siena of Kenosha (Kenosha, Wisconsin)
Congregation of the Sisters of Charity of the Incarnate Word (Houston, Texas)
Sisters of Mercy of the Americas, West Midwest Community (Omaha, Nebraska; formerly Auburn Regional Community of the Sisters of Mercy and Burlingame Regional Community of the Sisters of Mercy in California)
Sisters of St. Dominic, Congregation of the Most Holy Rosary (Adrian, Michigan)
Sisters of St. Francis of Penance and Christian Charity, St. Francis Province (Redwood City, California)
Sisters of the Third Order of St. Dominic, Congregation of the Most Holy Name (San Rafael, California)

COMPETITORS

Adventist Health
Banner Health
Community Health Systems
Ensign Group
HCA
Iasis Healthcare
John C. Lincoln Health Network
John Muir Health
Kaiser Permanente
Loma Linda University Medical Center
Los Angeles County Health Department
Memorial Health Services
Prospect Medical
Providence Health & Services
Shasta Regional Medical Center
St. Joseph Health System
Stanford University Medical
Sutter Health
Tenet Healthcare
UCSF Medical
Universal Health Services
Vanguard Health Systems
VITAS Healthcare

HISTORICAL FINANCIALS

Company Type: Not-for-profit

Income Statement

FYE: June 30

	REVENUE ($ mil.)	NET INCOME ($ mil.)	NET PROFIT MARGIN	EMPLOYEES
6/09	8,958	(126)	—	60,000
6/08	8,402	170	2.0%	50,000
6/07	7,477	891	11.9%	50,000
6/06	6,617	443	6.7%	—
6/05	6,002	348	5.8%	40,000
Annual Growth	**10.5%**	**—**	**—**	**10.7%**

Net Income History

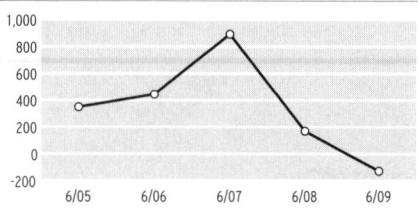

Cavaliers Operating Company

This business hardly has a carefree attitude towards roundball. The Cavaliers Operating Company owns and operates the Cleveland Cavaliers professional basketball team and its home court, Quicken Loans Arena. The Cavs joined the National Basketball Association in 1970 as part of an expansion that included the Portland Trail Blazers and Buffalo Braves (now the Los Angeles Clippers). Though losing records have been more the norm for the team in the past, things have been looking up for Cleveland since drafting high school sensation LeBron James in 2003. Quicken Loans founder Dan Gilbert has controlled the team since 2005; the family of original owner Gordon Gund continues to have a minority stake in the Cavs.

In addition to providing a much needed spark on the court, the arrival of James in Cleveland also helped spur increased ticket sales. The team clinched its first ever conference title in 2007, though the Cavs fell to the San Antonio Spurs in the NBA Finals.

Gilbert agreed in 2009 to sell a 15% stake in the basketball franchise to a group of Chinese investors led by Kenny Huang and Adrian Cheng. The influx of new capital will help the Cavs organization when it comes time to re-sign James to a new contract. Huang has brokered sports marketing deals in China involving the New York Yankees and Houston Rockets; Cheng's family controls New World Development, a diversified real estate conglomerate in Hong Kong.

With the Cavs' fortunes on the rise, the Gund family sold a majority stake in the team to Gilbert for about $365 million. He changed the name of the operating company from Cavaliers/Gund Arena Company later that year. Quicken Loans also took over naming rights to the team's home arena, which had formerly been known as Gund Arena.

In addition to the Gund family, the Cavs ownership group includes hip-hop star Usher.

EXECUTIVES

Chairman: Daniel B. (Dan) Gilbert
Vice Chairman: David B. Katzman, age 44
CEO: Mark Stornes
President: Len Komoroski
General Manager: Danny Ferry
Head Coach: Mike Brown
EVP: Roy Jones
SVP Communications: Tad Carper
EVP Corporate Sales and Broadcasting: Kerry Bubolz
SVP Marketing: Tracy Marek
VP Finance and Administration: John Wolf
Senior Director Broadcasting Services:
  Dave Dombrowski
Director Player Development and Assistant Coach:
  Chris Jent
Director Human Resources: Farrell Finnin

LOCATIONS

HQ: Cavaliers Operating Company, LLC
  1 Center Ct., Cleveland, OH 44115
Phone: 216-420-2000   **Fax:** 216-420-2101
Web: www.nba.com/cavaliers

The Cleveland Cavaliers play at 20,562-seat capacity Quicken Loans Arena in Cleveland.

PRODUCTS/OPERATIONS

Championship Titles
Eastern Conference Champions (2007)

COMPETITORS

Chicago Bulls
Detroit Pistons
Indiana Pacers
Milwaukee Bucks

CCA Global Partners

Business is "floor"ishing at CCA Global Partners. Formerly Carpet Co-op, the firm operates more than 3,800 floor covering and specialty retail stores in the US and abroad. Many stores operate under the Carpet One name; other names include Flooring America, ProSource, and International Design Guild (high-end showrooms). The world's largest floor covering retailer (with stores in the US, Canada, Australia, New Zealand, and South Africa), Carpet One is the exclusive US marketer of Bigelow and the Lees carpet brands. CCA Global has also made forays into bicycle and lighting products retailing, mortgage banking, and business services. Howard Brodsky and Alan Greenberg founded the co-op in 1984.

The company's BizUnite division serves organizations and their members through its Web-based B2B marketplace of more than 17,000 businesses. In a bid to attract more members, BizUnite in March 2009 acquired Minnesota-based MainStreet Business Services, which claims more than 130,000 member businesses. It became part of BizUnite, which made plans to expand the scope of services available to member companies.

CCA Global's Lenders One division operates as an aggregator of mortgage money. Its Lighting One division (bought by CCA in 2001) has about 100 locations selling lamps, ceiling fans, and accessories. The Bike Cooperative — a network of some 330 bicycle stores in 40-plus states — sells Giant brand bicycles, as well as other bicycle brands, parts, and accessories.

In 2006 the company added South Africa to its list of global sites when Durban-based Top Carpet & Tile, with 90 stores, joined the group.

In 2008 Rick Bennet, formerly of May Department Stores, joined Brodsky as co-CEO of CCA Global Partners.

EXECUTIVES

Chairman and Co-CEO: Howard Brodsky
Co-CEO and Director: Richard W. (Rick) Bennet III, age 56
President and Director: Sandy Mishkin
CFO: Jim Acker
Chief Product Officer: Charlie Dilks
Chief Marketing Officer: Dean P. Marcarelli
SVP National Accounts: Steve Pigman
SVP New Membership: Michael (Mike) Cherico, age 42
Chief Administrative Officer: Robert M. (Bob) Wilson
Executive Director, Nonprofits, CCA for Social Good:
  Laurie Cochran

LOCATIONS

HQ: CCA Global Partners
  4301 Earth City Expwy., St. Louis, MO 63045
Phone: 314-506-0000   **Fax:** 314-291-6674
Web: www.ccaglobalpartners.com

PRODUCTS/OPERATIONS

Selected Companies
Flooring Retail
  Carpet One Floor & Home
  Flooring America
  Flooring Canada
  International Design Guild
  ProSource Wholesale Floorcoverings
  Rug Décor
  Stone Mountain's Flooring Outlet
  The Floor Trader
  GCO Flooring Outlet

Bicycle Retail
  The Bike Cooperative
  The Biking Solution
Business Services
  BizUnite
Mortgage Banking
  Lenders One
Specialty Lighting
  Lighting One

COMPETITORS

Abbey Carpet
Home Depot
Lowe's
Menard
Performance Bike Shop

HISTORICAL FINANCIALS

Company Type: Cooperative

Income Statement				FYE: September 30
	REVENUE ($ mil.)	NET INCOME ($ mil.)	NET PROFIT MARGIN	EMPLOYEES
9/08	10,200	—	—	—
9/07	10,200	—	—	—
9/06	10,200	—	—	—
9/05	9,393	—	—	—
9/04	8,700	—	—	—
Annual Growth	4.1%	—	—	—

Revenue History

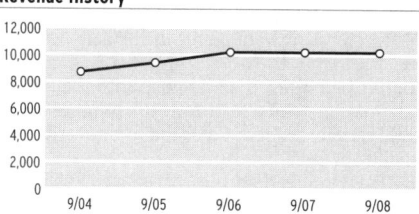

CDW Corporation

CDW Corporation takes more orders than Beetle Bailey. The company offers about 100,000 computer products, including notebook and desktop PCs, software, printers, servers, storage devices, networking tools, and accessories. Brands include Adobe, Apple, Cisco, Hewlett-Packard, Microsoft, Sony, ViewSonic, and Xerox, among others. Its Toronto-based subsidiary markets technology products to customers across Canada. Almost all of CDW's sales come from private business and public sector clients. The company was founded in 1984. It was acquired in 2007 by private equity firm Madison Dearborn Partners for about $7 billion.

CDW shareholders, including company founder and chairman emeritus Michael Krasny (who owned about 20% of CDW), received nearly $90 per share in cash from Madison Dearborn for their shares.

Since the acquisition, CDW has been evaluating its business lines and offerings. The company in 2009 sold the software division of IT solution provider Berbee Information Networks (which it had acquired three years prior) back to a group of its former managers. Berbee's other advanced technology products were added to

CDW's offerings for the corporate, education, government, and health care sectors.

The company continues to expand its public sector business, which accounts for about a third of sales, through its CDW Government subsidiary. The division sells exclusively to government (federal, state, and local) and education customers.

HISTORY

Michael Krasny started Computer Discount Warehouse at his kitchen table in 1984. Weary of selling used cars at his father's Chicago lot (though he did like using his programming skills to computerize the dealership), Krasny quit and had to sell his own computer to raise cash. A classified ad in the *Chicago Tribune* generated phenomenal response, and Krasny sold his computer almost immediately.

When the calls kept coming in, he bought more computers and sold them to people responding to the original ad, and his mail-order business was under way. Krasny chose new, stripped-down IBM clones, packaged them with monitors and printers, and advertised them as used computer systems. Because PCs were still in their infancy and because customers were lost in the technology, computer setup and repair became a large part of the early business.

CDW launched its first catalog in 1987. Figuring that some buyers would shy away from purchasing costly PC systems by mail, Krasny in 1990 opened his first retail showroom (one of two) in Chicago.

The company went public in 1993 after changing the name to CDW Computer Centers. By then it had intensified its push into the corporate market, which featured bulk purchases and solid repeat business. Sales that year nearly doubled from 1992.

CDW launched an Internet site in 1995. The next year it expanded its telemarketing-based sales strategy and began taking online orders. It also enlarged its Chicago showrooms.

Intense marketing and low prices boosted sales in 1997 with multimedia products, data storage devices, PCs, software, and video products as the fastest sellers. That year the company relocated its offices (and one of its showrooms) to a larger facility in Vernon Hills, Illinois. CDW pushed past the $1 billion mark for the first time in 1997, logging sales of nearly $1.3 billion. The following year the company formed CDW Government, a subsidiary set up to focus on sales to government and education institutions.

In May 2001 Krasny assumed the role of chairman emeritus; CEO John Edwardson added chairman to his duties. In May 2003 shareholders approved a decision to change the company name to CDW Corporation.

In October 2006 CDW completed the acquisition of privately held Berbee Information Networks (BIN) for $184 million. A year later, CDW was itself acquired by private equity firm Madison Dearborn Partners for about $7.3 billion. The company's shares were delisted on October 12, 2007.

In April 2009 CDW sold BIN back to a group of its former managers for an undisclosed sum.

EXECUTIVES

Chairman and CEO: John A. Edwardson, age 60
President and COO: Thomas E. (Tom) Richards, age 54
SVP and CFO: Ann E. Ziegler, age 51
SVP and Chief Coworker Services Officer:
 Dennis G. Berger, age 44

SVP, General Counsel, and Corporate Secretary; Secretary, CDW Government:
 Christine A. (Chris) Leahy, age 44
SVP and CIO: Jonathan J. (Jon) Stevens, age 39
SVP Operations: Douglas E. (Doug) Eckrote, age 44
VP Program Management, CDW Government, Inc.:
 Kevin P. Adams
VP Strategic Sales: Kenneth B. (Ken) Grimsley
VP Medium/Large Segment Sales:
 William T. (Bill) Weaver, age 55
VP Advanced Technology: Terry Swanson
VP Services: James J. (Norm) Lillis
VP and Chief Marketing Officer: Mark J. Gambill, age 49
VP Small Business: Maria M. Sullivan
VP and Controller: Virginia L. Seggerman, age 46
VP Financial Planning and Analysis: Collin Kebo
VP, Treasurer, and Assistant Secretary; Treasurer and Assistant Secretary, CDW Government:
 Robert J. (Bob) Welyki
VP Sales Planning and Operations: Anne B. Ireland
VP Product and Partner Management:
 Matthew A. (Matt) Troka
President, CDW Government, Inc.:
 Christina V. (Chris) Rother
Auditors: PricewaterhouseCoopers LLP

LOCATIONS

HQ: CDW Corporation
 200 N. Milwaukee Ave., Vernon Hills, IL 60061
Phone: 847-465-6000
Web: www.cdw.com

COMPETITORS

Amazon.com	Newegg
Apple Inc.	Office Depot
AT&T	OfficeMax
Austin Ribbon & Computer	PC Connection
Best Buy	PC Mall
Buy.com	Pomeroy IT
CompuCom	Softchoice
Costco Wholesale	Software House
Dell	Staples
Fry's Electronics	SunGard Availability
Gateway, Inc.	Services
GTSI	SunGard Higher Education
Hewlett-Packard	Systemax
HP Enterprise Services	Verizon
IBM	Wal-Mart
Insight Enterprises	Zones
Micro Electronics	

HISTORICAL FINANCIALS

Company Type: Private

Income Statement

FYE: December 31

	REVENUE ($ mil.)	NET INCOME ($ mil.)	NET PROFIT MARGIN	EMPLOYEES
12/08	8,070	—	—	6,850
12/07	8,100	—	—	6,900
Annual Growth	(0.4%)	—	—	(0.7%)

Revenue History

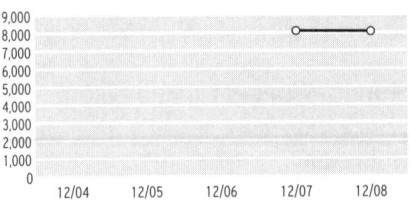

9,000			○———○	
8,000				
7,000				
6,000				
5,000				
4,000				
3,000				
2,000				
1,000				
0				
	12/04	12/05	12/06	12/07	12/08

Cellco Partnership

A strong alliance with a trusted partner can be the cornerstone of a great enterprise. While only time will tell how this union will fare as the telecommunications industry evolves, for now, Cellco Partnership is the #1 US wireless phone operator in terms of subscribers (ahead of rival AT&T Mobility). Serving more than 80 million consumers, business, and government customers nationwide under the Verizon Wireless brand, the joint venture is controlled by Verizon Communications (which owns 55% of the company); UK-based global communications giant Vodafone Group owns the remaining share. The company also offers mobile data services, including text messaging, multimedia content (V CAST), and Web access.

Formerly a provider of only wireline communications services, parent Verizon Communications continues to build its wireless business through acquisitions as it advances toward its goal of becoming a provider primarily of mobile services. Its growing wireless business accounts for half of total revenue.

In 2009 the company purchased Alltel in a $28.1 billion deal that made Verizon Wireless the leading US mobile carrier. In order to gain approval from the US Department of Justice for the acquisition, Verizon in 2009 exited about 100 US markets through the divestiture of assets located primarily in rural areas where Alltel also has operations. As part of this restructuring, AT&T paid about $2.3 billion for rural assets in 18 states. In a separate transaction later that year, AT&T agreed to sell certain wireless operations of Centennial Communications (located in Louisiana and Mississippi) to Verizon for $240 million upon the completion of AT&T's acquisition of Centennial.

In another smaller deal completed in mid-2008, Verizon Wireless bought regional competitor Rural Cellular for about $2.6 billion in cash and debt. The purchase increased Verizon's wireless customer base by more than 600,000. Rural Cellular offered cellular service in smaller markets under the Unicel brand in 12 states in the Midwest, the Pacific Northwest, the South, and the Northeast.

Verizon Wireless began operations in 2000 when former Baby Bell Bell Atlantic and Vodafone combined their US wireless assets. The company gained GTE's US wireless operations when Bell Atlantic bought GTE to form Verizon Communications that year.

EXECUTIVES

President, CEO, and Director: Lowell C. McAdam
COO: Daniel S. (Dan) Mead
CIO: Ajay Waghray
Chief Marketing Officer: John G. Stratton, age 47
SVP and CTO, Cellco Partnership and Rural Cellular:
 Anthony J. (Tony) Melone Sr., age 49
VP and CFO; VP, CFO, and Director, Rural Cellular:
 John Townsend, age 46
VP Legal and External Affairs, General Counsel, and Secretary: Steven E. Zipperstein, age 49
VP Customer Service Operations: Charlie Falco
VP Human Resources: Martha Delehanty, age 42
VP Workforce Development: Lou Tedrick
VP National Government Sales and Operations:
 Mark Harris
VP Corporate Communications: James J. (Jim) Gerace
VP Business Development, Cellco Partnership and Rural Cellular: Margaret P. (Molly) Feldman, age 51
Auditors: Deloitte & Touche LLP

HQ: Cellco Partnership
  1 Verizon Way, Basking Ridge, NJ 07920
Phone: 908-559-2000
Web: www.verizonwireless.com

PRODUCTS/OPERATIONS

Selected Services
Equipment sales
Location-based services
Mobile voice
Mobile Web
Paging
PCS (personal communications services)
Push-to-talk voice service
Ringback tones
Text and picture messaging
Wireless broadband
Wireless business services

COMPETITORS

AT&T Mobility
Centennial Communications
CenturyTel
Leap Wireless
Qwest Wireless
Sprint Nextel
T-Mobile USA
U.S. Cellular
Virgin Mobile USA

HISTORICAL FINANCIALS

Company Type: Joint venture

Income Statement				FYE: December 31
	REVENUE ($ mil.)	NET INCOME ($ mil.)	NET PROFIT MARGIN	EMPLOYEES
12/08	49,332	13,289	26.9%	85,800
12/07	43,882	10,860	24.7%	69,000
12/06	38,043	8,448	22.2%	67,000
12/05	32,301	6,152	19.0%	55,700
12/04	27,662	4,698	17.0%	49,800
Annual Growth	15.6%	29.7%	—	14.6%

2008 Year-End Financials
Debt ratio: 13.3%
Return on equity: —
Cash ($ mil.): —
Current ratio: —
Long-term debt ($ mil.): 9,938

Net Income History

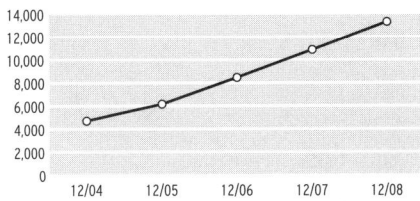

Center Oil

Center Oil's core business is peddling petroleum. The company is one of the largest private wholesale distributors of gasoline and other petroleum products to customers primarily in the eastern region of the US. Center Oil owns a dozen storage terminals capable of storing 2.8 million barrels of petroleum products. It also has access to 36 terminals in 10 states, as well as access to the Magellan, Texas Eastern, Kinder Morgan Chicago, and Kaneb pipeline systems. Its products are also distributed through a fleet of ships, barges, and trucks.

Diversifying his operations, president and CEO Gary Parker acquired a minority stake in ethanol producer Green Plains Renewable Energy Inc. in 2007, and in 2008 he formed a Center Oil ethanol subsidiary, Center Ethanol LLC.

Center Oil was established in 1986 by Parker. The company is one of the largest privately held companies in the St. Louis metropolitan area.

EXECUTIVES

President: Gary R. Parker, age 59
Secretary and General Counsel:
  Michael C. Aufdenspring
Manager Information Technology: Eric Pitts
Manager Finance: Brian Skoff
Systems Analyst: Kostadin Todorov
Controller: Joseph (Joe) Beck
Treasurer and Head Human Resources:
  Richard I. (Rick) Powers
Manager Operations and Scheduling, Supply and Distribution: Jerry Jost
Cash Management, Truck Sales: Lisa Wolff
Sales Manager, Truck Sales: Rob Kraeger

LOCATIONS

HQ: Center Oil Company
  600 Mason Ridge Center Dr., St. Louis, MO 63141
Phone: 314-682-3500   **Fax:** 314-682-3599
Web: www.centeroil.com

COMPETITORS

Apex Oil
Colonial Group
George Warren
Gulf Oil
U.S. Oil

HISTORICAL FINANCIALS

Company Type: Private

Income Statement				FYE: December 31
	REVENUE ($ mil.)	NET INCOME ($ mil.)	NET PROFIT MARGIN	EMPLOYEES
12/08	4,900	—	—	46

Central Grocers

In a city of big stores, Central Grocers helps neighborhood markets stay afloat. The member-owned cooperative wholesale food distributor supplies food items and general merchandise to more than 200 independent retail grocery stores in the Chicago area and in the northwest region of Indiana. It distributes products under both national brands and its own Centrella brand. The co-op also operates a number of stores under such banners as Strack & Van Til, Town & Country, Key Market, and the low-cost Ultra Foods chain. Central Grocers was founded in 1917.

Looking to expand its territory, the cooperative has announced plans to acquire rival wholesale distributor Certified Grocers. The combined operation will serve more than 440 stores in Illinois, Indiana, Iowa, and Wisconsin. In 2006 Central Grocers acquired about a dozen stores from regional supermarket chain Cub Foods. Almost half of those were converted to Ultra Foods locations.

CEO Joe Caccamo retired from Central Grocers in 2007 after 25 years of service. He was replaced by longtime veteran Jim Denges.

EXECUTIVES

President and CEO: James (Jim) Denges, age 62
CFO: Tim Kubis
Chief Technology Officer: Mark Brandes
VP and Assistant General Manager:
  Robert J. (Bob) Wagner
Director Meat: Wally Locke
Manager Human Resources: Annalee Robish
Controller: Jane T. Denges
Auditors: Deloitte & Touche LLP

LOCATIONS

HQ: Central Grocers, Inc.
  11100 Belmont Ave., Franklin Park, IL 60131
Phone: 847-451-0660   **Fax:** 847-288-8710
Web: www.central-grocers.com

COMPETITORS

Albertsons
ALDI
Associated Wholesale Grocers
C & S Wholesale
Certco
Certified Grocers Midwest
Dearborn Wholesale Grocers
Kroger
Meijer
Nash-Finch
Safeway
Schnuck Markets
SUPERVALU
Wal-Mart
Winkler Incorporated

HISTORICAL FINANCIALS

Company Type: Cooperative

Income Statement				FYE: Saturday nearest July 31
	REVENUE ($ mil.)	NET INCOME ($ mil.)	NET PROFIT MARGIN	EMPLOYEES
7/08	1,197	—	—	2,300

Central National-Gottesman

All the news that's fit to print (or at least some of it) shows up on a portion of Central National-Gottesman's (CNG) products. The papermaker distributes annually 4 million tons of goods, from wood pulp to paper, paperboard, and newsprint. Markets are tapped in 75-plus countries dotting the globe. In addition to North American operations, the company's international presence is established in about 20 offices, spanning Asia, Europe, and Latin America. The CNG community includes the Lindenmeyr family of companies, paper merchants in fine paper, papers for books, magazines and catalogs, specialized papers, and packaging grades. CNG is privately held by the fourth-generation of the founding Gottesman family.

The company breadth and depth of market penetration and product mix is central to its ability to defend itself against the global economic downturn. Although North American paper demand in waning, Central National-Gottesman is able to export to more promising opportunities in Asia, South America, and some in Europe.

The company's market share is supported by a roster of prominent suppliers, including paper industry leaders International Paper (#1) and Weyerhaeuser. Although it sources wood pulp on its own, Central National-Gottesman supplements its stock by gathering all types of wood from producers in Brazil and Argentina, Spain, and South Africa.

The company caters to customers with a wide slate of services. It offers sales, financing, transportation, and marketing research, as well as management and consulting expertise. Founded by European immigrants in 1886, Central National-Gottesman has evolved from a New York-based raw material papermaking source to rank among America's largest private companies.

EXECUTIVES

President and CEO: Kenneth L. Wallach
VP, Human Resources: Louise Caputo
Treasurer: Steven Eigen

LOCATIONS

HQ: Central National-Gottesman Inc.
3 Manhattanville Rd., Purchase, NY 10577
Phone: 914-696-9000   **Fax:** 914-696-1066
Web: www.cng-inc.com

COMPETITORS

Clifford Paper
International Paper
Midland Paper
RIS the paper house
Smurfit-Stone Container
Unisource

HISTORICAL FINANCIALS

Company Type: Private

Income Statement

FYE: December 31

	REVENUE ($ mil.)	NET INCOME ($ mil.)	NET PROFIT MARGIN	EMPLOYEES
12/08	3,500	—	—	925
12/07	3,000	—	—	1,000
12/06	2,700	—	—	850
12/05	2,300	—	—	850
12/04	2,000	—	—	775
Annual Growth	**15.0%**	**—**	**—**	**4.5%**

Revenue History

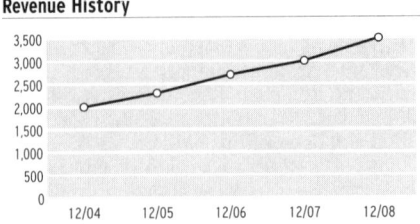

Central Parking

If you park your car in a central location, you might very well be doing business with Central Parking. A leading parking provider, the company oversees more than 2,500 facilities with about 1.2 million spaces, in about 40 states and Puerto Rico. Its facilities serve high-traffic locations such as airports, office buildings, and stadiums. Along with operating parking lots and garages, the company provides shuttle transportation and valet parking, plus parking meter enforcement and collection under contracts with cities. It also serves as a consultant for parking facility operators. A group of private equity firms bought Central Parking in May 2007.

The $726 million buyout — led by affiliates of Kohlberg & Co. LLC, Lubert-Adler LP, and Chrysalis Capital Partners LP — came amid an effort by Central Parking to enhance profitability by exiting smaller US markets and less-promising international locations. To focus on US markets, the company is shedding its international properties, starting with the sale in 2007 of operations in Europe, which had accounted for less than 5% of overall sales. In 2008 Central Parking sold its Canadian operations, which were only 2.5% of revenues. It plans to sell its South American properties as well.

To grow, Central Parking has been working to win contracts in major US metropolitan areas, particularly at airports, and on gaining national accounts from big customers, such as hotels and property management companies.

In 2008 the company sold 18 of its properties to the family of founder Monroe Carell for $65 million. The parking lots/facilities will be leased back to Central Parking. The sale continues the company's plan to shift from owning properties to managing them. The firm steadily is selling off the 130 properties it owns (about 5% of its parking lots) and anticipates that some of the lots will be developed instead of leased back to Central Parking.

EXECUTIVES

President and CEO: Emanuel J. Eads
EVP: Gregory J. (Greg) Stormberg
EVP: James H. Bond
SVP and CFO: John I. Hill
SVP and General Counsel:
 Johann R. (Chip) Manning Jr., age 46
SVP Human Resources: Donald N. Holmes
SVP: Gregory D. (Greg) Maxey
SVP: Alan J. Kahn
SVP: Robert L. Cizek
SVP: Hector Chevalier
President, USA Parking: William H. Bodenhamer Jr.
Secretary: Henry J. Abbott
Auditors: KPMG LLP

LOCATIONS

HQ: Central Parking Corporation
 2401 21st Ave. South, Ste. 200, Nashville, TN 37212
Phone: 615-297-4255   **Fax:** 615-297-6240
Web: www.parking.com

2008 Locations

	No. of properties
New York	316
California	278
Texas	192
Florida	167
Tennessee	167
Colorado	103
Louisiana	100
Ohio	87
Virginia	81
Alabama	76
New Jersey	74
Massachusetts	69
Washington, DC	69
Georgia	66
Missouri	66
Pennsylvania	55
Wisconsin	49
Illinois	48
North Carolina	48
Maryland	47
Minnesota	31
Washington	30
Nebraska	28
Mississippi	27
Oklahoma	25
Kentucky	24
Connecticut	22
Michigan	22
Arizona	21
West Virginia	19
Puerto Rico	13
Other states	39
Total	**2,459**

COMPETITORS

ABM Industries
Ace Parking
Diamond Parking
Impark
Macquarie Infrastructure Company
Parking Company of America
Standard Parking

Centric Group

This company makes sure the world has enough balloons, baggage, and beverages. Centric Group is a holding company for several manufacturing and distribution businesses. Its Betallic unit manufactures latex and Mylar balloons sold through florist shops and other gift retailers. The company's TRG Group, meanwhile, manufactures luggage and other travel bags under such brands as Callaway Golf and Victorinox. In addition, Centric serves commissaries at correctional facilities with snacks, beverages, and other food and nonfood items through its Keefe Group. The company was formed in 1974 as part of Enterprise Rent-A-Car and spun off in 1999. It is controlled by the Taylor family.

Longtime CEO Doug Albrecht retired early in 2008 and was replaced by a triumvirate including CFO John O'Connell, COO Jim Theiss, and chairman Andy Taylor (who also serves as CEO of Enterprise).

EXECUTIVES

Chairman: Andrew C. (Andy) Taylor, age 61
President and COO: Jim Theiss, age 50
Vice Chairman and CFO: John T. O'Connell, age 52
EVP and General Manager, Keefe Commissary Network: John Puricelli
President and General Manager, TRG Group: Nathan Schulte
VP and Corporate Controller: Vicki S. Altman
President and COO, Keefe Group: Jeff Donnelly
President and General Manager, Courtesy Products: Mark Schwarz

LOCATIONS

HQ: Centric Group, L.L.C.
1260 Andes Blvd., St. Louis, MO 63132
Phone: 314-214-2700 **Fax:** 314-214-2766
Web: www.centricgp.com

PRODUCTS/OPERATIONS

Selected Operations

Betallic (latex and Mylar balloon manufacturing)
Courtesy Products (hospitality beverage services and supplies)
Keefe Group
  Access Catalog Company
  Keefe Commissary Network (corrections facility commissary supplier)
  Keefe Supply Company (wholesale foodservice distribution)
TRG Group (travel baggage and athletic footwear manufacturing)

COMPETITORS

ABL Management
Amscan
ARAMARK
CTI Industries
Good Source
Guest Supply
Rawlings Sporting Goods
Samsonite
Tumi
US Balloon Manufacturing

HISTORICAL FINANCIALS

Company Type: Private

Income Statement				FYE: December 31
	ESTIMATED REVENUE ($ mil.)	NET INCOME ($ mil.)	NET PROFIT MARGIN	EMPLOYEES
12/08	820	—	—	2,422
12/07	750	—	—	2,300
12/06	700	—	—	2,000
12/05	600	—	—	1,600
Annual Growth	11.0%	—	—	14.8%

Revenue History

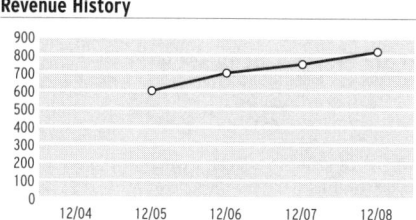

Ceridian Corporation

Problems with payroll? Trouble with taxes? Ceridian wants to help. The company provides payroll processing, tax filing, benefits administration, and other human resources services to employers mainly in the US but also in Canada and the UK. Ceridian's other business units, Comdata and Stored Value Solutions, issue and process payments for credit, debit, and stored value cards (gift cards and employee expense cards), primarily for companies in the trucking and retail industries. Investment firm Thomas H. Lee Partners and insurer Fidelity National Financial own Ceridian.

Ceridian generates human resources business through its sales force and via marketing alliances with consulting firms and other providers of outsourced business services.

In February 2009, Ceridian managed its own human resources by cutting 11% of its Stored Value Solutions subsidiary's workforce, citing a need to streamline operations.

Before it went private in 2007, the company grew by acquiring complementary businesses. It expanded its work-life offerings by buying Leade Health, a weight- and stress-management coaching company. Ceridian also bought Inter-Tax, a provider of fuel tax compliance services, to augment Comdata's transportation-related business.

EXECUTIVES

Chairman, President, and CEO: Kathryn V. (Kathy) Marinello, age 52
EVP Human Resources: Kairus K. Tarapore, age 47
EVP and CTO: Perry H. Cliburn, age 51
EVP and CFO: Gregory J. (Greg) Macfarlane, age 52
EVP, General Counsel, and Secretary: Michael W. Sheridan
EVP Quality and Service Operations: Michael F. Shea, age 43
EVP and President, Ceridian International: Jim Burns
SVP, Human Resources and Payroll Services: Steven Rodriguez
SVP U.S. Human Resource Solutions: Nancy L. Hanna
SVP Implementation: Liza Sayre

SVP Investor Relations and Business Development: Craig Manson
SVP Ceridian Tax Services: Webster Hill
SVP and Controller: Ralph T. Flees, age 41
VP, Marketing Communications: Keith Peterson
Chief People Officer: Jennifer Stacey
President, Comdata: Brett Rodewald, age 45

LOCATIONS

HQ: Ceridian Corporation
3311 E. Old Shakopee Rd., Minneapolis, MN 55425
Phone: 952-853-8100 **Fax:** 952-853-4430
Web: www.ceridian.com

PRODUCTS/OPERATIONS

Selected Business Units

Benefits
Ceridian Canada, Ltd.
Ceridian UK, Ltd.
Comdata
Human Resource Outsourcing
LifeWorks
Stored Value Solutions
US Payroll

Selected Products and Services

Compliance resources and services
Corporate health and wellness programs
Employee assistance programs
Employee benefits administration
Employee productivity management
Employee retention and rewards
Government solutions
Human resources management and HRO
Payroll processing and tax filing
Recruiting and screening services
Time and labor management

COMPETITORS

Administaff
ADP
Barrett Business Services
CBIZ
C.H. Robinson Worldwide
CompuPay.
Convergys
First Data
Fleetcor
Hewitt Associates
HP Enterprise Services
Northgate Information Solutions
Paychex
Sage Software
Spherion
TeamStaff
Ultimate Software
Wright Express

HISTORICAL FINANCIALS

Company Type: Private

Income Statement				FYE: December 31
	REVENUE ($ mil.)	NET INCOME ($ mil.)	NET PROFIT MARGIN	EMPLOYEES
12/08	1,695	—	—	8,776
12/07	1,700	—	—	9,177
Annual Growth	(0.3%)	—	—	(4.4%)

Revenue History

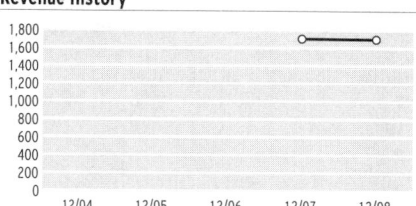

CH2M HILL Companies

Catchy, no. Descriptive, yes. CH2M HILL's name is culled from its founders — Cornell, Howland, Hayes, and Merryfield — plus HILL, from its first merger. The group is organized into three divisions: civil infrastructure, federal, and industrial. Its civil infrastructure group designs and builds water and wastewater systems, airports, highways, and other transportation infrastructures. Federal services include nuclear and environmental cleanup projects and government facility operations. Industrial operations include engineering, procurement, and construction for private-sector companies in the chemical, energy, and life sciences industries. Clients have included the US Department of Defense and the US Navy.

CH2M HILL provides its services to both domestic and international clients, although the US accounts for the vast majority of its revenues. The company's revenues are distributed among its three divisions, with the industrial segment accounting for nearly 50%.

The company has operations in more than 80 countries. Growth in its international markets, including Australia and the United Arab Emirates (where it is working on desalination plants), is what has helped spur increased revenues in its civil infrastructure group. The growth overseas has helped offset decreases in US projects due to the negative economic conditions at home.

In 2009 CH2M HILL announced the sale of the IT solutions division of its Enterprise Management Solutions business to CRITIGEN, a portfolio company of Golden Gate Capital. The sale allows the firm to focus on engineering, construction, and operations. It plans to partner with CRITIGEN for IT solutions through a three-year preferred provider agreement that is part of the sale.

On the federal front CH2M HILL won a $5.5 million contract from the Department of Energy in 2008 to help 25 American cities accelerate the adoption of solar energy. The company will work with city and government officials to help install clean solar energy technology by 2015.

CH2M HILL, along with partners Laing O'Rourke and Mace Ltd., won a $190 million contract to oversee construction on sports venues and infrastructures for the 2012 Olympic Games in London. CH2M HILL's team beat out other major rivals for the job: AMEC plc, Balfour Beatty plc and Jacobs Engineering Group; Bechtel Group; and Bovis Lend Lease, Kellogg Brown & Root, Capita Symonds, and Franklin & Andrews. Among CH2M HILL's responsibilities will be to make the 2012 Games the most environmentally friendly in history by using recycled construction materials, incorporating wind energy, and reducing carbon dioxide emissions.

The company also expects to see continued growth in its industrial segment partially due to key acquisitions in 2007 of two energy services companies, troubled Alaskan oil and gas services firm VECO and Colorado pipeline contractor Trigon EPC. The industrial segment also is being driven by several engineering, procurement, and construction contracts with major US utilities to build power generation facilities.

Founded in 1946, the company is owned by its employees.

EXECUTIVES

President and CEO: Lee A. McIntire, age 60, $2,698,636 total compensation
SVP, CFO, and Director: M. Catherine Santee, age 47, $900,042 total compensation
CIO: Robert (Bob) Bullock
Chief Accounting Officer: JoAnn Shea, age 44
SVP and Chief Human Resources Officer: John Madia
SVP: Michael C. (Mike) McKelvy, age 49
SVP and Director; Chairman CH2M Hill International, Ltd: Robert G. (Bob) Card, age 56, $4,517,948 total compensation
SVP and Director Operations, Environmental Services Business Group: Michael A. Szomjassy, age 58
SVP and Director; President, Energy and Chemicals Business Group: Garry M. Higdem, age 55, $2,043,673 total compensation
SVP and Director; President and Group Chief Executive, Civil Infrastructure Client Group: Mark A. Lasswell, age 54
SVP: Donald S. (Don) Evans, age 58, $2,126,278 total compensation
SVP and Director; President, Center for Project Excellence: Jacqueline C. Rast, age 47
Director External Communications: John Corsi
Chief Legal Officer: Margaret B. McLean
Auditors: KPMG LLP

LOCATIONS

HQ: CH2M HILL Companies, Ltd.
9191 S. Jamaica St., Englewood, CO 80112
Phone: 303-771-0900 **Fax:** 720-286-9250
Web: www.ch2m.com

2008 Sales

	% of total
US	82
International	18
Total	**100**

PRODUCTS/OPERATIONS

2008 Sales

	$ mil.	% of total
Industrial	2,586.1	46
Civil infrastructure	1,532.2	28
Federal	1,471.6	26
Total	**5,589.9**	**100**

Selected Subsidiaries

CH2M HILL Alaska, Inc.
CH2M HILL Canada, Inc.
CH2M HILL Constructors, Inc.
CH2M HILL Engineers, Inc.
CH2M HILL Hanford, Inc.
CH2M HILL, Inc.
CH2M HILL International, Ltd.
Operations Management International
VECO Corporation

COMPETITORS

AECOM
AMEC
Balfour Beatty
Bechtel
Black & Veatch
Bovis Lend Lease
ERM
Fluor
Foster Wheeler
Jacobs Engineering
KBR
MWH Global
Parsons Brinckerhoff
Parsons Corporation
Shaw Group
Tetra Tech
Tutor Perini
URS

HISTORICAL FINANCIALS
Company Type: Private

Income Statement

	REVENUE ($ mil.)	NET INCOME ($ mil.)	NET PROFIT MARGIN	EMPLOYEES
12/08	5,590	32	0.6%	24,000
12/07	4,376	66	1.5%	22,000
12/06	4,007	39	1.0%	17,000
12/05	3,152	82	2.6%	18,363
12/04	2,715	32	1.2%	14,000
Annual Growth	19.8%	(0.2%)	—	14.4%

FYE: December 31

2008 Year-End Financials

Debt ratio: 39.4%
Return on equity: —
Cash ($ mil.): —
Current ratio: —
Long-term debt ($ mil.): 151

Net Income History

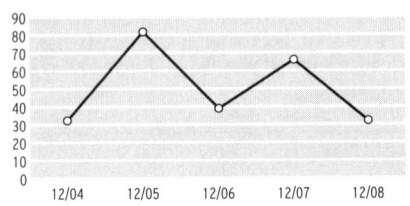

Charmer Sunbelt

The Charmer Sunbelt Group is one of the biggest swigs in its business sector. A leading wine and spirits wholesaler, the company operates through a number of joint ventures and subsidiaries including Empire Industries (New York), Premier Beverage (Florida), Reliable Churchill (Maryland), and Ben Arnold Beverage (South Carolina). Charmer Sunbelt also distributes nonalcoholic products such as bottled water. Division management bought the group from McKesson (drugs and sundries wholesaler) and took it private in 1988. CEO Charles Merinoff is the grandson of founder Herman Merinoff.

In 2007 the company combined Charmer Industries' metro New York operations with those of Peerless Importers to form a new entity, Empire Merchants.

Charmer operates in Alabama, Arizona, Colorado, Connecticut, Delaware, Florida, Illinois, Maryland, Mississippi, New Jersey, New York, North Carolina, Pennsylvania, South Carolina, Virginia, and the District of Columbia.

The company's name is a combination of C-H-A-R from Charles and the M-E-R from Merinoff.

EXECUTIVES

Vice Chairman and CEO: Charles (Charlie) Merinoff, age 52
EVP, COO, and CFO: Gene Luciano
EVP Sales and Marketing: Joe Davolio
Corporate VP and CIO: Bill Healey
Corporate VP Sales: Greg Baird
Corporate VP Marketing: Katherine Nicholls, age 42
Corporate Secretary: Steve Meresman

LOCATIONS

HQ: The Charmer Sunbelt Group
60 E. 42nd St., New York, NY 10165
Phone: 212-699-7000   **Fax:** 212-699-7099
Web: www.charmer-sunbelt.com

PRODUCTS/OPERATIONS

Selected Companies

Partnerships
  Alabama
    Alabama Sales Company, LLC
  Arizona
    Alliance Beverage Distributing Co.
  Colorado
    Beverage Distributors Corp.
  Delaware
    United Distributors of Delaware
  Massachusetts
    Commonwealth Wine & Spirits
  Mississippi
    Mississippi Sales Co., LLC
  New Jersey
    R&R Marketing, LLC
  New York
    Empire Merchants
    Empire Merchants North
  South Carolina
    Ben Arnold Beverage Co.
  Virginia
    Associated Distributors, LLC
Wholly Owned
  Connecticut
    Connecticut Distributors, Inc.
  Delaware
    Bacchus Importers, LTD
  District of Columbia
    Bacchus Importers, LTD
    Washington Wholesale Liquor Co. Inc.
  Florida
    Premier Beverage Co.
  Maryland
    Bacchus Importers, LTD
    Reliable Churchill
  North Carolina
    Prestige Wine Distributors, LLC
  Pennsylvania
    Capital Wine & Spirits Co.

COMPETITORS

Allied Beverage Group
Bacardi USA
Constellation Brands
Georgia Crown
Glazer's Wholesale Drug
Johnson Brothers
National Distributing
National Wine & Spirits
Southern Wine & Spirits
Tarrant Distributors
United States Beverage
W. J. Deutsch
Young's Market

Chevron Phillips Chemical

A coin toss determined whose name would go first when Chevron and Phillips Petroleum (now ConocoPhillips) formed 50-50 joint venture Chevron Phillips Chemical Company in 2000. Among the largest US petrochemical firms, the company produces ethylene, propylene, polyethylene, and polypropylene — sometimes used as building blocks for the company's other products such as pipe. Chevron Phillips Chemical also produces aromatics such as benzene and styrene, specialty chemicals such as acetylene black (a form of carbon black), and mining chemicals. The company has several petrochemicals joint ventures in the Middle East, including Saudi Chevron Phillips Company (50%) and Qatar Chemical Company (not quite 50%).

Chevron Phillips Chemical is the Western Hemisphere's largest producer of high-density polyethylene (HDPE) — used in blow/injection molding, plastic bags and pipes, and films. Chevron Phillips Chemical also is near the top in styrene, ethylene, and aromatics production.

Chevron Phillips Chemical Company LP is the US operating subsidiary of CPChem, which also includes foreign ventures, mainly those in Asia and the Middle East. Chevron Phillips Chemical Company LP accounts for most of its parent's revenues. Subsidiary Chevron Oronite produces fuel additives.

In 2008, Chevron Phillips Chemical combined its styrene and polystyrene business in the Americas with that of Dow Chemical to form a 50-50 joint venture. The JV, called Americas Styrenics, combined Dow's much-larger business with Chevron Phillips Chemical's ability to provide feedstocks for the production of styrene monomer and polystyrene.

EXECUTIVES

President and CEO: Greg C. Garland, age 51
SVP, CFO, and Controller: Greg G. Maxwell
SVP Manufacturing: Rick L. Roberts
SVP Specialties, Aromatics, and Styrenics: Mark Haney
SVP Olefins and Polyolefins: Timothy G. (Tim) Taylor
VP Information Technology and CIO: Peggy Colsman
VP Technology: Mary Jane Hagenson
VP Environmental Health and Safety: Charleen Dickson
VP Polyethylene: D. S. (Dave) Smith
VP Corporate Planning and Development:
  Mark E. Lashier
VP Human Resources: Chantal Veevaete
Styrenics General Manager; President and CEO, Americas Styrenics: Tim Roberts
General Manager Corporate Communications:
  Stan Sehested
Treasurer: Trevor Roberts
General Tax Counsel: Bill Stanley
Auditors: Ernst & Young LLP

LOCATIONS

HQ: Chevron Phillips Chemical Company LLC
10001 6 Pines Dr., The Woodlands, TX 77380
Phone: 832-813-4100   **Fax:** 800-231-3890
Web: www.cpchem.com

2008 Sales

	$ mil.	% of total
US	10,842	86
Other countries	1,804	14
Total	**12,646**	**100**

PRODUCTS/OPERATIONS

2008 Sales

	$ mil.	% of total
Olefins & polyolefins	9,134	72
Specialties, aromatics & styrenics	3,512	28
Total	**12,646**	**100**

Selected Products

Olefins and polyolefins
  Ethylene
  Polyethylene
  Polyethylene pipe
  Polypropylene
  Propylene
Aromatics and styrenics
  Benzene
  Cumene
  Cyclohexane
  Paraxylene
  Styrene
Specialty products
  Acetylene black
  Alpha olefins
  Dimethyl sulfide
  Drilling specialty chemicals
  High-purity hydrocarbons and solvents
  Mining chemicals
  Neohexene
  Performance and reference fuels
  Polyalpha olefins
  Polystyrene

Selected Joint Ventures

Americas Styrenics (50%)
Chevron Phillips Singapore Chemicals (Private) Limited (50%)
KR Copolymer, Co., Ltd. (60%, South Korea)
Qatar Chemical Company Ltd. (Q-Chem, 49%)
Saudi Chevron Phillips Company (50%)
Shanghai Golden Phillips Petrochemical Co. Ltd. (40%)

COMPETITORS

Dow Chemical	SABIC
DuPont	Sasol
ExxonMobil Chemical	Sterling Chemicals
KRATON	Sunoco Chemicals
LyondellBasell	Total Petrochemicals
NOVA Chemicals	Westlake Chemical

HISTORICAL FINANCIALS

Company Type: Joint venture

Income Statement

FYE: December 31

	REVENUE ($ mil.)	NET INCOME ($ mil.)	NET PROFIT MARGIN	EMPLOYEES
12/08	12,646	276	2.2%	4,800
12/07	12,986	719	5.5%	5,500
12/06	12,330	1,349	10.9%	5,150
12/05	11,038	853	7.7%	5,150
12/04	9,558	605	6.3%	5,300
Annual Growth	**7.2%**	**(17.8%)**	**—**	**(2.4%)**

2008 Year-End Financials

Debt ratio: 19.5%
Return on equity: 6.6%
Cash ($ mil.): —
Current ratio: —
Long-term debt ($ mil.): 810

Net Income History

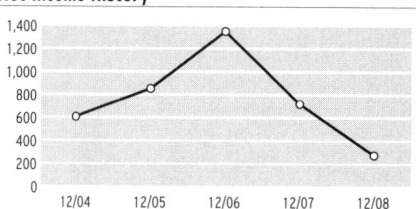

Chevy Chase Bank

Chevy Chase Bank is ready for prime time. The savings bank operates approximately 200 branches and 1,000 ATMs in the Washington, DC, area, and offers traditional deposit products such as checking and savings accounts, CDs, and IRAs, in addition to investment management services, insurance, and credit cards. Its loan portfolio is dominated by residential mortgages (more than 80% of all loans) and also includes consumer, commercial, and construction loans. In 2009 Capital One bought Chevy Chase Bank for some $520 million in cash and stock; the transaction created the largest retail bank network based in the DC area.

The bank now operates as a division of Capital One. It will be fully integrated into Capital One Bank over the course of a couple of years. No merger-related branch closures are planned.

B. Francis Saul II — who controls retail property owner Saul Centers — established Chevy Chase Bank in 1969. The company grew over the years through acquisitions including Government Services Savings and Loan and Gibralter Savings and Loan. Capital One was one of several larger banks that sought to acquire Chevy Chase.

EXECUTIVES

Chairman and CEO: B. Francis Saul II, age 76
Vice Chairman: Alexander R.M. Boyle
Vice Chairman: B. Francis Saul III, age 47
EVP and Chief Lending Officer: George P. Clancy Jr.
EVP and CFO: Stephen R. Halpin
EVP and CIO: Robert H. Spicer II
EVP and General Counsel: Thomas H. McCormick, age 58
SVP Human Resources: Russ McNish
CEO, Chevy Chase Trust and ASB Capital Management: Peter M. Welber
President, Chevy Chase Home Loans: Robert D. Broeksmit
Director Hispanic Banking: Enrique Carrillo

LOCATIONS

HQ: Chevy Chase Bank, F.S.B.
7501 Wisconsin Ave., Bethesda, MD 20814
Phone: 240-497-4600   **Fax:** 240-497-4110
Web: www.chevychasebank.com

PRODUCTS/OPERATIONS

2008 Sales

	$ mil.	% of total
Interest		
Loans	654.0	55
Securities	64.3	5
Other	4.0	—
Noninterest		
Net servicing fees	6.0	1
Other	455.8	39
Total	**1,184.1**	**100**

COMPETITORS

Bank of America
BB&T
Citibank
M&T Bank
PNC Financial
Sandy Spring Bancorp
StellarOne
SunTrust
TD Bank USA
Wells Fargo

CHG Healthcare

Medical practices without a doctor in the house look to CHG Healthcare Services to find them one. The company, formerly CompHealth Group, provides locum tenens (physician staffing) services, recruiting physicians in 35 specialties for temporary and permanent assignments at hospitals and medical practices throughout the US. It offers temporary placement of nurses and allied health professionals, including physician assistants, pharmacists, and radiology technicians. CHG Healthcare operates under the names CompHealth, Weatherby Locums, Destination Healthcare Staffing, Foundation Medical Staffing, and RN Network. In December 2006 investment firm J.W. Childs acquired the company for more than $300 million.

EXECUTIVES

President and CEO: Michael R. Weinholtz
COO: Donald D. (Don) DeCamp
CFO: Sean Dailey
Director Internet Services: Glen Thomson
VP Business Development: Brian Dunn
VP Marketing: John Genna
Corporate Communications and Public Relations: Mary Biljanic
Auditors: KPMG LLP

LOCATIONS

HQ: CHG Healthcare Services, Inc.
6440 South Millrock Dr., Ste. 175
Salt Lake City, UT 84171
Phone: 801-930-3000   **Fax:** 801-930-4517
Web: www.chghealthcare.com

COMPETITORS

AMN Healthcare
Cejka Search
Cross Country Healthcare
InteliStaf Healthcare
Medical Staffing Network
On Assignment
TeamStaff

Chicago Bulls

If you mess with these Bulls on the court, you might get the horns. Chicago Professional Sports owns and operates the Chicago Bulls professional basketball team, which boasts six NBA championships thanks to five-time MVP Michael Jordan. His charismatic presence not only set a high-water mark for Chicago between 1991 and 1998 but also helped increase the popularity of the league. The team was started by Dick Klein and joined the National Basketball Association in 1966. Real estate developer Jerry Reinsdorf has owned the Bulls since 1985. He also owns Chicago's United Center (along with Chicago Blackhawks owner the Wirtz Corporation) and the Chicago White Sox baseball team.

While the Bulls maintain a loyal following in the Windy City, Reinsdorf has shouldered much of the blame for the lack of championship performances since His Airness left the team in 1998. (Some still blame the owner and then general manager Jerry Krause for driving away Jordan and head coach Phil Jackson.)

Head coach Scott Skiles was replaced by Jim Boylan after a disappointing start to the 2007-08 season; Boylan was let go at the end of the campaign and replaced by first-year coach Vinny Del Negro. Skiles had led the Chicago bench for four seasons.

EXECUTIVES

Chairman: Jerry Reinsdorf, age 73
EVP Basketball Operations: John Paxson
EVP Business Operations: Steve Schanwald
SVP Financial and Legal: Irwin Mandel
Head Coach: Vinny Del Negro
Director Player Personnel: Gar Forman
Senior Manager Basketball Operations and Scout: Matt Lloyd, age 33
Assistant Coach and Advance Scout: Mike Wilhelm, age 40
Controller: Stu Bookman
Senior Director Public and Media Relations: Tim Hallam

LOCATIONS

HQ: Chicago Professional Sports Corporation
United Center, 1901 W. Madison St.
Chicago, IL 60612
Phone: 312-455-4000   **Fax:** 312-455-4189
Web: www.nba.com/bulls

The Chicago Bulls play at the 21,711-seat capacity United Center in Chicago.

PRODUCTS/OPERATIONS

Championship Titles
NBA Championship (1991-93, 1996-98)
NBA Eastern Conference Champions (1991-93, 1996-98)

COMPETITORS

Cavaliers
Detroit Pistons
Indiana Pacers
Milwaukee Bucks

Chick-fil-A

Beloved by bovines, Chick-fil-A operates one of the nation's largest fast-food chains that specializes in chicken dishes. Boasting more than 1,400 restaurants in almost 40 states, the chain offers chicken entrees, sandwiches, and salads, along with its popular waffle fries and fresh-squeezed lemonade. Its outlets are mostly freestanding units that offer drive-through service as well as dine-in seating, but the company also has a significant number of mall-based stores. Chick-fil-A also licenses its concept to foodservice and concessions operators. The chain was started in 1946 by chairman Truett Cathy; a devout Baptist, he insists on a policy that all Chick-fil-A restaurants be closed on Sundays.

Unlike most fast-food franchises, Chick-fil-A owns most of its restaurants and licenses franchisees to run the units for a fixed annual income plus a share in the profits. This unique arrangement lowers the initial cost to its franchisees and has resulted in less operator turnover than in other chains.

Chick-fil-A has been ramping up its expansion efforts the past few years, focusing especially on new free-standing units. It added more than 80 locations during 2008, this despite a slowing economy that forced other restaurant operators to shelve or contract their expansion plans. Looking to drive additional traffic to its eateries, the company has also been investing significantly in product development efforts to expand and refresh the chain's menu. New items rolled out in 2008 have included an expanded line of salads and new wrap-style sandwiches.

The company has been a big sponsor of athletic events, including the annual Chick-fil-A Bowl (formerly the Chick-fil-A Peach Bowl), one of the top postseason college football games. It also supports leadership training and scholarship programs through the WinShape Foundation.

In addition to its quick-service operations, the company operates two full-service restaurant concepts, Chick-fil-A Dwarf Houses and Truett's Grill.

HISTORY

Truett Cathy began his restaurant career in 1946 by opening a 24-hour diner called the Dwarf Grill (it only had 10 stools and four tables) in a suburb of Atlanta. It was there that he perfected a quick-cooked chicken sandwich. He ventured into the rapidly growing fast-food industry more than 20 years later, when in 1967 he convinced a local shopping mall to make room for the first Chick-fil-A unit. There he found a successful niche, and for nearly 20 years the company placed its units exclusively inside malls, especially in the South.

Chick-fil-A moved slowly at first, opening just six stores from 1968 to 1970. In 1974 it opened 14 new restaurants. It really hit its stride in the early 1980s, opening 101 units during the first two years of the decade (a store every eight days). Chick-fil-A Dwarf House, the chain's first full-service restaurant, opened in 1985.

As mall construction slowed and competition increased, the company began looking at alternatives. It began licensing in 1992, entering into agreements with Georgia Tech and Clemson University. The following year Chick-fil-A established its first drive-through-only outlet.

In an effort to extend its brand name, Chick-fil-A signed on as a sponsor for the Ladies Professional Golf Association in 1995 and college football's Peach Bowl in 1996. Also that year it opened its first airport store (at Atlanta's Hartsfield International) and expanded internationally with a unit in Durban, South Africa. In 1999 the company continued aggressive expansion, opening 88 new restaurants (56 of them standalone units).

Dan Cathy, son of the founder, was named president and COO of Chick-fil-A in 2001. In 2002 the company's number of freestanding units surpassed the number of its mall locations.

In early 2004 Chick-fil-A opened its first freestanding restaurant in Southern California. It also expanded its breakfast menu that year. In 2006 the company's sponsorship and marketing efforts got a boost when the Chick-fil-A Peach Bowl was renamed the Chick-fil-A Bowl.

EXECUTIVES

Chairman and CEO: S. Truett Cathy, age 88
President and COO: Dan T. Cathy, age 56
SVP Finance and CFO: James B. (Buck) McCabe
SVP Marketing and Chief Marketing Officer:
  Steve A. Robinson
SVP; President, Dwarf House: Donald M. (Bubba) Cathy
SVP Operations: Timothy P. (Tim) Tassopoulos
SVP Real Estate, Design, and Construction:
  Perry A. Ragsdale
VP Information Technology and CIO: Michael F. Erbrick
VP and Controller: Philip A. Barrett
VP Real Estate: Erwin C. Reid
VP Operations Services: Stephen G. Mason
VP and Assistant General Counsel, Real Estate Legal:
  B. Lynn Chastain
VP Service and Innovation: David B. Farmer
VP Training and Development: T. Mark Miller
VP Human Resources: Dee Ann Turner
VP Corporate Public Relations: Donald A. (Don) Perry
VP Business Analysis: Roger E. Blythe Jr.
Director Corporate Communications:
  Gregory B. Thompson

LOCATIONS

HQ: Chick-fil-A, Inc.
  5200 Buffington Rd., Atlanta, GA 30349
Phone: 404-765-8000
Web: www.chick-fil-a.com

COMPETITORS

AFC Enterprises
American Dairy Queen
Burger King
Chipotle
Church's Chicken
CKE Restaurants
Jack in the Box
McDonald's
Quiznos
Sonic Corp.
Subway
Wendy's/Arby's Group, Inc.
Whataburger
YUM!

HISTORICAL FINANCIALS

Company Type: Private

Income Statement

FYE: December 31

	REVENUE ($ mil.)	NET INCOME ($ mil.)	NET PROFIT MARGIN	EMPLOYEES
12/08	2,960	—	—	50,000
12/07	2,641	—	—	50,000
12/06	2,275	—	—	45,000
12/05	1,975	—	—	40,924
Annual Growth	14.4%	—	—	6.9%

Revenue History

	12/04	12/05	12/06	12/07	12/08

Children's Medical Center of Dallas

Sick kiddos in northern Texas who need specialized care don't have to travel far to find it. Children's Medical Center of Dallas treats children from birth to age 18 with various medical needs. Specialties include craniofacial deformities, cystic fibrosis, gastroenterology, and heart disease. Children's is also a major pediatric transplant center for bone marrow, heart, kidney, and liver. The hospital has nearly 500 beds and is the pediatric teaching facility for the University of Texas Southwest medical program. Children's also operates a network of some 50 outpatient clinics in and around Dallas.

The hospital also operates the county's only pediatric emergency room and is the only Level I trauma center for pediatrics in the state. Its Physicians for Children affiliate provides primary health care services to children living in Dallas County's underserved areas.

At any given time it seems Children's is building one thing or another. In the four-year period between 2001 and 2005 the center spent more than $250 million on new construction and expansion projects. Between 2009 and 2013 Children's plans to spend another $500 million on a whole range of new projects, including a new heart center, cancer center, surgical facilities, and an expansion of its Children's Legacy hospital campus in the nearby town of Plano.

Children's receives revenue from a mix of third-party payors including HMOs and PPOs, as well as Medicaid and Medicare and the Children's Health Insurance Program. Children's — which provides a hefty amount of charity care each year for the region's uninsured children — also relies heavily on private donations and fundraising efforts.

EXECUTIVES

Chairman: John L. Adams, age 64
Vice Chairman: Tom Baker
President and CEO: Christopher J. (Chris) Durovich
CFO: Ray Dziesinski
EVP Medical Affairs: Julio P. Fontán
SVP Administration: James W. (Jim) Herring
SVP Operations: Douglas G. (Doug) Hock
SVP Business Development and Ambulatory Services:
  Patricia U. (Pat) Winning
VP and CIO: Pamela Arora
VP Legal Affairs: Anne E. Long
VP Ancillary Services: Brett Daniel Lee
VP Public Affairs: Elizabeth F. (Betsy) MacKay
VP Facilities Management: Louis C. (Lou) Saksen
VP Ambulatory Services: Christopher Dougherty
VP Quality: Fiona Howard Levy
VP; Administrator, Children's Medical Center Legacy:
  David G. Biggerstaff
Chief Accounting Officer and Controller: Jerry Lee
Chief Nursing Officer: Mary Stowe
Auditors: Ernst & Young LLP

LOCATIONS

HQ: Children's Medical Center of Dallas
  1935 Motor St., Dallas, TX 75235
Phone: 214-456-7000   **Fax:** 214-456-2197
Web: www.childrens.com

Children's Medical Center Selected Locations

Children's Medical Center Dallas Main Campus
Children's Medical Center Legacy & Ambulatory Care
  Pavilion
Dallas Ambulatory Care Pavilion
Chase Bank Building Specialty Center
DeSoto Specialty Center
Irving Specialty Center
Mesquite Specialty Center

PRODUCTS/OPERATIONS

Children's Medical Center Selected Services

Allergy/Immunology/Asthma
Audiology
Cystic Fibrosis
Day Surgery
Dean Foods LEAN Families
Dermatology
Diabetes
Ear/Nose/Throat
Endocrinology
Gastroenterology
General Surgery
Genetics/Metabolism
International Adoption Medicine
Laboratory Services
Neurology
Nutrition
Obesity Program
Occupational Therapy
Ophthalmology
Orthodontics
Orthopaedics
Physical Therapy
Plastic Surgery
Pulmonary Function Lab
Pulmonology
Radiology
Rheumatology
Sleep Disorders
Speech Therapy
Trauma
Urology

COMPETITORS

Baylor University Medical Center
Cook Children's Health Care System
Dallas County Hospital District
Dell Children's Medical Center
HCA
Tenet Healthcare
Texas Children's Hospital

HISTORICAL FINANCIALS

Company Type: Not-for-profit

Income Statement				FYE: December 31
	REVENUE ($ mil.)	NET INCOME ($ mil.)	NET PROFIT MARGIN	EMPLOYEES
12/08	745	(3)	—	5,200
12/07	640	92	14.3%	4,800
12/06	580	88	15.2%	4,500
12/05	514	51	10.0%	—
12/04	448	44	9.9%	—
Annual Growth	13.6%	—	—	7.5%

Net Income History

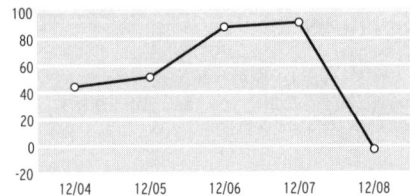

CHRISTUS Health

In CHRISTUS there is no east or west, but plenty of care nonetheless. The Catholic health care system operates more than 40 hospitals, including general hospitals and long-term acute care facilities (the latter under the Dubuis name). The majority of its operations are in Louisiana and Texas, but the organization also has facilities in Arkansas, Georgia, Missouri, New Mexico, and Utah, and in several states in Mexico. In addition to its acute care facilities, CHRISTUS Health runs outpatient centers, medical groups, home health and hospice agencies, and senior living facilities. Specialized services include oncology, pediatrics, rehabilitation, and women's and children's health care.

To make primary care a bit more accessible, the company is launching clinics within a handful of Texas Wal-Mart stores. It hopes that by offering affordable acute and preventative care, it can help reduce some trips to the emergency room for minor ailments like earaches and bladder infections.

Like many hospital companies (especially not-for-profit ones), the organization has struggled financially as a result of providing care for the indigent and for the growing ranks of uninsured. In 2006 it sold its money-losing St. Joseph Hospital in Houston to Hospital Partners of America (HPA), a company that allows doctors to take an ownership stake in its hospitals. It is taking a page from HPA's book in Houston, however, and is developing a small hospital there in partnership with doctors. CHRISTUS will own a majority of the planned hospital, which is slated to open in late 2009.

The company expanded into New Mexico with its 2008 merger with St. Vincent Regional Medical Center.

The organization's Mexico operations are a majority-owned partnership with Monterrey-based Muguerza and consist of seven hospitals. In 2007, the organization's main Monterrey facility became the first Mexican hospital to win accreditation from the Joint Commission International, a unit of the organization that certifies US hospitals. Because Mexican citizens overwhelmingly rely on public hospitals run by the national health care system, CHRISTUS Muguerza is marketing itself as a "medical tourism" destination, where Americans can go for cheaper and lower-hassle medical care.

CHRISTUS Health was formed through the 1999 merger of Incarnate Word Health System and Sisters of Charity Health System. Both systems have their roots in the religious order Sisters of Charity of the Incarnate Word, founded when three French nuns arrived in Texas in 1866 to care for the poor and sick.

EXECUTIVES

Chairman: Catherine Dulle
President, CEO, and Director: Thomas C. (Tom) Royer
SVP and Chief Medical Officer: John Gillean
SVP Business, Strategy, and Corporate Development:
  Peter Maddox
SVP Communications and Public Affairs:
  Linda McClung
SVP Patient- and Resident-Care Operations:
  Ernie W. Sadau
SVP and CFO: Jay Herron
SVP and CIO: George Conklin
SVP Human Resource Services: Mary Lynch
Corporate VP Business Development and Managed Care: Jeff Puckett
Director Strategic Marketing and Communications:
  Teri Cardenas
Director Public Affairs: Christie J. Fortune
Human Resources: Penny Welch

LOCATIONS

HQ: CHRISTUS Health
  Las Colinas Corporate Center II, 6363 N. Hwy. 161,
  Ste. 450, Irving, TX 75038
Phone: 214-492-8500   **Fax:** 214-492-8540
Web: www.christushealth.org

Selected Facilities

Mexico
  CHRISTUS Muguerza Alta Especialidad (Monterrey)
  CHRISTUS Muguerza Conchita (Monterrey)
  CHRISTUS Muguerza Del Parque (Chihuahua)
  CHRISTUS Muguerza Saltillo
  CHRISTUS Muguerza Sur (Monterrey)
US
  Arkansas
    Advance Care Hospital of Fort Smith (long-term
      acute care hospital)
    Advance Care Hospital of Hot Springs (long-term
      acute care hospital)
    Magnolia Hospital (Magnolia)
  Georgia
    Southern Crescent Hospital for Specialty Care (long-
      term acute care, Riverdale)
  Louisiana
    CHRISTUS St. Frances Cabrini Hospital (Alexandria)
    CHRISTUS Schumpert Bossier (Bossier City)
    CHRISTUS Coushatta Health Care Center
      (Coushatta)
    CHRISTUS St. Patrick Hospital (Lake Charles)
    CHRISTUS Schumpert Health System (Shreveport)
    Dubuis Hospital of Alexandria (long-term acute care
      hospital)
    Dubuis Hospital of Lake Charles (long-term acute
      care hospital)
    Dubuis Hospital of Shreveport (long-term acute care
      hospital)
    Natchitoches Parish Hospital (Natchitoches)
  Missouri
    Dubuis Hospital of St. Louis (Chesterfield)
  New Mexico
    CHRISTUS St. Vincent (Santa Fe)
  Texas
    Baptist St. Anthony's Health System (Amarillo)
    CHRISTUS Spohn Hospital Corpus Christi (Corpus
      Christi)
    CHRISTUS Spohn Hospital Alice (Alice)
    CHRISTUS Spohn Hospital Beeville (Beeville)
    CHRISTUS Spohn Hospital (Kleburg)
    CHRISTUS Hospital — St. Elizabeth (Beaumont)
    CHRISTUS Jasper Memorial Hospital (Jasper)
    CHRISTUS St. Catherine Hospital (Katy)
    CHRISTUS St. John Hospital (Nassau Bay)
    CHRISTUS St. Mary Hospital (Port Arthur)
    CHRISTUS Santa Rosa Hospital (San Antonio)
    CHRISTUS St. Michael Health System (Texarkana)
    Dubuis Hospital of Beaumont (long-term acute care
      hospital)
    Dubuis Hospital of Paris (long-term acute care
      hospital)
    Dubuis Hospital of Port Arthur (long-term acute
      care hospital)
    Dubuis Hospital of Texarkana (long-term acute care
      hospital)
  Utah
    CHRISTUS St. Joseph Villa (Salt Lake City)

COMPETITORS

Baylor Health
Community Health Systems
Harris County Hospital
HCA
Iasis Healthcare
Intermountain Health Care
Memorial Hermann Healthcare
Methodist Hospital System
Sisters of Mercy Health System
St. Luke's Episcopal Hospital
Tenet Healthcare
University of Utah Hospitals & Clinics
Vanguard Health Systems

HISTORICAL FINANCIALS

Company Type: Not-for-profit

Income Statement				FYE: June 30
	REVENUE ($ mil.)	NET INCOME ($ mil.)	NET PROFIT MARGIN	EMPLOYEES
6/08	3,168	—	—	25,000

Chugach Electric Association

Deriving its name from an old Eskimo tribal word, Chugach Electric Association generates, transmits, distributes, and sells electricity in Alaska's railbelt region. This area extends from the coastal Chugach Mountains into central Alaska and includes the state's two largest cities (Anchorage and Fairbanks). The member-owned cooperative utility has 530 MW of generating capacity from its natural gas-fired and hydro-electric power plants. Serving 80,300 metered retail locations, Chugach Electric, the largest electric utility in Alaska, also sells wholesale power to other municipal and cooperative utilities in the region.

Chugach Electric was formed in 1948 as a Rural Electrification Administration cooperative to create an electrical distribution system to meet the growing power needs of the Greater Anchorage region.

EXECUTIVES

Chairman: Rebecca Logan, age 45
Vice Chairman: Jim Nordlund, age 56
CEO: Bradley W. (Brad) Evans, age 54, $303,577 total compensation
SVP Finance and CFO: Michael R. (Mike) Cunningham, age 59, $330,318 total compensation
SVP Power Supply: Paul Risse, age 54, $215,790 total compensation
SVP Administration: David R. (Dave) Smith, age 62, $241,503 total compensation
SVP Strategic Planning and Corporate Affairs: Lee D. Thibert, age 53, $223,104 total compensation
VP Human Resources: Tyler E. Andrews, age 43, $106,571 total compensation
VP Power Delivery: Edward (Ed) Jenkin, age 48, $218,115 total compensation
Public Relations: Patti Bogan
Secretary and Director: Alex Gimarc, age 57
Treasurer and Director: P. J. Hill, age 64
Auditors: KPMG LLP

LOCATIONS

HQ: Chugach Electric Association, Inc.
5601 Electron Dr., Anchorage, AK 99518
Phone: 907-563-7494   **Fax:** 907-762-4678
Web: www.chugachelectric.com

PRODUCTS/OPERATIONS

2008 Sales

	$ mil.	% of total
Retail		
Residential	80.3	28
Commercial	77.2	27
Wholesale	109.4	38
Other	21.4	7
Total	**288.3**	**100**

HISTORICAL FINANCIALS

Company Type: Cooperative

Income Statement				FYE: December 31
	REVENUE ($ mil.)	NET INCOME ($ mil.)	NET PROFIT MARGIN	EMPLOYEES
12/08	288	6	2.2%	326
12/07	257	3	1.1%	348
12/06	268	10	3.7%	348
12/05	226	10	4.2%	356
12/04	201	8	3.8%	355
Annual Growth	9.4%	(4.2%)	—	(2.1%)

2008 Year-End Financials

Debt ratio: 202.5%
Return on equity: —
Cash ($ mil.): —
Current ratio: —
Long-term debt ($ mil.): 311

Net Income History

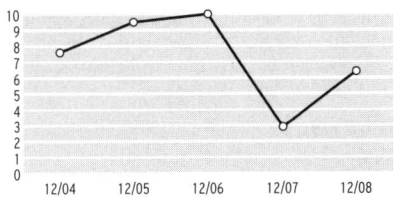

Citizens Bancorp

Citizens Bancorp is the holding company for Citizens Bank, which offers traditional banking services through about a dozen branches in western Oregon. Its retail offerings include regular savings and checking accounts, money market and NOW accounts, CDs, IRAs, and home mortgages. The bank also offers safe-deposit boxes and online banking and bill payment. It is mainly a business lender, with commercial mortgages making up the largest portion of its loan portfolio. Loans to farmers for land, operations, and equipment are a growing part of Citizens Bank's business.

EXECUTIVES

Chairman: Jock Gibson, age 67
EVP and COO, Citizens Bancorp and Citizens Bank: William F. (Bill) Hubel Jr., age 53
EVP and Chief Lending Officer, Citizens Bancorp and Citizens Bank: Steven R. (Steve) Terjeson, age 52
EVP and CFO, Citizens Bancorp and Citizens Bank: Lark E. Wysham, age 59

VP and Human Resources Manager, Citizens Bank: Bobbie Carter
President, CEO, and Director; President and CEO, Citizens Bank: William V. (Bill) Humphreys Sr., age 61
Auditors: Symonds, Evans & Company, P.C.

LOCATIONS

HQ: Citizens Bancorp
275 SW 3rd St., Corvallis, OR 97339
Phone: 541-752-5161   **Fax:** 541-757-3546
Web: www.citizensebank.com

PRODUCTS/OPERATIONS

2008 Sales

	$ mil.	% of total
Interest		
Loans	21.8	83
Securities	1.2	5
Other	0.2	1
Noninterest		
Service charges on deposit accounts	1.2	4
BankCard income	0.6	2
Other	1.3	5
Total	**26.3**	**100**

COMPETITORS

Bank of America
Cascade Bancorp
KeyCorp
Pacific Continental
Sterling Financial (WA)
Umpqua Holdings
U.S. Bancorp
Washington Federal
Wells Fargo

HISTORICAL FINANCIALS

Company Type: Private

Income Statement				FYE: December 31
	ASSETS ($ mil.)	NET INCOME ($ mil.)	INCOME AS % OF ASSETS	EMPLOYEES
12/08	381	5	1.3%	140
12/07	361	6	1.7%	132
Annual Growth	5.6%	(19.7%)	—	6.1%

2008 Year-End Financials

Equity as % of assets: —
Return on assets: 1.3%
Return on equity: —
Long-term debt ($ mil.): —
Sales ($ mil.): 26

Net Income History

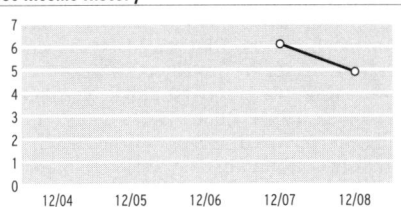

City University of New York

The City University of New York (CUNY) is the big "U" in the Big Apple. The college has 20 campuses in the five boroughs of New York City and is the US's largest urban university system. About 460,000 undergraduate, graduate, and continuing education students (from 164 countries) are enrolled at CUNY, which has 11 senior colleges, six community colleges, a doctoral-granting graduate school, a law school, the School of Professional Studies, and The Sophie Davis School of Biomedical Education. Its 1,400 academic programs range from specialized, career-oriented courses to traditional liberal arts curricula. CUNY employs some 6,100 full-time teaching faculty members.

CUNY has made some big changes, including tougher admission standards that critics feared would hurt the university's ethnic diversity, a hallmark of the school (enrollment numbers have proven otherwise). Notable CUNY alumni include novelist Oscar Hijuelos, General Colin Powell, comedian Jerry Seinfeld, and 11 Nobel laureates.

As with many public universities throughout the US, CUNY is enduring tough times economically. In order to free up the money to hire more full-time professors, the university has had to end a 10-year tradition of not charging four-year students for the last semester of their senior year.

CUNY opened its Graduate School of Journalism in September 2006.

HISTORY

The New York State Legislature created a municipal college system in New York City in 1926, forming the New York City Board of Higher Education to manage the operations of the City College of New York and Hunter College.

City College's roots were established in 1847 when New York passed a referendum creating the Free Academy, a tuition-free school. Hunter College was founded in 1870 as a women's college, and it was the first free teachers college in the US.

The Board of Higher Education authorized City College to create the Brooklyn Collegiate Center (a two-year men's college) in 1926; Hunter established a similar two-year women's branch in Brooklyn. Four years later the schools merged to create the Brooklyn College of the City of New York, the city's first public, coed liberal arts college. Other schools added to the municipal system included Queens College (1937), New York City Community College (1947), Staten Island Community College (1955), Bronx Community College (1957), and Queensborough Community College (1958).

The state legislature renamed New York City's municipal college system The City University of New York (CUNY) in 1961 and ordered its board of trustees to expand the system's facilities and scope. One of the first actions was to create a graduate school. CUNY chartered a number of new schools during the 1960s, including Richmond College (1965), York College (1966), Medgar Evers College (1968), and several community colleges. CUNY took over management of the New York State Institute of Applied Arts and Sciences (renamed New York City Technical College) in 1964 and

established the John Jay College of Criminal Justice. CUNY became affiliated with Mount Sinai School of Medicine in 1967.

Despite its expansion, the university system had difficulty keeping up with demand, particularly after 1970, when it established an open admissions policy for all New York City high school graduates. Richmond College and Staten Island Community College became the College of Staten Island in 1976. Both CUNY and the City of New York ran into serious financial problems in the mid-1970s, spelling the end of CUNY's tradition of free undergrad tuition for New York City residents. To increase state financial support for CUNY, the legislature signed the City University Governance and Financing Act in 1979.

The City University School of Law held its first classes in 1983. The following year the state board of regents authorized CUNY to offer a doctor of medicine degree. CUNY's law school received accreditation from the American Bar Association in 1992. Since abandoning the free enrollment policy in the 1970s, the university's tuition continued to increase. In 1992, after presenting a nearly $600 increase in tuition, CUNY initiated its "last semester free" program, whereby four-year students did not have to pay tuition for the last semester of their senior year.

After several years of budget cuts and steadily increasing enrollment, CUNY declared a state of financial emergency in 1995. The following year New York's Governor George Pataki proposed new budget cuts, and in 1997 he called for tuition hikes. CUNY's board of trustees introduced a resolution calling for the elimination of remedial education programs at the senior college level in 1998. The state Board of Regents approved the plan in 1999 (most remedial classes were phased out by 2001). Matthew Goldstein was appointed chancellor in 1999 and has worked to increase CUNY's budget to hire more full-time faculty.

EXECUTIVES

Chairperson: Benno C. Schmidt Jr.
Vice Chairperson: Philip A. Berry, age 59
Chancellor: Matthew Goldstein
Associate Vice Chancellor Technology and CIO: Brian Cohen
Executive Vice Chancellor and COO: Allan H. Dobrin
Senior Vice Chancellor University Relations and Secretary: Jay Hershenson
Senior Vice Chancellor Legal Affairs and General Counsel: Frederick P. Schaffer
Vice Chancellor Student Development: Garrie W. Moore
Vice Chancellor Research: Gillian Small
Vice Chancellor Labor Relations: Pamela S. Silverblatt
Vice Chancellor Facilities Planning, Construction, and Management: Iris Weinshall
Vice Chancellor Human Resources Management: Gloriana B. (Ginger) Waters
Vice Chancellor Budget and Finance: Ernesto Malave
University Dean, Academic Affairs: Jane E. Ashdown
University Dean and Special Counsel to the Chancellor: Dave Fields
University Dean, Undergraduate Education: Judith Summerfield
University Director Admission: Richard P. Alvarez
University Director Communications and Marketing: Michael Arena
Auditors: KPMG LLP

LOCATIONS

HQ: The City University of New York
535 E. 80th St., New York, NY 10075
Phone: 212-794-5555   **Fax:** 212-209-5600
Web: www.cuny.edu

The City University of New York has schools serving the Bronx, Brooklyn, Manhattan, Queens, and Staten Island boroughs of New York City.

PRODUCTS/OPERATIONS

Selected Senior Colleges
Bernard M. Baruch College
Brooklyn College
City College
City University School of Law at Queens College
The College of Staten Island
The Graduate School and University Center
Herbert H. Lehman College
Hunter College
John Jay College of Criminal Justice
Medgar Evers College
New York City College of Technology
Queens College
York College

Selected Community Colleges
Borough of Manhattan Community College
Bronx Community College
Hostos Community College
Kingsborough Community College
LaGuardia Community College
Queensborough Community College

HISTORICAL FINANCIALS
Company Type: School

Income Statement				FYE: June 30
	REVENUE ($ mil.)	NET INCOME ($ mil.)	NET PROFIT MARGIN	EMPLOYEES
6/09	1	—	—	33,642

Claire's Stores

If the difference between men and boys is the price of their toys, for young women and girls, it may be the price of their accessories. For thrifty, fashion-conscious females ages 3 to 27, Claire's Stores is the queen of costume jewelry, handbags, and hair bows. The company operates about 3,000 boutiques, primarily in malls, under the Claire's and Icing banners. The chain is present in all 50 US states, Puerto Rico, the US Virgin Islands, and Canada, as well as about 10 European countries. Founded by Rowland Schaefer and later run by his daughters, Bonnie and Marla Schaefer, Claire's Stores was sold to an affiliate of the New York-based private equity firm Apollo Management for about $3 billion in 2007.

Prior to the sale, the Schaefer family was the company's majority shareholder and controlled about a third of Claire's voting power. Apollo Advisors appointed Eugene Kahn, formerly the CEO of The May Department Stores, as the chain's chief executive, replacing co-CEOs Bonnie and Marla.

Declining sales attributed to the global economic downturn have pushed the company to shutter underperforming locations. In 2008 Claire's closed about 150 stores. In spite of slumping figures, the retailer continues to add shops at home and overseas. Claire's opened about 80 locations in 2008. It plans to add about 20 more company-owned stores to its global network in 2009.

Claire's has sought to extend its retail reach beyond the tween (ages 7 to 11) and teen markets by appealing to young girls (ages 3 to 5) through its Claire's Club brand and to the college set and young women entering the workforce (ages 18 to

27) through its Icing format. The retailer's jewelry and accessories (hair goods, handbags, small leather goods, and cosmetics) are typically priced between $2 and $24. Observing a shift in its customers' preferences, the company began offering more accessories and casual-dress items in stores in 2008. It has likewise been slimming its selection of costume jewelry and dress-up merchandise. Some two-thirds of Claire's products are imported from China.

EXECUTIVES

Chairman: Peter P. Copses, age 50
CEO and Director: Eugene S. (Gene) Kahn, age 58
President: James G. (Jim) Conroy, age 39
President, Europe: Kenny Wilson
EVP and General Merchandise Manager, North America: Denise Vujovich
EVP and General Merchandise Officer, Europe: Melanie Berry
EVP Corporate Merchandise, Trend and Product Development: Kirk Hanselman
SVP Information Technology: Donna Ruch
SVP Business Development and Planning: William Hoeller
SVP Store Operations, North America: Colleen Collins
SVP Human Resources, North America: MaryAnn Wagner
SVP and Managing Director, RSI: Chona Ponce
SVP and CFO: J. Per Brodin, age 47
SVP International: Bruce Marshall
SVP Human Resources and Logistics/Supply Chain: Joseph A. DeFalco
SVP, General Counsel, and Quality Assurance: Rebecca Orand
Auditors: KPMG LLP

LOCATIONS

HQ: Claire's Stores, Inc.
3 SW 129th Ave., Pembroke Pines, FL 33027
Phone: 954-433-3900   **Fax:** 954-433-3999
Web: www.clairestores.com

2009 Sales

	$ mil.	% of total
North America	907.5	64
International	505.5	36
Total	**1,413.0**	**100**

2009 Stores

	No.
North America	2,026
Europe	943
Total	**2,969**

PRODUCTS/OPERATIONS

2009 Sales

	% of total
Jewelry	51
Accessories	49
Total	**100**

2009 Stores

	No.
Company-owned	2,969
Joint venture	214
Franchise	196
Total	**3,379**

Selected Stores

Claire's
Icing

COMPETITORS

Alloy, Inc.
The Buckle
Charlotte Russe Holding
Charming Shoppes
Deb Shops
dELiA*s
Fingerhut
Forever 21
Hot Topic
Monsoon
Pacific Sunwear
Target
TJX Companies
Tween Brands
Urban Outfitters
Wal-Mart
Wet Seal

HISTORICAL FINANCIALS

Company Type: Private

Income Statement

	REVENUE ($ mil.)	NET INCOME ($ mil.)	NET PROFIT MARGIN	EMPLOYEES
			FYE: Saturday nearest January 31	
1/09	1,413	(644)	—	17,600
1/08	1,511	(43)	—	18,700
Annual Growth	**(6.5%)**	**—**	**—**	**(5.9%)**

Net Income History

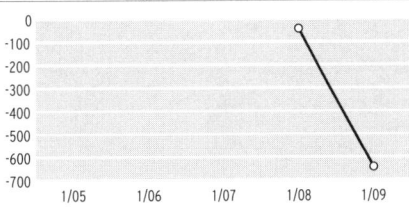

Clark Enterprises

Like Clark Kent, this firm holds some super powers. Privately owned Clark Enterprises has holdings in real estate, private equity, venture capital, construction companies, and other investments. Its real estate holdings include some 5 million sq. ft. of office space, 15,000 residential units, and 300,000 sq. ft. of warehouse space. The company's flagship subsidiary, The Clark Construction Group, has more than $4 billion in annual revenue and is a top US contractor that performs construction management, general contracting, design, and consulting services. Other Clark units include residential builder Seawright Homes, Clark Realty Capital, and highway construction company Shirley Contracting.

Chairman and CEO James Clark owns the company, which was founded in 1972. Its private equity and venture capital arm, CNF Investments, was founded in 1997. CNF, which focuses on early-stage and growth-stage companies, manages more than $170 million worth of investments in life sciences, oil and gas, technology, telecommunications, and alternative energy.

In the line of alternative energy solutions Clark Energy, an affiliate of Clark Realty Capital, partners with public and private clients to design and build projects that improve energy and water efficiency. Clark Energy was selected in 2009 to build a massive solar energy project for the Department of Defense. The project, which is the largest of its kind for the department, is in California and will power Fort Irwin and will serve as a pilot program for other military bases. Clark Realty Capital itself has a $5 billion Super Energy Savings Performance Contract with the US Department of Energy. The contract will include work on energy efficiency, renewable energy, and water efficiency projects at federally owned buildings and facilities.

EXECUTIVES

Chairman and CEO: A. James Clark
President and COO: Lawrence C. Nussdorf, age 62
EVP; Managing Director, CNF Investments LLC: Robert J. (Bob) Flanagan, age 52
SVP and General Counsel; Head, Legal, Acquisitions, Development and Repositioning Department: Rebecca L. Owen
SVP; Head, Wealth Management Department: Terri D. Klatzkin
President and CEO, Shirley Contracting: Michael Post
President, Seawright Homes: D. Stephen Seawright
President, Clark Realty Builders: Glenn Ferguson
President and CEO, Atkinson Construction: Scott Lynn
President, Clark Construction Group: Dan T. Montgomery
Chairman, Clark Construction Group: Peter C. Forster
President, Clark Realty Capital: Douglas (Doug) Sandor
Executive Assistant to President and Office Manager: Connie Pumphrey

LOCATIONS

HQ: Clark Enterprises, Inc.
7500 Old Georgetown Rd., 15th Fl.
Bethesda, MD 20814
Phone: 301-657-7100   **Fax:** 301-657-7263
Web: www.clarkenterprisesinc.com

PRODUCTS/OPERATIONS

Selected Subsidiaries

The Clark Construction Group, LLC. (commercial, institutional, and heavy construction)
Clark Reality Builders, LLC (residential building)
Clark Realty Capital, LLC (residential development)
Clark Realty Builders, LLC (dba Clark Energy)
Clark Realty Management, LLC (property management)
CNF Investments LLC (private equity investment)
Seawright Homes, LLC (single-family homes, high rise condos, rental apartments)
Shirley Contracting (highway and heavy construction)

COMPETITORS

Barton Malow
Bovis Lend Lease
Donohoe Companies
Fluor
Forest City Enterprises
Gilbane
Hensel Phelps Construction
Hunt Construction
Palomar Ventures
Peter Kiewit Sons'
RFE Investment Partners
Skanska
Turner Corporation
Whiting-Turner

HISTORICAL FINANCIALS

Company Type: Private

Income Statement

FYE: December 31

	REVENUE ($ mil.)	NET INCOME ($ mil.)	NET PROFIT MARGIN	EMPLOYEES
12/08	4,700	—	—	4,250
12/07	4,220	—	—	4,200
12/06	3,220	—	—	4,200
12/05	2,844	—	—	4,200
12/04	2,800	—	—	3,200
Annual Growth	13.8%	—	—	7.4%

Revenue History

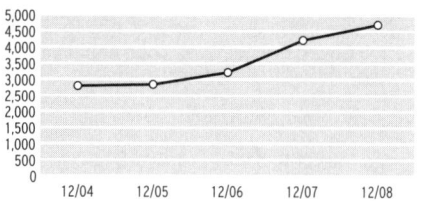

Clayton, Dubilier & Rice

Clayton, Dubilier & Rice (CD&R) specializes in turnaround situations. The private equity firm typically acquires noncore units of large corporations and works with existing management to improve operations. Since it was formed in 1978, CD&R has raised more than $11 billion in capital (including $4 billion for its latest fund), and has invested in more than 40 businesses in the US and Europe. In 2007 the company led an investor group that bought ServiceMaster, and joined with Bain Capital and The Carlyle Group to buy the wholesale construction supply business of The Home Depot for about $8.5 billion. Each firm owns a third of the unit, known as HD Supply.

In 2008 CD&R agreed to buy materials testing division Bodycote Testing Group from Bodycote International for $763 million.

Also in 2007 the company sold scientific/laboratory supplies distributor VWR International to Madison Dearborn Partners and UK foodservice supplier Brakes to Bain Capital. With Kohlberg Kravis Roberts, CD&R bought another food distributor, U.S. Foodservice, from Royal Ahold for more than $7 billion.

CD&R acquired acquired water-treatment specialist Culligan International and a 47.5% stake in Sally Beauty Holdings in 2006.

In 2005 the company teamed up with The Carlyle Group and Merrill Lynch Global Private Equity to buy Hertz from Ford Motor Company in a deal worth about $15 billion. Hertz went public in 2006, but CD&R retained a nearly 20% stake in the firm.

EXECUTIVES

Chairman: Joseph L. Rice III
President and CEO: Donald J. Gogel, age 59
Managing Partner: Kevin J. Conway, age 50
Senior Operating Partner: George W. Tamke, age 61
Special Partner: John Francis (Jack) Welch Jr.

General Partner, London: Huw Phillips
General Partner, London: Christian P. Rochat
General Partner, London: Roberto Quarta, age 60
General Partner, London: Fred Kindle, age 50
General Partner, London: David A. Novak
General Partner and Media Contact: Thomas C. Franco

LOCATIONS

HQ: Clayton, Dubilier & Rice, Inc.
375 Park Ave., 18th Fl., New York, NY 10152
Phone: 212-407-5200   **Fax:** 212-407-5252
Web: www.cdr-inc.com

Clayton, Dubilier & Rice has offices in London and New York.

PRODUCTS/OPERATIONS

Selected Portfolio Companies

Culligan International
HD Supply
Hertz Global Holdings
Sally Beauty Holdings
The ServiceMaster Company
U.S. Foodservice

COMPETITORS

Apollo Advisors
Bain Capital
Blackstone Group
The Carlyle Group
Equity Group Investments
HM Capital Partners
KKR
Leonard Green
Platinum Equity
Thomas H. Lee Partners
TPG
Wingate Partners

HISTORICAL FINANCIALS

Company Type: Private

Income Statement

FYE: December 31

	REVENUE ($ mil.)	NET INCOME ($ mil.)	NET PROFIT MARGIN	EMPLOYEES
12/08	1,100	—	—	15,500

ClubCorp USA

This company makes its green from the green — the golf green, that is. ClubCorp is one of the world's largest operators of golf courses and private clubs with more than 160 facilities throughout the US and in a small number of international locations. Its resorts and golf courses include such well known venues as Firestone Country Club (Akron, Ohio), The Homestead Club (Hot Springs, Virginia), and Mission Hills Country Club (Rancho Mirage, California). ClubCorp also operates private business and sports clubs. Robert Dedman started the company in 1957. It is owned by private equity firm KSL Capital Partners.

ClubCorp has been investing in improvements for its current properties while keeping an eye for new facilities to acquire. In 2008 it purchased Seville Golf & Country Club in Gilbert, Arizona,

and it opened a new water park at its Clubs of Kingwood in Texas.

KSL Capital acquired ClubCorp for about $1.8 billion in 2006. The investment firm already had investments in several resort properties, including the Doral Golf Resort in Florida and La Costa Resort and Spa in California. Eric Affeldt, a founding member of KSL Capital, took over as president and CEO of ClubCorp following the acquisition. As part of the deal, the Dedman family, which previously controlled 70% of the company, retained ownership of the historic Pinehurst Resort & Country Club in North Carolina.

HISTORY

Though his childhood in Depression-era Arkansas was dominated by intense poverty, ClubCorp founder Robert Dedman knew how to dream big. At a young age he vowed to become "very, very rich," and the scrappy Dedman embarked on achieving that goal by earning a college scholarship, obtaining a law degree, and eventually launching a flourishing Dallas law practice.

Dedman's law firm was successful, but he realized that it wouldn't bring him the $50 million he wanted to earn by age 50. In 1957 he formed Country Clubs, Inc., to venture into the country club business. At that time, doctors and lawyers working on a volunteer basis were managing most clubs, and Dedman believed his new company could bring professional management expertise to these facilities. The company opened its first country club, Dallas' Brookhaven Country Club, in 1957. Through the subsequent purchase of 20 more clubs, Country Clubs refined its management style, implementing unique practices such as reducing playing time on the golf course and developing specialized training for club staff.

In 1965 the company expanded into city and athletic clubs and assumed the Club Corporation of America name. The expansion drive that followed fueled a 30% growth rate that the company maintained from the 1960s through the 1980s. In 1985 the company was restructured and divided into a handful of separate companies owned by the newly formed Club Corporation International holding company.

In 1988 the company bought an 80% interest in Franklin Federal Bancorp. The bank's club properties had initially caught his eye, but Dedman also believed that the 400,000 members of his clubs might prove fertile ground for the marketing of financial services. In 1996, however, Club Corporation International sold the financial institution to Norwest. Although Franklin Federal was turning a profit, losses from investment in derivatives, coupled with the bank's inability to compete with larger competitors, prompted the company to sell the bank and refocus on its core club and resort business.

In 1996 Japanese cookie-maker Tohato sued the company, claiming that it intentionally mismanaged the Pinewild Country Club. Pinewild was owned by Tohato, managed by Club Corporation International, and located next door to Club Corporation International's Pinehurst Resort & Country Club. Tohato alleged that the company's mismanagement was part of a scheme to eventually buy Pinewild at a reduced price. The case was eventually settled, but the nasty legal wrangling that ensued cast a pall over the impending 1999 US Open at Pinehurst.

In 1998 the company was reincorporated as ClubCorp International, Inc. It expanded its international base that year by purchasing nearly

30% of PGA European Tour Courses. The company also entered into a joint venture with Jack Nicklaus to develop three dozen new golf courses.

The company shortened its moniker to ClubCorp in 1999. Among the additions ClubCorp made to its holdings that year were 22 properties acquired from The Meditrust Companies. The company also increased its ownership of Canadian club developer ClubLink to 25%. An influx of funds for further expansion came in 1999 after investment firm The Cypress Group took a stake. In 2001 the company sold its interests in ClubLink and PGA European Tour Courses.

Robert Dedman died in 2002. His son, Robert Dedman Jr., took over as CEO for a time, but relinquished those duties to president John Beckert in 2004. Two years later, the company was acquired by private equity firm KSL Capital Partners for $1.8 billion. As part of the deal, the Dedman retained ownership of the historic Pinehurst Resort & Country Club in North Carolina.

EXECUTIVES

President and CEO: Eric L. Affeldt, age 52
EVP and CIO: Daniel T. (Dan) Tilley
EVP and CFO: Curt McClellan
EVP Golf and Country Club Division: Mark Burnett
EVP People Strategy, General Counsel, and Secretary: Ingrid Keiser
EVP Sales and Marketing: Jamie Walters
EVP Business Development: David B. Woodyard
SVP Strategic Alliances and Global Sales: Mark Murphy
SVP Purchasing: William T. (Bill) Walden
SVP Business and Sports Club Division: Sean Laney
VP Golf Course Management: Douglas Miller
Auditors: Deloitte & Touche LLP

LOCATIONS

HQ: ClubCorp USA, Inc.
3030 LBJ Fwy., Ste. 600, Dallas, TX 75234
Phone: 972-243-6191   **Fax:** 972-888-7558
Web: www.clubcorp.com

PRODUCTS/OPERATIONS

Selected Clubs and Resorts

Country clubs and golf courses
Brookhaven Country Club (Dallas)
Country Club of Hilton Head (South Carolina)
Cozumel Country Club (Mexico)
Firestone Country Club (Akron, OH)
Golden Bear Golf Club at Indigo Run (Hilton Head, SC)
Greenbrier Country Club (Chesapeake, VA)
The Hills of Lakeway (Austin, TX)
Hunter's Green Country Club (Tampa)
Indian Wells Country Club (California)
Nags Head Golf Links (North Carolina)
Nicklaus Golf Club at LionsGate (Overland Park, KS)
Piedmont Golf Club (Haymarket, VA)

Resorts
Barton Creek Country Club (Austin, TX)
The Homestead Club (Hot Springs, VA)

Business and sports clubs
Boston College Club
Buckhead Club (Atlanta)
Capital Club Beijing
Citrus Club (Orlando, FL)
The City Clubs of Washington (Washington, DC)
City Club on Bunker Hill (Los Angeles)
Crescent Club (Memphis)
Nashville City Club (Tennessee)
One Ninety One Club (Atlanta)
Plaza Club (San Antonio)
Pyramid Club (Philadelphia)
Renaissance Club (Detroit)
Tower Club (Dallas)
University of Texas Club (Austin)

COMPETITORS

American Golf
Arnold Palmer Golf Management, LLC
Club Med
Eagle Golf
Four Seasons Hotels
Hilton Worldwide
Hyatt
KemperSports
Marriott
Starwood Hotels & Resorts
Troon Golf

HISTORICAL FINANCIALS

Company Type: Private

Income Statement				FYE: December 31
	REVENUE ($ mil.)	NET INCOME ($ mil.)	NET PROFIT MARGIN	EMPLOYEES
12/08	921	—	—	16,000
12/07	898	—	—	16,000
12/06	1,020	—	—	18,000
12/05	1,028	—	—	18,300
12/04	944	—	—	18,500
Annual Growth	(0.6%)	—	—	(3.6%)

Revenue History

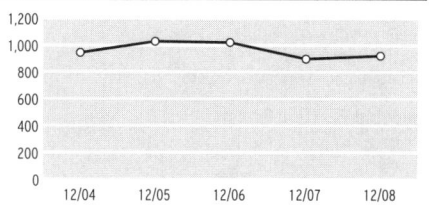

	12/04	12/05	12/06	12/07	12/08
1,200					
1,000					
800					
600					
400					
200					
0					

Coastal Pacific Food Distributors

If an army really does move on its stomach, then this company keeps the military in high gear. Coastal Pacific Food Distributors (CPF) is a leading wholesale food distributor serving the US armed forces in the western US and in the Far East. The company delivers a full line of groceries from three distribution centers in California and Washington to military bases, including US Army, Navy, Air Force, and Marine facilities. CPF also offers information system programming services for its customers to track sales and shipping. The company was founded in 1986.

EXECUTIVES

Chairman: Jerry Jared
Vice Chairman: David Jared
President: Frank Pecoraro
COO: Terrance Wood
CFO: William Ungerman
VP Finance: Monika Bertke
VP Distribution Systems: Timothy Tveitnes
VP Business Development: Jeffrey King
Treasurer: John Payne III

LOCATIONS

HQ: Coastal Pacific Food Distributors
1015 Performance Dr., Stockton, CA 95206
Phone: 209-983-2454   **Fax:** 209-983-8009
Web: www.cpfd.com

COMPETITORS

Advance Food
JTM Provisions
Nash-Finch
Richmond Wholesale Meat

HISTORICAL FINANCIALS

Company Type: Private

Income Statement				FYE: December 31
	REVENUE ($ mil.)	NET INCOME ($ mil.)	NET PROFIT MARGIN	EMPLOYEES
12/07	1,020	—	—	479

Coborn's, Incorporated

Coborn's hopes you'll shop buy at your convenience. The company runs about 25 Coborn's and Cash Wise Foods stores in Minnesota and South Dakota, another 30 shops under the Holiday, Little Dukes, and Save-A-Lot banners, and an online grocery shopping service CobornDelivers. It supplies its stores with baked goods, deli items, and meat from its own central bakery and manufacturing plant. Along with its grocery stores, the firm owns and operates convenience, liquor, and video stores, and pharmacies. Founded in 1921 when Chester Coborn started a single produce market, the company opened its first Cash Wise Foods store in 1979 and its first convenience store in 1986. Coborn's is owned by its employees.

In August 2008 Coborn's acquired the online grocery delivery service SimonDelivers, which was renamed CobornsDelivers and relaunched in October of the same year. (SimonDelivers survived the dot-com bust but ultimately succumbed to rising gas and food prices and shutdown in July 2008. Coborn's has offered its own Internet-based grocery order and delivery service since 2002.) In mid-2009 Coborn's extended its online delivery coverage to the Greater Twin Cities area.

Previous acquisitions include several Holiday Stationstores, purchased in 2006 from Minnesota-based Holiday Companies. Coborn's also bought the rights to the Save-A-Lot name from SUPERVALU in 2002 and opened its first Save-A-Lot deep discount store in Minnesota in 2004.

In mid-2007 Don Wetter stepped down as CEO of Coborn's after 33 years with the company. President Chris Coborn added the CEO title to his job description at that time.

EXECUTIVES

President and CEO: Chris Coborn
COO: Bob Thueringer
CFO: Curt Tillotson
Director Communications and Consumer Affairs: Steve Gottwalt
Director Human Resources: Greg Koenig
Controller: Jerome Schumacher

LOCATIONS

HQ: Coborn's, Incorporated
   1445 E. Hwy. 23, Bldg. A, St. Cloud, MN 56304
Phone: 320-252-4222   **Fax:** 320-252-0014
Web: www.cobornsinc.com

PRODUCTS/OPERATIONS

2008 Stores

	No.
Coborn's	26
Little Dukes	14
Holiday	12
Cash Wise Foods	8
Save-A-Lot	3
Total	**63**

COMPETITORS

Couche-Tard
Cub Foods
Kowalski's Markets
Kroger
Lunds
Wal-Mart

HISTORICAL FINANCIALS

Company Type: Private

Income Statement   FYE: December 31

	REVENUE ($ mil.)	NET INCOME ($ mil.)	NET PROFIT MARGIN	EMPLOYEES
12/08	1,020	—	—	6,500

Colliers International Property Consultants

No matter where your business lives, Colliers International can help you find the best commercial property, *propiedad, propriété,* or *eigentum*. An affiliation of independently owned commercial real estate firms, Colliers International is one of the world's largest commercial real estate dealers, with more than 290 offices in about 60 countries. Colliers International agencies provide property brokerage, investment sales, development, and management and consulting services to tenants, owners, and investors. Altogether, the group's member firms manage more than 670 million sq. ft. of space on six continents.

Among Colliers International's member firms are Colliers CRE, Colliers Hans Vestergaard (Denmark), and Colliers-EPMC (Belgium). Colliers Macauley Nicolls (based in Canada) is the largest member, with offices worldwide. Colliers Jardine, which traces its roots back to 1832, represents the Asia/Pacific region. US arms include Colliers Seeley and Colliers Houston.

EXECUTIVES

Chairman; President and CEO, Colliers Bennett & Kahnweiler Inc.: David Kahnweiler
COO: Margaret Kemp Carlson
CIO: Richard Secor

Chief Knowledge Officer; President Brokerage Services, USA: Craig Robbins
EVP USA: Dan Spiegel
EVP and USA Director of Research: Ross Moore
EVP Operations, U.S.: Carolyn J. Sidor
President and CEO, Colliers USA: Margaret Wigglesworth
President and CEO, Colliers Macaulay Nicolls, Inc.; Chairman USA Board: Doug P. Frye
CEO USA: Alan Oishi
President, Colliers Latin America: Chris McLernon
President, International: James W. (Jamie) Horne

LOCATIONS

HQ: Colliers International Property Consultants, Inc.
   50 Milk St., 20th Fl., Boston, MA 02109
Phone: 617-722-0221   **Fax:** 617-722-0224
Web: www.colliers.com

PRODUCTS/OPERATIONS

Selected Services

Consulting services
Corporate solutions
Development and project management
Facility management
Investment services
Location advisory
Management services
Property representation
Residential services
Retail services
Tenant representation
Valuation and appraisal services

Selected Practice Groups

Advanced technology
Hotels
Investment services
Law firm services
Life sciences/health care
Multi-family advisory
Multimodal
Not-for-profit

COMPETITORS

CB Richard Ellis
Coldwell Banker
Cushman & Wakefield
DTZ
Gale Company
Grubb & Ellis
JMB Realty
Jones Lang LaSalle
Marcus & Millichap
NRT LLC
Sherry FitzGerald
Trammell Crow Company

HISTORICAL FINANCIALS

Company Type: Private

Income Statement   FYE: December 31

	REVENUE ($ mil.)	NET INCOME ($ mil.)	NET PROFIT MARGIN	EMPLOYEES
12/08	1,600	—	—	12,700
12/07	1,600	—	—	10,092
Annual Growth	**0.0%**	**—**	**—**	**25.8%**

Revenue History

Colonial Group

Colonial Group presides over an empire of oil and gas and shipping-related companies in the southeastern US. The group provides storage and distribution services for liquid and dry bulk products including bulk chemicals, motor fuels, industrial fuel oil, and retail gas. It also provides ship bunkering, commercial shipping, and tug and barge services. Colonial Group also operates more than 70 gas stations and convenience stores in Georgia, North Carolina, and South Carolina through its Enmark Stations unit. In addition, subsidiary Georgia Kaolin Terminals provides storage facilities for customers in the US kaolin industry.

Colonial Group has established a number of complementary businesses to support and add value to its core petroleum products supply operations. The company's ocean terminals unit has more than 160 tanks with a total liquid fuels storage capacity of 3.4 million barrels. Subsidiary Compliance Systems helps shipping clients reduce port delays, increase safety and environmental awareness, and document good-faith efforts in ship safety and environmental compliance. Colonial Group operates a light oil products supply system (Colonial Caribbean) to serve the independent gasoline market in Puerto Rico.

EXECUTIVES

President: Robert H. Demere Jr., age 60
CFO: Francis A. (Frank) Brown, age 57
CTO: Bob May
VP Operations: William Baker
Director Human Resources: David (Dave) Deason
Employment Manager: Butch Almeida

LOCATIONS

HQ: Colonial Group Inc.
   101 N. Lathrop Ave., Savannah, GA 31415
Phone: 912-236-1331   **Fax:** 912-235-3881
Web: www.colonialgroupinc.com

PRODUCTS/OPERATIONS

Selected Subsidiaries

Chatham Towing Company, Inc. (tugboat and barge services)
Colonial Caribbean, Inc. (petroleum products supply, Puerto Rico)
Colonial Chemical Solutions, Inc. (products and services for food, chemical process, and basic chemical industries)
Colonial Energy, Inc. (natural gas supplies)
Colonial Marine Industries, Inc. (ship brokerage, chartering, and management)
Colonial Oil Industries, Inc. (oil pipelines and terminals)
Colonial Towing, Inc. (d/b/a Sun State Towing, tugboat and barge services)
Colonial Terminals, Inc. (liquid and dry bulk storage facilities)
Compliance Systems, Inc. (safety and compliance services)
Enmark Stations, Inc. (gas stations and convenience stores)
Georgia Kaolin Terminals, Inc. (marine terminal management)

COMPETITORS

Apex Oil
A.T. Williams
Center Oil
Jordan Oil Company
Mountain Empire Oil

Colorado Avalanche

This Avalanche is breaking loose on ice sheets across the National Hockey League. The Colorado Avalanche is a professional hockey team that represents the Denver area in the NHL and boasts two Stanley Cup championships, its last in 2001. With a popular following in the Rocky Mountain region, the team plays host at its Pepsi Center home arena. The franchise was founded in 1972 as the Quebec Nordiques of the World Hockey League and joined the NHL in 1979. It relocated to Colorado in 1995. Wal-Mart heir Stan Kroenke has owned the team and the Pepsi Center through his Kroenke Sports Enterprises since 2000. He also owns the Denver Nuggets basketball team.

After a poor showing during the 2007-08 season, the Avs fired general manager Francois Giguere and replaced head coach Joel Quenneville by promoting assistant Tony Granato behind the bench. Granato had previously coached the team for two seasons beginning in 2002 before being replaced by Quenneville in 2004. New general manager Greg Sherman, who was promoted during the off-season, later dismissed Granato.

Kroenke has been expanding his sports holdings internationally, becoming the largest shareholder in the UK's Arsenal Football Club in 2009. He also has a 40% stake in the St. Louis Rams football team.

EXECUTIVES

Owner: E. Stanley (Stan) Kroenke
President: Pierre Lacroix, age 50
General Manager: Greg Sherman, age 39
Head Coach: Joe Sacco
SVP Communications and Business Operations:
 Jean Martineau
VP Hockey Operations and Assistant General Manager:
 Craig Billington, age 42
Executive Director Hockey Administration:
 Charlotte Grahame
Director Player Personnel: Brad Smith
Director Player Development; General Manager, Lake Erie Monsters: David Oliver, age 38
Director Hockey Operations: Eric Lacroix
Head Equipment Manager: Mark Miller
Head Athletic Trainer: Matthew Sokolowski

LOCATIONS

HQ: Colorado Avalanche, LLC
 Pepsi Center, 1000 Chopper Circle
 Denver, CO 80204
Phone: 303-405-1100   **Fax:** 303-575-1920
Web: www.coloradoavalanche.com

The Colorado Avalanche play at the 18,000-seat capacity Pepsi Center in Denver.

PRODUCTS/OPERATIONS

Championship Trophies
Stanley Cup (1996, 2001)
Clarence S. Campbell Bowl (1996, 2001)
Presidents' Trophy (1997, 2001)

COMPETITORS

Calgary Flames
Edmonton Oilers
Minnesota Wild
Vancouver Canucks

Colt's Manufacturing

The Colt .45 may have won the West, but it took a New York investment firm stepping in with some cash to keep the company from waving the white flag (during a post-Cold War decline in weapons sales and tough foreign competition). Through the company's subsidiaries, Colt's Manufacturing makes handguns (Cowboy, Pocket Nine, Defender) and semiautomatic rifles (M-4). Colt's Manufacturing boasts more than a dozen distributors throughout Europe, Asia, and Australia. Founded in 1836 by Samuel Colt, the company is about 85%-owned by investment firm Zilkha & Co., which has been breathing new life into the company since 1994 when it bought the firm out of bankruptcy.

With the firearms industry taking cover from safety and health care expense-related lawsuits filed by cities and counties across the US, Colt's has been discontinuing a number of handguns it makes for the consumer market.

The company spun off its "smart gun" division as iColt, but the division closed soon thereafter. Another spinoff, small arms manufacturer Colt Defense, filed papers to go public in 2005, but the IPO did not go forward as planned.

Colt's inked a deal in 1999 for military rifles, which includes orders for exclusive production of the M-4 carbine extending through the year 2010. Colt's acquisition of Ultra Light Arms extended its reach into the popular sporting rifle business. And in recent years, Colt's has launched lines, such as the Colt Cowboy revolver and Pocket Nine pistol.

HISTORY

After waiting four years for a patent, Samuel Colt started the Patent Arms Manufacturing Company in 1836 to make his revolutionary handgun, a revolver. The newfangled gun was slow to catch on (the company went bankrupt in 1842), but it gained fame after being adopted by the Texas Rangers. The US Army delegated Capt. Samuel Walker to work with Colt to improve the design, and sales of the resulting "Walker Colt" enabled Colt to set up a factory in Hartford, Connecticut.

In 1851 the company became the first American manufacturer to open a plant in England. Patent Arms Manufacturing Company was renamed Colt's Patent Fire Arms Manufacturing Co. four years later. Colt was a millionaire when he died in 1862 at age 47.

Colt's introduced the six-shot Colt .45 Army Model, "the gun that won the West," in 1873. More products followed, including machine guns and automatic pistols designed by inventor John Browning. Colt's widow sold the firm to an investor group in 1901.

Business boomed during both world wars, but by the 1940s labor strife and outmoded equipment began to take a toll, and Colt's lost money during the last years of WWII. In 1955 the struggling firm was acquired by conglomerate Penn-Texas. In 1959 Colt's patented the M-16 rifle; in 10 years it sold a million units to the US military.

During the Vietnam War the company flourished, but the 1980s brought low-end competition and shrinking defense orders. Colt's sales were hurt when the US government replaced the Colt .45 as the standard-issue sidearm for the armed forces. A three-year strike prompted the Army to shift its M-16 contract to Belgium's FN Herstal in 1988.

Two years later Colt's was acquired by private investors and a Connecticut state pension fund and was renamed Colt's Manufacturing. Sales remained flat, however, forcing the company to seek bankruptcy protection in 1992. There Colt's remained until New York investment firm Zilkha & Co. bailed it out in 1994, reorganizing the company. The new management made an offer for rival FN Herstal in 1997, but the deal was blocked by the Belgian government and fell through. Late that year the company won a contract to supply M-4 rifles to the Army.

Colt's bought military weapons specialist Saco Defense, maker of MK 19 and Striker grenade launchers, in 1998. Also that year Steven Sliwa succeeded retiring CEO Ronald Stewart.

As US cities began suing Colt's and other makers of firearms in attempts to recover safety and health expenses attributed to gun violence, the company stepped up lobbying in 1999 and said it would increase gun safety efforts, including development of its "smart gun" technology.

A restructuring in 1999 ended most of Colt's consumer handgun business. It also spun off its smart gun technology as a separate company, iColt. Sliwa left to head iColt, and retired US Marine Lieutenant General William Keys was named president and CEO of Colt's. Also in 1999 Colt's bought Ultra-Light Arms, a maker of upscale hunting rifles, and said it would buy Heckler & Koch, a small arms manufacturer based in Germany. By 2000 the company had withdrawn iColt (investors didn't seem interested in a lawsuit laden industry) and stepped away from the Heckler & Koch deal. The company continues to focus on weapons for the military and police, but in 2001 it lost out to CAPCO Inc. in a bid for a contract to upgrade M16 rifles used by the Air Force.

EXECUTIVES

Chairman: Donald Zilkha
President and CEO: William M. (Bill) Keys
Director Materials: John Ibbotson
Director Human Resources: Mike Magouirk
Director Marketing: Mike Reissig

LOCATIONS

HQ: Colt's Manufacturing Company, LLC
 545 New Park Ave., West Hartford, CT 06110
Phone: 860-236-6311   **Fax:** 860-244-1442
Web: www.coltsmfg.com

PRODUCTS/OPERATIONS

Selected Brands
Colt Cowboy
Defender
M4
Pocket Nine

COMPETITORS

Browning Arms
Fabbrica D'Armi Pietro Beretta
Glock
Marlin Firearms
Mauser-Werke
Remington Arms
Ruger
SIG
Smith & Wesson Holding

Columbia Forest Products

Columbia Forest Products is one of North America's largest manufacturers of hardwood plywood, veneer, and laminated products as well as hardwood logs. The employee-owned company manufactures materials used to make cabinets, architectural millwork, commercial fixtures, and other wood products. Its rotary veneer is used by the cabinetry, door, furniture, and decorative plywood industries. Columbia specializes in Northern Appalachian hardwoods such as oak, ash, birch, and maple. The company sells its products to manufacturers, wholesale distributors, and mass merchandisers. Columbia Forest Products began in 1957 with a plywood plant in Oregon and has grown to operate around a dozen plants in the US and Canada.

Columbia also has a global operational network. It imports panel products from Indonesia, Malaysia, Taiwan, Africa, and other countries in South America and Europe.

In 2007 the company began retooling some of its operations. It sold several wood flooring plants to Mohawk Industries, one of its flooring distributors. The four plants — three in the US and one in Malaysia — had been operating at a loss. Later that same year Columbia also closed its Canadian particleboard plant, citing low prices, high energy costs, and reduced demand. However, it committed to spend $3 million on improvements to another hardwood mill that would allow it to increase production.

The company has made a commitment to environmental sustainability and safety. Columbia was ahead of the curve in 2005 when it phased out potentially toxic formaldehyde adhesives in its plywood manufacturing processes. The company's new glues (called PureBond) are based on a nontoxic soy-based adhesive. The company also is an exclusive distributor of adhesive producer Hercules' formaldehyde-free glues to the composite wood industry. In 2008 Columbia formed a partnership with Teragren to offer bamboo face veneers and formaldehyde-free hardwood plywood. Another partnership was formed that year with Weyerhaeuser to begin offering Lyptus hardwood — another non-toxic product.

Columbia was the first hardwood plywood company to be certified to Forest Stewardship Council (FSC) standards as well as California Air Resources Board (CARB) Airborne Toxic Control Measure's standards.

EXECUTIVES

Chairman: Arnold Curtis
President and CEO: Brad Thompson
EVP and CFO: Clifford (Cliff) Barry
EVP Columbia Flooring: Greg Pray
EVP Special Projects: Ed Woods
Director Marketing: Todd Vogelsinger
VP Northern Operations: Gary Gillespie
VP MIS: Frank Leipzig
VP Strategic Planning: Phill Guay
Human Resource Manager: Brian Kinsley

LOCATIONS

HQ: Columbia Forest Products Inc.
7820 Thorndike Rd., Greensboro, NC 27409
Phone: 336-605-0429
Web: www.columbiaforestproducts.com

PRODUCTS/OPERATIONS

Selected Products and Brands

Appalachian Traditions hardwood plywood
Aromatic cedar
Beaded panels
Columbia alder
Drawer sides
Europly (made from Polish birch)
FirstStep (pre-primed hardwood panels)
Hardwood logs (cherry, maple, poplar, red oak, walnut, white oak)
Hardwood plywood (aromatic cedar, decorative interior veneers and panels)
Hardwood veneers
Imported products
JayCore/KayCore (premium veneer core hardwood plywood)
Lyptus hardwood plywood
PLYprints (screen printed art by Alexander Girard)
Teragren bamboo hardwood plywood
UV Wood

COMPETITORS

Georgia-Pacific
Louisiana-Pacific
Norbord
Plum Creek Timber
Potlatch
Roseburg Forest Products
Sierra Pacific Industries
Temple-Inland
West Fraser Timber
Weyerhaeuser

HISTORICAL FINANCIALS

Company Type: Private

Income Statement				FYE: December 31
	REVENUE ($ mil.)	NET INCOME ($ mil.)	NET PROFIT MARGIN	EMPLOYEES
12/07	1,000	—	—	4,500
12/06	1,000	—	—	4,000
12/05	1,050	—	—	4,000
Annual Growth	(2.4%)	—	—	6.1%

Revenue History

Columbia Sussex

Columbia Sussex develops and manages more than 70 hotels and casinos in about 30 states. Its hotels operate under banners such as Hilton, Marriott, and Starwood. Its casinos are located in states such as Mississippi (Lighthouse Point), Louisiana (Amelia Belle), and Nevada (Lake Tahoe Horizon). CEO William Yung and his family own Columbia Sussex. Gaming affiliate Tropicana Entertainment filed for Chapter 11 in 2008. Columbia Sussex is not a part of the bankruptcy filing. However, the troubled Yung is losing more than $500 million from the bankruptcy, which is resulting in Tropicana canceling management-services contracts with Columbia Sussex worth more than $1 million a year. Yung founded the company in 1972.

Wimar Tahoe, the casino affiliate of Columbia Sussex that did business as Columbia Entertainment, turned heads in 2007 when it purchased Aztar Corporation, owner of the Las Vegas Tropicana, for about $2 billion. (After the deal, Wimar Tahoe took on the Tropicana identity and began operating as Tropicana Entertainment LLC.) The Columbia Sussex affiliate outbid several rivals, including Pinnacle Entertainment and Ameristar Casinos, in a bidding war for Aztar, a company valuable for its Tropicana, one of the last big redevelopment opportunities on the Vegas Strip. With the Aztar purchase, the number of casinos in Columbia's gaming affiliate increased to about a dozen. Despite the Tropicana bankruptcy filing and Yung's departure as Tropicana CEO, that company remains an affiliate of Columbia Sussex.

EXECUTIVES

President and CEO: William J. (Bill) Yung III
CFO: Theodore R. (Ted) Mitchel
Director Development: Joe A. Yung

LOCATIONS

HQ: Columbia Sussex Corporation
740 Centre View Blvd., Crestview Hills, KY 41017
Phone: 859-578-1100   **Fax:** 859-578-1154
Web: www.columbiasussex.com

PRODUCTS/OPERATIONS

Select Properties

Belle of Baton Rouge
Doubletree Hotel Birmingham
Crowne Plaza Richmond West
Hilton Crystal City at Washington Reagan National Airport
Jackson Marriott Downtown
Lake Tahoe Horizon Casino
Lighthouse Point Casino
Minneapolis Airport Marriott Bloomington
Sheraton Newark Airport Hotel
Westin Las Vegas

COMPETITORS

American Property Management
Ameristar Casinos
Boyd Gaming
Harrah's Entertainment
Hostmark Hospitality
Interstate Hotels
Isle of Capri Casinos
Janus Hotels
MGM MIRAGE
Pinnacle Entertainment
Station Casinos
Trump Resorts

HISTORICAL FINANCIALS

Company Type: Private

Income Statement				FYE: December 31
	REVENUE ($ mil.)	NET INCOME ($ mil.)	NET PROFIT MARGIN	EMPLOYEES
12/07	1,730	—	—	18,250

Columbia University

Predating the American Revolution, Columbia University (founded as King's College in 1754) is the fifth-oldest institution of higher learning in the US. With a student population of more than 24,900 and a main campus spread across 36 acres in Manhattan, Columbia's 15 schools and colleges grant undergraduate and graduate degrees in about 100 disciplines, including its well-known programs in journalism, law, and medicine. The Ivy League university's more than 3,500-member faculty has boasted nearly 70 Nobel laureates, including former Vice President Al Gore. Columbia, which operates four sites in New York City and one in Paris, also has a strong reputation for research.

Columbia has forged affiliations with nearby institutions such as Barnard College, Teachers College, Union Theological Seminary, and The Jewish Theological Seminary. Columbia-Presbyterian Medical Center, the result of more than 75 years of partnership between Columbia and New York Presbyterian Hospital, helped pioneer the concept of academic medical centers.

Columbia's list of alumni includes such luminaries as Yankee great Lou Gehrig, Supreme Court Justice Ruth Bader Ginsberg, and President Franklin Roosevelt. Columbia, with an endowment valued at about $5 billion, has dipped into the alumni well (and others sources) often over the past 10 years.

HISTORY

Created by royal charter of King George II of England, the university was founded in 1754 as King's College. Its first class of eight students met in a schoolhouse adjacent to Trinity Church (in what is now Manhattan). Some of the university's earliest students included Alexander Hamilton and John Jay. King's College was renamed Columbia College in 1784, a name that symbolized the patriotic mind-set of the age.

The college moved to 49th Street and Madison Avenue in 1849. The School of Law was founded in 1858, followed by the predecessor to the School of Engineering and Applied Science in 1864. The Graduate School of Arts and Sciences was established in 1880, and Columbia became affiliated with Barnard College in 1889.

Columbia College became Columbia University in 1896, and the following year it moved to its present location, the former site of the Bloomingdale Insane Asylum. Columbia continued to expand during the early 20th century. It added the School of Journalism in 1912 with funding from publishing magnate Joseph Pulitzer. Other additions included the School of Business (1916), the School of Public Health (1921), and the School of International and Public Affairs (1946).

Dwight Eisenhower became president of Columbia in 1948, retaining the position until becoming president of the US in 1953. During the late 1960s Columbia gained a reputation for student political action, and in 1968 students closed down the university for several days in protest of the Vietnam War.

Facing financial woes, an escalating New York City crime rate, and contention among its faculty, Columbia struggled to maintain its reputation during the 1970s and 1980s. With this challenge as a backdrop, the university continued to evolve, welcoming its first coed freshman class in 1983.

Still facing economic pressures and reductions in government research spending, Columbia was forced to cut costs, eliminating its linguistics and geography departments in 1991. George Rupp became Columbia's president in 1993. Columbia took over operation of the controversial Biosphere 2 laboratory in Arizona in 1996 (the university had been associated with the lab since 1994, when it formed a consortium with other universities to overhaul the ailing science experiment).

By the late 1990s Columbia had begun to recover from its financial and academic decline. Under the leadership of president Rupp, the university improved its fund-raising efforts and became more selective in student admissions. Microsoft founder Bill Gates donated $50 million to Columbia's School of Public Health in 1999 for research into the prevention of death and disability from childbirth in developing countries. That year Columbia created Morningside Ventures, a for-profit company focused on producing educational materials.

The university partnered in 2000 with the British Library, Cambridge University Press, London School of Economics, the New York Public Library, and the Smithsonian to form another for-profit venture, Fathom.com, a site offering online access to various scholarly resources from each institution. Although the Web site served more than 65,000 people, Fathom.com discontinued operations in 2003. Columbia refocused its online efforts through its Columbia Digital Knowledge Ventures (DKV), a Web site created in 2000, but updated to include e-learning tools in 2003.

In 2001 the National Science Foundation awarded Columbia a $90,000 grant to gather personal accounts and create an oral history piece on the World Trade Center attacks of September 11. In 2002 Columbia University received a pledge of $8 million from Bernard Spitzer for stem cell research to develop new treatments for Parkinson's disease and other neurological disorders. Also that year Lee Bollinger replaced Rupp as president.

EXECUTIVES

Chair: William V. (Bill) Campbell, age 69
Vice Chair: Philip L. Milstein
Vice Chair: Joan Edelman Spero, age 65
Vice Chair: Richard E. Witten
Vice Chair: Marilyn Laurie
President and Trustee: Lee C. Bollinger, age 62
Provost: Alan Brinkley
Chief of Staff: Kerri Jew
SEVP: Robert A. Kasdin, age 50
EVP Student and Administrative Services: Jeffrey F. Scott
EVP Research: David I. Hirsh
EVP Finance: Anne Rollow Sullivan
EVP Government and Community Affairs: Maxine F. Griffith
EVP University Development and Alumni Relations: Susan K. Feagin
EVP and Secretary: Jerome Davis
EVP Communications: David M. Stone
EVP Health and Biomedical Sciences; Dean, Faculties of Health Sciences and Medicine: Lee Goldman
VP and CIO, Columbia University Information Technology: Candace Fleming
VP Human Resources: Lucinda (Cindy) Durning
VP Arts and Sciences; Dean, Faculty of Arts and Sciences: Nicholas B. Dirks
Dean, Columbia Business School: R. Glenn Hubbard, age 51
Dean, Columbia Law School: David M. Schizer, age 38
General Counsel: Jane E. Booth
Auditors: PricewaterhouseCoopers LLP

LOCATIONS

HQ: Columbia University
2960 Broadway, New York, NY 10027
Phone: 212-854-1754   **Fax:** 212-749-0397
Web: www.columbia.edu

PRODUCTS/OPERATIONS

Schools, Colleges, and Affiliated Institutions

Undergraduate Schools
  Columbia College
  Engineering and Applied Science
  General Studies
    Postbaccalaureate Premedical Program
Graduate and Professional Schools
  Architecture, Planning and Preservation
  Arts
  Arts and Sciences
  Business
  Continuing Education
  Dental and Oral Surgery
  Engineering and Applied Science
  International and Public Affairs
  Journalism
  Law
  Medicine
  Nursing
  Public Health
  Social Work
Affiliated Institutions
  Barnard College
  Jewish Theological Seminary
  Teachers College
  Union Theological Seminary

CompuCom Systems

CompuCom Systems urges clients to leave the IT management to them. The company provides infrastructure management services encompassing desktops, servers, networks, data centers, and security. Its application services include consulting, implementation, and custom development. CompuCom also offers third-party hardware and software management services, handling the procurement, configuration, deployment, and support of products from such providers as Apple, Microsoft, IBM, Hewlett-Packard, and Sun Microsystems. The company markets primarily to medium and large enterprises in North America. Court Square Capital Partners acquired CompuCom for $628 million in 2007.

Court Square purchased CompuCom, along with the managed services business of Vanguard Managed Solutions, from Platinum Equity. It merged Vanguard and CompuCom after the acquisition.

In 2008 CompuCom purchased the North American operations of Netherlands-based IT services provider Getronics. The deal served to significantly increase CompuCom's presence in the US and Canada, as well as in Mexico.

EXECUTIVES

President and CEO: James W. Dixon
COO: Jeffrey E. Frick
CFO: Michael Simpson
CIO: John Douglas
CTO: David W. Hall
Chief Strategy Officer: John F. McKenna
SVP Remote Services: Richard (Dick) Boynton
SVP, Sales and Service Delivery: Kevin Shank
SVP, Human Resources: Joe Valdes
SVP ITO Business Development: Rocco Musumeche
SVP, Enterprise Sales: William D. (Bill) Barry
SVP Corporate Development: Timothy Shea
VP, Marketing: Jim Arnold
President, Application Services and Excell Data Division: Richard T. (Rick) Jorgenson
Corporate Communications Director: Stephanie Leonard

LOCATIONS

HQ: CompuCom Systems, Inc.
7171 Forest Ln., Dallas, TX 75230
Phone: 972-856-3600   **Fax:** 972-856-5395
Web: www.compucom.com

COMPETITORS

Accenture
Agilysys
ASI Computer Technologies
Avnet
Bell Industries
Bell Microproducts
Black Box
CDW
CompUSA
Computer Sciences Corp.
CSI Computer Specialists
Dimension Data
En Pointe
GTSI
Hewlett-Packard
High Point Solutions
HP Enterprise Services
IBM
Ingram Micro
Merisel
MicroAge
MoreDirect
New Age Electronics
Pomeroy IT
SARCOM, Inc.
Siemens AG
Softmart
Software House
Tech Data
Unisys
Westcon
ZT Group

HISTORICAL FINANCIALS

Company Type: Private

Income Statement

	REVENUE ($ mil.)	NET INCOME ($ mil.)	NET PROFIT MARGIN	EMPLOYEES
12/08	2,100	—	—	11,000
12/07	1,500	—	—	7,700
Annual Growth	40.0%	—	—	42.9%

FYE: December 31

Revenue History

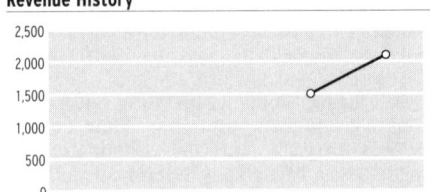

Conair Corporation

Counterintelligence has shown that Conair has a place in many bathrooms and kitchens. The company operates through several divisions, including personal care, hair goods, professional products, and Cuisinart & Waring, and has an international presence, particularly in Canada, Mexico, Asia, and Europe. Its personal care items, such as grooming and health and wellness appliances, are made under the names Interplak, Travel Smart, and Allegro. Conair's hair care unit makes brushes, mirrors, and Scünci accessories, while its Rusk subsidiary caters to salons. Conair's products are sold at discount chains, department stores, and mass merchants (Bed Bath & Beyond, Target, Wal-Mart) in the US and online internationally.

The company is a top-selling brand of hair accessories at food, drug, and discount retailers. To secure its spot at the top, Conair has been adding brand names, through acquisitions, to its portfolio. Having bought the Scünci hair accessories business, Conair has been expanding the Scünci brand into hair appliances and taking it to overseas markets. In 2007 Conair acquired Connecticut's Franzus Company to extend its reach into travel appliances and other items, as well as expand its market into Europe where Conair sells BaByliss haircare appliances.

To increase its domestic and international reach, Conair in September 2007 bought Allegro Manufacturing, based in California. The manufacturer of cosmetic and travel organizer bags had expanded into making diaper bags, bath items, small luggage, and pet accessories in recent years. The deal gave Conair a foothold in more than 20 countries where Allegro trades — such as London, Paris, Mexico City, Toronto, and Sydney — and ownership of Allegro's manufacturing plants in China and the Philippines.

Conair also manufactures and distributes hairstyling appliances (hair dryers, curling irons, and straightening irons) for teen girls marketed under teenage superstars Mary-Kate and Ashley Olsen's eponymous brand.

Lee Rizzuto, who founded Conair in 1959 with his parents, pleaded guilty to tax evasion in 2002.

EXECUTIVES

President: Ronald T. Diamond
CFO: Dennis Ling
SVP Finance: Pat Yannotta
SVP: Lee Rizzuto Jr.
SVP Administration: John Mayorek
VP, Treasurer and Assistant Secretary: John Vele
VP, General Counsel and Secretary: Ricard Margulies
VP Chemical Product Development: Lou Salce
VP Research and Development: Jules Nachtigal
VP Marketing, New Product Development: Martin A. Cohen
VP Advertising and Communications: Robert Dixon

LOCATIONS

HQ: Conair Corporation
1 Cummings Point Rd., Stamford, CT 06902
Phone: 203-351-9000
Web: www.conair.com

PRODUCTS/OPERATIONS

Selected Brands

BaByliss
Conair
ConairPro
Cuisinart
Grand Finale
Interplak
Jheri Redding
Pollenex
Rusk
Scünci
Waring

Selected Subsidiaries

Conair Consumer Products (Canada)
Continental Conair Ltd. (Hong Kong)

COMPETITORS

Alberto-Culver	Newell Rubbermaid
Claire's Stores	Philips Electronics
Global-Tech	Philips Oral
Goody Products	Procter & Gamble
Helen of Troy	Revlon
John Paul Mitchell	Salton
L'Oréal	Spectrum Brands
National Presto Industries	The Stephan Co.

HISTORICAL FINANCIALS

Company Type: Private

Income Statement

	REVENUE ($ mil.)	NET INCOME ($ mil.)	NET PROFIT MARGIN	EMPLOYEES
12/07	1,900	—	—	4,060
12/06	1,700	—	—	3,367
12/05	1,488	—	—	3,459
12/04	1,340	—	—	3,331
12/03	1,277	—	—	4,000
Annual Growth	10.4%	—	—	0.4%

FYE: December 31

Revenue History

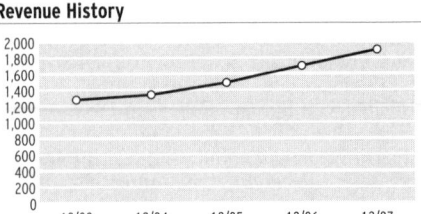

Concentra Inc.

Concentra concentrates on keeping employees healthy. The company's main business is providing occupational health care services through its network of more than 300 health care facilities and about 250 workplace clinics in 40 states. Services provided at the centers include pre-employment screening, injury and urgent care, wellness checks, vaccinations, lab tests, and physical therapy. It also operates mobile health clinics. The company's Auto Injury Solutions division provides a suite of services to property/casualty insurers, including bill review, claims processing, and other services related to auto injury cases. Concentra is owned by private equity firm Welsh, Carson, Anderson & Stowe.

Concentra has been paring down its operations geared towards insurers in order to focus on the provision of health care services. In 2007 it sold its workers' compensation services businesses to Coventry Health Care. The divested operations provided medical bill review, repricing, and pharmacy benefit management services to insurers.

The same year it spun off its Concentra Network Services division, which provided cost containment services to health insurers, into a newly formed company called Viant. And the previous year it sold First Notice Systems, at the time part of the Network Services unit, to The Innovation Group.

With those divestitures complete, Concentra is focusing its energies on managing and growing its health services business, providing occupational health services through its nationwide group of worksite clinics and stand-alone medical centers. It is expanding into the realm of urgent care as well, offering walk-in care to the general public at an increasing number of its medical centers.

The company has grown its portfolio of clinics by acquiring occupational health clinics and opening up centers of its own. In 2008 Concentra acquired two occupational health clinics from Trinity Regional Health System in Iowa and Illinois; it also bought centers in North Carolina and Missouri that year, and it purchased or constructed facilities in Alabama and Georgia in 2007. It had previously acquired Occupational Health + Rehabilitation, expanding its network by 27 locations into new markets in six states.

Former CEO Dan Thomas was named chairman of the board in 2007, and Jim Greenwood (previously executive vice president of corporate development) became CEO of Concentra.

EXECUTIVES

CEO: James M. (Jim) Greenwood, age 48
President and COO: W. Keith Newton
SVP and Chief Marketing Officer: John A. deLorimier
EVP and Chief Medical Officer: W. Tom Fogarty
EVP and CFO: Thomas E. (Tom) Kiraly, age 49
EVP, General Counsel, and Secretary: Mark A. Solls
SVP and National Therapy Director: Gary C. Zigenfus
SVP Sales and Account Management: Jay B. Blakey
SVP and CIO: Suzanne C. Kosub
SVP Human Resources and Compliance Officer:
Tammy S. Steele
President, Concentra Health Solutions:
A. Michael (Mike) McCollum
President, Auto Injury Services: Matthew K. Elges
President, Concentra Medical Centers: Ted Bucknam
Auditors: PricewaterhouseCoopers LLP

LOCATIONS

HQ: Concentra Inc.
5080 Spectrum Dr., Ste. 1200 West
Addison, TX 75001
Phone: 972-364-8000   **Fax:** 972-387-0019
Web: www.concentra.com

PRODUCTS/OPERATIONS

Selected Services

Auto injury solutions	Onsite employer clinics
Flu Shots	Physical therapy
Health and wellness	Preventative care
Injury and illness	Urgent care
Mobile medical units	Web portals
Occupational therapy	

COMPETITORS

Carle Clinic	Hooper Holmes
Crawford & Company	Intracorp
eScreen	Physiotherapy Associates
First Advantage	U.S. Physical Therapy
First Health Group	Walgreen

HISTORICAL FINANCIALS
Company Type: Private

Income Statement
FYE: December 31

	REVENUE ($ mil.)	NET INCOME ($ mil.)	NET PROFIT MARGIN	EMPLOYEES
12/08	826	—	—	11,281
12/07	832	—	—	—
12/06	1,299	—	—	11,585
12/05	1,155	—	—	11,285
12/04	1,102	—	—	10,370
Annual Growth	(7.0%)	—	—	2.1%

Revenue History

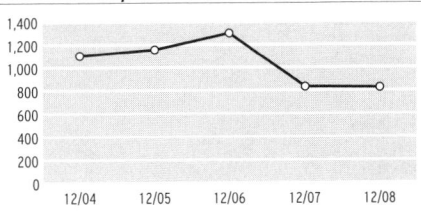

The Conference Board

The Conference Board is as serious as it sounds. The not-for-profit membership organization focuses on increasing the effectiveness of businesses through its nearly 110-member councils. It does research on corporate citizenship and governance, HR issues, and strategic planning and sponsors conferences, makes forecasts, and publishes economic reports and other products. In addition to research and executive action reports, it publishes *The Conference Board Review*, a magazine for senior executives, and newsletters for US, European, and Asian members. The organization traces its roots to 1916 when a group of business leaders banded together to bolster public confidence in business and quiet growing labor unrest.

EXECUTIVES

Chairman: Douglas R. Conant, age 58
Vice Chairman: Nandan M. Nilekani, age 54
Vice Chairman: Josef Ackermann, age 61
Vice Chairman: Ronald A. (Ron) Williams, age 59
Vice Chairman: Harry M. J. Kraemer Jr., age 54
CEO: Jonathan Spector
President: Gail D. Fosler, age 61
EVP and COO: Joan S. Dargery
SVP Human Resources and Chief Diversity Officer:
Toni L. Riccardi
VP and Chief Economist: Bart Van Ark
General Counsel and Corporate Secretary:
Sophia A. Muirhead
Executive Director, Research Communications and the Middle East, Europe: Andrew Tank
Program Director, Council on Corporate Compliance and Ethics: Donna Boehme
Trustee; President and CEO, The Conference Board of Canada: Anne Golden
Director Communications: Frank Tortorici
Auditors: Ernst & Young LLP

LOCATIONS

HQ: The Conference Board, Inc.
845 3rd Ave., New York, NY 10022
Phone: 212-759-0900   **Fax:** 212-980-7014
Web: www.conference-board.org

Connecticut Lottery

The Connecticut Lottery gives residents of the Constitution State a chance to amend their incomes. The organization operates a variety of scratch-off instant games and daily numbers games (Cash5, Play4). It also offers Classic Lotto twice-a-week jackpot games and the multistate Powerball Lottery. Revenues from the Connecticut Lottery are paid in prizes and to Connecticut's general fund, which finances services and programs in areas such as public health, public safety, and education. The Connecticut State Lottery began operating in 1971. It became a quasi-public corporation in 1996.

The company has given back more than $6.4 billion to the state's general fund since its founding. All total, it pays out about 60% of lottery revenue in prizes and about 30% to Connecticut's general fund. In 2008 players won more than $600 million in prize money, and the lottery provided $283 million to support the general fund. Medicaid was the largest recipient that year (receiving more than 20% of the proceeds).

EXECUTIVES

President and CEO: Anne Noble
VP Operations and Administration: Barbara A. Porto
VP Sales and Marketing: Paul Sternberg
Corporate Counsel and Director Government Affairs:
James F. McCormack
Director Information Systems: Michael J. Hunter
Director Communications and Public Relations:
Diane Patterson
Director Human Resources: Karen M. Mehigen
Director Security: Alfred W. Dupuis
Director Sales: Gloria G. Donnelly
Drawing Coordinator: Richard Wiszniak
Lottery Ambassador: Bill Hennessey
Coordinator, Primary Prevention Services:
Susan McLaughlin
Auditors: UHY LLP

LOCATIONS

HQ: Connecticut Lottery Corporation
777 Brook St., Rocky Hill, CT 06067
Phone: 860-713-2000   **Fax:** 860-713-2805
Web: www.ctlottery.org

PRODUCTS/OPERATIONS

2008 Sales

	$ mil	% of total
Scratch games	619.0	62
Powerball	98.2	10
Classic lotto	32.2	3
Other games	248.8	25
Total	**998.1**	**100**

Selected Games

Cash 5
Classic Lotto
Mid-day 3
Mid-day 4
Play 4
Powerball
Powerball Instant Millionaire
Scratch-off games

COMPETITORS

Loto-Québec
Mashantucket Pequot
Massachusetts State Lottery
New Hampshire Lottery
New Jersey Lottery
New York State Lottery
Pennsylvania Lottery

Consolidated Electrical Distributors

Wishing the world was on autopilot? Consolidated Electrical Distributors (CED) puts the power of technology at your fingertips. With over 500 US locations, the automation and electric control wholesaler is one of the major suppliers to offer proximity and photoelectric sensors and circuit breakers. Devices include alarms and buzzers, power supplies, transformers, switches, wiring, and motor and temperature controls. The company hooks up residential and commercial construction, industrial facilities, and factory automation. Founded as The Electric Corporation of San Francisco, CED has grown through acquisition of complementary distributors. It is owned by the Colburn family and operates under about 80 names.

Driving a large network of independently managed outlets affords CED considerable advantages of scale in the electrical distribution market. CED's position captures proximity to customer markets, reduced operating costs, competitive product prices, and attractive product line tie ups with major vendors such as 3M, General Electric, and Siemens. Although its sole US base of operations is exposed to economic swings, the breadth of its product assortment mitigates risk by catering to diverse industries — residential and non-residential — as well as increasing opportunities for cross-selling.

Recent acquisitions and associations have extended CED's market reach. In 2007 the company picked up US Electrical Services and its 11 wholesale distribution subsidiaries, and in 2008 Maurice Electrical Supply, an independent distributor located in Washington, DC, a key market. Tapping into the growing demand for eco-conscious electrical products, CED's Elevator Supply Division – West joined Power Efficiency Corporation (PEC). PEC, an energy company supplying green components for electric motors, opens the door for direct visibility of CED's energy efficient lineup.

EXECUTIVES

Chairman: Keith W. Colburn
President: H. Dean Bursch
VP and CFO: Jeff C. Wofford
VP and Secretary: David T. Bradford
VP Supplier Relations: Joe Huffman
Treasurer: John D. Parish
Manager, CED Long Beach: Scott Dutton
PC Manager: Mike Uggla

LOCATIONS

HQ: Consolidated Electrical Distributors, Inc.
31356 Via Colinas, Ste. 107
Westlake Village, CA 91362
Phone: 818-991-9000   **Fax:** 818-991-6842
Web: www.cedcareers.com

PRODUCTS/OPERATIONS

Selected Products

Adjustable-frequency drives
Circuit breakers
Control transformers
Load centers
Metering equipment
Motor control centers
Open starters/contractors
Panelboards
Power outlet panels
Pushbuttons
Relays
Safety switches
Starters
Switchboards
Switchgear
Timers
Transformers

COMPETITORS

Anixter International
Border States Electric
Electrocomponents
Fastenal
General Cable
Gexpro
Graybar Electric
HD Supply
Hubbell
Kirby Risk
McJunkin Red Man
McNaughton-McKay
North Coast Electric
OneSource Distributors
Premier Farnell
Rexel Canada
Rexel CLS
Rexel, Inc.
Sonepar USA
Stuart C. Irby
SUMMIT Electric Supply
Turtle & Hughes
United Electric Supply
Walters Wholesale Electric
WESCO International
W.W. Grainger

HISTORICAL FINANCIALS

Company Type: Private

Income Statement   FYE: December 31

	ESTIMATED REVENUE ($ mil.)	NET INCOME ($ mil.)	NET PROFIT MARGIN	EMPLOYEES
12/08	3,430	—	—	6,200
12/07	3,900	—	—	6,160
12/06	3,280	—	—	5,200
12/05	2,800	—	—	5,200
12/04	2,600	—	—	5,200
Annual Growth	7.2%	—	—	4.5%

Revenue History

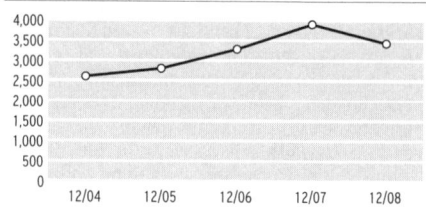

Consumers Union

Consumers Union of United States (CU) inspires both trust and fear. Best known for publishing *Consumer Reports* magazine, the independent not-for-profit also serves as a consumer watchdog through other print publications (newsletters and guides), TV and radio reports, and the Web (ConsumerReports.org). Its subscriber site rates products ranging from candy bars to cars. CU tests and rates thousands of products annually through its National Testing and Research Center, which conducts laboratory testing and survey research. CU accepts no advertising and derives income from the sale of *Consumer Reports* and other services, and from non-commercial contributions, grants, and fees.

CU has revamped its *Consumer Reports* publication with additional content and a new look aimed at improving the magazine's layout and organization. It has also launched a new magazine, *ShopSmart*, aimed at women who want a quick read on consumer items such as food, beauty products, and home and yard products. Expanding into health information, in 2008 CU launched its ConsumerReportsHealth.org Web site and the Consumer Reports Health Ratings Center.

In addition to those efforts, CU is looking to online's edgier world of blogs to attract audiences. The group acquired the consumer information site Consumerist from Gawker Media late in 2008. It continues the blog's snarky coverage of retail markups and shopper complaints.

In addition to its Testing and Research Center, the company has an Auto Test Center in East Haddam, Connecticut; and three advocacy offices, in Washington, DC; Austin, Texas; and San Francisco. The organization testifies before legislative and regulatory entities and files lawsuits on behalf of consumers. CU is governed by an 18-member board. Board members are elected by CU members and meet three times a year. To preserve its independence, CU does not permit its ratings or comments to be used commercially.

HISTORY

In 1926 engineer Frederick Schlink organized a "consumer club" (in White Plains, New York), which distributed lists of recommended and non-recommended products. The lists led to the founding of Consumers' Research and a magazine devoted to testing products.

Schlink moved the group to Washington, New Jersey, in 1933. In 1935 three employees formed a union. Schlink fired them. Faced with another strike that year, Schlink accused the strikers of being "Red" and responded with strikebreakers and armed detectives. The next year the strikers set up their own organization, the Consumers Union of United States (CU).

CU's first magazine, *Consumers Union Reports*, came out three months later and rated products that the fledgling organization could afford to test, such as soap and breakfast cereals. Subsequent issues focused on food and drug regulation and working conditions for women in textile mills.

The organization drew the wrath of both *Reader's Digest* and *Good Housekeeping* (which accused it in 1939 of prolonging the Depression). The next year the House Un-American Activities Committee put CU on its list of suspect organizations. CU cut staff and dropped "Union" from its magazine title, but circulation remained low until after WWII.

By 1950, however, Americans began consuming again, helping to boost circulation to almost 400,000. During the 1950s CU published a series of reports on the health hazards of smoking. In 1960 CU helped found the International Organization of Consumers Unions (now Consumers International) to foster the consumer movement worldwide. Rhoda Karpatkin was hired as publisher in 1974. During the 1970s CU established consumer advocacy offices in California, Texas, and Washington, DC.

Recession and an increase in mailing rates caused the organization to lose money in the early 1980s. CU looked to its readers, who donated more than $3 million. In 1984 the organization was hit by a 13-week strike by union members calling for more say in management.

In 1996 CU slapped "not acceptable" ratings on the Isuzu Trooper and the Acura SLX. The next year the National Highway Traffic Safety Administration declared that CU's testing procedure of the Trooper was flawed, but CU stood by its tests of the vehicle.

CU hit another bump in 1998 when it was compelled to retract a story on the nutritional value of Iams and Eukanuba pet food. Admitting its test results were incorrect, CU's retraction of the story was something of a rarity — its last retraction had occurred almost 20 years earlier when the organization retracted a story on condoms.

A legal dispute broke out in 1999 between CU and automakers Isuzu and Suzuki, which claimed negative reviews by *Consumer Reports* constituted defamation. The following year a jury found CU guilty of falsely reporting on the Isuzu but declined to impose fines on the publisher. (Suzuki eventually settled its case out of court in 2004.) Karpatkin announced she would step down as president in 2001 and was replaced by chairman James Guest. That same year CU agreed to license its content to Internet portal Yahoo!

Retailer Sharper Image (later TSIC) sued CU over an article unflattering to the company's popular air purifier device, but a judge threw out the suit in late 2004.

EXECUTIVES

Chair: Teresa Moran Schwartz
President and CEO: James A. (Jim) Guest
VP Executive Operations, and Chief of Staff:
Michael (Mike) D'Alessandro
SVP Information Products: John J. Sateja
VP and CFO: Richard B. (Rich) Gannon
VP and CTO: Rahul Belani
VP and General Counsel: Eileen B. Hershenov
VP External Affairs and Information Services:
Christopher (Chris) Meyer
VP Administration and Human Resources:
Richard (Rick) Lustig
VP Communications: Ken Weine
VP Publishing: Jerry Steinbrink
VP and Editorial Director: Kevin McKean
VP and Technical Director: Jeffrey A. (Jeff) Asher
Science and Policy Analyst: Kristi Wiedemann
Foundation Grants Officer: Robbin Blaine
Director, Business Planning and Analysis: JoAnne Boyd
Auditors: KPMG LLP

LOCATIONS

HQ: Consumers Union of United States, Inc.
101 Truman Ave., Yonkers, NY 10703
Phone: 914-378-2000   **Fax:** 914-378-2900
Web: www.consumersunion.org

PRODUCTS/OPERATIONS

2008 Sales

	$ mil.	% of total
Subscriptions	229.3	92
Contributions	17.5	7
Other	2.8	1
Investment income (loss)	(0.8)	—
Total	**248.8**	**100**

Content Areas

Autos
Food
Health Care
Money
Phones and Media
Product Safety

Selected Offerings

Magazines and newsletters
  Consumer Reports Magazine
  Consumer Reports Money Advisor (newsletter)
  Consumer Reports on Health (newsletter)
  ShopSmart
TV and radio
  Consumer Reports on TV (video segments)
  CR Radio (daily radio feature)
Web sites
  ConsumerReports.org

COMPETITORS

Better Business Bureaus
Consumers' Research
Hearst Magazines
International Data Group
J.D. Power
Kelley Blue Book
National Technical Systems
Reader's Digest
Reed Elsevier Group
Shopping.com
Underwriters Labs
Yelp

CONTECH

CONTECH Construction Products keeps the gutters going. The company makes, distributes, and installs civil engineering products related to environmental storm water, drainage, bridges, and earth stabilization, serving clients working on commercial, industrial, public, and large-scale residential projects. Products range from retaining walls and water-detention vaults to storm water pipes and bridges in a variety of types for vehicular or pedestrian use. CONTECH has dealers, distributors, or manufacturing plants in all 50 US states and a national sales organization of more than 350 people. Investment firm Apax Partners bought the company in 2006.

The acquisition included roughly $330 million and the assumption of $670 million in debt for a net cost of more than $1 billion. The deal poises CONTECH for further growth, both organically and through acquisitions. It has bought about 20 companies since 1999, including Thompson Culvert Company in Missouri and Tennessee-based Plateau Pipe in 2009. The most recent deals expand CONTECH's presence in southern and midwestern parts of the US. The company also has global aspirations, and in 2008 bought the rights to European SurfSep, giving CONTECH the ability to sell additional products in Europe's storm water runoff market.

The ability to grow internationally could attract investors. Also in 2008 new CEO Ron Keating announced plans to take CONTECH public within three to four years.

Members of management hold minority ownership interests in the recapitalized firm.

EXECUTIVES

President and CEO: Ronald C. (Ron) Keating
SVP and CFO: Jeffrey S. (Jeff) Lee
SVP and Chief Administrative and Development
  Officer: Michael M. Rafi
VP, Operations: Micheal (Mike) Mihelck
VP, General Counsel, and Secretary:
  Thomas D. (Tom) Singer
Regional VP, South Central Region: Andrew Sabados
President, Sales; Regional VP, Atlantic Region:
  Steve R. Spanagel
President, Manufacturing and Supply Chain:
  Mo Heshmati
President, Engineering and Customer Solutions and
  Marketing: Thomas P. Slabe
Director, Human Resources: Karen Luther
Chief Engineer: Darrell Sanders
Media Contact: Jessica Noll

LOCATIONS

HQ: CONTECH Construction Products Inc.
9025 Centre Pointe Dr., Ste. 400
West Chester, OH 45069
Phone: 513-645-7000   **Fax:** 513-645-7993
Web: www.contech-cpi.com

PRODUCTS/OPERATIONS

Selected Products and Brands

Bridges
  BEBO
  CON/SPAN
  CONTECH Structural Plate
  Continental
  Steadfast

Earth stabilization
  Armortec
  Keystone
  Tensar

Drainage
  A2 Liner PVC Pipe
  CORUX, aluminum pipe
  DuroMaxx, reinforced storm drain pipe
  Hel-COR, corrugated steel pipe
  SmoothCor, steel lined corrugated steel pipe
  Ultra FLO, smooth interior corrugated storm sewer
    pipe
Storm water management
  Enviropod
  Optimizer
  StormFilter
  StormScreen
  StormVault
  VortCapture
  VortSentry
  Vortechs

COMPETITORS

Advanced Drainage Systems
Charlotte Pipe & Foundry
Cretex
Hanson Pipe
Lafarge North America
Lehigh Cement
MANCO

ContiGroup Companies

Knowing its place on the food chain, ContiGroup Companies (CGC) focuses on meat production. CGC operates through subsidiary Wayne Farms, a major US poultry processor with 13 facilities and a capacity to process almost 2 million pounds of poultry a year. It also owns Continental Grain, which is headquartered in Belgium and trades grain worldwide. The company also operates Arlon, a private investment firm that manages three separate portfolios made up of diverse holdings. Chairman and CEO Paul Fribourg (a descendant of company founder Simon Fribourg) and his family own CGC.

CGC entered a joint venture, (Five Rivers Ranch Cattle Feeding) with Smithfield Foods in 2005. The two companies combined their respective feedlot operations to form a new entity, which operated 10 cattle feedlots with a capacity of more than 1 million head of beef cattle in Colorado, Idaho, Kansas, Oklahoma, and Texas.

After buying ContiGroup's 50% interest in Five Rivers in 2008, Smithfield Foods sold Five Rivers to Brazil's giant meat processor and exporter, JBS, as part of the sale of its beef operations to the Brazilian company.

The sale did not include any live cattle currently being raised at the lots. The cattle currently owned by Five Rivers will be transferred to a new 50-50 joint venture between Smithfield Foods and CGC, while live cattle currently owned by Smithfield Beef will be transferred to another subsidiary of Smithfield Foods. The live cattle will be raised by JBS after the deal is complete for a negotiated fee and then sold. Proceeds from the sale of the live cattle will be paid in cash to the Smithfield Foods/CGC joint venture and Smithfield Foods.

In 2007 Premium Standard Farms merged with Smithfield Foods. Contigroup (which owned about 39% of Premium at the time) now holds 9% of Smithfield.

Overseas, the company has extensive operations including ContiLatin in the Caribbean and Latin America. It owns feed and flour mills in the French West Indies; a flour mill in Haiti (as a joint venture with the Haitian government); a shrimp farm and hatchery in Ecuador; and poultry operations in Peru and Venezuela.

Through its ContiAsia operations, it has businesses in feed milling, animal husbandry, and poultry production and processing in China. Its Asian joint ventures include Conti Chia Tai International, a 50-50 joint venture with Charoen Pokphand, Thailand's largest agricultural company. It operates feed mills and premix plants.

The company's other Asian joint ventures include The Conti Feed (China) Group, which is majority owned by ContiGroup and includes five premix and feed production sites; the Great Wall Northeast Asia Corporation (in which CGC owns a minority interest) consisting of poultry processing plants, feed mills, broiler-breeder farms and hatcheries, and food manufacturing facilities; and ContiAsia Meat Merchandising, headquartered in Hong Kong, which sells frozen poultry, pork and other meat products.

HISTORY

Simon Fribourg founded a commodity trading business in Belgium in 1813. It operated domestically until 1848, when a drought in Belgium forced it to buy large stocks in Russian wheat.

As the Industrial Revolution swept across Europe and populations shifted to cities, people consumed more traded grain. In the midst of such rapid changes, the company prospered. After WWI, Russia, which had been Europe's primary grain supplier, ceased to be a major player in the trading game, and Western countries picked up the slack. Sensing the shift, Jules and Rene Fribourg reorganized the business as Continental Grain and opened its first US office in Chicago in 1921.

Throughout the Depression the company bought US grain elevators, often at low prices. Through its purchases, Continental Grain built a North American grain network that included major locations like Kansas City, Missouri; Nashville, Tennessee; and Toledo, Ohio.

In Europe, meanwhile, the Fribourgs were forced to endure constant political and economic upheaval, often profiting from it (they supplied food to Republican forces during the Spanish Civil War). When Nazis invaded Belgium in 1940, the Fribourgs were forced to flee, but they reorganized the business in New York City after the war.

Following the war, Continental Grain pioneered US grain trade with the Soviets. The company went on a buying spree in the 1960s and 1970s, acquiring Allied Mills (feed milling, 1965) and absorbing many agricultural and transport businesses, including Texas feedlots, a bakery, and the Quaker Oats agricultural products unit.

During the 1980s Continental Grain sold its baking units (Oroweat and Arnold) and its commodities brokerage house. Amid an agricultural bust, it formed ContiFinancial and other financial units.

Michel Fribourg stepped down as CEO in 1988 and was succeeded by Donald Staheli, the first outside CEO. The company entered a grain-handling and selling joint venture with Scoular

in 1991. Three years later Staheli added the title of chairman, and Michel's son Paul became president. Continental Grain sold a stake in ContiFinancial (home equity loans and investment banking) to the public in 1996.

That year Continental Grain and an overseas affiliate (Arab Finagrain) agreed to pay the US government $35 million, which included a $10 million fine against Arab Finagrain, to settle a fraud case involving commodity sales to Iraq.

Paul succeeded Staheli as CEO in 1997. The company bought Campbell Soup's poultry processing units that year, and in 1998 it bought a 51% stake in pork producer/processor Premium Standard Farms. Meanwhile, ContiFinancial diversified into retail home mortgage and home equity lending.

Continental Grain sold its commodities marketing business in 1999 to #1 grain exporter Cargill. With its grain operations gone, the company renamed itself ContiGroup Companies.

During 2000 ContiFinancial declared bankruptcy, and ContiGroup sold its Animal Nutrition Division (Wayne Foods) to feed manufacturer Ridley Inc. for $37 million. Later that year Premium Standard Farms doubled its processing capacity with the purchase of Lundy Packing Company. Chairman emeritus Michel Fribourg, the founder's great-great-grandson, died in 2001. That year ContiSea, the salmon and seafood processing joint venture between ContiGroup and Seaboard, was sold to Norway's Fjord Seafood, giving ContiGroup a significant share of Fjord.

To better focus on its food and agribusiness holdings, in 2003 ContiGroup sold off its ContiChem LPG business.

EXECUTIVES

Chairman and CEO: Paul J. Fribourg, age 55
EVP Investments: David A. Tanner
EVP Human Resources and Information Systems:
Teresa E. McCaslin
EVP and CFO; President, ContiInvestments:
Michael J. Zimmerman, age 59
SVP and Managing Director, ContiAsia:
Nicholas W. Rosa
VP and General Manager, ContiLatin: Brian G. Anderson
President and CEO, Wayne Farms: Elton H. Maddox

LOCATIONS

HQ: ContiGroup Companies, Inc.
  277 Park Ave., New York, NY 10172
Phone: 212-207-5930   **Fax:** 212-207-5499
Web: www.contigroup.com

COMPETITORS

ADM
Bachoco
Cagle's
Cargill
CHS
Land O'Lakes Purina Feed
Marubeni America
New Market Poultry
Perdue Incorporated
Petaluma Poultry
Pilgrim's Pride
Ridley Inc.
Rose Acre Farms
Tyson Foods

Cook Group

Cook Group makes sure your goose isn't cooked if you've got heart disease. Flagship subsidiary Cook Incorporated makes catheters, wire guides, stents, and other devices used in minimally invasive cardiac procedures. Cook Group operates a host of other medical subsidiaries that manufacture urological and gynecological devices, endoscopic accessories, and vascular products. Additionally, industrial parts manufacturers Sabin and K-Tube make plastic and metal parts used for medical and other industrial applications, and Cook Pharmica offers contract manufacturing services to the biotech industry. The company, one of the world's largest privately held medical device firms, was founded by William Cook in 1963.

Subsidiary Cook Incorporated (the company's original business) operates through four divisions: Diagnostic and Interventional (radiology, cardiology, and vascular surgery); Critical Care (emergency medicine, critical care medicine, and anesthesiology); Endovascular Therapy (endovascular treatment of aortic aneurysm); and Surgical (biologics for surgical applications).

In 2006 Cook Group took over the development of several cardiovascular device-related programs from AVI BioPharma. Among other things, it licensed AVI's NEUGENE technology for use in developing new drug-eluting stents.

Cook signed a development agreement with Cardica in 2007 to jointly design and manufacture an automated device used to close PFOs (patent foramen ovales), or holes in the heart. The following year, the company invested further in its research operations by expanding the facilities of subsidiary MED Institute, which conducts medical product design activities for the group.

With an eye towards reinvesting in its hometown of Bloomington, Indiana, Cook Group runs a number of non-medical businesses, including a real estate development firm that preserves important Bloomington buildings, an antique mall, and a historic inn. Cook Aviation, which provides fixed base operator services (fueling and aircraft care as well as concierge services) in Bloomington.

EXECUTIVES

Chairman: Steve Ferguson
President CEO: Kem Hawkins
EVP, Sales and Marketing: Pete Yonkman
SVP, Physician and Institutional Relations, Cook Medical: Jerry Williams
SVP, Business Development: Brian Bates
SVP and Global Strategic Business Unit Leader, Urology Division: Jerry French
VP, Surgical Division: Andy Cron
VP, Global Sales and Marketing, Cook Endoscopy: Barry Slowey
VP, Finance: David Breedlove
VP, Cook Critical Care: Bruce Gingles
VP, Systems Administration: Rick Snapp
VP and CIO: Chuck Franz
Global Director, Public Relations: David McCarty
VP, Engineering, Cook Medical: William S. Gibbons, age 33
President, Cook MyoSite: Carl Cook
President and CEO, Cook Biotech: Mark Bleyer

LOCATIONS

HQ: Cook Group Incorporated
750 Daniels Way, Bloomington, IN 47404
Phone: 812-339-2235   **Fax:** 800-554-8335
Web: www.cookgroup.com

PRODUCTS/OPERATIONS

Selected Subsidiaries
Cook Medical
  Cook Biotech Incorporated
  Cook Endoscopy
  Cook Incorporated
  Cook Ireland Ltd.
  Cook Pharmica
  Cook Urological Incorporated
  Cook Vascular Incorporated
  MED Institute, Inc.
  William Cook Europe ApS
  William A. Cook Australia Pty. Ltd.
Other
  CFC, Inc.
    Grant Street Inn
  Cook Aviation
  K-Tube Corporation
  Sabin Corporation

COMPETITORS

Abbott Labs
American Medical Systems
Angiotech Pharmaceuticals
Bard
Boston Scientific
CooperSurgical
Edwards Lifesciences
Endologix
Johnson & Johnson
LeMaitre Vascular
NMT Medical
Siemens Healthcare
Spectranetics
St. Jude Medical
Synovis Life Technologies

HISTORICAL FINANCIALS
Company Type: Private

Income Statement

	ESTIMATED REVENUE ($ mil.)	NET INCOME ($ mil.)	NET PROFIT MARGIN	EMPLOYEES	FYE: December 31
12/07	1,500	—	—	9,000	
12/06	1,500	—	—	6,300	
Annual Growth	0.0%	—	—	42.9%	

Revenue History

1,600				
1,400				
1,200				
1,000				
800				
600				
400				
200				
0				
12/03	12/04	12/05	12/06	12/07

Corbis Corporation

If a picture is worth a thousand words, then Corbis has lots to say. The company's archive of more than 100 million images is one of the largest in the world, along with that of rival Getty Images. Corbis licenses its images — contemporary and archival photography, art, illustrations, and footage — for commercial and editorial use in print and electronic media. Customers can find and license images via the company's Web site. Corbis also offers artist representation (matching photographers with assignments) and GreenLight rights services (securing rights to images controlled by third parties). Microsoft co-founder Bill Gates owns Corbis, which he founded in 1989.

Overall, Corbis has about 20 offices in about a dozen countries in the Asia/Pacific region, Europe, and North America. It does business in more than 50 countries altogether. Highlights of the Corbis archive include images from Ansel Adams, the Bettmann Collection, the Smithsonian Institution, and the Andy Warhol Foundation.

However, big-name collections like those of Corbis and Getty face a growing competitive threat from so-called microstock agencies, which receive images from amateur photographers and license them for as little as $1 apiece. (By contrast, the average cost of an image from the Corbis collection is about $250.) To keep up, Corbis in 2007 launched the SnapVillage online marketplace, where images cost between $1 and $50. In addition, Corbis is offering licensing options tailored for Internet and mobile phone applications, and in 2007 it expanded its image licensing business by buying Canada-based Veer.

In April 2009 Corbis launched Corbis Motion, a Web site featuring more than 300,000 video clips from companies including Paramount Pictures, Metro-Goldwyn-Mayer, National Geographic, Sony Pictures Entertainment, HBO Archives, and the Smithsonian Channel. About 150,000 of the clips are in high definition format.

To help generate new sales, Corbis is deploying business development teams in major media markets worldwide. At the same time, it is consolidating many of its customer service functions at centers in Europe and North America and closing some facilities in smaller markets. The changes were part of an effort to streamline the company's global sales organization. In September 2008 Corbis said it would eliminate 175 jobs over 12 months, adding to about 280 positions that were cut the year prior.

To capitalize on the growing demand to use "iconic content" in advertising and consumer products, Corbis rebranded its rights service division in 2008, renaming it GreenLight and expanding its offerings to include talent negotiation, rights clearances and other licensing activities involving celebrities, feature film and TV clips, music, and trademarks. Through GreenLight, Corbis represents the name, image and likeness rights to celebrities and historical figures including Albert Einstein, the Wright Brothers, and Steve McQueen.

The company's growth initiatives are being overseen by a new CEO. Steve Davis stepped down in 2007 after 10 years at the helm and president Gary Shenk succeeded him.

HISTORY

Bill Gates founded Interactive Home Systems (later Continuum Productions) in 1989 and began buying rights to digitize images from museums, archival collections, private collectors, and publications. The company changed its name to Corbis Corporation in 1995 and bought one of the world's largest collections of photos, the Bettmann Collection, which ranges from images of prehistoric cave drawings to the pre-1991 photo library of United Press International. That year it also bought the rights to Russia's Hermitage Museum collection (3 million works). Such moves prompted concern about the extent of Gates' control over world art treasures.

Corbis acquired exclusive rights to works from wilderness photographer Ansel Adams in 1996 (about 40,000 images). Also that year it reached a licensing agreement with the Mariners' Museum in Newport News, Virginia (with 650,000 photographic images). The company lost several key employees in 1997, including CEO Doug Rowan, during its struggle to pin down a strategic direction. Co-presidents Anthony Rojas and Steve Davis replaced Rowan.

In 1998 Corbis agreed to license the photographs of Jack Moebes, who captured the southern Civil Rights Movement of the 1960s. The company bought royalty-free digital image provider Digital Stock that year. The next year it more than doubled its collection when it acquired Sygma.

Corbis purchased TempSports (1.8 million images covering worldwide sports events) in 2000. It also launched a documentary film division. It continued to diversify its offerings the next year when it acquired moving image company Sekani.

Corbis opened Corbis Japan as a joint venture with Japanese image provider amana in 2002 to focus exclusively on the Japanese market, leveraging Corbis' own collection of international images with amana's Japanese image collection. That year the company also opened Corbis Germany.

Late in 2002 Corbis moved its headquarters from Bellevue, Washington, to Seattle. Rojas stepped down as co-president that year, leaving Davis in charge.

In 2005 Corbis purchased the Roger Richman Agency, a licensing agency representing deceased figures such as Albert Einstein, Sigmund Freud, the Marx Brothers, Steve McQueen, and Vivien Leigh. The acquisition of Roger Richman combined Corbis' existing historical archive images with the ability to secure the rights to license the persona of a dead celebrity; it also was a move toward expansion into the agency business.

After 14 years with Corbis, Davis left the company in 2007 to pursue other interests, and president Gary Shenk was promoted to CEO.

EXECUTIVES

Chairman: William H. (Bill) Gates III, age 53
CEO: Gary Shenk
CFO: Barry Allen
CTO: Rajiv Jain
SVP Networks: Nairn Nerland
SVP Corporate Development and General Counsel: Jim Mitchell
SVP Human Resources: Vivian Farris
VP Media Services: Drew MacLean
VP GreenLight: David Reeder
Senior Manager Creative Intelligence: Amber Calo
Director Communications: Dan Perlet
Auditors: Deloitte & Touche

LOCATIONS

HQ: Corbis Corporation
710 2nd Ave., Ste. 200, Seattle, WA 98104
Phone: 206-373-6000   **Fax:** 206-373-6100
Web: www.corbis.com

COMPETITORS

AG Interactive
Agence France-Presse
Associated Press
Broadcaster
Getty Images
Masterfile
National Geographic
New York Times
PR Newswire
Reuters
Rex Features
Sipa Press
Zuma Press

Cornell University

To excel at Cornell, you'll need every one of your brain cells. The Ivy League university has been educating young minds since its founding in 1865. Its more than 20,000 students can select undergraduate, graduate, and professional courses from 11 colleges and schools. In addition to its Ithaca, New York, campus the university has medical programs in New York City and Doha, Qatar. Cornell's faculty includes a handful of Nobel laureates, and the university has a robust research component studying everything from animal health to space to waste management; the university's 20 libraries hold more than 7 million volumes. Notable alumni include author E. B. White and US Supreme Court Justice Ruth Bader Ginsburg.

Cornell awarded the nation's first university degree in veterinary medicine and first doctorates in electrical engineering and industrial engineering. It awarded the world's first degree in journalism (and taught the first university course in that subject), and established the first four-year schools of hotel administration and industrial and labor relations.

EXECUTIVES

Chairman: Peter C. Meinig
Chairman Emeritus: Harold Tanner
Chairman Emeritus: Austin H. Kiplinger
Vice Chairman: Jan Rock Zubrow
Vice Chairman: David W. Zalaznick, age 53
Vice Chairman: Samuel C. Fleming, age 68
Vice Chairman: Robert S. Harrison
President: David J. Skorton
EVP Finance and Administration: Stephen T. (Steve) Golding
Interim Provost: David R. Harris
VP Financial Affairs and CFO: Joanne M. DeStefano
VP Student and Academic Services: Susan H. Murphy, age 57
VP Alumni Affairs and Development: Charles D. Phlegar
VP University Communications: Thomas W. Bruce
VP Human Resources: Mary G. Opperman
Chief Investment Officer: James Walsh
Dean, Students: Kent L. Hubbell
University Counsel and Secretary: James J. Mingle
University Librarian: Anne R. Kenney
Auditors: KPMG LLP

LOCATIONS

HQ: Cornell University
Cornell University Campus, Day Hall
Ithaca, NY 14853
Phone: 607-254-4636   **Fax:** 607-255-5396
Web: www.cornell.edu

PRODUCTS/OPERATIONS

Selected Undergraduate Colleges and Schools

College of Agriculture and Life Sciences
College of Architecture, Art, and Planning
College of Arts and Sciences
College of Engineering
School of Hotel Administration
College of Human Ecology
School of Industrial and Labor Relations

Selected Graduate and Professional Colleges and Schools

College of Veterinary Medicine
Graduate School
Johnson Graduate School of Management
Law School
Weill Graduate School of Medical Sciences (New York City)
Weill Medical College (Doha, Qatar)

HISTORICAL FINANCIALS

Company Type: School

Income Statement

FYE: June 30

	REVENUE ($ mil.)	NET INCOME ($ mil.)	NET PROFIT MARGIN	EMPLOYEES
6/08	2,826	—	—	15,558
6/07	2,678	—	—	—
6/06	2,504	—	—	14,226
6/05	2,546	—	—	14,073
6/04	2,510	—	—	13,677
Annual Growth	3.0%	—	—	3.3%

Revenue History

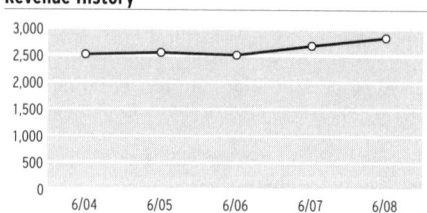

Corporation for Public Broadcasting

This organization is made possible by a grant from the federal government and by support from viewers like you. The Corporation for Public Broadcasting (CPB) is a private, not-for-profit corporation created by the federal government that receives appropriations from Congress to help fund programming for more than 1,000 locally owned public TV and radio stations. CPB-funded programs are distributed by the Public Broadcasting Service (PBS), National Public Radio (NPR), and Public Radio International (PRI). Funds are also used for research on media and education. CPB was created by Congress in 1967.

Funding for CPB has often been a political hot potato and a target for critics opposed to using government money for educational and cultural programming. Supporters, however, have been just as quick to promote the benefits of publicly funded news and informational programming that addresses groups and issues often ignored by commercial broadcasters.

HISTORY

As commercial radio began to fill the radio dial, the FCC in 1945 reserved 20 channels from 88 FM to 92 FM for noncommercial, educational broadcasts. The first public television station started broadcasting in 1953, and by 1965 there were 124 public TV stations across the country. To help allocate government funds to these public TV and radio stations, Congress created the Corporation for Public Broadcasting (CPB) in 1967. CPB created the Public Broadcasting Service (PBS) in 1969 and National Public Radio (NPR) in 1970.

CPB has always been politically controversial; critics have often charged it with elitism, cultural bias, and liberalism. When Republicans gained control of Congress in 1994, their laundry list of grievances included government cultural spending. They were foiled in their effort to eliminate funding for CPB, however, in part because of public support for public television. Congress still cut funding by $100 million, forcing CPB to reduce its staff by almost 25% and introduce performance criteria for stations seeking grant money, including listenership and community financial support minimums.

Robert Coonrod was promoted to CEO in 1997. The following year Congress approved additional funding to help public television's transition from analog to digital broadcasting. Frank Cruz was appointed chairman of CPB in 1999. At about the same time, increased funding for 2003 (funding is approved two years in advance) was threatened when it was discovered that some PBS stations were giving their mailing lists to the Democratic party for fund-raising purposes. Nevertheless, funding for CPB was increased in the 2001 budget.

In late 2001 businesswoman Katherine Milner Anderson was voted in as chairman, taking over for Cruz (who remained on the board). After serving two consecutive terms as chairman, Anderson was replaced by veteran journalist Kenneth Tomlinson in 2003.

CPB's funding was approved at $350 million for 2002 and $365 million for 2003. Coonrod left the company the following year. Former COO Kathleen Cox and CPB agreed to a one-year contract for her to serve as president and CEO. However, she left the post after nine months.

Chairman Tomlinson resigned in 2005 amid allegations that he violated CPB policies by using his position to get funding for programs with a conservative political view. That same year, former Republican National Committee co-chairwoman Patricia Harrison was named the new CEO of the CPB.

EXECUTIVES

Chairman: Ernest J. Wilson III
Vice Chairman: Beth Courtney
President and CEO: Patricia de Stacy (Pat) Harrison
CFO and Treasurer: William P. Tayman Jr.
EVP Corporate and Public Affairs: Michael Levy
EVP and COO: Vincent Curren
SVP Business Affairs: Steven J. Altman
SVP Radio: Bruce Theriault

SVP Education and Children's Content:
Susan T. Zelman
SVP System Development and Media Strategy:
Mark Erstling
SVP and General Counsel:
H. Westwood (West) Smithers Jr.
SVP Television Content: Ted A. Garcia
Corporate and Public Affairs: Louise Filkins
Inspector General: Kenneth A. Konz
Ombudsman: Ken A. Bode
Corporate Secretary: Teresa Safon
Auditors: PricewaterhouseCoopers LLP

LOCATIONS

HQ: Corporation for Public Broadcasting
401 9th St. NW, Washington, DC 20004
Phone: 202-879-9600   **Fax:** 202-879-9700
Web: www.cpb.org

Cox Enterprises

Cox Enterprises is a family-owned holding company with operations spanning cable TV, broadcasting, publishing, and auctions. Its flagship subsidiary, Cox Communications, is the #3 cable system operator (behind Comcast and Time Warner Cable) serving more than 6 million customers with TV, Internet, and digital phone services. Its Manheim unit is the largest wholesale vehicle auction company in the US, with about 145 locations. Cox's media operations, overseen by Cox Media Group, include Cox Newspapers (eight daily papers), Cox Television (about 15 local stations), and Cox Radio (more than 80 stations). Cox also owns a majority stake in AutoTrader.com, an online used car listing service.

The family of founder James Cox, now led by grandson and chairman James Kennedy, has been able to diversify its fortune through Cox Enterprises into holdings that span the country. However, unlike highly integrated media conglomerates such as Time Warner and Walt Disney, Cox's operations do not benefit as much from multi-purposed content and cross-promotion. Its focus on technology and telecommunications, though, does put the company in a position to capitalize on the rapidly converging digital media world.

The company's Cox Communications unit has focused on expanding the number of different services it delivers to subscribers. The cable company has been heavily marketing bundled service packages that include digital phone and broadband Internet access. It has also expanded video on demand (VOD) offerings. Cox Communications is also building a mobile communications network to offer cellular phone service and wireless broadband Internet access to its customers.

The Cox organization has also invested heavily in digital media and services in conjunction with its telecommunications infrastructure. The company has more than 100 online properties, including Web sites for its newspapers, television stations, and radio stations. It also owns online advertising network Adify Corporation which serves ads for a number of media Web properties, including sites owned by Forbes, Martha Stewart Living Omnimedia, and The Washington Post Company. Cox acquired the agency for $300 million in 2008.

Real world publishing, however, has not been so kind to the company. Its Cox Newspapers unit

has struggled along with the rest of the newspaper industry with declining readership and advertising revenue. In response, Cox put all but three of its papers up for sale and plans to use the proceeds to pay down debt and to fund new business investments. Its remaining properties, including the *Atlanta Journal-Constitution*, the *Palm Beach Post* (Florida), and the *Dayton Daily News*, plan to boost their online publishing efforts to expand readership. Cox is also selling its Valpak direct mail advertising unit.

Cox is divesting a portion of its cable programming business, agreeing in 2009 to sell a 65% stake in Travel Channel to Scripps Networks Interactive.

Company veteran Jimmy Hayes was tapped to replace James Kennedy as CEO of Cox Enterprises late in 2008. He was previously head of finance at Cox Communications. Kennedy, who remained chairman, had led the business since 1987.

HISTORY

James Middleton Cox, who dropped out of school in 1886 at 16, worked as a teacher, reporter, and congressional secretary before buying the *Dayton Daily News* in 1898. In 1905 he acquired the nearby *Springfield Press-Republican* and then took up politics, serving two terms in the US Congress (1909-1913) and three terms as Ohio governor (1913-1915; 1917-1921). He even ran for president in 1920 (his running mate was future President Franklin Roosevelt) but lost to rival Ohio publisher Warren G. Harding.

Once out of politics, Cox began building his media empire. He bought the *Miami Daily News* in 1923 and founded WHIO (Dayton, Ohio's first radio station). He bought Atlanta's WSB ("Welcome South, Brother"), the South's first radio station, in 1939 and added WSB-FM and WSB-TV, the South's first FM and TV stations, in 1948. Cox founded Dayton's first FM and TV stations (WHIO-FM and WHIO-TV) the next year, and *The Atlanta Constitution* joined his collection in 1950. Cox died in 1957.

The company continued to expand its broadcasting interests in the late 1950s and early 1960s. It was one of the first major broadcasting companies to expand into cable TV when it purchased a system in Lewistown, Pennsylvania, in 1962. The Cox family's broadcast properties were placed in publicly held Cox Broadcasting in 1964. Two years later its newspapers were placed into privately held Cox Enterprises, and the cable holdings became publicly held Cox Cable Communications. The broadcasting arm diversified, buying Manheim Services (auto auctions, 1968), Kansas City Automobile Auction (1969), and TeleRep (TV ad sales, 1972).

Cox Cable had 500,000 subscribers in nine states when it rejoined Cox Broadcasting in 1977. Cox Broadcasting was renamed Cox Communications in 1982, and the Cox family took the company private again in 1985, combining it with Cox Enterprises. The company also invested in upstart cable broadcaster Discovery Channel (now part of Discovery Communications) during the 1980s. James Kennedy, grandson of founder James Cox, became chairman and CEO in 1987.

Expansion became the keyword for Cox in the 1990s. The company merged its Manheim unit with the auto auction business of Ford Motor Credit and GE Capital in 1991. It also formed Sprint Spectrum in 1994, a partnership with Sprint, TCI (now part of AT&T), and Comcast to bundle telephone, cable TV, and other communications services (Sprint bought out Cox in

1999). Then, in one of its biggest transactions, Cox bought Times Mirror's cable TV operations for $2.3 billion in 1995 and combined them with its own cable system into a new, publicly traded company called Cox Communications.

To expand its online presence, the company formed Cox Interactive Media in 1996, establishing a series of city Web sites and making a host of investments in various Internet companies, including Career Path, ExciteHome, iVillage (later acquired by NBC Universal), MP3.com, and Tickets.com (now part of MLB Advanced Media).

In 2004, fed up with the demands of running a publicly traded cable company, Cox bought the 38% of Cox Communications that it didn't already own for $8.5 billion.

The company in 2007 exchanged Cox Communications' 25% stake in Discovery Communications for $1.3 billion in cash. The deal also included cable broadcaster the Travel Channel.

EXECUTIVES

Chairman, Cox Enterprises, Cox Communications, and Cox Radio: James C. Kennedy, age 61
Vice Chairman: G. Dennis Berry, age 64
President, CEO, and Director: Jimmy W. Hayes, age 56
EVP and CFO: John M. Dyer, age 54
SVP Human Resources and Administration: Marybeth H. Leamer
SVP Strategic Investments and Real Estate Planning: R. Dale Hughes
VP Supply Chain Services and Chief Procurement Officer: Michael J. (Mike) Mannheimer
VP Corporate Security: Robert R. (Bob) Brand
VP Internal Audit: Alexander R. (Alex) Stickney
VP and CIO: Gregory B. (Greg) Morrison
VP Public Policy and Regulatory Affairs: Alexandra M. Wilson
VP Corporate Communications and Public Affairs: Roberto I. Jimenez
VP Corporate Tax: Maria Friedman
VP Development: Robert N. (Bob) Redella
VP Government Affairs: Joab M. (Joey) Lesesne III
VP Legal Affairs, General Counsel, and Corporate Secretary: Andrew A. (Andy) Merdek
President, Cox Communications: Patrick J. (Pat) Esser
President, Cox Media Group and Cox Auto Trader: Sanford H. (Sandy) Schwartz, age 56
President and CEO, AutoTrader.com: Chip Perry
President and CEO, Manheim Auctions: Dean H. Eisner
President and Co-Founder, Adify: Russ Fradin
President, Cox Media Group, Reps: James J. (Jim) Monahan

LOCATIONS

HQ: Cox Enterprises, Inc.
6205 Peachtree Dunwoody Rd., Atlanta, GA 30328
Phone: 678-645-0000 **Fax:** 678-645-1079
Web: www.coxenterprises.com

PRODUCTS/OPERATIONS

2008 Sales

	% of total
Cox Communications	56
Manheim	23
Cox Media Group	14
Cox Auto Trader	6
Total	**100**

Selected Operations

Cox Communications (cable TV system operations)
Travel Channel (cable TV channel)
Manheim (wholesale automotive auctions)
Cox Media Group
Cox Newspapers
The Atlanta Journal-Constitution
Austin American-Statesman (Texas)
Dayton Daily News (Ohio)
JournalNews (Hamilton, OH)
The Middletown Journal (Ohio)
Palm Beach Daily News (Florida)
The Palm Beach Post (Florida)
Springfield News-Sun (Ohio)
Cox Radio
Cox Television
KFOX (FOX; El Paso, TX)
KICU (Ind.; San Jose, CA)
KIRO (CBS, Seattle)
KRXI (FOX; Reno, NV)
KTVU (FOX; Oakland, CA)
WFTV (ABC; Orlando, FL)
WHIO (CBS; Dayton, OH)
WJAC (NBC; Johnstown, PA)
WPXI (NBC, Pittsburgh)
WSB (ABC, Atlanta)
WSOC (ABC; Charlotte, NC)
WTOV (NBC; Steubenville, OH)
Cox Auto Trader (AutoTrader.com online used vehicle listings)

COMPETITORS

A. H. Belo
Advance Publications
AT&T
CBS Corp
Clear Channel
Columbus Fair Auto Auction
Comcast
Cumulus Media
DIRECTV
DISH Network
eBay
Entrade
McClatchy Company
Pittsburgh Independent Auto Auction
Ritchie Bros. Auctioneers
Verizon

HISTORICAL FINANCIALS

Company Type: Private

Income Statement				FYE: December 31
	REVENUE ($ mil.)	NET INCOME ($ mil.)	NET PROFIT MARGIN	EMPLOYEES
12/08	15,400	—	—	77,000
12/07	15,033	—	—	81,693
12/06	13,200	—	—	80,000
12/05	12,000	—	—	77,000
12/04	11,552	—	—	77,000
Annual Growth	**7.5%**	**—**	**—**	**0.0%**

Revenue History

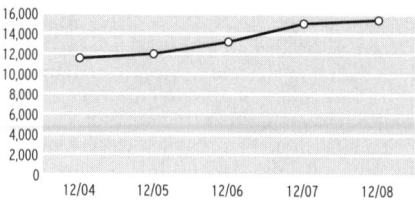

Crain Communications

These Crains have been whooping it up in the publishing business for a long time. Crain Communications is a leading publisher of trade journals and weekly business newspapers with about 30 titles serving audiences mostly in North America and Europe. Its portfolio covers such areas as the automotive industry (*Automotive News, AutoWeek*), the financial sector (*Business Insurance, InvestmentNews*), and media (*Advertising Age*). Crain also publishes business journals in four major US cities (Chicago, Cleveland, Detroit, and New York City). The family-owned company was started by G. D. Crain in 1916.

Crain Communications has built up its stable of trade journals over time, focusing on, and in most cases ultimately dominating, particular niche markets. Its *AutoWeek* and *Automotive News* are must-reads for anyone following the auto manufacturing industry, *Pensions & Investments* is the go-to source for financial services professionals, and *Advertising Age* (also known by the shortened moniker *AdAge*) is the bible for creatives and marketers.

Being a leader in its industry has not saved the company from the downturn in the economy, however. Print advertising, which has been on the decline for several years, took a sharp hit due to the recession. That downward trend has been exacerbated by the fact that many of the industries Crain covers, in particular the automotive sector, have also been struggling. In response, Crain was forced to institute a number of cost-cutting measures in 2009, including staff and salary cuts. The company also converted its *TelevisionWeek* magazine into TVWeek.com, a Web-only property, and it shuttered some other titles including *RCR Wireless News*.

HISTORY

G. D. Crain founded his publishing company in 1916 in Louisville, Kentucky, but quickly moved to Chicago. The firm produced two publications: *Class* (renamed *Business Marketing*) and *Hospital Management* (sold in the 1950s). In 1930 the company launched trade magazine *Advertising Age* and adopted the name Advertising Publications Inc.

Over time the company broadened its scope beyond advertising and in 1969 changed its name to Crain Communications. G. D. Crain led the company until his death in 1973. That year Rance Crain, G. D.'s elder son, became president; Crain's widow, Gertrude, became chairman; and Keith Crain (Rance's brother) was appointed vice chairman.

In 1986 Crain bought *Media World*, the UK's #1 media magazine at the time. By the early 1990s the company was publishing three magazines in Europe. It bought *RCR Radio Communications Report* (a wireless communications tabloid) in 1992.

Keith took Gertrude's place as chairman in 1997 after her 1996 death. In 1998 Crain introduced two publications: *Global Wireless* for the wireless communications industry and *InvestmentNews* for the financial planning industry.

The company bought *Automotive News International* in 1998, giving it a new presence in Asia and Latin America. In 1999 Crain acquired European media magazine *Media International* and turned it into a section of *Advertising Age International*. The following year it launched *BtoB*, a publication serving the business-to-business marketplace. The company advanced into Latin America in 2001, buying two Mexican business publications. (It closed the titles in 2007.)

In 2002 the company renamed its *Electronic Media* magazine *TelevisionWeek*.

EXECUTIVES

Chairman; Publisher and Editor-in-Chief, Automotive News, Automotive News Europe, and Crain's Detroit Business; Editor-in-Chief, Plastics News, Rubber & Plastics News, Tire Business, and Waste News; Editor-in-Chief, Automotive News: Keith E. Crain
President; Editor-in-Chief, Advertising Age, Crain's Chicago Business, Crain's New York Business, and TelevisionWeek: Rance E. Crain
EVP Operations: William A. (Bill) Morrow
SVP and Group Publisher: Gloria Scoby
CIO: Paul Dalpiaz
VP Finance: Thomas M. (Tom) Marantette Jr.
VP Manufacturing and Production: Dave Kamis
VP Human Resources: Laura Anger
VP; Group Publisher, Pensions & Investments, Business Insurance, Workforce Magazine, and Staffing Industry Analysts: Christopher (Chris) Crain, age 33
VP; Publishing and Editorial Director, The Ad Age Group: David S. Klein
VP; Publisher, Advertising Age and Creativity: Allison P. Arden
VP; Publisher, AutoWeek: K.C. Crain Jr.
VP; Publisher and Editorial Director, Automotive News; Group Publisher, Automotive News Europe: Peter Brown
VP; Publications Director, Rubber & Plastics News, Plastics News, Tire Business, ERJ, and Urethanes Technology; Publisher, Waste News: Robert S. (Bob) Simmons
Director, Corporate Communications: Colleen M. Robar

LOCATIONS

HQ: Crain Communications Inc
1155 Gratiot Ave., Detroit, MI 48207
Phone: 313-446-6000   **Fax:** 313-446-1616
Web: www.crain.com

Crain Communications has more than a dozen offices in Akron and Cleveland, Ohio; Boston; Chicago; Denver; Detroit; Irvine, Los Angeles, and San Francisco, California; Nashville, Tennessee; New York City; and Washington, DC, and in London, Munich, and Tokyo.

PRODUCTS/OPERATIONS

Selected Publications

Advertising Age
American Coin-Op
American Drycleaner
American Laundry News
Automobilwoche (Germany)
Automotive News
AutoWeek
BtoB
Business Insurance
Crain's Chicago Business
Crain's Cleveland Business
Crain's Detroit Business
Crain's Manchester Business (UK)
Crain's New York Business
Creativity
European Rubber Journal
InvestmentNews
Modern Healthcare
Pensions & Investments
Plastics News
Rubber & Plastics News
Tire Business
Urethanes Technology International
Waste & Recycling News
Workforce Management

COMPETITORS

Advanstar
American City Business Journals
The Detroit News
Dow Jones
Forbes
Gannett
Informa
Lebhar-Friedman
McGraw-Hill
New York Times
Nielsen Business Media
Penton Media
Reed Business Information
Tribune Company

Crete Carrier

Holding company Crete Carrier Corporation's flagship business, Crete Carrier, provides dry van truckload freight transportation services in the 48 contiguous states. It operates from some two dozen terminals, mainly in the midwestern and southeastern US. The company's Shaffer Trucking unit transports temperature-controlled cargo, and Hunt Transportation (no relation to J.B. Hunt Transport Services) hauls heavy equipment and other cargo on flatbed trailers. Overall, the companies operate more than 5,300 tractors and more than 12,400 trailers. Family-owned Crete Carrier was founded in 1966 by chairman Duane Acklie; president and CEO Tonn Ostergard is his son-in-law.

EXECUTIVES

Chairman: Duane W. Acklie
President and CEO: Tonn M. Ostergard
EVP and COO: Jack Peetz
EVP: Karel Znamenacek Jr.
VP Finance and CFO: Dean Troester
VP Transportation: Jon Huwe
VP Operations: Lee Hoffman
VP Company Fleets: Kerry Keari
VP Safety and Compliance: Ray Coulter
VP Sales and Marketing: Greg Breeden

LOCATIONS

HQ: Crete Carrier Corporation
400 NW 56th St., Lincoln, NE 68528
Phone: 402-475-9521   **Fax:** 402-479-2075
Web: www.cretecarrier.com

COMPETITORS

Arrow Trucking
Boyd Bros. Transportation
Celadon
Comcar
Con-way Truckload
Covenant Transportation
C.R. England
Heartland Express
J.B. Hunt
Landstar System
Prime Inc.
Schneider National
Swift Transportation
U.S. Xpress
Werner Enterprises

Crowley Maritime

Crowley Maritime has pushed and pulled its way into prominence as a leading tug and barge operator. The company's Liner Services unit provides scheduled transportation of containers, trailers, and other cargo, mainly between ports in the US, the Caribbean, and Central America. Other Crowley Maritime units transport oil and chemical products and oil field equipment and provide ship escort, marine salvage, logistics, and fuel distribution services. Overall, the company's fleet includes more than 210 vessels. Crowley Maritime is owned by members of the founding Crowley family, including chairman and CEO Thomas Crowley, and company employees. The company was founded in 1892.

In 2009, the company expanded its already wide array of offerings when it launched its first heavy-lift deck barge, used for hauling large industrial machinery such as drilling rigs. Crowley Maritime plans to build up to 13 of these barges by 2013.

EXECUTIVES

Chairman, President, CEO, and COO: Thomas B. (Tom) Crowley Jr., age 42
Vice Chairman and EVP: William A. (Bill) Pennella, age 64
SVP and General Manager, Logistics: Steve Collar
SVP and General Counsel: Michael Roberts
SVP and General Manager, Technical Services: Todd Busch
SVP and General Manager, Puerto Rico and Caribbean Services: Rob Grune
SVP and General Manager, Atlantic/Gulf Region: John Douglass
SVP and General Manager, Pacific/Alaska Region: Rockwell (Rocky) Smith
SVP and General Manager, Latin America Services: John Hourihan
VP and General Manager, Jensen Maritime: Jonathan Parrot
VP Government Relations and Projects: Jay Brickman
VP Salvage and Engineering: Dan Schwall
VP Marine Personnel: Cole Cosgrove
Director Corporate Communications: Mark Miller
Auditors: Deloitte & Touche LLP

LOCATIONS

HQ: Crowley Maritime Corporation
9487 Regency Sq. Blvd., Jacksonville, FL 32225
Phone: 904-727-2200   **Fax:** 904-727-2501
Web: www.crowley.com

PRODUCTS/OPERATIONS

Selected Services

Energy industry support services
Fuel sales and distribution
Liner services
Logistics
Ocean towing and transportation
Petroleum and chemical transportation
Project management
Salvage and emergency response
Ship assist and escort
Ship management
Vessel construction and naval architecture

COMPETITORS

A.P. Møller – Mærsk
APL
APL Logistics
Foss Maritime
Horizon Lines
Hornbeck Offshore
K-Sea Transportation
Lynden Incorporated
Sea Star Line
SEACOR
Tidewater Inc.
Trailer Bridge
UPS Supply Chain Solutions
U.S. Shipping
Washington Companies

HISTORICAL FINANCIALS

Company Type: Private

Income Statement				FYE: December 31
	REVENUE ($ mil.)	NET INCOME ($ mil.)	NET PROFIT MARGIN	EMPLOYEES
12/07	1,620	—	—	4,171

Crown Equipment

The jewels in the crown of Crown Equipment Corporation are electric and engine lift trucks used for maneuvering goods in warehouses and distribution centers. A market leader, the company's products include narrow-aisle stacking equipment, and powered pallet trucks. The engine lift truck line features forklifts with differing tons. Its equipment can move 4-ton loads and stack pallets nearly 45 ft. high. Crown Equipment sells its products globally through dealers and distributors. The company, founded in 1945 by Carl and Allen Dicke, has evolved from making temperature controls for coal furnaces to building 85% of the parts for its material-handling equipment. The Dicke family still controls Crown Equipment.

Riding the wave toward eco-friendly technology and practices, Crown has scored awards from the EPA for reducing its manufacturing waste, as well as a series of grants from the State of Ohio's Third Frontier Fuel Cell Program. The program provides $1 million to research, test, and develop new applications for fuel cells in lift trucks. Crown aims to qualify its lift trucks with fuel cell battery replacement power packs, eliminating the labor for replacing a depleted battery, battery-changing equipment, and room for charging and maintenance.

The spur toward "green" opportunities falls on the heels of inking a branding deal in 2008 with Komatsu Forklift USA that also promises to broaden Crown's customer base. Crown has agreed to sell Komatsu internal combustion lift trucks in the US and Canada. Its product portfolio has received an internal boost, too, with the introduction of a lineup of power-steering pallet trucks in 2009 and Web-based fleet management systems in 2007.

EXECUTIVES

Chairman and CEO: James F. Dicke II, age 61
President: James F. Dicke III, age 36
SVP Sales: James B. Ellis
SVP Manufacturing: David J. Besser
SVP: Donald E. Luebrecht
SVP: James D. Moran
VP and CFO: Kent W. Spille
VP Development and Information Services:
  Mark A. Manuel
VP Engineering: Timothy S. Quellhorst
VP Manufacturing Operations: David L. Beddow
VP Design Center: Michael P. Gallagher
VP and General Counsel: John G. Maxa
VP International Accounts: David J. Kerr
VP Human Resources: Randall W. (Randy) Niekamp
VP Branch Operations: David C. Moran
Controller: Craig Seitz
Auditors: Deloitte & Touche

LOCATIONS

HQ: Crown Equipment Corporation
  44 S. Washington St., New Bremen, OH 45869
Phone: 419-629-2311 **Fax:** 419-629-2900
Web: www.crown.com

PRODUCTS/OPERATIONS

Selected Products

Hand pallet trucks
Narrow-aisle reach trucks
Rider pallet trucks
Sit-down counterbalanced trucks
Stand-up counterbalanced trucks
Stockpickers
Tow tractors
Very narrow-aisle turret trucks
Walkie pallet trucks
Walkie stackers

COMPETITORS

Briggs Equipment	Linde Material Handling
Cascade Corp.	McNeilus Companies
Caterpillar	NACCO Industries
CLARK Material Handling	NACCO Materials Handling
Hyundai Heavy Industries	Nissan Forklift
Jungheinrich	Raymond Corp.
Komatsu	Toyota Material Handling

Cumberland Farms

Once a one-cow dairy, Cumberland Farms now operates a network of about 1,000 convenience stores and gas stations in about a dozen eastern seaboard states from Maine to Florida. The company operates its own grocery distribution and bakery operations to supply its stores, as well. Cumberland owns a two-thirds limited partnership in petroleum wholesaler Gulf Oil, giving it the right to use and license Gulf trademarks in Delaware, New Jersey, New York, most of Ohio, Pennsylvania, and the New England states. The first convenience-store operator in New England, Cumberland was founded in 1939 by Vasilios and Aphrodite Haseotes. The Haseotes' children, including chairman Lily Haseotes Bentas, own the company.

In March 2009 the company debuted a new prototype store in Farmington, Connecticut. The new store sports a redesigned blue-and-green logo, the first in 70 years, and emphasizes fresh foods, such as salads, fruit cups, yogurt, and hot

and cold sandwiches. Another such store is slated for the Connecticut markets and three for Massachusetts in the near future.

In August 2008 Joseph Petrowski was appointed CEO of the company and Bentas assumed the position of chairman.

The company's Wholesale Petroleum Division, its partnership with Gulf Oil, has given it a more than 300-strong network of franchised Gulf and Exxon gasoline stations.

EXECUTIVES

Chairman: Lily Haseotes Bentas
CEO: Joseph H. (Joe) Petrowski, age 54
SVP and CFO: Stephen Winslow
Chief Legal and Administrative Officer, General Counsel, and Corporate Secretary: Mark G. Howard
President and CEO, Gulf Oil: Ronald R. (Ron) Sabia
President and COO, Cumberland Farms Stores:
  Ari Haseotes
Real Estate, Massachusetts, Maine, Rhode Island, New Hampshire, Vermont, and Northern Connecticut:
  Rebecca Marks
Real Estate, Florida: John Tambakis
Recruiting and Staffing Supervisor: Stephen Dolinich
Manager, Fleet Administration Department:
  Edward Potkay

LOCATIONS

HQ: Cumberland Farms, Inc.
  100 Crossing Blvd., Framingham, MA 01702
Phone: 508-270-1400
Web: www.cumberlandfarms.com

PRODUCTS/OPERATIONS

Selected Operations

Convenience stores
Gas stations
Grocery distribution
Bakery operations
Gas wholesaler

COMPETITORS

7-Eleven	Golub
BP	Motiva Enterprises
Chevron	Racetrac Petroleum
DeMoulas Super Markets	Sheetz
Exxon Mobil	Stewart's Shops
Gate Petroleum	Stop & Shop
Getty Realty	Wawa, Inc.

CUNA Mutual

CUNA Mutual knows a thing or two about credit unions, having served them and their members since 1935. The company provides insurance (such as credit insurance and health benefit packages) for the credit unions themselves, as well as consumer products like homeowners and crop insurance that the institutions can offer to their members. Participants in CUNA Mutual's MemberCONNECT program, for instance, can offer auto and homeowners insurance provided jointly by CUNA and its partner Liberty Mutual. CUNA also provides credit unions with software and marketing support for bringing in new members and advisory services for growing their investments. It operates throughout the US and in some foreign markets.

Under CEO Jeff Post, CUNA Mutual has streamlined its business in response to a consolidating marketplace and revamped its sales and customer service operations. In addition to reducing its workforce and outsourcing some jobs, it opened a new customer operations center in Fort Worth and reorganized its sales team so that each of its credit union customer accounts has a single sales contact. It merged two of its insurance subsidiaries, CUNA Mutual Insurance Society and CUNA Mutual Life Insurance, in 2007 to realize tax savings, and further simplified by selling its IRA services division to Crump Group in 2009.

That same year the company sold its CUMIS Group subsidiary to Co-operators Life Insurance and Central 1 Credit Union for about $230 million as part of those same streamlining efforts. CUMIS provides a range of personal and commercial insurance products.

At the same time the company has been expanding its products and services offered to credit unions and their members. It introduced specialized crop insurance in partnership with Texas-based crop insurer Producers Ag Insurance Group (Pro Ag, 2006), and expanded its partnership with Liberty Mutual to offer workers' compensation insurance (2007). CUNA Mutual acquired a minority stake in Pro Ag in 2007. To build up its retirement plan products, in 2009 the company acquired CPI Qualified Plan Consultants, a third party administrator of employee benefits plans for small businesses.

CUNA Mutual established a new European headquarters in Dublin in 2008 and announced expansion plans in Europe. It has other international operations in Australia, Canada, and the Caribbean.

EXECUTIVES

Chairman: Loretta M. Burd
Vice Chairman: C. Alan Peppers
President, CEO, and Director: Jeff Post
EVP and COO: Robert (Bob) Trunzo
EVP and CFO: Gerald Pavelich
EVP and Chief Investment Officer: David Marks
EVP and Chief Administration and Operations Officer:
  David Lundgren
SVP and Group Leader Consumer Products:
  Andy Napoli
SVP Corporate and Legislative Affairs: Christopher Roe
SVP and CIO: Rick R. Roy
SVP and Chief Ethics and Compliance Officer:
  Steve Koslow
SVP Asset Accumulation Products: Kevin Thompson
SVP Strategy and Business Development: John Lass
VP Corporate Communications: Jim Buchheim
VP Human Resources and Talent Acquisition:
  Ryan Dull
Director Marketing Operations and Brand Management:
  Nancy Fisher
Auditors: Deloitte & Touche LLP

LOCATIONS

HQ: CUNA Mutual Group
  5910 Mineral Point Rd., Madison, WI 53705
Phone: 608-238-5851
Web: www.cunamutual.com

PRODUCTS/OPERATIONS

2008 Revenues

	$ mil.	% of total
Life & health premiums	1,280	44
Property/casualty premiums	894	31
Net investment income	373	13
Other	346	12
Total	**2,893**	**100**

2008 Operating Revenue

	% of total
Consumer products	54
Commercial products	14
International products	10
Asset accumulation	10
Crop insurance products	10
Service products	2
Total	**100**

COMPETITORS

Nexity
Online Resources
PrimeVest
U.S. Central

HISTORICAL FINANCIALS
Company Type: Mutual company

Income Statement				FYE: December 31
	REVENUE ($ mil.)	NET INCOME ($ mil.)	NET PROFIT MARGIN	EMPLOYEES
12/08	2,893	—	—	4,500
12/07	2,741	—	—	4,500
12/06	2,602	—	—	5,500
12/05	2,642	—	—	5,500
12/04	2,481	—	—	6,000
Annual Growth	**3.9%**	**—**	**—**	**(6.9%)**

Revenue History

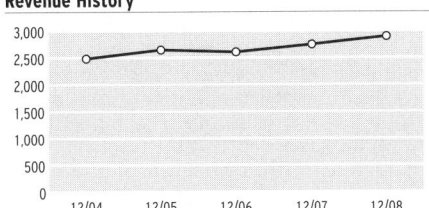

Curves International

Curves International is turning heads with its successful women's gym franchise. With more than 4 million members, the company operates one of the nation's fastest-growing franchise systems by targeting busy women with limited time for exercise. It franchises some 10,000 Curves for Women fitness centers worldwide (in the US and more than 70 additional countries). The centers offer 30-minute fitness workout sessions featuring strength and cardio training. The company was founded in 1992 when husband-and-wife Gary (CEO) and Diane Heavin opened a center in Harlingen, Texas. The company began franchise operations in 1995.

Most of the Curves locations are smaller than typical gym settings and are often located in strip mall store fronts. The company also offers the Curves Weight Management Plan, a diet program designed to raise metabolism and end the need for perpetual dieting. In addition, its Curves Complete is an online subscription program that provides customized meal plans, access to experts, and an online support group. Co-founder Diane Heavin publishes a magazine, called *diane*, which is available in Curves franchise locations.

Amidst a struggling US economy, Curves has been busy looking at international markets for growth. In 2009 the company, which has reported double-digit expansion overseas, opened franchises in Bulgaria, China, and Senegal. Outside North America, Japan is Curves' biggest market, with 744 locations. The company's concept could specifically appeal to Muslim countries, where religious custom often requires women and men exercise in separate public facilities. In 2008 Curves opened its first franchises in the Ukraine, Slovakia, Botswana, Bahrain, Qatar, and Saudi Arabia. Also that year the company sold franchises in Belgium, Finland, Jordan, and Malta.

EXECUTIVES

CEO: H. Gary Heavin, age 54
President and Head Marketing: Miner (Mike) Raymond
COO and Sales: Jim Johnson
CFO and Treasurer: Ronnie Glaesmann
CIO: Bob Kerr
SVP Legal Affairs and Chief General Counsel:
  Roger N. Schmidt
VP Health and Wellness Partnerships: Mark English
Secretary and General Counsel: Kevin D. Ayers
Director Interactive Marketing: Lisa Hendry
Director Curves Products: Chris Hendley
Director Continuing Education and Research:
  Cassie Findley
Manager In-Club Promotions and Partnerships:
  Nancy McEachern
Manager National Advertising: René Kekic
International Marketing Manager: Olga Yurchenko
Corporate Communications Manager: Becky Frusher
Human Resources Manager: Steffanie Huffstatler

LOCATIONS

HQ: Curves International, Inc.
  100 Ritchie Rd., Waco, TX 76712
Phone: 254-399-9285   **Fax:** 254-399-6623
Web: www.curves.com

PRODUCTS/OPERATIONS

Selected Web Sites

Curves.com (consumer site)
Curvesfoods.com (Curves Foods)
Curvescomplete.com (Curves Complete)
Mycurves.com (member site)

COMPETITORS

24 Hour Fitness
Bally Total Fitness
Contours Express
eDiets.com
Gold's Gym
Jazzercise
Jenny Craig
Lady of America
Weight Watchers International
YWCA

HISTORICAL FINANCIALS
Company Type: Private

Income Statement				FYE: December 31
	REVENUE ($ mil.)	NET INCOME ($ mil.)	NET PROFIT MARGIN	EMPLOYEES
12/08	2,000	—	—	—

Dairy Farmers of America

The members of the Dairy Farmers of America (DFA) are partners in cream. DFA is one of the world's largest dairy cooperatives, with some 18,000 members in 48 US states. With about 20 manufacturing sites located across the country, the co-op produces some 34% of the US milk supply from the annual pool of almost 62 billion pounds of milk its dairies contribute. (That's enough for 287 million glasses of milk every day.) Along with fresh and shelf-stable fluid milk, the co-op also produces cheese, butter, dried whey, dried milk powder, and other dairy products for industrial, wholesale, and retail customers worldwide. DFA is a major supplier to the #1 US dairy company, Dean Foods.

American dairy farmers have had to come to terms with consolidation in the retail industry, dissolving government milk price supports, and increased foreign competition. To better compete with other dairy processors and soften the swings of the commodity markets, DFA has invested heavily in facilities and joint ventures to process its fluid milk into value-added products and high-end dairy-based ingredients.

In order to invest in new strategic projects, in 2009 DFA sold its Dallas-based National Dairy Holdings to one of Mexico's powerhouse dairies, Grupo Lala. As part of the deal, DFA retained the Borden-branded cheese products, while the Borden milk operations became part of Lala.

DFA's sheer size makes it a frequent target of anti-trust investigations. Investigations have sought, for example, to determine if the cooperative manipulated milk and cheese prices (2008) and bullied farmers and smaller cooperatives to join it, and paid out below-market prices to its members (2006).

HISTORY

Mid-America Dairymen (Mid-Am), the largest of the cooperatives that merged to form Dairy Farmers of America (DFA), was born in 1968. At that time, several Midwestern dairy co-ops banded together to attack common economic problems, such as reduced government subsidies, price drops resulting from a rising milk surplus, dealer consolidation, and improvements in production, processing, and packaging. The merging organizations — representing 15,000 dairy farmers — were Producers Creamery Company (Springfield, Missouri), Sanitary Milk Producers (St. Louis), Square Deal Milk Producers (Highland, Illinois), Mid-Am (Kansas City, Missouri), and Producers Creamery Company of Chillicothe (north central Missouri).

During the early 1970s Mid-Am struggled with internal restructuring. Most dairy farmers and co-ops were hit hard by the energy crisis and the government's decision to allow increased dairy imports in 1973, the same year the US Justice Department filed an antitrust suit against Mid-Am. (A judge cleared the co-op 12 years later.)

In 1974 Mid-Am lost almost $8 million on revenues of $625 million, chalked up to record-high feed prices, a weakened economy, a milk surplus, and a massive inventory loss. Co-op veteran Gary Hanman was named CEO that year. Over the next two years, Mid-Am cut costs, sold corporate frills, downsized management, and began

marketing more of its own products under the Mid-America Farms label, thus reducing dependency on commodity sales.

Mid-Am expanded its research and development efforts throughout the 1980s. The co-op opened its services to farmers in California and New Mexico in 1993, and a series of mergers in 1994 and 1995 nearly doubled its size. In 1997 it purchased some of Borden's dairy operations, including rights to the valuable Elsie the Cow and Borden's trademarks.

Wary of falling milk prices, Mid-Am merged with Western Dairymen Cooperative, Milk Marketing, and the Southern Region of Associated Milk Producers at the end of 1997 to form DFA. Hanman moved into the seat of CEO at the new co-op. DFA began a series of joint ventures with the #1 US dairy processor, Suiza Foods (now Dean Foods).

DFA added California Gold (more than 330 farmers, 1998) and Independent Cooperative Milk Producers Association (730 dairy farmer members in Michigan and parts of Ohio and Indiana, 1999). In another joint venture with Suiza, in early 2000 DFA sold its 50% stake in the US's #3 fluid milk processor, Southern Foods, in exchange for 34% of a new company named Suiza Dairy Group.

After mollifying the government's antitrust fears, DFA acquired the butter operations of Sodiaal North America in 2000. It then molded all its butter businesses into a new entity, Keller's Creamery. However, another acquisition did not fare as well. The same year, DFA acquired controlling interest in Southern Belle Dairy only to have the merger challenged three years later by the Department of Justice. Arguing that the merger formed a monopoly in school milk sales in several states, the Department of Justice filed suit which a federal judge later dismissed.

During 2001 the cooperative went in with Land O'Lakes 50-50 to purchase a cheese plant from Kraft. Later in the year as Suiza Foods acquired Dean Foods (and took on its name), DFA sold back its stake in Suiza Dairy Group to the new Dean Foods. DFA then teamed up with a group of dairy investors to form a new 50-50 joint venture, National Dairy Holdings, which received 11 processing plants from Dean Foods as part of the exchange for Suiza Dairy.

Weak milk prices and a drop in demand during 2002 caused DFA's revenues to slide. DFA has typically grown by inviting smaller dairy co-ops to merge with it, including the Black Hills Milk Producers Cooperative in 2002. However, to better secure milk sources for its customers in the northeastern US, that same year DFA welcomed two regional co-ops, Dairylea and St. Albans, to join as members. The two co-ops remain as separate but affiliated organizations.

At the beginning of 2005 DFA acquired full ownership of what had been a joint venture in Keller's Creamery. Longtime president and CEO Hanman retired at the end of 2005; he was replaced by company veteran Rick Smith.

EXECUTIVES

Chairman: James P. (Tom) Camerlo
President and CEO: Richard P. (Rick) Smith
President, Dairy Food Products: Mark Korsmeyer
SVP Finance: David Meyer
SVP Legal and Administrative: David A. Geisler
SVP Accounting: Joel Clark
SVP Marketing and Industry Affairs: John J. Wilson
SVP Strategy and International Development:
  Jay Waldvogel

VP and COO, Southwest Area: David C. Jones
VP and COO, Western Area: David L. Parrish
VP and COO, Central Area:
  Randall S. (Randy) McGinnis
VP and COO, Mountain Area: Greg Yando
VP Human Resources: Annette Regan
VP Corporate Communications and Member Relations:
  Monica Coleman
VP Quality Assurance and Regulatory Affairs:
  James F. (Jim) Carroll
Auditors: Deloitte & Touche LLP

LOCATIONS

HQ: Dairy Farmers of America, Inc.
  10220 N. Ambassador Dr., Kansas City, MO 64153
Phone: 816-801-6455   **Fax:** 816-801-6456
Web: www.dfamilk.com

PRODUCTS/OPERATIONS

Selected Affiliate and Joint Venture Companies
Affiliate
  ASEP-TECH USA
  DairiConcepts
  Dairy.com
  Dietrich Milk
  Quality Milk

Joint Venture
  Hiland Dairy Foods
  Roberts Dairy
  Stemick Heritage Foods
  Wilcox Farms

Selected Brands
Borden (cheese)
Breakstone's (butter)
CalPro (whey protein concentrate)
Enricco (cheese)
Falfurrias (butter)
Golden (cheese)
Hotel Bar (butter)
Jacobo (cheese)
Keller's (butter)
Mid-America Farms (butter)
Plugra (butter)
Sport Shake (energy drink)

Selected Products
Butter
Cheese dips and sauces
Cheeses (Italian and American)
Condensed milk
Cream
Dehydrated dairy products
Dried whey products
Fluid milk
Infant formula
Nonfat dry milk powder
Shelf-stable nutritional beverages

COMPETITORS

Arla Foods	Humboldt Creamery
Associated Milk Producers	Kraft Foods
Berkeley Farms	Lactalis
California Dairies Inc.	Land O'Lakes
ConAgra	Leprino Foods
Darigold, Inc.	Marathon Cheese
Dean Foods	Mayfield Dairy Farms
Farmland Dairies	Northwest Dairy
Foremost Farms	Prairie Farms Dairy
Friendship Dairies	Quality Chekd
Garelick Farms	Saputo
Glanbia plc	Sargento
Great Lakes Cheese	Schreiber Foods

HISTORICAL FINANCIALS

Company Type: Cooperative

Income Statement

FYE: December 31

	REVENUE ($ mil.)	NET INCOME ($ mil.)	NET PROFIT MARGIN	EMPLOYEES
12/08	11,700	62	0.5%	4,000
12/07	11,100	—	—	4,000
12/06	7,899	—	—	4,000
12/05	8,909	—	—	—
12/04	8,954	—	—	—
Annual Growth	6.9%	—	—	0.0%

Revenue History

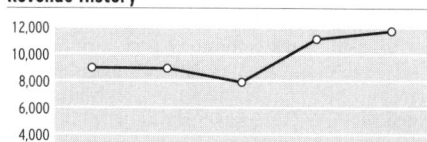

Revenue History chart, $ mil., 12/04 through 12/08.

Agri-Services Agency (health, dental, and group term life insurance; workers' compensation)
Dairy One (milk testing; herd records services; dairy management software and support; feedstuff, water, and manure analysis)
Eagle Dairy Direct (purchasing programs)
Empire Livestock Marketing Services (livestock marketing)

COMPETITORS

Agri-Mark
Associated Milk Producers
Dairy Farmers of America
Dean Foods
Foremost Farms
Garelick Farms
Keller's Creamery
Land O'Lakes
Quality Chekd

HISTORICAL FINANCIALS

Company Type: Cooperative

Income Statement

FYE: March 31

	REVENUE ($ mil.)	NET INCOME ($ mil.)	NET PROFIT MARGIN	EMPLOYEES
3/08	1,388	—	—	209

PRODUCTS/OPERATIONS

2008 Sales

	% of total
Retail	44
Foodservice	28
Ingredients	28
Total	**100**

COMPETITORS

ADM
American Italian Pasta
Barilla
Barilla America
Bay State Milling
Campbell Soup
ConAgra
Hodgson Mill
Horizon Milling
Italgrani
Kraft Foods
Nestlé
New World Pasta
Rossi Pasta

Dairylea Cooperative

Yes, *the farmer takes a wife*, then *hi-ho, the dairy-o*, the farmer takes membership in milk-marketing organizations such as Dairylea Cooperative. Owned by more than 2,300 dairy farmers in the northeastern US, Dairylea processes and markets 5.5 billion pounds of milk for its farmers annually to dairy-product customers including food manufacturers. Its Agri-Services holding company provides members with a full range of financial and farm-management services, as well as insurance. Its Empire Livestock Marketing unit operates eight regional livestock auction locations. Dairylea has a joint marketing venture (Dairy Marketing Services or DMS) with Dairy Farmers of America.

EXECUTIVES

Chairman and President: Clyde E. Rutherford
CEO: Gregory I. (Greg) Wickham
COO, Dairy Marketing Services: Brad Keating
CFO and Director, Human Resources: Edward Bangel
First VP, Board of Directors: Raymond J. Diebold
Second VP, Board of Directors and Secretary:
 William Beeman
VP, Finance: Ellen Gall
Treasurer and Director: David R. Chamberlain
Media Contact: Karen Cartier
Public Relations: Jennifer Huson

LOCATIONS

HQ: Dairylea Cooperative Inc.
 5001 Brittonfield Pkwy., East Syracuse, NY 13057
Phone: 315-433-0100   **Fax:** 315-433-2345
Web: www.dairylea.com

PRODUCTS/OPERATIONS

Selected Affiliates and Subsidiaries

Agri-Edge Development (farm management services)
Agri-Invest (investment services)
Agri-Max Financial Services (capital project and real estate financing; loans; cattle and farm equipment leasing)

Dakota Growers Pasta

Dakota Growers Pasta Company is trying to put an *al dente* in the noodle market. The company is a supplier of branded and private-label pasta products and flours to retail, foodservice, and food ingredient companies in North America. Its brand names include Dreamfields, Pasta Growers, Pasta Sanita, Primo Piatto, and Zia Briosa. It sells organic pasta under the Dakota Growers Pasta label. The company started out in 1991 as a wheat-farmers cooperative; it became a private corporation in 2002. Dakota Growers is the distributor for New World Pasta's Ronzoni, Prince, San Giorgio, and Mrs. Weiss pasta brands to the foodservice sector.

The company's products are distributed throughout the US. Customer U.S. Foodservice accounts for approximately 9% of its 2008 sales. Dakota Growers operates production plants in Minnesota and North Dakota.

Investment firm MVC Capital owns 10% of the company.

EXECUTIVES

Chairman: John S. (Jack) Dalrymple III, age 61
Vice Chairman: John D. Rice Jr., age 55
President and CEO: Timothy J. Dodd, age 54
CFO: Edward O. Irion, age 38
Auditors: Eide Bailly LLP

LOCATIONS

HQ: Dakota Growers Pasta Company, Inc.
 1 Pasta Ave., Carrington, ND 58421
Phone: 701-652-2855   **Fax:** 701-652-3552
Web: www.dakotagrowers.com

Dallas Cowboys

Proclaiming itself "America's Team," this football franchise certainly has the loyalty of many Texans. Dallas Cowboys Football Club operates the famed Dallas Cowboys professional football franchise, one of the most popular teams in the National Football League and the winner of five Super Bowl titles (a mark it shares with the San Francisco 49ers). The team was founded in 1960 by Clint Murchison Jr. and Bedford Wynne and competed for the NFL championship twice in that decade (losing both times to the Green Bay Packers). Dallas has been home to such Hall of Fame players as Troy Aikman, Michael Irvin, and Roger Staubach, as well as famed head coach Tom Landry. Oilman Jerry Jones has owned the team since 1989.

The Cowboys franchise has become one of the more financially successful teams in the NFL with the help of its legions of fans buying tickets and merchandise. To keep those fans coming through the turnstiles, Jones has spared little expense over the years acquiring talent for the Cowboys roster.

To expand the team's revenue-generating potential, the Cowboys moved into a new $1.12 billion retractable-roof stadium in 2009. Located in Arlington, Texas, the new facility seats 80,000 fans (expandable to 100,000 people for other events). The city of Arlington agreed to put up about $325 million of the cost. The new stadium replaced the team's aging Texas Stadium in nearby Irving, which had been one of the smaller venues in the league.

Jones expanded his sports and entertainment holdings further in 2008 when the Cowboys joined with the New York Yankees (owned by George Steinbrenner and his family) and Goldman Sachs to form Legends Hospitality Management. The contract foodservices provider boasts both the new Yankees Stadium and new Cowboys Stadium as primary clients but plans to expand to serve other major sports and events facilities.

EXECUTIVES

Owner, President, and General Manager:
Jerral W. (Jerry) Jones, age 67
EVP and Chief Sales and Marketing Officer:
Jerry Jones Jr., age 40
EVP, COO, and Director Player Personnel:
Stephen Jones, age 45
EVP Brand Management; President, Charities:
Charlotte Jones Anderson, age 43
Head Coach: Wade Phillips, age 62
Assistant Head Coach and Offensive Coordinator:
Jason Garrett, age 43
Director College and Pro Scouting: Tom Ciskowski
Director Public Relations: Rich Dalrymple

LOCATIONS

HQ: Dallas Cowboys Football Club, Ltd.
1 Cowboys Pkwy., Irving, TX 75063
Phone: 972-556-9900   **Fax:** 972-556-9304
Web: www.dallascowboys.com

The Dallas Cowboys play at 80,000-seat capacity
Cowboys Stadium in Arlington, Texas.

PRODUCTS/OPERATIONS

Championship Titles

Super Bowl Championships
Super Bowl XXX (1996)
Super Bowl XXVIII (1994)
Super Bowl XXVII (1993)
Super Bowl XII (1978)
Super Bowl VI (1972)
NFC Championship (1970-71, 1975, 1977-78, 1992-93,
1995)
NFC East Champions (1970-71, 1973, 1976-79, 1981,
1985, 1992-96, 1998, 2007)
NFL Eastern Conference Champions (1966-67)
NFL Capitol Division Champions (1967-69)

COMPETITORS

New York Giants
Philadelphia Eagles
Washington Redskins

HISTORICAL FINANCIALS

Company Type: Private

Income Statement   FYE: February 28

	REVENUE ($ mil.)	NET INCOME ($ mil.)	NET PROFIT MARGIN	EMPLOYEES
2/08	269	—	—	—
2/07	242	—	—	—
2/06	235	—	—	—
2/05	231	—	—	—
2/04	205	—	—	—
Annual Growth	7.0%	—	—	—

Revenue History

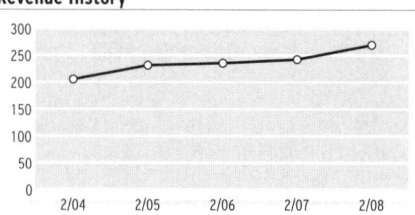

Dallas Mavericks

Sports fans in the Big D might make a fast break for this team. Dallas Basketball owns and operates the Dallas Mavericks professional basketball franchise, which joined the National Basketball Association in 1980. Dallas struggled to find success for much of its history but has become a regular contender for the playoffs under current owner Mark Cuban. A talented roster that included such players as Dirk Nowitzki and Josh Howard earned the franchise's first trip to the NBA Finals in 2006 (which resulted in a loss to the Miami Heat). The Dallas basketball team was formed by millionaire Donald Carter; Cuban, an Internet billionaire, has owned the Mavs since 2000.

Since becoming a franchise owner, Cuban has developed a reputation as an outspoken critic of game officiating and commissioner David Stern, and has been regularly fined by the league for his comments and courtside antics. His sometimes outrageous behavior has made him a popular figure among fans, however, and has helped raise the profile of the Mavericks.

Head coach Avery Johnson was let go from the team after the 2007-08 season; he had lead the team to four consecutive playoff appearances but only one appearance in the Finals. The Mavs later hired former Indiana Pacers coach Rick Carlisle as his replacement.

Cuban paid about $280 million to buy the team; he also shares ownership of Center Operating Company, which owns and operates the American Airlines Center, with Dallas Stars owner Tom Hicks. The forthright billionaire co-founded online broadcasting pioneer broadcast.com and sold it to Yahoo! for about $5 billion in 1999.

EXECUTIVES

Owner: Mark Cuban
President and CEO: Terdema L. Ussery II, age 50
President, Basketball Operations and General Manager:
Donnie Nelson
Head Coach: Rick Carlisle, age 50
SVP Human Resources: Buddy Pittman
SVP Corporate Sponsorships: George Killebrew
VP Marketing and Communications: Paul Monroe
VP Merchandising: Steve Shilts
VP and CFO: Floyd Jahner
VP Operations and Arena Development: Steve Letson
VP Ticket Sales and Services: George Prokos
Manager Player Relations and Manager Marketing Operations: Lesley Berry
Director Basketball Development: Rolando Blackman
Director Scouting: Amadou Gallo Fall
Director Broadcasting: Dave Evans
Director Production: Tom Ward
Director Technology and Information Systems:
Ken Bonzon

LOCATIONS

HQ: Dallas Basketball Limited
The Pavilion, 2909 Taylor St., Dallas, TX 75226
Phone: 214-747-6287   **Fax:** 214-752-3860
Web: www.dallasmavericks.com

The Dallas Mavericks play in the 21,041-seat capacity American Airlines Center in Dallas.

PRODUCTS/OPERATIONS

Championship Titles

Western Conference Champions (2006)

COMPETITORS

Houston Rockets
Memphis Grizzlies
New Orleans Hornets
San Antonio Spurs

D&H Distributing

D&H Distributing sells computer and electronics products in the US and Canada. Its product portfolio includes computers and peripherals, electronic components, data storage devices, printing and imaging equipment, software, mobile devices, gaming systems, home appliances, surveillance systems, and digital music players. Clients include small and large resellers and retailers, system builders, and college bookstores. D&H also targets schools and government agencies. Suppliers include Hewlett-Packard, Intel, and Microsoft. D&H Distributing is owned by its employees.

In 2008 the company reported significant growth in its gaming and home entertainment divisions, which distribute such products as digital music players, home theater systems, and high-definition gaming consoles. In the recessionary environment of 2009, D&H reported strong sales growth for digital cameras, DVD players, multifunction printers, netbook and notebook computers, and video capture systems.

D&H was founded in 1918 as a tire retreader; the company entered the electronics business in 1926, selling crystal radios. Dave Schwab and Harry Spector were the original D&H. The company has been employee-owned since 1999. D&H Canada ULC, its first international subsidiary, opened in 2007.

EXECUTIVES

Chairman and CEO: Israel (Izzy) Schwab
Co-President: Michael (Mike) Schwab
Co-President: Daniel (Dan) Schwab
President Emeritus: Gary Brothers
EVP and Treasurer: James F. (Jimmy) Schwab
VP Purchasing: Rob Eby
VP Marketing: Mary Campbell
VP and Controller: Robert J. Miller Jr.
VP Sales: Jeff Davis
Senior Director Purchasing: Tina Fisher
Director Purchasing Operations and Canada:
Mark Bowser
Director Credit and Financial Services: Joe Chaudoin
Manager Home Entertainment: John Alifano

LOCATIONS

HQ: D&H Distributing Co.
2525 N. 7th St., Harrisburg, PA 17110
Phone: 717-236-8001   **Fax:** 717-255-7838
Web: www.dandh.com

COMPETITORS

Agilysys	Presidio Technology
Arrow Electronics	Capital
ASI Computer	Sayers
Avnet	SED International
Elcom International	Sirius Computer Solutions
Electrograph Systems	Supercom
Ingram Micro	SYNNEX
Merisel	Tech Data
New Age Electronics	ZT Group

Dart Container

Dart Container is a world cup winner — not in soccer, but in foam cups and containers. It commands about half of the global market in foam cups! To make its products, Dart touts a secret molding method for expandable polystyrene. The foodservice lineup includes not just cups but lids, dinnerware, and cutlery, which is marketed through a global distribution network to hospitals, schools, and restaurants, as well as retailers. Self-sufficient, Dart builds its own molding machinery, and uses Dart trucks to deliver products from plants in the US, Canada, Mexico, Argentina, the UK, and Australia. Its recycled polystyrene is sold to manufacturers of such durables as insulation and egg cartons. Dart is family-owned.

Dart is maintaining its market presence by skirting the growing interest in sustainable practices, along with plugging the world's bottomless appetite for disposables and concern for hygiene. It has taken up manufacturing The Densifier, a one-ton machine used to recycle foam waste. These compactors are leased or sold to various organizations, institutions, and businesses. Moreover, the company runs commercial polystyrene-recycling plants in addition to eight drop-off recycling locations. Feeding demand for attractive convenience, the company began offering custom-graphic printing on its hot beverage cups under the Fusion brand name in 2008.

Dart however has tightened its operations under the recessionary pinch. In early 2009 the company laid off nearly 6% of its Mason, Michigan, workforce; the shrink was Dart's first since 2002. The hard choice was preceded by the company's $39.6 million investment to revamp two of its Pennsylvania warehouses and a manufacturing plant, which opened up 125 new jobs.

The king of cups is shaped as well by its history of secrecy. The Darts never patented the cup-making machine they developed; this allowed them to avoid revealing how it works. Most of the company's factory workers have never seen the machines, and Dart's salespeople are not allowed inside the plants. Internal management is equally circumspect. After years of legal battles in the 1990s and early 2000s, the Darts have reached an agreement regarding alleged discrepancies in the family inheritance. The terms of the settlement are, naturally, secret.

HISTORY

William F. Dart founded a Michigan firm to make steel tape measures in 1937. Dart's son William A. started experimenting with plastics in 1953, and in the late 1950s the two devised a cheap way to mold expandable polystyrene and built a cup-making machine. Dart Container was incorporated in Mason, Michigan, in 1960 and shipped its first cups that year. By the late 1960s the rising demand for plastic-foam products sparked an increase in R&D. In 1970 the company built a plant in Corona, California.

It was a family feud in the making in 1974, as William F. divided the business among his grandsons — Tom, Ken, and Robert — in separate trusts that named William A. trustee for all. Tom branched out in 1975 and founded oil and gas company Dart Energy, which was later absorbed into Dart Container. William F. died the next year. Following the oil market crash of the early 1980s, Tom went through a sticky divorce and admitted to cocaine abuse. His father temporarily removed him as head of Dart Energy in 1982, and the next year the entire family underwent group psychiatric counseling.

The family reorganized its assets in 1986, giving Ken and Robert the cup business and Tom the energy business plus $58 million in cash. In 1987 Ken began to swell the family fortune with a series of successful investments. Better tax rates motivated Dart family members to move to Sarasota, Florida, in 1989. They set up shop in an unmarked building behind a sporting-goods store. By the late 1980s Dart Container commanded more than 50% of the worldwide market for foam cups.

In 1990 the company paid $250,000 to settle a factory worker's minority discrimination lawsuit. The next year Ken bought 11% of the Federal Home Loan Mortgage Corp. (Freddie Mac), as well as portions of Salomon and Brazil's foreign debt. According to Tom, that year Ken also financed brain research in hopes of finding a way to keep his brain alive after the death of his body in an attempt to avoid future estate taxes.

Tom sued his brothers and father in 1992 for allegedly cheating him out of millions in trust money in the 1986 reorganization. Ken turned a $300 million investment into $1 billion by selling the Freddie Mac shares. The next year he and Robert renounced their US citizenship to avoid paying taxes. Ken also made a failed attempt to block the restructuring of Brazil's debt (of which Dart owned 4%). That year Ken's new $1 million Sarasota home was firebombed (the case remains unsolved), and Robert moved to Britain, where he soon filed for divorce.

Ken began hiring bodyguards, and he moved his family to the Cayman Islands in 1994. Dart then shelled out $230,000 to settle yet another discrimination case. In 1995 Tom was fired from Dart Energy, and Ken tried — and failed — to return to the US as a diplomat of Belize. In 1996 Tom accused Judge Donald Owens of being biased in favor of William A. The judge succumbed to the pressure in 1997 and removed himself from the proceedings, only to be ordered back on the case by Michigan's Court of Appeals. The lawsuit was settled in 1998 before going to trial, but the terms were kept secret. The following year saw yet another series of lawsuits for the container company. In 1999 Dart Container filed an appeal to an IRS demand to pay $31 million in back taxes from 1994 and late penalties. The legal wrangling continued through 2001, but in 2002 the company agreed to pay $26 million to settle the issue.

A slight shift in its operational practices occurred in 2005 when employees at the company's unionized Corona, California, plant voted to end its union contract. The move came as a result of management-style changes that valued worker input more than in the past. Also, in an effort to support operations at the Corona facility, Dart opened a new facility in Tijuana, Mexico, in 2007.

EXECUTIVES

Chairman: William A. Dart, age 81
CEO: Robert C. Dart, age 51
President: Kenneth B. Dart, age 54
VP Technology: Ralph MacKenzie
VP Administration and General Counsel:
James (Jim) Lammers
VP Manufacturing: Dan Calkins
VP Manufacturing: John M. Murray
Director Government Relations and Affairs:
Francis X. Liesman
Director Engineering: Dave Heisey
Treasurer: Kevin Fox
Director Sales: Robert Williams
Director Human Resources: Kenneth Petersen

LOCATIONS

HQ: Dart Container Corporation
500 Hogsback Rd., Mason, MI 48854
Phone: 517-676-3800 **Fax:** 517-676-3883
Web: www.dartcontainer.com

PRODUCTS/OPERATIONS

Selected Products

Clear containers
Container lids
Deli containers and lids
Dinnerware
Foam cups
Graphic-printed (custom or stock) hot beverage cups
Hinged containers
Paper cups and lids
Plastic cups and lids
Plastic cutlery

Selected Services

CARE (Cups Are REcyclable) Program (provides densifier to larger customers to compact their polystyrene, which Dart then picks up)
Foam-Recycling (four plants in Canada, Florida, Michigan, and Pennsylvania and drop-off sites in California, Florida, Georgia, Kentucky, Michigan, Pennsylvania, and Canada)
Recycla-Pak (provides small-volume businesses with cup-shipping containers that double as recycling bins)

COMPETITORS

Berry Plastics
Huhtamäki
NOVA Chemicals
Pactiv
Smurfit-Stone Container
Solo Cup
Sonoco Products
Temple-Inland
WinCup

HISTORICAL FINANCIALS

Company Type: Private

Income Statement				FYE: December 31
	ESTIMATED REVENUE ($ mil.)	NET INCOME ($ mil.)	NET PROFIT MARGIN	EMPLOYEES
12/08	1,400	—	—	8,500
12/07	1,540	—	—	5,840
12/06	1,510	—	—	5,640
12/05	1,388	—	—	5,200
12/04	1,250	—	—	5,000
Annual Growth	2.9%	—	—	14.2%

Revenue History

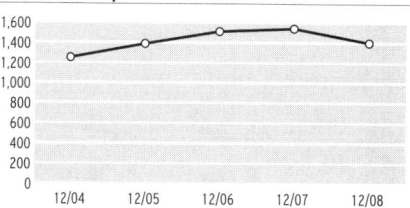

Datatel, Inc.

Datatel doesn't care if you're a Bruin, a Hurricane, or a Longhorn, as long as you've got data that needs managing. The company, which serves higher education institutions, makes software that manages information about students, finances, financial aid, human resources, and advancement. The company's software streamlines such processes as enterprise resource planning, e-recruitment, and alumni communications, serving more than 700 institutions throughout North America. Datatel was founded in 1968 by Ken Kendrick and Tom Davidson; they sold the company in 2005 to members of their executive team (backed by Thoma Cressey Equity Partners and Trident Capital). In 2009 Hellman & Friedman purchased Datatel.

Hellman & Friedman was joined by JMI Equity Fund and Datatel executives and employees in purchasing the company.

EXECUTIVES

President and CEO: John F. Speer III
CFO: Kevin M. Boyce, age 34
CTO: Thomas A. (Tom) Reynolds
Chief Client Officer: Elizabeth A. (Liz) Murphy
VP Product Management: Kyle J. Loudermilk
VP Sales: David J. Gutch
VP Finance: Virginia L. (Ginger) Piercy
VP Software Development: E. Joshua Dietrich
VP Professional Services: Mahesh Gidwani
Executive Director, Datatel Scholars Foundation:
 Jane Roth
Director Sales: Skip Steele
Director Marketing Communications: Peter Abzug
Director Product Management: Sue Kumpf

LOCATIONS

HQ: Datatel, Inc.
 4375 Fair Lakes Ct., Fairfax, VA 22033
Phone: 703-968-9000   **Fax:** 703-968-4573
Web: www.datatel.com

COMPETITORS

Blackbaud
Blackboard
Jenzabar
SunGard Higher Education

HISTORICAL FINANCIALS

Company Type: Private

Income Statement

	REVENUE ($ mil.)	NET INCOME ($ mil.)	NET PROFIT MARGIN	EMPLOYEES
				FYE: December 31
12/08	129	—	—	532
12/07	123	—	—	550
12/06	108	—	—	547
Annual Growth	9.2%	—	—	(1.4%)

Revenue History

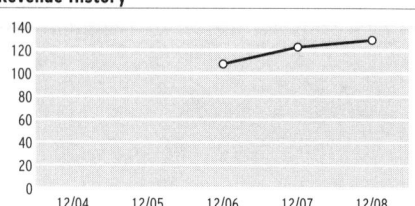

Davey Tree

Business at The Davey Tree Expert Company is as strong as an oak. The company's roots extend back to 1880 when John Davey founded the horticultural services firm, which branched into residential, commercial, utility, and other natural resource management services. With offices in the US and Canada, Davey's services include treatment, planting, and removal of trees, shrubs, and other plants; landscaping; tree surgery; and the application of fertilizers, herbicides, and insecticides. It also provides line clearing for public utilities, urban and utility forestry research and development, and environmental planning. Pacific Gas and Electric accounts for about 10% of sales. Davey has been employee-owned since 1979.

Acquisitions play a big part in Davey's growth strategy — the company has purchased some 30 companies since 2003. With the economic recession, the company's business may suffer as many residential and commercial customers cut back on landscaping expenses. But Davey's executives say the downturn won't affect the company's plans to continue picking up competitors that expand its services and geographic footprint.

Davey bought Ohio-based Monteleone Landscaping in February 2009 to bolster its commercial landscape unit. A year earlier, Davey acquired Tennessee-based utility tree trimming firm Wolf Tree Experts and The Care of Trees, an Illinois-based firm specializing in preserving trees in land developments.

EXECUTIVES

Chairman, President, and CEO: Karl J. Warnke, age 57, $1,349,997 total compensation
EVP Operations: Steven A. Marshall, age 57, $447,812 total compensation
EVP Operations: Patrick M. (Pat) Covey, age 45
EVP, CFO, and Secretary: David E. Adante, age 57, $575,544 total compensation
CIO: Tom Countryman
CTO: Roger C. Funk, age 64
SVP; General Manager, Davey Tree Surgery Company:
 Howard D. Bowles, age 65, $547,504 total compensation
SVP and General Manager, Residential and Commercial Services: C. Kenneth Celmer, age 62, $459,915 total compensation
VP and Controller: Nicholas R. Sucic, age 62
VP Personnel Recruiting and Development:
 Gordon L. Ober, age 59
Treasurer: Joseph R. Paul, age 47
Assistant Secretary and Counsel: Marjorie L. Conner, age 51
Manager Corporate Communications: Sandra Reid
Auditors: Ernst & Young LLP

LOCATIONS

HQ: The Davey Tree Expert Company
 1500 N. Mantua St., Kent, OH 44240
Phone: 330-673-9511   **Fax:** 330-673-9843
Web: www.davey.com

2008 Sales

	$ mil.	% of total
US	535.3	90
Canada	60.5	10
Total	**595.8**	**100**

PRODUCTS/OPERATIONS

2008 Sales

	$ mil.	% of total
Utility services	308.2	52
Residential & commercial services	249.5	42
Other	38.1	6
Total	**595.8**	**100**

Selected Tree Care Services

Cabling and bracing
Hazardous tree assessment
Insect and disease management
Large tree moving
Lightning protection
Root collar excavation
Removals and stump grinding
Shrub pruning
Tree cavity treatment
Tree pruning
Tree and shrub fertilization
Tree and shrub planting

COMPETITORS

Arbor Tree Surgery	TruGreen Landcare
Asplundh	UGL Unicco
Brickman	ValleyCrest Companies

HISTORICAL FINANCIALS

Company Type: Private

Income Statement

	REVENUE ($ mil.)	NET INCOME ($ mil.)	NET PROFIT MARGIN	EMPLOYEES
				FYE: December 31
12/08	596	19	3.2%	6,500
12/07	506	18	3.6%	5,600
12/06	468	14	3.0%	5,500
12/05	432	13	3.1%	5,200
12/04	399	12	3.1%	5,000
Annual Growth	10.6%	11.5%	—	6.8%

Net Income History

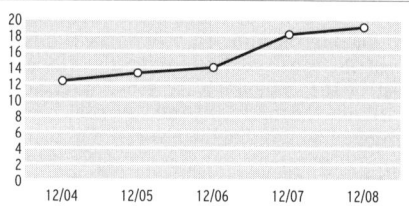

David and Lucile Packard Foundation

One of the wealthiest philanthropic organizations in the US, The David and Lucile Packard Foundation primarily provides grants to not-for-profit entities. The foundation focuses on operating in three areas: conservation and science; children, families, and communities; and population. The David and Lucile Packard Foundation boasts approximately $4.6 billion in assets. In 2009 the organization committed $100 million for the expansion of the Lucile Packard Children's Hospital at Stanford. The late David Packard (co-founder of Hewlett-Packard) and his wife, the late Lucile Salter Packard, created the foundation in 1964. Their children run the organization.

In 2006 it awarded about $225 million in national and international grants, with an extra focus on Northern California's Monterey, San Mateo, Santa Clara, and Santa Cruz counties.

EXECUTIVES

Chairman: Susan Packard Orr
Vice Chairman: Julie E. Packard
Vice Chairman: Nancy Packard Burnett
President and CEO: Carol S. Larson, age 51
VP and CFO: George A. Vera, age 65
VP and Director, Communications: Chris DeCardy
Chief Investment Officer: John H. Moehling
Director, Operations and Technology:
 Matthew D. (Matt) Sharp
Director, Population: Musimbi Kanyoro
Director, Children, Families, and Communities:
 Lois Salisbury
Director, Evaluation: Gale Berkowitz
Controller: Kenneth (Ken) Tsuboi
Director, Organizational Effectiveness:
 Stephanie McAuliffe
Director, Program-Related Investments:
 Mary Anne Rodgers
Director, Conservation and Science: Walter Reid
Auditors: PricewaterhouseCoopers LLP

LOCATIONS

HQ: The David and Lucile Packard Foundation
 300 2nd St., Los Altos, CA 94022
Phone: 650-948-7658   **Fax:** 650-948-5793
Web: www.packard.org

HISTORICAL FINANCIALS

Company Type: Foundation

Income Statement				FYE: December 31
	REVENUE ($ mil.)	NET INCOME ($ mil.)	NET PROFIT MARGIN	EMPLOYEES
12/08	99	(1,939)	—	—
12/07	591	252	42.6%	—
12/06	829	588	70.9%	—
12/05	646	462	71.4%	—
12/04	74	—	—	—
Annual Growth	7.3%	—	—	—

Net Income History

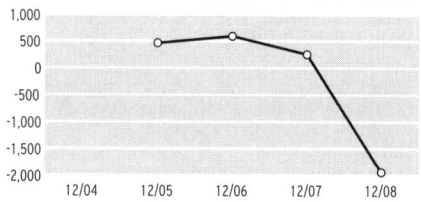

Davidson Companies

Employee-owned Davidson Companies offers investment banking, asset management, and travel services through five subsidiaries. The company's flagship firm, D.A. Davidson & Co., was founded in 1935 and offers investment banking services such as merger and acquisition advisory, capital raising, institutional sales and trading, and fundamental research. Davidson Companies provides brokerage, trust, wealth management, and financial planning services for private clients through Davidson Trust Co. and Davidson Investment Advisors. Davidson Travel is a full-service travel agency. Davidson Companies has more than 50 offices in some 15 states, though it is mainly active in the Northwest.

All together, Davidson Companies has approximately $25 billion of assets under management. Expanding its product offerings, the company introduced its first proprietary mutual fund in 2008.

The following year Davidson Companies added to its fixed income and public finance operations through the 2009 acquisition of Iowa-based Ruan Securities.

EXECUTIVES

Chairman: Ian B. Davidson, age 77
Vice Chairman: Vincent M. (Vinney) Purpura
President and CEO: William A. (Bill) Johnstone
SVP and COO: Tim Austin
SVP and CFO: Tom Nelson
**SVP, Chief Administrative Officer, and General
 Counsel:** Larry Martinez
**SVP, Chief Market Strategist, and Director, Private
 Client Research:** Fred Dickson
SVP and Director, Private Client Services:
 Jordan Werner
SVP; COO, Private Client Group: Michael Purpura
SVP Corporate Marketing; President, Davidson Travel:
 Michael Morrison
SVP and Director, Institutional Research: John Rogers
**SVP and Director, Fixed Income Capital Markets, D.A.
 Davidson:** Kreg Jones
VP and CIO: Donn A. Lassila
VP and Director, Human Resources: Dan McLaughlin
Associate VP, Public Relations: Jacquie Burchard
Auditors: KPMG LLP

LOCATIONS

HQ: Davidson Companies
 8 3rd St. North, Great Falls, MT 59401
Phone: 406-727-4200   **Fax:** 406-791-7238
Web: www.dadco.com

Selected Locations
Arizona
California
Colorado
Florida
Idaho
Illinois
Iowa
Kansas
Massachusetts
Minnesota
Missouri
Montana
Nebraska
Oklahoma
Oregon
Utah
Washington
Wyoming

COMPETITORS

Charles Schwab
Citigroup Global Markets
Edward Jones
Green Manning & Bunch
McAdams Wright
Piper Jaffray
Ragen MacKenzie

HISTORICAL FINANCIALS

Company Type: Private

Income Statement				FYE: September 30
	REVENUE ($ mil.)	NET INCOME ($ mil.)	NET PROFIT MARGIN	EMPLOYEES
9/08	230	—	—	—
9/07	212	—	—	—
9/06	187	—	—	—
9/05	109	—	—	866
9/04	121	—	—	800
Annual Growth	17.4%	—	—	8.3%

Revenue History

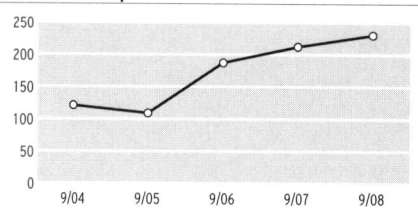

Dawn Food Products

They don't wait for the sun to come up at this company. The ovens are always fired up at Dawn Food Products. The company provides a comprehensive array of pre-baked and fully baked grain-based products, such as cakes, muffins, cookies, donuts, and artisan breads, as well as all the fixings for bakery production, including bases, fillings, flavorings, frozen dough, icings, ingredients, and mixes for other companies in the baking sector. Its customers include food manufacturers, foodservice companies, institutional bakeries, and restaurants. It also manufactures retail bakery goods, including Weight Watchers products.

Offering more than 4,000 products, Dawn has 20 manufacturing sites worldwide, including Canada, Mexico, Central and South America, and Europe. The company is owned and operated by the founding Jones family.

In 2004 the company acquired the bakery business of Bunge North America. It added California cookie-maker Countryside Baking to its list of holdings in 2006.

EXECUTIVES

Chairman: Ronald L. (Ron) Jones
Co-Chairman: Miles E. (Mike) Jones
CEO: Carrie L. Jones-Barber
VP, Distribution Services and Sales: Erik Riswick
VP, Principal Accounts: Richard L. (Rick) Dahlin
VP, Canadian Division: David Hawkins

President, U.S. Bakery Products: David (Dave) Kowal
President, Global Business Processes: Jerry Baglien
President, Global Resources: Tom Harmon
President, Dawn International: Ken Hall
Head, Asia-Pacific Region: Richard Kress
Head, Central America: Felipe Rodriguez
Manager, National Accounts: Sam Barber

LOCATIONS

HQ: Dawn Food Products, Inc.
 3333 Sargent Rd., Jackson, MI 49201
Phone: 517-789-4400   **Fax:** 517-789-4465
Web: www.dawnfoods.com

PRODUCTS/OPERATIONS

Selected Products

Batters
Breadings
Brownies
Cakes
 Crème
 Pound
Cinnamon rolls
Coatings
Cookies
Croissants
Danish
Donuts
Extracts, emulsions, and colors
Fillings
Frozen dough
Glazes
Ice cream bases
Ice cream toppings
Icings
 Butter cream
 Donut and pastry
 Specialty
Mixes
 Biscuit
 Pancake
 Scone
 Waffle
Mexican products
Muffins
Non-dairy icings, fillings, and toppings
Puff dough
Ready-to-finish donuts and cakes
Ready-to-sell cakes, donuts and muffins
Spreads and smears
Sweet dough
Toppings
 Dessert
 Ice cream

COMPETITORS

Alpha Baking	Heinemann's Bakeries
Awrey Bakeries	Hostess Brands
BakeMark	King Arthur Flour
Bell Flavors & Fragrances	King's Hawaiian
Best Brands	Maple Leaf Foods
Bimbo Bakeries	McCormick & Company
Blendex	Ottens Flavors
Bridgford Foods	Pepperidge Farm
Campagna Turano Bakery	Ralcorp Frozen Bakery
Chef Solutions	Products
Chelsea Milling	Rich Products
ConAgra Food &	Sara Lee North American
Ingredients	Retail
Denali Flavors	Sensient Dehydrated
Flowers Foods	Flavors
General Mills	Skinner Baking
George Weston	Smucker
George Weston Bakeries	Sterling Foods
Gonnella Baking	Tropical Nut & Fruit
Hayward Enterprises, Inc.	

HISTORICAL FINANCIALS

Company Type: Private

Income Statement

	REVENUE ($ mil.)	NET INCOME ($ mil.)	NET PROFIT MARGIN	EMPLOYEES
				FYE: December 31
12/07	1,370	—	—	3,950
12/06	1,250	—	—	4,000
12/05	1,110	—	—	3,850
Annual Growth	**11.1%**	**—**	**—**	**1.3%**

Revenue History

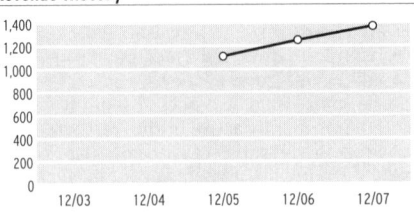

1,400				
1,200				
1,000				
800				
600				
400				
200				
0				
	12/03	12/04	12/05	12/06	12/07

Day & Zimmermann

 Day & Zimmermann offers services as distinct as day and night. Its family of companies provide engineering and construction, design, plant maintenance, security, staffing, munitions decommissioning, validation, and asset management services worldwide. A top global contractor, Day & Zimmermann provides operations, contract support, and maintenance services to US and foreign governments, as well as commercial customers. Its Day & Zimmermann NPS unit maintains half of the US's nuclear plants. Staffing subsidiary Yoh Services specializes in filling IT, engineering, and health care positions. Founded in 1901, Day & Zimmermann is owned and managed by the Yoh family, which has headed the firm for three generations.

 Day & Zimmerman works from more than 150 locations around the world and has completed projects in more than 75 countries.

 The firm has been busy expanding its services portfolio and geographic footprint by making acquisitions. In 2007 Day & Zimmermann became the primary service provider for nearly half of US nuclear power plants with the acquisition of Atlantic Services, Inc. The company also added to the Day & Zimmermann Security Services division when it bought Reliable Security Guard Agency Inc. Also in 2007 the company formed a joint venture with SAP services provider Dassian — Day & Zimmermann Dassian LLC — that markets project and contract management solutions.

 It also acquired the rest of American Ordnance — a munitions manufacturer and cleanup firm — that it didn't already own from General Dynamics.

 Not to be left out, Yoh Services acquired rival Sci-Tek Professionals, which places scientists in clinical and research positions.

 In 2008 Day & Zimmerman merged its Hawthorne Army Depot with Special Operations Consulting, a private security training firm, to train soldiers for deployment. Also that year Day & Zimmerman expanded its security services

presence in the Boston and Dallas areas when it bought South Shore Security Systems and a branch of Admiral Security Systems. Also that year the company added fabrication and machining to its capabilities when it acquired a machining facility in Mississippi.

EXECUTIVES

Chairman and CEO: Harold L. (Hal) Yoh III, age 49
SVP, General Counsel, and Secretary:
 William R. (Bill) Hamm
SVP West Region: Dan Cobb
VP Finance and CFO: Joseph W. (Joe) Ritzel
VP Planning and Strategy: Lisa Carr
VP Real Estate and Special Projects: Bob Fitzsimmons
VP Government Affairs: James (Jim) Hickey
VP Business Operations: Marcus Perdue
VP Human Resources: Diana M. Newmier
VP Human Resources: Silvana Battaglia
VP and CIO: Anthony J. Bosco Jr.
President and CEO, Yoh: William C. (Bill) Yoh, age 38
President and CEO, Commercial and Public:
 Joseph J. Ucciferro
President, Munitions: Michael H. Yoh
President, DZNPS: Gary McKinney
President, Engineering and Field Services:
 Michael J. (Mick) McAreavy
President, Power Services: Michael P. McMahon
President, Mason & Hanger: Ted Daniels
President, Security Services and Validation Services:
 John J. Sacht
President, Yoh Talent Solutions: Don Hanson
Auditors: Deloitte & Touche

LOCATIONS

HQ: The Day & Zimmermann Group
 1500 Spring Garden St., Philadelphia, PA 19130
Phone: 215-299-8000   **Fax:** 215-299-8030
Web: www.dayzim.com

PRODUCTS/OPERATIONS

Selected Subsidiaries

Defense Support Services DS2 (joint venture, equipment and facility maintenance)
Hawthorne Corporation (government services)
Mason & Hanger (architecture, engineering, and construction)
Yoh Services (temporary and long-term job placement in IT, medical, scientific, and other industries)

Selected Services

Commercial services
 Architecture, engineering, and plant services
 Maintenance and modification services
 Security services
 Talent and outsourcing services
 Validation services
Government services
 Architecture, engineering, and construction services
 DOD equipment maintenance and facilities services
 Facilities management and operations
 Munitions products
 Munitions logistics and demilitarization
 Security services
 Talent and outsourcing services

COMPETITORS

Adecco
Babcock & Wilcox Nuclear Power
Bechtel
CDI
Fluor
Jacobs Engineering
Manpower
McCarthy Building
Parsons Corporation
Peter Kiewit Sons'
URS
WS Atkins

HISTORICAL FINANCIALS

Company Type: Private

Income Statement

	REVENUE ($ mil.)	NET INCOME ($ mil.)	NET PROFIT MARGIN	EMPLOYEES
12/08	2,400	—	—	24,000
12/07	2,200	—	—	24,000
12/06	1,900	—	—	23,000
12/05	1,600	—	—	20,000
Annual Growth	14.5%	—	—	6.3%

FYE: December 31

Revenue History

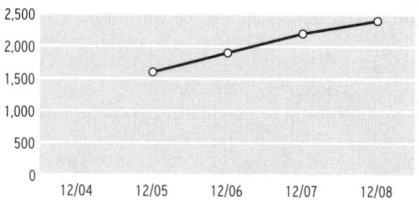

DeBruce Grain

Got a few bushels of wheat and no place to keep it? DeBruce Grain stores, handles, and sells grain and fertilizer for the agribusiness industry. The company owns and operates 20 grain elevators in seven US states, boasting a total storage capacity of more than 115 million bushels, nine fertilizer-distribution terminals, and eight retail fertilizer operations in Iowa, Nebraska, and Texas. DeBruce also markets wholesale fertilizer. The company also has a facility in Central Mexico (just northwest of Mexico City), which serves DeBruce's international customers. Owner and CEO Paul DeBruce founded the company in 1978.

DeBruce paid a $685,000 fine in relation to a 1998 explosion of its Haysville, Kansas, facility — at the time the largest grain elevator in the world. The explosion killed seven workers. It never reopened.

EXECUTIVES

CEO: Paul DeBruce
President: Larry Kittoe
CFO: Curt Heinz
General Director, DeBruce Grain De México: Cristopher Brown

LOCATIONS

HQ: DeBruce Grain, Inc.
4100 N. Mulberry Dr., Kansas City, MO 64116
Phone: 816-421-8182   **Fax:** 816-584-2350
Web: www.debruce.com

PRODUCTS/OPERATIONS

Selected Business Units

Creston Bean Processing LLC
DeBruce Feed Ingredients Inc.
DeBruce Fertilizer Inc.
DeBruce Grain Inc.
DeBruce Risk Services
DeBruce Transportation Inc.

Selected Elevator Locations

Indiana
New Carlisle
Iowa
Creston
Farragut
Joice
Lake Mills
Lenox
Shenandoah
Kansas
Abilene
Wichita
Kentucky
Owensboro

Nebraska
Fremont
Lexington
Nebraska City
Thumel
Oklahoma
Catoosa
Texas
Amarillo
Dimmitt
Etter
Plainview

COMPETITORS

ADM
Ag Processing
Bartlett and Company
Bunge Limited
Cargill
CHS
Farm Service Cooperative
Gold-Eagle Cooperative
Grain Processing Corporation
Heartland Co-op
Owensboro Grain
Scoular
Stewart Grain
West Central Co-op
Wheeler Brothers

Delaware North Companies

This company makes few concessions when it comes to selling hot dogs and sodas at the ball game. Delaware North is a leading provider of foodservices and hospitality at airports, sports stadiums, and tourist destinations throughout the US and in a handful of other countries. Its Sportservice division operates concessions at more than 50 major and minor league sporting arenas, while its Travel Hospitality Services division runs concessions and retail operations at more than 25 airports. In addition, Delaware North provides hospitality services at several tourist destinations, and it operates Boston's TD Garden arena. The family-owned company was founded in 1915 by brothers Charles, Louis, and Marvin Jacobs.

Delaware North's sports concessions unit boasts an impressive list of clients, including Busch Stadium in St. Louis, Soldier Field in Chicago, and famed Wembley National Stadium in the UK. Its parks and resorts division serves tourists at such destinations as the Grand Canyon, Kennedy Space Center Visitor Complex, and Yellowstone. In 2008 Sportservice inked a 10-year deal to provide concessions at the new stadium in the Meadowlands that will host the New York Giants and the New York Jets football teams. The 82,000-seat facility is slated to open in 2010.

The company has been eyeing expansion of its gaming operations, which includes a handful of pari-mutuel racetracks with casinos. In 2008 its

Gaming & Entertainment unit opened a greyhound racing track in Daytona Beach, Florida. Later that year it led a group in winning a bid to operate gaming machines at New York's Aqueduct Racetrack.

In Boston, meanwhile, Delaware North made changes at its hometown sports arena, renaming the facility TD Garden in 2009. The name change from TD Banknorth Garden coincides with a new branding effort by arena sponsor TD Banknorth, which became TD Bank following its 2008 merger with Commerce Bancorp. (The regional financial services giant is owned by Canada's Toronto-Dominion Bank, also known as TD Bank.)

In addition to running his family's concession and entertainment empire, CEO Jeremy Jacobs controls the Boston Bruins professional hockey team.

EXECUTIVES

Chairman and CEO: Jeremy M. Jacobs Sr.
President and COO: Charles E. (Chuck) Moran Jr., age 58
CFO: Karen L. Kemp
Executive Chef and Chief Culinary Ambassador: Roland Henin
EVP; Chairman, Sportservice: Jeremy M. Jacobs Jr.
EVP: Louis M. (Lou) Jacobs
VP, General Counsel, and Secretary: Bryan J. Keller
VP Corporate Communications and Public Relations: Wendy A. Watkins
VP Human Resources: Eileen Morgan
VP Financial Planning and Analysis: Stephen (Steve) Nowaczyk
VP Retail: Jeffrey (Jeff) Hess
VP and Controller: Bruce W. Carlson
VP Supply Management Services: Michael (Mike) Reinert
Chief Administrative Officer: Dennis J. Szefel

LOCATIONS

HQ: Delaware North Companies, Inc.
40 Fountain Plaza, Buffalo, NY 14202
Phone: 716-858-5000   **Fax:** 716-858-5479
Web: www.delawarenorth.com

PRODUCTS/OPERATIONS

Selected Operations

Hospitality services
Delaware North Companies Parks & Resorts (foodservices and lodging)
Delaware North Companies Sportservice (stadium foodservices and concessions)
Delaware North Companies Travel Hospitality Services (airport foodservices and concessions)
Other
Delaware North Companies Gaming & Entertainment (pari-mutuel racing and casino facilities)
TD Garden (sports and entertainment venue, Boston)

Selected Sports and Entertainment Arenas Served

Busch Stadium (St. Louis)
Cleveland Browns Stadium
Comerica Park (Detroit)
Edward Jones Dome (St. Louis)
HSBC Arena (Buffalo, New York)
Progressive Field (Cleveland)
Miller Park (Milwaukee)
Nationwide Arena (Columbus, Ohio)
PETCO Park (San Diego)
Ralph Wilson Stadium (Buffalo, New York)
Rangers Ballpark in Arlington (Texas)
Soldier Field (Chicago)
St. Pete Times Forum (Tampa)
US Cellular Field (Chicago)
Wembley National Stadium (London)

ARAMARK
Autogrill Group
Centerplate
Culinaire International
Guest Services
Legends Hospitality
Levy Restaurants
Ovations Food Services
SMG Management
Sodexo
SSP America

HISTORICAL FINANCIALS

Company Type: Private

Income Statement				FYE: December 31
	REVENUE ($ mil.)	NET INCOME ($ mil.)	NET PROFIT MARGIN	EMPLOYEES
12/08	2,200	—	—	50,000
12/07	2,000	—	—	40,000
12/06	2,040	—	—	50,000
12/05	2,000	—	—	40,000
12/04	1,700	—	—	30,000
Annual Growth	6.7%	—	—	13.6%

Revenue History

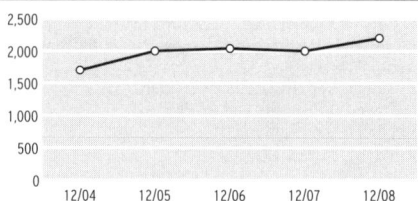

Deloitte Touche Tohmatsu

This company is "deloitted" to make your acquaintance, particularly if you're a big business in need of accounting services. Deloitte Touche Tohmatsu (dba Deloitte) is one of accounting's Big Four, along with Ernst & Young, KPMG, and PricewaterhouseCoopers. Deloitte operates through four business lines — audit, tax, consulting, and financial advisory services. In addition to audit and fiscal oversight services, Deloitte firms provide human resources and technology services. The group comprises some 150 independent firms in about 140 countries. Units include Deloitte & Touche (the US accounting arm) and Deloitte Consulting. Consulting and tax each account for about a quarter of Deloitte's revenues.

Deloitte's consulting arm grew through acquisitions in 2008. Its life sciences unit acquired Recombitant Capital (now operating as Deloitte Recap), which operates a life sciences subscription database and advisory services with 20 years of industry data. The company also acquired the assets of IT consultantcy Solbourne, which served corporate and public clients.

Also in 2008 Deloitte sold its grants and incentives division in the Netherlands and Belgium to PNO Consultants, allowing the group to focus on that region's auditing operations. The following

year, Deloitte purchased the North American public services practice of BearingPoint, which had filed for Chapter 11 bankruptcy protection. The $350 million deal increases Deloitte's presence in the growing government services market.

HISTORY

In 1845 William Deloitte opened an accounting office in London, at first soliciting business from bankrupts. The growth of joint stock companies and the development of stock markets in the mid-19th century created a need for standardized financial reporting and fueled the rise of auditing, and Deloitte moved into the new field. The Great Western Railway appointed him as its independent auditor (the first anywhere) in 1849.

In 1890 John Griffiths, who had become a partner in 1869, opened the company's first US office in New York City. Four decades later branches had opened throughout the US. In 1952 the firm partnered with Haskins & Sells, which operated 34 US offices.

Deloitte aimed to be "the Cadillac, not the Ford" of accounting. The firm, which became Deloitte Haskins & Sells in 1978, began shedding its conservatism as competition heated up; it was the first of the major accountancy firms to use aggressive ads.

The firm spent the 1980s and 1990s pursuing a strategy of using accountants and consultants in concert to provide seamless service in auditing, accounting, strategic planning, information technology, financial management, and productivity. In 1984 Deloitte Haskins & Sells tried to merge with Price Waterhouse, but the deal was dropped after Price Waterhouse's UK partners objected.

In 1989 Deloitte Haskins & Sells joined the flamboyant Touche Ross (founded 1899) to become Deloitte & Touche. Touche Ross's Japanese affiliate Ross Tohmatsu (founded 1968) rounded out the current name. The merger was engineered by Deloitte's Michael Cook and Touche's Edward Kangas, in part to unite the former firm's US and European strengths with the latter's Asian presence. Cook continued to oversee US operations, with Kangas presiding over international operations. Many affiliates, particularly in the UK, rejected the merger and defected to competing firms.

As auditors were increasingly held accountable for the financial results of their clients, legal action soared. In the 1990s Deloitte was sued because of its actions relating to Drexel Burnham Lambert junk bond king Michael Milken, the failure of several savings and loans, and clients' bankruptcies.

Nevertheless, in 1995 the SEC chose Michael Sutton, the firm's national director of auditing and accounting practice, as its chief accountant. That year Deloitte formed Deloitte & Touche Consulting to consolidate its US and UK consulting operations; its Asian consulting operations were later added to facilitate regional expansion. Deloitte Consulting became Deloitte's fastest-growing line, offering strategic and management consulting in addition to information technology and human resources consulting services.

Increasingly, Deloitte and its peers came under fire for their combined accounting/consulting operations; regulators and observers wondered whether accountants could maintain objectivity when they were auditing clients for whom they also provided consulting services.

The Asian economic crisis hurt overseas expansion in 1998, but provided a boost in restructuring consulting. In 1999 the firm sold its accounting staffing service unit (Resources Connection) to its managers and Evercore Partners, citing possible conflicts of interest with its core audit business. Also that year Kangas stepped down as CEO to be succeeded by James Copeland.

In 2001 the SEC forced Deloitte & Touche to restate the financial results of Pre-Paid Legal Services. In an unusual move, Deloitte & Touche publicly disagreed with the SEC's findings.

The accountancy put some old trouble to bed in 2003 when it agreed to pay $23 million to settle claims it had been negligent in its auditing of failed Kentucky Life Insurance, a client in the 1980s. Later that year the UK's High Court found Deloitte negligent in audits related to the failed Barings Bank; however, the ruling was considered something of a victory for the accountancy because it essentially cleared Deloitte of the majority of charges against it and effectively limited its financial liability in the matter.

Copeland retired from the global CEO's office that year and handed the reins over to Bill Parrett, who had formerly served as managing director for the US and the Americas. Parrett was succeeded in 2007 by Jim Quigley, who'd served as CEO of Deloitte's US arm.

EXECUTIVES

Chairman: John P. Connolly
CEO: James H. (Jim) Quigley, age 57
CFO: Jeffrey P. (Jeff) Rohr
Chief Information Officer: Wolfgang Richter
Chief Diversity Officer: James H. (Jim) Wall
Chief Knowledge Officer: Tracey Edwards
Executive Member and Country Leader, Netherlands: Roger J. M. Dassen
Executive Member and Country Leader, Japan: Ryoji Sato
Executive Member and Country Leader, United Kingdom: Martin J. A. Eadon
Executive Member and Country Leader, United States: Barry Salzberg, age 55
Global Managing Partner Consulting and Executive Member, US: Ainar D. Aijala Jr.
Global Managing Partner Financial Advisory Services and Executive Member, Canada: Frank Vettese
Global Managing Partner Strategic Client Program: Otmar Thoemmes
Global Brand and Marketing Director: Luis Gallardo
General Counsel: Philip Rotner
Chief Strategy Officer: Mumtaz Ahmed
Human Resources Operations: Peter May
Director Global PR and CEO Communications: Madonna Jarrett

LOCATIONS

HQ: Deloitte Touche Tohmatsu
1633 Broadway, New York, NY 10019
Phone: 212-489-1600   **Fax:** 212-489-1687
Web: www.deloitte.com/dtt

PRODUCTS/OPERATIONS

2008 Sales

	% of total
Audit	46
Consulting	23
Tax	22
Financial advisory services	9
Total	**100**

2008 Sales by Industry

	% of total
Financial services	23
Consumer business & transportation	19
Manufacturing	14
Telecommunications, media & technology	12
Energy & resources	8
Public sector	7
Life sciences	7
Real estate	5
Other	5
Total	**100**

Selected Products and Services

Audit
   Auditing services
   Global offerings services
   International financial reporting conversion services
Consulting
   Enterprise applications
   Human capital
   Outsourcing
   Strategy and operations
   Technology integration
Tax
   Corporate tax
   Global tax compliance
   Indirect tax
   International assignment services
   International tax
   M&A transaction services
   Research and development credits
   Tax publications
   Tax technologies
   Transfer pricing
Financial Advisory
   Corporate finance
   Forensic services
   Reorganization services
   Transaction services
   Valuation services
Other
   Enterprise Risk Services
     Capital markets
     Control assurance
     Corporate responsibility and sustainability
     Internal audit
     Regulatory consulting
     Security and privacy services
Merger and Acquisition Services

Selected Industry Specializations

Aviation and transport services
Consumer business
Energy and resources
Financial services
Life sciences and health care
Manufacturing
Public sector
Real estate
Technology, media, and telecommunications

COMPETITORS

Accenture
BDO International
Booz Allen
Boston Consulting
Capgemini
Ernst & Young Global
Grant Thornton International
HP Enterprise Services
KPMG
Marsh & McLennan
McKinsey & Company
PricewaterhouseCoopers
Towers Perrin

HISTORICAL FINANCIALS

Company Type: Partnership

Income Statement
FYE: May 31

	REVENUE ($ mil.)	NET INCOME ($ mil.)	NET PROFIT MARGIN	EMPLOYEES
5/08	27,400	—	—	165,000
5/07	23,100	—	—	146,600
5/06	20,000	—	—	135,000
5/05	18,200	—	—	121,283
5/04	16,400	—	—	115,000
Annual Growth	**13.7%**	**—**	**—**	**9.4%**

Revenue History

Delphi Automotive

Delphi has taken the long and winding road alone after being spun off from General Motors in 1999. One of the world's top makers of auto parts, Delphi makes nearly everything mechanical and electrical/electronic that goes into cars. Its primary business divisions include Electrical/Electronic Architecture (vehicle electrical systems), Powertrain (engine, fuel, and emissions systems), Electronics and Safety (sensors, security systems, seat belts, airbags, navigation and entertainment systems), and Thermal Systems (climate control, radiators, heat exchangers). In a deal that gave control of the company to its lenders, Delphi Automotive LLP (formerly Delphi Corp.) emerged from bankruptcy a private company in 2009.

The US Bankruptcy Court approved the plan to sell most of Delphi's assets to a group of the auto parts maker's lenders, led by Elliott Management and Silver Point Capital. The lenders forgave more than $3 billion in debt and agreed to invest an additional $900 million in the company. As part of the deal, GM will provide billions in loans to finance the restructuring and buy back four factories from Delphi, along with Delphi's global steering systems business. GM has already spent billions over the past four years making sure that Delphi, which makes a number of critical parts for GM, made it through restructuring.

Even with a vastly reduced workforce, fewer plants, and a significantly lighter debt load, Delphi faces the same challenges as other auto parts makers in the US. A severe downturn in the North American automotive market has meant less business from GM and other manufacturers in North America.

In late 2009 BeijingWest Industries Co. Ltd. bought Delphi's remaining global business in vehicle brakes and suspensions for about $100 million in cash. Delphi previously designated the business as non-core to its strategic plan. BeijingWest Industries is a new entity established by the Chinese government and two companies. Chinese state-owned steel maker

Shougang Group bought 51% of the Delphi business, while auto parts supplier Tempo Group has a 24% equity stake. The Chinese government also owns one-quarter of the business.

Delphi filed for Chapter 11 bankruptcy protection in 2005. The company expected to exit Chapter 11 by the end of 2007, but complications with lenders and potential investors pushed back the emergence from bankruptcy into 2008 and then into 2009.

Delphi had agreed to sell its steering systems operations to private equity firm Platinum Equity LLC in 2007. Although the US Bankruptcy Court approved the deal, the transaction was unwound by Delphi in 2009, with the company agreeing to sell its steering business back to GM.

The Obama administration's auto task force, however, did not approve of the terms for that proposed transaction, leaving the government, GM, and Delphi to negotiate further on refining the terms before presenting the deal to the bankruptcy court. In August 2009 the European Union approved GM's acquisition of Delphi's steering business, saying that it causes no antitrust problems in Europe.

Delphi then agreed to sell most of its global operations to Platinum Equity and certain assets of the steering systems business to GM, which itself went through a brief Chapter 11 reorganization in mid-2009. The US Bankruptcy Court held up those transactions, however, ruling that Delphi must conduct a court-supervised auction for the assets in question, after hearing objections to the GM/Platinum deal from Delphi's debtor-in-possession lenders. The court's decision once again delayed Delphi's possible exit from bankruptcy reorganization.

Delphi's survival response has taken several precarious turns. The company looked to sell off or shut down much of its US manufacturing base, even exiting certain component sectors such as chassis systems, brakes, and steering. Delphi cut more than 13% of its worldwide workforce during 2008. In another cost-trimming measure, Delphi worked to slash its stable of 2,850 suppliers to a lean group of about 750. Delphi's restructuring efforts also aimed to cut expenses by terminating the insurance benefits of 15,000 corporate retirees. The Delphi Salaried Retirees Association (DSRA) fought back, claiming that the benefits were vested by the company.

Offering a trickle of cash in 2008, Hephaestus Holdings, a unit of KPS Capital Partners that owns some small automotive suppliers, acquired Delphi's wheel bearings business, which was renamed Kyklos Bearing International, Inc. Delphi also sold the assets and inventory of its ride control business to Tenneco for about $19 million.

The company put most of its global suspension business up for sale too, hiring the firm of W.Y. Campbell & Company (part of Comerica) to handle the divestiture. The business makes the MagneRide suspension system, along with shock absorbers, struts, damper modules, and other products. Delphi later made public its desire to sell its automotive exhaust manufacturing operations. Any deal would include manufacturing facilities in Australia, China, India, Luxembourg, Mexico, Poland, South Africa, and the US. The company also elected to terminate its non-equity deal with Bosal International to provide exhaust systems. Delphi let its global exhaust business go to Katcon SA, a subsidiary of Mexico's Bienes Turgon SA, for $17 million. The US Bankruptcy Court endorsed the deal.

In 2007 Delphi reached definitive settlement and restructuring agreements with GM, resolving all outstanding issues between the companies, including the thorny problem of funding pension benefit programs for US employees. Delphi received temporary waivers of its minimum pension funding requirements from the IRS and the federal Pension Benefit Guaranty Corp., and will transfer $1.5 billion in net hourly pension obligations to GM's hourly employees pension plan, issuing a $1.5 billion note to GM. Among other provisions of the agreements, GM will get $2.7 billion in cash from Delphi to satisfy claims against the parts manufacturer.

EXECUTIVES

Chairman: Robert S. (Steve) Miller Jr., age 67
President, CEO, and Director: Rodney O'Neal, age 55, $3,165,937 total compensation
Chief Tax Officer: James P. Whitson, age 64
Chief Accounting Officer and Controller: Thomas S. Timko, age 40
EVP Global Business Services: Mark R. Weber, age 61, $1,854,756 total compensation
VP, General Counsel, and Chief Compliance Officer: David M. Sherbin, age 49
VP; President, Delphi Product and Service Solutions: Francisco A. (Frank) Ordoñez, age 58
VP; President, Delphi Steering: Robert J. Remenar, age 53
VP; President, Delphi Electronics and Safety and Delphi Asia Pacific: Jeffrey J. Owens, age 54
VP and CIO: Bette M. Walker, age 66
VP and CFO: John D. Sheehan, age 49, $676,554 total compensation
VP; President, Delphi Powertrain Systems and Delphi Europe, Middle East, and Africa: Ronald M. Pirtle, age 54, $1,622,997 total compensation
VP Human Resources Management: Kevin M. Butler, age 53
VP; President, Delphi Thermal Systems and Delphi Automotive Holdings Group: James A. Bertrand, age 51, $1,488,602 total compensation
VP; President, Delphi Electric/Electronic Architecture and Delphi Latin America: James A. Spencer, age 56
President, Secretary, and Treasurer, DPH Holdings: John C. Brooks
Secretary: Marjorie Harris Loeb, age 44
Auditors: Ernst & Young LLP

LOCATIONS

HQ: Delphi Automotive LLP
5725 Delphi Dr., Troy, MI 48098
Phone: 248-813-2000   **Fax:** 248-813-2670
Web: www.delphi.com

2008 Sales

	$ mil.	% of total
North America	7,671	43
Europe, Middle East & Africa	7,231	40
Asia/Pacific	2,021	11
South America	1,137	6
Total	**18,060**	**100**

PRODUCTS/OPERATIONS

2008 Sales

	$ mil.	% of total
Electrical/Electronic Architecture	5,649	31
Powertrain Systems	4,470	25
Electronics & Safety	4,048	22
Thermal Systems	2,121	12
Automotive Holding Group	1,348	8
Other	424	2
Total	**18,060**	**100**

2008 Sales by Customer

	$ mil.	% of total
GM & affiliates	5,525	31
Other customers	12,535	69
Total	**18,060**	**100**

Selected Divisions and Products

Electrical/Electronic Architecture
    Complete electronic architecture and components
Powertrain Systems
    Electronics controls
    Exhaust handling
    Fuel injection systems
Electronics and Safety
    Audio, entertainment, and communications components
    Body controls
    Displays
    Power electronics
    Safety systems
    Security systems
Thermal Systems
    Heating, ventilation, and air-conditioning systems
    Powertrain cooling and related technologies

COMPETITORS

ArvinMeritor
Autoliv
Continental Teves
Dana Holding
DENSO
Eaton
Federal-Mogul
Haldex
Honeywell International
ITT Corp.
Johnson Controls
Johnson Electric
JTEKT
Lear Corp.
LEONI
Magna International
Magneti Marelli Powertrain USA
Molex
Motorola, Inc.
NSK
Prestolite Electric
Robert Bosch
Senior plc
Sumitomo Electric
Tenneco
TRW Automotive
Tyco
Valeo
Visteon
Yazaki
ZF Friedrichshafen

HISTORICAL FINANCIALS

Company Type: Private

Income Statement

FYE: December 31

	REVENUE ($ mil.)	NET INCOME ($ mil.)	NET PROFIT MARGIN	EMPLOYEES
12/08	18,060	3,037	16.8%	146,600
12/07	22,283	(3,065)	—	169,500
12/06	26,392	(5,467)	—	171,400
12/05	26,947	(2,340)	—	184,200
12/04	28,622	(4,753)	—	185,200
Annual Growth	**(10.9%)**	**—**	**—**	**(5.7%)**

2008 Year-End Financials

Debt ratio: —
Return on equity: —
Cash ($ mil.): 959
Current ratio: 0.73
Long-term debt ($ mil.): 55

Net Income History

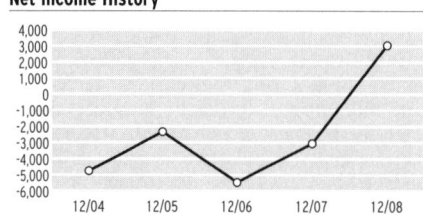

Delta Dental Plan

Delta Dental of California doesn't just help keep the mouths of movie stars clean. The not-for-profit company is a member of the Delta Dental Plans Association and has affiliates nationwide. Delta Dental of California provides dental coverage through HMOs, preferred provider plans (PPOs), and such government programs as the TRICARE Retiree Dental Program and California's Healthy Families Program. The company serves more than 17 million enrollees in California; its programs cover more than one-third of California residents. It also provides dental benefits administration support to employers.

Delta Dental of California has formed a holding company organization with other Delta Dental members, including Delta Dental of Pennsylvania and Delta Dental Insurance Company; together the affiliated companies serve more than 50 million members in some 15 states across the US.

EXECUTIVES

President and CEO: Gary D. Radine
EVP and Chief Legal Officer: Charles Lamont
EVP and CIO: Patrick S. Steele, age 55
EVP and CFO: Michael J. Castro
EVP and Chief Dental Officer: Marilynn Belek
EVP and COO; President, Delta Dental Insurance Company: Anthony S. (Tony) Barth, age 45
SVP Federal Services: Lowell Daun
SVP Sales and Marketing: Belinda Martinez
VP Sales: MohammadReza Navid, age 37
VP Public and Government Affairs: Jeff Album
VP and Enterprise Controller: Alicia Weber
VP Marketing: Eva Hoffman
VP Human Resources: Richard (Rick) Doering
VP Enterprise IT, Head of Applications Delivery and Enterprise Architecture: Hari Makkala

LOCATIONS

HQ: Delta Dental of California
100 1st St., San Francisco, CA 94105
Phone: 415-972-8300   **Fax:** 415-972-8466
Web: www.deltadentalins.com

COMPETITORS

Aetna
CIGNA
First Dental Health
Health Net
MetLife
SafeGuard Health Enterprises
WellPoint
Western Dental Services

HISTORICAL FINANCIALS

Company Type: Not-for-profit

Income Statement

FYE: December 31

	REVENUE ($ mil.)	NET INCOME ($ mil.)	NET PROFIT MARGIN	EMPLOYEES
12/08	5,900	—	—	3,600

DeMoulas Super Markets

The Demoulas supermarket chain is ripe with family history all rolled up into numerous Market Baskets. Demoulas Super Markets runs some 60 grocery stores under the Market Basket banner in Massachusetts and New Hampshire. One store still operates under the "DeMoulas" banner. The grocery retailer also manages real estate interests. Market Basket supermarkets are typically located in shopping centers with other retail outlets, including properties owned by the company through its real estate arm, Retail Management and Development (RMD), Inc. Begun as a mom-and-pop grocery store, the Demoulas sons transformed the chain into a traditional, yet modern, concept. The business is run by CEO Arthur Demoulas.

The company was founded in 1954 when brothers George and Telemachus "Mike" Demoulas bought their parents' mom-and-pop grocery. The men agreed that, upon one brother's death, the other would care for the deceased's family and maintain the firm's 50-50 ownership. In 1990 George's family alleged that Mike had defrauded them of all but 8% of the company's stock. The 10-year court battle was decided in favor of George's family, giving it 51% of the company. By then Mike had resigned as CEO; he died in 2003 at age 82.

The company is planning to tear down its last DeMoulas store, located in Salem, Massachusetts, and replace it with an 89,000-sq.-ft. Market Basket store.

EXECUTIVES

President: Arthur Demoulas
Director, Operations: Bill Marsden
EVP: James Miamis
VP, Grocery Sales and Merchandising: Joseph Rockwell
VP, Finance and Treasurer: Donald Mulligan
VP and Treasurer, Retail Management and Development Inc.: Michael Kettenbach
Coffee and Beverage Buyer: Jim Lacourse
Corporate Counsel: Sumner Darman
Payroll Administrator: Lucille Lopez

LOCATIONS

HQ: Demoulas Super Markets Inc.
875 East St., Tewksbury, MA 01876
Phone: 978-851-8000   **Fax:** 978-640-8390

2008 Stores

	No.
Massachusetts	35
New Hampshire	24
Total	**59**

PRODUCTS/OPERATIONS

Selected Banners
Market Basket
DeMoulas

COMPETITORS

Big Y Foods	Shaw's
BJ's Wholesale Club	Stop & Shop
Costco Wholesale	SUPERVALU
Cumberland Farms	Trader Joe's
Golub	Wal-Mart
Hannaford Bros.	Whole Foods
IGA	

HISTORICAL FINANCIALS
Company Type: Private

Income Statement
FYE: December 31

	REVENUE ($ mil.)	NET INCOME ($ mil.)	NET PROFIT MARGIN	EMPLOYEES
12/08	2,800	—	—	16,000
12/07	2,500	—	—	13,000
12/06	2,200	—	—	13,000
12/05	2,000	—	—	12,000
12/04	1,950	—	—	—
Annual Growth	9.5%	—	—	10.1%

Revenue History

Denver Nuggets

You might say this team has the perfect moniker when the name of the game is taking the rock to the hole. The Denver Nuggets professional basketball franchise was formed by trucking magnate J. W. "Bill" Ringsby in 1967 as the Denver Rockets (renamed in 1974), a charter member of the American Basketball Association. Since joining the National Basketball Association in 1976, the team has had little post-season success, although the signing of star forward Carmelo Anthony in 2004 has helped spur fan interest, giving a boost to attendance at the team's Pepsi Center arena. Wal-Mart heir Stan Kroenke has owned the team since 2000.

Through his Kroenke Sports Enterprises, Kroenke also owns the Colorado Avalanche professional hockey team and Denver's Pepsi Center. In addition, he is the largest shareholder in UK soccer team Arsenal Football Club and has a 40% stake in the St. Louis Rams football team.

EXECUTIVES

Owner: E. Stanley (Stan) Kroenke
Head Coach: George Karl, age 58
VP Player Personnel: Rex Chapman
VP Basketball Operations: Mark Warkentien, age 54
Director Player Services: Tim Dixon
Director Basketball Administration: Lisa Johnson
Advanced Scout: Chad Iske, age 31
Executive Assistant to the General Manager: Carol Williams
Assistant Coach/Player Development: Jamahl Mosley, age 29
Assistant Coach/Player Development: John Welch, age 46
Director Basketball Operations: Greg Knight, age 30
Director Media Relations: Eric Sebastian
Athletic Trainer and Traveling Secretary: Jim Gillen

LOCATIONS

HQ: Denver Nuggets Limited Partnership
1000 Chopper Circle, Denver, CO 80204
Phone: 303-405-1100   **Fax:** 303-575-1920
Web: www.nba.com/nuggets

COMPETITORS

Minnesota Timberwolves
Oklahoma City Thunder
Portland Trail Blazers
Utah Jazz

Desert Schools FCU

One of the largest credit unions in Arizona, Desert Schools Federal Credit Union operates about 60 branch locations in the Phoenix area, serving more than 325,000 members. Established in 1939 by a group of 15 teachers, the credit union offers banking products and services, including checking and savings accounts, IRAs, and CDs; it also provides online banking services. Subsidiary Desert Schools Financial Services sells insurance products and investment services. Membership is available to any individual living, working, or attending church or school in Gila, Maricopa, and Pinal counties.

EXECUTIVES

Chairman: Claudette M. Gronksi
President and CEO: Susan C. Frank
EVP: Jeffrey D. Meshey
SVP Retail Sales and Branch Operations: Carlos Pacheco
SVP Human Resources: David Strachan
SVP Strategic Direction and Operations: Lee Brice
VP Contact Center Operations: James (Jim) Lavery
VP and CFO: Mark Wiete
VP and CIO: Gary Laieski
VP Human Resources, Training and Development, and Quality: Jennifer Godel
Assistant VP Accounting and Payroll: Ann Prettyman
Assistant VP Finance/Secondary Marketing: Stephen Jordan
Assistant VP Marketing: Cathy Graham
Auditors: McGladrey & Pullen, LLP

LOCATIONS

HQ: Desert Schools Federal Credit Union
148 N. 48th St., Phoenix, AZ 85034
Phone: 602-433-7000
Web: www.desertschools.org

PRODUCTS/OPERATIONS

2008 Sales

	$ mil.	% of total
Interest		
Loans to members	154.5	66
Investments & cash equivalents	20.0	8
Noninterest		
Service charges & other fees	55.3	24
Net gains on sales of loans	3.4	1
Other	2.7	1
Total	**230.5**	**100**

COMPETITORS

Bank of America
Compass Bancshares
JPMorgan Chase
Marshall & Ilsley
Western Alliance
Zions Bancorporation

HISTORICAL FINANCIALS

Company Type: Not-for-profit

Income Statement

FYE: December 31

	ASSETS ($ mil.)	NET INCOME ($ mil.)	INCOME AS % OF ASSETS	EMPLOYEES
12/08	3,137	(39)	—	1,300
12/07	3,020	30	1.0%	1,300
12/06	2,885	40	1.4%	1,300
12/05	2,570	36	1.4%	1,134
12/04	2,212	28	1.3%	1,000
Annual Growth	9.1%	—	—	6.8%

2008 Year-End Financials

Equity as % of assets: —
Return on assets: —
Return on equity: —
Long-term debt ($ mil.): —
Sales ($ mil.): 231

Net Income History

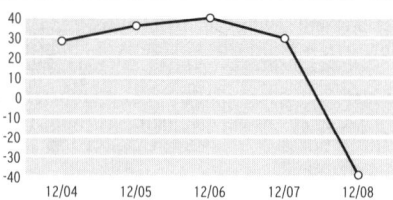

40				
30				
20				
10				
0				
-10				
-20				
-30				
-40				
	12/04	12/05	12/06	12/07	12/08

Dewey & LeBoeuf

International law firm Dewey & LeBoeuf has 1,400 lawyers in about 25 offices worldwide. One of the leading law firms headquartered in New York, Dewey & LeBoeuf's areas of expertise include antitrust, bankruptcy, government investigations, real estate, tax, and trade law, as well as mergers and acquisitions. The firm is the result of the October 2007 merger between law firms Dewey Ballantine and LeBoeuf, Lamb, Greene & MacRae. Dewey Ballantine was initially founded in 1909; the Dewey in the name refers to former partner Thomas Dewey, a three-term New York governor and two-time Republican presidential nominee in the 1940s. LeBoeuf, Lamb was established in 1929.

The LeBoeuf, Lamb transaction comes on the heels of a proposed merger that couldn't be completed. In late 2006 Dewey Ballantine was set to merge with San Francisco-based Orrick, Herrington & Sutcliffe; however, the deal fell through after key partners at Dewey left. The deal would have created Dewey Orrick, a firm with 1,500 lawyers and some $1 billion in annual revenue.

Still, the firm is satisfied with the results of the merger with LeBoeuf, Lamb, and by late 2008 it managed to fully integrate the two firms' managerial and technical infrastructure.

EXECUTIVES

Chairman: Steve H. Davis
Executive Director: Stephen DiCarmine
COO: Dennis D'Alessandro
CFO: Joel I. Sanders
CIO: Peter Owings

Chief Practice Services Officer: Herb Thomas
Chief Administrative Officer: Julia Sherlock
Chief Marketing Officer: Sophie Aldred
Chief Administrative Officer: Thomas F. Van Buskirk
Chief Human Resources Officer:
 Jason S. (Jay) Dinwoodie
Secretary: Carol A. McCrystal
Director of Information Technology: Eva Steiner
Director Pro Bono: Scot H. Fishman

LOCATIONS

HQ: Dewey & LeBoeuf LLP
 1301 Avenue of the Americas, New York, NY 10019
Phone: 212-259-8000   **Fax:** 212-259-6333
Web: www.deweyleboeuf.com

PRODUCTS/OPERATIONS

Selected Practice Areas

Antitrust
Bank and Institutional Finance
Bankruptcy Litigation
Business Solutions and Governance
Compensation, Benefits, and Employment
Competition/EU
Corporate Finance
Employment Litigation
Energy Litigation
Energy Regulatory
Environmental, Health, and Safety
Environmental Litigation
Insurance Regulatory
Insurance/Reinsurance
Intellectual Property Litigation
International Arbitration
International Litigation
International Trade
IT and IP Transactions
Legislative and Public Policy
Mergers and Acquisitions
Private Equity
Project Finance
Real Estate
Securities, Mergers and Acquisitions, and Corporate Governance Litigation
Sports Litigation
Structured Finance
Tax
Tax Controversy and Litigation
White Collar Criminal Defense and Investigations
Wealth Management

Selected Industry Experience

Insurance
Life Sciences and Health care
Media and Entertainment
Oil and Gas
Telecommunications
Utilities, Power, and Pipelines

COMPETITORS

Baker & McKenzie
Cleary Gottlieb
Cravath, Swaine
Davis Polk
Fried, Frank, Harris
Jones Day
Kirkland & Ellis
Shearman & Sterling
Skadden, Arps
White & Case
Willkie Farr

Dickinson Financial

Drop and give me a twenty. Dickinson Financial is the holding company for Bank Midwest, as well as a group of military banks: Armed Forces Bank, Armed Forces Bank of California, SunBank, Southern Commerce Bank, and Academy Bank. Bank Midwest operates about 70 branches in Kansas and Missouri. The military banking group operates from some 120 locations on or around military bases in about 20 states. The banks offer traditional deposit and lending products: savings, checking, money market, and retirement accounts; lines of credit; and CDs. The Dickinson family owns Dickinson Financial.

In 2009 the company arranged to sell Florida-based Southern Commerce Bank, which operates about a dozen branches, to NewStar Financial, which is applying to convert to a bank holding company. However, the buyer later terminated the deal after concluding that it would have difficulty integrating the acquisition.

Commercial real estate loans (including agricultural, construction, development, and multi-family residential loans) account for about two-thirds of Dickinson Financial's loan portfolio. Commercial, residential mortgage, and consumer loans make up the remainder.

EXECUTIVES

Chairman: Ann K. Dickinson
Vice Chairman: Amy Dickinson Holewinski
CEO: Paul P. Holewinski
President: Rick L. Smalley
SEVP: Daniel L. (Dan) Dickinson
EVP and COO: Tim C. Connealy
EVP, CFO, and Treasurer: Dennis P. Ambroske
EVP, General Counsel, and Secretary: John R. Cox
EVP: Donald C. Giles
SVP, Senior Counsel, and Assistant Secretary:
 Jane A. Dickinson Kress
VP: Douglas M. Neeb
VP: Eugene J. Twellman
VP: Stacey L. Lucas
VP: Burton K. Dickinson
VP: Cindy R. Buttress

LOCATIONS

HQ: Dickinson Financial Corporation
 1100 Main St., Ste. 350, Kansas City, MO 64105
Phone: 816-471-9800   **Fax:** 816-412-0022
Web: www.bankmw.com

COMPETITORS

Commerce Bancshares
UMB Financial
U.S. Bancorp
USAA

HISTORICAL FINANCIALS

Company Type: Private

Income Statement

FYE: December 31

	ASSETS ($ mil.)	NET INCOME ($ mil.)	INCOME AS % OF ASSETS	EMPLOYEES
12/08	6,080	(3)	—	2,226
12/07	5,579	105	1.9%	2,179
12/06	4,705	107	2.3%	2,002
12/05	4,022	76	1.9%	1,901
12/04	3,509	62	1.8%	1,726
Annual Growth	14.7%	—	—	6.6%

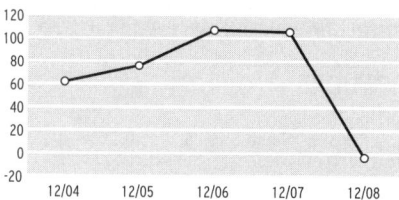
Discount Tire

Concerned about that upcoming "re-tire-ment"? Discount Tire Co., one of the largest independent tire dealers in the US, can provide several options. With about 780 company-owned stores in more than 20 states, the company sells such leading tire brands as Michelin, Goodyear, and Uniroyal, as well as wheels from Enkei, Konig, and TSW. Discount Tire operates mostly in the West, Midwest, Southwest, and Southeast. Some of the company's West Coast stores operate as America's Tire Co. because of a name conflict. Customers can search for tires by make and model on the company's Web site. Chairman and owner Bruce Halle founded the company in 1960 with six tires — four of them recaps.

The family-owned company is one of the fastest-growing tire dealers in the US. Indeed, 2008 marked a record year for expansion as Discount Tire added 50 stores in about 20 states. It is expected to match that figure again in 2009. One state that Discount Tire has targeted for expansion is Oklahoma. The company rolled in with its first store in 2008 and planned to open half a dozen more in the Oklahoma City area in 2009.

In addition to its bricks-and-mortar business, Discount Tire operates a mail-order and Internet division, Discount Tire Direct, for customers who do not live near a retail store.

EXECUTIVES

Chairman: Bruce T. Halle
Vice Chairman: Gary T. Van Brunt
CEO: Tom Englert
COO: Steve Fournier
CFO: Christian Roe
EVP and Chief Administrative Officer: Bob Holman

LOCATIONS

HQ: Discount Tire Co. Inc.
   20225 N. Scottsdale Rd., Scottsdale, AZ 85255
Phone: 480-606-6000   **Fax:** 480-951-8619
Web: www.discounttire.com

2009 Stores

	No.
Texas	210
California	121
Arizona	65
Michigan	58
Colorado	46
Illinois	30
Washington	29
North Carolina	26
Georgia	25
Florida	24
Minnesota	22
Nevada	21
Utah	21
Indiana	20
New Mexico	17
Ohio	12
Tennessee	11
Oregon	8
Oklahoma	7
South Carolina	6
Idaho	1
Wisconsin	1
Total	**781**

COMPETITORS

Bridgestone Retail Operations
Commercial Tire
Les Schwab Tire Centers
Monro Muffler Brake
Penske
Pep Boys
Sears
TBC
TCI Tire Centers
Tire Distribution Systems
VIP
Wal-Mart

HISTORICAL FINANCIALS

Company Type: Private

Income Statement

FYE: December 31

	REVENUE ($ mil.)	NET INCOME ($ mil.)	NET PROFIT MARGIN	EMPLOYEES
12/08	2,410	—	—	11,652
12/07	2,310	—	—	11,630
12/06	2,060	—	—	10,980
12/05	1,856	—	—	10,100
12/04	1,670	—	—	9,500
Annual Growth	**9.6%**	**—**	**—**	**5.2%**

Revenue History

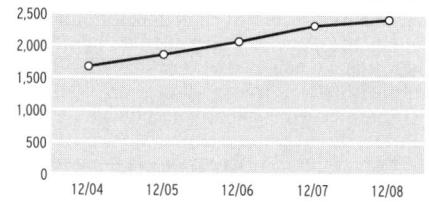

DLA Piper

One of the world's largest law firms, DLA Piper has about 3,500 lawyers operating in the US, Asia, Europe, and the Middle East. The firm's network of more than 65 offices spans about 30 countries. DLA Piper serves corporate clients through a broad range of practices divided into about a dozen key groups; specialties include mergers and acquisitions, intellectual property, regulatory and government affairs, and technology and media. Clients have included Life Technologies, British Midland Airways, and Trident Microsystems. The firm was formed in 2005 when Maryland-based Piper Rudnick merged with California-based Gray Cary Ware & Freidenrich and UK firm DLA.

Despite the global economic downturn, DLA Piper sees opportunities in the Middle East. In August 2009 the firm expanded its office in Abu Dhabi, United Arab Emirates, by adding a government relations practice to accommodate growth in that region. DLA Piper has new leadership in the Gulf Cooperation Council countries. In October 2009 the firm named Abdul Aziz Al-Yaquot as its regional partner in the Middle East. Abdul Aziz will oversee the firm's offices in Abu Dhabi, Bahrain, Saudi Arabia, Kuwait, Oman, and Qatar.

EXECUTIVES

Global Chairman: Francis B. Burch Jr.
Vice Chair, US Restructuring: Alan Solow
Partner; Vice Chair, Restructuring Practice Group and Head of West Coast Restructuring Practice: Karol K. Denniston
Joint CEO: Nigel Knowles
Joint CEO: Lee I. Miller
Executive Director: Stephen R. Colgate
Managing Partner, US: J. Terence (Terry) O'Malley
Chief Operations and Facilities: Alan E. Good
CFO: Raymond Dearchs
CIO: Donald P. Jaycox
Chief Risk Officer, US: William J. Campbell Jr.
Chief Marketing Officer: Jolene M. Overbeck
Chief People Officer, US: Clarissa Peterson
Global Chief People Officer: Robert Halton
Global CIO: Daniel Pollick

LOCATIONS

HQ: DLA Piper
   6225 Smith Ave., Baltimore, MD 21209
Phone: 410-580-3000   **Fax:** 410-580-3001
Web: www.dlapiper.com

PRODUCTS/OPERATIONS

Selected Practice Groups

Commercial contracts
Corporate
Employment, pensions, and benefits
Finance
Intellectual property
International arbitration
Litigation and arbitration
Product liability
Projects and infrastructure
Real estate
Regulatory and government affairs
Restructuring
Tax
Technology and media
White collar, corporate crime, and investigations

COMPETITORS

Baker & McKenzie	Jones Day
Cleary Gottlieb	Linklaters
Clifford Chance	Mayer Brown
Cooley Godward Kronish	Shearman & Sterling
Davis Polk	Sidley Austin
Freshfields	Skadden, Arps
Holland & Knight	Wilson Sonsini

HISTORICAL FINANCIALS

Company Type: Partnership

Income Statement
FYE: December 31

	REVENUE ($ mil.)	NET INCOME ($ mil.)	NET PROFIT MARGIN	EMPLOYEES
12/08	1,178	—	—	—
12/07	1,135	—	—	—
Annual Growth	3.8%	—	—	—

Revenue History

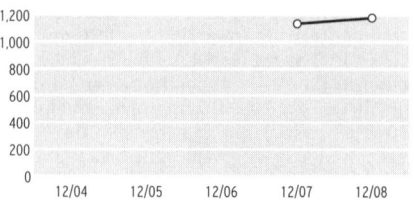

Do it Best

If you're building a house or fixing one up, you might as well Do it Best — at least that's the hope of one of the hardware industry's largest cooperatives. Do it Best boasts more than 4,100 member-owned stores in 47 countries worldwide, primarily in the US. Besides the usual tools and building materials, merchandise includes automotive items, bicycles, camping gear, housewares, office supplies, and small appliances. The co-op, whose buying power enables members to get retail items at competitive prices, also offers unifying branding programs using the Do it Best and Do it Center names. Do it Best (formerly Hardware Wholesalers) began in 1945; it bought the Our Own Hardware co-op in 1998.

Do It Best has been extending its reach internationally in recent years to grow. The company in 2008 added nine new international members, which brought 18 additional stores. Its international division also logged a third year of 18% average sales growth in 2008.

The company's RetailSTART! program provides market and site analysis, demographic research, project financing, inventory assistance, and project management for retailer-members who want to open more stores.

EXECUTIVES

Chairman: Mike Fujimoto
Vice Chairman: Pat Sullivan
President and CEO: Robert N. (Bob) Taylor, age 55
EVP and COO: David (Dave) Haist
VP Marketing: William (Bill) Zielke
VP Information Technology: Kay Williams
VP Merchandising: Steve Markley
VP Sales and Retail Development: Jay Brown
VP Finance: David W. (Dave) Dietz

VP Lumber and Building Materials: Quent Ondricek
VP Retail Logistics: John Snider
VP Human Resources and General Counsel:
  Daniel B. (Dan) Starr
Secretary and Director: Steve Phillips
Treasurer and Director: J. Johnson
Communications Manager: Kim Gonzalez

LOCATIONS

HQ: Do it Best Corp.
  6502 Nelson Rd., Fort Wayne, IN 46803
Phone: 260-748-5300　　**Fax:** 260-748-5620
Web: www.doitbestcorp.com

PRODUCTS/OPERATIONS

Selected Programs

ADpak (cutomizable advertising and merchandising
  program)
Do It Best Rental Center (tool and equipment rental)
INCOM Distributor Supply (industrial/commercial
  division)
Opportunity program (product management)

COMPETITORS

84 Lumber	Northern Tool
Ace Hardware	Orgill
Handy Hardware Wholesale	Sears
Home Depot	Sutherland Lumber
Lowe's	True Value
Menard	Wal-Mart

HISTORICAL FINANCIALS

Company Type: Cooperative

Income Statement
FYE: June 30

	REVENUE ($ mil.)	NET INCOME ($ mil.)	NET PROFIT MARGIN	EMPLOYEES
6/08	2,546	1	0.0%	—

Dot Foods

Dot Foods, the largest foodservice redistributor in the US, started out in business as one station wagon that hauled dairy goods around and went by the name of Associated Dairy Products. The company now owns more than 700 trucks (through its Dot Transportation division) that distribute some 70,000 products including food, flatware, serveware, and janitorial supplies from 500 manufacturers to its customers — more than 3,300 foodservice distributors. Dot has nine distribution facilities located across the country. Its edotfoods unit offers ordering and fulfillment services online. The company also sells food ingredients to dairies, bakeries, confectioners, meat processors, and other food manufacturers.

EXECUTIVES

Chairman: Patrick F. (Pat) Tracy
CEO and Director: John M. Tracy
President, COO, and Director: Joe Tracy
CFO: William H. (Bill) Metzinger
SVP, General Counsel, Secretary, and Director:
  James W. (Jim) Tracy, age 54
VP Information Technology: Mark Read
VP Retail: George Eversman
VP Marketing: Scott C. Stamerjohn

VP Sales: Michael J. (Mike) Duggan, age 58
VP Business Development: Michael A. (Mike) Buckley
VP Quality and Training: Jeff Bottorff
VP Human Resources: Matt Holt
VP Distribution Centers: John Long
VP Customer Development: Dick Tracy
Manager Corporate Communications: Bryan Hills
President, Tracy Family Foundation: Jean Buckley

LOCATIONS

HQ: Dot Foods, Inc.
  1 Dot Way, Mount Sterling, IL 62353
Phone: 217-773-4411　　**Fax:** 217-773-3321
Web: www.dotfoods.com

COMPETITORS

Associated Wholesalers
Bi-Rite Restaurant Supply
C.D. Hartnett
Federated Group
Gordon Food Service
MAINES
McLane Foodservice
Purity Wholesale Grocers
Reinhart FoodService
SYSCO

HISTORICAL FINANCIALS

Company Type: Private

Income Statement
FYE: December 31

	REVENUE ($ mil.)	NET INCOME ($ mil.)	NET PROFIT MARGIN	EMPLOYEES
12/08	3,100	—	—	3,248
12/07	2,810	—	—	3,168
12/06	2,490	—	—	2,916
12/05	2,164	—	—	2,746
12/04	1,930	—	—	2,500
Annual Growth	12.6%	—	—	6.8%

Revenue History

Dow Corning

Dow Corning knows about cooperation. The company began as a joint venture of chemical titan Dow and glass giant Corning in 1943 and ranks among the longest-lasting partnerships of its kind in the US. Dow Corning produces more than 7,000 silicone-based products such as adhesives, insulating materials, and lubricants for aerospace, automotive, and electrical uses. Because silicone does not conduct electricity, it is also used in its hard polycrystalline form (silicon) as the material on which semiconductors are built. Its products are also used in the production of photovoltaic cells used to produce solar energy. With plants worldwide, the company sells more than half of its products outside the US.

Through its Xiameter brand and Web site, Dow Corning sells products online to more than 80 countries. Launched in 2002, Xiameter serves customers that order in large volumes and require less customer service attention. Now Dow Corning (through both its eponymous brand and the Xiameter brand) achieves 30% of its sales online, more than twice the industry average.

The company announced in 2009 a shift in strategic focus that not only wants to further emphasize Xiameter but also to build on its environmental and sustainability offerings. It especially wants to devote investment to products relating to the solar energy industry. Key to that initiative is Dow Corning's majority ownership in the Hemlock Semiconductor Group; that company is investing $4.5 billion into solar energy R&D. (It owns 63% of Hemlock Semiconductor, with Shin Etsu and Mitsubishi Materials taking up the rest.) Dow Corning has also opened two solar energy applications centers, in the US and South Korea, since 2008.

Also in 2009 Dow Corning bought two chemical-grade silicon manufacturing facilities from Globe Specialty Metals for about $175 million. One of the plants is in Brazil; the other (of which Dow Corning actually bought 49%) is in the US.

HISTORY

Dow Corning was founded in 1943 as a joint venture between Dow Chemical and Corning Glass Works. Corning, founded by Amory Houghton in 1875, provided Thomas Edison with glass for the first light bulbs. It developed Pyrex heat-resistant glass in 1915.

Corning made its first silicone resin samples in 1938. It teamed with a group of Dow Chemical scientists who were also working on silicone products in 1940. Dow Chemical president Willard Dow and Corning Glass Works president Glen Cole shook hands on the idea of a joint venture in 1942, and 10 months later Dow Corning was formed. Its first product, the engine grease DOW CORNING 4, enabled B-17s to fly at 35,000 feet (a major contribution to the Allied war effort). In 1945 DOW CORNING 35 (an emulsifier used in tire molds) and Pan Glaze (which made baking pans stick-proof and easier to clean) were instant successes on the home front.

Dow Corning expanded rapidly in international markets and in 1960 set up Dow Corning International to handle sales and technical service in markets outside North America. By 1969 the company had operations worldwide.

Dow Corning's first breast implants went on the market in 1964. Over the next three decades, Dow Corning and other silicone makers sold silicone breast implants to more than a million women in the US. In the early 1980s breast-implant recipients began suing Dow Corning and other implant makers, claiming that the silicone gel in the implants leaked and caused health problems. Dow Corning, the leading implant maker, defended the devices as safe. The company stopped making implants in 1992, after the Food and Drug Administration called for a moratorium on silicone-gel implants.

In 1993 Baxter International, Bristol-Myers Squibb, and Dow Corning offered $4.2 billion to settle thousands of claims. The corporation declared bankruptcy in 1995 to buy time for financial reorganization. A federal judge stripped Dow Chemical of its protection from direct liability, and the company was later ordered to pay a Nevada couple $4.1 million in damages (other jurisdictions did not follow suit). Dow Corning sold its Polytrap polymer technology to Advanced Polymer, maker of polymer-based pharmaceutical delivery systems, in 1996. The following year the company sold Bisco Products, its silicone-foam business, to Rogers Corporation for $12 million.

Dow Corning's $3.7 billion bankruptcy reorganization plan, offered in 1997, allowed for $2.4 billion to be set aside to settle most implant lawsuits against the corporation. However, a federal bankruptcy judge found legal flaws in the proposal and refused to allow claimants to vote on it. In 1998 Dow Corning upped the ante to $4.4 billion — $3 billion to the silicone claimants and the rest to creditors.

Both sides later agreed to a $3.2 billion compensation package, and in 1999 the plan received approval from a bankruptcy judge and creditors. However, the settlement stalled when the judge ruled that women who disagreed with the settlement could sue Dow Chemical and Corning (Dow Corning appealed). Despite its court battles, in 2000 the company acquired the 51% of Universal Silicones & Lubricants (high-tech lubricants and silicone sealants) it did not own and renamed the company Dow Corning India.

In early 2004 a bankruptcy court judge ruled that the re-approved settlement would go through. The move allowed the money Dow Corning set aside for the settlement to be dispersed to claimants, and for the company to exit Chapter 11, which finally occurred in the middle of that year.

Moving outside its traditional position in polymeric silicones, the company acquired the holographic data storage business of Aprilis in 2006. The acquired division, now called DCE Aprilis, operates as a separate Dow Corning subsidiary.

EXECUTIVES

Chairman, President, and CEO: Stephanie A. Burns, age 55
EVP, Office of the CEO: Christopher J. (Chris) Bowyer
VP, General Counsel, and Secretary: Sue K. McDonnell
Executive Director and CIO: Abbe M. Mulders
Chief Marketing Officer and Executive Director, Marketing and Sales: Brian Chermside
Executive Director, Global Security: Kevin B. Kendrick
Executive Director, Environment, Health, and Safety: Peter Cartwright
VP and Executive Director, Manufacturing, Engineering, and Global Operations: James R. Whitlock
VP and General Manager, Specialty Chemicals; President, Asia Area: Jean-Marc Gilson
VP and Chief Human Resources Officer: Alan E. Hubbard
VP, CTO, and Executive Director, Science and Technology: Gregg A. Zank
VP and Chief Engineer: Brett W. Able
VP and CFO; President, Americas Area: Joseph D. (Don) Sheets
VP and General Manager, Core Products: Robert D. (Bob) Hansen
VP Strategic Programs: Allan C. (Harry) Ludgate
VP; VP Asia and President, Greater China: Thomas H. (Tom) Cook
Auditors: PricewaterhouseCoopers LLP

LOCATIONS

HQ: Dow Corning Corporation
2200 W. Salzburg Rd., Midland, MI 48686
Phone: 989-496-4000   **Fax:** 989-496-4393
Web: www.dowcorning.com

PRODUCTS/OPERATIONS

Selected Products and Applications

Aerospace
  Adhesives
  Encapsulants
  Exotic composite materials
  Greases
  High-purity fluids
  Primers
  Protective coatings
  Sealants
Automotive
  Body components
  Brake systems
  Chassis
  Electrical components
  Electronic components
  Engine/drivetrain
  Exterior lighting
  Fuel systems
Chemical and Material Manufacturing
  Auto appearance chemicals
  Industrial release agents
  Materials treatment
  Process aid antifoams
  Pulp manufacturing
Cleaning Products
  Dry cleaning
  Laundry detergents
  Polishes and hard surface cleaners
Coatings and Plastics
  Caulks
  Coatings
  Sealants
Electrical/Electronics
  Adhesives and sealants
  Conformal coatings
  Dielectric gels
  High-voltage insulators
  Hyperpure polycrystalline silicon
  Interlayer dielectric and passivation materials
  Liquid transformer fluid
  Silicone encapsulants
  Silicone grease for insulators
  Silicone RTV coating for insulators
  Silicone rubber insulators
  Thermally conductive adhesives
Food and Beverage
  Defoamers
  Packaging
Health Care
  Hydrocephalus shunts
  Pacemaker leads
  Tubing for dialysis
Paper Manufacturing and Finishing
  Release coatings for label-backing paper, pressure-sensitive adhesives, and paper coatings
Personal Care
  Materials for deodorants, cosmetics, and lotions
Plastics
Textiles
  Waterproofing agents

COMPETITORS

3M
Asahi Glass
Bayer MaterialScience
Bostik
Cytec Engineered Materials
Evonik Degussa
Formosa Plastics
H.B. Fuller
Hexcel
Honeywell Specialty Materials
Shin-Etsu Chemical
Wacker Chemie

HISTORICAL FINANCIALS

Company Type: Joint venture

Income Statement				FYE: December 31
	REVENUE ($ mil.)	NET INCOME ($ mil.)	NET PROFIT MARGIN	EMPLOYEES
12/08	5,450	739	13.6%	10,000
12/07	4,940	—	—	10,000
12/06	4,392	—	—	9,000
12/05	3,879	—	—	—
12/04	3,373	—	—	—
Annual Growth	12.7%	—	—	5.4%

Revenue History

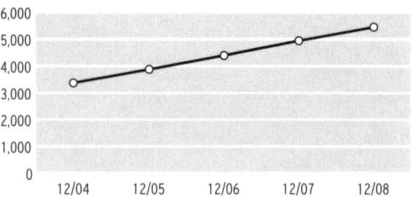

DPR Construction

From bio labs to wafer fabs, the projects of DPR Construction reflect the focus of its commercial building operations. The general contractor/construction manager builds projects for the biotechnology, pharmaceutical, health care, education, and semiconductor markets. DPR also specializes in corporate offices, entertainment facilities (theme parks and studios), energy efficient projects, and warehouse and distribution centers. Clients have included Apple, Banner Health, Pixar Animation, Scripps Research Institute, and the American Red Cross. President Doug Woods, CEO Peter Nosler, and secretary/treasurer Ron Davidowski (the D, P, and R) founded the company in 1990.

The company has gone green by completing several eco-friendly construction projects according to environmental standards. More than 40% of the company's projects are built to incorporate green building techniques or products, and one in four of its employees are Leadership in Energy and Environmental Design (LEED) certified.

DPR was named one of *Engineering News-Record*'s top green builders in 2008.

The company has 12 regional offices in Arizona, California, Florida, Georgia, Texas, and Virginia, and is headquartered in Redwood, California.

EXECUTIVES

President: Douglas E. (Doug) Woods
CFO: Gary Wohl
EVP: Jim Dolen
EVP: Eric Lamb
EVP: Peter A. Salvati
VP: Mike Ford
VP: George Pfeffer
Director Sustainable Construction: Ted van der Linden

Head, National Healthcare Core Market Group: Hamilton Espinosa
Head, National Advanced Technology Core Market Group: Mark Thompson, age 56
Head, National Biopharmaceutical Core Market Group: Michael Lynch
Project Executive: George Hurley
Marketing and Corporate Communications: Yumi Clevenger
Secretary and Treasurer: Ron J. Davidowski
Director Human Resources: Jorinne Jackson

LOCATIONS

HQ: DPR Construction, Inc.
1450 Veterans Blvd., Redwood City, CA 94063
Phone: 650-474-1450   **Fax:** 650-474-1451
Web: www.dprinc.com

PRODUCTS/OPERATIONS

Project Areas

Advanced Technology
Corporate Office
Education
Entertainment
Green Construction
Health Care
Life Sciences
Microelectronics
Retail

COMPETITORS

Austin Industries
Barnhill Contracting
Bechtel
Beck Group
Bovis Lend Lease
Clancy & Theys
Devcon Construction
Fluor
Hathaway Dinwiddie Construction
Hensel Phelps Construction
Hoffman Corporation
Jacobs Engineering
M. A. Mortenson
McCarthy Building
Pizzagalli Construction
Rudolph & Sletten
Skanska USA Building
Structure Tone
Swinerton
Turner Corporation
Webcor Builders
Whiting-Turner

HISTORICAL FINANCIALS

Company Type: Private

Income Statement				FYE: December 31
	REVENUE ($ mil.)	NET INCOME ($ mil.)	NET PROFIT MARGIN	EMPLOYEES
12/08	1,700	—	—	—
12/07	1,470	—	—	2,100
12/06	1,580	—	—	2,200
Annual Growth	3.7%	—	—	(4.5%)

Revenue History

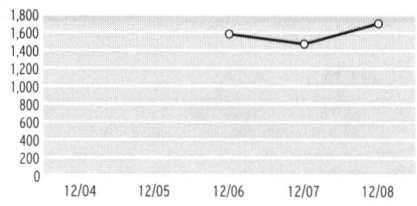

DreamWorks Studios

Stephen Spielberg has long since realized his dream. The filmmaker's DreamWorks Studios is a producer of movies and TV shows (*Tropic Thunder, Las Vegas*). Formerly owned by Paramount, it parted ways with that studio in 2008 and has formed a financing partnership with India's Reliance Entertainment. The company was founded in 1994 by Spielberg, animation guru Jeffrey Katzenberg, and recording industry maven David Geffen as an experiment in creating a diversified media firm. It struggled with any business beyond filmed entertainment, and later shed its other operations, including an arcade business and a music label. Money maker DreamWorks Animation was spun off to shareholders as a separate company in 2004.

The studio in 2009 sorted out its financing situation as an independent, private company (headed by Spielberg and his business partner, Stacey Snider) in the wake of a tumultuous credit market. Spielberg secured up to $825 million in financing — some $350 million is from Reliance, and another $150 million comes from Disney. The balance is from banks and other investors. Under its new partnership with Reliance, the studio will be able to fund its slate of five to six films a year for the next three years. (Geffen did not join the venture.) DreamWorks also switched distribution rights of its films from Paramount to Disney. Reliance will distribute the movies in India. Movies released under the new three-year partnership are scheduled for 2010. (DreamWorks had originally envisioned a five-year, $1.2 billion deal, but that fell through as a result of the economic downturn.)

Before settling its financing situation, DreamWorks released four films in 2009 (including *Hotels for Dogs*, *The Soloist*, and *The Uninvited* — none of which were breakout hits). The company's *Transformers: Revenge of the Fallen*, the sequel to the 2007 hit *Transformers* and a co-production with Paramount, opened in 2009. The movie was harshly reviewed by critics, but that didn't stop audiences from turning out in droves to see the spectacle of special effects.

DreamWorks principals and co-founders Spielberg and David Geffen left Paramount in 2008, at least partially as a result of DreamWorks feeling as though it hadn't been appreciated by Viacom (Paramount's parent company), despite the fact that DreamWorks played a large role in revitalizing Paramount the previous year with money-makers such as *Transformers*, *Norbit*, *Blades of Glory*, and *Disturbia*.

The divorce from Paramount follows more than two years of DreamWorks operating as part of that studio. Viacom bought DreamWorks for $1.6 billion and placed it under the purview of its Paramount subsidiary. To minimize the financial risk, Paramount sold the DreamWorks' library of about 60 films for $900 million to a private investment fund led by billionaire George Soros.

Katzenberg left the company to head DreamWorks Animation when that company was spun off. (The animation business made a name for itself with its hugely successful *Shrek* series, one of the most successful animated franchises of all time.) Paramount later lured former Universal Pictures chairman Stacey Snider into the fold as chairman and CEO of DreamWorks.

(She initially shared the chairman title with Geffen.) The move further cemented the turnaround of Paramount's executive suite, as Snider had a proven box office track record at Universal with such hits as *Meet the Fockers* and *The Bourne Supremacy*.

EXECUTIVES

Partner and Co-Chair: Steven Spielberg, age 62
Partner, Co-Chairman, and CEO: Stacey Snider
President and COO: Jeffrey (Jeff) Small
CFO: Larry Wasserman, age 34
Co-President, Production: Mark Sourian
Co-President, Production: Holly Bario
President, Marketing: Christine Birch
Co-Head, DreamWorks Television: Darryl Frank
Co-Head, DreamWorks Television: Justin Falvey
Head Corporate Communications: Chip Sullivan

LOCATIONS

HQ: DreamWorks Studios
   100 Universal City Plaza Dr., Bldg. 5121
   Universal City, CA 91608
Phone: 818-733-9300
Web: www.dreamworksstudios.com

PRODUCTS/OPERATIONS

Selected Films and Television Shows

DreamWorks Pictures
Almost Famous (2000)
American Beauty (1999)
Amistad (1997)
Antz (1998)
A Beautiful Mind (2001, co-produced with Universal Studios)
Blades of Glory (2007)
Catch Me if You Can (2002)
Chicken Run (2000, co-produced with Aardman Animation)
Collateral (2004, co-produced with Paramount Pictures)
Deep Impact (1998, co-produced with Paramount Pictures)
Disturbia (2007)
Dreamgirls (2006)
Galaxy Quest (1999)
Gladiator (2000, co-produced with Universal Studios)
House of Sand and Fog (2003)
Just Like Heaven (2005)
The Legend of Bagger Vance (2000)
Match Point (2005)
Memoirs of a Geisha (2005)
Minority Report (2002)
Mouse Hunt (1997)
Munich (2005)
Norbit (2007)
Old School (2003)
The Peacemaker (1997)
The Prince of Egypt (1998)
The Ring (2002)
The Ring Two (2005)
Road to Perdition (2002)
Road Trip (2000)
Saving Private Ryan (1998, co-produced with Paramount Pictures)
Seabiscuit (2003, co-produced with Paramount Pictures)
Shark Tale (2004)
Shrek (2001)
Shrek 2 (2004)
Sinbad: Legend of the Seven Seas (2003)
Small Time Crooks (2000)
The Terminal (2004)
Transformers (2007)
Tropic Thunder (2008)
War of the Worlds (2005, co-produced with Paramount Pictures)
What Lies Beneath (2000, co-produced with 20th Century Fox)
Win a Date with Tad Hamilton! (2004)

DreamWorks Television
Boomtown (2002-2003)
The Contender (2005)
Father of the Pride (2004)
Freaks and Geeks (1999-2000)
The Job (2001)
Las Vegas (2003-present)
Oliver Beene (2003)
Spin City (1996-2002)
Undeclared (2001)

COMPETITORS

Fox Filmed Entertainment
Legendary Pictures
Lionsgate
Lucasfilm
MGM
Miramax
Sony Pictures Entertainment
Universal Pictures
Warner Bros.

The Drees Company

The Drees Company, a leading homebuilder in Cincinnati, is one of the top private builders in the US. First-time home buyers and move-up customers may choose from homes that range from about $100,000 to more than $1 million. Drees also builds condominiums, town homes, and patio homes. It sells luxury homes through its Zaring Premier Homes division and more modest houses under the Marquis Homes name. The company purchases land to develop as homesites in Florida, Indiana, Kentucky, North Carolina, Ohio, Tennessee, Texas, and the Washington, DC, area. Drees also offers financing through its First Equity Mortgage subsidiary, which has closed more than $1 billion in loans over the years.

The company had been expanding through acquisitions such as the addition of the homebuilding assets of Zaring National in Cincinnati, Indianapolis, and Nashville, Tennessee, in 2000. It also bought Ausherman Homes (renamed Drees) in Frederick, Maryland (near Washington, DC). However, the economic recession has slowed such activities. The company's strategy is to invest in sales and marketing and sell and build homes for less money, while at the same time reducing its inventory of land. Drees also has been working to entice people into buying its homes. In 2009 it launched a new program that offers up to $15,000 to new buyers who lose their jobs.

A family-operated enterprise since its founding by immigrant Theodore Drees in 1928, the company is being run by the third generation of the Drees family.

EXECUTIVES

Chairman: Ralph A. Drees, age 74
President and CEO: David Drees, age 48
EVP, Secretary, and Treasurer: Lawrence G. (Larry) Herbst
EVP and CFO: Mark Williams
VP Human Resources: Effie McKeehan
VP Corporate Land: Rex Gordon
VP Marketing: Barbara Drees-Jones
VP Production: Jack Herbstreit
VP National Purchasing and Operations: David E. Metz, age 46
Director Information Systems: Mike Rulli
National Marketing Director: Patricia L. Kirk

LOCATIONS

HQ: The Drees Company
   211 Grandview Dr., Ste. 300
   Fort Mitchell, KY 41017
Phone: 859-578-4200   **Fax:** 859-341-5854
Web: www.dreeshomes.com

Division Office Locations

Austin (Texas)
Cincinnati (Fort Mitchell, KY)
Cleveland (North Canton, OH)
Dallas (Irving, TX)
Dayton (Centerville, OH)
Indianapolis (Indiana)
Jacksonville (Florida)
Nashville (Brentwood, TN)
Raleigh (North Carolina)
Washington, DC (Alexandria, VA)

COMPETITORS

D.R. Horton   M/I Homes
Fischer Homes   Pulte Homes
KB Home   The Ryland Group
Lennar

HISTORICAL FINANCIALS

Company Type: Private

Income Statement

	REVENUE ($ mil.)	NET INCOME ($ mil.)	NET PROFIT MARGIN	EMPLOYEES
3/08	833	—	—	750
3/07	1,105	—	—	900
3/06	1,120	—	—	1,226
3/05	1,183	—	—	1,339
3/04	978	—	—	1,200
Annual Growth	(3.9%)	—	—	(11.1%)

FYE: March 31

Revenue History

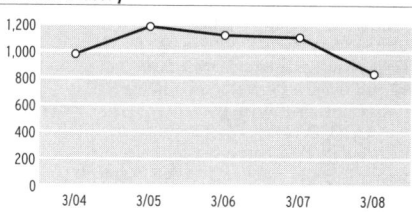

Dresser, Inc.

Is your energy business all dressed up with no place to flow? Not if Dresser can help it. The company, formerly Dresser Industries (and once a part of Halliburton), makes flow control products (valves, actuators, meters, fittings, and the like for oil and gas exploration), measurement systems (gas pumps and point of sale terminals made by business unit Dresser Wayne), power and compression systems (Waukesha engines, fuel testing systems), and infrastructure products (Roots blowers and compressors, piping systems, and pumps). Dresser serves companies in the oil and gas, power generation, water and wastewater, and other industries. The company has a presence in more than 100 countries.

Dresser has broadened its product lines and expanded geographically through acquisitions and partnerships. In 2009 it acquired iMeter, a

Netherlands-based maker of gas meters and instrumentation, bolstering its natural gas metering business with new products such as turbine meters, along with engineering and manufacturing operations in Europe. Dresser has also expanded its operations in Saudi Arabia through its Darvico joint venture with Al Rushaid Group; the JV is adding mobile valve maintenance and repair services that strenthen its valve manufacturing operations in the region.

At the same time, Dresser has added or expanded supplier agreements with Fluor (supplying control and pressure relief valves and related engineering design to Fluor projects globally); BP (retail fuel dispensers for service stations in Europe and North America); and TOTAL (supplying fuel dispensers in Europe). Supplier agreements give Dresser some protection from global economic ups and downs, as the company provides engineering and aftermarket services, in addition to equipment, for a specified period.

Acquisitions in 2007 included Dresser Piping Specialties' acquisition of Blackhawk Industries, a maker of fluid fittings, and Dresser Root's purchase of engineering and design firm ESCOR, which focuses on control systems for wastewater treatment systems, a core focus of Dresser Root. Dresser looks for small acquisitions that add new markets and products.

Dresser was acquired by an investment consortium led by Riverstone Holdings in mid-2007. Other members of the consortium include First Reserve Corporation and The Carlyle Group. First Reserve was already an investor, owning more than 90% of Dresser as of 2005 when Dresser announced plans for an IPO. After delays related to accounting problems, Dresser called off the IPO in 2006.

EXECUTIVES

President, CEO, and Director: John P. Ryan
EVP and CFO: Marty R. Kittrell, age 52
SVP Human Resources: Mark J. Scott
SVP and General Counsel: Linda Rutherford
VP Reengineering: Brian White
VP and CIO: Darren F. Whitney
VP Corporate Development: Scott Coleman
President, Power and Compression Segment:
  Barry Glickman
President, Infrastructure Solutions Segment:
  Daniel E. Jezerinac
President, Flow Technologies Segment:
  Thomas J. Laird
President, Measurement and Distribution Segment:
  Neil H. Thomas
Controller: David B. Brown
Corporate Secretary and Associate General Counsel:
  David M. Dolan
Treasurer: Richard T. Kernan
Auditors: PricewaterhouseCoopers LLP

LOCATIONS

HQ: Dresser, Inc.
  15455 Dallas Pkwy., Ste. 1100, Addison, TX 75001
Phone: 972-361-9800   **Fax:** 972-361-9903
Web: www.dresser.com

PRODUCTS/OPERATIONS

Selected Brands and Products

Andco	REDQ Regulators
Becker	Roots Blowers
Blackhawk	Roots Meters
Consolidated	Roots Provers
Masoneilan	Texstream Pumps
Mooney	Waukesha Engine
Piping Specialties	Wayne
RCS Actuators	

COMPETITORS

Cameron International	IDEX
Caterpillar	Ingersoll-Rand
CIRCOR International	ITT Corp.
Curtiss-Wright Flow	Kerr Machine
Control	Pentair
Danaher	Radiant Systems
Datamarine	Rotork
Elster American Meter	SPX
Emerson Electric	Tokheim
Flowserve	Tyco
Gilbarco	Velan

HISTORICAL FINANCIALS

Company Type: Private

Income Statement
FYE: December 31

	REVENUE ($ mil.)	NET INCOME ($ mil.)	NET PROFIT MARGIN	EMPLOYEES
12/08	2,240	—	—	6,500
12/07	2,000	—	—	6,400
12/06	1,830	—	—	6,100
12/05	1,700	—	—	6,500
12/04	1,992	—	—	8,800
Annual Growth	3.0%	—	—	(7.3%)

Revenue History

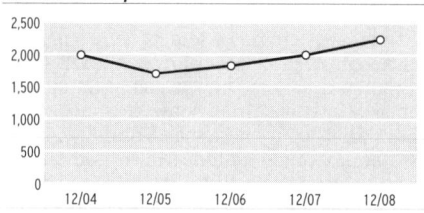

Drummond Company

Drummond does business from the ground down. The company operates the Shoal Creek underground coal mine in Alabama and the Pribbenow surface coal mine in Colombia. Drummond's ABC Coke unit produces foundry coke, which is used mainly in the automotive, construction, and sugar industries, at a plant in Alabama. It controls more than 2 billion tons of reserves and sells around 30 million annually. In addition, Drummond develops housing communities and office parks in Alabama, California, and Florida. H. E. Drummond began his company in 1935 on land homesteaded by his mother; eventually his five sons entered the business. The Drummond family still owns and manages the company.

EXECUTIVES

CEO: Garry N. Drummond Sr., age 67
CIO: John Fallis
EVP Mining: Richard Mullen
EVP and CFO: Jack Stilwell
EVP, General Counsel, and Assistant Secretary:
  Bruce C. Webster
VP Human Resources: Terry Whitt
VP Facilities Engineering: Gene Honeycutt
VP Mine Engineering and U.S. Operations: Mike Butts
President, Drummond, Ltd.: Augusto Jimenez
President, Drummond Coal Sales: George E. Wilbanks
President, ABC Coke Division: John M. Pearson

LOCATIONS

HQ: Drummond Company, Inc.
  1000 Urban Center Dr., Ste. 300
  Birmingham, AL 35242
Phone: 205-945-6300   **Fax:** 205-945-6440
Web: www.drummondco.com

PRODUCTS/OPERATIONS

Selected Operations

ABC Coke (coke plant, Alabama)
Liberty Park (real estate development, Alabama)
Mina Pribbenow (coal, Colombia)
Oakbridge (real estate development, Florida)
Puerto Drummond (port facilities, Colombia)
Rancho La Quinta (real estate development, California)
Shoal Creek Mine (coal, Alabama)

COMPETITORS

Alliance Resource	Peabody Energy
Arch Coal	Penn Virginia
CONSOL Energy	Sherritt International
Massey Energy	Walter Energy
Oxbow	Westmoreland Coal

HISTORICAL FINANCIALS

Company Type: Private

Income Statement
FYE: December 31

	REVENUE ($ mil.)	NET INCOME ($ mil.)	NET PROFIT MARGIN	EMPLOYEES
12/08	2,870	—	—	6,000
12/07	1,890	—	—	5,600
12/06	1,770	—	—	5,100
12/05	1,798	—	—	5,100
Annual Growth	16.9%	—	—	5.6%

Revenue History

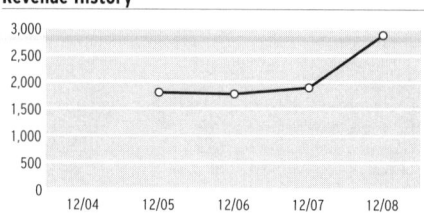

Duane Reade

Duane Reade is the Big Apple of drugstores. Named after the two streets where its first store was located, the company is the market leader in densely populated Manhattan. In all, the firm operates about 240 stores in New York and about a dozen in New Jersey. About 60% of the stores are in high-traffic Manhattan (giving the firm more sales per square foot than any other US drugstore chain). Duane Reade's stores vary greatly in size (500 to 12,700 sq. ft.). The company sells prescription drugs, but more than 50% of sales come from items such as over-the-counter medications, food and beverages, and health and beauty aids. Duane Reade is owned by the private equity group Oak Hill Capital Partners.

The deep recession in the US and layoffs on Wall Street have conspired to slow same-store sales growth at Duane Reade stores. To cope, it has been cutting costs, but not at the expense of positioning the chain for the future.

Under the leadership of chairman and CEO John Lederer, who joined the company in 2008 from the Canadian supermarket chain Loblaw, Duane Reade has assembled a new top management team, including a chief merchandising officer from Canada's Shoppers Drug Mart. Lederer is working on developing a new "urban drugstore box," exemplified by a recently renovated location at New York's Penn Station. The prototype — which features a larger pharmacy at the back of the store, wider aisles up front, and fresh foods cases with sandwiches and salads delivered daily — is the model for the firm's urban locations going forward. The company has introduced new in-store services, including professional tooth whitening, and diet planning. Duane Reade is also experimenting with ATM-like movie vending machines, coffee kiosks, and "Skin Wellness Centers" to boost sales. Currently the company operates Skin Wellness Centers in about 40 stores.

In 2008 Duane Reade opened 15 new stores, seven of which conform to the new prototype. By the end of 2009, about 30 stores will fit the new mold. The firm is also planning to expand its private-label offering. By the end of 2009, it expect to have added about 1,000 new items to its private-label menu of non-pharmacy products. Currently, Duane Reade stores offer more than 800 private-label products (including its "apt.5" line of cosmetics), which account for about 9% of non-pharmacy sales.

The firm buys most of its non-pharmacy products directly from manufacturers and distributes those items through its warehouses in New Jersey and Queens.

EXECUTIVES

Chairman and CEO: John A. Lederer, age 52
SVP and CFO: John K. Henry, age 59
SVP Pharmacy Operations: Frank V. Scorpiniti, age 38
SVP Store Operations: Charles R. (Chuck) Newsom, age 58
SVP, General Counsel, and Secretary: Phillip A. Bradley, age 54
SVP Human Resources and Administration: Vincent A. Scarfone, age 51
SVP and Chief Merchandising Officer: Joseph C. Magnacca, age 46
SVP Supply Chain: Mark W. Scharbo, age 45
VP Real Estate: Mark Bander
VP and CIO: Marc Saffer
VP Finance: Anthony M. Goldrick
VP and Controller: Chris A. Darrow
VP Asset Protection: William M. Knievel
VP Distribution: Donald L. Yuhasz
Auditors: KPMG LLP

LOCATIONS

HQ: Duane Reade Inc.
440 9th Ave., New York, NY 10001
Phone: 212-273-5700 **Fax:** 212-244-6527
Web: www.duanereade.com

2008 Stores

	No.
Manhattan	148
Brooklyn	31
Queens	27
Bronx	11
New Jersey	11
Staten Island	8
Nassau County, NY	8
Westchester County, NY	6
Suffolk County, NY	1
Total	**251**

PRODUCTS/OPERATIONS

2008 Sales

	$ mil.	% of total
Front-end	956.5	54
Pharmacy	817.5	46
Total	**1,774.0**	**100**

Selected Merchandise and Services

Automated teller machines
Cosmetics
Food and beverage items
Greeting cards
Health and beauty aids
Hosiery
Housewares
Lottery ticket sales
Nutritional products
Over-the-counter medications
Photo supplies
Photofinishing
Prescription drugs
Seasonal merchandise
Tobacco products
Vitamins

COMPETITORS

A&P
CVS Caremark
D'Agostino Supermarkets
drugstore.com
Rite Aid
Walgreen

HISTORICAL FINANCIALS

Company Type: Private

Income Statement

FYE: Saturday nearest December 31

	REVENUE ($ mil.)	NET INCOME ($ mil.)	NET PROFIT MARGIN	EMPLOYEES
12/08	1,774	(73)	—	6,800
12/07	1,687	(88)	—	6,700
12/06	1,585	(79)	—	6,100
12/05	1,590	(100)	—	6,100
12/04	1,598	(52)	—	6,300
Annual Growth	**2.6%**	**—**	**—**	**1.9%**

Net Income History

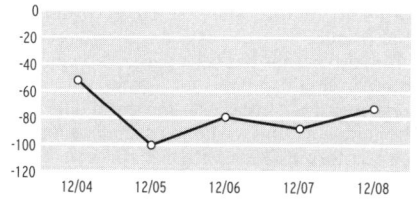

Duke University Health System

Antibodies inside ya dukin' it out? Better get to the Duke University Health System — no, no, not the campus infirmary, the Medical Center. At the core of the Duke University Health System is the Duke University Hospital. The system also includes two community hospitals in Durham (Durham Regional Hospital) and Raleigh (Duke Raleigh Hospital), North Carolina. Its network of medical facilities provides such services as primary and specialty care, home and hospice care, clinical research, and public education programs. The total capacity of all three hospitals combined is about 1,500 beds. The Duke University Health System is closely affiliated with the Duke University Medical School.

It is also affiliated with the Duke University School of Nursing. The three entities are all part of the Duke University Medical Center (research, educational, and clinical care facilities on the Duke campus), also known as Duke Medical.

The Health System works closely with the university's medical divisions to advance biomedical and general medical research and to train health care professionals in cutting-edge technologies and infrastructures.

The Duke University Health System was formed in 1998 to expand the core Medical Center operations and has since added the Durham and Raleigh facilities. It intends to expand further in its existing and additional territories. The system also plans to expand in areas such as cancer, vascular, and musculoskeletal care, as well as outpatient ambulatory care.

EXECUTIVES

Chair: Thomas M. Gorrie
President, CEO, and Director: Victor J. Dzau, age 63
Chief Patient Safety Officer: Karen Frush
SVP Clinical Affairs; CEO, Duke University Hospital: William J. Fulkerson Jr.
SVP, CFO, and Treasurer: Kenneth C. Morris
VP Medical Affairs; Vice Dean, Duke University School of Medicine: Michael Cuffe
VP Government and Community Affairs and External Relations, Duke University Medical Center and Duke University Health System: Gwynn Swinson
VP Administration; Associate Dean, Veteran Affairs, Duke University School of Medicine: Monte D. Brown
VP Ambulatory Care; Executive Director, Duke Private Diagnostic Clinic and Duke Patient Revenue Management Organization: Paul R. Newman
VP Duke Medicine Development and Alumni Affairs: Michael J. (Mike) Morsberger
VP Business Development and Chief Strategic Planning Officer; Vice Chancellor, Medical Center Integrated Planning, Duke University: Molly K. O'Neill
VP Diagnostic Services and CIO, Duke University Health System and Duke University Medical Center: Asif Ahmad
Dean, Duke University School of Nursing; Vice Chancellor, Academic Affairs Duke University: Nancy Andrews
President, Private Diagnostic Clinic: Carl E. Ravin
CEO, Durham Regional Hospital: Kerry Watson
CEO, Duke Raleigh Hospital: Douglas B. (Doug) Vinsel

LOCATIONS

HQ: Duke University Health System
3701 Duke Medical Center, Durham, NC 27706
Phone: 919-684-8111
Web: www.dukehealth.org

COMPETITORS

Carolinas HealthCare System
Cumberland County Hospital System
Danville Regional Medical Center
FirstHealth of the Carolinas
Morehead Memorial Hospital
Moses Cone Health
Novant Health
UNC Hospitals
University Health Systems of Eastern Carolina
Wake Forest University Baptist Medical Center
WakeMed

HISTORICAL FINANCIALS

Company Type: Private

Income Statement				FYE: June 30
	ESTIMATED REVENUE ($ mil.)	NET INCOME ($ mil.)	NET PROFIT MARGIN	EMPLOYEES
6/08	1,900	—	—	29,826
6/07	1,700	—	—	30,000
6/06	1,584	—	—	30,551
6/05	1,500	—	—	10,391
6/04	1,400	—	—	—
Annual Growth	7.9%	—	—	42.1%

Revenue History

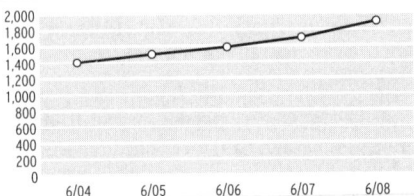

Dunavant Enterprises

King Cotton is alive and well in Memphis. Homegrown Dunavant Enterprises is one of the largest cotton traders in the world, handling more than 6 million bales of cotton per year. The company, which grew by selling aggressively to China and the Soviet Union, maintains cotton-buying offices in Africa, Asia, Australia, Europe, Latin America, and the southern US. Dunavant also maintains cotton ginning operations, which have a capacity of handling 700,000 bales (or more than 150,000 metric tons) of cotton every year. Dunavant Enterprises is owned by the Dunavant family and company employees.

The company has cotton warehouses in the US and Australia, and ginning operations in Zambia, Uganda, Mozambique, and Australia.

Dunavant also owns various real estate development companies and a truck-brokerage company. Dunavant was founded in 1960 by William Dunavant, his son Billy (who is allergic to cotton), and Samuel T. Reeves. (The elder Dunavant died shortly after the founding, and Reeves left in 1995 to form Pinnacle Trading.)

EXECUTIVES

Chairman: William B. (Billy) Dunavant Jr.
President and CEO: William B. Dunavant III
President, Dunavant of California: Roger Glaspey
Secretary and General Counsel:
 William (Bill) Stubblefield
Manager Human Resources: Mike Andereck

LOCATIONS

HQ: Dunavant Enterprises, Inc.
 3797 New Getwell Rd., Memphis, TN 38118
Phone: 901-369-1500 **Fax:** 901-369-1608
Web: www.dunavant.com

COMPETITORS

Calcot
Cargill
J.G. Boswell Co.
King Ranch
Plains Cotton
Plexus Cotton
Southwestern Irrigated Cotton
Staplcotn
Weil Brothers Cotton

Dunkin' Brands

Doughnuts and ice cream make sweet bedfellows at Dunkin' Brands. The company is a leading multi-concept quick-service franchisor that operates both the Dunkin' Donuts and Baskin-Robbins chains. It has more than 15,000 franchise locations operating in more than 40 countries. With more than 8,800 units in 30 countries (about 6,400 in North America), Dunkin' Donuts is the world's leading chain of doughnut shops. Baskin-Robbins is a top ice cream and frozen snacks outlet with its more than 6,000 locations (2,600 in the US). Dunkin' Brands is owned by a group of private investment firms including Bain Capital, The Carlyle Group, and Thomas H. Lee Partners.

Like other quick-service franchising businesses, Dunkin' Brands owns all the intellectual property connected to its restaurant concepts and licenses those brands to its franchise operators. It also controls how its franchisees operate their shops to ensure consistency in food quality and service throughout its chains. By using a franchising model, Dunkin' Brands has been able to expand its doughnut and ice cream concepts without the cost of new construction and operating expenses. Its growth has put the company in the same league as other big multi-concept outfits including Wendy's/Arby's Group and YUM Brands.

Dunkin' Brands has been particularly focused on expanding its chains into growing international markets such as Asia and the Middle East. The company's Baskin-Robbins chain is forging new territory in China, with plans to open 100 ice cream stores through 2018. About 100 Dunkin' Donuts outposts are slated to open in Taiwan by 2017. Meanwhile, the company is working with its Gulf region licensee, Galadari Ice Cream Company, to expand Baskin-Robbins' presence in several Middle East countries. Domestically, Dunkin' Brands is looking to push its concepts out of their core markets: Dunkin' Donuts has

long been a powerhouse in the Northeast, while Baskin-Robbins has a stronghold in California.

At the same time it is adding new franchise locations. Dunkin' Brands is working to upgrade and enhance its aging brands with new menu items. Dunkin' Donuts has focused its marketing efforts on coffee, taking on Starbucks and McDonald's in the morning java business. It also launched a line of sandwiches for breakfast and lunch in 2009 designed to drive additional traffic and boost sales. Baskin-Robbins, meanwhile, unveiled a line of iced drinks that same year, along with soft-serve ice cream.

Early in 2009, Nigel Travis replaced Jon Luther as CEO. He previously served as head of #3 pizza delivery chain Papa John's. Luther, who remained as chairman, had led Dunkin' Brands since 2003 when he was brought in from AFC Enterprises' Popeyes Chicken & Biscuits chain.

Formerly part of UK-based beverage maker Allied Domecq, Dunkin' Brands was acquired for $2.4 billion in 2006 by Bain Capital, The Carlyle Group, and Thomas H. Lee. The UK distiller had been acquired the previous year by French beverage maker Pernod Ricard, which then sold the restaurant business to focus on its core drinks operations.

EXECUTIVES

Chairman: Jon L. Luther, age 66
CEO: Nigel Travis, age 59
CFO: Kate S. Lavelle
CIO: Daniel J. (Dan) Sheehan
Chief Multibrand and New Market Entry Officer:
 Tom Wyczawski
Chief Legal Officer and General Counsel:
 Stephen (Steve) Horn, age 62
Chief Global Communications and Public Affairs Officer: Stephen J. (Steve) Caldeira, age 51
SVP and General Counsel: Richard J. (Rich) Emmett, age 52
SVP Human Resources: Christine Deputy
SVP Corporate Communications: Karen Raskopf
Executive Chef and Director Culinary Development:
 Stan Frankenthaler
Chief Creative and Innovation Officer:
 Joseph (Joe) Scafido
Chief Administrative Officer: Paul Leech
Chief Global Customer and Marketing Officer:
 John H. Costello, age 59
Executive Pastry Chef: Christopher Boos, age 47
Auditors: KPMG Audit Plc

LOCATIONS

HQ: Dunkin' Brands, Inc.
 130 Royall St., Canton, MA 02021
Phone: 781-737-3000 **Fax:** 781-737-4000
Web: www.dunkinbrands.com

COMPETITORS

Auntie Anne's
Burger King
Dairy Queen
FOCUS Brands
Freshëns
Kahala
Krispy Kreme
McDonald's
Mrs. Fields
Starbucks
Subway
Tim Hortons
Wendy's/Arby's Group, Inc.
YUM!

Duquesne Light Holdings

As energy markets deregulated, the venerable Duquesne Light Holdings (founded 1880) restructured PDQ. Its principal subsidiary, regulated utility Duquesne Light, distributes electricity to 580,000 customers in southwestern Pennsylvania. The company had divested non-core assets to concentrate on its power utility and energy services businesses; it changed its name in 2003 to mark the shift. In 2007 a consortium led by Macquarie Infrastructure Partners and Diversified Utilities and Energy Trust acquired Duquesne Light for about $3 billion in cash and debt.

EXECUTIVES

Chairman and CEO: Morgan K. O'Brien, age 48
SVP and CFO: Stevan R. Schott, age 45
SVP and Chief Strategic Officer: James E. Wilson, age 44
SVP and Chief Legal and Administrative Officer: Maureen L. Hogel, age 48
VP and Treasurer; President, DQE Financial: William F. Fields, age 58
Corporate Communications Representative: Joseph Vallarian
Auditors: Deloitte & Touche LLP

LOCATIONS

HQ: Duquesne Light Holdings, Inc.
411 7th Ave., Pittsburgh, PA 15219
Phone: 412-393-6000   **Fax:** 412-393-5517
Web: www.duquesnelight.com

COMPETITORS

Allegheny Energy	FirstEnergy
Dominion Resources	PPL Corporation
EQT Corporation	UGI
Exelon	

E. & J. Gallo Winery

E. & J. Gallo Winery brings merlot to the masses. The company is one of the world's largest winemakers, thanks in part to its inexpensive jug and box brands, including Carlo Rossi, Peter Vella, and Boone's Farm brands. The vintner owns seven wineries and about 20,000 acres of California vineyards. It is the leading US exporter of California wine, selling its some 60 brands in more than 90 countries across the globe. Among its premium wines and imports are those of Gallo Family Vineyards Sonoma Reserve and the Italian wine Ecco Domani. For those who prefer a little more kick to their imbibing, Gallo distills several lines of brandy and one gin label.

Gallo once only sold wine in the low-to-moderate price range, but now sells across a wide price range, from alcohol-added wines and wine coolers to upscale varietals that fetch more than $50 a bottle. It has successfully expanded premium wines such as Turning Leaf and Frei Brothers, which don't have the Gallo name on the label. It also imports wines from Argentina, Australia, France, Germany, Italy, New Zealand, South Africa, and Spain.

The company has tried new approaches to marketing its products, such as sponsoring pro volleyball tournaments. It also rebranded its California wines as the "Gallo Family Vineyards" and removed the Ernest & Julio tag from its packaging and advertising. In 2008 it began producing wines under the MARTHA STEWART VINTAGE label. Offering three varieties — chardonnay, cabernet sauvignon, and merlot — the label is a limited-release product consisting of 15,000 cases.

In addition to using its own grapes, Gallo buys the fruit from other Sonoma County growers. Its 2002 purchase of fellow Sonoma County vintner Louis M. Martini Winery marked the first time Gallo bought an entire winery rather than land or wine labels. Gallo invested about $1 million in capital improvements at the winery and ramped up production of cabernet under the Martini label. Along with brewing wine and spirits, Gallo makes its own labels and bottles at its subsidiary, Gallo Glass.

Founded in 1933, the company is still owned and operated by the Gallo family.

HISTORY

Giuseppe Gallo, the father of Ernest and Julio Gallo, was born in 1882 in the wine country of northwest Italy. Around 1900 he and his brother, Michelo (they called themselves Joe and Mike), traveled to America seeking fame and fortune in San Francisco. Both brothers became wealthy growing grapes and anticipating the growth of the market during Prohibition (homemade wine was legal and popular).

Giuseppe's eldest sons, Ernest and Julio, worked with their father from the beginning, but their relationship was strained. The father was reluctant to help his sons, particularly Ernest, in business. However, the mysterious murder-suicide that ended the lives of Giuseppe and his wife in 1933 eliminated that problem: The sons inherited the business their father had been unwilling to share.

From then on, Ernest ran the business end, assembling a large distribution network and building a national brand, while Julio made the wine and Joe Jr., the third, much younger, brother, worked for them. In the early 1940s Gallo opened bottling plants in Los Angeles and New Orleans, using screw-cap bottles, which then seemed more hygienic and modern than corks. Gallo lagged during WWII, when alcohol was diverted for the military. Under Julio's supervision, it upgraded its planting stock and refined its technology.

In an attempt to capitalize on the sweet wines popular in the 1950s, Gallo introduced Thunderbird, a fortified wine (its alcohol content boosted to 20%), in 1957. In the 1960s Gallo spurred its growth by heavily advertising and keeping prices low. It introduced Hearty Burgundy, a jug wine, in 1964, along with Ripple. Gallo introduced the carbonated, fruit-flavored Boone's Farm Apple Wine in 1969, creating short-term interest in "pop" wines.

The company introduced its first varietal wines in 1974. In the 1970s Gallo field workers switched unions, from the United Farm Workers to the Teamsters. Repercussions included protests and boycotts, but sales were largely unaffected. From 1976 to 1982 Gallo operated under an FTC order limiting its control over wholesalers. The order was lifted after the industry's competitive balance changed.

Through the 1970s and 1980s, Gallo expanded its production of varietals; in 1988 it began adding vintage dates to labels. But it also kept a hand in the lower levels of the market, introducing Bartles & Jaymes wine coolers.

Gallo began a legal battle in 1986 with Joe, who had been eased out of the business, over the use of the Gallo name. In 1992 Joe lost the use of his name for commercial purposes. Julio died the next year when his Jeep overturned on a family ranch.

In 1996 rival Kendall-Jackson sued Gallo for trademark infringement over Gallo's new wine brand, Turning Leaf, claiming Gallo copied its Vintner's Reserve bottle and label. A jury ruled in Gallo's favor in 1997; a federal appeals court supported that decision in 1998.

In 2000 Gallo announced plans to promote wine-cooler market leader Bartles & Jaymes with a new advertising campaign, although the category continued to wane. The next year, Gallo expanded the technological end of the wine business. Gallo's research team patented a number of tools licensed to winemakers around the world; one tool, for example, can diagnose a sick vine in a matter of hours, rather than years.

The purchase of Louis M. Martini Winery in Napa Valley in 2002 furthered Gallo's expansion into premium wines. In 2004 it bought the brand name and stocks of San Jose-based wine producer Mirassou Vineyards, one of the oldest wineries in California, and Santa Barbara company Bindlewood Weste Winery. In 2005 Gallo added Grape Links, Inc., maker of Barefoot Cellars, to its stable of holdings.

Ernest Gallo died in 2007 at the age of 97.

EXECUTIVES

Co-Chairman, President, and CEO: Joseph E. (Joe) Gallo, age 66
Co-Chairman: Robert J. (Bob) Gallo, age 74
Co-Chairman: James E. (Jim) Coleman, age 74
EVP and General Counsel: Jack B. Owens
VP and General Manager, Europe: Devinder Singh
VP Operations: Steven (Steve) Kidd
VP Sales and Administration: Peter Abate
VP and CIO: Kent Kushar
VP Marketing and Chief Marketing Strategist: Gerald (Gerry) Glasgow
VP North Coast Operations: Matt Gallo
VP Finance: Doug Vilas
VP Grower Relations: Gregory J. (Greg) Coleman, age 50
VP Gallo Glass: John Gallo, age 48
VP Supply Chain and Logistics: Ulli Thiersch
VP Strategic Planning and Public Relations: Susan Hensley
VP US Sales: Steve Sprinkle
VP Viticulture: Nick K. Dokoozlian
VP National Sales: Gary Ippolito
VP Communications: George Marsden
Director Winemaking: Gina Gallo
Director Global Consumer Relations: Marie Shubin
Director National Trade Development: Joseph (Joe) Farnan
Director Marketing: Stephanie Gallo, age 37
Director Wine Education and Hospitality: Patrick Dodd

LOCATIONS

HQ: E. & J. Gallo Winery
600 Yosemite Blvd., Modesto, CA 95354
Phone: 209-341-3111
Web: www.gallo.com

PRODUCTS/OPERATIONS

Selected Brands

Spirits
E. & J. VS Brandy
E. & J. VSOP Brandy
E. & J. XO Brandy
New Amsterdam Gin

Wine
Anapamu
André
Ballatore
Barefoot Bubbly
BarefootCellars
Bartles & Jaymes
Bella Sera
Black Swan
Boone's Farm
Bridlewood Estate Winery
Carlo Rossi
Cask & Cream
Clarendon Hills
Dancing Bull
DaVinci
Don Miguel Gascon
Ecco Domani
Frei Brothers
Frutézia
Gallo Family Vineyard Estate
Gallo Family Vineyard Single Vineyard
Gallo Family Vineyard Sonoma Reserve
Gallo Family Vineyard Twin Valley
Ghost Pines
Hornsby's
Indigo Hills
Liberty Creek
Livingston Cellars
Louis M. Martini
MacMurray Ranch
Marcelina
Martn Cõdax
Maso Canali
Mattie's Perch
McWilliam's
Mirassou
Peter Vella
Põlka Dot
Rancho Zabaco
Red Bicyclette
Red Rock Winery
Redwood Creek
Sebeka
Tisdale Vineyards
Turning Leaf
Turning Leaf Sonoma Reserve
Whitehaven
Wild Vines
William Hill Estate
Wycliff Sparkling

COMPETITORS

Asahi Breweries	LVMH
Bacardi	Newton Vineyard
Bacardi USA	Pernod Ricard
Bronco Wine Co.	Premier Pacific
Brown-Forman	Ravenswood Winery
Concha y Toro	Robert Mondavi Winery
Constellation Wines	Scheid Vineyards
Diageo	Sebastiani Vineyards
Diageo Chateau & Estate	Sunview Vineyards
Wines	Taittinger
Foster's Americas	Terlato Wine
Foster's Group	Trinchero Family Estates
GIV	UST llc
Heaven Hill Distilleries	Vincor
Kendall-Jackson	Wine Group
Kirin Holdings Company	

HISTORICAL FINANCIALS

Company Type: Private

Income Statement

FYE: December 31

	ESTIMATED REVENUE ($ mil.)	NET INCOME ($ mil.)	NET PROFIT MARGIN	EMPLOYEES
12/08	2,000	—	—	5,000
12/07	3,150	—	—	5,000
12/06	2,700	—	—	4,600
12/05	2,700	—	—	4,400
12/04	3,000	—	—	—
Annual Growth	(9.6%)	—	—	4.4%

Revenue History

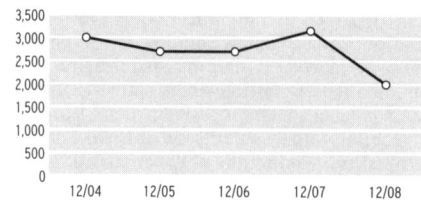

EBSCO Industries

Few portfolios are more diverse than that of EBSCO Industries (short for Elton B. Stephens Company). Among the conglomerate's more than 40 information services, manufacturing, and sales subsidiaries are magazine subscription and fulfillment firms, a fishing lure manufacturer, a rifle manufacturer, a specialty office and computer furniture retailer, and a real estate company. Its main businesses revolve around the publishing industry: EBSCO operates a subscription management agency and is one of the largest publishers of digital information. It has a database of more than 300,000 title listings from more than 78,000 publishers worldwide. The family of founder Elton B. Stephens Sr. owns the company.

EBSCO provides bulk subscription services for print and electronic journals, technical reports, books, and other publications to schools, libraries, and professional offices. The company offers sales, promotion, telemarketing, and fulfillment services to publishers, and it owns commercial printers and supplies bindery and packaging products. Its EBSCOhost is an online research service for universities, public libraries, and K-12 schools.

Among EBSCO's eclectic subsidiaries are PRADCO Fishing, which makes fishing lures; Valley Joist, which produces steel construction materials; Vulcan Industries, which makes point-of-purchase displays; Knight & Hale, which makes hunting accessories; specialty furniture makers H. Wilson and Luxor; and real estate unit EBSCO Development.

The acquisitive company's recent purchases include Hallmark Data Systems, a provider of subscription fulfillment services to business-to-business magazines; Lindy Little Joe, a sportfishing products company; and independent insurance agency ANB Insurance Services.

HISTORY

During the 1930s Elton B. Stephens Sr. put himself through college selling magazine subscriptions. Although he later earned a law degree, Stephens thought he could make more money selling magazines. Stephens and his wife, Alys, formed Military Service Co. in 1944 to sell magazines, binders, and display racks to the US military.

Early in his career Stephens suggested that he'd like to own five companies so that he'd have a fallback if one failed. He set about fulfilling his wish, forming Metal Fabricators and Finishers (now Vulcan Industries) in 1946, Vulcan Binder & Cover (now Vulcan Information Packaging) in 1947, and Vulcan Enterprises (now Directional Advertising Services) in 1954. In 1958 the Stephens' businesses were combined under the name EBSCO Industries, Inc. (the name is an acronym for Elton B. Stephens Company). In 1960 EBSCO acquired Chicago's Hanson-Bennett Magazine Agency, and in 1967 the company purchased Los Angeles' National Publications and binder manufacturer The Burkhardt Co. of Detroit.

Stephens retired as president of the company in 1971, and his son James took over. The following year EBSCO bought the Franklin Square Agency and Ziff-Davis' subscription service, doubling the volume of EBSCO Subscription Services. EBSCO started its Publisher Promotion and Fulfillment service and added operations in Europe in 1975.

EBSCO acquired Valley Joist (metal construction products) in 1976 and H. Wilson Co. (audiovisual and computer furniture) in 1977. EBSCO Curriculum Materials and EBSCO Reception Room Subscription Services were formed in 1979 and 1980, respectively. Purchases in 1980 included Metro Press (now EBSCO Graphics), National Billiard, and PRADCO (fishing lures).

In 1981 Elton began a second career at age 70 when he founded Alabama Bancorp.

Under James's direction, EBSCO continued to grow through acquisitions and startups. It bought Four Seasons (promotional clothing and other items, 1983) and NSC International (binding and laminating products, 1984). The company formed electronic database publisher EBSCO Electronic Information (now EBSCO Publishing, 1986) and bought Bomber Bait (1988).

After a short breather, the company acquired Luxor (school and library furniture) in 1992. That year the various Vulcan operations were combined in a new facility in Moody, Alabama. The company acquired Dynamic Information (later EBSCO Document Services) in 1994. The following year it bought Northeast Looseleaf (now part of Vulcan Information Packaging), and in 1996 it formed EBSCO Magazine Express.

The next year EBSCO bought Fred Arbogast, maker of the Jitterbug and Hula Popper fishing lures, and hunting game-call maker Knight & Hale. In 1998 the company bought Network Support, a Canadian maker of document imaging and management software, and closed down its document delivery unit. That year EBSCO Development Company was formed, beginning plans for Mount Laurel — a traditional neighborhood development. In 1999 EBSCO Publishing revealed Searchasaurus, an online search engine for children. The following year EBSCO formed EBSCOPrint.com to sell promotional products via the Internet.

In order to handle all its insurance needs in-house, in 2001 EBSCO acquired insurance firm S.S. Nesbitt & Co. In 2003 EBSCO acquired the European operations of RoweCom, an online service giving libraries access to more than 240,000 periodicals.

James Stephens announced in 2004 that he would step down as CEO in 2005 and appointed company executive Dixon Brooke Jr. (James's brother-in-law) as his replacement.

In 2005 EBSCO expanded its medicine and consumer health data with the acquisition of the assets of HealthGate Data's patient content repository business for $8.1 million in cash.

EXECUTIVES

Chairman: James T. (J.T.) Stephens
President and CEO: F. Dixon Brooke Jr.
VP and CFO: Richard L. (Rick) Bozzelli
VP and Chief Accounting Officer: Carol M. Johnson
VP and Director, Human Resources and Training:
John Thompson
VP and General Manager, Crown Products: Bob Bickert
VP Acquisitions: David Walker
**President, EBSCO Information Services and EBSCO
Book Services:** Allen Powell
President and General Manager, EBSCO Publishing:
Timothy R. (Tim) Collins

LOCATIONS

HQ: EBSCO Industries Inc.
5724 Hwy. 280 East, Birmingham, AL 35242
Phone: 205-991-6600   **Fax:** 205-995-1636
Web: www.ebscoind.com

PRODUCTS/OPERATIONS

Selected Operations

Information Services
  EBSCO Information Services (reference databases,
    online journals, and subscription services)
  EBSCO Publishing (database publishing and
    information retrieval services)
  EBSCO Subscription Services (subscription services
    for libraries and institutions)
Manufacturing
  EBSCO Media (commercial printer)
  Knight & Hale Game Calls
  Knight Rifles
  Luxor (specialty furniture for offices, schools, libraries,
    and health care facilities)
  PRADCO Outdoor Brands (fishing lures, fishing line,
    and related products)
  Valley Joist (steel joists, girders, and metal decks for
    the construction industry)
  Vitronic (promotional products)
  Vulcan Industries (point-of-purchase displays)
  Vulcan Information Packaging (binders, tabs, and
    packaging for albums, software, and videotapes)
  Wayne Industries (point-of-purchase advertising and
    signs)
Sales
  EBSCO Development Co. (real estate development)
  EBSCO Magazine Express (direct-marketing
    subscription agency)
  EBSCO Realty (real estate broker)
  EBSCO Reception Room Subscription Services
    (subscription services for professional offices)
  EBSCO TeleServices (telemarketing services)
  Military Service Company (producer and
    manufacturers' representative serving military base
    exchanges)
  NSC International (distribution of binding and
    laminating systems)
  Publisher Promotion and Fulfillment (promotion and
    fulfillment services)
  Publishers' Warehouse (publishers' warehousing and
    shipping service)
  S.S. Nesbitt & Co. (insurance)
  Vulcan Service (magazine subscription sales)

COMPETITORS

AMREP
APAC Customer Services
Bowne
Brunswick Corp.
Dai Nippon Printing
HALO Holding
Johnson Outdoors
McGraw-Hill
Quebecor
Reed Elsevier Group
Roanoke Bar Division
R.R. Donnelley
Scholastic
Simon Worldwide
Thomson Reuters
TRG Customer Solutions

Eby-Brown Company

Eby-Brown makes its money on such vices as munchies and nicotine. The company is a leading convenience-store supplier that distributes more than 11,000 products to about 12,000 customers in 28 states mostly east of the Mississippi. It operates eight distribution centers that supply such items as beverages, candy and snack foods, frozen and refrigerated foods, tobacco products, and general merchandise. In addition, the company offers advertising and promotion services for its customers. The family-owned Eby-Brown was founded in 1887 by the Wake family.

Looking to expand into the prepared foods segment, Eby-Brown in 2007 launched a new division called Wakefield Sandwich Company. The new unit supplies fresh, prepared sandwiches and breakfast sandwiches, along with related warmers and other display equipment.

EXECUTIVES

Co-President: Richard W. (Dick) Wake, age 55
Co-President: Thomas G. (Tom) Wake, age 49
CFO: Mark Smetana
CIO: Kevin Reilly
EVP Cigarette Purchasing: Jode Bunce
VP Business Development: Ron Coppel
Manager Human Resources: Steve Bundy
Auditors: Deloitte & Touche

LOCATIONS

HQ: Eby-Brown Company, LLC
280 W. Shuman Blvd., Ste. 280
Naperville, IL 60566
Phone: 630-778-2800   **Fax:** 630-778-2830
Web: www.eby-brown.com

Selected Distribution Locations

Baltimore
Eau Claire, WI
Montgomery, IL
Naperville, IL
Plainfield, IN
Rockmart, GA
Springfield, OH
Ypsilanti, MI

COMPETITORS

AMCON Distributing	H.T. Hackney
Atlantic Dominion	McLane
C & S Wholesale	Nash-Finch
Core-Mark	S. Abraham & Sons
GSC Enterprises	

Eddie Bauer

Nonagenarian Eddie Bauer is looking to the future with a focus on the past. The multi-channel retailer operates about 370 stores throughout North America, as well as a catalog and Web site. The company sells outerwear, apparel, and accessories for active outdoorsmen and women. It also licenses its name for eyewear, furniture, bicycles, and Ford SUVs and has stores in Japan through a joint venture there. A descendant of former top US direct retailer Spiegel, Eddie Bauer has struggled to find its niche in today's crowded marketplace. Eddie Bauer Holdings, formed in a reorganization in 2005, filed for Chapter 11 bankruptcy protection in June 2009 and was sold at auction to investment firm Golden Gate Capital (GGC).

The San Francisco-based private equity firm has a large stable of multi-channel retailers, including Express, J. Jill, and Orchard Brands. GGC retained Eddie Bauer's management and plans to keep most of its retail stores open. It is also on board with Eddie Bauer's pre-sale strategy of returning to its outdoor roots in an attempt to reconnect with customers. To that end, the company recently launched the First Ascent line of high-performance mountaineering gear and apparel, including backpacks, knives, and tents slated to be rolled out to about half the company's stores in the fall. The retailer's Heritage Collection will revive the "old" albeit updated Eddie Bauer look.

Prior to filing for bankruptcy, CEO Neil Fiske tried to right the company by closing stores, cutting jobs, freezing salaries, and even shrinking the size of its board to reduce costs. The cuts, designed to reduce expenses by up to $15 million, followed what Fiske described as a "brutal" fourth quarter for retailers.

EXECUTIVES

President: Neil S. Fiske Jr., age 47,
$3,163,452 total compensation
VP: Marv Toland, age 47, $455,527 total compensation
VP: Freya R. Brier, age 51

LOCATIONS

HQ: Eddie Bauer LLC
10401 NE 8th St., Ste. 500, Bellevue, WA 98004
Phone: 425-755-6544   **Fax:** 425-755-7696
Web: www.eddiebauer.com

PRODUCTS/OPERATIONS

2008 Stores

	No.
Eddie Bauer	255
Eddie Bauer Outlet	121
Total	**376**

2008 Sales

	$ mil.	% of total
Retail & outlet stores	697.1	68
Direct	274.2	27
Other (includes licensing, royalties & shipping)	52.1	5
Total	**1,023.4**	**100**

Selected Catalogs

Eddie Bauer (sportswear and accessories for men and
  women)
Eddie Bauer HOME (home furnishings and gifts)

Stores

Eddie Bauer
Eddie Bauer Outlet

COMPETITORS

Abercrombie & Fitch	L.L. Bean
American Eagle Outfitters	Macy's
AnnTaylor	Nordstrom
Chico's FAS	North Face
Coldwater Creek	Patagonia, Inc.
Columbia Sportswear	Phillips-Van Heusen
Dillard's	REI
The Gap	Sears
J. C. Penney	Talbots
J. Crew	Timberland
Lands' End	TJX Companies

HISTORICAL FINANCIALS

Company Type: Private

Income Statement				FYE: Saturday nearest December 31
	REVENUE ($ mil.)	NET INCOME ($ mil.)	NET PROFIT MARGIN	EMPLOYEES
12/08	1,023	(166)	—	7,427
12/07	1,044	(102)	—	9,629
12/06	1,013	(212)	—	9,613
12/05	1,059	38	3.6%	11,826
12/04	1,158	44	3.8%	—
Annual Growth	(3.0%)	—	—	(14.4%)

2008 Year-End Financials

Debt ratio: 326.2%
Return on equity: —
Cash ($ mil.): 60

Current ratio: 1.44
Long-term debt ($ mil.): 237

Net Income History

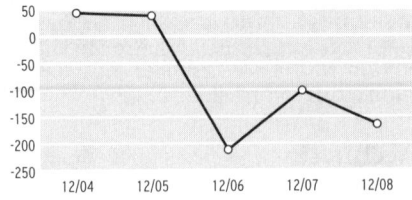

Edelman

If image truly is everything, then Edelman may be one of the most indispensable companies around. The public relations firm is the largest independent agency in the industry, conducting work for heavy hitters such as Wal-Mart and Microsoft. With more than 50 offices worldwide, the company provides its services to five industries through 18 practice areas (including financial communications and investor relations, corporate affairs, marketing, litigation, and public affairs). Edelman has fiercely guarded its independent status, despite the business world's ever-increasing trend toward consolidation. The company was founded in 1952 by chairman and owner Daniel Edelman.

The company owns one of Silicon Valley's leading PR firms, A&R Edelman (previously known as A&R Partners). The company bought A&R in 2006; the acquisition significantly augmented Edelman's global technology practice.

Years later, in late 2009, Edelman acquired Grassroots Enterprise, a digital grassroots advocacy firm specializing in creative and public relations strategies for national organizations, corporations, trade associations, and government agencies.

Although Edelman has been primarily a PR firm, the company also dabbles in advertising through its Blue unit. In addition, Edelman owns three other specialty agencies: First&42nd (management consulting), Bioscience Communications (medical education and publishing), and StrategyOne (research).

Edelman's independence is not without a price. The company competes with the PR segments of the large advertising and marketing conglomerates and must do so without the opportunities to raise capital that publicly held companies enjoy.

EXECUTIVES

Chairman: Daniel J. Edelman
President and CEO: Richard W. Edelman
CIO: Chris Scott
Chief of Staff: Derek Creevey
CFO, US: Michael Sloan
EVP Customer Publishing: Howard Lalli
EVP and General Manager San Francisco: Jay Porter
EVP and Director Editorial Services: Dan Santow
EVP and Director, U.S. Crisis & Issues Management: Harlan Loeb
EVP and Global Leader, Corporate Social Responsibility and Sustainability: Christopher (Chris) Deri
EVP and Creative Director: Camille DeSantis
EVP and Director, Financial Communications: Jeff Zilka
EVP Media Relations: Cheryl Cook
EVP Global Public Affairs: Anthony Blankley

LOCATIONS

HQ: Edelman
200 E. Randolph Dr., 63rd Fl., Chicago, IL 60601
Phone: 312-240-3000   **Fax:** 312-240-2900
Web: www.edelman.com

PRODUCTS/OPERATIONS

Practice Areas

Corporate
Design
Governance Advisors
Diversified Services
Crisis and Issues
Diversity Solutions
Editorial Services
Employee Management
Interactive Solutions
Financial and Investor Relations
Food
Litigation
Marketing
Public Affairs
Sports and Entertainment

Industries Served

Consumer Brands
Financial Services
Health
Industrial
Technology

COMPETITORS

Burson-Marsteller	Ketchum
Cohn & Wolfe	Manning Selvage
Euro RSCG	Ogilvy Public Relations
Fleishman-Hillard	Porter Novelli
Harrison, Elliott & Brown	Ruder Finn
Hill & Knowlton	Waggener Edstrom
Hoffman Agency	Weber Shandwick
KCSA	

Electro-Motive Diesel

What do manufacturer Electro-Motive Diesel (EMD) and 1970s band Grand Funk Railroad have in common? They both do the locomotion! EMD designs, builds, sells, and services diesel-electric locomotives for commercial railroad use, including commuter, freight, industrial, intercity passenger, and mining. The company has the largest installed base of diesel-electric locomotives in the world; its products are sold in more than 70 countries. EMD also provides diesel engines to the marine propulsion, oil drilling rigs, and power generation markets. The company was founded in 1922 as Electro-Motive Engineering. Formerly part of GM, the company is held by private-equity firms Greenbriar Equity and Berkshire Partners.

The company is struggling to take back market share from its biggest competitor, General Electric, which now captures more than 60% of the North American locomotive market. To this end, EMD is pushing installation of its Repower upgrade package on older locomotives. Replacing the original diesel engine, the package features a microprocessor-controlled locomotive engine technology that reduces emissions and maintenance costs, improves fuel efficiency and reliability, and extends the service life of the unit. In 2009 EMD introduced the upgrade on California Department of Transportation's Amtrak passenger trains, and Kansas City Southern locomotives and road switchers.

EMD is also guarding its long-held international relationships, particularly in the Middle East. The company looks to deliver 40 passenger locomotives by the third quarter of 2009 to Egyptian National Railways, a customer since the 1950s. EMD also inked a deal to supply the Saudi Railway Company with 25 heavy haul AC diesel electric locomotives. Another established customer in South Africa, Transnet Rail Engineering (TRE), has booked 50 locomotives. This deal calls for over 40% of the locomotive parts to come from South Africa, and for joint assembly by EMD and TRE employees. At about the same time, EMD laid off over 20% of its workforce at its headquarters in La Grange, Illinois. Early in 2009 the company cited weakening demand as the reason it shed about two-thirds of its London, Ontario, force.

EXECUTIVES

Chairman: Jerry Greenwald
President and CEO: John Hamilton
EVP and CFO: Michael P. O'Donnell, age 54
Regional Sales VP: Frank Ward
VP and Chief Mechanical Officer: Gary Griffiths
VP International Sales and Service: Albert Enste
Regional Director Sales, Europe: Frans Zoetmulder
Manager Commercial, Scotland: Russell Milne
Senior Manager, International Aftermarket Sales and Administration: Salvador E. Rangel

LOCATIONS

HQ: Electro-Motive Diesel, Inc.
9301 W. 55th St., La Grange, IL 60525
Phone: 800-255-5355   **Fax:** 708-387-6660
Web: www.emdiesels.com

Electro-Motive Diesel operates sales offices in China, Germany, India, and the US.

PRODUCTS/OPERATIONS

Selected Products

Locomotives
  Freight (JT42CWRM, SD70ACe, SD70M-2)
  Passenger (Euro 4000)
  Road-switcher (GP20D)

OEM Parts
  Diesel engines
  Digital video recorders
  Lash adjusters
  Valve bridges

COMPETITORS

Cummins Power Generation
GE
MISCOR Group
Sulzer

HISTORICAL FINANCIALS

Company Type: Private

Income Statement

FYE: December 31

	ESTIMATED REVENUE ($ mil.)	NET INCOME ($ mil.)	NET PROFIT MARGIN	EMPLOYEES
12/08	2,200	—	—	3,260
12/07	1,830	—	—	2,740
12/06	1,710	—	—	2,640
12/05	1,030	—	—	2,640
Annual Growth	28.8%	—	—	7.3%

Revenue History

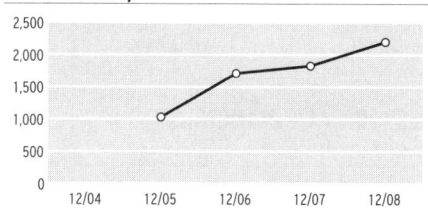

EmblemHealth, Inc.

EmblemHealth is the parent company of two not-for-profit health insurance companies, Group Health Incorporated (GHI) and the Health Insurance Plan of Greater New York (HIP). Collectively, the two health insurers cover some 4 million New Yorkers, primarily state government and New York City employees; the two companies cover upwards of 90% of Big Apple city workers and retirees. Both provide a variety of managed health plans to their members, including prescription drug and dental coverage, and Medicare plans. GHI and HIP joined together under the EmblemHealth banner in 2006, with the intention of merging into a single insurer that would convert to a for-profit, publicly traded company.

In 2008 EmblemHealth decided to delay conversion to for-profit status, citing challenging market conditions.

Under state law governing for-profit conversions, the company's stock would at first belong to the state, which would reap the benefits of the initial stock sale. But going public would give the combined insurers easier access to capital, which the companies believe would enhance their ability to compete against large national insurers. Not everyone is so sanguine about the potential public offering, however; the city of New York has opposed the conversion to for-profit status on the grounds that it might lead to higher premiums and lower benefits for city workers.

Along with its operations in New York, EmblemHealth offers health coverage in Connecticut and western Massachusetts through ConnectiCare, which has about a quarter of a million members. Additionally, its PerfectHealth subsidiary (acquired by HIP in 2006) specializes in consumer-driven health plans (that is, high-deductible plans coupled with a health savings account).

EXECUTIVES

Chairman and CEO: Anthony L. Watson, age 68
Vice Chairman: James F. Gill
Vice Chairman: Stuart H. Altman, age 71
President, COO, and Director: Frank J. Branchini

LOCATIONS

HQ: EmblemHealth, Inc.
  55 Water St., New York, NY 10041
Phone: 646-447-5000   **Fax:** 646-447-3011
Web: www.emblemhealth.com

PRODUCTS/OPERATIONS

2008 Revenue

	$ mil.	% of total
Earned premiums	8,553.2	98
Administrative services & other fees	114.8	1
Net investment income	81.1	1
Net realized loss on investments	15.5	—
Other	2.5	—
Adjustments	(155.0)	—
Total	**8,612.1**	**100**

COMPETITORS

Aetna
Affinity Health
AMERIGROUP New York
Capital District Physicians' Health Plan
CIGNA
Fidelis Care New York
Health Net
Healthfirst
HealthNow New York Inc.
Healthplex
Humana
Independent Health
Lifetime Healthcare
MVP Health Plan
UnitedHealth Group
WellPoint

HISTORICAL FINANCIALS

Company Type: Private

Income Statement

FYE: December 31

	REVENUE ($ mil.)	NET INCOME ($ mil.)	NET PROFIT MARGIN	EMPLOYEES
12/08	8,612	(117)	—	4,800
12/07	8,147	101	1.2%	5,400
12/06	7,781	239	3.1%	—
12/05	7,160	125	1.7%	—
Annual Growth	6.3%	—	—	(11.1%)

Net Income History

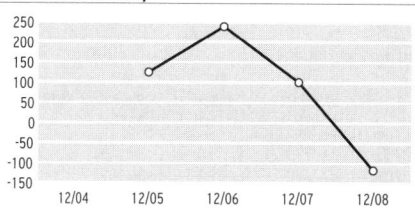

Emigrant Bank

Emigrant Bank has built its business around the huddled masses longing to save. The bank, which also has four regional Emigrant Savings Bank affiliates in the Bronx, Brooklyn, Queens, and Long Island, serves retail and commercial customers in the New York metropolitan area from some 35 branches. It offers online banking nationwide through its EmigrantOnline service. The bank provides standard products such as checking and savings accounts, CDs, IRAs, and credit and debit cards. New York Private Bank & Trust is Emigrant Bank's wealth management division; Emigrant Financial Services offers mutual funds and life insurance. Emigrant Mortgage originates home loans in about a dozen Eastern states.

One- to four-family residential mortgages account for the largest portion of Emigrant Bank's loan portfolio, followed by commercial mortgages, business loans, and multifamily residential mortgages.

The bank offers commercial real estate lending services through its Emigrant Funding unit. Emigrant Business Credit provides equipment financing. Emigrant Bank also has a Fine Art Financing division that lends money to clients using art or antiques as collateral. The bank's Emigrant Capital unit makes direct investments in private companies with annual sales between $20 million and $100 million.

One of the largest privately owned banks in the US, Emigrant Bank is controlled by the family of chairman and CEO Howard Milstein. It was founded by Irish emigrants in 1850.

EXECUTIVES

Chairman and CEO: Howard P. Milstein
SVP and Chief Credit Officer: Patricia Goldstein
SVP and Chief Marketing Officer: Ted Morehouse

LOCATIONS

HQ: Emigrant Bank
  5 E. 42nd St., New York, NY 10017
Phone: 212-850-4521   **Fax:** 212-850-4372
Web: www.emigrant.com

COMPETITORS

Astoria Financial
Bank of America
Capital One
Citigroup
Dime Community Bancshares
JPMorgan Chase
New York Community Bancorp
Signature Bank
TD Bank USA

HISTORICAL FINANCIALS
Company Type: Private

Income Statement
FYE: December 31

	REVENUE ($ mil.)	NET INCOME ($ mil.)	NET PROFIT MARGIN	EMPLOYEES
12/07	771	112	14.5%	809
12/06	640	162	25.3%	773
12/05	534	—	—	848
Annual Growth	20.2%	(30.6%)	—	(2.3%)

2007 Year-End Financials
Debt ratio: — Current ratio: —
Return on equity: 13.2% Long-term debt ($ mil.): 590
Cash ($ mil.): —

Net Income History

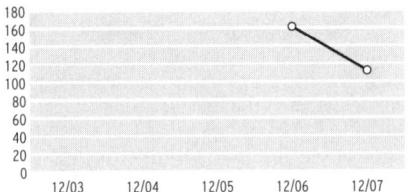

	12/03	12/04	12/05	12/06	12/07

Encyclopædia Britannica

Encyclopædia Britannica thinks it knows everything, and it probably does. In addition to its flagship 32-volume *Encyclopædia Britannica* (first published in 1768), the company publishes reference works (*Great Books of the Western World*), atlases (*Britannica's Student Atlas*), and other titles (*The American Presidency*). It publishes dictionaries (*Merriam Webster's Collegiate Dictionary*) through its Merriam-Webster subsidiary. The company's Britannica Online School Edition is a reference site for students and teachers. Most of the company's products are available online (Britannica.com), as well as on CD-ROM and DVD. Swiss financier Jacob Safra (a nephew of the late banking king Edmond Safra) owns the company.

Customers can buy print and interactive products through the company's online store, as well as via a variety of distributors. In addition to book and Web subscription sales, Britannica also earns revenue from advertising and licensing fees. Headquartered in Chicago, the company also has operations in Delhi, London, Paris, Seoul, Sydney, Taipei, Tel Aviv, and Tokyo, and has published works in 12 languages.

The company claims its flagship encyclopedia is the oldest reference work in the English language. Its contributors have included Albert Einstein, Sigmund Freud, Marie Curie, Bertrand Russell, T.H. Huxley, and George Bernard Shaw. Safra, a *Britannica* lover since childhood, led a group that paid $135 million for the struggling company in 1996.

HISTORY

Engraver Andrew Bell and printer and bookseller Colin Macfarquhar created the first edition of the *Encyclopædia Britannica* in Scotland, releasing the three-volume set in weekly installments between 1768 and 1771. Benjamin Franklin and John Locke were among early contributors. The second edition, completed in 1784, expanded to 10 volumes; the fourth (1809) contained 20. The ninth edition (1889) captured the scientific spirit of the age with articles by Thomas Henry Huxley and James Clerk Maxwell.

American businessmen Horace Hooper and Walter Jackson purchased the *Encyclopædia* in 1901 and established the Encyclopædia Britannica Company in the US. It published the first *Britannica Book of the Year* in 1913. Sears chairman Julius Rosenwald bought the company in 1920 and tried to market *Britannica* through Sears' retail operations, as well as with door-to-door sales. William Benton (of Benton & Bowles Advertising) bought the business from Sears in 1941 and built a nationwide sales force with a hard-sell reputation. Britannica released its first foreign-language encyclopedia, *Enciclopedia Barsa*, in 1957 and acquired dictionary publisher G. & C. Merriam in 1964.

When Benton died in 1974, he bequeathed the operation to the non-profit William Benton Foundation, the sole beneficiary of which was the University of Chicago. Britannica later bought out rival Compton's Encyclopedia in the mid-1970s. The 1989 CD-ROM release of *Compton's MultiMedia Encyclopedia* was a first for the industry, but Britannica sold Compton's NewMedia division to Chicago's Tribune Company in 1993 just before the CD-ROM market exploded. The company also promised not to release a competing multimedia version of Encyclopaedia Britannica for two years. Not realizing that the electronic revolution was upon them and reluctant to change its established and profitable door-to-door sales techniques, the conservative company fell behind challengers who offered CD-ROMs including Microsoft and its *Funk & Wagnalls* product (later relaunched as *Encarta*).

With book sales dwindling and heavy competition, Britannica cut its prices and ceased its door-to-door marketing in 1996 after Safra led the purchase of the company. It agreed to sell both its CD-ROM and print encyclopedias in retail stores in 1997, and lured publisher Paul Hoffman away from Walt Disney's successful *Discover* magazine. Britannica Internet Guide (BIG), a free Internet search engine, launched that year. Britannica added guest columns and other features to BIG in 1998 and renamed it eBlast (it changed the site's name again to Britannica the following year).

Encyclopædia Britannica Holdings (Safra's umbrella firm for the publisher) launched a sister firm, Britannica.com, in 1999 to oversee the company's electronic and Internet products and services. CEO Don Yannias resigned his post with the print company and took the reins of the new digital firm, allowing Hoffman to take over as the publisher's president. Britannica.com struggled with the rest of the Internet industry in 2000, laying off almost 25% of its staff.

In 2001 Yannias left the company entirely and was replaced by Ilan Yeshua, an executive from an Israeli educational technology firm. Later that year, the company integrated Britannica.com back into the encyclopedia unit of Encyclopædia Britannica, a move that involved severely downsizing the Web staff. Yeshua departed the company in 2003 and was replaced by Britannica executive Jorge Cauz.

EXECUTIVES

Chairman: Jacob E. (Jacqui) Safra
President: Jorge Cauz, age 47
EVP, Secretary, and General Counsel: William J. Bowe
SVP International: Leah Mansoor
SVP and Editor: Dale Hoiberg
SVP Corporate Development: Michael Ross
SVP Consumer Sales: Daniel W. (Dan) Smith, age 37
VP Operations and Finance: Richard Anderson
Executive Technology Director: Tom Lang
Direct Marketing Manager: Christine Hodgson
Corporate Communications Director: Tom Panelas
President and Publisher, Merriam-Webster: John Morse
Auditors: PricewaterhouseCoopers

LOCATIONS

HQ: Encyclopædia Britannica, Inc.
331 N. La Salle St., Chicago, IL 60610
Phone: 312-347-7159 **Fax:** 312-294-2104
Web: corporate.britannica.com

COMPETITORS

Answers Corporation	McGraw-Hill
Cengage Learning	Microsoft
Dow Jones	National Geographic
Editis	Pearson plc
Franklin Electronic Publishers	Random House
Google	Scholastic
Houghton Mifflin Harcourt	Time Inc.
LexisNexis	Wikimedia Foundation
	World Book

HISTORICAL FINANCIALS
Company Type: Private

Income Statement
FYE: December 31

	REVENUE ($ mil.)	NET INCOME ($ mil.)	NET PROFIT MARGIN	EMPLOYEES
12/08	50	—	—	439

Energy Future Holdings

Energy Future Holdings (formerly TXU) has seen the future and it works — powered by electricity. The company is the largest nonregulated retail electric provider in Texas (TXU Energy), with more than 2.2 million customers, and through its Luminant unit it has a generating capacity of more than 18,300 MW from its interests in nuclear and fossil-fueled power plants in the state. Energy Future Holdings has regulated power transmission and distribution operations through Oncor Electric Delivery. Oncor operates the largest distribution and transmission system in Texas, providing power to more than 3 million electric delivery points over more than 117,000 miles of transmission and distribution lines.

Energy Future Holdings' Luminant operations include 10,200 MW of natural gas, 2,300 MW of nuclear and 5,800 MW of coal-fueled generation capacity. It is also the largest purchaser of wind-generated electricity in Texas.

The company is seeking to increase efficiencies in its core operations and explore growth opportunities across its business lines.

In 2007 TXU was acquired in a $45 billion leveraged buyout by an investor group led by Goldman Sachs, Kohlberg Kravis Roberts, and Texas Pacific Group, and became Energy Future Holdings.

Diversifying its capital base, in 2008 the company sold a 20% stake in Oncor to an investor group led by Borealis Infrastructure Management for $1.2 billion.

HISTORY

The first North Texas electric power company was founded in Dallas in 1883. Another was built in 1885 in Fort Worth. From these and other small power plants, three companies grew to serve most of the state: Texas Power & Light (TP&L, incorporated in 1912), Dallas Power & Light (DP&L, 1917), and Texas Electric Service (TES, 1929). Texas Utilities Company, called TU, was formed in 1945 as a holding company for the three utilities.

In the 1940s TU began leasing large lignite coal reserves, and in 1952 formed Industrial Generating to mine lignite and operate a coal-fired power plant. TU, after pioneering lignite-burning technology in the 1960s, opened the first of nine large lignite units in 1971. In 1974 it began building the Comanche Peak nuclear plant near Fort Worth.

DP&L, TES, TP&L, and Industrial Generating joined in 1984 as Texas Utilities Electric (TU Electric). The mining company was renamed Texas Utilities Mining.

The Nuclear Regulatory Commission wouldn't license Comanche Peak in 1985, citing design and construction faults, but finally granted the license in 1990. TU bought out its construction partners after much wrangling over multibillion-dollar cost overruns.

In 1993 TU bought Southwestern Electric Service (now TXU SESCO), another Texas electric utility. Accounting changes resulted in a loss for TU in 1995. However, it did gain entry to the telecom arena, buying a 20% stake in the Texas operations of wireless PCS provider PrimeCo. (The company sold the PrimeCo stake in 1999.) TU expanded its telecom holdings in 1997 when it acquired phone company Lufkin-Conroe (now part of TXU Communications).

TU headed down under in 1996, buying Australian electric company Eastern Energy (now part of TXU Electricity). It purchased gas dealer ENSERCH (now TXU Gas), which brought substantial energy services and trading assets on board, including Texas' largest gas utility, Lone Star Gas.

Despite a windfall tax levied by the UK's Labor Party, TU bought British utility The Energy Group (now TXU Europe) for about $10 billion in 1998. Back in Texas the 1999 Legislature approved retail competition for the electric industry, beginning in 2002. Also in 1999 Texas Utilities restructured its operations and began using the name TXU Corp. It officially changed its name the next year.

In 2000 TXU acquired Norweb Energi, United Utilities' electricity and gas supply business, which added some 1.8 million electricity customers and 400,000 gas customers in the UK. TXU also contributed the stock of its telecommunications companies to Pinnacle One Partners in exchange for a 50% stake and about $960 million. Other efforts to reduce debt and streamline operations include TXU's sale of its natural gas

processing operations, UK gas metering business, and interests in a Czech utility and North Sea gas fields.

In 2001 TXU acquired a 50% stake in Stadtwerke Kiel, its first utility in Germany (where TXU Europe was already trading energy), and it agreed to sell two gas-fired power plants (2,300 MW) in Texas to Exelon for $443 million (completed in 2002). TXU Europe sold two UK power stations (3,000 MW) in 2001 and sold its Eastern Electricity distribution unit and its interest in joint venture 24seven in 2002.

In 2002 retail electric competition began in Texas, and TXU responded by separating TXU Electric's regulated and nonregulated operations. TXU Electric's name was changed to TXU US Holdings, which also took over TXU SESCO's electric operations.

TXU sold TXU Europe's retail supply and generation operations to UK utility Powergen in late 2002 due to poor market conditions. Shortly after, TXU Europe filed for bankruptcy protection, and TXU wrote off its investment in the unit. The following year, TXU sold the northeastern US gas marketing operations of TXU Energy to UGI.

Continuing with its effort to reduce debt and focus on core utility businesses, TXU sold subsidiary TXU Communications to private telecom firm Consolidated Communications and its TXU Fuel (gas transportation) unit to Energy Transfer Partners. The company sold TXU Gas to Atmos Energy for $1.9 billion in 2004; the transaction included the company's gas transportation and storage assets.

The company announced plans to form a wholesale energy marketing joint venture with Credit Suisse First Boston in 2004; however, the two firms later decided not to pursue the venture. Energy Future Holdings also outsourced its information technology functions to Capgemini Energy LP, a unit of Capgemini.

In 2006 the company teamed up with InfrastruX Group to form the InfrastruX Energy Services joint venture in a 10-year, $8.7 billion agreement to provide for utility infrastructure and management services.

EXECUTIVES

Chairman: Donald L. (Don) Evans, age 62
Vice Chairman: Michael S. (Mike) Greene, age 63, $2,054,299 total compensation
President, CEO, and Director: John F. Young, age 52
EVP and CFO: Paul M. Keglevic, age 55
EVP; Chief Executive, Luminant Construction: Charles R. (Chuck) Enze, age 55
EVP; EVP and Chief Commercial Officer, Luminant: Mac A. McFarland, age 39
EVP and General Counsel: Robert C. (Rob) Walters, age 51
EVP Human Resources and Administration: M. Rizwan (Riz) Chand, age 45
SVP and and Controller: Stanley J. (Stan) Szlauderbach, age 60
VP Government Affairs, TXU Energy: Carl S. Richie Jr.
VP Financial Reporting: Tim Hogan
President and CEO, TXU Energy: James A. (Jim) Burke, age 40, $2,059,293 total compensation
President and CEO, Luminant: David A. Campbell, age 40, $4,379,690 total compensation
Chairman and CEO, Oncor: Robert S. (Bob) Shapard, age 53
Chief Marketing Officer, TXU Energy: Dan Valentine
Manager Investor Relations: Bill Huber
Auditors: Deloitte & Touche LLP

LOCATIONS

HQ: Energy Future Holdings Corp.
    1601 Bryan St., Dallas, TX 75201
Phone: 214-812-4600
Web: www.energyfutureholdings.com

PRODUCTS/OPERATIONS

2008 Sales

	$ mil.	% of total
Unregulated		
Retail electric	6,328	50
Wholesale electric	3,329	26
Other	380	3
Regulated delivery	2,580	21
Adjustments	(1,253)	—
Total	**11,364**	**100**

COMPETITORS

AEP	Entergy
AEP Texas Central	First Choice Power
AEP Texas North	FPL Group
AES	Gexa Energy
Atmos Energy	Green Mountain Energy
Brazos Electric	Mirant
Calpine	NRG Energy
CenterPoint Energy	ONEOK
Direct Energy	RRI Energy
Duke Energy	Southwestern Electric
El Paso Electric	Texas Gas Transmission

HISTORICAL FINANCIALS

Company Type: Private

Income Statement

FYE: December 31

	REVENUE ($ mil.)	NET INCOME ($ mil.)	NET PROFIT MARGIN	EMPLOYEES
12/08	11,364	(9,838)	—	8,150
12/07	7,992	(637)	—	7,600
Annual Growth	42.2%	—	—	7.2%

Net Income History

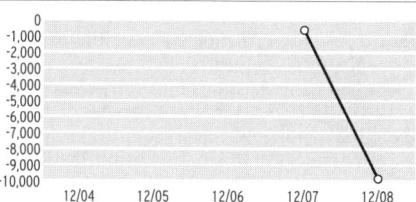

Enterprise Rent-A-Car

This Enterprise helps customers boldly go where they might not have gone before they rented a fresh set of wheels. A leading US car rental company, Enterprise Rent-A-Car maintains a fleet of about 714,000 vehicles from more than 7,000 locations — some 6,000 in the US and another 900 in Canada, Germany, Ireland, and the UK. Unlike rivals Hertz and Avis, which operate primarily from airports, Enterprise focuses on customers whose own cars are in the shop or need a rental for vacations or other occasions. In 2009 the company became a subsidiary of Enterprise Holdings following the integration of Vanguard Car Rental, former parent of the Alamo Rent A Car and National Car Rental brands.

The formation of Enterprise Holdings effectively brought together the Enterprise, Alamo, and National brands under one corporate umbrella. Vanguard had been purchased in 2007 and, until its integration, operated as a separate subsidiary. The Vanguard purchase strengthened Enterprise's airport business, where the Alamo and National brands operated more than 3,000 car rental locations.

Despite its boosted presence in airports, more than 90% of Enterprise's car rental business comes from customers in their home cities, as opposed to travelers. In addition to its primary car rental operations, Enterprise leases vehicles and manages fleets for other companies (Enterprise Fleet Services), rents trucks (from more than 90 locations), and sells used cars.

HISTORY

In 1957 Jack Taylor, the sales manager for a Cadillac dealership in St. Louis, hit on the idea that leasing cars might be an easier way to make money than selling them. Taylor's idea sounded good to his boss, Arthur Lindburg, who agreed to set Taylor up in the leasing business. In return for a 50% pay cut, Taylor received 25% of the new enterprise, called Executive Leasing, which began in the walled-off body shop of a car dealership.

In the early 1960s Taylor started renting cars for short periods as well as leasing them. When his leasing agents expressed annoyance with the rental operation, Taylor turned that business over to Don Holtzman. Holtzman realized that his 17-car rental operation was too little to take on industry giants like Hertz and Avis; instead, he concentrated on the "home city" or replacement market. He offered competitive rates to insurance adjusters who needed to find cars for policyholders whose vehicles were damaged or stolen.

Propelled by court decisions that required casualty companies to pay for loss of transportation, Taylor expanded from his St. Louis base in 1969 with a branch office in Atlanta. Since another car leasing outfit in Georgia was already named Executive, Taylor changed the name of his company to Enterprise Rent-A-Car.

The company expanded into Florida and Texas in the early 1970s, targeting garages and body shops that performed repairs for insured drivers. Oil price shocks of that period compelled Taylor to diversify his operations. In 1974 Enterprise acquired Keefe Coffee and Supply, a supplier of coffee, packaged foods, and beverages to prison commissaries. To service *FORTUNE* 1000 companies wanting to lease or buy more than 50 vehicles, the company started Enterprise Fleet Services in 1976.

Enterprise acquired Courtesy Products (coffee and tea for hotel guests) in 1980, and the following year sales reached the $100 million mark. It acquired ELCO Chevrolet in 1986, the same year it formed Crawford Supply (hygiene products for prisons). Taylor bought out the Lindburg family's interest in Enterprise the next year. In 1989 Enterprise raised its brand recognition with a national TV campaign that focused on an older and higher-income audience by showing its commercials exclusively on CBS. Also in the late 1980s, the company began targeting "discretionary rentals" to families with visiting relatives or with children home for the holidays.

Taylor's son, Andrew, became CEO of Enterprise in 1991, and sales topped $1 billion for the first time. By 1994 sales had passed $2 billion, and the company had expanded into Canada and the UK. By 1996 Enterprise had a fleet of more than 300,000 vehicles. That year it opened several locations in the UK. In 1997 the company opened locations in Ireland, Germany, Scotland, and Wales.

In 1998 Enterprise battled other rental firms over use of the advertising tagline, "We'll pick you up," which it had trademarked. Rent-A-Wreck lost a court case over the matter; Hertz settled with Enterprise over use of the phrase.

The company more than doubled the number of its airport locations in 1999 in an attempt to woo occasional travelers (rather than hard-core corporate fliers). Also that year the Taylor family split off their non-automotive operations (including companies involved in prison supplies, hotel amenities, a golf course, mylar balloons, and athletic shoes) as Centric Group.

In 2001 the company's COO, Donald Ross, became the first non-Taylor to be promoted to president after Jack Taylor was named chairman emeritus and Andrew gave up the president title to assume the company's chairmanship while remaining CEO.

In August 2007 Enterprise bought rival Vanguard Car Rental Group from Cerberus Capital Management. Vanguard managed the Alamo Rent A Car and National Car Rental brands. Enterprise completed the integration of Vanguard's operations in 2009.

EXECUTIVES

Chairman and CEO: Andrew C. (Andy) Taylor, age 61
Vice Chairman: Donald L. (Don) Ross, age 65
President and COO: Pamela M. (Pam) Nicholson, age 49
EVP and CSO: Greg R. Stubblefield
EVP North American Operations:
 Matthew G. (Matt) Darrah
EVP and CFO: William W. (Bill) Snyder
SVP and Chief Administrative Officer: Lee R. Kaplan
SVP Group Operations, West Coast: Dave Nestor
SVP Group Operations, Northeast: Rick Allen
SVP Group Operations, South Central: Dave Livon
SVP Human Resources: Edward (Ed) Adams
SVP Car Sales: Tim Walsh
SVP and CIO: Craig Kennedy
SVP Rental: Jim Runnels
SVP European Operations: James (Jim) Burrell
SVP Fleet Management and Car Sales:
 Steven E. (Steve) Bloom
VP Corporate Communications: Christy Conrad
VP Commercial Trucks: Allen Serfas
VP Marketing and Communications: Pat Farrell
President, Enterprise Rent-A-Car Foundation:
 Jo Ann Taylor Kindle
Auditors: Ernst & Young LLP

LOCATIONS

HQ: Enterprise Rent-A-Car Company
 600 Corporate Park Dr., St. Louis, MO 63105
Phone: 314-512-5000   **Fax:** 314-512-4706
Web: www.enterprise.com

PRODUCTS/OPERATIONS

Selected Operations

Enterprise Car Sales (used car sales)
Enterprise Fleet Services (vehicle leasing and fleet management services)
Enterprise Rent-A-Car
Enterprise Rent-A-Truck

COMPETITORS

Avis Budget	PHH Arval
Avis Europe	Rent-A-Wreck
Dollar Thrifty Automotive	Sixt
Hertz	

HISTORICAL FINANCIALS

Company Type: Subsidiary

Income Statement

FYE: July 31

	REVENUE ($ mil.)	NET INCOME ($ mil.)	NET PROFIT MARGIN	EMPLOYEES
7/08	10,100	—	—	65,000
7/07	9,500	—	—	66,700
7/06	9,000	—	—	75,700
7/05	8,230	—	—	61,000
7/04	7,400	—	—	57,300
Annual Growth	8.1%	—	—	3.2%

Revenue History

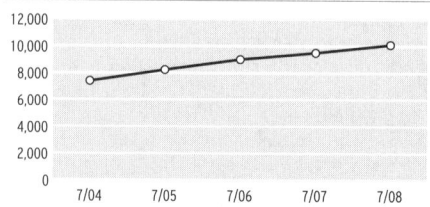

Environmental Protection Agency

Talk about an organization that's gone green. The US Environmental Protection Agency (EPA) develops and enforces environmental policy and regulations throughout the country. Besides working to ensure compliance with federal environmental rules, the agency provides support for state environmental protection efforts. In addition, the EPA conducts research on environmental issues through a network of laboratories. The agency was established in 1970, the same year as the first Earth Day, in response to growing concerns over air, water, and soil pollution. The agency is led by an administrator appointed by the US president.

The EPA's strategic plan, which it develops every five years (the current one will carry it through the year 2011), focuses on five main goals: clean air and global climate change, clean and safe water, land preservation and restoration, healthy communities and ecosystems, and compliance and environmental stewardship.

Its in-house team of engineers, scientists, legal experts, policy analysts, and computer specialists are working together to improve both the agency's data collection and analysis processes and its information technology capabilities. Key areas of focus include converting raw environmental data into information that top decision makers can understand and maximizing taxpayer dollars towards achieving EPA goals.

EXECUTIVES

Administrator: Lisa P. Jackson
Chief of Staff: Betty Wonkovich
Acting CFO: Maryann Froehlich
Director, Office of Administration: Renee Page
Director, Office of Transportation and Air Quality:
 Margo T. Oge
Director, Office of Human Resources: Rich Lemley
Acting Assistant Administrator, Office of Prevention, Pesticides, and Toxic Substances: James J. (Jim) Jones

Acting Assistant Administrator, Office of Enforcement and Compliance Assurance: Catherine R. McCabe

Acting Assistant Administrator, Office of Solid Waste and Emergency Response: Barry N. Breen

Acting Assistant Administrator, Office of Water: Michael H. Shapiro

Acting Assistant Administrator, Office of Research and Development: Lek Kadeli

Acting Assistant Administrator, Office of Administration and Resources Management: Craig E. Hooks

Acting Inspector General and Deputy Inspector General: Bill A. Roderick

Associate Administrator, Office of Homeland Security: Tom Dunne

Acting General Counsel: Patricia K. Hirsch

Acting Deputy Administrator and Acting Assistant Administrator, Office of International Affairs: Scott Fulton

Acting Assistant Administrator, Office of Air and Radiation: Elizabeth Craig

LOCATIONS

HQ: US Environmental Protection Agency
1200 Pennsylvania Ave. NW, Washington, DC 20460
Phone: 202-272-0167
Web: www.epa.gov

Ergon, Inc.

When it comes to work, Ergon (named after the Greek word for work) has it covered. Ergo, Ergon operates in six major business segments: asphalt and emulsions; information technology (embedded computing); oil and gas; real estate; refining and marketing; and transportation and terminaling. In addition to providing a range of petroleum products and services, the company manufactures and markets computer technology services and sells road maintenance systems, including emulsions and special coatings. Ergon also provides truck, rail, and marine transport services and sells residential and commercial real estate properties.

Ergon Asphalt and Emulsions is a leading innovator in the asphalt industry. It delivers high-performance, polymer-modified binders to asphalt suppliers throughout the inland waterways system via Ergon unit Magnolia Marine Transport. In 2007 the asphalt unit expanded its asset base and geographic coverage, acquiring Innovative Adhesives Company, a leading maker of specialty asphalt coatings and adhesives, located in Kansas City, Kansas.

In 2009 it expanded further, leasing 20 asphalt storage facilities in 10 states from SemGroup Energy Partners in a move that more than doubled Ergon Asphalt and Emulsions' production capacity.

EXECUTIVES

CEO: Leslie B. Lampton Sr.
CFO: A. Patrick (Pat) Busby
VP: Baxter Burns
VP Marine Operations, Magnolia Marine Transport: Roger Harris
VP Environment, Health, and Safety, Ergon Refining: Paul Young
President, Asphalt Division: Bill Lampton
Human Resources Manager: Daphne Williams
Director Communications: Jim Temple

LOCATIONS

HQ: Ergon, Inc.
2829 Lakeland Dr., Ste. 2000, Jackson, MS 39232
Phone: 601-933-3000   **Fax:** 601-933-3350
Web: www.ergon.com

PRODUCTS/OPERATIONS

Major Operations

Asphalt and Emulsions
Crafco, Inc.
Ertech, Inc.

Information Technology (Embedded Computing)
Diversified Technology, Inc.

Oil and Gas
Lampton-Love, Inc.

Real Estate
Ergon Properties, Inc.

Refining and Marketing
Ergon Refining, Inc.
Lion Oil Company

Transportation and Terminaling
Ergon Terminaling, Inc.
Ergon Trucking, Inc.
Magnolia Marine Transport Company

COMPETITORS

AmeriGas Partners
Ferrellgas Partners
Kirby Corporation
Koch Industries, Inc.
Marathon Oil

HISTORICAL FINANCIALS

Company Type: Private

Income Statement

FYE: December 31

	ESTIMATED REVENUE ($ mil.)	NET INCOME ($ mil.)	NET PROFIT MARGIN	EMPLOYEES
12/08	5,430	—	—	2,500
12/07	4,490	—	—	2,500
12/06	4,110	—	—	2,500
12/05	3,000	—	—	2,500
12/04	2,680	—	—	2,300
Annual Growth	19.3%	—	—	2.1%

Revenue History

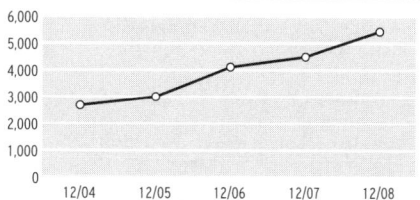

Ernst & Young Global

Accounting may actually be the *second*-oldest profession, and Ernst & Young is one of the oldest practitioners. Ernst & Young is also one of the world's Big Four accounting firms (third in revenue behind PricewaterhouseCoopers and Deloitte Touche Tohmatsu, ahead of KPMG). It has some 700 offices providing auditing and accounting services in 140 countries. The firm also provides legal services and services relating to emerging growth companies, human resources issues, and corporate transactions (mergers and acquisitions, IPOs, and the like). Ernst & Young has one of the world's largest tax practices, serving multinational clients that have to comply with multiple local tax laws.

Ernst & Young offers its services to a vast range of industries, including asset management, biotech, mining, and hotel and leisure. The company's financial reporting segment offers an IFRS/GAAP comparison so companies can compare and contrast the international and US accounting standards. Ernst & Young's tax business has grown as the economy has become increasingly globalized and companies face more complicated international compliance issues.

In 2008 the group restructured into five geographic areas, with divisions covering Europe, Middle East, India, and Africa; the Americas; Oceania; Japan; and the Far East. The structure allows the company to develop and strengthen its cross-country operations within integrated regions.

The company hands out an Entrepreneur of the Year award annually. In 2008 it was given to Dr. Jean-Paul Clozel, founder of Swiss pharmaceuticals company Actelion. The year before that, the award went to Cirque du Soleil founder Guy Laliberté.

HISTORY

In 1494 Luca Pacioli's *Summa di Arithmetica* became the first published text on double-entry bookkeeping, but it was almost 400 years before accounting became a profession.

In 1849 Frederick Whinney joined the UK firm of Harding & Pullein. His ledgers were so clear that he was advised to take up accounting, which was a growth field as stock companies proliferated. Whinney became a name partner in 1859 and his sons followed him into the business. The firm became Whinney, Smith & Whinney (WS&W) in 1894.

After WWII, WS&W formed an alliance with Ernst & Ernst (founded in Cleveland in 1903 by brothers Alwin and Theodore Ernst), with each firm operating on the other's behalf across the Atlantic. Whinney merged with Brown, Fleming & Murray in 1965 to become Whinney Murray. In 1979 Whinney Murray, Turquands Barton Mayhew (also a UK firm), and Ernst & Ernst merged to form Ernst & Whinney.

But Ernst & Whinney wasn't done merging. Ten years later, when it was the fourth-largest accounting firm, it merged with #5 Arthur Young, which had been founded by Scotsman Arthur Young in 1895 in Kansas City. Long known as "old reliable," Arthur Young fell on hard times in the 1980s because its audit relationships with failed S&Ls led to expensive litigation (settled in 1992 for $400 million).

Thus the new firm of Ernst & Young faced a rocky start. In 1990 it fended off rumors of collapse. The next year it slashed payroll, even thinning its partner roster. Exhausted by the S&L wars, in 1994 the firm replaced its pugnacious general counsel, Carl Riggio, with the more cost-conscious Kathryn Oberly.

In the mid-1990s Ernst & Young concentrated on consulting, particularly in software applications, and grew through acquisitions. In 1996 the firm bought Houston-based Wright Killen & Co., a petroleum and petrochemicals consulting firm, to form Ernst & Young Wright Killen. It also entered new alliances that year, including ones with Washington-based ISD/Shaw, which provided banking industry consulting, and India's Tata Consulting.

In 1997 Ernst & Young was sued for a record $4 billion for its alleged failure to effectively handle the 1993 restructuring of the defunct Merry-Go-Round Enterprises retail chain (it settled for $185 million in 1999). On the heels of a merger deal between Coopers & Lybrand and Price Waterhouse, Ernst & Young agreed in 1997 to merge with KPMG International. But Ernst & Young called off the negotiations in 1998, citing the uncertain regulatory process they faced.

The firm reached a settlement in 1999 in lawsuits regarding accounting errors at Informix and Avis Budget Group and sold its UK and southern African trust and fiduciary businesses to Royal Bank of Canada (now RBC Financial Group).

In 2000 Ernst & Young became the first of the (then) Big Five firms to sell its consultancy, dealing it to France's Cap Gemini Group for about $11 billion. The following year the UK accountancy watchdog group announced it would investigate Ernst & Young for its handling of the accounts of UK-based The Equitable Life Assurance Society. The insurer was forced to close to new business in 2000 because of massive financial difficulties.

Ernst & Young made headlines and gave competitors plenty to talk about in 2002 when closely held financial records were made public during a divorce case involving executive Rick Bobrow (who in 2003 abruptly retired as global CEO after just a year on the job).

Also in 2002 the firm allied with former New York City mayor Rudy Giuliani to launch a business consultancy bearing the Giuliani name. Ernst & Young later helped the venture to build its investment banking capabilities by selling its corporate finance unit (as well as its stake in Giuliani Partners) to that firm in 2004.

With the collapse of rival Andersen in 2002, Ernst & Young boosted its legal services, assembling some 2,000 lawyers in dozens of countries.

But the firm faced Andersen-style trouble of its own as client suits against auditors became more common in the wake of corporate scandals at Enron and other troubled companies. Both Avis Budget Group, Inc. (formerly Cendant) and HealthSouth sued Ernst & Young in connection with alleged accounting missteps in 2004.

In 2005 Ernst & Young's UK arm emerged victorious from a torrid legal battle with insurer Equitable Life, which in 2003 had sued the accountancy for professional negligence related to work performed when Ernst & Young was its auditor. Another highlight for that year was the fee bonanza fueled by changes in international accounting standards required by the Sarbanes-Oxley Act in the US.

EXECUTIVES

Chairman and CEO: James S. (Jim) Turley, age 54
Global COO: John Ferraro
Global Managing Partner, Quality and Risk Management: Victoria Cochrane
Global Managing Partner, Markets: John Murphy
Global Vice Chair, Strategy and Regulatory Affairs: Beth A. Brooke
Chairman and CEO, Canada: Lou P. Pagnutti
Global Managing Partner, Operations and Finance: Jeffrey H. (Jeff) Dworken
Global Managing Partner, EMEIA Integration: Patrick Gounelle
Global Managing Partner, People: Sam Fouad
Global Vice Chair, Transaction Advisory Services: Pip McCrostie
Global Vice Chair, Advisory: Norman Lonergan
Global Vice Chair, Tax: Mark A. Weinberger
Global Vice Chair, Assurance: Christian Mouillon
Global Director, Automotive: Michael S. (Mike) Hanley

LOCATIONS

HQ: Ernst & Young Global Limited
    Becket House, 1 Lambeth Palace Rd.
    London SE1 7EU, United Kingdom
Phone: 44-20-7951-2000   Fax: 44-20-7951-1345
US HQ: 5 Times Sq., New York, NY 10036
US Phone: 212-773-3000   US Fax: 212-773-6350
Web: www.ey.com

2008 Sales

	% of total
EMEIA	47
Americas	40
Far East	5
Japan	4
Oceania	4
Total	**100**

PRODUCTS/OPERATIONS

2008 Sales by Service Line

	$ mil.	% of total
Assurance & Advisory Business Services	16,600	63
Tax	6,700	26
Transaction Advisory Services	3,000	11
Adjustments	(1,800)	—
Total	**24,500**	**100**

Selected Services

Assurance and Advisory
    Actuarial services
    Audits
    Accounting advisory
    Business risk services
    Internal audit
    Real estate advisory services
    Technology and security risk services
Emerging Growth Companies
    Corporate finance services
    Mergers and acquisitions advisory
    Operational consulting
    Strategic advisory
    Transactions advisory
Human Capital
    Compensation and benefits consulting
    Cost optimization and risk management
    Transaction support services
Law
    Corporate and M&A
    Employment
    Finance
    Information technology services
    Intellectual property
    International trade and anti-trust
    Litigation and arbitration
    Real estate
Tax
    Global tax operations
    Indirect tax
    International tax

Transactions
    Capital management
    Corporate development advisory
    Financial and business modeling
    M&A advisory
    Post-deal advisory
    Strategic finance
    Transaction management
    Valuation

COMPETITORS

Baker Tilly International
BDO International
Crowe Horwath International
Deloitte
Grant Thornton International
KPMG
Moore Stephens International
PKF International
PricewaterhouseCoopers

HISTORICAL FINANCIALS

Company Type: Partnership

Income Statement

FYE: June 30

	REVENUE ($ mil.)	NET INCOME ($ mil.)	NET PROFIT MARGIN	EMPLOYEES
6/08	24,500	—	—	135,000
6/07	21,160	—	—	121,000
6/06	18,400	—	—	114,000
6/05	16,902	—	—	106,650
6/04	14,547	—	—	100,601
Annual Growth	**13.9%**	**—**	**—**	**7.6%**

Revenue History

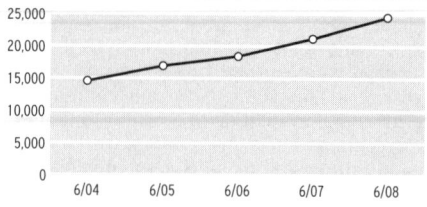

ESPN, Inc.

ESPN is a superstar of the sports broadcasting world. The company is the leading cable sports broadcaster, reaching about 100 million US homes with its stable of channels, including ESPN, ESPN2, and ESPN Classic. The 24-hour networks carry a variety of live sporting events, as well as news and analysis programs. ESPN also creates original programming for TV and radio and lends content for ESPN.com (operated by Disney Online), one of the most popular sports sites on the Internet. Its international operations extend the ESPN brand to another 190 countries. ESPN is 80% owned by Walt Disney (through ABC); media conglomerate Hearst has a 20% stake.

The network has become more than just a leading sports outlet on TV: ESPN's popularity is so vast it is a force to be reckoned with in popular culture, spurring catch phrases ("Boo-yah!") and launching athletes into celebrity status. Through ESPN Original Entertainment, the broadcaster has pushed into original programming with talk shows (*Pardon the Interruption*), series television, and specials.

To reach that stage, ESPN has worked tirelessly to extend its power and influence throughout sports and entertainment. It holds broadcasting contracts with Major League Baseball, the National Basketball Association, and the National Football League, as well as NASCAR and college sports conferences. In 2008 the cable sports channel inked a 15-year deal with the Southeastern Conference (SEC) worth more than $2 billion to air football and basketball games. It later outbid FOX to air the college football Bowl Championship Series, paying $125 million a year for four years to air the top games.

ESPN took over *Monday Night Football* from sister company ABC in 2006. ABC lost about $150 million a year on the venerable program, and the network decided it would fare better on cable. ESPN agreed to pay the NFL $1.1 billion a year for eight years for the broadcasting rights. ABC also turned over its sports programming arm (ABC Sports) to ESPN, which now airs games on ABC under the ESPN banner.

In addition to big-ticket sports, ESPN has been increasing its coverage of other sports leagues, including Major League Lacrosse and Major League Soccer. It also has an equity stake in the Arena Football League (acquired in 2006) and extended its AFL broadcasting contract for five more years. (Financially troubled, the AFL ceased operations and filed for bankruptcy during 2009.)

The company has also been expanding its influence into the international sports scene. In 2009 it acquired rights to air UK Premier League football matches. The rights to the games had been held by troubled Irish broadcaster Setanta Sports Holdings. ESPN plans to launch a new cable and satellite channel to carry the games, integrating content from ESPN America (formerly the North American Sports Network).

The network was launched in 1979 under the name Entertainment and Sports Programming Network; it adopted the new name — ESPN — in 1985.

EXECUTIVES

President ESPN, Inc and ABC Sports; Co-Chairman Disney Media Networks; Chairman ESPN, Inc:
George W. Bodenheimer, age 50
EVP Production: Norby Williamson
EVP Multimedia Sales: David Rotem
EVP Content: John Skipper
EVP Administration: Ed Durso
EVP News, Talent, and Content Operations:
Steve Anderson
EVP and Managing Director, ESPN International:
Russell Wolff
EVP and CTO: Chuck Pagano
EVP and Executive Editor: John Walsh
EVP Sales and Marketing: Sean H. R. Bratches
EVP and CFO: Christine Driessen
EVP Disney and ESPN Networks Affiliate US Sales and Marketing: David Preschlack
EVP Program Planning and Development: David Berson
EVP Multimedia Sales, ESPN Customer Marketing and Sales: Eric Johnson
EVP Programming and Acquisitions: John Wildhack
SVP Communications Counsel and Corporate Outreach: Rosa Gatti
Ombudsman: Donald Ohlmeyer, age 64

LOCATIONS

HQ: ESPN, Inc.
ESPN Plaza, 935 Middle St., Bristol, CT 06010
Phone: 860-766-2000   **Fax:** 860-766-2213
Web: espn.go.com

PRODUCTS/OPERATIONS

Selected Operations
Cable networks
ESPN (sporting events and news channel)
ESPN Classic (archival sports footage channel)
ESPN Deportes (Spanish-language sports network)
ESPN HD (high-definition channel)
ESPN2 (sporting events and news channel)
ESPN2 HD (high-definition channel)
ESPNEWS (24-hour sports news channel)
ESPNU (college sports)
ESPN Enterprises (new business venture development)
ESPN International
ESPN On Demand (video on demand programming)
ESPN Original Programming (original content for cable channels)
ESPN Radio
ESPN The Magazine (print magazine)

COMPETITORS

Big Ten Network
CBS
Comcast SportsNet
Fox Entertainment
Golf Channel
Madison Square Garden
NBC
NESN
Turner Broadcasting
VERSUS
YES Network

Estes Express Lines

Estes Express Lines is a multiregional less-than-truckload (LTL) freight hauler. (LTL carriers consolidate freight from multiple shippers into a single trailer.) The company operates a fleet of about 7,700 tractors and 22,000 trailers from a network of about 200 terminals throughout the US. Estes Express offers service in Canada through ExpressLINK alliance partner TST Overland Express; it works with other companies to offer service in the Caribbean and in Mexico. Founded by W.W. Estes in 1931, the company is owned and operated by the Estes family.

To supplement its LTL business, Estes Express offers airfreight forwarding, equipment leasing, expedited delivery, supply chain management, nationwide brokerage services, truckload transportation, and warehousing services.

Estes Express has gradually expanded its service territory over the years, and in 2008 the company opened terminals in the remaining states where it did not already have them: Iowa, Minnesota, Nebraska, North Dakota, South Dakota, and Wisconsin. Previously, Estes Express had served the upper Midwest through an alliance with Lakeville Motor Express.

EXECUTIVES

President and CEO: Robey W. (Rob) Estes Jr., age 57
EVP and COO: William T. (Billy) Hupp
EVP and COO, Estes Forwarding Worldwide:
 Scott Fisher
CFO and Treasurer: Gary D. Okes
VP Corporate Sales: Chuck Parker
VP Corporate Communications: Trish Garland
VP Human Resources: Thomas Donahue
VP Information Services: Hugh Camden
VP Safety: Curtis Carr
VP Safety: Paul J. Dugent
VP Operations, Estes Air Forwarding: Steve Mulloy
Director Operations Technology: Michael Lackey
Corporate Secretary: Stephen E. Hupp
Auditors: Joyner, Kirkham, Keel & Robertson, P. C.

LOCATIONS

HQ: Estes Express Lines, Inc.
3901 W. Broad St., Richmond, VA 23230
Phone: 804-353-1900   **Fax:** 804-353-8001
Web: www.estes-express.com

COMPETITORS

AAA Cooper Transportation
Arkansas Best
Averitt Express
Con-way Freight
FedEx Freight
Old Dominion Freight
Penske Truck Leasing
R+L Carriers
Ryder System
Saia
UPS Freight
Vitran
YRC Worldwide

HISTORICAL FINANCIALS

Company Type: Private

Income Statement   FYE: December 31

	REVENUE ($ mil.)	NET INCOME ($ mil.)	NET PROFIT MARGIN	EMPLOYEES
12/08	1,480	—	—	13,000
12/07	1,395	—	—	12,374
12/06	1,447	—	—	13,824
12/05	1,149	—	—	13,051
12/04	1,000	—	—	—
Annual Growth	10.3%	—	—	(0.1%)

Revenue History

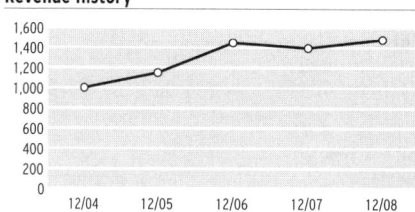

Euramax International

Euramax International takes aluminum to the max in the US and Europe. Through subsidiaries that include Amerimax Building Products, Amerimax Home Products, and Berger Building Products, the company makes roofs, walls, windows, doors, rain drainage systems, and patio covers out of such building materials as aluminum, fiberglass, steel, and vinyl. It also makes aluminum doors, windows, and sidewalls for RVs. Customers include residential and commercial building contractors, distributors, home centers, and RV manufacturers. Its Euramax Coated Products division consists of two European manufacturing plants that produce coil coating (or prepainting of metal products).

Euramax International was established in 1996 to acquire the fabricated products business of aluminum producer Alumax Inc. Since that time the company has grown organically and through several acquisitions to become a leading producer of steel roofing, siding, and trim for primarily commercial construction.

Today, it has a manufacturing and distribution network of more than 50 facilities, the majority of which are located in the US; one is located in Canada, while another eight are located in Europe.

Euramax International is controlled by Goldman Sachs & Co.

EXECUTIVES

President, CEO, and Director: Mitchell B. Lewis, age 46
VP, CFO, and Secretary: R. Scott Vansant, age 46
President, Amerimax Building Products: Nick E. Dowd, age 51
President, Gutter Suppliers and ADP: Scott R. Anderson, age 46
Auditors: Ernst & Young LLP

LOCATIONS

HQ: Euramax International, Inc.
5445 Triangle Pkwy., Ste. 350, Norcross, GA 30092
Phone: 770-449-7066   **Fax:** 770-449-7354
Web: www.euramax.com

PRODUCTS/OPERATIONS

Selected Products

Air filters
Bath & shower enclosures (aluminum)
Composite panels
Decorative skylights
Doors (aluminum, vinyl)
Fabricated metal
Grates & covers
Gutters
Patio covers
Rain drainage systems (metal, vinyl)
Recreational vehicle doors & sidewalls
Roofs (metal)
Signs
Snow guards
Soffit & fascia
Specialty coated coil
Trim coil
Walls (metal)
Windows (aluminum, vinyl)

Selected Subsidiaries

Amerimax Building Products
Amerimax Home Products, Inc.
Berger Building Products, Inc.
Coppercraft
Ellbee Limited
Euramax Canada, Inc.
Euramax Coated Products B.V.
Euramax Coated Products Ltd.
Euramax Industries S.A.
Fabral
Global Expanded Metals

COMPETITORS

American Buildings
Atwood Mobile
Butler Manufacturing
Design Components
Gibraltar Industries
NCI Building Systems

HISTORICAL FINANCIALS

Company Type: Holding company

Income Statement				FYE: Last Friday of December
	REVENUE ($ mil.)	NET INCOME ($ mil.)	NET PROFIT MARGIN	EMPLOYEES
12/07	1,300	—	—	3,471
12/06	1,210	—	—	3,300
12/05	1,068	—	—	3,200
12/04	965	—	—	2,700
12/03	744	—	—	2,600
Annual Growth	15.0%	—	—	7.5%

Revenue History

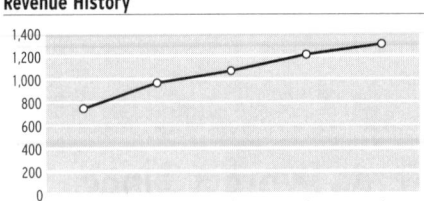

	12/03	12/04	12/05	12/06	12/07
1,400					
1,200					
1,000					
800					
600					
400					
200					
0					

Evergreen Holdings

Through subsidiary Evergreen International Aviation, Evergreen Holdings soars over green lands. Evergreen International Aviation itself operates through several units, including Evergreen International Airlines, which transports cargo for government and commercial customers with a fleet of Boeing 747 freighters. Evergreen Aviation Ground Logistics Enterprise provides ground handling services at US airports. Other Evergreen units offer helicopter transportation services; maintain, repair, and overhaul aircraft; sell and lease aircraft; and engage in farming. Del Smith, a former Air Force pilot and crop duster, owns a controlling stake in the company, which he founded in 1960.

Over the years the Air Force's Air Mobility Command has been a major customer of Evergreen International Airlines. The carrier hauls hazardous materials and other sensitive cargo for the Air Force; in addition, it transports general cargo for customers such as airlines and freight forwarders, often under ACMI (aircraft, crew, maintenance, and insurance) contracts.

Evergreen Holdings has stakes not only in the present and the future of aviation, but also in its past. A museum outside the company's headquarters houses Howard Hughes' *Spruce Goose* and other vintage aircraft.

EXECUTIVES

Chairman and CEO: Delford M. (Del) Smith, age 78
President and Director; President and Director, Evergreen International Aviation: Timothy G. Wahlberg, age 62
VP Planning, Military and Government Contracts: John Palo
President, Evergreen Helicopters: David Rath
President, Fixed Wing: Michael A. Hines
President, Evergreen Helicopters of Alaska: Sabrina Ford
President, Evergreen International Airlines and Systems LogistiX and Director, Evergreen International Aviation: Brian T. Bauer, age 39
President, Evergreen Helicopters International: Dan Blanchard
President, Evergreen Helicopters International: James A. Porter, age 61
Auditors: GHP Horwath, PC

LOCATIONS

HQ: Evergreen Holdings, Inc.
3850 Three Mile Ln., McMinnville, OR 97128
Phone: 503-472-9361   **Fax:** 503-472-1048
Web: www.evergreenaviation.com

PRODUCTS/OPERATIONS

Selected Subsidiaries and Affiliated Companies

Aviation
Evergreen International Aviation, Inc.
Evergreen International Airlines, Inc.
Evergreen Helicopters, Inc.
Evergreen Aviation Ground Logistics Enterprises, Inc. (EAGLE)
Evergreen Maintenance Center, Inc.
Evergreen Trade Inc.
Evergreen Systems Logistics, Inc.

Agriculture
Evergreen Agricultural Enterprises, Inc.
Evergreen Nursery
Evergreen Orchards and Vineyards

COMPETITORS

AAR Corp.
Air Methods
Air T
Air Transport Services Group
Aircraft Service International
Arrow Air
ASTAR Air Cargo
Atlas Air Worldwide
Bristow Group Inc
CHC Helicopter
GATX
GE Commercial Aviation Services
Goodrich Corp.
Grand Aire
Kalitta Air
Keystone Helicopter
Menzies Aviation
Mercury Air Group
PHI, Inc.
Servisair
Swissport USA, Inc.
WFS

Express Employment

When you need a worker fast, Express Employment Professionals delivers. Formerly known as Express Personnel Services, the professional staffing company provides work for some 350,000 employees from about 600 offices across Australia, Canada, South Africa, and the US. In addition to temporary staffing, it offers workplace services (consulting, training, development) through Express Business Solutions. Founded in 1983, the company is owned by founders William Stoller (vice chairman) and Robert Funk (CEO).

EXECUTIVES

Chairman and CEO: Robert A. Funk
Vice Chairman: William H. (Bill) Stoller
EVP Sales and Director: Robert E. (Bob) Fellinger
EVP Operations, CFO, and Director:
 Thomas N. Richards
SVP Administration and Human Resources: Carol Lane
SVP Franchise Support and Information Systems:
 Terri Weldon
SVP Sales: Cory Benton
SVP Zone Sales: Elaine Brink
VP Human Resources: Russ Moen
VP Franchising: Fred Bartliff
VP Public Relations and Corporate Communications:
 Jennifer Anderson
VP Corporate Accounting and Controller: Sharon Patric
VP Sales and Marketing: Linda Sasser
VP Franchise Systems: Harvey H. H. Homsey
Director Corporate Communications:
 Sean Taylor Simpson

LOCATIONS

HQ: Express Employment Professionals
 8516 Northwest Expwy., Oklahoma City, OK 73162
Phone: 405-840-5000   **Fax:** 405-717-5669
Web: www.expresspros.com

PRODUCTS/OPERATIONS

Selected Staffing Fields

Express Personnel
 General labor
 Government
 Health care
 Industrial
 Office and clerical
 Scientific
 Technical

Express Professional
 Accounting and financial
 Engineering and manufacturing
 Health care
 Human resources
 Information technology
 Sales and marketing
 Technical

COMPETITORS

Adecco
Administaff
ADP TotalSource
Barrett Business Services
Butler America
Kelly Services
Manpower
MPS
Randstad Holding
Robert Half
Spherion
Volt Information

HISTORICAL FINANCIALS
Company Type: Private

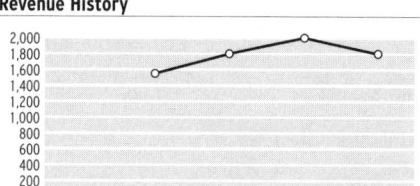

Income Statement				FYE: December 31
	REVENUE ($ mil.)	NET INCOME ($ mil.)	NET PROFIT MARGIN	EMPLOYEES
12/08	1,800	—	—	350,000
12/07	2,000	—	—	375,000
12/06	1,800	—	—	350,000
12/05	1,550	—	—	300,000
Annual Growth	5.1%	—	—	5.3%

Revenue History

(Revenue History chart showing values from 12/04 to 12/08, y-axis 0 to 2,000)

Express, LLC

Right from the runway is the Express way. Express operates about 550 stores in the US that sell trendy private-label apparel and accessories. (Its fashions are styled to have an international influence and modern appeal.) Express also sells denim and lingerie and operates an online store. Amid declining sales, Express has been closing stores and has converted about 500 of its locations to dual-gender outlets that carry both men's and women's fashions. Limited Brands, which launched Express in 1980, sold a majority stake in the chain to the San Francisco-based private equity firm Golden Gate Capital (GGC) in 2007.

More than 300 Express shops have closed their doors since 2005. Still the company is expanding abroad. In 2009 the retailer opened a pair of stores in the Middle East at the Dubai Mall and in Kuwait. In 2008 Express opened its first location in Hawaii.

Other specialty retailers, including Banana Republic and Brooks Brothers, have brought fragrances and personal care products to market in recent years in a bid to add more revenue and extend their brands. Express hopped on that bandwagon with the 2009 launch of a men's fragrance called Express Reserve.

GGC acquired a 75% interest in the chain in July 2007 for about $425 million. (Limited Brands retained a 25% stake in Express.) GGC kept the Express name, and the company remained based in Columbus, Ohio. However, GGC replaced Jay Margolis — who headed Express as president of Limited Brands' apparel group — with Michael Weiss as CEO. It is Weiss's second stint as head of Express. He had led the retailer for about two decades before retiring in 2004.

Sales at Express stores have declined in recent years, as have those of its former sister chain Limited Stores, which has also been sold to another private equity firm. Limited Brands said it sold both chains in order to focus on its better performing intimate apparel and personal care businesses (Victoria's Secret and Bath & Body Works). Express accounted for about 15% of Limited Brands' sales.

EXECUTiVES

President and CEO: Michael A. Weiss, age 68
CFO: Matt Mollering
EVP Marketing: Lisa A. Gavales

LOCATIONS

HQ: Express, LLC
 1 Limited Pkwy., Columbus, OH 43230
Phone: 614-415-4000   **Fax:** 614-415-7440
Web: www.expressfashion.com

COMPETITORS

Abercrombie & Fitch	Guess?
American Eagle Outfitters	J. C. Penney
AnnTaylor	Kenneth Cole
bebe stores	Kohl's
Charlotte Russe Holding	Macy's
Charming Shoppes	Target
Dillard's	TJX Companies
Donna Karan	Wet Seal
The Gap	

HISTORICAL FINANCIALS
Company Type: Private

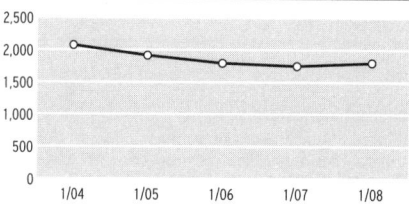

Income Statement				FYE: Saturday nearest January 31
	REVENUE ($ mil.)	NET INCOME ($ mil.)	NET PROFIT MARGIN	EMPLOYEES
1/08	1,800	—	—	—
1/07	1,749	—	—	—
1/06	1,794	—	—	—
1/05	1,913	—	—	—
1/04	2,071	—	—	—
Annual Growth	(3.4%)	—	—	—

Revenue History

(Revenue History chart showing values from 1/04 to 1/08, y-axis 0 to 2,500)

Factory Mutual Insurance

If you're looking to protect your corporation, turn your insurance dial to FM Global. Factory Mutual Insurance (operating as FM Global) provides commercial and industrial property/casualty insurance and a variety of risk management services. It provides specialized products for ocean cargo and machinery equipment, as well as property loss prevention engineering and research. FM Global operates through such subsidiaries as Affiliated FM Insurance, FM Global Cargo, and Mutual Boiler Re. In addition to the US, the company has offices in Asia, Australia, Canada, Europe, and South America.

FM Global operates a business model that promotes proactive loss prevention rather than actuarial loss predictions. The company helps its clients improve and strengthen facilities, minimizing the damage that can result from such events as fires, explosions, and hurricanes. Its engineering expertise is provided by FM Global Research Campus, a research and testing complex. The company's TSB Loss Control Consultants provides emergency response training for its customers.

EXECUTIVES

Chairman and CEO: Shivan S. Subramaniam
Vice Chairman: Ruud H. Bosman
EVP North and South America Insurance Operations:
Thomas A. Lawson
EVP: Jonathan W. Hall
SVP Information Services: Jeanne R. Lieb
SVP Investments: Paul E. LaFleche
SVP Claims: Gerardo L. Alonso
SVP Human Resources: Enzo Rebula
SVP International Division: Kenneth W. Davey
SVP Finance: Jeffrey A. Burchill
SVP Underwriting and Reinsurance: Carol G. Barton
SVP Marketing and Training:
Christopher (Chris) Johnson
SVP Engineering and Research: Brion E. Callori
SVP Law and Governmental Affairs: John J. Pomeroy
Senior Public Relations Consultant: Jamie Pachomski
Auditors: Ernst & Young LLP

LOCATIONS

HQ: Factory Mutual Insurance Company
1301 Atwood Ave., Johnston, RI 02919
Phone: 401-275-3000   **Fax:** 401-275-3029
Web: www.fmglobal.com

PRODUCTS/OPERATIONS

2008 Revenue

	$ mil.	% of total
Net premiums	2,943.8	88
Investment income	380.3	11
Fees	40.7	1
Total	**3,364.8**	**100**

Selected Subsidiaries

Affiliated FM Insurance Company
Corporate Insurance Services (insurance brokerage)
FM Approvals (third-party loss prevention certification services)
FM Global Cargo (cargo insurance, risk management)
FM Global Research
Mutual Boiler Re
TSB Loss Control Consultants, Inc.

COMPETITORS

ACE Limited
AIG
Allianz
Endurance Specialty
The Hartford
HSB Group
Nationwide
Specialty Underwriters' Alliance
Travelers Companies
Western World Insurance
XL Capital
Zurich Financial Services

HISTORICAL FINANCIALS

Company Type: Mutual company

Income Statement

FYE: December 31

	ASSETS ($ mil.)	NET INCOME ($ mil.)	INCOME AS % OF ASSETS	EMPLOYEES
12/08	11,307	(318)	—	5,000
12/07	13,030	928	7.1%	4,500
12/06	12,268	737	6.0%	4,900
12/05	11,090	635	5.7%	4,700
12/04	9,484	558	5.9%	4,700
Annual Growth	**4.5%**	**—**	**—**	**1.6%**

2008 Year-End Financials

Equity as % of assets: —   Long-term debt ($ mil.): —
Return on assets: —   Sales ($ mil.): 3,365
Return on equity: —

Net Income History

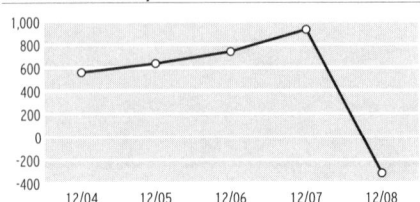

Fagen, Inc.

Although Fagen knows what the *dickens* is going on in the construction industry, it should not be confused with the character in *Oliver!* The company offers a range of commercial and industrial contracting and engineering services, including design/build, project management, and general contracting. Affiliate Fagen Engineering performs civil, structural, electrical, and mechanical design services. The company works across a variety of heavy industries and has completed such projects as power generation plants, water- and wastewater-treatment plants, manufacturing facilities, and housing.

Sectors served include auto manufacturing, pharmaceuticals, food processing, natural gas, rubber, and mining. Focusing on green energy, Fagen also works on ethanol plants and wind turbine projects.

The Fagen family owns the company.

EXECUTIVES

CEO: Ron Fagen
CFO: Jennifer A. Johnson, age 53

LOCATIONS

HQ: Fagen, Inc.
501 W. Hwy. 212, Granite Falls, MN 56241
Phone: 320-564-3324   **Fax:** 320-564-3278
Web: www.fageninc.com

COMPETITORS

Fluor
Jacobs Engineering
JGC
Skanska USA Building
SW&B Construction
URS
Washington Division

Fairview Health Services

Fairview Health Services is a not-for-profit health care system that serves Minnesota's Twin Cities and surrounding communities. Fairview Health Services is affiliated with the medical school of the University of Minnesota and counts among its seven hospitals the University of Minnesota Medical Center. All told, its hospitals house some 2,500 beds and provide comprehensive medical and surgical services. The integrated health system also operates a network of primary and specialty care clinics, retail pharmacies, and nursing homes; and it provides home health care and rehabilitation services.

Fairview is expanding with the construction of a new hospital in Maple Grove, just northwest of the Twin Cities, that is scheduled to open by the end of 2009. The organization opened a primary care and outpatient services center there (Maple Grove Medical Center) in 2007. The new hospital is being built in partnership with North Memorial Health Care.

Other construction efforts include a new Amplatz Children's Hospital facility, scheduled for completion in 2011. The children's medical center is part of the University of Minnesota Medical Center. In 2008 Fairview Health Services expanded through the acquisition of Columbia Park Medical Group, a multi-specialty medical group operating six clinics.

Mark Eustis became president and CEO of Fairview in 2007, replacing David Page.

EXECUTIVES

Chair: Jon R. Campbell
Vice Chair: Connie G. Weinman
President, CEO, and Director: Mark A. Eustis, age 56
SVP and CFO: James M. Fox
SVP and Chief Clinical Officer: Lois A. Lenarz
SVP and General Counsel: George Chresand
VP Public Policy: Mary C. Edwards
VP Strategy, Marketing, and Communication:
Mark Hansberry
President, Fairview Northland Care System: Mike Youso
President, Fairview Red Wing Care System:
Scott Wordelman
President, Fairview Range Care System: Larry Pfaff
President, Ebenezer Society: Mark Thomas
Chief Human Resources Officer: Paula H. Phillippe
Secretary and Director: Joanell Dyrstad
Auditors: Ernst & Young LLP

LOCATIONS

HQ: Fairview Health Services
2450 Riverside Ave., Minneapolis, MN 55454
Phone: 612-672-6000   **Fax:** 612-672-7186
Web: www.fairview.org

PRODUCTS/OPERATIONS

Selected Facilities

Fairview Lakes Medical Center (Wyoming)
Fairview Maple Grove Medical Center
Fairview Northland Medical Center (Princeton)
Fairview Red Wing Medical Center
Fairview Ridges Hospital (Burnsville)
Fairview Southdale Hospital (Minneapolis)
University of Minnesota Children's Hospital (Minneapolis)
University of Minnesota Medical Center (Minneapolis)

HISTORICAL FINANCIALS

Company Type: Not-for-profit

Income Statement				FYE: December 31
	REVENUE ($ mil.)	NET INCOME ($ mil.)	NET PROFIT MARGIN	EMPLOYEES
12/08	2,567	—	—	18,000

Federal Home Loan Bank of Atlanta

Where do banks in the southeastern US bank? Federal Home Loan Bank of Atlanta. More than 1,200 commercial banks, credit unions, insurance companies, and thrifts in the southeast bank at the institution, which calls itself FHLBank Atlanta. It's one of 12 Federal Home Loan Banks in the Federal Home Loan Bank System and is cooperatively owned by its member institutions, ranging in size from organizations with less than $5 million in assets to "super-regionals" with more than $125 billion. Institutions are required to purchase capital stock in the bank to be members. A government-sponsored enterprise, the bank funds residential mortgages and community development loans.

The bank's territory includes Alabama, Florida, Georgia, Maryland, North Carolina, South Carolina, Virginia, and Washington, DC.

An independent federal government agency, the Federal Housing Finance Board, supervises and regulates the bank.

EXECUTIVES

Chairman: Scott C. Harvard, age 54
Vice Chairman: James Thomas Johnson, age 62
President and CEO: Richard A. Dorfman, age 63, $1,840,886 total compensation
EVP and CFO: Steven J. Goldstein, age 57, $550,714 total compensation
EVP, General Counsel, Chief Strategy Officer, and Corporate Secretary: Jill Spencer, age 57, $1,192,461 total compensation
EVP and Chief Administrative Officer: Cathy C. Adams, age 49
EVP and Chief Credit Officer: Kirk R. Malmberg, age 48, $717,399 total compensation
EVP and Director Financial Management: W. Wesley (Wes) McMullan, age 45, $1,119,990 total compensation
SVP and Chief Information Officer: Robert Bennett
SVP and Director of Government and Industry Relations: Eric Mondres
SVP Financial Operations Management: Charlotte McRanie
SVP and Director Internal Audit: Richard A. Patrick
SVP and Treasurer: Andrew B. Mills
SVP and Controller: J. Daniel (Dan) Counce
Auditors: PricewaterhouseCoopers LLP

LOCATIONS

HQ: Federal Home Loan Bank of Atlanta
1475 Peachtree St., NE, Atlanta, GA 30309
Phone: 404-888-8000   **Fax:** 404-888-5648
Web: www.fhlbatl.com

PRODUCTS/OPERATIONS

2008 Sales

	$ mil.	% of total
Interest		
Advances	4,722.2	71
Other	1,911.0	29
Noninterest	(214.0)	—
Total	**6,419.2**	**100**

COMPETITORS

Fannie Mae
FHLB Chicago
Freddie Mac
Ginnie Mae
MoneyGram International

HISTORICAL FINANCIALS

Company Type: Member-owned banking authority

Income Statement				FYE: December 31
	ASSETS ($ mil.)	NET INCOME ($ mil.)	INCOME AS % OF ASSETS	EMPLOYEES
12/08	208,564	254	0.1%	383
12/07	189,746	445	0.2%	362
12/06	140,758	414	0.3%	349
12/05	143,239	344	0.2%	339
12/04	134,013	294	0.2%	—
Annual Growth	11.7%	(3.6%)	—	4.2%

2008 Year-End Financials

Equity as % of assets: —
Return on assets: 0.1%
Return on equity: —
Long-term debt ($ mil.): —
Sales ($ mil.): 6,419

Net Income History

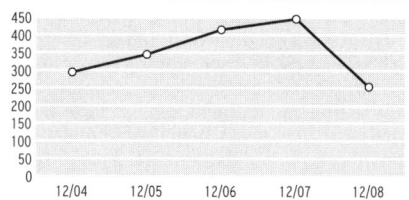

Federal Prison Industries

Some businesses benefit from captive audiences; this company benefits from captive employees. Federal Prison Industries (FPI), known by its trade name UNICOR, uses prisoners to make products and provide services, mainly for the US government. More than 21,000 inmates (almost 20% of the total eligible inmate population) are employed in over 100 FPI factories in prisons across the US. UNICOR, which is part of the Justice Department's Bureau of Prisons, manufactures products such as office furniture, clothing, beds and linens, electronics equipment, and eyewear. It also offers services, including data entry, bulk mailing, laundry services, recycling, and refurbishing of vehicle components.

UNICOR is self-supporting and is overseen by a governing board that is appointed by the President of the US. The mission of the FPI is to provide job training, job skills, and potential job opportunities to the inmates within the Federal Bureau of Prisons. Unlike most manufacturers these days that look to establish facilities in developing countries, UNICOR tries to leverage its low labor costs and actually looks for labor-intensive products to make. FPI is benefiting from a growing prison population and the cheap cost of its labor (pay ranges from 23 cents to $1.15 per hour). The following companies have moved production into prisons: Boeing, Microsoft, Starbucks, and Victoria's Secret, to name a few.

The FPI is an $800 million business which makes $150 million in automobile parts and over $100 million in office furniture. UNICOR is in alliance with a number of companies, some of which include: Filtration Services (commercial air filter service), HumanScale (ergonomic seating), and Titmus (protective eyewear). UNICOR is allowed to sell services, but not products, to the private commercial sector.

Federal law mandates that government buyers consider UNICOR products before they consider competing products from the private sector. Its largest customers include the US Departments of Defense (which buys nearly all of its furniture from UNICOR), Homeland Security, the Justice Department, and the Social Security Administration.

The Inmate Transition Branch of UNICOR conducts mock job fairs in the Federal correctional institutions to prepare inmates in their job searches. Over 7,000 company recruiters and representatives from community services and educational institutions have participated.

HISTORY

FPI was established by President Franklin Roosevelt in 1934 to teach job skills at men's and women's federal prisons. During WWII, 95% of FPI's output was dedicated to the war effort — the company's products included parachutes and munitions. In the late 1950s and early 1960s, FPI built or renovated structures at 18 of the 31 federal prisons. In 1974 it established regional sales offices, and in 1977 it took the name UNICOR.

Although self-supporting, UNICOR remained necessarily inefficient because of its goal to put as many inmates as possible to work. However, as the prison population increased, the company underwent rapid expansion and added skilled services in the 1980s.

UNICOR put its product catalog online in 1996. The next year the Senate authorized a study of ways to make UNICOR more competitive, after private businesses had complained that the booming prison population, low wages (23 cents to $1.15 per hour), and government preferential treatment gave UNICOR an unfair advantage. Legislation to force FPI to bid against the private sector for government contracts was brought before Congress in 1999; at the same time, a bill was introduced to allow the company to offer its products to the private sector. Meanwhile, FPI began selling services such as data entry to private-sector customers.

In 2003 Dell Computer dropped UNICOR as the vendor for its computer recycling program.

EXECUTIVES

Chairman: David D. Spears
Vice Chairman: Donald R. Elliott
CEO: Harley G. Lappin
COO: Paul M. Laird
CFO and Controller: Cathy Hawkins
Systems Administrator: Linda Burch
Chief, Strategic Business Development and Marketing:
 Robert Grieser
General Manager, Electronics Business Group:
 Brad Beus
General Manager, Services Business Group:
 Sheila Richardson
General Manager, Industrial Products Business Group:
 Germano Tavares
General Manager, Recycling Program: Robert J. Tonetti
General Manager, Office Furniture Business Group:
 Dan Moore
General Manager, Textiles Business Group:
 Marie-France Vareilles
General Manager, Fleet Solutions Business Group:
 Bill Bondy
General Counsel: Marianne Cantwell
Auditors: KPMG LLP

LOCATIONS

HQ: Federal Prison Industries, Inc.
 320 1st St. NW, Bldg. 400, Washington, DC 20534
Phone: 202-305-3500   **Fax:** 202-305-7340
Web: www.unicor.gov

PRODUCTS/OPERATIONS

2008 Sales

	% of total
Fleet Management & Vehicular Components	27
Electronics	26
Clothing & Textiles	24
Office furniture	15
Services	4
Industrial products	3
Recycling	1
Total	**100**

Selected Products

Clothing and textiles
 Apparel (law enforcement, medical, military, and
  institutional)
 Draperies and curtains
 Embroidery and screen printing on textiles
 Mattresses, bedding, linens, and towels
Electronics
 Electrical cables (both braided and cord assemblies)
 Electrical components and connectors
 Lighting systems
 Wire harness assemblies and circuit boards
Fleet management
 Fleet management customized services
 New-vehicle retrofit services
 Rebuilt and refurbished vehicle components
Industrial products
 Custom fabricated industrial products, lockers, and
  storage cabinets
 Dorm and quarters furnishings and packaged room
  solutions
 Industrial racking catwalks, mezzanines, and shelving
 License plates
 Optical eyewear (safety and prescription)
 Replacement filters
 Security fencing
Office furniture
 Casegoods and training table products
 Filing and storage products
 Office furniture and accessories
 Office system products
 Packaged office solutions
 Seating products
Recycling
 Recycling of electronic components
 Recycling activities

Services
 Assembly and packing services
 Call center and order fulfillment services
 Distribution and mailing services
 Document conversion
 Laundry services

COMPETITORS

Avnet
CPAC
Deere
Federal Signal
Haworth, Inc.
Herman Miller
HNI
Kimball International
Matthews International
Mine Safety Appliances
Molex
Steelcase
Tyco
WestPoint Home Inc

Federal Reserve System

Where do banks go when they need a loan? To the Federal Reserve System, which sets the discount interest rate, the base rate at which its member banks may borrow. Known as the Fed, the system oversees a network of 12 Federal Reserve Banks located in major US cities; these in turn regulate banks in their districts and ensure they maintain adequate reserves. The Fed also clears money transfers, issues currency, and buys or sells government securities to regulate the money supply. Through its powerful New York bank, the Fed conducts foreign currency transactions, trades on the world market to support the US dollar's value, and stores gold for foreign governments and international agencies.

By setting the discount rate and the federal funds rate (the rate at which banks borrow from each other), the Fed influences the pace of lending and, many believe, the pace of the economy. Fed board members are appointed by the US president and confirmed by the Senate for one-time 14-year terms, staggered at two-year intervals to prevent political stacking. Seven governors comprise the majority of the 12-person Federal Open Market Committee, which determines monetary policy. The five remaining members are reserve bank presidents who rotate in one-year terms, with New York always holding a place. Although the Fed enjoys significant political and financial freedom, the chairman is required to testify before Congress twice a year. National member banks must own stock in their Federal Reserve Bank, though it is optional for state-chartered banks.

A seven-member Board of Governors oversees the Fed's activities. The board was chaired by former Ayn Rand compadre Alan Greenspan from the Reagan administration until 2006. As chairman under four different presidents, Greenspan wielded more power than perhaps any Fed chief in history, and securities markets rose and fell on his every word. Greenspan was replaced by former chairman of President

George W. Bush's Council of Economic Advisers and Fed board member, Ben Bernanke. As his predecessor did during other economic downturns, Bernanke agressively cut the discount interest rate in an effort to jumpstart the economy.

However, in 2008 the US faced an economic crisis as severe as any seen since the Great Depression that claimed numerous victims, including Bear Stearns (the Fed brokered and assisted its purchase by JPMorgan Chase) and Lehman Brothers. Together with Secretary of the Treasury Henry Paulson, Bernanke pushed for the passage of a $700 billion rescue plan — the largest in history. Through the plan, the government will purchase toxic assets, including troubled mortgages and distressed properties.

The Fed also eased up its dollar swap facilities with top European central banks in an effort to provide liquidity and meet demand for the dollar overseas.

HISTORY

When New York's Knickerbocker Trust Company failed in 1907, it brought on a panic that was stemmed by J. P. Morgan, who strong-armed his fellow bankers into supporting shaky New York banks. The incident showed the need for a central bank.

Morgan's actions sparked fears of his economic power and spurred congressional efforts to establish a central bank. After a six-year struggle between Eastern money interests and populist monetary reformers, the 1913 Federal Reserve Act was passed. Twelve Federal Reserve districts were created, but New York's economic might ensured it would be the most powerful.

New York bank head Benjamin Strong dominated the Fed in the 1920s, countering the glut of European gold flooding the US in 1923 by selling securities from the Fed's portfolio. After he died in 1928, the Fed couldn't stabilize prices. Such difficulty, along with low rates encouraging members to use Fed loans for stock speculation, helped set the stage for 1929's crash.

During the Depression and WWII, the Fed yielded to the demands of the Treasury to buy bonds. But after WWII it sought independence, using Congress to help free it from Treasury demands. This effort was led by chairman William McChesney Martin, with the assistance of New York bank president Alan Sproul (also a rival for the chairmanship). Martin diluted Sproul's influence by governing by consensus with the other bank leaders.

The Fed managed the economy successfully in the postwar boom, but it was stymied by inflation in the late 1960s. In the early 1970s the New York bank also faced the collapse of the fixed currency exchange-rate system and the growth of currency trading. Its role as foreign currency trader became even more crucial as the dollar's value eroded amid rising oil prices and a slowing economy.

The US suffered from double-digit inflation in 1979 as President Jimmy Carter appointed New York Fed president Paul Volcker as chairman. Volcker, believing that raising interest rates a few points would not suffice, allowed the banks to raise their discount rates and increased bank reserve requirements to reduce the money supply. By the time inflation eased, Ronald Reagan was president.

During the 1980s and 1990s, US budget fights limited options for controlling the economy through spending decision, so the Fed's actions became more important. Its higher profile brought calls for more access to its decision-making processes. Alan Greenspan took over as chairman in 1987 after being designated by Reagan (and reappointed by presidents George H. W. Bush, Bill Clinton, and George W. Bush). He stepped down during the second Bush administration and was replaced by Ben Bernanke.

While the US economy seemed immune to the Asian currency crisis of 1997 and 1998, the Federal Reserve remained relatively quiescent. But when Russia defaulted on some of its bonds in 1998, leading to the near-collapse of hedge fund Long-Term Capital Management, the New York Federal Reserve Bank brokered a bailout by the fund's lenders and investors.

This led in 1999 to new guidelines for banks' risk management. The next year the Fed faced up to the Internet age, taking a look at e-banking supervision. After raising interest rates to stave off inflation during the go-go late 1990s, the Fed cut rates an unprecedented 11 times in 2001 (to a 40-year low of 1.75%) to help spur the flagging post-boom economy. Rate changes, and subsequent economic changes, continued with a low of 1% in 2003. In all, rates were adjusted a total of 18 times between 2002 and 2006.

EXECUTIVES

Chairman: Ben S. Bernanke, age 56
Vice Chairman: Donald L. Kohn, age 67
Director Information Technology: Maureen T. Hannan
President and CEO, Federal Reserve Bank of St. Louis: James B. Bullard, age 48
President and CEO, Federal Reserve Bank of New York: William C. Dudley, age 56
President, Federal Reserve Bank of Philadelphia: Charles I. Plosser, age 58
President, Federal Reserve Bank of Dallas: Richard W. Fisher
President and CEO, Federal Reserve Bank of Boston: Eric S. Rosengren, age 51
President, Federal Reserve Bank of San Francisco: Janet L. Yellen, age 63
President, Federal Reserve Bank of Minneapolis: Gary H. Stern
President and CEO, Federal Reserve Bank of Atlanta: Dennis P. Lockhart, age 60
President, Federal Reserve Bank of Kansas City: Thomas M. (Tom) Hoenig, age 63
President, Federal Reserve Bank of Cleveland: Sandra Pianalto, age 55
President, Federal Reserve Bank of Richmond: Jeffrey M. (Jeff) Lacker, age 54
President, Federal Reserve Bank of Chicago: Charles L. (Charlie) Evans, age 51
Inspector General: Elizabeth A. Coleman
Comptroller of the Currency: John C. Dugan, age 54
General Counsel, Legal Division: Scott G. Alvarez
Secretary: Jennifer J. Johnson
Director, International Finance Division: D. Nathan Sheets
Director, Banking Supervision and Regulation Division: Roger T. Cole
Director, Office of Board Members, and Assistant to the Board: Michelle A. Smith
Director, Research and Statistics Division: David J. Stockton
Director, Consumer and Community Affairs Division: Sandra F. Braunstein
Director, Monetary Affairs Division: Brian F. Madigan
Auditors: PricewaterhouseCoopers LLP

LOCATIONS

HQ: Federal Reserve System
20th Street and Constitution Avenue NW
Washington, DC 20551
Phone: 202-452-3000
Web: www.federalreserve.gov

Federal Reserve Banks
Atlanta
Boston
Chicago
Cleveland
Dallas
Kansas City, Missouri
Minneapolis
New York
Philadelphia
Richmond, Virginia
St. Louis
San Francisco

Feed The Children

Tuppence a bag might feed some birds, but it takes more to feed growing children. Feed The Children (FTC) is a not-for-profit Christian charity that distributes food, medicine, clothing, and other necessities. In the US, FTC accepts bulk contributions of surplus food from businesses, packages it in various ways at six main facilities nationwide, and distributes it to food banks, homeless shelters, churches, and other organizations that help feed the hungry. In more than 110 countries overseas FTC works with organizations such as schools, orphanages, and churches to provide food, medical supplies, clothing, and educational support to the needy. Larry and Frances Jones founded FTC in 1979.

In 2009 FTC's board fired Larry Jones as president and announced that COO and EVP Travis Arnold would take over the position in the interim. After giving up operational control in 2009, Jones had been embroiled in legal disputes with most of the board. He was also criticized for installing hidden microphones in the offices of the general counsel (a role filled by his daughter, Larri Sue Jones), CFO, and COO.

While FTC has focused its efforts on feeding children, the organization also concentrates on supplying them with support through outreach programs. FTC launched an educational initiative named H.E.L.P. (or Homeless Education and Literacy Program), which works with homeless outreach coordinators in elementary and middle schools to provide students with school supplies, books, and personal-care items, in addition to food.

The organization's FTC Transportation subsidiary picks up in-kind donations from corporate warehouses and distributes them to one of the charity's six regional distribution centers.

EXECUTIVES

Chairman: Dwight Powers
Interim President: Travis Arnold
CFO: Christy Tharp
EVP: Frances Jones
VP Human Relations: Richard Gray
VP Management Information Systems: Larry Correa
VP and General Counsel: Larri Sue Jones
VP International Public Relations: Steven Whetstone
Director: Leo B. Fundaro Jr.
Auditors: McGladrey & Pullen, LLP

LOCATIONS

HQ: Feed The Children, Inc.
333 N. Meridian Ave., Oklahoma City, OK 73107
Phone: 405-942-0228   **Fax:** 405-945-4177
Web: www.feedthechildren.org

Feld Entertainment

A lot of clowning around has helped Feld Entertainment become one of the largest live entertainment producers in the world. The company entertains people through its centerpiece, Ringling Bros. and Barnum & Bailey Circus, which visits about 90 locations. Feld also produces several touring ice shows, including Disney On Ice shows such as *High School Musical: The Ice Tour*. In addition, its Disney Live! produces live touring stage productions with Disney-themed stories and characters. Chairman and CEO Kenneth Feld, whose father, Irvin, began managing the circus in 1956, owns the company and personally oversees most of its productions. Ringling Bros. and Barnum & Bailey Circus made its first performance in 1871.

Feld Entertainment's circus, ice, and stage shows have played in more than 50 countries, and approximately 30 million people see the company's productions each year. Other Feld holdings include Hagenbeck-Wallace, a property, costume, and scenic design studio in Florida; and Feld Consumer Products, an international concessions operation with distribution facilities in Maryland.

In 2008 the company expanded with the purchase of Live Nation Motor Sports from concert producer Live Nation for some $175 million, creating Feld Motor Sports. The deal added car races and monster-truck events such as Monster Jam to Feld's operations.

Throughout its history, the company has engaged in some high-profile battles with animal rights activists who claim that the Ringling Bros. and Barnum & Bailey Circus' use of an elephant-herding tool known as a bullhook injures elephants. The company opened the Ringling Bros. and Barnum & Bailey Center for Elephant Conservation in 1995.

HISTORY

When five-year-old Irvin Feld found a $1 bill in 1923, he told his mother, "I'm going to buy a circus." He started by working the sideshows of traveling circuses, before settling in Washington, DC, in 1940. Feld, who was white, opened the Super Cut-Rate Drugstore in a black section of the segregated city with the backing of the NAACP. In 1944 he opened the Super Music City record store and started his own record company, Super Disc. Feld and his brother Israel also began promoting outdoor concerts. When rock and roll became popular in the 1950s, Feld promoted Chubby Checker and Fats Domino, among others.

Feld came a step closer to his dream in 1956 when he began managing the Ringling Bros. and Barnum & Bailey Circus for majority owner John Ringling North. North's circus traced its roots back to 1871 and P. T. Barnum's Grand Traveling Museum, Menagerie, Caravan, and Circus. Barnum's circus merged with James Bailey's circus in 1881, creating Barnum & Bailey. In 1907 Bailey's widow sold Barnum & Bailey to North's uncles, the Ringling brothers, who had started their circus in 1884. Among Feld's suggestions to North was moving the circus into air-conditioned arenas, saving $50,000 a week because 1,800 roustabouts were no longer needed to set up tents.

Feld continued to promote music acts, but he suffered a serious blow in 1959 when three of his stars — Buddy Holly, Ritchie Valens, and

J. P. Richardson (the Big Bopper) — died in a plane crash.

Feld's dream of owning a circus finally was realized in 1967 when he and investors paid $8 million for Ringling Brothers. He fired most of the circus' performers and opened a Clown College to train new ones. Feld bought a German circus the following year to obtain animal trainer Gunther Gebel-Williams (who then spent the next 30 years with Ringling Brothers). Feld split Ringling into two units in 1969, so he could book it in two parts of the country at the same time and double his profits. Feld took the company public that year.

Feld and the other stockholders sold the circus to Mattel in 1971 for $47 million in stock; Feld stayed on as manager and held on to the lucrative concession business, Sells-Floto. He persuaded Mattel to buy the Ice Follies, Holiday on Ice, and the Siegfried & Roy magic show in 1979. Mattel sold the circus back to Feld in 1982 for $22.5 million, along with the ice shows and the magic show. Feld died two years later, and his son Kenneth became head of the company. A chip off the old block, Kenneth fired almost all the circus performers when he took over.

In an attempt to leverage the Barnum & Bailey brand, the company opened four retail store locations in 1990, but the venture failed and the stores were closed two years later. A constant target of animal-rights activists, Feld began backing conservation efforts on behalf of the endangered Asian elephant and established the Center for Elephant Conservation in Florida in 1995. The next year the company changed its name to Feld Entertainment.

Under increasing pressure as the company's creative guru and managerial boss, Feld hired Turner Home Entertainment executive Stuart Snyder as president and COO in 1997, so he could focus on the creative side of the business. That focus produced Barnum's Kaleidoscope in 1999, an upscale version of the original circus, featuring specialty acts, gourmet food, plush seats, and audience interaction. Plus, for the first time since 1956, a Feld circus was performed under a tent. (The company later shut down the tour of the Kaleidoscope.) Snyder resigned later in 1999.

In an effort to inject new life into the 130-year-old Ringling Bros. and Barnum & Bailey Circus, Feld Entertainment launched two new marketing campaigns (one aimed at adults, the other at children) in 2001.

In 2001 a district court judge dismissed a complaint filed against the company by several animal activist groups that claimed that Feld Entertainment didn't comply with federal regulations regarding the care of Asian elephants. The lawsuit was reinstated in early 2003 due to a procedural technicality. A former Ringling Bros. employee is a co-plaintiff in the lawsuit.

Feld Entertainment's popular Siegfried & Roy show suffered a tragedy in 2003 when Roy Horn was mauled by a white tiger during a performance. He later suffered a stroke that left him partially paralyzed, and the Siegfried & Roy show is closed indefinitely.

In 2004 the company battled a potential ban on exotic animal acts in Denver. A 15-year-old student led the charge, getting the initiative on the ballot. Feld hired political consultants and handily defeated the measure by a 72% vote. In 2008 Feld acquired Live Nation Motor Sports.

EXECUTIVES

Chairman and CEO: Kenneth J. (Ken) Feld, age 61
President, COO, and Director: Michael Shannon
CFO and Director: Keith Senglaub
CTO: Neal Grunsey
EVP and General Counsel: Jerome S. (Jerry) Sowalsky
EVP: Nicole Feld
EVP: Alana Feld
SVP Consumer Products: Graeme Burman
SVP North America Event Marketing and Sales: Jeff Meyer
SVP International Sales and Business Development: Robert McHugh
SVP and Chief Marketing Officer: Vicki Silver
SVP and Chief Marketing Officer: Rob Desatnick
VP Creative Development: Jerry Bilik
VP Human Resources: Kirk McCoy
VP Corporate Communications: Stephen (Steve) Payne
VP Sponsorship and Strategic Alliances: Jason Bitsoff
VP Government Relations: Tom Albert
VP and Deputy General Counsel: Julie Alexa Strauss
VP Animal Stewardship: Bruce Read
President, Feld Motor Sports: Charlie Mancuso

LOCATIONS

HQ: Feld Entertainment, Inc.
8607 Westwood Center Dr., Vienna, VA 22182
Phone: 703-448-4000   **Fax:** 703-448-4100
Web: www.feldentertainment.com

PRODUCTS/OPERATIONS

Selected Attractions

Disney On Ice
  Finding Nemo
  High School Musical: The Ice Tour
  Magical Journey
  Monsters, Inc.
  Princess Classics
  The Incredibles
  Three Jungle Adventures
  Walt Disney's 100 Years of Magic
Feld Entertainment Motor Sports
  Monster Jam
Ringling Bros. and Barnum & Bailey Circus

COMPETITORS

CIE	NASCAR
Cirque du Soleil	On Stage Entertainment
Harlem Globetrotters	Renaissance Entertainment
HIT Entertainment	Six Flags
Indy Racing League	TBA Global
Live Nation	

Fellowes, Inc.

Fellowes (formerly Fellowes Manufacturing) produces office products that can organize or obliterate. The leading maker of paper shredders (Powershred, Micro-shred), it also makes computer and office accessories, such as ergonomic wrist rests, multimedia storage, and other accessories. As a licensee of Body Glove International (maker of high-tech surf and scuba gear), Fellowes offers fashionable Body Glove cases for mobile phones and iPods. Fellowes' products are sold through office retailers and mass merchants, as well as online. Still owned and run by the Fellowes family, the company was started in 1917 when Harry Fellowes paid $50 for Bankers Box, a maker of storage boxes for bank records.

The company has expanded its product offerings over the years through acquisitions and product innovations, including the addition of binding and laminating products to its business machines segment. Fellowes in 2006 expanded its record storage operations by acquiring the Perma corrugated storage box business from ACCO Brands.

Over the years Fellowes has grown its operations into about 15 countries by acquiring and opening facilities; it markets its products in another 10 nations worldwide through distribution partnerships. The company continued to expand internationally in 2007, opening joint ventures in China and Russia to increase global distribution of products. Its Chinese division has one of the largest shredder manufacturing facilities in the world.

EXECUTIVES

Chairman and CEO: James (Jamie) Fellowes
President, COO, and Director: Joseph T. (Joe) Koch
CFO: Brian Cooper
EVP Global Human Resources: Lyn Bulman
EVP and Chief Supply Chain Officer: James (Jim) Lewis
VP Corporate Marketing and Media Relations: Maureen Moore
President, Fellowes Europe: Andrea Davis

LOCATIONS

HQ: Fellowes, Inc.
1789 Norwood Ave., Itasca, IL 60143
Phone: 630-893-1600   **Fax:** 630-893-1683
Web: www.fellowes.com

PRODUCTS/OPERATIONS

Selected Products

Business machines
  Binding machines and supplies
  Cutters and trimmers
  Laminating machines and supplies
  Paper shredders and supplies
Desktop and office essentials
  Back supports
  Cleaning supplies
  Dust covers
  Foot supports
  Headsets
  Keyboard trays
  Mice, keyboards, and trackballs
  Monitor and CPU accessories
  Monitor/LCD enhancers
  Printer stands
  Surge protection
  Tool kits
  Wrist rests
Media labeling and storage
  CD storage
  CD wallets
  CD/DVD labeling
  DVD storage
  Multimedia storage
  Video storage
Mobile accessories
  Camera cases
  Cellular accessories
  Laptop accessories
  PDA accessories
  Tablet PC accessories
Records Storage
  Sorters
  Storage boxes
  Storage drawers

ACCO Brands
Cummins-American
Escalade
Esselte
Knape & Vogt
Newell Rubbermaid
Packaging Corp.

Paris Corporation
Peter Pepper Products
Relax the Back
Savin Corp.
Smead
Smurfit Kappa
Southern Container corp

FHC Health Systems

FHC Health Systems makes life just a little bit saner, providing behavioral health care services to millions of people through its operating subsidiaries. Its majority-owned subsidiary ValueOptions manages behavioral health care benefits offered by commercial and public health plans, serving some 23 million people. Through its Rx Innovations unit, the company provides institutional pharmacy services for long-term care facilities and other treatment centers. And FHC's FirstLab subsidiary offers drug testing and employment screening. FHC sold its Alternative Behavioral Services subsidiary, which offered residential psychiatric care and case management services, to Psychiatric Solutions for about $200 million.

Other businesses include the Corporation for Standards and Outcomes, which focuses on performance management for public programs.

In 2008 FHC sold a significant minority stake in ValueOptions to private equity firm Crestview Partners.

Chairman and CEO Ronald I. Dozoretz founded FHC Health Systems in 1983.

EXECUTIVES

Chairman and CEO; Chairman and CEO, FirstLab:
Ronald I. Dozoretz
EVP and CTO; CIO, ValueOptions: Bob Esposito
CEO, ValueOptions: Barbara B. Hill, age 56
COO, ValueOptions: Michele D. Alfano
VP Marketing and Communications, ValueOptions:
Anthony Davis
Chief Legal Officer and General Counsel, ValueOptions:
Paul Rosenberg
Chief Administrative Officer, ValueOptions: Tom Brown
Human Resources, ValueOptions: Larry Anderson

LOCATIONS

HQ: FHC Health Systems, Inc.
240 Corporate Blvd., Norfolk, VA 23502
Phone: 757-459-5100 **Fax:** 757-459-5219
Web: www.fhchealthsystems.com

PRODUCTS/OPERATIONS

Selected Subsidiaries

Corporation for Standards and Outcomes (CS&O, outcome and accountability software)
FirstLab (drug testing and employment screening services)
Rx Innovations (institutional pharmacy services)
ValueOptions (managed behavioral care)

COMPETITORS

Comprehensive Care
Horizon Health
Magellan Health
Mental Health Network

HISTORICAL FINANCIALS

Company Type: Private

Income Statement

FYE: December 31

	REVENUE ($ mil.)	NET INCOME ($ mil.)	NET PROFIT MARGIN	EMPLOYEES
12/07	1,300	—	—	4,500
12/06	1,400	—	—	4,549
12/05	1,600	—	—	8,100
12/04	1,500	—	—	8,500
12/03	1,300	—	—	8,198
Annual Growth	0.0%	—	—	(13.9%)

Revenue History

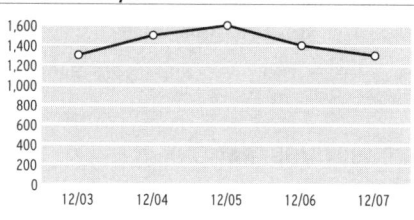

First Data Corporation

Paper, plastic, or Internet — First Data moves the money. The company covers virtually all the bases when it comes to transaction processing and funds transfer. Primary segments include commercial services and financial services (merchant and debit network processing, check verification, prepaid cards, statement and card processing), and First Data International. Through its integrated payment segment, the company also provides official checks and money orders, remote clearing, and similar services. Subsidiary TeleCheck provides paper check processing services, although the use of paper checks has been dropping steadily. Investment firm KKR bought First Data in 2007.

The deal valued First Data at some $29 billion. As part of the acquisition, the company announced plans to consolidate operations and close about a dozen offices. Following the acquisition by KKR, First Data merged its Commercial Services and Financial Institutions segments.

First Data is party to several joint ventures. In 2009 the company announced that it will hook up with Bank of America in a payment services venture to be called Banc of America Merchant Services. First Data, which is to own 48.5% of the new firm, will transfer the client base from its erstwhile Chase Paymentech joint venture with JPMorgan Chase. Bank of America will own 46.5% of Banc of America Merchant Services, while third-party investor Rockmount Investments will own the remainder.

The company moved its headquarters office back to Atlanta — near Banc of America Merchant Services and other payments industry companies, including customers — after some eight years of being headquartered in the Denver area. First Data maintained its Colorado office, which operates as its administrative headquarters.

In 2008 First Data strengthened its European business by forming card processing joint venture AIB Merchant Services with Allied Irish Banks, and through the acquisition of a 50% stake in the interbank processing business of multibank entity Trionis (formerly European Savings Banks Financial Services, or EUFISERV). Also that year First Data announced plans to buy prepaid gift card provider Interactive Communications, but purchase negotiations stalled and the company instead inked a distribution deal to sell InComm's cards.

First Data was also busy in 2007, with deals to acquire Brazilian payment processor Check Forte and Wells Fargo's Instant Cash business, which provides debit card and ATM processing services to community financial institutions in some 20 states.

EXECUTIVES

Chairman and CEO: Michael D. Capellas, age 55, $7,594,533 total compensation
EVP and CFO: W. Patrick (Pat) Shannon, age 46
EVP Human Resources: Peter W. Boucher, age 54
EVP and Chief Marketing Officer: John Elkins, age 57
EVP Communications: Grace Chen Trent, age 39, $1,772,582 total compensation
EVP Operations and Technology:
Robert P. (Bob) DeRodes, age 58
EVP, General Counsel, and Secretary:
David R. (Dave) Money, age 53
SVP and Controller: Raymond E. (Ray) Winborne Jr., age 41
SVP, Latin America and Canada: Benoit Culot
SVP Public Policy and Community Relations:
Joe Samuel
SVP, Asia/Pacific: Nigel Lee
SVP Investor Relations: Silvio Tavares
President, Retail and Alliance Services:
Edward A. (Ed) Labry III, age 46, $3,731,250 total compensation
President, International: David G. Yates, age 46, $2,448,996 total compensation
President, Financial Services: Kevin J. Schultz, age 51
Auditors: Ernst & Young LLP

LOCATIONS

HQ: First Data Corporation
5565 Glenridge Connector, NE, Atlanta, GA 30342
Phone: 303-967-8000 **Fax:** 303-967-7000
Web: www.firstdatacorp.com

PRODUCTS/OPERATIONS

2008 Sales

	$ mil.	% of total
Transaction & processing fees		
Merchant services	2,786.9	33
Card services	2,031.6	22
Check services	386.1	4
Other	580.7	7
Reimbursable debit network fees & other	2,100.7	24
Product sales & other	848.2	10
Investment income, net	77.1	—
Total	**8,811.3**	**100**

2008 Sales by Segment

	$ mil.	% of total
Merchant Services	4,127.8	48
Financial Services	2,788.2	30
International	1,827.4	19
Prepaid Services	228.6	2
Integrated Payments	43.1	—
Eliminations	(371.6)	—
Corporate, Other	167.8	1
Total	**8,811.3**	**100**

COMPETITORS

Atos Origin	Fiserv
Cardtronics	Global Payments
Deluxe Corporation	Litle & Co.
Discover	MasterCard
ECHO, Inc.	Total System Services
Elavon	US Postal Service
Fidelity National	Visa Inc
Information Services	

HISTORICAL FINANCIALS

Company Type: Private

Income Statement

FYE: December 31

	REVENUE ($ mil.)	NET INCOME ($ mil.)	NET PROFIT MARGIN	EMPLOYEES
12/08	8,811	(3,764)	—	26,600
12/07	8,051	159	2.0%	27,000
12/06	7,076	1,513	21.4%	29,000
Annual Growth	11.6%	—	—	(4.2%)

2008 Year-End Financials

Debt ratio: —
Return on equity: —
Cash ($ mil.): —
Current ratio: —
Long-term debt ($ mil.): 22,075

Net Income History

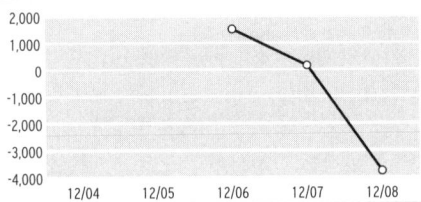

First Interstate BancSystem

This Treasure State bank wants to be your treasury. First Interstate BancSystem is the holding company for First Interstate Bank, First Western Bank, and The First Western Bank Sturgis, which have around 70 branches in Montana, South Dakota, and Wyoming. It offers individuals and businesses traditional banking services, including deposit accounts, insurance, and agricultural, consumer, commercial, and mortgage loan products. It also offers trust and wealth management services. Commercial real estate loans make up more than 25% of the bank's loan portfolio; other loans include farm and home loans.

In 2008 First Interstate acquired First Western Bank Sturgis, gaining a presence in South Dakota that includes nearly 20 branches. Later that year the company sold i_Tech, a provider of information processing services for financial institutions and ATMs, to Fiserv for approximately $40 million.

The Scott family, including brothers Thomas (chairman), James (vice chairman), and Homer (board member), controls First Interstate.

EXECUTIVES

Chairman: Thomas W. Scott, age 65
Vice Chairman: James R. Scott, age 59
President, CEO, and Director: Lyle R. Knight, age 63, $878,924 total compensation
COO: Gregory A. Duncan, age 54, $387,178 total compensation
EVP and Chief Credit Officer: Edward Garding, age 59, $373,180 total compensation
EVP and CFO: Terrill R. Moore, age 56, $342,859 total compensation
President, First Interstate Bank Wealth Management: Julie G. Castle, age 48, $715,426 total compensation
Auditors: McGladrey & Pullen, LLP

LOCATIONS

HQ: First Interstate BancSystem, Inc.
401 N. 31st St., Billings, MT 59116
Phone: 406-255-5390   **Fax:** 406-255-5160
Web: www.firstinterstatebank.com

PRODUCTS/OPERATIONS

2008 Sales

	$ mil.	% of total
Interest		
Loans, including fees	305.2	63
Securities	49.5	10
Other	1.3	—
Noninterest		
Service charges & fees	48.9	10
Gain on sale of nonbank subsidiary	27.1	5
Technology services	17.7	4
Wealth management	12.3	3
Loan origination & sales	12.3	3
Other	10.0	2
Total	**484.3**	**100**

HISTORICAL FINANCIALS

Company Type: Private

Income Statement

FYE: December 31

	ASSETS ($ mil.)	NET INCOME ($ mil.)	INCOME AS % OF ASSETS	EMPLOYEES
12/08	6,628	71	1.1%	1,771
12/07	5,217	69	1.3%	1,858
12/06	4,974	76	1.5%	1,608
12/05	4,562	55	1.2%	1,576
12/04	4,217	45	1.1%	1,574
Annual Growth	12.0%	11.7%	—	3.0%

2008 Year-End Financials

Equity as % of assets: —
Return on assets: 1.2%
Return on equity: —
Long-term debt ($ mil.): —
Sales ($ mil.): 484

Net Income History

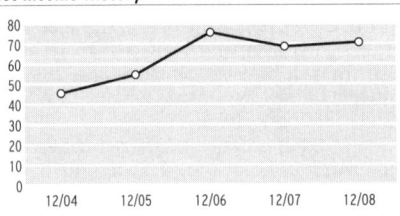

Flex-N-Gate

Flex-N-Gate makes metal and plastic automotive components and assemblies, such as bumpers, grilles, hinges, interior panels and pillars, latches, pedal systems, parking brakes, and running boards. The company also offers prototyping, mechanical assembly, and sequencing services. The company makes products for a wide range of car platforms; customers have included BMW, Chrysler, Ford, Honda, General Motors, Toyota, and Volvo. The company has more than 50 manufacturing and engineering facilities in Argentina, Canada, Mexico, Spain, and the US. Founded in 1956, president Shahid Khan has owned Flex-N-Gate since 1980.

Flex-N-Gate has been rapidly expanding its global manufacturing presence through acquisitions. In keeping with the company's strategy of growing its business by buying up distressed companies at fire-sale prices, in 2009 Flex-N-Gate acquired some of the bumper business of the bankrupt Meridian Automotive, including operations in Michigan and Indiana. In 2008 Flex-N-Gate acquired bankrupt molded plastics maker Blackhawk Automotive Plastics, expanding its interior plastics assemblies product lines.

The company name comes from Flex-N-Gate's first product: a stock rack for pickup trucks that included a roll-up rear gate. More recent offerings have included step bumpers with integrated tow hitches.

EXECUTIVES

President: Shahid Khan
VP Procurement: Bill Beistline
VP Operations: Kevin Hamilton
Director, Resin and Paint Procurement: Karen Costa
Director, Energy Management: Mellissa Kendall
Human Resources: Grace Clapper
Corporate Manager, Customer Service: M. Susan Puckett
Chief Representative and Purchasing Director, Asia: Bing Chen

LOCATIONS

HQ: Flex-N-Gate Corporation
1306 E. University Ave., Urbana, IL 61802
Phone: 217-278-2600   **Fax:** 217-278-2616
Web: www.flex-n-gate.com

COMPETITORS

A.G. Simpson
American Trim
Core Molding Technologies
Delphi Holdings
Dura Automotive
Johnson Controls
Magna International
Toledo Molding and Die
TRW Automotive

The Flintco Companies

After more than 50 years in business, The Flint Companies still has plenty of spark. The group provides general contracting, design services, and construction and project management in the US South, Midwest, and West. Subsidiaries Flintco, Inc. and Oakridge Builders, Inc. build commercial structures, such as correctional and health care facilities, casinos, museums, schools, stadiums, and parking garages. Among the largest Native American firms in the US, the family-owned company is led by Charles W. Flint III. His father, the late Charles W. Flint Jr., founded the firm in 1950 as an outgrowth of a 1908 company owned by Charles W. Flint Sr. that supplied wooden derricks.

With a controlled expansion strategy, The Flint Companies maintains offices in Arkansas, California, Missouri, New Mexico, Oklahoma, Tennessee, and Texas. It generally seeks mid-sized cities in which to operate, as opposed to larger cities where it is more difficult to establish personal relationships with clients. It has completed construction projects for Dell, The University of Memphis, the Institute of American Indian Arts, and the State of Oklahoma capitol building.

No stranger to the Sooner State, the firm is responsible for building much of Tulsa's city skyline, including the Mid-Continent Tower, First Place Tower, and the $178 million BOK Center, which is the largest single project Flintco has worked on to date.

EXECUTIVES

Chairman and CEO: Charles W. Flint III
President and COO: John R. Bates
SVP and CFO: David A. Dearing
VP and Area Manager, Springfield, Flintco: Jim Blose
VP Pre-Construction, Tulsa, Flintco: Rex Woods
VP Operations, Memphis, Flintco: Don Hutcherson
VP, Tulsa, Flintco: Lowell Heck
VP Pre-Construction, Memphis, Flintco:
Tim Weatherford
VP, Austin, Flintco: John A. Martin
President and CEO, The Flintco Companies:
Thomas E. (Tom) Maxwell, age 64
Division President, Albuquerque, Flintco: Ron Petty
Division President, The Flintco Companies:
David Kollmann
Division President, Memphis, Flintco: Kevin Moyes
Division President, Sacramento, Flintco: David Parkes
Division President, Oklahoma City, Flintco:
Mark Grimes

LOCATIONS

HQ: The Flintco Companies, Inc.
1624 W. 21st St., Tulsa, OK 74107
Phone: 918-587-8451   **Fax:** 918-582-7506
Web: www.flintco.com

PRODUCTS/OPERATIONS

Selected Projects
Construction management
Design/build
General contracting
Green construction
Preconstruction
Program & project management

COMPETITORS

Austin Commercial
Austin Industries
Barton Malow
Beck Group
Clark Construction Group
Duke Construction
FaulknerUSA
Hensel Phelps Construction
J. E. Dunn Construction
M. A. Mortenson
Manhattan Construction
Rooney Holdings
Turner Corporation

HISTORICAL FINANCIALS

Company Type: Private

Income Statement

	REVENUE ($ mil.)	NET INCOME ($ mil.)	NET PROFIT MARGIN	EMPLOYEES
12/08	1,559	—	—	900
12/07	1,290	—	—	1,089
Annual Growth	20.9%	—	—	(17.4%)

FYE: December 31

Revenue History

FMR LLC

FMR is *semper fidelis* (ever faithful) to its core business. The financial services conglomerate, better known as Fidelity Investments, is one of the world's largest mutual fund firms. Serving more than 20 million individual and institutional clients, Fidelity manages more than 400 funds and has more than $1.4 trillion of assets under management. It also operates a leading online discount brokerage and has more than 100 investor centers in the US and Canada, as well as locations in Europe and Asia. The founding Johnson family controls FMR; Abigail Johnson, CEO Ned Johnson's daughter and perhaps his successor (not to mention one of the richest women in America), is the company's largest single shareholder.

Fidelity's nonfund offerings include life insurance, trust services, securities clearing, and retirement services. It is one of the largest administrators of 401(k) plans, and the firm continues to grow this segment, which includes other services related to benefits outsourcing. The company had been reluctant to give direct investment advice to 401(k) plan participants, but under pressure from customers struck a formal agreement with Financial Engines, which now provides those services to Fidelity's clients.

FMR has private equity investments in telecommunications firm COLT Telecom Group and transportation company BostonCoach, among others. Like many institutional investors, Fidelity uses its clout to sway the boards of com-

panies in which it has significant holdings. In 2007 the company's Fidelity Equity Partners arm launched a $500 million buyout fund that targets middle-market firms involved in media, software, health care, and service industries in North America and Europe.

FMR also holds about a 15% stake in venerable British investment bank Lazard, which it acquired in 2005.

HISTORY

Boston money management firm Anderson & Cromwell formed Fidelity Fund in 1930. Edward Johnson became president of the fund in 1943, when it had $3 million invested in Treasury bills. Johnson diversified into stocks, and by 1945 the fund had grown to $10 million. In 1946 he established Fidelity Management and Research to act as its investment adviser.

In the early 1950s Johnson hired Gerry Tsai, a young immigrant from Shanghai, to analyze stocks. He put Tsai in charge of Fidelity Capital Fund in 1957. Tsai's brash, go-go investment strategy in such speculative stocks as Xerox and Polaroid paid off; by the time he left to form his own fund in 1965, he was managing more than $1 billion.

The Magellan Fund started in 1962. The company entered the corporate pension plans market (FMR Investment Management) in 1964, and the self-employed individual retirement market (Fidelity Keogh Plan) in 1967. It began serving investors outside the US (Fidelity International) in 1968.

Holding company FMR was formed in 1972, the same year Johnson gave control of Fidelity to his son Ned, who vertically integrated FMR by selling directly to customers rather than through brokers. In 1973 he formed Fidelity Daily Income Trust, the first money market fund to offer check writing.

Peter Lynch was hired as manager of the Magellan Fund in 1977. During his 13-year tenure, Magellan grew from $20 million to $12 billion in assets and outperformed all other mutual funds. Fidelity started Fidelity Brokerage Services in 1978, becoming the first mutual fund company to offer discount brokerage.

In 1980 the company launched a nationwide branch network and in 1986 entered the credit card business. The Wall Street crash of 1987 forced its Magellan Fund to liquidate almost $1 billion in stock in a single day. That year FMR moved into insurance by offering variable life, single premium, and deferred annuity policies. In 1989 the company introduced the low-expense Spartan Fund, targeted toward large, less-active investors.

Magellan's performance faded in the early 1990s, dropping from #1 performer to #3. Most of Fidelity's best performers were from its 36 select funds, which focus on narrow industry segments. FMR founded London-based COLT Telecom in 1993. In 1994 Johnson gave his daughter and possible heir apparent, Abigail, a 25% stake in FMR. She reportedly sold a significant portion of the stake in 2005.

Jeffrey Vinik resigned as manager of Magellan in 1996, one of more than a dozen fund managers to leave the firm that year and the next. Robert Stansky took the helm of the $56 billion fund, which FMR decided to close to new investors in 1997. Fidelity had a first that year when it went with an outside fund manager, hiring Bankers Trust (now part of Deutsche Bank) to manage its index funds.

FMR did some housecleaning in the late 1990s. It sold its Wentworth art galleries (1997) and *Worth* magazine (1998). Despite continued management turnover, it entered Japan and expanded its presence in Canada.

In 1999 the firm teamed with Internet portal Lycos (now part of Terra Networks) to develop its online brokerage. FMR opened savings and loan Fidelity Personal Trust Co. in 2000.

In 2006 the company announced that it would pay $42 million into its mutual funds after an internal investigation showed that some of its traders had allegedly guided business to brokers who had given the traders gifts. The SEC later slapped FMR with an $8 million fine.

EXECUTIVES

Chairman and CEO: Edward C. (Ned) Johnson III
President: Rodger A. Lawson, age 62
President, CIO: Roger T. Servison
CFO Fidelity Financial Services: Robert J. (Bob) Chersi
EVP Government Relations and Public Policy:
  James L. (J.J.) Johnson Jr., age 42
EVP Fidelity Personal Investments: Sanjiv Mirchandani
EVP Product Management, National Financial:
  Jody Meth
EVP Fidelity Human Resources: D. Ellen Wilson
EVP Defined Benefits: Jim MacDonald
President, Fidelity Real Estate: Sarah K. Abrams
President, Devonshire Investors: Timothy T. Hilton,
  age 56
**President, Asset Allocation Division, Strategic
  Advisors:** Boyce I. Geer
President, Fidelity Investments Canada Limited:
  Robert L. (Rob) Strickland, age 45
President and CEO, Pyramis Global Advisors:
  Kevin C. Uebelein
President, Fidelity Shared Services:
  Marvin W. (Marv) Adams, age 52
President, Fidelity Family Office Services: Ed Orazem
**President, Fidelity Investments Institutional Services
  Company:** Peter Cieszko
President, Fidelity Capital Market Services:
  Mark A. Haggerty
President, Fidelity Investments Institutional Products:
  Gerard (Gerry) McGraw
President, Fidelity eBusiness: Stephen A. Scullen III
**President, Institutional Platforms, Fidelity
  Institutional Products Group:** Charles G. Goldman,
  age 47
**President, Fidelity Personal and Workplace Investing;
  Director, FMR LLC:** Abigail P. (Abby) Johnson, age 47
COO Fidelity Investments Institutional Products:
  Mark Katzelnick
COO Asset Management: Jacques Perold
Manager, Fidelity Magellan Fund: Harry W. Lange,
  age 53
Managing Partner, Fidelity Ventures:
  Robert C. (Rob) Ketterson
General Counsel: Marc Gary
Director, Media Relations and Corporate Affairs:
  Chris Pepper
Auditors: PricewaterhouseCoopers LLP

LOCATIONS

HQ: FMR LLC
  82 Devonshire St., Boston, MA 02109
Phone: 617-563-7000   **Fax:** 617-476-6150
Web: www.fidelity.com

PRODUCTS/OPERATIONS

2008 Assets under Management

	% of total
Mutual funds	89
Trusts/other	11
Total	**100**

COMPETITORS

AllianceBernstein Holding
American Century
AXA Financial
Barclays
BlackRock
Charles Schwab
Citigroup
E*TRADE Financial
Goldman Sachs
John Hancock Financial Services
Marsh & McLennan
MassMutual
MetLife
Morgan Stanley
Principal Financial
Prudential
Putnam
Raymond James Financial
T. Rowe Price
TD Ameritrade
TIAA-CREF
UBS Financial Services
The Vanguard Group

HISTORICAL FINANCIALS
Company Type: Private

Income Statement

	REVENUE ($ mil.)	NET INCOME ($ mil.)	NET PROFIT MARGIN	EMPLOYEES
12/08	12,937	—	—	40,000
12/07	14,900	—	—	46,400
12/06	12,870	—	—	41,900
Annual Growth	0.3%	—	—	(2.3%)

FYE: December 31

Revenue History

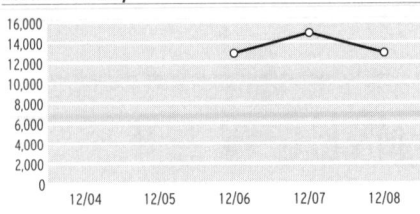

Foley & Lardner

Though most famous for its cheese, Wisconsin has another thing going for it: lawyers. Foley & Lardner, the largest and oldest law firm in Wisconsin, has nearly 1,000 lawyers and has expanded far beyond its Milwaukee base, with offices in more than 15 other US cities (including four in Florida and six in California). In addition, Foley & Lardner has international offices in Brussels, Shanghai, and Tokyo. The firm, founded in 1842, has one of the nation's leading health law practices and an increased focus on its intellectual property practice; other areas of expertise include business law, litigation, regulatory issues, and tax planning.

In mid-2008, Foley & Lardner opened an office in Shanghai. (It had already established a presence in China in the past, having conducted legal work for the Chinese government.) The firm hopes its specialized intellectual property practice will help separate itself from other law firms with an international presence.

EXECUTIVES

Chairman and CEO: Ralf-Reinhard (Ralf) Böer
Managing Partner: Stanley S. (Stan) Jaspan
Executive Director and COO: Darrell R. Ohlhauser
CFO: Tom L. Budde
CIO: Douglas D. (Doug) Caddell
Chief Marketing Officer: Kyle J. Heath
Chief Human Resources Officer: Marilyn L. Lagerman
**Chair, Intellectual Property Department and Partner,
  Chicago:** Sharon R. Barner
**Chair, Litigation Department and General Commercial
  Litigation Practice and Partner, Los Angeles:**
  Jon M. Wilson
**Chair, Business Law Department and Partner,
  Milwaukee:** Joseph B. (Joe) Tyson Jr.
**Chairman, Privacy, Security, and Information
  Management Practice:** Andy Serwin
Chairman, Litigation Department: Michael Tuteur
**Chair, Private Equity and Venture Capital Practice; Co-
  Chair, Life Sciences Team; and Partner, Boston:**
  Gabor Garai
**Chair, Regulated Industries Department and
  Government and Public Affairs Practice and Partner,
  Detroit:** George W. Ash
Senior Public Relations Manager: Jocelyn Brumbaugh
Director Administration and Operations:
  Joseph A. Shapiro

LOCATIONS

HQ: Foley & Lardner LLP
  777 E. Wisconsin Ave., Milwaukee, WI 53202
Phone: 414-271-2400   **Fax:** 414-297-4900
Web: www.foley.com

Office Locations

Boston
Brussels
Chicago
Detroit
Jacksonville, FL
Los Angeles
Madison, WI
Milwaukee
New York
Orlando, FL
Palo Alto, CA
Sacramento, CA
San Diego
San Francisco
Shanghai
Silicon Valley, CA
Tallahassee, FL
Tampa
Tokyo
Washington, DC

PRODUCTS/OPERATIONS

Selected Practice Areas

Antitrust
Appellate
Bankruptcy and Business Reorganizations
Construction
Consumer Financial Services Litigation
Corporate Compliance and Enforcement
Distribution and Franchise
Energy Regulation
Family Law
General Commercial Litigation
Immigration, Nationality, and Consular Law Services
Insurance and Reinsurance Litigation
Labor and Employment
Media Law
Securities Enforcement and Litigation
White Collar Defense

HISTORICAL FINANCIALS

Company Type: Partnership

Income Statement

FYE: January 31

	REVENUE ($ mil.)	NET INCOME ($ mil.)	NET PROFIT MARGIN	EMPLOYEES
1/08	720	—	—	2,621
1/07	668	—	—	2,527
1/06	611	—	—	2,405
1/05	543	—	—	2,305
1/04	523	—	—	—
Annual Growth	8.3%	—	—	4.4%

Revenue History

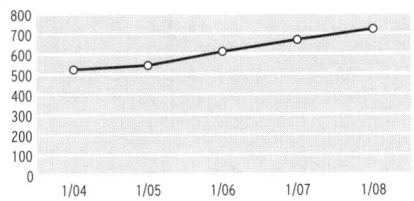

Follett Corporation

Not all kids like to read, but (fortunately for Follett) by the time they reach college, they don't have a choice. Follett is the #1 operator of US college bookstores, with more than 760 campus bookshops across the nation, as well as Canada. The company's business groups, which reach about 60 countries, also provide books and audiovisual materials to grade school and public libraries, library automation and management software, textbook reconditioning, and other services. Follett acquired its smaller online rival Varsity Group in 2008, complementing its own efollett.com Web site that sells new and used college textbooks. The Follett family has owned and managed the company for four generations.

Follett paid about $3.8 million to acquire publicly-held Varsity Group, based in Washington, DC. The company had made a name for itself as an online college retailer and provider of marketing services to colleges. Follett sought the virtual bookstore's e-commerce expertise to help it grow its online business.

To this end, Follett in November 2009 established Follett Virtual Bookstores, a business that caters to K-12 educational institutions with bookstore programs to manage and distribute course materials. The new business unit marries Follett's online and distribution savvy with the e-commerce finesse of Varsity Group. Follett, as part of the move, is rebranding the products and services provided by Follett Express Sales and Varsity Books under the Follett Virtual Bookstores name.

In addition to books, Follett's campus stores sell items such as clothing, school supplies, and software. The company has capitalized on the growing trend of universities farming out operations to independent operators.

HISTORY

Follett began in 1873 as a small bookstore opened by the Rev. Charles Barnes in his Wheaton, Illinois, home. By 1893 a recession had rocked the business, and Barnes sought investment from his wife's family, for which he gave up controlling interest. Sales topped $237,000 in 1899.

Initially hired by Barnes in 1901 to help move the store to a new location in Chicago, 18-year-old C. W. Follett stayed on as both salesman and stock clerk. Barnes retired the following year and left the business to his son William and his father-in-law, John Wilcox, who was a major shareholder. In 1917 C. W. bought into the company when William moved to New York (he started what became one of Follett's biggest competitors, Barnes & Noble), and he renamed it J. W. Wilcox & Follett Company. Wilcox died in 1923, and C. W. bought the Wilcox family shares and shortened the name to Wilcox & Follett.

C. W.'s sons were brought into the business, and each was instrumental in shaping the company's future. Garth created Follett Library Resources, a wholesale service for libraries. Dwight started the elementary textbook publishing division. But Robert would have the most influence: He began wholesaling college textbooks, which led to the establishment of Follett College Stores and Follett Campus Resources.

Wilcox & Follett expanded throughout the Depression. During WWII it began publishing kids' books, which were in demand because of a metal toy shortage. C. W. died in 1952 and Dwight took over. Five years later the firm organized into divisions; Follett was created as the parent company. During the 1960s Follett developed the first multiracial textbook series. Dwight built the company to $50 million in annual sales by 1977, when he retired. His son Robert succeeded him and led Follett through tremendous growth in the 1980s.

In 1983 the company sold its publishing division to Esquire Education Group; using funds from this sale, it began acquiring college bookstore chains such as Campus Services. In 1989 Follett developed Tom-Tracks, a computerized textbook system for college bookstores. A year later the company acquired Brennan College Service, adding 57 stores to its chain. Robert's son-in-law Richard Traut, named chairman in 1994, was the first person without the Follett name to hold that position. By 1994 Tom-Tracks had been installed in over 500 bookstores across the country. That year Follett introduced Sneak Preview Plus, a CD-ROM product designed to enhance the acquisition process in libraries.

The company acquired used-textbook reseller Western Textbook Exchange (1996), juvenile-book distributor Book Wholesalers (1997), and coursepack printer CAPCO (1998). In early 1998 Follett reorganized its corporate structure by market segments, establishing three divisions: the Elementary/High School Group, the Higher Education Group, and the Library Group. Later that year the Follett Campus Resources unit agreed to pay the University of Tennessee $380,000 after the school discovered that the firm had been underpaying students in

a book-buyback program for several years. Adding to its bevy of campus bookstores, it signed a contract the same year to build a $5 million bookstore at the University of Texas at Arlington.

Also in 1998 CFO Kenneth Hull replaced Richard Litzsinger as CEO. Follett launched efollett.com in early 1999 to sell college textbooks online. That year Hull became chairman upon Richard Traut's departure. In November 2000 Christopher Traut became CEO; Hull remained chairman.

In April 2001 Hull retired, and Mark Litzsinger succeeded him as chairman.

In April 2008, Follett acquired the online college textbook seller Varsity Group for about $3.8 million.

EXECUTIVES

Chairman: R. Mark Litzsinger
President and CEO: Christopher D. (Chris) Traut, age 44
EVP Human Resources: Richard Ellspermann
EVP Finance and CFO: Kathryn A. Stanton
VP and Chief Information Security Officer: Joe Agnew
President, Follett Educational Services: Todd Litzsinger
President, Follett Educational Distribution Group: Robert Mallo, age 48
President, Follett Software Company: Tom Schenck
President, Higher Education Group: Thomas A. (Tom) Christopher
President, BWI: John Nelson
President, Follett Technology Solutions and International Group: Chuck Follett, age 52
Director Marketing: Michael D. Campbell

LOCATIONS

HQ: Follett Corporation
2233 West St., River Grove, IL 60171
Phone: 708-583-2000   **Fax:** 708-452-9347
Web: www.follett.com

PRODUCTS/OPERATIONS

Selected Company Divisions

Elementary/High School Group
  Follett Educational Services (K-12 textbooks and workbooks)
  Follett Software Company (library automation)
  Follett Virtual Bookstores (K-12 bookstore programs)
Higher Education Group
Library Group
  Book Wholesalers, Inc. (BWI, public libraries)
  Follett International (international school libraries)
  Follett Library Resources (school libraries)
  VarsityBooks.com (online textbooks)

HISTORICAL FINANCIALS
Company Type: Private

Income Statement

FYE: March 31

	REVENUE ($ mil.)	NET INCOME ($ mil.)	NET PROFIT MARGIN	EMPLOYEES
3/08	2,500	—	—	10,000
3/07	2,520	—	—	8,000
3/06	2,370	—	—	8,300
3/05	2,000	—	—	10,000
3/04	1,899	—	—	10,000
Annual Growth	7.1%	—	—	0.0%

Revenue History

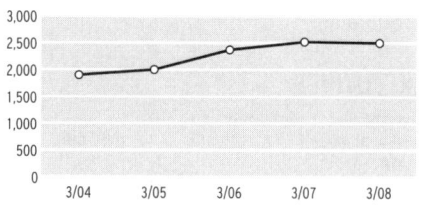

SVP, Financial Administration, Assistant Secretary and Assistant Treasurer: Joseph C. (Joe) Troilo
Secretary: Joseph J. Saker Jr.
Auditors: Amper, Politziner & Mattia, P.C.

LOCATIONS

HQ: Foodarama Supermarkets, Inc.
922 Hwy. 33, Bldg. 6, Ste. 1, Freehold, NJ 07728
Phone: 732-462-4700   **Fax:** 732-294-2322

COMPETITORS

A&P
Acme Markets
BJ's Wholesale Club
Costco Wholesale
Cumberland Farms
CVS Caremark
Food Circus Super Markets
Inserra Supermarkets
Kings Super Markets
Stop & Shop
Village Super Market
Walgreen
Wal-Mart
Wawa, Inc.
Wegmans

Foodarama Supermarkets

Foodarama Supermarkets thinks its customers deserve world-class grocery stores. A member of the Wakefern Food purchasing and distribution cooperative, the company operates about 25 ShopRite supermarkets in central New Jersey. The majority of Foodarama's stores are classified by the company as World Class, meaning they are larger than 50,000 sq. ft. and offer amenities such as international foods, in-store bakeries, kosher sections, snack bars, and pharmacies. Foodarama also operates two liquor stores, a garden center, a food processing facility (which supplies its stores with meat and prepared foods), and a bakery. The founding Saker family took the company private in 2006.

Foodarama owns nearly 16% of Wakefern Food, the New Jersey-based coop that owns the ShopRite name. Wakefern also supplies the Village Super Market and Inserra Supermarkets chains in New Jersey, New York, and Pennsylvania.

The company continues to upgrade older stores and plans to open new ones under its larger World Class store format.

The Sakers include Foodarama Chairman Joseph Saker and his son Richard, who has succeeded his father as president of the company. In mid-2006 a group led by Richard Saker launched a $25 million tender offer for the shares of the company it did not already own. In July of that year Foodarama shareholders gave the Saker bid a green light, tendering 91% of the outstanding shares of the company.

EXECUTIVES

President: Richard J. Saker
SVP Real Estate and Store Development: Edward Turkot
SVP and CFO: Thomas H. Flynn
SVP, Sales and Merchandising: Carl L. Montanaro
SVP, Operations: Thomas A. Saker

Ford Foundation

As one of the US's largest philanthropic organizations, the Ford Foundation can afford to be generous. The foundation offers grants to individuals and institutions around the world that work to meet its goals of strengthening democratic values, reducing poverty and injustice, promoting international cooperation, and advancing human achievement. The Ford Foundation's charitable giving has run the gamut from A (Association for Asian Studies) to Z (Zanzibar International Film Festival). The foundation has an endowment of more than $13 billion. Established in 1936 by Edsel Ford, whose father founded the Ford Motor Company, the foundation no longer owns stock in the automaker or has ties to the founding family.

The Ford Foundation gives to a variety of causes in one of three areas: Asset Building and Community Development (designed to help expand opportunities for the poor and reduce hardship); Peace and Social Justice (to promote peace and the rule of law, human rights, and freedom); and Knowledge, Creativity, and Freedom (aimed at strengthening education and the arts and at building identity and community).

The foundation has offices worldwide and is governed by an international board of trustees.

The Ford Foundation has offices in New York City, as well as Beijing; Cairo; Hanoi, Vietnam; Jakarta, Indonesia; Johannesburg; Lagos, Nigeria; Mexico City; Moscow; Nairobi, Kenya; New Delhi; Rio de Janeiro; and Santiago, Chile.

Luis Ubiñas joined the foundation as its ninth president in January 2008 from McKinsey & Company, where he was a director.

HISTORY

Henry Ford and his son Edsel gave $25,000 to establish The Ford Foundation in Michigan in 1936, followed the next year by 250,000 shares of nonvoting stock in the Ford Motor Company.

The foundation's activities were limited mainly to Michigan until the deaths of Edsel (1943) and Henry (1947) made the foundation the owner of 90% of the automaker's nonvoting stock (catapulting the endowment to $474 million, the US's largest).

In 1951, under a new mandate and president (Paul Hoffman, former head of the Marshall Plan), the Ford Foundation made broad commitments to the promotion of world peace, the strengthening of democracy, and the improvement of education. Early education program grants overseen by University of Chicago chancellor Robert Maynard Hutchins ($100 million between 1951 and 1953) helped establish major international programs (e.g., Harvard's Center for International Legal Studies) and the National Merit Scholarships.

Under McCarthyite criticism for its experimental education grants, the foundation in 1951 granted $550 million to noncontroversial recipients such as liberal arts colleges and not-for-profit hospitals. Public TV support became a foundation trademark that year when the organization's money set up the Radio and Television Workshop.

The Ford family and the Ford Foundation held sole ownership of the Ford company until 1956, when the company offered shares of its stock to the public. The foundation sold some 22% of its Ford Motor Company shares that year, and shed the rest over the next 20-plus years.

The 1950s saw the beginning of international work; begun in Asia and the Middle East (1950) and extended to Africa (1958) and Latin America (1959), the programs focused on education and rural development. The foundation also supported the Population Council and research in high-yield agriculture with The Rockefeller Foundation.

The Ford Foundation targeted innovative approaches to employment and race relations in the early 1960s. McGeorge Bundy (former national security adviser to President John Kennedy), named president of the foundation in 1966, increased the activist trend with grants for direct voter registration; the NAACP; public-interest law centers serving consumer, environmental, and minority causes; and housing for the poor.

The early 1970s saw support for black colleges and scholarships, child care, and job training for women; but by 1974 inflation, weak stock prices, and overspending had eroded assets. Programs were cut, but continued support for social justice issues led the conservative Henry Ford II to quit the board in 1976.

Under lawyer Franklin Thomas (named president in 1979), the Ford Foundation established the nation's largest community development support organization, Local Initiatives Support. Thomas, the first African-American to lead the foundation, was a catalyst in a series of meetings between white and black South Africans in the mid-1980s.

Thomas stepped down in 1996, and new president Susan Berresford, formerly EVP, consolidated the foundation's grant programs into three areas: Asset Building and Community Development; Peace and Social Justice; and Education, Media, Arts, and Culture. In the late 1990s the Ford Foundation was surpassed by various other foundations, and it had to relinquish its 30-year title as the biggest charitable organization in the US.

In 2000 the foundation announced its largest grant ever, the 10-year, $330 million International Fellowship Program to support graduate students studying in 20 countries.

After the September 11, 2001, terrorist attacks, the foundation joined other philanthropic organizations in providing disaster relief. It made grants of $10 million in New York and more than $1 million in Washington, DC.

Berresford retired in early 2008 after 12 years as president of the foundation. She was succeeded by Luis Ubiñas, formerly a director at McKinsey & Company.

EXECUTIVES

Chair: Kathryn S. Fuller, age 62
President and Trustee: Luis A. Ubiñas
CFO and Treasurer: Nicholas M. Gabriel
CTO: Mohamoud Jibrell
EVP, Secretary, and General Counsel: Barron M. Tenny
VP Communications: Marta L. Tellado
VP Peace and Social Justice Program: Maya Harris
VP Knowledge, Creativity, and Freedom:
 Alison R. Bernstein
VP Asset Building and Community Development:
 Pablo J. Farías
VP and Chief Investment Officer: Linda B. Strumpf
Director Administrative Services: Sandra L. Harris
Director Economic Development: Frank F. DeGiovanni
Director Human Resources: Bruce D. Stuckey
Manager Benefits and Compensation: Lisa A. Misakian
Manager Media Relations: Fiona Guthrie
Press Officer: Joseph Voeller
Comptroller and Director Financial Services:
 Nancy W. Kong
Auditors: PricewaterhouseCoopers LLP

LOCATIONS

HQ: Ford Foundation
 320 E. 43rd St., New York, NY 10017
Phone: 212-573-5000   **Fax:** 212-351-3677
Web: www.fordfound.org

PRODUCTS/OPERATIONS

Selected Programs

Asset Building and Community Development
 Community and Resource Development
 Economic Development

Knowledge, Creativity, and Freedom
 Education, Sexuality, Religion
 Media, Arts, and Culture

Peace and Social Justice
 Governance and Civil Society
 Human Rights

Foremost Farms

No jokes about "herd mentality," please. Foremost Farms USA (owned by some 2,700 dairy farmers in its founding state of Wisconsin and six other upper-midwestern states) is a major US dairy cooperative. The co-op's member/farmers' herds supply some 5 billion pounds of milk per year, which Foremost turns into dairy products for its customers. Taking the cheese-head description of its home-state's citizens seriously, the cooperative makes some 500 million pounds of cheese every year, along with butter and dairy-based ingredients. To reduce its dependence on commodity products, Foremost also manufactures value-added items, such as pharmaceutical-grade lactose and whey-based ingredients.

Getting out of the retail milk business in 2009, the company sold its milk-processing plants to Dean Foods. The sale included the Golden Guernsey Dairy and Morning Glory retail milk brands. The deal allowed Foremost to concentrate on the wholesale business of cheese, butter, and dairy-ingredients production.

The co-op operates 10 cheese plants, six dairy-ingredient plants, a butter plant, and two farm-milk transfer stations.

EXECUTIVES

Chairman: David Scheevel
First Vice Chairman: Bob Topel
Second Vice Chairman: Bob Prahl
President: David E. (Dave) Fuhrmann
VP Finance and CFO: Michael Doyle
VP Marketing and Technology: Douglas (Doug) Wilke
VP Member Services and Milk Marketing: Joseph Weis
VP Manufacturing: Mike Pronschinske
VP Human Resources, Safety, and Communications:
 Mike McDonald
Manager Product Development, Dairy Ingredients:
 Jenny Reuter
Manager Quality Systems: Dave Jelle
Manager Quality Systems: Tamara Fox
Manager Product Development, Cheese: Casey Baumler
Director Communications: Joan Behr
Director Technology: Brian Cords
Auditors: PricewaterhouseCoopers LLP

LOCATIONS

HQ: Foremost Farms USA, Cooperative
 E10889 Penny Ln., Baraboo, WI 53913
Phone: 608-355-8700   **Fax:** 608-355-8699
Web: www.foremostfarms.com

Foremost Farms serves farmers in Illinois, Indiana, Iowa, Michigan, Minnesota, Ohio, and Wisconsin.

PRODUCTS/OPERATIONS

Selected Products

Butter
Cheese
 American
 Asadero
 Brick
 Cheddar
 Colby
 Farmers cheese
 Havarti
 Monterey Jack
 Mozzarella
 Muenster
 Provolone
 Queso quesadilla
Ingredients
 Feed
 Food
 Nutritional
 Pharmaceutical
 Specialty

COMPETITORS

Associated Milk Producers
California Dairies Inc.
Century Foods
Dairy Farmers of America
Dairylea
Dean Foods
Kraft Foods
Land O'Lakes
Leprino Foods
MMPA
National Dairy Holdings
Prairie Farms Dairy
Quality Chekd
Saputo
Sargento
Schreiber Foods

HISTORICAL FINANCIALS
Company Type: Cooperative

Income Statement				FYE: December 31
	REVENUE ($ mil.)	NET INCOME ($ mil.)	NET PROFIT MARGIN	EMPLOYEES
12/08	1,600	—	—	1,370
12/07	1,600	—	—	1,400
12/06	1,246	—	—	1,523
12/05	1,419	—	—	1,540
Annual Growth	4.1%	—	—	(3.8%)

Revenue History

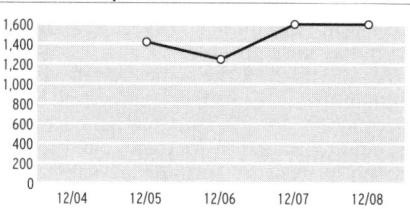

Forever 21

You don't have to be 21 or older to shop at Forever 21 stores — you just need your wallet. The fast-growing retailer operates some 450 mainly mall-based stores in the US and Canada under the Forever 21, Forever XXI, and For Love 21 banners. The chain, which helped pioneer fast fashion, offers cheap and chic apparel and accessories for women and junior girls. Most of its trendy apparel is private label and made in Southern California. Forever XXI stores are larger than classic Forever 21 shops and offer men's and women's fashions, as well as lingerie, footwear, cosmetic items, and other accessories. CEO Don Chang and his wife founded the company as Fashion 21 in 1984.

Forever 21 aims to open as many as 90 new stores per year. In a bid to open shops in 16 shuttered Gottschalks department stores, Forever 21 has offered $17.7 million to buy three locations and acquire leases. In 2008 the company acquired more than a dozen locations in California from retailer Mervyn's, which went out of business. Forever 21 was attracted to Mervyn's prime real estate. (Indeed, the company bid for the same sites back in 2004 when Mervyn's former parent Target Corp. was selling them, but lost at auction.) Additionally, in May 2009 Forever 21 agreed to buy three former Gottschalks stores and take over about a dozen of the bankrupt department store chain's leases. Farther from home, the company opened its first store in South Korea in the fall of 2008. Internationally, Forever 21 also has two stores in the United Arab Emirates and Singapore. It is also exploring expansion opportunities in Japan, China, Russia, and the UK.

The size of the retailer's stores has increased from about 15,000 square feet (on average) to include many 40,000-square-foot boutiques. Going forward, the company plans to construct even larger stores, eventually spanning 90,000 square feet and anchoring malls in select locations. The increase in scale matches Forever 21's aspiration to evolve from a purveyor of teen fashion to a youth-lifestyle retail concept. The chain also expanded into the market for plus-size apparel with a line of junior's plus-size clothing that launched in May 2009. The plus-size collection, named Faith 21, is sold on the company's Web site (forever21.com) and in the chain's larger stores.

Forever 21 has also grown by launching new concepts and acquiring other chains. The company bought 44 Rampage stores, valued at $14 million, from Charlotte Russe in late 2006. Also in 2006 Forever 21 launched Twenty One, a line of denim-based men's wear. Previously, in March 2005 the chain acquired the assets of bankrupt teen retailer Gadzooks for about $33 million. The purchase of 150 Gadzooks stores n 36 states greatly expanded Forever 21's retail presence. Also in 2005 it launched an accessories-only format, called For Love21, which has since grown to about a dozen locations. In mid-2003 the company extended its reach in the junior market by acquiring Reference Clothing Co. Reference had a similar product offering of inexpensive trendy clothes; all of its stores were converted into Forever 21 stores.

EXECUTIVES

CEO: Do Won (Don) Chang, age 49
SVP and CFO: Lawrence (Larry) Meyer
Head Buyer: Jin Sook Chang
Human Resources Manager: Kate Chun

LOCATIONS

HQ: Forever 21, Inc.
2001 S. Alameda St., Los Angeles, CA 90058
Phone: 213-741-5100   **Fax:** 213-741-5161
Web: www.forever21.com

COMPETITORS

Abercrombie & Fitch
American Eagle Outfitters
bebe stores
Catherines Stores
Charlotte Russe Holding
Charming Shoppes
Claire's Stores
dELiA*s
The Gap
H&M
Old Navy
Target
Urban Outfitters
Wal-Mart
Wet Seal
Zara

HISTORICAL FINANCIALS

Company Type: Private

Income Statement			FYE: December 31
	REVENUE ($ mil.)	NET INCOME ($ mil.)	NET PROFIT MARGIN	EMPLOYEES
12/08	1,700	—	—	—
12/07	1,300	—	—	—
12/06	1,050	—	—	—
Annual Growth	27.2%	—	—	—

Revenue History

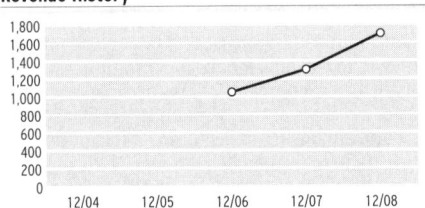

| | 12/04 | 12/05 | 12/06 | 12/07 | 12/08 |

Forstmann Little & Co.

Don't let the "Little" fool you: Buyout firm Forstmann Little & Co. has been home to some big names. The company, which specializes in telecommunications, technology, education, and health care investments, counts among its former advisory board members Donald Rumsfeld, Colin Powell, George Shultz, and Henry Kissinger. Since its founding in 1978, Forstmann Little has invested in about 30 companies, including former holdings Gulfstream Aerospace, General Instrument, Dr Pepper, and Revlon. Current holdings include IMG and 24 Hour Fitness. It is led by the surviving founding group member, Ted Forstmann.

The firm hit its heyday in the 1980s and 1990s, but was hurt by the telecom/Internet bust. It is still recovering from the ill-advised $2.5 billion investments in shaky telecom concerns McLeod USA and XO Communications (now controlled by corporate raider extraordinaire Carl Icahn).

However, in recent years the company raked in a handsome profit with the initial public offering of Citadel Broadcasting. It also unloaded its stakes in Yankee Candle and Community Health Systems.

EXECUTIVES

Senior Partner: Theodore J. (Ted) Forstmann, age 69
General Partner: Winston W. Hutchins
Chief of Staff: Margot Rohr McGinness

LOCATIONS

HQ: Forstmann Little & Co.
767 5th Ave., New York, NY 10153
Phone: 212-355-5656   **Fax:** 212-759-9059

PRODUCTS/OPERATIONS

Selected Investments

24 Hour Fitness (health and fitness clubs)
IMG (television production, distribution, and marketing and talent agency)

COMPETITORS

Apax Partners
Blackstone Group
Heico Companies
HM Capital Partners
KKR
Thomas H. Lee Partners
TPG
Vestar Capital Partners
Wingate Partners

HISTORICAL FINANCIALS

Company Type: Private

Income Statement			FYE: December 31
	REVENUE ($ mil.)	NET INCOME ($ mil.)	NET PROFIT MARGIN	EMPLOYEES
12/08	1,681	—	—	17,034

Forsythe Technology

Forsythe Technology believes it has the foresight to provide valuable business and information technology consulting services. The company helps businesses and government agencies manage their IT infrastructure, providing services ranging from strategy to implementation and support. It also provides leasing and other financial services. Serving clients from offices throughout the US and western Canada, the company works with vendors such as Cisco Systems and Sun Microsystems. Forsythe Technology customers have included Aflac and TriZetto. Chairman Richard Forsythe founded the company in 1971 as Forsythe McArthur Associates. Today the employee-owned company operates from about 50 offices in North America.

Forsythe has built its business and service portfolio in part through acquisitions. In 2008, the company acquired New England-based storage systems integrator More Group. The following year, through infrastructure integration subsidiary Forsythe Solutions Group, it bought IBM server and storage systems integrator Paragon Solutions Group. These two purchases made for a total of six acquisitions by Forsythe since 2001.

Efforts to push into new geographic markets included the establishment in 2008 of Forsythe Technology Canada. Aside from the Mississauga, Ontario-based headquarters of this subsidiary, the company's Canadian business grew during 2009 to include offices in Winnipeg, Calgary, Edmonton, and Vancouver.

EXECUTIVES

President, CEO, and Director; President and Director, Forsythe Solutions Group: William P. (Bill) Brennan, age 53
EVP, CFO, and Director: Albert L. (Al) Weiss
SVP and Chief Accounting Officer: Thomas R. (Tom) Ehmann, age 56
SVP Human Resources: Julie F. Nagle
SVP; Area Manager, Central Region; Sales Manager; and Director: Robert D. (Bob) Dvorak
SVP Sales Administration: Michelle M. Coffield, age 42
SVP, General Counsel, Secretary, and Director: R. Thomas (Tom) Hoffman
SVP and General Manager, Western Area; Sales Manager: Gregory P. (Greg) Fearing
SVP Emerging Technologies and Key Accounts and Director: Michael P. Conley, age 40
SVP Security Solutions: Stephen M. (Steve) Abbott
SVP Systems Solutions and Technology Products: Michael J. (Mike) Qualley
SVP Financial Services and Sales Manager: John D. Carcone
SVP Marketing and Sales Operations: James G. (Jim) Bindon
SVP and General Manager, Eastern Area; Sales Manager: David A. Fisher
SVP IT Strategy Solutions and Director: Cynthia L. (Cindy) Elzinga
VP and CIO: Daniel Rodgers
President and CEO, Paragon Solutions Group: Haydn Hirstine
Corporate Communications Manager: Kyra Auslander

LOCATIONS

HQ: Forsythe Technology, Inc.
7770 Frontage Rd., Skokie, IL 60077
Phone: 847-213-7000   **Fax:** 847-213-7922
Web: www.forsythe.com

COMPETITORS

Affiliated Computer	FAEF
Agilysys	GATX
ATEL Capital	GCI Systems
Black Box	HP Technology Solutions
Blackwell Consulting	IBM Global Services
CDW	ICON Capital
Computer Sciences Corp.	Keane
Datalink	Meridian Group
Dell	ORIX
Electro Rent	Sayers
ePlus	Unisys

HISTORICAL FINANCIALS
Company Type: Private

Income Statement
FYE: December 31

	REVENUE ($ mil.)	NET INCOME ($ mil.)	NET PROFIT MARGIN	EMPLOYEES
12/08	700	—	—	890
12/07	629	—	—	808
12/06	604	—	—	718
12/05	518	—	—	619
12/04	449	—	—	639
Annual Growth	11.7%	—	—	8.6%

Revenue History

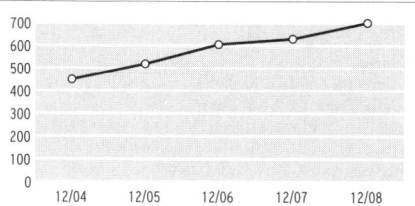

Foster Poultry Farms

It doesn't matter if Henny Penny is having hot flashes, Foster Poultry Farms never uses hormones (nor does it inject salt water into its birds to plump them up). The company is one of the leading poultry processors in the US with vertically integrated operations, taking chickens and turkeys from the incubator to grocers' meat cases, delis, and freezers. It sells poultry products mostly under the Foster Farms brand. In addition to the retail market, Foster Poultry Farms supplies customers in the foodservice industry, including restaurant and other hospitality operators. The family-owned company was started in 1939 by Max and Verda Foster. The Fosters also own and operate sister company Foster Dairy Farms.

Foster Poultry Farms has been expanding through targeted acquisitions. It purchased a chicken operation in Farmerville, Louisiana, from struggling Pilgrim's Pride in 2009. The $80 million deal included $40 million from the State of Louisiana, which pledged another $10 million toward equipment upgrades in order to save jobs at the plant.

Later in 2009 Foster acquired the Fernando's and El Extremo foodservice brands from ConAgra. Both brands offer ready-to-heat Mexican entrees and appetizers.

Foster Poultry Farms has operations in Alabama, Arkansas, California, Colorado, Louisiana, Oregon, and Washington.

EXECUTIVES
CEO: Ron Foster
SVP Supply Chain: Dan Huber
SVP Live Poultry Operations: Mike Pruitt
SVP and CIO: Dave Weinmeister
SVP Human Resources: Tim Walsh
SVP and General Counsel: Randy Boyce
SVP and CFO: John Landis
SVP Marketing: Bob Wangerien
SVP Retail Sales: Bob Kellert
VP Processing, Fresh Poultry: Richie King
Director Marketing: Ira Brill
Director Operations, Prepared Foods and Co-Packing: Armando Matus
Director Plant and Live Operations, Turkey: Yubert Envia
Treasurer: Regina King

LOCATIONS
HQ: Foster Poultry Farms
1000 Davis St., Livingston, CA 95334
Phone: 209-357-1121   **Fax:** 209-394-6342
Web: www.fosterfarms.com

PRODUCTS/OPERATIONS

Selected Products and Brands
Cooked frozen chicken
Cooked frozen turkey
Corn dogs
Fresh chicken
Fresh turkey
Hot dogs
Individually frozen chicken
Lunchmeat
Savory Servings

COMPETITORS

Bell & Evans	Perdue Incorporated
Butterball	Pilgrim's Pride
Cagle's	Plainville Farms
Cooper Farms	Raeford Farms
Eberly Poultry	Randall Foods
Fair Oaks Farms	Sanderson Farms
Hormel	Shelton's
Jennie-O	Tyson Foods
Murphy-Brown	Wayne Farms LLC
New Market Poultry	West Liberty Foods
Northern Pride	

HISTORICAL FINANCIALS
Company Type: Private

Income Statement
FYE: December 31

	ESTIMATED REVENUE ($ mil.)	NET INCOME ($ mil.)	NET PROFIT MARGIN	EMPLOYEES
12/08	2,000	—	—	10,000
12/07	1,890	—	—	10,000
12/06	1,800	—	—	10,500
12/05	1,730	—	—	10,000
12/04	1,660	—	—	10,000
Annual Growth	4.8%	—	—	0.0%

Revenue History

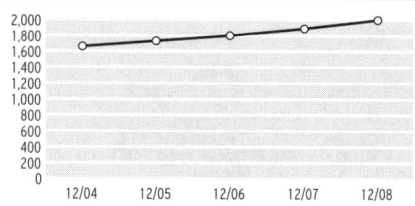

Frank Consolidated Enterprises

Frank Consolidated Enterprises believes that where there's a "Wheels" there's a way — to make money. A holding company for its Wheels subsidiary, the firm is a pioneer of the auto leasing concept, providing fleet management services — administrative, management, and financing services — to help clients maintain vehicle fleets. Overall, the company manages more than 270,000 vehicles. It operates in the US as Wheels and in other countries through Fleet Synergy International, an alliance of international fleet management and leasing companies. Wheels was founded in 1939 by a Chicago auto dealer named Zollie Frank. The Frank family owns and runs the company.

Wheels purchases and remarkets more than 120,000 vehicles every year. It serves a wide range of clients, although the bulk of its revenues comes from customers in the manufacturing and pharmaceutical industries and the wholesale and retail trade.

The company relies on innovation (especially of online services) and attention to clients' needs to keep its customers happy. In 2008 Wheels revamped its Wheels.com Web site, adding online Decisions Tools expense analysis and cost projection and the EcoWheels program to help clients meet their environmental goals. It also rolled out a new version of its FleetView program to provide more title and registration data and information.

EXECUTIVES
President and CEO: James S. (Jim) Frank
SVP Finance and Operations, CFO, and Director, Wheels: Mary Ann O'Dwyer, age 53
SVP Sales, Marketing, and Account Management, Wheels: Scott Pattullo
Senior Director Marketing: Stratford Dick
VP Sales, Wheels: Prentiss Harvey
VP International: Bill Robinson
VP Human Resources, Wheels: Joan Richards
VP IT and CIO: Steve Loos
VP Client Relations, Wheels: Norman Din
VP Customer Service Operations, Wheels: Christine Steinberg
VP International Sales, Wheels: Peter Egan
VP Finance, Wheels: Shlomo Y. Crandus
CEO, Fleet Logistics International: Peter Soliman

LOCATIONS
HQ: Frank Consolidated Enterprises, Inc.
666 Garland Place, Des Plaines, IL 60016
Phone: 847-699-7000   **Fax:** 847-699-6494
Web: www.wheels.com

COMPETITORS
Automotive Resources International
Donlen
Emkay
Enterprise Rent-A-Car
GE Fleet Services
Holman Enterprises
PHH Arval
Sixt

HISTORICAL FINANCIALS
Company Type: Private

Income Statement
FYE: August 31

	REVENUE ($ mil.)	NET INCOME ($ mil.)	NET PROFIT MARGIN	EMPLOYEES
8/08	2,000	—	—	600
8/07	2,000	—	—	600
8/06	1,890	—	—	602
8/05	1,733	—	—	551
8/04	1,600	—	—	550
Annual Growth	5.7%	—	—	2.2%

Revenue History

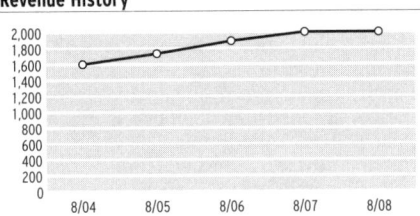

FreedomRoads, L.L.C.

"Home, home on the road, where the semis and the SUVs play. . ." That's how this company would sing it. Together with its Camping World subsidiary, the company sells and rents new and used RVs, along with other products for RV users, through more than 100 locations nationwide. The company offers more than 8,000 RV parts and accessories and also provides financing and maintenance services. It has grown by buying existing dealerships. To that end, the company acquired Sonny's Camp-N-Travel and in 2007 rebranded it as Camping World RV Sales. Chairman and CEO Marcus Lemonis founded FreedomRoads in 2003. It is owned, indirectly, by Steve Adams, chairman of RV products company Affinity Group.

EXECUTIVES

President and CEO, FreedomRoads:
 Marcus A. Lemonis, age 35
COO: Mark J. Boggess, age 53
CFO: Roger Nuttall
Chief Marketing Officer: Tamara Ward
EVP Business Development and General Counsel:
 Brent Moody, age 47
EVP and CIO: Matthew Baden
SVP and Chief Accounting Officer, RV Dealer Group:
 Karin Bell
SVP Communication and Marketing: Diana Ardelean
SVP Human Resources: Gene Schrecengost
President, E-Commerce: Kenneth Marshall, age 49
President, Retail Operations: John A. Sirpilla, age 42
President, RV Dealer Group: Craig Jensen
Division President, Southeast RV Group:
 Martin Zonnenberg
Division President, Mid-North RV Group, RV Dealer Group: Randy Thompson

LOCATIONS

HQ: FreedomRoads, L.L.C.
 250 Parkway Dr., Ste. 320, Lincolnshire, IL 60069
Phone: 847-808-3000 **Fax:** 847-808-7015
Web: www.freedomroads.com

COMPETITORS

Cruise America
General RV
Giant Inland Empire RV
La Mesa RV
Lazy Days RV Center

HISTORICAL FINANCIALS
Company Type: Private

Income Statement
FYE: December 31

	REVENUE ($ mil.)	NET INCOME ($ mil.)	NET PROFIT MARGIN	EMPLOYEES
12/07	1,650	—	—	4,000
12/06	1,600	—	—	3,500
12/05	1,500	—	—	3,200
12/04	1,200	—	—	—
Annual Growth	11.2%	—	—	11.8%

Revenue History

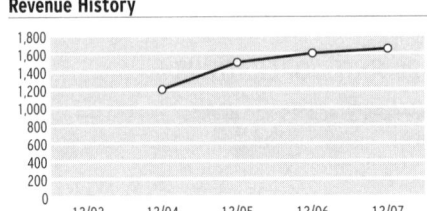

Freeman Decorating Services

Freeman Decorating Services knows there's no business like the trade show business. Doing business simply as Freeman, the firm stages thousands of conventions, corporate meetings, expositions, and trade shows every year and prepares exhibits for its clients. Its operations include event design and production, Party Time Rentals (equipment rental for events in Canada), and Stage Rigging (theatrical rigging). The company's Freeman Audio Visual unit specializes in providing audio and visual technology and equipment used for meetings and events. Freeman was founded by D.S. "Buck" Freeman in 1927; the company is owned by the Freeman family (including chairman Donald Freeman) and company employees.

In 2007 Freeman acquired Chicago-based ProActive, Inc., an event marketing and communications firm.

Freeman has about 65 offices in 40 cities in the US and Canada.

EXECUTIVES

Chairman: Donald S. Freeman Jr.
Vice Chairman: Carrie Freeman Parsons
CEO: Joseph V. (Joe) Popolo Jr.
President: John F. O'Connell Jr.
SEVP Executive Sales Group: Robert D. (Bob) Lozier
EVP and CFO: Ellis E. Moseley
EVP and CIO: Richard Maranville
EVP and Chief Sales Officer: Robert C. (Bob) Moore
EVP Customer Relations: Katy Wild
EVP and Chief Marketing Officer: Tony Purdy
EVP and Chief People Officer: Albert E. Chew III

EVP Operations: Jay Atherton
VP and General Counsel: Dawnn M. Repp
VP and Controller: Cheryl Farmer
VP and Treasurer: William H. (Bill) Baxley III
President, Freeman Audio Visual USA: Ken Sanders

LOCATIONS

HQ: Freeman Decorating Services, Inc.
 1600 Viceroy, Ste. 100, Dallas, TX 75235
Phone: 214-445-1000 **Fax:** 214-445-0200
Web: www.freemanco.com

PRODUCTS/OPERATIONS

Selected Operations

Freeman Decorating
 Budgeting
 Event design
 Rental furnishings and carpeting
 Sign and graphics production
 Theme decor
Freeman Exhibit
 Exhibit production and design
 Modular exhibit rental programs
Stage Rigging
 Theatrical rigging

Selected Clients

American Heart Association
Anheuser-Busch, Inc.
Mary Kay Cosmetics
Microsoft Corp.
National Association of Home Builders
National Automobile Dealers Association
National Cable TV Association
Republican National Convention
Starbucks Corp.
Texas Association of School Boards
Texas Instruments

COMPETITORS

Audio Visual Services Group
Champion Expo
Czarnowski
Exhibit Enterprises
Exhibitgroup/Giltspur
George P. Johnson
GES
GL events
Innovative Display & Design
Sparks Marketing Group
Viad
Virtual Meeting

HISTORICAL FINANCIALS
Company Type: Private

Income Statement
FYE: June 30

	REVENUE ($ mil.)	NET INCOME ($ mil.)	NET PROFIT MARGIN	EMPLOYEES
6/09	1,202	—	—	32,200
6/08	1,377	—	—	32,200
6/07	1,300	—	—	32,000
6/06	1,270	—	—	32,000
6/05	1,173	—	—	—
Annual Growth	0.6%	—	—	0.2%

Revenue History

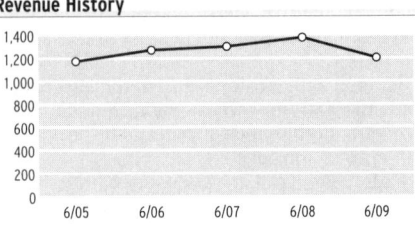

Freescale Semiconductor

Freescale Semiconductor just wants to be free. Freescale, formerly Motorola's Semiconductor Products Sector, is one of the oldest and most diverse makers of microchips in the world. It produces many different kinds of chips for use in automobiles, computers, industrial equipment, wireless communications and networking equipment, and other applications. The company's global client roster includes such blue-chip companies as Alcatel-Lucent, Bosch, Cisco Systems, Fujitsu, Hewlett-Packard, QUALCOMM, and Siemens, as well as former parent Motorola. Freescale nets about half of its sales from the Asia/Pacific region.

Following a strategic review in 2008 by CEO Rich Beyer and senior executives, Freescale is selling or spinning off certain product segments facing declining market demand. The company is focusing on the automotive, multimedia, and networking markets for growth; its remaining three product segments are Microcontrollers, Networking & Multimedia, and Radio Frequency, Analog & Sensors. Freescale reaches into patent licensing revenue and foundry services, too, which consist of contract manufacturing of semiconductors for other companies. Its shift has resulted in cutting operating expenses by reducing its workforce outside of those segments by at least 10% during 2009, eliminating more than 2,000 jobs. Manufacturing facilities in France, Japan, and the UK, have been shuttered, too.

Motorola's woes in the cellular handset market weigh heavily on Freescale. The former parent had accounted for more than 90% of sales in Freescale's cellular products segment. Freescale's total revenues have continued to dip, pressured by lower sales to Motorola. As a result, Freescale's cellular chipset products were placed on the sale rack. The lineup includes audio chips, baseband processors, power management devices, and radio-frequency (RF) transceivers; these products previously garnered about 20% of the company's sales. Freescale and Motorola subsequently amended their contractual obligations, relieving Motorola from meeting its prior minimum purchase commitments.

Although no buyer has appeared for the cellular chipset business, Abilis Systems, a Kudelski Group company, stepped up in the third quarter of 2009 to pick up Freescale's CMOS (complementary metal oxide semiconductor) modulators and silicon tuner product lines, part of Freescale's Digital Home Operations.

The deal fell on the heels of Freescale's acquisition of Austin-based chip maker, SigmaTel, for around $110 million in cash in 2008. While most of SigmaTel's products complement Freescale's offerings in digital multimedia applications, Freescale unloaded SigmaTel's multifunction printer product lines to Conexant. In addition, Motorola spun off its magnetoresistive random-access memory (MRAM) business, renamed EverSpin Technologies. Freescale, however, has retained an equity stake in EverSpin and perseveres in developing embedded products based on the MRAM technology.

Financially, Freescale's sales have been further weakened by the credit crisis and uncertain conditions in the world's 2008-09 economy. The company deals with a highly leveraged balance sheet, including almost $10 billion in debt.

Since 2006 Freescale has been owned by a group of private equity funds consisting of The Blackstone Group, The Carlyle Group, Permira Advisers, and Texas Pacific Group.

EXECUTIVES

Chairman and CEO: Richard M. (Rich) Beyer, age 60
SVP and General Manager, Networking and Multimedia and CTO: Lisa Su, age 39
SVP and Chief Sales and Marketing Officer: Henri Richard, age 51
SVP and General Manager, Cellular Products: Tom Deitrich, age 42
SVP and Chairman, Asia-Pacific: Joe Yiu
SVP Supply Chain: Alex Pepe, age 47
SVP and CFO: Alan Campbell, age 50
SVP and Chairman Europe, Middle East, and Africa (EMEA) Region: Denis Griot
SVP and General Manager Radio Frequency, Analog, and Sensors: Klaus Buehring, age 51
SVP and General Manager, Microcontroller Solutions: Reza Kazerounian, age 50
SVP Human Resources: Michel C. Cadieux, age 51
SVP Strategy and Business Transformation: Vivek Mohindra
VP and Acting General Counsel: John D. Holmes
VP and CIO: Sam Coursen
VP and Treasurer: Dave Stasse
VP and Chief Accounting Officer: Randy A. Hyzak
VP Operations: Fred Glasgow
Auditors: KPMG LLP

LOCATIONS

HQ: Freescale Semiconductor, Inc.
6501 W. William Cannon Dr., Austin, TX 78735
Phone: 512-895-2000
Web: www.freescale.com

Freescale Semiconductor has facilities in Denmark, France, Germany, Hong Kong, India, Ireland, Israel, Japan, Malaysia, Romania, Russia, the UK, and the US.

2008 Sales

	$ mil.	% of total
Asia/Pacific		
Singapore	1,430	28
Hong Kong	836	16
Japan	314	6
Taiwan	70	1
US	1,321	25
Europe		
Switzerland	882	17
France	62	1
Germany	53	1
UK	50	1
Other regions	208	4
Total	**5,226**	**100**

PRODUCTS/OPERATIONS

2008 Sales

	$ mil.	% of total
Microcontroller Solutions	1,630	31
Networking & Multimedia	1,161	22
Cellular Products	1,063	20
RF, Analog & Sensors	1,032	20
Other	340	7
Total	**5,226**	**100**

Selected Semiconductor Products

8-, 16-, and 32-bit microcontrollers (MCUs)
Analog
  Power management integrated circuits (ICs)
  Power switching ICs
  Network transceivers
Application-specific Standard Products (ASSPs)
  Digital video encoders
  Display drivers
Clock drivers
Digital signal processors
Embedded processors
Memory
  Content-addressable memory
  Magnetoresistive random-access memory (MRAM)
Networking processors
Radio-frequency
  Amplifier ICs and modules
  Transistors
Sensors
Wireless receivers and transmitters

COMPETITORS

AMD
Analog Devices
Atmel
Avago Technologies
Broadcom
Cavium Networks
Conexant Systems
Cypress Semiconductor
Fujitsu Microelectronics
IBM Microelectronics
Infineon Technologies
Intel
Linear Technology
LSI Corp.
Marvell Technology
Maxim Integrated Products
Microchip Technology
National Semiconductor
NVIDIA
NXP
Oki Semiconductor
ON Semiconductor
Qualcomm CDMA
Renesas Technology
RF Micro Devices
SANYO Semiconductor
Sensata
Silicon Labs
STMicroelectronics
Texas Instruments
VIA Technologies
Vishay Intertechnology
ZiLOG

HISTORICAL FINANCIALS

Company Type: Private

Income Statement

FYE: December 31

	REVENUE ($ mil.)	NET INCOME ($ mil.)	NET PROFIT MARGIN	EMPLOYEES
12/08	5,226	(7,913)	—	22,900
12/07	5,722	(1,607)	—	23,200
12/06	6,363	—	—	24,000
Annual Growth	**(9.4%)**	**—**	**—**	**(2.3%)**

Net Income History

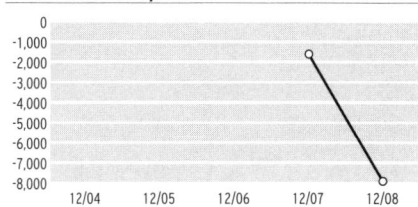

Friendly Ice Cream

Screaming ice cream lovers can soothe their pipes at Friendly's. Friendly Ice Cream operates a chain of more than 500 family-style restaurants in more than 15 states that specialize in frozen dairy treats. Among fan favorites are Friendly's Fribble shakes, the Royal Banana Split Sundae, and Chocolate Covered Berry Patch desserts. In addition to ice cream, the restaurants serve breakfast, lunch, and dinner — mostly traditional American fare such as sandwiches and burgers. Most of the chain's locations are company-operated. Friendly's also distributes ice cream and other frozen desserts through some 4,000 supermarkets and other retail sites. The company is owned by private equity firm Sun Capital Partners.

With the family-dining segment under pressure due to the recession, Friendly's has been focused mostly on cutting operating costs at its restaurants. Part of that effort includes a new express concept unveiled in 2008. The smaller fast-casual units offer a limited menu and are designed for areas that can't support a full-service restaurant. The company is also developing a quick-service concept focused on ice cream treats for high traffic areas such as airports and shopping malls.

Ned Lidvall, formerly head of Rock Bottom Restaurants, was appointed CEO in 2008, replacing George Condos who retired. Previously marketing chief at Dunkin' Donuts (one of the chains under the Dunkin' Brands umbrella), Condos had been appointed CEO in 2007 prior to Friendly's going private.

Sun Capital took the company private for almost $340 million in 2007 looking to reorganize the struggling restaurant chain. Friendly's later sold more than 160 properties in a sale-leaseback deal that netted about $40 million.

EXECUTIVES

President and CEO: Ned R. Lidvall, age 55
CFO: Steve Sanchioni
SVP Company Operations: John Bowie
VP Marketing: George (Skip) Weldon
VP Human Resources: Garrett J. Ulrich, age 58
General Counsel: Robert Sawyer Jr.
Senior Director Brand Marketing: Eileen Mastrio
Senior Director Investor Relations:
  Deborah (Debbie) Burns
Director Corporate Communications: Maura C. Tobias
Director Field Marketing: Jane Amico
Auditors: Ernst & Young LLP

LOCATIONS

HQ: Friendly Ice Cream Corporation
  1855 Boston Rd., Wilbraham, MA 01095
Phone: 413-731-4000   **Fax:** 413-731-4471
Web: www.friendlys.com

COMPETITORS

American Dairy Queen	Denny's
Ben & Jerry's	DineEquity
Bob Evans	Dreyer's
Brinker	Dunkin
Bruster's	Eat'n Park
Buffets Holdings	McDonald's
Carlson Restaurants	Nestlé
Carvel	NexCen Brands
Cold Stone Creamery	Perkins & Marie
Cracker Barrel	Callender's
Darden	Ruby Tuesday

Fry's Electronics

Trying to catalog all the things this superstore carries could fry your brain. Fry's Electronics is a leading big-box retailer of computers, consumer electronics, and appliances with some 35 stores in about 10 states. The retail chain's extensive inventory includes computer software and components, industry magazines, movies and music, refrigerators, washers and dryers, small appliances, stereo equipment, and televisions. Each store also typically stocks a variety of snacks and other impulse items. The technogeek's dream store began in 1985 as the brainchild of CEO John Fry (with brothers Randy and Dave) and EVP Kathy Kolder. The Fry brothers, who got their start at Fry's Food Stores, still own the company.

Its mammoth stores, some swallowing almost 200,000 sq. ft., cater to the intensely technical shopper. Fry's stores stock more than 50,000 low-priced electronic items and are known for their decor and displays. Each location follows a theme, from *Alice in Wonderland* to a UFO crash site. The selection ranges from silicon chips to potato chips, from *Byte* to *Playboy*, and high-speed PCs (plus software and peripherals) to hair dryers (and other health and beauty items).

In addition to its retail outlets, Fry's sells electronics online at Frys.com, replacing Outpost.com (its online subsidiary acquired in 2001). The company also offers dial-up and high speed Internet access services in more than 40 states.

Fry's stores' extensive inventories are said to be the company's strongest draw, unlike its speculated reputation for poor customer service. This reputation, combined with Fry's bemoaned system for returning items, has left the company a target of many gripe-filled Web sites.

HISTORY

The Fry brothers — David, John, and Randy — wear genes stitched of retailing. Their father, Charles, started Fry's Food Stores supermarket chain in the 1950s in South Bay, California. The 40-store chain was sold for $14 million in 1972 to Dillion (now part of grocery store giant The Kroger Co.) before Charles's progeny heard the retail calling.

Charles gave each of his sons $1 million from the sale of the supermarkets. His oldest, John, who had gained technical expertise while running the supermarket's computer system, convinced his siblings of the viability of a hard-core computer retail store. The brothers pooled their funds and in 1985 started the first in Sunnyvale, California, along with Kathryn Kolder (now EVP). They added a store in Fremont in 1988; the Palo Alto store was completed two years later.

John mixed his supermarket sales experience with a sharp marketing acumen, selling prime shelf space at smart prices to suppliers. He stocked the stores with everything for a computer user's survival and slashed prices. The first Los Angeles-area store opened in 1992; a second one opened the following year. Hiring an ex-Lucasfilm designer, John spent $1 million on each location, decorating stores like medieval castles, Mayan temples, Wild West saloons, and other individual fantasy themes.

In 1994 the Los Angeles computer retail market began to see increased competition from nationwide discount computer superstores. The next year Fry's responded by opening a new store in Woodland Hills with an *Alice in Wonderland* motif. It was the first Southern California Fry's Electronics store to offer appliances and an expanded music department.

The chain continued to gain notoriety for the contempt it seemed to show its customers. Local Better Business Bureaus started ranking Fry's "unsatisfactory" because the stores would not respond to complaints. Patrons with a beef were usually met by security guards, scores of hidden surveillance cameras, and employees who were promised bonuses for talking customers out of cash returns.

Still the company thrived, turning over its inventories twice as fast as competitors. One customer who sued Fry's for injuries allegedly received at the hands of store security guards went back for deals soon thereafter. Fry's went on an expansion frenzy in 1996, opening new California stores in Burbank, San Jose, and Anaheim. Moving beyond its Pacific roots, the company in 1997 spent $118 million to buy six of Tandy's failed Incredible Universe retail mega-outlets in Arizona, Oregon, and Texas. The company also won a legal battle with Frenchy Frys, a Seattle vending machine maker, for the right to own and use the frys.com URL. The company in 1998 continued to restructure its new stores into Fry's outlets.

Fry's opened a new store (complete with gushing oil derricks) in Houston in 2001. That year it pulled out of a deal to acquire all of the assets of technology products marketer Egghead.com and bought competitor Cyberian Outpost instead. In 2003 Fry's set up shop in Las Vegas; the entrance features a two-story neon slot machine.

In October 2006 the company (finally) launched Frys.com, although it has owned the domain name since 1997.

EXECUTIVES

CEO: John Fry
President: William R. (Randy) Fry
CFO and CIO: David (Dave) Fry
VP Business Development: Kathryn (Kathy) Kolder
Controller: Chris Scheiber
Legal Department Manager: Lisa McIntire
Community Relations Manager: Manuel Valerio

LOCATIONS

HQ: Fry's Electronics, Inc.
  600 E. Brokaw Rd., San Jose, CA 95112
Phone: 408-487-4500   **Fax:** 408-487-4741
Web: www.frys.com

PRODUCTS/OPERATIONS

Selected Products
Appliances (coffeemakers, blenders, vacuums)
Cameras
CD players
Computer components (hard drives, routers)
Computers (PCs, notebooks)
DVD players
DVDs
MP3 players
Office products (printers, copiers, fax machines)
PDAs
Software
Toys
Video games

COMPETITORS

Amazon.com	Hastings Entertainment
Apple Inc.	Newegg
Best Buy	Office Depot
Buy.com	PC Mall
CDW	RadioShack
CompUSA	Staples
Dell	Trans World Entertainment
GameStop	Wal-Mart
Gateway, Inc.	Zones

HISTORICAL FINANCIALS
Company Type: Private

Income Statement
FYE: December 31

	ESTIMATED REVENUE ($ mil.)	NET INCOME ($ mil.)	NET PROFIT MARGIN	EMPLOYEES
12/08	2,400	—	—	14,000
12/07	2,350	—	—	14,000
12/06	2,610	—	—	12,000
12/05	2,340	—	—	12,000
12/04	2,250	—	—	6,500
Annual Growth	1.6%	—	—	21.1%

Revenue History

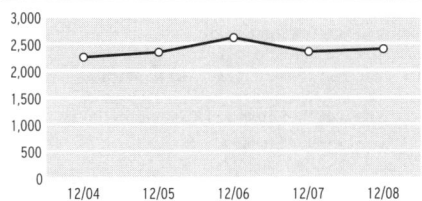

FXI-Foamex Innovations

Foam, sweet foam. FXI-Foamex International (formerly Foamex International) is one of North America's largest makers of flexible polyurethane and polymer foams for carpets and furniture. Products include mattresses, couches, car interior trim, and carpet cushions. Computer cabinets, industrial filters, and gaskets are a few of the uses for the products made by FXI's technical products division. FXI's customers include auto supplier Johnson Controls, as well as other major automobile and bedding manufacturers. The company emerged from Chapter 11 bankruptcy protection in 2007, after filing in 2005. Still beset by a heavy debt load, FXI entered Chapter 11 again in early 2009 and emerged in June of that year.

FXI restructured its debt under the Chapter 11 reorganization, while continuing day-to-day operations. Bank of America and MatlinPatterson Global Opportunities Partners III provided debtor-in-possession funding of up to $95 million to the company so it could continue to operate during the reorganization.

FXI sold its assets to MatlinPatterson Global Opportunities Partners and Black Diamond Capital Management for $155 million and the assumption of liabilities. The US bankruptcy court approved the proposed transaction in mid-2009, clearing the way for the company to emerge from Chapter 11 as a privately held firm. The new owners renamed the company FXI-Foamex Innovations.

Shortly after previously restructuring its finances, the company continued cost-cutting measures, including the 2007 sale of its 70% interest in Foamex Asia to its partner Hua Kee Company. (Foamex Asia was renamed Foamtec International.) Despite Foamex's desire to grow globally, the joint venture imposed certain noncompete restrictions that limited the company's ability to take advantage of other opportunities with more growth potential.

Foamex's first move toward growth since emerging from bankruptcy in 2007, however, was a domestic investment. In 2008 the company opened a fabrication and distribution plant in New Mexico. The motivation for the facility was to better serve its customers in the western US.

EXECUTIVES

President and CEO: John G. (Jack) Johnson Jr., age 68
EVP Automotive Products: Donald W. Phillips, age 43
EVP and CFO: Harold J. Earley
EVP and COO: David J. (Dave) Prilutski, age 55
SVP Human Resources: Michael V. Johnson
SVP Technical Products Business Management: Vincent A. Bonaddio
SVP Manufacturing: Ken Crawford
SVP Sales: Fred P. Rullo
SVP Research and Development: Chiu Chan
SVP Foam Products Business Management: Alvaro Vaselli
Auditors: KPMG LLP

LOCATIONS

HQ: FXI-Foamex Innovations
1400 N. Providence Rd., Ste. 2000, Media, PA 19063
Phone: 610-744-2300
Web: www.fxi.com

COMPETITORS

Advanced Materials	Latex International
American Excelsior	MTI Global
BBi Enterprises	Novagard Solutions
British Vita	Rieter Holding
Carpenter Co.	Sika Automotive
Crespi	Span-America Medical
Henry Company	UFP Technologies
Jason Incorporated	United Plastics
J.B. Poindexter	The Woodbridge Group

HISTORICAL FINANCIALS
Company Type: Private

Income Statement
FYE: Sunday nearest December 31

	REVENUE ($ mil.)	NET INCOME ($ mil.)	NET PROFIT MARGIN	EMPLOYEES
12/07	1,169	(47)	—	3,400
12/06	1,357	12	0.9%	4,000
12/05	1,312	(53)	—	5,000
12/04	1,266	(151)	—	5,500
12/03	1,305	(22)	—	5,100
Annual Growth	(2.7%)	—	—	(9.6%)

2007 Year-End Financials

Debt ratio: —	Current ratio: 1.69
Return on equity: —	Long-term debt ($ mil.): 528
Cash ($ mil.): 5	

Net Income History

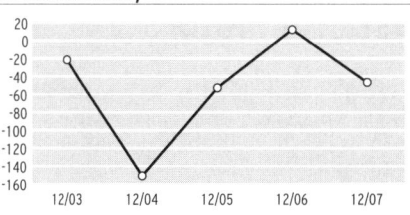

Gate Petroleum

Gate Petroleum swings many ways. The company runs a chain of about 225 Gate Food Post stores in Florida, Georgia, Kentucky, Louisiana, North Carolina, South Carolina, and Virginia that sell gas and groceries and offer fleet management services. The firm is also a wholesale fuel distributor to customers throughout the Southeast. The company is also active in the real estate and construction materials businesses. In Florida Gate owns several private clubs, office buildings, and business parks. Subsidiary Gate Concrete has plants in six states that make and sell concrete and building materials. CEO Herbert Peyton, who founded the company in 1960, owns the majority of Gate Petroleum Company.

Gate Petroleum's private clubs include the Epping Forest Yacht Club, the Ponte Vedra Inn & Club, and the Ponte Vedra Lodge & Club. It is also developing a huge residential and commercial complex in Jacksonville, Florida.

In February 2009 the company sold seven stores in North Carolina to Canada's Couche-Tard, which operates the Circle K chain of convenience stores in the US.

EXECUTIVES

Chairman and CEO; President, Gate Marketing Co.: Herbert H. (Herb) Peyton
VP, Development, Gate Marketing Co.: George Nail
VP, Finance: P. Jeremy Smith
VP, Real Estate; President GL National: Ken Wilson
VP, North Division, Gate Marketing Co.: John McMahon
VP, Payroll: Mary Ann Bright
Chairman, Gate Marketing Co.: Wayne Levitt
President, Gate Marketing Co.: Mitchell Rhodes
Director, Human Resources: Denise Gaitanzis

LOCATIONS

HQ: Gate Petroleum Company
9540 San Jose Blvd., Jacksonville, FL 32257
Phone: 904-737-7220   **Fax:** 904-732-7660
Web: www.gatepetro.com

PRODUCTS/OPERATIONS

Selected Operations

Gate Construction Materials (architectural and structural precast/prestressed concrete)
Gate Fuel Service (petroleum distribution)
Gate Petroleum Marketing (gas station/convenience stores)

COMPETITORS

7-Eleven	The Pantry
Chevron	Publix
Cumberland Farms	Racetrac Petroleum
Exxon Mobil	Royal Dutch Shell

General Motors

General Motors (GM) makes a wide portfolio of cars and trucks, with brands such as Buick, Cadillac, Chevrolet, and GMC. GM also produces cars through its GM Daewoo, Holden, Opel, and Vauxhall units. Financing and insurance business is primarily conducted by GMAC (GM currently owns about 10%). The century-old GM is experiencing historic financial challenges that threaten the company's longevity. The company received billions of dollars in loans from the Canadian and US governments as it restructured, negotiating concessions with its labor unions and jettisoning brands. The giant automotive manufacturer went through a brief Chapter 11 bankruptcy reorganization in 2009.

GM's bankruptcy reorganization was completed in 40 days. The company sold most of its global assets to a "New GM" entity to create a carmaker less burdened by debt and high costs for labor and retiree care. With the cooperation of the Canadian and US governments, its North American unions, and its unsecured bondholders, the "New GM" emerged from Chapter 11 with about $17 billion in debt, $8 billion of which is owed to government lenders. Other government loans were turned into equity in the new company. The US government owns about 61% of the "New GM," while the Canadian federal government and the Ontario provincial government together hold nearly 12%. The remainder is held by a UAW retiree health care trust, and by unsecured bondholders and unsecured creditors. The US government foresees a possible IPO for the restructured company in 2010.

Among other measures, GM will focus on its Buick, Cadillac, Chevrolet, Opel, and GMC brands, while discontinuing the HUMMER, Pontiac, Saab Automobile, and Saturn brands. The automaker plans to reduce its number of US dealerships by about 40%, closing more than 1,600 by the end of 2010.

The company is making 100 Chevrolet Volts in 2009 for test purposes. If all goes as planned, GM will produce 10,000 of the hybrids in 2010 and 60,000 in 2012. GM also announced a partnership with Segway to develop a two-wheeled, two-seat electric vehicle.

While it struggled mightily with its own finances, GM extended a helping hand to Delphi, the auto parts supplier it spun off in 1999. Delphi, which makes a number of critical parts for GM cars, filed for Chapter 11 in 2005 and emerged as a private company in 2009. As part of the private equity transaction, GM agreed to provide additional loans for restructuring to Delphi, as well as to buy four plants and Delphi's global steering business. Terms of the deal — including how much equity GM will hold in Delphi — were not announced.

GM's fortunes outside of North America are looking up. With the world's largest pool of potential drivers, China's automotive market is experiencing explosive growth and GM plans to spend $3 billion over the next couple of years in order to keep up with demand there. It also plans to double its production capacity and introduce new models, and has set up a financing venture with Chinese partner Shanghai Automotive Industry Corporation (SAIC).

After leading GM through a painful restructuring, CEO Rick Wagoner was forced to resign by the US government as a precondition for continued government aid. Frederick (Fritz) Henderson, the company's COO since 2006, took Wagoner's place. Henderson brought a blend of financial, operational, and international experience to his new assignment. In eight months on the job, Henderson brought GM out of bankruptcy and oversaw attempts to sell the company's non-core brands, with little success. In December 2009 Henderson resigned from all positions; he was replaced on an interim basis by chairman Ed Whitacre, while GM conducts an international search for a permanent replacement. Whitacre — the long-time CEO of AT&T until his retirement in 2007 — is known as a deal maker and a tough negotiator with a hands-on management style.

HISTORY

In the early years of the auto industry, hundreds of carmakers each produced a few models. William Durant, who bought a failing Buick Motors in 1904, reasoned that manufacturers could benefit from banding together and formed the General Motors Company in Flint, Michigan, in 1908.

Durant bought 17 companies (including Oldsmobile, Cadillac, and Pontiac) by 1910, the year a bankers' syndicate forced him to step down. In 1915 he regained control when he formed a company with racecar driver Louis Chevrolet. They soon formed GM Acceptance Corporation (GMAC, financing) and bought businesses including Frigidaire (sold in 1979) and Hyatt Roller Bearing.

With Hyatt came Alfred Sloan (president, 1923-37), who built GM into a corporate colossus via a decentralized management system. Unlike Ford — which offered cars in any color you liked as long as it was black — GM offered a range of models and colors; by 1927 it was the industry leader. It bought Vauxhall Motors (UK, 1925), merged with Adam Opel (Germany, 1931), added defense products for WWII, and diversified into home appliances and locomotives.

GM expanded with the nation in the post-war boom years; the good times rolled until Japanese automakers became established in the 1970s. GM spent much of the decade trying to emulate the Japanese while making its cars meet federal pollution-control mandates. CEO Roger Smith laid off thousands of workers.

GM bought Electronic Data Systems (1984), Hughes Aircraft (1986), and 50% of Saab Automobile (1989). GM launched the Saturn car in 1990; that year Robert Stempel became CEO. In 1992 GM made what was then the largest stock offering in US history ($2.2 billion), and Jack Smith replaced Stempel as CEO.

GM spun off Electronic Data Systems in 1996. In 1997 it sold the defense electronics business of Hughes Electronics to Raytheon.

UAW walkouts at two Michigan GM parts plants in 1998 forced the shutdown of virtually all of the company's North American production lines. In 1999 GM spun off Delphi and boosted its stake in small-truck partner Isuzu to 49%. The next year GM acquired the 50% of Saab Automobile that it didn't already own (from Investor AB).

President Rick Wagoner replaced Smith as CEO in June 2000. In 2001 GM paid about $600 million to double its stake in Suzuki to 20%. The following year GM took a 42% stake in South Korea's bankrupt Daewoo Motor (later increased to 51%).

In early 2006 GM's finance arm, GMAC, sold a 78% equity stake in its commercial mortgage business to a private equity consortium for about $9 billion. GM then sold a 51% stake in GMAC to a consortium of investors led by Cerberus Capital Management for $14 billion.

GM sold its Allison Transmission commercial and military business to The Carlyle Group and Onex Corp. for about $5.6 billion in 2007.

The company dodged a bullet in 2007 when the UAW, fighting for health care for retirees, ended a two-day strike — the first nationwide UAW strike against GM in more than 35 years. The two hammered out a deal creating a $50 billion independent health care trust (with GM ponying up most of the trust's funding).

For 2007 GM reported the largest annual loss in the history of the automotive industry — $38.7 billion.

EXECUTIVES

Chairman and Interim CEO:
Edward E. (Ed) Whitacre Jr., age 67
Vice Chairman Global Product Development:
Thomas G. Stephens, age 61
Vice Chairman Marketing and Communications:
Robert A. (Bob) Lutz, age 77
EVP and CFO: Ray G. Young, age 47
VP Information Systems and Services and Chief Information Officer: Terry Kline, age 47
Chief Tax Officer: Raymond P. (Ray) Wexler
Controller and Chief Accounting Officer:
Nicholas S. (Nick) Cyprus, age 55
Group VP; General Manager Vehicle Operations:
Nathan J. Porter
Group VP Global Manufacturing and Labor Relations:
Gary L. Cowger, age 62
Group VP; President, GM Latin America, Africa, and Middle East: V. Maureen Kempston-Darkes, age 60
Group VP Corporate Planning and Alliances and Secretary: John F. Smith Jr.
VP Engineering: Karl-Friedrich Stracke
VP Legal: Michael P. Millikin, age 61
VP Vehicle Sales, Service, and Marketing Operations:
Susan E. Docherty, age 46
VP Human Resources: Mary T. Barra
VP Global Product Planning:
Jonathan J. (Jon) Lauckner, age 51
VP Global Manufacturing Engineering: Eric R. Stevens, age 53
VP Communications: J. Christopher Preuss
VP Global Design: Edward T. (Ed) Welburn Jr., age 58
VP Global Purchasing and Supply Chain:
Robert E. (Bob) Socia, age 55
VP Global Public Policy and Government Relations:
Kenneth W. (Ken) Cole
VP Environment, Energy, and Safety Policy and Chief Environmental Officer: Elizabeth A. (Beth) Lowery, age 54
President, GM North America: Mark Reuss, age 46
President, International Operations:
Timothy E. (Tim) Lee, age 58
Corporate Secretary: Anne T. Larin
Treasurer: Walter G. Borst, age 47
Auditors: Deloitte & Touche LLP

LOCATIONS

HQ: General Motors Company
300 Renaissance Center, Detroit, MI 48265
Phone: 313-556-5000
Web: www.gm.com

2008 Sales

	$ mil.	% of total
North America		
US	75,382	51
Canada & Mexico	12,983	9
Europe		
UK	7,142	5
Germany	6,663	4
Italy	3,169	2
France	2,629	2
Russia	2,061	1
Spain	1,711	1
Sweden	1,195	1
Other countries	7,939	5
Latin America		
Brazil	8,329	6
Other countries	5,907	4
Asia/Pacific		
South Korea	7,131	5
Australia	3,355	2
Thailand	560	—
Other countries	1,401	1
Other regions	1,422	1
Total	**148,979**	**100**

PRODUCTS/OPERATIONS

2008 Sales

	$ mil.	% of total
Automotive		
GM North America	82,938	56
GM Europe	32,440	22
GM Latin America, Africa & Middle East	19,877	13
GM Asia Pacific	12,477	8
Financial services & insurance	1,247	1
Total	**148,979**	**100**

Selected Brands

Buick
Cadillac
Chevrolet
GMC
Holden
Isuzu
Opel
Vauxhall

COMPETITORS

BMW	Mitsubishi Motors
Chrysler	Navistar International
Daimler	Nissan
Fiat	Peugeot
Ford Motor	Renault
Fuji Heavy Industries	Suzuki Motor
Honda	Tata Motors
Hyundai Motor	Toyota
Kia Motors	Volkswagen
Land Rover	Volvo Car Corp.
Mazda	

HISTORICAL FINANCIALS

Company Type: Private

Income Statement
FYE: December 31

	REVENUE ($ mil.)	NET INCOME ($ mil.)	NET PROFIT MARGIN	EMPLOYEES
12/08	148,979	(30,860)	—	243,000
12/07	181,122	(38,732)	—	266,000
12/06	207,349	(1,978)	—	280,000
12/05	192,604	(10,458)	—	335,000
12/04	193,517	2,805	1.4%	324,000
Annual Growth	(6.3%)	—	—	(6.9%)

2008 Year-End Financials

Debt ratio: —
Return on equity: —
Cash ($ mil.): 14,053
Current ratio: 0.56
Long-term debt ($ mil.): 30,786

Net Income History

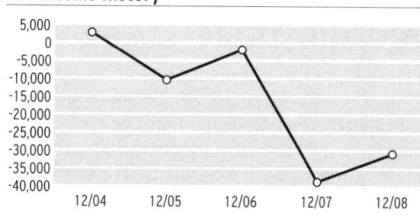

Revenue History

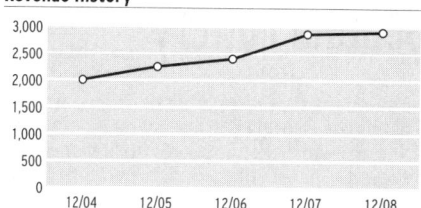

General Parts

Feel free to salute General Parts, distributor of replacement automotive parts, supplies, and tools for every make and model of foreign and domestic car, truck, bus, and farm or industrial vehicle. The firm operates the CARQUEST auto parts distribution network of some 40 distribution centers, and owns about 1,400 of CARQUEST's 3,400 auto parts stores across the US, Canada, and Mexico. The company sells its parts to DIY mechanics, professional installers, body shops, farmers, and fleet owners (commercial customers account for most sales). General Parts has traditionally grown through acquisitions. The company, founded in 1961 by college student Temple Sloan, owns CARQUEST Canada.

EXECUTIVES

Chairman and CEO: O. Temple Sloan Jr., age 70
President and COO: O. Temple Sloan III
CFO: John Gardner
EVP Product Management: Robert Blair
EVP Marketing and Merchandising: Dale Ward, age 59
EVP Store Group: Jerry Colley, age 52
SVP Marketing: Ray Birden
SVP Product Management; President, CARQUEST: Todd Hack
Chief People Officer: John Dibenedetto

LOCATIONS

HQ: General Parts, Inc.
2635 E. Millbrook Rd., Raleigh, NC 27604
Phone: 919-573-3000   **Fax:** 919-573-3551

COMPETITORS

Advance Auto Parts	Dorman Products
Applied Industrial Technologies	Hahn Automotive
Atwood Mobile	Keystone Automotive
AutoZone	Pep Boys
CSK Auto	Sears

HISTORICAL FINANCIALS

Company Type: Private

Income Statement
FYE: December 31

	ESTIMATED REVENUE ($ mil.)	NET INCOME ($ mil.)	NET PROFIT MARGIN	EMPLOYEES
12/08	2,910	—	—	16,800
12/07	2,870	—	—	18,000
12/06	2,400	—	—	24,500
12/05	2,250	—	—	23,000
12/04	2,000	—	—	20,000
Annual Growth	9.8%	—	—	(4.3%)

Genesis HealthCare

Genesis HealthCare Corporation cares for people when care is what counts. Genesis HealthCare operates about 200 assisted living and skilled nursing facilities in 13 states in the eastern US. Its facilities have about 26,000 beds total. Genesis HealthCare's rehabilitation division provides speech, physical, and occupational therapy services through contracts with health care providers in more than 20 states. The company also offers respiratory therapy, adult day care, Alzheimer's care, dialysis, and home and hospice care. Genesis HealthCare was taken private in 2007 by a group of private equity investors from Formation Capital and the private equity arm of real estate investment firm J. E. Roberts.

Genesis HealthCare has grown by developing its specialty services, including its transitional care facilities and rehabilitation contract services, as well as through acquisitions. In 2008 the company picked up a skilled nursing center in Massachusetts as well as one in Virginia and a nursing home/assisted living facility in Virginia.

In early 2007 investment firms Formation Capital and JER Partners announced a plan to purchase Genesis HealthCare. Fillmore Capital Partners countered with a higher offer, prompting Formation and JER to increase their offer, which was accepted in mid-2007.

EXECUTIVES

CEO: George V. Hager Jr., age 53
EVP and COO: Robert A. (Mike) Reitz, age 59
EVP and President, Central Area: Paul D. Bach
EVP and President, Northeast Area: Richard P. (Dick) Blinn, age 55
EVP and President, Southern Area: David C. (Dave) Almquist, age 55
SVP and CFO: Tom DiVittorio
SVP and CIO: Richard L. (Rich) Castor
SVP Administration: Richard (Rich) Pell Jr., age 61
Director Investor Relations: Lori Mayer
President, Genesis Rehab Services: Dan Hirschfeld
Auditors: KPMG LLP

LOCATIONS

HQ: Genesis HealthCare Corporation
101 E. State St., Kennett Square, PA 19348
Phone: 610-444-6350   **Fax:** 610-925-4000
Web: www.genesishcc.com

COMPETITORS

Golden Horizons
HealthSouth
Kindred Healthcare
Manor Care
Sunrise Senior Living

Georgia Lottery

You might say these games of chance are just peachy. The Georgia Lottery operates a number of instant-win ticket and lotto style games, including Cash 3, Fantasy 5, and Win for Life. It also takes part in the multi-state Mega Millions drawing game. Tickets are sold through more than 7,500 retailers throughout the state. Since it was established in 1993, the lottery has contributed more than $10 billion in proceeds to state education programs, including the HOPE Scholarship Program and Georgia's Prekindergarten Program.

EXECUTIVES

Chair: James F. (Jimmy) Braswell
President and CEO: Margaret R. DeFrancisco, age 60
CTO: Daniel Johnson
SVP Administration: Gerald Mecca
SVP Finance, Planning, and Development:
Joan Schoubert
SVP and General Counsel: Kurt Freedlund
VP Customer Operations: Teri Rosa
VP Human Resources: Douglas Parker
VP Sales: Jack Dimling
VP Marketing: James Hutchinson
VP Legal Affairs: Rosemarie Morse
VP Corporate Affairs: J.B. Landroche
VP Financial Management: Sharman Lomax
Media Relations Manager: Tandi Reddick
Auditors: Deloitte & Touche LLC

LOCATIONS

HQ: Georgia Lottery Corporation
250 Williams St., Ste. 3000, Atlanta, GA 30303
Phone: 404-215-5000   **Fax:** 404-215-8983
Web: www.galottery.com

HISTORICAL FINANCIALS
Company Type: Government-owned

Income Statement				FYE: June 30
	REVENUE ($ mil.)	NET INCOME ($ mil.)	NET PROFIT MARGIN	EMPLOYEES
6/08	3,519	—	—	279
6/07	3,422	—	—	266
6/06	2,960	—	—	260
6/05	2,922	—	—	—
6/04	2,710	—	—	—
Annual Growth	6.8%	—	—	3.6%

Revenue History

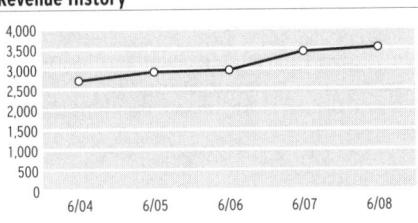

Georgia Tech

The Georgia Institute of Technology, commonly known as Georgia Tech, is one of the country's top engineering schools for both graduate and undergraduate students. The university also offers degrees in the Colleges of Architecture, Sciences, Computing, and Management, and the Ivan Allen College of Liberal Arts. It has an enrollment of more than 16,000 students. The school is also renowned for its scientific and technological research, receiving more than $355 million in research awards annually. Georgia Tech was founded in 1885 as the Georgia School of Technology.

EXECUTIVES

President: G. P. (Bud) Peterson
EVP Academic Affairs and Provost: Gary Schuster
EVP Administration and Finance:
Steven G. (Steve) Swant
SVP Administration and Finance: Robert K. Thompson
Senior Vice Provost Academic Affairs: Anderson Smith
Vice Provost Graduate and Undergraduate Studies:
Ray Vito
Vice Provost Academic Diversity: Gilda Barabino
Vice Provost Faculty and Academic Development:
Jack Lohmann
Associate Vice Provost Information Technology, Associate VP, and CIO: John K. Mullin
Director Public Relations: Lisa Grovenstein
Director Admissions: Rick Clark

LOCATIONS

HQ: Georgia Institute of Technology
225 North Ave. NW, Atlanta, GA 30332
Phone: 404-894-5051   **Fax:** 404-894-1277
Web: www.gatech.edu

Getty Images

With an eye out for the big picture, visual content provider Getty Images is a major supplier of creative (stock) and editorial still and moving images and illustrations, as well as music. It also offers photo services for corporate clients. The company targets four main markets: advertising and graphic design firms; editorial organizations, such as newspapers, magazines, and online publishers; corporate communications departments; and film and broadcast producers. Getty Images, which distributes its products online, has customers in more than 100 countries around the world; most of its sales come from outside the US. In mid-2008, Getty Images was acquired by private equity firm Hellman & Friedman.

Hellman & Friedman paid about $2.4 billion, including assumed debt, for the company. The deal was struck a few months after Getty Images had announced that it had hired advisers to help the company evaluate ways to increase shareholder value. Its profits and its share price had been slumping, in part because of increased competition from low-cost image providers.

Before it was taken private, Getty Images was expanding its image library quickly through acquisitions. In 2009 the company acquired Jupiterimages, a subsidiary of WebMediaBrands (formerly Jupitermedia), for $96 million. Through the deal, Getty picked up more than 10 million images under a plethora of brands that included Creatas Images, Liquid Library, Photos.com, Clipart.com, and AnimationFactory.com.

In 2007 Getty Images bought WireImage, a leading provider of celebrity- and entertainment-related images for editorial use, for about $200 million. Included in the deal were WireImage affiliates FilmMagic and Contour-Photos, along with the companies' parent, MediaVast. Also that year Getty Images entered the music licensing business by acquiring Pump Audio, provider of independent music used in advertising, broadcast, film, and other applications.

The transaction came on the heels of two acquisitions by Getty Images: Ireland-based Pixel Images, the parent company of visual content providers Stockbyte and Stockdisc, for $135 million; and iStockphoto, a company that deals mainly in micropayment transactions and makes images available for use for as little as $1, for $50 million. Getty Images is maintaining the Web sites for iStockphoto, Pump Audio, and WireImage as part of an effort to broaden its Web presence.

Besides acquisitions, the company's growth strategies have included boosting its presence in non-English speaking markets and strengthening its offerings in the micropayment market. With backing from Hellman & Friedman, Getty Images hopes to continue its expansion push.

EXECUTIVES

Chairman: Mark H. Getty, age 48
CEO and Director: Jonathan D. Klein, age 49
COO: Nicholas E. (Nick) Evans-Lombe, age 42
SVP and CFO: Jeff Dunn
SVP Editorial Imagery: Adrian Murrell
SVP Technology: Steve Heck
SVP Human Resources and Facilities: Lisa Calvert
SVP Business Development: Craig Peters
SVP and General Counsel: John J. Lapham, age 41
SVP Marketing: James C. (Jim) Gurke, age 53
SVP Sales, Europe: Lee Martin
SVP Sales, North America and Asia Pacific:
Michael D. Teaster, age 42
Senior Director Public Relations US: Bridget Russel
Auditors: PricewaterhouseCoopers LLP

LOCATIONS

HQ: Getty Images, Inc.
601 N. 34th St., Seattle, WA 98103
Phone: 206-925-5000   **Fax:** 206-925-5001
Web: www.gettyimages.com

COMPETITORS

AG Interactive
Agence France-Presse
Associated Press
Corbis
Masterfile
National Geographic
New York Times
PR Newswire
Reuters
Rex Features
Sipa Press
Zuma Press

Giant Eagle

Giant Eagle has its talons firmly wrapped around parts of Pennsylvania and Ohio. The grocery chain, a market leader in Pittsburgh and eastern Ohio, operates about 160 company-owned stores and some 60 franchised supermarkets, as well as about 150 GetGo convenience stores (which feature fresh foods and sell gas at discounted prices through the fuelperks! program). Many Giant Eagle stores feature video rental, banking, photo processing, dry cleaning services, and ready-to-eat meals. Giant Eagle is also a wholesaler to licensed stores and sells groceries to other retail chains. CEO David Shapira is the grandson of one of the men who founded the company in 1931. The founders' families own Giant Eagle.

In response to tough economic times and competition from discounters, Giant Eagle is restructuring and cutting prices on popular items, such as produce, chicken, ground beef, and prescription medication. The grocery chain's *Savings Squad* program has cut prices an average of 23% on 100-plus frequently purchased items. Giant Eagle is also cutting costs at the corporate level, eliminating about 80 positions at its headquarters in mid-2009 and another 45 store-level human resources jobs in September.

The supermarket chain, which also has limited operations in Maryland and West Virginia, has also shifted the start of its weekly sales specials from Sunday to Thursday to match its customers' changing shopping patterns and better compete with nontraditional grocery chains, such as Costco Wholesale and Wal-Mart.

As with other birds of the retailing feather, Giant Eagle's supermarkets carry private-label merchandise (Market District, Giant Eagle, and Value Time brands) and nonfood items; many have pharmacies.

The company's goal is to grow Giant Eagle food and drug sales through a combination of acquisitions and organic growth. To that end, in late 2006 Giant Eagle acquired nearly 20 stores in northeastern Ohio from rival TOPS Markets. Previous purchases include Giant Eagle's successful bid for the remaining assets of bankrupt discount drugstore chain Phar-Mor. It also acquired and converted eight Big Bear grocery stores in the Columbus area from bankrupt supermarket operator Penn Traffic.

HISTORY

When Joe Porter, Ben Chait, and Joe Goldstein sold their chain of 125 Eagle grocery stores in Pittsburgh to Kroger in 1928, the agreement stated that the men would have to leave the grocery business for three years. In retrospect, Kroger should have made the term last for the length of their lives, because in 1931 the three men joined the owners of OK Grocery — Hyman Moravitz and Morris Weizenbaum — and launched a new chain of grocery stores called Giant Eagle. Eventually, the chain would knock Kroger out of the Pittsburgh market.

Although slowed by the Great Depression, the chain expanded, fighting such large rivals as Acme, A&P, and Kroger for Pittsburgh's food

shoppers. The stores were mom-and-pop operations with over-the-counter service until they began converting to self-service during the 1940s. Store sizes expanded to nearly 15,000 sq. ft. in the 1950s. During that time Giant Eagle, with about 30 stores, launched Blue Stamps in answer to Green Stamps and other loyalty programs.

It phased out trading stamps in the 1960s in lieu of everyday low prices. To accommodate its growth, in 1968 Giant Eagle acquired a warehouse in Lawrenceville, Pennsylvania, that more than doubled its storage area. Also that year the firm opened its first 20,000-sq.-ft. Giant Eagle store.

During the inflationary 1970s Giant Eagle introduced generic items and began offering the Food Club line, a private-label brand, in conjunction with wholesaler Topco. It continued its expansion, and by 1979 it had become Pittsburgh's #1 supermarket chain, as chains such as Kroger, Acme, and A&P were leaving the city. In 1981 Giant Eagle, with 52 stores, acquired Tamarkin, a wholesale and retail chain in Youngstown, Ohio, part-owned by the Monus family. The purchase moved it into the franchise business, and later that year the first independent Giant Eagle store opened in Monaca (outside Pittsburgh).

The Tamarkin purchase brought together Mickey Monus and Giant Eagle CEO David Shapira, grandson of founder Goldstein. In 1982 they created Phar-Mor, a deep-discount drugstore chain (Wal-Mart's Sam Walton once said it was the only competitor he truly feared). From a single store in Niles, Ohio, Phar-Mor grew rapidly to 310 outlets in 32 states in the early 1990s.

Phar-Mor president Monus helped found the World Basketball League (WBL) in 1987 and became the owner of three teams. In 1992 an auditor discovered two unexplainable Phar-Mor checks to the WBL totaling about $100,000. Investigators soon uncovered three years of overstated inventories and a false set of books; Shapira (who was also CEO of Phar-Mor), Giant Eagle owners (which held a 50% stake in Phar-Mor until 1992), and other investors had been duped of more than $1 billion. Shapira fired Monus and other executives on July 31, 1992. The next day the WBL folded; about two weeks after that Phar-Mor filed for Chapter 11 bankruptcy. A mistrial in 1994 couldn't save Monus from prison; he was reindicted in 1995 and sentenced to 20 years (later reduced to 12).

Giant Eagle made its largest acquisition in 1997, paying $403 million for Riser Foods, a wholesaler (American Seaway Foods) with 35 company-owned stores under the Rini-Rego Stop-n-Shop banner.

In 2000 Giant Eagle opened several stores in Columbus, Ohio. The grocer moved into Maryland in 2001 when it acquired six Country Market stores in Maryland and Pennsylvania. Also in 2001, the grocer founded ECHO Real Estate Services Co. to develop retail, housing, and golf course projects.

In 2002 Giant Eagle was among the winning bidders for the remaining assets of bankrupt Phar-Mor. It acquired leases to 10 Phar-Mor stores and the inventory and prescription lists for 27 stores. In 2006 Giant Eagle acquired nearly 20 stores in northeastern Ohio from rival TOPS Markets.

In mid-2009 Giant Eagle closed four of its optical stores (launched in 2004) and ended a pilot program that allowed customers in six stores to scan their own groceries.

EXECUTIVES

Chairman, President, and CEO:
  David S. (Dave) Shapira, age 67
Vice Chairman: Raymond J. (Ray) Burgo
COO: John R. Lucot
EVP Sales: Laura S. Karet, age 40
EVP Human Resources: Michele M. Reuss
SVP and CIO: Russell (Russ) Ross
SVP Construction: Norman B. Weizenbaum
SVP Sustainability: Robert P. Garrity
SVP Retail Operations: Eugene W. (Gene) Tommasi
SVP and CFO: Mark J. Minnaugh
SVP Marketing: Brett L. Merrell
SVP Distribution and Logistics: Larry Baldauf
SVP Marketing, Market District: Kevin C. Srigley
SVP Real Estate and Asset Management:
  Michelle (Shelly) Sponholz
Director, Marketing: Rob Borella
Director, International Foods: David Atkins
General Counsel: Dan Shapira
Treasurer: Phillip Oliveri
President, Chestnut Ridge Beverage: Charley Price

LOCATIONS

HQ: Giant Eagle, Inc.
  101 Kappa Dr., Pittsburgh, PA 15238
Phone: 412-963-6200   **Fax:** 412-968-1617
Web: www.gianteagle.com

2009 Stores

	No.
Ohio	121
Pennsylvania	98
West Virginia	2
Maryland	2
Total	**223**

PRODUCTS/OPERATIONS

2009 Stores

	No.
Company-owned	158
Franchised	65
Total	**223**

Selected Private-Label Brands

Giant Eagle
Market District
Nature's Basket

Selected Services

Bakery
Banking services
Childcare
Deli department
Dry cleaning
Fresh seafood
Greeting cards
Pharmacy
Photo developing
Ready-to-eat meals
Ticketmaster outlet
Video rental

COMPETITORS

7-Eleven
Costco Wholesale
CVS Caremark
Giant Food
IGA
Kroger
Shop 'n Save
SUPERVALU
Target
Walgreen
Wal-Mart
Wegmans
Weis Markets
Whole Foods

Gibson Guitar

Real pickers put Gibson Guitar on a pedestal. Though it trails top guitar maker Fender, Gibson builds instruments that are held in unparalleled esteem by many guitarists, including top professional musicians. The company's most popular guitar is the legendary Les Paul. Gibson also makes guitars under such brands as Epiphone, Kramer, and Steinberger. In addition to guitars, the company manufactures pianos through its Baldwin unit, Slingerland drums, Tobias bass, Wurlitzer vending machines and jukeboxes, and Echoplex amplifiers, as well as many accessory items. Company namesake Orville Gibson began making mandolins in the late 1890s. Gibson Guitar is owned by executives Henry Juszkiewicz and David Berryman.

Gibson's core business continues to focus on challenging such rivals as Fender, Martin, and Taylor for a greater share of the guitar market. To get the word out about its products and to attract customers, the company has traditionally relied on word-of-mouth between players and endorsement deals with top-selling musicians. However, Gibson struck a lucrative marketing deal with Universal Studios in 2005, acquiring the naming rights to the 33-year-old Universal Amphitheatre at the company's Southern California theme park.

Through its acquisition of famous brand names, from Baldwin to Wurlitzer, and its reintroduction of others, such as Epiphone, Gibson has expanded its product lines beyond the core guitar market and continues to develop new products. Juszkiewicz sees a lot of potential in using technology to update designs that have not significantly changed since the 1950s. The firm introduced a digital guitar in 2004 that looks and feels like a conventional electric guitar but converts string vibrations into a data stream using its proprietary MaGIC (media-accelerated global information carrier) technology. Gibson also hopes to license MaGIC to manufacturers for use in consumer electronics.

Gibson's growth also has expanded the business from its Nashville roots and it now boasts a global presence. The company has a manufacturing plant in China to make Epiphone guitars and it has a majority stake in Baldwin Zhongshan China, a joint venture formed in 2004 with Zhongshan Yue Hua Piano and Musical Instruments. To strengthen its foothold in China and significantly expand its manufacturing capacity there, Gibson in late 2006 acquired a major player in China's piano market — Dongbei Piano Co., Ltd. Gibson renamed the firm Baldwin-Dongbei Piano & Musical Instruments Co., Ltd. In July 2006 Gibson acquired Deutsche Wurlitzer from Nelson Group Overseas after years of litigation between the two regarding use of the Wurlitzer name. The deal brings Wurlitzer Jukebox and Vending Electronics into Gibson's fold.

In mid-2007 the instrument manufacturer acquired Canada's Garrison Guitars, which is best known for the Griffiths Active Bracing System and its innovative guitar construction. Gibson plans to use the purchase to boost its median-priced guitar portfolio and grab a larger share of the acoustic guitar market. As part of the agreement, Gibson will expand Garrison's factory in Newfoundland.

Juszkiewicz and Berryman bought Gibson for $5 million in 1986.

HISTORY

In the 1880s shoe-store clerk Orville Gibson bought a small workshop and began making mandolins based on his own innovative design. He was soon making arch-top acoustic guitars, banjos, and lutes, and by the turn of the century demand outpaced supply. Gibson and a group of financiers established the Gibson Mandolin-Guitar Manufacturing Company in 1902. Gibson was given $2,500 for the right to use his surname; he died in 1918.

Gibson capitalized on the popularity of banjos in the 1920s and guitars in the 1930s. In 1941 guitarist and inventor Les Paul showed the company his new baby: an electric guitar. Gibson execs rejected the innovation immediately. During WWII the company made parts for the war effort, and in 1944 Chicago Musical Instruments (CMI) bought Gibson in preparation for the pent-up demand for guitars that would follow the war's end. In the meantime, Leo Fender had introduced the first commercially successful electric guitar: the Fender Telecaster. In response, Gibson Musical Instruments introduced the Les Paul model in 1952.

The rise of guitar-oriented rock 'n' roll during the 1950s and 1960s created unprecedented demand for guitars. In 1969 CMI and another company merged to form Norlin, whose lack of attention to manufacturing quality tarnished Gibson's good name. In 1986 Gibson guitar enthusiast (and Harvard MBA) Henry Juszkiewicz and his partner David Berryman bought the company for $5 million.

The two immediately replaced top management and began retooling Gibson's factories. From 1986 to 1996 the company grew a rock-solid 30% a year and acquired a slew of musical instrument makers, including Tobias Guitars in 1989. In 1996 it opened its first music cafe, originally called Henry's Coffeehouse and later named Gibson Cafe and Guitar Gallery, in Nashville, Tennessee.

Gibson continued making acquisitions in 1998, buying Opcode Systems (music production hardware and software) and Trace Elliot (amplifiers). After failing to meet expectations, it closed the Tobias division in 1998 (though it still produces guitars under the Tobias name). Also that year the company acquired another music cafe, Caffe Milano, in Nashville, but Gibson closed both of its cafes in 2000 after failing to make them profitable. That same year, however, the company opened music venue Gibson Bluegrass Showcase at Opry Mills shopping mall in Nashville.

In 2001 Gibson bought the assets of Baldwin Piano & Organ (the largest seller of acoustic pianos in the US), which was under bankruptcy protection. Gibson made it a subsidiary and changed its name to Baldwin Piano. The next year the company's technology division, Gibson Labs, introduced plans for the first digital electric guitar (introduced in 2004) along with technology partners 3Com, Xilinx, and AMD.

In 2003 the company formed its Gibson Audio division to create convergent products involving traditional electronics and digital technology. The group's first product, the Wurlitzer digital jukebox, was launched late that year.

Les Paul, the namesake for one of the company's top products, died at the age of 94 in August 2009.

EXECUTIVES

Chairman and CEO: Henry E. Juszkiewicz, age 55
President: David H. (Dave) Berryman
EVP Outreach Marketing: Caroline Galloway
SVP Sales and Marketing Administration:
  Roger Mitchell
VP Channel Sales: Kevin Van Pamel
President, Gibson China: Mark Klingspon
President, Gibson Europe: Anders Moeller
General Manager, Epiphone: Jim Rosenberg
General Manager, Custom Division:
  Richard (Rick) Gembar
General Manager, Gibson Acoustic: Doug Kofinke
Chief People Officer: Leah McGreary
Executive Director, Gibson Foundation: Nina Miller
Auditors: Grant Thornton

LOCATIONS

HQ: Gibson Guitar Corp.
  309 Plus Park Blvd., Nashville, TN 37217
Phone: 615-871-4500   **Fax:** 615-889-5509
Web: www.gibson.com

PRODUCTS/OPERATIONS

Selected Products

Amplifiers
Guitars
Pianos and consumer products
Other products
  Accessories
  Equipment
    Echoplex (sound processing equipment)
    Maestro (guitar effects pedals)
    Oberheim (sound processing equipment)

COMPETITORS

All A Cart Manufacturing
Allen Organ Company
C. F. Martin & Co.
Carvin
CASIO COMPUTER
Crane Co.
D'Addario
Ernie Ball
Fender Musical Instruments
Ford Gum & Machine Company
GHS
Harman International
Hoshino (U.S.A.)
Kawai
K.H.S. Musical Instrument
KMC Music
Korg
LaSiDo
Line 6
LOUD Technologies
The Music Link
Musicorp
Paul Reed Smith Guitars
Peavey Electronics
QSC Audio
Rickenbacker
Roland Corporation
Samick
St. Louis Music
Steinway
Taylor Guitars
US Music
Whirlpool
Yamaha

Gilbane, Inc.

Family-owned Gilbane has been the bane of its rivals for four generations, with a fifth generation on the way. Subsidiary Gilbane Building provides construction management, contracting, and design and build services to construct office buildings, manufacturing plants, schools, prisons, and more for the firm's governmental, commercial, and industrial clients. Landmark projects include work on the National Air and Space Museum, Baltimore's Inner Harbor project, and the World War II memorial and Capitol Visitors Center in Washington, DC. Another subsidiary, Gilbane Development Company, develops and finances public and private projects and acts as a property manager. William Gilbane founded the firm in 1873.

The company also includes Gilbane University, an in-house training program that offers more than 500 courses to assist new employees with construction and technical skills development. Gilbane spends millions each year to train its employees and views the investment as a way to attract and retain its workforce.

The company has more than 25 offices across the US.

EXECUTIVES

Chairman: Paul J. Choquette Jr., age 70
President and CEO; Chairman and CEO, Gilbane Building Company: Thomas F. (Tom) Gilbane Jr., age 61
VP and Regional Operations Manager, Delaware: Stephen J. O'Connor
VP: Robert C. Zerbe
VP; President and CEO, Gilbane Development: Robert V. Gilbane
VP; President and COO, Gilbane Building Company: William J. Gilbane Jr., age 62

LOCATIONS

HQ: Gilbane, Inc.
7 Jackson Walkway, Providence, RI 02903
Phone: 401-456-5800 **Fax:** 401-456-5936
Web: www.gilbaneco.com

PRODUCTS/OPERATIONS

Selected Markets

Convention/Cultural
Corporate
Criminal Justice
Education
Government
Healthcare
Life Sciences
Mission-Critical
Sports/Recreation
Transportation

COMPETITORS

Barton Malow	KBR
BE&K	M. A. Mortenson
Bechtel	McCarthy Building
Bernards Brothers	Parsons Corporation
Bovis Lend Lease	Skanska USA Building
Clark Enterprises	Structure Tone
Fluor	Swinerton
Hunt Construction	Turner Corporation
Jacobs Engineering	Whiting-Turner

HISTORICAL FINANCIALS

Company Type: Private

Income Statement				FYE: December 31
	REVENUE ($ mil.)	NET INCOME ($ mil.)	NET PROFIT MARGIN	EMPLOYEES
12/08	3,210	—	—	2,216
12/07	2,970	—	—	2,180
12/06	2,790	—	—	2,024
12/05	2,832	—	—	1,800
12/04	2,580	—	—	1,757
Annual Growth	5.6%	—	—	6.0%

Revenue History

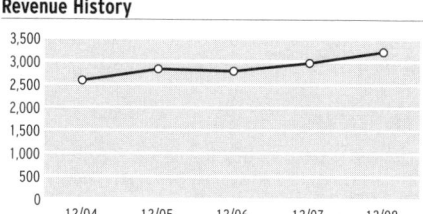

Glazer's Wholesale Drug Company

Glazer's Wholesale Drug, named during Prohibition when only drugstores and drug wholesalers could deal in liquor, is a wholesale distributor of alcoholic beverages. In Texas it is the largest company of its kind and one of the largest wine and spirits distributors in the US. The company distributes Budweiser Beer, Robert Mondavi wines, Brown-Forman and Bacardi spirits, and Diageo products. CEO Bennett Glazer and his family own Glazer's. The company's origins date back to the early 1900s when the Glazer family sold flavored soda water, which it distributed using horse-drawn wagons. Today Glazer owns and operates 43 offices in 11 US states.

Growth is Glazer's game. It began in earnest in 2003 when Glazer's bought a 50% stake in Union Beverage Co. (a subsidiary of National Wine & Spirits, Inc.) in order to gain a foothold in Illinois. Later that year, the company became the sole provider of Diageo brands in Dallas and Houston as part of Diageo's consolidation of its Texas distributors. Glazer's has been acquiring wholesalers and distributors in the Midwest, including Mid-Continent Distributor (Missouri). Glazer's expanded in Oklahoma, having bought Reliance Wine & Spirits Co. It also purchased Hirst Imports Co. In Arkansas, Glazer's consolidated three distributors: Little Rock-Silbernagel, Barrett Hamilton, and Strauss Distributors. In the Midwest it bought up Olinger Distributors. Its been scooping up smaller companies ever since, the most recent being the 2009 acquisition of Permian Distributing, which is located in Odessa, Texas, and serves 800 customers in west Texas.

Glazer's also plays with the big boys, forming joint ventures in order to grow its business. It has a strategic joint venture (formed in 2008) with Southern Wine & Spirits of America called

Southern/Glazer's Distributors of America, which covers wine and spirit distribution in 30 US states. It also has a joint venture with Charmer Sunbelt that goes by the name of Alliance Beverage Distributing Company of Arizona, which it entered into in order to get a foothold in The Grand Canyon State.

Founded in Dallas in 1933, the third generation of Glazers run this family-owned business.

EXECUTIVES

Chairman: R.L. Glazer
Chairman and CEO: Bennett J. Glazer
President: Jerry Cargill
EVP and COO: Mike Maxwell
EVP and CFO: Cary Rossel
EVP and Director: Mike Glazer
EVP and Director: Barkley J. Stuart
SVP Corporate Strategy and Business Intelligence: Louis Zweig
SVP Government Affairs: Richard Levi
SVP Marketing and Senior Consultant: Jim Reichardt
SVP Operations, Finance, and Administration: Phil Meacham
SVP Human Resources and Development: Kristin Snyder
SVP Wine: Dolph Parro
SVP Fine Wines: James Gunter
SVP Information Technologies and Supply Chain: Mike Adams

LOCATIONS

HQ: Glazer's Wholesale Drug Company, Inc.
14911 Quorum Dr., Ste. 400, Dallas, TX 75254
Phone: 972-392-8200 **Fax:** 972-702-8508
Web: www.glazers.com

States of Operation

Arizona
Arkansas
Illinois
Indiana
Iowa
Kansas
Louisiana
Mississippi
Missouri
Ohio
Oklahoma
Texas

PRODUCTS/OPERATIONS

Selected Operations

Advantage Wine Marketing
Alliance Beverage Distributing Company (joint venture with Charmer Sunbelt Arizona)
Glazer's Domains & Estates
In Vie
Olinger Distributing (joint venture with the Danny Romano family)
Permian Distributing Company

COMPETITORS

Ben E. Keith
Gambrinus
Georgia Crown
Hensley & Company
Johnson Brothers
National Distributing
National Wine & Spirits
Premier Beverage Company
Republic National Distributing Company
Southern Wine & Spirits
Sunbelt Beverage
Tarrant Distributors
Wirtz Corporation
Young's Market

HISTORICAL FINANCIALS

Company Type: Private

Income Statement

	ESTIMATED REVENUE ($ mil.)	NET INCOME ($ mil.)	NET PROFIT MARGIN	EMPLOYEES
12/08	3,000	—	—	5,500
12/07	3,150	—	—	5,900
12/06	3,000	—	—	5,800
12/05	2,900	—	—	5,800
12/04	2,800	—	—	5,800
Annual Growth	1.7%	—	—	(1.3%)

Revenue History

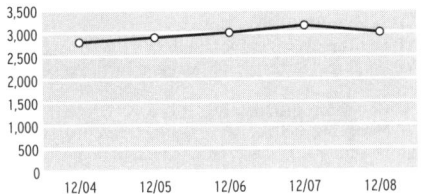

GNC Corporation

What's good for the customer is good for GNC Corporation (formerly General Nutrition Centers). With more than 6,600 stores throughout the US and Canada (including about 950 franchises and some 1,710 stores within Rite Aid drugstores) as well as franchise operations in about 45 foreign markets, GNC is the leading nutritional-supplements retail chain devoted solely to items such as vitamins and dietary products. The company also makes Rite Aid private-label products. GNC has been closing underperforming stores located in the US. GNC's online partner is drugstore.com. In 2007 Apollo Advisors sold the firm to Ontario Teachers' Pension Plan and Ares Management, a US private equity firm, for about $1.6 billion.

The vitamin maker and seller is benefiting from an aging US population, a greater focus on fitness and healthy living, and rising health care costs, which spur many consumers to take preventive measures, such as the use of alternative medicines and nutritional supplements. Still, the company is facing increased competition from mass merchants like Wal-Mart, which advertise low prices, natural and organic grocery chains (Whole Foods), and even traditional supermarkets and drugstores.

GNC has worked hard to shed its "muscle head" image by redesigning all of its US stores, which measure between 1,000 and 2,000 square feet. By attracting more women and seniors into its shops, the company hopes to increase its share of the nutritional supplement market. To that end, in April 2009 the company launched a new line of women's fitness, nutrition, and wellness products called GNC WELLbeING. The company has also pumped up its Web site, gnc.com, with e-commerce capabilities; the site is operated by GSI Commerce.

Aiming to extend the brand beyond its own brick-and-mortar establishments, GNC has been inking deals to build its boutiques within other stores. The Canada-based Forzani Group signed on in 2009 and looks to launch performance nutrition shops in Calgary. The GNC centers are expected to open in Forzani Group stores outside of Calgary in 2010. In 2007 Rite Aid extended its previous 1998 agreement to build GNC LiveWell stores-within-a-store. As part of the partnership extension, GNC will create 1,125 more stores within Rite Aid locations nationwide by the end of 2014. (By the end of 2008, Rite Aid had opened about 520 of the committed stores.)

GNC's private-label brands (about 48% of sales) include Mega Men and Pro Performance targeted at 18-to-49-year-old males and Body Answers, a diet product marketed to women. In addition to providing Rite Aid with private-label vitamins and nutritional supplements, GNC produces a line of co-branded vitamins and supplements for Rite Aid called PharmAssure.

EXECUTIVES

Chairman: Norman Axelrod, age 56
CEO and Director: Joseph (Joe) Fortunato, age 55, $3,042,776 total compensation
President, Chief Merchandising and Marketing Officer, and Director: Beth J. Kaplan, age 51, $2,122,402 total compensation
EVP and CFO: Michael Nuzzo, $211,321 total compensation
EVP Store Operations and Development: Tom Dowd, age 45, $804,212 total compensation
SVP, Chief Legal Officer, and Secretary: Gerald J. Stubenhofer Jr., age 39
SVP International Franchising: Reginald N. Steele, age 63
SVP Manufacturing: Michael Locke, age 63, $604,681 total compensation
SVP Merchandising: Robert M. (Bob) Kral, age 54
VP and Treasurer: J. Kenneth Fox, age 58, $490,973 total compensation
Auditors: PricewaterhouseCoopers LLP

LOCATIONS

HQ: GNC Corporation
300 6th Ave., Pittsburgh, PA 15222
Phone: 412-288-4600   **Fax:** 412-288-4764
Web: www.gnc.com

2008 Stores

	No.
US	
Company-owned	2,614
Franchised	954
Rite Aid	1,712
Canada	160
International franchises	1,190
Total	**6,630**

PRODUCTS/OPERATIONS

2008 Sales

	$ mil.	% of total
Retail	1,219.3	74
Franchise	258.0	15
Manufacturing & wholesale	179.4	11
Total	**1,656.7**	**100**

2008 Sales

	% of total
Vitamins, minerals & herbal supplements	42
Sports nutrition products	36
Diet products	13
Other	9
Total	**100**

Selected Proprietary Brand Names

Body Answers
Mega Men
Preventive Nutrition
Pro Performance
Ultra Mega

COMPETITORS

Alticor	Pfizer
Bactolac Pharmaceutical	Planet Organic Health
Bayer AG	Safeway
CVS Caremark	Shaklee
Duane Reade	Slim-Fast
Forever Living	Sunrider
Jenny Craig	Trader Joe's
Kroger	Tree of Life
Mannatech	United Natural
NAI	Vitamin Shoppe
Nature's Sunshine	Walgreen
NBTY	Wal-Mart
Nu Skin	Whole Foods

HISTORICAL FINANCIALS

Company Type: Private

Income Statement

FYE: December 31

	REVENUE ($ mil.)	NET INCOME ($ mil.)	NET PROFIT MARGIN	EMPLOYEES
12/08	1,657	55	3.3%	12,862
12/07	1,553	(32)	—	13,239
12/06	1,487	37	2.5%	12,707
12/05	1,318	18	1.4%	12,415
12/04	1,345	42	3.1%	13,618
Annual Growth	5.4%	7.1%	—	(1.4%)

Net Income History

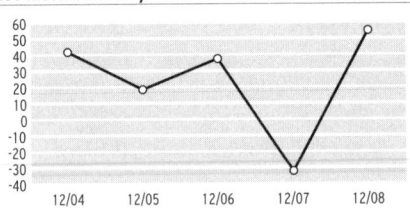

Go Daddy

Go Daddy, go! Go Daddy provides individuals and businesses with such Internet services as domain name registration and Web site hosting through its affiliates. It also offers related services and software for functions including e-mail, e-commerce, and Web-site creation. Touting discounted pricing on domain names and hosting services, Go Daddy has become the largest domain registrar accredited by ICANN (the international regulatory body for the public Internet) in the world, with more than 30 million domain names. The company has affiliates that address market niches in site registration and hosting, including Domains By Proxy and Wild West Domains. CEO Bob Parsons owns the company, which he founded in 1997.

Go Daddy expanded its Scottsdale, Arizona, offices in 2009 in order to make room for a growing number of employees. The company has experienced rapid growth in its short history in part due to high profile advertising campaigns which have included controversial Super Bowl commercials. Its 2009 Super Bowl ad featured Indy racing car driver and sometime swimsuit model Danica Patrick.

In addition to its core Web services, Go Daddy is also a leading host for the digital SSL (secure sockets layer) certificates that enable encrypted transmission of sensitive data such as credit card numbers and other personal information over the Web. The company sells and hosts the certificates for Web site owners to ensure that confidential information sent or received via a Web site is not intercepted by unauthorized viewers.

The company operates from eight facilities in the states of Arizona, Iowa, Colorado, and Washington, DC.

EXECUTIVES

Chairman and CEO: Robert R. (Bob) Parsons, age 58
President and COO: Warren J. Adelman, age 45
CFO: Michael J. Zimmerman, age 38
EVP: Barbara J. (Barb) Rechterman, age 45
VP Technical Operations and Chief Information Security Officer: Neil G. Warner, age 52
VP Corporate Administration: Nima Kelley
VP Customer Care Center: Miguel Lopez
VP Application Development: Wayne Thayer
VP Corporate Development and Policy: Timothy J. (Tim) Ruiz, age 54
VP Marketing: Theresa J. (Teri) D'Hooge, age 41
VP Custom Web Sites: Marianne Curran
VP Public Relations: Elizabeth Driscoll
VP Technology: Mike Chadwick
General Counsel and Corporate Secretary: Christine N. Jones, age 40
Auditors: Ernst & Young LLP

LOCATIONS

HQ: The Go Daddy Group, Inc.
 14455 N. Hayden Rd., Ste. 219
 Scottsdale, AZ 85260
Phone: 480-505-8800   **Fax:** 480-505-8844
Web: www.godaddy.com

PRODUCTS/OPERATIONS

Selected Services
Domain name registration, auctions, transfers
E-commerce tools
E-mail management
Security management
Web site development tools and hosting

COMPETITORS

Google	United Internet
Microsoft	Verio
Network Solutions	VeriSign
Register.com	Web.com Group Inc
Tucows	Yahoo!

Golden Horizons

GGNSC Holdings is a holding company doing business as Golden Horizons. The firm operates more than 300 skilled nursing facilities and more than 40 assisted living facilities under the Golden Living brand. The company's Golden Innovations unit oversees its subsidiary companies which provide contract rehabilitation therapy, hospice and home health care, health care staffing, group purchasing of health care products, and nursing facility design and construction services. Golden Innovation's companies serve more than 1,000 health care and nursing facilities in 37 states. Previously named Beverly Enterprises, GGNSC is owned by private equity firm Fillmore Capital Partners.

GGNSC still operates two Beverly Living Centers in Mississippi.

Beginning in early 2005 investor group Formation Capital, which owned 8% of Beverly, proposed a $1.5 billion takeover, but the unsolicited bid was rejected. Beverly then put itself on the auction block and a bidding war ensued between North American Senior Care and Formation Capital. However, it was Fillmore Capital that eventually won out with a bid of more than $2 billion. The company subsequently changed its name to Golden Horizons and rebranded all its company-owned operations under the "Golden" moniker.

In 2006 the company settled an investigation by the Justice Department, which had alleged that its erstwhile medical equipment subsidiary MK Medical had fraudulently billed Medicare and Medi-Cal (a California social service program) without doing the proper paperwork. The company agreed to pay $20 million to federal and state authorities to keep the issue from going to court.

EXECUTIVES

President and CEO: Neil Kurtz
EVP and Chief Administrative Officer: Lawrence (Larry) Deans, age 54
EVP and CFO: Richard D. Skelly Jr.
SVP, Controller, and Chief Accounting Officer: Belinda Marcotte
SVP and CIO: John Derr
SVP and Treasurer: Michael Morton
SVP Litigation: Paul Killeen
SVP Service Business Finance: Darlene Burch
SVP Skilled Nursing Facility: Kevin Roberts, age 56
SVP and Chief Legal Officer: David Beck, age 54
SVP Clinical Services and Quality of Life Programs: Andrea J. Ludington, age 63
SVP Government Relations & International Development: Jack MacDonald
SVP Sales and Marketing: Harold A. (Hal) Price
SVP Procurement; President, Ceres Purchasing: Ramon Rodriguez, age 48
SVP Human Resources & Administration: Michael Karicher, age 40
President and CEO, Golden Innovations: Cindy H. Susienka
President, AseraCare Hospice: Robert Donovan
President, Aegis Acute Rehab and Aegis Therapies: Martha J. Schram

LOCATIONS

HQ: GGNSC Holdings LLC
 1000 Fianna Way, Fort Smith, AR 72919
Phone: 479-201-2000   **Fax:** 479-201-1101
Web: www.goldenliving.com

PRODUCTS/OPERATIONS

Selected Subsidiaries
360 Healthcare Staffing
Aegis Therapies (contract rehabilitation therapy)
AseraCare Home Health
AseraCare Hospice
Ceres Purchasing Solutions (group purchasing organization)
Vizia Healthcare Design Group (design, construction, renovation of nursing care facilities)

COMPETITORS

Amedisys	Manor Care
Assisted Living Concepts	National HealthCare
Emeritus Corporation	Odyssey HealthCare
Extendicare REIT	Skilled Healthcare Group
Five Star Quality Care	Sun Healthcare
Genesis HealthCare	Sunrise Senior Living
Kindred Healthcare	VITAS Healthcare
Life Care Centers	

HISTORICAL FINANCIALS

Company Type: Private

Income Statement

FYE: December 31

	REVENUE ($ mil.)	NET INCOME ($ mil.)	NET PROFIT MARGIN	EMPLOYEES
12/08	2,580	—	—	41,000
12/07	2,490	—	—	41,000
12/06	2,500	—	—	40,000
Annual Growth	1.6%	—	—	1.2%

Revenue History

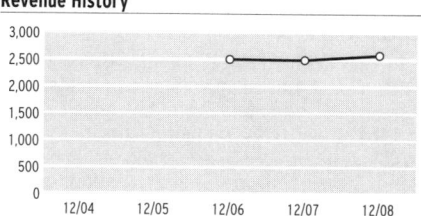

Golden State Foods

You might say this company helps make the Golden Arches shine. Golden State Foods is a leading foodservice supplier that primarily supplies McDonald's restaurants with more than 130 products, including beef patties, Big Mac sauce (which it helped formulate), buns, ketchup, and mayonnaise. It distributes goods to more than 20,000 quick-service eateries from 15 US distribution centers. In addition, the company runs a not-for-profit organization, the GSF Foundation, that supports local charities focused on helping children and families. Founded in 1947 by the late William Moore, Golden State Foods is controlled by Wetterau Associates, an investment group led by CEO Mark Wetterau.

The company is a supplier to McDonald's locations throughout the US and works closely with the fast-food giant to maintain standards. The two companies have enjoyed a long relationship that began in the 1950s and was later sealed with a handshake between Moore and fast-food pioneer Ray Kroc in the 1960s. As an indication of McDonald's loyalty to its suppliers, Golden State and McDonald's continue to do business without the benefit of a long-term contract. The company is McDonald's largest supplier of liquid products, its second largest distributor, and its third largest beef supplier in the US.

Golden State has a joint venture with Salinas, California-based grower, Taylor Fresh Foods, through which it supplies McDonald's with fresh produce. Taylor harvests some 800 million pounds of produce a year. It is the largest supplier of fresh produce to the fast-food industry in the US.

Golden State has seen higher sales recently due to the increased sales of its sauces and dressings, resulting from McDonald's growth in the Asian market. In addition the recent gourmet coffee push by McDonald's also has helped Golden State since it supplies the fast-food chain with coffee syrups and cream toppings.

And while the Golden Arches is the company's main customer, Golden State Foods has diversified its customer base in the past several years and now supplies other large fast-food chains, including Arby's, KFC, Popeyes, Subway, and Taco Bell.

Internationally, Golden State exports products to more than 50 countries and has facilities in Egypt and Australia. As a service to overseas customers, its food products can be adjusted to national and local tastes and traditions.

In addition to foodstuffs, the company also supplies its customers with access to raw materials and logistics, bulk-liquid-management, and other on-site services through its subsidiary, Golden State Service Industries.

HISTORY

In 1947 William Moore founded Golden State Meat, a small meat-supply business that served restaurants and hotels in the Los Angeles area. In 1954 he added several new clients to his business — franchisees of a new chain of hamburger stands called McDonald's that was founded in San Bernardino, California, in 1948. In 1961 Ray Kroc, a franchisee from Illinois, bought out the founding McDonald brothers, and the next year he moved to California to oversee a massive expansion in that state.

Moore and Kroc met, were mutually impressed, and became friends. Moore, at first, tried to get Kroc to buy him out, but Kroc's view of McDonald's did not include micromanaging its supply operations. He wanted to find suppliers the company could trust, and preferred smaller ones that weren't intent on breaking into the retail market. Golden State's relationship with McDonald's was sealed by a handshake between Kroc and Moore.

Moore and a partner bought a McDonald's franchise in 1965; two years later they had five. When Moore's partner died, McDonald's bought the units back for stock, which Moore later sold, using the proceeds to finance a new meat processing plant and warehouse. In 1969 Golden State Meat incorporated as Golden State Foods.

In 1972, after the new facilities were completed, Moore introduced the idea of total distribution. In addition to processing and distributing meat (by now delivered as frozen patties rather than fresh meat, which had limited delivery ranges in the 1950s and 1960s), Moore began supplying most of the needs of the McDonald's stores, making and delivering ketchup, mayonnaise, packaging, and syrup base for soft drinks. This allowed clients to reduce the number of weekly deliveries they received from as many as 30 to about three. The company went public in 1972, and two years later it dropped all of its other clients to cater exclusively to McDonald's.

Golden State grew in the 1970s, supplying a large share of the millions of McDonald's hamburgers sold every day. Moore died in 1978. Soon thereafter, a group of executives led by newly appointed CEO James Williams began exploring the possibility of taking the company private. In 1980, with backing from Butler Capital, they paid $29 million for the company, which then had sales of $330 million.

During the next decade Golden State expanded its relationship with McDonald's (and with the buying co-ops that supply stores operated by franchisees), opening facilities in other parts of the country. In 1990 the owners of Golden State tried to cash out by putting the company up for sale, but they withdrew it from the market within two years.

Golden State moved its headquarters from Pasadena to Irvine in 1992. In 1996 the company opened a distribution center in Portland, Oregon, and international expansion followed.

Yucaipa and Wetterau Associates, whose management hailed from a major Midwestern food wholesaler sold to SUPERVALU in 1992, bought Golden State in 1998 for about $400 million. The purchase represented Yucaipa's first significant acquisition outside the supermarket arena. James Williams, who had been with Golden State Foods for 38 years and served as its CEO for more than two decades, resigned in 1999. He was replaced by Mark Wetterau, a partner in Wetterau Associates along with his brother Conrad Wetterau.

In early 2004 Wetterau bought the 50% stake in Golden State Foods held by investor Ron Burkle and his Yucaipa investment firm for $110 million. During 2006 the company opened a new distribution center in City of Industry, California; the 270,000-sq.-ft. facility is the largest in the McDonald's supply chain. Golden State Foods also acquired two additional facilities from HAVI Group in Illinois and Wisconsin that year.

EXECUTIVES

Chairman, President, and CEO: Mark S. Wetterau, age 51
Vice Chairman: Michael L. (Mike) Waitukaitis
CFO: Richard D. (Rich) Moretti
CIO: Rhonda Sias
Corporate SEVP: Frank Listi
Corporate SVP; President, Distribution Group: Robert (Bob) Jorge
Corporate VP and General Counsel: John Page
Corporate VP Finance: Bill Sanderson
Corporate VP International: Phillip Crane
Corporate VP Human Resources: Steve Becker
Corporate VP; President, Liquid Products Group: John Pooley
Corporate VP; COO Conyers: Larry McGill
Group VP Meat Products Group: Wayne Morgan
Group VP, McDonald's Business: Paul Sestak
Group VP, National Accounts: Brian Dick
Group VP Distribution, West Region: Scott Thomas
Group VP Distribution, East Region: Tim Heskett
Senior Corporate Communications Director: Shellie Frey

LOCATIONS

HQ: Golden State Foods Corp.
18301 Von Karman Ave., Ste. 1100
Irvine, CA 92612
Phone: 949-252-2000   **Fax:** 949-252-2080
Web: www.goldenstatefoods.com

PRODUCTS/OPERATIONS

Selected Products

Bakery
  Buns
  Rolls
Liquid
  Dressings
  Jams
  Jellies
  Sauces
  Syrups
  Toppings
Meat
  Burrito fillings
  Chili
  Cooked beef
  Hamburger patties
  Taco meat

COMPETITORS

JR Simplot	Performance Food
Keystone Foods	Reyes Holdings
MAINES	Services Group of America
Martin-Brower	Shamrock Foods
McLane Foodservice	SYSCO
Meadowbrook Meat	UniPro Foodservice
OSI Group	U.S. Foodservice

HISTORICAL FINANCIALS

Company Type: Private

Income Statement

FYE: December 31

	REVENUE ($ mil.)	NET INCOME ($ mil.)	NET PROFIT MARGIN	EMPLOYEES
12/08	4,000	—	—	3,000
12/07	3,000	—	—	3,000
12/06	2,600	—	—	2,800
12/05	2,375	—	—	2,500
12/04	2,200	—	—	2,500
Annual Growth	**16.1%**	—	—	**4.7%**

Revenue History

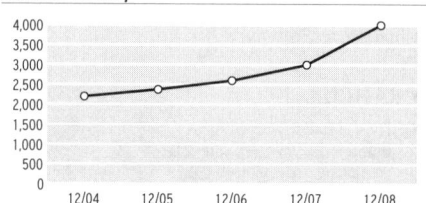

Golden State Warriors

These Warriors call the hardwood floor their battlefield. The Golden State Warriors professional basketball team has had a long and storied history since joining the Basketball Association of America (now the National Basketball Association) as a charter member in 1946. Originally formed as the Philadelphia Warriors by Eddie Gottlieb, the team moved to San Francisco in 1962 before relocating across the bay in 1971. Now playing host at Oracle Arena, the Warriors franchise boasts three league championships, its last in 1975. Former cable television system mogul Chris Cohan has controlled the franchise since 1995.

Playoff appearances have been few and far between for Oakland in recent years. However, the team did get a boost in 2006 when software giant Oracle agreed to a 10-year, $30 million naming rights deal for the Warriors' home arena. Previously the facility was known as Oakland Arena.

Cohan also managed to raise additional capital for his basketball franchise in 2004, selling a 20% stake in the team to four Silicon Valley businessmen. The new investors included Michael Marks (CEO of Flextronics), John Thompson (Symantec Corporation CEO), and venture capital investors Jim Davidson and Fred Harman.

EXECUTIVES

Owner and Managing Member: Christopher Cohan
President: Robert Rowell
EVP Basketball Operations: Chris Mullin, age 44
EVP Business Development: Neda Barrie
EVP Team Marketing: Travis Stanley

VP Finance: Dwayne Redmon
Head Coach: Don Nelson, age 69
Executive Director Public Relations: Raymond Ridder
Executive Director Broadcasting: Dan Becker
Executive Director Human Resources: Erika Brown
Director Athletic Development: Mark Grabow
Director Player Personnel: Mitch Richmond
Equipment Manager: Eric Housen
Pro Scout: Mike Riley

LOCATIONS

HQ: Golden State Warriors, LLC
1011 Broadway, Oakland, CA 94607
Phone: 510-986-2200   **Fax:** 510-452-0132
Web: www.nba.com/warriors

The Golden State Warriors play at the 19,596-seat capacity Oracle Arena in Oakland, California.

PRODUCTS/OPERATIONS

Championship Titles
NBA Champions (1947, 1956, 1975)
Western Conference Champions (1975)
Western Division Champions (1964, 1967)
Eastern Division Champions (1947-48, 1956)

COMPETITORS

Los Angeles Clippers
Los Angeles Lakers
Phoenix Suns
Sacramento Kings

Golub Corporation

Supermarket operator The Golub Corporation offers tasty come-ons such as table-ready meals, gift certificates, automatic discount cards, and a hotline where cooks answer food-related queries. Golub operates about 120 Price Chopper supermarkets in Connecticut, Massachusetts, New Hampshire, upstate New York, northeastern Pennsylvania, and Vermont. It also runs Mini Chopper service stations and convenience stores. Golub discontinued its HouseCalls home delivery service in 2001 but is giving home delivery another try. Brothers Bill and Ben Golub founded the company in 1932. Today the Golub family runs the company and owns 45% of the regional grocery chain; employees own slightly more than 50%.

Lewis Golub, chairman and former CEO of the company died in October 2009 at the age of 78. He was credited with establishing the company's employee ownership and profit sharing plans.

In a major expansion for the regional grocery chain, in late 2007 Golub announced that it planned to build as many as 30 new Price Chopper stores in the Northeast over the next three to four years.

EXECUTIVES

President and CEO: Neil M. Golub, age 72
CIO: Richard Bauer
EVP, Secretary and General Counsel:
William J. Kenneally
EVP and COO: Jerel T. (Jerry) Golub, age 51
SVP, Finance, Treasurer, and CFO: John J. Endres
SVP, Distribution and Transportation:
Renato (Ron) Cellupica
VP, Customer Analytics: Nancy Stanton
VP, Real Estate: Donald (Don) Orlando

VP, Strategic Initiatives: Jim Mizeur
VP, Risk Management: Anne Davis
VP, Store Operations, Price Chopper: David Golub, age 48
VP, Transportation: Thomas Bird
VP and Corporate Controller: Carol L. Cillis
VP, Human Resources: Margaret Davenport
VP, Public Relations and Consumer Services:
Mona J. Golub, age 45
Auditors: PricewaterhouseCoopers LLP

LOCATIONS

HQ: The Golub Corporation
501 Duanesburg Rd., Schenectady, NY 12306
Phone: 518-355-5000   **Fax:** 518-379-3536
Web: www.pricechopper.com

2009 Stores

	No.
New York	72
Vermont	15
Massachusetts	14
Pennsylvania	8
Connecticut	7
New Hampshire	3
Total	**119**

COMPETITORS

7-Eleven
A&P
ALDI
Big Y Foods
BJ's Wholesale Club
Costco Wholesale
Cumberland Farms
CVS Caremark
DeMoulas Super Markets
Gerrity's
Hannaford Bros.
Penn Traffic
Shaw's
Stop & Shop
Target
TOPS Markets
Wal-Mart
Wegmans

Goodman Global

While a good man may be hard to find, *this* Goodman makes it easy to find comfort with its residential and light commercial HVAC products. The company manufactures heating, ventilation, and air conditioning (HVAC) equipment, including split-system air conditioners and heat pumps, gas furnaces, packaged units, air handlers, and evaporator coils. Goodman operates seven plants in Texas, Tennessee, Arizona, Pennsylvania, and Florida. It sells products under the Goodman, Amana, and Quietflex brands through some 135 company-operated distribution centers and about 700 independent distributor locations throughout North America. Investment firm Hellman & Friedman bought the company in 2008.

Goodman Global had gone public in 2006, but another private equity firm, Apollo Advisors, held 40% of the company before it was sold to Hellman & Friedman.

The company focuses on placing its distribution centers in key states such as Texas and Nevada in order to access large markets in North

America. Goodman is looking to expand its distribution center footprint in targeted markets. Its centers and direct sales generate about 60% of revenues. Independent distributors account for the remaining 40% of sales.

In addition to independent distributors, Goodman Global's customers include contractors who install residential and light commercial HVAC products, national homebuilders, and other national accounts. The company sells to contractors mainly through its distribution network.

Historically, 20%-25% of Goodman's sales have been associated with residential new construction. However, a slowdown in the construction market has contributed to a decline in sales to that market.

Goodman Global was founded in 1975 by Harold Goodman to manufacture flexible duct for simplifying the installation of central air conditioning systems. The company entered the air conditioning equipment distribution business in 1980; two years later, it entered the air conditioning equipment manufacturing business.

EXECUTIVES

Chairman: Charles A. Carroll, age 58
President, CEO, and Director: David L. (Dave) Swift, age 50
EVP, Secretary, and General Counsel: Ben D. Campbell, age 52
EVP Human Resources: Donald R. King, age 52
EVP, CFO, and Director: Lawrence M. Blackburn, age 54
SVP Operations: William L. Topper, age 52
SVP and CIO: Terrance M. Smith, age 59
SVP Marketing: Gary L. Clark, age 46
SVP Independent Distribution: Peter H. Alexander, age 50
SVP Logistics and Business Development:
Samuel G. Bikman, age 40
SVP; President, Company Owned Distribution:
James L. Mishler, age 54
VP; President and General Manager, Quietflex:
Ardee Toppe, age 45
VP Engineering: Neelkanth S. Gupte, age 45
VP, Corporate Controller, and Treasurer: Mark M. Dolan, age 49
Auditors: Ernst & Young LLP

LOCATIONS

HQ: Goodman Global, Inc.
5151 San Felipe, Ste. 500, Houston, TX 77056
Phone: 713-861-2500   **Fax:** 713-861-3207
Web: www.goodmanglobal.com

2008 Sales by Geographic Region

	% of total
United States	95
Other countries	5
Total	**100**

PRODUCTS/OPERATIONS

Selected Brands
Amana
Goodman
Quietflex

COMPETITORS

Airwell-Fedders
Carrier
Lennox
Paloma Co.
Trane Inc.

HISTORICAL FINANCIALS

Company Type: Private

Income Statement

FYE: December 31

	REVENUE ($ mil.)	NET INCOME ($ mil.)	NET PROFIT MARGIN	EMPLOYEES
12/08	1,877	(40)	—	4,401
12/07	1,936	101	5.2%	—
12/06	1,795	58	3.2%	—
12/05	1,565	25	1.6%	—
12/04	1,318	48	3.6%	4,816
Annual Growth	9.3%	—	—	(2.2%)

Net Income History

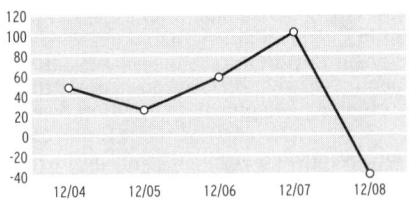

Goodwill Industries

Goodwill Industries International supports the operations of about 200 independent Goodwill chapters worldwide. Though most well known for its 2,250 thrift stores, the group focuses on providing rehabilitation, job training, placement, and employment services for people with disabilities and others. Goodwill is one of the world's largest providers of such services, as well as one of the world's largest employers of the physically, mentally, and emotionally disabled. Support for the organization's programs is generated primarily from sales of donated goods, both at the retail stores and through an online auction site, as well as from contract work and from government grants. Goodwill was founded in 1902.

The economic downturn has spurred more foot traffic at Goodwill's thrift stores while retailers, such as Target and Kmart, have logged declines. Compared to 2008, Goodwill's North American sales increased more than 6% during 2009. Along with this, though, Goodwill is seeing its donations dwindle while more clients approach the organization looking for help in finding a job.

The organization's online shopping and auction site, shopgoodwill.com (launched in 1999), has sold more than 3.5 million items and rang up more than $15 million in sales in 2008.

EXECUTIVES

Chairman: Raymond W. Bishop
President and CEO: Jim Gibbons
COO: Steve Krotonsky
VP Member Relations: Dave Barringer
Director Public Relations: Deborah Betsch
Manager Media Relations: Lauren Lawson
Auditors: Deloitte & Touche

LOCATIONS

HQ: Goodwill Industries International, Inc.
15810 Indianola Dr., Rockville, MD 20855
Phone: 301-530-6500   **Fax:** 301-530-1516
Web: www.goodwill.org

PRODUCTS/OPERATIONS

2008 Revenue

	% of total
Membership dues	49
Grants from government agencies	40
Program service fees	6
Contributions	2
Rental	1
Legacies & bequests	1
Investment income	1
Total	**100**

COMPETITORS

Amazon.com
craigslist
Google
Yahoo!

HISTORICAL FINANCIALS

Company Type: Not-for-profit

Income Statement

FYE: December 31

	REVENUE ($ mil.)	NET INCOME ($ mil.)	NET PROFIT MARGIN	EMPLOYEES
12/08	3,172	—	—	86,000
12/07	3,164	—	—	87,444
12/06	2,903	—	—	86,375
12/05	2,650	—	—	82,185
12/04	2,390	—	—	80,142
Annual Growth	7.3%	—	—	1.8%

Revenue History

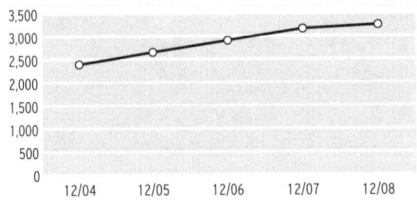

Gordon Food Service

This company caters to the tastes of American and Canadian restaurant operators alike. Gordon Food Service (GFS) is a leading foodservice supplier in North America with more than 15 distribution centers in the US and Canada. It offers more than 16,000 food and nonfood products (both nationally branded and private-label items) to some 45,000 customers in 15 US states and throughout Canada. It serves schools, restaurants, and other institutions. The company also sells food and supplies through more than 120 GFS Marketplace wholesale stores, which are open to the public, in five Midwestern states and Florida. Isaac VanWestenbrugge started the family-owned business in 1897.

EXECUTIVES

CEO: Dan Gordon
President: Jim Gordon
CFO: Jeff Maddox
EVP, US: Tony Groll
Director Marketing and Procurement, Canada: Todd Baker
Director Marketing and Procurement, US: Rob VanRenterghem
Director Sales, US: Paul LaLonde
Secretary and Treasurer: John Gordon Jr.
Customer Marketing Specialist: Ken Wasco
President, GFS Canada: Frank Geier

LOCATIONS

HQ: Gordon Food Service, Inc.
333 50th St. SW, Grand Rapids, MI 49501
Phone: 616-530-7000   **Fax:** 616-717-7600
Web: www.gfs.com

PRODUCTS/OPERATIONS

Selected Operating Units

Bridge Brand (Canada)
Distal (Canada)
GFS Marketplace (wholesale stores)
GFS Ontario
Gordon Food Service
M & S Food Service (Canada)
Neptune Food Service (Canada)

COMPETITORS

Ben E. Keith
Clark National
I Supply
MAINES
Mattingly Foods
McLane Foodservice
Meadowbrook Meat Company
Performance Food
Reinhart FoodService
Services Group of America
SYSCO
UniPro Foodservice
Unisource
U.S. Foodservice
Van Eerden

Goss International

Goss International always has some pressing news. The company manufactures web-offset printing presses and finishing systems for newspapers, commercial printers, and other high-volume print applications. Distribution of Goss presses, related parts, and services is driven through sales offices and plants in North America, Europe, and Asia. The company courts newspaper publishers in more than 120 countries, including *The Asahi Shimbun* (Japan), *The People's Daily* (China), the Moscow Newspaper Printing Plant (which prints *MK, Pravda,* and other Russian publications), and *The Financial Times* (UK). Investment firm Matlin Patterson Global Opportunities Partners and Shanghai Electric (Group) Corp. control the company.

Countering the 2008 and 2009 downturn in the publishing industry, the company is applying its high tech printing expertise to new markets. The company snagged a contract in late 2009 with Aeronautica Windpower, a provider of mid-scale wind turbines to public, commercial, industrial, and agricultural markets. Goss will manufacture nacelle assemblies, used in wind turbines to capture and convert wind energy into electricity.

The deal fell on the heels of several hard choices; Goss cut employee work days, initiated a round of layoffs, and consolidated production facilities in order to balance operating costs with dwindling orders. Sales in 2009 have, by and large, come from abroad. Among them, Goss sold one, and then a second press to China's Xi'an Daily Printing Center. Goss also received an order for equipment additions and enhancements from Greek newspaper publisher Naftemporiki P. Athanassiades & Co., and for a press from UK independent Newbury Weekly News Group. Other orders came from Italy, Russia, Venezuela, and Brazil.

Control of Goss also shifted in 2009. Regaining its financial footing, Goss sold off a hefty ownership stake (second only to that held by Matlin Patterson) to Shanghai Electric. The China-based owner is one of the Mainland's largest manufacturers of industrial equipment. Since 1993, subsidiary Shanghai Printing and Packaging Machinery and Goss have operated a joint venture, producing Goss web offset presses for the international market. Goss management received a face lift, too. Jochen Meissner took the helm as CEO, replacing Bob Brown who remains on the Goss board.

In the meantime, Goss is aiming to step ahead of its competition by enhancing its product portfolio through an array of patented improvements, as well as its customer training services. Goss publisher and printer customers can take an online course to learn how to use the company's various press and folder equipment. Goss is one of three companies that still manufacture web presses in the US; the others are Didde Press Systems (part of Stolle Machinery) and Web Press Corp.

EXECUTIVES

CEO: Jochen Meissner
CFO: Torben Rasmussen
SVP Global Sales: Dick Schultz
VP Sales: Doug Gibson
VP Sales: Graham Trevett
VP Americas Aftermarket: Wesley Clements
Manager Commercial Press Audits: Geoff Adamson
Director Business Development, Goss Lifetime Support, North and South America: John Gallagher
Director Sales: Don Pallotto
Manager Marketing: Cecilia Chou

LOCATIONS

HQ: Goss International Corporation
3 Territorial Ct., Bolingbrook, IL 60440
Phone: 630-755-9300   **Fax:** 630-755-9301
Web: www.gossinternational.com

PRODUCTS/OPERATIONS

Selected Products

Advertising-insert presses (C700, Magnum)
Aftermarket parts
Commercial presses (G18, G25, M16)
Large newspaper presses (Colorliner, Newsliner)
Small newspaper presses (Community, Universal)

COMPETITORS

Baldwin Technology
Dainippon Screen
FUJIFILM Graphic Systems U.S.A.
Heidelberger Druckmaschinen
Koenig & Bauer
Komori America
MAN
Manugraph DGM
MEGTEC Systems
Mitsubishi Heavy Industries
Pamarco Technologies
QuadTech
Quipp
Ryobi Ltd.

HISTORICAL FINANCIALS

Company Type: Private

Income Statement				FYE: December 31
	ESTIMATED REVENUE ($ mil.)	NET INCOME ($ mil.)	NET PROFIT MARGIN	EMPLOYEES
12/08	1,000	—	—	—
12/07	1,110	—	—	4,000
12/06	1,140	—	—	4,100
12/05	1,100	—	—	4,100
Annual Growth	(3.1%)	—	—	(1.2%)

Revenue History

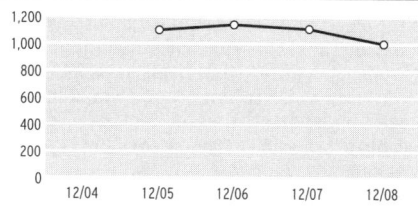

Gould Paper

Paper is as good as gold for Gould Paper, one of the largest privately owned distributors of printing and fine papers in North America. The company distributes and sells paper to multiple markets, from fine papers to commercial printing, lithography, newsprint, direct mail, catalogs, envelopes, and specialty papers. Gould supplies paperboard and packaging grades too, and drives paper converting operations. Its paperboard is used in packaging material for consumer and industrial products. Touting sales of 2 million tons of paper products annually, the company represents most major domestic and offshore mills.

In the US, Gould Paper took a hit in 2009 when printing concern National Hirschfeld filed for Chapter 11 bankruptcy protection. Its largest unsecured creditor, Gould Paper is owed $1.1 million. The loss came on the heels of another customer calling it quits, Tech Valley Printing, dba General Business Supply. With $5.9 million at stake, Gould Paper joined three other creditors in forcing Tech Valley into Chapter 7 bankruptcy. The company also saw publisher of hip-hop music and culture (and significant Gould Paper customer) Source Magazine file for Chapter 11 bankruptcy. The company has looked to shore up paper and printing

operations, specifically in the Southwest, Midwest, and Southeast markets. It scored the Dallas division of Sabin Robins Paper Company, merging it with subsidiary BRW Paper. Earlier, the company picked up Missouri-based Boone Paper Company, which also merged with the company's BRW Paper division, and Florida-based Southern Paper. It then snagged a deal with Domtar to lead distribution of North America's first antimicrobial office paper.

Looking to streamline its business, Gould Paper sold its Vancouver, Canada-based subsidiary to international distributor xpedx in 2009. Gould Paper (Canada) Ltd. distributed paper, ink and coating products through western Canada via Gould Paper outlets. (Purchased by Gould Paper in 2006, this unit originally comprised the western Canadian merchant operations of Cascades Resources.) The deal allows xpedx to expand its footprint in the Canadian market to Vancouver, Calgary, and Edmonton.

The company reaches as well across the UK, Finland, New Zealand, France, Russia, the Ukraine, Singapore, New Zealand, Hong Kong, China, and the Philippines. Clarifying its association, the corporate giant has renamed and rebranded several of its international divisions: Gould Publication Papers UK (formerly P3/Salehurst), Gould Paper Sales UK (formerly WWF), and Gould Papiers France (formerly Gallium EUL). Its Europe and Southeast Asia operations continue under the Price & Pierce nameplate.

Harry Gould, Sr. (father of chairman, president, CEO, and owner Harry Gould, Jr.) formed the company in 1924.

EXECUTIVES

Chairman and President: Harry E. Gould Jr.
EVP and CFO: Carl Matthews
VP and CIO: Robert (Bob) Bunsick
VP, Secretary, and Treasurer: Patrick Mullen
VP Sales: Joseph DeSopo
VP Operations, Business Products: Paul Collins
VP; President, Metro Division: Dean Marabeti
Director Human Resources: Barbara O'Grady
President, Gould Office Papers: Peter Tilearcio
President, Metro Division: Mike Trachtenberg
President, National: Mike Duncan
President, BRW Paper, Dallas: Gale Woellfer
President, BRW Paper, Kansas: Jim Rehor
President, Gould International: Bob Weill
President, Gould Business Products Division: Michael Negri
President, Distribution: Robert (Bob) Weil
President, Gould Paper (Canada): Jim Dunn

LOCATIONS

HQ: Gould Paper Corporation
11 Madison Ave., New York, NY 10010
Phone: 212-301-0000   **Fax:** 212-481-0067
Web: www.gouldpaper.com

COMPETITORS

Bradner Central
Cascades Inc.
Clifford Paper
Horizon Paper
Midland Paper
National Envelope
RIS the paper house
Sappi Fine Paper
Unisource
United Stationers
West Coast Paper
xpedx

HISTORICAL FINANCIALS

Company Type: Private

Income Statement

FYE: December 31

	REVENUE ($ mil.)	NET INCOME ($ mil.)	NET PROFIT MARGIN	EMPLOYEES
12/08	1,000	—	—	—
12/07	1,160	—	—	431
12/06	1,150	—	—	464
12/05	1,240	—	—	374
12/04	1,210	—	—	410
Annual Growth	(4.7%)	—	—	1.7%

Revenue History

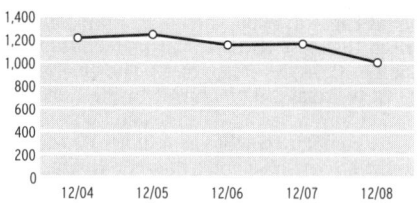

Goya Foods

Whether you call 'em *frijoles* or *habichuelas*, beans are beans, and Goya's got 'em, and lots more. Goya Foods produces approximately 1,600 Hispanic and Caribbean grocery items, including canned and dried beans, canned meats, fruit nectars, oils, olives, rice, seasonings and sauces, plantain and yucca chips, and frozen entrees. It sells many different types of rice and some 38 types of beans and peas. The company's brands include Goya and Canilla. It also sells beverages such as tropical fruit nectars and juices, tropical sodas, and coffee. Goya is owned and operated by one of the richest Hispanic *familias* in the US, the Unanues, who founded the company in 1936.

Goya has historically served the Hispanic communities in the northeastern US and Florida, having mostly Cuban, Dominican, and Puerto Rican customers. The company now has products geared toward the tastes of Hispanics in California and the Southwest who have roots in Mexico, the Caribbean, and Central and South America. An added plus is that the growing taste for ethnic foods across the US has fueled Goya's growth beyond its Hispanic roots. In addition, its "all-in-one-aisle" product placement in food stores has proven very successful.

Continued growth at Goya is a way of life for the company. However, it still faces competition from food giants such as Kraft Foods, which have lines of Hispanic specialty products. It's also challenged by food manufacturers located in Mexico, who are turning north to tap the pocketbooks of US consumers. Goya is one of the largest Hispanic-owned companies in the US.

Food retailers carrying Goya products in the US include Wal-Mart, H-E-B, Soriana, Chedraui, and Casa Ley. The company has 17 factories and 14 distribution centers located in the US, the Caribbean, and Spain. The company tailors its products to specific Hispanic markets. For example, in Miami, it emphasizes Cuban food. Attending to immigration patterns, it has introduced more foods popular in Central America, in keeping with the growth of that population in the US.

In 2007 Goya began distributing about 40 of its products in major Mexican cities, including Guadalajara, Monterrey, and Mexico City. The move marked the first time the company entered the Mexican food market. That year it also began marketing a line of organically grown beans; varieties include kidney, black, pinto, and navy beans, along with chickpeas.

Turning to markets farther afield, in 2008 the company entered into an agreement with Golden Dragon to market and distribute Goya products in China.

HISTORY

Immigrants from Spain by way of Puerto Rico, husband and wife Prudencio Unanue and Carolina Casal founded Unanue & Sons in New York City in 1936. The couple imported sardines, olives, and olive oil from Spain, but when the Spanish Civil War (1936-1939) interrupted supply lines, they began importing from Morocco.

In 1949 the company established a cannery in Puerto Rico; the Puerto Rican imports were distributed to local immigrants from the West Indies. Each of the couple's four sons eventually joined the family business, and in 1958 the firm relocated to Brooklyn. The company took its current name, Goya Foods, in 1962 when the family bought the Goya name — originally a brand of sardines — for $1.

The oldest Unanue son, CEO Charles, was fired from Goya in 1969 — and subsequently cut out of Prudencio's will — when he spoke out about an alleged tax evasion scheme. (Legal wrangling between Charles and the rest of the family continued into the late 1990s.) Goya moved to its present New Jersey headquarters in 1974.

Another son, Anthony, died in 1976, as did Prudencio. That year Joseph, another sibling, was named president and CEO. Along with his brother Francisco (Frank), president of Goya Foods de Puerto Rico, he began a cautious expansion campaign by adding traditional products to the company's existing line of Latin Caribbean and Spanish favorites.

Buoyed by the growing popularity of Mexican food, in 1982 Goya began distributing its products in Texas, targeting the region's sizable Mexican and Central American population. At first, the move proved a disaster. Goya's products were not suited to the Mexican palate, which generally preferred spicier food. Likewise, a similar strategy to capture a portion of Florida's huge Cuban market share initially met with only moderate success, but Goya persevered, eventually turning the tables in its favor.

During the 1980s the company also attempted to woo the non-Hispanic market. While Goya's cream of coconut — a key ingredient in piña coladas — found a broader market, its ad campaign featuring obscure actress Zohra Lampert did little to attract a large following of non-Hispanic customers.

Success in that market came in the 1990s. America's interest in the reportedly healthier "Mediterranean diet" boosted sales of Goya's extra-virgin olive oil. Recommendations for low-fat, high-fiber diets prompted the company's launch of the "For Better Meals, Turn to Goya" advertising campaign — its first in English — in 1992.

Three years later the company released a line of juice-based beverages. In 1996 Goya sponsored an exhibition of the works of the Spanish master Goya at the New York Metropolitan Museum of Art. Continuing its efforts to reach out to non-Hispanics and English-dominant Hispanics, in 1997 the company began including both English and Spanish on the front of its packaging.

To lure more snackers, the next year Goya added yucca (aka cassava) chips to its line. In 1999 Goya began packaging its frozen entrees in microwaveable trays. In 2001 it bought a new factory in Spain.

In 2002 Goya added 12 flavors (including guava, mandarin orange, and tamarind) to its line of Refresco Goya Fruit Sodas, thus joining the beverage industry trend toward offering more diverse flavors. In 2002, the president of the company's Puerto Rican division, Francisco J. Unanue, died.

In 2004 long-time chairman, CEO, and president Joseph Unanue and his son, COO Andy Unanue, were forced out of family-owned Goya by Joseph's two nephews, Robert I. and Francisco R. Unanue. Robert is now president and Francisco took over the Florida division of the company. Lawsuits to regain control of the company filed by Joseph followed but were eventually dropped.

In 2005 the company celebrated its 70th year in business and opened an online e-store.

EXECUTIVES

President: Robert I. (Bob) Unanue, age 55
SVP Purchasing, European Operations, and Marketing, Sales, and Advertising: Joseph F. Perez
VP Goya Foods Texas and General Manager, Goya Foods of California: Evelio Fernandez
VP Logistics and Operations: Peter J. Unanue
VP Operations Goya Foods Puerto Rico: Jorge Unanue
VP Traffic: Rebecca Rodriguez
VP Finance: Miguel Lugo
VP and General Manager, Goya Foods Puerto Rico: Carlos Unanue
VP and General Counsel: Carlos Ortiz
VP MIS: David Kinkela
VP Sales & Marketing: Conrad O. Colon
Director, Public Relations: Rafael Toro
Director, DSD Sales: John Hernandez
Director, Purchasing Goya Foods Florida: Tom Unanue
Director, Human Resources: Tony Rico
National Sales Manager: Eric Bray
Counsel: Sandra Gonzalez
President, Florida Division: Francisco R. (Frank) Unanue

LOCATIONS

HQ: Goya Foods, Inc.
100 Seaview Dr., Secaucus, NJ 07096
Phone: 201-348-4900   **Fax:** 201-348-6609
Web: www.goya.com

PRODUCTS/OPERATIONS

Selected Products

Beverages
  Café Goya
  Coconut water
  Refresco (fruit-flavored sparkling water)
  Malta (malt beverage)
  Nectars and juices (apple, apricot, banana, guanabana, guava, mango, passion fruit, papaya, peach, pear, pear/passion, pineapple, pineapple/guava, pineapple/passion, strawberry, strawberry/banana, tamarind, tropical fruit punch)
  Tropical sodas (apple, coconut, cola champagne, fruit punch, ginger beer, grape, guaraná, guava, lemon lime, mandarin orange, pineapple, strawberry, tamarind)

Foods and Other Products
Beans (black-eyed peas, chickpeas, lentils, refried)
Bouillon
Cookies
Cooking sauces
Cooking wine
Cornmeal
Devotional candles
Flour
Frozen convenience meals
Frozen vegetables
Masa harina
Marinades
Meat (chorizo, corned beef, potted, Vienna sausage)
Molé
Olive and other edible oils
Olives
Pasta
Plantain chips
Rice
Salsa
Savory snacks
Seafood (canned bonito, mackerel, pulpo, sardines, tuna)
Seasonings
Spices
Tomato sauce
Tortillas
Yucca chips

COMPETITORS

American Rice
Authentic Specialty Foods
Azteca Corn Products
B&G Foods
Birds Eye
Bolner's Fiesta Products
Bush Brothers
Campbell Soup
Casa de Oro Foods
Chiquita Brands
ConAgra
Del Monte Foods
Dole Food
Don Miguel Mexican Foods
Don Pancho Authentic Mexican Foods
Frito-Lay
General Mills
Grupo Bimbo
Heinz
Herdez
Hormel
Kraft Foods
La Flor
La Reina
La Tortilla Factory
McCormick & Company
Nestlé
Olé Mexican Foods
Patty King
Reser's Fine Foods
Riceland Foods
Riviana Foods
Ruiz Foods Inc.
Ruiz Mexican Foods
Taco Bell

HISTORICAL FINANCIALS

Company Type: Private

Income Statement
FYE: December 31

	ESTIMATED REVENUE ($ mil.)	NET INCOME ($ mil.)	NET PROFIT MARGIN	EMPLOYEES
12/08	1,300	—	—	3,000
12/07	1,260	—	—	3,000
12/06*	1,190	—	—	3,000
5/05	750	—	—	2,500
5/04	850	—	—	2,500
Annual Growth	**11.2%**	**—**	**—**	**4.7%**

*Fiscal year change

Revenue History

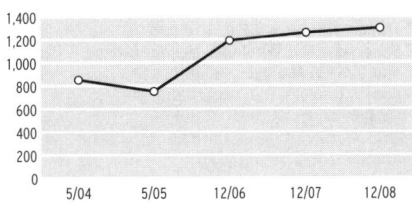

	5/04	5/05	12/06	12/07	12/08

Graham Packaging

Grocery stockers to mechanics can't keep their hands off Graham Packaging. No cookie-cutter, the company designs, manufactures, and sells blow-molded plastic containers for a diversity of goods, including food and beverages, automotive lubricants, and household and personal care products. Blue chip customers Clorox, Danone, Heinz, and PepsiCo are supplied through Graham Packaging's 80-plus manufacturing plants, which dot the globe. About one-third of plant operations are set on site at customers' production facilities. Graham Packaging is controlled by Blackstone Group and affiliates' 81% stake; in November 2009 the container company filed an initial public offering.

Graham Packaging's IPO objectives are clearly set on repaying some of its term loans. The company has contended with a series of losses; it has swerved to the red on an annual basis since 2003, and the burden of carrying $2.5 billion in debt has weighed down performance. Moreover, the worldwide credit crisis has crimped both debt refinancing options and renewal of credit and loan facilities. The company's fortunes have also taken a hit from the swing in availability and price of high-density polyethylene (HDPE), polyethylene terephthalate (PET), and other resins used in manufacturing, the costs of which can be difficult to pass on to established customers.

Persevering in 2009, the company is experiencing an uptick in net income, attributable to an improved sales program, bolstered market volumes, along with a lean manufacturing initiative. Graham Packaging is focusing on end markets where it can benefit from the conversion of metal, glass, and paperboard packaging to plastic. North American industries in food and beverage, and household goods lead in packaging makeovers, arenas where the company is well established. Graham Packaging generates about 60% of its revenues from such consumer consumables, predominantly in that geographic segment. In addition, the company has a market presence in Europe and South America, regions that are picking up their repackaging pace.

Looking to developing markets, in 2009 Graham Packaging acquired a minority interest in PPI Blowpack Pvt. Ltd., a privately held plastic container manufacturer based in Mumbai, India. The deal will boost Graham Packaging's market share in a promising region. In 2007 the company looked to grow its customer base by opening a plant in Turkey. The operation produces bottles for household products, dairy, and personal care goods, which are channeled to manufacturers in Europe and Asia. Simultaneously cutting costs, Graham Packaging closed its manufacturing plant in North Charleston, South Carolina.

EXECUTIVES

Chairman: Warren D. Knowlton, age 63, $3,550,101 total compensation
CEO: Mark S. Burgess, age 50, $2,011,971 total compensation
CFO: David W. Bullock, age 45
EVP and General Manager, Global Food and Beverage: Ashok Sudan, age 56, $934,741 total compensation
SVP Global Sourcing: Martin F. Sauer, age 54
SVP and General Manager of Household Chemical and Automotive, Personal Care/Specialty and South America: Peter T. Lennox, age 47, $628,855 total compensation
SVP Global Technology; General Manager, Proprietary Machinery Business Unit: David W. (Dave) Cargile, age 49
VP Global Marketing, Strategic Planning, and Investor Relations: Mark Leiden
Chief Human Resources Officer: David R. Nachbar, age 47
Chief Compliance Officer: Michael Korniczky
Director of Internal Audit: Robert Miller
Business Development Manager: Kapil Gami
Senior Project Manager: Phillip Sheets
Auditors: Deloitte & Touche LLP

LOCATIONS

HQ: Graham Packaging Company Inc.
2401 Pleasant Valley Rd., York, PA 17402
Phone: 717-849-8500   **Fax:** 717-848-4836
Web: www.grahampackaging.com

2008 Sales

	$ mil.	% of total
North America	2,195.0	86
Europe	274.2	11
South America	89.8	3
Total	**2,559.0**	**100**

PRODUCTS/OPERATIONS

2008 Sales

	$ mil.	% of total
Food & beverage	1,561.3	61
Household	491.6	19
Automotive lubricants	319.3	13
Personal care & specialty containers	186.8	7
Total	**2,559.0**	**100**

COMPETITORS

Amcor
Ball Corp.
Berry Plastics
Canal Corp.
Consolidated Container
Constar International
Plastipak Holdings
Rio Tinto Alcan
Ropak
Silgan

HISTORICAL FINANCIALS

Company Type: Private

Income Statement
FYE: December 31

	REVENUE ($ mil.)	NET INCOME ($ mil.)	NET PROFIT MARGIN	EMPLOYEES
12/08	2,559	(57)	—	7,400
12/07	2,471	(206)	—	7,800
12/06	2,500	(120)	—	8,400
12/05	2,473	(53)	—	8,900
12/04	1,353	(41)	—	8,600
Annual Growth	17.3%	—	—	(3.7%)

Net Income History

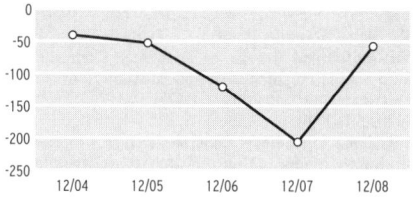

Grande Communications

Grande Communications' grand vision is to become a big player in Texas telecommunications. The company provides bundled telephone services, Internet access, and cable television to more than 140,000 residential and business customers over its own fiber-optic network. Grande Communications also provides wholesale communications services to other telecoms and ISPs. The company has operations in Austin-San Marcos, Corpus Christi, Dallas, Houston, Midland-Odessa, San Antonio, and Waco. Grande's investors include Whitney & Co. (22% of voting power), The Centennial Funds (17%), and Austin Ventures (7%).

Grande Communications expanded with the acquisition of broadband services provider ClearSource in 2002 and it expanded its fiber-optic network by purchasing assets from utility firms that are exiting the telecommunications market. These acquisitions include 3,000 fiber-miles of network from C3 Communications, a unit of American Electric Power (AEP). This purchase expanded the company's network from the Rio Grande Valley of South Texas to parts of Oklahoma, Arkansas, and Louisiana, and connects Texas' major markets, including Houston, Dallas, Austin, San Antonio, and Corpus Christi.

Grande Communications got a jump start on its operations in 2000 with the purchase of San Marcos, Texas-based integrated network services provider Thrifty Call.

EXECUTIVES

Chairman, President, and CEO: Roy H. Chestnutt, age 49
COO: W.K.L. (Scott) Ferguson Jr., age 50
CFO: Michael L. (Mike) Wilfley, age 53
VP and Controller: Deborah Riese Maus
VP Network Operations and Engineering: Brady Adams
VP Retail Operations: Mark Machen
VP Corporate Finance: Richard Robuck
VP Retail Operations: J. Lyn Findley
VP Human Resources: Kay Stroman
VP Enterprise and Wholesale Services: Jared P. Benson
VP and General Manager, Austin: Harris Bass
Treasurer: Douglas T. (Doug) Brannagan
General Manager, Waco: Matt Rohre
General Manager, Corpus Christi: Dottie Lane
Auditors: Ernst & Young LLP

LOCATIONS

HQ: Grande Communications Holdings, Inc.
401 Carlson Cir., San Marcos, TX 78666
Phone: 512-878-4000   **Fax:** 512-878-4010
Web: www.grandecom.com

PRODUCTS/OPERATIONS

Selected Services
Broadband Internet access
Cable TV
Local telephone access
Long-distance
Network services
  Data services
  Managed services
  Switched carrier services
Wholesale services

Selected Subsidiary
Grande Communications Networks, Inc.

COMPETITORS

AT&T
Cable One
CenturyTel
Charter Communications
Comcast Cable
Cox Communications
DIRECTV
DISH Network
Suddenlink Communications
Time Warner Cable
Verizon
Vonage

HISTORICAL FINANCIALS

Company Type: Private

Income Statement
FYE: December 31

	REVENUE ($ mil.)	NET INCOME ($ mil.)	NET PROFIT MARGIN	EMPLOYEES
12/08	205	(50)	—	785
12/07	197	(51)	—	831
12/06	190	(142)	—	810
12/05	195	(90)	—	835
12/04	179	(55)	—	873
Annual Growth	3.5%	—	—	(2.6%)

Net Income History

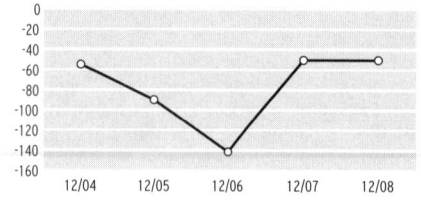

Grant Thornton International

Grant Thornton International is a kid brother to the Big Four. The umbrella organization of accounting and management consulting firms operates from more than 500 offices in more than 110 countries, making it one of the top second-tier companies that trail behind the biggest of the big guys (Deloitte Touche Tohmatsu, Ernst & Young Global, KPMG International, and PricewaterhouseCoopers). More than 60% of its member firms' clients are private companies. The company offers assurance, tax, business risk, corporate advisory, and other services to public and private companies. By virtue of the consolidation in the industry, Grant Thornton is the longest-lived, same-name network in the world.

Like other second-tier firms, the company concentrates its auditing efforts on mid-cap public, large private, and entrepreneurial companies, leaving the big boys to the Big Four. However, Grant Thornton has seen some doors opened by rules sparked by Enron and other scandals of the early 2000s: Mandates that companies use separate providers for auditing and some types of consulting and advisory have helped Grant Thornton step in with specialist services for clients who continued to use Big Four firms as their auditors.

Grant Thornton has been focusing on developing business in emerging markets, particularly in Asia, Europe, and Latin America. The accountancy is particularly keen to boost its presence in China and has been working with its US member firm, Grant Thornton LLP, to develop an independent, national Chinese firm.

Member firms have been working to increase cross-border cooperation by pooling resources and cutting costs. In 2008 a new global brand was introduced and some 99% of member firms began using the Grant Thornton corporate logo around the world. The move was made to help strengthen the company's brand recognition and stand out from competing firms.

HISTORY

Cameron, Missouri, accountant Alexander Grant founded Alexander Grant & Co. in 1924 with William O'Brien. They built their firm in Chicago and concentrated on providing services to midwestern clients.

In the 1950s and 1960s, the firm began expanding both domestically and internationally. Alexander Grant & Co. continued to focus on manufacturing and distribution companies.

In 1973 O'Brien died. In 1979 the company began publishing its well-known (and sometimes controversial) index of state business climates. An attempt to merge with fellow second-tier accounting firm Laventhol & Horwath failed that year. The next year Grant Thornton International was formed when Alexander Grant & Co. and its British affiliate, Thornton Baker, combined their offices around the world to form a network. The UK and US branches, however, kept their respective names.

The 1980s brought turmoil and change for the firm. Financial scandals led investors and the government to hold accounting firms liable for their audits. Along with the (then) Big Six, Alexander Grant & Co. was hit with several lawsuits alleging fraud and cover-ups. One case marred the firm's squeaky-clean image and caused dozens of clients to jump ship: Just days after Alexander Grant issued it a clean audit, a Florida trading firm was shut down by the SEC. Jilted investors sued to reclaim lost money; Alexander Grant settled for $160 million. Chairman Herbert Dooskin and other leaders also left the company; although they denied it was because of the scandal, their departures left Alexander Grant rudderless during a critical time.

Meanwhile, the company merged with Fox & Co. to create the US's #9 accounting firm. With scandal-scared partners leaving (and taking clients), Fox looked to the merger to shore up its reputation. But Alexander Grant's auditing troubles led some Fox partners and clients to flee from the merged company.

After the fallout from the lawsuits and the merger, the company began rebuilding, taking on new clients, reclaiming lost ones, and refocusing on midsized companies. In 1986 both Alexander Grant & Co. and Thornton Baker took the Grant Thornton name.

The early 1990s recession reduced accounting revenues but increased demand for management consulting. As political and economic barriers fell during the decade, Grant Thornton International grew. The firm entered emerging markets in Africa, Asia, Europe, and Latin America. In 1998 the Big Six became the Big Five; Grant Thornton added refugee firms and partners to its global network. In 1999 the firm's US branch entertained merger offers from H&R Block and PricewaterhouseCoopers, but instead announced plans to reposition itself as a corporate services firm to better compete.

In 2000 the company pulled out of its advisory position to companies involved in controversial diamond mining in war-torn portions of Africa. It also agreed to merge its UK operations with those of HLB Kidsons; the merged firm retained the Grant Thornton name.

The following year, after disagreements about strategy, US CEO Dom Esposito resigned. UK partner David McDonnell was named the global CEO. In 2002 Grant Thornton grew by picking up pieces of Andersen that fell away as a result of the Enron scandal. Andersen's fall also winnowed out Grant Thornton's competitors (at least in the numeric sense), as the Big Five became the Big Four.

Like Andersen before it, Grant Thornton felt the red-hot glare of unwanted media attention as Italian food giant Parmalat (a former auditing client) fell into bankruptcy amidst an Enron-style scandal in late 2003. Grant Thornton's Italian unit had remained the auditor for Parmalat subsidiary Bonlat, which played a central role in the unfolding scandal. The Italian affiliate, which has been expelled from Grant Thornton's global network, maintains it was a victim of fraud in the case. Parmalat in 2004 filed suit against the Italian accountancy, claiming two of its partners were involved in the fraud; the two also face criminal charges.

EXECUTIVES

CEO: David C. McDonnell
CEO, Grant Thornton LLP: Stephen Chipman
COO: Mike Starr
Executive Partner; CEO, Grant Thornton LLP:
Edward E. (Ed) Nusbaum, age 54

Global Leader Mergers and Acquisitions: Mike Hughes
Global Director Marketing Communications:
Jonathan (Jon) Geldart
Global Leader Specialist Advisory Services: David Fisher
Global Leader Tax Services: Ian Evans
Global Head Public Policy: April Mackenzie
Global Leader Privately Held Business Services:
Alex MacBeath
Global Leader Assurance Services: Ken Sharp
International Communications Manager:
Christine Hobart

LOCATIONS

HQ: Grant Thornton International Ltd
175 W. Jackson Blvd., 20th Fl., Chicago, IL 60604
Phone: 312-856-0200 **Fax:** 312-602-8099
Web: www.gti.org

2008 Member Fee Income by Region

	$ mil.	% of total
Europe, Middle East & Africa	1,817	46
Americas	1,775	45
Asia/Pacific	364	9
Total	**3,956**	**100**

PRODUCTS/OPERATIONS

Selected Services
Assurance
Corporate finance
Corporate recovery and business reorganization
International tax
PRIMA (people and relationship issues in management)

COMPETITORS

Baker Tilly International
BDO International
Deloitte
Ernst & Young Global
KPMG
McGladrey & Pullen
McKinsey & Company
Moore Stephens International
PricewaterhouseCoopers
RSM McGladrey

HISTORICAL FINANCIALS

Company Type: Not-for-profit

Income Statement FYE: September 30

	REVENUE ($ mil.)	NET INCOME ($ mil.)	NET PROFIT MARGIN	EMPLOYEES
9/08	3,956	—	—	30,662
9/07	3,461	—	—	27,861
9/06	2,772	—	—	24,577
9/05	2,454	—	—	22,066
9/04	2,092	—	—	20,486
Annual Growth	**17.3%**			**10.6%**

Revenue History

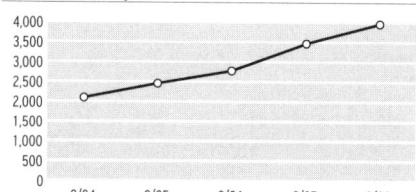

Graybar Electric

There's no gray area when it comes to Graybar Electric: it's one of the largest distributors of electrical products in the US. The employee-owned company pushes more than 1 million electrical, communications, and networking tools through 240-plus distribution centers. Its diversified lineup nets a myriad of wire, cable, and lighting products from thousands of manufacturers and suppliers, as well as a slate of supply chain management and logistics services. Affiliate Graybar Financial Services offers equipment leasing and financing. Graybar Electric caters to construction contractors, industrial plants, power utilities, and telecommunications providers, primarily in the US, and to some extent, US neighbors.

Throughout 2008-09, Graybar Electric has bravely confronted the global financial crisis. Although it has access to credit, its debt to equity ratio has inched up. Moreover, construction financing is harder to come by for its core customers. Electrical contractors account for about half of the company's sales. Graybar's results are also squeezed by its predominant US customer base, as well as cut-throat commodity price competition, especially for copper and steel-related products.

Graybar however has shored up its distribution networks — each comprising a main facility and supporting branch locations. Its scope of distribution is vital to responding to its more than 140,000 customers. To trim supply, distribution, and inventory costs, the company continues to implement state-of-the-industry operating technologies, such as an electronic data interchange and supplier-assisted inventory management system.

HISTORY

After serving as a telegrapher during the Civil War, Enos Barton borrowed $400 from his widowed mother in 1869 and started an electrical equipment shop in Cleveland with George Shawk. Later that year Elisha Gray, a professor of physics at Oberlin College who had several inventions (including a printing telegraph) to his credit, bought Shawk's interest in the shop, and the firm moved to Chicago, where a third partner joined.

The company incorporated as the Western Electric Manufacturing Co. in 1872, with two-thirds of the company's stock held by two Western Union executives. As the telegraph industry took off, the enterprise grew rapidly, providing equipment to towns and railroads in the western US.

Gray and his company missed receiving credit for inventing the telephone in 1875 when Gray's patent application for a "harmonic telegraph" reached the US Patent Office a few hours after Alexander Graham Bell's application for his telephone. However, the telephone and the invention of the light bulb in 1879 opened new doors for Western Electric. The company began to grow into a major corporation, selling and distributing a variety of electrical equipment, including batteries, telegraph keys, and fire-alarm boxes. By 1900 the firm was the world's #1 maker of telephone equipment.

Western Electric formed a new distribution business in 1926, Graybar Electric Co. (from

"Gray" and "Barton"), the world's largest electrical supply merchandiser. In 1929 employees bought the company from Western Electric for $3 million in cash and $6 million in preferred stock. During the 1930s it marketed a line of appliances and sewing machines under the Graybar name.

In 1941 the company bought the outstanding shares of stock from Western Electric for $1 million. Graybar Electric was a vital link between manufacturers and US defense needs during WWII. Its men and equipment wired the Panama Canal with telephone cable; it also helped the US military during the Korean conflict and the Vietnam War.

By 1980 Graybar Electric reached nearly $1.5 billion in sales. Business was hurt when construction slowed in the late 1980s and the early 1990s, and the company reorganized in 1991, closing regional offices and cutting jobs. Rebounding in 1992 as the US economy improved, Graybar acquired New Jersey-based Square Electric Co.

In 1994 the company acquired a minority interest in R.E.D. Electronics, a Canadian data communications and computer networking company, and realigned its operations into two business segments: electrical products and communications and data products.

In 1995 Graybar Electric formed the Solutions Providers Alliance with wholesale distributors Kaman Industrial Technologies, VWR Scientific Products, and Vallen Corporation. In 1996 AT&T's Global Procurement Group named the company as one of only three suppliers for its electrical products. The next year Graybar Electric upped its stake in one of its Canadian operations, Harris & Roome Supply Limited.

Graybar Electric in 1998 opened a subsidiary in Chile and formed a joint venture, Graybar Financial Services, with Newcourt Financial (formerly AT&T Capital). The next year Graybar Electric bought the Connecticut-based electrical wholesaler Frank A. Blesso, Inc., and it expanded its distribution partnership with wire and cable manufacturer Belden Electronics in 2000.

In 2001 Graybar opened a new distribution location in northeastern Pennsylvania. The following year Graybar increased its presence in the telecommunications industry when it inked a deal to distribute products made by Copper Mountain Networks, a US-based broadband equipment manufacturer.

The company received a five-year contract in 2003 from Los Angeles County to provide electrical supplies to local and state governments, school districts, and other tax-funded agencies participating in US Communities, a government buying cooperative established in 1999.

During 2004 Graybar won several contracts from the Defense Logistics Agency, worth a total of $195 million over two years. Also that year the company completed a multi-year project to implement an enterprise resource planning (ERP) system that linked its entire network of warehouses and distribution facilities.

Graybar signed a three-year supply contract in 2005 with Premier Purchasing Partners, a group purchasing organization for the health care industry.

In 2006 Graybar opened locations in Kent, Washington, and Wallingford, Connecticut.

EXECUTIVES

Chairman, President, and CEO: Robert A. Reynolds Jr., age 60, $2,022,792 total compensation
SVP, CFO, and Director: D. Beatty D'Alessandro, age 48, $790,172 total compensation
SVP Sales and Marketing, Electrical and Director: Richard D. Offenbacher, age 58, $802,693 total compensation
SVP US Business and Director: Dennis E. DeSousa, age 50, $893,578 total compensation
SVP Operations and Director: Lawrence R. (Larry) Giglio, age 54, $774,008 total compensation
SVP, Secretary, General Counsel, and Director: Matthew W. Geekie, age 47
SVP Sales and Marketing, Communication and Data and Director: Kathleen M. Mazzarella, age 49
VP and Controller: Martin J. Beagen, age 52
VP and Treasurer: Jon N. Reed, age 51
VP Human Resources: Beverly L. Propst
District VP, Chicago District and Director: Richard A. Cole, age 59
District VP, Richmond District and Director: Thomas S. Gurganous, age 59
District VP, Seattle District and Director: Kenneth B. Sparks, age 63
District VP, Tampa District and Director: Robert C. Lyons, age 52
President and CEO, Graybar Canada: Frank H. Hughes
Auditors: Ernst & Young LLP

LOCATIONS

HQ: Graybar Electric Company, Inc.
34 N. Meramec Ave., St. Louis, MO 63105
Phone: 314-573-9200   **Fax:** 314-573-9455
Web: www.graybar.com

Graybar Electric operates primarily in North America, with warehouses in California, Georgia, Illinois, Missouri, Ohio, Texas, and Virginia.

2008 Sales

	% of total
US	95
Other countries	5
Total	**100**

PRODUCTS/OPERATIONS

2008 Sales

	% of total
Electrical contractors	48
Voice & data communications	19
Commercial & industrial	19
Other	14
Total	**100**

Selected Products

Ballasts
Batteries
Cable
Conduit
Connectors
Emergency lighting
Enclosures
Fiber-optic cable
Fittings
Fluorescent lighting
Fuses
Hand tools
Hangers/fasteners
Heating and ventilating equipment
Industrial fans
Lighting
Lubricants
Paints
Patch cords
Smoke detectors
Testing and measuring instruments
Timers
Transfer switches
Transformers
Utility products
Wire

COMPETITORS

Anixter International
Asia Pacific Wire & Cable
Communications Supply
Communications Systems
Consolidated Electrical
Gexpro
Hagemeyer North America
HD Supply
HWC
Premier Farnell
Rexel Canada
Rexel, Inc.
Richardson Electronics
Sonepar USA
SUMMIT Electric Supply
Tech Data
United Electric Supply
WESCO International
W.W. Grainger

HISTORICAL FINANCIALS

Company Type: Private

Income Statement

	REVENUE ($ mil.)	NET INCOME ($ mil.)	NET PROFIT MARGIN	EMPLOYEES
12/08	5,400	87	1.6%	8,100
12/07	5,258	83	1.6%	8,600
12/06	5,009	57	1.1%	8,400
12/05	4,288	17	0.4%	7,800
12/04	4,080	14	0.3%	7,700
Annual Growth	**7.3%**	**58.1%**	**—**	**1.3%**

FYE: December 31

Net Income History

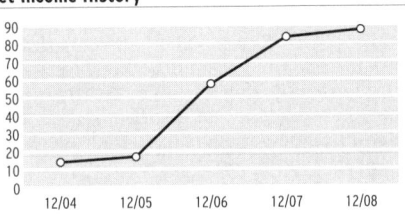

Great Lakes Cheese

Great Lakes Cheese understands the power of provolone, the charm of cheddar, and the goodness of gruyere. Based in Ohio, the firm manufactures and distributes natural and processed cheeses and cheese spreads, including varieties such as cheddar, Colby, Swiss, mozzarella, and provolone. It also makes the premium Adams Reserve New York Cheddar. Great Lakes packages shredded, chunked, and sliced cheese for deli, bulk, and foodservice sale under the Great Lakes, Adams Reserve, and private-label brands. With seven manufacturing plants, Great Lakes Cheese distributes its products, which are sold in deli and dairy cases, throughout the US.

In addition to its domestic production, Great Lakes imports cheese including havarti, blue, fontina from Denmark, gouda from Holland, emmentaler and gruyere from Switzerland, and jarlsberg from Norway. Its bulk products include blue, boursin, feta, goat, gorgonzola, grated Italian, and smoked cheeses.

Chairman Hans Epprecht, a Swiss immigrant, founded the firm in 1958 as a Cleveland bulk-cheese distributor. Epprecht and Great Lakes employees own the company.

EXECUTIVES

Chairman: Hans Epprecht, age 79
President and CEO: Gary Vanic
CFO: Russell (Russ) Mullins
Director IT: Suresh Babu
VP Procurement: Kurt L. Epprecht
VP Packaging: Richard (Dick) Metzler
VP Sales: William (Bill) Andrews
VP Human Resources: Beth Wendell
VP Supply Chain and Manufacturing: Craig Filkouski
VP and General Manager, Co-Packing Operations:
John W. Epprecht

LOCATIONS

HQ: Great Lakes Cheese Company, Inc.
17825 Great Lakes Pkwy., Hiram, OH 44234
Phone: 440-834-2500 **Fax:** 440-834-1002
Web: www.greatlakescheese.com

PRODUCTS/OPERATIONS

Selected Products

Domestic cheese
American
Cheddar
Colby
Cream
Hot pepper
Jack
Mozzarella
Provolone
Swiss
Imported cheese
Blue
Boursin
Brie
Emmenthaler
Feta
Fontina
Goat
Gorgonzola
Gouda
Gruyere
Havarti
Jarlsberg

COMPETITORS

American Milk Products
Associated Milk Producers
Bel Brands USA
BelGioioso Cheese
Cheesemakers, Inc.
Dairy Farmers of America
Ellsworth Cooperative
Kraft Foods
Land O'Lakes
Leprino Foods
Marathon Cheese
Original Herkimer County Cheese Company
Saputo
Saputo Cheese USA Inc.
Sargento
Schreiber Foods
Specialty Cheese Company
Swiss-American
Tillamook County Creamery Association
Tropical Cheese Industries
Uplands Cheese Company, Inc.
Warrnambool Cheese and Butter

HISTORICAL FINANCIALS

Company Type: Private

Income Statement

FYE: December 31

	REVENUE ($ mil.)	NET INCOME ($ mil.)	NET PROFIT MARGIN	EMPLOYEES
12/08	2,150	—	—	—
12/07	1,700	—	—	1,700
12/06	1,700	—	—	1,700
12/05	1,375	—	—	1,700
12/04	1,375	—	—	1,700
Annual Growth	11.8%	—	—	0.0%

Revenue History

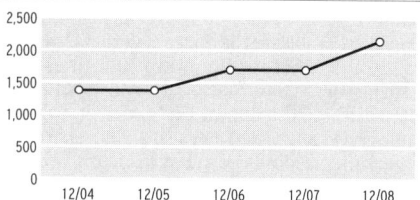

Greatwide Logistics

Greatwide Logistics Services brings together a world of freight transportation and logistics companies. The company's operating units, assembled through a series of acquisitions, provide dedicated transportation, in which drivers and equipment are assigned to a customer long-term; distribution logistics; truckload freight brokerage; and truckload freight transportation, largely via independent owner-operators. Greatwide calls upon a fleet of some 5,500 tractors and 1,700 trailers, and has 3.6 million sq. ft. of warehouse space in the US. Clients have included Target, Wal-Mart and IBM. In March 2009 Greatwide emerged from Chapter 11 bankruptcy protection after being acquired by an investor group.

The investor group was led by Centerbridge Capital Partners and affiliates of D.E. Shaw & Co. Greatwide, like other transportation and logistics companies, had been hit hard by the slowing economy and rising fuel prices. Greatwide received more than $73.6 million in financing to continue operating.

Greatwide intends to continue to cultivate relationships with agents that help market its services and truck owner-operators that help provide them. The company believes it can generate better investment returns by maintaining its asset-light business model than it could by investing extensively in transportation equipment and infrastructure.

In November 2009 Greatwide bought rival YRC Logistics' dedicated contract carriage business for $34 million. The purchase of YRC Logistics' customer contracts along with its trucks and trailers adds to Greatwide's offerings to the food and grocery, consumer products, steel and

automotive, and retail industries. About 600 workers will transfer to Greatwide from YRC.

Investcorp had owned the majority interest in Greatwide, and two other investment firms, Fenway Partners and Dallas-based Hicks Holdings, owned minority stakes. Fenway, which first invested in what is now Greatwide in 2000, sold most of its interest in the company to Investcorp and Hicks Holdings.

EXECUTIVES

Chairman: Leo H. Suggs, age 67
President, CEO, and Director: Raymond B. (Ray) Greer
CFO: Stephen P. (Steve) Bishop
CIO: Lloyd Boyd
SVP, General Counsel, and Secretary: John N. Hove
VP Business Development: James L. (Jim) Kitz
VP Human Resources, Dedicated Transport:
Kyle Killingsworth
Chief Risk Officer: Jeffery H. (Jeff) Lester
Chief Commercial Officer: Richard M. (Dick) Metzler
President and CEO, Freight Brokerage:
Douglas G. (Doug) Clark
President, Truckload Management: Joe Chandler
President, Distribution Logistics:
Vincent F. (Vin) Gulisano
President and COO, Dedicated Transport: John Simone

LOCATIONS

HQ: Greatwide Logistics Services, Inc.
12404 Park Central Dr., Ste. 300S, Dallas, TX 75251
Phone: 972-228-7300 **Fax:** 972-228-7328
Web: www.greatwide.com

COMPETITORS

Arrow Trucking
Boyd Bros. Transportation
CEVA Logistics U.S.
C.H. Robinson Worldwide
Crete Carrier
CRST Malone
J.B. Hunt
Landstar System
Ryder System
Schneider National
Swift Transportation
Transplace
UPS Supply Chain Solutions
U.S. Xpress
UTi Integrated Logistics
UTi Worldwide
Venture Logistics

HISTORICAL FINANCIALS

Company Type: Private

Income Statement

FYE: December 31

	REVENUE ($ mil.)	NET INCOME ($ mil.)	NET PROFIT MARGIN	EMPLOYEES
12/08	1,200	—	—	—
12/07	1,140	—	—	3,000
12/06	1,200	—	—	3,000
12/05	1,087	—	—	2,800
Annual Growth	3.4%	—	—	3.5%

Revenue History

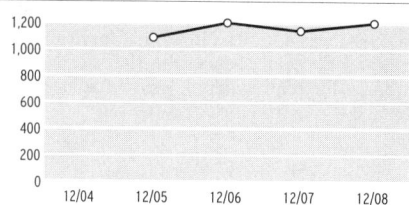

Green Bay Packers

On the frozen tundra of Lambeau Field, the Green Bay Packers battle for pride in the National Football League. The not-for-profit corporation owns and operates the storied Packers football franchise, which was founded in 1919 by Earl "Curly" Lambeau and joined the NFL in 1921. Home to such icons as Bart Starr, Ray Nitschke, and legendary coach Vince Lombardi, Green Bay boasts a record 12 championship titles, including three Super Bowl victories (its last in Super Bowl XXXI after the 1996 season). The team is also the only community-owned franchise in American professional sports with more than 112,000 shareholders. The shares do not increase in value nor pay dividends, and can only be sold back to the team.

Despite being in the smallest market of any team in the NFL, Green Bay has managed to thrive primarily because of its tight association with the community and rabid fan base. Regular season games have been sold out since 1960 and the waiting list for season tickets boasts about 81,000 names. The team has also benefited from NFL revenue sharing agreements that distribute revenue from national TV broadcasting deals to all the franchises in the league.

After a long, stable, and successful run that began in the early 1990s, Green Bay is adjusting to a new leadership in the front office and on the field. Mark Murphy replaced Bob Harlan as CEO at the beginning of 2008. Harlan had led the franchise for nearly 20 years before retiring, spearheading efforts during his tenure to upgrade and expand Lambeau Field. A former NFL player and NFL Players Association executive, Murphy previously served as athletic director at Northwestern University.

On the field, the Packers lost one of its biggest stars of recent history in 2008 when three-time MVP quarterback Brett Favre was traded to the New York Jets after retiring early that year and then attempting a comeback. He had led the team to a 13-3 regular season record the previous year, though a bid for the Super Bowl ended with a loss to the New York Giants in the NFC Championship game. Favre had played for Green Bay since 1992, winning one championship title and earning nearly every meaningful NFL passing record.

HISTORY

In 1919 Earl "Curly" Lambeau helped organize a professional football team in Green Bay, Wisconsin, with the help of George Calhoun, the sports editor of the *Green Bay Press-Gazette*. At 20 years old, Lambeau was elected team captain and convinced the Indian Packing Company to back the team, giving the squad its original name, the Indians. The local paper, however, nicknamed the team the Packers and the name stuck. Playing on an open field at Hagemeister Park, the team collected fees by passing the hat among the fans. In 1921 the franchise was admitted into the American Professional Football Association (later called the National Football League), which had been organized the year before.

The Packers went bankrupt after a poor showing its first season in the league and Lambeau and Calhoun bought the team for $250. With debts continuing to mount, *Press-Gazette* general manager Andrew Turnbull helped reorganize the team as the not-for-profit Green Bay Football Corporation and sold stock at $5 a share. Despite winning three straight championships from 1929-31, the team again teetered on the brink of bankruptcy, forcing another stock sale in 1935. With fortunes on and off the field dwindling, Lambeau retired in 1950 after leading the team to six NFL championships. A third stock sale was called for that year, raising $118,000. City Stadium (renamed Lambeau Field in 1965) was opened in 1957. In 1959 the team hired New York Giants assistant Vince Lombardi as head coach.

Under Lombardi, the Packers dominated football in the 1960s, winning five NFL titles with such players as Bart Starr and Ray Nitschke. The team defeated the Kansas City Chiefs in the first Super Bowl after the 1966 season. Lombardi resigned after leading Green Bay to victory over the Oakland Raiders in Super Bowl II. (Following his death in 1970, NFL commissioner Pete Rozelle named the league's championship trophy the Vince Lombardi trophy.)

The team again fell into mediocrity following the departure of Lombardi. Former MVP Starr was called upon to coach in 1974 but couldn't turn the tide before he was released in 1983. Forrest Gregg, another former Packer great, took over but was also unsuccessful in four seasons at the helm.

Bob Harlan, who had joined the Packers as assistant general manager in 1971, became president and CEO in 1989. He hired Ron Wolf as general manager in 1991, who in turn hired Mike Holmgren as head coach early the next year. With a roster including Brett Favre, Reggie White, and Robert Brooks, the Packers posted six straight playoff appearances and won its third Super Bowl (and 12th NFL title) in 1997. A fourth stock sale (preceded by a 1,000:1 stock split) netted the team more than $24 million.

After Holmgren resigned in 1999 (he left to coach the Seattle Seahawks), former Philadelphia Eagles coach Ray Rhodes tried to lead the team but lasted only one dismal season. In 2000 Mike Sherman, a former Holmgren assistant, was named the team's 13th head coach. Prompted by falling revenue, the team announced plans to renovate Lambeau Field, and voters in Brown County later approved a sales tax increase to help finance the $295 million project. (The work was completed in 2003.) The next year Wolf retired and coach Sherman added general manager to his title. The team also signed quarterback Favre to a 10-year, $100 million contract extension.

While Sherman managed to lead the team to the playoffs in four of his first five seasons, the Packers were a disappointing 2-4 in postseason play. The team hired Ted Thompson from Seattle in 2005 to take over the general manager duties. That season turned out to be one of the worst in recent team history, however, and Sherman was replaced as head coach by San Francisco 49ers assistant coach Mike McCarthy in 2006.

The Packers rebounded during the 2007 season, reaching the NFC Championship game. (Green Bay lost to the New York Giants.) That off-season in 2008, the Packers underwent a change in the front office as Harlan retired as CEO and was replaced by Mark Murphy, a former NFL player and athletic director at Northwestern University. Favre announced his retirement that same year but attempted a comeback during the summer; he was later traded to the New York Jets.

EXECUTIVES

Chairman Emeritus: Robert E. (Bob) Harlan, age 73
President, CEO, and Director: Mark H. Murphy, age 54
EVP, General Manager, and Director Football Operations: Ted Thompson, age 56
VP Administration and Player Finance: Russ Ball, age 50
VP Finance: Paul Baniel, age 48
VP Organizational and Staff Development: Betsy Mitchell
VP Administration and General Counsel: Jason Wied, age 37
Head Coach: Michael (Mike) McCarthy
Pro Personnel Coordinator: Autumn Thomas-Beenenga
Director Public Relations: Jeff Blumb
Director Information Technology: Wayne Wichlacz
Director Research and Development: Mike Eayrs, age 58
Director Marketing and Corporate Sales: Craig A. Benzel
Director Football Operations: Reggie McKenzie, age 46
Director College Scouting: John Dorsey, age 49
Director Player Development: Rob Davis, age 40
Director Football Administration and Communications: Mark Schiefelbein
Equipment Manager: Gordon (Red) Batty
Manager Human Resources: Nicole Ledvina
Manager Corporate Sales: Bill Hawker
Marketing Manager: Michelle Palubicki
Treasurer and Director: Larry L. Weyers, age 64
Secretary and Director: Peter M. Platten III, age 69
Auditors: Wipfli Ullrich Bertelson LLP

LOCATIONS

HQ: The Green Bay Packers, Inc.
Lambeau Field Atrium, 1265 Lombardi Ave.
Green Bay, WI 54304
Phone: 920-569-7500   **Fax:** 920-569-7301
Web: www.packers.com

The Green Bay Packers play at 72,928-seat capacity Lambeau Field in Green Bay, Wisconsin.

PRODUCTS/OPERATIONS

Championship Titles

Super Bowl Championships
  Super Bowl XXXI (1997)
  Super Bowl II (1968)
  Super Bowl I (1967)
NFL Championships (1929-31, 1936, 1939, 1944, 1961-62, 1965-67)
NFC Championships (1996-97)
NFC North Division (2002-04, 2007)
NFC Central Division (1972, 1995-97)
NFL Western Conference (1936, 1938-39, 1944, 1960-62, 1965-67)

COMPETITORS

Chicago Bears
Detroit Lions
Minnesota Vikings

HISTORICAL FINANCIALS

Company Type: Not-for-profit

Income Statement
FYE: March 31

	REVENUE ($ mil.)	NET INCOME ($ mil.)	NET PROFIT MARGIN	EMPLOYEES
3/09	248	—	—	268
3/08	241	—	—	189
3/07	218	—	—	200
3/06	208	—	—	150
3/05	200	—	—	150
Annual Growth	5.5%	—	—	15.6%

Revenue History

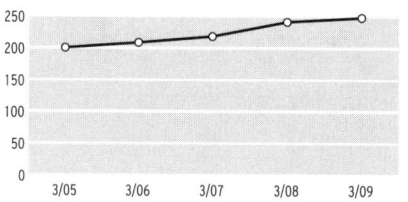

Greenberg Traurig

Greenberg Traurig is known for its entertainment practice, but show business isn't the firm's only legal business. Its 1,800-plus lawyers maintain a wide range of practices, including corporate and securities, intellectual property, labor and employment, litigation, and real estate. Clients have included Delta Air Lines, Lorimar Pictures, and Metromedia Company. The firm has about 30 offices, mainly in the US but also in Europe and the Asia/Pacific region. It extends its network in Europe and Asia via strategic alliances. Greenberg Traurig was founded in 1967 by Mel Greenberg.

EXECUTIVES

Chairman: Larry J. Hoffman
CEO: Cesar L. Alvarez, age 61
President: Richard A. Rosenbaum, age 54
President, Real Estate: Matthew B. (Matt) Gorson
COO, Global Practice Management: Sandy Grossman
VP and General Counsel: Richard G. Garrett
Chief Revenue Officer: Larry Harris
CIO: Jay Nogle
Chief Administrative Officer, Office Operations: Gregg Jones
Chief Recruitment Officer: Carol Allen
Chief Administrative Officer, Shared Services: Marty Miranda
Chief Marketing Officer: Jill Perry
Director Marketing and Communications: Laura Sinnott Peters
Director Human Resources: Karen Morita
Director Recruitment: Janet McKeegan
Chairman, Greenberg Traurig Maher: Paul Maher

LOCATIONS

HQ: Greenberg Traurig, LLP
1221 Brickell Ave., Miami, FL 33131
Phone: 305-579-0500   **Fax:** 305-579-0717
Web: www.gtlaw.com

PRODUCTS/OPERATIONS

Selected Practice Areas
ADA, Accessibility, Building & Life Safety Codes
Antitrust & Trade Regulation
Antitrust Litigation
Appellate
Automotive Dealerships
Aviation & Aircraft Finance
Business Reorganization & Bankruptcy
Class Action Litigation
Corporate & Securities
eDiscovery & eRetention
Energy & Natural Resources
Entertainment
Environmental
Executive Compensation & Employee Benefits
Export Controls
Financial Institutions
Franchising
Global
Global Trade
Globalization & Commercialization
Government Contracts
Governmental Affairs
Health Business
Hotel, Resort & Club
Immigration
Insurance Recovery & Advisory
Intellectual Property
International Dispute Resolution
Labor & Employment
Land Development
Life Sciences
Litigation
Products Liability & Mass Tort Litigation
Project & Infrastructure Finance
Public Finance
Public Infrastructure
Public Utility
Real Estate
Real Estate Investment Trust (REIT)
Real Estate Operations
Retail Industry
Securities & Shareholder Litigation
Structured Finance & Derivatives
Tax
Technology, Media & Telecommunications
Transportation
Trusts & Estates
Wealth Management
White Collar Criminal Defense

COMPETITORS

Akin Gump
Baker & Hostetler
Baker & McKenzie
Cravath, Swaine
Fulbright & Jaworski
Holland & Knight

Hughes Hubbard
Paul, Weiss, Rifkind
Proskauer Rose
Stroock
Vinson & Elkins

HISTORICAL FINANCIALS

Company Type: Partnership

Income Statement
FYE: December 31

	REVENUE ($ mil.)	NET INCOME ($ mil.)	NET PROFIT MARGIN	EMPLOYEES
12/08	1,204	—	—	—
12/07	1,200	—	—	—
Annual Growth	0.3%	—	—	—

Revenue History

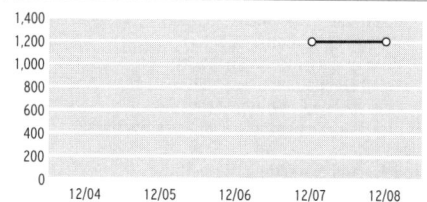

Grocers Supply

Need crackers in Caracas or vanilla in Manila? Grocers Supply Co. distributes groceries near and far. The company (not to be confused with fellow Texas distributor GSC Enterprises) supplies food, health and beauty items, household products, and school and office supplies to nearly 2,000 convenience stores and grocery retailers, as well as some 200 schools, within a 350-mile radius of Houston. The company's international division, meanwhile, ships supplies to oil company operations, US embassies, and other customers around the world. It also owns Fiesta Mart, a chain of ethnic food stores. Grocers Supply was founded by Joe Levit in 1923; his family, led by president Max Levit, continues to own the company.

Grocers Supply acquired nearly 40 grocery stores from Minyard Food Stores in 2008. The deal included the 23-unit Carnival Food Stores chain, most of which were converted to Fiesta Mart locations.

EXECUTIVES

President: Max S. Levit
COO: David D'Arezzo
CFO: Vicki Baum
SVP Financial Services: Jim Nelson
SVP Merchandising: Tom Becker
SVP Operations: Robert Hunt
VP Management Information Systems: Randy Cannon
VP Human Resources: Cindy Bradley
VP Real Estate: James Arnold
VP Sales: Jim Davenport
Auditors: PricewaterhouseCoopers

LOCATIONS

HQ: The Grocers Supply Co., Inc.
3131 E. Holcombe Blvd., Houston, TX 77021
Phone: 713-747-5000   **Fax:** 713-746-5611
Web: www.grocerssupply.com

COMPETITORS

Affiliated Foods
Associated Grocers, Inc.
Associated Wholesale Grocers
C & S Wholesale
GSC Enterprises
H-E-B

Kroger
McLane
Nash-Finch
Randall's
SUPERVALU
Wal-Mart

HISTORICAL FINANCIALS

Company Type: Private

Income Statement
FYE: December 31

	ESTIMATED REVENUE ($ mil.)	NET INCOME ($ mil.)	NET PROFIT MARGIN	EMPLOYEES
12/08	2,950	—	—	9,550
12/07	2,720	—	—	8,900
12/06	2,510	—	—	8,800
12/05	1,900	—	—	2,000
Annual Growth	15.8%	—	—	68.4%

Revenue History

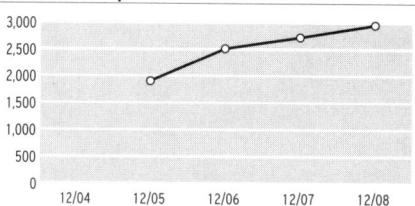

Group Health Cooperative

Group Health Cooperative gives new meaning to the term "consumer-driven health care." The organization is a not-for-profit managed health care group serving some half a million residents of Washington and Idaho. Governed by a board that its members elect, the co-op offers health insurance through its Group Health Options and KPS Health Plans subsidiaries, but it also provides medical care at its own facilities. It maintains a partnership with Group Health Permanente, a multispecialty medical group that provides care in those facilities. The co-op also partners with Kaiser Permanente to market its services, share knowledge, and offer reciprocal membership benefits.

Members may participate in a variety of group and individual health plans. Specialized services include mental health and substance abuse treatment, hospice services, women's health care, and emergency medicine. Group Health also offers Medicare Advantage and prescription drug plans, as well as state-funded health plans for low-income Washington residents.

Group Health operates about two dozen of its own primary care medical centers. It also owns a Seattle-area hospital (Central Hospital) and contracts with other hospitals in other communities to provide care.

The group closed a second Seattle-area inpatient facility (Eastside Hospital) in 2008 and is cutting costs (mostly through staff cuts) as a means to controlling rising health care costs and, by extension, plan premiums.

The system's Group Health Center for Health Studies engages in both government-funded and private grant-funded medical research.

Group Health Cooperative opened its doors in 1947.

EXECUTIVES

Chair: Jerry Campbell
Vice Chair: Bobbie Berkowitz
President and CEO: Scott Armstrong
CIO: Ernie Hood
Chief of Staff: Laura McMillan
EVP and CFO: Richard (Ric) Magnuson
EVP Public Affairs and Governance: Pam MacEwan
EVP and General Counsel: Rick Woods
EVP, Group Practice Division: Peter Morgan
EVP, Strategic Services and Quality: James Hereford
Interim EVP, Health Plan Division; Interim President, Group Health Options: Greg Swint
EVP, Group Health Permanente: Marc West
EVP, Health Plan Division: Robert O'Brien
President and CEO, Group Health Community Foundation: Laura Rehrmann
President, KPS Health Plans: Richard Marks
Auditors: Deloitte & Touche

LOCATIONS

HQ: Group Health Cooperative
521 Wall St., Seattle, WA 98121
Phone: 206-448-5600   **Fax:** 206-448-4010
Web: www.ghc.org

PRODUCTS/OPERATIONS

Selected Services

Adolescent Center (adolescent health services)
Alternative care (acupuncture, chiropractic services)
Behavioral health care
Consulting nurse service
Cosmetic dermatology
Emergency care
Eye care services
Hearing testing
Pharmacy services
Smoking cessation programs
Specialty care
Urgent care
Weight management programs

COMPETITORS

Aetna
CIGNA
Health Net
Premera Blue Cross
Regence
UnitedHealth Group

HISTORICAL FINANCIALS

Company Type: Cooperative

Income Statement				FYE: December 31
	REVENUE ($ mil.)	NET INCOME ($ mil.)	NET PROFIT MARGIN	EMPLOYEES
12/08	2,665	—	—	6,000

GSC Enterprises

GSC Enterprises brings the groceries to the grocery store. Doing business as Grocery Supply Company (not to be confused with Grocers Supply Co.), the wholesale distributor supplies more than 4,500 independent convenience stores, grocers, discounters, and other retailers and wholesalers with some 12,000 items. It distributes such items as beverages, dry goods, and prepared foods to customers in about 15 states, mostly in the Southwest, Southeast, and Midwest. In addition, its Fidelity Express division supplies equipment and services to allow smaller retailers to process money orders. Ken McKenzie, Curtis McKenzie, and Woodrow Brittain started GSC in 1947; the McKenzie family continues to own the company.

GSC in late 2008 sold three distribution facilities in Florida, Kansas, and Texas to Nash-Finch for about $80 million as part of an effort to focus on its retail food and financial services segments. The locations serviced primarily military commissaries.

EXECUTIVES

Chairman: Michael K. (Mickey) McKenzie
President and CEO: Michael J. Bain
VP Military Operations: Billy Key
VP Military Sales: Chris Pheiffer
VP Retail Operations: Ryan McKenzie
VP Finance and CFO: Kerry Law
VP Risk Management and Employee Services: Janet Price
VP Sales and Marketing: Steve Shing

Division Manager, Fidelity Express: Pat Odom
Division Manager, Grocery Supply Company: John Prickette
Corporate Counsel: Steve Rutherford
Corporate Controller: Robert Cody
Director Human Resources: Theresa Toland

LOCATIONS

HQ: GSC Enterprises, Inc.
130 Hillcrest Dr., Sulphur Springs, TX 75482
Phone: 903-885-7621   **Fax:** 903-885-6240
Web: www.grocerysupply.com

COMPETITORS

Affiliated Foods
Alex Lee
AMCON Distributing
Associated Wholesale Grocers
C & S Wholesale
Core-Mark
Eby-Brown
Grocers Supply
H.T. Hackney
McLane
Nash-Finch
SUPERVALU

HISTORICAL FINANCIALS

Company Type: Private

Income Statement			FYE: Saturday nearest December 31	
	REVENUE ($ mil.)	NET INCOME ($ mil.)	NET PROFIT MARGIN	EMPLOYEES
12/07	1,320	—	—	1,200
12/06	1,230	—	—	1,200
12/05	1,174	—	—	1,150
Annual Growth	6.0%	—	—	2.2%

Revenue History

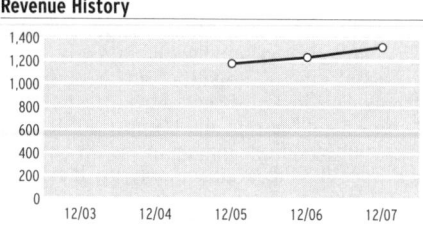

Guardian Industries

Giving its customers a break would never occur to Guardian Industries, one of the world's largest glassmakers. With more than 60 facilities on five continents, Guardian primarily produces float glass and fabricated glass products for the automobile and construction markets. It also makes architectural glass (mirrors), fiberglass, and automotive trim parts. Through its Guardian Building Products, the company operates one of largest building supply distribution centers in North America. Former president and CEO William Davidson took Guardian Industries public in 1968, buying it back in 1985. Ownership of the privately held company remains with the Davidson family.

Guardian faces off stiff industry competition by continuing to expand its international footprint and diverse portfolio of building materials. Its direction has gained traction primarily through investment in research and development and vigorous acquisitions. The company drives three major science and technology centers, each sited near manufacturing operations.

EcoGuard, a molybdenum-coated clear glass, was introduced in 2009 as part of its family of solar glass products. Other green material launches have been SunGuard SatinDeco for commercial exteriors, and ClimaGuard Satin Deco, for residential construction.

In the building products arena, Guardian's subsidiary Building Products Distribution, Inc. allied with Lapolla Industries, Inc. in 2009 to provide spray polyurethane foam for commercial and residential insulation end-uses. Bolstering its Guardian Automotive subsidiary, too, the company bought plastic, chrome-plating auto parts manufacturer Siegel-Robert Automotive in 2008. The acquisition enhances Guardian's leadership position in auto products with a well regarded brand. In addition, a partnership was formed with Sapa Fabricated Products, part of Indalex Holdings Finance, to plug Guardian ShowerGuard across North America.

Countering the risk in relying on demand from one market, the company has added operations in North America, Europe, the Middle East, Latin America, and Asia. Among many, manufacturing plants are positioned in Egypt (a stake in Egyptian Glass Company), as well as float glass plants and treatment facilities in Poland (2002), the UK (2003), Mexico (2004), and Russia and Brazil (2009). In addition to offering economies of scale, these sites serve local demand, catering to specific customer requirements, and keep costs controlled.

Davidson passed away in 2009. He is succeeded by a management team selected by Davidson during his 52 year tenure with Guardian. He was also the managing partner of the Detroit Pistons NBA team.

HISTORY

Guardian Glass Company began as a small maker of car windshields in Detroit in 1932 during the Great Depression. The company spent the 1930s and 1940s building its business to gain a foothold in glassmaking, historically one of the world's most monopolized industries. In 1949 PPG Industries and Libbey-Owens-Ford (now owned by the UK's Pilkington) agreed to stop their alleged monopolistic activity. William Davidson took over Guardian Glass from his uncle in 1957. As president, he tried to boost the enterprise's standing in the windshield niche, but PPG and Libbey-Owens-Ford refused to sell him raw glass. That year Guardian Glass filed for bankruptcy to reorganize.

The company emerged from bankruptcy in 1960 (the same year Pilkington developed the float process for glassmaking), and in 1965 it was hit with its first patent infringement lawsuit. Three years later the company went public, changed its name to Guardian Industries, and was refused a license to use Pilkington's float technology. Guardian began an aggressive acquisition strategy in 1969, and in 1970 it hired Ford Motor's top glass man (who knew the float process) and proceeded to build its first float-glass plant in Michigan. PPG sued Guardian in 1972. Davidson bought the Detroit Pistons in 1974. He applied a do-or-die style that was best illustrated by the 1979 firing of Pistons coach Dick Vitale, who claimed Davidson axed him on his own front doorstep while a curbside limo waited with the motor running.

In 1980 Guardian started making fiberglass and began hiring former workers from insulation maker Manville to duplicate that company's patented technology for fiberglass insulation. Manville successfully sued Guardian in 1981. Guardian opened a Luxembourg plant that year. Pilkington sued Guardian in 1983, but the case was settled out of court three years later. Davidson took Guardian private in 1985, and in 1988 he bought an Indiana auto trim plant. He also built The Palace of Auburn Hills sports arena in 1988.

The 1990s brought more international expansion for Guardian, with plants added in India, Spain, and Venezuela. It also set up a distribution center in Japan, a country known for its tight control of the glass industry. In 1992 Guardian bought OIS Optical Imaging Systems, a maker of computer display screens. Guardian moved its headquarters to Auburn Hills, Michigan, in 1995. Its 1996 purchase of Automotive Moulding boosted its position in the auto plastics and trim market.

Guardian booted its OIS Optical Imaging Systems unit in 1998, citing ongoing losses. That year the company's fiberglass subsidiary bought 50% of building materials buying group Builder Marts of America, giving Guardian a foothold in the markets for lumber and roofing products. Also in 1998 Davidson made a failed attempt to buy the Tampa Bay Lightning hockey team.

In 1999 Guardian bought Siam Guardian Glass Ltd. from Siam Cement Plc, the company's partner in Thailand. Davidson was able to acquire the Lightning NHL franchise that year. The next year Guardian acquired Cameron Ashley Building Products (renamed Ashley Aluminum), a distributor with more than 160 branches in the US and Canada. In 2002 the company expanded to Poland where it built a float glass plant; Guardian also opened float glass plants in the UK in 2003 and in Mexico in 2004.

In 2005 Guardian introduced ClimaGuard SPF, a residential glass product that blocks 99.9% of UV rays with no visible reduction in light transmission. The following year the company acquired the assets of Heartland Insulation.

William Davidson sold the Tampa Bay Lightning in 2008. He died in 2009 at the age of 86.

EXECUTIVES

Chairman; President, Glass Group: Russell J. Ebeid
EVP: Ralph J. Gerson
President, SRG Global and Director: Kevin Baird
President, Building Products Group and Director: Duane H. Faulkner
President, Automotive Glass Group and Director: D. James Davis
Group VP Finance, CFO, and Director: Jeffrey A. Knight
Group VP and Director: Peter Walters
VP and Director: Robert Gorlin
VP Human Resources: Bruce Cummings
Managing Director, Asian Operations: Chuck Croskey
Managing Director, Latin America: Mark LaCasse

LOCATIONS

HQ: Guardian Industries Corp.
2300 Harmon Rd., Auburn Hills, MI 48326
Phone: 248-340-1800   **Fax:** 248-340-9988
Web: www.guardian.com

PRODUCTS/OPERATIONS

Selected Products and Services

Architectural Glass
  Custom fabrication
  Float glass
  Insulating glass
  Laminated glass
  Mirrors
  Patterned glass
  Reflective coated glass
  Tempered glass
Automotive Systems
  Bodyside (mud flaps, wheel covers)
  Front and rear end (grilles, rub strips)
  Side window (door-frame moldings)
  Windshield (window-surround moldings)
Guardian Building Products
  Aluminum screen doors
  Carports
  Ceiling tile
  Door frames
  Doors
  Fiberglass insulation
  Formica
  Metal roofing
  Patio covers
  Plywood
  Rebar
  Sheetrock
  Storm doors
  Windows
Guardian Fiberglass
  Fiberglass insulation
Retail Auto Glass
  Auto glass
  Auto glass repair and replacement
  Insurance claim processing

COMPETITORS

Apogee Enterprises
Asahi Glass
AUTOGLASS
Belron US
Cardinal Glass
Corning
CRH
Dura Automotive
Johns Manville
Kalwall

Magna Mirrors
Nippon Sheet Glass
Owens Corning Sales
Pilkington Group
PPG Industries
Saint-Gobain
SCHOTT
United Glass
Vitro

HISTORICAL FINANCIALS

Company Type: Private

Income Statement

	ESTIMATED REVENUE ($ mil.)	NET INCOME ($ mil.)	NET PROFIT MARGIN	EMPLOYEES
12/08	5,600	—	—	19,000
12/07	5,470	—	—	19,000
12/06	5,330	—	—	19,000
12/05	5,000	—	—	19,000
Annual Growth	3.8%	—	—	0.0%

FYE: December 31

Revenue History

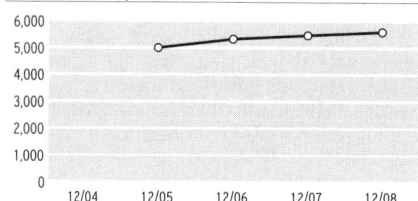

Guardian Life Insurance

When your guardian angel fails you, there's Guardian Life Insurance Company of America. The mutual company, owned by its policyholders, offers life insurance, disability income insurance, and — more recently — retirement programs to individuals and businesses. Guardian's employee health indemnity plans provide HMO, PPO, and dental and vision plans, as well as disability plans. In the retirement area, the company offers the Park Avenue group of mutual funds and annuity products, managed by its Guardian Investor Services. Guardian also offers estate planning and education savings programs.

To keep pace in the deregulated financial services area, the company has built up its wealth management capabilities to target baby boomers getting ready for retirement. Over the years it has created broker-dealer Park Avenue Securities and launched Guardian Trust Company to offer trust and investment management services. The company has also added long-term care insurance to its product line.

Guardian has also grown through acquisition, buying complementary firms, such as disability insurance specialist Berkshire Life Insurance (2001) and RS Investments (investment management, 2006).

HISTORY

Hugo Wesendonck came to the US from Germany in 1850 to escape a death sentence for his part in an abortive 1848 revolution. After working in the silk business in Philadelphia, he moved to New York, which was home to more ethnic Germans than any city save Berlin and Vienna.

In 1860 Wesendonck and other expatriates formed an insurance company to serve the German-American community. Germania Life Insurance was chartered as a stock mutual, which paid dividends to shareholders and policy owners. Wesendonck was its first president.

The Civil War blocked the company's growth in the South, but it expanded in the rest of the US and by 1867 even operated in South America.

After the Civil War, many insurers foundered from high costs. Wesendonck battled this by implementing strict cost controls and limiting commissions, allowing the company to continue issuing dividends and rebates on its policyholders' premiums.

In the 1870s Germania opened offices in Europe, and for the next few decades much of the company's growth was there. By 1910, 46% of sales originated in Europe. The company's target clientele in the US decreased between the 1890s and WWI as German immigration slowed, and its market share dropped from ninth in 1880 to 21st in 1910.

During WWI the company lost contact with its German business. Prodded by anti-German sentiment in the US, the company changed its name to The Guardian Life Insurance Company of America in 1917. After WWI the company began winding down its German business (a process that lasted until 1952).

In 1924 Guardian began mutualizing but could not complete the process until 1944 because of probate problems with a shareholder's estate.

After WWII, Guardian offered noncancelable medical insurance (1955) and group insurance (1957). The company formed Guardian Investor Services in 1969 to offer mutual funds; two years later it established Guardian Insurance & Annuity to sell variable contracts. In 1989 it organized Guardian Asset Management to handle pension funds.

In 1993, as indemnity health costs rose, the company moved into managed care via its membership in Private Healthcare Systems, a consortium of commercial insurance carriers offering managed health care products and services. This allowed Guardian to offer HMO and PPO products. It later sold its interest in Private Healthcare Systems to Multiplan in 2006.

Guardian entered a joint marketing agreement in 1995 with HMO Physicians Health Services, which contracts with physicians and hospitals in the New York tri-state area. In 1996 the company acquired Managed Dental Care of California and an interest in Physicians Health Services.

Facing deregulation and consolidation in the financial services area, as well as the demutualization of some of its largest competitors, Guardian in the late 1990s decided to add depth to its employee benefits lines and breadth to its wealth management lines.

In 1999 Guardian formed its broker-dealer subsidiary and received a thrift license to facilitate creation of a trust business. Acquisitions included Innovative Underwriters Services, Fiduciary Insurance Co. of America, and managed dental care companies First Commonwealth and First Choice Dental Network. In 2001 the company moved to boost its disability business with the purchase of Berkshire Life Insurance.

EXECUTIVES

President, CEO, and Director: Dennis J. Manning
EVP and COO: K. Rone Baldwin
EVP and Chief Investment Officer: Thomas G. Sorell
EVP and Chief Transformation Officer:
Gary B. Lenderink
EVP Individual Life and Disability: Deanna M. Mulligan, age 44
EVP Individual Products Distribution:
Margaret W. (Meg) Skinner
EVP Human Resources: John P. McCarthy
EVP Retirement Products and Services: Scott Dolfi
EVP Risk and Operational Excellence, CFO, and Director: Robert E. Broatch
EVP and Corporate Actuary: Armand M. de Palo
EVP, General Counsel, and Corporate Secretary:
Tracy L. Rich, age 57
SVP Corporate Finance and Treasurer: Barry Belfer
SVP and Chief Communications Officer:
Richard C. Jones
SVP and Corporate Controller: John Flannigan
SVP and Chief Actuary: Barbara L. Snyder
SVP Group Benefits: Jim Pogue
SVP and CIO: Frank Wander
SVP Group Pensions: Dennis P. Mosticchio
VP and General Counsel: John Peluso
President, Berkshire Life Insurance Company of America: Gordon Dinsmore
Auditors: PricewaterhouseCoopers LLP

LOCATIONS

HQ: The Guardian Life Insurance Company of America
7 Hanover Sq., New York, NY 10004
Phone: 212-598-8000   **Fax:** 212-919-2170
Web: www.guardianlife.com

Guardian Life Insurance Company of America has operations throughout the US.

PRODUCTS/OPERATIONS

2008 Revenues

	$ mil.	% of total
Premiums, annuity considerations & fund deposits	5,926	79
Net investment income	1,467	20
Other	79	1
Total	**7,472**	**100**

Selected Subsidiaries and Affiliates

Berkshire Life Insurance Company of America
First Commonwealth, Inc.
Guardian Baillie Gifford Limited
The Guardian Insurance & Annuity Company, Inc.
Guardian Investor Services LLC
Guardian Trust Company, FSB
Innovative Underwriters, Inc.
Managed Dental Care (California)
Managed DentalGuard, Inc. (New Jersey)
Managed DentalGuard, Inc. (Texas)
Park Avenue Life Insurance Company
Park Avenue Securities LLC

COMPETITORS

Aetna
AIG American General
Allstate
AXA Financial
Charles Schwab
CIGNA
Citigroup
CNA Financial
FMR
The Hartford
John Hancock Financial Services
Liberty Mutual
Lincoln Financial Group
MassMutual
MetLife
Mutual of Omaha
Nationwide
New York Life
Northwestern Mutual
Pacific Mutual
Principal Financial
Prudential
UBS Financial Services
UnitedHealth Group
Unum Group
USAA

HISTORICAL FINANCIALS

Company Type: Mutual company

Income Statement

	ASSETS ($ mil.)	NET INCOME ($ mil.)	INCOME AS % OF ASSETS	EMPLOYEES
12/08	28,973	437	1.5%	5,400
12/07	28,328	292	1.0%	5,000
12/06	26,719	376	1.4%	5,000
12/05	24,807	375	1.5%	5,000
12/04	23,336	286	1.2%	5,000
Annual Growth	5.6%	11.2%	—	1.9%

FYE: December 31

2008 Year-End Financials

Equity as % of assets: —   Long-term debt ($ mil.): —
Return on assets: 1.5%   Sales ($ mil.): 7,472
Return on equity: —

Net Income History

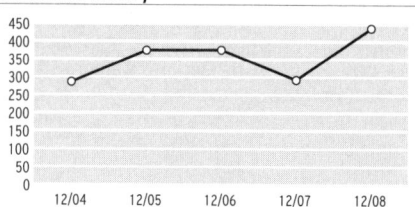

Guitar Center

What AutoZone is to the garage, Guitar Center is to the garage band. The nation's #1 retailer of guitars, amplifiers, drums, keyboards, and pro-audio equipment operates more than 210 stores in about 40 US states. Brands include Fender, Roland, Yamaha, and Sony. Stores also offer used and vintage instruments, computer hardware and software, and musician services (CD duplication, digital distribution). Its American Music Group division runs about 95 Music & Arts Center stores that sell and rent band and orchestral instruments. The music retailer acquired ailing Dennis Bamber in early 2007. Later that year Guitar Center was taken private by investment firm Bain Capital Partners (BCP) for about $2.1 billion.

No stranger to retailing, BCP has investments in companies such as Toys "R" Us, Michaels Stores, and Burlington Coat Factory.

After a decade of rapid growth as a public company, privately owned Guitar Center plans to slow the pace of new store openings, focusing instead on improving operations and internal efficiencies.

Operating in a highly fragmented industry (where the top five retailers account for about 25% of total sales), the company leverages its size to undersell — and sometimes flush out — its mostly mom-and-pop competitors. It also buys up ailing music retailers. To that end, Guitar Center's Musician's Friend subsidiary purchased all of the assets of bankrupt Dennis Bamber (dba The Woodwind & The Brasswind), including its inventory of band and orchestra instruments and music123.com and related Web sites for about $27 million in February 2007. Musician's Friend is the largest direct-response retailer of musical instruments in the US. Previous acquisitions include four Hermes Music stores in Texas in 2006. The stores were converted to carry the Guitar Center banner and strengthened the retailer's business with the Latino community.

Guitar Center stores range in size from 12,000 to 30,000 sq. ft., and the majority of the company's retail store customers are professional or aspiring musicians in large metropolitan areas. The company started opening smaller stores (8,000-10,000 sq. ft.) to cater to its secondary markets and operates about 35 stores under this format.

The company's original Hollywood store, founded in 1964, features the Rock Walk, a sidewalk tribute to 200 musicians and music pioneers.

HISTORY

"Ladies and gentlemen . . . the Beatles!" Ed Sullivan's introduction, barely audible over the hysterical screams of the audience, and the subsequent performance by the Fab Four sent American youths scurrying for electric guitars. Former car salesman Wayne Mitchell, who was running a chain of music stores at the time, was actually pushed into the fray. A supplier told him if he wanted to keep selling organs, he would have to stock the Beatles' signature Vox amplifiers, as well. Mitchell converted an old movie theater next door to his Hollywood shop, stocked it with Vox amps, and opened the first Guitar Center in 1964 on Sunset Boulevard.

Guitar Center opened its second store, in San Francisco, in 1972. Mitchell died in 1983, and former music products wholesaler Raymond Scherr acquired a majority interest in Guitar Center (reduced to about 8% after the company went public). Two years later the Hollywood Rock Walk was established in front of the original Guitar Center. It features cemented handprints and plaques honoring rock's most influential musicians and instrument makers and has become a tourist destination.

The company went public in 1997 (recapitalization the previous year created a $72 million loss). Guitar Center tripled in size between 1995 and 1998. It opened stores in highly populated areas buzzing with band activity, including Boston, Chicago, Los Angeles, and San Francisco.

In 1999 longtime employees Larry Thomas and Marty Albertson were named co-CEOs of the company. In addition to these titles, Thomas became chairman, and Albertson was named president. In June Guitar Center bought Musician's Friend, a leading catalog and Internet retailer of musical instruments, for $48.3 million (including more than $18 million in debt assumption). The company has converted seven of Musician's Friend's nine stores to Guitar Centers, and it is keeping the mail order and e-commerce business under the Musician's Friend moniker, which it operates as a separate business.

Guitar Center acquired New York-based American Music Group (12 band instrument retail stores, two mail-order catalogs, and a music accessory distributor) in April 2001 for almost $17 million. In 2002 American Music acquired M&M MUSIC, which operates five band instrument stores and serves more than 200 schools in the Southeast.

In January 2004 the company's direct response division, Musician's Friend, was named to Internet Retailer's Best of the Web 2004, as one of the country's top 50 retailing Web sites. In late 2004 chairman and co-CEO Larry Thomas stepped down in order to spend more time promoting music education. He remains on the board as chairman emeritus. Co-CEO and president Marty Albertson was named chairman and CEO.

In mid-2005 Guitar Center bought Maryland-based Music & Arts Center, a musical instrument chain that caters to beginners, and added it to its American Music Group division. The chain added 80-plus locations flying the Music & Arts Center banner. The following year Guitar Center bought four Hermes Music stores in Brownsville, Laredo, McAllen, and San Antonio, Texas, for about $11 million.

In February 2007 Guitar Center acquired all of the assets of Dennis Bamber (dba The Woodwind & The Brasswind) out of bankruptcy for about $30 million. Guitar Center itself was acquired by the private equity firm Bain Capital Partners in October 2007, and its shares were delisted from the NASDAQ stock exchange.

EXECUTIVES

Chairman and CEO: Marty P. Albertson
President and COO: Gregory A. (Greg) Trojan, age 49
EVP and CIO: John Zavada
EVP and CFO: Erick Mason
EVP Stores: Eugene (Gene) Joly
EVP Information Technology, Musician's Friend: Charles Hunsinger
EVP, Chief Administrative Officer, General Counsel, and Secretary: Leland (Lee) Smith
EVP and Chief Marketing Officer: Norman Hajjar

EVP Marketing, Musician's Friend: Stephen Zapf
EVP Merchandising: John Bagan
EVP International Development and Proprietary Brands: David Angress
SVP Human Resources: Dennis Haffeman
CEO, Musician's Friend: Craig Johnson
President and CEO, Music & Arts: Kenneth (Kenny) O'Brien, age 52
Auditors: KPMG LLP

LOCATIONS

HQ: Guitar Center, Inc.
5795 Lindero Canyon Rd.
Westlake Village, CA 91362
Phone: 818-735-8800   **Fax:** 818-735-8822
Web: www.guitarcenter.com

PRODUCTS/OPERATIONS

Selected Products and Brands

Accessories (cables, strings, microphones, picks, stands, straps)
Amplifiers (Ampeg, Crate, Fender, Marshall, Mesa Boogie, S.W.R., Vox)
Band and orchestral instruments and accessories (Blessing, Buffet, DEG, Gemeinhardt, Jupiter, Leblanc, Rico, Selmer, Schiller, Yamaha)
Computer-related recording products (monitors, sound cards, sound libraries, recording software)
Guitars (Fender, Gibson, Ibanez, Martin, Ovation, PRS, Taylor, Yamaha)
Keyboards (Alesis, Emu, Ensoniq, Korg, Kurzweil, Roland, Yamaha)
Percussion instruments (Drum Workshop, Pearl, Premier, Remo, Sabian, Tama, Yamaha, Zildjian)
Pro audio/DJ and recording equipment (Alesis, Digidesign, JBL, Mackie, Panasonic, Roland, Sony, Tascam, Yamaha)
Used and vintage products (instruments, technology products)

COMPETITORS

Best Buy
Costco Wholesale
Fletcher Music Centers
Full Compass Systems
Sam Ash Music
Schmitt Music
Sweetwater Sound
Target
Wal-Mart

HISTORICAL FINANCIALS

Company Type: Private

Income Statement				FYE: December 31
	ESTIMATED REVENUE ($ mil.)	NET INCOME ($ mil.)	NET PROFIT MARGIN	EMPLOYEES
12/08	2,300	—	—	9,540
12/07	2,300	—	—	9,540
Annual Growth	0.0%	—	—	0.0%

Revenue History

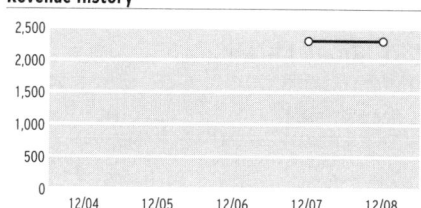

Gulf States Toyota

Even good ol' boys buy foreign cars from Gulf States Toyota (GST). One of only two US Toyota distributors not owned by Toyota Motor Sales (the other is JM Family Enterprises' Southeast Toyota Distributors), GST distributes Toyota, Lexus, and Scion brand cars, trucks, and sport utility vehicles in Arkansas, Louisiana, Mississippi, Oklahoma, and Texas. GST has expanded its vehicle processing center in Houston to handle Toyota Tundra pickup trucks built in nearby San Antonio. Founded in 1969 by its Chairman Thomas Friedkin, GST distributes new Toyotas, parts, and accessories to around 155 dealers in Texas and other states in the region. GST plans to move to a new headquarters in west Houston.

GST is moving ahead with the development of a new 16-acre corporate headquarters despite the crash in car sales. The Toyota distributor also plans to open a second vehicle processing center in Temple, Texas, in 2011. The new facility will be built in Temple's Rail Park at Central Pointe, offering access to the Burlington Northern Santa Fe railroad yard. It's expected to employ more than 500 people and process and ship about 100,000 Toyota and Scion vehicles annually via rail.

EXECUTIVES

Chairman: Thomas H. Friedkin
President and General Manager: Toby N. Hynes
CFO: Frank Gruen
SVP Marketing: J.C. Fassino
VP Sales Operations: Tom Bittenbender
VP Human Resources: Dominic Gallo
Director Administration: David Copeland
Media Relations: Frank Bianchi
Technical Capacity Manager: Don Cole
Marketing Support Senior Manager: Eric Williamson
Truck and Sport Utility Vehicle Marketing Manager: Rick Humphreys

LOCATIONS

HQ: Gulf States Toyota, Inc.
7701 Wilshire Place Dr., Houston, TX 77040
Phone: 713-580-3300   **Fax:** 713-580-3332

COMPETITORS

BMW
Daimler
David McDavid Auto Group
Ford Motor
General Motors
Honda North America
Kia Motors
Mazda
Nissan North America
Volkswagen
Volvo

HISTORICAL FINANCIALS

Company Type: Private

Income Statement				FYE: December 31
	ESTIMATED REVENUE ($ mil.)	NET INCOME ($ mil.)	NET PROFIT MARGIN	EMPLOYEES
12/08	5,100	—	—	1,200
12/07	5,700	—	—	1,275
12/06	4,600	—	—	1,200
12/05	4,600	—	—	1,200
12/04	4,000	—	—	3,500
Annual Growth	6.3%	—	—	(23.5%)

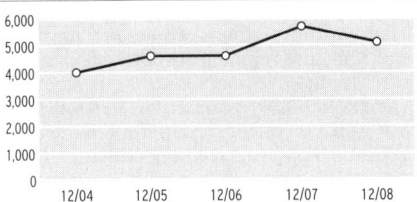

Revenue History

Guthy-Renker

What do Kathie Lee Gifford, Cindy Crawford, Victoria Principal, and Tony Robbins have in common? Each has starred in a program produced by Guthy-Renker, one of the largest infomercial producers in the US. The electronic retailing company pursues marketing opportunities through direct TV, cable and satellite, mail, and telemarketing. Its pitch people hawk a variety of goods and services, including skin care products and cosmetics such as Proactiv Solution (the company's primary category), fitness equipment, and motivational tapes. Guthy-Renker was founded in 1988 by co-CEOs Bill Guthy and Greg Renker, after being spun off from Guthy's Cassette Productions Unlimited (CPU).

Operators are standing by! Guthy-Renker renewed a $530 million contract with outsourcer EDS in 2008 to provide call center and customer service in the US, Canada, Australia, and New Zealand.

In 2007 the company bought RealtyTracker, an online real estate lead generator, and re-branded it as Guthy-Renker Home, LLC. The venture aims to utilize Guthy-Renker's experience with television to break into real estate marketing.

Guthy-Renker continues to expand its consumer brands product portfolio through acquisitions. In 2008 it paid $15 million to buy Scalp Med, a line of hair care products that stimulate hair growth. The next year it signed an agreement to begin promoting CyberDefender computer security software, its first foray into technology products.

EXECUTIVES

Founding Principal: Greg Renker
Founding Principal: William (Bill) Guthy
EVP and COO; Co-President, Guthy-Renker LLC: Kevin Knee
EVP; Co-President, Guthy-Renker LLC: Ben Van De Bunt
Director Public Relations: Corrie Murphy

LOCATIONS

HQ: Guthy-Renker Corporation
41-550 Eclectic St., Ste. 200
Palm Desert, CA 92260
Phone: 760-773-9022   **Fax:** 760-733-9016
Web: www.guthy-renker.com

PRODUCTS/OPERATIONS

Selected Infomercials

In an Instant skin care (hosted by Heidi Klum)
Malibu Pilates exercise program (hosted by Susan Lucci)
Meaningful Beauty skin care (hosted by Cindy Crawford)
Natural Advantage skin care (hosted by Kathie Lee Gifford)
Principal Secret skin care (hosted by Victoria Principal)
Proactiv Solution skin care (hosted by Elle Macpherson, Jessica Simpson, and Vanessa Williams)
Sheer Cover make-up (hosted by Leeza Gibbons)
Ultimate Edge motivational program (hosted by Tony Robbins)
Wen hair care (hosted by Melissa Gilbert)
Youthful Essence skin care (hosted by Susan Lucci)

COMPETITORS

Acorn International
Aloette
Avon
Bare Escentuals
Dynetech
Gaiam
HSN
QVC
Ronco
Thane International
ValueVision Media

HISTORICAL FINANCIALS

Company Type: Private

Income Statement				FYE: December 31
	ESTIMATED REVENUE ($ mil.)	NET INCOME ($ mil.)	NET PROFIT MARGIN	EMPLOYEES
12/08	1,500	—	—	—
12/07	1,800	—	—	—
12/06	1,500	—	—	825
12/05	1,500	—	—	825
Annual Growth	0.0%	—	—	0.0%

Revenue History

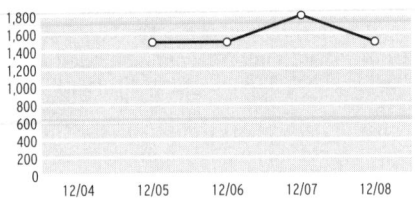

H Group Holding

Owned and operated by the Pritzkers, Chicago's financial super-family, H Group Holding is the holding company for Global Hyatt Corporation (hospitality operations) and Classic Residence senior communities. Since the death of Jay Pritzker in 1999, family squabbles over their vast (estimated $20 billion) fortune have led to talks of breaking up the empire and taking Hyatt public. The Pritzker portfolio also includes the credit bureau Trans Union, Pritzker Realty, and a stake in the Royal Caribbean cruise ship line. The family is active in philanthropic circles through the Pritzker Foundation.

In 2006 H Group Holding sold its Conwood tobacco company to cigarette giant Reynolds American, the #2 tobacco company in the US, for a reported $3.5 billion in cash.

In 2008 the Pritzker family sold 60% of industrial firm Marmon Holdings to Warren Buffet's Berkshire Hathaway for $4.5 billion. Marmon consists of more than 125 manufacturing and service companies.

EXECUTIVES

VP and Treasurer: John Stellato
Secretary: Harold S. (Hank) Handelsman
Director: Nicholas J. (Nick) Pritzker

LOCATIONS

HQ: H Group Holding, Inc.
71 S. Wacker Dr., Chicago, IL 60606
Phone: 312-873-4900   **Fax:** 312-873-4983

COMPETITORS

Equifax
Equity Group Investments
Four Seasons Hotels
GE
Henry Crown
Hilton Worldwide
Host Hotels & Resorts
ITT Corp.
Marriott
Starwood Hotels & Resorts

HISTORICAL FINANCIALS

Company Type: Private

Income Statement			FYE: December 31
	REVENUE ($ mil.)	NET INCOME ($ mil.)	NET PROFIT MARGIN	EMPLOYEES
12/08	4,921	—	—	42,000

Haights Cross Communications

Haights Cross Communications helps students buckle down on their studies. The company offers test preparation materials for the K-12 Education and library markets. Its imprints include Buckle Down, Coach, and Triumph Learning. It additionally publishes skills assessment products for math and reading students under the Options Publishing imprint. Haights Cross publishes audio books for public libraries and schools through its Recorded Books business. All total, the company offers more than 11,000 titles. It spent 2008 disposing of many of its assets, including supplemental education materials (competency tests, supplemental reading instruction, and skills assessments).

After a strategic review, the company in 2008 sold its Sundance Newbridge imprint to Rowman & Littlefield Publishing, a Maryland-based academic publisher; the unit contained K-12 Supplemental Education assets. That same year it sold its Oakstone Publishing business, which operated its Medical Education segment, to private equity firm Boston Ventures Management. Other restructuring activities in 2008 included the consolidation of several offices and job functions in order to cut costs and coordinate product development and sales and marketing activities. In addition, Haights Cross is in the process of undergoing a debt restructuring with its lenders.

The company's Recorded Books imprint offers a downloadable audiobook service to public libraries. As part of the service, libraries pay an annual subscription fee based on usage, and patrons can download audiobooks to their computer or portable device. Its Options Publishing unit includes intervention programs, used by students who have not achieved required skill levels in the traditional classroom setting. (Intervention settings include after-school, tutorial, and summer school environments.)

Haights Cross has approximately 88,000 customers, including educators and school systems, public and school libraries, and consumers. More than 80% of revenues come from schools, school districts, and school and public libraries.

EXECUTIVES

Chairman: Eugene I. (Gene) Davis, age 54
SVP and CFO: Mark Kurtz, age 44
SVP Finance and Planning and Treasurer:
Melissa L. Linsky, age 50
VP Content and Acquisitions, Recorded Books:
Troy Juliar
VP Sales and Marketing, Recorded Books: Matt Walker
VP Market Research: Julie Latzer
President and CEO, Triumph Learning: John A. Lawler, age 49
President, CEO, and Director; President, Haights Cross Operating: Paul J. Crecca, age 51
President, Recorded Books: Scott Williams, age 47
President, Buckle Down Publishing and Options Publishing: Thomas (Tom) Emrick
Auditors: Ernst & Young LLP

LOCATIONS

HQ: Haights Cross Communications, Inc.
10 New King St., Ste. 102, White Plains, NY 10604
Phone: 914-289-9400   **Fax:** 914-289-9401
Web: www.haightscross.com

PRODUCTS/OPERATIONS

2008 Sales

	$ mil.	% of total
Library	87.4	51
Test-prep & intervention	83.7	49
Total	**171.1**	**100**

Selected Product Lines

Buckle Down
  Practice tests
  Test-prep workbooks
Coach
  Complementary skills books
  Practice tests
  Test-prep workbooks
Options Learning
  Comprehensive assessments
  Reading kits
Recorded Books
  Audiobooks

Selected Subjects Covered

Language arts
Math
Science
Social studies

COMPETITORS

HarperCollins
Houghton Mifflin Harcourt
McGraw-Hill
National Geographic
Pearson Education
Random House
Scholastic
Simon & Schuster
Time Life

HISTORICAL FINANCIALS

Company Type: Private

Income Statement			FYE: December 31
	REVENUE ($ mil.)	NET INCOME ($ mil.)	NET PROFIT MARGIN	EMPLOYEES
12/08	171	(38)	—	542
12/07	232	64	27.4%	855
12/06	222	(73)	—	821
12/05	211	(44)	—	822
12/04	171	(26)	—	700
Annual Growth	0.0%	—	—	(6.2%)

Net Income History

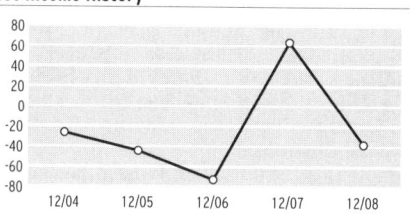

Hallmark Cards

As the #1 producer of warm fuzzies, Hallmark Cards is the Goliath of greeting cards. The company's cards are sold under brand names such as Hallmark, Shoebox, and Ambassador and can be found in more than 43,000 US retail stores. (About 3,500 stores bear the Hallmark Gold Crown name; the majority of these stores are independently owned.) Hallmark also offers electronic greeting cards, gifts, and flowers through its Web site. In addition to greeting cards, the company owns crayon manufacturer Crayola (formerly Binney & Smith), a controlling stake in cable broadcaster Crown Media, and Kansas City's Crown Center real estate development firm. Members of the founding Hall family own two-thirds of Hallmark.

While Hallmark has risen to the top tier in the industry, changes in the ways that people interact and communicate have created new challenges for the company. Sales have been fairly stagnant the past few years, leading Hallmark to continue to downsize its workforce as part of a cost-saving effort; in 2008 it consolidated production at two printing plants in Kansas, eliminating several jobs at plants in Arkansas, Ontario, and at its Sunrise Publications subsidiary in Indiana. The following year the company shuttered *Hallmark Magazine*, a women's lifestyle periodical launched in 2006.

Product development has been key for its traditional card business. Hallmark has had success with a line of musical cards (Cards With Sound) and now sells cards featuring short animated videos. The company has also teamed with DreamWorks Animation to launch interactive cards for children; the cards have flash drives that hold 3 interactive games featuring characters from *Madagascar: Escape 2 Africa*. The high-tech products, along with a new line of humorous cards, have helped boost the traditional card business.

Another of its makeover efforts has been an initiative to update its Gold Crown stores. The company hopes a new design and layout will reflect a homier image and differentiate the outlets from other retail shops.

Hallmark publishes products in more than 30 languages and distributes them in 100 countries across the globe.

HISTORY

Eighteen-year-old Joyce Hall started selling picture postcards from two shoe boxes in his room at the Kansas City, Missouri, YMCA in 1910. His brother Rollie joined him the next year, and the two added greeting cards to their line in 1912. The brothers opened Hall Brothers, a store that sold postcards, gifts, books, and stationery, but it was destroyed in a 1915 fire. The Halls got a loan, bought an engraving company, and produced their first original cards in time for Christmas.

In 1921 a third brother, William, joined the firm, which started stamping the backs of its cards with the phrase "A Hallmark Card." By 1922 Hall Brothers had salespeople in all 48 states. The firm began selling internationally in 1931.

Hall Brothers patented the "Eye-Vision" display case for greeting cards in 1936 and sold it to retailers across the country. The company aired its first radio ad in 1938. The next year it introduced a friendship card, displaying a cart filled with purple pansies. The card became the company's best-seller. During WWII Joyce Hall persuaded the government not to curtail paper supplies, arguing that his greeting cards were essential to the nation's morale.

The company opened its first retail store in 1950. The following year marked the first production of *Hallmark Hall of Fame,* TV's longest-running dramatic series and winner of more Emmy awards than any other program. Hall Brothers changed its name to Hallmark Cards in 1954 and introduced its Ambassador line of cards five years later.

Hallmark introduced paper party products and started putting *Peanuts* characters on cards in 1960. Donald Hall, Joyce Hall's son, was appointed CEO in 1966. Two years later Hallmark opened Crown Center, which surrounded company headquarters in Kansas City. Disaster struck in 1981 when two walkways collapsed at Crown Center's Hyatt Regency hotel, killing 114 and injuring 225.

Joyce Hall died in 1982, and Donald Hall became both chairman and CEO. Hallmark acquired Crayola Crayon maker Binney & Smith in 1984. It introduced Shoebox Greetings, a line of nontraditional cards, in 1986. Irvine Hockaday replaced Donald Hall as CEO the same year (Hall continued as chairman).

The company joined with Information Storage Devices in 1993 to market recordable greeting cards. The following year it acquired film production company RHI Entertainment, renaming the unit Hallmark Entertainment. Hallmark unveiled its Web site, Hallmark.com, in 1996 and began offering electronic greeting cards.

Hallmark's 1998 acquisition of UK-based Creative Publications boosted the company into the top spot in the British greeting card market. That same year it purchased Sunrise Publications. The following year the company acquired portrait studio chain The Picture People (sold in 2005) and

Christian greeting card maker DaySpring Cards. It also acquired a stake in cable channel Odyssey, which was later renamed the Hallmark Channel (now operated by Crown Media).

The company began testing overnight flower delivery in the US just in time for Valentine's Day 2000. Hockaday retired as president and CEO at the end of 2001; vice chairman Donald Hall Jr. took the additional title of CEO in early 2002.

Hallmark decided to move some of its IT operations in 2004 to Affiliated Computer Services in a seven-year deal worth $230 million; the Dallas-based company opened a center near the Hallmark headquarters to handle the work. Binney & Smith changed its name to Crayola in 2007.

EXECUTIVES

Chairman: Donald J. Hall, age 81
Vice Chairman, President, and CEO:
Donald J. (Don) Hall Jr., age 53
EVP and General Counsel: Brian E. Gardner, age 56
SVP and CIO: Michael W. (Mike) Goodwin
SVP Public Affairs and Communication: Steve Doyal, age 60
SVP Greetings: Steve Hawn
SVP Creative: Teri Ann Drake
SVP Party/Gift Presentation: John Sullivan
SVP Customer Development:
Stephen E. (Steve) Paoletti
SVP and Chief Merchandising Officer:
Lisa H. Macpherson
Group VP Operations: Margaret Keating
VP Marketing Strategy: Jay Dittmann
VP Business Development: Vince G. Burke
VP and Treasurer: Jeff McMillen
VP Logistics Solutions: Daniel S. (Dan) Krouse
VP Logistics Solutions: Pete Burney
President and CEO, Crayola: Mike Perry
President, Personal Expression Group: David E. Hall, age 46
President, Retail: Jack E. Moore Jr., age 54
Public Relations Director, Public Affairs and Communications: Julie O'Dell

LOCATIONS

HQ: Hallmark Cards, Inc.
2501 McGee Trafficway, Kansas City, MO 64108
Phone: 816-274-5111   **Fax:** 816-274-5061
Web: www.hallmark.com

PRODUCTS/OPERATIONS

Selected Brands

Keepsake (holiday ornaments and other collectibles)
Mahogany (products celebrating African-American heritage)
Nature's Sketchbook (cards and gifts)
Shoebox (greeting cards)
Sinceramente (Spanish-language greeting cards)
Tree of Life (products celebrating Jewish heritage)

Selected Subsidiaries

Crayola (crayons and markers)
Crown Center Redevelopment (retail complex)
Crown Media Holdings (pay television channels, 95%)
DaySpring Cards (Christian greeting cards)
Hallmark Insights (business and consumer gift certificates)
Halls Merchandising (department store)
Image Arts (discount greeting card distribution)
Irresistible Ink (handwriting and marketing service)
Litho-Krome (lithography)
William Arthur (invitations, stationery)

COMPETITORS

1-800-FLOWERS	Dixon Ticonderoga
123Greetings	Enesco
American Greetings	Faber-Castell
Amscan	International Greetings
Andrews McMeel Universal	iParty
BIC	MEGA Brands
Blyth	NobleWorks
Build-A-Bear	Party City
Clinton Cards	SPS Studios
CSS Industries	Taylor Corporation

HISTORICAL FINANCIALS

Company Type: Private

Income Statement				FYE: December 31
	REVENUE ($ mil.)	NET INCOME ($ mil.)	NET PROFIT MARGIN	EMPLOYEES
12/08	4,300	—	—	15,500
12/07	4,400	—	—	15,900
12/06	4,100	—	—	16,000
12/05	4,200	—	—	18,000
12/04	4,400	—	—	18,000
Annual Growth	(0.6%)	—	—	(3.7%)

Revenue History

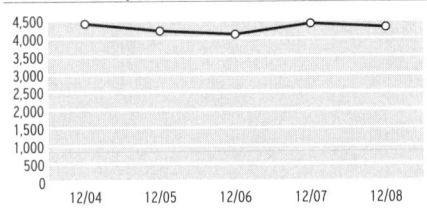

Harman Management

This company helped a colonel get started in the chicken business. Harman Management, one of the largest franchisees of KFC (a division of YUM! Brands), was founded by Leon Harman — the first person to buy a franchise from the chain's founder, Colonel Sanders. The company now has more than 330 fried chicken units in California, Colorado, Utah, and Washington, along with several locations co-branded with Taco Bell, Pizza Hut, and A&W units. Harman, who ran a cafe in Salt Lake City, was awarded his franchise in 1952. He coined the name Kentucky Fried Chicken and popularized the concept of selling the chicken in a bucket.

EXECUTIVES

Chairman Emeritus: Jackie Trujillo, age 73
Chairman and CEO: James D. (Jim) Olson
COO: Vern Wardle
VP Finance: James S. Jackson
VP Operations: James (Jim) Beglin
Director Information Systems: Jonathan Packer
Director Human Resources: Shawn Brady
Director Real Estate: Travis Gutke

LOCATIONS

HQ: Harman Management Corporation
199 1st St., Ste. 212, Los Altos, CA 94022
Phone: 650-941-5681   **Fax:** 650-948-7532

COMPETITORS

AFC Enterprises
American Dairy Queen
Arby's
Burger King
Chick-fil-A
Chipotle
Church's Chicken
CKE Restaurants
Del Taco
El Pollo Loco
Fresh Enterprises
In-N-Out Burgers
Jack in the Box
McDonald's
Quiznos
Subway
Wendy's International, Inc.

Harpo, Inc.

You might say this company puts the "O" in Oprah. Harpo controls the entertainment and media interests of talk-show host/actress/producer Oprah Winfrey. Its flagship *The Oprah Winfrey Show* is the highest-rated TV talk show in history and is seen in almost every US market and in 145 countries. Harpo also produces feature films (*Beloved,* which also starred Winfrey) and made-for-TV movies (*Their Eyes Were Watching God*), as well as radio content distributed by SIRIUS XM Radio. In addition, Harpo publishes *O, The Oprah Magazine* with Hearst Magazines, which boasts a circulation of about 2.3 million, and it publishes content online through Oprah.com. Winfrey started her production company in 1986.

With her media empire showing few signs of losing strength, Winfrey ranks among the top paid and most powerful celebrities in the entertainment world. She was also the first black woman to join the ranks of *Forbes* magazine's list of billionaires.

The crown jewel in Oprah's holdings by far is her talk show, which reaches more than 6 million viewers in the US each day, about three-fourths of whom are women. In 2009 Winfrey announced she would retire from the daytime talk business when *The Oprah Winfrey Show* ends its current syndication run in 2011. The show has been a staple of daytime TV schedules since it began syndication in 1986. It is syndicated through a partnership with CBS Television Distribution.

Harpo meanwhile continues to expand its portfolio of media holdings with new properties, such as *The Rachael Ray Show* starring Food Network star Rachael Ray. Launched in 2006, the show quickly gained a loyal following by pairing celebrity interviews and Ray's culinary talents. Harpo inked a deal with former *Playboy* Playmate and MTV star Jenny McCarthy in 2009 to develop a variety of projects including a new syndicated talk show. The company also produces the popular *Dr. Phil* show starring celebrity therapist Dr. Phil McGraw, as well as the *Dr. Oz* show, which offers viewers health and wellness tips.

Winfrey has also partnered with Discovery Communications to launch a new cable channel called OWN: The Oprah Winfrey Network. Operated through joint venture The Oprah Winfrey Network, OWN will replace Discovery's existing Discovery Health Channel when it launches in early 2011. Former MTV president Christina Norman was tapped to lead the new network.

HISTORY

Oprah Winfrey began her broadcasting career in 1973 at age 19 as a news anchor at Nashville's WTVF-TV. She became an evening news co-anchor in Baltimore in 1976, where she was recruited to co-host WJZ-TV's local talk show *People Are Talking*. She moved to Chicago in the early 1980s to host ABC affiliate WLS-TV's *AM Chicago,* which quickly became the city's top morning talk show. It was renamed *The Oprah Winfrey Show* in 1985.

Winfrey's performance in Steven Spielberg's *The Color Purple* in 1985 (her first-ever acting role) won her an Oscar nomination and boosted her ratings when *The Oprah Winfrey Show* debuted nationally in 138 cities the following year. The syndication deal with King World Productions was secured by her agent (later Harpo's president and COO) Jeffrey Jacobs. Harpo was founded that year.

Winfrey obtained full ownership of her program in 1988. Two years later Harpo Films was created, and Winfrey bought a Chicago studio to produce *Oprah,* becoming only the third woman to own her own production studio (Mary Pickford and Lucille Ball were the others). She introduced the popular Oprah's Book Club in 1996. Also that year Texas cattlemen filed a lawsuit claiming she had caused a drop in beef futures prices after a show on the UK outbreak of mad cow disease (Winfrey didn't emphasize that the disease had not appeared in the US). But jurors ruled in her favor in early 1998. Winfrey also renewed her contract that year until the 2001-2002 TV season.

In 1998 Winfrey agreed to produce original programming for Oxygen, a new cable network for women launched by Oxygen Media, in exchange for an equity stake. CBS bought King World in 1999, and the deal gave King World stockholder Winfrey a $100 million stake in CBS (later bought by Viacom and now part of CBS Corporation). The following year Winfrey, along with Hearst Magazines, launched her own magazine (*O, The Oprah Magazine*) that focuses on relationships, health, and fashion.

In 2002 the talk show diva decided that Oprah's Book Club would be an occasional, instead of a regular, segment on her TV program (much to the dismay of many book publishers). In addition, a spin-off talk show hosted by Dr. Phil McGraw (a regular on the Oprah show) premiered that year. In 2003 Winfrey announced that she was reviving her book club (with an emphasis on classic literature rather than books authored by contemporary writers). She also signed a contract to keep her TV program on the air into 2008. The next year Winfrey extended the contract even further, striking a deal to keep gabbing until 2011.

In 2006 Harpo launched another celebrity-hosted talk show, *The Rachael Ray Show* starring Food Network star Rachael Ray. Oxygen Media was acquired by NBC Universal the following year.

EXECUTIVES

Chairman: Oprah G. Winfrey, age 55
President: Tim Bennett
EVP Marketing and Development, Development Group: Harriet Seitler
EVP: Eric Logan
CFO: Douglas J. (Doug) Pattison
SVP Communications: Lisa Halliday
CEO, The Oprah Winfrey Network (OWN): Christina Norman
President, Harpo Films: Kate Forte
President Digital Media, The Oprah Winfrey Network (OWN): Robert A. Tercek
EVP Creative Development, Harpo Prods.: Valerie Schaer
SVP Scheduling, Acquisitions, and Strategy, The Oprah Winfrey Network (OWN): Jeffrey Meier
SVP Communications and Strategy, The Oprah Winfrey Network (OWN): Nicole Nichols
VP Integrated Marketing, The Oprah Winfrey Network (OWN): Meredith Momoda
VP Programming, The Oprah Winfrey Network (OWN): Timothy Kuryak
VP Programming, The Oprah Winfrey Network (OWN): Jill Dickerson
VP Operations, The Oprah Winfrey Network (OWN): Doug Levy
Executive Producer, The Oprah Winfrey Show: Sheri Salata
Co-Executive Producer, The Oprah Winfrey Show: Lisa Erspamer
Head Programming, The Oprah Winfrey Network (OWN): Jamila Hunter
General Counsel: William L. (Bill) Becker

LOCATIONS

HQ: Harpo, Inc.
110 N. Carpenter St., Chicago, IL 60607
Phone: 312-633-1000   **Fax:** 312-633-1976
Web: www.oprah.com

PRODUCTS/OPERATIONS

Selected Operations

Harpo Entertainment Group
  Harpo Films
    Amy & Isabelle (2001)
    Beloved (1998)
    Oprah Winfrey Presents: Before Women Had Wings (1997)
    Oprah Winfrey Presents: The Wedding (1998)
    Overexposed (1992)
    Their Eyes Were Watching God (2005)
    There Are No Children Here (1993)
  Harpo Productions
    Dr. Phil
    Oprah After the Show
    Oprah Winfrey Presents: David and Lisa (1998)
    Oprah Winfrey Presents: Tuesdays with Morrie (1999)
    The Oprah Winfrey Show
    The Rachael Ray Show
    The Women of Brewster Place (1989)
  Harpo Print
    O, The Oprah Magazine (joint venture with Hearst Corporation)
    O, At Home (periodic issues)
  Harpo Radio (satellite radio content)
  Harpo Video
Oprah's Angel Network (charitable organization)
Oprah's Book Club (reading club featured on *The Oprah Winfrey Show*)
Oprah Boutique (consumer products)
Oprah.com

HISTORICAL FINANCIALS
Company Type: Private

Income Statement

	REVENUE ($ mil.)	NET INCOME ($ mil.)	NET PROFIT MARGIN	EMPLOYEES
12/07	345	—	—	410
12/06	325	—	—	370
12/05	290	—	—	341
12/04	275	—	—	—
12/03	275	—	—	250
Annual Growth	5.8%	—	—	13.2%

FYE: December 31

Revenue History

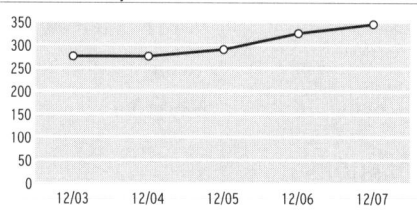

Harrah's Entertainment

Harrah's Entertainment likes to spread its bets. The world's largest gaming company, Harrah's owns, operates, and/or manages about 50 casinos (under such names as Bally's, Caesars, Harrah's, Horseshoe, and Rio), primarily in the US and the UK. Operations include casino hotels, dockside and riverboat casinos, and Native American gaming establishments. Harrah's acquired rival Caesars Entertainment for $9.4 billion in cash, stock, and debt. The deal cemented Harrah's as the world's #1 gaming company, jumping over the merged MGM MIRAGE/Mandalay combination. To appease regulators, Harrah's sold its Harrah's Tunica and East Chicago casinos to Colony Capital. The firm is owned by Apollo Advisors and TPG Capital. The company was acquired by Apollo and TPG in a deal worth some $30 billion in 2009.

The recession is hitting Harrah's hard. It has more than $24 billion worth of debt and is struggling to generate cash flow as fewer customers visit its casinos. In order to cut costs in 2009 it reduced managers' pay by 5% and has suspended contributions to employee retirement accounts.

The company's facilities boast more than 3 million sq. ft. of casino space and some 39,000 hotel rooms and suites. The company derives 70% of its revenues from gambling at its casinos.

Las Vegas properties include Harrah's Las Vegas, Rio All-Suite Hotel & Casino, Caesars Palace, Bally's Las Vegas, Flamingo Las Vegas, Paris Las Vegas, Imperial Palace Hotel & Casino, and Bill's Gamblin' Hall & Saloon. In 2009 the company filed an application to purchase the struggling Planet Hollywood Resort & Casino in Las Vegas, adding yet another Las Vegas location to its portfolio.

Harrah's also owns and operates the World Series of Poker tournament and brand, and manages three casinos on Indian reservations (Harrah's Phoenix Ak-Chin, near Phoenix, Arizona; Harrah's Cherokee Casino and Hotel in North Carolina; and Harrah's Rincon Casino and Resort, near San Diego, California). In Atlantic City, New Jersey, the company owns Harrah's Resort Atlantic City, Showboat Atlantic City, Caesars Atlantic City, and Bally's Atlantic City.

Internationally, the company's London Clubs subsidiary owns or manages eleven casinos in the UK, three in Egypt, and one in South Africa. It additionally owns the Macau Orient Golf, one of only two golf courses in Macau, China.

HISTORY

William Harrah and his father founded their first bingo parlor in Reno, Nevada, in 1937. Using the income from that business, Harrah opened his first casino, Harrah's Club, in downtown Reno in 1946. In 1955 and 1956 he bought several clubs in Stateline, Nevada (near Lake Tahoe). Harrah built the company by using promotions to draw middle-class Californians to his clubs.

During the 1960s the entrepreneur expanded his operations in Lake Tahoe, and in 1968 he built a 400-room hotel tower in Reno. Harrah's went public in 1971. After Harrah's death in 1978, the company expanded outside Nevada by building a hotel and casino in Atlantic City, New Jersey.

Holiday Inns bought Harrah's in 1980 for about $300 million. The hotelier already owned a 40% interest in River Boat Casino, which operated a casino next to a Holiday Inn in Las Vegas. When Holiday Inns acquired the other 60% of the casino/hotel in 1983, Harrah's took over its management. Holiday Inns became Holiday Corporation in 1985. The following year UK brewer Bass PLC put up $100 million for 10% of Holiday Corporation.

In 1990 Bass acquired the Holiday Inn hotel chain for $2.2 billion. The rest of Holiday Corporation, including Harrah's, was renamed Promus under chairman Michael Rose.

In the early 1990s Harrah's built a casino on Ak-Chin Indian land near Phoenix and opened riverboat casinos in Joliet, Illinois; Shreveport, Louisiana; and North Kansas City, Missouri. In 1995 Promus spun off its hotel operations as Promus Hotel Corporation and changed the name of its casino business to Harrah's Entertainment.

Also in 1995 Harrah's gambled and lost. Big. Its New Orleans casino was shelved even before it was finished — a victim of Louisiana's Byzantine politics. Eager for the right to build what would be a $395 million, 200,000-sq.-ft. casino in the heart of the city, Harrah's had made a number of ill-advised concessions to state and municipal officials. In the end the fiasco's price tag reached $900 million (only half of which went to casino construction costs), and Harrah's put the project into bankruptcy to stop the bleeding. (It resumed construction in 1999 and finally opened the casino at the end of the year.)

In 1997 Rose retired as chairman and was replaced by CEO Philip Satre. In 1998 Harrah's bought competitor Showboat, with properties in Las Vegas and Atlantic City, and management of a New South Wales, Australia, casino.

In early 1999 Harrah's bought Rio Hotel & Casino, which operates one upscale casino on the Las Vegas Strip, for about $525 million. In 2000 the company bought riverboat casino operator Players International for $425 million.

Harrah's purchased Harveys Casino Resorts, with four locations in Colorado, Iowa, and Nevada, for $675 million in 2001. (It sold the Colorado location in 2002.) The 452-room Harrah's Atlantic City hotel tower was opened in 2002. Also that year it began construction of a second, 800-room tower at its Atlantic City Showboat casino.

In 2004 Harrah's acquired casino operator Horseshoe Gaming for $1.45 billion. The purchase added properties to Harrah's portfolio (Hammond, Indiana; Bossier City, Louisiana; and Tunica, Mississippi). In order to gain regulatory approval for the purchase, Harrah's later sold its Harrah's Shreveport casino to Boyd Gaming for $190 million.

The following year Harrah's completed a monster-sized deal, the $9.4 billion acquisition of rival Caesars Entertainment, which rocketed the company to the top of the gaming world. In 2005 Harrah's bought the Imperial Palace, one of the last few independent casinos on the Las Vegas Strip, for $370 million.

The effects of Hurricane Katrina were felt at the company's Biloxi and Gulfport, Mississippi, locations, which suffered extensive damage. Harrah's sold the Gulfport location and rebuilt the Biloxi site, which re-opened in 2006. That year Harrah's sold its Flamingo Laughlin hotel-casino and an undeveloped land parcel in Atlantic City to American Real Estate Partners. It also purchased casino operator London Clubs International. London Clubs operates seven UK casinos, as well as two in Egypt and one in South Africa.

In 2008 the company ceased to be a publicly traded company after being bought out by two private equity firms.

EXECUTIVES

Chairman, President, and CEO: Gary W. Loveman, age 49
SVP and CTO: Katrina Lane
SVP Communications and Government Relations: Janis L. (Jan) Jones, age 59
SVP, Las Vegas Operations; SVP and General Manager, Rio All-Suite Hotel & Casino: Marilyn G. Winn
SVP and General Manager, Harrah's Laughlin: Wade Faul
SVP Human Resources: Mary H. Thomas, age 42
SVP and General Manager, Harrah's New Orleans Casino: Jim Hoskins
SVP, CFO, Treasurer, and Interim Chief Accounting Officer: Jonathan S. Halkyard, age 44
SVP and Chief Marketing Officer: David W. Norton, age 40
SVP and General Counsel: Stephen H. (Steve) Brammell, age 51
VP, Secretary, and Associate General Counsel: Michael D. Cohen
VP Community Reinvestment and Social Responsibility: Thom F. Reilly, age 48
VP Sports and Entertainment Marketing: Jeffrey N. Pollack
VP Public Policy and Communications: Marybel Batjer, age 53
VP Brand Management: Kris Hart
VP, Controller, and Chief Accounting Officer: Diane E. Wilfong, age 47
President, Northern Nevada Region: John Koster
President, Central Region: John Payne, age 40
President, Western Division: Thomas M. (Tom) Jenkin, age 54
President, Strategy and Development: Peter E. Murphy, age 47
Auditors: Deloitte & Touche LLP

LOCATIONS

HQ: Harrah's Entertainment, Inc.
1 Caesars Palace Dr., Las Vegas, NV 89109
Phone: 702-407-6000 **Fax:** 702-407-6037
Web: www.harrahs.com

PRODUCTS/OPERATIONS

2008 Sales

	$ mil.	% of total
Casino	8,092	69
Food & beverage	1,649	14
Rooms	1,271	11
Management fees	64	—
Other	668	6
Promotional allowances	(1,616)	—
Total	**10,127**	**100**

US Properties

Atlantic City, New Jersey
  Harrah's Atlantic City
  Showboat Atlantic City
  Bally's Atlantic City
  Caesars Atlantic City

Bossier City, Louisiana
  Louisiana Downs
  Horseshoe Bossier City

Chicago, Illinois area
  Harrah's Joliet (Illinois)
  Horseshoe Southern Indiana

Council Bluffs, Iowa
  Harrah's Council Bluffs
  Horseshoe Council Bluffs

Indiana
  Caesars Indiana

Kansas City, Missouri
  Harrah's North Kansas City

Lake Tahoe, Nevada
  Harrah's Lake Tahoe
  Harveys Lake Tahoe
  Bill's Lake Tahoe

Las Vegas, Nevada
  Harrah's Las Vegas
  Bally's Las Vegas
  Bill's Gamblin' Hall & Saloon
  Caesars Palace
  Flamingo Las Vegas
  Imperial Palace
  Paris Las Vegas
  Rio

Laughlin, Nevada
  Harrah's Laughlin

Reno, Nevada
  Harrah's Reno

Metropolis, Illinois
  Harrah's Metropolis

Mississippi Gulf Coast
  Grand Biloxi

New Orleans, Louisiana
  Harrah's New Orleans

St. Louis, Missouri
  Harrah's St. Louis

Tunica, Mississippi
  Harrah's Tunica
  Horseshoe Tunica

International Properties

Egypt
  London Club Cairo-Nile
  Rendezvous Cairo-Ramses

Ontario, Canada
  Casino Windsor

Punta del Este, Uruguay
  Conrad Punta del Este Resort and Casino

South Africa
  Emerald Safari

United Kingdom
  Golden Nugget
  Rendezvous Casino
  The Sportsman
  Fifty
  Rendezvous Brighton
  Rendezvous Southend-on-Sea
  Manchester235
  The Casino at the Empire
  Alea Nottingham
  Alea Glasgow

Other Operations

Casinos managed for Indian tribes
  Harrah's Ak-Chin (Phoenix, Arizona)
  Harrah's Cherokee (Cherokee, North Carolina)
  Harrah's Rincon (San Diego, California)
Racetracks
  Bluegrass Downs (Paducah, KY)
  Louisiana Downs (Bossier City)
  Turfway Park (50%; Simpson County, KY)
World Series of Poker

COMPETITORS

Ameristar Casinos	MGM MIRAGE
Boyd Gaming	Pinnacle Entertainment
Isle of Capri Casinos	Station Casinos
Kerzner International	Tropicana Entertainment
Las Vegas Sands	Trump Resorts
Mashantucket Pequot	Wynn Resorts

HISTORICAL FINANCIALS

Company Type: Private

Income Statement

FYE: December 31

	REVENUE ($ mil.)	NET INCOME ($ mil.)	NET PROFIT MARGIN	EMPLOYEES
12/08	10,127	(5,197)	—	80,000
12/07	10,825	619	5.7%	87,000
Annual Growth	(6.4%)	—	—	(8.0%)

Net Income History

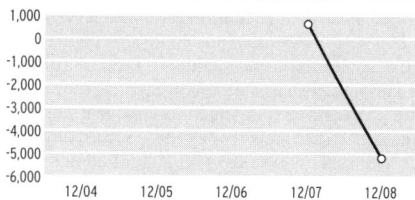

1,000				
0				
-1,000				
-2,000				
-3,000				
-4,000				
-5,000				
-6,000				
	12/04	12/05	12/06	12/07	12/08

Harvard Pilgrim Health Care

If Harvard Pilgrim Health Care were any more New England-centric, it would have to be located on Plymouth Rock. A leading provider of health benefits in Massachusetts, the not-for-profit organization also offers plans to residents of New Hampshire and Maine. It has more than 1 million members enrolled in its HMO, PPO, point-of-service, and Medicare Advantage plans. Those members have access to a regional network of about 135 hospitals and 28,000 doctors and other providers. Harvard Pilgrim Health Care also targets multi-state employers with its Choice Plus

and Options PPO plans, offered through a partnership with UnitedHealth.

In addition to its direct insurance offerings, the company provides third-party administrative services for self-insured plans. It has been growing this part of its business through acquisitions, including the purchases of regional third-party administrators Health Plans (in 2005) and Benefit Plan Management (2006).

Harvard Pilgrim Health Care upgraded the company's Medicare-related offerings in 2007, replacing its HMO plan with a Medicare Advantage private-fee-for-service plan (branded First Seniority Freedom), which it makes available in several Massachusetts and New Hampshire counties.

It has also begun enrolling Massachusetts residents in low-cost coverage plans as part of the state's mandate, passed in 2006, that requires every resident to have health insurance.

Charles Baker resigned as the company's CEO in mid-2009 to run for governor in Massachusetts. The company's COO Bruce Bullen replaced Baker after a short period of serving as interim CEO.

EXECUTIVES

Chairman: Barry L. Shemin
Interim President, Interim CEO, and Director:
Bruce M. Bullen
Interim COO and Chief Medical Officer:
Roberta Herman
CFO: James M. DuCharme
SVP Actuarial Services and Chief Actuary: Gary H. Lin
SVP Information Technology and Operations and CIO:
Deborah A. Norton
SVP and General Counsel: Laura S. Peabody
SVP Sales and Customer Service: Vincent (Vin) Capozzi
VP Corporate Compliance Programs: John J. Burke
VP Marketing: Dana Rashti
VP Financial Planning and Analysis: Jeffrey Hulburt
VP Network Services: Rick Weisblatt
VP Medical Management: Judith H. Frampton
VP Customer Service and Sales Operations:
Lynn A. Bowman
VP Benefits, Products, and Market Performance:
Vicki Coates
President, Health Plans: William R. (Bill) Breidenbach
Auditors: PricewaterhouseCoopers LLP

LOCATIONS

HQ: Harvard Pilgrim Health Care, Inc.
93 Worcester St., Wellesley, MA 02481
Phone: 617-509-1000 **Fax:** 617-509-7590
Web: www.harvardpilgrim.org

Harvard Pilgrim Health Care operates in Maine, Massachusetts, and New Hampshire.

PRODUCTS/OPERATIONS

Selected Products

Best Buy HSA PPO (high-deductible plan)
Choice Plus PPO (with UnitedHealth)
First Seniority Freedom (Medicare Advantage private-fee-for-service plan)
Harvard Pilgrim Core Coverage (HMO)
Harvard Pilgrim POS (point-of-service plan)
Harvard Pilgrim PPO (preferred provider organization)
Options PPO (with UnitedHealth)

COMPETITORS

Aetna	Fallon Community Health
Blue Cross and Blue Shield of Massachusetts	Health New England
CIGNA	MVP Health Plan
ConnectiCare	Neighborhood Health Plan
	Tufts Health Plan

HISTORICAL FINANCIALS
Company Type: Not-for-profit

Income Statement
FYE: December 31

	REVENUE ($ mil.)	NET INCOME ($ mil.)	NET PROFIT MARGIN	EMPLOYEES
12/08	2,591	48	1.9%	—
12/07	2,498	46	1.8%	—
12/06	2,488	71	2.8%	—
12/05	2,200	74	3.4%	—
12/04	2,300	39	1.7%	—
Annual Growth	3.0%	5.7%	—	—

Net Income History

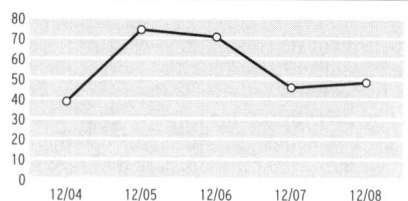

Harvard University

Many parents dream of sending their children to Harvard — and at more than $32,000 a year (undergraduate), some even dream of being able to afford it. Harvard, the oldest institution of higher learning in the US, is home to Harvard College (undergraduate studies) and 10 graduate schools including the Harvard Business, Law, and Medical schools. The Radcliffe Institute for Advanced Study at Harvard was created when Radcliffe College and Harvard University merged in 1999. Harvard has about 20,000 students, more than half of whom are enrolled in graduate or professional programs. Harvard's endowment of approximately $35 billion is the largest of any university in the world. (Yale ranks #2.)

It's usually a toss-up whether Harvard or one of its Ivy League rivals, Princeton or Yale, will rank at the top of the list of America's premiere schools or programs, but the university's reputation for academic excellence is well-founded. More than 40 Harvard faculty members have won Nobel Prizes over the years. Additionally, among Harvard's alumni are more than a half-dozen US presidents — John Adams, John Quincy Adams, Rutherford B. Hayes, Theodore Roosevelt, Franklin D. Roosevelt, John F. Kennedy, and George W. Bush.

Harvard's controversial and outspoken 27th president, Lawrence Summers, resigned at the end of the 2005-06 academic year. Derek Bok, who served as president of the university from 1971 to 1991, succeeded Summers on an interim basis. Radcliffe Institute dean Drew Faust was named as the school's 28th president (and first woman to hold the job) in 2007.

HISTORY

In 1636 the General Court of Massachusetts appropriated 400 pounds sterling for the establishment of a college. The first building was completed at Cambridge in 1639 and was named for John Harvard, who had willed his collection of about 400 books and half of his land to the school. The first freshman class had four students.

During its first 150 years, Harvard adhered to the education standards of European schools, with emphasis on classical literature and languages, philosophy, and mathematics. It established its first professorship in 1721 (the Hollis Divinity Professorship) and soon after added professorships in mathematics and natural philosophy. In 1783 the school appointed its first professor of medicine.

Harvard updated its curriculum in the early 1800s, after professor Edward Everett returned from studying abroad with reports of the modern teaching methods in Germany. The university established the Divinity School in 1816, the Law School in 1817, and two schools of science in the 1840s.

In 1869 president Charles Eliot began engineering the development of graduate programs in arts and sciences, engineering, and architecture. He raised standards at the medical and law schools and laid the groundwork for the Graduate School of Business Administration and the School of Public Health. Radcliffe College was founded as "Harvard Annex" in 1879, 15 years after a group of women had begun studying privately with Harvard professors in rented rooms.

Harvard's enrollment, faculty, and endowment grew tremendously throughout the 20th century. The Graduate School of Education opened in 1920, and the first undergraduate residential house opened in 1930. In the 1930s and 1940s, the school established a scholarship program and a general education curriculum for undergraduates. During WWII Harvard and Radcliffe undergraduates began attending the same classes.

A quota limiting the number of female students was abolished in 1975, and in 1979 Harvard introduced a new core curriculum. Princeton-educated Neil Rudenstine became president in 1991 and vowed to cut costs and to seek additional funding so that no one should be denied a Harvard education for financial reasons.

Harvard made dubious headlines during its 1994-95 academic year, enduring a bank robbery in Harvard Square, three student suicides, and one murder-suicide. The following year Harvard paid a fine of $775,000 after the US Attorney's Office claimed the school's pharmacy had not properly controlled drugs, including antidepressants and codeine cough syrup. The fine was the largest ever paid in the US under the Controlled Substance Act.

In 1998 Harvard's endowment fund acquired insurance services firm White River in one of the largest direct investments ever made by a not-for-profit institution. Also that year the school altered some of its graduation processes and introduced stress-reducing programs in the wake of another student suicide.

In 1999 Radcliffe College merged with Harvard, and the Radcliffe Institute for Advanced Study at Harvard was established. The following year Rudenstine stepped down as president; he was replaced by former US Treasury Secretary Lawrence Summers.

EXECUTIVES

President: Drew Gilpin Faust
EVP: Katherine N. (Katie) Lapp, age 52
Provost: Steven E. (Steve) Hyman
Senior Associate VP, Alumni Affairs and Development: Robert Cashion
VP Administration: Sally H. Zeckhauser
VP Alumni Affairs and Development: Tamara Rogers
VP Government, Community, and Public Affairs: Christine Heenan
VP Human Resources: Marilyn M. Hausammann
VP Finance and CFO: Dan Shore
VP and General Counsel: Robert I. Iuliano
VP Human Resources and Administration, Harvard Business Publishing: Robin Camara
VP Policy: A. Clayton Spencer
Treasurer: James F. Rothenberg
Secretary: Marc Goodheart
CEO, Harvard Business Publishing: David A. Wan
President and CEO, Harvard Management Company: Jane Mendillo
Director, Institute of Politics: Bill Purcell
Auditors: PricewaterhouseCoopers LLP

LOCATIONS

HQ: Harvard University
University Hall, Cambridge, MA 02138
Phone: 617-495-1000 **Fax:** 617-495-0754
Web: www.harvard.edu

PRODUCTS/OPERATIONS

Selected Programs and Schools

Undergraduate
  Harvard College
    Degree Programs
      Chemical and Physical Biology
      Environmental Science and Public Policy
      Social Studies
    Departments
      African and African-American Studies
      Earth and Planetary Sciences
      Economics
      History of Art and Architecture
      Molecular and Cellular Biology
      Organismic and Evolutionary Biology
      Sociology
    Schools
      School of Engineering and Applied Sciences
Graduate
  Graduate School of Arts and Sciences
  Graduate School of Design
  Graduate School of Education
  Harvard Business School
  Harvard Divinity School
  Harvard Law School
  Harvard Medical School
  Harvard School of Public Health
  John F. Kennedy School of Government
  School of Dental Medicine

HISTORICAL FINANCIALS
Company Type: School

Income Statement
FYE: June 30

	REVENUE ($ mil.)	NET INCOME ($ mil.)	NET PROFIT MARGIN	EMPLOYEES
6/08	3,482	—	—	15,302
6/07	3,211	—	—	14,865
6/06	3,000	—	—	13,000
6/05	2,801	—	—	18,000
6/04	2,598	—	—	15,000
Annual Growth	7.6%	—	—	0.5%

Revenue History

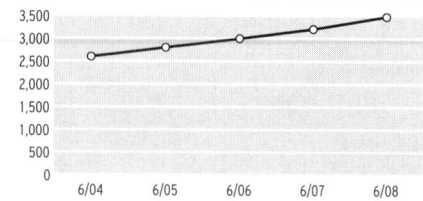

Haworth, Inc.

Designers at Haworth sit at their cubicles and think about . . . more cubicles. The company is one of the top office furniture manufacturers in the US, competing with top rivals Steelcase and HNI. Known for innovative design, it offers a full range of furniture, including partitions, desks, chairs, tables, and storage products. Brands include Monaco, Patterns, PLACES, and X99. The company operates about 60 showrooms worldwide and sells its products through more than 600 dealers. Dilbert and other long-suffering office drones have Haworth to thank for inventing the prewired partitions that make today's cubicled workplace possible. Haworth is owned by the family of Gerrard Haworth, who founded the company in 1948.

Amid the ailing economy, Haworth in 2009 relocated its wall and wood operations from Calgary, Canada, to Big Rapids and Holland, Michigan. (Haworth still maintains manufacturing facilities in Quebec.) The company is receiving about $20 million in tax credits over 13 years as part of the move. The new locations are expected to add about 1,400 new jobs in Michigan, where employers have been downsizing or moving out because of the recession.

As businesses close up shop, sales to the furniture maker's corporate clients are falling. To make up the difference, Haworth is marketing its collections to schools, hospitals, and local government agencies. It is also extending the range of its products beyond the cubicle. In 2009 it acquired a minority stake in Minnesota-based Tuohy Furniture, a maker of conference tables, lounge furniture, and storage units.

Also in 2009 Haworth sold the Falkridge Centre, a private executive retreat based in Calgary, to a regional energy executive for about $13 million. Spread across 13 acres of land, the compound has accommodated corporate chiefs, politicians, and celebrities over the years. Haworth had owned the property since it acquired SMED International in 2000.

EXECUTIVES

Chairman Emeritus: Richard G. (Dick) Haworth
Chairman: Matthew R. Haworth
President and CEO: Franco Bianchi
VP Global Marketing and Sales Support: Mabel Casey
VP European Operations: José Amaral
VP and General Manager, Asia Pacific and Emerging Markets: Frank Rexach
VP Global Sales: Todd James
VP Global Information Systems and Human Resources: Ann M. Harten
VP Business Groups, Global Architectural Interiors and Wood Solutions: Paul K. Smith
VP Global Quality and Continuous Improvement: Michael Valz
VP North America Operations: Kevin Bailey
VP Global Finance: John Mooney
Director Global Design: Jeff Reuschel
Director Sales Support: Phil Todd

LOCATIONS

HQ: Haworth, Inc.
1 Haworth Center, Holland, MI 49423
Phone: 616-393-3000   **Fax:** 616-393-1570
Web: www.haworth.com

PRODUCTS/OPERATIONS

Selected Products
Desks
Filing and storage units
Movable walls
Seating
Tables and conference furniture

COMPETITORS

ABCO Office Furniture
CFGroup
Global Group
Herman Miller
HNI
Inscape corp
KI
Kimball International
Knoll, Inc.
Neutral Posture
Norstar Office Products
Steelcase
Teknion
Trendway
Virco Mfg.

HISTORICAL FINANCIALS

Company Type: Private

Income Statement				FYE: December 31
	REVENUE ($ mil.)	NET INCOME ($ mil.)	NET PROFIT MARGIN	EMPLOYEES
12/08	1,650	—	—	7,500
12/07	1,660	—	—	8,000
12/06	1,480	—	—	8,000
12/05	1,400	—	—	7,500
12/04	1,260	—	—	7,500
Annual Growth	7.0%	—	—	0.0%

Revenue History

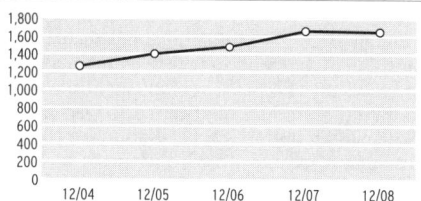

HCA Inc.

The largest for-profit hospital operator in the US, HCA (also known as Hospital Corporation of America) operates about 170 acute care, psychiatric, and rehabilitation hospitals in the US and abroad. It also runs about 100 ambulatory surgery centers, as well as diagnostic imaging, cancer treatment, and outpatient rehab centers that form health care networks in many of the communities it serves. The company has facilities in about 20 states, with about three-quarters of its hospitals located in the southern US (about 70 are in Florida and Texas). The hospital giant's HCA International operates a handful of hospitals and clinics in the UK.

The private investor group that owns HCA includes co-founder Thomas Frist Jr. (the largest shareholder), as well as Bain Capital, Kohlberg Kravis Roberts, the private equity arm of Merrill Lynch, and other members of HCA management.

Most of HCA's hospitals are in high-growth urban and suburban markets, and the vast majority are medical-surgical hospitals. (It has five psychiatric facilities and one rehabilitation hospital.)

The company plans to grow in its selected markets by acquiring hospitals and by luring patients to its existing facilities with high-quality care and a broad range of services. It is particularly interested in expanding its outpatient offerings, as well as specialty services in high-margin fields such as orthopedics and cardiology.

HCA also tries to take advantage of its national scale (and its position as the leading health care provider in many communities) to negotiate advantageous purchasing contracts, as well as favorable deals with managed care companies.

Thirty-year company veteran Jack Bovender Jr. retired as CEO at the end of 2008; he was succeeded by president and COO Richard Bracken. Bovender remains chairman of the board through 2009. Founder Frist relinquished his seat on the board to son William Frist shortly after Bovender announced his retirement.

EXECUTIVES

Chairman: Jack O. Bovender Jr., age 63, $12,173,602 total compensation
President, CEO, and Director: Richard M. Bracken, age 56, $4,639,779 total compensation
EVP and CFO: R. Milton Johnson, age 52, $3,847,136 total compensation
SVP and Chief Ethics and Compliance Officer: Alan R. Yuspeh, age 59
SVP and Controller: Donald W. (Don) Stinnett, age 53
SVP Development: V. Carl George, age 64
SVP Finance and Treasurer: David G. Anderson, age 62
SVP and CIO: Noel Brown Williams, age 53
SVP Internal Audit Services: Joseph N. (Joe) Steakley, age 54
SVP and Chief Development Officer: Joseph A. Sowell III
SVP and General Counsel: Robert A. (Bob) Waterman, age 55
SVP Human Resources: John M. Steele, age 53
VP Investor Relations: Mark Kimbrough
VP and Corporate Secretary: John M. Franck II
President, Western Group: Samuel N. (Sam) Hazen, age 48, $2,473,996 total compensation
President, Shared Services Group: Beverly B. Wallace, age 58, $3,556,331 total compensation
President, Clinical Services Group and Chief Medical Officer: Jonathan B. (Jon) Perlin, age 48
President, HCA International: Michael T. Neeb
Auditors: Ernst & Young LLP

LOCATIONS

HQ: HCA Inc.
1 Park Plaza, Nashville, TN 37203
Phone: 615-344-9551   **Fax:** 615-344-2266
Web: www.hcahealthcare.com

2008 Sales

	$ mil.	% of total
Western Group	12,118	43
Eastern Group	8,570	30
Central Group	6,740	24
Corporate & other	946	3
Total	**28,374**	**100**

US	No.
Florida	38
Texas	34
Tennessee	13
Georgia	11
Louisiana	10
Virginia	9
Colorado	7
Missouri	6
Utah	6
California	5
Kansas	4
Nevada	3
South Carolina	3
Idaho	2
Kentucky	2
New Hampshire	2
Oklahoma	2
Alaska	1
Indiana	1
Mississippi	1
UK	6
Total	**166**

PRODUCTS/OPERATIONS

2008 Sales

	% of total
Medicare	24
Uninsured	10
Medicaid	5
Managed Medicare	5
Managed Medicaid	3
Managed care & other insurers	53
Total	**100**

COMPETITORS

Adventist Health
Adventist Health System
Ascension Health
Banner Health
Baptist Hospital
Baylor Health
Catholic Health Initiatives
Catholic Healthcare West
Children's Medical Center of Dallas
CHRISTUS Health
Community Health Systems
Health Management Associates
HealthSouth
Kaiser Permanente
Psychiatric Solutions
SSM Health Care
Tenet Healthcare
Trinity Health (Novi)
Universal Health Services

HISTORICAL FINANCIALS

Company Type: Private

Income Statement

FYE: December 31

	REVENUE ($ mil.)	NET INCOME ($ mil.)	NET PROFIT MARGIN	EMPLOYEES
12/08	28,374	673	2.4%	191,000
12/07	26,858	874	3.3%	186,000
12/06	25,477	1,036	4.1%	186,000
Annual Growth	5.5%	(19.4%)	—	1.3%

2008 Year-End Financials

Debt ratio: —
Return on equity: —
Cash ($ mil.): —

Current ratio: —
Long-term debt ($ mil.): 26,585

Net Income History

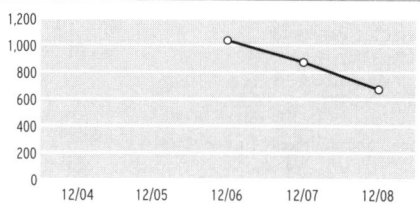

Health Care Service Corporation

Health Care Service Corporation (HCSC) has the Blues in Chicago and the Southwest. A licensee of the Blue Cross and Blue Shield Association, HCSC consists of four regional Blue health plans: Blue Cross Blue Shield of Illinois, Blue Cross and Blue Shield of Texas, Blue Cross and Blue Shield of New Mexico, and Blue Cross Blue Shield of Oklahoma. The mutually owned company provides group and individual health plans — including traditional indemnity plans, managed care programs, and Medicare supplemental coverage — to more than 12 million members, a majority of them in Illinois. Through some non-blue subsidiaries, HCSC sells life and disability insurance, as well as annuities.

Its life insurance companies include Fort Dearborn Life Insurance and Colorado Bankers Life Insurance. Together, the companies operate as the Preferred Financial Group.

The not-for-profit company has grown through strategic acquisitions of independent Blue Cross companies, as well as other health and insurance firms that complement the company's core product offerings. It began in the 1930s with its Blue Cross operations in Illinois but since 1998 has added Blue plans in Texas (1998), New Mexico (2001), and Oklahoma (2005). Its acquisition strategy has allowed HCSC to benefit from economies of scale.

HCSC has also been focused on better information technology as a means to improve health care costs. It has introduced online enrollment and health care management tools, as well as a comprehensive care management system (called Blue Care Connection) which integrates and analyzes data from claims forms, health care providers, and patients themselves, in order to reduce costs and inefficiencies. Additionally, in 2008 it acquired health care IT firm MEDecision, which provides health care management software and data analytics services to doctors and managed care companies.

Though the company has about half a million Medicare beneficiaries enrolled in supplemental health care plans, HCSC has been cautious about expanding into full-fledged Medicare Advantage plans. Its New Mexico, Oklahoma, and Texas operations do offer Medicare Advantage products in some markets, however.

In late 2008 the company expanded its Medicare operations when it acquired TMG Health, a third-party administrator of Medicare, Medicaid, and group retiree health plans that serves about 2 million members nationwide. Also in 2008 the company appointed Patricia Hemingway Hall, a long-time executive with HCSC, to the CEO post.

The following year the company expanded its dental plan subsidiary, Dental Network of America, by acquiring DenteMax from Blue Cross Blue Shield of Michigan.

HISTORY

The seeds of the Blue Cross organization were sown in 1929, when an official at Baylor University Hospital in Dallas began offering schoolteachers 21 days of hospital care for $6 a year. Fundamental to its coverage was a community rating system, which based premiums on the community's claims experience rather than subscribers' conditions.

In 1935 Elgin Watch Co. owner Taylor Strawn, Charles Schweppe, and other Chicago civic leaders pooled resources to form Hospital Services Corporation to provide the same type of coverage. (The firm adopted the Blue Cross symbol in 1939.) Employees of the Rand McNally cartography company were the first to be covered by the plan.

Soon, four similar plans were launched in other Illinois towns. Between 1947 and 1952, Hospital Services Corp. and these other four joined forces, offering coverage nearly statewide.

Meanwhile, Blue Shield physician's fee plans in several cities were incorporated as Illinois Medical Service. Hospital Services Corp. and Illinois Medical Service operated independently but shared office space and personnel.

A 1975 change in state legislation let the entities merge to become Health Care Service Corp. (HCSC), which offered both Blue Cross and Blue Shield coverage. Following the merger, the company's board of directors (which had been primarily composed of care providers) became dominated by consumers, which helped HCSC become more responsive to its members.

For the next six years, the state denied HCSC any rate increases, leaving it with a frighteningly low $12 million in reserves in 1982.

HCSC achieved statewide market presence in 1982 when it merged with Illinois' last independent Blue Cross plan, Rockford Blue Cross. In 1986, as managed care swept through the health care industry, only 14% of HCSC's members were enrolled in managed care plans. HCSC created its Managed Care Network Preferred point-of-service plan in 1991; the idea caught on with both employers and individuals and enrollment skyrocketed. By 1994 more than two-thirds of the firm's subscribers participated in some sort of managed care plan. That year it picked up Medicare payment processing for the state of Michigan.

In 1995 HCSC and Blue Cross and Blue Shield of Texas (BCBST) formed an affiliation they hoped would culminate in a merger giving the combined company $6 billion in sales and reserves of more than $1 billion. Texas consumer groups objected to the merger, claiming that Texas residents own BCBST and that Texans should be compensated for the transfer of ownership — especially since BCBST had received state tax breaks for decades in exchange for accepting all applicants. (A Texas judge ruled in favor of the merger in 1998.)

Citing high risks and low margins, HCSC in 1997 dropped its Medicare payment processing contract, which it had held for some 30 years. The next year HCSC agreed to pay $144 million after it pleaded guilty to covering up its poor performance in processing Medicare claims.

In 1998 HCSC acquired Blue Cross and Blue Shield of Texas.

In 2000 HCSC bought Aetna's NylCare of Texas, giving it large, profitable HMOs in Houston and Dallas. The next year it bested Anthem (now WellPoint) and Wellmark in wooing the troubled Blue Cross Blue Shield of New Mexico. And in 2005 it acquired Blue Cross and Blue Shield of New Mexico.

EXECUTIVES

Chairman: Milton Carroll, age 58
President and CEO: Patricia A. (Pat) Hemingway Hall, age 56
COO: Colleen F. Reitan, age 50
EVP Corporate Services: Tara Dowd Gurber
SVP, Chief Legal Officer, and Corporate Secretary: Deborah Dorman-Rodriguez
SVP and Chief Diversity Officer: Carolyn H. Clift
SVP and CIO: Brian Hedberg
SVP and CFO: Denise A. Bujack
SVP and Chief Actuary: Kenneth S. Avner
SVP and Chief Medical Officer: Paul B. Handel
President, Blue Cross and Blue Shield of Texas: Darren Rodgers
President, Blue Cross and Blue Shield of New Mexico: Elizabeth A. Watrin
President, Blue Cross and Blue Shield of Illinois: Paul S. Boulis
President, Blue Cross and Blue Shield of Oklahoma: Wyndham Kidd Jr.
President, Plan Operations: Martin G. Foster
Auditors: Ernst & Young LLP

LOCATIONS

HQ: Health Care Service Corporation
   300 E. Randolph St., Chicago, IL 60601
Phone: 312-653-6000   **Fax:** 312-819-1220
Web: www.hcsc.com

PRODUCTS/OPERATIONS

Selected Products and Services

Annuities
Dental insurance
Disability insurance
Indemnity insurance
Life insurance
Managed health care plans
Supplemental Medicare coverage
Prescription drug coverage

Selected Subsidiaries

Blue Cross and Blue Shield of Illinois
Blue Cross and Blue Shield of New Mexico
Blue Cross and Blue Shield of Oklahoma
Blue Cross and Blue Shield of Texas
Dental Network of America
Hallmark Services Corporation
Preferred Financial Group
   Colorado Bankers Life Insurance Company
   Fort Dearborn Life Insurance Co.

COMPETITORS

Aetna	Humana
Aflac	Kaiser Foundation
AMERIGROUP	Health Plan
CIGNA	MetLife
Coventry Health Care	Molina Healthcare
Guardian Life	Mutual of Omaha
Harmony Health Plan	New York Life
Health Alliance	Presbyterian Health Plan
Medical Plans	Prudential
Health Net	UnitedHealth Group
HealthMarkets	ValueOptions
HealthSpring	WellPoint

HISTORICAL FINANCIALS

Company Type: Mutual company

Income Statement

FYE: December 31

	REVENUE ($ mil.)	NET INCOME ($ mil.)	NET PROFIT MARGIN	EMPLOYEES
12/08	16,025	743	4.6%	17,500
12/07	14,348	866	6.0%	16,500
12/06	12,972	1,115	8.6%	16,500
12/05	11,714	1,146	9.8%	14,000
12/04	9,809	995	10.1%	—
Annual Growth	13.1%	(7.0%)	—	7.7%

Net Income History

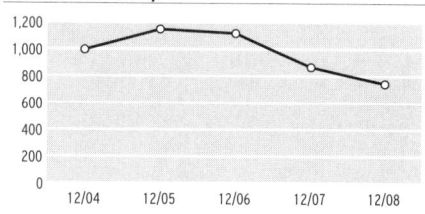

HealthMarkets, Inc.

HealthMarkets lets the self-employed shop for better insurance. The company offers health insurance through its MEGA Life and Health Insurance, Chesapeake Life Insurance Company, and Mid-West National Life Insurance Company of Tennessee to mostly self-employed individuals in about 45 states. It provides dental, vision, accident, and worker's compensation insurance; health care options include health spending accounts (HSAs) and high-deductible health plans (HDHPs). Other services include third-party administrative and distribution services for health care providers and reinsurance through the company's Zon Re subsidiary. A consortium led by the Blackstone Group owns HealthMarkets.

HealthMarkets is focusing on its businesses that serve the self-employed, and has exited other areas. In 2008 the company sold its life insurance businesses to Wilton Reassurance Company, and stopped offering Medicare Advantage products. The company announced plans in 2009 to form an independent life and health insurance agency (Insphere Insurance Solutions) to target small businesses and families. Insphere will be formed through a spinoff of part of HealthMarkets' sales organization in partnership with the Blackstone Group.

In 2008 the company was fined $20 million in connection with a multistate investigation by insurance regulators who said the company had problems with the training it provided to agents, disclosures to consumers, and claims and complaint handling. The investigation covered HealthMarkets' actions between 2000 and 2005 and was prompted by customer complaints in 29 states. The company, which admitted no wrongdoing, has agreed to corrective actions including notifying customers of complaint procedures. It faces another $10 million in fines if it doesn't meet all the settlement requirements.

HealthMarkets' legal woes didn't end there, however. The following year the company and two of its subsidiaries agreed to pay $17 million

to settle allegations that they used deceptive marketing practices in Massachusetts to lure self-employed people and small businesses into buying health plans with limited benefits, which it then failed to provide. HealthMarkets, along with subsidiaries MEGA Life and Health Insurance and Mid-West National Life Insurance, are also banned from conducting business (except for renewing existing plans) in Massachusetts for at least five years.

Blackstone Group holds just over half of the company, while Goldman Sachs has about a quarter and DLJ Merchant Banking Partners has 11%. Current and former management own the rest.

EXECUTIVES

Chairman: Chinh E. Chu, age 42
President, CEO, and Director: Phillip J. (Phil) Hildebrand, age 56, $3,832,713 total compensation
EVP and CFO: Steven P. (Steve) Erwin, age 66, $595,549 total compensation
EVP and General Counsel, HealthMarkets, The MEGA Life and Health Insurance Company, Mid-West National Life Insurance Company of Tennessee: Michael A. (Mike) Colliflower, age 54, $1,892,151 total compensation
EVP and Chief Administrative Officer: Anurag Chandra, age 32
EVP, HealthMarkets, The Mega Life and Health Insurance, and Mid-West National Life Insurance Company of Tennessee: Nancy G. Cocozza, age 45, $2,190,638 total compensation
EVP and and General Counsel: B. Curtis Westen, age 48
SVP Operations; SVP, Mid-West National Life Insurance Company of Tennessee: John E. Hunter
SVP and CIO; EVP, Mid-West National Life Insurance Company of Tennessee: Marc F. (Frank) Jackson
SVP and Chief Marketing Officer, HealthMarkets, MEGA Life and Health Insurance, and Mid-West National Life Insurance Company of Tennessee: Timothy (Tim) Roach
SVP and Chief Compliance Officer; SVP, Associate General Counsel, and Chief Compliance Officer, Mid-West National Life Insurance Company of Tennessee: Susan E. Dew
SVP HealthMarkets Agency Department: Jack V. Heller, $1,267,306 total compensation
SVP and Chief Investment Officer, HealthMarkets, MEGA Life and Health Insurance, and Mid-West National Life Insurance Company of Tennessee: Derrick A. Duke
SVP Human Resources: Vicki A. Cansler, age 54
Treasurer and Controller: Consuelo (Connie) Palacios
Auditors: KPMG LLP

LOCATIONS

HQ: HealthMarkets, Inc.
   9151 Boulevard 26, North Richland Hills, TX 76180
Phone: 817-255-5200   **Fax:** 817-255-5390
Web: www.healthmarkets.com

PRODUCTS/OPERATIONS

2008 Sales

	$ mil.	% of total
Premiums		
Health	1,262.4	88
Life	38.0	3
Investment income	60.2	4
Other income	80.1	5
Realized gains (losses)	(23.8)	—
Total	**1,416.9**	**100**

Selected Subsidiaries

Mid-West National Life Insurance Company of Tennessee
The Chesapeake Life Insurance Company
The MEGA Life and Health Insurance Company
ZON Re USA LLC (82.5%)

COMPETITORS

Aflac
Atlantic American
Guarantee Trust
HCSC
Torchmark
USHEALTH Group

HISTORICAL FINANCIALS

Company Type: Private

Income Statement

FYE: December 31

	REVENUE ($ mil.)	NET INCOME ($ mil.)	NET PROFIT MARGIN	EMPLOYEES
12/08	1,417	(54)	—	1,450
12/07	1,595	70	4.4%	2,000
12/06	2,147	238	11.1%	1,800
12/05	2,121	—	—	2,700
Annual Growth	(12.6%)	—	—	(18.7%)

Net Income History

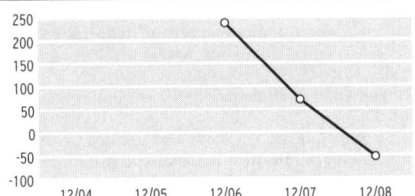

HealthNow New York

HealthNow New York provides health insurance and related services to about 1 million members in more than 50 counties in New York state. The company offers a wide range of Blue Cross and Blue Shield-branded products, including PPO, HMO, POS, and traditional indemnity health plans, primarily through its Blue Cross Blue Shield of Western New York and BlueShield of Northeastern New York subsidiaries. HealthNow also provides resources to help its members maintain and improve their health and avoid the pitfalls associated with unhealthy lifestyles. The company serves businesses large and small as well as individuals.

EXECUTIVES

Chair: John J. Canavan
Vice Chair: Donald K. Boswell, age 57
EVP Operations: Cheryl A. Howe
EVP and CFO: Stephen T. Swift
SVP Major and Administrative Services Only (ASO) Accounts: Lawrence F. Thompson
SVP and Chief Medical Officer: Cynthia Ambres
SVP Operations and General Business: Michael Giaquinto
SVP Human Resources: Thomas A. Fentner
SVP State and Federal Programs: Catherine M. Campbell
VP Healthcare Services: Karen Blount
VP and Chief Actuarial: Gerald Klopfer
VP and CIO: Paul Stoddard
VP Employee Relations: Melissa Tucker
VP and General Counsel: Kenneth J. Sodaro
VP, Controller, and Treasurer: Christopher Leardini

Senior Director Public Relations and Communications: Karen Merkel-liberatore
President, CEO, and Director, HealthNow New York, BlueCross BlueShield of Western New York, and BlueShield of Northeastern New York: Alphonso O'Neil-White

LOCATIONS

HQ: HealthNow New York, Inc.
1901 Main St., Buffalo, NY 14240
Phone: 716-887-6900   **Fax:** 716-887-8981
Web: www.healthnowny.com

COMPETITORS

Aetna
Capital District Physicians' Health Plan
CIGNA
excellus bluecross blueshield
Fallon Community Health Plan
Group Health
Group Health Plan
MVP Health Plan
UnitedHealth Group
WellPoint

HISTORICAL FINANCIALS

Company Type: Not-for-profit

Income Statement

FYE: December 31

	REVENUE ($ mil.)	NET INCOME ($ mil.)	NET PROFIT MARGIN	EMPLOYEES
12/08	2,271	—	—	2,200

Hearst Corporation

Like founder William Randolph Hearst's castle, The Hearst Corporation is sprawling. Through Hearst Newspapers, the company owns some 15 daily newspapers (such as the *San Francisco Chronicle* and the *Houston Chronicle*) and 50 weekly newspapers. Its Hearst Magazines publishes some 15 US consumer magazines (*Cosmopolitan, Esquire*) with nearly 200 international editions. Hearst has broadcasting operations through its Hearst Television subsidiary. Its Hearst Entertainment & Syndication unit includes syndication service King Features, newspaper production service Reed Brennan, and stakes in cable networks (A&E, ESPN). The Hearst Corporation is owned by the Hearst family, but managed by a board of trustees.

Hearst publishes information for automotive, electronic, pharmaceutical, and finance industries through its Hearst Business Media segment. Through its Hearst Interactive Media unit, the company makes strategic investments in online properties such as drugstore.com, and Gather. Hearst's top magazine title, *Cosmopolitan*, is published in about 35 languages and sold in more than 100 countries, making it the largest magazine franchise in the world. The company publishes magazines in the UK through subsidiary The National Magazine Company. Hearst also has interests in over 60 daily and 100 non-daily newspapers owned by MediaNews Group, which include the *Denver Post* and *Salt Lake Tribune*.

In a tough economic climate, especially for the print media world, Hearst has experienced a massive decline in newspaper and magazine advertising and newsstand sales. In 2009 the company published the last print editition of its *Seattle Post-Intelligencer*. It now operates a Web-only version, and is the largest American newspaper to make the leap from print to the exclusively digital format.

However, the company is working hard to offset these challenges by making progress on the digital media front. Hearst in 2008 partnered with MSN to launch online food destination Delish.com. Also that year the company partnered with real estate Web site Zillow.com and other newspaper companies to launch an online real estate advertising network.

The company is also boosting its involvement in television broadcasting; in 2009 it acquired the remaining shares it didn't already own in Hearst Television (formerly Hearst-Argyle). The business operates about 30 TV stations in about two dozen markets. Also in 2009 Hearst announced that its A&E plans to acquire cable network Lifetime Entertainment Services.

CEO Victor F. Ganzi resigned from his position in 2008. Vice chairman (and previous company head) Frank A. Bennack Jr. has reassumed the role of CEO.

Although the company no longer owns Hearst Castle (deeded to the State of California in 1951), it has extensive real estate holdings. Projects include the Hearst Ranch in San Simeon, California, and the Hearst Tower in New York.

Upon his death, William Randolph Hearst left 99% of the company's common stock to two charitable trusts controlled by a 13-member board that includes five family and eight non-family members. The will includes a clause that allows the trustees to disinherit any heir who contests the will.

HISTORY

William Randolph Hearst, son of a California mining magnate, started as a reporter — after being expelled from Harvard in 1884 for playing jokes on professors. In 1887 he became editor of the *San Francisco Examiner*, which his father had obtained as payment for a gambling debt. In 1895 he bought the *New York Morning Journal* and competed against Joseph Pulitzer's *New York World*. The "yellow journalism" resulting from that rivalry characterized American-style reporting at the turn of the century.

Hearst branched into magazines (1903), film (1913), and radio (1928). Also during this time it created the Hearst International News Service (it was sold to E.W. Scripps' United Press in 1958 to form United Press International). By 1935 Hearst was at its peak, with newspapers in 19 cities, the largest syndicate (King Features), international news and photo services, 13 magazines, eight radio stations, and two motion picture companies. Two years later Hearst relinquished control of the company to avoid bankruptcy, selling movie companies, radio stations, magazines, and, later, most of his San Simeon estate. (Hearst's rise and fall inspired the 1941 film *Citizen Kane*.)

In 1948 Hearst became the owner of one of the US's first TV stations, WBAL-TV in Baltimore. When Hearst died in 1951, company veteran Richard Berlin became CEO. Berlin sold off failing newspapers, moved into television, and acquired more magazines.

Frank Bennack, CEO since 1979, expanded the company, acquiring newspapers, publishing firms (notably William Morrow, 1981), TV stations, magazines (*Redbook*, 1982; *Esquire*, 1986), and 20% of cable sports network ESPN (1991). Hearst branched into video via a joint venture with Capital Cities/ABC (1981) and helped launch the Lifetime and Arts & Entertainment cable channels (1984).

In 1992 Hearst brought on board former Federal Communications Commission chairman Alfred Sikes, who quickly moved the company onto the Internet. In 1996 Randolph A. Hearst passed the title of chairman to nephew George Hearst (the last surviving son of the founder, Randolph died in 2000).

The company sold its book publishing operations to News Corp.'s HarperCollins unit in 1999. It also agreed to buy the *San Francisco Chronicle* from rival Chronicle Publishing. That deal was called into question over concerns that the *San Francisco Examiner* would not survive and the city would be left with one major paper. To resolve the issue, the next year Hearst sold the *Examiner* to ExIn (a group of investors affiliated with the Ted Fang family and other owners of the *San Francisco Independent*).

In mid-2002 Victor Ganzi took over as CEO and president following Bennack's retirement from these positions.

Hearst further expanded its potent stable of magazines in 2003 by purchasing *Seventeen* magazine from PRIMEDIA. Hearst also became a major player in yellow page publishing with its 2004 purchase of White Directory Publishers, one of the largest telephone directory companies in the US.

In 2006 Hearst backed MediaNews when that company paid $1 billion to acquire four newspapers (including the *San Jose Mercury News*, the *Contra Costa Times*, and the *St. Paul Pioneer Press)* from McClatchy. The following year Hearst purchased a 31% interest in 47 daily and 37 non-daily newspapers of MediaNews Group.

EXECUTIVES

Chairman: George R. Hearst Jr., age 81
Vice Chairman and CEO: Frank A. Bennack Jr., age 76
CFO: Mitchell Scherzer, age 47
EVP and Deputy Ground Head, Hearst Entertainment and Syndication: George Kliavkoff
SVP Finance, Hearst Newspapers: John M. (Jack) Condon
SVP; President, Entertainment & Syndication: Scott M. Sassa, age 50
SVP; President, Hearst Newspapers: Steven R. Swartz, age 46
SVP Finance and Administration: Ronald J. Doerfler, age 67
SVP and Digital Media, Hearst Newspapers: Lincoln Millstein
SVP, Chief Legal and Development Officer, Director, and Trustee: James M. Asher
VP; EVP and Deputy Group Head, Hearst Business Media: Steven A. Hobbs, age 49
VP; President and CEO, Hearst Magazines International; EVP, Hearst Magazines: George J. Green
VP and Special Assistant to the CEO: Neeraj Khemlani, age 38
President, San Francisco Chronicle and SFGate.com: Mark Adkins
President, Hearst Interactive Media: Kenneth A. Bronfin, age 49
President and CEO, Hearst Television: David J. Barrett, age 61
President, Hearst Business Media: Richard P. Malloch
President, Hearst Magazines: Cathleen P. (Cathie) Black, age 64
Chairman and Editorial Director, SmartMoney: Edwin A. Finn Jr.
Editor-at-Large, Hearst Newspapers and San Francisco Chronicle: Phil Bronstein
Executive Director Corporate Communications; VP Communications, Hearst Magazines: Paul Luthringer

LOCATIONS

HQ: The Hearst Corporation
300 W. 57th St., New York, NY 10019
Phone: 212-649-2000   **Fax:** 212-649-2108
Web: www.hearst.com

PRODUCTS/OPERATIONS

Selected Operations

Hearst Broadcasting
  Hearst Television
Hearst Business Media
  Black Book
  Diversion
  Electronic Products
  First DataBank
  MOTOR Magazine
Hearst Entertainment & Syndication
  A&E Television Networks (joint venture with ABC & NBC)
    A&E
    The Biography Channel
    The History Channel
    History Channel International
  ESPN (20%)
  King Features Syndicate
  Hearst Entertainment (content library and production operations)
  Lifetime Entertainment Services (with Walt Disney Company)
    Lifetime Movie Network
    Lifetime Online
    Lifetime Television
  Reed Brennan Media Associates (production services for newspapers)
Hearst Interactive Media
  Circles (online loyalty marketing programs)
  drugstore.com (online pharmacy site)
  Gather (social networking)
  Hire.com (job site)
Hearst Magazines
  Cosmopolitan
  Country Living
  Esquire
  Good Housekeeping
  Harper's BAZAAR
  House Beautiful
  Marie Claire
  O, The Oprah Magazine (with Harpo)
  Popular Mechanics
  Quick & Simple
  Redbook
  Seventeen
  SmartMoney (with Dow Jones)
  Teen
  Weekend
Hearst Newspapers
  Albany Times Union (New York)
  Houston Chronicle
  Huron Daily Tribune (Michigan)
  Laredo Morning Times (Texas)
  Midland Daily News (Michigan)
  San Antonio Express-News
  San Francisco Chronicle
Other Operations
  Real estate

COMPETITORS

Advance Publications	Liberty Media
Andrews McMeel Universal	McClatchy Company
Bauer Publishing (UK)	McGraw-Hill
Belo Corp.	Meredith Corporation
Bertelsmann	New York Times
Bloomberg L.P.	News Corp.
Cox Enterprises	Reader's Digest
Dennis Publishing	Reed Elsevier Group
Disney	Rodale
E. W. Scripps	Time Warner
Freedom Communications	Tribune Company
Gannett	Viacom
IPC Group	Washington Post
Lagardère	Yellow Book USA

HISTORICAL FINANCIALS

Company Type: Private

Income Statement				FYE: December 31
	ESTIMATED REVENUE ($ mil.)	NET INCOME ($ mil.)	NET PROFIT MARGIN	EMPLOYEES
12/08	4,810	—	—	20,000
12/07	4,380	—	—	17,070
12/06	4,520	—	—	17,062
12/05	4,550	—	—	17,016
12/04	4,000	—	—	16,667
Annual Growth	4.7%	—	—	4.7%

Revenue History

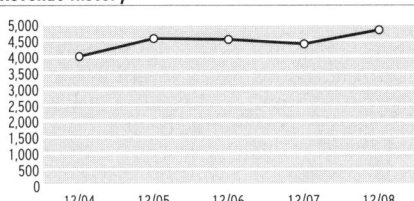

H-E-B

The Muzak bounces between Tejano and country, and the warm tortillas and marinated fajita meat are big sellers at H. E. Butt Grocery (H-E-B). Texas' largest private company and the #1 food retailer in South and Central Texas, H-E-B owns more than 300 supermarkets, including a growing number of large (70,000 sq. ft.) gourmet Central Market stores in major metropolitan areas and 80-plus smaller (24,000-30,000 sq. ft.) Pantry Foods stores, often in more rural areas. H-E-B also has about 30 upscale and discount stores in Mexico. The 100-year-old company is owned by the Butt family, which founded H-E-B in Kerrville, Texas, in 1905.

To cement its #1 spot in Central Texas and fend off Wal-Mart, which is expanding its supercenter presence in the region, H-E-B has begun opening huge H-E-B Plus stores, which range in size from 109,000 to nearly 200,000 sq. ft. and devote about 40% of their space to nonfood items, including casual furniture, cooking equipment, and electronics. The Wal-Mart-sized stores have opened in the San Antonio and Austin markets, where H-E-B has acquired stores from ailing rival Albertsons to bolster its position. H-E-B now operates some 45 stores in fast-growing Central Texas.

Since entering the Houston market in 2001, the Texas grocery chain has invested heavily to open about a dozen large combination food and drug stores, while closing some of its smaller Pantry supermarkets in the area. To gain an edge on its competition, H-E-B is incorporating aspects of its upscale Central Market format, including cafes, into the new Houston stores. To that end, in mid-July 2006 H-E-B opened its largest store in the Houston area: a 125,000-sq.-ft. combination H-E-B food and drug store and Central Market hybrid.

H-E-B currently operates eight Central Market stores in five Texas markets. The Texas grocery chain's newest format, Mi Tienda, debuted in Pasadena, Texas, in October 2006. The Hispanic-themed store features a Mexican-style bakery and other amenities designed to appeal to Latino shoppers.

H-E-B is familiar with the tastes of Latinos, as about half of its market is Hispanic. South of the border, the grocery company's Mexican subsidiary Supermercados Internacionales HEB has moved into Monterrey's more affluent neighborhoods, with stores operating under the H-E-B banner and the Economax name (a discount supermarket format).

More than 40% of the H-E-B stores have gasoline outlets, and about 190 have pharmacies, which are being remodeled to include drive-through windows and enlarged health and beauty aid selections. The retailer recently opened its first Payless Express shoe department in a Laredo store and has plans to open more.

In the fall of 2006 H-E-B launched a program to fill prescriptions for 500 generic drugs for $5 each. The move is an attempt to match rival Wal-Mart's $4 generic drug program. The company moved further into the medical arena with the introduction of in-store medical clinics run by RediClinic in select H-E-B locations.

The Texas grocer continues to build its H-E-B store brands. It has introduced a new line of baby products and extended its line of Central Market Organics and All Natural products to about 150 H-E-B stores.

HISTORY

Charles C. Butt and his wife, Florence, moved to Kerrville, in the Texas Hill Country, in 1905, hoping the climate would help Charles' tuberculosis. Since Charles was unable to work, Florence began peddling groceries door-to-door for A&P. Later that year she opened a grocery store, C. C. Butt Grocery. However, Florence, a dyed-in-the-wool Baptist, refused to carry such articles of vice as tobacco. The family lived over the store, and all three of the Butt children worked there. The youngest son, Howard, began working in the business full-time in his teens and took it over after WWI.

By adopting modern marketing methods such as price tagging (and deciding to sell tobacco), the Butts earned enough to begin expanding. In 1927 Howard opened a second store in Del Rio in West Texas, and over the next few years he opened other stores in the Rio Grande Valley. The company gained patron loyalty by making minimal markups on staples. It moved from Kerrville to Harlingen, Texas, in 1928 (it moved to Corpus Christi, Texas, in 1940 and to San Antonio in 1985).

The company began manufacturing foods in the 1930s and invested in farms and orchards. In 1935 Howard (who had adopted the middle name Edward) rechristened the chain the H. E. Butt Grocery Company (H-E-B). He put his three children to work for the company, grooming son Charles for the top spot after Howard Jr. took over the H. E. Butt Foundation from his mother.

While other chains updated their stores during the 1960s, H-E-B plodded. Howard Sr. resigned in 1971 and Charles took over, bringing in fresh management. But this was not enough. Studies showed that the reasons for its lagging market share were its refusal to stock alcohol and its policy of Sunday closing; it abandoned these policies in 1976. It also drastically undercut competitors, driving many independents out of business. H-E-B emerged the dominant player in its major markets.

H-E-B's first superstore, a 56,000-sq.-ft. facility offering general merchandise, photofinishing, and a pharmacy, opened in Austin, Texas, in 1979, and the company concentrated on building more superstores over the next decade.

In 1988 H-E-B launched its H-E-B Pantry division, which remodeled and built smaller supermarkets, mostly in rural Texas towns. Three years later it launched another format, the 93,000-sq.-ft. H-E-B Marketplace in San Antonio, which included restaurants. It also opened the upscale Central Market in Austin with extensive cheese, produce, and wine departments in 1994 (it later opened similar stores in San Antonio, Houston, and Dallas).

Chairman and CEO Charles retired as president in 1996, and James Clingman became the first non-family member to assume the office. That year H-E-B opened its first non-Texas store in Lake Charles, Louisiana. In 1997 it opened its first Mexican store in an affluent area of Monterrey, followed the next year by a discount supermarket there under the Economax banner. In 2001 H-E-B opened its first store — a Central Market — in the Dallas/Fort Worth area.

In 2002 the company also acquired five San Antonio stores from Albertsons and reopened them as H-E-B stores in August and September. Clingman retired in 2003.

In early 2004 H-E-B opened its first H-E-B Plus store in San Juan, Texas. In 2005 the Texas grocer celebrated its centennial.

EXECUTIVES

Chairman and CEO: Charles C. Butt, age 68
President: Robert D. (Bob) Loeffler
COO: Craig Boyan
CIO: Gavin L. Gallagher
EVP, Chief Merchant, Food Manufacturing, Procurement, and Merchandising: Steve Harper
EVP, Merchandising and Procurement and CFO: Martin Otto
SVP, Real Estate Facilities Alliance and Services: Todd Piland
SVP and General Merchandise Manager, San Antonio Region: Greg Souquette
SVP, General Manager, Central Texas: Jeff Thomas
SVP, Supply Chain and Logistics: Kenneth (Ken) Allen
SVP, Operations, Central Market, and Dallas-Fort Worth Region: Stephen Butt
SVP, Procurement and Merchandising Strategy: Harvey McCoy
Group VP, Manufacturing: Bob McCullough
Group VP, Marketing, Advertising, and Branding: Cory J. Basso
VP, Petroleum Marketing: James Aulds
VP, Innovation; VP, Procurement/Merchandising, Central Market: John Campbell
VP, Quality Assurance and Environmental Affairs: William (Bill) Fry, age 63
VP, Information Solutions: Shawn Sedate
VP, Public Affairs and Diversity: Winell Herron
VP, Meat Merchandising, Procurement, and Product Development: Randy Vaclavik
President, H-E-B Houston and Central Market Stores: Scott McClelland, age 52
Treasurer: Megan Rooney
Manager, Corporate Community Relations: Pablo Rodriguez

LOCATIONS

HQ: H. E. Butt Grocery Company
646 S. Main Ave., San Antonio, TX 78204
Phone: 210-938-8000   **Fax:** 210-938-8169
Web: www.heb.com

PRODUCTS/OPERATIONS

Selected Private Label Brands

Central Market All Natural
Central Market Organics
H-E-B Brand
Hill Country Fare

Selected Store Formats

Central Market (about 70,000 sq. ft., upscale supermarkets with expanded organic and gourmet foods; located in major metropolitan markets)
Economax (discount supermarkets, Mexico)
Gas 'N Go (gas stations)
H-E-B (large supermarkets)
H-E-B Marketplace (large supermarkets with specialty departments)
H-E-B Pantry (24,000-30,000 sq. ft., no-frills supermarkets with basic groceries; often located in rural or suburban areas)
H-E-B Plus (109,000-200,000 sq. ft., extensive nonfood sections)

COMPETITORS

7-Eleven
Brookshire Brothers
Chedraui
Comerci
Costco Wholesale
CVS Caremark
Fiesta Mart
Foodarama Supermarkets
Gerland's Food Fair
Grupo Corvi
IGA
Kmart
Kroger
Minyard Group
Randall's
Soriana
Target
Walgreen
Wal-Mart
Whole Foods

HISTORICAL FINANCIALS

Company Type: Private

Income Statement

FYE: October 31

	REVENUE ($ mil.)	NET INCOME ($ mil.)	NET PROFIT MARGIN	EMPLOYEES
10/08	15,000	—	—	68,000
10/07	13,500	—	—	63,000
10/06	12,400	—	—	60,000
10/05	11,500	—	—	60,000
10/04	10,500	—	—	60,000
Annual Growth	9.3%	—	—	3.2%

Revenue History

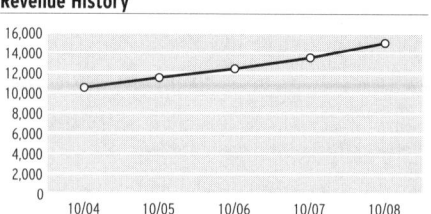

Heico Companies

Heico Companies specializes in buying distressed companies and turning them around. The firm, which typically invests for the long haul, owns interests in about 40 companies, several of them Rust Belt-based manufacturing concerns that founder Michael Heisley acquired during the 1980s. Many were bankrupt when they were bought. Heico's holdings include Davis Wire, Canadian steelmaker Ivaco, and heavy industrial equipment maker Pettibone. Heico also has interests in companies in the plastics, food, and telecommunications industries. Heisley, who launched Heico in 1979 with only $150,000, also controls the NBA's Memphis Grizzlies but is looking to sell his stake.

EXECUTIVES

Chairman Emeritus: Michael E. Heisley, age 68
Chairman: Emily Heisley Stoeckel
President and CEO: E. A. (El) Roskovensky
EVP and CFO: Lawrence G. Wolski

LOCATIONS

HQ: Heico Companies LLC
70 W. Madison St., Ste. 5600, Chicago, IL 60602
Phone: 312-419-8220   **Fax:** 312-419-9417

COMPETITORS

Blackstone Group
CD&R
HM Capital Partners
KKR
KPS Capital Partners
Leonard Green
Thomas H. Lee Partners
TPG
Wingate Partners

HISTORICAL FINANCIALS

Company Type: Private

Income Statement

FYE: December 31

	ESTIMATED REVENUE ($ mil.)	NET INCOME ($ mil.)	NET PROFIT MARGIN	EMPLOYEES
12/08	2,000	—	—	8,000
12/07	2,170	—	—	8,000
12/06	2,100	—	—	8,000
12/05	2,500	—	—	11,000
12/04	1,750	—	—	9,500
Annual Growth	3.4%	—	—	(4.2%)

Revenue History

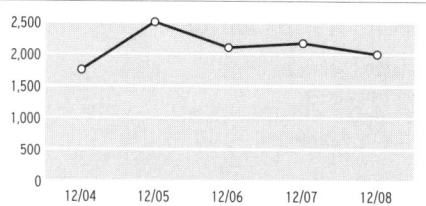

Heifer Project

It's not just a handout; it's a new way of life. Heifer Project International (known as Heifer International) runs more than 860 projects that help millions of impoverished families become self-sufficient. Recipients are located in 125 countries around the world, including 28 US states. The non-profit organization provides more than 25 different kinds of breeding livestock and other animals (bees, rabbits, ducks) that can be used for food, income, or plowing power, in addition to training in sustainable agriculture techniques. In exchange, the family agrees to pass on not only the animals' first female offspring to another needy family, but their knowledge, too.

In June 2009 Heifer International laid off 20% of its staff in the US and abroad. The charity citied declining donations as a result of the deep recession in the US as the reason for the layoffs. In March its board voted to freeze salaries.

In early 2008 Heifer International received a four-year more than $42 million grant from the Bill & Melinda Gates Foundation. The grant, which is the largest single grant to the foundation in its history, was dog-eared to fund a project to help poor rural East African farmers double their incomes by increasing the production of high-quality raw milk they can sell to dairies.

Despite the noteworthy donation, Heifer International saw a decline in donations in 2008 and continuing into 2009. As a result, the group initiated some cost-cutting measures in 2008, but that proved to be a Band-Aid for the group. In March 2009, it took more drastic measures and decided that it would lay off employees.

Heifer International was established in 1944 by Dan West who had worked helping feed the hungry during the Spanish Civil War.

EXECUTIVES

Chair: Stephen A. Mondora
Vice Chair: C. Douglas Smith
President and CEO: Jo Luck, age 68
COO: Steve Denne
EVP Global Learning and Action: Tanya Wright
EVP Marketing and Resource Development:
Steve Stirling
EVP Programs and Secretary: James (Jim) De Vries
EVP Finance and Administration, CFO, and Treasurer:
James Neal
Senior Director Marketing: Mike Matchett
Director Finance: Kit Smith
Auditors: BKD, LLP

LOCATIONS

HQ: Heifer Project International
1 World Ave., Little Rock, AR 72202
Phone: 800-422-0474   **Fax:** 501-907-2902
Web: www.heifer.org

Henkels & McCoy

When utilities, communications companies, or governments need the real McCoy to install or repair their transmission networks, they can call on specialty contractor Henkels & McCoy (H&M). The firm provides engineering, construction, and network development services globally. H&M also installs aerial and underground electrical distribution systems, gas transmission lines, and fiber-optic networks on electric transmission towers or along railroad rights-of-way. It has some 80 offices throughout the US. John Henkels Jr. and John McCoy founded H&M in Philadelphia in 1923 as a tree-trimming and landscaping firm. Employees and the Henkels family own H&M.

EXECUTIVES

Vice Chairman: Kenneth L. Rose
President and CEO: T. Roderick (Rod) Henkels
EVP and COO: Jonathon C. Schoff
SVP: William H. Boell
VP and CFO: Robert J. Delark
VP, General Counsel, and Secretary:
Christine A. Crawford
VP and Director, Power Operations: Ronald G. Jones
VP Market Planning and Business Development:
James A. Mulhern
Treasurer: Joseph C. Paulits IV
Manager Marketing Communications: Paul DeMara
Auditors: Ernst & Young

LOCATIONS

HQ: Henkels & McCoy, Inc.
985 Jolly Rd., Blue Bell, PA 19422
Phone: 215-283-7600   **Fax:** 215-283-7659
Web: www.henkels.com

Henkels & McCoy has about 80 offices throughout the US.

PRODUCTS/OPERATIONS

Selected Services

Communications
    Customized networks
    Detailed proposal creation
    Labor management
    Material logistics
    Status reports
Electric Transmission
    Aerial distribution
    Extra high voltage (EHV)
    Site analysis
    Storm restoration
    Substations
    Switching stations
    Underground distribution
Engineering
    Design
    Planning
    Project management
    Staffing
Gas Transmission
    Engineering
    Maintenance
    Pipeline installation
    Service line installation
General Construction
    Demolition
    Electrical systems
    Engineering
    Exterior finishes
    Foundations
    HVAC systems
    Interior finishes
    Mechanical systems
    Site preparation
    Steel erection

Henry Ford Health System

In 1915 automaker Henry Ford founded the hospital that forms the cornerstone of southeastern Michigan's not-for-profit Henry Ford Health System (HFHS), a hospital network that is also involved in medical research and education. The system's half-dozen hospitals — including the flagship Henry Ford Hospital, as well as Henry Ford Wyandotte Hospital and mental health facility Kingswood Hospital — hold more than 2,200 beds. HFHS also operates a 1,000-doctor-strong medical group, as well as nursing homes, hospice, and a home health care network. The system's Health Alliance Plan of Michigan provides managed care and health insurance to about 540,000 members.

Along with its hospitals, large and small, the system also operates more than 25 medical centers, and maintains partnerships with community health services.

While it is already far and away the largest health system in southeastern Michigan, HFHS has continued to grow. When Bon Secours Health System pulled out of Michigan in 2007, HFHS bought up its stake in upscale Cottage Hospital, which the two companies had held in a joint venture. That same year HFHS acquired full ownership of St. Joseph's Healthcare, a 435-bed hospital system headquartered in Clinton Township that it had previously operated through a joint venture with Trinity Health. HFHS subsequently changed the acquired system's name to Henry Ford Macomb Hospitals.

Fresh growth has also come in the form of new construction: HFHS built and opened a 300-bed acute care facility in West Bloomfield in 2009.

Affiliated with Wayne State University's School of Medicine, the health system is a leading education and research center, with ongoing research in areas such as stroke, heart disease, cancer, and diabetes. Wayne State and HFHS have agreed to expand their affiliation by increasing the number of medical students who train at Henry Ford, working together on research projects, and opening a new research center.

EXECUTIVES

Chair: Gary C. Valade
President Emeritus: Gail L. Warden, age 70
President, CEO, and Trustee: Nancy M. Schlichting, age 55

EVP and COO: Robert G. (Bob) Riney
EVP and Trustee; CEO, Henry Ford Medical Group:
 Mark A. Kelley
SVP and CFO: David E. Mazurkiewicz
SVP and Chief Revenue Officer: Stephen Hathaway
SVP Pathology and Laboratory Medicine:
 Richard J. Zarbo
SVP; President and CEO, Health Alliance Plan:
 William R. Alvin
SVP Marketing and Public Relations: Rose M. Glenn
SVP and Chief Human Resources Officer:
 Kathleen M. (Kathy) Oswald
SVP and CIO: Arthur A. Gross
SVP Clinical Affairs; Chairman, Department of Internal Medicine, Henry Ford Medical Group:
 John Popovich Jr.
SVP Strategic Business Development:
 William R. (Bill) Schramm
SVP Philanthropy: Gary E. Rounding
Chair, Biostatistics and Research Epidemiology:
 Christine Cole Johnson
SVP and Chief Quality Officer; Chief Medical Officer, Henry Ford Hospital: William A. Conway
VP Governance and Secretary: Edith L. Eisenmann
Chief Nursing Officer, Henry Ford Hospital and Health Network: Veronica M. Hall
Chief Diversity Officer: Randy D. Walker

LOCATIONS

HQ: Henry Ford Health System
 1 Ford Place, Detroit, MI 48202
Phone: 313-876-8700   **Fax:** 313-876-9243
Web: www.henryfordhealth.org

PRODUCTS/OPERATIONS

Selected Operations

Hospitals
 Henry Ford Cottage Hospital
 Henry Ford Hospital
 Henry Ford Macomb Hospitals
 Henry Ford West Bloomfield Hospital
 Henry Ford Wyandotte Hospital
 Kingswood Hospital (mental health care)
Other
 Greenfield Health Systems (dialysis provider)
 Health Alliance Plan of Michigan (health plan)
 Henry Ford Continuing Care (nursing homes)
 Henry Ford Health Products (medical supply retailer)
 Henry Ford Home Health Care
 Henry Ford Medical Group (physician's group)
 Hospices of Henry Ford

COMPETITORS

Blue Cross Blue Shield of Michigan
Crittenton Hospital
Detroit Medical Center
Garden City Hospital
HealthPlus of Michigan
McLaren Heath Care
OmniCare Health Plan
St. John Health
Total Health Care
Trinity Health (Novi)
University of Michigan Health System
William Beaumont Hospital

HISTORICAL FINANCIALS

Company Type: Not-for-profit

Income Statement

FYE: December 31

	REVENUE ($ mil.)	NET INCOME ($ mil.)	NET PROFIT MARGIN	EMPLOYEES
12/08	3,690	9	0.2%	21,500
12/07	3,470	106	3.0%	17,489
12/06	3,250	135	4.2%	16,000
12/05	3,049	112	3.7%	14,900
12/04	2,846	16	0.6%	13,000
Annual Growth	6.7%	(14.6%)	—	13.4%

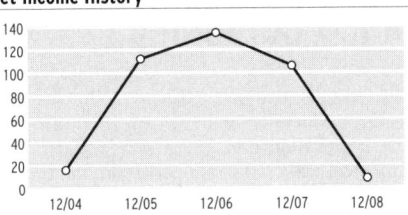

Hensel Phelps Construction

Hensel Phelps Construction builds it all, from the courthouse to the big house. The employee-owned general contractor provides a full range of development, preconstruction, and construction services for commercial, institutional, and government projects throughout the US and abroad. Its project portfolio includes prisons, airports, arenas, laboratories, government complexes, offices, and more. Major clients have included the US Army Corps of Engineers, IBM, United Airlines, The University of Texas, NASA, and Whole Foods. Hensel Phelps founded the eponymous company as a homebuilder in 1937.

Hansel Phelps has eight regional offices throughout the US. The company operates internationally, most often for US federal projects but also for foreign governments and private enterprises.

EXECUTIVES

Chairman and CEO: Jerry L. Morgensen
President and COO: Jeffrey (Jeff) Wenaas
EVP, Eastern Division: Mark T. Baugh
EVP, Pacific Division: Wayne S. Lindholm
EVP, Southern District: Michael J. Choutka
EVP, Central Division: Edwin L. Calhoun
VP International District: Ronald G. (Ron) Norby
VP and General Counsel: Eric L. Wilson
VP Finance and CFO: Stephen J. (Steve) Carrico
Auditors: KPMG LLP

LOCATIONS

HQ: Hensel Phelps Construction Co.
 420 6th Ave., Greeley, CO 80632
Phone: 970-352-6565   **Fax:** 970-352-9311
Web: www.henselphelps.com

PRODUCTS/OPERATIONS

Selected Services

Construction
 Construction waste management
 Quality control
 Scheduling
Post-construction
 Certificate of occupancy
 Commissiong and warranty programs
 LEED project certification
Preconstruction
 Design management
 Phasing plans
 Regulatory investigation
 Value engineering

COMPETITORS

Balfour Construction	McCarthy Building
C.F. Jordan	PCL Employees Holdings
CH2M HILL	Rooney Holdings
Clark Construction Group	Skanska USA Building
Fluor	Turner Corporation
Gilbane	Tutor Perini
Hunt Construction	Walbridge Aldinger
Jacobs Engineering	Walsh Group
KBR	Whiting-Turner
M. A. Mortenson	

HISTORICAL FINANCIALS

Company Type: Private

Income Statement

FYE: December 31

	REVENUE ($ mil.)	NET INCOME ($ mil.)	NET PROFIT MARGIN	EMPLOYEES
12/08	3,337	—	—	2,600
12/07	2,520	—	—	2,727
12/06*	2,130	—	—	2,534
5/05	1,728	—	—	2,324
5/04	1,800	—	—	2,500
Annual Growth	16.7%	—	—	1.0%

*Fiscal year change

Revenue History

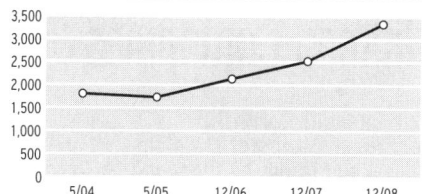

Hexion Specialty Chemicals

Hexion Specialty Chemicals is the world's largest thermosetting resins (or thermosets) maker, ahead of Georgia-Pacific. Thermosets add a desired quality (heat resistance, gloss, adhesion, etc.) to a number of different paints and adhesives. Hexion also is among the largest makers of formaldehyde and other forest product resins, epoxy resins, and raw materials for coatings and inks. In 2007 the company agreed to buy Huntsman for $10.5 billion. However, amid the general economic turmoil of 2008, Hexion pulled out of the transaction toward the end of that year. Apollo Management controls more than 90% of Hexion.

The company's business is divided into four segments. The Epoxy and Phenolic Resins unit is the largest, accounting for nearly half of sales. It sells its products to the auto, aerospace, electronics, and oil and gas industries. The next largest is the Formaldehyde and Forest Products Resins segment, whose products go into lumber, plywood, particle board, herbicides, and catalysts. The Coatings and Inks segment includes acrylic and polyester resins, versatic acids, and resins and additives for inks. These products are used in paints and coatings for the automotive, marine, construction, and maintenance industries as well as in printing inks.

The final unit is the company's smallest. The Performance Products segment makes encapsulated substrates used for oil field services as well as in foundries.

The offer for Huntsman came soon after LyondellBasell had bid $9.5 billion for Huntsman. That company eventually backed down, and Huntsman and Hexion agreed to the deal. In the months after the agreement, though, Huntsman's earnings continued to dip and the credit market continued to tank. Those factors led Hexion and Apollo to conclude that the combination of the two companies was no longer viable. They filed suit to break the agreement in mid-2008; Huntsman didn't agree with Hexion and Apollo's conclusion and filed a suit of its own, naming Apollo, rather than Hexion, as its target. The judgment, when it came, favored Huntsman, largely because Huntsman had backed out of the LyondellBasell deal to go with Apollo and Hexion. As a result, Apollo contributed $540 million to Hexion to help it finance the closing of the deal, but it wasn't enough. Toward the end of 2008, Huntsman, mollified perhaps by a substantial break-up fee, terminated the agreement, and the companies went their separate ways.

Apollo had formed Hexion in 2005 when it combined the former Borden Chemical, Resolution Performance Products, Resolution Specialty Materials, and Bakelite. All these companies had been owned by Apollo prior to Hexion's founding.

EXECUTIVES

Chairman, President, CEO, and Director: Craig O. Morrison, age 53, $1,712,242 total compensation
Vice Chairman: Marvin O. Schlanger, age 60
EVP; President, Forest Products Division: Dale N. Plante, age 51
EVP; President, Epoxy and Phenolic Division: Joseph P. (Jody) Bevilaqua, age 53, $848,967 total compensation
EVP; President, Coatings and Inks Division: Peter J. Hartland
EVP, CFO, and Director: William H. (Bill) Carter, age 55, $1,344,391 total compensation
EVP; President, Coatings and Inks: Sarah R. Coffin, age 56, $519,326 total compensation
EVP Procurement: Nathan E. Fisher, age 43
EVP Human Resources: Judith A. (Judy) Sonnett, age 52, $446,474 total compensation
EVP, Asia: Joseph Chan, age 53
EVP and General Counsel: Mary Ann Jorgenson, age 67
EVP Environmental Health and Safety: Richard L. Monty, age 61
SVP Finance and Treasurer: George F. Knight, age 52
VP and CIO: Kevin W. McGuire, age 48
VP Public Affairs: Peter F. (Pete) Loscocco
Director Investor Relations: John Kompa
Auditors: PricewaterhouseCoopers LLP

LOCATIONS

HQ: Hexion Specialty Chemicals, Inc.
180 E. Broad St., Columbus, OH 43215
Phone: 614-225-4000
Web: www.hexionchem.com

2008 Sales

	$ mil.	% of total
US	2,557	42
The Netherlands	1,222	20
Germany	494	8
Canada	276	5
Other countries	1,544	25
Total	**6,093**	**100**

PRODUCTS/OPERATIONS

2008 Sales

	$ mil.	% of total
Epoxy & Phenolic Resins	2,432	40
Formaldehyde & Forest Products Resins	2,033	34
Coatings & Inks	1,248	20
Performance Products	380	6
Total	**6,093**	**100**

COMPETITORS

Akzo Nobel	Dynea
Arizona Chemical	ExxonMobil Chemical
Arkema US	Georgia-Pacific
Ashland Inc.	MeadWestvaco
BASF SE	Mitsui Chemicals
Celanese	Nan Ya Plastics
DIC Corporation	Reichhold
Dow Chemical	

HISTORICAL FINANCIALS

Company Type: Private

Income Statement

FYE: December 31

	REVENUE ($ mil.)	NET INCOME ($ mil.)	NET PROFIT MARGIN	EMPLOYEES
12/08	6,093	(1,190)	—	6,800
12/07	5,810	(65)	—	6,400
12/06	5,205	(109)	—	6,900
12/05	4,470	(87)	—	7,000
12/04	2,019	(114)	—	6,900
Annual Growth	31.8%	—	—	(0.4%)

Net Income History

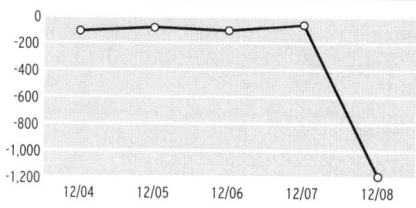

Highmark Inc.

Highmark has staked its claim as the largest health insurer in the Keystone state. A licensee of the Blue Cross and Blue Shield Association, the not-for-profit firm covers some 4 million people in central and western Pennsylvania, as well as the Lehigh Valley. It serves another 800,000 customers in West Virginia and other areas of Pennsylvania through affiliations and partnerships with other insurers, and it provides administrative and network-access services nationally. In addition, Highmark sells Medicare Advantage and prescription drug plans to seniors in both states. Other subsidiaries (not operating under the BCBS license) provide dental insurance, vision care, and other products and services nationwide.

Outside of its core Pennsylvania service areas (served through wholly owned subsidiaries Highmark Blue Cross Blue Shield, Keystone Health Plan West, and Highmark Blue Shield), the company manages the benefits of self-insured employers and provides third-party administrative and claims processing services to other BCBS plans.

After nearly two years of planning, Highmark and its Philadelphia-based neighbor Independence Blue Cross cancelled their plans to merge in early 2009, citing concerns that the deal would not receive regulatory approval. The merger would have created a massive health insurer covering more than half of Pennsylvania's population and was the subject of harsh criticism from Pennsylvania politicians, regulators, and other parties concerned that such a mega-company would stifle competition.

Despite the canceled merger plans, Highmark continues to co-market Blue-branded coverage in southeastern Pennsylvania with Independence Blue Cross under a previous collaboration agreement. The company operates similarly in the northeastern part of the state through a partnership with Blue Cross of Northeastern Pennsylvania. It works through affiliate Mountain State Blue Cross Blue Shield (in which it owns a controlling stake) to offer health plans in West Virginia.

Highmark plans to expand its health insurance operations by strengthening partnerships with other insurance companies and by increasing involvement in government health programs such as Medicare. It is also increasing its health plan offerings for individual consumers. The company is experiencing strong growth in its dental and vision care businesses, as well.

Highmark provides an impressive array of specialty services through its non-Blue subsidiaries. In the optical arena, subsidiaries include managed vision care organization Davis Vision, the Eye Care Centers of America chain of retail vision care centers, and eyewear manufacturer Viva. HM Insurance Group offers employer health risk solutions, such as stop-loss insurance and a limited-benefit medical plan, while United Concordia Companies provides dental coverage to around 8 million members across the US.

EXECUTIVES

Chairman: J. Robert Baum
President, CEO, and Director: Kenneth R. (Ken) Melani
EVP, CFO, Chief Administrative Officer, and Treasurer: Nanette P. (Nan) DeTurk
EVP Health Services: Deborah Rice
EVP Government Services: David M. O'Brien
EVP Subsidiary Business: Daniel J. (Dan) Lebish
EVP, Chief Marketing Officer, and Chief Strategy Officer: Thomas W. Kerr
EVP and Chief Medical Officer, HVHC, Inc.: Jeff Smith
SVP and Chief Audit Executive: Elizabeth A. Farbacher
SVP, Corporate Secretary, and General Counsel: Gary R. Truitt
SVP Community Affairs: Evan Frazier
President Operations, Mountain State Blue Cross Blue Shield: J. Fred Earley II
President and CEO, HVHC, Inc. and Chairman and CEO, Eye Care Centers of America: David L. Holmberg, age 50
Auditors: PricewaterhouseCoopers LLP

LOCATIONS

HQ: Highmark Inc.
Fifth Avenue Place, 120 5th Ave.
Pittsburgh, PA 15222
Phone: 412-544-7000   **Fax:** 412-544-8368
Web: www.highmark.com/hmk2

PRODUCTS/OPERATIONS

2008 Revenue

	$ mil.	% of total
Premiums	11,020	84
Vision revenue	1,077	8
Management services	626	5
Net investment income	160	1
Net realized gain (loss) on investments	(79)	—
Other	198	2
Total	**13,002**	**100**

Selected Subsidiaries and Affiliates

Blue Cross Blue Shield Licensee Companies
Highmark Blue Cross Blue Shield (health care plans, western Pennsylvania)
Highmark Blue Shield (health care plans, central Pennsylvania and the Lehigh Valley; also operates through partnerships in northeastern and southeastern Pennsylvania)
Highmark Health Insurance Company (Medicare Advantage plans, West Virginia)
Highmark Senior Resources, Inc. (Medicare Part D prescription drug plans, Pennsylvania and West Virginia)
Keystone Health Plan West, Inc. (HMO and Medicare Advantage plans, western Pennsylvania)
Mountain State Blue Cross & Blue Shield (controlled affiliate; health care plans, West Virginia)
Other Subsidiaries
Davis Vision, Inc. (vision insurance and ophthalmic laboratories)
Eye Care Centers of America, Inc. (retail vision care centers)
Gateway Health Plan (Medical Assistance coverage)
Highmark Foundation (community health charitable organization)
Highmark Medicare Services, Inc. (Medicare claims administration and financial management)
HM Insurance Group (stop-loss insurance, HMO reinsurance, and other health risk solutions)
Industrial Medical Consultants (physician workforce productivity services)
United Concordia Companies, Inc. (dental insurance)
Viva International Group (eyewear manufacturing)

COMPETITORS

Aetna
American United Mutual
AmeriChoice of Pennsylvania
Blue Cross of Northeastern Pennsylvania
Capital BlueCross
CIGNA
DeCare Dental
Delta Dental Plans
Dental Benefit Providers
DentaQuest
Emerging Vision
Geisinger Health System
Genworth Financial
HealthAmerica
Humana
Independence Blue Cross
Independence Holding
LensCrafters
National Vision
Pearle Vision
UPMC
U.S. Vision
Wal-Mart

HISTORICAL FINANCIALS

Company Type: Not-for-profit

Income Statement

FYE: December 31

	REVENUE ($ mil.)	NET INCOME ($ mil.)	NET PROFIT MARGIN	EMPLOYEES
12/08	13,002	94	0.7%	19,000
12/07	12,353	375	3.0%	18,500
12/06	11,084	398	3.6%	18,500
12/05	9,847	342	3.5%	12,000
12/04	9,118	311	3.4%	11,000
Annual Growth	**9.3%**	**(25.8%)**	**—**	**14.6%**

Net Income History

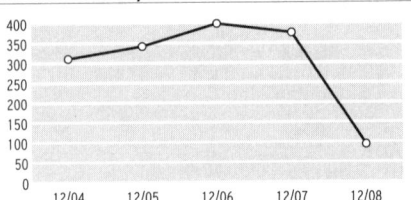

Hillman Companies

If you were to *label* it, the *key* to success — according to distributor The Hillman Companies — is doing things by the *numbers*. Operating through subsidiary The Hillman Group, it distributes small hardware such as fasteners, keys, signs, letters, numbers, and identification tags to home centers, hardware stores, pet stores, and grocery stores. Hillman distributes items from about 21,000 retail locations in over 58 countries worldwide. It also makes and distributes its own key duplication and engraving systems. Services offered include design and installation of merchandising systems and maintenance of appropriate in-store inventory levels. Customers include Wal-Mart, Home Depot, Lowe's, Sears, and PetSmart.

Hillman maintains a major presence in Canada, the Caribbean, Mexico, and Central and South America. Its fastener selection includes indoor and outdoor construction screws and a complete line of anchors and anchoring devices. It also offers rope and chain products and accessories, keys and key accessories, picture hanging accessories, and over 2,000 specialty items, ranging from furniture hardware and electrical accessories to plumbing, marine items, and merchandising displays.

In 2009 the company announced it would be closing its distribution center in New York, but said the impact of the facility closing was not material to company operations. The orders processed from this facility will be shifted to existing facilities in Ohio and Wisconsin. Hillman utilizes a third-party logistics provider to warehouse and ship customer orders in Mexico.

Fasteners still remain the core of Hillman's business. Some of the company's latest offerings include WallDog, which is an all-steel, one-piece screw anchor that features high-profile threads for easy fastening into drywall and masonry base materials. Its chrome fastener line is offered primarily to franchise and independent hardware stores, and is growing in popularity with the automotive and motorcycle industries.

Letters, Numbers and Signs includes utilitarian product lines that target both the homeowner and commercial user. Products include individual and/or packaged letters, numbers, signs, safety related products, driveway markers, and sign accessories.

Hillman markets its key-duplication system under brand names Axxess Precision the Hillman Key Program. The company also offers PC+Computerized Code Cutter, which is the only US-manufactured code cutter that can generate a key by tracing an original key. CreditCard Keys are made from DuPont Delrin plastic and serve as emergency spare keys. It also markets key accessories such as the Key Light, Valet KeyChain, Fanatix key identifiers, key coils, and key clips. Key Mates includes key chains, tags, lights, floats, holders, whistles, and other complementary items.

Engraving products offers Quick-Tag, which is a consumer-operated vending system that custom engraves and dispenses specialty products such as pet identification tags (VetScribe and PetScribe), military-style I.D. tags, holiday ornaments, and luggage tags. QuickScribe is a personalized engraving system via a touch-screen process.

The company's residential Builder's Hardware segment sells its newly developed product line to Canadian Tire, a Canadian retailer with 475 stores. The segment offers a variety of common household items such as coat hooks, door stops, hinges, gate latches, hasps, and decorative hardware. Hillman also offers a Faucet Repair Center display, which makes consumer guides and parts available in one location.

In late 2007 Hillman expanded its presence in Florida by purchasing All Points Industries, which specializes in distributing fasteners for hurricane protection. It plans to continue future growth through strategic acquisitions in existing or new markets.

Code Hennessy & Simmons owns almost 50% of the company's voting stock; the Ontario Teachers' Pension Plan controls about 28%; Hillman brothers, Max (Hillman Group CEO) and Richard (Hillman Group president), together hold about 8%.

EXECUTIVES

Chairman: Andrew W. Code, age 51
President, The Hillman Group:
Richard P. (Rick) Hillman, age 60,
$389,459 total compensation
CFO and Secretary; VP, CFO, and Secretary, The Hillman Group: James P. Waters, age 47,
$287,794 total compensation
SVP Operations, The Hillman Group: Ali Fartaj, age 41,
$304,469 total compensation
SVP National Account Sales, The Hillman Group:
Terry R. Rowe, age 55
SVP Engraving, The Hillman Group: George L. Heredia,
age 50, $309,996 total compensation
President, CEO, and Director; CEO, The Hillman Group: Max W. Hillman Jr., age 62,
$668,191 total compensation
Auditors: Grant Thornton LLP

LOCATIONS

HQ: The Hillman Companies, Inc.
10590 Hamilton Ave., Cincinnati, OH 45231
Phone: 513-851-4900   **Fax:** 513-851-4997
Web: www.hillmangroup.com

2008 Sales

	$ mil.	% of total
US	467.9	97
Canada	4.2	1
Mexico	3.4	1
Other countries	6.4	1
Total	**481.9**	**100**

PRODUCTS/OPERATIONS

2008 Sales

	$ mil.	% of total
Fasteners	261.5	54
Keys	80.8	17
Engraving	40.9	9
Threaded rod	37.3	8
Letters, numbers & signs	34.7	7
Code cutter	4.9	1
Builders hardware	1.6	—
Other	20.2	4
Total	**481.9**	**100**

Selected Products and Services

Anchors	Metal shapes
Bolts	Numbers
Brads	Nuts
Engraving	Picture hanging wire
Fasteners	Plumbing repair
Hasps	Rope and chain products
Hooks	Screws
In-store service	Signs
Keys	Tacks
Key duplication systems	Tags (luggage, military
Latches	I.D., pet)
Letters	Threaded rods
Merchandising systems	Washers

COMPETITORS

Applied Industrial Technologies
Crown Bolt
Dorman Products
Endries
Fastenal
Genuine Parts
Handy & Harman
Illinois Tool Works
Kwikset Corporation
Lawson Products
MNP Corp.
MSC Industrial Direct
NCH
Newell Rubbermaid

HISTORICAL FINANCIALS

Company Type: Private

Income Statement

FYE: December 31

	REVENUE ($ mil.)	NET INCOME ($ mil.)	NET PROFIT MARGIN	EMPLOYEES
12/08	482	(3)	—	1,996
12/07	446	(10)	—	2,055
12/06	424	(8)	—	1,897
12/05	383	(4)	—	1,853
12/04	352	(19)	—	1,794
Annual Growth	8.2%	—	—	2.7%

Net Income History

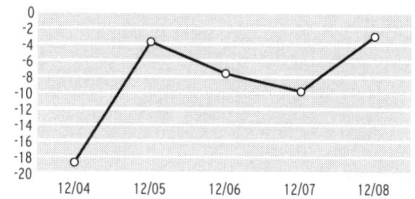

Hilton Worldwide

If you need a bed for the night, Hilton Worldwide (formerly Hilton Hotels) has a few hundred thousand of them. The company is one of the world's largest hoteliers, with a lodging empire that includes about 3,200 hotels and resorts in nearly 80 countries operating under such names as Doubletree, Embassy Suites, and Hampton, as well as its flagship Hilton brand. Many of its hotels serve the mid-market segment, though its Hilton and Conrad hotels offer full-service, upscale lodging. In addition, its Homewood Suites chain offers extended-stay services. The company franchises many of its hotels. Hilton is owned by private equity firm The Blackstone Group.

With its extensive portfolio of brands, Hilton seeks to serve multiple segments within the lodging sector. The company's largest chains, Hampton Inn and Hampton Inn & Suites, include about 1,600 locations and target mid-market travelers with moderately priced rooms and limited amenities. Nearly all its Hampton hotels are operated by franchisees or by the company under management contracts with third-party owners. At the other end of the scale, the company's Hilton and Conrad chains offer luxury services and distinctive locations, while its Waldorf-Astoria Collection is a prestigious collection of hotels inspired by the New York landmark. The company's Hilton Grand Vacations subsidiary operates more than 30 time-share vacation resorts located mostly in Florida.

Hilton expanded its portfolio in 2009 with the launch of its newest brand, Denizon Hotels, designed to cater to globally conscious modern travelers. It will operate as part of Hilton's Luxury & Lifestyle portfolio, which also includes the Waldorf Astoria, the Waldorf Astoria Collection, and Conrad Hotels & Resorts. (Development on Denizon Hotels was suspended later that year following a lawsuit from rival Starwood Hotels & Resorts charging that Hilton stole confidential and proprietary documents and used that information to help create Denizon.)

The company relocated its corporate headquarters from Beverly Hills, California, to the Washington, DC, area in 2009. The move was prompted by a desire to tap into local real estate and hospitality expertise. (The DC area is also home to rival Marriott, as well as smaller players such as Choice Hotels International, Host Hotels & Resorts, and Interstate Hotels & Resorts.) Also, the move put Hilton's HQ in closer proximity to other key corporate locations, including Dallas; Memphis; Orlando, Florida; and London. Following the relocation, the company changed its name to Hilton Worldwide to better reflect its global operations.

Blackstone took the company private in 2007 through a $26 billion buyout that included about $6 billion in assumed debt. It was the largest private equity buyout in the hotel industry. The private equity giant already owned such hotel assets as LaQuinta Inns and Suites (owned through LQ Management) and LXR Luxury Resorts & Hotels (operated by WHM). It is focusing on developing luxury brands, which has been the most competitive market in the hotel business.

HISTORY

Conrad Hilton got his start in hotel management by renting out rooms in his family's New Mexico home. He served as a state legislator and started a bank before leaving for Texas in 1919, hoping to make his fortune in banking. Hilton was unable to shoulder the cost of purchasing a bank, however, but recognized a high demand for hotel rooms and made a quick change in strategy, buying his first hotel in Cisco, Texas. Over the next decade he bought seven more Texas hotels.

Hilton lost several properties during the Depression, but began rebuilding his empire soon thereafter through the purchase of hotels in California (1938), New Mexico (1939), and Mexico (1942). He even married starlet Zsa Zsa Gabor in 1942 (they later divorced, of course). Hilton Hotels Corporation was formed in 1946 and went public. The company bought New York's Waldorf-Astoria in 1949 (a hotel Hilton called "the greatest of them all") and opened its first European hotel in Madrid in 1953. Hilton paid $111 million for the 10-hotel Statler chain the following year.

Hilton took his company out of the overseas hotel business in 1964 by spinning off Hilton International and began franchising the following year to capitalize on the well-known Hilton name. Barron Hilton, Conrad's son, was appointed president in 1966 (he became chairman upon Conrad Hilton's death in 1979). Hilton bought two Las Vegas hotels (the Las Vegas Hilton and the Flamingo Hilton) in 1970 and launched its gaming division. The company returned to the international hotel business with Conrad International Hotels in 1982 and opened its first suite-only Hilton Suites hotel in 1989.

Hilton expanded its gaming operations in the 1990s, buying Bally's Casino Resort in Reno in 1992 and launching its first riverboat casino, the Hilton Queen of New Orleans, in 1994. Two years later it acquired all of Bally Entertainment, making it the largest gaming company in the world. Also that year, Stephen Bollenbach, the former Walt Disney CFO who negotiated the $19 billion acquisition of Capital Cities/ABC, was named CEO — becoming the first non-family member to run the company.

Hilton formed an alliance with Ladbroke Group in 1997 (later Hilton Group, owner of Hilton International and the rights to the Hilton name outside the US) to promote the Hilton brand worldwide. With a downturn in the gambling industry translating into sluggish results in Hilton's gaming segment, the company spun off its gaming interests as Park Place Entertainment (later Caesars Entertainment, now owned by Harrah's) in 1998.

In 1999 Hilton made a massive acquisition with the $3.7 billion purchase of Promus Hotel Corp. Following an extended downturn in the hospitality business brought on by recession and post-9/11 fears about terrorism, Hilton began to invest in refurbishments for many of its properties and added about 150 locations in 2004.

Two years later the company re-unified the Hilton Hotels brand internationally by acquiring Hilton International from Hilton Group (now Ladbrokes) for about $5.7 billion.

In 2007 the company was acquired by The Blackstone Group, and Christopher J. Nassetta replaced Bollenbach as CEO. Hilton Hotels was renamed Hilton Worldwide in 2009.

EXECUTIVES

Chairman: William Barron Hilton, age 82
President and CEO: Christopher J. (Chris) Nassetta, age 46
CIO: Robert J. (Rob) Webb, age 39
EVP; CEO, Hilton Grand Vacations: Antoine Dagot
EVP; CEO, Americas and Global Brands:
Thomas L. (Tom) Keltner, age 62
EVP, General Counsel, and Corporate Secretary:
Madeleine A. Kleiner, age 57
EVP and CFO: Thomas C. (Tom) Kennedy, age 43
EVP and General Counsel: Richard M. (Rich) Lucas
EVP Americas Operations, Sales, and Revenue Management: Kenneth M. (Ken) Smith
EVP and Chief Human Resources Officer:
Matthew W. (Matt) Schuyler, age 43
SVP Real Estate and Asset Management:
Habib M. Enayetullah
SVP Hilton Brand Management: Jeffrey (Jeff) Diskin
SVP Sales and Development: Bob Dirks
SVP Development and Finance: Ted Middleton
SVP Architecture and Construction: Patrick Terwilliger
SVP Corporate Affairs: Marc A. Grossman
SVP Tax: W. Steven Standefer
SVP Customer Loyalty: Adam Burke
SVP Global Corporate Communications: Ellen D. Gonda
President, Middle East and Asia Pacific: Koos Klein
President, Conrad Hotels: Clem Barter
President, Hilton Grand Vacations: Mark Wang
President, Global Development and Real Estate:
Steven R. (Steve) Goldman, age 47
President, Global Operations; Interim Head Development: Ian R. Carter, age 47
Auditors: Ernst & Young LLP

LOCATIONS

HQ: Hilton Worldwide
7930 Jones Branch Dr., Ste. 1100
McLean, VA 22102
Phone: 703-883-1000
Web: www.hiltonworldwide.com

PRODUCTS/OPERATIONS

Selected Brands

Conrad Hotels & Resorts
Doubletree
Embassy Suites Hotels
Hampton Inn
Hampton Inn & Suites
Hilton
Hilton Garden Inn
Hilton Grand Vacations Club
Homewood Suites by Hilton

Selected Owned Hotels

Chicago's Palmer House Hilton
The Hilton Hawaiian Village on Waikiki Beach
Hilton San Francisco on Union Square
The New York Hilton
The Waldorf Astoria

COMPETITORS

Accor North America
Best Western
Carlson Hotels
Choice Hotels
Fairmont Raffles
Four Seasons Hotels
Hyatt
InterContinental Hotels
Marriott
Starwood Hotels & Resorts
Wyndham Worldwide

HISTORICAL FINANCIALS

Company Type: Private

Income Statement

FYE: December 31

	ESTIMATED REVENUE ($ mil.)	NET INCOME ($ mil.)	NET PROFIT MARGIN	EMPLOYEES
12/08	7,770	—	—	130,000
12/07	8,090	—	—	135,000
Annual Growth	(4.0%)	—	—	(3.7%)

Revenue History

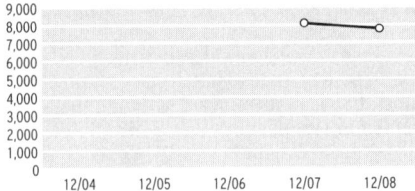

Hobby Lobby

If something wicker this way comes, Hobby Lobby Stores may be the source. The firm operates about 410 stores in more than 30 states and sells arts and crafts supplies, baskets, beads, candles, frames, home-decorating accessories, and silk flowers. It also has operations in China, Hong Kong, and the Phillippines, and it is the #3 craft and fabric retailer (behind Michaels Stores and Jo-Ann Stores). Sister companies, Crafts, Etc! and Hemispheres, supply Hobby Lobby stores with merchandise, received from its Oklahoma distribution facility. CEO David Green, who owns the company with his wife Barbara, founded Hobby Lobby in 1972 and operates it according to biblical principles, including closing stores on Sunday.

About a dozen new Hobby Lobby stores, also known as Hobby Lobby Creative Centers, opened in 2008, and the company has plans to open about twice that number in 2009. President Steven Green, the son of founder David Green, oversees finding new locations for the company, which typically sets up shop in second-generation retail sites (such as vacated supermarkets and superstores.) In addition to opening new stores, it recently expanded its 3.4 million sq. ft. of manufacturing, corporate office, and distribution space in Oklahoma City.

David Green's eldest son, Mart Green, heads up affiliate company Mardel, a maker of Christian Products, which is based at Hobby Lobby's Oklahoma facility. It operates about 30 stores located mostly in the Southwest. Crafts Etc! got its start in 1977 distributing arts and crafts supplies to Hobby Lobby, which it continues to do in addition to selling its products online directly to consumers. David and Barbara Green also founded Hemispheres, which imports and sells high-end furniture and home décor accessories from Europe and Asia. In addition to supplying Hobby Lobby with select imports, Hemispheres operates one store in Oklahoma and three in Texas.

David Green began making picture frames with his sons in 1970. The garage operation was called Greco Products. Two years later the first Hobby Lobby began operating in Oklahoma City.

EXECUTIVES

CEO: David Green
President and Director of Real Estate: Steven Green
SVP and CFO: John Cargill
SVP Operations: Ken Haywood
SVP Distribution: Bill Woody
VP Advertising: John Schumacher
VP Construction: Steve Seay
VP Legal: Peter Dobelbower
Assistant VP, Real Estate: Scott Nelson
Director of Recruiting: Bill Owens

LOCATIONS

HQ: Hobby Lobby Stores, Inc.
7707 SW 44th St., Oklahoma City, OK 73179
Phone: 405-745-1100   **Fax:** 405-745-1547
Web: www.hobbylobby.com

PRODUCTS/OPERATIONS

Selected Products

Arts and crafts supplies
Baskets
Candles
Cards
Furniture
Home accent pieces
Jewelry-making supplies
Model kits
Needlework
Party supplies
Picture frames and framing
Rubber stamping supplies
Scrapbooking supplies
Seasonal items
Sewing materials (fabric, patterns, notions)
Silk flowers
Toys
Wearable art

Selected Affiliates

Crafts, Etc! (online sales and wholesale distribution of domestic and imported arts, crafts, and jewelry-making and hobby materials to Hobby Lobby and other retailers)
Hemispheres (home furnishings and accessories stores)
HL Construction (remodels and redesigns sites to become Hobby Lobby stores)
Hong Kong Connection (China sourcing and buying office)
Mardel Christian Office & Educational Supply (Christian materials, office supplies, and educational products)

COMPETITORS

A.C. Moore
Burnes Home Accents
Family Christian Stores
Garden Ridge
Hancock Fabrics
HobbyTown USA
Jo-Ann Stores
Kirkland's
Longaberger
Michaels Stores
Old Time Pottery
Target
Wal-Mart

HISTORICAL FINANCIALS

Company Type: Private

Income Statement

FYE: December 31

	REVENUE ($ mil.)	NET INCOME ($ mil.)	NET PROFIT MARGIN	EMPLOYEES
12/08	1,800	—	—	18,000
12/07	1,800	—	—	18,000
12/06	1,620	—	—	17,500
12/05	1,500	—	—	17,000
12/04	1,400	—	—	16,000
Annual Growth	6.5%	—	—	3.0%

Revenue History

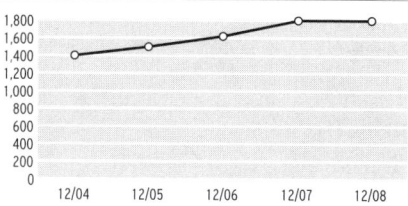

Hoffman Corporation

Hoffman cherishes a challenge — such as building the nation's deepest subway station in Portland, Oregon, or the snakelike, metal-clad Experience Music Project in Seattle. Through several subsidiaries (including flagship Hoffman Construction) the general contractor and construction manager builds civic, commercial, and industrial facilities, primarily in the northwestern US. It is a leading builder of semiconductor facilities and serves such sectors as education, health care, sports, transportation, industrial, and government. The group also provides electrical, surveying, concrete, and other services. Employees own the company, which was founded in 1922.

EXECUTIVES

Co-Chairman: Cecil W. Drinkward
Co-Chairman: Eric Hoffman
President and CEO: Wayne A. Drinkward
CFO: Scott W. Fredricks
VP Estimating: Richard (Dick) Silliman
VP Business Development and Marketing:
Barton (Bart) Eberwein
Director, Human Resources: Sheri Sundstrom
IT Manager: Anne Belle
Safety Director: Brian Clarke
Secretary: Dan D. Harmon
Purchasing Manager: Jon Grasle

LOCATIONS

HQ: Hoffman Corporation
805 SW Broadway, Ste. 2100, Portland, OR 97205
Phone: 503-221-8811   **Fax:** 503-221-8934
Web: www.hoffmancorp.com

PRODUCTS/OPERATIONS

Selected Markets

Athletic	Industrial
Civic	Laboratory
Cultural	Mixed-use
Education	Office
Health care	Technology
Hospitality	Transportation

COMPETITORS

Absher	McCarthy Building
Alberici	Peter Kiewit Sons'
Andersen Construction	Pizzagalli Construction
Bechtel	S.D. Deacon
Black & Veatch	Skanska USA Building
Bovis Lend Lease	Structure Tone
DPR Construction	Swinerton
Fluor	Turner Corporation
Gilbane	Washington Division
Hensel Phelps	Webcor Builders
Howard S. Wright Construction	Whiting-Turner

HISTORICAL FINANCIALS

Company Type: Private

Income Statement

FYE: December 31

	REVENUE ($ mil.)	NET INCOME ($ mil.)	NET PROFIT MARGIN	EMPLOYEES
12/08	1,209	—	—	—
12/07	1,190	—	—	971
12/06	1,600	—	—	920
Annual Growth	(13.1%)	—	—	5.5%

Revenue History

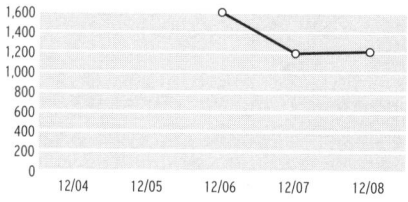

Holder Construction

Holder Construction Company's goal is to hold onto its clients' business. Boasting an 80% repeat customer rate, the firm provides commercial construction services, including computer modeling, planning and design, commissioning (which involves testing a facility's process systems), mechanical, electrical, and plumbing support, safety inspections and training, and environmental assessment. It serves as a general contractor, construction manager, and designer/builder on a variety of projects, from corporate offices and data technology centers to hotels and schools. Clients have included Mellon Financial, UPS, Emory University, and American Cancer Society.

Holder Construction also specializes in interior construction and renovation. Projects in this segment have included work on a University of Georgia marine laboratory, Cox Enterprises' headquarters office and heritage museum, and Zoo Atlanta's indoor resource center and outdoor panda and monkey exhibits.

Much of its work is done in the Southeast, but it has completed projects throughout the US, as well as Argentina, Brazil, and Costa Rica. The company has offices in Georgia, North Carolina, Virginia, and Arizona.

EXECUTIVES

Chairman and CEO: Thomas M. Holder
CFO: J. C. Pendrey
EVP: David (Dave) O'Haren
SVP: Bob Salmon

LOCATIONS

HQ: Holder Construction Company
3333 Riverwood Pkwy., SE, Ste. 400
Atlanta, GA 30339
Phone: 770-988-3000   **Fax:** 770-988-3042
Web: www.holderconstruction.com

COMPETITORS

Brasfield & Gorrie	Shelco
Choate Construction	Skanska USA Building
Hardin Construction	Turner Construction
Rodgers Builders	Winter Construction

HISTORICAL FINANCIALS
Company Type: Private

Income Statement				FYE: December 31
	REVENUE ($ mil.)	NET INCOME ($ mil.)	NET PROFIT MARGIN	EMPLOYEES
12/08	1,403	—	—	—
12/07	1,230	—	—	495
Annual Growth	14.1%	—	—	—

Revenue History

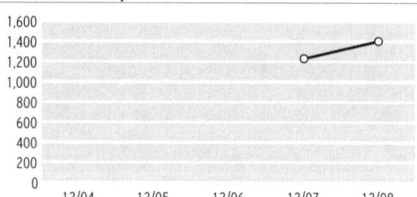

Holiday Companies

If your holiday involves a road trip across the central or western US, chances are you'll encounter a Holiday Stationstore. Holiday Companies operates about 400 convenience stores (about 100 of which are franchised) in a dozen states, from Michigan to Washington and Alaska under the Holiday Stationstores banner. The shops sell the company's own brand of Blue Planet gasoline (low-sulfur fuel available in Minnesota, South Dakota, and Wisconsin). The firm exited sporting goods retailing when its Gander Mountain chain (acquired in 1997) went public in 2004. Holiday Companies was founded in 1928 as a general store in a small Wisconsin town by two Erickson brothers, whose descendants still own and run the company.

EXECUTIVES

Chairman and CEO: Ronald A. (Ron) Erickson, age 72
President and COO: Brent G. Blackey, age 50
SVP Operations: Rick Johnson
VP and CIO: Randy Skare
VP Sales and Marketing: Brian Hooks
Vice Chairman and VP: Gerald Erickson
VP Merchandising: Dave Yamaguchi
VP Human Resources: Robert S. (Bob) Nye
VP Petroleum Supply and Distribution, Holiday Stationstores: Richard (Dick) Mills
Auditors: Ernst & Young LLP

LOCATIONS

HQ: Holiday Companies
4567 American Blvd., West
Bloomington, MN 55437
Phone: 952-830-8700   **Fax:** 952-830-8864
Web: holidaystationstores.com

COMPETITORS

7-Eleven	Kum & Go
Casey's General Stores	Marathon Petroleum
Couche-Tard	QuikTrip
Exxon Mobil	TravelCenters of America
Kroger	

HISTORICAL FINANCIALS
Company Type: Private

Income Statement				FYE: December 31
	ESTIMATED REVENUE ($ mil.)	NET INCOME ($ mil.)	NET PROFIT MARGIN	EMPLOYEES
12/08	2,000	—	—	4,600
12/07	2,000	—	—	4,600
12/06	1,820	—	—	4,410
12/05	1,742	—	—	4,200
12/04	1,310	—	—	4,000
Annual Growth	11.2%	—	—	3.6%

Revenue History

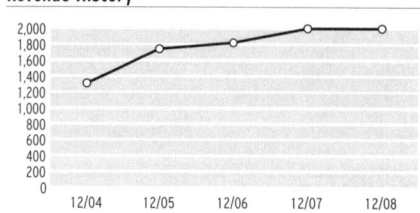

The Honickman Group

Honickman bottles its creative juices. The firm is one of the nation's largest privately owned bottlers — bottling and distributing soft drinks. It primarily sells and distributes Pepsi products in the New York City market, including its five boroughs and surrounding counties and in the Gloucester, Camden, and Burlington counties of southern New Jersey; it also sells and distributes Dr Pepper/7Up brands in an area stretching from New York City to the Virginia and North Carolina borders. In addition, Honickman offers such brands as AriZona, Glaceau Vitamin Water, and Evian.

EXECUTIVES

Chairman: Harold A. Honickman
CEO: Jeffrey A. (Jeff) Honickman, age 52
CFO: Walt Wilkinson
Data Processing: Gwen Dolceamore
President, Pepsi-Cola and Canada Dry: Robert Brockway
Corporate Safety Director: Jeffrey Brody
Director Human Resources: June Raufer

LOCATIONS

HQ: The Honickman Group
8275 Rte. 130, Pennsauken, NJ 08110
Phone: 856-665-6200   **Fax:** 856-661-4684
Web: www.honickmangroup.com/services.htm

PRODUCTS/OPERATIONS

Selected Brands

Dr Pepper/7UP Brands
  7UP
  A&W
  Canada Dry Ginger Ale
  Country Time
  Diet Rite
  Hawaiian Punch
  Mistic
  Nantucket Nectars
  RC Cola
  Snapple
  Stewart's
  Sunkist
  Tahitian Treat
  Welch's
  YooHoo
Pepsi Brands
  Aquafina
  Diet Mountain Dew
  Diet Pepsi
  Dole
  Gatorade
  Lipton Tea
  Mountain Dew
  Mug Root Beer
  Ocean Spray
  Pepsi Jazz
  Pepsi-Cola
  Sierra Mist
  SoBe
  Starbucks Frappuccino
  Tropicana
Other Brands
  AriZona Iced Tea
  Dr. Brown's
  Evian
  Fiji Water
  Glacéau Vitamin Water
  Hansen's Monster Energy
  Honest Tea
  Orangina
  Pennsylvania Dutch
  RockStar Energy
  Squirt
  Teany
  Liquid Lightning
  Huracan
  Vintage Water
  Volvic

COMPETITORS

Cott
G & J Pepsi-Cola Bottlers
National Beverage
Pepsi Bottling
Pepsi Bottling Ventures
Philadelphia Coca-Cola
Polar Beverages

HISTORICAL FINANCIALS
Company Type: Private

Income Statement
FYE: December 31

	ESTIMATED REVENUE ($ mil.)	NET INCOME ($ mil.)	NET PROFIT MARGIN	EMPLOYEES
12/07	1,330	—	—	5,000
12/06	1,280	—	—	5,000
12/05	1,215	—	—	5,000
12/04	1,130	—	—	5,000
12/03	1,100	—	—	5,000
Annual Growth	4.9%	—	—	0.0%

Revenue History

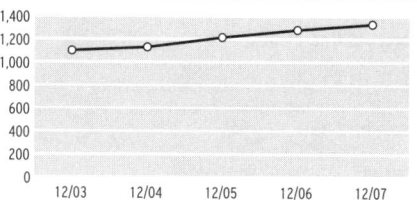

Horizon Healthcare

Horizon Healthcare Services is growing good health for Garden Staters. The company, dba Horizon Blue Cross Blue Shield of New Jersey, is New Jersey's top health insurance provider, serving about 3.6 million members. The not-for-profit company, a licensee of the Blue Cross and Blue Shield Association, offers traditional indemnity and managed care plans, including HMO, PPO, POS, and Medicare Advantage plans. It also provides dental and behavioral health coverage and manages workers' compensation claims through Horizon Casualty Services. Horizon Healthcare — which is led by CEO William Marino — is in the process of converting to a for-profit corporation.

The company has filed an application for conversion with New Jersey, and is creating an independent charitable foundation (as required by law) to receive 100% of the value of the company once it changes to publicly-held entity. Horizon Healthcare estimates that amount could be more than one billion dollars. The independent foundation is required by law to use that money "solely for the purposes of expanding access to quality, affordable health care" within New Jersey.

The change will give Horizon Healthcare access to capital markets that will help the company remain competitive in a changing health care environment.

Like all US health insurers, Horizon Healthcare is continually grappling with the problem of rising health care costs. Along with going public, the company is exploring a number of ways to keep expenses under control and remain competitive, including offering lower-cost, consumer-directed products (branded Horizon MyWay) which place more financial and decision-making responsibility on the policyholder.

The company is also trying to keep its members healthy through prevention programs that promote fitness, provide reminders for health screenings, and help members manage chronic diseases.

Horizon Healthcare's largest single account is New Jersey's State Health Benefits Program, which covers about 600,000 state government workers. The company also covers federal employees through the Blue Cross and Blue Shield (BCBS) Association's Federal Employee Program.

Horizon Healthcare has jumped on the Medicare prescription drug bandwagon, offering a Medicare Part D program through its Horizon NJ Health subsidiary, which has nearly 400,000 members. Other growing businesses within the company include its dental plan (which boasts more than a million members) and its workers' compensation managed care program, Horizon Casualty Services, which also provides personal injury protection.

Along with its portfolio of BCBS-associated subsidiaries, Horizon Healthcare provides managed care and traditional health plans through its non-BCBS licensed affiliates, Rayant Insurance Company of New York and Rayant Insurance Company of Pennsylvania.

It also offers life and disability insurance through Rayant Insurance Agency. Other Rayant companies include Rayant Healthcare Administrators and Rayant Dental Services. All of the Rayant companies offer their products to small to midsized businesses and other consumers in New York and Pennsylvania.

EXECUTIVES

Chairman: Vincent J. Giblin
President, CEO, and Director: William J. Marino, age 65
EVP and COO: Robert A. Marino
SVP Administration, CFO, and Treasurer: Robert J. Pures
SVP Market Business Units: Christopher M. Lepre
SVP Service: Jackie R. Jennifer
SVP, General Counsel, and Secretary: John W. Campbell
SVP Information Technology and CIO: Mark Barnard
SVP Healthcare Management; President and COO, Horizon Healthcare: Christy W. Bell
VP Human Resources: Margaret Coons
VP Clinical Affairs: Phillip M. Bonaparte
VP Healthcare Services: James F. Albano
VP Consumer and Senior Markets: Robert E. Meehan
VP Corporate Marketing and Communications: Lawrence B. Altman
VP Strategy and Development: Donna M. Celestini
VP Financial Planning and Analysis: David R. Huber
VP and Chief Medical Officer: Richard G. Popiel
President and CEO, Horizon NJ Health: Karen L. Clark
Director Public Affairs, Corporate Marketing, and Communications: Thomas W. Rubino
Auditors: PricewaterhouseCoopers LLP

LOCATIONS

HQ: Horizon Healthcare Services, Inc.
3 Penn Plaza East, Newark, NJ 07105
Phone: 973-466-4000   **Fax:** 973-466-4317
Web: www.horizon-bcbsnj.com

PRODUCTS/OPERATIONS

2008 Sales

	$ mil.	% of total
Insured premiums	7,588.7	95
Administrative service fee income	338.6	4
Other	36.7	1
Total	**7,963.0**	**100**

COMPETITORS

Aetna
AmeriHealth
CIGNA
Delta Dental Plans
Health Net
Healthfirst
Healthplex
Humana
Kaiser Foundation Health Plan
MetLife
Oxford Health
UnitedHealth Group
WellPoint

HISTORICAL FINANCIALS
Company Type: Not-for-profit

Income Statement
FYE: December 31

	REVENUE ($ mil.)	NET INCOME ($ mil.)	NET PROFIT MARGIN	EMPLOYEES
12/08	7,963	(45)	—	5,200
12/07	7,527	161	2.1%	5,200
12/06	6,730	180	2.7%	4,700
12/05	6,025	214	3.5%	4,400
12/04	5,504	173	3.1%	4,400
Annual Growth	9.7%	—	—	4.3%

Net Income History

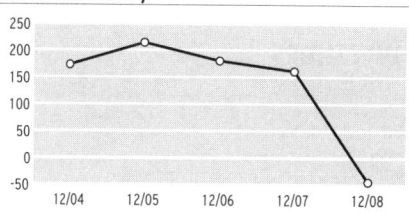

Horizon Media

Anxious to boost your media's magnitude? Horizon Media, one of the larger independent media buying shops, plans, coordinates, and negotiates deals across the media spectrum (television, radio, newspapers, billboards, and digital). The company's Eurizon subsidiary provides media services to European clients through offices in Amsterdam, and its membership in Columbus Media International partnership extends its reach worldwide. Horizon Media's client list has included NBC, Harrah's Entertainment Group, Panasonic, and Telemundo. The company has offices in California and New York. CEO and president Bill Koenigsberg founded Horizon Media in 1989.

Not content with just being a huge independent media buying shop, Horizon Media set its sights on the multinational networks when it formed Columbus Media International, a global media consortium with Canada's Cossette. Columbus Media was launched as an alternative to media services conglomerates such as Publicis and WPP. It conducts business across more than 25 global regions, including Russia, the Middle East, Latin America, and the Asia/Pacific region.

EXECUTIVES

President and CEO: William A. (Bill) Koenigsberg, age 53
EVP and CFO: Vinnie O'Toole
EVP and General Manager, Western Region: Zachary (Zach) Rosenberg
EVP, General Manager, and Director Marketing Services: Carl H. Kotheimer, age 58
EVP Human Resources: Eileen Benwitt
EVP and Managing Partner, Los Angeles: Serena Duff
EVP Marketing and Brand Strategy, New York: Gabrielle Magnani
EVP and Chief Media Negotiating Officer: Aaron Cohen, age 69
SVP Operations: Joyce FitzSimons
SVP Corporate Development: Jeff Andrews, age 60
SVP and CIO: Cliff Cree
SVP and Director Business Operations: Steven (Steve) Faske, age 54
SVP and Director Finance: Stewart Linder
SVP and Director Managing Director: Richard Simms
SVP and Director National TV: Louis Klidonas
SVP and Director Corporate Research: Brad Adgate, age 54
SVP and Account Group Head: Elyse Pollock
Director Corporate Communications: Jill Backlin

LOCATIONS

HQ: Horizon Media, Inc.
630 3rd Ave., New York, NY 10017
Phone: 212-916-8600   **Fax:** 212-916-8653
Web: www.horizonmedia.com

COMPETITORS

Aegis Group
Backchannelmedia
EarthQuake Media
Mediaedge
MPG
OMD
PGR Media
Starcom
Tower Media Advertising
ZenithOptimedia

HISTORICAL FINANCIALS

Company Type: Private

Income Statement

	ESTIMATED REVENUE ($ mil.)	NET INCOME ($ mil.)	NET PROFIT MARGIN	FYE: December 31 EMPLOYEES
12/08	2,000	—	—	475
12/07	1,800	—	—	—
Annual Growth	11.1%	—	—	—

Revenue History

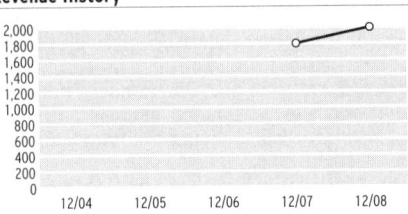

2,000	
1,800	
1,600	
1,400	
1,200	
1,000	
800	
600	
400	
200	
0	12/04 12/05 12/06 12/07 12/08

Houchens Industries

Houchens Industries is a supermarket of businesses as well as an operator of supermarkets. The diversified company runs about 170 grocery stores under the Houchens, Food Giant, IGA, Piggly Wiggly, and Buy Low banners. Its 215 Save-A-Lot discount grocery stores in a dozen states offer limited selections and cover 15,000 sq. ft. or less. Houchens also owns about 85 convenience stores and two dozen Tobacco Shoppe discount cigarette outlets, mostly in Kentucky and Tennessee. It sold cigarette maker Commonwealth Brands in 2007. Other businesses include construction, financial services, real estate, and recycling. Founded as BG Wholesale in 1917 by Ervin Houchens, the firm is 100% owned by its employees.

Employee owned since 1988, Houchens has amassed a diverse portfolio of some 30 businesses over the years through acquisitions. The conglomerate looks to buy assets that have sound management and a history of providing good cash flow that can be bought at a reasonable price. To that end, the company in 2009 purchased the 14-store family-run Whites Fresh Foods chain, which operates grocery stores in Tennessee and Virginia, and the Bowling Green, Kentucky-based two-store drug retailer Sheldon's Express Pharmacy, thereby expanding into the drugstore business. Houchens plans to leverage the acquisition to create a regional drugstore chain.

The Whites purchase follows the 2008 acquisition of Chicago-based Tampico Beverages, a maker of refrigerated juice drinks and punches sold in more than 36 countries, for an undisclosed amount. Tampico supplies beverages to grocery and convenience stores, as well as quick-serve restaurants. In June 2008 the firm acquired Buehler Foods, the operator of 22 BUY LOW grocery stores in Illinois, Indiana, and Kentucky. That purchase came on the heels of the addition of seven Cincinnati-area Save-A-Lot stores in May.

Houchens is the nation's largest Save-A-Lot licensee. True to its name, the chain focuses on lower-income shoppers and competes with other discount grocery operators, such as fast-growing ALDI. (Grocery retailer and wholesaler SUPERVALU is the parent company of Save-A-Lot.)

In March 2008 Houchens purchased the Kentucky-based brokerage and financial services firm J.J.B. Hilliard, W.L. Lyons, Inc. (Hilliard Lyons for short) from The PNC Financial Services Group to form a new company called HL Financial Services. In 2007 the company sold its Commonwealth Brands cigarette division to Britain's Imperial Tobacco for $1.9 billion. Houchens owned the business for about six years. In the grocery arena, Houchens acquired Food Giant Supermarkets, the operator of 90 Food Giant and Piggly Wiggly supermarkets in eight states, in mid-2004. In late 2004 the company also acquired Scotty's Contracting & Stone — a Central Kentucky highway-construction company — in a stock swap between the two employee-owned companies. Connected with the Scotty's transaction, Houchens also bought TS Trucking.

Other acquisitions made by the Houchens Insurance Group include the purchase of the assets of rival Synaxis Van Meter Insurance Agency Inc. and Employers Risk Services Inc., both in 2006.

EXECUTIVES

Chairman and CEO: James (Jimmie) Gipson, age 68
President: Spencer A. Coates
Information Systems Manager: Terry Cornell
CFO: Gordon Minter
Director Marketing and Merchandising: Alan Larsen
Director Benefits: Sharon Grooms

LOCATIONS

HQ: Houchens Industries, Inc.
700 Church St., Bowling Green, KY 42102
Phone: 270-843-3252   **Fax:** 270-780-2877
Web: www.houchensindustries.com

PRODUCTS/OPERATIONS

Selected Operations

American Sun Systems (tanning salon supplier)
Blake, Hart Taylor & Wiseman (insurance)
Buehler's Buy Low (grocery retail)
Food Giant (grocery retail)
Four Seasons (indoor tanning salons)
Hilliard Lyons (financial services)
Houchens Markets (grocery retail)
IGA (licensed, grocery retail)
Insurance Specialists (insurance)
Jr. Food Stores (convenience stores)
Save-A-Lot (licensed, grocery retail)
Scotty's (asphalt paving)
Sheldon's Express Pharmacy (drugstores)
Southern Recycling Inc. (recycling)
Stewart-Richey Construction, Inc. (construction management)
Tampico (juice)
TS Trucking (hauling)
Van Meter Insurance (insurance, benefits)
White's Fresh Foods (grocery retail)

COMPETITORS

7-Eleven
ALDI
Ameriprise
Charles Schwab
Citigroup
Cumberland Farms
CVS Caremark
Delhaize America
Dole Food
Dr Pepper Snapple Group
E*TRADE Financial
Edward D. Jones
Faygo
Florida's Natural
FMR
Goya
John Hancock Financial Services
Jugos del Valle USA
Kroger
K-VA-T Food Stores
Meijer
Mott's
Nestlé
Ocean Spray
Odwalla
Old Orchard
Raymond James Financial
Rite Aid
Sheetz
Sunkist
Sunny Delight
TD Ameritrade
Tree Top
Tropicana
Veryfine
Walgreen
Wal-Mart
Weis Markets
Welch's
Winn-Dixie

HISTORICAL FINANCIALS

Company Type: Private

Income Statement

FYE: September 30

	REVENUE ($ mil.)	NET INCOME ($ mil.)	NET PROFIT MARGIN	EMPLOYEES
9/08	2,500	—	—	16,826
9/07	2,000	—	—	12,000
9/06	1,890	—	—	10,500
9/05	2,360	—	—	11,487
9/04	2,005	—	—	9,229
Annual Growth	5.7%	—	—	16.2%

Revenue History

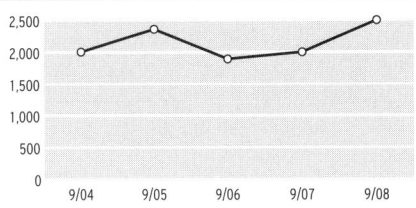

Houghton Mifflin

Alice Cooper's 1972 album *School's Out* probably doesn't get much play around the offices of Houghton Mifflin Holding Company. The firm does business through its Houghton Mifflin Harcourt Publishing Company subsidiary, a top publisher of textbooks for the K-12 markets. Houghton Mifflin Harcourt also offers trade and reference books for adults and children, such as the *American Heritage Dictionary*. In 2007 Houghton Mifflin acquired several businesses from Harcourt, another K-12 publisher, creating Houghton Mifflin Harcourt. It sold its College Division in 2008. Houghton Mifflin Holding Company is owned by Education Media and Publishing Group.

Irish private-equity concern Education Media Publishing Group was created from the reverse takeover by Barry O'Callaghan's Irish-based education software firm Riverdeep. An investment banker, O'Callaghan helped lead the buyout of Houghton Mifflin in 2006 and its subsequent acquisition of the Harcourt businesses. Education Media Publishing Group borrowed heavily to finance the two acquisitions, and Houghton Mifflin has been struggling with a heavy debt burden as a result. O'Callaghan was named CEO in 2009, replacing Tony Lucki who retired.

The company purchased the Harcourt businesses, including Harcourt Education, Harcourt Trade, and Greenwood-Heinemann, from Reed Elsevier in 2007. The $4 billion deal strengthened Houghton Mifflin's position in the US educational publishing market. (Reed Elsevier, meanwhile, sold other Harcourt brands, including international publishing business Harcourt Education Ltd., to education firm Pearson.) Houghton Mifflin later sold its College Division to Cengage Learning (formerly Thomson Learning) for $750 million in cash in order to become exclusively a publisher of K-12, trade, and reference titles.

EXECUTIVES

Chairman and CEO: Barry O'Callaghan
President and COO: Gerald T. Hughes
EVP and CFO: Michael Muldowney
EVP and General Counsel: Bill Bayers
EVP and Chief Human Resources Officer: Ciara Smyth
SVP and CIO: Paul Wilcox
SVP Operations: Greg DuMont
President, K-12 Publishers: Michael Lavelle
President, Houghton Mifflin Harcourt Trade and Reference Publishers: Gary Gentel
President, The Riverside Publishing Company: Richard Swartz
Auditors: PricewaterhouseCoopers LLP

LOCATIONS

HQ: Houghton Mifflin Holding Company Inc.
222 Berkeley St., Boston, MA 02116
Phone: 617-351-5000   **Fax:** 617-351-1105
Web: www.hmco.com

Houston Rockets

Houston basketball fans really blast off for this team. The Houston Rockets joined the National Basketball Association in 1967 as the San Diego Rockets, a franchise first awarded to Bob Breitbard. After moving to Houston in 1971, the team reached the NBA Finals twice before finally winning back-to-back championship titles in 1994 and 1995. The Rockets roster has been graced with such Hall of Fame players as Clyde Drexler, Moses Malone, and Hakeem Olajuwon. In 2003 the franchise took up residence at Houston's Toyota Center. Former Wall Street securities trader Leslie Alexander has owned the team since 1993.

While the Rockets have been perennial playoff contenders the past several years, the team has mostly failed to advance past the first or second round. At the end of the 2006-07 season, head coach Jeff Van Gundy was fired and replaced by former Sacramento Kings coach Rick Adelman. A former NBA player, Adelman had originally been drafted by the San Diego Rockets.

EXECUTIVES

Owner: Leslie L. Alexander, age 67
CEO: Thaddeus B. (Tad) Brown
CFO: Marcus Jolibois
General Manager: Daryl Morey
Head Coach: Rick Adelman, age 63
SVP Basketball Operations and Athletic Trainer: Keith Jones
VP Basketball Operations: Sam Hinkie
Director Player Development: Brett Gunning
Director Scouting: Gerald Madkins
Director Player Personnel: Gersson Rosas
Director Human Resources: Olga Piskor
Director Broadcasting: Joel Blank
Director Marketing Operations: Ken Sheirr
Director Information Technology and Telecommunications: Victor Tan
General Counsel: Rafael Stone
Manager Finance: Sue Feng
Equipment Manager: Anthony Nila

LOCATIONS

HQ: Houston Rockets
1510 Polk St., Houston, TX 77002
Phone: 713-758-7200   **Fax:** 713-758-7315
Web: www.nba.com/rockets

PRODUCTS/OPERATIONS

Titles

NBA Champions (1994-95)
Western Conference Champions (1981, 1986, 1994-95)

COMPETITORS

Dallas Mavericks
Memphis Grizzlies
New Orleans Hornets
San Antonio Spurs

Howard Hughes Medical Institute

The fortune that once belonged to a man afraid of germs and disease is now helping to fight them. The not-for-profit Howard Hughes Medical Institute (HHMI) is one of the largest private medical research organizations in the US. Unlike most such organizations, HHMI directly employs the researchers it funds (through a multibillion-dollar endowment) and provides needed equipment and facilities. Its 350 plus "investigators," as the institute calls them, include a dozen Nobel Prize winners. The organization concentrates primarily on such biomedical areas as cell biology, genetics, immunology, neuroscience, and structural biology. HHMI also supports science education through a grant program.

Founded in 1953 by Howard Hughes, the institute was the major beneficiary of the sale of Hughes Aircraft to General Motors and has an endowment of more than $17 billion.

That endowment has risen after dipping to about $10 billion in 2002. To sustain its giving power, the institute cut some programs, trimmed staff, and undertook other measures to reduce its annual budget.

HHMI also operates Janelia Farm, its own research campus complete with meeting and social gathering spaces for various research groups. The facility serves as a complement to the existing programs in place at more than 70 schools and labs throughout the US where its investigators typically work.

Robert Tjian, a biochemist at the University of California, Berkeley, succeeded Thomas R. Cech as president of HHMI in April 2009. Cech served as president since 2000.

EXECUTIVES

Chairman: Hanna H. Gray
President: Robert Tjian, age 50
VP and Chief Scientific Officer: Jack E. Dixon
VP Information Technology: Joseph D. Collins
VP and General Counsel: Craig A. Alexander
VP Finance and Treasurer: Edward J. Palmerino
VP Grants and Special Programs: Peter J. Bruns
VP Communications and Public Affairs: Avice A. Meehan
VP and Director, Janelia Farm Research Campus: Gerald M. Rubin
VP and Chief Investment Officer: Landis Zimmerman
VP Research Operations: David A. Clayton
Media Relations Specialist: Jennifer L. Michalowski
Information Officer: Jennifer B. Donovan
Auditors: Deloitte & Touche LLP

HISTORICAL FINANCIALS

Company Type: Foundation

Income Statement				FYE: August 31
	REVENUE ($ mil.)	NET INCOME ($ mil.)	NET PROFIT MARGIN	EMPLOYEES
12/08	3,029	—	—	3,000

Howard University

Howard University is a predominantly African-American university that enrolls some 10,600 students. The school offers nearly 80 undergraduate majors and about 100 graduate degrees in areas such as engineering, education, divinity, dentistry, law, medicine, history, political science, music, and social work. Notable alumni include choreographer Debbie Allen, former US Supreme Court Justice Thurgood Marshall, former New York City mayor David Dinkins, Nobel laureate Toni Morrison, and singer Roberta Flack. Established in 1867, the school was named after one of its founders, General Oliver O. Howard, a Civil War hero who was commissioner of the Freedman's Bureau.

EXECUTIVES

Chairman: Addison B. Rand, age 64
Vice Chairwoman: Renee Higginbotham-Brooks
President: Sidney A. Ribeau, age 61
SVP, CFO, and Treasurer: Sidney H. Evans Jr.
SVP Health and Sciences: Donald E. Wilson
SVP Strategic Planning, Operations, and External Affairs and CTO: Hassan Minor
SVP and Secretary: Artis G. Hampshire-Cowan
Acting SVP Academic Matters and Dean, School of Law: Kurt L. Schmoke, age 59
Vice Provost Student Affairs: Franklin D. Chambers II
Dean, School of Social Work: Cudore L. Snell
Dean, College of Arts and Sciences: James Donaldson
Dean, College of Business: Barron Harvey
Dean, College of Dentistry: Leo E. Rouse
Dean, Graduate School: Orlando L. Taylor
Dean, College of Engineering, Architecture, and Computer Sciences: James H. Johnson
Dean, School of Divinity: Alton B. Pollard III
Dean, School of Communications: Jannette L. Dates
Dean, Student Life and Activities: Tonya L. Guillory
Dean, School of Education: Leslie T. Fenwick
Dean, Residence Life: Charles J. Gibbs
Interim Dean, College of Medicine: Robert E. Taylor
Director Admissions: Linda Sanders-Hawkins
General Counsel: Norma Leftwich
President, Alumni Association: Kimberly Singleton

LOCATIONS

HQ: Howard University
   2400 6th St. NW, Washington, DC 20059
Phone: 202-806-6100
Web: www.howard.edu

HP Hood

HP Hood tries to cream its competition — with ice cream, sour cream, and whipping cream. The company, a leading US dairy producer, also makes fluid milk, cottage cheese, and juices. Its home turf is New England, where it is one of the few remaining dairies to offer home milk delivery. Hood's products are available at chain and independent food retailers and convenience stores, and to foodservice purveyors. In addition to its own brands, the company makes private-label, licensed, and franchise dairy products; Hood also owns regional dairy producers Kemps and Crowley Foods. The company operates more than 20 manufacturing plants throughout the US.

One of the company's most successful offerings is the Simply Smart line of fat-free and low-fat milks; another is the dairy beverage Calorie Countdown. Although introduced back in the low-carb diet craze, Calorie Countdown products continue to be popular.

Hood has been expanding its portfolio of brands and regional operations through a series of strategic acquisitions. It purchased California's Crystal Cream & Butter Co. in 2007, cementing its West Coast operations. The following year the company acquired the Brigham's ice cream brand and product lines. (An outside investment group acquired Brigham's chain of ice cream shops, striking a licensing deal with Hood to continue using the popular name.)

Hood's products are sold at such major food retailers along the East Coast as Price Chopper, Foodmart, Shaws, Stop & Shop, and Hannafords. Selected company and licensed products such as Lactaid, Stonyfield Farm Organic Milk, Southern Comfort Eggnog, and Hood Calorie Countdown are available nationally. In 2009 the company entered into an licensing agreement with Hershey to distribute and sell extended-shelf-life Hershey-flavored milks and milkshakes nationwide. Given Hershey's complete penetration in the US food sector, the agreement gave Hood the opportunity to become a truly national dairy company.

Harvey P. Hood founded the company in 1846 as a one-man milk-delivery service. The family of CEO John Kaneb controls the company.

EXECUTIVES

Chairman, President, and CEO: John A. Kaneb, age 74
EVP Sales: James F. (Jim) Walsh
CFO: Gary R. Kaneb
SVP Operations: H. Scott Blake
SVP and General Counsel: Paul C. Nightingale
SVP Research and Development, Engineering, and Procurement: Mike J. Suever
VP Marketing: Christopher S. (Chris) Ross
VP and Controller: James A. Marcinelli
VP Human Resources: Bruce W. Bacon
VP and Treasurer: Theresa M. Bresten
VP Operations Services: Francis V. Torgerson
VP Public Relations and Government Affairs: Lynne M. Bohan
VP Quality Systems and Regulatory Affairs: Margaret A. Poole
COO, Crowley Foods: Joseph (Joe) Cervantes
President and CEO, Kemps: James B. (Jim) Green
Director Information Systems: Jack Billiel

LOCATIONS

HQ: HP Hood LLC
   6 Kimball Ln., Lynnfield, MA 01940
Phone: 617-887-3000   **Fax:** 617-887-8484
Web: www.hood.com

PRODUCTS/OPERATIONS

Selected Products and Brands

Calorie Countdown
   Milk

Hood
   Cottage cheese
   Cream
   Eggnog
   Frozen novelties
   Ice cream
   Juice and drinks
   Milk
   Sour cream

Lactaid
   Milk

Simply Smart
   Cream
   Milk
   Sour cream

COMPETITORS

Agri-Mark
Associated Milk Producers
Ben & Jerry's
Coca-Cola North America
Dairy Farmers of America
Dean Foods
Dreyer's
Florida's Natural
Friendship Dairies
Garelick Farms
Gifford's
Guida's
Land O'Lakes
Maryland & Virginia Milk Producers
National Dairy Holdings
Odwalla
Old Orchard
Organic Valley
Stew Leonard's
Sunny Delight
Tree Top
Tropicana
Unilever
Veryfine
Welch's

HISTORICAL FINANCIALS

Company Type: Private

Income Statement				FYE: December 31
	ESTIMATED REVENUE ($ mil.)	NET INCOME ($ mil.)	NET PROFIT MARGIN	EMPLOYEES
12/08	2,200	—	—	4,500
12/07	2,300	—	—	4,500
12/06	2,500	—	—	5,400
12/05	2,300	—	—	5,000
12/04	2,300	—	—	4,850
Annual Growth	(1.1%)	—	—	(1.9%)

Revenue History

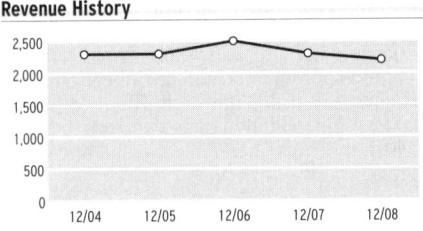

H.T. Hackney

The H.T. Hackney Company is a leading wholesale distributor of food products and other retail items serving more than 20,000 convenience stores and independent grocers in more than 20 states (mostly east of the Mississippi). The company supplies more than 25,000 items, including frozen food, tobacco products, health and beauty items, and deli products. In addition, it owns bottled water producer Natural Springs Water Group, and the company is involved in furniture manufacturing through subsidiary Holland House Furniture. Founded 1891, H.T. Hackney is owned by chairman and CEO Bill Sansom.

EXECUTIVES

Chairman and CEO: William B. (Bill) Sansom, age 67
VP and CFO: Mike Morton
VP Administration: Leonard Robinette
VP Sales and Marketing: Tommy Thomas

LOCATIONS

HQ: H.T. Hackney Company
502 S. Gay St., Knoxville, TN 37901
Phone: 865-546-1291   **Fax:** 865-546-1501
Web: www.hthackney.com

COMPETITORS

Alex Lee
Associated Wholesale Grocers
Atlantic Dominion
C & S Wholesale
Consolidated Companies
Consumer Product Distributors
Core-Mark
Eby-Brown
GSC Enterprises
McLane
Nash-Finch

HISTORICAL FINANCIALS

Company Type: Private

Income Statement

	REVENUE ($ mil.)	NET INCOME ($ mil.)	NET PROFIT MARGIN	EMPLOYEES
3/08	3,550	—	—	3,600
3/07	3,550	—	—	3,570
3/06	3,600	—	—	3,450
3/05	3,550	—	—	3,600
3/04	3,500	—	—	3,600
Annual Growth	0.4%	—	—	0.0%

FYE: March 31

Revenue History

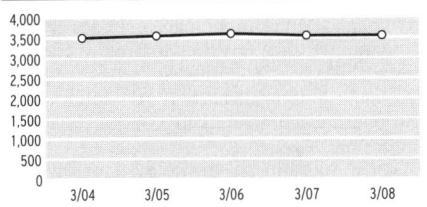

Hunt Consolidated

Hunt Consolidated is a holding company for the oil and real estate businesses of Ray Hunt, son of legendary Texas wildcatter and company founder H.L. Hunt. Founded in 1934 (reportedly with H.L.'s poker winnings), Hunt Oil is an oil and gas production and exploration company with primary interests in North and South America. Hoping to repeat huge discoveries in Yemen, Hunt Oil is exploring in Canada, Ghana, Iraq, Madagascar, and Oman. Hunt Realty handles commercial and residential real estate investment management activities. Other business include ranching, private equity investments and energy (refining and power interests).

Hunt Oil and its affiliates formed Hunt Consolidated as a holding company in order to better manage the Hunt family's diverse interests. The range of operations also helps protect the company's revenues from dependence on Hunt Oil's high risk/high return approach to exploration and production, and the boom and bust cycles of the oil and gas market.

In 2008 the company launched Hunt Ventures Fund I, L.P., to invest in early-stage IT companies. Hunt Consolidated is also investing in wind energy projects.

EXECUTIVES

Chairman, President, and CEO: Ray L. Hunt, age 65
SVP and CFO: Donald (Don) Robillard
SVP; President, Hunt Investment Corporation: Chris Kleinert
SVP Financial Administration: Harry Dombroski
SVP and General Counsel: W. Kirk Baker
SVP Corporate Development: Thomas A. (Tom) Meurer, age 67
SVP Corporate Affairs and International Relations: Rt. Hon. Jeanne L. Phillips
VP Environment, Health, and Safety: Scott Rolseth
VP and Tax Counsel: David Hernandez
VP and CIO: Kevin P. Campbell
VP Human Resources: Paul Hoffman
VP and Treasurer: Donna German
VP Tax: Wendy Finley
VP Global Security: Mike Pritchard
Manager Human Resources and Compensation: Dan Carrel
President, Hunt Power; SVP, Hunt Oil Company: Hunter Hunt, age 40

LOCATIONS

HQ: Hunt Consolidated Inc.
Fountain Place, 1445 Ross at Field, Ste. 1400
Dallas, TX 75202
Phone: 214-978-8000   **Fax:** 214-978-8888
Web: www.huntoil.com

PRODUCTS/OPERATIONS

Selected Subsidiaries and Affiliates

Hunt Oil Company (integrated oil company)
Hunt Oil Company of Canada
Hunt Power L.P. (utility projects and services)
Hunt Private Equity Group
Hunt Realty Corporation (acquires real estate and manages investments)
Hunt Refining Co. Inc.
Hunt Ventures, L.P. (diversified investments)
Yemen Hunt Oil Co.

COMPETITORS

Anadarko Petroleum	Murphy Oil
BP	Nexen
Exxon Mobil	Royal Dutch Shell
King Ranch	TOTAL
Lincoln Property	

HISTORICAL FINANCIALS

Company Type: Private

Income Statement

	ESTIMATED REVENUE ($ mil.)	NET INCOME ($ mil.)	NET PROFIT MARGIN	EMPLOYEES
12/08	2,870	—	—	3,000
12/07	2,120	—	—	3,000
12/06	2,130	—	—	3,000
12/05	2,300	—	—	3,000
Annual Growth	7.7%	—	—	0.0%

FYE: December 31

Revenue History

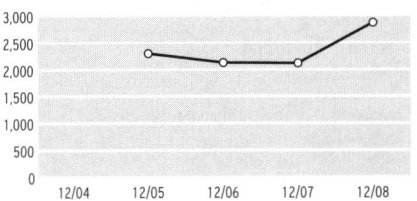

HVM L.L.C.

HVM's guests need not worry about wearing out their welcome. The company manages under contract more than 680 hotels throughout the US and Canada under the Extended Stay America, Extended Stay Deluxe, Homestead Studio Suites, StudioPLUS Deluxe Studios, and Crossland Economy Studios brands. A hybrid between a hotel and an apartment, its lodgings offer all-suite accommodations targeting both business and leisure travelers looking for a temporary place to call home. The rooms feature separate living and dining areas along with fully-equipped kitchens. Some properties also boast exercise centers, swimming pools, and wireless Internet access.

The Lightstone Group entered the lodging sector when it acquired the Extended Stay chain from The Blackstone Group in 2007. (Extended Stay is a separate business from HVM that is affiliated with, but not directly owned by the company.) The $8 billion deal was made at the peak of the commercial real estate market. Blackstone had formed the hotel business in 2004 after its acquisitions of Extended Stay America and Homestead Village.

In 2009 the debt-ridden Extended Stay filed for Chapter 11 bankruptcy as a result of a drastic decrease in corporate and leisure travel brought on by an economy in peril. HVM isn't involved in the filing, and states it will have no impact on the hotel chain's day-to-day operations.

Extended Stay is able to charge lower rates than hotels by eliminating room service and daily maid services.

EXECUTIVES

President and CEO: Gary A. DeLapp, age 50
SEVP Operations: Stephen T. (Steve) Woolridge
EVP Operations: Glen Shanor
EVP Operations: Tim Treadwell
EVP Human Resources: Marshall L. Dildy
EVP Operations: Terri Dombkowski
EVP Facilities Management and Purchasing:
  Roy G. (Ziggy) Clayton
EVP Sales and Marketing: Timothy B. (Tim) Groves
EVP Legal: Piero Bussani
EVP Accounting: Joseph (Joe) Rogers
EVP Operations: Victoria Plummer
EVP Finance and Chief Investment Officer: David Kim
EVP Revenue Management: John Kaufman

LOCATIONS

HQ: HVM L.L.C.
  100 Dunbar St., Spartanburg, SC 29306
Phone: 864-573-1600   **Fax:** 864-573-1695
Web: www.extendedstayhotels.com

PRODUCTS/OPERATIONS

Selected Hotel Brands

Crossland Economy Studios
Extended Stay Deluxe
Extended Stay America Efficiency Studios
Homestead Studio Suites
StudioPLUS Deluxe Studios

COMPETITORS

Choice Hotels
Country Inns & Suites
Hilton Worldwide
Hyatt
InterContinental Hotels

InTown Suites
Marriott
Travelodge
Wyndham Worldwide

HISTORICAL FINANCIALS

Company Type: Private

Income Statement				FYE: December 31
	REVENUE ($ mil.)	NET INCOME ($ mil.)	NET PROFIT MARGIN	EMPLOYEES
12/07	1,090	—	—	9,600

Hy-Vee, Inc.

Give Hy-Vee a high five for being one of the largest privately owned US supermarket chains, despite serving some modestly sized towns in the Midwest. The company runs about 225 Hy-Vee supermarkets in eight Midwestern states: Illinois, Iowa, Kansas, Minnesota, Missouri, Nebraska, South Dakota, and Wisconsin. About half of its stores are in Iowa, as are most of its 25-plus Hy-Vee (formerly Drug Town) drugstores. It distributes products to its stores through several subsidiaries, including Lomar Distributing (specialty foods) and Perishable Distributors of Iowa (fresh foods). Charles Hyde and David Vredenburg founded the employee-owned firm in 1930. It takes its name from a combination of its founders' names.

Hy-Vee is seeking to expand gradually in several key markets in the Midwest, including Chicago, Minneapolis, and Madison, Wisconsin.

To that end, the regional grocery chain opened its first supermarket in Madison in fall 2009, marking its entry into a new state for the first time in nearly 20 years. To cater to local tastes, the company says the 92,000-square-foot Madison store has the largest cheese selection of any Hy-Vee supermarket. Hy-Vee expects to open a second store in Madison in 2010. It has also announced that it will test a smaller format store (about 20,000-25,000 square feet, with no pharmacies) in selected locations.

Going beyond traditional grocery fare, the company has been focusing on adding Hy-Vee Gas convenience units (some 80 locations include these), wine and spirits stores, pharmacies, and Hy-Vee HealthMarket departments. The grocery retailer began selling prepaid mobile phones in late 2007. Many Hy-Vee stores also have seasonal garden centers. Store brands include Hy-Vee, Grand Selections, Health Market, and Midwest County Fare.

In a bid to get its customers to eat well, Hy-Vee employs more than 120 dietitians in its stores.

The company renamed its Drug Town stores Hy-Vee Drugstores to capitalize on Hy-Vee's strong brand recognition in the region. The company has begun opening walk-in medical clinics in its supermarkets through a partnership with Sioux City, Iowa-based Curaquick Clinics. The partnership dissolved in 2007 and Hy-Vee may find a replacement clinic company to continue to offer the service.

In late 2009 the regional grocery chain named 28-year-company-veteran Randall Edeker president of the company. Edeker succeeds Ric Jurgens, who has served as president since 2001. Jurgens remains chairman and CEO of Hy-Vee.

EXECUTIVES

Chairman, CEO, and COO: Richard N. (Ric) Jurgens
President: Randall B. Edeker, age 47
EVP: Raymond (Ray) Stewart
EVP: Ken Waller
SVP, CFO, and Treasurer: John Briggs
SVP Retail Operations: Randy Edeker, age 43
SVP Human Resources: Jane Knaack-Esbeck
SVP Corporate Procurement and Logistics: Ron Taylor
VP Marketing: Paula Correy, age 42
VP Distribution: Tod Hockenson
VP Petroleum Marketing, General Merchandise, and Pharmacy: Tom Watson
VP Perishables: Jon Wendel, age 45
VP Management Information Systems: Eric Smith
Assistant VP Information Technology: Cevin Anderson
Assistant VP Communications: Ruth Comer
Auditors: McGladrey & Pullen, LLP

LOCATIONS

HQ: Hy-Vee, Inc.
  5820 Westown Pkwy., West Des Moines, IA 50266
Phone: 515-267-2800   **Fax:** 515-267-2817
Web: www.hy-vee.com

PRODUCTS/OPERATIONS

Selected Subsidiaries

D & D Foods, Inc. (salads, dips, and meats)
Florist Distributing, Inc. (flowers, plants, and florist supplies)
Hy-Vee Weitz Construction, L.C. (construction)
Lomar Distributing, Inc. (specialty foods)
Midwest Heritage Bank, FSB (banking)
Perishable Distributors of Iowa, Ltd. (meat, fish, seafood, and ice cream)

COMPETITORS

ALDI
Associated Wholesale Grocers
Ball's Food
Casey's General Stores
CVS Caremark
Dahl's Foods
Fareway Stores
Kmart
Kroger
Nash-Finch
Niemann Foods
Rite Aid
Roundy's Supermarkets
Save-A-Lot Food Stores
SUPERVALU
Target
Walgreen
Wal-Mart

HISTORICAL FINANCIALS

Company Type: Private

Income Statement				FYE: September 30
	REVENUE ($ mil.)	NET INCOME ($ mil.)	NET PROFIT MARGIN	EMPLOYEES
9/08	6,200	—	—	55,000
9/07	5,600	—	—	54,000
9/06	5,840	—	—	52,000
Annual Growth	3.0%	—	—	2.8%

Revenue History

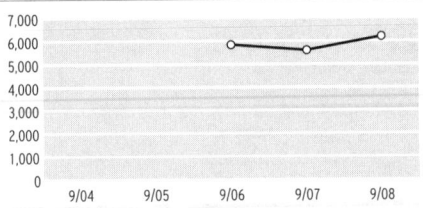

IAC North America

International Automotive Components Group North America (IAC North America) makes automobile interiors that are convenient, comfortable, and safe. The company designs and produces automotive consoles, instrument panels, interior trim designed for storage and safety (side airbags and sensors), exterior trim, door panels, and flooring for automobile manufacturing companies. Its customers include major manufacturers like Ford, GM, Honda, Toyota, and Volkswagen. The company operates around 40 manufacturing facilities located in the US, Mexico, and Canada. A privately-owned company, IAC North America is part of IAC Group, which also operates companies in Europe, Asia, and South America.

Lear Corporation's Interior Systems Division was sold and turned into IAC North America in 2007. The head of that Lear division, Jim Kamsickas, became IAC North America's president and CEO. Despite its exit from interior systems manufacturing, Lear still has a minority stake in IAC North America.

In addition to its operations in North America, IAC is also involved in two joint venture facilities in China.

EXECUTIVES

President and CEO: Jim Kamsickas
CFO: Jeff Vanneste
VP NA Commercial: John Smail
VP Product Engineering: Maurice Sessel
VP Human Resources: Robbie Bryan
VP, Secretary, and General Counsel: Janis N. Acosta
VP Operations: Jim Keppler

LOCATIONS

HQ: International Automotive Components Group
North America
5300 Auto Club Dr., Dearborn, MI 48126
Phone: 313-240-3000   **Fax:** 313-240-3100
Web: www.iacna.com

COMPETITORS

Faurecia Interior Systems
Key Plastics
Magna International
NYX Inc.
RFH Inc.
Summit Polymers
Visteon

HISTORICAL FINANCIALS

Company Type: Private

Income Statement

	REVENUE ($ mil.)	NET INCOME ($ mil.)	NET PROFIT MARGIN	EMPLOYEES
12/08	2,136	—	—	28,245

FYE: December 31

Iasis Healthcare

If you're sick in the suburbs, IASIS Healthcare provides a medical oasis. The company owns and operates about 15 acute care hospitals and one behavioral health facility (more than 2,600 beds total) in Arizona, Florida, Louisiana, Nevada, Texas, and Utah. IASIS also operates several outpatient facilities and other centers providing ancillary services, such as radiation therapy, diagnostic imaging, and ambulatory surgery. Its Health Choice Arizona subsidiary is a Medicaid managed health plan that serves about 145,000 individuals in Arizona. An investor group led by Texas Pacific Group owns the company.

IASIS is growing both by acquiring and building new facilities. It generally looks for hospitals that have between 100 and 400 beds and that are located in fast-growing urban and suburban areas.

The company purchased Glenwood Regional Medical Center in West Monroe, Louisiana, in 2007 and estimates it will spend $30 million on renovations at the facility in the first four years of owning it. It also built a new hospital in the Phoenix area (Mountain Vista Medical Center) that opened its doors in 2007, replacing the company's former Mesa General Hospital.

Also in 2007 IASIS acquired the Alliance Hospital in Odessa; the purchased facility was merged into the adjacent Odessa Regional Hospital, which IASIS already controlled, to form the Odessa Regional Medical Center.

In addition to expanding its portfolio of facilities, the company is adding services and upgrading equipment and facilities at its existing hospitals. Among other things, it looks to expand its higher-margin specialty medical and surgical offerings, add capacity to its emergency rooms, and upgrade diagnostic imaging and robotic surgical equipment. The company is constructing new patient towers to expand two of its Utah facilities.

EXECUTIVES

Chairman and CEO: David R. White, age 62
President and COO: Sandra K. McRee, age 53
CFO and Principal Financial Officer: W. Carl Whitmer, age 45
EVP Western Region: Paul Jenson, age 61
EVP Mountain Region: George Kirk Olsen, age 59
VP, Treasurer, and Chief Accounting Officer: John M. Doyle, age 48
VP Ethics and Business Practices: Peter Stanos, age 46
Secretary and General Counsel: Frank A. Coyle, age 45
Chief Quality Officer: John Cruickshank, age 52
Operations CFO: James Moake, age 40
President, Arizona Market: Dorothy Sawyer, age 59
CEO, Health Choice Arizona: Carolyn Rose, age 60
CFO, Texas and Louisiana Markets: Joe Minissale
CFO, Arizona and Nevada: Ruby Majhail, age 42
CFO, Utah Market: Steve King, age 42
CFO, Florida Market: Bashar Abunaser, age 41
Auditors: Ernst & Young LLP

LOCATIONS

HQ: IASIS Healthcare LLC
117 Seaboard Ln., Bldg. E, Franklin, TN 37067
Phone: 615-844-2747   **Fax:** 615-846-3006
Web: www.iasishealthcare.com

Selected Facilities

Davis Hospital and Medical Center (Layton, UT)
Glenwood Regional Medical Center (West Monroe, LA)
Jordan Valley Hospital (West Jordan, UT)
Memorial Hospital of Tampa (Tampa, FL)
Mountain Vista Medical Center (Mesa, AZ)
North Vista Hospital (Las Vegas, NV)
Odessa Regional Medical Center (Odessa, TX)
Palms of Pasadena Hospital (St. Petersburg, FL)
Pioneer Valley Hospital (West Valley City, UT)
St. Luke's Medical Center (Phoenix, AZ)
St. Luke's Behavioral Hospital (Phoenix, AZ)
Salt Lake Regional Medical Center (Salt Lake City, UT)
Southwest General Hospital (San Antonio, TX)
Tempe St. Luke's Hospital (Tempe, AZ)
The Medical Center of Southeast Texas (Port Arthur, TX)
Town & Country Hospital (Tampa, FL)

PRODUCTS/OPERATIONS

2008 Sales

	$ mil.	% of total
Acute care operations	1,523.8	74
Premiums (Health Choice)	541.7	26
Total	**2,065.5**	**100**

COMPETITORS

Aetna
Banner Health
BayCare Health System
Bayfront Health
Bon Secours Health
Catholic Healthcare West
CHRISTUS Health
Desert Springs Hospital
HCA
Humana
Intermountain Health Care
John C. Lincoln Health Network
MedCath
Northern Louisiana Medical Center
Tampa General Hospital
UnitedHealth Group
University Community Health
University Community Hospital
University Health System
University of Utah Hospitals & Clinics
Valley Hospital
Vanguard Health Systems
WellPoint

HISTORICAL FINANCIALS

Company Type: Private

Income Statement

FYE: September 30

	REVENUE ($ mil.)	NET INCOME ($ mil.)	NET PROFIT MARGIN	EMPLOYEES
9/08	2,066	36	1.8%	10,775
9/07	1,850	42	2.2%	10,826
9/06	1,626	40	2.4%	8,877
9/05	1,524	41	2.7%	8,800
9/04	1,387	(32)	—	9,000
Annual Growth	10.5%	—	—	4.6%

Net Income History

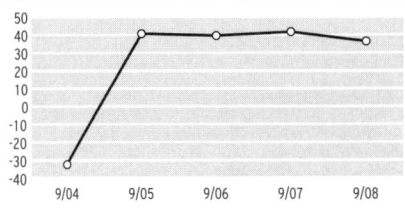

ICC Industries

ICC Industries is helping the world look brighter, smell better, and live healthier. The company trades basic and specialty chemicals globally. Operating through a number of subsidiaries, ICC Industries is an international maker of chemicals (Dover Chemical), plastics (Primex), and pharmaceutical products; it also distributes nutritional supplements and food ingredients. Its main subsidiary, ICC Chemical, is among the largest distributors in the US and maintains trading and marketing offices throughout the world. Other subsidiaries include Israeli flavors company Frutarom and the US plastics compounder and colorant producer O'Neil Color. The founding Farber family, including chairman John Farber, owns ICC.

EXECUTIVES

Chairman: John J. Farber, age 83
Vice Chairman: Sandra Farber
President: John Oram
VP and CFO: Blaise Sarcone
VP and General Counsel: Paul Falick
VP and Treasurer: Susan Abinder
President and CEO, Frutarom: Ori Yehudai, age 54
President, Dover Chemical Corporation:
 Dwain S. Colvin
President, Primex Plastics Corporation: Mike Cramer
**President and CEO, ICC Chemical and Fallek
 Chemical:** William Brunger

LOCATIONS

HQ: ICC Industries Inc.
 460 Park Ave., New York, NY 10022
Phone: 212-521-1700   **Fax:** 212-521-1970
Web: www.iccindustries.com

PRODUCTS/OPERATIONS

Selected Operations and Products

Azur S.A.
 Coatings
 Lacquers
 Paints
 Putties
 Synthetic resins
 Thinners
Dover Chemical Corporation
 Brominated and bromochlorinated flame retardants
 Chlorinated paraffins
 Lubricant additives
 Metallic stearates
 Organo-phosphites
 Specialty alkyl phenols
 Surfactants
Frutarom Industries Ltd. (37%)
 Botanicals
 Citrus derivatives
 Flavors for foods and beverages
 Natural flavor ingredients
 Protected amino acids
 Seasonings
 Spice oleoresins
Primex Plastics Corporation
 Plastic Sheets
 Antistatic, weatherable, conductive, and UV inhibited
  sheet
 Mono- and multilayer extruded and coextruded
  sheet (made from polystyrene, polyester,
  polyethylene, polypropylene, and acrylonitrile
  butadiene styrene)
 Print-grade sheet
 Polypropylene and polyethylene twin wall sheet
 Sheets produced under white room conditions
 Coral Plastics Enterprises Inc.
 Polystyrene and polystyrene light lens material
 O'Neil Color and Compounding Corp.
 Custom-color compounded resins
 Custom-color matched and standard color
  concentrates
 Custom compounding
 Mineral fillers
 Plastic additives (antiblocks, antistatic, ultraviolet
  inhibitors, and processing aids and flame
  retardants)
 Pace Industries, Inc.
 Polystyrene and polyolefin sheet for specialty
  industries
 Print-grade sheet
 Woodruff Corporation
 Custom packaging
 Reusable returnable containers
 Silk-screened indoor and outdoor signs

COMPETITORS

Ashland Distribution
Brenntag North America
Formosa Plastics
HELM U.S.
International Flavors
Lipo Chemicals
LyondellBasell
Nagase
R.T. Vanderbilt
Synthetech
Teva Pharmaceuticals
Univar USA

HISTORICAL FINANCIALS

Company Type: Private

Income Statement

FYE: December 31

	REVENUE ($ mil.)	NET INCOME ($ mil.)	NET PROFIT MARGIN	EMPLOYEES
12/07	1,800	—	—	1,700
12/06	1,370	—	—	1,525
12/05	1,342	—	—	1,700
Annual Growth	15.8%	—	—	0.0%

Revenue History

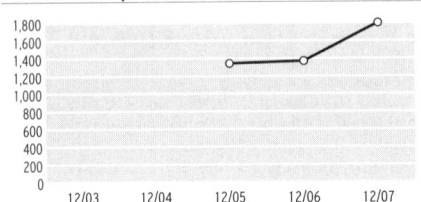

IGA, Inc.

IGA grocers are independent, but not alone. The world's largest voluntary supermarket network, IGA has 4,000-plus stores, including members in some 45 US states and more than 40 other countries on six continents. Collectively, its members are among North America's leaders in terms of supermarket sales. IGA (for either International or Independent Grocers Alliance, the company says) is owned by about 35 worldwide distribution companies, including SUPERVALU. Members can sell IGA-brand private-label products (over 2,300 items) and take advantage of joint operations and services, such as advertising and volume buying. Some stores in the IGA alliance, which primarily caters to smaller towns, also sell gas.

About two-thirds of IGA's total stores are located outside the US. As the first US grocer in China and Singapore, the company has plans for some 1,000 IGA-affiliated stores in China. IGA is also present in Europe, with operations in Poland and Spain. In 2008 it entered Russia followed by the opening of the first IGA on the island of Guam in 2009.

In 2006 the company reorganized by splitting itself into three companies: IGA USA, IGA Global, and the IGA Coca-Cola Institute. All three operate under IGA, Inc. As a result of the reorganization, Thomas Haggai became chairman and CEO of IGA International and Mark Batenic — formerly of Clemens Markets — joined the company as chairman, president, and CEO of IGA USA. (Previously, IGA realigned its corporate structure in 2001.)

By separating IGA's domestic stores from its stores overseas the company hopes to improve communications among IGA's US retailers.

One of Batenic's first moves was to establish a presence for IGA in San Francisco with the acquisition of eight supermarkets there from Ralphs Grocery.

IGA claims that it doesn't try to fight large chains such as Wal-Mart and Publix, instead preferring to keep the focus on its own niche of hometown and family-owned grocery stores.

HISTORY

IGA was founded in Chicago in 1926 by a group led by accountant Frank Grimes. During the 1920s chains began to dominate the grocery store industry. Grimes, an accountant for many grocery wholesalers, saw an opportunity to develop a network of independent grocers that could compete with the burgeoning chains. Grimes and five associates — Gene Flack, Louis Groebe, W. K. Hunter, H. V. Swenson, and William Thompson — created IGA.

Their idea was to "level the playing field" for independent grocers and chain stores by taking advantage of volume buying and mass marketing. IGA originally acted as a purchasing agent for its wholesalers but eventually passed that duty to the wholesalers. The group's first members were Poughkeepsie, New York-based grocery distributor W. T. Reynolds Company and the 69 grocery stores it serviced.

IGA focused on adding distributors and retailers, and it soon added wholesaler Fleming-Wilson (now Fleming Companies) and Winston & Newell (now SUPERVALU). In 1930 it hired Babe Ruth as a spokesman; other celebrity endorsers during the period included Jackie Cooper, Jack Dempsey, and Popeye. IGA also sponsored a radio program called the *IGA Home Town Hour*.

In 1945 the company introduced the Foodliner format, a design for stores larger than 4,000 sq. ft. The next year IGA introduced the 30-ft.-by-100-ft. Precision Store — designed so customers had to pass all the other merchandise in the store to get to the dairy and bread sections.

Grimes retired as president in 1951. He was succeeded by his son, Don, who continued to expand the company. Don was succeeded in 1968 by Richard Jones, head of IGA member J. M. Jones Co.

Thomas Haggai was named chairman of the company in 1976. A Baptist minister, radio commentator, and former CIA employee, Haggai had come to the attention of Grimes in 1960 when he praised Christian Scientists in one of his radio broadcasts. Grimes, a Christian Scientist, asked Haggai to speak at an IGA convention and eventually asked him to join the IGA board. Haggai, who became CEO in 1986, tightened the restrictions for IGA members, weeding out many of the smaller, low-volume mom-and-pop stores making up much of the group's network.

Haggai also began a push for international expansion. In 1988 the organization signed a deal with Japanese food company C. Itoh (now ITOCHU) to open a distribution outlet in Tokyo.

The 1990s saw expansion into Australia, Papua New Guinea, the Caribbean, China, Singapore, South Africa, and Brazil. IGA also expanded outside the continental US when it entered Hawaii. In 1993 IGA began an international television advertising campaign, a first for the supermarket industry. The next year the company launched its first line of private-label products for an ethnic food market, introducing several Mexican food products. In 1998 the group developed a new format for its stores that included on-site gas pumps.

SUPERVALU signed 54 independent grocery stores (primarily in Mississippi and Arkansas, and Trinidad in the Caribbean) to the IGA banner in August 1999.

With more than 60% of sales from international operations, IGA realigned its corporate structure in 2001, setting up IGA North America, IGA Southern Hemisphere/Europe/Caribbean, and IGA Asia, each with its own president.

IGA suffered the loss of Fleming (one of the grocery chain's principal wholesale distributors) and 300 stores in 2003. On the plus side, four Julian's Supermarkets on the Caribbean island of St. Lucia converted to IGA, giving IGA a presence in 45 countries worldwide.

The company's 2006 reorganization resulted in a three-way split that formed three separate companies (IGA USA, IGA Global, and IGA Coca-Cola Institute) operating under the IGA, Inc., name. In 2008 IGA expanded into Russia.

EXECUTIVES

Chairman and CEO: Thomas S. Haggai
VP Finance and CFO: John Collins
SVP Procurement and Private Brands: David S. Bennett
SVP Retail and Business Development: Doug Fritsch
VP Information Technology: Nick Liakopulos
VP Communications and Events: Barbara G. Wiest
Area Director: Ricky St. John
Area Director: Brian Horrigan
Area Director: Bill Overman
Area Director: Jim Griffin
New Area Director, Western US: Terry Carr
Director Private Brands: Wayne Altschul
Manager Marketing and Retail Programs: Heidi Huff
National Accounts Manager: Jim Collins
Editor, IGA Grocergram Quarterly: Ashley M. Page
Liaison: Richard Lukeman
President, IGA Coca-Cola Institute: Paulo Goelzer
CEO, IGA USA: Mark K. Batenic
Senior Director Marketing, Branding, and Business Development, IGA USA: Jim Walz

LOCATIONS

HQ: IGA, Inc.
8745 W. Higgins Rd., Ste. 350, Chicago, IL 60631
Phone: 773-693-4520   **Fax:** 773-693-4533
Web: www.iga.com

PRODUCTS/OPERATIONS

Selected Joint Operations and Services
Advertising
Community service programs
Equipment purchase
IGA Brand (private-label products)
IGA Grocergram (in-house magazine)
Internet services
Marketing
Merchandising
Red Oval Family (manufacturer/IGA collaboration on sales, marketing, and other activities)
Volume buying

COMPETITORS

A&P
Albertsons
Associated Wholesale Grocers
BJ's Wholesale Club
C & S Wholesale
Carrefour
Casino Guichard
Coles Group
Daiei
Dairy Farm International
Delhaize
George Weston
Hannaford Bros.
H-E-B
Ito-Yokado
Kroger
Meijer
Penn Traffic
Publix
Roundy's Supermarkets
Royal Ahold
Safeway
Spartan Stores
Wakefern Food
Wal-Mart
Winn-Dixie

HISTORICAL FINANCIALS
Company Type: Holding company

Income Statement

	REVENUE ($ mil.)	NET INCOME ($ mil.)	NET PROFIT MARGIN	EMPLOYEES
12/08	21,000	—	—	92,000
12/07	21,000	—	—	92,000
12/06	21,000	—	—	92,000
Annual Growth	0.0%	—	—	0.0%

FYE: December 31

Revenue History

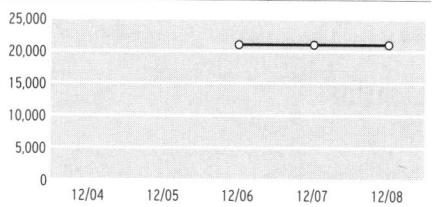

Ilitch Holdings

This holding company rules over a Caesar, tames Tigers, and takes flight on the ice. Ilitch Holdings controls the business interests of Mike and Marian Ilitch and their family, which includes the Little Caesars pizza chain, the Detroit Tigers baseball team, and the Detroit Red Wings hockey team. Subsidiary Olympia Entertainment owns Detroit's Fox Theatre and operates Comerica Park, Joe Louis Arena, and Cobo Arena. Additional holdings include Blue Line Foodservice Distribution, a leading supplier of food and equipment to restaurant operators (including Little Caesars operators), and an interest in the MotorCity Casino Hotel. The Ilitches started Little Caesars in 1959 and formed Ilitch Holdings in 1999.

While their entertainment and leisure holdings are vast, keeping the family business growing through a difficult economy has become a

challenge. The Ilitches had been investing in downtown real estate hoping to build a new hockey arena, but those plans have been put on hold due largely to the credit crisis that struck in late 2008. Their Olympia Entertainment unit, meanwhile, declined to renew its 30-year lease and operating agreement for both Joe Louis Arena and Cobo Arena in 2009; the company has announced plans to work with the city of Detroit to restructure those agreements.

Mike and Marian Ilitch parlayed their successful pizza franchise into an empire through a series of acquisitions. They purchased the Red Wings in 1982, the same year they acquired Olympia Entertainment. Ten years later they added the Tigers baseball team to their holdings.

EXECUTIVES

Chairman: Michael (Mike) Ilitch, age 80
Vice Chairwoman: Marian Ilitch
President and CEO: Christopher (Chris) Ilitch
CFO: Scott Fisher
CIO: Todd Seroka
VP Government Relations: Michael (Mike) McLauchlan
VP Corporate Communications: Karen Cullen
VP Human Resources: Joni C. Nelson
VP Tax Affairs: John M. Kotlar
Director Corporate Communications: Jennifer Haselhuhn

LOCATIONS

HQ: Ilitch Holdings, Inc.
2211 Woodward Ave., Detroit, MI 48201
Phone: 313-471-6600   **Fax:** 313-471-6094
Web: www.ilitchholdings.com

PRODUCTS/OPERATIONS

Selected Operations
Entertainment venues
  Olympia Entertainment
    Fox Theatre (Detroit)
  Uptown Entertainment (film theaters; Birmingham, Michigan)
Food services
  Blue Line Foodservice Distribution
  Champion Foods
  Little Caesars Pizza
Sports teams
  Detroit Red Wings (hockey)
  Detroit Tigers (baseball)

HISTORICAL FINANCIALS
Company Type: Holding company

Income Statement

	ESTIMATED REVENUE ($ mil.)	NET INCOME ($ mil.)	NET PROFIT MARGIN	EMPLOYEES
12/08	2,000	—	—	—
12/07	1,520	—	—	17,000
12/06	1,480	—	—	17,000
12/05	1,500	—	—	12,000
Annual Growth	10.1%	—	—	19.0%

FYE: December 31

Revenue History

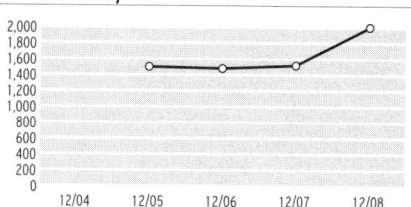

Indiana Pacers

This team sets the tempo on the basketball court. Pacers Basketball, which does business as Pacers Sports & Entertainment, owns and operates the Indiana Pacers professional basketball franchise of the National Basketball Association along with Indianapolis' Conseco Fieldhouse, the team's home arena. The franchise was formed in 1967 as a charter member of the American Basketball Association by a group of investors that included Richard Tinkman (who also helped found the ABA) and joined the NBA in 1976. Indiana has made just one appearance in the NBA Finals. The sports franchise is owned by shopping-center magnate Herbert Simon, who purchased the Pacers with his brother Melvin in 1983. Melvin Simon died in 2009.

The team has been under the leadership of head coach Jim O'Brien since 2007. He replaced Rick Carlisle at the end of that season after the Pacers failed to make the playoffs for the first time in a decade. Carlisle had coached the Pacers for four years, reaching the Eastern Conference finals in 2004. O'Brien was previously coach of the Philadelphia 76ers.

The following year, Herb Simon was named the new CEO of Pacers Sports after longtime team president Donnie Walsh resigned to take the top front office job with the troubled New York Knicks. Famed Hoosier State native and former Celtics star Larry Bird remained as head of basketball operations, while front office veteran David Morway was later promoted to general manager.

In addition to the NBA team, Pacers Basketball controls the Indiana Fever of the WNBA. The Simon family founded Simon Property Group, the top mall operator in the US.

EXECUTIVES

Co-Owner, Chairman, and CEO: Herbert (Herb) Simon, age 74
President: Jim Morris
COO: Rick Fuson
SVP Finance and CFO: Kevin Bower
SVP Marketing: Larry Mago
SVP and General Manager: David Morway
Head Coach: Jim O'Brien
President, Basketball Operations: Larry Bird, age 53
VP Operations: Tom Rutledge
VP Management Information Systems: Kevin Naylor
VP Marketing and Strategic Planning: Steve Gregory
VP Business Operations: Julie Graue
VP Corporate and Public Relations: Greg Schenkel
VP Human Resources: Donna Wilkinson
VP Player Relations: Sam Perkins
Executive Director, Pacers Foundation: Jami Marsh
Director Community Relations: Kelli Towles
Director Player Personnel: Mel Daniels
Director Scouting: Joe Ash

LOCATIONS

HQ: Pacers Basketball, LLC
    125 S. Pennsylvania St., Indianapolis, IN 46204
Phone: 317-917-2500   **Fax:** 317-917-2599
Web: www.nba.com/pacers

The Indiana Pacers play at the 18,345-seat capacity Conseco Fieldhouse in Indianapolis.

COMPETITORS

Cavaliers
Chicago Bulls
Detroit Pistons
Milwaukee Bucks

Indiana University

Indiana University has been schooling Hoosiers since 1820. With a total student population of some 100,000, the university offers more than 1,000 associate, baccalaureate, master's, professional, and doctoral degree programs at eight campuses: flagship institution IU-Bloomington; regional campuses in Fort Wayne, Gary, Kokomo, New Albany, Richmond, and South Bend; and an urban campus in Indianapolis that is operated jointly with Purdue University. An 1820 statute created the Indiana Seminary, the predecessor to Indiana University. In 1828 the legislature changed the name of the institution to Indiana College, and in 1838 it established Indiana University.

EXECUTIVES

President, Board of Trustees: Stephen L. Ferguson
President: Michael A. McRobbie
EVP and Chancellor, IU-Purdue University Indianapolis: Charles R. Bantz
EVP and Provost Indiana University Bloomington: Karen Hanson
VP and CFO: Neil D. Theobald
VP and Chief Administrative Officer: J. Terry Clapacs
VP and General Counsel: Dorothy J. Frapwell
VP Diversity, Equity, and Multicultural Affairs: Edwin C. Marshall
VP and Dean Walter J. Daly Professor, School of Medicine: D. Craig Brater
VP Information Technology: Bradley C. Wheeler
VP University Relations: Michael M. Sample
VP Institutional Development and Student Affairs: Charlie Nelms
Dean Library Services: Michele Russo
Treasurer: MaryFrances McCourt
Secretary: Robin Roy Gress
Executive Director Marketing: Lisa Townsend
Auditors: Indiana State Board of Accounts

LOCATIONS

HQ: Indiana University
    107 S. Indiana Ave., Bloomington, IN 47405
Phone: 812-855-4848   **Fax:** 812-855-9972
Web: www.indiana.edu

Indiana University has campuses in Bloomington, Fort Wayne, Gary, Indianapolis, Kokomo, New Albany, Richmond, and South Bend, Indiana.

Infor Global Solutions

Before manufacturers and distributors get products to the shelf, Infor gets software to their computers. Infor Global Solutions supplies enterprise software — that is software used for a wide range of business purposes. Whether managing inventories, tracking shipments, or working with customers, enterprise software can link disparate functions. Infor has a history of growing and changing its global enterprise software business with acquisitions and as a result can target customers in many industries. Among these are automotive, chemicals, consumer packaged goods, food and beverage processing, metal fabrication, and pharmaceuticals. Infor has offices in more than 100 countries.

Infor used a string of acquisitions to quietly become one of the leading vendors of business software. As a result, its product offerings cover a wide range of enterprise tasks. Resource planning, customer relationship management (CRM), and asset and supply chain management are some examples.

Its client list includes Bristol-Myers Squibb, Cargill, Coca-Cola Enterprises, GlaxoSmithKline, Grohe, Heinz, and TRW. Infor is backed by Golden Gate Capital and Summit Partners.

Golden Gate helped launch the company in 2002 when it worked with Parallax Capital Partners to buy the process manufacturing software business of Systems & Computer Technology. Formerly called Agilisys, the company became Infor after acquiring German enterprise resource planning software provider Infor Business Solutions AG in 2004.

In 2005 Infor purchased two providers of software for the manufacturing industry, MAPICS ($347 million) and Formation Systems. Its buying spree continued in 2006, when it snatched up asset management software supplier Datastream Systems ($216 million), enterprise software provider SSA Global Technologies ($1.36 billion), and financial and performance management software developers Systems Union Group and Extensity. The company expanded its offerings with the acquisitions of Workbrain (workforce management) and Hansen Information Technologies (enterprise applications for local government agencies) in 2007.

EXECUTIVES

Chairman and CEO: C. James (Jim) Schaper
EVP and CFO: Raghavan (Raj) Rajaji
CTO: Bruce Gordon
VP and CIO: Brian Rose
SVP and General Manager, EMEA: Benoit de la Tour
SVP, General Counsel, and Secretary: Gregory M. Giangiordano
SVP Latin America: Robert Faricy
SVP; President, Global Field Operations: Gregory (Greg) Corgan
SVP Human Resources: Glenn Goldberg
SVP Global Support: Marylon McGinnis
SVP Mergers & Acquisitions and Integration: Kevin Samuelson
SVP Strategic Planning and Alliances: Dennis Michalis
SVP and Chief Marketing Officer: Robert C. Humphrey
President, Customer Direct: Ken Walters
President, Asia Pacific: Lawrence Y. H. Chan
Manager, Public Relations: Cameron Smith

LOCATIONS

HQ: Infor Global Solutions, Inc.
    13560 Morris Rd., Ste. 4100, Alpharetta, GA 30004
Phone: 678-319-8000   **Fax:** 678-319-8682
Web: www.infor.com

COMPETITORS

American Software
AspenTech
CDC Corp.
CDC Software
Epicor Software
HP Enterprise Services
i2 Technologies
JDA Software
Lawson Software
Manhattan Associates
Microsoft
Oracle
QAD
RedPrairie
SAP

HISTORICAL FINANCIALS

Company Type: Private

Income Statement				FYE: May 31
	ESTIMATED REVENUE ($ mil.)	NET INCOME ($ mil.)	NET PROFIT MARGIN	EMPLOYEES
5/08	2,200	—	—	9,000
5/07	2,080	—	—	9,200
Annual Growth	5.8%	—	—	(2.2%)

Revenue History

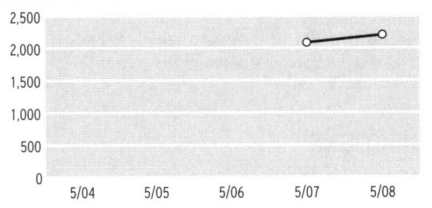

Ingram Entertainment

Companies selling books and CDs might get the star treatment, but Ingram Entertainment doesn't mind a supporting role. The company is one of the largest independent video, DVD, and computer game distributors in the US. In addition, Ingram distributes software, audio books, electronics, and used videos and games. From some 15 sales and distribution centers, Ingram serves more than 10,000 video stores, mass retailers, drugstores, and supermarkets. The company also operates AccessIngram.com, a business-to-business e-commerce site, and creates and maintains personalized Web sites for its customers through its MyVideoStore.com offering. Ingram Entertainment was spun off from family-owned Ingram Industries in 1997.

Ingram customers include leading retailers such as 7-Eleven, Amazon.com, Barnes & Noble, and Best Buy.

DVDs account for 75% of the company's sales.

EXECUTIVES

Chairman and President: David B. Ingram, age 46
EVP and CFO: William D. (Donnie) Daniel
EVP Purchasing and Operations: Robert W. (Bob) Webb
SVP Finance and Treasurer: Barbara Tucker
SVP and CIO: Mark D. Ramer
SVP Sales and Marketing: Bob Geistman
VP Sales: Bill Bryant
Auditors: PricewaterhouseCoopers

LOCATIONS

HQ: Ingram Entertainment Holdings Inc.
2 Ingram Blvd., La Vergne, TN 37089
Phone: 615-287-4000   **Fax:** 615-287-4982
Web: www.ingramentertainment.com

PRODUCTS/OPERATIONS

Products

Accessories
  Adapters
  Blank tapes
  Cleaning products
  Controllers
  Head cleaners
Audio books
DVDs
Electronics
Previously viewed videos
Video games
Videos

  Memory cards
  Repair kits
  Rewinders
  Security tags
  Storage cases

COMPETITORS

Alliance Entertainment
Baker & Taylor
E1 Distribution
East Texas Distributing
First Look Home
  Entertainment

Image Entertainment
MTI Home Video
Navarre
Rentrak
Source Interlink

HISTORICAL FINANCIALS

Company Type: Private

Income Statement				FYE: December 31
	REVENUE ($ mil.)	NET INCOME ($ mil.)	NET PROFIT MARGIN	EMPLOYEES
12/08	831	—	—	650
12/07	813	—	—	670
12/06	764	—	—	685
12/05	839	—	—	747
Annual Growth	(0.3%)	—	—	(4.5%)

Revenue History

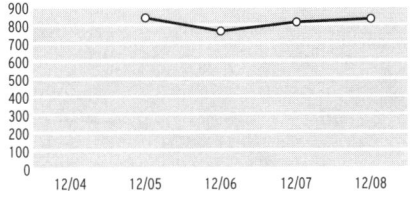

Ingram Industries

Ingram Industries is big in books and boats. The company distributes books and handles digital assets through Ingram Content Group, one of its operating divisions. Ingram Content Group consists of book wholesaler Ingram Book Group, digital content distributor Ingram Digital, and on-demand book printer Lightning Source, among other units geared toward Christian bookshops and libraries. Ingram Marine Group, which operates Ingram Barge, constitutes the company's other operating division. The nation's largest inland carrier, Ingram Barge ships grain, ore, and other goods via a fleet of about 4,000 barges and some 140 towboats. The Ingram family, led by chairman Martha Ingram, owns and runs Ingram Industries.

To better serve its customers and publishers, Ingram Industries in 2009 integrated its book distribution and digital services businesses under the corporate umbrella of Ingram Content Group. The new structure is intended to make Ingram's services more accessible and functional to its clientele.

Besides restructuring the content side of its business, Ingram Industries has also focused on building its boating operations. In 2008 Ingram Barge purchased 20 tank barges, the largest addition to its tank fleet in about 30 years. Tank barges carry oil and chemicals.

HISTORY

Orrin Ingram and two partners founded the Dole, Ingram & Kennedy sawmill in 1857 in Eau Claire, Wisconsin, on the Chippewa River, about 50 miles upstream from the Mississippi River. By the 1870s the company, renamed Ingram & Kennedy, was selling lumber as far downstream as Hannibal, Missouri.

Ingram's success was noticed by Frederick Weyerhaeuser, a German immigrant in Rock Island, Illinois, who, like Ingram, had worked in a sawmill before buying one of his own. In 1881 Ingram and Weyerhaeuser negotiated the formation of Chippewa Logging (35% owned by up-river partners, 65% by down-river interests), which controlled the white pine harvest of the Chippewa Valley. In 1900 Ingram paid $216,000 for 2,160 shares in the newly formed Weyerhaeuser Timber Company. Ingram let his sons and grandsons handle the investment and formed O.H. Ingram Co. to manage the family's interests. He died in 1918.

In 1946 Ingram's descendants founded Ingram Barge, which hauled crude oil to the company's refinery near St. Louis. After buying and then selling other holdings, in 1962 the family formed Ingram Corp., consisting solely of Ingram Barge. Brothers Bronson and Fritz Ingram (the great-grandsons of Orrin) bought the company from their father, Hank, before he died in 1963, and in 1964 they bought half of Tennessee Book, a textbook distributing company founded in 1935. In 1970 they formed Ingram Book Group to sell trade books to bookstores and libraries.

Ingram Barge won a $48 million Chicago sludge-hauling contract in 1971, but later the company was accused of bribing city politicians with $1.2 million in order to land the contract. The brothers stood trial in 1977 for authorizing the bribes; Bronson was acquitted, but the court convicted Fritz on 29 counts. Before Fritz entered prison (he served 16 months of a four-year sentence), he and his brother split their company. Fritz took the energy operations and went bust in the 1980s. Bronson took the barge and book businesses and formed Ingram Industries.

The new company formed computer products distributor Ingram Computer in 1982 and between 1985 and 1989 bought all the stock of Micro D, a computer wholesaler. Ingram Computer and Micro D merged to form Ingram Micro. In 1992 it acquired Commtron, the world's #1 wholesaler of prerecorded videocassettes, and merged it into Ingram Entertainment.

When Bronson died in mid-1995, his wife, Martha (the PR director), became chairman and began a restructuring. Ingram Industries closed its non-bookstore rack distributor (Ingram Merchandising) in 1995 and sold its oil-and-gas machinery subsidiary (Cactus Co.) in 1996. It spun off Ingram Micro in 1996, followed in 1997 by Ingram Entertainment. Ingram Industries purchased Christian books distributor Spring Arbor that year and also introduced an on-demand book publishing service (Lightning Print).

The company in late 1998 agreed to sell its book group to Barnes & Noble for $600 million, but FTC pressure killed the deal in mid-1999. With customers and competitors increasing distribution capacity in the western US, a resulting drop in business led Ingram Industries to cut more than 100 jobs at an Oregon warehouse in 1999. Also that year Martha Ingram, then chairman of the board, named her son, Orrin, as the company's president and CEO.

In early 2000 Ingram Industries renamed Lightning Print as Lightning Source. Also that year Ingram announced plans to distribute products other than books for e-tailers (starting with gifts). In March 2001 Ingram took over the specialty-book distribution for Borders.

In July 2002 Ingram completed its acquisition of Midland Enterprises LLC, a leading US inland marine transportation company that includes The Ohio River Company LLC and Orgulf Transport LLC. In an effort to streamline its distribution network, in mid-2002 Ingram Book Group consolidated its eight distribution centers into four super centers, including a new facility in Pennsylvania.

In late 2003 the company's Lightning Source subsidiary celebrated the printing of its 10 millionth book.

The company sold its Permanent General Insurance business (which covers high-risk drivers in about seven states) to Capital Z Financial Services Partners and PGC Holdings in late 2004.

Ingram Book acquired Coutts Information Services in late 2006, in order to boost its academic library supply business.

In 2008 Ingram Barge purchased 20 tank barges, the largest addition to its tank fleet in 30 years. Tank barges carry oil and chemicals.

EXECUTIVES

Chairman: John R. Ingram, age 48
SVP; CEO, Ingram Digital: Michael F. Lovett
COO, Ingram Digital: Kenton W. (Kent) Freeman
President and CEO, Ingram Content Group:
David (Skip) Prichard
President, Lightning Source and Lightning Source UK:
David Taylor
President and CEO; Chairman, Ingram Barge Company: Orrin H. Ingram II
Chief Strategy Officer, Ingram Content Group:
James R. Gray
Chief Commercial Officer, Ingram Content Group; President, Ingram Periodicals: Shawn Everson
SVP Global Operations, Lightning Source:
John F. Secrest
SVP and General Counsel, Lightning Source:
David Roland
SVP Finance, Lightning Source: Brian Dauphin
SVP Strategy and Business Development, Lightning Source: Larry Brewster

LOCATIONS

HQ: Ingram Industries Inc.
1 Belle Meade Place, 4400 Harding Rd.
Nashville, TN 37205
Phone: 615-298-8200   **Fax:** 615-298-8242
Web: www.ingrambook.com

PRODUCTS/OPERATIONS

Selected Operations

Ingram Marine Group
 Custom Fuel Services (provides midstream fueling services to inland marine operations)
 Ingram Barge (ships grain, ore, and other products)
 Ingram Materials (produces construction materials such as sand and gravel)

Ingram Content Group
 Coutts Information Services (book supply, collection management for libraries)
 Ingram Book Company (wholesaler of trade books and audiobooks)
 Ingram International (international distribution of books and audiobooks)
 Ingram Library Services (distributes books, audiobooks, and videos to libraries)
 Ingram Periodicals (direct distributor of specialty magazines)
 Lightning Source (on-demand printing and electronic publishing)
 Spring Arbor Distributors (products and services for Christian retailers)
 Tennessee Book Company (Tennessee school system textbook depository)

COMPETITORS

American Commercial Lines	Jim Pattison Group
Anderson News	Kirby Corporation
Baker & Taylor	Levy Home Entertainment
Flat World Knowledge	Media Source
Follett	Safeco
Hudson Group	Thomas Nelson
	Times Publishing Limited

HISTORICAL FINANCIALS

Company Type: Private

Income Statement

FYE: December 31

	ESTIMATED REVENUE ($ mil.)	NET INCOME ($ mil.)	NET PROFIT MARGIN	EMPLOYEES
12/08	2,160	—	—	5,400
12/07	2,100	—	—	5,700
12/06	1,810	—	—	5,200
12/05	2,539	—	—	5,200
12/04	2,310	—	—	5,767
Annual Growth	(1.7%)	—	—	(1.6%)

Revenue History

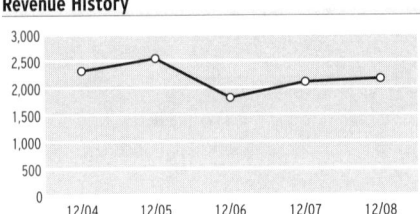

Inova Health System Foundation

Inova Health System Foundation provides financial support and assistance to the Inova Health System, which operates about 10 not-for-profit community hospitals in Northern Virginia. It also supports home health services, heart care programs, clinical research and trials, emergency and trauma centers, and nurse training. To raise funds for the hospital system, the foundation organizes special events such as galas, golf tournaments, and silent auctions. Donors can also make contributions through the Inova Web site. The foundation takes in about $20 million in contributions each year.

EXECUTIVES

Chairman: Fred Sachs
Manager Finance: Barbara Beard
VP: John Fay
Executive Director, Inova Fairfax Hospital Campus: Judy Bilicki
Manager, Inova Alexandria Hospital Foundation: Lori Powell
Manager, Inova Loudoun Hospital Foundation: Ginny Hamson
Executive Director, Inova Loudoun Hospital Foundation: Michelle Burke
Director Development, Annual Programs: Tim Cronen
Director Leadership Giving, Life with Cancer: Joanne Royaltey
Director Constituent Relations: Bonnie Roberts
Development Specialist, Annual Programs: Alexandra Obrand

LOCATIONS

HQ: Inova Health System Foundation
8110 Gatehouse Rd., Ste. 200E
Falls Church, VA 22042
Phone: 703-289-2072   **Fax:** 703-289-2073
Web: www.inova.org/get-involved/foundation

HISTORICAL FINANCIALS

Company Type: Not-for-profit

Income Statement

FYE: December 31

	REVENUE ($ mil.)	NET INCOME ($ mil.)	NET PROFIT MARGIN	EMPLOYEES
12/08	1,979	—	—	15,000

Inserra Supermarkets

The Big Apple need never be short of apples (or oranges, for that matter), thanks to Inserra Supermarkets. Inserra owns and operates about 20 ShopRite supermarkets and superstores in northern New Jersey and southeastern New York State (most are in Westchester and Rockland counties). Inserra's superstores feature bagel bakeries, cafes, and pharmacies. The regional grocery chain also offers banking services in selected stores through agreements with Poughkeepsie Savings Bank, Statewide Savings Bank, and others. Owned by the Inserra family, the retailer is one of more than 40 members that make up cooperative Wakefern Food, the owner of the ShopRite name.

The regional supermarket operator opened a new 70,000-sq.-ft. store in Lodi, New Jersey, in early 2008. The upscale store is one of Inserra's largest supermarkets and includes an upscale bakery department, floral section, fresh sushi, international gourmet cheeses, and full-service meat, seafood and pharmacy departments. Previously, it had closed a ShopRite supermarket in West Haverstraw, New York, in May 2007.

EXECUTIVES

Chairman, President, and CEO: Lawrence R. Inserra Jr.

LOCATIONS

HQ: Inserra Supermarkets, Inc.
   20 Ridge Rd., Mahwah, NJ 07430
Phone: 201-529-5900   **Fax:** 201-529-1189

COMPETITORS

A&P
D'Agostino Supermarkets
Food Circus Super Markets
Gristede's Foods
Hannaford Bros.
Key Food
King Kullen Grocery
Kings Super Markets
Stop & Shop
Trader Joe's
Western Beef

HISTORICAL FINANCIALS

Company Type: Private

Income Statement

FYE: December 31

	REVENUE ($ mil.)	NET INCOME ($ mil.)	NET PROFIT MARGIN	EMPLOYEES
12/08	1,050	—	—	—
12/07	1,050	—	—	3,500
12/06	1,030	—	—	4,000
12/05	1,030	—	—	4,000
Annual Growth	0.6%	—	—	(6.5%)

Revenue History

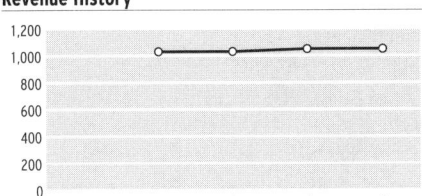

Insight Communications

As one of the ten largest US cable providers, Insight Communications has some inkling of what pay television and Internet subscribers want. The company's cable system serves about 700,000 consumer and business customers in the Midwest, with the bulk of its clients in Kentucky. Other key service areas include southern Indiana and Columbus, Ohio. Insight offers interactive digital video, video-on-demand, and such high-speed data services as cable Internet access and VoIP telephony services. The company has satellite offices and facilities in Indiana, Kentucky, and Ohio.

The company provides its enterprise customers with broadband data and video packages through its InsightBusiness division. It also offers Web hosting and IP-based voice telephony services.

Insight Communications was co-founded in 1985 by CEO Michael Willner and chairman Sidney Knafel.

EXECUTIVES

Chairman: Sidney R. Knafel
Vice Chairman and CEO: Michael S. Willner, age 55
President, COO, and Director: Dinesh C. (Dinni) Jain, age 43
EVP Central Operations and CTO: Hamid R. Heidary, age 51
EVP and CFO: John Abbot, age 45
EVP Operations, Insight Communications: Christopher (Chris) Slattery, age 40
SVP Programming and Video Services: Melani Griffith
SVP, Insight Media: Kevin Dowell
SVP Strategy and Operational Finance: Scott Schneiderman
SVP Communications: Sandra D. (Sandy) Colony
SVP Product Management: Paul Meltzer
SVP Field Operations: Gregory B. (Gregg) Graff
SVP Operations: John W. (Woody) Hutton
SVP Human Resources: Jim Morgan
SVP and Chief Accounting Officer: Daniel Mannino
SVP, General Counsel, and Secretary: Elliot Brecher, age 42
SVP Brand Strategy and Programming: Pamela Euler Halling
VP Marketing: Steven Eliasof

LOCATIONS

HQ: Insight Communications Company, Inc.
   810 7th Ave., New York, NY 10019
Phone: 917-286-2300   **Fax:** 917-286-2301
Web: www.insight-com.com

PRODUCTS/OPERATIONS

Selected Services

Basic, premium, and pay-per-view cable TV programming
Cable modem-based Internet access
Interactive digital video
Telephone services

COMPETITORS

AT&T
Cable One
Charter Communications
Comcast
Cox Communications
DIRECTV
DISH Network
Mediacom Communications
Rainbow Media
Time Warner Cable

HISTORICAL FINANCIALS

Company Type: Private

Income Statement

FYE: December 31

	REVENUE ($ mil.)	NET INCOME ($ mil.)	NET PROFIT MARGIN	EMPLOYEES
12/08	897	—	—	2,766
12/07	1,400	—	—	2,569
12/06	1,263	—	—	4,035
12/05	1,118	—	—	3,829
Annual Growth	(7.1%)	—	—	(10.3%)

Revenue History

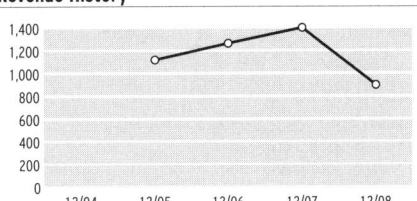

Intermountain Health Care

If you're whooshing down the side of one of Idaho's majestic mountains and take a nasty spill, Intermountain Health Care (IHC) will be there to save the day! From air ambulance services to urgent care clinics and general hospitals, IHC has all the tools to mend skiers (and non-skiers too) in Utah and southern Idaho. The not-for-profit health system operates some 20 hospitals, home health care agencies, dozens of physician and urgent care clinics, and rehabilitation centers. IHC was formed in 1975 when the Church of Jesus Christ of Latter Day Saints donated 15 hospitals to local communities. IHC is led by CEO Charles Sorenson, who replaced Bill Nelson when he retired after 33 years with the company.

Along with the full spectrum of physical health care services, IHC also offers comprehensive mental health and substance abuse programs for patients of all ages. The organization's spectrum of care includes acute inpatient, residential treatment, day treatment, chemical dependency inpatient/detoxification, and intensive outpatient programs.

IHC's more than two dozen hospitals have a combined total of some 2,300 beds. The hospitals range from general surgical to specialty care including orthopedic and pediatric facilities.

The organization conducts cancer research through its partnership with Huntsman Cancer Institute at the University of Utah. The two share data, best practices, funding, and co-conduct clinical trials. They also operate a number of cancer-specific treatment centers, including multi-disciplinary, tumor-specific clinics designed to provide one-stop service for cancer patients to meet with different cancer specialists on the same day, for a more comprehensive treatment plan.

EXECUTIVES

Chairman: Kem C. Gardner
Vice Chairman: Kent H. Murdock
President, CEO, and Trustee: Charles W. Sorenson
SVP and CFO: Bert R. Zimmerli
CIO: Marc Probst
SVP: Gregory P. Poulsen
SVP: Joseph R. (Joe) Horton

LOCATIONS

HQ: Intermountain Health Care, Inc.
   36 S. State St., Fl. 22, Salt Lake City, UT 84111
Phone: 801-442-2000   **Fax:** 801-442-3327
Web: www.ihc.com

Selected Hospitals

Alta View Hospital (Sandy, UT)
American Fork Hospital (American Fork, UT)
Bear River Valley Hospital (Tremonton, UT)
Cassia Regional Medical Center (Burley, ID)
Delta Community Medical Center (Delta, UT)
Dixie Regional Medical Center (St. George, UT)
Fillmore Community Medical Center (Fillmore, UT)
Garfield Memorial Hospital (Panguitch, UT)
Heber Valley Medical Center (Heber City, UT)
Intermountain Medical Center (Murray, UT)
LDS Hospital (Salt Lake City)
Logan Regional Hospital (Logan, UT)
McKay-Dee Hospital Center (Ogden, UT)
Orem Community Hospital (Orem, UT)
Primary Children's Medical Center (Salt Lake City)

Riverton Hospital (Riverton, UT)
Sanpete Valley Hospital (Mt. Pleasant, UT)
Sevier Valley Hospital (Richfield, UT)
The Orthopedic Specialty Hospital (Murray, UT)
Utah Valley Regional Medical Center (Provo, UT)
Valley View Medical Center (Cedar City, UT)

COMPETITORS

Aetna
Blue Cross
CHRISTUS Health
HCA
Iasis Healthcare
LifePoint Hospitals
Trinity Health (Novi)
UnitedHealth Group

HISTORICAL FINANCIALS

Company Type: Not-for-profit

Income Statement				FYE: December 31
	REVENUE ($ mil.)	NET INCOME ($ mil.)	NET PROFIT MARGIN	EMPLOYEES
12/08	3,049	—	—	23,000

International Data Group

International Data Group (IDG) is a publishing giant with digital appeal. The world's top technology publisher, IDG produces more than 300 magazines and newspapers (including *PC World* and *CIO*) in 85 countries and in dozens of languages. In addition to publishing, IDG provides technology market research through its IDC (International Data Corporation) unit, and the company also produces technology-focused industry events. The company offers career services through sites such as ITCareers.com, and operates 450 Web sites featuring technology content. Chairman Patrick McGovern founded IDG in 1964.

IDG produces more than 750 industry events, including Macworld Conference & Expo and LinuxWorld Conference & Expo. The company's IDC research unit has more than 900 analysts in more than 100 countries. Its IDG News Service is a 24-hour news organization that reports on IT news to the company's online network from bureaus around the world. In addition, IDG provides international brand marketing services for IT companies and media agencies through its IDG Global Services unit.

The company's IDG Ventures is a global family of venture capital funds affiliated with IDG. It has approximately $2 billion under management and a portfolio of more than 220 companies.

HISTORY

Patrick McGovern began his career in publishing as a paperboy for the *Philadelphia Bulletin*. As a teenager in the 1950s, McGovern was inspired by Edmund Berkeley's book *Giant Brains; or Machines That Think*. He later built a computer and won a scholarship to MIT. There he edited the first computer magazine, *Computers and Automation*. McGovern started market research firm International Data Corporation in 1964 after interviewing the president of computer pioneer UNIVAC. Three years later he launched *Computerworld,* and within a few weeks the eight-page tabloid had 20,000 subscribers. Combined under the name International Data Group, McGovern's company reached $1 million in sales by 1968.

Taking the "International" in its name to heart, IDG began publishing in Japan in 1971 and expanded to Germany in 1975. Following the collapse of communism, the company had 10 publications in Russia and Eastern Europe by 1990. That year two teenage hackers broke into the company's voice mail system and erased orders from customers and messages from writers. The prank cost IDG about $2.4 million. Also in 1990, IDG launched IDG Books Worldwide (renamed Hungry Minds in 2000), which hit it big the next year with *DOS for Dummies.*

With the technology boom of the 1990s, competition in tech publishing heated up. By 1993 several of IDG's magazines, including *InfoWorld, Macworld,* and *PC World,* began losing ad pages to rivals Ziff-Davis and CMP Media. To help stem advertiser attrition, IDG started an incentive program tied to its new online service. In 1995 IDG bought a stake in software companies Architect Software (now ExciteHome) and Netscape (now owned by America Online) as part of its move toward Internet-based services.

In 1996 IDG launched *Netscape World: The Web,* a magazine covering the Internet, and introduced more than 30 industry newsletters delivered by e-mail. The company also bought *PC Advisor,* the UK's fastest-growing computer magazine. IDG kicked off its online ad placement service, Global Web Ad Network, in 1997. That year IDG merged *Macworld* with rival Ziff-Davis' *MacUser* in a joint venture called Mac Publishing.

In 1998 IDG pledged $1 billion in venture capital for high-tech startups in China. It also introduced new publications in China, including a Chinese edition of *Cosmopolitan* (with Hearst Magazines) and *China Computer Reseller World.* Later that year the company launched *The Industry Standard* and spun off 25% of IDG Books to the public.

In 1999 it sold a 20% stake in Industry Standard Communications (renamed Standard Media International) to private investors and began laying plans for a possible spinoff in 2000. However, a weakening economy and slowing ad sales in 2000 quieted those plans.

The next year both Standard Media and Hungry Minds announced staff cuts and restructuring. IDG eventually sold its majority interest in Hungry Minds to John Wiley & Sons for about $90 million. Standard Media filed for bankruptcy and liquidated its assets, some of which were bought by IDG. The company also purchased Ziff Davis' 50% stake in their joint venture Mac Publishing. In 2002 IDG CEO Kelly Conlin left the business and was replaced by company executive Pat Kenealy, who had previously founded the now-defunct *Digital News* magazine.

EXECUTIVES

Chairman: Patrick J. (Pat) McGovern, age 71
CFO: Edward B. (Ted) Bloom
CEO, IDG Communications: Robert (Bob) Carrigan, age 43
VP Human Resources: Piper Sheer
VP Syndication, IDG Communications: Michael (Mike) Romoff

President and CEO, IDG Enterprise: Michael (Mike) Friedenberg
President, Connell Communications: Jim Connell
President, PC World/Macworld: Mike Kisseberth
President, IDG Strategic Marketing Services: Matthew (Matt) Yorke
President, GamePro Media: Marci Yamaguchi-Hughes
President, IDG Global Solutions: John P. O'Malley
President and CEO, IDC: Kirk S. Campbell, age 55
President and CEO, IDG International Publishing Services: David F. Hill
Editor-in-Chief, IDG News Service: Elizabeth Heichler
Director Communications and Marketing Programs, IDG Strategic Marketing Services: Howard Sholkin
Director Corporate Communications: Susanna Hinds
Auditors: Deloitte & Touche LLP

LOCATIONS

HQ: International Data Group, Inc.
1 Exeter Plaza, 15th Fl., Boston, MA 02116
Phone: 617-534-1200   **Fax:** 617-423-0240
Web: www.idg.com

PRODUCTS/OPERATIONS

Selected Operations

IDC (market research)
IDG Communications List Services
IDG Events & Conferences
IDG Global Solutions
IDG News Service
IDG Publications (periodical publishing)
IDG Recruitment Solutions (employment services)
IDG Research Services Group
IDG.net (online publications hub)

Selected Events

Bio-IT World Conference & Expo
CIO 100
ComNet Conference & Expo
DEMO
IDC Directions
LinuxWorld Conference & Expo
Macworld Conference & Expo

Selected Periodicals

Bio-IT World
Channel World
CIO
CSO
Computerworld
DigitalWorld
GamePro
InfoWorld
Macworld
Network World
PC World

COMPETITORS

1105 Media
Advanstar
CBS Interactive
Editis
Forrester Research
Freeman Decorating Services
Future plc
Gartner
IHS
The Nielsen Company
Penton Media
Red Herring
Reed Elsevier Group
SourceForge
SYS-CON Media
Tech Wire Media Group
TechTarget
UBM Technology
United Business Media
WebMediaBrands
Ziff Davis Media

International Specialty Products

If you've washed, shaved, and groomed, then you've probably shared a chemical experience with the folks at International Specialty Products (ISP). The company, also called ISP Chemco, makes about 400 types of specialty chemicals, including food and pharmaceutical ingredients, personal care, and fine chemicals, industrial chemicals (like butanediol for fibers and plastics), and minerals products. ISP also makes waterproofing agents, moisturizers, and preservatives for personal care products such as sunscreen and hair care products. The family of the company's late chairman, Samuel Heyman, controls ISP.

After watching the company's stock dive in 2002, Heyman took ISP private. After the transaction was complete, ISP went shopping. The company has bought many businesses, from smaller companies like Germinal, a South American food ingredients company, and UK oilfield chemicals producer Techwax, to divisions of multinational giants like BP.

International Specialty Products operates throughout North and South America, Europe, and Asia.

Heyman died late in 2009.

EXECUTIVES

President and CEO: Sunil Kumar
EVP, General Counsel, and Secretary:
Richard Weinberg, age 50
EVP Finance and Treasurer: Susan B. Yoss
SVP Sales and General Manager, Asia: Warren Bishop
SVP Sales and Commercial Director, Europe:
Roger J. Cope
SVP EMEA: Philip Strenger
SVP Supply Chain, and General Manager, Elastomers Business Unit: Melvin W. (Mel) Martin
SVP Specialty Chemicals, North America:
Catherine (Cathie) Joy
SVP and Commercial Director, Americas: Ron Brandt
SVP Global Marketing and Sales: Stephen R. Olsen
SVP Research and Development and Latin America:
Lawrence Grenner
SVP Operations, Specialty Chemicals Division:
Steven E. Post
VP and CIO: Ken Morris
VP Human Resources: Marianne Spencer
VP Corporate Development: Anthony Giorgio
Director Sales and Technical Service: Dale Henderson
Manager Communications: Michelle Evans
Auditors: KPMG LLP

LOCATIONS

HQ: International Specialty Products, Inc.
1361 Alps Rd., Wayne, NJ 07470
Phone: 973-628-4000   **Fax:** 973-628-4423
Web: www.ispcorp.com

PRODUCTS/OPERATIONS

Selected Products and Applications

Industrial chemicals
  Coatings
  Electronics cleaning
  High performance plastics
  Lubricating oil and chemical processing
Specialty chemicals
  Fine chemicals
    Specialized products (agricultural, biotechnology, imaging, and pharmaceutical markets)
    Flunixin Meglumine (animal analgesic)
    Milotane (cancer treatment)
    Pharmaceutical intermediates (cholesterol control, heart and kidney disease, and viral infections)
    Pheromones (used for insect control)
  Food and beverage
    Beer
    Cheese sauces
    Fruit fillings
    Health drinks
    Salad dressings
  Performance chemicals
    Acetylene-based polymers (agriculture, coatings, detergents, electronics, imaging, metalworking)
    Advanced materials (aerospace, defense, electronics, and powder metallurgy industries)
    Vinyl ether monomers
  Personal care
    Hair care
      Conditioning agent (hair conditioning rinses)
      Fixitive resins (holding power for gels, hairsprays, and mousses)
      Stabilizers (shampoo)
      Thickeners (shampoo)
    Skin care
      Adhesive (facial cleansing strips)
      Emollients (body and facial moisturizers)
      Moisturizers
      Preservatives
      Ultraviolet light absorbing chemicals
      Waterproofing agents (eyeliners and sun screen)
  Pharmaceutical
    Antiseptics
    Cough syrups
    Denture adhesives
    Injectable prescription drugs and serums
    Prescription and over-the-counter tablets
    Toothpastes
Minerals
  Colored roofing granules (asphalt roofing shingles)

COMPETITORS

3M
Albemarle
BASF SE
Cognis
CP Kelco
DuPont Canada
Evonik Degussa
Penford
Stepan
Yule Catto

HISTORICAL FINANCIALS

Company Type: Private

Income Statement

	REVENUE ($ mil.)	NET INCOME ($ mil.)	NET PROFIT MARGIN	EMPLOYEES
12/07	1,600	—	—	3,300
12/06	1,500	—	—	3,100
12/05	1,360	—	—	3,100
12/04	1,023	—	—	2,600
12/03	893	—	—	2,800
Annual Growth	15.7%	—	—	4.2%

FYE: December 31

Revenue History

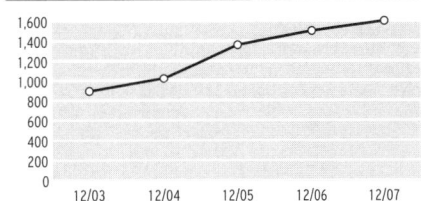

Interstate Batteries

Interstate Battery System of America offers a battery of batteries. The company can provide the electrical juice for everything from cellular phones and laptops to automobiles, boats, and lawn equipment. Interstate Battery has 300-plus distributors throughout North America; consumers can purchase Interstate Battery's products at more than 200,000 retail locations, including a growing number of Interstate All Battery Centers. The company makes the official replacement battery for the vehicles of companies such as Land Rover, Subaru, and Toyota. Interstate Battery sponsors the Joe Gibbs Racing team on the NASCAR circuit. Chairman Norm Miller owns the company.

Interstate sells batteries that carry its own brand as well as products with manufacturers' labels. Johnson Controls supplies Interstate's automotive line.

The company has grown its owned and franchised Interstate All Battery Center sales locations to more than 100 stores in the US, Canada, Puerto Rico, and the Dominican Republic.

The company was founded in Dallas in 1952 by John Searcy, who died in 2007. He started the company by selling replacement batteries in service stations on consignment. Searcy sold control of the company to Norm Miller in 1978.

EXECUTIVES

Chairman: Norm Miller
President and CEO: Carlos Sepulveda, age 51
VP All Battery and E-Commerce: Mickey Elam
VP Supply Chain Management: Chris Antoniou
VP Advertising and Public Relations: Scott Miller
VP Human Resources and Counsel: Chris Willis
VP Information Technology and CIO: Merv Tarde
VP Marketing: Dennis Brown
VP Accounting: Lisa Huntsberry
VP National Accounts: William (Billy) Norris
VP Independent Distributor Group: Jeff Haddock
VP Powercare and Interstate Owned Territories:
Walter (Walt) Holmes
Director Public Relations: Jane Koenecke

LOCATIONS

HQ: Interstate Battery System of America, Inc.
12770 Merit Dr., Ste. 400, Dallas, TX 75251
Phone: 972-991-1444   **Fax:** 972-458-8288
Web: www.ibsa.com

Interstate Battery System of America has distributors in Canada, the Dominican Republic, Guam, Jamaica, Puerto Rico, and the US.

PRODUCTS/OPERATIONS

Selected Applications

Automotive/truck
Calculators
Camcorders
Cellular phones
Chargers
Commercial equipment
Computers/laptops
Cordless phones
Cordless tools
Flashlights
Household batteries
Lawn and garden
Marine/RV
Medical equipment
Motorcycles
Pagers
Photo batteries
Radio batteries
Watches

Advance Auto Parts
AutoZone
Costco Wholesale
General Parts
Genuine Parts
O'Reilly Automotive
Pep Boys
Sears
Target
Universal Power Group
Wal-Mart

HISTORICAL FINANCIALS
Company Type: Private

Income Statement				FYE: April 30
	REVENUE ($ mil.)	NET INCOME ($ mil.)	NET PROFIT MARGIN	EMPLOYEES
4/08	1,500	—	—	1,415
4/07	1,000	—	—	1,275
4/06	1,000	—	—	1,400
4/05	755	—	—	1,251
4/04	700	—	—	900
Annual Growth	21.0%	—	—	12.0%

Revenue History

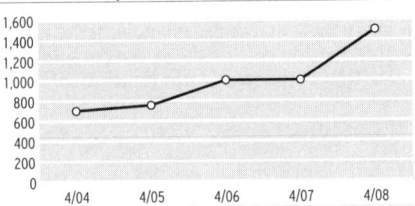

InterTech Group

The InterTech Group likes to interweave a wide variety of technology-driven manufacturing businesses with other activities, such as business services (image marketing, financial transaction services) and entertainment. The group, a holding company with more than 100 businesses worldwide, puts its primary focus on plastics and fiber products, including industrial protective wear and fabrics used by firefighters and astronauts (through its PBI Performance Products subsidiary). InterTech's RemGrit unit makes knives, saw blades, and various handheld tools. The company was founded in 1978 by the late Jerry Zucker, who in 2006 led the acquisition of Canada's Hudson's Bay Company, and is still owned by his family.

EXECUTIVES
Chairman and CEO: Anita Zucker
President: Jonathan M. Zucker, age 31
EVP and CFO: Brice Sweatt
EVP and COO: Jay Tiedemann
EVP and Chief Strategy Officer:
  Robert B. (Rob) Johnston

LOCATIONS
HQ: The InterTech Group, Inc.
  4838 Jenkins Ave., North Charleston, SC 29405
Phone: 843-744-5174   **Fax:** 843-747-4092
Web: www.theintertechgroup.com

HISTORICAL FINANCIALS
Company Type: Private

Income Statement				FYE: December 31
	ESTIMATED REVENUE ($ mil.)	NET INCOME ($ mil.)	NET PROFIT MARGIN	EMPLOYEES
12/08	3,800	—	—	16,000
12/07	3,450	—	—	16,000
12/06	3,830	—	—	16,000
12/05	3,500	—	—	14,500
Annual Growth	2.8%	—	—	3.3%

Revenue History

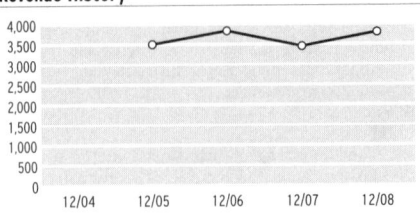

Iowa Health System

The Land Where the Tall Corn Grows is also the Land of Iowa Health System (IHS). The integrated health care system operates about 10 hospitals serving 70 communities throughout Iowa, as well as western Illinois and eastern Nebraska. IHS also manages clinics located in more than a dozen rural areas throughout Iowa and supports several rural hospitals. Founded in 1993, Iowa Health System has more than 3,000 licensed beds and a staff of some 450 physicians and other health care providers. The system's hospitals provide general medical-surgical care, as well as care in a number of medical specialties such as cardiovascular disease.

EXECUTIVES
Chair: Jim Hoffman
Vice Chair: Paula Arnell
President and CEO: Bill Leaver
EVP and CFO: Kevin Vermeer
VP and Chief Medical Officer: Alan S. Kaplan
VP and CIO: Joy M. Grosser
VP Public Relations and Communications: Cheri Bustos
VP and General Counsel: Denny Drake
Secretary and Director: Paul Brandt
Treasurer and Director: Bruce Sherman
Auditors: Deloitte & Touche LLP

LOCATIONS
HQ: Iowa Health System
  1200 Pleasant St., Des Moines, IA 50309
Phone: 515-241-6161   **Fax:** 515-241-6220
Web: www.ihs.org

COMPETITORS
Genesis Health System
Mercy Health Network
Regional Ventures
University of Iowa Hospitals and Clinics

HISTORICAL FINANCIALS
Company Type: Not-for-profit

Income Statement				FYE: December 31
	REVENUE ($ mil.)	NET INCOME ($ mil.)	NET PROFIT MARGIN	EMPLOYEES
12/08	1,875	—	—	18,923

Irvine Company

At The Irvine Company, everything goes according to plan — the *master* plan! The real estate investment company plans and designs office, retail, and residential villages in Los Angeles, Orange County, San Diego, and Silicon Valley. Its portfolio includes 400 office buildings, 40 retail centers, and 90 apartment communities, as well as several hotels, marinas, and golf clubs, not to mention The Irvine Ranch, one of the largest planned communities in the US. The ranch has some 260,000 residents and covers 93,000 acres, a drop from its original 120,000 acres back in the mid-1800s, when James Irvine bought out the debts of Mexican land-grant holders. Chairman Donald Bren, an American billionaire, owns the company.

The Irvine Company's portfolio includes Irvine Spectrum, one of the nation's largest high-tech research and business centers, encompassing some 40 million sq. ft. It also owns Irvine Apartment Communities, a residential management firm that owns and operates about 90 apartment complexes. The University of California, Irvine is built on company-donated land.

Bren has continued the 40-year-old master plan created by the Irvine Foundation (the former parent of The Irvine Company), which calls for gradual development of its rigorously planned communities. The plan — which has so far helped form the communities of Laguna Beach, Newport Beach, Orange, and Tustin, as well as centerpiece Irvine — has entered its final phase (set for completion around 2040), but the company faces increasing political opposition to its plans from area residents, who tend to become development-weary after they get their piece of The Irvine Ranch. In a move to prevent unchecked growth, the company has stopped selling desirable Irvine Spectrum land to small commercial building developers.

With most of its developments complete, The Irvine Company has increasingly focused on property investment and management. In addition to Irvine Spectrum, the company has been overseeing the development, marketing, leasing, and management of Fashion Island in Newport Beach, McCarthy Center in Silicon Valley, Symphony Towers in San Diego, and Fox Plaza in West Los Angeles.

Longtime Irvine Company CEO Michael McKee retired in 2008. The company is searching for a replacement.

HISTORY

A wholesale merchant in San Francisco during the gold rush, James Irvine and two others assembled vast holdings in Southern California in the mid-1800s by buying out the debts of Mexican and Spanish land-grant holders. Irvine bought his partners' shares in 1876 and passed the ranch of 120,000 acres to his son, James II, upon his death in 1886. Eight years later James II incorporated the ranch as The Irvine Company and began turning it into an agribusiness empire, shifting from sheep ranching to cash crop farming.

James II owned the ranch and company until the 1930s, when the death of his son, James III, prompted him to transfer a controlling interest in the company to the not-for-profit Irvine Foundation. James III's wife, Athalie, and daughter, Joan, inherited 22% of Irvine.

In 1959 company president Myford Irvine, a grandson of James I and uncle to Joan, was found dead from two shotgun wounds. Officials ruled it a suicide, but others weren't so sure.

With Athalie and Joan's encouragement, the company donated land in the early 1960s for construction of the University of California, Irvine. The company would continue contributing to educational and philanthropic causes as well as donating property for green space to improve Orange County's suburban areas.

The 1960s also saw the Irvine Foundation forming its definitive master plan for pre-arranged communities and marked the company's entry into the real estate development sector. The plan was designed to anticipate and control growth, with provisions for green space and a mix of pricing levels.

Super-rich firebrand Joan, who had long accused Irvine Foundation officers of serving their own interests at the expense of other stockholders, lobbied Congress in the late 1960s to change tax laws pertaining to the foundation. Along with a group of investors led by Donald Bren, Alfred Taubman, and Herbert Allen, Joan trumped a bid by Mobil Oil and in 1977 wrested control of the company from the foundation.

When California's real estate market went sour in 1983, Bren bought out his fellow shareholders, and increased his ownership stake from 34% to 95%. Joan returned to court to protest the price, gaining extra money when the court valued the land at $1.4 billion.

In 1993 Bren sought cash from his holdings by offering apartment developments as a real estate investment trust (REIT), Irvine Apartment Communities.

Orange County's record-setting bankruptcy in 1994 (the county lost $1.7 billion in risky investments) threatened the value of The Irvine Company's property portfolio, most of which is located in Orange County. Thanks in part to a frothy economy and settlements from brokerage firms, Orange County and The Irvine Company were spared another 1983-esque bust.

In 1996 Bren bought the company's remaining stock. As part of its expansion into R&D, retail, and office properties in the Silicon Valley area, The Irvine Company opened an office in San Jose the next year, followed by its Eastgate Technology Park in San Diego in 1998. An industrywide slide in REIT stock prices prompted Bren to take Irvine Apartment Communities private in 1999.

The company continued to expand its retail and office holdings into the aughts — including the purchase of Century City's Fox Plaza. In 2002 the Irvine City Council approved The

Irvine Company's plans to develop the last phase of the company's master plan (to be completed in 2040) — bringing over 12,000 homes, 730,000 sq. ft. of retail space, and 6.57 million sq. ft. of industrial space to the city's Northern Sphere area.

EXECUTIVES

Chairman: E. Valjean Wheeler
Chairman: Donald L. Bren, age 77
EVP, General Counsel and Secretary: Gregory P. (Greg) Lindstrom
SVP and CFO: Marc Ley, age 41
SVP Urban Planning and Design: Robert N. Elliott
President, Retail Properties: Keith Eyrich
President, Resort Properties: Ralph Grippo
President, Community Development: Daniel (Dan) Young
President, Office Properties Group: Richard I. (Rick) Gilchrist, age 64
President, Apartment Communities: Max L. Gardner, age 52

LOCATIONS

HQ: The Irvine Company
  550 Newport Center Dr., Newport Beach, CA 92660
Phone: 949-720-2000   **Fax:** 949-720-2218
Web: www.irvinecompany.com

PRODUCTS/OPERATIONS

Selected Divisions

Investment Properties Group
  Apartment communities
  Commercial land sales
  Office properties
  Resort properties (hotels, marinas, and golf courses)
  Retail properties
Irvine Community Development
  Agricultural operations
  Land sales and management
  Residential development sales

COMPETITORS

California Coastal Communities	The Koll Company
C.J. Segerstrom & Sons	Majestic Realty
Corky McMillin	MBK Real Estate
Douglas Company	Mission West Properties
D.R. Horton	Newhall Land
Intergroup	Rancho Mission Viejo
KB Home	Tejon Ranch
Kilroy Realty	Western National Group

It's Just Lunch

It's Just Lunch (IJL) doesn't offer high-tech hook-ups. The matchmaking service sets up busy, professional singles for lunch dates based on personal interviews instead of the much-maligned introduction videos or online dating pools. The company, which franchises more than 100 offices in Australia, Canada, the Caribbean, Europe, Singapore, and the US, charges singles around $1,000 for a series of dates (prices vary by location). It boasts having arranged more than 2 million dates since its inception. Founder Andrea McGinty established the company in 1991 after her fiancé jilted her weeks before their wedding. She sold IJL to The Riverside Company in 2006.

EXECUTIVES

Chairman: Matt Schaffer
CEO: Kevin Bazner
President and Chief Marketing Officer: Irene LaCota
SVP: Nancy Kirsch
VP: Jennifer Pannucci
VP: Melissa Brown
VP: Alana Beyer

LOCATIONS

HQ: It's Just Lunch International LLC
  75430 Gerald Ford Dr., Ste. 207
  Palm Desert, CA 92211
Phone: 760-779-0101   **Fax:** 760-779-9191
Web: www.itsjustlunch.com

Selected Franchise Locations

Albuquerque
Austin
Charlotte
Chicago
Madison
Minneapolis
New York City
San Antonio
St. Louis
St. Paul

COMPETITORS

eHarmony.com
Lavalife
Match.com
Spark Networks
Together Management Group
Yahoo!

Jacobs Entertainment

Jacobs Entertainment wants you to come out and play. The company operates The Lodge Casino and Gilpin Casino in Black Hawk, Colorado, and the Gold Dust West Casinos in Reno, Carson City, and Elko, Nevada. The company also has about 20 truck stop video gaming facilities throughout Louisiana; the Colonial Downs horseracing track in New Kent, Virginia; and eight satellite pari-mutuel wagering locations throughout Virginia. Chairman and CEO Jeffrey Jacobs owns 52% of the company; the Jacobs Family Economic and Control Trusts own 48%.

The company offers hotel rooms at its casino locations in Black Hawk, Reno, and Carson City.

In 2006 Jacobs Entertainment expanded with the purchase of Piñon Plaza in Carson City. The property was subsequently rebranded as Gold Dust West-Carson City. Also that year the company remodeled and improved the entrance and access to The Lodge Casino. Its Elko, Nevada, casino opened in 2007.

The company bought various parcels of land (or options to purchase land) on the Gulf Coast of Mississippi during 2008 for about $3 million and is exploring the feasibility of developing gaming, hotel, condominium, and parking facilities on them.

EXECUTIVES

President: Stephen R. Roark, age 61,
$590,816 total compensation
Chairman, CEO, Secretary, and Treasurer:
Jeffrey P. Jacobs, age 55, $2,152,500 total compensation
COO: Michael T. Shubic, age 55,
$437,094 total compensation
CFO: Brett A. Kramer, age 40,
$301,821 total compensation
EVP: Stanley Politano, $220,440 total compensation
EVP and General Counsel: Emanuel J. Cotronakis
President, Pari-Mutuel Wagering Operations:
Ian M. Stewart, age 54, $365,661 total compensation
Auditors: Deloitte & Touche LLP

LOCATIONS

HQ: Jacobs Entertainment, Inc.
17301 W. Colfax Ave., Ste. 250, Golden, CO 80401
Phone: 303-215-5200   **Fax:** 303-215-5219
Web: www.bhwk-hr.com

2008 Sales

	% of total
Louisiana	50
Colorado	26
Nevada	12
Virginia	12
Total	**100**

PRODUCTS/OPERATIONS

2008 Sales

	$ mil.	% of total
Gaming		
Casino	139.5	35
Truck stop	67.6	17
Pari-mutuel	38.7	10
Convenience store		
Fuel	97.0	25
Other	12.9	3
Food & beverages	30.7	8
Hotel	4.1	1
Other	5.7	1
Eliminations	(33.7)	—
Total	**362.5**	**100**

Selected Operations

Colonial Downs Racetrack
Gilpin Casino
Gold Dust West-Carson City
Gold Dust West-Elko
Gold Dust West-Reno
The Lodge Casino
Louisiana Truck Plazas

COMPETITORS

Ameristar Casinos
Boyd Gaming
Harrah's Entertainment
Isle of Capri Casinos
Magna Entertainment
MGM MIRAGE
Penn National Gaming
Pinnacle Entertainment
Station Casinos

HISTORICAL FINANCIALS

Company Type: Private

Income Statement				FYE: December 31
	REVENUE ($ mil.)	NET INCOME ($ mil.)	NET PROFIT MARGIN	EMPLOYEES
12/08	363	(4)	—	2,100
12/07	382	5	1.3%	2,200
12/06	339	(11)	—	1,100
12/05	234	(5)	—	1,585
12/04	190	5	2.6%	1,365
Annual Growth	**17.6%**	**—**		**11.4%**

Net Income History

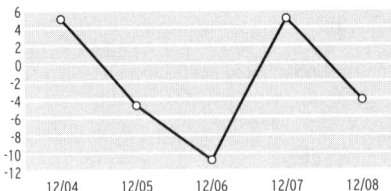

Jacuzzi Brands

Aaah, that feels good. Jacuzzi Brands makes the eponymous whirlpool baths, spas, and showers that soothe the aches and pains of customers in Europe, the Middle East, South America, and the US. Besides spas and baths, products include toilets and sinks, accessories such as bath pillows and heating kits, steam showers, and other Romanesque bathroom necessities. The company sells its products under brand names including Jacuzzi, Sundance, Zurn, Rainbow, and Astracast. Investment firm Apollo Management acquired Jacuzzi Brands for about $1.25 billion in 2007.

Immediately after the acquisition, Apollo sold Jacuzzi's institutional plumbing business, Zurn Industries, to its RBS Global (dba Rexnord) unit. The company now operates through its Jacuzzi Bath and Jacuzzi Spa divisions.

Later in 2007 Jacuzzi Brands entered the specialty mattress arena by forming a partnership with Thurmo-Pudic USA, which subsequently changed its name to Jacuzzi Sleep Systems.

EXECUTIVES

President and CEO: Thomas D. Koos
CFO: David Broadbent
VP and Global Controller: David Hellman
VP and General Council: Anthony Lovallo
President, Jacuzzi Luxury Bath, North America and Jacuzzi Spas International: Robert I. Rowan, age 49
EVP Sales, Jacuzzi Spas International: Jerry Pasley
SVP Operations, Jacuzzi Spas International:
Steve Purcell
Auditors: Ernst & Young LLP

LOCATIONS

HQ: Jacuzzi Brands Corporation
13925 City Center Dr., Ste. 200
Chino Hills, CA 91709
Phone: 909-606-1416
Web: www.jacuzzibrands.com

COMPETITORS

Clarion Bathware
Geberit
Kohler
Mansfield Plumbing
Moen
Ridgewood
Sanitec
TOTO
Villeroy & Boch

Jazzercise, Inc.

Jazzercise shows people how to shake their booties toward fitness. A leading fitness instruction operator, the company has more than 7,500 franchised instructors across the US and in more than 30 countries offering some 32,000 weekly fitness classes that blend jazz dancing with an aerobic workout. Jazzercise generates revenue through franchise fees, as well as the sale of clothing, books, and other merchandise. The company's JM DigitalWorks unit produces Jazzercise workout tapes and provides video production services to other clients. Its Jazzertogs division offers fitness apparel and accessories. CEO Judi Sheppard Missett, a professional dancer, founded Jazzercise in 1969 and began franchising in 1980.

While Jazzercise became closely associated with the music and fashion of the 1980s, the company's classes have kept up with the times. Instructors today incorporate Pilates, kick boxing, and weight training in the mix. To attract new class members, the company also offers some basic instruction through online videos.

EXECUTIVES

CEO: Judi Sheppard Missett, age 65
COO and CFO: Sally Baldridge
EVP: Shanna Missett Nelson, age 40
VP Sales: Kelly Sweeney
VP International Operations and Corporate Events:
Kenny Harvey
VP Technology and Distribution Services: Brad Jones
Senior Business Analyst: Kathy Missett

LOCATIONS

HQ: Jazzercise, Inc.
2460 Impala Dr., Carlsbad, CA 92010
Phone: 760-476-1750   **Fax:** 760-602-7180
Web: www.jazzercise.com

COMPETITORS

24 Hour Fitness
Bally Total Fitness
Butterfly Life
Contours Express
Crunch Fitness
Curves International
Gold's Gym
Healthy Inspirations
Lady of America
Merrithew
The Sports Club
Town Sports International Holdings
World Gym
YMCA
YWCA

HISTORICAL FINANCIALS

Company Type: Private

Income Statement				FYE: June 30
	REVENUE ($ mil.)	NET INCOME ($ mil.)	NET PROFIT MARGIN	EMPLOYEES
6/08	93	—	—	161

J.B. Poindexter & Co.

Got baggage issues? J.B. Poindexter can handle it. J.B. operates four units, manufacturing commercial truck bodies, multi-stop step vans, truck accessories, and specialty vehicles like limos and buses. Operating subsidiary Morgan makes van bodies for mounting on medium-duty truck chassis, used by businesses like Ryder and Penske. Morgan Olson supplies the bodies for vans often used for deliveries by UPS and Frito-Lay. Leer and LoRider branded pickup bed covers are made by a truck accessories unit. J.B.'s Specialty Manufacturing Group includes subsidiaries EFP (expandable foam plastics), Specialty Vehicle, and MIC (precision metal parts, casting, machining). Chairman and CEO John B. Poindexter owns the company.

The economic downturn and restricted access to credit have taken a toll on J.B. Poindexter. Particularly crippled have been the truck body, parts, and components segments tied to the transportation market. Sales to rental companies, such as AMERCO's U-Haul International; leasing companies, such as Penske Truck Leasing; and operators of fleets of delivery vehicles, such as FedEx and UPS, as well as truck dealers have experienced heavy deterioration. During 2008 the company moved to trim general and administrative, and labor costs, shedding about 14% of its workforce. Simultaneously, manufacturing operations were further consolidated to deliver more efficient processes.

However, the company's Specialty Manufacturing Division, which offers energy-related machining, fared better. Within this division, MIC Group acquired three precision machining operations in 2007: Richard's Manufacturing, Tarlton Supply Company, and Machine & Manufacturing I. Their specialties have expanded the company's slate of oil and gas exploration and production services. Earlier in 2006 J.B. Poindexter acquired Eagle Coach and combined its operations with Federal Coach (acquired in 2005) to create a Specialty Vehicle Group. This move gave the Specialty Manufacturing Division another arm, ramping up its product and service portfolio and opening the door to a niche commercial transportation market.

EXECUTIVES

Chairman, President and CEO: John B. Poindexter, age 64, $340,984 total compensation
VP Procurement: Michael Picone
VP Information Technology: Jay Krishnamurthy
VP Risk Management: Philip (Phil) Schull
VP Administration and Assistant Secretary: Larry T. Wolfe, age 60
President, Truck Accessories: Jim Donohue, age 52
President, Morgan Olson: Michael Ownbey, age 54
President, Morgan Truck Body: Norbert Markert, age 48, $904,732 total compensation
President, MIC Group: Nelson Byman, $640,469 total compensation
President, EFP: William (Bill) Flint Jr., age 59

LOCATIONS

HQ: J.B. Poindexter & Co., Inc.
1100 Louisiana, Ste. 5400, Houston, TX 77002
Phone: 713-655-9800   **Fax:** 713-951-9038
Web: www.jbpoindexter.com

PRODUCTS/OPERATIONS

2008 Sales

	$ Mil.	% of Total
Morgan Truck Body	233.9	33
Specialty Manufacturing	238.3	34
Truck Accessories	131.9	18
Morgan Olson	104.4	15
Adjustments	(2.1)	—
Total	**706.4**	**100**

Select Subsidiaries/Business Units

Morgan Olson, LLC
Morgan Truck Body, LLC
Specialty Manufacturing Division
  EFP, LLC
  MIC Group, LLC
  Specialty Vehicle Group
    Eagle Specialty Vehicles, LLC
    Federal Coach, LLC
Truck Accessories Group, LLC

COMPETITORS

Atia
Fleetwood Enterprises
FXI
Lund International
Master Precision
  Machining
RKI
Royal Truck Body
Supreme Industries
Utilimaster
Utility Trailer
Wabash National

HISTORICAL FINANCIALS

Company Type: Private

Income Statement

FYE: December 31

	REVENUE ($ mil.)	NET INCOME ($ mil.)	NET PROFIT MARGIN	EMPLOYEES
12/08	706	7	1.0%	3,795
12/07	792	(1)	—	4,227
12/06	795	8	1.0%	4,500
12/05	668	5	0.8%	4,000
12/04	585	10	1.7%	—
Annual Growth	**4.8%**	**(9.0%)**	**—**	**(1.7%)**

Net Income History

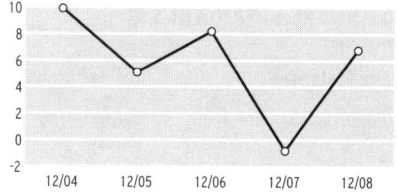

JCM Partners

At the northern end of the Golden State is where you'll find JCM Partners, which invests in, renovates, manages, markets, and sells multifamily residential and commercial real estate. The company also offers furnished corporate housing. JCM Partners owns about 45 properties, including apartment communities (containing a total of about 5,000 units), one multi-tenant office/retail property, office properties, and industrial properties. Nearly half of JCM Partners' residential properties are located in Sacramento County; the remainder are in San Joaquin, Solano, Stanislaus, and Contra Costa counties.

JCM runs Rent-One.com — an online apartment rental guide.

JCM Partners plans to continue to focus its portfolio on apartments, punctuated with commercial properties within the same geographical markets. The firm formed after a reorganization of IRM Corporation, which emerged from bankruptcy in 2000.

EXECUTIVES

Chairman: Michael W. Vanni, age 69
Vice Chairman: Marvin J. Helder, age 59
President, CEO, Secretary, and Manager: Gayle M. Ing
COO: Brian S. Rein, age 51
CFO: Robert Flaharty
Auditors: Moss Adams, LLP

LOCATIONS

HQ: JCM Partners, LLC
2151 Salvio St., Ste. 325, Concord, CA 94520
Phone: 925-676-1966   **Fax:** 925-676-1744
Web: www.rent-one.com

COMPETITORS

A.G. Spanos
Archstone
AvalonBay
BRE Properties
Equity Residential
Intergroup
Pacific Property Company
UDR

J. D. Heiskell & Company

Located in Tulare, California — along with about a third of a million dairy cows — feed maker J. D. Heiskell & Company has taken the real estate mantra to heart. But in addition to this location, location, location, Heiskell also has four other main mills in California, Idaho, and New Mexico, and a network of merchants that positions the company to be among the leading feed providers in the US. It purchases grain and other ingredients from farmers in the Midwest, markets grain nationwide, and ships feed products to customers throughout the country, though it focuses on the West Coast. The company, founded in 1886, is still controlled by descendants of founder Jefferson Davis Heiskell.

EXECUTIVES

Chairman: Scot Hillman
President and CEO: Duane (Butch) Fischer
EVP and COO: Ryan Pellett
EVP and CFO: Timothy J. (Tim) Regan
VP California Business Group: Robert Hodgen
VP Protein Products Group: Clark Jeary
VP and Whole Grains Manager: Randy W. Spiegel
VP Northwest and Southwest Business Groups: Todd Gearheart
VP Business Development: Charles Tsatsos
Corporate Counsel: Bret Hillman
Auditors: KPMG LLP

HQ: J. D. Heiskell & Company
116 W. Cedar St., Tulare, CA 93274
Phone: 559-685-6100   **Fax:** 559-686-8697
Web: www.heiskell.com

COMPETITORS

ADM
Ag Processing
Bartlett and Company
Cargill
CHS
Clarkson Grain Company
Columbia Grain

J.E. Dunn Construction Group

J.E. Dunn Construction Group prides itself on getting the job done. The firm, owned by descendants of founder John E. Dunn, consists of a group of construction companies, including flagship J. E. Dunn Construction and Atlanta-based R.J. Griffin & Company. The group builds institutional, commercial, and industrial structures around the US. It also provides construction and program management and design/build services. J. E. Dunn Construction, which ranks among the top 10 US general builders, was one of the first contractors to offer the construction management delivery method. Major projects it has completed include an IRS facility and the world headquarters for H&R Block, both in Kansas City, Missouri.

A bigwig particularly in the Midwest, J.E. Dunn won a major contract from the US Army Corps of Engineers to build a regional correctional facility at Fort Leavenworth, Kansas, that will replace smaller prisons in Texas, Kentucky, and Oklahoma. The facility is expected to open in 2010. The group regularly bids on federal government projects. Other projects include hospitals, casinos, condos, and schools.

EXECUTIVES

Chairman Emeritus: William H. Dunn Sr.
Chairman and Treasurer: Stephen D. (Steve) Dunn
President and CEO: Terrence P. (Terry) Dunn
EVP and CFO: Gordon E. Lansford III
EVP Purchasing and Warehouse Operations:
William H. (Bill) Dunn Jr.
EVP Marketing: Gregory E. Nook
EVP, General Counsel, and Secretary: Casey S. Halsey
SVP Risk Management: Robert L. Jacquinot
SVP Human Resources: Richard E. (Rick) Beyer
Corporate Communications Specialist: Danna Guffey

LOCATIONS

HQ: J.E. Dunn Construction Group, Inc.
1001 Locust St., Kansas City, MO 64106
Phone: 816-474-8600   **Fax:** 816-391-2510
Web: www.jedunn.com

PRODUCTS/OPERATIONS

Group Companies

JE Dunn Midwest
JE Dunn North Central
JE Dunn Northwest
JE Dunn Rocky Mountain
JE Dunn South Central
R.J. Griffin & Company

Selected Services

Preconstruction
Preconstruction estimating
Feasibility studies
Scheduling
Mechanical, electrical, plumbing review
Constructability review
Risk management
Market analysis
Quality control
Construction
LEED certification
Progress monitoring
Change order management
Quality control and testing
Labor relations
Post Construction
Commissioning
Lien releases
Operations and maintenance manuals
Final closeout
One-year walkthrough

COMPETITORS

Alberici
Bovis Lend Lease
Clark Enterprises
Hensel Phelps Construction
Hunt Construction
McCarthy Building
Skanska USA Building
Sundt
Turner Corporation
Tutor Perini
Washington Division
The Weitz Company, LLC
Whiting-Turner

HISTORICAL FINANCIALS

Company Type: Private

Income Statement				FYE: December 31
	REVENUE ($ mil.)	NET INCOME ($ mil.)	NET PROFIT MARGIN	EMPLOYEES
12/08	2,760	—	—	4,000
12/07	2,634	—	—	4,100
12/06	2,563	—	—	3,000
12/05	2,305	—	—	3,000
12/04	1,633	—	—	3,000
Annual Growth	14.0%	—	—	7.5%

Revenue History

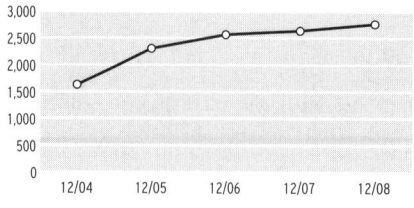

Jefferson Health System

This health care system's freedom-loving namesake might approve of its work to preserve the people's freedom of choice in health care. Jefferson Health System is a not-for-profit network that includes four health systems with hospitals, specialty clinics, and other medical facilities serving communities in the greater Philadelphia area. Members include the Thomas Jefferson University Hospital family (one of the system's founders), Main Line Health (the other founding organization), and Magee Rehabilitation, as well as affiliate Frankford Health Care System. The Jefferson network has some 2,400 beds and is affiliated with Thomas Jefferson University.

Former member Albert Einstein Healthcare Network broke off from the Jefferson Health Network in 2008 after the two organizations executed a formal separation agreement. The networks determined that their communities could be better served and their respective goals could be reached more effectively on an independent basis.

In 2007 Main Line Health expanded its operations by acquiring Riddle Memorial Hospital. Main Line Health is expanding Riddle's outpatient services, and it hopes to build another new hospital in the Philadelphia area.

EXECUTIVES

Chairman: Alfred W. Putnam Jr.
Vice Chairman: Jack F. Adler Jr.
President and CEO: Joesph T. Sebastianelli, age 60
SVP, CFO, and Treasurer: Kirk E. Gorman, age 58
SVP Payer Relations and General Counsel:
David F. Simon, age 54
President and Medical Director, Magee Rehabilitation Hospital: Guy Fried
President and CEO, Thomas Jefferson University Hospital: Thomas J. (Tom) Lewis, age 56
President and CEO, Frankford Health Care System:
Roy A. Powell, age 53
President and CEO, Main Line Health:
John J. (Jack) Lynch III

LOCATIONS

HQ: Jefferson Health System Inc.
259 N. Radnor-Chester Rd., Ste. 290
Radnor, PA 19087
Phone: 610-225-6200   **Fax:** 610-225-6254
Web: www.jeffersonhealth.org

PRODUCTS/OPERATIONS

2008 Sales

	$ mil.	% of total
Patient services	2,820.1	94
Investment income	24.7	1
Other	164.9	5
Total	**3,009.7**	**100**

Selected Members

Frankford Health Care System (affiliate, Philadelphia)
Magee Hospital for Convalescents (or Magee Rehabilitation, Philadelphia)
Main Line Health (Bryn Mawr, Pennsylvania)
Thomas Jefferson University Hospital System (Philadelphia)

COMPETITORS

Abington Memorial Hospital
Albert Einstein Healthcare Network
Crozer-Keystone Health System
Lancaster General
Lehigh Valley Hospital and Health Network
Memorial Hospital (PA)
Mercy Health System
North Philadelphia Health System
TUHS
University of Pennsylvania Health System
Virtua Health

HISTORICAL FINANCIALS

Company Type: Not-for-profit

Income Statement

	REVENUE ($ mil.)	NET INCOME ($ mil.)	NET PROFIT MARGIN	EMPLOYEES
				FYE: June 30
6/08	3,010	—	—	20,700

JELD-WEN, inc.

JELD-WEN can improve your outlook by providing new windows and doors for your home or by offering accommodations at a scenic resort. A leading manufacturer of windows and doors (some designed to withstand hurricane winds), JELD-WEN offers aluminum, vinyl, and wood windows; interior and exterior doors; garage doors; swinging and sliding patio doors; and door frames and moldings. It sells its products mainly in North America, Europe, and Australia. If you get tired of looking out your own doors and windows, JELD-WEN owns several resorts and communities in Oregon and Idaho, including Oregon's Eagle Crest Resort and Idaho's Silver Mountain Ski Resort.

JELD-WEN also has operations in marketing and advertising (through CMD Agency), stair parts manufacturing (part of JELD-WEN UK's offerings), and title and escrow services (AmeriTitle and JELD-WEN 1031).

In 2008 the company was the first manufacturer to offer interior and exterior doors made from western juniper. The overgrowth of juniper in the west has been linked to the disappearance of critical water springs in desert regions, and programs for the responsible removal of juniper have been offered by state and local governments.

To prove the quality and strength of its products, the company introduced the Reliable Lighthouse Restoration Initiative in 2004. JELD-WEN selects lighthouses (which are subjected to heavier wear-and-tear than the typical home) to restore; it donates its doors and windows to use in the projects. Lighthouses chosen for the program have included the New Canal Lighthouse in New Orleans, which was destroyed in Hurricanes Katrina and Rita, and the Umpqua River Lighthouse, the oldest in Oregon.

The company sold its 56-store home improvement outlet chain Grossman's (now Grossman's Bargain Outlet) to E.C. Barton in 2006.

Chairman Richard Wendt and his siblings founded JELD-WEN in 1960.

EXECUTIVES

Chairman: Richard L. Wendt, age 78
Vice Chair and EVP: Robert Turner
President and CEO: Roderick C. (Rod) Wendt
COO: Barry Homrighaus
CFO: R. Neil Stuart, age 54
SVP External Affairs: Ron Saxton

LOCATIONS

HQ: JELD-WEN, inc.
401 Harbor Isles Blvd., Klamath Falls, OR 97601
Phone: 541-882-3451   **Fax:** 541-885-7454
Web: www.jeld-wen.com

PRODUCTS/OPERATIONS

Selected Products

Doors
   Exterior (wood, custom fiberglass, fiberglass, and steel)
   Garage (wood composite)
   Interior (wood, custom-carved, molded, and flush)
   Patio (wood, vinyl, aluminum, and steel)
Millwork
   Columns
   Posts
   Spindles
   Stair parts
Windows
   Aluminum clad wood
   Energy-efficient
   Replacement
   Wood

Selected Resorts and Communities

Brasada Ranch (Oregon)
Chileno Bay Resort (Mexico)
Eagle Crest Resort (Oregon)
Ridgewater Properties (Oregon)
The Running Y Ranch Resort (Oregon)
Silver Mountain Ski Resort (Idaho)
Windmill Mills of America (Arizona and Oregon)

COMPETITORS

Andersen Corporation
Designer Doors
Great Lakes Window
Installux
Marshfield DoorSystems
MI Windows and Doors
NTK Holdings

Pella
Sierra Pacific Industries
Simonton Windows, Inc.
TRACO
Weather Shield Manufacturing
Wyndham Vacation

HISTORICAL FINANCIALS

Company Type: Private

Income Statement

	ESTIMATED REVENUE ($ mil.)	NET INCOME ($ mil.)	NET PROFIT MARGIN	EMPLOYEES
				FYE: December 31
12/08	2,900	—	—	20,000
12/07	3,160	—	—	23,750
12/06	3,160	—	—	23,750
12/05	2,600	—	—	25,000
12/04	2,300	—	—	21,000
Annual Growth	6.0%	—	—	(1.2%)

Revenue History

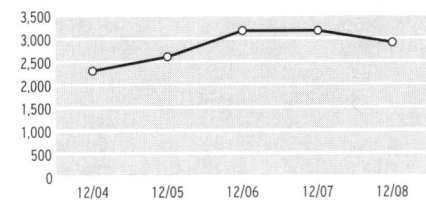

	12/04	12/05	12/06	12/07	12/08

J.F. Shea Co.

J.F. Shea didn't build Shea Stadium — but it could have. The real estate, engineering, and construction group provides services for civil engineering, commercial, and residential projects. Flagship division J.F. Shea Construction offers design/build services, while its civil engineering division builds tunnels and water treatment and storage facilities. Another group member, Shea Homes builds planned communities and other residences in about a half-dozen states. Shea Properties invests in and develops commercial real estate. Other divisions provide construction materials, foundation construction and machinery, and venture capital. The Shea family owns J.F. Shea, which was founded as a plumbing company in 1881.

J.F. Shea Construction has worked on engineering icons like the Hoover Dam and the Golden Gate Bridge. It also worked on San Francisco's urban transit system, the Bay Area Rapid Transit (BART).

More recent projects include the construction of a water purification and desalination project in Southern California (with Tetra Tech) and a tunnel and expansion project for the New York City subway system with a consortium that includes Skanska and Schiavone Construction.

EXECUTIVES

Chairman: John F. Shea
President and CEO: Peter O. Shea Jr., age 42
CFO and Secretary: James G. (Jim) Shontere
EVP: Edmund H. Shea Jr.
EVP; President, J.F. Shea Construction: Peter O. Shea
VP Taxes: Ron Lakey
Senior Technical Manager: Mike Little
Director, Finance: Andy Roundtree
Treasurer: Robert R. O'Dell
President and CEO, Shea Homes: Bert Selva

LOCATIONS

HQ: J.F. Shea Co., Inc.
655 Brea Canyon Rd., Walnut, CA 91789
Phone: 909-594-9500   **Fax:** 909-594-0917
Web: www.jfshea.com

PRODUCTS/OPERATIONS

Selected Group Members

BlueStar Resort & Golf (golf course in Scottsdale, Arizona)
J.F. Shea Construction, Inc. (commercial buildings, subways, and civil engineering projects)
JRedding Construction (sand, gravel, asphalt, and concrete products; highway construction)
Reed Manufacturing (concrete guns and pumps and concrete-placing equipment)
Shea Homes LP (developed and master-planned communities)
Shea Mortgage
Shea Properties LLC
Shea Ventures

COMPETITORS

Austin Industries
Bechtel
Black & Veatch
D.R. Horton
Fluor
Granite Construction
Hyundai Engineering
Jacobs Engineering
Lennar

Michael Baker
Parsons Corporation
Peter Kiewit Sons'
Shaw Group
Tutor Perini
Tutor-Saliba
URS
Washington Division
Zachry Inc.

HISTORICAL FINANCIALS

Company Type: Private

Income Statement

FYE: December 31

	REVENUE ($ mil.)	NET INCOME ($ mil.)	NET PROFIT MARGIN	EMPLOYEES
12/07	2,260	—	—	2,200
12/06	3,180	—	—	2,700
12/05	3,429	—	—	3,299
12/04	3,080	—	—	2,668
12/03	2,597	—	—	2,685
Annual Growth	(3.4%)	—	—	(4.9%)

Revenue History

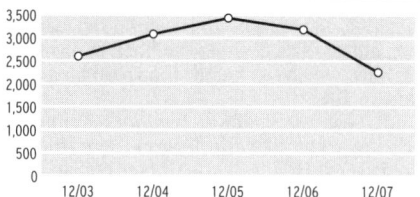

JM Family Enterprises

JM Family Enterprises is a family affair. JM, owned by the family of founder James Moran, is a holding company (Florida's second-largest private company, in fact, after Publix Super Markets) with about a dozen automotive-related businesses, including the world's largest-volume Lexus retailer, JM Lexus, in Margate, Florida. JM's major subsidiary, Southeast Toyota Distributors, is the nation's largest independent Toyota and Scion distribution franchise, delivering Toyota cars, trucks, and SUVs to more than 170 dealers in Alabama, Florida, Georgia, Texas, and Ohio. Company veteran Colin Brown serves as its CEO, following the 2007 retirement of chairwoman Pat Moran, daughter of the firm's founder.

Hard times for the auto industry and American consumers are hard times for JM Family enterprises, which in March 2009 said it would cut 500 jobs (about 11% of its workforce) and reduce pay for others as it attempts to ride out the plunge in new car sales. The layoffs affect all staff levels and extend to the company's subsidiaries.

Among JM Family's other subsidiaries, software marketer JM Solutions acquired Orlando-based DealerUps, a software firm specializing in customer-relations management, in January 2007 for an undisclosed sum. In January 2009 JM Solutions launched Inventory Optimization Services, a software program designed to provide dealer groups with advanced core inventory recommendations and services, including pricing analysis and recommendations based on local market sales and conditions.

JM&A Group provides insurance and warranty services to retailers nationwide. World Omni Financial handles leasing, dealer financing, and other financial services for 2,800 US auto dealers and is one of the largest auto finance firms in the US.

JM Family Enterprises is one of the largest woman-owned companies in the US and consistently ranks in the top half on *FORTUNE* magazine's 100 Best Companies to Work For list on

the strength of on-site medical, fitness, and day-care centers.

Pat Moran, who succeeded her father as chairman of the company, retired in early 2007. She remains a director of the diversified family-owned automotive firm. The chairman's post was eliminated upon her retirement.

HISTORY

Jim Moran first became visible as "Jim Moran, the Courtesy Man" in Chicago TV advertisements in the 1950s. At that time he ran Courtesy Motors, where he was so successful as the world's #1 Ford dealer that *Time* magazine put his picture on its cover in 1961.

Moran had entered the auto sales business after fixing up and selling a car for more than three times the price he had paid for it. That profit was much better than what he made at the Sinclair gas station he had bought, so he opened a used-car lot. Later, he moved to new-car sales when he bought a Hudson franchise (Ford had rejected him).

Seeing the promise of TV advertising, in 1948 Moran pioneered the forum for Chicago car dealers, not only as an advertiser and program sponsor but also as host of a variety show and a country/western music barn dance. The increased visibility positioned Moran as Hudson's #1 dealer, but the sales tactics at Courtesy Motors earned an antitrust suit that was settled out of court.

In 1955 Moran started with Ford and, with his TV influence as host of *The Jim Moran Courtesy Hour*, he became the world's #1 Ford dealer in his first month.

He moved to Florida in 1966 after being diagnosed with cancer and given one year to live. Successfully fighting the disease, he bought a Pontiac franchise and later started Southeast Toyota Distributors. In 1969 he formed JM Family Enterprises.

Legal problems cropped up in 1973 when the IRS investigated a Nassau bank serving as a tax haven for wealthy Americans. Moran and three Toyota executives were linked to the bank, and in 1978 Moran was indicted for tax fraud. When an immunity deal fell through, Moran pleaded guilty to seven tax fraud charges in 1984 and was sentenced to two years (suspended), fined more than $12 million, and ordered to perform community service. Moran's legal problems threatened his association with Toyota and were blamed for causing his stroke in 1983.

JM's legal problems continued in the 1980s, partly because of the imposition of auto import restrictions. To get more cars to sell, some Southeast Toyota managers encouraged auto dealers to file false sales reports. Some North Carolina dealers resisted and one sued, settling out of court for $22 million. Other dealers alleged racketeering and fraud on the part of Southeast Toyota, and by the beginning of 1994, JM had paid more than $100 million in fines and settlements for cases stretching back to 1988. In spite of that, Toyota renewed its contract with the company in 1993, a year ahead of schedule.

Pat Moran succeeded her father as JM president in 1992. Between 1991 and 1994 three suits were filed against Jim and Southeast Toyota alleging racism against blacks in establishing Toyota dealerships. All three suits were settled.

Jim teamed with Wayne Huizenga in 1996 to launch a national chain of used-car megastores under the name AutoNation USA, which Jim expected would draw buyers to his own auto deal-

erships. (AutoNation USA's first store was built just two blocks from JM's Coconut Creek Lexus Dealership.) Jim's interest in AutoNation USA was converted into a small percentage (less than 5%) of Republic Industries stock after Huizenga merged AutoNation into waste hauler Republic Industries (now called AutoNation) in 1997.

In late 1998 JM embarked on a national strategy to expand its presence outside the Southeast, establishing an office in St. Louis that handles indirect consumer leasing.

In 2000 Jim became honorary chairman while Pat was given the chairman position and continued as CEO; COO Colin Brown was named president. Also that year the company was named the 51st Best Company to Work For in the United States by *FORTUNE* magazine. The company's rank in the Best Company to Work For list rose to 20th place in 2001.

In March 2003 Brown assumed the CEO title, with Pat Moran continuing in the chairman position. In 2004 the company ranked first in the nation in dealer service contract satisfaction according to J.D. Power and Associates and sat at 25 on *FORTUNE*'s Best Company to Work For list.

In early 2007 Pat Moran retired. In April, founder and honorary chairman James Moran died at the age of 88.

EXECUTIVES

President and CEO: Colin Brown
EVP and CFO: Brent Burns
EVP; President, Southeast Toyota Distributors LLC: Ed Sheehy, age 48
EVP; President, World Omni Financial Corp.: Frank Armstrong
EVP; President JM & A Group: Forrest Heathcott
EVP, Chief Administrative Officer, and CIO; President, JM Service Center LLC: Ken Yerves
SVP and COO, JM&A Group: Ron Coombs
SVP and General Counsel: Carmen Johnson
VP and General Manager Sales and Field Service: T. Michael (Mike) Casey, age 53
Media Relations Manager: Ilisa Finkelman

LOCATIONS

HQ: JM Family Enterprises, Inc.
100 Jim Moran Blvd., Deerfield Beach, FL 33442
Phone: 954-429-2000 **Fax:** 954-429-2300
Web: www.jmfamily.com

JM Family Enterprises operates auto retail, distribution, leasing, and financing businesses across the US, mainly in Alabama, Florida, Georgia, and North and South Carolina.

PRODUCTS/OPERATIONS

Selected Subsidiaries

Finance and Leasing
  Centerone Financial Services
  World Omni Financial Corp.

Insurance, Marketing, Consulting, and Related Companies
  Courtesy Insurance Company
  Fidelity Insurance Agency, Inc.
  Fidelity Warranty Services, Inc.
  Jim Moran & Associates, Inc.
  JM&A Group (auto service contracts, insurance)
  J.M.I.C. Life Insurance Co.

Retail Car Sales
  JM Lexus

Software
  JMsolutions (customer relationship management software)

Vehicle Processing and Distribution
  SET Inland Processing
  SET Parts Supply and Distribution
  SET Port Processing
  SET Westlake Processing
  Southeast Toyota Distributors, LLC

COMPETITORS

AutoNation
CarMax
Ed Morse Auto
Gulf States Toyota
Hendrick Automotive
Holman Enterprises
Island Lincoln-Mercury
Penske Automotive Group

HISTORICAL FINANCIALS

Company Type: Private

Income Statement

FYE: December 31

	REVENUE ($ mil.)	NET INCOME ($ mil.)	NET PROFIT MARGIN	EMPLOYEES
12/08	10,100	—	—	4,000
12/07	12,200	—	—	4,700
12/06	11,100	—	—	4,600
12/05	9,400	—	—	4,300
Annual Growth	2.4%	—	—	(2.4%)

Revenue History

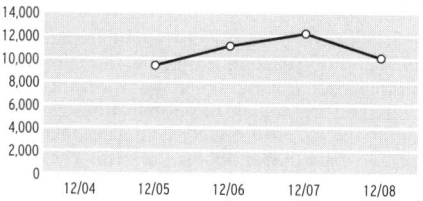

J.M. Huber

As great as toothpaste, paint, and tires may be, J.M. Huber claims to make them even better. Hard to believe, we know. Founded in 1890 by Joseph M. Huber and still owned by his heirs, the company makes specialty additives and minerals used to thicken and improve the cleaning properties of toothpaste, the brightness and gloss of paper, the strength and durability of rubber, and the flame-retardant properties of wire and cable. The diverse company also makes oriented strand board (a plywood substitute), explores for and produces oil and gas, and provides technical and financial services. Huber also makes hydrocolloids (thickeners for gums) through subsidiary CP Kelco.

Huber manages approximately 600,000 acres of timberlands in Maine and the southeastern US, and has oil and gas operations in Texas, Colorado, and Wyoming. The company's technology-based services and subsidiaries span from timber management (Huber Resources Corp.) to investment management (Demica and Shelterwood Financial Services).

In 2008 Huber sold its kaolin clay operations to private equity firm IMin Partners, which set it up as a stand-alone company called KaMin.

EXECUTIVES

President and CEO: Michael (Mike) Marberry
CFO: Jeffrey (Jeff) Prosinski
CIO: Vincent Solano
VP and General Counsel: Ed Castorina
VP Human Resources: Niall Mulkeen
VP Chief Communications and Public Affairs Officer: Robert (Bob) Currie
VP and General Manager, Huber Resources: Peter Triandafillou
President and CEO, Shelterwood Financial Services LLC: William Rankin
President, Huber Energy: Ralph Schofield
President, CP Kelco: Donald (Don) Rubright
President, Engineered Materials: Andy Trott
President, Huber Engineered Woods LLC: Brian Carlson
CEO, Demica: Phillip Kerle

LOCATIONS

HQ: J.M. Huber Corporation
  499 Thornall St., 8th Fl., Edison, NJ 08837
Phone: 732-549-8600   **Fax:** 732-549-7256
Web: www.huber.com

PRODUCTS/OPERATIONS

Selected Operations

Engineered Materials
  CP Kelco (food, pharmaceutical, household, and industrial gums; hydrocolloids for paper, food, hygiene, and industrial uses)
  Huber Engineered Materials (engineered minerals and specialty chemicals)
  Huber Engineered Woods (high-performance specialty wood composites)
Natural Resources
  Huber Energy (oil and gas acquisition, exploration, and production)
  Huber Timber (timberlands and forest acreage management)
Technology-Based Services
  Demica (trade receivables securitization)
  Huber Resources Corporation (yield maximization from timberlands)
  Shelterwood Financial Services LLC (investment management and business consulting)

COMPETITORS

ADM	Georgia-Pacific
Baker Hughes	Kerry Group
Danisco A/S	Minerals Technologies
Evonik Degussa	Occidental Petroleum

HISTORICAL FINANCIALS

Company Type: Private

Income Statement

FYE: December 31

	REVENUE ($ mil.)	NET INCOME ($ mil.)	NET PROFIT MARGIN	EMPLOYEES
12/08	2,000	—	—	4,200
12/07	2,100	—	—	4,500
12/06	2,220	—	—	5,000
12/05	2,300	—	—	5,000
12/04	2,400	—	—	5,000
Annual Growth	(4.5%)	—	—	(4.3%)

Revenue History

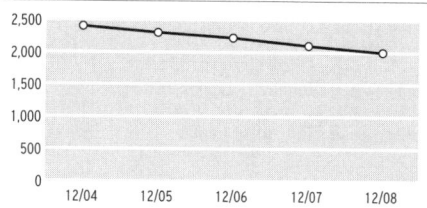

J M Smith Corporation

J M Smith Corporation has gone from corner drug store to serving drug stores and more. A holding company serving pharmacies and government agencies, the company consists of Smith Drug Company, Integral Solutions Group, QS/1 Data Systems, and Smith Premier Services. Smith Drug Company provides purchasing and distribution services for independent pharmacies, while QS/1 develops computer systems for medical equipment providers, institutional pharmacies, and related businesses. Smith Premier Service offers prescription benefit management services for employers and insurance carriers. Integral Solutions serves local government agencies providing hardware, software, forms and offering data processing services.

EXECUTIVES

Chairman and CEO: William (Bill) Cobb
CFO and Treasurer: James C. Wilson Jr.
Director, Human Resources: Rhonda Lockhart

LOCATIONS

HQ: J M Smith Corporation
  101 W. St. John St., Ste. 305
  Spartanburg, SC 29306
Phone: 864-542-9419   **Fax:** 864-582-6585
Web: www.jmsmith.com

COMPETITORS

Cardinal Health
Fiserv
HP Enterprise Services
Kinray
McKesson

Johnny Rockets

Hep cats still hang out at Johnny Rockets restaurants, where U-shaped counters, padded booths, table-top jukeboxes, and white uniforms salute the classic American diner. The Johnny Rockets Group operates and franchises more than 250 restaurants in about 30 states and 10 other countries that specialize in such classic diner fare as hamburgers, malts, fries, and apple pie. About two-thirds of the locations are operated by franchisees. The chain was founded by Ronn Teitelbaum, who opened the first Johnny Rockets on Los Angeles' fashionable Melrose Avenue in 1986. The company was acquired by RedZone Capital, an investment fund led by Washington Redskins owner Dan Snyder, in 2007.

Snyder purchased Johnny Rockets from Apax Partners with plans to fund an aggressive expansion campaign. With the deep pockets of its new owner, the chain announced plans to add 1,000 new locations by 2012. It also launched a new concept called Johnny Rockets Express, a smaller-format eatery designed for airports, malls, and other high-traffic locations. In addition, Johnny Rockets inked a deal with Six Flags (another business controlled by Snyder) to open more than 25 restaurants at its amusement parks.

Longtime CEO Michael Shumsky resigned in 2007 and was replaced by former Buffalo Wild Wings executive Lee Sanders.

Teitelbaum, who died of brain cancer in 2000, was an award-winning men's fashion retailer for nearly 20 years before he tried his hand at the restaurant business. He first sold Johnny Rockets in 1995 to an investor group led by Patricof & Co. (later Apax Partners).

EXECUTIVES

Chairman: Christopher J. (Chris) Ainley
CEO: Lee Sanders, age 55
CFO: John Fuller
SVP Franchise Sales: Dave Eberle
SVP International Development: Steve Devine
VP Franchise Operations: Chris Carver
Executive Director IT Systems: Paul Nishiyama
Executive Director Legal Services: Alan Hinson
Executive Director and Controller: Denise Campos
Director Corporate Operations: Chaz Dunham
Director Field Marketing: Lisa Bass
Director International Development: David Pettengill
Director Design and Construction: Mike Shotzbarger
Director Communications: Cozette Phifer
Director Human Resources: Terri Pattillo
Auditors: Ernst & Young LLP

LOCATIONS

HQ: The Johnny Rockets Group, Inc.
25550 Commercentre Dr., Ste. 200
Lake Forest, CA 92630
Phone: 949-643-6100   **Fax:** 949-643-6200
Web: www.johnnyrockets.com

COMPETITORS

BJ's Restaurants
Brinker
Bubba Gump Shrimp
California Pizza Kitchen
Carlson Restaurants
Cheesecake Factory
Darden
Denny's
DineEquity
Fuddruckers
Hard Rock Cafe
OSI Restaurant Partners
Planet Hollywood
Red Robin
Ruby Tuesday
Steak n Shake

HISTORICAL FINANCIALS

Company Type: Private

Income Statement   FYE: April 30

	REVENUE ($ mil.)	NET INCOME ($ mil.)	NET PROFIT MARGIN	EMPLOYEES
4/08	231	—	—	—
4/07	209	—	—	—
4/06	199	—	—	—
4/05	177	—	—	—
4/04	147	—	—	—
Annual Growth	12.0%	—	—	—

Revenue History

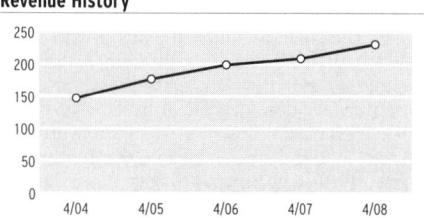

Johns Hopkins Health System

Johns Hopkins Health System, an affiliate of Johns Hopkins Medicine, provides health services to residents of the Baltimore area and to visitors from all over the world. The health system includes three hospitals: Johns Hopkins Hospital, Bayview Medical Center, and Howard County General Hospital.

The hospitals, affiliated with The Johns Hopkins University School of Medicine, offer an array of inpatient and outpatient health services that include general medicine, emergency/trauma care, pediatrics, maternity care, senior care, and clinics in numerous specialized areas of medicine. The system also includes an area network of primary care physicians and neighborhood clinics, and a home health agency.

EXECUTIVES

Chair: C. Michael Armstrong, age 70
Vice Chairman: A. B. Krongard, age 72
Vice Chairman: Edward D. Miller Jr., age 66
President and Trustee, Johns Hopkins Health System and The Johns Hopkins Hospital: Ronald R. Peterson, age 61
VP Innovation and Product Safety, Johns Hopkins Health System and The Johns Hopkins Hospital: Richard O. Davis
VP Supply Chain; VP General Services, The Johns Hopkins Hospital: Kenneth Grant
VP Facilities, Johns Hopkins Health System and The Johns Hopkins Hospital: Sally W. MacConnell
VP, Finance and Treasurer, Johns Hopkins Health System and The Johns Hopkins Hospital: Ronald J. Werthman
VP Operations Integration; EVP and COO, The Johns Hopkins Hospital: Judy A. Reitz
VP Management Systems and Information Services, Johns Hopkins Health System and The Johns Hopkins Hospital: Stephanie L. Reel
VP Human Resources, Johns Hopkins Health System and The Johns Hopkins Hospital: Pamela D. Paulk
VP and General Counsel and VP, HIPPA, Johns Hopkins Health System and The Johns Hopkins Hospital: Joanne E. Pollak
VP Corporate Compliance and Secretary, Johns Hopkins Health System and The Johns Hopkins Hospital: G. Daniel Shealer Jr.
VP Corporate Security, Johns Hopkins Health System and The Johns Hopkins Hospital: Harry Koffenburger
VP Marketing and Communications: Dalal Haldeman
Auditors: PricewaterhouseCoopers LLP

LOCATIONS

HQ: Johns Hopkins Health System
600 N. Wolfe St., Baltimore, MD 21287
Phone: 410-955-5000   **Fax:** 410-955-0890
Web: www.hopkinshospital.org

PRODUCTS/OPERATIONS

Selected Facilities

Bayview Medical Center
Howard County General Hospital
Johns Hopkins at Cedar Lane
Johns Hopkins at Greenspring Station
Johns Hopkins at Odenton
Johns Hopkins at White Marsh
Johns Hopkins Children's Center
Johns Hopkins Hospital
Johns Hopkins Outpatient Center

COMPETITORS

Anne Arundel Medical Center
Bon Secours Health
Carilion Clinic
Franklin Square Hospital Center
GBMC
Harbor Hospital
Levindale Hospital
LifeBridge Health
MedStar Health
Sinai Hospital of Baltimore
Union Memorial Hospital
University of Maryland Medical System

HISTORICAL FINANCIALS

Company Type: Private

Income Statement   FYE: June 30

	REVENUE ($ mil.)	NET INCOME ($ mil.)	NET PROFIT MARGIN	EMPLOYEES
6/08	2,439	—	—	13,000

Johnson Publishing

Snubbed by advertisers when he founded his company 60 years ago, the late John Johnson pushed his magazine company to the front of the pack. Led by its flagship publication, *EBONY,* family-owned Johnson Publishing Company is a black-owned global publishing firm. The company also publishes *JET* and operates the JPC Book Division. In addition, Johnson Publishing produces a line of cosmetics (Fashion Fair Cosmetics) marketed for African-American women, and each year it hosts the Ebony Fashion Fair, a traveling fashion show that raises money for scholarships and charities in cities across the US and Canada.

The company's book division features titles such as *The New Ebony Cookbook* and the more controversial *Forced Into Glory: Abraham Lincoln's White Dream.*

In 2007 the company further diversified, forming the EbonyJet Entertainment Group to oversee the creation and distribution of branded entertainment content through theatrical, broadcast, cable, and digital (video on demand and mobile) platforms. The following year the company teamed with YouTube to launch EbonyJet Television on YouTube. The channel offers news and entertainment content featuring notable African-American celebrities, politicians, and public figures.

Johnson Publishing is owned and controlled by family members of founder Johnson, who died in 2005. His daughter, Linda Johnson Rice is the company's chairman and CEO. His wife, Eunice, produces the Ebony Fashion Fair.

HISTORY

John H. Johnson launched his publishing business in 1942 while he was still in college in Chicago. The idea for a black-oriented magazine came to him while he was working part-time for Supreme Life Insurance Co. of America, where one of his jobs was to clip magazine and newspaper articles about the black community. Johnson used his mother's furniture as collateral to secure a $500 loan and then mailed $2 charter subscription offers to potential subscribers. He received 3,000 replies and used the $6,000 to print the first issue of *Negro Digest,* patterned after *Reader's Digest.* Circulation was 50,000 within a year.

Johnson started *Ebony* magazine in 1945 (which gained immediate popularity and is still the company's premier publication) and launched *Jet* in 1951, a pocket-sized publication containing news items and features. In the early days Johnson was unable to obtain advertising, so he formed his own Beauty Star mail-order business and advertised its products (dresses, wigs, hair care products, and vitamins) in his magazines. He won his first major account, Zenith Radio, in 1947; Johnson landed Chrysler in 1954, only after sending a salesman to Detroit every week for 10 years. For 20 years, *Ebony* and *Jet* were the only national publications targeting blacks in the US.

By the 1960s Johnson had become one of the most prominent black men in the US. He posed with John F. Kennedy in 1963 to publicize a special issue of *Ebony* celebrating the Emancipation Proclamation. US magazine publishers named him Publisher of the Year in 1972. Johnson launched *Ebony Jr!* (since discontinued) in 1973, a magazine designed to provide "positive black images" for black preteens. His first magazine, *Negro Digest* (renamed *Black World*), became known for its provocative articles, but its circulation dwindled from 100,000 to 15,000. Johnson retired the magazine in 1975.

Unable to find the proper makeup for his *Ebony* models, Johnson founded his own cosmetics business, Fashion Fair Cosmetics, that year, which carved out a niche beside Revlon (which introduced cosmetic lines for blacks) and another black cosmetics company, Johnson Products (unrelated) of Chicago. By 1982 Fashion Fair sales were more than $30 million.

The company got into broadcasting in 1972 when it bought Chicago radio station WGRT (renamed WJPC; that city's first black-owned station). It added WLOU (Louisville, Kentucky) in 1982 and WLNR (Lansing, Illinois; re-launched in 1991 as WJPC-FM) in 1985. By 1995, however, it had sold all of its stations.

Johnson and the company sold their controlling interest in the last minority-owned insurance company in Illinois (and Johnson's first employer), Supreme Life Insurance, to Unitrin (a Chicago-based life, health, and property insurer) in 1991. That year the company and catalog retailer Spiegel announced a joint venture to develop fashions for black women. The two companies launched a mail-order catalog called *E Style* in 1993 and an accompanying credit card the next year.

Johnson Publishing launched its South African edition of *Ebony* in 1995. Johnson was awarded the Presidential Medal of Freedom in 1996. The next year, however, circulation of *Ebony* fell 7% as mainstream magazines began covering black issues more thoroughly and a host of new titles appeared. In response, the company restructured its ventures and closed its *E Style* catalog. Johnson Publishing retired *Ebony Man* (launched in 1985) in 1998 and *Ebony South Africa* in 2000.

In 2002 John Johnson named his daughter Linda Johnson Rice as CEO; Johnson kept the title of chairman and publisher. John Johnson died at the age of 87 in 2005.

EXECUTIVES

Chairman and CEO: Linda Johnson Rice, age 51
Vice Chairman and General Counsel:
  June Acie Rhinehart
President and COO; President and COO Fashion Fair Cosmetics: Anne S. Ward, age 37
SVP Fashion Fair Cosmetics: J. Lance Clark
VP Multimedia Resources: Pamela Cash Menzies
VP and Director Manufacturing and Sales:
  Tammy E. Rollé
VP and Editorial Director, EBONY and JET Magazines:
  Bryan Monroe
Chief, Digital Strategy: Eric Easter
Director Information Technology: Eric Haynes
Director National Marketing: Raquel Graham Crayton
Director Corporate Communications: Wendy E. Parks
Secretary and Treasurer; Producer and Director,
  EBONY Fashion Fair: Eunice W. Johnson
Director Circulation: Robert S. Acquaye

LOCATIONS

HQ: Johnson Publishing Company, Inc.
820 S. Michigan Ave., Chicago, IL 60605
Phone: 312-322-9200   **Fax:** 312-322-0918
Web: www.johnsonpublishing.com

PRODUCTS/OPERATIONS

Selected Operations

Book publishing
  JBC Book Division

Fashion and beauty products
  Ebony Fashion Fair (traveling fashion show)
  Fashion Fair Cosmetics (color cosmetics, fragrances, skin care)

Magazines
  EBONY
  JET

Multimedia content
  EbonyJet Entertainment Group

COMPETITORS

Advance Publications	Hearst Magazines
Alberto-Culver	LFP
Avon	L'Oréal
BET	Mary Kay
Earl G. Graves	Meredith Corporation
Essence Communications	Revlon
Estée Lauder	Time Inc.
Forbes	

HISTORICAL FINANCIALS

Company Type: Private

Income Statement

FYE: December 31

	REVENUE ($ mil.)	NET INCOME ($ mil.)	NET PROFIT MARGIN	EMPLOYEES
12/07	453	—	—	503
12/06	458	—	—	1,100
12/05	496	—	—	1,707
12/04	498	—	—	—
12/03	489	—	—	2,000
Annual Growth	(1.9%)	—	—	(29.2%)

Revenue History

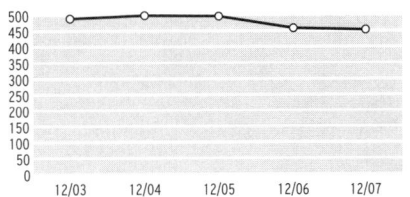

JohnsonDiversey, Inc.

The industrial-strength version of S.C. Johnson & Son, JohnsonDiversey split from the well-known company in 1999 to make commercial cleaning, hygiene, pest control, and food sanitation products for retailers, building service contractors, hospitality providers, and foodservice operators. It's the #2 global industrial and institutional cleaning products company behind Ecolab. JohnsonDiversey also provides safety and hygiene training and consulting. Europe generates more than half of the firm's sales, which span some 160 countries. Following a recapitalization deal in late 2009, the Johnson family controls 50% of the company while private equity firm Clayton Dubilier & Rice (CD&R) holds a 46% stake.

CD&R invested about $480 million in JohnsonDiversey in exchange for its share. Unilever, which controlled a third of the cleaning products manufacturer before the deal, unloaded most of its holdings but still retained a 4% stake in the recapitalized business. CD&R's investment was combined with nearly $1.5 billion in financing from about a dozen banks and some $250 million in seller financing from Unilever. JohnsonDiversey said it was seeking to refinance its debt ahead of its 2010 deadline largely because of banks' willingness to participate since the credit crisis. Also as part of the deal, the company will be simplifying its name to Diversey in early 2010.

JohnsonDiversey has been restructuring for the past few years by reducing its worldwide workforce, exiting its services to health and hospitality customers, and closing a number of factories. (The company operates about 30 manufacturing facilities in 25 countries.) As part of the restructuring plan, JohnsonDiversey sold specialty chemical maker DuBois Chemicals in October 2008 for about $70 million to private equity group Riverside Capital Appreciation Fund. The company also shed its Auto-Chlor branch operations, a unit that sold dishwashing systems and laundry and kitchen chemicals, for about $70 million in late 2007. A year earlier, JohnsonDiversey sold its Polymer unit, which made acrylic resins used in printing, packaging, and adhesives, to BASF.

Once known as S.C. Johnson Commercial Markets, the firm changed its name to JohnsonDiversey in 2002 after acquiring DiverseyLever, Unilever's industrial cleaning business.

EXECUTIVES

Chairman: S. Curtis (Curt) Johnson III, age 53,
  $4,126,431 total compensation
President, CEO, and Director: Edward F. (Ed) Lonergan,
  age 49, $4,938,636 total compensation
EVP and CFO: Joseph F. (Joe) Smorada, age 62,
  $2,224,803 total compensation
SVP and Chief Marketing Officer: Nabil Shabshab,
  age 43
SVP, General Counsel, and Secretary: Scott D. Russell,
  age 46
SVP Corporate Affairs and Director, Office of the
  President: John W. Matthews, age 49
SVP and Chief Scientific Officer, Research
  Development and Engineering:
  Stephen A. (Steve) Di Biase, age 56
SVP Global Human Resources: James W. (Jim) Larson,
  age 56
SVP Global Value Chain: Gregory F. Clark, age 55
VP and Corporate Treasurer: Lori P. Marin, age 47

VP Global Business Development: David S. Andersen, age 48
VP and CIO: Matt Peterson, age 45
VP and Corporate Controller: P. Todd Herndon, age 43
Regional President, Europe, Middle East, and Africa:
Pedro Chidichimo, age 50,
$1,850,671 total compensation
Regional President, Greater Asia Pacific:
Moreno G. Dezio, age 48,
$1,190,935 total compensation
Regional President, Japan: Sam Komoda
Regional President, Americas: John Alexander, age 44
Director, Americas Region and Global Funding:
Kathleen Powers
Auditors: Ernst & Young LLP

LOCATIONS

HQ: JohnsonDiversey, Inc.
8310 16th St., Sturtevant, WI 53177
Phone: 262-631-4001   **Fax:** 262-631-4282
Web: www.johnsondiversey.com

2008 Sales

	$ mil.	% of total
Europe	1,831.5	55
Americas		
North America	679.4	20
Latin America	263.0	8
Asia		
Japan	311.4	9
Asia/Pacific	251.7	8
Adjustments	(21.1)	—
Total	**3,315.9**	**100**

COMPETITORS

3M
Arrow-Magnolia
Clorox
Colgate-Palmolive
Dow Chemical
Ecolab
Kimberly-Clark
NCH
Procter & Gamble
Zep Inc.

HISTORICAL FINANCIALS

Company Type: Private

Income Statement

FYE: December 31

	REVENUE ($ mil.)	NET INCOME ($ mil.)	NET PROFIT MARGIN	EMPLOYEES
12/08	3,316	(12)	—	10,800
12/07	3,130	(87)	—	11,500
12/06	2,928	118	4.0%	11,000
12/05	3,310	(167)	—	12,000
12/04	3,169	14	0.4%	12,000
Annual Growth	**1.1%**	**—**	**—**	**(2.6%)**

Net Income History

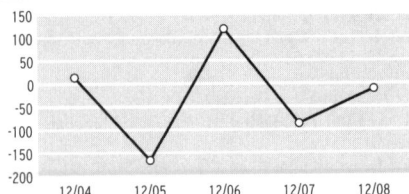

Jones Day

Legal leviathan Jones Day ranks as one of the world's largest law firms, providing counsel to about half of the *FORTUNE* 500 companies. It has some 2,400 attorneys in about 30 offices worldwide. Outside the US, Jones Day has offices in the Asia/Pacific region and in Europe. The firm's practice areas include capital markets, government regulation, intellectual property, real estate, and tax. Jones Day has counted Bridgestone/Firestone, General Motors, IBM, RJR Nabisco, and Texas Instruments among its clients. The firm traces its roots to the Cleveland law partnership founded by Edwin Blandin and William Rice in 1893.

In 2009 the company expanded its geographic reach when it merged with De Ovando y Martínez del Campo, a law firm based in Mexico City. During the same year, Jones Day opened an office in Dubai in order to penetrate the Middle East emerging market. The Dubai office has a focus on energy, finance, arbitration, and mergers and acquisition issues.

EXECUTIVES

Managing Partner: Stephen J. Brogan
Firmwide Hiring Partner: Gregory M. (Greg) Shumaker
Global Public Communications Manager:
David R. Petrou

LOCATIONS

HQ: Jones Day
North Point, 901 Lakeside Ave.
Cleveland, OH 44114
Phone: 216-586-3939   **Fax:** 216-579-0212
Web: www.jonesday.com

PRODUCTS/OPERATIONS

Selected Practice Areas

Antitrust and competition law
Banking and finance
Business restructuring and reorganization
Capital markets
Employee benefits and executive compensation
Energy delivery and power
Environmental, health, and safety
Government regulation
Health care
Intellectual property
International litigation and arbitration
Issues and appeals
Labor and employment
Mergers and acquisitions
Oil and gas
Private equity
Product liability and tort litigation
Real estate
Securities and shareholder litigation and SEC
enforcement
Tax
Trial practice

COMPETITORS

Akin Gump	Mayer Brown
Baker & McKenzie	McDermott Will & Emery
Cleary Gottlieb	Shearman & Sterling
Clifford Chance	Sidley Austin
Davis Polk	Skadden, Arps
Kirkland & Ellis	White & Case
Latham & Watkins	

HISTORICAL FINANCIALS

Company Type: Partnership

Income Statement

FYE: December 31

	REVENUE ($ mil.)	NET INCOME ($ mil.)	NET PROFIT MARGIN	EMPLOYEES
12/07	1,441	—	—	
12/06	1,310	—	—	4,977
12/05	1,285	—	—	4,850
Annual Growth	**5.9%**	**—**	**—**	**2.6%**

Revenue History

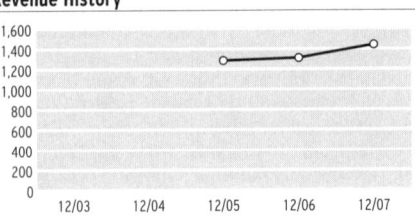

Jones Financial Companies

This isn't your father's broker. Well, maybe it is. The Jones Financial Companies is the parent of Edward Jones, an investment brokerage network catering to individual investors. Serving some 7 million clients, the "Wal-Mart of Wall Street" has thousands of satellite-linked offices in all 50 states (mainly in rural communities and suburbs), plus Canada and the UK. Brokers preach a conservative buy-and-hold approach, offering relatively low-risk investment vehicles such as government bonds, blue-chip stocks, and high-quality mutual funds. The company also sells insurance and engages in investment banking, underwriting and making markets for corporate securities and municipal bonds.

Edward Jones' network of more than 10,000 offices — many of them with a single financial advisor — makes it one of the largest brokerage networks in the world. The firm embraces technology, maintaining one of the industry's largest satellite networks (including a dish for each office).

Edwards Jones agreed to sell its UK operations, Edward Jones Limited, to Towry Law in 2009. Financial details were not disclosed. Edward Jones Limited had some 50,000 clients in the UK with assets under care of £1.5 billion ($2.5 billion).

Preferring to groom financial advisors internally, the firm accepts applicants with no previous experience, trains them extensively, and monitors investment patterns to prevent account churning and trading in risky low-cap stocks. Before they are given such luxuries as office space or assistants, new brokers must make 1,000 cold calls in their chosen community. Edward Jones' investment in training, backed by what's perceived to be old-school values and strong ethics, seems to be paying off: The firm is consistently ranked in the top 10 of *FORTUNE* magazine's "100 Best Companies to Work For."

The Jones Financial Companies' measured approach has also served it well during the economic downturn and the company has little exposure to risky investments like subprime mortgages or derivatives. It even added approximately 1,000 new financial advisors in 2008. The only major financial services firm still organized as a partnership, The Jones Financial Companies has said it has no plans to go public.

HISTORY

Jones Financial got its start in 1871 as bond house Whitaker & Co. In 1922 Edward D. Jones (no relation to the Edward D. Jones of Dow Jones fame) opened a brokerage in St. Louis. In 1943 the two firms merged.

Jones' son Edward "Ted" Jones Jr. joined the firm in 1948. Under Ted's leadership (and against his father's wishes), the company focused on rural customers, opening its first branch in the Missouri town of Mexico in 1955 and beginning its march across small-town America. Ted took over as managing partner in 1968, masterminding the company's small-town expansion. (The Wal-Mart comparison is apt; Ted Jones and Sam Walton were good friends.)

Almost from the start, the firm hammered home a conservative investment message focusing on blue-chip stocks and bonds. It expanded steadily throughout the years, adding offices with such addresses as Cedarburg, Wisconsin, and Paris, Illinois.

In the 1970s Edward D. Jones moved into underwriting with clients including Southern Co., Citicorp, and Humana. (It got burned in the mid-1980s on one such deal, when the SEC accused the company of fraud in a bond offering for life insurer D.H. Baldwin Co., which later filed for bankruptcy.)

The company's technological bent was spurred in 1978 after its Teletype network couldn't handle the demand generated by the firm's 220 offices. As a stopgap, the company nixed use of the Teletype for stock quotes, telling its brokers to call Merrill Lynch's toll-free number instead.

Managing partner John Bachmann took over from Ted Jones in 1980. (Bachmann started at the company as a janitor.) A follower of management guru Peter Drucker, Bachmann inculcated the company's brokers with Drucker's customer- and value-oriented principles.

Edward D. Jones began moving into the suburbs and into less-than-posh sections of big cities in the mid-1980s. In 1986 the company started a mortgage program, but the plan was never successful and was ended in 1988. The company weathered the 1987 stock market crash (many brokerages did not), albeit with thinner profit margins.

In 1990 Ted Jones died. The first half of the decade was a time of great expansion for the company as it doubled its number of offices. In 1993 the company opened an office in Canada.

In 1994 Jones Financial's acquisition of Columbia, Missouri-based thrift Boone National gave it the ability to offer trust and mortgage services to its clients, which helped sales as Jones started facing competition from Merrill Lynch in its small-town niche. The company's rapid expansion and relatively expensive infrastructure (all those one-person offices add up) began to eat at the bottom line, and in 1995 Bachmann stopped expansion so the firm could catch its breath.

In 1997 Edward Jones (which had unofficially dropped its middle "D" to boost name recognition) moved overseas, opening its first offices in the UK, a prime expansion target for the company. The next year the firm teamed up with Mercantile Bank to offer small-business loans. Jones resumed its expansionist push in 1999 and 2000, adding offices in all its markets.

In 2004 Edward Jones was one of several brokerage firms investigated for allegedly failing to disclose the incentives its brokers received for certain mutual fund sales. To settle the matter, the firm paid a $75 million penalty distributed to Edward Jones customers; also, managing partner Douglas Hill was required to step down in 2005 as part of an agreement with a US District Attorney investigating the matter.

The company sold its lone banking subsidiary, Boone National Savings and Loan, which had four branches in Columbia, Missouri, to Commerce Bancshares in 2006.

EXECUTIVES

CEO and Managing Partner: James D. (Jim) Weddle, age 55, $6,658,338 total compensation
CFO: Kevin Bastien, age 43
CIO: Vinny Ferrari
Chief Market Strategist: Alan F. Skrainka
General Partner, Client Solutions: Brett Campbell, age 49, $5,258,993 total compensation
General Partner, Legal and Compliance: James Tricarico Jr., age 56
Principal, Canadian Operations: Gary D. Reamey, age 53, $5,479,717 total compensation
Principal, United Kingdom Operations: Tim Kirley, age 54
Principal, Internal Audit: Tony Damico
Principal, Financial Advisor Training and Development: Dan Timm, age 50
Principal, Compliance: Pamela (Pam) Cavness
Principal, Service: Randy Haynes
Principal, Human Resources: Ken Dude
Auditors: PricewaterhouseCoopers LLP

LOCATIONS

HQ: The Jones Financial Companies, L.L.L.P.
12555 Manchester Rd., Des Peres, MO 63131
Phone: 314-515-2000   **Fax:** 314-515-2622
Web: www.edwardjones.com

2008 Offices

	No.
US	9,978
Canada	602
UK	298
Total	**10,878**

PRODUCTS/OPERATIONS

2008 Sales

	$ mil.	% of total
Commissions	1,586.6	41
Asset fees	1,067.9	27
Principal transactions	527.6	14
Account & activity fees	473.1	12
Interest & dividends	188.9	5
Investment banking	52.8	1
Adjustments	(37.9)	—
Total	**3,859.0**	**100**

COMPETITORS

Charles Schwab	Oppenheimer Holdings
Citigroup	Piper Jaffray
E*TRADE Financial	Raymond James Financial
FMR	T. Rowe Price
Legg Mason	TD Ameritrade
Morgan Stanley	UBS Financial Services
National Financial Partners	Wells Fargo Advisors

HISTORICAL FINANCIALS

Company Type: Partnership

Income Statement

FYE: December 31

	REVENUE ($ mil.)	NET INCOME ($ mil.)	NET PROFIT MARGIN	EMPLOYEES
12/08	3,859	312	8.1%	40,000
12/07	4,147	508	12.3%	38,100
12/06	3,518	391	11.1%	34,300
12/05	3,190	330	10.3%	32,400
12/04	2,891	217	7.5%	31,400
Annual Growth	**7.5%**	**9.5%**	**—**	**6.2%**

2008 Year-End Financials

Debt ratio: —   Current ratio: —
Return on equity: —   Long-term debt ($ mil.): 9
Cash ($ mil.): —

Net Income History

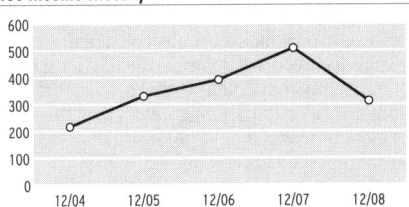

JR Simplot

J.R. Simplot hopes you'll have fries with that. Potato potentate J. R. "Jack" Simplot simply shook hands with McDonald's pioneer Ray Kroc in the mid-1960s, and his company's french fry sales have sizzled ever since. The company still remains the major french fry supplier for McDonald's and supplies Burger King, KFC, and Wendy's as well. It produces more than 3 billion pounds of french fries and hash browns annually, making it one of the world's largest processors of frozen potatoes. The company sells its potato products mainly to foodservice customers under the Simplot and private-label brands.

Along with potatoes, J.R. Simplot also produces fruits and vegetables under the RoastWorks and Simplot Classic labels. The company's spuds sprouted other businesses as well, including cattle ranches and feedlots (which use feed made from potato peels). Its AgriBusiness Group mines phosphates (for fertilizer and feed) and silica. The company's Turf and Horticulture Group produces grass and turf seed and fertilizer.

In 2008 the company acquired Washington State-based H&R Ag, an agricultural retailer that supplies crop nutrition and protection products to farmers. With operations in Washington and Oregon, H&R fits into the Simplot intended strategy to expand into new key products, services, and areas in the Northwest US.

In addition to the US, Simplot has foreign operations in Australia, Canada, China, Europe, Korea, Mexico, and Guatemala.

Founder Jack Simplot died in 2008. Officially retired from the company in 1994, he was one of the wealthiest people in America.

The company sponsors the Simplot Games, an athletic competition held each February at

Idaho State University. The games feature track-and-field events, in an indoor venue, for high school athletes from Canada and the US. Several participants have gone on to international competition as Olympians.

HISTORY

J.R. Simplot was born in Dubuque, Iowa, in 1909. His family moved to the frontier town of Declo, Idaho, about a year later. Frustrated with school and an overbearing father, Simplot dropped out at age 14 and moved to a local hotel, where he made money by paying cash for teachers' wage scrip, at 50 cents on the dollar. Simplot then got a bank loan using the scrip as collateral and moved into farming, first by raising hogs and then by growing potatoes. He met Lindsay Maggart, a leading farmer in the area, who taught him the value of planting certified potato seed, rather than potatoes.

Simplot purchased an electric potato sorter in 1928 and eventually dominated the local market by sorting for neighboring farms. By 1940 his company, J.R. Simplot, operated 33 potato warehouses in Oregon and Idaho. The company moved into food processing in the 1940s, first by producing dried onions and other vegetables for Chicago-based Sokol & Co. and later by producing dehydrated potatoes. Between 1942 and 1945 J.R. Simplot produced more than 50 million pounds of dehydrated potatoes for the US military. During the war the company also expanded into fertilizer production, cattle feeding, and lumber. It moved to Boise, Idaho, in 1947.

In the 1950s J.R. Simplot researchers developed a method for freezing french fries. In the mid-1960s Simplot persuaded McDonald's founder, Ray Kroc, to go with his frozen fries, a handshake deal that practically guaranteed Simplot's success in the potato processing industry. By the end of the 1960s, Simplot was the largest landowner, cattleman, potato grower, and employer in the state of Idaho. He also had established fertilizer plants, mining operations, and other businesses in 36 states, as well as in Canada and a handful of other countries.

During the oil crisis of the 1970s, J.R. Simplot began producing ethanol from potatoes. However, Simplot's empire-building was not without its rough edges. In 1977 he pleaded no contest to federal charges that he failed to report his income, and the next year he was forced to settle charges that he manipulated Maine potato futures.

The company entered the frozen fruit and vegetable business in 1983. Other ventures included using wastewater from potato processing for irrigation and using cattle manure to fuel methane gas plants. Simplot set up a Chinese joint venture in the 1990s to provide processed potatoes to McDonald's and other customers in East Asia.

The company bought the giant ZX cattle ranch near Paisley, Oregon, in 1994. Simplot retired from the board of directors that year to become chairman emeritus; Stephen Beebe was named president and CEO. The 1995 acquisition of the food operations of Pacific Dunlop (now Ansell) led to the creation of Simplot Australia, one of the largest food processors in Australia. Its 1997 stock swap with I. & J. Foods Australia enlarged the subsidiary's frozen food menu.

In 1999 the company sold its Simplot Dairy Products cheese business to France's Besnier Group, and it teamed with Dutch potato processor Farm Frites to enter new markets. In 2000 it bought the turf grass seed assets of AgriBioTech,

and added the US potato operations of Nestlé to its pantry.

The next year Simplot sold its Australian pudding maker Big Sister to the Fowlers Vacola Group and its Agrisource grain company to a private buyer. That same year Beebe retired and Lawrence Hlobik, president of the company's agribusiness unit, was named CEO. The company closed its only meat-processing plant in 2003.

After being out of the dehydrated potato business for more than 30 years, Simplot acquired the dehydrated potato granule business of Nestlé USA in 2004; in addition, it reached an agreement with Idaho Fresh-Pak to distribute that company's dehydrated potatoes. Also in 2004 the company began offering zero-gram trans-fat french fries, called Infinity Fries, for the food-service market.

In 2005 J. R. Simplot and his wife, Esther, donated their former hilltop home in Boise to the State of Idaho; the structure became the governor's mansion for the state, which previously didn't have an official residence for the governor's family.

Also that year, Simplot stopped producing fertilizer-grade ammonium nitrate; the material can be used to produce devastating explosions, as in the 1995 terrorist attack on the federal building in Oklahoma City.

EXECUTIVES

Chairman: Scott R. Simplot
President, CEO, and Director:
Lawrence S. (Larry) Hlobik
President AgriBusiness Group: Bill Whitacre, age 55
President AgriBusiness: Garrett Lofto
Public Relations Manager: David Cuoio
Manager Customer Focus Marketing: Meghan Swan
Manager Marketing Solutions, AgriBusiness:
Kristi Smith

LOCATIONS

HQ: J.R. Simplot Company
    999 Main St., Ste. 1300, Boise, ID 83702
Phone: 208-336-2110   **Fax:** 208-389-7515
Web: www.simplot.com

PRODUCTS/OPERATIONS

Selected Operating Groups

Agriculture Group
    Simplot Feed Ingredients
    Simplot Grower Solutions
    Simplot Plant Nutrients
Food Group
    Avocados
    Other fruits
    Potatoes
    Roastworks
    Vegetables
Industrial Group
    Simplot Industrial Products
    Simplot Silica Sand
Land and Livestock Group
    Simplot Cattle Feeding
    Simplot Farming Operations
    Simplot Ranching Operations
    Simplot Grain Facilities
    Western Stockmen's
Turf and Horticulture Group
    APEX Nursery Fertilizer
    BEST Turf Fertilizer
    Britz Fertilizer
    Jacklin Seed
    Simplot Partners

COMPETITORS

ADM	Heinz
Agri Beef	Idaho Supreme Potatoes
Bayer CropScience	King Ranch
Birds Eye	McCain Foods
Cactus Feeders	Michael Foods, Inc.
Calavo Growers	Monsanto Company
Cargill	Ore-Ida Foods, Inc.
CF Industries	Phosphate Holdings
ConAgra	PotashCorp
ContiGroup	Pro-Fac
Del Monte Foods	Scotts Miracle-Gro
Dow AgroSciences	Scoular
Fairmount Minerals	Seneca Foods
Friona Industries	Tejon Ranch
General Mills	U. S. Silica
Golden Belt Feeders	West Central Co-op
Golden State Foods	

Kaiser Permanente

Kaiser Permanente hopes to be a permanent leader in US health care. The not-for-profit entity is among the largest integrated health care systems in the US. The company offers health care services through a network of nearly 14,000 physicians belonging to Permanente Medical Groups; 32 medical centers and more than 400 medical offices that form the Kaiser Foundation Hospitals; and the Kaiser Foundation Health Plan, which covers some 8.7 million people (most of which are in California). Kaiser Permanente is primarily bi-coastal, active in California, Colorado, Georgia, Hawaii, Maryland, Ohio, Oregon, Virginia, Washington, and Washington, DC.

The company's empire is divided into geographic regions: Northern California Region; Southern California Region; Colorado Region; Georgia Region; Hawaii Region; Mid-Atlantic States Region (Maryland, Virginia, and Washington, D.C.); Ohio Region; and the Oregon/Washington Region. Although Kaiser Permanente owns hospitals only in California, Hawaii, and Oregon, it operates clinics in several states and provides services to its members in the other areas it operates through contracts with health care facilities. The company has an alliance with Group Health Cooperative that extends its network in the Pacific Northwest.

To better serve its roughly 3.3 million participants in Northern California (nearly 40% of its total enrollment), Kaiser Permanente reorganized its operations in the region, forming eight service areas, each with a major Kaiser-affiliated medical center at its core. The company is doling out a fair amount of money in the state, investing some $24 billion by 2014 to build new hospitals and bring its facilities up to earthquake safety codes.

In addition to providing health care plans and services, Kaiser Permanente conducts medical research and offers health education to the communities it serves. The organization is also something of a pioneer in health care administration: Its automated electronic medical records system is accessible to members and physicians and should help the company reap significant cost savings. Kaiser is spending some $3 billion over 10 years (from 2003 through 2013) on administrative technology. All of the company's facilities use the HealthConnect system for administration and business functions. In addition, all of Kaiser's outpatient clinics use electronic medical records; its hospitals are gradually implementing the system.

EXECUTIVES

Chairman and CEO: George C. Halvorson
EVP and CFO: Kathy Lancaster
EVP Health Plan Operations: Arthur M. Southam
EVP Health Plan and Hospital Operations:
  Bernard J. Tyson
SVP and Chief Diversity Officer: Ronald Knox
**SVP Brand Strategy, Communications, and Public
  Relations:** Diane G. Lofgren
SVP Customer Service and Program Management:
  Jerry Coy
SVP Quality and Care Delivery Excellence:
  Jed Weissberg
SVP Hospital Strategy and National Facilities:
  Christine L. Malcolm, age 59
SVP and CIO: Philip (Phil) Fasano
SVP and Chief Human Resources Officer: Paul Records
SVP National Sales and Account Management:
  Thomas A. Curtin Jr.
SVP Quality and Clinical Systems Support:
  Louise L. Liang
SVP, General Counsel, and Secretary:
  Steven (Steve) Zatkin
Executive Director, Permanente Federation:
  John H. Cochran Jr.
Auditors: KPMG LLP

LOCATIONS

HQ: Kaiser Permanente
  1 Kaiser Plaza, Oakland, CA 94612
Phone: 510-271-5800   **Fax:** 510-267-7524
Web: www.kaiserpermanente.org

Local Operating Markets

Colorado Region
  Boulder
  Colorado Springs
  Denver
Georgia Region
  Atlanta
Hawaii Region
  Hawaii
  Kauai
  Maui
  Oahu
Mid-Atlantic States Region
  Baltimore
  Northern Virginia
  Suburban Maryland
  Washington, D.C.
Northern California Region
  East Bay
  Fresno
  Golden Gate
  North East Bay
  South Bay
  Stanislaus County
  Valley
Ohio Region
  Akron
  Cleveland
Oregon/Washington
  Portland (includes Salem/Longview)
Southern California Region
  Coachella Valley
  Inland Empire
  Kern County
  Metropolitan Los Angeles/West Los Angeles
  Orange County
  San Diego County
  The Valleys
  Tri-Central
  Western Ventura County

COMPETITORS

Adventist Health
Aetna
Blue Cross
Catholic Health Initiatives
Catholic Healthcare Partners
Catholic Healthcare West
CIGNA
The Cleveland Clinic
HCA
Humana
Prince William Health System
Scripps health
St. Joseph Health System
Sutter Health
Swedish Health Services
Tenet Healthcare
UnitedHealth Group
ValleyCare Health System

HISTORICAL FINANCIALS

Company Type: Not-for-profit

Income Statement

FYE: December 31

	REVENUE ($ mil.)	NET INCOME ($ mil.)	NET PROFIT MARGIN	EMPLOYEES
12/08	40,300	—	—	167,300
12/07	37,800	—	—	159,766
12/06	34,400	—	—	156,853
12/05	31,100	—	—	148,884
12/04	28,000	—	—	140,356
Annual Growth	9.5%	—	—	4.5%

Revenue History

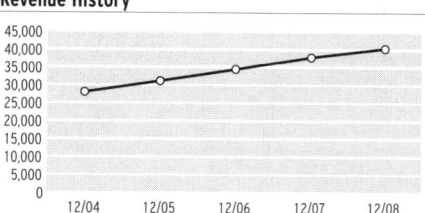

Keane Inc.

This company's customers are eager to have someone else take care of their technology systems. Keane is a leading provider of outsourcing and information technology consulting services. It manages enterprise information systems and provides system integration services for both private and public sector customers. Keane also offers a range of business process outsourcing (BPO) services, as well as application development, consulting, project management, and strategic staffing. The company, which does much of its business in the US, counts agencies of the federal government among its top customers.

In 2009 Keane bought part of financially beleaguered BearingPoint's North American commercial services business. The company also bought the New York City-based portion of BearingPoint's public sector business. The deal gives Keane a boost in its government segment, particularly in New York, where it will become a systems integration vendor to the city government.

Also that year, the company appointed John McCain as president and CEO.

EXECUTIVES

Chairman: Mani Subramanian
President and CEO: John W. McCain, age 49
EVP and CFO: Chris Setterington
EVP European Operations: Ian Miller
EVP Industry Solutions and Business Development:
  Sandeep Bhargava
**EVP Global Services, Client Management and Service
  Delivery:** Bob Gray
EVP and COO Global Client Management: Jim Puthuff
EVP; President, Keane India: Srikanth Rao
**EVP Global Services, Client Management and Service
  Delivery:** Jim Milde
EVP Products and Corporate Development:
  Marv Mouchawar
SVP Global Human Capital: Dean Williams
General Counsel: John M. Dick
Chief Marketing Officer: John Riley
Auditors: Ernst & Young LLP

LOCATIONS

HQ: Keane Inc.
  100 City Square, Boston, MA 02129
Phone: 617-241-9200   **Fax:** 617-241-9507
Web: www.keane.com

PRODUCTS/OPERATIONS

Selected Services

Outsourcing
  Business process outsourcing
  Enterprise applications outsourcing and maintenance
Development and integration
  Applications development
  Systems integration
Other
  Information technology consulting
  Staffing

COMPETITORS

Accenture	IBM Global Services
ADP	Infosys
Amdocs	McKinsey & Company
BearingPoint	Perot Systems
Booz Allen	Sapient
CIBER	SunGard Higher Education
Computer Sciences Corp.	Unisys
Convergys	Wipro Technologies
HP Enterprise Services	

HISTORICAL FINANCIALS

Company Type: Private

Income Statement

FYE: December 31

	REVENUE ($ mil.)	NET INCOME ($ mil.)	NET PROFIT MARGIN	EMPLOYEES
12/08	1,000	—	—	12,000
12/07	1,200	—	—	13,600
12/06	1,100	—	—	14,000
Annual Growth	(4.7%)	—	—	(7.4%)

Revenue History

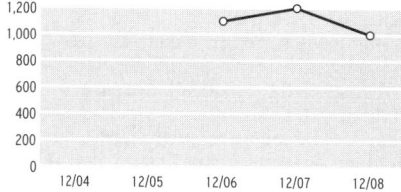

Kellogg Foundation

Charitable grants from W.K. Kellogg Foundation are grrrrrrrrreat! Founded in 1930 by cereal industry pioneer Will Keith Kellogg, the foundation provides more than $300 million in grants annually to programs focused on youth and education, health, food systems and rural development, and philanthropy and volunteerism. Most of its grants go to initiatives in the US, although it also makes grants throughout Latin America and Africa as well. The work of the W.K. Kellogg Foundation is supported by a related trust; together, the foundation and the trust have assets of more than $9 billion — mainly in Kellogg Company stock.

Charity really does begin at home for the W.K. Kellogg Foundation, which allocated about a quarter of its US grant money to activities in Michigan in 2008.

W.K. Kellogg Foundation is guided by its founder's desire "to help people help themselves" and prefers to support programs that offer long-term solutions rather than quick handouts.

Though they share a founder and a home city, the Kellogg Foundation and the Kellogg Company are governed independently.

HISTORY

Born in 1860, Will Keith Kellogg began his career with jobs as a stock boy and traveling broom salesman. He also worked as a clerk (and, later, bookkeeper and manager) at the Battle Creek Sanitarium, a renowned homeopathic hospital where his older brother, John Harvey Kellogg, was physician-in-chief. The brothers' experiments to improve vegetarian diets led to a happy accident in 1894 that resulted in the first wheat flakes. In 1906 W.K. Kellogg started the Battle Creek Toasted Corn Flake Company. Through marketing genius and innovative products, Kellogg's company became a leader in the industry.

A philanthropist by inclination, Kellogg established the Fellowship Corporation in 1925 to build an agricultural school and a bird sanctuary, as well as to set up an experimental farm and a reforestation project. He also gave $3 million to hometown causes, such as the Ann J. Kellogg School for disabled children, and for the construction of an auditorium, a junior high school, and a youth recreation center.

After attending a White House Conference on Child Health and Protection, Kellogg established the W.K. Kellogg Child Welfare Foundation in 1930. A few months later he broadened the focus of the charter and renamed the institution the W.K. Kellogg Foundation. That year the foundation began its landmark Michigan Community Health Project (MCHP), which opened public health departments in counties once thought too small and poor to sustain them. In 1934 Kellogg placed more than $66 million in Kellogg Company stock and other investments in a trust to fund his foundation.

During WWII the foundation expanded its programming to Latin America, funding advanced schooling for dentists, physicians, and other health professionals. After the war, it broadened its programming to include agriculture to help war-torn Europe. It funded projects in Germany, Iceland, Ireland, Norway, and the UK. Following Kellogg's death in 1951, the organization began providing support for graduate programs in health and hospital administration, as well as for rural leadership and community colleges.

During the 1970s the foundation lent its support to the growing volunteerism movement and to aiding the disadvantaged, with a special emphasis on programs for minorities. A review of operations in the late 1970s led the Kellogg Foundation to reassert its emphasis on health, education, agriculture, and leadership. The foundation also expanded its programs to southern Africa.

In 1986 the Kellogg Foundation began funding the Rural America Initiative — a series of 28 projects meant to develop leadership, train local government officials, and revitalize rural areas. William Richardson became president and CEO of the foundation in 1995, leaving his post as president of The Johns Hopkins University. Also during the 1990s, the foundation supported the Community-Based Public Health Initiative, which assisted universities in educating public health professionals by presenting community-based approaches to students and faculty.

In 1998 the organization announced a five-year, $55 million plan to bring health care to the nation's poor and homeless. Also that year it gave Portland State University a $600,000 grant to develop its Institute for Nonprofit Management. In 1999 the Kellogg Foundation started its first geographically based program, pledging $15 million in grants for development of Mississippi River Delta communities in Arkansas, Louisiana, and Mississippi. In 2001 the foundation pledged an additional $20 million to support economic growth in the region through the Emerging Markets Partnership. In 2002 the Kellogg Foundation awarded about $2 million in grants to SPARK (Supporting Partnerships to Assure Ready Kids) to help prepare low-income children for starting school. The organization funded a national campaign to improve men's health in 2003.

After a decade as president and CEO, Richardson stepped down in 2005. Sterling Speirn, who had led the San Mateo, California-based Peninsula Community Foundation since 1990, took over as president and CEO of the Kellogg Foundation in January 2006.

EXECUTIVES

Chairman: Cynthia H. Milligan, age 62
President and CEO: Sterling K. Speirn, age 61
Director Technology: Timothy L. Dechant
SVP Programs: James E. McHale
SVP, CFO, and Treasurer: La June Montgomery-Talley
SVP and Corporate Secretary: Gregory A. Lyman
Director Public Affairs: Dianne E. Price
Director Investments: Malcolm C. Goepfert
Director Human Resources: Norman (Norm) Howard
General Counsel and Assistant Corporate Secretary: Mary Carole Cotter
Auditors: Deloitte & Touche LLP

LOCATIONS

HQ: W.K. Kellogg Foundation
1 Michigan Ave. East, Battle Creek, MI 49017
Phone: 269-968-1611   **Fax:** 269-968-0413
Web: www.wkkf.org

2008 Grants

	$ mil.	% of total
US	254.6	83
Southern Africa	36.9	12
Latin America & the Caribbean	15.1	5
Total	**306.6**	**100**

Kellwood Company

Who would be one of the largest US apparel makers? Kellwood would. The firm generates most of its sales from women's wear, including its Koret and Sag Harbor lines. It also produces men's and children's clothes and accessories. Its other brands include My Michelle, Baby Phat, Phat Farm, Rewind, Vince, and XOXO. The company is a major supplier to department stores, as well as mass retailers, specialty boutiques, and catalogs. Kellwood also operates Vince and Sag Harbor brand outlet stores across the US. Kellwood has gained a foothold in new niches and grown through acquisitions, including Vince, Briggs New York, and Phat Fashions. It was taken private in 2008 by Sun Capital Partners and has been restructuring.

Kellwood became a portfolio company of the private equity firm — and its largest investment — in February 2008 following Sun Capital's second run at the apparel maker. (Kellwood had rejected a previous offer made in September 2007.) The purchase price was $542 million, about the same amount as the first offer.

In July 2008 retail veteran Michael Kramer was installed as president and CEO of Kellwood, succeeding Robert Skinner. Kramer hails from Abercrombie & Fitch, Apple Retail, and The Limited, among other firms. Kramer is charged with restructuring Kellwood and cutting its less profitable private-label and small-volume business, while dealing with the effects of a heavy debt load and a sharp drop in consumer spending, as a result of the deep recession in the US. Both have hurt Kellwood financially. Kellwood's bondholders agreed to extend the maturity date on some $140 million in debt from July 2009 to 2014. The extension ended weeks of negotiations, as failure to reach an agreement could have pushed the firm to file for Chapter 11 bankruptcy protection.

As part of its restructuring, Kellwood has exited many of its licensing deals, including deals with Accessory Network Group, Calvin Klein, Liz Claiborne, and Phillips-Van Heusen. Kellwood also halted operations of its Hollywould brand, an upscale contemporary line of women's footwear and apparel, in late 2008 after failing to find a buyer for that business. (Kellwood had acquired the brand for $5 million in 2006, aiming to expand its luxury segment.)

Soon after its purchase of Kellwood, Sun Capital sold the apparel maker's Gerber Childrenswear and Hanna Andersson businesses to Childrenswear LLC, an affiliate of the private equity firm, for $179 million in November. (Kellwood had acquired children's apparel maker and retailer Hanna Anderson in mid-2007 for about $175 million.) Sun Capital also separated Kellwood from its outdoor gear and apparel division American Recreation Products (acquired in 1989), and established American Recreation Products, which includes the Royal Robbins apparel brand, as a stand-alone company.

In mid-2009 Kellwood's licensed David Meister brand of better dresses, traditionally sold in better department stores, launched an e-commerce site.

Wal-Mart and Kohl's are two of Kellwood's largest customers.

EXECUTIVES

President and CEO: Michael W. Kramer, age 44
EVP, Secretary, and General Counsel: Keith Gyrpp
SVP Marketing and Brand Awareness: Eric Hunter
VP Strategy and Chief Marketing Officer:
George Sokolowski
VP and CIO: Michael M. Saunders
CEO, Vince: Rea Laccone
President, Vince: Christopher LaPolice
President, Modern Alliance Division: Arthur K. Gordon
President, Phat Fashions LLC: Kimora Lee Simmons
President, XOXO: Suzanne Desiderio
President, E*N*C: Penny Aschkenasy
President, My Michelle: Caren Belair
President, The Designer Alliance: Wendy R. Chivian
Chairman and Creative Director, The Designer Alliance:
David Meister
Senior Manager Corporate Communications:
Erin Haggerty

LOCATIONS

HQ: Kellwood Company
600 Kellwood Pkwy., Chesterfield, MO 63017
Phone: 314-576-3100   **Fax:** 314-576-3460
Web: www.kellwood.com

PRODUCTS/OPERATIONS

Selected Brands and Licenses

Baby Phat
Bice
Briggs New York
Democracy
Fabulosity
Jax
Jolt
Koret
My Michelle
Phat Farm
Rewind (girls/juniors sportswear)
Sag Harbor
Sangria
The Slimming Solution
Vince
XOXO (licensed)

COMPETITORS

Bernard Chaus	Perry Ellis International
Capital Mercury Apparel	Phillips-Van Heusen
Donna Karan	Polo Ralph Lauren
Fruit of the Loom	St. John Knits
Jones Apparel	Tommy Hilfiger
Levi Strauss	VF
Liz Claiborne	Warnaco Group
Oxford Industries	W.L. Gore

Kentucky Lottery

Kentucky Lottery operates a variety of instant-win and numbers games for the benefit of state educational programs. The lottery offers scratch-off and pull-tab games, as well as Pick 3, Pick 4, and Win for Life lotteries. In addition, Kentucky Lottery is part of the Multi-State Lottery Association and participates in that organization's multi-state Powerball drawing. Proceeds from the games go to a variety of programs, including the College Access Program, the Kentucky Educational Excellence Scholarship Program, and the Kentucky Tuition Grants Program, as well as Kentucky's General Fund. The Kentucky Lottery was established in 1989.

EXECUTIVES

Chairman: Keith Griffee
Vice Chairman: Ray DeSloover
President and CEO: Arthur L. (Arch) Gleason Jr.
EVP and COO: Margaret (Marty) Gibbs
SVP Information Technology: Gary Ruskowski
SVP Finance and Administration: Howard Kline
SVP Marketing and Sales: Steve Casebeer
SVP Internal Audit and Information Security:
Gale Vessels
SVP, General Counsel, and Corporate Secretary:
Mary Harville
SVP Security: Bill Hickerson
VP Systems Development: TH Morris
VP IT Operations: Brenda Reynolds
VP Human Resources: Church Saufley
Kentucky State Treasurer and Director:
Todd Hollenbach

LOCATIONS

HQ: Kentucky Lottery Corporation
1011 W. Main St., Louisville, KY 40202
Phone: 502-560-1500   **Fax:** 502-560-1670
Web: www.kylottery.com

COMPETITORS

Churchill Downs
Hoosier Lottery
Illinois Lottery
The Trump Organization
Virginia Lottery

Key Safety Systems

Key Safety Systems won't start your car, but it can protect your occupants. The company is a leading maker and seller of air bags and air bag components, including sensors and inflators. It also makes seat belts, steering wheels, and air bag webbing fabric. The company supplies air bags to most of the world's carmakers, including Ford, GM, Hyundai, and Volkswagen. Key Safety Systems also makes a line of automotive interior accessories, including automatic and manual shift knobs, parking brake handles, shift and brake boots, armrest covers, and pull handles. The company is controlled by private investment firm Crestview Partners.

Key Safety Systems' operational presence consists of more than 35 manufacturing, technical, and sales facilities in North America, Europe, and Asia. In 2008 it boosted its presence in Asia with the opening of a technical center in Japan to more closely serve automotive customers in that region. It joins the company's other technical centers in Shanghai, China; Frankfurt, Germany; and Detroit, Michigan, which are dedicated to prototype design, building, and testing.

EXECUTIVES

President and CEO: Jason Luo
SVP Global Human Resources: Larry Casey
SVP and CFO: Dave Smith
SVP Global Manufacturing and Quality: Jim Scarpa
SVP Global Sales and Marketing:
Ronald (Ron) Feldeisen Jr.
SVP Buiness Development, Specialty Business Group,
and Procurement: Greg Heald
SVP Legal Affairs and General Counsel:
Thomas M. (Tom) Dono Jr.
President, Hamlin Electronics: Antony Howell
President, Safety Products Business: Mark Wehner

LOCATIONS

HQ: Key Safety Systems, Inc.
7000 Nineteen Mile Rd., Sterling Heights, MI 48314
Phone: 586-726-3800   **Fax:** 586-726-4150
Web: www.keysafetyinc.com

PRODUCTS/OPERATIONS

Selected Products

Airbags
Armrest covers
Automatic and manual shift knobs
Electronic sensors
Inflators
Parking brake handles
Pull handles
Seat belts
Shift and brake boots
Steering wheels
Webbing fabric

COMPETITORS

Alpha Associates
Autocam
Autoliv
DENSO
International Textile Group
Nihon Plast
Robert Bosch
Sequa
Tokai Rika
TRW Automotive

HISTORICAL FINANCIALS

Company Type: Private

Income Statement

	REVENUE ($ mil.)	NET INCOME ($ mil.)	NET PROFIT MARGIN	EMPLOYEES
12/07	1,000	—	—	8,500
12/06	1,030	—	—	8,700
12/05	1,100	—	—	9,000
12/04	1,100	—	—	8,000
12/03	1,100	—	—	10,000
Annual Growth	(2.4%)	—	—	(4.0%)

FYE: December 31

Revenue History

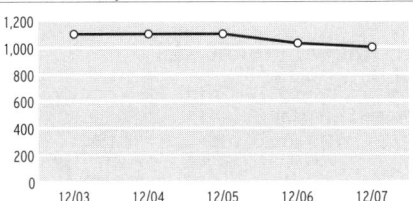

Keystone Foods

Beef is just one of the cornerstones of this food company. Keystone Foods is one of the largest makers of hamburger patties and processed poultry, with about 30 distribution and processing centers located throughout the world. A major supplier to McDonald's restaurants, Keystone serves about 30,000 restaurants worldwide with hamburgers, chicken wings, breast fillets, and chicken patties, as well as fish and pork products. Keystone also provides new product development services to its customers, as well as custom distribution and logistics services. Chairman Herb Lotman owns the company, which began as a beef-boning business in the 1960s.

EXECUTIVES

Chairman: Herbert (Herb) Lotman, age 75
President and CEO: Jerry Dean
EVP and CFO: John Coggins
SVP and Controller: Paul McGarvie
SVP USA Proteins: Gregg Berens
SVP Business Development: Ken Brown
VP, Keystone Europe: Patrice Botton
VP Research and Development: Chandler Horton
VP Global Risk Management: John Vantine
VP Information Technology: Charles Wallace
VP Quality Assurance and Food Safety: Dane Bernard
VP USA Distribution: Ken Wierman
**VP Corporate Engineering and Corporate Social
Responsibility:** Ed Delate
VP Human Resources and Communications:
 Jerry Gotro
Auditors: Ernst & Young LLP

LOCATIONS

HQ: Keystone Foods LLC
 300 Barr Harbor Dr., Ste. 600
 West Conshohocken, PA 19428
Phone: 610-667-6700   **Fax:** 610-667-1460
Web: www.keystonefoods.com

COMPETITORS

Cargill Meat Solutions
Golden State Foods
JBS
Kenosha Beef
Lopez Foods
Martin-Brower
McLane Foodservice
Meadowbrook Meat Company
OSI Group
Perdue Incorporated
Performance Food
Pilgrim's Pride
Sara Lee
Smithfield Foods
SYSCO
Tyson Foods
U.S. Foodservice

HISTORICAL FINANCIALS
Company Type: Private

Income Statement
FYE: December 31

	ESTIMATED REVENUE ($ mil.)	NET INCOME ($ mil.)	NET PROFIT MARGIN	EMPLOYEES
12/08	6,540	—	—	13,700
12/07	5,580	—	—	13,000
12/06	3,310	—	—	8,000
12/05	3,119	—	—	7,800
12/04	3,000	—	—	7,800
Annual Growth	21.5%	—	—	15.1%

Revenue History

Kinder Morgan

Kinder Morgan (formerly Knight) pipes in profits by operating 36,000 miles of natural gas pipelines in the US and Canada. The company also distributes natural gas to more than 1.1 million customers, primarily in the Midwest, and it operates gas-fired power plants along its pipelines. Through Kinder Morgan Management, it controls Kinder Morgan Energy Partners, which transports refined products and operates 170 terminals that handle coal, petroleum coke, and other materials. In 2007 chairman and CEO Richard Kinder, who owns 31% of the company, led a group of investors in taking Kinder Morgan private and adopted the Knight name. To take advantage of its better-known brand, it reverted to Kinder Morgan in 2009.

The company's strategy is focused on building and maintaining energy transportation and storage assets, which are central components to a growing natural gas and petroleum products infrastructure across North America. In 2009 it claimed leadership positions in petroleum product transportation, terminal operations, and coke and CO2 transportation.

After an acquisition spree in the early 2000s, Kinder Morgan has been selling assets in order to pay down debt and streamline its operations. In 2006 the company sold its US retail natural gas distribution and related operations for $710 million. In 2007 it sold Canada-based gas and petroleum products distributor Terasen Inc. to Fortis Inc. for approximately $3.2 billion. In 2008 Kinder Morgan sold 80% of its natural gas pipeline business segment to Myria Acquisition for $5.9 billion; it continues to operate these pipelines, however.

Kinder Morgan, formed in 1997 when Richard Kinder and William Morgan bought an Enron pipeline unit, expanded dramatically in 1999 through a reverse merger with troubled natural gas pipeline giant K N Energy.

EXECUTIVES

Chairman and CEO: Richard D. (Rich) Kinder, age 64,
 $660,389 total compensation
President and Director: C. Park Shaper, age 40,
 $1,747,940 total compensation
EVP and COO: Steven J. (Steve) Kean, age 47,
 $1,586,559 total compensation

VP and CFO: Kimberly A. (Kim) Dang, age 39,
 $731,188 total compensation
VP, General Counsel, and Secretary: Joseph Listengart,
 age 40, $1,264,001 total compensation
VP Corporate Communications: Larry S. Pierce
VP and Controller: Debra M. Witges
VP and CIO: Henry W. Neumann Jr.
VP and Chief Tax Officer: Jordan H. Mintz
VP; President, Retail: Daniel E. Watson, age 50
VP Human Resources and Administration:
 James E. Street, age 52
VP Corporate Development and Treasurer:
 David D. Kinder, age 34, $660,389 total compensation
President, Texas Intrastate Natural Gas Pipelines:
 Duane Kokinda
President, Natural Gas Pipelines: Tom Martin
President, Power: Paul R. Steinway
President, Gas Pipelines, West Region: Mark Kissel
President, Kinder Morgan Canada: Ian D. Anderson,
 age 51
Auditors: PricewaterhouseCoopers LLP

LOCATIONS

HQ: Kinder Morgan, Inc.
 500 Dallas St., Ste. 1000, Houston, TX 77002
Phone: 713-369-9000   **Fax:** 713-369-9100
Web: www.kindermorgan.com

2008 Sales

	$ mil.	% of total
US	11,804.2	98
Canada	269.3	2
Mexico & the Netherlands	21.3	—
Total	**12,094.8**	**100**

PRODUCTS/OPERATIONS

2008 Sales

	$ mil.	% of total
Kinder Morgan Energy Partners		
Natural gas pipelines	8,422.0	69
CO2	1,269.2	11
Terminals	1,172.7	10
Products pipeline	815.9	7
Kinder Morgan Canada	198.9	2
NGPL PipeCo.	132.1	1
Power	44.0	—
Other	40.0	—
Total	**12,094.8**	**100**

Selected Operations and Subsidiaries

Kinder Morgan Energy Partners, L.P.
 CO2 Pipelines
 Bulk Terminals
 Kinder Morgan Canada
 Natural Gas Pipelines
 Product Pipelines
Kinder Morgan Management, LLC
Kinder Morgan Retail Energy Services Company
Natural Gas Pipeline Company of America

COMPETITORS

Atmos Energy
Buckeye Partners
Canadian Utilities
CenterPoint Energy
Duke Energy
El Paso
Enterprise Products
Koch Industries, Inc.
Plains All American Pipeline
TransMontaigne
Williams Companies

HISTORICAL FINANCIALS

Company Type: Private

Income Statement

	REVENUE ($ mil.)	NET INCOME ($ mil.)	NET PROFIT MARGIN	EMPLOYEES
12/08	12,095	—	—	7,800
12/07	11,500	—	—	7,600
Annual Growth	5.2%	—	—	2.6%

FYE: December 31

Revenue History

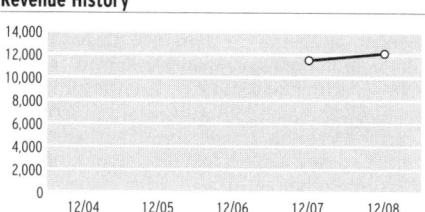

| | 12/04 | 12/05 | 12/06 | 12/07 | 12/08 |

(Y-axis: 0 to 14,000)

Kingston Technology

Kingston Technology cuts a regal figure in the realm of memory. The company is a top maker of memory modules — printed circuit boards loaded with DRAM or other memory chips that increase the capacity and speed of printers and computers. Kingston also makes flash memory cards used in portable electronic devices, such as digital still cameras, MP3 players, and wireless phones. Kingston takes on some manufacturing chores for customers through its sister company Payton Technology, which runs a specialized factory in China that tests and packages memory chips before assembling them into customized memory modules. Founders John Tu (president and CEO) and David Sun (COO) own Kingston.

Tu and Sun promote a casual atmosphere and treat employees as members of an extended family. (Their work cubicles are identical to their employees'.) Since 1996 they have given more than $100 million in bonuses to workers; in some cases the bonuses amounted to three times the employees' annual salaries.

Kingston is also known for its friendliness to business partners. It is sometimes the first to receive scarce components during shortages, thanks to its good supplier relations.

Sales of consumer electronics dramatically fell in 2008, due to the global recession, leading to a downturn in the semiconductor industry, especially in the DRAM business and the market for other memory products. Due to market conditions, memory prices fell throughout the year. As a result, Kingston shipped 41% more memory units in 2008 than the prior year, but lower prices meant that sales revenues for the year fell by $500 million from 2007, to $4 billion. While acknowledging the poor economic and market conditions, Kingston asserted it was financially secure to meet the challenges of 2009, with substantial cash reserves.

In 2009 Kingston Technology Europe signed an agreement with Staples to provide Kingston's DataTraveler Locker and DRAM products in Staples office products stores across Europe.

HISTORY

Kingston Technology was founded in 1987 by Shanghai-born John Tu and Taiwan-born David Sun, both of whom had moved to California in the 1970s. The pair met in 1982 and started a memory upgrade company called Camminton Technology in Tu's garage. Sales reached $9 million by 1986, when they sold the business to high-tech firm AST Research for $6 million. The two invested their money in stock market futures but suffered heavy losses when the market crashed in 1987.

That year PC makers were producing computers that lacked the memory needed to run the latest, hottest software, so Tu and Sun sprang into action. With just $4,000 in cash, they started another company that converted inexpensive, outdated chips into memory upgrades. Tu, who was educated in Europe, wanted to call the company Kensington after the gardens in London. A mouse pad company had that name, so Kingston was chosen.

Tu had doubts about the new company and bet Sun a Jaguar that it wouldn't survive the first year of operations. Sun won the car (which he later gave to a veteran employee who dreamed of owning one) and within two years the company sold nearly $40 million worth of products. In 1989 Kingston began making memory system upgrades; a year later it started producing processor upgrades.

The company was #1 on *Inc.* magazine's list of fastest-growing private US companies in 1992. The next year Kingston began marketing networking and storage products. Its vendor-friendly policy paid off that year, when demand for semiconductors far outstripped supply. Suppliers kept shipping to the company even when orders for other buyers were delayed.

In 1996 SOFTBANK paid $1.5 billion for 80% of the company, promising to preserve its culture and retain all management — including Tu and Sun — and employees. Sun and Tu set aside $100 million for employee bonuses.

In 1998 Kingston opened its first foreign manufacturing facilities, in Ireland and Taiwan. Also in 1998, in a unique arrangement suggesting that SOFTBANK overpaid when it bought Kingston, Tu and Sun agreed to forgo SOFTBANK's final $333 million payment. The following year Tu and Sun bought back SOFTBANK's stake for about $450 million. Also in 1999 the company opened a manufacturing plant in Malaysia.

After years of making computer storage devices, Kingston in 2000 formed a separate company, StorCase Technology, which specialized in storage equipment. The following year Kingston discontinued its Peripheral Products Division's offerings. Also in 2001 Kingston launched a joint venture (and opened a new plant) in China with computer maker China GreatWall Computer Shenzhen Company.

In 2002 the company inked a long-term deal with German chip heavyweight Infineon, under which Infineon supplied much of Kingston's DRAM needs and Kingston provided Infineon with contract manufacturing and engineering services. (In 2006 Infineon spun off its memory chip business as Qimonda, retaining majority ownership of the new venture.) In 2003 Kingston made a $50 million investment in DRAM maker Elpida Memory.

Annual revenues topped $2 billion for the first time in 2004. The following year Kingston formed a Japanese joint venture, Tera Probe,

with Elpida, Advantest, and Powertech Technology, to provide wafer testing services. Kingston's Japanese subsidiary invested ¥3 billion in Tera Probe, taking an equity stake of around 27%. Tera Probe was formed to serve Elpida and other Japanese semiconductor manufacturers.

Also in 2005 Kingston completed an expansion of its plant in Shanghai, increasing its production capacity from 1.5 million modules per month to 5 million modules per month. The company went over the $3 billion mark in sales for the year. Sales were $4.5 billion in 2007.

EXECUTIVES

President and CEO: John Tu, age 67
COO: David Sun
CFO: Koichi Hosokawa
Senior Technology Manager: Mark Tekunoff
SVP Sales and Marketing: Mike Sager
VP Sales: John Holland
VP Administration (HR): Daniel Hsu
Business Development Manager, Middle East and Africa: Antoine Harb
Digital Storage Product Manager: Mike Kuppinger

LOCATIONS

HQ: Kingston Technology Company, Inc.
  17600 Newhope St., Fountain Valley, CA 92708
Phone: 714-435-2600   **Fax:** 714-435-2699
Web: www.kingston.com

Kingston Technology has operations in Australia, China, France, Germany, India, New Zealand, Taiwan, the UK, the US, and Vietnam.

PRODUCTS/OPERATIONS

Selected Products

Flash memory cards (CompactFlash, DataFlash, MultiMediaCard)
Media readers (for data transfer between flash memory cards and PCs)
Memory modules and add-on boards
High-performance memory modules (HyperX)
Secure digital cards (for mobile and photo/video applications)
Solid-state drives (SSDNow)
Standard memory modules (ValueRAM)

COMPETITORS

Acer
Amkor
ASE Test
Buffalo Technology
Centon Electronics
Dataram
Elpida Memory
Entorian
Hynix
IM Flash Technologies
Imation
Lexar
MA Laboratories
Memorex
Micron Technology
Mosel Vitelic
Netlist
Numonyx
PNY Technologies
Samsung Electronics
SanDisk
Silicon Storage
SMART Modular Technologies
STEC
Unigen
Viking InterWorks
Wintec

HISTORICAL FINANCIALS

Company Type: Private

Income Statement

FYE: December 31

	REVENUE ($ mil.)	NET INCOME ($ mil.)	NET PROFIT MARGIN	EMPLOYEES
12/08	4,000	—	—	4,100
12/07	4,500	—	—	4,500
12/06	3,700	—	—	4,000
12/05	3,000	—	—	2,900
12/04	2,400	—	—	2,000
Annual Growth	13.6%	—	—	19.7%

Revenue History

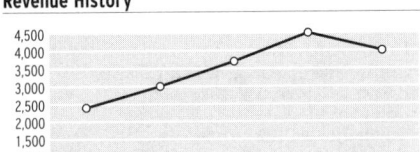

Kinray's billionaire CEO and owner, Rahr, also operates an informal lending system in which he finances local pharmacy owners looking to expand through acquisitions or to make up financial shortfalls. Rahr's lending activities have grown to about $30 million, with the tycoon charging prime plus 1% interest on loans of up to about $1 million.

EXECUTIVES

President and CEO: Stewart Rahr
EVP Operations: Lenny Romano
EVP Sales: Tom Pelizza
EVP and Director Data Processing: Casey Bruno
CFO: Howard B. Hirsch
VP Generic Sales and Business Development: Jean Kappes
VP Information Technology: Mikhail (Mike) Rapoport
VP and General Manager: Bill Bodinger
Director Credit and Accounts Recievable: Joe O'Sullivan

LOCATIONS

HQ: Kinray Inc.
152-35 10th Ave., Whitestone, NY 11357
Phone: 718-767-1234   **Fax:** 718-767-4388
Web: www.kinray.com

COMPETITORS

AmerisourceBergen
Amexdrug
Apothecary Products
Cardinal Health Pharmaceutical
H. D. Smith Wholesale Drug
The Harvard Drug Group
Imperial Distributors
McKesson
PSS World Medical
Quality King

HISTORICAL FINANCIALS

Company Type: Private

Income Statement

FYE: December 31

	REVENUE ($ mil.)	NET INCOME ($ mil.)	NET PROFIT MARGIN	EMPLOYEES
12/08	5,100	—	—	1,000
12/07	4,800	—	—	1,000
12/06	4,400	—	—	1,000
12/05	4,000	—	—	800
12/04	3,510	—	—	1,000
Annual Growth	9.8%	—	—	0.0%

Revenue History

Kinray Inc.

Kinray, the US's top private wholesale drug distributor, is nothing if not independent. It provides generic, branded, and repackaged drugs, health and beauty products, medical equipment, vitamins, and diabetes-care products. The distributor also offers about 800 private label products under the Preferred Plus Pharmacy brand. It serves more than 4,000 independent pharmacies, long-term care facilities, and specialty pharmacies in states stretching from Maine to Delaware, though Kinray is looking to supply generic drugs to pharmacies nationwide. The firm was founded in 1944 by Joseph Rahr. His son, CEO and president Stewart Rahr, has owned Kinray since 1975.

Like its bigger rivals McKesson, Cardinal Health, and AmerisourceBergen, Kinray had depended on speculative buying (the practice of stocking up on drugs it anticipated were about to go up in price) for much of its rapid growth. However, that mode of operation took a hit when Bristol-Myers Squibb was sued by the SEC over the practice several years ago.

The company also faces stiff competition from mail-order pharmacies, and in response has stepped up its online ordering capabilities with its Weblink system. The system allows pharmacies to view real-time pricing information; generate reports, invoices, and statements for inventory management; and order class 2 controlled drugs using Kinray's Controlled Substance Ordering System (CSOS).

Kinray is also focused on selling higher-margin generic drugs, a big part of its business, and private-label home health care products. In addition, the company offers merchandising and marketing programs, including retail pricing consultation, shelf-labeling, and promotional materials.

The company's stock of goods doesn't stop at medical supplies and prescription drugs. Other products include DVDs, fragrances, and household items (both branded and the private Preferred Plus Pharmacy label).

Knowledge Learning

Curious kids are learning while their parents are earning with the help of Knowledge Learning Corporation. The company operates more than 1,700 KinderCare, Knowledge Beginnings, and Children's Creative Learning early child care centers throughout the US; more than 300,000 students are enrolled in its centers. The group also offers before- and after-school care, summer camps, an online high school, and supplemental academic programs through its Champions division (formerly known as KLC School Partnerships). In 2007 Knowledge Learning Corporation acquired Children's Creative Learning Centers, an operator of onsite or adjacent child care centers for corporations, universities, and other entities.

In 2008 Knowledge Learning Corporation made an unsolicited bid to buy for-profit school operator Nobel Learning Communities, but lowered its offer from some $186 million to just over $140 million the following year. Nobel's board rejected the offer in 2009, saying it was too low.

Knowledge Learning Corporation rebranded its KLC School Partnerships division as Champions in 2009 in a move designed to change the image of the program. The Champions division, which serves mostly high school students, has three product lines: Champions Academy for math and reading skills; Champions Science Adventures for science skills; and Champions Extended Learning for after-school studies. Champions has more than 650 sites in 20 states.

Knowledge Learning Corporation is owned by Knowledge Universe, which also owns online education companies and student and teacher training firms in Singapore. Former junk-bond king Michael Milken co-founded Knowledge Universe and serves as its chairman.

EXECUTIVES

President and COO: Elanna S. Yalow
CFO: John A. (Jay) Muskovich
EVP and CIO: John R. Hnanicek
EVP and General Counsel: John Sims
EVP Human Resources: Donna J. Lesch
SVP Marketing and Business Development: Dan Frechtling
SVP Education and Training: Sharon Bergen
SVP Real Estate Development: Bill Robards
President, Knowledge Learning Corporation School Partnerships: Marcy Suntken

LOCATIONS

HQ: Knowledge Learning Corporation
650 NE Holladay St., Ste. 1400, Portland, OR 97232
Phone: 503-872-1300   **Fax:** 503-872-1349
Web: www.knowledgelearning.com

PRODUCTS/OPERATIONS

Selected Services
Backup child care
Child care consulting
Corporate discounts
Curriculum
 Creativity & imagination
 Mathematics
 Motor development
 Reading & language development
 Scientific discovery
 Social & emotional development
 Technology
Kindergarten
On-site care for children from infant through school age

COMPETITORS

Bright Horizons Family Solutions
Child Development Schools
Edison Learning
Imagine Schools
Kaplan
Learning Care Group
New Horizon
Nobel Learning Communities

HISTORICAL FINANCIALS

Company Type: Private

Income Statement

	ESTIMATED REVENUE ($ mil.)	NET INCOME ($ mil.)	NET PROFIT MARGIN	EMPLOYEES
12/07	1,620	—	—	42,000
12/06	1,550	—	—	41,000
12/05	1,654	—	—	41,000
Annual Growth	(1.0%)	—	—	1.2%

FYE: December 31

Revenue History

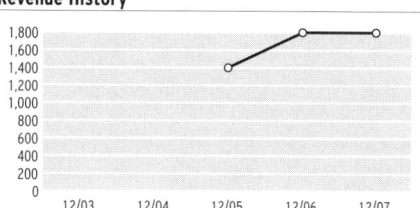

Koch Foods

Kids, always ready with a joke, ask why the chicken crossed the road. But it's you who should cross the road — to get to Koch Foods — because the company is ready with a whole hen house full of poultry products. It is one of the top chicken producers in the US, and its products include value-added fresh and frozen chicken, including chicken tenderloins, tenders, strips, boneless breasts, and wings, along with diced and pulled white and dark meat, and whole and whole cut-up chickens. Its customers include companies in the retail food and foodservice sectors throughout the US as well as overseas.

Starting out as a one-room chicken deboning and cutting operation, Koch Foods has grown into a full-service chicken producer mainly through acquisitions, including slaughtering plants and feed mills. The company's latest purchase was in 2006, when Koch closed on a $58 million deal for Alabama-based chicken processor, Sylvest Farms.

EXECUTIVES

President and CEO: Joseph C. (Joe) Grendys
CFO: Mark Kaminsky
Senior Director Marketing and Sales Support: Michael S. Lazarus

LOCATIONS

HQ: Koch Foods Incorporated
1300 W. Higgins Rd., Park Ridge, IL 60068
Phone: 847-384-5940   **Fax:** 847-384-5961
Web: www.kochfoods.com

COMPETITORS

Allen Family Foods
Barber Foods
Bell & Evans
Brakebush Brothers
Cagle's
Coleman Natural Foods
Cooper Farms
Empire Kosher Poultry
Fieldale Farms
Foster Farms
Hormel
Loggins Meat
Mountaire Farms
New Market Poultry
Northwestern Meat
O.K. Foods, Inc.
OSI Group
Perdue Incorporated
Petaluma Poultry
Pilgrim's Pride
Raeford Farms
Sanderson Farms
Townsends
Tyson Foods
Wayne Farms LLC

HISTORICAL FINANCIALS

Company Type: Private

Income Statement

	REVENUE ($ mil.)	NET INCOME ($ mil.)	NET PROFIT MARGIN	EMPLOYEES
12/07	1,800	—	—	14,000
12/06	1,800	—	—	8,000
12/05	1,400	—	—	7,500
Annual Growth	13.4%	—	—	36.6%

FYE: December 31

Revenue History

Koch Industries

Koch (pronounced "coke") Industries is the *real thing*, one of the largest (if not the largest) private companies in the US. Koch's operations are diverse, including refining and chemicals, process and pollution control equipment, and technologies; fibers and polymers; commodity and financial trading; and forest and consumer products (led by Georgia-Pacific LLC). Its Flint Hills Resources subsidiary owns three refineries that process 800,000 barrels of crude oil daily. Koch operates crude gathering systems and pipelines across North America as well as cattle ranches with a total of 15,000 head of cattle in Kansas, Montana, and Texas. Brothers Charles and David Koch control the company.

Koch's numerous subsidiary companies leverage capabilities such as its proprietary Market Based Management system, and a high level of operational, trading, transaction, and public sector skills, to create long-term value for its customers. The group has a presence in almost 60 countries.

The company has pursued a strategy of reinvesting about 90% of its earnings into acquisitions and investments (some $32 million over the past five years, including the $21 billion forest products giant Georgia Pacific.

Charles Koch released a book in 2007, *THE SCIENCE OF SUCCESS: How Market-Based Management Built the World's Largest Private Company*, outlining the company's philosophy.

HISTORY

Fred Koch grew up poor in Texas and worked his way through MIT. In 1928 Koch developed a process to refine more gasoline from crude oil, but when he tried to market his invention, the major oil companies sued him for patent infringement. Koch eventually won the lawsuits (after 15 years in court), but the controversy made it tough to attract many US customers. In 1929 Koch took his process to the Soviet Union, but he grew disenchanted with Stalinism and returned home to become a founding member of the anticommunist John Birch Society.

Koch launched Wood River Oil & Refining in Illinois (1940) and bought the Rock Island refinery in Oklahoma (1947). He folded the remaining purchasing and gathering network into Rock Island Oil & Refining (though he later sold the refineries).

After Koch's death in 1967, his 32-year-old son Charles took the helm and renamed the company Koch Industries. He began a series of acquisitions, adding petrochemical and oil trading service operations.

During the 1980s Koch was thrust into various arenas, legal and political. Charles' brother David, also a Koch Industries executive, ran for US vice president on the Libertarian ticket in 1980. That year the other two Koch brothers, Frederick and William (David's fraternal twin), launched a takeover attempt; but Charles retained control, and William was fired from his job as VP.

In a 1983 settlement Charles and David bought out the dissident family members for just over $1 billion. William and Frederick continued to challenge their brothers in court, claiming they had been shortchanged in the deal (the two estranged brothers eventually lost their case in 1998, and their appeals were rejected in 2000).

Despite this legal wrangling, Koch Industries continued to expand, purchasing a Corpus Christi, Texas, refinery in 1981. It expanded its pipeline system, buying Bigheart Pipe Line in Oklahoma (1986) and two systems from Santa Fe Southern Pacific (1988).

In 1991 Koch purchased the Corpus Christi marine terminal, pipelines, and gathering systems of Scurlock Permian (a unit of Ashland Oil). In 1992 the company bought United Gas Pipe Line (renamed Koch Gateway Pipeline) and its pipeline system extending from Texas to Florida.

To strengthen its engineering services presence worldwide, Koch acquired Glitsch International (a maker of separation equipment) from engineering giant Foster Wheeler in 1997. It also acquired USX-Delhi Group, a natural gas processor and transporter.

In 1998 Koch bought Purina Mills, the largest US producer of animal feed, and formed the KoSa joint venture with Mexico's Saba family to buy Hoechst's Trevira polyester unit. (Koch acquired the Saba family's stake in KoSa in 2001.) Lethargic energy and livestock prices in 1998 and 1999, however, led Koch to lay off several hundred employees, sell its feedlots, and divest portions of its natural gas gathering and pipeline systems. Purina Mills filed for bankruptcy protection in 1999 (later, it emerged from bankruptcy and held an IPO in 2000, and was acquired by #2 US dairy co-op Land O'Lakes in 2001).

William Koch sued Koch Industries in 1990, claiming the company had underreported the amount of oil purchased on US government and Native Americans lands. A jury found for William, but he, Charles, and David agreed to settle the case in 2001 — and sat down to dinner together for the first time in 20 years.

In other legal matters, in 2000 Koch agreed to pay a $30 million civil fine and contribute $5 million toward environmental projects to settle complaints over oil spills from its pipelines in the 1990s. The company agreed to pay $20 million in 2001 to settle a separate environmental case concerning a Texas refinery.

The company acquired INVISTA in 2004 for $4.2 billion and merged it with its KoSa unit. In 2005 SemGroup acquired all of Koch Materials Company's US and Mexico asphalt operations, and ONEOK, Inc. acquired the natural gas liquids businesses owned by several Koch companies.

In 2005 a Koch subsidiary completed the $21 billion acquisition of Georgia-Pacific.

EXECUTIVES

Chairman and CEO: Charles G. Koch, age 74
Vice-Chairman: Joseph W. (Joe) Moeller, age 66
President, COO, and Director:
 David L. (Dave) Robertson, age 47
CFO and Director: Steve Feilmeier
EVP and Director: Richard Fink
EVP Operations and Director: James L. (Jim) Mahoney
EVP and Director: David H. Koch, age 69
SVP Corporate Strategy: John C. Pittenger
SVP and General Counsel: Mark Holden
President, Koch Fertilizer, LLC: Steve Packebush
President, Koch Carbon, LLC: Steve Tatum
President, Koch Pipeline Company: Kim Penner
President, Koch Financial Corporation:
 Randall A. (Randy) Bushman
President, and COO Koch Chemical Technology Group:
 Robert (Bob) DiFulgentiz
President and COO, Flint Hills Resources:
 Bradley J. (Brad) Razook
President, Koch Supply & Trading: Steve Mawer
Controller: Richard Dinkel
Treasurer: David May
Communication Director: Melissa Cohlmia

LOCATIONS

HQ: Koch Industries, Inc.
 4111 E. 37th St. North, Wichita, KS 67220
Phone: 316-828-5500   **Fax:** 316-828-5739
Web: www.kochind.com

Koch Industries has operations in Argentina, Australia, Belgium, Brazil, Canada, China, the Czech Republic, France, Germany, India, Italy, Japan, Luxembourg, the Netherlands, Poland, South Africa, Spain, Switzerland, the UK, the US, and Venezuela.

PRODUCTS/OPERATIONS

Selected Operations

Refining & Chemicals
 Flint Hills Resources (formerly Koch Petroleum, crude oil, petrochemicals, and refined products)
 Koch Pipeline Co. LP

Process & Pollution Control Equipment & Technologies (specialty equipment and services for refining and chemical industry)
 Iris Power Engineering, Inc.
 The John Zink Company
 Koch-Glitsch, Inc.
 Koch Heat Transfer Group (formerly Brown Fintube Company)
 Koch Membrane Systems Inc.

Minerals
 Koch Mineral Services
  Koch Carbon LLC.
  Koch Exploration Company, LLC.

Fertilizers
 Koch Nitrogen Company
Fibers & Polymers
 INVISTA B.V.
Commodity & Financial Trading & Services
 Koch Financial Corp.
 Koch Supply & Trading
Forest & Consumer Products
 Georgia-Pacific LLC
Ranching
 Matador Cattle Co.
Business Development
 Koch Genesis Company (investment in noncore businesses)

COMPETITORS

AbitibiBowater
ADM
AEP
Ashland Inc.
Avista
BP
Cargill
CenterPoint Energy
Chevron
ConocoPhillips
ContiGroup
Duke Energy
Dynegy
Exxon Mobil
Gypsum Products
Imperial Oil
International Paper
Kimberly-Clark
King Ranch
Marathon Oil
Motiva Enterprises
Occidental Petroleum
OfficeMax
Packaging Corp. of America
Peabody Energy
PEMEX
PG&E Corporation
Royal Dutch Shell
Shell Oil Products
Smurfit-Stone Container
Southern Company
SUEZ-TRACTEBEL
Sunoco
Weyerhaeuser
Williams Companies

HISTORICAL FINANCIALS
Company Type: Private

Income Statement
FYE: December 31

	REVENUE ($ mil.)	NET INCOME ($ mil.)	NET PROFIT MARGIN	EMPLOYEES
12/08	100,000	—	—	70,000
12/07	98,000	—	—	80,000
12/06	90,000	—	—	80,000
12/05	80,000	—	—	80,000
12/04	40,000	—	—	30,000
Annual Growth	25.7%	—	—	23.6%

Revenue History

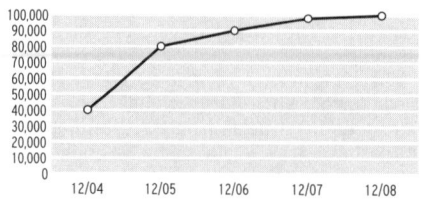

Kohler Co.

Kohler's profits are going down the drain, literally. The company makes bathroom and kitchen products — from toilets and baths to showers and sinks — under the names Kohler, Hytec, and Sterling. It also makes furniture under the names Baker and McGuire, as well as ceramic, stone, and mosaic tile under the brand Ann Sacks. Lesser-known operations include Kohler's manufacturing of small engines, generators, and power supplies for both consumer and industrial applications. Kohler's real estate operations include Destination Kohler, a resort in Wisconsin, and Old Course Hotel Golf Resort and Spa in Scotland. Chairman Herbert Kohler Jr. and his sister Ruth Kohler, grandchildren of the founder, control Kohler.

The slump in home sales in late 2008 and 2009 caused Kohler to contract. It instituted several cutbacks in its operation, including layoffs among both production and management employees, mainly in its global power, kitchen, and bath groups.

Renowned as a leader in bath and kitchen design and technology, the company continues to innovate within the industry, designing a "bathroom of the future," which features a digitally controlled shower system that offers 22 different body spray options at the touch of a button. Its Hatbox toilet combines a minimalist "tankless" design with powerful flushing capabilities. A handful of its toilets incorporate water-efficient design and use at least 20% less water than standard 1.6 gallon toilets.

Like any good three-headed giant, Kohler's other two business segments are also expanding. The company continues to seek and form joint ventures to market and sell its engine products overseas, especially in China, where it has a strong foothold. Through acquisitions of such companies as Lombardini Srl, Kohler's Global Power Group subsidiary makes further headway into European and North African markets.

On the real estate front, Kohler is planning to expand its hospitality business by opening its first day spa in the suburbs of Chicago. It will pair the spa with a Kohler retail store, selling some of the same equipment and bath fixtures used in the spa. The company sees this as an experiment full of synergistic opportunities. If successful, it plans to replicate the model in other markets.

HISTORY

In 1873, 29-year-old Austrian immigrant John Kohler and partner Charles Silberzahn founded Kohler & Silberzahn in Sheboygan, Wisconsin. That year they purchased a small iron foundry that made agricultural products for $5,000 from Kohler's father-in-law. In 1880, two years after Silberzahn left the firm, its machine shop was destroyed by fire.

The company introduced enameled plumbing fixtures in the rebuilt factory in 1883. The design caught on, and the business sold thousands of sinks, kettles, pans, and bathtubs. By 1887, when Kohler was incorporated, enameled items accounted for 70% of sales. By 1900 the 250-person company received 98% of its sales from enameled iron products. That year, shortly after John Kohler began building new facilities near Sheboygan (which later became the company village of Kohler), he died at age 56. More trouble followed: Kohler's new plant burned down in

1901, and two of the founder's sons died — Carl at age 24 in 1904 and Robert at age 35 in 1905.

Eldest surviving son Walter built a boarding hotel to house workers and introduced other employee-benefit programs. He also set up company-paid workers' compensation before the state made it law in 1917.

By the mid-1920s, when Kohler premiered colors in porcelain fixtures and added brass fittings and vitreous china toilets and washbasins to its line, it was the #3 plumbing-product company in the US. As a testament to the design quality of its products, Kohler items were displayed at the New York Museum of Modern Art in 1929. The company also began developing products that would grow in importance in later decades: electric generators and small gasoline engines. During the 1950s Kohler's engines virtually conquered Southeast Asia, where they were used to power boats, drive air compressors, and pump water for rice paddies in Vietnam and Thailand. While strikes against Kohler in 1897 and 1934 had been resolved quickly, a 1954 strike against the firm lasted six years. The strike gave Kohler the dubious honor of enduring the longest strike in US history.

Small-engine use grew in the US in the 1960s, and Kohler's motors were used in lawn mowers, construction equipment, and garden tractors.

The founder's last surviving son, Herbert (a child from John Kohler's second marriage), died in 1968. Under the leadership of Herbert's son Herbert Jr. (appointed chairman 1972), Kohler expanded its operations and began to develop its resort business in the US with the restoration of The American Club hotel (1981); it bought Sterling Faucet (1984), Knapp & Tubbs (1986), and Jacob Delafon (1986). Subsequent acquisitions have included Sanijura (bathroom furniture, France) in 1993, Osio (enamel baths, Italy) in 1994, Robern (mirrored cabinets) in 1995, Holdiam (baths, whirlpools, and sinks, France) in 1995, and Canac (cabinets, Canada) in 1996.

The company entered a growing plumbing market in China through four joint ventures formed in that country in 1996 and 1997. In 1998 several family and non-family shareholders claimed a reorganization plan unfairly forced them out and undervalued their stock. Legal battles over the stock's fair price continued in 1999, and a settlement was reached in 2000 that granted shareholders a fair price, and Herbert Jr. and his sister Ruth gained firm control of the company. Herbert reorganized the company and vowed it would never go public.

Following the tragedy of 9/11, Kohler quickly created a mobile showering unit with nine shower stalls and four sinks within an enormous semi-trailer to provide hot showers for workers and volunteers at the World Trade Center.

In 2002, Kohler and about 3,450 United Auto Workers (UAW) union members who worked at the company's Village of Kohler and Town of Mosel plants agreed on a five-year labor contract that called for increases in wages and benefits.

Kohler expanded its resort business internationally in 2004 by purchasing the world-renowned Old Course Hotel Golf Resort and Spa in St. Andrews, Scotland, along with Golf Resorts International (GRI), Limited.

The Global Power Group acquired Italian engine maker Lombardini Srl from Mark IV Industries in 2007, adding a diesel product line to its stable of offerings.

In 2008 Kohler acquired Mark David, a maker of upscale seating for the hospitality sector.

EXECUTIVES

Chairman and CEO: Herbert V. Kohler Jr., age 66
President, COO, and Director: David Kohler, age 42
SVP Human Resources: Laura Kohler
SVP Finance and CFO: Jeffrey P. Cheney
VP Hospitality and Real Estate: Alice Edland
VP Marketing, Fixtures: Mike Chandler
Group President, Kitchen and Bath: Jim Westdorp
President, Global Faucets: Jeffrey Mueller
President, Global Power Group:
   Richard J. (Dick) Fotsch, age 53
President, Engine Business: James Doyle, age 58
Consumer Segmentation Manager: Elisabeth Sutton
Communications, Kohler Global Power Group:
   Stephanie Dlugopolski
Public Relations, Kitchen and Bath Group: Todd Weber
Media Relations, Destination Kohler: Scott Silvestri
Marketing Director, Sterling Brand: Gordon Wuthich

LOCATIONS

HQ: Kohler Co.
   444 Highland Dr., Kohler, WI 53044
Phone: 920-457-4441   **Fax:** 920-457-1271
Web: kohlerco.com

PRODUCTS/OPERATIONS

Selected Operations

Engines
   Commercial turf equipment engines
   Consumer lawn and garden equipment engines
   Industrial, construction, and commercial equipment
      engines
   Recreational equipment engines
Furniture
   Baker Furniture
   McGuire Furniture Company
   Milling Road Furniture
Generators
   Kohler rental power
   Marine generators
   Mobile generators
   On-site power systems
      Automatic transfer switches
      Switchgear
   Residential generators
   Small business generators
Kitchen and bath products
   Cabinets and vanities
      Canac (bathroom cabinetry)
      Robern (lighting and mirrored bath cabinetry)
      Sanijura (vanities and other bath furniture)
   Plumbing products
      Jacob Delafon (bathtubs, faucets, lavatories, and
         toilets)
      Kallista (bathroom and kitchen sinks and faucets)
      Kohler (bath and shower faucets, baths, bidet
         faucets, bidets, body spa systems, glass showers
         and shower doors, kitchen and bathroom sinks
         and faucets, master baths, toilets, toilet seats,
         vanities, whirlpool baths)
      Sterling (bathing fixtures, faucets, sinks, tub/shower
         enclosures, vitreous china bath fixtures)
   Tile and stone products
      Ann Sacks (art tile, glazed tile, knobs and pulls,
         mosaics, terra cotta)
Real estate and hospitality (Destination Kohler)
   The American Club (resort hotel)
   Blackwolf Run golf course
   Golf Resorts International, Limited (Scotland)
   Inn on Woodlake
   Kohler Stables
   Kohler Waters Spa
   Old Course Hotel Golf Resort and Spa (Scotland)
   Riverbend (private club)
   River Wildlife
   The Shops at Woodlake Kohler
   Whistling Straits golf course

COMPETITORS

Armstrong World	Iberia Tiles
Industries	Jacuzzi Brands
Bassett Furniture	Klaussner Furniture
Black & Decker	Leggett & Platt
Briggs & Stratton	Masco
Carlson Companies	Moen
Chicago Faucet	Mueller Industries
Clarke Products	NIBCO
Crane Co.	Price Pfister
Crossville	Starwood Hotels & Resorts
Dal-Tile	Tecumseh Products
Elkay Manufacturing	TOTO
Geberit	Trane Inc.
Gerber Plumbing Fixtures	Waxman
Grohe	Yamaha
Honda	

HISTORICAL FINANCIALS

Company Type: Private

Income Statement				FYE: December 31
	ESTIMATED REVENUE ($ mil.)	NET INCOME ($ mil.)	NET PROFIT MARGIN	EMPLOYEES
12/08	5,500	—	—	30,000
12/07	5,230	—	—	32,000
12/06	5,000	—	—	33,000
12/05	3,000	—	—	31,000
12/04	3,000	—	—	28,000
Annual Growth	16.4%	—	—	1.7%

Revenue History

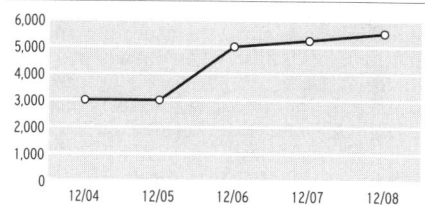

KPMG International

Businesses all over the world count on KPMG for accounting. KPMG is the smallest, yet one of the most geographically dispersed of accounting's Big Four firms, which also includes Deloitte Touche Tohmatsu, Ernst & Young, and PricewaterhouseCoopers. KPMG, a cooperative that operates as an umbrella organization for its global network of member firms, has organized its structure into three operating regions: the Americas (which includes KPMG LLC); Australia and Asia/Pacific; and Europe, the Middle East, South Asia, and Africa. Member firms' offerings include audit, tax, and advisory services. KPMG focuses on clients in such industries as financial services, consumer products, and government.

KPMG, which operates in more than 140 countries worldwide, is focusing its growth on the BRIC countries (Brazil, Russia, India, and China), as are many of its member firms' clients.

Increased spending on infrastructure has the company ramping up its advisory capabilities around the world. KPMG plans to tap its experience in building public-private partnerships in order to help finance infrastructure projects.

Another key issue KPMG is tackling is global accounting standards. The firm is a big proponent of International Financial Reporting Standards (IFRS). The set of global accounting practices have been adopted by more than 110 countries around the world, but KPMG would like to see that number grow. As countries make the shift, KPMG firms offer guidance and training.

HISTORY

Peat Marwick was founded in 1911, when William Peat, a London accountant, met James Marwick during an Atlantic crossing. University of Glasgow alumni Marwick and Roger Mitchell had formed Marwick, Mitchell & Company in New York in 1897. Peat and Marwick agreed to ally their firms temporarily, and in 1925 they merged as Peat, Marwick, Mitchell, & Copartners.

In 1947 William Black became senior partner, a position he held until 1965. He guided the firm's 1950 merger with Barrow, Wade, Guthrie, one of the US's oldest firms, and built its consulting practice. Peat Marwick restructured its international practice as PMM&Co. (International) in 1972 (renamed Peat Marwick International in 1978).

The next year several European accounting firms led by Klynveld Kraayenhoff (the Netherlands) and Deutsche Treuhand (Germany) began forming an international accounting federation. Needing an American member, the European firms encouraged the merger of two American firms founded around the turn of the century, Main Lafrentz and Hurdman Cranstoun. Main Hurdman & Cranstoun joined the Europeans to form Klynveld Main Goerdeler (KMG), named after two of the member firms and the chairman of Deutsche Treuhand, Reinhard Goerdeler. Other members were C. Jespersen (Denmark), Thorne Riddel (Canada), Thomson McLintok (UK), and Fides Revision (Switzerland).

Peat Marwick merged with KMG in 1987 to form Klynveld Peat Marwick Goerdeler (KPMG). KPMG lost 10% of its business as competing client companies departed. Professional staff departures followed in 1990 when, as part of a consolidation, the firm trimmed its partnership rolls.

In the 1990s the then-Big Six accounting firms all faced lawsuits arising from an evolving standard holding auditors responsible for the substance, rather than merely the form, of clients' accounts. KPMG was hit by suits stemming from its audits of defunct S&Ls and litigation relating to the bankruptcy of Orange County, California (settled for $75 million in 1998). Nevertheless, KPMG kept growing; it expanded its consulting division with the acquisition of banking consultancy Barefoot, Marrinan & Associates in 1996.

In 1997, after Price Waterhouse and Coopers & Lybrand announced their merger, KPMG and Ernst & Young announced one of their own. But they called it quits the next year, fearing that regulatory approval of the deal would be too onerous.

The creation of PricewaterhouseCoopers (PwC) and increasing competition in the consulting sides of all of the Big Five brought a realignment of loyalties in their national practices. KPMG Consulting's Belgian group moved to PwC and its French group to Computer Sciences Corporation. Andersen nearly wooed away KPMG's Canadian consulting group, but the plan was foiled by the ever-sullen Andersen Consulting group (now Accenture) and by KPMG's promises of more money. Against this background, KPMG sold 20% of its consulting operations to Cisco Systems for $1 billion. In addition to the cash infusion, the deal allowed KPMG to provide installation and system management to Cisco's customers.

Even while KPMG worked on the IPO of its consulting group (which took place in 2001), it continued to rail against the SEC as it called for relationships between consulting and auditing organizations to be severed. In 2002 KPMG sold its British and Dutch consultancy units to France's Atos Origin.

In 2003 the SEC charged US member firm KPMG L.L.P. and four partners with fraud in connection with alleged profit inflation at former client Xerox in the late 1990s. (In April 2005 the accounting firm paid almost $22.5 million, including a $10 million civil penalty, to settle the charges.)

KPMG exited various businesses around the globe during fiscal 2004, including full-scope legal services and certain advisory services, to focus on higher-demand services.

EXECUTIVES

Chairman; Chairman, KPMG L.L.P.:
Timothy P. (Tim) Flynn, age 52
Global Vice Chair, Risk and Compliance: Larry Leva
CEO and Global Board Member:
Michael P. (Mike) Wareing
Deputy Chairman: John B. Harrison, age 53
COO, ASPAC: Graeme Bailey
COO, Americas: Jack T. Taylor, age 57
Global Head, Audit: Henry Keizer, age 53
CEO, EMA: Jean-Paul Thill
Global Head, Insurance: Frank Ellenbuerger
Global Head, Financial Management: Jochen Pampel
Global Head, Tax: Loughlin Hickey
Global Head, Internal Audit, Risk and Compliance Services: Mike Nolan
Global Head, Advisory: Alan Buckle
Global Head, International Corporate Tax:
Wilbert Kannekens
Global Head, Citizenship and Diversity:
Lord Michael Hastings
Chairman, Americas Region; Deputy Chairman and CEO, KPMG L.L.P., and Global Board Member:
John B. Veihmeyer, age 53

LOCATIONS

HQ: KPMG International
Burgemeester Rijnderslaan 10
1185 MC Amstelveen, The Netherlands
Phone: 31-20-656-7890 **Fax:** 31-20-656-7700
US HQ: 3 Chestnut Ridge Road, Montvale, NJ 07645
US Phone: 201-307-7000 **US Fax:** 201-830-8617
Web: www.kpmg.com

2008 Sales

	% of total
Europe, Middle East & Africa	54
Americas	32
Asia/Pacific	14
Total	**100**

PRODUCTS/OPERATIONS

2008 Sales by Function

	$ mil.	% of total
Audit	10,690	47
Advisory	7,270	32
Tax	4,730	21
Total	**22,690**	**100**

2008 Sales by Industry Group

	$ mil.	% of total
Financial Services	5,680	25
Industrial Markets	5,550	25
Information, Communication & Entertainment	4,250	19
Infrastructure, Government & Healthcare	4,580	20
Consumer Markets	2,630	11
Total	**22,690**	**100**

Selected Services

Audit services
  Financial statement audit
  Internal audit services
Tax services
  Corporate and business tax
  Global tax
  Indirect tax
  Personal tax
Advisory services
  Audit support services
  Financial risk management
  Information risk management
  Process improvement
  Regulatory and compliance

Selected Industry Specializations

Consumer and industrial markets
  Consumer markets
    Consumer products
    Food and beverage
    Retail
  Industrial markets
    Chemicals and pharmaceuticals
    Energy and natural resources
    Industrial and automotive products
Financial services
  Banking
  Insurance
Infrastructure, government, and health care
  Building, construction, and real estate
  Funding agencies
  Government
  Health care
  Transportation
Information, communications, and entertainment
  Business services
  Communications
  Electronics
  Media
  Software

COMPETITORS

Aon	H&R Block
Bain & Company	Hewitt Associates
Baker Tilly	Marsh & McLennan
BDO International	McKinsey & Company
Booz Allen	PricewaterhouseCoopers
Deloitte	Towers Perrin
Ernst & Young	Watson Wyatt
Grant Thornton	

HISTORICAL FINANCIALS

Company Type: Partnership

Income Statement

FYE: September 30

	REVENUE ($ mil.)	NET INCOME ($ mil.)	NET PROFIT MARGIN	EMPLOYEES
9/08	22,690	—	—	136,896
9/07	19,810	—	—	123,322
9/06	16,880	—	—	112,795
9/05	15,690	—	—	103,621
9/04	13,440	—	—	93,983
Annual Growth	**14.0%**	**—**	**—**	**9.9%**

Revenue History

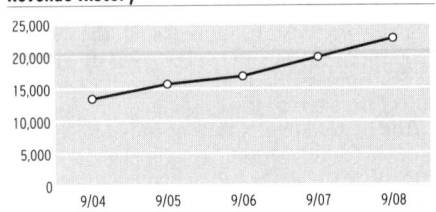

The Kraft Group

There's nothing cheesy about the diverse holdings of The Kraft Group. The family-owned firm (no relation to Kraft Foods) operates in four different industries. It owns paper and wood trader International Forest Products, along with several paper and packaging companies under the Rand-Whitney banner. Its sports holdings include the NFL's New England Patriots, the New England Revolution pro soccer team, and Gillette Stadium. The stadium-adjacent Patriot Place shopping center and private equity investment round out the company's activities. Founder, chairman, and CEO Robert Kraft and his family own the firm.

The $350 million Patriot Place opened in 2007 with a Bass Pro Shop, but quickly grew to a 1.3-million-sq.-ft. development with other retail and restaurants, as well as a museum dedicated to the Patriots, a movie theater, an outpatient health care center of Brigham and Women's Hospital, and a Renaissance Hotel by Marriott (scheduled to open in mid-2009).

In 2008 The Kraft Group sold its majority stake in Carmel Container Systems, Israel's largest packaging company, to Hadera Paper for $21 million. The group still has operations in more than 80 countries, with manufacturing and distribution facilities worldwide.

In 2006 the investment arm of The Kraft Group ventured into media holdings and put up a portion of the $20 million in funding for Plum TV, a network of cable TV stations aimed at high-net-worth individuals in eight cities, including Aspen, Colorado, and Martha's Vineyard, Massachusetts.

The Kraft Group began with the founding of International Forest Products in 1972. The company bought the Patriots for $172 million in 1994, and the New England Revolution was established a year later. Gillette Stadium, home to both teams, was finished in 2002 for $325 million.

EXECUTIVES

Chairman and CEO: Robert K. Kraft
President and COO: Jonathan A. Kraft
CFO: Michael Quattromani
CIO: Patricia Curley
EVP: Daniel A. Kraft
VP Business Development and External Affairs:
 Daniel Murphy

LOCATIONS

HQ: The Kraft Group
 1 Patriot Place, Foxborough, MA 02035
Phone: 508-698-4600   **Fax:** 508-698-1500
Web: www.thekraftgroup.com

COMPETITORS

Cascades Inc.
DeBartolo
Georgia-Pacific
Longview Fibre
Pactiv
Simon Property Group
Smurfit-Stone Container
Tegrant
Temple-Inland
Trammell Crow Company
Weyerhaeuser

HISTORICAL FINANCIALS

Company Type: Private

Income Statement

FYE: December 31

	REVENUE ($ mil.)	NET INCOME ($ mil.)	NET PROFIT MARGIN	EMPLOYEES
12/07	1,500	—	—	5,000
12/06	1,400	—	—	5,000
12/05	1,000	—	—	5,000
Annual Growth	22.5%	—	—	0.0%

Revenue History

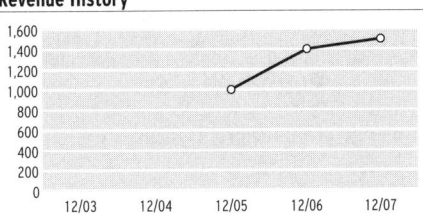

Kronos Incorporated

You won't ever catch Kronos taking a nap in the company supply closet. The company's Workforce Central systems collect attendance data and automatically post it to payroll. Kronos data collection systems keep track of factory production and labor hours. It also makes labor management analysis software and payroll processing applications. Kronos sells its products through its own salesforce and through an alliance with payroll service company ADP. The company focuses on the health care, manufacturing, government, retail, and hospitality markets. Kronos was acquired by an investment group led by private equity firm Hellman & Friedman in 2007.

In addition to Hellman & Friedman, technology investment specialist JMI Equity helped funded the transaction, which was valued at approximately $1.8 billion.

Kronos serves clients in more than 60 countries; customers have included Banner Health, the city of Orlando, Georgia-Pacific, IKEA, and Quantas Airways.

The company's acquisition strategy has included purchasing independent resellers and distributors of its products (which helps to quickly grow Kronos' customer base and boost its overall sales) and buying other software companies with applications that expand Kronos' product line. Purchases have included TimeWorks, Compu-Cash Systems, ClarityMatters, Unicru, SmartTime Software, and Deploy Solutions. Its most recent purchase was the 2009 acquisition of the Stromberg unit of Paychex.

Kronos has also broadened its service offerings and developed Web-based versions of its software, responding to the general trend in the software market of companies offering clients the choice of both installed and hosted versions of their software products.

Kronos has looked to international markets for growth in recent years, expanding its presence in the Asia/Pacific, the Middle East, Canada, Europe, and Latin America. Its European expansion has been fueled by the 2007 acquisition of

Captor, which provided workforce management software to Western European clients.

The company also works with partners, such as ADP, which offer Kronos products under their own branding.

EXECUTIVES

Chairman: Mark S. Ain, age 66
CEO and Director: Aron J. Ain, age 51
CFO: Mark V. Julien
Chief Administrative Officer:
 Charles T. (Charlie) Dickson, age 52
SVP Corporate Strategy and Chief Marketing Officer:
 James (Jim) Kizielewicz, age 46
SVP Products and Technology: Peter C. George, age 47
VP and General Counsel: Alyce Moore
VP Human Resources: Patrick J. (Pat) Moquin
VP Professional Services: Christopher R. Todd, age 39
VP Client Support Services: Michael Biery
VP Manufacturing: Lloyd B. Bussell, age 59
VP International Operations: Mick Adamson
VP North American Sales: John O'Brien
Senior Director, Corporate Communications:
 Michele Glorie
Auditors: Ernst & Young LLP

LOCATIONS

HQ: Kronos Incorporated
 297 Billerica Rd., Chelmsford, MA 01824
Phone: 978-250-9800   **Fax:** 978-367-5900
Web: www.kronos.com

PRODUCTS/OPERATIONS

Selected Products

Kronos iSeries Central (workforce management for IBM iSeries platform)
Workforce Central (process automation and workforce performance optimization suite)

COMPETITORS

Alphameric	Sage Software
Ceridian	Sandata Technologies
JDA Software	SAP
Lawson Software	Technical Difference
Navtech	Tempco
Northgate	TimeLink
Oracle	Ultimate Software
Replicon	WorkPlace Systems
Sage Group	Workscape

The Krystal Company

The Krystal Company is a fast-food gem of the South. The company's chain of about 400 restaurants in almost a dozen southern states are known for their petite, square hamburgers (what Northerners might call a Slyder). In addition, Krystal's menu features a larger-sized hamburger (B.A. Burger), chicken sandwiches (Krystal Chik), chili dogs (Chili Pup), and breakfast items. The company also sells its frozen burgers through grocery stores. More than 230 Krystal locations are company owned, while the rest are franchised. The chain got its start in 1932 when R.B. Davenport Jr. and J. Glenn Sherrill opened up shop in Chattanooga, Tennessee. It is controlled today by former CEO Philip Sanford.

Krystal's long history and strong association with the Southeast has made it a regional favorite. The company has relied strongly on that brand loyalty to help it compete with national chains such as McDonald's and Burger King. Taking a page from its Northern doppelgänger White Castle, Krystal has been focused on using social media sites such as Facebook and Twitter to maintain customer loyalty.

While it has yet to make significant investment in expansion outside the Southeast, the company has been slowly adding corporate-run locations to its chain. Krystal has also added some new menu items to boost business, including an energy drink called Krystal Blitz.

Krystal was a family-owned business until it went public in 1992. Sanford, a former Coca-Cola executive, led a buyout of the company five years later. He retired as CEO in 2003 and was replaced by former Wendy's franchise operator Fred Exum.

EXECUTIVES

Chairman: Andrew G. Cope, age 67
President and CEO: James F. (Fred) Exum Jr., age 52
EVP and CFO: James W. (Jim) Bear, age 64
SVP Administration: Michael C. Bass, age 62
VP Development: Bob Marshall
VP Franchise Division: Alan R. Wright
VP and CIO: David R. Reid
VP Real Estate: Dennis B. Bookwalter
VP Purchasing and Quality Assurance: Gloria Daniels
Director Advertising: Howard Curtis
Director Marketing: John Wolf
Director Company Operations: Howard A. Nelson
Director Research and Development: Becky Conner
Auditors: Ernst & Young LLP

LOCATIONS

HQ: The Krystal Company
1 Union Sq., Chattanooga, TN 37402
Phone: 423-757-1550   **Fax:** 423-757-5610
Web: www.krystal.com

COMPETITORS

American Dairy Queen	Hardee's
Back Yard Burgers	Jack in the Box
Bojangles'	McDonald's
Burger King	Sonic Corp.
Captain D's	Wendy's/Arby's Group
Checkers Drive-In	White Castle
Church's Chicken	YUM!

HISTORICAL FINANCIALS

Company Type: Private

Income Statement				FYE: Sunday nearest December 31
	REVENUE ($ mil.)	NET INCOME ($ mil.)	NET PROFIT MARGIN	EMPLOYEES
12/07	441	—	—	—
12/06	446	—	—	—
12/05	423	—	—	—
12/04	415	—	—	—
12/03	247	—	—	7,056
Annual Growth	15.6%			

Revenue History

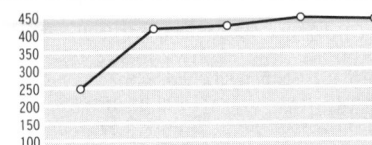

Kum & Go

Kum & Go brings convenience to America's heartland. The company's 430-plus stores in a dozen states throughout the Midwest offer beer, cigarettes, fountain drinks, coffee, snacks, and other items craved by late night shoppers and daytime commuters alike. The company also sells gasoline at most stores and even offers an ethanol blend (85% ethanol, 15% gasoline) at nine of its locations in Iowa, Minnesota, Missouri, and South Dakota. Corporate customers can take advantage of Kum & Go's fleet fueling service. In early 2009 the firm acquired the 37-store Cody's chain in southwest Missouri. Kum & Go, which was founded in 1959 by W.A. Krause & TS Gentle, gives 10% of annual profits to charity.

EXECUTIVES

CEO: Kyle Krause
CFO: Craig Bergstrom

LOCATIONS

HQ: Kum & Go, L.C.
6400 Westown Pkwy., West Des Moines, IA 50266
Phone: 515-226-0128
Web: www.kumandgo.com

COMPETITORS

7-Eleven
Allsup's
Chevron
Couche-Tard
Exxon Mobil
Kroger
Pilot Corporation
Racetrac Petroleum
Royal Dutch Shell
Walgreen

HISTORICAL FINANCIALS

Company Type: Private

Income Statement				FYE: December 31
	REVENUE ($ mil.)	NET INCOME ($ mil.)	NET PROFIT MARGIN	EMPLOYEES
12/08	2,030	—	—	3,895
12/07	1,720	—	—	3,672
12/06	1,450	—	—	3,805
12/05	1,430	—	—	3,660
Annual Growth	12.4%	—	—	2.1%

Revenue History

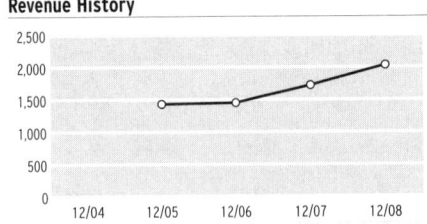

K-VA-T Food Stores

What do you call a chain of supermarkets in Kentucky, Virginia, and Tennessee? How about K-VA-T Food Stores? K-VA-T is one of the largest grocery chains in the region, with about 95 supermarkets under the Food City banner and another 10 Super Discount Foods locations. Originally a Piggly Wiggly franchise with three stores, K-VA-T was founded in 1955. It has expanded by acquiring stores from other regional food retailers, opening new stores, and adding services such as about 75 pharmacies, 55 Gas'N Go gasoline outlets, and banking. Its Food City Distribution Center provides warehousing and distribution services. The founding Smith family owns a majority of K-VA-T; employees own the rest of the company.

The company purchased eight BI-LO supermarkets in Tennessee in March 2006. The locations, acquired from C&S Wholesale, were quickly converted to the Food City label.

Food City is unique in its partnerships with local food product producers. In 2008 the company added products from regional Tennessee favorite Lay's Meats, following similar deals with a local bread company and ice cream company.

Jack C. Smith, founder and former chairman of K-VA-T, died in March 2007. His son Steven Smith is CEO of the company.

EXECUTIVES

President and CEO: Steven C. (Steve) Smith, age 51
EVP Operations: Jody Helms
EVP Merchandising and Marketing: Richard Gunn
EVP, Knoxville Division: John Jones
EVP, Tri-Cities Division: Johnny Cecil
SVP Finance and Administration, CFO, Secretary, and Treasurer: Robert L. Neeley
SVP and COO: Jesse A. Lewis
SVP Marketing: Thomas R. (Tom) Hembree
VP Pharmacy Operations: Don Clark
VP Information Systems: Paul Widener
VP and General Counsel: Charlie Fugate
VP In-Store Services: Don Mascola
VP Research and Real Estate: Lou Scudere
VP Human Resources: Donnie Meadows
VP Store Planning and Development: Don Smith

LOCATIONS

HQ: K-VA-T Food Stores, Inc.
201 Trigg St., Abingdon, VA 24210
Phone: 276-628-5503   **Fax:** 276-623-5440
Web: www.foodcity.com

2008 Stores

	No.
Tennessee	63
Virginia	27
Kentucky	13
Total	**103**

PRODUCTS/OPERATIONS

2008 Stores

	No.
Food City	94
Super Dollar Discount Foods	9
Total	**103**

Selected Departments

Bakery/Deli
Café
Dairy
Dry goods
Floral
Frozen foods

Gasoline
Meat
Pharmacy
Produce
Seafood
Video

Selected Services

Banking
Money orders
Party planning
Photo processing
Postage stamps

COMPETITORS

A&P
Alex Lee
Associated Wholesale
 Grocers
BI-LO
Costco Wholesale
Earth Fare
Food Lion
Harris Teeter

Houchens
Ingles Markets
Kroger
The Pantry
SUPERVALU
Target
Ukrop's Super Markets
Wal-Mart

HISTORICAL FINANCIALS

Company Type: Private

Income Statement

FYE: December 31

	REVENUE ($ mil.)	NET INCOME ($ mil.)	NET PROFIT MARGIN	EMPLOYEES
12/08	1,800	—	—	12,000
12/07	1,650	—	—	12,000
12/06	1,570	—	—	11,500
12/05	1,400	—	—	11,000
12/04	1,310	—	—	10,400
Annual Growth	8.3%	—	—	3.6%

Revenue History

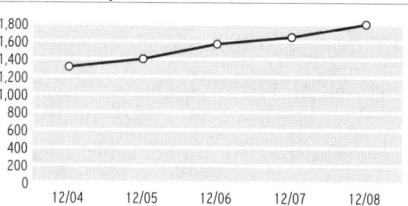

Lake Area Corn Processors

Lake Area Corn Processors produces ethanol and its byproduct, distillers grains, which are used in livestock feed. Through its Dakota Ethanol unit, the company produces about 50 million gallons of ethanol per year. Dakota Ethanol had worked in tandem with Broin Companies, a manufacturer of ethanol processing plants, until Lake Area Corn Processors bought out Broin's minority stake in Dakota Ethanol in 2006. The following year, the company acquired a stake in its ethanol distributor, Renewable Products Marketing Group. Lake Area Corn Processors is owned by its 1,000 members.

EXECUTIVES

Chairman: Ronald C. Alverson, age 57
Vice Chairman: Dale L. Thompson, age 61
CEO; General Manager, Dakota Ethanol: Scott Mundt, age 47, $168,214 total compensation
CFO: Robbi Buchholtz, age 38, $87,754 total compensation
Membership Coordinator, Dakota Ethanol: Alan May, age 52
Auditors: McGladrey & Pullen, LLP

LOCATIONS

HQ: Lake Area Corn Processors, LLC
 46269 S. Dakota Hwy. 34, Wentworth, SD 57075
Phone: 605-483-2676   **Fax:** 605-483-2681
Web: www.dakotaethanol.com

PRODUCTS/OPERATIONS

2008 Sales

	% of total
Ethanol	86
Distillers grains	14
Total	**100**

COMPETITORS

Abengoa Bioenergy
ADM
Badger State Ethanol
Cargill
Golden Grain
Little Sioux Corn Processors
Williams Companies

HISTORICAL FINANCIALS

Company Type: Private

Income Statement

FYE: December 31

	REVENUE ($ mil.)	NET INCOME ($ mil.)	NET PROFIT MARGIN	EMPLOYEES
12/08	112	(17)	—	38
12/07	104	18	17.4%	39
12/06	104	46	44.3%	39
12/05	80	11	13.6%	38
12/04	84	8	8.9%	38
Annual Growth	7.3%	—	—	0.0%

2008 Year-End Financials

Debt ratio: 13.9%
Return on equity: —
Cash ($ mil.): —

Current ratio: —
Long-term debt ($ mil.): 5

Net Income History

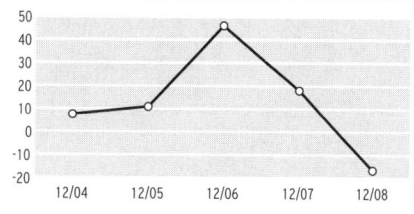

Land O'Lakes

Land O'Lakes butters up its customers, and shows you what life is like if everyone cooperates. Owned by and serving more than 7,000 dairy farmer members and 1,300 community cooperatives, Land O'Lakes is one of the largest dairy co-ops in the US (along with Dairy Farmers of America and California Dairies). It provides its members with wholesale fertilizer and crop protection products, seed, and animal feed. Its oldest and best known product, LAND O' LAKES butter, is the top butter brand in the US. Land O'Lakes also produces packaged milk, margarine, sour cream, and cheese. The co-op's animal-feed division, Land O'Lakes Purina Feed, is a leading animal and pet food maker.

In line with its strategy to concentrate on its crop protection products, in 2009 the company sold nine Agriliance retail stores to Agri-AFC and 11 more to the Tennessee Farmers Cooperative.

In 2007 the company sold its international cheese and protein operations (known as CPI) to Saputo Cheese USA for about $216 million. The sale included the Golden Valley Dairy Products cheese manufacturing and cut-and-wrap operations. The deal also included a long-term milks agreement, such that Land O'Lakes is the sole milk supplier for CPI.

Also in 2007 Land O'Lakes and CHS realigned the businesses of their 50-50 joint venture Agriliance in 2007, with CHS acquiring its crop-nutrients wholesale-products business and Land O'Lakes acquiring the crop-protection products business. The following year, Canadian ag cooperative La Coop fédérée purchased Agriliance's remaining retail agronomy operation.

Land O'Lakes also owns egg producer MoArk. (MoArk sold its liquid egg products operations to Golden Oval Eggs in 2006.) In addition, the company's subsidiary, Land O'Lakes Finance, provides financing services for beef, dairy, pork, and poultry producers.

Outside of the US, Land O'Lakes has taken aim at the largest emerging market, China, where the company is working to establish the Land O'Lakes brand of cheese and cultured dairy products in supermarkets.

The company operates 10 dairy-product manufacturing facilities throughout the US.

HISTORY

In the old days, grocers sold butter from communal tubs, and it often went bad. Widespread distribution of dairy products had to await the invention of fast, reliable transportation. By 1921 the necessary transportation was available. That year about 320 dairy farmers in Minnesota formed the Minnesota Cooperative Creameries Association and launched a membership drive with $1,375, mostly borrowed from the US Farm Bureau.

The co-op arranged joint shipments for members, imposed strict hygiene and quality standards, and aggressively marketed its sweet cream butter nationwide, packaged for the first time in the familiar box of four quarter-pound sticks. A month after the co-op's New York sales office opened, it was ordering 80 shipments a week.

Minnesota Cooperative Creameries, as part of its promotional campaigns, ran a contest in 1924 to name that butter. Two contestants offered the winning name — Land O'Lakes. The distinctive Indian Maiden logo first appeared about the same time, and in 1926 the co-op changed its name to Land O'Lakes Creameries. By 1929, when it began supplying feed, its market share approached 50%.

During WWII civilian consumption dropped, but the co-op increased production of dried milk to provide food for soldiers and newly liberated concentration camp victims.

In the 1950s and 1960s Land O'Lakes added ice cream and yogurt producers to its membership and fought margarine makers, yet butter's market share continued to melt. The co-op diversified in 1970 through acquisitions, adding feeds and agricultural chemicals. Two years later Land O'Lakes threw in the towel and came out with its own margarine. Despite the decreasing use of butter nationally, the co-op's market share grew.

Land O'Lakes formed a marketing joint venture, Cenex/Land O'Lakes Agronomy, with fellow co-op Cenex in 1987. As health consciousness bloomed in the 1980s, Land O'Lakes launched reduced-fat dairy products. It also purchased a California cheese plant, doubling its capacity. Land O'Lakes began ramping up its international projects at the same time: It built a feed mill in Taiwan, introduced feed products in Mexico, and established feed and cheese operations in Poland.

In 1997 the co-op bought low-fat cheese maker Alpine Lace Brands. Land O'Lakes took on the eastern US when it merged with the 3,600-member Atlantic Dairy Cooperative (1997), and it bulked up on the West Coast when California-based Dairyman's Cooperative Creamery Association joined its fold (1998).

During 2000 the co-op sold five plants to Dean Foods with an agreement to continue supplying the plants with raw milk. Also in 2000 Land O'Lakes combined its feed business with those of Farmland Industries to create Land O'Lakes Farmland Feed, LLC, with a 69% ownership. That same year, Land O'Lakes and CHS joined their agronomy operations to create a 50-50 joint venture, Agriliance LLC.

In late 2001 the company spent $359 million to acquire Purina Mills (pet and livestock feeds). Purina Mills was folded into Land O'Lakes Farmland Feed and, as part of the purchase, Land O'Lakes increased its ownership of the feed business to 92%. In 2004 it purchased the remaining 8%.

To take advantage of its nationally recognized brand, Land O'Lakes formed an alliance with Dean Foods in 2002 to develop and market value-added dairy products.

Exiting the meat business, Land O'Lakes sold its swine operations in 2005 to private pork producer Maschhoff West LLC for an undisclosed sum. That same year, it sold its interest in fertilizer manufacturer CF Industries. Long-time president and CEO Jack Gherty retired that year; he was replaced by Chris Policinski. In 2006 the company acquired 100% ownership of MoArk.

EXECUTIVES

Chairman: Peter (Pete) Kappelman, age 46
First Vice Chairman: Ronnie Mohr, age 60
President and CEO: Chris Policinski, age 50, $6,737,200 total compensation
EVP; COO, Seed Division: Mike Vande Logt, age 54
EVP; COO, Feed: Fernando J. Palacios, age 49, $2,226,173 total compensation
EVP; COO, Dairy Foods Value-Added: Steve Dunphy, age 51
EVP; COO, Crop Protection Products: Rodney (Rod) Schroeder, age 53
EVP; COO, Dairy Foods Industrial: Alan Pierson, age 58

EVP Ag Business Development and Member Services: David L. (Dave) Seehusen, age 62
SVP Corporate Marketing Strategy: Barry C. Wolfish, age 52, $1,809,881 total compensation
SVP and General Counsel: Peter S. Janzen, age 49, $1,837,233 total compensation
SVP Human Resources: Karen Grabow, age 59
SVP and CFO: Daniel E. (Dan) Knutson, age 52, $3,576,245 total compensation
SVP Corporate Strategy and Business Development: Jean-Paul (JP) Ruiz-Funes, age 51
SVP Public Affairs and Business Development: James D. (Jim) Fife, age 59
Secretary and Director: Douglas (Doug) Reimer, age 58
Director Corporate Communications: Lydia Botham
Auditors: KPMG LLP

LOCATIONS

HQ: Land O'Lakes, Inc.
4001 Lexington Ave., North, Arden Hills, MN 55112
Phone: 651-481-2222   **Fax:** 651-481-2000
Web: www.landolakesinc.com

PRODUCTS/OPERATIONS

2008 Sales

	$ mil.	% of total
Dairy foods	4,136.4	34
Feed	3,857.4	32
Agronomy	2,335.3	19
Seed	1,185.0	10
Layers	606.2	5
Eliminations	(81.0)	—
Total	**12,039.3**	**100**

Selected Brands and Products

Agronomy
  Winfield Solutions (wholesale crop protection products — adjuvants, fungicides, herbicides, insecticides, and seed treatments)
  Origin (micronutrients)
Animal feed
  Land O'Lakes Purina Feed
Bulk ingredients for manufacturers
  Non-fat dry milk powder
  Cheese
  Whey
Cheese
  Alpine Lace
  LAND O'LAKES
    New Yorker
Eggs
  Eggland's Best
  LAND O'LAKES All-Natural Farm Fresh Eggs
Other consumer dairy foods
  LAND O'LAKES
Seed
  CROPLAN GENETICS (alfalfa, corn, and soybean seed)
  FORAGE FIRST SEED (brassica, forage sorghum, grasses, herb, legume, and pasture mix seeds)
  Land O'Lakes Seed (alfalfa, canola, corn, grain sorghum, soybean, sugar beet, turf grass, and wheat seed)
  HYTEST SEED (alfalfa and corn seed)

Selected Dairy Foods

Butter
  Blends
  Flavored
  Light
  Salted
  Spreadable
  Whipped
  With Canola Oil
  Unsalted
Canola oil

Cheese
  American
  Cheddar
  Monterey Jack
  Mozzarella
  Parmesan
  Provolone
  Romano
Eggs
  All-natural
  Cage-free
  Nutritionally enhanced
  Organic
  Regular
Margarine

Selected Joint Ventures

Advanced Food Products (35%, with Bongrain, S.A.)
Agriliance LLC (50%, with CHS, Inc.)
Agronomy Company of Canada Ltd. (50%, with CHS, Inc.)

COMPETITORS

ADM	Kraft Foods
Agrium	Latham Seed Company
Associated Milk Producers	Mars Petcare
Barkley Seed	Michael Foods, Inc.
Blue Seal Feeds	Milk Specialties Company
Breeder's Choice	Monsanto Company
California Dairies Inc.	National Dairy Holdings
Cal-Maine Foods	NC Hybrids
Cargill	Nestlé Purina PetCare
ConAgra	Nestlé USA
Dairy Farmers of America	Northwest Dairy
Darigold, Inc.	Pfister Hybrid Corn
Dean Foods	Pioneer Hi-Bred
Fonterra	Prairie Farms Dairy
Foremost Farms	Rose Acre Farms
Frontier Agriculture	Royal Canin
Harris Moran	Sakata Seed
Hartz Mountain	Saputo
Hill's Pet Nutrition	Sargento
HP Hood	Schreiber Foods
Iams	Syngenta Seeds
Keller's Creamery	Unilever
Kent Feeds	Wilbur-Ellis

HISTORICAL FINANCIALS

Company Type: Cooperative

Income Statement

FYE: December 31

	REVENUE ($ mil.)	NET INCOME ($ mil.)	NET PROFIT MARGIN	EMPLOYEES
12/08	12,039	160	1.3%	9,100
12/07	8,925	164	1.8%	8,700
12/06	7,275	89	1.2%	8,500
12/05	7,557	129	1.7%	7,500
12/04	7,677	21	0.3%	8,000
Annual Growth	11.9%	65.3%	—	3.3%

Net Income History

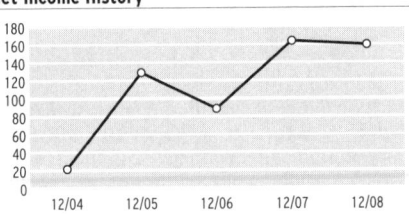

Latham & Watkins

Latham & Watkins' founders Dana Latham and Paul Watkins flipped a coin in 1934 to determine which of their names would go first on the law firm's shingle. From that coin toss, the firm has grown into one of the largest in the US and boasts more than 2,100 lawyers in almost 30 offices around the world, from Europe to Asia. Latham & Watkins organizes its practices into five main areas: corporate; environment, land, and resources; finance; litigation; and tax. The firm has counted companies such as Amgen, Time Warner Inc., and Morgan Stanley among its clients.

In an effort to expand globally in both leading and emerging financial, commercial, and regulatory capitals, Latham & Watkins is relocating some of its US and UK partners to the Middle East. By 2009 the law firm had already established a solid presence in three offices in the Gulf region — Abu Dhabi, Dubai, and Doha (capital city of Qatar) — to support cross-border mergers and acquisitions and other corporate finance deals, particularly between London and the Middle East.

EXECUTIVES

Chairman and Managing Partner: Robert M. (Bob) Dell
Vice Chairman and Chief Operating Partner: Mark E. Newell
Vice Chair, Tax and Benefits, Europe: Daniel Friel
COO: LeeAnn Black
CFO: Grant Johnson
CIO: Kenneth L. Heaps
Chief Real Estate and Facilities Officer: James E. Dow
Chief Administrative Officer: Wendy E. Ward
Chief Marketing Officer: Despina Kartson
Chief Human Resources Officer: Mimi A. Krumholz
Global Chair, Finance Department: David S. Heller
Global Recruiting Manager: Skip Horne
Director Global Public Relations and Communications: Geoff Burt

LOCATIONS

HQ: Latham & Watkins LLP
  885 3rd Ave., New York, NY 10022
Phone: 212-906-1200   **Fax:** 212-751-4864
Web: www.lw.com

PRODUCTS/OPERATIONS

Selected Practice Areas

Antitrust and competition
Appellate
Banking
Benefits and compensation
Communications
Company representation
Corporate finance
Employment law
Energy and natural resources
Entertainment, sports, and media
Environmental litigation
Environmental regulatory
Environmental transactional support
French practice
Gaming, hotels, and hospitality
German practice
Government contracts
Government relations
Greater China practice
Health care and life sciences

Insolvency
Insurance coverage litigation
Intellectual property, media, and technology
International dispute resolution
International tax
Investment and strategic ventures
Israeli practice
Italian practice
Land use
Latin American practice
Life sciences
Mergers and acquisitions
Outsourcing
Private equity
Private equity finance
Pro bono
Product liability and mass torts
Project finance
Public and tax-exempt finance
Public international law
Real estate
REITs
Scandinavian practice
Securities litigation and professional liability
Spanish practice
Stock options timing
Structured finance and securitization
Tax controversy
Tax-exempt organizations
Technology transactions
Transactional tax
Venture and technology
White collar and government investigations

COMPETITORS

Baker & McKenzie
Clifford Chance
Davis Polk
Dewey & LeBoeuf
Gibson, Dunn & Crutcher
Holland & Knight
Kirkland & Ellis
O'Melveny & Myers
Paul, Hastings
Ropes & Gray
Simpson Thacher
Skadden, Arps
Sullivan & Cromwell
Weil, Gotshal & Manges

HISTORICAL FINANCIALS

Company Type: Partnership

Income Statement

	REVENUE ($ mil.)	NET INCOME ($ mil.)	NET PROFIT MARGIN	EMPLOYEES
12/08	1,923	—	—	—
12/07	2,005	—	—	—
12/06	1,624	—	—	4,500
12/05	1,413	—	—	4,234
Annual Growth	10.8%	—	—	6.3%

FYE: December 31

Revenue History

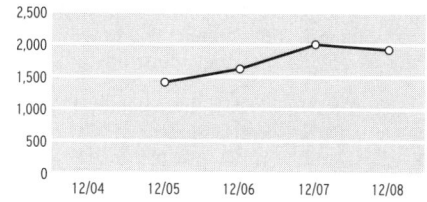

Laureate Education

If higher education is a matter of degrees, Laureate must be hot. The company provides full-time and working-adult career education through online and campus-based programs in 20 countries in Asia, the Americas, and Europe. Laureate's educational institutions offer more than 130 bachelor's, master's, and doctoral degree programs and specializations to a combined enrollment of more than 500,000. Students can earn degrees in areas such as business, hospitality management, law, engineering, and medicine. Laureate's Canter unit provides professional development and training for teachers. An investment group headed by chairman and CEO Douglas Becker owns the company.

Strong profits have allowed the company to aggressively expand its operations and build its collection of private universities around the world. In 2006 Laureate bought out Chilean partner Indeco (and its Ecuadorean subsidiary), and the following year it acquired Mexico's Universidad Valle del Bravo, adding five campuses and some 4,500 students. In early 2008 it took a 76% stake in German college BiTS and also bought INTI College in Malaysia.

The company also has expanded in Mexico and Latin America with the acquisition of Costa Rica-based universities Universidad Latina de Costa Rica and Universidad Americana and Mexican private university Universidad Tecnologica de Mexico (UNITEC). In 2008 the company expanded its stake in the Brazilian university Anhembi-Morumbi and plans to buy Faculdade Boa Viagem. The acquisitions are in line with Laureate's goal of having 100,000 college students in Brazil over the next few years.

Management took the company private in a leveraged buyout in 2007. According to its chairman, the move allowed it to expand in China, South Korea, and India.

EXECUTIVES

Chairman and CEO: Douglas L. (Doug) Becker, age 43
President and COO: Neal S. Cohen, age 49
EVP Corporate Operations: Daniel M. Nickel
EVP and CFO: Eilif Serck-Hanssen
SVP and Chief Accounting Officer: Amit Rai
SVP Education and Academic Quality and University Network Programs and Partnerships: Joseph D. Duffey
SVP and General Counsel: Robert W. (Bob) Zentz
VP Medicine and Health Sciences: Francisco Gutierrez
President, Latin America Operations: William C. (Bill) Dennis Jr.
President and CEO, Laureate Higher Education Group: Paula R. Singer
Media Relations: Debra B. Epstein
Auditors: Ernst & Young LLP

LOCATIONS

HQ: Laureate Education, Inc.
  650 S. Exeter St., Baltimore, MD 21202
Phone: 410-843-6100
Web: www.laureate-inc.com

PRODUCTS/OPERATIONS

Selected Operations

Online
Canter
National Technological University (NTU)
Walden University
Campus-based
Asia/Australia
Australian International Hotel School
Blue Mountains Hotel School
Les Roches Jin Jiang International Hotel
Management School
INTI Education Group
Sichuan Tianyi University
Xi'an Jiaotong-Liverpool University
Central America
Universidad Americana
Universidad de Desarrollo Profesional
Universidad del Valle de México
Universidad Interamericana de Costa Rica
Universidad Interamericana de Panama
Universidad Latina de Costa Rica
Universidad Latinoamericana de Ciencia y
Tecnología (ULACIT)
Universidad Technlogica de Mexico (UNITEC)
Europe
Business and Information Technology School (BiTS)
Centro Superior de Edificacion
Cyprus College
Ècole Centrale D'Electonique
Ècole Supérieure du Commerce Extérieur
European University Cyprus
Glion Institute of Higher Education
Institut Francais de Gestion (IFG)
Institute for Executive Development
Les Roches Hotel Management School
Les Roches Marbella
Universidad Europea de Madrid
South America
Business School Sao Paulo
Centro Universitario Do Norte
CIBERTEC
Escola Superior de Adminstracao Dereito e
Economia
Escuela Moderna de Musica (EMM)
Faculdad dos Guararapes
Instituto Tecnologico del Norte
Universidad Anhembi Morumbi
Universidad Andres Bello
Universidad de las Americas
Universidad Nacional Andrés Bello
Universidad Peruana de Ciencias Aplicadas
Universidad Potiguar
Universidad Privada del Norte (UPN)
United States
Kendall College
NewSchool of Architecture and Design (NSAD)

COMPETITORS

Apollo Group
Berlitz
Corinthian Colleges
DeVry
ITT Educational
PLATO Learning
Strayer Education

HISTORICAL FINANCIALS

Company Type: Private

Income Statement			FYE: December 31
	ESTIMATED REVENUE ($ mil.)	NET INCOME ($ mil.)	NET PROFIT MARGIN	EMPLOYEES
12/07	1,420	—	—	28,500

Lefrak Organization

Once a strictly New York City enterprise, the Lefrak Organization has branched out across the Hudson and around the world. The real estate development company is one of the US's largest private landlords, managing more than 200 apartment buildings (affordable and upscale) in New York, New Jersey, and more recently Los Angeles. The company also owns millions of square feet of commercial space, with new developments in London. Lefrak's office and retail holdings include its flagship office tower at 40 West 57th Street in midtown Manhattan, home to such tenants as Highbridge Capital Management, Nautica, and Wells Fargo. Still family-owned and run, Lefrak was founded in 1901.

The Lefrak Organization has developed property in New Jersey since 1995, focusing solely on the $10 billion mixed-use Newport in Jersey City. The 600-acre community of apartments, shopping centers, hotels, and office buildings sits on the Hudson River waterfront overlooking Lower Manhattan. It is one of the largest waterfront communities in the US. The company has built office towers on the site, and plans for further developments are under way. When completed, the development will include 9,000 apartment units and 9 million sq. ft. of commercial space.

Although the company has sold some of its older working-class apartment buildings in Queens and Brooklyn, Lefrak reportedly has no plans to sell its flagship residential development, the 5,000-unit LeFrak City in Queens, which has been home to successive waves of ethnic groups and working- and middle-class tenants.

However, the organization is expanding beyond New York in an attempt to diversify geographically, for the first time buying office buildings in Beverly Hills, California, and a development site on Hollywood Boulevard, which it plans to turn into a luxury high-rise apartment complex. In 2008 it continued its West Coast buying spree by acquiring a medical building in Beverly Hills. It also bought a minority stake in London developer Minerva in 2008.

In addition to real estate, The Lefrak Organization has holdings in oil and gas exploration and wind energy generation through its Lefrak Oil and Gas Organization Inc. (LOGO).

HISTORY

Harry LeFrak and his father Aaron came to the US from Palestine (or France — there are many conflicting versions of the LeFrak family history; Aaron's father Maurice is said to have been a developer there in the 1840s) around 1900. They began building tenements in Brooklyn's Williamsburg neighborhood to house the flood of immigrants then pouring into New York City.

In 1901 Harry and Aaron started what is now known as The Lefrak Organization. It diversified into glass, and for some time provided raw material for the workshops of Louis Comfort Tiffany. After WWI the glass factory was sold, and the company expanded into Brooklyn, where it developed housing and commercial space in Bedford-Stuyvesant, among other areas.

Samuel, Harry's son, began working in the business early, assisting tradesmen at building sites. He then attended the University of Maryland, and shunning a future career in dentistry

(family lore claims his left-handedness would have required special tools), returned to the business. Samuel's first project was a 120-unit apartment building in Brooklyn's Midwood — it was 1938, and he was 20 years old and still a university student.

During WWII the firm built camps and housing for the Army. After the war, business took off, as the company began building low-cost housing. Samuel took over the company in 1948. To keep costs down, Samuel bought clay and gypsum quarries, forests, and lumber mills and cement plants, eventually achieving 70% vertical integration of his operations. This included the creation of in-house architectural, engineering, and construction departments that handled all aspects of building the Lefrak empire's properties — from initial designs to general contracting — from the ground up.

The 1950s building boom was in part spurred by new laws in New York authorizing the issue of state bonds for financing low-interest construction loans, which Lefrak used to build more than 2,000 apartments in previously undeveloped coastal sections of Brooklyn. At its peak, Lefrak turned out an apartment every 16 minutes.

In 1960 Lefrak broke ground for LeFrak City, a 5,000-apartment development built on 40 acres in Queens (after four years of negotiations with the trustees of the William Waldorf Astor estate over the sale price — $6 million), which featured air-conditioned units and low rents.

The next decade brought a real estate slump that endangered the organization's next project, Battery Park. Lefrak issued public bonds to save it. Samuel also picked up a few more properties during this period, and he capitalized the "F" in his family name but not the company name. (He later said that he did this to distinguish himself from other Lefraks at his club who had been posted for nonpayment of dues, though a conflicting story states that his mother's French-born physician originally capitalized the "F" on Samuel's birth certificate.)

Samuel's son Richard became president of the company in 1975. Richard oversaw an even bigger project: the 600-acre Newport City development, begun in 1989 with plans for some 10,000 apartments and retail and commercial space.

The company bought 200 oil fields in 1994 to build up its reserves of gas and home-heating oil.

Meanwhile, LeFrak City had "turned," as its original Jewish occupants sought greener fields. As occupancy dropped, the company relaxed its tenant screening, and the development deteriorated (it was subsequently tagged "Crack City"). In the 1990s, however, it began attracting a mix of African, Jewish, and Central Asian immigrants, whose tightly knit communities improved safety and equilibrium.

Construction of the company's Newport project continued throughout the 1990s with construction of office buildings, apartments, and a hotel (completed in 2000) on the site. As a tight Manhattan office market drove up lease prices, Lefrak's new offices across the Hudson attracted companies in the finance and insurance sectors. Lefrak filled about 3 million sq. ft. in its Newport development during 1999 and 2000.

In 2001 the company's Gateway complex in Battery Park City was damaged in the World Trade Center terrorist attack. The tenants threatened a rent strike, prompting Lefrak to lower rents to compensate for the difficulties attributed to living near the site.

Samuel LeFrak died in 2003 at the age of 85.

EXECUTIVES

Chairman, President, and CEO: Richard S. LeFrak, age 63
Managing Director: Harrison LeFrak
Managing Director: James (Jamie) LeFrak
EVP and Chief Investment and Financial Officer: Richard N. Papert
CIO: Robert A. Brennan
SVP Development: Marsilia (Marcy) Boyle
SVP Marketing and Public Relations: Edward Cortese
SVP and General Manager: Charles J. Mehlman
SVP Construction and Engineering: Anthony Scavo
SVP Finance and Accounting: Judy Wortsmann
VP Commercial: Irwin Granville
VP Asset Management: Mitchell Ingerman
Assistant VP Human Resources and Administration: John Farrelly
General Counsel: Arnold S. Lehman
Auditors: Ernst & Young LLP

LOCATIONS

HQ: Lefrak Organization Inc.
40 W. 57th St., New York, NY 10019
Phone: 212-708-6600   **Fax:** 212-708-6641
Web: www.lefrak.com

Selected Properties

Commercial space
  Jersey City, NJ
    Newport development
  New York City (Manhattan)
    40 W. 57th St.
    30 W. 57th St.
    Gateway Plaza at Battery Park City
    James Tower
Residential apartments
  Jersey City, NJ
    Atlantic
    East Hampton
    James Monroe
    Presidential Plaza
    Riverside
    Southampton
    Towers of America
  New York City (Manhattan)
    Gateway Plaza at Battery Park City
  New York City (Queens)
    LeFrak City
Residential co-op properties
  New York City (Brooklyn)
    Bay Ridge
    Bensonhurst
    Flatbush
    Park Slope
    Sheepshead Bay
  New York City (Queens)
    Elmhurst
    Flushing
    Forest Hills
    Key Gardens
    Rego Park
    Woodside
Retail
  Jersey City, NJ
    Newport Centre Mall

PRODUCTS/OPERATIONS

Selected Operations

Energy
  Lefrak Oil & Gas Organization
Entertainment
  Lefrak Entertainment Company
Real estate
  Commercial properties
  Residential apartments
  Residential co-op properties
  Retail properties
Telecommunications
  Newport Telephone Company, Inc.

COMPETITORS

Alexander's
Apartment Investment and Management
Apollo Advisors
AvalonBay
Boston Properties
Centerline Capital Group
Durst Organization
Equity Office Properties
Equity Residential
Forest City Ratner
Grenadier
Helmsley Enterprises
Mack-Cali
Macklowe Properties
Silverstein Properties
SL Green Realty
Tishman
The Trump Organization
Vornado Realty
Witkoff Group

Leprino Foods

Don't try to butter up Leprino Foods — it's into mozzarella with a capital "M." The company is a worldwide leader in mozzarella making. It sells its mozzarella to pizza purveyors large and small, including powerhouses like Domino's, Papa John's, and Pizza Hut, as well as to food manufacturing companies. In addition to mozzarella, the company makes reduced-fat cheddar, reduced-fat Monterey Jack, string, and queso cheeses. Leprino's other products include dairy powders, such as whey protein concentrate and lactose for use in animal feeds, yogurt, baby formula, and baked goods. It is supplied by the nation's large dairy co-ops.

The company has a joint venture located in the UK called Glanbia Cheese with Irish cheese maker Glanbia. The joint venture makes Glanbia a top pizza-cheese maker in Europe. The world's largest food company, Nestlé, is a Leprino customer. It uses the company's products for manufacturing Hot Pockets and Stouffer's microwave pizzas.

Headquartered in Denver, Leprino has 11 cheese making sites in the US, located in California, Colorado, Michigan, Nebraska, New Mexico, and New York. Overseas, it operates two joint-venture plants in the UK.

Italian immigrant Michael Leprino Sr. founded the company in 1950. It is still owned and managed by the Leprino family. Indeed, company chairman, billionaire James Leprino, has been listed in the Forbes *The 400 Richest Americans.*

EXECUTIVES

Chairman: James Leprino, age 71
President: Larry Jensen
SVP Quality Assurance and Research and Development: Richard Barz
SVP People Development: Bradley (Brad) Olsen
SVP Production Operations: Tom Haggerty
SVP Sales and Marketing: Robert D. (Bob) Boynton
SVP Procurement, Logistics, and Business Development: Mike Reidy
SVP Administration and CFO: Ron Klump
VP and Controller: Paul Adams

LOCATIONS

HQ: Leprino Foods Company
1830 W. 38th Ave., Denver, CO 80211
Phone: 303-480-2600   **Fax:** 303-480-2605
Web: www.leprinofoods.com

COMPETITORS

Agri-Mark
Associated Milk Producers
Bel Brands USA
Century Foods
Crystal Farms Refrigerated Distribution Company
Ellsworth Cooperative
F. Cappiello Dairy Products
Foremost Farms
Great Lakes Cheese
Kraft Foods
Main Street Ingredients
Saputo
Sargento
Schreiber Foods
Sorrento Lactalis
Tate & Lyle

Les Schwab Tire Centers

If you need new tires after heeding Greeley's advice, go to Les Schwab Tire Centers. And it doesn't hurt that the owner wrote the bible of tire retailing: *Pride in Performance — Keep It Going.* Les Schwab Tire Centers prides itself on continued customer service. It sells batteries, custom wheels, and tires by name-brand and private-label manufacturers. The company also offers alignment, brake, and shock work at about 420 stores in Alaska, California, Idaho, Montana, Nevada, Oregon, Utah, and Washington. In 1952 late founder Les Schwab bought a tire shop that grew into the chain of Les Schwab Tire Centers. The firm is owned by Schwab's family.

Amid the US recession and slowed consumer spending, Les Schwab Tire Centers said in 2009 that its customers are increasingly opting for more-affordable private-label tires. Although the company carries such major brands as Goodyear and Michelin, it said most of its tire sales come from private-label manufacturers. These low-cost tires are mostly made in China, Mexico, and other international markets.

The company relocated its headquarters to Bend, Oregon, from Prineville, about 30 miles away, in 2008. The move to the larger town is intended to help Les Schwab Tire Centers attract and retain top executives.

CEO Dick Borgman added the role of chairman to his responsibilities when Phil Wick retired at the end of 2008. Wick had served the company for 40 years. Borgman took on the chief executive's position after succeeding founder Les Schwab, who died in 2007 at age 89.

EXECUTIVES

Chairman and CEO: Dick Borgman
CFO: Tom Freedman
VP Advertising and Marketing: Brian Capp
Director Human Resources: Jodie Hueske
Director Development: Dave Husk

LOCATIONS

HQ: Les Schwab Tire Centers
20900 Cooley Rd., Bend, OR 97701
Phone: 541-447-4136
Web: www.lesschwab.com

COMPETITORS

Advance Auto Parts	Goodyear Tire & Rubber
AutoZone	Pep Boys
Bridgestone Americas	Sears
Commercial Tire	TBC
CSK Auto	TCI Tire Centers
Discount Tire	Wal-Mart

HISTORICAL FINANCIALS

Company Type: Private

Income Statement

FYE: December 31

	REVENUE ($ mil.)	NET INCOME ($ mil.)	NET PROFIT MARGIN	EMPLOYEES
12/07	1,480	—	—	7,900
12/06	1,360	—	—	7,700
12/05	1,200	—	—	6,000
12/04	1,150	—	—	5,800
12/03	1,000	—	—	6,000
Annual Growth	10.3%	—	—	7.1%

Revenue History

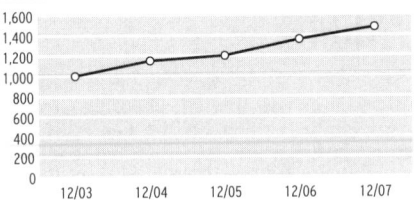

1,600	
1,400	
1,200	
1,000	
800	
600	
400	
200	
0	
	12/03 12/04 12/05 12/06 12/07

Leslie's Poolmart

Leslie's Poolmart is the big fish of pool product retailers. The company sells pool chemicals, cleaning and testing equipment, covers, and recreational items through more than 600 stores in some 35 states, mostly in Arizona, California, Florida, Georgia, and Texas. The company also sells its products through catalogs and its Web site. Leslie's makes chlorine tablets and repackages other chemicals to be sold under the Leslie name, as well. Pool chemicals, major equipment, and parts account for a majority of the company's sales. Founded in 1963, Leslie's is owned and operated by Leonard Green & Partners, which holds a more than 75% stake in the company.

The company concentrates on positioning its stores in an area that has a greater number of swimming pools. Its stores are found in strip malls or in freestanding sites near other retail traffic. The company generally draws its customers from a five-mile trade area.

Its Leslie's-branded products have brought in more sales revenue in recent years. In 2007 the brand generated about 40% of sales. Leslie's products accounted for about 48% of 2008 sales.

Leslie's Poolmart maintains a more than 7.5-million-address mailing list, which includes more than 90% of residential ground pools in the US.

EXECUTIVES

Chairman and CEO: Lawrence H. Hayward, age 54
President, COO, and Director: Michael L. Hatch, age 55
EVP, CFO, and Director: Steven L. Ortega, age 47
SVP Store Operations: Brian P. Agnew, age 43
SVP and CIO: Craig Wright
SVP Commercial, Service, and Logistics:
Rick D. Carlson, age 42
Auditors: Ernst & Young LLP

LOCATIONS

HQ: Leslie's Poolmart, Inc.
3925 E. Broadway Rd., Ste. 100, Phoenix, AZ 85040
Phone: 602-366-3999   **Fax:** 602-366-3934
Web: www.lesliespool.com

2008 Stores

	No.
California	134
Texas	108
Arizona	68
Florida	66
Georgia	24
New York	22
New Jersey	20
Pennsylvania	19
Nevada	17
Ohio	12
Connecticut	9
Louisiana	8
Missouri	8
Indiana	7
Massachusetts	7
Michigan	7
Oklahoma	7
Tennessee	7
Virginia	7
Alabama	6
Illinois	6
Maryland	6
North Carolina	5
Kentucky	4
South Carolina	4
Other states	16
Total	**604**

COMPETITORS

Home Depot	Pelican Sport Center
Keller Supply	Pool Corp.
Kmart	Target
Pacific Sands	Wal-Mart
Paddock Pool	

Levi Strauss

Levi Strauss & Co. (LS&CO.) strives to provide the world's casual workday wardrobe, inside and out. LS&CO., a top manufacturer of brand-name clothing globally, sells jeans and sportswear under the Levi's, Dockers, and Levi Strauss Signature names in more than 110 countries. It also markets men's and women's underwear and loungewear. Levi's jeans — department store staples — were once the uniform of American youth, but LS&CO. has been working to reconnect with the niche and expand outside the US. It has transformed its products portfolio to include wrinkle-free and stain-resistant fabrics used in making some of its Levi's and Dockers slacks. The Haas family (relatives of founder Levi Strauss) owns LS&CO.

Once solely an American icon, LS&CO. operates in mature markets in the Americas, Europe, and Asia/Pacific. It's also finding sales gains in Asia/Pacific and European markets, as its sales in the Americas remain lackluster. The company generates about half of its sales outside the US.

Despite its shifts in focus throughout the years, LS&CO. has come to rely heavily on its core Levi's label and less on its other brands. The Levi's brand accounted for 76% of the manufacturer's 2008 sales.

Through licensing deals the company has extended its reach into other niche markets. Through a licensing agreement with Delhi, India-based M&B Footwear, LS&CO. launched men's and women's casual shoes and sneakers. LS&CO., under license by Signature Apparel Group, added Levi-brand underwear and loungewear to its portfolio.

To give the company a boost when revenue was flat, LS&CO. had planned to put its popular Dockers brand up for sale. The company quickly took it off the block, however, deciding instead to reinvest in and revitalize the brand, which included a marketing campaign to position Dockers as a lifestyle brand for men and women. A 2006 deal with Perry Ellis International gave the Dockers brand another boost. Levi Strauss partnered with the firm to make and distribute Dockers-brand outerwear — including men's jackets, fleece items, and coats.

Looking to gain a more active role in its store business, LS&CO. in July 2009 bought the operating rights for more than 70 Levi's and Dockers Outlet locations from store operator Anchor Blue Retail Group, which had filed for bankruptcy.

Pinpointing 2006 as the best time to step down as the company's chief executive, Philip Marineau retired at the end of 2006. John Anderson, president of LS&CO.'s Asia/Pacific division and head of the firm's global supply chain unit, replaced Marineau as president and CEO.

HISTORY

Levi Strauss arrived in New York City from Bavaria in 1847. In 1853 he moved to San Francisco to sell dry goods to the gold rushers. Shortly after, a prospector told Strauss of miners' problems in finding sturdy pants. Strauss made a pair out of canvas for the prospector; word of the rugged pants spread quickly.

Strauss continued his dry-goods business in the 1860s. During this time he switched the pants' fabric to a durable French cloth called serge de Nimes, soon known as denim. He colored the fabric with indigo dye and adopted the idea from Nevada tailor Jacob Davis of reinforcing the pants with copper rivets. In 1873 Strauss and Davis produced their first pair of waist-high overalls (later known as jeans). The pants soon became *de rigueur* for lumberjacks, cowboys, railroad workers, oil drillers, and farmers.

Strauss continued to build his pants and wholesaling business until he died in 1902. Levi Strauss & Co. passed to four nephews who carried on their uncle's jeans business while maintaining the company's philanthropic reputation.

After WWII Walter Haas and Peter Haas (a fourth-generation Strauss family member) assumed leadership of LS&CO. In 1948 they ended the company's wholesaling business to concentrate on Levi's clothing. In the 1950s Levi's jeans ceased to be merely functional garments for workers: They became the uniform of American youth. In the 1960s LS&CO. added women's attire and expanded overseas.

The company went public in 1971. That year it added a women's career line and bought Koret sportswear (sold in 1984). By the mid-1980s profits declined. Peace Corps-veteran-turned-McKinsey-consultant Robert Haas (Walter's son) grabbed the reins of LS&CO. in 1984 and took the company private the next year. He also instilled a touchy-feely corporate culture often at odds with the bottom line.

In 1986 LS&CO. introduced Dockers casual pants. The company's sales began rising in 1991 as consumers forsook designer duds of the 1980s for more practical clothes. LS&CO. says seven out of every 10 American men own a pair of Dockers. However, LS&CO. missed out on the birth of another trend: the split between the fashion sense of US adolescents and their Levi's-loving, baby boomer parents.

In 1996 the company introduced Slates dress slacks. That year LS&CO. bought back nearly one-third of its stock from family and employees for $4.3 billion. Grappling with slipping sales and debt from the buyout, in 1997 LS&CO. closed 11 of its 37 North American plants, laying off 6,400 workers and 1,000 salaried employees; it granted generous severance packages even to those earning minimum wage.

In 1998, citing improved labor conditions in China, LS&CO. announced it would step up its use of Chinese subcontractors. Further restructuring added a third of its European plants to the closures list that year. LS&CO.'s sales fell 13% in fiscal 1998. The next year LS&CO. closed 11 of 22 remaining North American plants. It also unleashed several new jeans brands that eschewed the company's one-style-fits-all approach of old.

In 1999 Haas handed his CEO title to Pepsi executive Philip Marineau.

In April 2002 LS&CO. announced it would close six of its last eight US plants and cut 20% of its worldwide staff (3,300 workers). In September 2003 it cut another 5% of its global staff (650 workers). That month the company opened its first girls-only store, located in Paris. In December LS&CO. replaced CFO Bill Chiasson with an outside turnaround specialist.

EXECUTIVES

Interim Chairman: Richard L. Kauffman, age 54
President, CEO, and Director: R. John Anderson, age 57
EVP and CFO: Blake J. Jorgensen, age 49
SVP and Chief Supply Chain Officer: David Love, age 46
SVP Worldwide Human Resources: Cathleen L. Unruh, age 60
SVP and CIO: Tom Peck
SVP Corporate Affairs and General Counsel: Hilary K. Krane, age 45
SVP and President, Levi Strauss North America: Robert L. Hanson, age 45
SVP and President, Levi Strauss Asia/Pacific: Beng Keong (Aaron) Boey, age 47
SVP and Global Chief Marketing Officer, Levi's Brand: Jaime Cohen Szulc, age 47
SVP; President, Levi Strauss Europe: Armin Broger, age 47
SVP Strategy and Worldwide Marketing and Global Marketing Officer: Lawrence W. (Larry) Ruff, age 52
VP Finance, Levi Strauss North America: Mary Boland, age 51
VP Global Tax Department: Paul Smith
VP Marketing: Robert Cameron
VP, Controller, and Principal Accounting Officer: Heidi L. Manes, age 37
VP Corporate Affairs and Chief Communications Officer: Jill Nash
Investor Relations: Roger Fleischmann
Auditors: PricewaterhouseCoopers LLP

LOCATIONS

HQ: Levi Strauss & Co.
 1155 Battery St., San Francisco, CA 94111
Phone: 415-501-6000   **Fax:** 415-501-7112
Web: www.levistrauss.com

2008 Sales

	% of total
Americas	56
Europe	27
Asia/Pacific	17
Total	**100**

PRODUCTS/OPERATIONS

2008 Sales

	% of total
Levi's brand	76
Dockers brand	18
Levi Strauss Signature brand	6
Total	**100**

Selected Brand Names

Dockers
Dockers for Men
Dockers for Women
Levi's
Levi's 501
Levi's 505
Levi's Blue
Levi's Capital E
Levi's Red Tab
Levi's Silvertab
Levi's Vintage
Signature by Levis Strauss & Co.

COMPETITORS

Abercrombie & Fitch
adidas
American Eagle Outfitters
Benetton
Calvin Klein
Diesel SpA
Fast Retailing
Fruit of the Loom
FUBU
The Gap
Guess?
Haggar
Hugo Boss
J. C. Penney
J. Crew
Jockey International
Joe's Jeans
Jones Apparel
Kmart
Kohl's
Lands' End
Limited Brands
Liz Claiborne
Macy's
Nautica Apparel
NIKE
OshKosh B'Gosh
Oxford Industries
Perry Ellis International
Phillips-Van Heusen
Polo Ralph Lauren
Sean John
Sears
Target
Tommy Hilfiger
True Religion Apparel
Under Armour
VF
Victoria's Secret Stores
Wacoal
Wal-Mart
Warnaco Group

HISTORICAL FINANCIALS

Company Type: Private

Income Statement

	REVENUE ($ mil.)	NET INCOME ($ mil.)	NET PROFIT MARGIN	EMPLOYEES
11/08	4,303	229	5.3%	11,400
11/07	4,266	460	10.8%	11,550
11/06	4,107	239	5.8%	10,680
11/05	4,125	156	3.8%	9,635
11/04	4,073	30	0.7%	8,850
Annual Growth	**1.4%**	**65.7%**	**—**	**6.5%**

FYE: Last Sunday in November

Net Income History

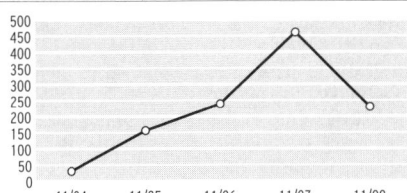

Liberty Media

Liberty Media takes the liberty of arranging its varied businesses as it pleases. The holding company comprises publicly traded Liberty Capital Group, Liberty Starz (formerly Liberty Entertainment), and Liberty Interactive Group. The arrangement effectively splits the fast-growing video and online commerce operations and the company's less robust telecommunications and entertainment businesses. Liberty Media's biggest holding, the QVC home-shopping network, falls under the Liberty Interactive umbrella, as does e-tailer Provide Commerce. Movie channel Starz Media and the Atlanta Braves both belong to Liberty Capital. In 2009 the company spun off most of its Liberty Entertainment unit, merging it with DIRECTV.

The move, first announced in 2008, gives both Liberty Media and the satellite TV provider greater flexibility to focus on other objectives. During the past few years, Liberty Media has made several attempts to simplify its structure through a variety of spinoffs, asset sales, acquisitions, and the formation of a third tracking stock. Whether it has succeeded is open to debate.

As part of the spinoff, Liberty Media turned over three regional sports networks, subsidiary FUN Technologies, and a 50% stake in the Game Show Network. It renamed its remaining Liberty Entertainment assets Liberty Starz. Chairman John Malone and his family retained about a 25% stake in the new DIRECTV organization.

Liberty Media adopted its present three-part structure in early 2008 when Liberty Capital spawned Liberty Entertainment. Liberty Entertainment was formed following Liberty Media's exchange in February 2008 of a 41% stake in The DIRECTV Group for its 16% stake in News Corp. (valued at more than $10 billion). Liberty Media had agreed back in late 2006 to swap its stake in News Corp. for a controlling interest in the satellite TV company, as well as three regional sports networks, and $465 million in cash.

In what's considered a pretty savvy deal on Malone's part, Liberty Media has invested $530 million in the form of high-interest loans in the satellite radio company SIRIUS XM Radio in exchange for an equity stake in the company and board representation. Liberty said the investment will be attributed to the Liberty Capital Group.

Malone's high volume of transactions during the past few years put him in hot water in June 2009, when it was announced by the Federal Trade Commission (FTC) that Malone had violated pre-merger competition rules by buying stock in Discovery Communications in 2005 and again in 2008 without properly disclosing the transactions. Malone, who had taken the recording error to the FTC voluntarily in 2008, has agreed to pay a $1.4 million penalty. Liberty Media had owned a 50% stake in Discovery Communications before it was spun off to Liberty's shareholders in July 2005.

What remains of Liberty Capital includes Liberty Media's minority investments in Time Warner and Sprint Nextel.

Unaffected by the 2008 reorganization is Liberty Interactive, whose holdings include about 24% of online travel firm Expedia and Bodybuilding.com, which it bought in January 2008. Later in the year, Liberty bought online party supply and costume seller Celebrate Express to combine with Buyseasons (acquired in 2006). The deal furthers Liberty's strategy of acquiring niche e-commerce businesses. Liberty Interactive also owns a majority voting stake (62%) in Barry Diller's Internet conglomerate IAC/InterActiveCorp. (In August 2008, however, IAC spun off several of its companies, reducing Liberty's voting interest to 30% in the four separate companies.)

The company's TruePosition unit, which supplies mobile-phone location equipment, won a permanent injunction in August 2008 that prohibits rival Andrew Corp. from marketing products that infringe on a US patent. The US district court adjusted downward a more than $45 million jury award to give TruePosition slightly more than $23 million and denied Andrew's bid for a new trial.

Outside North America, Liberty Media has operations in Europe, Asia, and South America.

EXECUTIVES

Chairman: John C. Malone, age 68,
$4,308,817 total compensation
President, CEO, and Director: Gregory B. (Greg) Maffei, age 48, $12,189,326 total compensation
EVP and General Counsel: Charles Y. Tanabe, age 58, $3,310,524 total compensation
SVP: Mark D. Carleton, age 49
SVP: Michael P. Zeisser, age 44
SVP Tax Strategy, Planning, and Compliance: Albert E. Rosenthaler, age 49, $2,107,627 total compensation
SVP and Controller: Christopher W. (Chris) Shean, age 44, $2,168,004 total compensation
SVP and Treasurer: David J. A. Flowers, age 54
VP, Deputy General Counsel, and Secretary: Pamela L. Coe
Chairman and CEO, Starz, LLC: Robert B. (Bob) Clasen, age 65
Auditors: KPMG LLP

LOCATIONS

HQ: Liberty Media Corporation
12300 Liberty Blvd., Englewood, CO 80112
Phone: 720-875-5400 **Fax:** 720-875-5401
Web: www.libertymedia.com

PRODUCTS/OPERATIONS

2008 Sales

	$ mil.	% of total
Interactive Group		
QVC	7,303	72
Corporate & other	776	8
Entertainment Group		
Starz Entertainment	1,111	11
Corporate & other	280	3
Capital Group		
Starz Media	321	3
Corporate & other	296	3
Adjustments	(3)	—
Total	**10,084**	**100**

Selected Consolidated Subsidiaries and Investments

Capital Group
Atlanta National League Baseball Club, Inc.
Leisure Arts, Inc.
Starz Media, LLC
TruePosition, Inc. (89%, wireless technology services)
WFRV and WJMN Televisions Station, Inc.

Starz Group
PicksPal, Inc.
Starz Entertainment, LLC
The DIRECTV Group, Inc. (54%, satellite-TV operator)
WildBlue Communications, Inc.

Interactive Group
Backcountry.com, Inc.
Bodybuilding.com, LLC
BuySeasons, Inc. (100%, online costume and party supply retail)
Expedia, Inc.
IAC/InterActiveCorp
Provide Commerce, Inc. (100%, e-commerce)
QVC (98%, home shopping network)

COMPETITORS

1-800-FLOWERS
Amazon.com
American Express
Blue Sky Studios
Comcast
Cox Communications
Dillard's
Disney
Disney Studios
DreamWorks
Fox Entertainment
FTD
Hallmark
Hearst Corporation
HSN
J. C. Penney
KaBloom
Macy's
NBC
NDS Group
Orbitz Worldwide
Oxygen Media
Pixar
priceline.com
Rainbow Media
Teleflora
Time Warner
Travelocity
Turner Broadcasting
Twentieth Century Fox
ValueVision Media
Viacom
Wal-Mart

Liberty Mutual

Boston boasts of baked beans, the Red Sox, and the Liberty Mutual Group. Liberty Mutual Holding is the parent company for the Liberty Mutual Group and its operating subsidiaries. Liberty Mutual is one of the top property/casualty insurers in the US and among the top 10 providers of automobile insurance. The company also offers homeowners' insurance and commercial lines for small to large companies. Liberty Mutual Group operates through four business divisions: Personal Markets, Commercial Markets, Agency Markets, and Liberty International. It distributes its products through a diversified blend of independent and exclusive agents, brokers, and direct sales.

True to its name, the company's Personal Market division offers personal lines property/casualty insurance including private auto and homeowners' insurance. Much of its new business comes from its relationships with affinity groups such as credit unions, employers, and professional and alumni associations.

The Commercial Markets division provides commercial property/casualty products. The division includes the National Market unit, which serves large businesses, and the Middle Market unit, serving midsized businesses. The Commercial Markets division also includes Liberty Mutual Property (commercial property coverage) and Group Market (group disability products and administration).

The Agency Markets division serves a balanced mix of small and midsized employers and individuals. It operates through smaller regional businesses as well as Summit Holding Southeast and Liberty Mutual Surety. To extend the division's geographical reach, Liberty Mutual acquired property/casualty insurer Ohio Casualty for $2.6 billion in 2007 and spent $6.3 billion to acquire Safeco in 2008. That deal gave the company a greater share of the West Coast markets, and the Safeco brand for new personal lines of insurance on a national basis.

Liberty's International division has grown in importance as part of a planned long-term expansion outside of the US. The International division includes operations that offer personal and commercial insurance to local markets in more than a dozen countries, and Liberty International Underwriters, which provides specialty commercial lines worldwide. To establish a presence in new markets, the company relies on both acquisitions of existing local businesses as well as start ups of new businesses.

The company's distribution strategy has shifted away from an in-house sales force, and into a blend of independent and exclusive agents, brokers, direct-response call centers, and the Internet. To that end, in early 2009 Liberty Mutual sold off its direct distribution business and Wausau agency brand to three brokers: Arthur J. Gallagher, Hub International, and USI Holdings. Simultaneously, Liberty Mutual also retired its Wausau Insurance brand.

HISTORY

The need for financial aid to workers injured on the job was recognized in Europe in the late 19th century but did not make its way to the US until a workers' compensation law for federal employees was passed in 1908. Massachusetts was one of the first states to enact similar legislation. Liberty Mutual was founded in Boston in 1912 to fill this newly recognized niche.

Liberty Mutual followed the fire insurance practice of taking an active part in loss prevention. It evaluated clients' premises and procedures and recommended ways to prevent accidents. The company rejected the budding industry practice of limiting medical fees, instead studying the most effective ways to reduce the long-term cost of a claim by getting the injured party back to work.

In 1942 the company acquired the United Mutual Fire Insurance Company (founded 1908, renamed Liberty Mutual Fire Insurance Company in 1949). The next year it founded a rehabilitation center in Boston to treat injured workers and to test treatments.

In the 1960s and 1970s, Liberty Mutual expanded its line to include life insurance (1963), group pensions (1970), and IRAs (1975).

Seeking to increase its national presence, the company formed Liberty Northwest Insurance Corporation in 1983. It continued expanding its offerings, with new subsidiaries in commercial, personal, and excess lines and, in 1986, by moving into financial services with the purchase of Stein Roe & Farnham (founded 1958).

The expansion/diversification strategy seemed to work. Earnings between 1984 and 1986 more than tripled. Then the downturn: Recession was followed by a string of natural disasters, and Liberty Mutual's income fell sharply between 1986 and 1988. In 1992 and 1993 the firm lost suits to Coors and Outboard Marine for failing to back them in environmental litigation cases.

Liberty Mutual gained a foothold in the UK in 1995 when it received permission to invest in a Lloyd's of London syndicate management company. In 1997 Liberty Mutual acquired bankrupt workers' comp provider Golden Eagle Insurance of California; the next year the firm bought Florida's Summit Holding Southeast. Mutual funds were also on the shopping list: Purchases included Société Générale's US mutual funds unit, led by international money dean Jean-Marie Eveillard.

In 1999 the company bought Guardian Royal Exchange's US operations. In a new international initiative that year, Liberty Mutual bought 70% of Singapore-based insurer Citystate Holdings as its foothold in Asia.

The company's diversification efforts included Liberty International, which expanded operations in such countries as Canada, Japan, Mexico, Singapore, and the UK. The company also grew its international presence in areas such as China and southern Europe.

Slumping property/casualty lines and the events of September 11 hit Liberty Mutual in 2001 (the company paid out some $500 million in claims). In 2001 and 2002 the company reorganized into a mutual holding company structure with its three principal operating companies (Liberty Mutual Insurance, Liberty Mutual Fire Insurance, and Employers Insurance Company of Wausau) each becoming separate stock insurance companies with Liberty Mutual Holding Company as the parent.

Strengthening its personal lines business, Liberty Mutual in 2003 bought Prudential's domestic property/casualty operations. The deal included some 1,400 Prudential agents, who were added to the company's distribution mix.

Hurricane-related losses totaled $1.5 billion in 2005, but were offset by nice returns from the company's investments that same year.

EXECUTIVES

Chairman, President, and CEO: Edmund F. (Ted) Kelly, age 63
EVP and Chief Investment Officer: A. Alexander Fontanes
SVP and CIO: James M. McGlennon
SVP and General Manager Technology Infrastructure: Baron Thrower
SVP and CFO: Dennis J. Langwell
SVP and General Counsel: Christopher C. Mansfield
SVP and Corporate Actuary: Robert T. Muleski
SVP Communications Services: Stephen G. Sullivan
SVP Human Resources and Administration: Helen E. R. Sayles
VP and Comptroller: John D. Doyle
VP and Secretary: Dexter R. Legg
VP and Manager External Relations: John Cusolito
VP and Treasurer: Laurance H. S. Yahia
President, Personal Lines: Timothy M. Sweeney, age 44
President, Liberty International: David H. Long, age 48
President, Commercial Lines: J. Paul Condrin III, age 48
President, Agency Markets: Gary R. Gregg
Auditors: Ernst & Young LLP

LOCATIONS

HQ: Liberty Mutual Holding Company Inc.
175 Berkeley St., Boston, MA 02116
Phone: 617-357-9500　　**Fax:** 617-350-7648
Web: www.libertymutual.com

PRODUCTS/OPERATIONS

2008 Revenues

	$ mil.	% of total
Premiums earned	25,524	87
Net investment income	2,880	10
Net realized investment losses	(330)	—
Fees & other revenues	781	3
Total	**28,855**	**100**

2008 Revenues

	$ mil.	% of total
Agency markets	8,245	29
International	7,049	24
Commercial markets	6,804	24
Personal markets	6,684	23
Other revenues	73	—
Total	**28,855**	**100**

Selected Subsidiaries and Affiliates

Liberty International
　Liberty ART SA (Argentina)
　Liberty Direct (Poland)
　Liberty Insurance Pte.Ltd. (Singapore)
　Liberty International Underwriters (LIU)
　Liberty Seguros (Brazil)
　Liberty Seguros SA (Colombia)
　Seguros Caracas de Liberty Mutual C.A. (Venezuela)
　Seker Sigorta A.S. (Turkey)
Domestic and Regional Companies
　America First Insurance
　Colorado Casualty
　Golden Eagle Insurance
　Indiana Insurance
　Liberty Northwest
　Montgomery Insurance
　Ohio Casualty
　Peerless Insurance
　Safeco Insurance
　Summit Holdings

COMPETITORS

ACE Limited	Progressive Corporation
AIG	State Farm
Allianz	Travelers Companies
Allstate	W. R. Berkley
Chubb Corp	White Mountains
CNA Financial	Insurance
The Hartford	Zurich Financial Services
MassMutual	

HISTORICAL FINANCIALS

Company Type: Mutual company

Income Statement				FYE: December 31
	ASSETS ($ mil.)	NET INCOME ($ mil.)	INCOME AS % OF ASSETS	EMPLOYEES
12/08	104,300	1,140	1.1%	45,000
12/07	94,679	1,518	1.6%	41,000
12/06	85,498	1,626	1.9%	39,000
12/05	78,824	1,027	1.3%	39,000
12/04	72,359	1,245	1.7%	38,000
Annual Growth	**9.6%**	**(2.2%)**	**—**	**4.3%**

2008 Year-End Financials

Equity as % of assets: —　　Long-term debt ($ mil.): —
Return on assets: 1.1%　　Sales ($ mil.): 28,855
Return on equity: —

Net Income History

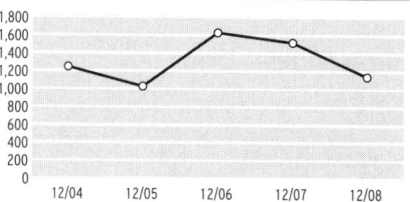

Life Care Centers

If you or a loved one has reached the Golden Age of retirement, there's a good chance Life Care Centers of America offers a service you can use. The company is a privately owned operator of more than 200 retirement and health care centers in 28 states. Its offerings include retirement communities, assisted-living facilities, and nursing homes (and even some campuses that provide all three in a continuum of care). In addition, Life Care operates centers specifically for people with Alzheimer's disease or related dementia. Some of Life Care's specialized services include home health care, adult day care, hospice, and wound care. Founder Forrest Preston opened his first center in 1970.

The company expands its network by leasing facilities from companies like Health Care REIT; buying existing facilities, such as the 2009 purchase of a county-owned nursing home in Dayton, Tennessee; and through new facility construction. Some of Life Care's facilities are operated by affiliate Century Park Associates.

Like most other health care providers, Life Care was affected negatively by the recession, and in 2009 announced it would close its Ocean View Convalescent Center, a skilled nursing and rehabilitation center in Long Beach, Washington. In announcing the closure, Life Care said it hadn't ruled out the possibility of shuttering additional facilities as long as the economy remains in recession.

EXECUTIVES

Chairman: Forrest L. Preston
President: Beecher Hunter
COO: Cathy Murray
CFO: Steve Ziegler
SVP Information Technology and CIO: Terry Leonard
SVP Human Resources: Jennie McClaren
SVP Clinical Services: Dee McCarthy
SVP Life Care Home Health: Christopher Mitchell
VP, Southeast Division: Michael Zomchek
VP Corporate Compliance: Gerald Webb
VP Human Resources: Peg Toohey
VP Treasurer and Payroll: Lisa Lay
Chief Corporate Compliance Officer: Sharon Coleman
Director Public Relations: Rob Alderman

LOCATIONS

HQ: Life Care Centers of America
3570 Keith St. NW, Cleveland, TN 37312
Phone: 423-472-9585   **Fax:** 423-476-5974
Web: www.lcca.com

COMPETITORS

Advocat
Amedisys
Assisted Living Concepts
Capital Senior Living
Emeritus Corporation
Golden Horizons
Kindred Healthcare
Manor Care
Merrill Gardens
National HealthCare
Regency Nursing and Rehabilitation
Res-Care
SavaSeniorCare
Skilled Healthcare Group
Sun Healthcare
Sunrise Senior Living

HISTORICAL FINANCIALS

Company Type: Private

Income Statement

	REVENUE ($ mil.)	NET INCOME ($ mil.)	NET PROFIT MARGIN	EMPLOYEES
12/08	2,290	—	—	31,000
12/07	2,120	—	—	31,153
12/06	2,050	—	—	30,000
12/05	1,957	—	—	30,000
12/04	1,800	—	—	40,000
Annual Growth	6.2%	—	—	(6.2%)

FYE: December 31

Revenue History

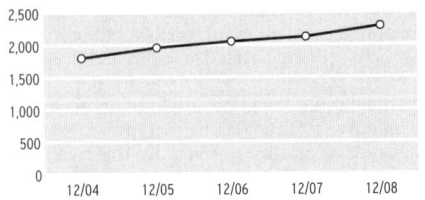

Lifetouch Inc.

When it's picture day at school and the kids are all lined up with new haircuts and scrubbed faces, odds are good that their toothy grins are directed at someone from Lifetouch. One of the largest US portrait photographers, employee-owned Lifetouch also runs about 700 photography studios inside J. C. Penney and Target stores across the nation. In addition, Lifetouch takes baby, family, business, and sports portraits; publishes church directories and yearbooks; and offers event digital imaging (which combines photography, graphics, and text), CD business imaging, and video production services. Lifetouch also operates more than 15 FLASH! Digital Portraits locations in malls in about 10 states. The firm operates in the US and Canada.

In early 2009 Lifetouch National Schools Studios, the company's school portrait business, acquired family-owned Bryn-Alan Studios. Tampa-based Bryn-Alan has operations in Florida, the Carolinas, Georgia, and Texas and specializes in photographing high school seniors. Shortly after the Bryn-Alan acquisition, Lifetouch National Schools Studios shuttered its production facility in Tulsa, Oklahoma, resulting in the loss of some 130 jobs. The closure was the result of the switch to digital photography, which rendered the Tulsa plant redundant. In 2009 the company's church directories business purchased another family-owned firm, Busson Photography. Based in Ohio, Busson Photography has operations in 25 states and caters to faith-based organizations. Previous major acquisitions include the North American school photography operations of yearbook and class rings designer Jostens in mid-2006. That purchase solidified Lifetouch's leadership position in the North American school photography sector.

The company's SmileSafe Kids Program allows Lifetouch to send portraits and pictures of missing children to the authorities when needed (and when authorized by the children's parents), 24 hours a day, 7 days a week.

Lifetouch was founded in 1936 as National School Studios.

EXECUTIVES

Chairman and CEO: Paul Harmel
SEVP: Jake Barker
EVP and COO: Bill Calpus
CFO: Randolph (Randy) Pladson
VP Administration: Ted Koenecke
President and COO; Lifetouch National School Studios: Ertugrul Tuzcu, age 52
Director Corporate Public Relations: Sara Thurin Rollin
Chairman Emeritus: Richard P. Erickson

LOCATIONS

HQ: Lifetouch Inc.
11000 Viking Dr., Ste. 400, Eden Prairie, MN 55344
Phone: 952-826-4000   **Fax:** 952-826-4557
Web: www.lifetouch.com

PRODUCTS/OPERATIONS

Selected Products and Services

Business portraits
Church directories
Church family portraits
Family portraits
Infant portraits
Preschool portraits
School portraits
Senior/graduation portraits
Sports portraits
Yearbooks

Selected Divisions

FLASH! Digital Portraits
Lifetouch Canada Inc.
Lifetouch Church Directories and Portraits Inc.
Lifetouch Development Inc. (special event photography at malls, business portraits, and video production)
Lifetouch National School Studios Inc. (school pictures)
Lifetouch Portrait Studios Inc. (in J. C. Penney and Target stores)
Lifetouch Publishing Inc. (school yearbooks)
Media Productions (produces videos)

COMPETITORS

Cherry Hill Photo
CPI Corp.
H Tempest Limited
Harris Connect
Olan Mills
Walsworth

L.L. Bean

With L.L. Bean, you can tame the great outdoors — or just look as if you could. The outdoor apparel and gear maker mails more than 200 million catalogs per year. L.L. Bean's library includes about 10 specialty catalogs offering products in categories such as children's clothing, fly-fishing, outerwear, sportswear, housewares, footwear, camping and hiking gear, and the Maine hunting shoe upon which the company was built. L.L. Bean also operates more than a dozen retail stores and some 15 factory outlets throughout the Northeast. In addition, it sells online through English- and Japanese-language Web sites. L.L. Bean was founded in 1912 by Leon Leonwood Bean and is controlled by his descendants.

From a pair of waterproof hunting boots L.L. Bean built a direct selling empire based on catalogs mailed out under some 60 different titles and advertising 16,000 products. Today, Web sales and a growing number of retail stores are contributing more to Bean's revenue. L.L. Bean's flagship store in Freeport, Maine (known by locals as "the Bean"), attracts 3 million visitors annually and is open 24 hours a day, 365 days a year. Maine's most famous retailer has been increasing its presence outside its home state, with stores in Connecticut, Maryland, Massachusetts, New Hampshire, New Jersey, New York, Pennsylvania, and Virginia. Beyond the East Coast, Bean is mining the Midwest for sales with a pair of stores in the Chicago area that opened in the fall of 2008. A third store in Massachusetts opened in July 2009. The company has set a target of 32 retail stores across the US by 2012.

But the recession in the US and a disappointing 2008 holiday selling season has Bean considering restructuring. Indeed, the retailer announced in April 2009 that it may lay off up to 240 workers due to lagging sales. To court budget-conscious shoppers, in February the company launched Bean Values, a campaign touting the price stability of many of its most popular items.

Amid losses, the retailer has exited the Japanese market after opening several retail stores there. L.L. Bean also plans to scale back the number of catalog titles it offers.

L.L. Bean's famous customer service is exemplified by its liberal return policies and perpetual replacement of the rubber soles of its Maine Hunting Shoe. The company also offers seminars and events on such topics as fly fishing, sea kayaking, and outdoor photography.

HISTORY

Leon Leonwood Bean started out as a storekeeper in Freeport, Maine. Tired of wet, leaky boots, he experimented with various remedies and in 1911 came up with the Maine Hunting Shoe, a boot with rubber soles and feet and leather uppers. It became his most famous product.

From its outset in 1912, Bean's company was a mail-order house. The first batch of boots was a disaster: Almost all of them leaked. But Bean's willingness to correct his product's defects quickly, at his own expense, saved the company.

Maine's hunting licensing system, implemented in 1917, provided the company with a mailing list of affluent recreational hunters in the Northeast, and that year Bean opened a showroom to accommodate the customers stopping by his Freeport workshop.

Bean cultivated the image of the folksy Maine guide, offering durable, comfortable, weather-resistant clothes and reliable camping supplies. In 1920 Bean built a store on Main Street in Freeport. L.L. Bean continued to grow and add products, even during the Depression, and sales reached $1 million in 1937.

During WWII Bean helped design the boots used by the US military, and his company manufactured them, thus remaining afloat as the war years and rationing brought cutbacks in materials and outdoor activities. He began keeping the retail store open 24 hours a day in 1951, noting that he had "thrown away the keys." Bean added a women's department three years later.

Sales rose to $2 million in the early 1960s and were at $4.8 million when Bean died in 1967 at age 94. (He had resisted growing the business bigger, saying, "I'm eating three meals a day; I can't eat four.") The new president was Bean's grandson Leon Gorman, who had started with L.L. Bean in 1960. His early attempts at updating the mailing operations (mailing labels typed by hand and correspondence kept in cardboard boxes) had been vetoed by his grandfather. Gorman brought in new people and made improvements, including automating the mailing systems, improving the manufacturing systems, and targeting new, nonsporting markets (like women's casual clothes).

L.L. Bean continued its transition by targeting more of its classic customer profile — upper-middle-class college graduates — and sales grew about 20% annually for most of the 1980s. By 1989, however, sales had slowed, and growth flattened as the national economy slumped and imitators carried away market share.

Unsolicited catalog orders had been coming in from Japan since the late 1980s, so in 1992 L.L. Bean began a joint venture with Seiyu and Matsushita Electric Industrial (now named Panasonic Corporation). Their first store opened that year (the company opened a catalog and service center in Japan in 1995). L.L. Kids began in 1993.

In 1996 the company began an online shopping service. Sparked by the success of its L.L. Kids division, which grew 300% in four years, the company opened a separate children's store in Freeport the next year. The company opened its second full-line store in 2000 near Washington, DC.

L.L. Bean veteran Chris McCormick was named president and CEO in May 2001; Gorman remained chairman. McCormick is the first person outside of the Bean family to head the company.

In January 2002 L.L. Bean laid off 175 employees (about 4% of its workforce); in early 2003 it cut about 500 more jobs and offered an early retirement program, which was accepted by an additional 200 employees.

In July 2004 L.L. Bean settled lawsuits filed against Atkins Nutritionals Inc. and Gevalia Kaffe, accusing those companies of using pop-up ads on Bean's Web site without its permission. The amount of the settlement was not disclosed.

EXECUTIVES

Chairman: Leon A. Gorman
President and CEO: Christopher J. (Chris) McCormick
SVP and COO: Bob Peixotto
SVP Retail: Ken Kacere
SVP Corporate Marketing: Steve Fuller
SVP and CFO: Mark Fasold
VP E-Commerce: Mary Lou Kelley
VP Human Resources: Martha Cyr
VP Card Services: Shawn Gorman
VP Merchandising: George Kiesewetter
VP L.L. Bean Signature: Chris Vickers
Chief Merchandising Officer: Fran Philip
Chief Retail Officer: Edward R. (Ed) Howell
Director Information Infrastructure: Stafford Soule
PR Spokesman: Rich Donaldson

LOCATIONS

HQ: L.L. Bean, Inc.
3 Campus Dr., Freeport, ME 04033
Phone: 207-552-3028   **Fax:** 207-552-3080
Web: www.llbean.com

2009 Stores

	No.
Illinois	2
Massachusetts	2
Pennsylvania	2
Connecticut	1
Maine	1
Maryland	1
New Hampshire	1
New Jersey	1
New York	1
Virginia	1
Total	**13**

PRODUCTS/OPERATIONS

Selected Catalogs

Corporate Sales (custom embroidered clothing and luggage)
Fly Fishing (equipment, outer wear, and accessories)
Home (linens, pillows, and decorating)
L.L. Bean
L.L. Bean Hunting
L.L. Bean: Everyday Adventures (women's yoga and fitness products)
Outdoor Discovery Schools (classes and symposiums)
Outdoors (seasonal outdoor wear and accessories)
Traveler (clothing, luggage, and accessories)

Selected Products

Home and garden accessories
Men's, women's, and children's casual apparel
Outer wear
Shoes and boots
Sports gear and apparel
Travel apparel and luggage

COMPETITORS

Abercrombie & Fitch	Macy's
American Eagle Outfitters	Nautica Apparel
Bass Pro Shops	Norm Thompson
Cabela's	North Face
Coldwater Creek	Orvis Company
Coleman	OshKosh B'Gosh
Columbia Sportswear	Patagonia, Inc.
Dillard's	Polo Ralph Lauren
Eddie Bauer llc	Redcats usa
Fast Retailing	REI
Foot Locker	Sara Lee
The Gap	Sears
J. C. Penney	Sports Authority
J. Crew	Sportsman's Guide
J. Jill Group	Talbots
Johnson Outdoors	Target
Lands' End	Timberland
Levi Strauss	Tommy Hilfiger

Los Angeles Clippers

Forget about tall ships, this team is interested in tall centers. LAC Basketball Club owns and operates the Los Angeles Clippers professional basketball franchise. The team joined the National Basketball Association in 1970 as the Buffalo Braves before moving west in 1978. Known as the San Diego Clippers, the team relocated to Los Angeles in 1984 and now plays host at the Staples Center with its division rival Los Angeles Lakers. Fans have yet to see the Clippers earn an NBA title or an NBA Finals appearance. Real estate magnate Donald Sterling has owned the franchise since 1981.

EXECUTIVES

Owner and Chairman: Donald T. Sterling
President: Andy Roeser
CFO: Ed Lamb
SVP Marketing and Sales: Carl Lahr
VP Marketing and Broadcasting: Christian Howard
VP Communications: Joe Safety
Head Coach and General Manager: Mike Dunleavy, age 55
Assistant General Manager: Neil Olshey
General Counsel: Bob Platt
Director of Communications: Rob Raichlen
Director of Community Relations and Player Programs: Denise Booth
Director of Sponsorship Sales: Chris Beyer
Director of Corporate Sales: Greg Flaherty
Assistant Director of Player Personnel: Gary Sacks

LOCATIONS

HQ: LAC Basketball Club, Inc.
Staples Center, 1111 S. Figueroa St., Ste. 1100, Los Angeles, CA 90015
Phone: 213-742-7500   **Fax:** 213-742-7570
Web: www.nba.com/clippers

The Los Angeles Clippers play at the 18,997-seat-capacity Staples Center in Los Angeles.

COMPETITORS

Golden State Warriors
Los Angeles Lakers
Phoenix Suns
Sacramento Kings

Los Angeles Kings

These Kings have yet to be crowned Stanley Cup champions. The Los Angeles Kings Hockey Club entered the National Hockey League in 1967 and has made just one appearance in the Stanley Cup finals. Led by the great Wayne Gretzky, the team reached the championship in 1993 but lost to the Montreal Canadiens. The franchise plays host at the Staples Center, which it shares with the title-laden Los Angeles Lakers basketball team. Denver billionaire Philip Anschutz and Los Angeles developer Edward Roski have owned the Kings since 1995. The partners also own the Staples Center and a minority stake in the Lakers.

After missing the playoffs for several seasons, the team brought in Terry Murray as head coach in 2008, replacing Marc Crawford. Murray previously coached the Florida Panthers.

Co-owner Anschutz controls an entertainment and media empire through his Anschutz Company, including Anschutz Film Group, movie theater chain Regal Entertainment, and the Los Angeles Galaxy soccer team. He and Roski acquired the Kings from Jeffrey Sudikoff and Joseph Cohen for about $110 million. The latter built the $375 million Staples Center in 1999 with the help of media giant News Corporation (Anschutz and Roski bought the media titan's 40% stake in the arena in 2004.)

The Los Angeles hockey franchise was first awarded to Jack Kent Cooke, one-time owner of both the Los Angeles Lakers and the Washington Redskins, and played in the LA Forum for most of its history. The height of success for the Kings came in the late 1980s and early 1990s, when the franchise managed to make a trade for Wayne Gretzky (The Great One), who had led the Edmonton Oilers to four Stanley Cup championships. Joining the the team in 1988, Gretzky led the Kings to five straight playoff berths culminating in a Stanley Cup Finals appearance in 1993 against the Canadiens, who won the series in five games. Gretzky stayed with Los Angeles until 1996, when he requested a trade to the St. Louis Blues.

EXECUTIVES

Governor: Timothy J. (Tim) Leiweke
President, General Manager, and Alternate Governor: Dean Lombardi, age 48
President, Business Operations and Alternate Governor: Luc Robitaille
COO and CFO: Dan Beckerman
Head Coach: Terry Murray, age 59
SVP Business Operations and Chief Marketing Officer: Chris McGowan, age 36
SVP Partnership Activation: Tracy Hartman
SVP Corporate Partnerships: Bill Pedigo
SVP Sales: Carola Ross
VP and Senior Counsel: John Keenan
VP Sales: Matt Rosenfeld
VP Communications and Broadcasting: Michael Altieri, age 43
Manager Human Resources: LaShawnda Mikhael
Director Team Operations: Marshall Dickerson
Pro Scout: Rob Laird
Head Equipment Manager: Darren Granger
Head Athletic Trainer: Chris Kingsley

LOCATIONS

HQ: The Los Angeles Kings Hockey Club LP
1111 S. Figueroa St., Ste. 3100
Los Angeles, CA 90015
Phone: 213-742-7100   **Fax:** 213-742-7296
Web: www.lakings.com

The Los Angeles Kings play at the 18,118-seat-capacity Staples Center in Los Angeles.

PRODUCTS/OPERATIONS

Championship Trophies
Clarence S. Campbell Bowl (1993)

COMPETITORS

Anaheim Ducks
Dallas Stars
Phoenix Coyotes
San Jose Sharks

Los Angeles Lakers

These Lakers can be found navigating the choppy waters of the National Basketball Association. The Los Angeles Lakers professional basketball franchise is one of the most popular and successful teams in the NBA, earning 15 championship titles since joining the league in 1949. The team was founded in 1947 as the Minnesota Lakers of the National Basketball League and moved to California in 1960. Its roster has included such Hall of Fame players as Kareem Abdul-Jabbar, Wilt Chamberlain, Earvin "Magic" Johnson, and Jerry West. The franchise has been controlled by real estate mogul Jerry Buss since 1979; billionaire Philip Anschutz, developer Edward Roski, and Magic Johnson also own minority stakes in the team.

Lakers fans are once again rooting for a winner after the team hit a rough patch and lost to the Boston Celtics in the 2008 NBA Finals. With head coach Phil Jackson at the helm and star player and former league MVP Kobe Bryant on the floor, the Lakers returned to the Finals in 2009 and beat the Orlando Magic to claim the franchise's 15th title (second all-time to the Celtics' 17). The win also gave Jackson his 10th championship as a head coach, the most in all of US professional sports.

The Lakers are a huge draw at Los Angeles' Staples Center, where the team boasts such celebrities as Denzel Washington and Jack Nicholson among its fan base.

Buss and his investors sold the Los Angeles Sparks of the WNBA to a local investment group led by Carla Christofferson and Katherine Goodman for $10 million in 2006.

HISTORY

The Los Angeles Lakers basketball team traces its roots to the Detroit Gems, a defunct franchise acquired for $15,000 by a group including Max Winter (later the first president of the Minnesota Vikings), Ben Berger, and Maurice Chalfen. Renamed the Minneapolis Lakers, the team joined the National Basketball League (NBL) in 1947 and, with the help of center George Mikan, won the league championship in

its first year. The team switched leagues the following season to the Basketball Association of America (BAA) and won that championship as well. The BAA and NBL merged to form the National Basketball Association (NBA) after that season, and the Lakers won the NBA's first championship in 1949. The team went on to win three straight NBA titles from 1952-54.

Berger and Chalfen sold the team to businessman Bob Short in 1957 for $150,000. With the team struggling and attendance lagging, Short decided to move the Lakers to Los Angeles in 1960. Stars Elgin Baylor and Jerry West helped the team rebound and reach the NBA finals six times in the 1960s; however, they lost each time to their archrivals, the Boston Celtics. Jack Kent Cooke bought the team from Short for $5 million in 1965, and the Lakers moved to their new arena, the Forum, in 1967. Center Wilt Chamberlain joined the team in 1968, but the Lakers didn't win an NBA title as an LA team until 1972 (against the Knicks).

In 1979 real estate tycoon Jerry Buss bought the Lakers, the Forum, and the Los Angeles Kings from Cooke (who also owned the Washington Redskins) for $67.5 million. Led by Kareem Abdul-Jabbar, Magic Johnson, and slick-haired coach Pat Riley, the Lakers won two NBA titles in the early 1980s and persevered twice during a new series of title bouts with rival Boston. The team earned its fifth NBA title that decade in 1988, the same year Buss sold the Los Angeles Kings.

Riley stepped down after the 1990 season, and in late 1991 Magic Johnson announced he was HIV-positive and retired. The loss was huge, and in 1994 the team missed the playoffs for the first time in almost 20 years. (Johnson also bought 5% of the team that year.) The Lakers signed center Shaquille O'Neal to a $120 million, seven-year contract and drafted 18-year-old guard Kobe Bryant in 1996. The next year saw the inaugural season of the NBA's sister league (literally), the Women's NBA (WNBA). Buss became owner of the Los Angeles Sparks. (He sold the women's basketball franchise to a local investment group in 2006.) Kings owners Philip Anschutz and Edward Roski bought 25% of the Lakers from Buss in 1998.

Buss sold the Forum in 1999, and the Lakers began the 1999-2000 season in the new $300 million Staples Center (built by Anschutz and Roski, which was what gave them their stake in the Lakers). After two consecutive sweeps out of the playoffs, the team in 1999 hired Phil Jackson, the cerebral head coach who led the Chicago Bulls to six NBA titles. The move immediately paid off as Jackson guided the Lakers, led by O'Neal and sharpshooter Bryant, to three straight championships between 2000 and 2002. In 2000 Jerry West retired from the franchise after 40 years as a player, coach, and front-office executive.

In 2003 the Lakers were booted from the playoffs in the second round. Future hall of famers Gary "The Glove" Payton and Karl "The Mailman" Malone signed with the team later that year in the hopes of winning a title. The move made the Lakers one of the most star-studded teams in NBA history, and though it gained a berth in the NBA Finals, the Lakers were thoroughly dominated in the championship series by the Detroit Pistons.

The team retooled in the off season and saw Jackson resign, O'Neal and Payton traded, and Malone opting out of his contract to become a free agent. The team hired former Houston

Rockets head coach Rudy Tomjanovich to replace Jackson. Bryant re-signed with LA to the tune of $136 million over seven years.

Tomjanovich quit the coaching game in 2005, and the team lured Phil Jackson out of retirement with a three-year, $30 million coaching contract. After three years of either missing the playoffs or exiting in the first round, the Lakers returned to the NBA Finals in 2008; however, the team fell to the Eastern Conference champion Celtics in six games. Fortunes turned around the next year when the team returned to the Finals and took down the Orlando Magic in five games. The win gave the franchise its 15th championship.

EXECUTIVES

Governor, President, and Majority Owner: Jerry Buss
CEO: Frank Mariani
EVP Basketball Operations and General Manager:
 Mitch Kupchak
EVP Business Operations and Alternate Governor:
 Jeanie Buss
Assistant General Manager: Ronnie Lester
Head Coach: Phil Jackson, age 64
SVP Finance and CFO: Joe McCormack
VP Player Personnel: Jim Buss
VP Public Relations: John Black

LOCATIONS

HQ: The Los Angeles Lakers, Inc.
 555 N. Nash St., El Segundo, CA 90245
Phone: 310-426-6000   **Fax:** 310-426-6115
Web: www.nba.com/lakers

PRODUCTS/OPERATIONS

Championship Titles
NBA Finals (1949-50, 1952-54, 1972, 1980, 1982, 1985, 1987-88, 2000-02, 2009)
NBA Western Conference (1972-73, 1980, 1982-85, 1987-89, 1991, 2000-02, 2004, 2008-09)
NBA Western Division (1951, 1953-54, 1962-63, 1965-66, 1969)
NBA Central Division (1950)
National Basketball League
 NBL Finals (1947)

COMPETITORS

Golden State Warriors
Los Angeles Clippers
Phoenix Suns
Sacramento Kings

Love's Travel Stops

If you're a trucker or RVer on the road, all you need is Love's. Love's Travel Stops & Country Stores operates more than 220 travel stop locations throughout a swath of about 35 states from California to Virginia, including convenience stores in Colorado, Kansas, New Mexico, Oklahoma, and Texas. Each travel stop includes a convenience store; a fast-food restaurant, such as Taco Bell or Subway; and gas outlets for cars, trucks, and RVs. The travel stops also provide shower rooms, laundry facilities, game rooms, and mail drops. Love's Travel Stops & Country Stores is owned by the family of CEO Tom Love, who founded the company in 1964.

Love's has entered the Iowa market with a store in Newton. The company adds about 15 locations a year, on average.

EXECUTIVES

Chairman and CEO: Tom Love
EVP and CFO: Doug Stussi
EVP Operations: Tom Edwards
VP Accounting: Shane Wharton
VP Human Resources: Kevin Asbury
VP and CIO: Jim Xenos
VP Construction and Environmental Compliance:
 Terry Ross
President Love's Operating Companies: Frank Love
President Love's Development Companies: Greg Love
Director Communications: Jenny Love Meyer
Director Marketing: Dave Frankenfield
Director Legal Services: Amy Guzzy
Director Sales: Don Van Curen

LOCATIONS

HQ: Love's Travel Stops & Country Stores, Inc.
 10601 N. Pennsylvania Ave.
 Oklahoma City, OK 73120
Phone: 405-751-9000   **Fax:** 405-749-9110
Web: www.loves.com

2008 Stores

	No.
Alabama	3
Arizona	9
Arkansas	5
California	4
Colorado	9
Florida	3
Georgia	7
Illinois	5
Indiana	4
Kansas	11
Kentucky	6
Louisiana	6
Mississippi	4
Missouri	5
Nevada	3
New Mexico	8
Ohio	5
Oklahoma	64
Oregon	2
Pennsylvania	3
South Carolina	3
Tennessee	7
Texas	33
Virginia	3
Wyoming	2
Other states	9
Total	**223**

COMPETITORS

7-Eleven	Pilot Corporation
Allsup's	Racetrac Petroleum
Chevron	Rip Griffin Truck Service
Common Cents	Royal Dutch Shell
Exxon Mobil	Stuckey's
E-Z Mart Stores	TravelCenters of America
Flying J	Valero Energy
Marathon Oil	Walgreen

HISTORICAL FINANCIALS

Company Type: Private

Income Statement

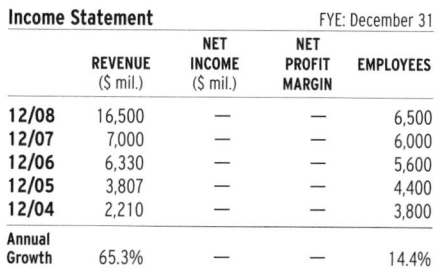

FYE: December 31

	REVENUE ($ mil.)	NET INCOME ($ mil.)	NET PROFIT MARGIN	EMPLOYEES
12/08	16,500	—	—	6,500
12/07	7,000	—	—	6,000
12/06	6,330	—	—	5,600
12/05	3,807	—	—	4,400
12/04	2,210	—	—	3,800
Annual Growth	**65.3%**	**—**	**—**	**14.4%**

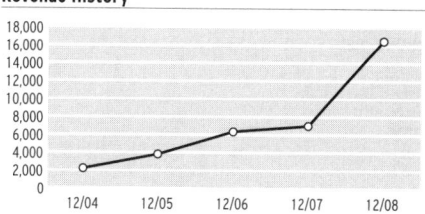

Lower Colorado River Authority

The stars at night may be big and bright, but more than one million people deep in the heart of Texas still need electricity from the Lower Colorado River Authority (LCRA). Serving more than 50 counties along the lower Colorado River from Central Texas' Hill Country to the Gulf of Mexico, the not-for-profit, state-run entity supplies wholesale electricity to more than 40 retail utilities (primarily municipalities and cooperatives). It operates three fossil-fuel powered plants and six hydroelectric dams that give it a production capacity of about 2,300 megawatts; it also purchases electricity from Texas wind farms. The LCRA provides water and wastewater utility services to more than 30 communities as well.

Founded by the Texas Legislature in 1934, the LCRA has pursued two complementary goals — providing reliable, low-cost utility and public services, and ensuring the protection of the area's natural resources. In the latter role, the LCRA owns or operates more than 40 public recreation areas comprising more than 16,000 acres; it also monitors the water quality of the lakes formed by its dams.

EXECUTIVES

Chair: Rebecca A. Klein
Vice Chair: Clayborne Nettleship
CEO and General Manager: Thomas G. Mason
CFO: Brady Edwards
Executive Manager, Wholesale Power: Don Kuehn
Executive Manager, Transmission Services:
 Ross Phillips
Executive Manager Water Services: Suzanne Zarling
Executive Manager External Affairs:
 Rebecca (Becky) Motal
Chief Administrative Officer: Christopher Kennedy
General Counsel: John Rubottom
Auditing Services: Charlie Johnson
Secretary and Director: Linda C. Raun
Manager State Governmental Affairs: Fred Aus
Manager Environmental Affairs: Henry Eby
Auditors: Deloitte & Touche LLP

LOCATIONS

HQ: Lower Colorado River Authority
 3700 Lake Austin Blvd., Austin, TX 78703
Phone: 512-473-3200
Web: www.lcra.org

PRODUCTS/OPERATIONS

2008 Sales

	$ mil.	% of total
Electric generation	1,064.1	90
Water & wastewater	62.5	5
Other	61.2	5
Total	**1,187.8**	**100**

Selected Subsidiaries and Affiliates

GenTex Power Corporation (power generation)
LCRA Transmission Services Corporation (power transmission services)

COMPETITORS

AEP
Brazos Electric
El Paso Electric
Energy Future
Entergy
ONEOK
Pedernales Electric
Southwest Water

HISTORICAL FINANCIALS

Company Type: Government-owned

Income Statement

FYE: June 30

	REVENUE ($ mil.)	NET INCOME ($ mil.)	NET PROFIT MARGIN	EMPLOYEES
6/08	1,188	51	4.3%	2,325
6/07	1,079	44	4.0%	2,244
6/06	1,045	26	2.5%	2,200
6/05	803	41	5.2%	2,200
6/04	694	34	5.0%	2,224
Annual Growth	**14.4%**	**10.3%**	—	**1.1%**

2008 Year-End Financials

Debt ratio: 288.0%
Return on equity: —
Cash ($ mil.): 113
Current ratio: 0.98
Long-term debt ($ mil.): 2,358

Net Income History

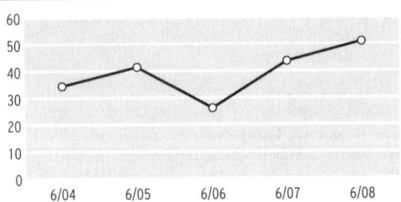

	6/04	6/05	6/06	6/07	6/08

Loyola University

Loyola University is a Jesuit, Catholic university with a reach that extends beyond the Windy City. In addition to its three Chicago-area campuses, the university also maintains an undergraduate campus in Italy and a study center in Beijing, China. Loyola University's more than 15,000 students can choose from about 70 undergraduate, 85 master's, 30 doctoral, and three professional degree programs. Notable alumni include actor Bob Newhart, writer Sandra Cisneros, and CNN-TV correspondent Susan Candiotti. Established in 1870 by a group of Jesuit priests, the university turned its medical center into a separate subsidiary in 1995.

EXECUTIVES

Chairman: Michael R. Quinlan, age 64
Vice Chair: William J. Hank
President and Trustee: Rev Michael J. Garanzini
Provost: Christine M. Wiseman
VP Strategic Capital Planning and Chief of Staff: Wayne F. Magdziarz
VP Public Affairs: Philip (Phil) Hale
VP Mission and Ministry: Lucien Roy
VP and General Counsel: Ellen K. Munro
VP Information Technology and Services and CIO: Susan M. Malisch
VP Finance, CFO, and Treasurer: William G. (Bill) Laird
VP Human Resources: Thomas M. (Tom) Kelly
VP Academic Affairs and Health Sciences: Paul K. Whelton
VP Student Affairs: Rev Richard P. Salmi
VP Marketing and Communication: Kelly Shannon
Dean Of Students: Jane F. Neufeld
Dean, Business Administration: Abol Jallivand
University Registrar: Clare Korinek
Director Alumni Relations: Nicole Meehan
Chief Investment Officer and Assistant Treasurer: Eric Jones
Auditors: Deloitte & Touche LLP

LOCATIONS

HQ: Loyola University Chicago
6525 N. Sheridan Rd., Chicago, IL 60626
Phone: 773-274-3000 **Fax:** 312-915-6455
Web: www.luc.edu

PRODUCTS/OPERATIONS

Selected Schools and Colleges

College of Arts and Sciences
Graduate School of Business
Institute of Pastoral Studies
School of Business Administration
School of Communication
School of Continuing and Professional Studies
School of Education
School of Law
School of Nursing
School of Social Work
Stritch School of Medicine
The Graduate School

LPL Investment Holdings

LPL Investment is the holding company for LPL Financial (formerly Linsco/Private Ledger), one of the largest brokerage firms in the US. The company offers technology, training, infrastructure, and research, as well as stocks, bonds, mutual funds, annuities, insurance, and other investment products and services to more than 11,000 independent financial advisors at some 6,500 branch offices across the US. It doesn't sell its own investment products, but provides access to those of other firms. LPL provides similar services to about 750 community banks and credit unions across the US. It also performs clearing and custody services for large financial institutions.

The Private Trust Company, an affiliate of LPL, manages assets for high-net-worth individuals and their families.

LPL nearly doubled its roster of bank and credit union clients with its 2007 purchase of UVEST Financial Services. Later that year the company acquired three broker-dealers from Pacific Life: Mutual Service Corporation, Associated Financial Group, and Waterstone Financial Group — adding some 2,200 independent brokers to its network.

Private equity firms Hellman & Friedman and TPG Capital each own approximately 40% of LPL.

EXECUTIVES

Chairman and CEO: Mark S. Casady, age 48, $1,854,949 total compensation
Vice Chairman: James S. (Jim) Putnam, age 54
President and COO: Esther M. Stearns, age 48, $1,042,758 total compensation
CIO: Christopher F. (Chris) Feeney, age 47
EVP and Chief Accounting Officer: Thomas D. Lux, age 51
EVP Strategic Development: Stephen Langlois
EVP Wealth Management; CEO, Private Trust Company: Christopher Poch, age 47
EVP and Head of National Sales: Jonathan Eaton
EVP; Head, Registered Investment Advisor: Gary Gallagher
EVP Corporate Marketing: Kandis Bates
Managing Director, Human Capital: Denise Abood
Managing Director, Research: Burt White
Managing Director and CFO: Robert J. Moore, age 47, $604,223 total compensation
Managing Director, Chief Investment Officer, and Chief Economist: Lincoln Anderson
Managing Director; President, Independent Advisor Services: William E. (Bill) Dwyer, age 51, $712,778 total compensation
Managing Director, General Counsel, and Secretary: Stephanie L. Brown, age 56
Managing Director and Chief Compliance Officer, Independent Advisor Services: Joseph P. Tuorto, age 51

LOCATIONS

HQ: LPL Investment Holdings Inc.
One Beacon St., Fl. 22, Boston, MA 02108
Phone: 617-423-3644
Web: lplfinancial.lpl.com

PRODUCTS/OPERATIONS

2008 Sales

	$ mil.	% of total
Commissions	1,640.2	53
Advisory fees	830.5	27
Asset-based fees	352.3	11
Transaction & other fees	240.5	8
Interest income	34.5	1
Other	19.1	—
Total	**3,117.1**	**100**

COMPETITORS

Ameriprise
Bank of America
Charles Schwab
Citigroup
E*TRADE Financial
Edward Jones
FMR
Morgan Keegan
Raymond James Financial
TD Ameritrade

HISTORICAL FINANCIALS

Company Type: Private

Income Statement

FYE: December 31

	REVENUE ($ mil.)	NET INCOME ($ mil.)	NET PROFIT MARGIN	EMPLOYEES
12/08	3,117	—	—	2,800
12/07	2,718	—	—	2,621
12/06	1,740	—	—	2,200
12/05	1,407	—	—	1,200
12/04	1,157	—	—	—
Annual Growth	28.1%	—	—	32.6%

Revenue History

Lucasfilm Ltd.

The Force is definitely with Emperor George Lucas. With three of the 20 highest-grossing movies of all time, Lucasfilm is one of the most successful independent movie studios in the history of film. Owned by filmmaker George Lucas (the brains behind the Star Wars and Indiana Jones films), Lucasfilm's productions have won about 20 Academy Awards. Its most recent film is 2008's Indiana Jones and the Kingdom of the Crystal Skull (in partnership with Paramount); 1999's Episode I — The Phantom Menace is Lucasfilm's biggest money-maker, with a gross of more than $920 million worldwide. Other subsidiaries in the Lucas empire are responsible for licensing, special effects, and software. Lucasfilm was created in 1971.

Lucasfilm consists of LucasArts (video games), special-effects house Industrial Light & Magic (ILM), Skywalker Sound, Lucas Licensing (consumer products), Lucas Online (e-commerce, news, and information), and Lucasfilm Animation (digitally animated feature films and television productions). The divisions are all housed under one roof at the Letterman Digital Arts Center at the Presidio, a former Army base in San Francisco.

The company has a presence in Asia with its Lucasfilm Animation Singapore. The unit, which produces digital animation for movies, television, and games, is majority owned by Lucasfilm. The remainder is held by a Singapore state-led consortium.

While audiences flocked to see Indiana Jones and the Kingdom of the Crystal Skull in 2008, the movie received mixed reviews and only came in third place at the box office that summer (it was beat by the breakout hits Dark Knight and Iron Man).

The final sequel to the Star Wars series, Episode III — Revenge of the Sith, was a box office hit, earning a whopping $50 million in its first day of release. An all-new Star Wars: The Clone Wars animated adventure from Lucasfilm Animation premiered in the summer 2008. Later

that year Lucasfilm partnered with Warner Bros. and Turner Broadcasting System to produce the television series Star Wars: The Clone Wars, which premiered on Cartoon Network.

HISTORY

After attending film school at the University of Southern California, George Lucas started his career as a documentary filmmaker, chronicling the production of Francis Ford Coppola's Finian's Rainbow in 1968. The two men became fast friends and founded American Zoetrope in 1969, which two years later released Lucas' feature film debut, the science-fiction film THX 1138 (a full-length version of a student film he made at USC). The film flopped, and Coppola went into production on The Godfather. Lucas left American Zoetrope and created his own company, Lucasfilm, in 1971.

Two years later Lucas released American Graffiti through Universal Pictures (with some financial help from Coppola). The film was a smash hit; it raked in $115 million in the US and made him a millionaire before the age of 30. It also gave him the clout to try and get his most ambitious project off the ground, a space opera called Star Wars. Universal, frustrated with cost overruns on Graffiti, wanted no part of Lucas' seemingly ridiculous idea, so he went to 20th Century Fox, which agreed to finance the $10 million film. Lucas gave up his directing fee for a percentage of the box-office take and all merchandising rights. He created Industrial Light & Magic (ILM) and Sprocket Systems (later Skywalker Sound) in 1975 to produce the visual and sound effects needed for the film.

Star Wars cost about $12 million, and almost everyone involved was sure it would bomb. Released in 1977, the movie shattered every box-office record, and the merchandising rights Lucas obtained made him a multimillionaire. With his take from Star Wars, Lucas was able to finance the film's sequel, The Empire Strikes Back (1980), out of his own pocket, meaning he would receive most of the profits (it grossed more than $220 million domestically). Lucasfilm's next production was Raiders of the Lost Ark (1981), directed by Lucas' friend Steven Spielberg. It went on to gross more than $380 million worldwide.

The next year Lucas began developing the THX sound system in preparation for the 1983 release of the third Star Wars film, Return of the Jedi (which hauled in more than $260 million domestically). He also founded LucasArts in 1982 to develop video games. Lucasfilm completed Skywalker Ranch (a facility housing many of its various companies in Marin County, California) in the mid-1980s and filled out the decade with two Raiders sequels — Indiana Jones and the Temple of Doom (1984, $333 million worldwide) and Indiana Jones and the Last Crusade (1989, $495 million worldwide).

Lucasfilm reorganized in 1993 by spinning off LucasArts into a separate subsidiary. Lucasfilm won local government approval to build an $87 million film studio near Skywalker Ranch in 1996, and the following year it re-released the Star Wars Trilogy to theaters with new special effects in celebration of the 20th anniversary, adding another $250 million to its take. Anticipating the release of the first of three prequels to the Star Wars Trilogy, Lucasfilm started signing marketing agreements in 1998 (including deals with Hasbro and Pepsi) that resulted in advance licensing of nearly $3 billion.

Star Wars: Episode I — The Phantom Menace opened in May 1999 and has grossed about $920 million worldwide (it finished its initial run second only to Titanic). Later in 1999 Lucas announced plans to develop a $250 million digital arts center at the old Presidio army base in San Francisco to house ILM, LucasArts, Lucas Online, Lucas Licensing, THX, and the George Lucas Educational Foundation (completed in 2005).

In 2002 Lucas spun off digital sound systems firm THX as an independent company. The next film in the Star Wars series, Episode II — Attack of the Clones, also opened that year. The following year the company formed its Lucasfilm Animation unit to create digitally animated feature films and television productions. The 2003 release of Lucasfilm's The Adventures of Indiana Jones: The Complete DVD Movie Collection made record-breaking sales.

The company hit gold again with the DVD release of the Star Wars Trilogy in 2004. In 2005 Lucasfilm released the third Star Wars movie, Episode III — Revenge of the Sith. Also that year the company opened its Letterman Digital Arts Center at the Presidio.

In 2008 Lucasfilm released the fourth film in the Indiana Jones series, Indiana Jones and the Kingdom of the Crystal Skull.

EXECUTIVES

Chairman: George W. Lucas Jr.
President and COO: Micheline (Mich) Chau, age 56
CTO: Richard Kerris
Chief Administrative Officer: Jan van der Voort
VP and General Manager, Skywalker Sound:
Glenn Kiser
VP and General Manager, Lucasfilm Animation:
Gail Currey
VP Finance and Chief Accounting Officer:
Steve Condiotti
President, Industrial Light and Magic: Chrissie England
President, LucasArts: Darrell Rodriguez
President, Lucas Licensing: Howard Roffman
General Counsel: David J. Anderman
Director Content Management Marketing and Head of Fan Relations: Steve Sansweet
Director Communications: Lynne Hale

LOCATIONS

HQ: Lucasfilm Ltd.
1110 Gorgas Ave., San Francisco, CA 94129
Phone: 415-662-1800
Web: www.lucasfilm.com

PRODUCTS/OPERATIONS

Selected Productions

American Graffiti (1973)
Howard the Duck (1986)
Indiana Jones and the Kingdom of the Crystal Skull (2008)
Indiana Jones and the Last Crusade (1989)
Indiana Jones and the Raiders of the Lost Ark (1981)
Indiana Jones and the Temple of Doom (1984)
Labyrinth (1986)
More American Graffiti (1979)
Radioland Murders (1994)
Raiders of the Lost Ark (1981)
Star Wars: Episode I — The Phantom Menace (1999)
Star Wars: Episode II — Attack of the Clones (2002)
Star Wars: Episode III — Revenge of the Sith (2005)
Star Wars: Episode IV — A New Hope (1977)
Star Wars: Episode V — The Empire Strikes Back (1980)
Star Wars: Episode VI — Return of the Jedi (1983)
Star Wars: The Clone Wars (2008)
Tucker: The Man and His Dream (1988)
Willow (1988)
The Young Indiana Jones Chronicles (1992-96, TV movies)

MA Laboratories

If you need a computer part, just ask your MA. Distributor MA Laboratories provides computer resellers and systems integrators with more than 5,000 computer-related products. MA Labs specializes in memory modules, but it supplies just about everything commonly found in or near a computer, including hard drives, motherboards, modems, power supplies, and graphics cards. Other products include monitors, software, GPS systems, network cards, digital cameras, notebook computers, wireless networking gear, digital music players, and accessories. MA Labs was founded in 1983 by owner and CEO Abraham Ma.

MA counts leading technology vendors such as 3Com, Advanced Micro Devices, Hewlett-Packard, IBM, Intel, Microsoft, Sony, and Toshiba among its suppliers.

The company is one of the largest privately held companies in the Bay Area.

EXECUTIVES

President and CEO: Abraham Ma
MIS Manager: Michael Ma
Business Development: Patrick Lai

LOCATIONS

HQ: MA Laboratories, Inc.
2075 N. Capitol Ave., San Jose, CA 95132
Phone: 408-941-0808   **Fax:** 408-941-0909
Web: www.malabs.com

PRODUCTS/OPERATIONS

Selected Products

CD and DVD drives
Computer components
Data storage
Digital cameras
Hard drives
Input/output cards
Memory
Modems
Monitors
Motherboards
Multimedia devices
Networking
Notebook computers and accessories
Printers
Processors
Software
Video cards

HISTORICAL FINANCIALS

Company Type: Private

Income Statement

FYE: December 31

	REVENUE ($ mil.)	NET INCOME ($ mil.)	NET PROFIT MARGIN	EMPLOYEES
12/07	2,000	—	—	1,200
12/06	1,500	—	—	1,000
12/05	1,200	—	—	600
Annual Growth	29.1%	—	—	41.4%

Revenue History

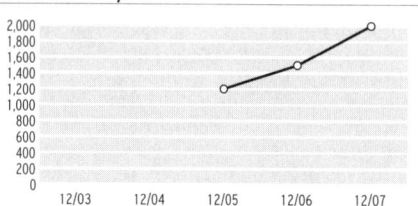

M. A. Mortenson

M. A. Mortenson Company is leaving its footprints all over the country. One of the largest builders in the US, with operations in 48 states, its design/build projects include the FedExForum, home of the NBA's Memphis Grizzlies, and the Walt Disney Concert Hall, home of the Los Angeles Philharmonic Orchestra. Besides its company projects group, Mortenson also has operations in biofuels and energy construction, targeting the growing renewable energy sector with projects including wind farms and biofuel facilities. Other construction ranges from real estate development to health care and government facilities. The family-owned company was founded in 1954 by M. A. Mortenson Sr., whose son now serves as chairman.

Its Mortenson China subsidiary, which was established in 2003, acts as a bridge between the West and East, facilitating the building process for western companies that are adding plants and operations in China. A recent project in the country includes building 150 learning centers for Disney, as the iconic company strives to provide English education in China.

EXECUTIVES

Chairman: M. A. Mortenson Jr.
President and CEO: Thomas F. (Tom) Gunkel
COO: Daniel L. (Dan) Johnson
Chief Investment Officer and Corporate Secretary:
 Mark A. Mortenson
EVP: David C. Mortenson

SVP and CFO: Sandra Sponem
SVP: John V. Wood
SVP: Thomas W. (Tom) Wacker
SVP: Paul I. Cossette
SVP Operations: Bradley C. (Brad) Funk
SVP: Robert J. Nartonis
SVP Administration: Paul V. Campbell
VP and General Manager: Timothy L. Maag
VP Project Development: Jerry Grundtner
VP Business Development: Patrick A. Burns
VP Controller and Chief Accounting Officer:
 William Patt
VP and Treasurer: Jennifer Facciani
VP and CIO: Cole Orndorff
VP Human Resources: Daniel R. (Dan) Haag
Auditors: Deloitte & Touche LLP

LOCATIONS

HQ: M. A. Mortenson Company
700 Meadow Ln. North, Minneapolis, MN 55422
Phone: 763-522-2100   **Fax:** 763-287-5430
Web: www.mortenson.com

PRODUCTS/OPERATIONS

Selected Services

Construction management
Design/build delivery
Engineering, procurement, and construction (EPC)
General contracting
Maintenance and operations
Planning
Preconstruction services
Program management
Project development
Turnkey construction

HISTORICAL FINANCIALS

Company Type: Private

Income Statement

FYE: December 31

	REVENUE ($ mil.)	NET INCOME ($ mil.)	NET PROFIT MARGIN	EMPLOYEES
12/08	2,684	—	—	2,200

MacAndrews & Forbes

Through MacAndrews & Forbes Holdings, financier Ron Perelman is focused on cosmetics and cash. The holding company has investments in an array of public and private firms, most notably cosmetics giant Revlon and M&F Worldwide, which deals in licorice flavors and financial products. It also has an influential role in entertainment, with significant stakes in Panavision, the top provider of cameras for movies and TV shows, and Deluxe Entertainment Services Group, the largest processor of motion picture film. MacAndrews & Forbes' other holdings include biotech firm SIGA Technologies, lottery system and gaming developer Scientific Games, and AM General, maker of Humvee and HUMMER vehicles.

Perelman is intent on reversing the fortunes of Revlon, which he has controlled since 1985. The company in 2009 boosted its holding in the cosmetics maker from about 60% to 80%.

Adding more companies to the mix, MacAndrews & Forbes acquired the data management business of Pearson for $225 million in 2008. As part of the agreement, the business is operated by MacAndrews & Forbes' Scantron testing unit. The data management business deal follows the company's 2007 acquisition of John H. Harland for nearly $2 billion, which was paired with its Clarke American unit.

Also in 2008 MacAndrews and Forbes unloaded its security services assets. It struck a deal with private equity firm Blackstone Group to take over its Allied Security business for $750 million.

HISTORY

Ron Perelman grew up working in his father's Philadelphia-based conglomerate, Belmont Industries, but he left at the age of 35 to seek his fortune in New York. In 1978 he bought 40% of jewelry store operator Cohen-Hatfield Industries. The next year Cohen-Hatfield bought a minority stake in MacAndrews & Forbes (licorice flavoring). Cohen-Hatfield acquired MacAndrews & Forbes in 1980.

In 1984 Perelman reshuffled his assets to create MacAndrews & Forbes Holdings, which acquired control of Pantry Pride, a Florida-based supermarket chain, in 1985. Pantry Pride then bought Revlon for $1.8 billion with the help of (convicted felon) Michael Milken. After Perelman acquired Revlon, he added several other cosmetics vendors, including Max Factor and Yves Saint Laurent's fragrance and cosmetic lines.

In 1988 MacAndrews & Forbes agreed to invest $315 million in five failing Texas savings and loans (S&Ls), which Perelman combined and named First Gibraltar (sold to BankAmerica, now Bank of America, in 1993). The next year MacAndrews & Forbes bought The Coleman Company, a maker of outdoor equipment.

With a growing reputation for buying struggling companies, revamping them, and then selling them at a higher price, Perelman bought Marvel Entertainment Group (Marvel Comics) in 1989 and took it public in 1991. That year he sold Revlon's Max Factor and Betrix units to Procter & Gamble for more than $1 billion.

MacAndrews & Forbes acquired 38% of TV infomercial producer Guthy-Renker and SCI Television's seven stations and merged them to create New World Television. That company was combined with TV syndicator Genesis Entertainment and TV production house New World Entertainment to create New World Communications Group, which Perelman took public in 1994. That year MacAndrews & Forbes and partner Gerald J. Ford bought Ford Motor's First Nationwide, the US's fifth-largest S&L at that time.

Subsidiaries Mafco Worldwide and Consolidated Cigar Holdings merged with Abex (aircraft parts) to create Mafco Consolidated Group in 1995. Following diminishing comic sales, Perelman placed Marvel in bankruptcy in 1996 and subsequently lost control of the company.

In 1997 First Nationwide bought California thrift Cal Fed Bancorp for $1.2 billion. In addition, Perelman sold New World to Rupert Murdoch's News Corp.

The next year Perelman orchestrated a $1.8 billion deal in which First Nationwide merged with Golden State Bancorp to form the US's third-largest thrift. Sunbeam Corp. (now American Household) bought Perelman's stake in Coleman that year, making Perelman a major American Household shareholder. Also in 1998 MacAndrews & Forbes bought a 72% stake in Panavision (movie camera maker, later increased to 91%), invested in WeddingChannel.com, and sold its 64% stake in Consolidated Cigar to French tobacco giant Seita (netting Perelman a smoking $350 million profit).

Still burdened by debt, Revlon sold its professional products business in 2000.

Perelman's stock in American Household was rendered worthless when the company initiated bankruptcy proceedings in February 2001. (It would emerge from bankruptcy, however, in December 2002.) He also was sued by angry shareholders after the board of M&F Worldwide, the licorice company he controls, bought Perelman's stock in Panavision at more than five times its market value. In order to settle the litigation surrounding the purchase, in 2002 M&F agreed to return Perelman's 83% stake in Panavision to Mafco. Golden State Bancorp also left the MacAndrews fold in 2002 when it was acquired by Citigroup.

MacAndrews & Forbes Holdings acquired Allied Security, the largest independent provider of contract security services and products in the US, from Gryphon Investors in February 2003 for an undisclosed sum.

Perelman's sale of The Coleman Company — in the late 1990s — helped the investor improve his cash flow later on. In his suit against Morgan Stanley, Perelman alleged that the investment bank withheld its knowledge of Sunbeam's accounting fraud when Perelman sold The Coleman Company to Sunbeam in 1998 for about $1.5 billion. Perelman's investment (he held 14.1 million shares of Sunbeam stock as part of the sale) later tanked as news broke of the accounting irregularities. Despite an attempt to settle the dispute with Morgan Stanley in 2003 for $20 million, Perelman took the bank to court and was awarded more than $1.5 billion in damages by a Florida jury in mid-2005.

It bought Deluxe Entertainment Services Group from The Rank Group for some $750 million in 2006. The purchase complements its majority stake in Panavision, the top provider of cameras for shooting movies and TV shows.

The firm sold WeddingChannel.com to The Knot in late 2006.

MacArthur Foundation

Granted, The John D. and Catherine T. MacArthur Foundation gives away a lot of money. With some $5.3 billion in assets, the private foundation issues more than $250 million in grants annually to groups and individuals working to improve the human condition. Its two primary programs are Human and Community Development (affordable housing, education reform, mental health) and Global Security and Sustainability (world peace, population reduction, conservation, human rights). The foundation also funds special initiatives and awards $500,000 MacArthur Fellowships to a variety of individuals. Since making its first grant in 1978, The John D. and Catherine T. MacArthur Foundation has distributed about $4 billion.

The John D. and Catherine T. MacArthur Foundation was established in 1978 after the death of billionaire John D. MacArthur. The foundation supports projects worldwide. Along with such organizations as The Rockefeller Foundation and The Andrew W. Mellon Foundation, it is a member of The Partnership for Higher Education in Africa.

Robert Gallucci, a career US diplomat and dean of Georgetown University's School of Foreign Service, was tapped to lead the foundation as president in July 2009. He succeeds the retiring Jonathan F. Fanton. The organization chose Gallucci for his experience in international affairs and decision-making ability.

HISTORY

The John D. and Catherine T. MacArthur Foundation was established by an eccentric billionaire who enjoyed making money more than spending it. MacArthur, one of the three richest men in the US at the time of his death, made a fortune after he bought Bankers Life and Casualty Company of Chicago and sold mail-order insurance at the end of the Depression. He later became the largest landowner in Florida.

To avoid paying taxes, MacArthur used most of his $2.5 billion estate to establish a foundation named after himself and his second wife. After MacArthur's death in 1978, the foundation's board of trustees found no guidelines other than a brief statement: "I figured out how to make the money; you fellows will have to figure out how to spend it."

Soon after the foundation began making fellowship awards, it became known as one of the more eccentric of large US foundations. Its MacArthur Fellows program provides so-called "genius-grants" ($500,000 paid out over five years); recipients have included a cartoonist and a rare-books binder. Critics argue that such money might be better spent on other programs.

In 1997 the foundation reorganized under two integrated programs — Human and Community Development and Global Security and Sus-

tainability — in an effort to unify its grant-making. It diversified its holdings in 1998 by selling nearly 15,000 acres of land in Florida. The following year Adele Simmons stepped down as president after a decade with the foundation; she was replaced by Jonathan Fanton, former president of the New York City-based New School for Social Research.

EXECUTIVES

Chairman and Director: Robert E. Denham, age 64
President: Robert L. Gallucci, age 63
VP and CFO: Marc P. Yanchura
CIO: Sharon Burns
VP General Program: Elspeth A. Revere
VP, General Counsel, and Assistant Secretary: Joshua J. Mintz
VP Program on Global Security and Sustainability: Barry F. Lowenkron
VP and Chief Investment Officer: Susan E. Manske
VP Public Affairs: Andrew Solomon
VP: Arthur M. Sussman
VP Program on Human and Community Development: Julia M. Stasch
Secretary: Elizabeth T. Kane
Director Finance and Tax: George B. Ptacin
Senior Advisor to the President: William E. Lowry
Associate VP Institutional Research and Grants Management: Richard J. Kaplan
Auditors: KPMG LLP

LOCATIONS

HQ: The John D. and Catherine T. MacArthur Foundation
140 S. Dearborn St., Ste. 1200, Chicago, IL 60603
Phone: 312-726-8000   **Fax:** 312-920-6258
Web: www.macfound.org

PRODUCTS/OPERATIONS

2008 Grants

	$ mil.	% of total
Global security & sustainability	101.3	40
Human & community development	89.4	35
General program	52.5	20
MacArthur Fellows program	12.3	5
Total	**255.5**	**100**

HISTORICAL FINANCIALS

Company Type: Foundation

Income Statement

FYE: December 31

	REVENUE ($ mil.)	NET INCOME ($ mil.)	NET PROFIT MARGIN	EMPLOYEES
12/08	53	(2,120)	—	173
12/07	662	—	—	173
Annual Growth	(92.0%)	—	—	0.0%

Revenue History

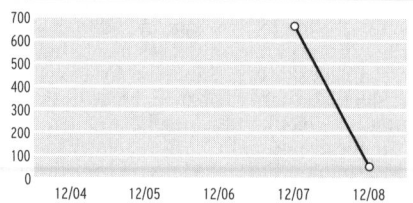

Main Street America

Who's your main insurance man? The Main Street America Group provides a range of personal and commercial property/casualty products including coverage for small and midsized businesses and individual auto and homeowners insurance plans. The company operates through its flagship subsidiary NGM Insurance, as well as its Old Dominion Insurance, MSA Insurance, and Main Street America Assurance businesses. Its Information Systems and Services Corporation offers third-party administration services such as broker management, policy processing, and underwriting services. Main Street America sells its products through more than 1,300 independent agents, primarily along the East Coast.

The company started out as National Grange Mutual Insurance in 1923 in New Hampshire. Since that time the company has expanded, and in 2005 it changed its corporate structure to that of a mutual insurance holding company.

Aiming to become a super-regional company, the company has expanded beyond its East Coast origins. In 2008 the firm entered the Michigan auto insurance market by acquiring Great Lakes Casualty Insurance.

Main Street America operates in about 20 states; primary markets include Connecticut, Florida, Massachusetts, New York, Pennsylvania, and Virginia.

The company also is expanding through new product offerings. Personal Auto MVP, a product offering multi-variable auto products, was launched in 2007. It also plans to expand its business owners' and commercial auto offerings.

EXECUTIVES

Chairman, President, and CEO: Thomas M. Van Berkel
EVP, CFO, and Treasurer: Edward J. (Ed) Kuhl
SVP Field Operations: Doug Eden
SVP Insurance Operations: Bill Anderson
SVP, General Counsel, and Secretary: Susan E. Mack
SVP Human Resources: Antonia (Toni) Porterfield
VP Claims: Mike Lancashire
VP Information Technology and CIO: Ron James
VP Internal Audit: Geof Molina
VP Commercial Lines: Henry Pippins
Regional President, New England: Steve Berry
VP and Chief Actuary: Ed Lotkowski
Auditors: Ernst & Young LLP

LOCATIONS

HQ: The Main Street America Group
4601 Touchton Rd., East, Ste. 3400
Jacksonville, FL 32246
Phone: 904-380-7281   **Fax:** 904-380-7244
Web: www.msagroup.com

PRODUCTS/OPERATIONS

2007 Written Premiums

	% of total
Commercial multiple peril	32
Private passenger auto	25
Commercial auto	14
Homeowners	13
Other lines	16
Total	**100**

COMPETITORS

ACE Limited
AIG
Allstate
American Family Insurance
American Financial Group
Arrowpoint Capital Corp.
Cincinnati Financial
Farmers Group
Fireman's Fund Insurance
GEICO
The Hartford
Liberty Mutual
Progressive Corporation
Prudential
Safeco
State Farm
Travelers Companies

MAINES Paper & Food Service

A lot of restaurants look to this main middle man to get their supplies. MAINES Paper & Food Service is a leading foodservice supplier in the US with about 10 distribution centers serving customers in more than 35 states. Stretching from the eastern seaboard to the upper Midwest, the company's distribution network supplies a wide range of products including fresh produce and meat products, dry goods, and beverages, as well as janitorial supplies, kitchen equipment, and food packaging. MAINES supplies both fast-food and casual dining establishments, convenience stores, schools, and other institutional foodservice operators. Floyd Maines started the family-owned business in 1919.

Like other wholesale supply operations, MAINES competes for business based on its ability to delivery quality products at the lowest possible cost. It operates in a highly fragmented business, meaning it faces competition from a wide range of local and regional suppliers as well as from national giants such as SYSCO, U.S. Foodservice, and Performance Food Group. Among its largest customers, MAINES supplies many Burger King locations.

Expanding its roster of customers, MAINES inked a deal in 2008 to become the primary supplier of Boston Market restaurants through a five-year partnership. It also started supplying more than 90 Applebee's locations operated by franchisee Thomas & King that same year.

In addition to its distribution network, MAINES operates four cash & carry locations under the name MaineSource Food & Party Warehouse. The outlets are located mostly in Eastern Pennsylvania and in Syracuse, New York.

EXECUTIVES

Co-Chairman: William R. (Bill) Maines
Co-Chairman: David J. Maines
President and CEO: Christopher (Chris) Mellon
COO: Terry Walsh
VP, MaineSource Food & Party Warehouse: Steve Ross
VP Human Resources: Stephanie Wyatt
VP Decision Support: Bill Kimler
VP National Accounts: Bill Savier
President, Corporate Park: Patrick (Pat) Lappin
Division President, Oakwood Facility: Dennis Kee
Division President, Farmingdale Facility:
 Mark Eisenberg
Division President, New England Facility: Mike DiLarso

LOCATIONS

HQ: MAINES Paper & Food Service Inc.
 101 Broome Corporate Pkwy., Conklin, NY 13748
Phone: 607-779-1200
Web: www.maines.net

COMPETITORS

Agar Supply
Ben E. Keith
Clark National
Gordon Food Service
Institution Food House
Jetro Cash & Carry
McLane Foodservice
Meadowbrook Meat
Performance Food
Reinhart FoodService
Services Group of America
SYSCO
UniPro Foodservice
U.S. Foodservice

HISTORICAL FINANCIALS

Company Type: Private

Income Statement

FYE: December 31

	REVENUE ($ mil.)	NET INCOME ($ mil.)	NET PROFIT MARGIN	EMPLOYEES
12/08	3,000	—	—	2,000
12/07	2,400	—	—	2,000
12/06	2,020	—	—	1,950
12/05	1,950	—	—	1,950
Annual Growth	15.4%	—	—	0.8%

Revenue History

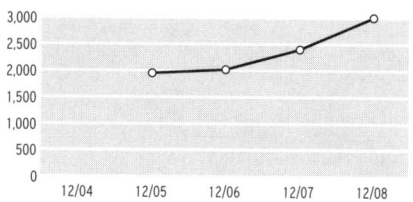

Major League Baseball

It may be the national pastime, but Major League Baseball (MLB) is also a big business. MLB runs the game of professional baseball and oversees 30 franchises in 28 cities. Each team operates as a separate business, but each is regulated and governed by MLB. The league sets official rules, regulates team ownership, and collects licensing fees for merchandise. It also sells national broadcasting rights and distributes fees to the teams. (Regional broadcast rights are held by each franchise.) MLB was formed when the rival National and American Leagues joined together in 1903.

Professional baseball has been riding a wave of renewed popularity and financial stability. A big reason for MLB's growth has been the increasing parity between teams, a result of the collective bargaining agreement (CBA) between the league and the MLB Players Association that enforces a luxury tax on teams with higher payrolls. Shifting some money from large market teams such as the New York Yankees and Boston Red Sox to the smaller markets has helped such franchises as the Milwaukee Brewers and Colorado Rockies remain competitive, ensuring higher ticket sales all around. (Renewed in 2006, the CBA remains in effect through 2011.)

MLB has also done a good job translating the nationwide popularity of baseball into revenue through broadcasting rights agreements. The league reached a new seven-year TV deal with FOX Broadcasting in 2006 worth $1.8 billion for a slate of regular-season games, one League Championship Series, and the World Series. TBS, a unit of Time Warner's Turner Broadcasting cable TV arm, also entered into separate seven-year deals worth a total of about $850 million to show baseball's other LCS and all the Division Series playoff games, along with more than 25 regular season contests. (Walt Disney's ESPN, meanwhile, kicked off an eight-year, $2.4 billion rights deal for regular-season games in 2006.)

The league's interactive media arm, MLB Advanced Media, has borne fruit in the form of subscription-based Internet audio and video broadcasts of out-of-market games. MLB also launched The MLB Network early in 2009. The new broadcast offering, a joint venture with cable and satellite operators Comcast, Cox Communications, DIRECTV, and Time Warner Cable, features subscription access to out-of-market games, along with news and other baseball programming.

MLB still faces the challenge posed by performance-enhancing drugs. An independent commission led by former Senator George Mitchell investigated the problem during 2007 and issued a report at the end of that year recommending a number of steps MLB should take to eliminate the use of steroids and other drugs. (The league has adopted some testing measures, but it has yet to find a suitable test for use of human growth hormones.)

Baseball owners awarded a three-year contract extension to commissioner Bud Selig in 2008 that will keep him in office through the 2012 season. He had announced plans to retire in 2009.

HISTORY

The first baseball team to field professional players was the Cincinnati Red Stockings (now the Cincinnati Reds) in 1869. Teams in Boston, New York City, and Philadelphia followed suit. In 1876 eight professional teams formed the National League. Competing leagues sprang up and folded, but Ban Johnson's Western League (formed in 1892) seized on territory abandoned by the National League in 1900 and began luring National League players with higher salaries. Renamed the American League, it also began drawing away fans. The two leagues agreed to join forces in 1903 by having their champions meet in the World Series.

The sport flourished until the "Black Sox" scandal of 1919, in which eight Chicago White Sox players were accused of taking bribes to throw the World Series. The owners hired Judge Kenesaw Mountain Landis as baseball's first commissioner in 1921 to clean up the game's image. He served until his death in 1944. A joint committee of owners and players introduced more reforms in 1947, including a player pension fund.

The players formed the Major League Baseball Players' Association (MLBPA) in 1954 and signed the first collective-bargaining agreement with the owners in 1968. The players called their first strike in 1972, a 13-day walkout that won an improved pension plan. They won the right to free agency in 1976; another seven-week strike interrupted the 1981 season.

Salary increases slowed, and the free agent market dried up in the mid-1980s, prompting the MLBPA to sue the owners for collusion. The owners agreed to a settlement of $280 million in 1990. Commissioner Fay Vincent resigned in 1992 after the owners effectively removed all power from the commissioner's office. An executive council of owners led by Milwaukee Brewers owner Bud Selig took control.

Prompted by the owners' decision to unilaterally restrict free agency and withdraw salary arbitration, the players started a 232-day strike in August 1994 that forced the cancellation of the World Series and stretched into the 1995 season. Revenue and income plummeted. Play resumed in 1995 when the owners and the MLBPA approved a new collective-bargaining agreement. Selig stepped down from the Brewers in 1998 to become the game's ninth commissioner.

Sweeping changes took place in 2000 when owners, who had voted the previous year to eliminate the American and National League offices (thus centralizing power with the commissioner's office), agreed to restore the "best interests of baseball" powers to the commissioner. This gave Selig full authority to redistribute wealth, block trades, and fine teams and players.

In 2004 Bob DuPuy was named president and COO of the league, replacing Paul Beeston, who resigned after talks over a new collective-bargaining agreement stalled. A new labor agreement was eventually reached in 2002, however, avoiding another players' strike. The new agreement enacted a luxury tax on teams with high payrolls, redistributing the money to small-market franchises.

Tokyo-based advertising giant Dentsu agreed to pay $275 million in 2003 for the right to broadcast MLB games in Japan. The following year MLB struck a $650 million broadcasting deal with XM Satellite Radio. Allegations about the use of performance enhancing drugs began to dominate the headlines in 2004 following a grand jury investigation of a California pharmaceuticals company. The flap over steroid use led to MLB implementing a tougher drug testing policy in 2005.

EXECUTIVES

Commissioner: Allan H. (Bud) Selig, age 75
President and COO: Robert A. (Bob) DuPuy, age 61
EVP Administration and CIO: John McHale Jr.
SVP Advertising and Marketing, and Chief Marketing Officer: Jacqueline Parkes
EVP Labor Relations and Human Resources: Robert D. (Rob) Manfred Jr.
EVP Business: Timothy J. (Tim) Brosnan
EVP Baseball Operations: Jimmie Lee Solomon
EVP Finance and CFO: Jonathan D. Mariner, age 54
SVP and General Counsel, Legal Business Affairs: Ethan Orlinsky
SVP Finance: Kathleen Torres
SVP Special Events: Marla Miller
SVP and General Counsel, BOC: Thomas J. (Tom) Ostertag
SVP Scheduling and Club Relations: Katy Feeney
SVP Media Relations: Richard (Rich) Levin
SVP Licensing: Howard Smith
SVP Club Relations: Phyllis Merhige
SVP Baseball Operations: Joe Garagiola Jr.
SVP Broadcasting: Chris Tully
SVP Corporate Sales and Marketing: John S. Brody
SVP International Business Operations: Paul Archey
VP Human Resources: Ray Scott
VP Public Relations: Patrick (Pat) Courtney
CEO, MLB Network: Anthony (Tony) Petitti
CEO, MLB Advanced Media: Robert A. (Bob) Bowman, age 54
Auditors: Deloitte & Touche LLP

LOCATIONS

HQ: Major League Baseball
245 Park Ave., 31st Fl., New York, NY 10167
Phone: 212-931-7800   **Fax:** 212-949-8636
Web: www.mlb.com

PRODUCTS/OPERATIONS

Major League Franchises

American League
Baltimore Orioles (1954)
    St. Louis Browns (1902)
    Milwaukee Brewers (1901)
Boston Red Sox (1901)
Chicago White Sox (1901)
Cleveland Indians (1915)
    Cleveland Spiders (1889)
Detroit Tigers (1900)
Kansas City Royals (1969, Missouri)
Los Angeles Angels of Anaheim (2005)
    Anaheim Angels (1965, California)
    Los Angeles Angels (1961)
Minnesota Twins (1961, Minneapolis)
    Washington Senators (1901; Washington, DC)
New York Yankees (1913, New York City)
    New York Highlanders (1903, New York City)
    Baltimore Orioles (1901)
Oakland Athletics (1968, California)
    Kansas City Athletics (1955, Missouri)
    Philadelphia Athletics (1901)
Seattle Mariners (1977)
Tampa Bay Rays (2007)
    Tampa Bay Devil Rays (1998)
Texas Rangers (1972, Arlington)
    Washington Senators (1961; Washington, DC)
Toronto Blue Jays (1977)

National League
Arizona Diamondbacks (1998, Phoenix)
Atlanta Braves (1966)
    Milwaukee Braves (1953)
    Boston Braves (1912)
    Boston Beaneaters (1883)
    Boston Red Stockings (1871)
Chicago Cubs (1903)
    Chicago Orphans (1898)
    Chicago Colts (1894)
    Chicago White Stockings (1871)
Cincinnati Reds (1866)
Colorado Rockies (1993, Denver)
Florida Marlins (1993, Miami)
Houston Astros (1964)
    Houston Colt .45s (1962)
Los Angeles Dodgers (1958)
    Brooklyn Dodgers (1890, New York)
Milwaukee Brewers (1970; switched from American League, 1998)
    Seattle Pilots (1969)
New York Mets (1962, New York City)
Philadelphia Phillies (1883)
Pittsburgh Pirates (1887)
St. Louis Cardinals (1900)
    St. Louis Brown Stockings (1882)
San Diego Padres (1969)
San Francisco Giants (1958)
    New York Giants (1883, New York City)
Washington Nationals (2004, Washington, DC)
    Montreal Expos (1969)

COMPETITORS

FIFA
Indy Racing League
Major League Soccer
NASCAR
NBA
NFL
NHL
PGA
PGA TOUR
World Wrestling Entertainment

HISTORICAL FINANCIALS

Company Type: Association

Income Statement				FYE: October 31
	REVENUE ($ mil.)	NET INCOME ($ mil.)	NET PROFIT MARGIN	EMPLOYEES
10/08	6,500	—	—	—
10/07	6,100	—	—	—
10/06	5,200	—	—	—
10/05	4,800	—	—	—
10/04	4,100	—	—	—
Annual Growth	12.2%	—	—	—

Revenue History

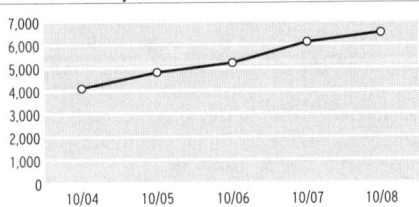

Manor Care

Manor Care is a lord of the manor in the nursing home kingdom. Operating as HCR Manor Care, the firm runs about 500 nursing homes, assisted living centers, and rehabilitation facilities in about 30 states. Its facilities, which operate under the names Heartland, ManorCare Health Services, and Arden Courts, provide not only long-term nursing care, but also rehabilitation services and short-term, post-acute care for patients recovering from serious illness or injury; many of them house special units for Alzheimer's patients. In addition to its nursing and assisted-living facilities, Manor Care offers hospice and home health care through offices across the US. It is owned by private equity firm The Carlyle Group.

Over the objections of the Service Employees International Union and some lawmakers, The Carlyle Group took Manor Care private in late 2007, in a deal worth about $6.3 billion.

In addition to its long-term care, hospice, and home health operations, Manor Care provides rehabilitation therapy at its own outpatient clinics, as well as third-party sites, such as schools, workplaces, and hospitals.

Manor Care gets most of its long-term care revenue from Medicare and Medicaid. In response to falling reimbursement rates, the company has shifted its focus to seeking out patients who require more complex care (over a shorter period of time) that is reimbursed at higher levels. This shift in patient mix has resulted in the growth of its post-acute business, which cares for patients recovering from chronic illness, serious injury, or surgery.

Manor Care also contracts with more than 200 managed care organizations nationally for providing post-hospital rehabilitation services.

The company continues to expand, investing more than $100 million in new construction, renovation, and expansions annually between 2006 and 2009.

HISTORY

The new Manor Care has its roots in an Ohio lumber company bought by the Wolfe family in the mid-1940s. Over the next two decades the business diversified into mortgages and real estate development. By 1975 the company (by then renamed Wolfe Industries) had begun acquiring nursing homes.

In 1981 Wolfe spun off its non-nursing home interests and created Health Care and Retirement Corporation of America (HCR) from what remained. HCR went public that year and continued making acquisitions.

Looking to diversify, glass and plastics maker Owens-Illinois bought HCR in 1984 and later added other health care operations, including long-term skilled nursing care, rehabilitation, and specialty care services. Owens-Illinois was taken private in a Kohlberg Kravis Roberts leveraged buyout in 1987; in 1991 HCR and related health care operations were sold to a group led by Paul Ormond, who had headed Owens-Illinois' health care business since 1986. Ormond took HCR public again that year.

HCR's acquisition strategy expanded to include partnerships and other ventures, as well as the opening of specialty units and the construction and development of new facilities. Under Ormond, HCR concentrated on attracting Medicare

and private-pay patients, who were more profitable than Medicaid (i.e., public aid) patients.

As part of the effort to diversify beyond nursing homes, HCR in the 1990s added vision care (forming Vision Management Services to provide financing and management for eye-related medical practices, 1991), short-term rehabilitation, home health care (Heartland Home Health Services, 1991; enlarged through the acquisition of Allan Home Health Care and Hospice, 1995), and pharmacy services (through a joint venture to supply nursing homes, 1994).

In 1997 the company acquired MileStone Healthcare, a top provider of program management services for subacute care and acute rehabilitation programs. But it was still not enough. The company's 1998 purchase of larger rival Manor Care more than doubled its size, although related costs hammered earnings.

The next year the company took the more widely recognized Manor Care name. It partnered with Alterra Healthcare (formerly Alternative Living Services) to build and operate Alzheimer's and assisted-living residences and to provide management services for about 30 assisted-living and Alzheimer's care residences located outside Manor Care's core operating areas.

Also in 1999 Manor Care was hit with a suit by Genesis Health Ventures, claiming that it had bought Vitalink, a nursing home pharmacy services company, from Manor Care with the understanding that service contracts with Manor Care homes would remain in effect for several years (the new Manor Care terminated the contracts soon after the merger). The company also faced regulatory and legal actions in several states over infractions of patient care rules.

In 2000 Manor Care nixed separate buyout bids led by chairman Stewart Bainum and another management group. It also bought the percentage of In Home Health (a home health care provider) that it didn't already own and absorbed the firm into its own operations. That year the company opened 10 new Alzheimer's assisted living centers.

The Carlyle Group bought the company in 2007 with the understanding that its existing management team would stay on to continue operating the business.

EXECUTIVES

Chairman, President, and CEO: Paul A. Ormond, age 59
EVP and COO: Stephen L. Guillard, age 59
VP and Chief Medical Officer: Mark J. Gloth
VP and Treasurer: Matthew S. Kang
VP and General Counsel: Richard A. Parr II, age 50
VP Information Services: Murry J. Mercier
VP and CFO: Steven M. Cavanaugh, age 38
VP Human Resources: Steven D. Spencer
VP Reimbursement: Barry A. Lazarus
VP Procurement: R. Michael Ferguson
VP Clinical Services: Joyce L. Smith
VP and General Manager, Central Division:
 Nancy A. Edwards, age 58
VP Marketing: L. Martin Grabijas
VP and Controller: John I. Remenar
Auditors: Ernst & Young LLP

LOCATIONS

HQ: Manor Care, Inc.
 333 N. Summit St., Toledo, OH 43604
Phone: 419-252-5500   **Fax:** 419-252-5554
Web: www.hcr-manorcare.com

Manor Care operates more than 500 facilities in 32 states.

PRODUCTS/OPERATIONS

Selected Services
Assisted-living facilities
Dementia care
Home health care and hospice
Post-acute care
Outpatient rehabilitation centers
Skilled nursing care

COMPETITORS

Advocat	HCA
Almost Family	Kindred Healthcare
Amedisys	Life Care Centers
American HomePatient	National HealthCare
Assisted Living Concepts	Odyssey HealthCare
Covenant Care	Regency Nursing
Emeritus Corporation	Skilled Healthcare Group
Extendicare REIT	Sun Healthcare
Five Star Quality Care	Sunrise Senior Living
Genesis HealthCare	Tenet Healthcare
Gentiva	Ventas
Golden Horizons	VITAS Healthcare

HISTORICAL FINANCIALS

Company Type: Private

Income Statement

FYE: December 31

	ESTIMATED REVENUE ($ mil.)	NET INCOME ($ mil.)	NET PROFIT MARGIN	EMPLOYEES
12/08	4,130	—	—	60,000
12/07	3,890	—	—	61,700
Annual Growth	6.2%	—	—	(2.8%)

Revenue History

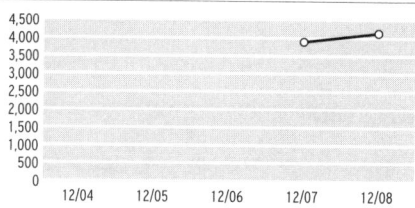

4,500				
4,000				
3,500				
3,000				
2,500				
2,000				
1,500				
1,000				
500				
0				
12/04	12/05	12/06	12/07	12/08

Mansfield Oil

Mansfield brings the oilfield to you. The fuel distribution company delivers more than 2 billion gallons of petroleum products every year to customers throughout the US, with the heaviest concentration east of the Mississippi. Customers include government agencies, resellers, and commercial and industrial users such as universities, airports, marinas, trucking firms, and retailers. Mansfield also sets up and maintains more than 600 retail locations and 900 supply locations. It also provides logistics, marketing support, and fuel equipment maintenance for its customers. The company was founded in 1957 by the Mansfield family; son Michael Mansfield is CEO.

Expanding its operations, in 2008 Mansfield bought the commercial and industrial business unit of TransMontaigne Product Services, a subsidiary of TransMontaigne.

In 2009 Mansfield boosted its renewables supply, acquiring C&N Companies, a leading marketer of ethanol.

EXECUTIVES

CEO: Michael F. Mansfield Sr.
President and COO: J. Alexander
EVP and CIO: Doug Haugh
EVP Operations: John Byrd
VP Midwest Marketing: Jim Stout
Director, Biofuels and Business Development:
  Bob Gray
Program Director: Mark Mixon

LOCATIONS

HQ: Mansfield Oil Company
  1025 Airport Pkwy. SW, Gainesville, GA 30501
Phone: 800-695-6626   **Fax:** 770-718-3053
Web: www.mansfieldoil.com

COMPETITORS

Center Oil
Colonial Group
Global Partners
Gulf Oil
SemGroup
Truman Arnold
U.S. Oil
World Fuel Services

HISTORICAL FINANCIALS

Company Type: Private

Income Statement			FYE: December 31	
	REVENUE ($ mil.)	NET INCOME ($ mil.)	NET PROFIT MARGIN	EMPLOYEES
12/08	5,100	—	—	—
12/07	5,100	—	—	285
12/06	2,652	—	—	226
12/05	2,100	—	—	220
Annual Growth	34.4%	—	—	13.8%

Revenue History

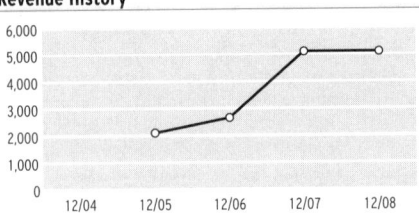

Marc Glassman

Marc Glassman is out to prove that low prices can lead to big things. The regional retailer operates about 60 discount stores, most of which are Marc's Deeper Discount Drug Stores in northeast Ohio, but also a half dozen Xpect Discount Drugs stores in Connecticut. The stores range in size from 18,000 sq. ft. to 48,000 sq. ft. More than 75% of the locations have pharmacies and offer a constantly changing mix of closeout and excess merchandise in some 20 categories, including clothing, cosmetics, housewares, toys, and tools. The company specializes in seasonal products (Christmas, Halloween, lawn and garden). Owner and chairman Marc Glassman founded the company in Middleburg Heights, Ohio, in 1979.

Despite competition from national giants Walgreen and CVS in the Cleveland market, Marc's has gained market share in recent years,

rising to 15% in 2007 up from 13% the previous year. To compete with the big chains and Wal-Mart, Marc's launched a low-price generic drug program in 2008 that sells a 3-day supply for $3.99 (a penny less than the big chains).

The chain also sells meat and produce in many of its stores, as well as other food items and pet products. It has been gradually expanding the amount of food in its merchandise mix over the past several years.

In late 2007 the firm began testing wall-to-wall carpet sales in several stores and later launched Marc's Carpet for Less kiosks in 25 stores in Ohio.

EXECUTIVES

Chairman: Marc Glassman
President: Kevin Yaugher
CFO: Beth Weiner
Human Resources Director: Shannon Oldenburgh

LOCATIONS

HQ: Marc Glassman, Inc.
  5841 W. 130th St., Parma, OH 44130
Phone: 216-265-7700   **Fax:** 216-265-7737
Web: www.marcs.com

2008 Stores	
	No.
Ohio	54
Connecticut	6
Total	**60**

COMPETITORS

ALDI
Big Lots
CVS Caremark
Discount Drug
Dollar General
Dollar Tree
Family Dollar Stores
Giant Eagle
Kmart
Medic Home Health Care
Medicine Shoppe
Rite Aid
Target
TOPS Markets
Walgreen
Wal-Mart

HISTORICAL FINANCIALS

Company Type: Private

Income Statement			FYE: December 31	
	ESTIMATED REVENUE ($ mil.)	NET INCOME ($ mil.)	NET PROFIT MARGIN	EMPLOYEES
12/07	1,130	—	—	6,850
12/06	1,060	—	—	6,850
Annual Growth	6.6%	—	—	0.0%

Revenue History

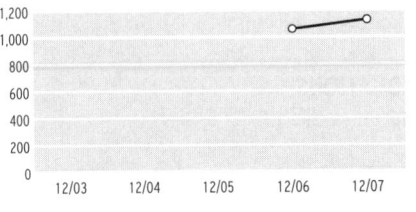

Maritz Inc.

Maritz may not *send* your employees on business trips, but it will still *motivate* them to go. The company designs employee incentive and reward programs (including incentive travel rewards) and customer loyalty programs, plans corporate trade shows and events, and also offers traditional market research services such as the creation of product launch campaigns. Its programs are designed to help its clients improve workforce quality and customer satisfaction. Subsidiaries and segments include Maritz Motivation, Maritz Research, Maritz Loyalty Marketing, and Maritz Travel.

One of Maritz's competitive strengths is its widely diversified customer base, which it hopes will make it less susceptible to regional or industry-specific economic downturns. Maritz owns offices in Canada, Germany, the UK, and the US. Its customers include a majority of the *Forbes* 500, including businesses residing in the automotive, financial services, health care, retail, pharmaceutical, telecommunications, and professional and business services industries.

Maritz expanded its product offerings and geographic reach in 2008 when it acquired Cascade Promotion Corporation, a marketing and fulfillment business operating out of Boston, Las Vegas, and St. Louis. With Cascade catering to the gaming and technology industries, the buyout also gave Maritz access to growing niche markets.

EXECUTIVES

Chairman and CEO: W. Stephen (Steve) Maritz, age 51
COO: Dennis Hummel
CFO: Rick Ramos
CIO: Gil Hoffman
Chief Sales Officer: William P. (Scott) Bush
Senior Executive, VP, and General Counsel:
  John Risberg
Senior Executive and VP Development: John McArthur
Chief Marketing Officer: Tim Rogers
VP and Group Executive, Maritz Learning and Maritz Research; President, Maritz Research:
  Michael Brereton, age 49
VP Research Division: Madhunika Raghavan
VP and Group Executive, Maritz Motivation and Maritz Loyalty Marketing; CEO, Maritz Motivation:
  Mike Donnelly
VP and Group Executive, Maritz Travel and Maritz Interactions; President, Maritz Travel: Christine Duffy
Group Executive; President, Maritz Learning:
  Brian Carlin
President, Maritz Interactions: Thom Casadonte

LOCATIONS

HQ: Maritz Inc.
  1375 N. Highway Dr., Fenton, MO 63099
Phone: 636-827-4000   **Fax:** 636-827-3312
Web: www.maritz.com

PRODUCTS/OPERATIONS

Selected Services
Marketing Research
  Custom marketing research
  Customer satisfaction and customer value analysis
  Data collection (focus groups, telephone interviews)
  Maritz Polls and Maritz Research Reports
  Syndicated buyer research
  Telecommunications research

Performance Improvement
  Communications
  e-Learning
  Fulfillment
  Internet consulting
  Loyalty marketing
  Measurement and feedback
  Rewards and recognition
Travel
  Consulting services
  Corporate travel management
  Group travel services
  Travel award programs

COMPETITORS

Franklin Covey	J.D. Power
Gallup	JTB Corp.
GiftCertificates.com	Motivcom
Harris Interactive	The Nielsen Company
IMS Health	ORC
Information Resources	TNS North America

HISTORICAL FINANCIALS

Company Type: Private

Income Statement

FYE: March 31

	REVENUE ($ mil.)	NET INCOME ($ mil.)	NET PROFIT MARGIN	EMPLOYEES
3/08	1,490	—	—	4,000
3/07	1,560	—	—	3,920
3/06	1,450	—	—	4,600
3/05	1,200	—	—	4,090
3/04	1,200	—	—	4,200
Annual Growth	**5.6%**	**—**	**—**	**(1.2%)**

Revenue History

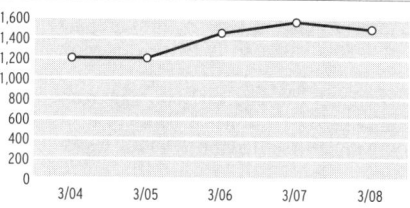

Marmon Group

With more monikers than most, The Marmon Group monitors a melange of more than 125 autonomous manufacturing and service companies. Marmon's manufacturing units make automotive components and trailers, food service equipment, wire and cable, industrial materials and components, consumer products, transportation equipment, building products, and water-treatment products. Services include marketing and distribution. Marmon is an international association of companies that operates about 250 facilities in more than 40 countries. Chicago's Pritzker family (owners of the Hyatt hotel chain) sold a 60% stake in The Marmon Group to Warren Buffett's Berkshire Hathaway for $4.5 billion in 2008.

For years the Pritzker family had been preparing a plan to break up The Marmon Group and divide it among heirs. An alternative to the breakup of the Marmon Group emerged when a buyer surfaced that had the experience — and the cash — to buy such an assemblage of diversified businesses all in one fell swoop. Of course, that buyer was none other than Warren Buffett's Berkshire Hathaway. The remaining 40% of the company will be acquired over the course of five to six years through staged acquisitions.

Marmon's largest operation is Union Tank Car. Along with a Canadian counterpart, Marmon owns over 90,000 rail cars valued in excess of $5 billion that are leased to shippers. Resulting revenues total about $7 billion.

The company functions through four business segments which offer both products and services: electrical components (wire and cable products), transportation equipment services (railroad tank car leasing, tank containers, and highway technologies), construction and industrial components (distribution services, metal fasteners, flow products, and construction services), and retail solutions (water treatment, food preparation equipment, and store fixtures).

Each Marmon company works under its own management, but shares services through a small corporate office (around 80 employees) that oversees and pulls together the conglomerate, and acts as combination CFO, tax lawyer, accountant, and broker to member companies. The company operates in China, North America, and the UK.

HISTORY

Although the history of The Marmon Group officially begins in 1953, the company's roots are in the Chicago law firm Pritzker and Pritzker, started by Nicholas Pritzker in 1902. Through the firm, the family made connections with First National Bank of Chicago, which A. N. Pritzker, Nicholas' son, used to get a line of credit to buy real estate. By 1940 the firm had stopped accepting outside clients to concentrate on the family's growing investment portfolio.

In 1953 A. N.'s son Jay used his father's connections to get a loan to buy Colson Company, a small, money-losing manufacturer of bicycles, hospital equipment, and other products. Jay's brother, Robert, a graduate of the Illinois Institute of Technology, took charge of Colson and turned it around. Soon Jay began acquiring more companies for his brother to manage.

In 1963 the brothers paid $2.7 million for about 45% of the Marmon-Herrington Company (whose predecessor, Marmon Motor Car, built the car that in 1911 won the first Indianapolis 500). The family now had a name for its industrial holdings — The Marmon Group.

It became a public company in 1966 when it merged with door- and spring-maker Fenestra. However, Jay began to take greater control of the group through a series of stock purchases, and by 1971 The Marmon Group was private once again.

A year earlier, in 1970, the group acquired a promising industrial pipe supplier, Keystone Tubular Service (which later became Marmon/Keystone). In 1973 Marmon began to acquire stock in Cerro Corp., which had operations in mining, manufacturing, trucking, and real estate; by 1976 the group had bought all of Cerro, thereby tripling its revenues. The brothers sold Cerro's trucking subsidiary, ICX, in 1977 and bought organ maker Hammond Corp., along with Wells Lamont, Hammond's glove-making subsidiary.

Marmon acquired conglomerate Trans Union in 1981. Trans Union brought many operations, including railcar and equipment leasing, credit information services, international trading, and water- and wastewater-treatment systems. In 1982 Jay acquired Ticketmaster (now a publicly traded company).

The Pritzkers made a foray into the airline business in 1984 by buying Braniff Airlines. After unsuccessfully bidding for Pan Am in 1987, they sold Braniff in 1988. Disappointments in other Pritzker businesses didn't slow Marmon, which added to its transportation equipment business in 1984 with Altamil, a maker of products for the trucking and aerospace industries.

To mark its 40th anniversary, the company sponsored a car, the Marmon Wasp II, at the 1993 Indianapolis 500. That year the Pritzkers sold 80% of Ticketmaster to Microsoft co-founder Paul Allen but retained a minority interest. Marmon sold Arzco Medical Systems in 1995, and Marmon/Keystone acquired Anbuma Group, a Belgian steel tubing distributor.

The Anbuma purchase and Marmon/Keystone's 1997 acquisition of UK tube distributor Wheeler Group exemplified Marmon's practice of building strength through acquisitions in its established markets. In 1998 Marmon purchased more than 30 companies and opened a business development office in Beijing.

Former Illinois Tool Works (ITW) chief John Nichols took over the Marmon CEO responsibilities from Robert Pritzker in 2001. The company again went to ITW when Nichols retired at the end of 2005, hiring former vice chairman Frank Ptak.

Also in 2005, the company spun off Trans Union, the consumer credit information services provider. Penny Pritzker, the independent Trans Union chairman, said that the separation would better allow the company to grow, as Trans Union is a technology and information company as opposed to Marmon's stable of manufacturing businesses. The Trans Union separation, however, served as a precursor to the decision to sell off the remainder of the Marmon Group companies in order to more easily divide the family holdings. Infighting among family members over the division of the family fortune began to intensify shortly after Jay's death in 1999.

Majority ownership of The Marmon Group was acquired by Berkshire Hathaway in 2008.

EXECUTIVES

President and CEO: Frank S. Ptak, age 65
SVP and CFO: Robert K. Lorch, age 63
SVP and General Counsel: Robert W. (Bob) Webb, age 70
President, Marmon Water LLC: John Goody
President, Marmon Flow Products LLC: Gary Ewing
President, Marmon Transportation Services LLC and Marmon Engineered Products: Kenneth Fischl, age 60
President, Marmon Industrial Companies LLC: Elwood (Woody) Petchel
President, Marmon Distribution Services LLC: Norman E. Gottschalk Jr., age 64
President, Marmon Wire and Cable LLC: Henry J. (Hank) West
President, Mamron Retail Services LLC: Anders Berggren
President, Marmon Highway Technologies LLC: Kelly E. Dier
Auditors: Ernst & Young LLP

HQ: The Marmon Group, LLC
181 W. Madison St., 26th Fl., Chicago, IL 60602
Phone: 312-372-9500   **Fax:** 312-845-5305
Web: www.marmon.com

PRODUCTS/OPERATIONS

Selected Companies by Sector

Building Wire (Cerro)
Construction Services (Sterling Crane)
Distribution Services (Bushwick Metals, Future Metals, M/K Express Company, Marmon/Keystone, Marmon/Keystone Canada)
Engineered Wire and Cable (Aetna Insulated Wire, Cable USA, Comtran, Dekoron Unitherm, Dekoron Wire & Cable, Harbour Industries, Hendrix Wire & Cable, Kerite, Owl Wire and Cable, RSCC Aerospace & Defense, RSCC Wire & Cable, TE Wire & Cable)
Flow Products (Anderson Copper and Brass, Cerro Flow Products, Penn Aluminum International)
Food Service Equipment (Catequip S.A. & Cat'Serv S.a.r.l., Prince Castle, Silver King Refrigeration, Unarco Industries)
Highway Technologies (Fleetline Products, Fontaine International, Fontaine Modification, Fontaine Spray Suppression, Fontaine Trailer, Hogebuilt, Marmon-Herrington, NU-LINE Products, Perfection, Triangle Suspension Systems, TSE Brakes, Webb Wheel Products)
Industrial Products (Atlas Bolt & Screw, Cerro E.M.S., Cerro Fabricated Products, Deerwood Fasteners International, EMC Traction, S.r.l., IMPulse NC, Koehler-Bright Star, Nylok, Pan American Screw, Robertson, Specialty Bolt & Stud, Wells Lamont Europe Industry)
Retail Store Fixtures (Darling (L.A.), Eden Industries (UK), Leader Metal Industry, Sloane Group, Store Opening Solutions, Streater, Thorco Industries, Wells Lamont Retail Group)
Transportation Services & Engineered Products (Enersul, Enersul Operations, Enersul Technologies, EXSIF Worldwide, Intermodal Transfer, McKenzie Valve & Machining, Penn Machine, Procor, Railserve, Trackmobile, Uni-Form Components, Union Tank Car, WCTU Railway)
Water Treatment (Amarillo Gear, Amarillo Wind Machine, Ecodyne Heat Exchangers, Ecodyne, Ecodyne Water Treatment, EcoWater Canada, EcoWater Systems Europe NV, EcoWater Systems, Graver Technologies, Graver Water Systems, KX Technologies)

COMPETITORS

Alcatel-Lucent
Balfour Beatty
Eaton
Illinois Tool Works
ITT Corp.
LEONI
Masco
Molex
Nexans
Superior Essex
Terex
USG
Wolverine Tube

Mars, Incorporated

Mars knows chocolate sales are nothing to snicker at. The company makes such worldwide favorites as M&M's, Snickers, and the Mars bar. Its other confections include 3 Musketeers, Dove, Milky Way, Skittles, Twix, and Starburst candy; Combos and Kudos snacks; Uncle Ben's rice; and pet food under the names Pedigree, Sheba, and Whiskas. It also owns the world's largest chewing gum maker, the Wm. Wrigley Jr. Company. The Mars family (including siblings and retired company CEO Forrest Mars Jr., chairman John Franklyn Mars, and VP Jacqueline Badger Mars) owns the highly secretive firm, making the family one of the richest in the US.

Sweet deals are the name of the game in the confectionery sector, and Mars' 2008 takeover of chewing gum giant Wrigley (valued at some $23 billion) brought together two iconic US companies, both of which already have a substantial worldwide presence. Mars acquired such well-known brands as Altoids, Life Savers, and Creme Savers, along with the best-selling chewing gum brands Spearmint, Juicy Fruit, Doublemint, and a host of others. Together, the companies benefit from greater global marketing and distribution muscle, as well as cost-savings in raw materials.

The deal, which took Wrigley private and left it a standalone subsidiary of Mars, was partially financed by Warren Buffett's Berkshire Hathaway, which owns a stake in Wrigley as a result.

Two weeks after the aquisition was final, Mars yanked Wrigley CEO and president William Perez and replaced him with a Mars 19-year veteran, Dushan "Duke" Petrovich. Petrovich carries the title of president, Mars having eliminated the CEO position at Wrigley. Perez received a severance package of some $25 million (including $10.5 million in cash).

Mars makes non-chocolate confections including breath mints such as AquaDrops, and snack foods like Combos and Kudos. It swallows a large bite of the pet-food market with its Royal Canin, Pedigree, and Whiskas brands. Pedigree has introduced a product called Wisdom Panel, which is a DNA test kit for dogs that determines the pet's breed mix. Mars' other brands include Uncle Ben's rice, Seeds of Change organic food, and the Klix and Flavia Beverage Systems.

Mars stays virtually debt-free and uses its profits for expansion. It has more than 130 factories in 75 countries and sells its products in more than 100.

HISTORY

Frank Mars invented the Milky Way candy bar in 1923 after his previous three efforts at the candy business left him bankrupt. After his estranged son, Forrest, graduated from Yale, Mars hired him to work at his candy operation. When Forrest demanded one-third control of the company and Frank refused, Forrest moved to England with the foreign rights to Milky Way and started his own company (Food Manufacturers) in the 1930s. He made a sweeter version of Milky Way for the UK, calling it a Mars bar. Forrest also ventured into pet food with the 1934 purchase of Chappel Brothers (renamed Pedigree). At one point he controlled 55% of the British pet food market.

During WWII Forrest returned to the US and introduced Uncle Ben's rice (the world's first brand-name raw commodity) and M&Ms (a joint venture between Forrest and Bruce Murrie, son of Hershey's then-president). The idea for M&M's was borrowed from British Smarties, for which Forrest obtained rights (from Rowntree Mackintosh) by relinquishing similar rights to the Snickers bar in some foreign markets. The ad slogan "Melts in your mouth, not in your hand" (and the candy's success in non-air-conditioned stores and war zones) made the company an industry leader. Mars introduced M&M's Peanut in 1954. It was one of the first candy companies to sponsor a television show — *Howdy Doody* in the 1950s.

Forrest merged his firm with his deceased father's company in 1964, after buying his dying half-sister's controlling interest. (He renamed the business Mars at her request.) The merger was the end of an alliance with Hershey, who had supplied Frank with chocolate since his Milky Way inception.

In 1968 Mars bought Kal Kan. In 1973 Forrest, then 69 years old, delegated his company responsibilities to sons Forrest Jr. and John. Five years later the brothers, looking for snacks to offset the dwindling candy market resulting from a more diet-conscious America, bought the Twix chocolate-covered cookie brand. During the late 1980s they bought ice-cream bar maker Dove Bar International and Ethel-M Chocolates, producer of liqueur-flavored chocolates, a business their father had begun in his retirement.

Hershey in 1988 surpassed Mars as the largest candy maker in the US when it acquired Mounds, Almond Joy, and other US brands from Cadbury Schweppes (now Cadbury). In response to the success of Hershey's Symphony Bar, Mars introduced its dark-chocolate Dove bar in 1991.

The company entered the huge confectionery market of India in 1989 by building a $10 million factory there. In 1996 the company opened a confectionery processing plant in Brazil.

Forrest Sr. died in 1999, spurring rumors that Mars would go public or be sold. Instead, the company dismantled most of its sales force, opting to use less costly food brokers. Forrest Jr. retired the same year, leaving brother John Franklyn as president and CEO.

In 2000 the company established a subsidiary, Effem India, to market Mars products in India. In 2003 Mars acquired French pet food producer Royal Canin. That year its Mexican subsidiary, Effem México SA de CV, merged with Mexican confectioner Grupo Matre to form a partnership to produce candy for Hispanic markets.

The company appointed two co-presidents, Peter Cheney and Paul Michaels, in 2004, leaving John Franklyn Mars as chairman. Cheney retired in 2005.

The company sold off its payment-processing subsidiary, MEI Conlux (which has headquarters in Pennsylvania and Japan) in 2006 to investment firms Bain Capital and Advantage Partners for more than $500 million.

Adding to its fast-growing pet-products sector, in 2006 Mars purchased dog-treat manufacturer S&M Nu Tec. Still barking up the pet-product tree, Mars acquired private-label dry pet food manufacturer Doane Pet Care Company that year as well. Doane's products are sold in the US and Europe.

The company discontinued brands in 2006, including Pop'ables and Cookies &, for an estimated $300 million savings, which it invested in advertising. The company introduced new Dove varieties and a dark chocolate version of M&Ms that year as well.

EXECUTIVES

Chairman: John F. Mars
President and CEO: Paul S. Michaels
Chief Science Officer: Harold Schmitz
EVP and CFO: Olivier Goudet
VP and General Manager, Mars Direct: Jim Cass
VP Technology: Richard Ware
VP Personnel and Organization: Aileen Richards
VP, Secretary, General Counsel: Alberto Mora
VP Small Outlet Sales, Masterfoods USA: Larry Lupo
VP Research and Development, U.S. Food: Mike Wilson
General Manager and CTO, Mars Botanical:
 Mary Wagner
President, Mars Snackfoods US: Todd R. Lachman
President, Wrigley Gum and Confections:
 Dushan (Duke) Petrovich, age 55
President, Petcare: Pierre Laubies
President, Mars Drinks and Developing Petcare:
 Martin Radvan
President, Symbioscience: Frank Mars
President, Snackfoods, Masterfoods Europe:
 Andy Weston-Webb
President, Food: Brian Camastral
President, Mars Nutrition for Health and Well-Being:
 James (Jamie) Mattikow
President, Chocolate: Grant Reid
Director Corporate Communications: Alison Clark

LOCATIONS

HQ: Mars, Incorporated
 6885 Elm St., McLean, VA 22101
Phone: 703-821-4900   **Fax:** 703-448-9678
Web: www.mars.com

PRODUCTS/OPERATIONS

Selected Products and Brands

Mars chocolate
 Dove
 Galaxy
 M&M's
 Mars
 Milky Way
 Skittles
 Snickers
 Starburst
 Twix

Mars drinks
 Flavia
 Klix

Mars foods
 Dolmio
 Ebly
 Masterfoods
 Seeds of Change
 Uncle Ben's

Mars pet care
 Cesar
 Pedigree
 Royal Canin
 Sheba
 Whiskas

Mars symbioscience
 Cocoapro
 MX
 Seramis
 Wisdom Panel

Wrigley
 Altoids
 Crème Savers
 Doublemint
 Extra
 Freedent
 Hubba Bubba
 Juicy Fruit
 Life Savers
 Orbit
 Skittles
 Starburst
 Winterfresh

COMPETITORS

American Italian Pasta
Barilla
Barry Callebaut
Breeder's Choice
Cadbury
Caribou Coffee
Chupa Chups
Colgate-Palmolive
ConAgra
Ezaki Glico
Farley's & Sathers
Fazer Konfektyr
Ferrara Pan Candy
Ferrero
General Mills
Ghirardelli Chocolate
Godiva Chocolatier
Green Mountain Coffee
Guittard
HARIBO
Harry London Candies
Heinz
Hershey
Hill's Pet Nutrition
Iams

Jelly Belly Candy
Kent Gida
Kraft Foods
Lindt & Sprüngli
Meiji Holdings
Nestlé
Nestlé Purina PetCare
Perfetti Van Melle
PETCO
Riviana Foods
Rocky Mountain Chocolate
Royal Cup Coffee
Russell Stover
S&D Coffee
Sara Lee International
 Beverage and Bakery
Sara Lee North American
 Foodservice
Smucker
Starbucks
SweetWorks
Tootsie Roll
Topps Company
Unilever
Upper Deck

HISTORICAL FINANCIALS

Company Type: Private

Income Statement				FYE: December 31
	REVENUE ($ mil.)	**NET INCOME** ($ mil.)	**NET PROFIT MARGIN**	**EMPLOYEES**
12/08	30,000	—	—	70,000
12/07	25,000	—	—	48,000
12/06	21,000	—	—	40,000
12/05	18,000	—	—	40,500
12/04	18,000	—	—	39,000
Annual Growth	**13.6%**	—	—	**15.7%**

Revenue History

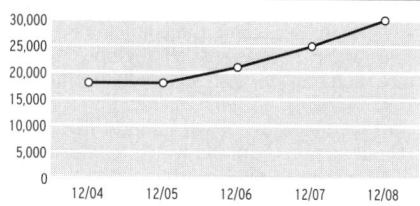

Marsh Supermarkets

Marsh Supermarkets is no backwater grocery chain. A leading retailer in Indianapolis, Marsh operates about 105 supermarkets under the Marsh Supermarkets, Marsh Hometown Markets, and O'Malia's Food Markets banners in central Indiana and western Ohio. About 40% of the stores have pharmacy departments. Its floral business — Marsh Floral Fashions — operates floral and gift departments inside Marsh stores.

Founded in 1931, the family of late founder Ermal Marsh sold the company in 2006 to an affiliate of the private equity firm Sun Capital Partners for about $325 million. The new owners in early 2009 sued former CEO and son of the founder Don Marsh, alleging fraud by diverting company funds for his personal use. Mr. Marsh has counter-sued, claiming the company owes him $2.1 million in salary and benefits.

Historically, Marsh has staked its reputation on high-quality goods and excellent customer service, but not necessarily low prices. However, with the onset of the deep recession in the US the regional supermarket chain began emphasizing value in an aggressive marketing campaign launched in spring 2009. As part of its value program, Marsh is offering 25% of the items in its stores at a reduced price (up from 15% in 2008). It is also emphasizing its lower-priced house brands, which include Food Club and Top Care.

Changes at the company since the September 2006 buyout by Sun Capital include the separation of the Marsh Supermarkets business from the 190-store Village Pantry convenience store chain as well as the 2007 sale of Marsh's Butterfield Foods commissary and McNamara Floral division; the conversion of all LoBill outlets to the Marsh Hometown Markets banner; the closure of several stores, including the upscale Arthur's Fresh Markets (launched 2004); and job cuts to free up capital to invest in its supermarkets. The grocery chain also sold off real estate including eight supermarkets to a Canadian real estate investment trust, H&R REIT, in November 2006 for about $88 million. (Marsh is leasing back the stores.) Overall, since the purchase by Sun Capital, about 80% of Marsh stores have been refurbished.

Previously, the company closed its Tuscan-style restaurant, Trios Di Tuscanos, and its Hispanic grocery store, Savin*$ Mercado, both in Indiana.

EXECUTIVES

Chairman, President and CEO: Frank Lazaran, age 49
COO: Bill Holsworth
EVP, Finance and Administration, and CFO:
 Douglas W. Dougherty, age 62
SVP, General Counsel, Secretary, and Director:
 P. Lawrence Butt, age 64
VP, Deli and Bakery Operations: Kent Tapley
VP, Food Safety and Sanitation: Scott Alkinburgh
VP, Incentives: Terence R. (Terry) Huser
VP, Corporate Controller: Mark A. Varner, age 56
President and COO, Supermarket Division:
 Daniel S. (Dan) Cross, age 50
President and COO, Village Pantry Division:
 Charles Barnard Jr., age 57
Senior Director, Pharmacy, General Merchandise, and HBC Merchandising: Don Rix
Auditors: Ernst & Young LLP

LOCATIONS

HQ: Marsh Supermarkets, Inc.
 333 S. Franklin Rd., Indianapolis, IN 46219
Phone: 317-594-2100   **Fax:** 317-594-2704
Web: www.marsh.net

PRODUCTS/OPERATIONS

2009 Stores

	No.
Marsh Supermarkets	99
O'Malia's	5
Total	**104**

COMPETITORS

ALDI
Costco Wholesale
Dollar General
Kroger
Meijer
Safeway

Save-A-Lot Food Stores
Spartan Stores
SUPERVALU
Target
Trader Joe's
Wal-Mart

Income Statement				FYE: Saturday nearest March 31
	REVENUE ($ mil.)	NET INCOME ($ mil.)	NET PROFIT MARGIN	EMPLOYEES
3/09	1,300	—	—	9,000

Mary Kay

Celebrating more than 40 years in business, Mary Kay is in the pink as one of the top direct sellers of beauty products in the US. It offers more than 200 products in six categories: body care, color cosmetics, facial skin care, fragrance, nail care, and sun protection. More than 1.8 million independent sales consultants demonstrate Mary Kay products in the US and some 35 other countries. Consultants vie for awards each year, ranging from jewelry to the company's trademark pink Cadillac (first awarded in 1969). The company also founded the Mary Kay Ash Charitable Foundation in 1996 to fund cancer research and domestic violence programs. The family of founder Mary Kay Ash owns most of the company.

Founded by a woman for women, Mary Kay has an overwhelmingly female independent sales force. Although the company stands by Mary Kay's original goal of providing financial and career opportunities for women, much of the company's executive population is male. Ash's son Richard Rogers (executive chairman) runs the company alongside David Holl (president and CEO).

Mary Kay works hard to retain the feel of a small company, despite its more than 1.8-million-strong independent sales force and the firm's growing international reach. As part of this initiative, each beauty consultant receives the option to buy his or her own Web site to use for selling to clients. More than 90% of its revenue is generated through online orders by the company's independent sales force.

During her lifetime Mary Kay Ash was known for her religious nature as well as her generosity. She founded the Mary Kay Ash Charitable Foundation in 1996; by 2006 the foundation had awarded $8 million in grants to cancer researchers and US women's shelters. Mary Kay Ash suffered a debilitating stroke in 1996 and died on Thanksgiving Day 2001.

HISTORY

Before founding her own company in 1963, Mary Kay Ash worked as a Stanley Home Products sales representative. Impressed with the alligator handbag awarded to the top saleswoman at a Stanley convention, Ash was determined to win the next year's prize — and she did. Despite that accomplishment and having worked at Stanley for 11 years, a male assistant she had trained was made her boss after less than a year on the job. Tired of not receiving recognition, Ash and her second husband used their life savings ($5,000) to go into business for themselves. Although her husband died of a heart attack shortly before the business opened, Ash forged ahead with the help of her two grown sons.

She bought a cosmetics formula invented years earlier by a hide tanner. (The mixture was originally used to soften leather, but the tanner noticed how the formula made his hands look younger, and he began applying the mixture to his face, with great results.) Ash kept her first line simple — 10 products — and packaged her wares in pink to complement the typically white bathrooms of the day. Ash also enlisted consultants, who held "beauty shows" with five or six women in attendance. Mary Kay grossed $198,000 in its first year.

The company introduced men's skin care products in 1964. Ash bought a pink Cadillac the following year and began awarding the cars as prizes in 1969. (By 1981 orders were so large — almost 500 — that GM dubbed the color "Mary Kay Pink.")

Ash became a millionaire when her firm went public in 1968. Mary Kay grew steadily through the 1970s. Foreign operations began in 1971 in Australia, and over the next 25 years the company entered 24 more countries, including nations in Asia/Pacific, Europe, and Central and South America.

Sales plunged in the early 1980s, along with the company's stock prices (from $40 to $9 between 1983 and 1985). Ash and her family reacquired Mary Kay in 1985 through a $375 million LBO. Burdened with debt, the firm lost money in the late 1980s. Mary Kay took a number of steps to boost sales and income, doing a makeover on the cosmetics line and advertising in women's magazines again (after a five-year hiatus) to counter its old-fashioned image. The company also introduced recyclable packaging and lipstick in a tube (replacing brush-on palettes). In 1989 Avon rebuffed a buyout offer by Mary Kay, and both companies halted animal testing.

In 1993 Mary Kay opened a subsidiary in Russia, which later became the company's fourth-largest international market (behind Mexico, China, and Canada). Ash suffered a debilitating stroke in 1996.

In 1998 Mary Kay began selling through retail boutiques in China because of a government ban on direct selling. Changing with the times, Mary Kay added a white sport utility vehicle and new shades of pink to its fleet of 10,000 GM cars that year.

Chairman John Rochon was named CEO in 1999. Also in 1999 Mary Kay launched *Women & Success* (a magazine for consultants) and Atlas (its electronic ordering system).

In June 2001 Richard Rogers, now the company chairman and son of Ash, replaced Rochon as CEO. A month later Mary Kay introduced the Velocity Products line, targeting girls ages 14 to 24. Ash died on Thanksgiving Day 2001.

Mary Kay Poland, headquartered in Warsaw, became the company's 34th international market in mid-2003.

In 2006 Rogers became executive chairman and David Holl, previously president and COO, was named president and CEO.

EXECUTIVES

Executive Chairman: Richard R. Rogers
President and CEO: David B. Holl, age 48
EVP Global Manufacturing: Dennis Greaney
EVP and CIO: Kregg Jodie
SVP Global Human Resources: Melinda Sellers
SVP Finance: Terry Smith
SVP, General Counsel, and Secretary: Nathan P. Moore
SVP Marketing: Rhonda Shasteen

VP International Market Development and Sales Support: Murray Smith
VP Sales Development: Greg Franklin
VP Government Relations: Anne Crews
VP Information Technology: Karen Calvert
VP Supply Chain Information Services and Technologies: Doug Voss
VP Global Corporate Communications: Randall G. Oxford
President, Mary Kay Greater China: Paul Mak
President, US: Darrell Overcash
President, Mary Kay Europe: Tara Eustace
Director Product Marketing: Lisa Cohorn

LOCATIONS

HQ: Mary Kay Inc.
16251 Dallas Pkwy., Addison, TX 75001
Phone: 972-687-6300   **Fax:** 972-687-1611
Web: www.marykay.com

PRODUCTS/OPERATIONS

Selected Product Lines

Body care
Cosmetics
Facial skin care
Fragrances (men's and women's)
Men's skin care
Nail care
Nutritional supplements for men
Nutritional supplements for women
Sun protection

COMPETITORS

Alberto-Culver	Johnson & Johnson
Alticor	L'Oréal
Avon	Merle Norman
Bath & Body Works	Murad, Inc.
BeautiControl	Nu Skin
Body Shop	Perrigo
Clarins	Procter & Gamble
Colgate-Palmolive	Reliv' International
Coty Inc.	Revlon
Dana Classic Fragrances	Schwarzkopf & Henkel
Del Laboratories	Scott's Liquid Gold
The Dial Corporation	Shaklee
Estée Lauder	Shiseido
Helen of Troy	Sunrider
Jafra	Unilever
John Paul Mitchell	

HISTORICAL FINANCIALS
Company Type: Private

Income Statement				FYE: December 31
	REVENUE ($ mil.)	NET INCOME ($ mil.)	NET PROFIT MARGIN	EMPLOYEES
12/08	2,600	—	—	5,000
12/07	2,400	—	—	5,000
12/06	2,250	—	—	4,500
12/05	2,200	—	—	4,000
12/04	1,900	—	—	3,600
Annual Growth	8.2%	—	—	8.6%

Revenue History

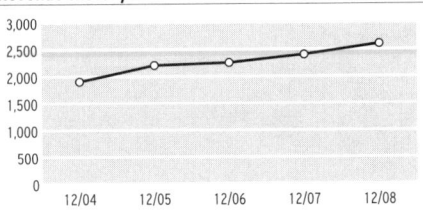

Maryland State Lottery

The Maryland State Lottery Agency runs that state's lottery system, offering a variety of scratch-off ticket games and such numbers games as Keno, Pick 3, and Pick 4. Maryland also participates in the multi-state Mega Millions lottery. The agency, which was created in 1973, distributes about 57% of its revenue as prizes and contributes more than 30% of funds to state-funded programs for education, human resources, and public health. (Some proceeds from the Mega Million game also goes to the Maryland Stadium Authority, which oversees several facilities including Camden Yards, home of Major League Baseball's Baltimore Orioles.)

Voters in 2008 approved a measure legalizing slot machine gaming in Maryland. The lottery commission will own or lease a planned 15,000 slot machines in the state. Taxes on the gaming operations are hoped to total about $600 million a year.

EXECUTIVES

Director: Buddy W. Roogow
Director Administration and Operations:
Richard Chavis
Deputy Director and CIO: John Gallagher
Assistant Director and CFO: Gina M. Smith
Director Systems and Programming: Zechariah Way
Director Communications: Carole Everett
Division Director, Product Development, Creative Services, and Research Division: Tracey Cohen
Director Creative Services: Jill Q. Baer
Director Policy and Development: Paul Dorsey
Principal Counsel: Robert T. Fontaine
Chief Security and Investigations:
Nathaniel (Nate) Smoot
Manager On-line Gaming System Management:
John Wood

LOCATIONS

HQ: Maryland State Lottery Agency
1800 Washington Blvd., Ste. 330
Baltimore, MD 21230
Phone: 410-230-8800   **Fax:** 410-230-8728
Web: www.msla.state.md.us

COMPETITORS

Multi-State Lottery
New Jersey Lottery
Pennsylvania Lottery
Virginia Lottery

HISTORICAL FINANCIALS

Company Type: Government-owned

Income Statement

FYE: June 30

	REVENUE ($ mil.)	NET INCOME ($ mil.)	NET PROFIT MARGIN	EMPLOYEES
6/08	1,673	—	—	200
6/07	1,577	—	—	200
6/06	1,500	—	—	188
6/05	1,486	—	—	179
6/04	1,395	—	—	150
Annual Growth	4.6%	—	—	7.5%

Revenue History

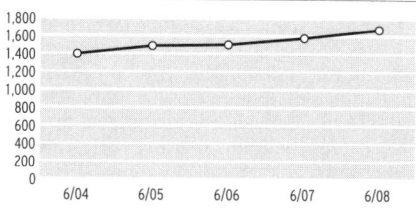

Mashantucket Pequot Tribal Nation

Mashantucket Pequot Tribal Nation (with roughly 700 members) has propelled itself from the depths of intense poverty to its lofty position as the wealthiest Native American tribe in the US. It owns and operates Foxwoods Resort Casino, one of the largest casinos in the world and, many believe, the most profitable. The complex offers more than 7,000 slot machines and some 400 gaming tables in six casinos, four hotels (Grand Pequot Tower, Great Cedar Hotel, Two Trees Inn, and MGM Grand at Foxwoods), about 30 restaurants, live entertainment, and a string of retail shops. Foxwoods opened the MGM Grand at Foxwoods in 2008. The project, which cost some $700 million, is Connecticut's third-largest casino.

MGM Grand is an 825-room hotel and casino. The property is also home to high-end retailers such as Dunhill and an Apple Reseller store and to celebrity chef restaurants such as Michael Schlow's Alta Strada Italian restaurant, Junior's Cheesecake of New York, and chef Tom Colicchio's Craftsteak. It is also home to the 4,000-seat MGM Grand Theater, which can draw bigger acts (such as Celine Dion) than its 1,400-seat Fox Theatre.

In addition to its gaming operations, the Mashantucket Pequot Tribal Nation owns the Foxwoods Development Company, a developer and manager of hospitality-related enterprises. Foxwoods Development Company holdings include Connecticut hotels and restaurants (Hilton Mystic, the Spa at Norwich Inn, and Randall's Ordinary), golf courses (Lake of Isles), and the five-story Mercantile building in Norwich, Connecticut. The Mashantucket Pequot Tribal Nation also operates the Mashantucket Pequot Museum and Research Center dedicated to the tribe's life and history.

HISTORY

Once a powerful tribe, the Pequots were virtually wiped out in the 17th century by disease and attacks from colonists. More than 350 years later, Richard "Skip" Hayward, a pipefitter making $15,000 a year, led the fight for federal recognition of his nearly extinct Mashantucket Pequot tribe. He was elected tribal chairman in 1975, and the US government officially recognized the tribe in 1983.

The Indian Gaming Regulatory Act of 1988 opened the door for legal gambling on reservations, but tribes still had to negotiate with state governments for authorization. Hayward hired

G. Michael "Mickey" Brown as a consultant and lawyer. Brown took the tribe's legal battle to the US Supreme Court, which eventually ruled that the Pequots could build a casino. When some 30 banks turned down the Pequots for a construction loan, Brown introduced Hayward and his tribe to Lim Goh Tong, billionaire developer of the successful Gentings Highlands Casino resort in Malaysia. Tong invested approximately $60 million, and the Foxwoods Casino opened in 1992.

Brown brought in Alfred J. Luciani to serve as president and CEO of Foxwoods. Luciani stayed less than a year, however, resigning because of what he called philosophical differences with tribe leadership. Brown took over as CEO in 1993. Although Foxwoods grew rapidly, Brown often wrestled with members of the tribal council over how the business should be run. The next year Brown rehired Luciani to oversee the development of the Grand Pequot Tower hotel.

Brown resigned and Luciani was fired in 1997 after it was revealed that Brown had not fully disclosed his ties with Lim Goh Tong and that, in 1992, Luciani had accepted a $377,000 loan from Gamma International, a vendor that provided keno services to Foxwoods. The Pequots considered these actions to be conflicts of interest. A new management team was brought in, and Floyd "Bud" Celey, a veteran of Hilton Hotels (now Hilton Worldwide), was appointed CEO.

The Pequots opened the Mashantucket Pequot Museum and Research Center in 1998. When tribal elections were held later that year, Kenneth Reels was elected chairman of the Pequot's tribal governing body, ousting Hayward from the position he had held for more than 20 years. Hayward was elected vice chairman. Mashantucket Pequot Gaming Enterprise concentrated on improving financial accountability in 1999, and the tribe began cutting costs by shuttering unprofitable holdings, including Pequot River Shipworks, its shipbuilding business.

Former COO William Sherlock replaced Celey as CEO in 2000. That year the first of two books (the second was published in 2001), which questioned the tribe's legitimacy, created some controversy for the group. The books claimed that the government was duped into giving them more land for their reservation than they were entitled to, and sparked a series of lawsuits from neighboring communities.

A federal audit in 2000 revealed that the tribe's pharmaceutical firm was giving discount drugs intended for Native Americans to its non-Native American employees.

In 2002 the tribe withdrew its application to annex 165 acres of land near its Foxwoods Resort Casino, ending nearly 10 years of legal battles.

EXECUTIVES

SVP Casino Marketing: Joseph C. Jimenez
SVP Administration: Bruce Kirchner
SVP Human Resources: Joanne Franks
SVP Property Marketing: Gary A. Borden
SVP Resort Operations: Barry J. Cregan, age 55
VP Human Resources, Foxwoods Resort Casino and the MGM Grand at Foxwoods: Stephen E. (Steve) Heise
VP Information Services: Brian Charette
VP Finance: Mark Ford
President, Foxwoods Development: Gary D. Armentrout
President, Mashantucket Pequot Gaming Enterprise:
Michael F. (Mike) Speller
General Manager, MGM Grand at Foxwoods:
Gillian Murphy
Chief Risk Management Officer:
Cynthia Sebastian-Welch
Director Public Affairs: William L. (Bill) Satti
Executive Director, Mashantucket Pequot Museum and Research Center: Kimberly Hatcher-White

LOCATIONS

HQ: Mashantucket Pequot Tribal Nation
39 Norwich-Westerly Rd., Ledyard, CT 06339
Phone: 860-312-3000 **Fax:** 860-396-3599
Web: www.foxwoods.com

PRODUCTS/OPERATIONS

Selected Holdings

Foxwoods Resort Casino (Mashantucket, CT)
Hilton Mystic (Mystic, CT)
Lake of Isles (golf courses, Mashantucket, CT)
Mashantucket Pequot Museum and Research Center
(Mashantucket, CT)
Mercantile Exchange Building (Norwich, CT)
Randall's Ordinary Inn (North Stonington, CT)
The Spa at Norwich Inn (Norwich, CT)

COMPETITORS

Connecticut Lottery
Harrah's Entertainment
Kerzner International
Mohegan Tribal Gaming Authority
New York State Lottery
Trump Resorts

Massachusetts Mutual Life Insurance

Massachusetts Mutual Life Insurance (aka MassMutual) is the flagship firm of the MassMutual Financial Group, a global organization of companies that provide financial services including life insurance, annuities, money management, and retirement planning. Founded in 1851, MassMutual's clients include individuals and businesses. The company also offers disability income insurance, long-term care insurance, structured settlement annuities, and trust services (through The MassMutual Trust Company). Other subsidiaries include OppenheimerFunds (mutual funds), Babson Capital Management (investor services), Baring Asset Management, and Cornerstone Real Estate Advisors (real estate investment management).

Like so many other insurance firms, MassMutual hopped on the financial services bandwagon to expand its product range. However, its management and policyholders have repeatedly reaffirmed their intention to keep MassMutual a mutual company despite the efforts of some policyholders. Also, the company doesn't seem too eager to throw out either the insurance baby or the bathwater — it has also reaffirmed its commitment to good old whole life insurance products and retirement income products.

MassMutual International has established subsidiaries in Asia, Europe, and South America where it is focused on new product development (the majority of sales come from products or channels developed within the last couple of years) and broadened distribution.

Stuart Reese stepped down as CEO at the end of 2009. MassMutual president Roger Crandall assumed the role of CEO; Reese remained with the company as a non-executive chairman.

HISTORY

Insurance agent George Rice formed Massachusetts Mutual in 1851 as a stock company based in Springfield. The firm converted to a mutual in 1867. For its first 50 years MassMutual sold only individual life insurance, but after 1900 it branched out, offering first annuities (1917) and then disability coverage (1918).

The early 20th century was rough on MassMutual, which was forced to raise premiums on new policies during WWI, then faced the high costs of the 1918 flu epidemic. The firm endured the Great Depression despite policy terminations, expanding its product line to include income insurance. In 1946 MassMutual wrote its first group policy, for Jack Daniel's maker Brown-Forman Distillers. By 1950 the company had diversified into medical insurance.

MassMutual began investing in stocks in the 1950s, switching from fixed-return bonds and mortgages for higher returns. It also decentralized and in 1961 began automating operations. By 1970 the firm had installed a computer network linking it to its independent agents. During this period, whole life insurance remained the core product.

With interest rates increasing during the late 1970s, many insurers diversified by offering high-yield products like guaranteed investment contracts funded by high-risk investments. MassMutual resisted as long as it could, but as interest rates soared to 20%, the company experienced a rash of policy loans, which led to a cash crunch. In 1981, with its policy growth rate trailing the industry norm, MassMutual developed new products, including some that offered higher dividends in return for adjustable interest on policy loans.

In the 1980s MassMutual reduced its stock investment (to about 5% of total investments by 1987), allowing it to emerge virtually unscathed from the 1987 stock market crash.

The firm changed course in 1990 and entered financial services. It bought a controlling interest in mutual fund manager Oppenheimer Management. MassMutual announced in 1993 that, with legislation limiting rates, it would stop writing new individual and small-group policies in New York.

The next year the company targeted the neglected family-owned business niche; in 1995 it sponsored the American Alliance of Family-Owned Businesses and rolled out new whole life products aimed at this segment. That year it bought David L. Babson & Company, a Massachusetts-based investment management firm, and opened life insurance companies in Chile and Argentina.

In 1996 MassMutual merged with Connecticut Mutual. It also acquired Antares Leveraged Capital Corp. (commercial finance) and Charter Oak Capital Management (investment advisory services). The next year MassMutual sold its Life & Health Benefits Management subsidiary.

Still in the mood to merge, the company entered discussions with Northwestern Mutual in 1998, but culture clashes terminated the talks. Also that year the company helped push through legislation that would allow insurers to issue stock through mutual holding companies, a move which MassMutual itself contemplated in 1999.

MassMutual expanded outside the US at the turn of the century. In 1999 it issued securities in Europe, opened offices in such locales as Bermuda and Luxembourg, and bought the Argentina operations of Jefferson-Pilot. A year later it expanded into Asia when it bought Hong Kong-based CRC

Protective Life Insurance (now MassMutual Asia). In 2001 the company entered the Taiwanese market, buying a stake in Mercuries Life Insurance (now MassMutual Mercuries Life Insurance) and acquiring Japanese insurer Aetna Heiwa Life (a subsidiary of US health insurer Aetna).

Also in 2001 MassMutual policyholders defeated a proposal by some to convert the company to stockholder ownership.

The company's board of directors terminated former CEO Robert O'Connell in 2005, citing a laundry list of reasons that included using company assets improperly and the use of retaliatory behavior against employees. Stuart Reese was named his replacement.

MassMutual acquired the operations of Baring Asset Management from ING Groep in 2005 to boost its financial services portfolio.

EXECUTIVES

Chairman and CEO: Stuart H. Reese
President, COO, and Director: Roger W. Crandall, age 44
EVP and General Counsel: Mark D. Roellig, age 53
EVP and CFO: Michael T. Rollings, age 45
EVP and Chief Investment Officer; Chairman and CEO, Babson Capital Management: Thomas M. (Tom) Finke
SVP and Chief Compliance Officer: Bradley J. Lucido, age 43
SVP Information Systems Organization: Marc A. Germain
SVP Strategic Communications and Community Responsibility: M. Trish Robinson
SVP and Chief Risk Officer: Elizabeth A. (Betsy) Ward, age 44
SVP Corporate Human Resources: Debra A. Palermino
SVP and General Auditor: Donald B. Robitaille
SVP and Chief Actuary: Isadore Jermyn
SVP, Secretary, and Deputy General Counsel: Stephen L. Kuhn
SVP and CIO: Robert J. (Bob) Casale, age 42

LOCATIONS

HQ: Massachusetts Mutual Life Insurance Company
1295 State St., Springfield, MA 01111
Phone: 413-744-1000 **Fax:** 413-744-6005
Web: www.massmutual.com

PRODUCTS/OPERATIONS

2008 Sales

	$ mil.	% of total
Premium income	13,716	71
Net investment income	5,164	27
Fees & other income	421	2
Total	**19,301**	**100**

Selected Subsidiaries and Affiliates

Babson Capital Management LLC
Baring Asset Management Limited (UK)
C.M. Life Insurance Company
Cornerstone Real Estate Advisers LLC (real estate equities)
Fuh Hwa Securities Investment Trust Co., Ltd. (Taiwan)
MassMutual Asia Ltd. (Hong Kong)
MassMutual Europe S.A. (Luxembourg)
MassMutual International, Inc.
MassMutual Life Insurance Co. (Japan)
MassMutual Mercuries Life Insurance Co., Ltd. (Taiwan)
The MassMutual Trust Company, FSB
MML Bay State Life Insurance Company
MML Investors Services, Inc.
OppenheimerFunds, Inc. (mutual funds)

HISTORICAL FINANCIALS

Company Type: Mutual company

Income Statement

FYE: December 31

	ASSETS ($ mil.)	NET INCOME ($ mil.)	INCOME AS % OF ASSETS	EMPLOYEES
12/08	125,086	239	0.2%	12,000
12/07	131,491	201	0.2%	12,000
12/06	122,155	810	0.7%	12,000
12/05	113,552	753	0.7%	10,000
12/04	108,216	335	0.3%	10,000
Annual Growth	3.7%	(8.1%)	—	4.7%

2008 Year-End Financials

Equity as % of assets: —
Return on assets: 0.2%
Return on equity: —
Long-term debt ($ mil.): —
Sales ($ mil.): 19,301

Net Income History

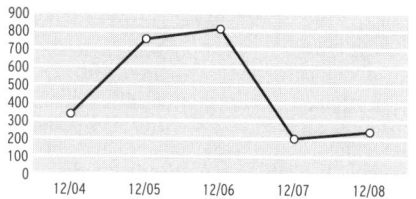

900				
800				
700				
600				
500				
400				
300				
200				
100				
0	12/04	12/05	12/06	12/07	12/08

Massachusetts State Lottery

For a lucky few, the Commonwealth lottery can create uncommon wealth. The Massachusetts State Lottery Commission operates several numbers games (Mass Cash, Cash Winfall, Mega Millions), as well as a variety of scratch-off games. Massachusetts also participates in the 12-state Mega Millions lottery. State law requires that at least 45% of lottery proceeds must go to pay prizes, while a maximum of 15% can be used for operating expenses. The remainder of the commission's take is distributed throughout Massachusetts to fund such local services as fire and police protection, as well as for education programs. The Massachusetts State Lottery Commission was created in 1971.

In an effort to boost sales of lottery tickets, the Massachusetts lottery has partnered with many of the state's popular sports teams to produce new game tickets. It struck licensing deals in 2009 with the Boston Red Sox baseball team and the New England Patriots football team to use their official logos on lottery tickets.

EXECUTIVES

Executive Director: Mark J. Cavanagh, age 54
CFO: Edward Bartley
Assistant Executive Director MIS: Paul Mandeville
Chief of Staff: Al Grazioso
Communications Director: Daniel L. (Dan) Rosenfeld
Assistant Executive Director Human Resources: Michael T. Coughlin
State Treasurer and Receiver General: Timothy P. (Tim) Cahill, age 50

LOCATIONS

HQ: Massachusetts State Lottery Commission
 60 Columbian St., Braintree, MA 02184
Phone: 781-849-5555   **Fax:** 781-849-5509
Web: www.masslottery.com

COMPETITORS

Connecticut Lottery	New Hampshire Lottery
Maine State Lottery	New York State Lottery
Multi-State Lottery	Vermont Lottery

Maverik Country Stores

Fillin' up your gas tank and your belly in the Wild West is a breeze, courtesy of Maverik Country Stores. The company operates about 170 gas station/convenience stores with an adventure theme in seven western US states: Arizona, Colorado, Idaho, Montana, Nevada, Utah, and Wyoming. The company also makes a television show called "Maverik Kick Start" that features a team that goes sky diving, river rafting, and on other adventures. Maverik Country Stores was founded by the late Reuel T. Call, who got into the petroleum business in the 1920s and considered himself a maverick (hence the company name).

EXECUTIVES

President and CEO: Mike Call
CFO: Spencer Hewlett
VP Marketing: Brad Call
VP Store Operations: Roger Green
Director of Marketing: Scott Shakespeare
Director of Merchandising: Tim Taylor

LOCATIONS

HQ: Maverik Country Stores, Inc.
 880 W. Center St., North Salt Lake, UT 84054
Phone: 801-936-5557   **Fax:** 801-936-1406
Web: www.maverik.com

HISTORICAL FINANCIALS

Company Type: Private

Income Statement

FYE: March 31

	REVENUE ($ mil.)	NET INCOME ($ mil.)	NET PROFIT MARGIN	EMPLOYEES
3/08	1,193	—	—	2,900

Mayer Brown

One of the world's largest law firms, Mayer Brown (formerly Mayer, Brown, Rowe & Maw) represents many of the companies in the *FORTUNE* 100 and the FTSE 100, as well as a number of leading banks. Major practice areas include appellate, corporate and securities, finance, litigation, real estate, and tax. Overall, Mayer Brown has about 1,800 lawyers in more than 20 offices in the Americas, Europe, and Asia. It significantly expanded its international reach in 2008 by combining with Hong Kong-based Johnson Stokes & Master (JSM), a 300-lawyer firm. Mayer Brown is made up of three partnerships — Mayer Brown LLP (located in the US), Mayer Brown International LLP (the UK), and JSM.

The firm's offices in Asia operate as Mayer Brown JSM. Affiliate Mayer Brown Consulting, headquartered in Beijing, advises clients on issues related to doing business in East Asia.

To simplify its global branding, the firm changed its name from Mayer, Brown, Rowe & Maw to Mayer Brown in September 2007. Before it acquired JSM, the law firm made moves to expand internationally when it opened its first office in Hong Kong and established an alliance with Ramón & Cajal, a Madrid-based law firm. It opened an office in São Paulo, Brazil, also at that time.

Mayer Brown traces its roots to a firm founded in 1881 in Chicago.

EXECUTIVES

Chairman: James D. Holzhauer
Global Vice Chairman: Paul Maher
Vice Chairman: Kenneth S. Geller
Executive Director: Steven R. Wells
CFO: Alan S. Cohen
CIO: Howard Niden
Chief Marketing Officer: Kathleen Reichert
Partner-in-Charge, Houston: Michael E. Niebruegge
Partner-in-Charge, Chicago: Frederick B. Thomas
Partner-in-Charge, Palo Alto: C. Cabell Chinnis Jr.
Partner-in-Charge, New York: Brian Trust
Partner-in-Charge, Los Angeles: James E. Tancula
Partner-in-Charge, Charlotte: Jonathan A. Barrett
Partner-in-Charge, São Paulo: Stephen Hood
Director Public Relations: Bob Harris
Director Human Resources: Coleen Callahan

LOCATIONS

HQ: Mayer Brown LLP
 71 S. Wacker Dr., Chicago, IL 60606
Phone: 312-782-0600   **Fax:** 312-701-7711
Web: www.mayerbrown.com

Selected Office Locations

Americas
 Charlotte, NC
 Chicago
 Houston
 Los Angeles
 New York
 Palo Alto, CA
 São Paulo
 Washington, DC
Asia
 Bangkok
 Beijing
 Guangzhou, Chian
 Hanoi, Vietnam
 Ho Chi Minh City, Vietnam
 Hong Kong
 Shanghai

Europe
  Berlin
  Brussels
  Cologne, Germany
  Frankfurt
  London
  Paris

PRODUCTS/OPERATIONS

Selected Practice Areas

Banking and finance
Corporate and securities
Environmental
Employment and benefits
Financial services regulatory and enforcement
Government/global trade
Intellectual property
Litigation and dispute resolution
Real estate
Restructuring, bankruptcy, and insolvency
Structured finance
Tax controversy
Tax transactions
Wealth management: trusts, estates, and foundations

COMPETITORS

Baker & McKenzie
Clifford Chance
DLA Piper
Hogan & Hartson
Jenner & Block
Jones Day
Kirkland & Ellis
Latham & Watkins
McDermott Will & Emery
Sidley Austin
Skadden, Arps
Sonnenschein Nath
Weil, Gotshal & Manges
White & Case
Winston & Strawn

HISTORICAL FINANCIALS

Company Type: Partnership

Income Statement			FYE: December 31
	REVENUE ($ mil.)	NET INCOME ($ mil.)	NET PROFIT MARGIN	EMPLOYEES
12/08	1,294	—	—	3,700
12/07	1,183	—	—	3,400
12/06	1,080	—	—	3,226
Annual Growth	9.5%	—	—	7.1%

Revenue History

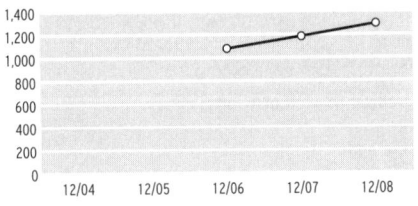

Mayer Electric Supply

Mayer Electric Supply helps light up those southern nights. The company, founded in 1930, distributes electrical supplies from more than 50 locations in the southeastern US. Mayer Electric's offerings include over 20,000 products made by leading manufacturers such as 3M, GE, Littelfuse, and Schneider Electric. These products include factory automation systems, controls and switches, fire and safety products, lighting fixtures, motors, power tools, and wire and cable. The company supplies customers in such industries as construction, manufacturing, and utilities. Chairman Charles Collat and his family own Mayer Electric.

Mayer Electric has operations in Alabama, Florida, Georgia, Mississippi, North Carolina, South Carolina, Tennessee, and Virginia, with strategic plans to expand further in the southeastern US.

EXECUTIVES

Chairman Emeritus: Charles A. Collat Sr.
Vice Chairman: Jim Summerlin
Chairman and CEO: Nancy Collat Goedecke
President: Wes Smith
CFO: David L. Morgan
EVP Sales and Marketing: Glenn Goedecke
Director, Corporate Marketing:
  W. Joseph (Joe) Llewellyn

LOCATIONS

HQ: Mayer Electric Supply Company Inc.
  3405 4th Ave. South, Birmingham, AL 35222
Phone: 205-583-3500   **Fax:** 205-322-2625
Web: www.mayerelectric.com

PRODUCTS/OPERATIONS

Selected Products

Ballasts
Batteries
Boxes
Cable and wire
Conduit
Factory automation products
Fans
Fasteners
Faucets
Fountains
Lenses
Lighting fixtures
Locks
Motors
Plumbing products
Terminal blocks
Tools
Transformers

COMPETITORS

Anixter International
Consolidated Electrical
Crescent Electric Supply
Gexpro
Graybar Electric
Independent Electric Supply
Rexel, Inc.
WESCO International
Wholesale Supply Group
W.W. Grainger

HISTORICAL FINANCIALS

Company Type: Private

Income Statement			FYE: December 31
	REVENUE ($ mil.)	NET INCOME ($ mil.)	NET PROFIT MARGIN	EMPLOYEES
12/08	680	—	—	900
12/07	670	—	—	1,000
12/06	505	—	—	1,000
12/05	507	—	—	900
12/04	507	—	—	900
Annual Growth	7.6%	—	—	0.0%

Revenue History

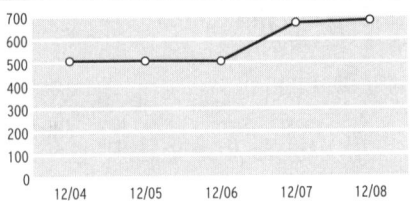

Mayo Foundation

Mayo can whip up a medical miracle. The not-for-profit Mayo Foundation for Medical Education and Research provides health care, most notably for complex medical conditions, through its renowned Mayo Clinic in Rochester, Minnesota. Other clinics are located in Arizona and Florida. The clinics' multidisciplinary approach to care attracts thousands of patients a year from around the globe, including such notables as the late Ronald Reagan and the late King Hussein of Jordan. The Mayo Health System operates a network of affiliated community hospitals and clinics in Minnesota, Iowa, and Wisconsin. The Mayo Foundation also conducts research and trains physicians, nurses, and other health professionals.

In addition to the Mayo Clinics, the foundation operates other hospitals, including Saint Marys Hospital and Rochester Methodist Hospital in Rochester and Mayo Clinic Hospital in Phoenix. It sold St. Luke's Hospital in Jacksonville to the St. Vincent's Health System in 2005, but leased the facility until 2008 when the construction of its new 200-bed hospital on the Mayo Clinic Jacksonville campus was completed.

The Mayo Health System affiliated network includes about five clinics in Iowa, some 25 clinics and hospitals in Wisconsin, and about 40 facilities in Minnesota. To manage its patient load, Mayo forms referral alliances with additional hospital groups, HMOs, and other organizations. The foundation's education programs include the Mayo School of Graduate Medical Education and the Mayo School of Health Sciences; some medical training programs are conducted through partnerships with universities including the University of Minnesota.

The company relies on private contributions, endowments, and grants to supplement funding for its operations and research programs. The foundation also publishes medical literature, commercializes medical technology, provides laboratory and research services, and invests in other medical startups to increase income. Reliance on these extra sources of income increased in 2008 as patient revenues fell due to economic conditions, reduced reimbursement levels from insurance sources, and shifting patient demographics.

In 2008 the foundation announced that it would phase out operations at its clinical trial services division in Rochester, which conducts product testing for pharmaceutical, biotech, and medical device firms, due to increased competition in the industry. The Mayo Collaborative Services division will instead focus on its medical lab testing and validation services segments. The Mayo Clinic in Florida continues to accept clinical trial contracts.

The Mayo Foundation dates back to a frontier practice launched by William Mayo in 1863. The foundation bases its philosophy of putting the patient first and investing in education and research on the founding family's medical practices.

HISTORY

In 1845 William Mayo came to the US from England. He was a doctor, veterinarian, river boatman, surveyor, and newspaper editor before settling in Rochester, Minnesota, in 1863.

When a tornado struck Rochester in 1883, Mayo took charge of a makeshift hospital. The Sisters of St. Francis offered to replace the hospital that was lost in the disaster if Mayo would head the staff. He agreed reluctantly. Not only were hospitals then associated with the poor and insane, but his affiliation with the sisters raised eyebrows among Protestants and Catholics.

Saint Marys Hospital opened in 1889. Mayo's sons William and Charles, who were starting their medical careers, helped him. After the elder Mayo retired, the sons ran the hospital. Although the brothers accepted all medical cases, they made the hospital self-sufficient, attracting paying patients by pioneering in specialization at a time when physicians were jacks-of-all-medical-trades.

This specialization attracted other physicians, and by 1907 the practice was known as "the Mayo's clinic." The brothers, in association with the University of Minnesota, established the Mayo Foundation for Medical Research (now the Mayo Graduate School of Medicine), the world's first program to train medical specialists, in 1915.

In 1919 the brothers transferred the clinic properties and miscellaneous financial assets, primarily from patient care profits, into the Mayo Properties Association (renamed the Mayo Foundation in 1964). Under the terms of the endowment, all Mayo Clinic medical staff members became salaried employees. In 1933 the clinic established one of the first blood banks in the US. Both brothers died in 1939.

Part of the association's mission was to fund research. In 1950 two Mayo researchers won a Nobel Prize for developing cortisone to treat rheumatoid arthritis. The foundation opened its second medical school, the Mayo Medical School, in 1972.

As insurers in the 1980s pressured to cut hospital admissions and stays, the foundation diversified with for-profit ventures. In 1983 Mayo began publishing the *Mayo Clinic Health Letter*, its first subscription publication for a general audience, and the *Mayo Clinic Family Health Book*. It also began providing specialized lab services to other doctors and hospitals. The addition

of Rochester Methodist Hospital (creating the largest not-for-profit medical group in the country) was also a response to financial pressures. Following the money south as affluent folks retired, the foundation opened clinics in Jacksonville (1986); Scottsdale, Arizona (1987); and in nearby Phoenix (1998).

Seeking to expand in its home market, Mayo in 1992 formed the Mayo Health System, a regional network of health care facilities and medical practices. In 1996 former patient Barbara Woodward Lips left $127.9 million to the foundation, the largest bequest in its history.

In the late 1990s the foundation increasingly looked to corporate partnerships to help defray costs and to expand research activities. In 1998 and 1999 Mayo boosted its presence overseas with nonmedical regional offices. Mayo scientists in 2000 announced they had regrown or repaired nerve coverings in mice; this type of damage in humans (caused by such conditions as multiple sclerosis) had been considered irreparable. The Mayo Foundation continues to push for breakthroughs in medical science.

EXECUTIVES

President and CEO, Mayo Clinic: Denis A. Cortese, age 65
CFO; Chair, Department of Finance, Mayo Clinic: Jeffrey W. Bolton
Secretary and Chief Legal Officer, Mayo Clinic: Jonathan J. Oviatt
VP and Chief Administrative Officer: Shirley A. Weis
President and CEO, Franciscan Skemp Healthcare: Robert E. Nesse
CEO, Mayo Clinic Rochester: Glenn S. Forbes
CEO, Mayo Clinic Arizona: Victor F. Trastek
CEO, Mayo Clinic Jacksonville: George B. Bartley
Director Center for Individualized Medicine Research: Franklyn G. Prendergast, age 63
Chief Administrative Officer, Mayo Clinic Rochester: Jeffrey O. (Jeff) Korsmo
Medical Director for Development, Mayo Clinic: John H. Noseworthy
Chairman Information Technology, Mayo Clinic: Abdul Bengali
Chairman, Department of Facilities and Systems Support Services, Mayo Clinic Rochester: Craig A. Smoldt
Chairman, Department of Development: James P. Lyddy
Chairman, Human Resources: Marita Heller
Auditors: Ernst & Young LLP

LOCATIONS

HQ: Mayo Foundation for Medical
    Education and Research
    200 1st St. SW, Rochester, MN 55905
Phone: 507-284-2511   **Fax:** 507-284-0161
Web: www.mayo.edu

Selected Locations and Affiliates
Direct Subsidiaries
  Arizona
    Mayo Clinic Hospital (Phoenix)
    Mayo Clinic Scottsdale
  Florida
    Mayo Clinic Hospital (Jacksonville)
    Mayo Clinic Jacksonville
  Minnesota
    Mayo Clinic Rochester
    Rochester Methodist Hospital
    Saint Marys Hospital (Rochester)
      Mayo Eugenio Litta Children's Hospital

Mayo Health System Affiliates
  Iowa
    Armstrong Clinic
    Decorah Clinic
    Lake Mills Clinic
    Franciscan Skemp Waukon Clinic
  Minnesota
    Albert Lea Medical Center
    Cannon Falls Medical Center
    Cannon Valley Clinic (Faribault)
    Fairmont Medical Center
    Fountain Centers Rochester
    Franciscan Skemp La Crescent Clinic
    Immanuel St. Joseph's (Mankato)
    Lake City Medical Center
    Springfield Medical Center
    St. James Medical Center
    Wabasha Clinic
    Waseca Medical Center
    Wells Clinic
  Wisconsin
    Luther Midelfort (Eau Claire)
    Luther Midelfort Chippewa Valley (Bloomer)
    Luther Midelfort Northland (Barron)
    Luther Midelfort Oakridge (Mondovi)
    Red Cedar Medical Center (Menomonie)
    Franciscan Skemp Arcadia Campus
    Franciscan Skemp Holmen Clinic
    Franciscan Skemp Lake Tomah Clinic
    Franciscan Skemp Onalaska Clinic
    Franciscan Skemp Prairie du Chien Clinic
    Franciscan Skemp Sparta Campus

PRODUCTS/OPERATIONS

2008 Sales

	$ mil.	% of total
Medical services	6,143.5	85
Grants & contracts	328.7	5
Return on investments	117.2	2
Contributions	114.3	1
Premiums	92.8	1
Other	425.3	6
Total	**7,221.8**	**100**

COMPETITORS

Allina Hospitals
Ascension Health
CentraCare Health
Children's Hospitals and Clinics of Minnesota
The Cleveland Clinic
Dana-Farber Cancer Institute
Detroit Medical Center
Fairview Health
Fox Chase Cancer Center
Gundersen Lutheran
HCA
Health Management Associates
Henry Ford Health System
Johns Hopkins Medicine
Memorial Sloan-Kettering
MeritCare Health System
Methodist Hospital System
North Memorial Health Care
Olmsted Medical
Park Nicollet Health Services
Rockefeller University
Rush System for Health
Sanford Health
Scottsdale Healthcare
Scripps health
SSM Health Care
Tenet Healthcare
Universal Health Services
University of Minnesota Medical Center
Wistar Institute

HISTORICAL FINANCIALS

Company Type: Not-for-profit

Income Statement

FYE: December 31

	REVENUE ($ mil.)	NET INCOME ($ mil.)	NET PROFIT MARGIN	EMPLOYEES
12/08	7,222	—	—	57,000
12/07	6,898	—	—	54,914
12/06	6,289	—	—	52,194
12/05	5,802	—	—	45,000
12/04	5,354	—	—	—
Annual Growth	7.8%	—	—	8.2%

Revenue History

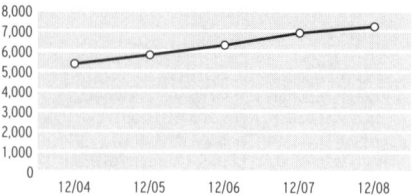

McCarthy Building Companies

A company that was in construction before Reconstruction, McCarthy Building Companies is one of the oldest privately held builders in the US. The general contractor and construction manager ranks among the top builders of health care and education facilities in the country. Contracts include heavy construction projects (bridges and water- and waste-treatment plants), commercial projects (retail and office buildings), and institutional projects (airports, schools, and prisons). Subsidiary MC Industrial handles energy, auto, and other manufacturing projects. Timothy McCarthy founded the firm in 1864. His great-grandson, Michael McCarthy, sold the firm to its employees in 2002.

McCarthy Building Companies' clients include Kaiser Permanente, California State University, and Bally's Casino Resort. Its projects include The Platinum condominium/hotel tower in Las Vegas, expansion at MD Anderson Cancer Center, and renovation and expansion of the National Baseball Hall of Fame and Museum in Cooperstown, New York.

Headquartered in Saint Louis, McCarthy Building Companies has offices in Newport Beach, San Francisco, Sacramento, and San Diego, California; Las Vegas; Phoenix; Salt Lake City; Dallas; and Atlanta. McCarthy is steadily building its presence across the US. In 2009 the company opened offices in Utah in an effort to grow in the Intermountain region and diversify its geographic footprint.

EXECUTIVES

Chairman and CEO: Michael D. (Mike) Bolen
President and COO: Derek W. Glanvill
CFO: J. Douglas (Doug) Audiffred, age 42
Southern California Division EVP and Leader San Diego Office: Ronald (Ron) Hall

Midwest Division EVP and Leader Atlanta Office: Kevin Kuntz
Midwest Division SVP, Laboratory/R&D Business Development: Walter R. (Bud) Guest
SVP, General Counsel, and Secretary: James A. Staskiel
VP Business Development: Jim Eaton
VP Laboratory/R&D Business Development, Midwest Division: Jim Contratto
Manager National Communications: Susan Garritano
Auditors: Ernst & Young LLP

LOCATIONS

HQ: McCarthy Building Companies, Inc.
1341 N. Rock Hill Rd., St. Louis, MO 63124
Phone: 314-968-3300 **Fax:** 314-968-4780
Web: www.mccarthy.com

PRODUCTS/OPERATIONS

Selected Markets

Commercial
Education K-12
Health care
Heavy/civil/transportation
Higher education
High performance/green
Hospitality/entertainment
Industrial
Parking structures
Science and technology

Selected Services

Negotiated general contracting
Construction management
Hard bid (lump sum contract for services)
Design/build
Construction management/general contracting

COMPETITORS

Alberici
Barton Malow
Bechtel
Bovis Lend Lease
Clayco
DPR Construction
Gilbane
HBE Corporation
Hensel Phelps
Korte
Peter Kiewit Sons'
Primus Builders
S. M. Wilson
Skanska
Swinerton
Turner Corporation
Tutor Perini

McJunkin Red Man Holding Corporation

No peddler of scrap, McJunkin Red Man is the largest North American pipeline of parts and supplies to energy and industrial markets. Operating from 200-plus sites in the US and Canada, the company distributes steel pipe, valves, and fittings, as well as drilling, electrical, and mining supplies. Oil and gas, power, pulp and paper, mining, and automotive industries are served. McJunkin Red Man offers technical support, too, along with storeroom management, investment recovery, and valve cleaning and rebuilding services. The company evolved from a merger, financed by Goldman Sachs, of McJunkin Corporation with oilfield supplier Red Man Pipe & Supply. PVF Holdings LLC owns a controlling interest in the company.

McJunkin Red Man has expanded its portfolio to include approximately 100,000 pipe, valve, and fitting products, and its geographic footprint, through acquisitions that complemented its core activities. Amidst the economic tough times, the company picked up sole control of Netherlands-based Transmark Fcx Group B.V., an international distributor of specialty valves and flow control equipment; the deal was finalized in the fall of 2009. Transmark has distribution portals in Northern Europe, Southeast Asia, Australia, Africa, and New Zealand. The company purchased LaBarge Pipe & Steel Co. in late 2008. The deal acquired capacity in supplying large-diameter carbon steel pipes, in high demand by North American oil and gas transmission, utility, industrial, and construction sectors.

In February 2009 the company moved its headquarters to Houston, Texas. It explained the importance of being in Houston, describing it as the "oil capital of the world."

Changes in McJunkin Red Man management have accompanied the company's growth. In 2008 the company tapped Andrew Lane, former Halliburton COO, as CEO. The role was previously held jointly by Red Man CEO Craig Ketchum and McJunkin CEO H. B. Wehrle III. Ketchum took the lead as chairman of McJunkin Red Man, and Wehrle remained chairman of PVF Holdings LLC, the majority shareholder of McJunkin Red Man, an entity controlled by Goldman Sachs.

EXECUTIVES

Chairman: L. Craig Ketchum, age 52
CEO: Andrew R. (Andy) Lane, age 49
EVP Supply Chain Management: Gary A. Ittner, age 57
EVP and CFO: James F. (Jim) Underhill, age 54
EVP Business Development: Rory M. Isaac, age 59
EVP Human Resources: Diana Morris
EVP Branch Sales and Operations: Jeffrey Lang, age 53
EVP Canadian Operations and Business Development: J. M. (Dee) Paige, age 56
EVP Branch Sales and Operations: Stephen D. (Steve) Wehrle, age 55
SVP Sales and Marketing (Upstream): Randy K. Adams, age 52
Senior Corporate VP, General Counsel, and Corporate Secretary: Stephen W. Lake, age 45
Auditors: Ernst & Young LLP

LOCATIONS

HQ: McJunkin Red Man Holding Corporation
835 Hillcrest Dr., Charleston, WV 25311
Phone: 304-348-5211 **Fax:** 304-348-4922
Web: www.mcjunkinredman.com

PRODUCTS/OPERATIONS

Selected Products

Carbon steel and corrosion-resistant fittings and flanges
  Buttweld
  Malleable iron fittings
  Pressure
Carbon steel pipe
  Grooved
  Beveled
  Threaded
  Coupled
  Plain end
  Seamless
Electrical products
  Conduit and channel
  Conveyor belt fasteners
  Insulating products
  Lighting, lamps, and ballasts
  Motors and motor controls
  Panelboards and switches
  Transformers
  Wire, cord, and cable

Engineered products
  Gaskets
  Pressure power pumps
  Steam traps
  Tylok tube fittings
  Victaulic tube fittings
Gas distribution and transmission products
  Gas fittings
  Meter parts
  Meter risers
  Meters and meter valves
  Polyethylene and steel pipe
  Protection products
  Regulators and parts
  Saddle tees and tapping tees
  Squeeze tools
  Transitions
  Valve and curb boxes
  Valves, clamps, and couplings
Stainless steel and corrosion-resistant tubular products
  Plastic-lined
  Seamless
  Welded
Valves
  Ball valves
  Bellows-sealed valves
  Butterfly valves
  Cast steel valves
  Check valves
  Gate valves
  Forged steel valves
  Globe valves
  Knife gate valves
  Plug valves
  Stainless steel valves
Other products
  Chains
  Compounds and paint
  Fasteners
  Hand tools
  Tape and Teflon

COMPETITORS

Applied Industrial Technologies
Blue Tee
Consolidated Electrical
Ferguson Enterprises
HD Supply
Piping & Equipment
Shaw Group
Würth Group
Wilson
WinWholesale
Wolseley
W.W. Grainger

HISTORICAL FINANCIALS
Company Type: Private

Income Statement			FYE: December 31
	REVENUE ($ mil.)	NET INCOME ($ mil.)	NET PROFIT MARGIN	EMPLOYEES
12/08	5,260	—	—	3,745
12/07	2,268	—	—	3,484
12/06	1,714	—	—	1,467
12/05	1,446	—	—	1,436
Annual Growth	53.8%	—	—	37.6%

Revenue History

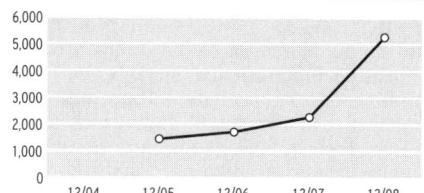

McKee Foods

When Little Debbie smiles up out of your lunch bag, you know you are loved. McKee Foods' Little Debbie is one of the US's best known brands of snack cakes, named for and featuring the smiling face of the four-year-old granddaughter of the company's late founders, O.D. and Ruth McKee. McKee also makes ready-to-eat breakfast cereals, granola, creme-filled cookies, crackers, and snack bars. There are more than 150 varieties of Little Debbie-brand snack packs. McKee's products are available in the US, Canada, and Mexico, as well as at US military commissaries around the world. The company is still owned and operated by the McKee family, including CEO Mike McKee.

In addition to Little Debbie, the company's brand names include Sunbelt and Fieldstone Bakery (foodservice only). McKee also owns Blue Planet Foods, which makes breakfast cereals, toasted oats, and other grain products under the Heartland brand name.

Product development is key in the highly competitive snack market, and McKee Foods steadily puts out offerings to keep it in the forefront of the snack-food world. In 2009 it introduced Little Debbie Chocolate Cupcakes in keeping with the new popularity of cupcakes and perhaps to compete with Hostess Cupcakes. Low prices and family packs of individually wrapped treats also continue to drive sales.

The company has operations in Arizona, Arkansas, Tennessee, and Virginia. In 2009 it shuttered and put up for sale its baking plant in Chattanooga, Tennessee — the plant that produced Little Debbie products. Production of Little Debbie was moved to the company's facilities in Arkansas and Collegedale, Tennessee.

EXECUTIVES

Chairman: R. Ellsworth McKee
President and CEO: Michael K. (Mike) McKee, age 47
EVP: Debra E. McKee-Fowler, age 53
EVP Sales and Marketing:
  Christopher T. (Chris) McKee, age 44
EVP Manufacturing: Russell E. (Rusty) McKee Jr.
VP and CFO: Barry S. Patterson
VP Collegedale Operations: Roger Fiske
VP Stuarts Draft Operations: Dawn Gillerman
VP Gentry Operations: Tim Broughton
VP Human Resources: Eva Lynne Disbro
Corporate Communications and Public Relations Manager: Mike Gloekler
Director Sales: Ed Hannah
Director Transportation: Renee Tracy
Director Marketing: Barry Anthony
Corporate Human Resources Manager: Mark Newsome

LOCATIONS

HQ: McKee Foods Corporation
  10260 McKee Rd., Collegedale, TN 37315
Phone: 423-238-7111   **Fax:** 423-238-7101
Web: www.mckeefoods.com

PRODUCTS/OPERATIONS

Selected Brands and Products
Fieldstone Bakery (foodservice)
  Breakfast cereals
  Breakfast pastries
  Cookies
  Granola
  Snack bars

Heartland (retail)
  Breakfast cereals
  Bulgar wheat
  Oat bran
  Pie crusts
  Steel-cut oats
Little Debbie (retail)
  Brownies
  Coffeecake
  Cookies
  Crackers
  Seasonal snacks
  Snack cakes
Sunbelt (retail)
  Cereal bars
  Fruit snacks
  Granola bars

COMPETITORS

Chattanooga Bakery   Lance Snacks
Flowers Foods   Otis Spunkmeyer
General Mills   Pepperidge Farm
Hostess Brands   Sara Lee 322
Interbake Foods   Tasty Baking
Kellogg U.S. Snacks   Voortman Cookies
Kraft Foods

HISTORICAL FINANCIALS
Company Type: Private

Income Statement			FYE: Friday nearest June 30
	REVENUE ($ mil.)	NET INCOME ($ mil.)	NET PROFIT MARGIN	EMPLOYEES
6/08	1,100	—	—	6,000
6/07	1,000	—	—	6,000
6/06	1,000	—	—	6,000
6/05	1,000	—	—	6,000
6/04	1,000	—	—	6,000
Annual Growth	2.4%	—	—	0.0%

Revenue History

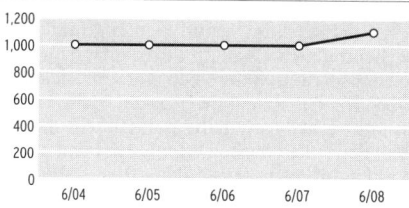

McKinsey & Company

One of the world's top management consulting firms, McKinsey & Company has about 90 offices in more than 50 countries around the globe. The company advises corporate enterprises, government agencies and institutions, and foundations on a variety of issues. It groups its practices into seven main areas: business technology, corporate finance, marketing and sales, operations, organization, risk, and strategy. McKinsey serves clients in numerous industry sectors, from automotive to high tech to telecommunications. Founded by James McKinsey in 1926, the company is owned by its partners.

McKinsey takes advantage of its global reach to gain business from multinational companies that want help in harmonizing their diverse operations. Toward that end, the firm aims to work collaboratively across its own organization, bringing together the work of multiple offices and practices on behalf of a single client.

In addition to being one of the oldest consulting firms, McKinsey is considered one of the most prestigious (along with Boston Consulting Group and Bain) as measured in surveys of aspiring consultants. Contributing to McKinsey's allure as an employer is the firm's network of 18,000-plus alumni, many of whom have been tapped for C-level jobs in the course of their careers. Alumni running companies, in turn, represent a potential source of business for the firm.

In July 2009 managing director Ian Davis stepped down as Dominic Barton, the firm's regional leader in Asia, was elected to the post by McKinsey's 400 or so senior partners. Davis served in the slot for two terms, the maximum allowed under McKinsey's policy.

HISTORY

McKinsey & Company was founded in Chicago in 1926 by University of Chicago accounting professor James McKinsey. The company evolved from an auditing practice of McKinsey and his partners, Marvin Bower and A. T. Kearney, who began analyzing business and industry and offering advice. McKinsey died in 1937; two years later Bower, who headed the New York office, and Kearney, in Chicago, split the firm. Kearney renamed the Chicago office A.T. Kearney & Co. (later acquired by Electronic Data Systems), and Bower kept the McKinsey name and built up a practice structured like a law firm.

Bower focused on the big picture instead of on specific operating problems, helping boost billings to $2 million by 1950. He hired staff straight out of prestigious business schools, reinforcing the firm's theoretical bent. Bower implemented a competitive up-or-out policy requiring employees who are not continually promoted to leave the firm.

The firm's prestige continued to grow during the booming 1950s along with demand for consulting services. Before becoming president in 1953, Dwight Eisenhower asked McKinsey to find out exactly what the government did. By 1959 Bower had opened an office in London, followed by others in Amsterdam; Düsseldorf, Germany; Melbourne; Paris; and Zurich.

In 1964 the company founded management journal *The McKinsey Quarterly*. When Bower retired in 1967, sales were $20 million and McKinsey was the #1 management consulting firm. During the 1970s it faced competition from firms with newer approaches and lost market share. In response, then-managing director Ronald Daniel started specialty practices and expanded foreign operations.

The consulting boom of the 1980s was spurred by mergers and buyouts. By 1988 the firm had 1,800 consultants, sales were $620 million, and 50% of billings came from overseas.

The recession of the early 1990s hit white-collar workers, including consultants. McKinsey, scrambling to upgrade its technical side, bought Information Consulting Group (ICG), its first acquisition. But the corporate cultures did not meld, and most ICG people left by 1993.

In 1994 the company elected its first managing director of non-European descent, Indian-born Rajat Gupta. Two years later the traditionally hush-hush firm found itself at the center of that most public 1990s arena, the sexual discrimination lawsuit. A female ex-consultant in Texas sued,

claiming McKinsey had sabotaged her career (the case was dismissed).

In 1998 McKinsey partnered with Northwestern University and the University of Pennsylvania to establish a business school in India. The following year graduating seniors surveyed in Europe, the UK, and the US named the company as their ideal employer.

Also in 1999 the company created @McKinsey to help "accelerate" Internet startups. The next year it increased salaries and offered incentives to better compete with Internet firms for employees. In 2001 the company expanded its branding business with the acquisition of Envision, a Chicago-based brand consultant.

Like its rivals in the consulting industry, McKinsey took a hit from the dot-com bust and the economic downturn of 2001 and 2002, as many companies were slower to sign up for costly long-term strategy consulting engagements, and mergers and acquisitions work dried up.

In 2003 Ian Davis was elected as managing director of the firm, succeeding Gupta, who had served as McKinsey's top executive for nine years. Davis had previously served as the head of the firm's UK office. Davis stepped down in July 2009 to make way for Dominic Barton, who was the firm's regional leader in Asia.

EXECUTIVES

Managing Director: Dominic Barton, age 46
Director External Relations, Germany: Kai Peter Rath
Director External Relations, Europe, Middle East, and Africa: Andrew Whitehouse
Director External Relations North and South America: Simon London
Director External Relations, UK: Andrea Minton Beddoes
Chairman, Americas: Michael Patsalos-Fox
Chairman, Europe, Middle East, and Africa: Robert Reibestein
Chairman, McKinsey Global Institute: Lenny Mendonca
Global Director Communications: Michael Stewart, age 59

LOCATIONS

HQ: McKinsey & Company
   55 E. 52nd St., 21st Fl., New York, NY 10022
Phone: 212-446-7000   **Fax:** 212-446-8575
Web: www.mckinsey.com

PRODUCTS/OPERATIONS

Selected Industry Practices

Automotive and assembly
Chemicals
Consumer packaged goods
Electric power and natural gas
Financial services
Health care payor and provider
High tech
Media and entertainment
Metals and mining
Petroleum
Pharmaceuticals and medical products
Private equity
Public sector
Pulp and paper
Retail
Social sector
Telecommunications
Travel infrastructure logistics

COMPETITORS

Accenture	ESource
A.T. Kearney	HP Enterprise Services
Bain & Company	IBM
BearingPoint	Mercer
Booz	Monitor Group
Booz Allen	Oliver Wyman
Boston Consulting	PA Consulting
Capgemini	Perot Systems
Computer Sciences Corp.	PRTM Management
Deloitte Consulting	Roland Berger

HISTORICAL FINANCIALS

Company Type: Private

Income Statement				FYE: December 31
	ESTIMATED REVENUE ($ mil.)	NET INCOME ($ mil.)	NET PROFIT MARGIN	EMPLOYEES
12/07	5,330	—	—	15,600
12/06	4,370	—	—	14,190
12/05	3,800	—	—	12,900
12/04	3,150	—	—	12,100
12/03	3,000	—	—	11,500
Annual Growth	15.5%	—	—	7.9%

Revenue History

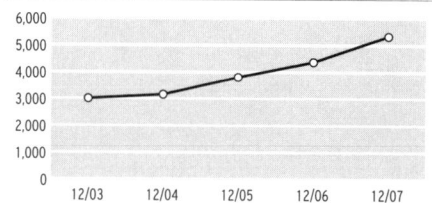

McWane, Inc.

As a manufacturer of fire hydrants, McWane is a friend to both firefighters and dogs. Orchestrated through five product groups, McWane's subsidiaries make a line of water distribution solutions including fire hydrants, cast-iron water and sewer pipes, fittings, and compressed air tanks. Its Amerex subsidiary is one of the world's largest makers of fire extinguishers. Subsidiary Manchester Tank makes pressure vessels, from huge propane cylinders to hand-held torches. M&H Valve Co., a maker of industrial valves for waste-water equipment and fire hydrants, has operated since 1854. Established in 1921, McWane continues as a closely held corporation, led by its founder's fourth generation, chairman Phillip McWane.

Over the years McWane has grown by acquiring troubled companies and turning them around with infusions of better equipment and streamlined management. Its expansions support a broad product portfolio, manufactured through a network of 25 facilities, 13 of which are iron foundries, in the US, Canada, Australia, and China. Moreover, McWane pipe products serve vital infrastructure markets, including drinking water and sanitation. The company has launched a new lineup of ductile iron utility poles and vehicle fire-suppression systems. Tying up with Janus Fire Systems, McWane added a division for fire protection products focused on foam and water-based fire extinguishers and hazard alarm devices.

Although the company asserts a worker safety record and its commitment to environmental responsibility (it recycles the equivalent of 800,000 cars in scrap iron per year), McWane and its former employees have attracted persistent regulatory scrutiny. More than 400 safety violations have been raised since 1995. In 2009 the company was fined $8 million for a series of US worker safety and environmental violations, charged in 2006. A prison sentence has been imposed on a former manager for dumping pollutants in the Delaware River and concealing safety violations. The company has also been fined $3 million for falsifying emissions tests.

EXECUTIVES

Chairman: C. Phillip McWane, age 51
President: G. Ruffner Page Jr.
EVP Ductile Iron Pipe Group: Dennis R. Charko
SVP and General Counsel: James M. Proctor II
SVP and CFO: Charles F. Nowlin
SVP Environmental, Health and Safety, and Human Resources: Jitendra Radia
VP Health and Safety: Barbara Wisniewski
VP Human Resources and Community Affairs: A.. Michelle Clemon
SVP McWane, Inc. and President, McWane Global: Michael C. Keel
Human Resources Manager, Tyler Pipe: Jim Rerich

LOCATIONS

HQ: McWane, Inc.
2900 Hwy. 280, Ste. 300, Birmingham, AL 35223
Phone: 205-414-3100   **Fax:** 205-414-3170
Web: www.mcwane.com

PRODUCTS/OPERATIONS

Selected Operations

Ductile Iron Pipe Group
  Atlantic States Cast Iron Pipe Company
  Canada Pipe Company, Ltd.
  Clow Water Systems Company
  McWane Cast Iron Pipe Company
  McWane Coal Sales
  McWane Poles
  Pacific States Cast Iron Pipe Company

Plumbing Group
  AB&I Foundry
  Anaco Inc.
  Bibby-Ste-Croix Companies
  Tyler Coupling
  Tyler Pipe Company
  Wade Inc.

Sales
  McWane International

Steel Fabrication Group
  Amerex Corporation
  Getz Manufacturing
  Janus Fire Systems
  Manchester Tank & Equipment

Valve and Hydrant Group
  American R/D
  Clow Canada
  Clow Valve Company
  Kennedy Valve Company
  M&H Valve Company

Waterworks Fittings Group
  Tyler Pipe
  Tyler Xian Xian
  Union Foundry Company

COMPETITORS

Aluminum Precision	ITT Corp.
American Cast Iron Pipe	McJunkin Red Man
Ameron	Mueller Water Products
Citation Corp.	Northwest Pipe
Eaton	SPX
Flowserve	SSAB North America
Henry Technologies	Watts Water Technologies

HISTORICAL FINANCIALS
Company Type: Private

Income Statement
FYE: December 31

	ESTIMATED REVENUE ($ mil.)	NET INCOME ($ mil.)	NET PROFIT MARGIN	EMPLOYEES
12/07	1,700	—	—	7,500
12/06	1,740	—	—	7,500
12/05	1,753	—	—	7,000
12/04	1,690	—	—	7,000
12/03	1,500	—	—	7,000
Annual Growth	3.2%	—	—	1.7%

Revenue History

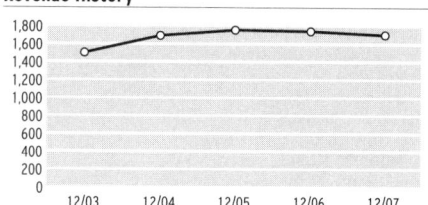

Meadowbrook Meat Company

What's on the menu at your favorite restaurant? Just ask Meadowbrook Meat Company, one of the largest privately owned foodservice distributors in the nation. The company specializes in providing food to more than 25,000 franchised restaurants, including Arby's, Burger King, Captain D's, Chick-fil-A, and Darden Restaurants (Red Lobster, Olive Garden). Meadowbrook fills customer orders through a nationwide network of more than 30 distribution centers. J. R. Wordsworth founded the company about 50 years ago as a retail food distributor. It made the transition to its present role in restaurant food distribution after Wordsworth's children bought the business in the 1970s.

EXECUTIVES

Chairman, President, and CEO: Jerry L. Wordsworth
EVP and COO: Jim K. Sabiston
CFO: Jeffrey M. (Jeff) Kowalk
Controller: Barry Adams
Executive Director National Accounts: Mike Burk
Executive Director Operations: Andy Blanton
Director Quality Assurance: Samuel Richardson
Director Human Resources: Tim Ozment
Director Purchasing: Mitch Brantley
Secretary and Treasurer: Debbie Wordsworth-Daughtridge

LOCATIONS

HQ: Meadowbrook Meat Company, Inc.
2641 Meadowbrook Rd., Rocky Mount, NC 27801
Phone: 252-985-7200   **Fax:** 252-985-7247

COMPETITORS

Alex Lee	McLane Foodservice
Ben E. Keith	Nash-Finch
Clark National	Performance Food
Golden State Foods	Reyes Holdings
Gordon Food Service	SYSCO
Keystone Foods	UniPro Foodservice
MAINES	U.S. Foodservice
Martin-Brower	

HISTORICAL FINANCIALS
Company Type: Private

Income Statement
FYE: December 31

	REVENUE ($ mil.)	NET INCOME ($ mil.)	NET PROFIT MARGIN	EMPLOYEES
12/07	5,500	—	—	3,400
12/06	5,200	—	—	3,400
12/05	4,964	—	—	3,000
12/04	4,800	—	—	3,500
12/03	4,744	—	—	3,500
Annual Growth	3.8%	—	—	(0.7%)

Revenue History

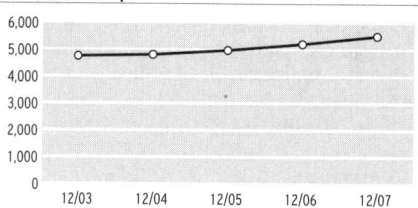

MediaNews Group

This company has part of the news media in its folds. MediaNews Group is one of the leading newspaper companies in the US with more than 60 daily papers serving markets in a dozen states. Its portfolio includes *The Denver Post, The Salt Lake Tribune*, and the *St. Paul Pioneer Press*, as well as Northern California newspapers the *Contra Costa Times* and the *San Jose Mercury News*. The papers boast a total circulation of about 2.5 million. In addition, MediaNews publishes about 100 non-daily newspapers and it operates a TV station in Anchorage, Alaska, along with four Texas radio stations. The company is owned by the families of vice chairman and CEO Dean Singleton and chairman Richard Scudder.

MediaNews has built its business through a series of acquisitions focused on creating newspaper clusters in specific markets, particularly in California, the Rocky Mountain region, and the Northeast. Its growth has also been helped by a variety of partnerships with other newspaper businesses. *The Salt Lake Tribune* is run under a joint operating agreement (JOA) with The Deseret News Publishing Company (part of Deseret Management and owner of the *Deseret News*). MediaNews also has a 60% interest in a partnership with Gannett that operates newspapers in Texas, New Mexico, and Pennsylvania.

With the newspaper industry struggling, MediaNews sold a group of papers in Connecticut including the *Connecticut Post* to media giant Hearst. The disposal came a year after the company had acquired several newspapers, including the *Monterey County Herald* and the *St. Paul Pioneer Press,* from Hearst in exchange for a 30% stake in MediaNews' newspaper operations outside the San Francisco area. MediaNews and Hearst had joined together in 2006 to acquire those papers along with *San Jose Mercury News* and the *Contra Costa Times* from McClatchy.

Detroit Media Partnership, the JOA that oversees circulation and ad selling for the company's *Detroit News* and its rival *Detroit Free Press* (owned by Gannett), took the bold step in 2009 of cutting home delivery of its papers to three times a week (twice a week for the *Detroit News*). The papers still distribute news online.

In the Denver market, meanwhile, MediaNews dissolved its JOA with E. W. Scripps, which co-produced both *The Denver Post* and the *Rocky Mountain News.* Scripps shuttered its paper in 2009 and sold its 50% stake in Denver Newspaper Agency (DNA) to MediaNews. The company also acquired from Scripps its Prairie Mountain Publishing, a community newspaper portfolio that includes the *Daily Camera* (Boulder, Colorado).

The company has also been focused on expanding its digital media distribution operations to take advantage of increased ad spending online. It operates more than 70 Web sites in conjunction with its local papers. The company is also partnered with Yahoo's HotJobs to sell listings on the online classified company's site. The deal also allows the company to sell access to HotJobs' resume database.

EXECUTIVES

Chairman: Richard B. Scudder, age 96
Vice Chairman and CEO: William D. (Dean) Singleton, age 58
President: Joseph J. (Jody) Lodovic IV, age 48
EVP and Chief Marketing and Sales Officer: Mark J. Winkler, age 49
SVP Operations: Anthony F. Tierno, age 64
SVP New Business Development; Interim Publisher, *Los Angeles Daily News*: Elizabeth A. (Liz) Gaier, age 44
SVP Circulation: Stephen M. (Steve) Hesse, age 61
Group VP, Bay Area News Group and President and Publisher, *San Jose Mercury News*: Michael (Mac) Tully, age 52
VP and CIO: David M. Bessen, age 55
VP and CFO: Ronald A. (Ron) Mayo, age 48
VP Human Resources: Charles M. Kamen, age 61
CEO, Detroit Media Partnership: Susie Ellwood
President and CEO, Los Angeles Newspaper Group: Fred Hamilton
President, MediaNews Group Interactive: Oliver Knowlton, age 51
President and CEO, California Newspapers: Steven B. (Steve) Rossi, age 60
Editor and Publisher, *Detroit Free Press*: Paul Anger
Treasurer: James L. McDougald, age 55
Secretary: Patricia (Pat) Robinson, age 67
Auditors: Ernst & Young LLP

LOCATIONS

HQ: MediaNews Group, Inc.
101 W. Colfax Ave., Ste. 1100, Denver, CO 80202
Phone: 303-954-6360   **Fax:** 303-954-6320
Web: www.medianewsgroup.com

PRODUCTS/OPERATIONS

Selected Operations
Newspapers
Bennington Banner (Vermont)
The Berkshire Eagle (Pittsfield, MA)
Brattleboro Reformer (Vermont)
Charleston Daily Mail (Charleston, WV)
Daily Breeze (Torrance, CA)
Daily News (Los Angeles)
The Denver Post
The Detroit News
The Monterey County Herald (California)
North Adams Transcript (Massachusetts)
Press-Telegram (Long Beach, CA)
St. Paul Pioneer Press
The Salt Lake Tribune
Sentinel & Enterprise (Fitchburg, MA)
The Sun (Lowell, MA)
Other
KLXK-FM (Breckenridge, TX)
KROO-FM (Breckenridge, TX)
KSWA-FM (Graham, TX)
KTVA-TV (CBS; Anchorage, AK)
KWKQ-FM (Graham, TX)

COMPETITORS

American City Business Journals
Freedom Communications
Gannett
Hearst Newspapers
McClatchy Company
New York Times
Philadelphia Media
Star Tribune
Tribune Company
Village Voice

Medical Information Technology

Medical Information Technology (MEDITECH) prescribes a good dose of software to cure health care disorders. Founded in 1969, MEDITECH provides software and services for managing hospitals, ambulatory care centers, doctors' offices, long-term care facilities, nursing homes, and home health care agencies in North America and the UK. The company's software includes applications for patient identification and scheduling, patient care management, clinical information management, long-term and ambulatory care, behavioral health, and financial and reimbursement management.

MEDITECH serves more than 2,200 hospital sites in Canada, the UK, and the US. CEO Neil Pappalardo controls 37% of the company.

EXECUTIVES

Chairman, CEO, and Director: A. Neil Pappalardo, age 66, $384,159 total compensation
Vice Chairman: Lawrence A. (Larry) Polimeno, age 67, $786,600 total compensation
President and COO: Howard Messing, age 56, $895,600 total compensation
CFO, Treasurer, and Clerk: Barbara A. Manzolillo, age 56, $334,600 total compensation
SVP Product Development: Robert G. Gale, age 62

VP Sales: Stuart N. (Stu) Lefthes, age 56, $647,600 total compensation
VP Marketing: Hoda Sayed-Friel, age 51
VP Product Development: Michelle O'Connor, age 43
VP Client Service: Joanne Wood, age 55
VP Technology: Christopher (Chris) Anschuetz, age 56
VP Implementation: Steven B. (Steve) Koretz, age 57
Marketing and Public Relations: Paul Berthiaume
Auditors: Ernst & Young LLP

LOCATIONS

HQ: Medical Information Technology, Inc.
MEDITECH Circle, Westwood, MA 02090
Phone: 781-821-3000   **Fax:** 781-821-2199
Web: www.meditech.com

PRODUCTS/OPERATIONS

Selected Software Products
Ambulatory care applications
   Emergency department management
   Prescription management
Behavioral health applications
Clinical applications
   Anatomical pathology
   Blood bank
   Imaging and therapeutic services
   Laboratory
   Microbiology
   Pharmacy
Decision support applications
   Budgeting and forecasting
   Cost accounting
   Data archiving
   Data repository
   Executive support system
   Faxing
   Integrated communication system
Financial management applications
   Accounts payable
   Fixed assets
   General ledger
   Materials management
   Payroll/personnel
   Staffing and scheduling
Long-term care information system
Patient care management applications
   Patient care system
   Patient education suite
   Physician care manager
   Physician practice management
Patient identification and scheduling applications
   Case mix management
   Community-wide scheduling
   Enterprise patient index and medical records
   Operating room management
   Registration
Reimbursement applications
   Authorization and referral management
   Billing/accounts receivable

COMPETITORS

Alteer
AMICAS
CareCentric
Cerner
CPSI
Eclipsys
Health Management Systems
Healthvision
iSOFT Group
McKesson
Mediware
MedPlus
NextGen
QuadraMed
Quality Systems
Siemens Healthcare
TriZetto

HISTORICAL FINANCIALS

Company Type: Private

Income Statement				FYE: December 31
	REVENUE ($ mil.)	NET INCOME ($ mil.)	NET PROFIT MARGIN	EMPLOYEES
12/08	398	36	9.0%	2,865
12/07	376	89	23.5%	2,872
12/06	345	87	25.3%	2,566
12/05	305	78	25.5%	2,500
12/04	281	71	25.4%	2,100
Annual Growth	9.1%	(15.9%)	—	8.1%

2008 Year-End Financials

Debt ratio: 0.0%
Return on equity: —
Cash ($ mil.): —
Current ratio: —
Long-term debt ($ mil.): 0

Net Income History

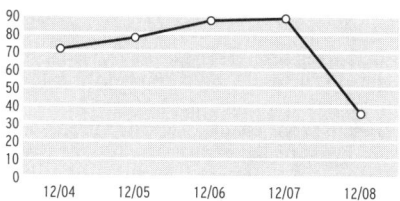

Medline Industries

When health care supplies are on the line, Medline Industries goes toe-to-toe with the bigger guns, selling more than 100,000 products. The family-owned company's catalog includes hospital furnishings, exam equipment, housekeeping supplies, and surgical gloves and garments. The firm manufactures and distributes health care products to customers including hospitals, long-term care facilities, physician practices, and home health providers. It also acts as a distributor for other manufacturers' products. In addition, Medline offers inventory and supply chain solutions for health care providers. Products are marketed by its more than 800 sales representatives through some 35 distribution centers in 20 countries.

The company manufactures a large number of the products it distributes; it also acts as a distributor for other products through partnerships with companies such as 3M. Medline also forms supply alliances with group hospital purchasing organizations such as Premier and Novation. The company is a primary supplier for some 250 hospitals and health care networks in the US.

Medline continues to expand its product line through acquisitions, partnerships, and product innovations. In 2007 the company acquired the Curad first-aid brand and related operations from Beiersdorf Inc.; it also launched a line of patient-lifting equipment. The following year Medline acquired Chester Packaging (formerly Chester Labs), a maker of liquid personal care, infection control, and diagnostic products.

Also in 2008 the company released a new line of pressure ulcer therapeutic mattresses and pads, and it purchased the Carrington line of wound care products from the now-defunct DelSite, which was exiting the wound care market. (Delsite later liquidated its remaining assets

through Chapter 7 bankruptcy.) Medline also acquired the Guardian Mobility (walking aids) and Guardian bath safety product lines from Sunrise Medical. The following year it agreed to acquire the UltraGard surgical textile operations of Precept Medical Products.

In addition, Medline has expanded its distribution capabilities by opening new warehouses. The company is also looking to expand into the pharmaceutical distribution market. The company has gained approval to conduct pharmacy distribution activities from some of its facilities in the US, and it is hoping to increase the number of accredited facilities.

Owned by the Mills family, Medline traces its roots to Northwest Garment Factory, started by the current owners' great-grandfather in 1910. Medline took shape as a medical products distributor in 1966.

EXECUTIVES

CEO: Charles N. (Charlie) Mills, age 47
President: Andy Mills
COO: Jim Abrams
SVP Corporate Sales: Tim Jacobson
VP National Accounts: Jack Hannemann
VP Human Resources: Joseph Becker
Group President, SPT, Anesthesia, OR: Tom Pistella
President, Health Care National Accounts: Scott Sibigtroth
President, Medline Personal Care Division: Dan Love
President, Durable Medical Equipment Division: Dave Jacobs
President, General Line National Accounts: Kurt Krieghbaum
President, Ready Care: Hunter Banks
President, Dermal Management Systems: Jonathan Primer
President, Operations: Bill Abington
President, Sales: Ray Swaback
Director Public Relations: Rebecca Hayne

LOCATIONS

HQ: Medline Industries, Inc.
1 Medline Place, Mundelein, IL 60060
Phone: 847-949-5500   **Fax:** 800-351-1512
Web: www.medline.com

PRODUCTS/OPERATIONS

Selected Products

Durable medical equipment (wheelchairs, beds, bath safety)
Face masks
Gloves
Housekeeping (microfiber mops)
Incontinence management
Isolation gowns
Prothrombin monitors (blood clot monitors)
Surgery sterile (surgical instruments, sterilization equipment)
Textiles (drapes, gowns, linens)
Wound and skin care

Selected Service Programs

ACCESS Consignment or ACCESS O.R. (inventory management)
Medline Select (hospital supply chain cost management)
MED-PACK (online tools)
Patient-Home Direct (home health agency supply management)
Physician-Office Direct (doctors' offices supply standardization)
Prime Vendor (expense reduction)
S.M.A.R.T. (cost management)
Super 60 Relief Service (backorder filling)
Surgery Center Supply Management (supply standardization)
Suture Control (inventory management)
TEXCAP (linen supply management)
Truecost (supply cost and logistics management)

COMPETITORS

3M Health Care
Bard
Becton, Dickinson
Bruno Independent Living Aids
Buffalo Supply
Cardinal Health
Covidien
Hill-Rom Holdings
Invacare
Johnson & Johnson
Kimberly-Clark
Kinetic Concepts
McKesson
Medical Action Industries
Molnlycke
Owens & Minor
Patterson Companies
Pride Mobility Products
PSS World Medical
Smith & Nephew
Sunrise Medical
Surgical Express
Terumo
Tri-anim

HISTORICAL FINANCIALS

Company Type: Private

Income Statement				FYE: December 31
	REVENUE ($ mil.)	NET INCOME ($ mil.)	NET PROFIT MARGIN	EMPLOYEES
12/08	3,190	—	—	6,800
12/07	2,830	—	—	6,000
12/06	2,460	—	—	4,422
12/05	2,000	—	—	4,892
12/04	1,940	—	—	4,500
Annual Growth	13.2%	—	—	10.9%

Revenue History

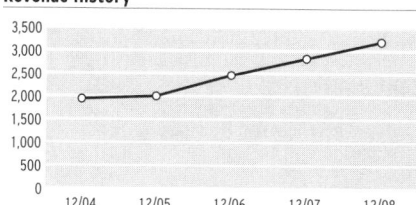

MedStar Health

Whether you're seeing stars or are just plain sickly, MedStar Health can cater to you. The not-for-profit organization runs nine hospitals and a number of other health care facilities in Maryland and the Washington, DC, area, including Union Memorial and Georgetown University Hospital. With some 2,800 beds and 5,000 affiliated physicians, MedStar has a comprehensive service offering, including acute and long-term sub-acute care, emergency services, home health care, and rehabilitation. It also operates emergency clinics and assisted living and nursing homes, maintains a primary care and specialist physician network (MedStar Physician Partners), and conducts research and medical education activities.

MedStar Health added a DC-area hospital in 2008 when it acquired Montgomery General Hospital, a 149-bed general acute care facility located in Montgomery County, Maryland. In

2009 the health network purchased St. Mary's Hospital, a not-for-profit medical center with 100 beds; the acquisition represented MedStar's growth into southern Maryland.

Also in 2008 MedStar formed a partnership with Rite Aid to establish walk-in health clinics in select Rite Aid pharmacies in the Baltimore and Washington, DC, markets.

The company was formed through the 1999 merger of Helix Health and Medlantic.

EXECUTIVES

Chairman: E. F. Shaw Wilgis
Vice Chairman: Edward J. Brody
President and CEO: Kenneth A. (Ken) Samet, age 51
EVP Baltimore: Carl J. Schindelar
EVP, Medical Affairs: William L. Thomas
EVP Finance and CFO: Michael J. Curran
EVP Corporate Services: Michael C. Rogers
SVP and CIO: Catherine Szenczy, age 54
SVP, Managed Care: Eric R. Wagner
SVP and General Counsel: Elizabeth A. Simpson
SVP, Integrated Operations: Steven S. Cohen
SVP Corporate Strategy and Business Development:
  Christine M. Swearingen
SVP Audit and Compliance: Alton F. Knight
Corporate VP Government Affairs: Pegeen Townsend
VP Corporate Human Resources: David Noe
Auditors: PricewaterhouseCoopers LLP

LOCATIONS

HQ: MedStar Health
  5565 Sterrett Place, 5th Fl., Columbia, MD 21044
Phone: 410-772-6500   **Fax:** 410-715-3905
Web: www.medstarhealth.org

Selected Facilities

Maryland
  Franklin Square Hospital Center (Baltimore)
  Good Samaritan Hospital (Baltimore)
  Harbor Hospital (Baltimore)
  Montgomery General Hospital (Olney)
  St. Mary's Hospital (Leonardtown)
  Union Memorial Hospital (Baltimore)

Washington, DC
  Georgetown University Hospital
  National Rehabilitation Hospital
  Washington Hospital Center

COMPETITORS

Adventist HealthCare
Anne Arundel Medical Center
Ascension Health
Bon Secours Health
Children's National Medical Center
Christiana Care
Civista Health
Inova
Johns Hopkins Health System
Levindale Hospital
University of Maryland Medical System
Valley Health
Virginia Hospital Center

HISTORICAL FINANCIALS

Company Type: Not-for-profit

Income Statement

FYE: June 30

	REVENUE ($ mil.)	NET INCOME ($ mil.)	NET PROFIT MARGIN	EMPLOYEES
6/08	3,502	—	—	23,000

Meijer, Inc.

Meijer (pronounced "Meyer") is a giant of retailing in the Midwest. The company's huge grocery and general merchandise stores average 200,000 to 250,000 sq. ft. each (or about the size of four regular grocery stores) and stock about 120,000 items, including Meijer private-label products. Meijer operates about 190 locations; about half of its stores are in Michigan, while the rest are in Illinois, Indiana, Kentucky, and Ohio. Customers can choose from 40-plus departments, including apparel, electronics, hardware, and toys. Most stores also sell gasoline, offer banking services, and have multiple in-store restaurants. Founder Hendrik Meijer opened his first store in 1934; the company is still family owned.

Although the discount superstore format is most often referred to in conjunction with its rival Wal-Mart, Meijer is its pioneer. But that hasn't stopped the world's #1 retailer from muscling in on Meijer's markets. Meijer is also facing increased pressure from warehouse club stores, drugstores, and supermarket chains, like Kroger, that are expanding in its markets. In response the chain has added fresh produce and meat departments to improve its grocery offering.

The retailer is also experimenting with smaller food-centered formats designed for more densely-populated locations, such as the Chicago suburbs. Meijer plans to open a 102,000-square-foot grocery-centered supercenter in Niles in early 2010. In 2009 the company announced it would be investing nearly $30 million to expand its Newport, Michigan, distribution center, which will span more than 1 million sq. ft. when completed. The expansion is anticipated to double the distribution center's capacity and enable it to serve nearly 60 additional stores.

Meijer has continued to innovate in the face of a difficult economy. In 2008 it introduced several new programs including Grocery by the Case (selling more than 2,000 products by the case via its Web site), Grocery Express (a personal shopping program that allows customers to shop online and have groceries delivered to their car), and Meijer Mealbox (a weekly meal planner tied to Meijer's coupons and promotions).

HISTORY

Dutch immigrant and barber Hendrik Meijer owned a vacant space next to his barbershop in Greenville, Michigan. Because of the Depression, he couldn't rent it out. So in 1934 he bought $338.76 in merchandise on credit and started his own grocery store, Thrift Market, with the help of his wife, Gezina; son, Fred; and daughter, Johanna; he made $7 the first day. Meijer had 22 competitors in Greenville alone, but his dedication to low prices (he and Fred often traveled long distances to find bargains) attracted customers. In 1935, to encourage self-service, Meijer placed 12 wicker baskets at the front of the store and posted signs that read, "Take a basket. Help yourself."

A second store was opened in 1942. The company added four more in the 1950s. In 1962 Meijer — then with 14 stores — opened the first one-stop shopping Meijer Thrifty Acres store, similar to a hypermarket another operator had opened in Belgium a year earlier. By 1964, the year that Hendrik died and Fred took over, three of these general merchandise stores were operating. The company entered Ohio in the late 1960s.

In the early 1980s Meijer bought 14 Twin Fair stores in Ohio and 10 in Cincinnati. But it sold the stores by 1987 after disappointing results. Meijer had greater success in Columbus, Ohio, where it opened one store that year and immediately captured 20% of the market. In 1988 the company began keeping most stores open 24 hours a day.

Meijer annihilated competitors in Dayton, Ohio, in 1991, when it opened four stores that year. The company entered the Toledo market in 1993 with four stores; after one year it had taken 11.5% of the market. A foray into the membership warehouse market was abandoned in 1993, just a few months after it began, when Meijer said it would close all seven SourceClubs in Michigan and Ohio.

The company entered Indiana in 1994, opening 16 stores in less than two years; it also reached an agreement with McDonald's to open restaurants in several stores. The first labor strike in Meijer's history hit four stores in Toledo that year, leading to pickets at 14 others. Union officials accused the company of using intimidation tactics by its hiring of large, uniformed men in flak jackets and combat boots as security guards. After nine weeks Meijer agreed to recognize the workers' newly attained union affiliation.

In 1995 the company opened 13 stores, including its first in Illinois. It reentered the Cincinnati market in 1996, announcing its opening of two new stores there by mailing 80,000 videos to residents. By the end of the year, Meijer had a total of five stores in Cincinnati and had entered Kentucky.

Meijer opened its first two stores in Louisville, Kentucky, in 1998. Meijer broke into the tough Chicago-area market with its first store in 1999.

The next year Meijer opened several "village-style" stores — scaled-down versions (about 155,000 sq. ft.) of its larger stores. Later in 2000 Meijer unveiled what it claimed was the largest superstore in North America. The 255,000-sq.-ft. behemoth (compared to a Wal-Mart Supercenter, which averages about 183,106 sq. ft.) features a gourmet coffee shop, a card shop, a bank open seven days a week, and restaurants serving pizza and sushi.

In February 2002 co-chairman Hank Meijer was named CEO, succeeding Jim McClean, who had run the company since 1999. The retailer launched a "reinvented superstore format" at six Dayton, Ohio-area stores in late 2002.

In 2003 Meijer eliminated about 350 jobs and opened two new stores. It also cut jobs — about 1,900 management positions — early the next year to become more efficient and competitive.

Larry Zigerelli was promoted from EVP of merchandising to president of the company in April 2005. He resigned in December citing personal reasons. Meijer opened about 10 stores in 2005. A year later, Meijer board member Mark Murray (formerly the president of Grand Valley State University) joined the company as president. (Co-CEOs Hank Meijer and Paul Boyer ran the grocery chain in the interim.) Boyer stepped down at the end of 2006, but remained on the executive board as vice chairman.

Meijer got into some hot water in Michigan in 2008, when it was fined by the secretary of state for campaign law violations. The company was fined for activities interfering with opposition to its planned big-box store in Acme Township.

EXECUTIVES

Chairman Emeritus: Fred Meijer, age 85
Co-Chairman and CEO: Hendrik G. (Hank) Meijer, age 57
Co-Chairman: Doug Meijer, age 51
Vice Chairman: Paul Boyer, age 57
President and Director: Mark A. Murray, age 54
EVP Merchandising: JK Symancyk
SVP, Human Resources and Government Relations: Brian Breslin
SVP, Finance and Administration, and CFO: Dan Webb
VP Human Resources: Karen Morris
VP, Drug Store: Nat Love
VP Brand and Product Development: Dave Clark
VP, Merchandise Planning and Supply Chain: Rick Keyes
VP Corporate Communications and Public Affairs: Stacie Behler
VP Talent Acquisition and Organizational Development: David Beach
VP Pricing, Consumer Insights, and Customer Database Marketing: Michael Ross
VP, Real Estate: Mike Kinstle
VP, Pharmacy Operations: Mike Major

LOCATIONS

HQ: Meijer, Inc.
2929 Walker Ave., NW, Grand Rapids, MI 49544
Phone: 616-453-6711   **Fax:** 616-791-2572
Web: www.meijer.com

2009 Stores

	No.
Michigan	100
Ohio	41
Indiana	28
Illinois	15
Kentucky	8
Total	**192**

PRODUCTS/OPERATIONS

Selected Meijer Store Departments

Apparel
Auto supplies
Bakery
Banking
Books
Bulk foods
Coffee shop
Computer software
Dairy
Delicatessen
Electronics
Floral
Food court
Gas station
Hardware
Health and beauty products
Home fashions
Jewelry
Lawn and garden
Music
Nutrition products
Paint
Pets and pet supplies
Pharmacy
Photo lab
Portrait studio
Produce
Service meat and seafood
Small appliances
Soup and salad bar
Sporting goods
Tobacco
Toys
Wall coverings
Wine

COMPETITORS

ALDI
Busch's
Costco Wholesale
CVS Caremark
Dollar General
Dominick's
Family Dollar Stores
Giant Eagle
Home Depot
IGA
Kmart
Kohl's
Kroger
Marsh Supermarkets
Retail Ventures
Roundy's Supermarkets
Sam's Club
Schnuck Markets
Schottenstein Stores
Spartan Stores
SUPERVALU
Target
Walgreen
Wal-Mart
Whole Foods

HISTORICAL FINANCIALS

Company Type: Private

Income Statement

FYE: January 31

	ESTIMATED REVENUE ($ mil.)	NET INCOME ($ mil.)	NET PROFIT MARGIN	EMPLOYEES
1/09	14,200	—	—	62,000
1/08	13,700	—	—	60,000
1/07	13,900	—	—	67,000
1/06	12,500	—	—	70,000
1/05	11,900	—	—	75,000
Annual Growth	4.5%	—	—	(4.6%)

Revenue History

Melaleuca, Inc.

Idaho may be known for potatoes, but *Melaleuca alternifolia* — better known as the tea tree — is Melaleuca's preferred flora. Founded in 1985 to market a tea tree oil formulation called Melaleuca Oil, the firm sells personal care products, cosmetics, household cleaning supplies, and vitamins directly to consumers through a network of sales representatives, catalogs, and its Web sites, but members only please. Melaleuca now sells more than 350 products, many of which are environmentally friendly and derived from natural ingredients, including tea tree oil. Tea tree oil is a powerful antiseptic and antifungal agent used for skin care, as well as the treatment of a variety of ailments, insect bites, boils, and wounds.

Melaleuca offers Internet and phone service, health savings plans, discounted travel, mortgages, and other services to its members. The company, which operates two manufacturing centers in eastern Idaho, sells its products throughout Asia, Europe, and North America. Melaleuca is rapidly expanding its international operations.

CEO Frank VanderSloot, a devout Mormon with 14 children, encourages sales representatives to engage in a frugal lifestyle and supports causes that espouse traditional family values.

EXECUTIVES

President and CEO: Frank L. VanderSloot, age 60
CFO and Treasurer: Thomas K. (Tom) Knutson
SVP Sales: Jeff Hill
VP Sales: Nathan R. (Nate) Blanchard
Human Resources: Jann Nielson
Director Corporate Relations: Damond R. Watkins
Secretary and Director: Allen Ball

LOCATIONS

HQ: Melaleuca, Inc.
3910 S. Yellowstone Hwy., Idaho Falls, ID 83402
Phone: 208-522-0700   **Fax:** 208-535-2362
Web: www.melaleuca.com

PRODUCTS/OPERATIONS

Selected Products

Health
  Daily needs
  Heart health
  Weight management
Body
  Bath and shower
  Hair care
  Lotions
  Perfume
  Shaving
  Sun care
Beauty
  Accessories
  Eyes
  Lips
  Nails
Home
  Laundry
  Cleansers
  Pet care
  Dish care
Kids
  Accessories
  Bath-time fun
  Oral hygiene
  Children's health
Medicine Cabinet
  Acne treatment system
  Dry skin care
  First aid
  Heartburn relief
Business Tools
  Brochures and flyers
  Forms
  Logo merchandise
  Product training and info
  Publications
  Tools for rapid growth

COMPETITORS

Amway
Avon
drugstore.com
Gaiam
Mary Kay
Pampered Chef
PartyLite Worldwide
Tupperware Brands

HISTORICAL FINANCIALS
Company Type: Private

Income Statement

FYE: December 31

	REVENUE ($ mil.)	NET INCOME ($ mil.)	NET PROFIT MARGIN	EMPLOYEES
12/08	887	—	—	—
12/07	859	—	—	2,400
12/06	795	—	—	—
12/05	719	—	—	—
Annual Growth	7.3%	—	—	—

Revenue History

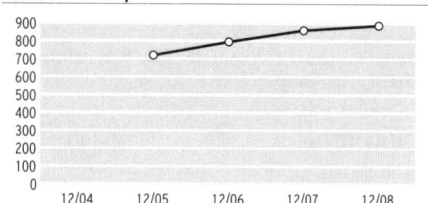

Memorial Hermann Healthcare System

Memorial Hermann Healthcare System is a Texas-sized operation. As Houston's largest not-for-profit health care system it includes 11 hospitals (one is a children's hospital) and dozens of specialty treatment centers. The system also operates three managed acute care hospitals and a retirement community. Through Memorial Hermann Regional Healthcare Services, the company is affiliated with more than 20 community hospitals and health centers, most serving rural areas within 150 miles of the Houston area. Other services and programs include substance abuse treatment, home health services, and diagnostic imaging. The organization was formed by the 1997 merger of two smaller systems.

The system also operates Houston's only burn center and Life Flight, the city's only air-ambulance, using helicopters to transports patients within a 150-mile radius around the city.

Memorial Hermann started a trend that's peaking as Houston, the nation's fourthlargest city, sprawls into the suburbs. Many hospitals that once confined themselves to the city's venerable downtown area, known as Texas Medical Center, have branched out to serve the population where it lives. Hermann Memorial opened five new hospitals from 2006 to 2009, all in suburbs and cities around Houston. Memorial Hermann Memorial City Medical Center is the latest, opened in late 2008.

EXECUTIVES

Chairman: James R. Montague, age 62
President and CEO: Daniel J. Wolterman
COO: Charles D. (Chuck) Stokes, age 55
SVP and CEO, Memorial Hermann Hospital: Juanita F. Romans, age 58
SVP Finance: Carrol Aulbaugh
Chief Medical Officer: John M. Zerwas
Chief Business Development Officer: David Whalen

LOCATIONS

HQ: Memorial Hermann Healthcare System
7737 Southwest Fwy., Ste. 200, Houston, TX 77074
Phone: 713-448-5555 **Fax:** 713-448-5665
Web: www.memorialhermann.org

PRODUCTS/OPERATIONS

Selected Facilities

Children's Memorial Hermann Hospital
Memorial Hermann Katy Hospital
Memorial Hermann Memorial City Medical Center
Memorial Hermann Northeast Hospital
Memorial Hermann Northwest Hospital
Memorial Hermann Southeast Hospital
Memorial Hermann Southwest Hospital
Memorial Hermann Sugar Land Health Center
Memorial Hermann — Texas Medical Center
Memorial Hermann The Woodlands Hospital
Memorial Hermann Wellness Center and Garden Spa
TIRR Memorial Hermann (Houston)
University Place Retirement Community and Nursing Center (Houston)

COMPETITORS

CHRISTUS Health
Harris County Hospital
HCA
M. D. Anderson Cancer Center
Methodist Hospital System
St. Luke's Episcopal Hospital
Tenet Healthcare
Texas Children's Hospital

HISTORICAL FINANCIALS
Company Type: Not-for-profit

Income Statement

FYE: June 30

	REVENUE ($ mil.)	NET INCOME ($ mil.)	NET PROFIT MARGIN	EMPLOYEES
6/08	2,841	—	—	16,500

Memphis Grizzlies

The sweetest honey for these Grizzlies is an NBA championship. Hoops, L.P. owns and operates the Memphis Grizzlies professional basketball franchise. Originally located in Vancouver and controlled by Arthur Griffiths (who also owned the Vancouver Canucks hockey club), the Grizzlies joined the National Basketball Association as an expansion team in 1995, forming the new Canadian wing of the league along with the Toronto Raptors. Chicago billionaire Michael Heisley acquired the franchise in 2000 and relocated the Grizzlies to Tennessee the following year. The team plays host at Memphis' FedExForum.

Looking to ensure the struggling Grizzlies would stay in Memphis, minority shareholders J.R. "Pitt" Hyde and Stanley Cates offered to buy-out Heisley in 2008, but the offer was turned down. The pair later reduced their holdings from 30% to less than 10%. Heisley, who controls buy-out firm Heico Companies, originally acquired control of the team for $160 million.

The team's finances have been buoyed somewhat since moving into the FedExForum in 2004. Local shipping giant FedEx ponied up $90 million as part of a 20-year sponsorship to put its name on the $300 million, publicly financed facility.

EXECUTIVES

Majority Owner: Michael Heisley Sr.
SVP Business Operations: Mike Redlick
SVP Broadcast: Randy Stephens
General Manager and VP Basketball Operations: Chris Wallace
Head Coach: Lionel Hollins
Senior Director Marketing and Communications: John Pugliese
Senior Director Information Technology: Mike Garrison
Director Human Resources: Arnetria Knowles
VP Basketball Operations and Team Programs: Dana Davis
Director of Scouting: Tony Barone Jr., age 36
Director Player Personnel: Tony Barone, age 61
Special Assistant to the General Manager: Kevin O'Neill
Executive Director, Grizzlies Foundation: Jenny Turner-Koltnow
President, Hoops, LP: Gene Bartow

LOCATIONS

HQ: Hoops, L.P.
191 Beale St., Memphis, TN 38103
Phone: 901-888-4667 **Fax:** 901-205-1235
Web: www.nba.com/grizzlies

The Memphis Grizzlies play at the 18,119-seat capacity FedExForum in Memphis.

COMPETITORS

Dallas Mavericks
Houston Rockets
New Orleans Hornets
San Antonio Spurs

Menard, Inc.

If sticks and stones break bones, what can two-by-fours and two-inch nails do? That is what Menard is wondering now that its biggest rivals (#1 home improvement giant The Home Depot and #2 Lowe's) are hammering away at its home turf. One of the largest home improvement chains in the Midwest, Menard has more than 220 stores in Illinois, Indiana, Iowa, Michigan, Minnesota, Missouri, Nebraska, North and South Dakota, Ohio, Wisconsin, and Wyoming. The stores sell home improvement products, such as floor coverings, hardware, millwork, paint, and tools. Unlike competitors, all the company's stores have full-service lumberyards. Menard is owned by president and CEO John Menard, who founded the company in 1972.

Although Menard outlets are typically smaller than those of Home Depot, they offer a similar selection of products by building large warehouses adjacent to stores and then quickly restocking merchandise when it's sold. The company's products are laid out on easy-to-reach, supermarket-styled shelves and have outdoor, drive-through lumber yards. To help keep expenses low and prices cheap, Menard's Midwest Manufacturing (MM) division makes some of its merchandise, including doors and trusses. MM operates about a half-dozen plants in five midwestern states that make metal roofing and siding, doors, decking, trusses, and other building materials.

The company is increasing its average store size to more than 220,000 sq. ft. It has opened its largest store ever — 250,000 sq. ft. — in Minnesota and is expanding 30-40 stores. Most of the company's new stores will be more than 200,000 sq. ft. Besides stocking hardware and building supplies, these new megastores will include garden centers and sell a large range of home appliances.

The family-owned chain does not release earnings, but the home improvement sector has clearly suffered as a result of the deep recession in the US and collapse of the housing market. Rival Home Depot has closed all of its EXPO Design Center stores and cut jobs, and Lowe's has scaled back its plans for new stores. Still the regional home improvement chain opened several new mega-stores in 2008.

In what may be a first for a home improvement chain, Menard has gotten into the business of residential real estate development with several large subdivisions either under construction or in the planning stages in Indiana and Illinois. The developments, situated on land near Menard stores, create a potential customer base among new homeowners and local builders.

In addition to billionaire founder John Menard, other family members are engaged in the chain's everyday operations. John Menard also owns Team Menard, an Indy car-racing team.

HISTORY

John Menard was the oldest of eight children on a Wisconsin dairy farm. To pay for attending the University of Wisconsin at Eau Claire, he and some fellow college students built pole barns in the late 1950s. Learning that other builders had trouble finding lumber outlets open on the weekends, Menard began buying wood in bulk and selling it to them. He added other supplies in 1960 and sold his construction business in 1970 as building supply revenues became his chief source of income.

He founded Menard in 1972 as the do-it-yourself craze was beginning, but he wanted an operation run more like mass merchandiser Target, with easy-to-reach shelves, wide aisles, and tile floors rather than the cold, cumbersome layout used by lumberyards. To realize that concept, Menard built warehouses and stockrooms behind the stores so he could restock merchandise quickly.

Menard's vision worked, and he began building his midwestern empire, often acquiring abandoned retail sites that were inexpensive and in good locations. By 1986 Menard was in Iowa, Minnesota, North and South Dakota, and Wisconsin, and by 1990 it had 46 stores. In the early 1990s Menard began enlarging its operations to serve the ever-growing number of stores, opening a huge warehouse and distribution center and a manufacturing facility that made doors, Formica countertops, and other products. Menard entered Nebraska in 1990 and opened its first store in Chicago the next year. By 1992 there were more than 60 stores.

That year Menard made the *National Enquirer* with a story about the firing of a store manager who had built a wheelchair-accessible home for his 11-year-old daughter with spina bifida, violating a company theft-prevention policy forbidding store managers to build their own homes. The company insisted that the man was fired in part because of poor work performance.

Menard continued to expand to new areas, operating stores in Indiana and Michigan by 1992. As it continued expanding in the Chicago area, it offered varying store formats, ranging from a full line of building materials to smaller Menards Hardware Plus stores. By 1994 Menard had 85 stores, many bigger than 100,000 sq. ft.

In 1995 and 1996 the company was plagued with lawsuits filed by customers charging false arrest and imprisonment for shoplifting. An on-duty police officer apprehending a shoplifting suspect at a store was even stopped and searched.

Competition also heated up during that time. The Home Depot's push into the Midwest — including opening several stores directly across the street from Menard — spurred Menard to fight back by lowering prices and opening nearly 40 stores. The fight forced smaller chains like Handy Andy out of business.

In 1997 Menard and his company were fined $1.7 million after dumping bags of toxic ash from its manufacturing facility at residential trash pick-up sites rather than at properly regulated outlets (it had been fined for similar violations in 1989 and 1994). In response to a price war initiated by Home Depot, in 1998 Menard dropped sales prices by 10%.

In 1999 competitor Lowe's began moving into Menard's biggest market, Chicago. Menard began opening larger stores in 2000 (about 162,000 sq. ft., or some 74,000 sq. ft. bigger than the older stores). In 2001 it began beefing up its lines of home appliances, adding more washers, dryers, dishwashers, refrigerators, and ranges.

In January 2005 the Internal Revenue Service ruled the company owed $5.5 million in back taxes and fines because it paid John Menard too high a salary in 1998. In 2009 the Court of Appeals for the Seventh Circuit reversed a tax court decision that Menard's compensation was unreasonable and therefore a nondeductible dividend. As a result, the company is off the hook for the back taxes.

EXECUTIVES

President and CEO: John R. Menard Jr., age 69
COO: Scott Collette
CIO: Dave Wagner
General Counsel: Rob Geske
VP Merchandise: Russ Raditke
Payroll Manager: Terri Jain

LOCATIONS

HQ: Menard, Inc.
    4777 Menard Dr., Eau Claire, WI 54703
Phone: 715-876-5911   **Fax:** 715-876-2868
Web: www.menards.com

PRODUCTS/OPERATIONS

Selected Operations

Menards (home improvement stores)
Midwest Manufacturing (product manufacturing)

COMPETITORS

84 Lumber	Sears
Ace Hardware	Sherwin-Williams
Carter Lumber	Stock Building Supply
Do it Best	Sutherland Lumber
Fastenal	True Value
Home Depot	Wal-Mart
Lowe's	WinWholesale

HISTORICAL FINANCIALS

Company Type: Private

Income Statement				FYE: January 31
	ESTIMATED REVENUE ($ mil.)	NET INCOME ($ mil.)	NET PROFIT MARGIN	EMPLOYEES
12/08	7,800	—	—	40,000

Merrill Corporation

Document services company Merrill is no relation to financial services giant Merrill Lynch, but the companies do share an interest in SEC paperwork. Through its transactional and compliance services segment, Merrill provides printing, distribution, and electronic processing of SEC filings and other documents related to corporate transactions. Merrill also handles documents used in litigation and in direct marketing. Customers come from the financial services, insurance, legal, and real estate industries. Founded in 1968, the firm operates from more than 70 offices in the US and 15 abroad. Affiliates of DLJ Merchant Banking Partners, a unit of investment firm Credit Suisse, own a majority stake in Merrill.

After acquiring litigation support provider WordWave in January 2006, Merrill reorganized its operations into four segments: legal solutions, marketing and communication solutions, transactional and compliance services, and other communications services.

The company has diversified beyond its traditional printing business through numerous acquisitions and strategic alliances to position itself as a business process outsourcing company. It sees growth opportunities in its legal solutions offerings, which include managing electronic data discovery, and in Merrill Datasite, which provides online hosting of documents related to mergers and acquisitions. In addition, Merrill is expanding geographically. In 2007 the company, through its WordWave subsidiary, acquired Sydney-based ComputerReporters, a provider of real-time and private reporting services to legal, corporate, and government clients. The acquisition followed WordWave's 2006 purchase of another Australian firm, Melbourne-based Court Recording Services, which does business in Australia and Hong Kong and offers similar services.

The company filed to go public in early 2006 but withdrew the offering in September 2007, citing adverse market conditions. Had the company completed the IPO, it would have been Merrill's second go-round as a public company. The company's stock was publicly traded from 1986 to 1999, when Merrill went private in a recapitalization backed by DLJ, then known as Donaldson, Lufkin & Jenrette.

Merrill employees own about 47% of the firm.

EXECUTIVES

Chairman and CEO: John W. Castro
President and COO: Rick R. Atterbury
Controller and Chief Accounting Officer:
  Katherine L. (Kathy) Miller
EVP Human Resources: Brenda J. Vale, age 44
EVP and General Counsel: Steven J. (Steve) Machov
EVP Strategy and Operations, Merrill Legal Solutions:
  Mark Kindy
EVP and CTO: John R. Stolle, age 60
EVP and CFO: Robert H. (Bob) Nazarian, age 56
EVP Global Marketing: Craig P. Levinsohn
SVP Marketing and Communication Solutions:
  Ken Lambert
President, Integrated Operations:
  Raymond J. (Ray) Goodwin
President, Translation Services: Claes Holm
President, Realty Services: Fred Thomas
President, Merrill DataSite: Ed Bifulk
President, Captioning Services (VITAC):
  Patricia (Pat) Prozzi
President, Transaction and Compliance Services:
  Pete Cronan
President, Financial Services and Brand Management:
  Mark A. Rossi
President, Legal Solutions and Director:
  B. Michael (Mike) James, age 51
President, Legal Solutions: Perry L. Solomon, age 58
President, Legal Solutions Sales: Allen J. (Al) McNee
Auditors: PricewaterhouseCoopers LLP

LOCATIONS

HQ: Merrill Corporation
  1 Merrill Cir., St. Paul, MN 55108
Phone: 651-646-4501   **Fax:** 651-646-5332
Web: www.merrillcorp.com

PRODUCTS/OPERATIONS

Selected Products and Services

Legal solutions
  Compliance and due diligence database
  Electronic discovery
  Litigation support
  Securities law database
Marketing and communication solutions
  Brand identity management
  Corporate identity materials
  Customer communications and packaged direct
    market programs
  Direct mail marketing collateral
Transaction and compliance services
  Document composition, filing, and printing
  Document hosting
  EDGAR filings
Other communications services
  Captioning
  Language translation
  Specialty printing

COMPETITORS

Applied Discovery
Bowne
Diebold
Harte-Hanks
IKON
IntraLinks
Kroll Ontrack
Lionbridge
Pitney Bowes
R.R. Donnelley
St Ives
Williams Lea
Xerox

The Methodist Hospital System

The not-for-profit Methodist Hospital System owns and operates several Houston-area hospitals, including the Methodist Hospital, San Jacinto Methodist Hospital, Methodist Sugar Land Hospital, and Methodist Willowbrook Hospital. The flagship Methodist Hospital has 900 beds and is known for innovations in urology and neurosurgery, among other specialties. The hospital is also affiliated with the Weil Cornell Medical College and the New York-Presbyterian Hospital, a center for medical education and research. The system also manages the Methodist Hospital Physician Organization and receives funding from the Methodist Hospital Foundation.

The Methodist Hospital System has about 1,350 beds total and also operates numerous international facilities in Latin America, Europe, and the Middle East. In addition, it operates the Methodist Hospital Research Institute, which conducts medical and clinical research and is undergoing expansion efforts. The main Methodist Hospital facility, which is located in Houston's Texas Medical Center complex, is also growing.

EXECUTIVES

Chairman: Ewing Werlein Jr.
Vice Chair: Ernest H. Cockrell, age 64
Vice Chair: David M. Underwood Sr.
President and CEO: Ronald G. (Ron) Girotto
EVP and COO: Marc L. Boom
EVP and CFO: John E. Hagale
EVP, The Methodist Hospital: Lynn Schroth
**SVP and Chief Nursing Executive, The Methodist
  Hospital:** Ann Scanlon McGinity
SVP Human Resources: Lauren Rykert
VP Human Resources: Carole Hackett
Director Public Relations: Stefanie Asin
Secretary: D. Gibson Walton
Treasurer: Carlton E. Baucum

LOCATIONS

HQ: The Methodist Hospital System
  6565 Fannin St., Ste. D200, Houston, TX 77030
Phone: 713-441-2221   **Fax:** 713-790-2605
Web: www.methodisthealth.com

PRODUCTS/OPERATIONS

US Hospitals

The Methodist Hospital (Houston)
Methodist Sugar Land Hospital (Sugar Land)
Methodist Willowbrook Hospital (Houston)
San Jacinto Methodist Hospital (Baytown)

COMPETITORS

CHRISTUS Health
Conroe Regional Medical Center
Dynacq Healthcare
HCA
HealthSouth
Mayo Foundation
Memorial Hermann Healthcare
Sisters of Mercy Health System
St. Luke's Episcopal Health System
Tenet Healthcare
Texas Health Resources
Tomball Regional
Universal Health Services

HISTORICAL FINANCIALS
Company Type: Not-for-profit

Income Statement

FYE: December 31

	REVENUE ($ mil.)	NET INCOME ($ mil.)	NET PROFIT MARGIN	EMPLOYEES
12/08	1,839	—	—	8,000

Metro-Goldwyn-Mayer

The name is Mayer. Metro-Goldwyn-Mayer (MGM). Home of the venerable and valuable James Bond franchise, MGM is a leading Hollywood moviemaker through its production units MGM Studios and United Artists (UA). Its feature films have included *Rocky Balboa, Quantum of Solace,* and *The Taking of Pelham 1 2 3.* Through MGM Television it produces TV shows such as *Stargate Universe* (on NBC Universal's Syfy channel) and the animated *Spaceballs* (G4). The company also owns one of the largest film libraries in the world, with about 4,000 titles, including the Bond and Pink Panther series. It distributes films on DVD through MGM Home Entertainment. Owned by a consortium led by Sony Corporation of America, MGM is up for sale.

In recent years MGM has been facing stiff competition from its rivals, which include bigger studio groups such as Fox Filmed Entertainment and Warner Bros. Entertainment. In response, MGM has reined in its production slate to just a few titles a year, most of which it produces in partnership with other studios. Its only release in 2009 was the remake of *Fame.* MGM has put more focus on its distribution business (though that activity has been rather lackluster, with recent mediocre titles such as *Soul Men* and *Hurricane Season* from The Weinstein Company's Dimension label). Instead, MGM has had better luck with exploiting its massive film library; the studio has won more than 200 Academy Awards over the years.

Without a string of hit films and challenged by a decline in the home entertainment market, MGM has been struggling financially. The company is burdened with a heavy debt load (nearly $4 billion), mostly the result of the buyout by Sony and its consortium partners, including Providence Equity Partners, Texas Pacific Group, and cable giant Comcast Corporation. After failing to turn the movie business around, Harry Sloan was ousted as CEO in 2009 (but remained as chairman) and was replaced by a triumvirate of Mary Parent (production chief), CFO Bedi Singh, and restructuring consultant Stephen Cooper. (The consortium had tapped Sloan to lead MGM following the buyout. He previously ran Lions Gate and SBS Broadcasting.) Later in 2009 MGM announced that it is seeking a buyer.

The studio scored with its 2008 James Bond film *Quantum of Solace,* co-produced with Sony's Columbia Pictures. The movie surpassed the previous Bond flick, *Casino Royale,* to become the franchise's top-grossing movie of all time at the North American box office. MGM's UA unit, meanwhile, tried to boost its output through a relationship with actor Tom Cruise, but the partnership's first release, 2007's *Lions for Lambs*, was a flop at the box office. UA later produced the Cruise vehicle *Valkyrie*, which fared better in 2008.

MGM continues to look for ways to diversify its business and capitalize on its library of films. It joined Viacom and Lions Gate in 2008 to form a premium pay TV joint venture called Epix that directly competes with HBO, Showtime, and Starz. The subscription channel, which launched in 2009, features movies and original TV series.

Sony and its consortium partners purchased MGM from Kirk Kerkorian for $4.8 billion, including $2 billion in debt, in 2005. The billionaire investor had taken control of MGM three times since the late 1960s, most recently in 1996.

HISTORY

Russian emigrant Louis B. Mayer started showing movies in a run-down theater outside Boston in 1907. After obtaining the New England distribution rights to D.W. Griffith's highly successful *Birth of a Nation* (1915), Mayer was flush with cash and left the theater business to start producing movies in Los Angeles. He founded Louis B. Mayer Pictures and began funding his own productions in 1918.

Theater chain owner Marcus Loew bought Metro Pictures in 1919. Frustrated with the lack of quality films coming from Metro, Loew proposed to buy Goldwyn Studios. Mayer wanted in on the deal and convinced Loew to make it a three-way merger. Metro-Goldwyn-Mayer was born in 1924, and Louis B. Mayer was head of the studio. Mayer ruled MGM with an iron fist and became the most powerful man in Hollywood during the 1930s and 1940s, guiding a firmament of stars including Clark Gable, Greta Garbo, and Judy Garland through a multitude of prestigious films such as *Ninotchka, The Wizard of Oz*, and *Gone With The Wind*.

After WWII, federal antitrust action forced movie companies to sell their theater chains. Despite successes such as *Singin' in the Rain*, MGM struggled. Mayer resigned under pressure in 1951 and died in 1957. By the end of the 1960s, MGM was faltering, while rival United Artists (UA) found itself prospering with the emergence of its James Bond series (*Dr. No*, 1962) and five best picture winners in the 1960s.

Financier Kirk Kerkorian bought MGM in 1970, sold off many of its assets, and used the MGM name and lion logo for a new Las Vegas casino, the MGM Grand. Film production slowed to a crawl in the 1970s, and UA bought MGM's distribution rights in 1973. But UA's success collapsed after the box-office disaster *Heaven's Gate*, and MGM swooped in and purchased UA and its 900 titles, including the coveted James Bond franchise, in 1981 for $380 million.

The new MGM/UA was only five years old when Kerkorian sold it to Ted Turner, who promptly sold most of the studio assets and the MGM logo back to Kerkorian for $780 million that same year. Pathé (then led by Giancarlo Paretti) bought what was left of MGM in 1990, but by 1992 Crédit Lyonnais foreclosed and took control.

In 1996 the French bank put the studio on the block. That year Kerkorian (for a third time) and a group led by MGM chairman Frank Mancuso and Australian broadcaster Seven Network bought MGM with a winning $1.3 billion bid.

The company went public in 1997 and focused on bulking up its catalog of movies. It paid $573 million, including debt, for the 2,200-title Metromedia library.

The next year Kerkorian bought out Seven Network's 25% interest. MGM also bought PolyGram's library of films from Seagram that year and won a crucial court battle with Sony Pictures Entertainment to maintain exclusive rights to James Bond.

In 2005 Kerkorian, yet again, sold MGM to a consortium of investors led by Sony Corporation of America (the other partners included Comcast, Texas Pacific Group, Providence Equity Partners, and DLJ Merchant Banking Partners).

The company later that year named former Lions Gate and SBS Broadcasting executive Harry Sloan CEO. After failing to turn the business around, however, Sloan was replaced by an executive committee in 2009. He remained chairman.

EXECUTIVES

Chairman: Harry E. Sloan
Vice Chairman and Member Office, CEO:
 Stephen F. (Steve) Cooper
Member Office, CEO; President Finance and Administration, and CFO: Bedi A. Singh, age 49
Member Office, CEO; Chairman, Worldwide Motion Picture Group: Mary Parent
SEVP: Charles Cohen
EVP Corporate Communications: Jeff Pryor
EVP Worldwide Digital Media: Douglas A. (Doug) Lee
EVP Consumer Products and Location Based Entertainment: Travis Rutherford
EVP Television Distribution: Joe Patrick
EVP Worldwide Television and Legal Affairs:
 Gerald Ament
EVP Theatrical Marketing MGM; President Marketing, United Artists: Michael Vollman
EVP Production: Cale Boyter
EVP Business and Legal Affairs: Ron Sufrin
EVP International Theatrical and Home Entertainment: Erik Lomis
EVP, Secretary, and General Counsel: Scott Packman
President, Theatrical Marketing: Perry Stahman
President, Domestic Theatrical Distribution:
 Clark Woods
President, MGM Networks: Bruce Tuchman
Co-President, Worldwide Television: Jim Packer
Co-President, Worldwide Television: Gary Marenzi
Auditors: Ernst & Young LLP

LOCATIONS

HQ: Metro-Goldwyn-Mayer Inc.
 10250 Constellation Blvd., Los Angeles, CA 90067
Phone: 310-449-3000 **Fax:** 310-449-8857
Web: www.mgm.com

PRODUCTS/OPERATIONS

Selected Films

Annie Hall (1977)
The Apartment (1960)
Barbershop (2002)
Be Cool (2005)
Dances with Wolves (1990)
Gone With the Wind (1939)
In the Heat of the Night (1967)
James Bond (franchise)
Legally Blonde (2001)
Marty (1955)
Midnight Cowboy (1969)
Miss Potter (2006)
Mister Brooks (2007)
The Nanny Diaries (2007)
Pink Panther (franchise)
Platoon (1986)
Rain Man (1988)
Rebecca (1940)
Rocky (franchise)
The Silence of the Lambs (1991)
The Taking of Pelham 1 2 3 (2009)
West Side Story (1961)
The Wizard of Oz (1939)

Selected Operations

MGM Consumer Products
MGM Distribution
MGM Home Entertainment
MGM Interactive (video games)
MGM Music (soundtracks)
MGM Networks
MGM Studios
MGM Television Entertainment
MGM Worldwide Television Distribution
United Artists

COMPETITORS

Disney Studios
Fox Filmed Entertainment
Lionsgate
Lucasfilm
Paramount Pictures
Universal Studios
Warner Bros.

Metromedia Company

This company has put its brand on both the dining and the energy sector. Metromedia is a holding company controlled by chairman John Kluge that owns steak buffet restaurant chains Ponderosa and Bonanza through its Homestyle Dining subsidiary. The company's energy holdings include Metromedia Energy, an independent energy marketer that provides natural gas procurement and energy management services to more than 10,000 commercial and industrial customers. Affiliate Metromedia Power offers electricity brokerage services to business customers in about a dozen states, mostly in the Northeast.

While Metromedia keeps a mostly low profile, the company's dining operations have been in the headlines because of the slumping economy. Formerly operating as Metromedia Steakhouses, the steak buffet subsidiary was forced to seek bankruptcy protection in 2008 citing declining sales due to weak consumer spending. It emerged the following year under the new name Homestyle Dining having closed or refranchised about 15 Ponderosa locations.

The recession took a heavier toll on Metromedia's other casual dining chains, Bennigan's Grill & Tavern and Steak & Ale. Those businesses, part of Metromedia Restaurant Group, were liquidated under Chapter 7 bankruptcy; 150 company-owned Bennigan's units and almost 60 Steak & Ale units (operated through S&A Restaurant Corp.) were closed. The Bennigan's brand and franchising rights were later sold to an affiliate of New York City-based private equity firm Atalaya Capital Management; the chain had more than 150 franchised units still operating.

HISTORY

German immigrant John Kluge, born in 1914, came to Detroit at age eight with his mother and stepfather. He later worked at the Ford assembly line. At Columbia University he studied economics and (to the chagrin of college administrators) poker, building a tidy sum with his winnings by graduation. Kluge worked in Army intelligence during WWII. After the war he bought WGAY radio in Silver Spring, Maryland, and went on to buy and sell other small radio stations.

Kluge began to diversify, entering the wholesale food business in the mid-1950s. In 1959 he purchased control of Metropolitan Broadcasting, including TV stations in New York and Washington, DC, and took it public. He renamed the company Metromedia in 1960.

Metromedia added independent stations — to the then-legal limit of seven — in other major markets, paying relatively little compared to network affiliate prices. The stations struggled through years of infomercials but thrived in the late 1970s and early 1980s. Metromedia's stock price rose from $4.50 in 1974 to top $500 in 1983. The company also acquired radio stations, the Harlem Globetrotters, and the Ice Capades.

In 1983 Kluge bought paging and cellular telephone licenses across the US. He later acquired long-distance carriers in Texas and Florida. In 1984 Metromedia went private in a $1.6 billion buyout and began to sell off its assets in 1985. It sold its Boston TV station to Hearst and its six other TV stations to Rupert Murdoch for a total of $2 billion. In 1986 Metromedia sold its outdoor advertising firm, nine of its 11 radio stations, and the Globetrotters and Ice Capades. Kluge then sold most of the company's cellular properties to SBC Communications (now AT&T Inc.). In 1990 it sold its New York cellular operations to LIN Broadcasting and its Philadelphia cellular operations to Comcast.

Building what Kluge envisioned as his steak house empire, the firm bought the Ponderosa steak house chain (founded in the late 1960s) in 1988 from Asher Edelman and later added Dallas-based USA Cafes (Bonanza steak houses, founded 1964) and S&A Restaurant Corp. (Steak & Ale, founded 1966; Bennigan's, founded 1976). Also in 1988 Kluge rescued friend Arthur Krim, whose Orion Pictures was threatened by Viacom, by buying control of the filmmaker.

Kluge's grand steak-house vision did not come to fruition. Increased competition squeezed profits at Ponderosa and Bonanza. The restaurant group also was plagued by management shake-ups, aging facilities, food-quality issues, and even bad press. (Bennigan's was ranked the worst casual-dining chain in the US in a 1992 *Consumer Reports* poll.)

In 1989 Kluge merged Metromedia Long Distance with the long-distance operations of ITT. Renamed Metromedia Communications in 1991, the company merged with other long-distance providers to become MCI WorldCom. (Kluge sold his 16% of MCI WorldCom to the public in 1995.)

Kluge created Metromedia International Group in 1995 by merging Orion Pictures, Metromedia International Telecommunications, MCEG Sterling (film and television production), and Actava Group (maker of Snapper lawn mowers and sporting goods — sold 2002). Metromedia Restaurant Group announced a $190 million refinancing agreement for S&A Restaurant Corp. in 1998 to expand and refurbish its restaurants; it closed 28 unprofitable restaurants that year and launched a franchise program to grow its Bennigan's and Steak & Ale chains.

Metromedia expanded its Bennigan's units in South Korea in 1999 and the next year announced it would build 65 new restaurants in the US and expand to more than 200 units internationally. In 2001 Verizon Communications invested nearly $2 billion in Metromedia unit Metromedia Fiber Network (MFN), but MFN was forced into Chapter 11 bankruptcy the following year. It blamed lower than expected demand for its metropolitan Internet services due to stiff competition, which drove down prices.

MFN (now AboveNet) emerged from bankruptcy in 2002 with a new owner. Kluge resigned from the Metromedia Fiber Network board that year and also stepped down from the Metromedia International Group board. In 2007, Metromedia divested its interest in Metromedia International Group, which was purchased by CaucusCom Ventures.

Metromedia's restaurant operations came under pressure in 2008 due to the recession. Its S&A Restaurant Corp. dissolved under Chapter 7, closing 150 company-owned Bennigan's units and almost 60 Steak & Ale units. Private equity firm Atalaya Capital Management later acquired the Bennigan's brand and franchising rights. The company's Metromedia Steakhouses, meanwhile, filed for Chapter 11 to reorganize its Ponderosa and Bonanza operations. Metromedia Steakhouses emerged from bankruptcy the following year under the new name Homestyle Dining.

EXECUTIVES

Chairman and President: John W. Kluge
EVP and General Partner: Stuart Subotnick, age 67
SVP Finance and Treasurer: Robert A. Maresca
SVP: Silvia Kessel
VP and Controller: David Gassler
Auditors: KPMG LLP

LOCATIONS

HQ: Metromedia Company
   21 Main St., Ste. 201, Hackensack, NJ 07601
Phone: 201-531-8000   **Fax:** 201-531-2804

COMPETITORS

AEP	Darden
Brinker	DineEquity
Carlson Companies	Exelon
Carlson Restaurants	Golden Corral
CenterPoint Energy	OSI Restaurant Partners

Metropolitan Transportation Authority

No Sigma Chi or Chi Omega chapter has anything on New York City's Metropolitan Transportation Authority (MTA) — it rushes millions of people every day. The largest public transportation system in the US, the government-owned MTA provides about 2.6 billion passenger trips and more than 300 million vehicles travel the MTA system annually. The MTA's New York City Transit Authority runs a fleet of some 6,300 buses in New York's five boroughs and, with about 8,900 rail and subway cars, it provides subway service to all but Staten Island and operates the Staten Island Railway. Other MTA units offer bus and rail service to Connecticut and Long Island and maintain the Triborough system of toll bridges and tunnels.

The MTA, a public-benefit corporation chartered by the New York Legislature in 1965, has battled persistent operating losses compounded by the economic downturn. The MTA has increased fares and tolls, taken advantage of low interest rates to restructure its debt, and trimmed operating costs. Faced with increasing expenses for pensions and disabled-accessible transportation services, the agency plans to cut about 360 maintenance, painting, and management jobs through retirements and reassignments.

The measures haven't been enough. In May 2009 the New York Legislature passed a $2.3 billion bailout package for the MTA, which outlines fare increases of 10% in 2009 and 7.5% in 2011 and 2013. Within days after the bailout was passed, CEO Elliot Sander stepped down. New York Governor David Paterson picked Jay Walder, a former executive with the London transit system and MTA's former CFO, to succeed Sander.

The MTA made a $4 million deal with Barclays in June 2009 to have the British bank's moniker added to the Atlantic Avenue-Pacific Street subway station in Brooklyn. The MTA also hopes to sell naming rights on its bus lines, bridges, and tunnels, and to expand other corporate sponsorship and advertising opportunities. In 2008 the agency reached a $1 billion deal with Related Companies for the rights to build a 26-acre office and apartment complex above railyards on Manhattan's West Side.

HISTORY

Mass transit began in New York City in the 1820s with the introduction of horse-drawn stagecoaches run by small private firms. By 1832 a horse-drawn railcar operating on Fourth Avenue offered a smoother and faster ride than its street-bound rivals.

By 1864 residents were complaining that horsecars and buses were overcrowded and that drivers were rude. (Horsecars were transporting 45 million passengers annually.) In 1870 a short subway under Broadway was opened, but it remained a mere amusement. Elevated steam railways were built, but people avoided them because of the smoke, noise, and danger from explosions. Cable cars arrived in the 1880s, and by the 1890s electric streetcars had emerged.

Construction of the first commercial subway line was completed in 1904. The line was operated by Interborough Rapid Transit (IRT), which leased the primary elevated rail line in 1903 and had effective control of rail transit in Manhattan and the Bronx. In 1905 IRT merged with the Metropolitan Street Railway, which ran most of the surface railways in Manhattan, giving the firm almost complete control of the city's rapid transit. Public protests led the city to grant licenses to Brooklyn Rapid Transit (later BMT), creating the Dual System. The two rail firms covered most of the city.

By the 1920s the transit system was again in crisis, largely because the two lines were not allowed to raise their five-cent fares. With the IRT and BMT in receivership in 1932, the city decided to own and operate part of the rail system and organized the Independent (IND) rail line. Pressure for public ownership and operation of the transit system resulted in the city's purchase of all of IRT's and BMT's assets in 1940 for $326 million.

In 1953 the legislature created the New York City Transit Authority, the first unified system. In 1968, two years after striking transit workers left the city in a virtual gridlock, the MTA began to coordinate the city's transit activities with other commuter services.

The 1970s and 1980s saw the city's transit infrastructure and service deteriorate as crime, accidents, and fares rose. But by the early 1990s a modernization program had begun to make improvements: Subway stations were repaired, graffiti was removed from trains, and service was extended. By 1994 the agency said subway crime was down 50% from 1990, and ridership had increased.

The MTA set up a five-year plan in 1995 to cut expenses by $3 billion. Only 18 months later and already two-thirds of the way to reaching the goal, the authority said it would cut another $230 million and return the savings to customers as fare discounts.

In 1998 the MTA capital program completed the $200 million restoration of the Grand Central Terminal. The next year the MTA ordered 500 new clean-fuel buses. But the agency suffered a setback when New York State's $3.8 billion Transportation Infrastructure Bond Act, which included $1.6 billion for MTA improvements, was rejected by voters in 2000.

MTA subway lines in lower Manhattan suffered extensive damage from the September 11, 2001, terrorist attacks that destroyed the World Trade Center's twin towers. The attacks left the MTA, which was already seeking billions of dollars for improvements, faced with $530 million worth of damage.

Confronted with a budget gap for the 2003 fiscal year, the MTA authorized the sale of nearly $2.9 billion worth of transportation bonds, the largest bond issue in the agency's history.

Angered by issues involving wage hikes, health care, retirement age, and pension costs, members of the Transportation Workers Union walked off the job mere days before Christmas in 2005. The strike was estimated to cause a loss of $300 million per day to the city. In the face of heavy fines, possible jail terms, and the growing ire of would-be commuters, the 33,000 striking union members agreed to go back to work without a contract after three days of picketing, and negotiations resumed. The MTA and the union later reached a contract agreement in which workers pay a portion of their health care costs.

EXECUTIVES

Chairman and CEO: Jay H. Walder
Vice Chairman: Andrew M. Saul, age 62
Vice Chairman: David S. Mack, age 67
COO: Susan L. Kupferman
President, MTA Bus Company and MTA Long Island Bus: Joseph Smith
President, MTA Long Island Rail Road:
Helena E. Williams
President, MTA Capital Construction:
Michael Horodniceanu
President, MTA New York City Transit:
Howard H. Roberts Jr.
President, Metro-North: Howard R. Permut
Deputy Executive Director and Director Security:
William A. Morange
Deputy Executive Director Administration:
Linda Kleinbaum
Deputy Executive Director General Counsel:
James B. Henly
Deputy Executive Director Corporate and Community Affairs: Christopher P. Boylan
Director Policy and Media Relations: Ernest Tollerson
Auditors: Deloitte & Touche LLP

LOCATIONS

HQ: Metropolitan Transportation Authority
347 Madison Ave., New York, NY 10017
Phone: 212-878-7000   **Fax:** 212-878-0186
Web: www.mta.info

PRODUCTS/OPERATIONS

Selected Operating Units

The Long Island Rail Road Company (MTA Long Island Rail Road)
Metro-North Commuter Railroad Company (MTA Metro-North Railroad)
Metropolitan Suburban Bus Authority (MTA Long Island Bus)
Metropolitan Transportation Authority Bus Company (MTA Bus)
Metropolitan Transportation Authority Capital Construction (MTA Capital Construction)
New York City Transit Authority (MTA New York City Transit)
Staten Island Rapid Transit Operating Authority (MTA Staten Island Railway)
Triborough Bridge and Tunnel Authority (MTA Bridges and Tunnels)

HISTORICAL FINANCIALS

Company Type: Government-owned

Income Statement

FYE: December 31

	REVENUE ($ mil.)	NET INCOME ($ mil.)	NET PROFIT MARGIN	EMPLOYEES
12/08	5,932	(963)	—	69,756
12/07	5,666	(66)	—	68,628
12/06	5,487	1,370	25.0%	67,457
12/05	5,198	397	7.6%	63,511
12/04	4,837	83	1.7%	63,604
Annual Growth	5.2%	—	—	2.3%

2008 Year-End Financials

Debt ratio: 148.0%   Current ratio: —
Return on equity: —   Long-term debt ($ mil.): 27,128
Cash ($ mil.): —

Net Income History

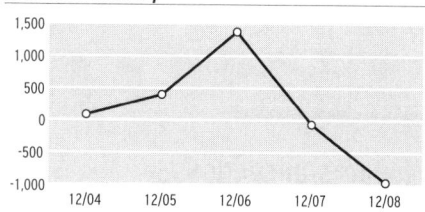

EXECUTIVES

Chairman: Joe Dent
Vice Chairman: Phil Becker
President and CEO: Bill Streeter
SVP, CFO, and Treasurer: Allen Floyd
SVP Corporate Operations: J. Brian Griffith
SVP Corporate and Member Services:
Janice Schuerman
VP Feed Division: Alan Wessler
VP Crop Protection, Seed and Farm Supply:
Ron Utterback
VP Plant Foods, Marketing, and Transportation Division: Charles (Charlie) Cott
Controller: Ernie Verslues
Executive Assistant and Assistant Secretary:
Larna Lavelle

LOCATIONS

HQ: MFA Incorporated
201 Ray Young Dr., Columbia, MO 65201
Phone: 573-874-5111   **Fax:** 573-876-5430
Web: www.mfaincorporated.com

COMPETITORS

ADM
Ag Processing
Andersons
Cargill
CHS
GROWMARK
Rabo AgriFinance
Wilbur-Ellis

MFA Incorporated

Begun in 1914 when seven Missouri farmers got together to buy 1,150 pounds of binder twine, the agricultural cooperative MFA today ties together 45,000 farmers in Missouri and adjacent states. MFA, one of the US's oldest regional co-ops, supplies its member/owners with manufacturing, distribution, financing, and purchasing services. It runs retail service centers and works with independent dealers. MFA produces and markets beef, dairy, horse, and swine feeds, as well as soybean, corn, wheat, grass, grain, and alfalfa seeds.

In addition to feed, the co-op also provides crop-protection services, animal-health products, and farm supplies. It also offers marketing services, and is the publisher of *Today's Farmer*, a magazine devoted to agriculture.

Miami Heat

Basketball is one hot property for this company. Basketball Properties owns and operates the Miami Heat professional basketball team, which joined the National Basketball Association as an expansion franchise in 1988. The team struggled to find success until 1995 when former Los Angeles Lakers coach Pat Riley came to Miami. However, it wasn't until 2006 that the Heat won its first NBA title with a roster that included another former Laker, Shaquille O'Neal, along with such stars as Dwyane Wade. The family of Carnival CEO Micky Arison has controlled the basketball franchise since its founding.

After a disappointing 2007-08 season, Riley stepped down as head coach and appointed Erik Spoelstra as his replacement. Spoelstra previously served as head of scouting for the Heat. The coaching change was a repeat performance of 2003 when Riley resigned as head coach to become president of the ball club (a title he still retains). The former Lakers coach had returned to the bench in 2005 after Stan Van Gundy quit the team. Miami defeated the Dallas Mavericks in six games to win the championship that season. O'Neal was later traded to the Phoenix Suns during the 2007-08 season.

Family scion Ted Arison, who died in 1999, was the primary financial backer of the expansion franchise, along with Broadway producer Zev Buffman and Hall of Fame basketball player Billy Cunningham.

EXECUTIVES

Managing General Partner: Micky Arison, age 59
President: Pat Riley, age 64
President, Business Operations: Eric Woolworth
EVP Sales: Stephen Weber
EVP Business Operations and CFO: Sammy Schulman
EVP and Chief Marketing Officer: Michael McCullough
EVP Heat Group Enterprises: Mike Walker
EVP and General Counsel: Raquel Libman
EVP; General Manager, AmericanAirlines Arena:
 Kim Stone
Head Coach: Erik Spoelstra
SVP Basketball Operations: Andy Elisburg
SVP and CIO: Tony Coba
VP Finance: Jeff Morris
VP Marketing: Jeff Craney
VP Human Resources: Sonia Harty

LOCATIONS

HQ: Basketball Properties, Ltd.
 AmericanAirlines Arena, 601 Biscayne Blvd.
 Miami, FL 33132
Phone: 786-777-1000   **Fax:** 786-777-1615
Web: www.nba.com/heat

The Miami Heat play at 19,600-seat capacity
AmericanAirlines Arena in Miami.

PRODUCTS/OPERATIONS

Championship Titles

NBA Champions (2006)
Eastern Conference Champions (2006)

COMPETITORS

Charlotte Bobcats
Hawks Basketball
Orlando Magic
Washington Wizards

Michael Foods

It's not meat and potatoes but poultry and potatoes at Michael Foods. The company is one of
the leading US producers of shell eggs and value-
added egg products (frozen, liquid, pre-cooked,
dried). It has other operations, but eggs account
for 70% of its sales. The spuds come in with its
Northern Star subsidiary, which pre-shreds and
mashes potatoes. The company's Crystal Farms
subsidiary packages and distributes cheese, butter and other dairy products. Michael's customers
include food processors, foodservice distributors,
and retail grocery stores throughout North
America, as well as in the Far East, South America, and Europe. Investment firm Thomas H. Lee
Partners owns almost 90% of the company.

Michael's other major subsidiaries include
M.G. Waldbaum Company and Papetti's Hygrade
Egg Products, Inc. (both make processed egg
products). Adding to its holdings in the specialty
egg product market, in 2008 it purchased organic and cage-free egg company, Mr. B's of Abbotsford, for about $9 million.

Its largest foodservice customers are SYSCO
(15% of sales) and U.S. Foodservice (13% of
sales); SUPERVALU is the Crystal Farms division's largest customer (38% of the divisions sales
and 9% of company sales). Its potato division's

largest customers include major foodservice distributors and major national food retailers.

About 26% of the company's egg needs are
supplied by its own eggs, the remainder being
purchased from third parties. Its laying barns,
housing some 10.8 million producing hens, are
located in Minnesota, Nebraska, and South
Dakota. In addition the production of some
16.5 million hens is under long-term supply
agreements and 16.7 million more are under
shorter-term agreements.

In 2009 the company named James E. Dwyer
Jr. as president and CEO. He replaced Gregg
A. Ostrander, who remained as chairman. Before
joining Michael, Dwyer worked for Ahold USA as
executive vice president of private brands and
e-commerce, as well as chief business development officer for Stop and Shop, a subsidiary of
Ahold USA.

EXECUTIVES

Chairman: Gregg A. Ostrander, age 56,
 $1,770,410 total compensation
Vice Chairman: John D. Reedy, age 62,
 $706,230 total compensation
President, CEO, and Director: James E. (Jim) Dwyer Jr.,
 age 51
SVP Operations and Supply Chain:
 Thomas J. (Tom) Jagiela, age 52,
 $464,012 total compensation
SVP and CFO: Mark W. Westphal, age 43,
 $609,329 total compensation
President, Crystal Farms: Mark B. Anderson, age 47
General Counsel and Secretary: Carolyn V. Wolski,
 age 51
Treasurer: Mark D. Witmer, age 51
Auditors: PricewaterhouseCoopers LLP

LOCATIONS

HQ: Michael Foods, Inc.
 301 Carlson Pkwy., Ste. 400
 Minnetonka, MN 55305
Phone: 952-258-4000   **Fax:** 952-258-4911
Web: www.michaelfoods.com

PRODUCTS/OPERATIONS

2008 Sales

	$ mil.	% of total
Egg products	1,265.6	70
Crystal Farms	413.7	23
Potato products	125.1	7
Total	**1,804.4**	**100**

Selected Brands

Egg products
 Abbotsford Farms
 All Whites
 Better n Eggs
 Broke N' Ready
 Canadian Inovatec
 Easy Eggs
 Excell
 Emulsa
 Inovatec
 Michael Foods
 Papett's
 Quaker State Farms
 Table Ready
Potato products
 Diner's Choice
 Farm Fresh
 Northern Star
 Simply Potatoes

Refrigerated distribution
 Crescent Valley
 Crystal Farms
 David's Deli
 Westfield Farms

Selected Products

Egg Products
 Dried eggs
 Egg substitutes
 Extended shelf-life liquid eggs
 Fresh eggs
 Frozen eggs
 Precooked eggs
Refrigerated distribution
 Bagels
 Butter
 Crystal Farms brand cheese
 Eggs
 Margarine
 Muffins
 Potato products
Refrigerated potato products
 Hash browns
 Mashed potatoes
 Specialty potato products

COMPETITORS

Bob Evans
Cal-Maine Foods
Cargill
ConAgra
Dairy Farmers of America
Golden Oval Eggs
Heinz
JR Simplot
Kraft Foods
Land O'Lakes
McCain Foods
Moark
Ore-Ida Foods, Inc.
Primera Foods
Reser's Fine Foods
Rose Acre Farms
Sargento
Sorrento Lactalis
Unilever

HISTORICAL FINANCIALS

Company Type: Private

Income Statement

FYE: Saturday nearest December 31

	REVENUE ($ mil.)	NET INCOME ($ mil.)	NET PROFIT MARGIN	EMPLOYEES
12/08	1,804	47	2.6%	3,790
12/07	1,468	28	1.9%	3,759
12/06	1,247	19	1.5%	3,875
12/05	1,243	39	3.1%	4,132
12/04	1,314	34	2.6%	3,897
Annual Growth	**8.3%**	**8.8%**	**—**	**(0.7%)**

Net Income History

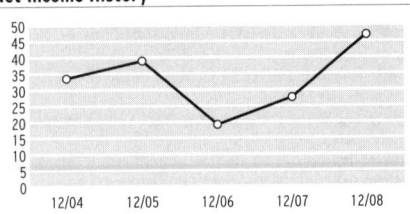

Michigan Education Special Services

There's a MESSA teachers in Michigan, and many of them get their health insurance from MESSA, or the Michigan Education Special Services Association. MESSA is a collective bargaining agency that structures and administers benefits plans for about 100,000 members of the Michigan Education Association (MEA), a union for school employees in the Wolverine State. The not-for-profit organization was founded in 1960. MESSA provides medical health plans through Blue Cross Blue Shield of Michigan; it also offers dental, vision, and prescription benefits.

EXECUTIVES

Executive Director: Cynthia Williams
Director Internal Operations and Facilities Services: Sue Kelly
Director Information Technology Support Services: Arjay Patrick
General Counsel and Director Business and Field Operations Division: Jeffrey Nyquist
Medical Director: Steve TePastte
Director Project Management Office: Charanya Girish
Director Benefits Administration: Bonnie Bloomquist
Director Field Services: Frank Musto
Director Communications and Government Relations: Gary Fralick
Director Marketing and Product Development: Richard (Dick) Ringstrom
Director Group Services: Jim Ponscheck

LOCATIONS

HQ: Michigan Education Special Services Association
1475 Kendale Blvd., East Lansing, MI 48826
Phone: 517-332-2581   **Fax:** 517-333-6252
Web: www.messa.org

HISTORICAL FINANCIALS

Company Type: Not-for-profit

Income Statement

FYE: June 30

	REVENUE ($ mil.)	NET INCOME ($ mil.)	NET PROFIT MARGIN	EMPLOYEES
6/08	1,244	365	29.3%	291
6/07	1,301	359	27.6%	322
6/06	1,355	269	19.8%	325
Annual Growth	(4.2%)	16.5%	—	(5.4%)

Net Income History

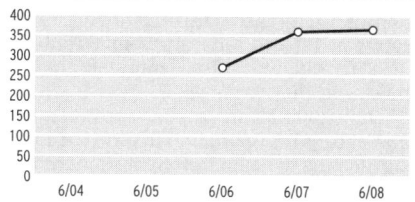

Michigan State University

The Spartan population is still growing today — in Michigan. With an enrollment of approximately 46,000 students, Michigan State University dominates the town of East Lansing. It offers more than 200 programs of study through 17 degree-granting colleges. Its research breakthroughs range from the cross-fertilization of corn in the 1870s to developing a top-selling anticancer drug in the 1960s. MSU was founded in 1855 as a land-grant college under the name Agricultural College of the State of Michigan. It became a full university a century later.

EXECUTIVES

Chairman: Joel I. Ferguson, age 70
Vice Chairperson: Melanie Foster
President: Lou Anna K. Simon
Vice Provost Libraries, Computing, and Technology: David A. Gift
VP Academic Affairs and Provost: Kim Wilcox, age 52
VP Finance and Operations and Treasurer: Fred L. Poston
VP Legal Affairs and General Counsel: Robert A. Noto
VP University Relations: Terry Denbow
Assistant VP, CFO, and Controller: David B. Brower
Assistant VP Human Resources: Brent Bowditch
Secretary: William R. Beekman
Auditors: KPMG LLP

LOCATIONS

HQ: Michigan State University
438 Administration Bldg., East Lansing, MI 48824
Phone: 517-355-6550   **Fax:** 517-355-9601
Web: www.msu.edu

PRODUCTS/OPERATIONS

Selected Colleges

College of Agriculture and Natural Resources
College of Arts and Letters
College of Communication Arts and Sciences
College of Education
College of Engineering
College of Human Ecology
College of Human Medicine
College of Law (affiliated)
College of Music
College of Natural Science
College of Nursing
College of Osteopathic Medicine
College of Social Science
College of Veterinary Medicine
James Madison College
The Eli Broad College of Business
The Eli Broad Graduate School of Management

Micro Electronics

There's nothing small about the way Micro Electronics sets up shop. The company has about 20 Micro Center computer retail stores, which operate in some 15 states, including California and Texas. The stores range up to 62,000 sq. ft., contain some 40,000 products organized in about a dozen specialized departments (an approach it calls "dedicated departments"), and sell video game consoles, as well. Micro Electronics sells its own brands of notebook and desktop computers under the WinBook and PowerSpec names. Micro Center Online is the company's e-commerce operation and Redemtech recycles IT equipment. Micro Center was founded in 1979 by John Baker.

With its faster-growing, larger rivals shuttering stores or closing up shop entirely, Micro Center's slow-growth plan (it has opened just 21 stores in 30 years) is looking measured and smart. The stores cater to tech enthusiasts with "Build Your Own" departments — where customers can build a computer from scratch — and "Knowledge Bars" up front where customers can speak with technicians. The chain distinguishes itself from its big-box competitors by stocking more products and employing a knowledgeable sales force. As a result, Micro Electronics is able to maintain a loyal customer base, such as Apple's (which happens to do quite a bit of business with Micro Electronics), without spending money on expensive advertising.

Other store departments include PCs (desktops, laptops), Macintosh computers, digital imaging (cameras, camcorders), hardware (monitors, printers, keyboards), accessories (memory, CD and DVD drives), The Game Room (game systems and games), and supplies (blank media, printer cartridges).

In 2006 Micro Electronics launched a gaming department at its stores; a mail-in rebate promotion helped the firm get a foothold in the niche.

EXECUTIVES

Chairman, President, and CEO; President, Micro Center: Richard M. (Rick) Mershad
COO: Peggy Wolfe
CFO: James Koehler
CIO: Misty Kuamoo
VP Retail Operations: Ralph Gilson
VP Business Development: Kevin Hollingshead
VP Retail Sales: Robert Demme
VP Retail Marketing: Mike Papai
VP Merchandising: Kevin Jones
President, Redemtech: Robert Houghton
Director Human Resources: Angie Miller
Director Visual Merchandising and Store Design: Matt Herman

LOCATIONS

HQ: Micro Electronics, Inc.
4119 Leap Rd., Hilliard, OH 43026
Phone: 614-850-3000   **Fax:** 614-850-3001
Web: www.microelectronics.com

2008 Stores

	No.
Ohio	3
California	2
Georgia	2
Illinois	2
Texas	2
Colorado	1
Kansas	1
Massachusetts	1
Maryland	1
Michigan	1
Minnesota	1
New Jersey	1
New York	1
Pennsylvania	1
Virginia	1
Total	**21**

PRODUCTS/OPERATIONS

Selected Operations

Micro Center
Micro Center Online
PowerSpec PC
Redemtech
WinBook
WinBook Computer Corporation

Selected Products

Accessories
  Cables
  Furniture
Books
Communications
  Handhelds
  PDAs
  Phones
Computers
  Desktops
  Notebooks
Digital imaging
  Camcorders
  Cameras
  Printers
Macintosh products
  Computers
  Notebooks
Peripherals
  Keyboards
  Monitors
  Printers
Software
Supplies
  Blank media
  Media storage
  Paper
  Printer cartridges
Upgrades
  Drives (CD, DVD)
  Memory

COMPETITORS

Amazon.com
Best Buy
Buy.com
CDW
Dell
Fry's Electronics
GameStop
Gateway, Inc.
Insight Enterprises
PC Connection
RadioShack
Systemax
Target
Wal-Mart

Midland Paper

Midland Paper Company (MPC) is a middle-man for the paper industry. The firm distributes coated, uncoated, bond, specialty, and other types of paper produced by such manufacturers as 3M, Boise Cascade, Domtar, and International Paper. It also sells packaging supplies and equipment and janitorial supplies, including mops and brooms, cleaners, and floor-care equipment. MPC distributes primarily to large companies that print books, magazines, and catalogs. Founded in 1907 as a paper supplier to Chicago's graphic arts industry, the company now operates warehouses and sales offices in California, Connecticut, Illinois, Minnesota, New York, North Dakota, and Wisconsin.

EXECUTIVES

President and CEO: E. Stanton (Stan) Hooker III
VP and COO: Michael Graves
VP and CFO: Ralph DeLetto
President, Midland Paper National: Jim O'Toole
Controller: George Koutsianelos
Corporate Credit Manager: Mari Fontana

LOCATIONS

HQ: Midland Paper Company Inc.
  101 E. Palatine Rd., Wheeling, IL 60090
Phone: 847-777-2700   **Fax:** 847-777-2552
Web: www.midlandpaper.com

COMPETITORS

Bradner Central
Central National-Gottesman
Clifford Paper
Gould Paper
RIS the paper house
Unisource
West Coast Paper
xpedx

HISTORICAL FINANCIALS

Company Type: Private

Income Statement

FYE: December 31

	REVENUE ($ mil.)	NET INCOME ($ mil.)	NET PROFIT MARGIN	EMPLOYEES
12/08	700	—	—	—
12/07	700	—	—	—
12/06	700	—	—	—
12/05	629	—	—	375
12/04	560	—	—	—
Annual Growth	**5.7%**	**—**	**—**	**—**

Revenue History

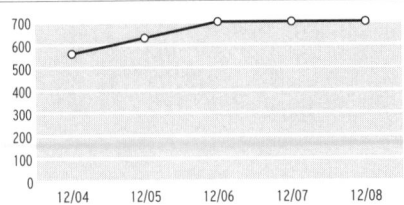

Midwest Research Institute

Midwest Research Institute (MRI) provides contract research services for government and private-sector clients in fields such as agricultural and food safety, analytical chemistry, biological sciences, energy, engineering, environment, health sciences, information technology, and national defense. The institute operates laboratories and agricultural research centers in Florida, Maryland, and Missouri. MRI also manages the US Department of Energy's National Renewable Energy Laboratory in Golden, Colorado. Work related to biological and chemical defense accounts for most of MRI's sales. The not-for-profit organization was founded in 1944.

EXECUTIVES

Chairman: Richard C. Green Jr.
Vice Chairman: James L. Spigarelli, age 66
President and CEO: Michael F. Helmstetter
EVP; Director National Renewable Energy Lab:
  Dan E. Arvizu
VP and CFO: Fred Cornwell
General Counsel and Corporate Secretary: Jeanie Latz

LOCATIONS

HQ: Midwest Research Institute
  425 Volker Blvd., Kansas City, MO 64110
Phone: 816-753-7600   **Fax:** 816-753-8420
Web: www.mriresearch.org

Milan Express Co.

It may sounds like a train from Rome, but this Milan Express is a trucking company from Tennessee. Milan Express provides less-than-truckload (LTL) and truckload freight transportation, as well as logistics and warehousing and distribution services. (LTL carriers consolidate freight from multiple shippers into a single truckload.) Although its service area ranges from Florida to Wisconsin, the company operates primarily in the Southeast and Midwest US with a fleet of about 960 trucks and tractors. It maintains about 530,000 sq. ft. of warehouse space. Tommy Ross, company chairman, founded Milan Express in 1969 to serve an 87-mile route between Memphis and Milan, Tennessee. The Ross family owns the company.

In July 2009 Milan Express partnered with New Century Transportation to form the Lightning Alliance, to haul LTL freight from the Midwest and Southeast to the Northeast. Beyond expanding Milan Express' geographic area, the deal makes New Century's services available to Milan Express' customers.

That same month, Milan Express formed another partnership to extend its territory, this time with Cavalier Transportation for transborder LTL, truckload, expedited, warehousing, and logistics services between the US and Canada.

EXECUTIVES

Chairman: Tommy W. Ross
President: John W. Ross
VP and CFO: Bruce F. Kalem
VP Operations: David Dallas
Network Administrator, MIS Department: Justin Story
VP Customer Service: Michelle Murphree
VP and COO, LTL Operations: Mark Leslie
VP Maintenance: Benny Page
VP Corporate Services: Jim Szopinski
VP Properties: Barry Jones
VP Administration: Ed Wright

LOCATIONS

HQ: Milan Express Co., Inc.
1091 Kefauver Dr., Milan, TN 38358
Phone: 731-686-7428   **Fax:** 731-686-8829
Web: www.milanexpress.com

PRODUCTS/OPERATIONS

Selected Services

Less-than-truckload
On-time expedited
Truckload
    Dedicated
    Flatbed
    Local region service
    Logistics
    Van
Warehousing and distribution

COMPETITORS

AAA Cooper Transportation
Arkansas Best
Averitt Express
Celadon
C.H. Robinson Worldwide
Con-way Freight
Con-way Truckload
Covenant Transportation
Crete Carrier
Estes Express
FedEx Freight
GENCO Distribution System
J.B. Hunt
Landstar System
Old Dominion Freight
Saia
Schneider National
Southeastern Freight Lines
Swift Transportation
UPS Freight
UPS Supply Chain Solutions
U.S. Xpress
USA Truck
Werner Enterprises
YRC Worldwide

HISTORICAL FINANCIALS

Company Type: Private

Income Statement

FYE: December 31

	REVENUE ($ mil.)	NET INCOME ($ mil.)	NET PROFIT MARGIN	EMPLOYEES
12/08	188	—	—	1,500
12/07	191	—	—	1,500
12/06	168	—	—	1,850
12/05	163	—	—	1,650
12/04	141	—	—	—
Annual Growth	7.5%	—	—	(3.1%)

Revenue History

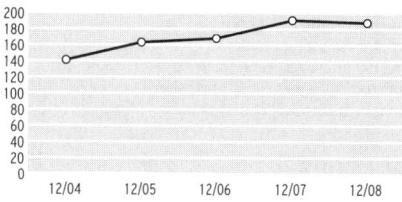

	12/04	12/05	12/06	12/07	12/08

Milliken & Company

Making tennis balls feel soft and Jell-O pudding taste smooth are just two of the things that Milliken & Company does. One of the world's largest private textile and chemical companies, Milliken produces more than 19,000 products, including carpets, apparel, automotive fabrics, mattress barriers, and wall coverings. It also makes chemicals and colorants that infuse such products as Crayola markers and liquid laundry detergent, make plastic food containers clear, and serve additional purposes in the automotive, consumer products, and turf markets. Milliken operates more than 55 plants globally and one of the largest textile research centers in the world. The Milliken family controls the company.

Seth Milliken and William Deering founded the company in 1865 as Deering Milliken Company, specializing in woolen fabrics. Seth's grandson, chairman Roger Milliken, has led the company since 1947.

Since then, the company has gone on to acquire Georgia-based Constantine LLC in October 2009. Constantine, which will join Milliken & Company's Floor Covering Division, makes broadloom and modular carpet tile, along with durable, hard surface flooring, primarily for commercial applications. The acquisition enhances Milliken's market share and portfolio in the architectural and design sector.

Also in October 2009 Milliken & Company, through one of its subsidiaries, completed the acquisition of the assets of Rebus, Inc. A chemical company located in Pennsylvania, Rebus produces custom-blended colorants and additives for plastic material applications.

The company also purchased Western Nonwoven's fire retardant barrier and geotextile businesses out of Chapter 11 bankruptcy. It gained the Paladin and Sandmat product lines in 2008, which helps Milliken expand into the nonwovens segment.

At the same time, dealing with a global economic crisis has led the company to resort to cost-cutting measures, including price hikes of up to 15% on most of its products.

HISTORY

Seth Milliken and William Deering formed a company in 1865 to become selling agents for textile mills in New England and the southern US. Deering left the partnership, and in 1869 he founded Deering Harvester (now Navistar).

Milliken set up operations in New York before the turn of the century, began buying the accounts receivable of cash-short textile mill operators, and invested in some of the companies.

In his position as agent and financier, Milliken was able to spot failing mills. He bought out the distressed owners at a discount and soon became a major mill owner himself. In 1905 Milliken and his allies waged a bitter proxy fight and court case to win control of two mills, earning Milliken a fearsome reputation.

H. B. Claflin, a New York dry-goods wholesaler that also operated department stores, owed money to Milliken. When Claflin went bankrupt in 1914, Milliken got some of the stores, which became Mercantile Stores. The Milliken family retained about 40% of the chain (sold to Dillard's in 1998).

Roger Milliken, grandson of the founder, became the president of the company in 1947 and has ruled with a firm hand. He fired brother-in-law W. B. Dixon Stroud in 1955, and none of Roger's children, nephews, or nieces has ever been allowed to work for the company. The workers at Milliken's Darlington, South Carolina, mill voted to unionize in 1956. The next day Milliken closed the plant, beginning 24 years of litigation that ended at the US Supreme Court. Milliken settled with its workers for $5 million.

In the 1960s the company introduced Visa, a finish for easy-care fabrics. Milliken launched its Pursuit of Excellence program in 1981; the program stressed self-managed teams of employees and eliminated 700 management positions. Tom Peters dedicated his 1987 bestseller, *Thriving on Chaos,* to Roger.

Away from that limelight, Milliken is (and has always been) a secretive, closely held business. In 1989 that secrecy and family control were threatened when members of the Stroud branch of the family sued the company in the Delaware courts and then sold a small number of shares to Erwin Maddrey and Bettis Rainsford, executives of Milliken competitor Delta Woodside. The courts ruled in favor of Milliken in 1992; Maddrey and Rainsford were required to sign confidentiality agreements before receiving Milliken information. Roger financially backed opponents of NAFTA in 1993.

Milliken is known by competitors for its unofficial motto: "Steal ideas shamelessly." Woven-filament maker NRB sued Milliken in 1997 for corporate spying and the following year industrial textile maker Johnston Industries filed a similar lawsuit. Milliken settled both cases out of court.

In 1999 Milliken began using its Millitron dye technology to produce residential carpets and rugs. It also introduced new brands of patterned rugs (including Royal Dynasty, Prestige, American Heritage). In 2000 the company built a manufacturing facility in South Carolina to expand its production of Millard-brand clarifying agents. Milliken closed its Union and Saluda plants in 2004.

EXECUTIVES

Chairman: Roger Milliken, age 93
President and CEO: Joe Salley, age 41
VP Human Resources: Brad Kendall
VP Quality & Milliken University: Craig Long
Director Public Affairs: Richard Dillard
Director Safety and Health: Wayne Punch
President, Milliken Chemical: John Rekers

LOCATIONS

HQ: Milliken & Company
920 Milliken Rd., Spartanburg, SC 29303
Phone: 864-503-2020   **Fax:** 864-503-2100
Web: www.milliken.com

PRODUCTS/OPERATIONS

Selected Products

Apparel
  Activewear
  Children's school uniforms
  Cheerleading apparel
  Fire retardant work wear
  Men's and women's wear
  Military uniforms

Automotive
  Airbags
  Interior fabrics (car seats, floor mats, side panels)

Chemicals
  Additives (antimicrobial agents, plastics additives)
  Carpet cleaner
  Coated products (extrusion coatings and composites, packaging systems)
  Colorants and tints (ClearTint, Liquitint, Palmer, Reactint, ViviTint)
  Elastomers
  Medical products
  Resin intermediates
  Specialty chemicals
  Textile chemicals (Lubestat, Syltint, Syn Lube, Syn Stat, Versatint)
  Turf maintenance chemicals

Carpets, coverings, and fabrics
  Area mats and rugs
  Carpets and carpet tiles
  Drapery fabrics
  Flame retardant mattress barrier materials
  Table linens
  Upholstery fabric
  Wall and floor coverings

COMPETITORS

Asahi Kasei	Johnston Textiles
BASF SE	Mohawk Industries
Beaulieu Group	Mount Vernon Mills
Conso International	Shaw Industries
Dixie Group	Springs Global
Dow Chemical	SWIFT GALEY
DuPont	Trelleborg Coated Systems
Guilford Mills	Unifi
Interface, Inc.	W.L. Gore
International Textile	

Milwaukee Bucks

A herd of basketball fans gather around these Bucks. The Milwaukee Bucks professional basketball franchise joined the National Basketball Association in 1968 and earned a championship title just three years later with the help of Hall of Fame player Lew Alcindor (later Kareem Abdul-Jabbar). The team has made one other appearance in the NBA Finals in 1974. Hometown fans support the Bucks at Milwaukee's aging Bradley Center. Local businessmen Wesley Pavalon and Marvin Fishman were originally awarded the basketball franchise. Wisconsin Senator Herb Kohl, whose family started the Kohl's department store chain, has owned the Bucks since 1985.

EXECUTIVES

President: Herb Kohl
VP Business Operations: John Steinmiller
CFO: Mike Burr
General Manager: John Hammond
Head Coach: Scott Skiles, age 45

Director Basketball Operations: John Horst
Director Corporate Sales: David Snyder
Director Public Relations: Dan Smyczek
Director Sales: Jim Grayson
Director of Player Personnel: Dave Babcock
Manager Equipment and Facilities: Dwayne Wilson
Manager Information Technology: Ron Kiepert

LOCATIONS

HQ: Milwaukee Bucks, Inc.
  Bradley Center, 1001 N. 4th St.
  Milwaukee, WI 53203
Phone: 414-227-0500   **Fax:** 414-227-0543
Web: www.nba.com/bucks

COMPETITORS

Cavaliers
Chicago Bulls
Detroit Pistons
Indiana Pacers

Minnesota Timberwolves

These wolves get basketball fans howling in the Twin Cities. Minnesota Timberwolves Basketball owns and operates the Minnesota Timberwolves professional basketball franchise, which joined the National Basketball Association as an expansion franchise in 1989. Playing host at the Target Center in Minneapolis, the Wolves have yet to claim an NBA Finals appearance. Local businessmen Harvey Ratner and Marv Wolfenson were first awarded the franchise; Glen Taylor, chairman of printing giant Taylor Corporation, led a group of investors who bought the team in 1995.

After failing to lead Minnesota to the playoffs for several years running, head coach and long-time executive Kevin McHale resigned from the Timberwolves in 2009. He had served as head of basketball operations for several seasons, ultimately hiring and then firing coach Randy Wittman, whom he then replaced on the bench during the 2008-09 season. McHale is best remembered as a member of the Boston Celtics.

The awarding of the basketball franchise to Minnesota marked the return of NBA action to the Land of 10,000 Lakes for the first time since 1960. That year the Minnesota Lakers moved to California to become the Los Angeles Lakers.

EXECUTIVES

Owner: Glen A. Taylor
CEO: Rob Moor
President: Chris Wright
President, Basketball Operations: David Kahn
General Manager: James (Jim) Stack
Head Coach: Kurt Rambis
Director of Finance: Peter Stene
VP Marketing: Jason LaFrenz
VP Communications: Ted Johnson
VP Client Development: Jeff Munneke
Director Corporate Sales: Chris Potenza
Director Player Personnel: Zarko Durisic
Head Athletic Trainer: Gregg Farnam
Community Relations Manager: Sarah Barthol

LOCATIONS

HQ: Minnesota Timberwolves Basketball
  Limited Partnership
  600 1st Ave. North, Minneapolis, MN 55403
Phone: 612-673-1600   **Fax:** 612-673-1699
Web: www.nba.com/timberwolves

The Minnesota Timberwolves play at the 23,500-seat capacity Target Center in Minneapolis.

COMPETITORS

Denver Nuggets
Oklahoma City Thunder
Portland Trail Blazers
Utah Jazz

Minnesota Wild

Fans of this team are Wild about hockey, you might say. Minnesota Wild Hockey Club owns and operates the Minnesota Wild professional hockey franchise. The team joined the National Hockey League in the expansion of 2000 (along with the Columbus Blue Jackets), filling the void left after the Minnesota North Stars moved to Texas in 1993 to become the Dallas Stars. An investment group led by Robert Naegele Jr. helped bring hockey back to the Twin Cities. Former Nashville Predators owner Craig Leipold acquired control of the team from Naegele in 2008.

After missing the 2008-09 post-season, the team fired president and general manager Doug Risebrough and replaced him with Chuck Fletcher, who had previously been assistant general manager with the Pittsburgh Penguins. Risebrough had led the Wild franchise since the team's inception. That same off-season, former San Jose Sharks assistant Todd Richards replaced head coach Jacques Lemaire who retired after eight seasons with the team.

Leipold, who sold the Preds to a group of Nashville businessmen for about $190 million in 2007, rejoined the ranks of NHL owners the following year when he purchased a 51% stake in the Minnesota team for $260 million. His Nashville franchise had struggled to build a fan base despite posting winning records and making the Stanley Cup playoffs three times since joining the league in 2001; Leipold claimed he lost about $70 million during the 2005-06 season.

Before starting the Nashville club in 1998, Leipold founded telemarketing firm Ameritel (later acquired by Convergys) and owned Rainfair Corporation, a maker of protective clothing that was sold to LaCrosse Footwear in 1996. His wife, Helen Johnson-Leipold, is CEO of outdoor equipment maker Johnson Outdoors and is part of the family that controls household products manufacturer S.C. Johnson & Son.

Former North Stars owner Norm Green — and NHL officials — drew the ire of Minnesota hockey fans when the Stars headed south for greener pastures in Dallas (where the franchise won its first Stanley Cup championship in 1999). Naegele and other investors, including Stanley Hubbard (CEO of Hubbard Broadcasting) and heirs of the Ordway family (early 3M investors), were awarded a new franchise for the Twin Cities market in 1997 as part of the league's expansion effort of the late 1990s.

EXECUTIVES

Owner: Craig L. Leipold
General Partner: Phil Falcone
Acting General Manager and Assistant General Manager, Hockey Operations: Tom Lynn, age 41
Assistant General Manager, Player Personnel: Tom Thompson, age 56
EVP and CFO: Pamela Wheelock
EVP: Matt Majka, age 49
VP Communications and Broadcast: Bill Robertson, age 48
Head Coach: Todd Richards, age 43
VP Corporate Sales and Service: Tom Garrity, age 45
Director Professional Scouting: Blair Mackasey, age 54
Director Hockey Operations: Chris Snow, age 28
Medical Director: Sheldon Burns, age 60
Player Development Coordinator: Barry MacKenzie, age 68

LOCATIONS

HQ: Minnesota Wild Hockey Club, LP
317 Washington St., St. Paul, MN 55102
Phone: 651-602-6000 **Fax:** 651-222-1055
Web: www.wild.com

The Minnesota Wild play at the 18,064-seat capacity Xcel Energy Center in St. Paul, Minnesota.

COMPETITORS

Calgary Flames
Colorado Avalanche
Edmonton Oilers
Vancouver Canucks

MITRE Corporation

The MITRE Corporation may not be able to cut perfect angles, but it can provide some fine systems engineering and information technology (IT) services. The not-for-profit organization develops, analyzes, and protects information systems for the US Department of Defense, the Internal Revenue Service, and the Federal Aviation Administration. MITRE's four Federally Funded Research and Development Centers (FFRDCs) provide such services as systems engineering, systems integration, and IT consulting. Founded in 1958 by former MIT researchers, MITRE also designs surveillance and reconnaissance systems and provides air traffic management services. It employs about 7,000 scientists, engineers, and support specialists.

EXECUTIVES

Chairman: James R. Schlesinger, age 80
Vice Chairman: Charles S. Robb
President, CEO, and Trustee: Alfred Grasso
SVP, CFO, and Treasurer: Mark W. Kontos
SVP, and General Manager, Center for Enterprise Modernization and IRS/VA Federally Funded Research and Development Center; Director, Homeland Security Center: Jason F. Providakes
Director, SVP, and General Manager, Center for Advanced Aviation System Development: Agam N. Sinha

SVP and Corporate Chief Engineer: Louis S. Metzger
SVP and General Manager, Command and Control Center: David H. Lehman
SVP and Director, Department of Defense Command, Control, Communications, and Intelligence Federally Funded Research and Development Center: Raymond Haller
SVP and General Manager, Center for Integrated Intelligence Systems: Robert F. Nesbit
VP and CIO: Robert A. Mikelskas
VP and CTO: Stephen D. Huffman
VP and Chief Human Resources Officer: Lisa R. Bender
VP, General Counsel, and Corporate Secretary: Sol Glasner
Director Corporate Communications and Knowledge Services: Catherine L. Crawford
Auditors: PricewaterhouseCoopers LLP

LOCATIONS

HQ: The MITRE Corporation
202 Burlington Rd., Bedford, MA 01730
Phone: 781-271-2000 **Fax:** 781-271-2271
Web: www.mitre.org

PRODUCTS/OPERATIONS

Selected Practice Areas

Acquisition and systems analysis
Aviation systems, safety, and security
Command and control
Cybersecurity
Emerging technologies
Enterprise systems engineering
Global networking
Healthcare transformation
Homeland security
Intelligence, surveillance, and reconnaissance
Large-scale enterprise transformation

Modern Woodmen

No need to pitch a tent to have Modern Woodmen in your camp. One of the largest fraternal benefit societies in the US, Modern Woodmen provides annuities and life insurance to more than 750,000 members through some 1,500 agents. The group, founded in 1883, is organized into "camps" (or chapters) that provide social, recreational, and service — as well as financial — benefits to members. Founder Joseph Cullen Root chose the society's name to compare pioneering woodmen clearing forests to men using life insurance to remove the financial burdens their families could face upon their deaths. Modern Woodmen offerings also include mutual funds, brokerage, and retirement and educational savings plans.

Subsidiaries MWA Financial Services Modern Woodmen Bank offer securities brokerage and retail banking services, respectively. All told, the company has about $8 billion in assets and $32.2 billion life insurance in force.

The organization claims more than 2,400 camps and nearly 800 youth clubs nationwide. In addition to financial services, the camps also offer social activities and community service opportunities for members and their families.

EXECUTIVES

President, CEO, and Director: W. Kenny Massey
Manager, Arkansas Agency and Director: Albert T. Hurst Jr.
General Counsel and Director: Darcy G. Callas
Investment Manager, Treasurer, and Director: Nick S. Coin
Corporate Communications Coordinator: Sharon K. Snawerdt
Public Relations Specialist: Kim Woodward
National Secretary and Director: Gerald P. Odean

LOCATIONS

HQ: Modern Woodmen of America
1701 1st Ave., Rock Island, IL 61201
Phone: 309-786-6481 **Fax:** 309-793-5547
Web: www.modern-woodmen.org

PRODUCTS/OPERATIONS

2008 Sales

	$ mil.	% of total
Premiums & other considerations		
Life & annuities	766.5	62
Other	4.9	—
Net investment income	458.9	37
Amortization of interest maintenance reserve	2.6	—
Other	13.3	1
Total	**1,246.2**	**100**

COMPETITORS

Allstate
Liberty Mutual
MassMutual
MetLife
Nationwide
New York Life
Northwestern Mutual
Prudential
Reliance Standard
State Farm
Thrivent Financial
Woodmen of the World

HISTORICAL FINANCIALS

Company Type: Not-for-profit

Income Statement

FYE: December 31

	ASSETS ($ mil.)	NET INCOME ($ mil.)	INCOME AS % OF ASSETS	EMPLOYEES
12/08	8,479	(7)	—	1,500
12/07	8,318	97	1.2%	1,500
12/06	7,929	99	1.3%	1,500
Annual Growth	3.4%	—	—	0.0%

2008 Year-End Financials

Equity as % of assets: —
Return on assets: —
Return on equity: —
Long-term debt ($ mil.): —
Sales ($ mil.): 1,246

Net Income History

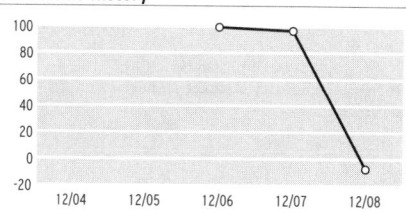

Mohegan Tribal Gaming Authority

The sun also rises at Mohegan Sun, a gaming and entertainment complex run by the Mohegan Tribal Gaming Authority for the Mohegan Indian tribe of Connecticut. The Native American-themed Mohegan Sun includes three casinos (Casino of the Earth, Casino of the Sky, and Casino of the Wind) which feature slot machines, game tables, horse race wagering, an arena, a cabaret, stores, restaurants, and a luxury hotel. The company also owns Pocono Downs, a horse racetrack in Pennsylvania. Gambling revenues go to the Mohegan Tribe, and are used for cultural and educational programs. The tribe has lived as a community for hundreds of years in what is today southeastern Connecticut, and has about 1,700 members.

In addition to operating casinos and hotels, the Mohegan Tribal Gaming Authority also owns the Connecticut Sun WNBA basketball team. Other operations include subsidiaries to assist the Cowlitz Indian Tribe of Washington and the Menominee Indian Tribe of Wisconsin to open casinos. The company has submitted proposals to co-develop gaming projects in New York and Kansas as well.

The company purchased Mohegan Sun at Pocono Downs, or Pocono Downs, from Penn National Gaming for $175 million in 2005. The Mohegan Tribal Gaming Authority is spending some $200 million renovating the facility by adding slot machines, gaming tables, restaurants and shops, and more parking. In 2007 the Mohegan Tribal Gaming Authority expanded into golf with the acquisition of Pautipaug Country Club in Connecticut. It purchased the golf course for some $4.7 million and renamed it Mohegan Sun Country Club at Pautipaug.

The company completed a major renovation (worth more than $110 million) at its Casino of the Wind in 2008. Included in the remodel were an additional 45,000 sq. ft. of gaming space, approximately 660 slot machines, nearly 30 table games, and a more than 40-table themed poker room, as well as approximately 20,000 sq. ft. of new dining and retail space. A similar renovation planned for its Casino of the Earth has been put on hold due to the national economic recession.

EXECUTIVES

Chairwoman: Marilynn R. (Lynn) Malerba, age 56
President and CEO: Mitchell Grossinger Etess
EVP and COO: Jeffrey E. (Jeff) Hartmann, age 46
CFO: Leo M. Chupaska, age 60
SVP Resort Operations Mohegan Sun: Gary S. Crowder
SVP Marketing Mohegan Sun: Anthony Patrone
SVP Information Systems and CIO Mohegan Sun:
 Daniel W. (Dan) Garrow
SVP Administration Mohegan Sun: Ray Pineault
SVP Sports and Entertainment Mohegan Sun:
 Paul S. Munick

VP Corporate Finance: Peter J. Roberti
VP Corporate Development: Paul Brody
VP Legal Administration: Michael J. Ciaccio
President and CEO Pocono Downs: Robert J. Soper, age 36
Medicine Woman and Tribal Historian:
 Melissa Tantaquidgeon Zobel
Treasurer and Director: William Quidgeon Jr., age 46
Auditors: PricewaterhouseCoopers LLP

LOCATIONS

HQ: Mohegan Tribal Gaming Authority
 1 Mohegan Sun Blvd., Uncasville, CT 06382
Phone: 860-862-8000   **Fax:** 860-862-7824
Web: www.mtga.com

PRODUCTS/OPERATIONS

2008 Sales

	$ mil.	% of total
Gaming	1,411	83
Food & beverage	104	6
Hotel	49	3
Retail & other	144	8
(Adjustments)	(136)	—
Total	**1,572**	**100**

2008 Sales

	$ mil.	% of total
Mohegan Sun	1,363	87
Pocono Downs	209	13
Total	**1,572**	**100**

Selected Holdings

Mohegan Basketball (Mohegan Sun WNBA team)
Mohegan Golf (Mohegan Sun Country Club at
 Pautipaug)
Mohegan Sun
 Casino of the Earth
 Casino of the Sky
 Casino of the Wind
 The Shops at Mohegan Sun
 Sky Hotel Tower
Mohegan Sun at Pocono Downs

HISTORICAL FINANCIALS

Company Type: Private

Income Statement

FYE: September 30

	REVENUE ($ mil.)	NET INCOME ($ mil.)	NET PROFIT MARGIN	EMPLOYEES
9/08	1,572	149	9.5%	11,575
9/07	1,620	173	10.7%	10,400
9/06	1,426	155	10.9%	10,400
9/05	1,332	24	1.8%	10,600
9/04	1,257	103	8.2%	10,300
Annual Growth	**5.8%**	**9.8%**	**—**	**3.0%**

Net Income History

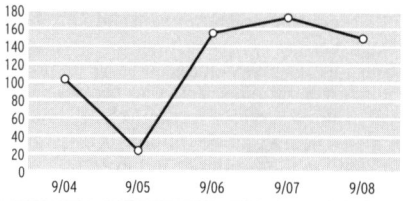

Momentive Performance Materials

Gathering momentum after its spinoff from General Electric, Momentive Performance Materials is ready to take on the world. The company manufactures silicone, quartz, and ceramic products for everything from adhesive labels to hair care products to pesticides. Silicone is used by makers of a vast array of products, both because of its ability to provide resistance to heat, UV rays, and chemical reactions, and because it allows for different levels of lubricity and adhesion. Its quartz and ceramic products go into semiconductors, cosmetics, and fiber optics. Created in 2006 after GE sold its former Advanced Materials unit to Apollo Management, the company operates globally through about 25 production plants.

When it was a part of GE the company had joint ventures with the likes of Bayer and Toshiba, but Momentive bought out its partners to prepare for its formation as a stand-alone company. It now serves companies as diverse as BASF, Lowe's, Motorola, and Unilever.

The silicones unit makes up the bulk of Momentive's business, accounting for just about 90% of sales. The company divides its global operations nearly equally among the Asia/Pacific region, Europe, and North America.

EXECUTIVES

Chairman: Joshua J. (Josh) Harris, age 44
President, CEO, and Director: Jonathan Rich, age 53, $847,409 total compensation
CFO: Anthony S. (Tony) Colatrella, age 53
CTO: Eric Thaler, age 48
Chief Commercial Officer: Michael D. (Mike) Modak, age 52
General Counsel, Secretary, and Director:
 Douglas A. Johns, age 51, $630,600 total compensation
Global Human Resources Leader: Edward Stratton, age 50, $588,685 total compensation
President and CEO, Silicones, Asia Pacific:
 Rachel Duan, age 38
Manager Global Business Development: Mark Irwin, age 44, $648,826 total compensation
Global Operations Leader: Joerg Krueger, age 45
Global EHS Leader: Edu Araujo, age 51
President and CEO, Global Sealants: Shawn Williams, age 45
President and CEO, Quartz: Raymond F. (Ray) Kolberg, age 47
President and CEO, Silicones Americas:
 Steven Delarge, age 51, $444,496 total compensation
President and CEO, Silicones, Europe, Middle East, Africa, and India: Ian Moore, age 49
Auditors: KPMG LLP

LOCATIONS

HQ: Momentive Performance Materials Inc.
 22 Corporate Woods Blvd., 2nd Fl.
 Albany, NY 12211
Phone: 518-533-4600   **Fax:** 518-533-4609
Web: www.momentive.com

2008 Sales

	$ mil.	% of total
Europe	933.7	35
US	824.1	31
Pacific	753.7	29
Mexico & Brazil	82.4	3
Canada	45.4	2
Total	**2,639.3**	**100**

PRODUCTS/OPERATIONS

2008 Sales

	$ mil.	% of total
Silicones	2,383.4	90
Quartz	255.9	10
Total	**2,639.3**	**100**

COMPETITORS

3M
Dow Corning
Evonik Degussa
SABIC Innovative Plastics
Saint-Gobain Ceramics & Plastics
Shin-Etsu Chemical
Tosoh
Wacker Chemie

HISTORICAL FINANCIALS

Company Type: Private

Income Statement

FYE: December 31

	REVENUE ($ mil.)	NET INCOME ($ mil.)	NET PROFIT MARGIN	EMPLOYEES
12/08	2,639	(997)	—	4,795
12/07	2,538	(254)	—	5,117
12/06	2,414	(37)	—	4,982
12/05	2,342	74	3.2%	—
12/04	2,228	67	3.0%	—
Annual Growth	**4.3%**	**—**	**—**	**(1.9%)**

Net Income History

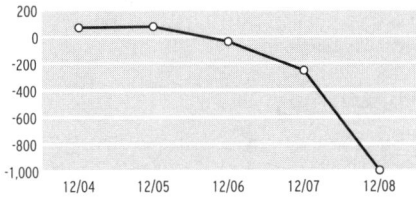

Montefiore Medical Center

The primary teaching hospital of the Albert Einstein College of Medicine, Montefiore Medical Center attends to the health care needs of the residents of the Bronx and nearby Westchester County. The health system has three main hospital campuses with more than 1,400 beds, as well as a children's hospital and centers for cancer, women's health, and cardiology. It also features two specialty outpatient facilities, which provide ambulatory and diagnostic services, and it operates a home health care agency and a network of dozens of primary and specialty care offices. Montefiore Medical Center also offers medical education programs in partnership with the Albert Einstein College of Medicine.

Founded in 1884 to treat tuberculosis patients, Montefiore Medical Center has a long history of responding to community health crises, including lead poisoning and AIDS. Montefiore opened

a community clinic in 2007 with the aim of vaccinating young women for HPV, a sexually transmitted disease that can cause cervical cancer.

In 2008 the health system acquired rival Bronx hospital Our Lady of Mercy Medical Center, which had filed for bankruptcy due largely to its inability to collect debts from indigent patients. Our Lady of Mercy, which now operates as the Montefiore North Division, has about 370 beds.

EXECUTIVES

President and CEO: Steven M. Safyer, age 60
SVP Network Development: Richard T. Celiberti
EVP Operations: Robert B. Conaty
EVP Finance: Joel A. Perlman
EVP Corporate: Donald L. Ashkenase
SVP and Special Advisor for Business Affairs: Stanley L. Jacobson
SVP Operations: Susan Green-Lorenzen
SVP and General Counsel: Christopher S. Panczner
SVP and Chief Medical Officer: Gary Kalkut
SVP Institutional Advancement and Chief Human Resources Officer: Milton C. Anderson
Auditors: Ernst & Young LLP

LOCATIONS

HQ: Montefiore Medical Center
111 E. 210th St., Bronx, NY 10467
Phone: 718-920-4321   **Fax:** 718-920-6321
Web: www.montefiore.org

PRODUCTS/OPERATIONS

Selected Facilities

Greene Medical Arts Pavilion
Montefiore Medical Group
Montefiore Medical Park
Montefiore Medical Specialists
Moses Division Hospital (or Henry and Lucy Moses Division)
Children's Hospital at Montefiore
North Division (formerly Our Lady of Mercy Medical Center)
Weiler Division Hospital (or Jack D. Weiler Hospital)

COMPETITORS

Beth Israel Medical Center
Bronx-Lebanon Hospital
Brooklyn Hospital Center
Catholic Healthcare System
Jamaica Hospital Medical Center
Lenox Hill Hospital
New York City Health and Hospitals
NewYork-Presbyterian Healthcare
Phelps Memorial Hospital Center
Saint Vincent Catholic Medical Centers

HISTORICAL FINANCIALS

Company Type: Not-for-profit

Income Statement

FYE: December 31

	REVENUE ($ mil.)	NET INCOME ($ mil.)	NET PROFIT MARGIN	EMPLOYEES
12/08	2,077	—	—	11,000

Morgan, Lewis & Bockius

Long a leading Philadelphia law firm, Morgan, Lewis & Bockius these days extends its reach well beyond the City of Brotherly Love to take in Boston, Brussels, and Beijing, as well as Paris and Pittsburgh. The firm has more than 20 offices overall. Of its 1,500 lawyers, about 800 are housed in New York, Philadelphia, and Washington, DC. The firm's multiple practice areas include business and finance, intellectual property, environment law, labor and employment, real estate, taxes, and litigation. Morgan, Lewis & Bockius was founded in 1873 by Charles Morgan Jr. and Francis Lewis.

EXECUTIVES

Chair of the Firm: Francis M. Milone
Executive Director: Francis X. Fee
Managing Partner, Operations: Thomas J. Sharbaugh
Director Practice Technology: Ellen J. Polhamus
Chief Human Resources Officer: Ellen H. Johnston
Chief of Marketing and Communications: Michael Baltes
Chief of Administrative Operations: Valerie D. Pearce
Chief of Practice Development: James K. (Jim) Dixon
General Counsel: Michael A. Bloom

LOCATIONS

HQ: Morgan, Lewis & Bockius LLP
1701 Market St., Philadelphia, PA 19103
Phone: 215-963-5000   **Fax:** 215-963-5001
Web: www.morganlewis.com

PRODUCTS/OPERATIONS

Selected Practice Areas

Antitrust
Business and finance
Employee benefits
Energy
Food and Drug Administration/Health care regulation
Intellectual property
Investment management
Labor and employment
Litigation
Personal law
Real estate
Tax

COMPETITORS

Akin Gump
Baker & McKenzie
Blank Rome
Cleary Gottlieb
Clifford Chance
Davis Polk
Dechert
DLA Piper
Duane Morris
Gibson, Dunn & Crutcher
Hogan & Hartson
Jones Day
K&L Gates
Kirkland & Ellis
Latham & Watkins
Mayer Brown
Pepper Hamilton
Reed Smith
Sidley Austin
Skadden, Arps
White & Case

Motiva Enterprises

Making money is a major motive behind Motiva Enterprises, which operates the eastern and southeastern US refining and marketing businesses of Shell Oil and Saudi Aramco. The company operates three refineries with a total capacity of 740,000 barrels a day, and it sells fuel at about 8,000 Shell-branded gas stations. It also has stakes in more than 40 refined product storage terminals in the East and Gulf Coast regions. Motiva and sister company Shell Oil Products US, which operates in the West and Midwest, together make up the #1 US gasoline retailer. Motiva is a 50-50 joint venture of Shell and Saudi Aramco.

In 2007 Motiva broke ground on a massive $7 billion refinery expansion in Port Arthur, Texas. The expansion, expected to be completed by 2012, will double the refinery's capacity to 600,000 barrels a day.

Motiva was formed in 1998 to combine the eastern and southeastern US refining and marketing businesses of Texaco, Shell Oil, and Saudi Aramco. Texaco and Saudi Aramco each owned 35% of Motiva, and Shell owned 30%. Texaco sold its stakes in Motiva (to Shell and Saudi Aramco) and Equilon (to Shell) to gain regulatory clearance to be acquired by Chevron. In 2002 Shell took full ownership of Equilon, which was renamed Shell Oil Products US.

HISTORY

Although Motiva was not created until the late 1990s, two of its key players, Texaco and Saudi Aramco, had been doing business together in various ventures since 1936. But they had never tried anything on the scale of the Star Enterprise joint venture approved by Texaco CEO James Kinnear and Saudi Oil Minister Hisham Nazer in late 1988. The deal, valued at nearly $2 billion, was the largest joint venture of its kind in the US.

The agreement to create Star Enterprise sprang, in part, from Texaco's tumultuous ride following its purchase of Getty Oil in 1983. Texaco was sued by Pennzoil for pre-empting Pennzoil's bid for Getty, and Pennzoil won a $10.5 billion judgment in 1985. Texaco filed for bankruptcy in 1987 and eventually settled with Pennzoil for $3 billion.

In 1988 Texaco emerged from bankruptcy after announcing a deal with Saudi Aramco at a stockholder meeting. Texaco got a much-needed injection of cash, and Saudi Aramco gained a steady US outlet for its supply of crude. The Saudis had been at odds with their OPEC partners for several years, and in late 1985 then-Saudi Oil Minister Sheikh Yamani and Saudi Aramco began increasing production, leading to an oil price crash in 1986. Nazer replaced Yamani and changed Saudi Aramco's strategy. To secure market share, the Saudis started signing long-term supply contracts.

The deal with Texaco gave Saudi Aramco a 50% interest in Texaco's refining and marketing operations in the East and on the Gulf Coast — about two-thirds of Texaco's US downstream operations — including three refineries and its Texaco-brand stations. In return, the Saudis paid $812 million cash and provided three-fourths of Star's initial inventory, about 30 million barrels of oil. They also agreed to a 20-year, 600,000-barrel-a-day commitment of crude. Each company named three representatives to Star's management.

The company soon initiated a modernization and expansion program: It acquired 65 stations, built 30 new outlets, and remodeled 172 during 1989. In 1994 the company began franchising its Texaco-brand Star Mart convenience stores. By mid-1995 it had sold 30 franchises.

Facing a more competitive oil marketing environment in the US, Shell Oil approached Texaco in 1996 with the possibility of merging some of their operations. In 1998 Shell and Texaco formed Equilon Enterprises, a joint venture that combined their western and midwestern refining and marketing activities.

Later that year Shell and Texaco/Saudi Aramco (Star Enterprises) formed Motiva to merge the companies' refining and marketing businesses on the East Coast and Gulf Coast. Shell and Texaco also formed two more Houston companies as satellite firms for Motiva and Equilon: Equiva Trading Company, a general partnership that provides supplies and trading services, and Equiva Services, which provides support services. Wilson Berry, the former president of Texaco Refining and Marketing, took over as CEO of Motiva.

In 1999 Motiva and Equilon together bought 15 product terminals from Premcor. To boost profits, the Motiva board appointed Texaco downstream veteran Roger Ebert as its new CEO in 2000, replacing Berry, who announced his resignation after a Motiva board meeting.

US government regulators in 2001 required that Texaco sell its Motiva and Equilon stakes in order to be acquired by Chevron. That year Texaco veteran John Boles replaced Ebert (who retired) as CEO. Shell and Saudi Aramco agreed to buy Texaco's stake in Motiva, and Shell agreed to buy Texaco's stake in Equilon. The deals were completed in 2002. Boles retired in 2004.

EXECUTIVES

President and CEO: Robert W. (Bob) Pease
CFO: Ronald Langan
VP Supply: Brian Smith
VP Services: John Kiappes
VP Human Resources and Corporate Services: Elaine Guarrero
VP Retail: Ian Sutcliffe
VP Refining: Rudy Goetzee
VP Commercial Marketing and Distribution: Ralph Grimmer
Chief Diversity Officer: John Jefferson
Media Relations Advisor: Karyn Leonardi-Cattolica
Manager Business Development and Product Exchanges: Mike Wallace
General Counsel: Lynda Irvine
Treasurer and Director Finance: James B. Castles

LOCATIONS

HQ: Motiva Enterprises LLC
700 Milam St., Houston, TX 77002
Phone: 713-277-8000
Web: www.motivaenterprises.com

COMPETITORS

7-Eleven
BP
CITGO
Exxon Mobil
Gulf Oil
Marathon Petroleum
Racetrac Petroleum
Sunoco
Valero Energy
Wawa, Inc.

Mountaire Corporation

These birds breathe the mountain air: Mountaire is a leading supplier of private-label chicken and value-added chicken products to supermarkets and foodservice customers worldwide. The company's chicken production business (Mountaire Farms) maintains breeding and chicken-processing facilities in Delaware, Maryland, and North Carolina. The company sells its products under names such as Black Label (aimed at the foodservice market), Blue Label (wholesale), and Bo-San Roasters (Asian market in the US). Mountaire Grain and Feed produces poultry feeds and operates grain elevators for corn, soybeans, wheat, and barley. Mountaire was founded in 1971, but the company's roots in the feed business date back to 1914.

EXECUTIVES

Chairman and CEO: Ronald M. (Ronnie) Cameron
CFO and Secretary: Alan H. Duncan
EVP and President, Mountaire Feeds: DeeAnn Landreth
VP Finance: Michael W. Lofton
President, Mountaire Farms and Mountaire Farms of Delaware: David L. (Dave) Pogge
Director Public Relations: Roger Marino
Auditors: Moore Stephens Frost

LOCATIONS

HQ: Mountaire Corporation
204 E 4th St, North Little Rock, AR 72114
Phone: 501-372-6524   **Fax:** 501-372-3972
Web: mountaire.com

COMPETITORS

Coleman Natural Foods	Perdue Incorporated
Cooper Farms	Pilgrim's Pride
Eberly Poultry	Raeford Farms
Fieldale Farms	Sanderson Farms
Foster Farms	Shelton's
Mar-Jac	Tyson Foods
MBA Poultry	Wayne Farms LLC
New Market Poultry	Zacky Farms
Northern Pride	

HISTORICAL FINANCIALS

Company Type: Private

Income Statement — FYE: October 31

	REVENUE ($ mil.)	NET INCOME ($ mil.)	NET PROFIT MARGIN	EMPLOYEES
10/08	1,211	—	—	6,000
10/07	1,150	—	—	—
Annual Growth	5.3%	—	—	—

Revenue History

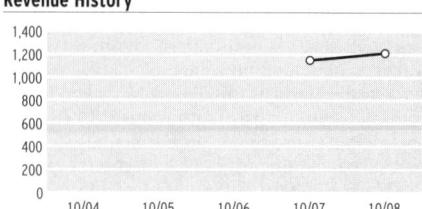

MTD Products

MTD Products wants to mow down its foes. The outdoor power equipment manufacturer makes walk-behind and tractor mowers, snow throwers, edgers, and tillers under the Cub Cadet, Bolens, McCulloch, White Outdoor, Yard-Man, and Yard Machines brands. Its Cub Cadet Commercial line is geared toward professional landscapers. In 2001 MTD bought the Troy-Bilt tiller and mower business from Garden Way, which had filed for bankruptcy. MTD sells its products through home improvement and farm supply stores, big-box retailers, and hardware shops. MTD was formed in 1932 by German immigrants Theo Moll, Emil Jochum, and Erwin Gerhard as the Modern Tool and Die Company. The Moll family, including CEO Robert Moll, owns MTD.

In October 2008 MTD shut down its production facility in Kitchener, Ontario, which produced snow throwers and lawnmowers, and consolidated its manufacturing in the US. The company blamed the high Canadian dollar and slow economy in the US.

In November 2005 MTD Products formed a 50-50 joint venture with transmission manufacturer Torotrak. The entity, called Infinitrak LLC, combines Torotrak's technology and MTD's manufacturing and distribution expertise to reach the outdoor power equipment market. Manufacturing of IVT units, sold under the Infinitrak brand name, began in 2006. The joint venture rolled out its Twin Toroidal Transmission (TTT) in April 2008 for the OPE and golf markets. Infinitrak is making plans to launch a second-generation product — the STT (Single Toroidal Transmission) — into the OPE market. MTD Products has manufacturing facilities in Europe and the US.

EXECUTIVES

Chairman: Theodore S. Moll, age 66
Vice Chairman: Hartmut Kaesgen
CEO: Robert T. Moll
President and COO: Jean Hlay
CFO: Jeff Deuch
EVP Product Development: Rory B. Bringhurst
EVP Operations and Global Sourcing: Roy G. Pullum
VP Operations: Randy Parish
Sales Director: Jason Mattern
Operations Manager: Jason Belsito
Director IT: Chip Moll
Director Health and Welfare: Fran Walsh
Director Marketing Communications, Mass Retail Group: Heidi Ketvertis

LOCATIONS

HQ: MTD Products Inc.
5965 Grafton Rd., Valley City, OH 44280
Phone: 330-225-2600   **Fax:** 330-273-4617
Web: www.mtdproducts.com

COMPETITORS

Alamo Group
Black & Decker
Blount International
Deere
Emak Group
Exmark Manufacturing
Honda
Toro Company

Mutual of America Life Insurance

Mutual of America Life Insurance may be the saving grace for a lot of folks in the not-for-profit sector. The company provides retirement savings to employees of not-for-profit organizations who are excluded from Social Security and other retirement programs. Mutual of America still serves that market, but also offers its employee-sponsored retirement plans, savings plans, and insurance products to private-sector organizations (typically small to midsized businesses) and direct to individual investors. The company has about $9 billion in assets under management.

Founded in 1945, Mutual of America and subsidiary Mutual of America Capital Management Corporation today provide products and services throughout the US via a network of more than 35 regional field offices.

EXECUTIVES

Chairman, President, and CEO: Thomas J. Moran, age 60
SEVP and Chief Marketing Officer: William S. Conway
SEVP and CFO; Chairman, President, and CEO, Mutual of America Institutional Funds: John R. Greed
EVP and CIO: Joan M. Squires
EVP and Chief Actuary: Jeremy J. Brown
EVP and Deputy General Counsel: Gregory A. Kleva Jr.
EVP Human Resources and Corporate Services: Daniel J. LeSaffre
EVP Administrative Technical Services: Jared Gutman
EVP Sales Operations: William Rose
EVP MIS Operations: Robert Giaquinto
EVP, Secretary, and Assistant to the Chairman: Diane M. Aramony
EVP External Affairs: Edward J. T. Kenney
EVP Corporate Finance and Treasurer: George L. Medlin
EVP and General Counsel: James J. Roth
Chairman and CEO, Mutual of America Foundation: Thomas Gilliam
President and COO, Mutual of America Capital Management: Amir Lear
Auditors: KPMG LLP

LOCATIONS

HQ: Mutual of America Life Insurance Company
320 Park Ave., New York, NY 10022
Phone: 212-224-1600   **Fax:** 212-224-2539
Web: www.mutualofamerica.com

PRODUCTS/OPERATIONS

2008 Sales

	$ mil.	% of total
Premium & annuity considerations	1,356.0	76
Net investment income	353.8	20
Separate account investment & administrative fees	44.1	3
Life & disability insurance premiums	15.3	1
Net other	3.7	—
Total	**1,772.9**	**100**

COMPETITORS

AIG Retirement Services
American United Mutual
Ameriprise
Catholic Order of Foresters
Charles Schwab
FMR
MFS
National Life Insurance
Principal Financial
TIAA-CREF

HISTORICAL FINANCIALS

Company Type: Mutual company

Income Statement

FYE: December 31

	ASSETS ($ mil.)	NET INCOME ($ mil.)	INCOME AS % OF ASSETS	EMPLOYEES
12/08	10,974	(54)	—	—
12/07	13,021	8	0.1%	—
12/06	12,442	17	0.1%	—
Annual Growth	(6.1%)	—	—	—

2008 Year-End Financials

Equity as % of assets: —
Return on assets: —
Return on equity: —
Long-term debt ($ mil.): —
Sales ($ mil.): 1,773

Net Income History

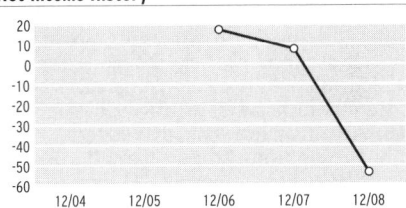

Mutual of Omaha

In the wild kingdom that is today's insurance industry, Mutual of Omaha Insurance Company wants to distinguish itself from the pack. The company provides individual, group, and employee benefits products through a range of affiliated companies. It offers Medicare supplement, disability, and long-term care coverage as well as life insurance and annuities through its United of Omaha Life Insurance unit. Its Mutual of Omaha Investor Services offers brokerage services, pension plans, and mutual funds, while the Mutual of Omaha Bank operates regionally. Mutual of Omaha, which is owned by its policyholders, offers its products through both its agency sales force and independent agents, as well as direct marketing.

Mutual of Omaha has remixed its health care insurance products. In 2007 it sold its employer-based group health business to Coventry Health Care, but it kept its employer-based life, disability, dental, and supplemental health coverage. It then launched its Medicare Supplement insurance products.

Taking advantage of changes in regulatory restrictions, Mutual of Omaha is expanding into banking through acquisitions. Its key markets are rapidly growing cities where it already has high numbers of insurance customers. Operating as Mutual of Omaha Bank, it provides commercial and personal banking through locations in nine states. The company intends to eventually offer Internet banking nationwide.

Like all insurance companies, Mutual of Omaha saw investment losses in 2008, but it was not badly shaken as it had not invested in the riskier products that undermined other companies.

The company's sponsorship of the long-running *Mutual of Omaha's Wild Kingdom,* introduced it to a generation of Americans. Recognizing that the connection remained strong, the company has revived the television series, which now runs on Discovery Communications' Animal Planet cable channel.

HISTORY

Charter Mutual Benefit Health & Accident Association got its start in Omaha, Nebraska, in 1909. A year later half of its founders quit, leaving a group headed by pharmaceuticals businessman H. S. Weller in charge. He tapped C. C. Criss as principal operating officer, general manager, and treasurer. Criss brought in his wife, Mabel, as well as his brother Neil to help run the business.

Formed to offer accident and disability protection at a time when there were many fraudulent benefit societies, Charter Mutual Benefit Health faced consumer resistance that slowed growth in its first 10 years. By 1920 it was licensed in only nine states. Experience helped it refine its products and improve its policies' comprehensibility. By 1924 the firm had more than doubled its penetration, gaining licensing in 24 states.

The US was nearing the depths of the Depression when Weller died in 1932. Criss succeeded him as president. The stock crash had brought a steep decline in the value of the firm's asset base, and premium income dropped (accompanied by an increase in claims). Even so, Mutual Benefit Health expanded its agency force, the scope of its benefits, and its operations. It went into Canada in 1935 and began a campaign to obtain licensing throughout the US.

By 1939 the company was licensed in all 48 states. During WWII it wrote coverage for civilians killed or injured in acts of war in the US (including Hawaii) and Canada. With paranoia running high and consumer goods in short supply, the insurance industry boomed during the war (and payouts on stateside act-of-war claims were low to nonexistent). Criss retired in 1949.

Gearing up its postwar sales efforts, in 1950 the company changed its name to Mutual of Omaha and adopted its distinctive chieftain logo. During the 1950s it added specialty accident and group medical coverage. In 1963 it made an advertising coup when it launched *Mutual of Omaha's Wild Kingdom.* Hosted by zoo director Marlin Perkins and, later, naturalist sidekick Jim Fowler, the show was one of the most popular nature programs of all time. Later that decade the company added investment management to its services.

Changes in the health care industry during the 1990s led Mutual of Omaha to de-emphasize its traditional indemnity products in favor of building managed care alternatives. In 1993 it joined with Alegent Health System to form managed care company Preferred HealthAlliance. Mutual of Omaha also stopped writing new major medical coverage in such states as California, Florida, New Jersey, and New York, where state laws made providing health care onerous. This led the company to cut its workforce by about 10% in 1996.

In 1999 it bought out Alegent's interest in their joint venture and entered the credit card business (offering First USA Visa cards). The firm also lifted its $25,000 limit for coverage of AIDS-related illnesses (its standard limit is $1 million); the company had been sued over the policy.

In the new millennium, the company enhanced its products targeted toward seniors as well as introducing more flexible personal health care plans.

Focusing on its core individual and employer-based lines, in 2003 the company sold the renewal rights to all of its Omaha Property and Casualty Co. (OPAC) policies to Fidelity National Financial. After all the actual operations had been transferred, in 2005 the UK's Beazley Group bought up the OPAC operating license. In 2006 Mutual of Omaha sold its innowave water purification subsidiary to Waterlogic International.

EXECUTIVES

Chairman and CEO; Chairman and CEO, United of Omaha Life Insurance Co.: Daniel P. (Dan) Neary, age 57
EVP, CFO, and Treasurer: David A. Diamond, age 53
EVP and Chief Investment Officer: Richard A. (Rick) Witt
EVP Customer Service: Madeline R. Rucker
EVP Group Benefit Services: Daniel P. Martin
EVP Corporate Services: Stacy A. Scholtz
EVP Information Services: Robert T. (Tim) Handren
EVP Individual Financial Services; President, United World Life Insurance: Michael C. (Mike) Weekly
EVP and General Counsel: Rich Anderl
SVP and Corporate Chief Actuary: Paul Ochsner
SVP and Medical Director: Tom Reeder
SVP Corporate Accounting: Mark Prauner
SVP Corporate Strategy: Pat Shiverdecker
Chairman and CEO, Mutual of Omaha Bank: Jeff Schmid
Director Human Resources, Mutual of Omaha Bank: Chuck Moomaw
Auditors: Deloitte & Touche LLP

LOCATIONS

HQ: Mutual of Omaha Insurance Company
Mutual of Omaha Plaza, Omaha, NE 68175
Phone: 402-342-7600   **Fax:** 402-351-2775
Web: www.mutualofomaha.com

PRODUCTS/OPERATIONS

2008 Revenues

	$ mil.	% of total
Health & accident	1,908.3	45
Life & annuity	1,322.6	31
Net investment income	909.7	22
Net realized investment losses	(133.7)	—
Other	65.9	2
Total	**4,072.8**	**100**

Selected Subsidiaries and Affiliates

Companion Life Insurance Company (insurance in New York)
Mutual of Omaha Investor Services, Inc. (mutual funds)
Omaha Financial Holdings (banking)
United of Omaha Life Insurance Company
United World Life Insurance Company

COMPETITORS

Aetna	MetLife
Allstate	New York Life
Assurant	Northwestern Mutual
CIGNA	Prudential
Guardian Life	State Farm
John Hancock Financial	Unum Group
MassMutual	USAA

HISTORICAL FINANCIALS

Company Type: Mutual company

Income Statement

FYE: December 31

	ASSETS ($ mil.)	NET INCOME ($ mil.)	INCOME AS % OF ASSETS	EMPLOYEES
12/08	21,246	47	0.2%	—
12/07	19,447	217	1.1%	—
12/06	19,008	166	0.9%	4,619
12/05	18,374	121	0.7%	5,053
12/04	18,540	125	0.7%	—
Annual Growth	**3.5%**	**(21.7%)**	**—**	**(8.6%)**

2008 Year-End Financials

Equity as % of assets: —   Long-term debt ($ mil.): 570
Return on assets: 0.2%   Sales ($ mil.): 4,073
Return on equity: —

Net Income History

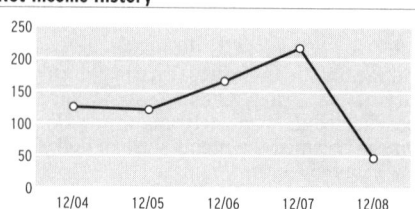

MWH Global

If it's wet, MWH Global will make it work. The energy and environmental engineering, construction, and water resource management firm specializes in water-related projects or "wet infrastructure." However, it also provides general building services for highway, bridge, airport, and industrial projects. MWH is active in nearly 40 countries and serves mainly the water, renewable energy, and infrastructure and industry markets. With some 200 offices around the globe, the firm has worked on wetlands restoration along the Danube in Bulgaria, wastewater treatment in Singapore, and hydroelectric facilities in South America. The employee-owned company formed after the 2001 merger of Montgomery Watson and Harza.

MWH has been working in New Orleans during the aftermath of Hurricane Katrina to help remove debris, clean the storm drains, and inspect the city's sewer and water infrastructure for damage. In 2008 that contract was expanded to include expediting the reconstruction of city facilities, including police and fire stations, recreation centers, libraries, and other municipal projects.

Other contracts include drought protection and water quality improvements in Nevada and work in the Florida Everglades with joint venture partner Jacobs Engineering. Overseas, it has worked on hydropower projects in Zambia, Uganda, Panama, and Pakistan.

Lately the company has been focusing on expansion, especially in South America, and especially its services for the mining industry. The company acquired a Peruvian groundwater consulting group in 2008, a move designed to bolster its mining services and water resources operations in South America and other markets.

MWH Global already has almost a dozen offices in the region.

MWH Global also has been growing in the Asia/Pacific region and the Middle East and Africa. In 2009 the company launched a new division to focus on opportunities in the Middle East.

The company has deep roots. Predecessor Watson Hawksley, Ltd., was founded in London in 1844.

EXECUTIVES

Chairman, CEO, and Director: Robert B. (Bob) Uhler
Vice Chairman and Chief Strategy Director:
 Donald L. Smith
President and COO: Alan J. Krause
CFO: David J. D. Harper
CIO: Micki C. Nelson
Chief People and Knowledge Officer: Vic Gulas
Corporate Counsel: Michael (Mike) Donnelly
President, Municipal & State Services, MWH Americas:
 Daniel (Dan) McConville
President, MWH Europe, Middle East, Africa and India:
 David Nickols
President and COO, MWH Soft, Inc.: Paul F. Boulos
President, MWH Business Solutions, MWH Americas, Inc.: Bruce K. Howard
President, MWH Constructors, MWH Americas:
 Joseph (Joe) Adams
President, Federal Services, MWH Americas:
 Gary M. Erickson
Auditors: PricewaterhouseCoopers LLP

LOCATIONS

HQ: MWH Global, Inc.
 380 Interlocken Crescent, Ste. 200
 Broomfield, CO 80021
Phone: 303-533-1900   **Fax:** 303-533-1901
Web: www.mw.com

PRODUCTS/OPERATIONS

Selected Services

Construction
Energy solutions
Facilities development
Government relations
Program management and management consulting
Mining
Research and testing
Risk assessment
Specialized consulting services
Technology
Transportation
Water and environment

COMPETITORS

AECOM
Bechtel
Black & Veatch
CH2M HILL
EA Engineering
Fluor
Foster Wheeler
GDF SUEZ
Jacobs Engineering
KBR
Peter Kiewit Sons'
Severn Trent
Shaw Group
Siemens Water Technologies
Tetra Tech
Washington Division
WS Atkins
Zachry Inc.

NAACP

The NAACP (National Association for the Advancement of Colored People) strives to ensure that all people are represented and have equal rights in American society and culture, regardless of race. The nation's oldest and largest civil rights organization, the group works via advocacy, education, and research, and it publishes the magazine *Crisis* and a quarterly newsletter *The NAACP Advocate*. It registers African Americans to vote, encourages academic achievement among high school students, and works with inmates to promote education and reduce recidivism. Sources of support include contributions and membership dues. The NAACP was founded in 1909 by a group that included W.E.B. Du Bois and Ida B. Wells-Barnett.

Benjamin Jealous became president and CEO of the association in September 2008. Previously president of San Francisco-based Rosenberg Foundation, Jealous has logged several years of experience at Amnesty International (directing its US Domestic Human Rights program) and the National Newspaper Publishers Association (as well as the *Jackson Advocate*).

EXECUTIVES

Chairman: Julian Bond
Vice Chairwoman: Roslyn M. Brock
President, CEO, and Director:
 Benjamin T. (Ben) Jealous, age 36
CFO: J. Linloy Cox
EVP: Steve Hawkins
SVP Advocacy and Director, Washington Bureau:
 Hilary O. Shelton
VP Field and Membership: Roger C. Vann
VP Stakeholder Relations: Rev Nelson B. Rivers III
National Director Field Organizing, Youth and College:
 Stefanie Brown, age 28
Director Field Organizing, Adult: Charles White Jr.
VP Communications: Leila McDowell
Interim General Counsel and Secretary: Angela Ciccolo
Treasurer and Director: Jesse Turner Jr., age 59
Manager Constituent Services Division:
 Audrey A. Lamyssaire

LOCATIONS

HQ: NAACP
 4805 Mount Hope Dr., Baltimore, MD 21215
Phone: 410-580-5777   **Fax:** 410-585-1310
Web: www.naacp.org

PRODUCTS/OPERATIONS

Selected Programs

Civic engagement
Criminal justice
Economic empowerment
Education
Health
Research

NASCAR

In the race for riches in the sports world, NASCAR is on the right track. The National Association for Stock Car Auto Racing oversees one of the most popular and fastest-growing spectator sports in the US. NASCAR runs more than 100 races each year in three racing circuits: the Nationwide, Craftsman Truck, and its signature Sprint Cup Series. The Sprint Cup draws millions of fans to the tracks each year. In addition to organizing and promoting the races, the association negotiates broadcast rights and licenses the NASCAR brand for merchandise. NASCAR was founded in 1948 by Bill France Sr. and is still owned by the France family.

While the sport of stock car racing continues to expand and grow, NASCAR is navigating through heavy traffic due to the economic recession. Attendance at race events has been declining as families have tightened their budgets for travel and entertainment, leading some tracks to lower ticket sales.

Most importantly, though, the organization is looking to ways to deal with troubles in the US auto industry. Car makers have historically played a big role in auto racing, but some manufacturers have been forced to cut or reduce their financial support of some racing teams. In response, NASCAR is looking for new ways to keep such companies as General Motors and Ford involved while eyeing other manufacturers for future support of the sport.

Meanwhile, the racing organization continues to work on expanding its fan base beyond the core audience of Southern white males to include more urban and female fans. The success of marketing auto racing to new audiences helped NASCAR negotiate a $4.4 billion TV contract with Disney's ABC and ESPN, Time Warner's TNT, and News Corp's FOX and the SPEED channel that began in 2007 and runs through 2014.

Also helping expand the popularity of the sport has been the construction of new race courses away from the South. The France family also controls publicly traded International Speedway Corporation (ISC), the largest racetrack operator in the US, which now has facilities in Chicago and New York.

NASCAR's premier racing circuit was renamed the Sprint Cup Series in 2008 as part of a sponsorship deal with telecommunications giant Sprint Nextel. The series had previously been called the NEXTEL Cup before the 2005 merger between Sprint and Nextel Communications, which had inked a 10-year, $750 million marketing partnership with NASCAR in 2003. That same racing season, NASCAR started using a new type of race car (dubbed "the car of tomorrow" while in development) that offers improved safety and performance, as well as lower costs.

HISTORY

Bill France Sr. founded the National Championship Stock Car Circuit (NCSCC) in 1947 as a place for ex-Prohibition-era moonshine runners to show off their driving skills. France, the son of a Washington, DC, banker, was a skilled mechanic and race car builder. In 1934 he moved his family to Daytona Beach, Florida, which was nirvana for race car drivers who used the hard beach as a speedway.

The City of Daytona Beach in 1938 approached France, who by then owned a successful gas station and mechanic shop frequented by racers, and asked him to organize a race. France rounded up drivers and solicited local businesses to donate prizes such as beer and cigars. The event drew 4,500 fans. He organized another race the following year and turned a profit of a few thousand dollars.

WWII interfered with France's racing career when he was drafted and sent to work in a shipyard. Upon his return, lacking the money to put another race together in Florida, he sponsored a national championship race for stock cars (cars with standard auto bodies not specially designed for racing) in North Carolina. Since there was no national body governing the races and setting rules, France's championship idea drew little enthusiasm. So in 1947 he formed the NCSCC and set up a point system for drivers and a fund for prize money. Seeking to expand NCSCC's powers, France in 1948 gathered 35 prominent racing figures from all over the US, and they organized to form the National Association for Stock Car Auto Racing (NASCAR), of which France was elected president.

France tirelessly promoted the sport with the help of racetrack owners wanting NASCAR to make their races official, and as a result the sport grew rapidly in the 1950s and 1960s. Racetrack owners began upgrading their facilities or building new ones with paved tracks to replace the older dirt tracks. France in 1957 convinced Daytona Beach to allow him to replace the city's original beach track with a 2.5-mile paved raceway. It opened two years later to a crowd of 42,000.

In 1972, as France got more involved in operating specific tracks and having less time to focus on NASCAR, he passed the business on to his son, Bill France Jr., who signed R.J. Reynolds as a major sponsor in 1971. NASCAR held the Winston 500 (the first incarnation of the Winston Cup series) in Talladega, Alabama.

The company's first televised race, the Daytona 500, aired on the CBS Television Network in 1979 and drew about 16 million viewers. Cable sports network ESPN also began airing races in 1981. NASCAR came into its own as a major sports player in 2000 when NBC, FOX, and Turner Broadcasting agreed to pay the company $2.4 billion for the circuit's broadcasting rights until 2006. (FOX later extended its agreement until 2008.) And the inherent danger of stock car racing began to hit home with the racing-related deaths of popular drivers such as Adam Petty in 2000 and Dale Earnhardt in 2001.

In 2003 Bill France Jr. handed reins of the company to son Brian France by promoting him to chairman and CEO. (Bill Jr. remained as vice chairman.) Also that year R.J. Reynolds dropped out as the sponsor for the Winston Cup series after more than 30 years with the race. Cell phone company Nextel (now Sprint Nextel) took over as the new sponsor with the signing of a 10-year, $750 million deal. (The race series was renamed the Sprint Cup in 2008.)

The following year NASCAR announced that its Busch racing series would hold a race in Mexico City during the 2005 season, marking the first points-paying international event in about 50 years. Later that same year NASCAR signed a new $4.4 billion broadcasting contract with Disney's ABC and ESPN, Time Warner's TNT, and News Corp's FOX and SPEED Channel. Bill France Jr. died in 2007.

EXECUTIVES

Chairman and CEO: Brian Z. France, age 46
Vice Chairman and EVP: James C. (Jim) France
President and Director: Mike Helton
EVP and Director: Lesa D. France Kennedy, age 47
Chief Marketing Officer: Steve Phelps
VP Racing Operations: Steve O'Donnell
VP Entertainment and Marketing:
 Bradley A. (Brad) Ball, age 59
General Counsel, Secretary, and Director:
 W. Garrett (Gary) Crotty, age 45

LOCATIONS

HQ: National Association for Stock Car
 Auto Racing, Inc.
 1801 W. International Speedway Blvd.
 Daytona Beach, FL 32114
Phone: 386-253-0611   **Fax:** 386-681-4041
Web: www.nascar.com

PRODUCTS/OPERATIONS

NASCAR Championships

Driver
 Bobby Allison (1983)
 Buck Baker (1956-57)
 Kurt Busch (2004)
 Red Byron (1949)
 Dale Earnhardt (1980, 1986-87, 1990-91, 1993-94)
 Bill Elliott (1988)
 Tim Flock (1952, 1955)
 Jeff Gordon (1995, 1997-98, 2001)
 Bobby Isaac (1970)
 Dale Jarrett (1999)
 Ned Jarrett (1961, 1965)
 Jimmie Johnson (2006-08)
 Matt Kenseth (2003)
 Alan Kulwicki (1992)
 Bobby Labonte (2000)
 Terry Labonte (1984, 1996)
 Benny Parsons (1973)
 David Pearson (1966, 1968-69)
 Lee Petty (1954, 1958-59)
 Richard Petty (1964, 1967, 1971-72, 1974-75, 1979)
 Bill Rexford (1950)
 Tony Stewart (2002, 2005)
 Herb Thomas (1951, 1953)
 Rusty Wallace (1989)
 Darrell Waltrip (1981-82, 1985)
 Joe Weatherly (1962-63)
 Rex White (1960)
 Cale Yarborough (1976-78)
Automobile
 Buick (1981-83)
 Chevrolet (1957, 1960-61, 1973, 1976-77, 1979-80, 1984-87, 1990-91, 1993-98, 2001, 2005-08)
 Chrysler (1954-56)
 Dodge (1966, 1970, 1974-75)
 Ford (1965, 1968-69, 1988, 1992, 1999, 2003-04)
 Hudson (1951-53)
 Oldsmobile (1949-50, 1958, 1978)
 Plymouth (1959, 1964, 1967, 1971-72)
 Pontiac (1962-63, 1989, 2000, 2002)

COMPETITORS

Automobile Racing Club of America
Indy Racing League
Major League Baseball
NBA
NFL
NHL
World Wrestling Entertainment

National Basketball Association

This league has the inside moves to score big with hoops fans. The National Basketball Association is one of the four major professional sports leagues in the US, with 30 teams representing 28 US markets and one in Canada. The NBA oversees the rules of the game and officiating, markets its teams and players, and regulates franchise ownership. It also licenses broadcasting rights and collects revenue from corporate sponsorships. In addition, the NBA operates the WNBA, a 14-team women's league; the NBA Development League for up-and-coming players; and NBA TV, a cable TV channel offering news, original programming, and live game broadcasts. The NBA was founded as the Basketball Association of America in 1946.

Professional basketball continues to be very popular and boasts a loyal fan base in many of its markets. Regular season attendance during the 2007-08 season dipped slightly from the record mark of more than 21.8 million set the previous year, but the league still managed to sell more than 90% of its seats for the fourth straight season. TV ratings also managed to tick upwards during 2008 after several seasons of stagnant viewership; a championship series between the Los Angeles Lakers and the Boston Celtics that season brought in the biggest television audience for the NBA Finals since 2004.

The association has been seeking a new star to replace Michael Jordan as the face of the NBA and has several contenders such as LeBron James (who plays for the Cleveland Cavaliers) and Carmelo Anthony (Denver Nuggets), yet the jury is still out on who will carry Jordan's torch for a new generation of fans.

Longtime broadcast partners ABC and ESPN (both owned by Walt Disney) and Time Warner's TNT signed on to a new eight-year, $7.4 billion TV deal that runs through 2016. The networks are hopeful that continued marketing efforts by the NBA will lead to more fan interest, though they are also praying for better match-ups in the playoffs to spur increased viewership.

The NBA is also looking outside the US for fans and possibly for expansion. In 2008 the league created NBA China to help spread professional basketball fever into the world's most populous country. ESPN, along with Bank of China and government-controlled Legend Holdings, acquired a 10% stake in the new business entity. Later that year, NBA China and Anschutz Entertainment Group (AEG; part of the Anschutz Company) inked a partnership to develop sports arenas throughout that country in an effort to spread the popularity of basketball.

Meanwhile, the league is making a concerted effort to expand its popularity in Europe through exhibition games against Euroleague teams and pre-season exhibition matches. The NBA has announced its intention to play regular-season games in London by 2012. It is also considering the possibility of creating an all European division to compete in the NBA regular season.

HISTORY

Dr. James Naismith, a physical education teacher at the International YMCA Training School in Springfield, Massachusetts, invented basketball in 1891. Naismith nailed peach baskets at both ends of the school's gym, gave his students a soccer ball, and one of the world's most popular sports was born.

In the beginning many YMCAs deemed the game too rough and banned it, so basketball was limited to armories, gymnasiums, barns, and dance halls. To pay the rent for the use of the hall, teams began charging spectators fees for admission, and leftover cash was divided among the players. The first pro basketball game was played in 1896 in Trenton, New Jersey.

A group of arena owners looking to fill their halls when their hockey teams were on the road formed the Basketball Association of America in 1946. It merged with the National Basketball League in 1949 to form the 17-team National Basketball Association (NBA).

Six teams dropped out in 1950. The league got an unexpected boost the next year when a point-shaving scandal rocked college basketball. The bad publicity for the college game made the pros look relatively clean, and it helped attract more fans. Another boost came through innovation when the league introduced the 24-second shot clock in 1954, which sped up the game and increased scoring.

Basketball came into its own in the late 1950s and 1960s, thanks to the popularity of such stars as Wilt Chamberlain, Bill Russell, and Bob Cousy. A rival league, the American Basketball Association (ABA), appeared on the scene in 1967 with its red, white, and blue basketball. Salaries escalated as the two leagues competed for players. The NBA and ABA merged in 1976.

By the early 1980s the NBA was suffering major image problems (drugs, fighting, racial issues) and began to wane in popularity. The league was resuscitated by exciting new players such as Magic Johnson, Larry Bird, and Michael Jordan, and in 1984, a new commissioner, David Stern. Although increased commercialism drove some purists crazy, big-name players and big-time rivalries helped sell the NBA's most important commodity — sport as entertainment.

Stern went to work cleaning up the league's image and financial problems, pushing through a strict anti-drug policy and a salary cap (the first such cap in major US sports). The NBA added its first two non-US teams in 1995, the Toronto Raptors and the Vancouver Grizzlies. (The Grizzlies moved to Memphis in 2001.)

On July 1, 1998, the NBA owners voted to lock out players, leading to the first work stoppage in the NBA's 52-year history. The dispute lasted six months, and the NBA's 1998-99 season was pared down to 50 games from the standard 82.

Concerned with the rash of players either leaving college early or skipping it entirely for the NBA, the league announced the formation of a developmental league (akin to baseball's minor leagues) in 2000, which started play in 2001.

The following year the league signed a new TV contract, a six-year, $4.6 billion deal with Walt Disney's ABC and ESPN, and Time Warner's Turner Sports. Also in 2002, the Charlotte Hornets relocated to New Orleans after the franchise failed to attract a loyal following in North Carolina. The vacancy allowed the league to grant its 30th franchise, the Charlotte Bobcats, to Robert Johnson, making the founder of BET the first African-American owner of a major sports team.

The year 2008 saw the suspension of basketball in Seattle when SuperSonics owner Clay Bennett relocated his franchise to Oklahoma City to become the Oklahoma City Thunder.

EXECUTIVES

Commissioner: David J. Stern, age 67
Deputy Commissioner and COO: Adam Silver
President, Global Marketing Partnerships and International Business Operations: Heidi J. Ueberroth, age 43
President League and Basketball Operations: Joel M. Litvin
EVP Business Affairs and General Counsel: William S. (Bill) Koenig
EVP Social Responsibility and Player Programs: Kathleen (Kathy) Behrens
EVP Marketing Partnerships: Mark A. Tatum
EVP Finance: Robert Criqui
EVP and General Counsel: Richard (Rick) Buchanan
EVP Events and Attractions: Ski Austin
EVP Basketball Operations: Stu Jackson
SVP and Chief Intellectual Property Counsel: Ayala Deutsch
SVP Referee Operations: Ronald L. Johnson
SVP Finance: Stephen O. (Steve) Richard
SVP Player Development: Michael A. Bantom
SVP Marketing Communications: Michael Bass
SVP Legal and Business Affairs: David Denenberg
President Women's National Basketball Association: Donna G. Orender, age 50
President NBA Development League: Dan Reed
Chief Basketball Operations and Player Relations: Reneé Brown

LOCATIONS

HQ: National Basketball Association, Inc.
Olympic Tower, 645 5th Ave., New York, NY 10022
Phone: 212-407-8000   **Fax:** 212-754-6414
Web: www.nba.com

PRODUCTS/OPERATIONS

Teams

Atlanta Hawks (1968)
  St. Louis Hawks (1955)
  Milwaukee Hawks (1951)
  Tri-Cities Blackhawks (Moline, Illinois; 1946; joined the NBA from the National Basketball League in 1949)
Boston Celtics (1946)
Charlotte Bobcats (North Carolina, 2004)
Chicago Bulls (1966)
Cleveland Cavaliers (1970)
Dallas Mavericks (1980)
Denver Nuggets (1974, joined the NBA from the American Basketball Association in 1976)
  Denver Rockets (1967)
Detroit Pistons (1957)
  Fort Wayne Pistons (1948, joined the NBA from the National Basketball League)
  Fort Wayne Zollner Pistons (Indiana, 1941)
Golden State Warriors (Oakland, 1971)
  San Francisco Warriors (1962)
  Philadelphia Warriors (1946)
Houston Rockets (1971)
  San Diego Rockets (1967)
Indiana Pacers (1967, joined the NBA from the American Basketball Association in 1976)
Los Angeles Clippers (1984)
  San Diego Clippers (1978)
  Buffalo Braves (New York, 1970)
Los Angeles Lakers (1960)
  Minneapolis Lakers (1947, joined the NBA from the National Basketball League in 1948)
Memphis Grizzlies (2001)
  Vancouver Grizzlies (1995)
Miami Heat (1988)
Milwaukee Bucks (1968)
Minnesota Timberwolves (1989)
New Jersey Nets (1977)
  New York Nets (1968, joined the NBA from the American Basketball Association in 1976)
  New Jersey Americans (1967)
New Orleans Hornets (2002)
  Charlotte Hornets (1988)
New York Knicks (1946)
Oklahoma City Thunder (2008)
  Seattle SuperSonics (1967)
Orlando Magic (1989)
Philadelphia 76ers (1963)
  Syracuse Nationals (1937, joined the NBA from the National Basketball League in 1949)
Phoenix Suns (1968)
Portland Trail Blazers (1970)
Sacramento Kings (1985)
  Kansas City Kings (1975)
  Kansas City-Omaha Kings (1972)
  Cincinnati Royals (1957)
  Rochester Royals (1945, joined the NBA from the National Basketball League in 1948)
San Antonio Spurs (1973, joined the NBA from the American Basketball Association in 1976)
  Dallas Chaparrals (1967)
Toronto Raptors (1995)
Utah Jazz (1979)
  New Orleans Jazz (1974)
Washington Wizards (1997)
  Washington Bullets (1974)
  Baltimore Bullets (1963)
  Chicago Zephyrs (1962)
  Chicago Packers (1961)

COMPETITORS

FIFA
Major League Baseball
Major League Soccer
NASCAR
NFL
NHL
PGA
PGA TOUR
World Wrestling Entertainment

National Cancer Institute

Established in 1937, the National Cancer Institute (NCI) supports and conducts research, training, information dissemination about what causes cancer, ways to prevent the disease, and how it can be treated. As a component of the National Institutes of Health (itself one of eight agencies comprising the Public Health Service), the National Cancer Institute falls under the purview of the Department of Health and Human Services. The organization operates a variety of its own programs and supports the research and medical centers of others; about half of its budget is allotted for funding research project grants. The NCI is pursuing an ambitious goal of eliminating cancer-related death and suffering by 2015.

Pointing to recent reports, the NCI announced that the US in 2007 recorded the steepest decline in cancer deaths since the nation began to invest in cancer research and care in 1971.

As it battles prostate cancer, NCI in early 2009 published results in the *New England Journal of Medicine* from a 17-year study. The study found that no fewer prostate cancer deaths occurred while six annual prostate-cancer screenings led to more diagnoses of the disease.

One primary goal of the NCI is to educate Americans about cancer risks, including those that can be prevented through changes in lifestyle. The institute publishes pamphlets and brochures, such as its *American Journal of Public Health: Young Adult Tobacco Cessation* and *Pap Tests: Things to Know*, and fact sheets the likes of *Access to Investigational Drugs: Questions and Answers*.

EXECUTIVES

Advisory Chair: Carolyn D. Runowicz
Director: John E. Niederhuber
Deputy Director: Alan Rabson
Executive Secretary: Joy Wiszneauckas
Director Office of Budget and Finance: Jim Dickens
Director Center for Biomedical Informatics and Information Technology: Ken H. Buetow
Director Division of Cancer Prevention: Peter Greenwald
Director Division of Cancer Biology: Dinah S. Singer
Director Center to Reduce Cancer Health Disparities: Sanya A. Springfield
Director Division of Cancer Control and Population Sciences: Robert T. Croyle
Director Division of Extramural Activities: Paulette S. Gray
Director Division of Cancer Epidemiology and Genetics: Joseph F. Fraumeni Jr.
Director Center for Cancer Research: Robert H. Wiltrout
Director Division of Cancer Treatment and Diagnosis: James Doroshow

LOCATIONS

HQ: National Cancer Institute
9000 Rockville Pike, Bethesda, MD 20892
Phone: 301-496-4000   **Fax:** 301-402-0601
Web: www.cancer.gov

National Football League

In the world of professional sports, the National Football League blitzes the competition. The organization oversees America's most popular spectator sport, acting as a trade association for 32 franchise owners. Among the league's functions, the NFL governs and promotes the game of football, sets and enforces rules, and regulates team ownership. It generates revenue mostly through marketing sponsorships, licensing merchandise, and by selling national broadcasting rights to the games. The teams operate as separate businesses but share a percentage of the league's overall revenue. Founded in 1920 as the American Professional Football Association, the league has been known as the NFL since 1922.

Like other sports organizations, the NFL depends primarily on revenue from broadcasters desperate to air games that will draw large audiences. The league has had little trouble demanding ever-increasing rights fees from television and radio networks, thanks to the growing popularity of football in America and around the world. CBS and News Corporation's FOX each pay more than $1.3 billion each year to show games on Sunday afternoons. NBC, part of NBC Universal, offers Sunday night games under a deal that pays the league about $600 million each season. The NFL aligned all of its broadcast network deals in 2009, extending them all through the 2013 campaign.

NFL games are distributed by cable networks and satellite TV providers as well, including ESPN and DIRECTV. Cable sports leader ESPN, owned by Walt Disney, took over the venerable *Monday Night Football* franchise from sister broadcast network ABC in 2006 and holds rights to the games through the 2013 season. DIRECTV offers games through its NFL Sunday Ticket package; that partnership was extended in 2009 with a $4 billion, four-year agreement that runs through the 2014 season.

The NFL is expanding its own NFL Network, a cable channel launched in 2003. The 24-hour football network offers news and analysis, as well as a package of regular season games on Thursday nights. The addition of regular season games in 2006 has helped the channel establish carriage agreements with many new cable systems.

The strength of football fandom has also translated into huge sales of licensed merchandise, from jerseys and caps to video games to every manner of trinket bearing the NFL emblem. The league gets more than $3 billion a year from licensed consumer products sales.

Making sure the league remains prosperous falls on the shoulders of commissioner Roger Goodell. To that end, his top priority is negotiating a settlement to the looming labor dispute between the team owners and the NFL Players Association. A new CBA must be enacted before the 2010 season to ensure labor peace. The last NFL players' strike was in 1987.

HISTORY

Descended from the English game of rugby, American football was developed in the late 1800s by Walter Camp, a player from Yale University who is generally credited with introducing new rules for downs and scoring. Professional teams sprang up in the 1890s, but football remained relatively unorganized until 1920, when George Halas and college star Jim Thorpe helped organize the American Professional Football Association. The new league featured 14 teams from the Midwest and East, including Halas' Staleys (now the Chicago Bears) and the Racine Cardinals (now the Arizona Cardinals). In 1922 the association changed its name to the National Football League.

The new league suffered many growing pains over the next decade, but by the 1930s the NFL had settled on 10 teams, including the Green Bay Packers (joined in 1921), the New York Giants (1925), and the Philadelphia Eagles (1933). Interest in the game remained somewhat regional, however, until the late 1940s and 1950s. In 1946 the Cleveland Rams moved to Los Angeles, and in 1950 the NFL expanded with three teams joining from the defunct All-American Football Conference. Television showed its potential in 1958 when that year's championship game, the first to be televised nationally, kept audiences riveted with an overtime victory by the Baltimore Colts (now the Indianapolis Colts) over the Giants. In 1962 the NFL signed its first league-wide television contract with CBS for $4.65 million.

The 1960s brought a new challenge in the form of the upstart American Football League (AFL). Concerned that the AFL would steal players with higher salaries and draw away fans, NFL commissioner Pete Rozelle negotiated a deal in 1966 to combine the leagues. That season concluded with the first AFL-NFL World Championship Game, which was renamed the Super Bowl in 1969. When the merger was completed in 1970, the new NFL sported 26 teams.

Football's popularity exploded during the 1970s, helped by the rise of franchise dynasties such as the Pittsburgh Steelers (four Super Bowl wins that decade) and the Dallas Cowboys (five NFC titles). In 1982 the Oakland Raiders moved to Los Angeles after a jury ruled against the NFL's attempts to keep the team in Oakland. The decision prompted other teams to relocate in search of better facilities and more revenue. (The Raiders returned to Oakland in 1995.) Rozelle stepped down in 1989 and was replaced by Paul Tagliabue.

During the 1990s the league expanded to 30 teams, adding the Carolina Panthers and Jacksonville Jaguars in 1995. That same year the Rams abandoned Los Angeles to begin life as the St. Louis Rams. The next year Art Modell moved his Cleveland Browns franchise to Baltimore to become the Ravens. (The city of Cleveland held onto the rights to the Browns name and history and the franchise was revived in 1999.) The Houston Oilers defected to Tennessee in 1997 and were later renamed the Titans. The next year brought new television deals worth $17.6 billion over eight years.

The NFL made plans for new expansion in 1999, awarding a franchise to Robert McNair of Houston. Named the Houston Texans, the team began play in 2002. In 2003 the league launched its own television channel, the NFL Network.

The NFL and the NFL Players Association reached an accord on a new six-year collective bargaining agreement in 2006. The league shut down its NFL Europa development league the following year as international expansion began to focus on scheduling selected regular season NFL games outside of the US. (The first such contest pitted the New York Giants against the Miami Dolphins at London's Wembley Stadium in 2007.)

EXECUTIVES

Commissioner: Roger Goodell
CFO: Anthony Noto, age 40
Chief Marketing Officer: Mark Waller
EVP Communications and Public Affairs: Joe Browne
EVP Player Programs: Harold R. Henderson
EVP Finance; President, Business Ventures: Eric P. Grubman
EVP, Chief Administrative Officer, and General Counsel: Jeff Pash
EVP Football Operations: Ray Anderson
EVP Media: Steve Bornstein
SVP Business Affairs: Frank Hawkins
SVP New Business and Product Development: Gene Goldberg
SVP Human Resources: Nancy Gill
SVP Partnership Marketing and Corporate Sales: Peter Murray
SVP Digital Media: Brian Rolapp
SVP Sales and Sponsorship: Keith G. Turner, age 50
SVP Media and Operations; COO, NFL Films: Howard Katz
SVP Public Relations: Greg Aiello
SVP Corporate Development: Neil Glat, age 42
Director Football Operations: Gene A. Washington, age 62
President, NFL Films: Steve Sabol
Auditors: Deloitte & Touche LLP

HQ: National Football League
280 Park Ave., 15th Fl., New York, NY 10017
Phone: 212-450-2000   **Fax:** 212-681-7599
Web: www.nfl.com

PRODUCTS/OPERATIONS

Teams

Arizona Cardinals (1994, Phoenix)
  Phoenix Cardinals (1988)
  St. Louis Cardinals (1960)
  Chicago Cardinals (1922)
  Racine Cardinals (1901, Chicago)
  Morgan Athletic Club (1898, Chicago)
Atlanta Falcons (1966)
Baltimore Ravens (1996)
Buffalo Bills (1959, joined the NFL from the AFL in
  1970, New York)
Carolina Panthers (1995; Charlotte, NC)
Chicago Bears (1922)
  Chicago Staleys (1921)
  Decatur Staleys (1920, Illinois)
Cincinnati Bengals (1968, joined the NFL from the AFL
  in 1970)
Cleveland Browns (1944, joined the NFL from the AAFC
  in 1950)
Dallas Cowboys (1960)
Denver Broncos (1959, joined the NFL from the AFL in
  1970)
Detroit Lions (1934)
  Portsmouth Spartans (1930, Ohio)
Green Bay Packers (1919, Wisconsin)
Houston Texans (2002)
Indianapolis Colts (1984)
  Baltimore Colts (1953)
Jacksonville Jaguars (1995, Florida)
Kansas City Chiefs (1963, joined the NFL from the AFL
  in 1970)
  Dallas Texans (1959)
Miami Dolphins (1966, joined the NFL from the AFL in
  1970)
Minnesota Vikings (1961, Minneapolis)
New England Patriots (1971; Foxboro, MA)
  Boston Patriots (1959, joined the NFL from the AFL in
  1970)
New Orleans Saints (1967)
New York Giants (1925)
New York Jets (1959, joined the NFL from the AFL in
  1970)
Oakland Raiders (1995, California)
  Los Angeles Raiders (1982)
  Oakland Raiders (1959, joined the NFL from the AFL
  in 1970)
Philadelphia Eagles (1933)
Pittsburgh Steelers (1940)
  Pittsburgh Pirates (1933)
St. Louis Rams (1995)
  Los Angeles Rams (1946)
  Cleveland Rams (1937)
San Diego Chargers (1961, joined the NFL from the AFL
  in 1970)
  Los Angeles Chargers (1959)
San Francisco 49ers (1946, joined the NFL from the
  AAFC in 1950)
Seattle Seahawks (1976)
Tampa Bay Buccaneers (1976)
Tennessee Titans (1998, Nashville)
  Tennessee Oilers (1997, Memphis)
  Houston Oilers (1959, joined the NFL from the AFL in
  1970)
Washington Redskins (1937; Washington, DC)
  Boston Redskins (1933)
  Boston Braves (1932)

Selected Business Units

NFL Charities
NFL Enterprises (media development)
NFL Films (highlight packages)
NFL Network (24-hour cable network)
NFL Properties (licensing, marketing, promotions, and
  publishing)

COMPETITORS

FIFA
Major League Baseball
Major League Soccer
NASCAR
NBA
PGA TOUR
World Wrestling Entertainment

HISTORICAL FINANCIALS

Company Type: Association

Income Statement

FYE: March 31

	REVENUE ($ mil.)	NET INCOME ($ mil.)	NET PROFIT MARGIN	EMPLOYEES
3/08	6,900	—	—	—
3/07	6,200	—	—	—
3/06	5,800	—	—	—
3/05	5,700	—	—	—
3/04	5,500	—	—	450
Annual Growth	**5.8%**	—	—	—

Revenue History

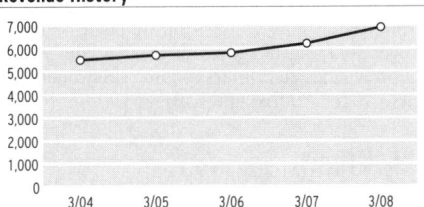

National Geographic Society

Still publishing its flagship *National Geographic* magazine, the not-for-profit National Geographic Society (NGS) has expanded into an array of venues to enhance our knowledge of the big blue marble. The NGS has staked claims in the worlds of television and the Web, as well as in book publishing and map-making. With News Corp., it operates the National Geographic Channel US, a cable channel that reaches about 65 million households worldwide. The NGS also supports geographic expeditions (it has funded more than 8,000 scientific research projects) and sponsors exhibits, lectures, and education programs. The NGS was founded in 1888, the year the first issue of *National Geographic* magazine was published.

Besides the award-winning *National Geographic* magazine, which has a circulation of some 8 million, the organization publishes several other magazines, including *National Geographic Traveler* and *National Geographic Kids*. As might be expected, the NGS's publishing operations are geographically diverse. *National Geographic* magazine is published in more than 30 local-language editions and has subscribers worldwide. Poor advertising prospects led the group in late 2009 to wind down regular publication of its *National Geographic Adventure* magazine, which was printed eight times a year and focused on adventure travel and eco-tourism. It still plans to publish special biannual issues of

National Geographic Adventure, however, and it will also maintain the brand online and in books. National Geographic had failed to sell the magazine because it was unwilling to leave its own name on the cover, and potential buyers weren't interested in a magazine simply titled *Adventure*.

Also outside the US, the organization owns 25% of National Geographic Channels International (NGCI). (News Corp. owns the rest.) NGCI, one of the fastest-growing cable networks around the globe, reaches more than 270 million households in some 165 countries.

The Society's National Geographic Entertainment (NGE) division has entered into a joint venture with Imagenation Abu Dhabi to produce 10 to 15 films by 2013.

As competition from relative newcomers, such as Discovery Communications, intensifies, the diversification of the NGS has been accelerating. The organization bought educational and English as a second language (ESL) publisher Hampton-Brown in February 2006. The next year it bought The Green Guide, publisher of an environment-oriented Web site and newsletter.

HISTORY

In 1888 a group of scientists and explorers gathered in Washington, DC, to form the National Geographic Society. Gardiner Greene Hubbard was its first president. The organization mailed the first edition of its magazine, dated October 1888, to 165 members. The magazine was clothed in a brown cover and contained a few esoteric articles, such as "The Classification of Geographic Forms by Genesis." The organization's tradition of funding expeditions began in 1890 when it sent geologist Israel Russell to explore Alaska. It began issuing regular monthly editions of *National Geographic* in 1896.

Following Hubbard's death in 1897, his son-in-law, inventor Alexander Graham Bell, became president. Aiming to boost the magazine's popularity, he hired Gilbert Grosvenor (who later married Bell's daughter) as editor. Grosvenor turned the magazine from a dry, technical publication to one of more general interest.

Under Grosvenor the magazine pioneered the use of photography, including rare photographs of remote Tibet (1904), the first hand-tinted colored photos (1910), the first underwater color photos (1920s), and the first color aerial photographs (1930).

The organization sponsored Robert Peary's trek to the North Pole in 1909 and Hiram Bingham's 1912 exploration of Machu Picchu in Peru. National Geographic expanded into cartography with the creation of a maps division in 1915. Grosvenor became president in 1920.

By 1930 circulation was 1.2 million (up from 2,200 in 1900). Grosvenor's policy of printing only "what is of a kindly nature . . . about any country or people" resulted in two articles that were criticized for their kindly portrayal of pre-war Nazi Germany (however, National Geographic maps and photographs were used by the US government for WWII intelligence). That policy eased over the years, and in 1961 a *National Geographic* article described the growing US involvement in Vietnam.

Grosvenor retired in 1954. His son Melville Bell Grosvenor, who became president and editor in 1957, accelerated book publishing with the first edition of *National Geographic Atlas of the World*. In addition, he created a film unit that aired its first TV documentary in 1965. Melville retired in 1967.

Melville's son Gilbert Melville Grosvenor took over as president in 1970. The organization debuted its *National Geographic Explorer* television series in 1985. National Geographic branched into commercial ventures in 1995 when it created subsidiary National Geographic Ventures to expand its presence on television, the Internet, maps, and retail. That same year the *National Geographic* magazine expanded circulation efforts internationally.

Grosvenor became chairman in 1996, and Reg Murphy took over as president. Murphy shook up the organization by laying off nearly a quarter of its staff and stepping up its profit-making activities. In 1997 National Geographic branched into cable television when it partnered with Fox, NBC, and BskyB to launch outside the US the National Geographic Channels International (NGCI).

John Fahey replaced Murphy as president in 1998. That same year National Geographic released *Mysteries of Egypt*, its first IMAX-style film. The following year National Geographic unveiled its *Adventure* magazine. The organization began offering *National Geographic* on newsstands for the first time in 1999. In 2001 National Geographic Channel US, a cable channel, was launched as a joint venture with Fox parent News Corp.

In 2002 National Geographic began to digitize thousands of its culture and nature images to sell online. That same year *National Geographic World,* a magazine for young people, became *National Geographic Kids*. The organization also began a literacy campaign that included *National Geographic Explorer* magazine and curriculum materials for classrooms.

EXECUTIVES

Chairman, National Geographic Society and Education Foundation: Gilbert M. Grosvenor, age 77
President and CEO: John M. Fahey Jr.
EVP; President, Magazine Group: John Q. Griffin
EVP Mission Programs: Terry D. Garcia
EVP and Secretary: Terrence B. (Terry) Adamson
EVP; President, National Geographic Enterprises: Linda Berkeley
EVP; President, Books and School Publishing: Nina A. Hoffman
EVP and Chief Cartographer, National Geographic Maps: Allen Carroll
EVP and CFO: Christopher A. Liedel
SVP Communications: Betty Hudson
SVP Human Resources: Thomas A. (Tony) Sabló
President, National Geographic Entertainment: David Beal
President, National Geographic Digital Media: John Caldwell
Chairman, National Geographic Ventures: Dennis Patrick
President, National Geographic Television: Michael Rosenfeld
President, Global Media Group: Timothy T. (Tim) Kelly
President, Distribution, National Geographic Cinema Ventures: Mark Katz
President, National Geographic Cinema Ventures: Lisa Truitt
President, National Geographic Films: Adam Leipzig
Editor in Chief, National Geographic Magazine: Chris Johns

LOCATIONS

HQ: National Geographic Society
1145 17th St. NW, Washington, DC 20036
Phone: 202-857-7000   **Fax:** 202-775-6141
Web: www.nationalgeographic.com

National Grape Cooperative

Well, of course grape growers want to hang out in a bunch! The more than 1,400 grower/owners who belong to the National Grape Cooperative Association harvest purple, red, and white grapes from almost 50,000 acres of vineyards in order to supply its wholly owned subsidiary Welch Foods. Welch's makes and sells juices, jams, and jellies under the Welch's and Bama brands. Other co-op products include fresh eating grapes, which are distributed by C.H. Robinson Worldwide, as well as dried fruit and frozen juice bars. National Grape Cooperative growers maintain vineyards in Pennsylvania, Michigan, New York, Ohio, Washington, and in Ontario, Canada.

Though jelly is a slowing market, new juice innovations, new packaging, and shelf-stable and single-serving products help drive sales at Welch's. Following the trend toward branded fresh produce, the Welch's logo appears on fresh grapes sold in grocery stores nationwide.

Top Welch's customers include US grocery giants Kroger, Publix, and Wal-Mart.

EXECUTIVES

President and Director: Randolph H. Graham
General Manager, COO, and Treasurer: Brent J. Roggie
Financial and Accounting Officer: Albert B. Wright III
First VP and Director: Joseph C. Falcone
Second VP and Director: James A. Schafer
Third VP and Director: Timothy E. Grow
Chief Legal Officer and Assistant Secretary: Vivian S. Y. Tseng
Secretary and Assistant Treasurer: Timothy A. Buss
President and CEO, Welch Foods: David J. Lukiewski, age 55
Auditors: KPMG LLP

LOCATIONS

HQ: National Grape Cooperative Association, Inc.
2 S. Portage St., Westfield, NY 14787
Phone: 716-326-5200   **Fax:** 716-326-5494
Web: www.nationalgrape.com

PRODUCTS/OPERATIONS

Selected Products
Bottled juices
Canned juices
Dried fruit
Fresh grapes
Frozen juices
Fruit juice bars
Fruit snacks
Jams
Jellies
Juice cocktails
Pourable concentrates
Preserves
Refrigerated juices
Single-serve juices
Sparkling juices

COMPETITORS

B&G Foods	Hansen Natural
Chiquita Brands	IZZE
Coca-Cola	Kraft Foods
Constellation Brands	Nestlé USA
Cranberries Limited	Ocean Spray
Del Monte Foods	PepsiCo
Dole Food	Procter & Gamble
Dr Pepper Snapple Group	Ralcorp
Ferolito, Vultaggio	Smucker
Fresh Del Monte Produce	Snapple
Goya	Tropicana

National Hockey League

Hockey is more than a cool sport for serious fans. The National Hockey League is one of the four major professional sports associations in North America, boasting 30 professional ice hockey franchises in the US and Canada organized into two conferences with three divisions each. The NHL governs the game, sets and enforces rules, regulates team ownership, and collects licensing fees for merchandise. It also negotiates fees for national broadcasting rights. (Each team controls the rights to regional broadcasts.) In addition, five minor and semi-pro hockey leagues also fly under the NHL banner. The league was organized in Canada in 1917.

Like other sports organizations, the NHL generates the bulk of its revenue through broadcasting fees, marketing sponsorships, and merchandise sales. Hockey remains the dominant spectator sport in Canada despite the fact that only six professional teams hail from the provinces, and there the NHL enjoys broadcasting partnerships with the Canadian Broadcasting Corporation (CBC) and The Sports Network (TSN; owned by CTVglobemedia). South of the border, however, the NHL enjoys a much smaller fan base than the National Football League and National Basketball Association, making it harder for the league to generate attention from national broadcasters.

The NHL's pact with broadcast network NBC, which extends through the 2010-11 season, is unique in sports as it offers the league a share of revenue from each game's advertising sales as opposed to a large sum paid up front for rights to the games. Cable sports network VERSUS (owned by Comcast), meanwhile, holds exclusive cable broadcast rights through 2011; that TV deal is worth more than $70 million a year.

To help expand its fan base in the US, the NHL operates its own cable sports channel — the NHL Network — which offers 24-hours of hockey news and features along with live coverage of some games.

Helping to secure the NHL's future growth is a collective bargaining agreement struck in 2005 that ended a season-long player lockout. The deal established a salary cap and revenue sharing between teams similar to the system used by the NFL. Many owners credited the leadership of commissioner Gary Bettman for holding the league together during the labor dispute and negotiating the new CBA.

The NHL commissioner still has his critics, though. Some continue to blame his expansion of the league into non-traditional markets far from its northern stronghold during the 1990s for the lack of US audience interest in the sport. The NHL was forced to purchase the Phoenix Coyotes out of bankruptcy in 2009 in order to save the franchise.

HISTORY

The National Hockey League traces its heritage to 1893, when the Stanley Cup (donated by Lord Stanley, Governor General of Canada) was first awarded to the Montreal Amateur Athletic Association hockey club of the Amateur Hockey Association of Canada. The National Hockey Association (NHA) became the first professional league to award the Cup in 1910. Five years later the NHA agreed to send its champion to play against the top team of the Pacific Coast Hockey Association (founded in 1911) for bragging rights to the Cup.

The onset of WWI siphoned away players, and with infighting intensifying among the NHA's owners, the association decided to disband in 1917. Later that year Frank Calder, a British scholar and former sports journalist who came to Canada to be a soccer player, helped form the National Hockey League (NHL) and appointed himself president. The league originally consisted of five teams from the NHA that played a 22-game schedule.

The league's first dynasty emerged in the form of the original Ottawa Senators (the team went under in 1934; the expansion Senators joined the league in 1992), which won four Cups from 1920 to 1927. The 1920s saw continued expansion — the Boston Bruins became the first US team in the league in 1925 — but the NHL remained amorphous as many teams joined up and dropped out during the decade.

The sport lost most of its talent to the military during WWII, forcing teams to field players who were often too young, too old, or who were barely able to skate. The league almost shut down, but the Canadian government encouraged play to continue, claiming it boosted national morale.

In the post-war years, the NHL consisted of just six teams: the Boston Bruins, the Chicago Blackhawks, the Detroit Red Wings, the Montreal Canadiens, the New York Rangers, and the Toronto Maple Leafs, known as the Original Six. The Canadiens began their three-decade domination of the NHL during this time, winning 17 championships from 1946 to 1979.

The league began expanding in 1967 when six US-based franchises were added to form the West Division, while the Original Six were placed in the East Division. More teams were added through the 1970s, and in 1979 the league absorbed four franchises from its rival professional league, the World Hockey Association (founded in 1972).

At the beginning of the 1980s the NHL consisted of 21 teams, including 15 franchises in the US. The NHL's shift towards the US market became more concrete when the league's headquarters moved from Montreal to New York City later in the decade. But Canadian fans still had reason to cheer as Wayne Gretzky (The Great One) and the Edmonton Oilers won five Stanley Cup titles from 1984 to 1990.

Late that year, Gary Bettman, formerly assistant commissioner of the National Basketball Association, was hired as the NHL's first real commissioner. Under his leadership, the NHL began expanding to more southern locations in the US. The league's growth was temporarily slowed in 1994, however, by the first major labor dispute in NHL history. Team owners began a player lockout that delayed the start of the season until early 1995, but they ultimately failed in their goal of implementing a salary cap.

In 1998 NHL team owners agreed to a $600 million, five-year television contract with Walt Disney's ABC and ESPN starting with the 2000-01 season. That season also marked further expansion as the Minnesota Wild and the Columbus Blue Jackets took to the ice.

In 2003 hockey returned to its roots with the outdoor Heritage Classic between the Edmonton Oilers and the Montreal Canadiens in minus-1 degree weather that drew record crowds.

EXECUTIVES

Commissioner: Gary B. Bettman, age 57
Deputy Commissioner: William L. (Bill) Daly
COO: John Collins, age 42
SEVP and Director of Hockey Operations: Colin Campbell
SEVP and CFO: Craig Harnett
SEVP Communications, Branding, Club Consulting, and Services: Ed Home
EVP Marketing: Brian Jennings
EVP and CTO: Peter DelGiacco
EVP Finance: Joseph DeSousa
EVP and General Counsel: David Zimmerman
SVP Broadcasting: John Shannon
SVP Communications: Bernadette Mansur
SVP Club Consulting and Services: Susan Cohig
SVP Events and Entertainment and NHL International and Business Affairs: Kenneth (Ken) Yaffe
Group VP Video Production and Programming: Ken Rosen
Group VP Media Operations and Planning: Patti Fallick
Group VP Media Relations: Frank Brown
Group VP Finance: Mary McCarthy
VP Public Relations and Player Development: Jamey Horan
VP Administration and Human Resources: Debbie Jordan
Director Corporate Communications: Michael Dilorenzo
Auditors: Ernst & Young LLP

LOCATIONS

HQ: National Hockey League
1185 Avenue of the Americas, 12th Fl.
New York, NY 10020
Phone: 212-789-2000   **Fax:** 212-789-2020
Web: www.nhl.com

PRODUCTS/OPERATIONS

Teams

Anaheim Ducks (2006)
  Mighty Ducks of Anaheim (1993, California)
Atlanta Thrashers (1999)
Boston Bruins (1924)
Buffalo Sabres (1970, New York)
Calgary Flames (1980, Alberta, Canada)
  Atlanta Flames (1972)
Carolina Hurricanes (1997, Raleigh)
  Hartford Whalers (1975, Connecticut, joined the NHL from the World Hockey League in 1979)
  New England Whalers (1971, Boston)
Chicago Blackhawks (1926)

Colorado Avalanche (1995, Denver)
  Quebec Nordiques (1972; Quebec City, Quebec, Canada; joined the NHL from the World Hockey League in 1979)
Columbus Blue Jackets (2000, Ohio)
Dallas Stars (1993)
  Minnesota North Stars (1967, Minneapolis)
Detroit Red Wings (1926)
Edmonton Oilers (1973; Alberta, Canada; joined the NHL from the World Hockey League in 1979)
  Alberta Oilers (1972; Edmonton, Alberta, Canada)
Florida Panthers (1993, Miami)
Los Angeles Kings (1967)
Minnesota Wild (2000, St. Paul)
Montreal Canadiens (1909)
Nashville Predators (1998)
New Jersey Devils (1982, East Rutherford)
  Colorado Rockies (1976, Denver)
  Kansas City Scouts (1974)
New York Islanders (1972, Unionville)
New York Rangers (1926, New York City)
Ottawa Senators (1992; Ontario, Canada)
Philadelphia Flyers (1967)
Phoenix Coyotes (1996)
  Winnipeg Jets (1972; Manitoba, Canada; joined the NHL from the World Hockey League in 1979)
Pittsburgh Penguins (1967)
St. Louis Blues (1967)
San Jose Sharks (1991, California)
Tampa Bay Lightning (1992)
Toronto Maple Leafs (1927)
  Toronto St. Patricks (1919)
  Toronto Arenas (1917)
Vancouver Canucks (1947, joined the NHL from the Western Hockey League in 1970)
Washington Capitals (1974; Washington, DC)

COMPETITORS

CFL
FIFA
Major League Baseball
Major League Soccer
NBA
NFL
PGA
PGA TOUR

HISTORICAL FINANCIALS

Company Type: Association

Income Statement

FYE: June 30

	REVENUE ($ mil.)	NET INCOME ($ mil.)	NET PROFIT MARGIN	EMPLOYEES
6/08	2,747	—	—	—
6/07	2,458	—	—	—
6/06	2,271	—	—	—
Annual Growth	10.0%	—	—	—

Revenue History

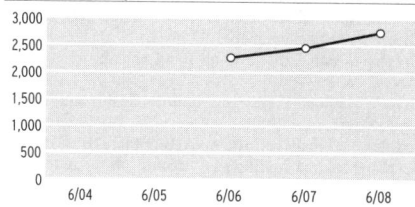

National Institutes of Health

The National Institutes of Health (NIH), through its research and the distribution of grants, seeks to understand disease inside and out. NIH is the government's main medical research entity and is part of the US Department of Health and Human Services. NIH comprises 27 institutes and centers covering every medical discipline, from general medical sciences to alternative therapies. The organization has nearly 6,000 scientists of its own and gives out some 50,000 grants to researchers at more than 3,000 universities, hospitals, and research labs in all 50 states. Among its vast array of projects, NIH has supported efforts to develop an AIDS vaccine, map human genetic variation, and study avian flu.

The history of the NIH began in an agency created by the federal government to check ship passengers coming into the country for signs of cholera and yellow fever. The NIH's predecessor, known as the Laboratory of Hygiene, used newfangled bacteriological methods to study infectious diseases in service of the public health. Today the NIH invests more than $30 billion each year in medical research.

One of the NIH's newer programs, Partners in Research, is designed to link scientists with community organizations to better communicate research results and make sure that the research being performed is meeting the health care needs of communities throughout the US. The NIH began handing out grants for Partners in Research in 2008.

EXECUTIVES

Director: Francis S. Collins
Deputy Director, Management and CFO: Colleen Barros
Center for Information Technology: John F. Jones
Director National Eye Institute: Paul A. Sieving
Director National Institute of Diabetes and Digestive and Kidney Diseases: Griffin P. Rodgers
Center for Scientific Review: Antonio Scarpa
Director NIH Clinical Center: John I. Gallin
Director Office of AIDS Research, Office of the Director: Jack Whitescarver
Director National Institute of Mental Health: Thomas R. Insel
Director Office of Research Facilities: Dan Wheeland
Director National Institute of Child Health and Human Development: Duane Alexander
Director National Institute of General Medical Sciences: Jeremy M. Berg
Director National Institute of Allergy and Infectious Diseases: Anthony S. Fauci
Director National Institute on Drug Abuse: Nora D. Volkow
Director National Center on Minority Health and Health Disparities: John Ruffin
Director National Institute on Aging: Richard J. Hodes
Director National Institute on Alcohol Abuse and Alcoholism: Ting-Kai (T. K.) Li
Director National Cancer Institute: John E. Niederhuber
Director Office of Communications and Public Liaison: John Burklow

LOCATIONS

HQ: National Institutes of Health
9000 Rockville Pike, Bethesda, MD 20892
Phone: 301-496-4000   **Fax:** 301-496-7422
Web: www.nih.gov

Federal Research Facilities
Frederick Cancer Research Center (Frederick, Maryland)
Baltimore Bayview Campus (Baltimore, Maryland)
National Institute of Environmental Health Sciences (Research Triangle Park, North Carolina)
Rocky Mountain Laboratories (Hamilton, Montana)

PRODUCTS/OPERATIONS

Selected Institutes and Centers
Center for Information Technology (CIT)
Center for Scientific Review (CSR)
John E. Fogarty International Center (FIC)
National Cancer Institute (NCI)
National Center for Complementary and Alternative Medicine (NCCAM)
National Center for Research Resources (NCRR)
National Center on Minority Health and Health Disparities (NCMHD)
National Eye Institute (NEI)
National Heart, Lung and Blood Institute (NHLBI)
National Human Genome Research Institute (NHGRI)
National Institute of Allergy and Infectious Diseases (NIAID)
National Institute of Arthritis and Musculoskeletal and Skin Diseases (NIAMS)
National Institute of Biomedical Imaging and Bioengineering (NIBIB)
National Institute of Child Health and Human Development (NICHD)
National Institute of Deafness and Other Communication Disorders (NIDCD)
National Institute of Dental and Craniofacial Research (NIDCR)
National Institute of Diabetes and Digestive and Kidney Diseases (NIDDK)
National Institute of Environmental Health Sciences (NIEHS)
National Institute of General Medical Sciences (NIGMS)
National Institute of Mental Health (NIMH)
National Institute of Neurological Disorders and Stroke (NINDS)
National Institute of Nursing Research (NINR)
National Institute on Aging (NIA)
National Institute on Alcohol Abuse and Alcoholism (NIAAA)
National Institute on Drug Abuse (NIDA)
National Library of Medicine (NLM)
NIH Clinical Center (CC)

National Life Insurance

One nation, under insurance, with financial security for all. National Life Group, the marketing name for National Life Insurance Company and its affiliated companies, is a mutually owned insurer dating back to 1848. Today, National Life Group offers a range of insurance and investment products throughout the US through its namesake National Life Insurance Company and other subsidiaries including Equity Services (insurance broker/dealer), Life Insurance Company of the Southwest (insurance and annuities), National Retirement Plan Advisors (a third-party administrator), Sentinel Asset Management, and Sentinel Financial Services company (mutual funds).

National Life distributes its products through a mix of both an internal career sales force and a network of independent agents. The company uses its NL Financial Alliance distribution arm to target wealthy customers while its Sentinel brand of funds are distributed by its Sentinel Financial Services company.

National Life's Private Client Group was spun off to management in 2004 and renamed Maple Capital Management. In 2006 the company sold off its American Guaranty & Trust subsidiary to Royal Bank of Canada.

EXECUTIVES

Chairman: Thomas H. MacLeay, age 59
President, CEO, and Director: Mehran Assadi
EVP and CFO: Edward J. (Ed) Parry III
EVP and Chief Marketing Officer: Vicent G. Vitiello
EVP, Chief People Officer, and Chief Legal Officer: Michele S. Gatto
EVP; President and CEO, Sentinel Investments: Christian W. Thwaites
SVP and CIO: Joel Conrad
SVP and Chief Investment Officer: Thomas H. (Tom) Brownell
SVP and General Counsel: Gregory D. Woodworth
VP Communications and Government Relations: Chris Graff
Auditors: PricewaterhouseCoopers LLP

LOCATIONS

HQ: National Life Insurance Company
1 National Life Dr., Montpelier, VT 05604
Phone: 802-229-3333   **Fax:** 802-229-9281
Web: www.nationallife.com

PRODUCTS/OPERATIONS

2008 Sales

	$ mil.	% of total
Investment income	575.8	47
Insurance premiums	322.5	26
Policy & contract charges	210.1	17
Mutual fund commissions & fee income	98.8	8
Other	19.6	2
Adjustments	(113.6)	—
Total	**1,113.2**	**100**

Selected Subsidiaries
Equity Services, Inc.
Life Insurance Company of the Southwest
National Life Insurance Company
National Retirement Plan Advisors Inc.
The Sentinel Companies

COMPETITORS
AIG American General
AXA Financial
FMR
John Hancock Financial Services
MassMutual
MetLife
Mutual of Omaha
New York Life
Ohio National
Pacific Mutual
Principal Financial
Prudential
Securian Financial
Sentry Insurance

HISTORICAL FINANCIALS

Company Type: Mutual company

Income Statement

FYE: December 31

	ASSETS ($ mil.)	NET INCOME ($ mil.)	INCOME AS % OF ASSETS	EMPLOYEES
12/08	15,210	15	0.1%	900
12/07	15,511	109	0.7%	900
12/06	15,009	111	0.7%	900
12/05	14,035	98	0.7%	—
12/04	12,796	86	0.7%	—
Annual Growth	4.4%	(34.9%)	—	0.0%

2008 Year-End Financials

Equity as % of assets: —
Return on assets: 0.1%
Return on equity: —
Long-term debt ($ mil.): —
Sales ($ mil.): 1,113

Net Income History

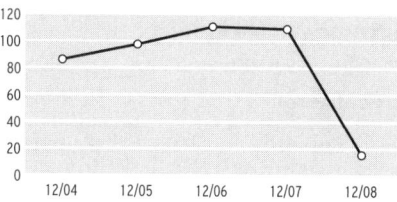

	12/04	12/05	12/06	12/07	12/08

National Wine & Spirits

This company acts as a kind of bartender to the nation's breadbasket. National Wine & Spirits is one of the Midwest's largest wine and liquor distributors. Serving 36,000 locations with its fleet of 350 delivery vehicles, the company distributes to restaurants, liquor stores, and beverage retailers in Indiana and Michigan. The distributor carries more than 120,000 products and its suppliers include Fortune Brands (Jim Beam), Diageo (Bailey's), and Beringer Blass Wine Estates. CEO James LaCrosse and director Norma Johnston own National Wine & Spirits, which was founded in 1934.

Major changes among suppliers of distilled spirits have National Wine & Spirits and other alcohol distributors across the country re-evaluating how they do business.

For example, Diageo conducted a state-by-state review to determine the companies that have exclusive rights to distribute its products. In Illinois it had not granted such rights to National Wine & Spirits; in addition, two other suppliers (including the now defunct Future Brands and Canandaigua Wine Company) ended the company's Illinois distribution rights. As a result, National Wine & Spirits scaled back operations and about 300 jobs in that state and formed a strategic alliance with Glazer's Wholesale Drug Company.

National sold its Illinois operations to Glazer's Wholesale Drug Company in 2006, effectively ending operations in that state. In 2007 the company acquired Michigan-based A.H.D. Vintners and L&L Wine & Liquor.

EXECUTIVES

Chairman, President, CEO, and CFO:
James E. LaCrosse, age 76
EVP Sales and Marketing: Gregory J. (Greg) Mauloff, age 57
EVP, COO, and Director: John J. Baker, age 39
Director; SVP Corporate Development and Fine Wine:
Catherine M. LaCrosse, age 42
VP Corporate Operations: Steven A. Null
VP Information Systems: Dwight P. Deming
VP Human Resources and Development:
Karin Lijana Matura

LOCATIONS

HQ: National Wine & Spirits, Inc.
700 W. Morris St., Indianapolis, IN 46206
Phone: 317-636-6092 **Fax:** 317-685-8810
Web: www.nwscorp.com

PRODUCTS/OPERATIONS

Selected Brands

Spirits
  Absolut Vodka
  Baileys
  Captain Morgan Rum
  Chivas Regal
  Courvoisier Cognac
  Cragganmore Single Malt
  Crown Royal
  Cuervo
  DeKuyper
  Frangelico
  Glenfiddich Single Malt Whiskey
  Glenmorangie
  Grand Marnier
  Hennessy Cognac
  J & B
  Jagermeister
  Jameson Irish Whiskey
  Jim Beam
  Johnnie Walker
  Kahlua
  Makers Mark
  Malibu Rum
  Sauza Tequila
  Seagram's Gin
  Smirnoff Vodka
  Stolichnaya
  Tanqueray
  Wild Turkey
Wine
  Acacia
  Almaden
  Arbor Mist
  Beaulieu Vineyard
  Beringer
  Blue Nun
  Bolla
  Chateau St. Jean
  Clos du Bois
  Columbia
  Dom Perignon
  Fetzer
  Fontana
  Inglenook
  Lindeman's
  Little Penguin
  Manischewitz
  Marcus James
  Moet & Chandon
  Monkey Bay
  Paul Masson Wine
  Penfolds
  Riunite
  Rosemount Estate
  Simi
  Stag's Leap
  Stella
  Sterling
  Taylor
  Vendange
  Veuve Clicquot
  Wild Horse

COMPETITORS

Constellation Brands
Georgia Crown
Glazer's Wholesale Drug
Johnson Brothers
National Distributing
Southern Wine & Spirits
Sunbelt Beverage

Nationwide Mutual Insurance

Call it truth in advertising — Nationwide Mutual Insurance Company has offices throughout the US. The company is a leading US property/casualty insurer that also provides life insurance through its Nationwide Financial Services subsidiary. In addition to personal and commercial property/casualty coverage, life insurance, and financial services, Nationwide also offers such specialty lines as professional liability, workers' compensation, agricultural insurance and loss-control, pet insurance, and other coverage. The company sells its products through such subsidiaries as ALLIED Group, Nationwide Agribusiness Insurance, GatesMcDonald, and Scottsdale Insurance.

As the US insurance industry has been mature for a long time, Nationwide has sought growth by moving into assorted niches, including specialty auto coverage, and financial services. The company launched its Nationwide Better Health program in 2006, and has grown it through acquisitions to provide health, productivity, and disease management services to employers.

Nationwide Financial Services received approval to expand its services to include full-service online and telephone banking in 2006. Operating as Nationwide Bank, the business has added deposit products and ATM access for its insurance, mortgage, and financial services customers. The company also established its Nationwide Advantage Mortgage business, which provides both mortgages and home equity loans. Consumers can access its services online and through Nationwide agents.

Nationwide Mutual sold off the London-based arm of its Gartmore Investment Management subsidiary to Gartmore's management and Hellman & Friedman LLC in 2006. Nationwide retained the US-based retail mutual-fund part of the business, changed its name to Nationwide Funds Group (NFG), and moved it under Nationwide Financial. However, in 2008 the company transferred NFG's active asset management business over to Aberdeen Asset Management.

Nationwide Financial Services was a publicly traded subsidiary from 1997 until early 2009 when, to simplify the group's ownership structure, Nationwide Mutual took it private in a $2.4 billion transaction.

Shortly after the Nationwide Financial transaction was completed, Nationwide Mutual named president and COO Steve Rasmussen into the CEO role, replacing Jerry Jurgensen, who left by mutual agreement with the board after nine years of service as chief executive.

HISTORY

In 1919 members of the Ohio Farm Bureau Federation, a farmers' consumer group, established their own automobile insurance company. (As rural drivers, they didn't want to pay city rates.) To get a license from the state, the company, called Farm Bureau Mutual, needed 100 policyholders. It gathered more than 1,000. Founder Murray Lincoln headed the company until 1964.

The insurer expanded into Delaware, Maryland, North Carolina, and Vermont in 1928 and began selling auto insurance in 1931 to city folks. It expanded into fire insurance in 1934 and life insurance the next year.

During WWII growth slowed, although the company had operations in 12 states and Washington, DC, by 1943. It diversified in 1946 when it bought a Columbus, Ohio, radio station. By 1952 the firm had resumed expansion and changed its name to Nationwide.

The company was one of the first auto insurance companies to use its agents to sell other financial products, adding life insurance and mutual funds in the mid-1950s. Nationwide General, the country's first merit-rated auto insurance firm, was formed in 1956.

Nationwide established Neckura in Germany in 1965 to sell auto and fire insurance. Four years later the company bought GatesMcDonald, a provider of risk, tax, benefit, and health care management services. It organized its property/casualty operations into Nationwide Property & Casualty in 1979.

The company experienced solid growth throughout the 1980s by establishing or purchasing insurance firms, among them Colonial Insurance of California (1980), Financial Horizons Life (1981), Scottsdale (1982), and, the largest, Employers Insurance of Wausau (1985). Wausau wrote the country's first workers' compensation policy in 1911.

Earnings were up and down in the 1990s as the company invested in Wausau and in consolidating office operations. Nationwide set up an ethics office in 1995, a time of increased scrutiny of insurance industry sales practices, and made an effort to hire more women as agents. In 1996 the Florida Insurance Commission claimed the company discriminated against customers on the basis of age, gender, health, income, marital status, and location. Nationwide countered that the allegations originated from disgruntled agents.

In 1997 the company settled a lawsuit by agreeing to stop its redlining practices (it avoided selling homeowners' insurance to urban customers with homes valued at less than $50,000 or more than 30 years old, which allegedly discriminated against minorities). It also dropped a year-old sales quota system that was under investigation.

As the century came to a close, Nationwide began to narrow its focus on its core businesses. It spun off Nationwide Financial Services so the unit could have better access to capital, and it expanded both at home and abroad through such purchases as ALLIED Group (multiline insurance), CalFarm (agricultural insurance in California), and AXA subsidiary PanEuroLife (asset management in Europe). The company's discrimination woes came back to haunt it in 1999, and it created a $750,000 fund to help residents of poor Cincinnati neighborhoods buy homes.

Although Nationwide Financial and its Strategic Investments segment underperformed in 2002, the company swung to a net profit, helped

in part by improved underwriting results by its insurance subsidiaries.

Nationwide and several other insurance companies were named in a series of lawsuits stemming from the aftermath of 2005's Hurricane Katrina. One suit alleged that prior to the natural disaster, insurance agents dissuaded their clients from purchasing flood insurance, and that the companies did not offer the full settlement amount to clients whose homes had been damaged by the storm surge of water. In one of the first lawsuits to be decided, the judge ruled in favor of Nationwide.

EXECUTIVES

President, CEO, and Director: Stephen S. (Steve) Rasmussen, age 56
EVP and Chief Marketing Officer: James R. (Jim) Lyski, age 46
EVP and Chief Human Resources: Gale V. King
EVP and CIO: Michael C. (Mike) Keller, age 49
EVP and CFO: Mark R. Thresher, age 52
EVP and Chief Legal and Governance Officer: Patricia R. (Pat) Hatler, age 54
EVP and Chief Administrative Officer; President, Nationwide Better Health: Terri L. Hill, age 49
SVP and Chief Investment Officer: Gail G. Snyder, age 54
SVP and Chief Strategy Officer: Matt Jauchius
CEO, NWD Investment Group: John Grady, age 47
President, Nationwide Bank: J. Lynn Greenstein
President, Nationwide Better Health: Holly Snyder
President and COO, Nationwide Insurance: Mark Pizzi
President and COO, Nationwide Financial: Kirt A. Walker, age 46
President and COO, Allied Insurance: W. Kim Austen, age 54
President and COO, Scottsdale Insurance: Michael D. (Mike) Miller
President and COO, Nationwide Direct and Customer Solutions: Lawrence A. (Larry) Hilsheimer, age 51
Chief Privacy Officer, Assistant VP, and Associate General Counsel: Kirk Herath
Chief Medical and Science Officer, Nationwide Better Health: Neil Gordon
Chief Diversity Officer: Candice R. Barnhardt
Assistant VP Corporate Communications: Joe Case
Treasurer: Harry H. Hallowell, age 48
Auditors: KPMG LLP

LOCATIONS

HQ: Nationwide Mutual Insurance Company
1 Nationwide Plaza, Columbus, OH 43215
Phone: 614-249-7111   **Fax:** 614-854-3676
Web: www.nationwide.com

PRODUCTS/OPERATIONS

Selected Subsidiaries and Affiliates

Property and casualty
American Marine Underwriters, Inc.
CalFarm Insurance Agency
Colonial County Mutual Insurance Company
DVM Insurance Agency, Inc.
Farmland Mutual Insurance Company
Nationwide Agribusiness Insurance Company
Scottsdale Insurance Company
Titan Insurance Company
Veterinary Pet Insurance Company
Victoria National Insurance Company

Life insurance and financial services
Nationwide Financial Services, Inc.
Nationwide Life Insurance Company
Nationwide Bank
Nationwide Retirement Solutions, Inc.
Pension Associates, Inc.
TBG Insurance Services Corp.

Asset management
Nationwide Asset Management Holdings, LTD.
Audenstar Limited
NWD Investment Management, Inc.
Strategic investments
GatesMcDonald & Company
Nationwide Advantage Mortgage Company

COMPETITORS

AIG	MassMutual
Allstate	MetLife
American Financial Group	New York Life
AXA Financial	Northwestern Mutual
Citigroup	Pacific Mutual
CNA Financial	Principal Financial
GEICO	Prudential
Guardian Life	State Farm
The Hartford	Travelers Companies
John Hancock Financial	USAA
Liberty Mutual	

HISTORICAL FINANCIALS

Company Type: Mutual company

Income Statement

FYE: December 31

	ASSETS ($ mil.)	NET INCOME ($ mil.)	INCOME AS % OF ASSETS	EMPLOYEES
12/08	161,090	1,994	1.2%	36,023
12/07	161,090	1,994	1.2%	36,000
12/06	160,009	2,113	1.3%	36,000
12/05	158,258	1,149	0.7%	35,000
12/04	157,371	1,010	0.6%	32,933
Annual Growth	0.6%	18.5%	—	2.3%

2008 Year-End Financials

Equity as % of assets: —
Return on assets: 1.2%
Return on equity: —
Long-term debt ($ mil.): —
Sales ($ mil.): 22,962

Net Income History

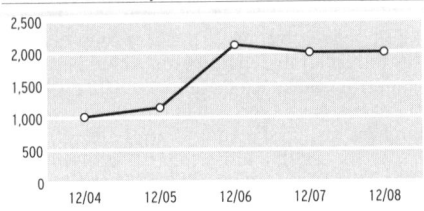

Navy Federal Credit Union

"Once a member, always a member," promises Navy Federal Credit Union (NFCU). This policy undoubtedly has helped NFCU become one of the nation's largest credit unions, claiming more than 3 million members who can retain their credit union privileges even after discharge from the armed services. Formed in 1933, NFCU provides a variety of banking services to all Department of Defense uniformed personnel, reservists, National Guard personnel, civilian employees, and contractors, as well as their families. NFCU offers checking, savings, and other deposit accounts, credit cards, insurance, investments, brokerage and trust services, and a variety of loans. It has more than 175 branch locations in the US and overseas.

During 2008 the previously Navy and Marine Corps-only credit union extended its membership offering to all armed forces branches including Army, Air Force, guard personnel, and all Department of Defense civilian workers and contractors on military installations.

In anticipation of an influx of members NFCU announced plans to open more than 100 new full-service branches by 2012. It added more than 20 in 2008 alone, most of them near Army and Air Force installations.

EXECUTIVES

Chairman: John A. Lockard
First Vice Chairman: Kenneth R. Burns
Second Vice Chairman: Bruce B. Engelhardt
COO: John R. Peden
CFO: Lauren D. Lloyd
Chief Innovation Officer: Dennis J. Godfrey
EVP Delivery Channels: Mary McDuffie
SVP Marketing and Development: Patricia Schneck
VP Regulatory Compliance and Public Policy:
  Bill Briscoe
VP Savings Products: Tisa Head
President and COO, Navy Federal Financial Group:
  Thomas Lee
President, CEO, Treasurer, and Director:
  J. Cutler Dawson Jr.
Public Relations Manager: Jennifer Sadler
Secretary and Director: David A. Gove
Auditors: PricewaterhouseCoopers LLP

LOCATIONS

HQ: Navy Federal Credit Union
  820 Follin Ln., Vienna, VA 22180
Phone: 703-255-8000   **Fax:** 703-255-8741
Web: www.navyfcu.org

COMPETITORS

Bank of America
Citibank
JPMorgan Chase
USAA
Wachovia Corp

HISTORICAL FINANCIALS

Company Type: Not-for-profit

Income Statement

FYE: December 31

	ASSETS ($ mil.)	NET INCOME ($ mil.)	INCOME AS % OF ASSETS	EMPLOYEES
12/08	36,399	82	0.2%	7,025
12/07	33,012	236	0.7%	7,000
12/06	27,122	402	1.5%	7,000
12/05	24,644	266	1.1%	—
12/04	22,897	274	1.2%	4,500
Annual Growth	12.3%	(26.1%)	—	11.8%

2008 Year-End Financials

Equity as % of assets: —
Return on assets: 0.2%
Return on equity: —
Long-term debt ($ mil.): —
Sales ($ mil.): 2,772

Net Income History

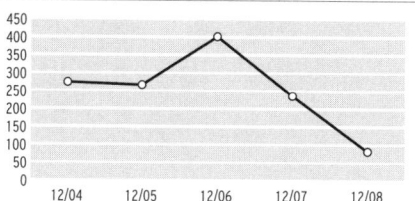

NBC Universal

Television, movies, and more fill the vastness of this entertainment company. NBC Universal (NBCU) is a leading media conglomerate anchored by its broadcast network NBC, with more than 200 affiliate stations (including 10 that are company-owned), and its Universal Studios film division. Other broadcasting operations owned by NBCU include Spanish-language network Telemundo and a portfolio of cable TV channels that includes Bravo, USA Network, Oxygen, and 24-hour news channel MSNBC. In addition to traditional media, NBCU owns online portal iVillage and has a stake in video site Hulu. Comcast, the country's #1 cable systems operator, is acquiring control of NBCU from industrial giant General Electric.

NBCU, like other media conglomerates such as Time Warner and News Corporation, is focused on using its vast distribution channels to maximize the profit potential of its creative content. However, the company has been beleaguered by uneven performance at the box office and low ratings for its broadcast network. The recession has also had a negative impact on advertising revenue and home entertainment DVD sales.

Looking to get its under-performing media operations off its books, GE agreed to cede control of NBCU to Comcast in 2009. The deal, valued at $30 billion, will see the cable TV company take a 51% stake in NBCU in exchange for $6.5 billion in cash and the contribution of several cable TV properties (E! Entertainment Television, The Golf Channel, VERSUS) valued at more than $7.2 billion. NBCU will also borrow more than $9 billion to distribute to GE; most of the borrowed cash will be used to buy back a 20% stake from French telecommunications giant Vivendi for $5.8 billion. GE will continue to own the remaining 49% of NBCU; the media operation will be managed by Comcast through a newly created division called Comcast Entertainment Group.

The cable systems operator agreed to the acquisition as a means of adding television and film content to its already formidable video distribution operation. When completed, the combination will allow Comcast to beef up its video-on-demand (VOD) offerings with both first-run and older movies from film imprints Universal Pictures and Focus Features. The deal will also diversify Comcast's revenue with more advertising-supported media.

Following its acquisition, however, Comcast will be faced with the task of turning around NBCU's fortunes. The company's NBC network has long been suffering as the fourth-ranked national broadcast network, hampered by an inability to find a break-out hit TV show. While newer shows such as *Heroes* and *The Office* have attracted loyal followings and some critical praise, their ratings are still dwarfed by hit programming from rivals CBS (*CSI: Crime Scene Investigation*) and FOX (*American Idol*). Renewed hopes of a turnaround came in 2009 when entertainment chief Ben Silverman (founder of Reveille Productions) departed NBC. NBC Universal Cable chairman Jeff Gaspin was promoted to lead all of NBCU's broadcast and cable operations as chairman of NBC Universal Television Entertainment.

Meanwhile in Hollywood, Universal Pictures has been plagued at the box office by more flops than hits. The studio flopped in 2009 with its re-imagined *Land of the Lost*, while 2008 releases

The Incredible Hulk and *The Mummy: The Tomb of the Dragon Emperor* also disappointed. As part of an effort to hold down production costs, the studio did strike a deal with Relativity Media in 2008 to co-finance a number of films through 2015. The following year the studio sold its Rogue Pictures imprint to Relativity for about $150 million.

Comcast will be acquiring a strong portfolio of cable channels, which has been one bright area in NBCU's broadcasting operations. USA has become one of the more popular general entertainment outlets on cable with popular reruns (*Law & Order: Special Victims Unit, House*) and successful original programming (*Burn Notice, Monk*), while Bravo has anchored its place in the reality-based TV niche with such hits as *Top Chef* and the *Real Housewives* franchise. NBCU's Syfy, meanwhile, is focused on using original programming in the science fiction and fantasy genres to build on its loyal following.

In addition to its wholly owned cable channels, NBCU is a partner in both The Weather Channel and A&E Television. NBCU joined with private equity firms Bain Capital and The Blackstone Group to acquire The Weather Channel from Landmark Communications for $3.5 billion in 2008. The deal added a popular cable property that reaches more than 95 million US homes, as well as the company's weather.com Web site and its audience of 30 million users. The Weather Channel operates as a separate entity managed by NBCU. Meanwhile, the company joined with cable joint venture partners Walt Disney and Hearst to combine A&E Television (AETN) and Lifetime Entertainment in 2009. NBCU continues to be a minority partner in the venture and will have the option of exiting, or may be bought out, from the joint venture over a period of 15 years.

NBCU has turned significant focus toward digital entertainment and online media distribution to capitalize on new technologies. The company has about a 30% stake in video streaming site Hulu, launched with News Corporation in 2008. The site has become a popular destination for streaming full-length TV episodes and some feature films. (Disney became a 30% partner in Hulu in 2009, adding content from ABC and other Disney-owned cable networks.)

NBC Universal was formed in 2004 through the merger of NBC (previously a wholly owned subsidiary of GE) and Vivendi Universal Entertainment. Jeff Zucker was promoted to replace Robert Wright as CEO in 2007. Zucker previously served as head of NBC Universal Television; Wright had led the NBC network and later NBC Universal for more than 20 years.

EXECUTIVES

President and CEO: Jeffrey A. (Jeff) Zucker, age 43
EVP TV Networks Distribution: Henry Ahn
EVP Strategic Partnership Group: Jay Linden
EVP Corporate Communications: Allison Gollust
EVP Diversity: Paula Madison
EVP and CTO: Darren Feher
EVP and Deputy General Counsel: Andrea R. Hartman
EVP Administration, NBC Universal Television Group, West Coast: Jerry Petry
EVP Entertainment Strategy and Programs: Ted Frank
EVP Corporate Sourcing: Marcia P. Haynes
EVP and General Counsel: Richard (Rick) Cotton
EVP and CFO: Lynn Calpeter
EVP Human Resources: Marc A. Chini
EVP, Universal Studios Partnerships: Stephanie Sperber
EVP Global Policy Strategies and Alliances:
  Cormac (Cory) Shields
EVP News, Promotion, and Original Content, NBC Universal Television Stations: Phyllis Schwartz

EVP Financial Planning & Analysis:
Christy Rupert Shibata
Chief Marketing Officer; President, The NBC Agency:
John Miller
SVP Corporate Communications and Media Relations:
Kathy Kelly-Brown
Chairman and CEO, Universal Parks & Resorts:
Thomas L. (Tom) Williams, age 61
Chairman, NBC Universal Sports and Olympics:
Dick Ebersol
Chairman Television Entertainment: Jeff Gaspin
Chairman, NBC Entertainment and Universal Media
Studios: Marc Graboff
President, Sales and Marketing: Michael J. Pilot
President, Digital Entertainment: Vivi Zigler
Auditors: KPMG LLP

LOCATIONS

HQ: NBC Universal, Inc.
30 Rockefeller Plaza, New York, NY 10112
Phone: 212-664-4444 **Fax:** 212-664-4085
Web: www.nbcuni.com

PRODUCTS/OPERATIONS

Selected Operations

Digital media
 Hulu (30%)
 iVillage
 nbc.com
Feature films
 Focus Features
 Universal Pictures
 Universal Studios Home Entertainment
Television networks and production
 Cable channels
  A&E Television Networks (25%)
  Bravo
  Chiller
  CNBC
  MSNBC
  mun2
  Oxygen
  Sleuth
  Syfy
  Universal HD
  USA Network
  The Weather Channel
 NBC Television Network
 NBC Universal Domestic Television Distribution
 NBC Universal International Television Distribution
 Telemundo
 Universal Media Studios
Television stations
 NBC
  KNBC (Los Angeles)
  KNSD (San Diego)
  KNTV (San Francisco)
  KXAS (Dallas)
  WCAU (Philadelphia)
  WMAQ (Chicago)
  WNBC (New York City)
  WRC (Washington, DC)
  WTVJ (Miami)
  WVIT (Hartford, CT)
 Telemundo
  KBLR (Las Vegas)
  KDEN (Denver)
  KHRR (Tucson, AZ)
  KMAS (Denver)
  KNSO (Fresno, CA)
  KSTS (San Francisco)
  KTAZ (Phoenix)
  KTMD (Houston)
  KVDA (San Antonio)
  KVEA (Los Angeles)
  KXTX (Dallas)
  WKAQ (Puerto Rico)
  WNEU (Boston)
  WNJU (New York)
  WSCV (Miami)
  WSNS (Chicago)
Universal Parks & Resorts (theme parks)

COMPETITORS

CBS Corp
Discovery Communications
Disney
Fox Entertainment
Lionsgate
MGM
Sony Pictures Entertainment
Time Warner
Univision
Viacom

HISTORICAL FINANCIALS

Company Type: Subsidiary

Income Statement

FYE: December 31

	REVENUE ($ mil.)	NET INCOME ($ mil.)	NET PROFIT MARGIN	EMPLOYEES
12/08	16,969	3,131	18.5%	—
12/07	15,416	3,107	20.2%	—
12/06	16,188	2,919	18.0%	—
12/05	14,689	3,092	21.0%	—
12/04	12,886	2,558	19.9%	—
Annual Growth	7.1%	5.2%	—	—

Net Income History

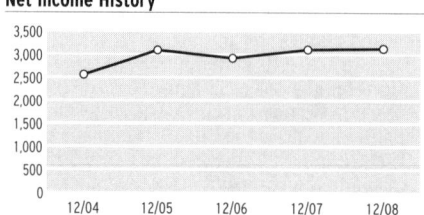

Nebraska Book

Nebraska Book Company (NBC) can help college students in the US and Canada with book learnin'. One of the largest textbook distributors in the US, NBC sells more than 6.8 million books annually and offers 108,000-plus titles. Its bookstores division operates about 260 bookstores on or adjacent to college campuses that sell new and used textbooks and other merchandise. NBC's Complementary Services unit provides education materials to students in private high schools, non-traditional colleges, and corporate and correspondence classes. Founded in 1915 as a single bookstore near The University of Nebraska, NBC also offers software for store management and WebPrism and CampusHub software for e-commerce.

The textbook company has grown its bookstores division through acquisitions and the opening new stores. In late 2007 it acquired nine new bookstores. In 2006, NBC bought College Book Stores of America, in a deal that practically doubled NBC's store count. College Book Stores of America kept its name and operates as a standalone business of NBC. Overall, the company has more than doubled the number of bookstores it operates since 2004.

Mark Oppegard, CEO of the company, promoted COO Barry Major to president and COO in September 2008. Investment firm Weston Presidio owns a controlling interest in the company.

EXECUTIVES

CEO and Director: Mark W. Oppegard, age 59,
$793,500 total compensation
President, COO, and Director: Barry S. Major, age 52,
$820,488 total compensation
Chief Technology Officer: Nathan D. Rempe, age 31
SVP, Complementary Services: Larry R. Rempe, age 61
SVP, College Bookstore Division: Robert A. (Rob) Rupe,
age 61, $292,680 total compensation
SVP, Textbook Division: Michael J. Kelly, age 51,
$280,835 total compensation
SVP Finance and Administration, CFO, Treasurer, and
Assistant Secretary: Alan G. Siemek, age 49,
$721,651 total compensation
VP Corporate Communications: Sue Riedman
General Information Textbook Division: Frank Condello
Human Resources: Melissa Kletchka
Corporate Administration: Mary Lockard
Marketing: Shane Jochum
Auditors: Deloitte & Touche LLP

LOCATIONS

HQ: Nebraska Book Company, Inc.
4700 S. 19th St., Lincoln, NE 68501
Phone: 402-421-7300 **Fax:** 800-869-0399
Web: www.nebook.com

PRODUCTS/OPERATIONS

2008 Sales

	$ mil.	% of total
Bookstore division	452.9	78
Textbook division	99.6	17
Complementary services	28.7	5
Total	**581.2**	**100**

COMPETITORS

Amazon.com
Barnes & Noble College Booksellers
Borders Group
Ecampus.com
Follett
MBS Textbook Exchange
Wal-Mart

HISTORICAL FINANCIALS

Company Type: Private

Income Statement

FYE: March 31

	REVENUE ($ mil.)	NET INCOME ($ mil.)	NET PROFIT MARGIN	EMPLOYEES
3/08	581	13	2.2%	3,400
3/07	544	13	2.3%	3,100
3/06	420	12	2.9%	2,900
3/05	402	14	3.4%	2,300
3/04	399	14	3.4%	2,500
Annual Growth	9.9%	(1.9%)	—	8.0%

Net Income History

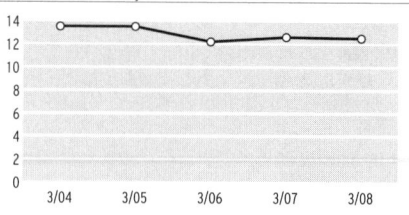

Neiman Marcus

Not for the faint of finances, Neiman Marcus department stores offer high-fashion, high-quality women's and men's apparel (from such labels as Chanel and Prada), shoes and accessories, fine jewelry, china, crystal, and silver. The Neiman Marcus Group operates some 40 Neiman Marcus stores in some 20 states and the District of Columbia, as well as two Bergdorf Goodman stores in New York City and some 30 Last-Call clearance centers that sell marked-down goods. Its mail-order business, Neiman Marcus Direct, distributes catalogs (which offer apparel, home furnishings, and gourmet foods) under the Neiman Marcus By Mail and Horchow names. The upscale retailer is owned by a pair of private equity firms.

Neiman Marcus — fondly known as "Needless Markups" — is among the retailers hardest hit by the plunge in demand for luxury goods and overall decline in consumer spending as a result of the deep recession in the US. Indeed, the company posted about a 21% drop in sales in fiscal 2009 vs. 2008. In response, the retailer has cut about 375 jobs, reduced salaries, and beginning in July 2009 shortened the number of hours its stores are open for business at about half of its 40 locations.

The firm is looking for growth outside its traditional markets, focusing on smaller enclaves of wealth scattered throughout the US. In 2009 Neiman's opened stores in Topanga, California, and Bellevue, Washington. Future stores are slated to open in Walnut Creek (2012) and San Jose (2013), California.

The retailer's caché can be attributed in part to the lavish customer service upscale shoppers have come to expect. It offers extravagant special events, one-of-a-kind items, and especially attentive salespeople. Customers (who tend to be older, affluent women) are often known by name and their needs are fastidiously met.

In a bid to appeal to the younger set, in 2006 Neiman's launched a retail concept called CUSP, a loft-like format (averaging 6,000 to 11,000 square feet) targeting at fashion savvy 25- to 45-year-old women. There are currently about a half a dozen CUSP stores in operation. The stores' main brands are Diane von Furstenberg, Seven For All Mankind, and BCBG Max Azria.

TPG Capital (formerly Texas Pacific Group) and Warburg Pincus LLC together in 2005 paid about $5.1 billion ($100 per share in cash) for the company, beating out other joint bids by Kohlberg Kravis Roberts & Co. and Bain Capital, and Thomas H. Lee Partners and The Blackstone Group.

HISTORY

When Herbert Marcus, his sister Carrie Marcus Neiman, and her husband, A. L. Neiman, sold their sales promotion business in Atlanta, they chose to take $25,000 in cash instead of the Missouri or Kansas franchise rights for a new drink called Coca-Cola (which later prompted family members to joke that their company was founded on poor business judgment since no one recognized the drink's potential). The three moved to Dallas, and in 1907 they used their cash and the contributions of other relatives to open Neiman Marcus, a store for "fashionable women."

The three owners were determined to have a specialty store unlike any in the entire South — one that sold ladies' millinery and outergarments that were stylish, high quality, and ready-to-wear (a new concept). Neiman Marcus was an immediate success that showed a profit its very first year.

In 1928 Herbert bought out the Neimans. Also that year the store added men's fashions. Herbert's son Stanley, who started the extravagant Neiman Marcus Christmas catalog and oversaw the company's expansion into new markets, ran the stores from 1952 to 1979.

Retailer Carter Hawley Hale bought the chain in 1969 but did not keep up the stores in the customary manner. As a result, sales and the chain's reputation as upscale and unique suffered throughout the 1970s and into the 1980s. In 1979 Stanley's son Richard continued the family's reign, becoming the company's chairman and CEO.

As part of its 1987 restructuring, Carter Hawley Hale spun off the Neiman Marcus stores. At that time General Cinema traded its interest in Carter Hawley Hale for a controlling 44% of The Neiman Marcus Group. In addition to the Neiman Marcus stores, The Neiman Marcus Group included New York City's exclusive Bergdorf Goodman and the mainstream chain Contempo Casuals. Tailor Herman Bergdorf and his partner, Edwin Goodman, founded Bergdorf Goodman in New York in 1901. Carter Hawley Hale bought the high-end retailer in 1972.

The Neiman Marcus Group bought Horchow Mail Order of Dallas, a retailer of personal and home upscale decorative items, in 1988. That year Richard resigned as CEO and ended 81 years of family management of the 22-store chain.

An offer in 1990 by General Cinema (later renamed Harcourt Education in 2003 and Houghton Mifflin Harcourt in 2008) to buy the rest of The Neiman Marcus Group was rejected.

It bought Chef's Catalog, which sells high-dollar cookware, in 1998. That year the company also began testing The Galleries of Neiman Marcus, a new, smaller store format selling fine jewelry and gifts. In November the company acquired 51% of Gurwitch Products (formerly Gurwitch Bristow Products), makers of Laura Mercier cosmetics. Also in 1998 Robert Smith was promoted to CEO of The Neiman Marcus Group; his father, Richard, remained chairman. (The two also head up Harcourt.)

In 1999 Richard's son-in-law, Brian Knez, was named co-CEO. Later that year Harcourt spun off most of its stake to its own shareholders, who are led by the Smith family. Also that year Neiman Marcus bought 56% of luxury handbag and accessories maker and retailer kate spade.

The company named co-CEOs Robert and Knez co-vice chairmen in February 2001 and appointed president and COO Burton Tansky CEO. Stanley Marcus, chairman emeritus of the company since 1975, died in early 2002 at the age of 96.

In 2004 the remainder of the company's The Galleries of Neiman Marcus stores shut down. In July 2005 the luxury retailer completed the sale of its private-label credit card business, which has about $525 million in accounts receivable, to HSBC Holdings for about $653 million. Under the terms of the deal, HSBC, one of the world's largest banks, will not sell the names of Neiman's 3 million credit card customers and Neiman's will continue to handle all dealings with cardholders. The purchase included the private-label credit card accounts of Neiman's Bergdorf Goodman subsidiary.

In 2006 the company sold kate spade to apparel giant Liz Claiborne for about $124 million.

EXECUTIVES

Chairman, President, and CEO: Burton M. (Burt) Tansky, age 71
EVP and CFO: James E. Skinner, age 55
EVP and General Merchandise Manager, Women's Apparel, Neiman Marcus Stores: Ann Stordahl
EVP Stores, Neiman Marcus: Neva L. Hall
EVP; President and CEO, Neiman Marcus Stores: Karen W. Katz, age 52
SVP and General Merchandise Manager, Neiman Marcus Stores: Lisa Kazor
SVP and CIO: Phillip L. Maxwell, age 61
SVP and General Merchandise Manager, Neiman Marcus Stores: Jonathan Joselove
SVP and General Merchandise Manager, Neiman Marcus Direct: Gerald Barnes
SVP Creative and Marketing, Neiman Marcus Stores: Steve Kornajcik
SVP and Director, Fashion Neiman Marcus Stores: Ken Downing
SVP and Chief Human Resources Officer: Marita O'Dea, age 60
SVP and General Counsel: Nelson A. (Tony) Bangs, age 56
SVP and General Merchandise Manager, Neiman Marcus Direct: Jeanie Galvin
SVP Properties and Store Development: Wayne A. Hussey, age 59
SVP Marketing and Customer Care, Neiman Marcus Direct: Jessica Weiland
SVP and Chief Marketing Officer: Wanda Gierhart
VP and Controller: T. Dale Stapleton
VP Corporate Communications, The Neiman Marcus Group: Ginger Reeder
VP Public Relations and Fashion Presentation: Gabrielle De Papp
President and CEO, Bergdorf Goodman: James J. (Jim) Gold
Auditors: Deloitte & Touche LLP

LOCATIONS

HQ: The Neiman Marcus Group, Inc.
1618 Main St., Dallas, TX 75201
Phone: 214-743-7600   **Fax:** 214-573-5320
Web: www.neimanmarcus.com

2009 Neiman Marcus Stores

	No.
Florida	7
Texas	7
California	6
Illinois	3
Massachusetts	2
New Jersey	2
Arizona	1
Colorado	1
District of Columbia	1
Georgia	1
Hawaii	1
Michigan	1
Minnesota	1
Missouri	1
Nevada	1
New York	1
North Carolina	1
Pennsylvania	1
Virginia	1
Washington	1
Total	**41**

PRODUCTS/OPERATIONS

2009 Stores

	No.
Neiman Marcus	41
Clearance Centers	28
CUSP	6
Bergdorf Goodman	2
Total	**77**

2009 Sales

	$ mil.	% of total
Department stores	2,991.3	82
Direct marketing	652.0	18
Total	**3,643.3**	**100**

2009 Sales

	% of total
Women's apparel	36
Women's shoes, handbags & accessories	21
Men's apparel & shoes	12
Designer & precious jewelry	11
Cosmetics & fragrance	11
Home furnishings & decor	7
Other	2
Total	**100**

Selected Operations

Catalogs (Horchow, Neiman Marcus By Mail)
Retail stores (Bergdorf Goodman, Last Call Clearance Centers, Neiman Marcus)

Selected Merchandise

Accessories
Children's apparel
China
Cosmetics
Crystal and silver
Decorative home items
Fine jewelry
Furs
Gift items
Gourmet foods
High-fashion women's and men's clothing
Shoes

COMPETITORS

AnnTaylor
Astor & Black
Barneys
Bloomingdale's
Brooks Brothers
Caché
DFS Group
Dillard's
Eddie Bauer llc
Estée Lauder
Henri Bendel
J. Crew
Lands' End
Nordstrom
Saks
Tiffany & Co.
Von Maur
Williams-Sonoma

HISTORICAL FINANCIALS

Company Type: Private

Income Statement				FYE: Saturday nearest July 31
	REVENUE ($ mil.)	NET INCOME ($ mil.)	NET PROFIT MARGIN	EMPLOYEES
7/08	4,601	—	—	18,000
7/07	4,390	—	—	17,900
7/06	4,390	—	—	17,900
7/05	4,106	—	—	17,200
Annual Growth	3.9%	—	—	1.5%

Revenue History

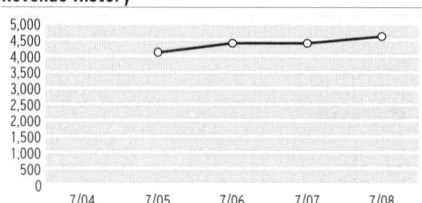

New Balance

New Balance Athletic Shoe runs on its everyman (and everywoman) appeal. Unlike its rivals, it shuns celebrity endorsers. By spotlighting lesser-known athletes the company claims to emphasize substance over style. The approach attracts Boomer jock clients who are less fickle than the teens chased by other shoemakers. Founded in 1906 to make arch supports, New Balance is known for its selection of shoe widths. Besides men's and women's shoes for running, crosstraining, basketball, tennis, hiking, and golf, the firm offers fitness apparel and kids' shoes and owns leather boot maker Dunham. Chairman Jim Davis bought New Balance on the day of the 1972 Boston Marathon.

The company appointed a new CEO in 2007. A former executive at Procter & Gamble, Gillette, and Tyson Foods, Robert DeMartini joined New Balance in April 2007 to bring a fresh perspective to the company, as Davis had been at the helm at New Balance for some 35 years. DeMartini brought with him more than 20 years of experience in sales, marketing, operations, and other areas. New Balance also hired him to bring in younger, more progressive management. As companies, such as Fila USA, are being bought out, New Balance and its rivals are jockeying for second-tier positions, under goliaths NIKE and adidas (which now owns Reebok).

Hiring DeMartini, who hails from companies with a global reach, will help New Balance get a foothold in overseas markets. While sales in the US have dropped from about $1.1 billion in 2004 to $995 million in 2007, New Balance has seen its revenue rise in its international business during the same time frame, albeit slightly, from $1.5 billion in 2004 to $1.63 billion in 2007. With the decline in the US economy in 2008, New Balance will be relying more on its global business to keep sales steady until the economy rebounds.

In addition to the company's namesake brand and its Dunham boots, New Balance's products portfolio includes PF Flyers footwear, Aravon shoes for comfort performance, Warrior hockey wear, and Brine, a leader in soccer, field hockey, volleyball, and lacrosse items. New Balance also makes apparel and accessories through licensing deals with the likes of Moretz Sports, Eyewear Designs, Fitness Quest, and Hickory Brands.

New Balance sells its products in more than 120 countries. Outside North America, the company operates in the UK, France, Germany, Sweden, Hong Kong, Singapore, Australia, New Zealand, Japan, Brazil, and South Africa. To emphasize its reach worldwide, New Balance in March 2009 launched a Total Fit global brand campaign to reinforce its expertise in running and its philosophy on how well a fitness shoe should fit. The campaign spans TV, print, and online mediums and targets potential customers 25 to 34 years old. New Balance is planning to launch the campaign in major international markets throughout 2009.

EXECUTIVES

Chairman: James S. (Jim) Davis, age 65
Vice Chairman and EVP Administration: Anne Davis
CEO: Robert T. DeMartini, age 48
President Emeritus and Advisor: John E. Larsen
EVP and CFO: John Withee
EVP International: Alan Hed, age 49
EVP Global Footwear Product and Marketing: Joseph (Joe) Preston
EVP Manufacturing: John Wilson
EVP North American Sales: Chris Quinn
EVP Apparel: Kerry Kligerman
EVP Commercial Opportunities: Herb Spivak
VP Global Design and Development: Jim Connors
VP and Treasurer: Alan Rosen
VP Corporate Human Resources: Carol O'Donnell
Corporate Communications Manager: Amy Vreeland

LOCATIONS

HQ: New Balance Athletic Shoe, Inc.
Brighton Landing, 20 Guest St., Boston, MA 02135
Phone: 617-783-4000　　**Fax:** 617-787-9355
Web: www.newbalance.com

PRODUCTS/OPERATIONS

Selected Brands

New Balance
Dunham
PF Flyers
Aravon
Warrior
Brine

COMPETITORS

adidas
ASICS
Brooks Sports
Converse
Fila USA
K-Swiss
Mizuno
NIKE
PUMA AG
Roots Canada
Saucony
Shoe Show

HISTORICAL FINANCIALS

Company Type: Private

Income Statement				FYE: December 31
	REVENUE ($ mil.)	NET INCOME ($ mil.)	NET PROFIT MARGIN	EMPLOYEES
12/08	1,640	—	—	4,000
12/07	1,630	—	—	2,800
12/06	1,550	—	—	2,800
12/05	1,540	—	—	2,800
12/04	1,400	—	—	2,600
Annual Growth	4.0%	—	—	11.4%

Revenue History

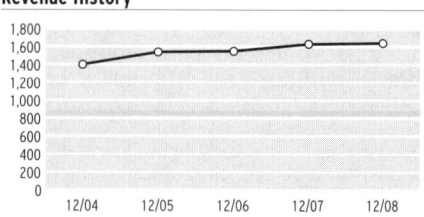

New England Alliance for Health

The New England Alliance for Health (NEAH) brings together physicians looking to improve health in the New England region. The alliance, formerly known as Dartmouth-Hitchcock Alliance, provides a wide range of health care services to residents of Massachusetts, New Hampshire, and Vermont through a network of about a dozen community hospitals, home health care agencies, and mental health centers. Each member of the alliance is an independently owned and operated not-for-profit organization with its own board of directors. Collaborative services provided by NEAH include procurement, human resources, information technology, and finance, as well as the coordination of facility policies and planning.

EXECUTIVES

President: Nancy Formella
COO: Stephen LeBlanc
CFO: Richard Showalter

LOCATIONS

HQ: New England Alliance for Health, LLC
1 Medical Center Dr., Lebanon, NH 03756
Phone: 603-650-5000   **Fax:** 603-650-8765
Web: www.neahllc.org

PRODUCTS/OPERATIONS

Selected Alliance Members

Massachusetts
  Cooley Dickinson Health Care

New Hampshire
  Mary Hitchcock Memorial Hospital (managing
    member, part of Dartmouth-Hitchcock Health)
  New London Hospital
  Upper Connecticut Valley Hospital
  Valley Regional Health Care
  VNA and Hospice of VT and NH
  Weeks Medical Center
  West Central Behavioral Health

Vermont
  Central Vermont Medical Center
  Mt. Ascutney Hospital and Health Center
  Northeastern Vermont Regional Hospital, Inc.

COMPETITORS

AMN Healthcare
Beth Israel Deaconess Medical Center
Boston Medical Center
Brigham and Women's Hospital
Broadlane
Cambridge Health Alliance
CareGroup
Caritas Christi
Children's Hospital Boston
Gentiva
Massachusetts General Hospital
MedAssets
Medical Staffing Network
Novation
Premier, Inc.
VHA
Winchester Healthcare

New Jersey Devils

These Devils make trouble for their opponents on the ice. The New Jersey Devils professional hockey team entered the National Hockey League in 1974 as the Kansas City Scouts and relocated to Colorado until it settled in the Garden State in 1982. A regular contender for the playoffs, it boasts three Stanley Cup championships, its last in 2003. The team has been owned since 2005 by an investment group led by Jeffrey Vanderbeek. The group purchased the Devils from uber-sports group YankeeNets (which had also owned the New York Yankees and the New Jersey Nets).

Head coach Brent Sutter resigned from the club in 2009 after leading the Devils to two consecutive post-season appearances. A veteran player with the Chicago Blackhawks and New York Islanders, he had been hired in 2007 to bring a more open and offensive style to the normally defensive New Jersey squad. Sutter had been the third person to work behind the team's bench in as many years. He was replaced by Jacques Lemaire, former head coach of the Minnesota Wild.

Looking to boost home attendance and gate receipts, the team relocated from its former home at the Meadowlands in 2007 to take up residence at the Prudential Center in Newark, New Jersey. The Devils helped finance part of the $380 million arena, with the rest of the project being funded through public money. Insurance giant Prudential Financial signed on to a $105 million, 20-year marketing deal that year to put its name on the facility.

EXECUTIVES

Chairman and Managing Partner:
  Jeffrey (Jeff) Vanderbeek, age 51
President, CEO, and General Manager:
  Louis A. (Lou) Lamoriello, age 67
SEVP and COO: Chris Modrzynski
EVP and CFO: Scott Struble
EVP: Peter S. McMullen
EVP Administration: Gordon Lavalette, age 46
EVP Hockey Operations and Director Scounting:
  David Conte, age 59
Head Coach: Jacques Lemaire
**SVP Hockey Operations; General Manager, Lowell &
  Scout:** Chris Lamoriello, age 33
SVP Information and Publications: Mike Levine, age 45
SVP Corporate Partnerships: Kenneth F. (Ken) Ferriter
SVP Facilities: Mark A. Gheduzzi
SVP and General Counsel: Joseph C. Benedetti
VP Marketing and Community Development: Jeff Longo
VP Hockey Operations: Steve Pellegrini
Director Communications: Jeff Altstadter
Equipment Manager: Rich Matthews, age 36

LOCATIONS

HQ: New Jersey Devils
  50 Rte. 120 North, East Rutherford, NJ 07073
Phone: 201-935-6050   **Fax:** 201-935-2127
Web: www.newjerseydevils.com

The New Jersey Devils play at the 17,625-seat capacity Prudential Center in Newark, New Jersey.

PRODUCTS/OPERATIONS

Championship Trophies

Stanley Cup (1995, 2000, 2003)
Prince of Wales Trophy (1995, 2000-01, 2003)

COMPETITORS

New York Islanders
New York Rangers
Philadelphia Flyers
Pittsburgh Penguins

New Jersey Nets

You might say this sports operator has a very appropriate name. New Jersey Basketball owns and operates the New Jersey Nets professional basketball team, a storied franchise of the National Basketball Association. Organized by Arthur Brown in 1967 as the New Jersey Americans of the American Basketball Association, the team won two ABA titles as the New York Nets with the help of Julius "Dr. J" Erving. It returned to the Garden State and joined the NBA in 1976. The team has yet to claim an NBA title. The Nets play host at The IZOD Center at the Meadowlands in New Jersey. New York real estate developer Bruce Ratner has owned the Nets since 2004; he has agreed to sell the team to Mikhail Prokhorov.

The richest man in Russia, Prokhorov agreed in 2009 to invest $200 million into the New Jersey basketball through his investment vehicle Onexim Group. The deal would give the billionaire an 80% stake in the Nets franchise and 45% of a planned $550 million arena in Brooklyn, New York. Prokhorov would become the first person outside North America to control an NBA franchise.

Ratner had announced big plans to move the team to Brooklyn after he acquired control of the team. Those plans included the basketball arena in the Atlantic Yards district, a nearly $5 billion real estate project being developed by Ratner's Forest City Enterprises. (The family-owned business owns a 21% stake in the Nets.) Construction of the controversial development was finally approved in 2008, but completion of the new arena has been delayed due to the recession and credit crisis. The Nets' current lease at The IZOD Center runs through 2010.

The new arena was supposed to have been designed by Frank Gehry, but Ratner later rejected the world famous architect's concept in favor of a more modest design from Kansas City's Ellerbe Becket. When completed, the facility will be called Barclays Center as part of a 20-year, $400 million naming rights deal signed with London-based financial services giant Barclays in 2007.

On the court, the Nets named general manager Kiki Vandeweghe as interim head coach early in the 2009 season. Vandeweghe, a former player who served as general manager of the Denver Nuggets until joining New Jersey in 2008, took over from Frank Lawrence, who was fired after a disastrous start to the campaign. Lawrence had coached the Nets for six and a half years.

Ratner purchased the Nets from Lewis Katz and Ray Chambers for about $300 million. The sale took place after the breakup of YankeeNets, a partnership that had controlled the Nets, the New York Yankees, and the New Jersey Devils.

EXECUTIVES

Principal Owner: Bruce C. Ratner, age 64
CEO: Brett Yormark
President: Rod Thorn
Interim Head Coach: Ernest M. (Kiki) Vandeweghe III, age 51
SVP and General Manager, Arena Operations: Alex Diaz
SVP Ticket Sales and Marketing: Fred Mangione
SVP and Chief Relationship Officer: Leo Ehrline
SVP and CFO: Charlie Mierswa
SVP and General Counsel: Jeff Gewirtz
VP Basketball Operations: Bobby Marks
VP Public Relations: Gary Sussman
Executive Director Human Resources: Kimberly Blanco
Director Player Personnel: Gregg Polinsky
Director Operations: Lewis Gibbons
Senior Director Information Technology: Mimi Viau
Athletic Trainer: Tim Walsh

LOCATIONS

HQ: New Jersey Basketball, LLC
390 Murray Hill Pkwy., East Rutherford, NJ 07073
Phone: 201-935-8888   **Fax:** 201-935-1088
Web: www.nba.com/nets

The New Jersey Nets play at 19,990-seat capacity IZOD Center in East Rutherford, New Jersey.

PRODUCTS/OPERATIONS

Championship Titles
Eastern Conference Champions (2002-03)

COMPETITORS

Boston Celtics
New York Knicks
Philadelphia 76ers
Toronto Raptors

New NGC

When it comes to work, New NGC is always *board*. The company, the second-largest gypsum wallboard manufacturer in the US (behind USG Corporation), does business as National Gypsum Company. It sells wallboard under the Gold Bond, Durabase, and SoundBreak brand names. The company also produces other building products such as joint treatment compounds (ProForm), cement board (PermaBase), plaster, and framing systems. Its testing services division tests acoustical, fire, and structural properties of building materials. National Gypsum, which has more than 20 plants in the US and Mexico, sells its products worldwide to the construction industry. Delcor Inc., a subsidiary of Golden Eagle Industries, owns the company.

Growing sales in Latin America prompted National Gypsum to open its first cement board pant in Mexico in 2008. The joint venture with Panel Rey is called PermaBase de Américas. The new plant allows the company to streamline distribution in Mexico and reduce shipping and customs fees.

The company also is targeting its marketing toward Latinos around the world as well as in the US, where about half of drywall installers are Hispanic.

The housing slump in 2008 forced National Gypsum to close some US plants and cut jobs.

EXECUTIVES

Chairman, President, and CEO: Thomas C. Nelson, age 46
SVP Manufacturing Operations and Engineering: Gerard (Jerry) Carroll
SVP Sales and Marketing: Craig Weisbruch
VP Human Resources: Nick Rodono
VP and General Counsel: Sam Schiffman
VP and CFO: William D. (Bill) Parmelee
Director Purchasing: Raymond Syracuse
Director Communications: Nancy H. Spurlock
Director Marketing: David Drummond
Auditors: PricewaterhouseCoopers LLP

LOCATIONS

HQ: New NGC, Inc.
2001 Rexford Rd., Charlotte, NC 28211
Phone: 704-365-7300   **Fax:** 800-329-6421
Web: www.nationalgypsum.com

PRODUCTS/OPERATIONS

Selected Products and Brands
Ceiling systems (Gridstone, Seaspray, and Hi-Strength)
Cement board (PermaBase)
Gypsum wallboard (Gold Bond, Durabase, Hi-Impact, and SoundBreak)
Joint compounds, spray textures, and tape (ProForm and Easy Finish)
Manufactured housing products (wallboard, ceiling board, spray texture, and construction guides)
Plaster, plaster base, and finishes
Prefinished gypsum wallboard and panels (Durasan, Kal-Kote, and Uni-Kal)
Shaftwall and area separation wall (H-Stud systems)
Wallboard and plaster base (Hi-Abuse and Hi-Impact)

COMPETITORS

American Gypsum
Eagle Materials
Gypsum Products
James Hardie Industries
Johns Manville
Lafarge North America
Temple-Inland
USG

HISTORICAL FINANCIALS

Company Type: Private

Income Statement				FYE: December 31
	ESTIMATED REVENUE ($ mil.)	NET INCOME ($ mil.)	NET PROFIT MARGIN	EMPLOYEES
12/07	1,100	—	—	2,800
12/06	1,850	—	—	2,800
12/05	1,700	—	—	2,800
Annual Growth	(19.6%)	—	—	0.0%

Revenue History

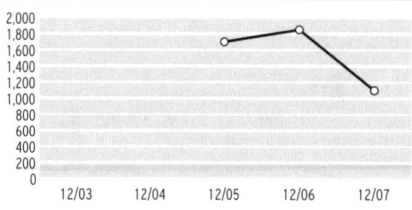

New Orleans Hornets

These Hornets are looking to sting their opponents on the basketball court. The New Orleans Hornets professional basketball team joined the National Basketball Association as the Charlotte Hornets in 1988 before moving from North Carolina to the Big Easy in 2002. During the 1990s the franchise was a perennial contender for the playoffs, but the team has yet to make an appearance in the NBA Finals. The team plays host at New Orleans Arena. George Shinn, who made his fortune building a network of for-profit schools, has controlled the franchise since its beginning.

While the Hornets have been thrilling fans in New Orleans with playoff appearances in 2008 and 2009, Shinn has been urging local officials to upgrade the facilities at New Orleans Arena. His inability to get a new arena in Charlotte forced him to move the franchise out of North Carolina. (A replacement franchise, the Charlotte Bobcats, was awarded to cable TV pioneer Robert Johnson in 2004.)

Team general manager Jeff Bower took over head coaching duties during the 2009-10 season after Byron Scott was fired in response to New Orleans' slow start. Bower, who was appointed GM in 2005, had previously served as an assistant under former head coach Tim Floyd. Scott had replaced Floyd on the bench in 2004.

The Hornets were forced to abandon their hometown during the 2005-06 season following the devastation from Hurricane Katrina. The team took up residence in Oklahoma City at the Ford Center that year. (That arena now serves as home court for the Oklahoma City Thunder.)

EXECUTIVES

Owner: George Shinn
Minority Owner: Gary Chouest
Executive Officer of the Board: Chad Shinn, age 29
President and COO: Hugh Weber
General Manager and Head Coach: Jeff Bower
EVP Business: Sam Russo
SVP Community Investment and External Affairs: Steve Martin
SVP Corporate Partnership and Broadcasting: Peter Goldsberry
VP Finance: Dan Crumb
VP Ticket Sales and Services: Kevin L. Terry
VP and General Counsel: Richard House
VP Corporate Strategic Development: Bill Bailey
VP Marketing: Matt Biggers
Director Business Development: Nathan Hubbell
Director Marketing: Jessica Richardson
Director Basketball Administration and Player Development: Andrew Loomis
Director Broadcasting: Lew Shuman
Director Corporate Communications: Michael Thompson
Director Human Resources: Donna Rochon

LOCATIONS

HQ: New Orleans Hornets
1250 Poydras St., Fl. 19, New Orleans, LA 70113
Phone: 504-593-4700
Web: www.nba.com/hornets

COMPETITORS

Dallas Mavericks
Houston Rockets
Memphis Grizzlies
San Antonio Spurs

New York City Health and Hospitals

New York City Health and Hospitals Corporation (HHC) takes care of the Big Apple. HHC has facilities in all five boroughs of New York City. As one of the largest municipal health service systems in the US, HHC operates a health care network consisting of 11 acute care hospitals (including Bellevue, the nation's oldest public hospital), community clinics, diagnostic and treatment centers, long-term care facilities, and a home health care agency. HHC also operates more than 80 community-based clinics and provides medical services to New York City's correctional facilities. In addition, it operates MetroPlus, a managed health care plan.

HHC is investing $1.2 billion program to improve its facilities over a five-year period. The health care system has worked on expansion projects for the Lincoln Medical & Mental Health Center, Harlem Hospital Center, and the Kings County Hospital Center.

HHC serves 1.3 million New Yorkers and nearly 400,000 who are uninsured. It provides medical, mental health, and substance abuse services through its 11 acute care hospitals, four skilled nursing facilities, six large diagnostic and treatment centers, and a chain of community based clinics.

HISTORY

The City of New York in 1929 created a department to manage its hospitals for the poor. During the Depression, more than half of the city's residents were eligible for subsidized care, and its public hospitals operated at full capacity.

Four new hospitals opened in the 1950s, but the city was already having trouble maintaining existing facilities and attracting staff (young doctors preferred private, insurance-supported hospitals catering to the middle class). Meanwhile, technological advances and increased demand for skilled nurses made hospitals more expensive to operate. The advent of Medicaid in 1965 was a boon for the system because it brought in federal money.

In 1969 the city created the New York City Health and Hospitals Corporation (HHC) to manage its public health care system — and, it was hoped, to distance it from the political arena. But HHC was still dependent on the city for funds, arousing criticism from those who had hoped for more autonomy. A 1973 state report claimed "the people of New York City are not materially better served by the Health and Hospitals Corporation than by its predecessor agencies."

City budget shortfalls in the mid-1970s led to cutbacks at HHC, including nearly 20% of staff. Later in the decade several hospitals closed and some services were discontinued. Ed Koch became mayor in 1978 and gained more control over HHC's operations. Struggles between his administration and the system led three HHC presidents to resign by 1981. That year Koch crony Stanley Brezenoff assumed the post and helped transform HHC into a city pseudo-department.

The early 1980s brought greater prosperity to the system. Reimbursement rates and collections procedures improved, allowing HHC to upgrade its record-keeping and its ambulatory and psychiatric care programs. In the late 1980s

sharp increases in AIDS and crack addiction cases strained the system and a sluggish economy decreased city funding. Criticism mounted in the early 1990s, with allegations of wrongful deaths, dangerous facilities, and lack of Medicaid payment controls. HHC lost patients to managed care providers, and revenues plummeted. In 1995 a city panel recommended radically revamping the system.

Faced with declining revenues and criticism from Mayor Rudolph Giuliani that HHC was "a jobs program," the company began cutting jobs and consolidating facilities in 1996. Under Giuliani's direction, HHC made plans to sell its Coney Island, Elmhurst, and Queens hospital centers. In 1997 the New York State Supreme Court struck down Giuliani's privatization efforts, saying the city council had a right to review and approve each sale. In 1998 Giuliani continued to seek to restructure HHC, and the agency itself contended it was making progress toward its restructuring goals, which were aimed at giving HHC more autonomy as well as more fiscal responsibility. In anticipation of a budget shortfall that year, the system laid off some 900 support staff employees. In 1999 the state court of appeals ruled HHC could not legally lease or sell its hospitals.

In 2000 HHC launched an effort to improve its physical infrastructure by beginning the rebuilding and renovation of facilities in Brooklyn, Manhattan, and Queens. The organization also began converting to an electronic (and thus more efficient) clinical information system. In 2001 HHC forged ahead with further restructuring initiatives. It introduced the Open Access plan, a cost-cutting measure designed to expedite the processes involved in outpatient visits.

In 2006 Mayor Michael Bloomberg committed $16 million in funds toward the treatment of those affected by exposure to toxic fumes and dust from the 2001 attacks on the World Trade Center. Together with the city, HHC established the WTC Environmental Health Center at Bellevue Hospital; treatment was made available at little or no charge to the patient.

EXECUTIVES

Chairman: Michael A. Stocker, age 67
Vice Chair: Rev Diane E. Lacey
President, CEO, and Director: Alan D. Aviles, age 57
CIO: Frances Pandolfi
EVP Medical and Professional Affairs: Ramanathan Raju
SVP Operations: Frank J. Cirillo
SVP and General Counsel: Richard A. Levy
SVP Corporate Planning, Community Health, and Intergovernmental Relations: LaRay Brown
SVP Facilities Development: Phillip W. Robinson
SVP Finance: Marlene Zurack
Executive Director, HHC Health and Home Care: Ann Frisch
Executive Director, MetroPlus Health Plan: Arnold Saperstein
Executive Director, Sea View Hospital Rehabilitation Center and Home: Angelo Mascia
Executive Director, Metropolitan Hospital Center: Meryl Weinberg
Executive Director, Coler-Goldwater Specialty Hospital and Nursing Facility: Claude Ritman
Executive Director, Harlem Hospital Center and Renaissance Health Care Network Diagnostic and Treatment Center: John M. Palmer
Executive Director, Elmhurst Hospital Center: Chris Constantino
Executive Director, Gouverneur Healthcare Services: Mendel Hagler
Senior Assistant VP, Corporate Communications and Marketing: Ana Marengo
Auditors: KPMG LLP

LOCATIONS

HQ: New York City Health and Hospitals Corporation
125 Worth St., Ste. 514, New York, NY 10013
Phone: 212-788-3321   **Fax:** 212-788-0040
Web: www.nyc.gov/html/hhc

HHC Networks

Central Brooklyn Family Health Network
  Dr. Susan Smith McKinney Nursing and
    Rehabilitation Center
  East New York Diagnostic & Treatment Center
  Kings County Hospital Center
Generations Plus Northern Manhattan Health Network
  Harlem Hospital Center
  Lincoln Medical and Mental Health Center
  Metropolitan Hospital Center
  Morrisania Diagnostic & Treatment Center
  Renaissance Health Care Network Diagnostic &
    Treatment Center
  Segundo Ruiz Belvis Diagnostic & Treatment Center
North Bronx Healthcare Network
  Jacobi Medical Center
  North Central Bronx Hospital
North Brooklyn Health Network
  Cumberland Diagnostic & Treatment Center
  Woodhull Medical and Mental Health Center
Queens Health Network
  Elmhurst Hospital Center
  Queens Hospital Center
South Brooklyn and Staten Island Health Network
  Coney Island Hospital
  Sea View Hospital Rehabilitation Center and Home
South Manhattan Healthcare Network
  Bellevue Hospital Center
  Coler-Goldwater Specialty Care and Nursing Facility
  Gouverneur Healthcare Services

COMPETITORS

Catholic Healthcare System
Columbia University
Cornell University
Lenox Hill Hospital
Memorial Sloan-Kettering
Montefiore Medical
Mount Sinai NYU Health
North Shore-Long Island Jewish Health System
NYU
Saint Vincent Catholic Medical Centers

New York Giants

It only seems natural that the Big Apple would have a big football team. New York Football Giants owns and operates the New York Giants professional football team, one of the oldest and most storied franchises in the National Football League. Started in 1925, the team has played for the league championship a record 18 times, winning seven titles including three Super Bowl championships. The Giants roster has included such Hall of Fame players as Frank Gifford, Sam Huff, Lawrence Taylor, and Y.A. Tittle. The team plays host at Giants Stadium at the Meadowlands in New Jersey, which it shares with the New York Jets. Tim Mara paid $500 to found the franchise; the Mara and Tisch families continue to control the team.

The Giants and Jets franchises are both awaiting the completion of a new stadium being built at the Meadowlands. The $1.3 billion privately financed facility, planned for opening in 2010, is envisioned to have seating for more than 82,500 spectators and will be part of a larger development project to create a sports, retail, and entertainment complex called Meadowlands Xanadu. The development is a partnership between the Giants, the New Jersey Sports and Exposition Authority, and Colony Capital. The Giants and Jets have called the Meadowlands home field since 1984.

Giants fans, meanwhile, are hoping for a return to the Super Bowl. Their team earned its last championship title at the end of the 2007 season. New York's previous Super Bowl wins had come under head coach Bill Parcells in 1986 and 1990.

Family patriarch Wellington Mara, the son of Tim Mara, died of cancer in late 2005. Robert Tisch became sole CEO of the organization but he also died of cancer three weeks later.

EXECUTIVES

President and CEO: John K. Mara, age 54
Director Information Technology Network and Systems: Justin Warren
Chairman and EVP: Steven (Steve) Tisch
SVP and General Manager: Jerry Reese
SVP and Chief Marketing Officer: Mike Stevens
Head Coach: Thomas R. (Tom) Coughlin, age 63
VP Communications: Pat Hanlon
VP Player Evaluation: Chris Mara
VP Medical Services: Ronnie Barnes, age 57
VP Giants Entertainment: Don Sperling
VP and CFO: Christine Procops
VP Media and Partnerships: Dan Lynch
VP Marketing: Rusty Hawley
CEO, The New Meadowlands Stadium: Mark Lamping
Assistant General Manager: Kevin Abrams
Director of Administration: Jim Phelan
Director Pro Personnel: David Gettleman
Director Research and Development: Raymond J. Walsh Jr.
Director of Public Relations: E. Peter John-Baptiste
Treasurer: Jonathan M. Tisch

LOCATIONS

HQ: New York Football Giants, Inc.
Giants Stadium, East Rutherford, NJ 07073
Phone: 201-935-8111   **Fax:** 201-935-8493
Web: www.giants.com

The New York Giants play at 78,741-seat capacity Giants Stadium in East Rutherford, New Jersey.

PRODUCTS/OPERATIONS

Championship Titles
Super Bowl Championships
Super Bowl XLII (2008)
Super Bowl XXV (1991)
Super Bowl XXI (1987)
NFL Championships (1927, 1934, 1938, 1956)
NFC Championships (1986, 1990, 2000, 2007)
NFC Eastern Division Champions (1986, 1989, 1990, 1997, 2000, 2005, 2008)
NFL Eastern Conference Champions (1956, 1958-59, 1961-63)
NFL East Division Champions (1933-35, 1938-39, 1941, 1944, 1946)

COMPETITORS

Dallas Cowboys
Philadelphia Eagles
Washington Redskins

HISTORICAL FINANCIALS

Company Type: Private

Income Statement

FYE: February 28

	REVENUE ($ mil.)	NET INCOME ($ mil.)	NET PROFIT MARGIN	EMPLOYEES
2/08	214	—	—	—
2/07	195	—	—	—
2/06	182	—	—	—
2/05	175	—	—	—
2/04	154	—	—	—
Annual Growth	**8.6%**	—	—	—

Revenue History

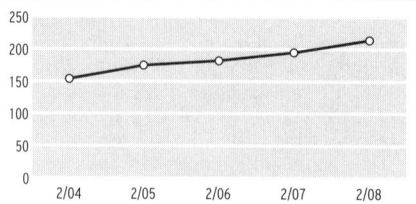

New York Islanders

These Islanders need to be surrounded by frozen water to be successful. Gotham's other hockey team, the New York Islanders entered the National Hockey League in 1972 and dominated the league in the early 1980s: The franchise won four consecutive Stanley Cup titles until its streak was ended in 1984 by the Wayne Gretzky-led Edmonton Oilers. More recently, the team has struggled on the ice, leading to a decline in ticket sales at Nassau Veterans Memorial Coliseum. Former CA executive Charles Wang has owned the Islanders franchise and its home arena since 2000.

The team's fortunes have been up and down the past few years under the leadership of general manager Garth Snow. A disappointing 2007-08 campaign led to the dismissal of head coach Ted Nolan after two seasons behind the bench; he had led the Isles to a post-season berth in his inaugural year. He was replaced with AHL Providence Bruins coach Scott Gordon.

Snow, a former goalie for the Islanders, joined the front office in 2006 replacing Mike Milbury after more than a decade. He had hired Nolan to replace Steve Stirling.

Wang, who founded CA as Computer Associates before leaving in 2002, and partner Sanjay Kumar, who served as CEO until 2004, bought the Islanders from Steven Gluckstern and Howard Milstein for about $190 million. Their relationship soured, however, and later unwound the partnership, leaving Wang in control of the franchise.

EXECUTIVES

Owner: Charles B. Wang, age 64
SVP Operations: Michael Picker
SVP Sales and Marketing: Paul Lancey
SVP Sports Properties: Mike Milbury, age 57
SVP and CFO: Arthur McCarthy
General Manager: Garth Snow
Head Coach: Scott Monroe

VP Marketing and Game Operations: Tim Beach
VP Corporate and Community Relations: Bill Kain
Director of Pro Scouting: Ken Morrow, age 44
Head Amateur Scout: Tony Feltrin, age 44
Assistant Coach: Jack Capuano

LOCATIONS

HQ: New York Islanders Hockey Club, L.P.
1535 Old Country Rd., Plainview, NY 11803
Phone: 516-501-6700   **Fax:** 516-501-6762
Web: www.newyorkislanders.com

The New York Islanders play at the 16,234-seat capacity Nassau Veterans Memorial Coliseum in Uniondale, New York.

PRODUCTS/OPERATIONS

Championship Trophies
Stanley Cup (1980-83)
Prince of Wales Trophy (1982-84)
Clarence S. Campbell Bowl (1978-79, 1981)

COMPETITORS

New Jersey Devils
New York Rangers
Philadelphia Flyers
Pittsburgh Penguins

New York Life Insurance

New York Life Insurance has been in the Big Apple since it was just a tiny seed. The company (the top mutual life insurer in the US) is adding products but retaining its core business: life insurance and annuities. New York Life has added such products and services as mutual funds for individuals. It also offers its investment management services to institutional investors. Other lines of business include long-term care insurance and special group policies sold through AARP and other affinity groups or professional associations. The company, through New York Life International, is also reaching out geographically, targeting areas such as Mexico and India where the life insurance markets are not yet mature.

After state legislators rejected a proposed company restructuring, New York Life announced it would not follow its rivals in demutualizing for fear of being gobbled up in a merger.

The insurer instead uses its considerable war chest to further expand its international operations — Asia and Latin America are major expansion targets, and sales growth in both regions has been rapid. It is also expanding its investment management operations through its New York Life Investment Management (mutual funds, group and individual retirement plans, college savings products).

While other big-name insurers in the mature US market are only aiming for high net-worth individual customers, New York Life is also casting its nets a bit lower to catch middle-income consumers and creating products to lure younger families.

HISTORY

In 1841 actuary Pliny Freeman and 56 New York businessmen founded Nautilus Insurance Co., the third US policyholder-owned company. It began operating in 1845 and became New York Life in 1849.

By 1846 the company had the first life insurance agent west of the Mississippi River. Although the Civil War disrupted southern business, New York Life honored all its obligations and renewed lapsed policies when the war ended. By 1887 the company had developed its branch office system.

By the turn of the century, the company had established an agent compensation plan that featured a lifetime income after 20 years of service (discontinued 1991). New York Life moved into Europe in the late 1800s but withdrew after WWI.

In the early 1950s the company simplified insurance forms, slashed premiums, and updated mortality tables from the 1860s. In 1956 it became the first life insurer to use data-processing equipment on a large scale.

New York Life helped develop variable life insurance, which featured variable benefits and level premiums in the 1960s; it added variable annuities in 1968. Steady growth continued into the late 1970s, when high interest rates led to heavy policyholder borrowing. The outflow of money convinced New York Life to make its products more competitive as investments.

The company formed New York Life and Health Insurance Co. in 1982. It acquired MacKay-Shields Financial, which oversees its MainStay mutual funds, in 1984. The company's first pure investment product, a real estate limited partnership, debuted that year. (When limited partnerships proved riskier than most insurance customers bargained for, investors sued New York Life; in 1996 the company negotiated a plan to liquidate the partnerships and reimburse investors.)

Expansion continued in 1987 when New York Life bought a controlling interest in a third-party insurance plan administrator and group insurance programs. The company also acquired Sanus Corp. Health Systems.

New York Life formed an insurance joint venture in Indonesia in 1992; it also entered South Korea and Taiwan. The next year it bought Aetna UK's life insurance operations.

In 1994 New York Life grew its health care holdings, adding utilization review and physician practice management units. Allegations of churning (agents inducing customers to buy more expensive policies) led New York Life to overhaul its sales practices in 1994; it settled the resulting lawsuit for $300 million in 1995. Soon came claims that agents hadn't properly informed customers that some policies were vulnerable to interest-rate changes and that customers might be entitled to share in the settlement. Some agents lashed out, saying New York Life fired them so it wouldn't have to pay them retirement benefits.

As health care margins decreased and the insurance industry consolidated, New York Life in 1998 sold its health insurance operations and said it would demutualize — a plan ultimately foiled by the state legislature.

In 2000 the company bought two Mexican insurance firms, including Seguros Monterrey, that nation's #2 life insurer. It received Office of Thrift Supervision permission to open a bank, New York Life Trust Company. Also that year the company created a subsidiary to house its asset management businesses and entered the Indian market through its joint venture with Max India. In 2002 New York Life entered into a joint life insurance venture with China's Haier Group.

EXECUTIVES

Chairman, President, and CEO:
Theodore A. (Ted) Mathas, age 42
**Vice Chairman and Chief Investment Officer;
Chairman, New York Life Investment Management:**
Gary E. Wendlandt, age 58
EVP and Chief Administrative Officer: Frank M. Boccio
EVP and Chief Distribution Officer, New York Life International: Eric B. Campbell
EVP; CEO, Greater China: Gary R. Bennett
EVP, New York Life Investment Management:
Patrick G. Boyle
EVP and COO, New York Life International:
Russell G. Bundschuh
EVP, New York Life Investment Management:
Frank J. Ollari
EVP and CFO: Michael E. Sproule
EVP; Chairman and CEO, New York Life International:
Richard L. (Dick) Mucci, age 58
EVP and CFO, New York Life International LLC:
Craig A. Merdian
EVP, Chief Legal Officer, and General Counsel:
Sheila K. Davidson
EVP, New York Life Investment Management:
Barry A. Schub
EVP; President and CEO, New York Life Investment Management: John Y. Kim, age 44
EVP US Life Insurance and Agency: Mark W. Pfaff
EVP Retirement Income Security:
Christopher O. (Chris) Blunt
SVP and General Cousel, New York Life International:
Maria G. Gutierrez
SVP, Deputy General Counsel, and Secretary:
Susan A. Thrope
SVP and CIO: Eileen T. Slevin
SVP Corporate Information and CTO: Sue Ericksen
First VP Human Resources: Dorothea Rodd
Chairman and CEO, MacKay Shields: Osbert M. Hood
CEO and Managing Director, Max New York Life:
Rajesh Sud
Auditors: PricewaterhouseCoopers LLP

LOCATIONS

HQ: New York Life Insurance Company
51 Madison Ave., New York, NY 10010
Phone: 212-576-7000   **Fax:** 212-576-8145
Web: www.newyorklife.com

PRODUCTS/OPERATIONS

2008 Sales

	$ mil.	% of total
Premiums	10,647	52
Investment income	7,918	39
Fees	960	5
Investment losses	(3,496)	—
Other	801	4
Total	**16,830**	**100**

COMPETITORS

AIG American General	MetLife
Allstate	Mutual of Omaha
American National	Northwestern Mutual
CIGNA	Principal Financial
CNA Financial	Prudential
Guardian Life	T. Rowe Price
The Hartford	TIAA-CREF
John Hancock Financial	UBS Financial Services
MassMutual	

HISTORICAL FINANCIALS

Company Type: Mutual company

Income Statement   FYE: December 31

	ASSETS ($ mil.)	NET INCOME ($ mil.)	INCOME AS % OF ASSETS	EMPLOYEES
12/08	188,908	(1,016)	—	15,000
12/07	198,383	1,497	0.8%	14,847
12/06	182,343	2,298	1.3%	13,580
12/05	168,865	855	0.5%	13,180
12/04	159,888	1,294	0.8%	12,650
Annual Growth	4.3%	—	—	4.4%

2008 Year-End Financials

Equity as % of assets: —
Return on assets: —
Return on equity: —
Long-term debt ($ mil.): —
Sales ($ mil.): 16,830

Net Income History

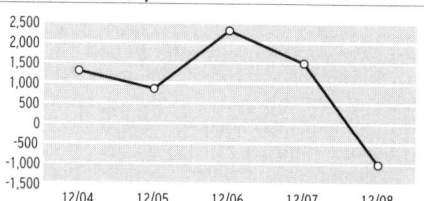

New York Power Authority

Question authority? Well, without question, authority for power lies in the Power Authority of the State of New York (commonly referred to as the New York Power Authority, or NYPA). The company generates and transmits more than 20% of New York's electricity, making it the largest state-owned public power provider in the US. It is also New York's only statewide electricity supplier. NYPA owns hydroelectric and fossil-fueled generating facilities (18 in total) that produce about 5,700 MW of electricity, and it operates more than 1,400 circuit-miles of transmission lines.

The authority sells power to government agencies, municipal systems, rural cooperatives, private companies, private utilities (for resale), and neighboring states. Its clients include some of the largest electricity users in the US, including the New York City government and the Metropolitan Transportation Authority. NYPA receives no state funds or tax credits. Instead, it finances new projects through bond sales.

Following its shift from a regulated monopoly to a competitor in an open power market, NYPA is aiming to grow by reducing the cost of the energy it provides and by developing electric transportation (such as electric cars) and other energy-efficiency projects, such as installing emergency power generators in metropolitan buildings. It is also working to improve the state's transmission grid and increase its generating capacity.

In 2008 the company began public hearings on renewing a long-term power contract with Alcoa involving supplying energy to the manufacturer's two facilities in Massena.

HISTORY

The Power Authority of the State of New York (aka New York Power Authority, or NYPA) was established in 1931 by Gov. Franklin Roosevelt to gain public control of New York's hydropower resources. The utility's major power plants came on line with the opening of the St. Lawrence-Franklin D. Roosevelt Power Project (1958) and the Niagara Power Project (1961). The Blenheim-Gilboa Pumped Storage Power Project opened in 1973.

In the mid-1970s NYPA shifted to nuclear power when it opened the James A. FitzPatrick Nuclear Power Plant (1975) and the Indian Point 3 Nuclear Power Plant (1976). The company then opened gas- and oil-powered plants: the Charles Poletti Power Project (1977) and the Richard M. Flynn Power Plant (1994).

In 1998 the authority allocated low-cost electricity to five companies that planned to invest $104 million in business expansions in western New York. The company suffered a loss in 1999 in part from reduced hydro generation and a drop in investment earnings. In 2000 NYPA sold its two nuclear plants (1,800 MW of capacity) to utility holding company Entergy for $967 million.

The company completed the installation of 11 gas-powered turbines at various locations in New York City and on Long Island in 2001; the program was initiated to prevent expected energy shortages that summer, but it also helped maintain power in areas of the city during the September 11 terrorist attacks.

EXECUTIVES

Chairman: Michael J. Townsend
Vice Chairman: Jonathan F. (Jon) Foster
President and CEO: Richard M. Kessel
COO: Gil C. Quiniones
EVP and Chief Engineer, Power Supply:
 Edward A. Welz
EVP and CFO: Joseph M. Del Sindaco
EVP and General Counsel: Terryl Brown Clemons
Acting EVP Corporate Services and Administration;
 SVP Enterprise Shared Services: Joan Tursi
SVP Transmission: Steven J. DeCarlo
Acting SVP Marketing and Economic Development:
 James F. Pasquale
SVP Energy Services and Technology:
 Angelo S. Esposito
SVP Public and Governmental Affairs: Paul F. Finnegan
SVP Corporate Planning and Finance: Donald A. Russak
SVP Energy Resource Management and Strategic
 Planning: William J. Nadeau
Auditors: Ernst & Young LLP

LOCATIONS

HQ: Power Authority of the State of New York
 123 Main St., Ste. 10-B, White Plains, NY 10601
Phone: 914-681-6200   **Fax:** 914-681-6949
Web: www.nypa.gov

PRODUCTS/OPERATIONS

2008 Sales

	$ mil.	% of total
Power sales	2,643	83
Wheeling charges	388	12
Transmission charges	154	5
Total	**3,185**	**100**

Selected Operations

Transmission Control Facility
 Frederick R. Clark Energy Center (Oneida County)
Fossil-Fueled Plants
 Charles Poletti Power Project (New York City)
 Richard M. Flynn Power Plant (Suffolk County)
 PowerNow! Turbines (11 units in New York City and
 Long Island)
Hydropower Plants
 Blenheim-Gilboa Pumped Storage Power Project
 (Schoharie County)
 Niagara Power Project (Niagara County)
 St. Lawrence-Franklin D. Roosevelt Power Project (St.
 Lawrence County)
Small Hydropower Plants
 Ashokan Project (Ulster County)
 Crescent Plant (Albany and Saratoga Counties)
 Gregory B. Jarvis Plant (Oneida County)
 Kensico Project (Westchester County)
 Vischer Ferry Plant (Saratoga and Schenectady
 counties)

COMPETITORS

CH Energy
Con Edison
Dynegy
Enbridge
Energy East
Entergy
National Grid USA
Rochester Gas and Electric
TransCanada

HISTORICAL FINANCIALS

Company Type: Government-owned

Income Statement

FYE: December 31

	REVENUE ($ mil.)	NET INCOME ($ mil.)	NET PROFIT MARGIN	EMPLOYEES
12/08	3,185	299	9.4%	1,559
12/07	2,906	235	8.1%	1,600
12/06	2,666	137	5.1%	1,600
12/05	2,506	58	2.3%	1,600
12/04	2,215	82	3.7%	1,600
Annual Growth	**9.5%**	**38.2%**	**—**	**(0.6%)**

2008 Year-End Financials

Debt ratio: 67.9%   Current ratio: —
Return on equity: —   Long-term debt ($ mil.): 1,744
Cash ($ mil.): —

Net Income History

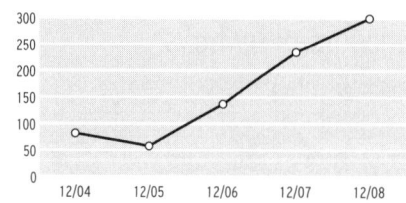

New York State Lottery

Winning the New York State Lottery could make you king of the hill, top of the heap. The New York State Lottery is one of the largest and oldest state lotteries in the US (only New Hampshire's lottery is older). It runs three jackpot, five daily, and about a dozen scratch-off games through retailers and online outlets. About a third of the lottery's revenue, or some $2 billion a year, goes to support New York State education. It also awards Leaders of Tomorrow scholarships to one eligible graduating senior from every public and private school in the state (provided they attend New York universities). The New York Lottery was established by the new state constitution passed in 1966.

The New York State Lottery has raised more than $30 billion for state educational programs since its inception. In addition to education, proceeds from the lottery have helped pay for the construction of New York City Hall, as well as bridges and roads for the state. It also sponsors the Empire State Games, an amateur athletic competition. The lottery returns more than half the money it takes in as prizes; 33% of sales go to aid education.

HISTORY

In the mid-1960s the New York state legislature succeeded in sending a lottery amendment to voters, and 60% of New Yorkers voted in favor of the amendment in 1966. Lottery sales began in 1967 with a raffle-style drawing game. In its first year of operation, the lottery contributed more than $26 million to the state's education fund.

New York introduced its first instant game in 1976, with sales topping $18 million the first week. The state debuted its six-of-six lotto game two years later. Sales were slow until 1981, when Louie "the Light Bulb" Eisenberg — the state's first lottery celebrity — won $5 million, the largest single-winner prize at that time.

GTECH won the contract to operate New York's lottery terminal sales in 1987. The Quick Pick option — through which a terminal chooses a player's numbers — was introduced in 1989, as was a new lotto game and the state's first online computer terminal game. Autoworker Antonio Bueti set a record for the largest individual prize, winning $35 million in 1990. A jackpot of $90 million was split among nine players in 1991.

Through the mid-1990s, however, lackluster lottery sales were blamed on the Persian Gulf War, the recession, and poor publicity. During 1993 and 1994 lottery management revamped the state's lottery infrastructure and redesigned some games. The investment paid off in October 1994 when lotto fever pushed a jackpot to $72.5 million. During the height of the frenzy, sales reached $46,000 a minute.

Quick Draw, a game in which players choose numbers every five minutes, was added in 1995. Sales of the game topped $1 million on the second day, and soon it was grossing nearly $12 million a week. Real estate mogul Donald Trump unsuccessfully sued to stop Quick Draw, claiming that it was more addictive than (his) casinos and would encourage organized crime. That year the New York State Lottery became the first to reach $3 billion in sales in a single year.

In 1996 the state pulled its Quick Draw advertising after critics complained it encouraged compulsive gambling. Lottery officials replaced enticing ads with advertising stressing the lottery's benefits to state education. The lottery was the subject of a sting operation that year led by Governor George Pataki to crack down on lottery vendors selling tickets to minors. In 1997 the lottery spawned its own game show with the debut of *NY Wired*, a half-hour weekly program pitting vendor representatives against each other for cash prizes given to audience members and schools.

With sales slipping, the state left longtime ad partner DDB Needham Worldwide (now DDB Worldwide) in 1998 and signed a $28 million contract with Grey Advertising (later Grey Group). Lottery director Jeff Perlee resigned the next year. He was replaced by Margaret DeFrancisco, who helped drum up sales with Millennium Millions, which paid out a record $100 million prize to Johnnie Ely, a cook from the South Bronx, on the eve of 2000. Two players shared a record $130 million jackpot later in the year.

After holding out for years, the New York legislature in late 2001 authorized a bill that would allow state residents to participate in the multi-state Powerball lottery. In 2002 the New York Lottery joined with the nine-state Big Game Group to launch the Mega Millions game, which replaced the Big Game established in 1996. By 2005, Mega Millions had 12 participating states and New York had nine winners in the game.

EXECUTIVES

Executive Director: Gordon Medenica
Deputy Director and Director Operations:
  Gardner S. Gurney
CIO: Ray Sestak
Director Video Game: Jim Nielsen
Director Sales and Marketing: Randall Lex
Director Human Resource Management:
  Lisa A. Fitzmaurice
Director Internal Audit: John R. McNulty
Director Communications: John E. Charlson
Director Research and Development: Tim Iacabucci
Director Administration: Frank Roddy
Director Lottery Game: Patrick K. Frament
Deputy Director and General Counsel:
  William J. (Bill) Murray
Senior Attorney: Julie Barker
Special Assistant: Susan E. Miller
Auditors: KPMG LLP

LOCATIONS

HQ: New York State Lottery
1 Broadway Center, Schenectady, NY 12301
Phone: 518-388-3300   **Fax:** 518-388-3403
Web: www.nylottery.org

PRODUCTS/OPERATIONS

2007 Revenue Allocation

	% of sales
Prizes	55
Aid to Education	33
Commissions for Traditional Lottery Facilities	6
Commissions for Video Gaming Facilities	3
Other	3
Total	**100**

COMPETITORS

Connecticut Lottery
Massachusetts State Lottery
Multi-State Lottery
New Hampshire Lottery
New Jersey Lottery
Pennsylvania Lottery
Vermont Lottery

New York University

Higher education is at the core of this Big Apple institution. The setting and heritage of New York University (NYU) make it one of the nation's most popular educational institutions. With more than 50,000 students attending its 14 schools and colleges, NYU is among the largest private schools in the US. Its Tisch School of the Arts is well regarded, and its law school and Leonard N. Stern School of Business are among the foremost in the country. NYU occupies five major centers in Manhattan; its Washington Square campus is in the heart of Greenwich Village. The school was founded in 1831. Notable alumni include former Federal Reserve Chairman Alan Greenspan and film producer Oliver Stone.

NYU is one of the largest employers in New York City, with more than 16,000 employees. International students make up about 10% of the school's student body. Undergraduate tuition for the university runs more than $37,000 per year.

HISTORY

New York University was founded by several prominent New Yorkers in 1831. The school held its first classes the following year in rented rooms on the corner of Beekman and Nassau streets, then moved to a building in Washington Square in 1835. It established its law school that year. NYU started its school of medicine in 1841, followed by the school of engineering and science (1854). Postgraduate studies in arts and science (its first coeducational program) began in 1886.

NYU's enrollment jumped from fewer than 2,000 in 1900 to 28,000 in 1930. After a lull during the Depression and WWII, the campus boomed again in the postwar years. During the 1950s the university began focusing on improving academics rather than on increasing enrollment. It created a school of the arts in 1965, and in the early 1970s it completed the Elmer Holmes Bobst Library. However, a cash crunch during that decade almost forced the school into bankruptcy.

President Jay Oliva took the reins in 1981 and focused on transforming NYU from a largely commuter college into a global university. The school began a campaign to raise $1 billion in 1984, but earmarked the funds for campus improvements rather than swelling its endowment. During the late 1980s NYU opened several new dormitories and conference spaces. In 1994 British historian and collector Sir Harold Acton bequeathed to the school his Tuscany estate — five art-filled villas overlooking Florence, Italy.

In 1996 NYU's Medical Center began talks with Mount Sinai Medical Center aimed at merging their hospitals and medical schools. The talks fell apart in early 1997, but the following year the two sides agreed to merge hospitals and keep their medical schools distinct. Also in 1998 NYU formed NYU On-Line, Inc., a for-profit subsidiary to develop and sell specialized Internet courses to other schools, training centers, and students; the venture was subsequently folded in late 2001.

During 1999 contributions to the school approached $250 million. That year, however, two upper-level school officials were fired following allegations of improper use of university money.

Oliva retired as president in 2002 and was replaced by John Sexton, former School of Law dean. In 2004 Sexton announced that NYU would give $1 million to New York City toward renovation of Washington Square Park (the school annually gives some $200,000 for the park's ongoing maintenance).

EXECUTIVES

Chairman: Martin Lipton
Honorary Vice Chair: Larry A. Silverstein, age 72
Honorary Vice Chair: Thomas S. Murphy
Vice Chair: Leonard A. Wilf
Vice Chair: Kenneth G. Langone, age 73
Vice Chair: William R. Berkley, age 63
President and Trustee: John E. Sexton, age 59
Provost: David W. McLaughlin
Chief of Staff and Deputy to the President: Diane C. Yu
Associate Provost and CIO: Marilyn McMillan
Dean, Tisch School of the Arts:
  Mary Schmidt Campbell
Dean, College of Arts and Science:
  Matthew S. Santirocco
Chair, Faculty Advisory Committee on Academic Priorities; Dean, Faculty of Arts and Science:
  Richard Foley
EVP: Michael C. Alfano, age 61
SVP Development and Alumni Relations:
  Debra A. LaMorte
SVP University Relations and Public Affairs:
  Lynne P. Brown
SVP, General Counsel, and Secretary: Bonnie Brier
SVP Finance and Budget: Martin S. Dorph
Chief of Staff to the EVP and VP for Administration:
  Steven Donofrio
VP Human Resources: Catherine M. Casey
Auditors: KPMG LLP

LOCATIONS

HQ: New York University
70 Washington Sq. South, New York, NY 10012
Phone: 212-998-1212   **Fax:** 212-995-4040
Web: www.nyu.edu

PRODUCTS/OPERATIONS

Selected Schools and Colleges

College of Arts and Science (founded 1832)
College of Dentistry (1865)
Courant Institute of Mathematical Sciences (1934)
Gallatin School of Individualized Study (1972)
Graduate School of Arts and Science (1886)
Leonard N. Stern School of Business (1900)
Robert F. Wagner Graduate School of Public Service (1938)
School of Continuing and Professional Studies (1934)
School of Law (1835)
School of Medicine (1841)
School of Social Work (1960)
Steinhardt School of Culture, Education, and Human Development (1890)
Tisch School of the Arts (1965)

New York Yankees

These Yanks are a big hit with New York baseball fans. New York Yankees Partnership owns and operates the New York Yankees professional baseball team, one of the most storied and popular clubs in Major League Baseball. The franchise boasts a record 27 World Series titles and 40 American League pennants, making it the most successful professional sports team in history. Along with that success, the Yankees organization has been associated with such sports icons as Babe Ruth, Lou Gehrig, Joe DiMaggio, and Mickey Mantle. Once known as the Highlanders, the Yankees have represented New York City since 1903. The Steinbrenner family, now led by George Steinbrenner's son Hal, has controlled the team since in 1973.

While the boys in pinstripes often appear to be in a class by themselves, the ball club is really no different from any other sports team. Ticket sales are the primary source of revenue, and the best way to get people in the stands is to win games. The big difference between the Yankees and other teams is that the franchise's ownership is willing to spend big for all-star talent to win those games, so much so that New York has perennially had the highest payroll in the majors.

One downside to all that free spending is that under MLB's collective bargaining agreement, the franchise has to give a percentage of its excess payroll back to the league to be distributed to smaller-market teams. The Yankees are the only franchise to be hit with the luxury tax each year since the agreement was struck in 2002; its 2008 payment was more than $26 million.

The Steinbrenners augmented their deep pockets with a new stadium in 2009 to help keep their team stocked with talent. The Yankees moved into a new Yankee Stadium across the street from the team's historic digs, better known as The House that Ruth Built. The $1.5 billion, 52,000-seat capacity facility features expanded space for luxury suites, restaurants, and other amenities to generate additional revenue for the franchise. The Yankee's original ballpark, built in 1923, is slated to be demolished to make way for a park.

The franchise also generates revenue from broadcasting deals, merchandise sales, and marketing partnerships. The Steinbrenners also control 60% of sports cable channel Yankees Entertainment & Sports (YES Network).

The team's roster of expensive and talented players, including Derek Jeter, Hideki Matsui, and Alex Rodriguez, has not always added up to championship titles, but in 2009 the Yanks won the World Series over the defending champion Philadelphia Phillies in six games. It was the first title for New York since 2000, a streak that led to the ousting of longtime skipper Joe Torre after an early post-season exit in 2007. Former Florida Marlins manager Joe Girardi replaced him.

The change in the dugout coincided with a change in front office leadership as the aging George Steinbrenner handed the reigns of daily responsibility to his sons Hank and Hal. (Hal, the younger sibling, formally replaced his father as controlling partner following the 2008 season; Hank remained as co-chairman of the team.)

HISTORY

Frank Farrell and Bill Devery purchased the Baltimore Orioles franchise (formed 1901) in 1903 for $18,000 and brought the team to New York. Known as the Highlanders, the team played at Hilltop Park. In 1913 the team changed its name to the Yankees, and two years later it was bought by Jacob Ruppert and Tillinghast L'Hommedieu Huston. (Ruppert bought out Huston in 1922.) The Yankees started down the path to greatness when they bought George Herman (Babe) Ruth from the Boston Red Sox for $125,000 in 1920. Three years later the team moved into Yankee Stadium. With icons such as Lou Gehrig (1923) and Joe DiMaggio (1936), the Yankees won 14 American League pennants and 10 World Series titles by 1943.

The club changed hands again in 1945 when Dan Topping, Del Webb, and Larry MacPhail bought the team for almost $3 million. The Yankees continued to collect championship titles throughout the 1950s and into the next decade. CBS bought 80% of the team in 1964 for more than $11 million. Coincidentally, the Yankees didn't win another pennant for 12 years. A partnership led by Cleveland shipbuilder George Steinbrenner bought the team from CBS in 1973. With slugger Reggie Jackson, the Yankees won three consecutive pennants and back-to-back World Series over the Los Angeles Dodgers (1977, 1978). But trouble between the meddling Steinbrenner and his managers (notably Billy Martin) helped quiet things during the 1980s.

The Yankees returned to championship form in 1996 under manager Joe Torre. The team set an AL record for most wins in the regular season (114) in 1998 and swept the San Diego Padres to win the World Series. The following year the Yankees repeated as champions, sweeping Atlanta in the 1999 World Series. The team increased its financial clout later that year by merging with pro basketball's New Jersey Nets. The resulting holding company, YankeeNets, attempted to form a cable network with IMG the following year, but MSG Network, which owned the rights to televise Yankee games, balked at the plan and won a ruling from the New York Supreme Court that ended the proposed partnership. Later in 2000 the Yankees won their third straight World Series title, defeating their cross-town rivals the New York Mets in the city's first Subway Series since 1956.

Putting its formidable wealth to good use, the Yankees signed star shortstop Derek Jeter to a 10-year, $189 million contract in early 2001. The team finally lost a World Series, to the Arizona Diamondbacks, that year The next year it launched the 60%-owned Yankees Entertainment & Sports cable channel. Reaching the World Series in 2003, the Yanks once again came up short, losing to the Florida Marlins. Later that year the Nets and Yankees dissolved their YankeeNets partnership. The following year, in an historic meltdown, the team won the AL East division title for the seventh year in a row but lost to the Boston Red Sox in the AL Championship Series. Boston went on to win the World Series for the first time in 86 years.

New York's post-season struggles continued in 2005 and 2006; despite a payroll hovering near $200 million, the Yankees were ejected from the playoffs after divisional series losses each year. The team lost again during the post-season in 2007, leading to the ouster of manager Torre.

EXECUTIVES

Principal Owner and Chairperson:
George M. Steinbrenner III, age 79
Managing General Partner and Co-Chairperson:
Harold Z. (Hal) Steinbrenner
General Partner and Co-Chairperson:
Henry G. (Hank) Steinbrenner
General Partner and Vice Chairperson:
Jennifer Steinbrenner Swindal
General Partner and Vice Chairperson:
Jessica Steinbrenner
Vice Chairperson: Joan Steinbrenner
President: Randy Levine
COO: Lonn A. Trost
SVP Marketing: Deborah A. (Debbie) Tymon
SVP Corporate and Community Relations: Brian Smith
SVP Baseball Operations: Mark Newman
SVP Strategic Ventures: Martin (Marty) Greenspun
SVP and Chief Security Officer: Sonny Hight
SVP Business Development: Jim Ross
SVP Corporate Sales and Sponsorships:
Michael J. Tusiani
SVP and General Manager: Brian Cashman
VP and CFO, Accounting: Robert Brown
VP and CFO, Financial Operations: Scott Krug
Team Manager: Joe Girardi
Director Human Resources: Betsy Peluso

LOCATIONS

HQ: New York Yankees Partnership
Yankee Stadium, E. 161st St. and River Ave.
Bronx, NY 10451
Phone: 718-293-4300   **Fax:** 718-293-8431
Web: newyork.yankees.mlb.com

The New York Yankees play at 52,325-seat capacity Yankee Stadium in Bronx, New York.

PRODUCTS/OPERATIONS

Championship Titles

World Series (1923, 1927-28, 1932, 1936-39, 1941, 1943, 1947, 1949-53, 1956, 1958, 1961-62, 1977-78, 1996, 1998-2000, 2009)
American League Pennant (1921-23, 1926-28, 1932, 1936-39, 1941-43, 1947, 1949-53, 1955-58, 1960-64, 1976-78, 1981, 1996, 1998-2001, 2003, 2009)

COMPETITORS

Baltimore Orioles
Boston Red Sox
Tampa Bay Rays
Toronto Blue Jays

HISTORICAL FINANCIALS

Company Type: Private

Income Statement

FYE: December 31

	REVENUE ($ mil.)	NET INCOME ($ mil.)	NET PROFIT MARGIN	EMPLOYEES
12/08	375	—	—	—
12/07	327	—	—	—
12/06	302	—	—	—
12/05	277	—	—	—
12/04	264	—	—	—
Annual Growth	9.2%	—	—	—

Revenue History

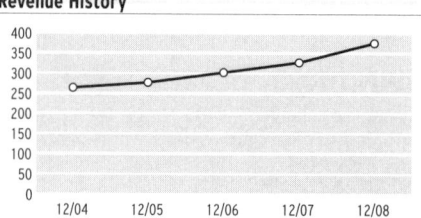

The Newark Group

The Newark Group is proof that one man's trash is another man's cash. The Group is a top producer and seller of paper goods from recycled paperboard and secondary fibers. It comprises three business units. A paperboard operation recovers some 3 million tons of paper annually, from corrugated containers to newspaper and mixed paper. A converted products unit manufactures laminated papers and graphic board, tube, core and related goods, and solidboard packaging. In Europe, an international unit makes corresponding products. Brands include Fiberwrap (paperboard), NewEx (graphicboard), NewForm (concrete forms), and Fortex (coverboard). Industry customers crisscross paper and packaging, printing and construction.

The Group's success is driven by sales prices for its waste paper and converted products, as well as consumer spending, balanced by mill production volume and operating costs, including recovered paper, energy, and transportation. Supported by 20 facilities, the paperboard business segment is the largest of the company's three operations, accounting for more than half of the company's sales. It involves the manufacture of recycled paperboard in several grades, and collection of recovered paper from various sources. Discarded packaging from large retailers is the biggest contributor to the recovered paper operation, accounting for more than 40%; industrial and other commercial customers account for about a third of its raw material.

The Group's next largest segment, converted products, supplies about 30% of the material used in its paperboard manufacturing. Accounting for nearly 30% of the company's sales, the converted products segment is responsible for making laminated and graphicboard products used for a range of products, such as game boards and book covers. It also makes tubes and cores, around which paper, tape, and textiles can be wrapped, and solidboard, which is used to make packaging for produce and other food goods. The Group's international segment oversees the paperboard and converted products operations at the company's six converting plants and three recycled paperboard mills.

Caught up in the recessionary wave of spiking costs and shrinking demand for everything from office supplies to appliances, 2008-09 demand for the paper recycler's lineup has plunged. The Group has shifted operations to compensate for its resulting overcapacity; it closed its Natick, Massachusetts mill in 2005, its sixth closure since 2001. In 2008, the Group pulled the plug on its #1 paper machine at a California mill, and subsequently shuttered two plants in New York, and one in California. Moreover, passing on the increased costs of raw material and energy by increasing its selling price has been stifled by the weak demand and fierce industry competition.

Adding to its woes, in 2009 the Group defaulted in paying the interest due on its debt, tripping a limited waiver and forbearance agreement by holders of the Group's notes. The agreement has been extended to allow the Group an opportunity to improve its capital position.

EXECUTIVES

Chairman, President, and CEO: Robert H. Mullen, age 56, $536,153 total compensation
Vice Chairman: Edward K. Mullen, age 86, $425,609 total compensation
SVP Converted Products: Philip B. Jones, age 60
SVP, Paperboard Mills: Richard M. Poppe, age 54, $363,988 total compensation
SVP European Operations: William D. (Bill) Harper, age 66, $431,452 total compensation
VP and Controller: Lynn M. Herro
VP and CFO: Joseph E. (Joe) Byrne, age 49, $325,923 total compensation
VP Human Resources: Carl R. Crook
VP, General Counsel, and Secretary: David Ascher, age 56
Auditors: Deloitte & Touche LLP

LOCATIONS

HQ: The Newark Group, Inc.
20 Jackson Dr., Cranford, NJ 07016
Phone: 908-276-4000   **Fax:** 908-276-2888
Web: www.newarkgroup.com

PRODUCTS/OPERATIONS

Selected Products

Recycled Fibers
  Corrugated products
  Envelopes
  Newspapers
  Printing grades
  Roll stock
Recycled Paperboard
  Boxboard
  Clay-coated folding board
  Separator stock
  Tube and core grades

COMPETITORS

Caraustar
Carter Holt Harvey
Eagle Materials
Georgia-Pacific
Graphic Packaging
Green Bay Packaging
International Paper
Oji Paper
Parsons & Whittemore
Rock-Tenn
Smurfit Kappa
Smurfit-Stone Container
Sonoco Products
Southern Container
Unipapel
Weyerhaeuser

HISTORICAL FINANCIALS

Company Type: Private

Income Statement

FYE: April 30

	REVENUE ($ mil.)	NET INCOME ($ mil.)	NET PROFIT MARGIN	EMPLOYEES
4/08	1,029	—	—	3,166
4/07	923	—	—	3,169
4/06	852	—	—	3,222
4/05	882	—	—	3,328
4/04	788	—	—	3,358
Annual Growth	6.9%	—	—	(1.5%)

Revenue History

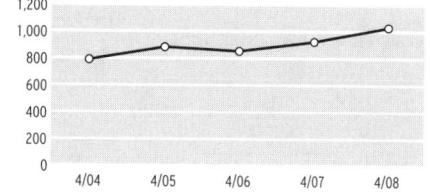

The Newton Group

The Newton Group, which operates as Strategic Products and Services (SPS), provides voice, data, and video networking services, including network design and installation, training, and technical support. Serving customers ranging from small businesses to multinational corporations, it integrates technology from Avaya, Cisco Systems, Extreme Networks, Juniper Networks, and Microsoft. In addition to design and installation, SPS provides phone, Internet, and other data services through partnerships with such carriers as AT&T. Established in 1988, the company has offices throughout New England and the Midwest, as well as the Mid-Atlantic and South Atlantic states.

EXECUTIVES

Chairman, President, and CEO: John N. Poole
COO: James R. (Jim) Felicetti
CTO and VP Emerging Technologies: Michael W. (Mike) Taylor
Director Marketing: Theresa Goodreau
VP Finance: Brian Crowe
VP Implementation Services: Ronald J. (Ron) Scavuzzo
VP Services and Operations: Nevelle R. (Vel) Johnson
VP Sales: James P. Maynard
Human Resources and Administration: Sue Mullen

LOCATIONS

HQ: The Newton Group, Inc.
300 Littleton Rd., Ste. 200, Parsippany, NJ 07054
Phone: 973-540-0600   **Fax:** 973-540-1221
Web: www.spscom.com

COMPETITORS

Altura Communication Solutions
Black Box
BT Global Services
Carousel Industries
CDW
CompuCom
Computer Design and Integration
HP Enterprise Services
MTM Technologies
Pomeroy IT
Software House
Unisys

HISTORICAL FINANCIALS

Company Type: Private

Income Statement

FYE: December 31

	REVENUE ($ mil.)	NET INCOME ($ mil.)	NET PROFIT MARGIN	EMPLOYEES
12/08	97	—	—	300
12/07	97	—	—	300
12/06	97	—	—	296
12/05	80	—	—	270
12/04	60	—	—	200
Annual Growth	12.8%	—	—	10.7%

Revenue History

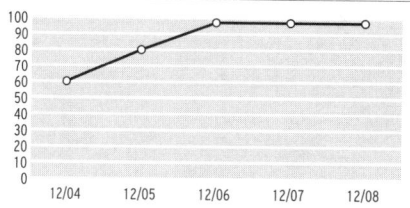

Noodles & Company

Forty lashes with a wet you-know-what if you don't like what this restaurant company offers. Noodles & Company operates and franchises more than 200 quick-casual restaurants in about 20 states that specialize in noodle entrees ranging in style from American to Asian to Mediterranean. The chain's menu includes noodle and vegetable bowls, soups, and green salads with pasta. Most of the eateries are company-owned. Founder Aaron Kennedy, a former brand manager at PepsiCo who opened the first Noodles & Company location in 1995, owns the company with a group of private investors.

Having expanded primarily through opening corporate-owned locations, Noodles & Company has been ramping up its franchising operation to accelerate its growth. Kevin Reddy, who previously worked for quick-casual restaurant operator Chipotle Mexican Grill, took over from Kennedy who stepped down as CEO in 2006.

EXECUTIVES

Chairman, President, and CEO: Kevin Reddy
CFO, COO, and Director: Keith Kinsey
EVP, General Counsel, and Secretary: Paul A. Strasen
Chief Administrative Officer: Dawn Voss
Creative Director: Susan Aust
Executive Chef: Ross Kamens
Director Marketing: Susan Shassetz
Director Corporate Communications: Jill Preston
Director Human Resources: Carol A. Nasta
VP Information Technology: David (Dave) Lehn
VP and Controller: Kathy Lockhart
VP Marketing: Dan Fogarty
VP Real Estate: Tim Mosbacher
VP Construction: Sam Herston
VP Supply Chain: Joe Gordan
VP Finance: Dave Boennighausen
VP Franchise Initiatives: Wayne Humphrey
Auditors: Deloitte & Touche

LOCATIONS

HQ: Noodles & Company
520 Zang St., Broomfield, CO 80021
Phone: 720-214-1900   **Fax:** 720-214-1934
Web: www.noodles.com

COMPETITORS

Café de Coral
California Pizza Kitchen
Camille's Sidewalk Cafe
Carlson Restaurants
CBC Restaurant
Chipotle
Einstein Noah Restaurant Group
Fresh Enterprises
Garden Fresh Restaurants
Moe's Southwest Grill
Panda Restaurant Group
Panera Bread
P.F. Chang's
Qdoba Restaurants

HISTORICAL FINANCIALS

Company Type: Private

Income Statement

FYE: December 31

	REVENUE ($ mil.)	NET INCOME ($ mil.)	NET PROFIT MARGIN	EMPLOYEES
12/07	130	—	—	4,500
12/06	115	—	—	3,900
12/05	106	—	—	3,000
12/04	90	—	—	3,000
12/03	70	—	—	2,100
Annual Growth	16.7%	—	—	21.0%

Revenue History

North Atlantic Trading Company

North Atlantic Trading Company is on the straight and narrow but it prefers its business path to incorporate plenty of Zig-Zags. Its North Atlantic Operating Company (NAOC), best known for its Zig-Zag brand of rolling papers, is a top importer and distributor of cigarette rolling papers in the US. NAOC also sells several styles of tobaccos, rolling machines, and accoutrements. North Atlantic Trading's National Tobacco subsidiary is a leading maker of chewing tobacco in the US on the strength of its bestselling Beech-Nut chaw, as well as Havana Blossom, Trophy, Stoker, and others. Chairman Thomas F. Helms Jr. owns about 49% of North Atlantic Trading.

The company's National Tobacco Company plans to shutter its tobacco manufacturing and distribution facility in Louisville, Kentucky, by the end of 2009. Production at the facility, which makes loose leaf tobacco, will be transferred to the company's Owensboro, Kentucky, plant under an agreement with Swedish Match North America.

The bearded icon emblazoned on the Zig-Zag label is that of a French soldier named Zouave. When his clay pipe broke, he rolled his tobacco in gunpowder paper. The company's primary brand gets its name from the process of interleaving papers in a zig-zag manner. The Braunstein Brothers were credited with having perfected this process in 1894.

EXECUTIVES

Chairman: Thomas F. Helms Jr., age 68
Vice Chairman: Jack Africk, age 80
President and CEO: Lawrence S. Wexler, age 54
SVP and CFO: Brian C. Harriss, age 60
SVP, General Counsel, and Secretary: James W. Dobbins, age 49
SVP, Market Planning and Strategy: James M. Murray, age 48
VP, Finance: Camilla Fentress
Auditors: McGladrey & Pullen, LLP

LOCATIONS

HQ: North Atlantic Trading Company, Inc.
777 Post Rd., Ste. 304, Darien, CT 06820
Phone: 203-202-9547   **Fax:** 230-656-3731
Web: www.zigzag.com

PRODUCTS/OPERATIONS

Selected Brands

Beech-Nut
Beech-Nut Wintergreen
Classic American Blend
Durango
Havana Blossom
Trophy
Zig-Zag

COMPETITORS

Altria
British American Tobacco
Conwood
Imperial Tobacco
Philip Morris USA
Reynolds American
Reynolds S.A.
Swedish Match
Swisher International
UST llc
Vector Group

HISTORICAL FINANCIALS

Company Type: Private

Income Statement

FYE: December 31

	REVENUE ($ mil.)	NET INCOME ($ mil.)	NET PROFIT MARGIN	EMPLOYEES
12/07	123	—	—	299
12/06	118	—	—	299
12/05	117	—	—	289
12/04	115	—	—	296
12/03	102	—	—	292
Annual Growth	4.9%	—	—	0.6%

Revenue History

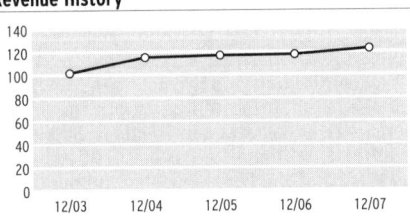

North Pacific Group

Paneling, poles, planks, pilings, and all, North Pacific Group is building on the construction industry. The company is one of North America's largest wholesale distributors of building materials. Through about 30 locations in 15 states, North Pacific sells wood, poles, flooring and roofing supplies, agricultural products, and food items. Customers include lumber yards, farm supply retailers, furniture makers, utility providers, and food manufacturers. The company was founded by Doug David in 1948. Employee-owned since David's 1986 retirement, North Pacific announced in mid-2009 that it has agreed to be acquired by an unnamed private equity firm.

The deal was announced as the company faced a downturn in the Oregon timber market. As part of the pending transaction, North Pacific will sell all of its stock to a "nationally recognized" firm, which to date remains unnamed. North Pacific anticipates that the deal will enable it to continue growing in the US and reduce its dependence on the banking industry. Wood products, such as lumber, millwork, and poles, have traditionally accounted for the majority of the company's sales. Yet it has been North Pacific's agricultural and food products that helped it to stay afloat amid the economic downturn.

EXECUTIVES

President and CEO: Jay A. Ross
CFO and Treasurer: Christopher D. Cassard
SVP, Southern Group: Frank Johnson
SVP, Industrial Wood Products: Jack Clark
SVP HR: Tacy Lind
SVP Commodity Products: Gregg Wilkinson
SVP, Specialty Products Business Unit: Kyle Burdick
SVP, Building Products Distribution: Tom Le Vere
VP Marketing: Monique Bauer
Auditors: KPMG LLP

LOCATIONS

HQ: North Pacific Group, Inc.
10200 SW Greenburg Rd., Portland, OR 97223
Phone: 503-231-1166   **Fax:** 503-238-2641
Web: www.north-pacific.com

PRODUCTS/OPERATIONS

Selected Products

Birdseed and grain seeds
Conventional and organic oils and vinegars
Decking, siding and flooring
Domestic and imported hardwoods
Engineered wood products
Ingredients and processed foods
Laminate panels
Manufactured housings, fencing, siding, and shingles
Moulding, timbers, blanks and cut stock
Plywood
Soil amendments: fertilizer, gypsum and limestone
Steel, aluminum and concrete poles
Wood poles and piling

COMPETITORS

ABC Supply	Louisiana-Pacific
Arthur Lumber	MAXXAM
Bradco Supply	McFarland Cascade
Building Materials	PrimeSource Building
Georgia-Pacific	Sierra Pacific Industries
Guardian Building	Simpson Investment
Products	Temple-Inland
Huttig Building Products	Weyerhaeuser

HISTORICAL FINANCIALS

Company Type: Private

Income Statement

FYE: December 31

	REVENUE ($ mil.)	NET INCOME ($ mil.)	NET PROFIT MARGIN	EMPLOYEES
12/08	1,000	—	—	626
12/07	1,200	—	—	780
12/06	1,200	—	—	769
12/05	1,232	—	—	813
12/04	1,450	—	—	862
Annual Growth	(8.9%)	—	—	(7.7%)

Revenue History

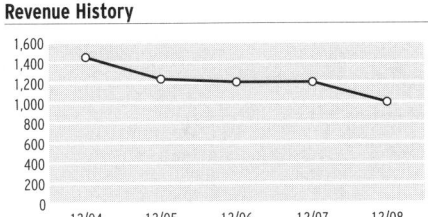

Northwestern Mutual Life Insurance

Keep an eye on the quiet ones. Northwestern Mutual Life Insurance, touting itself as "The Quiet Company," is one of the largest US life insurers with more than $1 trillion in individual policies in force. Its 7,000 representatives sell a lineup of life, disability, long-term care, and employee benefits products (health, dental, 401(k) plans). It also offers retirement products, including annuities and mutual funds, to a clientele of small businesses and prosperous individuals. Its institutional asset manager Frank Russell Company is known for the Russell 2000 stock index. Northwestern Mutual also offers brokerage and trust services through its investment services and wealth management subsidiaries.

While life insurance is generally not a glitzy industry, Northwestern Mutual takes staid and steady to another level. The company would "enter the 21st century as we left the 19th," according to former chairman and CEO James D. Ericson (who retired in mid-2001).

And, while it did reorganize to highlight its wealth management products, life insurance still accounts for the majority of the company's revenues. Northwestern Mutual also rode through an industry trend of demutualizing and remains committed to ownership by its more than 3 million policyholders. Being cautious and deliberate by nature served the company well during the economic turmoil of 2008 and 2009. With no debt and plenty of premiums squirreled away in low-risk investments, it spent the months of crisis calmly dusting off its triple-A ratings, paying out dividends, and attracting new agents.

One piece of housekeeping it attended to: in late 2008, the company agreed to pay as much as $92 million to settle a class action lawsuit filed in 2004. The plaintiffs alleged that the company's sales materials were misleading regarding certain term life and disability insurance policies. Northwestern Mutual maintained that it had acted fairly, but settled the case to limit its exposure to additional litigation expenses.

HISTORY

In 1854, at age 72, John Johnston, a successful New York insurance agent, moved to Wisconsin to become a farmer. Three years later Johnston returned to the insurance business when he and 36 others formed Mutual Life Insurance (changed to Northwestern Mutual Life Insurance in 1865). From the beginning, the company's goal was to become better, not just bigger.

The company continued to offer level-premium life insurance in the 1920s, while competitors offered new types of products. This failure to rise to new demands brought a decline in market share that lasted into the 1940s.

Northwestern Mutual automated in the late 1950s. In 1962 it introduced the Insurance Service Account, whereby all policies owned by a family or business could be consolidated into one monthly premium and paid with pre-authorized checks. In 1968 Northwestern Mutual inaugurated Extra Ordinary Life (EOL), which combined whole and term life insurance, using dividends to convert term to paid-up whole life each year. EOL soon became the company's most popular product.

Suffering from a low profile, in 1972 the insurer kicked off its "The Quiet Company" ad campaign during the summer Olympics. Public awareness of Northwestern Mutual jumped. But even in advertising, the company was staid; a revamped Quiet Company campaign made a return Olympic appearance 24 years later in another effort to raise the public's consciousness.

In the 1980s Northwestern Mutual began financing leveraged buyouts, gaining direct ownership of companies. Investments included two-thirds of flooring maker Congoleum (with other investors); it also bought majority interests in Milwaukee securities firm Robert W. Baird (1982) and mortgage guarantee insurer MGIC Investment (1985; later divested).

The firm stayed out of the 1980s mania for fast money and high-risk diversification. Instead, it devoted itself almost religiously to its core business, despite indications that it was a shrinking market.

In the early 1990s new life policy purchases slowed and the agency force declined — ominous signs, since insurers make their premium income on retained policies, and continued sales are crucial to growth. Northwestern Mutual reversed the trend, adding administrative support for its agents, using database marketing to target new customers, and increasing the cross-selling of products among existing customers. The result was a record-setting 1996.

With the financial services industry consolidating, Northwestern Mutual in 1997 moved into the mutual fund business by setting up its Mason Street Funds.

In the 1990s many large mutuals sought to demutualize, and in 1998 Northwestern Mutual, politically influential in Wisconsin, successfully lobbied for legislation to permit demutualization, citing the need to be able to move quickly in shifting markets.

To expand its wealth management services, in 1999 the company acquired Frank Russell Company, a pension management firm. The acquisition gave Northwestern Mutual a foothold in global investment management and analytical services (the Russell 2000 index). In 2001 the firm opened Northwestern Mutual Trust, a wholly owned personal trust services subsidiary.

In 2004 the employees of Robert W. Baird completed a buyback of Northwestern Mutual's stake in the firm.

EXECUTIVES

Chairman and CEO: Edward J. Zore, age 64
President and Trustee: John E. Schlifske, age 49
VP and CFO: Michael G. Carter, age 47
VP and Chief Actuary: David R. Remstad
CIO: Timothy G. Schaefer
EVP and Chief Administrative Officer: Marcia Rimai, age 53
EVP Insurance and Investment Products: Gregory C. Oberland, age 51
EVP, Chief Risk Officer, and Trustee: Gary A. Poliner, age 55
SVP Public Markets: Jefferson V. DeAngelis
SVP Real Estate: David D. Clark, age 57
SVP Agency Services: Christina H. Fiasca, age 54
SVP Enterprise Operations and Technology: Jean M. Maier, age 54
SVP and Chief Investment Officer: Mark G. Doll, age 59
SVP Product Distribution: Meridee J. Maynard, age 53
SVP Securities: Jeffrey J. Lueken, age 48
VP Human Resources: Susan A. Lueger, age 55
VP Communications and Corporate Affairs: Kimberley Goode
VP Marketing: Conrad C. York
General Counsel and Secretary: Raymond J. Manista, age 43
Auditors: PricewaterhouseCoopers LLP

LOCATIONS

HQ: The Northwestern Mutual Life Insurance Company
720 E. Wisconsin Ave., Milwaukee, WI 53202
Phone: 414-271-1444
Web: www.nmfn.com

PRODUCTS/OPERATIONS

2008 Sales

	$ mil.	% of total
Premiums	13,551	62
Investment Income	7,835	36
Other Income	537	2
Total	**21,923**	**100**

Selected Subsidiaries

Frank Russell Company
Northwestern Long Term Care Insurance Company
Northwestern Mutual Investment Services, LLC
Northwestern Mutual Wealth Management Company

COMPETITORS

AEGON USA
AIG American General
CIGNA
Citigroup
FMR
Genworth Financial
Guardian Life
The Hartford
ING
John Hancock Financial Services
MassMutual
MetLife
Mutual of Omaha
Nationwide
New York Life
Pacific Mutual
Principal Financial
Prudential
Sun Life
T. Rowe Price
TIAA-CREF

HISTORICAL FINANCIALS
Company Type: Mutual company

Income Statement
FYE: December 31

	ASSETS ($ mil.)	NET INCOME ($ mil.)	INCOME AS % OF ASSETS	EMPLOYEES
12/08	155,154	483	0.3%	5,000
12/07	156,547	1,000	0.6%	4,983
12/06	145,102	829	0.6%	4,800
12/05	133,057	924	0.7%	4,800
12/04	123,957	817	0.7%	4,700
Annual Growth	**5.8%**	**(12.3%)**	**—**	**1.6%**

2008 Year-End Financials

Equity as % of assets: —
Return on assets: 0.3%
Return on equity: —
Long-term debt ($ mil.): —
Sales ($ mil.): 21,923

Net Income History

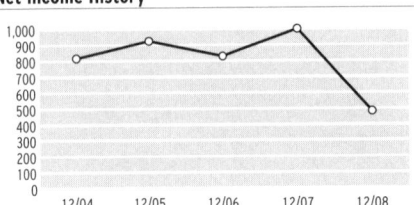

Northwestern University

What's NU? With its main campus in the Chicago suburb of Evanston, Northwestern University serves its 15,000 students through around a dozen schools and colleges such as the McCormick School of Engineering and Applied Sciences and the Medill School of Journalism. Its Chicago campus houses the schools of law and medicine, as well as several hospitals of the McGaw Medical Center. Faculty numbers around 2,500. Northwestern is home to several research centers, continuing education services, and community outreach programs; it has a branch in Qatar. It is the only private member of the Big 10 conference; varsity sports include baseball, football, basketball, and fencing.

Among Northwestern's top-ranked programs are its law school, medical school, and its engineering program. Its J. L. Kellogg Graduate School of Management consistently ranks among the nation's top five business schools by *Business Week* and *U.S. News & World Report*. Its prestigious journalism and drama programs produced such alumni as Charlton Heston, Gary Marshall, and Julia Louis-Dreyfus. Current US Supreme Court Justice John Paul Stevens is also a former Wildcat.

The school's endowment and other trust funds have swelled to around $6 billion, and it has exceeded its original Campaign Northwestern fundraising goal of $1 billion. The money is being used to increase endowment for student scholarships and fellowships, to help repair and build facilities, and to fund more faculty positions.

EXECUTIVES

President: Henry S. Bienen, age 69
Provost: Daniel I. Linzer, age 55
SVP Business and Finance: Eugene S. Sunshine
VP and Chief Investment Officer: Will McLean
VP Research: Joseph T. Walsh Jr.
VP Information Technology: Morteza A. Rahimi
VP Student Affairs: William J. Banis
VP Administration and Planning: Marilyn McCoy
VP and General Counsel: Thomas G. Cline
VP University Relations: Alan K. Cubbage
Dean, Northwestern University in Qatar: John D. Margolis
Associate Provost University Enrollment: Michael E. Mills
University Registrar: Patrick F. Martin
Auditors: Deloitte & Touche LLP

LOCATIONS

HQ: Northwestern University
633 Clark St., Evanston, IL 60208
Phone: 847-491-3741　　**Fax:** 847-491-8406
Web: www.northwestern.edu

PRODUCTS/OPERATIONS

Selected Undergraduate Colleges and Schools

Medill School of Journalism
Robert McCormick School of Engineering and Applied Sciences
School of Communication
School of Education and Social Policy
School of Music
Weinberg College of Arts and Sciences

Graduate and Professional Schools

Feinberg School of Medicine
Interdisciplinary Biological and Life Sciences
J.L. Kellogg School of Management
McCormick School of Engineering and Applied Science
Medill School of Journalism
School of Communication (Speech)
School of Education and Social Policy
School of Law
School of Music

Novant Health

Novant Health is a not-for-profit health system serving the eastern seaboard. The health system provides medical care to residents in more than 30 counties across North and South Carolina and Virginia. The system has about a dozen hospitals (with more than 3,000 beds), including Forsyth Medical Center (its largest facility with 960 beds in Winston-Salem, North Carolina) and the 530-bed Presbyterian Hospital in Charlotte, North Carolina. It also operates about 350 physician clinics and 100 outpatient diagnostic imaging centers (through subsidiary MedQuest), as well as nursing homes, rehabilitation and community outreach programs, and philanthropic foundations.

In addition to owning and operating facilities, Novant Health also provides facility management services for hospitals, including information technology and managed care efficiency. The health care network has been expanding its services in the region through partnerships and acquisitions.

Novant formed a strategic partnership with the Prince William Health System, which operates the 180-bed Prince William Hospital in Manassas, Virginia, in 2009. Prince William became an affiliated member of Novant Health, and in exchange will receive some $240 million from Novant to improve its facilities.

Also in 2009 the company increased its ownership of certain joint venture affiliates from partner Health Management Associates (HMA), giving Novant full ownership and management rights to two facilities in North and South Carolina (Upstate Carolina Medical Center and Franklin Regional Medical Center). The arrangement was a modification on the original partnership with HMA entered in 2007 in which Novant purchased minority stakes in seven hospitals in the Carolinas. Four of those have reverted to full HMA ownership.

In early 2008 Novant acquired and assumed the debt of Rowan Regional Medical Center, a 270-bed facility in central North Carolina. The deal extended the company's reach across the state, and linked two of its smaller regional clinics to the larger Rowan facilities.

The company acquired diagnostic imaging clinic operator MedQuest in 2007; the acquisition added about 100 facilities in over a dozen states. It also purchased the Brunswick Community Hospital in 2006.

Novant also grows by building new hospitals; it is currently constructing the Kernersville Medical Center, a 50-bed community hospital in the Winston-Salem area scheduled to open in 2010.

Novant Health was formed in 1997 by a merger of Carolina Medicorp, Presbyterian Healthcare, and Thomasville Medical Center.

EXECUTIVES

Chairman: John R. (Johnny) Belk, age 50
Vice Chairperson: Lisa Evans
President and Director: Paul M. Wiles
CFO, and President Ambulatory Services: Dean Swindle
EVP Finance: Fred Hargett
EVP Physician Services; President Novant Medical Group: Thomas H. (Hayes) Woollen
President Novant Core Markets: Carl Armato
President Acute Care Services: Gregory J. (Greg) Beier
Chief Medical Officer: Stephen L. Wallenhaupt
Chief Administrative Officer: Jacque Gattis
Secretary and Treasurer: Krista S. Tillman
Director: Randall Edwards

LOCATIONS

HQ: Novant Health, Inc.
2085 Frontis Plaza Blvd., Winston-Salem, NC 27103
Phone: 336-718-5000
Web: www.novanthealth.org

PRODUCTS/OPERATIONS

Selected Health Facilities

Brunswick Community Hospital (Supply, North Carolina)
Forsyth Medical Center (Winston-Salem, North Carolina)
Franklin Regional Medical Center (Louisburg, North Carolina)
Lake Norman Regional Medical Center (30%, venture with HMA; Mooresville, North Carolina)
Medical Park Hospital (Winston-Salem, North Carolina)
The Oaks at Forsyth (residental long-term care; Winston-Salem, North Carolina)
Presbyterian Hospital (Charlotte, North Carolina)
Presbyterian Hemby Children's Hospital
Presbyterian Hospital Huntersville (Huntersville, North Carolina)
Presbyterian Hospital Matthews (Charlotte, North Carolina)

Presbyterian Orthopaedic Hospital (Charlotte, North Carolina)
Prince William Hospital (managed affiliate; Manassas, Virginia)
Rowan Regional Medical Center (Salisbury, North Carolina)
Springwood Care Center (residental long-term care; Winston-Salem, North Carolina)
Thomasville Medical Center (Thomasville, North Carolina)
Upstate Carolina Medical Center (Gaffney, South Carolina)

COMPETITORS

Alamance Regional Medical Center
Bon Secours Health
Carilion Clinic
Carolinas HealthCare System
Carolinas Medical Center-NorthEast
CaroMont
Davis Regional Medical Center
Duke University Health System
Greenville Hospital System
New Hanover Health Network
Rex Healthcare
Riverside Health System (Virginia)
Sentara Healthcare
University Health Systems of Eastern Carolina
Wake Forest University Baptist Medical Center
WakeMed

HISTORICAL FINANCIALS

Company Type: Not-for-profit

Income Statement

FYE: December 31

	REVENUE ($ mil.)	NET INCOME ($ mil.)	NET PROFIT MARGIN	EMPLOYEES
12/08	2,887	—	—	12,500

NTK Holdings

Chill, bro. NTK Holdings is a breath of fresh air in the home HVAC market. Through subsidiary Nortek, the company makes air conditioning, heating, ventilation, and home technology products for the residential and commercial construction, do-it-yourself, remodeling, renovation, and manufactured housing markets. In addition to heating and air conditioning systems, NTK's wares include range hoods and other ventilation products, indoor air quality systems, lighting controls, and home entertainment system equipment. Products bear NTK's own brands (including Broan-NuTone), as well as such licensed names as Frigidaire, Maytag, and Westinghouse. NTK, along with its subsidiaries, filed for Chapter 11 bankruptcy in 2009.

NTK suffered as residential construction dwindled that year. The company also struggled under a mountain of debt. The move to reorganize and reduce debt followed a string of acquisitions. NTK bought several smaller companies to build its home technology and other divisions. In 2007 alone it acquired the assets of residential gate and garage door maker Allstar Corporation, bought security systems designer International Electronics, purchased the assets of security products maker Aigis Mechtronics, and bought

home subsystems (entertainment, security, climate control) firm Home Logic. The acquisitions were made with the aim of saving money and synergizing such operations as manufacturing, sourcing, distribution, sales and marketing.

With the downturn in the economy, NTK has slowed down spending on acquisitions and is focused on reducing costs. It moved some production operations to China, Poland, and Mexico, where labor costs are lower. As a result, manufacturing plants in California, Illinois, and Ohio were closed, as well as certain operations in Italy. Sales outside of the US (primarily to Canada and European countries) account for some 20% of revenues.

NTK Holdings is controlled by Thomas H. Lee Partners and company management. The company prepared itself for an IPO in 2006, but withdrew its registration statement the following year amidst the troubled financial markets.

EXECUTIVES

Chairman, President, and CEO: Richard L. Bready, age 64, $4,039,336 total compensation
VP and Treasurer: Edward J. Cooney, age 61, $482,052 total compensation
VP and CFO: Almon C. Hall III, age 62, $730,677 total compensation
VP, General Counsel, and Secretary: Kevin W. Donnelly, age 54, $571,419 total compensation
President, Nortek's CES Group: Eric Roberts
Director, Human Resources: Jane White
Auditors: Ernst & Young LLP

LOCATIONS

HQ: NTK Holdings, Inc.
50 Kennedy Plaza, Providence, RI 02903
Phone: 401-751-1600   **Fax:** 401-751-4610
Web: www.nortek-inc.com

2008 Sales

	% of total
US	79
Other countries	21
Total	**100**

PRODUCTS/OPERATIONS

2008 Sales

	$ mil.	% of total
Residential ventilation products	715.9	32
Residential HVAC products	524.5	23
Commercial HVAC products	515.2	23
Technology products	514.1	22
Total	**2,269.7**	**100**

Selected Brand Names

Air Conditioning and Heating Products

Cleanpak	Moducel
Colman	Qualitair
Cubit	Temtrol
Edenaire	Vapac
Governair	Venmar CES
Huntair	Ventrol
Mammoth	Webco

Home Technology Products

ATON	JobSite
Aigis	Linear
AllStar	M&S Systems
Channel Plus	Mighty Mule
Elan	Niles
GTO/PRO	OSCO
HomeLogic	Proficient Audio
ICS	SpeakerCraft
IEI	Sunfire
Imerge	Via
IntelliControl	Xantech

Residential Ventilation Products
Best
Broan
NuTone
Venmar
Zephyr

COMPETITORS

AAF-McQUAY	Johnson Controls
Carrier	Lennox
Duchossois Industries	Paloma Co.
GE Security	Trane Inc.
Goodman Manufacturing	

HISTORICAL FINANCIALS

Company Type: Private

Income Statement				FYE: December 31
	REVENUE ($ mil.)	NET INCOME ($ mil.)	NET PROFIT MARGIN	EMPLOYEES
12/08	2,270	(845)	—	8,800
12/07	2,368	(7)	—	9,800
12/06	2,218	58	2.6%	9,800
12/05	1,959	57	2.9%	8,600
12/04	1,679	(47)	—	7,700
Annual Growth	7.8%	—	—	3.4%

Net Income History

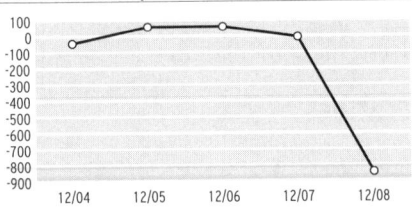

Nypro Inc.

Nypro is a real pro when it comes to injection molding. The company makes plastic parts used in devices that range from cell phones, electric razors, and seat belts to inkjet printer cartridges and personal computers. Nypro operates through three global units: Consumer & Electronics, Packaging, and Health Care. Although custom-precision plastic-injection molding is Nypro's core business, the company also offers assembly services to other manufacturers. Major customers include Dell, Nokia, and Procter & Gamble. The employee-owned company comprises about 50 businesses that span more than 15 countries.

One of the challenges the company has faced was getting its many business operations to work together smoothly. Amid the worldwide economic upheaval in 2009, the company decentralized its operations by creating three global business units, each with its own group president, to focus on customers in Nypro's primary markets. Diversification strategy was in Nypro's favor; though Consumer & Electronics experienced a decrease in sales of approximately 10% (2009 over 2008), the other two units posted increased revenues.

The restructuring reduced the corporate staff by around one-third. The company also bumped up investment in its strategic companies, including New Ventures Group (NVG) and Radius Product Development Group, as well as Nypro-branded NP Medical and Union Street Brand Packaging.

The company sold the plant operations and assets of Nypro Chihuahua (Juárez, Mexico) to Fortis Plastics; closed one of its four China-based injection molding sites and consolidated production; and announced the shuttering of its Corvallis, Oregon, plant — all in 2009. Concomitantly, it entered new markets such as solar and clean technology. Nypro became a key partner when it invested $1 million in Toronto-based Morgan Solar in 2009. Morgan Solar, which has designed and developed a solar panel called the Sun Simba HCPV (designed for electric utilities), needs Nypro's manufacturing and product assembly processes to produce the light-guide solar optics (LSO) for its photovoltaic panel. Nypro will also provide the final testing of the LSOs.

Chairman Gordon Lankton joined Nypro (then known as Nylon Products, Inc.) in 1962 as general manager and co-owner. He acquired the rest of the company in 1969. In 1998 Lankton sold the firm to Nypro's employee stock ownership plan (ESOP).

EXECUTIVES

Chairman: Gordon B. Lankton
President, CEO, and Director:
Theodore E. (Ted) Lapres III
CFO and Chief Strategy Officer:
James R. (Jim) Buonomo
Corporate VP, General Counsel, and Secretary:
James W. (Jim) Peck
Corporate VP Human Resources and Organizational Development: Ann S. Liotta
Corporate VP and Chief Marketing Officer:
Steven E. Callahan
Corporate VP Healthcare: Stephen J. (Steve) Glorioso
Corporate VP, Global Engineering and Technology:
Greg G. Adams
Corporate VP Consumer and Electronics:
Louis (Lou) Gaviglia
Corporate VP, China and India: Nelson Ngais
President, Americas: Raymond S. (Ray) Grupinski
Director Corporate Communications: Al Cotton
Auditors: PricewaterhouseCoopers LLP

LOCATIONS

HQ: Nypro Inc.
101 Union St., Clinton, MA 01510
Phone: 978-365-9721   **Fax:** 978-368-0236
Web: www.nypro.com

PRODUCTS/OPERATIONS

Selected Markets

Automotive
Air bag covers
Bezels
Covers and trim
Door handles
Shift consoles
Steering wheels
Consumer/industrial
Adhesives
Electrical components
Fasteners
Fitness
Lawn and garden
Photography
Small and large appliances
Sporting goods
Storage
Tools
Contract manufacturers

Electronics/telecommunications
Assemblies and disposable cartridges
Consumer electronic products
Hard disk drive components
Laptop computer components and assemblies
Mechanical printer components
Mobile phones
Health care
Collection containers
Contact lenses
Drug containers
Drug syringes
Inhalers
Lancing devices
Petri dishes
Pipettes
Surgical instruments
Test tubes
Packaging
Beverage containers
Cosmetics
Food storage
Hair and personal care
Kitchen and bath products

Selected Services

Assembly
Automation
Contract manufacturing
Decoration and finishing technologies
Injection molding
Metal fabrication
Mold design and fabrication
Product design and development
Program management

COMPETITORS

Berry Plastics
Blue Star Plastics
Cascade Engineering
Deswell
Hoffer Plastics
MXL Industries
NN Inc.
Omni Industries Holdings
Protomold Company
Toledo Molding and Die
Trend Technologies
Tuthill

HISTORICAL FINANCIALS

Company Type: Private

Income Statement				FYE: June 30
	REVENUE ($ mil.)	NET INCOME ($ mil.)	NET PROFIT MARGIN	EMPLOYEES
6/08	1,164	4	0.3%	18,000
6/07	1,106	18	1.7%	18,000
6/06	1,066	5	0.5%	17,000
6/05	729	17	2.4%	15,000
6/04	627	16	2.5%	—
Annual Growth	16.7%	(30.5%)	—	6.3%

Net Income History

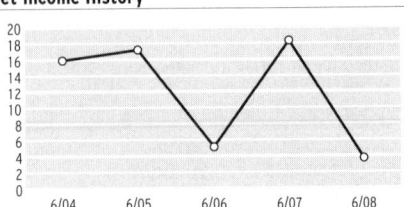

Oakland Raiders

Fighting under the silver and black Jolly Rodger, these Raiders are looking to plunder some treasure on the gridiron. The Oakland Raiders professional football team is one of the more storied franchises in the National Football League. Founded in 1960 as a charter member of the American Football League, the team played in the second Super Bowl between the rival leagues (losing to the Green Bay Packers) before joining the NFL in 1970. The franchise has since won three championship titles (its last in 1984). Over the years, Oakland has been home to such Hall of Fame players Marcus Allen, Howie Long, and Jim Otto, as well as legendary head coach John Madden. Al Davis has run the team since 1972.

In 2007 Davis raised some additional capital for his football franchise by selling a 20% stake to outside investors, including David Abrams, Dan Goldberg, and Paul Leff. Through a settlement the previous year, Davis had gained a 30% stake owned by the family of E.J. McGah, one of the team's founders.

The Raiders have been on a downward trajectory since reaching the Super Bowl in 2003, where the team lost to the Tampa Bay Buccaneers. In 2008 head coach Lane Kiffin was fired shortly after the season began; assistant Tom Cable, who served as interim head coach that season, officially took over as the Raiders' fifth head coach in seven years. Kiffin, a former University of Southern California assistant, had replaced Art Shell following the 2006 campaign.

In 2008 software company McAfee declined to renew its naming rights sponsorship with the Raiders home stadium, which reverted back to its original name of Oakland-Alameda County Coliseum. The company had originally entered into the naming rights deal in 1998 when it was known as Network Associates.

Davis, who served as Raiders head coach in the early 1960s and later helped negotiate the merger of the two rival football leagues as commissioner of the AFL, has been something of a thorn in the side of the NFL and a lightning rod for critics for many years. Unable to get concessions from Oakland for a new stadium, he proposed moving the Raiders to Los Angeles in 1980 but was blocked by the league. He later sued the NFL and won the right to relocate, but then returned the team to the Bay Area in 1995 when the City of Angels backed out of a new stadium deal. In recent years he has also filed unsuccessful lawsuits against the Carolina Panthers and the Buccaneers for trademark infringement.

EXECUTIVES

Owner: Al Davis
CEO: Amy Trask
CFO: Marc Badain
Head Coach: Tom Cable, age 44
Marketing: Colin Allen
Technology: Tom Blanda
Director Football Development: Mark Jackson
Director Public Relations: Mike Taylor
General Counsel: Jeff Birren

LOCATIONS

HQ: The Oakland Raiders
 1220 Harbor Bay Pkwy., Alameda, CA 94502
Phone: 510-864-5000   **Fax:** 510-864-5160
Web: www.raiders.com

PRODUCTS/OPERATIONS

Championship Titles
Super Bowl Championship
 Super Bowl XVIII (1984)
 Super Bowl XV (1981)
 Super Bowl XI (1977)
AFC Championship (1976, 1980, 1983, 2002)
AFC Western Division Champions (1970, 1972-76, 1983, 1985, 1990, 2000-02)
AFL Championship (1967)
AFL Western Division Champions (1967-69)

COMPETITORS

Denver Broncos
Kansas City Chiefs
San Diego Chargers

HISTORICAL FINANCIALS

Company Type: Private

Income Statement

FYE: June 30

	REVENUE ($ mil.)	NET INCOME ($ mil.)	NET PROFIT MARGIN	EMPLOYEES
6/08	205	—	—	—
6/07	189	—	—	—
6/06	171	—	—	—
6/05	169	—	—	—
6/04	149	—	—	—
Annual Growth	8.3%	—	—	—

Revenue History

Ocean Spray Cranberries

Ocean Spray Cranberries transformed that quivering red Thanksgiving side dish to beverages, cereals, and snacks. Known for its blue-and-white wave logo, Ocean Spray is the largest producer of canned, bottled, and shelf-stable juice drinks in the US. A cooperative owned by about 600 cranberry and 50 grapefruit growers in North America, the company produces its line of juice drinks by blending the cranberries with other fruits ranging from apples to tangerines. It also offers other cranberry products (fresh and dried berries, sauces, trail mixes, instant oatmeal, and snack bars), as well as fresh grapefruit and grapefruit juice.

To expand beyond the berry's traditional role, Ocean Spray has turned the fruit into a chewy snack (Craisins), and cranberries now show up in co-branded cookies and cereal. It has also introduced a "white juice" made from pre-ripened cranberries that have a less tart taste. Promotional efforts have been aided by research showing that cranberry juice can reduce urinary tract infections and fight stomach ulcers. In 2009, the company introduced a line of pomegranate juice drinks (pomegrante being one of the latest "superfruits" touted for its antioxidant properties).

Ocean Spray's Ingredient Technology Group processes fruit into ingredients for food and beverage manufacturers. The co-op has production facilities in Massachusetts, New Jersey, Wisconsin, Nevada, Texas, and Florida. Its growers are located in British Columbia, Florida, Massachusetts, New Jersey, Oregon, and Wisconsin.

HISTORY

Ocean Spray Cranberries traces its roots to Marcus Urann, president of the Cape Cod Cranberry Company. In 1912 Urann, who became known as the "Cranberry King," began marketing a cranberry sauce that was packaged in tins and could be served year-round. Inspired by the sea spray that drifted off the Atlantic and over his cranberry bogs, Urann dubbed his concoction Ocean Spray Cape Cod Cranberry Sauce.

It didn't take long for other cranberry growers to make their own sauces, and rather than compete, the Cranberry King consolidated. In 1930 Urann merged his company with A.D. Makepeace Company and with Cranberry Products, forming a national cooperative called Cranberry Canners. During the 1940s it added growers in Wisconsin, Oregon, and Washington and, to reflect its new scope, changed its name to National Cranberry Association.

Canadian growers were added to the fold in 1950. Urann retired in 1955, and two years later the co-op introduced its first frozen products. To take advantage of the popular Ocean Spray brand name, in 1959 the company changed its name to Ocean Spray Cranberries.

Two weeks before Thanksgiving that year, the US Department of Health mistakenly announced that aminotriazole, a herbicide used by some cranberry growers, was linked to cancer in laboratory rats. Sales of what consumers called "cancer berries" plummeted, and Ocean Spray nearly folded. However, the US government came to the rescue with subsidies in 1960, and the company stayed afloat.

The scare convinced Ocean Spray it needed to cut its dependence on seasonal demand, and it began to diversify more aggressively into the juice business, introducing a heavily promoted new line of juices blending cranberries with apples, grapes, and other fruits.

Ocean Spray allowed Florida's Indian River Ruby Red grapefruit growers to join the co-op in 1976. The company acquired Milne Food Products, a manufacturer of fruit concentrates and purees, in 1985, and three years later it signed a Japanese distribution deal.

To maintain its edge in a growing but increasingly competitive market, Ocean Spray automated plants and allied with food giants to create cranberry-flavored treats such as cookies (Nabisco, 1993) and cereal (Kraft Foods, 1996). In 1998 it unsuccessfully sued to block PepsiCo's purchase of juice maker Tropicana on grounds that it would interfere with PepsiCo's distribution of Ocean Spray's drinks. Ocean Spray also introduced a line of 100% juice blends to compete with rivals such as former co-op member Northland Cranberries.

Bumper harvests from 1997 through 1999 led to lower cranberry prices. As a result, in 1999 the company announced its third round of layoffs since 1997 (bringing the total to 500, or nearly one-fifth of its workforce). It also suspended its practice of buying back the stock of its growers, who must buy shares to join the co-op.

Amid criticism that it has been unable to compete effectively with for-profit rivals, Ocean Spray hired former Pillsbury executive Robert Hawthorne as CEO in 2000. Grower-owners voted not to explore a sale of the company at its 2001 annual meeting, a vote of confidence for the new management. Ocean Spray also sold its interest in Nantucket Allserve (Nantucket Nectars) to Cadbury Schweppes, which folded Nantucket's brands into its Snapple unit. (Cadbury later spun off its beverage assets, which became Dr Pepper Snapple Group.)

In 2002 Hawthorne resigned. Barbara Thomas, a board member and former president of Warner Lambert's consumer health care division, was named interim CEO. She left the position in 2003 and was replaced by company president and COO Randy Papadellis.

In 2003 rival Northland made a cash and stock bid to take over the juice business of Ocean Spray. The company rejected the offer the same month. Upset by their lack of input in the decision, cranberry growers voted to revamp the Ocean Spray board, reducing its size from 15 to 12 members and keeping just three of the board's previous members. Soon after, Ocean Spray laid off about 60 people, including several executives.

In 2004 the cooperative nearly revamped its board a second time in one year to again increase input from membership. As a compromise, the cooperative returned the size of its board to 15 members. Seven of the members were considered "compromise" candidates that would bring "additional viewpoints" to the Board.

Rounding out a busy year, in 2004 Ocean Spray settled an antitrust lawsuit filed by Northland Cranberries and Clermont, Inc. As part of the settlement, Ocean Spray agreed to purchase Northland's production plant and pay more than $5 million to buy eight of Northland's cranberry marshes in Wisconsin. The agreement also stipulated that Ocean Spray would make cranberry concentrate for Northland.

In 2005 it sold a fruit-processing facility in Vero Beach, Florida.

EXECUTIVES

President and CEO: Randy C. Papadellis, age 51
SVP and COO, Domestic: Kenneth G. (Ken) Romanzi, age 49
SVP, CFO, and Treasurer: Timothy C. (Tim) Chan, age 57
VP Operations: Michael (Mike) Stamatakos
VP, Human Resources and Organization Development: Katie Morey
VP International: Peter Patkowski, age 55
Public Relations: Kelly Kass
Director, Cooperative Development: Arun Hiranandani
PR Specialist: Sharon Newcomb
Senior Manager, Corporate Communications: Chris Phillips
Senior Corporate Communications Specialist: Denise Perry
Auditors: Deloitte & Touche

LOCATIONS

HQ: Ocean Spray Cranberries, Inc.
   1 Ocean Spray Dr., Lakeville-Middleboro, MA 02349
Phone: 508-946-1000   **Fax:** 508-946-7704
Web: www.oceanspray.com

PRODUCTS/OPERATIONS

Selected Products and Brands
Juice
   Cranberry Premium 100%
   Grapefruit Premium 100%
Juice Drinks
   Blueberry
   Blueberry Pomegranate
   Cranberry
   Cranergy Energy
   Cran-Pomegranate
   Grapefruit
   Ruby Pomegranate Grapefruit
   White Cranberry
Other
   Craisins
   Craisins Trail Mix
   Fresh cranberries
   Fresh grapefruits
   Intant oatmeal
   Jellied sauce
   Whole berry sauce

COMPETITORS

A. Duda & Sons	Freshco
Arcade Industries	Jamba
Cherry Central	Jugos del Valle USA
Cooperative,	Mariani Packing
Chiquita Brands	Meridian Nut Growers
Cliffstar	Naked Juice
Coca-Cola	National Grape Cooperative
Coloma Frozen Foods	Nestlé USA
Cranberries Limited	Odwalla
Dole Food	Old Orchard
Dundee Citrus Growers	Roll International
Edinburg Citrus	Shoreline Fruit
Ferolito, Vultaggio	Sunsweet Growers
Florida's Natural	Tampico Beverages
Fresh Del Monte Produce	Tropicana

Oglethorpe Power

Much ogled, not-for-profit Oglethorpe Power Corporation is one of the largest electricity cooperatives in the US, with contracts to supply wholesale power to 38 member/owners (making up most of Georgia's electric distribution cooperatives) until 2025. Oglethorpe Power's member/owners, which also operate as not-for-profits, serve about 4.1 million residential, commercial, and industrial customers. The company has a generating capacity of more than 4,744 MW from fossil-fueled, nuclear, and hydroelectric power plants. In addition, Oglethorpe purchases power from other suppliers, and it markets power on the wholesale market.

Oglethorpe has stakes in 24 generating units. In 2008 Oglethorpe members Cobb EMC, Jackson EMC, and Sawnee EMC accounted for 13%, 11%, and 10% of Oglethorpe's total revenues.

In 2009 the company acquired the Heard County Power Generation Facility in Georgia from Dynegy for $105 million. It also acquired the 318 MW Hartwell Peak Generating Plant from International Power.

Part of Oglethorpe's future power generating needs is for renewable power sources, as the power producer, like other utilities, seeks to lower its carbon emissions. In 2009 the company acquired 55 acres of land in Warren County on which it plans to build a 100 MW biomass plant.

EXECUTIVES

Chairman and At-Large Director: Benny W. Denham, age 78
Vice Chairman; Member Director (Group 4): J. Sam L. Rabun, age 77
President and CEO: Thomas A. (Tom) Smith, age 54, $706,209 total compensation
EVP External Relations and Member: William F. (Billy) Ussery, age 44, $309,696 total compensation
EVP and CFO: Elizabeth Bush (Betsy) Higgins, age 40, $407,183 total compensation
EVP and COO: Michael W. (Mike) Price, age 48, $408,552 total compensation
SVP and General Counsel: Charles W. (Chuck) Whitney
SVP Governmental Affairs: W. Clayton (Clay) Robbins, age 62, $272,534 total compensation
SVP Plant Operations: James A. (Jim) Messersmith
SVP Strategic Initiatives: George B. Taylor Jr.
VP Human Resources: Jami G. Reusch, age 46, $221,235 total compensation
Director Public Relations: Greg Jones
Auditors: PricewaterhouseCoopers LLP

LOCATIONS

HQ: Oglethorpe Power Corporation
   2100 E. Exchange Place, Tucker, GA 30084
Phone: 770-270-7600   **Fax:** 770-270-7325
Web: www.opc.com

PRODUCTS/OPERATIONS

2008 Sales

	$ mil.	% of total
Members		
Energy	646.1	52
Capacity	591.6	48
Non-members	1.1	—
Total	**1,238.8**	**100**

Member/Owners
Altamaha Electric Membership Corporation
Amicalola Electric Membership Corporation
Canoochee Electric Membership Corporation
Carroll Electric Membership Corporation
Central Georgia Electric Membership Corporation
Coastal Electric Membership Corporation (dba Coastal Electric Cooperative)
Cobb Electric Membership Corporation
Colquitt Electric Membership Corporation
Coweta-Fayette Electric Membership Corporation
Diverse Power Incorporated, an Electric Membership Corporation (formerly Troup Electric Membership Corporation)
Excelsior Electric Membership Corporation
Grady Electric Membership Corporation
GreyStone Power Corporation, an Electric Membership Corporation
Habersham Electric Membership Corporation
Hart Electric Membership Corporation
Irwin Electric Membership Corporation
Jackson Electric Membership Corporation
Jefferson Energy Cooperative, an Electric Membership Corporation
Lamar Electric Membership Corporation
Little Ocmulgee Electric Membership Corporation
Middle Georgia Electric Membership Corporation
Mitchell Electric Membership Corporation
Ocmulgee Electric Membership Corporation
Oconee Electric Membership Corporation
Okefenoke Rural Electric Membership Corporation
Pataula Electric Membership Corporation
Planters Electric Membership Corporation
Rayle Electric Membership Corporation
Satilla Rural Electric Membership Corporation
Sawnee Electric Membership Corporation
Slash Pine Electric Membership Corporation
Snapping Shoals Electric Membership Corporation
Sumter Electric Membership Corporation
Three Notch Electric Membership Corporation
Tri-County Electric Membership Corporation
Upson Electric Membership Corporation
Walton Electric Membership Corporation
Washington Electric Membership Corporation

COMPETITORS

AGL Resources
FPL Group
MEAG Power
Progress Energy
PS Energy
Southern Company
TVA

HISTORICAL FINANCIALS

Company Type: Cooperative

Income Statement

FYE: December 31

	REVENUE ($ mil.)	NET INCOME ($ mil.)	NET PROFIT MARGIN	EMPLOYEES
12/08	1,239	19	1.6%	176
12/07	1,151	19	1.7%	160
12/06	1,129	18	1.6%	161
12/05	1,170	18	1.5%	160
12/04	1,313	17	1.3%	168
Annual Growth	(1.4%)	2.9%	—	1.2%

Net Income History

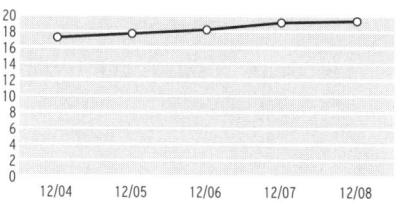

Ohio State University

The first student body of The Ohio State University (OSU) had 24 students. Today the school has around 54,000 at its flagship Columbus campus, edging out Arizona State and the University of Florida for the nation's largest campus in terms of enrollment. OSU also has four regional campuses and two agricultural institutes. Its approximately 3,100 regular and research faculty members offer instruction in some 165 undergraduate and more than 230 graduate programs. The colleges and schools range from the Austin E. Knowlton School of Architecture to the College of Medicine and Public Health to the Fisher College of Business. OSU was established in 1870 as Ohio Agricultural and Mechanical College.

Noteworthy university alumni include astronaut Nancy Sherlock Currie, golfer Jack Nicklaus, author John Jakes, and Olympian Jesse Owens.

Ohio State University has campuses in Columbus, Lima, Mansfield, Marion, and Newark. It has two agricultural centers in Wooster and a freshwater biological field station (the Franz Theodore Stone Laboratory) on Gibraltar Island in Put-in-Bay Harbor on Lake Erie.

The school had an endowment of almost $2.1 billion in 2008.

HISTORY

In 1870 the Ohio legislature, prompted by Governor Rutherford B. Hayes, agreed to establish the Ohio Agricultural and Mechanical College in Columbus on property provided by the Morrill Act of 1862 (the land-grant institution act, which gave land to states and territories for the establishment of colleges).

After a heated battle over whether the college should teach only agricultural and mechanical arts or foster a broad-based liberal arts curriculum, the college opened in 1873 offering agriculture, ancient languages, chemistry, geology, mathematics, modern languages, and physics courses. Two years later the school appointed its first female faculty member. Ohio State University became the school's name in 1878; that year it graduated its first class. The next year OSU graduated its first female student.

OSU grew dramatically, adding schools of veterinary medicine (1885), pharmacy (1885), law (1891), and dairy sciences (1895). It awarded its first Masters of Arts degree in 1886.

The university continued to expand in the early 20th century, with enrollment surpassing 3,000 in 1908; by 1923 it had reached 10,000. New schools were added in education (1907), medicine and dentistry (1913), and commerce and journalism (1923). During WWI Ohio State designated part of its campus as training grounds and established the only college schools in the nation for airplane and balloon squadrons. Ohio Stadium was dedicated in 1922.

During the Great Depression, Ohio State cut back salaries and course offerings. In the 1940s the school geared for war once again by establishing radiation and war research labs, as well as programs and services for students who were drafted. OSU captured its first national football championship in 1942.

The 1950s ushered in the era of legendary OSU football coach Woody Hayes. Hayes led his beloved Buckeyes to three national championships and nine Rose Bowl appearances before he was discharged for striking a Clemson player in 1978. The 1950s also saw the addition of four regional campuses at Lima, Mansfield, Marion, and Newark.

In the early 1960s the university was engaged in internal free-speech battles. By the end of that decade, enrollment had surpassed 50,000. OSU opened its School of Social Work in 1976.

In 1986 OSU and rival Michigan shared the Big 10 football conference title. Enrollment at OSU topped 54,000 in 1990 but then began declining. In response, the university tried to cut costs and beef up revenues. One way was through alliances: In 1992 it teamed with research group Battelle to develop a testing system for new drugs for the Food and Drug Administration. But when more savings were needed in 1995-96, the university began streamlining operations, merging journalism and communications, and consolidating several university veterinary departments. However, it also approved the creation of a new school of public health to provide education in environmental health, epidemiology, and health care management and financing.

But sports were not forgotten, and in 1996 OSU broke ground on the $84 million Schottenstein Center, a multipurpose facility for the university's basketball and ice hockey teams. In 1997 president Gordon Gee announced that he was leaving OSU for Brown University. The next year William Kirwan from the University of Maryland came on board as president.

In 2000 the university's "Affirm Thy Friendship" campaign came to a close. It increased OSU's endowment from $493 million in 1993 to $1.3 billion in 2000. In 2002 Kirwan stepped down and Karen Holbrook took over as president.

Ohio State won the national football championship in early 2003. The Buckeyes made it to the BCS championship game following the 2006 football season, only to be defeated by the #2-ranked Florida Gators. In 2007 Gordon Gee returned as president.

EXECUTIVES

Chairman: Leslie H. Wexner, age 71
Vice Chairman: Jo Ann Davidson
President: E. Gordon Gee, age 65
CIO: Kathleen Starkoff
EVP and Provost: Joseph A. Alutto, age 67
SVP University Development: Peter Weiler
SVP Outreach and Engagement: Joyce Beatty
SVP Health Sciences and CEO, OSU Medical Center: Steve G. Gabbe
SVP Government Affairs: Curt Steiner
SVP University Communications: Thomas (Tom) Katzenmeyer
SVP Research: Robert T. McGrath
SVP Administration and Planning: Jeff Kaplan
SVP Business and Finance: William J. (Bill) Shkurti
VP Office of Student Life: Javaune Adams-Gaston
VP and Chief Investment Officer: Jonathan D. Hook
VP and General Counsel: Christopher M. Culley
VP and Executive Dean: Bobby D. Moser
Chief of Staff: Kelly Des Roches
Assistant to the President and Operations Director: Kate Wolford
Secretary: David O. Frantz
Associate VP Human Resources: Larry M. Lewellen
Auditors: Deloitte & Touche LLP

LOCATIONS

HQ: The Ohio State University
Enarson Hall, 154 W. 12th Ave.
Columbus, OH 43210
Phone: 614-292-3980   **Fax:** 614-292-0154
Web: www.osu.edu

PRODUCTS/OPERATIONS

Selected Colleges and Schools

Austin E. Knowlton School of Architecture
College of Biological Sciences
College of Dentistry
College of Education
College of Education and Human Ecology
College of Engineering
College of Food, Agricultural, and Environmental Sciences
College of Human Ecology
College of Humanities
College of Law
College of Mathematical and Physical Sciences
College of Medicine and Public Health
College of Nursing
College of Optometry
College of Pharmacy
College of Social and Behavioral Sciences
College of Social Work
College of the Arts
College of Veterinary Medicine
Graduate School
John Glenn School of Public Affairs
Max M. Fisher College of Business
Michael E. Moritz College of Law
School of Allied Medical Professions
School of Biomedical Science
School of Communication
School of Environment and Natural Resources
School of Music
School of Natural Resources
School of Public Health
University College

Oklahoma City Thunder

This team is causing a big noise in Oklahoma. Professional Basketball Club owns and operates the Oklahoma City Thunder of the National Basketball Association. Previously known as the Seattle SuperSonics, the franchise was started by Sam Schulman and joined the NBA in 1967. Its roster boasted such Hall of Fame talent as Lenny Wilkins, who later coached Seattle to its first and only championship title in 1979. Oklahoma businessman Clay Bennett purchased the SuperSonics from a group led by Starbucks founder Howard Schultz in 2006 and relocated the franchise to Oklahoma City two years later.

The relocation deal struck between Bennett and Seattle gave the city rights to the SuperSonics name, history, and colors. The deal also ended a long-running dispute over building a new sports facility to replace Seattle's KeyArena. Bennett, with the backing of the NBA, had insisted the aging arena was unfit for a professional basketball franchise to survive. (Schultz, in fact, claimed losses of about $60 million over five years when he sold the team.) However, the two parties could not come to an agreement on public funding for a new building.

With its new name in place, the franchise took up residence at Oklahoma City's Ford Center. Before becoming a team owner, Bennett had helped negotiate a deal to temporarily relocate the New Orleans Hornets to the Ford Center in 2005 after Hurricane Katrina. He later led the $350 million acquisition of the SuperSonics.

Professional Basketball Club had also owned the Seattle Storm WNBA franchise but Bennett sold that team in 2008 for about $10 million to a local group of investors led by Anne Levinson, who previously served as Deputy Mayor of Seattle. The Storm's new ownership group, calling itself Force 10 Hoops, included Microsoft executives Lisa Brummel and Dawn Trudeau.

EXECUTIVES

Chairman: Clayton I. (Clay) Bennett
EVP and Chief Administrative Officer: Danny Barth
EVP and General Manager: Sam Presti, age 31
Head Coach: Scott Brooks
SVP and Executive Producer: Ken Adelson
SVP Ticket Sales and Services: Brian M. Byrnes
SVP Guest Relations: Pete Winemiller
VP Human Resources: Katy Semtner
VP Business Development: John R. Croley
VP Communications and Community Relations: Dan Mahoney
Director Medical Services: Donnie Strack
Director Pro Player Personnel: Bill Branch, age 40
Director Team Operations: Marc St. Yves
Director College/International Player Personnel: Rob Hennigan

LOCATIONS

HQ: Professional Basketball Club, LLC
2 Leadership Sq., 211 N. Robinson Ave., Ste. 300
Oklahoma City, OK 73102
Phone: 405-208-4800   **Fax:** 405-429-7900
Web: www.nba.com/thunder

The Oklahoma City Thunder play at the 19,599-seat capacity Ford Center in Oklahoma City.

COMPETITORS

Denver Nuggets
Minnesota Timberwolves
Portland Trail Blazers
Utah Jazz

Old Dominion Electric

Ol' Virginny and neighboring states get power from Old Dominion Electric Cooperative, which generates and purchases electricity for its 12 member distribution cooperatives. These in turn serve nearly 550,000 customers in four northeastern states. The member-owned power utility has more than 2,000 MW of generating capacity from nuclear and fossil-fueled power plants and diesel generators; it purchases the remainder of its power from neighboring utilities and power marketers. Old Dominion transmits power to its members through the systems of utilities and transmission operators in the region. It also provides power to TEC Trading, a wholesale company also owned by the distribution cooperatives.

Old Dominion was organized in 1948 to identify new electric power sources for its growing member systems. It initially planned to build a power plant in 1949 but this plan fell through and the utility remained inactive until energy costs surged during the 1970s. From 1976 on Old Dominion has been serving its members' power supply needs by purchasing wholesale power and selling it to them at cost.

In 2008 the company's largest revenue contributor — Northern Virginia Electric Cooperative — renegotiated its wholesale supply agreement with Old Dominion, allowing it to seek supply from other sources.

As part of an energy diversification strategy, in 2008 the company signed a long-term contract with AES to purchase up to 70 MW of wind power.

EXECUTIVES

Chairman: James M. Reynolds, age 61
Vice Chairman: Frederick L. Hubbard, age 68
President and CEO: Jackson E. (Jack) Reasor, age 56, $606,700 total compensation
SVP, Accounting and Finance and Secretary: Terri Young
SVP Power Supply: Lisa D. Johnson, age 43, $332,088 total compensation
SVP and CFO: Robert L. (Bob) Kees, age 56, $428,432 total compensation
VP Information Technology: B. Lee McDaniel, age 56, $205,497 total compensation
VP, Finance: Lynn Maloney
VP Human Resources: Elissa Ecker, age 49, $245,314 total compensation
VP, Member and External Relations: John C. Lee Jr.
VP, Engineering and Operations: Ken Alexander
VP, Power Supply Planning: Rick Beam
Secretary and Treasurer: Gregory W. (Greg) White
Auditors: Ernst & Young LLP

LOCATIONS

HQ: Old Dominion Electric Cooperative
4201 Dominion Blvd., Glen Allen, VA 23060
Phone: 804-747-0592   **Fax:** 804-747-3742
Web: www.odec.com

Old Dominion Electric Cooperative operates in Delaware, Maryland, Virginia, and West Virginia.

PRODUCTS/OPERATIONS

2008 Sales

	$ mil.	% of total
Member cooperatives		
Northern Virginia Electric Cooperative	272.1	26
Rappahannock Electric Cooperative	201.4	19
Delaware Electric Cooperative	100.1	10
Other cooperatives	391.8	38
Nonmember cooperatives	75.3	7
Total	**1,040.7**	**100**

HISTORICAL FINANCIALS
Company Type: Cooperative

Income Statement
FYE: December 31

	REVENUE ($ mil.)	NET INCOME ($ mil.)	NET PROFIT MARGIN	EMPLOYEES
12/08	1,041	12	1.1%	104
12/07	963	16	1.7%	101
12/06	818	21	2.6%	103
12/05	738	12	1.6%	83
12/04	589	12	2.1%	84
Annual Growth	**15.3%**	**(0.6%)**	**—**	**5.5%**

2008 Year-End Financials

Debt ratio: 8.7%
Return on equity: —
Cash ($ mil.): —
Current ratio: —
Long-term debt ($ mil.): 91

Net Income History

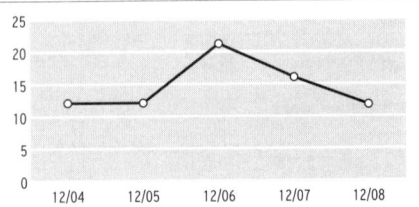

O'Melveny & Myers

O'Melveny & Myers has gotten used to playing the role of legal guardian angel. The firm is one of the oldest in Los Angeles, and over the years it has developed strong ties to the media and entertainment industries. Among its clients have been such leading players as Walt Disney, Sony Pictures Entertainment, and Time Warner. Besides entertainment and media law, O'Melveny & Myers' practice areas include labor and employment, intellectual property and technology, and venture capital litigation. The firm has more than 1,000 lawyers located in about a dozen offices worldwide. O'Melveny & Myers was founded in 1885.

After being nominated by President Obama, partner Alejandro Mayorkas became the director of US Citizenship and Immigration Services in August 2009. Before working at O'Melveny & Myers, Mayorkas was the US Attorney for the Central District of California.

In 2008 the firm expanded its Asia practice by opening an office in Singapore and forming an Asia strategic capital and finance group. The office is focusing on finance, restructuring and distressed investment, private equity, mergers and acquisitions, and capital markets.

EXECUTIVES

Chair: Arthur B. Culvahouse Jr.
Vice Chair: Robert E. (Bob) Willett
COO: Bruce A. Boulware
Managing Director, Finance: Peter J. Cyffka
Managing Director, Information: Jeffrey S. Rovner
Managing Director, Adversarial: Paul R. Covey
Chair, Strategic Counseling Practice: Thomas E. (Tom) Donilon
Chair, Labor and Employment Practice: Framroze (Fram) Virjee
Chair, Appellate Practice: Walter Dellinger

Chair, Business Trial and Litigation Practice:
Daniel (Dan) Petrocelli
Chair, Project Development and Real Estate Practice:
Gregory (Greg) Thorpe
Secretary and Partner, Corporate Finance and Capital Markets: Maritza U. B. Okata
Director Global Communications: John Buchanan
Director Marketing: Suzanne Donnels

LOCATIONS

HQ: O'Melveny & Myers LLP
400 S. Hope St., Los Angeles, CA 90071
Phone: 213-430-6000   **Fax:** 213-430-6407
Web: www.omm.com

Selected Office Locations

Beijing
Brussels
Century City, CA
Hong Kong
London
Los Angeles
New York
Newport Beach, CA
San Francisco
Shanghai
Silicon Valley (Menlo Park, CA)
Singapore
Tokyo
Washington, DC

PRODUCTS/OPERATIONS

Selected Practice Areas

Antitrust and competition
Appellate
Aviation
Broker-dealer regulation and compliance
Business tax
Business trial and litigation
Capital markets
China practice
Class actions, mass torts, and aggregated litigation
Clean energy technology
Climate change
Corporate finance
Corporate practice
Derivatives and structured products
Electronic discovery and document retention
Emerging technology
Energy and natural resources
Entertainment and media
Entertainment and media litigation
Environmental law
ERISA litigation
Executive compensation and employee benefits
Foreign corrupt practices act
Health care and life sciences
Insurance and reinsurance
Intellectual property and technology
International arbitration
International trade
Investment adviser regulation and compliance
Investment funds
Japan practice
Korea practice
Labor and employment
Latin America
Life sciences
Mergers and acquisitions
Political law
Products liability and mass torts
Project development and infrastructure
Real estate
Restructuring
Securities enforcement
Securities litigation
Securitization
South Asia and Southeast Asia practice
Strategic counseling
Tax controversy
Telecommunications
Transactional intellectual property
Venture capital litigation
White collar defense and corporate investigations

COMPETITORS

Akin Gump
Baker & McKenzie
Bingham McCutchen
Davis Polk
Gibson, Dunn & Crutcher
Greenberg Glusker
Latham & Watkins
Morrison & Foerster
Munger, Tolles & Olson
Paul, Hastings
Pillsbury Winthrop Shaw Pittman
Skadden, Arps
Sullivan & Cromwell

O'Neal Steel

O'Neal Steel has an angle on the steel industry. One of the US's leading metals service companies, O'Neal sells a full range of metal products — including angles, bars, beams, coil, pipe, plate, and sheet — made from steel, aluminum, brass, and bronze. The company operates about 75 facilities throughout the US as well as in Canada and Mexico; it also markets to Europe and the Asia/Pacific region, offering such metal-processing services as forming, laser cutting, machining, plasma cutting, tube bending, and sawing. Founded by Kirkman O'Neal in 1921 in Alabama, the company has expanded largely through acquisitions. It is still owned and run by the O'Neal family.

O'Neal has added a number of companies in the latter half of the decade, acquiring Pennsylvania-based metals service center TW Metals; metal services center Timberline Steel; supply chain management company Supply Dynamics, and service center TAD Metals, which focuses on aluminum and stainless steel.

EXECUTIVES

Chairman: Craft O'Neal
President and CEO: Bill Jones
CIO: Michael (Mike) Gooldrup
EVP and COO: Holman Head
EVP and CFO: Mary Valenta
VP and CIO, TW Metals: Aldo Miceli
VP Human Resources: Shawn Smith
VP and CFO, TW Metals: Kirk Moore
VP Sales and Marketing, TW Metals:
Robert L. (Bob) Mraz
VP Human Resources, TW Metals: Patricia H. Wilson
President and CEO, TW Metal: Jack Elrod
President, Metal West: Terry Taft
Director Marketing: Henley Smith

LOCATIONS

HQ: O'Neal Steel, Inc.
744 41st St. North, Birmingham, AL 35222
Phone: 205-599-8000   **Fax:** 205-599-8037
Web: www.onealsteel.com

PRODUCTS/OPERATIONS

Selected Products

Alloy bars
Coil
Cold finished bars
Grating
Hot rolled bars
Pipe
Structural shapes
Tubing

Selected Processing Services

Coil processing
Cutting
Forming
Machining
Notching
Punching and drilling
Rolling
Sawing
Shearing
Tube bending
Welding

COMPETITORS

A. M. Castle
Metals USA
Quanex Building Products
Reliance Steel
Russel Metals
Ryerson
SSAB North America
Worthington Industries

HISTORICAL FINANCIALS

Company Type: Private

Income Statement

FYE: December 31

	REVENUE ($ mil.)	NET INCOME ($ mil.)	NET PROFIT MARGIN	EMPLOYEES
12/08	2,930	—	—	4,400
12/07	2,440	—	—	4,400
12/06	2,300	—	—	4,300
12/05	1,600	—	—	3,700
Annual Growth	22.3%	—	—	5.9%

Revenue History

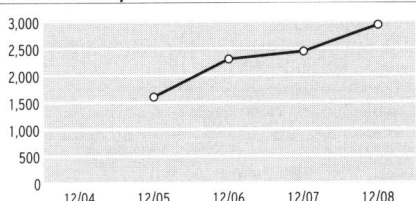

Orlando Magic

This organization hopes to work a little voodoo on the basketball court. The Orlando Magic is a professional basketball franchise that joined the National Basketball Association in 1989. A surprising upstart, Orlando made its first playoff appearance in 1994 with the help of star center Shaquille O'Neal and reached the NBA Finals the following season, losing to the Houston Rockets in four games. (O'Neal left the following year to join the Los Angeles Lakers.) Founded by local businessman Jim Hewitt, the team holds court at Orlando's Amway Arena; the family of Amway co-founder Rich DeVos has owned the Magic through RDV Sports since 1991.

The team brought in Steve Van Gundy to be head coach in 2007 following an aborted attempt to hire University of Florida basketball coach Billy Donovan. During his inaugural season, Orlando reached the second round of the NBA playoffs. The Magic won its second conference title in 2009 by defeating LeBron James and the Cleveland Cavaliers in six games. However, they lost in the NBA Finals to the Los Angeles Lakers.

Orlando began construction of a new events facility in 2008 that will serve as the future home of the Magic. The team plans to move into the $480 million arena for the 2010 season. Michigan-based direct-sales company Amway took over naming rights at Orlando's current arena in 2006 with a four-year deal that pays the city about $1.5 million each year. Previous named sponsor TD Waterhouse had let its naming deal run out after it was acquired by Ameritrade to become TD AMERITRADE.

Through RDV Sports, the DeVos family owns the RDV Sportsplex entertainment and fitness center. They previously owned the WNBA Orlando Miracle. (Sold in 2002, the team now competes as the Connecticut Sun.)

EXECUTIVES

Owner and Chairman: Richard M. (Rich) DeVos Sr., age 83
President and CEO: Bob Vander Weide, age 50
COO: Alex Martins
CFO: Jim Fritz
General Manager: Otis Smith
Head Coach: Stan Van Gundy, age 50
SVP Corporate Relationships: Jack Swope
SVP: Pat Williams, age 69
VP Information Technology: Jason Coleman
VP Business Strategy: Charles Freeman
VP Communications: Joel Glass
VP Community Relations and Government Affairs: Linda Landman-Gonzalez
VP Corporate Partnerships: Chip Bowers
VP Marketing and Ticket Sales: Chris D'Orso
VP Human Resources and Administrative Services: Audra Hollifield
Director Communications: George Galante
Director Broadcasting: Kevin Cosgrove
Director Marketing: Stephanie Mellenberndt

LOCATIONS

HQ: Orlando Magic, Ltd.
8701 Maitland Summit Blvd., Orlando, FL 32810
Phone: 407-916-2400   **Fax:** 407-916-2830
Web: www.nba.com/magic

The Orlando Magic play at the 17,519-seat capacity Amway Arena in Orlando, Florida.

PRODUCTS/OPERATIONS

Championship Titles
Eastern Conference Champions (1995, 2009)

COMPETITORS

Charlotte Bobcats
Hawks Basketball
Miami Heat
Washington Wizards

OSF Healthcare System

OSF Healthcare helps patients feeling oh, so frail. OSF Healthcare System includes seven acute care hospitals and two long-term care facilities, with some 1,600 beds (as well as more than 1,000 beds in its network of affiliates). The system's primary care physician network consists of about 250 physicians at 50 locations. Subsidiary OSF Home Care provides hospice, home visit, and equipment services, and OSF Saint Francis provides ambulance, pharmacy, and health care management services. Serving Illinois and Michigan, the system is a subsidiary of the Sisters of The Third Order of St. Francis.

OSF sold its OSF Healthplans subsidiary to Humana in 2008. OSF Healthplans offered managed care programs to employers and Medicare recipients in a number of central and northern Illinois counties and served about 80,000 people.

EXECUTIVES

Chairperson: Sister Judith Ann Duvall
Vice Chairperson and CEO: James M. Moore
President, Treasurer, and Director: Sister Diane Marie McGrew
CFO and SVP Finance and Accounting: Daniel Baker
SVP Quality Improvement: Sister Joan Marie Paris
SVP Materials Management: Larry M. Brown
SVP Engineering: Mike Chihoski
SVP Human Resources: Bruce F. Mehl
SVP Compliance and Privacy: John R. Evancho
SVP Legal Services and Director: Vance C. Parkhurst
SVP Managed Care: Mary E. Breeden
SVP Mission Integration and Corporate Ethicist: Joseph J. Piccione
SVP Marketing and Communications: James G. Farrell
Secretary: Sister Theresa Ann Brazeau
Management Information Systems and CIO: Michael B. Nauman
Director: Sister Mary Ellen Flannery
Director and Director, Medical Services: Gerald J. McShane
Auditors: KPMG LLP

LOCATIONS

HQ: OSF Healthcare System
800 NE Glen Oak Ave., Peoria, IL 61603
Phone: 309-655-2850   **Fax:** 309-655-6869
Web: www.osfhealthcare.org

PRODUCTS/OPERATIONS

Selected Facilities
OSF Holy Family Medical Center (Monmouth, IL)
OSF Saint Anthony Medical Center (Rockford, IL)
OSF Saint Clare Home (Peoria Heights, IL)
OSF Saint Francis Medical Center (Peoria, IL)
OSF Saint James — John W. Albrecht Medical Center (Pontiac, IL)
OSF Saint Mary Medical Center (Galesburg, IL)
OSF St. Francis Hospital (Escanaba, MI)
OSF St. Joseph Medical Center (Bloomington, IL)

COMPETITORS

Centegra Health System
Covenant HealthCare
Memorial Health System
SwedishAmerican Health System
University of Michigan Health System

HISTORICAL FINANCIALS
Company Type: Not-for-profit

Income Statement   FYE: September 30

	REVENUE ($ mil.)	NET INCOME ($ mil.)	NET PROFIT MARGIN	EMPLOYEES
9/08	1,482	—	—	4,007

OSI Industries

You might say a steady diet of red meat has made this company big and strong. OSI Industries (doing business as OSI Group) is one of the largest suppliers of meat products to foodservice operators. Through its operating companies, OSI provides a variety of beef, pork, and poultry products, including beef patties, hot dogs, sausages, bacon, and chicken nuggets. It has long been a supplier of beef to fast-food chain McDonald's. In addition, OSI offers contract manufacturing and packaging services for other food processors; it has more than 40 manufacturing facilities around the world. The company traces its roots to a family meat market started by Otto Kolschowsky.

EXECUTIVES

Chairman, President, and CEO: Sheldon (Shelly) Lavin
President and COO: David G. (Dave) McDonald, age 44
EVP and CFO: William J. (Bill) Weimer Jr.
EVP, Americas Zone: Kevin R. Scott
EVP, General Counsel, and Secretary: William S. Lipsman
SVP Sales: Ron Bree
VP Finance, Americas Zone: Patricia A. Peterson
VP, Treasurer, and Assistant Secretary: Sherry DeMeulenaere
Assistant VP Human Resources: Mike Diaz

LOCATIONS

HQ: OSI Industries, LLC
1225 Corporate Blvd., Aurora, IL 60504
Phone: 630-851-6600   **Fax:** 630-692-2340
Web: www.osigroup.com

COMPETITORS

Cargill Meat Solutions
Golden State Foods
Hormel
JBS
Keystone Foods
Lopez Foods
Perdue Incorporated
Pilgrim's Pride
Sanderson Farms
Sara Lee North American Retail
Smithfield Foods
Tyson Foods

HISTORICAL FINANCIALS

Company Type: Private

Income Statement

FYE: December 31

	ESTIMATED REVENUE ($ mil.)	NET INCOME ($ mil.)	NET PROFIT MARGIN	EMPLOYEES
12/08	3,000	—	—	9,200
12/07	4,620	—	—	22,000
12/06	4,200	—	—	20,500
12/05	4,000	—	—	19,738
12/04	3,400	—	—	—
Annual Growth	(3.1%)	—	—	(22.5%)

Revenue History

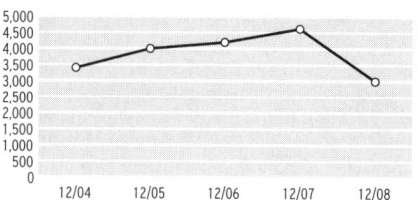

OSI Restaurant Partners

Peel back the layers of this restaurateur and you'll find more than a bloomin' steakhouse. OSI Restaurant Partners is the #2 casual-dining company in terms of revenue (behind Darden Restaurants) with nearly 1,500 locations in the US and 20 other countries. Its flagship Outback Steakhouse chain boasts more than 970 outposts offering steak, chicken, and seafood in Australian-themed surroundings. OSI Restaurants also operates the Carrabba's Italian Grill chain, along with Bonefish Grill and Fleming's Prime Steakhouse. A small number of the restaurants are franchised. Kangaroo Holdings, a group including co-founders Chris Sullivan and Bob Basham and private equity firm Bain Capital, owns the company.

OSI Restaurants has developed along the same lines as other multi-concept dining businesses, using its restaurant concepts to target different segments of the dining market. Outback Steakhouse and Carrabba's are designed to appeal to the casual steak and Italian dining segments, respectively, while Bonefish Grill offers mid-market seafood fare. Fleming's, meanwhile, is a player in the upscale dining sector.

With the recession taking a heavy toll on the casual dining industry, OSI Restaurants has been focused primarily on reducing costs through negotiations with suppliers and other improvements in its supply chain. The company has also been working to cut labor costs. To help with top line growth, OSI introduced a new menu of lower-priced items to drive additional traffic to its flagship Outback Steakhouse chain.

In addition to those restructuring moves, OSI has been looking to offload some of its developing chains to focus on its core dinnerhouses. The company sold its Cheeseburger in Paradise concept for $2 million to a group led by that chain's president, Steve Overholt. The gourmet burger chain had grown to almost 40 locations. That disposal came after OSI sold a majority stake in its Lee Roy Selmon's business to co-founders Sullivan and Bob. A Southern-style comfort food concept, Lee Roy Selmon's had a half-dozen units. Other concepts being looked at for disposal include Roy's (Hawaiian-inspired dishes created by chef Roy Yamaguchi) and Blue Coral Seafood.

Liz Smith was brought in as CEO in 2009, replacing Bill Allen, who retired. She previously served as president of Avon Products.

EXECUTIVES

Chairman: A. William (Bill) Allen III, age 49, $4,121,228 total compensation
President, CEO, and Director: Elizabeth A. (Liz) Smith, age 46
EVP and Chief Officer Legal and Corporate Affairs: Joseph J. Kadow, age 52, $1,178,782 total compensation
EVP and Chief Brand Officer: Jody L. Bilney, age 47, $1,176,884 total compensation
EVP and Chief Development Officer: Richard L. Renninger, age 41
SVP and CFO: Dirk A. Montgomery, age 45, $1,339,230 total compensation
SVP and Chief Procurement Officer: Irene Wenzel
SVP Construction: Steven C. (Steve) Stanley
SVP Equipment and Design: Lindon Richardson
VP Public Relations: Stephanie L. Amberg
President, Outback Steakhouse: Jeff Smith, age 46
President, Roy's: Mark D. Running
President, Fleming's Prime Steakhouse and Wine Bar; President, Blue Coral Seafood & Spirits: C.H. (Skip) Fox
President, Bonefish Grill: John W. Cooper, age 55
President, Carrabba's Italian Grill: Steven T. (Steve) Shlemon, age 49
President, Outback Steakhouse International: Michael W. Coble, age 60
Chef and Founder, Roy's: Roy Yamaguchi
Auditors: PricewaterhouseCoopers LLP

LOCATIONS

HQ: OSI Restaurant Partners, LLC
2202 N. West Shore Blvd., Ste. 500
Tampa, FL 33607
Phone: 813-282-1225
Web: www.osirestaurantpartners.com

2008 Locations

	No.
US	
Florida	215
California	84
Texas	74
North Carolina	63
Virginia	63
Ohio	53
Georgia	51
New York	45
Pennsylvania	43
New Jersey	42
Maryland	41
Tennessee	40
South Carolina	39
Michigan	38
Arizona	35
Colorado	30
Illinois	30
Indiana	29
Alabama	24
Massachusetts	21
Louisiana	20
Washington	20
Kentucky	17
Missouri	17
Nevada	17
Oklahoma	14
Wisconsin	13
Connecticut	12
Kansas	12
Arkansas	11
Minnesota	10
Iowa	8
Mississippi	8
Nebraska	8
Oregon	8
West Virginia	8
Hawaii	7
Idaho	7
Other states	32
International	182
Total	**1,491**

PRODUCTS/OPERATIONS

2008 Sales

	$ mil.	% of total
Restaurants	3,939.4	99
Other	23.4	1
Total	**3,962.8**	**100**

2008 Locations

	No.
Company-owned	1,323
Franchised	146
Joint venture	22
Total	**1,491**

2008 Locations

	No.
Outback Steakhouse	978
Carrabba's Italian Grill	238
Bonefish Grill	149
Fleming's Prime Steakhouse	61
Cheeseburger in Paradise	38
Roy's	26
Blue Coral Seafood & Spirits	1
Total	**1,491**

COMPETITORS

Applebee's
Brinker
Carlson Restaurants
Cheesecake Factory
Darden
Del Frisco's Restaurant
Hooters
McCormick & Schmick's
Ruby Tuesday
Ruth's Hospitality
Texas Roadhouse

Income Statement				FYE: December 31
	REVENUE ($ mil.)	NET INCOME ($ mil.)	NET PROFIT MARGIN	EMPLOYEES
12/08	3,963	—	—	105,000
12/07	4,167	—	—	—
Annual Growth	(4.9%)	—	—	—

Revenue History

(Line graph showing revenue history from 12/04 to 12/08, with values around 4,000 at 12/07 and declining slightly to 12/08)

Oxbow Corporation

Oxbow's Koch is bullish on coke. The diversified firm's Oxbow Carbon unit markets and distributes coke, coal, petroleum, and carbon products and other commodities to power producers, refineries, and industrial manufacturers. Oxbow is the world's top marketer of petroleum coke, which is used in power generation, cement kilns, sugar mills. and aluminum manufacturing. The company also trades gypsum, bauxite, and clinker. Oxbow also owns a highly productive coal mine which produces 6.5 million tons of coal annually. Oxbow is controlled by William Koch, an America's Cup winner who founded Oxbow in 1983 after being ousted from the family business (Koch Industries) by brothers Charles and David.

EXECUTIVES

President and CEO: William I. (Bill) Koch
CFO and Director: Zachary K. Shipley
EVP, Petcoke Supply and Optimization: David Nestler
EVP, Oxbow Calcined Petcoke Business: Eric Johnson
EVP, General Counsel, and Director:
  Richard P. Callahan
VP Human Resources: Kathy Flaherty
President, Oxbow Gas: Brian Mock
President, Gunnison Energy: Brad Robinson
President, Oxbow Steel International: Ron Saca
President and COO, Oxbow Carbon and Minerals:
  Brian Acton
President, Oxbow Mining: Jim Cooper
Director Corporate Communications: Brad Goldstein
Auditors: PricewaterhouseCoopers LLP

LOCATIONS

HQ: Oxbow Corporation
  1601 Forum Place, Ste. 1400
  West Palm Beach, FL 33401
Phone: 561-697-4300   **Fax:** 561-697-1876
Web: www.oxbow.com

COMPETITORS

Alliance Resource	Koch Industries, Inc.
Arch Coal	Massey Energy
Black Hills	Peabody Energy
CONSOL Energy	Westmoreland Coal
Drummond Company	

Income Statement				FYE: December 31
	REVENUE ($ mil.)	NET INCOME ($ mil.)	NET PROFIT MARGIN	EMPLOYEES
12/08	4,500	—	—	1,100
12/07	3,400	—	—	1,200
12/06	1,600	—	—	800
12/05	1,300	—	—	800
Annual Growth	51.3%	—	—	11.2%

Revenue History

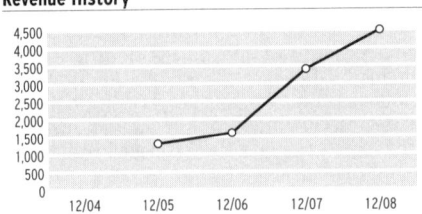

Pabst Brewing

The Pabst Brewing Company is a 19th-century brewer retooled for the 21st century. Pabst, founded in Milwaukee in 1844, today is something of a "virtual" brewer. The company actually owns no breweries, but instead, it pays other brewers, such as G. Heileman Brewing and Stroh Brewery, to actually manufacture the beers, while Pabst retains the ownership and marketing of its brands (including Pabst Blue Ribbon, Blatz, Pearl, Lone Star, Old Milwaukee, Old Style, Schlitz, and Colt 45). Pabst Brewing is owned by the private group Kalmanovitz Charitable Trust.

Pabst's market share can't compare with those of the nation's top brewing giants, but its Pabst Blue Ribbon is enjoyed by rebel beer drinkers who resist the mass marketing of Pabst's rivals.

In 2009 Kevin Kotecki resigned as CEO; he was replaced by John J. Lennon. Lennon was most recently the president of International Beverage Holdings USA and has held the position of president and CEO at both Pyramid Breweries and Beck's North America.

HISTORY

The Pabst Brewing Company was founded in 1844 in Milwaukee, Wisconsin, by Jacob Best and his four sons. Expansion came 10 years later when Jacob's son, Philip, opened a sales office in Chicago.

Philip's daughter, Maria, married Frederick Pabst in 1862, and he bought a half interest in the brewing company two years later. Pabst went on to become the company's president, and under his direction the brewery began selling nationwide.

Pabst was the #1 beer in the US through the turn of the century, registering sales throughout the US, across Europe, and as far afield as China. By the 1970s Pabst fell to #3. Its decline was attributed to its failure to introduce new brands. In 1983 Pabst acquired Olympia Brewing Co. (founded 1896).

In a 1985 takeover, Paul Kalmanovitz and his S&P Company acquired Pabst. Kalmanovitz

---

plowed the profits of Pabst and other beer interests into real estate until he died in 1987. His wife, Lydia, died seven years later. After her death, relatives attempted to gain larger shares of the estate, charging, among other things, that trustees of the Kalmanovitz family had influenced her to change her will and had kept her isolated.

Financial information obtained from court filings revealed that Pabst was losing money. S&P closed the antiquated Milwaukee plant in 1996 and farmed all Pabst production out to rival brewer Stroh, throwing about 400 Pabst workers out of their jobs. In 1998 S&P moved Pabst Brewing back to Milwaukee via a five-year contract with Miller Brewing.

In 2001 the company agreed to move production of the Pabst-owned brands to Miller Brewing's plant in Fort Worth, Texas. Pabst's historic Pearl brewery in San Antonio shut down that year as well. In 2003 Pabst had about 3% of the US beer-drinking market, still exceeding many premium imports such as Heineken and Guinness.

In 2006 the company moved its corporate headquarters from San Antonio to the Chicago suburb of Woodridge, Illinois. The state is one of Pabst's largest markets.

EXECUTIVES

Chairman: Bernard Orsi
CEO: John J. Lennon, age 54
COO: James P. (Jim) Walter
CFO: William (Bill) Wolz
CTO: Dave Meinz
Chief Sales Officer: Abbott Wolfe
Chief Marketing Officer: Brad Hittle
VP Human Resources: Susan Lundquist
VP Network Development: Richard Bartlett
VP and General Counsel: Yeoryios Apallas
Director, Management Information Systems:
  Linda Ramos

LOCATIONS

HQ: Pabst Brewing Company
  9014 Heritage Pkwy., Ste. 308, Woodridge, IL 60517
Phone: 630-972-3830
Web: www.pabstbrewingco.com

PRODUCTS/OPERATIONS

Selected Breweries and Brands

F&M Schaefer Brewing Co.
  Schaefer Beer

G. Heileman Brewing Co.
  Carling's Black Label Beer
  Blatz Beer
  Champale Malt Beverage
  Colt 45 Malt Liquor
  Coqui 900 Premium Malt Liquor
  Kingsbury Beer
  National Bohemian Beer
  Old Style Beer
  Schmidt Beer
  Special Export Beer
  Stag Beer

Jos. Schlitz Brewing Co.
  Old Milwaukee Beer
  Schlitz Beer

Lone Star Brewing Co.
  Lone Star Beer

McSorley's Ale House
  McSorley's Ale

Narragansett Brewing Co.
  Haffenreffer Private Stock Malt Liquor

Pabst Brewing Co.
  Jacob's Best Beer
  Olympia Genuine Draft Style Beer
  Pabst Blue Ribbon Beer

Pearl Brewing Co.
  Ballantine Beer
  Country Club Malt Liquor
  Falstaff Beer
  Pearl Beer
Piel Bros.
  Piels Light Beer
Rainier Brewing Co.
  Rainier Beer
Southampton Bottling, LLC
  Southampton Ales and Lagers
Specialty Brewing Co.
  Ice Man Malt Liquor
St. Ides Brewing Co.
  St. Ides High Gravity Malt Liquor
Stroh Brewery Co.
  Schlitz Malt Liquor
  Silver Thunder Malt Liquor
  Stroh's Beer

COMPETITORS

Anchor Brewing
Anheuser-Busch
Big Rock Brewery
Boston Beer
Breckenridge Brewery
Carlsberg
City Brewing Company
Constellation Brands
Craft Brewers Alliance
Flying Dog Brewery
Gambrinus
Grupo Modelo
Heineken
Jacob Leinenkugel
Labatt
Lancaster Brewing Co.
Lion Brewery
Massachusetts Bay Brewing
Molson Coors
New Belgium Brewing
Pyramid Breweries
Rheingold
Rogue Ales
SABMiller
Shipyard Brewing
Sierra Nevada
Stone Brewing
Stoudt's Brewing
Victory Brewing
Weyerbacher Brewing

Pacific Coast Building Products

Protecting Ronald Reagan's papers *and* propping up the San Francisco art world would seem like a tall order, but Pacific Coast Building Products does both. The building materials manufacturer and distributor made roof tiles for Reagan's presidential library and concrete blocks for the San Francisco Museum of Modern Art. Through its subsidiaries, it sells building products for residential, commercial, and industrial construction to builders and contractors in the western US. Pacific Coast Building Products also provides services, such as roofing and insulation. The late Fred Anderson (father-in-law of president and CEO David Lucchetti) founded the company as Anderson Lumber in 1953; his family owns the firm.

EXECUTIVES

Chairman: James B. Thompson
President and CEO: David J. Lucchetti
CFO: Darren Morris
CIO: Mike O'Dell
EVP: Dave Pringle
VP Human Resources: Mark Ingram
Director Marketing: Elaine Keane
Director Community Relations: Megan Vincent
Manager Human Resources: Kimberly Bright

LOCATIONS

HQ: Pacific Coast Building Products, Inc.
  10600 White Rock Rd., Bldg. B, Ste. 100
  Rancho Cordova, CA 95670
Phone: 916-631-6500   **Fax:** 916-631-6690
Web: www.paccoast.com

PRODUCTS/OPERATIONS

Selected Subsidiaries, Divisions, and Activities

Contracting
  Alcal Roofing, Waterproofing, and Insulation (installation and service of commercial and residential insulation, roofing, waterproofing)
  Arcade Insulation (installation and service of commercial and residential insulation)
Distribution
  Anderson Lumber (framing packages, including decks, doors, millwork, joists, paneling, plywood, particle board, lumber)
  Anderson Truss (roof and floor trusses, I-joists)
  Diamond Pacific (building products from lumber to paint, plus Keystone Retaining Wall Systems)
  Pacific Supply (brick, roofing materials, masonry, drywall, stucco products, acoustical ceiling products, insulation, pipes, waterproofing and coatings, tools and equipment)
  P.C. Wholesale (mill-direct shipments of lumber, sheet goods, i-joists, siding, and other wood products for large, high-volume projects)
Manufacturing
  Basalite Concrete Products (dry mixes, fences and wall systems, paving stones, retaining walls, structural block, garden products, stucco)
  Gladding, McBean (clay, terra cotta, architectural pottery, roof tile)
  H.C. Muddox (brick, clay, stone products; flue liners; pool coping; glass block)
  Interstate Brick (brick, stone veneer, flue liners, glass brick)
  PABCO Gypsum (drywall)
  PABCO Roofing Products (asphalt roofing shingles)
Transportation
  Material Transport (fleet for transporting product and raw materials between various divisions)
  Pacific Coast Jet Charter, Inc. (charter jet and turboprop service throughout Western Hemisphere)

COMPETITORS

84 Lumber
ABC Supply
Building Materials Holding
Dixieline ProBuild
Georgia-Pacific
Guardian Building Products Distribution
HD Supply
Huttig Building Products
Lowe's
Pavestone
USG

Pacific Mutual

Life insurance is "alive and whale" at Pacific Mutual Holding. The company's primary operating subsidiary, Pacific Life Insurance (whose logo is a breaching whale), is a top California-based life insurer. Lines of business include a variety of life insurance products for individuals and businesses; annuities and mutual funds geared to individuals and small businesses; management of stable value funds, fixed income investments, and other investments for institutional clients and pension plans; and real estate investing. Additionally, its Aviation Capital Group subsidiary provides commercial jet aircraft leasing. The company is owned by its Pacific Life shareholders and led by CEO James Morris.

Major operating subsidiaries of Pacific Mutual Holding include mutual fund and annuities distribution network Pacific Select Distributors; Pacific Asset Funding, which provides trade financing and related services; and College Savings Bank, which offers a variety of college savings vehicles.

Pacific Life has expanded its European operations by acquiring the International Life Reinsurance segment of Scottish Re Group. The $70 million buy — renamed Pacific Life Re — bolstered Pacific Life's reinsurance offerings to insurance and annuity providers in the UK and Ireland, as well as some markets in Asia.

The company has been selling off some of its broker/dealer businesses, excluding its Pacific Select operations. For example, Pacific Mutual sold its minority stake in Pacific Investment Management Company (PIMCO), a major investment management firm, for $288 million to PIMCO's majority-owner, insurance giant Allianz. It had already sold smaller chunks of its PIMCO stake to Allianz in previous years.

Pacific Mutual Holding Company was created in 1997 following a conversion to a mutual holding company structure. Pacific LifeCorp is the intermediate stockholding company, which owns 100% of Pacific Life and can take on outside capital funding (though it has not done so).

HISTORY

The Pacific Mutual Life Insurance began business in 1868 in Sacramento, California, as a stock company. Its board was dominated by California business and political leaders, including three of the "Big Four" who created the Central Pacific Railroad (Charles Crocker, Mark Hopkins, and Leland Stanford) and three former governors (Stanford, Newton Booth, and Henry Huntley Haight). Stanford (founder of Stanford University) was the company's first president and policyholder.

By 1870 Pacific Mutual Life was selling life insurance throughout most of the western US. Expansion continued in the early 1870s into Colorado, Kentucky, Nebraska, New York, Ohio, and Texas. In 1873 the company ventured into Mexico but sold few policies. It had better luck in China, accepting its first risk there in 1875, and in Hawaii, where it started business two years later. In 1881 Pacific Mutual Life moved to San Francisco.

Leland Stanford died in 1893. The eponymous university and Stanford's widow, though rich in assets, found themselves struggling through a

US economic depression. The benefit from Stanford's policy kept the university open until the estate was settled.

In 1905 Conservative Life bought the firm. The Pacific Mutual Life name survived the acquisition just as its records survived the fire that ravaged San Francisco after the 1906 earthquake. Pacific Mutual Life then relocated to Los Angeles.

The company squeaked through the Depression after a flood of claims on its noncancellable disability income policies forced Pacific Mutual Life into a reorganization plan initiated by the California insurance commissioner (1936). After WWII, Pacific Mutual Life entered the group insurance and pension markets.

After 83 years as a stock company and an eight-year stock purchasing program, Pacific Mutual Life became a true mutual in 1959.

Pacific Mutual Life relocated to Newport Beach in 1972. During the 1980s it built up its financial services operations, including its Pacific Investment Management Co. (PIMCO, founded 1971). The company was in trouble even before the stock crash of 1987 because of health care costs and over-investment in real estate. That year it brought in CEO Thomas Sutton, who sold off real estate and emphasized HMOs and fee-based financial services.

In the 1990s the firm cut costs and increased its fee income. PIMCO Advisors, L.P. was formed in 1994 when PIMCO merged with Thomson Advisory Group. The merger gave Pacific Mutual Life a retail market for its fixed-income products, a stake in the resulting public company, and sales that offset interest-rate variations and changes in the health care system.

In 1997 the company assumed the corporate-owned life insurance business of failed Confederation Life Insurance; it also merged insolvent First Capital Life into Pacific Life as Pacific Corinthian Life. That year Pacific Mutual Life, which became Pacific Mutual Holding, became the first top-10 US mutual to convert to a mutual holding company, thus allowing it the option of issuing stock to fund acquisitions. Because the firm remained partially mutual, however, policyholders retained ownership but got no shares of Pacific LifeCorp, its new intermediate stockholding company.

To compete with such one-stop financial service behemoths as Citigroup, Pacific Mutual began selling annuities through a Compass Bank subsidiary in 1998. The next year it bought controlling interests in broker-dealer M.L. Stern and investment adviser Tower Asset Management. In 2000 the world's #2 insurer, Allianz, bought all of PIMCO Advisors (now Allianz Global Investors of America) other than the interest retained by Pacific Mutual when it spun off the investment manager. (Pacific Mutual gradually sold its holdings in the firm, and thus its stake in Pacific Investment Management Company, through sales to Allianz.)

Pacific Mutual Holding sharpened its focus on individuals and small businesses in 2001 with the sale of its reinsurance unit to what is now Scottish Re.

With its focus so firmly on life insurance, Pacific Life sold its group health insurance business (which included medical, dental, and life policies) to PacifiCare in 2005.

In 2007 the company formed Pacific Asset Management to act as a third-party manager for structured credit transactions.

EXECUTIVES

Chairman, President, and CEO; President and CEO, Pacific Life Insurance Company: James T. (Jim) Morris, age 49
EVP and CFO: Khanh Tran, age 52
SVP Human Resources: Anthony J. Bonno
CEO, College Savings Bank: Gilbert S. Johnson
President and CEO, M.L. Stern & Co.: Milford L. (Mickey) Stern
Group Managing Director and CEO, Aviation Capital Group: R. Stephen Hannahs
Managing Director, Pacific Asset Funding: Robert G. Denhert
Chairman and CEO, Pacific Select Group: Gerald W. (Bill) Robinson
Auditors: Deloitte & Touche LLP

LOCATIONS

HQ: Pacific Mutual Holding Company
700 Newport Center Dr., Newport Beach, CA 92660
Phone: 949-219-3011
Web: www.pacificlife.com

PRODUCTS/OPERATIONS

2008 Sales

	$ mil.	% of total
Policy fees & insurance premiums	2,103	39
Net investment income	2,029	38
Aircraft leasing	571	11
Investment advisory fees	255	5
Other	403	7
Adjustments	(1,351)	—
Total	**4,010**	**100**

Selected Products and Services

Life Insurance Division
  Indexed universal life
  Interest-sensitive whole life
  Joint and last-survivor life
  Term life
  Universal life insurance
  Variable universal life
Annuities and Mutual Fund Division
  529 College savings plans
  Individual(k) programs
  Mutual funds
  Small business 401(k) plans
  Variable annuities
Investment Management Division
  Fixed income investments
  Funding agreements
  High-yield and money market advisory
  Private equity investments
  Single premium group annuity contracts
  Stable value products
  Structured settlement annuities
Aircraft Leasing Division
  Aircraft asset management for third-party financial institutions
  Aircraft and aviation-related joint venture investments
  Commercial jet aircraft for lease to airlines
Other products and services
  Asset funding
    Invoice discounting
    Refinancing and re-factoring of accounts receivable
    Revolving credit facilities
    Structured trade finance facilities
  Real estate services
    Commercial mortgage-backed securities
    Equity real estate properties and funds
    Fixed-rate and floating-rate mortgage loans
    REIT debt

COMPETITORS

AXA Financial	Mutual of Omaha
Boeing Capital	Nationwide
CIT Transportation Finance	New York Life
Great-West Life	Northwestern Mutual
Guardian Life	Penn Mutual
Hartford Life	Principal Financial
John Hancock Financial	Prudential
Lincoln Financial	StanCorp Financial
MassMutual	Travelers Companies
MetLife	USAA

HISTORICAL FINANCIALS

Company Type: Mutual company

Income Statement

FYE: December 31

	ASSETS ($ mil.)	NET INCOME ($ mil.)	INCOME AS % OF ASSETS	EMPLOYEES
12/08	96,983	(289)	—	—
12/07	111,024	647	0.6%	2,800
12/06	99,346	614	0.6%	2,900
12/05	86,977	542	0.6%	3,100
12/04	77,137	540	0.7%	—
Annual Growth	5.9%	—	—	(5.0%)

2008 Year-End Financials

Equity as % of assets: —
Return on assets: —
Return on equity: —
Long-term debt ($ mil.): —
Sales ($ mil.): 4,010

Net Income History

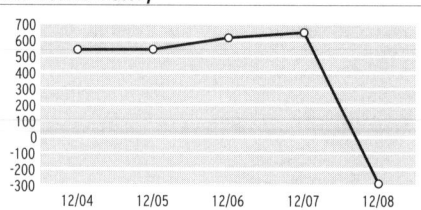

Palmetto Bancshares

Since the palmetto is South Carolina's state tree, does that make Palmetto Bancshares that state's official bank? Palmetto Bancshares is the holding company for The Palmetto Bank, which operates about 40 full- and limited-service branches mostly in upstate South Carolina. Its offerings include checking, savings, and money market accounts; IRAs; and CDs. Loans secured by commercial real estate account for the largest portion of its loan portfolio, with single-family residential mortgages at a distant second. The Palmetto Bank also provides financial planning, trust, and brokerage services, plus bond, mutual fund, and annuity sales. It's been serving South Carolinians since 1906.

A group of about 17 officers and directors controls approximately 15% of Palmetto Bancshares, led by chairman and CEO Leon Patterson who owns about 9%.

EXECUTIVES

Chairman and CEO: L. Leon Patterson, age 68, $501,107 total compensation
EVP and Chief Credit Officer: William (Jack) McElveen Jr., age 46
SEVP, Palmetto Bancshares and The Palmetto Bank: Lee S. Dixon, age 43
SEVP, Palmetto Bancshares and The Palmetto Bank: Samuel L. (Sam) Erwin, age 41
Treasurer; EVP, The Palmetto Bank: Ralph M. Burns III, age 58
EVP and Chief Credit Officer, The Palmetto Bank: W. Michael Ellison, age 56, $196,687 total compensation
EVP, The Palmetto Bank: Teresa W. Knight, age 54, $190,129 total compensation
SVP, COO, and CTO, Palmetto Bank: Edward M. Simpson, age 53
SVP and CFO, Palmetto Bank: Lauren S. Greer, age 34
SVP and Commercial Relationship Manager, The Palmetto Bank: Robert A. (Rob) Hrubala
SVP, The Palmetto Bank: Cindi S. Adams
Vice Chairman, Retail Banking, The Palmetto Bank: George A. (Andy) Douglas Jr., age 57, $285,546 total compensation
Secretary: Teresa M. Crabtree
Auditors: Elliott Davis LLC

LOCATIONS

HQ: Palmetto Bancshares, Inc.
301 Hillcrest Dr., Laurens, SC 29360
Phone: 864-984-4551   **Fax:** 864-984-8415
Web: www.palmettobank.com

COMPETITORS

Bank of America
BB&T
Community Capital
Community First Bancorp
First Citizens Bancorporation
First National Bancshares
First South Bancorp (NC)
First South Bancorp (SC)
GrandSouth Bancorporation
Peoples Bancorporation
Provident Community Bancshares
South Financial Group
Southern First Bancshares
Wachovia Corp

HISTORICAL FINANCIALS

Company Type: Private

Income Statement

FYE: December 31

	ASSETS ($ mil.)	NET INCOME ($ mil.)	INCOME AS % OF ASSETS	EMPLOYEES
12/08	1,370	14	1.0%	415
12/07	1,248	16	1.3%	409
12/06	1,153	15	1.3%	400
12/05	1,075	14	1.3%	387
12/04	996	12	1.2%	374
Annual Growth	8.3%	3.0%	—	2.6%

2008 Year-End Financials

Equity as % of assets: —
Return on assets: 1.0%
Return on equity: —
Long-term debt ($ mil.): 52
Sales ($ mil.): 97

Net Income History

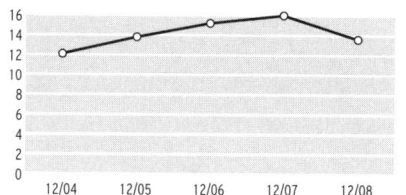

| | 12/04 | 12/05 | 12/06 | 12/07 | 12/08 |

Panda Restaurant Group

This Panda certainly has food on its mind. Panda Restaurant Group is a leading quick-service restaurant operator with more than 1,200 Panda Express locations in more than 35 states, Puerto Rico, and Japan. The chain offers Asian-themed food primarily in high-traffic locations, including malls, airports, and sporting arenas. The company also runs almost 30 mall-based Hibachi-San outlets that offer a quick-service Japanese grill menu. For patrons looking for full-service dining, Panda Restaurants has a handful of Panda Inn branded units in California. The company is owned by the family of co-chairman Andrew Cherng, who opened the first Panda Inn location in 1973.

Where other restaurant operators have mostly failed, Panda Restaurants has succeeded in creating a nationwide chain of Asian food outlets, a feat made more impressive by the fact that the company does not have a full-scale franchising effort. (A small number of locations are licensed to such foodservice operators as SSP America.) However, by owning and operating the vast majority of its restaurants, Panda Restaurants has been able to maintain strict training and food quality standards.

In the food court arena, Panda Express must contend against major fast-food chains such as Taco Bell and KFC (both part of YUM! Brands) and McDonald's. The brand also fits within the growing fast-casual category, however, along with such heavyweights as Chipotle Mexican Grill and Panera Bread.

Cherng opened the first Panda Inn with his father (a master Szechuan chef) in Pasadena, California, in 1973. A decade later they opened the first Panda Express in a California mall.

EXECUTIVES

Co-Chairman: Andrew Cherng
Co-Chairman: Peggy Tsiang Cherng, age 61
CEO: Thomas E. (Tom) Davin, age 51
CFO: John F. Theuer
Chief Marketing Officer: Glenn Lunde
Chief People Officer: Linda Brandt
EVP Restaurant Development: Kim Ellis
SVP Operations Support and Innovation: Larry Behm
SVP Information Systems: William Yu
VP Operations: Stanley Liu
VP Real Estate: David Landsberg
General Counsel: Mike Wilkinson
Executive Chef, Panda Inn: Sun-Fu Huang
Executive Chef, Panda Express: Andy Kao

LOCATIONS

HQ: Panda Restaurant Group, Inc.
1683 Walnut Grove Ave., Rosemead, CA 91770
Phone: 626-799-9898   **Fax:** 626-372-8288
Web: www.pandarg.com

COMPETITORS

ABP Corporation	Kahala
AFC Enterprises	L&L Hawaiian Barbecue
Burger King	McDonald's
Café de Coral	Moe's Southwest Grill
Chick-fil-A	Quiznos
Chipotle	Sbarro
CKE Restaurants	Subway
Einstein Noah	Wendy's/Arby's Group, Inc.
Fazoli's	YUM!
Jack in the Box	

Parsons Corporation

Parsons provides engineering, construction, and management services for corporate, industrial, institutional, and government projects all over the world. It designs and builds power plants, dams, commercial buildings; provides environmental remediation services including hazardous materials cleanup; and adds improvements to airports, rail systems, bridges, and highways. Its Commercial Technology (PARCOMM) unit serves corporate and government clients with a wide variety of capabilities including design, development, management, and support services. Other units include Parsons Water & Infrastructure, Parsons Infrastructure & Technology, and Parsons Transportation. The employee-owned group was founded in 1949.

Parsons competes in every major region — and many major industries — of the world. Its client roster includes telecom carriers, equipment manufacturers, government agencies, pharmaceutical firms, defense contractors, and transportation agencies. Parsons participates in such initiatives as the US Army's program to develop alternative technologies for the destruction of chemical weapons. The group has had decades of experience internationally in infrastructure restoration, including work in Bosnia-Herzegovina and Kosovo.

Parsons is participating in the $4.5 billion renovation of the Pentagon, the largest design/build office renovation project in the US. Through a joint venture, the company provides project and construction management services for the renovation, which is the first major upgrade for the site since its construction. Other recent projects include the construction of a mock village in California for the US Army to test equipment designed to detect improvised explosive devices (IEDs) in war zones.

Parsons has grown throughout its history by acquiring businesses with new capabilities or serving new sectors. In 2009 the company acquired analytic services provider McMunn Associates, which has done work for the Department of Defense, Department of Energy, and other government agencies. Other purchases include the wireless telecommunications services company Alaris Group, pharmaceuticals and biotechnology construction firm MW Consultants, and bridge engineering group Finley McNary Engineers.

HISTORY

Ralph Parsons, the son of a Long Island fisherman, was born in 1896. At age 13 he started his first business venture, a garage and machine shop, which he operated with his brother. After a stint in the US Navy, Parsons joined Bechtel as an aeronautical engineer. The company changed its name to Bechtel-McCone-Parsons Corporation in 1938. However, Parsons later sold his shares in that company and left in 1944 to start his own design and engineering firm, the Ralph M. Parsons Co., after splitting with partner John McCone (who later headed the CIA).

Parsons Co. expanded into the chemical and petroleum industries in the early 1950s. During that decade it oversaw the building of several natural gas and petroleum refineries overseas, including the world's largest, in Lacq, France.

In the early 1960s the company began working in Kuwait, which later proved to be one of its biggest markets. By 1969 Parsons had built oil refineries for all of the major oil companies, designed launch sites for US missiles, and constructed some of the largest mines in the world. In 1969 the company went public. With annual sales of about $300 million, it ranked second only to Bechtel in the design and engineering field. Ralph Parsons died in 1974.

The company built oil and gas treatment and production plants in Alaska in the 1970s and reorganized itself into The Parsons Corporation and RMP International in 1978. It went private in 1984 as The Parsons Corporation, taking advantage of a new tax law that favored corporations with employee stock ownership plans (ESOPs). Not all employees were happy, though. Several groups sued, maintaining that the plan disproportionately benefited executives, and that the buyout left the ESOP with all of the debt but no decision-making power. A Labor Department investigation later exonerated Parsons executives.

Parsons had just finished work on a power plant in Kuwait when Iraq invaded in 1990. Several employees were detained by the Iraqis but were released shortly before the Persian Gulf War. Two years later the company returned to Kuwait to rebuild some of the country's demolished infrastructure.

James McNulty, who had led the company's infrastructure and technology group, replaced Leonard Pieroni as CEO in 1996 after Pieroni died in a plane crash in Bosnia.

Parsons restructured in 1997 to focus on energy, transportation, and infrastructure projects. In 1999 Parsons was chosen to manage construction of a $5 billion refinery in Bahrain, a $1.4 billion gas plant in Saudi Arabia, and a $1 billion polyethylene project in Abu Dhabi.

Parsons partnered with TRW in 2000 to create TRW Parsons Management & Operations to bid on the DOE's Yucca Mountain site in Nevada, a potential repository for the US's high-level radioactive waste and spent nuclear fuel. It also was awarded a three-year contract to help rebuild the war-torn Serbian province of Kosovo and the next year was awarded a similar contract for Bosnia-Herzegovina.

In 2001 the company won a US Federal Aviation Agency contract to upgrade air traffic control towers and other equipment and systems, a contract that had been held by rival Raytheon since 1988. That year the company's joint venture with construction giant Fluor was awarded a contract to design and do engineering work for the first offshore oil field in Kazakhstan.

In 2002 Parsons completed construction of the Parsons Fabrication Facility as part of the US Army's push for alternative methods of chemical weapons disposal.

In 2004 the Parsons' joint venture with Kellogg Brown & Root won a controversial defense contract for oil field and refinery engineering, construction, and maintenance in Iraq.

Parsons was selected to provide engineering management support for Russia's Chemical Weapons Destruction Complex in 2006.

The company ran into trouble in war-torn Iraq in 2007. The army cancelled the remainder of a $70 million contract to build 20 hospitals in Iraq, due to performance problems with the construction. The company maintained (and an investigation supported) that the problems stemmed from mismanagement by the Army Corps of Engineers. It then lost a $99 million contract to build a prison in northern Iraq.

McNulty retired in 2008, and Charles Harrington took over the helm as both chairman and CEO.

EXECUTIVES

Chairman and CEO: Charles L. (Chuck) Harrington, age 50
Vice Chairman, EVP, Chief Risk Officer, and Special Assistant to the CEO: Curtis A. (Curt) Bower
SVP and General Counsel: Clyde E. (Sonny) Ellis Jr.
SVP and East Division Manager, Water and Infrastructure: Kevin E. Kelly
VP Government Relations: Larry G. Shockley
VP and Program Manager, Water and Infrastructure: Robert P. (Bob) Vilker
VP Safety: Andrew D. Peters
VP Government Relations: Margareth C. Harper
Group Executive, Development and Strategy: James R. (Jim) Shappell
VP Global Shared Services: John D. Thomas
VP Corporate Relations: Erin M. Kuhlman
VP Human Resources: David R. Goodrich
President, Parsons Transportation Group: Thomas E. Barron
President, Water and Infrastructure: Richard N. (Rich) Wankmuller
President, Parsons Infrastructure & Technology Group: Todd K. Wager
President, Commercial Technology: Michael M. (Mike) Walsh
Group Executive, Operations and Risk: Thomas L. (Tom) Roell

LOCATIONS

HQ: Parsons Corporation
100 W. Walnut St., Pasadena, CA 91124
Phone: 626-440-2000   **Fax:** 626-440-2630
Web: www.parsons.com

PRODUCTS/OPERATIONS

Selected Markets and Services

Parsons Commercial Technology
  Advanced manufacturing
  Commercial facilities
  Data management services
  Educational facilities
  Entertainment
  Healthcare
  Industrial environmental remediation
  Life sciences
  Mission critical facilities
  Telecommunications
  Vehicle inspection and compliance
  Wireless telecommunications systems
Parsons Infrastructure and Technology
  Community relations
  Construction
  Construction management
  Design
  Engineering
  Estimating
  Operations
  Operator training
  Procurement

Program management
Start-up and operations
Parsons Transportation
  Aviation
  Bridges
  Highways
  Railroads
  Revenue collection and management systems
  Systems engineering
  Transportation consumer services
  Transportation planning
  Tunneling
  Urban Transit
Parsons Water and Infrastructure
  Biosolids management
  Combined sewer overflows
  Construction/Construction management
  Desalination and membrane technology
  Design-build
  Emergency response support
  Environmental planning and restoration
  Master planning
  Ocean outfalls
  Operations and maintenance
  Storm water management
  Utility tunneling
  Wastewater collection systems
  Wastewater treatment
  Water resources
  Water supply and pipelines

COMPETITORS

ABB	Layne Christensen
AECOM	Lend Lease
ARCADIS	Louis Berger
BE&K	M. A. Mortenson
Bechtel	Michael Baker
Black & Veatch	Mott MacDonald
Bouygues	Paragon Project Resources
Day & Zimmermann	Pernix Group
Fluor	Peter Kiewit Sons'
Foster Wheeler	RailWorks
Gilbane	RBF Consulting
Granite Construction	Shaw Group
Halliburton	Technip
Hill International	TIC Holdings
HOCHTIEF	Turner Corporation
Hyundai Engineering	Tutor-Saliba
Jacobs Engineering	URS
Kaiser Group	Vecellio & Grogan
KBR	Washington Division

HISTORICAL FINANCIALS

Company Type: Private

Income Statement

FYE: December 31

	REVENUE ($ mil.)	NET INCOME ($ mil.)	NET PROFIT MARGIN	EMPLOYEES
12/08	3,400	—	—	11,500
12/07	3,600	—	—	11,500
12/06	2,710	—	—	11,500
12/05	3,000	—	—	11,600
12/04	1,990	—	—	10,000
Annual Growth	14.3%	—	—	3.6%

Revenue History

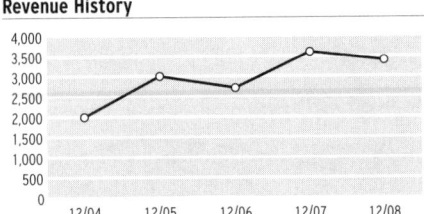

Partners HealthCare System

Partners HealthCare System is looking out for the health of the Bay State. Founded by Brigham and Women's Hospital and Massachusetts General Hospital, Partners HealthCare now includes six community hospitals and other health care centers. Functioning as an umbrella, the system offers acute, primary and specialist health care, and other services. Other ventures include the Harvard Clinical Research Institute and the Dana-Farber/Partners CancerCare (a collaboration with the Dana-Farber Cancer Institute). Partners HealthCare System also includes home health and hospice services and long-term care facilities. Its rehabilitation facilities include the Spaulding Rehabilitation Hospital Network.

Partners Community HealthCare is a management services organization that provides support for a physician network encompassing more than 4,500 practitioners. Partners HealthCare also sponsors community health outreach programs. Community hospitals affiliated with Partners include McLean Hospital, Newton-Wellesley Hospital, North Shore Medical Center, and the Martha's Vineyard Hospital.

Brigham and Women's and Massachusetts General are both teaching hospitals for Harvard's Medical School. The Harvard Clinical Research Institute is a partnership between the Harvard Medical School, Partners HealthCare, and CareGroup. Partners HealthCare also conducts research with Harvard through the Center for Genetics and Genomics.

EXECUTIVES

Chairman: John M. (Jack) Connors Jr., age 66
President, CEO, and Trustee: James J. Mongan
COO: Thomas P. Glynn, age 61
Chief Development Officer: Allen Peckham
Chief of Staff: Robin M. Jacoby
Chief Scientific Officer: Dennis A. Ausiello
VP Finance: Peter K. Markell, age 53
VP and CIO: John P. Glaser
VP Business Planning and Market Development: Lynne J. Eickholt
VP and General Counsel: Brent L. Henry
VP Human Resources: Dennis D. Colling
VP Public Affairs: Lee A. Chelminiak
VP Research Ventures and Licensing: Christopher H. (Chris) Colecchi
VP Corporate Development and Treasury Affairs: Jay B. Pieper, age 65
Director Communications: Richard W. Copp Jr.

LOCATIONS

HQ: Partners HealthCare System, Inc.
Prudential Tower, 800 Boylston St., Ste. 1150
Boston, MA 02199
Phone: 617-278-1000   **Fax:** 617-278-1049
Web: www.partners.org

PRODUCTS/OPERATIONS

Selected Member Institutions

Brigham and Women's Hospital
  Brookside Community Health Center
  Faulkner Hospital
Dana-Farber/Partners CancerCare (joint venture)
Harvard Clinical Research Institute (joint venture)
Harvard-Partners Center for Genetics and Genomics (joint venture)
Martha's Vineyard Hospital

Massachusetts General Hospital
  Charlestown HealthCare Center
  Chelsea HealthCare Center
  MGH Back Bay Health Center
  North End Community Health Center
  Revere HealthCare Center
McLean Hospital (mental health and chemical dependency)
MGH Institute of Health Professions
Nantucket Cottage Hospital
Newton-Wellesley Hospital
North Shore Medical Center
  North Shore Children's Hospital
  Salem Hospital
  Union Hospital
Partners Community HealthCare, Inc.
Partners Continuing Care
  Boston Center for Rehabilitative and Subacute Care
  Clark House Nursing Center at Foxy Hill Village
  North End Rehabilitation and Nursing Center
  Partners Hospice
  Partners Home Care
  Rehabilitation Hospital of the Cape and Islands
  Shaughnessy-Kaplan Rehabilitation Hospital
  Spaulding Rehabilitation Hospital Network
  Youville Hospital and Rehabilitation Center

COMPETITORS

Baystate Health
Boston Medical Center
Cambridge Health Alliance
Cape Cod Healthcare
Care New England
Caritas Christi
Children's Hospital Boston
Milford Regional Medical Center
Northeast Health System
Southcoast Hospitals Group
Universal Health Services
Vanguard Health Systems

HISTORICAL FINANCIALS

Company Type: Not-for-profit

Income Statement

	REVENUE ($ mil.)	NET INCOME ($ mil.)	NET PROFIT MARGIN	EMPLOYEES
9/08	6,478	—	—	16,981

FYE: September 30

Paul, Hastings, Janofsky & Walker

Paul, Hastings, Janofsky & Walker has built a solid reputation in employment law, and over the years companies such as United Parcel Service and Hughes Aircraft have turned to the firm for its expertise in the field. With about 1,300 attorneys, Paul Hastings also practices in such areas as intellectual property, litigation, mergers and acquisitions, and real estate. Paul Hastings operates from about 20 offices, not only in the US but also in Europe and the Asia/Pacific region. The firm was founded in 1951; it adopted its current name in 1962.

EXECUTIVES

Chairman: Seth M. Zachary
Managing Partner: Greg M. Nitzkowski
CIO: Stova Wong
Chair, Tax Department: Douglas A. Schaaf
Chair, Private Equity Practice Group and Partner, Costa Mesa: William J. Simpson
Chair, Real Estate Department and Partner, Los Angeles: Philip N. Feder
Chair, Employment Law Department and Partner, Los Angeles: Nancy L. Abell
Chair, Corporate Department and Partner, Los Angeles: Robert A. Miller Jr.
Managing Partner, San Diego and Chair, National Securities Litigation Practice Group: William F. Sullivan
Global Chairman, Litigation Department and Partner, Washington, DC: James D. (Jamie) Wareham
Chief Administrative Officer: Adam Norris
Chief Business Development and Marketing Officer: Meg Sullivan
Managing Director Diversity and Global Talent: Anton Mack
Director Public Relations: Eileen King
Director Information Services: Deborah (Debby) Hein
Partner, Employment Department: Bo Cooper
Partner and Chair, Global Restructuring Practice: Luc Despins

LOCATIONS

HQ: Paul, Hastings, Janofsky & Walker LLP
515 S. Flower St., 25th Fl., Los Angeles, CA 90071
Phone: 213-683-6000   **Fax:** 213-627-0705
Web: www.paulhastings.com

PRODUCTS/OPERATIONS

Selected Practice Areas

Affordable housing and tax credits
Antitrust and competition
Appellate litigation
Asset securitization and structured finance
Banking and financial institutions
Bankruptcy litigation
Base realignment and closures
Class actions
Commercial leasing and sales leaseback
Copyright
Corporate
Counseling and preventive advice
Disaster mitigation
E-discovery
Employment class actions
Employment law
Employment litigation
Environmental law
ERISA, employee benefits, and executive compensation
Estate planning and probate
Finance and restructuring
Financial litigation
Financial services
Foreign corrupt practices act
Government affairs
Government contracts litigation
Immigration
Intellectual property
Intellectual property transactions and licensing
International arbitration
International employment law
International trade and export controls
Investment management
Labor/management relations
Land use
Leveraged finance
Litigation
Mergers and acquisitions
Patent litigation
Patent preparation and prosecution
Payment systems
Political risk and international trade credit insurance
Private equity
Private investment funds
Product liability and toxic tort
Project development and finance

Purchase and sale of non-performing loans
Real estate
Real estate acquisitions and dispositions
Real estate equity investments and joint ventures
Real estate finance
Real estate capital markets
Real estate litigation
Real estate restructuring and reorganization
Regulatory compliance
Restructuring
Securities finance and capital markets
Securities litigation and enforcement
Sustainability and global climate change
Tax advisory
Trade secrets
Trademark
White collar, internal investigations, and corporate
  governance

COMPETITORS

Baker & McKenzie	Orrick
DLA Piper	Perkins Coie
Gibson, Dunn & Crutcher	Pillsbury Winthrop Shaw
Jones Day	Pittman
Latham & Watkins	Seyfarth Shaw
Littler Mendelson	Skadden, Arps
Morrison & Foerster	Wilson Sonsini
O'Melveny & Myers	

HISTORICAL FINANCIALS

Company Type: Partnership

Income Statement

FYE: January 31

	REVENUE ($ mil.)	NET INCOME ($ mil.)	NET PROFIT MARGIN	EMPLOYEES
1/08	976	—	—	2,500
1/07	814	—	—	2,500
1/06	667	—	—	2,650
1/05	609	—	—	—
1/04	537	—	—	—
Annual Growth	16.1%	—	—	(2.9%)

Revenue History

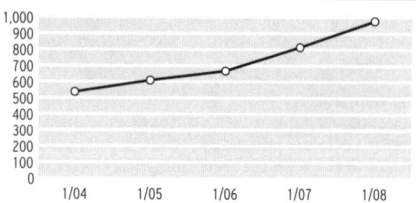

PBS

You might say these shows get a lot of public support. Public Broadcasting Service (PBS) is a non-profit organization that provides educational and public interest programming to more than 350 member public TV stations in the US. In addition to such programs as *NOVA*, *This Old House*, and *Masterpiece Theatre*, it provides related services such as distribution, fundraising support, and technology development. PBS gets its revenue from underwriting, membership dues, federal funding (including grants from the not-for-profit Corporation for Public Broadcasting), royalties, license fees, and product sales. The organization was founded in 1969 to provide cultural and educational programming.

While PBS — and its federal funding — regularly finds itself caught in the crossfire between liberal and conservative political groups, supporters of the non-profit trumpet the benefits of publicly funded television programming created to serve groups often overlooked by commercial broadcasters. PBS's children's programming and news shows such as *Frontline* and *PBS NewsHour* (formerly *The NewsHour with Jim Lehrer*) are often touted as examples of how public broadcasting can fill voids left by the major networks.

Being publicly supported has not spared PBS from the downturn in the economy, however. The recession has led to declining federal funds and has made it harder for the network to raise additional underwriting support from corporations. In response, PBS has been focused on cutting production costs while maintaining quality programming. That effort included some job cuts in 2009.

The organization has also been looking to capitalize on new distribution channels to get its programming to the public. PBS sells its programs on DVD and through Apple's iTunes store. It has also ramped up its online video efforts.

EXECUTIVES

Chair: John E. Porter
General Vice Chair: Robert J. Flowers
Professional Vice Chair: Peter Frid
President, CEO, and Director: Paula A. Kerger
COO: Michael D. Jones
CTO: John McCoskey
Chief Content Officer: John L. Boland
CFO and Treasurer; SVP, Corporate Services: Barbara L. Landes
SVP and Chief TV Programming Executive: John F. Wilson
SVP Interactive: Jason Seiken
SVP PBS Ventures: Andrew L. Russell
SVP Programming Services: Pat Hunter
SVP Children's Media and PBS Brand Management: Lesli Rotenberg
SVP, General Counsel, and Corporate Secretary: Katherine Lauderdale
SVP Education: Robert M. Lippincott
SVP Station Services: Joyce Herring
Auditors: BDO Seidman, LLP

LOCATIONS

HQ: Public Broadcasting Service
  2100 Crystal Dr., Arlington, VA 22202
Phone: 703-739-5000   **Fax:** 703-739-8495
Web: www.pbs.org

PRODUCTS/OPERATIONS

Selected Programming

Antiques Roadshow
Austin City Limits
Barney
Evening at Pops
Frontier House
Frontline
Great Performances
In The Mix
Juila Child: Lessons with Master Chefs
Live from Lincoln Center
Masterpiece Theatre
Mister Rogers' Neighborhood
MotorWeek
Mystery!
Nature
NOVA
NOW
P.O.V.

PBS NewsHour
Reading Rainbow
Sesame Street
Teletubbies
This Old House
Victory Garden
Washington Week
ZOOM

COMPETITORS

ABC, Inc.
BBC Worldwide
CBS
Current Media
Discovery Communications
Disney ABC Cable
Fox Entertainment
HBO
MTV Networks
NBC
NBC Universal Cable
Rainbow Media
Scripps Networks
Turner Broadcasting

P.C. Richard & Son

P.C. Richard & Son aims to beat out Best Buy. The family-owned company has about 50 electronics stores in the New York City area. P.C. Richard sells home electronics (DVD players, TVs), computers and appliances (microwaves, vacuum cleaners), and entertainment systems (portable electronics, video games, satellites). P.C. Richard also sells its wares online. In 2003 the company acquired the name, trademark, and customer lists of bankrupt electronics chain Nobody Beats The Wiz. Founded in 1909 by Dutch immigrant milkman and jack-of-all-trades Peter Christiään Richard as a hardware store, the firm is operated by fourth-generation Richard family members.

The regional consumer electronics chain plans to expand beyond New York City and Long Island to the north and west. To that end, P.C. Richard opened its first store in Westchester County in 2008. It also opened its first location in Staten Island in fall 2007, making its coverage of New York's five boroughs complete. To aid its expansion, P.C. Richard is developing a tract of land along the New Jersey Turnpike to improve its distribution operations.

About half of the company's locations house design centers for high-end appliances from manufacturers such as Bosch, Miele, Sub-Zero, and Viking.

EXECUTIVES

CEO: Gary Richard
President: Gregg Richard
CTO: Chuck Fichtner
EVP: Peter Richard II
VP and CFO: Tom Pohmer
Manager Operations: Peter Richard III
Director Human Resources: Bonni Rondinello

LOCATIONS

HQ: P.C. Richard & Son
  150 Price Pkwy., Farmingdale, NY 11735
Phone: 631-843-4300   **Fax:** 631-843-4309
Web: www.pcrichard.com

PRODUCTS/OPERATIONS

Selected Products

Appliances
Camcorders
Cameras
Home office
Mobile
Portable electronics
Televisions
Vacuums
Video games

COMPETITORS

Best Buy
J & R Electronics
Lowe's
Sears
Sixth Avenue Electronics
Wal-Mart

Pella Corporation

Call Pella more practical than romantic; it can't make a window to your soul, but it can make windows for your house. Since the mid-1920s, Pella has designed, manufactured, and installed window and door products made from wood, vinyl, and fiberglass for construction and remodeling in the residential and commercial sectors. Many of its windows are energy efficient. Pella operates a nationwide network of stores and also sells its products through retailers in the US and Canada, as well as distributors in Asia, Mexico, Central America, the Caribbean, Russia, the Middle East, and the UK. Do-it-yourselfers can find its windows and patio doors at such stores as Lowe's. Descendants of founder Pete Kuyper own Pella.

Pella was founded in 1925 as the Rolscreen Company. The company was named after its first product, a roll-up window screen. Updated in design, the patented Rolscreen insect screen still remains a popular product.

In 2008 Pella was affected by the downturn in residential building, forcing it to close manufacturing plants in Tucson, Arizona, and Story City, Iowa. In addition, layoffs were announced at several of its US manufacturing plants, including its facility in Sioux City, Iowa.

Mel Haught retired as CEO in late 2009. He was succeeded by company executive Pat Meyer, who joined Pella in 1990.

EXECUTIVES

Chairman: Charles (Charlie) Farver
President and CEO: Pat Meyer
SVP and CFO: David Smart
VP Human Resources: Karin Peterson
IT Supply Chain Manager: Peter Genheimer
Corporate Public Relations: Kathy Krafka Harkema
Pella Corporation Sponsorships: Leanna Hafften

LOCATIONS

HQ: Pella Corporation
102 Main St., Pella, IA 50219
Phone: 641-628-1000   **Fax:** 641-628-6070
Web: www.pella.com

PRODUCTS/OPERATIONS

Selected Products

Doors
Fiberglass
Hinged patio
Sliding patio
Steel entry
Storm door
Windows
Angled
Awning
Bay/bow
Casement
Curved
Double-hung
Fixed
Garden
Single-hung
Sliding
Special (skylight)

Selected Brands

Architect Series
Centera by Pella
Designer Series
Encompass by Pella
Pella Impervia
ProLine
ThermaStar
Vinyl by Pella
Pella Entry Door Systems

Selected Materials

Fiberglass
Steel
Vinyl
Wood

COMPETITORS

Andersen Corporation
Atrium Companies
Designer Doors
GBO
Great Lakes Window
International Aluminum
JELD-WEN
Marshfield DoorSystems
MI Windows and Doors
NTK Holdings
Ply Gem
Sierra Pacific Industries
Silver Line Building Products
Simonton Windows, Inc.
Thermal Industries
Therma-Tru
Tomkins
TRACO
Weather Shield Manufacturing

Penn Mutual Life Insurance

Founded in 1847, Penn Mutual Life Insurance offers life insurance, annuities, and investment products and services. Its core product line consists of life insurance every which way, including traditional life insurance products (term life, whole and universal life) and a variety of fixed and variable annuities. The company sells its products through several channels, using both independent and captive agents, as well as broker/dealers. Two of its financial services subsidiaries — broker/dealer Hornor, Townsend & Kent and Janney Montgomery Scott — also distribute Penn Mutual products. Additionally, the company provides trust services to individuals and institutions through The Pennsylvania Trust Company.

EXECUTIVES

Chairman, President, and CEO: Robert E. Chappell, age 64
EVP and CFO: Peter J. Vogt
EVP and Chief Marketing Officer: Eileen C. McDonnell
EVP Technology and Service Operations: Terry Ramey
EVP and Chief Investment Officer: Peter M. Sherman
SVP and Chief Human Resources: Edward F. Clemons
SVP Career Agency System: William D. Gruccio
SVP Product Management Department: David O'Malley
SVP and General Auditor: Nina M. Mulrooney
SVP Retail Distribution: Ralph L. Crews
SVP and Treasurer: Barbara S. Wood
VP Corporate Communications: Patricia Beauchamp
President and CEO, Janney Montgomery Scott: Timothy C. (Tim) Scheve, age 51
President and CEO, Hornor, Townsend & Kent: Michelle Barry
Managing Corporate Counsel and Secretary: Frank Best

LOCATIONS

HQ: The Penn Mutual Life Insurance Company
600 Dresher Rd., Horsham, PA 19044
Phone: 215-956-8000   **Fax:** 215-956-7699
Web: www.pennmutual.com

PRODUCTS/OPERATIONS

2008 Sales

	$ mil.	% of total
Premiums	493.8	36
Investment income	388.8	28
Other	499.3	36
Total	**1,381.9**	**100**

Selected Subsidiaries and Affiliates

Hornor, Townsend & Kent, Inc. (securities broker/dealer)
Independence Capital Management, Inc. (in-house asset management)
Janney Montgomery Scott LLC (securities brokerage)
The Pennsylvania Trust Company (investment advisory and trust services)

COMPETITORS

AEGON USA
Aetna
AIG
American National Insurance
AXA Financial
Erie Family Life Insurance
The Hartford
ING Americas
John Hancock Financial Services
Manulife Financial
MassMutual
MetLife
Midland National Life
Nationwide Financial
New York Life
OM Financial
Pacific Mutual
Primerica
Protective Life
Protective Life and Annuity Insurance
Prudential
Securian Financial
Security Benefit Group
Sentry Insurance
TIAA-CREF
Union Central

HISTORICAL FINANCIALS

Company Type: Mutual company

Income Statement

FYE: December 31

	ASSETS ($ mil.)	NET INCOME ($ mil.)	INCOME AS % OF ASSETS	EMPLOYEES
12/08	12,628	43	0.3%	1,800
12/07	14,480	137	0.9%	3,000
12/06	14,082	145	1.0%	3,000
12/05	13,092	112	0.9%	—
12/04	14,251	137	1.0%	550
Annual Growth	(3.0%)	(25.2%)	—	34.5%

2008 Year-End Financials

Equity as % of assets: —
Return on assets: 0.3%
Return on equity: —
Long-term debt ($ mil.): —
Sales ($ mil.): 1,382

Net Income History

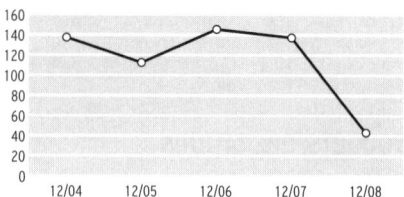

Pennsylvania Lottery

Even if they don't become millionaires, senior citizens in Pennsylvania can still benefit from the state lottery. Established in 1971, Pennsylvania Lottery proceeds (more than $18 billion raised since inception) are dedicated to programs geared toward seniors (property-tax relief, rent rebates, reduced-cost transportation, co-pay prescriptions). Proceeds also fund more than 50 Area Agencies on Aging across Pennsylvania. State law mandates that at least 40% of lottery proceeds must be awarded in prizes, and about 30% must be used for benefit programs. Games range from the traditional Powerball to daily-wagering game Big 4.

Powerball sales are down, and instant ticket sales (with lower profit margins), are increasingly accounting for a larger portion of total game sales. In 2008 Pennsylvania Lottery launched Quinto (mid-day and evening), the first five-digit numbers game introduced in the US. It also planned to launch two more Millionaire Raffles games in 2009 and 2010. In addition to new and revised games, the lottery is rolling out new equipment, promotions, and retailer and consumer incentive programs in order to increase sales.

The Pennsylvania Lottery is the sixth-largest lottery in the country in sales; it ranks fifth in the amount of proceeds it grants to programs.

EXECUTIVES

Executive Director: Ed Trees
Deputy Executive Director Administration and Finance: Walt Rubel
Deputy Executive Director Retail Operations: Tom Blaskiewicz
Deputy Executive Director Marketing and Product Development: Drew Svitko
Director Marketing: Rob Shelton
Director Finance and Administration: Damon Baltimore
Director Security: Jim Morgan
Director, Retail Operations: Bob Siodlowski
Director Research and Development: Cal Heath
Director Product Delivery: David Alicea
Press Secretary, Pennsylvania Lottery and Pennsylvania Department of Revenue: Stephanie Weyant

LOCATIONS

HQ: The Pennsylvania Lottery
1200 Fulling Mill Rd., Ste. 1, Middletown, PA 17057
Phone: 717-702-8000   **Fax:** 717-702-8024
Web: www.palottery.state.pa.us

The Pennsylvania Lottery has offices throughout Pennsylvania in Clearfield, Erie, Harrisburg, Lehigh, Middletown, Philadelphia, Pittsburgh, and Wilkes-Barre.

PRODUCTS/OPERATIONS

2008 Contributions

	% of total
Prizes	59
Benefit programs	30
Retailer & vendor commissions	8
Operating expenses	3
Total	**100**

COMPETITORS

Connecticut Lottery
Maryland State Lottery
Multi-State Lottery
New Jersey Lottery
New York State Lottery
Ohio Lottery
Virginia Lottery

HISTORICAL FINANCIALS

Company Type: Government-owned

Income Statement

FYE: June 30

	REVENUE ($ mil.)	NET INCOME ($ mil.)	NET PROFIT MARGIN	EMPLOYEES
6/08	3,089	928	30.0%	—
6/07	3,076	949	30.9%	—
6/06	3,070	965	31.4%	—
6/05	2,645	852	32.2%	—
6/04	2,352	817	34.7%	—
Annual Growth	7.1%	3.2%	—	—

Net Income History

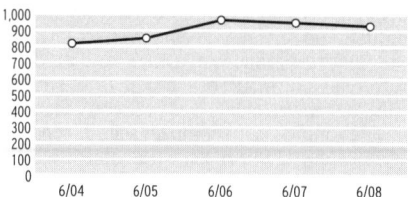

Pension Benefit Guaranty Corporation

Underfunded pension plans give PBGC the heebie-jeebies. The Pension Benefit Guaranty Corporation, or PBGC — itself operating at a multi-billion-dollar deficit — was set up to promote the growth of defined-benefit pension plans, provide payment of retirement benefits, and keep pension premiums as low as possible. The government agency protects the pensions of more than 34 million workers and monitors employers to ensure that plans are adequately funded. The agency receives no tax funds; its income is generated by insurance premiums paid by employers, investments, and assets recovered from terminated plans. The corporation was created by the Employee Retirement Income Security Act of 1974.

Insurance premiums paid by employers go into two programs: single-employer (about 28,800 pension plans) and multi-employer (some 1,540 pension plans under collective bargaining agreements that involve several unrelated employers). Employers pay about $8 per employee in the multi-employer plans and about $31 per employee for single-employer programs (plus a flat fee per $1,000 of unfunded vested benefits in underfunded plans).

PBGC terminates pension plans when it determines that a company can no longer pay benefits; it can take a portion of a company's assets to ensure that pension obligations are met. When PBGC takes over a failed plan, it pays each individual pensioner covered by the plan up to $54,000 annually.

Many companies have moved from traditional defined-benefit pension plans to so-called defined contribution plans, usually reducing the benefits of long-time workers in the process. Workers and their advocates criticize the switched plans, but they don't come under PBGC's jurisdiction unless they fail.

In 2009 the agency's Inspector General issued a report critical of former PBGC Director Charles Millard. The report alleged that Millard made improper contact with individuals at three companies who were under review to be hired as strategic investment partners for the agency. It alleged that Millard sent emails and made phone calls to individuals at BlackRock, Goldman Sachs, and JP Morgan while they were in line to be hired to manage real estate and private equity investments at PBGC. All three companies were ultimately hired, but their contracts will likely be canceled and rebid.

Millard, who served as agency director from 2007 to early 2009, declined to testify before a Congressional committee investigating the matter. He could face criminal charges in the matter.

The hiring of outside advisers was part of a controversial plan by Millard to shift PBGC's investments from bonds to stocks, private equity, and real estate to reduce the agency's deficit, which was $11 billion in late 2008. However, instead of cutting the deficit, the timing of the change to more volatile investments came just before the economy collapsed in 2008, adding to the problem. By May 2009 PBGC's deficit had tripled. The agency's board voted to return to a more conservative investment portfolio.

HISTORY

The Employment Retirement Income Security Act (ERISA) of 1974 established the Pension Benefit Guaranty Corporation (PBGC) to protect workers' pension benefits. The poor economy of the day guaranteed PBGC plenty of business. By 1975 more than 1,000 companies were unable to meet pension obligations. Other companies tried to avoid entering the system by terminating their plans before a 1996 deadline; the Supreme Court in 1980 upheld PBGC's contention that these companies were obligated to pay benefits to vested workers.

ERISA's provisions initially let companies voluntarily terminate their plans by paying PBGC a portion of their assets; many companies took this route until Congress limited the provision. Pensions faced a new threat in the late 1980s, as many buyout deals were structured to use company pension plans as part of their funding; Congress put a stop to that practice in 1990.

Companies found themselves caught between conflicting requirements of the PBGC (ever watchful for underfunded pension plans) and the IRS (which penalized overfunded plans). PBGC's deficit grew as it took on more and more pension payment liabilities; companies continued to jeopardize plans by using funds for other purposes. On behalf of 40,000 workers, PBGC in 1988 sued companies that allegedly terminated their plans illegally between 1976 and 1981 (the suit was settled in 1995 for $100 million).

In 1989 new director James Lockhart began airing PBGC's plight, claiming that the pension system would follow the savings and loan industry into collapse. In the early 1990s his predictions seemed reasonable; PBGC's deficit was driven sky-high by such bankruptcies as Pan Am (1991), TWA, and Munsingwear (1992). Under Lockhart's guidance, the PBGC began publishing the "iffy fifty" — the 50 most underfunded pensions in the country.

Martin Slate succeeded Lockhart in 1993 and toned down the Chicken Little rhetoric, although that year PBGC announced that underfunding had nearly doubled between 1987 and 1992. Help arrived in the form of 1994's Retirement Protection Act, which put some teeth into pension laws. Under the reforms, PBGC required some employers to notify workers and retirees about the funding of their plans; it also changed the rules for annual reporting to the PBGC. The next year President Clinton vetoed the budget bill, which would have allowed companies to take money from their pension plans.

Slate died in 1997 and David Strauss took over. After two decades in the red, PBGC in 1998 marked its third consecutive year in the black. The organization was sued by several former Pan Am workers who claimed PBGC had shorted their benefits.

In 1999 PBGC defended itself against critics who claimed it took too long to determine benefits from bankrupt companies and often required pensioners to repay thousands of dollars that had been paid in estimated benefits.

PBGC recorded a string of losses beginning in 2002, the largest in the single-employer programs; the agency had an $11 billion deficit in 2003, primarily due to terminated pension plans. Posting a $23.5 billion deficit in 2004 prompted the government to create a plan to protect the agency from going bankrupt. Losses decreased slightly over the years, but by 2007, PBGC was still more than $13 billion in the red. Strauss resigned that year. Vincent Snowbarger was appointed acting director in 2009.

HOOVER'S HANDBOOK OF PRIVATE COMPANIES 2010

EXECUTIVES

Acting Director and Deputy Director Operations:
Vincent (Vince) Snowbarger
COO: Richard H. Macy
CFO: Patricia Kelly
CIO: Patsy A. Garnett
Chief of Staff: George Koklanaris
Chief Management Officer: Stephen E. Barber
Chief Insurance Program Officer: Terrence M. Deneen
Director, Budget Department: Henry R. Thompson
Director, Benefits Administration and Payment Department (BAPD): Bennie Hagans
Chief Counsel: Israel Goldowitz
Director, Department of Insurance Supervision and Compliance (DISC): Joseph House
Director, Communications and Public Affairs Department (CPAD): Timothy M. Murtaugh
Director, Human Resources Department (HRD):
Arrie Etheridge
Director, Procurement Department (PD): Susan Taylor
Director, Strategic Planning and Evaluation Department (SPED): Wilmer Graham
General Counsel: Judith R. Starr
Director, Contracts and Controls Review Department (CCRD): Martin O. Boehm
Director, Policy, Research, and Analysis Department (PRAD): David Gustafson
Director, Legislative and Regulatory Department:
John R. Hanley
Director Facilities and Services Department (FASD):
Patricia Davis

LOCATIONS

HQ: Pension Benefit Guaranty Corporation
1200 K St. NW, Washington, DC 20005
Phone: 202-326-4000   **Fax:** 202-326-4042
Web: www.pbgc.gov

Penske Corporation

Penske, headed by race-car legend Roger Penske, appears to be on the right track as a diversified transportation firm. Penske is a partner with GE Equipment Management in Penske Truck Leasing, a commercial truck rental operation with about 200,000 vehicles at some 1,000 locations. Penske owns about 40% of publicly traded auto dealer Penske Automotive Group (formerly United Auto Group), which runs 310 franchised dealerships in some 20 states, Germany, Puerto Rico, and the UK. Through Penske Motor the company sells cars in California. Truck-Lite makes safety lights for boats, buses, cars, commercial trucks, construction equipment, and recreational vehicles. Roger Penske is the majority owner of the company.

Other Penske interests include: Michigan-based DAVCO, a leader in Class 8 heavy duty diesel powered truck fuel-heater/water separators and filter systems, and QEK Global Solutions, a provider of vehicle management services such as fleet planning and management; and logistics service provider Penske Logistics.

Penske just can't seem to resist that new car smell. The company has sold its racetrack interests and upped its stake in Penske Automotive Group (PAG). Roger Penske personally visited most of PAG's dealerships to help return the chain to profitability. He now heads PAG.

Penske souped up its Penske Truck Leasing unit with the purchase of Rollins Truck Leasing, which was the US's third-largest truck rental and leasing player.

Penske is also a lead investment partner in Transportation Resource Partners, which is part of a group that acquired automotive component maker Autocam in 2004.

HISTORY

As a teen Roger Penske earned money by repairing and reselling cars. At 21 he entered his first auto race; he was running second when his car overheated. His winning ways, however, were soon apparent, and in 1961 *Sports Illustrated* named him race car driver of the year.

Nonetheless, in 1965 Penske went looking for a day job. With a $150,000 loan from his father, he bought a Chevrolet dealership in Philadelphia and retired from racing to avoid loading his balance sheet with steep life-insurance premiums for the CEO. Penske teamed with driver Mark Donohue in 1966 to form the Penske Racing Team. Donohue died in a crash in 1975, but team Penske continued.

In 1969 Penske started a regional truck-leasing business, incorporated under the name Penske. The company established auto dealerships in Pennsylvania and Ohio in the early 1970s. In 1975 the company bought the Michigan International Speedway. Penske and fellow racing team owner Pat Patrick started the race-sponsoring organization Championship Auto Racing Teams (CART) in 1978.

In 1982 Penske's truck-leasing business formed a joint venture with rental company Hertz to form Hertz Penske Truck Leasing. Penske expanded its auto dealerships in the 1980s by acquiring dealerships in California, including Longo Toyota in 1985.

Racing legend Al Unser Sr. surprised Indy 500 watchers in 1987 by driving a car borrowed from an exhibition in a hotel lobby to a first-place finish for the Penske Racing Team.

In 1988 Penske bought 80% of GM's Detroit Diesel engine-making unit, which had a market share of only 3% and had lost some $600 million over the previous five years. Penske trimmed $70 million from the unit's budget by firing 440 salaried employees, streamlining manufacturing processes, and cutting administration expenses. Detroit Diesel's market share doubled in its first two years as a Penske unit. Also in 1988 Penske purchased Hertz's stake in Hertz Penske Truck Leasing, which it later combined with the truck-rental division of appliance maker General Electric to create Penske Truck Leasing.

By 1993 Detroit Diesel's market share had grown to more than 25%. That year the engine maker went public. Penske bought 860 Kmart auto centers for $112 million in 1995. The company's racing business, Penske Motorsports, went public in 1996, but Penske retained a 55% stake in the company. Also that year Penske bought Truck-Lite, Quaker State's automotive lighting unit.

Penske Truck Leasing formed Penske Logistics Europe in 1997 to offer information systems and other integrated logistics services on that continent. The next year it formed a logistics joint venture with Brazil-based Cotia Trading to serve US-based clients in the South American market, and Penske Logistics Europe opened a pan-European transport routing center in the Netherlands.

Penske sold its Penske Motorsports operations, which included racetracks in California, Michigan, North Carolina, and Pennsylvania, to International Speedway in 1999. The same year Penske invested about $83 million for a 38%

stake in car retailer United Auto Group and Roger Penske became CEO of Penske. In 2000 the company sold its 48.6% stake in Detroit Diesel to Daimler AG.

The following year Penske Corp. added three additional dealerships. Later in 2001 Penske Truck Leasing acquired Rollins Truck Leasing (then the US's third-largest player behind Ryder and Penske) for $754 million.

After Kmart filed Chapter 11 early in 2002, Penske expressed a "wait and see" strategy about the fate of its Penske Auto Centers business. Later that year Penske's Truck-Lite Industries bought Federal-Mogul's lighting business for $23 million.

Early in April 2002 Penske had waited long enough, and didn't like what it saw. It closed its 560-plus Penske Auto Centers at Kmart locations nationwide.

In 2007 Penske Corporation renamed two of its companies: United Auto Group changed its name to Penske Automotive Group, taking the name of the company's California auto dealership, which changed its name to Penske Motor Group.

The company sold its 50% stake in Italy's VM Motori, which specializes in the design and production of diesel engines, to Russian automaker GAZ Group in September 2008.

EXECUTIVES

Chairman and CEO: Roger S. Penske, age 72
EVP and CFO: J. Patrick Conroy
EVP: Walt Czarnecki
EVP, Penske Automotive Group, Eastern Region: Bernie Wolfe, age 53
EVP, Administration: Paul F. Walters, age 63
VP: Tim Cindric
VP, Human Resources: Randall W. Johnson
President, Penske Logistics: Vince Hartnett
Managing Director, Sytner Group: Gerard Nieuwenhuys, age 47
President and Director; Vice Chairman and President, Penske Automotive Group: Robert H. Kurnick Jr., age 47
Chairman, Truck-Lite, Inc.; Managing Partner, Transportation Resource Partners: Richard J. Peters, age 61
Director, Communications: Randy Ryerson

LOCATIONS

HQ: Penske Corporation
2555 Telegraph Rd., Bloomfield Hills, MI 48302
Phone: 248-648-2000   **Fax:** 248-648-2525
Web: www.penske.com

PRODUCTS/OPERATIONS

Selected Subsidiaries and Affiliates

Davco Technology, LLC (fuel filters and engine accessories)
Penske Automotive Group, Inc. (about 40%, retail auto sales)
Penske Motor Group (retail auto sales, California)
Penske Truck Leasing Co. LP (joint venture with GE Equipment Management, truck rental and leasing)
QEK Global Solutions (fleet and vehicle management services)
Truck-Lite Co., Inc. (automotive lighting)

COMPETITORS

AMERCO	Mack Trucks
Asbury Automotive	Navistar International
AutoNation	PACCAR
Daimler	Ryder System
Fiat	Sonic Automotive
General Motors	Trailer Fleet Services
Group 1 Automotive	Volvo
Isuzu	

Pepper Construction

Pepper Construction Group spices up the construction business with a little of this and a pinch of that. The construction operations of The Pepper Companies provide general contractor and construction management services for sectors including health care, retail, commercial, hotels, malls, and schools. Projects include the 29,000-sq.-ft. ape habitat at the Lincoln Park Zoo, 900,000-sq.-ft. of new or renovated space at Central DuPage Hospital, and more than a dozen Galyan's outdoor stores throughout the Midwest. Pepper Environmental Technologies provides hazardous waste services. Stanley F. Pepper founded the company in Chicago in 1927; the group is owned by his family and employees of the firm.

The Pepper Companies formed Pepper Construction Group in 2000 to combine its construction assets. It has divisions in Illinois, Indiana, Ohio, and Texas. Health care clients account for the largest share (28%) of Pepper Construction's business, followed by the entertainment and education sectors.

The company's extensive list of clients includes UBS, Indiana University, University of Notre Dame, Texas Heart Institute, and NASA.

Green building has become a large part of Pepper Construction's operations. It's Green Team of certified professionals have helped construct more than 2.9 million sq. ft. of eco-friendly space.

EXECUTIVES

Chairman and CEO: J. David (Dave) Pepper II, age 46
Chairman Emeritus: Richard S. Pepper
EVP and General Counsel: Thomas M. O'Leary
SVP and CFO: Joel D. Thomason
SVP Human Resources: John Beasley
President and COO, Pepper Construction Company: Kenneth A. (Ken) Egidi
President, Pepper Construction Company of Ohio: Paul Francois
President, Pepper-Lawson Construction in Texas: Paul E. Lawson
President, Pepper Construction Company of Indiana: William J. (Bill) McCarthy
SVP Marketing; President, Pepper Environmental Technologies: Richard H. (Rich) Tilghman
Director Communications: Shannon Ghera

LOCATIONS

HQ: Pepper Construction Group, LLC
643 N. Orleans St., Chicago, IL 60610
Phone: 312-266-4700   **Fax:** 312-266-2792
Web: www.pepperconstruction.com

PRODUCTS/OPERATIONS

2009 Sector and Service Breakdown

	% of total
Health care	28
Entertainment	14
Education	14
Retail	10
Interiors	8
Hospitality	6
Corporate Headquarters	5
Industrial	5
Water Works	4
Institutional	3
Commercial	1
Environmental, parking deck & other	2
Total	**100**

COMPETITORS

Barton Malow
Bovis Lend Lease
Bulley & Andrews
C. G. Schmidt
Charles Pankow Builders
Clark Enterprises
Gilbane
Graycor
M. A. Mortenson
McCarthy Building
Power Construction
Turner Corporation
Walbridge Aldinger
Walsh Group

Perceptive Software

Perceptive hopes your company is receptive to its document management tools. The company provides software and services that companies use to manage documents, workflows, and other enterprise content. Its ImageNow software suite includes tools for document and content capture, integration, imaging, Web publishing, and workflow management. The company's customers have included Asante Health System, Georgia Tech, Novant Health, and Vassar College. Perceptive has technology alliances with such companies as Canon, Hewlett-Packard, IBM, Microsoft, Oracle, SAP, and Sun Microsystems.

Perceptive markets its ImageNow suite and other imaging and document management applications directly and through resellers and system integrators worldwide.

EXECUTIVES

President and CEO: Scott Coons
CFO: Eric J. Bur
EVP Sales and Strategic Alliances: Tim Helton
EVP Marketing and Communications: Cary DeCamp
VP Professional Services: Patrick Kearney
VP Corporate Finance: Marjorie (Marge) Adair
VP Information Technology: Lynne Wilson
VP Technical Services: Brent Flanders
Director Human Resources: Susie Coultis
Director Sales: Dennis Cunningham
Manager Corporate Communications: Sherlyn Manson
Media Contact: Paul Arnhold

LOCATIONS

HQ: Perceptive Software, Inc.
22701 W. 68th Terrace, Shawnee, KS 66226
Phone: 913-422-7525   **Fax:** 913-422-3820
Web: www.imagenow.com

COMPETITORS

EMC
Hyland Software
Omtool
Open Text
Standard Register
Streamline Health Solutions

Perdue Incorporated

Chickens are always on the menu at this company. Perdue Incorporated is one of the largest poultry (chicken and turkey) producers in the US. The company operates live production and processing facilities in about 15 US states through its some 2,250 contracted poultry farmers. The Perdue Farms division processes and packs 3 billion pounds of chicken and 268 million pounds of turkey a year. Perdue sells poultry through retail food outlets and to foodservice customers, most of which are located in the eastern half of the US; the company also exports worldwide. Its Perdue Agribusiness unit processes grain for animal feed and pet food ingredients, makes vegetable oils, and manufactures fertilizer and renewable fuel.

Perdue continues to strengthen its position in the consumer poultry market with new product innovations such as frozen and full-cooked poultry products designed for busy families (and FUN SHAPES Nuggets for the kids). It has responded to consumer concerns about food quality, trumpeting its "Farm-to-Fork" production and processing capabilities, as well as its antibiotic-free products. It also offers safe-food handling tips on its Web site.

James Perdue — like his father, Frank, before him — appears in the company's advertisements. Perdue produces its own breed of chicken, the skin of which is a distinct yellow color, resulting from a diet that includes marigold petals. Arthur Perdue started the family-owned business in 1920.

HISTORY

If asked which came first, the chickens or the eggs, the Perdue family will tell you the eggs did. Arthur Perdue, a railroad express worker, bought 23 layer hens in 1920 and started supplying the New York City market with eggs from a henhouse in his family's backyard in Salisbury, Maryland. His son Frank joined the business in 1939.

The Perdues sold broiling chickens to major processors, such as Swift and Armour, in the 1940s and pioneered chicken crossbreeding to develop new breeds. The family started contracting with farmers in the Salisbury area in 1950 to grow broilers for them. Frank became president of the company in 1952. The next year it began mixing its own feed.

Frank persuaded his father to borrow money to build a soybean mill in 1961. (Arthur had not willingly gone into debt in his previous 40-plus years in the poultry industry.) The soybean mill was part of Frank's plan to vertically integrate the company — with grain storage facilities, feed milling operations, soybean processing plants, mulch plants, hatcheries, and 600 contract chicken farmers — to counter the threat of processors buying chickens directly from farmers rather than through middlemen like the Perdues. To differentiate their products, the Perdue name was applied to packages on retail meat counters in 1968.

Two years later the company began a breeding and genetic research program. During the following years Frank transformed himself from country chicken salesman to media poultry pitchman when the company decided to use him as spokesperson in its print, radio, and TV ads. Catchy slogans ("It takes a tough man to make a tender chicken") combined with Frank's whiny voice and sincere face helped sales. As Perdue Farms expanded geographically into new eastern markets such as Philadelphia, Boston, and Baltimore, it acquired the broiler facilities of other processors.

In 1983 James Perdue, Frank's only son, joined the company as a management trainee. In 1984 Perdue added processors in Virginia and Indiana and introduced turkey products. Two years later it acquired Intertrade, a feed broker, and FoodCraft, a food equipment maker. However, after enjoying a rising demand for poultry by a health-conscious society in the 1970s and early 1980s, the company found its sales leveling off in the late 1980s. When North Carolina fined Perdue for unsafe working conditions in 1989, the company increased its emphasis on safety.

James, who had become chairman of the board in 1991, replaced his folksy father in 1994 as the company's spokesman in TV ads. In the early 1990s Perdue's management determined future sales growth lay in foodservice and international sales; therefore, the poultry company quietly began laying the groundwork to support these new markets.

Perdue launched its Cafe Perdue entree meal kits in 1997. The following year it purchased foodservice poultry processor Gol-Pak and, through a joint venture, opened a poultry processing plant in Shanghai, China.

Settlements to chicken catchers and line workers in 2001 and 2002 cost the company over $12 million in back wages. Also in 2002 Perdue announced it would be shuttering a deboning plant purchased only three years earlier. During 2003 the company started work on a new research and development facility in Salisbury, Maryland. In January 2004 Perdue purchased a poultry processing facility from competitor Cagle's, Inc.

Frank Perdue died in 2005. He was 84.

EXECUTIVES

Chairman and CEO: James A. (Jim) Perdue
Chief Marketing Officer, Perdue Farms: John Bartelme
SVP and CFO: Eileen F. Burza
SVP Retail Sales: Steve Evans
SVP Operations and Supply Chain Management:
Clint Rivers
VP International: Carlos Ayala
VP Supply Chain Management: Lester Gray
VP Corporate Communications: Luis A. Luna
VP and CIO: Sandy Rasel
VP Foodservice Sales and Marketing: Charlie Carrigan
VP Foodservice Marketing: Bernie McGorry
VP Sales and Marketing, Deli and Frozen Foods:
Andrew (Andy) Seymour
VP Human Resources: Robert H. (Rob) Heflin

President, Perdue AgriBusiness:
Richard L. (Dick) Willey
President, Foodservice Division:
James B. (Jim) Leighton, age 53
President, Perdue Food Products:
J. Michael (Mike) Roberts
**Chief Medical Officer and Head, Perdue Wellness
Program:** Roger Merrill
Director Military Sales and Value Added: Mitch Boswell

LOCATIONS

HQ: Perdue Incorporated
31149 Old Ocean City Rd., Salisbury, MD 21804
Phone: 410-543-3000   **Fax:** 410-543-3532
Web: www.perdue.com

PRODUCTS/OPERATIONS

Selected Poultry Products

Fresh poultry
  Chicken parts
  Cornish hens
  Ground chicken
  Roasters and turkeys
  Rotisserie chicken
  Seasoned chicken
  Skinless, boneless poultry cuts
  Turkey breasts
  Turkey burgers
  Turkey franks
  Turkey sausage
Fully cooked poultry
  Breaded chicken breasts
  Chicken cutlets
  Chicken nuggets
  Chicken tenderloins
  Chicken wings
  Pan-roasted turkey
  Roasted bone-in chicken
  Rotisserie-style chicken
Other products
  Pet food ingredients
  Vegetable oils

COMPETITORS

Butterball	Peco Foods
Cagle's	Pilgrim's Pride
Cooper Farms	Sanderson Farms
Foster Farms	Tyson Foods
Hormel	Wayne Farms LLC
Jennie-O	West Liberty Foods
OSI Group	Zacky Farms

Performance Food

When it's time to eat out, Performance Food Group (PFG) delivers. The #3 broadline foodservice distributor in the US (behind SYSCO and U.S. Foodservice), PFG supplies more than 68,000 products to restaurants, hotels, and other hospitality operators through its 18 distribution facilities. Its Customized Distribution division serves specifically chain restaurants such as Cracker Barrel and Ruby Tuesday through about 10 facilities around the country. Its subsidiary Vistar is a leading supplier of specialty foods for both foodservice and vending operators. The company was taken private in 2008 by The Blackstone Group and Wellspring Capital Management.

With the $1.3 billion buyout, PFG was merged with Colorado-based Vistar (which was already controlled by Blackstone) to create a giant in the foodservice distribution industry with tentacles reaching into several markets. The combined business continues to operate under the PFG name, however, each unit maintains its own headquarters. George Holm, who headed Vistar, was named CEO for PFG following the going-private deal.

For PFG's broadline foodservice supply division, the focus has been on expanding the range of products it distributes to existing customers while improving margins. The division's customers include franchisees of such chains as Burger King, Popeyes (owned by AFC Enterprises), and Subway. It also serves contract foodservice operators, such as Compass Group USA. The company also expanded its broadline division in 2009 with the acquisition of Somerset Food Service, a regional supplier in Kentucky.

The company's custom distribution segment, meanwhile, has been looking primarily to add new customers. In 2007 the company struck a deal to supply the O'Charley's casual dining chain.

HISTORY

Robert Sledd began working for his family's Taylor & Sledd food distribution business in 1974 and became president a decade later. In 1987, fearing that his family's business would be swallowed up in the ongoing consolidation of the foodservice industry, Sledd convinced his father, Hunter, to spin off their Richmond, Virginia-based Pocahontas Foods business and put him in charge, along with Robert's University of Tennessee fraternity brother and longtime friend, Michael Gray.

As part of the spinoff, Pocahontas merged with Caro Produce & Institutional Foods, which distributed produce in Texas and Louisiana. The company acquired Tennessee-based distributors Kenneth O. Lester Company and Hale Brothers in 1988 and 1989, respectively.

In 1991 the company changed its name from Pocahontas Foods to Performance Food Group (PFG). Although the company's name was different, its policy of growth by acquisition remained the same and PFG continued gobbling up distributors. That year PFG acquired B&R Foods, based in Tampa. The company continued to make acquisitions that expanded its market share in the South, including New Orleans distributor Loubat-L. Frank in 1992 and another Tennessee distributor, Hale of Summit Distributors, in 1993. That year the company offered its stock to the public for the first time.

Along with its aggressive consumption, PFG felt a burp in 1994 in the form of stunted profits and disappointing earnings. In what should have been the newly public company's salad days, PFG's performance was stifled by difficulties at its pre-cut salad plant and by rising labor and warehousing costs. As a result, the company's stock price plunged 66% at the end of 1994.

Undaunted, the company brought in new salad-making equipment and continued on its industry-consolidating course the next year. PFG acquired Atlanta's Milton's Food and North Carolina-based Cannon Food in 1995.

In 1996 PFG expanded its service in the Southwest with the acquisition of Texas distributor McLane Foodservice-Temple (now operating as Performance Food Group of Texas). Buoyed by solid growth in sales, the company made additional acquisitions in 1997, including Georgia's W.J. Powell, and its first foray into the Northeast, AFI Food Service.

The company grew internally in 1998 with the construction of distribution centers in Tennessee and Texas as well as its acquisition of Affiliated Paper Companies of Alabama and regional food distributor Virginia Food Service Group. In 1999 the company moved into the New England market when it bought NorthCenter Foodservice (Maine), and it expanded into custom-cut steaks when it bought State Hotel Supply Company and Nesson Meat Sales.

PFG continued to bulk up its broadline service when it acquired Carroll County Foods in 2000. Seeing the future in pre-cut salads and vegetables, the company purchased Dixon Tom-A-Toe (1999) and Redi-Cut Foods (2000). It also bought Empire Seafood Holding in 2001, doubling its seafood sales. That year Gray was promoted to CEO and PFG also bought Springfield Foodservice, a leading foodservice distributor in New England. The company then bought the largest independent fresh-cut produce processor in the US, Fresh Express.

In 2002 the acquisitions continued when in May PFG acquired Arkansas-based Quality Foods, which serves customers in Arkansas, Louisiana, Mississippi, Missouri, Oklahoma, Tennessee, and Texas. In July PFG acquired two foodservice distribution companies: Middendorf Meat, which specializes in custom-cut steaks, and Illinois-based Thoms-Proestler Co., which serves customers in Illinois, Indiana, Iowa, and Wisconsin. In October its Pocahontas Foods USA subsidiary acquired All Kitchens, a privately owned Idaho company, for $15.6 million.

In 2004 Gray left PFG and Sledd took over as chairman and CEO. The company sold its Fresh Express produce division the following year to Chiquita Brands International for $855 million. Steven Spinner was promoted from president and COO to succeed Sledd as CEO in 2006; Sledd remained as chairman.

PFG was taken private in 2008 by The Blackstone Group and Wellspring Capital Management for $1.3 billion. The deal also involved merging PFG's existing foodservice supply business with Vistar, a Colorado-based distributor of specialty foods for foodservice and vending operators. That same year George Holm became president and CEO of the company.

EXECUTIVES

Chairman: Robert C. Sledd, age 56
CEO: George L. Holm
EVP: Mac Pearce
SVP and Chief Human Resources Officer:
  Charlotte L. Perkins, age 50
SVP and President and CEO, Customized Division:
  Thomas (Tom) Hoffman, age 69
SVP and CFO: John D. Austin, age 47
SVP Broadline Operations: Joseph J. (Joe) Paterak Jr., age 57
President, Somerset Food Service: Mac Godby
President, Performance Foodservice, Somerset:
  Tommy Jones
Auditors: KPMG LLP

LOCATIONS

HQ: Performance Food Group Company
  12500 W. Creek Pkwy., Richmond, VA 23238
Phone: 804-484-7700   **Fax:** 804-484-7701
Web: www.pfgc.com

PETCO Animal Supplies

PETCO Animal Supplies is a holding company for PETCO Animal Supplies Stores, which is the second-largest US retailer of specialty pet supplies. The company boasts more than 950 stores in all 50 states, making it the only pet store to cover the entire US market. The company is barking up the tree of rival PetSmart, which leads the market. PETCO Animal Supplies holding company was formed in early 2005 to create a foundation for the firm's upcoming growth strategies. The holding company also changed the name of its operating subsidiary. In 2006 two buyout firms — Texas Pacific Group and Leonard Green & Partners — took PETCO private in a deal worth $1.8 billion.

Growing its retail operations by adding Hawaii as its 50th state in 2008 has been a top priority to PETCO. Despite a looming recession in the US, the retailer opened store No. 1,000 in 2009, putting the company in line with its primary competitor.

EXECUTIVES

CEO: James M. Myers
CIO: Herman Nell
EVP and Chief Merchandising Officer:
  David E. (Dave) Bolen
EVP and CFO: Michael E. (Mike) Foss
SVP Business Development: William M. Woodard
VP Pet Services New Growth: Taylor Phillips
VP Pet Services: John Dunn
VP Animal Care: Marcie Whichard
VP Corporate Communications: Kevin Whalen
Executive Director, PETCO Foundation: Paul Jolly
Director Veterinary Medicine: Thomas Edling
Field Director National Pet Services: John Cheney
Director Communications: Don Cowan
Secretary: Darragh J. Davis
Auditors: KPMG LLP

LOCATIONS

HQ: PETCO Animal Supplies, Inc.
  9125 Rehco Rd., San Diego, CA 92121
Phone: 858-453-7845
Web: www.petco.com

PRODUCTS/OPERATIONS

Selected Store Services

Dog training
DNA breed testing
Grooming
Pet photography
Self-service dog wash
Vaccinations

Peter Kiewit Sons'

Peter Kiewit Sons' is a heavyweight in the heavy construction industry. The general contractor and its subsidiaries has a breadth of expertise, building everything from roads and dams to high-rise office towers and power plants throughout the US and Canada. Its transportation projects, which include bridges, rail lines, airport runways, and mass transit systems, account for a majority of its sales. Kiewit also serves the oil and gas, electrical, power, and waterworks industries. Public contracts, most of which are awarded by government agencies, are handled by its Kiewit Federal Group. The company, also an owner of coal mines, is owned by current and former employees and Kiewit family members.

As a leader in construction in the transportation sector, Kiewit is responsible for several notable highway and bridge projects, from replacing a segment of the San Francisco-Oakland Bay Bridge Skyway to upgrading the Sea-to-Sky Highway between Vancouver and Whistler, British Columbia. Water supply and dam projects include the Olivenhain and East dams in California, underground storage tanks for the Hollywood Hills Quality Improvement Project, and an intake valve at Lake Mead in Nevada.

Peter Kiewit Sons' also has steadily built its expertise working on environmentally sensitive projects in the power sector. Through its Kiewit Power Engineers Co., the company has been contracted by Plutonic Energy Corporation and GE Energy Financial Services to work on one of British Columbia's largest renewable energy projects, building six hydroelectric projects with intakes, penstocks, and a transmission line that will reduce dependence on non-renewable imported energy. The firm is working with the local Native American community, First Nations, creating jobs to help complete the project. Kiewit also has experience working on wind energy farms in Canada.

The company's mining operations (Kiewit Mining Group) include ownership of coal mines in Texas, Montana, and Wyoming and management of two additional mines, all of which are surface mines.

Subsidiary Kiewit Offshore Services fabricates complex offshore oil production platforms at a facility in Texas. The company counts many of the world's largest oil companies as its clients. Another subsidiary, Kiewit Energy Group, focuses on the petroleum refining business.

In 2008 the group acquired TIC Holdings, a heavy industrial construction and engineering firm based in Colorado. The deal put two of the largest North American construction companies under the same ownership.

HISTORY

Born to Dutch immigrants, Peter Kiewit and brother Andrew founded Kiewit Brothers, a brickyard, in 1884 in Omaha, Nebraska. By 1912 two of Peter's sons worked at the yard, which was named Peter Kiewit & Sons. When Peter Kiewit died in 1914, his son Ralph took over, and the firm took the name Peter Kiewit Sons'. Another son, Peter, joined Ralph at the helm in 1924 after dropping out of Dartmouth, and later took over.

During the Depression, Kiewit managed huge federal public works projects, and in the 1940s it focused on war-related emergency construction projects.

One of the firm's most difficult projects was top-secret Thule Air Force Base in Greenland, above the Arctic Circle. For more than two years 5,000 men worked around the clock, beginning in 1951; the site was in development for 15 years. The company won a contract in 1952 to build a $1.2 billion gas diffusion plant in Portsmouth, Ohio. It also became a contractor for the US interstate highway system (begun in 1956).

Peter Kiewit died in 1979, after stipulating that the largely employee-owned company should remain under employee control and that no one employee could own more than 10%. His 40% stake, when returned to the company, transformed many employees into millionaires. Walter Scott Jr., whose father had been the first graduate engineer to work for Kiewit, took charge. Scott made his mark by parlaying money from construction into successful investments.

When the construction industry slumped, Kiewit began looking for other investment opportunities, and in 1984 it acquired packaging company Continental Can Co. (selling off non-core insurance, energy, and timber assets). Continental was saddled with a 1983 class action lawsuit alleging that it had plotted to close plants and lay off workers before they were qualified for pensions. In 1991 Kiewit agreed to pay $415 million to settle the lawsuit. In the face of a consolidating packaging industry, the company sold Continental in the early 1990s.

In 1986 Kiewit loaned money to a business group to build a fiber-optic loop in Chicago; by 1987 it had launched MFS Communications to build local fiber loops in downtown districts. In 1992 Kiewit split its business into two pieces: the construction group, which was strictly employee-owned; and a diversified group, to which it added a controlling stake in phone and cable TV company C-TEC in 1993. That year Kiewit took MFS public; by 1995 it had sold all its shares, and the next year MFS was bought by telecom giant WorldCom.

In 1996 Kiewit assisted CalEnergy (now MidAmerican Energy) in a hostile $1.3 billion takeover of the UK's Northern Electric. Kiewit got stock in CalEnergy and a 30% stake in the UK electric company, all of which it sold to CalEnergy in 1998.

That year Kiewit spun off its telecom and computer services holdings into Level 3 Communications. Scott, who had been hospitalized the year before for a blood clot in his lung, stepped down as CEO, and Ken Stinson, CEO of Kiewit Construction Group, took over.

In 1999 Kiewit acquired a majority interest in Pacific Rock Products, a construction materials firm in Canada. Kiewit spun off its asphalt, concrete, and aggregates operations in 2000 as Kiewit Materials. Also that year the company created Kiewit Offshore Services to focus on construction for the offshore drilling industry. In 2001 the company acquired marine construction firm General Construction Company (GCC).

Kiewit made history in 2002 for the fastest completion of a project of its type when it completed the rebuilding of Webbers Falls I-40 Bridge in Oklahoma at the end of July. (The bridge had collapsed in May after being hit by a pair of barges, resulting in 14 fatalities.)

Kiewit underwent a changing of the guard at the end of 2004, when 22-year veteran Bruce Grewcock took the reins as the company's fourth CEO since its founding. Stinson stayed on as the company's chairman.

EXECUTIVES

Chairman Emeritus: J. Walter (Walter) Scott Jr., age 77
Chairman: Kenneth E. (Ken) Stinson, age 66
President and CEO: Bruce E. Grewcock, age 54
EVP; EVP, Kiewit Corporation and Kiewit Pacific Co.: Richard W. Colf, age 64
EVP and Division Manager and Director; EVP, Kiewit Corporation, Kiewit Construction, Kiewit Pacific Co., and Kiewit Western Co.: R. Michael Phelps, age 54
EVP: Douglas E. Patterson, age 56
EVP and Division Manager; EVP, Kiewit Corporation and Kiewit Construction; President, Gilbert Industrial Corp.: Scott L. Cassels, age 49
SVP and Hawaii Area Manager, Kiewit Building Group; VP Kiewit Pacific: Lance K. Wilhelm
SVP, General Counsel, and Secretary: Tobin A. Schropp, age 45
SVP and CFO: Michael J. Piechoski, age 53
VP and Treasurer: Ben E. Muraskin, age 43
VP Human Resources and Administration: Michael Gary
Division Manager, VP, and Director; SVP, Kiewit Corporation; President, Kiewit Mining Group: Christopher J. Murphy, age 53
Division Manager and Director; SVP, Kiewit Corporation and Kiewit Construction; President, Kiewit Energy Group: Thomas S. Shelby, age 49
President, Kiewit Engineering Co. (KECo): Gary Pietrok
CEO, Kiewet Federal Group: Kirk R. Samuelson, age 50
Leader, Structural Design Team, Keiwit Engineering Co.: Dave Sinsheimer
Leader, Structural Design Team, Keiwit Engineering Co.: Dave Anderson
Auditors: KPMG LLP

LOCATIONS

HQ: Peter Kiewit Sons', Inc.
    Kiewit Plaza, 3555 Farnam St., Omaha, NE 68131
Phone: 402-342-2052   **Fax:** 402-271-2939
Web: www.kiewit.com

PRODUCTS/OPERATIONS

Selected Subsidiaries and Affiliates

Ben Holt Company
Bighorn Walnut, LLC
Buckskin Mining Company
CMF Leasing Co.
Continental Alarm & Detection Company
Continental Fire Sprinkler Company
General Construction Company
Gilbert Central Corp.
Gilbert Industrial Corporation
Gilbert Network Services, L.P.
Gilbert/Healy, L.P.
Global Surety & Insurance Co.
GSC Atlanta, Inc.

GSC Contracting, Inc.
Guernsey Construction Company
KES Inc.
KiEnergy, Inc.
Kiewit Power Engineers (formerly Bibb and Associates)
KT Developers, LLC
KT Mining Inc.
Lac De Gras Excavation Inc.
Mass. Electric Construction Canada Co.
Mass. Electric Construction Co.
Mass. Electric Construction Venezuela, S.A.
Mass. Electric International, Inc.
MECC Rail Mexicana, S.A. de C.V.
Midwest Agencies, Inc.
Mission Materials Company
Seaworks, Inc.
Servitec de Sonora, S.A. de C.V.
TIC Holdings, Inc.
Twin Mountain Construction II Company
V. K. Mason Construction Co.
Walnut Creek Mining Company

COMPETITORS

ABB
Ames Construction
Balfour Beatty Infrastructure
Bechtel
Black & Veatch
Bovis Lend Lease
CH2M HILL
Fluor
Foster Wheeler
Granite Construction
Halliburton
Hubbard Group
Jacobs Engineering
KBR
Lane Construction
Parsons Corporation
Raytheon
Rio Tinto plc
Skanska USA Civil
Turner Corporation
Tutor Perini
Tutor-Saliba
Walsh Group
Washington Division
Whiting-Turner
Williams Companies

HISTORICAL FINANCIALS

Company Type: Private

Income Statement				FYE: Last Saturday in December
	REVENUE ($ mil.)	NET INCOME ($ mil.)	NET PROFIT MARGIN	EMPLOYEES
12/08	8,000	—	—	15,000
12/07	6,200	—	—	15,000
12/06	5,049	—	—	14,700
12/05	4,145	—	—	14,500
12/04	3,352	—	—	14,000
Annual Growth	24.3%	—	—	1.7%

Revenue History

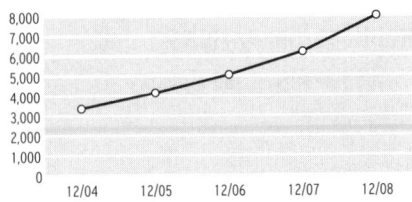

Phoenix Suns

These Suns give life to desert basketball fans. Suns Legacy Partners owns and operates the Phoenix Suns professional basketball team, which plays host at US Airways Center. The National Basketball Association franchise was awarded to businessman Richard Bloch in 1968 and fronted by investors such as Tony Curtis and Henry Mancini. Phoenix has reached the NBA Finals twice (the last time in 1993) but has yet to win a championship title. An investment group led by real estate executive Robert Sarver owns the team; former owner Jerry Colangelo remains as the team's chairman.

Since the resignation of head coach Mike D'Antoni at the end of the 2007-08 season, the Suns have struggled on the court. Terry Porter, who replaced D'Antoni, was fired midway through the 2008-09 season and replaced by Alvin Gentry. D'Antoni had led Phoenix to four straight post-season appearances but left to take the top coaching job with the New York Knicks.

Sarver, chairman of Western Alliance Bancorporation, ponied up a record $400 million for the team in 2004. Colangelo had owned the Suns since 1987; he also lost control of the Arizona Diamondbacks baseball team in 2004. Rick Welts was later promoted to president and CEO in 2009.

EXECUTIVES

Chairman: Jerry J. Colangelo, age 69
Vice Chairman: Samuel S. (Sam) Garvin
President and CEO: Rick Welts
Managing Partner: Robert Sarver
President, Basketball Operations and General Manager: Steve Kerr, age 44
Head Coach: Alvin Gentry
SEVP: Dick Van Arsdale, age 66
SEVP: Harvey Shank, age 63
EVP Finance and Administration: Jim Pitman, age 44
SVP Marketing Partnership: Lynn Agnello
SVP and General Counsel: Jason Rowley
SVP Business Development: John Walker
SVP Basketball Operations: David Griffin
SVP Broadcasting: Al McCoy
SVP Facility Management: Alvan Adams
SVP; Executive Director, Phoenix Suns Charities: Thomas (Tom) Ambrose, age 61
VP Information Services: William Bolt
VP Human Resources: Peter Wong
Senior Director Marketing: Niki Adams
Director Public Relations: Jamie Morris
Director Community Relations: Cassidy Kersten
Director of Human Resources: Karen Rausch

LOCATIONS

HQ: Suns Legacy Partners, L.L.C.
201 E. Jefferson St., Phoenix, AZ 85004
Phone: 602-379-7900 **Fax:** 602-379-7990
Web: www.nba.com/suns

The Phoenix Suns play at 18,422-seat capacity US Airways Center in Phoenix.

PRODUCTS/OPERATIONS

Championship Titles

Western Conference Champions (1976, 1993)

COMPETITORS

Golden State Warriors
Los Angeles Clippers
Los Angeles Lakers
Sacramento Kings

Pilot Corporation

Pilot offers a salve to those suffering from white-line fever. Its Pilot Travel Centers LLC, which operated as a joint venture until October 2008, runs about 305 truck stops in some 40 states. Each features restaurant chains such as Subway, Pizza Hut, and Taco Bell. Pilot has fuel islands large enough to service several 18-wheelers at a time and private showers. Pilot Truck Care Centers provide TLC for big rigs. The firm also owns and operates about 40 convenience stores under the Pilot Food Mart banner in Tennessee. James Haslam II got Pilot off the ground in 1958 as a gas station that sold cigarettes and soft drinks; now his son, CEO James Haslam III, pilots the firm. The Haslam family owns the company.

As a leading supplier of diesel fuel to the trucking industry, Pilot supplies about 10% of the truck diesel fuel used in US.

Pilot's convenience store business has shrunk from about 65 stores in three states to less than 40 shops — all in Tennessee but for a single location in Kentucky — in recent years. In 2006 the firm sold 10 Pilot Food Mart shops in the Knoxville, Tennessee, area. The sale followed the previous divestment of all of the company's stores in Virginia and West Virginia. Pilot entered the convenience store business in 1976 and opened its first travel center in 1981. Travel centers became the company's focus as Pilot built a nationwide network through organic growth and acquisitions.

In 2001 the company entered into a joint venture agreement with Marathon Petroleum Company (formerly Marathon Ashland Petroleum) to form Pilot Travel Centers (PTC). In 2003 PTC acquired Williams Travel Centers. Private equity firm CVC Capital Partners acquired the approximately 50% stake in PTC forming an equal governance partnership with parent company Pilot Corporation.

EXECUTIVES

Chairman: James A. Haslam II
CFO: Mitch D. Steenrod
EVP Direct Sales and Development: Mark A. Hazelwood
SVP, Operations: Ken Parent
CEO; President, Pilot Travel Centers LLC: James A. (Jimmy) Haslam III, age 55
Director, Merchandising: Tim Purcell

LOCATIONS

HQ: Pilot Corporation
5508 Lonas Rd., Knoxville, TN 37909
Phone: 865-588-7487 **Fax:** 865-450-2800
Web: www.pilotcorp.com

PRODUCTS/OPERATIONS

Selected Operations

Convenience stores (groceries, gas and diesel, and assorted merchandise)
Travel centers (groceries, showers, gas and diesel, restaurants, and assorted merchandise)

COMPETITORS

7-Eleven
Chevron
Couche-Tard
Exxon Mobil
Flying J
Love's Country Stores
Motiva Enterprises
Rip Griffin Truck Service Center
Royal Dutch Shell
Stuckey's
TravelCenters of America
Wawa, Inc.

HISTORICAL FINANCIALS

Company Type: Private

Income Statement				FYE: December 31
	REVENUE ($ mil.)	NET INCOME ($ mil.)	NET PROFIT MARGIN	EMPLOYEES
12/08	1,014	—	—	900

Pinnacle Foods

Pinnacle Foods has a mouthful of big-name brands. The company produces North American grocery store staples such as Mrs. Butterworth's, Log Cabin, and Country Kitchen (syrup, pancake mixes); Duncan Hines (baking mixes); Lender's (bagels); Van de Kamp's and Mrs. Paul's (fish sticks, anyone?); Vlasic and Milwaukee's (pickles); Chef's Choice (frozen skillet meals); and Celeste (frozen pizza). Pinnacle has grown by buying well-known brands and then expanding those brand lines by adding new products. In 2009 it increased its frozen foods holdings significantly with the 2009 purchase of Birds Eye Foods.

Pinnacle was acquired in 2007 by the Blackstone Group for some $2 billion in cash and assumed debt.

As a result of the merger, the company changed its name to Pinnacle Foods Finance. Former Kraft Foods CEO Roger Deromedi became Pinnacle's chairman. Jeffrey Ansell, a 25-year veteran of Procter & Gamble, was appointed as new CEO. Ansell resigned in mid-2009; he was replaced by Bob Gamgort, the former North American president of candy giant Mars.

At the close of 2009 Pinnacle acquired Birds Eye Foods from a holding company controlled by Vestar Capital Partners, Pro-Fac Cooperative, and members of Birds Eye Foods' management in a deal that was paid for by Blackstone. Birds Eye is the US's #1 frozen vegetable and #2 frozen bagged meal maker. The deal makes Pinnacle Foods a leader in both the frozen and shelf-stable business segments, adding Birds Eye's frozen meals and vegetables, as well as pie fillings, snacks, soups, and salad dressings to its holdings.

The company distributes its products in Canada and the US to supermarket and other retail food outlets. It also sells through club stores, as well as the private-label, military, and food service channels; it has a product-development center in St. Louis and seven warehouse and manufacturing plants — two in Illinois and one each in Arkansas, Delaware, Michigan, Iowa, and Tennessee.

Wal-Mart is the company's largest customer and accounted for 23% of its 2008 sales.

EXECUTIVES

Chairman: Roger K. Deromedi, age 55
CEO: Robert J. (Bob) Gamgort
EVP and CFO: Craig D. Steeneck, age 51, $1,203,697 total compensation
EVP and Chief Customer Officer: Chris Kiser, age 46, $415,180 total compensation
EVP Supply Chain and Operations: Edward L. (Ed) Sutter, age 51
EVP Human Resources: John L. Butler
SVP and Chief Marketing Officer: Sally Genster Robling, age 52
SVP and Treasurer: Lynne M. Misericordia, age 45, $334,099 total compensation
SVP, General Counsel, and Secretary: M. Kelley Maggs, age 57, $364,340 total compensation
VP, Deputy General Counsel, and Assistant Secretary: John F. Kroeger, age 53
Auditors: PricewaterhouseCoopers LLP

LOCATIONS

HQ: Pinnacle Foods Finance LLC
1 Old Bloomfield Ave., Mountain Lakes, NJ 07046
Phone: 973-541-6620
Web: www.pinnaclefoodscorp.com

2008 Sales

	% of total
US	95
Canada	5
Total	**100**

PRODUCTS/OPERATIONS

2008 Sales

	$ mil.	% of total
Dry foods	915.3	59
Frozen foods	641.1	41
Total	**1,556.4**	**100**

Selected Brands

Appian Way
Armour (licensed from Smithfield Foods)
Aunt Jemima (frozen breakfasts only, licensed from The Quaker Oats Company)
Celeste
Duncan Hines
Grabwich
Hawaiian Bowls
Hearty Hero
Hungry-Man (licensed from Campbell Soup Company)
Lenders
Log Cabin
Lunch Bucket
Milwaukee's
Mrs. Butterworth's
Mrs. Paul's
Open Pit
Snack'mms
Swanson (licensed from Campbell Soup Company)
Van de Kamp's
Vlasic

COMPETITORS

American Seafoods
B&G Foods
Campbell Soup
Chelsea Milling
ConAgra
General Mills
Gilster-Mary Lee
Gorton's
Goya
Heinz
High Liner Foods
Hormel
Hostess Brands
Icelandic USA
Kellogg
Kraft Foods

Mt. Olive Pickle
Nestlé
Nippon Suisan Kaisha
Pacific Seafood Group
PepsiCo
Red Chamber Co.
Rich Products
Sara Lee North American Retail
Schwan's
Smucker
StarKist
Thai Union
Trident Seafoods
Unilever

HISTORICAL FINANCIALS

Company Type: Subsidiary

Income Statement				FYE: Last Sunday in December
	REVENUE ($ mil.)	NET INCOME ($ mil.)	NET PROFIT MARGIN	EMPLOYEES
12/08	1,556	(29)	—	3,000
12/07	1,515	(115)	—	3,100
12/06	1,442	34	2.4%	3,100
12/05	1,256	(43)	—	2,700
12/04	511	(25)	—	2,600
Annual Growth	32.1%	—	—	3.6%

Net Income History

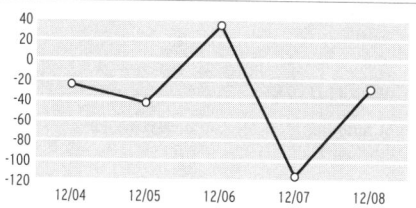

Pittsburgh Glass Works

Pittsburgh Glass Works (formerly PPG Auto Glass) can't help you if you've got a chip on your shoulder, but its business is to be all over a chip in your car's windshield. It supplies automotive OEM windshields, rear and side windows, sunroofs, and assemblies to automakers such as Daimler, as well as replacement auto glass products for use in aftermarket applications. It also provides insurance claim services through its LYNX Services subsidiary, glass management software through its GTS unit, and e-business solutions through its GLAXIS division. Former parent PPG Industries sold its controlling interest in the firm to an affiliate of funds managed by Kohlberg & Company in 2008 for about $270 million.

PPG Industries retained a 40% stake in the company, which was renamed Pittsburgh Glass Works when the deal closed in late September 2008. (Previously, PPG Industries had agreed in September 2007 to sell PPG Auto Glass to a California-based private equity firm, Platinum Equity, for about $500 million, but the offer was rescinded later in the year.)

Amid a decline in orders for auto glass, Pittsburgh Glass Works decided to close facilities in

Oshawa, Ontario, and Evart, Michigan, in early 2009, resulting in about 300 layoffs. Two assembly plants in Newark, Delaware, and Cambridge, Ontario, were slated to close later in the year. The company also negotiated wage cuts with employees in Evansville, Pennsylvania.

EXECUTIVES

President: Marc E. Talbert
VP Customer Service and Strategic Initiatives:
  H. Lee (Lee) St. John
Territorial Sales Director, East: Robert C. Taylor
Territorial Operations Director, West:
  Thomas P. (Tom) Moerdyke
Territorial Operations Director, North:
  Michael T. Zimmer
Director, Glass Alliance Programs: Glenn Davis
Director, Process Improvements: Jeffrey W. Smith
Manager, Human Resources: Diana M. Jaden
Controller: David Nazakis

LOCATIONS

HQ: Pittsburgh Glass Works LLC
  1 PPG Place, Pittsburgh, PA 15272
Phone: 412-434-3131   **Fax:** 412-434-3001
Web: www.ppgautoglass.com

PRODUCTS/OPERATIONS

Selected Businesses
GLAXIS
GTS Services
LYNX Services
PPG AutoGlass
PROSTARS

COMPETITORS

ABRA Auto Body   Henderson Glass
All Star Glass   Mygrant
Belron US

HISTORICAL FINANCIALS

Company Type: Private

Income Statement				FYE: December 31
	REVENUE ($ mil.)	NET INCOME ($ mil.)	NET PROFIT MARGIN	EMPLOYEES
12/07	1,010	—	—	4,400

Pittsburgh Penguins

These Penguins do their thing on the ice in downtown Pittsburgh, not the Antarctic. The Lemieux Group owns and operates the Pittsburgh Penguins professional hockey franchise. The team has represented the Steel City in the National Hockey League since 1967 and boasts back-to-back Stanley Cup championships in 1991 and 1992. The team won a third title in 2009. Popular through good times and bad, fans root for the Pens at Pittsburgh's Mellon Arena, better known to locals as "The Igloo." Legendary forward Mario Lemieux, who played for Pittsburgh during the 1990s, has controlled the franchise since 1999.

While Pittsburgh continues to focus on improvements in talent on the ice, the franchise is also building a new facility to replace Mellon Arena, the oldest rink in the NHL, in order to boost its finances. Construction on the $320 million Consol Energy Center began in 2008; it is being funded partly through proceeds the state gets from slot machine casinos, with the team also contributing to the construction. Local coal mining giant CONSOL Energy agreed to a 21-year naming rights deal in 2008. The Pens hope to have the facility completed for the 2010 season.

While they await the new arena, fans are enjoying a resurgence of their Pens on the ice. Young stars such as Sidney Crosby, Evgeni Malkin, and Jordan Staal have re-energized the stands and helped Pittsburgh earn back-to-back trips to the Stanley Cup finals in 2008 and 2009; both times the Pens faced the Detroit Red Wings and successfully overcame the opposition in seven games in 2009. The team's post-season campaign that year was led by coach Dan Bylsma, who had replaced Michel Therrien earlier in the 2008-09 season after Pittsburgh got off to a slow start. Therrien had coached the Penguins since 2005.

The current state of affairs is in stark contrast to the instability and uncertainty that has visited Pittsburgh hockey in the past. The Penguins were under bankruptcy protection in 1975 (when the IRS padlocked the offices) and then again when the team was forced to declare bankruptcy in 1998 under previous owner Howard Baldwin. Lemieux, who had retired in 1997 after leading the team to two of its championship titles, saved the club the next year by rolling over nearly $30 million owed to him into an ownership bid. The Hall of Fame player resigned his position as governor of the club in 2000 to rejoin the team on the ice, scoring 35 goals in 43 games to take the Pens into the playoffs the following year. (Pittsburgh was eliminated by the New Jersey Devils in the Eastern Conference finals.)

Baldwin had helped form the New England Whalers of the World Hockey League (which joined the NHL in 1979 and became the Carolina Hurricanes) and later owned a stake in the Minnesota North Stars (now the Dallas Stars) before buying control of the Penguins in 1991 from Edward DeBartolo, Sr.

EXECUTIVES

Chairman: Mario Lemieux, age 44
CEO: Ken Sawyer
President: David Morehouse, age 46
EVP and General Manager: Ray Shero, age 46
Assistant General Manager: Chuck Fletcher, age 40
Head Coach: Dan Bylsma, age 38
Senior Director Team Operations and Communications:
  Frank Buonomo
Senior Advisor Hockey Operations: Ed (E.J.) Johnston
Director Hockey Administration: Jason Botterill
Director Pro Scouting: Dan MacKinnon
Director Amateur Scouting: Jay Heinbuck
Director Communications: Jennifer Bullano

LOCATIONS

HQ: Lemieux Group LP
  1 Chatham Center, Ste. 400, Pittsburgh, PA 15219
Phone: 412-642-1300   **Fax:** 412-642-1859
Web: www.pittsburghpenguins.com

The Pittsburgh Penguins play in 16,940-seat capacity Mellon Arena in Pittsburgh.

PRODUCTS/OPERATIONS

Championship Trophies
Stanley Cup (1991-92, 2009)
Prince of Wales Trophy (1991-92, 2008-09)
Presidents' Trophy (1993)

COMPETITORS

New Jersey Devils
New York Islanders
New York Rangers
Philadelphia Flyers

Pittsburgh Steelers

Pittsburgh Steelers Sports has forged a championship tradition in Steel Town. The company owns the Pittsburgh Steelers football franchise, which has won a record six Super Bowl titles, its last coming at the end of the 2008 season. During the 1970s under head coach Chuck Noll, the team dominated the National Football League by winning four titles with the help of such stars as Terry Bradshaw and Lynn Swann. Founded in 1933 as the Pirates, the football team (renamed in 1940) claimed winning seasons only eight times during its first 40 years. Dan Rooney, son of late team founder Art Rooney, and his son Art Rooney II lead a group that owns the Steelers.

The Rooney family is noted for its steady and stable management of the football franchise, illustrated in part by the fact that the team has had just three head coaches since the mid-1960s. Before he resigned following the 2006 season, Bill Cowher boasted the longest tenure of any active head coach in the NFL. Mike Tomlin, a former assistant with the Minnesota Vikings and Tampa Bay Buccaneers, led Steelers Nation to a sixth championship title just two years after replacing Cowher.

The family brought in outside investors in 2009, however, prompted by league rules about ownership of gaming enterprises. (Some in the Rooney family have an interest in racing tracks in New York and Florida.) Those new investors included James Haslam, head of Pilot Travel Centers, Pittsburgh's Paul family, which controls manufacturer Ampco-Pittsburgh, and film producer Thomas Tull. Others with a minority stake in the team include Bruce Rauner, chairman of private equity firm GTCR Golder Rauner, the family of video game executive Paul Sams (Blizzard Entertainment), and former Steelers player John Stallworth.

The Pittsburgh Steelers play host at Heinz Field, a $244 million stadium that replaced aging Three Rivers Stadium when it opened in 2001. Local condiment maker H. J. Heinz poured out $57 million for the naming rights.

EXECUTIVES

Chairman: Daniel M. (Dan) Rooney
President: Arthur J. (Art) Rooney II, age 56
VP: Arthur J. Rooney Jr.
Head Coach: Mike Tomlin
Player Development: Ray Jackson
Pro Personnel Coordinator: Doug Whaley
Director Business: Mark Hart
Director Football Operations: Kevin Colbert
Director Marketing: Tony Quatrini
Manager Information Technology: Scott Phelps
Manager Corporate Sales and Marketing: Kathy Wallace
Manager Marketing and Community Relations:
Lynne Molyneaux
Human Relations and Office Coordinator:
Geraldine Glenn

LOCATIONS

HQ: Pittsburgh Steelers Sports, Inc.
3400 S. Water St., Pittsburgh, PA 15203
Phone: 412-432-7800 **Fax:** 412-432-7878
Web: www.steelers.com

The Pittsburgh Steelers play at the 65,050-seat capacity Heinz Field in Pittsburgh.

PRODUCTS/OPERATIONS

Championship Titles

Super Bowl Championships
Super Bowl XLIII (2009)
Super Bowl XL (2006)
Super Bowl XIV (1980)
Super Bowl XIII (1979)
Super Bowl X (1976)
Super Bowl IX (1975)

AFC Championship (1974-75, 1978-79, 1995, 2005, 2008)
AFC North Division Champions (2002, 2004, 2007-08)
AFC Central Division Champions (1972, 1974-79, 1983-84, 1992, 1994-97, 2001)

COMPETITORS

Baltimore Ravens
Cincinnati Bengals
Cleveland Browns

HISTORICAL FINANCIALS

Company Type: Private

Income Statement

FYE: March 31

	REVENUE ($ mil.)	NET INCOME ($ mil.)	NET PROFIT MARGIN	EMPLOYEES
3/08	216	—	—	—
3/07	198	—	—	—
3/06	187	—	—	—
3/05	182	—	—	—
3/04	159	—	—	—
Annual Growth	**8.0%**	—	—	—

Revenue History

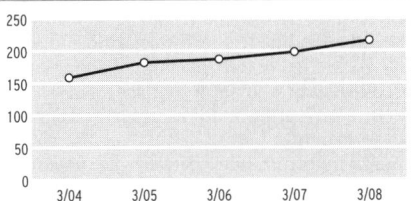

	3/04	3/05	3/06	3/07	3/08
250					
200					
150					
100					
50					
0					

Plastipak Holdings

Plastipak likes to keep things bottled up! Through its subsidiary, Plastipak Packaging, the company makes 9 billion-plus plastic containers a year for consumer products' manufacturers. Containers hold beverages (soft drinks, water, juices, and beer); cleansers (laundry soap, and household cleaners); processed foods (coffee creamer, salad dressing); health and personal care (mouthwash, perfume); and industrial and automotive goods (motor oil, windshield washer fluid). The company is among the largest users of polyethylene terephthalate (PET), and high-density polyethylene (HDPE) bottle resin. Plastipak has facilities in the US, Europe, and South America. Privately held, it is owned by the Young family.

Plastipak has benefited from proprietary packaging relationships with major consumer products companies such as Procter & Gamble, Reckitt Benckiser, Kraft Foods, Quaker Oats, Kroger, and Tropicana. Within the carbonated and non-carbonated market, Plastipak bottles are used for high profile waters such as Pepsi's Aquafina. The company supplies wide-mouth containers for Procter & Gamble's liquid laundry detergents like Tide, and household products such as Bounce. Plastipak's sustainable packaging for Kraft Foods has won notice too; its lightweight PET salad dressing bottle improves the product's shelf and pallet footprint. Automotive customers are another key market; Plastipak deals with the container needs of companies like Castrol, SOPUS Products, and Chevron/Texaco.

Timing and location work in Plastipak's favor; plants are located near the filling sites of many of its customers. Meeting the call for reduced cost, on-time transportation, Plastipak Packaging is supported by a private fleet of trucks from an affiliated subsidiary, Whiteline Express. Clean Tech, a recycling affiliate, produces Post Consumer Recycled (PCR) PET materials for use in Plastipak's new food and beverage containers. Plastipak Holdings also controls TABB Realty, and packaging interests in Brazil, Czech Republic, Slovakia, and Luxembourg.

EXECUTIVES

Chairman, President, and CEO: William C. Young
CIO: David Daugherty, age 53
VP, Packaging Development: Richard Darr, age 59
VP, Product Supply: J. Ronald Overbeck, age 60
VP, Human Resources: Renee Naud
VP, International Sales and Marketing: Frank Pollock, age 53
VP, Finance; CFO, Treasurer, and Assistant Secretary:
Michael J. Plotzke, age 51
VP, Operations and Manufacturing: William A. Slat, age 58
VP, Controller and Strategic Operation Planning:
Pradeep Modi, age 53
VP, Sales and Marketing: Gene W. Mueller, age 51
Corporate Legal Counsel and Secretary:
Leann M. Underhill, age 63
President, Clean Tech: Thomas Busard, age 57
Auditors: Grant Thornton LLP

LOCATIONS

HQ: Plastipak Holdings, Inc.
41605 Ann Arbor Rd., Plymouth, MI 48170
Phone: 734-455-3600 **Fax:** 734-354-7391
Web: www.plastipak.com

PRODUCTS/OPERATIONS

Selected Operations

Package development services
Plastic container manufacturing
High-density polyethylene (HDPE) resins
Polyethylene terephthalate (PET)
Technology licensing and equipment
EXI-PAK preform over-molding process technology (employs multi-layer, barrier, and post-consumer plastic technologies in PET bottles)
G.E.M. PAK container molding system

Selected Subsidiaries

Clean Tech, Inc.
Plastipak Packaging, Inc.
Whiteline Express, Ltd.

COMPETITORS

Amcor
Ball Corp.
Consolidated Container
Constar International
Crown Holdings
DuPont Liquid Packaging Systems
Graham Packaging
Husky Injection Molding Systems
NOVAPAK
Owens-Illinois
Silgan

Platinum Equity

Platinum Equity thinks the companies it buys are just precious. The investment firm typically seeks to acquire units that large corporations are looking to divest; these companies usually have established brands and customer bases, and most importantly, recurring revenues. Platinum Equity also looks for acquisitions as strategic add-ons to its portfolio companies, which have operations worldwide. It focuses on such sectors as manufacturing, distribution, and communications. Founder and CEO Tom Gores, who started Platinum Equity in 1995, is the brother of Alec Gores, who founded another investment firm, Gores Technology Group. The company has made more than 80 acquisitions since its founding.

Its current portfolio includes holdings in some two dozen firms.

In 2009 Platinum Equity acquired the failing San Diego Union-Tribune newspaper from Copley Press. The Union-Tribune, like many metropolitan newspapers, suffered losses from a major drop in advertising in recent years. Shortly after the deal closed, the paper announced plans to lay off 18% of its staff.

Also that year, the firm purchased the wire harness and electrical distribution business of Alcoa; a majority stake in Canvas Systems, a provider of used IT equipment; and The Geesink Norba Group from Oshkosh Corporation. Rebranded GEESINKNORBA, the company is based in Emmeloord, The Netherlands, and is a leading European manufacturer of refuse collection vehicles.

Later in 2009, though, Platinum Equity lost a bid to take control of auto parts maker Delphi. That same year, it acquired Pomeroy IT Solutions, a provider of information technology solutions and services.

In 2008, as part of its focus on the metals and manufacturing industries, Platinum Equity bought SCM Metal Products, a maker of copper-based powder and pastes and copper oxide powders, from Gibraltar Industries. Other acquisitions in 2008 included Maxim Crane Works and Covad Communications.

Platinum Equity bought the wireless communications project management business of WFI Government Services in 2007 for a reported $24 million. It also acquired Strategic Distribution and steel and metal processor Ryerson that year.

EXECUTIVES

Chairman and CEO: Tom T. Gores, age 44
CFO: Mary Ann Sigler, age 54
Partner, General Counsel, and Secretary:
 Eva M. Kalawski, age 54
Principal: Roger House
Principal: Michael Scott
Principal: Mark Barnhill
Principal: Bryan L. Kelln, age 43
Principal: Robert (Bob) Wymbs
Principal: Louis Samson
Principal: Matt Young
Principal: Stephen T. (Steve) Zollo

LOCATIONS

HQ: Platinum Equity, LLC
 360 N. Crescent Dr., South Bldg.
 Beverly Hills, CA 90210
Phone: 310-712-1850   **Fax:** 310-712-1848
Web: www.platinumequity.com

PRODUCTS/OPERATIONS

Selected Portfolio Companies

3B The Fibreglass Company
Acument Global Technologies
Advogent
Altura Communication Solutions
Americatel Corporation
Broadleaf Logistics Company
Covad Communications Group
Data2Logistics
DAUM Commercial Real Estate Services
DCA Services
DyStar
iET Solutions
Matrix Business Technologies
Maxim Crane Works
NextiraOne Mexico
OVISO Manufacturing
PEAK Technologies
Ryerson, Inc
SCM Metal Products
Strategic Distribution, Inc.
Tecumseh Power Company
Turf Care Supply Corp.
USRobotics
Vanguard Networks
WFI Deployment
Wheel Pros

COMPETITORS

Apollo Advisors
Behrman Capital
CD&R
The Gores Group
HM Capital Partners
Hummer Winblad

KKR
Madison Dearborn
Thomas H. Lee Partners
TPG
Welsh, Carson, Anderson
 & Stowe

HISTORICAL FINANCIALS

Company Type: Private

Income Statement				FYE: December 31
	REVENUE ($ mil.)	NET INCOME ($ mil.)	NET PROFIT MARGIN	EMPLOYEES
12/08	27,500	—	—	60,000
12/07	13,500	—	—	50,000
12/06	8,000	—	—	45,000
12/05	8,000	—	—	45,000
12/04	8,000	—	—	45,000
Annual Growth	36.2%	—	—	7.5%

Revenue History

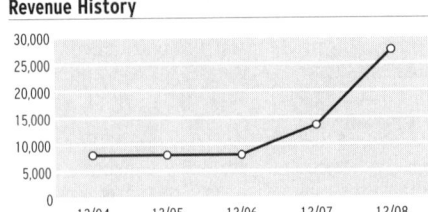

Port Authority of New York and New Jersey

The Port Authority of New York and New Jersey bridges the sometimes-troubled waters between the two states and helps with many of the region's other transportation needs. The bi-state agency operates and maintains airports, tunnels, bridges, a commuter rail system, shipping terminals, and other facilities (such as the World Trade Center complex) within the Port District, an area surrounding the Statue of Liberty. A self-supporting public agency, the Port Authority receives no state or local tax money. It relies on tolls, fees, and rents. Airport operations account for the majority of its revenue. The two governors each appoint six of the 12 members of the agency's board and review the board's decisions.

The Port Authority's facilities include such international symbols of transportation and commerce as the George Washington Bridge, the Holland and Lincoln tunnels, and LaGuardia and John F. Kennedy airports. The Port Authority Trans-Hudson (PATH) rapid-transit system provides commuter rail service between New York and New Jersey.

The World Trade Center was among the agency's most visible assets before its twin towers and much of the rest of the complex were destroyed in the terrorist attacks of September 11, 2001. The Port Authority is working with other agencies, government officials, and real estate interests on the rebuilding of the 16-acre site in Lower Manhattan, which will include skyscraper One World Trade Center (which will be New York City's tallest building when completed) and five other office towers, the World Trade Center Transportation Hub, and the National September 11th Memorial and Museum.

The Port Authority is working with New Jersey Transit and the New Jersey Turnpike Authority on the Mass Transit Tunnel (MTT), a new, almost four-mile tunnel beneath the Hudson River. Work started in June 2009 on the MTT — the first such project in 100 years. The MTT will double the rail capacity between New Jersey and New York. The agencies have committed $5.7 billion toward the $8.7 billion undertaking while the federal government will contribute $3 billion to the project plus $130 million in federal stimulus money. The MTT is set to be completed by 2017.

Christopher Ward was named executive director in 2008. The Port Authority's fourth leader since the September 11 attacks, Ward served as a port authority executive from 1997 to 2002.

HISTORY

New York and New Jersey spent much of their early history fighting over their common waterways. In 1921 a treaty creating a single, bi-state agency, the Port of New York Authority, was ratified by the New York and New Jersey state legislatures. The agency struggled at first, although its early projects, such as the Goethals Bridge (1928, linking Staten Island to New Jersey), were far from timid.

It merged with the Holland Tunnel Commission in 1930, which brought a steady source of revenue. In 1931 the George Washington Bridge (spanning the Hudson River from Manhattan to New Jersey) was completed. The Lincoln Tunnel (also linking Manhattan to New Jersey) opened in 1937.

After WWII the Port Authority broadened its focus to include commercial aviation. In 1947 the agency took over LaGuardia Airport, and the next year it dedicated the New York International Airport (renamed John F. Kennedy International Airport in 1963).

As trucking supplanted railroads in the late 1950s, The Port Authority experimented with more-efficient ways of transferring cargo. In 1962 it built the first containerport in the world. That year the agency acquired a commuter rail line connecting Newark to Manhattan, which became the Port Authority Trans-Hudson (PATH).

In the early 1970s the Port Authority completed the World Trade Center. The agency changed its name to The Port Authority of New York and New Jersey in 1972 to reflect its role in mass transit between the two states. Critics, however, frequently assailed the agency for inefficiency and pork-barrel politics. In 1993 terrorists detonated a truck bomb in one of the World Trade Center towers, but within a year the building had largely recovered.

George Marlin became executive director in 1995. He cut operating expenses for the first time since 1943 and through budget cuts and layoffs, saved $100 million in 1996 and avoided hikes in tolls and fares. He stepped down in 1997, and Robert Boyle took the post. That year the agency broke ground on the $1.2 billion Terminal 4 at JFK International Airport.

In 1998 the Port Authority authorized a $930 million design and construction contract for a light-rail line to JFK International Airport. New York City mayor Rudolph Giuliani proposed legislation in 1999 to place the Port Authority's LaGuardia and JFK airports under City Hall jurisdiction.

An 18-month standoff between the governors of New York and New Jersey regarding disputes over leases and agency spending was settled in 2000, which allowed the Port Authority to move forward with projects that had been blocked. Also in 2000 Boyle announced plans to resign. Neil Levin, New York's state insurance superintendent and a former Goldman Sachs vice president, replaced him the next year.

After the Port Authority and Vornado Realty Trust in 2001 failed to finalize an agreement for Vornado to lease the World Trade Center, the Port Authority that year signed a 99-year, $3.2 billion deal to lease portions of the World Trade Center's office space to a group led by Silverstein Properties while leasing the retail space to Westfield America.

Less than two months later, on September 11, 2001, the World Trade Center's twin towers were destroyed when terrorists hijacked passenger jets and flew them into the buildings. Levin was killed, and 83 other Port Authority employees were listed as dead or missing.

The cleanup of the World Trade Center site, known as "Ground Zero," was completed in 2002, eight months after the attacks. In 2003 the Port Authority reopened the PATH rail station at the World Trade Center site. Construction of the World Trade Center Transportation Hub, intended to serve PATH, subway, and ferry passengers and aid in the economic development of Lower Manhattan, began in 2005.

To keep up with anticipated increases in air traffic, the Port Authority in 2007 took over the operating lease for Stewart International Airport in Newburgh, New York, about 70 miles north of Manhattan.

EXECUTIVES

Chairman: Anthony R. Coscia
Vice Chairman: Henry R. Silverman, age 68
Executive Director: Christopher O. (Chris) Ward
COO: Ernesto L. Butcher
CFO: A. Paul Blanco
CTO: Diana E. Beecher
Chief Administrative Officer: Louis J. LaCapra
Chief Engineer: Francis J. Lombardi
Inspector General: Robert E. Van Etten
General Counsel: Darrell Buchbinder
Director Office of Business and Job Opportunity: Lash Green
Director Human Resources: Mary Lee Hannell
Director Engineering: Peter Zipf
Acting Director Office of Emergency Management: Brian P. Lacey
Director Treasury: Anne Marie Mulligan
Director Procurement: Lillian D. Valenti
Director Planning: Richard W. Roper
Director Marketing: Kevin Kirchman
Director Government and Community Affairs: Tina Lado
Director Management and Budget: Michael G. Massiah
Director Public Safety and Superintendent of Police: Samuel J. Plumeri Jr.
Director World Trade Center Redevelopment: Richard Gladstone
Director Aviation: William R. DeCota
Director Office of Investigations: Michael Nestor
Director Rail Transit: Michael P. DePallo
Secretary: Karen E. Eastman
Auditors: Deloitte Touche Tohmatsu

LOCATIONS

HQ: The Port Authority of New York and New Jersey
225 Park Ave. South, New York, NY 10003
Phone: 212-435-7000   **Fax:** 212-435-6670
Web: www.panynj.gov

PRODUCTS/OPERATIONS

2008 Sales

	$ mil.	% of total
Air terminals	2,025.9	57
Interstate transportation	1,102.7	31
Port commerce	201.3	6
Economic & waterfront development	108.6	3
World Trade Center	89.1	3
Total	**3,527.6**	**100**

Selected Operations

Air terminals
  Downtown Manhattan Heliport (New York)
  John F. Kennedy International Airport (New York)
  LaGuardia Airport (New York)
  Newark Liberty International Airport (New Jersey)
  Stewart International Airport (New York)
  Teterboro Airport (New Jersey)
Interstate transportation
  Bayonne Bridge (Staten Island to Bayonne, NJ)
  George Washington Bridge (Manhattan to Ft. Lee, NJ)
  George Washington Bridge Bus Terminal
  Goethals Bridge (Staten Island to Elizabeth, NJ)
  Holland Tunnel (Manhattan to Jersey City, NJ)
  Lincoln Tunnel (Manhattan to Union City, NJ)
  Outerbridge Crossing (Staten Island to Perth Amboy, NJ)
  Port Authority Bus Terminal (Manhattan)
  The Port Authority Trans-Hudson System (PATH, rail transportation between New York and New Jersey)
Port commerce
  Auto Marine Terminal (Bayonne, NJ)
  Brooklyn-Port Authority Marine Terminal (New York)
  Elizabeth-Port Authority Marine Terminal (New Jersey)
  Howland Hook Marine Terminal (New York)
  Port Newark (New Jersey)
  Red Hook Container Terminal (New York)
Economic and waterfront development
  Bathgate Industrial Park (Bronx, NY)
  Essex County Resource Recovery Center (municipal waste-to-energy electric generation plant; Newark, NJ)
  Hoboken South (mixed-use waterfront development, New Jersey)
  Industrial Park at Elizabeth (New Jersey)
  Newark Legal & Communications Center (office development, New Jersey)
  Queens West (mixed-use waterfront development, New York)
  The Teleport (communications center; Staten Island, NY)
  World Trade Center

HISTORICAL FINANCIALS

Company Type: Government agency

Income Statement

	REVENUE ($ mil.)	NET INCOME ($ mil.)	NET PROFIT MARGIN	EMPLOYEES
12/08	3,528	806	22.9%	7,127
12/07	3,192	248	7.8%	7,128
12/06	3,039	200	6.6%	7,181
12/05	3,001	223	7.4%	7,194
12/04	2,865	264	9.2%	7,267
Annual Growth	**5.3%**	**32.2%**	**—**	**(0.5%)**

FYE: December 31

Net Income History

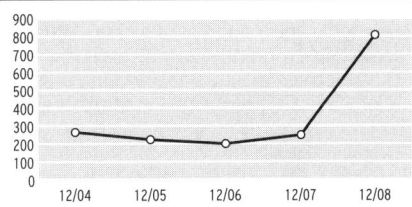

Portland Trail Blazers

This enterprise has opened a path for basketball fans in the Beaver State. Trail Blazers, Inc., owns and operates the Portland Trail Blazers professional basketball franchise, which plays host at Portland's Rose Garden Arena. The team boasts three NBA Finals appearances (its last in 1992), winning one championship in 1977. The Blazers joined the National Basketball Association in 1970 as an expansion franchise awarded to Harry Glickman, a local journalist turned sports promoter. Microsoft co-founder Paul Allen, who also owns the Seattle Seahawks, has controlled the team since 1988.

Blaming the terms of the team's lease at the Rose Garden for financial losses, Allen in 2007 purchased the sports arena he helped bankroll in 1995. (He had sold the bankrupt facility to creditors in 2004.) The team is now soliciting a corporate sponsor to buy the naming rights to the building.

With its finances starting to shape up, Portland is also hoping for a resurgence on the court. Former NIKE executive Larry Miller was hired to lead the front office in 2007; the team finished that season with a .500 record, its best mark since 2004.

In addition to the Seahawks and Trail Blazers, Allen controls a portfolio of technology investments through Vulcan Inc.

EXECUTIVES

Chairman and Owner: Paul G. Allen, age 56
President: Larry G. Miller, age 60
General Manager: Kevin Pritchard
Assistant General Manager: Tom Penn
Head Coach: Nate McMillan, age 45
SVP and General Counsel: Michael (Mike) Fennell
SVP and CFO: Gregg M. Olson
SVP Business Affairs: J. E. Isaac
VP Marketing: Michele Daterman
VP Community Relations: Traci Rose
VP Ticket Sales and Service: Brad Stith
VP and CIO: Chris Dill
VP Communications: Cheri Hanson
VP Blazers Broadcasting and Production: Dick Vardanega
VP Human Resources: Traci Reandeau
Director Basketball Operations: Brad Weinrich
Director Marketing: Traci Richardson
Mascot Coordinator: Jack Dellert

LOCATIONS

HQ: Trail Blazers, Inc.
1 Center Ct., Ste. 200, Portland, OR 97227
Phone: 503-234-9291   **Fax:** 503-736-2194
Web: www.nba.com/blazers

The Portland Trail Blazers play at the 20,630-seat capacity Rose Garden Arena in Portland, Oregon.

PRODUCTS/OPERATIONS

Championship Titles

NBA Championship (1977)
Western Conference Champions (1977, 1990, 1992)

COMPETITORS

Denver Nuggets
Minnesota Timberwolves
Oklahoma City Thunder
Utah Jazz

Pricewaterhouse-Coopers International

Not merely the firm with the longest one-word name, PricewaterhouseCoopers (PwC) is also one of the world's largest accounting firms. PwC was formed when Price Waterhouse merged with Coopers & Lybrand in 1998, bypassing then-leader Andersen. With some 770 offices in more than 150 countries, the accountancy provides clients with services in three business lines: assurance (including financial and regulatory reporting), tax, and advisory. The umbrella entity for the PwC worldwide network of member firms is one of accounting's Big Four, along with Deloitte Touche Tohmatsu, Ernst & Young, and KPMG. PwC provides services in some capacity for most of the world's largest companies as well as smaller businesses.

PwC puts its heft to good use: Non-North American clients make up nearly two-thirds of the firm's sales. The company has expanded in developing economies, including Brazil, China, India, and Russia. Member firms are locally owned and operated.

The accounting business as a whole got a boost from the implementation of such regulatory and financial reporting rules as the International Financial Reporting Standards (IFRS) and the Sarbanes-Oxley Act. The industry has faced criticism for the practice of mark-to-market accounting, which many say contributed to the global economic crisis in 2008. PwC stands behind the practice as the best accounting method of complex financial instruments.

In 2007 US arm PricewaterhouseCoopers agreed to pay a whopping $225 million to settle a class-action lawsuit related to the Tyco International financial scandal. The suit asserted that the auditors should have uncovered a $5.8 billion overstatement of earnings during the four years ending in 2002. The fraud sent Tyco top executives to prison.

In 2009 PwC acquired the North American commercial services business of the bankrupt firm BearingPoint. PwC Advisory, its Japanese subsidiary, acquired BearingPoint's consulting practice in that country.

HISTORY

In 1850 Samuel Price founded an accounting firm in London and in 1865 took on partner Edwin Waterhouse. The firm and the industry grew rapidly, thanks to the growth of stock exchanges that required uniform financial statements from listees. By the late 1800s Price Waterhouse (PW) had become the world's best-known accounting firm.

US offices were opened in the 1890s, and in 1902 United States Steel chose the firm as its auditor. PW benefited from tough audit requirements instituted after the 1929 stock market crash. In 1935 the firm was given the prestigious job of handling Academy Awards balloting. It started a management consulting service in 1946. But PW's dominance slipped in the 1960s, as it gained a reputation as the most traditional and formal of the major firms.

Coopers & Lybrand, the product of a 1957 transatlantic merger, wrote the book on auditing. Lybrand, Ross Bros. & Montgomery was formed in 1898 by William Lybrand, Edward Ross, Adam Ross, and Robert Montgomery. In 1912 Montgomery wrote *Montgomery's Auditing*, which became the bible of accounting.

Cooper Brothers was founded in 1854 in London by William Cooper, eldest son of a Quaker banker. In 1957 Lybrand joined up to form Coopers & Lybrand. During the 1960s the firm expanded into employee benefits and internal control consulting, building its technology capabilities in the 1970s as it studied ways to automate the audit process.

Coopers & Lybrand lost market share as mergers reduced the Big Eight accounting firms to the Big Six. After the savings and loan debacle of the 1980s, investors and the government wanted accounting firms held liable not only for the form of audited financial statements but for their veracity. In 1992 the firm paid $95 million to settle claims of defrauded investors in MiniScribe, a failed disk-drive maker. Other hefty payments followed, including a $108 million settlement relating to the late Robert Maxwell's defunct media empire.

In 1998 Price Waterhouse and Coopers & Lybrand combined PW's strength in the media, entertainment, and utility industries, and Coopers & Lybrand's focus on telecommunications and mining. But the merger brought some expensive legal baggage involving Coopers & Lybrand's performance of audits related to a bid-rigging scheme involving former Arizona governor Fife Symington.

Further growth plans fell through in 1999 when merger talks between PwC and Grant Thornton International failed. The year 2000 began on a sour note: An SEC conflict-of-interest probe turned up more than 8,000 alleged violations, most involving PwC partners owning stock in their firm's audit clients.

As the SEC grew ever more shrill in its denunciation of the potential conflicts of interest arising from auditing companies that the firm hoped to recruit or retain as consulting clients, PwC saw the writing on the wall and in 2000 began making plans to split the two operations. As part of this move, the company downsized and reorganized many of its operations.

The following year PwC paid $55 million to shareholders of MicroStrategy Inc., who charged that the audit firm defrauded them by approving the client firm's inflated earnings and revenues figures.

The separation of PwC's auditing and consulting functions finally became a reality in 2002, when IBM bought the consulting business. (The acquisition took the place of a planned spinoff.)

Like the other members of the Big Four, PwC picked up business and talent as scandal-felled Andersen was winding down its operations in 2002. The former Andersen organization in China and Hong Kong joined PwC, accounting for about 70% of the approximately 3,500 Andersen alumni that came aboard.

In 2003 former client AMERCO (parent of U-Haul) sued PwC for $2.5 billion, claiming negligence and fraud in relation to a series of events that led to AMERCO restating its results. The suit was settled for more than $50 million the following year.

PwC endured a two-month suspension in Japan in 2006 after three partners of its firm there were implicated in a fraud investigation involving a PwC client, Kanebo. To distance itself from the scandal, PwC's existing Japanese firm was renamed and a second firm was launched.

EXECUTIVES

Chairman: Dennis M. Nally, age 56
Global Leader Operations: Paul Boorman
Global Assurance Leader: Donald A. McGovern
Global Board Member, Hong Kong: Carrie Yu
Global General Counsel: Javier H. Rubinstein
Global Leader for Risk and Quality: Pierre Coll
Global Leader, Advisory Services: Juan Pujadas
Global Leader, Public Policy and Regulation:
Peter L. Wyman
**Global Leader, People and Culture, Brand and
Communications:** Moira Elms
**Global Leader, Tax; Managing Partner,
PricewaterhouseCoopers, UK:** Richard Collier-Keywood
Global Leader, Strategy: Anthony P.D. Harrington
Global Leader, Global Strategic Sourcing:
Edgardo Pappacena
Global Leader, Clients and Markets: Donald V. Almeida
Regional Marketing Director: Cynara Tan
Chairman, India: Gautam Banerjee
Chairman, Regional Asia Board: Silas S.S. Yang
Chairman and Senior Partner US: Robert E. Moritz
Director, Communications: Mike Davies

LOCATIONS

HQ: PricewaterhouseCoopers International Limited
300 Madison Ave., New York, NY 10017
Phone: 646-471-4000   **Fax:** 813-286-6000
Web: www.pwcglobal.com

PricewaterhouseCoopers has more than 770 offices in 150 countries.

2008 Sales

	% of total
Europe	
Western Europe	45
Central & Eastern Europe	3
North America & the Caribbean	33
Asia	9
Australasia & Pacific Islands	5
Middle East & Africa	3
South & Central America	2
Total	**100**

PRODUCTS/OPERATIONS

2008 Sales

	% of total
Assurance	49
Tax	27
Advisory	24
Total	**100**

2008 Sales by Industry

	% of total
Industrial products	22
Investment management	12
Banking & capital markets	11
Retail & consumer	10
Energy, utilities & mining	8
Technology	7
Insurance	5
Entertainment & media	5
Professional services	4
Pharmaceuticals	4
Government & public service	4
Automotive	3
Information & communications	3
Health care	2
Total	**100**

Selected Products and Services

Audit and assurance
  Actuarial services
  Assistance on capital market transactions
  Corporate reporting improvement
  Financial accounting
  Financial statement audit
  IFRS reporting
  Independent controls and systems process assurance
  Internal audit
  Regulatory compliance and reporting
  Sarbanes-Oxley compliance
  Sustainability reporting

Crisis management
 Business recovery services
 Dispute analysis and investigations
Human resources
 Change and program effectiveness
 HR management
 International assignments
 Reward
Performance improvement
 Financial effectiveness
 Governance, risk, and compliance
 IT effectiveness
Tax
 Compliance
 EU direct tax
 International assignments
 International tax structuring
 Mergers and acquisitions
 Transfer pricing
Transactions
 Accounting valuations
 Advice on fundraising
 Bid support and bid defense services
 Commercial and market due diligence
 Economics
 Financial due diligence
 Independent expert opinions
 Mergers and acquisitions advisory
 Modeling and business planning
 Post deal services
 Private equity advisory
 Privatization advice
 Project finance
 Public company advisory
 Structuring services
 Tax valuations
 Valuation consulting

COMPETITORS

Bain & Company
Baker Tilly International
BDO International
Booz Allen
Boston Consulting
Deloitte
Ernst & Young Global
Grant Thornton International
H&R Block
Hewitt Associates
KPMG
Marsh & McLennan
McKinsey & Company
Towers Perrin
Watson Wyatt

HISTORICAL FINANCIALS

Company Type: Partnership

Income Statement

FYE: June 30

	REVENUE ($ mil.)	NET INCOME ($ mil.)	NET PROFIT MARGIN	EMPLOYEES
6/08	28,185	—	—	155,693
6/07	25,150	—	—	146,767
6/06	21,986	—	—	142,162
6/05	18,998	—	—	130,203
6/04	16,283	—	—	122,471
Annual Growth	14.7%	—	—	6.2%

Revenue History

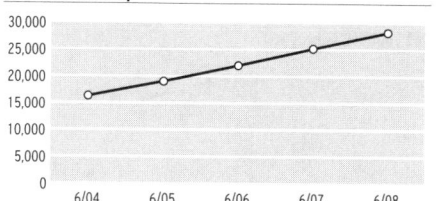

Princeton University

This prince's kingdom is covered with ivy. Princeton University, a member of the Ivy League, an elite group of top-ranked schools in the northeast US, is a research university offering degrees in 35 departments. It has more than 7,000 students (4,900 undergraduates and 2,300 graduate students), more than half receiving financial aid. One of the US's richest universities (behind Harvard, Yale, and Texas), Princeton has an endowment of more than $10 billion. The highly selective school admits about 10% of its total applicants. Nobel prize winners associated with Princeton include Woodrow Wilson (Princeton's president before becoming US president), writer Toni Morrison, and physicist Richard Feynman.

Princeton is loosely affiliated with the Institute for Advanced Study where Albert Einstein once taught.

Founded in 1746, Princeton is the fourth-oldest college in the nation. It was housed in Nassau Hall, which contained the entire college for nearly half a century. Nassau Hall served as the temporary capitol of the US in 1783.

EXECUTIVES

Chairman, Executive Committee: Stephen A. Oxman
Vice Chairman, Executive Committee: Dennis J. Keller, age 67
President and Trustee: Shirley M. Tilghman, age 62
Provost: Christopher L. Eisgruber
EVP: Mark Burstein
VP Human Resources: Lianne Sullivan-Crowley
VP Development: Brian J. McDonald
VP, Secretary, and Trustee: Robert K. Durkee
VP Finance and Treasurer: Christopher McCrudden
VP Information Technology and CIO: Betty Leydon
Dean, Undergraduate Students: Kathleen Deignan
Dean, Faculty: David P. Dobkin
Dean, Graduate School: William B. Russel
Dean, Admissions: Janet Lavin Rapelye
Dean, College: Nancy Weiss Malkiel
University Librarian: Karin A. Trainer
General Counsel: Peter G. McDonough
President, Princeton University Investment Co.: Andrew K. Golden
Auditors: Deloitte & Touche LLP

LOCATIONS

HQ: Princeton University
1 Nassau Hall, Princeton, NJ 08544
Phone: 609-258-3000   **Fax:** 609-258-1301
Web: www.princeton.edu

PRODUCTS/OPERATIONS

Select Councils, Institutes, and Centers

Bendheim Center for Finance
Center for Migration and Development
Center for the Study of Religion
Council of the Humanities
Council on Science and Technology
Davis Center for Historical Studies
James Madison Program in American Ideals and Institutions
Lewis-Sigler Institute for Integrative Genomics
Liechtenstein Institute on Self-Determination
Princeton Environmental Institute (PEI)
Princeton Institute for International and Regional Studies (PIIRS)
Princeton Institute for the Science and Technology of Materials (PRISM)
Princeton Writing Program
Program of Freshman Seminars in the Residential Colleges
Program in Law and Public Affairs
Program in Neuroscience
University Center for Human Values

Printpack, Inc.

And that's a wrap! Printpack wraps its array of flexible and rigid packaging around salty snacks, confections, baked goods, and cereal, as well as tissues and paper towels. The company's packaging includes plastic film, aluminum foil, metalized films, and paper with specialized coatings, as well as cast and blown monolayer and co-extruded films. Its sustainable lineup is marketed under the Natura brand. Blue chip clients are Frito-Lay, Georgia-Pacific, General Mills, and Quaker Oats. Printpack manufactures packaging at more than 25 plants in the US, UK, Mexico, Poland, and China. For over half a century the Love family has owned the company; Dennis Love, the son of Printpack's founder, serves as president.

Printpack caters to the appetites of both consumer goods and industrial manufacturers for ever more attractive, functional, less expensive packaging. Offering thermoformed structures to stand-up pouches, extruded films to nine-color rotogravure printing, and a myriad of wraps, the company — the second-largest flexible package-maker in the US — has the diverse needs of its customers literally covered. Moreover, in the highly competitive packaging arena, Printpack bows to industry acclaim; it has won numerous packaging awards that place it in a favored manufacturer status, engendering customer loyalty, spotlighting product quality, as well as opening up new market opportunities.

Stepping up to high customer expectations, Printpack, for example, rolled out in 2009 a shrink film offering, branded NeoAffinia, to target a variety of shrink sleeve label applications. Touted for its product differentiated, consumer preferred finish, the film is also marketed as an improved light barrier product that is cost efficient, eco friendly (providing more film per pound), and a one-size-fits-all-shapes claim. Its Seal-It division (acquired in 2006) introduced the first all body shrink sleeve label in 2008 for an Integrated BioPharma subsidiary's lineup of nutraceutical products. The green packaging eliminated the need for box containers and sported shelf-appeal labels.

Operations are tracking the company's product growth as well. In fall 2009 Printpack launched construction of a $52 million replacement plant in Bloomington, Indiana. Its expansion gained public support along with a 10-year, $2.8 million tax abatement. Geographically, the company made significant steps towards increasing its presence in Latin America in 2007 when it acquired Mexican flexible package maker Grupo Industrial Plastico (GIPSA).

EXECUTIVES

Chairman: Gay M. Love, age 80
President, CEO, and Director: Dennis M. Love, age 53
VP, General Counsel and Secretary: Gray McCalley Jr.
VP Human Resources: Rick Williams
VP and General Manager: John N. Stigler, age 62
VP Finance and CFO: R. Michael Hembree, age 60
VP Technology and Support: Terrence P. Harper, age 51
VP, General Manager, and Director: James E. Love III, age 53
VP and General Manager: James J. Greco, age 67
VP and General Manager: Michael A. Fisher, age 63
Treasurer and Assistant Secretary: Dave Kenny
Auditors: PricewaterhouseCoopers LLP

LOCATIONS

HQ: Printpack, Inc.
2800 Overlook Pkwy. NE, Atlanta, GA 30339
Phone: 404-691-5830 **Fax:** 404-699-7122
Web: www.printpack.com

PRODUCTS/OPERATIONS

Selected Products

Freshgard Films
Matte Finishes
MetalWhite
Re-Seal It
Shrink Labels
Showpack Flat Bottom Bags
Stand-Up Pouches
Stickpack
Viscopack

COMPETITORS

AEP Industries
Alcoa
Bemis
Exopack
FlexSol Packaging
Madeco

Pliant Corporation
PMC Global
Reynolds Food Packaging
Sealed Air Corp.
Tetra Pak

Pro-Build Holdings

Pro-Build Holdings is big and lumbering but it isn't unwieldy. Pro-Build is the nation's largest supplier of building materials to professional builders, contractors, and project-oriented consumers, serving customers through 10 regional brands. The company boasts more than 550 locations in 42 states, consisting of more than 470 lumber yards and dozens of truss plants, millwork shops, and wall panel plants. Services include installation, delivery, and manufacturing. The company's regional brands include The Contractor Yard, Dixieline Lumber, F.E. Wheaton, Strober Building Supplies, and U.S. Components.

Pro-Build announced a major reorganization in 2009 with a new regional structure and the adoption of a shared services operations model. The firm expanded from four to six regions to bring its operations closer to its major customers to reduce shipping and overhead costs. Its shared services model was also designed to reduce costs associated with back office operations.

In 2008 Pro-Build acquired Wisconsin building supply business Big Buck Builders Supply, Ohio-based Khempco Building Supply, CTX Builders Supply, and others. It also bought the lumber business of Home Depot's supply operations that year, after Home Depot Supply was sold.

EXECUTIVES

Chairman: Paul L. Mucci
Vice Chairman: Frederick M. (Fred) Marino
CEO: Paul W. Hylbert Jr.
COO: William J. Myrick
CFO: Thomas W. Ryan
CIO: Michael Seay
SVP Manufacturing: Lonnie Bernardoni
SVP Supply Chain: Paul J. Dodge
SVP Human Resources: John Spenard
President ProBuild Midwest: Doug Ossefoort
President Pro-Build Southwest: Joe Lawrence
President ProBuild Northwest: Ed Waite

President Pro-Build South Central:
James (Jim) Cavanaugh
President Pro-Build Southeast: Buddy Ables
President Market Development; President, Northeast:
Joseph (Joe) Todd
Director Marketing and Communications:
Carolyn Atkinson

LOCATIONS

HQ: Pro-Build Holdings Inc.
7595 Technology Way, 5th Fl., Denver, CO 80237
Phone: 303-262-8500
Web: www.pro-build.com

COMPETITORS

84 Lumber
ABC Supply
Building Materials Holding
HD Supply

Lowe's
PrimeSource Building
Structural Wood Products

HISTORICAL FINANCIALS

Company Type: Private

Income Statement				FYE: December 31
	REVENUE ($ mil.)	NET INCOME ($ mil.)	NET PROFIT MARGIN	EMPLOYEES
12/08	4,400	—	—	13,204
12/07	5,000	—	—	17,000
12/06	5,960	—	—	16,640
12/05	5,700	—	—	12,790
Annual Growth	(8.3%)	—	—	1.1%

Revenue History

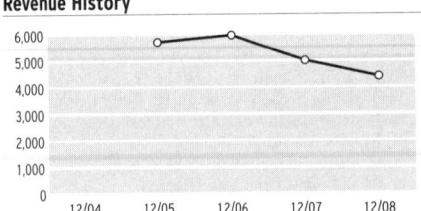

Professional Veterinary Products

Cats and dogs count on PVPL to supply them with products during those sometimes anxious vet visits. Professional Veterinary Products, Ltd. (PVPL) wholesales and distributes pharmaceuticals and supplies to licensed veterinarians. The company carries more than 20,000 products from about 350 manufacturers, ranging from diagnostic equipment to animal identification tags. It boasts two subsidiaries: Exact Logistics (distributes to other animal-health firms) and ProConn (supplies products directly to the consumer). The company was founded by a group of veterinarians in 1982. PVPL says that even its telesales staff has field experience — phones are manned by veterinary techs and others with animal science degrees.

The company launched an online store and home delivery service in 2007 called Vets First Choice. The service helps veterinarians by allowing their customers to order products online and improve compliance with doctor's orders.

PVPL distributes its products to its shareholders, as well as non-shareholder customers. Non-shareholders comprise some 70% of sales. PVPL has distribution centers in Kentucky, Nebraska, Pennsylvania, and Texas.

In January 2009 Dr. Lionel Reilly, PVPL's president and CEO, retired and was replaced by Stephen Price. Price had held the title of COO at the company since February 2006.

EXECUTIVES

Chairman: Amy L. Hinton, age 44
Vice Chairman: G.W. Buckaloo Jr., age 62
President and CEO: Stephen J. Price, age 50,
$309,162 total compensation
CFO: Tara Chicatelli, age 34
VP Technology: Leon Thomas
VP People: Chris McGonigle
VP Supply Chain: Jaime Meadows
VP Sales and Marketing: Daryl E. Schraad
Secretary: Tom Latta, age 65
Auditors: Quick & McFarlin, P.C.

LOCATIONS

HQ: Professional Veterinary Products, Ltd.
10077 S. 134th St., Omaha, NE 68138
Phone: 402-331-4440 **Fax:** 402-331-8655
Web: www.pvpl.com

PRODUCTS/OPERATIONS

2009 Sales

	$ mil.	% of total
Wholesale distribution	294.4	84
Direct customer services	55.5	16
Logistics	.3	—
Adjustments	(50.5)	—
Total	**299.7**	**100**

COMPETITORS

Animal Health International
Drs. Foster & Smith
FarmVet
IVESCO
Lambriar Animal Health
MWI Veterinary Supply
Patterson Companies
PETCO
PetMed
PetSmart
TW Medical
United Pharmacal

HISTORICAL FINANCIALS

Company Type: Private

Income Statement				FYE: July 31
	REVENUE ($ mil.)	NET INCOME ($ mil.)	NET PROFIT MARGIN	EMPLOYEES
7/09	300	(4)	—	337
7/08	340	1	0.4%	361
7/07	343	2	0.7%	341
7/06	369	2	0.7%	350
7/05	387	3	0.6%	327
Annual Growth	(6.2%)	—	—	0.8%

Net Income History

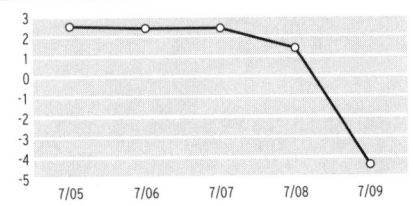

Promega Corporation

Promega helps researchers plumb the depths of the life sciences. The company sells more than 2,000 products that allow scientists to conduct various experiments in gene, protein, and cellular research. Its reagents and other goods fall into more than two dozen categories, including DNA and RNA purification, genotype analysis, protein expression and analysis, and DNA sequencing. Promega has branches in about a dozen countries around the world. The firm sells its products directly and through more than 50 distributors. Customers include academic, pharmaceutical, and clinical labs, as well as government agencies and energy and chemical companies.

Subsidiary Terso Solutions provides inventory management services, primarily through the PromegaExpress product management system, which directly ties stored products to automatic inventory controls.

Promega is continuously growing its product offerings through research efforts; R&D spending accounts for more than 10% of annual revenues. The company also licenses its technologies to other biotech firms.

Promega is owned by investors and employees.

EXECUTIVES

Chairman, President, and CEO:
William A. (Bill) Linton, age 61
VP and CTO: Randall (Randy) Dimond
VP Finance and CFO: Laura Francis
Manager Corporate Communications: Penny Patterson
Director Information Technology: Jeff Christopher
Auditors: Ernst & Young LLP

LOCATIONS

HQ: Promega Corporation
 2800 Woods Hollow Rd., Madison, WI 53711
Phone: 608-274-4330   **Fax:** 608-277-2516
Web: www.promega.com

PRODUCTS/OPERATIONS

Selected Product Categories
Cellular Analysis
 Apoptosis
 Automation-robotics
 Cell viability
 Drug discovery
 Gene expression and reporter assays
 Immunological detection
 In-vitro toxicology
 Signal transduction
 Transfection
Genetic Identity
Genomics
 Automation-robotics
 Cloning
 DNA and RNA purification
 Electrophoresis
 Food and GMO testing
 Genotype analysis
 In-vitro transcription
 Microarrays
 Plant biotechnology
 Reverse transcription and cDNA synthesis
 RNA interference
 Sequencing
Proteomics
 Electrophoresis
 Gene expression and reporter assays
 Mutagenesis
 Protein interactions
 Protein expression and analysis
 RNA interference
 Transfection

COMPETITORS

Beckman Coulter
Becton, Dickinson
Life Technologies Corporation
QIAGEN
Roche Diagnostics
Siemens Healthcare
Sigma-Aldrich
Stratagene
Transgenomic

HISTORICAL FINANCIALS

Company Type: Private

Income Statement   FYE: December 31

	REVENUE ($ mil.)	NET INCOME ($ mil.)	NET PROFIT MARGIN	EMPLOYEES
12/08	220	—	—	920
12/07	220	—	—	920
12/06	200	—	—	911
12/05	175	—	—	850
12/04	170	—	—	755
Annual Growth	**6.7%**	**—**	**—**	**5.1%**

Revenue History

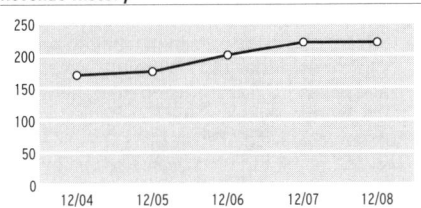

Providence Health & Services

Sisterhood is powerful in health care. Sponsored by two congregations of nuns — the Sisters of Providence and the Sisters of the Little Company of Mary — Providence Health & Services (through Providence Health System) operates more than 25 hospitals and dozens of other health facilities in five states in the western US. Its hospitals, nursing homes, and clinics are located in Alaska, California, Montana, Oregon, and Washington. All together, the system has more than 5,000 acute care beds and some 2,000 long-term care beds. The organization also provides health insurance to hundreds of thousands of people through Providence Health Plans and offers subsidized housing for the low-income elderly and disabled.

In addition to its health care and housing operations, Providence Health & Services operates a small Catholic university in Great Falls, Montana, called University of Great Falls, and a private

high school — aptly named Providence High School — in Burbank, California.

As the US economy began to falter and eventually crash in 2008, and families began to lose their jobs and health insurance, Providence Health & Services' charity care reached record highs. In 2008 the system provided the most free and discounted care it has given in its entire history. Nearly $180 million in charity care was provided in 2008, about 20% more than in the prior year.

Since the majority of the system's revenues (40%) come from commercial payors (private insurance), it feels a pinch when people begin to lose coverage, not only in increased charity care, but also through a drop in overall revenue. However, it still has other revenue sources, including Medicare payments, which make up about 30% and Medicaid payments about 8%. The rest of Providence Health's income comes from a mix of other payors and additional operating revenue.

The Sisters of Providence were founded in 1843 in Montreal. Their work in the US began in 1856, when five members of the order established a mission in what was then Washington Territory.

EXECUTIVES

Chairman: Kay Stepp
President and CEO: John F. Koster, age 58
EVP: Greg Van Pelt
SVP Mission Leadership: John O. (Jack) Mudd
SVP and CFO: Michael (Mike) Butler
SVP and Chief Administrative Officer: Jan Jones
SVP and Chief Medical Quality Officer: Keith I. Marton
VP and CIO: John Kenagy
VP Public Affairs: Chuck Hawley
VP and General Counsel, Legal Affairs:
 Jeffrey W. (Jeff) Rogers
VP Governance and Strategic Planning:
 Claudia Haglund
VP Advocacy and Development: Michael J. Madden
VP and Chief Executive, Oregon Region:
 Russ Danielson
VP and Chief Executive, Alaska Region: Al Parrish
VP and CEO, Washington/Montana Region:
 John Fletcher
VP and CEO, Southern California Region:
 Arnold R. (Arnie) Schaffer
Auditors: KPMG LLP

LOCATIONS

HQ: Providence Health & Services
 1801 West Bay Drive NW, Ste. 206
 Olympia, WA 98502
Phone: 425-525-3355
Web: www.providence.org

2008 Operating Revenue

	% of total
Commercial payors	39
Medicare	28
Medicaid	8
All other payors	5
Premium revenue	15
Other operating revenue	5
Total	**100**

Selected Hospital Facilities

Alaska
 Providence Alaska Medical Center (Anchorage)
 Providence Kodiak Island Medical Center (Kodiak)
 Providence Seward Medical Center (Seward)

California
 Providence Saint Joseph Medical Center (Burbank)
 Providence Holy Cross Medical Center (Mission Hills)
 Little Company of Mary Hospital (Torrance)
 San Pedro Peninsula Hospital (San Pedro)

Montana
St. Joseph Medical Center (Polson)
St. Patrick Hospital (Missoula)
Oregon
Providence Hood River Memorial Hospital (Hood River)
Providence Medford Medical Center (Medford)
Providence Milwaukie Hospital (Milwaukie)
Providence Newberg Hospital (Newberg)
Providence Portland Medical Center (Portland)
Providence St. Vincent Medical Center (Portland)
Providence Seaside Hospital (Seaside)
Washington
Deer Park Hospital (Deer Park)
Holy Family Hospital (Spokane)
Mount Carmel Hospital (Colville)
Providence Centralia Hospital (Centralia)
Providence Everett Medical Center (Everett)
Providence St. Peter Hospital (Olympia)
Sacred Heart Medical Center (Spokane)
St. Joseph's Hospital (Chewelah)
St. Mary Medical Center (Walla Walla)

PRODUCTS/OPERATIONS

2008 Licensed Beds

	No. of Beds
Acute	
Washington/Montana Region	2,218
California Region	1,357
Oregon Region	1,350
Alaska Region	389
Long-term care	
Washington/Montana Region	787
California Region	611
Alaska Region	243
Oregon Region	186
Total	**7,141**

COMPETITORS

Adventist Health	Legacy Health System
Banner Health	Memorial Health Services
Catholic Healthcare West	PeaceHealth
Centra Health, Inc.	Sutter Health
CHRISTUS Health	Tenet Healthcare
HCA	

HISTORICAL FINANCIALS

Company Type: Not-for-profit

Income Statement				FYE: December 31
	REVENUE ($ mil.)	NET INCOME ($ mil.)	NET PROFIT MARGIN	EMPLOYEES
12/08	7,026	(764)	—	45,000
12/07	6,348	434	6.8%	45,000
12/06	5,821	348	6.0%	45,220
12/05	4,365	249	5.7%	47,572
12/04	4,021	382	9.5%	33,940
Annual Growth	**15.0%**	**—**	**—**	**7.3%**

2008 Year-End Financials

Debt ratio: 29.4%
Return on equity: —
Cash ($ mil.): —
Current ratio: —
Long-term debt ($ mil.): 1,149

Net Income History

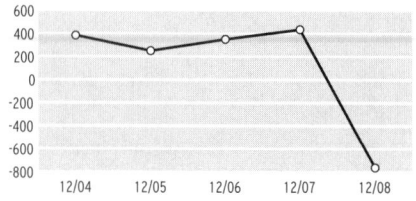

Publishers Clearing House

If your doorbell rings unexpectedly, it's probably just your neighbor stopping by for a chat. But it *could be* the Publishers Clearing House (PCH) Prize Patrol letting you know that you've won $10 million. PCH is one of the world's largest direct marketing organizations. Once known primarily for its magazines (and PCH giveaways), the company now makes most of its money from direct mail offerings for household items, personal care products, entertainment, collectibles, and food items in the US, the UK, and Canada. About half of the company's profits goes to charities. PCH was founded in 1953 by Harold and LuEsther Mertz and is still owned largely by the charitable foundations established by the Mertz family.

In a bid to extend its reach into the virtual world in recent years, PCH acquired Mill Valley, California-based Blingo, an Internet search engine that tempts users with the chance to win instant prizes with each search they perform. With PCH's backing, Blingo offers prizes ranging from movie tickets, gift cards, new cars, big screen plasma TVs, $5,000 in cash, and more to fortunate Web surfers.

Another effort to capture the attention of digital age consumers is PCH's partnership in early 2009 with social media site TriviaTown.com to develop an iPhone application that offers a free trivia game. Players with enough points for correct answers get to spin the "PCH Winning Wheel" for cash and prizes. PCH also is using social networking sites Twitter, MySpace, and Facebook to reach a younger generation of customers.

Over the years, PCH has been plagued by con artists using its name in phony prize-notification letters and bogus phone calls. The company, which always notifies winners of $10,000 or more in person and never charges fees to collect prizes, has countered the scam by urging people to call its Consumer Affairs division to verify authenticity of prize notifications.

EXECUTIVES

Chairman: Robin B. Smith, age 67
President and CEO: Andy Goldberg
CFO: Rick Busch
EVP: Deborah Holland
SVP: Todd Sloane
Senior Director Consumer and Privacy Affairs: Christopher L. Irving

LOCATIONS

HQ: Publishers Clearing House
382 Channel Dr., Port Washington, NY 11050
Phone: 516-883-5432   **Fax:** 516-767-4567
Web: www.pch.com

PRODUCTS/OPERATIONS

Selected Sources of Revenue

Magazines
Merchandise
pch.com
International

COMPETITORS

Amazon.com	Lillian Vernon
Amazon.co.uk	Reader's Digest
Avon	Synapse Group
EBSCO	Time Inc.
Google	Yahoo!

HISTORICAL FINANCIALS

Company Type: Private

Income Statement				FYE: December 31
	REVENUE ($ mil.)	NET INCOME ($ mil.)	NET PROFIT MARGIN	EMPLOYEES
12/07	620	—	—	—

Publix Super Markets

Publix Super Markets tops the list of privately owned supermarket operators in the US. By emphasizing service and a family-friendly image over price, Publix has grown faster and been more profitable than Winn-Dixie Stores and other rivals. More than two-thirds of its 1,000 stores are in Florida, but it also operates in Alabama, Georgia, South Carolina, and Tennessee. Publix makes some of its own bakery, deli, and dairy goods, and many stores house pharmacies and banks. The firm also operates liquor stores, convenience stores, and Crispers restaurants in Florida. Founder George Jenkins began offering stock to Publix employees in 1930. Employees own about 30% of Publix, which is still run by the Jenkins family.

The fast-growing grocer opened its 1,000th supermarket in early 2009 and plans to open approximately 40 more stores this year, including about a dozen locations acquired from Albertsons. While the purchase of Albertsons' Florida stores eliminated one rival, Publix is facing increased competition from Winn-Dixie, following its stint in bankruptcy; Sweetbay; and supercenter operator Wal-Mart. (Low-cost ALDI is also expanding in Florida.) Aggressive price cutting by Publix and its rivals in response to the downturn in the Florida economy is putting a squeeze on profits. In the Atlanta market, Publix is facing increased heat from Kroger.

To stay on top of the competitive Florida grocery market, Publix keeps up with national trends in grocery retailing. In 2009 the company teamed up with NCR to install DVD rental kiosks in its supermarkets, saving customers a trip to the video store and giving Netflix a bit of competition. In 2007 it began offering free antibiotics at its 680-plus in-store pharmacies. The grocery chain also fills other generic prescriptions for $4 (upon customer request), thereby matching Wal-Mart's low-cost generic drug program. To better serve its Latino customers, Publix has launched its own line of pre-packaged Hispanic foods, including frozen plantains and ready-to-eat black beans. It also launched a Hispanic-themed format called Publix Sabor in 2005, which operates two stores in Miami.

In 2007 the company launched a new store format called GreenWise Market (the name Publix had already given its store-within-a-store natural/organic sections and private-label line of specialty foods) to court more health-conscious consumers and compete with national organic chains, such as Whole Foods.

In addition to grocery stores, Publix also operates liquor stores next to about 75 of its supermarkets in Florida. Other ventures include its majority-owned restaurant chain Crispers in Florida. Currently, the soup-salad-and-sandwich chain operates about 40 locations.

HISTORY

George Jenkins, age 22, resigned as manager of the Piggly Wiggly grocery in Winter Haven, Florida, in 1930. With money he had saved to buy a car, he opened his own grocery store, Publix, next door to his old employer. The small store (named after a chain of movie theaters) prospered despite the Depression, and in 1935 Jenkins opened another Publix in the same town.

Five years later, after the supermarket format had become popular, Jenkins closed his two smaller locations and opened a new, more modern Publix Market. With pastel colors and electric-eye doors, it was also the first US store to feature air conditioning.

Publix Super Markets bought the All-American chain of Lakeland, Florida (19 stores), in 1944 and moved its corporate headquarters to that city. The company began offering S&H Green Stamps in 1953, and in 1956 it replaced its original supermarket with a mall featuring an enlarged Publix and a Green Stamp redemption center. Publix expanded into South Florida in the late 1950s.

As Florida's population grew, Publix continued to expand, opening its 100th store in 1964. Publix was the first grocery chain in the state to use bar-code scanners; all its stores had the technology by 1981. The company beat Florida banks in providing ATMs, and during the 1980s opened debit card stations.

Publix continued to grow in the 1980s, safe from takeover attempts because of its employee ownership. In 1988 it installed the first automated checkout systems in South Florida, giving patrons an always-open checkout lane.

In 1989, after almost six decades, "Mr. George" — as founder Jenkins was known — stepped down as chairman in favor of his son Howard. (George died in 1996.)

In 1991 Publix opened its first store outside Florida, in Georgia, as part of its plan to become a major player in the Southeast. Publix entered South Carolina in 1993 with one supermarket; it also tripled its presence in Georgia to 15 stores.

The United Food and Commercial Workers Union began a campaign in 1994 against alleged gender and racial discrimination in Publix's hiring, promotion, and compensation policies.

Publix opened its first store in Alabama in 1996. That year a federal judge allowed about 150,000 women to join a class-action suit filed in 1995 by 12 women who had sued Publix, charging that the company consistently channeled female employees into low-paying jobs with little chance for good promotions. The case, which at the time was said to be the biggest sex discrimination lawsuit ever, was set to go to trial, but in 1997 the company paid $82.5 million to settle and another $3.5 million to settle a complaint of discrimination against black applicants and employees.

Publix promised to change its promotion policies, but two more lawsuits alleging discrimination against women and blacks were filed in 1997 and 1998. The suit filed on behalf of the women was denied class-action status in 2000. Later that year the company settled the racial discrimination lawsuit for $10.5 million. Howard Jenkins stepped down as CEO in mid-2001; his cousin Charlie Jenkins took the helm.

In 2002 Publix entered the Nashville, Tennessee, market with the purchase of seven Albertsons supermarkets, a convenience store, and a fuel center. In 2004 Publix became the majority owner of Crispers.

In 2007 the chain began offering seven popular antibiotics free at some 685 Publix Pharmacies. The drugs account for almost 50% of the generic pediatric prescriptions filled at Publix.

CEO Charlie Jenkins Jr. retired at the end of March 2008. Jenkins was succeeded by his cousin and Publix president Ed Crenshaw. In September Publix completed the roughly $500-million acquisition of 49 Albertsons stores in Florida.

EXECUTIVES

Chairman: Charles H. (Charlie) Jenkins Jr., age 65, $540,093 total compensation
Vice Chairman: Hoyt R. (Barney) Barnett, age 65
CEO and Director: William E. (Ed) Crenshaw, age 58, $795,466 total compensation
President: Randall T. (Todd) Jones Sr., age 46, $646,539 total compensation
CFO and Treasurer: David P. Phillips, age 49, $634,007 total compensation
SVP and CIO: Laurie Z. Douglas, age 45, $540,093 total compensation
SVP: R. Scott Charlton, age 50
SVP, General Counsel, and Secretary:
John A. Attaway Jr., age 50, $456,031 total compensation
SVP: John T. Hrabusa, age 54
VP Manufacturing: Michael R. (Mike) Smith, age 49
VP Real Estate, Crispers: Cliff Wiley
VP Risk Management: Marc Salm, age 48
Director Marketing and Advertising: Kevin Lang
Director Marketing and Research: Mark Lang
Assistant Secretary and Executive Director Publix Super Markets Charities: Sharon A. Miller, age 65
Chairman and CEO, Crispers Restaurants: Ron Fuller
Auditors: KPMG LLP

LOCATIONS

HQ: Publix Super Markets, Inc.
3300 Publix Corporate Pkwy., Lakeland, FL 33811
Phone: 863-688-1188 **Fax:** 863-284-5532
Web: www.publix.com

2008 Supermarkets

	No.
Florida	713
Georgia	176
South Carolina	42
Alabama	37
Tennessee	25
Total	**993**

PRODUCTS/OPERATIONS

2008 Stores

	No.
Supermarkets	993
Liquor stores	73
Crispers restaurants	41
Pix convenience stores	10
Total	**1,117**

Selected Supermarket Departments

Bakery	Health and beauty care
Banking	Housewares
Dairy	Meat
Deli	Pharmacy
Ethnic foods	Photo processing
Floral	Produce
Groceries	Seafood

Foods Processed

Baked goods
Dairy products
Deli items

COMPETITORS

ALDI	The Pantry
BI-LO	Rite Aid
Costco Wholesale	Ruddick
CVS Caremark	Sedano's
IGA	Sweetbay
Ingles Markets	Walgreen
Kerr Drug	Wal-Mart
Kmart	Whole Foods
Kroger	Winn-Dixie
Nash-Finch	

HISTORICAL FINANCIALS

Company Type: Private

Income Statement			FYE: Last Saturday in December	
	REVENUE ($ mil.)	NET INCOME ($ mil.)	NET PROFIT MARGIN	EMPLOYEES
12/08	24,110	1,090	4.5%	144,000
12/07	23,194	1,184	5.1%	144,000
12/06	21,820	1,097	5.0%	140,000
12/05	20,745	989	4.8%	134,000
12/04	18,686	819	4.4%	128,000
Annual Growth	6.6%	7.4%	—	3.0%

Net Income History

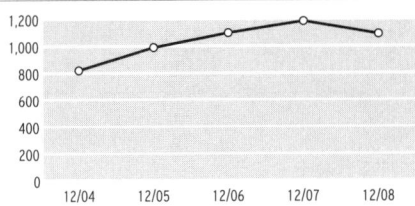

Purity Wholesale Grocers

This company gets the goods to grocers at a discount. Purity Wholesale Grocers (PWG) is a leading secondary wholesaling company that distributes broadline grocery products, health and beauty care items, pharmaceutical products, dairy foods, and dry goods to small retailers across the country. It takes advantage of discounts granted to large wholesalers and retailers (and of the promotional pricing offered in certain regions) and passes those cost savings on to its customers. PWG supplies grocery chains, drugstores, and convenience stores. In addition, PWG offers online sourcing services that also help retailers find bargains. The company is owned by Jeff Levitetz, who founded PWG in 1982.

EXECUTIVES

Chairman: Jeffrey A. (Jeff) Levitetz, age 52
President: Alan Rutner
President: David Groomes
VP Accounting and Controller: Tom Jankus
VP Human Resources: Karen L. McGrath

LOCATIONS

HQ: Purity Wholesale Grocers, Inc.
5400 Broken Sound Blvd. NW, Ste. 100
Boca Raton, FL 33487
Phone: 561-994-9360   **Fax:** 561-241-4628
Web: www.pwg-inc.com

PRODUCTS/OPERATIONS

Selected Operating Companies
American Wholesale Grocers
Purity Wholesale Grocers
Super Marketing
Supreme Distributors

COMPETITORS

Amexdrug	Imperial Distributors
Associated Wholesale	Kroger
Grocers	McLane
C & S Wholesale	Nash-Finch
Dot Foods	SUPERVALU
Eby-Brown	Wal-Mart
H.T. Hackney	

HISTORICAL FINANCIALS
Company Type: Private

Income Statement
FYE: June 30

	REVENUE ($ mil.)	NET INCOME ($ mil.)	NET PROFIT MARGIN	EMPLOYEES
6/08	1,000	—	—	500
6/07	1,000	—	—	500
6/06	1,200	—	—	500
6/05	1,000	—	—	350
6/04	1,700	—	—	425
Annual Growth	(12.4%)	—	—	4.1%

Revenue History

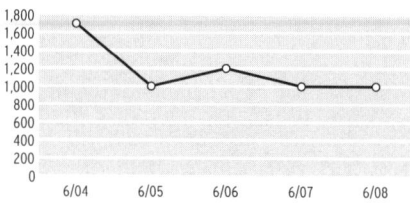

Quad/Graphics, Inc.

Your mailbox may be filled with Quad/Graphics' handiwork. A leading US printing company, Quad/Graphics produces catalogs, magazines, books, direct mail, and other commercial material. The company offers a full range of services, including design, photography, desktop production, printing, binding, wrapping, distribution, and related software. At its 10 printing facilities, about half of which are in Wisconsin, the company has produced catalogs for the likes of Bloomingdale's and L.L. Bean, books for National Geographic, and magazines such as *People*, *Newsweek*, and *Sports Illustrated*. Company employees and members of the founding Quadracci family own and run Quad/Graphics.

The company is diversifying beyond its core catalog and magazine printing services in a bid

to grow the business. In 2008 Quad/Graphics invested $25 million to expand its direct-mail division, which had previously been a smaller contributor. The move helped the company to acquire digital presses and envelope inserters and to update other features of its production center. As demand has fallen for printing services, Quad/Graphics in 2009 laid off about 550 plant workers nationwide. The company linked the workforce reduction to dwindling sales of catalogs and other media.

It has likewise extended its reach into Europe to strengthen its presence, acquiring Ireland-based Vigitek in 2008. Vigitek, whose scanners and inspection systems detect printing defects, was renamed QuadTech following the purchase. In 2007 the company bought Poland-based Winkowski, a leading commercial printer. Quad/Graphics later renamed the unit QuadWinkowski, and appointed Tom Frankowski, a veteran of its US manufacturing operations, as the unit's president. In addition to its European business lines, Quad/Graphics maintains partnerships with printers in Argentina and Brazil.

Quad/Graphics is widely recognized in the US as a good place to work. The company has provided on-site day care centers, health clubs, and medical clinics. In addition, it has sponsored sports leagues, awarded college scholarships to employees' children, and offered interest-free auto loans. Quad/Graphics' Windhover Foundation supports social, cultural, and educational projects. Besides Wisconsin, the firm's US operations include printing plants in Georgia, Nevada, New York, Oklahoma, and Virginia.

EXECUTIVES

President, CEO, and Director: J. Joel Quadracci
SVP and CFO: John C. Fowler
SVP Sales and Administration: David A. Blais
SVP Manufacturing; President, QuadWinkowski: Thomas J. (Tom) Frankowski
VP Customer Service: Ron Nash
VP Finishing Operations: Bill Graushar
VP Employee Services: Emmy M. LaBode
VP and Treasurer: Kelly Vanderboom
VP Press Operations: Tim Sands
VP and General Counsel: Andy Schiesl
VP Distribution: David (Dave) Riebe
VP Information Systems and Infrastructure; President, QuadDirect: Steve Jaeger

LOCATIONS

HQ: Quad/Graphics, Inc.
N63 W23075 State Hwy. 74, Sussex, WI 53089
Phone: 414-566-6000   **Fax:** 414-566-4650
Web: www.qg.com

PRODUCTS/OPERATIONS

Selected Services
Binding and finishing
Color correction
Defect detection
Design
Desktop production
Direct mailing
Imaging and photography
Ink jetting
Integrated circulation
Mailing and distribution
Mailing list management
Printing
Scanning

COMPETITORS

Angstrom Graphics
Arandell
Brown Printing
Cenveo
Consolidated Graphics
Dai Nippon Printing
Merrill
R.R. Donnelley
Toppan Printing
World Color Press

HISTORICAL FINANCIALS
Company Type: Private

Income Statement
FYE: December 31

	REVENUE ($ mil.)	NET INCOME ($ mil.)	NET PROFIT MARGIN	EMPLOYEES
12/08	2,000	—	—	11,000
12/07	2,050	—	—	12,000
12/06	2,030	—	—	12,000
12/05	1,950	—	—	12,000
Annual Growth	0.8%	—	—	(2.9%)

Revenue History

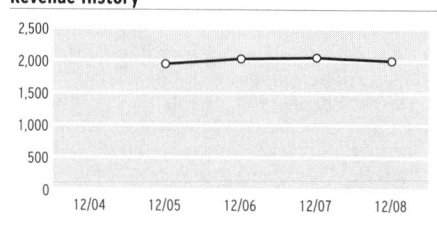

Quality King Distributors

Quality King Distributors rules a gargantuan gray-market empire. It buys US name-brand OTC pharmaceutical and branded personal care products that have been exported to overseas markets, re-imports them, then sells them below suggested retail prices. The practice, deeply disliked by US manufacturers, has been ruled legal by the Supreme Court. Quality King distributes its products to pharmacy and grocery chains, grocery distributors, and wholesale clubs throughout the US. Subsidiary QK Healthcare distributes branded and generic prescription pharmaceuticals. Bernard Nussdorf and his wife Ruth founded Quality King in 1961 in Long Island, New York. The Nussdorf family still owns the company.

EXECUTIVES

Chairman and CEO: Glenn H. Nussdorf
COO: Marc Garrett
EVP: Michael W. Katz, age 61
VP Human Resources: Olga Lancaster
General Counsel: Alfred Paliani
Director Sales: Michael Ross

LOCATIONS

HQ: Quality King Distributors Inc.
2060 9th Ave., Ronkonkoma, NY 11779
Phone: 631-737-5555   **Fax:** 631-439-2388
Web: www.qkd.com

COMPETITORS

AmerisourceBergen
Apothecary Products
Cardinal Health
The Harvard Drug Group
Imperial Distributors
Kinray
McKesson

QuikTrip Corporation

QuikTrip provides a quick fix for those on the go. QuikTrip (QT) owns and operates some 525 gasoline/convenience stores in nine states, mostly in the central US. QT stores, which average 4,200 to 5,000 sq. ft., feature the company's own QT brand of gas and diesel fuel, as well as brand-name beverages, candy, and tobacco, and QT's Quik 'n Tasty and HOTZI lines of sandwiches. QT's 15-plus travel centers offer scales, food, fuel, showers, and other services for truckers. The firm's FleetMaster program offers commercial trucking companies detailed reports showing drivers' product purchases, amounts spent, and odometer readings. QT was co-founded in 1958 by chairman Chester Cadieux. His son Chet runs the company.

In mid-2009 QuikTrip and another Tulsa-based company Magellan Midstream Partners tried to acquire the refined petroleum unit of SemGroup LP out of bankruptcy, but were outbid by Noble Americas Corp., a subsidiary of the Hong Kong-based Noble Group.

QuikTrip is remodeling stores and expanding its hot and cold beverage selection. The icy "Koolee," introduced in 1963, has been phased out and replaced by a frozen carbonated beverage called a Freezoni, available in seven flavors. More than 70% of the food products sold at QT stores are delivered by its QT Distribution (QTD) subsidiary. QTD has warehouses in Arizona, Georgia, and Phoenix.

The company recently opened several upscale, high-volume (capable of handling 120 cars per hour) car washes in Tulsa and Wichita, Kansas. QuikTrip operates convenience stores in Arizona, Georgia, Illinois, Iowa, Kansas, Missouri, Nebraska, Texas, and its home state of Oklahoma.

EXECUTIVES

Chairman, President, and CEO:
Chester (Chet) Cadieux III, age 42
VP and CFO: Sandra J. (Sandi) Westbrook
SVP Store Operations: Mike Stanford
VP Operations Systems: Ron Jeffers
VP Finance and Treasurer: Paula Cotten
VP Marketing: James (Jim) Denny
VP Human Resources: Kimberly (Kim) Owen
Director Real Estate: Rodney Loyd
Manager Real Estate: Alan Renner
Manager Public and Government Affairs:
Mike Thornbrugh
Corporate Fleet Sales Manager: Bill Friggel

LOCATIONS

HQ: QuikTrip Corporation
4777 S. 129th East Ave., Tulsa, OK 74134
Phone: 918-615-7900   **Fax:** 918-615-7377
Web: www.quiktrip.com

PRODUCTS/OPERATIONS

2008 Stores

	No.
Convenience stores	524
Travel centers	17
Total	**541**

COMPETITORS

7-Eleven	E-Z Mart Stores
Casey's General Stores	Krause Gentle
Chevron	Motiva Enterprises
CITGO	Racetrac Petroleum
Couche-Tard	Valero Energy
Exxon Mobil	

HISTORICAL FINANCIALS

Company Type: Private

Income Statement				FYE: April 30
	REVENUE ($ mil.)	NET INCOME ($ mil.)	NET PROFIT MARGIN	EMPLOYEES
4/08	7,700	—	—	10,745
4/07	8,300	—	—	10,500
4/06	6,740	—	—	10,062
4/05	7,157	—	—	8,500
4/04	4,051	—	—	7,000
Annual Growth	17.4%	—	—	11.3%

Revenue History

Quintiles Transnational

Quintiles Transnational has plenty to CRO about. One of the world's top contract research organizations (CROs), with operations in more than 50 countries, it helps drug and medical device companies develop and sell their products. The firm provides a comprehensive range of clinical trials management services, including patient recruitment, data analysis, laboratory testing, and regulatory filing. Its consulting unit offers strategic advice at every stage of drug discovery and development, and its Innovex subsidiary is a contract sales organization providing sales personnel to promote approved products. An investment group led by founder and CEO Dennis Gillings owns the company.

Additionally, the company provides financing and partnering support through its NovaQuest unit, which invests in client companies (either through cash or services) in return for royalties on sales of approved products.

Quintiles Transnational has been taking advantage of the growing demand for outsourced clinical development services, as belt-tightening pharma and biotech companies look to trim costs even as they are desperate to find and develop new products. The company has focused efforts on developing services that help its clients reduce risk and time-to-market. It established a joint venture with Thermo Fisher Scientific called Cenduit, for example, which helps control clinical trials costs by automating delivery of supplies, among other things. And in 2007 it acquired Eidetics, a company that helps drug companies collect and analyze data that is used at various decision-making junctures in the drug development process. To expand its oncology development services, Quintiles acquired Targeted Molecular Diagnostics in 2008.

Because Quintiles' customers and alliance partners tend to be larger firms, it has not been pinched as hard by the softened credit market. Smaller biotech firms, which have had a hard time attracting fresh capital to continue their research, account for only a fraction of the company's revenues.

The company sold much of its preclinical services business, which provided services like toxicology testing and chemistry services, to Aptuit, in order to focus on its core clinical (i.e., human testing) services. However, it still offers early-stage testing services to its clients through a continuing partnership with Aptuit.

HISTORY

Quintiles was founded by Dennis Gillings, a British biostatistician who had worked with Hoechst (now part of Sanofi-Aventis) on data analysis in the 1970s. Gillings set up Quintiles (Quantitative Information Technology In The Life and Economic Sciences) in 1982 at the University of North Carolina, where he was then teaching. The company grew as drug companies began outsourcing some of the more irksome tasks of drug development. Quintiles went public in 1994.

Quintiles used the proceeds of the IPO to expand its health economics segment with the purchases of Benefit International (1995) and Lewin Group (1996). These purchases introduced the company to such new clients as governments and HMOs. Quintiles' 1996 purchase of Innovex (unrelated to the computer hardware maker of the same name) made it the world's largest CRO. The buying spree continued in 1997 and 1998. Among the purchases were some intended to strengthen Quintiles' marketing services (Data Analysis Systems Inc., Q.E.D. International, and France-based Serval). The firm also formed new collaborations with such academic research organizations as Johns Hopkins Medicine.

In 1999 Quintiles expanded its marketing arm with the purchase of Pharmaceutical Marketing Services (parent of the leading pharmaceuticals industry research company, Scott-Levin) and jumped headlong into data mining with its purchase of ENVOY — which processed insurance claims. Quintiles found the core business uninspiring and sold it to Healtheon (now Emdeon, formerly WebMD) the next year. But it kept rights to ENVOY's stream of treatment, outcome, and insurance data, gleaned from health care providers, hospitals, payers, and pharmacies — a treasure house of information useful to salespeople and health providers.

The company continued in 2000 to add offices in Europe, Asia, and Latin America. The company also opened additional offices in the US and Europe to help Japanese pharmaceutical companies market their products in those regions. Late in the year, Quintiles bought the clinical development unit of Pharmacia.

In 2001 Quintiles became embroiled in a legal dispute with WebMD involving the availability of data associated with ENVOY; the company challenged WebMD's efforts to withhold such data. The two companies settled the squabble later that year and agreed to sever all ties. Also in 2001 Quintiles streamlined operations and cut about 5% of its workforce.

The future of the CRO came into question at the end of 2002. Gillings presented the company with a buyout offer; he planned to take the company private so he could pursue a new growth strategy Wall Street would surely find risky. The board rejected that offer in October 2002, but it opened up an auction. Some leading equity firms reportedly made offers, but Gillings — with backing from Blackstone Group and BANK ONE's One Equity Partners (now part of JPMorgan Chase) — placed another offer for Quintiles and won the prize in April 2003. Some five months later, Quintiles went private.

In 2005 Quintiles sold three business units — preclinical services, pharmaceutical sciences, and clinical trial supplies — to privately held Aptuit for $125 million. It made the sale in order to focus efforts on its core clinical-stage services.

In late 2007 Quintiles made changes in its ownership structure: CEO Gillings, TPG Capital, and Temasek Holdings stayed in while others opted out and Bain Capital and 3i joined in the investment group.

EXECUTIVES

Chairman and CEO: Dennis B. Gillings, age 64
CFO: Mike Troullis
Chief Administrative Officer: Mike Mortimer, age 45
Chief Medical and Scientific Officer:
Christopher H. Cabell
EVP and CIO: William R. Deam
EVP Corporate Development: Ronald J. (Ron) Wooten
EVP Strategic Business Partnerships and Customer Relationship: Derek M. Winstanly
SVP Clinical Research Strategies; Managing Director, Quintiles Public Health and Government Services: Oren Cohen
SVP Communication and Patient Recruitment: David (Dave) Coman
SVP Global Marketing and Chief Marketing Officer: Millie Tan
VP Global Staffing: Dave Cooper
VP Business Development: Matt Eberhart
Practice Leader, Market Access, US: John Doyle
Practice Leader, Product Development and Commercialization, US: Adrian McKerney
Practice Leader, Regulatory and Quality and Product Development and Commercialization, Europe: Jim Featherstone
President, iGuard: Hugo Stephenson
President, Innovex: Richard D. (Rich) Pilnik, age 52
Senior Director Corporate Communication: Mari Mansfield
Auditors: PricewaterhouseCoopers LLP

LOCATIONS

HQ: Quintiles Transnational Corp.
4820 Emperor Blvd., Durham, NC 27703
Phone: 919-998-2000   **Fax:** 919-998-9113
Web: www.quintiles.com

PRODUCTS/OPERATIONS

Selected Products and Services

Contract sales services (Innovex)
Financing and partnering solutions (NovaQuest)
Product development services
  Biostatistics
  Central laboratory services
  Clinical pharmacology
  Data management
  Patient and investigator recruitment
  Phase I-III clinical trial design
  Regulatory services

COMPETITORS

Covance
ICON
IMS Health
Kendle
MDS
PAREXEL
PDI, Inc.
Pharmaceutical Product Development
PharmaNet Development Group
PRA International
Quest Diagnostics

HISTORICAL FINANCIALS

Company Type: Private

Income Statement				FYE: December 31
	REVENUE ($ mil.)	NET INCOME ($ mil.)	NET PROFIT MARGIN	EMPLOYEES
12/08	2,800	—	—	23,000
12/07	2,700	—	—	21,000
12/06	2,530	—	—	18,000
12/05	2,399	—	—	16,000
12/04	2,146	—	—	16,986
Annual Growth	6.9%	—	—	7.9%

Revenue History

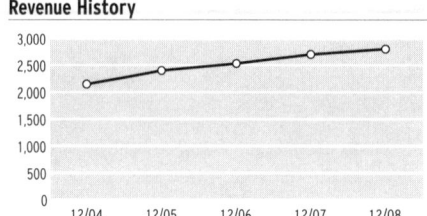

RaceTrac Petroleum

RaceTrac Petroleum hopes it's a popular pit stop for gasoline and snacks in the Southeast. The company owns more than 525 gas stations and convenience stores in about a dozen states under the RaceTrac and RaceWay names. (RaceWay stores are operated by independent contractors.) The chain plans to grow by adding between 35 and 45 new locations annually. Carl Bolch founded RaceTrac in Missouri in 1934. His son, chairman and CEO Carl Bolch Jr., moved the company into high-volume gas stations with long, self-service islands that can serve as many as two dozen vehicles at one time. RaceTrac's convenience stores sell fresh deli food and offer some fast-food fare. The Bolch family owns the company.

EXECUTIVES

Chairman and CEO: Carl E. Bolch Jr.
President: Max Lenker
CFO: Robert J. Dumbacher
SVP, Operations: Ben Tison
VP, Human Resources: Allison Moran

LOCATIONS

HQ: RaceTrac Petroleum, Inc.
3225 Cumberland Blvd., Ste. 100, Atlanta, GA 30339
Phone: 770-431-7600
Web: www.racetrac.com

COMPETITORS

7-Eleven   Gate Petroleum
Chevron   Motiva Enterprises
Couche-Tard   The Pantry
Cumberland Farms   Pilot Corporation
Exxon Mobil   QuikTrip
E-Z Mart Stores

HISTORICAL FINANCIALS

Company Type: Private

Income Statement				FYE: December 31
	REVENUE ($ mil.)	NET INCOME ($ mil.)	NET PROFIT MARGIN	EMPLOYEES
12/08	6,680	—	—	4,454
12/07	5,520	—	—	3,812
12/06	4,900	—	—	4,039
12/05	4,969	—	—	3,962
Annual Growth	10.4%	—	—	4.0%

Revenue History

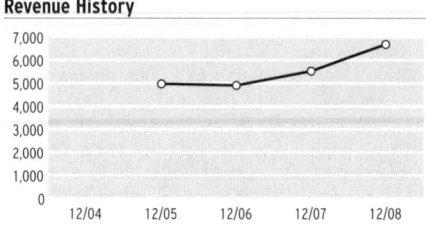

Raley's

Raley's has to stock plenty of fresh fruit and great wines — it sells to the people that produce them. The company operates about 135 supermarkets and larger-sized superstores in California and northern Nevada. In addition to its 85 flagship Raley's Superstores, the company operates about 20 Bel Air Markets (in the Sacramento area), Nob Hill Foods (an upscale Bay Area chain with about two-dozen locations), and about five discount warehouse stores under the Food Source banner in Northern California. Raley's stores typically offer groceries, natural foods, and liquor, as well as in-store pharmacies. Founded during the Depression by Thomas Porter Raley, the company is owned by Tom's daughter Joyce Raley Teel.

The regional grocery chain is shopping for a new CEO following the resignation of William Coyne in October 2009. Coyne, who held the top job at Raley's since 2003, departed amid tough times for both the grocery chain and economy in California. (Dave Clark, the company's COO, is filling in on an interim basis.) Raley's is being squeezed between non-traditional grocery operators, such as Wal-Mart and WinCo Foods on the low end, and more upscale chains like Whole Foods and grocery giant Safeway.

In response to rising food prices, the dismal state of the California economy, and the stubborn perception of Raley's as a full-service retailer with high prices, the grocery chain launched "Your Ticket to Savings" in September 2008. The program is designed to call attention to sale items, temporary price reductions, less expensive private brands, and more. However, the chain's attempts to market itself as a value retailer, haven't resonated with customers who increasingly are shopping elsewhere.

Raley's has also struggled to expand beyond its core market in California. It has a relatively small footprint in Nevada, and in 2007 it sold its 10 stores in New Mexico to Albertsons, thereby exiting that market. Raley's said the sale will allow it to better focus on its core markets in Northern California, the Bay Area, and northern Nevada.

EXECUTIVES

Co-Chairman and Owner: Joyce Raley Teel, age 73
Co-Chairman: James E. (Jim) Teel
Interim CEO and COO: David B. (Dave) Clark
SVP and CFO: Don Ball
SVP, Sales and Merchandising: Joel Barton
SVP and CIO: Eric F. G. Wilson
SVP, Human Resources: Jeffrey D. Szczesny
Chief Marketing Officer: Michelle Cervantez
General Counsel: Jennifer Crabb
VP, Real Estate: Kent Haggerty
VP, Pharmacy and General Merchandise:
  Flint Pendergraft
Nutrition Specialist: Earline Griffith
Communications Specialist: Jennifer Ortega
Manager, Consumer Affairs: Nancy McGagin
Senior Director, Facilities: Edward (Ed) Estberg

LOCATIONS

HQ: Raley's
  500 W. Capitol Ave., West Sacramento, CA 95605
Phone: 916-373-3333 **Fax:** 916-371-1323
Web: www.raleys.com

2009 Stores

	No.
California	120
Northern Nevada	14
Total	**134**

PRODUCTS/OPERATIONS

2009 Stores

	No.
Raley's	85
Nob Hill	23
Bel Air	21
Food Source	5
Total	**134**

COMPETITORS

Andronico's Market
Costco Wholesale
Food 4 Less Holdings
Grocery Outlet
Kroger
Lunardi's Super Market
Ralphs Grocery
Safeway
Save Mart
Trader Joe's
Wal-Mart
Whole Foods
WinCo Foods

HISTORICAL FINANCIALS

Company Type: Private

Income Statement				FYE: June 30
	ESTIMATED REVENUE ($ mil.)	NET INCOME ($ mil.)	NET PROFIT MARGIN	EMPLOYEES
6/08	3,400	—	—	15,000
6/07	3,450	—	—	15,500
6/06	3,200	—	—	15,500
6/05	3,370	—	—	16,600
6/04	3,300	—	—	16,500
Annual Growth	**0.7%**	**—**	**—**	**(2.4%)**

Revenue History

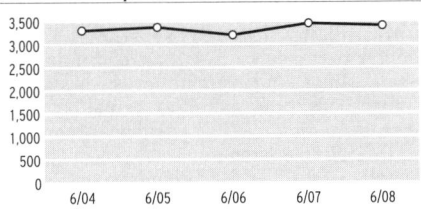

Rand McNally

You might say this mapmaker lets you know where you stand. Rand McNally, the largest commercial mapmaker in the world, is famous for its top-selling flagship product, the *Rand McNally Road Atlas*. In addition, the company publishes *The Thomas Guide* map books and educational products for classrooms, as well as travel-related software (StreetFinder Wireless) and online map content. It also makes commercial mileage and routing software for the transportation industry (IntelliRoute). The company sells its products online and through some 50,000 retail outlets. William Rand and Andrew McNally established the business in 1868; Rand McNally is owned by private equity firm Patriarch Partners.

The company's popular road atlas and other printed product continue to form the core of Rand McNally's business, but the company is focused on remaking itself for the digital age. To compete with Google Maps (from search giant Google) and other online services, Rand McNally has expanded its offerings to include trip and travel services, traffic reports, and a travel blog. Its RandMcNally.com features 1 million additional home addresses and over 22,000 more miles of roads that it claims are not found on other online maps and directions services. Rand McNally is also focused on consumer and commercial GPS devices.

The company's push to develop new products is being fueled by capital from Patriarch Partners, which purchased Rand McNally in late 2007. It later installed former video game executive Dave Muscatel as CEO.

HISTORY

Rand McNally was founded by William Rand and Andrew McNally in 1868 when they bought the job-printing department of the *Chicago Tribune*. Originally focused on printing railroad tickets and schedules, the partners published their first book, a Chicago business directory, in 1870.

In 1872 the company printed its first map for the *Railway Guide*. Rand McNally later expanded into publishing paperback novels (popular among train travelers), and by 1891 annual sales topped $1 million.

During the 1890s McNally bought Rand's share of the business, and the company branched into printing school textbooks. Rand McNally's first photo auto guide was issued in 1907, and the company introduced its first complete US road atlas in 1924.

When Hitler invaded Poland in 1939, Rand McNally's New York stock of European maps sold out in one day. WWII necessitated the revision of a number of maps — a challenge that the company continued to face throughout the 20th century.

Although the company abandoned adult fiction and nonfiction in 1914, it re-entered the field in 1948 when a company official persuaded explorer Thor Heyerdahl to write a book for the company about his adventures. First published in 1950, Heyerdahl's *Kon-Tiki* sold more than a million copies in its first six years.

Rand McNally produced its first four-color road atlas in 1960, and during the 1970s it began publishing travel guides for Mobil Oil. The next decade the company published several new road atlases to fill the void created when gas stations discontinued their practice of giving away free road maps. Rand McNally sold its textbook publishing business to Houghton Mifflin in 1980, and five years later it began computerizing its cartography operation.

In 1993 the company acquired Allmaps Canada Limited (now Rand McNally Canada). It introduced *TripMaker*, a CD-ROM vacation-planning program, the next year. Also in 1994 Rand McNally won a contract to create maps for a *Reader's Digest* atlas. The company debuted its StreetFinder street-level software in 1995 and created its Cartographic and Information Services division in 1996. It also established a Web site that year.

The next year, as part of a plan to focus on mapmaking and providing geographic information, Rand McNally sold a number of its subsidiaries (Book Services Group, DocuSystems Group). AEA Investors bought a controlling interest in the company later in 1997, bringing an end to more than 140 years of McNally family control (though it did retain a minority stake). While Rand McNally was still profitable, the sale to AEA underscored the challenges facing the company: Growth in earnings had slowed, and technological changes (Internet maps and software) had altered the mapmaking industry.

Rand McNally expanded in 1999 with acquisitions of mapmakers Thomas Bros. Maps and King of the Road Map Service. Later that year Henry Feinberg resigned as chairman and CEO. Richard Davis was appointed CEO, and John Macomber became chairman.

In 2000 the company relaunched its Web site with additional trip planning capabilities. Also that year it became the primary North American distributor of *National Geographic* maps, and COO Norman Wells replaced Davis as CEO.

In 2001 Michael Hehir was named CEO, Wells replaced Macomber as chairman, and Macomber remained as a director on the board. In 2003 Rand McNally filed for Chapter 11 bankruptcy protection. The company exited bankruptcy within two months, with buyout firm Leonard Green & Partners as its new majority owner. Also that year

Hehir left the company, and Allstate executive Robert Apatoff was named CEO. Wells was replaced by Peter Nolan, a managing partner at Leonard Green & Partners.

Product development efforts languished as Rand McNally focused on fixing its balance sheet. Late in 2007 private equity firm Patriarch Partners purchased the company. Former video game executive Dave Muscatel later took over as CEO.

EXECUTIVES

President and CEO: Dave Muscatel
EVP Digital Products and Services: Andreas Hecht
SVP and CTO: Ken Levin
SVP Geographic Information Services: Joel Minster
SVP and CFO: Norman Smagley, age 48
VP National Travel Marketing: Kendra Ensor
VP New Products and Strategy: Alan Yefsky
VP Sales, Enterprise: Dennis FitzPatrick
Editorial Director: Laurie Borman
Director Supply Chain: Warren Luk
Director Educational Publishing: Pat Riley

LOCATIONS

HQ: Rand McNally & Company
9855 Woods Dr., Skokie, IL 60077
Phone: 847-329-8100   **Fax:** 800-934-3479
Web: www.randmcnally.com

PRODUCTS/OPERATIONS

Selected Products

Commercial Trucking Products
  IntelliRoute
  MileMaker
  Motor Carriers' Road Atlas
Consumer Products
  Children's Products
  Reference Maps and Books
  Road Atlases
    Motor Carriers' Road Atlases
    The Rand McNally Road Atlas Line
  Road and Street Maps
  Software
    StreetFinder
  Street Guides (street-level detail)
  Thomas Guides (spiral-bound format)
Educational Products
Online Business Locator
Wireless Products
  Mobile Travel Tools
  Rand McNally Traffic

COMPETITORS

American Automobile Association (AAA)
American Educational Products
Avalon Travel Publishing
Axion
DeLorme
ESRI
Expedia
Fodor's
Globe Pequot
Google
Lonely Planet
MapQuest
Michelin
Multimap.com
National Geographic
Pitney Bowes Software
R. L. Polk
Yahoo!

Randolph-Brooks Federal Credit Union

Randolph-Brooks Federal Credit Union (RBFCU) provides deposit and lending services, including checking and savings accounts and loans for homes, cars, education, and consumer goods. Serving more than 280,000 members, RBFCU has about 30 Texas locations in San Antonio, Austin, and nearby communities. Other products offered by the credit union include business loans, MasterCard credit cards, and term certificates. Through its Randolph Brooks Services Group subsidiary, the credit union offers investment and insurance products such as mutual funds, IRAs, annuities, dental benefits, home warranties, roadside assistance programs, and financial planning services.

Another subsidiary, Randolph Brooks Insurance Agency, offers auto, home, and personal property insurance to members, while Randolph Brooks Title Company provides title insurance and settlement services.

The credit union opened in 1952 to serve military personnel stationed at Randolph Air Force Base near San Antonio.

EXECUTIVES

Chairman: Fred Walters
President: Randy Smith
SVP Planning and Marketing: John Kelly
SVP Information Systems: Ron Freerking
SVP Finance: Jimmy O. Junkin
VP Consumer Lending: Mark Sekula

LOCATIONS

HQ: Randolph-Brooks Federal Credit Union
Creswell Center, 1 Randolph Brooks Pkwy.
Live Oak, TX 78233
Phone: 210-945-3333   **Fax:** 210-945-3764
Web: www.rbfcu.org

PRODUCTS/OPERATIONS

2008 Sales

	$ mil.	% of total
Interest		
Loans	107.4	50
Investments	52.0	24
Noninterest		
Fees	35.5	17
Other	20.3	9
Total	**215.2**	**100**

COMPETITORS

Bank of America
Compass Bancshares
Cullen/Frost Bankers
JPMorgan Chase
Regions Financial
San Antonio Federal Credit Union
SSFCU
Wells Fargo

HISTORICAL FINANCIALS

Company Type: Not-for-profit

Income Statement

FYE: December 31

	ASSETS ($ mil.)	NET INCOME ($ mil.)	INCOME AS % OF ASSETS	EMPLOYEES
12/08	3,144	38	1.2%	901
12/07	2,952	36	1.2%	810
12/06	2,542	33	1.3%	736
12/05	2,380	35	1.5%	—
12/04	2,234	26	1.2%	—
Annual Growth	8.9%	9.3%	—	10.6%

2008 Year-End Financials

Equity as % of assets: —
Return on assets: 1.2%
Return on equity: —
Long-term debt ($ mil.): —
Sales ($ mil.): 215

Net Income History

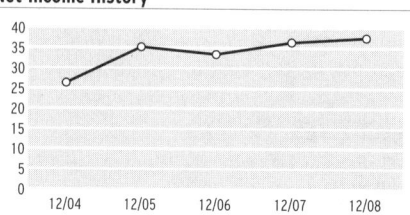

RBS Global

RBS Global is the parent company of Rexnord LLC, whose subsidiaries manufacture power transmission and conveying equipment, such as drives, gears, bearings, chains, and couplings for the aerospace, construction, chemicals, energy, mining, material handling, marine, and petrochemical industries, to name a few. Brand names include Cartriseal, Falk, MB, Link-Belt, Marbett, and Rexnord. Its Water Management business (AquaSense, Zurn, and EcoVantage brands) designs and makes water products for conservation, safety, and control for the commercial construction market. In 2006 The Carlyle Group sold RBS Global to Apollo Management for about $1.8 billion. The US accounts for about 70% of the company's sales.

RBS Global's Power Transmission division operates over 30 manufacturing and warehouse facilities and four repair facilities, and represents around 70% of the company's total sales. It produces conveying equipment, which includes engineered elevators, steel and roller chains, and related components. The company makes light, medium, and heavy duty gears and gear drives, as well as offers general gearing, service, and repair. The products are marketed to industries involved in heavy, large-scale manufacturing.

Between 2007 and 2009 the company made several acquisitions to develop and expand its Water Management division into the water and wastewater markets, especially hydropower, industrial, and municipal environments. In 2009 RBS Global acquired the stock of Fontaine-Alliance and its affiliates (Fontaine) for over $24 million. Fontaine manufactures stainless steel slide gates and other flow control products. The company also purchased GA Industries, a manufacturer of automatic valves (control, check, and air), for over $3 million in cash, and

Zurn Industries, a former business of Jacuzzi Brands, which makes plumbing products for the non-residential water control product market, for about $942 million in cash. The company sees the expanding renovation and repair market for this area as a potential business opportunity. Water Management has 22 manufacturing and warehousing facilities in North America, which generate around 30% of company sales. Products include point drains and drainage systems, interceptors, and hydrants. PEX is the company's polyethylene tubing line used in water and radiant heating systems.

RBS Global's special component products are part of three product lines: electric motor brakes, small-scale power transmission components, and security devices for utility companies. This area is run by three companies: Stearns, W.M. Berg, and Highfield.

The company derives more than half of its gear sales from replacement, or aftermarket, parts. RBS Global, operating under the Rexnord, RBS Global, and Falk names, sells its products globally through more than 2,000 OEMs and more than 400 industrial distributors that operate through more than 2,400 branches. The company owns and operates about 50 manufacturing facilities and four repair facilities worldwide.

Disasters have played a crucial role in the history of Falk, which was founded in 1856 as the Bavaria Brewery, on the site of the company's main plant in Milwaukee. Fires twice destroyed the brewery, in 1889 and again in 1892, forcing the Falk family to sell the business to Frederick Pabst (of Pabst Brewing fame). Herman Falk, a son of the founder, eventually found his way into the cast-welding business, shaping and joining rails for railroad lines. The Falk company got into the foundry business in 1899 and went on to become a leading manufacturer of gears for steam turbines and other machinery. Sundstrand Corporation (now Hamilton Sundstrand) acquired Falk in 1968.

EXECUTIVES

Chairman: George M. Sherman, age 67
President, CEO, and Director: Todd A. Adams, age 38, $766,976 total compensation
EVP and Acting CFO; EVP and Secretary, Rexnord: George C. Moore, age 54, $914,068 total compensation
VP and General Counsel: Patricia (Patty) Whaley
Auditors: Ernst & Young LLP

LOCATIONS

HQ: RBS Global, Inc.
4701 W. Greenfield Ave., Milwaukee, WI 53214
Phone: 414-643-3000   **Fax:** 414-643-3078
Web: www.rexnord.com

2009 Sales

	$ mil.	% of total
US	1,435.3	76
Europe	249.4	13
Other regions	197.3	11
Total	**1,882.0**	**100**

PRODUCTS/OPERATIONS

2009 Sales

	$ mil.	% of total
Power transmission	1,321.7	70
Water management	560.3	30
Total	**1,882.0**	**100**

Selected Products and Brands

Aerospace bearings and seals
  Cartriseal
  PSI bearing
  Shafer bearing
  Tuflite
Brakes
  Industrial electromechanical
Couplings
  Elastomeric
  Flexible disc
  Fluid fixed-fill
Industrial Chains
  Conveyor components
  Engineered chain
  Flattop
  MatTop chain
  Roller
  TableTop
Gears Drives
  Link-Belt
  Prager
  Rex
Industrial bearings
  Ball bearings
  Cylindrical bearings
  Filament and sleeves
  Roller bearings
Special components
  Electric motor brakes
  Miniature mechanical power transmission
    components
  Security devices for utility companies
Water management (Zurn)
  Backflow preventers
  Chemical drainage systems
  Commercial brass faucets and valves
  Fire system valves
  Hydrants
  Interceptors
  Linear drainage systems
  Plumbing systems (PEX)
  Point drains
  Radiant heating systems (PEX)
  Relief valves
  Thermostatic mixing valves (Aqua-Guard)

COMPETITORS

A. O. Smith
Baldor Electric
Crane Co.
Emerson Electric
Geberit
Habasit America
JTEKT
Kaydon
Kohler
MINEBEA
Moen
NSK
NTN
RBC Bearings
Regal Beloit
Renold
Rockwell Automation
Schaeffler
SKF
Sloan Valve
Solus Industrial Innovations
TB Wood's
Timken
Trane Inc.
Uponor
Watts Water Technologies

HISTORICAL FINANCIALS

Company Type: Private

Income Statement

FYE: March 31

	REVENUE ($ mil.)	NET INCOME ($ mil.)	NET PROFIT MARGIN	EMPLOYEES
3/09	1,882	0	0.0%	6,200
3/08	1,854	41	2.2%	7,400
3/07	1,256	3	0.2%	7,100
3/06	1,416	(17)	—	5,800
3/05	811	22	2.7%	5,680
Annual Growth	**23.4%**	**(63.1%)**	**—**	**2.2%**

Net Income History

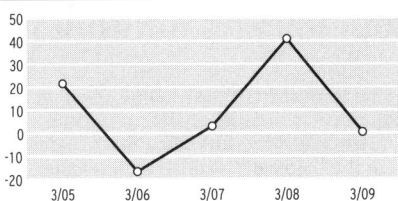

RDO Equipment

RDO Equipment herds Deere in a big way. It sells and rents new and used trucks and heavy equipment to customers in the agriculture and construction industries. The largest independent dealer of John Deere equipment, RDO operates about 60 locations in 10 states. About 10 locations are dedicated Vermeer dealerships, while its RDO Truck Centers offer heavy-duty Volvo, GMC, Isuzu, and Mack trucks. In addition, the company provides maintenance and repair services as well as replacement parts. Chairman Ronald Offutt founded the company in 1968.

EXECUTIVES

Chairman: Ronald D. Offutt
CEO: Christi J. Offutt
CFO: Steven B. Dewald
SVP Special Projects: Larry E. Scott
VP Organizational Development: Gean Zimmerman
Precision Product Manager: Brian Verkuehlen
Director Information Systems: Dave Green
Director HR: Ryan Johnson
Secretary: Allan F. Knoll
Treasurer and Assistant Secretary: Thomas K. (Tom) Espel
Auditors: PricewaterhouseCoopers LLP

LOCATIONS

HQ: RDO Equipment Co.
700 Seventh St. South, Fargo, ND 58103
Phone: 877-444-7363   **Fax:** 701-239-8741
Web: www.rdoequipment.com

2009 Locations

	No.
North Dakota	11
California	10
Minnesota	10
Arizona	7
Texas	6
Oregon	4
South Dakota	4
Montana	3
Washington	2
Total	**57**

Income Statement				FYE: January 31
	REVENUE ($ mil.)	NET INCOME ($ mil.)	NET PROFIT MARGIN	EMPLOYEES
1/09	1,105	—	—	1,500

Real Mex Restaurants

This company is a real *combinación grande*. Real Mex Restaurants operates and franchises more than 220 Mexican restaurants in California and more than a dozen other states. Its flagship El Torito chain has about 80 locations offering full-service Mexican dining, while its chain of about 100 Chevys Fresh Mex (operated through Chevys Restaurants) provide a more laid-back cantina atmosphere. Real Mex also operates more than 30 full-service Acapulco restaurants featuring California-Mexican cuisine. Smaller concepts include Casa Gallardo and Las Brisas. About 190 of the restaurants are company-owned. Real Mex is owned by private equity firm Sun Capital Partners.

The recession has slowed consumer spending on such things as entertainment and dining out, creating difficult conditions for casual dining chains. Real Mex has been focused on cost cutting and efficiency measures to help prop up its bottom line and pay down its significant debt load. It is also investing in new marketing efforts to drive additional traffic to its restaurants. In addition, the company is trying to boost sales of its Real Mex Foods unit, which primarily supplies Mexican food ingredients to other restaurant operators, as well as its own chains. The foodservice supply subsidiary accounts for more than 5% of sales.

The El Torito banner, which includes about 10 El Torito Grill restaurants, had originally been operated by doomed restaurateur Prandium, which sold the Mexican concept to private equity firm Bruckmann, Rosser, Sherrill & Co. (BRS) in 2000. Real Mex was formed to build a portfolio of dining concepts, and it acquired Chevys in 2005 along with the Fuzio Universal Pasta chain (sold in 2007). Sun Capital — which also owns bagel outlet Bruegger's Enterprises, Italian chain Fazoli's, Garden Fresh, and Souper Salad — acquired the company in 2006.

In 2009 Richard Rivera was named CEO, replacing Frederick Wolfe who had resigned late the previous year. Rivera previously served as an executive with Darden Restaurants and operated T.G.I. Friday's locations franchised from Carlson Restaurants.

EXECUTIVES

Chairman, President, and CEO:
 Richard E. (Dick) Rivera, age 62
EVP and CFO: Steven (Steve) Tanner, age 58,
 $382,958 total compensation
SVP and Chief Marketing Officer: Lowell Petrie, age 58
SVP Information Technology: John Koontz
SVP Human Resources: Steven K. (Steve) Wallace,
 age 53, $214,447 total compensation
SVP Operations, Chevys: Nicholas (Nick) Mayer, age 47

SVP Operations, El Torito and Acapulco:
 Raymond (Ray) Garcia, age 54
SVP Research and Development and Executive Chef:
 Roberto (Pepe) Lopez, age 53,
 $226,033 total compensation
VP and Controller: Kathleen Burkett
President, Real Mex Foods: Carlos Angulo, age 48,
 $346,371 total compensation
Secretary: Madelaine Morrow
Auditors: Grant Thornton LLP

LOCATIONS

HQ: Real Mex Restaurants, Inc.
 5660 Katella Ave., Ste. 100, Cypress, CA 90630
Phone: 562-346-1200 **Fax:** 562-346-1469
Web: www.realmexrestaurants.com

2008 Locations

	No.
US	
California	157
Missouri	13
Illinois	6
Arizona	5
New Jersey	5
Oregon	5
Florida	4
Maryland	4
New York	4
Virginia	4
Washington	3
Louisiana	2
Nevada	2
Indiana	1
Minnesota	1
South Dakota	1
International	
Japan	6
Turkey	2
Total	**225**

PRODUCTS/OPERATIONS

2008 Sales

	$ mil.	% of total
Restaurants	509.0	92
Franchising & other	44.7	8
Total	**553.7**	**100**

2008 Restaurant Sales

	% of total
El Torito	42
Chevys	38
Acapulco	15
Other	5
Total	**100**

2008 Locations

	No.
Company-owned	190
Franchised	35
Total	**225**

Selected Restaurants

Acapulco Mexican Restaurants
Casa Gallardo Mexican Restaurant
Chevys Fresh Mex
El Paso Cantina
El Torito
El Torito Grill
Las Brisas
WhoSong & Larry's

COMPETITORS

Applebee's	Darden
BJ's Restaurants	Hooters
Brinker	OSI Restaurant Partners
Carlson Restaurants	P.F. Chang's
Cheesecake Factory	Romacorp
Chipotle	Ruby Tuesday

HISTORICAL FINANCIALS
Company Type: Private

Income Statement				FYE: Last Sunday in December
	REVENUE ($ mil.)	NET INCOME ($ mil.)	NET PROFIT MARGIN	EMPLOYEES
12/08	554	(177)	—	12,085
12/07	565	(24)	—	12,701
12/06	565	(14)	—	12,769
12/05	534	13	2.5%	—
12/04	327	14	4.2%	—
Annual Growth	**14.1%**	**—**	**—**	**(2.7%)**

Net Income History

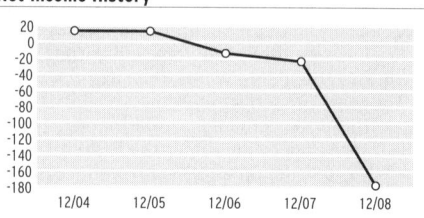

Realogy Corporation

Realogy Corporation is all about keeping it real. The company is one of the biggest names you've never heard of in the real estate business. Instead, it operates through the names you *have* heard of: Century 21, Coldwell Banker, Sotheby's International Realty, and ERA. The company also licenses the Better Homes and Gardens brand from Meredith Corporation. Realogy has nearly 16,000 offices (more than 900 are company-owned) in nearly 90 countries. Besides its bread and butter of residential real estate and corporate relocation, it also offers title settlement and research through Title Resource Group. Domus Holding (an affiliate of Apollo Advisors) acquired Realogy for a reported $9 billion.

As with the rest of the real estate industry, Realogy has been affected by the downturn in the housing market in 2007 and 2008, with revenues sliding for the third straight year. Realogy's mounting debts and liquidity needs have forced the Apollo Group to pledge up to $150 million for its faltering company. The emergency cash (if Realogy deems it's needed) will help the company stay afloat.

Because Internet searches for homes have dramatically increased over the years, the company has made the decision to move away from traditional print marketing and put a greater emphasis on the Web. Its Openhouse.com site lists open houses around the country; in 2008 Prudential Realty signed a deal to provide a feed of its open house events to the site.

That year the company also took a stake in Century 21 China Real Estate, an independently owned firm that franchises the Century 21 name. China's growing middle class is spurring the growth of homeownership in the country.

Realogy was spun off from Avis Budget Group (formerly Cendant) in 2006.

EXECUTIVES

Chairman, President, and CEO: Richard A. Smith, age 55, $2,792,395 total compensation
EVP and Chief Administrative Officer: David J. (Dave) Weaving, age 42
EVP, CFO, and Treasurer: Anthony E. (Tony) Hull, age 50, $1,230,520 total compensation
EVP, General Counsel, and Secretary: Marilyn J. Wasser, age 53
SVP Corporate Compliance and Ethics: Elisabeth W. (Liz) Gehringer
SVP Corporate Communications: Mark Panus
SVP, Chief Accounting Officer, and Controller: Dea Benson, age 53
VP Human Resources, Realogy Franchise Group: Tanya Reu
President and CEO, Better Homes and Gardens Real Estate: Sherry A. Chris
President and CEO, Title Resource Group: Donald J. (Don) Casey, age 47
President and CEO, NRT: Bruce G. Zipf, age 52, $1,126,655 total compensation
President and CEO, Sotheby's International Realty Affiliates: Michael R. Good
President and CEO, Realogy Franchise Group: Alexander E. (Alex) Perriello III, age 61, $1,031,521 total compensation
President and CEO, Century 21: Thomas R. (Tom) Kunz
President and CEO, Cartus Corporation: Kevin J. Kelleher, age 54, $796,664 total compensation
President and CEO, Coldwell Banker Real Estate: James R. (Jim) Gillespie
President and COO, Coldwell Banker Commercial Affiliates and COO, Coldwell Banker Real Estate: Richard W. (Rick) Davidson
Director Corporate Communications: Kathy Borruso
Auditors: PricewaterhouseCoopers LLP

LOCATIONS

HQ: Realogy Corporation
1 Campus Dr., Parsippany, NJ 07054
Phone: 973-407-2000   **Fax:** 973-407-7004
Web: www.realogy.com

PRODUCTS/OPERATIONS

2008 Sales

	$ mil.	% of total
Gross commission income	3,483	74
Service revenue	737	16
Franchise fees	323	7
Other	182	4
Total	**4,725**	**100**

Selected Subsidiaries

Better Homes and Gardens Real Estate
Century 21
Coldwell Banker
Coldwell Banker Commercial
ERA
Sotheby's International Realty

COMPETITORS

CB Richard Ellis
Cushman & Wakefield
Draper and Kramer
First American
Grubb & Ellis
GVA Advantis
HomeServices
Investors Title
John L. Scott Real Estate
Jones Lang LaSalle
LandAmerica Financial Group
Prudential Connecticut
RE/MAX
SIRVA
Weichert Realtors
ZipRealty

HISTORICAL FINANCIALS

Company Type: Private

Income Statement

FYE: December 31

	REVENUE ($ mil.)	NET INCOME ($ mil.)	NET PROFIT MARGIN	EMPLOYEES
12/08	4,725	(1,912)	—	11,400
12/07	5,967	(841)	—	7,500
12/06	6,492	365	5.6%	14,600
12/05	7,139	627	8.8%	9,000
12/04	6,549	618	9.4%	—
Annual Growth	**(7.8%)**	**—**	**—**	**8.2%**

2008 Year-End Financials

Debt ratio: —
Return on equity: —
Cash ($ mil.): —
Current ratio: —
Long-term debt ($ mil.): 6,213

Net Income History

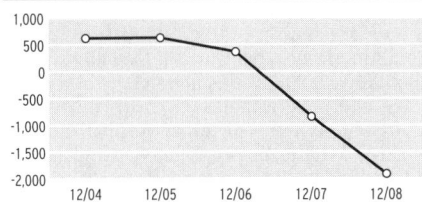

Red Apple Group

Red Apple Group sells more than just apples in the Big Apple. Subsidiary United Refining, which processes 70,000 barrels of oil a day, distributes fuel to about 370 Country Fair, Red Apple Food Marts, and/or Kwik Fill branded gas stations/convenience stores in New York, Pennsylvania, and Ohio. Red Apple controls Gristede's Foods, a leading New York City supermarket chain. It also has real estate, aircraft leasing, and newspaper operations. The Red Apple Group is owned by Greek immigrant entrpreneuer CEO John Catsimatidis, who, in a classic rags-to-riches story, started his business empire with one small grocery store in Manhattan.

With the ups there have been some downs, however. In the the early 2000s the company lost out to Russian oil giant LUKOIL in a $5 billion bid to acquire East Coast gasoline retailer Getty Petroleum Marketing.

A master of picking up and revitalizing struggling companies, Catsimatidis, though his Red Apple Group, acquired Gristede's in 1986, and the Sloan's retail chain between 1991 and 1993. United Refining was rescued from bankruptcy by Catsimatidis in 1986.

EXECUTIVES

Chairman, President, and CEO, Red Apple Group and Gristede's Foods; Chairman and CEO, United Refining Company: John A. Catsimatidis, age 61
President and COO, United Refining: Myron L. Turfitt, age 58

LOCATIONS

HQ: Red Apple Group, Inc.
823 11th Ave., New York, NY 10019
Phone: 212-956-5803   **Fax:** 212-247-4509
Web: www.jacny.com

COMPETITORS

7-Eleven
A&P
Ahold USA
D'Agostino Supermarkets
Getty Petroleum Marketing
Hess Corporation
King Kullen Grocery
Motiva Enterprises
Pathmark Stores
Sunoco
TOTAL
Wakefern Food

Red Chamber Co.

Ahoy there, matey! Red Chamber doesn't actually *catch* fish and other seafood, but it does almost everything else. A major North American seafood supplier, Red Chamber imports, exports, and processes a boatload of finfish (basa, catfish, cod, haddock, swodfish, halibut, tuna, mahi-mahi, orange roughy, perch, pollock, and salmon), as well as oysters, octopus, lobster, scallops, mussels, crab, surimi (imitation crab), and squid. It offers raw frozen and cooked white and black tiger shrimp. Red Chamber started as a small family-owned restaurant in Los Angeles.

Red Chamber has processing facilities on both US coasts and operates storage facilities throughout the US. It has a cold storage capacity of more than 60 million pounds of seafood.

EXECUTIVES

Co-Chairman: Shan Chun Kou
Co-Chairman: Shu Chin Kou
President: Ming Bin Kou
EVP and CFO: Ming Shin Kou
SVP: Tony Neves
President, Neptune Foods: Howard Choi
President, OFI Markesa International: Brent Church

LOCATIONS

HQ: Red Chamber Co.
1912 E. Vernon Ave., Vernon, CA 90058
Phone: 323-234-9000   **Fax:** 323-231-8888
Web: www.redchamber.com

COMPETITORS

Alaska Seafood Company
Alaskan Leader Fisheries
American Seafoods
Bumble Bee Foods
Chicken of the Sea
Fishhawk Fisheries
Gorton's
Icelandic Group
Kyokuyo
Maruha Nichiro
Morey's Seafood
Nippon Suisan Kaisha
North Pacific Seafoods
Ocean Beauty Seafoods
Orca Bay Seafoods
Pacific Seafood Group
Peter Pan Seafoods
StarKist
Trident Seafoods

Red Cross

A specialist in dealing with events beyond its control, The American Red Cross offers disaster relief, shelter, and other humanitarian services through more than 700 chapters nationwide. Although it was chartered by Congress in 1905, the American Red Cross isn't a government agency. The not-for-profit charitable organization relies on the efforts of about 1 million volunteers. Aside from helping victims of about 70,000 disasters large and small each year, the American Red Cross teaches CPR and first aid courses; provides support for US military personnel; and maintains some of the largest blood and plasma banks nationwide. The group is a member of the International Red Cross and Red Crescent Movement.

The American Red Cross, which has endured several disasters of its own making in recent years, got a new leader in 2008 when Gail McGovern joined the organization. McGovern succeeded Mary Elcano, who served as interim CEO and president following the resignation of former Internal Revenue Service chief Mark Everson in late 2007. (It was disclosed that Everson had had an inappropriate relationship with a female subordinate.) Everson had succeeded Marsha Evans, who resigned in 2005 amid criticism of her handling of hurricane relief efforts following Gulf Coast hurricanes Katrina, Rita, and Wilma.

McGovern, a former Harvard business professor and business executive, is expected to bring stronger finance and management skills, as well as stability, to the job.

To fund its activities, the American Red Cross relies largely on its biomedical operation, which supplies blood and tissue to some 3,000 hospitals. Corporate, foundation, and individual donations, along with grants from organizations such as the United Way, account for most of the rest of its revenue.

In the years since the September 11, 2001, terrorist attacks, the organization has been engaged in a campaign to raise the nation's emergency preparedness, both for government agencies and for individuals.

HISTORY

The Red Cross traces its start to a trip made in 1859 by Jean-Henri Dunant, a Swiss businessman. Dunant was traveling in northern Italy when he saw the aftermath of the Battle of Solferino — 40,000 dead or wounded troops, left without help. He published a pamphlet three years later calling for the formation of international volunteer societies to aid wounded soldiers.

In 1863 a five-member committee (including Dunant) formed the International Committee of the Red Cross in Geneva. Delegates of 16 countries attended the first conference, which resulted in the formation of national Red Cross societies across Europe. A red cross on a white background (the reverse of the Swiss flag) was chosen as the organization's symbol; the Red Crescent symbol was added in 1876 by Muslim relief workers during the Russo-Turkish War. In 1864 the group's principles were codified into international law — initially signed by 12 nations — through the first Geneva Convention.

Clara Barton, famous for her aid to soldiers during the US Civil War, learned about the Red Cross when she assisted with relief efforts during the Franco-Prussian War (1870-71). After the war, Barton returned home and persuaded Congress to support the Geneva Convention. In 1881 she and some friends founded the American Association of the Red Cross, with the first chapter in Dansville, New York. The US signed the Geneva Convention in 1882.

Barton soon expanded the Red Cross' mission to include aiding victims of natural disasters. The group received a congressional charter in 1905, making it responsible for providing assistance to the US military and disaster relief in the US and overseas. Membership soared during WWI as the number of chapters jumped from 107 to 3,864, and volunteers from the US and other nations served with the armed forces in Europe. After the war, the American Red Cross helped refugees in Europe, recruited thousands of nurses to improve the health and hygiene of rural Americans, and provided food and shelter to millions during the Depression.

The Red Cross established its first blood center, in New York's Presbyterian Hospital, in 1941. During WWII the American Red Cross again mobilized massive relief efforts. At home, volunteers taught nutrition courses, served in hospitals, and collected blood.

In 1956 the Red Cross began research to increase the safety of its blood supply. It also continued to provide assistance during natural disasters, as well as during the Korean and Vietnam Wars and other US military conflicts.

During the 1980s the Red Cross was criticized for moving too slowly to improve testing of its blood supply for the HIV virus. Elizabeth Dole, named the organization's president in 1991, reorganized the blood collection program.

In 1997 HemaCare settled a blood-product-pricing lawsuit against the Red Cross without disclosing terms. In 1999 Dole resigned to make a bid for the US presidency in 2000 (she later dropped out of the race). Dole was succeeded by Dr. Bernadine Healy, a former dean of the Ohio State University College of Medicine and the first physician to head the association.

The mission of the American Red Cross was highlighted after the 2001 terrorist attacks on New York City and Washington, DC, gaining praise for its quick response immediately afterwards. Donations made to the Red Cross specifically for the September 11 victims and their families amounted to about $1 billion. The group drew criticism, however, over a proposal to use some donations for a blood bank reserve instead of it all going to families of those killed and injured in the attacks. Amid the controversy, Healy was given her walking papers.

General Counsel Harold Decker was tapped to replace Healy at the end of 2001. That year the FDA announced that the Red Cross had failed to be in compliance with safety laws in its blood collection program, despite being under a consent decree since 1993. The American Red Cross appointed Marsha Johnson Evans CEO in 2002.

In 2005 the organization announced a termination of its tissue programs to concentrate on disaster relief. The same year the FDA slapped the Red Cross with a $3.4 million fine for mishandling blood products after the government

agency picked up 135 unsafe blood distributions. Later in the year, CEO Evans stepped down and biomedical services EVP John McGuire was named interim chief; he served until 2007, when Everson took over the position. Everson left the Red Cross in late 2007.

Gail McGovern, a Harvard Business School professor and former holder of management positions at AT&T and Fidelity Investments, was named CEO in April 2008.

EXECUTIVES

Chairman: Bonnie McElveen-Hunter, age 59
President and CEO: Gail J. McGovern, age 57
COO: Kevin M. Brown
CFO: Brian Rhoa
EVP Chapter and International Operations: R. Alan McCurry
EVP Biomedical Services: John F. McGuire
SVP and Chief Diversity Officer: Floyd W. Pitts
SVP Disaster Services: Joseph C. (Joe) Becker
SVP Communications: Roger K. Lowe
SVP Operations, Biomedical Services: William F. Moore
SVP International Services: David Meltzer, age 49
Chief Marketing Officer: Peggy Dyer
Chief Development Officer: Jeffrey T. (Jeff) Towers
Chief Nurse and Director Disaster Health and Disaster Mental Health: Sharon A. R. Stanley
Chief Public Affairs Officer: Suzanne (Suzy) DeFrancis
Chief Medical Officer: Richard Benjamin
General Counsel and Corporate Secretary: Mary S. Elcano
VP Disaster Operations: Armond Mascelli
VP Communication and Marketing: Brian McArthur
National Chair, Volunteers: Kathryn A. Forbes
Senior Director Disaster Services: Trevor Riggen
Corporate Ombudsman: Kevin Jessar
Auditors: KPMG LLP

LOCATIONS

HQ: The American National Red Cross
2025 E St. NW, Washington, DC 20006
Phone: 202-303-4498
Web: www.redcross.org

PRODUCTS/OPERATIONS

Selected Programs and Services

Biomedical services
  Blood
  Clinical services
  Plasma
  Testing
Disaster relief

Health and safety services
  Care giving and babysitting
  CPR training
  First aid
  Lifeguard training
  Swimming lessons
  Youth programs

Community services
  Food and nutrition
  Homeless shelters
  Hospitals and nursing homes
  Senior services
  Transportation services

Military services
  Counseling
  Emergency communications
  Financial assistance
  Veterans services

HISTORICAL FINANCIALS

Company Type: Not-for-profit

Income Statement

FYE: June 30

	REVENUE ($ mil.)	NET INCOME ($ mil.)	NET PROFIT MARGIN	EMPLOYEES
6/08	3,204	(665)	—	35,000
6/07	3,175	39	1.2%	35,000
6/06	6,009	539	9.0%	35,000
6/05	3,919	445	11.4%	35,000
6/04	3,092	34	1.1%	—
Annual Growth	0.9%	—	—	0.0%

Net Income History

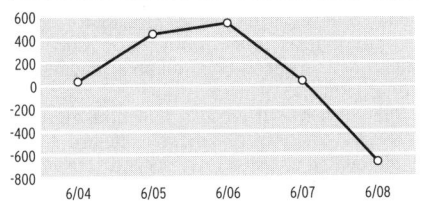

The Regence Group

The Regence Group is the health care king of the Northwest, operating the largest group of Blue Cross Blue Shield companies in the region. Through its subsidiaries, Regence BlueCross BlueShield of Oregon, Regence BlueShield (select areas of Washington), Regence BlueCross BlueShield of Utah, and Regence BlueShield of Idaho, the company provides health insurance products to some 3 million members through a network composed of tens of thousands of providers. Subsidiary offerings include individual and group medical, vision, and dental plans and pharmacy benefits management services. Regence Life & Health Insurance provides life, disability, and short-term medical insurance.

Another subsidiary, Asuris Northwest Health, serves 40,000 members in eastern Washington. Asuris, which is not affiliated with Blue Cross Blue Shield, provides health care coverage to individuals and commercial members.

Although it faces stiff competition, The Regence Group has decided to remain not-for-profit. The company's strategy for remaining competitive consists of consolidating operations, upgrading the company's information technology infrastructure, and deploying new health insurance products. It also promotes wellness programs for its members; for example, the company has introduced an interactive Web site through which members can obtain medical information, give feedback on providers, create personal health records to track medical history, and access educational and wellness tools.

The Regence Group has also initiated pharmacy education programs designed to encourage the use of generic medications and help consumers understand all the alternatives available to them. The intended goal is that the increased use of generic medications will lead to a reduction in health care costs.

The company has also enhanced its technology platform by participating as a minority investor in Apax Partners' $1.2 billion acquisition of billing systems and process management services firm TriZetto Group.

EXECUTIVES

Chair: Jack G. Strother
Vice Chair: William G. Marsh
President, CEO, and Director: Mark B. Ganz, age 48
EVP and Chief Marketing Executive: Mohandas (Mohan) Nair
EVP Corporate Services and Chief Legal Officer: Kerry E. Barnett
EVP Health Care Operations: William C. (Bill) Barr
SVP Enterprise Program Management: Jo Anne C. Long
SVP Health Care Services: John M. Stellmon
SVP and CIO: Cheron R. Vail
SVP Finance and CFO: Steven L. (Steve) Hooker
VP and Chief of Staff, Office of the President: Margaret M. (Peggy) Maguire
President, Regence BlueShield, Oregon: Jared L. Short
President, Regence BlueShield of Idaho: Scott Kreiling
President, Regence BlueShield, Washington: Jonathan Hensley
President, Regence BlueCross BlueShield, Utah: Scott Ideson
Auditors: Deloitte & Touche LLP

LOCATIONS

HQ: The Regence Group
200 SW Market St., Suite 1500, Portland, OR 97201
Phone: 503-225-5221 **Fax:** 503-225-5274
Web: www.regence.com

PRODUCTS/OPERATIONS

Selected Subsidiaries

Asuris Northwest Health
Regence BlueCross BlueShield of Oregon
Regence BlueCross BlueShield of Utah
Regence BlueShield of Idaho
Regence BlueShield (Washington)
Regence Life and Health

COMPETITORS

Aetna
BEST Life
CIGNA
Delta Dental Plans
First Choice Health
Group Health Cooperative (Puget Sound)
Health Net
Humana
Kaiser Foundation Health Plan
Molina Healthcare
Premera Blue Cross
UnitedHealth Group

HISTORICAL FINANCIALS

Company Type: Not-for-profit

Income Statement

FYE: December 31

	REVENUE ($ mil.)	NET INCOME ($ mil.)	NET PROFIT MARGIN	EMPLOYEES
12/08	8,930	(22)	—	6,300
12/07	8,372	155	1.9%	7,500
12/06	7,551	241	3.2%	6,000
Annual Growth	8.7%	—	—	2.5%

Net Income History

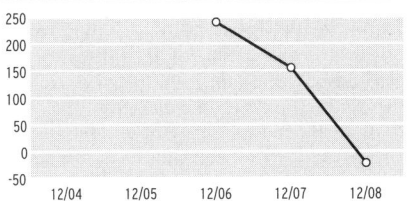

REI

Outdoor gear and clothing from Recreational Equipment, Inc. (REI) outfits everyone from mountain climbers to mall walkers. It's the nation's largest consumer cooperative, with more than 3 million members. Through more than 80 outlets in 27 states, REI sells high-end gear, clothing, and footwear (including private-label goods) for outdoor activities such as climbing, kayaking, and skiing, as well as for hiking, bicycling, and camping. The company also repairs gear, and it sells merchandise online and through occasional catalogs. Its travel service, REI Adventures, offers trips such as cycling the Alps, sea kayaking Costa Rica, and hiking New Zealand. Climbers Lloyd and Mary Anderson formed REI in 1938.

REI's community and environmental involvement includes youth program support and community service, and the group designates a portion of its operating budget to environmental restoration projects. Through its partnership with US Bank (a subsidiary of U.S. Bancorp), the company offers members the REI Visa card.

REI stores feature product demonstrations, educational seminars, and gift registries. The company's MSR (Mountain Safety Research) subsidiary makes mountaineering equipment, outdoor clothing, and camping products. Customers can become co-op members by paying a one-time fee; its privileges include getting about 10% of their annual purchases refunded in the form of patronage dividends.

In 2005 former president and CEO Dennis Madsen retired. He had joined the company as a stockroom clerk when he was 17 years old. Sally Jewell, REI's COO, was named as new CEO and president.

HISTORY

Lloyd Anderson founded REI in his Seattle garage in 1938 with his wife, Mary, and 23 other mountain climbers who were looking for high-quality mountaineering equipment at low prices. Uncomfortable about making money off of his friends, Anderson formed a co-op, returning a portion of the profits to its members. REI's first retail location (opened in 1944 in the back of a Seattle gas station) consisted of three shelves of Army surplus items. The company did not hire its first full-time employee until 1953.

Growth was slow yet steady. In 1971 the company operated one store; by 1983 REI had grown to seven stores with several additional product lines and a catalog business. That year Wally Smith became the company's CEO.

REI benefited from the growing interest in outdoor activities, expanding to 17 stores in 13 states in 1987. By 1991, when it built its first distribution center, REI had 27 stores in 16 states. The co-op reached for a new frontier in 1996 when it began selling on the Internet. It launched its REI-Outlet.com Web site in 1998 to sell discounted merchandise, and began a Japanese retail Web site in 1999. Also in 1999 REI decided to scale back its catalog mailings and focus instead on e-commerce. Smith, who grew the company from 9 to 54 stores during his 17-year reign, retired in early 2000 and was replaced by COO Dennis Madsen, a 34-year company veteran.

In 2000 the co-op rankled its rank and file when it moved its manufacturing operations to Mexico and closed its fleece-manufacturing subsidiary, Thaw. Also that year the company opened its first international location in Tokyo, but ended up closing the store and shutting down the Japanese Web site in 2001.

The company was named to *FORTUNE*'s "100 Best Companies" list for the sixth year in a row in 2003. It made the list again the next year, ranking 24th. In 2005 REI broke into the top 10 with a #9 ranking. Madsen retired in 2005 and was replaced by Sally Jewell.

In late 2007 REI opened a second distribution center. The first outside its home state, the new 520,000-sq.-ft. facility in rural Bedford, Pennsylvania, will supply about a third of the company's stores and help it grow in the East, South, and Midwest.

EXECUTIVES

Chairman: Anne V. Farrell
Vice Chairman: Ivar Chhina
President, CEO, and Director: Sally Jewell
CFO and Chief Administrative Officer: Brad Johnson
EVP Merchandising and Marketing: Matt Hyde
EVP Sales, Service, Store Development, and Logistics:
  Brian Unmacht
SVP Legal, General Counsel, and Secretary:
  Catherine Walker
SVP Human Resources: Michelle Clements
VP Marketing: Tom Vogl
VP Merchandising: Angela Owen
VP REI Gear and Apparel: Lee Fromson
VP E-Commerce and Web Strategy: Brad Brown
VP Public Affairs: Michael Collins
VP Information Technology: Bill Baumann
VP Logistics and Distribution: David Presley
Regional VP Retail Stores, Midwest and East Region:
  Janet Hopkins
Regional VP Retail Stores, Western Region:
  Tim Spangler
Director Store Development: Dean Iwata
Director Product Integrity: Kevin Myette
Director Direct Sales: Noel Nelson
Auditors: Grant Thornton LLP

LOCATIONS

HQ: Recreational Equipment, Inc.
  6750 S. 228th St., Kent, WA 98032
Phone: 253-891-2500   **Fax:** 253-891-2523
Web: www.rei.com

PRODUCTS/OPERATIONS

Selected Products and Services

Bicycles and accessories
Books and maps
Camping gear
Canoes, kayaks, and related gear
Climbing gear
Clothing (children's, men's, and women's)
Fitness gear
Footwear
Gift registry
Racks (bike, boat, and ski mounts)

REI repair service
Sleeping bags
Snow sports gear
Tents
Travel accessories

COMPETITORS

Academy Sports & Outdoors
Bass Pro Shops
Big 5
Cabela's
Campmor
Dick's Sporting Goods
Eastern Mountain Sports
Hibbett Sports
Johnson Outdoors
Lands' End
L.L. Bean
Olympia Sports
Orvis Company
Patagonia, Inc.
Performance Bike Shop
Sport Chalet
Sports Authority
Sportsman's Guide
Sportsman's Warehouse

HISTORICAL FINANCIALS
Company Type: Cooperative

Income Statement			FYE: December 31
	REVENUE ($ mil.)	NET INCOME ($ mil.)	NET PROFIT MARGIN	EMPLOYEES
12/08	1,435	15	1.0%	10,000
12/07	1,342	41	3.1%	10,000
12/06	1,182	40	3.4%	8,000
12/05	1,022	33	3.2%	8,000
12/04	888	25	2.8%	6,500
Annual Growth	12.7%	(13.0%)	—	11.4%

Net Income History

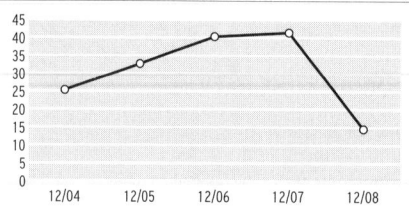

But Related bounced back with development plans that are taking it beyond South Beach. The company created a new subsidiary, Related International, and announced it would invest $1 billion in Mexico real estate projects through 2009, specifically developments in tourist locales such as Acapulco, Cabo San Lucas, and Playa del Carmen. It is also eyeing locations in Panama, Argentina, Uruguay, and the Caribbean for possible projects. It entered a joint venture with Meritage Hospitality Group in 2008 to create a luxury resort in the Bahamas.

In late 2008 the company formed Related Asset Advisors to assist financial institutions with troubled real estate assets. The new affiliated company offers asset management and sales and leasing advice. Earlier that year Related launched a $1 billion fund aimed at buying up mortgages and property from other developers, lenders, and property owners.

The economic downturn and housing price slump led to a glut of condos in Miami during 2008. Related was stuck renting out some of the units it could not sell and delaying further development on some projects.

EXECUTIVES

Chairman and CEO: Jorge M. Pérez, age 59
EVP: Bill Thompson
EVP: Roberto S. Rocha
EVP: Joyce Bronson
EVP and COO: Matthew J. (Matt) Allen
SVP: Oscar A. Rodríguez
SVP: Barbara Salk
VP Construction: Jim M. Werbelow
VP: R. Lee Hodges
VP: Carlos Rosso
Manager Communications: Leah Weatherspoon

LOCATIONS

HQ: The Related Group
  315 S. Biscayne Blvd., Miami, FL 33131
Phone: 305-460-9900   **Fax:** 305-460-9911
Web: www.relatedgroup.com

COMPETITORS

American Invsco
DYL Group
Goldfield
Opus South
Stiles
Turnberry Associates

HISTORICAL FINANCIALS
Company Type: Private

Income Statement			FYE: December 31
	REVENUE ($ mil.)	NET INCOME ($ mil.)	NET PROFIT MARGIN	EMPLOYEES
12/07	1,250	—	—	450
12/06	1,400	—	—	—
12/05	3,200	—	—	—
Annual Growth	(37.5%)	—	—	—

Revenue History

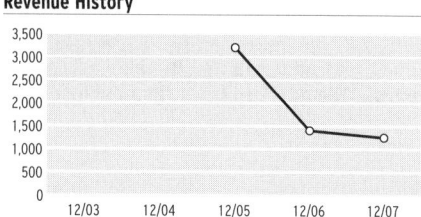

The Related Group

Florida's skyline is only getting higher thanks to The Related Group. The real estate company develops and builds luxury condominiums and mixed-use properties, with 70,000 residential units under its belt throughout the state. Its portfolio includes $10 billion worth of developments, including Miami residential projects such as the Trump Towers and Icon Brickell, as well as the St. Regis Resort and Residences, which it developed with Starwood Hotels & Resorts. Related operates several divisions covering construction, property management, and mortgage services. The company was founded in 1979 by chairman and CEO Jorge M. Pérez, who was once named as one of *TIME* magazine's 25 most influential Hispanics.

The Related Group has ventured out of Miami with mixed success. It made a move on Las Vegas, announcing plans for the 11-tower Las Ramblas condo resort (to be backed by actor George Clooney and nightclub owner Rande Gerber). However, it ultimately sold the property on which Las Ramblas was to be built because of rising construction costs. The company attributed the project's demise to taking on a market — casino resort versus residential — that was less familiar territory.

Remy International

They keep the big wheels turning. Remy International (formerly Delco Remy International) revs up cars and light- and heavy-duty trucks. The manufacturer and distributor offers an electrical lineup of starter motors and alternators and hybrid transmission components. Most parts are sold under the Delco Remy brand, debuted in 1918. The company claims the top spot for remanufacturing starters and alternators for the automotive aftermarket in North America. Its roster of OEM customers includes General Motors, and aftermarket concerns Advance Auto Parts and AutoZone. Collectively, these three account for around 40% of sales. In 2008 Fidelity National, a title insurance company, picked up a 47% stake in Remy.

The cyclical exposure to risk inherent in manufacturing and distributing auto and heavy-duty electrical parts has pushed the company to offer more remanufacturing and aftermarket services. Remy International steps over to third-party core acquisition services as well, selling component cores to other remanufacturers. These cores are usually non-functioning auto parts, reclaimed at the time of replacement for remanufacture and re-use. Through Western Reman Industrial, the company remanufactures locomotive, marine, and industrial engines. Capitalizing on eco-friendly trends, the company is also moving further into peddling hybrid electric motor parts, including transmission assemblies and motor modules to Hyundai, BMW, and GM.

Experience in the auto parts business has been a hard teacher. Early in 2007 Remy sold its light and medium truck diesel engine and parts remanufacturing operations to Caterpillar. Later that year, crushed by a lack of cash, Remy International voluntarily filed for Chapter 11 bankruptcy protection. However, the company outlined a strategy for the restructuring of its debt prior to filing. Its foresight made the process faster and cheaper. Remy International emerged from chapter 11 late 2007, and did so with access to about $330 million in financing. The company has been successful in keeping its loan covenants.

EXECUTIVES

President, CEO, and Director: John H. Weber
SVP and Chief Human Resources Officer:
Gerald T. (Jerry) Mills
SVP and CFO: Fred Knechtel
Legal General Counsel: Quinn Williams
Chief Procurement Officer: David R. Muir
President, Aftermarket: Jay Sanchez
President, Remy Inc.: Jay Pittas
President and Managing Director, Europe Aftermarket:
Philippe James
Auditors: Ernst & Young LLP

LOCATIONS

HQ: Remy International, Inc.
2902 Enterprise Dr., Anderson, IN 46013
Phone: 765-778-6499 **Fax:** 765-778-6404
Web: www.remyinc.com

PRODUCTS/OPERATIONS

Selected Products

Alternators
Fuel systems
Gears
Hybrid Electric Transmission Assembly
Hybrid Motor Modules, Truck / SUV
Power steering systems
Starters
Water pumps

COMPETITORS

Cummins	Mitsubishi Motors
Dana Holding	Motorcar Parts
Federal-Mogul	Prestolite Electric
General Parts	Robert Bosch
Genuine Parts	Valeo
Hahn Automotive	

HISTORICAL FINANCIALS
Company Type: Private

Income Statement				FYE: December 31
	REVENUE ($ mil.)	NET INCOME ($ mil.)	NET PROFIT MARGIN	EMPLOYEES
12/08	1,101	(6)	—	—
12/07	1,129	31	2.7%	7,300
12/06	1,422	(123)	—	6,900
12/05	1,229	(97)	—	7,971
12/04	1,051	56	5.4%	6,800
Annual Growth	1.2%	—	—	2.4%

2008 Year-End Financials

Debt ratio: 460.0%   Current ratio: —
Return on equity: —   Long-term debt ($ mil.): 345
Cash ($ mil.): —

Net Income History

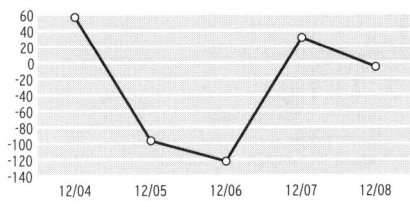

The Renco Group

Renco Group is a holding company for a diverse bunch of businesses. Its AM General subsidiary (a joint venture with Ronald Perelman's MacAndrews & Forbes Holding) makes the HUMVEE, an extra-wide, all-terrain vehicle used by the military, and the HUMMER, the HUMVEE's civilian counterpart. Renco Steel and Baron Drawn Steel manufacture, fabricate, and distribute steel. Other Renco Group companies include Doe Run, the world's #2 lead smelter; Unarco Material Handling, which makes racks and systems for warehouses; and US Magnesium. The company is owned by industrialist Ira Rennert.

In 2008 Renco set up a subsidiary, called Inteva Products, to acquire Delphi's interiors and closures business for just more than $100 million. Those operations serve the automotive industry (making instrument panels, cockpits, and door modules and latches) and give Inteva a global manufacturing presence, which includes more than 15 facilities worldwide.

Renco lost control of WCI Steel (now called Severstal Warren) when that company emerged from Chapter 11 bankruptcy protection in 2006.

EXECUTIVES

Chairman and CEO: Ira L. Rennert, age 74
VP: Ari Rennert
VP Finance; VP Finance and CFO, Renco Steel:
Roger L. Fay
President, Unarco Material Handling: Gary Slater
President and CEO, US Magnesium: Michael H. Legge
President and CEO, Doe Run: A. Bruce Neil
President, Baron Drawn Steel: Timothy J. (Tim) Dillon
President and CEO, AM General:
James A. (Jim) Armour, age 65
President, Doe Run Peru: Juan Carlos Huyhua

LOCATIONS

HQ: The Renco Group Inc.
30 Rockefeller Plaza, New York, NY 10112
Phone: 212-541-6000 **Fax:** 212-541-6197
Web: www.rencogroup.net

PRODUCTS/OPERATIONS

Selected Subsidiaries

AM General (manufactures the HUMVEE and the HUMMER, and diesel engines)
Baron Drawn Steel (cold-drawn steel bar producer)
Doe Run Company (lead smelter)
Inteva Products (automotive interior and closure products)

COMPETITORS

AK Steel Holding	RSR Corporation
Ford Motor	United States Steel
Robert Bosch	

Research Triangle Institute

Pythagoras would find a happy home among the scientists at Research Triangle Institute. Operating mainly under its trade name, RTI International, the not-for-profit enterprise conducts research in such areas as advanced technologies, environmental resources, and medicine. It provides such services as certification and materials testing, as well as software used in laboratories and research projects. Primarily serving the federal government, RTI International offers analytical perspectives on public policy and has more than 2,800 researchers working in offices around the world. Duke University, North Carolina State University, and the University of North Carolina at Chapel Hill established RTI in 1958.

RTI International's main clients are the Department of Health and Human Services and the US Agency for International Development; both agencies collectively accounted for more than 60% of the institute's revenue in 2007.

The company operates out of eight US offices, six non-US offices, and an international subsidiary named RTI Health Solutions headquartered in Ottawa, Canada.

EXECUTIVES

Chairman: Earl Johnson Jr.
President, CEO, and Governor: Victoria F. Haynes, age 61
EVP and CFO: James J. (Jim) Gibson
EVP International Development Group:
 Lon E. (Bert) Maggart
EVP Social and Statistical Sciences: E. Wayne Holden
EVP International Development Group:
 Ronald W. (Ron) Johnson
EVP Science and Engineering Group: Satinder K. Sethi
SVP RTI Health Solutions: Allen W. Mangel
SVP, General Counsel, and Corporate Secretary:
 G. Edward (Eddie) Story
SVP Human Resources and Corporate Affairs:
 Lorena K. Clark
VP, Treasurer, and Chief Risk Officer: E. Ward Sax
VP Survey and Computing Sciences: Timothy J. Gabel
VP Molecular Epidemiology, Genomics, Environment, and Health: Claude Hughes
VP and CIO: David Roseberry
VP and COO, International Development Group:
 Lisa J. Gilliland
VP Corporate Affairs: Sally S. Johnson
VP Environmental Sciences: Terrence K. Pierson
VP Health Sciences, Biostatistics: Alan H. Staple

LOCATIONS

HQ: Research Triangle Institute
 3040 Cornwallis Rd.
 Research Triangle Park, NC 27709
Phone: 919-541-6000   **Fax:** 919-541-5985
Web: www.rti.org

PRODUCTS/OPERATIONS

Selected Research Areas

Advanced technology
 Aerospace and defense
 Auditory prosthesis research
 Contamination control
 Energy technology
 Information technology
 Nanotechnology
 Semiconductors
 Technology assisted learning
 Technology commercialization and policy
 Thermoelectrics
Drug discovery and development
 Bioassays
 Chemical synthesis and characterization
 Chemoinformatics
 Clinical trials
 Drug design and synthesis
 Drug metabolism and pharmacokinetics
 General chemistry support
 Natural products chemistry
 Proteomics
 Therapeutic outcomes and safety
 Toxicology services
Economic and social development
 Crime and justice
 Economic development and technology
 Environment and natural resource management
 Public utilities and infrastructure
Education and training
 Adult education
 Disability policy and programs
 Elementary and secondary education
 Family and early childhood
 International education policy and systems
 Postsecondary education
 Technology assisted learning
Environment and natural resources
 Air, water, and land resources
 Energy and the environment
 Environmental and natural resource economics
 Environmental chemistry and toxicology
 Environmental information systems
 Management and engineering
 Measurement and monitoring
 Policies and regulations
 Risk management

Health
 Communication and education
 Health and the environment
 Health behaviors and interventions
 Health care access
 Health economics
 Genetics, proteomics, and bioinformatics
 Special populations
 Therapeutic outcomes and safety
International development
 Democratic governance
 Education
 Environmental management
 Financial systems
 Health
 Information and communication technology

Resurrection Health Care

They may not raise the dead, but Resurrection Health Care does help people get back up on their feet. Resurrection Health Care is Chicago's largest Catholic health care system. The system consists of eight acute care hospitals with about 2,300 beds, nine long-term care and rehabilitation facilities, a home health care company, and dozens of health care outpatient facilities and community clinics. Specialized services include home health, cancer treatment, pediatrics, cardiac care, and oncology. The system also offers a variety of wellness programs. Resurrection Health Care is sponsored by the Sisters of the Holy Family of Nazareth and the Sisters of the Resurrection.

EXECUTIVES

President and CEO: Sandra Bennett Bruce, age 64
EVP Finance: Tom Capobianco
SVP Mission: Robert T. Bulger
SVP Human Resources: Paul Skiem
VP Corporate Compliance: Julia Ward
Director Web Marketing: Judith Singer
Director Marketing and Public Relations: Steve Sonn

LOCATIONS

HQ: Resurrection Health Care
 7435 W. Talcott Ave., Chicago, IL 60631
Phone: 773-774-8000   **Fax:** 773-990-7626
Web: www.reshealth.org

PRODUCTS/OPERATIONS

Selected Hospitals

Holy Family Medical Center (Des Plaines)
Resurrection Medical Center (Chicago)
Our Lady of the Resurrection Medical Center (Chicago)
Saint Francis Hospital (Evanston)
Saint Joseph Hospital (Chicago)
Saints Mary and Elizabeth Medical Center (Chicago)
West Suburban Medical Center (Oak Park)
Westlake Hospital (Melrose Park)

COMPETITORS

Advocate Health Care
Alexian Brothers Health System
Children's Memorial Hospital
Covenant Ministries
Gottleib Memorial Hospital
Loyola University Health System
Mercy Hospital and Medical Center
Mount Sinai Hospital
NorthShore University HealthSystem
Northwest Community Healthcare
Northwestern Memorial HealthCare
Rush-Copley Medical Center
Silver Cross Hospital
Sinai Health System
St. Bernard Hospital and Health Care Center
University of Chicago Medical Center

HISTORICAL FINANCIALS

Company Type: Not-for-profit

Income Statement

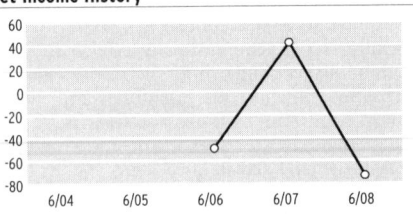

	REVENUE ($ mil.)	NET INCOME ($ mil.)	NET PROFIT MARGIN	EMPLOYEES
6/08	1,688	(73)	—	14,409
6/07	1,708	42	2.5%	14,853
6/06	1,525	(49)	—	15,050
Annual Growth	5.2%	—	—	(2.2%)

FYE: June 30

Net Income History

60				
40				
20				
0				
-20				
-40				
-60				
-80				
	6/04	6/05	6/06	6/07	6/08

Reyes Holdings

Reyes Holdings has a grip on two things that are complementary — food and beer. The company is a leading food and beverage wholesale distributor, serving customers throughout the US, Canada, and Latin America. Its The Martin-Brower Company is a leading supplier of both food and non-food products for the McDonald's restaurant chain. Its Reinhart FoodService is another top foodservice supplier with more than 20 locations. One of the top beer distributors in the US, Reyes Holdings operates about a dozen distribution facilities through subsidiaries Premium Distributors of Virginia, Chicago Beverage System, and California's Harbor Distributing. Co-chairmen Chris Reyes and Jude Reyes founded the company in 1976.

Reyes Holdings grew to be a leader in the distribution business largely through acquisitions, a strategy it continues to follow today. Its Reinhart FoodService unit expanded its territory into the southeastern US in 2008 through the acquisition of The IJ Company. The following year, Martin-Brower purchased Metroplex Holdings, a supplier of McDonald's restaurants in New York and New Jersey, and in Ireland.

The Reyes family started the business when it bought a Schlitz distributorship in Chicago. The company expanded into food distribution with the 1998 acquisition of Martin-Brower.

EXECUTIVES

Co-Chairman: M. Jude Reyes, age 54
Co-Chairman: J. Christopher (Chris) Reyes, age 55
EVP Business Development: Dean H. Janke
EVP: James Reyes, age 46
SVP and CFO: Daniel P. (Dan) Doheny
SVP Corporate Finance: Peter A. (Pete) Swan
SVP: Richard F. (Dick) Strup
SVP Business Development: Kristin A. Hayes
SVP, General Counsel, and Secretary:
 Nicholas L. (Nick) Giampietro
CIO: Anjoo Rai-Marchant
VP Human Resources: Jeff Carlsen
VP Finance: Joseph (Joe) DeJean
VP and Treasurer: Kurt J. Roemer

LOCATIONS

HQ: Reyes Holdings LLC
 9500 W. Bryn Mawr Ave., Ste. 700
 Rosemont, IL 60018
Phone: 847-227-6500   **Fax:** 847-227-6550
Web: www.reyesholdings.com

PRODUCTS/OPERATIONS

Selected Operations

Beverage distribution
 Chicago Beverage System
 Gate City Beverage Distributors (Indio, CA)
 Harbor Distributing (Anaheim, CA)
 Lee Distributors (Charleston, SC)
 Premium Distributors of Maryland (Frederick)
 Premium Distributors of Virginia (Chantilly)
 Premium Distributors of Washington, DC

Food distribution
 Martin-Brower
 Reinhart FoodService (LaCrosse, WI)

COMPETITORS

Alex Lee
Anderson-DuBose
Atlantic Dominion
Clark National
Glazer's Wholesale Drug
Golden State Foods
Gordon Food Service
Jordano's
Keystone Foods
Liquid Investments
McLane Foodservice
Meadowbrook Meat Company
National Wine & Spirits
Performance Food
Republic National Distributing Company
Sunbelt Beverage
SYSCO
U.S. Foodservice
Wirtz Corporation

HISTORICAL FINANCIALS

Company Type: Private

Income Statement				FYE: December 31
	REVENUE ($ mil.)	NET INCOME ($ mil.)	NET PROFIT MARGIN	EMPLOYEES
12/08	11,000	—	—	10,300
12/07	10,100	—	—	8,700
12/06	8,400	—	—	8,000
12/05	7,266	—	—	7,200
12/04	5,076	—	—	—
Annual Growth	21.3%	—	—	12.7%

Revenue History

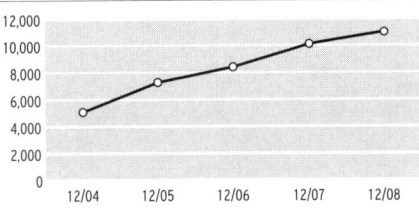

Reynolds and Reynolds

Auto dealers might want to test drive enterprise software from The Reynolds and Reynolds Company. Reynolds provides software and services designed for the automotive retail industry (both dealerships and automakers), including applications to manage sales and service programs, loyalty programs, and procurement systems. It also offers customer relationship management (CRM) applications and document management systems. In addition, Reynolds provides its customers with a range of professional technology services, including consulting, design, integration, and training.

Recurring sales from maintenance and support services have helped the company weather downturns in the auto industry. In addition to its proprietary software, Reynolds offers third-party products from vendors such as IBM. The company is focused on growing its portfolio of integrated information systems for CRM, procurement, and sales through internal development, acquisitions, and partnerships.

Unlike its larger rivals that serve customers in many industries, Reynolds has focused on a single market with products specifically tailored for the auto industry. However, the company is also looking for opportunities to extend its reach into adjacent markets, such as commercial equipment, marine and power sports, and vehicle care.

Outside of North America, the company provides its products and services though UK-based Kalamazoo and DCS Automotive, companies which it acquired in 2001 and 2006, respectively.

EXECUTIVES

Chairman and CEO: Robert T. (Bob) Brockman
President: Rob Nalley
EVP: Dan Agan
VP Product Marketing: Jon Strawsburg
Director Data Services: Bob Schaefer
Director Compliance: Terrence O'Loughlin
Media Contact: Thomas P. (Tom) Schwartz
Auditors: Deloitte & Touche LLP

LOCATIONS

HQ: The Reynolds and Reynolds Company
 1 Reynolds Way, Kettering, OH 45430
Phone: 937-485-2000   **Fax:** 937-485-8971
Web: www.reyrey.com

PRODUCTS/OPERATIONS

Selected Software

Dealership management systems (ERA and POWER)
Document solutions
OEM and third party integration (RCI and RFI)

COMPETITORS

Accenture
Activant Solutions
ADP
Arkona
BearingPoint
Cobalt Group
Computer Sciences Corp.
DealerTrack
Deloitte Consulting
GXS
Hewlett-Packard
HP Enterprise Services
IBM
Microsoft
Oracle
SAP

HISTORICAL FINANCIALS

Company Type: Private

Income Statement			FYE: December 31
	ESTIMATED REVENUE ($ mil.)	NET INCOME ($ mil.)	NET PROFIT MARGIN	EMPLOYEES
12/07	1,730	—	—	6,000
12/06	1,600	—	—	6,500
Annual Growth	8.1%	—	—	(7.7%)

Revenue History

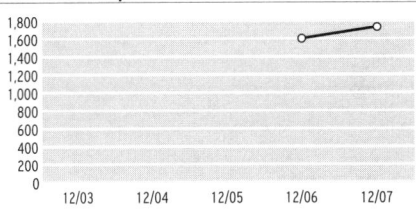

Riceland Foods

Riceland Foods is ingrained in the marketing and milling business. The agricultural cooperative markets rice, soybeans, and wheat grown by its 9,000 member-owners, who farm in Arkansas, Louisiana, Mississippi, Missouri, and Texas. One of the world's leading rice millers, Riceland sells long-grain, brown, and wild rice; flavored rices; and rice-based meal kits (under the Riceland name, as well as private labels). Its customers include grocery retailers and foodservice and food manufacturing companies. The co-op also makes edible oil and processes soybeans, bran, and lecithin, and it supplies rice bran and hulls to petfood makers and to livestock farmers as feed and bedding products.

In addition to being a leader in rice milling, it is a major soybean processor. Riceland's milled soybean customers include poultry, catfish, and livestock producers in the southern and southwestern US.

Established in 1921, the co-op produces and processes more than 125 million bushes of grain a year and markets its products throughout the US and overseas.

EXECUTIVES

Chairman: Thomas C. (Tommy) Hoskyn
President and CEO: K. Daniel (Danny) Kennedy, age 50
VP and CFO: Harry E. Loftis
VP International Rice Marketing: Terry Harris
VP Research: Don McCaskill
VP Corporate Communications and Public Affairs:
 Bill J. Reed
VP Commodity Operations: Scott Gower
VP Soybean and Grain Procurement and Marketing:
 John B. Ruff
Management Director, Commodity Operations:
 Bennie B. Lackey Jr.
Director Marketing, Food Ingredients: Dan Meins

LOCATIONS

HQ: Riceland Foods, Inc.
 2120 S. Park Ave., Stuttgart, AR 72160
Phone: 870-673-5500   **Fax:** 870-673-3366
Web: www.riceland.com

PRODUCTS/OPERATIONS

Selected Consumer Brands and Products

Broccoli & Cheese Rice N Easy Mix
Chicken Rice Mix Rice N Easy Mix
Extra Long Grain Rice
Jasmine Rice
Long Grain & Wild Mix Rice N Easy Mix
Long Grain Rice
Natural Brown Rice
Plump & Tender Medium Grain Rice
Rice Bran Oil
Riceland GOLD
Riceland GOLD Perfected
Saffron Yellow Rice N Easy Mix
Spanish Rice Mix Rice N Easy Mix

COMPETITORS

AarhusKarlshamn
American Rice
Cereal Byproducts
CHS
Connell Company
Ebro Puleva
Farmers' Rice Cooperative
Farmers Rice Milling
Goya
JFC International
Lotus Foods
Louis Dreyfus Group
Pacific International Rice Mills
Producers Rice Mill
Riviana Foods
Specialty Rice

HISTORICAL FINANCIALS

Company Type: Cooperative

Income Statement

FYE: July 31

	REVENUE ($ mil.)	NET INCOME ($ mil.)	NET PROFIT MARGIN	EMPLOYEES
7/08	1,226	—	—	1,750
7/07	947	—	—	1,900
7/06	937	—	—	1,900
7/05	956	—	—	1,900
7/04	951	—	—	1,900
Annual Growth	6.6%	—	—	(2.0%)

Revenue History

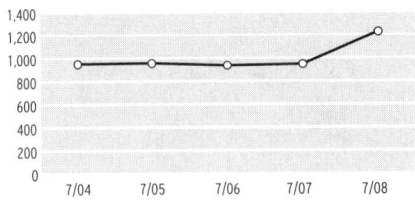

Rich Products

Starting in 1945 with "the miracle cream from the soya bean," Rich Products has grown from a niche maker of soy-based whipped toppings and frozen desserts to a major US frozen foods manufacturer. The company has developed other products, such as Coffee Rich (non-dairy coffee creamer). It has expanded its product line to include frozen bakery and pizza doughs and ingredients for the foodservice and in-store bakery markets, plus appetizers, baked goods, seafood, and barbecue meat. Rich Products markets more than 2,000 frozen food items that are available in about 70 countries; it has manufacturing facilities throughout the US and around the world.

In a move to expand its health and wellness offerings, Rich Products acquired GLP Free Manufacturing, a maker of gluten-free baked goods, in 2007.

The Rich family, through its Rich's Entertainment Group, owns the Buffalo Bisons, the Jamestown Jammers, and the Wichita Wranglers minor-league baseball teams. It also owns and operates a number of catering operations and restaurants in New York and Florida through its Be Our Guest group. In addition, the family owns a corporate and leisure travel management and event-planning business called The Travel Team; Roar Logistics, which offers truck and rail shipping solutions; and the Palm Beach National Gold & Country Club.

EXECUTIVES

Chairman; Co-Chairman, Rich Products, Canada:
 Robert E. (Bob) Rich Jr., age 68
Vice Chairman; President, Rich's Entertainment Group:
 Melinda R. (Mindy) Rich, age 51
President, CEO, and Director:
 William G. (Bill) Gisel Jr., age 56
EVP and CFO: James (Jim) Deuschle
EVP and Chief Administrative Officer:
 Maureen O. Hurley
SVP and General Counsel: Jill Bond
SVP Procurement: William V. Gillmore
SVP and CIO: Paul Klein
VP International Human Resources: Judy Campbell
VP Communications: Dwight Gram
Marketing Director: Gary Duszynski
Group President, International Business Group:
 Kevin R. Malchoff
Group President, North America Business Group:
 Richard M. Ferranti
President, Foodservice & In-Store Bakery Divisions:
 Ray Burke
President, Consumer Brands Division: Jack C. Kilgore
Chairman, Europe: George Thomopoulos
Public Relations: Lisa Texido

LOCATIONS

HQ: Rich Products Corporation
 1 Robert Rich Way, Buffalo, NY 14213
Phone: 716-878-8000   **Fax:** 716-878-8765
Web: www.richs.com

PRODUCTS/OPERATIONS

Selected Products

Appetizers
Bagels
Barbecue meat
Beverage concentrates
Bread and rolls
Brownies
Cakes
Cheesecakes
Donuts
Dough
 Bread
 Cookie
 Pizza
Dry Mixes
Eclairs and puffs
Fillings
Frozen shrimp and other seafood
Icings
Italian specialties
 Meatballs
 Pepperoni
Mini desserts
Muffins
Pies
Pudding
Sweet rolls
Topping
 On-top topping
 Prewhipped topping
 Ready-to-whip topping

COMPETITORS

BakeMark
Campbell Soup
ConAgra
Dawn Food Products
Dean Foods
General Mills
Gonnella Baking
Gorton's
Heinz

Hom/Ade Foods
Kraft Foods
Maple Leaf Bakery
Nestlé
Pinnacle Foods
Ralcorp
Sara Lee
Schwan's
Windsor Foods

HISTORICAL FINANCIALS

Company Type: Private

Income Statement

FYE: December 31

	REVENUE ($ mil.)	NET INCOME ($ mil.)	NET PROFIT MARGIN	EMPLOYEES
12/08	2,800	—	—	7,300
12/07	2,650	—	—	7,200
12/06	2,400	—	—	6,500
12/05	2,500	—	—	7,000
12/04	2,100	—	—	6,500
Annual Growth	7.5%	—	—	2.9%

Revenue History

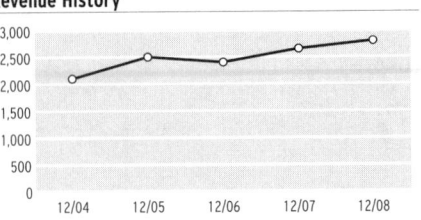

Richards Group

For The Richards Group every day is brand new. The independent advertising agency specializes in creating loyalty for its customers' brands through marketing, public relations, and sales promotions. Services include creating company or product names and inventing corporate identities, as well as graphic design, packaging, analytics, digital marketing, and marketing for certain niches, including sports, entertainment, and minorities. Founded by Stan Richards in 1965, the group builds brand awareness through everything from print ads to employee uniform design. It has molded the public's perception of such brands as Amstel Light, Fruit of the Loom, GameStop, Motel 6, The Home Depot, and Red Lobster.

At a time when advertising firms are losing clients because of the economic downturn, The Richards Group won an important victory in 2008 when long-time client Home Depot decided to stick with the agency. Home Depot sifted through proposals from more than 20 ad agencies before selecting The Richards Group to create a refreshed campaign for the home improvement giant. The Richards Group fended off competition for the $580 million Home Depot account from global advertising powerhouses including Interpublic's Hill, Holliday; Omnicom's GSD&M Idea City; and WPP Group's JWT.

EXECUTIVES

Principal and Creative Director: Stan Richards, age 70
CFO: Scot Dykema
Principal and Head of Brand Managemnt:
Diane Fannon
Public Relations: Katie Myers

LOCATIONS

HQ: The Richards Group, Inc.
8750 N. Central Expwy., Ste. 100, Dallas, TX 75231
Phone: 214-891-5700   **Fax:** 214-891-5230
Web: www.richards.com

COMPETITORS

Burrell Communications
Carmichael Lynch
C-K
Corporate Branding
Crispin Porter
Doner
Fallon Worldwide
Goodby, Silverstein
GSD&M Idea City
Hill, Holliday
JWT
Landor
Lee Tilford Agency
Leo Burnett
Martin
Martin Agency
McKinney
MQ&C
Ogilvy & Mather
Publicis & Hal Riney
TBWA Worldwide
TM Advertising
TracyLocke
Williams

HISTORICAL FINANCIALS
Company Type: Private

Income Statement

FYE: December 31

	REVENUE ($ mil.)	NET INCOME ($ mil.)	NET PROFIT MARGIN	EMPLOYEES
12/08	167	—	—	620
12/07	166	—	—	700
12/06	160	—	—	684
12/05	148	—	—	657
12/04	100	—	—	—
Annual Growth	13.7%	—	—	(1.9%)

Revenue History

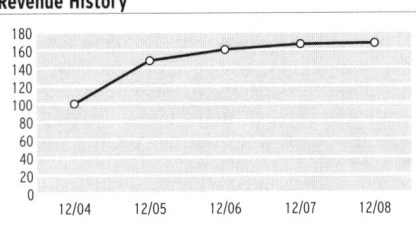

RNDC Texas

RNDC Texas, LLC (also known as Republic National Distributing Company) is one of the largest distributors of wine and spirits in the US (right up there with big-boys like Charmer Sunbelt), serving 18 US states and Washington, DC. It operated as the Republic Beverage Company until 2007, when it combined its operations with most of those of National Distributing (National retained the Georgia and New Mexico territories). Prior to this most recent expansion, RNDC was already growing; it formed partnerships with the operations of the Naifeh family (Oklahoma), Hertz (the Southeast), and United Distillers (Nebraska), as well as acquiring a 50% stake in Alliance Wine and Spirits (Alabama).

The company began life with the combination of the Goldring and Block families' beverage distributorships. The families agreed in 2005 to merge their wine and spirits wholesaling companies and to use the Republic Beverage name at all of their locations, which included Arizona, Alabama, Louisiana, Mississippi, and Texas.

In 2006, just prior to joining forces with National Distributing, the company acquired SODAK Distributing Company of South Dakota, Congress Distribution of North Dakota, and Kentucky's Horizon Wine and Spirits.

EXECUTIVES

President: Thomas (Tom) Cole
CFO: Paul Fine
Chief Administrative Officer: Greg Johnson

LOCATIONS

HQ: RNDC Texas, LLC
8045 Northcourt Rd., Houston, TX 77040
Phone: 832-782-1000   **Fax:** 832-782-1010
Web: www.rndc-usa.com

Republic Beverage Company has operations in Alabama, Arizona, Kentucky, Louisiana, Mississippi, Nebraska, North Carolina, North Dakota, South Dakota, Oklahoma, Texas, Virginia, and West Virginia.

COMPETITORS

Ben E. Keith
Constellation Brands
Gambrinus
Glazer's Wholesale Drug
National Wine & Spirits
Southern Wine & Spirits
Sunbelt Beverage

HISTORICAL FINANCIALS
Company Type: Private

Income Statement

FYE: December 31

	ESTIMATED REVENUE ($ mil.)	NET INCOME ($ mil.)	NET PROFIT MARGIN	EMPLOYEES
12/08	4,400	—	—	5,000
12/07	4,320	—	—	6,000
12/06	4,000	—	—	4,000
12/05	1,600	—	—	3,000
Annual Growth	40.1%	—	—	18.6%

Revenue History

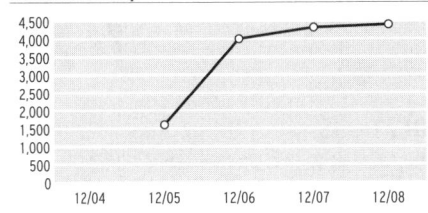

Robert W. Baird & Co.

Employee-owned Robert W. Baird & Co. brings midwestern sensibility to the high-flying world of investment banking. A subsidiary of Baird Holding Company, the company offers brokerage, asset management, and investment banking services to middle-market corporations, institutional clients, and wealthy individuals and families. Its investment banking activities include underwriting and distributing corporate securities, mergers and acquisition advisory, and institutional sales and trading. The company also conducts equity research on more than 600 US firms. It has more than 100 offices in the US, Asia, and Europe, where it owns 48% of Baird UK.

More than half of Robert W. Baird's locations are wealth management offices in the US. The company manages about 10 bond and equity mutual funds; Baird Advisors manages fixed-income investments, while Baird Investment Management handles the equities side. Robert W. Baird also invests in private equity and venture capital.

In 2008 the company turned to the East for its fortunes as its private equity group opened an office in China, hoping to capitalize on the country's expanding business-friendly environment. The outpost will focus on small, high-growth businesses that have been overlooked by other venture capitalists. The company has also expanded its investment banking operations in Shanghai and Hong Kong.

Founded in 1919, Robert W. Baird had been majority-owned by Northwestern Mutual since 1982. However, employees bought back the company's stock in a series of purchases that culminated in 2004.

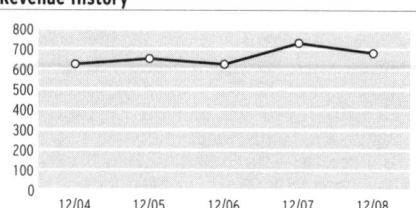
Robert Wood Johnson Foundation

The Robert Wood Johnson Foundation uses its wealth to improve your health. The foundation is the nation's largest charitable organization devoted exclusively to health care issues. The group awards grants for programs that address such problems as health care quality and coverage, childhood obesity, and addiction prevention and treatment. In addition, the Robert Wood Johnson Foundation supports efforts to improve health care for vulnerable populations and to help recruit, develop, and retain health care workers. Established in 1972, the foundation has an endowment of more than $9 billion. Looking at a shortage of trained nurses in 2009, the foundation is working to offset declines.

The Robert Wood Johnson Foundation and the New Jersey Chamber of Commerce Foundation partnered in May 2009 to fund a major new initiative formed to ensure that New Jersey's future nursing workforce will be able to meet health care demands. Spanning five years, the $22 million project focuses on boosting the number of nurse faculty in the state.

The foundation awards more than 900 grants and contracts each year for projects that improve health and health care in the US. Investments in the infrastructure of the public health care system and in disease prevention have gained importance for the foundation, particularly in light of a shift in government priorities toward issues such as the threat of bioterrorism.

The foundation's founder and namesake, Robert Wood Johnson, endowed the organization with stock in his family's business — health care products conglomerate Johnson & Johnson.

HISTORY

Robert Wood Johnson took control of his family's health care products company, Johnson & Johnson, in 1932. Deeply concerned about corporate responsibility, he urged other corporate leaders to embrace philanthropy and set out his principles in a pamphlet called *Try Reality* (1935). He launched the Johnson Foundation in 1936, putting his words into action. The organization went nationwide in 1972 and was renamed The Robert Wood Johnson Foundation in honor of its founder, who had died in 1968 and bequeathed $1.2 billion in stock as an endowment.

The foundation began tackling the issue of terminal care in the late 1980s, seeking ways to improve the quality of care for dying patients. In 1987 it released its first forecast regarding the future of health care, which warned that the US government should adopt a national health care policy. Dr. Steven Schroeder was tapped to lead the Johnson Foundation in 1990. One year later, the foundation adopted a health reform initiative designed to help states analyze ways to increase health coverage.

In 1994 the Johnson Foundation bought airtime on NBC for a debate on national health care; despite the fact that NBC News crafted the program's content, some Republican officials questioned the foundation's impartiality because it had participated in First Lady Hillary Clinton's task force on health care. As managed-care practices increased in 1998, the foundation doubled

the amount it would give for proposals to enhance the patient-provider relationship.

In 1999 the foundation embarked on a plan to address the issue of uninsured individuals in the US. The same year chairman Sidney Wentz stepped down and was replaced by former Johnson & Johnson vice chairman Robert Campbell. In 2000 the Johnson Foundation began a three-year drive to inform parents of ways they can obtain health insurance for their children. At the beginning of 2001, Johnson family member Robert Wood Johnson IV was named to the foundation's board. Later that year the Johnson Foundation committed $100 million to Faith in Action, a faith-based volunteer effort that addresses the needs of the chronically ill. In late 2002 Risa Lavizzo-Mourey became president and CEO when Steven Schroeder retired after leading the foundation for 12 years.

Chairman Robert Campbell retired in 2005; Thomas Kean, a former New Jersey governor and president of Drew University, was selected as his replacement.

EXECUTIVES

Chairman: Thomas H. (Tom) Kean, age 73
President, CEO, and Trustee: Risa J. Lavizzo-Mourey, age 54
Chief of Staff and Special Advisor to the President/CEO: Calvin Bland
CFO and Treasurer: Margaret H. (Peggi) Einhorn
Chief Investment Officer: Brian S. O'Neil
SVP and Director, Health Care Group: John R. Lumpkin
SVP and Director Health Group: James S. Marks
VP and Chief Learning Officer: Robert G. Hughes
VP, General Counsel, and Secretary: Katherine Hatton
VP National Program Affairs: Peter Goodwin
VP Information Technology: Albert O. Shar
VP Communications: David J. Morse
VP Human Resources and Administration: David L. Waldman
VP Research and Evaluation: David C. Colby
Senior Counsel: James C. Ingram
Director Foundation Services: Kristine Nasto
Director National Program Affairs: Rona Smyth Henry
Director Philanthropy Applications and Analytics: Joseph P. Calabrese
Director Public Affairs: Adam M. Coyne
Auditors: PricewaterhouseCoopers LLP

LOCATIONS

HQ: Robert Wood Johnson Foundation
Route 1 and College Road East
Princeton, NJ 08543
Phone: 609-452-8701 **Fax:** 609-627-6422
Web: www.rwjf.org

PRODUCTS/OPERATIONS

Selected Programs

Human capital (recruitment, development, and retention of health care workers)
New Jersey
Pioneer (research and development)
Targeted
Addiction prevention and treatment
Childhood obesity
Coverage
Disparities (access to health care)
Nursing
Public health
Quality health care
Tobacco use and exposure
Vulnerable populations

HISTORICAL FINANCIALS

Company Type: Foundation

Income Statement

FYE: December 31

	REVENUE ($ mil.)	NET INCOME ($ mil.)	NET PROFIT MARGIN	EMPLOYEES
12/07	1,632	1,040	63.7%	—
12/06	1,251	770	61.5%	—
12/05	1,041	—	—	—
12/04	1,506	—	—	—
12/03	601	—	—	—
Annual Growth	28.4%	35.0%	—	—

Net Income History

1,200				
1,000				
800				
600				
400				
200				
0				
	12/03	12/04	12/05	12/06	12/07

Rock Bottom Restaurants

When you reach this Rock Bottom, you'll find a warm meal and craft brewed beers waiting. Rock Bottom Restaurants operates about 100 eateries and brew pubs across the US, including its flagship pizzeria chain Old Chicago and its Rock Bottom Restaurant & Brewery pub chain. Its pizzerias, found in Colorado, Minnesota, and 20 other states, feature deep-dish, Chicago-style pizza and more than 110 different brands of beer. Rock Bottom's smaller brew pub chain offers fish, pasta, and meat, plus a variety of microbrews produced on the premises. In addition to its corporate-run units, the company has a small number of franchised Old Chicago locations. Chairman Frank Day opened the first Old Chicago restaurant in 1976.

Rock Bottom was a pioneering force in the microbrew restaurant movement, distinguishing itself from other casual dining chains by offering unique restaurant themes, heartier menu items, and a wide selection of beer. With a somewhat higher price point than other operators in the sector, the company has been hurt by the downturn in the economy and slowing consumer spending.

In addition to its flagship chains, Rock Bottom has a small number of steakhouse restaurants operating under the name ChopHouse & Brewery. It also runs the Walnut Brewery in Boulder, Colorado, and a couple of Sing Sing piano bars.

Frank Day returned to the CEO post in 2008 after Ned Lidvall and two other top executives resigned. Lidvall had been promoted to the top post in 2001. Day had taken the company private in 1999.

EXECUTIVES

Chairman, President, and CEO: Frank B. Day, age 74
SVP Development and Old Chicago Franchising: Buck Warfield
CFO and SVP Corporate Performance Management: Brian T. Armstrong
SVP Brewery Division: Ted E. Williams
SVP Old Chicago Division: Gary B. Foreman
VP Legal: Doug Christman
VP Human Resources: Robin Manley
VP Purchasing and Supply Chain Management: Maryanne Rose
VP Operations, Brewery Division: Eliot J. Hermanson
VP Franchise Operations: Tom Lund
Brewery Operations Director: Kevin Reed
Loyalty Programs Director: Brian Lambert
Culinary Research and Development Director: Mike Thom
Marketing and Public Relations Director: Marilyn Davenport

LOCATIONS

HQ: Rock Bottom Restaurants, Inc.
248 Centennial Pkwy., Ste. 100
Louisville, CO 80027
Phone: 303-664-4000   **Fax:** 303-664-4197
Web: www.rockbottomrestaurantsinc.com

COMPETITORS

Applebee's
BJ's Restaurants
Brinker
Bubba Gump Shrimp
Carlson Restaurants
Cheesecake Factory
Damon's
Darden
Famous Dave's
Fox & Hound Restaurant
Gordon Biersch
Granite City
Hillstone Restaurant Group
Hooters
Johnny Rockets
OSI Restaurant Partners
P.F. Chang's
Planet Hollywood
Romacorp
Ruby Tuesday
Uno Restaurants

HISTORICAL FINANCIALS

Company Type: Private

Income Statement

FYE: December 31

	REVENUE ($ mil.)	NET INCOME ($ mil.)	NET PROFIT MARGIN	EMPLOYEES
12/08	312	—	—	6,914
12/07	306	—	—	7,500
12/06	283	—	—	7,000
12/05	275	—	—	7,200
12/04	266	—	—	7,000
Annual Growth	4.1%	—	—	(0.3%)

Revenue History

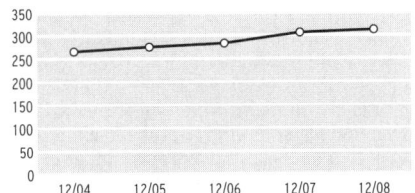

350				
300				
250				
200				
150				
100				
50				
0				
	12/04	12/05	12/06	12/07	12/08

Rockefeller Foundation

The Rockefeller Foundation, established in 1913, is one of the oldest private charitable organizations in the US. It supports grants, fellowships, and conferences for programs that concentrate on identifying and alleviating need and suffering worldwide. These programs (or themes) include initiatives to foster fair implementation of health care, job opportunities for America's urban poor, creative expression through the humanities and arts, and agricultural policies that ensure food distribution to people in developing countries. An additional theme — global inclusion — serves as a connection between the foundation's other programs and as a way to ensure that poor people benefit from global trade increases.

Outside North America, the Rockefeller Foundation concentrates its efforts in eastern and southern Africa and in Southeast Asia.

The foundation maintains no ties to the Rockefeller family or its other philanthropies. An independent board of trustees sets program guidelines and approves all expenditures.

HISTORY

Oil baron John D. Rockefeller, one of America's most criticized capitalists, was also one of its pioneer philanthropists. Before founding The Rockefeller Foundation in 1913, he funded the creation of The University of Chicago (with $36 million over a 25-year period) and formed organizations for medical research (1901), the education of southern African-Americans (1903), and hookworm eradication in the southern US.

Rockefeller turned the control of the foundation over to his son John D. Rockefeller Jr. in 1916. The younger Rockefeller separated the foundation from the family's interests and established an independent board. (The board later rejected a proposal from John Sr. to replace school textbooks that he claimed promoted Bolshevism.)

In the mid-1920s the foundation started conducting basic medical research. In 1928 it absorbed several other Rockefeller philanthropies, adding programs in the natural and social sciences and the arts and humanities. During the 1930s the foundation developed the first effective yellow fever vaccine (1935), continued its worldwide battles against disease, and supported pioneering research in the field of biology. Other grants supported the performing arts in the US and social science research. During WWII it supplied major funding for nuclear science research tools (spectroscopy, X-ray diffraction).

After the war, with an increasing number of large public ventures modeled after the foundation (e.g., the UN's World Health Organization) taking over its traditional physical and natural sciences territory, the organization dissolved its famed biology division in 1951. The following year emphasis swung to agricultural studies under chairman John D. Rockefeller III. The organization took wheat seeds developed at its Mexican food project to Colombia (1950), Chile (1955), and India (1956); a rice institute in the Philippines followed (1960). The Green Revolution sprouted 12 more developing-world institutes.

In the 1960s the foundation began dispatching experts to African and Latin American universities in an effort to raise the level of training at those institutions. The long bear market of the

1970s caused the foundation's assets to drop to a low of $732 million (1977).

In 1990 the organization set up the Energy Foundation, a joint effort with the the Pew Charitable Trusts and the MacArthur Foundation, to explore alternate energy sources.

In the mid-1990s the Republican-led Congress launched three probes into the foundation and several other not-for-profits over allegations of political activities that could jeopardize their tax status.

In 1998 Gordon Conway, a British agricultural ecologist, became the foundation's 12th (and first non-US) president. He implemented a retooling of the organization's programs in 1999. He also led an effective campaign against bioengineering giant Monsanto's (now part of Pfizer) plan to market "sterile seeds" that do not regenerate. In 2000 James Orr, one of the foundation's board members and CEO of Boston's United Asset Management Corporation, succeeded Alice Ilchman as the organization's chairman.

The foundation pledged $5 million for disaster relief efforts in New York City following the September 11 terrorist attacks in 2001. The Rockefeller Foundation launched a multi-year initiative to promote fair intellectual-property policies to the poor the following year.

Conway retired from the foundation at the end of 2004; former University of Pennsylvania president Judith Rodin was named as his successor.

EXECUTIVES

Chairman: James F. (Jim) Orr III, age 65
President: Judith (Judy) Rodin, age 64
COO: Peter Madonia
CFO: Ellen Taus, age 50
CTO: Fernando Mola-Davis
Treasurer and Chief Investment Officer: Donna J. Dean
VP Research and Evaluation: David J. Jhirad, age 61
VP Foundation Initiatives: Darren Walker
Managing Director Grants Management and Assistant General Counsel: Pamela Foster
General Counsel and Corporate Secretary: Shari L. Patrick
Director Communications: Peter Costiglio
Director Human Resources: Samantha H. Gilbert, age 46
Auditors: Deloitte & Touche LLP

LOCATIONS

HQ: The Rockefeller Foundation
420 5th Ave., New York, NY 10018
Phone: 212-869-8500   **Fax:** 212-764-3468
Web: www.rockfound.org

HISTORICAL FINANCIALS

Company Type: Foundation

Income Statement				FYE: December 31
	REVENUE ($ mil.)	NET INCOME ($ mil.)	NET PROFIT MARGIN	EMPLOYEES
12/07	478	—	—	158
12/06	474	—	—	158
12/05	344	—	—	174
12/04	368	—	—	—
12/03	586	—	—	212
Annual Growth	(5.0%)	—	—	(7.1%)

Revenue History

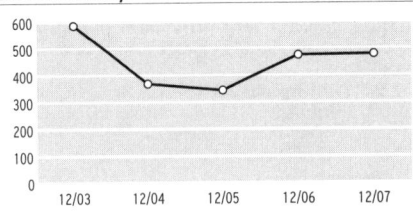

Roll International

It's Wonderful over at Stewart and Lynda Resnick's eclectic empire, Roll International. Its holdings include POM Wonderful, the hip and trendy pomegranate juice with its distinctive bulbous bottle, as well as the hip and trendy water bottler, FIJI Water. More mundane but no less important to its bottom line are the company's other holdings, which include Teleflora, the largest flower-delivery service in the US; Paramount Farms, the world's largest grower and supplier of almonds and pistachios; and Paramount Citrus, a leading producer of fresh lemons and oranges. Roll also owns deep-sea cargo shipper Neptune Pacific Line, along with Suterra, a maker of environmentally friendly pest-control products.

In 2008 Mr. Resnick and Los Angeles businessman and entrepreneur, Selim K. Zilkha, formed of a 50-50 joint venture (Jatropha Farm) with Global Clean Energy Holdings in order to commercialize a renewable, alternate energy source. The venture intends to acquire and develop raw land in the State of Yucatan in Mexico in order to grow jatropha (*Jatropha curcas*) trees. The fruit and seeds of the trees, which are not edible and are not grown as a food crop, are to be made into oil for use as biomass, biodiesel, or feedstock.

Beyond biomass, things can get a little nuts at Roll. The company's Paramount Farms unit harvests more than 30,000 acres of pistachios and 40,000 acres of almonds every year. After processing, they're sold under the Sunkist and Everybody's Nuts brand names. Paramount also makes private-label nut products.

Out on the rest of the back forty is another of the Resnicks' farming operations — Paramount Citrus. Its fruit is the bounty of 30,000 acres of navel and Valencia oranges, lemons, and Clementine mandarins. Paramount's Delano, California, processing plant is one of North America's largest orange and lemon packing operations.

The company's pomegranate juice is advertised as a source of antioxidants, and its ad campaigns play upon the fruit's supposed age-defying attributes, with slogans like "The pomegranate is 5,000 years old. Drink it and you will be, too."

Also on Roll's roster is FIJI Water, which the company acquired in 2004. Founded in 1998, FIJI's premium (and premium-priced) water is sourced from an artesian aquifer on the island of Fiji. It is distributed throughout the world.

Dipping into shipping, Neptune Pacific runs a fleet of four deep-sea tankers and container vessels that ship agricultural grains and liquid commodities throughout the Pacific Ocean region.

Last but not least, Suterra makes pheromone traps and lures under the CheckMate brand. The products are used by fruit farmers to control vineyard pests in a non-chemical way, since pheromones interrupt insect mating cycles.

EXECUTIVES

Co-Chairman: Lynda R. Resnick
Co-Chairman, President, and CEO; Co-Chairman and CEO, Teleflora; President, Paramount Farms: Stewart A. Resnick, age 71
SVP and Chief Tax Officer: Jordan P. Weiss
SVP and CFO: Robert W. Bryant
SVP and Chief Legal Officer: Craig B. Cooper
VP Corporate Communications: Rob Six

LOCATIONS

HQ: Roll International Corporation
11444 W. Olympic Blvd., 10th Fl.
Los Angeles, CA 90064
Phone: 310-966-5700   **Fax:** 310-914-4747
Web: www.roll.com

PRODUCTS/OPERATIONS

Company Holdings

FIJI Water Company LLC (bottled water)
Neptune Pacific Line (ocean liners and bulk shipping)
Paramount Citrus (lemon and orange production)
Paramount Farms (almond and pistachio production)
POM Wonderful, LLC (fresh pomegranates and pomegranate juice)
Suterra LLC (pest-control products)
Teleflora LLC (floral wire service)

COMPETITORS

1-800-FLOWERS
AgraQuest
Bayer CropScience
Blue Diamond Growers
Calcot
Cargill
Chemtura
Coca-Cola
COSCO Group
Danone Water
Diamond Foods
Dole Food
DuPont Agriculture & Nutrition
Ferolito, Vultaggio
Florida's Natural
Frito-Lay
FTD Group
Fuze Beverage
Golden West Nuts
Inventure
IZZE
J & J Snack Foods
Kraft Foods
Lance Snacks
Maersk Line
Martha Stewart Living
Naked Juice
Nestlé Waters
OceanFreight
PepsiCo
Polar Beverages
Primex International
Stewart & Jasper Orchards
Sugar Foods
Sun Growers
SunWest Foods
Syngenta Crop Protection
Tejon Ranch
Tropicana

HISTORICAL FINANCIALS
Company Type: Private

Income Statement				FYE: December 31
	ESTIMATED REVENUE ($ mil.)	NET INCOME ($ mil.)	NET PROFIT MARGIN	EMPLOYEES
12/08	2,010	—	—	3,765
12/07	1,980	—	—	3,714
12/06	1,430	—	—	2,596
12/05	1,479	—	—	2,685
Annual Growth	10.8%	—	—	11.9%

Revenue History

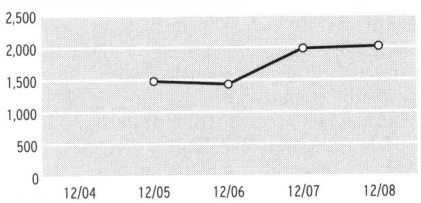

Rooney Holdings

Film star Mickey isn't the only Rooney to get his act together. Rooney Holdings, through Manhattan Construction and other subsidiaries, builds hospitals, schools, government buildings, roads and bridges, and sports facilities including the Dallas Cowboys Stadium and Reliant Stadium in Houston. Rooney's family of companies offer construction management, general contracting, and design/build services in the US, Mexico, Central America, and the Caribbean. The family-owned company also operates an insurance agency and manufactures electronics through OAI Electronics.

Rooney Holdings was formed in 1984 to acquire Manhattan Construction Company, which was founded by patriarch L. H. Rooney in 1896. Current CEO Francis Rooney III served as the US ambassador to the Catholic Church's Holy See.

Rooney looked to Florida in 2008 and bought Kraft Construction — a big commercial and residential builder in that state. The acquisition was made in order to expand Manhattan's geographic reach. But it may have been ill-timed, as Florida's construction industry took a big economic hit. Shortly after the acquisition Kraft was forced to make job cuts.

EXECUTIVES
Chairman and CEO: L. Francis Rooney III
VP Information Technology: Duwayn Anderson
VP Administration: Jackie Proffitt
CEO, Hope Lumber: James (Jim) Cavanaugh
CFO and Chief Administrative Officer: Kevin P. Moore
Manager Human Resources, Hope Lumber: Bill Vogt
Auditors: Hogan & Slovacek

LOCATIONS
HQ: Rooney Holdings, Inc.
1400 Gulf Shore Blvd. N., Ste. 184
Naples, FL 34102
Phone: 239-403-0375   **Fax:** 239-403-0316
Web: www.rooneybrothers.com

PRODUCTS/OPERATIONS

Subsidiaries
Manhattan Construction Company
  Cantera Concrete Company
  Kraft Construction Company
  Manhattan Road & Bridge
OAI Electronics, Inc.
Rooney Insurance Agency, Inc.

COMPETITORS
Austin Industries
Barton Malow
Bechtel
Beck Group
Fluor
Foster Wheeler
Hensel Phelps
Jacobs Engineering
M. A. Mortenson
Siemens Corp.
Skanska USA Building
Turner Corporation
Washington Division

Roseburg Forest Products

With roots in a Depression-era sawmill, Roseburg Forest Products has branched out with a comprehensive line of wood products. Formed in 1936, the company produces specialty panels (melamine, particleboard, and vinyl laminates), engineered wood products (joists, beams, and rimboards), and plywood products such as siding and concrete forming. Its products are available through dealers, home centers, and wholesale distributors. Roseburg manages some 750,000 acres of timberland in northern California and southern Oregon. Heirs of philanthropist Kenneth Ford, who established the Ford Family Foundation, own the company. Allyn Ford, Kenneth's son, is chairman, president, and CEO.

In 2006 the company bought around a half-dozen particleboard plants in the southeastern US from Georgia-Pacific, raising its profile nationally. But Roseburg was hurt in 2008 when a local short-line railroad in Oregon shut down, raising the company's shipping costs by as much as $2 million annually. However, new plans to reopen the line were made in 2009. The company was struck by the decline in home construction in 2008 and was forced to reduce production, cut jobs, and close some plants.

Roseburg has plans to create a $15 million power plant, which will burn wood scrap to generate power at one of its California veneer manufacturing facilities.

EXECUTIVES
Chairman, President, and CEO: Allyn C. Ford
COO: Charles E. (Chuck) Ulik, age 48
CIO: Dan Coyle
VP Composite Manufacturing: Darrell Keeling
VP Solid Wood Manufacturing: Dave Weak
VP Finance and CFO: Robert L. (Bob) Desrochers
VP Engineering: Bill Randles
VP Sales and Marketing: J. Ray Barbee
VP Human Resources: Hank Snow
Controller: Jeff Groom

LOCATIONS
HQ: Roseburg Forest Products Co.
10599 Old Hwy. 99 S., Dillard, OR 97432
Phone: 541-679-3311   **Fax:** 541-679-9543
Web: www.rfpco.com

Facilities and Locations
1 medium-density fiberboard plant, SC
1 sawmill, OR
1 engineered wood products plant, OR
1 wood-chip export terminal, OR
1 softwood veneer plant, CA
3 plywood plants, OR
3 melamine plants, MS, MT, SC, and OR
1 panel cut-to-size facility, MS
6 particleboard plants, OR, MT, MS, GA, and SC

PRODUCTS/OPERATIONS

Selected Products
Engineered Wood
  Beams
  Columns
  Headers
  Joists
  Rimboard
  Underlayment
Lumber
  Douglas fir
  Hemlock/white fir
  Pine
  Premier stud
Plywood and Particleboard Products
  Concrete forming
  Industrial grades
  Medium-density overlay
  Sanded fir plywood
  Sheathing
  Siding
  Superply
  Underlayment
Specialty Panels
  Melamine
  Shelving
  Vinyl laminates

COMPETITORS
Boise Cascade
Columbia Forest Products
Georgia-Pacific
Hampton Affiliates
Louisiana-Pacific
MAXXAM
Potlatch
Sierra Pacific Industries
Simpson Investment
Weyerhaeuser

HISTORICAL FINANCIALS
Company Type: Private

Income Statement				FYE: December 31
	REVENUE ($ mil.)	NET INCOME ($ mil.)	NET PROFIT MARGIN	EMPLOYEES
12/07	1,300	—	—	3,800
12/06	1,100	—	—	3,900
12/05	1,162	—	—	3,650
Annual Growth	5.8%	—	—	2.0%

Revenue History

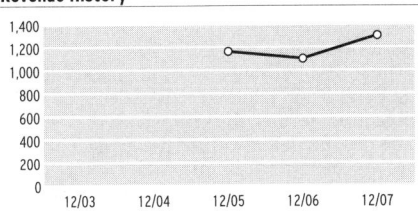

Rotary International

The rotary phone may be a thing of the past, but Rotary International and its more than 1.2 million members are still going strong. The service organization is made up of more than 32,000 clubs in some 200 countries and territories worldwide. Rotary service projects are intended to alleviate problems, such as disease, hunger, illiteracy, poverty, and violence. Grants from the Rotary Foundation support the group's efforts. Along with its service projects, Rotary aims to promote high ethical standards in the workplace. Membership in Rotary clubs is by invitation; each club strives to include representatives from major businesses, professions, and institutions in its community.

Rotary was founded in 1905. The organization's name arose from the early practice of rotating meetings among members' offices.

As it enters its second century in operation, Rotary has chosen the eradication of polio as its top priority. The Bill & Melinda Gates Foundation is helping Rotary meet these new goals. Other goals include expanding internationally and increasing the diversity of the organization's membership. Rotary International began admitting women to its clubs in 1989. It now counts more than 145,000 female members.

HISTORY

On February 23, 1905, lawyer Paul Harris met with three friends in an office in Chicago's Unity Building. Inspired by the fellowship and tolerance of his boyhood home in Wallingford, Vermont, Harris proposed organizing a men's club to meet periodically for the purpose of camaraderie and making business contacts. The new endeavor was organized as the Rotary Club of Chicago and had 30 members by the end of the year.

As additional clubs followed, the organization assumed its role as a civic and service organization (the installation of public comfort stations in Chicago's City Hall was one of its first projects). At the first convention of the National Association of Rotary Clubs in 1910, Harris was elected president. International clubs soon followed, and by 1921 there were Rotary clubs on six continents.

In 1932, while struggling to revive a company with financial difficulties, Rotarian Herbert Taylor devised a statement of business ethics that later became the Rotarian mantra. Taylor's "4-Way Test" consisted of the following questions: "Is it the truth? Is it fair to all concerned? Will it build goodwill and better friendships? Will it be beneficial to all concerned?"

During WWII Rotary clubs promoted war relief and peace fund efforts. Following WWII the clubs assisted in efforts to aid refugees and prisoners of war. The extent of Rotarian involvement in international issues became clear when 49 members assisted in drafting the United Nations Charter in 1945.

The first significant contributions to The Rotary Foundation followed Harris' death in 1947. These funds formed the bedrock for the foundation's programs, and in 1965 the foundation created its Matching Grants and Group Study Exchange programs. Rotary International also welcomed younger members in the 1960s by creating its Interact and Rotaract clubs in 1962 and 1968, respectively.

The largest meeting of Rotarians occurred in 1978, when almost 40,000 members attended the organization's Tokyo convention. But controversy was fast approaching the male-only organization. In 1978 a California Rotary club defied the male-only requirement and admitted two women. Claiming that the club had violated the organization's constitution, Rotary International revoked the club's charter. A lengthy court battle ensued, and a series of appeals landed the issue on the docket of the US Supreme Court. In 1987 the court ruled that the all-male requirement was discriminatory. Two years later Rotary International officially did away with its all-male status.

In the 1990s membership in Rotary clubs grew, but at a slower pace than in the organization's past. Mary Wolfenberger was appointed the organization's first female CFO in 1993 (resigned 1997). In 1998 Rotary International joined with the United Nations to launch a series of humanitarian service projects in developing areas. In 1999 the organization spearheaded events to help flood victims in North Carolina and refugees in the Balkans. In 2000 the group created a program specializing in peace and conflict resolution. Rotary International established its first Internet-based Rotary club in early 2002. Also that year the group founded the Rotary Centers for International Studies, which selects 70 scholars a year to participate in a master's-level peace studies program.

In addition to celebrating its 100th anniversary in 2005, the organization awarded grants in Sudan and Indonesia to stop polio, and assisted victims of the tsunami that struck Southeast Asia at the end of the year.

EXECUTIVES

President: Dong Kurn Lee
President-elect: John Kenny
Vice President: Monty J. Audenart
Treasurer: Bernard L. Rosen
General Secretary: Edwin H. (Ed) Futa
Auditors: Deloitte & Touche LLP

LOCATIONS

HQ: Rotary International
  1 Rotary Center, 1560 Sherman Ave.
  Evanston, IL 60201
Phone: 847-866-3000   **Fax:** 847-328-8281
Web: www.rotary.org

PRODUCTS/OPERATIONS

Selected Programs
Educational programs
  Ambassadorial Scholarships
  Grants for University Teachers
  Group Study Exchange (GSE)
  Rotary World Peace Scholarships
Humanitarian grants
  Discovery Grants
  Grants for Rotary Volunteers
  Matching Grants
  New Opportunities Grants
  Peace Program Grants
PolioPlus Program
  Polio Eradication Advocacy
  Polio Eradication Private Sector Campaign
  PolioPlus Partners

Roundy's Supermarkets

If you live in Wisconsin, you can probably find one of these grocery stores right 'round the corner. Roundy's Supermarkets owns and operates more than 150 grocery stores in Wisconsin and Minnesota under the names Pick 'n Save, Copps Food Center, and Rainbow Foods. The company also operates Metro Market, a smaller-format store concept in Milwaukee that specializes in gourmet foods and features an in-store cafe. In addition to its retail operations, Roundy's has three distribution centers that serve a small number of independent grocers, as well as its own stores. Founded in 1872 by a partnership that included Judson Roundy, the company is owned by private-equity firm Willis Stein & Partners.

Once a major food distributor in the Midwest, Roundy's has been shedding its wholesale operations to concentrate on its retail businesses. To that end, the regional grocery chain acquired five Jewel-Osco stores in the Milwaukee market from its rival SUPERVALU in early 2007 and reopened them as Pick 'n Save stores in February. Roundy's is exploring entering the Chicago market.

In 2006 Roundy's CEO Robert Mariano said he expected the company's capital structure to change in the near future. Chicago-based Willis Stein, which bought Roundy's for $750 million in 2002, has a track record of holding its acquisitions for five years. The regional supermarket chain has been reported to be on or off the block since mid-2007. Among the rumored potential buyers is Safeway, the owner of Chicago's Dominick's chain.

HISTORY

Migration from the eastern US and overseas was boosting Milwaukee's ranks when William Smith, Judson Roundy, and Sidney Hauxhurst formed grocery wholesaler Smith, Roundy & Co. in 1872. Smith left the firm in 1878 for his first of two terms as Wisconsin's governor, and William Peckham joined the enterprise, which was then renamed Roundy, Peckham & Co. Two years later Charles Dexter joined the company, by then operating in five midwestern states and running a manufacturing business.

The wholesaler became Roundy, Peckham & Dexter Co. in 1902, following the death of Hauxhurst (Roundy died in 1907). The company introduced its first private-label product — salt — in 1922. In 1929 Dexter (then 84) came up with a plan to publicize the Roundy's name by handing out cookbooks that called for the company's goods.

Roy Johnson, who joined the company in 1912, was named president near the end of the Depression. In the 1940s the wholesaler acquired smaller companies in the region. The company became Roundy's in 1952 when Roundy, Peckham & Dexter was bought by a group comprising hundreds of Wisconsin grocery retailers. Johnson remained head of the new company until his death in 1962. James Aldrich led the company for the next 11 years.

In 1970 Roundy's started Insurance Planners, which offered insurance to retailers. Vincent Little became president of the company in 1973. Two years later Roundy's began a real estate subsidiary (Ronco Realty) and opened its first Pick 'n Save Warehouse Food store.

The company expanded in the mid-1980s through the purchase of distributors. But expansion hurt profits, and dividends were suspended in 1984 and 1985. In the late 1980s several Pick 'n Save stores opened throughout Wisconsin and other midwestern states. Owners grew suspicious of Little's accounting practices and the special treatment given a Roundy's-owned store run by his son, and in 1986 they forced him out of his president and CEO positions. John Dickson replaced him.

By 1994 Pick 'n Save had vastly upgraded its image — one store sold $1,000 cognac and featured an $18,000 cappuccino machine. However, sales dropped off for the third straight year. COO Gerald Lestina was named CEO in 1995, replacing Dickson, who continued as chairman. Dickson died later that year.

Roundy's did not pay its members a dividend in 1995 as it made an effort to offset losses in Michigan and Ohio. To ease those losses, in 1997 the company closed 12 poorly performing stores in those states. A year later a fire destroyed its Evansville, Indiana, warehouse; the company rebuilt the facility in 1999. Also in 1999 Roundy's purchased three supermarkets in Indiana from Kroger and The John C. Groub Company.

The Mega Marts and Ultra Mart chains, which together operate 24 Pick 'n Save stores, primarily in Wisconsin, were acquired by Roundy's in 2000. In 2001 Roundy's launched an online grocery shopping service, called Pick 'n Save Online Shopping, in two test stores in Wisconsin (the plan was eventually scuttled). Also in 2001 the company purchased its competitor, The Copps Corporation, acquiring 21 stores in north and central Wisconsin and a wholesale business that distributes to retailers in Wisconsin and northern Michigan. Chicago-based Willis Stein & Partners bought Roundy's in 2002 for $750 million.

In 2003 Roundy's purchased the Hopkins, Minnesota-based Rainbow Foods supermarket chain for $121.5 million from Fleming Companies Inc., a Texas-based wholesaler and retailer.

Dale Riley, who had been hired to revitalize Roundy's flagging Minnesota Rainbow Food chain, resigned in 2004 after a year on the job. That year the company closed its distribution operations in Illinois.

Nash Finch bought Roundy's wholesale food distribution operations in Westville, Indiana, and Lima, Ohio, as well as two Ohio retail stores for about $225 million in 2005.

EXECUTIVES

Chairman and CEO: Robert A. (Bob) Mariano, age 59
EVP and CFO: Darren W. Karst
EVP Operations: Donald S. (Don) Rosanova
Group VP Merchandising and Procurement: Donald G. (Don) Fitzgerald
Group VP Sales and Marketing: Ronald (Ron) Cooper
Group VP Legal, Risk, and Treasury: Edward G. (Ed) Kitz
Group VP Human Resources: Colleen J. Stenholt
Group VP IT and Business Process Excellence: John W. Boyle
Group VP Retail Operations and Customer Satisfaction: Gary L. Fryda
Director Public Affairs: Vivian King
Director Communications: Lynn Guyer

LOCATIONS

HQ: Roundy's Supermarkets, Inc.
875 E. Wisconsin Ave., Milwaukee, WI 53202
Phone: 414-231-5000   **Fax:** 414-231-7939
Web: www.roundys.com

PRODUCTS/OPERATIONS

Selected Operations

Retail grocery stores
  Copps Food Center
  Pick 'n Save
  Rainbow Foods
Wholesale food distribution

COMPETITORS

ALDI
Costco Wholesale
Cub Foods
Hy-Vee
IGA
Kroger
Piggly Wiggly Midwest
Wal-Mart

HISTORICAL FINANCIALS

Company Type: Private

Income Statement				FYE: Saturday nearest December 31
	REVENUE ($ mil.)	NET INCOME ($ mil.)	NET PROFIT MARGIN	EMPLOYEES
12/08	3,900	—	—	19,000
12/07	4,000	—	—	21,000
12/06	3,620	—	—	21,000
12/05	3,700	—	—	21,000
12/04	4,777	—	—	21,855
Annual Growth	(4.9%)	—	—	(3.4%)

Revenue History

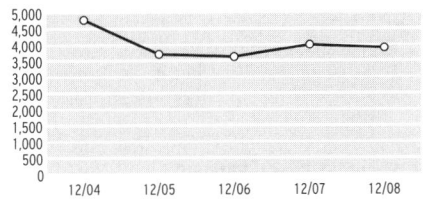

Russell Stover

For Russell Stover Candies, life really *is* a box of chocolates. The largest US maker of boxed chocolates is protecting its sweet position. And while boxed chocolates, such as the Whitman Sampler, are its, well, bread and butter, the company also sells bagged and individually wrapped hard candies and jellies. It offers sugar-free candy, including a sugarless version of Pangburn's Millionaires. Russell Stover's candies are sold by more than 70,000 retail outlets in all 50 US states and Puerto Rico, and in more than 20 other countries, including Canada and the UK. The company also operates some 45 Russell Stover Candies retail stores in the US. Co-presidents and brothers, Tom and Scott Ward, own the company.

Faced with growing competition as the big boys like The Hershey Company and Mars invaded the boxed-chocolate arena, the company countered with other products, including candy bars and bagged chocolate pieces similar to M&Ms called Color Me Candies.

It markets to younger customers through the use of licensed characters, such as Beanie Babies, in conjunction with its chocolate products. Its Whitman's division sells candy under license from Weight Watchers; the Russell Stover division offers a line of low-carb candies called Net Carb and Private Reserve upscale chocolate.

EXECUTIVES

Co-President: Scott H. Ward, age 52
Co-President and COO: Thomas S. (Tom) Ward, age 50
COO: Dan Trott
CFO: David S. (Dave) Shapland
SVP Operations: Mark Frame
SVP Logistical Operations: Garry Willenbrink
SVP Administration: Paul R. Billington
SVP Finance: Curtis Scholz
SVP Human Resources: Robinn S. Weber
SVP and Chief Marketing Officer: Mark Sesler
VP Information Systems: Stan Stohr
VP Advertising and Public Relations: John O'Hara
VP Retail: Angela Ellsworth

LOCATIONS

HQ: Russell Stover Candies Inc.
4900 Oak St., Kansas City, MO 64112
Phone: 816-842-9240   **Fax:** 816-561-4350
Web: www.russellstover.com

PRODUCTS/OPERATIONS

Selected Products

Almond Delights
Assorted Chocolates
Butterscotch Buttons
Caramels
Cherry Cordials
Chocolate Covered Nuts
Cinnamon Buttons
French Chocolate Mints
Fruit-Flavored Jellies
Lemon Sour Wedges
Millionaires
Miniature Chocolates
Mint Patties
Orange Patties
Pecan Delights
Root Beer Barrels
Sugar Free Milk Chocolate
Toasted South Seas Coconut
Toffee
Traditional S'mores Candy Bar
Truffles

COMPETITORS

Anthony-Thomas Candy	Jelly Belly Candy
Asher's Chocolates	Just Born
Barry Callebaut	Laura Secord
Betsy Ann Candies	Lindt & Sprüngli
Cadbury	Mars, Incorporated
Chase General	Nestlé
Dynamic Confections	Perfetti Van Melle
Endangered Species Chocolate	Purdy's Chocolates
Ferrero	Rocky Mountain Chocolate
Ghirardelli Chocolate	See's Candies
Godiva Chocolatier	Sherwood Brands
Guittard	The Sweet Shop USA
Harry London Candies	Tootsie Roll
Hershey	World's Finest Chocolate
	Zachary Confections

Rutgers University

Rutgers University offers undergraduate and graduate degrees from more than two dozen schools and colleges on three campuses (Camden, Newark, and New Brunswick/Piscataway). Notable alumni include actors James Gandolfini and Calista Flockhart. Rutgers has more than 50,000 students and some 2,500 faculty members. The university's 27 degree-granting units offer majors in more than 100 fields, including business and law. Founded in 1766 as Queen's College, the university was the colonies' eighth institution of higher education. The name was changed in 1825 to honor Revolutionary War hero and alumnus Colonel Henry Rutgers. Despite the name, Rutgers is the publicly funded state university system of New Jersey.

EXECUTIVES

Chair: Anthony J. DePetris
Vice Chair: Mark P. Hershhorn
Vice Chair: Robert L. Stevenson
President and Trustee: Richard L. McCormick, age 61
EVP Development and Alumni Relations and President, Rutgers University Foundation: Carol P. Herring
EVP Academic Affairs: Philip Furmanski
SVP Finance and Administration and Treasurer: Bruce C. Fehn
VP Research and Graduate and Professional Education: Michael J. Pazzani
VP Undergraduate Education: Barry V. Qualls
VP and General Counsel: Jonathan R. Alger
VP Public Affairs: Jeannine F. LaRue
VP Alumni Relations: Donna Thornton
VP Student Affairs: Gregory S. Blimling
Secretary: Leslie A. Fehrenbach
Interim VP Information Technology and CIO: Donald E. Smith
Auditors: KPMG LLP

LOCATIONS

HQ: Rutgers, The State University of New Jersey
83 Somerset St., New Brunswick, NJ 08901
Phone: 732-932-4636   **Fax:** 732-932-8060
Web: www.rutgers.edu

PRODUCTS/OPERATIONS

Selected Colleges and Schools

Camden College of Arts & Sciences
College of Nursing, Newark Campus
Cook College, New Brunswick/Piscataway Campus
Ernest Mario School of Pharmacy, New Brunswick/Piscataway Campus
Graduate School, Camden
Rutgers Business School, Newark and New Brunswick/Piscataway Campuses
School of Criminal Justice, Newark Campus
School of Management and Labor Relations, New Brunswick/Piscataway Campus

Ryan Companies US

Ryan Companies US is a commercial real estate development and property management company that offers design/build construction services and facilities management as well as financing. The group works on office, industrial, retail, hospitality, medical, public-sector, and mission-critical projects nationwide. The property management unit manages more than 10 million sq. ft. of property valued at more than $700 million. Ryan customers have included CitiGroup, Nationwide, Reader's Digest, and Target. Francis and Russell Ryan began the enterprise in 1938 as a small northern Minnesota lumber company. It is in its third generation of leadership by the Ryan family.

EXECUTIVES

CEO: James R. (Jim) Ryan
President: Patrick G. (Pat) Ryan
EVP: John P. Kelly
EVP, Minnesota Region: Mike Cairl
VP and CFO: Timothy M. (Tim) Gray
VP Development, Urban-Mixed Use, Corporate Build-to-Suit, and Hotel Development: Collin Barr
VP and Division Manager: Chuck Carefoot
VP Industrial Development, Industrial Site Selection and Planning: Tim Hennelly
VP Development, Southwest: Todd Holzer
VP Development, Des Moines Office: Douglas (Doug) Dieck
VP Development, Historic Renovation: Rick Collins

LOCATIONS

HQ: Ryan Companies US, Inc.
50 S. 10th St., Ste. 300, Minneapolis, MN 55403
Phone: 612-492-4000   **Fax:** 612-492-3000
Web: www.ryancompanies.com

PRODUCTS/OPERATIONS

Selected Services

Asset, property, and facility management
Construction
  Specialty concrete
Design/build
  Land acquisition
  Legal and code requests
  Scheduling
Development
  Brownfield projects
  Gaining government approvals
  Pre-construction
  Redevelopment
  Site renovations
  Site selection
Financing
Leasing

Selected Clients

3M
Allied Signal
AT&T
Deere & Company
Carlson Companies
EDS
Liberty Diversified Industries
Motorola
Qwest
State of Minnesota
Target
Toro Company
University of Minnesota
U.S. Bancorp
Veritas Software

COMPETITORS

Adolfson & Peterson, Inc.
Bovis Lend Lease
CB Richard Ellis
Duke Realty
Jones Lang LaSalle
Opus Corp.
Trammell Crow Company
Weis Builders

Ryerson Inc.

Ryerson has a heart of steel. A distributor and processor of metals, the company offers its customers steel products (carbon, stainless, and alloy), aluminum, brass, copper, and nickel alloys. It buys bulk metal products (in sheets, bars, and other forms) from metal producers and processes them into smaller lots to meet the specifications of its customers — machine shops, fabricators, metal producers, and machinery makers. The company also offers pipes, valves, and fittings; metal roofing, flooring, and grating products; and fabrication services. Ryerson has facilities in the US and Canada, as well as a joint venture in China. Private investment firm Platinum Equity owns Ryerson.

The company raised its ownership interests in the Chinese joint venture, called VSC Ryerson, in 2009. Ryerson had owned 40% of the JV since its formation in 2006, but the company raised that stake to 80% in hopes of accelerating growth in the country. It also divested itself of its stake in an Indian joint venture with Tata Steel, selling its 50% for about $50 million.

HISTORY

In 1893 eight partners purchased used steel-making machinery from bankrupt Chicago Steel and established Inland Steel in the Chicago Heights, Illinois, area. Eight years later the Lake Michigan Land Company offered 50 acres to any company that would spend $1 million to develop it by building an open-hearth steel mill. Inland raised the money and built Indiana Harbor Works.

Inland grew and in 1916 expanded to meet the steel demands of WWI. After the war Inland began producing rails (1922). During the Depression years, Inland turned out tinplate and steel sheet used in consumer goods. In 1931 the company, under chairman L. E. Block, built plants to make strip, sheet, and plate steel. It moved into steel warehousing in 1935, buying Joseph T. Ryerson & Son, a Chicago-based metal processor. Inland also bought Wilson & Bennett Manufacturing (later renamed Inland Steel Containers) in 1939. Inland manufactured armor during WWII, and after the war it expanded its rolling mills.

Inland became a billion-dollar company in 1966. The 1970s brought a steel boom, but when the party ended in the 1980s, the firm suffered large losses. Inland reorganized in 1986 as a holding company to separate its steel-manufacturing operations from its more profitable distribution division. The company also acquired J.M. Tull Metals from Bethlehem Steel.

Inland entered into joint ventures with Nippon Steel in 1987 and 1989 to build and operate a cold-rolling mill (I/N Tek, 60%-owned) and a coating facility (I/N Kote, 50%). Inland ceased making structural steel that year.

In 1994 the company formed Inland International and created a service center joint venture (Ryerson de Mexico) with Mexico's #1 steelmaker, Altos Hornos de Mexico. Two years later the company combined its Ryerson and Tull operations and sold the public a 13% stake in Ryerson Tull.

In 1997 Inland Steel inked a deal with Tata Steel, the flagship of India's Tata conglomerate, to process steel in that country. That year Ryerson Tull (87% owned by Inland) acquired Thypin Steel, a US distributor of carbon and stainless-steel products. Inland sold its Inland Steel Company to Ispat International for $1.4 billion in 1998.

Inland Steel Industries acquired the rest of its Ryerson Tull subsidiary in 1999 and adopted the name Ryerson Tull for the company. Also in 1999 Ryerson Tull bought Washington Specialty Metals, which operates metal service centers that specialize in stainless steel, to boost its market share over 10%. The purchase added to Ryerson Tull's expansion of the specialty metals group, the company's single-largest product area. Despite the growth, slumping steel prices industrywide and weakness in the US manufacturing sector caused Ryerson Tull's profits to plunge by 90% in 1999 compared to its previous year.

In 2000 Ryerson Tull sold its 50% interest in Ryerson de México to its partner in the Altos Hornos de México joint venture. That year Ryerson Tull closed its coil processing facility in Minnesota and a metal service center in Texas. In December 2001 the company sold its subsidiary, Ryerson Industries de Mexico, S.A. de C.V., to Grupo Collado. It also stopped operations of its Internet steel marketplace, MetalSite.

As part of the company's continuing restructuring plan, Ryerson Tull sold off its Emeryville, California, service center for about $12 million in 2002. In 2003 Ryerson Tull formed a joint venture with G. Collado S.A. de C.V. to expand its services in Mexico. The following year, Ryerson Tull acquired J&F Steel, a carbon flat-rolled processor and subsidiary of Arcelor, for approximately $55 million. In 2005 Ryerson purchased Integris Metals from joint venture partners Alcoa and BHP Billiton for $640 million. Following full integration of the acquired company, Ryerson Tull changed its name to just plain Ryerson.

Early in 2007, amid shareholder unrest, the company postponed its annual meeting, in part, to ward off a proxy fight for control of the Board. Ryerson's board of directors announced that it would review its strategic alternatives, which meant it would look for someone to buy the company. Cue private equity groups: Platinum Equity moved in on Ryerson in the middle of 2007 with its offer to take the publicly traded company private. The $2 billion selling price included assumed debt.

EXECUTIVES

CEO: Stephen E. (Steve) Makarewicz, age 61
COO: Matthias Heilmann
EVP and CFO: Terence R. (Terry) Rogers, age 48
Chief Procurement Officer: Leslie Norgren
VP Marketing: Patti Buckland
VP International; President and CEO VSC, Ryerson China Limited: Frank Muñoz
VP Finance and Treasurer: Brian Deck
President, Ryerson Canada: Michael L. Whelan
Sales Manager: Timothy Farrell
Auditors: Ernst & Young LLP

LOCATIONS

HQ: Ryerson Inc.
2621 W. 15th Place, Chicago, IL 60608
Phone: 773-762-2121   **Fax:** 773-762-0437
Web: www.ryerson.com

PRODUCTS/OPERATIONS

Selected Products

Alloy steel	Carbon steel
Aluminum	Nickel alloys
Brass and copper	Stainless steel

COMPETITORS

A. M. Castle	Olympic Steel
AK Steel Holding	O'Neal Steel
Allegheny Technologies	Reliance Steel
Blue Tee	Rio Tinto Alcan
Commercial Metals	Steel Technologies
Empire Resources	Sumitomo Metal Industries
Kreher Steel	Worthington Industries
Metals USA	

HISTORICAL FINANCIALS

Company Type: Private

Income Statement				FYE: December 31
	REVENUE ($ mil.)	NET INCOME ($ mil.)	NET PROFIT MARGIN	EMPLOYEES
12/08	5,310	27	0.5%	4,600
12/07	6,002	57	0.9%	—
12/06	5,909	72	1.2%	—
Annual Growth	(5.2%)	(38.2%)	—	—

2008 Year-End Financials

Debt ratio: 280.5%   Current ratio: —
Return on equity: —   Long-term debt ($ mil.): 965
Cash ($ mil.): —

Net Income History

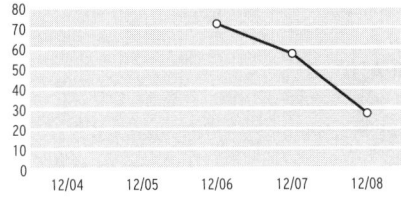

Sabre Holdings

Sabre Holdings has cut itself a huge slice of the travel reservations industry pie. Used by travel agencies worldwide to book airline tickets, rental cars, hotel reservations, and cruise/tour packages, the Sabre system is the world's #1 computerized travel reservation system. Individual consumers make travel plans using the company's Travelocity Web site (among the leaders of online travel services). The company also owns lastminute.com which gives it a significant travel presence in Europe. Sabre is owned by private equity groups Silver Lake Partners and Texas Pacific Group.

Other key brands within the Sabre network include GetThere (offers business travel reservation technology), SynXis (provider of reservation management services to thousands of hotels), and TRAMS Marketing Alliance (promotional services provider targeting the leisure travel industry).

In a joint venture with Spanish-based software developer Amadeus, Sabre provides a multichannel payment processing solution for the global travel and tourism industry called Moneydirect. Over 8,000 customers use Moneydirect to securely manage more than $2 billion annually in global travel payments.

Through Sabre Airline Solutions, the company offers software and services used by airlines and airports to help manage their operations. Adding to its Airline Solutions unit, in 2008 Sabre acquired Flight Dimensions International, which provides real-time tracking, reporting, and display of en-route aircraft. Sabre also bought EB2 International Limited, which supplies e-commerce software products and services to airlines.

To bolster its Travel Network business, in 2008 Sabre acquired BidStork, a tool travel agents can use to negotiate with hoteliers, and the travel software assets of Voxel Soluções em Informatica, which allowed Sabre to develop its business in Brazil.

Sabre, an acronym for Semi-Automated Business Research Environment, was established in 1996. AMR, American Airlines' parent company, developed Sabre and spun off its 83% stake to AMR shareholders in 2000.

EXECUTIVES

Chairman, President, and CEO:
Michael S. (Sam) Gilliland
CTO: Robert Wiseman
CIO: Barry Vandevier
EVP and CFO: Mark K. Miller
EVP Corporate Business Development:
Jeffery M. Jackson, age 53
EVP and Group President, Sabre Travel Network and Sabre Airline Solutions: Thomas (Tom) Klein
EVP and General Counsel: David A. Schwarte
EVP Human Resources: Paul G. Rostron
SVP Corporate Communications: Al Comeaux
SVP Product and Solutions Development:
Sara Garrison
SVP Government Affairs: Bruce J. Charendoff
SVP; President, Airline Products and Services, Sabre Airline Solutions: Stephen M. (Steve) Clampett
President and General Manager, Sabre Hospitality Solutions: Felix Laboy
President and CEO, Travelocity: Hugh W. Jones
President and General Manager, SynXis: Scott Alvis
SVP and Chief Marketing Officer, Sabre Travel Network and Sabre Airline Solutions: Greg Webb
SVP and Chief Marketing Officer, Travelocity:
Jeffrey (Jeff) Glueck
Director Corporate Social Responsibility:
Barbara Anderson
Auditors: Ernst & Young LLP

LOCATIONS

HQ: Sabre Holdings Corporation
3150 Sabre Dr., Southlake, TX 76092
Phone: 682-605-1000
Web: www.sabre-holdings.com

2008 Sales

	% of total
US	62
Europe	21
Other countries	17
Total	**100**

PRODUCTS/OPERATIONS

Selected Products and Services

Cubeless (internal social networking for employers)
IgoUgo.com (online travel community)
Jurni Network (offline travel agency consortium)
Moneydirect (joint venture with Amadeus, travel payment system)
Sabre Airline Solutions (technology development and consulting services)
Sabre Travel Network (sales of travel-related products and services)
SynXis (reservation management system for hotels)
Travelocity.com (online travel reservation service for individual consumers)
  lastminute.com (European online travel services)
  Travelocity Business (travel service available for corporations and business travelers)
  Zuji (online travel company for Asia/Pacific)

COMPETITORS

Amadeus IT
American Express
Carlson Companies
Expedia
Pegasus Solutions
priceline.com
Travelport

HISTORICAL FINANCIALS

Company Type: Private

Income Statement

FYE: December 31

	REVENUE ($ mil.)	NET INCOME ($ mil.)	NET PROFIT MARGIN	EMPLOYEES
12/08	2,900	—	—	9,000
12/07	3,000	—	—	9,000
Annual Growth	(3.3%)	—	—	0.0%

Revenue History

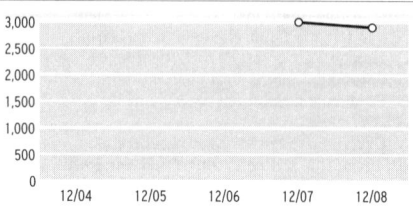

	12/04	12/05	12/06	12/07	12/08
3,000					
2,500					
2,000					
1,500					
1,000					
500					
0					

Sacramento Kings

These Kings hold court on the hardwood. The Sacramento Kings professional basketball team is one of the oldest franchises in the National Basketball Association, taking the court for the first time in New York as the Rochester Royals in 1945. Les Harrison started the team and coached the Royals to an NBA title in 1951, the only championship in the franchise's history. Afterward, the club turned vagabond and was known variously as the Cincinnati Royals, the Kansas City-Omaha Kings, and the Kansas City Kings until Gregg

Lukenbill bought the team and moved it to Sacramento, California, in 1985. Brothers Joe and Gavin Maloof bought the team in 1998 through their Maloof Sports and Entertainment.

In 2006 the City of Sacramento agreed to foot part of the bill to construct a new arena for the Kings to replace the aging ARCO Arena. The Maloof family plans to contribute money as well, but negotiations continue about where to build such an arena. Some had feared the Maloofs would move their team to Las Vegas if a new arena deal couldn't be hammered out.

After a slow start in 2008, the Kings ousted Reggie Theus as head coach, naming former assistant Kenny Natt as interim coach for the season. Theus, a former Sacramento player and coach at New Mexico State, had been hired the previous year to replace Eric Musselman. Paul Westphal was named head coach in 2009.

In addition to the Kings, the Maloof brothers own the Sacramento Monarchs of the WNBA as well as the ARCO Arena both teams share. The Maloofs, whose family fortune was built through the Joe G. Maloof & Co. liquor distributorship, also own the Palms Casino Hotel in Las Vegas.

EXECUTIVES

Co-Owner: Gavin Maloof
Co-Owner: Joe G. Maloof
President: John Thomas
President, Basketball Operations: Geoff Petrie
Head Coach: Paul Westphal
SVP Arena Services: Mark Stone
SVP Strategic Alliances: Tom Hunt
SVP Business Operations: John Rienhart
VP Marketing, Brand Development, and Monarchs Business Operations: Danette Leighton
VP Arena Programming: Mike Duncan
VP Human Resources: Donna Ruiz
VP Finance: Ruth Hill
VP Basketball Operations: Wayne Cooper
VP Business Communications: Mitch Germann
Director Player Personnel and TV Color Analyst: Jerry Reynolds
Director, Operations: Devon Shea

LOCATIONS

HQ: Sacramento Kings
  ARCO Arena, 1 Sports Pkwy.
  Sacramento, CA 95834
Phone: 916-928-0000   **Fax:** 916-928-8109
Web: www.nba.com/kings

The Sacramento Kings play at the 17,317-seat capacity ARCO Arena in Sacramento, California.

PRODUCTS/OPERATIONS

Championship Titles

NBA Championship (1951)
Western Division Champions (1951)

COMPETITORS

Golden State Warriors
Los Angeles Clippers
Los Angeles Lakers
Phoenix Suns

St. Joseph Health System

When young men (and women) heeding the advice to go west find themselves in need of health care, St. Joseph Health System can meet their needs. The health care network operates 14 hospitals, three home health agencies, clinics, hospices, and other health care delivery organizations throughout California and in eastern New Mexico and western Texas. In its primary market of California, the health system has more than 2,500 beds at nine hospitals. Its Covenant Health System unit operates in Texas and New Mexico with more than 1,100 beds in its network of some 50 primary care facilities.

The health care system was founded with the establishment of St. Joseph Hospital in Eureka, California, in 1920. St. Joseph Health System is a ministry of The Sisters of St. Joseph of Orange.

St. Joseph is already one of the largest health systems on the West Coast, but that hasn't kept it from continuing to grow. In 2009 the system added the 300-bed Mission Hospital Laguna Beach in Orange County, California, to the organization. That same year, St. Joseph's Covenant Health division also expanded by opening the Covenant Women's & Children's Hospital (the first of its type in the region).

EXECUTIVES

Chairman: Sister Katherine (Kit) Gray
President, CEO, and Director: Deborah A. Proctor
EVP and COO: Joseph (Joe) Randolph
EVP and Chief Medical Officer: Elliot B. Sternberg
EVP: Sister Jayne Helmlinger
SVP and CFO: Darrin Montalvo
SVP and CIO: Larry Stofko
SVP Communications and Marketing: Adriana P. Lynch
SVP Strategic Implementation: Annette M. Walker
SVP and Chief Administrative Officer: Susan Whittaker
SVP Governance: Sister Suzanne Sassus
SVP and Chief Human Resources Officer: William J. (Bill) Murin
SVP Physician Practice Operations: C. R. Burke
SVP Ministry Integrity: Margaret Hambleton
SVP Community Health: Azhar Qureshi
SVP and General Counsel: Shannon Dwyer
SVP Theology and Ethics: John (Jack) Glaser
VP Corporate Communications: Kevin Andrus
VP Marketing: James Hartung

LOCATIONS

HQ: St. Joseph Health System
  500 S. Main St., Ste. 1000, Orange, CA 92868
Phone: 714-347-7500   **Fax:** 714-347-7540
Web: www.stjhs.org

Selected Operations

Northern California
  Petaluma Valley Hospital
  Redwood Memorial Hospital
  Santa Rosa Memorial Hospital
  St. Joseph Home Care Network of Northern California
  St. Joseph Hospital
  Queen of the Valley Hospital
Southern California
  Mission Hospital
  St. Joseph Health System Home Health Agency
  St. Joseph Hospital
  St. Jude Medical Center
  St. Mary Medical Center
  Mission Hospital

West Texas/Eastern New Mexico
  Covenant Health System
    Covenant Children's Hospital
    Covenant Hospital Levelland
    Covenant Hospital Plainview
    Covenant Medical Center
    Covenant Medical Center — Lakeside

COMPETITORS

Adventist Health
Arrowhead Medical Center
Banner Health
Catholic Health Initiatives
Catholic Healthcare West
Cedars-Sinai Medical Center
Citrus Valley Health Partners
City of Hope
HCA
Kaiser Permanente
Loma Linda University Medical Center
Los Angeles County Health Department
Memorial Health Services
Pasadena Hospital Association
Prospect Medical
Scripps health
Sutter Health
Tenet Healthcare
Western Medical Center — Santa Ana

HISTORICAL FINANCIALS

Company Type: Not-for-profit

Income Statement				FYE: June 30
	REVENUE ($ mil.)	NET INCOME ($ mil.)	NET PROFIT MARGIN	EMPLOYEES
6/08	3,944	—	—	21,500

St. Louis Blues

With no championship title to call their own, St. Louis hockey fans have been singing the blues for a long time. St. Louis Blues Hockey Club operates a professional ice hockey team that entered the National Hockey League in 1967 but has yet to capture a Stanley Cup championship. Despite many playoff appearances, St. Louis boasts just two appearances in the final round of the NHL playoffs during back-to-back seasons in 1969 and 1970. The franchise plays host at St. Louis' Scottrade Center. An investment group led by former New York Knicks president Dave Checketts has owned the Blues since 2006.

Checketts, who was also formerly the CEO of Madison Square Garden (which oversees both the Knicks and the New York Rangers, in addition to their historic home venue), bought the team through Sports Capital Partners along with Dean Howes, Mike McCarthy, and Ken Munoz. The group, which owns Real Salt Lake of Major League Soccer, purchased the franchise and its arena from Bill Laurie and his wife Nancy (daughter of Wal-Mart founder James "Bud" Walton) for about $150 million.

Following the acquisition of the Blues, Sports Capital Partners negotiated an arena naming rights deal with local stock brokerage firm Scottrade, renaming the team's home ice Scottrade Center. It was previously called Savvis Center under a long-term marketing deal with Savvis Communications.

The Lauries, who had acquired the team in 1999, put the Blues up for sale in 2005 during the labor lockout that forced cancellation of the 2004-05 season. When hockey resumed in 2005, the Blues struggled early in the season, prompting the Lauries to sell off much of the team's talent to reduce expenses while awaiting an offer on the franchise.

Sidney Salomon, Jr., and his son Sidney Salomon III were first awarded the hockey franchise in St. Louis. The 1967 NHL expansion also saw the addition of such teams as the Los Angeles Kings, Minnesota North Stars (now the Dallas Stars), the Philadelphia Flyers, and the Pittsburgh Penguins.

EXECUTIVES

Chairman and Governor: David W. (Dave) Checketts, age 53
Vice Chairman and Alternate Governor: Michael (Mike) McCarthy
Alternate Governor: Kenneth W. Munoz
President, Hockey Operations: John Davidson
Head Coach: Andy Murray, age 58
EVP and Chief Marketing Officer: David Bullock
EVP Corporate Sponsorship and Sales: Mark Toffolo
Executive Assistant to President and General Manager: Donna Lembke
SVP Finance and Administration: Phil Siddle
SVP and General Manager: Larry Pleau, age 62
SVP Sales: Todd Lambert
SVP Business Development: Eric Stisser
VP Hockey Operations: Al MacInnis
VP Player Personnel: Doug Armstrong, age 44
VP Public Relations: Mike Caruso
Director Human Resources: Val Brinker
CEO, St. Louis Blues Enterprises: Peter C. McLoughlin, age 52

LOCATIONS

HQ: St. Louis Blues Hockey Club, L.P.
Scottrade Center, 1401 Clark Ave.
St. Louis, MO 63103
Phone: 314-622-2500   **Fax:** 314-622-2582
Web: www.stlouisblues.com

The St. Louis Blues play at 19,250-seat capacity Scottrade Center in St. Louis.

PRODUCTS/OPERATIONS

Championship Titles

Clarence S. Campbell Bowl (1969-70)
Presidents' Trophy (2000)

COMPETITORS

Chicago Blackhawks
Columbus Blue Jackets
Detroit Red Wings
Nashville Predators

Salt River Project

One of the US's largest government-owned utilities, Salt River Project (SRP) provides Phoenix with two types of currents: electric and water. Electricity comes from the Salt River Project Agricultural Improvement and Power District, a political subdivision of the State of Arizona that has a generating capacity of 8,094 MW and distributes power to about 929,000 homes and businesses. The district also sells excess power to wholesale customers. Water comes from the Salt River Valley Water Users' Association, a private firm that delivers almost 1 million acre-ft. of water per year to residents and agricultural irrigators; the association also operates dams, canals, reservoirs, and wells in its service area.

SRP's mission is to provide the basic infrastructure — water and power services — to ensure the viability of residential communities and businesses in the Salt River Valley. The company owns or has stakes in eleven major power generating plants fueled by diverse sources, including nuclear, hydro, coal, biomass, and natural gas.

In 2008 the company settled a Clean Air Act case with the federal government, agreeing to install pollution controls at its Coronado Generating Station (for some $400 million) and paying a $950,000 fine.

SRP was founded in 1903 under the Natural Reclamation Act.

EXECUTIVES

President: John M. Williams Jr.
VP: David Rousseau
Associate General Manager, Environmental, Human Resources, Land, Risk Management, and Telecom Services: Richard M. Hayslip
Corporate Treasurer: Steven J. Hulet
Assistant General Manager and CIO: Barbara Hoffnagle
Manager Public Affairs: Peter M. Hayes
Corporate Counsel: Jane D. Alfano
Associate General Manager, Water Group: John F. Sullivan
Corporate Secretary: Terrill A. Lonon
Associate General Manager, Commercial and Customer Services and CFO: Mark B. Bonsall
Associate General Manager, Power, Construction, and Engineering Services: David G. Areghini
Associate General Manager, Public and Communications Services: D. Michael Rappoport
General Manager: Richard H. Silverman
Auditors: PricewaterhouseCoopers LLP

LOCATIONS

HQ: Salt River Project
1521 N. Project Dr., Tempe, AZ 85281
Phone: 602-236-5900   **Fax:** 602-236-4423
Web: www.srpnet.com

PRODUCTS/OPERATIONS

2008 Sales

	$ mil.	% of total
Electric		
Retail	2,212.8	81
Wholesale & other electric	512.0	18
Water	14.3	1
Total	**2,739.1**	**100**

HISTORICAL FINANCIALS

Company Type: Government-owned

Income Statement

FYE: April 30

	REVENUE ($ mil.)	NET INCOME ($ mil.)	NET PROFIT MARGIN	EMPLOYEES
4/08	2,739	232	8.5%	4,431
4/07	2,631	466	17.7%	4,388
4/06	2,522	426	16.9%	4,328
4/05	2,252	363	16.1%	4,336
4/04	2,077	112	5.4%	4,300
Annual Growth	7.2%	19.9%	—	0.8%

Net Income History

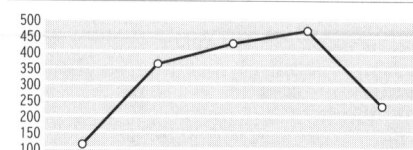

Salvation Army

Battling to provide social services, The Salvation Army is more than 4 million strong — including some 3.4 million registered volunteers. Its Christian faith-based programs assist alcoholics, drug addicts, the homeless, the elderly, prison inmates, people in crisis, and the unemployed through offerings, such as community centers, housing facilities, and rehabilitation centers. It also provides disaster-relief services. Overall, the organization serves more than 35 million people a year and provides in excess of 60 million meals. The US organization is a unit of the London-based Salvation Army, which oversees activities in more than 100 countries. US operations began in 1880.

The organization's structure incorporates both church and military themes. In the US, it is organized into four regional commands. Its 3,600-plus US officers, who are also ordained ministers, are expected to wear their uniforms at all times and to work full-time for The Salvation Army. They receive no salary; instead, they are provided with room and board and given a limited stipend. Reporting to the officers of the US organization are more than 107,000 soldiers, or lay members. Before joining the organization as a soldier, one must agree to avoid gambling, debt, and profanity, as well as alcohol, tobacco, and recreational drugs.

In addition, The Salvation Army counts about 413,000 US members, or adherents — people who consider the organization to be their church.

Ringing bells at Christmas is just one of the ways The Salvation Army raises money. Besides cash dropped into red kettles, the group receives donations in response to direct mail campaigns; gifts from companies, foundations, and individuals; and fees from government agencies for providing social services under contract.

HISTORY

William Booth (1829-1912) started preaching the gospel as a Wesleyan Methodist in the UK, but the church expelled him because he insisted on preaching outside and to everyone, including the poor. In 1865 he moved to the slums of London's East End and attracted large crowds with his volatile sermons. Opposition to his message of universal salvation for drunks, thieves, prostitutes, and gamblers often caused riots. In fact, the first women in the organization wore bonnets designed with a dual purpose in mind — warmth and protection from flying objects.

At a meeting in 1878, a sign was used referring to the "Salvation Army." Booth adopted the reference as both the name and the style of his organization. Members became soldiers, evangelists were officers, and Booth was referred to as "General." Prayers became knee drills, and contributions were called cartridges.

The Salvation Army marched across the Atlantic to the US in 1880, led by seven women and one man. Women have always played an active role in the Salvation Army, both as officers and soldiers. Booth's wife, Catherine Mumford, was a leading suffragette, and Booth advocated equal rights for women.

In 1891 a crab pot was placed on a San Francisco street to collect donations, with a sign reading "Keep the Pot Boiling." The idea led to the Salvation Army's Christmas kettle program.

During WWI the organization became famous for the doughnuts that it served the doughboys fighting on the front lines. After some internal dissension, The Salvation Army took its only public political stance in 1928 with the endorsement of Herbert Hoover for his support of Prohibition during his presidential campaign. The charity opened its first home for alcoholics in 1939, in Detroit.

After WWII The Salvation Army began using such radio and TV programs as *Heartbeat Theater* and *Army of Stars* to spread its message.

Over the years The Salvation Army has provided assistance to victims of hurricanes, floods, and earthquakes. Volunteers rendered almost 70,000 service hours in the aftermath of the Oklahoma City bombing in 1995, counseling more than 1,600 victims and family members, helping with funeral arrangements, and providing food, clothing, and travel assistance. Indicative of the organization's readiness and extensive reach, its volunteers were helping victims in Guam within minutes of the 1997 Korean Air plane crash. The Salvation Army was quickly on the scene after a

Jonesboro, Arkansas, shooting incident in 1998 when four students and one teacher were killed by fellow students. Late that year the organization received the largest donation in its history — $80 million from Joan Kroc, wife of McDonald's co-founder Ray Kroc.

In 2000 the organization initiated a major reform by allowing officers to marry outside the ranks. After the September 11 attacks in 2001, The Salvation Army provided assistance to rescue workers and families affected by the tragedy through its Disaster Relief Fund.

Joan Kroc left The Salvation Army $1.5 billion in 2003. The money was earmarked for construction of community centers modeled on one in San Diego named for her and her husband. By 2006 plans were underway to build community centers in Atlanta, Honolulu, Phoenix, and San Francisco.

EXECUTIVES

Chairman National Advisory Board: Robert J. (Rob) Pace, age 47
Commissioner (National Commander): Israel L. Gaither, age 65
Commissioner (National President of the Women's Ministries): Eva D. Gaither
Commissioner (Southern Territory): Maxwell Feener
Commissioner (Western Territory): Philip (Phil) Swyers
General (International Director): Shaw Clifton
Commissioner (Eastern Territory): Lawrence R. Moretz
Commissioner (Central Territory): Kenneth Baillie
Director Territorial Public Relations: Andrew Burditt
National Chief Secretary: David Jeffrey

LOCATIONS

HQ: The Salvation Army
615 Slaters Ln., Alexandria, VA 22313
Phone: 703-684-5500　　**Fax:** 703-684-3478
Web: www.salvationarmyusa.org

PRODUCTS/OPERATIONS

2008 Income

	% of total
Contributions	36
Sales to the public	12
Donations in kind	10
Government funds	9
Program service fees	4
United Way & similar funding organizations	2
Other income	27
Total	**100**

Selected Services

Alcohol and drug treatment centers
Clinics and hospitals
Convalescent homes
Counseling
Crisis counseling
Disaster services
Food distribution centers
Handicapped housing
Homeless shelters
Human trafficking awareness and eradication
Institutes for the blind
Leprosy clinics
Military canteens and hostels
Nurseries and day care centers
Occupational centers
Prison ministry
Probation housing
Refugee centers
Science and trade schools
Student housing
Welfare aid

Sammons Enterprises

Sammons Enterprises summons its revenues from several sources. The diversified holding company's operations include the Sammons Financial Group, which offers life insurance and financial services, and its Briggs Equipment business, which offers heavy equipment sales and rentals. Its insurance and financial group includes Midland National Life Insurance, North American Company for Life and Health Insurance, and Sammons Annuity Group. Sammons Enterprises also owns The Grove Park Inn Resort in Asheville, North Carolina. The company's list of partially owned holdings runs the range from real estate investments to oilfield suppliers. It prefers to invest in companies that have strong employee-ownership programs.

Sammons Enterprises is large enough to operate its own equity fund, SRI Ventures, LLC, which invests in real estate. It holds assets nearing $40 billion.

The company holds an interest in North American Technologies Group's Tie Tek unit, which supplies railroad ties.

Sammons Enterprises continues to grow and is eyeing the life sciences and health care industries as possible expansion areas.

The late Charles Sammons, an orphan who became a self-made billionaire philanthropist (despite never attending college), founded the company in 1962 to consolidate his already varied holdings. His estate still owns the company, and his widow, Elaine Sammons, served as chairman until her death in 2009.

EXECUTIVES

Chairman: Elaine D. Sammons
CEO: Robert W. (Bob) Korba, age 64
President: Dave Sams
SVP Organizational Development, Sammons Financial Group: Brian P. Rohr
SVP, Secretary, and General Counsel: Heather Kreager
SVP and CFO: Darron Ash
SVP Human Resources, Sammons Financial Group: C. Michael Haley
SVP Operations, Sammons Financial Group: Robert R. Tekolste
VP and Treasurer: Pamela (Pam) Doeppe
VP, Sammons Realty Corporation, SRI Ventures LLC: Mark Brandenburg
VP Organization Development: Mike Costello
Director General: Fernando Malvido
Auditors: PricewaterhouseCoopers LLP

LOCATIONS

HQ: Sammons Enterprises, Inc.
5949 Sherry Ln., Ste. 1900, Dallas, TX 75225
Phone: 214-210-5000   **Fax:** 214-210-5099
Web: www.sammonsenterprises.com

PRODUCTS/OPERATIONS

Selected Subsidiaries

Wholly Owned
Briggs Construction Equipment, Inc.
Midland National Life Insurance Company
North American Company for Life and Health Insurance Company
Sammons Annuity Group
Sammons Corporate Markets Group
SRI Ventures LLC
The Grove Park Inn Resort & Spa

Partially Owned
iSECUREtrac
Ocular LCD, Inc.

COMPETITORS

CNH Global
Deere
MetLife
NES Rentals
New York Life
Principal Financial
Prudential
United Rentals

HISTORICAL FINANCIALS

Company Type: Private

Income Statement				FYE: December 31
	REVENUE ($ mil.)	NET INCOME ($ mil.)	NET PROFIT MARGIN	EMPLOYEES
12/08	2,800	—	—	4,000
12/07	3,375	—	—	4,300
12/06	2,560	—	—	4,500
12/05	2,400	—	—	3,491
12/04	2,200	—	—	3,290
Annual Growth	6.2%	—	—	5.0%

Revenue History

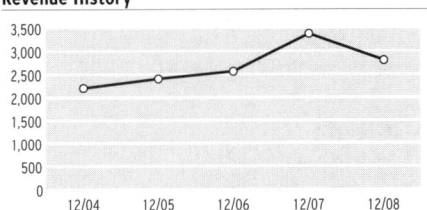

San Antonio Spurs

South Central Texas basketball fans hardly need to be prodded to root for this team. The San Antonio Spurs professional basketball franchise was formed by Bob Folsom in 1967 as the Dallas Chaparrals of the American Basketball Association. The team moved to San Antonio in 1973 and joined the National Basketball Association when the leagues merged in 1976. The Spurs boast four NBA championship titles, its last in 2007. Peter Holt, whose family owns statewide Caterpillar dealership Holt CAT, has controlled the team since 1996. He also owns the San Antonio Silver Stars of the WNBA.

San Antonio won its fourth NBA title by sweeping the Cleveland Cavaliers in four games. A perennial playoff contender, the team's later efforts to reach the final round again have been thwarted by the Los Angeles Lakers (in 2008) and the Dallas Mavericks (2009).

The Spurs home arena changed its name from SBC Center to AT&T Center in 2006 after its corporate sponsor, SBC Communications, changed its name to AT&T. The company acquired the naming rights under a 20-year, $40 million marketing deal. The publicly financed $180 million facility was built in 2002.

EXECUTIVES

Chairman and CEO: Peter M. Holt
EVP Business Operations: Russ Bookbinder
EVP Finance and Corporate Development: Rick A. Pych
SVP and General Manager: R. C. Buford
SVP Broadcasting: Lawrence Payne
SVP Marketing and Sales, Spurs Sports & Entertainment: Frank Miceli
Head Coach: Gregg Popovich, age 60
VP Finance: Lori Warren
VP and Assistant General Manager: Dennis Lindsey
VP Community Relations: Alison Fox
VP Human Resources: Paula Winslow
VP Sales: Joe Clark
VP Marketing: Bruce Guthrie
Director Basketball Operations: Rob Hennigan
Director of Pro Player Personnel: Dell Demps
Auditors: Ernst & Young

LOCATIONS

HQ: San Antonio Spurs LLC
1 AT&T Center Pkwy., San Antonio, TX 78219
Phone: 210-444-5000   **Fax:** 210-444-5100
Web: www.nba.com/spurs

The San Antonio Spurs play at the 18,797-seat capacity AT&T Center in San Antonio.

PRODUCTS/OPERATIONS

Championship Titles
NBA Champions (1999, 2003, 2005, 2007)
Western Conference Champions (1999, 2003, 2005, 2007)

COMPETITORS

Dallas Mavericks
Houston Rockets
Memphis Grizzlies
New Orleans Hornets

San Jose Sharks

Here's a team hockey fans can sink their teeth into. The San Jose Sharks professional hockey franchise represents the San Francisco Bay Area in the National Hockey League, having joined as an expansion team in 1991. Despite some success in reaching the playoffs the past several years, fans are still waiting for an appearance in the Stanley Cup finals. The team plays host at HP Pavilion, affectionately known as "The Shark Tank." George and Gordon Gund, former owners of the Cleveland Cavaliers, were originally awarded the NHL franchise; Silicon Valley Sports & Entertainment, an investment group led by veteran sports executive Greg Jamison, has owned the team since 2002.

Despite playing far from the more hockey-fertile regions in the North, the Sharks have built a strong following in the Bay Area thanks to the team's success in reaching the playoffs in recent years. The 2008-09 season saw the team capture first place in its division for the second consecutive year. The feat also marked San Jose's fourth straight post-season appearance since the lockout that scuttled the 2004-05 season.

The team and its home arena are operated through Silicon Valley Sports & Entertainment (SVS&E), a marketing and facilities management business that also operates Sharks Ice (the team's practice rink), the Worcester Sharks of the American Hockey League, and the San Jose Stealth professional lacrosse team. SVS&E also handles marketing and merchandising for the Sharks.

Jamison previously worked for the Dallas Mavericks and Indiana Pacers before joining the Sharks organization in 1993. He eventually rose to become president of the team before leading the $80 million buyout. The Gund family, which also owned the Minnesota Stars (now the Dallas Stars) continues to own a small stake in the franchise.

EXECUTIVES

President and CEO: Greg Jamison, age 58
EVP Business Operations: Malcolm Bordelon, age 50
EVP and General Manager, Sharks: Doug Wilson
EVP and General Manager, HP Pavilion at San Jose: Jim Goddard, age 60
EVP and CFO: Charles (Charlie) Faas, age 49
EVP and General Counsel: Don Gralnek, age 63
Head Coach: Todd McLellan
VP Finance: Ken Caveney, age 41
VP and Assistant General Manager, Sharks: Wayne Thomas, age 61
VP Sales and Marketing: Kent Russell, age 51
VP Corporate Partnerships: Eric Mastalir
Senior Director Communications: Ken Arnold
Director Human Resources: Cathy Chandler
Director Information Technology: Uy Ut
Controller: Stephanie Reitz

LOCATIONS

HQ: San Jose Sharks, LLC
525 W. Santa Clara St., San Jose, CA 95113
Phone: 408-287-7070 **Fax:** 408-999-5797
Web: www.sjsharks.com

The San Jose Sharks play at the 17,496-seat capacity HP Pavilion in San Jose, California.

PRODUCTS/OPERATIONS

Selected Trophies
Presidents' Trophy (2009)

COMPETITORS

Anaheim Ducks
Dallas Stars
Los Angeles Kings
Phoenix Coyotes

Sandia National Laboratories

Sandia stands for national security. Established in 1945 as part of the Manhattan Project, Sandia National Laboratories performs research and development related to national security and defense. Its focus is nuclear weapons systems research, but the lab also performs nonproliferation assessments, infrastructure assurance, and other research and development on such topics as energy and environmental technologies and economic competitiveness. Sandia National Laboratory's recent duties have expanded to combat terrorism, aid homeland security, and support US military in Afghanistan and Iraq. A part of the US Department of Energy, Sandia is operated by Lockheed Martin. Its annual budget is about $2.2 billion.

Sandia National Laboratories has facilities in Albuquerque, New Mexico, and Livermore, California; a rocket launch range in Kauai, Hawaii;

and additional operations in New Mexico, Nevada, Texas, and Washington, DC.

There has been discussion by the Obama administration about moving Sandia and its sister lab, Los Alamos, into the Defense Department as a budget cutting move. New Mexico's Congressional delegation strongly opposes the move and vowed to fight the effort.

EXECUTIVES

President and Laboratories Director: Thomas O. (Tom) Hunter
EVP, Deputy Laboratories Director, and COO: Alton D. (Al) Romig Jr.
VP Business Operations and CFO: Matthew J. O'Brien
EVP and Deputy Laboratories Director for Integrated Technologies and Systems: Joan B. Woodard, age 56
EVP and Deputy Laboratories Director for the Nuclear Weapons Program; VP, California Laboratory: Paul J. Hommert
VP, General Counsel, and Corporate Secretary: Elizabeth D. (Becky) Krauss
VP and Principal Scientist: Gerold (Gerry) Yonas
Group Manager, Public Relations and Communications: Michael D. DeWitte
VP Weapons Engineering and Product Realization: Carolyne Hart
VP Integrated Security and Chief Security Officer: Richard J. Detry
Director Human Resources: Karen G. Gillings

LOCATIONS

HQ: Sandia National Laboratories
1515 Eubank Blvd. SE, Albuquerque, NM 87123
Phone: 505-845-0011 **Fax:** 505-844-1120
Web: www.sandia.gov

PRODUCTS/OPERATIONS

Selected Operations
Defense Systems and Assessments
  C3ISR (Command, Control, Communication, Intelligence, Surveillance and Reconnaissance)
  Integrated Military Systems for Missile Defense and Strike Systems
  Complex Adaptive Systems (e.g., Robotics)
  System-Level Modeling and Simulation
  Homeland Defense and Force Protection
  Science and Technology Products
Energy and Infrastructure Assurance
  Enhance the safety of energy and other critical infrastructures
Homeland Security
Nonproliferation
  Supporting treaty verification with other countries
  Creating new technologies for aircraft and satellites to detect proliferation activities
  Working with the former Soviet Union to safely manage nuclear materials from dismantled weapons systems
  Enhancing nuclear, chemical, and biological weapon proliferation detection capabilities
  Developing physical security technologies, including entry-control devices and electronic monitoring
Nuclear Weapons
  Enhance the capabilities of radiation-hardened microelectronics to address national security issues
  Develop advanced simulation and computing capabilities to model the entire nuclear weapon lifecycle
  Deliver advanced robotics systems to monitor proliferation activities, clean up hazardous sites, and disassemble old munitions
  Improve the methods and practices used to support product delivery
  Incorporate pulsed power technology into defense applications
  Develop distributed information systems for the nuclear weapons complex

Science, Technology, and Engineering
  Aerospace Engineering
  BioScience and Technology
  Combustion, Chemical, and Plasma Sciences
  Data Instrumentation / Telemetry
  Directed Energy
  Electromechanical Components / Firing Sets
  Energy System and Environmental Characterization
  Environmental Remediation Systems
  Gas Transfer Systems
  GeoSciences
  Intelligence Technologies and Assessments
  Pulsed Power
  Radars
  Radiation Effects Science
  Remote Sensing and Satellite Systems
  Stockpile Surety and Analysis
  Stockpile Surveillance
  Systems Data Exploitation and Information Technologies
  System Performance Assessment
  Test Ranges / Facilities / Readiness
  Transportation Materials Management
  Weapon Engineering / Design

COMPETITORS

Argonne National Laboratory

SAS Institute

Don't talk back to this company about business intelligence. SAS (pronounced "sass"), the world's largest privately held software company, is a leader in the market for business analytics, data warehousing, and data mining software used to gather, manage, and analyze enormous amounts of corporate information. Clients such as Air France and the US Department of Defense use its software to find patterns in customer data, manage resources, and target new business. Founded in 1976, SAS also offers industry-specific integrated software and support packages. CEO James Goodnight owns about two-thirds of the company; co-founder and EVP John Sall owns the remainder.

SAS has expanded its core business intelligence product line with such offerings as financial management software and marketing automation and analysis applications. The company has also worked closely with its more than 600 strategic partners such as Teradata and Accenture to integrate its software with their offerings. SAS serves more than 45,000 customers (including 92 of the top 100 *FORTUNE* Global 500 companies) from about 400 offices worldwide.

In 2008 the company acquired IDeaS Revenue Optimization, a provider of revenue management software for the hospitality industry. That year SAS also purchased Teragram, a text mining and natural language processing technology provider.

Known for its tight-knit community, SAS offers its employees perks including on-site child-care centers, cafeterias, exercise facilities, walking trails, and a health care center.

EXECUTIVES

CEO: James H. (Jim) Goodnight
EVP, SAS Americas: Carl Farrell
EVP: John P. Sall
EVP EMEA and Asia/Pacific: Mikael Hagström
SVP and CFO: Don Parker
SVP and SAS Fellow: Allan Russell

SVP and Chief Marketing Officer: Jim Davis
SVP and CTO: Keith V. Collins
VP Human Resources: Jennifer Mann, age 38
VP and Chief Accounting Officer: David Davis
VP and General Counsel: John Boswell
VP Information Technology and CIO: Suzanne Gordon
VP Operations, Asia/Pacific: David Hughes
VP Alliances and Product Marketing: Russ Cobb
Corporate Public Relations: Beverly Brown

LOCATIONS

HQ: SAS Institute Inc.
100 SAS Campus Dr., Cary, NC 27513
Phone: 919-677-8000   **Fax:** 919-677-4444
Web: www.sas.com

2008 Sales

	% of total
EMEA	45
Americas	43
Asia/Pacific	12
Total	**100**

PRODUCTS/OPERATIONS

2008 Sales by Industry

	% of total
Financial services	42
Government	15
Services	11
Health & life sciences	8
Communications	7
Other industries	17
Total	**100**

Selected Software

Customer relationship management
  Credit analysis
  Customer interaction management
  Customer retention
  Customer segmentation management
Data analysis
Data mining
Data warehousing
E-commerce
Enterprise performance management
  Balanced score card reporting
Experimental design
Financial management
  Activity-based management
  Forecasting
  Planning and budgeting
Human resources management
Information technology systems management
  Cost management
  Resource optimization
  Security management
Project planning and management
Quality improvement
  Warranty analysis
Risk management
Statistical analysis

COMPETITORS

Actuate
AngossSoftware
CA, Inc.
Cognos
Fair Isaac
IBM
Information Builders
Kalido
Lawson Software
Microsoft
MicroStrategy
Oracle
SAP
SPSS
Sybase
Teradata

HISTORICAL FINANCIALS

Company Type: Private

Income Statement

FYE: December 31

	REVENUE ($ mil.)	NET INCOME ($ mil.)	NET PROFIT MARGIN	EMPLOYEES
12/08	2,260	—	—	11,019
12/07	2,150	—	—	10,737
12/06	1,900	—	—	10,027
12/05	1,680	—	—	10,000
12/04	1,530	—	—	9,528
Annual Growth	**10.2%**	**—**	**—**	**3.7%**

Revenue History

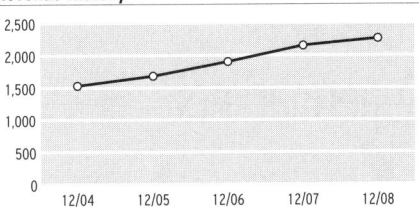

Sauder Woodworking

Sauder Woodworking takes the fear out of furniture and makes furniture for the God-fearing. The company is the top US maker of ready-to-assemble (RTA) furniture (ahead of Bush Industries and O'Sullivan Industries) and, through Sauder Manufacturing, is also a top manufacturer of church furniture and institutional seating. The company's RTA products include such items as computer workstations, desks, entertainment centers, and wardrobes. Sauder's products are sold through retailers in more than 70 countries. Sauder acquired Progressive Furniture, which makes fully assembled furniture, in 2001. The company was founded in 1934 by Erie Sauder and is still family owned and operated.

From its struggling rival O'Sullivan, Sauder strategically purchased the company's intellectual property, which included O'Sullivan's name, patents, and certain product drawings. As part of the deal, which was inked in 2007, Sauder also inherited O'Sullivan's licensing agreement to make Coleman-branded garage storage products.

After its O'Sullivan deal, Sauder in 2008 phased out domestic production of laminate and veneer bedroom pieces at its Progressive division. Due to stale sales, the company also exited its upscale Royal Patina line, which it bought in 2005. In 2008 Sauder whittled down its number of SKUs from approximately 1,100 products to about 700 to reduce costs.

Sauder, in recent years, has been quick to realign its companies or exit underperforming ones for improved efficiencies. Sauder merged the sales and marketing operations for two of its business units — Studio RTA and Sauder RTA — in 2006 to create operational efficiencies. Sauder also sold its subsidiary Archbold Container, maker of corrugated packaging and displays, to Green Bay Packaging in mid-2005.

EXECUTIVES

Chairman: Maynard Sauder, age 76
President and CEO: Kevin J. Sauder, age 48
EVP Marketing and Sales: John D. Yoder
EVP Finance and CFO: Arnold Moshier
EVP Operations: Garrett Tinsman
VP Human Resources: Steve Webster
VP Engineering: Dan Sauder
VP Supply Chain Management: David K. Yoder
Design Team Head: Doug Krieger
Marketing Director: Michael (Mike) Lambright
President, Progressive Furniture: Dan Kendrick
President, Studio RTA: Bob Hughes

LOCATIONS

HQ: Sauder Woodworking Co.
502 Middle St., Archbold, OH 43502
Phone: 419-446-2711   **Fax:** 419-446-3692
Web: www.sauder.com

PRODUCTS/OPERATIONS

Selected Furniture Products

Bedroom
Entertainment
Kitchen/Utility
Office/Computer
Shelving/Storage

Selected Subsidiaries

Sauder Manufacturing Company (furniture for houses of worship, colleges, universities, and health care facilities)
Studio RTA (imports and distributes home office, entertainment, and art and hobby RTA furniture)
Progressive Furniture (makes and imports traditional solid wood, veneered, and laminate furniture)
Historic Sauder Village (history museum for the founding settlers of northwestern Ohio)

COMPETITORS

Bassett Furniture	Haworth, Inc.
Bush Industries	Herman Miller
Chromcraft Revington	HNI
Cost Plus	IKEA
DMI Furniture	Pier 1 Imports
Dorel Industries	Stanley Furniture
Furniture Brands	Steelcase

HISTORICAL FINANCIALS

Company Type: Private

Income Statement

FYE: December 31

	REVENUE ($ mil.)	NET INCOME ($ mil.)	NET PROFIT MARGIN	EMPLOYEES
12/08	570	—	—	2,200
12/07	700	—	—	2,700
12/06	700	—	—	3,400
12/05	730	—	—	3,400
12/04	750	—	—	4,000
Annual Growth	**(6.6%)**	**—**	**—**	**(13.9%)**

Revenue History

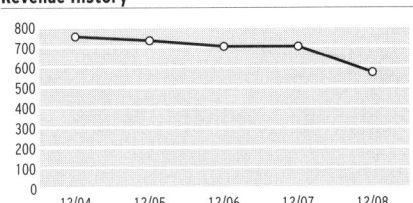

SavaSeniorCare

SavaSeniorCare operates about 190 skilled nursing and assisted living facilities in some two dozen states. The company provides health care, rehabilitation, physical therapy, and daily living assistance, as well as help with dementia and respiratory and intravenous therapy. SavaSeniorCare owns, leases, or subleases the facilities through third parties (including Mariner Health Care). The company's SavaSeniorCare Administrative Services unit provides its properties with support services, including human resources, financial services, IT, compliance, legal, and risk management.

EXECUTIVES

Chairman: Leonard Grunstein, age 57
President: Tony Ogolsby
EVP Human Resources and Risk Management:
L. Scott Bardowell
EVP Audit and Compliance: Brent A. Snelgrove
EVP and General Counsel: Stefano M. Miele
SVP and CIO: Julie D. Purcell
VP and Controller: Robert M. Lyle
VP Real Estate and Associate General Counsel:
Annaliese (Nan) Impink

LOCATIONS

HQ: SavaSeniorCare, LLC
1 Ravinia Dr., Ste. 1400, Atlanta, GA 30346
Phone: 770-829-5100   **Fax:** 770-393-8054
Web: www.savaseniorcare.com

COMPETITORS

Advocat
Brookdale Senior Living
Catholic Healthcare Partners
Extendicare REIT
Golden Horizons
HCA
Kindred Healthcare
Life Care Centers
Manor Care
National HealthCare
Omnicare
RehabCare
Signature HealthCARE
Skilled Healthcare Group
Sun Healthcare
Sunrise Senior Living
Tenet Healthcare

HISTORICAL FINANCIALS

Company Type: Private

Income Statement				FYE: December 31
	ESTIMATED REVENUE ($ mil.)	NET INCOME ($ mil.)	NET PROFIT MARGIN	EMPLOYEES
12/07	1,270	—	—	22,000
12/06	1,200	—	—	23,368
12/05	1,160	—	—	23,673
Annual Growth	4.6%	—	—	(3.6%)

Revenue History

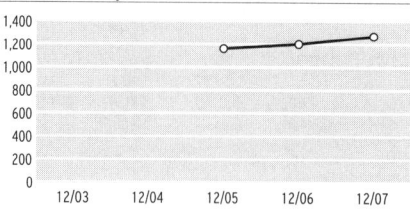

Save Mart Supermarkets

Save Mart Supermarkets is an even bigger wheel in the California grocery business now that it has doubled in size as a result of its acquisition of 132 Albertsons supermarkets in northern California and Nevada. A sponsor of the NASCAR Toyota/Save Mart 350, the company now operates about 250 grocery stores in northern and central California and Nevada. About half of the locations house in-store pharmacies. Its supermarkets and warehouse stores operate under the Save Mart Supermarkets, S-Mart, Lucky, and FoodMaxx names. Save Mart also owns distributor SMART Refrigerated Transport. CEO Robert Piccinini owns most of Save Mart, which was founded in 1952 by his father, Mike Piccinini, and uncle, Nick Tocco.

The grocery chain converted most of the Albertsons stores it acquired in February 2007 to the Save Mart banner. (The remaining former Albertsons stores took on the resurrected Lucky Stores banner and FoodMaxx name.) Along with the supermarkets, Save Mart also purchased two distribution centers and division offices in California from Albertsons. The deal transformed Save Mart into the second-largest California-based grocer, after Safeway. The Albertsons purchase also added more than 75 in-store pharmacies to Save Mart's operations.

After a big year in 2007, Save Mart opened only three new stores in 2008, all with pharmacies.

Save Mart's distribution arm SMART Refrigerated Transport trucks dry groceries, frozen foods, ice, and novelties to the company's own stores and those operated by other retailers. The grocery chain also owns and operates Yosemite Wholesale Warehouse in Merced and Yosemite Advertising in Modesto. It is also a voting partner in Super Store Industries, which owns and operates a distribution center, dairy, and ice cream plant.

The chain has been trying out different formats, including an upscale prototype with its own coffeehouse and expanded offerings of ethnic and organic foods and its popular private-label salad mix line, Fresh Favorites.

Save Mart grew its sales and store count in 2003 with the acquisition of 25 Food 4 Less stores from bankrupt grocery distributor Fleming Companies, which were quickly converted to the FoodMaxx banner. The grocery chain has also been adding to its real estate holdings with the purchase of two shopping centers in Fresno and Visalia, California, in mid-2004 and early 2005, and the purchase of four stores from rival Ralphs Grocery Co.

EXECUTIVES

Chairman and CEO: Robert M. (Bob) Piccinini
President and COO: Steve Junqueiro
CFO: Steve Ackerman
Chief Administrative Officer: Mike Silveira
VP Center Store: Robert Dyer
VP Real Estate: Ray Cipolla
VP Corporate Communication and Development:
Wendy Kennedy
VP Distribution: Kathy McKenna
VP Marketing: John Kelly
VP Fresh: Rick Smith
VP Strategic Development: Cecil Russell
VP Operations, Coastal Region: Woody Hunter
VP Food Maxx: Frank Capps
VP Engineering: Ray Agah
Director Community Affairs and Public Relations:
Alicia Rockwell

LOCATIONS

HQ: Save Mart Supermarkets
1800 Standiford Ave., Modesto, CA 95350
Phone: 209-577-1600   **Fax:** 209-577-3857
Web: www.savemart.com

PRODUCTS/OPERATIONS

2009 Stores

	No.
Save Mart	124
Lucky	75
FoodMaxx	44
S-Mart Foods	7
Total	**250**

COMPETITORS

Costco Wholesale
Raley's
Ralphs Grocery
Rite Aid
Safeway
Target
Trader Joe's
Vons
Wal-Mart

HISTORICAL FINANCIALS

Company Type: Private

Income Statement				FYE: December 31
	REVENUE ($ mil.)	NET INCOME ($ mil.)	NET PROFIT MARGIN	EMPLOYEES
12/08	5,100	—	—	21,000
12/07	5,100	—	—	23,000
12/06	5,000	—	—	25,000
12/05	2,500	—	—	10,500
12/04	2,194	—	—	9,417
Annual Growth	23.5%	—	—	22.2%

Revenue History

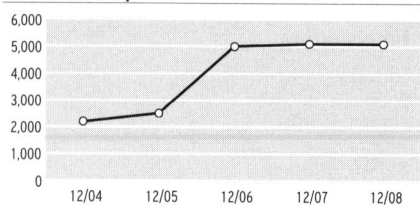

Sbarro, Inc.

Sbarro lends an Italian flavor to that great American innovation, the shopping mall. The company operates and franchises nearly 1,100 cafeteria-style Italian-food stands across the US and more than 40 other countries. Serving pizza, pasta entrees, and salads, Sbarro's units are typically found in high-traffic locations, such as malls, airports, and toll-road rest areas. The company owns and operates more than 500 locations, while the rest of the chain is operated by franchisees. Sbarro also sells its sauces through select locations. The late Gennaro Sbarro, with his wife Carmela, started the business in 1954; the Sbarro family sold the company to private equity firm MidOcean Partners in 2007.

In addition to its mall-based quick service restaurants, Sbarro has about 80 free-standing locations. It has also been branching out into the full-service dining sector through a small number of Carmela's of Brooklyn casual-dining units.

Sbarro has been expanding its chain mostly through additional franchising agreements. During 2008 it added more than 50 new locations. Meanwhile, the company has been focused on maintaining expense controls due to the rising cost of food ingredients and slower consumer spending during the recession.

The Sbarro family originally took the company private for almost $390 million in 1999. They sold the business to MidOcean for about $450 million.

EXECUTIVES

Chairman, President, and CEO: Peter J. Beaudrault, age 54, $583,000 total compensation
President, Business Development and Corporate VP: Anthony J. Missano, age 50, $374,000 total compensation
President, Franchise Development: John Brisco
VP and CFO: Daniel G. (Dan) Montgomery, age 44
CIO: Richard Guariglia
SVP Operations: Randy Jones
SVP Operations: Jim Kelbaugh
VP Operations, Domestic Franchise: Mike Dumelle
VP Operations, International Franchise: Stephen O'Connor
VP Operations, Southeast Region: Jim McCann
VP Operations, Southwest Region: Tony Martin
VP Franchise Development and Support Services: William J. Vetter
General Counsel and Secretary: Stuart M. Steinberg, age 52, $5,000 total compensation
Auditors: PricewaterhouseCoopers LLP

LOCATIONS

HQ: Sbarro, Inc.
401 Broadhollow Rd., Melville, NY 11747
Phone: 631-715-4100   **Fax:** 631-715-4197
Web: www.sbarro.com

2008 Locations

	No.
US	
New York	74
California	72
Florida	64
Ohio	41
Illinois	36
Pennsylvania	34
Virginia	29
Massachusetts	25
Michigan	24
Texas	24
New Jersey	23
Minnesota	22
Georgia	21
Nevada	21
North Carolina	21
Maryland	19
Washington	15
Connecticut	14
Missouri	14
Tennesee	12
Kentucky	11
Arizona	10
Wisconsin	10
South Carolina	8
Alabama	7
Colorado	7
Iowa	7
Louisiana	7
Oklahoma	7
Oregon	7
Utah	7
Arkansas	6
Indiana	6
Washington, DC	6
Other states	41
International	57
Total	**809**

PRODUCTS/OPERATIONS

2008 Sales

	$ mil.	% of total
Restaurants	343.3	96
Franchising	15.8	4
Total	**359.1**	**100**

2008 Locations

	No.
Franchised	566
Company-owned	509
Joint venture	16
Total	**1,091**

COMPETITORS

AFC Enterprises
Arby's
Burger King
California Pizza Kitchen
Chick-fil-A
Church's Chicken
CiCi Enterprises
CKE Restaurants
Dairy Queen
Fazoli's
Galardi Group
Kahala
McDonald's
Nathan's Famous
Noble Roman's
Panda Restaurant Group
Pizza Inn
Quiznos
Subway
Uno Restaurants
Wendy's International, Inc.
YUM!

HISTORICAL FINANCIALS

Company Type: Private

Income Statement

FYE: Sunday nearest December 31

	REVENUE ($ mil.)	NET INCOME ($ mil.)	NET PROFIT MARGIN	EMPLOYEES
12/08	359	(91)	—	5,500
12/07	359	(30)	—	5,400
12/06	350	10	2.8%	8,000
12/05	349	1	0.4%	5,500
12/04	349	(4)	—	6,500
Annual Growth	**0.7%**	**—**	**—**	**(4.1%)**

2008 Year-End Financials

Debt ratio: 782.9%
Return on equity: —
Cash ($ mil.): —
Current ratio: —
Long-term debt ($ mil.): 346

Net Income History

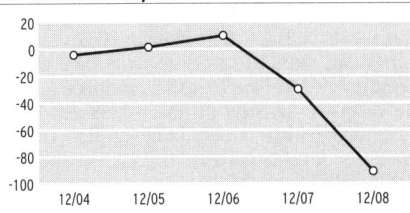

S.C. Johnson

S.C. Johnson & Son helped to replace the flyswatter with the spray can. The company is one of the world's largest makers of consumer chemical products, including Glade, Mr. Muscle, Raid, Pledge, Brise, Drano, Fantastik, Kabbikiller, OFF!, Scrubbing Bubbles, Saran, Shout, Vanish, Windex, and Ziploc. S.C. Johnson peddles its products in more than 110 countries. The founder's great-grandson and once one of the richest men in the US, Samuel Johnson, died in 2004. His immediate family owns about 60% of S.C. Johnson; descendants of the founder's daughter own about 40%. Chairman Dr. Fisk Johnson assumed the title of CEO when president, CEO, and director Bill Perez left for Nike in late 2004.

Many of S.C. Johnson's products have been and remain top sellers in their markets. However, after seeing its Edge and Skintimate shave preparation brands lose market share to rival P&G's Gillette, the company in June 2009 sold the two brands to Energizer, which already competes with P&G in the razors business with its Schick-Wilkinson Sword unit.

The company's commercial products division (Johnson Wax Professional and Johnson Polymer) was spun off as a private company owned by the Johnson family.

In recent years, consumers have avoided use of some plastic storage containers for fear that they contain biphenyl A (BPA). S.C. Johnson in September 2008 attempted to head off speculation and possible reduced sales of its plastic wraps by announcing that its Ziploc and Saran products do not contain BPA.

The company boasts operations in more than 70 countries, including Canada, Australia, Costa

Rica, Mexico, and Puerto Rico. For three years since 2006 *Working Mother* magazine has recognized S.C. Johnson as one of the 100 best companies for working mothers.

HISTORY

Samuel C. Johnson, a carpenter whose customers were as interested in his floor wax as in his parquet floors, founded S.C. Johnson in Racine, Wisconsin, in 1886. Forsaking carpentry, Johnson began to manufacture floor care products. The company, named S.C. Johnson & Son in 1906, began establishing subsidiaries worldwide in 1914. By the time Johnson's son and successor, Herbert Johnson, died in 1928, annual sales were $5 million. Herbert Jr. and his sister, Henrietta Lewis, received 60% and 40% of the firm, respectively. The original section of S.C. Johnson's headquarters, designed by Frank Lloyd Wright and called "the greatest piece of 20th-century architecture" in the US, was finished in 1939.

In 1954, with $45 million in annual sales, Herbert Jr.'s son Samuel Curtis Johnson joined the company as new products director. Two years later it introduced Raid, the first water-based insecticide, and soon thereafter, OFF! insect repellent. Each became a market leader. The company unsuccessfully attempted to diversify into paint, chemicals, and lawn care during the 1950s and 1960s. The home care products segment prospered, however, with the introduction of Pledge aerosol furniture polish and Glade aerosol air freshener.

After Herbert Jr. suffered a stroke in 1965, Samuel became president. In 1975 the firm banned the use of the chlorofluorocarbons (CFCs) in its products, three years before the US government banned CFCs. Samuel started a recreational products division that was bought by the Johnson family in 1986. That company went public in 1987 as Johnson Worldwide Associates, with the family retaining control.

The company launched Edge shaving gel and Agree hair products in the 1970s but had few products as successful in the 1980s. It moved into real estate with Johnson Wax Development (JWD) in the 1970s, but sold JWD's assets in the late 1980s.

S. Curtis Johnson, Samuel's son, joined the company in 1983. In 1986 S.C. Johnson bought Bugs Burger Bug Killers, moving into commercial pest control; in 1990 it entered into an agreement with Mycogen to develop biological pesticides for household use.

In 1993 it bought Drackett, bringing Drano and Windex to its product roster along with increased competition from heavyweights such as Procter & Gamble and Clorox. That year S.C. Johnson sold the Agree and Halsa lines to DEP. In 1996 it launched a line of water-soluble pouches for cleaning products that allow work to be done without touching hazardous chemicals. President William Perez became CEO the next year (and left in late 2004 to become president, CEO, and director of Nike, Inc.).

S.C. Johnson bought Dow Chemical's Dow-Brands unit, maker of bathroom cleaner (Dow), plastic bags (Ziploc), and plastic wrap (Saran Wrap), for $1.2 billion in 1998. It then sold off other Dow brands (cleaners Spray 'N Wash, Glass Plus, Yes, and Vivid) to the UK's Reckitt & Colman to settle antitrust issues.

A year later S.C. Johnson sold its skin care line, including Aveeno, to health care products maker Johnson & Johnson, and spun off its commercial products unit as a private firm owned by the Johnson family. Boosting its home cleaning line, in 1999 it introduced two new products: AllerCare (for dust mite control) and Pledge Grab-It (electrostatically charged cleaning sheets).

In 2000 S.C. Johnson pulled its AllerCare carpet powder and allergen spray from store shelves after some consumers had negative reactions to the fragrance additive in the products. That year H. Fisk Johnson succeeded his father (who became chairman emeritus) as chairman.

In 2001 the company was fined $950,000 for selling banned Raid Max Roach Bait traps in New York after agreeing to pull them from store shelves. Also that year S.C. Johnson's Japanese subsidiary agreed to buy that country's leading drain cleaner brand, Pipe Unish, from Unicharm.

In October 2002 the company acquired the household insecticides unit of German drug giant Bayer Group for $734 million. The following year S.C. Johnson invested in Karamchand Appliances Private Limited, which owns India's second-leading insect control brand *AllOut*.

Chairman emeritus Samuel C. Johnson died in May 2004 at the age of 76. Chairman Dr. Fisk Johnson became CEO of the company again in late 2004.

In June 2009 S. C. Johnson sold its Edge and Skintimate pre-shave brands to Energizer Holdings for an aggregate purchase price of $275 million.

EXECUTIVES

Chairman and CEO: H. Fisk Johnson
EVP and CFO: W. Lee McCollum, age 59
EVP, Worldwide Human Resources: Gayle P. Kosterman
EVP, Worldwide Corporate and Environmental Affairs: Jane M. Hutterly
SVP, Worldwide Manufacturing and Procurement: Darcy D. Massey
SVP, New Products: Gregory J. (Greg) Barron
VP, Marketing Services: Patricia Penman
VP Global Environmental and Safety Actions: Scott Johnson
VP, North American Sales: Darwin Lewis
VP and General Manager, Mexico and Central America: Eduardo Ortiz-Tirado
VP Global Public Affairs and Communications: Kelly M. Semrau
VP and Group Managing Director, Europe: Filippo Meroni
VP and Corporate Treasurer: William H. Van Lopik
VP, Human Resources Asia Pacific: Jeffrey M. (Jeff) Waller
VP and CIO: Mark H. Eckhardt
President, North America: David L. (Dave) May

LOCATIONS

HQ: S.C. Johnson & Son, Inc.
1525 Howe St., Racine, WI 53403
Phone: 262-260-2000   **Fax:** 262-260-6004
Web: www.scjohnson.com

PRODUCTS/OPERATIONS

Selected Products and Brands

Air Care
  Air freshener (Glade, Glade Duet)
Home Cleaning
  Bathroom/drain (Drano, Scrubbing Bubbles, Vanish)
  Cleaners (Fantastik, Windex, Windex Multi-Surface Cleaner with Vinegar)
  Floor care (Pledge, Johnson)
  Furniture care (Pledge, Pledge Wipes, Pledge Grab-it Dry Dusting Mitts)
  Laundry/carpet care (Shout)

Home Storage
  Plastic bags (Ziploc)
  Plastic wrap (Handi-Wrap, Saran Wrap)
Insect Control
  Insecticides (Raid, Raid Max)
  Repellents (Deep Woods OFF!, OFF!, OFF! Mosquito Lamp, OFF! Skintastic)

COMPETITORS

3M
Alticor
Blyth
Church & Dwight
Clorox
Colgate-Palmolive
Dow Chemical
DuPont
Henkel Corp.
IWP International
Procter & Gamble
Reckitt Benckiser
Shaklee
Unilever
Yankee Candle

HISTORICAL FINANCIALS

Company Type: Private

Income Statement

FYE: Friday nearest June 30

	REVENUE ($ mil.)	NET INCOME ($ mil.)	NET PROFIT MARGIN	EMPLOYEES
6/08	8,000	—	—	12,000
6/07	8,750	—	—	12,000
6/06	7,000	—	—	12,000
6/05	6,500	—	—	12,000
6/04	6,500	—	—	12,000
Annual Growth	5.3%	—	—	0.0%

Revenue History

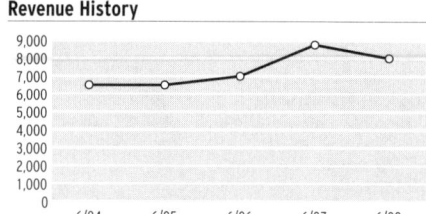

SCAN Health Plan

With a goal of allowing seniors to live independently in their own homes longer, SCAN Health Plan provides Medicare Advantage HMO health insurance to more than 110,000 seniors in seven counties of southern California. In addition to medical and prescription drug coverage, the not-for-profit organization offers transportation services for doctor visits, personal care assistance, caregiver relief, and home meal delivery, among other services. The company partnered with health care management company INSPIRIS to provide similar services to SCAN members in the Phoenix, Arizona, market. SCAN Health Plan was founded by seniors as the Senior Care Action Network in 1977.

SCAN has a network of more than 135 hospitals and 14,000 local physicians. That network expanded in 2009 when St. Joseph Health System and St. Jude Medical Center joined the group, adding nearly 1,000 additional primary care physicians to the SCAN network.

Also in 2009 SCAN Health Plan joined with six Arizona health insurers to form the Arizona Association of Health Plans. The group's aim is to increase access to health care to the state's residents.

EXECUTIVES

Chairperson: Colleen A. Cain
CEO: David (Dave) Schmidt
CFO: Dennis Eder
CIO: Merlin L. (Roy) Swackhamer, age 59
SVP Health Care Services: Deborah A. Miller
SVP Network Management: Elizabeth S. Russell
SVP and Compliance Officer:
  Rebecca Mauritson Learner
SVP Human Resources: Marc J. Radner
SVP Business Development: Henry W. (Hank) Osowski
SVP Service Operations/Marketing: Sherry L. Stanislaw
SVP, General Counsel, and Secretary:
  Douglas A. (Doug) Jaques
SVP Sales/Membership: Roger L. Lapp
Chief Medical Officer: Timothy (Tim) Schwab
Director Public and Government Affairs: Thomas Dey
President and CEO, The SCAN Foundation:
  Bruce A. Chernof
President, SCAN Health Plan Arizona:
  Thomas (Tom) Lescault

LOCATIONS

HQ: SCAN Health Plan
  3800 Kilroy Airport Way, Ste. 100
  Long Beach, CA 90806
Phone: 562-989-5100   **Fax:** 562-989-5200
Web: www.scanhealthplan.com

Selected Counties and Locations

Kern
Los Angeles
Long Beach
Orange
Riverside
San Bernardino
San Diego
Ventura

COMPETITORS

Aetna
Anthem Blue Cross
CIGNA
Health Net of California
Humana
Kaiser Foundation Health Plan
Molina Healthcare
UnitedHealth Group

HISTORICAL FINANCIALS
Company Type: Not-for-profit

Income Statement				FYE: December 31
	REVENUE ($ mil.)	NET INCOME ($ mil.)	NET PROFIT MARGIN	EMPLOYEES
12/08	1,563	—	—	857

Scarborough Research

Scarborough Research provides marketing research studies for 80 local markets that delve into more than 2,000 consumer research topics such as lifestyle, home improvement, demographics, and travel. The company's more than 3,500 clients include the media, ad agencies, and sports teams. Its specialized services include Hispanic market research and custom analytics (helping clients better read customer data and make decisions based on that data). The company is a joint venture of marketing research firms Arbitron and The Nielsen Company. Scarborough Research was founded in 1975 and was originally developed as a newspaper measurement tool.

EXECUTIVES

President and CEO: Robert L. (Bob) Cohen
EVP and Director Sales: Steve Seraita
EVP Research: Gregg Linder
SVP Human Resources: Debbie Morisie
SVP Print and Internet Sales: Gary A. Meo
SVP Television: Cheryl Greenblatt
SVP Radio, Sports Marketing, and Outdoor Media:
  Howard Goldberg
VP Advertiser Marketing Services: Alisa Joseph
VP Marketing and Communications: Deirdre McFarland
VP and CFO: David Reifer
VP Cable and Out-of-Home Services: Carol Edwards

LOCATIONS

HQ: Scarborough Research
  770 Broadway, New York, NY 10003
Phone: 646-654-8400   **Fax:** 646-654-8450
Web: www.scarborough.com

COMPETITORS

Edison Media Research	Kantar Group
GfK NOP	Mediamark
Iconoculture	ORC
International	TNS Custom
Demographics	Zogby

HISTORICAL FINANCIALS
Company Type: Joint venture

Income Statement				FYE: December 31
	REVENUE ($ mil.)	NET INCOME ($ mil.)	NET PROFIT MARGIN	EMPLOYEES
12/08	69	—	—	—
12/07	65	—	—	—
12/06	61	—	—	—
12/05	56	—	—	—
12/04	55	—	—	—
Annual Growth	6.0%	—	—	—

Revenue History

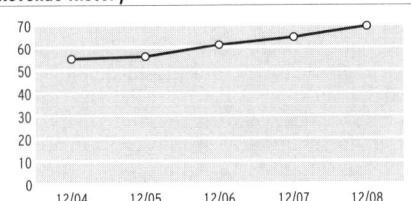

Schneider National

If you think that's the Great Pumpkin behind you on the highway, look again. With its signature bright-orange fleet of about 15,300 tractors and 38,800 trailers, Schneider National is one of the largest truckload carriers in the US. The company's Schneider National Carriers unit provides truckload service throughout North America, including one-way van, dedicated, expedited, regional, and bulk freight transportation. The company also offers intermodal service, in which it arranges the transportation of freight by multiple methods, such as road and rail. It has a fleet of some 8,200 intermodal containers. Subsidiary Schneider Logistics offers supply chain management services.

Schneider National announced in February 2009 that its revenues grew in 2008 — unusual news as transportation companies battled against mounting losses caused by unprecedented heights in fuel prices followed by an economic downturn. Demand for freight has slipped dramatically and Schneider National isn't immune. To hedge against future losses, the company is suspending pay increases, deferring funding for retirement plans and 401(k) matching, requiring its 6,600 office workers to take an unpaid furlough for one week, and cancelling holiday pay for drivers.

Not content to rely on its signature nationwide truckload business, in 2008 Schneider National began offering regional freight hauling in the western US and then the south-central US. It hopes the new business will be able to take advantage of increased demand for short-haul transportation services. In addition, Schneider National has been working to strengthen its intermodal business, and it has entered China's domestic logistics services market.

Schneider National is known for being an early adopter of new transportation technology — it was one of the first carriers to link all its trucks by two-way satellite. The company has been recognized for a pioneering trailer-tracking system that uses wireless networks, global positioning units, and sensors in order to keep closer track of shipments.

Chairman and former CEO Don Schneider, son of the company's founder, is among its shareholders, but he doesn't disclose how much of the company he owns.

HISTORY

A. J. "Al" Schneider bought a truck in 1935 with money earned from selling the family car. He drove the truck for three years, got another, and then leased them both to another firm. Becoming general manager of Bins Transfer & Storage in 1938, Schneider bought the company that year and changed the name to Schneider Transport & Storage. In 1944 Schneider stopped storing household goods and continued as an intrastate carrier in Wisconsin through the 1950s, transporting food and household goods. The Interstate Commerce Commission granted its first interstate license to Schneider in 1958.

Al's son Donald joined the company as general manager in 1961, and in 1962 the company dropped "Storage" from its name to become Schneider Transport. The 1960s also saw the first of many acquisitions. Donald became CEO in 1973, overseeing more acquisitions and the creation of Schneider National as a holding company for the organization. Donald also saw to the installation of computerized control systems, the first of many technical innovations Schneider would use in its trucks.

With the Motor Carrier Act's passage in 1980, restrictions eased and interstate shipping opened up. Schneider (and its competitors) saw the sky as the limit and founded Schneider Communications, a long-distance provider, in 1982. Eager to escape the Teamsters' thrall but choosing not to go head-to-head with the powerful union, Schneider formed Schneider National Carriers as a nonunion company out of three 1985 acquisitions, which signed on new recruits, while Schneider Transport remained unionized. Schneider focused on guaranteeing on-time delivery in the deregulated market: In 1988 Schneider became the first trucking company to install a satellite-tracking system in its trucks, setting the industry standard.

Schneider further expanded its services in the 1990s, starting with Schneider Specialized Services for carrying difficult items. It moved into Canada and Mexico in 1991. By 1993 some two-thirds of *FORTUNE* 500 companies used Schneider, and the company formed Schneider Logistics to help companies streamline their shipping operations. It sold Schneider Communications to Frontier Communications in 1995. The company moved into Europe in 1997.

It continued buying other US trucking firms, including Landstar Poole and Builder's Transport (both in 1998), mainly to acquire their drivers for its expanding fleet. In 1999 Schneider acquired the glass-transportation business of A. J. Metler & Rigging.

In 2000 Schneider acquired the freight payment services of Tranzact Systems and further boosted its e-commerce offerings via alliances with ContractorHub.com and Paperloop.com. The company also made plans to spin off Schneider Logistics and sell part of it to the public, but unfavorable market conditions put the IPO on hold. Schneider added expedited services to its portfolio in 2001 to provide time-definite delivery in Canada, Mexico, and the US.

Christopher Lofgren's promotion to president and CEO in 2002 made him the first person outside the founding family to lead Schneider National.

The company enhanced its intermodal business in 2005 when Schneider Logistics acquired American Port Services, a provider of transloading services — moving freight from one mode of transportation to another — at several key US ports.

EXECUTIVES

Chairman: Donald J. (Don) Schneider, age 69
Vice Chairman and Secretary: Thomas A. (Tom) Gannon
President and CEO: Christopher B. (Chris) Lofgren, age 50
EVP and CIO: Judith A. (Judy) Lemke
EVP Sales, Marketing, and Customer Service: Steve Matheys
SVP Enterprise Sales: Dan Van Alstine
VP Safety and Driver Training: Don Osterberg
VP Enterprise Recruiting: Rob Reich
VP Sales Regional Client Group: Greg Sanders
VP Technology Services: Paul Mueller
VP Human Resources: Tim Fliss
VP International, Schneider Logistics: John Ferguson
VP and General Manager, Schneider Regional: Marc Rogers
VP Commercial Operations, Intermodal: Jim Van Hefty
Manager Public Relations: Janet Bonkowski
President, Schneider Logistics: Thomas I. (Tom) Escott
President, Intermodal: Bill Matheson
President, Truckload: Mark Rourke

LOCATIONS

HQ: Schneider National, Inc.
   3101 S. Packerland Dr., Green Bay, WI 54306
Phone: 920-592-2000   **Fax:** 920-592-3063
Web: www.schneider.com

COMPETITORS

Burlington Northern	Norfolk Southern
C.H. Robinson	Pacer Transportation
Con-way Inc.	Penske
Crete Carrier	Ryder System
CSX	Swift Transportation
DHL	Union Pacific
Expeditors	UPS
J.B. Hunt	U.S. Xpress
Landstar System	Werner Enterprises
Menlo Worldwide	

HISTORICAL FINANCIALS

Company Type: Private

Income Statement
FYE: December 31

	REVENUE ($ mil.)	NET INCOME ($ mil.)	NET PROFIT MARGIN	EMPLOYEES
12/08	3,700	—	—	21,400
12/07	3,400	—	—	22,216
12/06	3,700	—	—	21,600
12/05	3,500	—	—	20,000
12/04	3,200	—	—	20,000
Annual Growth	**3.7%**	**—**	**—**	**1.7%**

Revenue History

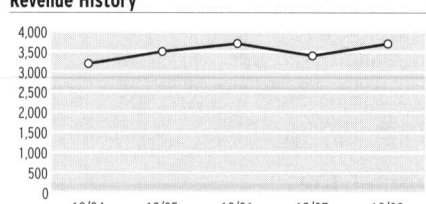

Schnuck Markets

If you'll meet me in St. Louis, then chances are there'll be a Schnucks in sight. The region's largest food chain, Schnuck Markets operates 100-plus stores, mostly in the St. Louis area, but also in other parts of Missouri and in Illinois, Indiana, Iowa, Mississippi, Tennessee, and Wisconsin. All stores offer a full line of groceries, and most have pharmacies, video rental outlets, in-store banking, and florist shops. Although most stores operate under the Schnucks banner, the company also runs about a half a dozen Logli supermarkets in Illinois and Wisconsin, and a specialty pharmacy. Founded in 1939, the company is owned by the Schnuck family and run by CEO Scott Schnuck and president and COO Todd Schnuck.

While Schnuck Markets does most of its business in the suburbs, the grocery chain in August 2009 opened a new urban prototype store — named Culinaria — in the heart of downtown St. Louis. Measuring a modest 23,000 sq. ft., the store is about a third of the size of a traditional Schnuck supermarket. Culinaria is a full-service grocery store with specialty food items and a coffee bar and wine shop. If all goes well, the company may open Culinaria stores in other urban markets. The company is also tinkering with its traditional store format in suburban Des Peres, Missouri, where it has opened a new replacement store that includes a cooking school, an expanded selection of prepared foods for in-store dining or take out, and other innovations. While the two new stores opened in the second half of 2009, overall the company is cutting back on new store development during the economic downturn and is instead focusing on improving operations across its 100-plus stores.

In recent years, the grocery chain has been focused on improving its pricing to fend off rival Wal-Mart Stores, whose supercenters have grown to be the leading seller of groceries in the US. To that end, Schnuck Markets has lowered prices on some 10,000 items in many of its stores in the St. Louis and Springfield, Illinois, markets, adopting an everyday-low-price strategy associated with Wal-Mart. Also in response to Wal-Mart, which operates about 55 supercenters in Schnuck's markets, Schnuck pharmacies have begun offering free supplies of some antibiotics to customers. Schnuck's announcement came about a year after Wal-Mart began selling about 150 generic medications for $4.

In July 2009 Schnuck Markets reorganized its top management with Scott Schnuck turning over responsibility for day-to-day stores operations to his younger brother Todd, who added the COO title to his president's duties. Scott has been CEO since 2006 when longtime chief executive Craig Schnuck, another brother, stepped aside to oversee growth planning and government affairs.

EXECUTIVES

Chairman and CEO: Scott C. Schnuck, age 59
President and COO: Todd R. Schnuck, age 49
CFO: David Bell, age 42
Chief Talent and Strategy Officer: Richard (Rick) Frede, age 56
VP, Human Resources: Janice Rhodes
VP, Bakery: Bill Mihu
VP, Shopping Center Development: Mark Schnuck
VP, Produce: Michael (Mike) O'Brien
VP, Information Technology: Mark Zimmerman
VP, Logistics: Steve Carroll, age 53
VP, Center Store: Robert (Bob) Watson
VP, Supermarket Development: David G. (Dave) Fontana, age 54
VP, Merchandising: Lori Caster
VP, Store Operations: Ryan J. Cuba, age 41
Secretary and General Counsel: Mary Moorkamp, age 47
Director, Information Technology: Jim Mueller
Director, Communications: Lori Willis

LOCATIONS

HQ: Schnuck Markets, Inc.
   11420 Lackland Rd., St. Louis, MO 63146
Phone: 314-994-9900   **Fax:** 314-994-4465
Web: www.schnucks.com

COMPETITORS

7-Eleven
Associated Wholesale Grocers
CVS Caremark
Dierbergs Markets
Dominick's
Hy-Vee
Kmart
Kroger
Meijer
SUPERVALU
Walgreen
Wal-Mart

HISTORICAL FINANCIALS
Company Type: Private

Income Statement				FYE: October 31
	REVENUE ($ mil.)	NET INCOME ($ mil.)	NET PROFIT MARGIN	EMPLOYEES
10/08	2,500	—	—	15,000
10/07	2,500	—	—	15,500
10/06	2,400	—	—	15,000
10/05	2,300	—	—	15,000
10/04	2,200	—	—	16,000
Annual Growth	3.2%	—	—	(1.6%)

Revenue History

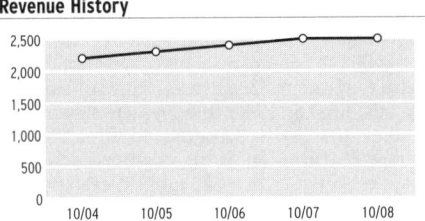

Schottenstein Stores

Schottenstein Stores is where the Schottenstein family keeps its retail holdings. The investment firm owns interests in a host of retail businesses, including a majority holding in Retail Ventures (the operator of some 300 DSW shoe warehouse stores). Schottenstein Stores also owns Value City Furniture (about 130 superstores located primarily in the eastern US), about 15% of casual clothing chain American Eagle Outfitters (some 1,100 mall stores in the US and Canada), and retail liquidator SB Capital Group, as well as 50 shopping centers. Chairman and retail magnate Jay Schottenstein is the largest shareholder in American Eagle, DSW, and Retail Ventures.

Retail Ventures unloaded off-price retailing veteran Filene's Basement to an affiliate of liquidation company Buxbaum Group in April 2009. The holding company, which didn't record any net proceeds from the sale, said the discount retailer faced "significant" liquidity issues as a result of its plan to shutter 11 of its 36 Filene's Basement department stores. (Filene's Basement was eventually plucked out of Chapter 11 bankruptcy protection by rival Syms Corp in mid-2009.) Retail Ventures also sold its majority stake in its money-losing Value City Department Stores chain to VCHI Acquisition Co. in January 2008 after putting it up for sale in late 2006. With 113 locations, Value City Department Stores accounted for nearly 45% of Retail Ventures' sales. Value City Department Stores filed for Chapter 11 bankruptcy protection later in the year and is liquidating.

In August 2008 Schottenstein purchased Steuben Glass from Corning. As part of the deal, Corning retained a 19.9% stake in the upscale glassmaker, which was renamed Steuben Glass LLC. Schottenstein acquired the ailing crystal maker to breathe life back into the longtime company and pair it with other luxury brands in the Schottenstein Luxury Group, a growing portfolio of brands that includes luxe handbag maker Judith Leiber and the Italian fashion brand Shiró. Schottenstein Stores, best known for its discount brands, began its foray into the luxury market in 2007.

The Schottenstein retailing empire's DSW (formerly Shonac Corp.) retail shoe business went public in mid-2005. The Schottensteins still control fast-growing DSW through Retail Ventures, which owns 93% of the footwear retailer.

The SB Capital Group provides retail consulting services and purchases retail assets, including inventory, equipment, receivables and real property. It operates worldwide with offices in New York, Ohio, Canada, and the UK.

The company launched American Signature Furniture stores in 2002 and is expanding throughout the Southeast. American Signature operates about two dozen midpriced to high-end furniture stores in Florida, Georgia, Maryland, Tennessee, and Virginia. The company also owns five factories, where most of its stores' merchandise is made.

Schottenstein Stores is part of a consortium of investors led by Cerberus Capital Management that acquired some 660 stores, distribution centers, and offices from the Albertsons chain of supermarkets and drugstores in mid-2006.

EXECUTIVES

Chairman and CEO; Chairman and CEO, American Eagle Stores; CEO, Value City Furniture; Chairman and CEO, DSW: Jay L. Schottenstein, age 54
Vice Chairman and CFO: James B. Flaws
Chairman, Retail Ventures; SVP: Jeffry D. Swanson
SVP Real Estate: Michael S. Schiff
VP Real Estate: Jeffrey M. (Jeff) Schottenstein, age 68
VP Human Resources: Shelley Zajic
VP Corporate Affairs: Michael Broidy
VP Construction and Store Planning: Mark Wright
General Counsel: Irwin A. Bain
President, SB Capital Group: David Bernstein
President, Value City Department Stores, Value City Furniture, and American Signature Home: David W. Thompson
President and CEO, Retail Ventures: Heywood Wilansky, age 61
Managing Director, SB Capital Group: Robert Raskin
Managing Director, SB Capital Europe: Bob Marsh

LOCATIONS

HQ: Schottenstein Stores Corporation
1800 Moler Rd., Columbus, OH 43207
Phone: 614-221-9200   **Fax:** 614-449-0403

COMPETITORS

Abercrombie & Fitch
Ashley Furniture
Brown Shoe
Collective Brands
Ethan Allen
Fitz and Floyd
The Gap
Gordon Brothers Group
J. C. Penney
Kmart
La-Z-Boy
Lenox Corp
Liquidation World
Macy's
Oneida
Rooms To Go
Royal Doulton
Sears
Shoe Carnival
Swarovski
Target
Tiffany & Co.
TJX Companies
Wal-Mart

HISTORICAL FINANCIALS
Company Type: Private

Income Statement				FYE: December 31
	ESTIMATED REVENUE ($ mil.)	NET INCOME ($ mil.)	NET PROFIT MARGIN	EMPLOYEES
12/07	1,300	—	—	8,050
12/06	1,230	—	—	7,600
Annual Growth	5.7%	—	—	5.9%

Revenue History

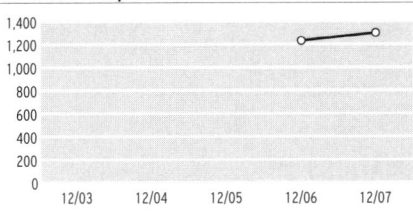

Schreiber Foods

If you order cheese on your burger at the drive-thru, you might well get a taste of a product made by Schreiber Foods. The company is a major supplier of the cheese used on hamburgers by US fast-food restaurants, along with K-12 schools, colleges and universities, and health care providers. Schreiber produces primarily private-label processed and natural cheeses, and dairy ingredients for food retailers, retailers, foodservice distributors, and other food manufacturers. It does offer a few of its brands for retail sale, including American Heritage and Cooper. The company has bought up smaller cheese operations to expand its geographic reach and is now a leading US private-label cream cheese maker.

In addition to cheese and dairy ingredients, the company offers its customers such services as category management, risk management, vendor managed inventory (VMI), packaging and design, and supply chain management.

Schreiber Foods has cheese production facilities in Arizona, Georgia, Missouri, Nebraska, Pennsylvania, Tennessee, Texas, Utah, and Wisconsin, as well as in Brazil, China, Germany, India, and Mexico. It counts among its customers Subway, Safeway, Weight Watchers, and Wal-Mart.

CEO David Pozniak retired in 2008; he was replaced by Mike Haddad, who had been president and COO of Schreiber Foods Sales since 2006. (Pozniak died in May 2009.)

Schreiber owns and operates Capri Packaging, which offers flexible film structures and packaging solutions. It also owns Green Bay Machinery, a manufacturer of extruders and other equipment for processing cheese.

Founded in 1945, Schreiber opted in 1999 to transfer its ownership into an employee stock-ownership plan.

EXECUTIVES

Chairman: Larry P. Ferguson
CEO and Director: Mike Haddad
SVP Foodservice Sales: John O'Connor
SVP Supply Chain Management: Steve Shelley
VP Education and Community Relations:
  Nancy Armbrust
VP Retail: Staci Kring
VP Engineering: Mark W. Peterson
VP Finance and CFO: Matt Mueller
VP Information Services and CIO: Tom Andreoli
VP and General Counsel: Jerry Smyth
VP International Operations: Helmut Felder
VP Industrial & Regulatory Affairs: Deborah A. Van Dyk
President, Yogurt Division: Dan LaValley
Director, Retail Branded Deli-Specialty:
  Robert Willardson
Product Management: Karen Lancelle
Treasurer: Bob Pruess

LOCATIONS

HQ: Schreiber Foods Inc.
  425 Pine St., Green Bay, WI 54301
Phone: 920-437-7601   **Fax:** 920-437-1617
Web: www.schreiberfoods.com

PRODUCTS/OPERATIONS

Selected Cheese Brands and Products

Foodservice
  Clearfield (natural and processed cheese)
  LaFeria (natural and processed cheese)
  Lov-It (butter blends)
  Menu (imitation and substitute cheese)
  Raskas (cream cheese)
  Redy-Cut (natural and processed cheese)
  School Choice (natural and processed cheese)
  Schreiber (natural, processed, and cream cheese)
Retail
  American Heritage (natural, processed, specialty, and
    imitation cheese)
  Cooper (natural and processed cheese)
  Old York (natural and processed cheese)
  Cuba (natural and processed cheese)

Selected Ingredient Products

Condensed skim milk
Cream cheese
Imitation cheese formulas
Processed cheese formulas
Substitute cheese formulas
Sweetened condensed milk

Selected Subsidiaries

Capri Packaging (packaging films)
Green Bay Machinery Co., Inc. (cheese slicing and
  wrapping equipment)

COMPETITORS

Ampac Packaging
APW Wyott Foodservice
  Equipment
Associated Milk Producers
Barry-Wehmiller
Bel Brands USA
BelGioioso Cheese
Bongrain
Butter Buds Food
  Ingredients
Carlisle Companies
Carlisle FoodService
Dairy Farmers of America
Darigold, Inc.
Dover Corp.
Exopack
Foremost Farms
Fromageries Bel
Gencor Industries
Great Lakes Cheese

Hiland Dairy
Kraft Foods
Land O'Lakes
Leprino Foods
Letica
Marathon Cheese
PrimeSource FoodService
Rexam
Saputo
Sargento
Sartori Foods
Southern Film Extruders
Tetra Pak Cheese and
  Powder Systems
Tillamook County
  Creamery Association
Toyo Seikan Kaisha
Warrnambool Cheese and
  Butter

Schwan Food

Frozen pizza is the flashy part of The Schwan Food Company. With well-known pizza brands such as Tony's, Red Baron, and Freschetta, the company is one of the top frozen pizza makers in the US, along with Kraft Foods. Schwan is also a big supplier to the institutional frozen-pizza market and has operations in more than 50 countries worldwide. But pizza isn't the only slice of the company's revenue — its core business is a fleet of some 6,000 home-delivery trucks. Schwan delivers casseroles, ice cream, and frozen foods to homes throughout the lower US, as well as in Mexico. The family of late founder Marvin Schwan owns the company.

Alfred Schwan (brother of Marvin) retired as chairman in 2009 after 15 years in the post. He was replaced by long-time board member and former president of Ecolab, Allan L. Schuman.

President and CEO Lenny Pippin, who had been with the company since 1999, resigned unexpectedly in 2008. Greg Flack, president of the company's global consumer brands division, was named Schwan's new leader.

With its unintentionally retro-hip bright yellow-gold freezer delivery trucks (the company calls the color Inca Gold), Schwan is definitely cool, both temperature-wise and customer-wise. It maintains a home-delivery system that brings some 400 frozen food products directly to customers in all the US mainland states. Orders can include bagels, pancakes, or Schwan's ice cream, which has a devoted following.

The company's Salina, Kansas, facility is one of the world's largest frozen pizza-manufacturing plants. If you laid all the pepperoni that Schwan uses in a year end to end, it would stretch from New York City to Los Angeles. In addition to the US pizza market, Schwan sells Chicago Town pizzas in Western Europe and supplies schools and other institutional cafeterias with frozen pizza and sandwiches. Its foodservice group serves health care facilities, public and private schools and universities, chain restaurants, and convenience stores.

In conjunction with its Red Baron pizza brand, Schwan owned and operated the #1 civilian airshow act in the world, featuring the Red Baron Stearman Squadron, a formation aerobatics team that performed using vintage Stearman biplanes. However, in 2007 it refocused its Red Baron marketing program and retired the squadron, which had performed for 28 years.

The Schwan family is notoriously secretive (Marvin Schwan himself gave no interviews after 1982).

HISTORY

Paul Schwan bought out his partner in their dairy in 1948 and began manufacturing ice cream using his own recipes. His son, Marvin Schwan, made deliveries for the dairy for a few years. After attending a two-year college, Marvin came back in 1950 to work at the dairy full-time. Two years later he began using his delivery experience to take advantage of the increase in homes with freezers. He bought an old truck for $100 and began a rural route selling ice cream to farmers. He quickly developed a loyal customer base and expanded to two routes the following year.

In the 1960s the company diversified with two acquisitions: a prepared sandwich company and

a condensed fruit juice company. A new holding company, Schwan's Sales Enterprises, was established in 1964. Schwan's began delivering pizza the next year. Paul died in 1969.

Deciding that frozen pizza was not a fad, Marvin bought Kansas-based Tony's Pizza in 1970 and quickly rose to the top of the new industry. In the late 1970s Schwan's entered the commercial leasing business, and it later added more leasing companies under the Lyon Financial Services umbrella (sold 2000).

The company entered the institutional-pizza market in the mid-1980s and bought out competitors Sabatasso Foods and Better Baked Pizza. Schools liked Schwan's use of their government surplus cheese to make pizzas, which the company then sold to the schools at a discount.

In 1992 the company bought two Minnesota-based food companies: Panzerotti, a stuffed pastry business, and Monthly Market, a specialty retailer that sells groceries to fund-raising groups. It also began selling its pizzas in the UK. The next year Schwan's bought Chicago Brothers Frozen Pizza, a San Diego-based company specializing in deep-dish pizza.

Marvin died of a heart attack in 1993 at age 64, with his worth estimated at more than $1 billion. The previous year he had willed two-thirds of the company's stock to a charitable Lutheran trust, which was to be bought out by Schwan's after his death. In 1994 his brother Alfred, and Marvin's friend Lawrence Burgdorf made arrangements to have the company repurchase the foundation's shares for a total of $1.8 billion. But Marvin's four children filed a lawsuit in 1995 against their uncle and Burgdorf over the action. They claimed the men did not have the financial health of the company at heart and were divided in their loyalty. The children, on the other hand, were called money-hungry and callous to their father's last wishes. (The case was settled in 1997, but no information was released.)

In 1994 more than 200,000 people in 28 states contracted salmonella food poisoning after eating *E. coli*-tainted Schwan's ice cream. The company's insurance company eventually paid out nearly $1 million to about 6,000 affected customers in exchange for their signed releases promising they would not sue Schwan's.

Lenny Pippin became the company's fourth CEO in 1999, replacing Alfred, who stayed on as chairman. Schwan's exited the Canadian market at the end of 1999 due to perennial losses. In 2000 Schwan's introduced irradiated frozen ground-beef patties, and struck an agreement with another company to electronically pasteurize some of its products.

The company changed its name from Schwan's Sales Enterprises to The Schwan Food Company in early 2003. Also in 2003 Schwan acquired the frozen-dessert business of Mrs. Smith's Bakeries from Flowers Foods for $240 million in cash. Flowers retained the frozen bread and roll dough segment of Mrs. Smith's.

The company was forced to recall more than 350,000 pounds of products in 2005 because they might have contained glass fragments. The recalled products, which were manufactured at Schwan's Minh plant in Pasadena, Texas, and were distributed to food stores nationwide and purchased by the federal school lunch program, included eggrolls, pizza twists, and tacos.

Later in 2005 Schwan acquired Canadian company T&N Foods (frozen pizza, bread products). In 2006 it acquired Hollywood, Florida-based wholesale appetizer company Holiday Foods.

EXECUTIVES

Chairman: Allan L. Schuman, age 74
President, CEO, COO, and Director:
  Gregory D. (Greg) Flack
EVP Finance and CFO: James P. (Jim) Dollive, age 57
EVP and Chief Human Resources Officer:
  Scott Peterson
EVP Administration and General Counsel:
  Brian R. Sattler
SVP Information Services and CIO:
  Kathleen (Kate) McNulty
SVP and Chief Strategy and Marketing Officer:
  Yvonne La Penotiere
SVP and Controller: Bernadette M. Kruk
SVP Product and Market Strategy: Kristy Griffin
VP Food Safety and Quality: Jeff Varcoe
President Home Service: Scott McNair
President Consumer Brands, Europe: John M. Beadle
President Food Service: Mark Jansen
President Global Supply Chain:
  Douglas J. (Doug) Olsem
Public Relations: Peggy Connot

LOCATIONS

HQ: The Schwan Food Company
  115 W. College Dr., Marshall, MN 56258
Phone: 507-532-3274   **Fax:** 507-537-8226
Web: www.theschwanfoodcompany.com

PRODUCTS/OPERATIONS

Selected Consumer Brands

Asian Sensations (frozen Asian foods)
Big Daddy's (frozen pizza)
Chicago Town (frozen pizza and ready meals)
Edward's Fine Foods (desserts)
Freschetta (frozen pizza)
Larry's (frozen potato side dishes)
Mrs. Smith's (bakery)
Red Baron (frozen pizza)
Tony's (frozen pizza)
Wolfgang Puck (licensed, frozen pizza)

COMPETITORS

Bellisio Foods
Ben & Jerry's
Blue Bell
ConAgra
Cuisine Solutions
DineWise
Domino's
Dreyer's
FreshDirect
Heinz
Kraft Foods
Kraft North America
Little Caesar's
McLane Foodservice
MyWebGrocer
Nash-Finch
Nation Pizza Products
Nestlé
Nestlé USA
Omaha Steaks
On-Cor Frozen Foods
Overhill Farms
Papa John's
Peapod, LLC
Performance Food
Pinnacle Foods
Southern Foods
Stefano Foods
SYSCO
U.S. Foodservice
YUM!

HISTORICAL FINANCIALS

Company Type: Private

Income Statement

FYE: December 31

	ESTIMATED REVENUE ($ mil.)	NET INCOME ($ mil.)	NET PROFIT MARGIN	EMPLOYEES
12/08	3,530	—	—	18,000
12/07	3,300	—	—	22,000
12/06	3,500	—	—	22,000
12/05	3,375	—	—	22,000
Annual Growth	1.5%	—	—	(6.5%)

Revenue History

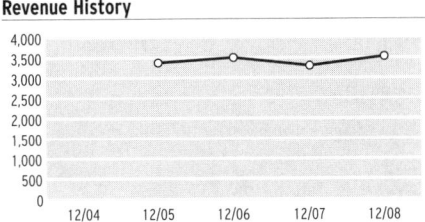

Schwarz Paper

Schwarz Supply Source (formerly Schwarz Paper Company) began as a local paper supplier, and over its 100-year history it has evolved into a global supply chain management services provider. Corporations around the world in the retail, restaurant, food packaging, moving and self-storage, and mailing and parcel industries rely on Schwarz for procurement of such supplies as bags, boxes, cleaning equipment, first aid, office furniture, packing materials, and paper products. The company also offers inventory planning and management, distribution and warehousing, and specialty printing. Customers have included The Gap and McDonald's.

Chairman Andrew McKenna Sr. (also chairman of McDonald's) owns the company. McKenna became the president of Schwarz Paper in 1964.

The company was founded in 1907 as a small store in Chicago providing paper and packaging supplies to other local businesses. It has since expanded its operations across North America and into Europe and the Pacific Rim.

EXECUTIVES

Chairman: Andrew J. (Andy) McKenna Sr., age 79
CEO: Christopher J. Donnelly
President: Andrew J. (Andy) McKenna Jr., age 51
EVP and Chief Administration Officer: Louis M. DeRose
EVP and CFO: Warren J. Kelleher
SVP Human Resources: Susan H. Bondy
VP Sales and Marketing: Paul Frantz
VP Inventory Management: Bruce B. Barton
VP and CIO: Jean A. Luber
VP Distribution: Kevin T. Hourican
Auditors: Deloitte & Touche

LOCATIONS

HQ: Schwarz Paper Company
  8338 Austin Ave., Morton Grove, IL 60053
Phone: 847-966-2550   **Fax:** 847-966-1271
Web: www.schwarz.com

PRODUCTS/OPERATIONS

Selected Services

Inventory management
Logistics and freight management
Print management
Sourcing and procurement
Specialty printing and converting
Warehousing and fulfillment
Web ordering, tracking, and reporting

COMPETITORS

3M
Bunzl Distribution USA
McLane Foodservice
Menasha Packaging
Packaging Dynamics
SupplyOne
Unisource
xpedx

Scottrade, Inc.

One of the largest online brokerages in the US, Scottrade offers low-cost trading in stock, bonds, options, mutual funds, and exchange-traded funds (ETFs) to consumers, with transactions handled in real time. Customers can trade online via the company's Scottrade, Scottrader, and ScottradeELITE platforms, as well as by phone or wireless device. The company also maintains a network of brokers at more than 425 branch offices in nearly all 50 states, with concentrations on both coasts. It also offers certificates of deposit, individual retirement accounts, and Coverdell education savings accounts. Scottrade, which has more than 1.5 million active accounts, is controlled by founder and CEO Rodger Riney.

Scottrade also offers a Chinese trading platform for customers in China, Hong Kong, Taiwan, and the US. Scottrade Chinese includes translated market news and research reports. Scottrade has also been mulling potential expansion into Europe, but so far it has been content to grow domestically, where its branch network far outstrips those of rivals TD AMERITRADE and E*TRADE.

Scottrade continues to expand its brick-and-mortar branch system — in recent years to the tune of around 50 new locations annually — as a means to attract and satisfy customers who prefer face-to-face interaction. Commensurately, its ranks of investment advisors are also growing. Despite the expense of the branch network, the company is able to maintain its discount pricing of $7 per trade.

Founded as Scottsdale Securities in 1980, the company put its name on the St. Louis Blues' hockey arena (now known as Scottrade Center) in 2006. It was one of the largest advertising outlays to date for the company, which previously focused its marketing efforts on active traders on the Web. Scottrade has since added TV spots to its repertoire, reaching out beyond financial news channels.

EXECUTIVES

Founder, President, and CEO: Rodger O. Riney, age 63
Executive Director Operations:
 Catherine (Cathy) Maher
CFO: Ron Wiese
CTO: Joan Albeck
CIO: Ian Patterson
Chief Administrative Officer: Jane Wulf
Chief Marketing Officer: Chris X. Moloney
EVP and Chief Legal Counsel, Scottrade Bank:
 Patricia Milon
Director Public Relations: Kelly Doria
Director Corporate Communication: Craig Ransom

LOCATIONS

HQ: Scottrade, Inc.
 12800 Corporate Hill Dr., St. Louis, MO 63131
Phone: 314-965-1555 **Fax:** 314-543-6222
Web: www.scottrade.com

COMPETITORS

Charles Schwab
E*TRADE Financial
FMR
Merrill Lynch
optionsXpress
ShareBuilder
Siebert Financial
Stifel Financial
T. Rowe Price
TD Ameritrade
The Vanguard Group

The Scoular Company

It's a grind, and at the Scoular Company, that's a good thing. The company is best known for buying, selling, storing, handling, and transporting agricultural products (mainly grains) worldwide. It deals in the mainstays of farming — corn, hay, millet, rice, sorghum, soybeans, and wheat — and gets them where they need to go. It transports these products via rail, truck, barge, and seagoing container vessels. The company's other divisions offer fishmeal products for farmanimal, pet, and aquaculture feeds, ingredients for food manufacturers, and truck freight brokering. Scoular has customers in Asia, Africa, Europe, and North and South America.

Company services include bagging, blending, cleaning, containerizing, organic certification, packaging, sorting, sourcing, and storage. It also offers risk management and transportation logistics services.

Scoular serves customers in the aquaculture, flour milling, food processing and manufacturing, grain production, industrial ag processing, livestock feeding and manufacturing, pet food manufacturing, and renewable fuels sectors.

Adding four grain-handling facilities in the Mississippi Delta region, in 2008 the company acquired the assets of the McAlister Grain Company. That year it also acquired the assets of Hancock Elevator, which comprised 14 Iowa grainhandling facilities.

In 2009 Charles (Chuck) Elsea was named CEO, replacing the retiring Randall Linville. Elsea is a 28-year veteran of Scoular.

Founded in 1892 to run grain elevators, Scoular is employee owned.

EXECUTIVES

Chairman: Marshall E. Faith
CEO: Charles (Chuck) Elsea
President: David M. Faith
COO: Robert (Bob) Ludington
SVP Asset Management and Business Development:
 John M. Heck
SVP, Secretary, Communication, and General Counsel:
 Joan C. Maclin
SVP Operations: Todd McQueen
VP Finance and Treasurer: Roger L. Barber
VP Performance Management and Human Resources:
 Theresa A. Ruby
VP Accounting and Control Officer: Randall Foster
VP Asset Management and Loss Control: Tom DiGiorgio
VP Information Technology: Jim Konz
Director Human Resources: Yvonne Lutz

LOCATIONS

HQ: The Scoular Company
 2027 Dodge St., Omaha, NE 68102
Phone: 402-342-3500 **Fax:** 402-342-5568
Web: www.scoular.com

PRODUCTS/OPERATIONS

Selected Customer Industries and Services

Aquaculture (global supply chain solutions)
Container and Vessel Transportation (freight, forwarding, logistics, and documentation between North America and the Pacific Rim)
Flour Milling (shipping)
Food Manufacturing and Processing (conventional, organic, and functional ingredients, co-packing)
Grain Production (marketing, buying, storing, handling, and shipping programs)
Industrial Ag Processing (feedstock supply, byproduct marketing, and crush risk management)
Livestock Feeding and Feed Manufacturing (risk management, grain and feed ingredient delivery)
Pet Food Manufacturing (ingredients)
Rail, Truck, and Barge Transportation (logistics for shipping agricultural products)

Selected Products

Bakery meal
Barley
Beet pulp
Citrus
Corn gluten
Corn (yellow and white)
Cottonseed
Fats and oils
Hay
Hominy
Hulls
Millet
Oats
Proteins (animal, dairy, marine, vegetable, and wet pet)
Rice hulls
Sorghum
Soybeans
Specialty food ingredients
Specialty pet-food ingredients
Wheat (durum, hard red winter, soft red winter, hard red spring, and white)

COMPETITORS

ADM	DeBruce Grain
Ag Processing	Excel Maritime Carriers
AGRI Industries	GROWMARK
Andersons	Louis Dreyfus Group
Bartlett and Company	Southern States
Bunge Limited	TBS International
Cargill	TORM
CHS	

Scripps Health

Scripps Health has its medical script down pat. The not-for-profit hospital group serves the San Diego area through about a half dozen acute-care hospitals with some 1,400 beds and 20 outpatient clinic locations. The system also offers home health care and operates community outreach programs. Its hospitals, along with outpatient Scripps Clinic and Scripps Coastal Medical Center locations, include more than 2,600 affiliated general practice and specialty physicians. Scripps Health is affiliated with The Scripps Research Institute, which performs biomedical research. The Scripps Foundation for Medicine and Science serves as a fundraiser for both the hospital group and the research institute.

In 2008 Scripps Health acquired the Sharp Mission Park Medical Group and added it to its Scripps Mercy Medical Group; the combined entity operates as Scripps Coastal Medical Center and has 10 outpatient health clinics and an associated network of physicians. Also that year, the company opened the Scripps Clinical Research Center to support drug and medical device development.

Scripps Health also expands its operations through construction efforts. The company is expanding its Scripps Memorial Hospital Encinitas campus by adding an emergency and inpatient care wing, as well as outpatient facilities. It is also expanding emergency room facilities at the main Scripps Mercy Hospital campus in San Diego. The health network also plans to add a new cardiovascular center by 2015; the heart center is the first step in a plan to replace the Scripps Memorial Hospital La Jolla campus.

Scripps Health was founded by Ellen Browning Scripps in 1924 when the Scripps Memorial Hospital and Scripps Metabolic Clinic opened in La Jolla. Scripps Green Hospital opened in 1977, and the Scripps Memorial Hospital Encinitas campus was added through the purchase of San Dieguito Hospital in 1978. Scripps Mercy Hospital, which was first established in 1890 in San Diego, joined the Scripps network in 1995, and the Scripps Mercy Hospital Chula Vista campus was acquired in 2004.

EXECUTIVES

Chairman: Richard Vortmann
President and CEO: Christopher D. Van Gorder
Chief Medical Officer: A. Brent Eastman
EVP and CFO: Richard Rothberger
SVP and Chief Development Officer: John B. Engle
SVP, Strategic Planning and Business Development:
 June Komar
SVP Human Resources: Victor V. (Vic) Buzachero
SVP, General Counsel, and Secretary:
 Richard R. Sheridan
SVP and CEO, Scripps Clinic: Larry J. Harrison
SVP and CEO, Scripps Home Health Care Services:
 Mary Lou Carraher
President and CEO, Scripps Howard Foundation:
 Mike Philipps
Director Corporate Public Relations: Don Stanziano

LOCATIONS

HQ: Scripps Health
 4275 Campus Point Ct., San Diego, CA 92121
Phone: 858-678-7000 **Fax:** 858-678-6767
Web: www.scripps.org

PRODUCTS/OPERATIONS

2008 Sales

	$ mil.	% of total
Patient service	1,667.2	85
Capitation premium	202.1	10
Net assets released	17.3	1
Other	67.2	4
Total	**1,953.8**	**100**

Selected California Facilities

Scripps Clinic (outpatient centers)
Scripps Coastal Medical Center (outpatient centers, formerly Scripps Mercy Medical Group)
Scripps Green Hospital (La Jolla)
Scripps Memorial Hospital Encinitas
Scripps Memorial Hospital La Jolla
Scripps Mercy Hospital (San Diego)
Scripps Mercy Hospital Chula Vista

COMPETITORS

Adventist Health
Cedars-Sinai Medical Center
Grossmont Hospital
HCA
Kaiser Permanente
Kindred Healthcare
Mayo Foundation
Palomar Pomerado Health
Paradise Valley Hospital
Rady Children's Hospital
Sharp HealthCare
St. Joseph Health System
Tenet Healthcare
Tri-City Healthcare District
UCSD Medical

HISTORICAL FINANCIALS

Company Type: Not-for-profit

Income Statement

FYE: September 30

	REVENUE ($ mil.)	NET INCOME ($ mil.)	NET PROFIT MARGIN	EMPLOYEES
9/08	1,954	—	—	11,000

Securian Financial

After 125 years of being in business, Minnesota Mutual felt secure enough to change its name to Securian Financial Group. The company still operates through its subsidiary Minnesota Life which offers individual and group life and disability insurance and annuities, as well as retirement services. Other subsidiaries include Securian Financial Services which, along with Advantus Capital Management, offers mutual funds, institutional asset management, trust services, and annuity and retirement plans. It also offers a small amount of property/casualty coverage nationwide. The company was founded in 1880 and restructured as a mutual holding company in 2005.

Life insurance is not the most dynamic product in the marketplace, so before the economy curdled, Securian began expanding its financial services units. It acquired several smaller firms, including Maryland-based Capital Financial Group and its H. Beck securities broker-dealer business in 2008. It used the new companies to extend its geographic reach across the US.

The company has also steadily been expanding its property/casualty product lines — which were nonexistent before 2005. While they are still a tiny portion of its overall revenues, property/casualty products sold through banks and credit unions are the fastest growing portion of Securian's business.

EXECUTIVES

Chairman and CEO: Robert L. Senkler
President and Vice Chairman: Randy F. Wallake
SVP and Chief Investment Officer: David M. Kuplic
EVP Group Insurance: James E. Johnson
EVP and CFO: Warren J. Zaccaro
SVP Broker-Deal and Trust: George I. Connolly
SVP Human Resources and Corporate Services: Keith M. Campbell
SVP Individual Distribution Management: Wilford J. Kavanaugh
SVP Financial Institution Group: Christopher M. Hilger
SVP Retirement: Bruce P. Shay
SVP and CIO: Jean Delaney Nelson
SVP; Chief Investment Officer, Advantus Capital Management: Christopher R. Sebald
SVP Group Insurance: Robert M. Olafson
SVP and General Counsel: Dwayne C. Radel
VP Investment Law and Chief Compliance Officer: Vicki L. Bailey
VP and Chief Medical Director: George N. Battis Jr.
VP Human Resources: Kathleen L. (Kathy) Pinkett
VP, Treasurer, and Controller: David J. LePlavy
VP and Actuary: Leslie J. Chapman
Auditors: KPMG LLP

LOCATIONS

HQ: Securian Financial Group, Inc.
400 Robert St. North, St. Paul, MN 55101
Phone: 651-665-3500   **Fax:** 651-665-4488
Web: www.securian.com

PRODUCTS/OPERATIONS

2008 Revenues

	$ mil.	% of total
Premiums	1,906.7	59
Net investment income	553.9	17
Policy & contract fees	503.6	15
Commission income	136.5	4
Finance charge income	53.3	2
Net realized investment losses	(497.6)	—
Other	89.1	3
Total	**2,745.5**	**100**

COMPETITORS

AIG American General	Nationwide Life Insurance
American United Mutual	New York Life
Conseco	Northwestern Mutual
COUNTRY Financial	Pacific Mutual
Guardian Life	Prudential
MetLife	Torchmark
National Western	

HISTORICAL FINANCIALS .

Company Type: Private

Income Statement

FYE: December 31

	ASSETS ($ mil.)	NET INCOME ($ mil.)	INCOME AS % OF ASSETS	EMPLOYEES
12/08	21,686	(259)	—	5,000
12/07	26,644	207	0.8%	5,000
12/06	25,631	179	0.7%	5,000
12/05	23,435	186	0.8%	5,000
12/04	21,929	137	0.6%	5,000
Annual Growth	**(0.3%)**	**—**	**—**	**0.0%**

2008 Year-End Financials

Equity as % of assets: —	Long-term debt ($ mil.): —
Return on assets: —	Sales ($ mil.): 2,746
Return on equity: —	

Net Income History

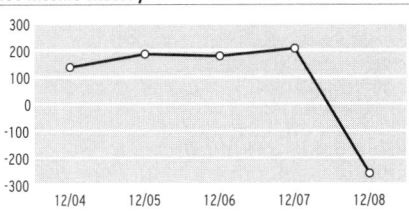

Seminole Electric Cooperative

This Seminole is not only a native Floridian, but it has also provided electricity in the state since 1948. Seminole Electric Cooperative generates and transmits electricity for 10 member distribution cooperatives that serve 1.7 million residential and business customers in 46 Florida counties. Seminole Electric has more than 2,100 MW of primarily coal-fired generating capacity (but with some natural gas and nuclear power generation, too). The cooperative also buys electricity from other utilities and independent power producers, and it owns about 350 miles of transmission lines.

In 2008, as part of Florida's push for more power generation from renewable sources, Seminole Electric boosted its portfolio of green energy to more than 100 MW.

Seminole Electric was formed to aggregate the power demands of its members and is governed by a board of trustees representing the 10 member utilities. The cooperative built its first power plant in the 1970s.

EXECUTIVES

President, Board of Trustees: Mal Green
EVP and General Manager: Timothy S. Woodbury
SVP Operations: Floyd (Joe) Welborn
SVP Strategic Services: Michael P. Opalinski
Assistant General Manager and CFO: John W. Geeraerts
Director Information Systems: William C. Cross
VP, Board of Trustees: Robert W. Strickland
VP Bulk Power and Generation Planning: Trudy S. Novak
VP Administration: Savino (Al) Garcia
Secretary and Treasurer: Malcolm V. Page
Senior Director Corporate Compliance and Risk Management: Thomas H. Turke
Director Operations: Steven R. (Steve) Wallace
Auditors: PricewaterhouseCoopers LLP

LOCATIONS

HQ: Seminole Electric Cooperative, Inc.
16313 N. Dale Mabry Hwy., Tampa, FL 33618
Phone: 813-963-0994   **Fax:** 813-264-7906
Web: www.seminole-electric.com

447

PRODUCTS/OPERATIONS

Members

Central Florida Electric Cooperative
Clay Electric Cooperative
Glades Electric Cooperative
Lee County Electric Cooperative
Peace River Electric Cooperative
Sumter Electric Cooperative
Suwannee Valley Electric Cooperative
Talquin Electric Cooperative
Tri-County Electric Cooperative
Withlacoochee River Electric Cooperative

COMPETITORS

Duke Energy	JEA
Florida Power & Light	Progress Energy
Florida Public Utilities	Southern Company
FPL Group	TECO Energy

HISTORICAL FINANCIALS

Company Type: Cooperative

Income Statement

FYE: December 31

	REVENUE ($ mil.)	NET INCOME ($ mil.)	NET PROFIT MARGIN	EMPLOYEES
12/08	1,290	12	0.9%	505
12/07	1,210	11	0.9%	484
12/06	1,173	14	1.2%	482
12/05	1,080	6	0.6%	477
12/04	897	2	0.3%	468
Annual Growth	9.5%	49.9%	—	1.9%

2008 Year-End Financials

Debt ratio: 1,147.4%
Return on equity: —
Cash ($ mil.): —
Current ratio: —
Long-term debt ($ mil.): 1,348

Net Income History

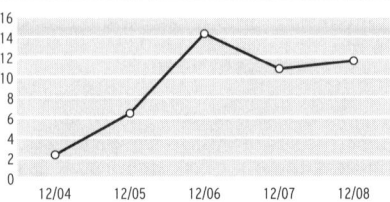

Sentara Healthcare

Health care's a beach for Sentara Healthcare. The not-for-profit organization operates a network of hospitals and other health facilities primarily in the coastal Hampton Roads area of southeastern Virginia. The system includes eight acute care hospitals housing a total of more than 1,900 beds; one of the hospitals, Sentara Norfolk, includes a dedicated cardiac hospital with more than 100 beds. In addition to its acute care facilities, Sentara Healthcare operates several outpatient care facilities, as well as nursing homes, rehab centers, and medical practices. Its Optima Health unit provides HMO coverage and other health insurance products to about 350,000 Virginians.

The medical system also operates a multispecialty physicians group. The Sentara Medical Group has more than 380 primary care and specialty physicians with practices located throughout southeastern Virginia.

Though it's already one of the largest health care organizations in the state, Sentara is not resting on its laurels. The system continues to grow through acquisitions, construction (both expansions and new buildings), and mergers.

In mid-2009 the company expanded its home health services by acquiring Bath Community House Home Health and Hospice of the Highlands, and subsequently gave it the less-lengthy moniker of Sentara Highlands Home Health. Following that acquisition Sentara operates home care offices in seven cities in Virginia and in Elizabeth, North Carolina.

Sentara also acquired the 180-bed Potomac Hospital (now operating as Sentara Potomac Hospital) in Woodbridge through a merger transaction in 2009, expanding its hospital operations into northern Virginia. The agreement was made, in part, to keep Potomac Hospital from going under in the face of continuing economic pressure. As part of the agreement, Sentara will invest in the hospital's infrastructure and establish a community health foundation to help address the medical needs of the area's residents.

Sentara is also building an eighth acute care hospital, scheduled to open in 2010, to be located on Sentara's existing Princess Anne outpatient campus. The 120-bed, $145 million Sentara Princess Anne Hospital will encompass five stories and offer comprehensive surgical procedures, intensive care, advanced cardiac care, and a maternity center.

EXECUTIVES

CEO: David L. Bernd
President and COO: Howard P. Kern
Chief Medical Officer: Gary R. Yates
SVP System Development: Vicky G. Gray
SVP; President, Sentara Peninsula Region:
Kenneth M. (Ken) Krakaur
SVP Managed Care; President, Sentara Health Plans:
Michael M. Dudley
SVP and CFO: Robert A. (Rob) Broerman
VP Materials Management: Carl Manley
VP and CIO: Bertram S. (Bert) Reese
VP Human Resources: Michael V. (Mike) Taylor
VP Reinventing and Decision Support:
Douglas M. (Doug) Thompson
Director Government Relations and Advocacy:
Sandra Miller
Director Public Relations: Emma Inman

LOCATIONS

HQ: Sentara Healthcare
6015 Poplar Hall Dr., Norfolk, VA 23502
Phone: 757-455-7540   **Fax:** 757-455-7964
Web: www.sentara.com

Selected Locations

Facilities in operation
Sentara Bayside Hospital (Virginia Beach, VA)
Sentara CarePlex Hospital (Hampton, VA)
Sentara Heart Hospital (Norfolk, VA)
Sentara Leigh Hospital (Norfolk, VA)
Sentara Norfolk General Hospital (Norfolk, VA)
Sentara Obici Hospital (Suffolk, VA)
Sentara Potomac Hospital (Woodbridge, VA)
Sentara Virginia Beach General Hospital (Virginia Beach, VA)
Sentara Williamsburg Regional Medical Center (Williamsburg, VA)
Facilities under construction
Sentara Princess Anne Hospital (Virginia Beach, VA)
Sentara Obici Bed Tower
Orthopaedic Hospital at Sentara CarePlex
Sentara Saint Luke's Health Campus (Phase 1)

PRODUCTS/OPERATIONS

Selected Services

Cancer
Cardiac (Heart)
Digestive (Colorectal)
Home Care
Imaging
Maternity
Neurosciences
Rehabilitation
Seniors
Thoracic
Transplant
Trauma/Emergency Services
Urology
Vascular
Weight Loss Surgery
Women's

COMPETITORS

Bon Secours Health
Carilion Clinic
Children's Hospital of The King's Daughters
Franklin Hospital Corp.
Novant Health
Riverside Health System (Virginia)
Wake Forest University Baptist Medical Center

Sentry Insurance

Ever vigilant for its policyholders, Sentry Insurance (with the famous Minuteman statue as its logo) offers a variety of insurance products, including auto, homeowners, and other property/casualty lines, as well as life and annuities. The mutual company (owned by its policyholders) offers individual and family coverage through several subsidiaries nationwide. Sentry Insurance also provides specialized insurance to businesses of all sizes, including manufacturers and retailers. The company's Sentry Equity Services offers mutual fund services through its Sentry Fund. Formerly named Hardware Mutual, Sentry Insurance was founded in 1904 to provide insurance to members of the Wisconsin Retail Hardware Association.

Sentry Insurance has offices from coast to coast and scattered throughout the US. Subsidiaries include Parker Centennial Assurance, Dairyland Insurance, Middlesex Insurance, and Sentry Life Insurance.

Sentry Insurance has expanded through a few acquisitions, such as the buy of ALF Insurance Agency. One of Sentry's brokerage partners, ALF continues to operate as an independent agency and sell other companies' products through about 15 Michigan locations.

The Farm Equipment Manufacturers Association gives Sentry Insurance an exclusive endorsement as a recommended insurance provider. The company works with a number of other member groups to create insurance programs, including Business Technology Association, Industrial Supply Association, and Power Transmission Distributors Association.

EXECUTIVES

Chairman and CEO: Dale R. Schuh
EVP Business Products: Jim Clawson
SVP and Treasurer: William J. Lohr
SVP Information Technology: Jim Stitzlein
SVP Investments: Jim Weishan
VP Business Products Systems: Don Olson
VP Information Technology: Greg Pfluger
VP, General Counsel, and Corporate Secretary:
William M. O'Reilly
VP National Accounts: Dan Revai
VP Finance: Michael Zimmer
VP Human Resources: Joe Fritzsche
VP and Chief Actuary: Janet Fagan
VP Business Products Claims: Tom Whittington
VP Transportation: Michael Williams
VP Life and Health: Mark Hackl
VP Specialty Cycle and Corporate Planning: Pete Anhalt
Auditors: PricewaterhouseCoopers

LOCATIONS

HQ: Sentry Insurance
1800 North Point Dr., Stevens Point, WI 54481
Phone: 715-346-6000   **Fax:** 715-346-7516
Web: www.sentry.com

PRODUCTS/OPERATIONS

Selected Subsidiaries

Dairyland Insurance Company
Middlesex Insurance Company
Parker Centennial Assurance Company
Patriot General Insurance Company
Sentry Aviation Services, Inc.
Sentry Casualty Company
Sentry Equity Services, Inc.
Sentry Life Insurance Company
Sentry Lloyds of Texas
Sentry Select Insurance Company

COMPETITORS

AIG	New York Life
Allstate	Penn Mutual
Badger Mutual	Progressive Corporation
CIGNA	Prudential
CNA Financial	State Farm
GEICO	Travelers Companies
MetLife	USAA
Nationwide	

HISTORICAL FINANCIALS

Company Type: Mutual company

Income Statement

FYE: December 31

	REVENUE ($ mil.)	NET INCOME ($ mil.)	NET PROFIT MARGIN	EMPLOYEES
12/07	2,588	306	11.8%	—
12/06	2,626	262	10.0%	—
12/05	1,987	—	—	—
12/04	2,213	—	—	—
12/03	2,088	—	—	4,400
Annual Growth	5.5%	16.6%	—	—

Net Income History

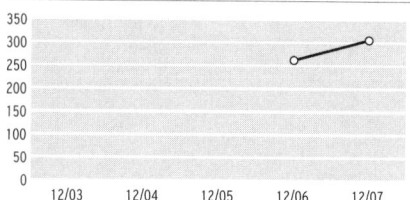

Sequa Corporation

Sequa's sequel is a sleek new beginning. Having divested itself of its formal apparel and chemical businesses, Sequa has turned its eye to its four main businesses, which comprise three operating segments. Chromalloy Gas Turbine is the largest unit in the Aerospace segment; it makes and repairs jet engine parts for airlines and other customers. Sequa's Automotive unit, which includes ARC Automotive and Casco Products, makes airbag inflators, sensors, and car cigarette lighters. Its Metal-Coatings unit, Precoat Metals, makes coatings for building products. In 2007 the company was bought out by The Carlyle Group in a deal valued at about $2.7 billion.

The company has focused its business plan on aviation, automotive, and chemical coatings, and divested itself of peripheral companies.

In 2008 the company sold its specialty chemical unit Warwick International (bleach activator manufacturer) for approximately $230 million to Close Brothers Private Equity in the UK. That same year Sequa sold its formal wear label After Six to The Anderson Group; terms were not disclosed. It also sold its printing machinery company MEGTEC Systems to Hamilton Robinson Capital Partners for about $90 million.

Citing a downturn in demand for metal buildings, Sequa announced in early 2009 its plans to shutter its Precoat Metals processing plant in Pennsylvania; production will not be transferred to any of the unit's eight other facilities. The economic slowdown in the airline and automotive industries prompted the company to make staff cuts at its Chromalloy and ARC Automotive plants.

Sequa is focusing on operations that have a strong technological component. Chromalloy Gas Turbine provides aftermarket services to the airline, military aviation, marine, and industrial gas turbine industries. ARC Automotive and Casco Products serve customers such as DaimlerChrysler, Ford, General Motors, Hyundai, and Volkswagen, among others. Precoat Metals provides decorative and protective coatings to coiled steel for use in construction projects. It uses plasma spray overlay coatings for turbine applications, and has invested more than $75 million in electron beam vapor deposition.

In October 2008 Dr. Martin Weinstein retired as CEO of Sequa, but will continue as a senior consultant, focusing primarily on technology development. Effective January 2009 Armand Lauzon (former COO) assumed the position of CEO.

HISTORY

Sequa Corporation began in 1929 from the merger of five firms: George H. Morrill Co. (1840), Sigmund Ullman Co. (1861), Fuchs & Lang Manufacturing (1871), Eagle Printing Ink (1893), and American Printing Ink (1897). Founded as General Printing Ink Corp., it specialized in making ink for news, letterpress, and lithographic printing. It also made lithographic machines and supplies.

Although the company's units competed against each other in the 1930s, they managed to stay profitable during the Depression. General Ink bought four firms in 1945 and, to reflect its expanding interests, changed its name to Sun Chemical Corp. More acquisitions followed over the next few years. By 1950 Sun had formed seven divisions.

The growth turned out to be too much, too soon, however. In 1954 Sun consolidated into three groups: chemicals; graphic arts; and waterproofing, paints, and product finishing. Norman Alexander became Sun's president in 1957. A research program began in 1960, and Sun spent much of the next decade expanding abroad and diversifying its product line.

In 1972 Sun entered the auto parts industry when it bought Standard Kollsman Industries. Sun's expansion in the late 1970s established subsidiaries in Bermuda, Chile, and Panama. The company initiated a takeover attempt in 1979 by buying 5% of diversified Chromalloy American. By 1980 Sun was the #1 world producer of printing inks, and by 1982 it had acquired 36% of Chromalloy. Also that year Alexander became Sun's CEO.

Sun itself became a takeover target in 1986, as Dainippon Ink and Chemicals tried to buy it. Alexander refused and upped his ownership in Sun to 47%. He sold the company's graphic arts unit to Dainippon later that year and used the proceeds to buy the rest of Chromalloy. Sun's 1987 purchase of Atlantic Research Corp. (ARC; rocket motors) was the impetus to rename itself Sequa Corporation, to reflect a shift in focus from chemical to military products.

Sales skyrocketed until 1990, but post-Cold War cutbacks dealt Sequa a financial blow. In the next several years it dumped about half a dozen divisions and cut its workforce in half. In 1996 ARC won a contract to make rocket motors for missiles used on Canadian, NATO, and US fighter planes.

Sequa bought TEC Systems (web press products) in 1997 and merged it with MEG, its French auxiliary press equipment division, to form MEGTEC Systems. Sequa sold its Northern Can Systems unit, a maker of easy-open can lids. It initiated major layoffs at MEGTEC in 1998 and sold its Sequa Chemicals unit to GenCorp for $108 million. That year ARC became the sole owner of its former joint venture, Bendix Atlantic Inflator Co.; it was renamed Atlantic Research Automotive Products Group.

In 1999 Sequa paid $13 million for Thermo Fibertek's Thermo Wisconsin unit, which supplies the US process and printing industries with continuous process dryers, air-pollution control equipment, and other specialty products. Sequa planned to combine the unit with its MEGTEC Systems. That year Sequa won a seven-year $10.1 billion contract to repair military aircraft for the US Air Force. The company acquired metal can machinery maker Formatec Tooling Systems in 2000.

In early 2002 Sequa reported a record fourth-quarter loss for 2001. The loss was largely related to cost-cutting measures and environmental remediation. Late in 2002 Sequa acquired Pacific

Gas Turbine, an airplane engine overhaul business. The next year Sequa sold the propulsion business of its ARC unit for about $133 million. Sequa kept ARC's automotive business.

Focusing on its core operations of aviation, automotive, and chemical coatings, Sequa divested a number of its extraneous companies over the next several years. Some such companies include Stolle Machinery Company, Warwick International, After Six, and MEGTEC Systems.

EXECUTIVES

Chairman: Peter J. Clare, age 44
CEO and Director; President, Chromalloy Gas Turbine: Armand F. Lauzon Jr.
CFO: Donna Costello, age 36
VP Human Resources: John Bollman
VP, General Counsel, and Secretary: Steven R. Lowson
VP and Treasurer: James P. Langelotti, age 48
VP External Affairs: David G. Albert
VP Marketing and Corporate Communications: Andrew Farrant
President and CEO, ARC Automotive and Casco Products: Ali El-Haj
President and General Manager, Precoat Metals: Gerard M. Dombek, age 56
Auditors: KPMG

LOCATIONS

HQ: Sequa Corporation
200 Park Ave., New York, NY 10166
Phone: 212-986-5500   **Fax:** 212-370-1969
Web: www.sequa.com

PRODUCTS/OPERATIONS

Selected Subsidiaries and Operations

Aerospace
  Chromalloy Gas Turbine Corporation (jet aircraft engine repair and manufacture)
Automotive
  ARC Automotive, Inc. (airbag inflators)
  Casco Products (automotive cigarette lighters, climate control and fluid sensors, and power outlets)
Metal Coatings
  Precoat Metals (protective and decorative coatings for steel and aluminum)

COMPETITORS

AAR Corp.
Autoliv
Autoliv ASP, Inc.
Ball Corp.
Barnes Group
Dover Corp.
GE
General Magnaplate
Honeywell International
Nippon Kayaku
Pratt & Whitney
Raytheon
Rolls-Royce
Special Devices
Valspar

HISTORICAL FINANCIALS

Company Type: Private

Income Statement

FYE: December 31

	ESTIMATED REVENUE ($ mil.)	NET INCOME ($ mil.)	NET PROFIT MARGIN	EMPLOYEES
12/08	2,250	—	—	10,340
12/07	1,960	—	—	10,000
Annual Growth	14.8%	—	—	3.4%

Revenue History

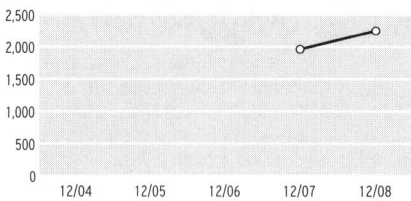

	12/04	12/05	12/06	12/07	12/08
2,500					
2,000					
1,500					
1,000					
500					
0					

ServiceMaster

ServiceMaster merrily mows, scrubs, sprays, and trims. A giant in its industry, the company serves millions of commercial and residential customers in the US and around the world with housecleaning, termite and pest control, and landscape maintenance services. Its best-known brands include Merry Maids, Terminix, and TruGreen LawnCare. The TruGreen Companies provides landscaping services to commercial clients. ServiceMaster Clean cleans carpets and flooring for residential and commercial clients. Its AmeriSpec division inspects homes, American Home Shield provides home warranty plans, and Furniture Medic repairs and restores furniture. ServiceMaster is owned by investment firm Clayton, Dubilier & Rice.

Under its new owners, ServiceMaster has been working to improve the results of its business, in which the TruGreen and Terminix segments make up about 75% of sales. Most of the company's businesses, including TruGreen and Terminix, operate through company-owned branches. However, Merry Maids primarily franchises its units, and American Home Shield operates through a network of independent real estate brokers, who sell the service, and subcontractors, who perform the work.

ServiceMaster hopes to improve performance in its more than 5,500 service centers by centralizing some administrative functions (payroll and accounts receivable, for instance) and freeing the branch locations to focus on customer service and employee care. At the same time, since 2008 ServiceMaster has focused its efforts on restructuring to cut down costs and optimize its organizational structure. This process has involved reducing its work force, shutting down several centers or offices, and outsourcing certain business functions to third parties.

ServiceMaster also has been divesting noncore operations, and in 2008 the company sold its InStar Services Group, a contractor that specializes in disaster recovery services, to private equity firm BlackEagle Partners. Two years earlier, ServiceMaster sold its American Mechanical Services and American Residential Services units, the latter of which included ARS Service Express and Rescue Rooter brands.

Firmly rooted in religion, the company's name reflects both its business focus and its Christian credo of "Service to the Master."

EXECUTIVES

Chairman and CEO; Interim President, TruGreen LawnCare: J. Patrick (Pat) Spainhour, age 58, $2,824,757 total compensation
SVP and CFO: Steven J. (Steve) Martin, age 45, $822,798 total compensation
SVP and CIO: Daniel J. (Dan) Marks, age 44
SVP and General Counsel: Greer G. McMullen, $935,093 total compensation
SVP Innovation and Process Improvement: Reggie Crenshaw, age 39
SVP Corporate Strategy and Marketing: Jim Kunihiro, age 42
SVP and Controller: David W. Martin, age 44
SVP and Treasurer: Mark W. Peterson, age 54
SVP Human Resources: Jed L. Norden, age 58
VP Corporate Communications: Pete Tosches, age 43
President and COO, American Home Shield/AmeriSpec: David J. (Dave) Crawford, age 51
President and COO, Merry Maids: Laura J. Hendricks, age 46
President and COO, Terminix International: Thomas G. (Tom) Brackett, age 42, $943,794 total compensation
President and COO, ServiceMaster Clean, Furniture Medic, and AmeriSpec: Michael M. (Mike) Isakson, age 55, $766,712 total compensation
President and COO, TruGreen LandCare: Richard A. (Rick) Ascolese, age 55
Auditors: Deloitte & Touche LLP

LOCATIONS

HQ: The ServiceMaster Company
860 Ridge Lake Blvd., Memphis, TN 38120
Phone: 901-597-1400   **Fax:** 630-663-2001
Web: www.servicemaster.com

PRODUCTS/OPERATIONS

2008 Sales

	$ mil.	% of total
TruGreen LawnCare	1,094.7	33
Terminix	1,093.9	33
American Home Shield	588.0	18
TruGreen LandCare	316.4	9
Other	218.4	7
Total	**3,311.4**	**100**

Selected Consumer Services

American Home Shield (warranty and service contracts)
AmeriSpec (home inspections)
Furniture Medic (on-site furniture repair, restoration)
Merry Maids (housecleaning)
ServiceMaster Clean (commercial and residential cleaning, disaster restoration, carpet cleaning)
Terminix (commercial and residential pest control)
TruGreen LandCare (landscape maintenance)
TruGreen LawnCare (commercial and residential lawn, tree, and shrub care)

COMPETITORS

ABM Industries	Maid Brigade
Balboa Insurance	Maid to Perfection
BELFOR USA Group	MaidPro
The BMS Enterprises	Maids International, Inc.
Brickman	Molly Maid
Davey Tree	Orkin, Inc.
Dwyer Group	Rentokil Initial
Ecolab	Scotts Miracle-Gro
First American	Servpro Industries
Home Buyers Warranty	Stanley Steemer
HomeServices	UGL Unicco
ISS A/S	ValleyCrest Companies

HISTORICAL FINANCIALS

Company Type: Private

Income Statement

FYE: December 31

	REVENUE ($ mil.)	NET INCOME ($ mil.)	NET PROFIT MARGIN	EMPLOYEES
12/08	3,311	(126)	—	27,000
12/07	3,357	(42)	—	29,000
Annual Growth	(1.3%)	—	—	(6.9%)

Net Income History

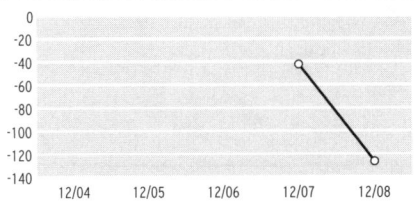

| | 12/04 | 12/05 | 12/06 | 12/07 | 12/08 |

Services Group of America

Supplying American restaurants with food is the primary service of this company. Services Group of America (SGA) is one of the leading foodservice suppliers in the country. Subsidiary Food Services of America distributes a wide range of food and nonfood items to foodservice operators in 15 mostly western states through nine distribution facilities. It also has specialist subsidiaries such as Amerifresh (fresh produce), Ameristar Meats, and Systems Services of America (chain restaurants). In addition, SGA offers event planning services through Event Services of America, while its Development Services of America manages the company's commercial real estate. SGA was founded in 1985 by chairman Thomas Stewart.

EXECUTIVES

Chairman and CEO: Thomas J. (Tom) Stewart, age 65
President and COO: Peter Smith
CFO: Jim Keller
SVP and Chief Merchandising Officer, Food Services of America: Scott Bixby
VP, Corporate Communications: Gary L. Odegard
President, Food Services of America — Spokane, WA: Mike George

LOCATIONS

HQ: Services Group of America, Inc.
  16100 N. 71st St., Ste. 400, Scottsdale, AZ 85255
Phone: 480-927-4000   **Fax:** 480-927-4299
Web: www.servicesgroupofamerica.com

COMPETITORS

Clark National
Golden State Foods
Gordon Food Service
MAINES
McLane Foodservice
Meadowbrook Meat
Performance Food
Reinhart FoodService
Shamrock Foods
SYSCO
UniPro Foodservice
U.S. Foodservice

Shamrock Foods

You might say this company is milking the foodservice distribution business for all it's worth. Shamrock Foods is a major foodservice supplier that also owns one of the largest dairy operations in the southwestern US — Shamrock Farms. The company's distribution business supplies food and related products to restaurants and institutional foodservice operators in the intermountain states of the western US through its three distribution centers. Sister company Shamrock Farms, with more than 10,000 cows, produces and distributes a full line of dairy products including milk, ice cream, and cottage cheese.

In 2006 the company expanded its foodservice distribution operations with the acquisition of DPI Southwest, one of the regional operating units of wholesaler DPI Specialty Foods. The deal added a new distribution facility in Albuquerque, New Mexico, to its Phoenix and Denver operations.

Founded in 1920 as a mom-and-pop dairy, Shamrock Foods is still owned and operated by the founding McClelland family.

EXECUTIVES

Chairman and CEO: Norman McClelland
President and COO: Kent McClelland
CIO: Rob Baxter
SVP and General Manager, Arizona Foods Division: Larry F. Yancy
SVP and CFO: F. Phillips (Phil) Giltner III
SVP and General Manager, Colorado Foods Division: Kent Mullison
SVP and General Manager, Dairy Division: Michael Krueger
VP Human Resources: Robert (Bob) Beake

LOCATIONS

HQ: Shamrock Foods Company
  5080 N. 40th St., Ste. 400, Phoenix, AZ 85009
Phone: 602-477-2500
Web: www.shamrockfoods.com

PRODUCTS/OPERATIONS

Selected Brands and Products

Brickfire Bakery Cookies
Bountiful Harvest
  Canned Fruits and vegetables
  French Fries
  Frozen Fruits and vegetables
Cobblestone Market
  Cheese
  Corned Beef
  Pastrami
  Pot Roast
  Prime Rib
  Refrigerated Salads
  Roast Beef
  Sliced Meats
Hidden Bay
  Breaded shrimp
  Gulf shrimp
  Norwegian seafood
  Scallops
  Seafood steaks and fillets
  Surimi
  Tiger shrimp
!Intros!
  Breaded cheese sticks
  Breaded vegetables
  Onion rings
  Stuffed jalapenos
Katy's Kitchen
  Canned Puddings
  Cheese sauce
  Cookies
  Cooking wines
  Dessert toppings
  Pie filling
  Pudding mixes
Markon First Crop
  Fresh fruits and vegetables
  Table-ready fruits and juices
ProPak
  Disposable paper products
Ridgeline Coffee
San Pablo
  Canned and frozen peppers and chilies
  Canned beans
  Canned tomatoes
  Cheese sauce
  Guacamole
  Refried beans
  Salsa
  Tortillas
Shamrock Farms
  Butter
  Cottage cheese
  Cream cheese
  Eggs
  Half and half
  Heavy whipping cream
  Ice cream
  Milk
  Sour cream
Smart Source
  Canned fruits and vegetables
  Canned puddings
  French fries
  Frozen vegetables
Trescerro Coffee
Trifoglio
  Artichokes
  Balsamic vinegar
  Extra virgin olive oils
  Imported pasta
  Pear tomatoes
  Premium cheese
  Premium sausage
  Veal

COMPETITORS

C & S Wholesale
California Dairies Inc.
Dairy Farmers of America
Dean Foods
Land O'Lakes
McLane

Meadowbrook Meat
Nash-Finch
Performance Food
Services Group of America
SYSCO
U.S. Foodservice

Sheetz, Inc.

You might say Sheetz is to the convenience store business what Wal-Mart is to discount shopping. Noted for being exceptionally large (stores average 4,200 sq. ft., nearly twice the size of the average 7-Eleven, but new stores are as large as 5,000 sq. ft.), Sheetz stores sell groceries, fountain drinks, baked goods, and made-to-order sandwiches and salads, self-service car washes, as well as discount gas and cigarettes. The company operates more than 365 combination convenience stores and gas stations, mostly in Pennsylvania, but also in five other states (Maryland, North Carolina, Ohio, Virginia, and West Virginia). Founded in 1952 by Bob Sheetz, the company is owned and run by the Sheetz family.

With about 200 of its 365 stores located in one of the two US states (the other is Colorado) to prohibit beer sales by convenience stores, Sheetz has been lobbying to change the law. But a ruling by the State Supreme Court of Pennsylvania in mid-2009 revoking the company's liquor license at its convenience restaurant in Altoona, doesn't bode well for the future of beer sales by convenience stores in Pennsylvania. The company recently launched its freemybeer.com campaign for customers to sign an online petition requesting that the law be changed. Sheetz stores in other states sell beer.

Sheetz has gone far beyond traditional convenience store fare at locations in Altoona, Pennsylvania, and Raleigh, North Carolina. The two "convenience restaurants" are twice the size of a typical Sheetz store and have fried chicken, soups, salads, and pizza, in addition to sandwiches, on the menu. The stores seat about 50 people. In 2007 Sheetz began selling beer and malt-based coolers at the Altoona location, but stopped after the 2009 court ruling.

In July 2008 the chain launched its Sheetz Bros. Kitchen business. The 140,000-sq.-ft. commissary supplies Sheetz's stores with baked goods and prepared foods.

Increasing convenience is a priority at Sheetz stores. The company has begun installing gas machines that accept paper money at the pump, eliminating the walk inside for drivers on the go. To court the Starbucks crowd, Sheetz has added made-to-order espressos, cappuccinos, lattes, and mochas to its coffee menu. The company has installed Sheetz Bros. Coffeez counters with touch-screen ordering systems in all of its stores.

EXECUTIVES

Chairman: Stephen G. (Steve) Sheetz, age 61
President and CEO: Stanton R. (Stan) Sheetz, age 53
EVP Finance and Store Development:
Joseph S. (Joe) Sheetz
EVP Marketing: Louie Sheetz
EVP Petroleum Supply: Mike Lorenz
EVP Distribution and Sheetz Bros. Kitchen: Ray Ryan
VP Human Resources: Stephanie Hoover
VP and General Counsel: R. Michael (Mike) Cortez
VP Operations: Travis Sheetz
VP Information Technology: Jim Wenner
Director Corporate Information Technology:
George Medairy

LOCATIONS

HQ: Sheetz, Inc.
5700 6th Ave., Altoona, PA 16602
Phone: 814-946-3611 **Fax:** 814-946-4375
Web: www.sheetz.com

2009 Stores

	No.
Pennsylvania	203
Virginia	57
Maryland	28
West Virginia	28
Ohio	27
North Carolina	23
Total	**366**

PRODUCTS/OPERATIONS

Selected Products

Breakfast sandwiches
Burgerz and hot dogz
Coffeez
Cupo'ccino
Deli sandwiches
Dot'z Bakery items
Grilled chicken sandwiches
Hot and cold Subz
Nachoz
Pretzel meltz
Saladz
Wrapz

COMPETITORS

7-Eleven	Kroger
BP	Motiva Enterprises
Couche-Tard	Starbucks
Cumberland Farms	Sunoco
Exxon Mobil	Uni-Marts
Giant Eagle	Wawa, Inc.

Sherwood Food Distributors

Where's the beef? It might be on a truck owned by Sherwood Food Distributors. One of the largest meat and poultry wholesale distributors in the US, the company ships more than 12 million pounds of meat every week from packing facilities to grocery retailers, food manufacturers, and foodservice suppliers in the Midwest and southeastern US. It has five distribution centers in Florida, Georgia, Michigan, and Ohio, and operates a fleet of more than 150 trucks. Sherwood Food Distributors was formed in 1987 through the merger of the food distribution operations of Orleans International and Regal Packaging.

EXECUTIVES

CEO and Managing Partner: Earl Ishbia
EVP Corporate Affairs: Gary Karp
EVP Ohio Operations: Robert Lipson
EVP Inventory Management: Joel Ishbia
EVP Operations: Jim Gell
EVP Strategic Planning: Lon Makanoff
EVP and CFO: Jason Ishbia
EVP Sales and Marketing: Howard Ishbia

LOCATIONS

HQ: Sherwood Food Distributors
12499 Evergreen Rd., Detroit, MI 48228
Phone: 313-659-7300 **Fax:** 313-659-7506
Web: www.sherwoodfoods.com

COMPETITORS

Atlantic Premium Brands
C & S Wholesale
Colorado Boxed Beef
McLane
Nash-Finch
Quirch Foods
SUPERVALU
Wolverine Packing

ShopKo Stores

Rather than be a jack-of-all-retailing-trades across the country, Shopko Stores is content to concentrate on a limited product range in a few regions of the US. The company operates about 135 Shopko discount stores and half a dozen Shopko Express Rx drugstore outlets in about a dozen states throughout the Midwest, Mountain, and Pacific Northwest regions. Instead of offering a watered-down selection of many retail categories, it focuses on popular, higher-margin categories such as casual apparel, health and beauty items, and housewares. Most Shopko stores have optical centers and pharmacies. The company was taken private in 2005 by an affiliate of private investment firm Sun Capital Partners.

Shopko Stores has a new top shopkeeper: W. Paul Jones was promoted from the positions of president and chief merchandising officer to chairman and CEO in April 2009. Prior to joining Shopko in 2007, Jones logged 20 years at May Department Stores, Kohl's, and Sears. He succeeded Michael McDonald who left the company to join shoe retailer DSW. Sun Capital recruited McDonald from Carson Pirie Scott in May 2006.

Pharmacies and optical centers are big business for Shopko, which fills more than 11.5 million pharmacy prescriptions and sells 530,000 pair of eyeglasses each year, making it one of the nation's top 15 optical companies. Its optometrists perform in-store eye exams and prescribe correctional lenses, most of which are made in the company's optical laboratory and in 80-plus in-store finishing labs. The retailer is also rolling out health clinics in select locations in a partnership with Medical Marts Group. Shopko is expanding its network of stand-alone Shopko Express Rx drugstores, adding three locations in the Green Bay area in 2008.

Payless ShoeSource operates shoe departments (through a licensing agreement) in every Shopko store.

HISTORY

Chicagoan James Ruben moved to Green Bay, Wisconsin, and opened the first Shopko there in 1962. While other discounters crowded around major metro areas, Ruben saw the value potential in smaller markets and set up his stores in such locations. Shopko focused on male consumers, with most of its goods in the hardlines segment, which includes sporting goods and automotive parts. Ruben soon expanded into Michigan and had annual sales of $41 million by the end of the decade.

Shopko Stores was acquired by SUPERVALU, one of the US's biggest food wholesalers, in 1971. That year it became one of the first discounters to offer pharmacies at its stores; it also opened its tenth store. SUPERVALU was a hands-off parent and allowed store managers to select their own merchandise lines, which led to a merchandise shift toward housewares and clothing during the 1970s. By 1977, with 21 stores, Shopko surpassed $100 million in sales.

The company began offering in-store eye exams (in addition to selling eyeglasses) in 1978. Shopko's strong growth continued, and by 1984 it ran 39 stores, mostly in Minnesota, Nebraska, and Wisconsin, but also in three other Upper Midwest states. Bitten by Horace Greeley's "Go West" spirit, Shopko entered Montana and Idaho in 1986 and Utah in 1988. That year, with 87 stores, sales hit the billion-dollar mark.

Wal-Mart had become the proverbial 800-lb. gorilla by the middle of the 1980s, though, and Shopko set up a special task force in 1986 to figure out how not to get squashed. Executives realized that Shopko couldn't compete on price and decided instead to become strong where Wal-Mart was weak and to stay out of the ring when outmatched.

The ribbon on Shopko's 100th store was cut in 1990, and the company's 1991 figures attest to its health at the time: It was eighth among the US's discount chains in sales but second in profits. In 1991 SUPERVALU made Dale Kramer Shopko's president and CEO; it then spun the company off to the public, retaining a 46% stake. Shopko also began remodeling its stores, giving the chain a more upscale image.

In 1993 Shopko created ProVantage Health Services to offer prescription benefit management and mail-order pharmacy services. It soon added vision benefit management through a network of 4,500 eye care practitioners. Shopko supplemented its retail health offerings by acquiring Bravell (1995, claims management) and a division of United Wisconsin Insurance Company (1996, vision benefit management).

Shopko tested four Vision Advantage standalone optical outlets in Ohio in 1997 but closed them a year later. It also abandoned a proposed merger with discount drug chain Phar-Mor after both companies' stocks plummeted. Also in 1997 SUPERVALU sold its 46% stake in Shopko, and the company purchased 19 Penn-Daniels stores (two were closed, and 17 Jacks stores, mostly in Iowa and Illinois, were converted to the ShopKo banner in 1998).

In 1999 the firm spun off ProVantage to the public, retaining a 70% stake. Shopko then acquired Pamida Holdings (about 160 small-town discount stores) for $375 million including debt. In 2000 Shopko sold its ProVantage stake to drug maker Merck for $222 million and bought the 49-store P.M. Place Stores discount chain for $22 million. Later that year the company opened 56 additional Pamida stores. In 2001 Shopko closed more than 20 low-performing stores in seven states and cut about 2,500 jobs.

In April 2002 president and CEO William Podany resigned and was replaced by vice chairman Jeffrey Girard as interim CEO. In September Shopko launched in-store Urbanology shops offering home furnishings (including neon wall clocks, candles, and furry pillows) and fashion accessories targeted to the Generation Y market.

Sam Duncan (formerly president of Fred Meyer Stores) joined the company as its new chief executive the following month.

In 2004 Girard resigned as the vice chairman.

Duncan resigned in 2005 following the announcement of the pending acquisition by GHJ&M. That December, Shopko stock was delisted from the NYSE following the completion of the acquisition of the company by an affiliate of investment firm Sun Capital Partners. The deal valued the retailer at about $29 per share.

Michael MacDonald, from a Saks division, was appointed chairman and CEO in May 2006.

In March 2008 the company opened its first new store in six years.

McDonald resigned as CEO in March 2009 to lead the discount shoe retailer DSW. He was succeeded in April by W. Paul Jones, the company's president and chief merchandising officer.

EXECUTIVES

CEO: W. Paul Jones
EVP and COO: Michael J. Bettiga
EVP and Chief Merchandising Officer: Jill Soltau
CTO and VP Ecommerce: Ray Petersen
SVP and CIO: Tammy Hermann, age 41
SVP Merchandise Support: Jack Ingersoll
SVP, General Merchandise Manager, Hardlines and Home: Rod Ghormley
SVP Store Operations: Douglas McHose
SVP Marketing: Jack Mullen
VP Application and Integration Services: Jeffrey Herkert, age 44
VP Store Operations: Greg Morris
VP HR: Sara Stensrud
VP Loss Prevention: Annette McKeough
VP Pharmacy Services: Greg Ahmann
VP Financial Planning and Analysis: Dave Krivoshia
VP and Controller: Mary Meixelsperger
VP and General Counsel: Peter G. Vandenhouten
VP Advertising: Kathy Friedland-Howard, age 45
VP and Treasurer: Gary Gibson
Director of Corporate Communications: John Vigeland
Senior Corporate Counsel, Real Estate: David Crist, age 50
Auditors: Deloitte & Touche LLP

LOCATIONS

HQ: Shopko Stores Operating Co., LLC
700 Pilgrim Way, Green Bay, WI 54307
Phone: 920-429-2211   **Fax:** 920-429-4799
Web: www.shopko.com

PRODUCTS/OPERATIONS

2009 Stores

	No.
ShopKo	136
ShopKo Express Rx	6
Total	**142**

Selected Retail Merchandise

Hardlines
  Automotive
  Candy
  Electronics
  Furniture
  Greeting cards and gift wrap
  Health and beauty aids
  Home entertainment products
  Home textiles
  Household supplies
  Housewares
  Lawn and garden products
  Music/videos
  Seasonal goods
  Small appliances
  Snack foods
  Sporting goods
  Toys

Softlines
  Accessories
  Apparel
  Cosmetics
  Jewelry
  Shoes

COMPETITORS

Best Buy
Big Lots
Blue Cross Blue Shield of Michigan
Costco Wholesale
CVS Caremark
Dollar Tree
Duckwall-ALCO
Family Dollar Stores
J. C. Penney
Kmart
Kohl's
LensCrafters
Sears
Target
Thrifty White
TJX Companies
Walgreen
Wal-Mart

Sidley Austin

Sidley Austin aims to be a one-stop shop for large and small businesses, government agencies, and individuals needing legal help. The firm's 1,800-plus lawyers practice in a wide range of areas from about 15 offices in the US, Europe, and the Asia/Pacific region. Sidley focuses on business transactions and litigation, and the firm's geographic diversity enables it to handle multinational matters. Sidley took its modern form in 2001 when Chicago-based Sidley & Austin (founded by Norman Williams and John Thompson in 1866) merged with New York-based Brown & Wood (established in 1914). The combined firm was known as Sidley Austin Brown & Wood until 2006, when it changed to Sidley Austin.

President Barack Obama met his wife, Michelle, at Sidley Austin's Chicago office in 1988. The future president was a summer associate at the firm where the future first lady was working as a full-time associate.

Sidley Austin boasts several high-profile former government lawyers among its current ranks, including Roger Martella Jr., former general counsel to the US Environmental Protection Agency; Daniel Price, former assistant to the president and deputy national security advisor for International Economic Affairs; Jonathan Cohn, former deputy assistant attorney general; Peter Goodloe, former legislative counsel and parliamentarian for the House Committee on Energy and Commerce; and David Hill, former general counsel of the US Department of Energy.

EXECUTIVES

Chairman, Management Committee: Charles W. Douglas
Chairman, Executive Committee: Thomas A. Cole
Vice Chairman, Management Committee: Theodore N. Miller
Executive Director: Timothy Bergen
CIO: Nancy Karen
Partner, Commercial Litigation and Regulatory Practice, Hong Kong: Alan Linning

Partner: Peter D. Keisler
Director Training: Joy Heath Rush
Director Human Resources: Michael Prapuolenis
Director Marketing: Janet Zagorin
Controller: Christian Cooley
Counsel, Intellectual Property Litigation: Karin Norton,
age 46

LOCATIONS

HQ: Sidley Austin LLP
1 S. Dearborn St., Chicago, IL 60603
Phone: 312-853-7000   **Fax:** 312-853-7036
Web: www.sidley.com

PRODUCTS/OPERATIONS

Selected Practice Areas

Alternative dispute resolution
Antitrust
Automotive safety litigation and regulation
Banking and financial transactions
Canada
China
College and university law
Communications
Corporate
Corporate reorganization and bankruptcy
Corporate/securities
Employee benefits
Employment and labor
Energy
Environmental
European Union law
Financial institutions
Food and drug
General appellate
Government contracts
Government relations
Health care
Hong Kong corporate finance
Immigration
Information law and privacy
Insurance
Insurance corporate practice
Intellectual property
International investment funds
International trade and dispute resolution
Investment company and investment adviser
Investment products and derivatives
Latin America
Litigation
London transactional practice
Postal services practice
Privacy, data protection, and information security
Private clients, trusts, and estates
Pro bono
Project finance
Public finance
Real estate
Religious institutions
Securities enforcement
Securitization and structured finance
Tax

COMPETITORS

Baker & McKenzie
Clifford Chance
Jones Day
Kirkland & Ellis
Latham & Watkins
Mayer Brown
McDermott Will & Emery
Morgan, Lewis
Shearman & Sterling
Skadden, Arps
Sullivan & Cromwell
Weil, Gotshal & Manges
White & Case

HISTORICAL FINANCIALS
Company Type: Partnership

Income Statement

FYE: December 31

	REVENUE ($ mil.)	NET INCOME ($ mil.)	NET PROFIT MARGIN	EMPLOYEES
12/08	1,490	—	—	—
12/07	1,386	—	—	—
12/06	1,247	—	—	3,806
12/05	1,124	—	—	3,585
Annual Growth	9.8%	—	—	6.2%

Revenue History

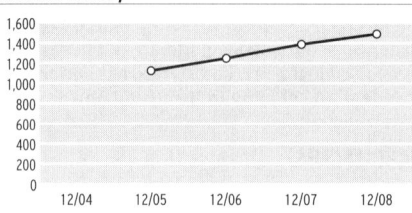

Sierra Club

Take a hike with the Sierra Club. The Sierra Club promotes outdoor activities and environmental activism on both the local and national levels through political lobbies, education, outings, and publications. The club's more than 1.3 million members are organized into state and regional chapters throughout the US and Canada. Sierra Club publishes books, calendars, *SIERRA* magazine, and *The Planet,* an activist newsletter. Its current issues are smart energy solutions, clean water, stopping commercial logging in national forests, ending sprawl, and protecting wetlands. The group was founded in 1892 by naturalist John Muir.

Organizations within the Sierra Club focus on bringing people to the wilderness. Youth program Building Bridges to the Outdoors gives inner-city children access to nature experiences. The program's motto is "No child will be left inside." Sierra Club Outings organizes trips from Tahoe to Tibet that cover a range of interests, including backpacking, canoeing, and sailing. The group also coordinates excursions for activists, families, and seniors. The Sierra Club's diversity programs focus on engaging people of wide-ranging ethnicities and cultures. It has established Ecocentro as an outreach to the Latino community on issues concerning the environment and family health.

EXECUTIVES

Executive Director: Carl Pope
President: Robbie Cox
VP: Robin Mann
Treasurer: Joni Bosh
Secretary: Sanjay Ranchod
National Press Secretary: David Willett
Director: Larry Fahn
Auditors: KPMG LLP

LOCATIONS

HQ: Sierra Club
85 2nd St., 2nd Fl., San Francisco, CA 94105
Phone: 415-977-5500   **Fax:** 415-977-5799
Web: www.sierraclub.org

Sierra Pacific Industries

Sierra Pacific Industries (SPI) isn't your run-of-the-mill company. SPI owns and manages about 2 million acres of timberland in California and Washington. Through its network of sawmills the company produces millwork, lumber and wood-fiber products, fencing, aluminum-clad and wood patio doors, and windows. SPI also operates cogeneration plants that recycle wood waste into electricity for its plants; excess electricity is sold to local energy service providers. In addition to the timber business, the company is involved in residential and commercial real estate. SPI traces its roots to the late 1920s when it was founded by R. H. "Curly" Emmerson. The Emmerson family continues to own and operate SPI.

The company distributes its products by truck, train, and boat. SPI oversees a fleet of about 250 trucks and operates Eureka Dock facility on Humboldt Bay in Eureka, California, to serve its own shipping needs as well as those of other California sawmills. SPI also owns the Quincy Railroad.

Recognizing that some of its acquired land tracts are better suited for residential or commercial development than for growing trees, SPI has moved into property development. A few of its projects include forested subdivisions and a regional business park.

SPI has not gone unscathed during the economic downturn. In 2009 it closed three sawmills and one of its biomass-fueled electric power plants in California. The closures stemmed from a difficult lumber market and reduced harvests on nearby national forest land.

EXECUTIVES

President: A. A. (Red) Emmerson
CTO: Steve Gaston
VP Financial: Mark Emmerson
VP Sales and Marketing: George Emmerson
Real Estate: Gary Blanc
Director Government Affairs: Mark Pawlicki
Manager Equipment Sales: Gary Morgan
President, Sierra Pacific Foundation:
Carolyn Emmerson Dietz

LOCATIONS

HQ: Sierra Pacific Industries
19794 Riverside Ave., Anderson, CA 96007
Phone: 530-378-8000   **Fax:** 530-378-8109
Web: www.spi-ind.com

PRODUCTS/OPERATIONS

Selected Products
Aluminum-clad windows and doors
Cedar fencing
Chips for pulp mills
Decorative bark
Dimension lumber
Douglas Fir timbers
Mouldings and millwork
Poles
Shavings for particleboard
Wood windows and doors

COMPETITORS

Andersen Corporation
GBO
Georgia-Pacific
Hampton Affiliates
Harvey Industries
International Paper
Kolbe & Kolbe
Louisiana-Pacific
North Pacific Group
Plum Creek Timber
Potlatch
Roseburg Forest Products
Silver Line Building Products
Storey Sawmill
Tumac Lumber
VELUX
Western Forest Products
Weyerhaeuser

HISTORICAL FINANCIALS
Company Type: Private

Income Statement

FYE: December 31

	ESTIMATED REVENUE ($ mil.)	NET INCOME ($ mil.)	NET PROFIT MARGIN	EMPLOYEES
12/07	1,010	—	—	4,400
12/06	1,350	—	—	3,900
12/05	1,570	—	—	4,000
12/04	1,500	—	—	3,600
12/03	1,400	—	—	3,600
Annual Growth	(7.8%)	—	—	5.1%

Revenue History

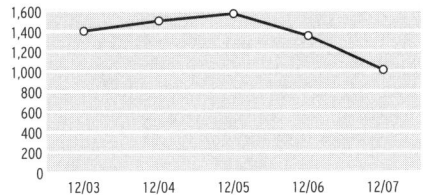

Sigma Plastics

The plastic sheeting and stretch film business is not Greek to Sigma Plastics. Growing through acquisitions, the conglomerate (one of the largest of its kind in North America) produces plastic film and sheet for industrial, institutional, and government markets. Subsidiary Alpha Industries and its 15 sister subsidiaries, including Beta, Epsilon, and Omega, make plastic film and bags for dry cleaners, grocers, and retailers, as well as food service, health care, janitorial, industrial packaging, lodging, and safety industries. Sigma Plastics manufactures its wide range of plastic products on 700 extrusion lines at its four North American plants and one in Canada. Chairman Alfred Teo owns the company.

The company maintains its practice of adding new territory to its business empire by purchasing struggling competitors and funding their growth. Sigma Plastics acquired the majority ownership in specialty film maker ISO Poly Films in early 2009. ISO Poly's business lines — extruding multilayer films and pouches for the food-packaging industry's produce, liquids, and other products — reportedly supply a more

recession-proof market than some of Sigma Plastics' existing ones. Alfred Teo is taking the reins as chairman of ISO Poly Films.

The ISO Poly score comes on the heels of picking up the customs film plant of Allied Extruders in mid-2007. The deal gave Sigma Plastics an additional 80,000-sq.-ft. facility for making specialty films, also for the food packaging industry.

Singapore-born and China-raised Alfred Teo founded Sigma Plastics (as Sigma Extruding) in 1978. In mid-2006 Teo pleaded guilty in a US federal court to securities fraud unrelated to Sigma Plastics. Teo was sentenced to serve 30 months in federal prison. He served 11 months and returned to day-to-day management of Sigma Plastics in late 2008. Teo still faces a civil lawsuit filed by the Securities and Exchange Commission related to insider trading.

Teo's son, Mark Teo, assumed leadership of the company as president and chief operating officer. The patriarch's other sons, Alan, Alfred Jr., and Andrew, also serve in the management of Sigma Plastics.

EXECUTIVES

Chairman and CEO: Alfred S. Teo, age 63
President, Stretch Film: Bob Nocek
EVP Stretch Film: Per Nylen
Northeast Region Sales Manager Stretch Film: Michael Richwalder
Central Region Sales Manager Stretch Film: Chuck Magee
Southwest Region Sales Manager Stretch Film: Jim Love
Western Region Sales Manager Stretch Film: Bruce Gustafson

LOCATIONS

HQ: Sigma Plastics Group
Page & Schuyler Aves., Bldg. #5
Lyndhurst, NJ 07071
Phone: 201-507-9100   **Fax:** 201-507-0447
Web: www.sigmaplastics.com

COMPETITORS

AEP Industries	Paragon Films
Bemis	Pliant Corporation
Berry Plastics	Raven Industries
DuPont	Sealed Air Corp.
Exopack	Sonoco Products
Inteplast	Spartech
Pactiv	

HISTORICAL FINANCIALS
Company Type: Private

Income Statement

FYE: October 31

	REVENUE ($ mil.)	NET INCOME ($ mil.)	NET PROFIT MARGIN	EMPLOYEES
10/08	1,800	—	—	5,000
10/07	1,580	—	—	5,000
Annual Growth	13.9%	—	—	0.0%

Revenue History

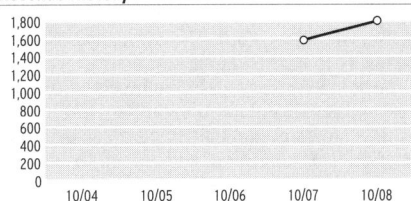

Simmons Bedding

Simmons sleeps tight as one of the top three US mattress makers alongside rivals Sealy and Serta. The company, founded by Zalmon Simmons in 1870, makes mattresses and accessories to serve a range of customers looking for luxury, eco-friendly, and memory-foam products. It makes its products under the Beautyrest, DeepSleep, BeautySleep, ComforPedic, Natural Care, and Simmons labels. Simmons sells its products across North America through more than 15,500 furniture outlets, department stores, and specialty shops. It also operates a handful of World of Sleep shops. In November 2009 the company filed for Chapter 11 and plans to be acquired by a private equity consortium as part of its reorganization.

Declining consumer spending amid the US recession prompted Simmons to restructure its operations and debt. Through the reorganization plan, the company looks to slash its liabilities in half, from about $1 billion. It also obtained about $35 million in debtor-in-possession financing. The bankruptcy is not expected to interfere with operations, and Simmons expects to emerge from Chapter 11 in January 2010. The private equity consortium, which includes investment firm Ares Management and Teachers' Private Capital (the investment unit of the Ontario Teachers' Pension Plan), will acquire Simmons for $760 million. (Ares Management and Teachers' Private Capital also own competitor Serta, which they plan to continue operating as a separate entity.)

To weather the economic downturn that hit many manufacturers during 2008, Simmons implemented a two-fold strategy. First, it pared down its operations: By 2009 the company had cut its salaried workforce by 20%. The reduction extended to all levels and divisions of the company and included voluntary and involuntary layoffs. Also, Simmons shuttered its manufacturing facilities in Mableton, Georgia, and Bramalea, Ontario, in 2008. Second, the company raised prices on its products in the US and Canada across most of its lines. Simmons had logged about a 9% decline in overall sales volumes as consumer spending slowed that year. While its Canadian products sold better in 2008 than the company had expected, the increases weren't enough to turn the tide. The company was hoping to offset sales volume declines by selling its mattresses at slightly higher prices.

Simmons makes most of its revenue through wholesale sales of its innerspring mattresses. The manufacturer partners with other US and Canadian manufacturers by licensing its brand names for bedding accessories, furniture, and air beds. For items sold outside the region, Simmons enlists third-party manufacturers to produce its branded goods.

In addition to its manufacturing and licensing operations, Simmons distributes mattresses and other bedding to the hospitality industry (Starwood Hotels, La Quinta, Best Western) and to government agencies. Starwood's Westin properties promotes its Heavenly Bed, which is a Simmons Beautyrest mattress produced under private label. The company also boasts supply agreements with Leggett & Platt, Foamex, and National Standard Company.

Looking to extend its reach into memory foam products and chase after rival Tempur-Pedic's share of that niche of the market, Simmons in

2007 bought Comfor Products, which makes and markets the Comfor-Pedic line of mattresses. The company was founded as Industrial Rubber & Supply and has been manufacturing foam products for more than 60 years. Simmons retained Comfor Product's headquarters near Seattle. The deal has allowed Simmons to leverage Comfor Products' foam mattress capabilities and expand its specialty sleep unit, which is anchored by the Simmons Natural Care line of latex mattresses.

The executive suite at Simmons is showing some worn carpet: Gary Matthews lasted less than a year, leaving in May 2007. The next year, in September 2008, Simmons chairman and CEO Charlie Eitel resigned and was replaced by Steve Fendrich. Fendrich had joined the mattress company in January 2008 as its president and COO, reporting to Eitel. Eitel remains vice chairman.

THL Bedding (a holding of Thomas H. Lee Partners) bought Simmons in 2003 for about $1.1 billion. THL owns 71% of Simmons, while Fenway Partners Capital Fund holds a stake of about 9%.

EXECUTIVES

Vice Chairman: Charles R. (Charlie) Eitel, age 59, $1,021,308 total compensation
President and COO: Stephen G. (Steve) Fendrich, age 48, $617,950 total compensation
EVP and CFO: William S. Creekmuir, age 54
EVP Sales: Dominick Azevedo, $519,181 total compensation
EVP Marketing: Timothy F. (Tim) Oakhill, age 47, $382,086 total compensation
EVP General Counsel: Kristen K. McGuffey, age 44
EVP Human Resources: Kimberly A. Samon, age 42
SVP Sales Operations and Development: Bradley (Brad) Hill
SVP Manufacturing: Robert Ballard
SVP Manufacturing: Tom Burns
SVP Technical Services: Robert M. Carstens, age 43
SVP and Controller: Mark F. Chambless, age 52
VP Credit Services: Tom Brkanovic
President Specialty Products: Scott Smalling
Auditors: PricewaterhouseCoopers LLP

LOCATIONS

HQ: Simmons Company
1 Concourse Pkwy., Ste. 800, Atlanta, GA 30328
Phone: 770-512-7700   **Fax:** 770-392-2560
Web: www.simmons.com

2008 Sales

	% of total
Domestic, including Puerto Rico	88
Canada	12
Total	**100**

PRODUCTS/OPERATIONS

Selected Brands

Advanced Pocketed Coil
BackCare
Beautyrest
Beautyrest Black
Comfor-Pedic
DeepSleep
Pocketed Coil
Simmons

COMPETITORS

1800Mattress.com
Aero Products International
Comfortaire
J. C. Penney
King Koil
Mattress Giant
Premier Bedding Group
Restonic Mattress
Sealy
Sears
Select Comfort
Serta
Spring Air
Tempur-Pedic

HISTORICAL FINANCIALS

Company Type: Private

Income Statement

FYE: Last Saturday in December

	REVENUE ($ mil.)	NET INCOME ($ mil.)	NET PROFIT MARGIN	EMPLOYEES
12/08	1,029	(492)	—	2,800
12/07	1,127	24	2.1%	3,800
12/06	962	48	5.0%	3,300
12/05	855	3	0.4%	3,000
12/04	870	25	2.8%	3,300
Annual Growth	**4.3%**	**—**		**(4.0%)**

2008 Year-End Financials

Debt ratio: —   Current ratio: —
Return on equity: —   Long-term debt ($ mil.): 13
Cash ($ mil.): —

Net Income History

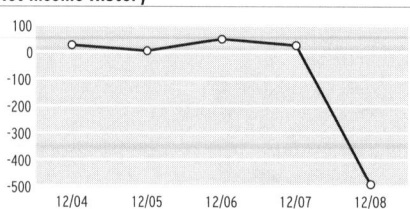

Sinclair Oil

Way out west, where fossils are found, brontosaur signs appear all 'round. They belong to Sinclair Oil's more than 2,600 service stations and convenience stores in 21 western and midwestern US states. The company also operates three oil refineries, pipelines, exploration operations, and a trucking fleet, all in the western US. It owns a 71,500-barrels-per-day refinery in Rawlins, Wyoming, a 20,000-barrels-per-day unit in Casper, Wyoming, and a 75,000-barrels-per-day refinery in Tulsa, Oklahoma.

A diversified company, Sinclair also owns the Grand America Hotel, the Little America hotel chain, and two ski resorts (Sun Valley in Idaho and Snowbasin in Utah). The company is owned and led by R. Earl Holding.

The company was looking to invest $1 billion to expand capacity at its Tulsa refinery to 115,000 by 2010. However, in 2009 Sinclair decided that cash was a better option, and agreed to sell the refinery to Holly Corporation for $128.5 million in return for a long-term supply agreement.

When Harry Sinclair set up his namesake exploration and production company in 1916, it was the largest oil independent in the US mid-continent, and sold some 33,000 barrels a day. Imprisoned for seven months in 1929 for refusing to answer questions from senators regarding his lucrative oil contracts with the government-owned Teapot Dome properties, Sinclair subsequently built Sinclair Oil into an industry giant. R. Earl Holding acquired the major surviving refining and marketing assets of the company in 1976.

EXECUTIVES

Chairman: R. Earl Holding
President and CEO: Peter M. Johnson
EVP Operations: Kevin Brown
SVP Marketing: Bud Blackmore
VP Government Relations: Clint Ensign
VP Finance and Treasurer: Charles Barlow
General Manager Retail: Larry Rogers
Regional Manager: Dalton Kehlbeck
Manager Real Estate: Mark London
Auditors: PricewaterhouseCoopers LLP

LOCATIONS

HQ: Sinclair Oil Corporation
550 E. South Temple, Salt Lake City, UT 84102
Phone: 801-524-2700   **Fax:** 801-524-2880
Web: www.sinclairoil.com

Sinclair Oil's operations include marketing offices, refineries, trucking terminals, and Little America hotels and resorts throughout the western US.

PRODUCTS/OPERATIONS

Selected Operations

Oil and gas (exploration, marketing, pipelines, product terminals, refineries, service stations, trucking)
Little America Hotels & Resorts
Grand America Hotel (Salt Lake City)
Little America hotel chain (Arizona, Utah, Wyoming)
Snowbasin (Utah) and Sun Valley (Idaho) ski resorts
The Westgate Hotel (San Diego)

COMPETITORS

Avis Budget	Marriott
BP	Royal Dutch Shell
ConocoPhillips	Vail Resorts
Exxon Mobil	Valero Energy
Hilton Worldwide	Winter Sports

HISTORICAL FINANCIALS

Company Type: Private

Income Statement

FYE: December 31

	ESTIMATED REVENUE ($ mil.)	NET INCOME ($ mil.)	NET PROFIT MARGIN	EMPLOYEES
12/08	7,750	—	—	7,000
12/07	7,000	—	—	7,000
12/06	6,800	—	—	7,000
12/05	5,600	—	—	7,000
12/04	3,950	—	—	7,000
Annual Growth	**18.4%**	**—**	**—**	**0.0%**

Revenue History

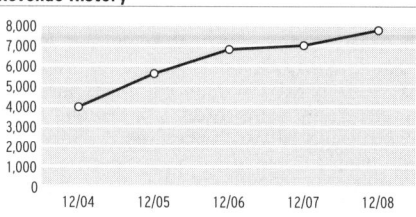

Sisters of Charity of Leavenworth Health System

In 1858 a group of Catholic sisters arrived in Kansas, then still a territory, and began teaching and tending the sick. In 1864 the sisters opened a private hospital, establishing the foundation for what would eventually be the Sisters of Charity of Leavenworth Health System (SCLHS). Today, the not-for-profit health care organization operates nine hospitals and four clinics throughout California, Colorado, Kansas, and Montana, with a total of more than 2,000 beds. Its facilities include acute care, extended care, and rehabilitation services. True to its name, the organization's facilities continue to provide health services to low-income and uninsured people.

Exempla is a joint venture between SCLHS and the Lutheran-sponsored Community First Foundation. The independently-run three-hospital system objected to a plan for SCLHS to buy out its partner, citing the Catholic ethical and religious directives that SCLHS would impose on the hospitals. In mid-2009 binding arbitration blocked the sale of Exempla to SCLHS, but SCLHS may eventually take full ownership without an exchange of cash payment.

Faced with reduced revenues due to economic pressures, SCLHS is working to centralize its business offices to increase efficiency.

EXECUTIVES

Chair: Sister Doris Gottemoeller
President, CEO, and Director: William M. Murray
EVP and COO: Mary Jo Gregory
VP and General Counsel: Edward L. Barker
VP Sponsorship: Sister Judith Jackson
VP Strategy and Business Development and Chief Strategy Officer: Jill Willen Kennelly
VP Human Resources: Irma Napoli
VP Information Services and CIO: Robert A. Boysen
VP Finance and CFO: Michael D. Rowe
VP Quality and Safety: Peter Wong
Chief Clinical Transformation Officer: Richard Lopes

LOCATIONS

HQ: Sisters of Charity of Leavenworth Health System
9801 Renner Blvd., Ste. 100, Lenexa, KS 66219
Phone: 913-895-2800   **Fax:** 913-895-2900
Web: www.sclhsc.org

Selected Facilities
California
  Saint John's Health Center (Santa Monica)
Colorado
  Exempla Saint Joseph Hospital (Denver)
  Marillac Clinic (Grand Junction)
  St. Mary's Hospital and Medical Center (Grand Junction)
Kansas
  Duchesne Clinic (Kansas City)
  Marian Clinic (Topeka)
  Providence Medical Center (Kansas City)
  St. Francis Health Center (Topeka)
  Saint John Hospital (Leavenworth)
  Saint Vincent Clinic (Leavenworth)
Montana
  Holy Rosary Healthcare (Miles City)
  St. James Healthcare (Butte)
  Saint Vincent Healthcare (Billings)

COMPETITORS
Billings Clinic
Brotman Medical Center
Catholic Health Initiatives
Cedars-Sinai Medical Center
Denver Health and Hospital Authority
Presbyterian/St. Luke's Medical Center
Shawnee Mission Medical Center
Sisters of Mercy Health System
Stormont-Vail HealthCare
Truman Medical Centers
University of Colorado Hospital
University of Kansas Medical Center

HISTORICAL FINANCIALS
Company Type: Not-for-profit

Income Statement				FYE: December 31
	REVENUE ($ mil.)	NET INCOME ($ mil.)	NET PROFIT MARGIN	EMPLOYEES
12/08	1,832	—	—	10,770

Sisters of Mercy Health System

Not to be confused with the goth rock band of the same name, *this* Sisters of Mercy provides a range of health care and social services through its network of facilities and service organizations. The organization operates nearly 20 acute care hospitals (including one specialty heart hospital) with some 4,000 licensed beds in seven states throughout the South and Midwest. Its hospital groups include facilities for nursing homes, medical practices, and outpatient centers. Sisters of Mercy Health System also runs health outreach organizations in Louisiana, Mississippi, and Texas; and its for-profit Mercy Health Plans offers managed health plans, primarily in Arkansas, Missouri, and Texas.

The organization's outreach efforts include Mercy Ministries of Laredo, a group providing primary health care and social services to residents of Laredo, Texas. It had previously owned a hospital system in Laredo (formerly known as Mercy Health Center), but sold the system to Community Health Systems.

In New Orleans, Sisters of Mercy sponsors Mercy Family Center, a mental health services provider, and in Mississippi it funds a health care advocacy group.

In recent years the hospital has undergone a number of expansions and has established several new outpatient services in multiple locations throughout its service area. In 2008 alone, the hospital invested about $445 million in facility replacements, renovations, expansions, and information technology implementations.

The organization was founded by the Sisters of Mercy of the St. Louis Regional Community in 1986 and operated under that model until 2008, when its sponsorship was transferred from the Sisters of Mercy of the St. Louis Regional Community to a new entity, Mercy Health Ministry. The shift to the new sponsorship organization was made to allow lay members to join the Sisters of Mercy in sponsoring the ministry. It also reflects the growing number of lay people holding executive positions at the system's hospitals and on the board of directors.

Sisters of Mercy named Lynn Britton as its president and CEO in 2009. Britton, who had served as senior vice president since 2004, replaced John Sullivan, who was CEO for about two years.

EXECUTIVES

Chairman: Ronald B. (Ron) Ashworth
President and CEO: Lynn Britton
EVP and COO: Michael (Mike) McCurry
EVP Finance: James R. Jaacks
SVP and CFO: Randall J. (Randy) Combs
SVP and General Counsel: Philip Wheeler
SVP Regional Markets, Oklahoma; President and CEO, St. John's Mercy Health Care: Denny DeNarvaez, age 53
SVP Regional Markets, Arkansas and Kansas; President and CEO, St. John's Health System: Kim Day
VP and CIO: Will Showalter
VP Clinical Safety and Chief Medical Officer: Glenn Mitchell
VP Market Development: Nikki Viner
VP Corporate Communications: Barbara W. (Barb) Meyer
VP Human Resources: Anthony D. (Tony) Kinslow
Senior Communications Specialist: Nichole (Niki) Burgdorf

LOCATIONS

HQ: Sisters of Mercy Health System
14528 S. Outer Forty Dr., Ste. 100
Chesterfield, MO 63017
Phone: 314-579-6100   **Fax:** 314-628-3723
Web: www.mercy.net

Selected Service Units and Subsidiaries
Mercy Health Plans
Mercy Health System of Kansas
  Mercy Health Center (Fort Scott)
  Mercy Hospital (Independence)
  Mercy Physician Group
Mercy Health System of Northwest Arkansas
  Mercy Health Center (Bentonville)
  Mercy Medical Clinics
  St. Mary's Hospital (Rogers)
Mercy Health System of Oklahoma
  Mercy Health Center (Oklahoma City)
  Mercy Health Network (clinics, Oklahoma City)
  Mercy Memorial Health Center (Ardmore)
  Oklahoma Heart Hospital (Oklahoma City)
  Southern Oklahoma Physician Hospital Organization (Ardmore)
Mercy Ministries of Laredo (Laredo, TX)
St. Edward Mercy Health Network (Arkansas)
  Health Point Physician Hospital Organization (Fort Smith)
  Mercy Hospital of Scott County (Waldron)
  Mercy Hospital/Turner Memorial (Ozark)
  Mercy Medical Group
  Mercy Northside Clinic (Fort Smith)
  North Logan Mercy Hospital (Paris)
  St. Edward Mercy Medical Center (Fort Smith)
St. John's Health System (Missouri)
  St. John's Clinic
  St. John's Home Care
  St. John's Hospital (Springfield)
  St. John's Hospital-Aurora (Aurora)
  St. John's Hospital-Berryville (Berryville)
  St. John's Hospital-Cassville (Cassville)
  St. John's Hospital-Lebanon (Lebanon)
  St. John's Mercy Villa
  St. John's St. Francis Hospital (Mountain View)
St. John's Mercy Health Care (Missouri)
  St. John's Mercy Medical Group (St. Louis)
  St. John's Mercy Hospital (Washington)
  St. John's Mercy Medical Center (Creve Coeur)
St. Joseph's Mercy Health Center (Arkansas)
  St. Joseph's Mercy Health Center (Hot Springs, AR)

COMPETITORS

Ascension Health
Baptist Health (Arkansas)
Barnes-Jewish Hospital
BJC HealthCare
Christian Hospital
CHRISTUS Health
Community Health Systems
HCA
INTEGRIS Health
Lester E. Cox Medical Centers
MedCath
Memorial Hospital (Illinois)
RehabCare
Saint Luke's Health System
Shawnee Mission Medical Center
Sisters of Charity of Leavenworth
SSM Health Care
St. Anthony's Medical Center
St. John's Mercy Health Care
St. Luke's Hospital
St. Vincent Health System
Tenet Healthcare
Universal Health Services

HISTORICAL FINANCIALS

Company Type: Not-for-profit

Income Statement

FYE: June 30

	REVENUE ($ mil.)	NET INCOME ($ mil.)	NET PROFIT MARGIN	EMPLOYEES
6/08	3,748	55	1.5%	29,500
6/07	3,654	68	1.9%	28,000
6/06	3,580	46	1.3%	29,500
6/05	3,247	56	1.7%	29,100
6/04	3,003	—	—	26,000
Annual Growth	5.7%	(0.4%)	—	3.2%

Net Income History

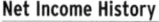
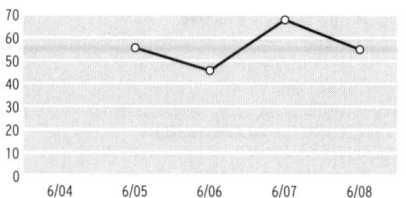

Sitel Corporation

When businesses need a little help in taking care of their customers, teleservices company Sitel (formerly ClientLogic) wants to be there. The company is a leading provider of business process outsourcing (BPO) services related to customer care. Its offerings include customer acquisition, back-office processing, collections, and technical support. It operates from more than 155 facilities in about 30 countries around the world. The former ClientLogic expanded significantly in 2007 when it acquired larger rival SITEL; the combined company then changed its name to Sitel. Canadian investment company Onex owns a controlling stake in Sitel.

In early 2008 Sitel launched call centers in Managua, Nicaragua, and Berlin. Later that year it expanded its operations in Managua by opening another call center specializing in customer service, technical support, and sales and back office services.

The former ClientLogic paid about $472 million for SITEL, which before the deal ranked behind only Convergys and TeleTech Holdings among US teleservices providers. To focus on its teleservices operations, ClientLogic sold its Columbus, Ohio-based fulfillment business to distribution company Innotrac in October 2006.

The new Sitel traces its roots to Buffalo, New York-based Upgrade Corp. of America, which was founded by Ronald Schreiber and Jordan Levy. Upgrade (later known as SOFTBANK Services Group) marketed software upgrades for such clients as Microsoft. It was acquired in 1998 by Onex and merged with North Direct Response to create ClientLogic.

EXECUTIVES

Chairman: Seth M. Mersky
President and CEO: David E. Garner
Global COO: Bert Quintana
Global CFO: Patrick Dupuis, age 46
CIO: Mandy Edwards
Global Chief Sales and Marketing Officer:
  Donald B. (Don) Berryman, age 50
Global Chief Marketing Officer: Amit Shankardass
Chief Legal Officer and Secretary: David Beckman
Chief Human Resources Officer: Michael Wellman
Auditors: PricewaterhouseCoopers LLP

LOCATIONS

HQ: Sitel Corporation
  3102 West End Ave., Ste. 1000, Nashville, TN 37203
Phone: 615-301-7100 **Fax:** 615-301-7150
Web: www.sitel.com

PRODUCTS/OPERATIONS

Selected Products and Services

Back-office processing
  Catalog services
  eCommerce services
  Order and payment processing
  Rebate processing activities
Customer acquisition
  Database management
  Inbound sales
  Lead generation
  Order taking
  Outband sales
  Subscription renewals
Customer care
  Account change
  Billing information
  Investor inquiries
  Loyalty clubs
  Repeat purchases
  Up-selling/cross-selling
  Warranty calls
Risk management
  Credit activation
  Disaster prevention and recovery
  Property recovery
Technical support
  Corporate help desk
  Hardware and software support
  Internet support
  PC/server support
  Troubleshooting
  Warranty and post warranty

COMPETITORS

Accenture	ICT Group
Affiliated Computer Services	NCO
	PeopleSupport
APAC Customer Services	StarTek
Computer Sciences Corp.	Sykes Enterprises
Concentrix	Teleperformance
Convergys	TeleTech
HP Enterprise Services	West Corporation
IBM Global Services	Wipro Technologies

HISTORICAL FINANCIALS

Company Type: Private

Income Statement

FYE: December 31

	REVENUE ($ mil.)	NET INCOME ($ mil.)	NET PROFIT MARGIN	EMPLOYEES
12/08	1,700	—	—	60,000
12/07	1,700	—	—	66,000
12/06	749	—	—	67,000
12/05	715	—	—	22,000
12/04	562	—	—	20,300
Annual Growth	31.9%	—	—	31.1%

Revenue History

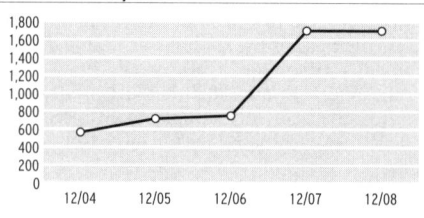

Skadden, Arps

Have you heard about the law firm that sued the business-information publisher for a profile that opened with a wickedly clever lawyer joke? Neither have we, and we would like to keep it that way. Skadden, Arps, Slate, Meagher & Flom, a leading US law firm and one of the largest in the world, has some 2,000 attorneys in some 25 offices around the globe, from Boston to Beijing and from London to Los Angeles. The firm is best known for its work in mergers and acquisitions, corporate restructuring, and corporate finance, but it represents businesses in a wide variety of practice areas, including intellectual property and litigation. Skadden was founded in 1948.

Skadden has worked for a number of *FORTUNE* 500 companies. High-profile clients have included JPMorgan Chase and State Farm, as well as Arcelor, Merrill Lynch, and Toshiba.

Over the years Skadden has grown organically rather than by merging with other firms. The New York office is the firm's largest, but offices outside the US have been growing faster. As part of its plan to expand outside the US, Skadden opened offices in Shanghai and São Paulo in 2008 — giving the firm greater access to growing markets less affected by the economic downturn.

EXECUTIVES

Executive Partner: Eric J. Friedman, age 44
Managing Director: Earle Yaffa
CFO: Noah J. Puntus
CTO: Harris Z. Tilevitz
Senior Director: Carol A. Sawdye
Managing Attorney: Robert Abrams
Corporate Deputy Legal Practice Partner:
  Thomas H. Kennedy
Chief Administrative Officer: Laurel E. Henschel
Senior Partner, Corporate Practice: Roger S. Aaron
**Global Head, Real Estate Investment Trust Practice
  Group:** Barnet Phillips IV
Director Marketing and Business Development:
  Sally J. Feldman
Director Human Resources: Vaughn Burke
Corporate Partner: Joseph H. Flom

LOCATIONS

HQ: Skadden, Arps, Slate, Meagher & Flom LLP
  4 Times Sq., New York, NY 10036
Phone: 212-735-3000   **Fax:** 212-735-2000
Web: www.skadden.com

PRODUCTS/OPERATIONS

Selected Practice Areas

Alternative dispute resolution
Antitrust
Appellate litigation and legal issues
Banking and institutional investing
Biological and chemical technology diligence and
  transactions
CFIUS
Class action litigation
Climate change
Communications
Consumer financial services enforcement and litigation
Corporate compliance programs
Corporate finance
Corporate governance
Corporate restructuring
Crisis management
Derivative financial products, commodities, and futures
Energy and infrastructure projects
Energy regulation and litigation
Environmental
Environmental litigation
European Union/international competition
Executive compensation and benefits
Exempt and nonprofit organizations
False Claims Act defense
Financial institutions
Financial institutions regulation and enforcement
Foreign Corrupt Practices Act defense
Franchise law
Gaming
Government contract disputes
Government enforcement and white collar crime
Health care
Health care and life sciences
Information technology and e-commerce
Insurance
Intellectual property and technology
International law and policy
International litigation and arbitration
International tax
International trade
Investment management
Labor and employment law
Lease financing
Litigation
Mass torts and insurance litigation
Media and entertainment
Mergers and acquisitions
Outsourcing
Patent and technology litigation and counseling
Pharmaceutical, biotechnology, and medical device
  licensing
Political law
Private equity
Private equity funds
Pro bono
Public policy

Real estate
Real estate investment trusts
Russia and CIS
Securities enforcement and compliance
Securities litigation
Sports
Structured finance
Tax
Tax controversy and litigation
Trademark, copyright, and advertising litigation and
  counseling
Trusts and estates
UCC and secured transactions
Utilities mergers and acquisitions

COMPETITORS

Baker & McKenzie	O'Melveny & Myers
Clifford Chance	Shearman & Sterling
Davis Polk	Sidley Austin
Gibson, Dunn & Crutcher	Sullivan & Cromwell
Jones Day	Wachtell, Lipton
Kirkland & Ellis	Weil, Gotshal & Manges
Latham & Watkins	White & Case
Mayer Brown	WilmerHale
McDermott Will & Emery	

HISTORICAL FINANCIALS

Company Type: Partnership

Income Statement

FYE: December 31

	REVENUE ($ mil.)	NET INCOME ($ mil.)	NET PROFIT MARGIN	EMPLOYEES
12/08	2,200	—	—	4,500
12/07	2,170	—	—	4,721
12/06	1,850	—	—	4,520
12/05	1,610	—	—	4,400
Annual Growth	11.0%	—	—	0.8%

Revenue History

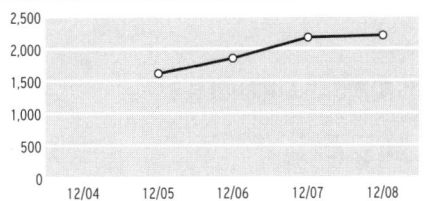

Smart & Final

Smart & Final caters to caterers — as well as small businesses, restaurants, and individual households in the western US. Its 280-plus non-membership warehouse stores stock groceries, party supplies, paper products, cleaning supplies, and more, in bulk sizes and quantities. The stores operate under the Smart & Final and Cash & Carry names in urban and suburban areas in Arizona, California, Idaho, Nevada, Oregon, and Washington, as well as northern Mexico. It also operates about 35 Henry's Farmers Markets and Sun Harvest stores. Once a foodservice operator, Smart & Final left that business to focus on its retail operations. Smart & Final is owned by an affiliate of the private equity firm Apollo Management.

France's Casino Guichard-Perrachon sold its majority stake in the retailer to Apollo Management for $813 million in May 2007. Following the ownership change, former Ralphs Grocery executive George Golleher succeeded Etienne Snollaerts as CEO of the company. In October of the same year Apollo acquired 35 Henry's Farmers and Sun Harvest stores in California and Texas from Whole Foods Market for about $166 million. The stores, which Whole Foods acquired when it bought Wild Oats Markets, joined the Smart & Final chain but continue to operate under their own banners.

Following the change in ownership, Smart & Final began opening larger stores (between 25,000 and 30,000 square feet), which will allow the chain to stock more product for both business and household customers. The company is also emphasizing value with its "wall of values" in-store sections, to better compete with rival SAM'S CLUB and other discounters. On the merchandise front, the retailer is expanding its range of grocery products and is offering more fresh produce and other perishables. A perishables warehouse acquired in the Whole Foods deal has allowed the chain to improve its perishables offering.

Smart & Final also operates about 50 stores under the Smart Foodservice Cash & Carry name. The stores carry a broad range (more than 13,000 products) of restaurant-quality food, foodservice supplies, and culinary equipment. Smart & Final also operates about a dozen stores in Mexico under a joint venture agreement with the operators of Calimax, a major grocery store chain there.

The company was founded in 1871 in Los Angeles as the Hellman-Haas Grocery Company. It later took the names of subsequent owners J. S. Smart and H. D. Final.

EXECUTIVES

Chairman and CEO: George G. Golleher, age 61
SVP and CFO: Richard N. (Rick) Phegley, age 51
SVP Human Resources: Jeff D. Whynot, age 51
SVP Supply Chain: C. Marie Robinson, age 40
SVP Information Services: Sherry Archer
SVP General Counsel, and Secretary:
  Donald G. Alvarado, age 53
SVP Cash & Carry Stores: Martin J. Trtek
SVP Store Operations: Timothy M. Snee, age 54
Group VP Buying: Diana Godfrey
VP, Controller, and Chief Accounting Officer:
  Richard A. Link, age 52
VP Real Estate: Anthony V. Bernardini
Auditors: Ernst & Young LLP

LOCATIONS

HQ: Smart & Final Inc.
  600 Citadel Dr., Commerce, CA 90040
Phone: 323-869-7500   **Fax:** 323-869-7868
Web: www.smartandfinal.com

2008 Stores

	No.
US	270
Mexico	13
Total	**283**

PRODUCTS/OPERATIONS

2008 Stores

	No.
Warehouse	197
Cash & Carry	50
Henry's Farmers Market	28
Sun Harvest	8
Total	**283**

Selected Products

Beverages
Candy
Delicatessen products
Fresh meats
Fresh produce
Frozen and refrigerated foods
Janitorial supplies
Paper products
Party supplies
Restaurant equipment
Snacks
Tobacco

COMPETITORS

Costco Wholesale
Ralphs Grocery
Sam's Club
Save Mart
Stater Bros.
Trader Joe's
Vons

HISTORICAL FINANCIALS

Company Type: Private

Income Statement			FYE: Sunday nearest December 31
	ESTIMATED REVENUE ($ mil.)	NET INCOME ($ mil.)	NET PROFIT MARGIN	EMPLOYEES
12/08	2,400	—	—	5,300
12/07	2,300	—	—	6,200
Annual Growth	4.3%	—	—	(14.5%)

Revenue History

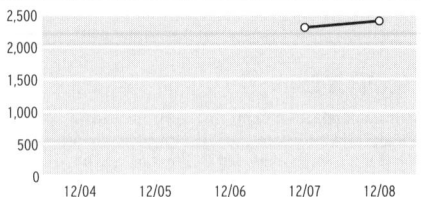

SmithGroup, Inc.

SmithGroup is the oldest continuously practicing architectural and engineering firm in the US. Founded in 1853 in Detroit by architect Sheldon Smith, the firm partnered with engineers in 1907 to become one of the first multidisciplinary firms in the country. Formerly known as Smith, Hinchman & Gryllis, it influenced the skyline of Detroit with structures like the Guardian, Penobscot, and Buhl buildings. The group also offers planning and consulting services and has 10 offices across the US. It targets the office, research, education, health care, technologies, and cities and communities markets.

SmithGroup's projects include the Providence Saint Joseph Medical Center in Burbank, California; the Smithsonian Institution's National Museum of the American Indian; and the US Arid-Land Agricultural Research Center in Maricopa, Arizona. The firm also was chosen to create a master plan for Indiana University.

Industry trends have led SmithGroup to build more and more environmentally friendly structures. The company joins other architects and engineers who are Leadership in Energy and Environmental Design certified.

In 2008 SmithGroup teamed with landscape architects JJR to create a joint studio dedicated to urban design, planning, and landscape architecture in Washington, DC.

EXECUTIVES

Chairman: David R. H. King
President and CEO: Carl Roehling
COO: Randal (Randy) Swiech
CFO: Russell (Russ) Sykes
VP: William Loftis
VP: Juhee Cho
VP and Director, Human Resources:
    Edward (Ed) Dodge
Leader, Los Angeles and San Francisco: Jim Hannon
Leader, Washington and Raleigh: Hal Davis
Corporate Marketing Director: Susan Arneson

LOCATIONS

HQ: SmithGroup, Inc.
    500 Griswold St., Ste. 1700, Detroit, MI 48226
Phone: 313-983-3600   **Fax:** 313-983-3636
Web: www.smithgroup.com

COMPETITORS

Carter & Burgess
Einhorn Yaffee
Gensler
Leo A Daly
RTKL Associates
Skidmore Owings
Syska Hennessy
URS

HISTORICAL FINANCIALS

Company Type: Private

Income Statement			FYE: December 31
	REVENUE ($ mil.)	NET INCOME ($ mil.)	NET PROFIT MARGIN	EMPLOYEES
12/08	166	—	—	800
12/07	148	—	—	800
12/06	144	—	—	800
12/05	132	—	—	800
12/04	116	—	—	800
Annual Growth	9.5%	—	—	0.0%

Revenue History

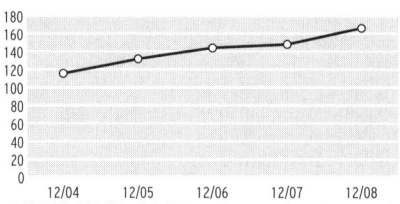

Smithsonian Institution

The Smithsonian Institution has many hats, from the one worn by Harrison Ford in the *Indiana Jones* movies to the one worn by Abraham Lincoln the night he was assassinated. One of the world's leading cultural institutions, the Smithsonian houses more than 136 million pieces in 19 museums and galleries, most of which are on the National Mall in Washington, DC. Some 24 million people every year view the Smithsonian's exhibits on art, music, TV and film, science, history, and other subjects. Admission to all but one of the Smithsonian's facilities is free; only the Cooper-Hewitt, National Design Museum in New York charges admission. The Smithsonian receives about 80% of its funding from the federal government.

The Smithsonian's exhibits display items such as the Declaration of Independence, the ruby slippers worn by Judy Garland in *The Wizard of Oz*, and the Wright brothers' first airplane. Along with its museums and galleries, the Smithsonian also operates the National Zoo and nine research facilities.

A board of regents that includes the vice president and the chief justice of the US, six members of Congress, and nine private citizens leads the institution. Patty Stonesifer, former CEO of the Bill & Melinda Gates Foundation, joined the board as its new leader in January 2009. Stonesifer has been a member of the board since 2001.

Other recent leadership changes at the Smithsonian include a new secretary (or CEO). G. Wayne Clough became the 12th secretary of the Smithsonian in mid-2008. Prior to his appointment, Clough, an academic, served as president of the Georgia Institute of Technology for 14 years. He succeeded Lawrence Small, who resigned under pressure in March 2007 amid criticism of his spending practices. Clough's aim is to expand the Smithsonian's global relevance.

After a 10-month delay The Smithsonian Channel debuted in September 2007. The new television unit is a joint venture between the museum and Showtime Networks. The launch had been delayed in part because the unit, Smithsonian Networks LLC, changed its business plan to become a 24-hour, high-definition channel in response to changing industry demands instead of starting with on-demand video, as originally planned. The new channel is operating solely as a high-definition channel on DirecTV.

An estimated $2.5 billion is needed to fund extensive maintenance and repair projects at the Smithsonian.

HISTORY

English chemist James Smithson wrote a proviso to his will in 1826 that would lead to the creation of the Smithsonian Institution. When he died in 1829, he left his estate to his nephew, Henry James Hungerford, with the stipulation that if Hungerford died without heirs, the estate would go to the US to create "an Establishment for the increase and diffusion of knowledge among men." Hungerford died in 1835 without any heirs, and the US government inherited more than $500,000 in gold.

Congress squandered the money after it was received in 1838 but, perhaps feeling pangs of guilt, covered the loss. The Smithsonian was finally created in 1846, and Princeton physicist Joseph Henry was named its first secretary. That year it established the Museum of Natural History, the Museum of History and Technology, and the National Gallery of Art. The Smithsonian's National Museum was developed around the collection of the US Patent Office in 1858. The Smithsonian continued to expand, adding the National Zoological Park in 1889 and the Smithsonian Astrophysical Observatory in 1890.

The Freer Gallery, a gift of industrialist Charles Freer, opened in 1923. The National Gallery was renamed the National Collection of Fine Arts in 1937, and a new National Gallery, created with Andrew Mellon's gift of his art collection and a building, opened in 1941. The Air and Space Museum was established in 1946.

More museums were added in the 1960s, including the National Portrait Gallery in 1962 and the Anacostia Museum (exhibits and materials on African-American history) in 1967. The Kennedy Center for the Performing Arts was opened in 1971. The Collection of Fine Arts was renamed the National Museum of American Art, and the Museum of History and Technology was renamed the National Museum of American History in 1980.

The Smithsonian placed its first-ever contribution boxes in four of its museums in 1993.

A planned exhibit featuring the *Enola Gay* — the plane that dropped the atomic bomb on Hiroshima — created a firestorm in 1994 with critics charging that the exhibit downplayed Japanese aggression and US casualties in WWII. The original exhibit was canceled in 1995, the director of the Air and Space Museum resigned, and a scaled-down version of the exhibit premiered. In 2004 the exhibit attracted more protestors, prompting Smithsonian officials to evacuate and temporarily close the museum.

Large contributions from private donors continued in the 1990s; the Mashantucket Pequot tribe gave $10 million from its casino operations in 1994 for the Smithsonian's planned American Indian museum, and prolific electronics inventor Jerome Lemelson donated $10.4 million in 1995. The museum celebrated its sesquicentennial in 1996 amid news that $500 million in repairs were needed over the next 10 years.

California real estate developer Kenneth Behring gave the largest cash donation ever to the museum in 1997 — $20 million for the National Museum of Natural History. Short of funds, the Smithsonian had to cut back on its 150th anniversary traveling exhibit that year. The Smithsonian announced a $26 million renovation for the National Museum of Natural History in 1998. Two years later Behring quadrupled his record-breaking 1997 donation of $20 million by giving $80 million to the National Museum of American History. Catherine Reynolds withdrew most of her $38 million gift in 2002 after the Smithsonian Institution refused to implement her ideas for an exhibit at the National Museum of American History.

The National Museum of the American Indian opened on the National Mall in 2004.

Secretary Lawrence Small resigned under pressure in March 2007 amid criticism of his spending practices. Cristián Samper, director of the Smithsonian's National Museum of Natural History, was named acting secretary. A report on the matter issued by the Smithsonian in June said its Board of Regents failed to provide the oversight that might have prevented Small's extravagant spending.

In July 2008 G. Wayne Clough became the 12th secretary of the Smithsonian.

EXECUTIVES

Chairman Board of Regents:
Patricia Q. (Patty) Stonesifer, age 52
Vice Chairman Board of Regents: Alan G. Spoon, age 57
Secretary: G. Wayne Clough, age 67
CFO: Alice Collier Maroni
CIO: Ann Speyer
Editor-in-Chief, Smithsonian Magazine: Carey Winfrey
Ombudsman: Chandra P. Heilman
Comptroller: Andrew J. Zino
General Counsel: John E. Huerta
Under Secretary Finance and Administration:
Alison McNally
Director Human Resources: James Douglas
Director Investments: Amy Chen
Director Communications and Public Affairs:
Evelyn S. Lieberman
Director Special Events and Protocol: Nicole L. Krakora
Treasurer: Sudeep Anand
President and Director of Media, Smithsonian Enterprises: Tom Ott
Smithsonian Inspector General: Anne Sprightley Ryan
Auditors: KPMG LLP

LOCATIONS

HQ: Smithsonian Institution
1000 Jefferson Dr. SW, Washington, DC 20560
Phone: 202-633-1000
Web: www.si.edu

PRODUCTS/OPERATIONS

Selected Museums and Research Centers

Anacostia Museum and Center for African American History and Culture
Archives of American Art
Arthur M. Sackler Gallery and Freer Gallery of Art
Arts and Industries Building
Center for Folklife and Cultural Heritage
Conservation and Research Center
Cooper-Hewitt, National Design Museum (New York)
Hirshhorn Museum and Sculpture Garden
National Air and Space Museum
National Museum of African Art
National Museum of American History
National Museum of Natural History
National Museum of the American Indian
National Museum of the American Indian George Gustav Heye Center (New York)
National Portrait Gallery
National Postal Museum
National Zoological Park
Smithsonian American Art Museum and Renwick Gallery
Smithsonian Astrophysical Observatory
Smithsonian Center for Latino Initiatives
Smithsonian Center for Materials Research and Education
Smithsonian Environmental Research Center (SERC)
Smithsonian Institution Building (The Castle)
Smithsonian Museum Conservation Institute
Smithsonian Tropical Research Institute

Soave Enterprises

Soave Enterprises is suave enough to manage multiple lines of business. The company's wide-ranging interests are divided into four main industries: real estate (residential and industrial development), auto dealerships, beer distribution, plus a catch-all diversified holdings group that includes businesses ranging from waste collection and transportation to scrap metals processing, as well as units engaged in hydroponic tomato gardening and taxi services. The bulk of Soave's operations are in Michigan. President and CEO Anthony Soave, who founded the company in 1961, owns Soave Enterprises.

In 2005 Soave Enterprises teamed up with longtime auto parts professional Bill Wild to form Parts Galore, a Michigan-based self-service, used auto parts retail chain.

In 2008 the company's Ferrous Processing & Trading unit took in the disassembled metal structures from Detroit's legendary Tiger Stadium to size or shred before being sold to be remelted. The recycled materials will be used in everything from new appliances to cars.

EXECUTIVES

President and CEO: Anthony L. Soave, age 69
EVP and Director: Yale Levin
SVP, CFO, and Director: Michael L. Piesko
SVP and Director: Michael D. (Mike) Hollerbach
SVP and Director: Kathleen B. McCann
President, Soave Automotive Group:
Marion N. Battaglia
President, CEO, and COO, Ferrous Processing and Trading: Howard Sherman
Secretary and Senior Counsel: Bryant M. Frank
Treasurer: Richard T. Brockhaus
Corporate Director Human Resources: Marcia K. Moss

LOCATIONS

HQ: Soave Enterprises L.L.C.
3400 E. Lafayette St., Detroit, MI 48207
Phone: 313-567-7000   **Fax:** 313-567-0966
Web: www.soaveenterprises.com

COMPETITORS

Continental Motors
David J. Joseph
KB Home
Lennar
OmniSource
Republic Services
Russ Darrow
The Ryland Group
Schnitzer Steel
Steel Technologies
Tang Industries
Waste Management

HISTORICAL FINANCIALS

Company Type: Private

Income Statement

FYE: December 31

	REVENUE ($ mil.)	NET INCOME ($ mil.)	NET PROFIT MARGIN	EMPLOYEES
12/08	2,220	—	—	1,972
12/07	1,770	—	—	2,200
12/06	1,630	—	—	2,450
12/05	1,500	—	—	2,601
12/04	1,610	—	—	2,556
Annual Growth	8.4%	—	—	(6.3%)

Revenue History

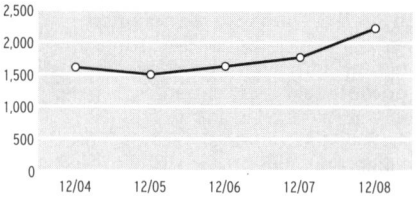

Software House

Software House International (SHI) wants to put computer products in houses across the globe. The company distributes more than 100,000 hardware and software products from suppliers such as Adobe, Cisco, Hewlett-Packard, Lenovo, McAfee, IBM, Microsoft, Oracle, Samsung, and Xerox. SHI also offers professional services such as application development, asset and lifecycle management, product procurement, systems integration, and training. The company serves enterprise, corporate, public sector, and health care customers worldwide. Clients have included Bank of America, Boeing, and Merrill Lynch. SHI was founded in 1989.

The company operates from locations in the US, Canada, the UK, France, and Hong Kong. SHI claims that a customer retention rate of 99% and a focus on operational efficiency has enabled it to expand from a small regional reseller to a global enterprise with more than $3 billion in annual revenue.

EXECUTIVES

Chairman: Koguan Leo
President and CEO: Thai Lee, age 51
CTO: Kevin Clements
VP Finance and Corporate Secretary: Paul Ng
VP Information Technology: Sam Mourad
Controller: Akif Nizam
Senior Director Operations and Quality: Bernadette Ulrich
Director Marketing and Event Planning: Janet Valvano
Director Hardware and Advanced Solutions: Bill Wyckoff
Director Public Sector Sales: Katie O'Kane
Director Software and Licensing: Patrick Hart
Director Purchasing: Vincent (Vince) Casale
Director Facilities: Steve Alt
Director Human Resources: Michael Haluska

LOCATIONS

HQ: Software House International
33 Knightsbridge Rd., Piscataway, NJ 08854
Phone: 732-764-8888   **Fax:** 732-764-8889
Web: www.shi.com

PRODUCTS/OPERATIONS

Selected Services

Application development
Asset management
Contract staffing
Desktop installation
E-commerce
Network consulting
Security management
Systems integration
Technical support

COMPETITORS

Agilysys	Computacenter
Arrow Electronics	Electrograph Systems
ASI Computer	Ingram Micro
Avnet	Insight Enterprises
Azlan Group	Merisel
Bell Microproducts	Morse plc
CDW	Tech Data
CompuCom	

HISTORICAL FINANCIALS

Company Type: Private

Income Statement

FYE: December 31

	REVENUE ($ mil.)	NET INCOME ($ mil.)	NET PROFIT MARGIN	EMPLOYEES
12/08	3,000	—	—	1,000
12/07	2,330	—	—	1,000
12/06	2,230	—	—	1,000
12/05	2,051	—	—	1,000
Annual Growth	13.5%	—	—	0.0%

Revenue History

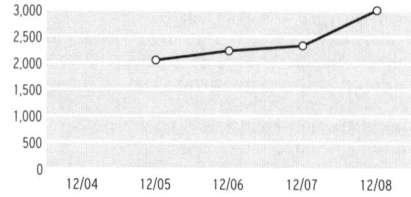

Solae, LLC

Solae mixes up its products and its ownership. Formed as a joint venture between DuPont and Bunge Limited in 2003, Solae develops, makes, and markets soy-based food ingredients. With more than 3,500 customers in 80 countries across the globe, the company manufactures soy protein that is used in a variety of beverages and meatless foods (V8 Splash smoothies, Gardenburgers, Mori-Nu nondairy pie fillings and pudding mixes, and Yves Veggie Cuisine deli slices and hotdogs). In addition to soy products for use in the food and beverage sectors, Solae makes soy-based polymers for use by makers of coated paper and paperboard.

Solae has a partnership with Chinese meat processor Henan Luohe Shineway Industry Group to expand its soy-processing production in that country. The company renamed all of its lecithin products Solec Soy Lecithin in order to improve customer recognition.

Adding to its meat-replacement manufacturing capabilities and offerings, in 2007 the company purchased the soy protein product line (including the Prolisse brand) from Cargill. That same year, Solae entered into a collaborative agreement with food-ingredient company Senomyx to develop flavor ingredients to enhance the taste of soy proteins.

The company has experienced rising costs for soy-protein manufacturing and materials, and in 2005 Solae exited the soy isoflavone business when it sold its global isoflavone business to Archer Daniels Midland.

Solae's products are used in four sectors of the food-manufacturing industry: meat and poultry, consumer food, nutritional, and dairy-alternative companies.

DuPont owns 72% of Solae; Bunge owns the remaining 28%.

EXECUTIVES

Chairman: Craig F. Binetti, age 54
CEO: Torkel Rhenman
SVP Global Sales, Specialty Business: Gregory P. Warner
VP and CFO: Steven W. (Steve) Fray
VP and General Counsel: Cornel B. Fuerer
VP Meat Solutions, Lecithin, and DuPont Soy Polymer: Darren Haar
VP Global Strategy and Marketing, Specialty Business: Michele Fite
VP Human Resources and Communications: Patricia K. (Patty) Fish, age 48
VP Global Operations: Paul Bossert Jr.
VP Six Sigma and Facilities: R. Michael (Mike) Reed
Senior Director Research and Development: Phil Kerr
Senior Director Technology and Implementation: Sarah Martin

LOCATIONS

HQ: Solae, LLC
4300 Duncan Ave., St. Louis, MO 63110
Phone: 314-659-3000   **Fax:** 314-659-5749
Web: www.solae.com

PRODUCTS/OPERATIONS

Selected Soy Products

Fibers
Industrial polymers
Lecithins
Protein concentrates
Protein isolates

COMPETITORS

ADM
Ag Processing
Cargill
Carolina Soy
Central Soya
CHS
US Soy

HISTORICAL FINANCIALS

Company Type: Joint venture

Income Statement

FYE: December 31

	REVENUE ($ mil.)	NET INCOME ($ mil.)	NET PROFIT MARGIN	EMPLOYEES
12/08	1,000	—	—	2,400
12/07	1,000	—	—	3,500
12/06	1,000	—	—	3,500
12/05	1,000	—	—	3,000
12/04	800	—	—	3,000
Annual Growth	5.7%	—	—	(5.4%)

Revenue History

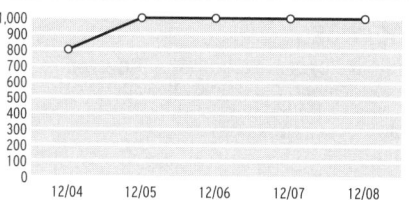

Solo Cup

Solo Cup married a Sweetheart but kept its own name. Solo Cup acquired Sweetheart Holdings, and today is a key player in the disposable consumer products industry. The company makes single-use cups, plates, cutlery, take-out containers, and the like under both brand names. Solo Cup's plastic, paper, and foam items are sold through retailers and food service distributors around the world, then used and thrown away by consumers. In addition to typical disposables, Solo also makes specialty party supplies, upscale disposable products, and plastic and paper packaging for snack food and dairy product manufacturers. The company, which has facilities in the Americas and Europe, gets most of its sales in the US.

Sales to food service distributors such as Sysco and Bunzl and food chains such as Starbucks and McDonald's account for about 80% of the company's sales. Solo Cup also serves consumer retail outlets, including supermarkets, warehouse clubs, and dollar stores.

A bad economic environment led Solo Cup to announce cost-cutting plans in 2008 that include a reduction in its corporate workforce (amounting to just under 10%) and the planned closing of one of its Illinois manufacturing facilities sometime in 2009. The company also plans to relocate its headquarters employees to one building rather than the three buildings they currently occupy.

EXECUTIVES

Chairman: Kevin A. Mundt, age 55
Chairman Emeritus: Robert L. Hulseman, age 76
President, CEO, and Director: Robert M. Korzenski, age 54, $751,716 total compensation
COO: George Chappelle, age 48
EVP Human Resources, General Counsel, and Secretary: Jan Stern Reed, age 49, $462,853 total compensation
EVP and CFO: Robert D. Koney Jr., age 52, $391,962 total compensation

EVP Supply Chain and Logistics: Thomas A. Pasqualini, age 51, $456,757 total compensation
SVP Operations: Peter J. Mendola, age 52
SVP and CIO: Robert J. Fronberry, age 54
SVP Consumer Sales and Marketing: Steven J. Jungmann, age 45
SVP Foodservice Sales and Marketing: Malcolm S. Simmonds, age 46, $328,893 total compensation
Auditors: KPMG LLP

LOCATIONS

HQ: Solo Cup Company
1700 Old Deerfield Rd., Highland Park, IL 60035
Phone: 847-831-4800 **Fax:** 847-579-3245
Web: www.solocup.com

2008 Sales

	$ mil.	% of total
US	1,511.1	82
Other countries	335.9	18
Total	**1,847.0**	**100**

PRODUCTS/OPERATIONS

2008 Sales

	$ mil.	% of total
Food service	1,536.7	83
Consumer	310.3	17
Total	**1,847.0**	**100**

Selected Products

Cold cups, lids, and straws
Cutlery
Dinnerware
Doilies
Fluted/Bakery products
Food containers
Hot cups and lids
Napkins
Paper plates, bowls, and cups
Placemats
Plastic plates, bowls, cups, lids, deli, and food containers
Portion cups
Specialty tabletop disposables
Tablecovers

COMPETITORS

American Greetings
Amscan
Berry Plastics
Dart Container
Dopaco
Dover Industries Limited
Georgia-Pacific
Huhtamäki
International Paper
Klöckner Pentaplast
Pactiv
WinCup

HISTORICAL FINANCIALS

Company Type: Private

Income Statement

FYE: December 31

	REVENUE ($ mil.)	NET INCOME ($ mil.)	NET PROFIT MARGIN	EMPLOYEES
12/08	1,847	(12)	—	7,100
12/07	2,106	68	3.2%	8,700
12/06	2,490	(373)	—	11,500
12/05	2,432	(19)	—	12,000
12/04	2,116	(50)	—	11,500
Annual Growth	(3.3%)	—	—	(11.4%)

2008 Year-End Financials

Debt ratio: 2,290.8%
Return on equity: —
Cash ($ mil.): —
Current ratio: —
Long-term debt ($ mil.): 717

Net Income History

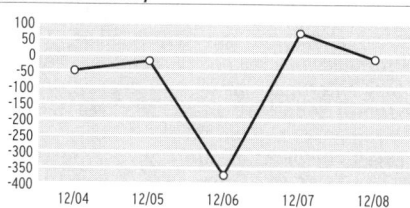

Source Interlink Companies

Whether you relax by listening to 50 Cent, watching Disney's latest, or reading *The Economist*, Source Interlink wants to have a hand in the transaction. A major distributor of magazines in the US and Canada, the firm also markets music CDs, DVDs, and video games to retailers through its Alliance Entertainment subsidiary. Major customers include Barnes & Noble, which accounts for about 20% of sales. In addition to distribution, Source Interlink publishes special-interest magazines, such as *Motor Trend, Soap Opera Digest,* and *Stereophile*. It also owns and produces content for about 90 Web sites. The company filed for Chapter 11 bankruptcy protection in April 2009 and emerged in June as a privately held company.

Under its reorganization plan, Source Interlink rid itself of about $1 billion in debt related to its acquisition of PRIMEDIA's Enthusiast Media division. The PRIMEDIA division was home to more than 70 magazines and 90 Web sites. Despite the filing, Source Interlink plans to continue promoting its Enthusiast assets, including Automotive.com, a car sales lead generator, and other branded sites. It intends to increase the sites' niche content offerings and targeted advertising. To this end, the company has introduced *LOWRIDER Mobile*, the first of its lifestyle magazines formatted for reading on Apple's iPhone and other mobile devices. Also slated for mobile launch are *Super Street, Import Tuner,* and *Soap Opera Digest*.

Source Interlink joined rival Anderson News in January 2009 in demanding that magazine publishers pay an extra 7 cents for each copy of a magazine delivered to retailers (regardless of the number of copies sold by those retailers). Together, the two firms are believed to control more than 50% of the nation's magazine wholesale distribution to retailers. Within months of making their demands known, Source Interlink and Anderson News settled and secured distribution agreements with Time, American Media, Hudson News, and other companies.

As a leading magazine distributor in the US, Source Interlink buys from producers and resells to retailers. In February 2009 the company added Wal-Mart, Kroger, and Bashas' supermarkets to its roster of retail customers.

Besides helping to supply the items on the rack, Source Interlink manages front-end displays, provides sales data, processes rebate claims, and installs store fixtures and displays. Its media business sells advertising in its enthusiast publications and sells the publications through newsstands and other retailers.

Previously focused on magazine distribution, Source Interlink expanded its offerings to include CDs and DVDs when it acquired Alliance Entertainment in 2005.

In October 2008 Greg Mays took over as Source Interlink's CEO and chairman of the board. In addition to serving as a director for the company since 2005, he has logged time on the boards of A&P and Simon Worldwide. Mays has also managed companies for investment firm Yucaipa.

AEC Associates, an affiliate of Yucaipa, owns about 40% of Source Interlink's shares.

EXECUTIVES

Chairman and CEO: Gregory (Greg) Mays, age 62
President, COO, and Director: James R. (Jim) Gillis, age 56
CFO: Marc Fierman, age 48
Chief Administration Officer: William D. (Bill) Bailey, age 62
Chief Legal Officer, General Counsel, and Secretary: Douglas J. Bates, age 51
President, Source Interlink Media Digital: Greg Goff
President, Distribution: Alan Tuchman, age 50
President, Media: Steven (Steve) Parr, age 49
Director, Financial Reporting and Treasury: Jason P. Adams
Auditors: BDO Seidman, LLP

LOCATIONS

HQ: Source Interlink Companies, Inc.
27500 Riverview Center Blvd., Ste. 400
Bonita Springs, FL 34134
Phone: 239-949-4450   **Fax:** 239-949-7623
Web: www.sourceinterlink.com

PRODUCTS/OPERATIONS

2008 Sales

	$ mil.	% of total
CD & DVD fulfillment	1,021.0	45
Magazine fulfillment	950.3	42
Media	252.9	11
In-store services	44.6	2
Adjustments	(14.6)	—
Total	**2,254.2**	**100**

Selected Customers

Amazon.com
Ahold USA
Barnes & Noble
Best Buy
Borders Group
Circuit City
Fry's
Hastings
Kroger
Meijers
Sears
Target
Walgreens
Wal-Mart

COMPETITORS

Anderson News
Audit Bureau
Baker & Taylor
E1 Distribution
Image Entertainment
Information Resources
Ingram Book Group
Ingram Entertainment
Jim Pattison Group
Kable Media Services
Navarre

HISTORICAL FINANCIALS

Company Type: Private

Income Statement

FYE: January 31

	REVENUE ($ mil.)	NET INCOME ($ mil.)	NET PROFIT MARGIN	EMPLOYEES
1/08	2,254	(28)	—	8,500
1/07	1,855	(25)	—	7,500
1/06	1,528	13	0.8%	7,000
1/05	357	12	3.4%	2,473
1/04	333	10	3.0%	1,082
Annual Growth	**61.3%**	**—**	**—**	**67.4%**

2008 Year-End Financials

Debt ratio: 328.3%   Current ratio: 0.96
Return on equity: —   Long-term debt ($ mil.): 1,361
Cash ($ mil.): 36

Net Income History

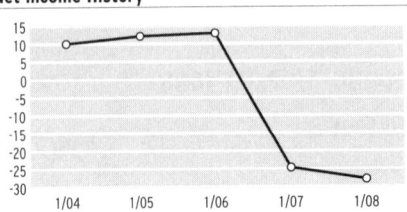

South Carolina Public Service Authority

Someone's got to turn on those bright lights in the big city — and in the small cities, too. South Carolina Public Service Authority, known as Santee Cooper (after two interconnected river systems), provides wholesale electricity to 20 co-operatives and two municipalities that serve more than 625,000 customers in South Carolina. It directly retails electricity to 155,000 customers. One of the largest US state-owned utilities, Santee Cooper operates in all 46 counties in South Carolina and has interests in power plants (fossil-fueled, nuclear, and hydroelectric) that give it 5,100 MW of generating capacity. The Santee Cooper Regional Water System distributes water to 125,000 consumers in the state.

The $48.2 million Santee Cooper project (55% federal loan and 45% federal grant), which connected the Santee and Cooper rivers and established hydroelectric dams and a transmission grid, began to generate electricity for the first time in 1942.

In the last three years the company has begun to invest heavily in solar, wind, and other renewable energy sources. In 2008 the Santee Cooper Board expanded its renewables program by authorizing the utility to contract for purchased biomass-generated power.

EXECUTIVES

Chairman: O. L. Thompson
First Vice Chairman: G. Dial Dubose
Second Vice Chairman: Clarence Davis
President and CEO: Lonnie N. Carter
EVP and CFO: Elaine G. Peterson
EVP and COO: Bill McCall Jr.
SVP and General Counsel: Jim Brogdon Jr.

SVP Corporate Services: Rennie M. (R. M.) Singletary III
SVP Generation: Maxie C. Chaplin
SVP Power Delivery: Terry L. Blackwell
VP Corporate Communications: Laura G. Varn
VP Corporate Planning and Bulk Power: Suzanne H. Ritter
VP Retail Operations: Zack W. Dusenbury
VP Engineering and Construction Services: Thomas L. Kierspe
VP Fossil and Hydro Generation: Lewis P. (Phil) Pierce
VP Business Services and Treasurer: Jeffrey Armfield
VP Planning and Power Supply: S. Thomas (Tom) Abrams
VP Human Resource Management: W. Glen Brown Jr.
Corporate Secretary and Associate General Counsel: Pamela J. Williams
Auditors: Cherry, Bekaert & Holland, LLP

LOCATIONS

HQ: South Carolina Public Service Authority
1 Riverwood Dr., Moncks Corner, SC 29461
Phone: 843-761-8000   **Fax:** 843-761-7060
Web: www.santeecooper.com

PRODUCTS/OPERATIONS

2008 Sales

	$ mil.	% of total
Electricity	1,568.3	99
Water	5.7	—
Other	12.3	1
Total	**1,586.3**	**100**

COMPETITORS

Delmarva Power
Dominion Resources
Duke Energy
E.ON U.S.
Florida Public Utilities
Memphis Light
North Carolina Electric Membership
Progress Energy
PS Energy
SCANA
TVA
Utilities, Inc.

HISTORICAL FINANCIALS

Company Type: Government-owned

Income Statement

FYE: December 31

	REVENUE ($ mil.)	NET INCOME ($ mil.)	NET PROFIT MARGIN	EMPLOYEES
12/08	1,586	82	5.1%	1,850
12/07	1,465	86	5.9%	1,700
12/06	1,413	88	6.2%	1,700
12/05	1,350	135	10.0%	1,700
12/04	1,151	79	6.8%	1,734
Annual Growth	**8.3%**	**0.9%**	**—**	**1.6%**

2008 Year-End Financials

Debt ratio: 246.8%   Current ratio: —
Return on equity: —   Long-term debt ($ mil.): 3,929
Cash ($ mil.): —

Net Income History

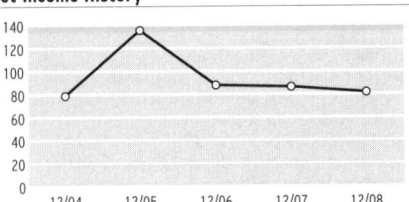

Southeastern Freight Lines

Less-than-truckload (LTL) carrier Southeastern Freight Lines hauls freight throughout the southern US with a fleet of about 2,700 tractors and 7,850 trailers. (LTL carriers consolidate freight from multiple shippers into a single truckload.) Southeastern Freight Lines operates from a network of about 75 terminals in a dozen states, plus Puerto Rico, and the US Virgin Islands. Through partnerships with other carriers, including A. Duie Pyle, Dayton Freight, and Oak Harbor Freight Lines, Southeastern Freight Lines provides service throughout the US, Mexico, and Canada. Southeastern Freight Lines is controlled by the Cassels family, which also owns truckload carrier G&P Trucking.

To attract additional business, Southeastern Freight Lines has been building out its network of service centers. In 2008 it began offering service in Mexico, and built a 30,000-sq.-ft. warehouse across the border in nearby Laredo, Texas.

Although the company continues to concentrate on its core territory, the new facilities allow Southeastern Freight Lines to offer next-day service to additional markets within its home region. The company opened terminals in Texas and Arkansas during 2007 and a new $4 million terminal in Virginia in 2008.

EXECUTIVES

CEO: W. T. Cassels Jr.
President: W. T. (Tobin) Cassels III
SVP Quality and Human Resources: David Scoggins
SVP Corporate Planning and Development: Braxton Vick
SVP Operations: Rick Toburen
SVP Sales and Marketing: Mike Heaton
SVP Finance: Russ Burleson
Regional VP Operations: Richard Bogan
VP Transportation: Steve Palmer
VP Management Information Systems: Dave Robinson

LOCATIONS

HQ: Southeastern Freight Lines, Inc.
420 Davega Rd., Lexington, SC 29073
Phone: 803-794-7300   **Fax:** 803-794-8131
Web: www.sefl.com

COMPETITORS

AAA Cooper Transportation
Arkansas Best
Averitt Express
Benton Express
Con-way Freight
Estes Express
FedEx Freight
Old Dominion Freight
Saia
UPS Freight
Wilson Trucking
YRC Worldwide

HISTORICAL FINANCIALS

Company Type: Private

Income Statement

FYE: December 31

	REVENUE ($ mil.)	NET INCOME ($ mil.)	NET PROFIT MARGIN	EMPLOYEES
12/08	740	—	—	6,800
12/07	730	—	—	6,800
12/06	711	—	—	6,800
12/05	648	—	—	6,000
12/04	546	—	—	6,000
Annual Growth	**7.9%**	**—**	**—**	**3.2%**

Revenue History

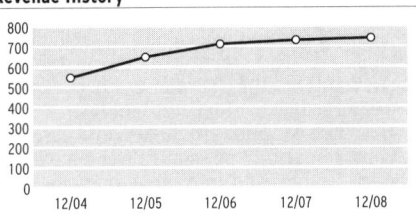

Southern States Cooperative

Founded to provide affordable, high-quality seed for Virginia farmers, Southern States Cooperative has grown into an agricultural powerhouse, serving its approximately 300,000 members, mainly in the mid-Atlantic and southern US states. The co-op makes and/or offers just about everything agricultural to its farmer/owners, including animal feed and fertilizer; seed processing; grain marketing; diesel, propane, and home-heating services; wholesale farm supplies; and even bib overalls. Its Southern States and Garden South stores sell farm supplies, garden products, and fuel through some 1,200 retail outlets in 23 states. Other services include crop financing, crop services, and an aquaculture program.

Demographic shifts are taking place in Southern States' region, among them urban sprawl, which continues to spread into rural areas. The cooperative has had increasing numbers of rural, rural-lifestyle, and suburban customers looking for the same crop-growing services and advice it provides to its members/farmers. In order to answer this need and target its sales growth in this new consumer segment, in 2007 the co-op began a multiyear relationship with GE Money's Sales Finance unit, which provides financing options through GE Money's private-label credit program.

EXECUTIVES

Chairman: John B. East
President and CEO: Thomas R. Scribner
EVP and CFO: Leslie Newton
SVP Retail Operations: Jobie Miller
SVP and General Merchandising Manager: Todd Fleer
SVP Commodities: Gregory Adlich
VP Retail Operations: Donnie Dunbar
VP and General Merchandising Manager, Crops: Dannie Dillon
VP Credit: Anne Clingenpeel

VP and General Manager, Agway: Grant Sanborn
VP, General Counsel, and Secretary: Kim Bram
VP Insurance Services and Risk Management: Wendy Tate
VP and General Merchandising Manager, Feed: Jim Moore
VP Information Systems: Karen Lankford
VP and Controller: Philip Miller
VP Finance and Treasurer: Fred Jezouit
Auditors: PricewaterhouseCoopers LLP

LOCATIONS

HQ: Southern States Cooperative, Incorporated
6606 W. Broad St., Richmond, VA 23230
Phone: 804-281-1000   **Fax:** 804-281-1413
Web: www.southernstates.com

PRODUCTS/OPERATIONS

Selected Facilities and Operations

Cotton gin
Crop-protection warehouses
Farm-supply distribution centers
Feed mills
Fertilizer plants
Fertilizer terminals
Grain-elevator retail facilities
Peanut purchasing facilities
Turf warehouses

COMPETITORS

ADM
Ag Processing
Alabama Farmers Cooperative
Andersons
Cargill
CHS
Corn Products International

DeBruce Grain
GROWMARK
Miles Enterprises
Rabo AgriFinance
Scoular
Tennessee Farmers Co-op
Wilbur-Ellis

HISTORICAL FINANCIALS

Company Type: Cooperative

Income Statement

FYE: June 30

	REVENUE ($ mil.)	NET INCOME ($ mil.)	NET PROFIT MARGIN	EMPLOYEES
6/08	2,104	—	—	4,000

Southern Wine & Spirits

Fueled by alcohol, Southern Wine & Spirits of America brews up market dominance. The firm is the #1 US distributor of wine and spirits. It represents more than 1,500 wine, beer, and spirits suppliers from around the world, offering some 5,000 different brands. With more than 200,000 customers, the company ships more than 70 million cases a year and has operations in 30 US states. Southern Wine & Spirits imports products include Grolsch and Steinlager beers; cigars, such as Don Diego and Montecristo; and nonalcoholic beverages, including Clamato and Rose's Lime Juice.

Through a joint venture with the Odom company, the distributor does business in the "control states" of Alaska, Idaho, Montana, Oregon, Utah, Washington, and Wyoming. (Control states are those that regulate the sale of alcohol through a monopoly.)

Southern Wine & Spirits of America was founded in Florida in 1968.

EXECUTIVES

Chairman and CEO: Harvey R. Chaplin, age 80
President and COO: Wayne E. Chaplin, age 53
EVP and Treasurer: Steven R. Becker
SVP, CIO, and Managing Director, Business Solutions Group: Barry J. Goldberg
EVP and General Manager: Brad Vassar, age 51
EVP, Spirits: Rodolfo A. (Rudy) Ruiz, age 60
SVP; President, Wine Division: Melvin A. (Mel) Dick, age 73
SVP Sales and Marketing: Kevin Fennessey
SVP Human Resources: W. Michael Head, age 59
Chairman and CEO, Lauber Imports: Ed Lauber
President, Lauber Imports: Mark Lauber

LOCATIONS

HQ: Southern Wine & Spirits of America, Inc.
1600 NW 163rd St., Miami, FL 33169
Phone: 305-625-4171 **Fax:** 305-625-4720
Web: www.southernwine.com

PRODUCTS/OPERATIONS

Selected Products
Beer
Cigars
Nonalcoholic beverages and mixes
Spirits
Wines

COMPETITORS

Altadis
Bacardi
Banfi Vintners
Ben E. Keith
Constellation Brands
Geerlings & Wade
Georgia Crown
Glazer's Wholesale Drug
Johnson Brothers
National Distributing
National Wine & Spirits
Rémy Cointreau
Sunbelt Beverage
Synergy Brands
Topa Equities
UST llc
Wirtz Corporation
Young's Market

HISTORICAL FINANCIALS
Company Type: Private

Income Statement
FYE: December 31

	REVENUE ($ mil.)	NET INCOME ($ mil.)	NET PROFIT MARGIN	EMPLOYEES
12/08	8,400	—	—	11,000
12/07	8,300	—	—	10,300
12/06	6,980	—	—	10,300
12/05	6,500	—	—	10,300
12/04	5,500	—	—	—
Annual Growth	11.2%	—	—	2.2%

Revenue History
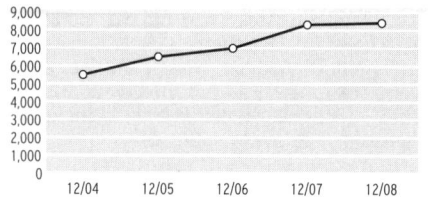

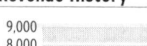

Southwire Company

Southwire hopes everyone's cable-ready. One of the world's largest cable and wire manufacturers, Southwire makes building wire and cable, utility and industrial power cable, cord products, telecommunications cable, and copper and aluminum rods. The company provides engineering, machining, and fabrication services, as well as electronic inventory management. It also offers copper products, such as bare copper and line wire, to the semiconductor market. Southwire customers include building contractors, utility companies, and OEMs in the areas of automotive, electrical, appliances, and industrial equipment. Founded in 1950 by Roy Richards Sr. (the chairman's father), Southwire is owned by the Richards family.

Southwire continues to build on its core operations, but also to develop a diverse range of products and expand into niche markets. The company has expanded its base of operations into Asia and Europe, but continues to focus on the North American market.

In 2009 Southwire broadened its product offerings with the acquisition of privately held Maxis, a maker of tools and equipment used to install wire and cable products. The acquisition adds research and development capabilities for Southwire, and fits with its strategy of focusing on ways to improve the safety of electrical installations through new products.

In 2008 the company acquired certain assets of Centrilift (a division of Baker Hughes) pertaining to pumps used for mining, water, and petroleum industries. Also that same year, the company purchased CableTech Global, a cable manufacturing business owned by General Chemical Performance Products, for over $9 million.

Southwire has entered into a joint agreement with 3M to produce aluminum conductor composite reinforced high voltage overhead conductor. Additionally, the company has been working with American Superconductor, Consolidated Edison, and the Department of Homeland Security to develop surge-suppressing superconductor cable, which is being used to develop more secure power systems in areas such as New York City.

Southwire operates through three divisions. Its Energy division supplies wire and cable products to the electric power distribution industry, while the Electrical division provides building wire products for commercial and industrial buildings, as well as houses. The OEM division addresses the needs of its OEM market for wire, cable, copper rod, and aluminum rod, which is used in automotive, HVAC, lighting, home appliance, industrial equipment, and military applications.

EXECUTIVES

Chairman: Roy Richards Jr.
President and CEO: Stuart Thorn
EVP Finance and CFO: J. Guyton Cochran Jr.
EVP and President, Electrical Division: Jack Carlson
EVP Human Resources: Michael R. (Mike) Wiggins
EVP Operations: Jeff Herrin
EVP and President, Energy: Charlie Murrah
EVP, General Counsel, and Corporate Secretary: Floyd Smith
SVP Information Technologies Services: Phil Tuggle
SVP and President, OEM Division: Norman Adkins
SVP; President, SCR: Will Berry
SVP Research and Development: Vince Kruse
Director, Healthcare: Lisa Evans
Manager, Communications: Gary Leftwich

LOCATIONS

HQ: Southwire Company
1 Southwire Dr., Carrollton, GA 30117
Phone: 770-832-4242
Web: www.southwire.com

PRODUCTS/OPERATIONS

Selected Products
Aluminum rod
Building wire (copper, aluminum)
Communication cable
Copper rod
Electrical wire and cable
Flexible conduit section
Flexible cord
High voltage cable
Magnet wire
Pumps
Specialty wire
Transit cable
Wire-making machinery

COMPETITORS

AFC Cable
Alcatel-Lucent
Alpine Group
Andrew Corporation
Anixter International
Belden
Carlisle Companies
Corning
Driver-Harris
Encore Wire
Freeport-McMoRan
General Cable
Hitachi Cable
Hubbell
International Wire
IRCE
Nexans
OFS BrightWave
Rio Tinto Alcan
Sumitomo Electric
Superior Essex
SWCC SHOWA
Volex

HISTORICAL FINANCIALS
Company Type: Private

Income Statement
FYE: December 31

	REVENUE ($ mil.)	NET INCOME ($ mil.)	NET PROFIT MARGIN	EMPLOYEES
12/08	4,600	—	—	4,000
12/07	4,980	—	—	4,200
12/06	4,900	—	—	4,108
12/05	3,200	—	—	4,180
12/04	2,200	—	—	3,600
Annual Growth	20.2%	—	—	2.7%

Revenue History
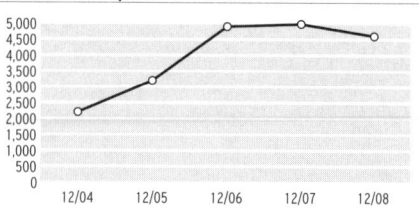

HOOVER'S HANDBOOK OF PRIVATE COMPANIES 2010

Spectrum Health System

Spectrum Health is a regional health system serving western Michigan. The not-for-profit health network features over a half-dozen hospitals with some 2,000 beds; most of the hospitals operate under the Spectrum Health name. Residents and visitors to the area can also access Spectrum Health through its more than 140 service sites, which include urgent care centers, primary care physician offices, community clinics, rehabilitation and other outpatient facilities, and continuing care residences and services for the elderly. The health system also operates Priority Health, a health plan with about 470,000 members.

Spectrum Health was formed through the 1997 merger of Blodgett Hospital and Butterworth Hospital. Kent Community Hospital joined the organization in 1999, and the United Memorial Health System (Kelsey Hospital and United Hospital) became a member in 2003.

The company began construction on a new 14-story building for the Helen DeVos Children's Hospital in 2006; the facility is scheduled to open in 2010.

In 2007 Priority Health acquired Michigan insurance provider Care Choices, adding 120,000 members to its system.

EXECUTIVES

President and CEO: Richard C. (Rick) Breon
EVP; President, Spectrum Health Hospitals:
Matthew G. (Matt) Van Vranken
EVP and CFO: Michael P. (Mike) Freed
SVP System Quality: John J. Byrnes
SVP Human Resources: Daniel C. (Dan) Oglesby
SVP and CIO: Patrick O'Hare
SVP Strategy and Business Development: John Mosley
Chief Medical Officer: Richard Freeman
President, Helen DeVos Children's Hospital:
Robert H. (Bob) Connors
President and CEO, Priority Health:
Kimberly K. (Kim) Horn
President, Spectrum Health Medical Group:
James M. Tucci
President, Spectrum Health Continuing Care:
Jeffrey Lemon
President, Blodgett Hospital: James (Jim) Wilson, age 53
General Counsel: David Leonard
Auditors: Ernst & Young LLP

LOCATIONS

HQ: Spectrum Health System
100 Michigan St. NE, Grand Rapids, MI 49503
Phone: 616-391-1774   **Fax:** 616-391-2780
Web: www.spectrum-health.org

PRODUCTS/OPERATIONS

2008 Sales

	$ mil.	% of total
Health plan	1,370.9	53
Hospital, continuing care & physician services	1,163.7	45
Investment income	16.9	1
Other	44.0	1
Total	**2,595.5**	**100**

Selected Operations

Helen DeVos Children's Hospital (Grand Rapids)
Priority Health (managed care plans)
Spectrum Health Blodgett Hospital (Grand Rapids)
Spectrum Health Butterworth Hospital (Grand Rapids)
Spectrum Health Continuing Care (long-term, rehabilitative, skilled nursing, and home health care)
Spectrum Health Kent Community Campus (Grand Rapids)
Spectrum Health Reed City Hospital (Reed City)
Spectrum Health Special Care Hospital (Grand Rapids)
Spectrum Health United Memorial
  Kelsey Hospital (Lakeview)
  United Hospital (Greenville)

COMPETITORS

Battle Creek Health System
Bay Regional Medical Center
Borgess Health
Bronson Healthcare
Covenant HealthCare
Munson Healthcare
Sheridan Community Hospital
Zeeland Community Hospital

HISTORICAL FINANCIALS

Company Type: Not-for-profit

Income Statement

FYE: June 30

	REVENUE ($ mil.)	NET INCOME ($ mil.)	NET PROFIT MARGIN	EMPLOYEES
6/08	2,596	(11)	—	14,400
6/07	2,322	185	8.0%	14,400
6/06	2,103	90	4.3%	14,400
6/05	1,932	65	3.4%	14,400
6/04	1,868	—	—	14,000
Annual Growth	**8.6%**	**—**	**—**	**0.7%**

Net Income History

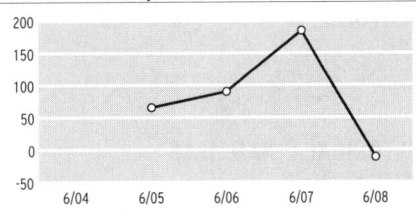

Sports Authority

Are you gonna argue with The Sports Authority? Now get in there and buy a StairMaster . . . or some cleats . . . or a basketball! The #1 US sporting goods chain (with more than 450 stores in 45 states), The Sports Authority sells sports equipment, general merchandise, shoes, bikes, and apparel, with a focus on premium brands. It also has an online store. The company's 2003 merger with Gart Sports (owner of the Sportmart and Oshman's chains) marked a major consolidation in the sporting goods retail industry with the merged company coming out on top. Senior managers of The Sports Authority together with an investor group led by Leonard Green & Partners took the company private in 2006.

After a decade at the top and more than 20 years with the company, executive John Doug Morton stepped down as CEO in 2009. Morton handed over the day-to-day operations of the company to an interim executive operating committee, which comprises a trio of C-level executives, and retained his title as chairman. The company enlisted the help of Herbert Mines Associates to search for a permanent CEO.

Following its merger with Gart Sports, the combined entity became known as The Sports Authority (TSA). As a result of a major rebranding effort, all the retailer's stores now operate under the Sports Authority nameplate. (Previously, TSA operated stores under the Sports Authority, Gart Sports, Oshman's, and Sportmart banners.) During the two years before it went private, the sporting goods chain invested heavily in closing and repositioning stores and remerchandising those that remained to achieve a consistent look. It also adopted a new game plan: to court customers willing to pay full price. To that end, TSA adopted Gart Sports' emphasis on stocking premium brands in categories such as apparel, fitness, footwear, golf, and team sports.

With its rebranding, remerchandising, and remodeling efforts behind it, TSA has returned to opening new stores. In 2008 the company opened about 40 new stores, including locations in Alaska, California, Florida, and Hawaii, and plans to add about 20 more in 2009. (The new stores range in size between 42,000 square feet and 50,000 square feet.) While not recession-proof, the sporting goods retail industry is faring relatively well in the current economic downturn, with categories such as team uniforms and running and camping gear outperforming golf and fitness equipment.

Many TSA stores also rent winter sports equipment, including skis and snowboards. The stores will also tune up your bike.

EXECUTIVES

Chairman: John D. (Doug) Morton, age 58
President: David J. (Dave) Campisi, age 53
EVP and COO: Greg A. Waters, age 48
CFO, Chief Administrative Officer, and Treasurer:
Thomas T. Hendrickson, age 54
EVP, Chief Marketing Officer, and Chief Strategy Officer: Jeffrey (Jeff) Schumacher
EVP Human Resources: Kerry M. Sims, age 51
EVP, General Counsel, and Secretary:
Nesa E. Hassanein, age 56
Auditors: Deloitte & Touche LLP

LOCATIONS

HQ: The Sports Authority, Inc.
1050 W. Hampden Ave., Englewood, CO 80110
Phone: 303-200-5050
Web: www.sportsauthority.com

PRODUCTS/OPERATIONS

Merchandise Categories

Athletic and active apparel
Athletic and active footwear
Fitness sports
Golf clubs and equipment
Outdoor sports
Recreational sports
Winter sports

COMPETITORS

Academy Sports & Outdoors	Hibbett Sports
Bass Pro Shops	J. C. Penney
Big 5	Kmart
Cabela's	Lands' End
Chick's	L.L. Bean
Christy Sports	Loncor Resources
Costco Wholesale	Modell's
Dick's Sporting Goods	Olympia Sports
Dunham's	Performance Bike Shop
Eastern Mountain Sports	REI
Edwin Watts Golf	Scheels
Finish Line	Sears
Foot Locker	Sport Chalet
Gander Mountain	Target
Golf Galaxy	Wal-Mart
Golfsmith	West Marine

HISTORICAL FINANCIALS

Company Type: Private

Income Statement

FYE: Saturday nearest January 31

	REVENUE ($ mil.)	NET INCOME ($ mil.)	NET PROFIT MARGIN	EMPLOYEES
1/08	2,980	—	—	15,825
1/07	2,740	—	—	14,586
1/06	2,509	—	—	14,300
1/05	2,436	—	—	15,000
1/04	1,760	—	—	17,000
Annual Growth	14.1%	—	—	(1.8%)

Revenue History

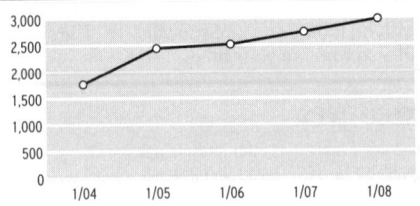

Spring Air International

Spring Air International (SAI) is calling you to bed. The successor of mattress maker Spring Air Company, SAI controls the Spring Air brand globally. The newly-formed firm has about 10 licensees in the US and about 10 abroad. The original Spring Air was founded in 1926 by mattress innovator Francis Karr, who introduced an offset coil that adjusts to sleepers' weights. It merged with its largest licensee, Florida-based Consolidated Bedding, and folded in other licensees in 2007. In May 2009 the company abruptly ceased operations, and in June emerged under new ownership and management as SAI. Spring Air brand products are sold worldwide through furniture retailers, department stores, and bedding stores.

The deep recession in the US has made making and retailing mattresses difficult. It led to significant turmoil at the mattress maker and ultimately to its rebirth as a licensor. SAI is led by president Rick Robinson, who plans to rebuild the business by focusing on local markets.

To achieve this goal, the company first plans to strengthen its nationwide production capabilities. In July 2009 SAI added a half-dozen US li-

censees to its roster. The move allows the firm to operate through nearly 10 manufacturing centers and almost 15 distribution facilities across the US.

In May the former ownership of Spring Air closed the company's nine corporate-owned plants. Ed Bates, former owner of the plant in Chelsea, Massachusetts, subsequently reacquired and reopened the Massachusetts plant and created SAI as the new worldwide licensor and holder of Spring Air brands.

EXECUTIVES

Chairman: Michael Michienzi
President: Rick Robinson, age 53
SVP Sales, (Columbus, OH and Dallas): Chad Megard
SVP Sales (Lacey, WA and Salt Lake City): Charles Dietiker
SVP Sales (Los Angeles): Howard Glant
SVP: Eric Spitzer
VP Human Resources: Katie Sems
Director Manufacturing Services: Bill Frame

LOCATIONS

HQ: Spring Air International LLC
70 Everett Ave., Ste. 507, Chelsea, MA 02150
Phone: 617-884-2300 **Fax:** 617-884-2818
Web: www.springair.com

PRODUCTS/OPERATIONS

Selected Collections

Back Supporter
ComfortFlex
Four Seasons
Posture Comfort

COMPETITORS

Sealy
Select Comfort
Serta
Simmons Bedding
Tempur-Pedic

HISTORICAL FINANCIALS

Company Type: Private

Income Statement

FYE: December 31

	REVENUE ($ mil.)	NET INCOME ($ mil.)	NET PROFIT MARGIN	EMPLOYEES
12/07	650	—	—	3,100
12/06	649	—	—	3,100
12/05	638	—	—	3,100
12/04	619	—	—	—
Annual Growth	1.6%	—	—	0.0%

Revenue History

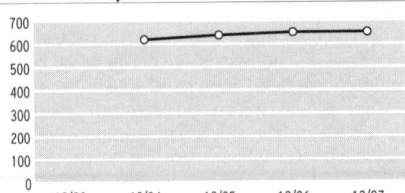

SRI International

With *BusinessWeek* magazine calling SRI International "Silicon Valley's soul," the not-for-profit think tank ponders advances in biotechnology, chemicals and energy, computer science, electronics, and public policy — and ways to commercialize those advances. SRI focuses on technology research and development, business strategies, and issues analysis. It has patents and patent applications in such areas as information sciences, software development, communications, robotics, and pharmaceuticals. SRI's clients have included Visa, Samsung, NASA, and the US Department of Defense. Originally founded in 1946 as Stanford Research Institute, SRI became fully independent of Stanford University in 1970.

The organization has conceived such innovations as the computer mouse, magnetic encoding for checks, and high-definition television, not to mention some of the foundations of personal computing, the Internet, and stealth technology. Its 1,400 employees (including about 600 scientists and researchers) work at research centers worldwide.

SRI's for-profit subsidiary the Sarnoff Corporation was formed in 1942 as RCA Laboratories. Formerly a unit of General Electric and gifted to SRI in 1987, Sarnoff specializes in creating and commercializing electronic, biomedical, and information technologies. SRI and Sarnoff together have spun off about two dozen companies.

HISTORY

In the 1920s Stanford University professor Robert Swain envisioned a research center devoted to chemistry, physics, and biology. Swain received support from university president Ray Lyman and alumnus Herbert Hoover, but the Great Depression and WWII postponed the venture. Finally, in 1946, the Stanford Research Institute was formed in conjunction with the university. That year the David Sarnoff Research Center invented the color TV tube under the wing of RCA Laboratories.

During Stanford Research's early years, it worked on such projects as logistics for Disneyland, magnetic ink for character recognition, and strategies for combating air pollution. The think tank was the focus of student protests in the 1960s because of its defense work. In 1969 Stanford Research Institute was one of four nodes on the first computer network, the ARPANET. It became fully independent in 1970 as SRI International.

During the 1960s and 1970s SRI won large contracts from the US Department of Defense for research in such areas as radar, speech recognition, and noise cancellation technologies. It got a tremendous boost in 1987 when longtime client General Electric gave SRI the Sarnoff Research Center (as a tax write-off) plus $250 million in business, along with $65.2 million in cash.

In 1993 SRI founded Pangene to commercialize gene cloning and analysis technology. The next year it founded GeneTrace to develop genetics-related products for biomedical research, and Nuance Communications to commercialize speech-recognition products. Intuitive Surgical, which develops minimally invasive surgical technologies, was formed in 1995.

SRI developed two key components for use in an improved mail sorting program, which the

US Postal Service announced in 1997 it would use to save millions in processing costs. The David Sarnoff Research Center changed its name to Sarnoff Corporation that year. SRI joined Motorola in 1997 to make semiconductors for digital TVs.

In 1998 SRI and the National Science Foundation teamed to develop innovative science and math teaching programs. The following year SRI began working with network equipment leader Cisco Systems and the US Army to develop a voice and multimedia communications system for the military. In 2001 SRI partnered with SPEEDCOM Wireless to co-develop wireless technology.

In order to complement its biosciences division, SRI bought Quality Clinical Labs (QCL) a few years later. QCL was a California-based clinical pathology analysis center specializing in clinical hematology and chemistry evaluations.

EXECUTIVES

Chairman: Samuel H. Armacost, age 70
President, CEO, and Director: Curtis R. Carlson
SVP and CFO: Thomas J. Furst
VP Information and Computing Sciences Division: William Mark
VP Engineering and Systems Division: John W. Prausa
VP Ventures and Strategic Programs: Norman D. Winarsky
VP Strategic Business Development: Stephen J. (Steve) Ciesinski
VP Biosciences Division: Walter H. Moos, age 54
VP Physical Sciences Division: Eric Pearson
VP Policy Division: Dennis Beatrice
VP Legal and Business Affairs and General Counsel: Richard Abramson
VP Human Resources: Jean E. (Jeanie) Tooker
VP Corporate and Marketing Communications: Alice R. Resnick
Director Science and Technology Policy: David Cheney
Director: John J. Young Jr.
Auditors: PricewaterhouseCoopers LLP

LOCATIONS

HQ: SRI International
333 Ravenswood Ave., Menlo Park, CA 94025
Phone: 650-859-2000   **Fax:** 650-326-5512
Web: www.sri.com

PRODUCTS/OPERATIONS

Selected Research Areas

Automation and robotics
Automotive and commercial equipment technologies
Chemistry, materials, and applied physics
Communications
Defense and intelligence
Homeland defense and national security
Information science and software development
Medical devices
Product engineering
Pharmaceutical services
Policy
Sensors and measurement systems

COMPETITORS

Aerospace Corporation	MITRE
Battelle Memorial	PAREXEL
Bayer Corp.	Quintiles Transnational
CACI International	RAND Corporation
Charles Stark Draper	Research Triangle Institute
Laboratory	Southwest Research
DaVinci Institute	Institute
DuPont	Teknowledge
Kendle	University of California
LECG	Wellcome Trust
MIT	Westat

HISTORICAL FINANCIALS

Company Type: Not-for-profit

Income Statement

FYE: December 31

	REVENUE ($ mil.)	NET INCOME ($ mil.)	NET PROFIT MARGIN	EMPLOYEES
12/08	490	—	—	2,100
12/07	450	—	—	1,600
12/06	411	—	—	1,400
12/05	286	—	—	1,400
Annual Growth	**19.7%**	**—**	**—**	**14.5%**

Revenue History

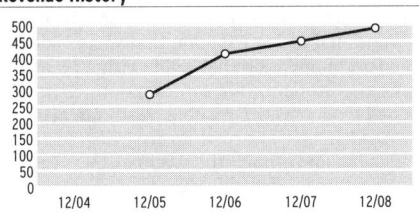

SSM Health Care

The mission of SSM Health Care System began with five nuns who fled religious persecution in Germany in 1872 only to arrive in St. Louis in the midst of a smallpox epidemic. They formed their first hospital there in 1877. Today the not-for-profit system, sponsored by the Franciscan Sisters of Mary, owns or manages some 20 acute care hospitals with about 4,400 licensed beds. The company also operates physicians' practices and two nursing homes, and it offers rehabilitation, home health care, hospice, and skilled nursing services. Its facilities are located in Illinois, Missouri, Oklahoma, and Wisconsin.

SSM Health Care System has about 5,000 physicians on its medical staff. In addition to providing health care services, the company owns an interest in Wisconsin-based health plan provider Premier Medical Insurance Group and in the Wisconsin Integrated Information Technology & Telemedicine System (WIITTS), which manages patient information for regional providers.

In 2008 the company sold the MetroSouth Medical Center (MSMC, formerly St. Francis Hospital & Health Center) to MSMC Investors. The facility was put up for sale in 2007 due to recurring financial losses. SSM had nearly exhausted its efforts to offload the hospital and had announced plans to shut down the facility before the deal with MSMC was announced.

SSM Health Care is expanding in fast-growth territories — it is constructing a new 50-bed acute care hospital (St. Mary's Janesville) in Wisconsin to be opened in 2011. The company also completed construction of the new SSM St. Clare Health Center in St. Louis in 2009; that hospital replaces the SSM St. Joseph Hospital of Kirkwood. In 2009 it formed a partnership with Select Medical to build a rehabilitation hospital (as well as to jointly operate existing therapy locations) in St. Louis. In addition, SSM Health Care is installing electronic medical record systems at all of its facilities.

EXECUTIVES

Chairman and CEO: Sister Mary Jean Ryan
President and COO: William P. Thompson
SVP Human Resources: Steven M. (Steve) Barney
SVP Strategic Development: Paula J. Friedman
SVP Finance: Kris A. Zimmer
SVP Mission and External Affairs: Dixie L. Platt
SVP and CIO; President, SSM Information Center: Thomas K. (Tom) Langston
VP Organizational Effectiveness: A. Dawn Runge
VP Communications: Suzy Farren
Interim Regional President and System VP, St. Mary's Good Samaritan: Jerry Lefert
VP Ethics: Michael (Mike) Panicola, age 35
Regional President SSM Health Care of Oklahoma and System VP: Chris Howard
Regional President and System VP; President SSM Health Care-St. Louis: James M. Sanger
Regional President; System VP St. Mary's Good Samaritan: Phillip P. Gustafson
President, SSM St. Joseph Health Center: Gaspare Calvaruso, age 41
President and CEO, SSM Health Care of Wisconsin: Mary C. Starmann-Harrison

LOCATIONS

HQ: SSM Health Care System Inc.
477 N. Lindbergh Blvd., St. Louis, MO 63141
Phone: 314-994-7800   **Fax:** 314-994-7900
Web: www.ssmhc.com

PRODUCTS/OPERATIONS

2008 Sales

	% of total
Patient services	95
Net assets released	1
Other	4
Total	**100**

Selected Facilities

Illinois
St. Mary's Good Samaritan (joint sponsorship, Mt. Vernon and Centralia)

Missouri
St. Francis Hospital & Health Services (Maryville)
St. Mary's Health Center (Jefferson City)
SSM Cardinal Glennon Children's Hospital (St. Louis)
SSM DePaul Health Center (Bridgeton)
SSM St. Clare Health Center (St. Louis)
SSM St. Joseph Health Center (St. Charles)
SSM St. Joseph Health Center (Wentzville)
SSM St. Joseph Hospital West (Lake St. Louis)
SSM St. Mary's Health Center (St. Louis)

Oklahoma
Bone & Joint Hospital (Oklahoma City)
St. Anthony Hospital (Oklahoma City)
Unity Health Center (affiliate, Shawnee)

Wisconsin
Boscobel Area Health Care (managed, Boscobel)
Columbus Community Hospital (affiliate, Columbus)
St. Clare Hospital and Health Services (Baraboo)
St. Clare Meadows Care Center (Madison)
St. Mary's Care Center (Madison)
St. Mary's Hospital (Madison)
Stoughton Hospital (affiliate, Stoughton)

HISTORICAL FINANCIALS

Company Type: Not-for-profit

Income Statement				FYE: December 31
	REVENUE ($ mil.)	NET INCOME ($ mil.)	NET PROFIT MARGIN	EMPLOYEES
12/08	2,682	—	—	24,000

Stanford University

Prospectors panning for gold in higher education can strike it rich at Stanford University. The school is one of the premier educational institutions in the US, boasting respected programs in business, engineering, law, and medicine, among others. The school serves more than 19,700 students and has about 1,000 faculty members. A private institution, Stanford supports its activities through a $17 billion endowment, one of the largest in the US. The university was established in 1885 by Leland Stanford Sr., who made his fortune selling provisions to California gold miners. Leland Sr. and his wife, Jane, founded the school in memory of their son, Leland Jr., who died of typhoid at age 15.

Stanford is also widely recognized as one of the top US research universities, and sports a host of laboratories and research centers, including the Stanford Institute for Economic Policy Research and the Stanford Linear Accelerator Center. Its faculty members include around 20 Nobel Prize winners, a handful of Pulitzer Prize winners, and around 20 National Medal of Science winners.

The university has received sizable donations from notable alumni such as Jerry Yang (co-founder of Yahoo!), Charles Schwab, Texas billionaire Robert Bass, and William Hewlett (of Hewlett-Packard, who has since died). The gift by the Hewlett Foundation of $400 million is the largest in university history.

HISTORY

In 1885 Leland Stanford Sr. and his wife, Jane, established Leland Stanford Junior University in memory of their son Leland Jr., who had died of typhoid at age 15. Stanford made his fortune selling provisions to California gold miners and as a major investor in the Central Pacific Railroad, one of the two companies that built the first transcontinental railway. It was Stanford who connected the tracks laid eastward by Central Pacific and westward by Union Pacific with a gold railway spike in 1869. He also served as California's governor and as a US senator.

The Stanfords donated more than 8,000 acres of land from their own estate to establish an unconventional university, one that was coeducational and nondenominational, with a focus on preparing students for a profession. Stanford opened its doors in 1891 to a freshman class of 559 students. It awarded its first degrees four years later, and among the graduates was future US president Herbert Hoover.

Leland Stanford Sr. died in 1893, and in 1903 Jane Stanford turned the university over to the trustees. After weathering significant damage in 1906 from the Great San Francisco Earthquake, the university established a law school in 1908 and its medical school five years later.

During WWI the university mobilized half of its students into the Students' Army Training Corps. The School of Education was established in 1917, followed by the School of Engineering and Graduate School of Business eight years later. In 1933 a rule limiting the number of women admitted to Stanford was abolished.

Wallace Sterling, who became president of the university after WWII, initiated the transformation of Stanford into a world-class institution with a reputation for teaching and research. Under Sterling the university initiated development on the Stanford Research Park.

In 1958 Stanford opened its first overseas campus (near Stuttgart, Germany), and the Stanford Medical Center was completed the following year. The university created a computer science department in 1965 and two years later opened the Stanford Linear Accelerator Center dedicated to physics research.

Donald Kennedy became president in 1980. The next year students voted to abandon the university's official mascot, the "Indians," in response to concerns raised by Native American students. The nickname "Cardinal" was adopted in its place. The term refers to the school's color, cardinal red.

Also during Kennedy's tenure, it was revealed that Stanford had overcharged the Office of Naval Research for indirect costs associated with research. The scandal led to Kennedy's resignation in 1992, and in 1994 the Office of Naval Research and the university settled a related lawsuit for $1.2 million and a stipulation that Stanford had not committed any wrongdoing. Gerhard Casper succeeded Kennedy as president.

In 1997 Stanford and the University of California at San Francisco combined their teaching hospitals in a public/private merger. Two years later, after the controversial experiment had harmed both hospitals' financial pictures, the merger was terminated, and the two hospitals agreed to go their separate ways.

In 1999 Casper announced his intention to resign as president. The school tapped provost John Hennessy as his replacement. Soon after his appointment in 2000, Hennessey launched a campaign to raise $1 billion. Former Stanford professor and Netscape co-founder Jim Clark donated $150 million later that year to support Stanford's biomedical engineering and sciences program. The school also launched a new company, SKOLAR, which developed an online search engine for the medical industry.

EXECUTIVES

President: John L. Hennessy, age 56
Provost: John W. Etchemendy
VP Development: Martin Shell
VP Public Affairs: David Demarest
VP Land, Buildings, and Real Estate: Robert Reidy
VP and General Counsel: Debra Zumwalt
VP Alumni Affairs and President, Stanford Alumni Association: Howard Wolf
VP Business Affairs and CFO: Randall S. (Randy) Livingston, age 55
Associate VP and Director University Communications: Alan Acosta
Dean School of Law: Larry D. Kramer
Director Stanford Linear Accelerator Center: Prof Persis Drell
Dean Graduate School of Business: Robert L. (Bob) Joss, age 68
Controller: Susan Calandra
Vice Provost and Dean Research: Ann M. Arvin
Vice Provost Undergraduate Education: John Bravman
Vice Provost Graduate Education: Patricia Gumport
Executive Director Information Technology Services: Bill Clebsch
Executive Director Human Resources: Diane Peck
Auditors: PricewaterhouseCoopers LLP

LOCATIONS

HQ: Stanford University
655 Serra St., Stanford, CA 94305
Phone: 650-723-2300   **Fax:** 650-725-0247
Web: www.stanford.edu

PRODUCTS/OPERATIONS

Selected Schools

Undergraduate
  School of Earth Sciences
  School of Engineering
  School of Humanities and Sciences

Graduate
  School of Business
  School of Earth Sciences
  School of Engineering
  School of Education
  School of Humanities and Sciences
  School of Law
  School of Medicine

Selected Interdisciplinary Research Centers

Alliance for Innovative Manufacturing at Stanford
Center for Computer Research in Music and Acoustics
Center for Integrated Facility Engineering
Center for Integrated Systems

Selected Laboratories, Centers, and Institutes

Center for Research on Information Storage Materials
Center for the Study of Language and Information
Edward L. Ginzton Laboratory
Institute for International Studies
Institute for Research on Women and Gender
John and Terry Levin Center for Public Service and Public Interest Law
Stanford Center for Buddhist Studies
Stanford Humanities Center
Stanford Institute for Economic Policy Research
W.W. Hansen Experimental Physics Laboratory

Selected Medical Research Facilities

Center for Biomedical Ethics
Center for Research in Disease Prevention
Human Genome Center
Richard M. Lucas Center for Magnetic Resonance Spectroscopy & Imaging
Sleep Disorders Center

Other Selected Research Facilities

Hoover Institution on War, Revolution and Peace
Hopkins Marine Station
Martin Luther King Jr. Papers Project
Stanford Linear Accelerator Center

Staple Cotton Cooperative

Get some new cotton underwear for a gift? Chances are a member of the Staple Cotton Cooperative Association (Staplcotn) grew the cotton your new skivvies are made of. Most of the co-op's yield is sold to the US textile industry to make men's knit underwear, T-shirts, sheets, towels, and denim. Staplcotn sells some 3 million bales of cotton annually both domestically and overseas. It serves its more than 11,000 members in 45 states. The co-op's Stapldiscount unit offers members low-interest loans for equipment, buildings, and land. Staplcotn has 14 regional offices in six states and 16 warehouses in three states.

Staplcotn's US customers include such clothing giants as Fruit of the Loom, Levi Strauss, and Hanes. Although the co-op's cotton is sold mainly to domestic customers, a decrease in demand for cotton in the US has led Staplcotn to look toward foreign sales, mainly in Asia.

The cooperative was founded in 1921 by Mississippi cotton producer Oscar Bledsoe and 10 other growers.

EXECUTIVES

Chairman; Chairman, Stapldiscount: Ben Lamensdorf
President, CEO, and Director; President and CEO, Stapldiscount: Woods E. Eastland
EVP; EVP, Stapldiscount: Meredith B. Allen
VP and CFO; VP and CFO, Stapldiscount: Charles Robertson
VP Sales Operations: David C. Camp
VP and COO, Stapldiscount: J. D. Hoover
VP Systems and Controls; VP Systems and Controls, Stapldiscount: L. A. (Larry) Gnemi
VP Warehousing: Shane Stephens
VP Human Resources; VP Human Resources, Stapldiscount: Russell Robertson
VP Cotton Services: Sterling P. Jones
VP and COO, Stapldiscount: Tom Dillard
General Counsel and Secretary; General Counsel and Secretary, Stapldiscount: Kenneth E. Downs
Senior Director North American Sales: Frederick Barrier

LOCATIONS

HQ: Staple Cotton Cooperative Association
214 W. Market St., Greenwood, MS 38930
Phone: 662-453-6231   **Fax:** 662-453-4622
Web: www.staplcotn.com

COMPETITORS

Alabama Farmers Cooperative
Calcot
Cargill
Dunavant Enterprises
International Cotton Marketing
JB Cotton
J.G. Boswell Co.
King Ranch
Louis Dreyfus Group
Noble Group Limited
Olam
Plains Cotton
Southern States
Tennessee Farmers Co-op
Weil Brothers Cotton

HISTORICAL FINANCIALS
Company Type: Cooperative

Income Statement				FYE: August 31
	REVENUE ($ mil.)	NET INCOME ($ mil.)	NET PROFIT MARGIN	EMPLOYEES
8/08	932	—	—	201

State Farm Mutual Automobile Insurance

Like an enormous corporation, State Farm is everywhere. The leading US personal lines property/casualty company (by premiums), State Farm Mutual Automobile Insurance Company is the #1 provider of auto insurance. It also is the leading home insurer and offers nonmedical health and life insurance through its subsidiary companies. Its products are marketed via some 17,000 agents in the US and Canada. Competition has increased with the fall of barriers between the banking, securities, and insurance industries. State Farm's efforts to diversify include a federal savings bank charter (State Farm Bank) that offers consumer and business loans.

The company also established itself as a financial services provider in 1999, and its mutual funds have since built up $4.6 billion in assets. However, insurance is still its main source of income. And, while State Farm already insures 15% of the automobiles on US roads, it is scrambling to hang on to that much while attempting to grab an even larger portion of the pie.

State Farm still insures more than 20% of the single-family homes in the US, but the insurer stopped writing new homeowners policies in some 15 states in an effort to improve profitability. Citing that it spends $1.20 for every dollar it earns in Florida, in 2008 the company filed for permission to raise its homeowners rates. When Florida insurance regulators denied the request in 2009, State Farm announced that it would discontinue writing new homeowners and other property policies in the state.

Hurricanes Katrina, Wilma, and Rita brought State Farm customer claims totaling $6.3 billion in property and casualty losses. For residents along the Gulf Coast, at first it seemed like State Farm would stay put. However, as the claims keep rolling in, the company has rewritten its underwriting guidelines to limit its risk. New homeowner policies in places such as New Orleans now have steeper deductibles and less coverage, and the company has completely stopped offering new homeowners and commercial property policies in the state of Mississippi.

A quieter problem looms ahead for the company's future: Its aging agency force is readying for retirement, and fewer younger agents are signing up to sell insurance. It is an industry-wide trend that State Farm is addressing with more aggressive recruitment efforts.

Since its founding, the group's companies have been run by only two families, the Mecherles (1922-54) and the Rusts (1954-present).

HISTORY

Retired farmer George Mecherle formed State Farm Mutual Automobile Insurance in Bloomington, Illinois, in 1922. State Farm served only members of farm bureaus and farm mutual insurance companies, charging a one-time membership fee and a premium to protect an automobile against loss or damage.

Unlike most competitors, State Farm offered six-month premium payments. The insurer billed and collected renewal premiums from its home office, relieving the agent of the task. In addition, State Farm determined auto rates by a simple seven-class system, while competitors varied rates for each model.

State Farm in 1926 started City and Village Mutual Automobile Insurance to insure nonfarmers' autos; it became part of the company in 1927. Between 1927 and 1931 it introduced borrowed-car protection, wind coverage, and insurance for vehicles used to transport schoolchildren.

State Farm expanded to California in 1928 and formed State Farm Life Insurance the next year. In 1935 it established State Farm Fire Insurance. George Mecherle became chairman in 1937, and his son Ramond became president. In 1939 George challenged agents to write "A Million or More (auto policies) by '44." State Farm saw a 110% increase in policies.

During the 1940s State Farm focused on urban areas after most of the farm bureaus formed their own insurance companies. In the late 1940s and 1950s, it moved to a full-time agency force. Homeowners coverage was added to the insurer's offerings under the leadership of Adlai Rust, who led State Farm from 1954 until 1958, when Edward Rust took over. He died in 1985; his son Edward Jr. currently holds the top spot.

Between 1974 and 1987 the insurer was hit by several gender-discrimination suits (a 1992 settlement awarded $157 million to 814 women). State Farm has since tried to hire more women and minorities.

Serial disasters in the early 1990s, including Hurricane Andrew and the Los Angeles riots, proved costly. The 1994 Northridge earthquake alone generated more than $2.5 billion in claims and contributed to a 72% decline in earnings. State Farm — the top US home insurer since the mid-1960s — canceled 62,500 residential policies in South Florida in 1996 to cut potential hurricane loss an estimated 11%. In response, Florida's insurance regulators rescinded a previously approved rate hike. That year the company agreed to open more urban neighborhood offices to settle a discrimination suit brought by the Department of Housing and Urban Development, which accused State Farm of discriminating against potential customers in minority-populated areas.

Legal trouble continued. In 1997 State Farm settled with a California couple who alleged the company forged policyholders' signatures on forms declining coverage and concealed evidence to avoid paying earthquake damage claims. That year a policyholder sued to keep State Farm from "wasting company assets" on President Clinton's legal defense against Paula Jones' sexual harassment charges (Clinton held a State Farm personal liability policy).

Relations with its sales force already rocky, State Farm in 1998 proposed to reduce up-front commissions and cut base pay in favor of incentives for customer retention and cross-selling. Reduced auto premiums and increased catastrophe claims from across the US eroded State Farm's bottom line that year. A federal thrift charter obtained in 1998 let the company launch banking operations the next year.

In 2000 the company was hit with a class-action lawsuit about its denial of personal-injury claims; previous suits had been individual cases. In 2002 State Farm Indemnity, the company's auto-only New Jersey subsidiary, withdrew from the Garden State's auto insurance market but began phasing back into the market in 2005.

Like all reinsurers, State Farm's reinsurance business was tested by the 2005 hurricane season. It underwrote losses of $2.8 billion.

EXECUTIVES

Chairman and CEO: Edward B. (Ed) Rust Jr., age 58
Vice Chairman, CFO, and Treasurer: Michael L. Tipsord
Vice Chairman and Chief Agency and Marketing Officer: Michael C. Davidson
Vice Chairman and Chief Administrative Officer: James E. (Jim) Rutrough
EVP, General Counsel, and Secretary: Kim M. Brunner
EVP: Brian V. Boyden
EVP: Barbara Cowden
EVP: Deborah Traskell
EVP: Willie G. Brown
EVP: William K. (Bill) King
SVP, Texas: Mike Wey
SVP, Florida: Joe Formusa
SVP, Heartland: James Thompson
SVP, Mid-Atlantic: Duane Farrington
SVP, California: Rand Harbert
SVP, Mid-America: Paul Smith
SVP, Southern: Robert (Bob) Trippel
SVP, Great Lakes: Mary Crego
SVP, Central: Lee Baumann
SVP, Canada: Bob Cooke
SVP, Great Western: Dave Gonzales
SVP, Northeast: Brian Carlson
SVP, Pacific Northwest: Harold Gray
VP Health: Susan D. Waring
VP Agency: Craig Allen
VP Enterprise Internet Solutions: Ann Baughan
President, State Farm Bank: Mike Smith
SVP, State Farm Mutual; President and CEO, State Farm General: Gregory (Greg) Jones
Auditors: PricewaterhouseCoopers LLP

LOCATIONS

HQ: State Farm Mutual Automobile Insurance Company
1 State Farm Plaza, Bloomington, IL 61710
Phone: 309-766-2311   **Fax:** 309-766-3621
Web: www.statefarm.com

PRODUCTS/OPERATIONS

Selected Subsidiaries

State Farm Bank, FSB
State Farm Fire and Casualty Company (homeowners, boat owners, and commercial insurance)
State Farm Florida Insurance Company (homeowners and renters insurance)
State Farm General Insurance Company (property insurance)

State Farm Indemnity Company (auto insurance in New Jersey)
State Farm Investment Management Corp
State Farm Life and Accident Assurance Company
State Farm Life Insurance Company
State Farm Lloyds, Inc.
State Farm VP Management Corp

COMPETITORS

Allstate	MetLife
American Family	Nationwide
Berkshire Hathaway	Philadelphia Insurance
CNA Financial	Progressive Corporation
COUNTRY Financial	Prudential
GEICO	Torchmark
GMAC Insurance	USAA
The Hartford	W. R. Berkley
Liberty Mutual	

HISTORICAL FINANCIALS

Company Type: Mutual company

Income Statement				FYE: December 31
	REVENUE ($ mil.)	NET INCOME ($ mil.)	NET PROFIT MARGIN	EMPLOYEES
12/08	61,300	(542)	—	68,600
12/07	61,600	5,460	8.9%	68,000
12/06	60,500	5,320	8.8%	68,000
12/05	59,200	3,240	5.5%	79,200
12/04	58,800	5,300	9.0%	79,200
Annual Growth	1.0%	—	—	(3.5%)

Net Income History

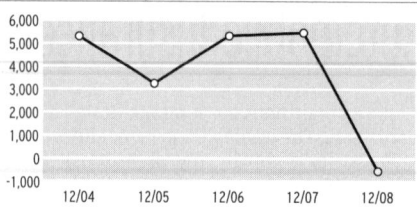

State University of New York

SUNY days are ahead for many New Yorkers seeking higher education. With an enrollment of more than 420,000 students, The State University of New York (SUNY) is vying with California State University System for the title of largest university system in the US. Most students are residents of New York State (about 40% of all New York State high school graduates enroll at SUNY institutions). SUNY maintains 64 campuses around the state, including four university centers, 13 university colleges, 30 community colleges, eight technical colleges, two medical centers, and colleges of ceramics and optometry.

Offering more than 7,600 degree and certificate programs, SUNY confers some 80,000 diplomas each year, including nearly 14,000 post-graduate degrees.

HISTORY

The State University of New York was organized in 1948, but it traces its roots back to several institutions founded in the 19th century. In 1844 the New York state legislature authorized the creation of the Albany Normal School, which was charged with educating the state's secondary school teachers. Two years later, the University of Buffalo was chartered to provide academic, theological, legal, and medical studies. More normal schools later were founded between 1861 and 1889 in Brockport, Buffalo, Cortland, Fredonia, Geneseo, New Paltz, Oneonta, Oswego, Plattsburgh, and Potsdam.

In the early 1900s the state established several agricultural colleges, including schools in Canton (1907), Alfred (1908), Morrisville (1910), Farmingdale (1912), and Cobleskill (1916). New York also set up several schools as units of Cornell University, including colleges of veterinary medicine (1894), agriculture (1909), home economics (1925), and industrial and labor relations (1945).

After WWII, veterans began to fill US colleges and universities, taking advantage of the GI Bill to secure a college education. The legislature set up SUNY in 1948 to consolidate 29 institutions under a single board of trustees charged with meeting the growing demand. The board coordinated the state colleges into a single body and established four-year liberal arts colleges, professional and graduate schools, and research centers. During the 1950s and 1960s, new campuses were created at Binghamton, Stony Brook, Old Westbury, Purchase, and Utica/Rome, and enrollment began to take off, jumping from 30,000 in 1955 to 63,000 in 1959.

By the early 1970s SUNY had more than 320,000 students at 72 institutions. But budget constraints later that decade led to higher tuition, reduced enrollment goals, and employment cutbacks. In 1975 eight New York City community colleges were transferred to City University. SUNY's enrollment began growing again during the 1980s, reaching more than 400,000 by 1990. Early in the decade, the institution began implementing SUNY 2000, a plan that called for increasing access to education and diversifying undergraduate studies. Following his election in 1994, Governor George Pataki proposed more than $550 million in cuts to the SUNY system.

In 1997 John Ryan replaced Thomas Bartlett as chancellor. The following year SUNY became the exclusive sponsor of The College Channel, a guide to colleges and college life aimed at high-school juniors and seniors and broadcast by PRIMEDIA's Channel One. In 1999 the governor's budget director, Robert King, was named chancellor to replace the retiring Bartlett. King challenged SUNY administrators and the state to increase levels of funding to help keep the university competitive against other top-flight institutions. In 2000 SUNY faced rising budget shortfalls at its teaching hospitals, in part because money was being siphoned off to other areas. That year King announced a set of initiatives to raise an additional $1.5 billion in federal research grants and $1 billion in private donations over five years.

King retired as the university's chancellor in June 2005. Nancy Zimpher became the university's first female chancellor in 2009. The university had been without a permanent leader since 2007 when John Ryan resigned.

Stater Bros.

Stater Bros. has no shortage of major-league rivals, operating in the same crowded Southern California markets as Kroger-owned Ralphs and Safeway-owned Vons. Stater Bros. Holdings operates about 165 full-service Stater Bros. Markets in some six counties, primarily in the Riverside and San Bernardino areas. About 25 of the regional chain's grocery stores host Super Rx Pharmacies. The grocery chain, which sold its milk-producing operation (Santee Dairies) to Dean Foods in 2009, plans to use the proceeds to invest in real estate and other growth opportunities. Founded in 1936 by twin brothers Leo and Cleo Stater, Stater Bros. is owned by chairman and CEO Jack Brown through La Cadena Investments.

Competition from the grocery giants and the purchase of stores from Albertsons has put a strain on the company's profits. To distinguish itself from rivals, the chain refuses to offer promotional games and frequent shopper cards, boasting everyday low prices and chainwide temporary price reductions (called Stater Savers) instead. Stater Bros. is bracing itself for intense competition from Wal-Mart and SAM'S CLUB stores, which are becoming more common in the area. To better compete with Wal-Mart, the regional grocery chain cut prices on more than 10,000 products in all of its stores in mid-2009. Also, its Super RX Pharmacy locations began offering up to a 14-day supply of selected antibiotics free to customers in fall 2009, and generic drugs for $4 per prescription in mid-2008.

Stater Bros. Holdings is the largest privately held supermarket chain in Southern California. The company plans to open three to six new stores per year. The firm opened a new distribution center on the site of its new corporate headquarters in San Bernardino in September 2008. With the cost of the new distribution center behind it, Stater Bros. plans to use its free cash to reduce debt and possibly acquire some sites for future supermarkets.

HISTORY

In 1936, at age 23, Cleo Stater and his twin brother, Leo, mortgaged a Chevrolet to make a down payment on a modest grocery store where Cleo had been working for five years in their hometown of Yucaipa, California. Later that year the brothers bought their second grocery in the nearby community of Redlands. Their younger brother, Lavoy, soon joined them to help build the company. In 1938 the brothers opened the first Stater Bros. market in Colton; by 1939 they had a chain of four stores.

The small, family-owned grocery chain continued to grow. In 1948 Stater Bros. opened its first supermarket (which was several times larger than its other stores and had its own parking lot) in Riverside. By 1950 the company had 12 stores.

Stater Bros. consolidated its offices and warehouse in Colton in the early 1960s and continued its expansion into nearby communities. By 1964 it operated 27 supermarkets in 18 cities in Los Angeles, Orange, Riverside, and San Bernardino counties. In 1968 the brothers sold the company's 35 stores to Long Beach, California-based petroleum services provider Petrolane for $33 million. Lavoy succeeded Cleo as president.

As a division of Petrolane, Stater Bros. kept growing. In the 1970s the company introduced a new store design that expanded sales area but required less land and a smaller building. The number of stores more than doubled (to over 80) between 1968 and 1979, when Lavoy retired.

Ron Burkle, VP of Administration for Petrolane, and his father, Joe, president of Stater Bros., attempted to buy the chain for $100 million in 1981. Infuriated by the low bid, Petrolane fired Ron and demoted his father, who left that year. Jack Brown was named president in his place. Petrolane sold the chain in 1983 to La Cadena Investments, a private company that included Brown and other top Stater Bros. executives.

Leo died in 1985. That year the company went public to reduce debt from the 1983 LBO and to provide funds for an extensive expansion plan. It also incorporated as Stater Bros. Inc. In 1986 a proxy fight for control of the company erupted between Brown's La Cadena group and chairman Bernard Garrett, who owned about 41% of Stater Bros. Brown had been suspended as president and CEO (Joe Burkle returned in his place), but Los Angeles-based investment firm Craig Corp. bought Garrett's stake, and Brown returned; he was later elected chairman. That year Stater Bros. also became a co-owner in Santee Dairies with Hughes Markets (now part of Kroger).

The next year Craig and Stater Bros. executives took the grocery chain private again. Burkle bought a 9% stake in Craig in 1989 through Yucaipa Capital Partners. Also in 1987 Craig reduced its stake in Stater Bros., transferring some stock to La Cadena. Stater Bros. Holdings was created as a parent company for the grocery chain.

Stater Bros. expressed an interest in buying rival Alpha Beta stores when they were put up for sale, but Yucaipa Companies bought them in 1991. Craig considered selling its stake in Stater Bros. in 1992; it finally sold its half of the company to La Cadena in 1996.

In 1999 Stater Bros. acquired 33 Albertsons and 10 Lucky stores, as well as one store site. (The FTC required Albertsons to sell the stores in order to acquire American Stores, Lucky's parent.) The acquisition and the early retirement of debt resulted in its 1999 losses. In September 2001 company co-founder Cleo Stater died.

In early 2002 the company announced a partnership with Krispy Kreme Doughnuts to offer the treats at selected Stater Bros. supermarkets. In 2003 Stater Bros. introduced Topco private-label brand merchandise in its stores.

In 2004 Santee Dairies became a wholly owned subsidiary of Stater Bros. when the grocery chain acquired Kroger's 50% stake in the operation.

Stater Bros. sales rose by about 5% during a four-and-a-half-month-long strike by employees of rivals Albertsons, Kroger, and Vons. The dispute, which diverted shoppers from those stores to Stater Bros. markets, ended in March 2004. In October Don Baker was promoted to president and COO of Stater Bros. Previously, Baker was EVP and COO of the company.

Jim Lee replaced Baker as president and COO of the regional grocery chain in 2006. In 2007 the company moved its headquarters to the site of the former Norton Air Force Base in San Bernardino. In 2009 Stater Bros. sold its milk-processing division, Santee Dairies, to Dean Foods, America's largest dairy and home to Alta Dena and Horizon Organic dairy brands.

EXECUTIVES

Chairman and CEO: Jack H. Brown, age 70
Vice Chairman: Thomas W. Field Jr., age 75
President and COO: James W. (Jim) Lee, age 57
EVP Marketing: Dennis L. McIntyre, age 48
EVP Retail Operations and Administration:
George Frahm, age 55
EVP and CFO: Phillip J. (Phil) Smith, age 61
VP Corporate Affairs: Susan Atkinson
VP Finance: Dave Harris
VP Produce Division: Roger Schroeder
Secretary and Director: Bruce D. Varner, age 72
Auditors: Ernst & Young LLP

LOCATIONS

HQ: Stater Bros. Holdings Inc.
301 S. Tippecanoe Ave., San Bernardino, CA 92408
Phone: 909-733-5000   **Fax:** 909-733-3930
Web: www.staterbros.com

2009 Stores

	No.
San Bernardino County	51
Riverside County	46
Orange County	30
Los Angeles County	26
San Diego County	10
Kern County	2
Total	**165**

PRODUCTS/OPERATIONS

Selected Departments and Products

Bakery
Dairy products
Delicatessen
Floral
Fresh produce
Frozen foods
General merchandise
Health and beauty aids
Liquor
Meats
Pharmacy
Seafood

COMPETITORS

Arden Group	Tesco
Costco Wholesale	Trader Joe's
Ralphs Grocery	Vons
Sam's Club	Walgreen
Save Mart	Wal-Mart
Smart & Final	Whole Foods

Stephens Inc.

Those who bristle at the carrying-on of those highfalutin Wall Street bankers may take some comfort in Stephens — one of the largest investment banking firms based outside New York City. The company, founded in 1933, offers a variety of services, including advice for IPOs and mergers and acquisitions, as well as public financing, institutional stock and bond trading, insurance brokerage and advisory services, and equity research. It also provides asset management for individual and institutional investors. Chairman, president, and CEO Warren Stephens, the nephew of founder Witt Stephens, acquired 100% of the outstanding stock of Stephens in 2006.

With Warren Stephens at the helm (he succeeded his father Jack as CEO in 1986), the firm

has maintained a relatively low profile as it has pursued more business outside Arkansas. Positioning itself as an independent alternative to larger, scandal-ridden Wall Street firms, the company operates some 25 offices mainly in the southern and eastern US as well as an office in London.

In 2006 the company separated its investment banking and related financial services (to remain under the aegis of Stephens Inc. and Warren Stephens) from its private equity operations, which adopted the moniker The Stephens Group.

EXECUTIVES

Chairman, President, and CEO: Warren A. Stephens, age 52
COO and Director: Curt Bradbury
CFO: Mark Doramus
CFO Stephens Capital Partners: Kathy Riley Bryant
SEVP Private Client Group: Greg Feltus
EVP Management Information Systems: John Green
EVP Accounting: Zoe Hines
EVP and Senior Managing Director, Stephens Cori Capital Advisors: Stormy Byorum
EVP and General Counsel: David Knight
EVP Research: Nik Fisken
EVP and Investment Advisor: Larry Middleton
EVP Human Resources: Ellen Gray
EVP Private Client Group: Kevin Scanlon
EVP Capital Management: Warren Simpson
EVP Telecommunications and Media and Co-Head Investment Banking: Kenny Gunderman, age 36
EVP Public Finance: Mark McBryde
President, Stephens Insurance: Marty Rhodes
Auditors: Deloitte & Touche LLP

LOCATIONS

HQ: Stephens Inc.
111 Center St., Little Rock, AR 72201
Phone: 501-377-2000   **Fax:** 501-377-2470
Web: www.stephens.com

Selected Offices

Atlanta	Little Rock, AR
Austin, TX	London
Baton Rouge, LA	Memphis, TN
Boston	Miami, FL
Charlotte, NC	Nashville, TN
Chicago	New Haven, CT
Columbia, SC	New York
Conway, AR	Richmond, VA
Dallas	Ridgeland, MS
Fayetteville, AR	St. Petersburg, FL
Hot Springs, AR	Texarkana, TX
Houston, TX	Washington, DC
Jonesboro, AR	

COMPETITORS

Canaccord Adams
Charles Schwab
Citigroup Global Markets
Deutsche Bank Alex. Brown
Fox-Pitt Kelton Cochran Caronia Waller
Goldman Sachs
Greenhill
Houlihan Lokey
Jefferies Group
KBW
Merrill Lynch
Morgan Keegan
Morgan Stanley
Piper Jaffray
SWS Group

HISTORICAL FINANCIALS

Company Type: Private

Income Statement

FYE: December 31

	REVENUE ($ mil.)	NET INCOME ($ mil.)	NET PROFIT MARGIN	EMPLOYEES
12/08	1,835	—	—	—

Stewart's Shops

I scream, you scream, we all scream for Stewart's ice cream — especially if we live in upstate New York or Vermont, home to nearly 330 Stewart's Shops. The chain of convenience stores sell more than 3,000 products, including dairy items, groceries, food to go (soup, sandwiches, hot entrees), beer, gasoline, and, of course, ice cream. In addition to its retail business, the company owns about 100 rental properties, including banks, hair salons, and apartments, near its stores. Stewart's Shops, formerly known as Stewart's Ice Cream Company, was established in 1945. The founding Dake family owns about two-thirds of the company; employee compensation plans own the rest.

Stewart's Shops makes its own ice cream — more than 50 flavors, both hand-dipped and packaged — and dairy products. Recognized for its quality products, the company relies on a group of about 50 farmers in New York to supply its milk. The company, which makes about 75% of the items it sells, also offers private-label goods and national brands in its stores.

EXECUTIVES

Chairman: William (Bill) Dake, age 69
President: Gary C. Dake, age 48
Treasurer: David A. Farr
SVP: Nancy Trimbur
Director, HR: Jim Botch
Director, Marketing and Public Relations:
Susan Law Dake

LOCATIONS

HQ: Stewart's Shops Corp.
2907 Rte. 9, Ballston Spa, NY 12020
Phone: 518-581-1200   **Fax:** 518-581-1209
Web: www.stewartsicecream.com

PRODUCTS/OPERATIONS

Selected Products and Services

Automated Teller Machines (ATMs)
Beer
Dairy products
Food to go
Gasoline
Groceries
Hand-dipped ice cream
Lottery sales
Packaged ice cream
Rental properties
Soda

COMPETITORS

7-Eleven	Kroger
Ben & Jerry's	Pathmark Stores
Cumberland Farms	Penn Traffic
Exxon Mobil	Royal Ahold
Golub	Sunoco
Hannaford Bros.	TravelCenters of America

HISTORICAL FINANCIALS

Company Type: Private

Income Statement				FYE: Last Sunday in December
	REVENUE ($ mil.)	NET INCOME ($ mil.)	NET PROFIT MARGIN	EMPLOYEES
12/08	1,000	—	—	4,000
12/07	1,000	—	—	3,800
12/06	1,000	—	—	3,800
12/05	1,023	—	—	4,000
Annual Growth	(0.8%)	—	—	0.0%

Revenue History

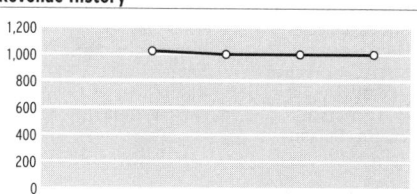

Structure Tone

Structured to set the right tone for its clients, The Structure Tone Organization develops commercial, industrial, and institutional properties for clients around the world. Active in the US, the UK, and Asia, the firm provides preconstruction, general contracting, construction management, and project management services for building construction, interior fit-outs and renovations, and infrastructure upgrades. Affiliates include construction management and services firms Constructors & Associates in Texas, Pavarini Construction in Florida and Connecticut, and New York's Pavarini McGovern. Lewis Marino and Patrick Donaghy, whose families now own the company, founded Structure Tone in 1971.

The Structure Tone Organization has completed a wide variety of projects, including academic facilities, broadcast studios, condos, government facilities, museums, and research and development labs.

The company's diverse portfolio and accumulation of long-standing clients help it weather ups and downs in the economy.

EXECUTIVES

Chairman: James K. Donaghy
Vice Chairman: Brian M. Donaghy
CEO: Robert W. Mullen
President: Anthony M. Carvette
CFO: Brett A. Phillips
EVP, Pavarini McGovern: William (Bill) Frederick
EVP and Secretary: John T. White
EVP: Michael Neary
SVP Human Resources: Robert (Bob) Yardis

VP Information Technology: Terrence Robbins
VP Marketing: Robin Malacrea
CEO, Pavarini McGovern: Eric McGovern

LOCATIONS

HQ: The Structure Tone Organization
770 Broadway, New York, NY 10003
Phone: 212-481-6100   **Fax:** 212-685-9267
Web: www.structuretone.com

PRODUCTS/OPERATIONS

Selected Sectors

Academia
Broadcast and media
Commercial
Cultural and entertainment
Financial
Government
Health care
Hospitality
Interiors
Law
Mission critical
Non-profit
Parking structures
Residential
Retail
Life Sciences

COMPETITORS

Bovis Lend Lease
Clark Enterprises
Devcon Construction
DPR Construction
Foster Wheeler
Gilbane
HRH Construction
Hunt Construction
Opus Corp.
PCL Employees Holdings
Peter Kiewit Sons'
Skanska USA Building
Tishman
Turner Corporation
Tutor Perini
Walsh Group
Washington Division

HISTORICAL FINANCIALS

Company Type: Private

Income Statement				FYE: October 31
	REVENUE ($ mil.)	NET INCOME ($ mil.)	NET PROFIT MARGIN	EMPLOYEES
10/08	3,100	—	—	1,450
10/07	3,330	—	—	1,650
10/06	3,160	—	—	1,670
10/05	2,592	—	—	1,450
10/04	1,950	—	—	1,200
Annual Growth	12.3%	—	—	4.8%

Revenue History

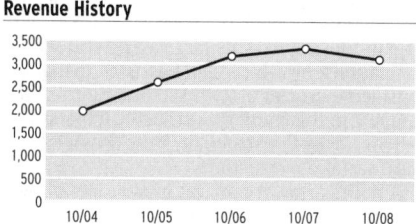

Subway

You don't have to go underground to catch this Subway. Doctor's Associates operates the Subway chain of sandwich shops, the second-largest quick-service chain behind McDonald's. It boasts more than 31,000 locations in 90 countries, with more US locations than the Golden Arches. Virtually all Subway restaurants are franchised and offer such fare as hot and cold sub sandwiches, turkey wraps, and salads. Subways are located in freestanding buildings, as well as in airports, convenience stores, sports facilities, and other locations. Doctor's Associates is owned by co-founders Fred DeLuca and Peter Buck, who opened the first Subway in 1965.

The national focus on healthy eating habits and the fast food industry has benefited the Subway chain greatly in recent years, and the company continues to tout the health benefits of its sandwiches over traditional burgers and fries. Its poster boy for weight loss, Jared Fogle, continues to be a focus for much of Subway's marketing campaign to get consumers to move away from fatty fast food.

The company's success also stems in part from its attractiveness to franchisees. With a low initial franchise cost and simple operations (minimum space requirements and little on-site cooking), the chain has been one of the fastest-growing franchises in the world. Subway surpassed 21,000 locations in the US in 2007. The following year the chain reached 1,300 locations in the UK and Ireland, surpassing the number of McDonald's restaurants in those countries as well.

The downside to this trend has been increasing competition in the healthy dining market. Quiznos, the company's main rival in the sub sandwich game, has been focused on expanding its own footprint of franchised outlets while mounting an aggressive advertising effort to steal away consumers. Some pizza chains, such as Domino's, have also been expanding into the sandwich segment. At the same time, McDonald's and other fast food giants have been adding healthier items to their menus.

While keeping its competitors at bay, Subway has been focused on new menu items in an effort to increase business during the evening hours. During 2008 the company began promoting foot-long subs to drive additional traffic to its restaurants, and Subway continues to market its toasted sandwiches as a dinner alternative.

HISTORY

In 1965 17-year-old Fred DeLuca dreamed of becoming a doctor and worked as a stock boy in a Bridgeport, Connecticut, hardware store to earn college tuition. It wasn't enough, so he cornered family friend Peter Buck at a backyard barbecue and asked for advice. Buck, a nuclear physicist, suggested DeLuca open a submarine sandwich shop and put up $1,000 to get him started.

As the summer of 1965 was coming to an end, DeLuca rented a small location in a remote area of Bridgeport, opened Pete's Super Submarines, and there he sold foot-long sandwiches. On the first day the sandwiches were so popular that DeLuca hired his own customers to work behind the counter; by the end of the day, he had sold out of all his supplies. The sandwiches continued to be popular for a while, but within a few months the shop started losing money, and DeLuca and

Buck found that selling submarine sandwiches was a seasonal business. They decided they could create an illusion of success by opening a second location and then a third. The third store was finally successful, partly because of its more visible location and increased marketing and partly because of a new name — Subway.

DeLuca and Buck had set a goal of 32 shops opened by 1975, but they had only 16 by 1974. They realized that the only way they could reach their goal in one year was to license the Subway name. The first franchise opened that year in Wallingford, Connecticut, and they opened 32 by the end of 1975. The partners hit 100 by 1978, then 200 by 1983, and DeLuca set a new goal: 5,000 Subway shops by 1994. The first international Subway opened in Bahrain in 1984, and DeLuca achieved his goal of 5,000 shops by 1990.

During the 1990s DeLuca experimented with several other franchise concepts, including We Care Hair (budget styling salons), Cajun Joe's (spicy fried chicken), and Q Burgers, but none of these ventures fared as well as his sandwich empire. As Subway grew, however, controversy surrounding its treatment of franchisees began to surface. A Federal Trade Commission investigation of the company was dropped in 1993, but Subway continued to battle franchisees complaining about broken contracts, market oversaturation (and, therefore, too much competition and self-cannibalization), and what the franchisees viewed as unreasonably high royalty fees.

In spite of its franchising troubles, Subway kept growing. It expanded into Russia and China in the mid-1990s, and opened its 11,000th restaurant in 1995. In 1997 Subway inked deals with the Army, Navy, and Air Force exchange services to bring Subway units to military bases. Two years later the company opened its 14,000th restaurant in Mount Gambier, Australia, an event that coincided with Subway's renewed push to expand internationally.

The company got some unexpected publicity in 1999 when 22 year-old Jared Fogle claimed that he dropped 245 pounds from his 425-pound frame by subsisting on a diet of Subway turkey sandwiches. Subway helped Fogle extend his 15 minutes of fame by featuring him and his oversized pants in a TV commercial. (The company has since built an entire campaign around Fogle, which features other weight watchers attributing their success to Jared and Subway.) Subway introduced its largest menu initiative ever in 2000 when it unveiled its Subway Selects Gourmet Sandwiches, adding 13 items to the menu. In April 2001 the company opened its 15,000th store.

Also that year Buck retired as chairman but stayed on as a member of the board of directors. Becoming one of the fastest-growing franchises in the world, Subway expanded from 16,000 locations in 2002 to more than 22,000 stores by the end of 2004.

All US Subway outlets switched from Pepsi to Coke products in 2005. Two years later the chain surpassed 21,000 locations in the US.

EXECUTIVES

President: Frederick A. (Fred) DeLuca, age 61
CTO: Thys Van Hout
Chief Marketing Officer: Bill Schettini
VP Purchasing: Dennis Clabby
VP Operations: Millie Shinn
CEO, Subway Development Corporation of Washington: Larry Feldman
President and CEO, Subway Independent Purchasing Cooperative: Jan Risi
President, Subway Development Corporation of Washington: Alan Warmund
CEO, Subway Franchisee Advertising Trust: Jeff Moody
SVP and Chief Marketing Officer, Subway Franchisee Advertising Fund Trust: Tony Pace
Director Research and Development: Suzanne Greco
Controller: David Worroll
Coordinator Public Relations: Les Winograd

LOCATIONS

HQ: Doctor's Associates Inc.
325 Bic Dr., Milford, CT 06461
Phone: 203-877-4281 **Fax:** 203-876-6674
Web: www.subway.com

COMPETITORS

AFC Enterprises	Jack in the Box
Burger King	McDonald's
Chick-fil-A	Papa John's
Chipotle	Quiznos
Church's Chicken	Sonic Corp.
CKE Restaurants	Wendy's/Arby's Group, Inc.
Dairy Queen	YUM!
Domino's	

Suffolk Construction

The bricks are being laid at Suffolk Construction. The company provides general contracting, construction management, preconstruction, and design/build services in the public and private sectors to automotive, education, health care, retail, and assisted living clients across the US. Suffolk builds both commercial and residential buildings such as universities, senior housing, hotels, corporate offices, and retail stores. Major clients include Penske Automotive Group, Harvard University, and Boston Medical Center. The firm is owned by president and CEO John Fish, whose family has been in construction for four generations. It was founded in 1982 and operates in California, Florida, Virginia, and Boston.

Already a successful builder in New England, Suffolk Construction is working to expand nationally. It plans to merge with William A. Berry & Son, another Massachussets-based builder. Together, the companies have some $3.2 billion of work in the pipelines, including biomedical and health care projects, which are a specialty of Berry's.

To counteract the downturn in the residential market, Suffolk restructured its Florida division in West Palm Beach into four business units. That division is expected to reach $500 million in gross billings by 2012 by focusing on building more schools, biotechnology labs, and health care facilities, rather than residences. Particularly in Florida, with its large aging and senior populations, health care and assisted living are considered crucial growth sectors. Suffolk will compete in this market with such companies as Balfour Beatty Construction, Moss & Associates, and Coastal Construction.

Suffolk's array of projects in a variety of sectors help keep the company thriving even in challenging times.

EXECUTIVES

Chairman, President, and CEO: John F. Fish
EVP and Chief Accounting Officer: Michael (Mike) Azarela
VP, Human Resources: Zoe Damplo
General Manager, Mid-Atlantic: Reg Arnold
Corporate Controller: George E. Mastaby
General Manager, Retail and Interiors: Mike DiNapoli
General Manager, Commercial: Jeff Gouveia
General Manager, Institutional: Mark L. DiNapoli
General Manager, South East: Rex B. Kirby
General Counsel: Robert V. Lizza
General Manager, West Coast: David Cavecche
Auditors: McGladrey & Pullen, LLP

LOCATIONS

HQ: Suffolk Construction Company, Inc.
65 Allerton St., Boston, MA 02119
Phone: 617-445-3500 **Fax:** 617-541-2128
Web: www.suffolkconstruction.com

COMPETITORS

Balfour Construction	Pepper Construction
Bovis Lend Lease	Swinerton
Clark Enterprises	Turner Corporation
Coastal Construction	Tutor Perini
DooleyMack	Walsh Group
Kraus-Anderson	Whiting-Turner
McCarthy Building	

HISTORICAL FINANCIALS

Company Type: Private

Income Statement

FYE: August 31

	REVENUE ($ mil.)	NET INCOME ($ mil.)	NET PROFIT MARGIN	EMPLOYEES
8/08	1,570	—	—	800
8/07	1,220	—	—	700
8/06	1,207	—	—	710
8/05	1,200	—	—	709
Annual Growth	**9.4%**	**—**	**—**	**4.1%**

Revenue History

Sun Coast Resources

Breaking the glass ceiling with large containers of Texas tea, woman-owned Sun Coast Resources buys refined oil and sells it to third-party customers such as convenience stores, school districts, and companies in the construction industry. Sun Coast Resources serves customers (including the US Coast Guard) in the southern and southwestern US. The company's transportation services unit (an extensive truck fleet with more than 300 drivers) delivers gasoline and diesel fuels, marine and aviation fuels, and lubricants. The supplier also provides on-site and fleet fueling, petroleum tanks, and generator fueling services. Sun Coast carries a full line of Chevron oils and lubricants.

Other Sun Coast services include additive packages, bulk storage and warehousing, a computerized fleet tracking system, and customized schedule and deliveries (from 50 to 8,600 gallons per load).

The company was founded in 1985 by president and CEO Kathy Lehne with $2,000 in start-up capital.

In 2008 the company received the Chevron Lubrication Marketer Diamond Award, an honor reserved for the oil giant's top marketers. That year Sun Coast distributed more than 1.5 million gallons of Chevron lubricants, placing it as the fourth-largest Chevron marketer in the US.

EXECUTIVES

President and CEO: Kathy Lehne
Director Operations: Bill Tilger
CFO: Deniese Palmer-Huggins
VP Sales and Marketing: Kyle Lehne
VP Supply Logistics: Diana Durand
Secretary and Treasurer: Lisa Smith
Director IT: Bryan Frazier
Director Safety: Stratton Williams
Senior Managing Director Trading: Steve Boyd
Auditors: Melton & Melton LLP

LOCATIONS

HQ: Sun Coast Resources Inc.
6922 Cavalcade, Houston, TX 77028
Phone: 713-844-9600   **Fax:** 713-844-9696
Web: www.suncoastresources.com

Sun Coast Resources serves customers in Arkansas, Florida, Kansas, Louisiana, Mississippi, Missouri, New Mexico, Oklahoma, and Texas.

PRODUCTS/OPERATIONS

Selected Products

Petroleum Products
 Aviation gasoline
 High sulfur diesel fuel
 Jet fuel
 Kerosene
 Lubricants
 Marine fuels
 Mid-grade fuel
 Low sulfur diesel fuel
 Premium low sulfur diesel fuel
 Premium unleaded gasoline
 Unleaded gasoline
Oils and Lubricants
 Automatic transmission fluid
 Chain oils
 Food-grade oils
 Fuel Additives
 Gear oils
 Greases
 Heat transfer oils
 Hydraulic oils
 Metal-working oils
 Motor oils
 Refrigeration oils
 Solvents and chemicals

COMPETITORS

George Warren
J.A.M. Distributing
Martin Resource Management
Mercury Air Group
SMF Energy

Company Type: Private

Income Statement			FYE: December 31
	REVENUE ($ mil.)	NET INCOME ($ mil.)	NET PROFIT MARGIN	EMPLOYEES
12/08	1,064	—	—	585

Sun Products

The Sun Products Corporation (formerly Huish Detergents) believes sunlight is truly the best disinfectant. The company makes laundry detergents and household cleaning products, such as floor and glass cleaners, oxygenated stain removers, prewash formulas, antibacterial soaps, bleach, and fabric softeners under the Sun brand name. It's also one of the largest US contract manufacturers of private-label brands for major retailers and makes personal care products under the White Rain brand. The company expanded in 2008 when its parent Vestar Capital Partners acquired Unilever's North American laundry brands (All, Wisk, Sunlight, Surf, and Snuggle) and merged the two businesses to form The Sun Products Corporation.

Vestar, which acquired Huish Detergents in April 2007, paid $1.45 billion for the Unilever brands sold in the US, Canada, and Puerto Rico. The deal closed in September 2008 and the combined operation was renamed The Sun Products Corporation at that time. The purchase added Unilever's manufacturing plant in Baltimore and greatly expanded the company's stable of brands. Indeed, Sun Products is now the second-largest producer of fabric care products in North America, behind Procter & Gamble.

Following the transaction, Neil DeFeo (former chairman and CEO of defunct Playtex Products) was named CEO of the new company and the firm moved its corporate headquarters from Salt Lake City, Utah to Wilton, Connecticut. The company maintained its R&D facility in Salt Lake City and two others located in Trumbull, Connecticut and Toronto, Canada. Sun Products also has manufacturing plants Salt Lake City; Bowling Green, Kentucky; Dyersburg, Tennessee; and Houston, Texas.

EXECUTIVES

CEO: Neil P. DeFeo, age 62
President: David P. (Dave) Lundstedt
Chief Marketing Officer: Robert F. (Bob) Waldron
EVP and CFO: Kris J. Kelley, age 49
EVP; General Manager, Branded Products:
 William H. (Bill) Littlefield
SVP, General Counsel, and Secretary: Beth P. Hecht
SVP Human Resources: Gretchen R. Crist, age 41

LOCATIONS

HQ: The Sun Products Corporation
60 Danbury Rd., Wilton, CT 06897
Phone: 203-254-6700   **Fax:** 203-256-0585
Web: www.sunproductscorp.com

PRODUCTS/OPERATIONS

Selected Products
Antibacterial soaps
Bleach
Dish detergents
Fabric softeners
Floor cleaners
Glass cleaners
Laundry detergents
Oxygenated stain removers
Prewash formulas

COMPETITORS

Church & Dwight
Clorox
Henkel
Procter & Gamble
S.C. Johnson

HISTORICAL FINANCIALS
Company Type: Private

Income Statement			FYE: December 31
	ESTIMATED REVENUE ($ mil.)	NET INCOME ($ mil.)	NET PROFIT MARGIN	EMPLOYEES
12/08	2,000	—	—	3,200
12/07	2,000	—	—	3,000
Annual Growth	0.0%	—	—	6.7%

Revenue History

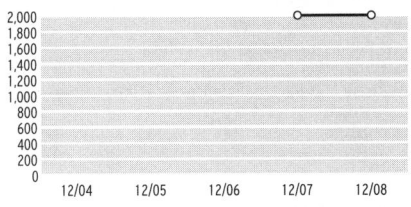

PRODUCTS/OPERATIONS

Selected Products

(see above)

The Sundt Companies

Sundt has put its stamp on the Southwest. Through Sundt Construction and other subsidiaries, The Sundt Companies offers construction management, general contracting, and design/build services for its commercial, government, and industrial clients. Sundt's projects include commercial buildings, military bases, light rail, airports, and schools, among others. The company has overseen some notable projects: It developed the top-secret town of Los Alamos, New Mexico (where the first atomic bomb was built), and in the 1970s it relocated the London Bridge to Arizona. Sundt Companies was founded in 1890 by Norwegian immigrant carpenter Mauritz Sundt; it is now employee-owned.

EXECUTIVES

Chairman and CEO: J. Doug Pruitt
President, COO and Director: David S. (Dave) Crawford
EVP, CFO, and Director: Raymond C. (Ray) Bargull
EVP, Building Division: Jon Wald

SVP, Chief Administrative Officer, and Director:
Richard B. Condit
SVP, General Counsel, and Director: Randy Nye
SVP and Manager, Federal Division:
Ronald (Ron) Brown
SVP and Heavy Civil Division Manager:
G. Michael (Mike) Hoover
SVP, Building Division: Eric H. Hedlund
SVP and Heavy Civil Division Manager, California:
Todd West
SVP and Pre-Construction Manager, Heavy Civil Division: Dee Fedrick
VP and Pre-Construction Manager, Heavy Civil Division: Mike Berry
VP and Operations Manager, Heavy Civil Division:
Matt O'Connell
VP Special Projects and Business Development Manager, Heavy Civil Division: John Carlson
VP and Operations Manager, Heavy Civil Division:
Robert Fedrick
VP and Business Development Manager, Building Division: Richard S. Parker

LOCATIONS

HQ: The Sundt Companies, Inc.
2620 S. 55th St., Tempe, AZ 85282
Phone: 480-293-3000
Web: www.sundt.com

The Sundt Companies and its subsidiaries have offices in Dallas; Novato, Sacramento, and San Diego, California; Reno, Nevada; and Phoenix, Tempe, and Tucson, Arizona.

PRODUCTS/OPERATIONS

Selected Services

Build-to-suit
Construction manager at risk (CMAR)
Construction/program manager
Design-bid-build/general contractor (DBB)
Preconstruction
Subcontractor
Job order contractor (JOC)

COMPETITORS

Austin Industries
Charles Pankow Builders
CORE Construction
DPR Construction
Granite Construction
Hunt Companies
Hunt Construction
Kitchell
McCarthy Building
Meadow Valley
O'Neil Industries
Peter Kiewit Sons'
Swinerton
Tutor Perini
The Weitz Company, LLC

HISTORICAL FINANCIALS

Company Type: Private

Income Statement

FYE: September 30

	REVENUE ($ mil.)	NET INCOME ($ mil.)	NET PROFIT MARGIN	EMPLOYEES
9/08	1,100	—	—	—

SunGard Data Systems

Just about every financial services company under the sun relies on SunGard Data Systems. A majority of all Nasdaq trades pass through SunGard's investment support systems, which banks, stock exchanges, mutual funds, insurance companies, governments, and others use for transaction processing, asset management, securities and commodities trading, and investment accounting. SunGard provides business continuity, managed information technology, and professional services for businesses that rely on information resources. SunGard, which also offers higher education and public sector administrative systems, serves more than 25,000 customers in 70 countries, including the world's 25 largest financial services firms.

Operating in a variety of markets to a global customer base (none of whom account for more than 8% of SunGard's total sales) insulates the company from short-term revenue fluctuations that other competitors who focus on only one product or market may experience.

Its Financial Systems (FS) segment offers more than 50 software brands used by financial services firms, corporate and government treasury departments, and energy companies to automate the securities trading and portfolio and asset management processes. SunGard's FS customers use its products and services to manage over $25 trillion in investments and process over 5 million transactions each day.

SunGard's Higher Education and Public Sector Systems divisions serve higher education institutions, state and local governments, and not-for-profit organizations with over 30 products used for enterprise planning and administration functions. More than 1,600 colleges, universities, and foundations use SunGard's Higher Education offerings in managing their daily operations.

Its Availability Services (AS) segment provides standby services for business continuity and disaster recovery functions. SunGard's AS segment serves more than 10,000 businesses of all sizes, primarily in North America and Europe.

The company has traditionally been very acquisitive, a trend that continued in 2008 with the purchase of six companies (Advanced Portfolio Technologies, Strohl Systems Group, Delphi Technologies, the corporate payments division of Payformance Corporation, and the disaster recovery business of an undisclosed French company) for a collective $721 million. SunGard also acquired Zurich-based Genix Systems in 2009 in a move to build its banking unit. Genix specialized in software for small and midsized private banks.

HISTORY

When Philadelphia-based Sun Company in 1983 shifted focus from its computer disaster recovery services business in favor of its oil-related operations, the subsidiary's founder and president, John Ryan, led a group of New York investment bankers in a leveraged buyout for $19 million. They changed the name to SunGard Data Systems, providing IBM mainframe users with disaster recovery services through four operating subsidiaries in California, Illinois, North Carolina, and Pennsylvania.

By 1985 half of sales came from financial processing and software development services. In 1986 SunGard went public and reached profitability on revenues of $70 million. That year former US Air Force pilot and IBM salesman James Mann, who joined SunGard after the buyout in 1983, was named chairman and CEO.

SunGard acquired four more companies in 1987, including Devon International, whose CEO, Cristóbal Conde, went on to launch SunGard's trading systems division in 1990 and became the company's president in 2000. The acquisition also marked SunGard's first expansion overseas.

SunGard grew rapidly in the early 1990s through acquisitions, mostly in the area of data recovery. By 1993, sales had eclipsed $380 million. Two years later SunGard entered the health care information systems market with the acquisitions of Intelus Corporation and MACESS (later renamed SunGard Workflow Solutions).

Propelled by 12 more acquisitions in 1997, including risk management software maker Infinity Financial Technology, SunGard reached $1 billion in sales in 1998. By the following year its focus had shifted toward providing software for asset management and trade execution to financial services companies. The strategy paid off; nearly 70% of all 1999 trades on the Nasdaq exchange were supported by SunGard software. Among its acquisitions that year was life insurance and pension software specialist FDP.

In 2001 SunGard entered into a bidding war with Hewlett-Packard for Comdisco's computer services operations, eventually purchasing the business for about $850 million.

In 2003 the company completed nine acquisitions. Most notably, it spent $159 million to acquire Caminus, a provider of commodity trading software for the global energy industry, in order to grow its SunGard Trading and Risk Systems unit; it bought UK-based insurance and government software maker Sherwood International in order to expand SunGard Insurance Systems; and it spent $121 million to buy public sector software maker H.T.E., which became part of the SunGard Higher Education and Public Sector Systems segment. SunGard's acquisition spree continued into 2004: the company further expanded its Higher Education and Public Sector segment with its $590 million purchase of Systems & Computer Technology (now SunGard SCT) and its purchase of Collegis, a provider of information technology services for higher education.

In 2004 SunGard sold its Brut subsidiary, which operates the Brut ECN alternative electronic trade-execution system, to Nasdaq for about $190 million in cash. Also that year, the company announced that it would spin off its Availability Services disaster recovery division as a separate, publicly traded company, but it canceled those plans after it agreed to be taken private.

In 2005 a group of seven private investment firms — Silver Lake Partners (lead investor), Bain Capital, The Blackstone Group, GS Capital Partners, Kohlberg Kravis Roberts & Co., Providence Equity Partners, and Texas Pacific Group — acquired SunGard Data Systems for about $11.3 billion.

In 2006 and 2007 the company made more than 20 acquisitions throughout Europe, Asia, and North America. Those deals included boosting its availability services division with the acquisition of managed hosting services provider VeriCenter, as well as purchasing Aceva Technologies, a provider of credit and collections software.

EXECUTIVES

Chairman: Glenn H. Hutchins, age 53
Vice Chairman: Till M. Guldimann, age 59
President, CEO, and Director: Cristóbal I. (Cris) Conde, age 48, $7,455,286 total compensation
SVP Finance and CFO: Michael J. Ruane, age 55, $2,231,141 total compensation
SVP and Chief Marketing Officer: Brian Robins, age 50
SVP Corporate Development: Richard C. Tarbox, age 56
SVP Legal and General Counsel: Victoria E. Silbey, age 45
SVP Human Resources and Chief Human Resources Officer: Kathleen Asser Weslock, age 53
Division CEO, SunGard Financial Systems: Harold C. Finders, age 53, $2,149,472 total compensation
Division CEO, SunGard Financial Systems: James E. (Jim) Ashton III, age 50, $1,898,079 total compensation
CEO, SunGard Higher Education: Ron Lang
CEO, Public Sector: Gilbert O. (Gil) Santos, age 49
CEO, Availability Systems: Eric A. Berg, age 46
President K-12 Education, SunGard Public Sector: Frank W. Lavelle, age 59
President Local Government, SunGard Public Sector: Maj. Thomas V. Huber
President SunGard Insurance Systems iWORKS: Gregory S. (Greg) Webber
Corporate Communications: Suzanne DeFruscio
Auditors: PricewaterhouseCoopers LLP

LOCATIONS

HQ: SunGard Data Systems Inc.
680 E. Swedesford Rd., Wayne, PA 19087
Phone: 484-582-2000   **Fax:** 610-225-1120
Web: www.sungard.com

PRODUCTS/OPERATIONS

2008 Sales

	$ mil.	% of total
Financial Systems	3,078	55
Availability Services	1,567	28
Higher Education	540	10
Public Sector Systems	411	7
Total	**5,596**	**100**

Selected Products

BondMaster (interest and principal payments management systems)
BrokerWare (customer relationship management)
eTreasury (online cash management)
EXPEDITER (online mutual funds processing)
Investment support systems
  Asset management
  Banking and treasury
  Brokerage and execution
  Investor accounting
  Public sector
  Risk and derivatives
MINT (standardized messaging implementation)
Network Trade Model (XML-based data sharing between trading systems)
SunGard Transaction Network (financial services firm trade processing exchange)

Selected Services

Application service processing
Business continuity (on-site and remote disaster recovery)
Collocation application hosting
Consulting
Data center outsourcing
Private network access
Training
Web hosting

COMPETITORS

ADP
Advent Software
Bloomberg L.P.
DST Systems
First Data
Fiserv
HP Enterprise Services
IBM
Jack Henry
Merrill Lynch
Misys
Morgan Stanley
Reuters

HISTORICAL FINANCIALS

Company Type: Private

Income Statement

FYE: December 31

	REVENUE ($ mil.)	NET INCOME ($ mil.)	NET PROFIT MARGIN	EMPLOYEES
12/08	5,596	(242)	—	20,000
12/07	4,901	(60)	—	17,900
12/06	4,323	(118)	—	16,600
12/05	4,002	117	2.9%	15,000
12/04	3,180	454	14.3%	13,000
Annual Growth	**15.2%**	**—**		**11.4%**

Net Income History

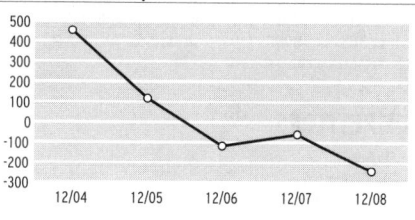

Sunkist Growers

Perhaps the US company least susceptible to an outbreak of scurvy among its employees, Sunkist Growers is an agricultural cooperative owned by California and Arizona citrus growers who farm some 300,000 acres. Sunkist offers traditional and organic fresh oranges, lemons, limes, grapefruit, and tangerines worldwide. The company also makes cut fruit in jars and juice. Fruit that doesn't meet fresh market standards is turned into juices, oils, and peels for use in food products made by other manufacturers. Its customers include food retailers and manufacturers and foodservice operators.

The cooperative's seasonal citrus includes Meyer lemons, mandarin oranges, clementine oranges, and tangelos. It offers Sunkist Fruit Gems (gummie candies), made for the company by the Jelly Belly Candy Company.

Sunkist is one of the most recognized brand names in the world; through licensing agreements, its name appears on beverages and other products, from vitamins to candy, soda to pistachios. In 2008 long-time president and CEO Tim Lindgren retired. He was replaced by Sunkist veteran Russ Hanlin.

HISTORY

Sunkist Growers was founded in the early 1890s as the Pachappa Orange Growers, a group of California citrus farmers determined to control the sale of their fruit. Success attracted new members, and in 1893 the Southern California Fruit Exchange was born. The name "Sunkissed" was coined by an ad copywriter in 1908, and it was soon reworked into "Sunkist" and registered as a trademark, becoming the first brand name for a fresh produce item. Eventually the co-op renamed itself after its popular brand: It became Sunkist Growers in 1952. Sunkist began licensing its trademark to other companies in the early 1950s.

As early as 1916, efforts to increase citrus consumption included designing and marketing glass citrus juicers and encouraging homemakers to "Drink an Orange." The co-op also promoted the practice of putting lemon slices in tea or water and funded early research on the health benefits of vitamins (vitamin C in particular). In 1925 tissue wrappers gave way to stamping the Sunkist name directly on each piece of fruit.

Although Sunkist pioneered bottled orange juice in 1933, its juice marketing efforts were never as successful as those of its Florida competitors. Florida oranges are drippy and dowdy and thus better suited for juicing. Capitalizing on this aspect, Florida growers dominated the market for fresh and frozen juice.

In 1937 Congress created a system of citrus shipment quotas and limits (known as "marketing orders") that ultimately proved most beneficial to large citrus cooperatives. By the early 1990s the marketing order system was under political attack, and in 1992 the Justice Department filed civil prosecution against Sunkist, alleging that the co-op had reaped unfair extra profits by surpassing its lemon shipment limits. In 1994, after much legal wrangling, the quotas were abolished and the Justice Department dropped its case against Sunkist.

Inconveniently warm weather and increasing competition from imported citrus marked the harvests of 1996. That year the co-op had trouble maintaining discipline among its members; some undercut Sunkist price levels, while others flooded the market to sell their fruit at the higher early market prices, creating a supply surplus. Also that year the co-op relinquished the marketing of all Sunkist juices in North America to Florida-based Lykes Bros. in a licensing agreement.

The co-op agreed in 1998 to distribute grapefruit from Florida's Tuxedo Fruit, providing Sunkist with a winter grapefruit supply and increasing its year-round consumer a-peel. Also in 1998 Russell Hanlin, Sunkist president and CEO since 1978, was succeeded by Vince Lupinacci. Lupinacci, who had held positions with Pepsi and Six Flags, became the first person from outside the citrus business to hold Sunkist's top post.

In 1998 the company sold 90 million cartons of fresh citrus — the greatest volume in its history — despite increased competition from imported Latin American, South African, and Spanish crops, a damaging California freeze, and the ill effects of *El Niño*. The next year production was almost halved because of adverse weather.

Lupinacci resigned in 2000, citing personal and family reasons. Chairman emeritus James Mast then took the helm as acting president. Although the company grew its market through exports to China in 2000, its profits were squeezed that year by increasing foreign competition, a citrus glut, and lessened demand. In mid-2001 Jeff Gargiulo replaced Mast as Sunkist's president and CEO.

In 2003 Sunkist formed a joint venture with Coastal Berry Co. to market strawberries under the Sunkist label year-round. (Coastal Berry's president and CEO John Gargiulo and Sunkist's former president and CEO Jeff Gargiulo are brothers.) Also that year Sunkist began offering pre-cut bagged fruit to retail customers and restaurants in order to keep up with a changing market and consumer demand.

In retrospect, 2006 was an eventful year for Sunkist. The co-op's largest producer and 16-year-member Paramount Citrus Association left the organization. In addition, chairman and CEO David Krause stepped down and president Jeff Gargiulo left the company. Krause was replaced as chairman by Nicholas Bozick, president of produce grower/packer Richard Bagdasarian, Inc. Sunkist veteran and former president of Fruit Growers Supply Company, Timothy Lindgren, was appointed president and CEO.

And, citing expense as the determining factor, the co-op discontinued marketing berries (strawberries, blueberries, and raspberries) in 2006.

Lindgren retired in 2008; Russell Hamlin was named president and CEO.

EXECUTIVES

Chairman: Nicholas L Bozick
Vice Chairman: Craig Armstrong
Vice Chairman: Mark G. Gillette
Vice Chairman: James P. Finch
President and CEO: Russell L. (Russ) Hanlin II
SVP Corporate Relations and Administration:
  Michael J. (Mike) Wootton
SVP Law and General Counsel: Charles L. Woltmann
VP and CFO: Richard G. French
VP Citrus Juice and Oil Business: Ted R. Leaman III
VP Sales and Marketing: Kevin P. Fiori
VP Human Resources: John R. McGovern
Managing Director, Sunkist Global:
  Michael (Mike) Nomoto
Director of Foodservice Sales: Bruce Simmons
Director Business Development: Brian Slagel
Director Domestic Sales: Mark Tompkins
Director Corporate Communications: Claire H. Smith
Corporate Secretary: John Caragozian
Auditors: Moss Adams, LLP

LOCATIONS

HQ: Sunkist Growers, Inc.
  14130 Riverside Dr., Sherman Oaks, CA 91423
Phone: 818-986-4800   **Fax:** 818-379-7405
Web: www.sunkist.com

2008 Fresh Fruit Sales

	% of total
Domestic	73
Export	27
Total	**100**

COMPETITORS

Alico	Naked Juice
Chiquita Brands	Ocean Spray
Coca-Cola	Odwalla
Del Monte Foods	Old Orchard
Dole Food	Silver Springs
Dundee Citrus Growers	Snapple
Florida's Natural	South Beach Beverage
Fresh Del Monte Produce	Southern Gardens Citrus
Great Western Juice	Sunny Delight
Hansen Natural	Tree Top
IZZE	Tropicana
Lake Placid Groves	Vitality Foodservice
Louis Dreyfus Citrus	Welch's
Mott's	

Super Center Concepts

Super Center Concepts is big on superlatives as well as groceries. One of the largest independently owned grocery supercenter chains in Southern California, the company operates more than 30 outlets under the Superior Grocers banner. The regional grocery chain has continued to expand, in spite of operating in the super-competitive supercenter market where it competes with national chains including Wal-Mart and Costco Wholesale. The stores sell name-brand and private-label merchandise in the traditional grocery departments (produce, meat, bakery), and offer services such as check cashing and money orders. The first Superior Super Warehouse opened in Los Angeles in 1981.

EXECUTIVES

President: Mimi R. Song, age 47
CFO: Bill Cote
EVP: Marie Song
SVP, Operations: Phil Lawrence
Director, Risk Management: Cris Nunez

LOCATIONS

HQ: Super Center Concepts, Inc.
  15510 Carmenita Rd., Santa Fe Springs, CA 90670
Phone: 562-345-9000   **Fax:** 562-345-9052
Web: superiorgrocers.com

COMPETITORS

Albertsons
Arden Group
Costco Wholesale
Food 4 Less Holdings
Ralphs Grocery
Save Mart
Scolari's Food and Drug
Stater Bros.
Target
Vons
Wal-Mart
WinCo Foods

HISTORICAL FINANCIALS

Company Type: Private

Income Statement				FYE: December 31
	REVENUE ($ mil.)	NET INCOME ($ mil.)	NET PROFIT MARGIN	EMPLOYEES
12/07	969	—	—	4,700
12/06	916	—	—	4,000
12/05	789	—	—	3,900
Annual Growth	**10.9%**	**—**	**—**	**9.8%**

Revenue History

(Revenue History chart showing values from 12/03 to 12/07, with data points at 12/05 ≈ 789, 12/06 ≈ 916, 12/07 ≈ 969)

Sutherland Lumber

They are in a Southern state of mind at Sutherland Lumber. The company operates more than 65 lumber and home improvement stores in 13 states, primarily in the southern and southwestern US. Sutherland's stores range in size from 50,000 to more than 140,000 sq. ft. They sell lumber, paints, tools, and building packages for houses, sheds, garages, and farm buildings. In addition, the stores sell lawn and garden equipment, plumbing supplies, and materials for hobbies and crafts. The company, which is owned and operated by the Sutherland family, was founded in 1917 to supply Oklahoma farmers with building materials.

The company revised its business model in 2005 to better compete with big-box retailers. In this regard, it opened a design center for contractors, homeowners, and builders at its store at 2701 S. College Avenue in Fort Collins, Colorado. In 2009 it acquired a 15,000-sq.-ft. building, and announced plans to consolidate its College Avenue and Prospect Road stores into a new destination store.

EXECUTIVES

CEO and CFO: Steve Scott
President and CEO, Housemart.com:
  Chris Sutherland Jr.

LOCATIONS

HQ: Sutherland Lumber Company, L.P.
  400 Main St., Kansas City, MO 64111
Phone: 816-756-3000   **Fax:** 816-756-3594
Web: www.sutherlands.com

COMPETITORS

84 Lumber
Ace Hardware
Amazon.com
Do it Best
Foxworth-Galbraith Lumber
Handy Hardware Wholesale
Home Depot
Lowe's
McCoy Corp.
Menard
National Home Centers
True Value

HISTORICAL FINANCIALS

Company Type: Private

Income Statement				FYE: December 31
	ESTIMATED REVENUE ($ mil.)	NET INCOME ($ mil.)	NET PROFIT MARGIN	EMPLOYEES
12/07	1,070	—	—	2,140
12/06	1,180	—	—	2,300
12/05	1,100	—	—	2,400
Annual Growth	**(1.4%)**	**—**	**—**	**(5.6%)**

Revenue History

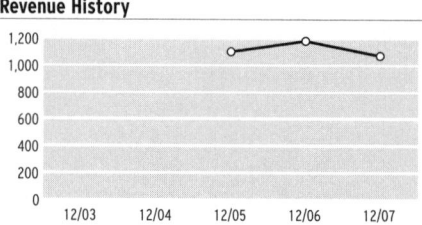

(Revenue History chart showing values from 12/03 to 12/07, with data points at 12/05 ≈ 1,100, 12/06 ≈ 1,180, 12/07 ≈ 1,070)

Sutter Health

Whether you drink too much in Wine Country, hit some rough waters off the Marin Headlands, or trip during a hike through the redwood forest, it's likely Sutter Health is just a stone's throw away. The Northern Californian not-for-profit health care system is one of the nation's largest. After being formed more than a decade ago through the merger of Sutter Health and California Healthcare System, Sutter Health now caters to residents of more than 100 communities from the Bay Area to the Central Valley. Its services are provided through about 3,500 affiliated doctors from a host of health care facilities, including more than 25 acute care hospitals, home health/hospice networks, and skilled nursing facilities.

In late 2008 Sutter Health reorganized its governance structure into five geographic regions throughout Northern California. Each region was given its own physician organization board to oversee all of the Sutter-affiliated medical facilities and hospitals in that area. The reorganization plan was implemented to replace the more than 50 existing hospital and physician organization boards that were in place throughout the network. The regional boards will also charter entity-based committees to focus on local matters such as quality and community benefit.

Despite an uncertain economy in 2009, Sutter Health earmarked about $1 billion for capital spending throughout the year. Undertakings include major medical center construction projects in Burlingame and Sacramento and design and entitlement processes for seismic-replacement hospitals (to make them earthquake safe) in Oakland and San Francisco. Sutter Health is also moving forward with plans to build new hospitals in Castro Valley and Santa Rosa.

Sutter Health operated six Express Care clinics in Rite Aid stores near Sacramento until 2009, when the system closed half of them to focus on the three remaining clinics — which charge a flat fee of $65 for basic health care services. Sutter Health intends to redirect resources from the closed clinics to expand services at its busiest locations in and around the Capital City.

EXECUTIVES

Chairman: Jim Gray, age 64
President, CEO, and Director: Patrick E. (Pat) Fry
VP Communications: Bill Gleeson
President and CEO, Eden Medical Center:
George Bischalaney
CEO, Memorial Medical Center: James E. Conforti
CEO, Sutter Coast Hospital: Eugene F. Suksi
CEO, Sutter Delta Medical Center: Gary Rapaport
CEO, Sutter Tracy Community Hospital:
Dave Thompson
CEO, Marin General Hospital: David Bradley
CEO, Sutter Health Sacramento-Sierra Region:
Sarah Krevans
Chair, Sutter Lakeside Hospital: Bill Kearney
Chair, Memorial Hospitals Association: Richard M. Beal
President, California Pacific Medical Center:
Martin Brotman
President, Central Valley Region; President, Memorial Hospitals Association: David P. Benn
Director Communications: Karen Garner
Auditors: Ernst & Young LLP

LOCATIONS

HQ: Sutter Health
2200 River Plaza Dr., Sacramento, CA 95833
Phone: 916-733-8800 **Fax:** 916-286-6841
Web: www.sutterhealth.org

Hospitals

Alta Bates Summit Medical Center (Berkeley, Oakland)
California Pacific Medical Center (San Francisco)
Eden Medical Center (Castro Valley)
Kahi Mohala (Ewa, HI)
Marin General Hospital (Greenbrae)
Memorial Hospital Los Banos (Los Banos)
Memorial Medical Center (Modesto)
Menlo Park Surgical Hospital
Mills-Peninsula Health Services (Burlingame)
Novato Community Hospital (Novato)
Sutter Amador Hospital (Jackson)
Sutter Auburn Faith Hospital (Auburn)
Sutter Coast Hospital (Crescent City)
Sutter Davis Hospital (Davis)
Sutter Delta Medical Center (Antioch)
Sutter Lakeside Hospital (Lakeport)
Sutter Maternity & Surgery Center of Santa Cruz
Sutter Medical Center (Sacramento)
Sutter Medical Center of Santa Rosa
Sutter Roseville Medical Center
Sutter Solano Medical Center (Vallejo)
Sutter Tracy Community Hospital (Tracy)

COMPETITORS

Adventist Health
Catholic Healthcare West
HCA
Kaiser Permanente
Memorial Health Services
Odyssey HealthCare
Providence Health & Services
Stanford University Medical
Tenet Healthcare
UCSF Medical

HISTORICAL FINANCIALS

Company Type: Not-for-profit

Income Statement				FYE: December 31
	REVENUE ($ mil.)	NET INCOME ($ mil.)	NET PROFIT MARGIN	EMPLOYEES
12/08	8,281	186	2.2%	47,892
12/07	7,651	—	—	44,828
12/06	7,258	—	—	43,139
12/05	6,663	—	—	43,139
12/04	6,280	—	—	—
Annual Growth	7.2%	—	—	3.5%

Revenue History

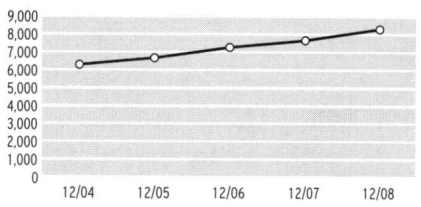

Swagelok Company

With sales partners worldwide, Swagelok has to speak many languages, *fluidly*. The company makes fluid system components, which include plug, pinch, and radial diaphragm valves, regulators, filters, flexible tubing, and welding systems. Its products are used in the instrumentation, oil and gas, power, petrochemical, food and beverage, alternative fuels, and semiconductor industries, as well as by pharmaceuticals research companies. Swagelok also offers custom kitting, made-to-order products, and third-party sourcing services. It has more than 200 sales and service locations in nearly 60 countries. Founded in 1947 by Fred Lennon in his kitchen, Swagelok is still controlled by the Lennon family.

Swagelok is expanding its product base through the introduction of new equipment and through acquisitions that add to existing product lines or expand applications. In 2008 the company bought the assets of Coreflex LLC, a manufacturer of hose products for biopharmaceutical and semiconductor applications. Swagelok also bought the assets of Hy-Level Industries (now Swagelok Hy-Level Company) to enhance its fluid systems offerings for automotive applications in 2007.

The company also continues to expand its portfolio of services. In 2008 Swagelok bought Plant Support and Evaluations Inc. (PSE), a provider of engineering, audits, project management, and training services for evaluating compressed-air, condensate, and steam systems; PSE was renamed Swagelok Energy Advisors, Inc.

In order to market a new process developed by the company, Swagelok in 2007 formed Swagelok Technology Services Company to commercialize its SAT12 metals surface enhancement heat-treatment process, a way to extend the life of a part by increasing hardness and improving corrosion resistance. Swagelok Technology Services provides the customized service.

EXECUTIVES

President and CEO: Arthur F. (Art) Anton, age 51
CFO: Frank J. Roddy
VP Operations: Michael F. Neff
VP and CIO: Matthew P. (Matt) LoPiccolo
VP Marketing: Michael R. Butkovic
VP Customer Service: David E. O'Connor
VP Human Resources: James L. (Jim) Francis
VP Corporate Communications: Franziska H. Dacek
VP Continuous Improvement and Quality:
Wil Christensen
VP Distributor Support: Sylvie A. Bon, age 49
VP Engineering: David H. Peace

LOCATIONS

HQ: Swagelok Company
29500 Solon Rd., Solon, OH 44139
Phone: 440-248-4600 **Fax:** 440-349-5970
Web: www.swagelok.com

PRODUCTS/OPERATIONS

Selected Products

Filters
Fittings
Flexible tubing
Gauges
Hoses
Leak detectors
Lubricants and sealants
Manifolds

Pressure gauges
Quick connects
Regulators
Sample cylinders
Thermometers and thermowells
Tube benders and cutters
Valves
Weld systems

COMPETITORS

CIRCOR International	Precision Castparts
Crane Co.	Shaw Group
Dover Corp.	SPX
IMI plc	T3 Energy Services
ITT Corp.	Tyco Flow Control
McJunkin Red Man	Watts Water Technologies

HISTORICAL FINANCIALS
Company Type: Private

Income Statement
FYE: December 31

	ESTIMATED REVENUE ($ mil.)	NET INCOME ($ mil.)	NET PROFIT MARGIN	EMPLOYEES
12/08	1,300	—	—	4,000
12/07	1,300	—	—	4,000
12/06	1,100	—	—	3,300
12/05	1,000	—	—	3,000
Annual Growth	9.1%	—	—	10.1%

Revenue History

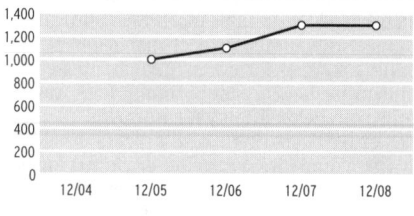

Swift Transportation

Swift, but within the speed limit, truckload carrier Swift Transportation hauls freight such as building materials, paper products, and retail merchandise throughout the US and in Mexico. The company operates a fleet of about 18,000 tractors and 48,000 trailers from a network of about 40 terminals. Its services include dedicated contract carriage, in which drivers and equipment are assigned to a customer long-term. Besides standard dry vans, Swift's fleet includes refrigerated, flatbed, and other specialized trailers, as well as about 5,800 intermodal containers. Chairman and CEO Jerry Moyes owns the company, which he founded in 1966, took public, and took private again in 2007.

Moyes took the company private by buying the 61% of Swift that he and his family didn't already own. His bid valued the carrier at about $2.7 billion, including some $330 million in assumed debt. Along with taking full ownership, Moyes took over as CEO, a position he had held for many years before stepping down in 2005 as part of an executive succession plan.

With Moyes in the driver's seat once again, Swift continues to concentrate on regional routes rather than long hauls. The company does offer transcontinental van service, but the shorter routes that are Swift's bread and butter help the company retain drivers and keep costs low.

Over the years Swift has worked to grow by selling more services to its large customers and by taking advantage of the trend among shippers toward outsourcing of transportation functions. Major customers have included Wal-Mart and Lowe's. Swift also has expanded its intermodal service, in which the company handles pick up and delivery of shipping containers transported by rail.

EXECUTIVES

Chairman and CEO: Jerry C. Moyes, age 64
President and COO: Richard Stocking
EVP Business Transformation: Chad E. Killebrew
EVP and CFO: Ginnie Henkels
EVP Eastern Region: Kenneth C. (Ken) Runnels
EVP Intermodal: Mark Young
EVP Western Region: Rodney K. Sartor
VP and CIO: Mike Ruchensky
VP and Corporate Controller: Cary Flanagan
VP Procurement and Shop Operations: Michele Calbi
VP and General Counsel: James Fry
Director Financial Reporting and SEC Compliance: Brad Stewart
Auditors: KPMG LLP

LOCATIONS

HQ: Swift Transportation Co., Inc.
2200 S. 75th Ave., Phoenix, AZ 85043
Phone: 602-269-9700 **Fax:** 623-907-7380
Web: www.swifttrans.com

COMPETITORS

Comcar
Covenant Transportation
Crete Carrier
CRST International
Heartland Express
J.B. Hunt
Knight Transportation
Landstar System
Schneider National
Universal Truckload Services
U.S. Xpress
Werner Enterprises

HISTORICAL FINANCIALS
Company Type: Private

Income Statement
FYE: December 31

	REVENUE ($ mil.)	NET INCOME ($ mil.)	NET PROFIT MARGIN	EMPLOYEES
12/08	3,400	—	—	19,700
12/07	3,270	—	—	21,900
Annual Growth	4.0%	—	—	(10.0%)

Revenue History

Swinerton Incorporated

Swinerton is building up the West just as it helped rebuild San Francisco after the 1906 earthquake. The construction group, formerly Swinerton & Walberg, builds commercial, industrial, and government facilities, including resorts, subsidized housing, public schools, Hollywood soundstages, hospitals, and airport terminals. Through its subsidiaries, Swinerton offers general contracting and design/build services, as well as construction and program management. It also provides property management for conventional, subsidized, and assisted living residences. The employee-owned company, which has expanded in the past decade in the Northwest and Southwest, traces its family tree to 1888.

Swinerton offices are located throughout California, and in Colorado, Hawaii, Texas, New Mexico, and Washington.

Swinerton takes environmental stewardship to heart. As one of the top waste-reducing companies in California, Swinerton employs green building construction and design practices to conserve resources, reduce waste, and create healthier environments. The company's own headquarters building in San Francisco received Gold LEED-EB (Leadership in Energy & Environmental Design for Existing Buildings) certification from the U.S. Green Building Council.

EXECUTIVES

Chairman: Gordon W. Marks
CEO: Michael (Mike) Re
President: Jeffrey C. (Jeff) Hoopes
EVP and Co-COO: Charles P. (Charlie) Kuffner
EVP, Secretary, and General Counsel: Luke P. Argilla
EVP and COO: Gary J. Rafferty
SVP and CIO: Lucille (Luci) Morris-Tyndall
SVP and Los Angeles Division Manager, Swinerton Builders: Frank Foellmer
VP and CFO: Linda G. Showalter
VP Community Relations: Charles (Rick) Moore
VP and Director Human Resources: Brenda Reimche
President, William P. Young Construction: Jay Kuhre
President, Lyda Swinerton Builders: Jack Dysart
President, Harbison-Mahony-Higgins Builders (HMH): David Higgins Jr.
President, Swinerton Property Services: Sue Twitchel
President, Swinerton Management and Consulting: Terry Bush
National Marketing Director: Mark Gudenas
Auditors: PricewaterhouseCoopers

LOCATIONS

HQ: Swinerton Incorporated
260 Townsend St., San Francisco, CA 94107
Phone: 415-421-2980 **Fax:** 415-984-1204
Web: www.swinerton.com

Swinerton has offices in California, Colorado, Hawaii, New Mexico, Texas, and Washington.

PRODUCTS/OPERATIONS

Selected Projects

One Lincoln Park Residential, Denver
deYoung Museum, San Francisco
Jet Propulsion Laboratory Flight Project Center, Pasadena, CA
Santa Fe Civic Center
St. Jude SW Tower, Fullerton, CA

HISTORICAL FINANCIALS

Company Type: Private

Income Statement				FYE: December 31
	REVENUE ($ mil.)	NET INCOME ($ mil.)	NET PROFIT MARGIN	EMPLOYEES
12/08	1,871	—	—	1,300
12/07	1,993	—	—	1,300
12/06	1,680	—	—	1,260
12/05	1,830	—	—	1,450
12/04	1,840	—	—	1,450
Annual Growth	0.4%	—	—	(2.7%)

Revenue History

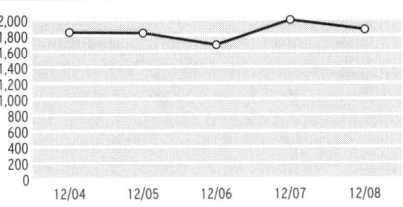

TA Delaware

Automakers do a lot of leaning on TA Delaware for their metal stampings and engineered assemblies. The company's products include body structures and assemblies (body pillars, roof rails); lower vehicle frames and structures (pickup and SUV full-frame assemblies); complex body-in-white assemblies (front and rear floor pan assemblies); chassis modules (axle assemblies); and suspension components (control arms, spring and shock towers). TA's largest customers include Ford Motor, General Motors, Honda, and Volkswagen. Struggling financially, TA filed for bankruptcy protection from creditors in 2005; it emerged from Chapter 11 and was acquired by Cerberus Capital Management in 2007.

The global downturn in the automotive industry is hitting suppliers of auto parts particularly hard, as the big automakers downsize operations, especially in North America. TA customers Chrysler and GM are hanging on, thanks to loans from the Canadian and US governments, while Ford has a healthier balance sheet but is still losing money. Since TA Delaware has already been through a bankruptcy reorganization, it may be better financially prepared to survive in the recessionary environment.

Between 2001 and 2005 TA was riding high with a big backlog of fresh business. During this time the company reorganized its North American operations to tighten capacity and reduce costs. But events conspired to undermine TA's efforts. Starting in 2004 rising steel prices, production cuts among key customers, and high costs associated with program launches created a liquidity crisis leading to the bankruptcy filing in 2005.

The company got a tighter rein on costs and has its eye on incremental organic growth. TA also is capturing more business from outside Detroit, which takes advantage of the company's substantial global footprint.

In 2007 the Cerberus private equity group bought the company (the same year it bought majority ownership of Chrysler in what proved to be a bad bet on the auto industry). Shortly after the transaction was completed, the company's name was changed from Tower Automotive to TA Delaware, Inc.

EXECUTIVES

Chairman: Daniel Ajamian
Vice Chairman: Rande Somma
President and CEO: Mark Malcolm
COO: Mike Rajkovic
EVP and CFO: Jim Gouin
SVP and Corporate Controller: Jeffrey L. (Jeff) Kersten
SVP Global Purchasing: Paul Radkoski, age 49
SVP Global Human Resources: William R. (Bill) Cook
President, International: Gyula Meleghy, age 53
President, Americas: D. William (Bill) Pumphrey, age 49
Auditors: Deloitte & Touche LLP

LOCATIONS

HQ: TA Delaware, Inc.
27175 Haggerty Rd., Novi, MI 48377
Phone: 248-675-6000   **Fax:** 248-675-6494
Web: www.towerautomotive.com

PRODUCTS/OPERATIONS

Selected Products

Body Structures and Assemblies
  Body pillars
  Heavy-truck frame rails
  Intrusion beams
  Light-truck frames
  Parcel shelves
  Roof rails
  Side sills
Lower Vehicle Frames and Structures
  Automotive engine cradles
  Cross members
  Floor pan components
  Pickup truck and SUV full frames
Chassis Modules and Systems
  Axle assemblies
  Front and rear structural suspension modules/systems
Complex Body-in-White Assemblies
  Door/pillar assemblies
  Front and rear floor pan assemblies
Suspension Components
  Control arms
  Spring/shock towers
  Suspension links
  Track bars
  Trailing axles
Other Products
  Heat shields
  Precision stampings

COMPETITORS

A.G. Simpson	Midway Products Group
American Axle	Midwest Stamping
ArvinMeritor	Noble International
Benteler Automotive	Norstar Founders
Boler	Ogihara America
Cosma International	SANLUIS
Dana Holding	Shiloh Industries
Kalamazoo Fabricating	Sypris Solutions
KTH Parts	Talon
KUO	T.J.T.
Lydall	Visteon
Magna International	Winnebago

HISTORICAL FINANCIALS

Company Type: Private

Income Statement				FYE: December 31
	REVENUE ($ mil.)	NET INCOME ($ mil.)	NET PROFIT MARGIN	EMPLOYEES
12/07	2,500	—	—	11,000

Tastefully Simple

Taste buds get the Tupperware treatment at Tastefully Simple. The company promotes its line of gourmet soups, dips, desserts, and convenience foods through in-home parties where attendees can taste products alongside friends and family prior to purchasing them. Its standard food items range in price from $4.99 for beer bread mix to $41.99 for a large gift pack. Many items are ready-to-eat, while others require only one or two additional ingredients. Tastefully Simple boasts more than 28,000 sales representatives in all 50 US states, and it buys its products from specialty food vendors. Jill Blashack Strahan and Joani Nielson founded the company in 1995. CEO Blashack Strahan owns about 70% of Tastefully Simple.

To keep its inventory fresh and create buzz among its in-home consultants, Tastefully Simple maintains about 30 standard products and introduces some 20 new items each season. Its seasonal items typically include soups, sauces, dressings, desserts, and beverages. Consultants are not required to carry inventory, and they receive help peddling Tastefully Simple products by being supplied with recipe cards, available to customers, that use the company's products.

EXECUTIVES

President and CEO: Jill Blashack Strahan, age 50
COO: Joani Nielson
CFO: Rick Miller
Chief Legal Officer: Christy Caspers
VP Organizational Effectiveness: Theresa Moberg
VP Marketing: Jennifer Panchenko
VP Team Relations: Edgar F. Timberlake
VP Information Systems: Peter Bellavance
Team Leader, Sales: Barbara Lopez
Communication Senior Lead: Lynn Grueneich
Trainer and Facilitator: Lisa DeKrey
Director Business Development:
  John Richard Verhaeghe

LOCATIONS

HQ: Tastefully Simple, Inc.
  1920 Turning Leaf Ln. SW, Alexandria, MN 56308
Phone: 320-763-0695   **Fax:** 320-763-2458
Web: www.tastefullysimple.com

PRODUCTS/OPERATIONS

Selected Products

Beer bread
Chili mix
Corn and black bean salsa
Creamy wild rice soup
Dips
Dried tomato garlic pesto
Fudge brownies
Fudgy popcorn
Honey mustard
Marinara sauce
Potato cheddar soup
Pretzels
Raspberry salsa
Spinach artichoke ball
Sweet pepper jalapeño jam

COMPETITORS

Fingerhut
Harry & David Holdings
Pampered Chef
Trader Joe's
Tupperware Brands

HISTORICAL FINANCIALS

Company Type: Private

Income Statement

	REVENUE ($ mil.)	NET INCOME ($ mil.)	NET PROFIT MARGIN	EMPLOYEES
12/08	144	—	—	350
12/07	138	—	—	300
12/06	120	—	—	300
12/05	110	—	—	300
12/04	123	—	—	311
Annual Growth	4.0%	—	—	3.0%

FYE: December 31

Revenue History

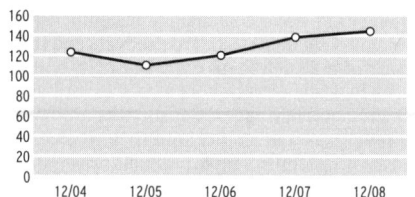

Tauber Oil

No petrochemical product is taboo for oil refiner and marketer Tauber Oil. The company markets refined petroleum products, natural gas, carbon black feedstocks, liquefied petroleum gases, chemicals, and petrochemicals (including benzene, styrene monomer, and methanol). It buys and sells about 225,000 barrels of petroleum products a day. Tauber Oil is one of the US's leading suppliers of feedstocks for reforming and olefin cracking. Subsidiary Tauber Petrochemical was created in 1997 to beef up the company's international petrochemical business. Tauber Oil, which is owned by David and Richard Tauber, maintains a fleet of more than 500 rail cars to supply its customers.

Unlike most other oil and gas marketers, Tauber Oil does not rely on a financial speculation strategy (the buying and selling of contracts for petroleum products). The company primarily plays the role of the middleman and more than 90% of the company businesses involves the actual delivery of petroleum products and gas liquids.

Tauber Oil was founded in 1953 by O. J. Tauber Sr. He gained his oil and petroleum products trading experience working for a small Houston refinery called Eastern States Refining.

EXECUTIVES

Owner and Principal: David W. Tauber, age 59
Owner and Principal: Richard E. Tauber
VP, Finance: Stephen E. Hamlin
VP, Blending Components: John J. Wakefield Jr.
VP, Natural Gas Liquids: Chadwick Verhoff
VP, Public Relations: Connie Kubiak
VP, Tauber Petrochemical: Robert D. Mackenzie
VP, Marketing Mid-Continent: Michael Swallow
VP, Tauber Petrochemical: Steven M. Elliott
VP, Intermediate and Heavy Feedstocks:
  Gerald M. Appelstein
VP, Tauber Petrochemical: J. Scott Podsednik
VP, Intermediate and Heavy Feedstocks:
  Kevin A. Wilson
VP, Natural Gas Liquids: John A. Ratcliffe
VP, International Marketing, Carbon Black Feedstocks:
  Kavan J. Mehta
VP, Transportation and Marketing, Residual Fuels and Blending Components: Jan Hicks
VP, Supply and Marketing, Carbon Black Feedstocks:
  Robert C. (Bobby) Combs
Auditors: Mohle, Adams, Till, Guidry & Wallace, LLP

LOCATIONS

HQ: Tauber Oil Company
  55 Waugh Dr., Ste. 700, Houston, TX 77007
Phone: 713-869-8700   **Fax:** 713-869-8069
Web: www.tauberoil.com

PRODUCTS/OPERATIONS

Selected Products

Natural Gas Liquids
  Butane
  Ethane
  Isobutane
  Propane
Petrochemicals
  Benzene
  Methanol
  MTBE
  Styrene monomer
  Toluene
  Xylene

Refined
  Aviation jet fuel
  Kerosene
  Low sulfur diesel
  No. 2 fuel oil

COMPETITORS

Exxon Mobil
George Warren
Global Partners
Tesoro
Valero Energy

Taylor Corporation

The pleasure of your presence is big business to the Taylor Corporation. One of the holding company's largest businesses is Carlson Craft, a leading printer of invitations and related material for weddings and other special events. Other Taylor units provide business cards and stationery, greeting cards (Current USA), marketing communications products, and promotional items, along with other commercial printing services. Overall, Taylor's operations include more than 100 companies that do business throughout North America and in Europe. Chairman Glen Taylor, majority owner of the NBA's Minnesota Timberwolves, has assembled the company from acquisitions, starting with Carlson Craft in 1975.

The company has been steadily strengthening its position since then. In July 2008 Taylor purchased Interprise Software Systems International, a developer of scalable software solutions for businesses, by Taylor's Services and Technology division. The firm's Print Craft unit in June bought the assets of Litho Express, which makes packaging for CDs and DVDs. In April Taylor's Current USA subsidiary acquired catalog and online gift and home decor retailer Lillian Vernon out of bankruptcy.

The company moved three of its custom-printing brands (Carlson Craft Business Solutions, Regency, Label Works) under the Navitor umbrella in 2007. Navitor aims to improve its printed offerings through the combined business operations.

EXECUTIVES

Chairman: Glen A. Taylor
President and CEO: Jean M. Taylor, age 46
CFO: Tom Johnson
CIO: Jeff Eccles
Chief Human Resources Officer: Donna DiMenna
Chief Administrative Officer and General Counsel:
  Greg Jackson
EVP: Steven Singer
EVP: Ron Hoffmeyer
EVP: Colleen R. Willhite
EVP: Mark Deterding
VP Sales and Customer Loyalty: Todd Alexander
President, ADG Promotional Products: Bill Mahre

LOCATIONS

HQ: Taylor Corporation
  1725 Roe Crest Dr., North Mankato, MN 56003
Phone: 507-625-2828   **Fax:** 507-625-2988
Web: www.taylorcorp.com

COMPETITORS

American Achievement
American Greetings
BCT International
Champion Industries
CSS Industries
Hallmark
Quad/Graphics
R.R. Donnelley
World Color Press

HISTORICAL FINANCIALS

Company Type: Private

Income Statement				FYE: December 31
	ESTIMATED REVENUE ($ mil.)	NET INCOME ($ mil.)	NET PROFIT MARGIN	EMPLOYEES
12/07	1,700	—	—	12,500
12/06	1,700	—	—	15,000
12/05	1,706	—	—	15,000
12/04	1,600	—	—	15,000
12/03	1,400	—	—	14,220
Annual Growth	5.0%	—	—	(3.2%)

Revenue History

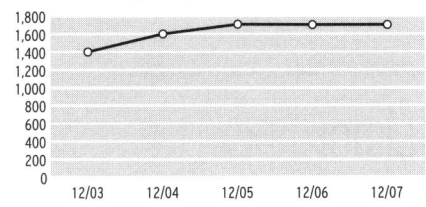

Teacher Retirement System of Texas

T is for Texas and teachers, too. The Teacher Retirement System (TRS) of Texas provides retirement, health care, and other benefits to educators and other employees of the Lone Star State's more than 1,000 independent public school districts, as well as universities, community colleges, junior colleges, and medical and dental schools. TRS serves more than 1.2 million active and retired members with more than $81 billion under management in its pension trust fund; almost two-thirds of that is invested in domestic and international equities. In 2007 the company added hedge funds to its investment mix despite the risk, and divested holdings in companies that do business in Iran, at the behest of Texas lawmakers.

Following outrage at the Texas Legislature over investment bonuses paid at other state trust funds, the TRS Board of Trustees voted in 2009 to defer some $2.5 million in bonuses due more than 80 employees in the investment division. The fund lost 27% in 2008 during a downturn in the economy.

TRS was established in 1936 and had just 38,000 members its first year. In the beginning, the fund was limited to investing in government and municipal bonds.

Teamsters

One of the largest and best-known labor unions in the US, the International Brotherhood of Teamsters has 1.4 million members. The Teamsters represents workers in some 20 industry sectors, including airlines, freight, parcel delivery, industrial trades, and public service. More than 200,000 of the union's members are employees of package delivery giant United Parcel Service. Besides negotiating labor contracts with employers on behalf of its members, the union oversees pension funds and serves as an advocate in legislative and regulatory arenas. The union and its affiliates have about 1,900 local chapters in the US and Canada, including about 475 Teamsters locals. The Teamsters union was founded in 1903.

Teamsters chief James P. Hoffa (son of assumed-dead union leader Jimmy Hoffa) is working to improve the union's image after implementing ethics policies aimed at rooting out internal corruption and ties to organized crime. Hoffa, first elected in 1998, wants the Teamsters to police themselves and to put an end to the government supervision under which the union has operated since 1989.

The Teamsters have packed up and moved out from under the AFL-CIO umbrella and joined fellow unions Unite Here (textile, hotel, and restaurant workers), Service Employees International (SEIU), United Food and Commercial Workers, and others in the rival Change to Win Coalition. The group hopes to reverse the decline of labor jobs and union membership in the US by focusing its time and money on recruiting rather than on participating in political campaigns. Other key issues for Change to Win include health care, immigration, and retirement security.

HISTORY

Two rival team-driver unions, the Drivers International Union and the Teamsters National Union, merged to form the International Brotherhood of Teamsters in 1903. Led by Cornelius Shea, the Teamsters established headquarters in Indianapolis. Daniel Tobin (president for 45 years, starting in 1907) demanded that union locals obtain executive approval before striking. Membership expanded from the team-driver base, prompting the union to add Chauffeurs, Stablemen, and Helpers to its name (1909).

Following the first transcontinental delivery by motor truck (1912), the Teamster deliverymen traded their horses for trucks. The union then recruited food processing, brewery, and farm workers, among others, to augment Teamster effectiveness during strikes. It joined the American Federation of Labor in 1920.

Until the Depression the Teamsters was still a small union of predominantly urban deliverymen. Then Farrell Dobbs, a Trotskyite Teamster from Minneapolis, organized the famous Minneapolis strikes in 1934 to protest local management's refusal to allow the workers to unionize. Workers clashed with police and National Guard units for 11 days before management acceded to the workers' demands. The strikes demonstrated the potential strength of unions, and Teamsters membership swelled. Although union power ebbed during WWII, the union continued to grow. It moved its headquarters to Washington, DC, in 1953.

The AFL-CIO expelled the Teamsters in 1957 when Teamster ties to the mob became public during a US Senate investigation. New Teamsters boss Jimmy Hoffa eluded indictment and took advantage of America's growing dependence on trucking to negotiate the powerful National Master Freight Agreement (1964). Hoffa also organized industrial workers. He used a union pension fund to make mob-connected loans and was later convicted of jury tampering and sent to prison. In 1975, four years after his release, Hoffa vanished without a trace and is believed to have been the victim of a Mafia hit.

The Teamsters rejoined the AFL-CIO in 1987 and the following year settled a racketeering lawsuit filed by the US Justice Department by allowing government appointees to discipline corrupt union leaders, help run the union, and oversee its elections. The election of self-styled reformer Ronald Carey in 1991 (he received 49% of the vote) seemed to portend real changes for the union; each of his six predecessors had been accused of or imprisoned for criminal activities. However, membership dropped by 40,000 in both 1991 and 1992.

Carey won re-election as union president in 1996 over rival, and son of former boss Jimmy Hoffa, James P. Hoffa (whom Carey accused of having ties to organized crime). A 15-day strike by the Teamsters' UPS employees in 1997 led to the delivery company's agreement to combine part-time jobs into 10,000 new full-time positions. That year Carey's re-election was overturned amid a campaign finance investigation that netted guilty pleas from three Carey associates, and the Teamsters leader was disqualified from running for re-election in 1998. Carey was officially expelled from the Teamsters by the federal government, and Hoffa won the 1998 election over Tom Leedham (who was backed by the union's reform wing).

Promising to fight corruption, Hoffa hired former federal prosecutor Edwin Stier and several former FBI agents to help him operate Project RISE (respect, integrity, strength, and ethics), a new in-house anti-corruption program. In 2002 the union began lobbying against plans to allow Mexican trucking companies to transport goods across the US.

In 2005 the Teamsters joined four other unions representing more than 5 million workers to call for sweeping reform in the AFL-CIO. They released a proposal to revitalize the labor movement by focusing on growth and empowerment. When AFL-CIO president John Sweeney failed to heed their calls, the Teamsters joined the Service Employees International Union in boycotting the umbrella group's annual convention and joining the Change to Win Coalition.

EXECUTIVES

General President: James P. (Jim) Hoffa, age 68
Director, Information Systems Department: David Gormley
Director Department of Federal Legislation and Regulation: Lisa Kinard
Director, Drive Accounting Department: Colleen Brady
Director, Training and Development Department: Cynthia Impala
Director, Economics and Contracts Department: Jim Kimball
Director, Communications Department: Bret Caldwell
Director, Capital Strategies Department: Carin Zelenko
Director, Organizing Department: Jeff Farmer
Director, Strategic Research and Campaigns Department: Iain Gold
Director, Accounting and Budget Department: Mitzi Montemore
Director Safety and Health Department: LaMont Byrd
Director Human Rights Commission: Antonio Christian
Department for Retiree Affairs: Edgar A. Scribner
Director, Affiliates and Automated Records Department: Hollis Hypes
General Secretary and Treasurer: C. Thomas (Tom) Keegel
General Counsel: Bradley T. Raymond
VP, Canada; President, Teamsters Canada: Robert Bouvier
Press Secretary: Galen Munroe

LOCATIONS

HQ: International Brotherhood of Teamsters
25 Louisiana Ave. NW, Washington, DC 20001
Phone: 202-624-6800   **Fax:** 202-624-6918
Web: www.teamster.org

PRODUCTS/OPERATIONS

Trade Divisions

Airline
Bakery and Laundry
Brewery and Soft Drink
Building Material and Construction
Carhaul
Dairy
Food Processing
Freight
Graphic Communications
Industrial Trades
Motion Picture and Theatrical Trade
Newspaper, Magazine, and Electronic Media
Parcel and Small Package
Port
Public Services
Rail
Solid Waste
Tankhaul
Trade Show and Convention Centers
Warehouse

Tekni-Plex, Inc.

Combining packaging technology with a modicum of complexity, Tekni-Plex manufactures packaging, industrial materials, specialty resins, and tubing products for the food, health care, and consumer industries. The company's consumer packaging division makes foam egg cartons and plates, poultry and meat processing trays, pharmaceutical blister films, closure liners, and aerosol and pump packaging components. Its tubing products division manufactures irrigation and garden hoses, medical tubing, and pool and vacuum hoses. Tekni-Plex also makes PVC compounds and recycled PET (plastic) used in a variety of industrial products. Oaktree Capital Management and Avenue Capital Group of New York own 80% of the company.

Tekni-Plex's subsidiary operating brands, including American Gasket & Rubber Company, Colorite, Dolco Packaging, Natvar, PurePlast, and Swan, underpin the company's hopes for international recognition. In 2009 Tekni-Plex's European subsidiary, Tekni-Plex Europe NV, picked up an established closure manufacturer, Top-Seals Dichtungseinlagen GmbH. Specializing in liners and gaskets, the German-based acquisition improves Tekni-Plex's ability to court European packaging customers.

In 2008 the company looked to bolster its manufacturing foothold in the Asia/Pacific markets; Tekni-Plex expanded compounding operations in Suzhou, China, and opened a subsidiary in India. The move was countered by closing three Dolco facilities in Tennessee, California, and Ohio. Tekni-Plex has opted to preserve some locations in the US, as well as in Canada, Hong Kong, Belgium, Italy, Northern Ireland, and Argentina.

Shifts in 2008 included a financial restructuring, forced by Tekni-Plex's default on a $20 million interest payment. Approximately $340 million of debt was sold to private equity firms Avenue Capital Group and Oaktree Capital Management. In exchange, the investors scored majority ownership. Paul J. Young was named CEO, succeeding Dr. F. Patrick Smith, who retired.

EXECUTIVES

CEO: Paul J. Young
CFO: Robert M. Larney, age 58
SVP and General Counsel: Michael Zelenty
SVP Colorite Division: Miguel Nistal
SVP Dolco Packaging: Norm Patterson
SVP Europe: Luc Vercruyssen
SVP Pharmaceutical and International: Michael Franklin
VP Procurement: Daniel C. Mullock, age 54
VP Human Resources: Joe Bruno
Auditors: BDO Seidman, LLP

LOCATIONS

HQ: Tekni-Plex, Inc.
1150 1st Ave., Ste. 501, King of Prussia, PA 19406
Phone: 484-690-1520
Web: www.tekni-plex.com

PRODUCTS/OPERATIONS

Selected Products

Aeration Tubing
Closure Liners
Egg Cartons
Foam Packaging
Garden Hose
Pharmaceutical Packaging Films
Processor Trays
PVC Industrial Compounds
PVC Medical Compounds
PVC Medical Tubing
PVC Specialty Resins
Rubber Components
Rubber Seals, Gaskets, Stoppers, and Syringe Plungers
Silicone Replacement Tubing
Specialty Packaging

COMPETITORS

Crown Holdings
Pactiv
RPC Group
Sealed Air Corp.
Sonoco Products
Teknor Apex
Winpak

Teknor Apex

Teknor Apex is no retread. At least not any longer. Founded in 1924 as a tire distributor and retreader, Teknor Apex has sold off those assets to concentrate on chemicals, plastic, and rubber. The company has seven divisions that provide chemicals (plasticizers and toll compounding), garden hoses, rubber (custom mixing and molding of rubber compounds), specialty compounding (custom thermoplastic compound manufacturing and toll compounding of plastics), color concentrates for plastics (Teknor Color Company), thermoplastic elastomers, and vinyl (custom PVC compounds). The founding Fain family owns a controlling interest.

The company is broadening its technology base as well as its geographic reach. Chem Polymer, its wholly owned subsidiary in the UK, was purchased in 2004. It makes specialty compounds for glass fiber, flame retardants, and other items. In 2008 the company established a European holding company to house all of its compounding businesses on the continent. At that time Teknor Apex said it would stop using the Chem Polymer business name and rebrand those operations as Teknor Apex too.

EXECUTIVES

President and CEO: Jonathan D. Fain
CFO: James E. Morrison
EVP: Bertram M. Lederer
SVP, Manufacturing: William (Bill) Murray
VP and Business Manager, Vinyl Division: Lou Cappucci
VP and Business Manager, Thermoplastic Elastomer Division: Suresh Swaminathan
VP and Business Manager, Hose Division: Jack McGrath

VP and Business Manager, Teknor Color Division: Jonathan C. Riley
VP Human Resources: Laurie Meisner
VP, Business Development: Robert S. Brookman
President, Chem Polymer U.S.: Scott Fleming
General Manager, Chem Polymer UK: Russell Livesey
Manager, Corporate Marketing Communications: Sandra L. (Sandy) Hopkins
Treasurer: Edward Massoud

LOCATIONS

HQ: Teknor Apex Company
 505 Central Ave., Pawtucket, RI 02861
Phone: 401-725-8000   **Fax:** 401-725-8095
Web: www.teknorapex.com

PRODUCTS/OPERATIONS

Selected Products and Services

Chemicals and Colorants
 Color concentrates
 Custom compounds
 Dry colors
 High-performance colors
 Plasticizers (trimellitates, adipates, phthalates, sebacates, and azelates)
 Pulverized colors
 PVC compounds
 Thermoplastic elastomers
Garden Hose Products
 Cord, hose, and rope organizers
 Residential and commercial hoses
Rubber Products
 Custom rubber mixing
 Custom rubber molding

COMPETITORS

DuPont
GLS
PMC Global
PolyOne
RB Rubber
Spartech
Tekni-Plex
Vulcan International
Yule Catto

Temple University

Temple University, part of Pennsylvania's Commonwealth System of Higher Education, has four campuses in the Philadelphia area, as well as campuses in Tokyo and Rome and educational programs in China, Greece, France, Israel, and the UK. More than 34,000 students are enrolled in Temple's 17 schools and colleges. Temple's Health Sciences Center includes Temple University Hospital and schools that teach medicine and dentistry. Its Tyler School of Art will relocate from the Elkins Park campus to a modern facility on the main campus in 2009. After the move Temple plans to sell the 12-acre Elkins Park property. Dr. Russell Conwell founded the institution in 1884 and it was incorporated as Temple University in 1907.

EXECUTIVES

Chairman: Patrick J. (Pat) O'Connor
Vice Chair: Anthony J. Scirica
President: Ann Weaver Hart, age 60
Provost, EVP Academic Affairs, and Professor of Surgery: Lisa F. Staiano-Coico

Chief Communications Officer: Mark Eyerly
SVP Government Community and Public Affairs: Kenneth (Ken) Lawrence Jr.
University Counsel, Secretary, and SVP: George E. Moore
VP Human Resources: Deborah Hartnett
VP Student Affairs: Theresa A. Powell
VP Computing, Financial Services and CIO: Timothy C. O'Rourke
Controller: Frank P. Annunziato
Director Communications: Ray Betzner
Auditors: Deloitte & Touche LLP

LOCATIONS

HQ: Temple University
 1801 N. Broad St., Philadelphia, PA 19122
Phone: 215-204-7000   **Fax:** 215-204-4403
Web: www.temple.edu

Tenaska, Inc.

Tenaska is tenacious when it comes to producing and selling energy. The employee-owned company is a top natural gas marketer in North America (selling or managing more than 2 trillion cu. ft. of natural gas a year though Marketing Ventures/Tenaska Marketing Canada); it is also a leading independent power producer, trading and marketing electricity (including renewable energy). Its Tenaska Power Services unit — which is promoting the use of clean coal technology — develops, owns, or operates 10 generating plants with 6,800 MW of capacity in the US. Other operations include fuel supply, biofuels development, oil and gas exploration and production, power transmission, and gas transportation contracting.

Diversifying its portfolio to gain access to more revenue streams, in 2008 Tenaska formed a number of oil and gas businesses, including Tenaska Resources (gas exploration and production), Tenaska Drilling Services (drilling rigs in the Marcellus Shale gas play), and Tenaska Midstream Services. In 2008 Tenaska's biofuels unit (Tenaska BioFuels) acquired Edible Oil Marketing, an Omaha-based biodiesel and vegetable oil marketing and trading company.

In order to capture a share of the growing renewables market, in 2008 the company also made its first investments in wind and solar energy.

In 2006 its Tenaska Power Fund unit acquired InfrastruX Group for $275 million and also acquired 3,145 MW of natural gas-fired generation assets from Constellation Energy for $1.6 billion.

Tenaska was founded in 1987 by CEO Howard Hawks and EVP Thomas Hendricks.

EXECUTIVES

Co-Founder, Chairman, and CEO; Chairman, Tenaska Capital Management: Howard L. Hawks
Co-Founder and EVP; Vice Chairman, Tenaska Capital Management: Thomas E. (Tom) Hendricks
CFO: Jerry K. Crouse
EVP Corporate Investments: Michael F. (Mike) Lawler
EVP: Ronald N. Quinn
SVP, Gas Marketing, North: Terry K. Cameron
SVP, Power Marketing: Kevin R. Smith
SVP, Gas Marketing, West: Mark J. Whitt
SVP, Gas Marketing, South: David N. Schettler
VP and General Counsel: Drew J. Fossum
CEO and Senior Managing Director, Tenaska Capital Management: Paul G. Smith, age 51

President and CEO, Business Development Group: David G. Fiorelli
President, Tenaska Power Services: Trudy A. Harper
President and CEO, Engineering and Operations Group: Michael C. (Mike) Lebens, age 57
President, Tenaska Marketing Ventures and Tenaska Marketing Canada: Fred R. Hunzeker

LOCATIONS

HQ: Tenaska, Inc.
 1044 N. 115th St., Ste. 400, Omaha, NE 68154
Phone: 402-691-9500   **Fax:** 402-691-9526
Web: www.tenaska.com

PRODUCTS/OPERATIONS

Selected Subsidiaries

Tenaska BioFuels (biofuels)
Tenaska Capital Management LLC (asset management)
Tenaska Drilling Services (drilling rigs)
Tenaska Marketing Canada (gas marketing)
Tenaska Marketing Ventures (gas marketing)
Tenaska Midstream Services (midstream equipment and services)
Tenaska Power Services Co. (power marketing)
Tenaska Resources (gas exploration and production)

COMPETITORS

AES
BP
Calpine
Chevron
ConocoPhillips
Covanta
Edison Mission Energy
El Paso
Exxon Mobil
International Power
Mirant
NRG Energy
RRI Energy
Sempra Energy
Shell Oil

HISTORICAL FINANCIALS

Company Type: Private

Income Statement

	REVENUE ($ mil.)	NET INCOME ($ mil.)	NET PROFIT MARGIN	EMPLOYEES
				FYE: December 31
12/08	16,000	—	—	700
12/07	11,600	—	—	624
12/06	8,700	—	—	569
12/05	10,000	—	—	550
12/04	6,670	—	—	500
Annual Growth	24.5%	—	—	8.8%

Revenue History

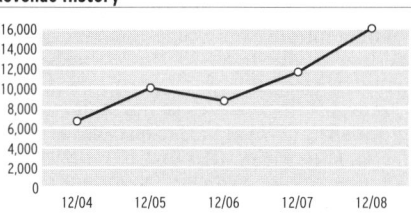

Tennessee Valley Authority

The Tennessee Valley Authority (TVA) may not be an expert on Tennessee attractions like Dollywood and the Grand Ole Opry, but it is an authority on power generation. TVA is the largest publicly owned power producer in the US, with more than 35,000 MW of generating capacity. Its facilities include 11 fossil-powered plants, 29 hydroelectric dams, three nuclear plants, and six combustion turbine plants. The federal corporation transmits electricity to about 160 local distribution utilities, which in turn serve some 9 million consumers, as well as industrial facilities and government agencies, in most of Tennessee and neighboring parts of Alabama, Georgia, Kentucky, Mississippi, North Carolina, and Virginia.

The TVA also manages the Tennessee River system for flood control and navigation.

Most of TVA's power comes from traditional generation sources, but the company is also exploring alternative energy technologies. It has developed nearly 20 solar, wind, and methane gas facilities. Government appropriations for the authority ceased in 1999; since that time the company has funded its activities almost entirely from the sale of electricity. The TVA is, however, exempt from federal and state income taxes. Nonetheless, it is working on reducing a $20 billion-plus debt load.

In 2008 a holding pond at TVA's coal-burning Kingston Fossil Plant failed and dumped some 5.4 million cu. yd. of fly ash over 400 acres in eastern Tennessee's Roane County. The slide knocked down utility poles and trees, and damaged at least a dozen homes (some beyond repair). Although nobody was hurt, some residents were cut off by the spill, prompting officials to build a new road. The flooding was the pond's third reported incident in six years.

TVA has an agreement to produce tritium, a radioactive gas that boosts the power of nuclear weapons, for the US Department of Energy at its Watts Bar nuclear plant. The company also plans to add three more nuclear plants by 2020 and is working with the DOE to reprocess waste from its existing plants.

HISTORY

In 1924 the Army Corps of Engineers finished building the Wilson Dam on the Tennessee River in Alabama to provide power for two WWI-era nitrate plants. With the war over, the question of what to do with the plants became a political football.

An act of Congress created the Tennessee Valley Authority (TVA) in 1933 to manage the plants and Tennessee Valley waterways. New Dealers saw TVA as a way to revitalize the local economy through improved navigation and power generation. Power companies claimed the agency was unconstitutional, but by 1939, when a federal court ruled against them, TVA had five operating hydroelectric plants and five under construction.

During the 1940s TVA supplied power for the war effort, including the Manhattan Project in Tennessee. During the postwar boom between 1945 and 1950, power usage in the Tennessee Valley nearly doubled. Despite adding dams, TVA couldn't keep up with demand, so in 1949 it began building a coal-fired unit. Because coal-fired plants weren't part of TVA's original mission, in 1955 a Congressional panel recommended the authority be dissolved.

Though TVA survived, its funding was cut. In 1959 it was allowed to sell bonds, but it no longer received direct government appropriations for power operations. In addition, it had to pay back the government for past appropriations.

TVA began to build the first unit of an ambitious 17-plant nuclear power program in Alabama in 1967. However, skyrocketing costs forced it to raise rates and cut maintenance on its coal-fired plants, which led to breakdowns. In 1985 five reactors had to be shut down because of safety concerns.

In 1988 former auto industry executive Marvin Runyon was appointed chairman of the agency. "Carvin' Marvin" cut management, sold three airplanes, and got rid of peripheral businesses, saving $400 million a year. In 1992 Runyon left to go to the postal service and was replaced by Craven Crowell, who began preparing TVA for competition in the retail power market.

TVA ended its nuclear construction program in 1996 after bringing two nuclear units on line within three months, a first for a US utility. The next year it raised rates for the first time in 10 years, planning to reduce its debt. In response to a lawsuit filed by neighboring utilities, it agreed to stop "laundering" power by using third parties to sell outside the agency's legally authorized area.

In 1999 the authority finished installing almost $2 billion in scrubbers and other equipment at its coal-fired plants so that it could buy Kentucky coal along with cleaner Wyoming coal. That year, however, the EPA charged TVA with violating the Clean Air Act by making major overhauls on some of its older coal-fired plants without getting permits or installing updated pollution-control equipment. It ordered TVA to bring most of its coal-fired plants into compliance with more current pollution standards. The next year TVA contested the order in court, stating compliance would jack up electricity rates.

TVA was fined by the US Nuclear Regulatory Commission in 2000 for laying off a nuclear plant whistleblower. Crowell resigned in 2001, and Glenn McCullough Jr. was named chairman; he served in that role until May 2005. He was replaced by Bill Baxter (who served until March 2006) and then by William Sansom.

EXECUTIVES

President and CEO: Tom D. Kilgore, age 60
COO: William R. (Bill) McCollum Jr., age 57
SVP and Treasurer: John M. Hoskins, age 53
EVP Financial Services and CFO:
Kimberly (Kim) Scheibe-Greene, age 42
Chief Nuclear Officer and EVP, Nuclear Power Group:
Preston D. Swafford, age 48
Chief People and Performance Officer:
John M. Thomas III, age 45

EVP PowerSystem Operations:
Robin E. (Rob) Manning, age 52
EVP Customer Resources: Kenneth R. Breeden, age 60
EVP Power Supply and Fuels: Van M. Wardlaw, age 48
EVP Fossil Power Group: John J. McCormick Jr., age 47
EVP Administrative Services and Chief Administrative Officer: John E. Long Jr., age 56
EVP TVA Nuclear and Chief Nuclear Officer:
William R. (Bill) Campbell Jr., age 57
EVP, General Counsel, and Secretary:
Maureen H. Dunn, age 59
SVP Corporate Responsibility and Diversity, Ombudsman, Chief Ethics and Compliance Officer, and External Ombudsman: Peyton T. Hairston Jr., age 53
General Manager, Global Business and Community Development: Heidi T. Smith
General Manager, Economic Development Information and Technical Services: Ray Knotts
Freedom of Information Act Officer: Denise Smith
Privacy Act Officer: Mark R. Winter
Communications Contact: Brooks Clark
Auditors: Ernst & Young LLP

LOCATIONS

HQ: Tennessee Valley Authority
400 W. Summit Hill Dr., Knoxville, TN 37902
Phone: 865-632-2101   **Fax:** 888-633-0372
Web: www.tva.gov

2008 Sales

	$ mil.	% of total
Electricity sales		
Tennessee	6,389	62
Alabama	1,410	14
Kentucky	1,192	12
Mississippi	923	9
Georgia	238	2
North Carolina	50	—
Virginia	37	—
Other revenues	143	1
Total	**10,382**	**100**

PRODUCTS/OPERATIONS

2008 Sales

	$ mil.	% of total
Electricity sales		
Municipalities & cooperatives	8,659	84
Industries directly served	1,472	14
Federal agencies & other	121	1
Other revenues	130	1
Total	**10,382**	**100**

HISTORICAL FINANCIALS

Company Type: Government-owned

Income Statement   FYE: September 30

	REVENUE ($ mil.)	NET INCOME ($ mil.)	NET PROFIT MARGIN	EMPLOYEES
9/08	10,382	817	7.9%	11,584
9/07	9,244	383	4.1%	12,013
9/06	9,175	329	3.6%	12,600
9/05	7,794	85	1.1%	12,703
9/04	7,533	386	5.1%	12,742
Annual Growth	**8.3%**	**20.6%**	**—**	**(2.4%)**

Net Income History

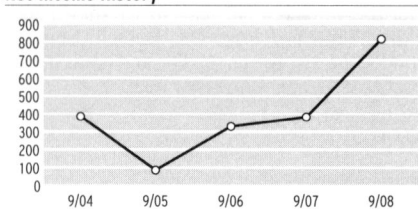

Texas A&M University System

Everything is bigger in Texas, even its universities. With over 100,000 students at nine institutions, The Texas A&M University System ranks among the largest in the US. Its flagship school at College Station is well known not only for its programs in engineering and agriculture, but also for its long-held traditions and school spirit. Other system institutions include Tarleton State University and Prairie View A&M. The system also runs seven state extension agencies and a health sciences center. Texas A&M was founded in 1876 as the Agricultural and Mechanical College of Texas. The A&M system was formed in 1948; it is funded in part by a state endowment (shared with the University of Texas).

Flagship Texas A&M in College Station is the largest campus in the university system, with an enrollment of about 46,500 students. Its campus is home to the George Bush Presidential Library Center, which opened in 1997.

At about 2,000 members, A&M's Corps of Cadets (commonly referred to as "the Corps") remains the largest uniformed body of students in the nation outside the US service academies.

In the wake of a bonfire collapse which took the lives of 12 students in 1999, Texas A&M has been charged by outsiders with trying to conceal its own involvement in the accident. Still others have called on Texas A&M to loosen some of its traditions. However, the school, students, and alumni have all stood fast against the tide of pressure. Texas A&M has embarked on a 20-year mission to renovate its facilities and secure status as a top public university.

EXECUTIVES

Chairman: John D. White
Chancellor: Michael D. (Mike) McKinney, age 58
Chief of Staff: Janet Smalley
Provost and EVP: Jeffrey S. Vitter
EVP Operations: H. Russell Cross
VP Finance and CFO: Terry A. Pankratz
VP and Associate Provost for Information Technology: Pierce E. Cantrell Jr.
Vice Chancellor Academic Affairs: Frank B. Ashley III
Vice Chancellor for Research: Brett Giroir
President, Texas A&M University - Commerce: Dan R. Jones
President and Vice Chancellor for Health Affairs, Health Science Center: Nancy W. Dickey
President, Texas A&M University - Texarkana: Carlisle Baxter Rathburn III
Interim President, Texas A&M University: R. Bowen Loftin
President, Prairie View A&M University: George C. Wright
President, Texas A&M International University: Ray M. Keck
President, Tarleton State University: F. Dominic Dottavio
President, Texas A&M University - Corpus Christi: Flavius C. Killebrew
Director of Communications: Rod Davis
General Counsel: Andrew L. Strong
Auditors: Texas State Auditor

LOCATIONS

HQ: The Texas A&M University System
A&M System Bldg., 200 Technology Way, Ste. 2043
College Station, TX 77845
Phone: 979-458-6000 **Fax:** 979-458-6044
Web: www.tamus.edu

PRODUCTS/OPERATIONS

Selected Texas A&M University System Components

Health Science Center
  Baylor College of Dentistry
  College of Medicine
  College of Nursing
  Graduate School of Biomedical Sciences
  Institute of Biosciences and Technology
  Irma Lerma Rangel College of Pharmacy
  School of Rural Public Health
State Agencies
  Texas Agricultural Experiment Station
  Texas Cooperative Extension
  Texas Engineering Experiment Station
  Texas Engineering Extension Service
  Texas Forest Service
  Texas Transportation Institute
  Texas Veterinary Medical Diagnostic Laboratory
Universities
  Prairie View A&M University
  Tarleton State University
  Texas A&M International University
  Texas A&M University
  Texas A&M University - Commerce
  Texas A&M University - Corpus Christi
  Texas A&M University - Kingsville
  Texas A&M University - Texarkana
  West Texas A&M University

Texas Lottery

The Texas Lottery Commission hopes to have the eyes of Texans watching the lotto jackpot. The Texas Lottery Commission oversees one of the country's largest state lotteries, which has pumped more than $15 billion into state coffers since its inaugural in 1991. More than 60% of lottery sales are paid out in prize money, while almost 30% goes to the state's Foundation School Fund; the remainder goes to retailer commissions and administrative costs. The lottery offers numbers games and several instant-win games sold through grocery stores, gas stations, and convenience stores. In addition, Texas participates in Mega Millions, a multistate lottery game.

With its popularity running high, the Texas lottery returned $1 billion to the state each year from 2005 through 2007. A downturn in the economy, however, has dragged down lottery sales. In response, the lottery commission added some new numbers games and increased the Lotto Texas from 50 to 54 numbers to increase jackpots.

HISTORY

A state lottery had been an issue in Texas for years before it was discussed in earnest in the mid-1980s. Falling oil and gas revenue had plunged the state into a recession, raising the specter of tax increases. In 1985 the state budget had a shortfall of $1 billion; that figure tripled by 1987. Adding fuel to the fire, the Texas Supreme Court ruled in 1989 that Texas had to change the way it funded public schools to avoid penalizing poor school districts. The ruling forced the state to seek new sources of revenue. In 1991 Gov. Ann Richards called a special session of the legislature to deal with the fiscal crisis, and House Bill 54 was passed, creating the state lottery. The measure was approved by 64% of voters.

In May 1992 Richards bought the symbolic first ticket at an Austin feed store (it was not a winner). Fourteen hours later Texans had spent nearly $23 million on tickets — breaking the California Lottery's first-day sales record — and had won $10 million in prizes. More than 102 million tickets were sold the first week. GTECH was awarded a five-year contract that year for lotto operations. Lotto Texas started in November with a winner taking nearly $22 million. By the end of the year, lotto sales in Texas had topped $1 billion. In its first 15 months, it contributed $812 million to the state's coffers.

In March 1994 five winners split a record $77 million jackpot. By that autumn, sales from the lottery's beginning had surpassed $5 billion. In November a Mansfield, Texas, gas station owner picked up the largest single-winner jackpot, $54 million. By the end of 1994, Texas had the largest state lottery in the US. Cumulative sales topped $8 billion in mid-1995. In its first 37 months of operation, the Texas Lottery contributed $2.5 billion to the state's general fund. Cash 5 debuted that year, and instant ticket vending machines were installed at some sites.

In 1996 lottery director Nora Linares was dismissed following allegations that one of her friends received $30,000 from GTECH as a "hunting consultant." When a GTECH official was convicted in New Jersey of taking kickbacks from a lobbyist, questions were raised concerning payments to GTECH's Texas lobbyist, former Texas Lt. Gov. Ben Barnes. In 1997 Texas canceled its contract with GTECH to operate the lottery through 2002 and reopened bidding; GTECH filed suit to enforce the contract. Executive director Lawrence Littwin later was dismissed by the commission. Littwin sued GTECH, claiming the company had gotten him fired (the case was settled in 1999). Linda Cloud, his replacement, reinstated GTECH's contract. That year the Texas Legislature voted to increase the amount going to the state and to reduce prize payouts.

Lottery sales fell sharply in 1998, due in part to the reduced prize money. To combat suffering sales, the legislature reversed itself the next year and restored the level of prize payouts. The commission proposed lengthening the odds of winning to create larger jackpots, but public outcry scuttled the plan. In 2000 the commission agreed to change the wording on its scratch tickets after a San Antonio College professor and his students argued that breaking even is not winning.

The following year it introduced its first new lottery game in about three years, Texas Two Step, and discontinued Texas Million following slumping sales. It also changed its Lotto Texas game so that customers must match six numbers out of 54 numbers instead of 50. The extra four numbers changed the odds of winning from about one in 16 million to one in 26 million. The game was changed again in 2003 to a two-field game where players first select five numbers out of 44, and then select one number from a second field of 44. The new game has changed the odds of winning the jackpot to one in 48 million, while the odds of winning any prize have changed from one in 71 to one in 57.

EXECUTIVES

Chairman: James A. Cox Jr.
Executive Director: Anthony J. Sadberry
Deputy Executive Director: Gary Grief
Director Governmental Affairs: Nelda Treviño
Director Charitable Bingo Operations: Phil Sanderson
Director Lottery Operations: Michael Anger
Director Media Relations: Robert Heith
Director Enforcement: James (Jim) Carney
Director Human Resources: Janine Mays
Director Internal Audit: Catherine Melvin
Director Administration: Michael (Mike) Fernandez
General Counsel: Kimberly (Kim) Kiplin
Controller: Kathy Pyka
Security Director, Lottery Operations: Brenda Pisana
Manager Financial Accounting and Reporting:
 Benito (Ben) Navarro
Manager Information Resources: Joan Kotal
Manager Support Services: Toni Erickson
Manager Facilities: Vince Devine
Manager Audit, Charitable Bingo Operations:
 Debbie Parpounas
Manager Drawings and Validations, Lottery Operations:
 Robert Barnett
**Manager Advertising and Promotions, Lottery
 Operations:** Ray Page
Auditors: Maxwell Locke & Ritter LLP

LOCATIONS

HQ: Texas Lottery Commission
 611 E. Sixth St., Austin, TX 78701
Phone: 512-344-5000   **Fax:** 512-344-5080
Web: www.txlottery.org

Thomas Nelson

Thomas Nelson's psalm of success comes straight from the Good Book. Considered the world's top commercial publisher of Christian-related materials, it produces about 10 major Bible translations in the English language, as well as biblical reference products, including commentaries, help texts, and study guides. In addition, Thomas Nelson publishes religious and inspirational titles by authors such as Max Lucado and John Eldredge. The company also hosts inspirational conferences (Women of Faith) and is a leading producer of Christian-oriented and family-focused products for adults and children, including books and games, and audio, video, and CD-ROM materials. Thomas Nelson became a private company in 2006.

The company's products are distributed through Christian and general bookstores, mass merchandisers, and by direct marketing to consumers via direct mail, telemarketing, conferences, and the Internet.

Cable veteran Leo Hindery and his private equity investment firm InterMedia Partners and its subsidiary Faith Media took Thomas Nelson private in a $473 million buyout deal in 2006.

Going against industry standards, the company eliminated its more than 20 imprints in early 2007 as part of its "One Company" initiative, instead putting all of its books under one brand and its publishing functions into consumer categories. As part of the initiative,

Thomas Nelson began using a single strategy for all of its nonfiction books, combining two nonfiction units into one.

In 2008 the company cut some 55 jobs (about 10% of its workforce) as a result of the weak economy. The cuts affected nearly every department at Thomas Nelson.

EXECUTIVES

President and CEO: Michael S. (Mike) Hyatt, age 53
EVP and Chief Live Events Officer: Mary Graham
EVP and Chief Sales Officer: Mark Schoenwald
EVP and CFO: Stuart M. Bitting
EVP and Chief Service Officer: Vance Lawson, age 50
EVP and Chief Publishing Officer:
 Tamara L. (Tami) Heim
SVP; Publisher, Fiction: Allen Arnold
SVP; Publisher, Corporate Brands: Brian Hampton
SVP; Publisher, Bibles: Wayne Hastings
SVP; Publisher, Specialty: Tod Shuttleworth
SVP; Group Publisher, Non-Fiction Trade Book Group:
 David Moberg
VP Customer Service: Mike Mitchell
VP Facilities Administration: Scott Holloway
VP Human Resources: Jim Thomason
VP; Publisher, Thomas Nelson Family Entertainment:
 Dan Lynch
VP Information Systems: Rick Proctor
VP Distribution: Joel Beasley
Director Corporate Communications: Lindsey Nobles
Auditors: KPMG LLP

LOCATIONS

HQ: Thomas Nelson, Inc.
 501 Nelson Place, Nashville, TN 37214
Phone: 615-889-9000   **Fax:** 615-391-5225
Web: www.thomasnelson.com

PRODUCTS/OPERATIONS

Selected Books

Anchored in Love (John Carter Cash)
Every Day Deserves a Chance (Max Lucado)
Get Out of That Pit (Beth Moore)
Inside My Heart (Robin McGraw)
It's All About Him (Denise Jackson)
On the Move (Bono)
One Minute Wellness (Dr. Ben Lerner)
Talent Is Never Enough (John C. Maxwell)
Ten Tortured Words (Stephen Mansfield)
The Great Bird Flu Hoax (Dr. Joseph Mercola)
The Ransomed Heart (John Eldredge)
You Are Captivating (Stasi Eldredge)
Winning With People (John C. Maxwell)

Selected Bible Editions

International Children's Bible
King James Version
New American Bible
New American Standard Bible
New Century Version
New King James Version
New Living Translation
New Revised Standard Version
Revised Standard Version, Catholic Edition

Selected Children's Titles

Adventures in Odyssey
Bibleman
Buginnings
God's Kids Worship
Hermie and Friends
Jacob's Gift
Just in Case You Ever Wonder
Just Like Jesus for Tweens
Wally McDoogle series
Wemmicks

COMPETITORS

Baker Publishing
Beliefnet
Courier Corporation
Deseret Management
Guideposts
Integrity Media
R. B. Pamplin
Salem Communications
Standex
Tyndale House Publishers
Zondervan

Thorntons Inc.

Fill 'er (and you) up at Thorntons. Kentucky's largest privately owned corporation, Thorntons operates about 160 Thorntons and QuickCafé & Market convenience stores and gas stations in Connecticut, Illinois, Indiana, Kentucky, Ohio, and Tennessee. It also operates a single travel plaza and eight car wahes. Through wholly owned subsidiary Thornton Transportation, the company distributes its own fuel and operates a river bulk storage terminal. The chain is focusing on high-margin items such as sandwiches, doughnuts and gourmet coffee to boost sales. The family-owned and -operated company was co-founded in 1971 by namesake and chairman James H. Thornton and is run by his son CEO Matt Thornton.

In 2007 Thorntons entered the Tennessee market. It announced plans to add four stores there in 2009, bringing its Tennessee store count to 10 locations. Overall, the chain had plans for a half-dozen new stores in 2009, including one in the Chicago area, where Thorntons already has a strong presence.

Thorntons recently introduced CornerMarkets, convenience stores that offer shoppers a greater grocery selection, and Subworks, a proprietary food program that allows customers to order sandwiches and other fresh food via a touch-screen menu.

EXECUTIVES

CEO: Matt Thornton
CFO: Christopher (Chris) Kamer
Director Operations: Shawn Kendrick
Director IT: David Caudill
EVP Human Resources: Brenda Stackhouse
Regional VP Operations: Sam Picone
VP and General Counsel: David Bridgers
VP Construction and Environmental Concerns:
 Eric Zoph
VP Marketing: John Zikias
VP Petroleum Supply and Distribution: Jeff Gallic
VP Store Operations: Tony Harris
Senior Manager Petroleum Supply and Distribution:
 Patty Leonhardt
Manager Advertising: Kelly Ogburn
Controller: Lennie Kamer

LOCATIONS

HQ: Thorntons Inc.
 10101 Linn Station Rd., Ste. 200
 Louisville, KY 40223
Phone: 502-425-8022   **Fax:** 502-327-9026
Web: www.thorntonsinc.com

2009 Stores

	No.
Kentucky	53
Illinois	52
Indiana	30
Ohio	22
Tennessee	6
Connecticut	4
Total	**167**

COMPETITORS

7-Eleven
Chevron
Couche-Tard
Exxon Mobil
Kroger
The Pantry
Speedway SuperAmerica

HISTORICAL FINANCIALS

Company Type: Private

Income Statement

FYE: September 30

	REVENUE ($ mil.)	NET INCOME ($ mil.)	NET PROFIT MARGIN	EMPLOYEES
9/08	1,900	—	—	2,500
9/07	1,520	—	—	2,500
9/06	1,250	—	—	1,900
9/05	1,018	—	—	1,897
Annual Growth	**23.1%**	**—**	**—**	**9.6%**

Revenue History

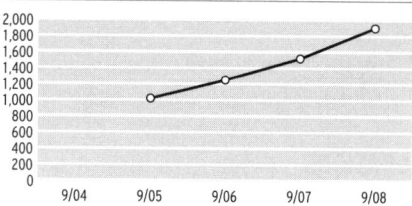

Thrivent Financial

The Spirit moved Aid Association for Lutherans (AAL) to merge with Lutheran Brotherhood and form a new entity, christened Thrivent Financial for Lutherans. The fraternal benefit society now includes nearly 3 million members, and brings under one steepled roof more than $70 billion in assets under management. Individuals and congregations that become members can shop for life insurance, mutual funds, bank and trust services (through Thrivent Financial Bank), and other financial services. Thrivent Financial, which operates all over the US, has nearly $160 billion in life insurance in force. The company also supports three separate foundations which contribute to charitable causes.

EXECUTIVES

Chairman, President, and CEO: Bruce J. Nicholson, age 63
Vice Chairman: Kurt M. Senske
SVP and Chief Investment Officer: Russell W. (Russ) Swansen
SEVP and COO: Bradford L. (Brad) Hewitt
EVP Marketing and Products: Pamela J. (Pam) Moret

EVP Field Distribution; President, Thrivent Investment Management: James A. (Jim) Thomsen
SVP and CFO: Randall L. (Randy) Boushek
SVP Marketing: Timothy J. Lehman
SVP and Chief of Staff and Administration: Jon M. Stellmacher
SVP: David Francis
SVP, General Counsel, and Secretary: Teresa J. (Terry) Rasmussen
SVP and CIO: Holly J. Morris
SVP Communications: Marie A. Uhrich
SVP Financial Services Operations; SVP Thrivent Investment Management: David M. (Dave) Anderson
Director Community Relations: Stacy Hanley
Director Public Relations: Brett Weinberg
Auditors: Ernst & Young LLP

LOCATIONS

HQ: Thrivent Financial for Lutherans
4321 N. Ballard Rd., Appleton, WI 54919
Phone: 612-340-7000   **Fax:** 800-205-8348
Web: www.thrivent.com

PRODUCTS/OPERATIONS

2008 Revenues

	$ mil.	% of total
Premium income & contract proceeds	3,818	60
Net investment income	2,322	36
Other	273	4
Total	**6,413**	**100**

COMPETITORS

Citigroup
ELCA Board of Pensions
FMR
MetLife
Modern Woodmen
New York Life
Northwestern Mutual
Royal Neighbors Of America
Security Benefit Group
State Farm
TIAA-CREF

HISTORICAL FINANCIALS

Company Type: Not-for-profit

Income Statement

FYE: December 31

	ASSETS ($ mil.)	NET INCOME ($ mil.)	INCOME AS % OF ASSETS	EMPLOYEES
12/08	49,470	(315)	—	2,926
12/07	53,474	391	0.7%	—
12/06	52,539	524	1.0%	—
12/05	50,816	522	1.0%	—
12/04	56,750	488	0.9%	2,676
Annual Growth	**(3.4%)**	**—**	**—**	**2.3%**

2008 Year-End Financials

Equity as % of assets: —
Return on assets: —
Return on equity: —
Long-term debt ($ mil.): —
Sales ($ mil.): 6,413

Net Income History

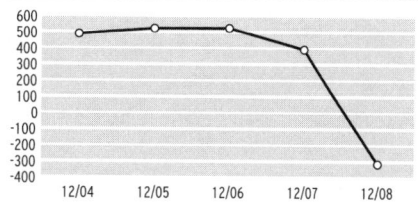

TIAA-CREF

It's punishment enough to write the name once on a blackboard. Teachers Insurance and Annuity Association — College Retirement Equities Fund (TIAA-CREF) is one of the largest, if not longest-named, private retirement systems in the US, providing for more than 3.5 million members of the academic, cultural, medical, and research communities and for investors outside academia's ivied confines. It also serves institutional investors. TIAA-CREF's core offerings include financial advice, investment information, retirement plans and accounts, annuities, life insurance, brokerage, and trust services (through TIAA-CREF Trust). The system, a not-for-profit organization, also manages a line of mutual funds.

TIAA-CREF is one of the nation's heftiest institutional investors, with some $400 billion in assets under management, and it has not been afraid to throw its weight around corporate boardrooms. The organization is known for active and choosy investing and is a vocal critic of extravagant executive compensation packages. It invests with an eye toward social responsibility, as well, taking into account companies' policies and practices toward such issues as human rights, labor, and global warming.

In 2006 TIAA-CREF bought Kaspick & Company, which manages planned giving assets for colleges, universities, and other not-for-profits. The acquisition makes the system the largest provider of such services in the US. TIAA-CREF also owns one of the nation's largest portfolios of real estate investments.

HISTORY

With $15 million, the Carnegie Foundation for the Advancement of Teaching in 1905 founded the Teachers Insurance and Annuity Association (TIAA) in New York City to provide retirement benefits and other forms of financial security to educators. When Carnegie's original endowment was found to be insufficient, another $1 million reorganized the fund into a defined-contribution plan in 1918. TIAA was the first portable pension plan, letting participants change employers without losing benefits and offering a fixed annuity. The fund required infusions of Carnegie cash until 1947.

In 1952 TIAA CEO William Greenough pioneered the variable annuity, based on common stock investments, and created the College Retirement Equities Fund (CREF) to offer it. Designed to supplement TIAA's fixed annuity, CREF invested participants' premiums in stocks. CREF and TIAA were subject to New York insurance (but not SEC) regulation.

During the 1950s TIAA led the fight for Social Security benefits for university employees and began offering group total disability coverage (1957) and group life insurance (1958).

In 1971 TIAA-CREF began helping colleges boost investment returns from endowments, then moved into endowment management. It helped found a research center to provide objective investment information in 1972.

For 70 years retirement was the only way members could exit TIAA-CREF. Their only investment choices were stocks through CREF or a one-way transfer into TIAA's annuity accounts based on long-term bond, real estate, and mortgage investments. In the 1980s CREF indexed its funds to the S&P average.

By 1987's stock crash, TIAA-CREF had a million members, many of whom wanted more protection from stock market fluctuations. After the crash, Clifton Wharton (the first African-American to head a major US financial organization) became CEO; the next year CREF added a money market fund, for which the SEC required complete transferability, even outside TIAA-CREF. Now open to competition, TIAA-CREF became more flexible, adding investment options and long-term-care plans.

John Biggs became CEO in 1993. After the 1994 bond crash, TIAA-CREF began educating members on the ABCs of retirement investing, hoping to persuade them not to switch to flashy short-term investments and not to panic during such cyclical events as the crash.

In 1996 it went international, buying interests in UK commercial and mixed-use property. TIAA-CREF filed for SEC approval of more mutual funds in 1997. Although federal tax legislation took away TIAA-CREF's tax-exempt status in 1997, the change was made without decreasing annuity incomes for the year.

The status change let TIAA-CREF offer no-load mutual funds to the public in 1998. A trust company and financial planning services were added; all new products were sold at cost, with TIAA-CREF waiving fees. TIAA-CREF in 1998 became the first pension fund to force out an entire board of directors (that of sputtering cafeteria firm Furr's/Bishop's). Also that year TIAA-CREF's crusade to curb "dead hand" poison pills (an antitakeover defense measure) found favor with the shareholders of Bergen Brunswig (now AmerisourceBergen), Lubrizol, and Mylan Laboratories.

Biggs retired in 2002 and was succeeded by Herbert Allison. In 2008 Allison retired; he was replaced by Roger Ferguson.

EXECUTIVES

Chairman: Ronald L. Thompson, age 58
President, CEO, and Director: Roger W. Ferguson Jr., age 58
EVP and Chief Legal Officer: Brandon Becker
EVP Public Affairs: I. Steven (Steve) Goldstein
EVP Risk Management: Erwin W. Martens
EVP Human Resources and Corporate Services: Dermot J. O'Brien
EVP Individual Client Services; President, TIAA-CREF Individual & Institutional Services: Maliz E. Beams, age 53
EVP and CTO: Susan S. Kozik
EVP and CFO: Georganne C. Proctor, age 52
EVP Asset Management; CEO Teachers Advisors and TIAA-CREF Investment Management: Scott C. Evans
EVP and Head of Fixed Income and Real Estate: John A. Somers
EVP Technology and Operations: Cara L. Schnaper
EVP Product Development and Management: Edward Van Dolsen
EVP and Chief Institutional Development and Sales Officer: Bertram L. Scott, age 57
SVP and General Counsel: Jonathan Feigelson
SVP Marketing and Advertising: Jamie DePeau
VP and Corporate Secretary: E. Laverne Jones
VP and Treasurer: Gary Chinery
Senior Managing Director and Chief Strategy Officer: Keith Stock, age 56
Senior Managing Director and Chief Investment Officer: Edward J. Grzybowski
Chairman, President, and CEO, TIAA-CREF Life Insurance: Bret L. Benham

LOCATIONS

HQ: Teachers Insurance and Annuity Association — College Retirement Equities Fund
730 3rd Ave., New York, NY 10017
Phone: 212-490-9000   **Fax:** 212-916-4840
Web: www.tiaa-cref.org

PRODUCTS/OPERATIONS

Selected Mutual Funds
Bond
Bond Index
Bond Plus
Equity Index
Growth & Income
High-Yield
Inflation-Linked Bond
International Equity
Large-Cap Growth
Large-Cap Value
Lifecycle Retirement Income Fund
Managed Allocation
Mid-Cap Growth
Mid-Cap Value
Money Market
Real Estate Securities
Short-Term Bond
Small-Cap Equity
Social Choice Equity
Tax-Exempt Bond

COMPETITORS

Aetna
Ameriprise
AXA Financial
CalPERS
Charles Schwab
CIGNA
Citigroup
FMR
John Hancock Financial Services
JPMorgan Chase
MassMutual
MetLife
New York Life
Northwestern Mutual
Principal Financial
Prudential
T. Rowe Price
USAA
VALIC
The Vanguard Group

HISTORICAL FINANCIALS

Company Type: Private

Income Statement

FYE: December 31

	REVENUE ($ mil.)	NET INCOME ($ mil.)	NET PROFIT MARGIN	EMPLOYEES
12/08	12,740	(3,060)	—	7,500
12/07	13,187	1,465	11.1%	7,500
12/06	12,378	3,453	27.9%	5,500
12/05	11,703	1,878	16.0%	5,500
12/04	10,864	540	5.0%	6,000
Annual Growth	4.1%	—	—	5.7%

Net Income History

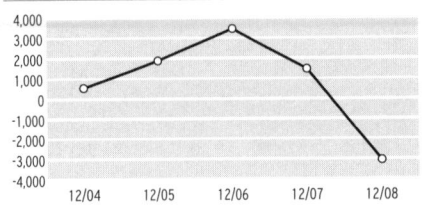

Tillamook County Creamery Association

Hoping to put its name on the map in more ways than one, Tillamook County Creamery Association has developed a reputation for making cheese. The cooperative, also known as Tillamook Cheese, manufactures dairy products including butter, ice cream, sour cream, and yogurt, but most of its production is devoted to cheddar cheese. It does, however, make other cheeses, including colby, jack, mozarella, and Swiss. Tillamook cheese products are available thoughout the US. The co-op is owned by some 130 dairy farmers in and around Tillamook County, Oregon.

Tillamook butter can be found throughout the western US and in selected eastern locations. Tillamook ice cream, yogurt, and sour cream are available in Oregon, Washington, and Northern California.

The cooperative was founded in 1909 when 10 farmers consolidated their cheese manufacturing operations.

EXECUTIVES

Chairman and Secretary: Rick Godinho
President and CEO: Harold G. M. Strunk
VP Finance and CFO: Don Desjarlais, age 53
VP Member Relations and Public Affairs: Mark Wustenberg
VP Sales and Marketing: Jay Allison
Director Marketing: Kathy Holstad
Director Information Technology: Steve Burge

LOCATIONS

HQ: Tillamook County Creamery Association
4175 Hwy. 101 North, Tillamook, OR 97141
Phone: 503-815-1300   **Fax:** 503-842-6039
Web: www.tillamookcheese.com

PRODUCTS/OPERATIONS

Selected Products and Brands
Butter and Sour Cream
  Fat-free sour cream
  Light sour cream
  Premium sour cream
  Sweet cream butter
  Sweet cream unsalted butter

Cheese
  Colby
  Colby jack
  Flavored cheese
  Kosher medium cheddar
  Medium cheddar
  Monterey jack
  Mozzarella
  Pepper jack
  Reduced-fat medium cheddar
  Reduced-fat monterey jack
  Sharp cheddar
  Shredded cheese
  Sliced cheese
  Smoked cheddar
  Special reserve extra-sharp cheddar
  Swiss
  Vintage white extra-sharp cheddar
  Vintage white medium cheddar

Ice Cream
  Banana Split
  Bubble Gum
  Caramel Butter Pecan
  Caramel Toffee Crunch
  Chocolate
  Chocolate Peanut Butter
  Coffee Almond Fudge
  Cookie Dough
  Cookies and Cream
  Espresso Mocha
  French Vanilla
  Marionberry Pie
  Mint Chocolate Chip
  Mountain Huckleberry
  Old-Fashioned Vanilla
  Oregon Black Cherry
  Oregon Strawberry
  Rocky Road
  Tillamook Mudslide
  Udderly Chocolate
  Vanilla Bean
  Wild Mountain Blackberry

Yogurt
  Baked Apple
  Cherry
  Cherry Vanilla
  Country Orange Cream
  Cranberry-Raspberry
  French Vanilla Bean
  Key Lime
  Lemon Squeeze
  Light Dark Cherry
  Light Marionberry
  Light Mountain Huckleberry
  Light Oregon Boysenberry Pomegranate
  Light Oregon Strawberry
  Light Peach
  Light Raspberry
  Light Vanilla Bean
  Marionberry
  Mountain Huckleberry
  Northwest Berry Patch
  Orchard Harvest
  Oregon Strawberry
  Passion Fruit
  Peach
  Raspberry
  Strawberry Lemonade
  Vanilla Bean
  Watermelon

COMPETITORS

Agri-Mark	Guida's
American Milk Products	Hiland Dairy
Associated Milk Producers	HP Hood
Bel Brands USA	Kraft Foods
BelGioioso Cheese	Land O'Lakes
Ben & Jerry's	Leprino Foods
Brewster Dairy	Marathon Cheese
California Dairies Inc.	Maryland & Virginia Milk
Cheesemakers, Inc.	Producers
Crystal Farms	Organic Valley
Dairy Farmers of America	Prairie Farms Dairy
Darigold, Inc.	Saputo
Dean Foods	Sargento
Dreyer's	Swiss Valley Farms
Ellsworth Cooperative	Swiss-American
Friendly Ice Cream	United Dairy Farmers
Great Lakes Cheese	Wells' Dairy

HISTORICAL FINANCIALS

Company Type: Cooperative

Income Statement

FYE: December 31

	REVENUE ($ mil.)	NET INCOME ($ mil.)	NET PROFIT MARGIN	EMPLOYEES
12/08	449	—	—	650
12/07	382	—	—	650
12/06	326	—	—	650
12/05	309	—	—	650
12/04	309	—	—	650
Annual Growth	9.8%	—	—	0.0%

Revenue History

Tishman Realty & Construction

Tishman Realty & Construction is an immigrant story of massive proportions. Founded by Julius Tishman, who emigrated from Poland in 1885 and began building tenements in 1898, it is now one of the nation's leading property development and management companies, offering a full menu of real estate services including design, construction supervision, and property management. Since its inception, the company has built about 300 million sq. ft. of all types of buildings. High-profile projects handled by the company include Disney World's EPCOT Center, Madison Square Garden, the ill-fated World Trade Center (and the future Freedom Tower), and Chicago's John Hancock Center. It is still owned by the Tishman family.

Recent projects include the Henry Miller's Theater in New York City (Broadway's first green theater), a new headquarters for literary and talent agency William Morris in Los Angeles, and reconstruction of the historic clock tower at Hoboken Ferry Terminal in New Jersey. The Henry Miller Theater is part of more than 50 million sq. ft. of green projects built or currently being built by Tishman. Affiliate Tishman Sustainability Corporation consults clients who are building sustainable properties.

Other affiliates include Tishman Technologies, which equips buildings with data and communications infrastructure, and Tishman Hotel & Realty, which provides construction management and financial and property management services for hospitality and retail space.

Former CEO John Tishman expanded the company beyond its Big Apple origins, most notably through a partnership with the Walt Disney Company to build hotels and theme parks in Florida. Among the company's completed non-New York projects are the Dolphin and Swan hotels at Disney's EPCOT Center, the Sheraton Chicago Hotel & Towers, and the Westin Rio Mar Beach Resort & Casino in Puerto Rico.

HISTORY

Julius Tishman escaped the Russian attacks on Jews pogroms of the late 19th century by emigrating to the US in 1885. Five years later he opened a store in Newburgh, New York. In 1898, as eastern European immigrants inundated New York City, Tishman began building tenements on the Lower East Side. He named his business Julius Tishman & Sons. By the 1920s the firm had moved uptown and upscale, building luxury apartment buildings. The firm went public in 1928 as Tishman Realty & Construction, with the family retaining an ownership stake. Julius was chairman; son David was CEO.

The pitfalls of going public were soon obvious. The offering raised less than $2 million, not enough to finance projects, and because the stock market favored profit generation over asset appreciation, the company was undervalued. When the Depression hit, David's involvement as a director of the Bank of the United States and the family's participation in bad loans made by the bank forced the firm to sell assets. Tishman's lenders, including insurer Metropolitan Life, took over some of its buildings, leaving the firm to manage them. In the 1930s and 1940s the company focused mainly on managing its properties. It continued its construction operations on a contract basis for the Federal Housing Authority.

After WWII, Tishman moved away from residential development and into office construction. Meanwhile, David's younger brothers Paul and Norman began jockeying for position to replace him as CEO; in 1948 David chose Norman to succeed him (Paul resigned to form his own construction company). A nephew, John, became head of the firm's construction arm.

By the early 1950s Tishman had moved into management and leasing services and expanded nationally, opening offices in Chicago and Los Angeles. In 1962 David relinquished his chairmanship to Norman, who was in turn replaced as CEO by his brother Bob. Under Bob's leadership, Tishman divested residential properties to focus on office space, mostly company-owned.

In 1972 the company completed the World Trade Center complex, including twin 110-story towers which were then the tallest buildings in the world. The iconic structures stood more than 1,300 feet above Manhattan until they collapsed as a result of the September 11 terrorist attacks in 2001.

Tishman was hit hard by recession in the 1970s. In 1976 Bob took the company private again, selling off the firm's New York assets, and split the company into Tishman Speyer Properties (headed by Bob and son-in-law Jerry Speyer); Tishman Management and Leasing (now part of Grubb & Ellis); and Tishman Realty & Construction (headed by John and promptly bought by the Rockefeller Center Corporation).

John Tishman bought back Tishman Realty & Construction in 1980 and steered it into high-profile partnerships with the likes of the Walt Disney Company. He also added project management and real estate financial services to his company's repertoire and continued to take part in highly visible construction projects.

Since the late 1990s Tishman's major projects have centered around revitalization efforts of Times Square and 42nd Street in New York City — including the construction of 4 Times Square (Condé Nast building), 3 Times Square (Reuters America headquarters), and E Walk, a mixed-use entertainment and retail center.

EXECUTIVES

Chairman and CEO: Daniel R. (Dan) Tishman
Vice Chairman; Chairman and CEO, Tishman Hotel & Realty LP: John A. Vickers
CFO: Frank Beck
EVP, Estimating: Bill Endres
EVP, Tishman Technologies: Richard O. Blackman
EVP, Tishman Technologies and Tishman Construction: John Krush
EVP, Tishman Technologies Corporation: Ronald H. Bowman Jr.
EVP, Tishman Interiors: Vincent Piscopo
EVP, Tishman Technologies: Joseph B. Ryan Jr.
EVP and Regional Manager, Tishman Construction Corporation of Illinois: James E. McLean
EVP and Regional Manager, Tishman Construction Corporation of Washington, DC: Stephen H. Dalton
EVP and Regional Manager, New Jersey and Pennsylvania: Edward J. (Ed) Cettina
SVP, Tishman Real Estate Services: Charles A. Wojcik
SVP, Tishman Construction Corporation of New York: James Raved
SVP, Tishman Technologies: William (Bill) Stanton
SVP and General Counsel: Linda Christensen Sjogren
SVP, Tishman Real Estate Services: Paul Diamond
SVP, Corporate Relations: Richard M. Kielar
President, Tishman Realty Corp.: William J. Sales
President and CEO, Tishman Real Estate Services: Joseph J. Simone
President, Construction Operations: Peter A. (Pete) Marchetto
President, Corporate Operations: John T. Livingston

LOCATIONS

HQ: Tishman Realty & Construction Co., Inc.
666 5th Ave., 38th Fl., New York, NY 10103
Phone: 212-399-3600 **Fax:** 212-739-7065
Web: www.tishman.com

PRODUCTS/OPERATIONS

Selected Subsidiaries
Tishman Advisory Services
Tishman Hotel & Realty LP
Tishman Interiors Corporation
Tishman Sustainability Corporation
Tishman Technologies Corporation

COMPETITORS

Bovis Lend Lease
CB Richard Ellis
Cushman & Wakefield
E.W. Howell
Forest City Ratner
Gilbane
Grubb & Ellis
JMB Realty
Jones Lang LaSalle
Lefrak Organization
Lincoln Property
Trammell Crow Company
The Trump Organization
Tully Construction
Turner Construction
Witkoff Group

HISTORICAL FINANCIALS

Company Type: Private

Income Statement

FYE: December 31

	REVENUE ($ mil.)	NET INCOME ($ mil.)	NET PROFIT MARGIN	EMPLOYEES
12/08	4,690	—	—	970
12/07*	3,560	—	—	1,051
6/06	2,510	—	—	1,000
6/05	2,458	—	—	857
6/04	2,000	—	—	900
Annual Growth	23.7%	—	—	1.9%

*Fiscal year change

Revenue History

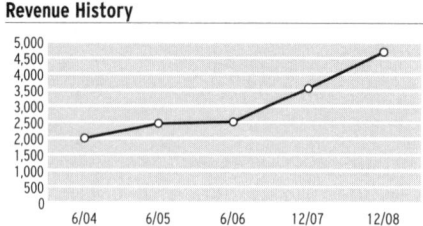

Topa Equities

Holding company Topa Equities casts a wide net. Owned by John Anderson, Topa has about 40 businesses involved in auto dealerships, beer distribution, insurance, real estate, and more. Topa's beverage operations include Ace Beverage, Mission Beverages, and Paradise Beverages; the firm dominates the Hawaiian beer market. Brands sold include all major US brews and leading US imports, including Guinness, Heineken, and Anheuser-Busch InBev products. Anderson started in 1956 as a distributor of Hamm's beer. UCLA's Anderson School of Business, to which Anderson donated $15 million, is named for him.

EXECUTIVES

Chairman, President, and CEO: John E. Anderson Sr., age 91
VP: Robin N. Platt
VP: Gary Clopp
VP and Director Leasing: Darren Bell
VP Topa Properties: Christine Thompson
VP, CFO, and Treasurer, Topa Insurance: Daniel Sherrin
VP Commercial Lines, Topa Insurance: Larry Esposito
VP: Carol T. Shain
Assistant VP and CIO, Topa Insurance: Rob Livingston
President, Topa Properties: Steven D. Morton
President and CEO, Topa Insurance: Noshirwan Marfatia
President, Topa Management Company: Paul R. Gienger
Director Human Resources, Topa Insurance: William Robinson

LOCATIONS

HQ: Topa Equities, Ltd.
1800 Avenue of the Stars, Ste. 1400
Los Angeles, CA 90067
Phone: 310-203-9199 **Fax:** 310-557-1837
Web: www.topa.com

COMPETITORS

Beauchamp Distributing
Constellation Brands
Glazer's Wholesale Drug
Reyes Holdings
Southern Wine & Spirits

HISTORICAL FINANCIALS

Company Type: Private

Income Statement

FYE: December 31

	REVENUE ($ mil.)	NET INCOME ($ mil.)	NET PROFIT MARGIN	EMPLOYEES
12/07	1,200	—	—	2,133
12/06	1,210	—	—	2,295
12/05	1,202	—	—	2,318
12/04	1,120	—	—	2,298
12/03	1,056	—	—	2,278
Annual Growth	3.2%	—	—	(1.6%)

Revenue History

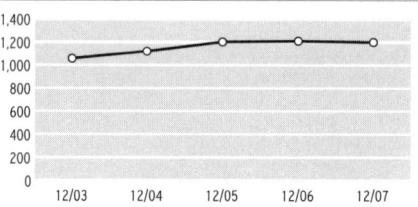

Towers Perrin

Refusing to live in an ivory tower, this company aims to offer practical advice. One of the leading management consulting firms in the world, Towers Perrin serves major enterprises — including most of the *FORTUNE* 1,000 — across a broad span of industries. The firm divides its service offerings into two main categories: human capital, which includes human resources consulting practices related to issues such as benefits, compensation, and workforce effectiveness; and risk and financial services, which includes several practices related to insurance issues. Its Tillinghast unit provides consulting services for insurance companies. In June 2009 Towers Perrin announced it was merging with rival firm Watson Wyatt.

The mega deal with Watson Wyatt — valued at $3.5 billion — will create a new publicly listed company called Towers Watson & Co. Mark Mactas, Towers Perrin's chairman and CEO, is tapped for the role of president while John Haley, the top executive at Watson Wyatt, will serve as its new CEO. As one of the world's largest HR consultancies, the combined company will boast annual sales of around $3.2 billion and specialize in three main service areas: employee benefits, talent and rewards, and risk and financial services.

Towers Perrin takes advantage of its global reach to pitch its services to multinational enterprises. It has offices and alliance partners throughout the Americas, the Asia/Pacific region, and Europe. Months before the merger with Watson Wyatt was announced, Towers Perrin launched operations in the Middle East, a region it considers a key market ripe for growth, particularly for expanding its risk and human capital management services.

Towers Perrin, which is owned by its partners, was established in 1934.

EXECUTIVES

Chairman and CEO: Mark Mactas
CFO: Robert G. (Bob) Hogan
Managing Director, Human Capital Group:
 Jim Foreman
SVP Towers Perrin Capital Markets: James Doona
SVP Towers Perrin Capital Markets: Rick Miller
General Counsel and Secretary: Kevin Young
**Managing Director, Risk and Financial Services
 Businesses:** Patricia L. (Tricia) Guinn
Managing Director, Human Capital Group:
 Donald L. (Don) Lowman

LOCATIONS

HQ: Towers Perrin
 1 Stamford Plaza, 263 Tresser Blvd.
 Stamford, CT 06901
Phone: 203-326-5400   **Fax:** 203-326-5499
Web: www.towersperrin.com

PRODUCTS/OPERATIONS

Selected Services

Human Capital
 Actuarial consulting
 Executive compensations
 Health and welfare
 HR function effectiveness
 Mergers, acquisitions, and restructuring
 Research and surveys
 Retirement
 Total rewards effectiveness
 Workforce effectiveness
Risk and Financial
 Actuarial consulting
 Enterprise risk management
 Financial modeling
 Insurance consulting
 Mergers, acquisitions, and restructuring
 Reinsurance
 Retirement risk solutions

COMPETITORS

Accenture
Aon
A.T. Kearney
Bain & Company
Benecon Group
Booz Allen
Boston Consulting
Deloitte
Drake Beam Morin
Ernst & Young Global
Gallup
Hewitt Associates
HR Solutions
KPMG
Marsh & McLennan
McKinsey & Company
PricewaterhouseCoopers
Right Management
Watson Wyatt

HISTORICAL FINANCIALS

Company Type: Private

Income Statement				FYE: December 31
	REVENUE ($ mil.)	NET INCOME ($ mil.)	NET PROFIT MARGIN	EMPLOYEES
12/08	1,766	—	—	6,412
12/07	1,570	—	—	6,232
12/06	1,420	—	—	5,484
12/05	1,410	—	—	5,171
12/04	1,620	—	—	7,827
Annual Growth	2.2%	—	—	(4.9%)

Revenue History

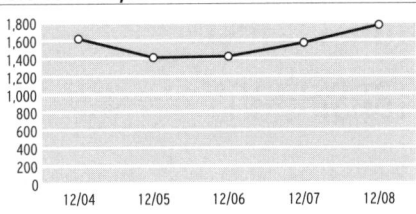

TPG Capital

Yee-haw! Let's round us up some LBOs! TPG Capital, also known as Texas Pacific Group, has staked its claim on the buyout frontier. The firm, which does not get involved in the day-to-day operations of its portfolio companies, usually holds onto its investments for at least five years, although consistent moneymakers may be kept indefinitely. It is not picky about the industries in which it invests. Acting in concert with other private equity firms, TPG has stakes in notable enterprises such as Avaya, Biomet, Energy Future Holdings, Freescale Semiconductor, Metro-Goldwyn-Mayer, Neiman Marcus, Sabre Holdings, SunGard Data Systems, Univision, and Aleris International.

Boasting more than $45 billion of capital under management, TPG is considering raising as little as a relatively meager $1 billion for its latest fund, to the dismay of some investors. (TPG amassed some $14 billion for a Texas-sized buyout fund in 2006.) Co-founder and partner David "Bondo" Bonderman, known for turning around Continental Airlines, has traditionally adhered to the "bigger is better" model of investing, but TPG believes that the market for massive deals is becoming oversaturated and that midsized firms are ripe for the picking.

However, the company isn't exactly walking the talk just yet. Working with Apollo Management and Northwest Airlines, respectively, TPG closed an approximately $28 billion purchase of Harrah's Entertainment and acquired Midwest Air Group for some $450 million in early 2008; TPG sold Midwest to Republic Airways for $31 million the following year.

TPG hasn't gone through the economic downturn unscathed, either. In 2008 the firm lost some $1.3 billion when Washington Mutual failed; TPG was part of an investor group that had given WaMu a $7 billion capital infusion but it wasn't enough to prevent the thrift's collapse. Early the following year, TPG suffered another loss when debt-ridden portfolio company Aleris International filed for Chapter 11 bankruptcy

protection. The aluminum sheet maker had been hit with a drop in product demand, compounded by a lack of liquidity and the global credit crisis.

With KKR, the company bought electric company TXU (now Energy Future Holdings) in 2007 for some $45 billion, including debt, in one of the largest buyouts in history. Also that year TPG joined with GS Capital Partners to buy telecommunications giant ALLTEL for nearly $25 billion. (The investment firms are seeing a rapid return on the investment: They are selling ALLTEL to Verizon Wireless for $28.1 billion.) Also, with Silver Lake Partners, TPG acquired telecom equipment maker Avaya for more than $8 billion.

TPG's European investments include UK retailer Debenhams (with CVC Capital Partners) and German bathroom fixtures manufacturer Grohe. TPG sold luxury brand Bally International to LABELUX in 2008. Newbridge, a joint venture with Blum Capital Partners before TPG bought full control, took a 17% share of China-based Shenzhen Development Bank in a landmark foreign investment in mainland China. A deal to sell the stake to Ping An Insurance is under review; if approved, TPG will gain some $1.35 billion from the investment.

TPG's venture capital affiliate, TPG Growth, specializes in telecommunications and technology companies.

EXECUTIVES

Founding Partner: David Bonderman, age 66
Founding Partner: James G. (Jim) Coulter, age 49
Senior Partner and Chief Investment Officer:
 Jonathan J. Coslet
Partner, Operations: Richard W. (Dick) Boyce, age 55
Partner and CFO: John E. Viola
Partner and Managing Director, TPG Growth:
 Sing Wang
Partner, European Portfolio Companies:
 Vincenzo Morelli, age 54
Parnter and Managing Director, Europe:
 Philippe Costeletos, age 42
Partner and General Counsel: Clive Bode
Partner, Investor Relations: Jamie Gates
Partner and Managing Director, TPG Japan:
 Jun Tsusaka
Partner, Greater China, Eurasia, India and SE Asia:
 Stephen Peel
Partner and Managing Director, China: Mary X.H. Ma,
 age 56
**Senior Adviser, Global Investment Strategies,
 Technology Sector:** Kevin B. Rollins, age 56
Senior Advisor, Health Care Sector:
 Leonard D. Schaeffer, age 63

LOCATIONS

HQ: TPG Capital, L.P.
 301 Commerce St., Ste. 3300
 Fort Worth, TX 76102
Phone: 817-871-4000   **Fax:** 817-871-4001
Web: www.texaspacificgroup.com

COMPETITORS

AEA Investors
Apollo Advisors
Bain Capital
Berkshire Hathaway
Blackstone Group
The Carlyle Group
CD&R
Haas Wheat
HM Capital Partners
KKR
Silver Lake Partners
Thomas H. Lee Partners

Transammonia, Inc.

Fertilizers, liquefied petroleum gas (LPG), and petrochemicals form the lifeblood of international trader Transammonia. The company trades, distributes, and transports these commodities around the world. Transammonia's fertilizer business includes ammonia, phosphates, and urea. Its Sea-3 subsidiary imports and distributes propane to residential, commercial, and industrial customers in the northeastern US and Florida. The Trammochem unit trades in petrochemicals, specializing in aromatics, methanol, methyltertiary butyl ether (MTBE), and olefins. Trammo Petroleum trades oil products including gasoline, heating oil, jet fuel, and naphtha. Formed in 1965, Transammonia is owned by founder Ronald Stanton.

Transammonia was founded in 1965 as an international ammonia trader. It branched into fertilizer merchandising and trading in 1967, LPG trading in 1978, and petrochemicals trading in 1987.

EXECUTIVES

Chairman and CEO: Ronald P. Stanton
CIO: Benjamin Tan
SVP and CFO: Edward G. Weiner
Director Human Resources: Marguerite Harrington

LOCATIONS

HQ: Transammonia, Inc.
320 Park Ave., New York, NY 10022
Phone: 212-223-3200 **Fax:** 212-759-1410
Web: www.transammonia.com

PRODUCTS/OPERATIONS

Major Subsidiaries
Sea-3 (liquefied propane)
Trammo Gas (LPG)
Trammo Petroleum (crude oil and oil products)
Trammochem (petrochemicals)
Transammonia (fertilizers)

COMPETITORS

Cargill
CF Industries
ConAgra
Dynegy
HELM
Magellan Midstream
Terra Industries
Yara

HISTORICAL FINANCIALS

Company Type: Private

Income Statement				FYE: December 31
	REVENUE ($ mil.)	NET INCOME ($ mil.)	NET PROFIT MARGIN	EMPLOYEES
12/08	11,200	—	—	380
12/07	8,339	—	—	330
12/06	5,430	—	—	347
12/05	6,059	—	—	301
12/04	5,340	—	—	296
Annual Growth	20.3%	—	—	6.4%

Revenue History

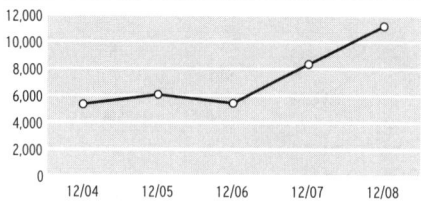

TransPerfect Translations

You pick the language, or languages, and TransPerfect Translations International will aim to get your message through. In addition to translation and interpretation, the company offers services such as document management, multicultural marketing, staffing, subtitling, and voice-over work. Its network of translators can handle more than 100 languages. TransPerfect does much of its work for law firms and corporate legal departments; it also draws customers from industries such as advertising, financial services, information technology, and retail. Clients have included American Express, Credit Suisse, Exxon Mobil, and Jones Day. TransPerfect was founded in 1992.

TransPerfect acquired Overtaal, a Dutch translation and language training company, in mid-2008, expanding the company's European operations. Later that year, TransPerfect bought Milwaukee-based Iverson Language Associates, a technical translation services company, and India-based Quagnito Solutions, a localization and content management company. Expanding its footprint globally, TransPerfect also opened new office locations in Arizona, Berlin, Dubai, Milan, and Prague.

EXECUTIVES

Co-CEO: Phil Shawe
Co-CEO: Elizabeth (Liz) Elting, age 43
COO: Roy B. Trujillo
CIO: Yu-Kai Ng
CTO: Mark Hagerty
SVP Global Sales: A. Brooke Christian
VP Global Production: Mark Peeler
VP Sales, US: Kevin Obarski
VP Legal Technology: Jordan Ellington
VP Corporate Strategy: Michael Sank
VP European Operations: Angela O'Sullivan
VP Quality Systems; President, Crimson Life Sciences Division: Marc H. Miller
President, TransPerfect Deposition Services: Stewart I. Edison
President, TransPerfect Document Management: Steven R. Kaplan
Communications Manager: Jacquelyn Lane

LOCATIONS

HQ: TransPerfect Translations International, Inc.
3 Park Ave., 39th Fl., New York, NY 10016
Phone: 212-689-5555 **Fax:** 212-689-1059
Web: www.transperfect.com

PRODUCTS/OPERATIONS

Selected Services
Brand research
Court reporting
Document management
Graphic services
Interpretation
Linguistic validation
Multilingual typesetting
Multicultural marketing
Software localization
Staffing
Subtitling
Technical writing
Translation
Virtual data rooms
Voice-overs
Web site globalization

COMPETITORS

Albors & Associates
ALT Services
Eclipse Translations
JLS Language Corporation
Linguistic Systems
Lionbridge

HISTORICAL FINANCIALS

Company Type: Private

Income Statement				FYE: December 31
	REVENUE ($ mil.)	NET INCOME ($ mil.)	NET PROFIT MARGIN	EMPLOYEES
12/08	205	—	—	1,100
12/07	156	—	—	800
12/06	113	—	—	600
12/05	100	—	—	500
12/04	50	—	—	250
Annual Growth	42.3%	—	—	44.8%

Revenue History

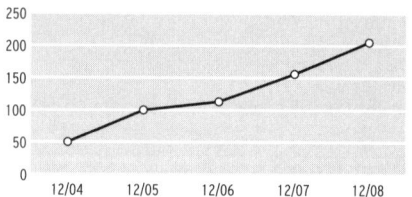

TransUnion LLC

TransUnion makes sure those past-due student loan bills follow you across the country. The firm is one of the three major consumer credit reporting agencies (the others are Experian and Equifax) that lenders use to help determine a borrower's creditworthiness. Combining technology with analysis, the company combats fraud and facilitates credit transactions between businesses and consumers by maintaining credit histories of more than 500 million people in about 30 countries. TransUnion also provides risk management services, insurance credit information, and real estate information services. Subsidiary TransUnion Interactive helps consumers protect and improve their credit ratings via its TrueCredit.com site.

The company provides services for industries including banking, real estate, health care, retail, insurance, automotive, collections, communications, and tenant screening. Clients use TransUnion to collect overdue payments, check credit histories, and make overall business decisions. For example, TransUnion gives landlords access to screening tools in order to assess a prospective tenant's credit history.

The company is aggressively building upon and expanding its international footprint, especially in Asia and Africa. In 2008 TransUnion sharpened its focus on Asia by teaming with D&B to form D&B TransUnion Analytic and Decision Centre. The deal combined D&B's business information and insight with TransUnion's technical expertise and resources in the region. The joint venture offers data-driven consulting services, risk management, analytics and scoring, and fraud and identity management for the credit industry throughout the Asia/Pacific region.

TransUnion already has a foothold in Asia, as it is the technology provider and shareholder of Credit Information Bureau India Limited (CIBIL), India's first credit reporting company. Together, TransUnion and CIBIL launched a new credit scoring model for individual borrowers in 2007.

Previously a member of the Pritzker family-owned Marmon Group since 1981, TransUnion was spun off in 2005. Its new parent company, TransUnion Corp., is also owned by the Pritzkers. The spinoff followed a series of squabbles over the Pritzker family fortune. TransUnion was founded in 1968 by the Union Tank Car Company, a railcar leasing operation.

EXECUTIVES

President and CEO: Siddharth N. (Bobby) Mehta, age 49
CFO: S. Allen Hamood
EVP Global Analytics and Decisioning:
 Wilbert P. Noronha
EVP and CIO: Peter Hoversten
EVP Human Resources: Mary Krupka
VP Corporate Affairs and Consumer Education:
 Colleen Ryan
President, Consumer Services: Mark Marinko
President, U.S. Information Services:
 Jeffrey (Jeff) Hellinga
President, International: Andrew Knight
Leader Healthcare Vertical, U.S. Information Services:
 Milton G. Silva-Craig, age 41
Corporate General Counsel: John W. Blenke
Senior Director Corporate Communications:
 Clifton M. O'Neal

LOCATIONS

HQ: TransUnion LLC
 555 W. Adams St., Chicago, IL 60661
Phone: 312-258-1717   **Fax:** 312-466-8385
Web: www.transunion.com

PRODUCTS/OPERATIONS

Selected Services

Business
 Collections
 Credit reporting
 Fraud and identity management
 Marketing
 Rental screening
 Risk management
Consumer
 Credit dispute investigation
 Credit monitoring
 Credit reports
 Fraud and identity theft

COMPETITORS

Equifax
Experian Americas
Kroll Factual Data
Moody's

HISTORICAL FINANCIALS

Company Type: Private

Income Statement

FYE: December 31

	REVENUE ($ mil.)	NET INCOME ($ mil.)	NET PROFIT MARGIN	EMPLOYEES
12/07	1,200	—	—	4,000
12/06	1,200	—	—	4,100
12/05	1,140	—	—	4,100
12/04	1,000	—	—	4,000
Annual Growth	**6.3%**	**—**	**—**	**0.0%**

Revenue History

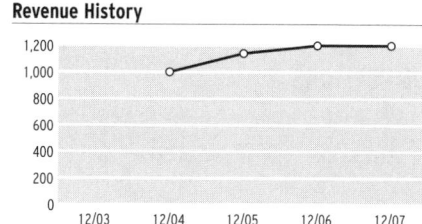

Travelport Limited

Travelport will find you a safe port in the perilous seas of travel services. The company's global distribution system (GDS) segment consists of computerized reservation systems providers Worldspan and Galileo, and Gullivers Travel Associates, a wholesale distribution business for travel agents. Its GDS segment operates in 160 countries, providing services to more than 950 travel suppliers and 60,000 travel agencies. Through Travelport's network, the agencies can access about 430 airlines, 280 hotel chains, 25 car rental companies, 400 cruise lines and tour operators, and 15 rail networks. Travelport also owns a 48% stake in Orbitz Worldwide, an online travel services provider.

Former parent Cendant (now Avis Budget Group) assembled its travel services businesses under the Travelport banner, then sold the company to private equity firm The Blackstone Group for $4.3 billion.

The financial clout that Blackstone carries has helped Travelport expand its operations and made it easier for the company to act on investment opportunities. At the same time, however, Blackstone has been moving to cut costs in the company's operations, and about 10% of Travelport's workforce has been laid off since Blackstone bought the company.

As part of an effort to gain market share, Travelport acquired reservation firm Worldspan for $1.4 billion in August 2007. The deal was viewed as a major step toward consolidation in the reservation systems industry, because Worldspan was a major competitor of Travelport's own Galileo unit. The deal greatly enhanced both companies' product offerings and significantly

expanded their customer base. Shortly after the acquisition, Travelport integrated all its travel reservations businesses underneath the "Travelport GDS" umbrella; it also appointed a senior management team (taken from the top executives of those businesses) to lead the Travelport GDS business.

Travelport is looking to the Middle East, Asia/Pacific and Eastern Europe regions for growth, opening new offices and beefing up distributor relationships and agreements in those areas. Travelport raised cash in 2007 with an IPO of a minority stake in Orbitz. Proceeds were used to pay down debt.

EXECUTIVES

Chairman: Paul C. (Chip) Schorr IV, age 41
President, CEO, and Director: Jeff Clarke, age 47, $5,438,336 total compensation
Deputy CEO: Gordon A. Wilson, age 43, $1,594,147 total compensation
EVP, Chief Administrative, Compliance, and Ethics Officer, and General Counsel: Eric J. Bock, age 43, $1,617,488 total compensation
EVP and CFO: Philip Emery, age 45
EVP Human Resources: Jo-Anne Kruse, age 42
EVP Operations and Chief Re-engineering Officer: Patrick J. (Pat) Bourke III, age 50
Chief Marketing Officer: Jon Hall
SVP and Chief Communications Officer: Elliot Bloom
SVP and Chief Accounting Officer: Simon Gray, age 41
SVP Government Affairs: Dirk Vande Beek
Vice Chairman, Travelport GDS: Bob Coggin
President and CEO, GTA: Kenneth (Ken) Esterow, age 44, $1,466,231 total compensation
President and Managing Director Americas, Travelport GDS: Travis Christ
CEO IT Services & Software, Travelport GDS: Susan J. (Sue) Powers
General Counsel, Travelport GDS: Tad Ostrowski
Director Corporate Communications: Kate Aldridge
Auditors: Deloitte & Touche LLP

LOCATIONS

HQ: Travelport Limited
 Morris Corporate Center III, 400 Interpace Pkwy.
 Bldg. A, Parsippany, NJ 07054
Phone: 973-939-1000   **Fax:** 973-939-1096
Web: www.travelport.com

PRODUCTS/OPERATIONS

2008 Sales

	$ mil.	% of total
Travelport GDS	2,171	86
GTA	356	14
Total	**2,527**	**100**

COMPETITORS

Amadeus IT
American Express
Carlson Wagonlit
Expedia
Holidaybreak
HotelConnect
Hotwire, Inc.
Kuoni Travel
lastminute.com
Pegasus Solutions
Prestige Travel
priceline.com
Sabre Holdings
TravelSky Tech
TUI Travel

HISTORICAL FINANCIALS

Company Type: Private

Income Statement

FYE: December 31

	REVENUE ($ mil.)	NET INCOME ($ mil.)	NET PROFIT MARGIN	EMPLOYEES
12/08	2,527	(179)	—	5,500
12/07	2,780	(436)	—	6,100
12/06	2,550	(2,327)	—	8,000
Annual Growth	(0.5%)	—	—	(17.1%)

Net Income History

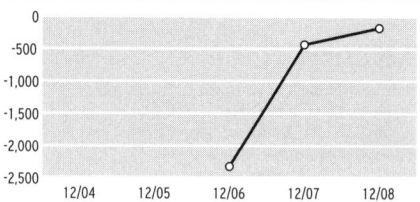

Tree Top

Tree Top stands tall in the nation's apple juice market. The cooperative's approximately 1,400 members grow and harvest about 450,000 tons of apples each year to make apple juice and cider. The co-op produces the Tree Top brand of apple juice, blended fruit juices, and applesauce. It also produces dehydrated, and frozen fruit products for food manufacturers worldwide through its ingredient unit. Tree Top customers include retailers and distributors in 30 states. The cooperative operates five production facilities (four in the state of Washington and one in southern California).

Tree Top's apple juice and cider account for the majority of its sales. The company has focused on growing markets by introducing new product lines including blended juices and flavored applesauce, bagged fresh apple slices and trim, a low-cal fortified fruit drink.

The company faces stiff competition from such beverage giants Coca-Cola, PepsiCo, and Dr Pepper Snapple Group, which continually unveil new juices and other noncarbonated beverage products.

Tree Top produces and sells a wide variety of bulk dried, chilled, frozen apple, and frozen cherry products as ingredients and are used by food manufacturers in such products as baked and frozen desserts, cold and hot cereals, yogurt, fruit fillings, and fruit smoothies.

The company owns Northwest Naturals, a juice concentrate maker for the beverage industry. In 2008 it acquired Sabroso, a maker of fruit purees, dried fruit flakes, and other fruit ingredient preparations.

EXECUTIVES

Chairman: Tom Auvil
President and CEO: Tom Stokes, age 57
SVP Sales and Marketing: Dan Hagerty, age 47
SVP Field Services: Lindsay Buckner, age 57
SVP Ingredient and Foodservice Sales: Tom Hurson
VP Human Resources: Scott Washburn
VP Finance and CFO: John Wells, age 48
VP Operations: Berry Wright, age 60
VP Legal Services: Nancy Smith Buck, age 58
Auditors: Moss Adams, LLP

LOCATIONS

HQ: Tree Top, Inc.
220 E. 2nd Ave., Selah, WA 98942
Phone: 509-697-7251   **Fax:** 509-697-0421
Web: www.treetop.com

PRODUCTS/OPERATIONS

Selected Brands and Products

Consumer products
  Applesauce
  Apple slices
  Cider
  Flat fruit
  Juice
    Orchard blends
    Premium blends
    Tree Top frozen juice concentrate
    Three Apple Reserve
Ingredient Products
  Apple (dried, chilled, frozen, and concentrate)
  Cherry (dried, chilled, frozen, and concentrate)

COMPETITORS

Chiquita Brands	National Beverage
Coca-Cola	National Grape Cooperative
Cranberries Limited	Ocean Spray
Del Monte Foods	Odwalla
Dole Food	Old Orchard
Dominion Citrus	PepsiCo
Hansen Natural	Sun-Rype
Knouse Foods	Tropicana
Mott's	Veryfine
Naked Juice	Welch's

Tri Marine International

Before it's eaten as a salad, casserole, or steak, tuna must first be captured — and that's where Tri Marine International comes in. Operating and selling in countries around the world, Tri Marine was the #1 North American seafood supplier in 2008 (Trident Seafoods was #2). The company is a major supplier of raw albacore, raw light meat (skipjack, yellowfin, bigeye, and bluefin), cooked, and processed tuna. Its operations includes a fleet of some 10 refrigerated cargo ships that sail the Pacific and Indian oceans, as well as both contracted and affiliated fishing boats. It also operates eight processing plants located around globe.

In addition to its tuna-related operations, Tri Marine also supplies squid, mackerel, and sardines. To compliment its fishing and processing operations, the company coordinates marketing, trading, logistics, and international finance activities with its buyers.

EXECUTIVES

Chairman and CEO: Renato Curto
CFO: Steve Farno
Commercial Manager, Value Added Products: Rick Heroux
Commercial Manager, Mexico: Joe Gligo
Commercial Manager, Korea, Philippines, Western and Central Pacific: Joe Hamby
Commercial Manager, Latin America: Peter Trutanich

Commercial Manager, Europe, Kenya, Middle and Near East: Carlo Mango
Commercial Manager, Spain, Portugal, Africa, and Indian Ocean: Alfonso Beitia
Commercial Manager, Thailand, Vietnam, and Maldives: Marco D'Agostini
Commercial Manager, China and Taiwan: Clifford Chen
Commercial Manager, US, American Samoa, and New Zealand: Anthony Vuoso

LOCATIONS

HQ: Tri Marine International, Inc.
10500 N.E. 8th St., Ste. 1888, Bellevue, WA 98004
Phone: 425-688-1288   **Fax:** 425-688-1388
Web: www.trimarinegroup.com

COMPETITORS

Bumble Bee Foods	Peter Pan Seafoods
Chicken of the Sea	Princes Limited
Fishhawk Fisheries	Qualy-Pak Specialty Foods
Kyokuyo	Red Chamber Co.
Maruha Nichiro	S.K. Foods
Nippon Suisan	StarKist
Ocean Beauty Seafoods	Trident Seafoods
Pacific Seafood Group	

HISTORICAL FINANCIALS

Company Type: Private

Income Statement

FYE: December 31

	REVENUE ($ mil.)	NET INCOME ($ mil.)	NET PROFIT MARGIN	EMPLOYEES
12/08	1,150	—	—	—
12/07	925	—	—	—
Annual Growth	24.3%	—	—	—

Revenue History

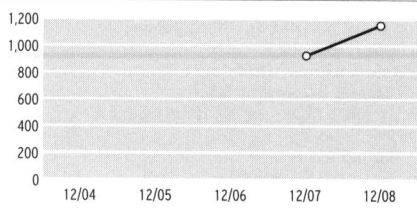

Trinity Capital

Trinity Capital is the holding company for Los Alamos National Bank, which operates four offices in Los Alamos, Santa Fe, and White Rock, New Mexico. A loan office is located in Albuquerque and the company plans to grow in that market. The bank was founded in 1963 to serve the scientific community that developed in the area as a result of the development of the atomic bomb. It offers a range of standard deposit and lending services. Real estate loans, including commercial mortgages, residential mortgages, and construction loans make up more than 80% of the company's loan portfolio. Trinity Capital also has divisions that offer financial advice, mutual funds, title insurance, and real estate appraisal services.

EXECUTIVES

Chairman: Robert P. Worcester, age 62
Vice Chairman: Stanley D. Primak, age 58
CFO; VP and CFO, Los Alamos National Bank:
Daniel R. Bartholomew, age 43
President, CEO, and Director; Chairman and CEO, Los Alamos National Bank and Trinity Guaranty:
William C. Enloe, age 60
Secretary and Director; President and Chief Administrative Officer, Los Alamos National Bank:
Steve W. Wells, age 53
Auditors: Moss Adams, LLP

LOCATIONS

HQ: Trinity Capital Corporation
1200 Trinity Dr., Los Alamos, NM 87544
Phone: 505-662-5171   **Fax:** 505-662-0329
Web: www.lanb.com

PRODUCTS/OPERATIONS

2008 Sales

	$ mil.	% of total
Interest		
Loans, including fees	78.7	82
Investment securities	2.9	3
Other	1.6	2
Noninterest		
Loan & other fees	2.6	3
Mortgage servicing fees	2.5	3
Gain on sale of loans	2.0	2
Service charges on deposits	1.7	2
Trust fees	1.1	1
Other	1.6	2
Total	**94.7**	**100**

COMPETITORS

Bank of America
BOK Financial
First State Bancorporation

HISTORICAL FINANCIALS

Company Type: Private

Income Statement   FYE: December 31

	ASSETS ($ mil.)	NET INCOME ($ mil.)	INCOME AS % OF ASSETS	EMPLOYEES
12/08	1,418	8	0.6%	269
12/07	1,380	13	1.0%	271
12/06	1,359	10	0.8%	269
12/05	1,244	12	1.0%	260
12/04	1,080	10	1.0%	271
Annual Growth	7.0%	(6.3%)	—	(0.2%)

2008 Year-End Financials

Equity as % of assets: —   Long-term debt ($ mil.): 26
Return on assets: 0.6%   Sales ($ mil.): 95
Return on equity: —

Net Income History

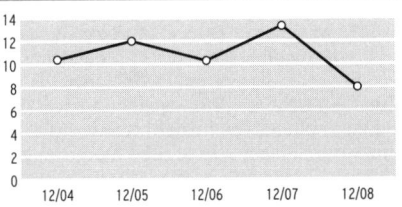

Trinity Health

One of the largest Catholic health care systems in the US, Trinity Health runs about 45 hospitals and has nearly 400 outpatient facilities, as well as nursing homes, senior living facilities, home health agencies, and hospice programs. Of the hospitals, it owns more than 30 and manages about a dozen for third parties. Its Trinity Senior Living Communities subsidiary operates nearly 35 long-term care facilities for seniors, and its Trinity Health International unit provides consulting, training, and other assistance to hospitals worldwide. Trinity Health has facilities in seven mostly midwestern states. Catholic Health Ministries sponsors the organization.

The organization's facilities in Iowa (Mercy Health Network) are a joint venture between Trinity Health and Catholic Health Initiatives.

In 2007 Trinity Health sold its stake in Michigan's St. Joseph's Healthcare (located in Clinton Township) to its joint-venture partner in the enterprise, Henry Ford Health System.

Trinity Health is really more of a duo than a trio: The not-for-profit company is the result of a coupling between Mercy Health Services and Holy Cross Health System.

EXECUTIVES

Chairman: Patrick G. Hays, age 66
Vice Chairman: Lawrence D. (Larry) Damron, age 62
President, CEO, and Director: Joseph R. Swedish
EVP and Chief Administrator Officer:
Debra A. (Deb) Canales
EVP and Chief Clinical Officer:
P. Terrence (Terry) O'Rourke
EVP Trinity Institute of Health and Community Benefit: Daniel G. (Dan) Hale
SVP; Chief Development Officer and Interim CFO:
Mary D. Szymanski
SVP Patient Care Services and Chief Nursing Officer:
Gay Landstrom
SVP Clinical Quality and Patient Safety: Paul F Conlon
SVP Information Services and Program Management:
Paul Browne
SVP Supply Chain and Capital Projects Management:
Louis J. (Lou) Fierens II
SVP Governance and Sponsorship:
Sister Catherine DeClercq
SVP, Treasurer, and Chief Investment Officer:
James W. Bosscher
VP Corporate Communications and Public Relations:
Stephen M. Shivinsky
Auditors: Deloitte & Touche LLP

LOCATIONS

HQ: Trinity Health
27870 Cabot Dr., Novi, MI 48377
Phone: 248-489-5004   **Fax:** 248-489-6039
Web: www.trinity-health.org

Selected Operations

California
Saint Agnes Medical Center (Fresno)
Idaho
Saint Alphonsus Regional Medical Center (Boise)
Indiana
Saint Joseph Regional Medical Center (South Bend)
Iowa
Mercy Health Network (Des Moines)
Maryland
Holy Cross Hospital (Silver Spring)

Michigan
Battle Creek Health System
Mercy General Health Partners (Muskegon)
Mercy Hospital (Cadillac)
Mercy Hospital (Grayling)
Mercy Hospital (Port Huron)
Saint Mary's Health Care (Grand Rapids)
Saint Joseph Mercy Health System (Ann Arbor)
St. Joseph Mercy Oakland (Pontiac)
St. Mary Mercy Hospital (Livonia)
Trinity Health International (Farmington Hills)
Ohio
Mount Carmel Health System (Columbus)

COMPETITORS

Amedisys
Ascension Health
Detroit Medical Center
HCA
Henry Ford Health System
Hospice of Michigan
Johns Hopkins Medicine
Mayo Foundation
MedStar Health
Memorial Hospital & Health System
Odyssey HealthCare
OhioHealth
St. Luke's Health System
VITAS Healthcare
William Beaumont Hospital

HISTORICAL FINANCIALS

Company Type: Not-for-profit

Income Statement   FYE: June 30

	REVENUE ($ mil.)	NET INCOME ($ mil.)	NET PROFIT MARGIN	EMPLOYEES
6/08	6,300	—	—	44,500
6/07	6,110	—	—	44,000
6/06	6,050	—	—	45,800
6/05	5,715	—	—	44,950
6/04	5,287	—	—	44,100
Annual Growth	4.5%	—	—	0.2%

Revenue History

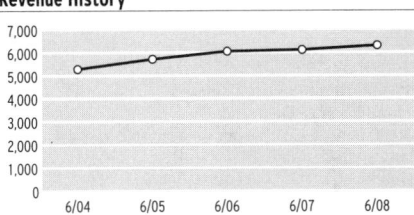

Tri-State Generation and Transmission

OK, so it covers four states, but who's counting? Tri-State Generation and Transmission Association supplies wholesale electricity to 44 rural distribution utilities that serve more than 1.4 million customers (more than 592,920 meters) in Colorado, Nebraska, New Mexico, and Wyoming (New Mexico was a late addition to the association's service region). The member-owned cooperative has a generating capacity of 3,536 MW from its interests in fossil-fueled power plants, and it operates 5,200 miles of transmission lines. Tri-State Generation and Transmission also purchases power and sells its excess supply to other utilities.

In 2009, as part of its push to develop green energy sources to cut carbon emissions, the company teamed up with First Solar, Inc., agreeing to develop a 30 MW solar power plant in northeastern New Mexico. The project is the largest photovoltaic project undertaken by an electric cooperative.

Tri-State Generation and Transmission was formed in 1952 by its member cooperatives and public power districts. It entered New Mexico through its 2000 acquisition of Plains Electric Generation and Transmission Cooperative.

EXECUTIVES

Chairman: Harold (Hub) Thompson
Vice Chairman: Rick Gordon
EVP and General Manager: J. M. Shafer
SVP and CFO: Charles L. (Chuck) Yetzbacher
SVP, Corporate Services: Mike McInnes
SVP, Generation and Power Management: Ken Anderson
SVP, External Affairs and Member Relations:
  Robert (Mac) McLennan
SVP, Transmission: Joel Bladow
SVP, General Counsel: Ken Reif
Corporate Secretary: Gerald Lorenz
Treasurer: Jerry Underwood
Auditors: Ernst & Young LLP

LOCATIONS

HQ: Tri-State Generation and
  Transmission Association, Inc.
  1100 W. 116th Ave., Westminster, CO 80234
Phone: 303-452-6111   **Fax:** 303-254-6007
Web: www.tristategt.org

PRODUCTS/OPERATIONS

2008 Sales

	% of total
Members	73
Non-members	24
Other	3
Total	**100**

Member Systems

Big Horn Rural Electric Company
Carbon Power & Light, Inc.
Central New Mexico Electric Cooperative, Inc.
Chimney Rock Public Power District
Columbus Electric Cooperative, Inc.
Continental Divide Electric Cooperative, Inc.
Delta-Montrose Electric Association
Empire Electric Association, Inc.
Garland Light & Power Company
Gunnison County Electric Association, Inc.
High Plains Power, Inc.
High West Energy, Inc.
Highline Electric Association
Jemez Mountains Electric Cooperative, Inc.
K.C. Electric Association, Inc.
Kit Carson Electric Cooperative, Inc.
La Plata Electric Association, Inc.
Midwest Electric Cooperative Corporation
Mora-San Miguel Electric Cooperative Corporation
Morgan County Rural Electric Association
Mountain Parks Electric, Inc.
Mountain View Electric Association, Inc.
Niobrara Electric Association, Inc.
Northern Rio Arriba Electric Cooperative, Inc.
Northwest Rural Public Power District
Otero County Electric Cooperative, Inc.
Panhandle Rural Electric Membership Association
Poudre Valley Rural Electric Association, Inc.
Roosevelt Public Power District
San Isabel Electric Association, Inc.
San Luis Valley Rural Electric Cooperative, Inc.
San Miguel Power Association, Inc.
Sangre De Cristo Electric Association, Inc.
Sierra Electric Cooperative, Inc.
Socorro Electric Cooperative, Inc.
Southeast Colorado Power Association
Southwestern Electric Cooperative, Inc.
Springer Electric Cooperative, Inc.
United Power, Inc.

Wheat Belt Public Power District
Wheatland Rural Electric Association, Inc.
White River Electric Association, Inc.
Wyrulec Company
Y-W Electric Association, Inc.

COMPETITORS

Basin Electric Power
El Paso Electric
Nebraska Public Power
Omaha Public Power
PNM Resources
Xcel Energy

HISTORICAL FINANCIALS

Company Type: Cooperative

Income Statement				FYE: December 31
	REVENUE ($ mil.)	NET INCOME ($ mil.)	NET PROFIT MARGIN	EMPLOYEES
12/08	1,060	—	—	2,477

True Value

To survive against home improvement giants such as The Home Depot and Lowe's, True Value (formerly TruServ) is relying on the true value of service. Formed by the merger of Cotter & Company (which was the supplier to the True Value chain) and ServiStar Coast to Coast, the retailer-owned hardware cooperative serves some 5,400 retail outlets (down from nearly 7,200 in 2001), including its flagship True Value hardware stores. The co-op sells home improvement and garden supplies, as well as appliances, housewares, sporting goods, and toys. Members use the Taylor Rental, Grand Rental Station, Home & Garden Showplace, Induserve Supply, and other banners. True Value also manufactures its own brand of paints.

The merger of Cotter & Company and ServiStar Coast to Coast (operator of Coast to Coast and ServiStar hardware stores, most of which converted to the True Value banner) gave members — many of them mom-and-pop outlets — more buying clout to compete against the do-it-yourself mega-retailers, plus retail advice and advertising support. True Value has been growing its business in the rental and maintenance, repair, and operation (MRO) arenas, and has resumed supplying lumber and building materials. (The company sold its lumber and building materials business in 2000.) At the store level, True Value has been developing "lite" or smaller versions of its signature programs, such as Platinum Paint Shop, for the co-op's stores (more than half) that are less than 6,000 sq. ft.

True Value's smaller in-town locations have taken a beating at the hands of the big-box hardware chains, as is reflected in the steep decline in store count over the past decade. But rising gas prices, shoppers' ambivalence toward the big-box shopping experience, and improvements in True Value's retail operation may bode well for the co-op's future. Indeed, 2008 marked the first time in over a decade where revenue from new stores exceeded lost revenue from terminated stores. The company credits its new Destination True Value

(DTV) format for the turnaround. The flexible format features a "racetrack" layout for convenient shopping and allows owners to customize their stores to the local market. It is slated to be rolled out to another 100 retail stores in 2009.

Outside the US the company serves about 700 stores in more than 50 countries.

HISTORY

Noting that hardware retailers had begun to form wholesale cooperatives to lower costs, John Cotter, a traveling hardware salesman, and associate Ed Lanctot started pitching the wholesale co-op idea in 1947 to small-town and suburban hardware retailers, and by early 1948 they had enrolled 25 merchants for $1,500 each. Cotter became chairman of the new firm, Cotter & Company.

The co-op created the Value & Service (V&S) store trademark in 1951 to emphasize the advantages of an independent hardware store. Acquisitions included the 1963 purchase of Chicago-based wholesaler Hibbard, Spencer, Bartlett, giving Cotter 400 new members and the well-known True Value trademark, which soon replaced V&S signs. Four years later Cotter broadened its focus by buying the General Paint & Chemical Company (Tru-Test paint). The V&S name was revived in 1972 for a five-and-dime store co-op, V&S Variety Stores.

In 1989 Cotter died and Lanctot retired. (Lanctot died in October 2003.) By 1989 there were almost 7,000 True Value Stores. Cotter moved into Canada in 1992 by acquiring hardware distributor and store operator Macleod-Stedman (275 outlets).

Juggling variety-store and hardware merchandise and delivering very small amounts of merchandise to a lukewarm co-op membership did not allow for economies of scale, so in 1995 the company quit its manufacturing operations and its US variety stores.

Two years later Cotter formed TruServ by merging with hardware wholesaler ServiStar Coast to Coast. ServiStar had its origins in the nation's first hardware co-op, American Hardware Supply, which was founded in Pittsburgh in 1910 by M. R. Porter, John Howe, and E. S. Corlett. By 1988, the year it changed its name to ServiStar, the co-op topped $1 billion in sales.

ServiStar expanded in the upper Midwest and on the West Coast in 1990 when it acquired the assets of the Coast to Coast chain (founded in 1928 as a franchise hardware store in Minneapolis). Merging its 1992 acquisition of Taylor Rental Center with its Grand Rental Station stores in 1993 made ServiStar the #1 general rental chain.

President Don Hoye became CEO of the company in 1999. That year TruServ slashed 1,000 jobs and declared it would convert all its hardware store chains to the True Value banner. But TruServ lost $131 million in 1999 over bookkeeping gaffes, and co-op members received no dividends. Of 2,800 ServiStar dealers, only 1,900 raised the True Value flag. Others either declined to switch or were never offered the change because other True Value stores already shared their market area. In addition, stores began deserting the co-op because of inventory and other problems.

As competition continued to increase in 2001, the company was facing falling sales, lawsuits from shareholders, and accusations by retailers of unfair practices intended to pressure them into adopting the cooperative's flagship True Value banner. TruServ also had to confront a $200 million loan default. It made cuts in its corporate staff and divested its Canadian interests. In July 2001 Hoye resigned. The company's CFO and COO, Pamela Forbes Lieberman, was named the new CEO that November.

TruServ, under SEC investigation for alleged inventory, accounting, and other internal-control problems, was one of several companies that failed in 2002 to meet a government requirement to swear by their past financial results. In March 2003 TruServ settled the SEC's allegations, without admitting or denying them.

Lieberman resigned in November 2004. Director Thomas Hanemann was named interim CEO. TruServ changed its name to True Value in January 2005. In June 2005 Hanemann turned over the reins to Sears veteran Lyle Heidemann, who joined True Value as its new president and CEO. In December 2005 the company sold its oil-based paint manufacturing operation in Chicago to Blackhawk/Halsted for about $10 million.

In 2007 True Value added more than 100 new stores in the US and experienced modest growth overseas. Also in 2007 the company launched its new store format, called Destination TrueValue.

The year 2008 marked the first time in over a decade where revenue from new stores exceeded lost revenue from terminated stores.

EXECUTIVES

Chairman; CEO, Krueger's True Value, Neenah, WI: Brian A. Webb
President, CEO, and Director: Lyle G. Heidemann, age 64
SVP and Chief Merchandising Officer: Michael Clark
SVP and CFO: David A. (Dave) Shadduck
SVP and CIO: Leslie A. Weber
SVP Human Resources, General Counsel, and Secretary: Cathy C. Anderson
SVP Logistics and Supply Chain Management: Stephen Poplawski
VP Retail Growth: Mark Flowers
VP and Controller: Donald J. (Don) Deegan
VP and Corporate Treasurer: Barbara L. Wagner
VP Retail and Specialty Businesses Development: Fred L. Kirst, age 55
VP Marketing: Carol Wentworth, age 49
VP Retail Finance: Jon Johnson
Director; CEO, Campbell's True Value, Madison, ME: Brent A. Burger
Director; CEO, Shively True Value Hardware, Saratoga, WY: Michael S. Glode, age 58
Director; CEO, True Value Hardware House, Annapolis, MD: Kenneth A. Niefeld, age 65
Director; CEO, Welch's True Value Hardware, South Royalton, VT: Charles M. Welch, age 57
Auditors: PricewaterhouseCoopers LLP

LOCATIONS

HQ: True Value Company
8600 W. Bryn Mawr Ave., Chicago, IL 60631
Phone: 773-695-5000 **Fax:** 773-695-6516
Web: www.truevaluecompany.com

PRODUCTS/OPERATIONS

2008 Sales

	$ mil.	% of total
Hardware	1,932.2	96
Paint manufacturing & distribution	80.5	4
Total	**2,012.7**	**100**

Selected Operations

Grand Rental Station (general rental)
Home & Garden Showplace (nursery and giftware)
Induserve Supply (commercial and industrial)
Party Central (parties and corporate events)
Taylor Rental (general rental)
True Value (hardware)

COMPETITORS

84 Lumber
Ace Hardware
Akzo Nobel
Benjamin Moore
Do it Best
Fastenal
Home Depot
Kmart
Lowe's
McCoy Corp.
Menard
Northern Tool
Orgill
Reno-Depot
Sears
Sherwin-Williams
Stock Building Supply
Sutherland Lumber
United Rentals
Valspar
Wal-Mart

HISTORICAL FINANCIALS

Company Type: Cooperative

Income Statement				FYE: December 31
	REVENUE ($ mil.)	NET INCOME ($ mil.)	NET PROFIT MARGIN	EMPLOYEES
12/08	2,013	64	3.2%	3,000
12/07	2,041	64	3.1%	3,000
12/06	2,050	73	3.6%	3,000
12/05	2,043	48	2.3%	2,800
12/04	2,024	43	2.1%	2,800
Annual Growth	(0.1%)	10.4%	—	1.7%

Net Income History

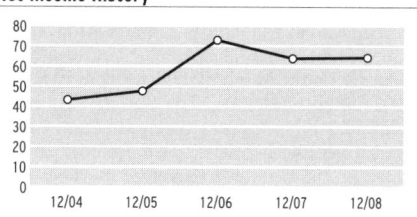

Truman Arnold

It is not jibber jabber — this jobber gets the job done by distributing wholesale petroleum across the US. Truman Arnold Companies (TAC) markets and distributes more than 1 billion gallons of petroleum products a year to customers located in 48 states in the US through its TAC Energy subsidiary. Its TAC Terminals unit operates two major petroleum terminals in Arkansas (with 1.3 million barrels of capacity). Through its TAC Air unit, the company offers fixed-based operations (FBO), including aircraft fueling, hanger, and ground transportation services, through 13 general aviation facilities in the US. The company also operates two Road Runner convenience stores and has interests in real estate and ranching.

TAC's four divisions — Aviation Services, Wholesale Petroleum Marketing, Branded Petroleum Marketing, and Petroleum Terminal Services, operate independently but take advantage of shared management and technical resources.

Aviation Service has been a growth area. The company expanded its FBO business through the acquisition of Cherokee Aviation in 2005. It opened its 12th FBO location in 2007, in Raleigh-Durham, and its 13th in 2009, in the Spirit of St. Louis Airport, in Chesterfield, Missouri.

The family-owned and -operated company was founded in 1964 by Texarkana businessman Truman Arnold. It once operated a chain of 125 Road Runner convenience stores in eight states, before selling this network to Total Petroleum in 1989. TAC revived the brand in 2003.

EXECUTIVES

Chairman: Truman Arnold
President and CEO: Gregory A. (Greg) Arnold
SVP and General Counsel: James (Jim) Day
SVP and CFO: Steve McMillen
VP and CIO: Michael Davis
VP, Aviation Division (TAC Air): Daniel A. (Danny) Walsh
VP, Terminal Services (TAC Energy): Benny Webb
VP, Trading and Supply: Tom Knight
Director, Marketing: Jennifer Green
Director, Human Resources: Denny Peterson

LOCATIONS

HQ: Truman Arnold Companies, Inc.
701 S. Robison Rd., Texarkana, TX 75501
Phone: 903-794-3835 **Fax:** 903-831-4056
Web: www.trumanarnoldcompanies.com

COMPETITORS

Atlantic Aviation
Getty Petroleum Marketing
Gulf Oil
Million Air
Signature Flight
SMF Energy
Sun Coast Resources
Warren Equities

The Trump Organization

The Trump Organization knows all about gilding the lily. Run by flamboyant, modern-day King Midas/media czar Donald Trump, The Trump Organization owns several pieces of high-end real estate in the Big Apple. Properties include Trump International Hotel & Tower, Trump Tower, and 40 Wall Street. It also owns and operates hotels, resorts, residential towers, and golf courses in major US markets and abroad. Trump Organization also has a stake in Trump Entertainment Resorts, which owns and operates the Trump Taj Mahal, Trump Plaza, and Trump Marina casinos in New Jersey's Atlantic City. Together with NBC, Trump additionally owns the Miss USA, Miss Teen USA, and Miss Universe beauty pageants.

The Trump Organization depends heavily on (or succeeds in spite of, depending on your perspective) the fortunes of its founder, Donald Trump. The author of numerous books including *Think Like a Billionaire* and *The Art of the Deal* is renowned for setting up real estate partnerships in which other firms put up most of the cash while he retains most of the control.

He keeps himself in the public eye with the reality television show *The Apprentice*, in which aspiring moguls compete for a spot in his companies, and its *Celebrity Apprentice* spinoff. The Donald even has a signature line: "You're fired!" and a signature move: the cobra — the hand motion he makes when axing a contestant. He has splashed his famous moniker, now trademarked, not just on buildings, but also water, vodka, restaurants, a university, a magazine, and more. Trump's three adult children, Donald Jr., Ivanka, and Eric, have all taken executive roles with the company and are primed to carry on the Trump legacy.

In 2008 The Trump Organization opened the Trump International Hotel & Tower Chicago at the site formerly leased by the *Chicago Sun-Times*. The company originally intended to make it the world's tallest building but those plans were scrapped after the terrorist attacks on New York City's World Trade Center in 2001. The Trump Organization also teamed up with Irongate Capital Partners to build Trump International Hotel & Tower Waikiki in Hawaii, expected to open in 2009.

The company has battled environmental groups opposing the planned development of a $2 billion golf course and resort in Scotland. The proposed project is located within a Site of Special Scientific Interest, an aread designated for protection for natural or geological reasons by the UK government. Trump has received preliminary approval for the development.

In 2009 Trump's casino venture hit more troubles and filed for Chapter 11 bankruptcy. Trump also resigned from its board. Later that same year Trump, along with his daughter, Ivanka, reached a deal with creditors in the bankruptcy and abandoned their bid to regain control of the Atlantic City casinos. Under the deal the casinos will continue to use the Trump name and Trump, himself, could receive up to a 10% stake in the reorganized gaming company.

HISTORY

The third of four children, Donald Trump was the son of a successful builder in Queens and Brooklyn. After graduating from the Wharton School of Finance in 1968, his first job was to turn around a 1,200-unit foreclosed apartment complex in Cincinnati that his father had bought for $6 million with no money down. Managing the Cincinnati job gave Trump a distaste for the nonaffluent; he wanted to get to Manhattan to meet all the right people.

Operating as The Trump Organization, he took options on two Hudson River sites in 1975 for no money down and began lobbying the city to finance his construction of a convention center. The center was built, but not by Trump, who nevertheless got about $800,000 and priceless publicity. He and hotelier Jay Pritzker turned the Commodore Hotel near Grand Central Station into the Grand Hyatt Hotel in 1975.

In 1981 he built the posh Trump Tower on Fifth Avenue and proceeded to wheel and deal himself into 1980s folklore. In 1983 he joined with Holiday Inn to build the Trump Casino Hotel (now Trump Plaza) in Atlantic City using public-issue bonds (he bought out Holiday Inn's interest in 1986), and he bought the Trump Castle from Hilton in 1985. In 1987 he ended up with the unfinished Taj Mahal in Atlantic City, then the world's largest casino, after a battle with Merv Griffin for Resorts International (Griffin won). He bought the Plaza Hotel in Manhattan

in 1988, and the Eastern air shuttle (renamed the Trump Shuttle) the next year.

As the 1990s dawned, though, Trump's balance sheet was loaded with about $3 billion in debt. Trump's 70 creditor banks consolidated and restructured his debt in 1990. In 1995 Trump formed Trump Hotels & Casino Resorts and took it public. He also paid a token $10 for 40 Wall St. (now home to American Express). The next year he sold his half-interest in the Grand Hyatt Hotel to the Pritzker family and unloaded more than $1.1 billion in debt by selling the Taj Mahal and Trump's Castle to Trump Hotels. That year Trump bought the Miss Universe, Miss USA, and Miss Teen USA beauty pageants.

In 1997 he published *The Art of the Comeback*, a follow-up to *The Art of the Deal* (1987), and started work on Trump Place, a residential development on New York's Upper West Side. He teamed with Conseco in 1998 to buy the famed General Motors Building for $800 million. In 1999 he began building the Trump World Tower — a 90-story residential building near the United Nations complex.

The following year Trump and publisher Hollinger International announced plans to transform the former riverfront headquarters of the *Chicago Sun-Times* into a residential and commercial development. Hollinger sold its stake in the venture to Trump in 2004.

In 2002 Trump dumped his stake in the Empire State Building. He was also ordered by the courts — after a lengthy legal battle — to sell his 50% stake in the General Motors Building to co-owner Conseco; the two parties agreed to sell the building. Trump ventured into reality television as the star and executive producer of *The Apprentice* in 2004.

In mid-2005 the Trump Organization and a group of investors sold a parcel of land and three buildings on the Manhattan waterfront to Extell Development Corp. and The Carlyle Group for about $1.8 billion. Later that year The Donald inked a deal with Nakheel, a developer in the United Arab Emirates, to develop resort destinations in the Middle East, including a $600 million high-rise in Dubai's ritzy Palm resort.

EXECUTIVES

Chairman and President: Donald J. Trump, age 62
EVP and COO: Matthew F. Calamari
EVP and CFO: Allen Weisselberg
EVP Development and Acquisitions:
Donald J. Trump Jr.
EVP and General Counsel: Bernard Diamond
EVP Construction: Andrew Weiss
EVP Development and Acquisitions: Eric Trump
EVP and Assistant General Counsel: Jason Greenblatt
EVP Golf Course Development: Vincent Stellio
EVP and COO, Trump National Golf Club: Dan Scavino
EVP Global Licensing: Cathy Hoffman Glosser
SVP and Controller: Jeffrey McConney
VP Strategic Marketing: Selma Langer
VP Media Relations and Human Resources:
Norma Foerderer
VP Real Estate Development and Acquisitions:
Ivanka M. Trump, age 27
VP Development: Jill Cremer
CEO, Trump Entertainment Resort: Mark Juliano, age 54
CEO, Trump Financial: David Brecher
President, Trump University: Michael W. Sexton

LOCATIONS

HQ: The Trump Organization
725 5th Ave., New York, NY 10022
Phone: 212-832-2000 **Fax:** 212-935-0141
Web: www.trump.com

PRODUCTS/OPERATIONS

Selected Holdings
40 Wall Street (The Trump Building, Manhattan)
The Estates at Trump National (Los Angeles)
Mar-A-Lago (private club; Palm Beach, FL)
Miss Teen USA pageant
Miss Universe pageant
Miss USA pageant
Trump International Golf Club West Palm Beach, FL
Trump International Hotel & Tower (Ft. Lauderdale, FL)
Trump International Hotel & Tower Chicago
Trump International Hotel & Tower New York
Trump International Hotel & Tower Colts Neck, NJ
Trump National Golf Club Westchester (NY)
Trump Parc (Manhattan)
Trump Tower at City Center, Westchester (NY)
Trump Towers Atlanta
Trump Towers, Sisli, Istanbul

COMPETITORS

Boston Properties
Brookfield Properties
Diageo
Durst Organization
Helmsley Enterprises
HKR International
Hyatt
Icahn Enterprises
Lefrak Organization
Marriott
Ritz-Carlton
Rockefeller Group International
Starwood Capital
Taconic Investment Partners
Vornado Realty
Witkoff Group

Trustmark Mutual Holding Company

One no longer has to be a brother or a railway employee to benefit from Trustmark Mutual's offerings. Established in 1913 as the Brotherhood of All Railway Employees to provide disability coverage to railroad workers, the company still administers benefits to workers across the US. Now it operates through subsidiaries including Trustmark Group Benefits (group medical, dental, disability, and life insurance for larger employers), Starmark (employee benefits for smaller employers), and CoreSource (customized employee benefits for companies that self-fund). Trustmark Mutual Holding is owned by its policyholders.

Other Trustmark Mutual companies include: Trustmark's Disability Advisors, which offers employers disability claim management services; Trustmark Affinity Markets, which creates customized health insurance programs for associations and affinity organizations; and Trustmark Voluntary Benefit Solutions which provides life, disability, dental, accident, and critical illness coverage to the voluntary benefits market.

Despite its already hefty roster of businesses, the company continues to expand its services through acquisitions. In 2008 Trustmark Mutual acquired Health Contact Partners, which operates a telephone call center for customers seeking health care information.

That same year the company acquired the group health insurance arm of Destiny Health Insurance and brought the division under the Trustmark umbrella. The buy expanded Trustmark Mutual's group insurance offerings in Illinois.

EXECUTIVES

Chairman: J. Grover Thomas Jr.
President and CEO: David M. McDonough
EVP and CFO: J. Brink Marcuccili
EVP Affinity Markets, Trustmark Group Benefits and Starmark: Warren R. Schreier
EVP CoreSource and Voluntary Benefit Solutions: Christopher J. (Chris) Martin
SVP Investments: Jerry Hitpas
SVP: Nancy Eckrich
SVP and General Counsel: Sara Lee Keller
SVP Human Resources and Corporate Communication: Kate Martiné, age 56
SVP The Sentinel Group and Business Development: Julie M. Malida
SVP and COO CoreSource: Paul Lotharius
VP Group Sales, Marketing, and Administration: David J. Meyer
VP and Medical Director: Deborah Y. Smart
VP Internal Audit and Compliance: John Hester, age 43
Second VP Finance: Yasmin Thompson
Second VP Human Resources: Tracy Rhomberg
Second VP Communications: Patton Hollow
President FMH Benefit Services: Ben Frisch, age 39

LOCATIONS

HQ: Trustmark Mutual Holding Company
400 Field Dr., Lake Forest, IL 60045
Phone: 847-615-1500   **Fax:** 847-615-3910
Web: www.trustmarkinsurance.com

COMPETITORS

Aetna
Aflac
Assurant Employee Benefits
Assurant Health
Blue Cross
CIGNA
Citigroup
Humana
Mutual of America
ULLICO
UnitedHealth Group
WellPoint

HISTORICAL FINANCIALS

Company Type: Mutual company

Income Statement

FYE: December 31

	REVENUE ($ mil.)	NET INCOME ($ mil.)	NET PROFIT MARGIN	EMPLOYEES
12/07	983	39	4.0%	2,400
12/06	1,101	111	10.1%	2,152
12/05	1,120	—	—	2,358
12/04	1,160	—	—	—
12/03	1,131	—	—	3,000
Annual Growth	(3.4%)	(64.8%)	—	(5.4%)

Net Income History

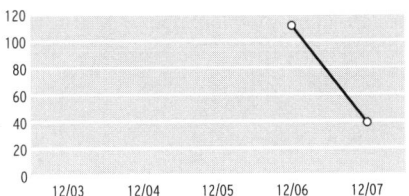

TTX Company

TTX keeps the railroad industry in the US and Canada chugging along by leasing railcars. Railroad operators often opt to lease railcars rather than buy them in order to be more nimble in adjusting to changes in demand. TTX's fleet of more than 210,000 railcars includes three types: intermodal, designed to carry shipping containers; autorack, for vehicles; and general use, for items such as lumber, steel, and farm and construction equipment. Its operations are supported by the Southeastern Repair Division with facilities in Florida and South Carolina. TTX is owned by the largest US and Canadian railroads, which are also the company's main customers.

The company was originally formed in 1955 as Trailer Train by the Pennsylvania Railroad to supply affordable rail freight cars. Eventually, the Department of Transportation's Surface Transportation Board (formerly the Interstate Commerce Commission), the government regulatory agency responsible for rail transportation, sanctioned TTX's current operating structure. That structure allows major railroads to share the ownership and the use of equipment owned by TTX. Although ownership percentages have changed over the years, all owners share the same level of access to equipment and services that TTX offers. The fleet pool-like structure also gives TTX an edge over other rail equipment lessors because its customers are its shareholders. As such, increased profits are not the company's primary goal, and costs can be kept to a minimum.

TTX's equipment department keeps equipment upgraded and maintained through its company-owned repair facilities. The company also offers fleet management and services including purchasing new equipment and parts for repair, maintenance, and modification. Intermodal terminal repair sites are located throughout the US. Its information technology segment allows the company to monitor each car, track its movements, and record the maintenance history for quality control.

EXECUTIVES

President, CEO, and Director: Thomas F. Wells
SVP Law and Administration: Patrick B. Loftus
VP and Chief Information Officer: Bruce G. Schinelli
VP Equipment: Sharon Harmsworth
VP Human Resources and Labor Relations: Brian R. Powers
VP Fleet Management: Patrick J. Casey
VP and CFO: Kathleen M. Savard
Controller: Donald J. Schaffer
Assistant Treasurer: John G. Rainsford
Communications Director: Sara Lorenzo
Assistant General Counsel and Assistant Secretary: Anne E. Treadway
Auditors: KPMG LLP

LOCATIONS

HQ: TTX Company
101 N. Wacker Dr., Chicago, IL 60606
Phone: 312-853-3223   **Fax:** 312-984-3790
Web: www.ttx.com

PRODUCTS/OPERATIONS

Selected Markets Served

Agricultural industry
Automobile industry
Construction industry
Intermodal market
Lumber industry
Military
Steel industry

COMPETITORS

Andersons
CIT Transportation Finance
GATX
Genesee & Wyoming
Greenbrier Companies
Pioneer Railcorp
XTRA Corp.

HISTORICAL FINANCIALS

Company Type: Private

Income Statement

FYE: December 31

	REVENUE ($ mil.)	NET INCOME ($ mil.)	NET PROFIT MARGIN	EMPLOYEES
12/07	1,118	—	—	1,800
12/06	1,156	—	—	1,707
12/05	1,134	—	—	1,670
12/04	1,015	—	—	—
Annual Growth	3.3%	—	—	3.8%

Revenue History

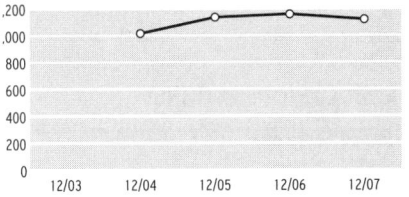

Tube City IMS

Tube City IMS can do just about anything with industrial leftovers. The company provides outsourced raw material procurement and post-production services that help steel mills profit from scrap. A major scrap metal broker, Tube City purchases more than 6 million tons of scrap annually from the likes of U.S. Steel and AK Steel. It also offers a host of pre-production material handling, scrap management, and scrap preparation services. Tube City's post-production services include material and product handling, co-product processing, and metal recovery. It also provides slag handling, metal recovery, and high-speed flame cutting to the steel industry. Canadian investment firm Onex owns Tube City IMS.

Wellspring Capital Management had acquired International Mill Service (IMS) and Tube City LLC in 2004; it then merged them to form Tube City IMS. It filed to take the company public in 2006. Before the public offering went through, however, Onex Corporation came in (allied with company management) to purchase Tube City.

The company operated both Tube City LLC and IMS as separate entities until the beginning of 2008, when the company merged the two units. The move consolidated operations into one unit called Tube City IMS, LLC. Later in 2008 the company acquired UK steel service center Hanson Resource Management. Tube City IMS wants Hanson to assist the company's other European operations.

Tube City, originally known as Tube City Iron & Metal, derives its name from the town of McKeesport, the site of its original plant. McKeesport was nicknamed Tube City because it was home to a large steel tube mill run by U.S. Steel.

EXECUTIVES

Chairman: I. Michael Coslov, age 67
President, CEO, and Director: Joseph Curtin, age 63
COO; President and COO, Mill Services:
Raymond S. (Ray) Kalouche
EVP, General Counsel, and Secretary:
Thomas E. (Tom) Lippard
SVP and CFO: Daniel E. Rosati
VP, Treasurer, and Principal Accounting Officer:
Kirk Peters
VP Financial Operations and Corporate Controller:
Electa Boyle
President and COO, Raw Materials and Optimization:
J. David Aronson
Manager Media Relations: James C. (Jim) Leonard
Auditors: Ernst & Young LLP

LOCATIONS

HQ: Tube City IMS, LLC
12 Monongahela Ave., Glassport, PA 15045
Phone: 412-678-6141   **Fax:** 412-678-2210
Web: www.tubecityims.com

Tube City IMS Corporation primarily operates in the US, though it also is active in Serbia and Slovakia.

PRODUCTS/OPERATIONS

Selected Services

Post-production
Co-product processing, metal recovery, and sales
Material handling and product handling
Pre-production
Material handling, scrap management, and scrap preparation
Raw materials optimization
Raw materials procurement

COMPETITORS

Aleris International
Commercial Metals
David J. Joseph
Edw. C. Levy
Harsco
Keywell
OmniSource
Sims Metal Management

HISTORICAL FINANCIALS

Company Type: Private

Income Statement

FYE: December 31

	REVENUE ($ mil.)	NET INCOME ($ mil.)	NET PROFIT MARGIN	EMPLOYEES
12/08	2,900	—	—	3,000
12/07	1,670	—	—	2,600
12/06	1,376	—	—	2,400
12/05	1,123	—	—	2,250
12/04	199	—	—	—
Annual Growth	95.4%	—	—	10.1%

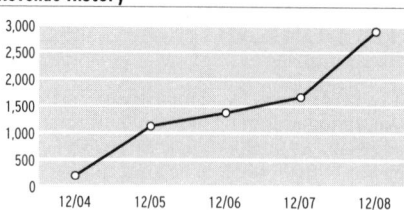

Revenue History

Tufts Associated Health Plans

Getting good health care becomes a little less rough with Tufts. Tufts Associated Health Plans is a leading New England health insurer operating as Tufts Health Plan. The company provides medical coverage to hundreds of thousands of members in Massachusetts and (to a lesser degree) Rhode Island. Its products include HMO, PPO, and point-of-service plans for both employers and individuals, as well as Medicare Advantage plans for retirees. With partner CIGNA, Tufts also offers a nationwide health network called CareLink for multi-state employers. The company, founded in 1979, is led by CEO James Roosevelt Jr.

Tuft's health care network includes some 85 hospitals and more than 20,000 doctors. Its plans also include consumer-directed products such as health savings accounts and health care reimbursement accounts.

The company began operating in Rhode Island in 2009 with a PPO suite of plans. After surpassing its initial membership goals, Tuft's decided later that year to expand its Ocean State offerings to include HMO plans.

Like most managed health care companies, Tufts has worked to control medical costs while still adding members and encouraging quality care. It has embraced the practice of "evidence-based medicine," encouraging standardized best practices among its providers.

It has also implemented disease management programs for chronic illnesses like diabetes and chronic heart failure. It expanded its disease management programs, which help members manage their illnesses in ways that hopefully prevent big and costly interventions, through a partnership with Healthways.

Additionally, Tufts has introduced the My Wellness Plan, a set of online tools that, among other things, give members access to health information, reminds them about prescription renewals, and helps them with getting claims resolved.

On the provider side, Tufts works to build its network of participating medical professionals by providing services designed to streamline their practices and reduce administrative costs. The company's e-Access for Providers includes online self-service options such as direct claims submission, interactive voice response systems for obtaining authorizations, and electronic remittance advice.

EXECUTIVES

Chairman: Davey S. Scoon, age 62
Vice Chairman: David Green
President, CEO, and Director: James Roosevelt Jr., age 63
COO: Thomas A. (Tom) Croswell
SVP Sales and Client Services: Brian P. Pagliaro
SVP and CFO: Umesh Kurpad
SVP Operations and CIO: Tricia Trebino
SVP Marketing, Product Development, and Strategy:
Robert D. (Rob) Egan
SVP and Chief Medical Officer: Allen J. Hinkle, age 58
SVP Human Resources, General Counsel, and Senior Compliance Officer: Lois Dehls Cornell
VP Communications: Patti Embry-Tautenhan
VP Secure Horizons: Patricia Blake

LOCATIONS

HQ: Tufts Associated Health Plans, Inc.
705 Mt. Auburn St., Watertown, MA 02472
Phone: 617-972-9400
Web: www.tuftshealthplan.com

PRODUCTS/OPERATIONS

Selected Health Plans

Advantage HMO
Advantage PPO
Advantage Saver (high-deductible plan with health savings account)
CareLink (national network PPO, with CIGNA)
EPO Choice Copay (exclusive provider organization)
HMO Choice Copay (tiered provider network)
Navigator Choice (PPO)
Tufts Health Plan Medicare Preferred (HMO or private-fee-for-service Medicare plan)
Tufts Medicare Complement (supplemental Medicare coverage)

COMPETITORS

Aetna
Blue Cross and Blue Shield of Massachusetts
ConnectiCare
Fallon Community Health Plan
Harvard Pilgrim
Health New England
MVP Health Plan
Neighborhood Health Plan
UnitedHealth Group

HISTORICAL FINANCIALS

Company Type: Not-for-profit

Income Statement

FYE: December 31

	REVENUE ($ mil.)	NET INCOME ($ mil.)	NET PROFIT MARGIN	EMPLOYEES
12/08	2,300	19	0.8%	—
12/07	2,200	110	5.0%	—
12/06	1,900	78	4.1%	—
12/05	1,900	79	4.1%	—
12/04	2,100	28	1.3%	—
Annual Growth	2.3%	(9.6%)	—	—

Net Income History

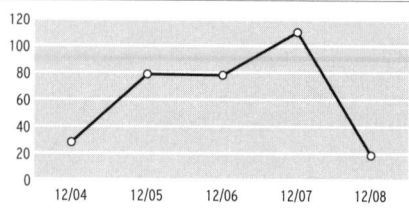

Turner Industries

Turner Industries does the heavy lifting for heavy industry. The company is a major US provider of industrial construction, contract maintenance, and outsourcing. Its customers include oil refiners, petrochemical companies, power generators, and pulp and paper mills. Through its equipment and specialty services divisions, the group provides more than 50 services including scaffolding equipment rental, environmental remediation, heavy hauling and rigging, water treatment, pipe fabrication, welding, and tank cleaning. Turner Industries also offers material management, training workshops, and staffing services. The late Bert Turner founded the family-owned company in Baton Rouge, Louisiana, in 1961.

The company's bread and butter is the oil and gas industry, which also is Louisiana's economic mainstay. Turner also has a big presence in neighboring Texas and Alabama. With such a strong tie to the Gulf Coast region and the petrochemical industry, Turner is susceptible to natural disasters. The company was hurt by Hurricane Katrina in 2005, but added some 3,000 workers after the hurricane to cope with the cleanup, rebuilds, and restoration.

Business continues to boom for Turner Industries, which has annual revenue at about $1.8 billion. Most of the industry's growth is fueled by manufacturers that upgrade plants and facilities. Turner also is expanding its fabrication and administration facilities in Texas and Alabama.

In order to keep up with that growth and strengthen its work force, the company also is building a new 20,000-sq.-ft. training and recruiting facility near Baton Rouge.

EXECUTIVES

Chairman and CEO: Roland M. Toups
Vice Chairman and COO: Thomas H. Turner
VP Finance, CFO, Secretary, and Treasurer:
Lester J. (Les) Griffon Jr.
VP Business Development and Marketing:
Stephen M. Toups
General Counsel: John H. Fenner
President, Pipe Fabrication Division:
Robert L. (Bob) Pearson
President, Equipment and Specialty Services Division:
Davis J. Lauve
President, Maintenance and Turnarounds Division:
Joseph W. (Billy) Guitreau
President, Construction Division:
Donald L. (Don) McCollister
Director Internal Audit: Leslie Thompson
Director Marketing: Tobie Craig
Director Corporate Safety and Health: Michael Phelps
Auditors: Postlethwaite & Netterville

LOCATIONS

HQ: Turner Industries Group, L.L.C.
8687 United Plaza Blvd., 5th Fl.
Baton Rouge, LA 70809
Phone: 225-922-5050 **Fax:** 225-922-5055
Web: www.turner-industries.com

PRODUCTS/OPERATIONS

Selected Services
Construction
Contract maintenance
Environmental remediation
Equipment rental
Heat exchanger bundle extraction and cleaning
Heavy hauling

Hydroblasting and lancing
Painting and blasting
Petrochemical wastewater treatment construction and project management
Pipe fabrication and bending
Preventive maintenance
Project management
Procurement
Rigging
Scaffolding
Specialty welding
System integration
Tank cleaning
Turnarounds and shutdowns

Selected Industries
Chemical processing
Manufacturing plants
Metals and mining
Power generation
Pulp and paper
Oil and gas
Refining

COMPETITORS

ABB
Aker Solutions
APi Group
Aquilex HydroChem
Austin Industries
BE&K
Bechtel
Black & Veatch
Brock Group
CH2M HILL
Chicago Bridge & Iron
Fluor
Foster Wheeler
Halliburton
Jacobs Engineering
McDermott
Parsons Corporation
Performance Contractors
Peter Kiewit Sons'
Philip Services
Rust Constructors
Shaw Group
Yates Companies
Zachry Inc.

HISTORICAL FINANCIALS
Company Type: Private

Income Statement
FYE: December 31

	REVENUE ($ mil.)	NET INCOME ($ mil.)	NET PROFIT MARGIN	EMPLOYEES
12/08	1,772	—	—	15,000
12/07	1,604	—	—	15,000
12/06	1,410	—	—	13,300
12/05	900	—	—	12,000
12/04	816	—	—	12,000
Annual Growth	21.4%	—	—	5.7%

Revenue History

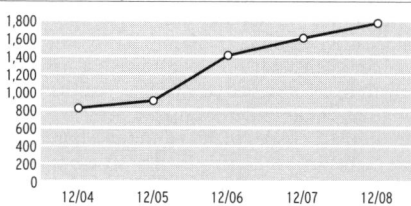

Ty Inc.

Take some fabric, shape it like an animal, fill it with plastic pellets, and you, too, could own luxury hotels. That's the lesson taught by Ty Warner, sole owner of Ty Inc., the company behind Beanie Babies and their worldwide cult following — popular with kids and adults alike. Since 1993 Ty has produced more than 365 different Beanie Babies with colorful names such as McLucky the bear (current) and Cheeks the baboon (retired). Other products include Beanie Buddies (bigger versions of traditional Beanies), Ty Classics (stuffed animals), Ty Girlz (cloth dolls), and Bow Wow Beanies (pet toys). Beanie bucks enabled Warner to buy a half-dozen luxury hotels (mostly in New York and California).

Ty's marketing smarts have kept Beanies popular for years rather than for a single holiday season, à la Furby or Tickle Me Elmo. The company limits production so that supply never outstrips demand, keeping only 40 or 50 Beanie Babies in circulation at any one time. Ty's "retirement" of a Beanie can cause its price among collectors to skyrocket from its $5-$7 retail debut to hundreds or even thousands of dollars. Also, rather than flood the market with Beanies through the likes of Toys "R" Us and Wal-Mart, Ty sells them only through specialty toy and gift retailers.

Historically, the firm doesn't advertise, relying instead on the word of mouth that is rampant in Beanie culture. Books, magazines, newsletters, and Web sites stoke collectors' enthusiasm. This collectors' market — which Ty frowns upon (officially, anyway) — shows signs of fading, however.

Deciding to capitalize on a new market of young consumers who likely aren't familiar with its core product, the company launched Beanie Babies 2.0 in 2008. The newer Beanie Babies plushes come with a secret code that allows owners to access the online Beanie Baby world. The company's move is to compete head to head with Webkinz plushes, which also have a secret code and a partnering Web site.

Knowing that online worlds for toys are becoming increasingly popular with today's youth, Ty also launched a line of cloth dolls named Ty Girlz in 2007. The dolls come with passwords to an online world where users can interact with other Ty Girlz doll owners.

HISTORY

Ty Warner, the son of a plush-toy salesman, started his toy career selling stuffed animals to specialty shops for stuffed-bear manufacturer Dakin. Warner left Dakin in 1980, moved to Europe for a few years, and in the mid-1980s returned to the US and founded Ty Inc. The company first designed a line of understuffed Himalayan cats.

Beanie Babies first debuted at a 1993 trade show. In January 1994 the first nine Beanies went on sale — at prices low enough for kids to afford — in Chicago specialty stores. As Warner had learned at Dakin, selling stuffed animals through specialty retailers rather than through mass merchandisers meant bigger profits for suppliers and longer-term popularity. By 1995 there were about 30 different Beanies, and Ty's estimated sales were $25 million.

The popularity of Beanies exploded in 1996, first in the Midwest, then the East Coast, and then across the US. By midyear, Beanies — and the public's mania for getting them before they sold out — were receiving widespread media coverage. Ty heightened the frenzy among collectors when it started announcing Beanie retirements on its Web site in 1997.

That same year, McDonald's got on the bandwagon: The fast-food giant issued some 100 million "teenie" Beanie Babies in a Happy Meal promotion. McDonald's ran out of the toys and had to end the promotion early, causing a public relations mess. McDonald's doubled its toy order in 1998 and teamed up with Ty again in 1999 and 2000.

In 1998 Warner paid $10 million for a 7% stake in marketing company Cyrk. In return, Cyrk developed the Beanie Babies Official Club, which turned stores that sell Beanies into "official headquarters" offering club membership kits. Ty introduced its Attic Treasures and Beanie Buddies lines that year.

By spring 1998 Beanies had become a customs issue at the Canadian border, where Ty's limit of one imported Beanie per person into the US resulted in tears and fisticuffs. (The company later raised the personal limit to 30.) That summer the crowds at Major League Baseball games featuring Beanie giveaways were 26% bigger than average.

Warner bought the Four Seasons hotel in New York City in 1999. He also provided auditing documents and correspondence to *The New York Post* indicating that Ty had 1998 profits of more than $700 million — more than Hasbro and Mattel combined.

After an August 1999 announcement that it would retire the Beanies at the end of the year, the company held a New Year's vote to determine their fate. In the most shocking outcome since *Rocky IV*, the public voted overwhelmingly in favor of continuing the Beanies. Ty introduced its humanoid Beanie Kids line in early 2000. Later that year Warner bought the Four Seasons Biltmore Hotel and the San Ysidro Ranch — the hostelry where JFK and Jackie honeymooned; both are near Santa Barbara, California.

In 2001 Ty debuted its pre-teen Beanie Boppers (boy and girl dolls designed for kids from 8 to 12 years of age). To round out his Four Seasons Hotels and Coral Casino properties in California, in 2003 Warner purchased nearby Sandpiper Golf Course. Also that year, the Beanie Baby celebrated its 10th anniversary, and Ty marked the event with the introduction of the Decade Beanie Baby.

In 2008 the company introduced Beanie Babies 2.0, plush animals that come with codes to an online world where owners can interact with other Beanie owners.

EXECUTIVES

Chairman and CEO: H. Ty Warner
CFO: Richard Jeffrey
SVP Sales: Tania Lundeen
Interactive Creative Director: Michael Rezac
Marketing Manager: Dana Scott-Turkovich

LOCATIONS

HQ: Ty Inc.
280 Chestnut Ave., Westmont, IL 60559
Phone: 630-920-1515   **Fax:** 630-920-1980
Web: www.ty.com

PRODUCTS/OPERATIONS

Selected Products

Baby Ty
Beanie Babies
Beanie Babies 2.0
Beanie Buddies
Bow Wow Beanies
Pinkies
Pluffies
Ty Classics
Ty Girlz

COMPETITORS

Aurora World
Build-A-Bear
Disney Online
Enesco
Ganz
Gund
Hasbro
Kid Brands
Manhattan Group
Mattel
Nakajima USA
North American Bear
Sanrio
Simba Dickie Group
Vermont Teddy Bear

Unified Grocers

These grocers are unified in their purpose of stocking the shelves. Unified Grocers is a leading wholesale distributor that serves about 3,000 independent grocers, cash and carry outlets, and major grocery chains mostly in the western US through more than a dozen distribution centers. It offers some 80,000 items to its members and non-member stores, including meat, dairy goods, fresh produce, general merchandise, and specialty items. The company sells national brands, as well as such private labels as Cottage Hearth, Golden Creme, and Western Family. Unified Grocers boasts more than 2,000 member stores. The cooperative was formed in 1922 as Certified Grocers of California.

In addition to its core wholesale distribution business, Unified Grocers offers its customers such services as liability insurance, financing, and other support services. It also owns more than 20% of Western Family Foods, a distributor of private-label goods sold under the Western Family and Shurfine brands. The cooperative's largest customer, cash and carry warehouse operator Smart & Final, accounts for about 10% of sales.

Expanding its number of store locations has helped drive wholesale volumes for Unified Grocers, and its perishable goods division has seen growth in the past few years. However, the company has come under increased pressure from the number of supercenters and discount grocers in its territory. It acquired Seattle-based Associated Grocers in 2007 for $40 million as part of an expansion effort.

HISTORY

Certified Grocers of California evolved from a group of 15 independent Southern California grocers that formed a purchasing cooperative in 1922 to compete against large grocery chains. Certified Grocers of California incorporated in 1925 and issued stock to 50 members.

The co-op merged with a small retailer-owned wholesale company called Co-operative Grocers in 1928. It acquired Walker Brothers Grocery in 1929 and nearly tripled the previous year's sales. By 1938 the co-op had grown to 310 members and 380 stores, and sales passed $10 million.

Certified launched a line of private-label products under the Springfield name in 1947. In the early 1950s it added nonfood items and began processing its own private-label coffee and bean products. The co-op added delicatessen items in 1956. During the 1960s and 1970s, Certified added a meat center, a frozen food and deli warehouse, a produce distribution center, a creamery, a central bakery, and a specialty foods warehouse.

In 1989 the co-op opened several membership warehouse stores called Convenience Clubs. The Save Mart and Boys Markets chains left the fold in 1991. The co-op lost about 30% of its business during the next two years, including the Bel Air and Williams Bros. chains. After disappointing returns, in 1992 Certified sold its warehouse stores, cut staff, and consolidated warehouses.

CFO (and former Atlantic Richfield executive) Al Plamann was appointed CEO in 1994, succeeding Everett Dingwell. In 1996 the co-op began to convert its customers' older retail stores to Apple Markets in Southern California. Revenues began to dip in 1997 as the result of reduced purchases from some supermarkets and the sale the previous year of one of its subsidiaries, Hawaiian Grocery Stores.

Member chain Stumps converted to the Apple Markets banner in 1998. Faced with a declining customer base, in 1999 Certified merged with United Grocers of Oregon to form Unified Western Grocers.

Dr. R. Norton, F. L. Freeburg, and A. C. Brinckerhoff founded United Grocers of Oregon in 1915 as a way for grocers in Portland to cooperate in purchasing merchandise. By the next year the co-op had 35 members. In the 1950s United formed a trucking department and established a general merchandise division. It also grew rapidly in the 1950s through acquisitions, buying Northwest Grocery Company and the Fridegar Grocery Company. In 1963 United formed its frozen food department when it purchased Raven Creamery.

By 1975 the company's Northwest Grocery Company subsidiary had 14 Cash and Carry warehouses that sold goods to small grocers and restaurants. In 1995 United bought California food distributor Market Wholesale. Three years later the company sold its Cash and Carry warehouse-style stores to Smart & Final.

Upon completion of the merger in 1999, Certified's president and CEO, Plamann, was named to head the new organization. Soon after, Unified consolidated warehouse operations, eliminated duplicate personnel, and combined its private labels. Also in 1999 the company acquired California-based Gourmet Specialties.

The next year it bought the specialty foods business of J. Sosnick and Son, another California company, and Central Sales of Washington State. The company attributed net losses during 2001 to delays in moving the source for northern California specialty merchandise from southern to northern California and to the costs of entering the Washington marketplace, among other factors.

In 2002 Unified closed seven retail stores in Northern California and Oregon (under the Apple Markets and SavMax Foods banners) that accounted for sales of about $140 million as part of its plan to reduce debt and focus on wholesaling. In 2003 the co-op sold or closed all 12 of its company-owned SavMax Foods stores as part of its plan to exit its unprofitable retail business and focus on its wholesale division (99% of total sales).

As part of an expansion effort, Unified acquired Associated Grocers, a Seattle-based wholesale cooperative, for about $40 million. It later changed its name to Unified Grocers.

EXECUTIVES

Chairman: Richard L. (Dick) Wright, age 71
First Vice Chairman: Peter J. O'Neal, age 63
Second Vice Chairman: Terry H. Halverson, age 58
President and CEO: Alfred A. (Al) Plamann, age 67
EVP, General Counsel, and Secretary:
Robert M. Ling Jr., age 52
EVP, Chief Marketing Officer, and Chief Procurement Officer: Philip S. (Phil) Smith, age 59
EVP Finance and Administration and CFO:
Richard J. (Rich) Martin, age 64
SVP Finance and Treasurer: Christine Neal, age 56
SVP Retail Support Services and Perishables:
Daniel J. (Dan) Murphy, age 63
SVP Operations: Rodney L. (Rod) Van Bebber, age 54
SVP Sales: Joseph L. (Joe) Falvey, age 49
VP and CIO: Gary S. Herman
VP Marketing: Dirk T. Davis
VP Credit: Carolyn S. Fox
VP Accounting and Chief Accounting Officer:
Randall G. (Randy) Scoville, age 49
VP Procurement: Robert (Bob) Lutz
VP Manufacturing: John C. Bedrosian
VP Human Resources: Donald E. (Don) Gilpin
VP Insurance: Joseph A. (Joe) Ney, age 61
VP Real Estate: Gary C. Hammett
Auditors: Deloitte & Touche LLP

LOCATIONS

HQ: Unified Grocers, Inc.
5200 Sheila St., Commerce, CA 90040
Phone: 323-264-5200   **Fax:** 323-265-4006
Web: www.unifiedgrocers.com

PRODUCTS/OPERATIONS

2008 Sales

	$ mil.	% of total
Wholesale distribution	4,091.5	99
Insurance	28.4	1
Other	1.8	—
Adjustments	(16.9)	—
Total	**4,104.8**	**100**

COMPETITORS

Associated Food
Associated Wholesale Grocers
C & S Wholesale
IGA
Kroger
McLane
Nash-Finch
Safeway
SUPERVALU
URM Stores
Wal-Mart

HISTORICAL FINANCIALS
Company Type: Cooperative

Income Statement

	REVENUE ($ mil.)	NET INCOME ($ mil.)	NET PROFIT MARGIN	EMPLOYEES
			FYE: Saturday nearest September 30	
9/08	4,105	17	0.4%	3,496
9/07	3,133	14	0.5%	2,900
9/06	2,954	16	0.5%	2,800
9/05	2,867	11	0.4%	2,800
9/04	3,040	7	0.2%	2,900
Annual Growth	**7.8%**	**23.8%**	**—**	**4.8%**

Net Income History

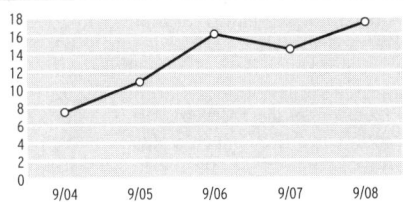

UniGroup, Inc.

Moving people's possessions has made many of UniGroup's companies household names. The company transports household goods and other items in more than 100 countries through subsidiaries United Van Lines and Mayflower Transit and a network of affiliates. The movers' operations are supported by UniGroup units such as Trans Advantage, which sells and leases trucks and trailers and provides moving supplies; UniGroup Worldwide UTS, which coordinates international moves; and Vanliner Group, which offers insurance to movers. Subsidiary Allegiant Move Management offers relocation management and assistance. UniGroup is owned by agents of United Van Lines and Mayflower Transit and by the company's senior executives.

In response to competition from companies such as PODS, which deliver storage containers to customers and then provide transportation and storage services, UniGroup has rolled out a similar offering, SAM (for Store and Move).

EXECUTIVES

Chairman and CEO: H. Daniel (Dan) McCollister
President and COO: Richard H. (Rich) McClure
CFO: James G. (Jim) Powers
CIO: Randall C. (Randy) Poppell
SVP Human Resources: Cathy Malear
SVP and Chief Marketing Officer:
Stephan (Steve) Burkhardt
VP Sales and Marketing: Casey P. Ellis
General Counsel: Jan R. Alonzo
President and CEO, Transportation Services Group; President and COO, United Van Lines and Mayflower Transit: Patrick (Pat) Larch
President, SAM Store and Move: Tom McCormick
President, Vanliner Group: Gale Preston
Manager, Marketing and Communications, UniGroup Worldwide: Liona Potrikus
President, UniGroup Worldwide: Michael Kranisky
Director Marketing Communications: Jennifer Bonham

LOCATIONS

HQ: UniGroup, Inc.
1 Premier Dr., Fenton, MO 63026
Phone: 636-305-5000   **Fax:** 636-326-1106
Web: www.unigroupinc.com

COMPETITORS

AMERCO
Atlas World Group
Bekins
Budget Rent A Car
Door To Door Storage, Inc.
Graebel
National Van Lines
Penske Truck Leasing
PODS Enterprises
Ryder System
SIRVA

HISTORICAL FINANCIALS
Company Type: Private

Income Statement

	REVENUE ($ mil.)	NET INCOME ($ mil.)	NET PROFIT MARGIN	EMPLOYEES
			FYE: December 31	
12/08	2,000	—	—	1,100
12/07	2,200	—	—	1,350
12/06	2,300	—	—	1,350
12/05	2,200	—	—	1,350
12/04	2,000	—	—	1,350
Annual Growth	**0.0%**	**—**	**—**	**(5.0%)**

Revenue History

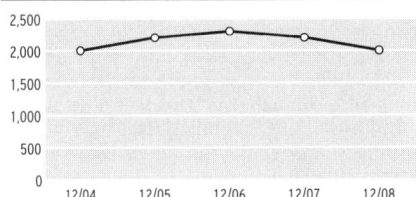

Unisource Worldwide

This company has a singular mission to distribute paper to North America. Unisource Worldwide is a leading distributor of paper products and other supplies, providing commercial printing and business imaging paper and specialty paper products though more than 100 distribution centers. Its offerings include ink jet and laser paper, Xerox paper, and toner cartridges, in addition to coated and uncoated commercial printing paper. Unisource also distributes packaging supplies (corrugated papers, foam and bubble sheeting), packaging systems (pallet systems, shrink packaging systems), and cleaning supplies and equipment. The company is 60%-owned by Bain Capital; paper manufacturer Georgia-Pacific owns about 40%.

In addition to its traditional distribution business, Unisource offers paper supply services to publishers and other commercial operators through its Websource paper brokerage. Its Rollsource unit specializes in business forms and products for customers in the direct mail industry. The company also sells retail paper products online and operates about 40 retail stores in nearly 20 states under the Paper Plus banner.

HISTORY

Tinkham Veale II, a mechanical engineer from Cleveland, got help from his father-in-law, A. C. Ernst of Ernst & Ernst accounting firm, to buy a stake in a prosperous engineered goods manufacturer in 1941. Veale retired at age 37 to breed and race horses. He invested his earnings, became a millionaire by 1951, and joined the board of Alco Oil and Chemical. In 1960 he and his associates formed a holding company, V & V Associates, and bought a large minority share in Alco.

Renamed Alco Chemical two years later, the company bought four fertilizer companies, and in 1965 (by then renamed Alco Standard) it merged with V & V Associates, which had stakes in machinery producers. At the helm, Veale implemented the partnership strategy that would serve Alco for 25 years: He bought small, privately owned companies, usually in exchange for cash and Alco stock, and let the owners continue to run them.

The company took advantage of several Supreme Court antitrust decisions in the 1960s that forced papermakers to divest marketing companies acquired in the 1950s. Alco acquired Garrett-Buchanan of Philadelphia and Monarch Paper in 1968 as the basis for its national paper distribution network. After acquiring other paper distributors, the company formed a paper distributor unit called Unisource. Veale brought in former Kimberly-Clark executive Ray Mundt in 1970 to guide the growing division. Unisource's profitability prompted Alco to enter other distribution businesses, including pharmaceuticals, hospital supplies, steel products, foodservice equipment, and liquor.

Alco also acquired several manufacturers (plastics, machinery, rubber, and chemicals), but they were not as prosperous. By 1981, with large warehouses and computerized ordering and delivery systems, Unisource was the most efficient, cost-effective distributor in the US. It continued to buy distributors, such as Saxon Industries (1984), an international paper seller valued at $378 million.

Mundt succeeded Veale as chairman two years later and switched Alco's focus to office products and paper distribution, eliminating seven divisions. In the 1990s Mundt oversaw a restructuring that included installing a state-of-the-art distribution software system across the network and consolidating the company's service center operations (Mundt cut Unisource's locations by half). He also expanded the supply products offered to include disposable paper and plastic supplies, packaging systems, and sanitary maintenance equipment in order to offset cyclical downturns in the paper market.

Unisource continued to grow, acquiring more than 40 companies (including 15 in Mexico) in fiscal 1996, and eventually accounting for 70% of Alco's revenues. In late 1996 Alco (which soon after became IKON Office Solutions) spun off Unisource Worldwide with Mundt as its chairman and CEO. The next year Unisource bought National Sanitary Supply (the #1 specialized distributor of sanitary maintenance supplies in the US) and 13 other companies (mostly supply systems). It also sold its $300 million grocery systems operation to Bunzl in 1997.

In 1998 the company announced a restructuring plan that included reducing its US workforce by 15% and cutting its number of distribution facilities almost in half (it took a $370 million charge for the year). Also that year Unisource divested its businesses in Mexico, where the economy was too uncertain.

In early 1999 Unisource agreed to be acquired by UGI Corporation, majority shareholder of AmeriGas Partners, the largest US propane distributor. However, UGI shares fell shortly after the offer, reducing the value of the deal. Georgia-Pacific made an unsolicited bid that Unisource couldn't refuse and the $1.2 billion deal was completed later that year. Unisource became the sole authorized distributor of Ecolab's Professional Products-branded janitorial supplies in 2001.

The next year Georgia-Pacific sold a 60% stake in the company to Bain Capital. It also sold 38 of Unisource's warehouses to Cardinal Capital Partners, which leased them back to the company. Unisource acquired paper broker Graphic Communications in 2003 and merged it with Websource, its existing paper brokerage division.

Al Dragone was named CEO in 2004.

The company sold its converting and manufacturing facility in Jacksonville, Florida, to Cardinal UniJax, LLC in 2006.

EXECUTIVES

CEO: Allan (Al) Dragone, age 53
CFO and Chief Administrative Officer: John Sills
SVP Marketing & Communications: Edward I. Farley
SVP and CIO: Tim Kutz
SVP Sales West: Steve Topor
SVP Sales East: Darin Tang
SVP Sales Central: Glenn Barton
Corporate VP Sustainability: Nancy C. Geisler
VP Strategic Development: Jeff Hederick
General Counsel: Jennifer Williams
Senior Director Corporate Communications: Kevin Feeney
President Unisource Canada: Bruce Bond
President Paper: Kenneth Winterhalter
President Supply Chain: Jeff Rudy
President Strategic Solutions: Thomas (Tom) Pitera
Auditors: Ernst & Young LLP

LOCATIONS

HQ: Unisource Worldwide, Inc.
6600 Governors Lake Pkwy., Norcross, GA 30071
Phone: 770-447-9000   **Fax:** 770-734-2000
Web: www.unisourcelink.com

PRODUCTS/OPERATIONS

Selected Products

Envelopes, computer paper, and specialty paper
Computer paper (blank and proprietary grades)
Envelopes (mailing, shipping, commercial)
Specialty products (engineering rolls, labels)
Facility supplies and equipment
Production supplies (degreasers, work wear)
Sanitary supplies and equipment (can liners, matting systems)
Packaging
Case erecting, packaging, and sealing systems (case packers, gummed tapes)
Case and pallet coding systems (ink jet printers, label materials)
Packaging supplies (foam and bubble sheeting)
Pallet unitization systems (conveyers, stretch films)
Shrink packaging, bundling, bagging, and overwrapping systems
Printing papers
Coated and uncoated sheet-fed papers
Premium text, cover, and writing papers
Uncoated and coated web papers

Specialty businesses
Paper Plus (smaller orders of paper, packaging, and supplies)
Rollsource (paper conversion to forms, direct mail)
Websource (large web paper orders)

COMPETITORS

Bradner Central	Midland Paper
Central National-	Office Depot
Gottesman	OfficeMax
Domtar	RIS Paper Company
Ecolab	Schwarz Paper
Gould Paper	S.P. Richards
International Paper	Staples
Katy Industries	United Stationers
Menasha	Weyerhaeuser

HISTORICAL FINANCIALS
Company Type: Private

Income Statement				FYE: Saturday nearest December 31
	REVENUE ($ mil.)	NET INCOME ($ mil.)	NET PROFIT MARGIN	EMPLOYEES
12/08	5,000	—	—	6,000
12/07	5,300	—	—	6,500
12/06	6,000	—	—	6,400
12/05	6,000	—	—	7,000
12/04	6,000	—	—	8,500
Annual Growth	(4.5%)	—	—	(8.3%)

Revenue History

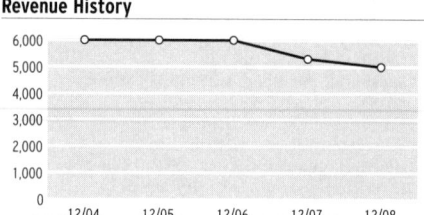

United Components

United Components, Inc. (UCI) might not bring together all the parts of an automobile, but it's got a good start. UCI was formed by The Carlyle Group in 2003 after it acquired the operations of several auto parts companies from UIS. UCI's component divisions include Airtex Products (fuel pumps and cooling systems), ASC Industries (cooling systems, water pumps), Champion Laboratories (oil, fuel, and air filters), and Wells Manufacturing (engine management products). Building on current relationships, UCI increased the number of product lines sold at AutoZone (which represents 29% of sales). The company makes most of its sales in North America.

Other customers include Advance Auto Parts, CARQUEST, and O'Reilly Automotive. Nearly 90% of sales are to the aftermarket segment.

Among UCI's challenges in 2009 are the severe downturn in the North American automotive industry, due to the credit crisis and the recession. The company's dependence on AutoZone also could be a liability if that retailer loses sales to competitors. UCI could be negatively impacted if Chrysler and/or General Motors were to go into bankruptcy protection from creditors, a prospect the Obama administration is dangling over those automakers as it directs the restructuring of the industry.

UCI divested non-core operations in an effort to achieve a more ideal and profitable product mix.

In 2006 UCI added to its water pump business with the acquisition of water pump manufacturer ASC Industries. Later that year the company sold its Pioneer and Neapco business units. Pioneer went to entrepreneur Doran Arad, and Neapco was sold to the division's senior management and a private investor group. The sales are part of UCI's efforts to focus on its core businesses.

To that same end, later in 2006 UCI sold its Flexible Lamps division (a maker of commercial vehicle lighting systems in the UK) for about $39 million to an affiliate of Truck-Lite Co.

EXECUTIVES

Chairman: David L. Squier, age 63
President, CEO and Director: Bruce M. Zorich, age 55, $656,968 total compensation
VP Human Resources: Mike Malady
VP Sales and Marketing: Curtis Draper
VP Global Procurement: Tom Blackerby
VP and General Counsel: Keith A. Zar
Auditors: Grant Thornton LLP

LOCATIONS

HQ: United Components, Inc.
14601 Hwy. 41 North, Evansville, IN 47725
Phone: 812-867-4156   **Fax:** 812-867-4157
Web: www.ucinc.com

2008 Sales

	$ mil.	% of total
US	735.1	84
Mexico	32.9	4
Canada	30.1	3
UK	12.3	1
France	9.8	1
Spain	5.2	1
Germany	5.0	1
Venezuela	4.6	—
Other countries	45.4	5
Total	**880.4**	**100**

PRODUCTS/OPERATIONS

2008 Sales

	% of total
Filtration products	42
Fuel products	25
Cooling products	17
Engine management products	16
Total	**100**

COMPETITORS

Affinia Group
BorgWarner
CLARCOR
Cummins
Dana Holding
Delphi Holdings
DENSO
Federal-Mogul
Honeywell International
Magna International
Robert Bosch
Standard Motor Products

HISTORICAL FINANCIALS

Company Type: Private

Income Statement

	REVENUE ($ mil.)	NET INCOME ($ mil.)	NET PROFIT MARGIN	EMPLOYEES
12/08	880	10	1.1%	4,900
12/07	970	38	3.9%	5,200
12/06	906	(9)	—	5,200
12/05	1,009	(5)	—	6,200
12/04	1,027	31	3.0%	6,900
Annual Growth	**(3.8%)**	**(24.7%)**	**—**	**(8.2%)**

FYE: December 31

2008 Year-End Financials

Debt ratio: 160.7%
Return on equity: —
Cash ($ mil.): —
Current ratio: —
Long-term debt ($ mil.): 418

Net Income History

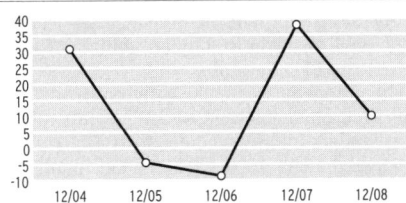

United Way Worldwide

Where there's a will, there's a Way. United Way Worldwide unites some 1,800 United Way organizations that extend to about 45 countries and territories. The group works to raise money for charitable causes. In 2009 it merged its United Way of America network of almost 1,300 organizations with its United Way International group. While its specific priorities are set by local entities, United Way Worldwide tends to focus on helping children achieve their potential, promoting financial stability, and improving access to health care. Major recipients of it contributions have included American Cancer Society, Big Brothers/Big Sisters, Catholic Charities, Girl Scouts, Boy Scouts, and The Salvation Army, among others.

United Way Worldwide raises money primarily through an annual campaign conducted in workplaces. Its organizations also receive US government grants and corporate contributions. The group launched a new campaign in 2008 named LIVE UNITED, which is meant to enlist the help of volunteers and donors to become part of change.

Each of its organizations is an independent entity governed by local volunteers. United Way Worldwide acts as a global services and training center that supports its network with services, such as advertising and research. Organizations, in turn, support United Way Worldwide with membership dues.

For many years, the organization has raised money through workplace payroll deductions. Layoffs nationwide in 2008 spurred United Way Worldwide to make more realistic goals, given that fewer workers were bringing home paychecks. United Way Worldwide's focus shifted from managing fundraising goals to having what

it calls "impact goals." To this end, in 2008 the organization launched a 10-year plan to cut dropout rates and improve the health and financial stability of families.

HISTORY

The first modern Community Chest was created in 1913, laying the foundation for the practice of allocating funds among multiple causes. Five years later, representatives from 12 fundraising organizations met in Chicago and established the American Association for Community Organizations, the predecessor of the present-day United Way. By 1929 more than 350 Community Chests had been established.

Payroll deductions for charitable contributions debuted in 1943. In 1946 the United Way's predecessor organization initiated a cooperative relationship with the American Federation of Labor and the Congress of Industrial Organizations (which merged to become the AFL-CIO in 1955); the two groups agreed to provide services to members of organized labor. (The relationship continues today, with the organizations collaborating on projects such as recruiting members of organized labor to lead health and human services organizations.)

The Uniform Federal Fund-Raising Program was created by order of President Dwight Eisenhower in 1957, enabling federal employees to contribute to charities of their choice. (The program later evolved into the Combined Federal Campaign.) Six years later Los Angeles became the first city to adopt the United Way name when more than 30 local Community Chests and United Fund organizations merged. The national organization, which had been operating under the United Community Funds and Councils (UCFCA) name, adopted the United Way of America (UWA) name in 1970. It established its headquarters in Alexandria, Virginia, the next year.

Congress made its first grant for emergency food and shelter to the private sector in 1983, and UWA was selected as its fiscal agent. UWA created its Emergency Food and Shelter National Board Program the same year. In 1984 UWA created the Alexis de Tocqueville Society to solicit larger donations from individuals (it attracted such members as Bill Gates and Walter Annenberg).

In 1992 William Aramony, UWA's president for more than two decades, resigned after coming under fire for his lavish expenditures. Former Peace Corps head Elaine Chao was tapped to replace him, and in 1995 Aramony was sentenced to seven years in prison for defrauding the organization of about $600,000. Former UWA CFO Thomas Merlo and Stephen Paulachak (former president of a UWA spinoff) were convicted on related charges. After four years spent burnishing UWA's tarnished image, Chao resigned in 1996 and was succeeded the next year by Betty Beene, who had served as CEO of the Tri-State United Way.

In an effort to stress the manner in which its local organizations benefit their communities, UWA launched a brand-initiative campaign in 1998. The following year UWA's local organization in Santa Clara, California, found itself in serious financial straits when donations began slipping despite its location in the wealthy Silicon Valley. Infoseek founder Steve Kirsch and Microsoft founder Bill Gates chipped in $1 million and $5 million, respectively, to help keep the organization afloat.

Beene, who drew the ire of some chapters for suggesting a national pledge-processing center and national standards, stepped down in January 2001. That same year UWA began funneling more funds into smaller community projects instead of national charities. In 2002 Brian Gallagher took over as president and CEO.

In the aftermath of Hurricane Katrina in 2005, UWA teamed up with the Red Cross and Salvation Army to form a Coordinated Assistance Network to address the needs of evacuees by providing emergency and recovery services.

Looking to unite its international and American entities and let others know about its global reach, the organization kicked off a brand campaign in 2008. The new LIVE UNITED campaign also included a name change for the organization to United Way Worldwide.

EXECUTIVES

Chairman: William G. (Bill) Parrett, age 64
President and CEO: Brian A. Gallagher, age 50
COO: Joseph V. Haggerty
CFO: Robert E. Berdelle, age 52
Chief of Staff: Brian J. G. Lachance
EVP, Center for Community Leadership and Community Impact Leadership: Stacey D. Stewart
Executive Director, International Network and EVP Investor Relations: Atul Tandon
EVP Brand Leadership: Cynthia Round
EVP Strategic Alliances and Inclusiveness: Deborah W. (Debbie) Foster
VP Public Relations: Del Galloway
Director Public Relations: Sally (Sal) Fabens
Auditors: Ernst & Young LLP

LOCATIONS

HQ: United Way Worldwide
    701 N. Fairfax St., Alexandria, VA 22314
Phone: 703-836-7112   **Fax:** 703-683-7840
Web: www.liveunited.org

PRODUCTS/OPERATIONS

Selected Recipients

Big Brothers/Big Sisters
Catholic Charities
American Cancer Society
Girl Scouts
Boy Scouts

HISTORICAL FINANCIALS

Company Type: Not-for-profit

Income Statement			FYE: December 31
	REVENUE ($ mil.)	NET INCOME ($ mil.)	NET PROFIT MARGIN	EMPLOYEES
---	---	---	---	---
12/08	66	9	13.3%	304
12/07	66	6	8.6%	207
12/06	68	(6)	—	186
12/05	74	15	20.1%	174
12/04	45	(4)	—	181
Annual Growth	10.5%	—	—	13.8%

Net Income History

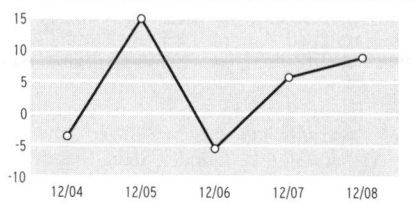

Universal Hospital Services

The yearning for medical equipment is universal, as Universal Hospital Services (UHS) well knows. Founded in 1939, the company leases movable medical equipment to hospitals and care providers from 80 sales and distribution offices across the US. It has a pool of more than 200,000 pieces of equipment in specialty areas such as critical care, monitoring, respiratory therapy, and newborn care. UHS' programs include the Asset Management Partnership, which supplies, maintains, manages, and tracks equipment for customers. The company also sells new and used equipment and disposable supplies, and it provides equipment maintenance services. In 2007 UHS was acquired by an affiliate of Bear Stearns for $712 million.

The company was previously controlled by leveraged buyout specialist J.W. Childs; other shareholders included equity firm The Halifax Group and members of UHS' management.

EXECUTIVES

Chairman Emeritus: David E. Dovenberg, age 64
Chairman and CEO: Gary D. Blackford, age 51
EVP and COO: Timothy W. Kuck, age 51
EVP and CFO: Rex T. Clevenger, age 51
EVP Sales and Marketing: Jeffrey L. Singer, age 47
SVP National Accounts: Steve Heintze
SVP Information and Strategic Resources: David G. Lawson, age 52
SVP Human Resources and Development: Walter T. Chesley, age 54
SVP and General Counsel: Diana J. Vance-Bryan, age 52
VP, Controller, and Chief Accounting Officer: Scott M. Madson, age 48
VP Asset Optimization: Phil Zeller
VP Marketing: Mary Rapaport
VP Technical Services: John Ainsworth
VP Strategic Partnerships: Daren Kneeland
Auditors: Deloitte & Touche LLP

LOCATIONS

HQ: Universal Hospital Services, Inc.
    7700 France Ave. South, Ste. 275, Edina, MN 55435
Phone: 952-893-3200   **Fax:** 952-893-0704
Web: www.uhs.com

PRODUCTS/OPERATIONS

2008 Sales

	% of total
Medical equipment outsourcing	77
Technical & professional services	16
Medical equipment sales & remarketing	7
Total	**100**

COMPETITORS

Hill-Rom
Kinetic Concepts
Medline Industries
Owens & Minor
PSS World Medical

HISTORICAL FINANCIALS

Company Type: Private

Income Statement			FYE: December 31
	REVENUE ($ mil.)	NET INCOME ($ mil.)	NET PROFIT MARGIN	EMPLOYEES
---	---	---	---	---
12/08	289	(24)	—	1,451
12/07	264	(64)	—	1,318
12/06	225	0	0.0%	1,274
12/05	216	(2)	—	1,139
12/04	200	(4)	—	1,188
Annual Growth	9.7%	—	—	5.1%

2008 Year-End Financials

Debt ratio: 280.1%   Current ratio: —
Return on equity: —   Long-term debt ($ mil.): 528
Cash ($ mil.): —

Net Income History

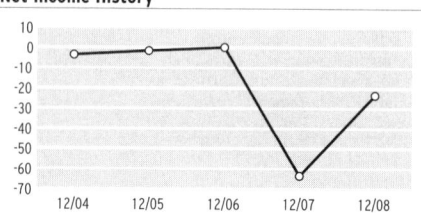

University of Alabama System

Students in the Heart of Dixie can choose from among three campuses overseen by The University of Alabama system. The flagship Tuscaloosa campus, created in 1936, offers more than 200 degree programs to more than 25,000 students. The University of Alabama at Birmingham offers nearly 140 degree programs and has an enrollment of more than 16,000 students; it is also home to the university's school of medicine and a 900-bed hospital. The system's Huntsville campus has about 7,000 students enrolled in its five colleges and graduate school. Each campus offers bachelor's, master's, and doctoral degree programs. The University of Alabama was founded in Tuscaloosa in 1831 as the state's first public university.

EXECUTIVES

Chancellor: Malcolm Portera, age 63
Vice Chancellor Financial Affairs: C. Ray Hayes
Vice Chancellor System Relations: Kellee Reinhart
Vice Chancellor Academic Affairs: Charles R. Nash
President, The University of Alabama in Huntsville: David B. (Dave) Williams
President, The University of Alabama at Birmingham: Carol Z. Garrison
President, The University of Alabama: Robert E. Witt
Coordinator Information Systems: Kim Thoma Bailey
Human Resources Generalist: Jon Garner
Director Financial Operations: Stan Acker
General Counsel: Ralph H. Smith II
Secretary and Executive Assistant to the Chancellor: Michael A. Bownes
General Auditor: Newt Hamner
Auditors: KPMG LLP

LOCATIONS

HQ: The University of Alabama System
401 Queen City Ave., Tuscaloosa, AL 35401
Phone: 205-348-5861   **Fax:** 205-348-9788
Web: www.uasystem.ua.edu

PRODUCTS/OPERATIONS

Selected Colleges and Schools

The University of Alabama (Tuscaloosa)
Capstone College of Nursing
College of Arts and Sciences
College of Communication
College of Community Health Sciences
College of Continuing Studies
College of Education
College of Engineering
College of Human Environmental Sciences
Culverhouse College of Commerce and Business
Administration
Graduate School
School of Law
School of Social Work

The University of Alabama at Birmingham
School of Arts and Humanities
School of Business
School of Dentistry
School of Education
School of Engineering
School of Health Related Professions
School of Medicine
School of Natural Sciences and Mathematics
School of Nursing
School of Optometry
School of Public Health
School of Social and Behavioral Sciences

The University of Alabama in Huntsville
College of Administrative Science
College of Engineering
College of Liberal Arts
College of Nursing
College of Science
School of Graduate Studies

University of California

The University of California (UC) system has some 220,000 students at its 10 campuses (which include four law schools and five medical schools) located in Berkeley, Davis, Irvine, Los Angeles, Merced, Riverside, San Diego, San Francisco, Santa Barbara, and Santa Cruz. The schools, with more than 180,000 faculty and staff, offer areas of study in more than 150 disciplines ranging from the arts to bioengineering. UC also operates three US Department of Energy research labs in California and New Mexico. The system has an $18 billion annual operating budget.

Funding was cut by $813 million in 2009 as the state of California suffered its own budget crisis. In response to the cuts, the university and its campuses plan to initiate staffwide furloughs, cut hiring, raise student fees, and reduce or cut academic programs.

In the wake of the 1996 approval of California's Proposition 209, which eliminated state affirmative-action programs, enrollment of minorities and the hiring of female faculty both dropped in the UC system. To help restore minority admissions to pre-Prop 209 levels, UC guarantees admission to the top 4% of students at each California high school and operates outreach programs aimed at low-income students.

In 2009 the system's board of regents expanded eligibility requirements for incoming freshmen, based on high school performance scores. The move did not expand the number of freshman admissions — it just increased the pool of applicants — but it was a response to criticism that the system was not doing enough to encourage minority applicants.

HISTORY

The founders of California's government provided for a state university in the state's constitution in 1849. The origins of the College of California, opened in Oakland in 1869, date back to the Contra Costa Academy, a small school established by Yale alumnus Henry Durant in 1853. Durant ran Contra Costa, and then the college, until 1872. Women were allowed to enter the school in 1870. The college moved to Berkeley and graduated its first class (12 men) in 1873.

As California's economy and population grew, so did its university system. Renamed University of California (UC) in 1879, it had 1,000 students by 1895. Agriculture, mining, geology, and engineering were among its first fields. A second campus was established at Davis in 1905, followed by campuses in San Diego (1912) and Los Angeles (1919).

The Depression brought cutbacks in funding for UC, but the system rebounded in the 1940s. It opened its fifth campus (Santa Barbara) in 1944, and during WWII it also began gaining recognition for research. Between 1945 and 1965 enrollment quadrupled, spurred by GI Bill-sponsored veterans and a population shift to the West. The state legislature formulated the Master Plan for Higher Education in 1960, which reorganized university administration and established admission requirements. Campuses were established at Irvine and Santa Cruz in 1965.

The first of several important demonstrations in the 1960s at UC Berkeley came in 1964 over the university's attempts to ban political activity on a strip of UC-owned land. The People's Park riot of 1969, touched off when UC tried to close a parcel of land in Berkeley that students had turned into a kind of playground for the counterculture, left one dead and more than 50 wounded. Aware of the changing demographics of its student body, especially its growing Asian enrollment (28% in 1990), UC Berkeley gave the chancellor's job to Chang-Lin Tien in 1990 — the first person of Asian descent to hold that position at a major US university (Tien served as chancellor until 1997). A California recession in the early 1990s resulted in budget cuts for UC. Strapped for cash, the university launched a for-profit entity in 1992 to tap its extensive library of patents.

UC San Diego chancellor Richard Atkinson succeeded Jack Peltason as UC president in 1995, the same year the UC Board of Regents approved a new campus — the university's 10th — in the San Joaquin Valley. That year it voted to phase out race- and sex-based affirmative action. The board, in an effort to be competitive with other top universities in recruiting faculty, voted to offer health benefits to the partners of gay employees in 1997. Also that year UC created the California Digital Library and began putting its library collection online.

Entrepreneur Alfred Mann donated $100 million to UCLA in 1998 for biomedical research. Also that year admissions of non-Asian-American minorities to the fall freshman classes of UCLA and UC Berkeley fell sharply. The following year

the UC system began guaranteeing admission to the top 4% of students in each of the state's high schools. UC took some heat in 1999 and 2000 for two separate instances of security breaches at the Los Alamos National Laboratory.

Robert Dynes, previously chancellor of UC San Diego, became president of the UC system in October 2003. In 2008 he was replaced by Mark G. Yudof, former chancellor of The University of Texas System.

EXECUTIVES

President: Mark G. Yudof, age 64
Acting Chief of Staff: John Sandbrook
Interim Provost and EVP Academic Affairs:
Robert D. Grey
EVP: Bruce B. Darling
EVP Business Operations: Katherine Lapp
SVP Chief Compliance and Audit Officer: Sheryl Vacca
**Chief Investment Officer and VP Investments and
Acting Treasurer of the Regents:** Marie N. Berggren
VP Student Affairs: Judy K. Sakaki
VP Finance: Anne C. Broome
Associate VP Communications: Lynn Tierney
Acting Associate VP Human Resources and Benefits:
John Cammidge
General Counsel and VP Legal Affairs:
Charles F. Robinson
VP Research and Graduate Studies:
Steven V.W. Beckwith
Chancellor, University of California Riverside:
Timothy P. White
Chancellor, University of California Berkeley:
Robert J. Birgeneau, age 67
Chancellor, University of California Irvine:
Michael V. Drake
Chancellor, University of California Santa Cruz:
George R. Blumenthal
Chancellor, University of California Santa Barbara:
Henry T.Y. Yang
Chancellor, University of California Merced:
Sung-Mo (Steve) Kang, age 64
Chancellor, University of California Los Angeles:
Gene D. Block
Chancellor, University of California San Francisco:
J. Michael Bishop
Chancellor, University of California San Diego:
Marye Anne Fox
**Associate VP Information Resources and
Communications and CIO:** David Ernst
Secretary and Chief of Staff to the Regents:
Diane M. Griffiths
Auditors: PricewaterhouseCoopers LLP

LOCATIONS

HQ: University of California
1111 Franklin St., Oakland, CA 94607
Phone: 510-987-0700   **Fax:** 510-987-0894
Web: www.universityofcalifornia.edu

Campuses

UC Berkeley
UC Davis
UC Irvine
UC Los Angeles
UC Merced
UC Riverside
UC San Diego
UC San Francisco
UC Santa Barbara
UC Santa Cruz

PRODUCTS/OPERATIONS

Department of Energy Laboratories

Ernest Orlando Lawrence Berkeley National Laboratory (Berkeley, CA)
Lawrence Livermore National Laboratory (Livermore, CA)
Los Alamos National Laboratory (New Mexico)

University of California, Davis

If you want to grow grapes and make wine in Napa Valley or Sonoma County, you might want to swing by the University of California, Davis (UC Davis) first. The school offers a wide variety of agricultural programs; its Viticulture and Enology department provides professional education for aspiring winemakers. Located between Sacramento and San Francisco, UC Davis has professional schools in education, law, business, medicine, and veterinary medicine. UC Davis enrolls more than 30,000, including about 4,100 graduate students. It was originally known as the University Farm School, and accepted its first students at its new campus in the town of Davisville (later changed to Davis) in 1909.

The California Legislature in 1905 authorized the establishment of a state agricultural college, and a 778-acre farm near the state capital was purchased the following year.

The first classes were held in 1908 for local farmers, and the first official class, which included students from the University of California at Berkeley, convened in January of 1909. The school that became UC Davis was administratively tied to UC Berkeley for decades, before gaining its status as an independent university in 1959.

Davis had long been the largest campus in the UC system, at 5,300 acres, but the new University of California, Merced campus in the Central Valley has since surpassed it with more than 7,000 acres.

The university became part of US legal history in 1974, when Allan Bakke sued UC regents to gain admission to UC Davis' School of Medicine, saying he was the victim of reverse racial discrimination. In 1978 the US Supreme Court set the precedent for affirmative action when it ruled that race could be lawfully considered in college admissions.

EXECUTIVES

Chancellor: Linda Katehi
Executive Vice Chancellor and Provost: Enrique Lavernia
Vice Provost Undergraduate Studies: Patricia (Pat) Turner
Vice Provost University Outreach and International Programs: William B. Lacy
Vice Provost Information and Educational Technology and CIO: Peter M. Siegel
Vice Chancellor Human Health Sciences and Dean, UC Davis School of Medicine: Claire Pomeroy
Vice Chancellor Resource Management and Planning: John A. Meyer
Vice Chancellor Student Affairs: Fred Wood
Vice Chancellor Research: Barry M. Klein
Vice Chancellor University Relations: Beverly (Babs) Sandeen
Vice Chancellor Administration: Stan E. Nosek
Interim Associate Vice Chancellor Business Services: Andy Lamb
Associate Vice Chancellor Finance and Controller: J. Michael Allred
Associate Vice Chancellor Safety Services: Jill Blackwelder Parker
Associate Vice Chancellor Human Resources: Karen Hull
University Librarian: Marilyn J. Sharrow

LOCATIONS

HQ: University of California, Davis
1 Shields Ave., Davis, CA 95616
Phone: 530-752-1011   **Fax:** 530-752-2400
Web: www.ucdavis.edu

PRODUCTS/OPERATIONS

2008 Revenues

	$ mil.	% of total
Medical center	938	34
State government	619	23
Federal government	315	12
Student fees & tuition	304	11
Sales & services	266	10
Private gifts, grants & contracts	138	5
Auxiliary enterprises	93	3
Local government & other	49	2
Total	**2,722**	**100**

University of California, San Diego

Established in 1912 and a full university since 1961, the University of California at San Diego (UCSD) is a scientific powerhouse. Its faculty currently boasts five Nobel laureates, three National Medal of Science winners, and eight MacArthur Fellows (the "genius awards"). The university is home to the San Diego Supercomputer Center, the Scripps Institution of Oceanography, and the UCSD Medical Center, among other research organizations. With an enrollment of more than 22,500 students, UCSD has six undergraduate colleges as well as graduate and medical schools. The school is one of the ten campuses in the University of California System.

UCSD has one Pulitzer Prize and nine Nobel Prize winners, in addition to nine MacArthur "genius" awardees on its faculty. It is home to the Institute on Global Conflict and Cooperation and the California Institute for Information Technology and Telecommunications.

EXECUTIVES

Chancellor: Marye Anne Fox, age 61
Senior Vice Chancellor Academic Affairs: Paul Drake
Associate Chancellor and Chief Diversity Officer: Sandra Daley
Vice Chancellor Marine Sciences; Director, Scripps Institution of Oceanography; Dean, Graduate School of Marine Sciences: Tony D. Haymet
Vice Chancellor Student Affairs: H. E. (Penny) Rue
Vice Chancellor Health Sciences and Dean, School of Medicine: David A. Brenner
Vice Chancellor External and Business Affairs; President, UCSD Foundation: Steven W. Relyea
Vice Chancellor, Research: Arthur B. Ellis
Associate Chancellor and Chief of Staff: Clare Kristofco
Controller and Assistant Vice Chancellor, Business and Financial Services: Donald (Don) Larson
Assistant Vice Chancellor Admissions and Enrollment Services: Mae Brown
Assistant Vice Chancellor Human Resources: Thomas R. Leet
Dean, Graduate Studies: Kim Barrett
Dean, Randy School of Management: Robert S. Sullivan, age 64
Dean, Jacons School of Engineering: Frieder Seible
Dean, Division of Arts and Humanities: Seth Lerer
Dean, Division of Social Sciences: Jeffrey Elman

Dean, Division of Physical Sciences: Mark H. Thiemens
Executive Director University Communications and Public Affairs: Jeff Gattas
Chief Campus Counsel: Daniel W. Park
University Librarian: Brian E. C. Schottlaender

LOCATIONS

HQ: University of California, San Diego
9500 Gilman Dr., La Jolla, CA 92093
Phone: 858-534-2230
Web: www.ucsd.edu

PRODUCTS/OPERATIONS

Colleges

Earl Warren College
Eleanor Roosevelt College
John Muir College
Revelle College
Sixth College
Thurgood Marshall College

Schools and Divisions

Division of Arts and Humanities
Division of Biological Sciences
Division of Physical Sciences
Division of Social Sciences
Graduate School of International Relations and Pacific Studies
Graduate Studies and Research
Jacobs School of Engineering
Preuss School
School of Management
School of Medicine
School of Pharmacy and Pharmaceutical Sciences
Scripps Institution of Oceanography
UCSD Extension
UCSD Healthcare

University of Chicago

The University of Chicago ranks among the world's most esteemed major universities. It has an enrollment of around 15,000 students, some two-thirds of which are graduate students. The school's undergraduate branch offers a core curriculum based on the Great Books; students can choose from majors in about 50 areas. Among its graduate programs are the University of Chicago Law School and Graduate School of Business, both of which consistently rank in the top 10 according to *U.S. News & World Report*. The school is associated with more than 80 Nobel Prize recipients including Enrico Fermi, Milton Friedman, and Saul Bellow. Founded in 1890 by John D. Rockefeller, the university has an endowment of about $4.8 billion.

The University of Chicago has steadfastly stood its ground against trendiness in education curricula. All students take courses that expose them to the social, biological, and physical sciences, as well as humanities, mathematics, and language. While the university's list of those who graduated is impressive, the list of those who did not is equally prominent, including Oracle's Larry Ellison and author Kurt Vonnegut.

Students attending the university study primarily at its 200-acre main campus on the South Side of Chicago, but the university's Graduate School of Business also maintains campuses in downtown Chicago, London, Paris, and Singapore. Among its many affiliated institutions are the University of Chicago Hospitals and Health

System, the Argonne National Laboratory, and the Yerkes Observatory. The University of Chicago Press, founded in 1892, is the largest university press in the US.

HISTORY

The University of Chicago took its name from the first U of C, a small Baptist school that operated from 1858-1886. The school, incorporated in 1890, was born when William Rainey Harper, the man who was to become the University's first president, convinced Standard Oil's John D. Rockefeller to provide a founding gift of $600,000. Members of the American Baptist Education Society chipped in another $400,000, and department store owner Marshall Field donated the land for the campus.

The university opened in 1892 with a faculty of 103 and 594 students. As it grew, the university took over property that had been used in the Columbian Exposition of 1892-93, eventually surrounding the fair's former midway. (The school's football team later earned the nickname "Monsters of the Midway" while being coached by the legendary Amos Alonzo Stagg; this was before withdrawing from intercollegiate play in 1939. Legend has it that the university retains the right to rejoin the Big Ten.)

Only four years after its founding, the university's enrollment of 1,815 exceeded Harvard's. By 1907, 43% of its 5,000 students were women. Robert Maynard Hutchins, president from 1929 to 1951, revolutionized the university and American higher education by insisting on the study of original sources (the Great Books) and competency testing through comprehensive exams. He organized the college and graduate divisions into their present structure, reaffirming the role of the university as a place for intellectual exploration rather than vocational training. In 1942 the U of C ushered in the nuclear age when Enrico Fermi created the first controlled nuclear chain reaction in the school's abandoned football stadium.

From the 1950s through the 1970s, the university purchased and restored Frank Lloyd Wright's famed Robie House and built the Joseph Regenstein Library (1970). In 1978 Hanna Holborn Gray became the first woman to be named president of a major university. Gray abolished the decade-old Lascivious Costume Ball, a major social event (some would say the only social event) at the university. Hugo Sonnenschein succeeded Gray in 1993. The beginning of his tenure coincided with a period of financial difficulty for the school as increases in costs outpaced revenue growth. In 1996 Sonnenschein announced plans to boost enrollment by as much as 30% in order to invigorate the school's finances.

U of C graduate and former professor Myron Scholes shared the Nobel Prize in economics in 1997. The next year the school announced plans for a $35 million athletics center to be named after Gerald Ratner, a former student who donated $15 million toward construction of the facility. The university later signed an agreement to supply content to UNext.com (now Cardean Learning Group), an Internet distance-learning startup founded by trustee Andrew Rosenfield. (This agreement was controversial within the university community.) Cardean University, UNext.com's online university, began operating in 2000.

Sonnenschein resigned in 2000 and was replaced by Don Randel, former provost of Cornell University. That year the University of Chicago Graduate School of Business opened a campus in Singapore, and U of C economist James Heckman was awarded the Nobel Prize for his work in microeconomics.

Don Randel stepped down as president in 2006 to become president of the Andrew W. Mellon Foundation. Robert Zimmer, previously provost at Brown University, was named his successor.

EXECUTIVES

Chairman: James S. Crown, age 56
Provost: Thomas A. Rosenbaum
President and Trustee: Robert J. (Bob) Zimmer
SVP University Resources, Development, and Alumni Relations: Randy L. Holgate
VP Administration and CFO: Nim Chinniah
VP Communications: Julie Peterson
VP and Chief Investment Officer: Peter D. A. Stein
VP Research and National Laboratories: Donald H. Levy
VP Development and Alumni Relations: Ronald J. Schiller
VP University Relations and Dean, College Enrollment: Michael C. Behnke
VP and Dean, Students at the University: Kimberly Goff-Crews
VP and CIO: Gregory A. (Greg) Jackson
VP and General Counsel: Beth A. Harris
VP Medical Affairs; Dean, Biological Sciences Division and the Pritzker School of Medicine; CEO, The University of Chicago Medical Center: James L. Madara
Dean, Graham School of General Studies: Daniel Shannon
Dean, Graduate School of Business: Edward A. (Ted) Snyder, age 55
Dean, Divinity School: Richard Rosengarten
Dean, Law School: Saul Levmore
Dean, The College: John W. Boyer
Dean, Harris School of Public Policy: Susan Mayer
Dean, School of Social Services Administration: Jeanne Marsh
Director Argonne National Laboratory: Robert (Bob) Rosner
Director Fermi National Accelerator Laboratory: Piermaria J. Oddone
University Secretary: David Fithian
Auditors: KPMG LLP

LOCATIONS

HQ: The University of Chicago
5801 S. Ellis Ave., Chicago, IL 60637
Phone: 773-702-1234   **Fax:** 773-702-4155
Web: www.uchicago.edu

PRODUCTS/OPERATIONS

Selected Undergraduate Majors

African and African American Studies
Ancient Studies
Art History
Biological Chemistry
Cinema and Media Studies
Classical Studies
Early Christian Literature
East Asian Languages and Civilization
English Language and Literature
Geographical Studies
Geophysical Sciences
Germanic Studies
History
History, Philosophy, and Social Studies of Science and Medicine
International Studies
Jewish Studies
Latin American Studies
Medieval Studies
Music

Near Eastern Languages and Civilizations
Physics
Political Science
Psychology
Public Policy Studies
Religion and the Humanities
Romance Languages and Literatures
Russian Civilization
Sociology
South Asian Languages and Civilizations
Visual Arts

Selected Affiliated Institutions

Argonne National Laboratory
Chapin Hall Center for Children
Consortium on Chicago School Research
Institute for Mind and Biology
University of Chicago Hospitals and Health System
Yerkes Observatory

Selected Graduate Schools and Programs

Divinity School
Graduate School of Business
Harris Graduate School of Public Policy Studies
Law School
Pritzker School of Medicine
School of Social Service Administration

University of Illinois

The log cabins that used to dot the landscape in the Land of Lincoln have given way to the three campuses of the University of Illinois. Established as a land grant institution in 1867, the university has grown to include campuses in Chicago, Springfield, and Urbana-Champaign. Its roughly 70,000 students (a majority of whom study at the main Urbana-Champaign campus) can choose from more than 150 undergraduate programs and more than 100 graduate and professional programs. The Urbana-Champaign campus is the site of the National Center for Supercomputing Applications (which developed Mosaic, the basis for popular Internet browsers such as Netscape Navigator).

In 2007 U of I launched its $10 Global Campus program. The online virtual campus allows students to receive degrees for less than one-half of the cost of residential degrees. Global Campus offers career-oriented programs in psychology, business administration, nursing, and environmental sustainability. Master's degrees also are available in education, public administration, and more. However, after two years university officials began considering whether or not to shut it down after it attracted only a few hundred students.

EXECUTIVES

Chairman: Christopher G. Kennedy
President: B. Joseph White, age 61
VP, CFO, and Comptroller: Walter Knorr
VP Academic Affairs: Mrinalini C. (Meena) Rao
VP Technology and Economic Development: Avijit Ghosh
Assistant VP Human Resources: Maureen M. Parks
Senior Associate VP Business and Finance: Doug Beckmann
Senior Associate VP Planning and Administration: Douglas H. Vinzant
Chancellor, UI Springfield: Richard D. Ringeisen
Chancellor, UI Urbana-Champaign: Richard Herman
Chancellor, UI Chicago: Paula Allen-Meares

University Counsel: Thomas R. Bearrows
Controller: Patrick M. Patterson
President and CEO, University of Illinois Alumni
  Association: Loren R. Taylor
Executive Director Governmental Relations:
  Richard M. (Rick) Schoell
Executive Director University Relations: Thomas Hardy
Director, Institute of Government and Public Affairs:
  Robert F. Rich
Auditors: BKD, LLP

LOCATIONS

HQ: University of Illinois
    108 Henry Administration Bldg., Urbana, IL 61801
Phone: 217-333-1000   Fax: 217-244-2282
Web: www.uillinois.edu

The University of Illinois has campuses in Chicago,
Springfield, and Urbana-Champaign, as well as health
professions sites and continuing education centers
throughout the state.

PRODUCTS/OPERATIONS

Selected Colleges and Instructional Units

College of Agricultural, Consumer and Environmental
  Sciences
College of Applied Life Studies
College of Business
College of Communications
College of Education
College of Engineering
College of Fine and Applied Arts
College of Law
College of Liberal Arts and Sciences
College of Medicine at Urbana-Champaign
College of Veterinary Medicine
Division of General Studies
Graduate School of Library and Information Science
Institute of Labor and Industrial Relations
School of Social Work

HISTORICAL FINANCIALS
Company Type: School

Income Statement

FYE: June 30

	REVENUE ($ mil.)	NET INCOME ($ mil.)	NET PROFIT MARGIN	EMPLOYEES
6/08	3,900	—	—	24,513
6/07	3,680	—	—	24,276
6/06	3,200	—	—	24,276
6/05	3,192	—	—	23,660
6/04	2,900	—	—	23,483
Annual Growth	7.7%	—	—	1.1%

Revenue History

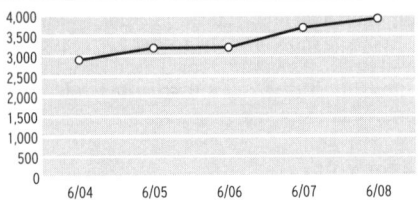

	6/04	6/05	6/06	6/07	6/08

University of Iowa Hospitals and Clinics

University of Iowa Hospitals and Clinics partners with the University of Iowa Roy J. and Lucille A. Carver College of Medicine and the
University of Iowa Physicians group practice organization to make up the University of Iowa
Health Care network. The organization provides
residents of the Hawkeye State with an acute
care hospital serving a variety of inpatient and
outpatient needs, including more than 200
health care specialties. The facility also houses
the Children's Hospital of Iowa and the Holden
Comprehensive Cancer Center. The health care
system, founded in 1898, has some 680 beds.

EXECUTIVES

CEO: Kenneth P. (Ken) Kates
Interim COO: Eric Dickson
CFO: Kenneth L. (Ken) Fisher
CIO: L. Carmen
Associate Director and Chief Administrative Officer:
  Timothy M. Gaillard
Associate Director and Legal Counsel:
  William W. Hesson
Chief of Staff: Eva Tsalikian
Head, Graduate Medical Education: M. Wilson
Head, Ambulatory Clinics: J. Swenning
Head, Heart and Vascular Care Center: D. Montchal
Joint Office for Marketing and Communications:
  D. Lundell
Joint Office for Marketing and Communications:
  S. McGauvran-Hruby
Associate VP Nursing and Chief Nursing Officer:
  Ann Williamson
Community Relations: C. Scheetz
Clinical Staff Office: C. Geyer
Medical Director Clinical Quality, Safety, and
  Performance Improvement: Charles M. Helms

LOCATIONS

HQ: University of Iowa Hospitals and Clinics
    200 Hawkins Dr., Iowa City, IA 52242
Phone: 319-356-1616   Fax: 319-384-7099
Web: www.uihealthcare.com/uihospitalsandclinics

PRODUCTS/OPERATIONS

Selected Centers

Holden Comprehensive Cancer Center
James A. Clifton Center for Digestive Diseases
University of Iowa Children's Hospital
University of Iowa Family Care
University of Iowa Heart and Vascular Center
University of Iowa Neurosciences
University of Iowa Sports Medicine
University of Iowa Weight Loss

COMPETITORS

Genesis Health System
Iowa Health System
Mercy Health Network
Regional Ventures

University of Kentucky

Kentucky knows bluegrass and basketball.
Perennial basketball powerhouse The University
of Kentucky (UK) has an enrollment of approximately 27,000 in about 20 colleges and schools.
It offers more than 100 undergraduate majors
and more than 100 graduate degree programs,
including master's, doctoral, first professional,
and post-doctoral programs. It confers some
5,500 degrees annually. UK also operates the Albert B. Chandler Hospital. A public university
and research institution, the school was founded
in 1865 as the Agricultural and Mechanical College of the Kentucky University.

EXECUTIVES

Chairman: Mira S. Ball
Vice Chairman: Stephen P. Branscum
President: Lee T. Todd Jr., age 62
Provost: Kumble R. Subbaswamy
Trustee: James F. Hardymon, age 75
EVP Finance and Administration: Frank A. Butler
EVP Health Affairs: Michael Karpf
VP Research: James W. Tracy
VP Information Technology: Eugene R. Williams
VP Student Affairs: Patricia S. Terrell
Dean, Libraries: Carol Pitts Diedrichs
Interim Dean, College of Arts and Sciences:
  Philip Harling
Interim Dean, College of Law: Louise Graham
Interim Dean, College of Education: Rosetta Sandidge
Dean, Graduate School: Jeannine Blackwell
Dean, College of Medicine: Jay Perman
Dean, College of Engineering: Thomas W. Lester
Dean, Gatton College of Business and Economics:
  Devanathan Sudharshan
Dean, College of Agriculture: M. Scott Smith
Dean, College of Pharmacy: Kenneth Roberts
Dean, College of Public Health: Stephen Wyatt
Treasurer: Marc A. Mathews
Secretary: Pamela Robinette May
General Counsel: Barbara W. Jones
Auditors: Deloitte & Touche LLP

LOCATIONS

HQ: The University of Kentucky
    410 Administration Dr., Lexington, KY 40506
Phone: 859-257-9000   Fax: 859-257-1760
Web: www.uky.edu

PRODUCTS/OPERATIONS

Selected Colleges and Schools

College of Agriculture
College of Arts and Sciences
College of Communications and Information Studies
College of Dentistry
College of Design
College of Education
College of Engineering
College of Fine Arts
College of Health Sciences
College of Law
College of Medicine
College of Nursing
College of Pharmacy
College of Public Health
College of Social Work
Gatton College of Business and Economics
Graduate School
Martin School of Public Policy and Administration
Patterson School of Diplomacy and International
  Commerce

University of Louisville

This Louisville Slugger has hit a few out of the park, as well. Living up to its mandate by the Kentucky General Assembly to be a "preeminent metropolitan research university," the University of Louisville (U of L) is home to the first self-contained artificial heart implant and the first successful hand transplant. A major focus of the university is health care, and the University of Louisville Hospital is a part of the school's medical programs. U of L offers associate, baccalaureate, master's, professional, and doctorate degrees, as well as certificates in some 170 fields of study. It has more than 22,000 students enrolled in 12 colleges and schools on three campuses.

The origins of the University of Louisville date back to 1798 with a meeting to establish Jefferson Seminary, which didn't open its doors until 1813 and closed 16 years later. Subsequent incarnations eventually led to the creation of the University of Louisville in 1846.

EXECUTIVES

President: James R. Ramsey, age 60
EVP and Provost: Shirley C. Willihnganz
EVP Health Affairs: Larry N. Cook
Acting EVP Research: William M. Pierce
VP Information Technology and CIO: Priscilla Hancock
VP Administration and Business Affairs:
  Larry L. Owsley
VP Student Affairs: Tom Jackson Jr.
VP Finance: Michael J. Curtin
Associate VP Communications and Marketing:
  John Drees
Director James Graham Brown Cancer Center:
  Donald Miller
Dean, University Libraries: Hannelore B. Rader
Bursar: Don Barnett
University Counsel: Angela Koshewa
Controller and Treasurer: Larry W. Zink
University Registrar and Director Enrollment Services:
  Kathleen Otto
**Chairman, Department of Surgery, U of L School of
  Medicine:** Kelly M. McMasters, age 48
**Director Communications for Development and
  Alumni:** Andrea Blair
Auditors: BKD, LLP

LOCATIONS

HQ: University of Louisville
   2301 S. 3rd St., Grawemeyer Hall, Rm. 108
   Louisville, KY 40292
Phone: 502-852-5555   **Fax:** 502-852-4337
Web: www.louisville.edu

University of Maryland Medical System

What began with a single University Hospital has grown to become The University of Maryland Medical System (UMMS) spanning ten general, specialty, and community hospitals. UMMS serves Baltimore and the mid-Atlantic region with more than 1,700 acute care and long-term care beds and addresses such specialties as trauma care, coma emergence, kidney and pancreas transplants, orthopedic rehabilitation, stroke intervention, and pediatric care. The system also includes community clinics to address mental health, rehabilitation services, and primary care. UMMS was established in 1984.

In 2009 UMMS announced it had formed an affiliation with Upper Chesapeake Health System, with plans to eventually merge the systems by 2013. As part of the deal, Upper Chesapeake Health System — which owns hospitals in Bel Air and Havre de Grace in Maryland — has ended a financial agreement it had with St. Joseph Medical Center, which held a minority share in Upper Chesapeake Health System. UMMS made the move to address doctor shortages and add services to Hartford County.

EXECUTIVES

Chairman: Stephen A. Burch, age 59
President and CEO: Robert A. Chrencik
SVP Corporate Operations: Jerry Wollman
SVP and CFO: Henry J. Franey
SVP and Chief Medical Officer: Glenn F. Robbins
SVP and Chief Medical Informatics Officer:
  Mark Kelemen
SVP and CIO: Jon P. Burns
SVP Facilities Planning, Design, and Construction:
  Rick E. Dunning
SVP Government and Regulatory Affairs:
  Donna L. Jacobs
SVP and General Counsel: Megan M. Arthur
SVP External Affairs and Development:
  Mark L. Wasserman
**SVP Network Development; Associate Dean, University
  of Maryland School of Medicine:** John W. Ashworth III
VP Corporate Communications and Public Affairs:
  Joan S. Shnipper

LOCATIONS

HQ: University of Maryland Medical System
   250 W. Pratt St., Baltimore, MD 21201
Phone: 410-328-6732   **Fax:** 410-328-1931
Web: www.umms.org

PRODUCTS/OPERATIONS

Selected Facilities

Baltimore Washington Medical Center
Chester River Health System
   Chester River Hospital Center
   Chester River Home Care & Hospice
   Chester River Manor
Kernan Hospital
Maryland General Hospital
Mt. Washington Pediatric Hospital
Shore Health System
   Dorchester General Hospital
   The Memorial Hospital at Easton
The University of Maryland Hospital for Children
The University of Maryland Medical Center
University Specialty Hospital

COMPETITORS

Ascension Health
Bon Secours Health
Christiana Care
Franklin Square Hospital Center
GBMC
Johns Hopkins Health System
LifeBridge Health
MedStar Health

HISTORICAL FINANCIALS

Company Type: Not-for-profit

Income Statement

	REVENUE ($ mil.)	NET INCOME ($ mil.)	NET PROFIT MARGIN	EMPLOYEES
6/08	1,960	—	—	10,000

FYE: June 30

University of Michigan

Michigan — it's shaped like a mitten, and higher education fits the state like a glove. The University of Michigan has been a leader in that state's education effort since its founding in 1817. With some 57,000 students and about 6,600 faculty members scattered across three campuses in Ann Arbor, Dearborn, and Flint, the university's diverse academic units span such areas of study as architecture, education, law, medicine, music, and social work. Notable alumni include the late President Gerald Ford (the university is home to the Gerald R. Ford Library and the Ford School of Public Policy) and playwright Arthur Miller. In addition to state funding, the university is supported by a $7.5 billion endowment.

The University of Michigan was founded in Detroit but moved to Ann Arbor in 1837. There are seven museums on campus — including the Museum of Art, the Exhibit Museum of Natural History (with a planetarium), and the Kelsey Museum of Archaeology — as well as the Nichols Arboretum and the Mattaei Botanical Gardens.

The university maintains one of the largest health care complexes in the world through its Hospitals and Health Centers division. It is made up of 40 health centers and 120 outpatient clinics around the state. In 2007 the university sold its M-CARE managed health care benefits arm to Blue Cross Blue Shield of Michigan for about $250 million. The sale also included a separate joint venture between the university and Blue Cross Blue Shield of Michigan, which will commission research and projects aimed at improving health care around the state.

In 2008 UM announced that it will buy Pfizer's former 170-acre campus near Ann Arbor for some $108 million. The space will help the university expand its research in health, biomedical sciences, and other fields.

EXECUTIVES

President: Mary Sue Coleman, age 65
Chief Information Technology Security Officer:
  Paul Howell
EVP Medical Affairs; CEO, Health System:
  Ora H. Pescovitz, age 51
EVP Academic Affairs and Provost: Teresa A. Sullivan

EVP and CFO: Timothy P. (Tim) Slottow
VP Research: Stephen R. Forrest, age 58
VP and Secretary: Sally Jo Churchill
VP and General Counsel: Suellyn Scarnecchia
VP Government Relations: Cynthia H. Wilbanks
Associate VP and Chief Human Resource Officer:
  Laurita E. Thomas
Associate VP Student Affairs and Dean, Students:
  Laura Blake Jones
Senior Vice Provost Academic Affairs: Lester P. Monts
**Vice Provost Academic Affairs, Graduate Studies and
  Dean, Horace H. Rackham School of Graduate
  Studies:** Janet A. Weiss
Vice Provost Academic Information: John L. King
Vice Provost Academic and Faculty Affairs: Lori Pierce
Vice Provost Academic and Budgetary Affairs:
  Phil Hanlon
Director Public Affairs: Kelly E. Cunningham
Director Community Relations: James A. (Jim) Kosteva
Auditors: PricewaterhouseCoopers LLP

LOCATIONS

HQ: The University of Michigan
  3074 Fleming Administration Bldg.
  Ann Arbor, MI 48109
Phone: 734-764-1817   **Fax:** 734-764-4546
Web: www.umich.edu

PRODUCTS/OPERATIONS

Selected Academic Units

Architecture and urban planning
Art and design
Business administration
Dentistry
Education
Engineering
Kinesiology
Law
Literature, science, and the arts
Medicine
Music
Natural resources and environment
Nursing
Pharmacy
Public health
Public policy
Social work

VP Human Resources: Carol Carrier
VP and Chief of Staff: Kathryn F. Brown
Associate VP Information Technology and CIO:
  Stephen P. Cawley
Associate VP Finance and Controller: Michael D. Volna
Vice Provost Undergraduate Education:
  Robert McMaster
Vice Provost Faculty and Academic Affairs:
  Arlene Carney
Vice Provost Student Affairs: Gerald Rinehart
Vice Provost; Dean, Graduate School: Gail Dubrow
Dean, Medical School: Deborah Powell
University Librarian: Wendy Pradt Lougee
General Counsel: Mark B. Rotenberg
Director Communications: Lori Ann Vicich
Director Budget, Human Resources and Payroll:
  Jill Merriam
Auditors: Deloitte & Touche LLP

LOCATIONS

HQ: University of Minnesota
  234 Morrill Hall, 100 Church St. SE
  Minneapolis, MN 55455
Phone: 612-625-5000   **Fax:** 612-626-1693
Web: www.umn.edu

PRODUCTS/OPERATIONS

Selected Colleges and Schools

Carlson School of Management
Center for Allied Health Programs
College of Food, Agricultural, and Natural Resource
  Science
College of Biological Sciences
College of Continuing Education
College of Design
College of Education and Human Development
College of Liberal Arts
College of Pharmacy
College of Veterinary Medicine
Graduate School
Hubert H. Humphrey Institute of Public Affairs
Institute of Technology
Law School
Medical School
School of Dentistry
School of Nursing
School of Public Health

VP Finance and Administration:
  Natalie R. (Nikki) Krawitz
VP Human Resources: Elizabeth (Betsy) Rodriguez
VP Research and Economic Development:
  Michael F. Nichols
VP Government Relations: Stephen C. Knorr
Chancellor, UM-Rolla: John F. Carney III
Chancellor, UM-St. Louis: Thomas F. (Tom) George
Chancellor, UM-Columbia: Brady J. Deaton
CEO, University of Missouri Health Care:
  James H. Ross
General Counsel: Stephen J. Owens
Secretary: Kathleen M. Miller
Auditors: KPMG LLP

LOCATIONS

HQ: University of Missouri System
  1100 Carrie Francke Dr., Columbia, MO 65211
Phone: 573-882-2121   **Fax:** 573-882-2721
Web: www.umsystem.edu

PRODUCTS/OPERATIONS

Selected Colleges and Schools

College of Agriculture, Food and Natural Resources
  School of Natural Resources
College of Arts and Sciences
  School of Music
College of Education
  School of Information Science and Learning
  Technologies
College of Engineering
College of Human Environmental Sciences
  School of Social Work
College of Veterinary Medicine
Graduate School
  Harry S. Truman School of Public Affairs
School of Health Professions
School of Journalism
School of Law
School of Medicine
Sinclair College of Nursing
Trulaske College of Business
  School of Accountancy

University of Minnesota

More than 65,000 students come seeking higher education in the Land of 10,000 Lakes. A major land grant university system, the University of Minnesota (U of M) offers undergraduate and graduate degrees in some 370 academic fields. It has some 4,000 faculty members. The university's Twin Cities campus, with about 50,000 students, ranks among the largest in the country in terms of enrollment. U of M serves additional students through campuses in Crookston, Duluth, Morris, and Rochester. The university was founded as a prep school in 1851 and became a land grant institution in 1867.

EXECUTIVES

Chairman: Patricia S. Simmons
President: Robert H. (Bob) Bruininks
SVP Health Sciences: Frank B. Cerra
SVP Academic Affairs and Provost:
  E. Thomas (Tom) Sullivan
SVP System Academic Administration: Robert J. Jones
VP, CFO, and Treasurer: Richard H. Pfutzenreuter
VP Research: R. Timothy (Tim) Mulcahy

University of Missouri

Education isn't just for show in the Show Me State. The University of Missouri (UM), founded in 1839, educates more than 64,000 students at four campuses and through a statewide extension program; about a quarter of students are in graduate or professional programs. The university's campuses include flagship UM-Columbia (home to nearly 30,000 students, some 20 schools and colleges, and the University of Missouri Health Sciences Center), UM-Kansas City, UM-St. Louis, and the Missouri University of Science and Technology (aka Missouri S&T, formerly UM-Rolla). Nicknamed "Mizzou," the University of Missouri System has more than 7,500 faculty members.

EXECUTIVES

Chairman: Cheryl D. S. Walker
Vice Chairman: Buford M. (Bo) Fraser
President: Gary D. Forsee, age 59
EVP: Gordon H. Lamb
VP Information Technology: Gary K. Allen

University of Nebraska

The University of Nebraska has sprouted four campuses out in the fields of the Cornhusker State. Founded in 1869, the state university system offers bachelor's, master's, and doctoral degrees in such programs as agriculture, business, education, and engineering at its campuses in Kearney, Lincoln, and Omaha. The university's Medical Center in Omaha trains doctors, performs research, and is affiliated with a 700-bed teaching hospital. The University of Nebraska also operates research and extension services across the state. Nearly 47,000 students attend classes in the university system.

EXECUTIVES

President: James B. (J. B.) Milliken
EVP and Provost: Linda Pratt
VP University Affairs: Peter G. (Pete) Kotsiopulos
VP and General Counsel: Joel D. Pedersen
VP Business and Finance: David E. Lechner
**Associate VP University Affairs and Director
  Governmental Relations:** Ron Withem
Assistant VP and Director Human Resources:
  Ed Wimes
Assistant VP Communications and Marketing:
  Sharon Stephan
CIO: Walter Weir

Director, University Communications: Meg Lauerman
Chancellor, Kearney Campus:
 Douglas A. (Doug) Kristensen
Chancellor, Omaha Campus: John Christensen
Chancellor, Lincoln Campus: Harvey S. Perlman
Chancellor, Medical Center: Harold M. Maurer
Auditors: KPMG LLP

LOCATIONS

HQ: The University of Nebraska
 3835 Holdrege St., Lincoln, NE 68583
Phone: 402-472-2111 **Fax:** 402-472-1237
Web: www.nebraska.edu

PRODUCTS/OPERATIONS

University Campuses
The University of Nebraska at Kearney
The University of Nebraska-Lincoln
The University of Nebraska Medical Center
The University of Nebraska at Omaha

Selected Colleges and Programs
Agricultural Science and Natural Resources
Architecture
Arts and Sciences
Business Administration
Dentistry (University of Nebraska Medical Center)
Engineering and Technology
Fine and Performing Arts
Graduate Studies
Human Resources and Family Science
Law
Medicine (University of Nebraska Medical Center)
Nursing (University of Nebraska Medical Center)
Pharmacy (University of Nebraska Medical Center)
Teachers College

COMPETITORS

Kansas State University
Oklahoma State
The University of Kansas
University of Missouri
University of Oklahoma
University of Wyoming

University of New Mexico

With some 26,000 students attending its main campus in Albuquerque, The University of New Mexico is most renowned for its schools of medicine, law, and education. Nearly 7,000 additional students attend one of the school's four branches located around the northern part of the state at Taos, Los Alamos, Gallup, and Valencia. Through its eight schools and colleges, the university offers 100 bachelor's degrees, some 70 master's degrees, about 40 doctorate degrees, and a variety of certificates and education specializations. UNM was founded in 1889. Its annual budget tops $2 billion.

In 2006 UNM agreed to purchase a new site for a campus in Rio Rancho. In addition to housing a new UNM campus, the university reached an agreement with rival New Mexico State University to include some of its specialized degree programs, including hotel and restaurant management, natural resource management, and agricultural programs.

EXECUTIVES

President: David J. Schmidly
EVP Academic Affairs and Provost: Reed Dasenbrock
**EVP Health Sciences, Dean School of Medicine, and
 Associate VP Clinical Affairs:** Paul B. Roth
VP Student Affairs: Eliseo (Cheo) Torres
**Interim VP Advancement and Interim President, UNM
 Foundation:** Michael Kingan
Associate VP Development: Walt Miller
**Associate VP College Enrichment and Outreach
 Programs:** Tim Gutierrez
**Associate VP Alumni Relations and Executive Director
 UNM Alumni:** Karen Abraham
Associate VP and Director Human Resources:
 Susan A. Carkeek
Vice Provost Undergraduate Education: Peter White
**Vice Provost Graduate Education and Dean Graduate
 Studies:** Amy Wohlert

LOCATIONS

HQ: The University of New Mexico
 1 University Hill NE, Albuquerque, NM 87131
Phone: 505-277-0111 **Fax:** 505-277-6686
Web: www.unm.edu

HISTORICAL FINANCIALS
Company Type: School

Income Statement
FYE: June 30

	REVENUE ($ mil.)	NET INCOME ($ mil.)	NET PROFIT MARGIN	EMPLOYEES
6/08	1,841	—	—	20,210
6/07	1,678	—	—	20,140
6/06	1,573	—	—	19,683
6/05	1,485	—	—	19,662
Annual Growth	7.4%	—	—	0.9%

Revenue History

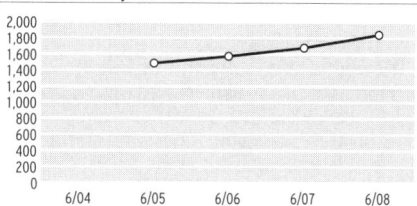

University of Pennsylvania

The University of Pennsylvania was founded by Benjamin Franklin when he had a little down time between establishing a country and experimenting with lightning. Since opening its doors to students in 1751, the Ivy League university has accumulated a notable list of accomplishments, including the creation of the first medical school in the US and the invention of the ENIAC computer. The university has about 24,000 students that pursue their studies in four undergraduate schools and a dozen graduate and professional schools, including the renowned Wharton School and the Annenberg School for Communications. Former president Judith Rodin was the first female to head an Ivy League university.

EXECUTIVES

President: Amy Gutmann
Provost: Ronald J. Daniels
**EVP University of Pennsylvania Health System and
 Dean School of Medicine:** Arthur H. Rubenstein,
 age 71
EVP: Craig Carnaroli
SVP and General Counsel: Wendy S. White
VP Development and Alumni Relations: John H. Zeller
VP and Chief of Staff: Greg Rost
VP Human Resources: John J. Heuer
VP Finance and Treasurer: Scott R. Douglass
VP Information Systems and Computing:
 Robin H. Beck
VP University Communications: Lori Doyle
Dean, School of Nursing: Afaf I. Meleis
Interim Dean, Graduate School of Education:
 Stanton Wortham
Dean, Wharton School: Thomas S. Robertson
Dean, School of Arts and Sciences:
 Rebecca W. Bushnell
Dean, Annenberg School for Communication:
 Michael X. Delli Carpini
Dean, School of Law: Michael A. Fitts
Secretary: Leslie Laird Kruhly
Comptroller: John F. Horn
Auditors: PricewaterhouseCoopers LLP

LOCATIONS

HQ: The University of Pennsylvania
 3451 Walnut St., Philadelphia, PA 19104
Phone: 215-898-5000 **Fax:** 215-898-9659
Web: www.upenn.edu

PRODUCTS/OPERATIONS

Selected Schools
Annenberg School for Communication
The College at Penn (School of Arts and Sciences)
Graduate School of Education
Graduate School of Fine Arts
Law School
School of Arts and Sciences
School of Dental Medicine
School of Engineering and Applied Science
School of Medicine
School of Nursing
School of Social Work
School of Veterinary Medicine
The Wharton School

University of Rochester

The buzz about the University of Rochester is music to some ears. The private, upstate New York institution is nationally recognized for its programs in medicine, engineering, and business, and its Eastman School of Music (founded by Eastman Kodak founder George Eastman) is one of the top music schools in the US. The university, which has an endowment of more than $1.7 billion, offers about more than 200 academic majors and about 30 master's and doctoral degree programs to more than 9,000 undergraduate and graduate students. Founded as a Baptist-sponsored institution in 1850, the university is nonsectarian today.

EXECUTIVES

Chairman: Edmund (Ed) Hajim
President and Trustee: Joel Seligman, age 59
Provost and EVP: Ralph W. Kuncl

SVP Health Sciences; CEO, University of Rochester
  Medical Center: Bradford C. Berk
SVP and Dean, Robert L. & Mary L. Sproull Dean of
  the Faculty of Arts, Sciences, and Engineering:
  Peter Lennie
SVP and Chief Advancement Officer:
  James D. (Jim) Thompson
SVP Administration and Finance, CFO, and Treasurer:
  Ronald J. Paprocki
SVP Institutional Resources: Douglas W. Phillips
VP Communications: Bill Murphy
VP and General Counsel: Sue S. Stewart, age 66
VP, General Secretary, and Senior Advisor to the
  President, and University Dean: Paul J. Burgett
Vice Provost and CIO: David E. Lewis
Dean, School of Medicine and Dentistry:
  David S. Guzick
Dean, School of Nursing: Dorothy Parker
Dean, Eastman School of Music: Douglas A. Lowry
Dean, Hajim School of Engineering and Applied
  Sciences: Robert A. Clark
Dean, College of Arts, Science and Engineering:
  Richard Feldman
Dean, Margaret Warner Graduate School of Education
  and Human Development: Raffaella Borasi
Dean, William E. Simon School of Business
  Administration: Mark Zupan, age 49
Auditors: PricewaterhouseCoopers LLP

LOCATIONS

HQ: University of Rochester
    200 Administration Bldg., Rochester, NY 14627
Phone: 585-275-3221   Fax: 585-461-1046
Web: www.rochester.edu

PRODUCTS/OPERATIONS

Selected Schools and Colleges
Eastman School of Music
School of Arts and Sciences
School of Engineering and Applied Sciences
School of Medicine and Dentistry
School of Nursing
Simon School of Business
Warner School of Education

HISTORICAL FINANCIALS
Company Type: School

Income Statement

	REVENUE ($ mil.)	NET INCOME ($ mil.)	NET PROFIT MARGIN	EMPLOYEES
6/08	2,419	—	—	18,531
6/07	2,295	—	—	18,000
6/06	2,143	—	—	17,696
6/05	1,977	—	—	17,075
6/04	1,809	—	—	16,554
Annual Growth	**7.5%**	**—**	**—**	**2.9%**

Revenue History
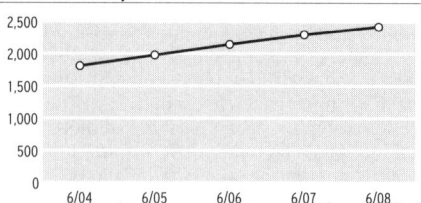

| | 6/04 | 6/05 | 6/06 | 6/07 | 6/08 |

University of Southern California

This Trojan horse, filled with more than 33,000 students, is more than welcome at the University of Southern California (USC). Founded in 1880, the private university (with a Trojan mascot) grew up with the city of Los Angeles, and is one of the largest private employers in the city. California's oldest research university, USC is recognized for distinguished programs in fields including business, engineering, film, law, medicine, public administration, and science. The university has two campuses in Los Angeles and additional centers and programs elsewhere in California and Washington, DC.

Notable alumni include Marion Morrison (also known as John Wayne), who played tackle on the school's football team, and the first man on the moon, Neil Armstrong. Directors George Lucas and Robert Zemeckis are both USC film school graduates.

HISTORY

Los Angeles was still a frontier town when a diverse group of local citizens, led by Judge Robert Maclay Widney, established the University of Southern California in 1880 (early rules for students included a prohibition against carrying guns to class). But Los Angeles grew quickly, and USC grew with it. By 1910 the university had most of its major programs in place, including law and medical schools. During the 1920s USC established the nation's first school of international relations (1924) and offered the first degree in cinema (1929).

The end of WWII and the GI Bill brought a major increase in enrollment, forcing the university to expand. Some 50 new buildings were added in the 1950s and 1960s, and another 37 were begun or completed in the 1970s. The university started increasing its fund-raising efforts in the 1980s. Steven Sample became president in 1991 and secured hundreds of millions in donations over the course of the decade, including a $110 million grant in 1999 from the W.M. Keck Foundation for USC's School of Medicine.

USC was named 1999 college of the year by *Time* magazine and the *Princeton Review*.

EXECUTIVES

Chairman: Edward P. (Ed) Roski Jr.
President and Trustee: Steven B. Sample, age 68
EVP and Provost: Chrysostomos L. (Max) Nikias, age 56
SVP University Relations: Martha Harris
Interim SVP and CFO: Robert Abeles, age 63
SVP Administration: Todd R. Dickey
Associate SVP Alumni Relations: Scott Mory
VP Student Affairs: Michael L. Jackson
CIO: Ilee Rhimes
General Counsel and Secretary: Carol M. Amir
Dean, USC School of Architecture: Qingyun Ma
Dean, School of Fine Arts: Ruth E. Weisberg
Dean, School of Theatre: Madeline Puzo
Dean, USC Gould School of Law: Robert K. Rasmussen
Dean, USC Libraries: Catherine Quinlan
Dean, Keck School of Medicine of USC:
  Carmen A. Puliafito
Dean, USC Marshall School of Business:
  James G. Ellis, age 62
Dean, USC College of Letters, Arts, and Sciences:
  Howard Gillman

Dean, USC Annenberg School for Communication:
  Ernest J. Wilson III
Dean, School of Cinematic Arts: Elizabeth M. Daley
Auditors: PricewaterhouseCoopers LLP

LOCATIONS

HQ: The University of Southern California
    University Park Campus, Los Angeles, CA 90089
Phone: 213-740-2311   Fax: 213-740-5229
Web: www.usc.edu

PRODUCTS/OPERATIONS

Selected Schools
Annenberg School for Communication
College of Letters, Arts and Sciences
Davis School of Gerontology
Gould School of Law
Graduate School
Keck School of Medicine
Leventhal School of Accounting
Marshall School of Business
Roski School of Fine Arts
Rossier School of Education
School of Architecture
School of Cinematic Arts
School of Dentistry
School of Pharmacy
School of Policy, Planning, and Development
School of Social Work
School of Theatre
Thornton School of Music
Viterbi School of Engineering

University of Texas System

These students are hooked on higher education. The University of Texas System runs nine universities throughout the Lone Star State with a total enrollment of more than 190,000 students, making it one of the largest university systems in the US. Its flagship Austin campus, with some 50,000 students, ranks as one of the nation's largest student populations (neck-and-neck with the main campuses at Ohio State and the University of Minnesota). UT also runs six health institutions, including four medical schools. Its approximately $15 billion endowment fund (managed by the University of Texas Investment Management Co.) is the country's third largest (after Harvard and Yale).

Established in 1876, UT Austin opened in 1883. The UT System was formally organized in 1950.

HISTORY

The Texas Declaration of Independence (1836) admonished Mexico for having failed to establish a public education system in the territory, but attempts to start a state-sponsored university were stymied until after Texas achieved US statehood and fought in the Civil War. A new constitution in 1876 provided for the establishment of "a university of the first class," and in 1883 The University of Texas (UT) opened in Austin. Eight professors taught 218 students in two curricula: academics and law.

The school's first building opened in 1884, and in 1891 the university's medical school opened in

Galveston. By 1894 UT-Austin had 534 students and a football team. UT opened a Graduate School in 1910 and various other colleges over the years. The university added its first academic branch campus when the Texas State School of Mines and Metallurgy (opened in 1914 in El Paso) became part of the system in 1919.

UT's financial future was secured in 1923 when oil was found on West Texas land that had been set aside by the legislature as an education endowment. The income from oil production, as well as the proceeds of surface-use leases, became the Permanent University Fund (PUF), from which only interest and earnings on the revenues can be used: two-thirds by UT and one-third by Texas A&M University. UT continued to grow, thanks to the PUF, which topped $100 million by 1940.

UT sported the black eye of racial prejudice (as did many other institutions at the time) when it refused to admit Heman Sweatt, a black student, to its law school in 1946. The Supreme Court ordered UT to admit him in 1950, the same year the UT System was officially organized. Sixteen years later, in one of the nation's most highly publicized crimes, Charles Whitman killed 14 people and wounded 31 others with a high-powered rifle fired from atop the UT-Austin administration tower. The observation deck wasn't closed until 1975, however, after a series of suicides. (It was later reopened in 1999.)

In the meantime, UT added a medical center in Dallas and several graduate schools in Austin. The 1960s through the 1980s were a time of geographic expansion for the system as it absorbed other institutions, started several new campuses, and expanded its network of medical centers. In 1996 the UT System became the first public university to establish a private investment management company (University of Texas Investment Management Co.) to invest PUF money (by that time over $9 billion) and other funds.

The race issue reared its head again in 1996 when a Federal court ruled in the Hopwood decision (named for the plaintiff) that the UT System could no longer use race to determine scholarships and admissions. Minority enrollments declined the following year, prompting the Texas Legislature to enact a law granting admission to the top 10% of graduates from any Texas high school to the state university of their choice.

Chancellor William Cunningham announced plans in 2000 to expand the UT System by 100,000 students over the decade. After he resigned that year, R. D. Burck took over as his successor. In 2001 UT received a $50 million donation, the largest gift in its history, from Texas businessman and Minnesota Vikings owner Red McCombs. The following year Burck stepped down and was replaced by Mark Yudof, former president of the University of Minnesota. Dr. Francisco Cigarroa replaced Yudof as chancellor in 2009.

EXECUTIVES

Chairman: H. Scott Caven Jr.
Vice Chairman: James R. Huffines, age 58
Vice Chairman: Robert B. Rowling, age 56
Chancellor: Francisco G. Cigarroa
Executive Vice Chancellor for Academic Affairs:
David B. Prior
Executive Vice Chancellor Business Affairs:
Scott C. Kelley
Vice Chancellor Finance and Business Development:
Philip R. Aldridge
Vice Chancellor Strategic Management:
Geri H. Malandra
Vice Chancellor External Relations: Randa S. Safady

Vice Chancellor Federal Relations: William H. Shute
Vice Chancellor for Governmental Relations:
Barry McBee
Vice Chancellor and General Counsel: Barry D. Burgdorf
Vice Chancellor Administration: Tonya M. Brown
Associate Vice Chancellor and CIO: Marg Knox
Associate Vice Chancellor, Controller, and Chief Budget Officer: Randy Wallace
Associate Vice Chancellor Research:
Arjuna (Arjun) Sanga
General Counsel, Board of Regents:
Francie A. Frederick
Director Technology and Information Services:
Sheila Ochner
Director Community and Donor Relations:
Melissa Jackson
Auditors: Deloitte & Touche LLP

LOCATIONS

HQ: The University of Texas System
601 Colorado St., Austin, TX 78701
Phone: 512-499-4200   **Fax:** 512-499-4215
Web: www.utsystem.edu

PRODUCTS/OPERATIONS

Selected Institutions

Academic Institutions
The University of Texas at Arlington (established 1895)
The University of Texas at Austin (1883)
The University of Texas at Brownsville (1991)
The University of Texas at Dallas (1961)
The University of Texas at El Paso (1914)
The University of Texas-Pan American (Edinburg; 1927)
The University of Texas of the Permian Basin (Odessa; 1969)
The University of Texas at San Antonio (1969)
The University of Texas at Tyler (1971)

Health Institutions
The University of Texas Health Science Center at Houston (established 1972)
The University of Texas Health Science Center at San Antonio (1959)
The University of Texas Health Science Center at Tyler (1977)
The University of Texas M.D. Anderson Cancer Center (Houston, 1941)
The University of Texas Medical Branch at Galveston (1891)
The University of Texas Southwestern Medical Center at Dallas (1943)

University of Washington

The University of Washington (UW) is Husky indeed, with an enrollment of some 40,000 students. Founded in 1861 as the Territorial University of Washington, UW (pronounced "U-dub" by those on campus) has smaller branches in Tacoma and Bothell in addition to its main Seattle campus. The university, whose mascot is a Husky, offers undergraduate, graduate, and professional degree programs in some 150 fields of study at more than 15 schools and colleges. It also operates a health sciences center and an academic medical center, which includes the University of Washington Medical Center and Harborview Medical Center.

EXECUTIVES

President: Mark A. Emmert, age 56
Provost and EVP: Phyllis M. Wise, age 61
SVP Finance and Facilities: V'Ella Warren
VP Medical Affairs; Dean, School of Medicine:
Paul G. Ramsey
VP University Advancement:
Constance H. (Connie) Kravas, age 62
VP Minority Affairs and Vice Provost Diversity:
Sheila E. Lange
VP Human Resources: Mindy Kornberg
Executive Vice Provost: Doug Wadden
Vice Provost Undergraduate Academic Affairs: Ed Taylor
Vice Provost Student Life: Eric Godfrey
Vice Provost Academic Personnel: Cheryl A. Cameron
Vice Provost Information Management: Sara Gomez
Vice Provost Research: Mary Lidstrom
Dean and Vice Provost Graduate School:
Gerald (Jerry) Baldasty
Auditors: KPMG LLP

LOCATIONS

HQ: University of Washington
Schmitz Hall, 1410 NE Campus Pkwy.
Seattle, WA 98195
Phone: 206-543-2100
Web: www.washington.edu

The University of Washington has campuses in Bothell, Seattle, and Tacoma, Washington.

PRODUCTS/OPERATIONS

Selected Schools and Colleges

College of Architecture and Urban Planning
College of Arts and Sciences
College of Education
College of Engineering
College of the Environment
College of Forest Resources
College of Ocean and Fishery Sciences
Daniel J. Evans School of Public Affairs
The Graduate School
Information School
Michael G. Foster School of Business
School of Dentistry
School of Law
School of Medicine
School of Nursing
School of Pharmacy
School of Public Health and Community Medicine
School of Social Work

HISTORICAL FINANCIALS

Company Type: School

Income Statement

FYE: June 30

	REVENUE ($ mil.)	NET INCOME ($ mil.)	NET PROFIT MARGIN	EMPLOYEES
6/08	2,853	—	—	28,198
6/07	2,590	—	—	28,188
6/06	2,420	—	—	27,958
6/05	2,298	—	—	27,695
6/04	2,263	—	—	26,750
Annual Growth	6.0%	—	—	1.3%

Revenue History

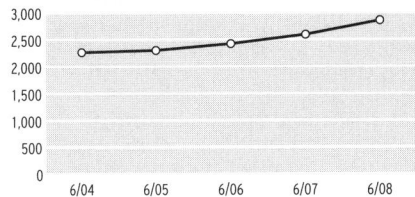

University of Wisconsin

There is no School of Cheese in the University of Wisconsin System, but there are 13 four-year universities, 13 two-year campuses, and a statewide extension program. The University of Wisconsin System is one of the largest public university systems in the US, with more than 170,000 students. Its top school is the University of Wisconsin at Madison, which offers more than 400 undergraduate majors, master's degree programs, and doctoral programs to some 42,000 students. The system's other major campus is the University of Wisconsin at Milwaukee, with about 28,000 students.

Nearly one-quarter of the UW System's annual budget comes from state funds. Student fees, federal grants, fund raising, and other sources account for the remainder.

HISTORY

When Wisconsin became a state in 1848, its constitution called for the establishment of a state university. A board of regents was named, and it first established a preparatory school because regents felt Wisconsin's secondary schools were not advanced enough to prepare students for university studies. The school began classes in 1849 with 20 students in the Madison Female Academy Building. The University of Wisconsin's first official freshman class began studies in the fall of 1850. A campus was established a mile west of the state capitol in Madison. By 1854, when it held its first commencement (with two graduates), the school had 41 students.

Enrollment dipped during the Civil War (all but one of the school's senior class joined the army) but soon rebounded, and by 1870 the university had almost 500 students. Meanwhile, it established a school of agriculture (1866) and a school of law (1868). The state established normal schools (teachers colleges) in Platteville (1866), Whitewater (1868), Oshkosh (1871), and River Falls (1874).

There was also a teachers' course for women at the university in Madison. However, when John Bascom became president in 1874, he transformed the university into a truly coeducational institution, putting women "in all respects on precisely the same footing" with the men.

While the university at Madison remained Wisconsin's primary seat of learning, the state continued to establish normal schools. It opened institutions in Milwaukee (1885), Superior (1893), Stevens Point (1894), La Crosse (1909), and Eau Claire (1916). The nine normal schools eventually became a system of state colleges called Wisconsin State Universities.

The university at Madison also continued to grow, and by the late 1920s it had almost 9,000 students. WWII brought a drop in enrollment, but afterward it took off, jumping from about 7,000 in 1945 to over 22,000 by the late 1950s. The University of Wisconsin-Milwaukee branch was founded in 1956. Other branch campuses were established in Green Bay (1965) and Kenosha (1968).

The Madison campus became a focal point for student protests during the Vietnam War. Events came to a head in 1970 when President Fred Harrington resigned during a four-day standoff between students and the National Guard. War protesters also placed a bomb outside Sterling Hall, which housed the Army Math Research Center; the explosion killed one student and injured three others.

The state legislature merged the University of Wisconsin and the Wisconsin State Universities in 1971 to create The University of Wisconsin System.

EXECUTIVES

Regent President: Mark J. Bradley
Regent Vice President: Charles Pruitt
President: Kevin P. Reilly
SVP Academic Affairs: Rebecca R. Martin
SVP Administration and Fiscal Affairs:
 Thomas K. (Tom) Anderes
VP Finance and Administrative Services:
 Ruth Anderson
Associate VP Learning and Information Technology:
 Edward (Ed) Meachen
Associate VP Financial Administration: Glen R. Nelson
Associate VP Budget and Planning: Freda J. Harris
Associate VP Human Resources: Alan Crist
Assistant VP Communications and External Relations:
 Kristine Andrews
Registrar: Sue Moore
Controller: D. Jeff Arnold
Secretary: Judith A. Temby
General Counsel: Patricia A. Brady
**Executive Director Communications and External
 Relations:** David F. Giroux
Director Human Resources Information Services:
 Sue Chamberlain
Auditors: State of Wisconsin Legislative Audit Bureau

LOCATIONS

HQ: The University of Wisconsin System
 Van Hise Hall, 1220 Linden Dr., Madison, WI 53706
Phone: 608-262-2400 **Fax:** 608-262-3985
Web: www.uwsa.edu

PRODUCTS/OPERATIONS

Four-Year Campuses

UW-Eau Claire
UW-Green Bay
UW-La Crosse
UW-Madison
UW-Milwaukee
UW-Oshkosh
UW-Parkside
UW-Platteville
UW-River Falls
UW-Stevens Point
UW-Stout
UW-Superior
UW-Whitewater

Two-Year Colleges

UW-Baraboo/Sauk County
UW-Barron County
UW-Fond du Lac
UW-Fox Valley
UW-Manitowoc
UW-Marathon County
UW-Marinette
UW-Marshfield/Wood County
UW-Richland
UW-Rock County
UW-Sheboygan
UW-Washington County
UW-Waukesha

University of Wisconsin-Madison

The University of Wisconsin-Madison, the largest campus of the University of Wisconsin System, offers academic programs in more than 100 fields of study. UW-Madison offers about 8,000 courses in areas such as computer science, psychology, English, nursing, journalism, and art. The university, which offers bachelor's, master's, doctoral, and professional degrees, has an enrollment of more than 41,000 students and has about 2,000 faculty members. Its extracurricular activities include more than 600 clubs and student organizations. Resident undergraduate tuition and fees cost about $17,200. Wisconsin's first governor, Nelson Dewey, established the university in 1848.

Notable alumni include US Vice President Dick Cheney, novelist Joyce Carol Oates, and architect Frank Lloyd Wright. The university's students come from all the states in the US and abroad.

A decline in state funding, once its primary source of revenue, has led the university to rely more on tuition, federal and private grants, and auxiliary enterprises to fund its programs.

EXECUTIVES

Chancellor: Carolyn A. (Biddy) Martin
Provost and Vice Chancellor for Academic Affairs:
 Patrick V. Farrell
Vice Chancellor Administration: Darrell Bazzell
Vice Chancellor Research; Dean, Graduate School:
 Martin Cadwallader
CIO and Vice Provost for Information Technology:
 Ron Kraemer
**Associate Vice President Academic and Student
 Services:** Ronald M. Singer
Registrar: Joanne E. Berg
Dean, School of Business: Michael M. Knetter, age 48
Director Admissions: Robert A. Seltzer
Director Libraries and Senior Academic Librarian:
 Kenneth L. (Ken) Frazier
Director Purchasing: Michael R. Hardiman
Director Financial Aid: Susan E. Fischer
Director Educational Placement and Career Services:
 Steve Head
President and CEO, Wisconsin Alumni Association:
 Paula Bonner

LOCATIONS

HQ: The University of Wisconsin-Madison
 Van Hise Hall, 1220 Linden Dr., Madison, WI 53706
Phone: 608-263-2400 **Fax:** 608-262-3985
Web: www.wisc.edu

Univision
Communications

Some Spanish-speaking Americans have a singular vision when it comes to watching TV. Univision Communications is the leading Spanish-language broadcaster in the US with a portfolio of television and radio operations. It runs the top-rated Univision network, carried by more than 1,400 broadcast and cable affiliates, as well as sister networks TeleFutura and Galavisión. The company also owns and operates nearly 40 full-power TV stations and more than 20 low-power stations. Its Univision Radio division boasts about 70 stations. Univision was founded in 1961 as Spanish International Network. It is controlled by a group of private investment firms led by TPG Capital and Thomas H. Lee Partners.

In addition to its traditional broadcasting operations, Univision distributes content online and to mobile handheld devices. It also owns 50% of TuTv, a joint venture with Grupo Televisa that distributes a handful of digital TV networks to the US market.

The Univision network continues to rank as the #1 TV destination for Spanish-language speakers in the US, which puts it just behind the four main broadcast networks in the key 18-49 audience demographic. Univision has benefited in the past from advertisers eager to reach the growing Hispanic population, a segment that has seen its buying power increase markedly over the past decade, but the recession has led to decreasing ad revenue. In response, the company cut several hundred jobs early in 2009 in an effort to reduce operating expenses.

Early in 2009 Univision settled a dispute with Televisa over royalty payments for TV shows produced by the Mexican media company. The two companies agreed to leave in place a licensing agreement that runs through 2017. For Univision, the deal means it can continue to air its most popular telenovelas.

Univision was taken private in 2007 for about $12.3 billion (plus the assumption of $1.4 billion in debt). While the deal was a victory for former CEO Jerrold Perenchio, who led the growth of the company and owned a 10% stake, it has left the company struggling with debt.

Following the going-private transaction Joe Uva was installed as Univision's new CEO. A veteran of the entertainment and media business, Uva formerly oversaw sales and marketing for several units at Time Warner's Turner Broadcasting subsidiary. He left his post as CEO at OMD Worldwide, one of the media buying agencies of advertising conglomerate Omnicom Group.

EXECUTIVES

President and COO: Ray Rodriguez, age 58, $2,676,710 total compensation
CEO and Director: Joseph (Joe) Uva, age 53, $3,199,110 total compensation
SEVP, CFO, and Chief Strategy Officer: Andrew W. (Andy) Hobson, age 47, $3,832,557 total compensation
EVP and General Counsel: C. Douglas Kranwinkle, age 67, $6,988,923 total compensation
EVP Distribution Sales and Marketing, Univision Networks: Tonia O'Connor, age 37
EVP Sales, Univision Network: Judy Kenny
SVP Univision Network Sales: Carlos Deschapelles

SVP and Chief Accounting Officer: Peter H. Lori, age 43, $527,172 total compensation
SVP Business Affairs: Glenn A. Dryfoos
VP Corporate Communications: Mónica Talán
VP Investor Relations: Diana M. Vesga
President, Advertising Sales: David Lawenda, age 42
President, Univision Television Station Group: Joanne Lynch
President, Univision Studios: Luis Fernandez
President and COO, Univision Radio: Gary B. Stone
President, Univision Networks: Cesar Conde, age 35
President, Television Station Group: Terry Mackin, age 50
Auditors: Ernst & Young LLP

LOCATIONS

HQ: Univision Communications Inc.
605 Third Ave., 12th Floor, New York, NY 10158
Phone: 212-455-5200   **Fax:** 212-867-6710
Web: www.univision.com

Selected Radio Markets

Albuquerque, NM
Austin, TX
Chicago
Dallas
El Paso, TX
Fresno, CA
Houston
Las Vegas
Los Angeles
McAllen, TX
Miami
New York City
Phoenix
San Antonio
San Diego
San Francisco

PRODUCTS/OPERATIONS

2008 Sales

	$ mil.	% of total
Television	1,563.7	77
Radio	414.1	21
Interactive media	42.5	2
Total	**2,020.3**	**100**

Selected Operations

Television networks
  Galavisión
  TeleFutura
  Univision
Univision Radio
Univision Online

COMPETITORS

ABC, Inc.
CBS Corp
Clear Channel
Discovery Communications
Entravision
Fox Entertainment
Liberman Broadcasting
NBC
SIRIUS XM
Spanish Broadcasting
Telemundo Communications
Televisa
Turner Broadcasting
TV Azteca

HISTORICAL FINANCIALS
Company Type: Private

Income Statement
FYE: December 31

	REVENUE ($ mil.)	NET INCOME ($ mil.)	NET PROFIT MARGIN	EMPLOYEES
12/08	2,020	(5,127)	—	4,107
12/07	2,073	(248)	—	4,282
Annual Growth	(2.5%)	—	—	(4.1%)

Net Income History

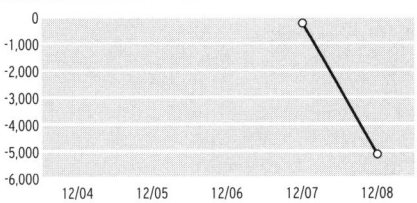

Uno Restaurants

It shouldn't be a surprise that Uno Restaurant Holdings thinks its pizza is numero uno. The company operates and franchises more than 200 Uno Chicago Grill restaurants in about 30 states and a handful of other countries. Known for their deep-dish, Chicago-style pizza, the casual-dining spots also serve pasta, seafood, and sandwiches. About 120 locations are company-owned, while the rest are franchised. Through subsidiary Uno Foods, the company also sells branded food products to airlines, hotels, supermarkets, and theaters. Ike Sewell opened the first Pizzeria Uno in Chicago in 1943. Uno Restaurants is controlled by private equity firm Centre Partners Management.

The company is looking to expand its chain of restaurants through increased franchising, both in the US and abroad. As part of that strategy, Uno Restaurants launched Uno Due Go, a new quick-service concept designed for high-traffic locations such as airports and shopping malls. The company is also working to increase its consumer products business.

Its expansion plans are being bolstered by the investment of Centre Partners Management, which acquired its controlling stake in Uno Restaurants in 2005.

EXECUTIVES

Chairman Emeritus: Aaron D. Spencer, age 77
CEO: Frank W. Guidara, age 61
COO: Roger L. Zingle, age 55
EVP; President, Uno Foods: Alan M. Fox, age 61
SVP Marketing: Richard K. (Rick) Hendrie
SVP and CFO: Louie Psallidas
SVP Franchise Development: Jack G. Crawford
SVP New Concept Development: James T. (Jamie) Strobino
SVP and General Counsel: George W. Herz II, age 53
SVP Operations: William J. (Bill) Golden
SVP Human Resources and Training: Roger C. Ahlfeld
SVP, Uno Foods: Charles J. Kozubal
VP and Controller: Dino Georgakopoulos
VP Information Systems: Alan D. LaBatte
VP Food and Beverage and Executive Chef: Christopher S. (Chris) Gatto
Auditors: Ernst & Young LLP

LOCATIONS

HQ: Uno Restaurant Holdings Corp.
100 Charles Park Rd., Boston, MA 02132
Phone: 617-323-9200   **Fax:** 617-218-5376
Web: www.unos.com

COMPETITORS

Applebee's
Bertucci's Corp.
BJ's Restaurants
Brinker
BUCA
California Pizza Kitchen
Carino's Italian Grill
Carlson Restaurants
Cheesecake Factory
Darden
Famous Famiglia
OSI Restaurant Partners
Papa Gino's Holdings
Rock Bottom Restaurants
Ruby Tuesday
Sbarro

U.S. Central Federal Credit Union

U.S. Central Federal Credit Union is a cooperative "central bank" for a network of about 30 corporate credit unions. These, in turn, represent nearly 7,900 credit unions nationwide. U.S. Central performs a variety of liquidity and cash management functions, such as funds transfer, settlement services, risk management, and custody services. Subsidiary CU Investment Solutions provides investment advisory and brokerage services to the corporate credit unions, while its majority-owned Corporate Network eCom offers bill payment and technology services to the network and its members. U.S. Central Federal Credit Union was seized and placed in conservatorship by federal regulators in 2009.

The intervention came after the credit union's portfolio of mortgage-related securities deteriorated. The National Credit Union Administration (NCUA) had already supplied some $1 billion in capital from its insurance fund to prop up U.S. Central after the company warned of heavy losses for fiscal 2008. The following year, the NCUA appointed James Nance as U.S. Central's CEO, but replaced him later that year, citing strategic differences. He was succeeded by the company's general counsel, Francois Henriquez, on an interim basis.

The NCUA will continue to operate U.S. Central until its financial status regains stability. The member accounts of U.S. Central are guaranteed under the NCUA Share Guarantee Program through the end of 2010.

Among the company's other subsidiaries, Charlie Mac (formerly Network Liquidity Accep-

tance Company), works as a liquidity facility by purchasing loans originated by credit unions. Its Network Financial Services provides electronic data transfer services and access to electronic forms, operational reports, and other information for credit unions.

EXECUTIVES

Interim President and CEO: François G. Henriquez II
EVP Correspondent Services: Marcie Haitema
SVP and CFO: Kathryn (Kathy) Brick
SVP and CIO: Charles Troutman
Auditors: Ernst & Young LLP

LOCATIONS

HQ: U.S. Central Federal Credit Union
9701 Renner Blvd., Ste. 100, Lenexa, KS 66219
Phone: 913-227-6000   **Fax:** 913-227-6250
Web: www.uscentral.coop

PRODUCTS/OPERATIONS

Selected Subsidiaries and Affiliates

Charlie Mac LLC (formerly Network Liquidity Acceptance Company, correspondent banking)
Corporate Network eCom LLC (87%, electronic billing and technology services)
CU Investment Solutions, Inc. (formerly U.S. Central Capital Markets, Inc.; brokerage and advising services for member credit unions)
Network Financial Services, LLC (common trust fund, file-switching service, and electronic information exchange)

COMPETITORS

CUNA Mutual
CUSO Financial Services
Elavon
Fidelity National Information Services
First Data
PSCU Financial Services
WesCorp

HISTORICAL FINANCIALS

Company Type: Cooperative

Income Statement

FYE: December 31

	REVENUE ($ mil.)	NET INCOME ($ mil.)	NET PROFIT MARGIN	EMPLOYEES
12/08	1,596	(4,831)	—	250
12/07	2,599	(51)	—	250
12/06	1,948	63	3.2%	250
12/05	1,224	59	4.8%	250
12/04	756	50	6.6%	250
Annual Growth	20.5%	—	—	0.0%

Net Income History

U.S. Foodservice

A lot of food services in the US would suffer without this company. U.S. Foodservice is the #2 foodservice supplier in the country (behind SYSCO), serving some 250,000 customers from more than 70 distribution facilities. The company supplies restaurants, hotels, schools, and other foodservice operators with a wide variety of food products, including canned and dry foods, meats, frozen foods, and seafood. It also distributes kitchen equipment and cleaning supplies among other nonfood supplies. U.S. Foodservice distributes both national brand products and its own private labels. Tracing its roots to 1853, the company is owned by private equity firms KKR & Co. and Clayton, Dubilier & Rice.

U.S. Foodservice has been investing in acquisitions and other expansion efforts to grow its business, adding a handful of new distribution centers during 2007 and 2008 to increase capacity. It also acquired the broadline distribution division of Clark National in 2008.

Meanwhile, the company's North Star Foodservice division, which serves mostly quick-service chain restaurants, has been reorganizing with a focus on improving efficiency. The unit has closed and consolidated some branches while investing in new information technology. U.S. Foodservice has also been expanding its proprietary food brands distributed through its Monarch Foods unit.

KKR and Clayton, Dubilier joined together in 2007 to purchase U.S. Foodservice from Dutch food retail giant Royal Ahold for about $7.1 billion. The private equity firms announced plans to invest heavily in turning around the distribution business. The deal also allowed Royal Ahold to focus on its core supermarket business.

By shedding U.S. Foodservice, the supermarket operator also hoped to recover from an accounting scandal that embroiled the business from the time it acquired the distributor in 2000. Following the $3.6 billion deal, federal investigators began reviewing accounting irregularities at the company and later brought charges and some convictions against several former executives and suppliers.

HISTORY

U.S. Foodservice has its origins in several different operations. The oldest part, Monarch Foods, dates back to 1853 and was an early foodservice distribution innovator. The Chicago-based company helped supply pioneers heading West and brought items to the Midwest, such as California oranges and imported teas.

Some 50 years later Scottish immigrant C. C. Pearce started Pearce-Young-Angel (PYA) with two mules, two wagons, and a 3,000-sq.-ft. warehouse in Columbia, South Carolina. The company became a produce supplier to independent grocers in the Carolinas and diversified into beer, becoming the exclusive distributor for Anheuser-Busch in the two states. PYA switched to wholesaling products to institutions, such as nursing homes, restaurants, and schools.

Consolidated Foods (now Sara Lee) acquired Monarch in 1946 and merged it with PYA in 1967, spinning off its Anheuser-Busch unit simultaneously. The Pearce family continued to manage both operations, and under their leadership PYA/Monarch grew from sales of about

$100 million to about $3 billion. The southeastern division of the company (primarily the old PYA operations) maintained its lead as the #1 regional food distributor, but the northern division (primarily the old Monarch operations) was #3, behind SYSCO and Kraft. Sara Lee, which wanted all its business segments to be #1 or #2, decided it would keep the southeastern operations but dispose of the northern ones.

In 1989 James Miller (former CEO of U.S. Foodservice) led other managers in a $317 million LBO, acquiring 12 distribution centers in the Northeast and Midwest, then quickly selling three of them. Miller and associates got 11% of the new company, JP Foodservice, while Sara Lee took 47% (sold 1996) and institutional investors got the rest. Heavily in debt, JP Foodservice (which took its name from the initials of the first names of two senior stockholders) lost $33 million over the next five years before becoming profitable in 1995.

JP Foodservice went public in 1994; its IPO raised $80 million to help with its expansion strategy of acquiring smaller distributors. After spending $350 million on several acquisitions in 1996, the company spent $1.4 billion the next year to buy Rykoff-Sexton. Saul E. Rykoff started that company in 1911 as S.E. Rykoff & Co. It went public in 1972 and acquired John Sexton & Co. from Beatrice Group in 1983. When purchased by JP Foodservice, Rykoff-Sexton had twice the sales of JP. Rykoff-Sexton moved the company into markets in the Southeast, as well as into Texas and California.

In early 1998 JP changed its name to U.S. Foodservice. Also that year the company acquired New York-based J.H. Haar & Sons and California-based Joseph Webb Foods. In 2000 U.S. Foodservice was itself acquired for about $3.6 billion by Royal Ahold, becoming a subsidiary of its Ahold USA unit.

U.S. Foodservice gained access to 21 new US markets by acquiring Alliant Exchange, the parent of Alliant Foodservice in 2001.

The discovery of massive accounting irregularities at the company led its Dutch parent in 2002 to report a $1.41 billion loss, which Royal Ahold attributed to special charges related to overstated profits at U.S. Foodservice. Royal Ahold attributed the scheme to inflate vendor rebates to two U.S. Foodservice managers who resigned. Founder and CEO of U.S. Foodservice James Miller also resigned and Robert Tobin, a member of Royal Ahold's supervisory board and former chairman and CEO of Stop & Shop, was named interim CEO. In all, the company's five most senior managers left U.S. Foodservice in the wake of the accounting scandal. Twenty more employees were suspended in 2003 as the investigation into the accounting scandal continued.

Lawrence S. Benjamin joined U.S. Foodservice as its new CEO. In 2004 the company hired two executives who specialize in corporate turnarounds to run its purchasing and marketing efforts.

That same year, Royal Ahold settled civil charges with the Securities and Exchange Commission and later paid $1.1 billion to settle a class-action lawsuit brought by shareholders. Federal prosecutors, however, brought charges against several former executives and suppliers, alleging that they played a role in the accounting fraud. Former CFO Michael Resnick pleaded guilty to charges of conspiracy in 2006.

Royal Ahold sold the company to private equity firms Kohlberg Kravis Roberts (KKR) and Clayton, Dubilier & Rice for about $7.1 billion in 2007. Also that year Robert Aiken replaced Benjamin as CEO.

EXECUTIVES

President and CEO: Robert (Bob) Aiken
CFO: Al Swanson
Chief Human Resources Officer: Dave Esler
EVP Business Development: David Schreibman
SVP and Deputy General Counsel: Juliette Pryor
SVP Information Systems: Rod Harris
VP Corporate Communications: Kim Brown
President, West Region: Gene Steffes
President, Southeast Region: Bob Stout
President, Monarch Foods: Pat Mulhern
President, North Star Foodservice: Keith Campbell
President, Alliant Logistics: Mike Frank
President, North Region: Stuart Schuette
Auditors: Deloitte & Touche Accountants

LOCATIONS

HQ: U.S. Foodservice, Inc.
9399 W. Higgins Rd., Rosemont, IL 60018
Phone: 847-720-8000   **Fax:** 847-720-8099
Web: www.usfoodservice.com

COMPETITORS

Ben E. Keith
Clark National
Edward Don
Foodbuy
Golden State Foods
Gordon Food Service
Keystone Foods
MAINES
Martin-Brower
McLane Foodservice
Meadowbrook Meat Company
Performance Food
Reinhart FoodService
Services Group of America
SYSCO
UniPro Foodservice

HISTORICAL FINANCIALS

Company Type: Private

Income Statement

FYE: Saturday nearest December 31

	REVENUE ($ mil.)	NET INCOME ($ mil.)	NET PROFIT MARGIN	EMPLOYEES
12/08	19,810	—	—	26,000
12/07	20,200	—	—	27,160
12/06	25,357	—	—	27,630
12/05	17,613	—	—	28,286
12/04	20,692	—	—	28,658
Annual Growth	(1.1%)	—	—	(2.4%)

Revenue History

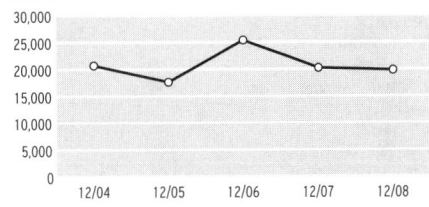

U.S. Oil

Smitten with the oil distribution business, the founding Schmidt family owns and operates U.S. Oil Co. The company supplies refined oil products to US residents in the Midwest, and does a lot more. In addition to the wholesale distribution of oil products (its largest revenue generator), the company operates gas stations, and installs gas pumps, tanks, and other petroleum-related equipment. It also provides plumbing and HVAC services, operates a research laboratory for environmental analysis, collects used waste oil to be processed into burner fuel, and has a metal custom manufacturing unit.

U.S. Oil Co. was established in the 1950s as Schmidt Oil by the sons of local fuel distributor Albert Schmidt, who landed his first job in the oil business in 1923.

EXECUTIVES

Chairman: Thomas A. (Tom) Schmidt
President and CEO: John Schmidt
CFO: Paul Bachman
CIO: Mark Duening
General Counsel: Marjorie Young
Director Human Resources: Lori Hoersch
Director Safety and Risk Management: Tom Titzkowski

LOCATIONS

HQ: U.S. Oil Co., Inc.
425 S. Washington St., Combined Locks, WI 54113
Phone: 920-739-6101   **Fax:** 920-788-0531
Web: www.usoil.com

PRODUCTS/OPERATIONS

Selected Operations

Design Air (heating and air conditioning equipment)
Express Convenience Centers (gas stations and car washes)
U.S. Custom Manufacturing (tube bending and fabrication)
U.S. Lubricants (motor oil and related products)
U.S. Petroleum Equipment — New (petroleum-related equipment installation)
U.S. Petroleum Equipment — Used (petroleum-related equipment installation)
U.S. Petroleum Laboratory (environmental and used oil testing and analysis)
U.S. Petroleum Operations (gasoline, fuel oil, and natural gas)
U.S. Tire & Exhaust (exhaust pipe manufacturing and autoparts distribution)

COMPETITORS

Apex Oil
Marathon Oil
Motiva Enterprises
Quality State Oil Company
Sunoco

US Oncology

US Oncology has got the backs (and the back offices) of medical oncologists across the US. The company, which is majority-owned by investment firm Welsh, Carson, Anderson & Stowe, provides management and support services to some 450 oncology practices and treatment centers throughout the US. It provides a comprehensive management offering, including billing, recruiting, data management, drug purchasing, and accounting. It also offers a separate drug purchasing service, negotiating prices with pharmaceutical and biotech companies for specialty cancer drugs and distributing them to client practices. Additionally, US Oncology helps its affiliate practices expand into full-fledged cancer treatment centers.

US Oncology has helped develop about 80 such cancer centers, and it has ownership stakes in about half of those. It also manages some 15 radiation clinics. The company provides development capital and shepherds its medical practices through the process of negotiating regulatory issues, building the facilities, and setting up operations. For independent practitioners, the company either offers a comprehensive management package or select offerings on a fee-for-service basis. Clients can also elect to only participate in the group purchasing and distribution segment.

Along with its services aimed at cancer doctors, the company serves pharmaceutical and biotechnology firms by designing and supervising cancer-related clinical trials. It enlists its affiliated physicians in the trials, thus giving them access to the latest available treatments. The company also provides services to insurance companies to help them avoid unnecessary care costs.

US Oncology has several ongoing initiatives to enhance the quality and efficiency of the care it provides, including the Innovent Oncology project, which offers new patient support services and an oncology-specific electronic record-keeping system. The company wants to continue to expand its network of affiliated practices, which already includes some 1,200 doctors in more than 450 locations. It has also been expanding its drug distribution and mail-order operations, and it plans to grow its offerings for pharmaceutical companies.

In early 2008 long-time CEO Dale Ross resigned and was replaced by company president Bruce Broussard. Ross remained with US Oncology as executive chairman.

Investment firm Welsh, Carson, Anderson & Stowe (WCAS) owns about 80% of the company. Directors Scott Mackesy and Russell Carson are general partners of WCAS.

EXECUTIVES

Chairman, President, and CEO: Bruce D. Broussard, age 46
Vice Chairman: Lloyd K. Everson, age 65
EVP and COO: Glen C. Laschober, age 55
EVP and Chief Administrative Officer: Frank A. Saputo
EVP and CFO: Michael A. (Mike) Sicuro, age 50
EVP Human Resources: David Bronsweig, age 49
VP and General Manager Research and Personalized Science Services: Stephen Smith
VP Pharmaceutical Distribution: Rolando de Cardenas
VP Finance and Chief Accounting Officer: Kevin F. Krenzke
Marketing Communications Manager: Cara Heiman
Auditors: PricewaterhouseCoopers LLP

LOCATIONS

HQ: US Oncology, Inc.
10101 Woodloch Forest, The Woodlands, TX 77380
Phone: 281-863-1000
Web: www.usoncology.com

PRODUCTS/OPERATIONS

2008 Sales

	$ mil.	% of total
Pharmaceutical services	2,486.7	48
Medical oncology services	2,251.4	44
Cancer center services	367.1	7
Research & other services	59.0	1
Adjustments	(1,860.0)	—
Total	**3,304.2**	**100**

2008 Sales

	$ mil.	% of total
Products	2,224.7	67
Services	1,079.5	33
Total	**3,304.2**	**100**

Selected Subsidiaries

AccessMed, LLC
Cancer Treatment Associates of Northeast Missouri, Ltd., LP
Colorado Cancer Centers, L.L.C.
Greenville Radiation Care, Inc.
Metropolitan Integrated Cancer Care, LCC
Oncology, LLC
Oncology Rx Care Advantage, LP
Oncology Today, LP
Oregon Cancer Center, Ltd.
Physician Reliance Network, LLC
RMCC Cancer Center, LLC
SelectPlus Oncology, LLC
Southeast Texas Cancer Centers, LP
The Carroll County Cancer Center, LP
TOPS Pharmacy Services, Inc.
Unity Oncology, LLC
US Oncology Integrated Solutions, LP
US Oncology Pharmaceutical Services, LLC
US Oncology Reimbursement Solutions, LLC
US Oncology Research, LLC
US Oncology Specialty, LP

COMPETITORS

AmerisourceBergen
AmSurg
Apria Healthcare
Aptium Oncology
BioScrip
Cardinal Health
Caremark Pharmacy Services
Covance
Express Scripts
Gentiva
InSight Health
Magellan Health
Mayo Foundation
McKesson
Medco Health
Memorial Sloan-Kettering
OnCure Medical
Orion HealthCorp
PAREXEL
Pharmaceutical Product Development
Quintiles Transnational
Radiation Therapy Services
RadNet
SDI Health
Sheridan Healthcare
Sterling Healthcare
Symbion
United Surgical Partners

HISTORICAL FINANCIALS

Company Type: Private

Income Statement

FYE: December 31

	REVENUE ($ mil.)	NET INCOME ($ mil.)	NET PROFIT MARGIN	EMPLOYEES
12/08	3,304	(413)	—	9,600
12/07	3,001	(35)	—	9,000
12/06	2,811	26	0.9%	8,600
12/05	2,519	31	1.2%	8,300
12/04	2,260	48	2.1%	—
Annual Growth	**10.0%**	**—**	**—**	**5.0%**

2008 Year-End Financials

Debt ratio: —
Return on equity: —
Cash ($ mil.): —
Current ratio: —
Long-term debt ($ mil.): 1,518

Net Income History

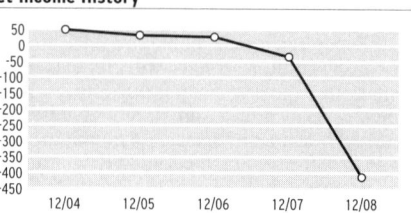

US Postal Service

The United States Postal Service (USPS) handles cards, letters, and packages sent from sea to shining sea. The USPS delivers 203 billion pieces of mail a year (at an average of 667 million per day) to some 149 million addresses in the US and its territories. The independent government agency relies on postage and fees to fund operations. Though it has a monopoly on delivering the mail, the USPS faces competition for services such as package delivery. The US president appoints nine of the 11 members of the board that oversee the USPS. The presidential appointees select the postmaster general, and together they name the deputy postmaster general; the two also serve on the board.

A challenge for the agency is the growing use of the Internet, which has led to lower volume of some types of mail. To keep pace, the USPS has worked to gain delivery business generated by online shopping. The agency also is investing in the development of the Intelligent Mail Barcode, a mini-GPS system for tracking mail. In 2009 the USPS introduced its new mobile phone application allowing phone users to locate post offices, track and confirm packages, and look up ZIP codes.

At the same time the agency is looking to technical advancements, it is also attentively working to cut costs. In 2008 USPS reduced its workforce by more than 20,000 positions through attrition and by cutting hours of operation at some of its 32,000-plus post offices and other retail and delivery facilities. Transportation is also a major expense for the agency, and high fuel prices have pumped up costs for operating the agency's 221,000 vehicles.

With an eye on its bottom line, the USPS has accelerated the pace of its rate increases. Between January 2006 and May 2009 the price of a first-class stamp went from 37 cents to 44 cents. To cater to customers who get stuck with some of the out-of-date stamps, USPS introduced a new concept in April 2007 — the Forever Stamp. The Liberty Bell-imaged stamp is sold at the same price as a first-class stamp but it can then be used, as the name says, forever, even as the price of first-class postage goes up.

The USPS was given some flexibility in setting rates, as well as some new restrictions, by the Postal Accountability and Enhancement Act of 2006, considered the farthest-reaching postal reform legislation since the agency became independent in 1970. The goal of the law was to enable the USPS to adopt some private-sector management practices in order to ensure the agency's long-term financial health and to preserve universal mail service. Among the short-term effects of the legislation was a requirement that the agency pay into a new fund for retiree health benefits. The $5.6 billion payment caused the USPS to record a loss in 2007, the agency's first since 2002.

Affected by the skyrocketing fuel prices (which increased costs by more than $500 million) and diminished demand for its postal and shipping services, the USPS recorded another loss in 2008.

HISTORY

The second-oldest agency of the US government (after Indian Affairs), the Post Office was created by the Continental Congress in 1775 with Benjamin Franklin as postmaster general. The postal system came to play a vital role in the development of transportation in the US.

At that time, postal workers were riders on muddy paths delivering letters without stamps or envelopes. Letters were delivered only between post offices. Congress approved the first official postal policy in 1792: Rates ranged from six cents for less than 30 miles to 25 cents for more than 450. Letter carriers began delivering mail in cities in 1794.

First based in Philadelphia, in 1800 the Post Office moved to Washington, DC. In 1829 Andrew Jackson elevated the position of postmaster general to cabinet rank — it became a means of rewarding political cronies. Mail contracts subsidized the early development of US railroads. The first adhesive postage stamp appeared in the US in 1847.

Uniform postal rates (not varying with distance) were instituted in 1863, the year free city delivery began. The start of free rural delivery in 1896 spurred road construction in isolated US areas. Parcel post was launched in 1913, and new mail-order houses such as Montgomery Ward and Sears, Roebuck flourished.

The famous pledge beginning "Neither snow nor rain . . ." — not an official motto — was first inscribed at the main New York City post office in 1914. Scheduled airmail service between Washington, DC, and New York City began in 1918, stimulating the development of commercial air service. The ZIP code was introduced in 1963.

As mail volume grew, postal workers became increasingly militant under work stress. (Franklin's pigeonhole sorting method had barely changed.) A work stoppage in the New York City post office in 1970 spread within nine days to 670 post offices, and the US Army was deployed to handle the mail. Later that year the

Postal Reorganization Act was passed. The new law established a board of governors to handle postal affairs and choose the postmaster general, who became CEO of an independent agency, the US Postal Service (USPS). The next year USPS negotiated the first US government collective-bargaining labor contract. Express mail service began in 1977.

In 1995 USPS launched Global Package Link, a program to expedite major customers' shipments to Canada, Japan, and the UK. The next year it overhauled rates, cutting prices for larger mailers who prepared their mail for automation and raising prices for small mailers who didn't.

Postmaster General Marvin Runyon — whose six-year tenure took the agency from the red into the black — retired in 1998 and was succeeded by USPS veteran William Henderson. The next year a one-cent hike in the price of first-class postage took effect. (Another one-cent increase took effect in 2001, and the rate rose once again the following year.) USPS in 1999 contracted with outside vendors to enable customers to buy and print stamps online.

In 2001 USPS formed a strategic alliance with rival FedEx through which FedEx agreed to provide air transportation for USPS mail, in return for the placement of FedEx drop boxes in post offices. Henderson stepped down in 2001, and EVP Jack Potter was named to replace him. That year several postal workers in a Washington, DC, branch were exposed to anthrax-tainted letters.

Potter launched a series of cost-cutting programs, which together with rate increases enabled the USPS to post a profit in 2003 — the agency's first year in the black since 1999.

EXECUTIVES

Chairman: Alan C. Kessler
Vice Chairman: Carolyn Lewis Gallagher
Postmaster General, CEO, and Governor:
  John E. (Jack) Potter
Deputy Postmaster, COO, and Governor:
  Patrick R. Donahoe
Acting Chief Postal Inspector: William R. Gilligan
President, Shipping and Mailing Services Division:
  Robert F. Bernstock, age 58
EVP and CIO: Ross Philo
EVP and Chief Human Resources Officer:
  Anthony J. (Tony) Vegliante
EVP and CFO: Harold Glen Walker
SVP and General Counsel: Mary Anne Gibbons
SVP Strategy and Transition: Linda A. Kingsley
SVP and Managing Director, Global Business:
  Paul Vogel
SVP Mailing Services: David B. Shoenfeld
SVP Customer Service: Stephen M. (Steve) Kearney
SVP Operations: William P. (Bill) Galligan
SVP Intelligent Mail and Address Quality:
  Thomas G. (Tom) Day
VP and Treasurer: Robert J. Pedersen
VP and Controller: Lynn Malcolm
VP Corporate Communications: Mitzi R. Betman
Secretary: Julie S. Moore
Judicial Officer: William A. Campbell
Auditors: Ernst & Young LLP

LOCATIONS

HQ: United States Postal Service
  475 L'Enfant Plaza SW, Washington, DC 20260
Phone: 202-268-2500   **Fax:** 202-268-4860
Web: www.usps.com

PRODUCTS/OPERATIONS

2008 Sales

	$ mil.	% of total
First-Class Mail	38,179	51
Standard Mail	20,586	27
Periodicals	2,295	3
Package Services	1,845	3
Shipping Services	8,382	11
Other Mailing Services	3,645	5
Total	**74,932**	**100**

HISTORICAL FINANCIALS

Company Type: Government agency

Income Statement

FYE: September 30

	REVENUE ($ mil.)	NET INCOME ($ mil.)	NET PROFIT MARGIN	EMPLOYEES
9/08	74,932	(2,806)	—	663,238
9/07	74,973	(5,142)	—	684,762
9/06	72,650	900	1.2%	696,138
9/05	69,907	1,445	2.1%	704,716
9/04	68,996	3,065	4.4%	707,485
Annual Growth	**2.1%**	**—**	**—**	**(1.6%)**

Net Income History

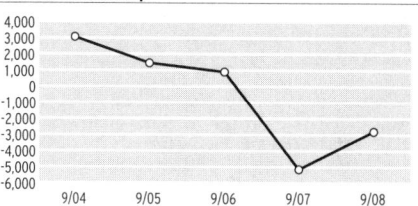

U.S. Premium Beef

U.S. Premium Beef (USPB) likes to see things through from start to finish, or at least from the ranch to the plate. USPB sends cattle from producers' ranches in 37 states, through feedlots, and off to National Beef Packing Company, the beef processor it owns. From there, some of the company's better steaks head to the Kansas City Steak Company, a foodservice distributor that it partially owns, which supplies high-end steakhouses and restaurants. The rest of its value-added and branded beef is boxed and sold to food retailers and foodservice distributors throughout the US. The company, founded in 1997, also operates a mail-order business for its products.

In 2008 USPB agreed to sell National Beef to Brazil's meat giant, JBS. However, in October 2008 the US Department of Justice filed a motion to block the sale of National Beef on antitrust grounds and in 2009 the deal fell through.

National Beef has three processing plants located in Liberal and Dodge City, Kansas, and Brawley, California. The company also owns National Carriers, a 1,000-unit refrigerated trucking operation.

EXECUTIVES

Chairman: Mark Gardiner
Vice Chairman: John Fairleigh
CEO: Steven D. (Steve) Hunt, age 50
COO: Stan Linville
Treasurer: Danielle Imel
Chief Reporting and Compliance Officer: Scott Miller

Secretary: Duane Ramsey
Director Field Operations: Brian Bertelsen
Director Operations: Lisa Phillips
Director Marketing: Tracy Thomas
Director Communications: Bill Miller

LOCATIONS

HQ: U.S. Premium Beef LLC
12200 N. Ambassador Dr., Kansas City, MO 64163
Phone: 816-713-8800 **Fax:** 816-713-8810
Web: www.uspremiumbeef.com

PRODUCTS/OPERATIONS

Selected Brands and Products

Black Canyon Angus Beef
Black Canyon Premium Reserve
Certified Angus Beef
Certified Hereford Beef
Certified Premium Beef
NatureSource Natural Angus Beef
Naturewell Natural Beef
Vintage Natural Beef

COMPETITORS

Buckhead Beef	JBS USA
Cactus Feeders	Jobbers Meat Packing
Cargill Meat Solutions	Kenosha Beef
Chicago Meat Authority	L&H
Clougherty Packing	Laura's Lean Beef Co.
Ellison Meat Company	Maverick Ranch
Freedman Meats	Omaha Steaks
Fremont Beef	Sam Kane Beef Processors
Greater Omaha Packing	Tyson Foods
Indiana Packers	Wolverine Packing

HISTORICAL FINANCIALS

Company Type: Private

Income Statement			FYE: Last Saturday of August	
	REVENUE ($ mil.)	**NET INCOME** ($ mil.)	**NET PROFIT MARGIN**	**EMPLOYEES**
8/08	5,847	—	—	8,900

U.S. Xpress

U.S. Xpress Enterprises hopes customers find it x-ceptional. The company's truckload transportation units, led by flagship U.S. Xpress, provide medium- to long-haul service throughout North America, as well as regional service in the midwestern, southeastern, and western US. It also offers dedicated contract carriage, in which drivers and equipment are assigned to a customer long-term, and expedited freight hauling. Subsidiary Xpress Global Systems provides less-than-truckload freight hauling, warehousing, and distribution services. Overall, the company's fleet includes about 8,500 trucks and 26,000 trailers. Co-chairmen and co-founders Patrick Quinn and Max Fuller own the company.

U.S. Xpress Enterprises' truckload transportation units account for the vast majority of the company's overall sales. In addition, U.S. Xpress Enterprises owns a minority stake in Transplace, a provider of transportation management and other logistics services.

The company has extended its reach by investing in regional truckload carriers. U.S. Xpress Enterprises owns controlling stakes in Arnold Transportation Services and Total Transportation of Mississippi, as well as minority interests in Richmond, Virginia-based Abilene Motor Express and Duncan, South Carolina-based C&C Transportation. In late 2008 U.S. Xpress Enterprises also bought a 47% stake in Smith Transport, a truckload carrier owning 850 tractors and 3,000 trailers in the eastern US.

U.S. Xpress Enterprises hopes to achieve profitable growth by allocating its assets efficiently among the different types of truckload transportation the company provides. It has seen strong growth in its dedicated services segment. Also, the company differentiates itself from competitors with a couple of expedited service offerings. Its "near airfreight" service uses teams of drivers on long-haul routes to compete with airfreight at lower costs, and its intermodal rail business involves contracting with railroads to move customers' freight on high-speed trains for less than the cost of over-the-road hauling.

The company's customers typically include retailers, manufacturers, and other transportation companies.

EXECUTIVES

Co-Chairman, CEO, and Secretary: Max L. Fuller, age 56
Co-Chairman, President, and Treasurer: Patrick E. Quinn, age 62
EVP Finance and CFO: Ray M. Harlin, age 59
EVP Operations and COO: Jeffrey S. (Jeff) Wardeberg, age 46
SVP and General Manager, Dedicated Services Business Unit: William K. Farris, age 54
VP Sales and Marketing: Bob Poulos
VP and General Manager, Xpress Direct: William E. Fuller
VP and General Manager, International SBU: Patrick Brian Quinn
VP and General Counsel: Lisa M. Pate
President, Smith Transport: Barry Smith
President, U.S. Xpress Inc.: John White
President, Xpress Global Systems: John Bowes
President, Arnold Transportation: Thomas M. (Tom) Glaser
Auditors: Ernst & Young LLP

LOCATIONS

HQ: U.S. Xpress Enterprises, Inc.
4080 Jenkins Rd., Chattanooga, TN 37421
Phone: 423-510-3000 **Fax:** 423-510-3318
Web: www.usxpress.com

COMPETITORS

CEVA Logistics U.S.
Con-way Freight
Covenant Transportation
Crete Carrier
Estes Express
Heartland Express
J.B. Hunt
Knight Transportation
Landstar System
Ryder System
Saia
Schneider National
Swift Transportation
Universal Truckload Services
UPS Supply Chain Solutions
Werner Enterprises

HISTORICAL FINANCIALS

Company Type: Private

Income Statement			FYE: December 31	
	REVENUE ($ mil.)	**NET INCOME** ($ mil.)	**NET PROFIT MARGIN**	**EMPLOYEES**
12/08	1,600	—	—	8,000
12/07	1,510	—	—	10,885
Annual Growth	6.0%	—	—	(26.5%)

Revenue History

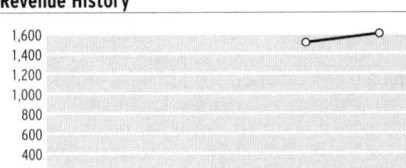

USAA

USAA has a decidedly military bearing. The mutual insurance company serves 7.2 million member customers, primarily military personnel, military retirees, and their families. Its products and services include property/casualty and life insurance, banking, discount brokerage, and investment management. USAA relies largely on technology and direct marketing to sell its products, reaching clients via the telephone and Internet. The company's USAA Alliance Services unit provides discount shopping (floral, jewelry, and home and auto safety items), and travel and delivery services to its members. Its USAA Real Estate division serves institutional and corporate customers with real estate development.

On average, members use five of the company's different products, and the company has begun tying its auto insurance rates to the number of products a member uses as well as how long they have held insurance with USAA.

To drive growth, the company broadened its eligibility guidelines in 2008. As a result, USAA is projecting its membership to nearly double. In another attempt to increase revenue, the company has entered new markets by making efforts to target people less affluent than military officers. At present, nearly 50% of its members are the grown children and grandchildren of people who have served in the military.

In recent years USAA has streamlined operations by reducing staff and closing down divisions (including mailing, printing, and information technology offices). However, during 2008 the company began making greater efforts to recruit and hire employees with military experience.

HISTORY

In 1922 a group of 26 US Army officers gathered in a San Antonio hotel and formed their own automobile insurance association. The reason? As military officers who often moved, they had a hard time getting insurance because they were considered transient. So the officers decided to insure each other. Led by Major William Garrison, who became the company's first president, they formed the United States Army Automobile Insurance Association.

In 1924, when US Navy and Marine Corps officers were allowed to join, the company changed its name to United Services Automobile Association. By the mid-1950s the company had some 200,000 members. During the 1960s the company formed USAA Life Insurance Company (1963) and USAA Casualty Insurance Company (1968).

Robert McDermott, a retired US Air Force brigadier general, became president in 1969. He cut employment through attrition, established education and training seminars for employees, and invested in computers and telecommunications (drastically cutting claims-processing time). McDermott added new products and services, such as mutual funds, real estate investments, and banking. Under McDermott, USAA's membership grew from 653,000 in 1969 to more than 3 million in 1993.

During the 1970s, in an effort to go paperless, USAA became one of the insurance industry's first companies to switch from mail to toll-free (800) numbers. In the early 1980s the company introduced its discount purchasing program, USAA Buying Services. In 1985 it opened the USAA Federal Savings Bank. USAA began installing an optical storage system in the late 1980s to automate some customer service operations.

McDermott retired in 1993 and was succeeded by Robert Herres. The following year USAA Federal Savings Bank began developing a home banking system, offering members information and services over advanced screen telephones provided by IBM.

In the early 1990s USAA's real estate activities increased dramatically. In 1995 USAA restructured its interest in the Fiesta Texas theme park in San Antonio in order to focus on previously developed properties in geographically diverse areas. That year Six Flags Theme Parks (now Six Flags, Inc.) assumed operation and management of Fiesta Texas (which purchased it from USAA in 1998).

In 1997 USAA began including enlisted military personnel as members. It also started to experiment with a "plain English" mutual fund prospectus. In 1998 USAA also began offering Choice Ride in Orlando, Florida. For about $1,100 per quarter and a promise not to drive except in emergencies, the pilot program provided 36 round trips and a 90% discount on car insurance, in hopes of keeping older drivers from unnecessarily getting behind the wheel.

Also in 1998, as part of its new Financial Planning Network, USAA began offering retirement and estate planning assistance aimed at 25- to 55-year-olds for a yearly $250 fee. In 1999 claims doubled largely due to the impact of Hurricane Floyd and spring hail storms hitting military communities in North Carolina and Virginia.

USAA also moved in 1999 to consolidate its customers' separate accounts (such as mutual fund holdings, stocks and bonds, and life insurance products) into one main account to strengthen customer relationships and reduce operational costs. The next year, after completing a number of technology projects, it laid off workers for the first time in its history.

In 2002, Robert Herres resigned as chairman and was succeeded by CEO Robert Davis. The next year the company saw increased sales and an improved net income thanks to a rebounding stock market and membership growth.

Robert Davis stepped down as chairman and CEO in 2007 and was replaced by John Moellering (chairman) and Joe Robles (CEO).

EXECUTIVES

Chairman: Lt. Gen. John H. Moellering
President and CEO: Maj. Gen. Josue (Joe) Robles Jr., age 63
CFO: Kristi A. Matus, age 40
EVP and Chief Marketing Officer: Roger V. Chacko
EVP, General Counsel, and Corporate Secretary: Steven A. Bennett
EVP Enterprise Business Operations: S. Wayne Peacock
EVP People Services: Elizabeth D. (Liz) Conklyn
EVP Corporate Communications: Wendi E. Strong
SVP Information Technology and CIO: Greg Schwartz
SVP Claims Service: Ken Rosen
President, USAA Federal Savings Bank: F. David Bohne
President, USAA Financial Services Group: Christopher W. Claus
President, USAA Property & Casualty Insurance Group: Stuart Parker
Auditors: Ernst & Young LLP

LOCATIONS

HQ: USAA
9800 Fredericksburg Rd., San Antonio, TX 78288
Phone: 210-498-2211
Web: www.usaa.com

PRODUCTS/OPERATIONS

2008 Revenues

	$ mil.	% of total
Insurance premiums	9,641	75
Fees, sales & loan income	2,008	15
Services & contractual income on securitizations	368	3
Investment return	254	2
Real estate investment income	171	1
Other revenue	470	4
Total	**12,912**	**100**

COMPETITORS

Allstate	John Hancock Financial
American Financial	Liberty Mutual
AXA Financial	MetLife
Berkshire Hathaway	Mutual of Omaha
Charles Schwab	Nationwide
Chubb Corp	New York Life
CIGNA	Northwestern Mutual
Citigroup	Pacific Mutual
Farmers Group	Prudential
GEICO	State Farm
Guardian Life	T. Rowe Price
The Hartford	

HISTORICAL FINANCIALS

Company Type: Mutual company

Income Statement

FYE: December 31

	ASSETS ($ mil.)	NET INCOME ($ mil.)	INCOME AS % OF ASSETS	EMPLOYEES
12/08	68,296	423	0.6%	21,900
12/07	67,177	1,855	2.8%	22,000
12/06	60,269	2,330	3.9%	22,000
12/05	51,038	1,388	2.7%	21,900
12/04	46,482	1,597	3.4%	21,000
Annual Growth	**10.1%**	**(28.3%)**	**—**	**1.1%**

2008 Year-End Financials

Equity as % of assets: —
Return on assets: 0.6%
Return on equity: —
Long-term debt ($ mil.): —
Sales ($ mil.): 12,912

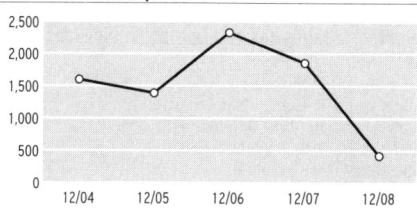

ValleyCrest Companies

ValleyCrest Companies hits pay dirt with plant care. The company uses its green thumb to provide landscape construction and maintenance, irrigation, golf course construction, lawn care, nurseries, and site engineering. ValleyCrest grows more than 2 million trees (for relocation), maintains indoor and outdoor gardens, and restores wetlands. It also franchises landscape maintenance services. Michael Dell, founder of Dell, controls ValleyCrest with a 51% stake. Founded in 1949 as a small neighborhood landscape retail nursery, ValleyCrest now has more than 100 offices worldwide. Notable clients have included the Nixon Presidential Library, Centennial Olympic Park in Atlanta, and Caesars Palace in Las Vegas.

Over the years the company has grown through acquiring regional landscaping businesses. In 2007 it bought Tropics North Landscaping, a landscaping maintenance firm based in Florida. Months later it bought Scapes, based in Atlanta.

In mid-2008 ValleyCrest acquired Pine Ridge Landscaping based in Virginia. The deal strengthened the company's presence in the lucrative Washington, DC-metro area. A few months earlier, it snatched up Concepts in Greenery (based in Florida) and Second Nature (a landscape maintenance firm located in South Carolina).

EXECUTIVES

Chairman and Co-CEO: Burton S. (Burt) Sperber
President and Co-CEO: Richard A. Sperber
EVP and CFO: Andrew J. (Andy) Mandell
SVP People Development: Steven Phillips
SVP, ValleyCrest Landscape Maintenance: David L. (Dave) Hanson
SVP Asset and Risk Management: Michael L. (Mike) Dingman
VP Human Resources: Raúl Díaz de León
VP and CIO: John D. Johnston
VP and Corporate Controller: Anthony (Tony) Garruto
President, ValleyCrest Tree Company: Robert L. Crudup Jr.
President, ValleyCrest Landscape Maintenance: Roger J. Zino
President, ValleyCrest Golf Course Maintenance: Gregory A. (Greg) Pieschala
President, ValleyCrest Landscape Development: Thomas C. (Tom) Donnelly, age 52
President, U.S. Lawns: Kenneth L. (Ken) Hutcheson

LOCATIONS

HQ: ValleyCrest Companies
24151 Ventura Blvd., Calabasas, CA 91302
Phone: 818-223-8500   **Fax:** 818-223-8142
Web: www.valleycrest.com

PRODUCTS/OPERATIONS

Selected Subsidiaries and Operating Divisions
U.S. Lawns
ValleyCrest Design Group
ValleyCrest Golf Course Maintenance
ValleyCrest Landscape Development
ValleyCrest Landscape Maintenance
ValleyCrest Tree Company

COMPETITORS

Davey Tree
Excel Landscape
FirstService
Griffin Land & Nurseries
Hines Horticulture
Skinner Nurseries
TruGreen Landcare

Vance Publishing

Does your pig need a new hairdo? Vance Publishing can help. The company publishes about 20 trade magazines serving a wide range of professionals, from beauticians (*Modern Salon*) to farmers (*Ag Professional*). It also publishes titles for woodworkers (*Wood & Wood Products*), farmers (*The Grower*), furniture retailers (*Residential Lighting*), and supermarket retailers (*Produce Merchandising*). The company — owned by the family of Herbert Vance, who founded it in 1937 — also provides custom publishing and research services, and invests in Internet ventures related to the industries it serves.

Vance's food and agriculture publications are organized under a unit called Food 360, while its Interiors Media Group includes trade titles related to decorating and design. Its third division, the Salon group, publishes titles for salon and spa professionals.

In 2009 Vance sold its *Residential Lighting* and *Hospitality Lighting* magazines and a related Web site to trade publisher Scranton Gillette Communications. Also that year the company ceased publication of two other titles, *Design & Decor* and *Furniture Style*. The company made the divestitures in order to increase its focus on its remaining core markets.

EXECUTIVES

Chairman: William C. (Bill) Vance
President: Peggy Walker
VP and Publishing Director, Produce:
 Donald P. Ransdell
VP eMedia: Tom Denison
VP and Publishing Director, Interiors Media Network:
 Ned Bardic
VP Human Resources and Facilities: Loreen Muzik
VP and Publishing Director, Protein: Cliff Becker Jr.
VP Publication Services: Mike Morgan
VP and Group Publisher, Interiors Media Network:
 Laura Didier
Group Publisher, Interiors Media Network:
 Julie M. Smith
Group Publisher, Salon Media: Scot Stevens

LOCATIONS

HQ: Vance Publishing Corporation
 400 Knightsbridge Pkwy., Lincolnshire, IL 60069
Phone: 847-634-2600 **Fax:** 847-634-4379
Web: www.vancepublishing.com

COMPETITORS

Ascend Media
August Home Publishing
Fairchild Fashion Group
Farm Journal
Hanley Wood
Lebhar-Friedman
Nielsen Business Media
Penton Media
Questex Media
Rodale
Watt Publishing

Vanderbilt University

The house that Cornelius built, Vanderbilt University was founded in 1873 with a $1 million grant from industrialist Cornelius Vanderbilt. The university's endowment has grown to more than $3 billion, and the school is a haven for more than 12,000 students and nearly 3,000 full-time faculty. Vanderbilt offers undergraduate and graduate programs in areas such as education and human development, engineering, and the arts and sciences. The university has 10 schools and colleges; its Owen Graduate School of Management and its medical school rank near the top of national surveys. A major research university, Vanderbilt receives millions of dollars annually in sponsored awards and grants to fund its facilities.

For its first 40 years of existence, Vanderbilt was under the auspices of the Methodist Episcopal Church, South. The Vanderbilt Board of Trust severed its ties with the church in 1914 after a dispute with the bishops over who would appoint university trustees.

EXECUTIVES

Chairman: Martha R. Ingram, age 73
Vice Chairman: Dennis C. Bottorff, age 64
Vice Chairman: Darryl D. Berger
Chancellor; Provost and Vice Chancellor for Academic Affairs: Nicholas S. Zeppos
Executive Associate Vice Chancellor, Development and Alumni Relations: Robert L. Early
Assistant Vice Chancellor, Information Technology Services: Matt Hall
Vice Chancellor University Affairs, General Counsel, and Secretary: David Williams II
Vice Chancellor Investments: Mathew Wright
Vice Chancellor Health Affairs: Harry R. Jacobson, age 61
Vice Chancellor Administration and CFO:
 Lauren J. Brisky, age 58
Associate Provost, Enrollment Management; Dean, Admissions: Douglas L. Christiansen
Associate Provost; Dean, Students: Mark Bandas
Associate Provost, Faculty: Timothy P. McNamara
Associate Vice Chancellor Finance and Controller:
 Betty Price
Associate Provost, Research and Graduate Education:
 Dennis G. Hall
Associate Provost, Undergraduate Education:
 Lucius T. Outlaw Jr.
Secretary of the Board: William W. Bain Jr.
Interim Chief Human Resources Officer:
 Lenon Coleman
Dean, Peabody College: Camilla Benbow
Dean, School of Law: Edward Rubin
Dean, Owen Graduate School of Management:
 Jim Bradford
Auditors: KPMG LLP

LOCATIONS

HQ: Vanderbilt University
 2201 West End Ave., Nashville, TN 37235
Phone: 615-322-7311
Web: www.vanderbilt.edu

PRODUCTS/OPERATIONS

Selected Schools and Colleges
Blair School of Music
College of Arts and Science
Divinity School
Graduate School
Law School
Owen Graduate School of Management
Peabody College of Education and Human Development
School of Engineering
School of Medicine
School of Nursing

Vanderbilt University Medical Center

The Vanderbilt University Medical Center (VUMC) is one of the top health care organizations in the country, with its network of hospitals, outpatient centers, clinics, and specialty institutes. Its medical education programs train hundreds of doctors and nurses each year, and the center's Vanderbilt Clinic receives nearly 700,000 annual patient visits. Its Vanderbilt University Hospital, together with the clinic, has more than 800 beds. VUMC also boasts a children's hospital, a psychiatric hospital, a veterans' health facility, and a rehabilitation hospital, as well as a biomedical research center and the Vanderbilt-Ingram Cancer Center, a National Cancer Institute Comprehensive Cancer Center.

EXECUTIVES

Chairman: Edward G. Nelson, age 77
SVP and CFO: J. Richard Wagers
Chief Marketing Officer: Jill D. Austin
CEO, Vanderbilt Clinic; Executive Director, Vanderbilt Medical Group: David R. Posch
Executive Director and CEO, Vanderbilt University Hospital: Larry M. Goldberg
Executive Director Research Operations:
 John F. Manning Jr.
Chief of Staff, Research: Andrea Baruchin
Chief Nursing Officer and Director Patient Care Services, Vanderbilt University Hospital:
 Marilyn A. Dubree
Vice Chancellor for Health Affairs and Director:
 Harry R. Jacobson, age 61
Associate Vice Chancellor for Research: Jeffrey R. Balser
Associate Vice Chancellor for Clinical Affairs; Chief Medical Officer, Vanderbilt Medical Group:
 C. Wright Pinson
Dean, School of Medicine: Steven G. Gabbe
Dean, School of Nursing: Colleen Conway-Welch, age 65
Director News and Public Affairs: William N. Hance

LOCATIONS

HQ: Vanderbilt University Medical Center
21st Ave. South and Medical Center Dr.
Nashville, TN 37232
Phone: 615-322-5000
Web: www.mc.vanderbilt.edu

COMPETITORS

Baptist Hospital
Blount Memorial Hospital
Community Health Systems
Erlanger Health System
HCA
LifePoint Hospitals
Middle Tennessee Medical Center
Southern Hills

The Vanguard Group

If you buy low and sell high, invest for the long term, resist the urge to panic, and generally disapprove of those whippersnappers at Fidelity, then you may end up in the Vanguard of the financial market. The Vanguard Group offers individual and institutional investors a line of popular mutual funds and brokerage services. Claiming more than $1.2 trillion of assets under management, the firm is battling FMR (AKA Fidelity) for the title of largest retail mutual fund manager on the planet. Vanguard's fund options include more than 200 stock, bond, mixed, and international offerings, as well as variable annuity portfolios; its Vanguard 500 Index Fund is one of the largest in the US.

The company is known as much for its puritanical thriftiness and conservative investing as for its line of index funds, which track the performance of such groups of stock as the S&P 500. Retired company founder John Bogle is sometimes derisively called "St. Jack" for his zealous criticism of industry practices, but the company's reputation for being squeaky clean appears to have kept it unscathed by the mutual fund industry scandals of recent years.

Unlike other fund managers, Vanguard is set up like a mutual insurance company. The funds (and by extension, their more than 9 million investors) own the company, so fees are low to nonexistent; funds are operated on a tight budget so as not to eat into results. The company spends next to nothing on advertising, relying instead on strong returns and word-of-mouth. And despite its no-broker, no-load background, Vanguard has developed cheap ways to dole out advice, especially through the use of toll-free numbers and the Internet and by quietly touting its online brokerage service.

In 2008 Vanguard joined the government's money-market guarantee program, which was designed to keep nervous investors from emptying their funds by safeguarding deposits. The program ended the following year, signalling growing confidence in the economy as well as the relative security of money-market funds.

Also in 2008 John Brennan retired as CEO but remained chairman of Vanguard. William McNabb, formerly the managing director of Vanguard's institutional investor group, succeeded Brennan as CEO.

HISTORY

A distant cousin of Daniel Boone, Walter Morgan knew a few things about pioneering. He was the first to offer a fund with a balance of stocks and bonds, serendipitously introduced early in 1929, months before the stock market collapsed. Morgan's balanced Wellington fund (named after Napoleon's vanquisher) emerged effectively unscathed.

John Bogle's senior thesis on mutual funds impressed fellow Princeton alum Morgan, who hired Bogle in 1951. Morgan retired in 1967 and picked Bogle to replace him. That year Bogle engineered a merger with old-school investment firm Thorndike, Doran, Paine and Lewis. After culture clashes and four years of shrinking assets, the Thorndike-dominated board fired Bogle, who appealed to the mutual funds and their separate board of directors. The fund directors decided to split up the funds and the advisory business.

Bogle named the fund company The Vanguard Group, after the flagship of Lord Nelson, another Napoleon foe. Vanguard worked like a cooperative; mutual fund shareholders owned the company, so all services were provided at cost. Wellington Management Company remained Vanguard's distributor until 1977, when Bogle convinced Vanguard's board to drop the affiliation. Without Wellington as the intermediary, Vanguard sold its funds directly to consumers as no-load funds (without service charges). In 1976 the company launched the Vanguard Index 500, the first index fund. These measures attracted new investors in droves.

Vanguard rode the 1980s boom. Its Windsor fund grew so large the company closed it, launching Windsor II in 1985. Vanguard weathered the 1987 crash and began the 1990s as the US's #4 mutual fund company. The actively managed funds of FMR (better known as Fidelity), most notably its Magellan fund, led the market then. The retirement of legendary Magellan manager Peter Lynch and the fund's consequential underperformance spurred a rush to index funds. Vanguard moved up to #2.

Vanguard played against type in 1995 when it introduced the Vanguard Horizon Capital Growth stock fund, an aggressively managed fund designed to vie directly with Fidelity's funds.

In 1997 Vanguard added brokerage services and began selling its own and other companies' funds on the Internet to allow clients to consolidate their financial activities. In 1998 Bogle passed the chairmanship to CEO John Brennan, a soft-spoken technology wonk. Morgan died that year at age 100.

Investors' feathers were ruffled when 70-year-old Bogle announced that corporate age limits would force him to leave the board of directors at the end of 1999. (Bogle retains an office at Vanguard headquarters and remains popular on the speaker circuit.)

Despite Vanguard's stated commitment to the little guy, by late 2002 the company was forced to mitigate realities of the economy and started courting investors with bigger bankrolls; it also raised fees for some customers with smaller accounts.

In another concession to changing times, the company began managing exchange-traded funds (ETFs) in 2001. Within a decade, Vanguard became the third-largest ETF sponsor in the US, thanks largely to its low fees.

EXECUTIVES

Chairman: John J. (Jack) Brennan, age 54
President, CEO, and Director:
F. William (Bill) McNabb III, age 51
Chief Investment Officer: George U. (Gus) Sauter
General Counsel: Heidi Stam
Managing Director and CIO: Paul Heller
Managing Director, International Operations:
James M. Norris
Managing Director, Strategy and Finance Group:
Glenn Reed
Managing Director, Human Resources:
Kathleen C. Gubanich
Managing Director, Planning and Development Group:
Michael S. Miller
Managing Director, Institutional Investor Group:
R. Gregory Barton
Managing Director, Retail Investor Group:
Mortimer J. (Tim) Buckley
Principal Education Markets Group: Alba Martinez

LOCATIONS

HQ: The Vanguard Group, Inc.
100 Vanguard Blvd., Malvern, PA 19355
Phone: 610-648-6000   **Fax:** 610-669-6605
Web: www.vanguard.com

PRODUCTS/OPERATIONS

Selected Funds

500 Index Fund
Admiral Treasury Money Market Fund
Balanced Index Fund
California Long-Term Tax-Exempt Fund
Developed Markets Index Fund
Diversified Equity Fund
Dividend Appreciation Index Fund
Emerging Markets Stock Index Fund
Energy Fund
Equity Income Fund
European Stock Index Fund
Explorer Fund
Extended Market Index Fund
Federal Money Market Fund
Florida Long-Term Tax-Exempt Fund
FTSE Social Index Fund
Global Equity Fund
GNMA Fund
Growth and Income Fund
Growth Equity Fund
Growth Index Fund
Health Care Fund
High-Yield Corporate Fund
High-Yield Tax-Exempt Fund
Inflation-Protected Securities Fund
Intermediate-Term Bond Index Fund
Intermediate-Term Investment-Grade Fund
Intermediate-Term Tax-Exempt Fund
Intermediate-Term Treasury Fund
International Explorer Fund
International Growth Fund
International Value Fund
Large-Cap Index Fund
LifeStrategy Conservative Growth Fund
LifeStrategy Growth Fund
LifeStrategy Income Fund
LifeStrategy Moderate Growth Fund
Limited-Term Tax-Exempt Fund
Long-Term Bond Index Fund
Long-Term Investment-Grade Fund
Long-Term Tax-Exempt Fund
Long-Term Treasury Fund
Massachusetts Tax-Exempt Fund
Mid-Cap Growth Fund
Mid-Cap Index Fund
Mid-Cap Value Index Fund
New Jersey Long-Term Tax-Exempt Fund
New York Long-Term Tax-Exempt Fund
Ohio Long-Term Tax-Exempt Fund
Pacific Stock Index Fund
Pennsylvania Long-Term Tax-Exempt Fund
Precious Metals and Mining Fund
Prime Money Market Fund
PRIMECAP Fund

REIT Index Fund
Short-Term Bond Index Fund
Short-Term Federal Fund
Short-Term Treasury Fund
Small-Cap Growth Index Fund
Strategic Equity Fund
Target Retirement 2010 Fund
Target Retirement 2015 Fund
Target Retirement 2020 Fund
Target Retirement 2025 Fund
Target Retirement 2030 Fund
Target Retirement 2035 Fund
Target Retirement 2040 Fund
Target Retirement 2045 Fund
Target Retirement 2050 Fund
Tax-Exempt Money Market Fund
Total Bond Market Index Fund
Total International Stock Index Fund
Total Stock Market Index Fund
Treasury Money Market Fund
U.S. Growth Fund
U.S. Value Fund
Value Index Fund

COMPETITORS

AIG
AllianceBernstein
American Century
AXA Financial
BlackRock
Charles Schwab
FMR
Franklin Resources
Invesco
Invesco Aim
Janus Capital
Legg Mason
MFS
Principal Financial
Putnam
T. Rowe Price
TIAA-CREF
USAA

Vanguard Health Systems

Vanguard Health Systems wants to lead the way to better health care. The company operates more than a dozen for-profit acute care hospitals located in mostly affluent urban and suburban markets in Arizona, Illinois, Massachusetts, and Texas; all told, the hospitals have more than 4,000 licensed beds. The company's hospital systems generally include outpatient facilities and medical office buildings that form local health care networks providing a continuum of care. Vanguard also runs three managed health care plans that serve more than 200,000 members in Arizona and Illinois. The Blackstone Group owns a majority stake in the company.

In order to focus on its four core markets, the company sold three Southern California hospitals to Prime Healthcare Services. It still owns two surgery centers in California, however.

The company's managed care operations include Phoenix Health Plan, a Medicaid managed care plan serving more than 130,000 members in the Phoenix area, and MacNeal Health

Providers, an organization affiliated with the company's Chicago-area facility MacNeal Hospital. Its third health plan, Abrazo Advantage, provides Medicare Advantage and prescription drug plans to Phoenix-area Medicare members who are also eligible for Medicaid.

Like most hospital operators, the company hopes to attract customers by providing high quality care, recruiting good doctors, and expanding its services. It particularly looks to add high-margin services in areas such as cardiology and orthopedics and to increase its hospitals' ability to offer private rooms.

Vanguard Health looks to selectively acquire additional facilities, both in its existing markets and in others that fit its preferred profile: struggling not-for-profits located in fast-growing and generally affluent urban and suburban areas.

The system's hospitals have a fairly diverse payor mix. The biggest single source of income comes from managed care plans (about 35%), Medicare and Medicaid account for 25% and 8%, respectively, with the remainder being made up of commercial payors and self-pay patients.

Vanguard Health has begun expanding its hospitalist programs. Hospitalists help coordinate care between specialist physicians and the nursing staff, and are available to provide one-on-one patient care on a 24-hour-a-day, 7-day-a-week basis. Many health care providers believe the presence of a hospitalist program and staff increases the quality of patient care, thereby making the hospital more attractive to potential patients. Vanguard will increase its hospitalist programs throughout 2010.

Blackstone acquired its majority stake in the company from Morgan Stanley Capital Partners, which retains a minority interest. Chairman and CEO Charles Martin also holds about 7% of the company.

EXECUTIVES

Chairman and CEO: Charles N. (Charlie) Martin Jr., age 66
Vice Chairman: Keith B. Pitts, age 52
President and COO: Kent H. Wallace, age 54
EVP, CFO, and Treasurer: Phillip W. Roe, age 48
EVP, Secretary, and General Counsel:
Ronald P. (Ron) Soltman, age 63
EVP: Joseph D. (Joe) Moore, age 62
EVP Strategy and Innovation and Chief Transformation Officer: Bradley A. Perkins
EVP and Chief Medical Officer: Mark R. Montoney, age 52
SVP and Chief Information Officer: Deanna L. Wise, age 40
SVP, Controller, and Chief Accounting Officer:
Gary D. Willis, age 44
SVP and Chief Nursing Executive: Jana S. Stonestreet, age 56
SVP Operations: Graham Reever, age 45
SVP Market Strategy and Government Affairs:
Reginald M. Ballantyne III, age 65
SVP Human Resources: Larry L. Fultz, age 54
SVP and Chief Development Officer:
Harold H. Pilgrim III, age 48
Director Investor Relations: Aaron Broad
Auditors: Ernst & Young LLP

LOCATIONS

HQ: Vanguard Health Systems, Inc.
20 Burton Hills Blvd., Ste. 100, Nashville, TN 37215
Phone: 615-665-6000   **Fax:** 615-665-6099
Web: www.vanguardhealth.com

Selected Facilities

Arrowhead Hospital (Phoenix)
Baptist Medical Center (San Antonio)
Louis A. Weiss Memorial Hospital (Chicago)
MacNeal Hospital (Chicago)
Maryvale Hospital (Phoenix)
MetroWest Medical Center-Framingham Union Hospital (Framingham, MA)
MetroWest Medical Center-Leonard Morse Hospital (Natick, MA)
North Central Baptist Hospital (San Antonio)
Northeast Baptist Hospital (San Antonio)
Paradise Valley Hospital (Phoenix)
Phoenix Baptist Hospital (Phoenix)
Southeast Baptist Hospital (San Antonio)
St. Luke's Baptist Hospital (San Antonio)
Saint Vincent Hospital at Worcester Medical Center (Worcester, MA)
West Valley Hospital (Phoenix)

PRODUCTS/OPERATIONS

2009 Sales

	$ mil.	% of total
Acute care services	2,522	79
Health plans	678	21
Total	**3,200**	**100**

COMPETITORS

Advocate Health Care
Banner Health
Blue Cross Blue Shield of Arizona
Catholic Healthcare West
CHRISTUS Health
Community Health Systems
Covenant Ministries
Essent Healthcare
John C. Lincoln Health Network
Massachusetts General Hospital
Methodist Healthcare System
Partners HealthCare
Rush System for Health
Tenet Healthcare
Universal Health Services
University Health System
WellGroup HealthPartners

HISTORICAL FINANCIALS

Company Type: Private

Income Statement

				FYE: June 30
	REVENUE ($ mil.)	NET INCOME ($ mil.)	NET PROFIT MARGIN	EMPLOYEES
6/09	3,200	29	0.9%	19,200
6/08	2,791	(1)	—	18,500
6/07	2,581	(133)	—	18,000
6/06	2,653	13	0.5%	19,500
6/05	2,269	(78)	—	19,000
Annual Growth	**9.0%**	**—**	**—**	**0.3%**

Net Income History

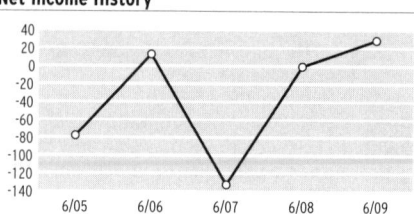

Varolii Corporation

Varolii makes sure customers and employees get the message. The company provides automated contact and notification software. Its products and services help client companies manage their interactions, contacting customers and employees via e-mail, fax, telephone, or instant messaging devices. Varolii provides applications designed to handle collections, customer service, customer retention, and business continuity. It targets customers in the communications, financial services, government, health care, insurance, transportation, and utilities sectors.

Formerly called PAR3 Communications, the company acquired competitor EnvoyWorldWide, a provider of notification services for business continuity and emergency communications, in 2005. The company changed its name to Varolii in 2007, the year it filed to go public. Citing unfavorable market conditions, Varolii withrew its IPO in 2008.

EXECUTIVES

President, CEO, and Director: Nicholas A. Tiliacos, age 54
EVP Field Operations: Jeffrey J. Read, age 39
CFO: John J. Flavio, age 61
CTO: Derrick Mar
Chief Security Officer: Vern Cole
VP and General Counsel: Jeff Shelby, age 43
VP and General Manager, Business Continuity: Steve H. Zirkel
Senior Director Project Management: Kate McArdle
Senior Director Marketing: Kael Kelly
Director Contact Center Solutions: Mary Bartels
Director Decisioning Products and Strategy: Randal Hisatomi
Director Healthcare Solutions: Marc Lawrence
Auditors: PricewaterhouseCoopers LLP

LOCATIONS

HQ: Varolii Corporation
821 2nd Ave., 10th Fl., Ste. 1000, Seattle, WA 98104
Phone: 206-902-3900   **Fax:** 206-902-3902
Web: www.varolii.com

HISTORICAL FINANCIALS

Company Type: Private

Income Statement

	REVENUE ($ mil.)	NET INCOME ($ mil.)	NET PROFIT MARGIN	EMPLOYEES
12/07	68	(5)	—	287
12/06	51	(5)	—	251
12/05	30	(1)	—	144
12/04	16	(1)	—	81
Annual Growth	61.3%	—	—	52.5%

FYE: December 31

2007 Year-End Financials

Debt ratio: (10.3%)   Current ratio: —
Return on equity: —   Long-term debt ($ mil.): 3
Cash ($ mil.): —

Net Income History

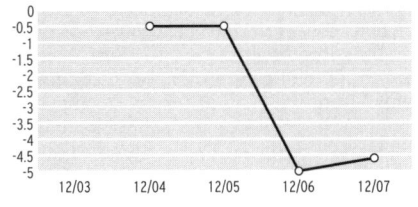

Vertis, Inc.

Vertis (dba Vertis Communications) provides marketing services from conception through design, production, and distribution for thousands of clients, including grocery stores, retail chains, newspapers, and ad agencies. Vertis' services include market research, media planning, advertising production, digital production, and fulfillment services. It produces newspaper inserts such as color comics, TV magazines, and supplements and provides direct mail, package design, interactive marketing, and media planning services to clients in the US and the UK. Producing more than 30 billion advertising inserts per year, it operates from 100 locations worldwide. In late 2008 Vertis acquired rival ACG Holdings.

After the acquisition was completed in October 2008, ACG Holdings (which conducts business through its American Color Graphics unit) became a wholly owned subsidiary of Vertis, but within months Vertis had absorbed ACG Holdings' operations. The deal greatly enhanced Vertis' printing offerings and also helped to alleviate debt. (In order to restructure for the acquisition, Vertis voluntarily filed for Chapter 11 bankruptcy protection in July 2008 and emerged a few months later in October.) The combined company has about 8,000 employees and serves more than 3,000 clients.

Following the acquisition, Vertis closed printing plants in Baltimore; Chicago; San Antonio, Texas; and Sylacauga, Alabama, to streamline its operations. Other Vertis Communications offerings include digital services, online marketing, and strategic consulting, as well as direct mailing, response management, Internet integration, and database management.

The company adopted the Vertis Communications brand in 2006, capping a series of moves to diversify its services. It began relying less and less on its traditional commercial printing business in the late 1990s as it expanded into areas of marketing and advertising. Later it consolidated its three primary divisions (all the better to create cross-selling opportunities), took itself private, moved its headquarters from New York City to Baltimore (headquarters of its TC Advertising division), and changed its name from Big Flower Holdings to Vertis.

In 2009 CEO Mike DuBose was replaced by Quincy Allen, a 25-year veteran from Xerox.

EXECUTIVES

CEO: Quincy L. Allen, age 48
CFO: Barry C. Kohn, age 53
CIO: Richard Guetzloff
Chief Legal Officer: David Glogoff
Chief Marketing Officer: Kathy L. Calta, age 50
SVP and General Manager, Premedia and Technology Groups: Michael (Mike) Kucharski
SVP and General Manager, Inserts: Douglas L. (Doug) Mann, age 45
SVP Human Resources: Carmen Allen
SVP Sales, Direct Marketing Group: Scott Berry
SVP Sales, Advertising Inserts: Steve Wohlert
VP Communications: Grace Platon
President, Direct Marketing: Charles (Chuck) Miotke, age 55
Auditors: Deloitte & Touche LLP

LOCATIONS

HQ: Vertis, Inc.
250 W. Pratt St., 18th Fl., Baltimore, MD 21201
Phone: 410-528-9800   **Fax:** 410-528-9287
Web: www.vertisinc.com

PRODUCTS/OPERATIONS

Selected Products and Services

Ad Technology Services
Consulting services
Digital content management
Digital photography, compositing, and retouching
Graphic design and animation
In-store displays and billboards
Media planning and placement software
Newspaper advertisement development
Response management, warehousing, and fulfillment services

Direct Marketing Services
Automated digital fulfillment services
Customized one-to-one marketing programs
Data design, collection, management
Direct mail production
Effectiveness measurement
Mailing management services

Retail and Newspaper Services
Ad insert programs for retailer and manufacturers
Consumer research
Creative services for ad insert page layout and design
Digital advertising design and transmission
Freight and logistics management
Newspaper products including TV magazines, comics, and supplements

COMPETITORS

Acxiom
Communisis
Harte-Hanks
News America Marketing
Polestar Group
Quad/Graphics
R.R. Donnelley
Schawk
Sleepeck Printing
Valassis
World Color Press

HISTORICAL FINANCIALS

Company Type: Private

Income Statement

	REVENUE ($ mil.)	NET INCOME ($ mil.)	NET PROFIT MARGIN	EMPLOYEES
12/07	1,365	(327)	—	5,800
12/06	1,469	(26)	—	5,800
12/05	1,510	(173)	—	6,300
12/04	1,645	(11)	—	8,000
12/03	1,586	(96)	—	8,000
Annual Growth	(3.7%)	—	—	(7.7%)

FYE: December 31

Net Income History

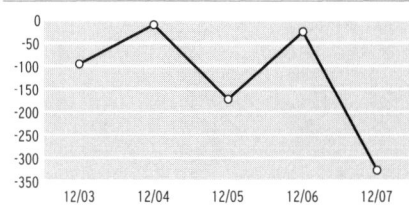

Vertrue Incorporated

Vertrue is all set to hook you up with the love of your life, or at least some discounts. The company markets membership programs offering discounts on financial services, health and dental care, travel, and other consumer products and services. Vertrue partners with companies such as credit card issuers, banks, direct-response TV advertisers, and retailers to market its membership programs. The company's personals business, Lavalife, provides Web and phone-based personals services to about 2 million members; it generates revenue by selling credits needed for romantics to interact with other lonely hearts. In 2007 Vertrue was acquired by an investment group that included the company's management team.

With the assumption of debt, the buyers paid about $855 million for Vertrue. Besides company executives, the investor group included One Equity Partners and Rho Ventures.

Other Vertrue units include My Choice Medical Holdings, which connects consumers with medical professionals in the fast-growing cosmetic surgery market, and Coverdell, a subsidiary which acts as a full-service marketing agency that markets insurance to banks. In addition, its Neverblue unit is an online marketing company focusing on lead generation and client acquisition services that caters to the Canadian market.

EXECUTIVES

President and CEO: Gary A. Johnson, age 52
EVP Health and Insurance Services:
Vincent DiBenedetto, age 51
SVP and CFO: Lorraine DiSanto
SVP Corporate Development: David Schachne, age 44
SVP and Chief Marketing Officer: Jay Sung
SVP and General Counsel: George Thomas
Auditors: PricewaterhouseCoopers LLP

LOCATIONS

HQ: Vertrue Incorporated
20 Glover Ave., Norwalk, CT 06850
Phone: 203-324-7635   **Fax:** 203-674-7080
Web: www.vertrue.com

COMPETITORS

AARP
Access Plans
Affinion Group
American Automobile Association (AAA)
Costco Wholesale
eHarmony.com
Hospitality Marketing Concepts
Match.com
Passport Unlimited
Provell
Q Interactive
Rewards Network
Sam's Club
Student Advantage
USAA

ViewSonic Corporation

ViewSonic has a display for every occasion. The company makes cathode ray tube (CRT) and LCD computer displays, including the Pro Series for high-end computer-aided design, desktop publishing, and graphic design; the X and Graphics lines for consumers and businesses; and the E2, Optiquest, and Value Series for budget-minded buyers. ViewSonic also offers LCD TVs, LCD projectors, tablet PCs, and digital photo frames. ViewSonic sells directly and through resellers and distributors to consumer, corporate, government, and education customers. Chairman and CEO James Chu, ViewSonic's majority owner, founded the company in 1987.

A leading provider of displays, ViewSonic has managed to hold its own in an industry where Asian giants such as NEC, Samsung, and Sony vie for market share. The company is on top of the latest trends in its markets, introducing a "pico projector" (a miniature unit weighing just two pounds, based on the DLP chip made by Texas Instruments), moving into the smartphone display business, unveiling the VieBook netbook computer, and selling all-in-one PCs that look like standard computer monitors but house all the elements of a full PC. ViewSonic also is addressing the cloud computing market.

ViewSonic filed to go public in 2007, but poor market conditions caused the company to withdraw its registration the following year.

EXECUTIVES

Chairman and CEO: James Chu
CFO: Sung Yi
VP Sales, Americas: Brian Igoe
VP and General Manager, Global Products and Solutions: Michael Sun
VP and General Manager, ViewSonic North America: Jeff Volpe
Managing Director, Asia/Pacific and MEA: Alan Chang
Managing Director, China: Rebecca Tsen
Auditors: Deloitte & Touche LLP

LOCATIONS

HQ: ViewSonic Corporation
381 Brea Canyon Rd., Walnut, CA 91789
Phone: 909-444-8888   **Fax:** 909-468-1240
Web: www.viewsonic.com

PRODUCTS/OPERATIONS

Selected Products

Digital photo frames
Digital signage
LCD projectors
LCD TVs
Monitors (cathode ray tube, LCD)
Tablet PCs

COMPETITORS

Acer	Panasonic Corp
Apple Inc.	Philips Electronics
BenQ	Planar Systems
Dell	Proview
Fujitsu	Samsung Electronics
Gateway, Inc.	Sharp Corp.
Hewlett-Packard	Sony
InFocus	THOMSON
INNOLUX	Toshiba
LG Display	TPV Technology
Mitsubishi Corp.	Victor Company of Japan
NEC	VIZIO
NEC Display Solutions	

HISTORICAL FINANCIALS

Company Type: Private

Income Statement				FYE: December 31
	REVENUE ($ mil.)	NET INCOME ($ mil.)	NET PROFIT MARGIN	EMPLOYEES
12/07	1,600	—	—	900
12/06	1,589	—	—	786
12/05	1,200	—	—	647
12/04	1,104	—	—	807
12/03	1,075	—	—	743
Annual Growth	10.5%	—	—	4.9%

Revenue History

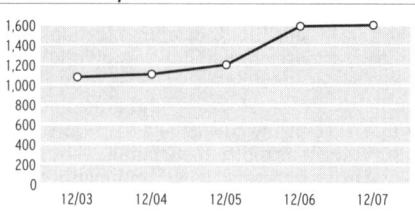

Visant Holding Corp.

Visant Holding is a real class act. Through its Jostens Scholastic unit, the company provides school-related affinity products, such as class rings and graduation items, mostly to North American high schools and colleges. It also makes championship rings for professional sports and specialty markets. Its Jostens Memory Book unit makes and markets yearbooks to US middle and high schools and universities. Visant's Marketing and Publishing Services group produces advertising and direct marketing materials for the fragrance, cosmetics, and personal care markets, as well as the direct marketing sector. It also makes book covers for educational publishers. Visant bought Rennoc's team outerwear business in July 2009.

The acquisition allows Visant to be a leader in letter jacket manufacturing and distributing overnight, as Rennoc has logged more than 50 years in that niche of the awards market. The deal also gives Visant a foot in the door with sports dealers. As part of the purchase, Visant plans to continue to sell Rennoc products through existing Rennoc-specific independent sales channels, which primarily cater to the sporting goods dealer network. The assets acquired will operate within Visant's Scholastic segment and are complementary to its Neff Motivation subsidiary, which was purchased in 2007. Neff Motivation provides custom award programs and apparel, including chenille letters and letter jackets.

Looking to build upon its publishing operations, Visant in 2008 acquired book component printer Phoenix Color for about $220 million. Phoenix Color was then combined with Visant's own book cover printing operation — known as Lehigh Lithographers — to form Lehigh Phoenix. (The Phoenix Color purchase complements Visant's 2007 deals for book component supplier Visual Systems and yearbook producer Publishing Enterprises.) Soon after the Phoenix

Color transaction was completed, Visant shuttered its plant in Pennsauken, New Jersey, allowing the two companies to combine their printing facilities in order to reduce costs and streamline operations.

Closing the New Jersey facility was also part of Visant's greater restructuring efforts undertaken that year. In addition to right-sizing production, the company in 2008 laid off about 400 employees across all segments, amounting to nearly 10% of the workforce. It also streamlined sales, administrative, and support functions. Even though sales have remained steady, the company anticipates rolling out additional cost-cutting measures in the years ahead.

The company was formed in 2004 through the consolidation of Jostens, Von Hoffmann, and Arcade. It has since sold off its Von Hoffmann business to R.R. Donnelley & Sons (in May 2007) for more than $410 million as well as its Jostens Photography business.

Visant is controlled by Kohlberg Kravis Roberts & Co. and DLJ Merchant Banking Partners.

EXECUTIVES

Chairman, President, and CEO: Marc L. Reisch, age 53
VP Finance: Paul B. Carousso, age 39
VP, General Counsel, and Secretary: Marie D. Hlavaty, age 45
President and Chief Executive Officer, Jostens Group: Timothy M. Larson, age 35
Auditors: Deloitte & Touche LLP

LOCATIONS

HQ: Visant Holding Corp.
357 Main St., Armonk, NY 10504
Phone: 914-595-8200
Web: www.visant.net

PRODUCTS/OPERATIONS

2008 Sales

	$ mil.	% of total
Marketing & Publishing Services	501.2	37
Scholastic	472.4	34
Memory Book	392.0	29
Total	**1,365.6**	**100**

COMPETITORS

American Achievement
Coral Graphic Services
Herff Jones
Walsworth

HISTORICAL FINANCIALS

Company Type: Holding company

Income Statement

FYE: December 31

	REVENUE ($ mil.)	NET INCOME ($ mil.)	NET PROFIT MARGIN	EMPLOYEES
12/08	1,366	46	3.4%	5,645
12/07	1,270	155	12.2%	5,691
12/06	1,187	48	4.0%	5,096
Annual Growth	**7.3%**	**(1.8%)**	**—**	**5.2%**

2008 Year-End Financials

Debt ratio: 1,089.4%
Return on equity: —
Cash ($ mil.): —
Current ratio: —
Long-term debt ($ mil.): 1,414

Net Income History

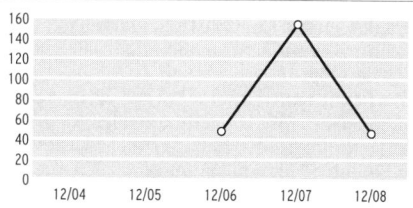

VIZIO, Inc.

VIZIO has done for HDTVs what Dell did for PCs and Southwest Airlines did for air travel: sell them for less. The company sells low-cost flat panel and plasma LCD HDTVs. It has gone head to head with Japanese giants such as Sony and Samsung, but its products are made in China and Taiwan. Each year VIZIO has logged large revenue gains by selling quality televisions for hundreds, if not thousands, of dollars less than its competitors. The company was founded by CEO William Wang in 2003 and, initially, its TVs were only sold at membership retailers such as Costco Wholesale, BJ's Wholesale Club, and Sam's Club. Since then it has extended its reach to discount retailers Wal-Mart and Sears.

VIZIO's low-cost business model and partnerships with high-volume retailers, such as Wal-Mart, has paid off for the company, which in 2009 was named the #1 shipper of LCD TVs in the US. While TVs are VIZIO's bread and butter, it also makes Blue-Ray disc players and other consumer electronics products.

Wang is a former electronics executive who tried to help the PC maker Gateway branch out into the television market. Wang says VIZIO maintains a low overhead by not keeping a lot of inventory and by selling no-frills TVs that don't have a lot of features. The company also keeps costs low by not spending a lot on advertising. The firm only has about 160 full-time employees at its headquarters in California, most of whom work in customer service and technical support.

VIZIO also controls the design and marketing of its products and partners with contract manufacturers to make TVs less expensively than its competitors. Its collaboration with AmTran Technology Co., based in Taipei, has proven to be an integral part of the success of both VIZIO and AmTran. AmTran, which has an ownership stake in VIZIO, generates some 80% of its revenue from sales to VIZIO, while VIZIO relies on AmTran as a supplier for most of its TVs.

In early 2009 VIZIO filed an antitrust and unfair competition suit against Japan's Funai Electronics Co. alleging that the distributor of digital televisions unlawfully restrained trade and monopolized the market for the licensing of technology used to interpret and retrieve information from a digital TV broadcast signal, as well as the market for digital TV sets and receivers. In August Funai rejected VIZIO's claims and sought dismissal of the antitrust suit.

EXECUTIVES

COO: Elson Chang
CEO and CTO: William Wang
VP and CFO: Kyle Wescoat
VP Management Information Systems: Eunice Tseng

VP New Products: John Schindler
VP Operations: Rob L. Brinkman
VP Partner Management: John Morriss
VP Sales: Laynie Newsome
Director Marketing: Jason Maciel
Human Resources Manager: Wendy Hershman

LOCATIONS

HQ: VIZIO, Inc.
39 Tesla, Irvine, CA 92618
Phone: 949-428-2525
Web: www.vizio.com

PRODUCTS/OPERATIONS

Selected Products

Cables and other accessories
Blue-ray disc players
HDTVs
HD Home theater systems

COMPETITORS

Funai Electric
LG Electronics
Panasonic Corp
Philips Electronics
Samsung Electronics
Sony
Westinghouse

HISTORICAL FINANCIALS

Company Type: Private

Income Statement

FYE: December 31

	REVENUE ($ mil.)	NET INCOME ($ mil.)	NET PROFIT MARGIN	EMPLOYEES
12/08	2,010	—	—	118
12/07	1,970	—	—	105
Annual Growth	**2.0%**	**—**	**—**	**12.4%**

Revenue History

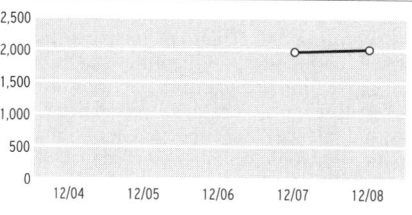

Volunteers of America

There's a volunteer everywhere you look at Volunteers of America, a national faith-based organization that provides community-level human services to more than 2 million people a year. It works to help abused and neglected children, at-risk youth, disabled people, the homeless, people with substance abuse problems, the elderly, and prisoners and former prisoners. The group operates from about 40 offices across the US and counts more than 70,000 volunteers in its ranks. It receives government grants as well as support from the public. Volunteers of America was organized in 1896 by Ballington and Maud Booth. Name sound familiar? Ballington's father, William Booth, founded the Salvation Army.

EXECUTIVES

Chairman: C. David Kikumoto, age 59
Vice Chairman: Don Conley
President and CEO: Charles W. Gould
EVP Community Engagement: Jatrice Martel Gaiter
EVP and General Counsel: David T. Bowman
EVP Strategy: Rosemarie A. (Rose) Rae
Secretary and Director: Nancy B. Gofus, age 52
Treasurer and Director: Maury Reiter
Director; President, Volunteers of America of Wyoming and Montana: Jeff Holsinger
Director; President and CEO, Volunteers of America Greater Sacramento and Northern Nevada: Leo McFarland
Director; President and CEO, Volunteers of America Greater New York: Richard Motta
Director; President and CEO, Volunteers of America of Oregon: Kay Dean Toran
Director; President and CEO, Volunteers of America Serving Minnesota: Michael Weber
Director; President and CEO, Volunteers of America Colorado Branch: Dianna Kunz
Director; VP Organizational Planning and Growth, Volunteers of America of Western Washington: Karen Kipling

LOCATIONS

HQ: Volunteers of America
1660 Duke St., Alexandria, VA 22314
Phone: 703-341-5000   **Fax:** 703-341-7000
Web: www.voa.org

Vulcan Inc.

Even with all his Vulcan logic, could Spock invest like *this*? Brainy billionaire Paul Allen organizes his business and charitable ventures under Vulcan Inc. The firm includes the Microsoft co-founder's remaining stake in the industry-defining juggernaut, as well as holdings in dozens of companies involved in technology, life sciences, multimedia, energy, and real estate. Portfolio holdings include stakes in SpaceShipOne, Vulcan Capital, and Charter Communications. Allen also owns two professional sports teams, the NBA's Portland Trail Blazers and the NFL's Seattle Seahawks, as well as interests in several charitable organizations.

Vulcan's charities support the arts, medical research, land conservation, and other causes. Allen, who co-founded Microsoft with Bill Gates, promotes a "wired world" vision, in which everyone is united through interconnecting communications, entertainment, and information systems. CEO Jody Patton, Allen's sister, oversees both his business and charitable ventures.

In 2007 the company joined a joint venture to acquire banks in the Southeast. Vulcan developed a group of low-cost apartments in 2008 to serve Seattle residents making below the median income.

Vulcan expanded its sports empire in 2008 by becoming a part-owner of the Seattle Sounders, an expansion team in Major League Soccer. The team plays its home games at Qwest Field, also owned by Vulcan.

In early 2009 Vulcan laid off some 50 employees to cut its total work force to about 600 employees in response to economic conditions. A spokesman said Vulcan was postponing or canceling some projects but would not specify which ones.

HISTORY

Paul Allen and Bill Gates first worked together on computer projects as schoolmates in Seattle. They developed a program to determine traffic patterns and launched Traf-O-Data, an operation that failed because the state provided the information for free. When Allen saw an article on the MITS Altair 8800 minicomputer in 1975, the two realized it needed a simplified programming language to make it useful. They offered MITS a modified version of BASIC they had written for Traf-O-Data. The company set them up in an office in Albuquerque, New Mexico. They then began their biggest collaboration of all: Microsoft. While Gates concentrated on business, Allen focused on technical issues.

They moved to Bellevue, a Seattle suburb, in 1979. The next year IBM asked them to create a programming language for a PC project. Allen bought Q-DOS (quick and dirty operating system) from Seattle Computer; the pair tweaked it and renamed it MS-DOS. Allen and Gates made a key decision to structure their contract with IBM to allow clones. They also helped design many aspects of the original IBM PC.

Allen developed Hodgkin's disease in 1982. Facing his own mortality, he ended his daily involvement in Microsoft (keeping a chunk of the company and a board seat) and began to play more (traveling and playing the electric guitar). With his cancer in remission in 1985, Allen founded multimedia software company Asymetrix. The next year he set up Vulcan to hold his diversified interests and Vulcan Ventures. He also began helping startups, indulging his interests (buying the NBA's Portland Trail Blazers in 1988 and donating some $60 million to build a museum honoring his musical idol, Jimi Hendrix, and other Pacific Northwest artists). He has also funded Seattle-area civic improvements.

In 1990 Allen hired William Savoy to help organize his finances; Savoy later became president of Vulcan Ventures. Seeing a need for more R&D in the US, Allen in 1992 started Interval Research. He also invested in America Online (sold 1994). In 1993 Allen bought 80% of Ticketmaster (sold 1997), and in 1995 he invested in DreamWorks SKG, the multimedia company of Steven Spielberg, Jeffrey Katzenberg, and David Geffen.

Allen made a rare buy outside the entertainment and high-tech worlds through a 1996 investment in power turbine maker Capstone Turbine. To prevent the Seattle Seahawks from moving to California, Allen bought the team in 1997 and made plans for a new stadium. He consolidated his management operations under Vulcan and dissolved Paul Allen Group (founded 1994), keeping Vulcan Ventures.

Allen moved into cable in 1998 and 1999; his Charter Communications eventually became the #4 US cable firm. In 1999 several Allen investments (Charter Communications, Vulcan Ventures, RCN, High Speed Access, and Go2Net) joined to form wired-world venture Broadband Partners.

In 2000 it was nearly impossible to ignore Allen's influence on Seattle as several major projects took shape or were completed, including the new Seahawks' arena, the Experience Music Project, and the renovation of a 90-year-old train station as part of a complex that includes Vulcan's new headquarters. That year he provided a $100 million infusion to struggling Oxygen Media. In 2001 Vulcan Ventures bought sports games Web site operator Small World Media to boost its sports holdings, which was later folded

into the online fantasy sports operations of another Allen holding, *The Sporting News*, which was later sold.

Tech-boom losses accounted for only about 5% of Allen's portfolio, but things looked very bleak indeed in 2002 when the US attorney's office began investigating Charter Communications — for accounting irregularities. Four former executives were later indicted for fraud in 2003. Long-time right-hand man Bill Savoy left the firm that year; Savoy had overseen Vulcan's tech investments for more than a decade.

In late 2003 Allen began to restructure his holdings, dumping remaining unprofitable holdings (including RCN), and laying off many employees, including Savoy. TechTV was sold to Comcast in 2004; the network was merged into Comcast's existing gaming and technology network, G4.

EXECUTIVES

Chairman: Paul G. Allen, age 56
President and CEO: Jo Lynn (Jody) Allen Patton, age 51
EVP, Finance: Denise K. Fletcher, age 60
EVP, Legal and General Counsel: Bill McGrath
SVP, Business Operations, Major League Soccer Team: Gary Wright
VP, Technology: Chris Purcell
VP, Tax: Bruce Lowry
VP, Corporate Communications: Steven C. Crosby
VP, Design and Construction: Ray Colliver
VP, Paul G. Allen Family Foundation and Collections: Susan Coliton
VP, Media Development: Richard E. Hutton
VP, Real Estate Development: Ada M. Healey
VP, Corporate Development and Operations: Denise Wolf
President, Vulcan Capital: Christopher M. (Chris) Temple

LOCATIONS

HQ: Vulcan Inc.
505 5th Ave. South, Ste. 900, Seattle, WA 98104
Phone: 206-342-2000   **Fax:** 206-342-3000
Web: www.vulcan.com

PRODUCTS/OPERATIONS

Selected Holdings

Allen Institute for Brain Science
Audience (telecommunications audio)
Charter Communications (TV system)
Cinerama (movie theater, Seattle)
Digeo (interactive television)
DrumCore (drum software and workstation)
Ember (wireless networking systems)
Experience Music Project (EMP, music museum, Seattle)
Flying Heritage Collection (WWII aircraft exhibit, Arlington, WA)
The Hospital (music, art, and film facility, London)
IntraPace (development of an endoscopically delivered pacemaker for treating obesity)
Laureate Education, Inc.
Makena Capital Management
Portland Trail Blazers (professional basketball franchise)
PTC Therapeutics (small molecule drugs)
Redfin (online real estate services)
Rose Garden (sports and entertainment arena)
Science Fiction Museum and Hall of Fame (Seattle)
Seattle Seahawks (professional football franchise)
Seattle Sounders (professional soccer franchise)
Silvercrest Asset Management Group
SpaceShipOne (privately built spacecraft)
Vulcan Energy (formerly Plains Resources, oil and gas pipeline, transportation, and storage)
Vulcan Productions (independent film production company)
ZoomInfo (search engine focusing on people, companies, and relationships)

COMPETITORS

Accel Partners	KKR
Benchmark Capital	Kleiner Perkins
Blackstone Group	Matrix Partners
The Carlyle Group	MSD Capital
Draper Fisher Jurvetson	Platinum Equity
Equity Group Investments	SOFTBANK
Hummer Winblad	Thomas H. Lee Partners
IVP	The Trump Organization

VyStar Credit Union

VyStar provides a galaxy of financial services from more than two dozen locations in northeastern Florida. The credit union offers traditional banking services including deposit accounts and loans; its VyStar Financial Group subsidiary specializes in financial management and insurance services to members and nonmembers alike. The credit union's loan portfolio consists of home mortgage, automobile, personal, and credit card loans. Membership in VyStar is available to all who live or work in one of 15 area counties. Founded in 1952 as Jax Navy Federal Credit Union to serve those stationed at the Naval Air Station in Jacksonville, VyStar now boasts approximately 350,000 members.

EXECUTIVES

Chairman: George R. Berry
Vice Chairman: Esther T. Schultz
President and CEO: Terry R. West
CIO: Terry L. Mayne
Chief Lending Officer: Kathryn Bonaventura
EVP and CFO: John H. Turpish
EVP and COO: Richard G. Alfirevic
SVP Human Resources: Robert L. Davis
SVP Business Services: Joseph Nowland
SVP Member Services: Randy Swift
SVP Risk Management: Raymond Ritoch
SVP Marketing and Planning: Judith T. Walz
VP Accounting: Joan M. Hill
VP Mortgages: Lori Allen
VP Business Services: Katrena Pitts
Secretary: P. Kem Siddons
Treasurer: Ralph R. Story
Auditors: Nearman, Maynard, Vallez, CPAs and Consultants, P.A.

LOCATIONS

HQ: VyStar Credit Union
4949 Blanding Blvd., Jacksonville, FL 32210
Phone: 904-777-6000 **Fax:** 904-908-2488
Web: www.vystarcu.org

PRODUCTS/OPERATIONS

2008 Sales

	$ mil.	% of total
Interest		
Loans	155.3	61
Investments & cash equivalents	40.4	16
Noninterest		
Commissions	29.2	11
Service charges & other fees	26.8	11
Other	3.1	1
Total	**254.8**	**100**

COMPETITORS

Bank of America
BB&T
Compass Bancshares
SunTrust
Wachovia Corp

HISTORICAL FINANCIALS

Company Type: Not-for-profit

Income Statement				FYE: December 31
	ASSETS ($ mil.)	NET INCOME ($ mil.)	INCOME AS % OF ASSETS	EMPLOYEES
12/08	3,687	(10)	—	1,100
12/07	3,337	18	0.6%	1,100
12/06	3,169	22	0.7%	1,059
12/05	2,995	21	0.7%	1,000
12/04	2,852	17	0.6%	900
Annual Growth	6.6%	—	—	5.1%

2008 Year-End Financials

Equity as % of assets: —
Return on assets: —
Return on equity: —
Long-term debt ($ mil.): 320
Sales ($ mil.): 255

Net Income History

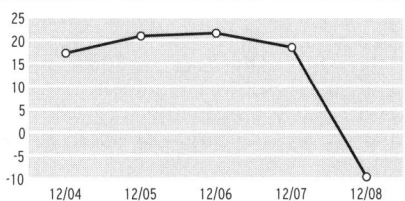

Waffle House

Don't look for pancakes at the Waffle House, because it doesn't serve 'em. The #2 family-style restaurant chain (behind Denny's) has more than 1,500 diners known for eggs, grits, waffles, and their famous "scattered, smothered, and covered" hash browns. In addition to day starters, the menu features T-bone steaks, cheeseburgers, and other sandwiches. Waffle House units are typically free standing, designed to resemble 1950s-style diners, and open 24 hours a day. They can be found in more than two dozen states, mostly in the South. The company operates more than 700 units and franchises the rest. Joe Rogers Sr., father of CEO Joe Rogers Jr., started the family-owned business with partner Tom Forkner in 1955.

Waffle House continues to expand slowly through a mix of franchising and new corporate-run locations, but the chain has yet to stray far from its core market in the South. That concentration has made the brand an institution along southern highways where it competes with Denny's, IHOP (owned by DineEquity), and Cracker Barrel.

Despite its popularity, Waffle House has not been immune to the effects of rising food costs and a slowing economy, however. Two of the company's largest franchisees, Northlake Foods in Florida and Tennessee-based SouthEast Waffles, were forced to file for bankruptcy during 2008. Together, the two businesses operated more than 250 stores. Early the next year, Waf-

fle House took over more than 110 locations from Northlake.

The chain has developed close relationships with food suppliers to serve exclusively Coca-Cola soft drinks, Minute Maid orange juice, and Heinz condiments. It also boasts several celebrities among its fans, including Britney Spears, running back Emmitt Smith, and actor Billy Bob Thornton.

HISTORY

Joe Rogers Sr. and Tom Forkner opened the first Waffle House restaurant on Labor Day, 1955, in Avondale Estates, Georgia. Rogers and Forkner based their restaurant's strategy on simple Southern cooking and low overhead. Little has changed at the Waffle House — the same black-on-yellow signs hang over each restaurant, and the menu could serve as a time capsule from 1955 (prices aside).

Joe Rogers Jr. became CEO in 1973. He built a reputation for management skills, establishing a rigorous training program for store managers and instituted incentive-based compensation in an effort to retain employees.

In 1981 the US Department of Labor took exception to the company's practice of paying inordinately low wages to restaurant managers who also served as cooks. The company won the case in 1983 and has since become tight-lipped about its operations.

Waffle House had another scrape with the law in 1997. A US district judge found the company guilty of sexual harassment and "egregious conduct" against a former human resources employee. The judge ordered the company to pay $8.1 million in damages. The following year Waffle House showed signs of rethinking its tight-lipped stance when it hired a public relations firm.

Waffle House's largest franchisee, Northlake Foods, was hit by a racial discrimination suit in 1999. Five African-American men alleged that they were denied service by a white cook at an Atlanta-area restaurant. Also that year a Waffle House waitress in Mobile, Alabama, won $10 million from a lottery ticket left by a customer as a tip. Four of her co-workers won a share in the winnings after demonstrating in court that the employees had a "share the wealth" agreement.

In 2000 the company found itself the subject of another race-related lawsuit when a manager said he was ordered to fire black employees in order to have the restaurant's staff reflect the racial makeup of its mostly white town. The following year a federal judge ordered Waffle House franchisee Treetop Enterprises to pay nearly $3 million to 125 employees who worked more than 80 hours a week despite allegedly being hired to work 53-hour weeks.

In 2003 and 2004 Waffle House faced more racial-discrimination lawsuits in five states, including Georgia. The company celebrated its 50th anniversary in 2005.

EXECUTIVES

Founder: Tom Forkner
Chairman and CEO: Joe W. Rogers Jr., age 62
President and COO: Bert Thornton
VP Public Relations and Marketing: Pat Warner
VP Human Resources: Will Mizell
VP Advocacy: Don Balfour
Media Contact: Kelly Thrasher

Wakefern Food

Some might say you aren't shopping right if you don't get your groceries from stores supplied by this company. Wakefern Food is the largest member-owned wholesale distribution cooperative in the US, supplying groceries and other merchandise to a chain of more than 200 ShopRite supermarkets in five eastern states. The company supplies both national brand and private-label products (ShopRite, Chef's Express, Readington Farms) to its member stores; Wakefern also offers advertising, merchandising, insurance, and other business support services. The co-op, which boasts more than 40 members, was founded by seven grocers in 1946 and rebranded the individual stores with the ShopRite name five years later.

While the ShopRite chain boasts a loyal following in its core markets, the supermarkets have been feeling the pinch from rivals in the price-competitive grocery business. It is especially feeling pressure from non-supermarket chains such as Wal-Mart, CVS/Caremark, and Wawa.

The cooperative added to its footprint in 2007 when it acquired about 10 underperforming retail locations from Stop & Shop. The stores, located mostly in South Jersey, were rebranded under the ShopRite banner.

HISTORY

Wakefern Food was founded in 1946 by seven New York- and New Jersey-based grocers: Louis Weiss, Sam and Al Aidekman, Abe Kesselman, Dave Fern, Sam Garb, and Albert Goldberg (the company's name is made up of the first letters of the last names of first five of those founders). Like many cooperatives, the association sought to lower costs by increasing its buying power as a group.

They each put in $1,000 and began operating a 5,000-sq.-ft. warehouse, often putting in double time to keep both their stores and the warehouse running. The shopkeepers' collective buying power proved valuable, enabling the grocers to stock many items at the same prices as their larger competitors.

In 1951 Wakefern members began pooling their resources to buy advertising space. A common store name — ShopRite — was chosen, and each week co-op members met to decide which items would be sale priced. Within a year, membership had grown to over 50. Expansion became a priority, and in the mid-1950s co-op members united in small groups to take over failed supermarkets. One such group, called the Supermarkets Operating Co. (SOC), was formed in 1956. Within 10 years it had acquired a number of failed stores, remodeled them, and given them the ShopRite name.

During the late 1950s sales at ShopRite stores slumped after Wakefern decided to buck the supermarket trend of offering trading stamps (which could then be exchanged for gifts), figuring that offering the stamps would ultimately lead to higher food prices. The move initially drove away customers, but Wakefern cut grocery prices across the board and sales returned. The company did embrace another supermarket trend: stocking stores with nonfood items.

The co-op was severely shaken in 1966 when SOC merged with General Supermarkets, a similar small group within Wakefern, becoming Supermarkets General Corp. (SGC). SGC was a powerful entity, with 71 supermarkets, 10 drugstores, six gas stations, a wholesale bakery, and a discount department store. Many Wakefern members opposed the merger and attempted to block the action with a court order. By 1968 SGC had beefed up its operations to include department store chains as well as its grocery stores. In a move that threatened to break Wakefern, SGC broke away from the co-op, and its stores were renamed Pathmark.

Wakefern not only weathered the storm, it grew under the direction of chairman and CEO Thomas Infusino, elected shortly after the split. The co-op focused on asserting its position as a seller of low-priced products. Wakefern developed private-label brands, including the ShopRite brand. In the 1980s members began operating larger stores and adding more nonfood items to the ShopRite product mix. With its number of superstores on the rise and facing increased competition from club stores in 1992, Wakefern opened a centralized, nonfood distribution center in New Jersey.

In 1995, 30-year Wakefern veteran Dean Janeway was elected president of the co-op. The company debuted its ShopRite MasterCard, co-branded with New Jersey's Valley National Bank, in 1996. The following year the co-op purchased two of its customers' stores in Pennsylvania, then threatened to close them when contract talks with the local union deteriorated. In 1998 Wakefern settled the dispute, then sold the stores.

The company partnered with Internet bidding site priceline.com in 1999, offering customers an opportunity to bid on groceries and then pick them up at ShopRite stores. Big V, Wakefern's biggest customer, filed for Chapter 11 bankruptcy protection in 2000 and said it was ending its distribution agreement with the co-op. In July 2002, however, Wakefern's ShopRite Supermarkets subsidiary acquired all of Big V's assets for approximately $185 million in cash and assumed liabilities.

Infusino retired in May 2005 after 35 years with Wakefern Food. He was succeeded by former vice chairman Joseph Colalillo.

EXECUTIVES

Chairman and CEO: Joseph S. (Joe) Colalillo, age 48
President and COO: Dean Janeway
CFO: Doug Wille
EVP: Joseph Sheridan
SVP and CIO: Natan Tabak
VP Logistics: Pete Rolandelli
VP Information Services Division: Alan Aront
VP Human Resources: Ann Burke
VP Merchandising and Advertising: Bill Crombie
VP Corporate and Consumer Affairs: Karen Meleta
Director Advertising: Karen McAuvic
Director Wholesale Division: Dave Baer
Director Private Label Branding: Loren Weinstein
Director Consumer Affairs: Cheryl Macik

LOCATIONS

HQ: Wakefern Food Corporation
600 York St., Elizabeth, NJ 07207
Phone: 908-527-3300 **Fax:** 908-527-3397
Web: www.shoprite.com

COMPETITORS

A&P	Krasdale Foods
Acme Markets	Stop & Shop
C & S Wholesale	SUPERVALU
CVS Caremark	Wal-Mart
IGA	Wawa, Inc.

HISTORICAL FINANCIALS

Company Type: Cooperative

Income Statement				FYE: September 30
	REVENUE ($ mil.)	NET INCOME ($ mil.)	NET PROFIT MARGIN	EMPLOYEES
9/08	10,600	—	—	50,000
9/07	9,900	—	—	50,000
9/06	7,500	—	—	50,000
9/05	7,239	—	—	50,000
9/04	7,116	—	—	50,000
Annual Growth	10.5%	—	—	0.0%

Revenue History

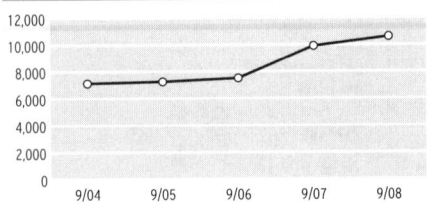

Walsh Group

The Walsh Group erects walls, halls, malls, and more. Operating through Walsh Construction and Archer Western Contractors, the group provides design/build, general contracting, and construction services for industrial, public, and commercial projects throughout the US. Walsh provides complete project management services, from demolition and planning to general contracting and finance. The company is involved in the construction of bridges, highways, water treatment facilities, airports, hotels, convention centers, correctional facilities, and commercial, industrial, and residential buildings; it also renovates and restores buildings. The Walsh family still owns the firm, founded in 1898.

EXECUTIVES

Chairman and CEO: Matthew M. Walsh
President; President, Walsh Construction:
Daniel J. Walsh
CFO, Secretary, and Treasurer: Larry J. Kibbon
VP Business Development: Patrick M. Donley
Human Resources Manager: Rhonda Hardwick
Auditors: Wolf & Company, P.C.

LOCATIONS

HQ: The Walsh Group
929 W. Adams St., Chicago, IL 60607
Phone: 312-563-5400   **Fax:** 312-563-5420
Web: www.walshgroup.com

PRODUCTS/OPERATIONS

Selected Projects

Airports
Athletic facilities
Bridges
Conference centers
Correctional facilities
Data centers
Educational facilities
Entertainment
Government
Health care
High rise residential
Highways and bridges
Hotels
Interiors
Laboratories
Parking garages
Renovations
Retail centers
Senior housing
Treatment plants
Warehouse and distribution

COMPETITORS

APAC
Bechtel
Black & Veatch
Bovis Lend Lease
Brasfield & Gorrie
C. G. Schmidt
CH2M HILL
Flatiron Construction
Fluor
Granite Construction
Hunt Companies
Hunt Construction
Jacobs Engineering
James McHugh
Lane Construction
McCarthy Building
MWH Global
Peter Kiewit Sons'
Skanska
TIC Holdings
Turner Corporation
Vecellio & Grogan

HISTORICAL FINANCIALS

Company Type: Private

Income Statement

FYE: December 31

	REVENUE ($ mil.)	NET INCOME ($ mil.)	NET PROFIT MARGIN	EMPLOYEES
12/08	3,530	—	—	10,300
12/07	3,600	—	—	10,500
12/06	2,900	—	—	6,000
12/05	2,335	—	—	5,000
12/04	1,955	—	—	4,200
Annual Growth	15.9%	—	—	25.1%

Revenue History

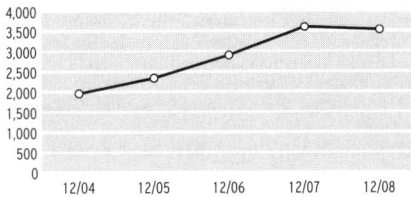

Warren Equities

Warren Equities fills car tanks and stomachs in the US Northeast. The holding company sells fuel and groceries from more than 300 Xtra Mart brand service stations and convenience stores from Maine to Virginia. Warren's distribution companies supply those stores, as well as independent outlets, with gasoline, grocery, and tobacco products. Other Warren companies trade and store petroleum, provide environmental testing services, and make promotional signs and clothing. Founder Warren Alpert's foundation gives annual grants to medical researchers. Alpert died in 2007. His last gift was a $100 million gift to the medical school at Brown Universtity.

Warren Alpert set up the company in 1950 after Standard Oil awarded him a distributorship. Over time, Alpert built Warren Equities into the holding company for wholesale and retail businesses.

EXECUTIVES

Chairman and CEO: Herbert (Herb) Kaplan
Vice Chairman: Edward M. Cosgrove
President and COO: August (Gus) Schiesser
CFO and Treasurer: John T. Dziedzic
EVP: Jeffery A. (Jeff) Walker
Controller and Assistant Treasurer: Richard J. Sawicki
Director Human Resources: Thomas (Tom) Palumbo

LOCATIONS

HQ: Warren Equities, Inc.
27 Warren Way, Providence, RI 02905
Phone: 401-781-9900   **Fax:** 401-461-7160
Web: www.warreneq.com

PRODUCTS/OPERATIONS

Major Subsidiaries

Drake Petroleum Company, Inc. (wholesale gasoline)
Warex Terminals Corporation (wholesale marketing)
Xtra Mart Convenience Stores (convenience stores)

COMPETITORS

7-Eleven
BP
Casey's General Stores
Crown Central
Cumberland Farms
Getty Petroleum Marketing
Global Partners
Motiva Enterprises
Sunoco
SUPERVALU
Wawa, Inc.

Washington Capitals

This company rules over hockey in the nation's capital. Lincoln Holdings, through Lincoln Hockey, owns and operates the Washington Capitals professional hockey franchise, which joined the National Hockey League in 1974. The team was founded by Abe Pollin, the late owner of the Washington Wizards, and has reached the Stanley Cup finals just once, losing to the Detroit Red Wings in 1998. Washington plays host at the Verizon Center, in which Lincoln Holdings owns a 45% stake. The group also owns the Washington Mystics WNBA and a 45% stake in the Wizards. Ted Leonsis, former vice chairman of AOL, has controlled the hockey franchise since 1999.

The Caps made a return to the playoffs at the end of the 2007-08 season, ending a four-year drought that had drawn the ire of fans. The improvement came in part because of Alexander Ovechkin, a top prospect from Russia who joined the team in 2005. The Caps had also hired Bruce Boudreau as head coach during that season, replacing longtime coach Glen Hanlon.

Lincoln Holdings got into the basketball business in 2005 when the group purchased the Mystics from Washington Sports & Entertainment. Dr. Sheila Johnson, a co-founder of BET Holdings and a partner in Lincoln Holdings, was named president of the women's basketball team, becoming the first black woman to run a WNBA franchise.

Pollin, a fixture on the Baltimore and DC area sports scene since 1964, died in 2009. He had been the longest-tenured owner in the NBA.

Other investors in Lincoln Holdings include team president Dick Patrick and Capital One Financial chairman Richard Fairbank.

EXECUTIVES

Chairman: Theodore J. (Ted) Leonsis, age 52
President: Richard M. (Dick) Patrick
CFO: Ellen Folts
SVP and Chief Marketing Officer: Tim McDermott
VP Communications and Chief Communications Officer: Kurt Kehl
VP and General Manager: George McPhee
Head Coach: Bruce Boudreau, age 54
Assistant General Manager and Director Player Personnel: Brian MacLellan
Director Office Administration and Executive Assistant: Michelle Trostle
Director Marketing: Joseph Dupriest
Director Corporate Partnerships: John Greeley
Director Ticket Operations: Christopher Sheap
Information Technology Manager: Brian McPartland
Manager Community Relations: Elizabeth Wodatch

LOCATIONS

HQ: Lincoln Holdings LLC
627 N. Glebe Rd., Ste. 850, Arlington, VA 22203
Phone: 202-266-2200   **Fax:** 202-266-2360
Web: www.washingtoncaps.com

The Washington Capitals play in the 18,277-seat capacity Verizon Center in Washington, DC.

PRODUCTS/OPERATIONS

Championship Trophies

Prince of Wales Trophy (1998)

COMPETITORS

Atlanta Thrashers
Carolina Hurricanes
Florida Panthers
Tampa Bay Lightning

HISTORICAL FINANCIALS

Company Type: Private

Income Statement
FYE: July 31

	REVENUE ($ mil.)	NET INCOME ($ mil.)	NET PROFIT MARGIN	EMPLOYEES
7/08	73	—	—	—
7/07	66	—	—	—
7/06	63	—	—	—
7/05	0	—	—	—
7/04	61	—	—	—
Annual Growth	4.6%	—	—	—

Revenue History

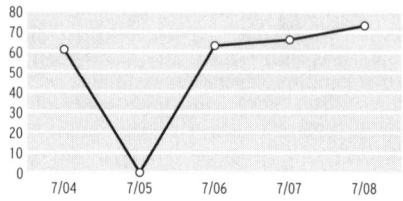

Washington Companies

Crossing the Delaware was the feat of one Washington, but traversing several industries is The Washington Companies' accomplishment. The group's activities include aviation technology, construction and mining, heavy equipment sales, marine transportation, and rail transportation. Seaspan International, one of the group's marine transportation units, is a leading Canadian tug and barge operator. (The group's containership operations have been spun off as Seaspan Corp.) Other affiliates include Montana Resources, which mines and mills copper and other minerals, and Montana Rail Link, which offers freight transportation. Billionaire Dennis Washington owns controlling stakes in all of the group's companies.

Although Dennis Washington's ownership stakes unite The Washington Companies, separate boards of directors and management teams oversee the individual companies under the group's umbrella. One of the companies, Washington Corporations, handles administrative functions for other companies in the group.

EXECUTIVES

Chairman: Dennis R. Washington, age 75
President, Coast Engine and Equipment:
David S. (Dave) Swanson
President and CEO, Aviation Partners Boeing:
John R. Reimers
President and CEO, Envirocon: Jack Gilbraith
President, Southern Railway of British Columbia:
Frank J. Butzelaar
President, Washington Development: Paul W. Keiper
President; President, Washington Corporations:
Lawrence R. (Larry) Simkins
President, Montana Rail Link: Thomas J. Walsh

CEO, Washington Marine Group:
Jonathan P. Whitworth, age 42
President, Montana Resources: Rolin P. Erickson
Chairman and CEO, Aviation Partners; Chairman, Aviation Partners Boeing: Joseph (Joe) Clark
President, Modern Machinery: Brian Sheridan
EVP, Washington Marine Group; President, Marine Division: Kevin N. Irvine
Director, Human Resources, Washington Corporations:
Jon Barlow
Director, Government and Corporate Affairs, Washington Corporations: Mike Halligan

LOCATIONS

HQ: The Washington Companies
101 International Way, Missoula, MT 59808
Phone: 406-523-1300   **Fax:** 406-523-1399
Web: www.washcorp.com

PRODUCTS/OPERATIONS

Selected Operating Units

Aviation technology
Aviation Partners, Inc. (develops and markets high-performance wingtips for jet industry)
Construction and mining
Envirocon, Inc. (remediation, reclamation, and construction)
Montana Resources, Inc. (mining and milling)
Heavy equipment sales
Modern Machinery, Inc.
Marine transportation
Norsk Pacific Steamship
Seaspan Coastal Intermodal, Ltd.
Seaspan International Ltd. (Canada)
Washington Marine Group Shipyards
Rail transportation
Montana Rail Link, Inc.
Southern Railway of British Columbia Ltd. (SRY, Canada)
Real estate and professional services
Washington Corporations (administrative services for group companies)
Washington Development (oversees real estate transactions of group companies)

COMPETITORS

Alexander & Baldwin
APL
ASARCO
Canadian Pacific Railway
Crowley Maritime
Evergreen Marine
Freeport-McMoRan
Union Pacific

HISTORICAL FINANCIALS

Company Type: Group

Income Statement
FYE: December 31

	REVENUE ($ mil.)	NET INCOME ($ mil.)	NET PROFIT MARGIN	EMPLOYEES
12/07	1,900	—	—	4,300
12/06	1,700	—	—	4,300
12/05	1,300	—	—	4,100
Annual Growth	20.9%	—	—	2.4%

Revenue History

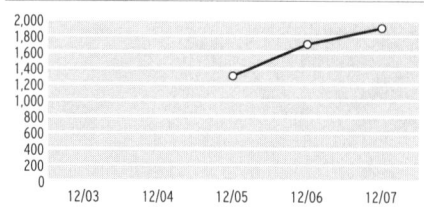

Wawa, Inc.

It's not baby talk — when folks say they need to go to the Wawa; they need groceries. Wawa runs some 570 Wawa Food Markets in Delaware, Maryland, New Jersey, Pennsylvania, and Virginia. Wawa stores are noted for their coffee and their salad and deli offerings, including hoagie sandwiches; more than 250 stores sell gas. Unlike many convenience store chains, Wawa has its own dairy, supplying Wawa stores and about 1,000 hospitals, schools, and other institutions. The company opened its first store in 1964, but its roots go back to an iron foundry begun in 1803 by the Wood family; food operations began in 1902 when George Wood started a dairy in Wawa, Pennsylvania. The Wood family owns 52% of the company.

Howard Stoeckel succeeded chairman Richard Wood as CEO of the company in January 2005. Stoeckel is the first non-family member to lead Wawa.

To weather the recession the convenience-store operator put aside an aggressive new store opening plan, and instead focused on maintaining its headcount and emphasizing value and value-added services in stores. To that end, Wawa has stuck with its no-fee ATM policy, been actively refurbishing stores and investing in technology, new products, and its employees, all in a bid to maintain sales.

Wawa continues to work to expand its line of private-label foods and other merchandise in an effort to differentiate itself from its competition. It offers a large selection of fresh food, including ready-to-eat salads and produce. Since the launch of its own brand of bottled water in 2004, the company has introduced about 300 packaged items, including candy, yogurt, and tea — under the Wawa label.

In mid-2006 the convenience-store operator opened its first airport location at the Northeast Philadelphia Airport.

Wawa is the Lenni Lenape word for the Canada goose that was found in the Delaware Valley, hence the goose on Wawa's logo. Employees own about 28% of Wawa.

EXECUTIVES

Chairman: Richard D. (Dick) Wood Jr.
Vice Chairman, President, and CEO:
Howard B. Stoeckel, age 63
EVP and COO: David Johnston
CIO: Suzanne Keenan
Chief Marketing Officer: Carol E. Jensen
Chief People Officer: Harry McHugh
VP Supply Chain: Jim Bluebello
Director Information Technology Business Solutions:
John Cunningham
Director Food Service: Michael (Mike) Sherlock
Product Manager: Jane Coleman
Manager Public Relations: Lori Bruce
Manager Real Estate Technology:
Michael C. (Mike) McCabe

LOCATIONS

HQ: Wawa, Inc.
260 W. Baltimore Pike, Red Roof, Wawa, PA 19063
Phone: 610-358-8000   **Fax:** 610-358-8878
Web: www.wawa.com

PRODUCTS/OPERATIONS

Selected Products and Private-Label Brands

Bakery (Wawa)
Cold beverages (Wawa)
Hoagies (Built-to-Order, Shorti)
Hot breakfast
    Coffee (Freshly Brewed Coffee)
    Hash browns
    Hot breakfast sandwiches (Sizzli)
Party platters
Ready-to-eat foods (Wawa Express)
Sides
Soups

Wawa Dairy Division

Products
    100% orange juice (All Florida)
    Butter
    Buttermilk
    Cappuccino
    Cottage cheese
    Cream cheese
    Eggs
    Fruit juices and drinks
    Half and half
    Ice cream mixes
    Margarine
    Milk (including lactose-free, chocolate, and
      strawberry)
    Non-dairy coffee blend
    Shakes
    Sour cream
    Spring water (Deer Park)
    Tea
    Whipping cream
    Yogurt (Dannon)
Customers
    Bakeries
    Colleges
    Hospitals
    Hotels
    Nursing homes
    Restaurants
    School districts
    Universities
    Wawa Food Markets

COMPETITORS

7-Eleven
A&P
Chevron
Cumberland Farms
Exxon Mobil
Foodarama Supermarkets
Genuardi's
Getty Realty
Hess Corporation
Kroger
Motiva Enterprises
Sheetz
Subway
Village Super Market
Warren Equities
Wegmans

HISTORICAL FINANCIALS

Company Type: Private

Income Statement
FYE: December 31

	REVENUE ($ mil.)	NET INCOME ($ mil.)	NET PROFIT MARGIN	EMPLOYEES
12/08	5,700	—	—	16,000
12/07	5,050	—	—	16,426
12/06	4,670	—	—	16,866
12/05	3,905	—	—	15,999
Annual Growth	13.4%	—	—	0.0%

Revenue History

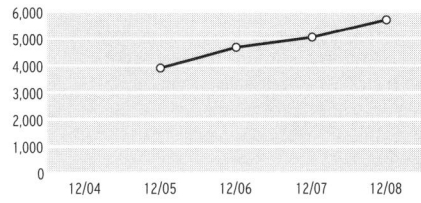

COMPETITORS

Arnold Worldwide	JWT
BBDO Detroit	Leo Burnett
Campbell Mithun	Martin Agency
Campbell-Ewald	Publicis USA
C-K	Richards Group
Deutsch, Inc.	Saatchi & Saatchi
Euro RSCG	TBWA Worldwide
Fallon Worldwide	Team One
GSD&M Idea City	Wieden and Kennedy
Hill, Holliday	Young & Rubicam

W. B. Doner & Company

This company brings marketing skills to the party. W. B. Doner & Company, which does business as Doner, is the largest independent advertising agency in the US, boasting a client roster that includes UPS, Mazda, Minute Maid, and Coleman. It provides creative ad development and campaign management services, along with media planning and buying. Founded by Wilfred Broderick Doner in 1937, the firm has created classic campaigns for such customers as Timex ("Takes a licking and keeps on ticking") and Klondike Bar ("What would you do for a Klondike Bar?"). It is controlled by a management group that includes chairman and CEO Alan Kalter and vice chairman Barry Levine.

Over the years, Doner has picked up several top brands as clients, including Hotels.com (under Expedia) and Lexmark. It also struck a chord with its Mr. Six campaign for theme park operator Six Flags. Going forward, Doner plans to grow by expanding its interactive marketing and online advertising services and catering to new and emerging social media channels such as Facebook and Twitter.

In the US, Doner has offices in Cleveland; Detroit; Dallas; and Newport Beach, California. Internationally, the firm has facilities in Canada and in the UK, where it operates under the banner Doner Cardwell Hawkins.

EXECUTIVES

Chairman and CEO: Alan Kalter
Vice Chairman and CFO: H. Barry Levine
EVP and Chief Marketing Officer: James Ward
EVP and Chief Creative Officer: Rob Strasberg
EVP and Chief Strategy Officer: David DeMuth
SVP and Chief Digital Officer: Brett Groom
EVP and Chief Media Officer: Greg Clausen
EVP and Account Management Director: Greg Gerfen
EVP and Account Management Director: Lisa Nardone
EVP and Account Management Director: Pete Spender
EVP and Account Management Director: Kevin Weinman
EVP and Account Management Director: Monica Tysell
EVP and Director Operations: Sue Guise
EVP and General Manager, Direct: Ted Thompson
Director Human Resources: Carol Cothern
President, Newport Beach: Tim Blett

LOCATIONS

HQ: W. B. Doner & Company
    25900 Northwestern Hwy., Southfield, MI 48075
Phone: 248-354-9700   **Fax:** 248-827-0880
Web: www.wbdoner.com

Webloyalty.com

Webloyalty.com offers services such as consumer membership programs for companies that are looking to garner better relationships with its customers. The company serves e-commerce, travel, and other fee-based Web sites by providing travel discounts and promotional offers on entertainment, retail merchandise, and home computer protection software seamlessly (Webloyalty sends the offers out but they are branded with the clients' Web site), building customer loyalty. Established in 1999, Webloyalty is owned by private equity firm General Atlantic LLC.

The company's business strategy involves expanding internationally into key markets involving savvy online communities. In mid-2007 Webloyalty opened its first office overseas, in London. The following year it opened a new office in Paris (consumers shopping online in France now have the option to join its "Remises & Réductions" promotional program). The company plans to open an additional office in Germany in the future.

EXECUTIVES

CEO: Richard J. (Rick) Fernandes, age 51
President: Vincent R. D'Agostino
CTO: Gary Cacace
SVP Account Management: Eli Chalfin
SVP Finance: Gina Carey
SVP Business Development: Matt Gilbert
SVP Marketing: Martin Isaac
SVP Information Technology and Operations:
  Jeffrey Kendall
SVP and General Counsel: Sloane Levy
SVP Corporate Development and Corporate Marketing:
  David Lynch
Managing Director, Europe: Martin Child

LOCATIONS

HQ: Webloyalty.com, Inc.
    101 Merritt 7, 4th Fl., Norwalk, CT 06851
Phone: 203-846-3300   **Fax:** 203-846-4100
Web: webloyalty.com

COMPETITORS

Advantex Marketing International
Affinion Group
Loyaltyworks
Maritz Loyalty Marketing
OneCause
Synapse Group

HISTORICAL FINANCIALS

Company Type: Private

Income Statement

FYE: December 31

	REVENUE ($ mil.)	NET INCOME ($ mil.)	NET PROFIT MARGIN	EMPLOYEES
12/07	193	—	—	330
12/06	144	—	—	300
12/05	109	—	—	220
12/04	86	—	—	175
12/03	55	—	—	—
Annual Growth	36.6%	—	—	23.5%

Revenue History

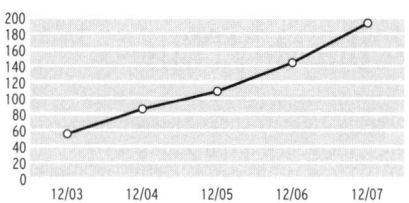

| 12/03 | 12/04 | 12/05 | 12/06 | 12/07 |

Weekley Homes

A subdivision home developed to *your* taste? Weekley Homes can do it. Doing business as David Weekley Homes, the company is one of the largest privately owned homebuilders in the US. It builds annually around 4,600 single-family detached homes that range from about 1,500 sq. ft. to 5,000 sq. ft. Weekley builds homes from hundreds of floor plans and offers custom options and upgrades. Prices range from the $100,000s to the $800,000s; the average home price is $275,000. The company has planned communities in major cities in the West, Southeast and Mid-Atlantic. Chairman and owner David Weekley founded the company in 1976.

As with most builders in the nation, David Weekley Homes has been affected by the subprime mortgage collapse as well as the general oversupply of new housing. The company has been hit with high foreclosure rates in its Florida, Denver, and Dallas markets, although other regions have not been as badly affected.

To combat the decline in sales, the company cut prices (its average home price has dropped) and added incentives.

EXECUTIVES

Chairman: David M. Weekley
CEO: John Johnson
CFO: Stuart M. Bitting
CIO: Heather Humphrey
VP Human Resources: Michael (Mike) Brezina
VP Supply Chain Services: Bill Justus
VP Marketing: Natalie Harris
VP Operations: Mike Humphrey
VP Design: Bob Rhode
Director Finance: John Bena
Communications Coordinator: Vicki Cassidy
Communications Coordinator: Cindy Haynes
Auditors: Ernst & Young LLP

LOCATIONS

HQ: Weekley Homes L.P.
1111 N. Post Oak Rd., Houston, TX 77055
Phone: 713-963-0500   **Fax:** 713-963-0322
Web: www.davidweekleyhomes.com

Selected Markets

Arizona
  Phoenix
Colorado
  Denver
Florida
  Jacksonville
  Orlando
  Palm Coast
  Panama City
  Tampa
Georgia
  Atlanta
North Carolina
  Charlotte
  Raleigh
South Carolina
  Bluffton/Hilton Head
  Charleston
Texas
  Austin
  Dallas/Ft. Worth
  Houston
  San Antonio

COMPETITORS

Beazer Homes
Choice Homes
D.R. Horton
Highland Homes
Hovnanian Enterprises
KB Home
Lennar
M.D.C.
Mercedes Homes
M/I Homes
NVR
Pulte Homes
Rottlund
The Ryland Group
Standard Pacific
Toll Brothers

HISTORICAL FINANCIALS

Company Type: Private

Income Statement

FYE: December 31

	REVENUE ($ mil.)	NET INCOME ($ mil.)	NET PROFIT MARGIN	EMPLOYEES
12/08	982	—	—	—
12/07	1,300	—	—	1,221
12/06	1,500	—	—	1,446
12/05	1,272	—	—	1,466
Annual Growth	(8.3%)	—	—	(8.7%)

Revenue History

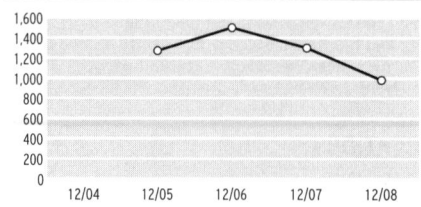

| 12/04 | 12/05 | 12/06 | 12/07 | 12/08 |

Wegmans Food Markets

One name strikes fear in the hearts of supermarket owners in New York, New Jersey, Pennsylvania, and now, Maryland and Virginia: Wegmans Food Markets. The regional grocery chain owns about 75 stores, but they are hardly typical. Much larger than most supermarkets (up to 160,000 sq. ft.), they offer specialty shops such as huge in-store cafes, cheese shops with some 300 different varieties, sub shops, and French-style pastry shops. The company is known for its gourmet cooking classes and an extensive employee-training program. Founded in 1916, today Wegmans is one of the largest private companies in the US. The grocery chain is owned and run by the family of founder John Wegman.

Former chairman Robert B. Wegman (who died in April 2006) stepped down as CEO of the company in January 2005 and was succeeded by his son Danny Wegman. Concurrently, Colleen Wegman, Danny Wegman's daughter, was named president of the grocery chain. Under the father-daughter team, Wegmans has been expanding, but mostly outside of New York state. In 2009 the grocery chain opened stores in Maryland and Virginia and has announced plans to enter the Massachusetts market in 2011. The chain is also evaluating the Connecticut market.

In response to the weakening economy and in anticipation that wholesale food prices will fall, Wegmans lowered prices on hundreds of products in November 2008. Many of the reduced items are Wegmans' private label brand and are in the bakery, meat, produce, deli, and general grocery departments. To emphasize its commitment to health, Wegmans in early 2008 stopped selling cigarettes and other tobacco products.

Wegmans has landed on *FORTUNE* magazine's list of the "100 Best Companies to Work For," in each of the past 11 years and captured the #1 spot in 2005.

Citing competition from national home improvement chains Home Depot and Lowe's, Wegmans closed all 14 of its Chase-Pitkin Home and Garden Centers in 2005. (Chase-Pitkin employed 507 full-time and 1,660 part-time workers.)

EXECUTIVES

Chairman and CEO: Daniel R. (Danny) Wegman
President: Colleen Wegman, age 34
EVP Operations: Jack DePeters
SVP and CFO: James (Jim) Leo
SVP Real Estate Development: Ralph Uttaro
SVP, Syracuse Division: Shari Constantine
SVP Human Resources: Gerald Pierce
SVP Consumer Affairs: Mary Ellen Burris
Secretary and General Counsel: Paul S. Speranza Jr.
CIO: Donald (Don) Reeve
VP Store Operations, Human Resources: Kevin Stickles
VP Wine: Nicole Wegman
VP Seafood: Carl Salamone
VP Produce: Dave Corsi
Buyer Kosher Products: Ellen Campbell
Director Media Relations: Jo Natale
Director Managed Care: John B. Carlo

LOCATIONS

HQ: Wegmans Food Markets, Inc.
1500 Brooks Ave., Rochester, NY 14603
Phone: 585-328-2550
Web: www.wegmans.com

2008 Stores

	No.
New York	48
Pennsylvania	12
New Jersey	7
Virginia	4
Maryland	1
Total	**72**

PRODUCTS/OPERATIONS

Selected Products and Operations

Asian foods
Bath and body
Bulk foods
Cheeses
Coffee/cappuccino Bar
Cooking classes
Deli
Dry cleaning
European bread bakery
Floral department
Food from around the world
Gift and fruit baskets
Kosher deli
Market café
Meat service
Nature's Marketplace (organic health and food items)
Organic produce
Pasta Station
Pharmacy
Photo processing and photo enlarging
Photocopies
Pizza Primo
Ready-to-cook meat and seafood
Rotisserie
Rug Doctor carpet cleaner rental
Seafood
Sub sandwiches
Sushi bar
UPS parcel service
Video player and game system rentals
Videos and DVDs
WKids Fun Center
Wokery

COMPETITORS

A&P
Foodarama Supermarkets
Genuardi's
Giant Eagle
Giant Food Stores
Golub
IGA
Penn Traffic
Safeway
SUPERVALU
TOPS Markets
Wal-Mart
Wawa, Inc.
Weis Markets

HISTORICAL FINANCIALS

Company Type: Private

Income Statement

FYE: December 31

	REVENUE ($ mil.)	NET INCOME ($ mil.)	NET PROFIT MARGIN	EMPLOYEES
12/08	4,800	—	—	37,000
12/07	4,500	—	—	37,602
12/06	4,100	—	—	35,798
12/05	3,800	—	—	35,000
12/04	3,600	—	—	32,000
Annual Growth	**7.5%**	**—**	**—**	**3.7%**

Revenue History

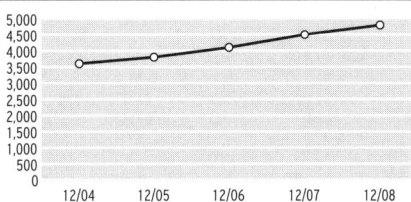

Weil, Gotshal & Manges

The seeds of today's Weil, Gotshal & Manges may have been planted in New York, but over the years the law firm's branches have spread far and wide. Founded in 1931, the firm has more than 1,300 lawyers at about 20 offices in the US, Europe and the Asia/Pacific region. Weil Gotshal maintains a full range of business-oriented practices, which it organizes into five main areas: business finance and restructuring, corporate, litigation and regulatory, tax, and trusts and estates. Clients have included CBS Broadcasting, General Electric, and HM Capital Partners. Weil Gotshal has served as lead law firm in the cleanup of bankrupt Lehman Brothers, whose Chapter 11 filing in 2008 shocked the financial world.

EXECUTIVES

Chairman: Stephen J. Dannhauser
Executive Director: David Strumeyer
CFO, Finance and Accounting: Norman W. LaCroix
Corporate Partner: E. Norman Veasey
Corporate Partner: Glenn D. West
CIO: Ian M. Miller
Products Liability and Mass Tort Practice Group: Michael J. (Mike) Lyle, age 45
Litigation Counsel: John M. Ryan
Director Attorney Programs and Resources: Lisa I. Cuevas
Director Human Resources, Human Capital: Michael R. (Mike) Lewis
Director Global Diversity: Meredith Moore
Director Attorney Development: Sara B. Littauer

LOCATIONS

HQ: Weil, Gotshal & Manges LLP
767 5th Ave., New York, NY 10153
Phone: 212-310-8000   **Fax:** 212-310-8007
Web: www.weil.com

PRODUCTS/OPERATIONS

Selected Practice Areas

Business finance and restructuring
Corporate
  Banking and finance
  Capital markets
  Corporate governance
  Mergers and acquisitions
  Private equity
  Real estate transactions and finance
  Structured finance/derivatives
Litigation and regulatory
  Antitrust/competition
  Appellate
  Bankruptcy litigation
  Complex commercial litigation
  Employment
  Financial services
  Global dispute resolution
  Intellectual property and media
  International trade
  Patent appellate
  Patent litigation
  Product liability/mass tort/environmental
  Securities/corporate governance
Tax
Trusts and estates

COMPETITORS

Cleary Gottlieb
Clifford Chance
Cravath, Swaine
Paul, Weiss, Rifkind
Proskauer Rose
Shearman & Sterling

Sidley Austin
Simpson Thacher
Skadden, Arps
Sullivan & Cromwell
Wachtell, Lipton
White & Case

HISTORICAL FINANCIALS

Company Type: Partnership

Income Statement

FYE: December 31

	REVENUE ($ mil.)	NET INCOME ($ mil.)	NET PROFIT MARGIN	EMPLOYEES
12/08	1,231	—	—	—
12/07	1,175	—	—	—
12/06	1,050	—	—	2,800
12/05	1,017	—	—	3,000
Annual Growth	**6.6%**	**—**	**—**	**(6.7%)**

Revenue History

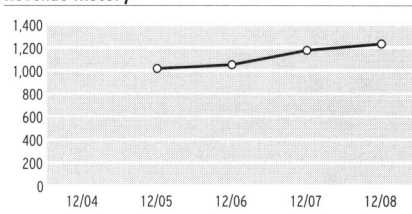

The Weitz Company

It took wits for The Weitz Company to become a top US general building contractor. Founded in 1855 by carpenter Charles H. Weitz, the company was run by the Weitz family for four generations before becoming employee-owned. It provides general contracting, construction management, and design/build services, constructing everything from office buildings, industrial plants, senior communities, and schools to hotels, golf courses, supermarkets, and malls. Weitz builds supermarkets and warehouse/distribution centers through its Hy-Vee Weitz unit.

Weitz affiliate companies go beyond the construction industry. Through subsidiaries, the company offers construction products distribution, insurance, home security solutions, and document management services. Its capital resources group provides funding to developers and owners for various building projects.

Its 2006 acquisition of Miller/Watts Constructors increased Weitz's presence in the heavy engineering and military design/build fields.

EXECUTIVES

Chairman: Glenn H. De Stigter
President and CEO: Craig Damos
COO: Len Martling
CFO and Treasurer: Don Blum
CIO: Mark Federle
SVP Human Resources: Kris Jensen
SVP: Larry Mohr
SVP, General Counsel, and Secretary: David Strutt
SVP, Weitz Senior Living: Fran Snook
VP Business Development: Clay Wells
President, Southwest Division: Mike Bontrager
President, Rocky Mountain Division: Bill Hornaday
President, Kansas City Division: Radd Way
President, Iowa Division: Mike Tousley
President, Weitz Golf International: Greg Carlson
President and Business Development Manager, Hy-Vee Weitz: Brad Strehlow
Auditors: KPMG Peat Marwick

LOCATIONS

HQ: The Weitz Company, LLC
400 Locust St., Ste. 300, Des Moines, IA 50309
Phone: 515-698-4260   **Fax:** 515-697-5968
Web: www.weitz.com

PRODUCTS/OPERATIONS

Selected Subsidiaries
A+ Communications & Security/A+ Home Solutions
Capital Resources Group
Construction Products Distributors
Data Builder, Inc.
Hy-Vee Weitz Construction
Weitz Agricultural Services
Watts Constructors
Weitz Florida
Weitz Golf International
Weitz Industrial Services Group
Weitz Iowa
Weitz Rocky Mountain
Weitz Senior Living
Weitz Southwest

COMPETITORS

Barton Malow
Bovis Lend Lease
Brasfield & Gorrie
Charles Pankow Builders
Choate Construction
Clark Enterprises
Gilbane
Graycor
Hunt Construction
J. E. Dunn Construction
Miron Construction
Peter Kiewit Sons'
Skanska
Structure Tone
Sundt
Turner Corporation
Walsh Group
Whiting-Turner

HISTORICAL FINANCIALS
Company Type: Private

Income Statement

	REVENUE ($ mil.)	NET INCOME ($ mil.)	NET PROFIT MARGIN	EMPLOYEES
12/08	1,560	—	—	—
12/07	1,614	—	—	—
12/06	1,450	—	—	2,313
12/05	1,111	—	—	2,024
12/04	1,006	—	—	—
Annual Growth	11.6%	—	—	14.3%

FYE: December 31

Revenue History

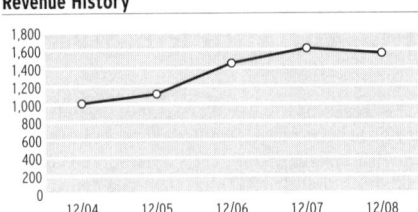

West Suburban Bancorp

As its name would indicate, West Suburban Bancorp provides banking services out in the *burbs*. West Suburban Bancorp is the holding company for West Suburban Bank, a community-oriented institution with about 40 branches serving Chicago's western suburbs. It offers personal and business deposit products such as checking, savings, and money market accounts, and certificates of deposit, as well as loan products including commercial, consumer, and home mortgage loans. Rounding out its offerings are Visa debit, credit, and gift cards; electronic banking; and investment and trust services offered through West Suburban Financial Services.

West Suburban Bancorp also runs an insurance agency, West Suburban Insurance Services, which offers auto, home, life, and major medical insurance, and a travel agency, Travel With West Suburban.

West Suburban Bank sold subsidiary Prepaid Solutions USA, a provider of prepaid and debit cards to primarily under-banked customers, to private equity firm Navigation Capital Partners in 2009.

EXECUTIVES

Chairman, CEO, and VP; SVP Marketing, West Suburban Bank: Kevin J. Acker, age 59, $468,120 total compensation
COO; President and Director, West Suburban Bank: Keith W. Acker, age 59, $362,466 total compensation
President, CFO, and Director; SVP and Comptroller, West Suburban Bank: Duane G. Debs, age 52, $362,937 total compensation
VP; Commercial and Consumer Lending, West Suburban Bank: Michael P. Brosnahan, age 59, $280,657 total compensation

LOCATIONS

HQ: West Suburban Bancorp, Inc.
711 S. Meyers Rd., Lombard, IL 60148
Phone: 630-629-4200   **Fax:** 630-629-0278
Web: www.westsuburbanbank.com

COMPETITORS

AJS Bancorp	Fort Dearborn Life
American Chartered	Harris Bankcorp
Bank of America	Marquette National
Best Travel & Tours	MB Financial
Citibank	Northern Trust
Corporate Travel Management	Old Second Bancorp
	Sammons Financial
Fifth Third	Taylor Capital
First Midwest Bancorp	U.S. Bancorp

HISTORICAL FINANCIALS
Company Type: Private

Income Statement

	REVENUE ($ mil.)	NET INCOME ($ mil.)	NET PROFIT MARGIN	EMPLOYEES
12/08	124	17	13.6%	627
12/07	136	23	17.3%	616
12/06	129	25	19.8%	610
12/05	113	26	22.6%	616
12/04	98	24	24.3%	613
Annual Growth	6.1%	(8.2%)	—	0.6%

FYE: December 31

Net Income History

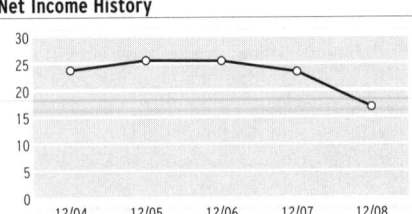

Western & Southern Financial

Whether cowboy or Southern belle, if it's insurance and investment advice you seek, Western & Southern Financial Group wants to be your destination. Through its subsidiaries the company offers a variety of life insurance products and annuities; accident and supplemental health coverage; and mutual funds (Constellation family of funds) and other investment management products and services. The company's financial services include mutual fund administration, trust services, financial advisory, and real estate development. The mutually owned company is licensed in most states and the District of Columbia. Western & Southern was founded in 1888 and is led by CEO John Barrett.

The company's customer base is wide and varied. It consists of moderate-, middle- and upper-income families; affluent individuals; independent advisors, financial planners, and consultants; corporations; financial institutions; small and mid-sized businesses; real estate investors; and foundations, endowments, and universities. Western & Southern tends to grow its business and customer base by launching new products aimed at filling gaps in its existing areas of operation.

Western & Southern Financial Group operates more than a dozen subsidiaries that offer everything from cancer insurance to funds and annuities. Some of the company's subsidiaries include Western & Southern Life Insurance, which provides whole life products, and Western-Southern Life Assurance, which provides universal life and term insurance and annuities.

On the financial side, IFS Financial Services provides investment advisory, securities brokerage, and annuity products. Its Touchstone Advisors subsidiary offers a series of funds and annuities. Integrated Fund Services provides third-party administration for independent mutual funds.

For affluent clients seeking investment advice, Western & Southern operates Fort Washington Investment Advisors — which includes Todd Investment Advisors — to manage private equity assets for corporate and government institutions and wealthy individuals; it has more than $29 billion under management.

Other divisions include Columbus Life Insurance, Integrity Life Insurance, Lafayette Life Insurance, and Eagle Realty Group (commercial real estate investment and management).

EXECUTIVES

Chairman, President, and CEO: John F. Barrett, age 59
SVP and CFO: Robert L. Walker
SVP and CIO: Clint D. Gibler
SVP, Insurance Operations: Constance M. Maccarone
SVP and Chief Actuary: Nora E. Moushey
SVP and General Counsel: Donald J. Wuebbling
SVP, Corporate Financial Planning: Edward S. Heenan
SVP, Special Projects: Carroll R. Hutchinson
SVP, Human Resources: Noreen Hayes
VP and Chief Compliance Officer: Michael R. Moser
VP and CTO: Douglas Ross
VP and Chief Risk Officer: David T. Henderson
VP and Chief Underwriter: Keith W. Brown
VP and Medical Director: Keith T. Clark
VP and Treasurer: James J. (Jim) Vance
VP, Public Relations and Corporate Communications: Michael J. Laatsch
Chairman, Todd Investment Advisors: Robert P. Bordogna
Chairman Emeritus, Todd Investment Advisors: Bosworth M. Todd
Auditors: Ernst & Young

LOCATIONS

HQ: Western & Southern Financial Group
400 E. 4th St., Cincinnati, OH 45202
Phone: 513-629-1800   **Fax:** 513-629-1220
Web: www.westernsouthern.com

PRODUCTS/OPERATIONS

2008 Assets

	$ mil.	% of total
Investments		
Debt securities	19,728.2	64
Equity securities	1,381.6	4
Other invested assets	4,492.3	14
Other general account assets	3,885.3	13
Assets held in separate accounts	1,552.5	5
Total	**31,040**	**100**

2008 Sales

	$ mil.	% of total
Insurance premiums, product charges & other	902.1	35
Net investment income	1,507.7	56
Net realized investment gains	(473.8)	—
Other income	237.2	9
Total	**2,173.2**	**100**

Selected Subsidiaries and Affiliates

Columbus Life Insurance Company
  Capital Analysts Incorporated
Eagle Realty Group, LLC
Fort Washington Investment Advisors, Inc.
  Todd Investment Advisors, Inc.
IFS Financial Services, Inc.
  Touchstone Advisors, Inc.
  Touchstone Securities, Inc.
  W&S Financial Group Distributors, Inc.
Integrity Life Insurance Company
  National Integrity Life Insurance Company
The Lafayette Life Insurance Company
The Western and Southern Life Insurance Company
  Western-Southern Life Assurance Company

COMPETITORS

AEGON USA
AIG American General
CNA Financial
Guardian Insurance and Annuity
Jackson National Life
John Hancock Financial Services
Liberty Mutual
Lincoln Financial Group
MetLife
Nationwide Life Insurance
Northwestern Mutual
Penn Mutual
Phoenix Companies
Principal Financial
Protective Life
Prudential
Securian Financial
Security Benefit Group
Sentry Insurance

HISTORICAL FINANCIALS

Company Type: Private

Income Statement
FYE: December 31

	ASSETS ($ mil.)	NET INCOME ($ mil.)	INCOME AS % OF ASSETS	EMPLOYEES
12/08	31,040	(49)	—	4,000
12/07	32,752	365	1.1%	4,000
12/06	32,158	306	1.0%	4,000
12/05	30,764	268	0.9%	—
12/04	27,466	210	0.8%	—
Annual Growth	**3.1%**	**—**	**—**	**0.0%**

2008 Year-End Financials

Equity as % of assets: —   Long-term debt ($ mil.): 515
Return on assets: —   Sales ($ mil.): 2,173
Return on equity: —

Net Income History

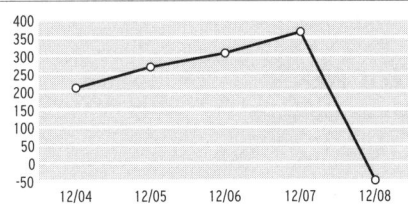

Whataburger

Fans of this chain know they can get quite a burger at the place with the orange and white roof. Whataburger Restaurants is a leading regional hamburger chain with more than 700 outlets in Texas and about 10 other states. The restaurants are typically open 24 hours a day and serve burgers and fries along with chicken sandwiches, salads, and a breakfast menu. Nearly 600 of the restaurants are company-owned. Loyal Whataburger fans can also don the company's line of apparel sporting the chain's logo. The late Harmon Dobson founded the family-owned chain in Corpus Christi, Texas, in 1950.

Despite the fact that Whataburger has a much smaller presence than its national competitors, the chain continues to be a powerful player in its native Texas because of the intense loyalty of its customers. It continues to expand mostly through new franchising agreements, though in 2008 the company acquired its largest franchisee, Barrand. The Texas-based operator had run about 50 Whataburger restaurants located in northeast Texas and the Florida Panhandle.

Whataburger moved its headquarters from Corpus Christi to San Antonio in 2009. The relocation is part of an effort to manage costs as the hamburger chain expands.

EXECUTIVES

Chairman and CEO: Thomas E. (Tom) Dobson, age 59
President and COO: Preston L. Atkinson
EVP: John M. (Mike) McLellan
Group Director Finance and Accounting: Ed Nelson
CIO: Karen H. Bird
VP Business Risks and Reporting: Jim Langenkamp
VP Operations: Byron E. (Buddy) Reno
VP Human Resources: Marianne Dowdy
VP Supply and Services: Dino Del Nano
VP Brand Management: Todd A. Coerver
VP Strategic Planning: Rodney J. (Rod) Martin
VP Property and Facilities: James G. Turcotte
Director Marketing: Rich Scheffler
Director Training and Development: Bill Adams
Director Communications: Pam Cox
Auditors: KPMG LLP

LOCATIONS

HQ: Whataburger Restaurants LP
300 Concord Plaza, San Antonio, TX 78216
Phone: 210-476-6000
Web: www.whataburger.com

COMPETITORS

AFC Enterprises
American Dairy Queen
Arby's
Burger King
Chick-fil-A
Church's Chicken
Jack in the Box
Jason's Deli
Krystal
McDonald's
Quiznos
Schlotzsky's
Sonic Corp.
Subway
Taco Bueno
Taco Cabana
Wendy's International, Inc.
YUM!

Wheaton Franciscan Services

Wheaton Franciscan Services (WFSI) is the parent company for more than 100 health care, housing, and social service organizations in Colorado, Illinois, Iowa, and Wisconsin. Through its Wheaton Franciscan Healthcare division, WFSI operates 15 hospitals including Affinity Health System, Marianjoy, Rush Oak Park Hospital, and United Hospital System. Its Franciscan Ministries division provides affordable housing units including assisted living facilities and housing for people living with HIV/AIDS. WFSI also includes home health agencies and physician offices. The health system was founded in 1983 and is sponsored by The Franciscan Sisters, Daughters of the Sacred Hearts of Jesus and Mary.

In 2008 the company completed construction on a new $90 million hospital facility in Franklin, Wisconsin. The Franklin Hospital provides emergency, surgery, imaging, and primary and specialty care.

EXECUTIVES

Chair: Joseph W. Lewis, age 74
President, CEO, and Director; President and CEO, Wheaton Franciscan Healthcare: John D. Oliverio
SVP and COO, Wheaton Franciscan Medical Group: Robert De Vita
SVP and CFO: William H. Blum
SVP and CIO: Gregory A. (Greg) Smith
SVP Mission Services: Terrance P. McGuire
SVP Human Resources: David A. Smith
SVP and General Counsel: Richard J. Canter
SVP and Chief Administrative Officer: Jon L. Wachs
VP Communications and Public Relations: Anne Ballentine
VP Payer Contracting and Relations: Coreen Dicus-Johnson
VP Strategic Planning: Abigail L. Navti
Chief Medical Officer, Wheaton Franciscan Healthcare: Stephen Cardamone

LOCATIONS

HQ: Wheaton Franciscan Services, Inc.
26 W. 171 Roosevelt Rd., Wheaton, IL 60189
Phone: 630-462-9271   **Fax:** 630-462-4977
Web: www.wfhealthcare.org/Wheaton

PRODUCTS/OPERATIONS

Selected Operations
Franciscan Ministries, Inc. (housing in Colorado, Illinois, Iowa, and Wisconsin)

Illinois
Marianjoy Rehabilitation Hospital (Wheaton)
Rush Oak Park Hospital (Oak Park)

Iowa
Covenant Medical Center (Waterloo)
Mercy Hospital (Oelwein)
Sartori Memorial Hospital (Cedar Falls)

Wisconsin
Affinity Health System (affiliated system)
Calumet Medical Center (Chilton)
Mercy Medical Center (Oshkosh)
St. Elizabeth Hospital (Appleton)
All Saints Hospital (Racine)
Elmbrook Memorial Hospital (Brookfield)
Franklin Hospital (Franklin)
St. Francis Hospital (Milwaukee)
St. Joseph Hospital (Milwaukee)
United Hospital System, Inc. (affiliated system)
Kenosha Medical Center (Kenosha)
St. Catherine's Medical Center (Pleasant Prairie)
Wisconsin Heart Hospital (Wauwatosa)

COMPETITORS

Alden Management Services
Elmhurst Memorial Healthcare
FHN
Froedtert Hospital
Hospital Sisters Health System
KishHealth
Loyola University Health System
Rockford Health System
SwedishAmerican Health System

White & Case

One of the world's largest law firms, White & Case has buoyed its global reputation by establishing some 35 offices in locations spanning the US, Latin America, Europe, the Middle East, Africa, and Asia. It has some 2,100 lawyers overall. With the firm's global reach as its cornerstone, White & Case offers expertise in such areas as bankruptcy, corporate, intellectual property, litigation, project finance, and tax. The firm's client list has included major multinational companies such as Deutsche Bank, Royal Ahold, and Wal-Mart. White & Case was founded in 1901.

Feeling the strain of the economic downturn, in April 2009 White & Case laid off 200 lawyers and about 200 other staff members. This follows a round of layoffs in November 2008 of 70 lawyers and 100 staff. More cuts may be on the horizon: White & Case says it will ultimately shed 15%-20% of its global partnership.

To avoid some layoffs, White & Case and other big firms have redeployed lawyers to overseas to markets less affected by the global economic recession. In April 2009 White & Case shifted some of its London-based attorneys to its South Africa office in Johannesburg. The move also joins a trend of global law firms ramping up legal services in Africa. Besides South Africa, White & Case is focusing its efforts in Africa on specific countries including Angola, Kenya, Mozambique, Nigeria, and Uganda.

The job cuts and shifts come on the heels of a reorganization in the management structure at White & Case. After a four-month review by management consultancy McKinsey & Company, in December 2008 White & Case decided the firm needs a more regional approach and a focus on its global practice areas.

EXECUTIVES

Chairman: Hugh Verrier
COO: Gregory J. Dolan
CFO: Steve Wrede

LOCATIONS

HQ: White & Case LLP
1155 Avenue of the Americas, New York, NY 10036
Phone: 212-819-8200   **Fax:** 212-354-8113
Web: www.whitecase.com

PRODUCTS/OPERATIONS

Selected Practice Areas
Antitrust/competition
Asset finance
Bank advisory
Bank finance
Banking
Capital markets/securities
Climate change, renewable energy, and clean technology
Construction and engineering
Corporate
Energy, infrastructure, and project finance
Environmental
European Union
Executive compensation and employee benefits
Financial restructuring and insolvency
Global equity-based compensation
India
Insurance
Intellectual property
International arbitration
International trade
Investment funds
Islamic finance
Labor, employment, and immigration law
Latin America
Legislative/law reform
Litigation
Mergers and acquisitions
Outsourcing
Privacy
Private clients
Private equity
Privatization
Public finance
Public international law
Real estate
Securitization
Sovereign
Tax
Technology
Telecommunications, media, and technology
Trade and commodity finance
White collar

COMPETITORS

Akin Gump	Jones Day
Baker & McKenzie	Latham & Watkins
Bryan Cave	Mayer Brown
Clifford Chance	Milbank, Tweed
Cravath, Swaine	Morgan, Lewis
Debevoise & Plimpton	Pillsbury Winthrop Shaw
Denton Wilde Sapte	Pittman
Dewey & LeBoeuf	Proskauer Rose
DLA Piper	Sidley Austin
Eversheds	Skadden, Arps
Freshfields	Weil, Gotshal & Manges
Holland & Knight	

HISTORICAL FINANCIALS
Company Type: Partnership

Income Statement

	REVENUE ($ mil.)	NET INCOME ($ mil.)	NET PROFIT MARGIN	EMPLOYEES
12/08	1,467	—	—	—
12/07	1,373	—	—	—
12/06	1,185	—	—	4,372
12/05	1,046	—	—	4,541
Annual Growth	11.9%	—	—	(3.7%)

FYE: December 31

Revenue History

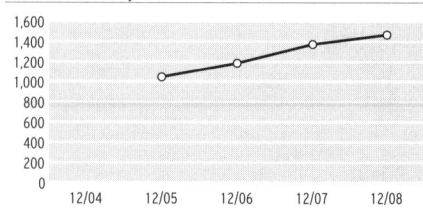

White Castle

The treasure room of this fast food fortress contains Slyders. White Castle System owns and operates more than 400 hamburger joints known for their little square burgers called Slyders. The meat patty is steamed over a bed of onions rather than grilled, and served on a steamed bun with a single slice of pickle. Patrons typically consume a sack of Slyders at a time. White Castle restaurants can be found in about a dozen states, primarily in the Midwest. The company also sells frozen Slyders through supermarket chains. The first fast food chain in the US, White Castle was founded by Walter Anderson and real estate broker E. W. "Billy" Ingram in 1921. The Ingram family continues to control the company.

Little has changed at White Castle over the years, from its Slyders to its castle-shaped buildings, which has helped the chain establish strong loyalty among both customers and employees. Growth for the chain has been slow, however, due to the fact that the company does not franchise its restaurants. Yet change is slowly creeping into the mix at White Castle: The handful of new units it builds each year are now incorporating a slightly updated interior design. White Castle also sells branded items (caps, mugs, and shirts) to keep its loyal fans happy and engaged.

In addition to its hamburger business, White Castle System owns PSB Company, a subsidiary that makes metal products and equipment, including fixtures and cooking tools used at the company's restaurants. PSB also makes lawn spreaders under the PrizeLAWN brand.

EXECUTIVES

Chairman, President, and CEO:
 Edgar Waldo (Bill) Ingram III, age 58
VP, CFO, and Treasurer: Russell (Russ) Meyer
VP, Corporate Relations: Jamie Richardson
VP, Marketing and Site Development: Kim Kelly-Bartley
VP, General Counsel, and Secretary: G. Roger Post
VP, Assistant Secretary, and Corporate Counsel:
 Nicholas W. Zuk
VP and General Manager, White Castle Distributing:
 Rob Camp
Assistant VP, Training and Human Resources:
 John Kelley
**Senior Director of Information Services and
 Information Technology:** Don Long
Director, Real Estate: Rob Albert
Director, Human Resources: Heather Ward
Director of Benefits: Fred G. Gunderson
Director of Restaurant Operations: Lisa Ingram
Supervisor, Communications: Deborah P. Cline

LOCATIONS

HQ: White Castle System, Inc.
 555 W. Goodale St., Columbus, OH 43215
Phone: 614-228-5781   **Fax:** 614-464-0596
Web: www.whitecastle.com

COMPETITORS

AFC Enterprises
American Dairy Queen
Arby's
Back Yard Burgers
Burger King
Checkers Drive-In
Chick-fil-A
Church's Chicken
Culver's
Hardee's
Jack in the Box
Krystal
McDonald's
Quiznos
Sonic Corp.
Subway
Wendy's International, Inc.
YUM!

Whiting-Turner Contracting

Whiting-Turner Contracting knows that in the construction industry you have to fish or cut bait. The employee-owned firm provides construction management, general contracting, and design/build services, primarily for large commercial, institutional, and infrastructure projects in the US. A key player in retail construction, the company also undertakes such projects as biotech cleanrooms, theme parks, educational facilities, stadiums, and corporate headquarters for such clients as AT&T and General Motors. Whiting-Turner Contracting has some 30 locations throughout the US. G. W. C. Whiting and LeBaron Turner founded the company in 1909 to build sewer lines.

Whiting-Turner Contracting's project portfolio includes the Joseph B. Whitehead Building at Emory University, Vanderbilt Hall at Yale University, and a vaccine facility at Chesapeake Biological Laboratories, Inc. Projects for the firm's hometown of Baltimore have included the city's convention center and Harborplace.

EXECUTIVES

President: Willard Hackerman
SEVP Finance and CFO: Charles A. (Chuck) Irish
SVP (New Haven, Connecticut): Daniel (Dan) Bauer
SVP (Baltimore): Gino J. Gemignani
SVP (Irvine, California): Len Cannatelli Jr.
SVP (Washington, DC/Bethesda, Maryland):
 Richard L. Vogel Jr.
Auditors: PricewaterhouseCoopers LLP

LOCATIONS

HQ: The Whiting-Turner Contracting Company
 300 E. Joppa Rd., Baltimore, MD 21286
Phone: 410-821-1100   **Fax:** 410-337-5770
Web: www.whiting-turner.com

The Whiting-Turner Contracting Company has offices in California, Colorado, Connecticut, Delaware, Florida, Georgia, Maryland, Massachusetts, Nevada, North Carolina, New Jersey, New York, Ohio, Pennsylvania, Texas, Virginia, and Washington, DC.

PRODUCTS/OPERATIONS

Selected Services
Construction management (at-risk or agency)
Design/build
General contracting
Preconstruction

Selected Markets
Biotechnology and pharmaceutical
Cleanroom and high-technology
Education
Entertainment
Health care
Industrial and manufacturing
Lodging and hospitality
Mission-critical facilities
Offices and headquarters
Retail
Senior living
Sports
Warehouse and distribution

COMPETITORS

Barton Malow
Bechtel
Bovis Lend Lease
Choate Construction
Clark Enterprises
DPR Construction
Fisher Development
Fluor
Gilbane
Hensel Phelps Construction
Hoffman Corporation
Jacobs Engineering
J.E. Dunn Construction Group
Kitchell
McCarthy Building
Peter Kiewit Sons'
Simon Property Group
Skanska
Suffolk Construction
Swinerton
Turner Corporation
Tutor Perini
The Weitz Company, LLC

HISTORICAL FINANCIALS
Company Type: Private

Income Statement

	REVENUE ($ mil.)	NET INCOME ($ mil.)	NET PROFIT MARGIN	EMPLOYEES
12/08	4,150	—	—	2,300
12/07	3,970	—	—	2,200
12/06	3,340	—	—	1,900
12/05	3,066	—	—	1,700
12/04	2,620	—	—	1,600
Annual Growth	12.2%	—	—	9.5%

FYE: December 31

Revenue History

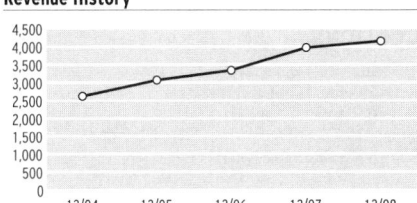

Wilbur-Ellis Company

Seed 'em, weed 'em, and feed 'em could be the motto of San Francisco's Wilbur-Ellis Company. Through its agribusiness and feed divisions, Wilbur-Ellis sells animal feed, fertilizer, insecticides, seed, and farm machinery in North America. Subsidiary Connell Bros. exports and distributes industrial chemicals and animal feed throughout the Pacific Rim. Additionally, Wilbur-Ellis provides consulting, pesticide spraying, and other agriculture-related services. It also owns Knox McDaniel, a supplier of vitamin and mineral premix products for farm animals in the western US. In addition to distribution in the US, Wilbur-Ellis exports its products to Canada and Pacific Rim countries.

The company implements a strategy of acquiring successful companies and integrating them into its existing operations. Examples of these acquisitions include Brayton Chemicals, Harricros Chemicals, Tide Products, Tex-Ag Company, John Taylor Fertilizers, Soilserve, Willamette Seed Company, Integra Seed, John Pryor Fertilizers, and the Olson Seed Company.

Continuing to grow, its recent acquisitions include Knox McDaniel (2001), Hughtson Chemical (2004), and Ag Supply (2007). In 2008 it purchased Ripon Farm Service, a farm management company and farm product retailer in California. The following year Connell Bros. acquired Newson International, a Chinese maker of fine chemicals and ingredients for personal care products.

Wilbur-Ellis has operations in Australia, China, India, Indonesia, Japan, Korea, Malaysia, New Zealand, the Philippines, Singapore, Taiwan, Thailand, Vietnam, and Hong Kong.

Brayton Wilbur Sr. and Floyd Ellis founded the company in 1921 as a fish-oil supplier; it is still owned by the Wilbur family.

EXECUTIVES

Chairman: Herbert B. Tully
Vice Chairman: Carter P. Thacher, age 83
President and CEO: John P. Thacher
EVP Agribusiness Division: Daniel R. (Dan) Vradenburg
VP, Treasurer, and CFO: James D. Crawford
VP National Marketing and Supplier Relations: James M. (Jim) Loar
VP Feed Division: Ronald G Salter
VP and General Counsel: William R. Sawyers, age 40
CIO: Jerry Coupe
Director Human Resources: Anne E. Cleary
President, Connell Bros: Theodore L. (Ted) Eliot III
President, Connell Bros, Korea: M.H. Oh
President, Connell Bros, Japan: Ken Kanai
Auditors: Hood & Strong

LOCATIONS

HQ: Wilbur-Ellis Company
345 California St., 27th Fl.
San Francisco, CA 94104
Phone: 415-772-4000   **Fax:** 415-772-4011
Web: www.wilbur-ellis.com

PRODUCTS/OPERATIONS

Selected Products and Services

Agribusiness Division
  Agricultural chemicals
  Fertilizers
  Fungicides
  Herbicides
  Insecticides
  Machinery
  Pesticides
  Seed protectants
  Seed treatments
  Sprayers
  Supply-chain management
Connell Bros. Division
  Industrial chemicals
Feed Division
  Aquaculture products
  Feed ingredients
  Food oils
  Forage products
  Pet food
Professional Products
  Forestry
    Fungicides
    Herbicides
  Golf
    Fungicides
  Landscape
    Fungicides
  Nursery/Greenhouse
    Fungicides
  Vegetation Management
    Selective and nonselective growth regulators

COMPETITORS

ADM
Ag Processing
AGRI Industries
Agrium
Andersons
BASF SE
Bayer CropScience
Cargill
CF Industries
CHS
Corn Products International

Dow AgroSciences
DuPont
Frontier Agriculture
Goulding Chemicals
GROWMARK
JR Simplot
Land O'Lakes Purina Feed
Monsanto Company
Southern States
Terra Industries

HISTORICAL FINANCIALS

Company Type: Private

Income Statement

FYE: December 31

	REVENUE ($ mil.)	NET INCOME ($ mil.)	NET PROFIT MARGIN	EMPLOYEES
12/08	2,577	—	—	2,500
12/07	2,012	—	—	2,500
12/06	1,710	—	—	2,500
12/05	1,632	—	—	2,500
Annual Growth	16.4%	—	—	0.0%

Revenue History

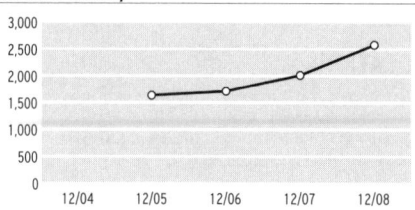

William Beaumont Hospital

William Beaumont Hospital draws on a rich history of pioneering medical research to serve the health needs of southeastern Michigan and advance healing techniques nationwide. William Beaumont Hospital consists of three hospitals with more than 1,700 beds in suburban Detroit. Other facilities include nursing homes, a home health care agency, a research institute, and primary and specialty care clinics, as well as rehabilitation, cardiology, and cancer centers. The hospitals are affiliated with the medical schools of institutions including the University of Michigan and Wayne State University.

William Beaumont Hospital is also partnering with Oakland University to open a new medical school focused on both education and research. The two organizations project that the Oakland University William Beaumont School of Medicine will open in 2010. The medical school is being added to the Beaumont Hospital Royal Oak campus, which is the system's largest facility with nearly 1,100 beds. In addition, the 360-bed Beaumont Hospital Troy facility is undergoing an expansion project that will include new emergency, critical care, and ambulatory care facilities.

The health system traces its roots to Dr. William Beaumont, an army doctor who conducted groundbreaking research on the human digestive system on Mackinac Island, Michigan, in the 1820s. The first Beaumont Hospital was opened in Royal Oak in 1955, and the Troy facility was opened in 1977.

The system's third hospital was added in 2007 when William Beaumont Hospital bought Bon Secours Hospital (located in the Detroit area) from Bon Secours Health System, as well as Bon Secours' Michigan nursing homes. The 290-bed hospital was renamed Beaumont Hospital Grosse Pointe.

EXECUTIVES

Chairman: Thomas G. Denomme, age 69
Vice Chairman: Stephen R. Howard
President and CEO: Kenneth J. Matzick
EVP and COO: Eugene F. Michalski
EVP and Chief Medical Officer: Ananias C. Diokno
SVP and Hospital Director, Beaumont Hospital, Troy, Michigan: Tom Brisse
SVP and Hospital Director, Beaumont Grosse Pointe: Richard Swaine
SVP and Hospital Director, Beaumont Royal Oak: John D. Labriola
VP Operations: Christine Stesney-Ridenour
VP Marketing and Public Affairs: Mike Killian
Director Legal Affairs: Terese Farhat
Secretary: Gale R. Colwell
Treasurer: William R. James

LOCATIONS

HQ: William Beaumont Hospital
3601 W. 13 Mile Rd., Royal Oak, MI 48073
Phone: 248-898-5000   **Fax:** 248-551-1555
Web: www.beaumonthospitals.com

PRODUCTS/OPERATIONS

Selected Facilities

Beaumont Hospital, Grosse Pointe
Beaumont Hospital, Royal Oak
Beaumont Hospital, Troy
Beaumont Medical Centers
Evergreen Health and Living Center (Southfield)
Shelby Nursing Center
ShorePointe Nursing Care Center (Grosse Pointe)
ShorePointe Village Assisted Living (Grosse Pointe)
West Bloomfield Nursing Center
Woodward Hills Nursing Center (Bloomfield Hills)

COMPETITORS

Crittenton Hospital
Detroit Medical Center
Henry Ford Health System
Mayo Foundation
McLaren Heath Care
Mount Clemens Regional Medical Center
Oakwood Healthcare
St. John Health
Trinity Health (Novi)
University of Michigan Health System

HISTORICAL FINANCIALS

Company Type: Private

Income Statement

FYE: December 31

	REVENUE ($ mil.)	NET INCOME ($ mil.)	NET PROFIT MARGIN	EMPLOYEES
12/08	2,061	—	—	18,050

William Lyon Homes

William Lyon's compass is pointed due west. That's where the homebuilder and its joint venture partners construct single-family detached and attached homes. California accounts for about 65% of its closings, ahead of both Arizona and Nevada. The builder operates some 30 sales locations and targets entry-level and move-up buyers. Homes range in price from about $75,000 to more than $1.7 million, and average $300,000. The company and its partners also control about 11,000 lots for development. Subsidiary William Lyon Financial Services (formerly known as Duxford Financial) offers loan and home financing services. Chairman William Lyon and family own 100% of the company.

Like other big domestic homebuilders, William Lyon Homes has been no stranger to the slow housing market. In 2008 its backlog consisted of about $80 million of homes sold under sales contracts that have not yet closed. Because of decreased home orders and high cancellation rates in all but its California market, the company slashed its workforce by about 25% and sold properties in 10 communities for about $90 million in order to increase its cash.

The losses continued into 2009, with development down by half in the first quarter and losses ballooning to $69 million. The number of homes built dropped from 371 to 182, and the average price dropped by more than $70,000.

EXECUTIVES

Chairman and CEO: William Lyon Sr., age 85
President and COO: William H. (Bill) Lyon Jr., age 35
SVP and President, Arizona Division:
  W. Thomas Hickcox, age 56
SVP and President, Nevada Division: Mary J. Connelly, age 57
SVP Finance: Richard S. Robinson, age 62
VP Human Resources: Maureen Singer
VP Tax and Internal Audit: Cynthia E. Hardgrave, age 60
VP and President, Northern California: Gary L. Galindo
VP and President, Southern California: Brian W. Doyle
VP Development and Operations: Matthew R. Zaist
VP Corporate Controller, Secretary, and Interim CFO:
  Colin T. Severn, age 38
Auditors: Windes & McClaughry Accountancy Corporation

LOCATIONS

HQ: William Lyon Homes
  4490 Von Karman Ave., Newport Beach, CA 92660
Phone: 949-833-3600   **Fax:** 949-476-2178
Web: www.lyonhomes.com

2008 Homes Sales by Region

	$ mil.	% of total
Southern California	323.4	62
Northern California	95.0	18
Nevada	58.4	11
Arizona	49.2	9
Total	**526.0**	**100**

PRODUCTS/OPERATIONS

2008 Sales

	$ mil.	% of total
Home sales	468.5	89
Lots, land & other sales	39.4	8
Construction services	18.1	3
Total	**526.0**	**100**

COMPETITORS

Beazer Homes
Capital Pacific
Corky McMillin
D.R. Horton
KB Home
Lennar
M.D.C.
Meritage Homes
The Ryland Group
Shapell Industries
Standard Pacific
Toll Brothers

HISTORICAL FINANCIALS

Company Type: Private

Income Statement

FYE: December 31

	REVENUE ($ mil.)	NET INCOME ($ mil.)	NET PROFIT MARGIN	EMPLOYEES
12/08	526	(112)	—	421
12/07	1,105	(349)	—	632
12/06	1,492	75	5.0%	730
12/05	1,856	191	10.3%	977
Annual Growth	**(34.3%)**	—	—	**(24.5%)**

2008 Year-End Financials

Debt ratio: 278.3%
Return on equity: —
Cash ($ mil.): —
Current ratio: —
Long-term debt ($ mil.): 476

Net Income History

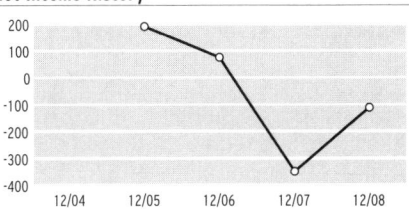

Williamson-Dickie Manufacturing

Appreciated by both the working class and the sophomore class, Williamson-Dickie Manufacturing makes Dickies-brand khaki pants, bib overalls, jeans, women's and children's apparel, and Workrite safety uniforms. It also makes apparel and footwear for work and outdoor use under the Kodiak and Terra names. Its work clothes, originally tailored for the blue-collar set, have come back into fashion with teens, which account for a growing portion of sales. Its products are sold worldwide through retailers (Academy, Wal-Mart), directly to businesses, and through its Work Authority stores. It was founded in 1922 by the Williamson family, which still owns the company. Dickies acquired Kodiak Group Holdings in April 2008.

Based in Canada, Kodiak Group Holdings makes and distributes work and outdoor footwear under the Kodiak and Terra brand names. The purchase allows Dickies to extend its reach into Canada and gives the company another brand that's just as rich in history as its own. As part of the agreement, Kodiak became a unit of Dickies, which has retained the Kodiak name, licensing program, and Work Authority stores in Canada.

Dickies workwear is sold in all 50 states and worldwide in countries such as Australia, Russia, Chile, Japan, Iceland, Canada, South Africa, Europe, and Mexico.

EXECUTIVES

Chairman, President, and CEO: Philip C. Williamson
Vice Chairman: Gail Williamson-Rawl
CFO: Randy Teuber
EVP Human Resources: Marett Cobb
SVP Marketing and Merchandising: Tad Uchteman
VP Marketing: Chris Prokopeas
VP Licensing: Michael Penn
VP Marketing and Operations, Canada: Bill McFarlane
Director Public Relations: Misty Otto

LOCATIONS

HQ: Williamson-Dickie Manufacturing Company
  509 W. Vickery Blvd., Fort Worth, TX 76104
Phone: 866-411-1501   **Fax:** 817-877-5027
Web: www.dickies.com

PRODUCTS/OPERATIONS

Selected Brand Names

Dickies
Workrite
Kodiak
Terra

COMPETITORS

Carhartt
Fruit of the Loom
FUBU
Levi Strauss
OshKosh B'Gosh
Phat Fashions
Tommy Hilfiger
VF

HISTORICAL FINANCIALS

Company Type: Private

Income Statement

	ESTIMATED REVENUE ($ mil.)	NET INCOME ($ mil.)	NET PROFIT MARGIN	EMPLOYEES
12/07	1,100	—	—	4,160
12/06	1,100	—	—	4,160
12/05	1,102	—	—	4,160
Annual Growth	(0.1%)	—	—	0.0%

Revenue History

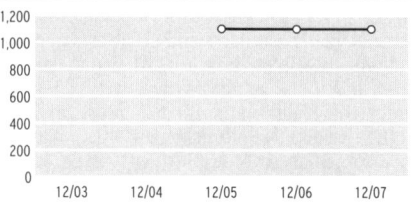

Wilson Sonsini

You might say these lawyers can get downright technical. Wilson Sonsini Goodrich & Rosati (WSGR) is one of the largest law firms in the US specializing in representing high-tech corporations. Its client roster has included several big Silicon Valley names, such as Apple Computer, Hewlett-Packard, and Sun Microsystems. WSGR has advised hundreds of clients on their IPOs and has been involved in more than 700 merger and acquisition transactions (valued at more than $300 billion) in the last five years. The firm has hundreds of lawyers working across seven offices in the US and one in Shanghai. It was founded in 1961.

Other practice areas include antitrust and trade regulation, intellectual property, corporate finance, fund services, and wealth management.

WSGR rode high during the high-tech boom, collecting large fees and paying out large bonuses. The cooling of the sector has meant making some cutbacks, but the firm continues to grow and has an eye out for business in Europe and Asia (the company opened its Shanghai office in 2005).

It has also capitalized on industry consolidation by doing more merger and acquisition work and is garnering more non-tech clients such as Hasbro and Monaco RV.

In August 2009 partner John Roos stepped down as CEO to become the US ambassador to Japan. Roos was replaced by Steven Bochner, who has been with Wilson Sonsini Goodrich & Rosati since 1981.

EXECUTIVES

Chairman: Larry W. Sonsini, age 68
Vice Chairman: Jeffrey D. (Jeff) Saper
CEO: Steven E. (Steve) Bochner
VP, Finance: Sunil Bhardwaj
VP, Information Services: Phillip Hoare
VP, Marketing: Courtney Chiang Dorman
General Counsel: Donald E. (Don) Bradley
Partner: Elton Satusky
Partner, Corporate and Securities: Rezwan Pavri
Partner, Intellectual Property: Michael Hostetler
Partner, Employee Benefits and Compensation: M. Madeleine Boshart
Partner, Intellectual Property: Effie Toshav
Partner, Tax Practice: Jonathan Zhu
Partner, Corporate and Securities: Nathaniel Gallon
Partner, Corporate and Securities: Melissa Hollatz
Senior Director, Human Resources and Office Administration: Stacey Layzell
Senior Director, Professional Services: Chris Boyd
Director, Attorney Recruiting and Retention: Carol A. Timm
Librarian: Liza MacMorris

LOCATIONS

HQ: Wilson Sonsini Goodrich & Rosati
650 Page Mill Rd., Palo Alto, CA 94304
Phone: 650-493-9300   **Fax:** 650-493-6811
Web: www.wsgr.com

PRODUCTS/OPERATIONS

Selected Practice Areas

Antitrust and trade regulation
Commercial litigation
Corporate finance
Corporate law and governance
Employee benefits and compensation
Employment law and litigation
Fund services
Intellectual property
Counseling and patents
Intellectual property litigation
Internal investigations
Life sciences
Mergers and acquisitions
Real estate and environmental
Securities litigation
Tax
Technology transactions
Trademarks, copyrights, and advertising
Venture capital
Wealth management
White collar crime

Industry Specializations

Communications and networking
Clean technology and renewable energy
Electronics and computer hardware
Financial institutions
Information service providers
Life sciences
Media and entertainment
Retail and consumer products and services
Semiconductors
Software
Venture capital

COMPETITORS

Cooley Godward Kronish
DLA Piper
Fenwick & West
Morrison & Foerster
Orrick
Perkins Coie

HISTORICAL FINANCIALS

Company Type: Partnership

Income Statement

FYE: January 31

	REVENUE ($ mil.)	NET INCOME ($ mil.)	NET PROFIT MARGIN	EMPLOYEES
1/08	531	—	—	—
1/07	460	—	—	—
1/06	412	—	—	—
1/05	382	—	—	—
1/04	387	—	—	—
Annual Growth	8.2%	—	—	—

Revenue History

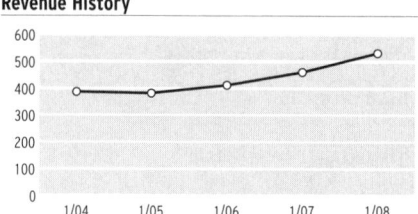

WinCo Foods

WinCo Foods isn't just big on self-service — it's giant. Inside the immense stores (average size is 90,000 sq. ft.) of this mostly employee-owned supermarket chain, customers shop for food in bulk and bag their own groceries. The company's 70 stores is six western states also feature pizza shops, bakeries, health and beauty products, and organic foods. WinCo Foods, formerly known as Waremart Foods, was renamed as a shortened version of "winning company." The name is also an acronym for its states of operation, which include Washington, Idaho, Nevada, California, and Oregon. Founded in 1968, employees, past and present, own most of the company.

WinCo's long-held low-price, no-frills strategy has paid off despite the rise of Wal-Mart supercenters in its markets. The discount supermarket operator is one of the few grocery chains known to match or beat Wal-Mart on price. Thriving in a sour economy, the company is expanding, adding a pair of stores in Utah and another in California in fall 2009. To support its growth in Utah, the company opened a distribution center in Boise, Idaho, in September 2009. The 750,000-sq.-ft. facility has the capacity to supply up to 28 stores in Idaho, eastern and central Washington, and Utah. Several more stores are planned for the Utah market.

EXECUTIVES

President, CEO, and Director: Steven Goddard
EVP and COO: Rich Charrier
EVP Finance, CFO, and Director: Gary R. Piva
SVP Real Estate Development and Construction: Kelly Adams
VP Information Technology: Glen Reynolds
VP Produce Operations: Greg Haag
VP Retail Development: Morgan Randis
VP Grocery Purchasing: Kay Kerr
VP Labor and Human Resources: Valerie Davis
VP Food Safety and Compliance: Alan Malone
VP and Controller: Del Ririe
VP Engineering: David Van Etten

VP General Merchandising: Richard Whitten
VP Merchandising and Retail Pricing: Gary Kintz
VP Distribution: Jim Parker
VP Public and Legal Affairs: Michael (Mike) Read

LOCATIONS

HQ: WinCo Foods, Inc.
650 N. Armstrong Place, Boise, ID 83704
Phone: 208-377-0110   **Fax:** 208-377-0474
Web: www.wincofoods.com

2009 Stores

	No.
California	29
Oregon	16
Washington	12
Idaho	9
Nevada	2
Utah	2
Total	**70**

PRODUCTS/OPERATIONS

Selected Store Departments

Bakery
Bulk foods (more than 500 items)
Delicatessen
Fresh meat
Health and beauty aids
Organic products
Pizza shop
Produce
Seafood

COMPETITORS

Albertsons	Raley's
Associated Food	Rosauers Supermarkets
Associated Wholesale	Safeway
Grocers	Stater Bros.
Costco Wholesale	Trader Joe's
Fred Meyer Stores	Unified Grocers
Haggen	Wal-Mart
PCC Natural Markets	

EXECUTIVES

President and CEO: Richard W. (Rick) Schwartz
COO: Monte L. Salsman
CFO: Jack W. Johnston
CIO: Steven L. Hangen
CTO: Jeffrey C. (Jeff) Dana
Regional VP, Eastern Region:
Ronald H. (Ron) Bohannon
Regional VP, Central Region: Michael G. Souders
Regional VP, Western Region: Steven M (Steve) Coen
VP Finance: Ward Allen
VP Vendor Relations: Roger E. (Eddie) Gibbs
VP Capital Management: Robert C. (Bob) Guiney
VP Sourcing Services: Paul H. Donarum
President, Noland Company: Jack Osenbaugh
Director, Corporate Communications:
Steven B. (Steve) Edwards

LOCATIONS

HQ: WinWholesale Inc.
3110 Kettering Blvd., Dayton, OH 45439
Phone: 937-294-6878   **Fax:** 937-293-9591
Web: www.winholesale.com

PRODUCTS/OPERATIONS

Selected Businesses

Noland Company (wholesale distributor of plumbing, electrical, HVAC, and mechanical equipment and supplies)
Winair (heating, ventilation, air conditioning, and refrigeration)
Windustrial (industrial pipes and valves)
Winfastener (specialty fasteners)
Winlectric (electrical supplies and products)
Winnelson (plumbing)
Winpump (pumps and accessories)
Wintronic (electronic parts and equipment)
Winwater Works (waterworks and utility supplies)

COMPETITORS

Fastenal	Johnstone Supply
Ferguson Enterprises	Lowe's
Gensco	MSC Industrial Direct
Groeniger & Company	Watsco
Hajoca Corporation	W.W. Grainger
HD Supply	

EXECUTIVES

Chairman: William Rockwell (Rocky) Wirtz, age 57
CFO: Max Mohler
VP; President, DeLuca Liquor and Wine: Ray Novell
VP Human Resources: Cindy Krch
Director Sales, Wine, Wirtz Beverage Minnesota:
David Duncan
General Manager, Wine, Wirtz Beverage Nevada:
David Scott
Controller: Linda Bescalli

LOCATIONS

HQ: Wirtz Corporation
680 N. Lakeshore Dr., 19th Fl., Chicago, IL 60611
Phone: 312-943-7000   **Fax:** 312-943-9017
Web: www.judgedolph.com

PRODUCTS/OPERATIONS

Selected Operating Companies

Callison Distributing
Coors of Las Vegas
DeLuca Liquor & Wine, Ltd.
Edison
Griggs, Cooper & Company
Hawkeye Wine & Spirits Inc.
Judge & Dolph, Ltd.
Mark VII Distributors
Nevada Wine Agents
Silver State Liquor and Wine
Wirtz Realty Corporation

COMPETITORS

Columbus Blue Jackets	National Wine & Spirits
Detroit Red Wings	Reyes Holdings
Gambrinus	Southern Wine & Spirits
Georgia Crown	St. Louis Blues
Glazer's Wholesale Drug	Sunbelt Beverage
Johnson Brothers	Tarrant Distributors
Nashville Predators	Young's Market
National Distributing	

WinWholesale

You Win some, you Win some more. So it goes for WinWholesale. The company owns all or part of more than 540 small to medium-sized wholesale distributors in 40-plus states that sell plumbing, heating, air-conditioning, electrical, and other supplies to contractors and other professional customers. The companies are easily recognizable by their Win-prefixed names, such as Columbia Winnelson, Salt Lake Windustrial, and Dayton Winfastener. The exception to the naming scheme is the company's Noland Co. subsidiary (acquired in 2005), which operates about 70 locations in the Southeast under the Noland brand. WinWholesale supports all of its companies with bulk purchasing, warehousing, accounting, and data processing.

Virginia-based Noland is a wholesale distributor of plumbing, electrical, HVAC, and mechanical equipment and supplies.

The fast-growing company, which traces its roots back to 1875 and operated as Primus Inc. for more than 40 years, is expanding via acquisitions and adding new locations. The company changed its name to WinWholesale in 2004.

Wirtz Corporation

Wirtz does it best on ice. The company owns the Chicago Blackhawks hockey team and is partnered with Jerry Reinsdorf, of the Chicago Bulls basketball team, in ownership of the United Center, where both sports teams play. It also owns and operates liquor distributorships, including Judge & Dolph, among the largest distributors in Illinois, and Wisconsin-based Edison through the Wirtz Beverage Group. Judge & Dolph owns the rights to distribute some key Diageo brands such as Crown Royal, Johnny Walker, J&B, and Tanqueray. President and CEO William Wirtz died in 2007; his eldest son, Rocky, took over management of the company.

The firm also owns beverage interests in Wisconsin and Nevada, and real estate interests, through Wirtz Realty Corporation, in Illinois, Mississippi, Texas, and Florida.

Arthur Wirtz (father of the late William Wirtz) founded the family-controlled empire in 1922.

World Wide Technology

World Wide Technology (WWT) has a broad view of its business. The company primarily provides such IT services as network design and installation, systems and application integration, and procurement. It also offers a range of Web-based products and services, including e-commerce systems development, order tracking, and catalog management. WWT serves businesses in the automotive, retail, and telecommunications industries, as well as government agencies. Top clients include Dell, the State of Missouri, and the State of Alaska. WWT was co-founded in 1990 by chairman David Steward and CEO Jim Kavanaugh.

Successful strategic partnerships with technology leaders including Cisco Systems and Hewlett-Packard and important contract wins, such as a seven year deal with NASA signed in 2007, have contributed to WWT's steady growth over the past several years. The company's sales more than tripled between 2002 and 2008. World Wide Technology bought St. Louis-based Server Centric Consulting in 2009. The deal served to expand the company's data center operations. Previous expansions included new facilities in Arizona and Nevada.

EXECUTIVES

Chairman: David L. Steward, age 57
CEO: James P. (Jim) Kavanaugh
President: Joseph G. (Joe) Koenig
CFO: Thomas W. (Tom) Strunk
VP Professional Services: Matt Horner
VP Human Resources: Ann W. Marr
VP Business Strategy: Robert M. (Bob) Olwig
President and COO, Telcobuy.com: Mark J. Catalano

LOCATIONS

HQ: World Wide Technology, Inc.
60 Weldon Pkwy., St. Louis, MO 63043
Phone: 314-569-7000   **Fax:** 314-569-8300
Web: www.wwt.com

COMPETITORS

Accenture
Computer Sciences Corp.
Dell
Hewlett-Packard
IBM Global Services
Perot Systems
Unisys

HISTORICAL FINANCIALS

Company Type: Private

Income Statement

FYE: December 31

	REVENUE ($ mil.)	NET INCOME ($ mil.)	NET PROFIT MARGIN	EMPLOYEES
12/08	2,560	—	—	1,100
12/07	2,500	—	—	1,100
12/06	2,100	—	—	1,050
12/05	1,800	—	—	1,030
12/04	1,400	—	—	—
Annual Growth	16.3%	—	—	2.2%

Revenue History

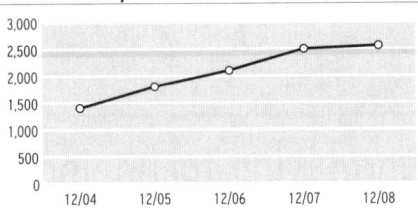

| | 3,000 |
| 2,500 |
| 2,000 |
| 1,500 |
| 1,000 |
| 500 |
| 0 |
| 12/04 12/05 12/06 12/07 12/08 |

Wyle Laboratories

Wyle Laboratories provides engineering, testing, life cycle management, clinical health services, operations support, and other technical support services to clients in such industries as aerospace, life sciences, telecommunications, and transportation. Besides serving commercial and industrial clients, the company is also a large government contractor, working with various branches of the Department of Defense and NASA. Founded in 1949 as a testing laboratory, Wyle Laboratories operates more than 40 facilities around the country with about 3,800 employees. It owns fellow government contractor Wyle Information Systems Group. In June 2009 private equity firm Court Square Capital Partners bought Wyle Laboratories.

Court Square bought the company for an undisclosed amount from turnaround firm Littlejohn & Co., which bought Wyle in 2003. Under Littlejohn's ownership, Wyle Laboratories expanded its research and testing capabilities when it acquired the aeronautics services business of General Dynamics in 2005, and it bought RS Information systems in early 2008 and renamed the company Wyle Information Systems Group.

Wyle's nonmilitary clients include Virgin Galactic, part of the Virgin Group which hopes to become the world's first provider of commercial space tourism. Virgin Galactic contracted Wyle to provide chief medical officer, medical data analysis, and program management services for its maiden space flight.

EXECUTIVES

Chairman, President, and CEO: George R. Melton
SVP and CFO: Dana P. Dorsey
SVP: Roger Wiederkehr
SVP: Jim Neu
VP Human Resources: Patti Robinson
VP and Controller: Doug Van Kirk
VP and CIO: Greg Burner
Group President, Integrated Science and Engineering Group: Bob Ellis
Group President, Aerospace Group: Brent M. Bennitt
Manager Corporate Communications: Dan Reeder

LOCATIONS

HQ: Wyle Laboratories, Inc.
1960 E. Grand Ave., Ste. 900, El Segundo, CA 90245
Phone: 310-563-6800   **Fax:** 310-563-6850
Web: www.wylelabs.com

PRODUCTS/OPERATIONS

Selected Services

Acoustics research and consulting
Acquisition program management
Aerospace cost estimating and analysis
Clinical and occupational health services
Design and construction of advanced test equipment
Earned Value Management (EVM)
Foreign military sales case management
Information technology
Life cycle management
Life sciences research
Non-destructive inspection
Science and mission integration
Space flight hardware development and fabrication
Space launch and operations support
Space medical operations
Systems engineering
Telemetry and data systems
Test and evaluation
Test pilot and test aircrew services
Testing services, including dynamics, climatics, fluid flow, and structural

COMPETITORS

Bureau Veritas
Exponent
Intertek
National Technical Systems
Orbital Research
SGS
SRI International

HISTORICAL FINANCIALS

Company Type: Private

Income Statement

FYE: December 31

	REVENUE ($ mil.)	NET INCOME ($ mil.)	NET PROFIT MARGIN	EMPLOYEES
12/08	800	—	—	3,800

Yale New Haven Health System

Yale New Haven Health System is a health care haven for residents of Southern Connecticut, Southwestern Rhode Island, and parts of New York's Westchester County. The company operates Yale-New Haven Hospital, Greenwich Hospital, and Bridgeport Hospital (and has a contract relationship with The Westerly Hospital in Rhode Island), as well as a children's hospital and a psychiatric care facility. In addition to its health care services, Yale New Haven Health System provides such managed care services as network contracting, as well as disease management programs. The system is affiliated with Yale University's medical school. The system was formed in 1995 and has a grand total of more than 1,500 beds.

EXECUTIVES

President and CEO: Marna P. Borgstrom
EVP and COO, Yale-New Haven Hospital: Richard D'Aquila
EVP; President and CEO, Greenwich Hospital and Greenwich Health Care System: Frank A. Corvino
EVP Strategy and System Development: Gayle L. Capozzalo
EVP; President and CEO, Bridgeport Hospital and Southern Connecticut Health System: Robert J. (Bob) Trefry
EVP Finance and Corporate Services; CFO and SVP, Finance, Yale-New Haven Hospital: James M. Staten
SVP and CIO: Mark L. Andersen
SVP Human Resources; SVP Human Resources Yale-New Haven Hospital: Kevin Myatt
SVP Payer Relations: William S. Gedge
SVP Medical Affairs; Chief of Staff and SVP, Medical Affairs, Yale-New Haven Hospital: Peter N. Herbert
VP Corporate Business Services: David Wurcel

LOCATIONS

HQ: Yale New Haven Health System
789 Howard Ave., New Haven, CT 06519
Phone: 203-688-4608   **Fax:** 203-688-3774
Web: www.yalenewhavenhealth.org

COMPETITORS

Bristol Hospital
Danbury Health Systems
Hartford Health Care
Health Quest
Hospital of Central Connecticut
Memorial Sloan-Kettering
New Milford Hospital
NewYork-Presbyterian Hospital
Saint Francis Hospital and Medical Center
Stamford Health
University of Connecticut Health Center
Waterbury Hospital
Westchester Medical Center

HISTORICAL FINANCIALS

Company Type: Not-for-profit

Income Statement

FYE: September 30

	REVENUE ($ mil.)	NET INCOME ($ mil.)	NET PROFIT MARGIN	EMPLOYEES
9/08	1,800	—	—	12,176
9/07	1,589	—	—	12,666
9/06	1,478	—	—	11,610
Annual Growth	10.4%	—	—	2.4%

Revenue History

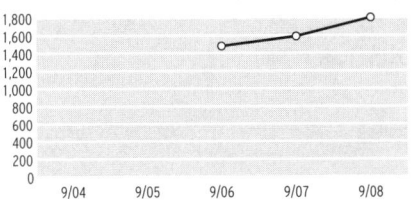

Yale University

What do former President George W. Bush and actress Meryl Streep have in common? They are Yalies. Yale University is one of the nation's most prestigious private liberal arts institutions, as well as one of its oldest (founded in 1701). Its more than $22 billion endowment ranks second only to Harvard's in the US. Yale comprises an undergraduate college, a graduate college, and more than a dozen professional schools. Programs of study include architecture, law, medicine, and drama. Its 12 residential colleges (a system borrowed from Oxford) serve as dormitory, dining hall, and social center. The school has around 11,250 students and some 3,600 faculty members.

EXECUTIVES

President: Richard C. Levin, age 61
Chief Investment Officer: David F. Swensen, age 56
Associate Vice President and Chief Financial Officer: Gwendolyn Sykes
Associate VP and Chief Human Resources Officer: Robert P. Schwartz
Associate Vice President and Chief Procurement Officer: John Mayes
VP and Secretary: Linda K. Lorimer, age 57
VP and General Counsel: Dorothy K. Robinson, age 58
CIO and Director Information Technology Services: Philip Long
Provost; Dean, Yale College: Peter Salovey
Dean, School of Medicine: Robert J. Alpern, age 58
Dean, School of Nursing: Margaret Grey
Dean, Divinity School: Harold W. Attridge
Dean, Yale Law School: Harold H. Koh
Associate Dean and Dean Student Affairs, Yale College: W. Marichal Gentry
Director Marketing and Communications: Ellen Lewis
Auditors: PricewaterhouseCoopers LLP

LOCATIONS

HQ: Yale University
246 Church St., New Haven, CT 06520
Phone: 203-432-2331   **Fax:** 203-432-2334
Web: www.yale.edu

PRODUCTS/OPERATIONS

Colleges and Schools

Graduate School of Arts and Sciences
Professional schools
  School of Architecture
  School of Art
  Divinity School
  School of Drama
  School of Engineering & Applied Science
  School of Forestry & Environmental Studies
  Law School
  School of Management
  School of Medicine
  School of Music
  School of Nursing
  School of Public Health
  Institute of Sacred Music
Yale College (undergraduate studies)

Yankee Candle

While most Yankees are good at warming their homes, the ones at The Yankee Candle Company are also good at making their homes smell like Egyptian Cotton or Home Sweet Home. It makes and sells candles, known for their burning longevity and strong smells — in more than 150 fragrances. It also sells candleholders, accessories, and dinnerware. Yankee Candle's products are sold by about 17,500 gift shops nationwide, as well as internationally in about 20 countries. Yankee Candle operates about 420 stores in 43 states, mostly in malls, and sells online and through catalogs. Madison Dearborn Partners acquired Yankee Candle in 2007 for $1.6 billion. A new CEO took over in October 2009.

Former chairman and CEO Craig Rydin handed over the title of CEO to Harlan Kent, the company's president and COO, on October 1, 2009. Rydin serves as executive chairman through October 1, 2010, and as a non-executive chairman thereafter.

Yankee Candle was banking on future growth as part of Madison Dearborn, but the downturn in the US economy and dismal climate for retailers is leading to cuts. As part of a restructuring plan, the company closed its Illuminations retail stores and halted its consumer direct business in April 2009. It also plans to shutter a single underperforming Yankee Candle shop.

Yankee Candle's Housewarmer and Country Kitchen candles, its core product, come in many different fragrances and a variety of sizes and shapes. Its signature style is a lidded jar. Yankee Candle's 90,000-sq.-ft. flagship store in South Deerfield, Massachusetts, attracts more than 2.5 million tourists a year.

EXECUTIVES

Chairman: Craig W. Rydin, age 57,
  $1,562,310 total compensation
President, CEO, and Director: Harlan M. Kent, age 46,
  $864,620 total compensation
SVP Marketing and Innovation:
  Richard R. (Rick) Ruffolo, age 41,
  $528,746 total compensation
SVP Wholesale Division: Michael Thorne, age 44
SVP and General Counsel: James A. Perley, age 46
SVP Retail: Stephen (Steve) Farley, age 54,
  $580,695 total compensation
SVP Supply Chain: Paul J. Hill, age 54
SVP Human Resources: Martha S. LaCroix, age 43
Auditors: Deloitte & Touche LLP

LOCATIONS

HQ: The Yankee Candle Company, Inc.
16 Yankee Candle Way, South Deerfield, MA 01373
Phone: 413-665-8306   **Fax:** 413-665-4815
Web: www.yankeecandle.com

PRODUCTS/OPERATIONS

Selected Products

Jar candles (3.7 oz., 14.5 oz., 22 oz.)
Kindle Candles (unscented wax for fire starters)
Samplers (votive candles for sampling fragrances)
Scented Ionic pillars (grooved candles)
Scented tea lights (small, scented candles in clear cups)
Standard pillars (scented and unscented)
Tapers (scented and unscented, the oldest style of candles)
Tart Warmers (white, unscented candles for potpourri pots)
Textured pillars (scented and unscented)
Wax Potpourri Tarts (scented wax without wicks used in potpourri pots)

COMPETITORS

American Greetings	Lancaster Colony
Avon	Procter & Gamble
Bath & Body Works	Reckitt Benckiser
Blyth	S.C. Johnson
The Dial Corporation	Target
Faultless Starch	Unilever
Human Pheromone Sciences	Wal-Mart

Yates Companies

The Yates Companies operates an extended family of construction firms, comprising W.G. Yates & Sons Construction (the largest of the group), Yates Electrical Division, Mississippi-based JESCO, and Tennessee-based Blaine Construction. The group provides a broad range of construction-related services, including engineering, electrical and mechanical construction, millwrighting, and steel fabrication. It operates mostly in the Southeast and along the East Coast. Completed projects include casinos, sports facilities, schools, and military facilities. William Yates Jr. co-founded the family-owned company in 1963 with his father, the late William Gully Yates. W.G. Yates Jr. now leads the company.

EXECUTIVES

Chairman, President, and CEO:
  William G. (Bill) Yates Jr., age 67
CFO and Treasurer: Marvin Blanks III
EVP and President, W.G. Yates & Sons:
  William G. Yates III, age 36
VP and General Counsel: Kenny Bush
Controller: Brandon Dunn
President, JESCO: Jerry Stubblefield
President, Blaine Construction: Dorman Blaine

LOCATIONS

HQ: The Yates Companies, Inc.
1 Gully Ave., Philadelphia, MS 39350
Phone: 601-656-5411   **Fax:** 601-656-8958
Web: www.wgyates.com

COMPETITORS

Brasfield & Gorrie
Choate Construction
Clark Enterprises
Fluor
Hunt Construction
Jacobs Engineering
J.E. Dunn Construction Group
Turner Corporation
Tutor Perini
Whiting-Turner

HISTORICAL FINANCIALS

Company Type: Private

Income Statement

FYE: December 31

	REVENUE ($ mil.)	NET INCOME ($ mil.)	NET PROFIT MARGIN	EMPLOYEES
12/07	1,980	—	—	8,000
12/06	2,240	—	—	8,000
12/05	1,761	—	—	8,000
12/04	1,440	—	—	6,000
12/03	1,100	—	—	4,500
Annual Growth	15.8%	—	—	15.5%

Revenue History

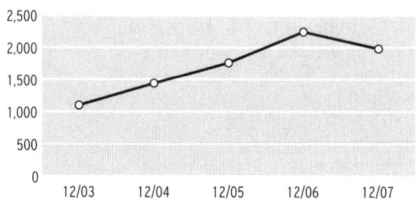

YMCA

A not-for-profit community service organization, YMCA of the USA assists the more than 2,600 individual YMCAs across the country and represents them on both national and international levels. Local YMCAs are leading providers of child care in the US. The facilities also offer programs in areas such as aquatics, arts and humanities, education of new immigrants, health and fitness, and teen leadership. Overall, YMCAs serve about 21 million people across the US, which includes about 10 million children under the age of 17. The first YMCA in the US was established in 1851 as an outgrowth of the YMCA movement launched by George Williams in the UK in 1844.

Although YMCA stands for Young Men's Christian Organization, the organization's programs are open to all. The organization is one of the largest providers of well-being programs in the nation and it promotes healthy living through its programs, such as YMCA Activate America.

YMCA of the USA regularly partners with the Centers for Disease Control and Prevention to operate the CDC Steps Program.

EXECUTIVES

Chairman: Ken Colloton
Chairman-Elect: Ulice Payne Jr., age 53
President and CEO: Neil Nicoll
SVP and Chief Innovation Officer: Lynne Vaughan
SVP Large YMCA Resources: Michael Weil
SVP and General Counsel: Angela Williams
SVP and COO: Kent Johnson
SVP and CFO: Jim Mellor
SVP and Chief Government Affairs Officer: Audrey Tayse Haynes
VP Certification and Membership Standards / Small and Mid-Size YMCA Resources: Fred Hauser
VP YMCA Resources: Larry Kameya
VP and Chief Development Officer: Monique Hanson
VP Membership and Programming: Roz Hamby
VP Diversity and Inclusion: David Thomas
VP Training and Leadership Development: Terri Radcliff
Advisor to President and CEO: Tom Craine
President, National YMCA Employee Benefits Plan: Steve Gustavson
Director International: Selma Zaidi
Director Knowledge Management: Stefan LaFloer
Director Activate America: Jonathan Lever

LOCATIONS

HQ: YMCA of the USA
101 N. Wacker Dr., Chicago, IL 60606
Phone: 312-977-0031 **Fax:** 312-977-9063
Web: www.ymca.net

PRODUCTS/OPERATIONS

Selected YMCA Programs

Aquatics
Arts and humanities
Camping
Child-care
Community development
Family
Health and fitness
International
Older adults
SCUBA
Sports
Teen leadership

Young's Market

Although no longer young, Young's Market Company, founded in 1888, is in high spirits. The company is a major US supplier of alcoholic beverages; its customers are located in California, Arizona, and Hawaii. Young's Market distributes wine and liquors for Bacardi, Brown-Forman, and Rémy Contreau, among other domestic and foreign distillers and winemakers. In California it distributes wines of Brown-Forman's Sonoma-Cutter Vineyards. The Underwood family, relatives of the founding Young family, bought the company in 1990. The third generation of the family currently operates the company, with Jeff and Chris Underwood serving as co-presidents.

The company's domestic wines also include those of Sonoma Coast Vineyards and Silverado Vineyards. Its imports include Grant Burge Wines, Morey-Blanc, and House of Delamotte.

EXECUTIVES

Co-President: John Klein
Co-President and COO: Christopher (Chris) Underwood
Co-President and COO: Jeffrey V. (Jeff) Underwood
EVP and CFO: Dennis J. Hamann
EVP and General Counsel: Donald (Don) Robbins
EVP Young's Columbia Oregon: Andy Lytle
EVP Marketing and Internal Operations, Southwest: Ashley Burnette
EVP Sales and Business Development, California: Chris Nicks
EVP Operations, Southwest: Bob Richardson
SVP and CIO: Karen Eaton
SVP Strategic Human Resources: Valerie Gart
President and CEO, Young's Holdings: Paul A. Vert

LOCATIONS

HQ: Young's Market Company, LLC
2164 N. Batavia St., Orange, CA 92865
Phone: 714-283-4933 **Fax:** 714-283-6175
Web: www.youngsmarket.com

COMPETITORS

Beauchamp Distributing
Glazer's Wholesale Drug
Harbor Distributing
Johnson Brothers
Republic National Distributing Company
Southern Wine & Spirits
Sunbelt Beverage

Yucaipa Companies

Yucaipa has a hungry eye for picking out ripe bargains in different industries, but made its name with grocery stores. The investment company, which was formed in 1986, forged its reputation as the ultimate grocery shopper, executing a series of grocery chain mergers and acquisitions involving such companies as Fred Meyer, Ralphs, and Jurgensen's that put the company on the supermarket map. It currently owns stakes in about 35 companies, including SUPERVALU and A&P, but sold its interest in organic market Wild Oats to Whole Foods in 2007. Yucaipa's chairman, billionaire and former grocery store bag boy Ron Burkle, is a prominent Democratic activist and fundraiser.

Former president Bill Clinton has served as an advisor to, and was a high-profile investor in, Yucaipa, but cashed out his interest in order to avoid any conflicts with the 2008 presidential bid of wife Hillary.

Burkle, who also owns a significant stake in the NHL's Pittsburgh Penguins, made headlines in 2006 when he set up a sting to catch New York *Post* columnist Jared Paul Stern allegedly trying to extort some $200,000 from Burkle to keep him off the gossip page.

Yucaipa's portfolio also includes Piccadilly Restaurants, about a 20% stake in Simon Worldwide, and half of Alliance Entertainment (a distributor of music, videos, and games). Building its portfolio of temperature-controlled warehousing and distribution business, Yucaipa bought Americold Realty Trust from Vornado Realty Trust for $220 million in 2008, and a 49% stake in VersaCold Logistics from Eimskip the following year, with an option to acquire the rest.

Also in 2008 Yucaipa's Aloha Airlines shut down business and filed for bankruptcy after high fuel prices, competition, and dwindling support from investors caught up with it. Yucaipa took over a lawsuit first filed by Aloha Airlines against former competitor Mesa Air Group, which operates its go! fleet in Hawaii. The lawsuit accused Mesa of using confidential business information about Aloha in order to better compete with them. The two entities settled the lawsuit and initially Mesa agreed to pay Yucaipa more than $6 million over 10 years to use the Aloha name and rebrand its go! fleet. Yucaipa also was awarded a minority stake in Mesa. However, a bankruptcy judge later invalidated the sale of the Aloha brand and logo because the sale was not held publicly.

HISTORY

Ronald Burkle launched his career in the grocery industry as a bag boy at his dad's Stater Bros. grocery store. By age 28 Burkle had moved up to SVP of administration, but he was fired after botching a buyout of the company in 1981.

Burkle and former Stater Bros. colleagues Mark Resnik and Douglas McKenzie founded Yucaipa (named after Burkle's hometown of Yucaipa, California) in 1986 when they bought Los Angeles gourmet-grocery chain Jurgensen's. The next year Yucaipa bought Kansas-based Falley's, which had 20 Food 4 Less stores in California.

In 1989 Yucaipa merged with Breco Holding, operator of 70 grocery stores, and bought Northern California's Bell Markets. It acquired ABC Markets in Southern California in 1990. The next year the company bought the 142-store chain Alpha Beta. Thirty-six Yucaipa stores were damaged in the 1992 Los Angeles riots, but Yucaipa rebuilt, working with unions to keep workers employed until the stores were operational.

The company acquired the 28-store Smitty's Super Valu chain (now Fred Meyer Marketplace) in 1994. The following year Yucaipa bought the 70-year-old family-owned chain Dominick's Finer Foods. Later in 1995 Yucaipa's Food 4 Less chain merged with Los Angeles competitor Ralphs Grocery (founded in 1873 by George Ralphs), making Yucaipa #1 in Southern California.

Yucaipa sold Smitty's to Utah-based Smith's in 1996, acquiring a minority stake in Smith's (Burkle became Smith's CEO). Dominick's went public in 1996, and Yucaipa retained a minority stake. The next year Fred Meyer bought Smith's for $1.9 billion. Burkle became the acquired company's chairman, and Yucaipa gained a 9% interest in Fred Meyer.

In 1998 Fred Meyer bought Ralphs and 155-store Quality Food Centers (QFC). Yucaipa and Wetterau Associates, a management firm,

bought Golden State Foods, giving Yucaipa a 70% stake in the McDonald's food supplier. Yucaipa sold Dominick's to Safeway.

After Kroger bought Fred Meyer in 1999, Yucaipa turned away from the consolidating grocery industry and moved into cyberspace. That year Burkle and former Walt Disney president Michael Ovitz launched CheckOut Entertainment Network, which operated CheckOut.com, an entertainment Web site at which Web surfers could buy books, music, and video games. Yucaipa hired Richard Wolpert, former president of Disney Online, to oversee its Internet and technology activities.

Yucaipa added to its portfolio in 1999 by taking stakes in GameSpy (online games), Talk City (later LiveWorld, online chat service), OneNetNow (online communities), ClubMom (Web site for mothers), and Cyrk (now Simon Worldwide, promotional marketing). Yucaipa also bought music, video, and games distributor Alliance Entertainment. The company also holds a minority stake in Simon Worldwide.

Music and video retailer Wherehouse Entertainment became a 50%-owner of CheckOut.com after it merged its online retailing operations with CheckOut.com in 1999. (As the Internet economy faltered, Yucaipa sold CheckOut.com in 2001.)

In 2000 the company digressed from its focus on the Web to invest in Kole Imports, an importer of merchandise sold in discount stores.

Yucaipa sold its stakes in grocery distributor Fleming and discount retailer Kmart in 2001 before both companies crashed into bankruptcy.

EXECUTIVES

Managing Partner: Ronald W. (Ron) Burkle, age 56
CFO: Lori Crawford
Legal: Robert P. Bermingham
Partner: Edward (Ed) Renwick, age 41
Partner: Erika Paulson, age 35
Partner: Steven L. Mortensen
Partner: Carlton J. Jenkins, age 53
Partner: Ira Tochner, age 47
Investor Relations and Corporate Communications:
Frank Quintero

LOCATIONS

HQ: The Yucaipa Companies LLC
9130 W. Sunset Blvd., Los Angeles, CA 90069
Phone: 310-789-7200   **Fax:** 310-228-2873
Web: www.yucaipaco.com

COMPETITORS

Bain Capital
Berkshire Hathaway
Blackstone Group
The Carlyle Group
HM Capital Partners
KKR
Leonard Green
Thomas H. Lee Partners
TPG

Zachry Holdings

Zachry plans, builds, and maintains major facilities in the power, cement, and nuclear sectors. The holding company for Zachry Engineering and Zachry Industrial, the company builds and maintains power and chemical plants, cement and paper mills, refineries, roadways, railways, dams, airfields, and pipelines, primarily in the Lone Star State. Zachry Engineering performs a variety of design tasks for transportation projects, power plants, and refineries. Its Industrial Services subsidiary provides maintenance, construction, and consulting work for plants in the pulp and paper, chemical, refining, and power generations industries. The Zachry family owns the firm, which was founded by H.B. Zachry in 1924.

In 2008 Zachry reorganized, and folded its Zachry construction subsidiary into Zachry Engineering. Company executives said that streamlining its structure would enable it to pursue contracts in the growing ethanol and nuclear markets, among others.

Also that year Zachry expanded geographically by acquiring Southerland Associates, an engineering, construction, and fabrication services company based in Charlotte, North Carolina. The deal gave Zachry a permanent presence in the southeast US. Zachry also plans to develop a regional employment and training center in Charlotte.

Zachary acquired Groton, Connecticut-based Proto-Power Corporation, a full-service engineering firm that provides engineering, design, and project management services to the nuclear power industry, in 2009. Proto-Power was renamed Zachary Nuclear Engineering, and adds design service capabilities to its subsidiary, Zachary Nuclear Inc.

EXECUTIVES

Chairman: H. Bartell Zachry Jr.
CEO and Director: John B. Zachry, age 47
President, COO, and Director: David S. Zachry
SVP and Manager, Power: Robert J. (Bob) Kalt
SVP Finance and Director: D. Kirk McDonald
SVP Corporate Development: Kenneth A. (Ken) Oleson
SVP: Edward R. (Ed) Bardgett, age 66
SVP Corporate Business Development:
Keith D. Manning
SVP, Controller, and Director: Joe J. Lozano
VP Heavy Construction: Fred Lueck
VP Corporate Risk Management: Timothy A. (Tim) Watt
VP and Chief Estimator: Ray Wenz
VP Information Technology: Norman Thurow
VP Civil Group: Steve Zander
VP Administration, Accounting, and Director:
Charles Ebrom
VP, General Counsel, Secretary and Director:
Murray L. Johnston Jr.
VP Employee Relations: Stephen L. (Steve) Hoech
VP Community Relations: Cathy Obriotti Green
Treasurer: Gonzalo O. Ornelas
Director Public Affairs: Victoria Waddy
Auditors: Ernst & Young

HQ: Zachry Holdings, Inc.
527 Logwood Ave., San Antonio, TX 78221
Phone: 210-475-8000   **Fax:** 210-475-8060
Web: www.zhi.com

COMPETITORS

Aker Solutions
Alberici
APAC
Austin Industries
Barton Malow
Bechtel
Black & Veatch
Fluor
Foster Wheeler
Gilbane
Granite Construction
Hensel Phelps Construction
Hoffman Corporation
Holloman
Jacobs Engineering
KBR
M. A. Mortenson
McCarthy Building
MWH Global
Parsons Corporation
Peter Kiewit Sons'
Polysius
Shaw Group
Sumitomo Mitsui
TIC Holdings
Turner Industries
Washington Division
Williams Brothers Construction

HISTORICAL FINANCIALS

Company Type: Private

Income Statement

FYE: December 31

	ESTIMATED REVENUE ($ mil.)	NET INCOME ($ mil.)	NET PROFIT MARGIN	EMPLOYEES
12/08	2,800	—	—	15,500
12/07	2,188	—	—	11,500
12/06	1,660	—	—	14,000
12/05	1,175	—	—	12,000
12/04	966	—	—	9,096
Annual Growth	30.5%	—	—	14.3%

Revenue History

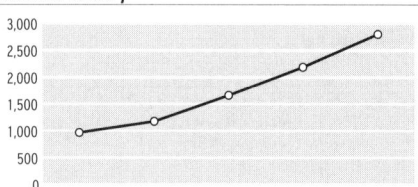

ZelnickMedia

Entertainment is big business for ZelnickMedia Corporation. The firm owns and manages a variety of media businesses and focuses its investments on television advertising, online gaming, direct marketing and e-commerce, recorded music, and media-related technology, among other sectors. Holdings include in-flight catalogue publisher and marketer SkyMall, online gaming developer Arkadium, video game publisher Take-Two Interactive Software, and market research firm OTX. ZelnickMedia serves its portfolio companies in either an advisory or management capacity. The company was created in 2001 by Strauss Zelnick, the former CEO of BMG Entertainment (now Sony Music Entertainment).

Zelnick took charge of one of his firm's most prized possessions, Take-Two, in 2008. That year, with Zelnick at the helm as executive chairman, the maker of the popular video game series, *Grand Theft Auto*, rebuffed a hostile $2 billion takeover bid by rival Electronic Arts.

ZelnickMedia has typically partnered with other finance firms on deals. However, it raised new capital in 2008 and assembled its own private equity fund, ZM Capital, to make new investments in a market filled with undervalued properties. In 2009 the company invested in infomercial distributor, Cannella Response. ZelnickMedia continues to search for opportunities in interactive entertainment, marketing services, market research, and advertising-related businesses with exposure to the Internet.

EXECUTIVES

CEO: Strauss Zelnick, age 51
Director, Finance and Operations: Brian D. Motechin
Partner: Benjamin Shriner
Partner: Justin Landau
Partner: Billy Ingram
Partner: Clemens Dornemann
Partner: Jordan Turkewitz
Partner: Andrew E. Vogel, age 36
Partner: Scott Siegler
Partner: Jim Friedlich
Partner: Benjamin (Ben) Feder, age 46
Partner: Karl Slatoff, age 39
Partner: Seymour Sammell

LOCATIONS

HQ: ZelnickMedia Corporation
19 W. 44th St., 18th Fl., New York, NY 10036
Phone: 212-223-1383   **Fax:** 212-223-1384
Web: www.zelnickmedia.com

PRODUCTS/OPERATIONS

Portfolio Companies

Advisory
Arkadium (online gaming developer)
OTX (aka Online Testing Exchange, consumer market research)
Skymall, Inc. (catalog sales)
Managed
Cannella Response Television, Inc. (infomercials)
Columbia Music Entertainment (Japan, music direct retailer)
ITN Networks (national media sales)
Naylor, Inc. (B2B media services for advertising, printing, and publishing industries)
Take-Two Interactive Software, Inc. (entertainment hardware, software, and accessories)

COMPETITORS

ABRY Partners
Allen & Company
Audiolux
Benchmark Capital
Bertelsmann
CCMP Capital
Demand Media
News Corp. Digital Media
Platinum Equity
WPP

Hoover's Handbook of

Private Companies

The Indexes

Index by Industry

ENERGY & UTILITIES

Ergon, Inc. 183

Electric Utilities

Associated Electric Cooperative 59
Bonneville Power Administration 94
Chugach Electric Association 133
Duquesne Light Holdings 175
Energy Future Holdings 180
New York Power Authority (Power Authority of the State of New York) 365
Oglethorpe Power 376
Old Dominion Electric 378
Salt River Project 433
Seminole Electric Cooperative 447
South Carolina Public Service Authority 464
Tri-State Generation and Transmission 499

Independent/Merchant Power Production

Tenaska, Inc. 487

Oil & Gas Exploration & Production

Arctic Slope Regional Corporation 53
Belden & Blake 78
Hunt Consolidated 255

Oil & Gas Refining, Marketing & Distribution

Apex Oil 51
Center Oil 125
Colonial Group 138
Koch Industries 285
Mansfield Oil 311
Motiva Enterprises 344
Red Apple Group 415
Sinclair Oil 456
Sun Coast Resources 476
Tauber Oil 484
Truman Arnold 501
U.S. Oil 523
Warren Equities 537

Oil & Gas Transportation & Storage

Kinder Morgan 282

ENVIRONMENTAL SERVICES & EQUIPMENT

Solid Waste Services & Recycling

America Chung Nam 40
Soave Enterprises 461

FINANCIAL SERVICES

Accounting

Deloitte Touche Tohmatsu 162
Ernst & Young Global 183
Grant Thornton International 220
KPMG International 287
Pricewaterhouse-Coopers International 402

Asset Management

AllianceBernstein L.P. 35
CalPERS (California Public Employees' Retirement System) 109
Capital Group Companies 111
FMR LLC 195
Mutual of America Life Insurance 345
Teacher Retirement System of Texas 485
TIAA-CREF (Teachers Insurance and Annuity Association - College Retirement Equities Fund) 491
The Vanguard Group 529

Investment Banking

Robert W. Baird & Co. 423
Stephens Inc. 474

Investment Firms

APi Group 51
Berwind Corporation 81
The Carlyle Group 115
Castle Harlan 117
Clayton, Dubilier & Rice 136
Forstmann Little & Co. 200
H Group Holding 230
Heico Companies 243
Platinum Equity 399
TPG Capital 495
Vulcan Inc. 534
Yucaipa Companies 552
ZelnickMedia 554

Lending

AgFirst Farm Credit Bank 30
AgriBank, FCB 31

Outsourced Financial Products & Services Marketing

LPL Investment Holdings 304

Securities Brokers & Traders

Davidson Companies 159
Jones Financial Companies 276
Scottrade, Inc. 445

Transaction, Credit & Collections

First Data Corporation 193
TransUnion LLC 496
U.S. Central Federal Credit Union 522

FOOD

Candy & Confections

Mars, Incorporated 314
Russell Stover 429

Canned & Frozen Foods

JR Simplot 277
Rich Products 422
Schwan Food 444

Dairy Products

California Dairies Inc. 106
Dairy Farmers of America 154
Foremost Farms 199
Great Lakes Cheese 222
HP Hood 254
Land O'Lakes 291
Leprino Foods 295
Michael Foods 336
Schreiber Foods 443
Tillamook County Creamery Association 492

Fish & Seafood

American Seafoods 44
Red Chamber Co. 415
Tri Marine International 498

Flavorings, Spices & Other Ingredients

Solae, LLC 462

Food Wholesale Distributors

Affiliated Foods 26
Alex Lee 33
Associated Food Stores 60
Associated Wholesale Grocers 62
Associated Wholesalers 63
Bozzuto's Inc. 99
C & S Wholesale Grocers 110
Central Grocers 125
Coastal Pacific Food Distributors 137
Eby-Brown Company 177
Grocers Supply 225
GSC Enterprises 226

H.T. Hackney 255
Purity Wholesale Grocers 407
Sherwood Food Distributors 452
Unified Grocers 506
Wakefern Food 536

Foodservice

ARAMARK Corporation 52
Ben E. Keith 79
Centric Group 127
Delaware North Companies 161
Dot Foods 168
Golden State Foods 213
Gordon Food Service 216
MAINES Paper & Food Service 309
Meadowbrook Meat Company 325
Performance Food 393
Services Group of America 451
Shamrock Foods 451
U.S. Foodservice 522

Grains

Bartlett and Company 72
Dakota Growers Pasta 155
Dawn Food Products 159
McKee Foods 323
Pinnacle Foods 397
Riceland Foods 421

Meat Products

ContiGroup Companies 146
Foster Poultry Farms 201
Keystone Foods 282
Koch Foods 285
Mountaire Corporation 344
OSI Industries 380
Perdue Incorporated 393
U.S. Premium Beef 525

Sauces & Condiments

Goya Foods 218

Sugar & Sweeteners

American Crystal Sugar 41

FOUNDATIONS

Bill & Melinda Gates Foundation 82
David and Lucile Packard Foundation 158
Ford Foundation 198
Howard Hughes Medical Institute 253
Inova Health System Foundation 262
Kellogg Foundation (W.K. Kellogg Foundation) 280
MacArthur Foundation (The John D. and Catherine T. MacArthur Foundation) 308
Robert Wood Johnson Foundation 424
Rockefeller Foundation 425

GOVERNMENT

Federal Reserve System 190
Tennessee Valley Authority 488

US Federal

Environmental Protection Agency (US Environmental Protection Agency) 182
Pension Benefit Guaranty Corporation 390
Sandia National Laboratories 436

US Local/County/City

New York City Health and Hospitals 363

US State/Regional

California State Board of Equalization 107
Lower Colorado River Authority 303

HEALTH CARE

Health Care Products

Bausch & Lomb 75
Biomet, Inc. 83
Cook Group 147
Medline Industries 327
Universal Hospital Services 510

Health Care Services

Adventist Health System 24
Advocate Health Care 25
Allina Hospitals 37
Ardent Health 54
Ascension Health 56
Banner Health 70
Baptist Health South Florida 71
BayCare Health System 76
Blue Cross and Blue Shield Association 86
Blue Cross and Blue Shield of Florida 87
Blue Cross and Blue Shield of Kansas City 88
Blue (LA) (Blue Cross and Blue Shield of Louisiana) 89
Blue Cross and Blue Shield of Massachusetts 89
Blue Cross Blue Shield of Michigan 90
Blue Cross (NC) (Blue Cross and Blue Shield of North Carolina) 91
Blue Cross (SC) (Blue Cross and Blue Shield of South Carolina) 91
Bon Secours Health System 94
California Physicians' Service 106
CareGroup, Inc. 112
Catholic Health East 118
Catholic Health Initiatives 119
Catholic Healthcare Partners 120
Catholic Healthcare West 121
Children's Medical Center of Dallas 131
CHRISTUS Health 132
Concentra Inc. 143
Delta Dental Plan (Delta Dental of California) 164
Duke University Health System 173
EmblemHealth, Inc. 179
Fairview Health Services 188
FHC Health Systems 193
Genesis HealthCare 207
Golden Horizons (GGNSC Holdings LLC) 213
Group Health Cooperative 226
Harvard Pilgrim Health Care 235
HCA Inc. 237
Health Care Service Corporation 238
HealthMarkets, Inc. 239
HealthNow New York 240
Henry Ford Health System 244
Highmark Inc. 245
Horizon Healthcare 251
Iasis Healthcare 257
Intermountain Health Care 263
Iowa Health System 266
Jefferson Health System 270
Johns Hopkins Health System 274
Kaiser Permanente 278
Life Care Centers 299
Manor Care 311
Mayo Foundation 320
MedStar Health 327
Memorial Hermann Healthcare System 330
The Methodist Hospital System 332
Michigan Education Special Services 337
Montefiore Medical Center 343
New England Alliance for Health 361
Novant Health 372
OSF Healthcare System 380

Partners HealthCare System 387
Providence Health & Services 405
The Regence Group 417
Resurrection Health Care 420
St. Joseph Health System 432
SavaSeniorCare 438
SCAN Health Plan 440
Scripps Health 446
Sentara Healthcare 448
Sisters of Charity of Leavenworth
  Health System 457
Sisters of Mercy Health System 457
Spectrum Health System 467
SSM Health Care 469
Sutter Health 481
Trinity Health 499
Tufts Associated Health Plans 504
University of Iowa Hospitals and
  Clinics 514
University of Maryland Medical
  System 515
US Oncology 524
Vanderbilt University Medical
  Center 528
Vanguard Health Systems 530
Wheaton Franciscan Services 544
William Beaumont Hospital 546
Yale New Haven Health System 550

INDUSTRIAL MANUFACTURING

Marmon Group 313

Fluid Control Equipment, Pump, Seal & Valve Manufacturing
Dresser, Inc. 171
Swagelok Company 481

Glass & Clay Product Manufacturing
Guardian Industries 226

Industrial Contract Manufacturing
Federal Prison Industries 189

Industrial Machinery & Equipment Distribution
Hillman Companies 246
McJunkin Red Man Holding
  Corporation 322

Industrial Machinery & Equipment Manufacturing
Amsted Industries 47
Barry-Wehmiller 72
Goss International 216
RBS Global 412

Lighting & Other Fixture Manufacturing
Advanced Lighting Technologies 23

Material Handling Equipment Manufacturing
Crown Equipment 152

Metal Fabrication
Euramax International 186

Packaging & Container Manufacturing
Berry Plastics 80
Dart Container 157
Graham Packaging 219
Plastipak Holdings 399
Printpack, Inc. 403
Solo Cup 463
Tekni-Plex, Inc. 486

Paper & Paper Product Manufacturing
Appleton Papers 52
Central National-Gottesman 126
The Kraft Group 289
The Newark Group 369

Rubber & Plastic Product Manufacturing
Advanced Drainage Systems 22
FXI-Foamex Innovations 205
Nypro Inc. 374
Sigma Plastics 455

Textile Manufacturing
Beaulieu Group 76
Milliken & Company 339

Wire & Cable Manufacturing
Southwire Company 466

INSURANCE

CUNA Mutual 152

Insurance Brokers
AmWINS Group 49

Life Insurance
American United Mutual
  Insurance 46
Guardian Life Insurance 228
Massachusetts Mutual Life
  Insurance 318
Modern Woodmen 341
National Life Insurance 354
New York Life Insurance 364
Northwestern Mutual Life
  Insurance 371
Pacific Mutual 383
Penn Mutual Life Insurance 389
Sammons Enterprises 435
Securian Financial 447
Thrivent Financial 491
Western & Southern Financial 542

Property & Casualty Insurance
American Family Insurance 42
Auto-Owners Insurance Group 66
Factory Mutual Insurance 187
Liberty Mutual 298
Main Street America 308
Mutual of Omaha 345
Nationwide Mutual Insurance 355
Sentry Insurance 448
State Farm Mutual Automobile
  Insurance 471
Trustmark Mutual Holding
  Company 502
USAA 526

LEISURE

Carlson Companies 114
Ilitch Holdings 259
It's Just Lunch 267

Entertainment
AMC Entertainment 39
Feld Entertainment 191

Gambling
Connecticut Lottery 143
Georgia Lottery 208
Harrah's Entertainment 234
Jacobs Entertainment 267
Kentucky Lottery 281
Maryland State Lottery 317
Mashantucket Pequot Tribal
  Nation 317
Massachusetts State Lottery 319
Mohegan Tribal Gaming
  Authority 342
New York State Lottery 366
Pennsylvania Lottery 390
Texas Lottery 489

Lodging
Best Western 81

Columbia Sussex 140
Hilton Worldwide 247
HVM L.L.C. 255

Restaurants & Cafes
Chick-fil-A 130
Dunkin' Brands 174
Friendly Ice Cream 204
Harman Management 232
Johnny Rockets 273
The Krystal Company 289
Metromedia Company 333
Noodles & Company 370
OSI Restaurant Partners 381
Panda Restaurant Group 385
Real Mex Restaurants 414
Rock Bottom Restaurants 425
Sbarro, Inc. 439
Subway (Doctor's Associates Inc.) 475
Uno Restaurants (Uno Restaurant
  Holdings Corp.) 521
Waffle House 535
Whataburger 543
White Castle 545

Sports & Recreation
24 Hour Fitness 16
Anaheim Ducks 49
Atlanta Spirit 64
Boston Red Sox 97
Carolina Hurricanes 116
Cavaliers Operating Company 122
Chicago Bulls (Chicago Professional
  Sports Corporation) 130
ClubCorp USA 136
Colorado Avalanche 139
Curves International 153
Dallas Cowboys 155
Dallas Mavericks (Dallas Basketball
  Limited) 156
Denver Nuggets 165
Golden State Warriors 214
Green Bay Packers 224
Houston Rockets 253
Indiana Pacers (Pacers Basketball,
  LLC) 260
Jazzercise, Inc. 268
Los Angeles Clippers (LAC Basketball
  Club, Inc.) 301
Los Angeles Kings 302
Los Angeles Lakers 302
Major League Baseball 309
Memphis Grizzlies (Hoops, L.P.) 330
Miami Heat (Basketball Properties,
  Ltd.) 335
Milwaukee Bucks 340
Minnesota Timberwolves 340
Minnesota Wild 340
NASCAR (National Association for
  Stock Car Auto Racing, Inc.) 347
National Basketball Association 348
National Football League 350
National Hockey League 352
New Jersey Devils 361
New Jersey Nets (New Jersey
  Basketball, LLC) 361
New Orleans Hornets 362
New York Giants (New York Football
  Giants, Inc.) 363
New York Islanders 364
New York Yankees 368
Oakland Raiders 375
Oklahoma City Thunder (Professional
  Basketball Club, LLC) 378
Orlando Magic 379
Phoenix Suns (Suns Legacy Partners,
  L.L.C.) 396
Pittsburgh Penguins (Lemieux Group
  LP) 398
Pittsburgh Steelers 398
Portland Trail Blazers (Trail Blazers,
  Inc.) 401

Sacramento Kings 432
San Antonio Spurs 435
San Jose Sharks 435
St. Louis Blues 433
Washington Capitals (Lincoln
  Holdings LLC) 537

MEDIA

Cox Enterprises 149
Hearst Corporation 240
NBC Universal 357

Film & Video
DreamWorks Studios 170
Ingram Entertainment 261
Lucasfilm Ltd. 305
Metro-Goldwyn-Mayer 332

Information Collection & Delivery
Associated Press 61
Bloomberg L.P. 85
EBSCO Industries 176

Music
Bad Boy Worldwide Entertainment
  Group 67

Publishing
Advance Publications 21
Advanstar Communications 23
American Media 43
Bureau of National Affairs 103
Consumers Union 144
Crain Communications 150
Encyclopædia Britannica
  (Encyclopaedia Britannica, Inc.) 180
Haights Cross Communications 231
Hallmark Cards 231
Houghton Mifflin 253
International Data Group 264
Johnson Publishing 274
MediaNews Group 325
Rand McNally 411
Thomas Nelson 490
Vance Publishing 528

Television
Allbritton Communications 34
Corporation for Public
  Broadcasting 148
ESPN, Inc. 184
Harpo, Inc. 233
PBS (Public Broadcasting
  Service) 388
Univision Communications 521

MEMBERSHIP ORGANIZATIONS

AARP 17
Academy of Motion Pictures (Academy
  of Motion Picture Arts and
  Sciences) 19
Academy of Television Arts &
  Sciences 19
AFL-CIO 28
American Bar Association 40
American Library Association 43
American Medical Association 44
Boy Scouts of America 98
Broadcast Music, Inc. 101
The Conference Board 143
NAACP 347
Rotary International 428
Sierra Club 454
Teamsters (International Brotherhood
  of Teamsters) 485

Index by Headquarters

Index of Executives

A

Aaron, Roger S. 459
Abate, Peter 175
Abbot, John 263
Abbott, Henry J. 126
Abbott, Michael 473
Abbott, Stephen M. 200
Abeles, Jon C. 120
Abeles, Robert 518
Abell, Nancy L. 387
Abinder, Susan 258
Abington, Bill 327
Able, Brett W. 169
Ables, Buddy 404
Abood, Denise 304
Abraham, Karen 517
Abrams, Jim 327
Abrams, Robert 459
Abrams, S. Thomas 464
Abrams, Sarah K. 196
Abramson, Richard 469
Abunaser, Bashar 257
Abzug, Peter 158
Acheson, Eleanor D. 48
Acheson Luther, Lisa 88
Acker, Jim 123
Acker, Kevin J. 542
Acker, Stan 510
Ackerman, Steve 438
Ackermann, Josef 143
Acklie, Duane W. 151
Acosta, Alan 470
Acosta, Janis N. 257
Acquaye, Robert S. 275
Acton, Brian 382
Adair, Marjorie 392
Adams, Alvan 396
Adams, Barry 325
Adams, Bill 543
Adams, Brady 220
Adams, Cathy C. 189
Adams, Cindi S. 385
Adams, Clint B. 54
Adams, Edward 182
Adams, Greg G. 374
Adams, Jason P. 464
Adams, John L. 131
Adams, Joseph 347
Adams, Kevin P. 124
Adams, Marvin W. 196
Adams, Mike (Bechtel) 77
Adams, Mike (Glazer's Wholesale
  Drug) 211
Adams, Paul 295
Adams, Richard C. 74
Adams, Stephen 28
Adams, Tom 99
Adams-Gaston, Javaune 377
Adamson, Geoff 217
Adamson, Mick 289
Adamson, Terrence B. 352
Adante, David E. 158
Adelman, Warren J. 213

Adgate, Brad 252
Adkins, Mark 241
Adkins, Norman 466
Adler, Jack F. Jr. 270
Adlich, Gregory 465
Afable, Mark V. 43
Affeldt, Eric L. 137
Africk, Jack 370
Agah, Ray 438
Agan, Dan 421
Agnello, Lynn 396
Agnew, Brian P. 296
Agnew, Joe 197
Agostinelli, D. D. 65
Ahearn, Joseph 307
Ahlfeld, Roger C. 521
Ahmad, Asif 173
Ahmann, Greg 453
Ahmaogak, Mary Ellen 54
Ahmed, Mumtaz 162
Ahn, Henry 357
Aiello, Greg 350
Aijala, Ainar D. Jr. 162
Aiken, Robert 523
Ain, Mark S. 289
Ainley, Christopher J. 274
Ainsworth, John 510
Ajamian, Daniel 483
Albano, James F. 251
Albeck, Joan 446
Alber, Michael J. 33
Alberici, John S. 32
Albert, David G. 450
Albert, Rob 545
Albert, Tom 192
Albertson, Marty P. 229
Album, Jeff 164
Alderman, Rob 300
Aldred, Sophie 166
Aldridge, Philip R. 519
Alexander, Craig A. 253
Alexander, Duane 354
Alexander, J. (Mansfield Oil) 312
Alexander, Jimmy (Ace Hardware) 20
Alexander, Ken 378
Alexander, Peter H. 215
Alfano, Jane D. 433
Alfano, Michele D. 193
Alfirevic, Richard G. 535
Alger, Jonathan R. 430
Alic, James M. 23
Alifano, John 156
Alire, Camila A. 43
Alkinburgh, Scott 315
Allbritton, Barbara B. 34
Allbritton, Robert L. 34
Alldian, David P. 92
Allen, A. William III 381
Allen, Barry 148
Allen, Carmen 531
Allen, Carol 225
Allen, Colin 375
Allen, Craig 472
Allen, Gary K. 516

Allen, Jim 31
Allen, Kenneth 242
Allen, Matthew J. 418
Allen, Meredith B. 471
Allen, Paul G. 401, 534
Allen, Quincy L. 531
Allen, Rick 182
Allen, Ward 549
Allen Patton, Jo Lynn 534
Allen-Meares, Paula 513
Allison, Jay 492
Almeida, Butch 138
Almeida, Donald V. 402
Almquist, David C. 207
Alonso, Gerardo L. 188
Alpern, Robert J. 551
Alpert, Theodore S. 23
Alston, John 102
Alt, Steve 462
Altieri, Michael 302
Altman, Lawrence B. 251
Altman, Steven J. 149
Altman, Stuart H. 179
Altman, Vicki S. 127
Altschul, Wayne 259
Altstadter, Jeff 361
Alutto, Joseph A. 377
Alvarado, Donald G. 459
Alvarez, Cesar L. 225
Alvarez, Richard P. 134
Alvarez, Scott G. 191
Alverson, Ronald C. 291
Alvin, William R. 244
Alvis, Scott 431
Amaral, José 237
Amberg, Stephanie L. 381
Ambres, Cynthia 240
Ambrosini, Robert P. 104
Ambroske, Dennis P. 166
Amedro, Daniel E. 53
Amendola, Michael 116
Ament, Gerald 333
Amerson, Leon T. 30
Amico, Jane 204
Andereck, Mike 174
Anderl, Rich 346
Andersen, David S. 276
Andersen, Mark L. 550
Anderson, Ann S. 89
Anderson, Barbara 431
Anderson, Bill 308
Anderson, Brian G. 146
Anderson, Charlotte Jones 156
Anderson, Dave (Peter Kiewit
  Sons') 395
Anderson, David G. (HCA) 237
Anderson, David M. (Thrivent
  Financial) 491
Anderson, David R. (American Family
  Insurance) 43
Anderson, Douglas 114
Anderson, Duwayn 427
Anderson, Ian D. 282
Anderson, Jarrett 122

Anderson, Jennifer 187
Anderson, John E. Sr. (Topa
  Equities) 494
Anderson, Jonathan (Blue Cross and
  Blue Shield of Florida) 88
Anderson, Ken 500
Anderson, Larry 193
Anderson, Lee R. Sr. 51
Anderson, Lincoln 304
Anderson, Maggie 84
Anderson, Mark B. 336
Anderson, Milton C. 343
Anderson, Richard 180
Anderson, Ross B. 31
Anderson, Ruth 520
Anderson, Scott R. 186
Anderson, Steve 185
Andoga, James R. 66
Andreassen, Inge 45
Andreoli, Tom 444
Andrews, Jeff 252
Andrews, Nancy 173
Andrews, Tyler E. 133
Andrews, William 223
Andrus, Kevin 432
Anger, Laura 151
Anger, Michael 490
Anger, Paul 326
Angress, David 229
Anhalt, Pete 449
Annunziato, Frank P. 487
Anschuetz, Christopher 326
Anthony, Barry 323
Anton, Arthur F. 481
Antonello, Michael 44
Antoniou, Chris 265
Apallas, Yeoryios 382
Appel, Gary B. 117
Appelstein, Gerald M. 484
Apperson, Kevin 34
Appleby, C. G. 96
Aramony, Diane M. 345
Araujo, Edu 342
Arbuckle, Katherine A. 94
Archer, Sherry 459
Archey, Paul 310
Archila, Juan Carlos 100
Ardelean, Diana 202
Arden, Allison P. 151
Areghini, David G. 433
Arena, Michael 134
Argilla, Luke P. 482
Arison, Micky 336
Armacost, Samuel H. 469
Armato, Carl 373
Armbrust, Nancy 444
Armentrout, Gary D. 317
Armfield, Jeffrey 464
Armour, James A. 419
Armstrong, Brian T. 425
Armstrong, C. Michael 274
Armstrong, Craig 480
Armstrong, David J. 94
Armstrong, Frank 272

Armstrong, Scott 226
Arnell, Paula 266
Arneson, Susan 460
Arnold, Allen 490
Arnold, D. Jeff 520
Arnold, Gregory A. 501
Arnold, James (Grocers Supply) 225
Arnold, Jim (CompuCom) 142
Arnold, Ken 436
Arnold, Reg 476
Arnold, Steve 63
Arnold, Travis 191
Arnold, Truman 501
Aronowitz, Alan B. 112
Aront, Alan 536
Arora, Pamela 131
Arsenault, Lisa 104
Arthur, Megan M. 515
Arthur, Warren J. 60
Arvin, Ann M. 470
Arvizu, Dan E. 338
Asbury, Kevin 303
Ascher, David 369
Aschkenasy, Penny 281
Ascolese, Richard A. 450
Ash, Darron 435
Ash, George W. 196
Ash, Joe 260
Ash, Scott 119
Ashby-Johnson, Roderick 26
Ashdown, Jane E. 134
Asher, Jeffrey A. 145
Ashley, Garrett P. 107
Ashline, Michael 98
Ashworth, Ronald B. 457
Asin, Stefanie 332
Asplundh, Christopher B. 59
Asplundh, Scott M. 59
Asser Weslock, Kathleen 479
Astrup, Thomas S. 42
Atefi, Bahman 33
Atherton, Jay 202
Atkins, C. Richard 89
Atkins, David 209
Atkins, George W. P. 41
Atkinson, Carolyn 404
Atkinson, Preston L. 543
Atkinson, Susan 474
Attaway, John A. Jr. 407
Atterbury, Rick R. 332
Attridge, Harold W. 551
Aubee, Debi 97
Audenart, Monty J. 428
Audiffred, J. Douglas 322
Aufdenspring, Michael C. 125
Aulbaugh, Carrol 330
Aulds, James 242
Aurik, Johan 64
Aus, Fred 303
Auslander, Kyra 200
Austen, W. Kim 356
Austin, Catherine 70
Austin, J. Paul 90
Austin, John D. 394
Austin, Russell P. 74
Austin, Ski 349
Austin, Tim 159
Austin, Wanda M. 26
Auvil, Tom 498
Avner, Kenneth S. 239
Axelrod, Norman 212
Ayala, Carlos 393
Aycock, Ben 116
Ayers, Kevin D. 153
Ayers, Mark H. 29
Azarela, Michael 476

B

Babcock, Dave 340
Babu, Suresh 223
Babyak, Barry 66

Bach, Paul D. 207
Bachman, Paul 523
Backlin, Jill 252
Backus, Harroll 18
Bacon, Bruce W. 254
Badain, Marc 375
Baden, Matthew 202
Baer, Dave 536
Baer, Jill Q. 317
Bagan, John 229
Baglien, Jerry 159
Bahn, Tom 108
Baich, Jim 22
Baile, Charles C. 59
Bailey, A. Robert D. 75
Bailey, Bill (New Orleans Hornets) 362
Bailey, Graeme 288
Bailey, Kevin 237
Bailey, William D. (Source
    Interlink) 464
Baillie, Kenneth 434
Bailly, Bruce W. 82
Bain, Mark 69
Bain, Michael J. 226
Baird, Greg 128
Baird, Kevin 227
Baker, Arlene Holt 29
Baker, Carmen 114
Baker, Dave 92
Baker, James A. III (Baker Botts) 70
Baker, James A. IV (Baker Botts) 70
Baker, John J. 355
Baker, Thomas M. (Army and Air Force
    Exchange) 56
Baker, Todd 216
Baker, Tom (Children's Medical Center
    of Dallas) 131
Baker, W. Kirk 255
Baker, William 138
Balagna, Jeffrey A. 114
Baldauf, Larry 209
Baldridge, Sally 268
Baldwin, K. Rone 228
Balfour, Don 535
Ball, Allen 329
Ball, Billy 17
Ball, Bradley A. 348
Ball, Don 411
Ball, Mira S. 514
Ball, Russ 224
Ballantyne, Reginald M. III 530
Ballentine, Anne 544
Baltes, Michael 343
Baltimore, Damon 390
Baltz, Jeffrey D. 51
Bander, Mark 173
Banerji, Shumeet 96
Bangel, Edward 155
Bangs, Nelson A. 359
Baniel, Paul 224
Banis, William J. 372
Banks, Hunter 327
Bantom, Michael A. 349
Bantz, Charles R. 260
Barabino, Gilda 208
Baratz, Alan E. 67
Barbee, J. Ray 427
Barber, Sam 160
Bardgett, Edward R. 553
Bardic, Ned 528
Bario, Holly 171
Barker, Edward L. 457
Barlow, Charles 456
Barnard, Charles Jr. 315
Barnard, Mark 251
Barner, Mark D. 57
Barner, Sharon R. 196
Barnes, Gerald 359
Barnes, Ronnie 364
Barnett, Don 515
Barnett, Hoyt R. 407
Barnett, Robert 490
Barney, Robin T. 84

Barney, Steven M. 469
Barnhill, Mark (Platinum Equity) 400
Barnhill, Mark L. (Belden & Blake) 78
Barone, Tony (Memphis Grizzlies) 330
Barone, Tony Jr. (Memphis
    Grizzlies) 330
Barr, Collin 430
Barr, William C. 417
Barra, Mary T. 206
Barrett, David J. 241
Barrett, John F. (Western & Southern
    Financial) 543
Barrett, Jonathan A. (Mayer
    Brown) 319
Barrett, Kim 512
Barrett, Philip A. 131
Barrie, Neda 214
Barrier, Frederick 471
Barringer, Dave 216
Barron, Gregory J. 440
Barron, Thomas E. 386
Barros, Colleen 354
Barry, Clifford 140
Barry, Lisa 23
Barry, Michelle 389
Barry, William D. 142
Barsa, Paul 99
Bartelme, John 393
Bartels, Mary 531
Barter, Clem 248
Barth, Anthony S. 164
Barth, Danny 378
Bartholomew, Dana 66
Bartholomew, Daniel R. 499
Bartlett, Mark R. 90
Bartlett, Paul D. Jr. 72
Bartlett, Richard 382
Bartley, Edward 319
Bartley, George B. 321
Bartliff, Fred 187
Bartolo, Lynn 107
Bartolomei, Lee A. 23
Barton, Bruce B. 445
Barton, Carol G. 188
Barton, Dominic 324
Barton, Glenn 508
Barton, Jeremy 97
Barton, Joel 411
Barton, R. Gregory 529
Baruchin, Andrea 528
Barz, Richard 295
Bass, Harris 220
Bass, Lisa 274
Bass, Michael 349
Basso, Cory J. 242
Bastien, Kevin 277
Bates, Brian 147
Bates, John R. 195
Bates, Kandis 304
Bates, Mark 33
Batjer, Marybel 234
Battaglia, Marion N. 461
Battaglia, Silvana 160
Baucum, Carlton E. 332
Baudhuin, Robert J. 35
Bauer, Brian T. 186
Bauer, Daniel 545
Bauer, Gerhard 75
Bauer, Richard 215
Baugh, Mark T. 244
Baughan, Ann 472
Baum, J. Robert 246
Baum, Vicki 225
Bauman, William J. 20
Baumann, Lee 472
Baumhoer, Patrick A. 59
Baumler, Casey 199
Baxley, William H. III 202
Baxter, Joanne 71
Baxter, Rob 451
Baze, Zach 39
Bazner, Kevin 267
Beach, David 329

Beach, Tim 364
Beadle, John M. 445
Beagen, Martin J. 222
Beal, David 352
Beal, Greg 19
Beal, Richard M. 481
Beall, Robert M. II 76
Beam, Rick 378
Beams, Maliz E. 492
Beard, Barbara 262
Bearrows, Thomas R. 514
Beasley, Joel 490
Beasley, John 392
Beatrice, Dennis 469
Beatty, Joyce 377
Beauchamp, Patricia 389
Beauchamp, Philip K. 76
Beauchine, Fay 114
Beaudrault, Peter J. 439
Beazley, Eric 100
Bechtel, Riley P. 77
Bechtel, Stephen D. Jr. 77
Beck, David 213
Beck, Frank 494
Beck, Joseph 125
Beck, Robin H. 517
Becker, Brandon 492
Becker, Cliff Jr. 528
Becker, Dan 215
Becker, Douglas L. 293
Becker, Joseph 327
Becker, Phil 335
Becker, Russell 51
Becker, Steve (Golden State Foods) 214
Becker, Steven R. (Southern Wine &
    Spirits) 466
Becker, Tom 225
Becker, William L. 233
Beckerman, Dan 302
Beckmann, James K. Jr. 57
Beckwith, Steven V.W. 511
Beddow, David L. 152
Bedrosian, John C. 507
Beecher, Diana E. 401
Beeken, David 50
Beekman, William R. 337
Beeler, Ralph B. 80
Beeman, William 155
Beeson, Thomas 97
Behler, Stacie 329
Behm, Larry 385
Behnke, Michael C. 513
Behr, Joan 199
Beier, Gregory J. 373
Beistline, Bill 194
Beitia, Alfonso 498
Belair, Caren 281
Belani, Rahul 145
Belek, Marilynn 164
Belfield, Pat 101
Beliveau, Bernie M. 51
Belk, H. W. McKay 79
Belk, John R. 79, 373
Belk, Thomas M. Jr. 79
Bell, Darren 494
Bell, David 442
Bell, Karin 202
Bell, Stanley R. 93
Bellavance, Peter 484
Beller, Marti 27
Belsito, Jason 345
Benedetti, Joseph C. 361
Bennack, Frank A. Jr. 241
Bennet, Richard W. III (CCA Global
    Partners) 123
Bennett, Clayton I. 378
Bennett, David S. 259
Bennett, Gary R. 365
Bennett, Gwen 76
Bennett, Richard (Best Western
    International) 82
Bennett, Robert 189
Bennett, Steven A. 527

Callori, Brion E. 188
Calo, Amber 148
Calpeter, Lynn 357
Calpus, Bill 300
Calvert, Karen 316
Calvert, Lisa 208
Camara, Robin 236
Camastral, Brian 315
Cambern, Donn 19
Camden, Hugh 185
Camerlinck, Bryan R. 88
Camerlo, James P. 154
Cameron, Cheryl A. 519
Cameron, Ian 62
Cameron, Robert 297
Cameron, Ronald M. 344
Cameron, Terry K. 487
Cammidge, John 511
Camp, David C. 471
Camp, Rob 545
Campbell, Alan 203
Campbell, Ben D. 215
Campbell, Beth 82
Campbell, Catherine M. 240
Campbell, Colin 353
Campbell, David A. (Energy Future) 181
Campbell, David K. (Boston University) 98
Campbell, Ellen 540
Campbell, Eric B. 365
Campbell, Jerry 226
Campbell, John (H-E-B) 242
Campbell, John B. (Ag Processing) 29
Campbell, John W. (Horizon Healthcare) 251
Campbell, Jon R. (Fairview Health) 188
Campbell, Judy 422
Campbell, Keith (U.S. Foodservice) 523
Campbell, Keith M. (Securian Financial) 447
Campbell, Kevin P. 255
Campbell, Kirk S. 264
Campbell, Mary 156
Campbell, Michael (Baker & McKenzie) 69
Campbell, Michael D. (Follett) 197
Campbell, Paul V. 306
Campbell, William J. Jr. (DLA Piper) 167
Campbell, William R. Jr. (TVA) 488
Campbell, William V. (Columbia University) 141
Campsey, David 26
Canavan, Francis 78
Canavan, John J. 240
Cancro, Lawrence C. 98
Cannady, Samuel 94
Cannatelli, Len Jr. 545
Cannon, Fred 101
Cannon, James W. Jr. 70
Cannova, Laurie 68
Canter, Richard J. 544
Cantrell, Pierce E. Jr. 489
Cantwell, Marianne 190
Capasso, John 119
Capellas, Michael D. 193
Capobianco, Tom 420
Capozzalo, Gayle L. 550
Capp, Brian 295
Capps, Frank 438
Cappucci, Lou 486
Capuano, Jack 364
Caputo, Louise 126
Caracappa, Joe 110
Caragozian, John 480
Carcone, John D. 200
Card, Robert G. 128
Cardamone, Stephen 544
Cardenas, Teri 132
Carefoot, Chuck 430
Carey, Gina 539
Cargill, John 249

Carkeek, Susan A. 517
Carleton, Mark D. 298
Carlile, Thomas E. 93
Carlin, Brian 312
Carlisle, Rick 156
Carlo, John B. 540
Carlsen, Jeff 421
Carlson, Brian (J.M. Huber) 273
Carlson, Brian (State Farm) 472
Carlson, Bruce W. 161
Carlson, Greg 542
Carlson, Jack (Southwire) 466
Carlson, Jeanne H. 90
Carlson, John (Sundt) 478
Carlson, Margaret Kemp 138
Carlson, Rick D. 296
Carlucci, David 21
Carlyle, Randy 49
Carmen, L. 514
Carnaroli, Craig 517
Carney, James (Texas Lottery) 490
Carney, James J. (Blue Cross and Blue Shield of Louisiana) 89
Carney, John F. III 516
Carousso, Paul B. 533
Carper, Tad 123
Carper, Thomas C. 48
Carr, Curtis 185
Carr, Lisa 160
Carr, Terry 259
Carrel, Dan 255
Carrico, Stephen J. 244
Carrigan, Charlie 393
Carrigan, Robert 264
Carrillo, Enrique 130
Carroll, Allen 352
Carroll, Charles A. 215
Carroll, Gerard 362
Carroll, James F. 154
Carroll, Kathleen 62
Carroll, Matt 70
Carroll, Milton 239
Carroll, Steve 442
Carstens, Robert M. 456
Carter, Bobbie 133
Carter, Herbert L. 107
Carter, Ian R. 248
Carter, Lonnie N. 464
Carter, Mary D. 50
Carter, Michael G. 372
Carter, William H. 245
Cartier, Karen 155
Cartin, James 63
Cartwright, Peter 169
Caruso, Thomas (Blue Tee) 92
Caruso, Thomas J. (ADESA) 21
Carvette, Anthony M. 475
Casadonte, Thom 312
Casady, Mark S. 304
Casale, Robert J. 318
Casale, Vincent 462
Casebeer, Steve 281
Casey, Donald J. 415
Casey, Larry 281
Casey, Patrick J. 503
Casey, Sister Juliana M. 119
Cashman, Brian 368
Casnelli, Chris 51
Cass, Jim 315
Cassels, Scott L. 395
Cassels, W. T. III (Southeastern Freight Lines) 465
Cassels, W. T. Jr. (Southeastern Freight Lines) 465
Cassidy, Vicki 540
Castellini, Richard 112
Caster, Lori 442
Castle, John K. 117
Castle, Julie G. 194
Castles, James B. 344
Castorina, Ed 273
Castro, John W. 332
Castro, Michael J. 164

Catalano, Mark J. 550
Cathy, Dan T. 131
Cathy, Donald M. 131
Cathy, S. Truett 131
Catsimatidis, John A. 415
Caudill, David 490
Cauz, Jorge 180
Cavallaro, Leonard A. 46
Cavanagh, Mark J. 319
Cavanaugh, James 404, 427
Cavanaugh, Steven M. 311
Cavecche, David 476
Caven, H. Scott Jr. 519
Caveney, Ken 436
Cavness, Pamela 277
Cawley, Stephen P. 516
Cazadd, Kristine 107
Celestini, Donna M. 251
Celiberti, Richard T. 343
Cellupica, Renato 215
Celmer, C. Kenneth 158
Cerra, Frank B. 516
Cervantes, Joseph 254
Cestaro, David 105
Chacko, Roger V. 527
Chadwick, Mike 213
Chalfin, Eli 539
Chamberlain, David R. 155
Chamberlain, Sue 520
Chambers, Franklin D. II 254
Chambless, Mark F. 456
Chambrello, Michael R. 307
Chan, Chiu 205
Chan, Joseph 245
Chand, M. Rizwan 181
Chandler, Joe 223
Chandler, Mike 287
Chandra, Anurag 239
Chandraraj, Girisha 101
Chang, Do Won 200
Chang, Elson 533
Chaplin, Harvey R. 466
Chaplin, Maxie C. 466
Chaplin, Wayne E. 466
Chapman, Leslie J. 447
Chapman, Rex 165
Chapman, Robert H. 72
Chappell, Robert E. 389
Chappelle, George 463
Charendoff, Bruce J. 431
Charette, Brian 317
Charko, Dennis R. 325
Charles, Lee D. 70
Charlson, John E. 367
Charlton, R. Scott 407
Charlton, Scott 110
Chase, Barbara 19
Chastain, B. Lynn 131
Chau, Bernard W. 26
Chau, Micheline 305
Chaudoin, Joe 156
Chavis, Richard 317
Checketts, David W. 433
Chelminiak, Lee A. 387
Chen, Amy 461
Chen, Bill 58
Chen, Bing 194
Chen, Clifford 498
Chen, Henry 58
Cheney, David 469
Cheney, Jeffrey P. 287
Cheng, Eva 38
Cherico, Michael 123
Chermside, Brian 169
Cherng, Andrew 385
Cherng, Peggy Tsiang 385
Chersi, Robert J. 196
Chestnutt, Roy H. 220
Cheung, Teresa 40
Cheung, Yan 40
Chevalier, Hector 126
Chew, Albert E. III 202
Chhina, Ivar 418

Chicatelli, Tara 404
Chidichimo, Pedro 276
Chieffe, Thomas N. 60
Chihoski, Mike 380
Chilvers, Dick 49
Chiminski, John R. 118
Chin Kou, Shu 415
Chinnis, C. Cabell Jr. 319
Chipman, Patti 59
Chipman, Stephen 221
Chirico, Jim 67
Chivian, Wendy R. 281
Chlapaty, Joseph A. 22
Cho, Juhee 460
Choe, Martha 83
Choi, Howard 415
Choquette, Paul J. Jr. 211
Chou, Cecilia 217
Chouest, Gary 362
Chrastka, John F. 43
Chrencik, Robert A. 515
Chresand, George 188
Chrestman, Flossie 54
Chris, Sherry A. 415
Christ, Travis 497
Christen, Bob 83
Christensen, Wil 481
Christensen Sjogren, Linda 494
Christman, Doug 425
Christopher, Jeff 405
Christopher, Thomas A. 197
Chu, Chinh E. 239
Chu, James 532
Chu, Judy 107
Chubb, Sarah 22
Chun, Kate 200
Chupaska, Leo M. 342
Church, Brent 415
Churchill, Sally Jo 516
Ciaccio, Michael J. 342
Ciccolo, Angela 347
Cicero, Frank 17
Cichowski, Lorraine 62
Ciesinski, Stephen J. 469
Cieszko, Peter 196
Cillis, Carol L. 215
Cindric, Tim 392
Cinelli, Michael A. 70
Ciniello, Leonard P. 27
Cinotti, Carolyn 97
Ciolino, Paul T. 47
Cipolla, Ray 438
Cirillo, Frank J. 363
Ciskowski, Tom 156
Cizek, Robert L. 126
Cizik, Robert 23
Clabby, Dennis 476
Clampett, Stephen M. 431
Clancy, George P. Jr. 130
Clapper, Grace 194
Clare, Peter J. 450
Clark, A. James 135
Clark, Alison 315
Clark, Brian 58
Clark, Carol A. 104
Clark, Dave (Meijer) 329
Clark, David B. (Raley's) 411
Clark, David D. (Northwestern Mutual) 372
Clark, Don 290
Clark, Douglas G. 223
Clark, Gary L. 215
Clark, J. Lance 275
Clark, Jack 371
Clark, Joe (San Antonio Spurs) 435
Clark, Joel (Dairy Farmers of America) 154
Clark, Joseph (Washington Companies) 538
Clark, Karen L. 251
Clark, Kim 26
Clark, Laya 44
Clark, Michael 501

Jones, Donald G. 24
Jones, Eric 304
Jones, Frances 191
Jones, Greg (Oglethorpe Power) 376
Jones, Gregg (Greenberg Traurig) 225
Jones, Gregory (State Farm) 472
Jones, Hugh W. 431
Jones, James J. 182
Jones, Jan (Providence Health &
  Services) 405
Jones, Janis L. (Harrah's
  Entertainment) 234
Jones, Jerral W. (Dallas Cowboys) 156
Jones, Jerry Jr. (Dallas Cowboys) 156
Jones, John F. 354
Jones, Joy 62
Jones, Kevin 337
Jones, Kreg 159
Jones, Larri Sue 191
Jones, Michael D. 388
Jones, Miles E. 159
Jones, Paul 453
Jones, Philip B. 369
Jones, Randall T. Sr. (Publix) 407
Jones, Randy (Sbarro) 439
Jones, Richard C. 228
Jones, Robert J. 516
Jones, Ronald G. (Henkels &
  McCoy) 243
Jones, Ronald L. (Dawn Food
  Products) 159
Jones, Roy 123
Jones, Stephen 156
Jones, Tracie 49
Jones-Barber, Carrie L. 159
Jordan, Debbie 353
Jordan, Nicole 58
Jordan, Stephen 165
Jorge, Robert 214
Jorgensen, Blake J. 297
Jorgenson, Mary Ann 245
Jorgenson, Richard T. 142
Joselove, Jonathan 359
Joseph, Alisa 441
Joseph, Charles S. 88
Joseph, Robert H. Jr. 36
Joss, Robert L. 470
Jost, Jerry 125
Joy, Catherine 265
Joyner, David S. 106
Judd, Richard 76
Juliano, Mark 502
Julien, Mark V. 289
Junck, Mary E. 62
Jung, Ronnie G. 485
Jungmann, Steven J. 463
Junkin, Jimmy O. 412
Junqueiro, Steve 438
Jura, James J. 59
Jurgens, Richard N. 256
Justus, Bill 540
Juszkiewicz, Henry E. 210

K

Kacere, Ken 301
Kacmarcik, James 82
Kadeli, Lek 183
Kadow, Joseph J. 381
Kaegi, John 88
Kaesgen, Hartmut 345
Kahle, Rita D. 20
Kahn, Alan J. 126
Kahn, David 340
Kahn, Eugene S. 135
Kahnweiler, David 138
Kalawski, Eva M. 400
Kaleak, George T. 54
Kalkut, Gary 343
Kalouche, Raymond S. 504
Kalt, Robert J. 553
Kalter, Alan 539

Kamener, Larry 97
Kamer, Lennie 490
Kameya, Larry 552
Kaminsky, Mark 285
Kamis, Dave 151
Kammer, Randy 88
Kamsickas, Jim 257
Kanai, Ken 546
Kane, Elizabeth T. 308
Kaneb, John A. 254
Kang, Matthew S. 311
Kang, Sung-Mo 511
Kanin, Fay 19
Kannekens, Wilbert 288
Kanter, Donna 19
Kanyoro, Musimbi 159
Kao, Andy 385
Kaplan, Alan S. 266
Kaplan, Herbert 537
Kaplan, Lee R. 182
Kaplan, Richard J. 308
Kaplan, Steven R. 496
Kappelman, Peter 292
Kappes, Jean 284
Karen, Nancy 453
Karet, Laura S. 209
Karicher, Michael 213
Karl, George 165
Karmanos, Jason 116
Karmanos, Peter Jr. 116
Karol, Tom 99
Karp, David J. 96
Karp, Gary 452
Karpf, Michael 514
Karst, Darren W. 429
Kartson, Despina 293
Kasdin, Robert A. 141
Kashuba, Glen A. 84
Kasi, Srinandan 62
Kass, Kelly 376
Kastner, Richard J. 88
Katehi, Linda 512
Kates, Kenneth P. 514
Katz, Howard 350
Katz, Marc D. (Burlington Coat
  Factory) 105
Katz, Mark (National Geographic) 352
Katz, Michael W. 408
Katzelnick, Mark 196
Katzenmeyer, Thomas 377
Katzman, David B. 123
Kauffman, Richard L. 297
Kaufman, John 256
Kavanaugh, James P. 550
Kavanaugh, Wilford J. 447
Kazerounian, Reza 203
Kazor, Lisa 359
Kean, Steven J. 282
Kean, Thomas H. 424
Keane, Elaine 383
Keari, Kerry 151
Kearney, Patrick 392
Kearns, Jim 38
Keating, Brad 155
Keating, John 113
Keating, Ronald C. 145
Kebo, Collin 124
Keck, Ray M. 489
Kee, Dennis 309
Keegel, C. Thomas 486
Keel, Michael C. 325
Keeley, Brian E. 71
Keeley, John 99
Keeling, Darrell 427
Keenan, John 302
Keenan, Suzanne 538
Kees, Robert L. 378
Keglevic, Paul M. 181
Kehl, Kurt 537
Kehlbeck, Dalton 456
Keiper, Paul W. 538
Keiser, Ingrid 137
Keisler, Peter D. 454

Keith, Claudia 107
Keith, Robert M. 36
Keith, Tricia A. 90
Keizer, Henry 288
Kekic, René 153
Kelbaugh, Jim 439
Kelemen, Mark 515
Kelleher, Kevin J. 415
Kelleher, Warren J. 445
Keller, Bryan J. 161
Keller, Dennis J. 403
Keller, Jim 451
Keller, Michael C. 356
Keller, Sara Lee 503
Keller, Steven E. 26
Kellert, Bob 201
Kelley, Barbara M. 75
Kelley, Kris J. 477
Kelley, Mary Lou 301
Kelley, Nima 213
Kelley, Vicki 69
Kelln, Bryan L. 400
Kelly, Daniel J. 43
Kelly, Edmund F. 299
Kelly, John (Randolph-Brooks Federal
  Credit Union) 412
Kelly, John (Save Mart) 438
Kelly, John P. (Ryan Companies
  US) 430
Kelly, Kael 531
Kelly, Kathleen 57
Kelly, Kevin E. 386
Kelly, Michael J. 358
Kelly, Patricia 391
Kelly, Stephen E. 74
Kelly, Sue 337
Kelly, Thomas M. 304
Kelly, Timothy T. 352
Kelly, William M. 92
Kelly-Bartley, Kim 545
Kelly-Brown, Kathy 358
Kemp, Karen L. 161
Kempston-Darkes, V. Maureen 206
Kendall, Brad 339
Kendall, Jeffrey 539
Kendall, Mellissa 194
Kendrick, Dan 437
Kendrick, Kevin B. 169
Kendrick, Shawn 490
Kenneally, William J. 215
Kennedy, Christopher (LCRA) 303
Kennedy, Christopher G. (University of
  Illinois) 513
Kennedy, Craig 182
Kennedy, James C. (Cox
  Enterprises) 150
Kennedy, James M. (Associated
  Press) 62
Kennedy, John W. 88
Kennedy, K. Daniel 422
Kennedy, Kathleen 19
Kennedy, Kevin J. 67
Kennedy, Samuel 98
Kennedy, Thomas C. (Hilton
  Worldwide) 248
Kennedy, Thomas H. (Skadden,
  Arps) 459
Kennedy, Wendy 438
Kenney, Anne R. 148
Kenney, Edward J. T. 345
Kenny, Dave 403
Kenny, John 428
Kent, Harlan M. 551
Keppler, Jim 257
Kerger, Paula A. 388
Kerin, Andrew C. 53
Kerle, Phillip 273
Kern, Howard P. 448
Kern, Paul J. 307
Kernan, Richard T. 172
Kerr, Bob 153
Kerr, David J. 152
Kerr, Phil 462

Kerris, Richard 305
Kersten, Cassidy 396
Kersten, Jeffrey L. 483
Kessel, Richard M. 366
Kessel, Silvia 334
Kessler, Alan C. 525
Kesteloot, Hendrick 117
Ketchum, L. Craig 322
Kettenbach, Michael 165
Ketterson, Robert C. 196
Keup, Gregory J. 51
Key, Billy 226
Keyes, Rick 329
Keys, William M. 139
Khalighi, Dar 45
Khan, Shahid 194
Khemlani, Neeraj 241
Khichi, Samrat S. 118
Kiappes, John 344
Kidd, Steven 175
Kidd, Wyndham Jr. 239
Kielar, Richard M. 494
Kierspe, Thomas L. 464
Kiesewetter, George 301
Kikumoto, C. David 534
Kilgore, Tom D. 488
Killebrew, Chad E. 482
Killebrew, Flavius C. 489
Killebrew, George 156
Killeen, Paul 213
Killen, James C. Jr. 34
Killingsworth, Cleve L. Jr. 89
Kim, David 256
Kim, Michael C. 64
Kimball, Jim 486
Kimball, Walker 77
Kimbrough, Mark 237
Kimler, Bill 309
Kimmel, Steve 34
Kinard, Lisa 486
Kinder, David D. 282
Kinder, Jacquelyn 119
Kinder, Richard D. 282
Kindle, Fred 136
Kindy, Mark 332
King, David L. (Associated
  Materials) 60
King, David R. H. (SmithGroup) 460
King, Donald R. 215
King, Edward (California State Board of
  Equalization) 107
King, Edward M. (Boston
  University) 98
King, Eileen 387
King, Gale V. 356
King, Jeffrey 137
King, John L. 516
King, Regina 201
King, Richard L. (Associated Food) 60
King, Richie (Foster Farms) 201
King, Steve 257
King, Thomas H. 37
King, Tim 102
King, Vivian 429
King, William K. 472
Kingan, Michael 517
Kingsbury, Thomas A. 105
Kingsley, Chris 302
Kingsley, Linda A. 525
Kinkela, David 218
Kinser, Dennis 63
Kinsley, Brian 140
Kinslow, Anthony D. 457
Kinstle, Mike 329
Kinzie, Jack L. 70
Kipling, Karen 534
Kiplinger, Austin H. 148
Kiraly, Thomas E. 143
Kirby, Rex B. 476
Kirchman, Kevin 401
Kirchner, Bruce 317
Kirk, Patricia L. 171
Kirk, Randy 37

Muñoz, Frank 431
Munro, Ellen K. 304
Muraskin, Ben E. 395
Murdock, Kent H. 263
Murin, William J. 432
Murken, Geoff 73
Murphree, Michelle 339
Murphy, Bill 518
Murphy, Christopher J. 395
Murphy, Corrie 230
Murphy, Daniel (The Kraft Group) 289
Murphy, Daniel J. (Unified Grocers) 507
Murphy, Elizabeth A. 158
Murphy, Jeremiah T. 30
Murphy, John 184
Murphy, Mark 137
Murphy, Peter E. 234
Murphy, Ronald H. 59
Murphy, Susan H. 148
Murray, Bob 49
Murray, Cathy (Life Care Centers) 300
Murray, James M. 370
Murray, John M. 157
Murray, Kathy (ABC Supply) 18
Murray, Peter 350
Murray, William 486
Murrell, Adrian 208
Murtaugh, Timothy M. 391
Musacchio, Robert A. 44
Muscatel, Dave 412
Music, Terry 41
Muskovich, John A. 284
Musto, Frank 337
Musumeche, Rocco 142
Muzik, Loreen 528
Myatt, Bob 45
Myatt, Kevin 550
Myers, Glen 38
Myers, James M. 394
Myers, Thomas 101
Myette, Kevin 418
Myrick, William J. 404

N

Nachtigal, Jules 142
Nachtwey, Peter H. 116
Nadeau, William J. 366
Nagle, Julie F. 200
Nahrgang, Jim 73
Nail, George 205
Nair, Mohandas 417
Nakis, Dominic J. 25
Nalley, Rob 421
Nally, Dennis M. 402
Napoli, Andy 153
Napoli, Irma 457
Napolitano, Fernando Flavio 96
Nardone, Lisa 539
Nartonis, Robert J. 306
Nash, Jill 297
Nash, Ron 408
Nassetta, Christopher J. 248
Nasto, Kristine 424
Natale, Jo 540
Naud, Renee 399
Nauman, Michael B. 380
Navarro, Benito 490
Navarro, Richard J. 33
Navti, Abigail L. 544
Naylor, Kevin 260
Nazarian, Robert H. 332
Neal, Christine 507
Neal, Grant R. 51
Neal, James 243
Neal, Jeffrey T. 24
Neary, Daniel P. 346
Neary, Michael 475
Neeb, Douglas M. 166
Neeb, Michael T. 237
Neeley, Robert L. 290

Neely, Alfred G. 53
Neff, Michael F. 481
Negri, Michael 217
Neil, A. Bruce 419
Neilson, Gary L. 96
Nell, Herman 394
Nelms, Charlie 260
Nelson, David R. 30
Nelson, Donnie 156
Nelson, Ed (Whataburger) 543
Nelson, Edward G. (Vanderbilt University Medical Center) 528
Nelson, Howard A. 290
Nelson, Jean Delaney 447
Nelson, Jim 225
Nelson, John 197
Nelson, Joni C. 259
Nelson, Marilyn Carlson 114
Nelson, Micki C. 347
Nelson, Noel 418
Nelson, Robert C. 70
Nelson, Scott W. 24
Nelson, Shanna Missett 268
Nelson, Thomas C. (AARP) 18
Nelson, Thomas C. (New NGC) 362
Nelson, Tom (Davidson Companies) 159
Nelson, William C. 88
Nemeth, Ken 63
Nerland, Nairn 148
Nesbit, Robert F. 341
Nesse, Robert E. 321
Nestor, Dave 182
Nestor, Michael 401
Nettleship, Clayborne 303
Neu, Jim 550
Neubauer, Joseph 53
Neufeld, Jane F. 304
Neumann, Henry W. Jr. 282
Neves, Tony 415
Newbold, Michael 110
Newcomb, Sharon 376
Newhouse, Donald E. 22
Newhouse, Samuel I. Jr. 22
Newhouse, Steven 22
Newman, Mark 368
Newman, Paul R. 173
Newmier, Diana M. 160
Newsom, Charles R. 173
Newsome, Laynie 533
Newsome, Mark 323
Newton, Leslie 465
Newton, Richard Y. III 56
Newton, W. Keith 143
Ney, Joseph A. 507
Ng, Yu-Kai 496
Ngais, Nelson 374
Nguyen-Phuong, Lam 111
Nicholls, Katherine 128
Nichols, Kenneth L. 20
Nichols, Michael F. 516
Nichols, Scott G. 98
Nicholson, Bruce J. 491
Nicholson, Pamela M. 182
Nick, Jerry 102
Nickel, Daniel M. 293
Nickols, David 347
Nicksa, Gary W. 98
Nicol, Ron 97
Nicoll, Neil 552
Niden, Howard 319
Niebruegge, Michael E. 319
Niederhuber, John E. (National Cancer Institute) 350
Niederhuber, John E. (NIH) 354
Niefeld, Kenneth A. 501
Niekamp, Randall W. 152
Nielsen, Jim 367
Nielson, Jann 329
Nielson, Joani 484
Nieuwenhuys, Gerard 392
Nightingale, Paul C. 254
Nikias, Chrysostomos L. 518

Nila, Anthony 253
Nilekani, Nandan M. 143
Nishiyama, Paul 274
Nistal, Miguel 486
Nitschke, Ken 109
Nitzkowski, Greg M. 387
Nizam, Akif 462
Nobers, Jeff 17
Noble, Anne 143
Nobles, John E. 105
Noe, David 328
Nogle, Jay 225
Nolan, Mike 288
Noll, Jessica 145
Nook, Gregory E. 270
Norby, Ronald G. 244
Norden, Jed L. 450
Nordlund, Jim 133
Nordyke, Greg 102
Norgren, Leslie 431
Norman, Paul E. 95
Norris, Adam 387
Norris, James M. 529
Norris, William 265
Norton, David W. 234
Norton, Deborah A. 235
Norton, Karin 454
Nosek, Stan E. 512
Noseworthy, John H. 321
Notkin, Shelby 111
Noto, Anthony 350
Noto, Robert A. 337
Novak, David A. 136
Novak, Trudy S. 447
Novell, Ray 549
Novelly, P. Anthony 51
Nowaczyk, Stephen 161
Nowland, Joseph 535
Nowlin, Charles F. 325
Noyes, Don 60
Nugent, Nancy 23
Null, Steven A. 355
Nunez, Cris 480
Nusbaum, Edward E. 221
Nussdorf, Glenn H. 408
Nussdorf, Lawrence C. 135
Nuttall, Roger 202
Nye, Robert S. 250
Nylen, Per 455
Nyquist, Jeffrey 337

O

Oakhill, Timothy F. 456
Obarski, Kevin 496
Obendorf, Steven E. 47
Ober, Gordon L. 158
Oberland, Gregory C. 372
Obert, Steve 49
Obray, Robert 60
O'Brien, David M. 246
O'Brien, Dermot J. 492
O'Brien, John 289
O'Brien, Karen L. 43
O'Brien, M. Elizabeth 120
O'Brien, Matthew J. 436
O'Brien, Michael 442
O'Brien, Morgan K. 175
O'Brien, Shelbie 23
O'Callaghan, Barry 253
Ochner, Sheila 519
O'Connell, John F. Jr. (Freeman Decorating Services) 202
O'Connell, John T. (Centric Group) 127
O'Connell, Matt 478
O'Connor, David E. 481
O'Connor, John J. 473
O'Connor, Maureen K. 91
O'Connor, Michelle 326
O'Connor, Patrick J. 487
O'Connor, Stephen (Sbarro) 439
O'Connor, Stephen J. (Gilbane) 211

Oddone, Piermaria J. 513
O'Dea, Marita 359
Odean, Gerald P. 341
Odegard, Gary L. 451
O'Dell, Julie 232
O'Dell, Mike 383
Odom, Pat 226
O'Donnell, Michael P. 178
O'Donnell, Steve 348
O'Dwyer, Mary Ann 201
Oeltjen, Edward 47
Offutt, Christi J. 413
Offutt, Ronald D. 413
Oge, Margo T. 182
Ogilvie, Scott 77
Oglesby, Daniel C. 467
Ogolsby, Tony 438
Oh, M.H. 546
O'Hara, John 429
O'Hare, Patrick 467
O'Haren, David 250
Ohle, David 34
Ohlhauser, Darrell R. 196
Ohlmeyer, Donald 185
Oishi, Alan 138
O'Kane, Katie 462
Okata, Maritza U. B. 379
O'Keane, Brian J. 31
Okes, Gary D. 185
Olafson, Robert M. 447
Oldenburgh, Shannon 312
O'Leary, Thomas M. 392
Olemaun, Forrest 54
Oleson, Kenneth A. 553
Oliva, Harvey 73
Oliver, David 139
Ollari, Frank J. 365
O'Loughlin, William B. 87
Olsem, Douglas J. 445
Olsen, Bradley 295
Olsen, Davin 116
Olsen, George Kirk 257
Olsen, Stephen R. 265
Olsen-Clark, Kim 43
Olson, Don 449
Olson, Gregg M. 401
Olson, James D. 232
Olson, Jayme D. 113
Olwig, Robert M. 550
O'Malley, David 389
O'Malley, J. Terence 167
O'Malley, John P. 264
Ondricek, Quent 168
O'Neal, Clifton M. 497
O'Neal, Craft 379
O'Neal, Peter J. 507
O'Neal, Rodney 164
O'Neill, Kevin 330
O'Neill, Michael 101
O'Neill, Molly K. 173
O'Neil-White, Alphonso 240
Opperman, Mary G. 148
O'Quinn, Marvin 122
Oram, John 258
Oran, Ron 102
Orand, Rebecca 135
Orange, Satia M. 43
Orazem, Ed 196
Ordoñez, Francisco A. 164
O'Reilly, William M. 449
Orender, Donna G. 349
Orfanos, Natalia 30
Orlando, Donald 215
Orleck, Sarah 105
Orlinsky, Ethan 310
Ormond, Paul A. 311
Orndorff, Cole 306
Ornelas, Gonzalo O. 553
O'Rourke, Michael 120
O'Rourke, Timothy C. 487
Orr, James F. III 426
Orr, Susan Packard 159
Orsi, Bernard 382

Wendel, Jon 256
Wendell, Beth 223
Wender, Justin B. 117
Wendlandt, Gary E. 365
Wendt, E. Lisa 90
Wendt, Richard L. 271
Wendt, Roderick C. 271
Wenner, Jim 452
Wentworth, Carol 501
Wenz, Ray 553
Wenzel, Gregory G. 96
Werbelow, Jim M. 418
Werlein, Ewing Jr. 332
Werner, David 80
Werner, Jordan 159
Werner, Thomas C. 98
Werthman, Ronald J. 274
Wessler, Alan 335
West, Henry J. 313
West, Marc 226
West, P. G. 82
West, Richard P. 107
West, Terry R. 535
West, Todd 478
Westbrook, Sandra J. 409
Weston-Webb, Andy 315
Westphal, Mark W. 336
Wetterau, Mark S. 214
Wexler, Lawrence S. 370
Wexler, Raymond P. 206
Wexner, Leslie H. 377
Wey, Mike 472
Weyhrich, Todd 105
Whalen, David 330
Whalen, Kevin 394
Whaley, Patricia 413
Wharton, Shane 303
Wheeland, Dan 354
Wheeler, Arnold F. 72
Wheeler, Bradley C. 260
Wheeler, E. Valjean 267
Wheeler, Penny Ann 37
Wheeler, Steven B. 96
Wheelock, Pamela 341
Whelan, Michael L. 431
Whelton, Paul K. 304
Whetstone, Steven 191
Whichard, Marcie 394
Whitacre, Bill 278
Whitacre, Edward E. Jr. 206
Whitcomb, Laurel 19
White, B. Joseph 513
White, Brian 172
White, Burt 304
White, David R. 257
White, Gregory W. 378
White, Henry F. Jr. 40
White, Jane 373
White, John (U.S. Xpress) 526
White, John D. (Texas A&M) 489
White, John T. (Structure Tone) 475
White, Mark 70
White, Timothy P. 511
White, Tracy 64
White, Wendy S. 517
White, William 82
Whitehouse, Andrew 324
Whiteley, Larry L. 73
Whitescarver, Jack 354
Whitesell, Shirley J. 47
Whitlock, James R. 169
Whitmer, W. Carl 257
Whitney, Charles W. 376
Whitney, Darren F. 172
Whitson, James P. 164
Whitt, Mark J. 487
Whitt, Terry 172
Whittington, Tom 449
Whitworth, Jonathan P. 538
Whynot, Jeff D. 459
Wiard, Nancy Bradley 19
Wickham, Gregory I. 155
Widener, Paul 290

Wider, John 18
Widmann, Janet 106
Wiebe, Robert L. 122
Wiedemann, Kristi 145
Wiedenkeller, Keith 39
Wiederkehr, Roger 550
Wieland, Robert A. 37
Wierman, Ken 282
Wiese, Ron 446
Wiest, Barbara G. 259
Wiete, Mark 165
Wiggins, Michael R. 466
Wiggins, Stephen K. 91
Wigglesworth, Margaret 138
Wight, Marshall A. 70
Wigington, Daryl 80
Wilansky, Heywood 443
Wilbanks, George E. 172
Wilcox, Kim 337
Wilcox, Paul 253
Wild, Katy 202
Wildhack, John 185
Wiles, Paul M. 373
Wiley, Cliff 407
Wilf, Leonard A. 367
Wilfley, Michael L. 220
Wilgis, E. F. Shaw 328
Wilhelm, Lance K. 395
Wilhelm, Mike 130
Wilke, Douglas 199
Wilkerson, Mark A. 46
Wilkins, Dominique 64
Wilkinson, Donna 260
Wilkinson, Gregg 371
Wilkinson, Joseph E. 59
Wilkinson, Mike 385
Wilkinson, Scott 64
Wilkinson, Walt 250
Wille, Doug 536
Willen Kennelly, Jill 457
Willenbrink, Garry 429
Willett, David 454
Willett, Robert E. 378
Willetts, Kent E. 52
Willey, Richard L. 393
Willhite, Colleen R. 484
Williams, Angela 552
Williams, Benjamin R. 122
Williams, Bob (Atlanta Spirit) 64
Williams, Carol 165
Williams, Cynthia 337
Williams, Daphne 183
Williams, David II (Vanderbilt
    University) 528
Williams, David B. (Appleton
    Papers) 52
Williams, David B. (University of
    Alabama) 510
Williams, Dean 279
Williams, Eugene R. 514
Williams, Helena E. 335
Williams, Jerry 147
Williams, Jim 45
Williams, John M. Jr. 433
Williams, Kay 168
Williams, Mark (Drees) 171
Williams, Mark E. (Best Western) 82
Williams, Michael (Anaheim Ducks) 49
Williams, Michael (Sentry
    Insurance) 449
Williams, Noel Brown 237
Williams, Pat 380
Williams, Rick 403
Williams, Robert (Dart Container) 157
Williams, Ronald A. 143
Williams, Scott 231
Williams, Shawn 342
Williams, Thomas L. 358
Williams, Virgil 56
Williams LaVelle, Vance 67
Williamson, Ann 514
Williamson, Blake J. 88
Williamson, Eric 230

Williamson, Norby 185
Williamson, Philip C. 547
Willis, Chris 265
Willis, Lori 442
Willner, Michael S. 263
Wilmoski, Scott 63
Wilson, Alexandra M. 150
Wilson, D. Ellen 196
Wilson, Danette K. 88
Wilson, Donald E. 254
Wilson, Doug 436
Wilson, Dwayne 340
Wilson, Eric F. G. (Raley's) 411
Wilson, Eric L. (Hensel Phelps
    Construction) 244
Wilson, Ernest J. III 149, 518
Wilson, Gordon A. 497
Wilson, J. Bradley 91
Wilson, James (Spectrum Health) 467
Wilson, James C. Jr. (J M Smith) 273
Wilson, James E. (Duquesne Light
    Holdings) 175
Wilson, John (New Balance) 360
Wilson, John F. (PBS) 388
Wilson, John J. (Dairy Farmers of
    America) 154
Wilson, Jon M. (Foley & Lardner) 196
Wilson, Keith A. 26
Wilson, Ken (Gate Petroleum) 205
Wilson, Kenny (Claire's Stores) 135
Wilson, Kevin A. 484
Wilson, Lowell D. 29
Wilson, Lynne 392
Wilson, M. 514
Wilson, Mike 315
Wilson, Modena H. 44
Wilson, Robert M. 123
Wilson, Roger G. 87
Wilson, Thomas 45
Wiltrout, Robert H. 350
Wimes, Ed 516
Winarsky, Norman D. 469
Winborne, Raymond E. Jr. 193
Windle, Bill 64
Winemiller, Pete 378
Winfield, Hank M. 111
Winfrey, Carey 461
Winfrey, Oprah G. 233
Winkler, Matthew 86
Winn, Marilyn G. 234
Winning, Patricia U. 131
Winograd, Les 476
Winslow, Paula 435
Winslow, Stephen 152
Winstanly, Derek M. 410
Winterlind, Fredrik 85
Wirthlin, Dave 60
Wirtz, William Rockwell 549
Wise, Joan S. 18
Wiseman, Christine M. 304
Wiseman, Robert 431
Wisniewski, Barbara 325
Wiszniak, Richard 143
Witczak, Janet 100
Witges, Debra M. 282
Withee, John 360
Withey, Howard G. 85
Witmer, Mark D. 336
Witt, Anne 48
Witt, Richard A. 346
Witt, Robert E. 510
Witten, Richard E. 141
Wodatch, Elizabeth 537
Woellfer, Gale 217
Wofford, Jeff C. 144
Wohl, Gary 170
Wohlert, Steve 531
Wojcik, Charles A. 494
Wojcik, Paul N. 104
Wolf, Denise 534
Wolf, G. Van Velsor Jr. 41
Wolf, Howard 470
Wolf, John (Cavaliers) 123

Wolf, John (Krystal) 290
Wolfe, Bernie 392
Wolfe, Peggy 337
Wolfe, Thomas F. 28
Wolff, Lisa 125
Wolff, Russell 185
Wolfish, Barry C. 292
Wolford, Kate 377
Wolkow, Mike 61
Wollman, Jerry 515
Wolski, Carolyn V. 336
Wolski, Lawrence G. 243
Wolterman, Daniel J. 330
Woltmann, Charles L. 480
Wolz, William 382
Womack, Walt 105
Wong, D. M. 26
Wong, Peter (Phoenix Suns) 396
Wong, Peter (Sisters of Charity of
    Leavenworth) 457
Wong, Stova 387
Wonkovich, Betty 182
Wood, Fred 512
Wood, Joanne 326
Wood, John V. 306
Wood, Melissa 105
Wood, Philip W. 473
Wood, Richard D. Jr. 538
Wood, Robert H. 99
Wood, Terrance 137
Woodard, Joan B. 436
Woodard, M. Rufus Jr. 103
Woodard, William M. 394
Woodcock, Kris 58
Woods, Douglas E. 170
Woods, Ed 140
Woods, Rex 195
Woods, Rick 226
Woodward, Kim 341
Woodworth, Gregory D. 354
Woody, Bill 249
Woodyard, David B. 137
Woollen, Thomas H. 373
Woolridge, Stephen T. 256
Woolworth, Eric 336
Wooten, Ronald J. 410
Wootton, Michael J. 480
Worcester, Robert P. 499
Wordelman, Scott 188
Wordsworth, Jerry L. 325
Wordsworth-Daughtridge, Debbie 325
Wories, John Jr. 47
Wormington, John R. 26
Worroll, David 476
Wortham, Stanton 517
Wray, John 122
Wrede, Steve 544
Wright, Alan R. 290
Wright, Albert B. III 352
Wright, Berry 498
Wright, Chris 340
Wright, Craig 296
Wright, Ed 339
Wright, Gary 534
Wright, George C. 489
Wright, Joseph R. Jr. 307
Wright, Linus D. 485
Wright, Mark 443
Wright, Mathew 528
Wright, Richard L. 507
Wright, Stephen J. 94
Wright, Tanya 243
Wright, Vicente 108
Wuebbling, Donald J. 543
Wulf, Jane 446
Wurcel, David 550
Wustenberg, Mark 492
Wuthich, Gordon 287
Wyatt, Stephanie 309
Wyatt, Stephen 514
Wyckoff, Bill 462
Wyczawski, Tom 174
Wyman, Peter L. 402